Oxford Dictionary of National Biography

Volume 27

Oxford Dictionary of National Biography

IN ASSOCIATION WITH

The British Academy

From the earliest times to the year 2000

Edited by

H. C. G. Matthew

and

Brian Harrison

Volume 27

Hickeringill–Hooper

OXFORD

UNIVERSITY PRESS

OXFORD
UNIVERSITY PRESS

Great Clarendon Street, Oxford OX2 6DP

Oxford University Press is a department of the University of Oxford.
It furthers the University's objective of excellence in research, scholarship,
and education by publishing worldwide in

Oxford New York

Auckland Bangkok Buenos Aires Cape Town
Chennai Dar es Salaam Delhi Hong Kong Istanbul Karachi
Kolkata Kuala Lumpur Madrid Melbourne Mexico City Mumbai Nairobi
São Paulo Shanghai Taipei Tokyo Toronto

Oxford is a registered trade mark of Oxford University Press
in the UK and in certain other countries

Published in the United States
by Oxford University Press Inc., New York

British Library Cataloguing in Publication Data
Data available

Library of Congress Cataloging in Publication Data
Data available: for details see volume 1, p. iv

ISBN 0-19-861377-6 (this volume)
ISBN 0-19-861411-X (set of sixty volumes)

Text captured by Alliance Phototypesetters, Pondicherry
Illustrations reproduced and archived by
Alliance Graphics Ltd, UK
Typeset in OUP Swift by Interactive Sciences Limited, Gloucester
Printed in Great Britain on acid-free paper by
Butler and Tanner Ltd,
Frome, Somerset

LIST OF ABBREVIATIONS

1 General abbreviations

AB	bachelor of arts
ABC	Australian Broadcasting Corporation
ABC TV	ABC Television
act.	active
A$	Australian dollar
AD	*anno domini*
AFC	Air Force Cross
AIDS	acquired immune deficiency syndrome
AK	Alaska
AL	Alabama
A level	advanced level [examination]
ALS	associate of the Linnean Society
AM	master of arts
AMICE	associate member of the Institution of Civil Engineers
ANZAC	Australian and New Zealand Army Corps
appx *pl.* appxs	appendix(es)
AR	Arkansas
ARA	associate of the Royal Academy
ARCA	associate of the Royal College of Art
ARCM	associate of the Royal College of Music
ARCO	associate of the Royal College of Organists
ARIBA	associate of the Royal Institute of British Architects
ARP	air-raid precautions
ARRC	associate of the Royal Red Cross
ARSA	associate of the Royal Scottish Academy
art.	article / item
ASC	Army Service Corps
Asch	Austrian Schilling
ASDIC	Antisubmarine Detection Investigation Committee
ATS	Auxiliary Territorial Service
ATV	Associated Television
Aug	August
AZ	Arizona
b.	born
BA	bachelor of arts
BA (Admin.)	bachelor of arts (administration)
BAFTA	British Academy of Film and Television Arts
BAO	bachelor of arts in obstetrics
bap.	baptized
BBC	British Broadcasting Corporation / Company
BC	before Christ
BCE	before the common (*or* Christian) era
BCE	bachelor of civil engineering
BCG	bacillus of Calmette and Guérin [inoculation against tuberculosis]
BCh	bachelor of surgery
BChir	bachelor of surgery
BCL	bachelor of civil law
BCnL	bachelor of canon law
BCom	bachelor of commerce
BD	bachelor of divinity
BEd	bachelor of education
BEng	bachelor of engineering
bk *pl.* bks	book(s)
BL	bachelor of law / letters / literature
BLitt	bachelor of letters
BM	bachelor of medicine
BMus	bachelor of music
BP	before present
BP	British Petroleum
Bros.	Brothers
BS	(1) bachelor of science; (2) bachelor of surgery; (3) British standard
BSc	bachelor of science
BSc (Econ.)	bachelor of science (economics)
BSc (Eng.)	bachelor of science (engineering)
bt	baronet
BTh	bachelor of theology
bur.	buried
C.	command [identifier for published parliamentary papers]
c.	*circa*
c.	*capitulum pl. capitula*: chapter(s)
CA	California
Cantab.	Cantabrigiensis
cap.	*capitulum pl. capitula*: chapter(s)
CB	companion of the Bath
CBE	commander of the Order of the British Empire
CBS	Columbia Broadcasting System
cc	cubic centimetres
C$	Canadian dollar
CD	compact disc
Cd	command [identifier for published parliamentary papers]
CE	Common (*or* Christian) Era
cent.	century
cf.	compare
CH	Companion of Honour
chap.	chapter
ChB	bachelor of surgery
CI	Imperial Order of the Crown of India
CIA	Central Intelligence Agency
CID	Criminal Investigation Department
CIE	companion of the Order of the Indian Empire
Cie	Compagnie
CLit	companion of literature
CM	master of surgery
cm	centimetre(s)

Cmd	command [identifier for published parliamentary papers]
CMG	companion of the Order of St Michael and St George
Cmnd	command [identifier for published parliamentary papers]
CO	Colorado
Co.	company
co.	county
col. *pl.* cols.	column(s)
Corp.	corporation
CSE	certificate of secondary education
CSI	companion of the Order of the Star of India
CT	Connecticut
CVO	commander of the Royal Victorian Order
cwt	hundredweight
$	(American) dollar
d.	(1) penny (pence); (2) died
DBE	dame commander of the Order of the British Empire
DCH	diploma in child health
DCh	doctor of surgery
DCL	doctor of civil law
DCnL	doctor of canon law
DCVO	dame commander of the Royal Victorian Order
DD	doctor of divinity
DE	Delaware
Dec	December
dem.	demolished
DEng	doctor of engineering
des.	destroyed
DFC	Distinguished Flying Cross
DipEd	diploma in education
DipPsych	diploma in psychiatry
diss.	dissertation
DL	deputy lieutenant
DLitt	doctor of letters
DLittCelt	doctor of Celtic letters
DM	(1) Deutschmark; (2) doctor of medicine; (3) doctor of musical arts
DMus	doctor of music
DNA	dioxyribonucleic acid
doc.	document
DOL	doctor of oriental learning
DPH	diploma in public health
DPhil	doctor of philosophy
DPM	diploma in psychological medicine
DSC	Distinguished Service Cross
DSc	doctor of science
DSc (Econ.)	doctor of science (economics)
DSc (Eng.)	doctor of science (engineering)
DSM	Distinguished Service Medal
DSO	companion of the Distinguished Service Order
DSocSc	doctor of social science
DTech	doctor of technology
DTh	doctor of theology
DTM	diploma in tropical medicine
DTMH	diploma in tropical medicine and hygiene
DU	doctor of the university
DUniv	doctor of the university
dwt	pennyweight
EC	European Community
ed. *pl.* eds.	edited / edited by / editor(s)
Edin.	Edinburgh

edn	edition
EEC	European Economic Community
EFTA	European Free Trade Association
EICS	East India Company Service
EMI	Electrical and Musical Industries (Ltd)
Eng.	English
enl.	enlarged
ENSA	Entertainments National Service Association
ep. *pl.* epp.	*epistola(e)*
ESP	extra-sensory perception
esp.	especially
esq.	esquire
est.	estimate / estimated
EU	European Union
ex	sold by (*lit.* out of)
excl.	excludes / excluding
exh.	exhibited
exh. cat.	exhibition catalogue
f. *pl.* ff.	following [pages]
FA	Football Association
FACP	fellow of the American College of Physicians
facs.	facsimile
FANY	First Aid Nursing Yeomanry
FBA	fellow of the British Academy
FBI	Federation of British Industries
FCS	fellow of the Chemical Society
Feb	February
FEng	fellow of the Fellowship of Engineering
FFCM	fellow of the Faculty of Community Medicine
FGS	fellow of the Geological Society
fig.	figure
FIMechE	fellow of the Institution of Mechanical Engineers
FL	Florida
fl.	*floruit*
FLS	fellow of the Linnean Society
FM	frequency modulation
fol. *pl.* fols.	folio(s)
Fr	French francs
Fr.	French
FRAeS	fellow of the Royal Aeronautical Society
FRAI	fellow of the Royal Anthropological Institute
FRAM	fellow of the Royal Academy of Music
FRAS	(1) fellow of the Royal Asiatic Society; (2) fellow of the Royal Astronomical Society
FRCM	fellow of the Royal College of Music
FRCO	fellow of the Royal College of Organists
FRCOG	fellow of the Royal College of Obstetricians and Gynaecologists
FRCP(C)	fellow of the Royal College of Physicians of Canada
FRCP (Edin.)	fellow of the Royal College of Physicians of Edinburgh
FRCP (Lond.)	fellow of the Royal College of Physicians of London
FRCPath	fellow of the Royal College of Pathologists
FRCPsych	fellow of the Royal College of Psychiatrists
FRCS	fellow of the Royal College of Surgeons
FRGS	fellow of the Royal Geographical Society
FRIBA	fellow of the Royal Institute of British Architects
FRICS	fellow of the Royal Institute of Chartered Surveyors
FRS	fellow of the Royal Society
FRSA	fellow of the Royal Society of Arts

FRSCM	fellow of the Royal School of Church Music	ISO	companion of the Imperial Service Order
FRSE	fellow of the Royal Society of Edinburgh	It.	Italian
FRSL	fellow of the Royal Society of Literature	ITA	Independent Television Authority
FSA	fellow of the Society of Antiquaries	ITV	Independent Television
ft	foot *pl.* feet	Jan	January
FTCL	fellow of Trinity College of Music, London	JP	justice of the peace
ft-lb per min.	foot-pounds per minute [unit of horsepower]	jun.	junior
FZS	fellow of the Zoological Society	KB	knight of the Order of the Bath
GA	Georgia	KBE	knight commander of the Order of the British Empire
GBE	knight or dame grand cross of the Order of the British Empire	KC	king's counsel
GCB	knight grand cross of the Order of the Bath	kcal	kilocalorie
GCE	general certificate of education	KCB	knight commander of the Order of the Bath
GCH	knight grand cross of the Royal Guelphic Order	KCH	knight commander of the Royal Guelphic Order
GCHQ	government communications headquarters	KCIE	knight commander of the Order of the Indian Empire
GCIE	knight grand commander of the Order of the Indian Empire	KCMG	knight commander of the Order of St Michael and St George
GCMG	knight or dame grand cross of the Order of St Michael and St George	KCSI	knight commander of the Order of the Star of India
GCSE	general certificate of secondary education		
GCSI	knight grand commander of the Order of the Star of India	KCVO	knight commander of the Royal Victorian Order
		keV	kilo-electron-volt
GCStJ	bailiff or dame grand cross of the order of St John of Jerusalem	KG	knight of the Order of the Garter
		KGB	[Soviet committee of state security]
GCVO	knight or dame grand cross of the Royal Victorian Order	KH	knight of the Royal Guelphic Order
		KLM	Koninklijke Luchtvaart Maatschappij (Royal Dutch Air Lines)
GEC	General Electric Company		
Ger.	German	km	kilometre(s)
GI	government (*or* general) issue	KP	knight of the Order of St Patrick
GMT	Greenwich mean time	KS	Kansas
GP	general practitioner	KT	knight of the Order of the Thistle
GPU	[Soviet special police unit]	kt	knight
GSO	general staff officer	KY	Kentucky
Heb.	Hebrew	£	pound(s) sterling
HEICS	Honourable East India Company Service	£E	Egyptian pound
HI	Hawaii	L	lira *pl.* lire
HIV	human immunodeficiency virus	l. *pl.* ll.	line(s)
HK$	Hong Kong dollar	LA	Lousiana
HM	his / her majesty('s)	LAA	light anti-aircraft
HMAS	his / her majesty's Australian ship	LAH	licentiate of the Apothecaries' Hall, Dublin
HMNZS	his / her majesty's New Zealand ship	Lat.	Latin
HMS	his / her majesty's ship	lb	pound(s), unit of weight
HMSO	His / Her Majesty's Stationery Office	LDS	licence in dental surgery
HMV	His Master's Voice	*lit.*	literally
Hon.	Honourable	LittB	bachelor of letters
hp	horsepower	LittD	doctor of letters
hr	hour(s)	LKQCPI	licentiate of the King and Queen's College of Physicians, Ireland
HRH	his / her royal highness		
HTV	Harlech Television	LLA	lady literate in arts
IA	Iowa	LLB	bachelor of laws
ibid.	*ibidem*: in the same place	LLD	doctor of laws
ICI	Imperial Chemical Industries (Ltd)	LLM	master of laws
ID	Idaho	LM	licentiate in midwifery
IL	Illinois	LP	long-playing record
illus.	illustration	LRAM	licentiate of the Royal Academy of Music
illustr.	illustrated	LRCP	licentiate of the Royal College of Physicians
IN	Indiana	LRCPS (Glasgow)	licentiate of the Royal College of Physicians and Surgeons of Glasgow
in.	inch(es)		
Inc.	Incorporated	LRCS	licentiate of the Royal College of Surgeons
incl.	includes / including	LSA	licentiate of the Society of Apothecaries
IOU	I owe you	LSD	lysergic acid diethylamide
IQ	intelligence quotient	LVO	lieutenant of the Royal Victorian Order
Ir£	Irish pound	M. *pl.* MM.	Monsieur *pl.* Messieurs
IRA	Irish Republican Army	m	metre(s)

m. *pl.* mm.	membrane(s)
MA	(1) Massachusetts; (2) master of arts
MAI	master of engineering
MB	bachelor of medicine
MBA	master of business administration
MBE	member of the Order of the British Empire
MC	Military Cross
MCC	Marylebone Cricket Club
MCh	master of surgery
MChir	master of surgery
MCom	master of commerce
MD	(1) doctor of medicine; (2) Maryland
MDMA	methylenedioxymethamphetamine
ME	Maine
MEd	master of education
MEng	master of engineering
MEP	member of the European parliament
MG	Morris Garages
MGM	Metro-Goldwyn-Mayer
Mgr	Monsignor
MI	(1) Michigan; (2) military intelligence
MI1c	[secret intelligence department]
MI5	[military intelligence department]
MI6	[secret intelligence department]
MI9	[secret escape service]
MICE	member of the Institution of Civil Engineers
MIEE	member of the Institution of Electrical Engineers
min.	minute(s)
Mk	mark
ML	(1) licentiate of medicine; (2) master of laws
MLitt	master of letters
Mlle	Mademoiselle
mm	millimetre(s)
Mme	Madame
MN	Minnesota
MO	Missouri
MOH	medical officer of health
MP	member of parliament
m.p.h.	miles per hour
MPhil	master of philosophy
MRCP	member of the Royal College of Physicians
MRCS	member of the Royal College of Surgeons
MRCVS	member of the Royal College of Veterinary Surgeons
MRIA	member of the Royal Irish Academy
MS	(1) master of science; (2) Mississippi
MS *pl.* MSS	manuscript(s)
MSc	master of science
MSc (Econ.)	master of science (economics)
MT	Montana
MusB	bachelor of music
MusBac	bachelor of music
MusD	doctor of music
MV	motor vessel
MVO	member of the Royal Victorian Order
n. *pl.* nn.	note(s)
NAAFI	Navy, Army, and Air Force Institutes
NASA	National Aeronautics and Space Administration
NATO	North Atlantic Treaty Organization
NBC	National Broadcasting Corporation
NC	North Carolina
NCO	non-commissioned officer
ND	North Dakota
n.d.	no date
NE	Nebraska
nem. con.	*nemine contradicente*: unanimously
new ser.	new series
NH	New Hampshire
NHS	National Health Service
NJ	New Jersey
NKVD	[Soviet people's commissariat for internal affairs]
NM	New Mexico
nm	nanometre(s)
no. *pl.* nos.	number(s)
Nov	November
n.p.	no place [of publication]
NS	new style
NV	Nevada
NY	New York
NZBS	New Zealand Broadcasting Service
OBE	officer of the Order of the British Empire
obit.	obituary
Oct	October
OCTU	officer cadets training unit
OECD	Organization for Economic Co-operation and Development
OEEC	Organization for European Economic Co-operation
OFM	order of Friars Minor [Franciscans]
OFMCap	Ordine Frati Minori Cappucini: member of the Capuchin order
OH	Ohio
OK	Oklahoma
O level	ordinary level [examination]
OM	Order of Merit
OP	order of Preachers [Dominicans]
op. *pl.* opp.	opus *pl.* opera
OPEC	Organization of Petroleum Exporting Countries
OR	Oregon
orig.	original
OS	old style
OSB	Order of St Benedict
OTC	Officers' Training Corps
OWS	Old Watercolour Society
Oxon.	Oxoniensis
p. *pl.* pp.	page(s)
PA	Pennsylvania
p.a.	per annum
para.	paragraph
PAYE	pay as you earn
pbk *pl.* pbks	paperback(s)
per.	[during the] period
PhD	doctor of philosophy
pl.	(1) plate(s); (2) plural
priv. coll.	private collection
pt *pl.* pts	part(s)
pubd	published
PVC	polyvinyl chloride
q. *pl.* qq.	(1) question(s); (2) quire(s)
QC	queen's counsel
R	rand
R.	Rex / Regina
r	recto
r.	reigned / ruled
RA	Royal Academy / Royal Academician

RAC	Royal Automobile Club		Skr	Swedish krona
RAF	Royal Air Force		Span.	Spanish
RAFVR	Royal Air Force Volunteer Reserve		SPCK	Society for Promoting Christian Knowledge
RAM	[member of the] Royal Academy of Music		SS	(1) Santissimi; (2) Schutzstaffel; (3) steam ship
RAMC	Royal Army Medical Corps		STB	bachelor of theology
RCA	Royal College of Art		STD	doctor of theology
RCNC	Royal Corps of Naval Constructors		STM	master of theology
RCOG	Royal College of Obstetricians and Gynaecologists		STP	doctor of theology
RDI	royal designer for industry		*supp.*	supposedly
RE	Royal Engineers		suppl. *pl.* suppls.	supplement(s)
repr. pl. reprs.	reprint(s) / reprinted		*s.v.*	*sub verbo* / *sub voce*: under the word / heading
repro.	reproduced		SY	steam yacht
rev.	revised / revised by / reviser / revision		TA	Territorial Army
Revd	Reverend		TASS	[Soviet news agency]
RHA	Royal Hibernian Academy		TB	tuberculosis (*lit.* tubercle bacillus)
RI	(1) Rhode Island; (2) Royal Institute of Painters in Water-Colours		TD	(1) *teachtaí dála* (member of the Dáil); (2) territorial decoration
RIBA	Royal Institute of British Architects		TN	Tennessee
RIN	Royal Indian Navy		TNT	trinitrotoluene
RM	Reichsmark		trans.	translated / translated by / translation / translator
RMS	Royal Mail steamer		TT	tourist trophy
RN	Royal Navy		TUC	Trades Union Congress
RNA	ribonucleic acid		TX	Texas
RNAS	Royal Naval Air Service		U-boat	*Unterseeboot*: submarine
RNR	Royal Naval Reserve		Ufa	Universum-Film AG
RNVR	Royal Naval Volunteer Reserve		UMIST	University of Manchester Institute of Science and Technology
RO	Record Office		UN	United Nations
r.p.m.	revolutions per minute		UNESCO	United Nations Educational, Scientific, and Cultural Organization
RRS	royal research ship		UNICEF	United Nations International Children's Emergency Fund
Rs	rupees		unpubd	unpublished
RSA	(1) Royal Scottish Academician; (2) Royal Society of Arts		USS	United States ship
RSPCA	Royal Society for the Prevention of Cruelty to Animals		UT	Utah
Rt Hon.	Right Honourable		*v*	verso
Rt Revd	Right Reverend		v.	versus
RUC	Royal Ulster Constabulary		VA	Virginia
Russ.	Russian		VAD	Voluntary Aid Detachment
RWS	Royal Watercolour Society		VC	Victoria Cross
S4C	Sianel Pedwar Cymru		VE-day	victory in Europe day
s.	shilling(s)		Ven.	Venerable
s.a.	*sub anno*: under the year		VJ-day	victory over Japan day
SABC	South African Broadcasting Corporation		vol. *pl.* vols.	volume(s)
SAS	Special Air Service		VT	Vermont
SC	South Carolina		WA	Washington [state]
ScD	doctor of science		WAAC	Women's Auxiliary Army Corps
S$	Singapore dollar		WAAF	Women's Auxiliary Air Force
SD	South Dakota		WEA	Workers' Educational Association
sec.	second(s)		WHO	World Health Organization
sel.	selected		WI	Wisconsin
sen.	senior		WRAF	Women's Royal Air Force
Sept	September		WRNS	Women's Royal Naval Service
ser.	series		WV	West Virginia
SHAPE	supreme headquarters allied powers, Europe		WVS	Women's Voluntary Service
SIDRO	Société Internationale d'Énergie Hydro-Électrique		WY	Wyoming
sig. *pl.* sigs.	signature(s)		¥	yen
sing.	singular		YMCA	Young Men's Christian Association
SIS	Secret Intelligence Service		YWCA	Young Women's Christian Association
SJ	Society of Jesus			

2 Institution abbreviations

All Souls Oxf.	All Souls College, Oxford	Garr. Club	Garrick Club, London
AM Oxf.	Ashmolean Museum, Oxford	Girton Cam.	Girton College, Cambridge
Balliol Oxf.	Balliol College, Oxford	GL	Guildhall Library, London
BBC WAC	BBC Written Archives Centre, Reading	Glos. RO	Gloucestershire Record Office, Gloucester
Beds. & Luton ARS	Bedfordshire and Luton Archives and Record Service, Bedford	Gon. & Caius Cam.	Gonville and Caius College, Cambridge
Berks. RO	Berkshire Record Office, Reading	Gov. Art Coll.	Government Art Collection
BFI	British Film Institute, London	GS Lond.	Geological Society of London
BFI NFTVA	British Film Institute, London, National Film and Television Archive	Hants. RO	Hampshire Record Office, Winchester
		Harris Man. Oxf.	Harris Manchester College, Oxford
BGS	British Geological Survey, Keyworth, Nottingham	Harvard TC	Harvard Theatre Collection, Harvard University, Cambridge, Massachusetts, Nathan Marsh Pusey Library
Birm. CA	Birmingham Central Library, Birmingham City Archives	Harvard U.	Harvard University, Cambridge, Massachusetts
Birm. CL	Birmingham Central Library	Harvard U., Houghton L.	Harvard University, Cambridge, Massachusetts, Houghton Library
BL	British Library, London	Herefs. RO	Herefordshire Record Office, Hereford
BL NSA	British Library, London, National Sound Archive	Herts. ALS	Hertfordshire Archives and Local Studies, Hertford
BL OIOC	British Library, London, Oriental and India Office Collections	Hist. Soc. Penn.	Historical Society of Pennsylvania, Philadelphia
BLPES	London School of Economics and Political Science, British Library of Political and Economic Science	HLRO	House of Lords Record Office, London
		Hult. Arch.	Hulton Archive, London and New York
		Hunt. L.	Huntington Library, San Marino, California
BM	British Museum, London	ICL	Imperial College, London
Bodl. Oxf.	Bodleian Library, Oxford	Inst. CE	Institution of Civil Engineers, London
Bodl. RH	Bodleian Library of Commonwealth and African Studies at Rhodes House, Oxford	Inst. EE	Institution of Electrical Engineers, London
		IWM	Imperial War Museum, London
Borth. Inst.	Borthwick Institute of Historical Research, University of York	IWM FVA	Imperial War Museum, London, Film and Video Archive
Boston PL	Boston Public Library, Massachusetts	IWM SA	Imperial War Museum, London, Sound Archive
Bristol RO	Bristol Record Office		
Bucks. RLSS	Buckinghamshire Records and Local Studies Service, Aylesbury	JRL	John Rylands University Library of Manchester
		King's AC Cam.	King's College Archives Centre, Cambridge
CAC Cam.	Churchill College, Cambridge, Churchill Archives Centre	King's Cam.	King's College, Cambridge
		King's Lond.	King's College, London
Cambs. AS	Cambridgeshire Archive Service	King's Lond., Liddell Hart C.	King's College, London, Liddell Hart Centre for Military Archives
CCC Cam.	Corpus Christi College, Cambridge		
CCC Oxf.	Corpus Christi College, Oxford	Lancs. RO	Lancashire Record Office, Preston
Ches. & Chester ALSS	Cheshire and Chester Archives and Local Studies Service	L. Cong.	Library of Congress, Washington, DC
		Leics. RO	Leicestershire, Leicester, and Rutland Record Office, Leicester
Christ Church Oxf.	Christ Church, Oxford		
Christies	Christies, London	Lincs. Arch.	Lincolnshire Archives, Lincoln
City Westm. AC	City of Westminster Archives Centre, London	Linn. Soc.	Linnean Society of London
CKS	Centre for Kentish Studies, Maidstone	LMA	London Metropolitan Archives
CLRO	Corporation of London Records Office	LPL	Lambeth Palace, London
Coll. Arms	College of Arms, London	Lpool RO	Liverpool Record Office and Local Studies Service
Col. U.	Columbia University, New York		
Cornwall RO	Cornwall Record Office, Truro	LUL	London University Library
Courtauld Inst.	Courtauld Institute of Art, London	Magd. Cam.	Magdalene College, Cambridge
CUL	Cambridge University Library	Magd. Oxf.	Magdalen College, Oxford
Cumbria AS	Cumbria Archive Service	Man. City Gall.	Manchester City Galleries
Derbys. RO	Derbyshire Record Office, Matlock	Man. CL	Manchester Central Library
Devon RO	Devon Record Office, Exeter	Mass. Hist. Soc.	Massachusetts Historical Society, Boston
Dorset RO	Dorset Record Office, Dorchester	Merton Oxf.	Merton College, Oxford
Duke U.	Duke University, Durham, North Carolina	MHS Oxf.	Museum of the History of Science, Oxford
Duke U., Perkins L.	Duke University, Durham, North Carolina, William R. Perkins Library	Mitchell L., Glas.	Mitchell Library, Glasgow
		Mitchell L., NSW	State Library of New South Wales, Sydney, Mitchell Library
Durham Cath. CL	Durham Cathedral, chapter library		
Durham RO	Durham Record Office	Morgan L.	Pierpont Morgan Library, New York
DWL	Dr Williams's Library, London	NA Canada	National Archives of Canada, Ottawa
Essex RO	Essex Record Office	NA Ire.	National Archives of Ireland, Dublin
E. Sussex RO	East Sussex Record Office, Lewes	NAM	National Army Museum, London
Eton	Eton College, Berkshire	NA Scot.	National Archives of Scotland, Edinburgh
FM Cam.	Fitzwilliam Museum, Cambridge	News Int. RO	News International Record Office, London
Folger	Folger Shakespeare Library, Washington, DC	NG Ire.	National Gallery of Ireland, Dublin

NG Scot.	National Gallery of Scotland, Edinburgh
NHM	Natural History Museum, London
NL Aus.	National Library of Australia, Canberra
NL Ire.	National Library of Ireland, Dublin
NL NZ	National Library of New Zealand, Wellington
NL NZ, Turnbull L.	National Library of New Zealand, Wellington, Alexander Turnbull Library
NL Scot.	National Library of Scotland, Edinburgh
NL Wales	National Library of Wales, Aberystwyth
NMG Wales	National Museum and Gallery of Wales, Cardiff
NMM	National Maritime Museum, London
Norfolk RO	Norfolk Record Office, Norwich
Northants. RO	Northamptonshire Record Office, Northampton
Northumbd RO	Northumberland Record Office
Notts. Arch.	Nottinghamshire Archives, Nottingham
NPG	National Portrait Gallery, London
NRA	National Archives, London, Historical Manuscripts Commission, National Register of Archives
Nuffield Oxf.	Nuffield College, Oxford
N. Yorks. CRO	North Yorkshire County Record Office, Northallerton
NYPL	New York Public Library
Oxf. UA	Oxford University Archives
Oxf. U. Mus. NH	Oxford University Museum of Natural History
Oxon. RO	Oxfordshire Record Office, Oxford
Pembroke Cam.	Pembroke College, Cambridge
PRO	National Archives, London, Public Record Office
PRO NIre.	Public Record Office for Northern Ireland, Belfast
Pusey Oxf.	Pusey House, Oxford
RA	Royal Academy of Arts, London
Ransom HRC	Harry Ransom Humanities Research Center, University of Texas, Austin
RAS	Royal Astronomical Society, London
RBG Kew	Royal Botanic Gardens, Kew, London
RCP Lond.	Royal College of Physicians of London
RCS Eng.	Royal College of Surgeons of England, London
RGS	Royal Geographical Society, London
RIBA	Royal Institute of British Architects, London
RIBA BAL	Royal Institute of British Architects, London, British Architectural Library
Royal Arch.	Royal Archives, Windsor Castle, Berkshire [by gracious permission of her majesty the queen]
Royal Irish Acad.	Royal Irish Academy, Dublin
Royal Scot. Acad.	Royal Scottish Academy, Edinburgh
RS	Royal Society, London
RSA	Royal Society of Arts, London
RS Friends, Lond.	Religious Society of Friends, London
St Ant. Oxf.	St Antony's College, Oxford
St John Cam.	St John's College, Cambridge
S. Antiquaries, Lond.	Society of Antiquaries of London
Sci. Mus.	Science Museum, London
Scot. NPG	Scottish National Portrait Gallery, Edinburgh
Scott Polar RI	University of Cambridge, Scott Polar Research Institute
Sheff. Arch.	Sheffield Archives
Shrops. RRC	Shropshire Records and Research Centre, Shrewsbury
SOAS	School of Oriental and African Studies, London
Som. ARS	Somerset Archive and Record Service, Taunton
Staffs. RO	Staffordshire Record Office, Stafford
Suffolk RO	Suffolk Record Office
Surrey HC	Surrey History Centre, Woking
TCD	Trinity College, Dublin
Trinity Cam.	Trinity College, Cambridge
U. Aberdeen	University of Aberdeen
U. Birm.	University of Birmingham
U. Birm. L.	University of Birmingham Library
U. Cal.	University of California
U. Cam.	University of Cambridge
UCL	University College, London
U. Durham	University of Durham
U. Durham L.	University of Durham Library
U. Edin.	University of Edinburgh
U. Edin., New Coll.	University of Edinburgh, New College
U. Edin., New Coll. L.	University of Edinburgh, New College Library
U. Edin. L.	University of Edinburgh Library
U. Glas.	University of Glasgow
U. Glas. L.	University of Glasgow Library
U. Hull	University of Hull
U. Hull, Brynmor Jones L.	University of Hull, Brynmor Jones Library
U. Leeds	University of Leeds
U. Leeds, Brotherton L.	University of Leeds, Brotherton Library
U. Lond.	University of London
U. Lpool	University of Liverpool
U. Lpool L.	University of Liverpool Library
U. Mich.	University of Michigan, Ann Arbor
U. Mich., Clements L.	University of Michigan, Ann Arbor, William L. Clements Library
U. Newcastle	University of Newcastle upon Tyne
U. Newcastle, Robinson L.	University of Newcastle upon Tyne, Robinson Library
U. Nott.	University of Nottingham
U. Nott. L.	University of Nottingham Library
U. Oxf.	University of Oxford
U. Reading	University of Reading
U. Reading L.	University of Reading Library
U. St Andr.	University of St Andrews
U. St Andr. L.	University of St Andrews Library
U. Southampton	University of Southampton
U. Southampton L.	University of Southampton Library
U. Sussex	University of Sussex, Brighton
U. Texas	University of Texas, Austin
U. Wales	University of Wales
U. Warwick Mod. RC	University of Warwick, Coventry, Modern Records Centre
V&A	Victoria and Albert Museum, London
V&A NAL	Victoria and Albert Museum, London, National Art Library
Warks. CRO	Warwickshire County Record Office, Warwick
Wellcome L.	Wellcome Library for the History and Understanding of Medicine, London
Westm. DA	Westminster Diocesan Archives, London
Wilts. & Swindon RO	Wiltshire and Swindon Record Office, Trowbridge
Worcs. RO	Worcestershire Record Office, Worcester
W. Sussex RO	West Sussex Record Office, Chichester
W. Yorks. AS	West Yorkshire Archive Service
Yale U.	Yale University, New Haven, Connecticut
Yale U., Beinecke L.	Yale University, New Haven, Connecticut, Beinecke Rare Book and Manuscript Library
Yale U. CBA	Yale University, New Haven, Connecticut, Yale Center for British Art

3 Bibliographic abbreviations

Adams, *Drama* — W. D. Adams, *A dictionary of the drama*, 1: *A–G* (1904); 2: *H–Z* (1956) [vol. 2 microfilm only]

AFM — J O'Donovan, ed. and trans., *Annala rioghachta Eireann | Annals of the kingdom of Ireland by the four masters*, 7 vols. (1848–51); 2nd edn (1856); 3rd edn (1990)

Allibone, *Dict.* — S. A. Allibone, *A critical dictionary of English literature and British and American authors*, 3 vols. (1859–71); suppl. by J. F. Kirk, 2 vols. (1891)

ANB — J. A. Garraty and M. C. Carnes, eds., *American national biography*, 24 vols. (1999)

Anderson, *Scot. nat.* — W. Anderson, *The Scottish nation, or, The surnames, families, literature, honours, and biographical history of the people of Scotland*, 3 vols. (1859–63)

Ann. mon. — H. R. Luard, ed., *Annales monastici*, 5 vols., Rolls Series, 36 (1864–9)

Ann. Ulster — S. Mac Airt and G. Mac Niocaill, eds., *Annals of Ulster (to AD 1131)* (1983)

APC — *Acts of the privy council of England*, new ser., 46 vols. (1890–1964)

APS — *The acts of the parliaments of Scotland*, 12 vols. in 13 (1814–75)

Arber, *Regs. Stationers* — F. Arber, ed., *A transcript of the registers of the Company of Stationers of London, 1554–1640 AD*, 5 vols. (1875–94)

ArchR — *Architectural Review*

ASC — D. Whitelock, D. C. Douglas, and S. I. Tucker, ed. and trans., *The Anglo-Saxon Chronicle: a revised translation* (1961)

AS chart. — P. H. Sawyer, *Anglo-Saxon charters: an annotated list and bibliography*, Royal Historical Society Guides and Handbooks (1968)

AusDB — D. Pike and others, eds., *Australian dictionary of biography*, 16 vols. (1966–2002)

Baker, *Serjeants* — J. H. Baker, *The order of serjeants at law*, SeldS, suppl. ser., 5 (1984)

Bale, *Cat.* — J. Bale, *Scriptorum illustrium Maioris Brytannie, quam nunc Angliam et Scotiam vocant: catalogus*, 2 vols. in 1 (Basel, 1557–9); facs. edn (1971)

Bale, *Index* — J. Bale, *Index Britanniae scriptorum*, ed. R. L. Poole and M. Bateson (1902); facs. edn (1990)

BBCS — *Bulletin of the Board of Celtic Studies*

BDMBR — J. O. Baylen and N. J. Gossman, eds., *Biographical dictionary of modern British radicals*, 3 vols. in 4 (1979–88)

Bede, *Hist. eccl.* — *Bede's Ecclesiastical history of the English people*, ed. and trans. B. Colgrave and R. A. B. Mynors, OMT (1969); repr. (1991)

Bénézit, *Dict.* — E. Bénézit, *Dictionnaire critique et documentaire des peintres, sculpteurs, dessinateurs et graveurs*, 3 vols. (Paris, 1911–23); new edn, 8 vols. (1948–66), repr. (1966); 3rd edn, rev. and enl., 10 vols. (1976); 4th edn, 14 vols. (1999)

BIHR — *Bulletin of the Institute of Historical Research*

Birch, *Seals* — W. de Birch, *Catalogue of seals in the department of manuscripts in the British Museum*, 6 vols. (1887–1900)

Bishop Burnet's History — *Bishop Burnet's History of his own time*, ed. M. J. Routh, 2nd edn, 6 vols. (1833)

Blackwood — *Blackwood's [Edinburgh] Magazine*, 328 vols. (1817–1980)

Blain, Clements & Grundy, *Feminist comp.* — V. Blain, P. Clements, and I. Grundy, eds., *The feminist companion to literature in English* (1990)

BL cat. — *The British Library general catalogue of printed books* [in 360 vols. with suppls., also CD-ROM and online]

BMJ — *British Medical Journal*

Boase & Courtney, *Bibl. Corn.* — G. C. Boase and W. P. Courtney, *Bibliotheca Cornubiensis: a catalogue of the writings … of Cornishmen*, 3 vols. (1874–82)

Boase, *Mod. Eng. biog.* — F. Boase, *Modern English biography: containing many thousand concise memoirs of persons who have died since the year 1850*, 6 vols. (privately printed, Truro, 1892–1921); repr. (1965)

Boswell, *Life* — *Boswell's Life of Johnson: together with Journal of a tour to the Hebrides and Johnson's Diary of a journey into north Wales*, ed. G. B. Hill, enl. edn, rev. L. F. Powell, 6 vols. (1934–50); 2nd edn (1964); repr. (1971)

Brown & Stratton, *Brit. mus.* — J. D. Brown and S. S. Stratton, *British musical biography* (1897)

Bryan, *Painters* — M. Bryan, *A biographical and critical dictionary of painters and engravers*, 2 vols. (1816); new edn, ed. G. Stanley (1849); new edn, ed. R. E. Graves and W. Armstrong, 2 vols. (1886–9); [4th edn], ed. G. C. Williamson, 5 vols. (1903–5) [various reprs.]

Burke, *Gen. GB* — J. Burke, *A genealogical and heraldic history of the commoners of Great Britain and Ireland*, 4 vols. (1833–8); new edn as *A genealogical and heraldic dictionary of the landed gentry of Great Britain and Ireland*, 3 vols. [1843–9] [many later edns]

Burke, *Gen. Ire.* — J. B. Burke, *A genealogical and heraldic history of the landed gentry of Ireland* (1899); 2nd edn (1904); 3rd edn (1912); 4th edn (1958); 5th edn as *Burke's Irish family records* (1976)

Burke, *Peerage* — J. Burke, *A general [later edns A genealogical] and heraldic dictionary of the peerage and baronetage of the United Kingdom* [later edns *the British empire*] (1829–)

Burney, *Hist. mus.* — C. Burney, *A general history of music, from the earliest ages to the present period*, 4 vols. (1776–89)

Burtchaell & Sadleir, *Alum. Dubl.* — G. D. Burtchaell and T. U. Sadleir, *Alumni Dublinenses: a register of the students, graduates, and provosts of Trinity College* (1924); [2nd edn], with suppl., in 2 pts (1935)

Calamy rev. — A. G. Matthews, *Calamy revised* (1934); repr. (1988)

CCI — *Calendar of confirmations and inventories granted and given up in the several commissariots of Scotland* (1876–)

CCIR — *Calendar of the close rolls preserved in the Public Record Office*, 47 vols. (1892–1963)

CDS — J. Bain, ed., *Calendar of documents relating to Scotland*, 4 vols., PRO (1881–8); suppl. vol. 5, ed. G. G. Simpson and J. D. Galbraith [1986]

CEPR letters — W. H. Bliss, C. Johnson, and J. Twemlow, eds., *Calendar of entries in the papal registers relating to Great Britain and Ireland: papal letters* (1893–)

CGPLA — *Calendars of the grants of probate and letters of administration* [in 4 ser.: England & Wales, Northern Ireland, Ireland, and Éire]

Chambers, *Scots.* — R. Chambers, ed., *A biographical dictionary of eminent Scotsmen*, 4 vols. (1832–5)

Chancery records — chancery records pubd by the PRO

Chancery records (RC) — chancery records pubd by the Record Commissions

CIPM	*Calendar of inquisitions post mortem*, [20 vols.], PRO (1904–); also *Henry VII*, 3 vols. (1898–1955)
Clarendon, *Hist. rebellion*	E. Hyde, earl of Clarendon, *The history of the rebellion and civil wars in England*, 6 vols. (1888); repr. (1958) and (1992)
Cobbett, *Parl. hist.*	W. Cobbett and J. Wright, eds., *Cobbett's Parliamentary history of England*, 36 vols. (1806–1820)
Colvin, *Archs.*	H. Colvin, *A biographical dictionary of British architects, 1600–1840*, 3rd edn (1995)
Cooper, *Ath. Cantab.*	C. H. Cooper and T. Cooper, *Athenae Cantabrigienses*, 3 vols. (1858–1913); repr. (1967)
CPR	*Calendar of the patent rolls preserved in the Public Record Office* (1891–)
Crockford	*Crockford's Clerical Directory*
CS	Camden Society
CSP	*Calendar of state papers* [in 11 ser.: domestic, Scotland, Scottish series, Ireland, colonial, Commonwealth, foreign, Spain [at Simancas], Rome, Milan, and Venice]
CYS	Canterbury and York Society
DAB	*Dictionary of American biography*, 21 vols. (1928–36), repr. in 11 vols. (1964); 10 suppls. (1944–96)
DBB	D. J. Jeremy, ed., *Dictionary of business biography*, 5 vols. (1984–6)
DCB	G. W. Brown and others, *Dictionary of Canadian biography*, [14 vols.] (1966–)
Debrett's Peerage	*Debrett's Peerage* (1803–) [sometimes *Debrett's Illustrated peerage*]
Desmond, *Botanists*	R. Desmond, *Dictionary of British and Irish botanists and horticulturists* (1977); rev. edn (1994)
Dir. Brit. archs.	A. Felstead, J. Franklin, and L. Pinfield, eds., *Directory of British architects, 1834–1900* (1993); 2nd edn, ed. A. Brodie and others, 2 vols. (2001)
DLB	J. M. Bellamy and J. Saville, eds., *Dictionary of labour biography*, [10 vols.] (1972–)
DLitB	Dictionary of Literary Biography
DNB	*Dictionary of national biography*, 63 vols. (1885–1900), suppl., 3 vols. (1901); repr. in 22 vols. (1908–9); 10 further suppls. (1912–96); *Missing persons* (1993)
DNZB	W. H. Oliver and C. Orange, eds., *The dictionary of New Zealand biography*, 5 vols. (1990–2000)
DSAB	W. J. de Kock and others, eds., *Dictionary of South African biography*, 5 vols. (1968–87)
DSB	C. C. Gillispie and F. L. Holmes, eds., *Dictionary of scientific biography*, 16 vols. (1970–80); repr. in 8 vols. (1981); 2 vol. suppl. (1990)
DSBB	A. Slaven and S. Checkland, eds., *Dictionary of Scottish business biography, 1860–1960*, 2 vols. (1986–90)
DSCHT	N. M. de S. Cameron and others, eds., *Dictionary of Scottish church history and theology* (1993)
Dugdale, *Monasticon*	W. Dugdale, *Monasticon Anglicanum*, 3 vols. (1655–72); 2nd edn, 3 vols. (1661–82); new edn, ed. J. Caley, J. Ellis, and B. Bandinel, 6 vols. in 8 pts (1817–30); repr. (1846) and (1970)
DWB	J. E. Lloyd and others, eds., *Dictionary of Welsh biography down to 1940* (1959) [Eng. trans. of *Y bywgraffiadur Cymreig hyd 1940*, 2nd edn (1954)]
EdinR	*Edinburgh Review, or, Critical Journal*
EETS	Early English Text Society
Emden, *Cam.*	A. B. Emden, *A biographical register of the University of Cambridge to 1500* (1963)
Emden, *Oxf.*	A. B. Emden, *A biographical register of the University of Oxford to AD 1500*, 3 vols. (1957–9); also *A biographical register of the University of Oxford, AD 1501 to 1540* (1974)
EngHR	*English Historical Review*
Engraved Brit. ports.	F. M. O'Donoghue and H. M. Hake, *Catalogue of engraved British portraits preserved in the department of prints and drawings in the British Museum*, 6 vols. (1908–25)
ER	The English Reports, 178 vols. (1900–32)
ESTC	*English short title catalogue, 1475–1800* [CD-ROM and online]
Evelyn, *Diary*	*The diary of John Evelyn*, ed. E. S. De Beer, 6 vols. (1955); repr. (2000)
Farington, *Diary*	*The diary of Joseph Farington*, ed. K. Garlick and others, 17 vols. (1978–98)
Fasti Angl. (Hardy)	J. Le Neve, *Fasti ecclesiae Anglicanae*, ed. T. D. Hardy, 3 vols. (1854)
Fasti Angl., 1066–1300	[J. Le Neve], *Fasti ecclesiae Anglicanae, 1066–1300*, ed. D. E. Greenway and J. S. Barrow, [8 vols.] (1968–)
Fasti Angl., 1300–1541	[J. Le Neve], *Fasti ecclesiae Anglicanae, 1300–1541*, 12 vols. (1962–7)
Fasti Angl., 1541–1857	[J. Le Neve], *Fasti ecclesiae Anglicanae, 1541–1857*, ed. J. M. Horn, D. M. Smith, and D. S. Bailey, [9 vols.] (1969–)
Fasti Scot.	H. Scott, *Fasti ecclesiae Scoticanae*, 3 vols. in 6 (1871); new edn, [11 vols.] (1915–)
FO List	*Foreign Office List*
Fortescue, *Brit. army*	J. W. Fortescue, *A history of the British army*, 13 vols. (1899–1930)
Foss, *Judges*	E. Foss, *The judges of England*, 9 vols. (1848–64); repr. (1966)
Foster, *Alum. Oxon.*	J. Foster, ed., *Alumni Oxonienses: the members of the University of Oxford, 1715–1886*, 4 vols. (1887–8); later edn (1891); also *Alumni Oxonienses … 1500–1714*, 4 vols. (1891–2); 8 vol. repr. (1968) and (2000)
Fuller, *Worthies*	T. Fuller, *The history of the worthies of England*, 4 pts (1662); new edn, 2 vols., ed. J. Nichols (1811); new edn, 3 vols., ed. P. A. Nuttall (1840); repr. (1965)
GEC, *Baronetage*	G. E. Cokayne, *Complete baronetage*, 6 vols. (1900–09); repr. (1983) [microprint]
GEC, *Peerage*	G. E. C. [G. E. Cokayne], *The complete peerage of England, Scotland, Ireland, Great Britain, and the United Kingdom*, 8 vols. (1887–98); new edn, ed. V. Gibbs and others, 14 vols. in 15 (1910–98); microprint repr. (1982) and (1987)
Genest, *Eng. stage*	J. Genest, *Some account of the English stage from the Restoration in 1660 to 1830*, 10 vols. (1832); repr. [New York, 1965]
Gillow, *Lit. biog. hist.*	J. Gillow, *A literary and biographical history or bibliographical dictionary of the English Catholics, from the breach with Rome, in 1534, to the present time*, 5 vols. [1885–1902]; repr. (1961); repr. with preface by C. Gillow (1999)
Gir. Camb. opera	*Giraldi Cambrensis opera*, ed. J. S. Brewer, J. F. Dimock, and G. F. Warner, 8 vols., Rolls Series, 21 (1861–91)
GJ	*Geographical Journal*

Gladstone, *Diaries*	*The Gladstone diaries: with cabinet minutes and prime-ministerial correspondence*, ed. M. R. D. Foot and H. C. G. Matthew, 14 vols. (1968–94)
GM	*Gentleman's Magazine*
Graves, *Artists*	A. Graves, ed., *A dictionary of artists who have exhibited works in the principal London exhibitions of oil paintings from 1760 to 1880* (1884); new edn (1895); 3rd edn (1901); facs. edn (1969); repr. [1970], (1973), and (1984)
Graves, *Brit. Inst.*	A. Graves, *The British Institution, 1806–1867: a complete dictionary of contributors and their work from the foundation of the institution* (1875); facs. edn (1908); repr. (1969)
Graves, *RA exhibitors*	A. Graves, *The Royal Academy of Arts: a complete dictionary of contributors and their work from its foundation in 1769 to 1904*, 8 vols. (1905–6); repr. in 4 vols. (1970) and (1972)
Graves, *Soc. Artists*	A. Graves, *The Society of Artists of Great Britain, 1760–1791, the Free Society of Artists, 1761–1783: a complete dictionary* (1907); facs. edn (1969)
Greaves & Zaller, *BDBR*	R. L. Greaves and R. Zaller, eds., *Biographical dictionary of British radicals in the seventeenth century*, 3 vols. (1982–4)
Grove, *Dict. mus.*	G. Grove, ed., *A dictionary of music and musicians*, 5 vols. (1878–90); 2nd edn, ed. J. A. Fuller Maitland (1904–10); 3rd edn, ed. H. C. Colles (1927); 4th edn with suppl. (1940); 5th edn, ed. E. Blom, 9 vols. (1954); suppl. (1961) [see also *New Grove*]
Hall, *Dramatic ports.*	L. A. Hall, *Catalogue of dramatic portraits in the theatre collection of the Harvard College library*, 4 vols. (1930–34)
Hansard	*Hansard's parliamentary debates*, ser. 1–5 (1803–)
Highfill, Burnim & Langhans, *BDA*	P. H. Highfill, K. A. Burnim, and E. A. Langhans, *A biographical dictionary of actors, actresses, musicians, dancers, managers, and other stage personnel in London, 1660–1800*, 16 vols. (1973–93)
Hist. U. Oxf.	T. H. Aston, ed., *The history of the University of Oxford*, 8 vols. (1984–2000) [1: *The early Oxford schools*, ed. J. I. Catto (1984); 2: *Late medieval Oxford*, ed. J. I. Catto and R. Evans (1992); 3: *The collegiate university*, ed. J. McConica (1986); 4: *Seventeenth-century Oxford*, ed. N. Tyacke (1997); 5: *The eighteenth century*, ed. L. S. Sutherland and L. G. Mitchell (1986); 6–7: *Nineteenth-century Oxford*, ed. M. G. Brock and M. C. Curthoys (1997–2000); 8: *The twentieth century*, ed. B. Harrison (2000)]
HJ	*Historical Journal*
HMC	Historical Manuscripts Commission
Holdsworth, *Eng. law*	W. S. Holdsworth, *A history of English law*, ed. A. L. Goodhart and H. L. Hanbury, 17 vols. (1903–72)
HoP, *Commons*	*The history of parliament: the House of Commons* [*1386–1421*, ed. J. S. Roskell, L. Clark, and C. Rawcliffe, 4 vols. (1992); *1509–1558*, ed. S. T. Bindoff, 3 vols. (1982); *1558–1603*, ed. P. W. Hasler, 3 vols. (1981); *1660–1690*, ed. B. D. Henning, 3 vols. (1983); *1690–1715*, ed. D. W. Hayton, E. Cruickshanks, and S. Handley, 5 vols. (2002); *1715–1754*, ed. R. Sedgwick, 2 vols. (1970); *1754–1790*, ed. L. Namier and J. Brooke, 3 vols. (1964), repr. (1985); *1790–1820*, ed. R. G. Thorne, 5 vols. (1986); in draft (used with permission): *1422–1504, 1604–1629, 1640–1660*, and *1820–1832*]
IGI	*International Genealogical Index*, Church of Jesus Christ of the Latterday Saints
ILN	*Illustrated London News*
IMC	Irish Manuscripts Commission
Irving, *Scots.*	J. Irving, ed., *The book of Scotsmen eminent for achievements in arms and arts, church and state, law, legislation and literature, commerce, science, travel and philanthropy* (1881)
JCS	*Journal of the Chemical Society*
JHC	*Journals of the House of Commons*
JHL	*Journals of the House of Lords*
John of Worcester, *Chron.*	*The chronicle of John of Worcester*, ed. R. R. Darlington and P. McGurk, trans. J. Bray and P. McGurk, 3 vols., OMT (1995–) [vol. 1 forthcoming]
Keeler, *Long Parliament*	M. F. Keeler, *The Long Parliament, 1640–1641: a biographical study of its members* (1954)
Kelly, *Handbk*	*The upper ten thousand: an alphabetical list of all members of noble families*, 3 vols. (1875–7); continued as *Kelly's handbook of the upper ten thousand for 1878* [1879], 2 vols. (1878–9); continued as *Kelly's handbook to the titled, landed and official classes*, 94 vols. (1880–1973)
LondG	*London Gazette*
LP Henry VIII	J. S. Brewer, J. Gairdner, and R. H. Brodie, eds., *Letters and papers, foreign and domestic, of the reign of Henry VIII*, 23 vols. in 38 (1862–1932); repr. (1965)
Mallalieu, *Watercolour artists*	H. L. Mallalieu, *The dictionary of British watercolour artists up to 1820*, 3 vols. (1976–90); vol. 1, 2nd edn (1986)
Memoirs FRS	*Biographical Memoirs of Fellows of the Royal Society*
MGH	Monumenta Germaniae Historica
MT	*Musical Times*
Munk, *Roll*	W. Munk, *The roll of the Royal College of Physicians of London*, 2 vols. (1861); 2nd edn, 3 vols. (1878)
N&Q	*Notes and Queries*
New Grove	S. Sadie, ed., *The new Grove dictionary of music and musicians*, 20 vols. (1980); 2nd edn, 29 vols. (2001) [also online edn; see also Grove, *Dict. mus.*]
Nichols, *Illustrations*	J. Nichols and J. B. Nichols, *Illustrations of the literary history of the eighteenth century*, 8 vols. (1817–58)
Nichols, *Lit. anecdotes*	J. Nichols, *Literary anecdotes of the eighteenth century*, 9 vols. (1812–16); facs. edn (1966)
Obits. FRS	*Obituary Notices of Fellows of the Royal Society*
O'Byrne, *Naval biog. dict.*	W. R. O'Byrne, *A naval biographical dictionary* (1849); repr. (1990); [2nd edn], 2 vols. (1861)
OHS	Oxford Historical Society
Old Westminsters	*The record of Old Westminsters*, 1–2, ed. G. F. R. Barker and A. H. Stenning (1928); suppl. 1, ed. J. B. Whitmore and G. R. Y. Radcliffe [1938]; 3, ed. J. B. Whitmore, G. R. Y. Radcliffe, and D. C. Simpson (1963); suppl. 2, ed. F. E. Pagan (1978); 4, ed. F. E. Pagan and H. E. Pagan (1992)
OMT	Oxford Medieval Texts
Ordericus Vitalis, *Eccl. hist.*	*The ecclesiastical history of Orderic Vitalis*, ed. and trans. M. Chibnall, 6 vols., OMT (1969–80); repr. (1990)
Paris, *Chron.*	*Matthaei Parisiensis, monachi sancti Albani, chronica majora*, ed. H. R. Luard, Rolls Series, 7 vols. (1872–83)
Parl. papers	*Parliamentary papers* (1801–)
PBA	*Proceedings of the British Academy*

Pepys, *Diary* — *The diary of Samuel Pepys*, ed. R. Latham and W. Matthews, 11 vols. (1970–83); repr. (1995) and (2000)

Pevsner — N. Pevsner and others, Buildings of England series

PICE — *Proceedings of the Institution of Civil Engineers*

Pipe rolls — *The great roll of the pipe for . . .*, PRSoc. (1884–)

PRO — Public Record Office

PRS — *Proceedings of the Royal Society of London*

PRSoc. — Pipe Roll Society

PTRS — *Philosophical Transactions of the Royal Society*

QR — *Quarterly Review*

RC — Record Commissions

Redgrave, *Artists* — S. Redgrave, *A dictionary of artists of the English school* (1874); rev. edn (1878); repr. (1970)

Reg. Oxf. — C. W. Boase and A. Clark, eds., *Register of the University of Oxford*, 5 vols., OHS, 1, 10–12, 14 (1885–9)

Reg. PCS — J. H. Burton and others, eds., *The register of the privy council of Scotland*, 1st ser., 14 vols. (1877–98); 2nd ser., 8 vols. (1899–1908); 3rd ser., [16 vols.] (1908–70)

Reg. RAN — H. W. C. Davis and others, eds., *Regesta regum Anglo-Normannorum, 1066–1154*, 4 vols. (1913–69)

RIBA Journal — *Journal of the Royal Institute of British Architects* [later *RIBA Journal*]

RotP — J. Strachey, ed., *Rotuli parliamentorum ut et petitiones, et placita in parliamento*, 6 vols. (1767–77)

RotS — D. Macpherson, J. Caley, and W. Illingworth, eds., *Rotuli Scotiae in Turri Londinensi et in domo capitulari Westmonasteriensi asservati*, 2 vols., RC, 14 (1814–19)

RS — Record(s) Society

Rymer, *Foedera* — T. Rymer and R. Sanderson, eds., *Foedera, conventiones, literae et cuiuscunque generis acta publica inter reges Angliae et alios quosvis imperatores, reges, pontifices, principes, vel communitates*, 20 vols. (1704–35); 2nd edn, 20 vols. (1726–35); 3rd edn, 10 vols. (1739–45); facs. edn (1967); new edn, ed. A. Clarke, J. Caley, and F. Holbrooke, 4 vols., RC, 50 (1816–30)

Sainty, *Judges* — J. Sainty, ed., *The judges of England, 1272–1990*, SeldS, suppl. ser., 10 (1993)

Sainty, *King's counsel* — J. Sainty, ed., *A list of English law officers and king's counsel*, SeldS, suppl. ser., 7 (1987)

SCH — Studies in Church History

Scots peerage — J. B. Paul, ed. *The Scots peerage, founded on Wood's edition of Sir Robert Douglas's Peerage of Scotland, containing an historical and genealogical account of the nobility of that kingdom*, 9 vols. (1904–14)

SeldS — Selden Society

SHR — *Scottish Historical Review*

State trials — T. B. Howell and T. J. Howell, eds., *Cobbett's Complete collection of state trials*, 34 vols. (1809–28)

STC, 1475–1640 — A. W. Pollard, G. R. Redgrave, and others, eds., *A short-title catalogue of . . . English books . . . 1475–1640* (1926); 2nd edn, ed. W. A. Jackson, F. S. Ferguson, and K. F. Pantzer, 3 vols. (1976–91) [see also Wing, *STC*]

STS — Scottish Text Society

SurtS — Surtees Society

Symeon of Durham, *Opera* — *Symeonis monachi opera omnia*, ed. T. Arnold, 2 vols., Rolls Series, 75 (1882–5); repr. (1965)

Tanner, *Bibl. Brit.-Hib.* — T. Tanner, *Bibliotheca Britannico-Hibernica*, ed. D. Wilkins (1748); repr. (1963)

Thieme & Becker, *Allgemeines Lexikon* — U. Thieme, F. Becker, and H. Vollmer, eds., *Allgemeines Lexikon der bildenden Künstler von der Antike bis zur Gegenwart*, 37 vols. (Leipzig, 1907–50); repr. (1961–5), (1983), and (1992)

Thurloe, *State papers* — *A collection of the state papers of John Thurloe*, ed. T. Birch, 7 vols. (1742)

TLS — *Times Literary Supplement*

Tout, *Admin. hist.* — T. F. Tout, *Chapters in the administrative history of mediaeval England: the wardrobe, the chamber, and the small seals*, 6 vols. (1920–33); repr. (1967)

TRHS — *Transactions of the Royal Historical Society*

VCH — H. A. Doubleday and others, eds., *The Victoria history of the counties of England*, [88 vols.] (1900–)

Venn, *Alum. Cant.* — J. Venn and J. A. Venn, *Alumni Cantabrigienses: a biographical list of all known students, graduates, and holders of office at the University of Cambridge, from the earliest times to 1900*, 10 vols. (1922–54); repr. in 2 vols. (1974–8)

Vertue, *Note books* — [G. Vertue], *Note books*, ed. K. Esdaile, earl of Ilchester, and H. M. Hake, 6 vols., Walpole Society, 18, 20, 22, 24, 26, 30 (1930–55)

VF — *Vanity Fair*

Walford, *County families* — E. Walford, *The county families of the United Kingdom, or, Royal manual of the titled and untitled aristocracy of Great Britain and Ireland* (1860)

Walker rev. — A. G. Matthews, *Walker revised: being a revision of John Walker's Sufferings of the clergy during the grand rebellion, 1642–60* (1948); repr. (1988)

Walpole, *Corr.* — *The Yale edition of Horace Walpole's correspondence*, ed. W. S. Lewis, 48 vols. (1937–83)

Ward, *Men of the reign* — T. H. Ward, ed., *Men of the reign: a biographical dictionary of eminent persons of British and colonial birth who have died during the reign of Queen Victoria* (1885); repr. (Graz, 1968)

Waterhouse, *18c painters* — E. Waterhouse, *The dictionary of 18th century painters in oils and crayons* (1981); repr. as *British 18th century painters in oils and crayons* (1991), vol. 2 of *Dictionary of British art*

Watt, *Bibl. Brit.* — R. Watt, *Bibliotheca Britannica, or, A general index to British and foreign literature*, 4 vols. (1824) [many reprs.]

Wellesley index — W. E. Houghton, ed., *The Wellesley index to Victorian periodicals, 1824–1900*, 5 vols. (1966–89); new edn (1999) [CD-ROM]

Wing, *STC* — D. Wing, ed., *Short-title catalogue of . . . English books . . . 1641–1700*, 3 vols. (1945–51); 2nd edn (1972–88); rev. and enl. edn, ed. J. J. Morrison, C. W. Nelson, and M. Seccombe, 4 vols. (1994–8) [see also *STC, 1475–1640*]

Wisden — *John Wisden's Cricketer's Almanack*

Wood, *Ath. Oxon.* — A. Wood, *Athenae Oxonienses . . . to which are added the Fasti*, 2 vols. (1691–2); 2nd edn (1721); new edn, 4 vols., ed. P. Bliss (1813–20); repr. (1967) and (1969)

Wood, *Vic. painters* — C. Wood, *Dictionary of Victorian painters* (1971); 2nd edn (1978); 3rd edn as *Victorian painters*, 2 vols. (1995), vol. 4 of *Dictionary of British art*

WW — *Who's who* (1849–)

WWBMP — M. Stenton and S. Lees, eds., *Who's who of British members of parliament*, 4 vols. (1976–81)

WWW — *Who was who* (1929–)

Hickeringill, Edmund (*bap.* **1631**, *d.* **1708**), Church of England clergyman and religious controversialist, was born in Aberford (near Leeds) where he was baptized on 19 September 1631. His father, Edmund Hickhorngill, the subject of a public proclamation in 1638 for absenting himself from church, was a recusant and the favoured servant of the papist Sir John Gascoigne. After attending Pocklington School, Yorkshire, on 17 June 1647 Hickeringill was admitted as pensioner to St John's College, Cambridge, where some of the principles he would later display were, perhaps, instilled by his tutor Zachary Cawdrey. After the Restoration Cawdrey, although a conforming and beneficed Anglican minister, was nevertheless considered 'guilty of sinfull popularity and coaxing the Dissenters Party' in Chester, and produced a discourse on conformity to the established church, 'on principles granted by the Non-Conformists' (Bodl. Oxf., MS Tanner 34, fols. 26–7). Hickeringill graduated BA in 1651 and on Lady day was intruded as junior fellow into Gonville and Caius College by the parliamentary committee for regulating the universities—probably at the instigation of his tutor. Despite a mission to London by the master, William Dell, 'to reverse if possible the Orders' (C. Brooke, *History of Caius College*, 1985, 133), Hickeringill proceeded MA in midsummer 1652. On 24 August, having undertaken adult baptism, he was admitted to the communion of Thomas Tillam's newly founded Baptist congregation at Hexham in Northumberland, and on 20 December the church 'ordained brother Hickhorngill a minister, and their messenger in Scotland' (Underhill, 251). He arrived at Dalkeith on 30 December whence, having been handed over by General Monck to be chaplain in Robert Lilburne's regiment of horse, on 8 January 1653 he began a series of letters to the Hexham congregation relating his progress.

Apostasy to ordination, 1653–1664 Hickeringill soon perceived that to elements within the rank and file his position as chaplain was a 'chief stumbling-block' from the way of God, and desired of Lilburne some other employment 'whereby I might live without making the gospel burdensome' (Underhill, 308). In March 1653 he joined a Baptist congregation at Leith, but by May his religious opinions were in turmoil: he became a Quaker and went missing. He returned to Dalkeith on 12 July 'in a swaggering garb', declaring that his devotion was worn threadbare, and that he had 'left his religion in England' (Underhill, 330). The Hexham congregation excommunicated their 'alas! deluded' messenger, but it was reported that Hickeringill—a 'desperate atheist'—cared 'not a fig' for this sentence (ibid., 328, 330, 331). 'Full of joy in his God', he propounded 'no other rule to himself but his reason' (ibid., 331). Despite resuming his chaplaincy, he nevertheless omitted from his duties any sacerdotal functions, so that he 'would neither pray nor preach, otherwise than by common discourse', and was granted instead a military commission as lieutenant to Captain Gascoigne in Colonel Daniell's regiment (Underhill, 331). Although his links with the Baptists were apparently severed, his religious mission did not end here. In Gelsland, Hickeringill was one of a number of 'Military Independent Officers',

Edmund Hickeringill (*bap.* 1631, *d.* 1708), by Joseph Nutting, pubd 1707 (after James Jull)

men of 'more Witt and Ingenuity then solidity and serious Religion', who 'in their Buff-Coats and Armour' preached in vacant cures around Carlisle. A hostile account of their ministry, noting their capacity for sowing schism, commented that they 'talked to the people what they saw fitt' (Nightingale, 1.376).

By his own account Hickeringill remained four years in Scotland, where he was 'governor and deputy governor' of Finlarig and Meikleour castles, Perthshire, and was 'one of the first and last justices of the peace that ever were in Scotland' (Hickeringill, *Works*, 3.29). Entering next into foreign service, he accepted a commission as captain under Major-General Fleetwood, then ambassador to Sweden. He departed Hull for Hamburg with a company of 125 mercenaries, was made governor of Buckstaho, a Swedish garrison in Bremen, and was present at the siege of Elsinor. He sailed to Spain and Portugal, was active throughout the West Indies, and made a stay in Jamaica (*Letters to Thoresby*, 2.10–12). Prompted to return to England at the Restoration, Hickeringill curried favour by drafting and publishing in 1661 an account of Jamaica dedicated to Charles II. In reward Charles made him secretary of state for Jamaica under Baron Windsor 'then going governour', a post worth £1000 a year. Awaiting departure for the Caribbean, however, Hickeringill performed an enigmatic volte-face: why he 'left the Secretaries place (so very profitable and honourable) to be a Divine, I do not know', puzzled his editor (E. Hickeringill, *Jamaica Viewed*, 1705, preface). He was 'persuaded into orders' by Robert Sanderson, bishop of Lincoln, nicknamed (Hickeringill claimed) the 'presbyterian bishop' (Hickeringill, *Works*, 2.379). Sanderson and Gilbert Sheldon, the bishop of London, apparently considered him particularly suited, in the wake of the St Bartholomew's day ejections, to minister to the burgeoning nonconformity in Colchester, Essex (*Letters to Thoresby*, 2.15). Following brief preferment as vicar of St Peter's there, Hickeringill was instituted on 21 October 1662 to the neighbouring rectory of All Saints, which he would hold until his death, and on 22 October to the vicarage of Boxted, 10 miles to the north. He settled in nearby Wickes and married; his wife's name was Mary, and they had four daughters and two sons, Thomas and Matthias.

Conduct as a minister Following his ordination Hickeringill swiftly signalled his loyalty to the royal supremacy but also his dissidence from episcopal authority. In a sermon on 30 January 1662 he likened the royal martyr to the biblical figure of Naboth, an innocent vintner stoned to death for blasphemy. Yet at the same time in Boxted he began a habit of adapting Church of England ceremonial to his own standards. In 1664 he was prosecuted in the court of arches by a number of the village's dissenting (probably Quaker) parishioners for omitting to recite the Thirty-Nine Articles before his congregation in the words and manner stipulated by the Act of Uniformity. Reciting the articles before his congregation, Hickeringill had interjected into the ceremony a list of heterodox beliefs which contradicted the established articles, so as to underscore the divisiveness of the church's liturgy. The irony of nonconformist parishioners' stipulating precise adherence to the Anglican rubric is a symptom of Hickeringill's equivocal relationship with the orthodox communion. In pursuing a local policy of comprehension, which undermined the national religious settlement, he won over moderate nonconformists but alienated more uncompromising dissidents. By 1663 his dispensation to hold the Boxted living was withdrawn, and his relations with his dissenting parishioners had descended into a series of violent skirmishes. Abandoning Boxted in 1664, he received a new presentation to All Saints under the great seal of England. His turbulent reputation did not diminish: in 1668 he was ejected from his house near Wickes in Essex, where he was perpetual curate, by a clamorous uprising of more than forty people from three villages, and the same year the Colchester borough assembly advised the bishop of London that he was 'not a man of peaceable and quiet temper', and thus not suitable for presentation to an additional living (Essex RO D/b5, Gb5, fol. 10). In 1673 he appeared as pamphleteer with an attack against Andrew Marvell's *Rehearsal Transpros'd* and the philosophy behind

religious separatism. 'For all our worship of God; prayers, praises, and preachings, observing Lords Days and Sacraments', asked Hickeringill, 'Is He the better for them?' (E. Hickeringill, *Gregory, Father Greybeard*, 1673, 67). Dissenters placed empty doctrine before the king's laws; instead, he proposed that adherence to a minimalist creed could make all fanatics good conformists. He dramatized this theme on 9 May 1680 when, in a caustic sermon before the lord mayor, Sir Robert Clayton, in the Guildhall chapel, London, he hurled the curse of Meroz on all who, like his bishop, Henry Compton, slighted the law by allowing latitude to dissenters. This sharp reproach, which Hickeringill acknowledged was contrary to his 'natural tenderness and inclination' towards nonconformists, displayed instead his antipathy towards the meddling of bishops in civil affairs; a symptom of which, he claimed, was that English clergymen treated as a piece of apocrypha the best example of loyalty in the Bible. For Hickeringill, concerned with the political status of doctrines and beliefs, all rebellion came cloaked in religious dress. He challenged both bishops and nonconformists, who concurred that domination was founded in grace.

This enmity with his diocesan was to shape Hickeringill's subsequent career: through litigation or print he was in almost constant dispute with the forces of ecclesiastical authority. Compton set aside the tithes of St Botolph's, Colchester, which had (since 1544) been enjoyed by the rectors of All Saints, in favour of a more compliant clergyman. Ignoring the edict, Hickeringill established himself in open competition with his local rival for church business: he poached tithes, proposed to 'rout' a neighbouring cleric from his livings for a £20 fee, offered to marry at reduced rates and without banns or licence, and intercepted funeral processions in order to read the service. He posed as a barrister, teaching his neighbours how to avoid the exactions of the spiritual courts, and between 1680 and 1683 unleashed a virulent print attack on episcopacy and the legality of church courts. Compton pursued him with a stream of litigation: on 3 March 1681 Hickeringill was tried, before Judge Baron Weston at Chelmsford assizes, on an indictment of twenty-four charges of barratry. He mounted his own defence, and in a display of legal acumen trounced the prosecution's rising star, Sir George Jeffreys. The case was dismissed, although the tory press reported his conviction for perjury. Compton next had him cited to the court of arches to answer charges relating to his deviant ministerial conduct around Colchester, but when he appeared before Sir Robert Wiseman on 8 June 1681, he adopted the sectarian gesture of refusing to remove his hat, and would speak only in Greek, the language (he claimed) of the canon law. When a court official grabbed the offending headgear, Hickeringill snatched it back, and upon the announcement that his carriage amounted to a non-appearance, he denounced the arches as 'no Court of Law', and threatened to prosecute Wiseman according to statute for citing him outside his own diocese (Hickeringill, *Works*, 1.176). Wiseman stopped the proceedings. Upon a second appearance on 21 November Hickeringill submitted a written defence, which four days later was allowed. The consequence of his Erastian protest was, on 8 February, to be bound over to good behaviour in king's bench, for 'his unmannerly deportment before the Court of Civil Law' (*CSP dom.*, *9 Feb 1682*).

Compton settled the score by prosecuting Hickeringill for slander, 'scandalum magnatum', under the statute 2 Ric. II c. 5. The cleric had defamed his bishop with 'several false news and horrible lyes' (Hickeringill, *Scandalum magnatum*, 8) at an Easter election of parish officials, although in his defence Hickeringill claimed to have been quoted out of context. Furthermore, he had failed to address his superior with the customary epithet of 'Right Reverend Father in God'. He subsequently compounded his insubordination by using the occasion of his trial, at Chelmsford assizes on 8 March, as a public platform to derogate the 'Black Regiment' of bishops (ibid., 15). Jeffreys, again counsel for the prosecution, elicited a conviction and a £2000 fine against Hickeringill, which Compton earmarked for the rebuilding of St Paul's. For celebrating clandestine marriages Hickeringill was suspended for three years. In the aftermath he sent (and then published) a letter to Compton which, purportedly seeking an accommodation through flattery, in fact boldly restated the grounds of his original dissidence. He refused to pay the fine and, offering to pay Compton's legal costs, challenged a retrial. Finally, on 27 June 1684, Hickeringill received restoration and exemption from the punishment upon a public recantation in the court of arches of the 'scandalous, erroneous, and seditious principles' of several of his publications (Luttrell, 1.312). The dean of the arches offered to Sancroft 'to burne with mine owne hands' each of the books in public (Bodl. Oxf., MS Tanner 32, fol. 70). The fine's remission, however, came too late to secure Hickeringill a £20,000 fortune: his uncle Dr Troutbeck, Charles II's surgeon in the north and sometime translator of Erastus, had altered the disposal of his estate, 'lest any of the lawn-sleeves should lay their fingers on't' (Hickeringill, *Works*, 3.117). Hickeringill's redemption was short-lived. His sermon in 1685 on Philippians 2: 10—'At the name of Jesus, every knee shall bow'—was a pretext for the tory recorder of Colchester and activist against nonconformity, Sir John Shaw, to complain to his friend the chancellor of the diocese. Hickeringill was charged with preaching against Anglican ceremonial, and peremptorily suspended. Petitions to the king, and a letter of 'apology and defence' to Sancroft—in which he compared the Romanist doctrine of infallibility with the Church of England's prescriptions on ceremonies and matters 'indifferent', and made a strong historical defence of dissent within a fallible church—were to no avail (Bodl. Oxf., MS Tanner 32, fol. 232). Only in 1688, 'about a month before the Dutch landed', was he recalled (Hickeringill, *Works*, 2.380).

On 15 January 1691 Hickeringill became chaplain to the whig Edward Howard, earl of Carlisle, and the following day was granted dispensation to hold the vicarage of Fingringhoe, adjoining Colchester. In *The Survey of the Earth* (1705) he implicated the Church of England in a long historical tradition where true religion was supplanted by superstition: the common prayer in particular was cited as containing pagan beliefs. Though Hickeringill was now old, Compton had him cited before the ecclesiastical court for its authorship in November (Luttrell, 5.607), and, perhaps as a consequence, in March 1706 Hickeringill published a *Letter Concerning Barretry, Forgery and the Danger and Malignity of Partial Judges and Jurymen*. In 1707 he was tried for forgery in his capacity as tax assessor for the parish of Wickes. For altering the rate books, and 'as a specimen of his morality', he was fined £400. 'He carried himself with that indecency to the court', noted Hearne, 'that he was thought to be mad' (Hearne, *Collectanea*, 2.33). His final court appearance, on 1 November, was in queen's bench on an information against him for writing libels.

Hickeringill died at his home, Pond Hall, near Wickes, on 30 November 1708. Buried in his church of All Saints, he suffered a final indignity when the lengthy epitaph on his tombstone was defaced. The words 'Reverendus admodum Dominus' ('a master greatly to be respected') and praise of his military ability and literary success were erased—Colcestrians believed—by Compton.

Writings and historical significance Hickeringill used print culture as an alternative forum for articulating his resistance to episcopal ecclesiology. He was the author of some thirty individual tracts, for which he became notorious; the 'great scribbler of the nation'. The odium he incurred, from the likes of the censor Sir Roger L'Estrange, was premised upon his skill at political disguise: throughout his pamphlets he intruded a critique of ecclesiological pretensions and practice in the form of protestant orthodoxy. *Naked Truth the Second Part* (1681), taking its name though not its theme from Bishop Herbert Croft's work, denounced all independent ecclesiastical jurisdiction. The church's power was defined by *regnum*, but its courts operated under the myth of a *jus divinum*: they were relics of popery. Hickeringill used his scholarly research into history and law to underpin a practicable assault on priestly authority. He taught, for example, that it was not 'sacrilege' for parishioners to withhold tithes (*Naked Truth*, 29–30). Similar themes appeared in his *The Test or Tryal of the Goodness and Value of Spiritual Courts* (1683), where readers were urged to take no notice of their summons to the church court. At the pamphlet's end, to prevent extortion, appeared a 'just table' of clerical fees with the slogan 'And no more!'.

At the same time Hickeringill launched theological and dogmatic attacks on established church practice, exposing and undermining the cultural foundations of sacerdotal authority. *The Black Non-Conformist* (1682) revealed church ceremonial to be intimate with political power. There was a characteristic dose of rationalism: the historical appearance of bishops in the world was commensurate with the invention of ceremonies and eschatological supernaturalism. The central charge—that English bishops were nonconformists, as practising popish ceremonies contrary to the king's ecclesiastical laws—was extended in his *Ceremony-Monger* (1689). Prelates maintained the ignorance of Anglican congregations by imposing blind devotion and implicit faith. It was this concentration on the whiggish theme of 'priestcraft' which distinguished his thinking from Reformation ecclesiology. The *Lay Elder* (1695) went beyond Erastianism, in suggesting that the distinction between the laity and a priestly caste itself was fraudulent, without historical or scriptural pedigree. Central to its priestcraft was the church's monopoly on interpreting scripture. In *Priestcraft; its Character and Consequences* (1705?) he undermined inerrant and inspired exegesis, by exposing the variations and contradictions of scriptural texts. For his description of the corruption of the Bible from primitive Christian purity through its duplicitous transmission by priests, he was charged by some with blasphemy. This notion of an overarching clerical conspiracy, mapped out over centuries, was a core theme in contemporary and later deist tracts. Hickeringill's bad press denotes a coarse appeal: in *Reformator Vapulans* (1691) Tom Brown portrayed him (negatively) as a popular oracle.

Hickeringill is an ambiguous figure: his position as conforming clergyman of the Church of England sits ill at ease with his conduct and writing. Contemporaries portrayed him as an opportunist who 'would change note or coat if it was possible to get into some fatter pastures' (*Observations on Meroz*, 1680, 26). In 1710 his writings were read out in open court during the state trial of Henry Sacheverell, as evidence that the church was in danger from a blasphemous coven of 'false brethren' (*Trial of Henry Sacheverell*, 216). In historiography his example has been used to illustrate the evolution of a tradition of interregnum puritan thought into deism after the Restoration (Emerson, 396–7). Hickeringill here represents a cadre of figures who, having lost their faith, marginalized a seam of radical thought that had previously been central to national discourse. Yet Hickeringill promoted his writings as remedial rather than revolutionary, and throughout his trials was concerned to preserve his status as a true and sincere clergymen. More recently it has been suggested that, rather than demonstrating the peripheral nature of heterodox beliefs, Hickeringill's conduct (parochially, in print, and in the courts) illustrates the difficulty for the ruling élite in making routine the acts of conformity which symbolized religious order. Hickeringill used the authority of clerical office as a platform for both dissent, and the fabrication of order and compliance. Orthodoxy in Hickeringill's case was not a category of doctrinal authenticity that could be imposed by his superiors, but was attempted in a process of negotiation between the agencies of priest, laity, and ecclesiastical institution.

J. L. C. McNulty

Sources E. Hickeringill, *Works*, 3 vols. (1716) • E. Hickeringill, *Miscellaneous tracts* (1707) • E. Hickeringill, *Scandalum magnatum* (1682) • E. B. Underhill, ed., *Records of the Churches of Christ, gathered at Fenstanton, Warboys, and Hexham, 1644–1720*, Hanserd Knollys Society (1854) • [J. Hunter], ed., *Letters of eminent men, addressed to Ralph Thoresby*, 2 vols. (1832) • Bodl. Oxf., MSS Tanner • quarter session records, Essex RO, QS/R 400 • LPL, Court of Arches MSS, Bbb 497 •

J. A. I. Champion and J. L. C. McNulty, 'Making orthodoxy in Restoration England: the trials of Edmund Hickeringill, 1662–1710', *Negotiating authority*, ed. M. Braddick and J. Walter [forthcoming] • J. L. C. McNulty, 'An anticlerical priest: Edmund Hickeringill and the context of priestcraft', MPhil. diss., U. Cam., 1998 • Venn, *Alum. Cant.* • R. Newcourt, *Repertorium ecclesiasticum parochiale Londinense*, 2 vols. (1708–10) • P. Morant, *The history and antiquities of the most ancient town and borough of Colchester in the county of Essex* (1748) • N. Luttrell, *A brief historical relation of state affairs from September 1678 to April 1714*, 6 vols. (1857) • R. L. Emerson, 'Heresy, the social order and English deism', *Church History*, 37 (1968), 389–403 • *The trial of Henry Sacheverell* (1710) • B. Nightingale, *The ejected of 1662 in Cumberland and Westmorland: their predecessors and successors*, 1 (1911) • J. E. B. Mayor and R. F. Scott, eds., *Admissions to the College of St John the Evangelist in the University of Cambridge*, 3 vols. in 4 pts (1882–1931) • 'Subsidy roll of the wapentake of Skyracke', *Publications of the Thoresby Society: Miscellanea*, 1 (1897) • J. Lister, ed., *West Riding sessions records*, 2, Yorkshire Archaeological Society, 54 (1915) • parish register, Aberford, near Leeds, 19 Sept 1631 [baptism]

Archives GL, MS 912, box 1. vi | Bodl. Oxf., Tanner MSS • Essex RO, QS/R 400

Likenesses J. Nutting, line engraving (after J. Jull), BM; repro. in Hickeringill, *Miscellaneous tracts* [see illus.] • Roffe, stipple (after J. Jull), BM; repro. in R. Page, *Lives of eminent and remarkable characters … of Essex, Suffolk and Norfolk* (1820)

Hickes, Francis (1565/6–1631), translator, was probably born in Shipston, Worcestershire, the son of Richard Hickes (d. 1621) and Anne Ingram. His father is said by Wood to have been an arras-weaver (Wood, *Ath. Oxon.*, 2.490). Hickes matriculated at St Mary Hall, Oxford, on 27 March 1579, aged thirteen, and took his BA on 30 April 1583. After graduation he appears to have spent most of his life in Barcheston, Warwickshire, and Shipston, where he devoted himself to translations from Greek into English. Probably about 1593, he married Elizabeth Munday, daughter of Thomas Munday, of Bagshot, Surrey; they had four children. Elizabeth died in 1616 and was buried at Barcheston on 25 May.

None of Hickes's works was published during his lifetime, but in 1634 his *Certain Select Dialogues of Lucian, together with his True History* was published in Oxford, with additions by his son Thomas [see below]. Thomas described his father as 'no profest scoller' but 'a true lover of Schollers, and Learning', whose translations were '[h]is studie or rather his recreation' (Hickes and Hickes, sig. A3r). Two more translations from Greek are extant in manuscript: 'The history of the wars of Peloponnesus, in 8 books, written by Thucydides the Athenian' and 'The history of Herodian, beginning from the reign of the emperor Marcus'. These manuscripts were presented to the library of Christ Church, Oxford, by Thomas Hickes, and are still held among the library's collections.

Hickes is said by Wood to have died in a kinsman's house at Sutton in Gloucestershire on 9 January 1631, and to have been buried in the chancel of the parish church at Brailes, Worcestershire (Wood, *Ath. Oxon.*, 2.491). There is, however, no reference to his burial in the Brailes parish registers, and no will survives.

Wood writes that Hickes's son **Thomas Hickes** (1598/9–1634) was born in Shipston in the parish of Tredington in Worcestershire (Wood, *Ath. Oxon.*, 2.584), but there is no record of his birth in the Tredington or Shipston parish registers. Thomas matriculated at Balliol College, Oxford, on 13 December 1616, aged seventeen, and took his BA on 11 May 1620 and his MA on 23 January 1623. In 1630 he became a chaplain at Christ Church, Oxford, an appointment attributed by Wood to the patronage of Brian Duppa, then dean of Christ Church and vice-chancellor of Oxford University (ibid.). Hickes's edition of his father's translation of Lucian is dedicated to Duppa, with the assurance that Hickes is 'so farre indebted to your favours, that my thankfulnesse cannot willingly omit the occasion of expressing itself' (sig. A2r). As well as the dialogues translated by Francis, this volume includes Thomas's *Life of Lucian, Gathered out of his Own Writings*, and his notes on his father's translations. In his letter 'To the honest and judicious reader' Hickes hints at plans to publish more of his father's works 'to propagate his owne memorie, which may chance to last longer in this small monument of his owne raising (or in some larger hereafter) than in the hardest marble posteritie can erect him' (sig. A3v). His own notes to the dialogues, which testify to an extensive knowledge of Greek literature, are justified as an attempt to make his father's translations comprehensible even to 'the meanest capacities ... otherwise, the English, would be to many, almost as much Greeke as the Originall' (ibid.).

Wood records that in addition to his proficiency in Greek, Thomas Hickes had a reputation as a good poet and an excellent limner (Wood, *Ath. Oxon.*, 2.584); he contributed Latin verses to the Oxford volume, *Camdeni insignia* (1624). Thomas Hickes died, unmarried, at Christ Church on 16 December 1634, and was buried in Christ Church Cathedral. No monument to him survives.

GILLIAN WRIGHT

Sources F. Hickes and T. Hickes, *Certain select dialogues of Lucian, together with his true history* (1634) · Wood, *Ath. Oxon.*, new edn, vol. 2 · Foster, *Alum. Oxon.* · dean's admission register, Christ Church Oxf. · parish register, Warks. CRO [marriage, parents; burial, wife] · private information (2004) [librarian and archivist, Christ Church, Oxford] · A. T. Butler, ed., *The visitation of Worcestershire, 1634*, Harleian Society, 90 (1938)
Archives Christ Church Oxf., MSS 156, 157

Hickes, Gaspar (1605–1677), clergyman and ejected minister, son of a Berkshire clergyman, matriculated at Trinity College, Oxford, on 26 October 1621, aged sixteen, graduating BA in 1625 and proceeding MA in 1628. He was ordained priest at Bristol on 24 December 1626 and in 1628 appears to have been beneficed. Instituted vicar of Launceston on 23 September 1630, he was also vicar of Lavnells from 1630 to 1636, and, resigning Launceston, from 1632 vicar of Landrake: all of these livings were in Cornwall, and the last was in the home parish of Francis Rous, the godly former MP. At an unknown date Hickes married, but little is known about his wife, Julian. Probably through the influence of Sir John Maynard and of Rous, then MP for Truro, on 20 April 1642 Hickes was named to parliament as one of the two Cornish divines whose advice should be sought on ecclesiastical matters. As the royalists gained ascendancy in Cornwall, he retired to London; he was a member of the Westminster assembly of divines

from July 1643, and in October 1644, as one of the 'plundered ministers', was placed in possession of the vicarage of Tottenham, which was worth less than £50. Additionally a grant of £100 per annum was assigned to him out of the revenues of St Paul's chapter in the parish.

While known for his preaching, Hickes went into print only when commanded and as a result only three of his sermons survive. In his fast sermon *Glory and Beauty of God's Portion* (1644) Hickes encouraged the Commons towards militant action, reminding them that 'the prophecies in the Revelation seem to foreshew that the ruine of Antichrist shall in a good part be brought to pass by the sword' (p. 42). Hickes used his funeral sermon of 26 June 1645 for William Strode as an opportunity to further encourage godly parliamentarians: *The Life and Death of David* (1645), dedicated to Sir Edward Barkham and Lady Barkham, emphasizes the need for action, saying, 'You that live, while ye have time and strength, work on' (p. 26). The following January he warned the House of Lords against growing secure amid success in a fast sermon, *The Advantage of Afflictions* (1646). Hickes later returned to Landrake, and as the leading presbyterian divine in the county was appointed in 1654 assistant to the commissioners for Cornwall for ejecting scandalous ministers and schoolmasters. In October 1658 he was a member of the Cornish Association. Dispossessed of his benefice in 1662, Hickes continued to minister in the area. At some point after 1670 he was prosecuted under the Conventicle Act for unlawful preaching. When the justice of his own district refused to convict he was taken further west, where he was convicted and fined £40. He appealed, but without any result beyond increasing the substantial costs of the proceedings. He was granted a licence as a presbyterian in April 1672. In 1677 he died, and was buried in the porch of the parish church on 10 April, when many of the 'godly party' attended. In his will dated 9 February 1674 Hickes left bequests to his brother Edward and 'the children of my brothers and sisters', and his estate first to his wife and then to Gaspar Geffrey. The suggestion that Gaspar Hickes (d. 1714), captain of a Yarmouth man-of-war, was a possible son (Laughton, 141) is thus unlikely.

MARK ROBERT BELL

Sources A. F. Robbins, 'Jasper Hickes, M.A., vicar of Launceston, Launcells, and Landrake', *Notes and Gleanings*, 3 (1890), 158–160 · [J. Hickes], *A true and faithful narrative, of the unjust and illegal sufferings, and oppressions of many Christians* (1671) · *Memoirs relating to the Lord Torrington*, ed. J. K. Laughton, CS, new ser., 46 (1889), 141–2, 193 · *The nonconformist's memorial ... originally written by ... Edmund Calamy*, ed. S. Palmer, [3rd edn], 1 (1802), 352–3 · J. F. Wilson, *Pulpit in parliament: puritanism during the English civil wars, 1640–1648* (1969) · *CSP dom.*, 1671–2 · *Reg. Oxf.*, vol. 2/2–3 · Wood, *Ath. Oxon.*, new edn, 3.1107–8 · Boase & Courtney, *Bibl. Corn.*, 1.237–8 · Foster, *Alum. Oxon.* · *Calamy rev.* · index of Devonshire wills and administrations, Devon RO
Wealth at death £722 4s.: will, 14 April 1677

Hickes, George (1642–1715), bishop of the nonjuring Church of England and antiquary, was born at Moorhouse, Newsham, in the parish of Kirby Wiske near Thirsk in Yorkshire, on 20 June 1642, the second son of William Hickes, originally of Ness in the parish of Stonegrave,

George Hickes (1642–1715), by Robert White, 1703

Yorkshire, a landowning farmer at Moorhouse, and his wife, Elizabeth Kay (or Key), daughter of George Kay, rector of nearby Topcliffe. Hickes was the fourth child of seven and had two brothers, an elder brother, John *Hickes (1633–1685), later a nonconformist minister, and Ralph Hickes (c.1651–1711), who became a physician. After some time at school in Thirsk, Hickes, when aged about ten, was sent to the free school of Northallerton where he was taught by the royalist schoolmaster Thomas Smelt. The devotional writer John Kettlewell, later Hickes's close friend, was also a pupil of Smelt's at Northallerton. Smelt taught and reinforced the loyalist principles traditionally adhered to by the family of Hickes's mother. To his later friend and biographer, Hilkiah Bedford, Hickes remembered in admiration that:

> He [Smelt] was wont to take all occasions from the Classick Authors to instill into his upper boys due notions of the sacred Majesty of Kings, & the wickedness of Usurpers, as his scholar G. H. us'd frequently to mention, particularly what he us'd to say of Agathocles in Justin's *History* by whom they all understood that he meant the then Protector. In his upper Class which read Homer, he us'd to take occasion from that Author to speak of Kings as God's Ministers & Vice-gerents, & not the People's, to whom they were not accountable. (Bedford, 2)

Hickes was to suffer considerably from his father's adherence to Cromwell and often felt he had to compensate for this 'sin' of rebellion 'by doing the utmost in his power through the whole course of his life to serve the Royal cause & that of the Church, which had been so much disserv'd by his father' (ibid., 5). In 1658 Hickes went to live with his brother John, then minister of Saltash, Cornwall,

and was bound apprentice to a Plymouth merchant. However, John realized his younger brother's 'genius was to learning, & not to trade' (ibid., 3). After consulting George Hughes, rector of Plymouth, John advised his father to send George to Oxford, where he entered St John's College as a battler in April 1659.

Early career: the Restoration, Oxford scholars, travel abroad, and the church in Scotland Under the puritan president, Thankful Owen, Hickes refused to take sermon notes or attend young scholars' meetings for spiritual exercises, his royalist Anglicanism making him despair of a university education. Attending the visitation following the restoration of Charles II, however, Hickes decided to stay at Oxford and migrated to Magdalen College as servitor to Henry Yerbury, one of the restored fellows. On 24 February 1663 he graduated BA, after which he migrated to Magdalen Hall. On 23 May 1664 he obtained the Yorkshire fellowship of Lincoln College, and he proceeded MA on 8 December 1665. He became deacon on 10 June and priest on 23 December the next year. From about 1665 to 1673 Hickes worked as a tutor of Lincoln College. He was incorporated at Cambridge on 8 July 1668. It was during this early period of some seven years at Lincoln that he laid the foundations for his later career as a leading philologist and Anglo-Saxon scholar.

At Lincoln College, Hickes met the linguistic scholar Thomas Marshall, who had been appointed a fellow in 1668 after his publication, together with his teacher Francis Junius (François du Jon), of the Gothic and Anglo-Saxon versions of the gospels, including Marshall's *Observationes in evangeliorum versiones perantiquas duas, Gothicas scil. et Anglo-Saxonicas* (Dordrecht, 1665). Marshall, in correspondence, also introduced Hickes to John Fell, canon and dean of Christ Church and vice-chancellor of the university. Fell, a strong university man and renovator of the university press, together with other scholars that he grouped around him (Edward Bernard, Samuel Clarke, Henry Dodwell, John Pearson, and others), was responsible for a revival of patristic, historical, and philological learning. In the early 1670s he commissioned Marshall, then living in the Netherlands, to acquire punches, matrices, and type for the newly built printing house, the Sheldonian Theatre. Through Fell, and also on the advice of Hickes, Marshall subsequently became rector of Lincoln in 1672. In those years a need began to be felt for a new Anglo-Saxon dictionary and grammar (William Somner's *Dictionary*, including Aelfric's grammar, of 1659, was hardly available at the time). Among his other language studies Marshall set to work on such a grammar (Bodl. Oxf., MS Marshall 78). Inevitably Hickes was influenced by and indebted to these efforts by Junius, Fell, and Marshall.

However, for the time being Hickes's interest in philology was cut short when he fell seriously ill and was advised to rest. To recuperate he travelled abroad in October 1673, accompanying one of his former Lincoln College students, Sir George Wheler, a royalist scholar and traveller, on part of his grand tour. At Wheler's invitation Hickes visited Paris, Blois, Montpellier, Nîmes, Marseilles, Lyons, and Geneva among other places. In Paris Hickes met the eminent protestant scholar Henri Justell who (before the revocation of the edict of Nantes) told Hickes 'many secret matters, particularly that of the intended persecution of the Hugonots, & of a design in Holland & England to extirpate the Royal Family of the Stewarts' (Bedford, 8). Through Hickes, Justell, secretary to Louis XIV and later Charles II's librarian at St James's, presented his father's valuable late sixth-century manuscripts of acts and canons of the early church to the Bodleian Library (MSS e Museo 100–102). At Geneva the Anglican Hickes refused the protestant sacrament from François Turretin because he doubted its validity. However, his sermon *The True Notion of Persecution* (1681) shows that Hickes also felt somewhat sympathetic to the cause of the persecuted Huguenots whom he did not wish to associate with the English dissenters. *A Letter from beyond the Seas to One of the Chief Ministers of the Non-Conforming Party* (1674) was Hickes's anonymous letter to his dissenting brother John, written from Saumur. Hickes returned to England in 1674.

Hickes proceeded BD at Oxford on 14 May 1675 while he was rector of St Ebbe's Church. In the same year his friend John Kettlewell was elected fellow of Lincoln College, largely through his influence. He preached a sermon (published as *Peculium Dei*, 1681) at St Mary's 'to confute the many dangerous doctrines & opinions antient & modern, grounded upon the misunderstanding of the Jewish Oeconomy & the Mosaick Law' (Bedford, 33), for which he was praised by Richard Allestree, regius professor of divinity, and Kettlewell. In August 1676 Hickes met the learned and controversial John Maitland, second earl and first duke of Lauderdale, who offered him a chaplaincy. Maitland, who had considerable influence on King Charles II, was on his way to Edinburgh as secretary of state for Scotland to safeguard constitutional affairs against the interests of the Scots covenanters and defend the re-established episcopal church against Scottish presbyterianism. After consulting John Fell, by then bishop of Oxford, Hickes accepted the position despite some misgivings concerning Maitland's debauched courtly lifestyle. In Scotland it was Hickes's task to introduce the liturgy and support Maitland's policies. Thus Maitland commissioned Hickes's *Ravillac redivivus* (1678), an account of the trial of the covenanter James Mitchell, who had attempted to assassinate James Sharpe, the archbishop of St Andrews. Through Sharpe, Hickes was offered a DD at St Andrews for this work. That same year Hickes together with Alexander Burnet, archbishop of Glasgow, reported to the court in London on Scottish ecclesiastical affairs.

Besides these official duties Hickes continued to pursue philology and antiquarian interests—as is evident, for example, from his correspondence with Thomas Smith, then chaplain to Sir Joseph Williamson, secretary of state. Williamson founded a collegiate lectureship in Saxon studies at Queen's College, Oxford, for William Nicolson in 1679. Hickes also appears to have studied Hebrew to be able to discuss 'Rabbinical learning' (*Remarks*, 1.268) with Maitland. His *Ravillac* also betrayed his steady interest in Anglo-Saxon etymology and English dialects. Hickes stayed for some time with Maitland at Ham House, Surrey, where he met William Hopkins, prebendary of Worcester, who was improving the cathedral library at Worcester and who had visited Sweden to study the septentrional languages.

On 13 September 1679 Hickes married Frances Marshall (*c*.1633–1714), daughter of Charles Mallory of Rainham, Essex, and widow of John Marshall, citizen of London. Frances had a royalist background. They had no children. On 17 December that year Hickes was created Oxford DD. He was at the beginning of a promising career in the established church.

A career in defence of the Restoration church, 1680–1687 For the next seven years Hickes preached and published on ecclesiastical controversies and developed his patristic scholarship. In the aftermath of the Popish Plot Hickes preached several sermons in the prevailing anti-Catholic climate, among them *The Spirit of Popery Speaking out of the Mouths of Phanatical Protestants* (1680) for which, as well as for his service in Scotland, he was given a prebendary of Worcester by the king. Also in 1680 Archbishop Sancroft presented him to the vicarage of All Hallows Barking. In the next year Hickes gave up his fellowship of Lincoln, becoming chaplain to Charles II. *A Sermon Preached on the 30th of Jan* (1682) on the Anglican doctrines of divine right, passive obedience, and non-resistance caused consternation among dissenters in the church of St Mary-le-Bow and publication was resisted (unsuccessfully) by the court of aldermen. In the same year, 1682, a work was published of seminal importance to the revival of Anglican patristic theology and scholarship which was deeply to influence Henry Dodwell, Hickes, and the nonjuring movement after the revolution of 1688. To the nonjurors John Fell's edition of St Cyprian showed that the principles of primitive Christianity (the Cyprianic principles) paralleled those of the post-Reformation episcopal Church of England envisioned as a divine society with independent jurisdiction in spiritual matters. Also in 1682 Hickes's sermon *A Discourse of the Sovereign Power* was answered by *Julian the Apostate* (1682) by the nonconformist Samuel Johnson. Hickes was becoming aware of increasing opposition to his Restoration principles, especially from John Tillotson, then dean of Canterbury. At Sancroft's request Hickes answered Johnson with *Jovian* (1683). In these years (1681–4), in the aftermath of the exclusion crisis, the influential commission for ecclesiastical promotions elected bishops and deans who could be trusted to be loyal to the king's brother and heir, James, duke of York. Hickes was promoted to the deanery of Worcester in August and installed on 13 October 1683. He declined the bishopric of Bristol the following year.

In 1685 Thomas Marshall died and Hickes wished to succeed him as rector of Lincoln College. He obtained Fell's support but was not elected. According to Anthony Wood, John Radcliffe thought Hickes 'a turbulent man and that if he should be rector they should never be at quiet' (*Life and*

Times, 3.142). In April that year Hickes attended the coronation of the Catholic King James II. The year ended tragically for him when on 6 October his brother John was executed for his involvement in Monmouth's rebellion. Hickes had tried but failed to obtain a pardon. After his father's 'sin' of rebellion, he had to contend once again in a most personal way with the moral forces of familial love and belief in non-resistance. In 1686 Hickes resigned All Hallows and became rector of Alvechurch, near Worcester. His Stuart loyalties were firm, but so was his anti-Catholicism. Early that year he had preached a sermon, *An Apologetical Vindication of the Church of England* (published 1687), for which he was summoned to the king. Hickes had cast suspicion on the so-called strong box papers, but James proved to him that Charles II's papers on his conversion to Catholicism were genuine. James proceeded with his campaign to put Catholics in Oxford colleges. After Fell's death the Catholic convert John Massey succeeded to the deanery of Christ Church, and at Magdalen a Catholic president was appointed. In 1687 Hickes opposed the declaration of indulgence that granted full freedom of religious observance to Catholics and protestant dissenters. When Bishop William Thomas of Worcester was ill Hickes publicly declared that he would not summon the chapter to elect a Catholic successor on his death.

Religion and politics: the Saxon scholarship of an outlaw, 1688–1699

> [Hickes] was no sooner settled at Worcester but being then about 45 years of age he apply'd himself to the study of the ancient Septentrional Languages, of which by indefatigable pains he made himself a perfect Master in one year, & at the same time compiled his Anglo-Saxon & Moeso-Gothick Grammar. (Bedford, 22)

For Hickes the affairs of English politics and religion came together with his historical and linguistic studies in the years leading up to the revolution of 1688–9. One of Fell's earlier cherished plans had been a publication of Junius's Old English–Latin dictionary, based on the Junius manuscripts which had come to the Bodleian in 1677 together with the Junius fount of type. The dictionary was to be accompanied by Marshall's Saxon grammar. After Marshall's death this task devolved upon William Nicolson, who had copied the Junius manuscripts with a view to publication but had left for Cumberland in 1681 (Nicolson's copy would come to the Bodleian in Fell's collection in 1686). According to Hickes's later friend, the Saxonist Edward Thwaites, Fell subsequently assigned the grammar to Hickes. At Worcester, where the cathedral library was rich in Saxon charters and where his association with William Hopkins was renewed, Hickes continued his philological studies and mastered Anglo-Saxon. Hickes now had access to the newly acquired Junius manuscripts at Oxford and was influenced by Junius's ideas about the history of the Germanic languages. With the encouragement and support of Arthur Charlett, delegate of Oxford University Press, and the scholar John Mill, Hickes's Old English grammar was printed (using Junius's type) and published at Oxford as *Institutiones grammaticae Anglo-Saxonicae et*

Moeso-Goethicae (1689); yet not without Mill's drastic curtailment of Hickes's dedication to the by then suspended Archbishop Sancroft. In the following decade ecclesiastical and scholarly interests were combined and inextricably connected in Hickes's life in a manner characteristic both of antiquarian research in general and of Hickes's methods as one of its leading proponents. Hickes 'belonged in a sense to an age earlier than that in which he lived, since his mind, encyclopedic in its range, refused to specialize and so entangled his learning with his life, that it is difficult to regard him solely as an historian or philologist, or solely as a divine' (Douglas, 78).

With the confusion among scholars, clergy, and lawyers attending the unprecedented circumstance after the revolution of both a king *de facto* (William) and a king *de jure* (James II), several ideological theories on the settlement and kingship were expounded. Hickes's *Institutiones* was undertaken as he wrote later 'purely out of zeale to make known the Language, Customes, Laws, and manners of our ancestres, and so to set our English antiquities in a good light' (Harris, *Chorus of Grammars*, 402). Nevertheless Hickes made a political statement by presenting in the same work a Saxon coronation oath (copied from Bodl. Oxf., Junius MS 60) as historical evidence of divinely ordained kingship that invalidated, in his view, whig historians' arguments about the 'original contract' between the king and his people as a basis of good government, a contract which justified resistance (or even active rebellion) if a king proved to be a tyrant.

On 1 August 1689 Hickes was, as dean of Worcester, suspended for refusing to take the oath of allegiance to William and Mary. On 1 February 1690 he was deprived but remained in possession until May 1691 when William Talbot was granted the deanery by King William. Hickes refused to accept his deprivation and wrote a claim of right which he pinned over the entrance to the choir in Worcester Cathedral. Soldiers took the document down and sent it to Daniel Finch, second earl of Nottingham and secretary of state. A warrant for high misdemeanour was issued after a debate in the council. Hickes's house was searched but Hickes had gone into hiding in London; he was outlawed on 11 August 1691.

In the following years Hickes further pursued his philological studies in correspondence with Arthur Charlett, Edmund Gibson (who published his edition of the *Anglo-Saxon Chronicle* in 1692), and William Nicolson, thinking of an expanded second edition of the *Institutiones*. He also contributed to the nonjurors' defence of the deprived bishops. Among other tracts he countered William Sherlock's influential ideas about divine providence (*The Case of Allegiance due to Sovereign Princes*, 1691), which propagated acceptance of and loyalty to William III by the providential right of a non-hereditary king, in his anonymous *Vindication of Some among Ourselves Against the False Principles of Dr. Sherlock* (1692), a legitimist defence of hereditary monarchy. In May 1693 Sancroft, wishing to continue the apostolic succession among nonjurors, sent Hickes to James II at St Germain to obtain permission to appoint suffragans in line with Henrician statute. Delayed by illness

Hickes finally returned to London on 4 February 1694. He was secretly consecrated suffragan bishop of Thetford on 24 February 1694 by the deprived bishops William Lloyd of Norwich, Francis Turner of Ely, and Thomas White of Peterborough. (A second nonjuror, Thomas Wagstaffe, was consecrated suffragan bishop of Ipswich.) When Gilbert Burnet attacked the deprived bishops in his funeral sermon on Archbishop Tillotson, Hickes published *Some Discourses upon Dr. Burnet and Dr. Tillotson* (1695), once more anonymously. Hickes's depreciation of his adversary Tillotson gave great offence.

During the years of his persecution Hickes lived in insecure and impoverished circumstances. He suffered from ill health and was frustrated by a lack of progress in his scholarship, being forced to move about the country to hide from the authorities. Friends such as Charlett supplied him with books. Hickes stayed at Bagshot with the Jacobite Colonel Grymes (James Grahme or Graham) and worked on an answer to Burnet's *Reflections on … 'Some Discourses'* (1696), with which Burnet had continued his argument against the deprived bishops, until in February the assassination plot broke out and he was forced to leave Bagshot (Grahme was arrested 3 March). Hickes stayed in various places, notably at Shottesbrooke with the Jacobite Francis Cherry for three months in the summer of 1696. A later friend, the nonjuror antiquary Thomas Hearne, remembered:

> the house was one night (about twelve a Clock I think) beset, on purpose to apprehend him, but he got out at a back door, passed through the Gardens into the Church Yard & escaped safe to Bagshot to Collonel Grymes's, & his wife followed. (*Remarks*, 10.237)

Subsequently Hickes stayed at Ambrosden with White Kennett, then vicar of Ambrosden and rector of Shottesbrooke, for five weeks in June–July 1696. He lived in a house at Sandford and after a period of illness and fever moved to Gloucester Green, Oxford, where he composed his *Declaration … Concerning the Faith and Religion in which he Lived and Intended to Die* (published posthumously, 1743). In 1697 he went to live with the Jacobite antiquary William Brome at Ewithington in Herefordshire, where he stayed for more than a year. In 1698 Hickes was back in London and living in Ormond Street, where he would remain for the rest of his life. It was this troublesome decade in Hickes's life which saw the production of his most important and influential work of scholarship, the *Thesaurus* (1703–5). In May 1699 Chancellor John Somers obtained an act of council for Hickes by which the attorney-general was ordered to cause a writ of *nolle prosequi*, to be entered to cease all proceedings against him.

Linguarum veterum septentrionalium thesaurus grammatico-criticus et archaeologicus 'If the work of Junius had been in part the mainspring of this [Anglo-Saxon] movement, its leader was to be Hickes, and the enthusiastic scholars who were to surround him all wore in some measure the livery of his majestic mind' (Douglas, 65). In the 1690s Hickes's *Institutiones* gradually grew from a grammar (it had already included Runólfur Jónsson's Old Icelandic grammar and Edward Bernard's 'Etymologicon Britannicum'), via an

idea about a second edition with additional studies, to a full-blown history of the English language and a monumental work of Old English and medieval Germanic culture and history, archaeology, numismatics, philology, and bibliography, for which he enlisted the scholarly assistance and expertise of a range of English, Swedish, and Danish scholars. It was to be called *Linguarum veterum septentrionalium thesaurus grammatico-criticus et archaeologicus*.

Continuing with his philological and linguistic studies of Old English, Gothic, Dutch, Francic, and later Old Icelandic, Hickes ever widened his scope and developed insights into the interrelated northern languages. This interest from his Oxford days became a passion now that he was in his fifties. 'For as I take it', he explained to Charlett in 1694,

> there are four old origenall European languages the Greek, the Sclavonick, the Gothick, and the Celtick, or ancient Brittish, and he that understands them all, as an ingenious Welshman that hath learned Greek, may easily do, will be able to illustrate the Harmony of Languages ancient, and modern, Latin also comprehended, because it is little els, but Greek. He will also thereby be enabled to illustrat many things in antiquity, which yet ly in darknesse, and the discoverys he will find himself able to make in these thinges will be so delightfull to him, that he will scarse be sensible of his paines. (Harris, *Chorus of Grammars*, 151)

Together at Ambrosden in 1696, Hickes worked with White Kennett, who had been pursuing his own antiquarian studies for his *Parochial Antiquities* (1695), on an 'Etymologicon Anglicanum'. Correspondences with Nicolson, Gibson, Hopkins, and Thomas Smith continued and through Charlett, Hickes was introduced to Humfrey Wanley, then an assistant at the Bodleian and later Harley's librarian and a leading Saxonist and palaeographer. In fact, Wanley was to become more of a co-author, with contributions throughout the *Thesaurus* and fully responsible for the *Catalogue* of Anglo-Saxon manuscripts which eventually appeared as volume 2.

Many others became involved. The connoisseur Sir Andrew Fountaine (assisted by Ralph Thoresby) contributed an essay on Anglo-Saxon and Anglo-Danish coins and William Elstob his edition of the *Sermo Lupi*. The Scandinavian Christian Worm offered assistance when at Oxford in 1696–7, and though he left England rather abruptly he remained an important influence on Hickes's pursuit of runic materials. Contacts with Danish and Swedish scholars, among them Jonas Nicolaus Salan, Petrus N. Salan, and Johann Peringsköold the elder, who sent a catalogue of manuscripts in the Antikvitetsarkiv, Uppsala, were established mostly through the correspondence of Edward Thwaites. Thwaites, professor of Greek and an inspiring teacher of Old English at Queen's College, Oxford, was responsible for much of the proofreading, the production of the book at Oxford University Press, the finances (the project was published by subscription), and the distribution of the *Thesaurus*.

Hickes improved Jónsson's Old Icelandic grammar for the *Thesaurus* and expanded his Anglo-Saxon grammar with six new chapters, which:

deserve a full-length study in themselves, constituting as they do the first history of the English language and a remarkably early survey of Old English literature and poetics. Hickes's sensitivity ranged far beyond the merely linguistic, and his understanding of early Germanic poetry was extraordinary for the time.   (Harris, *Chorus of Grammars*, 79)

In 1699 Hickes began his 'Dissertatio epistolaris' (for vol. 1), a remarkable study to which other Saxonists also contributed and in which Hickes argued the use of philology for the understanding of pre-conquest history, the Saxon laws, and the institutions of the country. Its discourse on the charters and the methodology needed to ascertain their authenticity (Wanley's contributions were crucial here) inaugurated the study of diplomatic for England (as Mabillon had done for France). Thus the work of Hickes and his co-workers in the field provided a 'chorus of grammars', a corpus of historical linguistics and comparative philology as well as the sources of history and the critical apparatus needed for historical and literary scholarship to make a great leap forward. It would take about a century, however, before scholarship would again attain Hickes's erudition and technical level.

'Bonus pastor' of the remnant of the Church of England, 1700–1715   After the *Thesaurus* was finally published, and after the preparation of the *Conspectus brevis* (1708) nominally by William Wotton, but mostly executed by Hickes himself in order to boost the sales of the *Thesaurus*, Hickes's studies in Saxon and medieval Germanic philology were exhausted and he consciously stopped his efforts. During the reign of Queen Anne he continued as a patristic scholar, a nonjuror controversialist (with regular contributions to the renewed political debate on the succession question after he obtained the *nolle prosequi*), and a 'bonus pastor' to the nonjuring community which now faced an additional oath of abjuration of the hereditary Stuart, James, the Pretender. He offered important moral support to, among others, the antiquary Thomas Hearne. Especially after the death of William Lloyd, deprived bishop of Norwich, when Henry Dodwell and the Shottesbrooke nonjurors returned to the established church in 1710 Hickes was intent on leading, as bishop, pastor, and theologian, what he considered was the surviving remnant of the true apostolic church.

Hickes's theology, like Dodwell's, based itself on Cyprianic principles and sacerdotal power. Yet where Dodwell's ultimate concern was with the church as a society receiving sacramental grace through apostolic succession and independent of secular power, John Kettlewell and Hickes insisted on a vision of the apostolic church which excluded not only Roman Catholics and presbyterians but also the great majority of Anglicans who no longer adhered to its doctrines of divine hereditary monarchy, passive obedience, and non-resistance. In this confessional and sectarian model (though it adopted Dodwellian principles), the consecration of new nonjuror bishops, and therefore separation, continued to be justified. Hickes published his views in such works as *Two treatises: one of the Christian priesthood, the other of the dignity of the*

episcopal order (1707, an answer to the deist Matthew Tindal's *Rights of the Christian Church*, 1706), and *The Constitution of the Catholic Church and the Nature and Consequences of Schism* (published posthumously by Nathaniel Spinckes, 1716). After Wagstaffe's death Hickes was the only nonjuror bishop left, and it became necessary to consecrate new bishops to ensure the succession and the continuity of the surviving remnant of the Anglican church. Three new bishops, Samuel Hawes, Nathaniel Spinckes, and Jeremy Collier, were consecrated by Hickes and two Scottish bishops, James Gadderar and Archibald Campbell, at St Andrew's, Holborn, on Ascension day 1713. After Hickes's death his *Constitution* provoked attacks on the nonjurors from White Kennett (*A Second Letter to the Lord Bishop of Carlisle*, 1716), Benjamin Hoadly, and Nathaniel Marshall in the wider context of the Bangorian controversy.

Hickes's life was plagued with spells of severe illness. In addition, his wife, Frances, in the early 1700s suffered from a long debilitating disease. She died on 3 December 1714. Hickes died of stone on 15 December 1715 at Westminster. He was buried in St Margaret's churchyard, Westminster, on 18 December. He bequeathed his manuscripts and letters to the nonjuror Hilkiah Bedford, his closest friend since the death of Kettlewell. A sale catalogue of his books was published in 1716. According to Hearne, Hickes desired Bedford to write his biography, which Bedford started but left unfinished. A number of Hickes's works were published after his death, among them Francis Lee's *Memoirs of the Life of Kettlewell* (1718) with an introduction by Hickes and based on materials and reminiscences of Robert Nelson and Hickes.

The emphasis in studies about Hickes from the days of his biographer Bedford to late twentieth-century scholarship has clearly shifted from a preoccupation with the churchman and nonjuror to one with the Anglo-Saxon scholar. No doubt posterity owes most to Hickes's achievements as a Saxon scholar, even more so because the discipline declined and much of the early Saxonists' expertise was lost for most of the remaining part of the eighteenth century. Hickes's *Thesaurus*, as R. L. Harris proves, remains a landmark of scholarship today. But as David Douglas has observed, the importance of Hickes needs to be recognized as combining in one remarkable man religious and theological thought on the one hand, and often (but not exclusively) religiously motivated and high-principled antiquarian scholarship on the other. This combination was characteristic not only of Hickes as a leading philologist but of many contemporary antiquarian scholars of the Augustan age, although few equalled the versatility and depth of Hickes's learning.   THEODOR HARMSEN

Sources Bodl. Oxf., MSS Ballard, MSS Cherry, MSS Rawlinson, incl. Rawlinson K (Hearne-Smith) · *A chorus of grammars: the correspondence of George Hickes and his collaborators on the 'Thesaurus linguarum septentrionalium'*, ed. R. L. Harris (1992) · H. Bedford, account of Hickes's life and works, Bodl. Oxf., MS Eng. misc. e. 4 [contd in MS Eng. hist. b. 2, fols. 52–7] · *Remarks and collections of Thomas Hearne*, ed. C. E. Doble and others, 11 vols., OHS, 2, 7, 13, 34, 42–3, 48, 50, 65, 67, 72 (1885–1921) · J. H. Overton, *The nonjurors: their lives, principles, and writings* (1902) · J. C. Findon, 'The nonjurors and the Church of England, 1689–1716', DPhil diss., U. Oxf., 1978 · D. C.

Douglas, *English scholars, 1660–1730*, 2nd edn (1951), chaps. 3–5 · R. L. Harris, 'George Hickes, White Kennett, and the inception of the *Thesaurus linguarum septentrionalium*', *Bodleian Library Record*, 11 (1983), 169–86 · J. A. W. Bennett, 'Hickes' thesaurus: a study in Oxford book production', *English Studies*, new ser., 1 (1948), 28–45 · *Letters of Humfrey Wanley: palaeographer, Anglo-Saxonist, librarian, 1672–1726*, ed. P. L. Heyworth (1989) · M. Goldie, 'The nonjurors, episcopacy, and the origins of the convocation controversy', in E. Cruickshanks, *Ideology and conspiracy: aspects of Jacobitism, 1689–1759* (1982), 15–35 · D. Fairer, 'Anglo-Saxon studies', *Hist. U. Oxf.* 5: *18th-cent. Oxf.*, 807–29 · V. H. H. Green, *The commonwealth of Lincoln College, 1427–1977* (1979), 275–91 · J. A. W. Bennett, 'The history of Old English and Old Norse studies in England from the time of Francis Junius till the end of the eighteenth century', DPhil diss., U. Oxf., 1938, 43–122 · T. H. B. M. Harmsen, *Antiquarianism in the Augustan age: Thomas Hearne, 1678–1735* (2000) · W. D. Macray, *Annals of the Bodleian Library, Oxford*, 2nd edn (1890); facs. edn (1984) · E. N. Adams, *Old English scholarship from 1566–1800* (1917); repr. (1970), 75–90 · T. A. Birrell, 'The Society of Antiquaries and the taste for Old English, 1705–1840', *Neophilologus*, 50 (1966), 107–17 · J. M. Levine, *The battle of the books: history and literature in the Augustan age* (1991), chap. 11 · T. Lathbury, *A history of the nonjurors: their controversies and writings; with remarks on some of the rubrics in the Book of Common Prayer* (1845) · W. B. Gardner, 'George Hickes and his *Thesaurus*', *N&Q*, 200 (1955), 196–9 · C. T. Berkhout and N. McC. Gatch, eds., *Anglo-Saxon scholarship: the first three centuries* (1982) · K. Dekker, *The origins of Old Germanic studies in the Low Countries* (1999), 339–43 · P. Bayle and others, *A general dictionary, historical and critical*, 6 (1738), 153–62 · G. M. Yould, 'The career and writings of Dr. George Hickes, nonjuror (1642–1715)', BD diss., U. Oxf., 1968, Bodl. Oxf., MS BD d. 2 · W. B. Gardner, 'Life of George Hickes', PhD diss., Harvard U., 1946 · *Bibliotheca Hickesiana, or, A catalogue of the library of the late reverend Dr George Hickes, … which will begin to be sold on Thursday, March 15, 1716*, by Nath. Noel … Bookseller [1716] · H. Carter, *A history of the Oxford University Press*, 1: *To the year 1780* (1975) · J. Maskell, 'George Hickes the nonjuror', *N&Q*, 6th ser., 12 (1885), 401–3 · W. Newton, *The life of the right reverend Dr White Kennett, late lord bishop of Peterborough* (1730) · M. Murphy, 'Edward Thwaites, pioneer teacher of English', *Durham University Journal*, 73 (1981), 153–9 · Wood, *Ath. Oxon.*, new edn · *The life and times of Anthony Wood*, ed. A. Clark, 5 vols., OHS, 19, 21, 26, 30, 40 (1891–1900) · A. Chalmers, *New and general biographical dictonary*, 11 vols. (1761) · *Biographia Britannica, or, The lives of the most eminent persons who have flourished in Great Britain and Ireland*, 7 vols. (1747–66) · Foster, *Alum. Oxon.* · will, PRO, PROB 11/549, sig. 238 · parish register, Kirby Wiske, 20 June 1642, N. Yorks. CRO [baptism] · *DNB*

Archives Bodl. Oxf., biographical papers · Bodl. Oxf., commonplace book · Bodl. Oxf., corresp. and papers · Bodl. Oxf., letters, MSS Rawl. D. 844 and D. 1234 · LPL, catalogue, MS 3171 · LPL, papers · Yale U., Beinecke L., letters and papers | BL, Cotton MSS · BL, Harley MSS · BL, Hickes and White Kennett papers, Lansdowne MSS 1033, 1034 · BL, papers relating to the Pretender, Add. MS 33286 · BL, corresp. with Hans Sloane, etc., Sloane MSS 50, 63 · BL, Stowe MSS · BL, Wanley–Hickes corresp., MS loan 29 · Bodl. Oxf., Ballard MSS · Bodl. Oxf., corresp. with Hilkiah Bedford, MS Rawl. lett. 42 · Bodl. Oxf., letters to Sir William Boothby, MS Eng. hist. d. 1 [copies] · Bodl. Oxf., corresp. with other scholars, esp. Francis Brokesby, Henry Dodwell, Thomas Smith, MSS Rawl. letters · Bodl. Oxf., corresp. with William Brome and Richard Rawlinson, Ballard MSS 31, 41 · Bodl. Oxf., letters to Arthur Charlett, Ballard MS 12 · Bodl. Oxf., letters to Thomas Hearne, MSS Rawl. lett. 7, 15 · Bodl. Oxf., Junius MSS · Bodl. Oxf., corresp. and papers of nonjurors · Bodl. Oxf., MSS Rawl. K (Hearne–Smith) · Bodl. Oxf., letters to Thomas Smith, Smith MSS 50, 63 · Bodl. Oxf., letters to Thomas Turner, MSS Rawl. lett. 91–92 · Bodl. Oxf., corresp. and papers, incl. corresp. with White Kennett, MS Eng. hist. b. 2 · LPL, notebook of John Leake jun.; corresp. on nonjurors with copies of letters of Francis Brokesby quoting Cherry's views on the nonjuring schism, MS 2522

Likenesses R. White, line engraving, 1703, NPG, BM; repro. in G. Hickes, *Linguarum veterum septentrionalium thesaurus*, 2 vols. [*see illus.*] · oils (after R. White), Bodl. Oxf. · portrait, Worcester Cathedral; repro. in Harris, *Chorus*, frontispiece · version (after oil painting), Lincoln College, Oxford

Wealth at death see will, 23 Nov 1713, PRO, PROB 11/549, sig. 238

Hickes, John (1633–1685), clergyman, ejected minister, and rebel, was born at Moorhouse Farm in Newsham, near Kirby Wiske, Yorkshire, the son of William Hickes of Stonegrave, Yorkshire, and his wife, Elizabeth Kay of Topcliffe, Yorkshire. After being educated at Thirsk he graduated BA from Trinity College, Dublin, in 1655, was a fellow there, and in 1656 became minister at Ballyroan, Queen's county. On 2 October 1657 he was appointed curate at Saltash, Cornwall, and, beginning in 1659, he also served as rector of nearby Stoke Damerel, Devon, following the death of German Gouldson (Goldstone). He was ejected from Stoke Damerel prior to 17 November 1660, when a new rector was installed, and subsequently from Saltash, where his successor subscribed under the Act of Uniformity on 5 August 1662. Hickes remained at Saltash, and was one of six dissenting ministers living there in 1665. Following the passage of the File Mile Act, he moved to Kingsbridge, Devon, where he associated with the dissenting ministers James Birdwood, Christopher Jellinger, and Edmund Tucker. He and his first wife, Abigail (1632–1675), daughter of John Howe, minister of Loughborough, Leicestershire, and sister of the presbyterian minister John Howe, had five children: John; William, who became rector of Broughton Gifford, Wiltshire; Abigail, who was baptized at Saltash on 1 December 1667; Catherine; and Elizabeth, wife of the martyrologist John Tutchin.

After justices in Devon and Cornwall began enforcing the 1670 Conventicle Act, Hickes chronicled some of their activities in *A True and Faithful Narrative, of the Unjust and Illegal Sufferings*, published anonymously in 1671. Calling for royal intervention, he denounced informers as unreliable witnesses, argued that meetings held openly were not seditious conventicles, insisted that penal laws be applied justly and rationally, and asserted that religious persecution harmed the country's economy. Having been charged with murder after a magistrate died, allegedly as the result of forcibly dispersing a conventicle in his house, Hickes went into hiding between 11 September 1670 and February 1671. When the king saw Hickes's *Narrative* he was irate, but in December 1671 Thomas Blood, whom Hickes would have met in Ireland, intervened on his behalf. On 2 January 1672 Charles II pardoned Hickes and such dissidents as Ralph Alexander, Robert Perrott, Nicholas Lockyer, and Blood's son for all acts of treason and other crimes committed since 29 May 1660.

For much of 1672 Hickes remained in London, assisting numerous dissenters to obtain licences under the declaration of indulgence; of his 515 applications (282 from Devon), 86 were successful. Most of those he helped were presbyterians and congregationalists, though at least one, Adam Pearse of Exeter, was a Baptist. Many were from the south-west but others were from as far away as Yorkshire,

Northumberland, and Lancashire. Hickes acquired a general licence for himself as a presbyterian on 2 April, and licences for his house at Kingsbridge on 11 April, a new meeting-house there on 30 September, and (if actually issued) his house at Hatton Garden, London, on 23 December. On 6 April 1672 he and Thomas Martin of Plymouth presented the king with a declaration of thanks from seventy-two nonconforming ministers in Devon, and he probably wrote or influenced similar statements from Cornwall and Wiltshire. Hickes also persuaded Charles to remit a third of the fines levied on dissenters in the west for holding conventicles.

The persecution deeply impressed Hickes, who addressed it again in the epistle to *A Discourse of the Excellency of the Heavenly Substance* (1673), in which he protested that nonconformists suffered more at the hands of fellow protestants than did Catholics. He also noted that during the preceding decade he had been forced to find employment outside the ministry and had found little opportunity to study. After the indulgence was cancelled he continued to preach, and in August 1673 was fined £20 for doing so at Exeter. On 4 July 1674 the bishop of Exeter, Anthony Sparrow, noting that he had persuaded the lord keeper to restore a JP dismissed because of Hickes's complaints, protested to the chancellor that Hickes was disturbing the peace. By 1675 Hickes was ministering to a congregation at Portsmouth, where magistrates disrupted his conventicle on 14 October 1677 and fined the owner of the house. Following the death of his first wife in 1675, he married a widow, Elizabeth Mills (*d. c.*1705), the daughter of John Moody, a Portsmouth maltster, and his wife, Elizabeth Arnold. They had two children, Elizabeth (*b.* 1678), who married Captain Luke Spicer of the Royal Navy, and James (*b.* 1679). In 1681 or 1682 Hickes moved to Keynsham, Somerset.

Convinced that Monmouth was Charles II's legitimate heir, Hickes joined the duke at Shepton Mallet, Somerset, on 24 June 1685. He later insisted that he had not recruited men for Monmouth's forces or recommended that the duke assume the title of king at Taunton. When the rebellion collapsed, he and the attorney Richard Nelthorpe fled, taking shelter with Dame Alice Lisle at Moyles Court, Ellingham, on the edge of the New Forest. There they were captured by Colonel Thomas Penruddocke. Hickes was tried by George Jeffreys and his colleagues on 23 September. As he faced execution, having been convicted of aiding the rebels, he told his wife that he would die because he had defended protestantism and English liberties. After efforts by his brother George *Hickes, dean of Worcester, to obtain royal mercy failed, Hickes was executed at Glastonbury on 6 October 1685. A month later his brother-in-law, Daniel Moody, a master gunner in the Royal Artillery, petitioned for his sister's estate, valued at £100 per annum plus £2000 in goods, which had been forfeited when Hickes was convicted. The latter, Moody claimed, had employed sinister artifices to persuade his father to make a will favouring his sister.

RICHARD L. GREAVES

Sources *CSP dom.*, 1671–3 · G. L. Turner, ed., *Original records of early nonconformity under persecution and indulgence*, 3 vols. (1911–14) · Bodl. Oxf., MS Tanner 42, fol. 110 · *Calamy rev.*, 260 · St J. D. Seymour, *The puritans in Ireland, 1647–1661* (1912) · [J. Tutchin], *A new martyrology*, 3rd edn (1689) · 'The Conventicle Act in operation', *Transactions of the Congregational Historical Society*, 6 (1913–15), 174–5 · *Walker rev.*, 113 · W. A. Shaw, ed., *Calendar of treasury books*, 8, PRO (1923), 404–5 · R. Clifton, *The last popular rebellion: the western rising of 1685* (1984) · P. Earle, *Monmouth's rebels: the road to Sedgemoor, 1685* (1977) · *The last speech of … Mr John Hicks, who was executed at Glassenbury, Octob. 1685* [1685]

Archives Bodl. Oxf., Tanner MS 42, fol. 110 · PRO, state papers domestic, SP 29

Likenesses J. Hopwood, stipple, BM, NPG; repro. in E. Calamy, *Nonconformist's memorial* (1802)

Wealth at death property worth £100 p.a., plus £2000 in goods; forfeited when convicted of treason: *Calendar of treasury books*, vol. 8, pt 1, pp. 404–5

Hickes, Sir Michael (1543–1612), administrator, was born on 21 October 1543, the first of six children of a mercer, Robert Hickes or Hicks (*d.* 1557), of the White Bear, Cheapside, London, and Julian (*d.* 1592), daughter of William Arthur of Somerset. The Hickes family had a long history as yeomen in neighbouring Gloucestershire, and it seems likely that Robert married before digging up his west country roots and setting off for London, where he established a retail mercery. Michael had five younger brothers, though only two, Clement and Baptist *Hicks (1551?–1629), survived until manhood. Their father died in 1557 and his will reveals a moderate prosperity which enabled Michael to go up to Trinity College, Cambridge, in 1559.

It is not clear how long Hickes stayed at Trinity—he did not graduate—but he was certainly in residence in 1562. It was no doubt largely through his years at Trinity that Hickes acquired the extensive knowledge of the classics that enabled him to sprinkle his later correspondence with Latin epigrams. During the 1560s Trinity College was an important centre of puritanism at Cambridge. Thomas Cartwright, one of the leaders of the early Elizabethan puritan movement, was a fellow there while Hickes was in residence, and the two men got to know each other. Hickes's closest friends at university, men like Vincent Skinner and John Stubbe, were also puritans, and it is clear that he shared their religious views. In March 1565 he was admitted to Lincoln's Inn, where Stubbe and Skinner had preceded him. He maintained his interest in the law long after he had ceased to be a student. In 1577, four years after his entry into Lord Burghley's service, he received a call to the bar, though there is no evidence that he ever practised as a lawyer.

In 1573 Hickes entered the household of William Cecil, Lord Burghley, and embarked on a career which led to political influence and personal affluence. Four years later, serving alongside Henry Maynard, he became one of Burghley's two principal secretaries. He was patronage secretary, helping his master to deal with the flood of requests for favours and assistance which assailed Burghley from all corners of the land. Hickes dealt with suits of a very varied nature: requests for wardships, petitions from towns, university patronage, assistance with official government business, matters connected with the country's customs administration, legal requests, ecclesiastical causes, and petitions connected with building operations in London. The range of these suits to Hickes reflected his master's role as chief minister of the crown, a position which gave Burghley the greatest role in the distribution of the queen's patronage.

Hickes's position as middleman gave him great opportunities to extract gratuities from grateful clients. They knew that favours had to be paid for, and sometimes promised large sums, as much as £100, for Hickes's help. It is probable in fact that during the 1590s he 'received more gratuities than any other servant in England' (Neale, 76). Hickes sat in four parliaments during his years as Burghley's secretary—those of 1584, 1589, 1593, and 1597—but we have certain knowledge of only one speech which he made in the Commons, and there is no indication that he ever played a prominent role in the house. He was almost certainly the author of the so-called *Anonymous Life* of Burghley, published within a few years of the latter's death and the most important literary source for his career.

During his years in Burghley's service Hickes forged a firm friendship with his master's younger son and political heir, Robert Cecil. In the 1590s the two men, working sometimes behind Burghley's back, resorted to a number of dubious practices in their dealings with suitors, and the personal and political friendship between the two continued into James I's reign. After 1608 their friendship cooled, though at the very end of Cecil's life the old intimacy was renewed. Early in 1612 a multiplicity of distressing symptoms suggested that Cecil was terminally ill. Towards the end of April it was decided that he should take the waters at Bath, and Hickes accompanied him in the role of close friend, staying with him until his death on 24 May.

In December 1594 Hickes married Elizabeth Parvish (*née* Colston), the prosperous widow of a London merchant, who bore him two sons, William and Michael, and a daughter, Elizabeth. She had a life interest in her late husband's country house at Ruckholt in Essex and Hickes spent much of his later life there, devoting a good deal of his time to local administration. He was feodary of Essex (the local representative of the court of wards) between 1598 and 1601; receiver-general of crown lands in Essex, Hertfordshire, London, and Middlesex between 1603 and 1604; and chief steward of nine royal manors in Essex after 1608. From 1609 until 1612 he once more played a role in central administration as a deputy in the alienations office, which dealt with the fines levied on those who wished to sell freehold land or land held in chief of the crown.

Both Queen Elizabeth and James I visited Ruckholt, the former in 1597 and the latter in 1604. Shortly after James's visit Hickes was knighted, on 6 August 1604. He died at Ruckholt on 15 August 1612 of a 'burning ague' (*Letters of John Chamberlain*, 1.379), and was buried at Leyton church, Essex. At the time of his death he owned property in London, Nottinghamshire, and Gloucestershire, and he had,

during his lifetime, made considerable sums from the profits of office holding and from the moneylending activities which he undertook for many years.

A. G. R. SMITH

Sources BL, Lansdowne MSS, 46–112 • A. G. R. Smith, *Servant of the Cecils: the life of Sir Michael Hickes, 1543–1612* (1977) • HoP, *Commons, 1558–1603* • A. G. R. Smith, 'The secretariats of the Cecils, c.1580–1612', *EngHR*, 83 (1968), 481–504 • S. E. Hicks Beach, *A Cotswold family: Hicks and Hicks Beach* (1909) • will, PRO, PROB 11/120, sig. 110 • inquisition post mortem, PRO, C 142/327/132 • J. Hurstfield, *The queen's wards: wardship and marriage under Elizabeth I* (1958) • *The letters of John Chamberlain*, ed. N. E. McClure, 2 vols. (1939) • M. Hickes, *The 'Anonymous life' of William Cecil, Lord Burghley*, ed. A. G. R. Smith (1990) • J. E. Neale, *The Elizabethan political scene* (1958) • J. Nichols, *The progresses, processions, and magnificent festivities of King James I, his royal consort, family and court*, 1 (1828), 454
Archives BL, Lansdowne MSS • Hatfield House, Hertfordshire, Salisbury MSS
Likenesses portrait, repro. in Smith, *Servant of the Cecils*, facing p. 32
Wealth at death lands in London, Gloucestershire, and Nottinghamshire; plus considerable capital: will, PRO, PROB 11/120, sig. 110; PRO, C 142/327/132; Lansdowne MSS

Hickes, Thomas (1598/9–1634). *See under* Hickes, Francis (1565/6–1631).

Hickey, Diarmuid [*name in religion* Antony] (1586–1641), Franciscan friar, was born in the diocese of Killaloe in Thomond, Ireland. The O'Hickeys were hereditary physicians to the O'Briens of Thomond and lived on both sides of the Shannon estuary. Other details survive concerning his background. He used the name 'Dermitius Thadaei … filius' showing that his father's name was Tadhg. His brother Cormac was archdeacon of Killaloe and prior of Inis Cathaigh (Scattery Island in the estuary), and he wrote to him in Irish in 1626 naming other family members, possibly seven other brothers and one sister: Turlough, Una, Tadhg, Brian, Conor, Richard, Andrew, and James; Cormac was then staying with Richard and his family at Dunmoylan in north Limerick. Antony Hickey was, on one occasion, listed among the Franciscans from Connaught, while Bonaventure Baron said he was 'Tuamensis' meaning, perhaps, from the diocese of Tuam; Hickey had, in fact, lived near Tuam town. He himself said that he grew up with his cousin Malachy O'Queely, later archbishop of Tuam, who came from Drinagh, co. Clare.

Hickey studied in Paris with O'Queely. He attended the Irish College at Douai and, when twenty-one, joined the Irish Franciscans at the recently founded St Anthony's College, Louvain, on 1 November 1607, as one of the first novices there. He received orders up to the diaconate at Malines in March–April 1609, and the priesthood on 6 March 1610. He attended the general chapter at Rome in 1612 as a respondent defending theological theses. He taught theology at St Anthony's, Louvain, was on the house council in 1616, and was *praeses* or acting superior in 1617. He taught philosophy at Aix-la-Chapelle and theology at Cologne for some part of the years 1617–19, but was in Louvain in February 1618 when he signed an approbation for Aodh Mac Aingil's (Hugh MacCaughwell's) *Sgáthán Shacramainte na hAithrighe*.

In 1619 Hickey was called to Rome to assist Luke Wadding, at the friary of San Pietro in Montorio, in his project of restoring the literary and historical glory of the Franciscan order. One of the best Irish theologians of his day, Hickey answered the attacks on the Franciscans that had appeared in the *Annales ecclesiastici*, volumes 13 and 14, of Abraham Bzovius OP, continuator of Baronius, published at Rome in 1616–17. Hickey's lengthy response, *Nitela Franciscanae religionis*, was completed before January 1626, but not published until 1627, under the name Dermitius Thadaei. A few years later he and Wadding were faced with the hostility of Patrick Cahill and Paul Harris to the religious of Ireland. On 22 June 1625 he became the first lecturer at the newly opened St Isidore's College in Rome, and later became a consultor for Roman congregations concerned with the doctrine of the immaculate conception of the Blessed Virgin Mary, the revision of the Roman breviary, and the ritual of the Greek church. He was also an agent at Rome for some Irish ecclesiastics. He edited three volumes of the works of Angelo del Paz OFM (who had died in the friary at San Pietro in Montorio in 1596) with Wadding, who thought very highly of him, and edited volumes 9, 10, and 12, on *Quaestiones in lib. IV sententiarum*, for Wadding's edition of John Duns Scotus. He left manuscript commentaries on Scotus, on moral and ascetical theology, on the immaculate conception, and on the stigmata of St Catherine of Siena. When he was appointed definitor-general in 1639 he was described as a jubilate lector of Ireland and minister provincial of Scotland. He was a large and amiable man, a favourite conciliator, beloved by all including Pope Urban VIII, who lamented his death on 26 June 1641 at St Isidore's at the age of fifty-five: he had struck his ankle on a step and a fatal infection had set in. He was buried in St Isidore's, and Wadding wrote his epitaph.   IGNATIUS FENNESSY

Sources A. F. Allison and D. M. Rogers, eds., *The contemporary printed literature of the English Counter-Reformation between 1558 and 1640*, 2 vols. (1989–94) • F. Haroldus, *Vita Fratris Lucae Waddingi* (1931) • B. Baronius, *Opuscula prosa et metro* (1668) • B. Jennings, *Michael O Cleirigh, chief of the four masters, and his associates* (1936) • B. Jennings, ed., *Wadding papers, 1614–38*, IMC (1953) • B. Jennings and C. Giblin, eds., *Louvain papers, 1606–1827*, IMC (1968) • G. Cleary, *Father Luke Wadding and St Isidore's College, Rome* (1925), 73–8 • J. Brady, 'The Irish colleges in the Low Countries', *Archivium Hibernicum*, 14 (1949), 66–91 • C. Giblin, 'The Processus datariae and the appointment of Irish bishops in the 17th century', *Father Luke Wadding: commemorative volume*, ed. Franciscan Fathers dún Mhuire, Killiney (1957), 508–616 • C. Giblin, 'Hickey, Antony', *New Catholic encyclopedia* (1967–89) • C. M. Perusino, *Chronologia historico-legalis seraphici ordinis fratrum minorum sancti patris Francisci*, 3/2 (Rome, 1752), 7 • F. J. Biggar, 'The Irish in Rome in the seventeenth century', *Ulster Journal of Archaeology*, new ser., 5 (1898–9), 115–38, esp. 126 • *Report on Franciscan manuscripts preserved at the convent, Merchants' Quay, Dublin*, HMC, 65 (1906)
Archives Archivio Vaticano, Vatican City, archives of Propaganda Fide • St Isidore's College, Rome, archives, MS 2/19
Likenesses E. di Como, fresco, 17th cent., St Isidore's College, Rome • portrait; formerly at St Isidore's College, Rome; now lost

Hickey, Emily Henrietta (1845–1924), writer and schoolteacher, was born on 12 April 1845 at Castle Macmine, co. Wexford, Ireland (home of her mother's Stewart ancestors), the second of two daughters of Canon John Stewart Hickey and his wife, a Newton-King related to the Stewarts of Stewart Lodge, co. Carlow. She was the granddaughter of the Revd William *Hickey (1787–1875), a philanthropist and writer under the pseudonym of Martin Doyle; her ancestral heritage was Anglo-Irish and Scottish. The family home was in Goresbridge, co. Carlow. Educated at home in early childhood, Emily Hickey attended day school at ten and boarding-school at thirteen. At twenty she published a poem in the *Cornhill Magazine* and shortly after, some narrative poems in *Macmillan's Magazine*, and it became her ambition to be a writer.

Happily for that ambition, the Macmillans invited Emily Hickey to visit and introduced her to their literary circle. Determined to pursue her career in London, she took whatever employment was available to young women at that time: private teacher, secretary, governess, companion. She also took full advantage of the opportunities that London offered. She studied with Andrew Lang and, via correspondence, earned a first-class honours certificate from Cambridge. She attended the lectures of F. J. Furnivall, who was so impressed with her work that he helped her obtain an appointment as lecturer in the London Collegiate School for Girls, where she taught for eighteen years—work for which she was put on the civil pension list. As a member of Furnivall's circle, she took part in Shakespearian readings, where it was remarked that 'her voice was singularly musical and her intonation faultless' (Dinnis, 26). Through Furnivall Hickey met Robert Browning, who admired her poetry and remained a friend until his death. She edited and annotated his 'Strafford' and with Furnivall founded the Browning Society; her role as honorary secretary was celebrated in a fine caricature by Max Beerbohm.

Emily Hickey continued to write, publishing four volumes of poetry between 1881 and 1901. She translated Anglo-Saxon and French verse, and also wrote essays and criticism. Her interest in social problems brought her to know Conrad Roden Noel and to write on his work, and she also became interested in home rule; her blank-verse essay 'Michael Villiers' addressed Irish problems. Her work appeared in major periodicals in America, England, and Ireland.

In the mid-1890s ill health sent Emily on a trip to France, Germany, and Switzerland, the only recorded journey that took her away from the British Isles. Switzerland inspired a series of nature verses, which with other works of this period were published in 1896. On her return to England she dedicated herself to social causes and became an active Anglo-Catholic. On 22 July 1901 she joined the Roman Catholic church, and for a time she wrote for the Catholic Truth Society. Her poetry became devotional and her prose dedicated to Catholic concerns; after her conversion she retracted her first three collections of verse (*A Sculptor*, 1881, *Verse-Translations*, 1891, and *Michael Villiers*), as they had expressed ideas at odds with her newly adopted beliefs. English critics largely ignored her post-conversion work; American and Irish continued to print and comment favourably upon it. In 1912 Pope Pius IX awarded her the gold cross 'pro ecclesia et pontifice'. It was hung in the church of St Thomas à Becket.

In the last two years of Emily Hickey's life her health and sight failed, but she continued to write until she died on 9 September 1924 at the Hospital of St John and St Elizabeth in London. She left a poem, 'At Eventide', to be published after her death.

In retrospect Emily Hickey's is the story of a talented woman who was able to be independent and successful in acquiring higher education and literary reputation. Her biography, together with a selection of her poetry, was published in 1927 by her literary executor, Enid Dinnis. It is as objective a record as a friend and co-religionist can be expected to give, but does not, however, have the last word on Emily's literary reputation. Dinnis wrote,

> Little by little the brilliant essayist, the erudite student of early English texts, the spoiled child of Victorian verse-makers and co-founder of the Browning Society, receded from the world of letters … she remained a Victorian to the end.   (Dinnis, 47)

Interest in Emily Hickey's work has been more lasting than this; in 1982 the musical setting of her translation of the Irish 'His Home and his Own Country' was included in *Seven Irish Songs*, and the late twentieth century also saw something of a revival of critical attention to her work.

CATHARINE WEAVER MCCUE

Sources E. Dinnis, *Emily Hickey* (1927) · *Irish Book Lover*, 14 (1924), 138 · Blain, Clements & Grundy, *Feminist comp.*, 519–20 · G. Watson, ed., *New CBEL* (1969–77), index, vol. 5 · G. A. Cevasco, ed., *The 1890s: an encyclopedia of British literature, art, and culture* (1993) · A. Furlong, 'Emily Hickey', *Irish Monthly*, 53 (1925), 16–20 · R. Hogan, ed., *Dictionary of Irish literature*, rev. edn, 1 (1996), 546–7 · *CGPLA Eng. & Wales* (1924)
Wealth at death £4945 2s. 9d.: probate, 20 Oct 1924, *CGPLA Eng. & Wales*

Hickey, John (1751–1795). *See under* Hickey, Thomas (1741–1824).

Hickey, Thomas (1741–1824), portrait painter and traveller, was born in Dublin in May 1741, the second son of Noah Hickey, a confectioner in Capel Street there. Between 1753 and 1756 he studied at the Royal Dublin Society Schools, where he won several prizes. His earliest portraits, chalk drawings of 1758 and 1759, are in the National Gallery of Ireland, Dublin. In April 1762 George Dance reported him in Rome 'a very agreeable young man' (Ingamells, 496) who had been recommended by one Captain Smith and William Dance (a miniaturist, brother of George). He was still there in April 1765, living in the strada Felice, and in May 1765 he visited Naples. He was said to have been one of those artists who paid court to Angelica Kauffman (who was in Rome from January 1763 to June 1765). In May 1767 he was back in Dublin, where he exhibited with the Society of Artists during 1768–70, before moving to London. He exhibited portraits at the Royal Academy (1772–6), and in 1775 his sitters included the duke of Cumberland and the actress Mrs Abington (Garrick Club, London). In December 1776 he moved to

Bath for two years, where he painted two full-length portraits of masters of ceremonies, William Dawson and William Brereton (both engraved).

On 26 March 1780 Hickey received permission from the East India Company to go to India, and on 6 July Sir Joshua Reynolds wrote on his behalf to Warren Hastings, recommending 'a very ingenious young painter' who wished 'to make a trial of his own abilities' (Archer, 206). Hickey sailed from Portsmouth on 27 July but the convoy of five vessels was captured by the French and Spanish on 9 August. Hickey was taken to Cadiz but released as a non-combatant; he made his way to Lisbon where, for three years, he established a profitable practice as a portrait painter. In 1782 he was living in 'four handsome rooms on the ground floor of Mrs Williams' hotel' (*Memoirs*, 2.386). The elegant *Girl Leaning on a Piano* in the Tate collection belongs to this period. At the close of 1783 he left Lisbon and arrived at Calcutta in March 1784.

For three years Hickey had considerable success, living in 'a large handsome house in the most fashionable part' (*Memoirs*, 3.202) and enjoying the patronage of the attorney William Hickey (who was not related). The *Indian Lady* of 1787 (National Gallery of Ireland, Dublin), possibly Jemdanee, William Hickey's *bibi*, remains one of his finest pictures. Late in 1786 the painter John Zoffany returned to Calcutta, and Hickey's practice declined. He turned to compiling a *History of Ancient Painting and Sculpture*, the first, and only, volume of which was published in 1788; future volumes, the *Calcutta Chronicle* announced in February 1789, would have to await further research by the author in Europe. From February 1789 Hickey had some success in Madras, but he was back in Calcutta by 1790. In January 1791 he sailed home.

Hickey again encountered a lack of business, although he was able to exhibit the portrait of a nobleman at the Royal Academy in 1792. He was preparing to return to India in February when he received an invitation from Lord Macartney, whose portrait he had previously painted, to accompany him on a diplomatic mission to Peking (Beijing). The mission lasted from September 1792 to September 1794, during which Hickey entertained Macartney with shrewd and clever conversation, but devoted more time to writing than to drawing or painting.

On his return, Hickey spent four years in London and Dublin, without any marked success. Early in 1798 he returned for the last time to India with his two daughters (but nothing is recorded of his marriage). They had left London by 23 February 1798 and arrived at Madras later in the year. The Anglo-Mysore wars, establishing British ascendancy in southern India, were then in their final throes; in May 1799 Tipu Sultan was slain and Seringapatam was taken. Hickey found himself the only portrait painter on the spot and his services were urgently sought. He made chalk drawings of fifty-five British officers (Stratfield Saye House, Hampshire) which were much admired, and he intended to paint a series of large history paintings describing the last Mysore war, which never materialized. Portraiture took up all his time: in 1799 he painted a full-length portrait of Lord Mornington, the British supreme commander, for the Exchange at Madras (Apsley House, London); a series of sixteen Indian dignitaries for Government House, Calcutta, was completed in 1805, and there were many portraits of British inhabitants, of which the full-length of William Kirkpatrick (National Gallery of Ireland, Dublin) was perhaps the most accomplished.

In 1804, when a history of the East India Company was being contemplated, Hickey unsuccessfully proposed himself as the company's historical and portrait painter with responsibility for describing the different Indian inhabitants and their surroundings. In May 1807 he moved to Calcutta where he stayed five years, although only one portrait has been identified from this period. In December 1812 he was invited back to Madras, where he settled with his elder daughter. He was much employed in repairing paintings and few of his portraits survive from these years. The last was of the celebrated Indologist the Abbé Dubois in 'Bramanical costume', painted in 1823 (Madras Literary Society). Hickey died at Madras in May 1824 at the age of eighty-three.

Throughout his restless career Hickey never quite attained eminence as a painter, and he was frequently concerned over his prospects. Though his drawings could be vigorous, his paintings, particularly the whole-length presentation pieces, tended to be wooden; 'combination & general effect are the great difficulties', wrote Lord Sydenham in 1800, 'and we are yet to know whether Mr Hickey possesses these requisites' (Archer, 221). It is, however, apparent that Hickey's personal charm and erudition, quite apart from his extensive experience of the world, considerably helped his social progress.

John Hickey (1751–1795), sculptor, fourth son of Noah Hickey, younger brother of Thomas, was born in Dublin on 7 November 1751. He entered the Royal Dublin Society Schools in 1764, before becoming a pupil of the wood carver Richard Cranfield in Dublin. In 1776 he went to England, enrolling at the Royal Academy Schools, where he obtained a gold medal in 1778. From 1777 to 1794 he exhibited regularly at the Royal Academy, his subjects including, besides mythological scenes, busts of his patron Edmund Burke (1785 and 1791, the earlier sent to India and included in Thomas Hickey's portrait of William Hickey in the National Gallery of Ireland), and of Mrs Siddons as Cassandra (1786). In 1786 he was appointed sculptor to the prince of Wales, and the following year he exhibited at the Royal Academy a model for a colossal figure of Time for Carlton House. A list of monuments executed between 1775 and 1790 is given by Gunnis. He died in London on 13 January 1795 'owing to having lain three days in a damp bed' (Farington, *Diary*, 2.295), and the contents of his studio were sold at Christies on 15 March 1798.

JOHN INGAMELLS

Sources M. Archer, *India and British portraiture, 1770–1825* (1979), 205–33 · A. Crookshank and the Knight of Glin [D. Fitzgerald], *The painters of Ireland, c.1660–1920* (1978), 88–90 · J. Ingamells, ed., *A dictionary of British and Irish travellers in Italy, 1701–1800* (1997), 496–7 · Farington, *Diary*, 1.282; 2.292, 294; 3.698, 938, 984 · R. Gunnis, *Dictionary of British sculptors, 1660–1851* (1953); new edn (1968) · *Memoirs of William Hickey*, ed. A. Spencer, 2–3 (1918–23), vol. 2, p. 386; vol. 3, p. 202 · Graves, *RA exhibitors* · A. Crookshank and the Knight of Glin [D. Fitzgerald], eds., *Irish portraits, 1660–1860* (1969), 54–5 [exhibition catalogue, Dublin, London, and Belfast, 14 Aug 1969 – 9 March 1970]

Hickey, William (1749–1827), lawyer in India and memoirist, was born in St Alban's Street, Pall Mall, Westminster, on 30 June 1749, the eighth child of Joseph Hickey (c.1712–1794), an Irishman, a successful London attorney, and his wife, Sarah Boulton (1720–1768), whose family were landed property owners in Yorkshire. Joseph was evidently an indulgent parent, whose efforts to advance William's career were largely wasted on what was, by his own account, an exceptionally wayward adolescent. William went to Westminster School from 1757 until he left in 1763, as he himself put it, 'most deservedly in high disgrace'. By then his disinclination for systematic work or study, his capacity to spend money, and what he called his 'propensity to women' were all well developed (*Memoirs*, ed. Quennell, 24). A succession of scandals finally persuaded his father that William must seek his fortune overseas. In 1769 he obtained a cadetship in the East India Company's army at Madras and made the journey to India, but, seeing no prospect of advancement there, returned to London via China. An attempt in 1775 to set him up in Jamaica was no more enduring. In 1777, however, he was packed off to India again, this time to Calcutta, where, with the exception of an interval of two years in London managing a parliamentary petition, he was to remain until he retired in 1808.

For some thirty years Hickey practised as an attorney at the supreme court established in 1774 in the capital of the new British empire in India to administer English law to the inhabitants of Calcutta and to British subjects in Bengal generally. In addition Hickey served for some years as deputy to the sheriff of Calcutta and became clerk to Sir Henry Russell, ultimately chief justice of the supreme court. Although in his style of living he remained for many years something of a rake, his career in Calcutta appears to have been a success. He built up a large practice, relying especially on 'native' clients, and earned enough money to enable him to live in a very opulent way, even if he did not save any considerable fortune. He prided himself on being a very well-esteemed member of the British community. He was known as the Gentleman Attorney and the company he kept 'always was the best' (*Memoirs*, ed. Quennell, 234). Fearing for his health, he reluctantly left India in 1808. Little is known of his retirement in Britain. He settled at first in Beaconsfield, moving to London in 1817.

Any assessment of Hickey's career and of his personality depends almost entirely on a single source provided by Hickey himself: his 742 pages of memoirs written shortly after his return to Britain. Little is otherwise known about him. No collection of his own papers survives, nor is there much about him in the letters of others. At least two portraits of him can, however, be definitely identified; one was painted in India by Thomas Hickey (no relation to William) and another by William Thomas was exhibited at the Royal Academy in 1820.

The memoirs are extremely detailed, yet Hickey states

that he wrote them almost entirely from memory, having only a few documents available to him and those mostly from his later years. By strict standards, therefore, the memoirs must contain much that can be regarded only as fiction. For instance, Hickey includes many conversational passages that purport to be verbatim records, but must be reconstructions of what he thought was appropriate to have been said on the occasion. Nevertheless, the memoirs undeniably deal with real people, places, and events. Subject to many small mistakes, the memoirs stand up well to cross-checking with other records. They therefore constitute a significant historical source, above all in bringing to life the British community in Calcutta.

For Hickey, however, the memoirs were evidently much more than a mere record of past events. In them he tried to recreate the characters of people who had meant much to him. In some cases he was brilliantly successful, as with the 'irresistibly attracting and engaging' (*Memoirs*, ed. Quennell, 126) (but also outrageously insensitive) Robert Pott, his friend for thirty years. The main character of the memoirs is of course ultimately their author, and, although he ostensibly denied this, they constitute his apologia. In them he presents himself as a 'pickle', that is as a self-confessed reprobate, who made good. Even at his worst he implies that he never transcended the ultimate standards of gentlemanly conduct and human decency— or at least never did so without sincere repentance.

Hickey never married. Being, as he freely admitted, of an 'amorous disposition', among innumerable liaisons he formed a number of enduring relationships with women. One of these, Charlotte Barry (1762–1783), took the name of Mrs Hickey. After Charlotte's death the great love of Hickey's life was Jemdanee, one of his Indian mistresses, with whom he had a son, who died in infancy. His death date is unknown, but his burial was recorded on 10 February 1827 at St John the Evangelist, Smith Square, Westminster. Prior to his death he had been living nearby in Holywell Street. P. J. MARSHALL

Sources *Memoirs of William Hickey*, ed. A. Spencer, 4 vols. (1913–25), esp. notes to vol. 4, pp. 481–96 · *Memoirs of William Hickey*, ed. P. Quennell (1960); new edn (1975) · William Hickey's memoirs, BL OIOC, MS Eur. G. 118 · Bengal births, marriages, burials, BL OIOC, N/1/2 · M. Archer, *India and British portraiture, 1770–1825* (1979) · private information (2004)
Archives BL OIOC, memoirs, MS Eur. G. 118
Likenesses W. Thomas, oils, 1819, NPG · A. W. Davis, portrait (W. Hickey?), repro. in Archer, *India and British portraiture* · T. Hickey, oils, NG Ire.
Wealth at death £13,000 on return from India; £11,643 received from India in 1810: *Memoirs*, ed. Spencer, 483, 496

Hickey, William [*pseud.* Martin Doyle] (**1787–1875**), writer and philanthropist, was born in Murragh, co. Cork, the eldest son of Ambrose Hickey DD, rector of Murragh. After spending five terms at Trinity College, Dublin (1804–5), he was admitted a pensioner of St John's College, Cambridge, on 7 March 1806 and then became a scholar there. His father was admitted fellow-commoner at the same college three days later. Hickey took a BA at both Cambridge and Dublin in 1809, and took an MA at Dublin in 1832.

In 1811 Hickey was ordained, and he became curate of Dunleckny in the diocese of Leighlin. In 1813 he married Henrietta Maria, only daughter of John Steuart, of Steuart's Lodge, co. Carlow. He moved in 1820 to become vicar of Bannow, in the diocese of Ferns. While there he built a glebe house, restored the fabric of the church, and with Thomas Boyce of Bannow House founded Bannow agricultural school on a farm of 40 acres. With Boyce he also established the South Wexford Agricultural Society, the first of its kind in Ireland. In 1826 Hickey moved to the rectory of Kilcormick, where he built a new church and a schoolhouse, and initiated the building of roads and bridges. In 1831 he was advanced to the rectory of Wexford, and finally, in 1834, to Mulrankin. He was also rural dean of Tacumshane.

Hickey was concerned about the poor condition of the Irish farmer. As early as 1817 he produced a pamphlet entitled *State of the Poor in Ireland*. His first substantial work on farming was written, like his subsequent publications, under the pseudonym of Martin Doyle. It was originally issued in the *Wexford Herald* in the form of letters to the editor, as 'Hints to small farmers', and after publication in a collected form in 1830 it passed through many editions, of which the last appeared in 1867. For the rest of his life a steady stream of practical handbooks on agriculture and gardening appeared. His many publications included *Hints to Small Holders on Planting and on Cattle* (1830), *Practical Gardening* (1833), *A Cyclopaedia of Practical Husbandry* (1839), *Small Farms: a Practical Treatise Intended for Persons Inexperienced in Husbandry* (1855), and *Cottage Farming* (1870). Hickey also contributed regularly to several periodicals, including *Blackwood's Agricultural Magazine*, the *Gardeners' Chronicle*, and *Chambers's Journal*. With Edmund Murphy he launched the *Irish Farmer's and Gardener's Magazine* in 1834. He also edited *The Illustrated Book of Domestic Poultry* (1854).

Hickey was a member of the Royal Dublin Society, and was awarded their gold medal in recognition of his services to Ireland. He also received a pension from the Royal Literary Fund. He died comparatively poor on 24 October 1875 at Mulrankin.

GORDON GOODWIN, rev. ANNE PIMLOTT BAKER

Sources A. J. Webb, *A compendium of Irish biography* (1878) · Venn, *Alum. Cant.* · Boase, *Mod. Eng. biog.* · *Alumni Dublinienses* (1935) · IGI
Likenesses J. Kirkwood, etching (after drawing by C. Grey), repro. in *Dublin University Magazine* (April 1840), 374–6

Hickie, Sir William Bernard (**1865–1950**), army officer, was born on 21 May 1865, eldest of eight children of Colonel James Francis Hickie (1833–1913) of Slevyre, Terryglass, co. Tipperary, and his wife, Lucila Larios y Tashara (*d.* 1880), fourth daughter of Pablo Eustaquio Larios, y Herreros de Tejada, y las Heras Saenz de Tejada, of Castile. Hickie was educated first at Oscott College and later (*c.*1884–5) at the Royal Military College, Sandhurst; he was commissioned in 1885 into his father's regiment, the Royal Fusiliers, and in 1899 attended the Staff College, Camberley, graduating early because of the Second South African War. He spent almost two years on active service in South Africa, latterly in command of a mobile column; the experience proved invaluable, and he ended the war a brevet lieutenant-colonel.

There followed various staff appointments, and from 1909 to 1912 Hickie had command of the 1st Royal Fusiliers. In 1914, now a brigadier-general, he served briefly on the staff of the British expeditionary force's (BEF) 2nd corps and then as commander of 13th brigade (5th division), taking part in the battles of Mons, Le Cateau, and La Bassée before being evacuated sick in October. In April 1915 he took charge of 53rd brigade (18th division), and in December assumed command of the 16th (Irish) division as a major-general. His new appointment was politically highly sensitive. The division was formed around a core of national volunteers, Irish nationalism's response to Carson's Ulster Volunteer Force, and represented nationalism's major contribution to the war effort. Its performance and treatment were therefore under constant scrutiny: fortunately Hickie, a Roman Catholic and supporter of home rule, possessed the professionalism and political awareness to manage successfully the sometimes conflicting pressures of operational necessity and political expectation.

Hickie proved a popular and capable leader, his division earning a reputation for aggression and élan. He commanded it on the Somme in September 1916 at the capture of Ginchy; in the successful Messines offensive in June 1917; in the failure, in appalling conditions, at Ypres in August; and in attacks near Bullecourt in November during the Cambrai offensive. During this period the BEF made considerable progress in developing its operational techniques, but at heavy cost. A particular problem for Hickie was a growing shortage of Irish replacements, partly reflecting increasing nationalist disenchantment with the war; but he met the challenge of integrating non-Irish soldiers into his division with considerable success. In February 1918 he was invalided home ill, so being spared his division's destruction in the German spring offensive. He retired in 1921.

Hickie was a good-looking, intelligent man, charming and articulate; though popular with women, he never married. Competent and resourceful, he typified the army's better divisional commanders during the difficult period of 1916–17, helping to lay the foundations of the BEF's full tactical coming of age in 1918. In retirement he worked tirelessly for Irish ex-servicemen, serving as president of the British Legion in Ireland for many years; and from 1925 to 1935 he was a member of the Irish Free State senate. He was made CB in 1914, and knighted in 1918. Hickie died in Dublin on 3 November 1950 and was buried in Terryglass.   NICHOLAS PERRY

Sources T. Denman, *Ireland's unknown soldiers* (1992) • *The Times* (4 Nov 1950) • *Irish Times* (4 Nov 1950) • *Royal Fusiliers Chronicle* (March 1951) • private information (2004) • Burke, *Gen. Ire.* (1958) • J. E. Edmonds, ed., *Military operations, France and Belgium, 1914*, 2, History of the Great War (1925) • J. E. Edmonds, ed., *Military operations, France and Belgium, 1915*, 1, History of the Great War (1927) • J. E. Edmonds, ed., *Military operations, France and Belgium, 1916*, 2, History of the Great War (1938) • J. E. Edmonds, ed., *Military operations, France and Belgium, 1917*, 2, History of the Great War (1948) • J. E. Edmonds, ed., *Military operations, France and Belgium, 1917*, 3, History of the Great War (1948)

Archives priv. coll.

Likenesses photograph, repro. in H. C. O'Neill, *The royal fusiliers in the Great War* (1922)

Hickman, Sir Alfred, first baronet (1830–1910), iron and steel manufacturer, was born on 3 July 1830 in Tipton, Staffordshire, the younger son in the family of two sons and one daughter of George Rushbury Hickman (1795–1854), ironmaster and colliery owner of Tipton, and his wife, Mary (d. 1872), daughter of Benjamin Haden of Old Hall, Tipton. He left King Edward VI School, Birmingham, at the age of sixteen, and soon joined his father's business, which included the Groveland ironworks and Moat colliery in Tipton. In 1850 he married Lucy Owen Smith (c.1829–1914), only daughter of William Smith, civil engineer, of Portsea, Hampshire, formerly from Staffordshire. Of their sixteen children, twelve (five sons and seven daughters) survived childhood. One son, Brigadier-General Thomas E. Hickman, was Unionist MP for Wolverhampton South 1910–18, and for Bilston 1918–22, and a daughter, Mary, married Sir William Christie, the astronomer royal.

After his father's death in 1854 Hickman continued in partnership with his brother, George Haden Hickman, but in 1862 the partnership was dissolved, and in 1867 he bought the Spring Vale blast furnaces in Bilston, and modernized them to make the firm a leading producer of pig iron in the Black Country. One of the first to see the potential of the new basic Bessemer steelmaking process, licensed in 1879, Hickman, together with other Black Country ironmasters, organized a trial of the new process in 1881 to see whether local pig iron was suitable for conversion into steel. The original Bessemer process, described to the British Association for the Advancement of Science in 1856, did not work with ores with a high phosphorus content, but in the new process the phosphorus was removed in the slag. Impressed by the results, Hickman bought three Bessemer converters and formed the Staffordshire Steel and Ingot Company, with a steel works next to his blast furnaces at Bilston. Production began in 1884, and in 1897 he amalgamated the steel works and the blast furnaces into one company, Alfred Hickman Ltd. By 1900 Alfred Hickman Ltd was producing 3000 tons of iron and 1500 tons of steel annually, and employed over 2000 workmen. Expansion continued as he installed the latest machinery, including, in 1903, one of the earliest gas engines used in England, and in 1907–8 electrically driven reversing motors. His rolling mills came to be regarded as among the best in the world. In order to ensure a good supply of raw materials, Hickman bought collieries near Nuneaton and ironstone quarries near Banbury. He also profited greatly from the sale of the by-products of the steelmaking process, selling slag for use as railway ballast and ground slag to farmers for use as fertilizer. He supplied slag to the Tar Macadam Syndicate Ltd (later Tarmac Ltd), and in 1904 supplied land and capital for Tarmac Ltd to build a plant at Bilston. In 1905 Hickman became chairman of Tarmac Ltd. For many years he went into his works daily, and remained active in Alfred Hickman Ltd until his death, when he was succeeded as chairman by his son, Edward. The firm was taken over by

Stewarts and Lloyds in 1920, and the name disappeared in 1925. Hickman had played an important part in the development of steel production in the Black Country, and helped to postpone the decline of heavy industry in the area.

In addition to his role as the 'Iron King of South Staffordshire' (*Wolverhampton Chronicle*, 16 March 1910), Hickman was Conservative MP for Wolverhampton West 1885–6 and 1892–1906, and was so popular that the Liberals did not bother to contest the seat until 1906. In parliament he was the leading spokesman for the industrialists of the Black Country, campaigning in particular for lower freight charges, but he was also concerned with the welfare of the industrial workers, although his bill introducing loans to help workmen buy their houses failed to win approval. He was deeply concerned about the effect of foreign tariffs on British industry, and served on the iron and steel committee of Joseph Chamberlain's tariff commission in 1904.

Hickman played a leading part in trades organizations such as the South Staffordshire Ironmasters Association and the Wolverhampton chamber of commerce, and he became an authority on the transport problems faced by heavy industries in the midlands. While chairman of the Wolverhampton chamber of commerce he tried to persuade the railway companies to reduce their freight charges, and, with the newly opened Manchester Ship Canal in mind, he proposed that the canal between Wolverhampton, Birmingham, and London, belonging to the Grand Junction Canal Company, be enlarged. This was turned down by the local councils because of the expense. He was also chosen by the iron and hardware trades to put their case to the Board of Trade enquiry into railway rates and canal tolls.

In Wolverhampton, Hickman was president of the Wolverhampton Wanderers Football Club, and he also gave the city 25 acres for a park in 1893, known as Hickman Park. He managed to combine his life as a steel magnate and MP with the lifestyle of a country gentleman. He was a JP for Staffordshire, built a large house, Wightwick Hall, near Wolverhampton, became a member of the Albrighton hunt, and rented a sporting estate in Scotland, as well as maintaining a London home at 22 Kensington Palace Gardens.

Hickman was knighted in 1891 and made a baronet in 1903. He died on 11 March 1910 at Wightwick Hall from complications following typhoid fever, and was succeeded in the baronetcy by his grandson, Alfred Edward Hickman (1885–1947). He was buried on 14 March in Penn parish churchyard, near Wolverhampton.

ANNE PIMLOTT BAKER

Sources G. R. Morton and M. Le Guillon, 'Alfred Hickman Ltd, 1866–1932', *West Midlands Studies*, 3 (1969), 1–30 · R. Trainor, 'Hickman, Sir Alfred', *DBB* · R. H. Trainor, *Black Country élites: the exercise of authority in an industrialised area, 1830–1900* (1993) · N. Mutton, 'Sir Alfred Hickman … the man on a tricycle', *Wolverhampton and West Midlands Magazine*, 24 (1975) · W. K. V. Gale, *The Black Country iron industry*, 2nd edn (1979) · W. K. V. Gale, *The British iron and steel industry: a technical history* (1967) · J. C. Carr and W. Taplin, *History of the British steel industry* (1962) · *The Times* (12 March 1910) · *The Times* (15 March 1910) · J. Lawrence, *Speaking for the people: party, language and popular politics in England, 1867–1914* (1998)
Archives British Steel Records Centre, Irthlingborough, Northamptonshire, east midlands region, Alfred Hickman Ltd MSS · University of Sheffield, corresp. with W. A. S. Hewins
Likenesses photograph, *c*.1911, repro. in E. Woolley, *Bilston on old picture postcards* (1993), 18 · portrait, Dudley Art Gallery; repro. in Trainor, 'Hickman, Sir Alfred' · portrait, repro. in Morton and Guillon, 'Alfred Hickman Ltd', 1
Wealth at death £1,000,000: probate, 22 March 1910, *CGPLA Eng. & Wales*

Hickman, Charles (1648–1713), Church of Ireland bishop of Derry, was the son of William Hickman of Barnack, Northamptonshire, and his wife, Abigail (*d.* 1699). He was educated at Westminster School and at Christ Church, Oxford, where he graduated BA (1671), MA (1674), BD (1684), and DD (1685). Thereafter he held a series of prestigious appointments: chaplain to Charles II's illegitimate son Charles, duke of Southampton; chaplain to Baron Chandos, whom he might have accompanied on his embassy to Constantinople in 1680; and chaplain to the lord lieutenant of Ireland in 1684. He was rector of Farnham Royal, Buckinghamshire, during 1688–1703, and from July 1692 lecturer at St James's Church, Westminster, as well as serving as chaplain-in-ordinary to William and Mary, and later Anne. He was appointed bishop of Derry in 1703 (patent 19 March, consecrated 11 June). Henry Cotton says that Hickman was chaplain to the earl of Rochester, lord lieutenant from 1701 to 1703, which would account for his promotion to an Irish bishopric at this time. However, the official order for his appointment (*CSP dom.*, 1703–4, 283) identifies him simply as one of the queen's chaplains-in-ordinary.

Hickman became a prominent spokesman for the high-church party that emerged in Ireland in the years following his appointment. Addison, reporting in 1709 on proceedings in convocation, claimed that Hickman and Bishop Thomas Lindsay of Killaloe were 'the two firebrands … who have a great influence on the majority of their own order and many of the lay gentlemen of the kingdom' (*The Letters of Joseph Addison*, ed. W. Graham, 1941, 168). Comments by Hickman's predecessor at Derry, William King, though not mentioning him by name, imply that he was non-resident (TCD, MS 750/4/1, pp. 311, 326). King also complained that Hickman had 'entirely rooted up and destroyed a large flourishing wood, which I with care and cost had planted whilst at Londonderry' (C. S. King, *A Great Archbishop of Dublin*, 1906, 228). Hickman published volumes of collected sermons in 1706 and 1713, as well as several single sermons. In 1703 he married Anne, daughter of Sir Roger Burgoyne of Aynhoe, Northamptonshire, who predeceased him. They had one daughter, Anne. He died at Fulham on 28 November 1713 and was buried in the south aisle of Westminster Abbey.

S. J. CONNOLLY

Sources Foster, *Alum. Oxon.* · Wood, *Ath. Oxon.*, new edn · H. Cotton, *Fasti ecclesiae Hibernicae*, 6 vols. (1845–78) · J. L. Chester, ed., *The marriage, baptismal, and burial registers of the collegiate church or abbey*

of St Peter, Westminster, Harleian Society, 10 (1876) · *VCH Buckinghamshire*, 3.230 · *CSP dom.*, 1703–4, 283 · TCD, MS 750/4/1
Archives BL, letters to John Ellis, Add. MSS 28884–28894 · TCD, corresp. with William King
Likenesses M. Dahl, oils, Christ Church Oxf. · S. Gribelin, line engraving (after A. Russell), BM, NPG; repro. in C. Hickman, *Sermons*, 2 vols. (1724)

Hickman, Francis (*b.* 1662/3), classical scholar, was the fourth son of Sir William Hickman, baronet, of Gainsborough, Lincolnshire, and Elizabeth, daughter of John Nevile of Mattersey, Nottingham. In 1676 he became a king's scholar at Westminster School, and in 1681, aged eighteen, entered Christ Church, Oxford. In 1685 he graduated BA, and MA in 1688. He became a nonjuror at the revolution of 1688, but did not lose his student's place at Christ Church, because, according to Anthony Wood, his name was not mentioned in the Act of Deprivation. In 1693 Hickman delivered the Bodleian oration at Oxford University. His only known literary remains are two Latin poems in the 1741 *Musae Anglicanae* (edited by Vincent Bourne, vol. 2, 108–13), upon the death of Charles II and upon an exploit of the duke of Ormond in Ireland. Hickman also co-operated with Francis Atterbury's 1682 Latin translation of John Dryden's *Absalom and Achitophel*. The date of his death is unknown.

T. E. JACOB, *rev.* PHILIP CARTER

Sources Wood, *Ath. Oxon.*, new edn, 4.666 · J. Welch, *The list of the queen's scholars of St Peter's College, Westminster*, ed. [C. B. Phillimore], new edn (1852), 190–91 · *The private correspondence of Dr Francis Atterbury and his friends* (1768)

Hickman, Henry (*bap.* 1629, *d.* 1692), clergyman, ejected minister and religious controversialist, was baptized on 19 January 1629 at Old Swinford, Worcestershire, the son of Richard Hickman (*d.* 1656/7), a clothier, and his wife, Rose, *née* Male. With substantial assistance from his uncle Henry Hickman, a salter of London, he was educated at St Catharine's College, Cambridge, where he graduated BA in 1648. Hickman then entered Magdalen College, Oxford, becoming a demy on 29 October 1648. On 5 March 1649 he was admitted as a fellow by the parliamentary visitors; on 14 March 1650 he was incorporated BA and proceeded MA the same day. Licensed as a preacher, he was lecturer at Brackley, Northamptonshire, by the time he arrived at Steane about 1650 or 1651 to teach logic to Nathaniel Crewe, later Baron Crewe of Steane and bishop of Durham.

Hickman was friendly with John Spilsbury, also a fellow of Magdalen, vicar of Bromsgrove, Worcestershire from 1654 to 1660, and with Richard Baxter. On 12 September 1653 Hickman was appointed vicar of Brackley; on 7 January 1654 he wrote to Baxter that 'I have withdrawn myself from the university' to officiate there, and that he did not intend to involve himself in the controversies which Baxter's works were stimulating (Keeble and Nuttall, 1.122–3). He was, however, unable to suppress his taste for theological battle. In a university disputation of 1657, having obtained Baxter's advice on the validity of Catholic ordination, Hickman argued that 'the Church of Rome, for aught he knew, was a true church'; this did not find favour

with Vavasor Powel, who at All Saints, Oxford, on 15 July 1657, riposted that 'the Pope would provide him with a mitre and the Devil with a frying-pan' (*Calamy rev.*). In May 1657 Hickman was invited to become pastor of Stoke Newington but he declined in the hope of a benefice close to his college; he was admitted rector of St Aldates, Oxford, on 29 July 1657, and proceeded BD on 29 May 1658. On 20 July 1659 Hickman wrote thanking Baxter for his book, probably *The Holy Commonwealth*, remarking that he could not tell whether most to admire his 'judgement or your courage' (Keeble and Nuttall, 1.401). Baxter wrote to William Mewe on 6 September 1659 that 'my friend' Hickman was his only active ally in refuting their various opponents (ibid., 1.407–8).

Of Hickman's voluminous polemical writings, sometimes issued anonymously or under the pseudonym Theophilus Churchman, the exchanges with Thomas Pierce and Peter Heylin are perhaps most notable. In the first preface to Pierce's *An Impartial Inquiry into the Nature of Sin* (1660) the author denounced Hickman as a brother in spirit of 'the rigid scotized thorow paced Presbyterians', accusing him of holding the heresy of some high Calvinists that God was the author of sin, and of thus 'laying the foundation of perfect Libertinism and Rantism'. Hickman replied to Pierce in *A justification of the fathers and the schoolmen that they are not self condemned for denying the positivity of sin* (1659). In *Plus ultra* (1661) and other works he also challenged Peter Heylin's version of the history of English protestantism. He was outraged, for example, that Heylin should 'lay his pelagian eggs in the nest of our first reformers', and denounced as unreliable William Barlow's anti-puritan account of the Hampton Court conference of 1604 (*A Review of the Certamen epistolare*, 1659). Hickman also ill-advisedly questioned the legality of Heylin's marriage.

After the restoration of Charles II in 1660 Hickman lost his post at St Aldates and was ousted from his university fellowship on 6 August 1662. At a dinner with the diarist Samuel Pepys on 21 August 1662 he complained bitterly of the high-handed ejections initiated by vengeful returned Anglican fellows. Soon afterwards he crossed to the Netherlands and took refuge with Matthew Newcomen, the ejected lecturer of Dedham, acting as an assistant preacher in the English church at Leiden in 1664. A Henry Hickman appears under the date 13 July 1663 as a student of the University of Leiden. On 26 March 1666, however, his name featured on a list of English subjects whom the government sought to have returned to stand trial for their activities during the interregnum. Hickman did return, but seems not to have been dealt with severely. However, he quickly became involved in a long and labyrinthine struggle in the court of chancery against Alice Hickman, over the estate of her husband Henry, his uncle and former benefactor. In 1666–7 Hickman became a tutor in the house of William Strode, of Barrington, Somerset, a presbyterian and former MP, with a salary of £10 a year 'and his diet' (Reade, *Gleanings*, 55). Strode died in December 1666, leaving £2500 and an additional £1000 due on a mortgage to his daughter Joanna. On 30 November 1667

Hickman, then of St James's, Clerkenwell, was licensed to marry Joanna (*d.* 1692), who was then aged twenty-six; this presaged the launch of another lawsuit. On 24 November 1668 the couple filed a petition in chancery against her brothers for claims under her father's will. In response William Strode alleged that after his father's death Joanna and Henry had removed gold and other valuable property from the house, and he further accused Hickman of secretly marrying Joanna to get her fortune. It was probably after his marriage that Hickman opened a school at Dusthorp, near Bromsgrove, Worcestershire, to which Oliver Heywood and Adam Martindale sent their sons. He probably lived at the nearby parish of Belbroughton (where John Tristram, his sister's husband, was the patron); he baptized a son, William, there on 28 October 1668. Probably about this time he founded a library at Stourbridge grammar school.

Hickman returned to the Netherlands in 1674 and became pastor of the English church at Leiden. Here it was expected that he would place himself under the discipline of the Dutch classis, but 'no action was taken because Hickman could not understand the Dutch language, and it was decided to wait "until Hickman understands Dutch better"' (Sprunger, 416). On 18 April 1675, as pastor of the English church in the city, he was admitted to study medicine at Leiden University. On 19 March 1683, at the office of the public notary in Leiden, Henry and Joanna Hickman willed that most of their estate should pass to their children, making special arrangements for property in Warwickshire and for Hickman's library. They both died in Leiden in 1692, Henry about Michaelmas, and Joanna a few weeks later. On 10 March 1693 the prerogative court of Canterbury granted the administration of their estate to their son William, who the following week made his own will before returning to the Netherlands.

STEPHEN WRIGHT

Sources *Calamy rev.* · A. L. Reade, *Reades of Blackwood Hill* (1906) · A. L. Reade, *Johnsonian gleanings*, 6 (1927) · *Calendar of the correspondence of Richard Baxter*, ed. N. H. Keeble and G. F. Nuttall, 2 vols. (1991) · K. Sprunger, *Dutch puritanism* (1982) · W. Steven, *The history of the Scottish church, Rotterdam* (1832, 1833) · M. Burrows, ed., *The register of the visitors of the University of Oxford, from AD 1647 to AD 1658*, CS, new ser., 29 (1881) · Venn, *Alum. Cant.* · Pepys, *Diary* · E. Peacock, *Index of English speaking students who have graduated at Leyden* (1883) · J. R. Bloxam, *A register of the presidents, fellows … of Saint Mary Magdalen College*, 8 vols. (1853–85) · Foster, *Alum. Oxon.* · Wood, *Ath. Oxon.*, new edn · N. Crewe, *An examination of the life and character of Nathaniel Lord Crewe* (1790) · R. W. Innes Smith, *English-speaking students of medicine at the University of Leyden* (1932) · will, 10 March 1693, PRO, PROB 11/414, sig. 53

Archives DWL, corresp. with Richard Baxter

Wealth at death substantial, incl. landed property and an advowson in Warwickshire: will, PRO, PROB 11/414, sig. 53

Hickman, Henry (1800–1830), promoter of anaesthesia, was born at Lady Halton in the parish of Bromfield, Shropshire, on 27 January 1800. He was the fifth son and seventh child in the family of eight sons and five daughters of John Hickman, farmer (also clerk of the course at Ludlow races), and his wife, Sarah, daughter of Benjamin Hill, yeoman, of Stanton Lacy. From 1819 he sometimes inserted Hill after Henry, although this was not a baptismal name.

Henry Hickman (1800–1830), by unknown artist

His early education, apprenticeship, and hospital attendance are unknown save for a surviving fair-copy notebook dated 1816–18, containing extracts from textbooks and a record of attendance for two weeks at Brookes's school of anatomy, London. In November 1819 Hickman matriculated at Edinburgh, registered with the university, and joined the Royal Medical Society, but he did not graduate. In 1820, although under age, he became MRCS. On 29 May 1821 Hickman married Eliza Hannah, daughter of Benjamin Gardner, a farmer, of Leigh Court, near Worcester; they had one son and three daughters.

Hickman set up practice as a surgeon in Ludlow. Advertising for an apprentice he promised instruction in the different branches of the profession and access to his museum. In May 1824, however, before moving to Shifnal, near Telford, he auctioned some of the natural history specimens. Commercial directories listed him as physician in Shifnal.

In February 1824 Hickman wrote to T. A. Knight FRS, suggesting the use of suspended animation to tranquillize fear and relieve suffering during surgical operations. He reported standard surgical procedures on animals, rendered insensible under a bell glass by denying them fresh air or by administering carbon dioxide, without evidence of pain and with full recovery. Usually haemorrhage was trifling and healing clean; he attributed the latter to the antiputrescent properties of carbon dioxide. The origins of his inspiration, twenty years before Horace Wells discovered nitrous oxide anaesthesia, are unknown. Suggestions that Hickman experimented with nitrous oxide remain unsubstantiated.

In August 1824 Hickman produced a pamphlet entitled

A letter on suspended animation, containing experiments showing that it may be safely employed during operations on animals, with a view of ascertaining its probable utility in surgical operations on the human subject, addressed to T. A. Knight esq. of Downton Castle, Herefordshire, one of the presidents of the Royal Society. The next line (overscored on the only surviving copy) reads: '… and read before it by Sir Humphrey Davy'—an event which did not take place. The text was also reproduced in the *Shrewsbury Chronicle*; *The Lancet* responded in 1826 with a scathing letter, under the heading 'Surgical Humbug', signed 'Antiquack'.

In 1828 Hickman appealed to Charles X, king of France, for the collaboration of the king's medical schools with his experiments on insensibility produced by 'introduction of certain gases into the lungs'; these were ridiculed by the Académie de Médecine. On his return to England, Hickman practised in Tenbury Wells, Worcestershire. He died at Tenbury Wells on 2 April 1830 and was buried at Bromfield three days later. DENIS SMITH, *rev.*

Sources W. D. A. Smith, 'A history of nitrous oxide and oxygen anaesthesia, pt 4: Hickman and the "introduction of certain gases into the lungs"', *British Journal of Anaesthesia*, 38 (1966), 58–72 · W. D. A. Smith, 'A history of nitrous oxide and oxygen anaesthesia, pt 4B: further light on Hickman and his times', *British Journal of Anaesthesia*, 42 (1970), 347–53, 445–58 · W. D. A. Smith, 'A history of nitrous oxide and oxygen anaesthesia', *British Journal of Anaesthesia*, 50 (1978), 519–30, 623–7, 853–61 · W. D. A. Smith, *Henry Hill Hickman, M.R.C.S. (1800–1830)* (1981) · F. F. Cartwright, *The English pioneers of anaesthesia: Beddoes, Davy, and Hickman* (1952) · *Souvenir: Henry Hill Hickman centenary exhibition, 1830–1930*, Wellcome Historical Medical Museum (1930) · *The Lancet* (4 Feb 1826), 646
Archives Wellcome L.
Likenesses oils, Wellcome L. · portrait, priv. coll. [*see illus.*]

Hickman, Rose. *See* Throckmorton, Rose (1526–1613).

Hickmott, Harold Edward (1881–1947), motor bus operator, was born on 8 May 1881 at Marden, Moorgate Grove, Rotherham, Yorkshire, the son of Edward Hickmott, master grocer, and his wife, Rebecca, *née* Dawes. Nothing else is known about his early life; but Hickmott trained as an engineer at the Vickers naval dockyard, Barrow in Furness, before moving to Brighton to join the management of Southdown Motor Services, in the fledgeling motor omnibus industry. During the First World War, Hickmott served in the Royal Flying Corps, becoming a major, a rank he was unwilling to relinquish during his subsequent civilian career.

Hickmott left the forces in 1919, hoping to make a big splash in the passenger transport business. With the assistance of two friends from Yorkshire, Hickmott acquired James Hodson's suburban bus service in Preston, Lancashire, and founded Ribble Motor Services Ltd in June 1919, a company with an initial capital of £20,000. Britain stood on the brink of a bus mania. New bus routes spilled out from the towns into the countryside, where buses competed with the railways, while in urban areas private bus operators sought to challenge the municipal tramways. British Automobile Traction, an offshoot of the country's largest private sector tramways company,

British Electric Traction, purchased Ribble in 1920. Hickmott could afford to be satisfied with this new arrangement as he retained managerial control. He was managing director of Ribble from 1920 until 1944, and finally retired from the board in 1946.

As a subsidiary of British Automobile Traction, Ribble could draw upon a large reservoir of capital, providing the company with a significant advantage over most of its neighbours. Commanding forces befitting a general, Major Hickmott surveyed the map of north-west England, and planned his attack. Hickmott's victims among the region's small bus firms were offered fair terms, but those who resisted being taken over faced a ruinous fare-cutting war. These tactics did not work against stronger rivals, such as the London Midland and Scottish Railway (LMS), and the corporation transport departments, such as Liverpool, Wigan, and Preston, whose networks had a degree of legal protection. Hickmott entered into collusive agreements with LMS and the corporations, and in the 1930s he was a staunch advocate of co-ordination between road and rail services, and private and public sector transport undertakings. One of Hickmott's greatest coups was a market sharing agreement, commencing in 1931, between the railways, municipal tramways, and major bus companies on Merseyside. Ribble's territory in the 1930s stretched from Liverpool to Carlisle, and the company became Britain's largest operator of express coach services. In 1939 Ribble owned 1055 vehicles, and its issued capital was £1,400,000.

Hickmott was called Hicky by those not required to call him major. In a photograph taken in 1939 he comes across as square-jawed, tight-lipped, and bespectacled; keeping a firm grip on his drink, he exudes a steely determination. Another photograph shows him sporting a military moustache, and staring piercingly, but not coldly, into the camera (his eyes were blue). The managing director of Crosville Motor Services described Hickmott in his prime as a 'large cockerel scratching vigorously in the bran' (Crosland-Taylor, 282), and later in life as an elderly viking. Hickmott was regarded with respect and affection by his equals. Less is known about the attitude of his inferiors, although Ribble had a reputation as a paternalistic employer. Ribble was a disciplined, but overly bureaucratic, organization in Hickmott's day. The senior staff corridor at head office in Preston was known as the quarterdeck, and loyalty was rewarded more liberally than efficiency, as was the norm in transport undertakings.

Determination and good fortune were the twin secrets of Hickmott's rise to fame in the world of the omnibus. Following its takeover by British Automobile Traction, Ribble's destiny was virtually assured. At the very least, however, Hickmott had the ability to make the most of a winning hand, and his contemporaries believed him to be one of the sharpest thinkers in the passenger transport industry. Hickmott retired to the Sherwood House Hotel, Newton St Cyres, Devon, where, following a stroke, he died on 19 August 1947. He was buried in Newton St Cyres. JOHN SINGLETON

Sources W. J. Crosland-Taylor, 'Pioneers of the bus industry: Major H. Hickmott', *Bus and Coach*, 34 (1962), 282–4 · T. B. Maund, *Ribble*, 1 (1993) · *Lancashire Evening Post* (20 Aug 1947) · H. E. Hickmott, 'The development and future of Lancashire's road passenger transport', *Transport in Lancashire: papers and proceedings* [Manchester 1938] (1938), 31–42 · J. Singleton, 'Ribble Motor Services and co-operation in the inter-war bus industry', *Journal of Transport History*, 3rd ser., 16 (1995), 117–33 · CGPLA *Eng. & Wales* (1947) · b. cert. · d. cert.
Likenesses Leyland Motors Ltd, photograph, 1939, repro. in Crosland-Taylor, 'Pioneers of the bus industry', 282 · photograph, priv. coll.; repro. in Maund, *Ribble*, 144
Wealth at death £52,534 8s. 7d.: probate, 4 Dec 1947, CGPLA *Eng. & Wales*

Hicks. For this title name *see* Terriss, Ellaline [(Mary) Ellaline Hicks, Lady Hicks] (1871–1971).

Hicks, Amelia Jane [Amie] (**1839/40–1917**), socialist and trade unionist, was born in 1839 or 1840, the daughter of a Chartist. Little is known of her early life. She married William John Hicks, a pianoforte maker, and they had six children. In 1865 they emigrated to Auckland, New Zealand, where Amie was employed in rope making.

The family returned to England in the early 1880s, and set up home in West Hampstead; this marked the beginning of Amie's involvement in socialist politics. By the spring of 1883 Amie, William, and their daughter, Margaretta, had joined H. M. Hyndman's Democratic Federation, renamed the Social Democratic Federation (SDF) in the following year. Amie, along with two other women (Eleanor Marx and Mrs Hyndman), was elected onto the SDF executive committee in 1884 and 1885. She played an active role in socialist affairs as an open-air speaker and lecturer. In the free-speech campaign of 1885 she was fined £20 for a breach of the peace while addressing a crowd in Dod Street, and she also took part with her son Alfred, a compositor, in the unemployed agitation of 1885–6. She stood unsuccessfully as an SDF candidate for the London school board in 1885 and 1888, giving her occupation as 'accoucheuse' (midwife).

In 1888 Amie Hicks moved to Kentish Town and for the next two decades lived in a variety of homes in nearby Camden Town. She became involved in the labour unrest in London between 1888 and 1890, which led to a shift in the focus of her activities away from socialist politics towards women's labour issues. None the less, she continued to attend SDF meetings, and her links with the party were maintained through Margaretta Hicks, who stood as an SDF candidate for the board of guardians in St Pancras in 1904, set up the women's paper *The Link* in 1911, and became the first woman organizer of the British Socialist Party (successor to the SDF) in 1914.

In 1889 Amie Hicks became involved in a new organization, the Women's Trade Union Association (WTUA), which aimed to help female workers in the East End to form trade unions. She worked closely with Clementina Black, who had been secretary of the Women's Trade Union League, and Clara James, assistant secretary of the association, who was already a close friend. After convening a meeting of rope makers in 1889 Amie was elected secretary of a newly formed East London Ropemakers'

Union, a position she held for ten years. Along with Clara James she pressurized the royal commission on labour to hear female witnesses, and in 1891 the two women were invited to give evidence about the work conditions for rope makers and confectionery workers. Amie noted that conditions for women were so bad in east London that an employer had only to say he wanted some work done, fix his own rate of pay, and he would always find women glad to take it. She appealed, therefore, for the appointment of women factory inspectors, for the medical inspection of women's work, government regulation of profit and wages, and amendments to the Employers' Liability Act.

The difficulties of organizing 'sweated' workers convinced the leaders of the WTUA that they should redirect their energies into a new organization, the Women's Industrial Council (WIC), established in 1894. The new group sought to undertake systematic enquiry into the conditions of working women, to influence public opinion, and to lobby for government policies which would improve women's employment position. Amie Hicks served on the executive of the WIC from its foundation until 1908. She was president of the Clubs' Industrial Association (CIA), which represented forty-five working girls' clubs and was intended to strengthen links between a predominantly middle-class leadership and working women. With her 'hands on' industrial experience and working-class background Amie Hicks had a better understanding of factory girls and what would appeal to them than many more philanthropically minded club workers. The association aimed to encourage leadership among working-class girls, to develop domestic ideals, and to improve physical conditions. Clara James, for example, ran classes in physical drill. The organizers hoped that working girls would take an active interest in civic life and Amie Hicks arranged lectures on industrial, social, and educational topics. She believed that this would enable working women to understand industrial law which might encourage them to assist factory inspectors. She also emphasized the need for training and education since she argued that this would enable women workers to demand better pay and to understand the benefits of trade unionism.

Amie Hicks was joined in her work for the WIC by her daughter Frances Amelia Hicks (sometimes called Amy), who was secretary of the London Tailoresses' Society. Frances was elected to the London Trades Council executive in 1893, joined the technical education board of the London County Council in February 1894, and was appointed the first secretary of the WIC on £100 a year in 1895. She held this post for only six months, resigning on her marriage to Henry James, a mariner, in September 1895. She continued, however, as secretary of the organizations committee of the WIC, of which her mother was chair, and gave lectures on technical education and the Factory Acts. She wrote two essays, 'Dressmakers and tailoresses' (in F. Galton, ed., *Workers on their Industries*, 1896) and 'Factory girls' (in A. Reid, ed., *The New Party*, 1895). She later joined the Women's Labour League and was secretary of the St Pancras branch in 1907.

Amie Hicks's work for the WTUA and WIC brought her

into contact with women from varied social backgrounds who were interested in improving women's work conditions. She opened her home to trade unionists and socialists such as Margaret Bondfield who later acknowledged her influence and support. In an account of the life of Clara James, Mrs Gilchrist Thompson, a member of the WIC, claimed that Clara 'came under the influence of a heroic Labour leader, Mrs Amie Hicks, who, when I came to know her, typified to me what must have been the aspect of one of the minor prophets—denouncing the greed and cruelty of the society of his day' (Bondfield, 32–3). It was in Amie Hicks's garden that Mrs Thompson found out from the young Margaret Gladstone that she was to marry Ramsay MacDonald, who later claimed that Amie was one of the two women who most inspired his wife. He described her as 'a woman of some note as a socialist worker, with a strong motherly face, a firm independent character, a great store of good simple common sense, and above all the mother of children who doated [sic] upon her and admired her' (MacDonald, 137).

During the 1890s Amie Hicks had a considerable reputation as a speaker on subjects relating to working women. She was appointed a delegate with John Burns and David Holmes (of the Weavers' Union) to the American Convention of Labour in 1894. A serious illness on arrival in America prevented her from attending the convention, but she addressed a strike meeting in Boston and lectured to the Twentieth Century Club on women and the labour movement.

She attended the Socialist and Trade Union International Congress in London in 1896, where she presented a resolution calling for the prohibition of women working in factories for six weeks before and after confinement and for a maternity grant. She attended the 1897 Conference on Home Work and read a paper on 'child-bearing women' at the International Conference of Women held in London in June 1899. She was also a member of the London Reform Union, a non-party-political organization which was concerned with moral and social reforms, better housing, and improvements in the municipal government of London.

Amie Hicks continued her association with the WIC until 1910, after which she became vice-president of the National Association of Girls' Clubs, which was formed in 1911 from an amalgamation of the girls' clubs and rest rooms committees of the National Union of Women Workers and the CIA. Amie Hicks appears to have spent her last years living with her daughter, Margaretta, at 21 Rochester Square, St Pancras. She died, after a long illness, in the Middlesex Hospital on 5 February 1917. There was an 'In memoriam' tribute to her in the WIC journal, *Women's Industrial News*, which recorded her 'personal note of sympathy for the particular case ... her passionate sense of justice and ... her eager, youthful spirit' (*WIN*, April 1917), but there were no obituaries in the general press. And yet Amie Hicks was a well-known figure in the trade union and socialist movements and one of the few working-class women to achieve prominence as an organizer and speaker. JUNE HANNAM

Sources J. Bellamy and J. A. Schmiechen, 'Hicks, Amelia (Amie) Jane', *DLB*, vol. 4 • M. G. Bondfield, *A life's work* [1948] • H. W. Lee and E. Archbold, *Social-democracy in Britain: fifty years of the socialist movement*, ed. H. Tracey (1935) • J. R. MacDonald, *Margaret Ethel MacDonald* (1912) • Y. Kapp, *Eleanor Marx*, 2 (1976) • B. L. Hutchins, *Women in modern industry* (1915) • *Women's Industrial News* (April 1917) • B. Drake, *Women in trade unions* (1920) • E. Mappen, *Helping women at work: the Women's Industrial Council, 1889–1914* (1985) • d. cert.

Hicks, Baptist, first Viscount Campden (1551?–1629), mercer and moneylender, was the third son of Robert Hicks (d. 1557), a rich London citizen. He was probably educated at St Paul's School, and then at Trinity College, Cambridge. He was brought up in, and inherited, his father's flourishing mercer's business at the White Bear in Cheapside. The influence of his elder brother, Sir Michael *Hickes (1543–1612), a secretary to Lord Burghley and an intimate of Robert Cecil (later the earl of Salisbury), provided him with opportunities to supply the court with silks and mercery, as well as to make loans to the crown and to courtly persons, among them the earl and countess of Shrewsbury, the earls of Pembroke and Montgomery, Lord Chandos, Anthony and Francis Bacon, and Sir Fulke Greville.

Baptist Hicks complained more than once to his brother about his undeserved reputation for hard dealing, 'when others ... goe away with the gaines and yet byte to the bone' (BL, Lansdowne MS 89, no. 32). He was one of the most important individual lenders to the early Stuart kings, his loans to whom amounted to at least £33,000, not including some of his contributions to syndicated loans, which cannot be precisely quantified, nor the extended credit which he gave for silks and luxury items for the royal household and wardrobe. About this last involvement he expressed concern in a letter to his brother on 9 January 1607: 'I would to god that I had never procured yt' (BL, Lansdowne MS 90, no. 3). In 1609 he obtained a lucrative concession as one of a number of contractors for the purchase and resale of royal lands. His importance to the crown was demonstrated in November 1611, and on other occasions, when royal intervention was instrumental in saving him from serving as alderman.

In 1584 Hicks married Elizabeth, daughter of Richard May, merchant tailor of London. According to Stow, each of their two daughters and coheirs had a fortune of £100,000 (Stow, 760–61). Soon after 1608 Hicks purchased the manor of Campden in Gloucestershire, where he erected a noble mansion near the church; the 'outside' of the house was said to have cost him £29,000. The building was destroyed during the civil war. In 1612 he became involved in a long but ultimately successful dispute with Lionel Cranfield (later the earl of Middlesex), over the profits of the rectory of Campden. In 1611–12 he built at his own cost a sessions house in Clerkenwell for the Middlesex magistrates. This became known as Hicks Hall.

Knighted in 1603, shortly after James I's accession, Hicks was one of the first knighted citizens to continue keeping shop after being honoured. On 1 July 1620 he was created a baronet. He served as MP for Tavistock in the parliament of 1621, and for Tewkesbury in the parliaments of 1624,

Baptist Hicks, first Viscount Campden (1551?–1629), attrib. Paul van Somer

1625, 1626, and 1628. In 1625 he was appointed a deputy lieutenant for Middlesex, and on 5 May 1628 he was raised to the peerage as Baron Hicks of Ilmington, Warwickshire, and Viscount Campden of Campden, Gloucestershire. The titles were inherited by special remainder by his son-in-law, Edward, Baron Noel.

Campden died in London on 18 October 1629, aged seventy-eight, and was buried, on 4 November 1629, in Campden church, where a magnificent monument of black and white marble was erected, with reclining effigies of himself and his wife (who survived him). His epitaph stated that he gave £10,000 to charitable uses, though a later estimate reckoned this sum at £7058. Among the parish churches to benefit from his generosity were those of Campden, Tewkesbury, Hampstead, his City church of St Lawrence Jewry, and Kensington, where in 1612 he had built another country house conveniently near the City. Other benefactions included the building of a market house, the endowment of twelve almshouses in Campden, and bequests for the poor, both there and in Kensington.   ROBERT ASHTON

Sources BL, Lansdowne MSS, exec. vols. 88–90 · BL, Harleian MS 3796, fol. 22 · Exchequer of receipt, order books, PRO, E403/2727–8, 2731–3, 2738, 2741, 2745–6 · state papers, domestic, James I, PRO, SP 14–15, 26/103, 32/68, 36/42, 38/46–7, 60, 20/67 · *CSP dom.*, 1625–6 · Close rolls, James I, PRO, 6 Jac. I, pts 41, 43; 7 Jac. I, pt 29 · *APC, 1621–*

1623, 1625–1626 · Collected sign manual warrants, James I, PRO, Jac. I, vol. 8, no. 15 · *Calendar of the manuscripts of the most hon. the marquess of Salisbury*, 18, HMC, 9 (1940) · R. Ashton, *The crown and the money market, 1603–1640* (1960) · R. Ashton, 'Usury and high finance in the age of Shakespeare and Jonson', *Renaissance and Modern Studies*, 4 (1960), 14–39 · GEC, *Peerage* · J. Stow, *The survey of London*, ed. A. M. [A. Munday] and others, rev. edn (1633), 760–1 · S. E. Hicks Beach, *A Cotswold family: Hicks and Hicks Beach* (1909) · W. K. Jordan, *The charities of London, 1480–1660: the aspirations and achievements of the urban society* (1960) · A. B. Beaven, ed., *The aldermen of the City of London, temp. Henry III–[1912]*, 2 vols. (1908–13) · A. G. R. Smith, *Servant of the Cecils: the life of Sir Michael Hickes, 1543–1612* (1977) · S. Rudder, *A new history of Gloucestershire* (1779) · C. Whitfield, 'Lionel Cranfield and the rectory of Campden', *Transactions of the Bristol and Gloucestershire Archaeological Society*, 81 (1962), 98–118 · memorial tomb, Chipping Campden church, Gloucestershire

Archives BL, Lansdowne MSS, Hicks MSS · NRA, priv. coll., commonplace book

Likenesses attrib. P. van Somer, oils; formerly Middlesex Guildhall, London [*see illus.*] · tomb effigy, Chipping Campden church, Gloucestershire

Hicks, David Nightingale (1929–1998), interior designer and author, was born on 25 March 1929 at The Hamlet, Little Coggeshall, Essex, the second son of Herbert Hicks (1863–1941), stockbroker, and his wife, Iris Elsie Platten, a former actress. After a happy early childhood he became a pupil at Charterhouse School, but did not enjoy the experience, leaving on the advice of his housemaster before he was due to take the school certificate. He decided on a career in art and design, so enrolled at the Central School of Arts and Crafts in London before undertaking his national service in the Royal Army Educational Corps, where he taught art for two years from 1949 to 1951. Afterwards he returned to the Central School, then travelled for a year around Europe before taking up a six-month job with the advertising firm J. Walter Thompson in 1954.

Hicks married Lady Pamela Carmen Louise Mountbatten (b. 1929), the daughter of Earl Mountbatten of Burma and Lady Edwina Mountbatten, on 13 January 1960 at Romsey Abbey. The couple had two daughters, Edwina and India, and one son, Ashley, during their thirty-eight-year marriage. His father-in-law and mother-in-law had been influential themselves in the world of interior design during the 1930s, combining European modernism with transatlantic glamour in their London residence.

Hicks embarked on his glittering career as an interior designer in 1954 when his mother moved from Essex into a new house in South Eaton Place, Belgravia, London, and invited her son to redesign the interior. Photographs of the makeover were published in the leading lifestyle magazine *House and Garden* during that year. The combination of strong colours such as scarlet, black, and cerulean blue in the library, the accent on crisp outline, and the detailed table-top arrangements or 'tablescapes', all characterize Hicks's design work. The article attracted the attention of Mrs Rex Benson, former wife of the publisher Condé Nast, and the pair worked together on some modest commissions during the early 1950s.

In 1956 Hicks entered a business partnership with the antique dealer Tom Parr. They opened their own shop,

Hicks and Parr, located on Lowndes Street off Belgrave Square, London, in 1958, and Hicks's unique style began to make an impact. In 1959 the partnership ended and Parr went on to run the decorating firm of Colefax and Fowler while Hicks opened his own shop, David Hicks Ltd, on Lowndes Street in 1959. From this base he ran his retail and decorating business, undertaking commissions for London flats and country houses owned by aristocratic patrons. The show-window displays, which changed weekly, presented objects from around the world in uncompromising arrangements and attracted much notoriety among his upper-class client base.

During the early 1960s Hicks contributed to the renaissance in British culture at a time when British pop groups, fashion designers, photographers, and models dominated the international scene. He was featured in *David Bailey's Box of Pin-Ups* in 1965 as one of the young style gurus based in 'swinging London'. His first marital home, in Britwell Salome in Oxfordshire, which dated back to 1728, underwent the Hicks treatment. This began with a classical re-creation of eighteenth-century interiors, but he soon branched out into more adventurous colour combinations and furniture arrangements. It included combinations of pink, orange, and aubergine or contrasting green, lurid yellow, and scarlet. The library had matt black walls, and white ceiling and woodwork, with the books bound in crimson, scarlet, and vermilion. These interiors were featured in his second book, *David Hicks on Living—with Taste*, published in 1968. Hicks wrote eight books on various aspects of interior design between 1966 and 1987. All were lavishly illustrated and featured his own schemes, with information on how to achieve a similar effect. They also included Hicks's strong opinions on design, for example:

> I dislike brightly coloured front doors—they are more stylish painted white, black or other dark colours. I hate wrought iron. I loathe colour used on modern buildings—it should be inside. I do not like conventional standard lamps—I prefer functional floorstanding reading lights. Function is just as important as aesthetics ... Function dictates design. (Hicks, *Living with Design*, 252–3)

In 1969 Hicks designed his most prestigious interior to date, that of the Q4 nightclub on the *Queen Elizabeth II* ocean liner. This featured walls covered with grey flannel, offset by silver borders and bright red screens to be drawn across the windows at night. Other commissions, in London, included the Raffles nightclub in Chelsea and beauty salons for Helena Rubenstein Ltd. The growth in Hicks's reputation led to the foundation of David Hicks Marketing Ltd in 1970, with branch offices opening in Switzerland, France, Belgium, Germany, Pakistan, and Australia. He expanded into furniture design, textiles, ceramic tiles, and clothing, employing a wide range of designers worldwide. He designed clothing and fashion accessories for the Association of Japanese Manufacturers from 1977 and womenswear collections from 1982. One of his trademarks was his use of bold, geometrically patterned carpets and textiles—particularly influential in American

interior decoration. The leading post-war interior decorator Billy Baldwin proclaimed that Hicks had 'revolutionised the floors of the world with his small-patterned and striped carpeting' (M. J. Pool, ed., *20th Century Decorating, Architecture and Gardens*, New York, 1980, 10).

Hicks continued to design for the aristocracy as well as undertaking official state commissions in the 1970s and 1980s. The connections made through his marriage to Lady Pamela Mountbatten plus his suave good looks enhanced his career. Clients included Princess Anne, the prince of Wales, President Nkrumah of Ghana, and the sultan of Oman. He also received commissions to decorate the library of the British embassy in Washington and offices for Aeroflot. His interest in architectural design grew, and in his late fifties he designed a Palladian villa in Portugal for himself and his family.

David Hicks's contribution to the world of design was honoured in 1970 with a Design Council award. In 1977 he followed in the footsteps of his grandfather and father by becoming a master of the Worshipful Company of Salters. David Hicks died at his home, The Grove, Brightwell Baldwin, Oxfordshire, on 29 March 1998. He was survived by his wife. ANNE MASSEY

Sources J. West, 'David Hicks', *Encyclopedia of interior design*, ed. J. Banham (1997), 560–62 · D. Hicks, *David Hicks on decoration* (1966) · D. Hicks, *David Hicks on living—with taste* (1968) · D. Hicks, *David Hicks on bathrooms* (1970) · D. Hicks, *David Hicks on decoration with fabrics* (1971) · D. Hicks, *Living with design* (1979) · D. Hicks, *Style and design* (1987) · S. Calloway, *Twentieth-century decoration: the domestic interior from 1900 to the present day* (1988) · M. Hampton, *Legendary decorators of the twentieth century* (1992) · A. Massey, *Interior design of the twentieth century*, 2nd edn (2001) · Burke, *Peerage* (1999) · b. cert. · *CGPLA Eng. & Wales* (1998) · *The Times* (31 March 1998) · *The Guardian* (1 April 1998) · *The Independent* (2 April 1998) · *Daily Telegraph* (1 April 1998)
Archives V&A, corresp. and papers
Likenesses Lee, photograph, 1960, Hult. Arch. · K. Saunders, photograph, repro. in *The Guardian* · photograph, repro. in *The Times* · photograph, repro. in *Daily Telegraph* · photograph, repro. in *The Independent*
Wealth at death £59,844 gross, £55,844 net: probate, 1998, *CGPLA Eng. & Wales*

Hicks, Edward Lee (1843–1919), bishop of Lincoln, was born at 15 Ship Street, Oxford, on 18 December 1843, the elder son of Edward Hicks, a tradesman, and his wife, Catherine Pugh (1812–1897). Both his parents were well read, Liberals in politics, and low-church evangelicals in religion. After attending a private school in St John's Street, he was a day boy at Magdalen College School, Oxford (1855–61), from where he won a scholarship at Brasenose College, Oxford. He depended upon financial support to pursue his studies for his father's business was not a success. Among his friends at Brasenose was Henry Bazely, 'the Oxford evangelist', whose memoir he later wrote (1886). After gaining firsts in classical moderations (1863) and *literae humaniores* (1866), and winning the Craven scholarship (1867) and university Latin essay prize (1868), he was elected by open examination to the first fellowship at Corpus Christi College to be tenable by a layman.

From 1866 to 1873 Hicks was a classical tutor at Corpus,

Edward Lee Hicks (1843–1919), by James Russell & Sons

where the intellectual life of the senior common room was particularly vigorous. John Ruskin was in residence and exercised a strong influence upon him. Chance, however, seems to have led him to take up the academic work for which he was best-known. Laid up after an accident, which forced him to use crutches for several years, he began to study Greek inscriptions. He soon recognized their importance for ancient history, at a time when most English scholars still regarded literary sources as paramount, and with the encouragement of Sir Charles Newton spent his vacations working on the British Museum's collections.

Despite the free-thinking atmosphere of Corpus, and his own drift away from the evangelicalism of his home, Hicks decided to take holy orders (deacon 1870, priest 1871). In 1873 he accepted the Corpus living of Fenny Compton, Warwickshire. Before the colleges awarded research fellowships, the incumbency of a small, rural parish continued to offer fuller opportunities than the university for writing scholarly work. During his time at Fenny Compton he edited *The Collection of Greek Inscriptions in the British Museum* (1874–90). His *Manual of Greek Historical Inscriptions* (1882) became a standard textbook. On 19 September 1876 he married Agnes Mary, daughter of the Revd Edwin Trevelyan Smith, sometime vicar of Cannock, Staffordshire, with whom he had four sons and two daughters.

Hicks was a conscientious country clergyman, organizing weekly prayer meetings, mothers' meetings, district visitors, and support for foreign missions. The plight of farm workers during the agricultural depression led him to support their campaign for land reform, and he set aside some of his own glebe for small-holdings. It was the rural labourers' example in setting up a temperance society in the parish which converted him, in December 1877, to the cause of restricting the consumption of alcohol. He saw abstinence from drink as essential to improving social conditions, became a teetotaller, and joined the United Kingdom Alliance for the Total Suppression of the Liquor Traffic. For the rest of his life he was a tireless campaigner for temperance reform. He was a close associate of Sir Wilfrid Lawson, president of the alliance, and on the latter's death in 1906 became its honorary secretary. He also wrote for *Alliance News*, and addressed temperance meetings. When a heckler charged him with 'trying to rob the poor man of his beer', he replied that he was 'trying to prevent beer robbing the poor man' (*Life and Letters*, 200). Within the alliance he urged the objective of local option (that is, permitting localities to vote on whether to ban the drink trade) rather than the extreme option of complete prohibition, while he pressed the more cautious Church of England Temperance Society to take a bolder position against the sale of liquor.

The fall in the value of tithe, which made it difficult for him to support his family from his clerical income, caused Hicks to leave Fenny Compton in 1886, when he was elected principal of Hulme Hall, Manchester, a Church of England hall of residence for students at Owens College, Manchester. There he attempted to generate some of the collegiate ethos with which he was familiar from his Oxford days, and sought to interest science students in the humanities. He continued his own researches in epigraphy and gave lectures on classical archaeology at Owens College.

In 1892 Bishop Moorhouse appointed him to a canonry of Manchester Cathedral attached to the living of St Philip's, Salford, a slum parish with a population of 10,000. He set about evangelizing non-churchgoers by promoting Church Army missions and holding open-air services in the most deprived areas. He saw it as part of his clerical duty to work towards improving living conditions, and he was a strong critic of slum landlords. He contributed the introduction to a work of social investigation among the most disadvantaged, *Five Days and Five Nights as a Tramp among Tramps* (1904). His concern for the welfare of female millworkers, associated with his support for the 'social' (sexual) purity movement, led him to set up a club for them. As president of the Lancashire and Cheshire Band of Hope Union, a temperance organization, he championed the Anti-Footing League, which campaigned to end the custom in factories of requiring individuals to purchase drink for collective consumption on special occasions.

Hicks opposed the Second South African War, and his sermon on the subject, preached on 21 January 1900, was published by the Manchester Transvaal Peace Committee as *The Mistakes of Militarism*. From 1904 to 1910 he wrote a column under the pseudonym Quartus for the *Manchester Guardian*, a Liberal paper edited by his old Corpus pupil C. P. Scott. His other journalism included contributions to *The Commonwealth*, the organ of the Christian Social Union. He was not, however, identified with any single party within the church. He was quite conservative in matters of ritual, insisting on decency and decorum in services and resisting the complaints of ultra-protestants against what they regarded as high Anglican practices in Manchester Cathedral. Although sympathetic to the modernist movement in biblical criticism, he was no latitudinarian. While, throughout his ministry, he set great store by maintaining good relations with nonconformists and admired their zeal for social and moral reform, he disliked evangelical theology. He was also deeply suspicious of Roman Catholicism (his father-in-law and his youngest son were converts to Rome), regarding papal authority as a threat to freedom. A collection of his sermons and addresses was published as *Addresses on the Temptation* (1903).

Hicks's outspoken radicalism delayed his promotion to a bishopric until March 1910 when, overruling the opposition of the archbishop of Canterbury (Randall Davidson), the prime minister, H. H. Asquith, offered him the bishopric of Lincoln in succession to Edward King. Asquith acknowledged his 'broadminded conception of the true functions of a chief pastor of the Church under democratic conditions' (*Life and Letters*, 136). Enthroned in June 1910, Hicks announced that his 'sympathies lay with the friends of democratic reform' (*Diaries*, 2), and though this caused him to be regarded with some suspicion in the diocese, 'his humour, courtesy, tolerance, and lightly-worn learning' (*DNB*) won over opponents. His ideals were set out in his visitation charge, *Building in Troublous Times* (1912). The diary which he kept during his Lincoln years, published in 1993, records his energetic work visiting the parishes in his rural diocese. He continued the evangelizing of his Salford period, appointing the controversial figure of John Wakeford to promote this object.

The First World War, in which he lost his eldest son, shattered many of Hicks's hopes for moral and spiritual regeneration. In 1910 he had accepted the presidency of the Church of England Peace League, which advocated arbitration in international disputes and opposed militarism. On 2 August 1914 he 'pleaded for British neutrality' in an address to a Church Army service on the sands at Cleethorpes (*Diaries*, 88) and he was a signatory to the declaration in favour of neutrality published on the following day. But within days he argued that the war was necessary to defeat Prussian militarism, a position he described in his *The Church and the War* (1915), originally published in the *Political Quarterly* (December 1914), where he also looked forward to a post-war settlement in which the independence of small states would be guaranteed, foreign policy would be subject to democratic control, and peace would be secured by international arbitration. He sheltered Belgian refugees in his episcopal palace. His view of the private manufacture and trade in arms, like

that in drink, as an evil of plutocracy strengthened his loathing of materialism. He sympathized with conscientious objectors, in whom he saw parallels with the early Christians. While he contested the idea that war engendered the highest form of self-sacrifice, he initially detected signs that the war might create favourable conditions for collectivist social reform. He was therefore particularly depressed by the Conservative reaction evident in the general election of December 1918.

In his family life Hicks was unusual among his generation in believing that girls should have the same educational opportunities as boys; his younger daughter, who attended Somerville College, Oxford, was given the choice of pursuing a career or remaining a 'home-daughter' with her parents. He was strongly in favour of women's suffrage, both because of his belief in the equality of the sexes and because he thought that women voters would add strength to the temperance cause. Maude Royden regarded it as a coup when, in 1912, as bishop of Lincoln, he was persuaded to accept the presidency of the Church League for Women's Suffrage, a suffragist organization which relied on prayer and education to further its aims. He wanted to see women on the same footing as men in the lay councils of the church, attended a sermon by Maude Royden at the City Temple (18 March 1917), and permitted Edith Picton-Turbervill to preach in a church in his diocese, though in April 1919 he resigned the presidency when the league passed a resolution in favour of admitting women to the priesthood.

Hicks suffered a stroke early in 1919 and resigned his see to take effect from 1 September, but died as bishop of Lincoln at Lincoln Lodge, Manor Road, Worthing, Sussex, on 14 August 1919. Four days later, by his wish, he was cremated at Golders Green crematorium—'even in death your father was ahead of his generation', a mourner told his son (*Life and Letters*, 220)—and his ashes placed in Lincoln Cathedral.   M. C. Curthoys

Sources *The life and letters of Edward Lee Hicks*, ed. J. H. Fowler (1922) · *The diaries of Edward Lee Hicks, bishop of Lincoln, 1910–1919*, ed. G. Neville, Lincoln RS, 82 (1993) · *DNB* · A. Wilkinson, *The Church of England and the First World War* (1978) · S. Fletcher, *Maude Royden: a life* (1989) · B. Heeney, *The women's movement in the Church of England, 1850–1930* (1988)
Archives Claremont Colleges, California, Honnold/Mudd Library, corresp. · Lincs. Arch., diaries; official corresp.
Likenesses James Russell & Sons, photograph, NPG [*see illus.*] · G. Manton, portrait, Old Palace, Lincoln · photograph, repro. in Fowler, ed., *Life and letters of Edward Lee Hicks*, frontispiece
Wealth at death £1707 2s. 7d.: probate, 6 Jan 1920, *CGPLA Eng. & Wales*

Hicks, (Ernest) George (1879–1954), trade unionist and politician, was born at Vernham Dean, Hampshire, on 13 May 1879, the fourth of the nine children of William Hicks, bricklayer, and his wife, Laura Beckingham Clarke. Hicks attended the village school but left at the age of eleven to work with his father. He went to London in 1896 and joined the Pimlico branch of the Operative Bricklayers' Society. Appointed national organizer in 1912, he succeeded in recruiting a large number of new members for his union and was elected general secretary in 1919.

That year he also became president of the newly formed National Federation of Building Trades Operatives.

Hicks pushed ahead long-delayed plans to amalgamate the building trade unions. Adopting the slogan 'More unity and fewer unions', he succeeded in uniting the bricklayers' two unions and the Operative Stonemasons' Society into the Amalgamated Union of Building Trade Workers, of which he was first general secretary from 1921 to 1940. Over the same period he was a member of the general council of the Trades Union Congress. In his early days with the bricklayers' union Hicks had been a strong supporter of industrial unionism, akin to syndicalism, and he continued to hold militant left-wing views. But as chairman of the TUC in 1926–7, in the period after the failure of the general strike, he emphasized the need to maintain industrial peace.

Hicks was a ready and humorous speaker, and an effective propagandist for trade unionism. He was much in demand as a campaigner for the Labour Party and very active in a wide range of committee work, on international delegations, and in involvement with working-class education. He was elected as the Labour member of parliament for East Woolwich in 1931 and retained his seat until his retirement in 1950. He was parliamentary secretary to the Ministry of Works from November 1940 until May 1945. He was not invited to serve in the Labour administration formed in July 1945. He was appointed CBE in 1946, having declined in 1945 the prime minister's offer to submit his name for a knighthood.

There was a Rabelaisian flavour about Hicks: fat and red-faced in middle age, he indulged, not always wisely, a fondness for eating and drinking and the broad joke. He was twice married: first, on 29 August 1897, to Kate Louise (d. 24 June 1934), daughter of William Bennett, carpenter, with whom he had one son and two daughters; and second, on 1 October 1938, to Emma Ellen, daughter of James William Arden, stevedore, and widow of Alfred Ellis. He died at his home at 41 Elmbridge Avenue, Surbiton, on 19 July 1954. He was survived by his second wife.

ERIC DE NORMANN, rev. MARC BRODIE

Sources private information (1971) • personal knowledge (1971) • *The Times* (20 July 1954) • *WWBMP* • *The Labour who's who* (1927)
Likenesses W. Stoneman, photograph, 1945, NPG • M. Zulauski, portrait; in possession of the Amalgamated Union of Building Trade Workers in 1971 • photographs, Trades Union Congress, London
Wealth at death £8154 7s. 11d.: probate, 1954, *CGPLA Eng. & Wales*

Hicks, George Dawes (1862–1941), philosopher, was born at Column House, Shrewsbury, on 14 September 1862, the eldest of the six children of Christopher Hicks (d. 1888), solicitor, and his wife, Victoria, daughter of John Samuel Dawes, of Smethwick Hall, near Birmingham. In 1866 the family left Shrewsbury, and by 1869 they had settled in Guildford. Hicks was sent to a preparatory school, Castle School, kept by Robert Lydgate, and in 1876 he won a scholarship to the Royal Grammar School, Guildford, where he remained until 1880. He then studied law in his father's office, but he soon formed a desire to enter the

Unitarian ministry, and went to Owens College, Manchester, in 1883. After graduating in philosophy with first-class honours in 1888, he continued to study the subject at Manchester College, initially in London and then in Oxford. From 1891 he studied at Leipzig, gaining his PhD in 1896 with a thesis on Kant which was published the following year. While there he was involved also in psychological and physiological research which attested to a lifelong interest in natural science.

From 1897 to 1903 Hicks was minister at Unity Church, Islington. During this period he lectured for the London School of Ethics and Sociology and was closely involved in the Aristotelian Society. His marriage in 1902 to Lucy Katherine Garrett (d. 1908), daughter of William Henry Garrett, who was of independent means, brought him easier financial circumstances which enabled him to resign his ministry and settle in Cranmer Road, Cambridge, in 1903, presumably so as to be able to devote himself to philosophy.

In 1904 Hicks was appointed to the chair of moral philosophy at University College, London. He continued to live in Cambridge, travelling to London several times weekly, and he also gave some lectures in Cambridge. He obtained the degree of BA, Cambridge, by research in 1909, and that of LittD, Manchester, in 1904. In 1923 he married Frances Jane Bovill (d. 1935), widow of E. C. Aguggia and daughter of a schoolmaster, John Langley Whitty. This marriage, like his first, was childless. He retired from his chair in 1928. In 1927 he was elected FBA. He was president of the Aristotelian Society in 1913 and Hibbert lecturer in 1931.

As a philosopher Hicks united two very different qualities: immense learning and real independence of mind. Combined with his remarkable command of the German language (his first published work was written in German) these made him an authority on Kant, as well as on Berkeley, and he was a complete master of the history of philosophy. The range and breadth of his learning are well exhibited in the surveys of recent philosophical literature which, over a long period, he contributed twice in each year to the *Hibbert Journal*, of which he was sub-editor.

Hicks's reputation as an original thinker rests on his theory of knowledge. His starting point was Kant, and to the end of his life he always looked back to Kant; but after a short period of neo-Hegelianism, he tended steadily towards the realistic theory of his final years. In this development he was much influenced by the arguments of James Ward and G. E. Moore, and perhaps by the example of his first teacher Robert Adamson, who in his later period began to work out a realistic theory.

Hicks's final views are set out in his collection of essays called *Critical Realism* (1938), a name which he claimed to be the first to use, although it later became the description applied by some American epistemologists to their own theory. His theory rests essentially on a distinction between the act of knowing and the object known; this position is, of course, common to all realists. But while insisting that it is always the object that we know, he distinguishes further between the content of the object and the apprehended content. There are many difficulties in this theory, of all of which he was well aware, and he attempted in his essay 'On the nature of images' to meet one of the most serious. Whatever the difficulties, the whole theory is a strikingly original and penetrating piece of work.

Though an affectionate and courteous man, Hicks was on the whole of a retiring disposition, and most of his energies were given to thinking and teaching. In spite of his apparently frail physique he had a passion for mountaineering, although at the age of sixty-nine he complained to a friend that his climbing days were almost over. Bereavement, ill health, and disappointment arising from his belief that he had not been accorded the recognition which was his due, overcast his later years. He died at his home, 9 Cranmer Road, Cambridge, on 16 February 1941, and was buried on the 19th in Cambridge cemetery. Despite W. G. de Burgh's prediction that 'Hicks will be recognized as a pioneer who shaped … the materials for an enduring synthesis in the theory of knowledge' (Burgh, 431), his ideas have not attracted attention in the decades following his death.

ALAN DORWARD, rev. C. A. CREFFIELD

Sources W. G. de Burgh, 'George Dawes Hicks', *PBA*, 27 (1941), 405–31 · S. V. Keeling, *Mind*, new ser., 50 (1941), 306–9 · J. Passmore, *A hundred years of philosophy* (1957) · A. Quinton, 'Dawes Hicks, George', *Biographical dictionary of twentieth-century philosophers*, ed. S. Brown and others (1996), 171 · personal knowledge (1959) · private information (1959) · CGPLA Eng. & Wales (1941)
Archives Harris Man. Oxf., corresp. and papers relating to *Hibbert Journal* · LUL, lecture notes
Likenesses photograph, repro. in de Burgh, 'George Dawes Hicks'
Wealth at death £10,187 15s. 6d.: probate, 8 July 1941, CGPLA Eng. & Wales

Hicks, Henry (1837–1899), geologist and alienist, was born at St David's, Pembrokeshire, on 26 May 1837, the son of Thomas Hicks (b. 1807), surgeon, and Anne (d. 1884), daughter of William Griffiths of Carmarthen. He was educated at the cathedral chapter school at St David's and at Guy's Hospital, where he became MRCS (in 1862) and an Apothecaries' licentiate. (He also took an MD from St Andrews in 1878.) He began practice at St David's and on 2 February 1864 married Mary, daughter of P. D. Richardson, vicar of St Dogwell's. In 1871 he moved to Hendon as a general practitioner, but subsequently began to specialize in psychiatric medicine and opened a clinic for female patients, eventually transferring to spacious premises at Hendon Grove.

In the 1860s Hicks undertook the care of the palaeontologist John Salter, who had resigned from the geological survey under a cloud with incipient mental illness. Hicks and his patient found a common interest in geology and collaborated in several investigations in Pembrokeshire. Important finds of Lower Palaeozoic fossils were made, and Hicks and Salter began to establish the idea of there also being Precambrian rocks at St David's which had once formed an island in a Cambrian sea and around which the Cambrian strata had been deposited. This idea

was developed with claims of Precambrians in the Malvern hills, north Wales, and elsewhere.

Hicks was a follower to some extent of the ideas of 'chemical geology' of the North American geologist T. S. Hunt, according to which one might, from chemical principles, deduce a series of chemical processes occurring in the earth's early oceans which had led to the formation of strata in a determinate sequence. Such ideas were poorly received in Britain, and Hicks found himself at odds with the scientific establishment in the persons of Andrew Ramsay and Archibald Geikie concerning the rocks of St David's, and specifically whether the crystalline rocks of Salter's Precambrian 'island' were or were not intrusive. In this controversy, Hicks's opponents accused him of invoking faults too readily to account for his field observations, and he was also charged with making correlations between distant rocks on the basis of insufficient lithological resemblances.

Besides doing much work on the Lower Palaeozoic rocks of south Wales, with numerous fossil finds, especially near Llanfirn farm, Abereiddi Bay (today the type area for the 'Llanvirnian' division of the Ordovician), Hicks divided the claimed Precambrian rocks of Pembrokeshire into three lithological units, 'Dimetian', 'Pebidian', and 'Arvonian', which could also be recognized in north Wales; however, this threefold division had few supporters. With his interest in Precambrian rocks, Hicks also participated in the so-called highlands controversy, concerned with the age and structure of the rocks of the north-west highlands of Scotland. It was Hicks who, in 1878, reopened the question, which had been settled in favour of the views of the survey officers Roderick Murchison and Archibald Geikie, developed in the 1860s. Though Hicks did not solve the structural problem successfully, his role in the debate was undoubtedly significant.

Hicks also wrote on Pleistocene geology, in which he became interested when mammalian remains were discovered in the valley below his house in Hendon. Following excavations in cave deposits in north Wales, he concluded that there was evidence of preglacial humans in that part of the world. This suggestion, like many of his other ideas, quickly involved him in controversy. His other main research interest had to do with the so-called 'Morte Slates', near Ilfracombe. He visited this area in 1890, discovering fragmentary fossils, which he took to be Silurian. His suggestion—which has not been accepted subsequently, the rocks being regarded as Upper Devonian—was that the rocks had been emplaced by thrusting into younger strata. However, his work on the area was incomplete at the time of his death.

One of the best-known amateur geologists of his day, Hicks was renowned for his skill at finding fossils and his forceful expression of controversial views. He was secretary of the Geological Society in 1890–93 and president in 1896–8, having been awarded the society's Bigsby medal in 1883. He was president of the Geologists' Association in 1883–5 and was elected FRS in 1885. Besides his geological and medical work, Hicks involved himself in sanitary and educational matters, in church affairs, and in Conservative Party organization. He died unexpectedly of heart disease at Hatchcroft House, Hendon, on 18 November 1899, being survived by his widow and three daughters.

DAVID OLDROYD

Sources T. G. B. [T. G. Bonney], *PRS*, 75 (1905), 106–9 • W. Whitaker, *Quarterly Journal of the Geological Society*, 56 (1900), lviii–lix • [W. Whitaker], *Geological Magazine*, new ser., 4th decade, 6 (1899), 574–5 • D. R. Oldroyd, 'The Archaean controversy in Britain: pt 1—the rocks of St David's', *Annals of Science*, 48 (1991), 407–52 • D. R. Oldroyd, 'The Archaean controversy in Britain: pt 3—the rocks of Anglesey and Caernarvonshire', *Annals of Science*, 50 (1993), 523–84 • D. R. Oldroyd, *The highlands controversy: constructing geological knowledge through fieldwork in nineteenth-century Britain* (1990), 173–8 • P. N. Pearson and C. J. Nicholas, 'Defining the base of the Cambrian: the Hicks–Geikie confrontation of April 1883', *Earth Sciences History*, 11 (1992), 70–80 • H. B. Woodward, *Nature*, 61 (1899–1900), 109–10 • *CGPLA Eng. & Wales* (1900) • m. cert. • *DNB*
Archives NL Wales, geological notes • NL Wales, MS of unpublished book 'The oldest rocks in the British Isles', MS 444OC • U. Cam., Sedgwick Museum of Earth Sciences, Sedgwick Club archives | U. Edin. L., corresp. with Sir Charles Lyell
Likenesses Fradelle, photograph, U. Cam., Sedgwick Museum of Earth Sciences, Sedgwick Club archives; repro. in Pearson and Nicholas, 'Defining the base of the Cambrian' • caricature, U. Cam., Sedgwick Museum of Earth Sciences, Sedgwick Club archives • double portrait, photograph (H. Hicks? with J. Salter), repro. in A. Wheeler and J. H. Price, eds., *From Linnaeus to Darwin: commentaries on the history of biology and geology* (1985), 70
Wealth at death £18,338 11s. 8d.: resworn probate, April 1901, *CGPLA Eng. & Wales* (1900)

Hicks, James Joseph (1837–1916), manufacturer of scientific instruments, was born on 4 November 1837 at Ross Carbery, co. Cork, one of three children of George Hicks and Gillian Coakley. His father worked in the Coakleys' flax mill and may have held a little land, but the family was poor and James was sent to London to live with another branch of the Coakley family. In 1852 he was apprenticed to L. P. Casella of Hatton Garden, London, a philosophical glass-blower, where by 1860 he had risen to the status of foreman. This date marks also the first of many patents filed by Hicks, principally relating to meteorological and clinical thermometers, but covering other items such as barometers, hydrometers and radiometers, aneroid barometers, and various medical appliances utilizing aneroid pressure capsules. In 1862 he established his own wholesale business at 8 Hatton Garden and on 19 June married Emma Sarah Robertson, a milliner, with whom he had a son and two daughters.

It seems likely that in 1861, in Casella's shop, Hicks had made the first clinical thermometer. In 1878, as an independent manufacturer, he acquired partial rights in Luigi Peroni's lens-front tube patent, after which his workforce swelled from about a dozen men to fifty-four employed on clinical thermometers alone, and annual sales rose to about 500 gross, of which a quarter went to the United States. In 1882, to stop infringement of his patent, Hicks went to New York to prosecute what turned out to be the biggest patent lawsuit yet contested between British and American parties. Hicks won this case, and, subsequently, others of a similar nature. By the end of his working life,

he claimed to have manufactured 13 million clinical thermometers, which he supplied throughout the empire.

Hicks also became well known for his aneroid barometers, aimed at the large market which opened to British manufacturers when Vidi's original patent expired in 1861. He produced these in all sorts and sizes, from the popular pocket aneroids to accurate instruments which could register over a wide pressure range, for use as surveying barometers. The mountaineer Edward Whymper and Henry Watkin of the Royal Artillery collaborated with him on the improvement of high-altitude aneroids, while his reputation for precision led to his being approached by various medical men, who saw the aneroid as a means of measuring blood pressure. Under their guidance various sphygmomanometers were patented and sold on the specialist market. The firm catered to the developing science of meteorology, the growing use of industrial control instruments, and to military needs, by the provision of scientific, industrial, and domestic thermometers, barometers, and pressure gauges, and many other types of apparatus. Some, like the Crookes radiometers, were the joint product of scientific knowledge and the glass-blowing skills available in Hicks's workshops; others were aimed at new markets, for which he sometimes lacked understanding; his forays into the manufacture of aeronautical instruments, for example, were unsuccessful.

In 1892 Hicks expanded his manufacturing capacity by building a large factory a short distance from Hatton Garden, eventually employing some 350 men. A benevolent paternalism ruled; his men fielded cricket and football teams, and enjoyed winter social events and summer outings, joined by Hicks and his son, George, who served as his manager. To market his huge and varied output, which was always aimed at wholesale and government buyers, Hicks travelled the world, visiting the United States, South Africa, China, and Australia. He was represented at many of the international and domestic trade fairs, for example, at the annual brewery trades fairs, at Meteorological Society and Royal Geographical Society exhibitions, and at Royal Society conversaziones. He wrote, or had written on his behalf, articles in the popular and scientific press describing his new products. He was admitted a member of the Spectaclemakers' Company in 1898 and sat on its trades council, which was endeavouring to regulate the practice of ophthalmic opticians.

Hicks was a staunch Roman Catholic, a prominent and generous member of the church of St John the Evangelist at Islington, which served the local Irish community. In 1898 he joined other London Catholics on a pilgrimage to Rome, where he presented Pope Leo XIII with medical instruments and a gilt aneroid. In December that year the pope created him a knight of St Gregory. In 1901 he travelled again to Rome to install meteorological apparatus at the Vatican observatory, and in 1906 he presented and fitted up a similar set of apparatus at the patriarchal seminary in Venice. He gave more than £1000 towards the building of Westminster Cathedral and built and endowed a church and presbytery in north London.

In 1911 Hicks sold his business to W. and F. Stanley of

Great Turnstile, Holborn, and although he remained nominally a director until his death, his son severed all connections with the trade. Hicks's wife died in 1899; he himself died at Margate, Kent, on 24 October 1916 and was buried at St Augustine's Abbey in Ramsgate.

ANITA McCONNELL

Sources A. McConnell, *The life and times of James Joseph Hicks (1837–1916): "King of the clinicals"* (1998) • private information (2004) • *The Optician*, 1–49 (1891–1955) [many references throughout] • d. cert. • m. cert.
Likenesses photograph, repro. in *The Optician*, 7 (17 May 1894), 77 • sketch, repro. in *The Optician*, 16 (6 Oct 1898), 182
Wealth at death £36,583: resworn probate, 2 Jan 1917, *CGPLA Eng. & Wales*

Hicks, Sir John Richard (1904–1989), economist, was born in Warwick on 8 April 1904, the eldest of the three children and only son of Edward Hicks, editor and part proprietor of the *Warwick and Leamington Spa Courier*, of Leamington Spa, and his wife, Dorothy Catherine Stephens, who was one of five children of a nonconformist minister. There was an intellectual tradition on both sides of his family, particularly that of his mother, where there was a connection with the political scientist Graham Wallas. Hicks received much intellectual stimulus from the head of his preparatory school, Grey Friars, near Leamington Spa—more stimulus, probably, than he received from his public school, Clifton College. None the less he acquitted himself perfectly adequately at Clifton, and in 1922 won a scholarship to Balliol College, Oxford, to study mathematics, in which he gained a first in moderations in 1923. His undergraduate contemporaries realized that his abilities were something out of the ordinary, as did his tutors. But he was not well taught, at least on the economics side of the new philosophy, politics, and economics school (to which he moved at the end of his first year). Something went seriously wrong with his performance in his final examinations, in which he obtained a second class (1925). His failure to get a first came as a serious set-back, and he was unsuccessful too in the All Souls fellowship examination.

Hicks tried for some months to follow his father's profession as a journalist, on the *Manchester Guardian*; but that was not congenial. In 1927 he obtained a BLitt (under the supervision, surprisingly, of G. D. H. Cole). He then made the decisive step in his life: in 1926 he moved to a teaching position at the London School of Economics (LSE), as a lecturer. His years there were the most important ones in his intellectual development. Hicks was the most eminent economic theorist of his generation in Britain. He was an economist's economist, much less well known to politicians and civil servants and to the general public than many other economists esteemed far less highly by their peers. Primarily, he was a conceptualizer. Concepts that he introduced were later used every day by economists who had almost forgotten their origin: income-effect / substitution-effect, 'Hicks-neutral' technical progress, the portfolio approach to the demand for money, 'fix-price / flex-price', and a host of others. He was not an ivory-tower economist: he believed the purpose of economic theory

Sir John Richard Hicks (1904–1989), by Walter Stoneman, 1953

was to be useful. But he himself was more a toolmaker than a tool-user. His contribution did not lie in establishing specific empirical conclusions or policy recommendations. The book of his that came nearest to seeking to establish a definite conclusion was something of a *jeu d'esprit*, *A Theory of Economic History* (1969).

There is no school of Hicksian economics, although Hicks did have in his own mind a consistent system of thought, which evolved over the years, but which already by the time of the publication of *Value and Capital* (1939)— his most important book—was reasonably comprehensive in its scope. Hicks might perhaps have found congenial the genre of an earlier epoch: the comprehensive treatise, revised through several editions. As it was, he was unusual among modern economic theorists in putting forward many of his chief ideas in books, nearly twenty of them, ranging over almost the whole of economic theory, rather than in articles, though his collected articles also amounted to three substantial volumes. Among his articles were 'Mr Keynes and the classic' (*Econometrica*, 1937), which shaped economists' understanding of the Keynesian system for decades to come, and 'A suggestion for simplifying the theory of money' (*Economica*, 1935), which anticipated part of that system.

It may be conjectured that Hicks's approach was affected by the nearly complete *tabula rasa* that he brought to the LSE as a result of the weakness of his economic education in Oxford. He felt that he had to work things out for himself, almost from first principles, into his own consistent system of thought. That is not to say that his system of thought did not owe much to the great economists of the past—continental rather than British. The ideas of his contemporaries were also grist to his mill; but their status was no higher than that. 'I could not understand what others were doing,' he said, 'unless I could re-state it in my own terms.' His writings give an occasional impression of vanity. But the vanity was not for himself but on behalf of his work.

Hicks's later work continued to attract very serious attention. But with the vast proliferation in the literature of the subject, it inevitably seemed less innovative than what he had done in the golden years at the LSE. In addition, although the contemporary development of economic theory took its impetus in no small part from value and capital, he was out of sympathy with much of it. He wrote, about his successors, largely American:

> I have disappointed them, … I have felt little sympathy with the theory for theory's sake, which has been characteristic of one strand of American economics; nor with the idealisation of the free market, which has been characteristic of another; and I have little faith in the econometrics on which they have largely relied to make their contact with reality.

At the LSE, but not later, Hicks worked in close association with others of his own age and standing—R. G. D. Allen, Nicholas Kaldor, A. P. Lerner, and several others, as well as the more senior Friedrich von Hayek. In later years he gave encouragement and discerning help to his graduate students, relatively few in number. They came mainly from overseas, particularly Italy. Hicks left the LSE in 1935 to go to Cambridge as a university lecturer and fellow of Gonville and Caius College. In Cambridge Dennis Robertson became a good friend, and so remained until Robertson's death. But unfortunately the already powerful Keynesian school in the faculty made clear that it had room for only one god in the pantheon of economic theory: it was not interested in what Hicks was doing. So Hicks was glad to take the chair of political economy in Manchester in 1938, where he stayed until 1946. A fellowship in the newly established Nuffield College in Oxford then offered an attractive opportunity, with fewer administrative responsibilities; he held this post until 1958. The LSE may have been the place that left its strongest intellectual imprint, but Oxford was where by far the largest part of his long life was spent. He moved to All Souls as Drummond professor of political economy in 1952, a post he held until 1965. In all he was a fellow of All Souls for thirty-five years. He was greatly devoted to the college. He was a very active delegate of the Oxford University Press.

Hicks received innumerable academic honours, in addition to his fellowship of the British Academy (1942) and his knighthood (1964). He was the first British scholar to win the Nobel prize in economics (1972); he gave the proceeds to the appeal then in progress for the new LSE library. He was an honorary fellow of the LSE (1969) and of Gonville and Caius (1971).

In 1935 he married an assistant lecturer at the LSE, Ursula Kathleen, the daughter of William Fisher Webb, solicitor, of Dublin. For the rest of his life, until her death in 1985, they were seldom separated, even for a few days.

Their marriage was unusual by conventional standards and there were no children. Their characters were entirely unalike: he was shy, she was outgoing; she was direct, he was subtle. But she protected him and organized their lives; and their loyalty to each other was unswerving. They were both obsessive travellers. Hicks died suddenly, of a heart attack, on 20 May 1989 in the house at Blockley, Gloucestershire, which had been his principal home for many years.   R. C. O. MATTHEWS, *rev.*

Sources D. Helm, *The economics of John Hicks* (1984) · *The Times* (18 July 1985) [obit. of Lady Hicks] · *The Times* (22 May 1989) · *The Independent* (25 May 1989) · private information (1996) · personal knowledge (1996)

Archives BLPES, corresp. with the editors of the *Economic Journal* · JRL, letters to *Manchester Guardian* | CAC Cam., corresp. with R. G. Hawtrey · King's AC Cam., letters to Joan Violet Robinson · Trinity Cam., corresp. with Sir D. H. Robertson

Likenesses W. Stoneman, photograph, 1953, NPG [*see illus.*] · portrait, All Souls Oxf.

Hicks, Sir Michael. *See* Hickes, Sir Michael (1543–1612).

Hicks, Robert Drew (1850–1929), classical scholar, was born at Aust, Gloucestershire, on 29 June 1850, the eldest son of William Hicks, a head clerk in the post office at Bristol, and his wife, Frances Oldland. He was educated at Bristol grammar school, and in 1870 entered Trinity College, Cambridge, of which he was elected a scholar in 1872. He was bracketed sixth classic in the tripos of 1874, and in the same year obtained a second class in the moral sciences tripos. In 1876 he was elected fellow of his college, a position which he held until his death, and from 1884 to 1900 was lecturer in classics. In 1894 Hicks married Bertha Mary, daughter of Samuel Heath, farmer, of Thornton Curtis, Lincolnshire, and sister of Sir Thomas Little Heath and Robert Samuel Heath, the mathematicians. They had one son and one daughter. In 1900 Hicks became blind, but, helped by his wife and by a few friends, he continued to pursue his laborious and fruitful studies in the classics with indomitable courage. In 1928 the honorary degree of DLitt was conferred on him by Manchester University. He died at his home, Fossedene, Mount Pleasant, Cambridge, on 8 March 1929.

In 1894 Hicks published an edition of five books of Aristotle's *Politics*, based on the edition of the German scholar, Franz Susemihl, but including much original work of his own. In 1899, in collaboration with Richard Dacre Archer-Hind, he edited a volume of *Cambridge Compositions* in Greek and Latin. He contributed the section on chronology and on the later philosophical schools to the Cambridge *Companion to Greek Studies* (1905) and that on philosophy to the *Companion to Latin Studies* (1910). In 1907 Hicks published his chief work, a monumental edition of Aristotle's *De anima*. In 1910 he published *Stoic and Epicurean*, and in 1925 a text and translation of Diogenes Laertius in the Loeb Classical Library which remains the standard edition. In 1921 he prepared a *Concise Latin Dictionary* in braille type.

Hicks must be accounted one of the most learned students of Greek philosophy in his generation. His *magnum opus*, packed as it is with detailed discussions of the text and interpretation of the *De anima*, and showing knowledge of the whole literature of the subject, would have been a remarkable achievement for anyone; considered as the work of a blind man, it is much more remarkable. His other works are slighter in character, but are models of clear and judicious presentation, and worthy of the high reputation for scholarship which Hicks enjoyed. As a teacher, he would take endless trouble to deal with the difficulties of his students, and his wide reading and tenacious memory made him an oracle to whom they seldom appealed in vain. When he became blind, he wrote out many of his favourite philosophical works in braille, and a friend relates how he found him in bed reading Aristotle with his fingers under the bedclothes. It may be added that, although no performer, he was passionately devoted to music.   DAVID ROSS, rev. RICHARD SMAIL

Sources *The Times* (9 March 1929) · Venn, *Alum. Cant.* · CGPLA Eng. & Wales (1929)
Wealth at death £16,876 5s. 6d.: probate, 2 May 1929, CGPLA Eng. & Wales

Hicks, Sir (Edward) Seymour George (1871–1949), actor, theatre manager, and author, was born at La Fontaine, Queen's Road, St Helier, Jersey, on 30 January 1871, one of three sons among the four children of Lieutenant Edward Percy Hicks (*d. c.*1884) of the 42nd highlanders and his wife, Grace Gertrude Seymour. The absence of tax on tobacco and brandy may have been part of Jersey's attraction to retired army officers, but the young Seymour's greatest delight was, as he later rather tactlessly recalled in the presence of the prince of Wales, being nursed on the knee of Lillie Langtry (daughter of William Le Breton, dean of Jersey). Hicks's education at Prior Park College, Bath, and Victoria College, Jersey, had been intended to prepare him for a career in the army, but after his appearance—aged nine—as Buttercup in *HMS Pinafore* he never thought of being anything other than what he called 'a facer of the footlights' (Hicks, *Me and my Missus*, 9). At least Hicks made his professional début in a play with a military title: *In the Ranks* at the Grand Theatre, Islington, on 11 November 1887.

In 1888 Hicks secured an engagement with the Kendals, with whom he toured in England and America for two years; he was an eager and quick-witted apprentice of the formidable Madge, whom he described as a mistress of technique, and her husband William, an astute businessman whose forte was light comedy. The youthful Hicks also found time to write his first play (of sixty), a transpontine melodrama entitled *This World of Ours*, which was staged at the Theatre Royal, Brighton, on 20 July 1891 with Violet and Irene Vanbrugh in the cast. It ran for only a week, but the Vanbrugh connection served Hicks well when at Irene's recommendation he adopted a Scottish accent and went to see James Barrie, who gave him the part of Andrew McPhail, the young Scottish medical student, in *Walker, London* at Toole's Theatre (25 February 1892); thanks in no small measure to Hicks's own success it ran for over 600 performances. Despite this, the actor William Terriss did not regard Hicks as a suitable match for his only daughter, Ellaline *Terriss (1871–1971), cabling her from America: 'Stop this nonsense' (Terriss, *Ellaline Terriss*, 46). Undeterred, the couple married at Brentford register office on 3 October 1893, beginning one of the longest partnerships in the history of the theatre.

The next month (25 November 1893), in collaboration with Charles Brookfield, Hicks created at the Court Theatre what is recognized as the first real revue in London: *Under the Clock*. The subject matter was almost entirely theatrical, with unsparing imitations (many by Brookfield) of the leading actors of the day. Hicks sang and danced on the stage for the first time; as a result George Edwardes immediately offered him a three-year contract at the Gaiety Theatre, where he had already recruited Ellaline. First the golden couple fulfilled an engagement in *Cinderella* in New York, before inaugurating a landmark period at the Gaiety. It began on 11 August 1894 with a revival of the 1885 burlesque *Little Jack Shepherd* by H. Pottinger Stephens and William Yardley but, as Macqueen Pope suggests, this was intended 'chiefly to throw additional light and *réclame* upon the production designed to follow it' on 24 November (Macqueen Pope, 318): *The Shop Girl*, the first real musical comedy.

Hicks had persuaded Edwardes that the juvenile leads should be young and sprightly rather than sentimental. Furthermore he introduced into his role as Charles Appleby (the impecunious medical student of good family) a song which he had picked up (not for nothing was he dubbed 'Stealmore Tricks') in America, entitled 'Her golden hair was hanging down her back'; Hicks's rendition of it was a personal triumph. *The Girl* (13 July 1896), in which Hicks did not appear, failed, but he was back with *The Circus Girl* (5 December 1896) in which Ellaline Terriss's big number, 'Just a Little Bit of String', was much admired by the prince of Wales. Unhappily, before the successful run ended Ellaline Terriss had been rendered childless (the loss of a baby), fatherless (William Terriss's murder on 16 December 1897), and motherless (Mrs Terriss did not survive her husband long), but by 21 May 1898 she was in *A Runaway Girl* as the orphan Winifred Grey, the role Hicks had written for her.

True to its title *A Runaway Girl* was a runaway hit, but ever one to seek fresh challenges, Hicks went on to play the duc de Richelieu in *A Court Scandal* (Court, 24 January 1899), a perfect Mad Hatter in *Alice in Wonderland* (Vaudeville, 12 December 1900), Scrooge in J. B. Buckstone's play of that name (Vaudeville, 3 October 1901), Valentine Brown in J. M. Barrie's *Quality Street* (Vaudeville, 17 September 1902), and Edmund Kean in a one-act play by Gladys Buchanan Unger. Then with Cosmo Hamilton he wrote his phenomenal Vaudeville success *The Catch of the Season* (Vaudeville, 9 September 1904) which, in his own words, 'introduced the famous "Gibson Girls" to the grateful youth of the day' (Hicks, *Me and my Missus*, 192).

Hicks, who was keenly interested in the great actors of the past and collected props and other memorabilia, was fascinated by Edmund Kean; he sought out Kean's former call-boy at the Richmond Theatre, but the old man's recollections of the great romantic actor were limited to his description of him as 'a very strange gentleman' (Hicks,

Me and my Missus, 204). It was in one of Kean's most celebrated roles that Hicks made his only incursion into the Shakespearian repertory: as Richard III in a condensed version for Sir Oswald Stoll at the Coliseum. Hicks's own fortunes as a theatre owner began well enough with the Aldwych (1905), followed by the Hicks (later the Globe, later renamed the Gielgud) and the Queen's, but fluctuated considerably until in 1915 he found himself with nothing in the world but responsibilities and a £10 note. Fortunately he had kept his hand in as an actor and playwright, in both of which capacities he worked unstintingly throughout the First World War, to which both of his brothers fell victim. Hicks himself was rejected for military service, but he had set the example to his profession by arranging the first concert party at the front in December 1914.

After the war Hicks maintained a busy and successful career not only in England, but also in Australia, New Zealand, South Africa, and Canada. A long-standing success, which drew audiences throughout the 1920s and into the 1930s, was *The Man in Dress Clothes* (Garrick, 22 March 1922), his own adaptation from the French. As Lucien d'Artois, a role in which he was painted by Maurice Codner RA, Hicks was said to be more French than any Frenchman, investing a thin script with his incomparable verve as a comic actor. His association with French theatre brought Hicks the award of chevalier of the Légion d'honneur in 1931; his knighthood followed in 1935. Thus when President Lebrun of France visited London in the summer of 1939 Hicks was a natural choice for the command performance in his honour. He paired up with Sacha Guitry, with whom he already had a close link, but their playlet *You're Telling me*, which subsequently ran at the Coliseum, put the relationship under strain as the two consummate artistes tried to dry each other up.

In May 1939 Hicks and Basil Dean were summoned to the Home Office, where the lord privy seal, Sir John Anderson, discussed with them the creation of the organization which was to be known as ENSA (Entertainments National Service Association). On 11 September 1939 ENSA, with Hicks as controller, took over Drury Lane Theatre. In 1941 Hicks, together with Ellaline Terriss, led the 'New Arrivals' concert party to the Middle East, where in Palestine they were reunited with their now-widowed daughter Betty and her son. Thereafter Hicks undertook a lecture tour through Africa under the auspices of the British Council, returning home in 1946. After the war the couple lived at The Courtyard, part of their daughter's home at Fleet in Hampshire. Sir Seymour continued as president of Denville Hall as he had been since 1935 and as a member of the Garrick Club as he had been since 1900. Game to the last, he took part in a radio programme a month before his death. He died at his home, on 6 April 1949. On that night one of his films (about all of which he was rather self-deprecating) was being shown on television. His wife outlived him and her own centenary, dying on 16 June 1971.

Seymour Hicks was the author of several volumes of memoirs, the title of one of which, *Chestnuts Reroasted* (1924), reflects their rather repetitive content. However, he had real gifts as a writer, and his portrait of the 1890s entitled *Vintage Years: when King Edward the Seventh was Prince of Wales* (1943) is a wonderfully vivid evocation of the decade with its lovely women, well-turned phrases, sporting life, luxuries old and new, and above all its unsurpassable theatre to which the many-talented Seymour Hicks contributed so much and the spirit of which he personally upheld through the first five decades of the twentieth century.   RICHARD FOULKES

Sources S. Hicks, *Me and my missus* (1939) • S. Hicks, *Hail fellow well met* (1949) • S. Hicks, *Vintage years: when King Edward VII was prince of Wales* (1943) • E. Terriss, *Ellaline Terriss, by herself and with others* [1928] • E. Terriss, *Just a little bit of string* (1955) • *The Times* (7 April 1949) • *The Times* (21 April 1949) • *The Stage* (7 April 1949) • F. L. M. Corbet and others, *A biographical dictionary of Jersey*, [2] (1998) • W. Macqueen-Pope, *Gaiety: theatre of enchantment* (1949) • A. Nicoll, *A history of late nineteenth century drama, 1850–1900*, 2 vols. (1946) • A. Nicoll, *English drama, 1900–1930* (1973) • E. Dudley, *The gilded lily* (1958) • *Who's who in the theatre* • B. Hunt and J. Parker, eds., *The green room book, or, Who's who on the stage* (1906–9) • *CGPLA Eng. & Wales* (1950) • m. cert. • d. cert.
Archives University of Georgia, Athens, corresp. and papers | FILM BFI NFTVA, performance footage | SOUND BL NSA, recorded talk
Likenesses J. Beagles and Co., photograph, 1890–99, NPG • Ellis and Walery, photograph, 1890–99, NPG • A. Ellis, photograph, 1894, NPG • M. Beerbohm, caricature, drawing, 1900, U. Texas • H. Coster, photographs, 1930–39, NPG • M. Codner, oils, *c*.1931, Garr. Club; repro. in Terriss, *Just a little bit of string* • photographs, repro. in Hicks, *Me and my missus* • photographs, repro. in Hicks, *Hail fellow well met* • photographs, repro. in Hicks, *Vintage years* • photographs, repro. in Terriss, *Ellaline Terriss* • photographs, repro. in Terriss, *Just a little bit of string*
Wealth at death £1099 0s. 7d.: probate, 19 May 1950, *CGPLA Eng. & Wales*

Hicks, William (*bap.* 1621, *d.* 1660), religious writer, was baptized at Kerris in the parish of Paul, Cornwall, on 2 January 1621, the son of Nicholas Hicks, gentleman. He was educated partly at grammar school in Exeter, Devon, and partly at Liskeard, Cornwall, and was then sent to Oxford. He matriculated commoner from Wadham College on 9 March 1638, where he attended the courses in logic and philosophy but from where he did not graduate.

In early 1642 Hicks's name appeared near the head of those who subscribed to the protestation in Paul. According to the hostile Anthony Wood:

> he was by his relations put in arms against the king, and in short time became so fanatical in his opinion that he was esteemed by some to be little better than an anabaptist. So that being looked upon as a zealous brother for the cause, he was made a captain in the trained-bands, and became very forward against those of the loyal party. (Wood, *Ath. Oxon.*, new edn, 1813–20, 3.489)

Hicks's own writings suggest that by the late 1650s he was indeed a Baptist, citing in support of belief in the truth of Christ's promised second coming and the thousand-year rule of the saints 'the general consent of most of the Baptized Churches for it, as may appear in a Confession of Faith of divers Churches in Wiltshire, Glocester, Somerset, Dorset, and Devon' (Hicks, 'Quinto-Monarchiae', epistle dedicatory). Hicks shared the millenarian enthusiasm and widespread interest in the books of Daniel and Revelation of the 1640s and 1650s. The millennium was the theme of Hicks's book, published in 1659 and re-issued in 1661, *Apokalypsis apokalypseos, or, Revelation Revealed: being a Practical Exposition on the Revelation of St John*. The doggerel motto beneath his frontispiece portrait placed Hicks firmly within the mainstream of protestant millenarian writing, conjuring the names of Thomas Brightman, Joseph Mede, and John Napier:

> Though Brightman, Napeir, Mede are gone to rest,
> Their Sp'rite yet lives redoubled in thy Breast:
> Yee, that have cast th'Apocalyps to ground,
> Because so dark, mysterious and profound,
> Why take it up againe, and use this Glasse,
> Twill then no longer for a Mystrie passe.

Hicks, like his predecessors, held the pope to be Antichrist:

> The work of this present generation for all Christian
> Worthies to set their hands and heart to, being (as I conceive)
> if not to the downfal of the Throne of the Beast, yet at least
> to the Eclipsing of the Austrian Sun, the great Pillar of the
> Antichristian State.   (Hicks, *Revelation Revealed*, epistle
> dedicatory, sig. a2)

However, as is revealed by the essay which formed the second part of the book (with a separate title-page, dedication, and epistle to the reader, but thereafter with pagination continuous with the rest of the volume), he was an opponent of the radical Fifth Monarchists. In 'Quinto-Monarchiae … or a friendly complyance between Christ's monarchy, and the magistrates', he sought to demonstrate how their misreading of the biblical texts led them to a presumptuous belief in the role of the saints in bringing about the second coming. They had misunderstood many of the prophecies, applying to the present times passages which 'rather wholly relate to that most happy and glorious Millenary Kingdom of Christ, wherein Christ, with all his Saints shall reigne and triumph over all their Enemies, before the end and final Judgement' ('Quinto-Monarchiae', 'To the Christian reader'). Until that time the duty of the saints was not to rule—or to usurp or overthrow the Christian magistrate, who had his own duties in the struggle against Antichrist—but to struggle against sin and popery through the spiritual weapons of prayer and the Bible. The millennium was approaching, but not yet come, and its timing was in God's hands alone. The Fifth Monarchists:

> not weighing the various dispensations of God's Providence,
> through heedlessness, or the temptations of the Evil One …
> [they] are carried out to the opposing of Magistracy, an
> Ordinance of God, that they may bring about (as they
> conceive) the predeterminate Counsels of God's commands
> … Revealed things pertain unto us; but unrevealed things
> (times and seasons) pertain unto God until the times of their
> manifestation come.   ('Quinto-Monarchiae', epistle
> dedicatory)

Appropriately, given Hicks's respect for magistracy, *Revelation Revealed* was dedicated to a recent lord mayor of London, Sir Richard Chiverton, whose family came from Kerris. Even more significantly, 'Quinto-Monarchiae' was dedicated to his fellow Baptist, Colonel Robert Bennet, governor of nearby St Michael's Mount and a powerful

and loyal subject of the protectorate in Cornwall who was 'a clear example of a religious radical who was relatively moderate and pragmatic in his politics' (A. Woolrych, *Commonwealth to Protectorate*, 1982, 220).

Wood reported the rumour—current in Cornwall and in Exeter College, Oxford, he claimed—that Hicks was not actually the author of *Revelation Revealed*: that he had found the manuscript of the book among the papers of his dead kinsman Alexander Harry, sometime fellow of Exeter College, Oxford, and rector of Roche, Cornwall, and published it under his own name. Hicks died at Kerris at the beginning of March 1660, and was buried in the parish church at Paul on 3 March; the administration of his estate was granted to his widow, Margaret, in July.

JOHN S. MACAULEY

Sources Wood, *Ath. Oxon.*, new edn, 3.489–90 • J. S. Macaulay, 'William Hicks', Greaves & Zaller, *BDBR*, 2.88 • Foster, *Alum. Oxon.* • will, grant of administration, PRO, PROB 6/36, fol. 96v • T. L. Stoate, ed., *The Cornwall protestation returns* (1974) • W. Hicks, *Revelation revealed: being a practical exposition on the Revelation of St John, whereunto is annexed a small essay, entituled, Quinto-Monarchiae* (1659), (1661), esp. separate epistles dedicatory to the two works • T. L. Stoate, ed., *Cornwall hearth tax and poll taxes, 1660–1664* (1981) • IGI [parish registers of Paul, Cornwall]
Archives DWL, corresp. with Richard Baxter
Likenesses D. Loggan, line engraving, BM, NPG; repro. in Hicks, *Revelation revealed* (1659)

Hicks, William (*fl. c.*1630–1682), editor of miscellanies, was generally known as Captain Hicks, and identified himself on title-pages as a native of Oxford. In 1671 he described himself as a resident of Shipton-on-Cherwell, 'some four short miles from Oxford' (W. Hicks, 'To the reader', *Oxford Drollery*, 1671). Though the titles *Oxford Drollery* and *Oxford Jests* may have led readers to assume 'that they were written by a scholastical wit', according to Wood he was born in St Thomas's parish, Oxford, 'of poor and dissolute parents', and was 'bred a tapster'. In the 1640s he 'became a retainer to the family of Lucas in Colchester' (presumably the household of Sir John Lucas, who became Lord Lucas in 1645) and later served as 'clerk to a woodmonger in Deptford' (Wood, *Ath. Oxon.*, 3.490). Evidently he had enough education to be able to make jokes about Latin grammar and vocabulary in *Grammatical Drollery* (1682). Hicks was awarded the title of captain at the time of the Restoration as reward for 'training the young men, and putting them in a posture of defense'. Wood describes him as 'a sharking and indigent fellow while he lived in Oxon, and a great pretender to the art of dancing (which he forsooth would sometimes teach)' and dismisses his writings as 'little trivial matters meerly to get bread, and make the pot walk' (ibid., 3.490).

Oxford Jests was published in 1671 (Wood mentions a 1669 edition, not extant) and reprinted in 'refined and enlarged' editions in 1684 and later; a second collection by Hicks, *Coffee-House Jests* (1677), was even more popular, with five editions by 1688. The second of Hicks's compilations to be published ('I now appear a second time in Print', he says in the rhyming preface to the reader) was *Oxford Drollery; being new poems, and songs. The first part, composed by W. H. The second and third parts being, upon several* occasions, made by the most eminent and ingenious wits of the said university (1671). Hicks's own poems, described by the *Dictionary of National Biography* as 'often somewhat licentious', largely consist of comic songs to existing tunes, with titles such as 'The New Scolding Wife'. Poets included in parts two and three include Richard Lovelace, John Suckling, and William Cartwright. *London Drollery, or, The wits academy, being a select collection of the newest songs, lampoons, and airs alamode* (1673), another miscellany edited by Hicks, includes an exchange of poems, 'On Captain Hicks his Curiosities of Nature: by a Young Lady' and Hicks's 'Answer to Madam E. C. upon her Curious Art in Cutting Figures in Paper'. A later collection of verse (this time mostly of Hicks's own composition) is an amusing Latin primer, *Grammatical Drollery, consisting of poems & songs. Wherein the rules of the nouns & verbs in the accedence are pleasantly made easie* (1682). 'The Battle of the Verbs' is representative:

Incipio doth begin the battle …
Poor *timeo* is afraid, and *fugio* shuns
The Battle, *sequor* follows, *curro* runs.

Several miscellaneous poems ('A Mock-Song to Beauty', for example) are also included in the volume.

WARREN CHERNAIK

Sources Wood, *Ath. Oxon.*, new edn, 3.490 · *DNB* · Wing, *STC*

Hicks, William [*called* Hicks Pasha] (1831–1883), army officer, was born on 29 April 1831, and entered the Bombay army as ensign in December 1849. He served as lieutenant (1856) with the 1st Beluchi battalion in the campaign of 1857–9, as staff officer in the Punjab movable column, and with General Penny in the Rohilkhand campaign, subsequently serving under Lord Clyde. Promoted captain in 1861 he served in the Abyssinian expedition of 1867–8 as brigade major in the 1st division, attaining the rank of lieutenant-colonel in 1875, and honorary colonel in 1880.

Recommended by Valentine Baker Pasha, then commanding the Egyptian gendarmerie, Hicks was dispatched in February 1883 to command the Egyptian army in the Sudan in the suppression of the Mahdi's revolt. When he left Cairo on 7 February with a staff of European officers, the British government and its representatives in Egypt were criticized for allowing him to depart on so hazardous an enterprise with only some ten to twelve thousand troops, many of whom had taken part in the recent rebellion under Arabi Pasha. Hicks reached Berber by way of Suakin, and from there proceeded up the Nile to Khartoum, where he joined his army. A reconnaissance under Colonel the Hon. J. Colborne to Kawa showed the proximity of the enemy, and on Hicks's arrival there an advance into Sennar was resolved on. On 24 April they marched, five thousand strong, with four Nordenfeldt guns, upon Jebel ʿAin, and on the way met, on 29 April, a Mahdist force of four or five thousand. Hicks's force won a victory so decisive that, on arriving at Jebel ʿAin in June, no enemy was to be found. The province of Sennar was deserted by the Mahdi's troops; the chiefs were assembled and addressed by Hicks with tact in a spirit of conciliation.

William Hicks [Hicks Pasha] (1831–1883), by unknown engraver, pubd 1883

With the situation apparently tranquil, the army returned to Khartoum.

Later in the year the Mahdi's influence was rapidly spreading in the direction of al-ʿUbayd, and Hicks determined to advance to the attack, a decision subsequently much criticized. On 9 September, with more than ten thousand men of low military quality, he left Omdurman and ascended the White Nile to Dueim, from there striking across the desert to al-ʿUbayd. Against his will, he was accompanied on his desert march by large bodies of Arabs or Sudanese, who apparently had the approval of the Egyptian governor-general of the Sudan. These men were undoubtedly in league with the Mahdi, while Hicks's chief guide, as afterwards appeared, was in communication with the enemy. On 1 November Hicks and his army, without water and lost in forest country unknown to them, were betrayed into an ambush at Kashgil, where the enemy, commanded by the Mahdi, fired on the Egyptians from a dense cover. Despite extreme thirst, the Egyptians fought for three days. On 5 November their ammunition gave out, and the Mahdists charged the Egyptians and speared the wounded as they lay. Hicks led his mounted staff in a final charge in which he and his comrades were all killed. Following this débâcle, Charles George Gordon was sent to the Sudan to superintend the withdrawal of remaining European and Egyptian forces. Hicks was survived by his wife, Sara Sophia.

STANLEY LANE-POOLE, *rev.* M. G. M. JONES

Sources J. Colborne, *With Hicks Pasha in the Soudan* (1884) · *The Times* (17 Jan 1884) · *The Times* (7 Feb 1884) · *The Times* (8 March 1884) · *Army List* · *Hart's Army List* · Boase, *Mod. Eng. biog.* · earl of

Cromer [E. Baring], *Modern Egypt*, 1 (1908) • A. Milner, *England in Egypt*, new edn (1894) • *CGPLA Eng. & Wales* (1884)

Archives U. Durham L., diary and corresp. relating to service in India, Abyssinia, and Sudan

Likenesses engraving, pubd 1883, NPG [*see illus.*]

Wealth at death £625 12s. 11d.: administration, 27 June 1884, *CGPLA Eng. & Wales*

Hicks, William Joynson- [*nicknamed* Jix], **first Viscount Brentford** (1865–1932), politician, was born in Canonbury, London, on 23 June 1865, the eldest son of Henry Hicks (*b.* 1840), merchant, of Benhill and later of Plaistow Hall, Kent, and his wife, Harriett (*d.* 1931), daughter of William Watts of Oadby, Leicestershire. Educated at Merchant Taylors' School, London (1875–81), he took the pledge at the age of fourteen and never wavered in his abstinence from alcohol.

Solicitor and MP Articled to a London solicitor, Hicks built up a considerable practice from 1888 onwards, helped by his father's connections as deputy chairman of the London General Omnibus Company and as a prominent member of the City common council, the omnibus company using him in its numerous claims cases; the law firm he founded was still operating in 1989, when a partner, David Lester, published *Joynson-Hicks on UK Copyright*, a guide to the 1988 Copyright Act.

While on holiday in Italy Hicks met the Joynson family, and on 12 June 1895 married Grace Lynn (*d.* 1952), the only child of Richard Hampson Joynson of Bowdon, Cheshire, silk manufacturer and leading Manchester notable, prominent in Manchester Conservative and evangelical circles. In 1896 he added Joynson to his surname and began cultivating local Conservative and charitable connections associated with his father-in-law, being adopted as one of Manchester's Conservative candidates in 1898; he was defeated by Charles Swann in the general election of 1900 and by Winston Churchill in 1906, scarcely endearing himself to the wealthy, cosmopolitan Manchester élite by his antisemitic speeches. At this point he was becoming known, with his publication in 1906 of *The Law of Heavy and Light Mechanic Traction on Highways*, as something of an oddity, a fiercely traditional evangelical lawyer with an interest in the latest technology. As well as early motors cars, of which he owned a succession, he was fascinated by telephones and aeroplanes, and acquired a good grasp of their working. His interest in cars led him to become chairman of the Motor Union in 1907, a motorists' pressure group, and he presided over its merger with the Automobile Association in 1911, serving as chairman until 1922; one of his first actions was to assert the legality of the AA's patrols warning member-motorists of police speed traps, a position which in the 1920s he presumably preferred not to remember. His mechanical interests were also reflected in his presidencies of the Lancashire Commercial Motor Users' Association, the National Threshing Machine Owners' Association, and the National Traction Engine Association, altogether less conventional positions than that of treasurer of the Zenana Bible and Medical Mission or his membership of the finance committee of the YWCA.

William Joynson-Hicks, first Viscount Brentford (1865–1932), by Walter Stoneman, 1925

In 1908 Joynson-Hicks briefly captured the headlines by defeating Winston Churchill in a by-election in North-West Manchester in 'the most brilliant, entertaining and hilarious electoral fight of the century' (Blythe, 25), another oddity for a traditionalist since it was common form to allow a cabinet minister, obliged by law to seek re-election on appointment, to be returned unopposed at the necessary by-election. It was in this election that a supporter was inspired to coin the nickname Jix, which carried instant recognition—whether of approval, ridicule, or disgust—for the rest of his life. It was also in this election that there were the first of many subsequent exposures of his narrow-minded Conservative populism. He referred to Keir Hardie as a 'leprous traitor' whose object was 'that all the Ten Commandments should be swept away', and in return H. G. Wells sent an open letter to Labour sympathizers in Manchester saying that Jix 'represents absolutely the worst element in British political life … an entirely undistinguished man … and an obscure and ineffectual nobody' (Churchill, *Churchill*, 2.255; Churchill, *Companion*, pt 2, 780).

The publicity and fame of the triumph in 1908 was short-lived. Joynson-Hicks lost the Manchester seat in January 1910, stood unsuccessfully for Sunderland in December 1910, and then re-entered the Commons unopposed in a by-election at Brentford in March 1911; in the 1918 election he was elected for Twickenham, a seat he held until 1929. In the Commons he set about cultivating a reputation as an expert on motors and aviation, and during the First World War acquired some influence as a well-informed back-bencher. His incessant needling of ministers on aircraft design and production and methods of attacking Zeppelins with special bombs culminated in the unabashed barbarity of his pamphlet *The Command of the Air* (1916); it advocated indiscriminate bombing of open towns, especially Berlin, in order to terrorize the complacent German bourgeoisie, and went a long way towards securing him a baronetcy in 1919. That looked like the end of his political career, and in 1920 he went on an extended trip to the Sudan and India, making a point of visiting Amritsar, an inspection which convinced him that Reginald Dyer had been completely justified in ordering the massacre, and that the secretary of state for India, E. S. Montagu, was hopelessly pro-Indian. The visit also confirmed his earlier view that 'it is said at missionary meetings that we conquered it [India] to raise the level of the Indians. That is cant. … We hold it as the finest outlet for British goods in general, and for Lancashire cotton goods in particular' (Blythe, 28).

Puritanical home secretary Political events, however, took a surprising course, and at fifty-seven Joynson-Hicks's ministerial career unexpectedly began. He was so outspoken, and his views were often so embarrassingly extreme, that there had been no danger of his being identified with support for the Lloyd George coalition government, so that he was in an excellent position to profit from its downfall in 1922 and even to play a small part in bringing it about. This was so small that historians have not bothered to notice it, but Bonar Law did, and in quick succession made Jix parliamentary secretary to the department of overseas trade, postmaster-general, and paymaster-general. In 1923 Baldwin, as prime minister, was even shorter of trustworthy front-benchers untainted by records of supporting his rivals, and accelerated the rise of Jix by making him first financial secretary to the Treasury and then minister of health. After the short interlude of the first Labour government Jix returned to office in 1924 as home secretary and remained at the Home Office until his retirement from the Commons in 1929. Some regarded this as a 'leap in the dark', although by 1924 his extreme puritanism and illiberalism should have been sufficiently obvious.

Thus all of a sudden Joynson-Hicks found himself co-equal with party notables such as Austen Chamberlain, Winston Churchill, Birkenhead, and Curzon, all with more ministerial experience than himself. Such eminence went to his head, and already by October 1925 'the most amazing stories about Jix and his aspirations to the Premiership' were circulating in the Commons' smoking room (*Amery Diaries*, 1.421). In August 1928 Beaverbrook—perhaps not the most reliable of political commentators—thought that Jix 'is the only possible successor to Baldwin' (Gilbert, *Churchill*, 5.1318–19), and as late as October 1931 urged Jix 'to set up an alternative Tory Shadow Cabinet, which is badly needed' (*Amery Diaries*, 2.187). Most of Jix's senior colleagues regarded these pretensions as ridiculous, merely confirming their view that he was the joker in the Baldwin pack, a figure of fun who served to

divert and amuse the public. Possibly, however, Beaverbrook was closer to the mark in taking him seriously: 'He is one of those curious products you sometimes get in politics,' he wrote to Mackenzie King, 'a man who is thought a fool by his colleagues, a fine fellow by the private member, and a romantic hero by the chairman of the local Conservative Association' (Gilbert, *Churchill*, 5.1318–19).

Three elements contributed to Joynson-Hicks's bizarre reputation: his seemingly inexhaustible capacity for the absurd; his unabashed appeal to the most illiberal prejudices of popular Conservatism; and, usually overlooked by his detractors, his occasional paradoxical, often unintentional, flashes of enlightenment. He was the most prudish, puritanical, and protestant home secretary of the twentieth century. He led the campaign to suppress the hedonistic permissiveness of metropolitan life in the 1920s, attempting to stem 'the flood of filth coming across the Channel' by rooting out the pornography of *The Well of Loneliness*, D. H. Lawrence's books and pictures, works on birth control, the translation of the *Decameron*, sundry publications condemned as 'pseudo-sociological', and the like, the policy being defended in his 1929 pamphlet *Do We Need a Censor?* In this he recounted how he had got the police to stamp out indecency in Hyde Park, so that it might be possible for 'a man to take his daughter for a walk' there, and made indirect reference to his part in forcing the British publisher to make an expurgated edition of *Lady Chatterley's Lover*, while vehemently denying that he had tried 'to establish a dictatorship in the realm of literature and morals' (Joynson-Hicks, *Do We Need a Censor?*, 7, 9–19). He was mocked in the weeklies for being too unintelligent to recognize literary merit in books he condemned as tending to deprave the public, and was praised in the popular press. His most publicized and farcical moral policing was the attempt to shut down, or sanitize, the night clubs which had mushroomed in central London after 1918, where he smelled unbridled and unmentionable vice, much of which was only doubtfully against the law, and a great deal of drinking out of hours, which decidedly was. A succession of police raids produced embarrassing lists of members of fashionable society found in night clubs, and he came to be seen as playing cat and mouse with Kate Meyrick, 'the undisputed night club queen of London' (Blythe, 37), who was in and out of prison at least three times for licensing law offences, and whose 'release parties' were champagne celebrations featured in the popular press. The raids were satirized by A. P. Herbert in a one-act play, *Two Gentlemen of Soho* (1927).

The prayer book, the Arcos raid, and equal rights for women Joynson-Hicks's greatest triumph came when, defying his leader's wishes, he almost single-handedly routed the massed ranks of the bishops over the revised prayer book, the fruit of years of painstaking and agonizing discussion within the Anglican establishment. Jix had been president of the evangelical National Church League since 1921 and knew a papist when he saw one. In magnificent oratory not heard since the 1850 'papal aggression', and reminiscent of the seventeenth-century Titus Oates and Exclusion Bill rantings, Jix denounced the 1927 prayer book as a thinly disguised attempt to undo the Reformation and prepare for a return to Rome. Rather implausibly likened to John Hampden or Oliver Cromwell, Jix led an otherwise unholy alliance of ultra-protestant tories, Liberals, and nonconformist Labour MPs to a decisive rejection of the book in the Commons, and to a repeat performance when the slightly changed 'deposited book' was presented to the house in 1928, the litmus test for popish practices being the provisions for the 'reservation' of the sacraments, implying belief in transubstantiation. Several prominent Anglicans felt that disestablishment was the only possible response to what they saw as unwarranted interference with matters of doctrine and liturgy by a motley crew of ignorant politicians, many of whom were not Anglicans and, possibly, not even Christians. Jix pressed home his attack by publishing a booklet, *The Prayer Book Crisis*, correctly predicting that the ecclesiastical élite would fight shy of disestablishment for fear of losing the church's endowments and salaries. It turned out to be a pyrrhic victory, however, since the bishops authorized the permissive use of the revised prayer book even though it had no statutory sanction; thus the 1928 version came to be generally adopted, probably illegally.

This episode did something to moderate the hostility of some of those on the left who had been outraged by Joynson-Hicks's behaviour as home secretary, not simply by his censorious stance but also by his stridently anti-union line in the general strike and his obsessive pursuit of communists thereafter. He instigated a notorious police raid on the offices of the Soviet trade delegation, Arcos, in 1927, against the wishes of the foreign secretary, searching for a non-existent secret document alleged to have been stolen, in the hope, quickly realized, of provoking a rupture in diplomatic relations; virtually mimicking the Soviet government he staged a show trial of Harry Pollitt and a dozen leading communists, using the antisubversion statutes of the 1790s. He became extremely popular with the police, and when he retired they raised a subscription for his portrait to hang in Scotland Yard. Yet there was also an unexpected liberal streak in his performance. He devoted some time to developing the borstal system for more enlightened treatment of young offenders. Although he sided with his old opponent Winston Churchill during the general strike and over India, he parted company when Churchill wanted to crush the newfangled greyhound-racing, countering the proposition that totalizators were good for horse-racing but bad for 'this, new degeneracy'—'these animated roulette boards', as Churchill put it—with the barbed remark that that 'savours more of my rather puritanical views than those of your broadminded self' (Gilbert, *Churchill*, 5.1142–5). Joynson-Hicks declined to support one law for the rich and another for the poor, and in the Commons argued that greyhound-racing was positively good for the working class by drawing people away from the pubs. Largely by accident he became the hero of the shop assistants by pushing through the 1928 Shops Act which prohibited working later than 8 p.m. and provided for one halfholiday during the week. He removed the absurdity of the theatre licensing laws which prohibited the sale of chocolates during the first interval of any performance, but allowed it in the second interval.

Above all, entirely by accident Joynson-Hicks rounded off his political career by becoming a champion of women's rights. Off the cuff and without any cabinet discussion he declared in debate (20 February 1925) on a private member's bill that Baldwin's statement in the election campaign of 1924 that the Unionists were in general in favour of equal political rights for all was a pledge 'for equal rights at the next election. I will say quite definitely that means that no difference will take place in the ages at which men and women will go to the poll at the next election' (*Hansard 5C*, 180, 1925, 1504). Churchill commented:

> It may well happen that the whole course of history will have been deflected by the chance utterances in the pressure of a debate of a single Minister speaking beyond Cabinet authority during a Friday afternoon on a Private Member's Bill. (Gilbert, *Churchill*, 5.962–3)

It may well be that after 1832, or more certainly after 1867, universal adult suffrage lay in the logic of history: Jix has the distinction, nevertheless, of giving history a helping hand, for without his unpremeditated undertaking it must be doubtful whether the Baldwin government would have found it necessary or expedient to activate the 'flapper vote' by removing the age limit of thirty, set in 1918, and enfranchising women aged twenty-one and over in the 1928 Reform Act, of which Joynson-Hicks, as home secretary, moved the second reading (29 March 1928). Wisely, Jix did not stand for re-election in the ensuing general election of 1929 in which his party lost power, being rewarded with a peerage as Viscount Brentford.

Jix With the tories in opposition Joynson-Hicks continued for a short while to be the leader-in-waiting of the extreme right, but his health quickly ebbed and he died on 8 June 1932 at his country home, Newick Park, Sussex, and was succeeded in the title by his elder son, Richard Cecil. A throwback to—or prolongation of—an unmistakable type of stern late Victorian evangelical, in his unvarying uniform of top hat and frock coat, there was enough comic light relief to his censorious demeanour for 'the public, always at war with one or other of his opinions, to regard him with genuine, if jesting, affection' (*The Times*, 9 June 1932, leader). Lord Bridgeman thought him altogether too much of a buffoon—'There is something of the comedian in him, which is not intentional, but inevitably apparent, which makes it hard to take him as seriously as one might' (*Diaries and Letters*, 233). Leo Amery was more charitable—'Poor Jix is dead', he noted in his diary. 'He was a very likeable fellow and as S. B. [Baldwin] once said "he may have said many foolish things but rarely did one"' (*Amery Diaries*, 2.240). Churchill delivered an epitaph which summed up tory opinion: 'The worst that can be said about him is that he runs the risk of being most humorous when he wishes to be most serious' (Churchill, *Churchill*, 2.114). A not inconsiderable politician in his time, Jix has also failed to overcome the risk of not being taken seriously by historians.   F. M. L. THOMPSON

Sources *The Times* (9 June 1932) · *The Times* (1908–32) · W. Joynson-Hicks, *Do we need a censor?* (1929) · W. Joynson-Hicks, *The prayer book crisis* (1928) · W. Joynson-Hicks, *The command of the air* (1916) · R. S. Churchill, *Winston S. Churchill*, 2: *Young statesman, 1901–1914* (1967) · R. Churchill, *Companion*, pt 2 (1967) · M. Gilbert, *Winston S. Churchill*, 5: *1922–1939* (1976) · M. Gilbert, *Companion* (1979) · *The Leo Amery diaries*, ed. J. Barnes and D. Nicholson, 1 (1980) · *Hansard 5C* (1924); (1927), 211.2540–50; (1928), 218.1197–211 · R. Blythe, 'The salutary tale of Jix', *The age of illusion* (1963) · *The modernisation of conservative politics: the diaries and letters of William Bridgeman, 1904–1935*, ed. P. Williamson (1988) · *Parliament and politics in the age of Baldwin and MacDonald: the Headlam diaries, 1923–1935*, ed. S. Ball (1992) · H. A. Taylor, *Jix, Viscount Brentford* (1933) · *WWW* · *DNB* · H. Barty-King, *The AA: a history of the first 75 years of the Automobile Association, 1905–1980* (1980) · *CGPLA Eng. & Wales* (1932)
Archives NRA, priv. coll., papers | HLRO, corresp. with Beaverbrook · HLRO, letters to Ralph Blumenfeld
Likenesses W. Stoneman, photograph, 1925, NPG [*see illus.*] · A. S. Cope, oils, 1929, Scotland Yard, London · B. Partridge, caricature drawing, V&A; repro. in *Punch* (21 May 1928) · photographs, repro. in Taylor, *Jix*
Wealth at death £67,661 5s. 7d.: probate, 13 Aug 1932, *CGPLA Eng. & Wales*

Hicks, William Mitchinson (1850–1934), physicist and campaigner for higher education, was born on 23 September 1850 in Launceston, Cornwall, the son of Samuel Hicks, a schoolmaster, and Elizabeth Mitchinson. He went to school at Nelson House, Devonport, and was also tutored privately. He was awarded a scholarship and entered St John's College, Cambridge, to read mathematics in 1869, graduating in 1873 as seventh wrangler. In 1876 he took his MA and was elected a fellow of St John's.

In 1873 Hicks was the first research student to take up postgraduate studies in mathematical and experimental physics under James Clerk Maxwell at the newly founded Cavendish Laboratory. Hicks valued the opportunity to research and experiment with a minimum of training and the maximum of encouragement prevalent under Maxwell at that time in the Cavendish. He went on to develop the mathematics of vortices and invented toroidal functions. At the time physicists were investigating these mechanical and dynamical models as possible explanations for the stability of the atom and the periodicity of chemical behaviour. Hicks's work, recognized for both its advances in mathematics and the promise it held for explaining chemical periodicity, was published in a series of papers in the *Transactions of the Royal Society* (1881–5).

Hicks left St John's in 1883 to take up the position of principal and professor of physics and mathematics at Firth College, Sheffield. He married Ellen Perrin (*d.* 9 Nov 1920) on 13 July 1887. They had two sons, Eric, who became a physician, and Basil, killed in action in 1915. At Sheffield, Hicks's work changed from mainly research to principally teaching and administration. He did a small amount of research in the measurement of alternating currents and the electrolysis of iron. In 1892, on the appointment of a professor of mathematics, he became professor of physics and principal of the college. In 1905 he became, for a brief time, the first vice-chancellor of the University of Sheffield, but returned later that year to the position of professor of physics until his retirement in 1917. His scientific interests at this stage were in theories relating to movement of the ether and from 1912 he threw himself into the task of finding mathematical relationships between the frequencies of spectral lines independent of any theory. He was awarded the Adams prize in 1921 for his work on the analysis of spectra. This work continued until his death.

Hicks was elected to the Royal Society in 1885 and served three times as a committee member. He regularly attended British Association meetings and gave a paper summarizing developments in hydrodynamics in 1880 and in 1895 a paper on vortices. He acted as secretary to section A for several years and chaired it in 1895. He also maintained close contact with Cambridge. He had been awarded the Hopkins prize in 1885 in recognition of his work on the mathematics of vortices and he became one of the three judges for the award of this prize. In 1891 Cambridge honoured Hicks with a ScD. He was awarded the Royal Society's royal medal in 1912 in recognition of his work in physical science and especially for his work on hydrodynamics and vortex motions. In addition to his many papers he published a textbook on dynamics and a treatise on spectral analysis and was working on the proofs of a book about spectra at his death. He corresponded nationally and internationally with scientists and mathematicians about their subjects and also within Britain on higher education.

A national campaign for state funding of higher education in the provinces was started by Hicks and Ramsay after the British Association meeting in 1884. Both men acted as secretaries to a committee of regional higher education colleges and, with allies from Cambridge and Oxford, lobbied for state funding of higher education in the regions. This national campaign resulted in the first, small amount of government funding in 1889. University College, Sheffield, as it had by then become, received £1200—a third of its income.

When Hicks went to Firth College the classes and enrolments were small and the college was in danger of becoming insolvent. He worked tirelessly to ensure that local higher education was maintained through subscriptions and endowments from wealthy local industrialists and gentry, a task described in a local magazine as labouring on stony ground. As a result of his perseverance and powers of persuasion the technical school, medical school, and Firth College amalgamated to form University College, Sheffield, in 1897 and the University of Sheffield was inaugurated in 1905. Hicks served only a few months as vice-chancellor by mutual consent; the council of the university had wished him to be the first vice-chancellor as a sign of respect for his part in the formation of the university, but he, at fifty-four, wanted to return to teaching and researching physics.

Hicks was respected and admired nationally and internationally for his scientific work and nationally for his campaigns for regional higher education. He was respected and liked by colleagues and peers for his courteous and open manner. While he was quiet, he was persistent, and his prodigious scientific and educational achievements testify to his selflessness. He was genuinely liked by his students. He retired in 1917 and moved to Crowhurst, Sussex, in 1919, where he died at the Crowhurst Hotel on 17 August 1934. He was buried at Crowhurst four days later.   MICK NOTT

Sources S. R. Milner, *Obits. FRS*, 1 (1932–5), 393–9 • *Daily Independent* [Sheffield] (20 Aug 1934) • *Sheffield Telegraph* (20 Aug 1934) • *The Eagle*, 48 (1934–5), 193–4 • A. W. Chapman, *The story of a modern university: a history of the University of Sheffield* (1955) • E. W. Chapman, 'William Mitchinson Hicks', *University of Sheffield Gazette*, 57 (1977) • W. M. Hicks, *Local colleges and higher education for the people* (1886) • annual reports of Firth College, University of Sheffield • Venn, *Alum. Cant.* • *South Yorkshire, Derbyshire, Nottinghamshire, and Lincolnshire Notes and Queries, A Quarterly Magazine*, 2/4 (1901), 265 • d. cert. • notes and cuttings, St John Cam.
Archives University of Sheffield | St John Cam., letters to Sir J. Larmor
Likenesses A. S. Cope, University of Sheffield • cartoon, repro. in *South Yorkshire … Notes and Queries* • photograph, repro. in *Daily Independent*
Wealth at death £12,826 12*s.* 9*d.*: probate, 27 Oct 1934, *CGPLA Eng. & Wales*

Hicks, William Robert (1808–1868), asylum superintendent and humorist, was born at Bodmin, Cornwall, on 1 April 1808, the son of William Hicks (*d.* 1833), a schoolmaster of Bodmin, and Sarah, daughter of William and Margaret Hicks. He was educated under his father until 1824, and then under a Mr Harvey at Plymouth. From 1832 to 1840 he kept a boys' boarding-school in Honey Street and on the Castle Hill, Bodmin, and was noted for his extensive knowledge of mathematics. In 1834 he became clerk of the Bodmin board of guardians and superintendent registrar. In that same year, he married Elizabeth, daughter of George Squire of Stoke Damerel, Devon.

In 1840 Hicks was appointed domestic superintendent of the Cornwall County Lunatic Asylum, clerk of the asylum, and clerk to the committee of visitors at Bodmin, and soon after was also named clerk to the highway board. The earl of Devon later procured for him the additional situation of auditor of the metropolitan district asylums. When Hicks became connected with the Bodmin asylum he found the old system of management prevailing, and, in conjunction with the medical superintendent, introduced more humane modern methods. One patient who was chained in a dark cell as a dangerous lunatic turned out to be a wit and a philosopher. He was found to be harmless, and employed to take care of the pigs and do other useful work. In 1865–6 Hicks was mayor of Bodmin, when he revived the custom of beating the bounds of the town (Maclean, 229).

Hicks was a witty speaker, and especially famous for telling a story. He was popular in Cornwall and Devon, and had an established reputation in London, being known as the 'Yorick of the West'. His memory was excellent, and he was an admirable mimic. His wit, musical talent, and good taste in art made him a favourite in society, especially in company with his old friend George Wightwick, the architect. Many of Hicks's narratives were in the Cornish dialect, but he was equally adept in the Devon, as well as in the peculiar talk of the miners. Among his best-known

stories were 'The Coach Wheel', 'William Rabley', 'The Gallant Volunteer', and 'The Dead March in *Saul*'. His best-known story, 'The Jury', referred to the trial in 1817 of Robert Sawle Donnall, accused of poisoning his mother-in-law, when each of the jurors gave a different and ludicrous reason for acquitting the prisoner. On 31 December 1860 Hicks resigned his connection with the lunatic asylum, retiring on a full pension. He died at Westheath (a residence which he himself had built), Bodmin, on 5 September 1868, and was buried at Bodmin cemetery on 9 September. He was survived by his wife who married her second husband, J. Massey, in 1876.

G. C. BOASE, *rev.* CHARLES BRAYNE

Sources G. C. Boase, *Collectanea Cornubiensia: a collection of biographical and topographical notes relating to the county of Cornwall* (1890) • *West Briton* (10 Sept 1868), 4 • J. C. Young, *A memoir of C. M. Young*, 2 (1871), 301–8 • A. Hayward, *Morning Post* (8 Sept 1868), 5 • Boase & Courtney, *Bibl. Corn.*, 1.238 • J. Maclean, *The parochial and family history of the deanery of Trigg Minor in the county of Cornwall*, 1 (1873), 229 • W. F. Collier, ed., *Tales and sayings of William Robert Hicks*, 3rd edn (1893) • *N&Q*, 6th ser., 4 (1881), 367
Likenesses W. Iago, lithographic chalk caricature, 1888 (after Sandercock of Bodmin) • J. Kirkwood, etching (after C. Grey), repro. in *Dublin University Magazine*, 15 (April 1840), 374–6 • portrait, repro. in W. F. Collier, ed., *W. R. Hicks: a memoir* (1888)
Wealth at death under £1500: administration, 19 Oct 1868, *CGPLA Eng. & Wales*

Hickson [*married name* Butler], **Joan Bogle** (1906–1998), actress, was born on 5 August 1906 at 26 Cranford Terrace, Northampton, the only child of Alfred Harold Squire Hickson (*b.* 1874), shoe manufacturer, and his wife, Edith Mary Thorpe Bogle (*c.*1878–1958). Her mother helped, with her sisters, to run the Castle Park School in Northampton. Joan was sent away to school, to Oldfield at Swanage in Dorset, one of the first co-educational schools. At five she saw a West End pantomime, *Cinderella*, and knew at once that she wanted to be an actress: 'I was utterly entranced and asked my parents to move as near to the theatre as possible. I knew immediately that the life I wanted was there' (*The Independent*). During the First World War she would sing as her mother played the piano to entertain wounded soldiers at home. With no encouragement from her family, she trained for the stage at the Royal Academy of Dramatic Art (RADA).

On leaving RADA in 1927, Hickson made her first stage appearance on a provincial tour as Lady Shoreham in *His Wife's Children*, and made her first London appearance in 1928 as the maidservant in a version of Henry James's *The Tragic Muse* at the Arts Theatre. She spent two years in a succession of light West End comedies by Ian Hay and P. G. Wodehouse, and then joined the Oxford Playhouse company, where she stayed for three seasons from 1931 to 1933. The company was run by Stanford and Thea Holme, and situated in a former museum of stuffed animals on the Woodstock Road. Hickson remained grateful for the opportunities and challenges of weekly repertory, where she learned her trade and honed her unique and impeccable sense of comic timing. After this and before the Second World War she had a steady London career in a run of thrillers and comedies, including playing the leading role

Joan Bogle Hickson (1906–1998), by unknown photographer, 1949

in Philip King's farce *See How They Run* (1944), and an unlikely Emma Hamilton in *Rain before Seven* (1949). When Hickson played Madame Henry, a clairvoyant, in *Murder Gang* in 1935, James Agate had already noticed the 'brilliance of her assumptions of gentility … she set the house deliriously rocking' (*Daily Telegraph*). Perhaps she was never fully challenged: she remained dismissive of her talent and said, 'I wasn't beautiful so there were plenty of character roles. I never did any Shakespeare, I'm far too superficial for that. I just act instinctively' (ibid.). But however stereotypical the character, Hickson would bring wit and humanity to the part, and was held in huge esteem both within her profession and beyond. On 29 October 1932 Hickson married Eric Norman Butler (1902–1967), physician, the son of Thomas Harrison Butler (1871–1945), eye surgeon and yacht designer, and his wife, Ellen Reid (d. 1945). They had a son and a daughter.

Hickson made her screen début in *Trouble in Store* in 1933, a short film vehicle for the Scottish comedian James Finlayson. During the 1940s and 1950s she continued to appear in the film studios by day and the theatre at night, establishing herself as an indispensable character actress with a gallery of nosy landladies, doting or overbearing mothers or mothers-in-law, sniffy housekeepers, eccentric aunts, barmaids, and hospital sisters. In a film career that spanned sixty years she appeared in more than 100 films. They included several for the Boulting brothers, *The Guinea Pig* (1948) (where she repeated her stage role), as the landlady in *Seven Days to Noon* (1950), *The Card* (1952), *Doctor*

in the House (1954) and one of its sequels, and several of the 'Carry On' series.

Hickson made no theatre appearances between 1956 and 1967, and then scored a huge success as Grace in Peter Nichols's *A Day in the Death of Joe Egg* in London and New York, repeating the role in the film version in 1970. She made her National Theatre début in 1974 in Nichols's *The Freeway*, staying there for *Blithe Spirit*, and although she was perfect as Mrs Bradman she would have been a glorious Madame Arcati. Also at the National she played Delia in Alan Ayckbourn's *Bedroom Farce*, where her duet with Michael Gough, as an elderly couple munching pilchards on toast in bed while their family disintegrates around them, was hugely acclaimed, culminating in Tony awards for them both when they took it to Broadway in 1978.

While working in the theatre and on film she also managed to appear regularly on radio (in the late forties and early fifties as Mrs Gage, the cockney charwoman, in five series of *The Bell Family*) and on television (from 1963 to 1966 as the housekeeper in the series *Our Man at St Mark's*). Hickson was seventy-eight when she auditioned for and was chosen to play Miss Jane Marple, Agatha Christie's spinster sleuth, for the BBC. She played Miss Marple in twelve television films, finishing only when Hickson decided to retire at eighty-six. In 1946 she had appeared on stage in Christie's *Appointment with Fear*. Christie had seen her and written to her, 'I hope that one day you will play my dear Miss Marple' (*The Guardian*). It was said that Miss Marple was loosely based on one of Christie's aunts, as a small and delicate woman, far closer to the febrile and birdlike Hickson than was the previous distinguished but overbearing occupant of the role, Margaret Rutherford (Hickson had appeared in one of Rutherford's Marple films, as yet another housekeeper). Hickson was the definitive Miss Marple; ever watchful, neat, calm, and unflappable, with a cup of tea in one hand and a crocodile-skin handbag in the other, she personified 'justice in a hand-knitted cardigan' (*The Independent*). When Hickson was made an OBE in 1987, the honour was long overdue, and came directly from one of Miss Marple's greatest fans, Elizabeth II.

Hickson and her husband lived a quiet village life, at odds with the world of theatre and film, and Hickson said that her husband 'had no interest in the theatre. I don't think he ever came to see my work. After the show I would get on the train, go home and become Mrs Butler again. It was rather nice having two lives'. Her husband died in 1967. 'I never really got over it, but my work was an enormous help. You simply have to go on' (*Daily Telegraph*). Hickson never completely retired, recording talking books of Miss Marple mysteries almost to the end. She died in Colchester General Hospital on 17 October 1998.

ALEX JENNINGS

Sources b. cert. · m. cert. · d. cert. · *The Times* (19 Oct 1998) · *Daily Telegraph* (19 Oct 1998) · *The Independent* (19 Oct 1998) · *The Guardian* (19 Oct 1998) · I. Herbert, ed., *Who's who in the theatre*, concise 16th edn (1978) · D. Quinlan, *Illustrated directory of film character actors* (1989) · private information (2004)
Likenesses photograph, 1949, News International Syndication [*see illus.*]

Hickson, William Edward (1803–1870), author and educationist, was born in Westminster, London, on 7 January 1803, the son of William Hickson and his wife, Matilda, *née* Underhill. His father became a wealthy boot and shoe manufacturer with a wholesale business at 20 West Smithfield, London. Between 1806 and 1812 the business moved to Northampton, where the family were active in the Baptist Sunday school movement. Hickson's account of his own youthful years recorded that he was 'a pupil of Joseph Lancaster; a Sunday School teacher; a Bible Christian … an enthusiastic promoter of Co-operative Associations. Editor in 1826 of the first Co-operative Magazine published in this country' (*Tracts for Inquirers*, No. 1). However, no details of his formal schooling have yet been found, though he was much influenced by his grandfather (another William) who died in 1822. The reference to Lancaster probably only concerns a lecture given in the Hickson home in 1810. As eldest son Hickson entered the family business, but he also attended meetings of the Aldersgate Street Literary and Scientific Society, and formed friendships with other young London radicals, including John Stuart Mill. On 15 September 1830 he married Jane Brown (*d.* January 1871); they had no children.

A pioneer of musical education, Hickson opposed John Hullah and his 'fixed doh' method of teaching sight singing, and advocated instead beginning with melodies themselves. *The Singing Master* (1836) contained instructions for teaching singing both for schools and for families; a lecture delivered on 29 May 1838 before members of the Sunday School Union on the use of singing as part of the moral discipline of schools was published later that year. *Part Singing, or, Vocal Harmony for Choral Societies and Home Circles* appeared in 1842, *A Musical Gift from an Old Friend* in 1859.

Hickson served on the royal commission appointed in 1837 to inquire into the condition of the unemployed handloom weavers, and in 1840 wrote a separate report which advocated the repeal of the corn laws and the promotion of national education. In 1849 he produced a substantial pamphlet which sought to refute the population theories of Thomas Malthus. He argued not only that the valley of the Mississippi could provide sufficient corn and cotton to feed and clothe the whole population of Europe, but also that moral and physical problems could be overcome by developing human intelligence.

Hickson was a leading member of the Central Society of Education, and of its committee of management. In 1837 the society published, anonymously, his *Schools for the Industrious Classes*, which advocated a central board for education, model and normal schools for training teachers, and the separation of religious and secular instruction. In 1839 he undertook a tour in Belgium, Holland, and north Germany to study their national school systems, and in the following year his report on the tour was published in pamphlet form under the title *Dutch and German Schools*.

In 1840 Hickson gave up his business career and purchased the radical quarterly, *The Westminster Review*, which he also edited, writing many of the articles himself. Educational reform took pride of place, but other prominent concerns included child labour, the repeal of the corn laws, the condition of women, and municipal, legal, and medical malpractice. After 1846, when the title was changed to *The Westminster and Foreign Quarterly Review*, Hickson's crusading tone was moderated, and in 1851 he sold the *Review* to John Chapman for £300.

Although in his later years Hickson (who had in 1836 been a founder member of the Reform Club) remained interested in reform questions, as evidenced by his *Tracts for Inquirers*, published in 1867, he also became concerned with metaphysical issues. He suffered from asthma for many years and died at his home, Manor House, Fairseat, Stansted, Kent, on 22 March 1870. RICHARD ALDRICH

Sources Boase, *Mod. Eng. biog.* · R. T. Van Arsdel, 'Hickson, William Edward', *BDMBR*, vol. 3, pt 1 · R. Aldrich, 'W. E. Hickson and the *Westminster Review*, 1840–1851', *Biography and education: some eighteenth and ninteenth century studies*, ed. R. Lowe (1980) · *Wellesley index*, vol. 3 · R. Ely, *In search of the Central Society of Education* (1982) · W. A. C. Stewart and W. P. McCann, *The educational innovators*, 2 vols. (1967–8) · W. E. Hickson, *Tracts for inquirers* (1867) · B. Rainbow, *The land without music: musical education in England, 1800–1860* (1967) · d. cert. · *CGPLA Eng. & Wales* (1870) · census returns, 1861

Archives Devon RO, Buckland and Gordon family MSS · UCL, Chadwick MSS

Wealth at death under £5000: probate, 5 April 1870, *CGPLA Eng. & Wales*

Hide, Mary Edith [Molly] (1913–1995), cricketer and farmer, was born in Shanghai, China, on 24 October 1913, the elder of two children of Arthur Hide and his wife, Edith, *née* Jansen. Her father ran a business in China and she was four years old when the family returned to England. At her local school in Haslemere, Surrey, a games mistress instilled an enthusiasm for cricket. Hide moved on to Wycombe Abbey School and then became the first woman to gain a diploma in agriculture at Reading University. For most of her career she combined playing cricket with working on and then managing the 200 acre family farm at Haslemere.

Hide was the epitome of women's cricket. She played in the very first test match, for England against Australia in Brisbane in 1934, and took over the captaincy of her country in 1937. During the next seventeen years she became England's most successful captain and when she was laid to rest at the age of eighty-one it was as a universally revered figure. Tall and calm, Hide was a masculine type of character. She led from the front and expected nothing less than total commitment from her teams. Some did not find her sufficiently encouraging but there was always total respect for a colleague who set high standards and knew what she was doing.

A classic right-hand bat, Hide defied her parents by taking her place in the 1934–5 touring team to Australia and New Zealand. When she planned to return for the 1939 tour they insisted she should not 'go gallivanting' again. In the event the Second World War intervened, the tour was cancelled, and Hide accepted full responsibility for the upkeep of the family farm for four years. Hide's first innings on that pioneering 1934–5 tour was a century, against Western Australia, and she recorded the first of her two test centuries when England moved on to Christchurch in New Zealand. Played in February 1935 it was New Zealand's first test match and Hide (110) and Betty Snowball (189) put on 235 runs for the second wicket in only 142 minutes. This was of course a world record and it remained the only record of those trailblazing days to survive to the end of the twentieth century. Hide was twenty-one when she undertook that tour and quickly emerged as a young player with a great future. Not only did she contribute steady scores, but her bowling success was also substantial. She delivered off spin but, as captain, did not make the full use of her own talent. A return of thirty-six international wickets, at an average of 15.25 runs, included at least two test winning performances.

When 1937 came around and it was time for Australia to embark on the return tour of England, Hide was a natural choice to lead her country. Her philosophy drew the crowds and 5000 turned up for the first test at Northampton. Hide's main objective was to try and play bright, attractive cricket, and obtain a definite result. She was not afraid of defeat and as captain of England in all home and overseas tour years from 1937 to 1954, eleven test matches in all, she won four times. Only England's original captain, Betty Archdale, had a better win ratio, three out of four played. No other England captain has, however, won more matches than Hide, despite, as the years ticked by and the game progressed, the fact that many more matches were played.

Hide was delighted with the attention women's cricket received during her years as captain. Looking back on the 1949 tour to Australia she recalled what a thrill it was playing on such grounds as Sydney, the Adelaide Oval, and the Western Australia Cricket Association ground in Perth: all test match venues today. The third test in Sydney was especially memorable. Amid a glut of runs Hide scored 63 and 124 not out, after which her portrait was hung in the pavilion. This match was also the first time that women had been allowed to use the men's dressing rooms in the main pavilion.

As befitted her pioneering instinct Hide was also one of the first two women to enter another holy of cricketing holies, Lord's. Along with Amy Bull, Hide was invited by the Marylebone Cricket Club, then the game's governing body and based at St John's Wood in London, to join an MCC committee and discuss the future of cricket. Hide had been retired over twenty years when women were first allowed to play at Lord's: a one-day international between England and Australia in 1976. It took another twenty-three years and much public debate before women were accepted as members of the MCC.

Hide's last test match was against New Zealand at the Oval in London in 1954. That match was drawn, but England had won the first test and thus the series was theirs. Hide finished with a test batting average of 36.33, her highest score in an aggregate of 872 runs being her 124 not out at the Sydney cricket ground.

As well as captaining England, Hide turned out for her local club and Surrey, and large crowds flocked to Mitcham Green whenever she was playing. She was totally committed to cricket and on her retirement from active service became a selector, manager, and administrator for both Surrey and England. She stepped in as president of the Women's Cricket Association when Mary Duggan died on the eve of the 1973 world cup. It was the biggest undertaking in the history of women's cricket. England had invited six teams to contest the very first world cup, for men or women. England won and Hide was, of course, delighted.

As well as playing lacrosse for England, Hide was, for many years, secretary of the Peper Harow Park fly-fishers club. On her death one member remarked that 'the mark Molly Hide left on the river-bank is indelible' (*The Independent*, 16 Sept 1995). The same could certainly be said of cricket. Shortly before her death she handed over her England blazer and badges to the Women's Cricket Association archivist for safekeeping. She was always extremely proud of her contribution to the history of women's cricket. She died, unmarried, on 10 September 1995, at Clare Park, Crondall, Hampshire, of cancer. Her remains were cremated, and her memorial service, at St Bartholomew, Haslemere, on what would have been her eighty-second birthday—24 October 1995—was overflowing with those wishing to pay tribute to a sporting legend.

CAROL SALMON

Sources Women's Cricket Association archives • R. H. Flint and N. Rheinberg, *Fair play: the story of women's cricket* (1976) • J. L. Hawes, *Women's test cricket: the golden triangle, 1934–84* (1987) • *The Independent* (13 Sept 1995) • *The Independent* (16 Sept 1995) • *The Times* (14 Sept 1995) • d. cert.

Archives Women's Cricket Association archives

Likenesses photograph, repro. in *The Independent* (13 Sept 1995) • photograph, repro. in *The Times*

Wealth at death £496,187: probate, 3 Jan 1996, *CGPLA Eng. & Wales*

Hide, Thomas (1524–1597), religious controversialist, was born at Newbury in Berkshire. He became a scholar of Winchester College aged thirteen and then went to New College, Oxford, where he became a fellow in 1543, graduating BA in October 1545 and MA in 1549. He resigned his fellowship of New College in 1550 and in 1551 succeeded William Everard as headmaster of Winchester College. He was made a canon of Winchester, to which benefice he was presented by the king and queen, being installed on 23 June 1557. After Elizabeth's accession, however, he was forced to resign his offices. Identified as a favourer of the old religion, he was ordered to the custody of the lord treasurer by the ecclesiastical commissioners in 1561. He fled to join the exile community at Louvain, and lived there for some years; William (later Cardinal) Allen commended his abilities in a letter dated 1579. Then he moved to Douai, where he boarded with the widow of John Fowler, who had been chief printer to the English Catholic exiles at Louvain. When Thomas Harding died in 1572, Hide was appointed executor of his will with Thomas Bayley, and was bequeathed Harding's best gold ring, a gold portague, and £5.

Hide is known chiefly for the work *A Consolatorie Epistle to the Afflicted Catholikes* (labelled Louvain, 1579, although in fact secretly published at Greenstreet House, East Ham). In this work he attempted to comfort his Catholic countrymen by arguing that persecution was a blessing, since it stirred up their faith, where long years of peace had caused it to become corrupted. He compared the state of the church to that of the apostles on board ship when a storm arose, and tried:

> briefly to shew to the persecuted Catholikes of our time, that if now they find al possible oppressions under heresie and tyrannie, it may not seeme straunge unto them, if they consider how Christes shippe was covered with the waves, how the Church hath bene persecuted even from her infancie. (sig. Aiijr)

Hide spoke of suffering as a great gift, and the trials of persecution as a mark of the true church, observing that those 'who so hath not the gifte to suffer, ought to seeke it by prayer and penance' (sig. Aviv). He also reflected the mood of many Elizabethan Catholics at the time by emphasizing devotion to the church above loyalty to family or obedience to any ruler: 'Kings, Princes, and Potentates of the World, be the servantes of God, God is their master, we maye not obey the servant against the master' (sig. Biijr). He died on 9 May 1597, and was buried in the lady chapel of St James's Church in Douai.

L. E. C. WOODING

Sources J. Strype, *Annals of the Reformation and establishment of religion … during Queen Elizabeth's happy reign*, new edn, 1 (1824), 414 · T. F. Kirby, *Winchester scholars: a list of the wardens, fellows, and scholars of … Winchester College* (1888), 121, 130 · *Fasti Angl., 1541–1857*, [Canterbury], 99 · Wood, *Ath. Oxon.*, new edn, 1.659 · H. Rashdall and R. S. Rait, *New College* (1901), 112 · H. de Vocht, 'Thomas Harding', *EngHR*, 35 (1920), 233–44 · A. F. Allison and D. M. Rogers, eds., *The contemporary printed literature of the English Counter-Reformation between 1558 and 1640*, 2 (1994), 86 · Gillow, *Lit. biog. hist.*, 3.526–7

Hieover, Harry. *See* Bindley, Charles (1795/6–1859).

Hieron, Samuel (*bap.* 1572, *d.* 1617), Church of England clergyman and devotional writer, was born in London and baptized at St Peter-le-Poer on 10 August 1572, the son of Roger Hieron, Heron, or Herryn, schoolmaster and later vicar of Epping, Essex, who was a friend of John Foxe the martyrologist. Initially taught by his father, in July 1584 he was admitted to Eton College, where he became a king's scholar in 1586. On 24 August 1590 he was admitted to King's College, Cambridge, where he was elected a fellow in 1593 and graduated BA in 1595. Encouraged and financially assisted in his studies by Sir Francis Barrington of Barrington Hall, Essex, Hieron also benefited much, according to his biographer John Quick, from the godly atmosphere then prevailing at Cambridge. As a result, according to his other biographer, Robert Hill, when he first preached in the college chapel 'he seemed rather a Bachelor of Divinity than a Bachelor of Arts, rather a Divine of forty, than one of four and twenty' (Quick, 56).

Ordained deacon in London on 21 December 1595, Hieron became a notable preacher in the city: exactly where is unknown, but he later acknowledged in *The Christians Journall* (1609) Barrington's 'kind watering' of his 'first endeavours in the Ministerie' (A2). He once delivered a sermon in the Chapel Royal at Whitehall which Queen Elizabeth, punning on their respective names as 'heron'

and 'mountain', reputedly considered to have soared higher than that of the previous preacher, George Montaigne. However, he declined offers of preferment in the city churches and at the inns of court and returned to Cambridge to proceed MA in 1598. The following year he resigned his fellowship and on the presentation of Henry Savile, as provost of Eton, was on 4 July instituted to the vicarage of Modbury, Devon. About this time he married Mildred, whose other name is unknown: their first child, Roger, was baptized at Modbury probably in March 1600; five further sons and three daughters were baptized there between 1601 and 1616.

Hieron rapidly established a pioneering preaching ministry which drew a large cross-section of south Devon society, and which was respectfully remembered in the later seventeenth century as having laid the foundation of a vigorous tradition of puritan nonconformity in the area. Its hallmarks are evident in his earliest printed works, *The Preachers Plea* and *An Answere to a Popish Ryme, Lately Scattered Abroad in the West*, which appeared in 1604. The former proclaims the saving and sanctifying work of sermons through a 'homely and coarse discourse' between a minister and a pious man; the latter seeks to make the protestant response to Catholics' criticisms accessible through simple verse. Both carry learned marginal notes, but in the conviction that 'plain-ness' was 'the best eloquence' (*Truths Purchase*, 1606, dedication) Hieron deliberately reined himself in: 'I have bound myselfe to studye so to speake, as that I may not exceed the conceit of common hearers' he explained in the dedication to *The Spirituall Sonneshipe* (1611).

Implacable against wicked popes, 'carnall Cardinals' (*An Answere*, C2v), the mass—'a grosse device, defaming Christ' (ibid., C1v)—and Roman idolatry, Hieron rejected the charge of sectarianism, and clung to the Church of England:

> We doe not hang on Calvins sleeve
> Nor yet on Zwinglius we beleeve
> And Puritanes we doe defye
> If right the name you do apply
> All giddy Sects among us crept
> We wish out of our Church were swept;
> (ibid., B3)

Yet, although his works confirm that 'he was not absolutely against the use of a Forme of prayer' (Quick, 59), in his Sunday morning and afternoon services 'he never confined himself to the use of the publick liturgy, nor did he at all conforme unto the Ceremonys' (ibid., 60). On one occasion when he wore a surplice the adverse reaction of his congregation was reported to have induced him to abandon it altogether. Such practices, together with his conviction, as expressed in *The Dignitie of Scripture* (1607), that nothing must be added to scripture, and his promotion in the west country of the millenary petition, five times led to his suspension by the normally moderate bishop of Exeter, William Cotton. Each time Sir William Strode went to London to plead on his behalf; each time, according to Quick, he returned with a discharge and a new preaching licence. Similarly, friends in Plymouth arranged for the printing and distribution of his clandestine *A defence of the ministers reasons for refusall of subscription to the Book of Common Prayer and of conformitie* [1607].

That Hieron not only remained at Modbury but also very publicly prospered seems to have been due both to an inherent loyalty to the national church, whatever its shortcomings in his eyes, and to the formidable array of local and non-local notables who promoted his ministry. A 1615 sermon proclaimed that he rejoiced to be a son of 'our English church … wherein, it shall be my glorie and my crown in the day of Christ, to have been employed as a minister' (Wolffe, 96). The very many patrons, friends, and fellow workers for the gospel revealed in dedications to his publications included: William Herbert, earl of Pembroke and lord warden of the stannaries of Devon, to whom he sometimes acted as chaplain; Robert Rich, Lord Rich; the Champernownes of Modbury; local magistrates like Sir Ferdinando Gorges; Lady Strode and Lady Hele, both his spiritual daughters, the latter being a convert from Catholicism; Sir John Poyntz, 'one of his majesty's pensioners'; and Laurence Chaderton and Roger Goad, respectively masters of Emmanuel College and King's College, Cambridge. As Hieron explained in a funeral sermon for Henry Sommaster of Pensford, reproduced in *Three Sermons* (1607), magistrates and ministers were joint leaders of the people in the fight for the maintenance of religion. On the other hand, as he asserted in a Gunpowder Plot commemoration address issued in *Three Sermons* (1609), those who professed true religion yet were adversaries to its life and power were as much enemies as were the papists.

Hieron published extensively, with the first of several major collections of his works appearing, apparently on his own initiative, in 1614. However, it was his *A Helpe unto Devotion* (1608), which became a cornerstone of contemporary piety and made him a household name. Here the pastor who acknowledged 'that set formes of Prayer are very distastfull to many' who considered them 'a kind of confining and limiting of Gods Spirit', dismissed not just the 'fondnesse' of those 'who scarce count it praying, unlesse it bee by a booke', but also 'their carelesness, who labor not to attaine to an ability of commending their personall occasions … unto God'. Not prescriptively, but as a manual in orderly and effective intercession, to assist 'stammering and lisping tongues' to develop into 'tongues as fined silver … plainly and distinctly to speake the language of Canaan', he offered template prayers for everyday occasions and moods (foreword). His final prayer 'For the Whole State' gave thanks for prolonged peace, for the light of the Gospel and for freedom from the 'miserable bondage of Romish and Antichristian tyrannie' (p. 239), although continued watchfulness was necessary to counter the 'many Locusts' and 'continual spawn of new conspirators', that 'come dayly out of that Pit of Rome' (p. 258). It called on God not only to furnish 'everie place … with a Pastor after thine own heart' but, more provocatively, to 'restraine and reforme the greedinesse of those which muzzle their mouthes that should tread out the corne, and bring forth food of life to thy people' (p. 256).

In 1615 Sir William Strode established a lecture at Modbury itself, the one place stubbornly resistant to Hieron's energetic and persuasive oratory, but by this time his health was being progressively undermined by the stone and by gout. In the aftermath of a crowded lecture at Plympton on a hot day in May 1617 he succumbed to a chill, but according to Quick it was heart disease which, after four weeks' illness, killed him at Modbury on 17 June; he was buried in the church there the same day. The funeral sermon, preached by Hieron's closest ministerial friend, John Barlow, lecturer at Plymouth, was published as *Mr Hierons Last Farewell* (1618); the funeral charges were paid by Lady Hele, who also gave his widow an annuity and provided for some of his children. Several of his sons became clergymen, but it was his grandson and namesake Samuel Hieron (d. 1686), ejected rector of Feniton, Devon, and licensed presbyterian preacher, who followed most closely in his footsteps and who helped ensure, through his friendship with Quick, that the reputation of the 'Star of the West', the proto-nonconformist of the Jacobean church, was kept alive not just locally but among the godly at large. VIVIENNE LARMINIE

Sources J. Quick, 'The life of Mr Samuell Hieron, the Star of the West', in 'Icones sacrae Anglicanae', DWL · S. G. Harris, 'Samuel Hieron: a Devonshire vicar in the reigns of Elizabeth and James I', *Report and Transactions of the Devonshire Association*, 24 (1892), 77–85 · Venn, *Alum. Cant.* · W. Sterry, ed., *The Eton College register, 1441–1698* (1943), 171 · IGI [parish registers of St Peter-le-Poer, London, and of Modbury, Devon] · *Calamy rev.*, 262 · Foster, *Alum. Oxon.* · M. Wolffe, *Gentry leaders in peace and war: the gentry governors of Devon in the early seventeenth century* (1997) · M. Stoyle, *Loyalty and locality: popular allegiance in Devon during the English civil war* (1994) · STC, 1475–1640 · I. Green, *The Christian's ABC* (1996), 664–5 · I. Green, *Print and protestantism in early modern England* (2000)

Hiffernan, Paul (1719?–1777), writer and playwright, is said to have been born in Dublin, although he intentionally obscured the details of his life. He attended a grammar school, a Dublin seminary to prepare him for Roman Catholic ordination, and finally a college in the south of France, where ultimately he took a degree in medicine from the University of Montpellier. Hiffernan returned to Dublin before 1748, and was known thereafter as 'the doctor' (and as Gallows Paul). The quintessential new author by profession, gregarious and entertaining, Hiffernan scrounged his dinners and hawked his works around his friends but never divulged where he lived; his letters were directed to coffee houses. Two works, both published in Dublin in 1739, *The Enthusiasm. A Poem. With a Character of Dr. Jonathan Swift* and *The Poet, a Poem*, both by 'Mr. P. H.', have been attributed to Hiffernan.

In Ireland Hiffernan attempted unsuccessfully to practise medicine, but being a notorious drunkard, he instead turned to literature. He was engaged by government to attack the popular opposition candidate Charles Lucas in a periodical, *The Tickler*, that first appeared on 18 February 1748 and lasted for seven influential numbers. In it Hiffernan exhibited a characteristic bent toward scurrility and abuse. A counterattack, *The Marrow of the Tickler's Works*, appeared in 1748, as did *A Faithful Narrative of the Barbarous and Bloody Murder of P—l H—Ff—n*. The pamphlet *A Letter of Thanks to the Barber* by 'Mr. Francis Liberty: A Freeman and Citizen of Dublin', published in March 1748, was attributed in annotation to the Tickler. Hiffernan's ambitious *Reflections on the Structure, and Passions of Man* (1748), in which he also considered the transitoriness of life, was published without enhancing the author's reputation.

Hiffernan attempted to achieve success in the theatre and in 1750 his comedy *The Self-Enamour'd, or, The Ladies Doctor* was acted at the City Theatre, Capel Street, and published in Dublin. In Dublin in 1752 he published his *Remarks on an Ode on the Death of his Royal Highness Frederick, Prince of Wales*: the ode the work of William Dunkin, the remarks scurrilous.

But by the end of 1753, 'in some danger of his life' as he reported (*European Magazine*, February 1794, 112), Hiffernan moved to England, and on 21 January commenced a new periodical, *The Tuner*, in which he savaged a number of new tragedies. He also began work as a translator. He published his *Miscellanies in Prose and Verse* (1755), but fame continued to be elusive. Now a pamphleteer and paragraph writer, Hiffernan's formal publications slowed but he continued to entertain and keep the friends on whom he sponged through dining, subscription collecting, hawking his books, and occasional blackmail. He wrote only when reduced by absolute necessity.

On 24 April 1756 Hiffernan's two-act farce, *The Maiden Whim, or, The Critical Moment*, played once (the prompter's review: 'O Sad!') for his benefit, at Drury Lane. Fearing critical reprisals, he published in the *Daily Advertiser* on the day of the performance the egregious lie that he had never hurt a playwright by savaging a play during its run. In 1761 Hiffernan published in honour of the new queen *The Wishes of a Free People: a Dramatic Poem*, and produced a farce, 'The New Hippocrates', acted just once at Drury Lane on 1 April (prompter: 'wretched, but went off quietly'); it went unpublished and unappreciated. The bookseller Tom Davies credits Hiffernan with the attack on Bute, *Scotchman be Humble* (1763). In 1764 he published *The Earl of Warwick*, 'a very indifferent translation of Monsieur de la Harpe's play' (Genest, 4.457–8). The play was never produced, but when Thomas Francklin's translation of the same play had a triumphant run at Drury Lane in 1766, Hiffernan responded with violence, issuing a new edition (1767) of his play in which he criticized the taste of the managers. Hiffernan then went on to attack Garrick in his *A Letter from the Rope-Dancing Monkey in the Hay-Market to the Acting Monkey of Drury Lane*. Garrick capitulated, produced *The National Prejudice* for Hiffernan on 6 April 1768 (one performance), and helped him achieve a splendid subscription for his *Dramatic Genius, in Five Books* (1770), which apotheosized Garrick. In 1770 Hiffernan engaged in a polemical war with Samuel Foote, who refused to employ him at the Haymarket Theatre as playwright and was so harassed for subscriptions by Hiffernan that Foote dubbed him a common thief. In retaliation Hiffernan published a critique, *Foote's Prologue Detected* (1770), and prepared a letter inciting the public to tear down his theatre.

Garrick successfully interceded. In 1772 during Garrick's polemical war with William Kenrick, Hiffernan provided on Garrick's behalf manifold newspaper paragraphs, verses, and pamphlets (most notably *The Recantation and Confession of Doctor Kenrick, LLD*). Hiffernan also at various times coached candidates for the stage and attempted public lectures in anatomy. In 1774 *The Heroine of the Cave*, a tragedy left at his death by Henry Jones and completed by Hiffernan, opened at Drury Lane on 19 March.

Thereafter, suffering from the liver disease that killed him, Hiffernan survived on the charity of Foote, Garrick, and others. He died on 12 June 1777 at his lodgings, variously thought to be a small court off St Martin's Lane or near Westminster Bridge. 'His education was certainly liberal, and his knowledge of letters extensive', reported the *Freeman's Journal* on 24 June, but his reviews were invariably contemptuous and it was

> a fact easily ascertained, that he never distinguished himself as a Writer; unless, indeed, a peculiar quaintness of phraseology, a remarkably vulgar train of thinking, and as remarkably vulgar a mode of expressing his thoughts, can be allowed to be the proper pretensions to distinction among Authors. (*Westminster Magazine*)

BETTY RIZZO

Sources 'Table talk', *European Magazine* (Feb 1794), 110–14 · 'Table talk', *European Magazine* (March 1794), 179–84 · *Westminster Magazine* (June 1777), 286–7 · T. Davies, *Memoirs of the life of David Garrick*, 2 vols. (1808), 1.283–92 · T. P. Kirkpatrick, 'A note on the life and writings of Paul Hiffernan', *Irish Book Lover*, 19 (1931), 11–21 · R. R. Madden, *The history of Irish periodical literature*, 2 vols. (1867), 1.315–30 · *The private correspondence of David Garrick*, ed. J. Boaden, 2 vols. (1831–2), 1.390–92; 2.353 · *The letters of David Garrick*, ed. D. M. Little and G. M. Kahrl, 2 (1963), 692, 703–4, 791–2, 859 · Genest, *Eng. stage*, 4.457–8, 566, 611; 5.168, 405–7 · *Morning Chronicle* (July 1772) · *Monthly Review* (May 1759), 463 · *Monthly Review* (Nov 1761), 396 · *Monthly Review* (March 1764), 240 · *Monthly Review* (Jan 1767), 67–8 · D. E. Baker, *Biographia dramatica, or, A companion to the playhouse*, rev. I. Reed, new edn, rev. S. Jones, 3 vols. in 4 (1812), 1.333; 2.183, 300, 361; 3.72–3, 78, 145–6, 413 · S. Trefman, *Sam. Foote, comedian* (New York, 1971), 190–91, 224 · G. W. Stone and G. M. Kahrl, *David Garrick, a critical biography* (Illinois, 1979), 586 · *Freeman's Journal* (24 June 1777) · A. Chalmers, ed., *The general biographical dictionary*, new edn, 17 (1814), 462

Higbert. *See* Hygeberht (*d.* in or after 803).

Higden, Henry (*bap.* 1645), author and lawyer, the son of John Higden (*b. c.*1610) and his wife, Joane, *née* Durden (*b. c.*1610), was baptized at St Mary Putney, Surrey, on 28 August 1645. After attending Westminster School he was admitted to the Middle Temple in April 1665; he was called to the bar in 1686. 'A Person known to all the conversable part of the Town, for his Pleasant and Facetious Company' (Gildon, 72), he published his lively translation of the thirteenth satire of Juvenal in 1686. His version of Juvenal's tenth satire appeared a year later, with commendatory verses by John Dryden, Aphra Behn, and Elkanah Settle. Higden defended free translation against Thomas Shadwell's attacks, writing that his aim was to give 'Life and Spirit to his Author, by making him English, in a Modish and Familiar way' (H. Higden, *A Modern Essay on the Tenth Satyr of Juvenal*, 1687).

Higden's comedy *The Wary Widdow* received a disastrous single performance in 1693, soon after the success of Congreve's *The Old Batchelor*. According to *The Poetical Register* (1719), 'the Author having contriv'd to make so much drinking of Punch in the Play, that the Actors got drunk, and were unable to go through with it, the Audience was dismiss'd at the Close of the Third Act' (Jacob, 138). In his indignant preface to the play text Higden did not mention drunkenness, but blamed the faction against him for turning the theatre into a bear-garden by 'hissing, mimicking, ridiculing, and Cat-calling', the management for spending no money on the production, and the actors for not learning their lines. His play had been cut by the master of the revels, when audiences were lapping up the obscenities of 'the Baudy Batchelour' and Dryden's *The Kind Keeper*. In his *Table-Talk*, Tom Brown remarked that Harry Higden included a great deal of eating in his comedy because authors always wrote about what they liked best. Higden's poverty during the legal long vacation, when his rooms at the Temple contained only 'a Rug, two Blankets, a Joint-Stool and a Tin-Candlestick', are described in *Letters from the Dead to the Living* (*Works*, 2.177). His later career is obscure; in the late 1690s Gildon did not know whether Higden was living or not.

OLIVE BALDWIN and THELMA WILSON

Sources [C. Gildon], *The lives and characters of the English dramatick poets … first begun by Mr Langbain* [1699] • [G. Jacob], *The poetical register, or, The lives and characters of the English dramatick poets*, [1] (1719) • H. Higden, *The wary widdow, or, Sir Noisy Parratt* (1693) • *The works of Mr Thomas Brown*, ed. J. Drake, 3rd edn, 4 vols. (1715), vols. 1–2 • W. Van Lennep and others, eds., *The London stage, 1660–1800*, pt 1: 1660–1700 (1965) • W. B. Bannerman, ed., *The parish register of Putney*, 1 (privately printed, Croydon, 1913) • *Old Westminsters*, vol. 1 • H. A. C. Sturgess, ed., *Register of admissions to the Honourable Society of the Middle Temple, from the fifteenth century to the year 1944*, 1 (1949)

Higden, Ranulf (*d.* 1364), Benedictine monk and chronicler, appears to have been a Cheshire man, although little is known about his life. According to a colophon in one copy of his chronicle (Bodl. Oxf., MS Laud misc. 619) he entered the abbey of St Werburgh, Chester, in 1299. There is no evidence that he studied at a university, or travelled much outside Chester. The one reliable fact for the later years of his life is that in 1352 he was summoned by Edward III to appear at court with his chronicles. A note in the Laud manuscript suggests that he died in 1364 after living over sixty years in religion.

Higden's major writing was his universal chronicle, in seven books, known as the *Polychronicon*. Apart from the *Polychronicon* he wrote a guide to sermon literature entitled the *Ars componendi sermones*, the *Speculum curatorum*, which was an aid to preaching, and a number of minor works including a collection of Latin sermons. Although his name has been associated with the Chester cycle of Whitsuntide plays there is no evidence that he was in any way connected with them. His reputation rests almost entirely upon the *Polychronicon*. That work offered to the educated and learned audience of fourteenth-

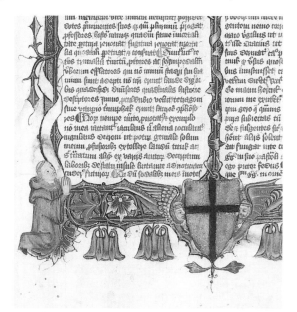

Ranulf Higden (*d.* 1364), manuscript illumination [kneeling, left]

century England a clear and original picture of world history based upon medieval tradition, but with a new interest in antiquity, and with the early history of Britain related as part of the whole. Higden's historical narrative is particularly notable for its description of the Roman world. An interest in the ancient world had been developing for some time in fourteenth-century England. Higden was clearly aware of this, for he says that at the request of his fellow monks he changed his plan of writing a history of his own country and decided to enlarge the scope of his work. A further feature of his account is the description of the world contained in the first book of the *Polychronicon*. Through the medium of John Trevisa's translation this section of Higden's work proved to be one of the most popular parts of his chronicle. To illustrate this description Higden included a world map in the later versions of his chronicle. The most elaborate copy, which may be the closest one to the original, is found in BL, Royal MS 14 C.ix.

The *Polychronicon* went through a number of editions in Higden's lifetime. The Latin text survives in a short, an intermediate, and a long version. Although it was once thought that the intermediate version was the original one, it is clear from Higden's autograph copy in the Huntington Library (Hunt. L., MS 132) that the short version of the text written soon after 1327 is the earliest, and that the narrative was then expanded into the later and longer accounts. A medieval text was rarely completed and Higden was still revising his chronicle at the time of his death.

In the sixteenth and seventeenth centuries John Bale and Humfrey Wanley supposed that the short version of the text was the work of one Roger of Chester who called his compilation *Polycratica* as opposed to *Polychronicon*. The shorter work, they believed, was incorporated into the longer one. The name Roger of Chester does not, however, occur in any contemporary script, and there is no justification, as the editors of the Rolls Series edition themselves stated, for supposing that the short version represents the work of anyone other than Higden himself. Wanley was further misled into thinking that a text found in BL, Harley MS 655, was also the work of the apocryphal Roger of Chester. This text is simply a form of the *Polychronicon* taken from the short version which adds passages from the later books of the *Historia aurea* of John Tynemouth.

The Latin text of the *Polychronicon* survives in over 100 manuscripts testifying to its immense appeal. Many cathedral churches and larger religious houses possessed copies. In the later middle ages copies were also owned by individual clerics as well as by parish churches, Oxford and Cambridge colleges, members of the nobility, and the wealthier merchants of London. The influence of the *Polychronicon* is most clearly seen, however, in the continuations that were added to its text during the second half of the fourteenth century. As regards chronicle writing, that period may be termed the age of the *Polychronicon* continuation. The first continuation from 1340 to 1377 was a standard account which went through a number of versions. Its importance lies in the fact that it covers a period when there are few first-rate contemporary chronicles, due to the fact that several writers, notably Adam Murimuth, Robert of Avesbury, and Geoffrey Baker, ended their work in the 1340s and 1350s.

One important continuation covering the years 1348–81 was written by **John Malvern** (*d.* in or before 1414?), chronicler and monk, of Worcester, who is probably to be identified with the sacrist of that name who became prior of Worcester in 1395 and died before November 1414. What is known as the Rolls Series A continuation of the *Polychronicon* (1348–81) is ascribed to John Malvern in Cambridge, Corpus Christi College, MS 197A. Although in the Corpus manuscript Malvern is credited with the continuation from 1346, it seems certain that his work only began in 1348, and that the text from 1346 to 1348 was by an unknown author.

Malvern's continuation borrows from the final version (E) of the first *Polychronicon* continuation (1340–77), and from Walsingham's text as printed in the *Chronicon Angliae*. It contains none the less some original material, and achieved a certain popularity towards the end of the fourteenth century, when it was used to follow the main text of the *Polychronicon* in a number of manuscripts.

Several of the major chronicles of Richard II's reign were also written as *Polychronicon* continuations. One of these is Walsingham's contemporary history for the years 1376–7, the so-called 'scandalous chronicle' which was once found continuing a *Polychronicon* now divided between Bodl. Oxf., MS Bodley 316, and BL, Harley MS 3634. The Westminster chronicle (1381–94) was a continuation of three other works, including Malvern's chronicle, which were themselves continuations of the *Polychronicon*. The chronicle of Adam Usk (1377–1421) also follows a text of Higden's work. The most popular continuation covering Richard's reign was the *Vita Ricardi secundi* (1377–1402),

the work of two monks of Evesham, which was sometimes used to form an eighth book of the *Polychronicon*. In addition several religious houses added their own brief additions to Higden's text.

The influence of the *Polychronicon* extended beyond these continuations. The English translations of the Latin text increased knowledge of the work among a lay audience. The first translation of the *Polychronicon* was made by John Trevisa during the 1380s. A second translation, made in the fifteenth century, is found in a single manuscript, BL, Harley MS 2261. Although fewer manuscripts of Trevisa's translation survive than copies of the Latin original, it would be wrong to underestimate its influence, for many copies of Trevisa's version in lay households may have failed to survive. The influence of Higden's chronicle is also to be seen in the work of chroniclers like the author of the *Eulogium historiarum* who attempted to model their writings upon the *Polychronicon*. Although the influence of the *Polychronicon* was to decline at the close of the middle ages, the universal outlook that it reflected lived on among the writers and antiquaries of the Tudor age.

JOHN TAYLOR

Sources *Polychronicon Ranulphi Higden monachi Cestrensis*, ed. C. Babington and J. R. Lumby, 9 vols., Rolls Series, 41 (1865–86) · J. Taylor, *The universal chronicle of Ranulf Higden* (1966) · A. Gransden, *Historical writing in England*, 2 (1982), 43–57 · A. Gransden, 'Silent meanings in Ranulf Higden's *Polychronicon* and in Thomas Elmham's *Liber metricus de Henrico quinto*', *Medium Aevum*, 46 (1977), 231–40, esp. 231–3, 238–9 · V. H. Galbraith, 'An autograph manuscript of Ranulph Higden's *Polychronicon*', *Huntington Library Quarterly*, 23 (1959–60), 1–18 · J. G. Edwards, 'Ranulf, monk of Chester', *EngHR*, 47 (1932), 94 · D. Woodward, 'Medieval *mappaemundi*', *The history of cartography*, ed. J. B. Harley and D. Woodward, 1 (1987), 286–358 · G. B. Stow, ed., *Historia vitae et regni Ricardi Secundi* (1977) · Bodl. Oxf., MS Laud misc. 619 · obedientiary rolls, Worcester · *Report of the Deputy Keeper of the Public Records*, 44 (1883), 556
Archives BL, Royal MS 14 C.ix · Bodl. Oxf., MS Laud misc. 619 · Hunt. L., MS 132
Likenesses manuscript illumination, Bodl. Oxf., MS Bodley 316, fol. 8 [*see illus.*]

Higden, William (1662/3–1715), Church of England clergyman, was perhaps the son of Lawrence Higden of Corfe Castle, Dorset, clergyman. Though Higden had previously matriculated at St Edmund Hall, Oxford, on 23 February 1681, aged eighteen, on 5 April 1682 he matriculated sizar at King's College, Cambridge, and it was at Cambridge that he graduated BA in 1684 and proceeded MA in 1688. He became curate of Camberwell, Surrey, where in 1688 he preached the funeral sermon for the wife of the rector, Richard Parr. Higden contributed to a translation of Tacitus's life of Agricola which was published in 1698.

At the revolution of 1688 Higden became a nonjuror, but later took the oaths of allegiance to Queen Anne about 1708, and in 1709 published a defence of his actions in *A View of the English Constitution*, which went through several editions. In it he offered a variety of precedents from common and statute law which he felt justified giving allegiance to the king *de facto*. Like many jurors Higden tried to differentiate his arguments from those used to support the Rump Parliament, but particularly in the later parts of the *View* he did lapse into discussing allegiance purely in terms of the relationship between protection and obedience, a very common argument in the engagement controversy of the 1650s. His work attracted a number of replies from leading nonjurors, including Charles Leslie, George Harbin, Theophilus Downes, and Henry Gandy, partly, it seems, in response to the contemporary opinion that Higden's work was unanswerable.

Thomas Hearne claimed that Higden was created DD in 1710 in return for his efforts. Certainly publishing the *View* seems to have done his career no harm. He preached at court on the anniversary of Charles I's death in 1711, and in the same year became rector of St Paul's, Shadwell. In May 1713 he was made a prebendary of Canterbury Cathedral. However, some time before taking the oaths Higden had been in lengthy correspondence in the summer of 1707 with Samuel Hawes (a future nonjuring bishop) about ending the nonjuring schism, so his decision cannot be seen as mere opportunism. The debate between them focused on two particular issues in the relationship between nonjurors and the established (and to them schismatic) church of the settlement of 1689. The first was the problem raised by the apparent inconsistency in the nonjuring position over accepting into occasional communion with them conformists (significantly, Higden had written on this theme in *The Case of the Admission of Occasional Conformists to the Holy Communion* in 1705, republished in 1715 with a title adapted to make dissenters the explicit target of the work). The second was whether nonjurors should end their breach when the last bishop lawfully ordained before the revolution died or (as George Hooper had done in 1703) conformed. Did the demands of the Christian communion override formal questions raised by the revolution of 1688–9 about the relationship between church and state? Higden felt that it did, citing that 'our Blessed Saviour & his Apostles held communion with the High Priests who were advanced by the Civil Power' (MS Rawl. D844, fol. 47r). It seems best to take Higden at his word in his preface to the *View*, where he put his change of heart down to his worrying away at doubts which had arisen in his mind about his original decision. Parts of the book, he explained, were reworked from letters he had written in answer to objections raised by friends to his new position.

Higden died in London on 28 August 1715 and was buried on 5 September in the Broadway Chapel, St Margaret's, Westminster. Although his *View* was roundly attacked in his lifetime, it seems to have had a lasting legacy. John Wesley referred to the work as 'one of the best-wrote books I have ever seen in the English tongue' (Hynson, 69), and it has been suggested that Higden's writing was fundamental to shaping the Methodist leader's political outlook.   EDWARD VALLANCE

Sources Venn, *Alum. Cant.* · *DNB* · *Remarks and collections of Thomas Hearne*, ed. C. E. Doble and others, 11 vols., OHS, 2, 7, 13, 34, 42–3, 48, 50, 65, 67, 72 (1885–1921), vol. 2, p. 284; vol. 3, p. 93 · W. Higden, *A view of the English constitution* (1709) · L. O. Hynson, 'Human liberty as divine right: a study in the political maturation of John Wesley', *Journal of Church and State*, 25 (1983), 58–85 · Samuel Hawes correspondence, Bodl. Oxf., MSS Rawl. D844, D845, D890 · private information (2004) [librarian, Westminster]
Archives Bodl. Oxf., Rawl. MSS

Higdon [*née* Schollick]**, Annie Catharine** [Kitty] (1864–1946), schoolmistress, was born on 30 December 1864 at Poolton cum Seacombe, Cheshire, the daughter of Samuel Schollick, a foreman shipwright, and his wife, Jane. She became a certificated elementary teacher, and when she married on 11 July 1896 was residing at Shepton Mallet, Somerset. Her husband, Thomas George Higdon [*see below*], was a fellow teacher. Early in married life the couple moved to London, and on 14 April 1902 took up joint posts at Wood Dalling council school in Norfolk. Annie Higdon, known as Kitty, was the head teacher and her husband an uncertificated assistant. As Christian socialists with strong egalitarian views they were dedicated to improving the lot of their pupils, many of whom came from poor labouring families. Kitty was deeply critical of the widespread illegal employment of children on the land. A confirmed pacifist, she taught her pupils to abhor cruelty to animals. She did much to promote the children's welfare by purchasing food, clothing, and footwear for them out of her own pocket. She also provided equipment for the school and conducted cookery classes in her own kitchen.

In 1907 Thomas Higdon, with his wife's backing, became actively involved in promoting agricultural trade unionism. In what was regarded as almost a rural revolution, Thomas Higdon's efforts led to the election of labourers to the parish council in 1910, to which the Higdons were also elected, though Kitty retired without taking office. These developments, and Kitty Higdon's continuing demands for improvements to the fabric of the school, led to friction with the managers, many of whom were farmers. In December 1908 and July 1910 official inquiries into the couple's conduct were instituted under the aegis of Norfolk education committee. Although a threat of dismissal was withdrawn, they were transferred to Burston and Shimpling council school, where they took up duty on 1 February 1911. Their political activities and social concerns again led to clashes with their managers. After Thomas Higdon helped local labourers to oust sitting members at the parish council elections, himself heading the poll, the managers requested in November 1913 Norfolk education committee to remove Kitty Higdon from her post on disciplinary grounds. After an inquiry, the committee asked her to seek alternative employment; when she took no action she and her husband were dismissed as from 31 March 1914.

Kitty Higdon was an excellent teacher, as reports by the school inspectors make clear. On 1 April 1914, as a protest against her dismissal, sixty-six of the seventy-two children on the register, with the support of their parents, came out on strike. As the dispute went on, it drew support from trade unions and other national labour organizations. Public meetings were held on Burston Green, addressed by leading political figures. The Higdons, meanwhile, began to teach the striking children, at first in the open air and then in a temporary 'strike school' held in a former carpenter's shop. A national campaign was launched to raise funds for a purpose-built property, and between April 1916 and December 1917 £1662 was raised, with the miners' union alone subscribing £401. The new building was opened on 13 May 1917 amid great celebrations.

By 1919 the strike school still had forty pupils and throughout the 1920s and much of the 1930s it continued to prosper, drawing children not only from the immediate vicinity but from the wider community. Among them were two Russian boys, the sons of members of the Russian trade delegation in London. Kitty Higdon laid great emphasis on the inculcation of civic values, and older pupils were taken to trade union and political rallies. In a grudging tribute to the couple's sincerity, the Board of Education described them as 'persons who conceive themselves to have a "mission"'. The school building, described by the Higdons as the 'centre of a new living movement of educational and social activity', was used for meetings in support of various educational and socialist causes.

The school remained open until shortly after Thomas Higdon's death in August 1939. Its eleven pupils were then transferred to Burston council school and Kitty Higdon entered a retirement home at Swainsthorpe, near Norwich, where she died on 24 April 1946. She was buried in Burston churchyard.

Thomas George Higdon (1869–1939), schoolmaster, was born on 21 August 1869 at East Pennard, Somerset, a younger son of Dennis Higdon, a farm labourer, and his wife, Ann. He became a teacher on the basis of an Oxford local senior certificate and, after his marriage in 1896, taught at St James's and St Peter's School, Piccadilly, London, where he remained from 1899 until he and his wife moved to Wood Dalling. An outspoken critic of child employment on the land, his firm political beliefs and farm labouring background led to a close involvement in the agricultural trade union movement in Norfolk. He joined the union's executive committee in 1914 and, except for the period 1924–7, continued to serve until 1938. He acted as union treasurer from 1916 to 1920, and in 1917 was appointed a member of the agricultural industry's first central wages board. He was the author of at least two pamphlets. The first, *Bodies without Abodes* (n.d., c.1912), was a fictional account of labouring life and the tied cottage system; the second, *The Burston Rebellion* (n.d., c.1916), examined events surrounding the school strike of 1 April 1914.

Thomas Higdon died at Mill Green, Burston, on 17 August 1939, after a long illness. Appropriately the simple funeral service five days later was conducted in the strike school, before his burial in the village churchyard. The school building, under the care of trustees, was still in existence in the 1990s.   PAMELA HORN

Sources *Eastern Daily Press* (4 May 1946) · *The Burston strike school: the story of the longest strike in history*, Trustees of Burston strike school [1991] · B. Edwards, *The Burston school strike* (1974) · Burston and Shimpling council school file, PRO, ED.21.12712 B · Burston school file, headquarters of the National Union of Teachers, London · b. cert. · b. cert. [Thomas George Higdon] · m. cert. · d. cert. · d. cert. [Thomas George Higdon] · *Land Worker*, 20/244 (Sept 1939) [obit. of Thomas George Higdon]
Archives Norfolk RO, C/ED 2/120 · Norfolk RO, C/ED 3/237 · Norfolk RO, C/ED 4/41 · Norfolk RO, C/ED 5/27 · PRO, ED 21/12712B
Likenesses photograph, trustees of the Burston Strike School · photograph (Thomas George Higdon), trustees of the Burston Strike School · photographs, repro. in T. G. Higdon, *The Burston rebellion* (1984) · photographs, repro. in Edwards, *Burston school strike* · photographs (Thomas George Higdon), repro. in T. G. Higdon, *The Burston rebellion* (1984) · photographs (Thomas George Higdon), repro. in Edwards, *Burston school strike*
Wealth at death £1516 3s. 2d.: administration, 1 Aug 1947, *CGPLA Eng. & Wales*

Higdon, Thomas George (1869–1939). *See under* Higdon, Annie Catharine (1864–1946).

Higford, William (1580/81–1657), writer on conduct, was born in Dixton, Alderton parish, Gloucestershire, one of five children of John Hugford (d. 1616), whose family owned the manor, and his wife, Dorothea, daughter of William Rogers. William (who adopted the spelling Higford) matriculated at Oriel College, Oxford, on 14 January 1597 but later transferred to Corpus Christi College, which his father and grandfather had both attended. Here he studied under Sebastian Benefield and 'by the benefit of good discipline and natural parts, he became a well qualified gentleman' (Wood, *Ath. Oxon.*, 3rd edn, 3.429), gaining his BA in February 1599. He returned to Dixton and married Mary (d. 1657), daughter of Sir John Meulx of Kingston, Isle of Wight, with whom he had seven children.

Through the patronage of Grey Brydges, fifth Baron Chandos, he was appointed a JP. Wood describes him as a zealous puritan but his anthologist, Clement Barksdale, rector of Sudeley, contends that Higford held fast to the Elizabethan church, 'warping neither to Rome nor Amsterdam' (*Harleian Miscellany*, 9.582). This is not necessarily reliable either, since Barksdale was a firm Anglican, but Higford's writings show only conventional protestant piety and give fulsome praise to the Chandos and Tracy families, both of whom were royalist in the civil war. Higford died at Dixton on 6 April 1657, in his seventy-seventh year, and was buried in Alderton church.

Barksdale collated some of Higford's writings and published them posthumously as *Institutions, or, Advice to a Grandson* (1658). The recipient of this advice was John (b. 1627), son of Higford's son John (b. 1607), who married in 1626 Frances Scudamore (1608–1688) but predeceased his father. Higford clearly felt responsible for his grandson's upbringing. *Institutions* was reprinted in 1660, republished in 1666 as *The Institution of a Gentleman in III Parts*, and reprinted by Thomas Park in *The Harleian Miscellany* in 1812. The book draws on a wide-ranging classical knowledge to advise Higford's young grandson on such matters as preserving the estate, religion, education, how to act towards friends and servants, and drawing attention to the key virtues of justice, temperance, fortitude, and prudence. Knox suggests that Higford's work is largely derivative, but has the merit of offering a broad curriculum and praises the benefits of foreign travel and the acquisition of a foreign language. Wood records that Higford left behind other 'matters fit for the press … which being not understood by his children were lost' (Wood, *Ath. Oxon.*, 3rd edn, 3.429).   ANDREW WARMINGTON

Sources Wood, *Ath. Oxon.*, new edn, 3.429 • R. Atkyns, *The ancient and present state of Gloucestershire* (1714) • S. Rudder, *A new history of Gloucestershire* (1779) • H. M. Knox, 'A little known contribution to English courtesy education', *British Journal of Educational Studies*, 5/1 (1956), 67–71 • private information (2004) [Society of Genealogists]

Higginbottom, Frederick James (1859–1943),

journalist, was born on 21 October 1859 at Accrington, Lancashire, the son of Matthew Fielding Higginbottom, a mathematics tutor, and his wife, Margaret, *née* Sykes. After a private education in Liverpool, Higginbottom began his career in journalism with the *Southport Daily News*, at the age of fifteen. He had learned enough by 1879 to take up the editorship of the *Southport Visiter*, described in his memoirs as a 'social paper' but offering scope to develop his skills as a political reporter. By 1881 Higginbottom's enterprise had attracted the attention of the Press Association; the London-based news agency sent him to Dublin in 1882, where he remained as its special correspondent for almost ten years. His reporting during an especially troubled phase of Anglo-Irish relations established the Press Association as the principal supplier of Irish news for the London and provincial press. In 1884 Higginbottom married Ann Elizabeth (d. 1922), daughter of Edwin H. Neville.

On returning to London, Higginbottom served briefly as a parliamentary correspondent for a Dublin paper and, in 1892, founded the London Press Exchange, which flourished as an advertising-cum-news agency servicing the requirements of provincial newspapers. He also began his long association with the *Pall Mall Gazette*, the London evening newspaper made famous by W. T. Stead in the 1880s but by Higginbottom's time rather past its prime in terms of influence and circulation. It is clear from his memoirs that he felt most comfortable as a member of the parliamentary press lobby; he stayed there as the *Pall Mall Gazette's* political correspondent until 1900. After a short stay at the *Daily Chronicle*, Higginbottom returned to the *Gazette*, succeeding Sir Douglas Straight as editor in April 1909. His two years in the post represent the pinnacle of his career. He maintained the paper's 'independent Conservative' stance, backing resistance to the Parliament Bill in 1911. Though this earned the gratitude of the Conservative faction, who opposed 'wobbling and scuttling', it did not arrest the decline of the *Gazette*, which was reported to be losing about £20,000 a year, with sales dipping below 10,000. Under Higginbottom's editorship, the paper was, according to one description, 'undistinguished but workmanlike' (Scott, 392–3).

By the end of 1911 Waldorf Astor, owner of the *Pall Mall Gazette*, was seeking an editor who could offer more than a safe pair of hands. Higginbottom moved aside for J. L. Garvin, whose work at the *Observer* he had recommended to Astor; the transition appears to have been without acrimony. Higginbottom was re-employed as parliamentary correspondent at the same salary. Apart from an interlude as director of press intelligence for the Ministry of National Service in 1917–18, he remained a parliamentary correspondent for the rest of his career, which concluded with an attachment to the *Daily Chronicle* from 1919 to 1930. He died suddenly at his home, The Lawn, Briston, Norfolk, on 12 May 1943.

Higginbottom took pride in being a working journalist. His connection with the Institute of Journalists, dating from its foundation in 1890, allowed him to campaign for appropriate professional standards and, through stewardship of the institute's provident fund, to show a concern for the welfare of journalists who had fallen on hard times. Even after his retirement Higginbottom continued to contribute to the institute's *Journal*. At the end of his life he was engaged in debate with those who favoured an academic training for journalists; characteristically, Higginbottom preferred a more practical apprenticeship beginning 'in a provincial newspaper office, where the pupil learns something of all departments and a good deal of some' (*Journal*, March 1943).   DILWYN PORTER

Sources F. J. Higginbottom, *The vivid life: a journalist's career* (1934) • *The Times* (14 May 1943) • *The Times* (15 May 1943) • *The Times* (22 May 1943) • *The Journal* [Institute of Journalists], 31/300–04 (1943) • S. E. Koss, *The rise and fall of the political press in Britain*, 2 vols. (1981–4) • J. W. Robertson Scott, *The life and death of a newspaper* (1952) • A. J. Lee, *The origins of the popular press in England, 1855–1914* (1976) • D. Griffiths, ed., *The encyclopedia of the British press, 1422–1992* (1992) • WWW
Archives Col. U., Henry Cust MSS • U. Reading, Aston MSS
Wealth at death £9877 1s. 8d.: probate, 11 Sept 1943, *CGPLA Eng. & Wales*

Higgins, Ambrose. *See* O'Higgins, Ambrosio, marquess of Osorno in the Spanish nobility (c.1721–1801).

Higgins, Bryan (c.1741–1818), medical practitioner and chemist, was born in Sligo, Ireland, the son of Bryan Higgins (d. 1777), medical practitioner; little is known about his education. As his family, eminent in medicine, was Roman Catholic, he probably attended irregular 'hedge schools'. It was customary for Irish Catholic students to go abroad for higher education, and on 5 October 1765 he enrolled at the University of Leiden 'at the age of 24' (Wheeler and Partington, 51), passing the medical examination on 2 November and defending his thesis ten days later. Where he had studied medicine is thus not known. He practised medicine in London, but saw the entrepreneurial possibilities of chemistry.

About 1770 Higgins married Jane, daughter and heir of J. Welland of London, and in 1774 opened a school of practical chemistry with a laboratory in Greek Street, Soho. The laboratory was 30 ft long, extensively equipped with furnaces and several thousand glass vessels; large chimneys were built to carry off the fumes of chemical reactions. Josiah Wedgwood's showroom was nearby, and so was Sir Joseph Banks's house in Soho Square: it was a fashionable area, and Higgins clearly possessed charm and social grace, which recommended him to the scientifically minded gentry of Hanoverian London. He became a friend of Samuel Johnson and of James Boswell, and Benjamin Franklin and Edward Gibbon were among his auditors. Joseph Priestley had attended Higgins's lectures, and bought chemicals from him, but became an enemy following a dispute over experiments on air, in which Higgins accused Priestley of stealing experiments from other chemists. Priestley retaliated by making an attack on Higgins's character, portraying him in a pamphlet as socially inferior and sycophantic.

In 1775 Higgins published the first of several syllabuses of his lectures; copies of these were forwarded by Jean de Magellan (1722–1790) to Lavoisier in Paris. In 1776 he published experiments on the freezing of sea water, and on 8 January 1779 he patented a cement composed of sand, slaked lime, limewater, and bone ash—a cement he claimed was cheap and durable. He promoted it in a book published in the following year, describing the experiments leading to its production. In 1786 Higgins published his best-known work, *Experiments and observations relating to acetous acid, fixable air, dense inflammable air, oils and fuels*. The work, associated with his lectures, shows his concern both with the practicalities of heating and lighting systems, and also with the nature of matter and its relation to heat and light. These were Newtonian concerns typical of the day, but Higgins's reasoning was acute and original. He believed that the particles composing airs were hard and globular, surrounded by atmospheres of fire. They might acquire polarity, and definite repulsive and attractive forces were associated with them; these forces were 'saturated' in compounds. His nephew William *Higgins developed these ideas further, and both Higginses have been seen as precursors of John Dalton, although his theory was much more testable and had a rather different basis.

In 1788 Higgins had published analyses of mineral waters, an important business at that period. In November 1793 he issued proposals for a society, and on 25 January 1794 established the Society for Philosophical Experiments and Conversations. The first chairman was Field Marshal Conway; Charles, third earl of Stanhope, was a member; and Thomas Young acted as Higgins's assistant. The subscription was 5 guineas, and the society met weekly at 8 p.m., over a period of six months, at Higgins's house in Greek Street. The society's *Minutes* were published in 1796. Although short-lived, the society demonstrated the demand, and the gentlemanly support, for scientific knowledge in London, which was later exploited by the Royal Institution.

Presumably through the influence of his highly placed associates, in 1796 Higgins was appointed at £1000 per annum, later increased to £1400, to improve sugar and rum in Jamaica, and went to Spanish Town, from where he returned in 1801. His *Observations and Advices* in this profitable technology was published between 1797 and 1803. Before leaving London, he had sold his apparatus and after his return does not seem to have been very active in chemistry, though in 1803 he did advise the Royal Institution about its laboratory, at the suggestion of Humphry Davy.

Higgins died in 1818 at Walford in Staffordshire. He had made his career in an atmosphere of chemical and technical progress and optimism, where devising oil lamps which looked like candles, and heating systems based on warm air, went with and were as important as performing chemical analyses and syntheses. DAVID KNIGHT

Sources A. Thackray, 'Higgins, Bryan', *DSB* · T. S. Wheeler and J. R. Partington, *The life and work of William Higgins, chemist, 1763–1825* (1960) · *DNB* · J. Priestley, *Philosophical empiricism: containing remarks on a charge of plagiarism respecting Dr H—s* (1775)
Wealth at death wealthy: Wheeler and Partington, *Life and work of William Higgins*, 2, 28

Higgins, Charles Longuet (1806–1885), benefactor, was born at Turvey Abbey, Bedfordshire, on 30 November 1806. He was the eldest son of John Higgins (1768–1846) of Turvey Abbey and Theresa (d. 1845), eldest daughter of Benjamin Longuet of Louth and Bath, a gentleman of Huguenot descent. The family had strong links with the evangelical movement, and the parish church at Turvey had evangelical links. He was taught at home and matriculated at Trinity College, Cambridge, as a pensioner on 14 November 1825.

At Cambridge Higgins was impressed by the piety of the Revd Charles Simeon, the evangelical revivalist, and developed a taste for natural history and music, though he was an undistinguished scholar. He graduated BA in 1830 and proceeded to an MA in 1834. Although he had hoped to become a clergyman he relinquished the idea in deference to his father's wishes, and was admitted a student of Lincoln's Inn on 16 November 1830. He was not called to the bar, and from 1836 to 1838 studied medicine at St Bartholomew's Hospital. Having qualified as a doctor, he carried on a general medical practice at Turvey.

When his father died in 1846, Higgins succeeded to the family property. The following year he built a village school, to which he added a museum in 1852. He also restored the church (1852–4) and erected more than sixty comfortable cottages. On 26 June 1853 he married Helen Eliza, daughter of Thomas Burgon of the British Museum. They had no children. Although Higgins never formally renounced his evangelical background, his increasing interest in high-church Anglicanism can be felt in the hymn-book which he compiled for general use in the Church of England and his paper on hymnology, afterwards published, which he read to the church congress at Nottingham in 1871. He was a JP and deputy lieutenant of Bedfordshire, and he delivered lectures on natural history and other subjects. Higgins died at Turvey Abbey on 23 January 1885, survived by his wife.

WILLIAM HUNT, *rev.* MARK CLEMENT

Sources J. W. Burgon, *Lives of twelve good men*, [new edn], 2 (1889)
Archives Beds. & Luton ARS, Longuet-Higgins MSS
Wealth at death £5176 0s. 10d.: resworn probate, March 1886, *CGPLA Eng. & Wales* (1885)

Higgins, Edward John (1864–1947), Salvation Army officer, was born on 26 November 1864 at 10 Church Street, Highbridge, Somerset, the son of Edward Higgins, saddler and harness maker, and his wife, Martha Deacon (d. 1870). After the death of his mother Higgins was brought up by his maternal grandparents, while his father pursued business interests elsewhere. Both father and son were keen Methodists. He was educated at a small private school in Burnham and then at Dr Morgan's Grammar School, Bridgwater. At the age of fifteen he went to work for a Highbridge provision merchant, but was already a Sunday school teacher. His father, who had opened a boot and shoe shop in Reading, Berkshire, in 1881 became a commissioner in the Salvation Army.

Early in 1882, after attending a meeting at which General William Booth preached, Edward Higgins himself became a Salvationist, and he thereafter devoted the rest of his life to the cause. After moving to Reading he became a soldier in the Salvation Army and experienced the hurly-burly of open-air evangelism. He later recalled the first time he spoke to a Saturday night meeting: 'I stumbled and stuttered, and at last sat down, feeling in my heart that I would never do it again' (Harris, 15). Yet he persevered and became a fluent, forceful, and persuasive speaker.

Higgins had much business acumen and a gift for organization, which secured for him the rapid promotion which may have startled some of his less energetic colleagues. He served in various positions of increasing seniority in Twyford, Durham, and Darlington, personally selling copies of the *War Cry* and the *Young Soldier* in public houses. While based in Penarth, near Cardiff, on 2 April 1888 he married another Salvationist, Catherine (*d.* 1952), daughter of David Price, a building contractor. The couple had four sons and three daughters. Higgins subsequently became a staff captain, in charge of training young officers in Oxfordshire and Buckinghamshire.

In 1896 Higgins was sent to the United States, with the rank of colonel, as chief secretary to General Frederick St George de Latour Booth-Tucker, and he did much to establish the Salvation Army there on a firm footing. This appointment was followed by one in which he was directly concerned with the army's foreign affairs, so he had to handle many problems arising from the peculiar difficulties which beset colleagues carrying out the Salvation Army's mission abroad. There its intentions were often questioned, its aims often misunderstood or misinterpreted. But Higgins's tact, his skill in negotiation, and his patience in counsel stood the army in good stead and contributed much to its success in maintaining its evangelizing campaign in many lands. Such work, however, was not all done from a desk in London. He travelled widely with both General Booth and his son William Bramwell Booth. In 1911 he became British commissioner, and as such was responsible for the army's evangelical work at home. For his services during the First World War he was appointed CBE in 1920. In December 1918 he became chief of staff, a position in which he was, as all earlier holders of the office had been, the leader's right-hand man and confidential agent.

In 1928 there developed a crisis within the Salvation Army. Some members of the high council, an authoritative group of senior officers, had long felt that, for many reasons, a change in command was desirable, and that the system whereby a retiring general was able to nominate his successor was outmoded in a changing world. The council met in London to consider what they should do, within the fairly wide limits of their powers. Discussion was protracted. Bramwell Booth offered to surrender the right to nominate his successor, but declined to resign his own office. Eventually on 13 February 1929 the high council, by a very large majority, and after hearing a mass of evidence and speeches by counsel, declared Bramwell Booth 'unfit for the office of General of the Salvation Army', removed him therefrom, and recorded that their resolution was based upon the state of his health. These events, while they did not lack some of the essential qualities of drama, also had their pathos. In all of them Higgins took a leading part. It is for this principally that he will be remembered within and without the ranks of the Salvation Army. Having deposed the leader and destroyed the dynastic principle at a stroke, the high council immediately elected Higgins to the generalship by a majority of twenty-five over the other candidate. This was Commander Evangeline Booth, herself prominent in the move to depose her brother; she eventually succeeded Higgins as general.

Higgins took office knowing that the problems he must now face dwarfed any with which he had been called upon to grapple earlier. The drastic action in which he had very actively shared so recently did not gain the immediate or unanimous support of all senior officers or of the whole of the rank and file. It had, however, been taken only after profound and prayerful thought, and after the co-operation of Bramwell Booth and his supporters had been vigorously sought. For a time it seemed as if the Salvation Army might falter in its march. Higgins and his staff, however, initiated further reforms which were concerned with the powers of the general, the status and duties of officers, and the fundamental constitution of the organization, to introduce into it a more democratic spirit.

The Salvation Army Act was subsequently passed by parliament and became law in 1931. It provided that subsequent generals would be elected by a high council; and that the assets of the movement, previously held by the general, would be transferred to the Salvation Army Trustee Company. Generals also were obliged to retire on reaching the age of seventy.

Higgins's retirement in 1934 was marked by a presentation in the Royal Albert Hall at which their royal highnesses the duke and duchess of York were present. Subsequently Higgins went to live in the United States, and died in New York on 14 December 1947.

RONALD CARTON, *rev.* ROBERT BROWN

Sources W. G. Harris, *Storm pilot: the story of the life and leadership of General Edward J. Higgins* (1981) · H. Begbie, *Life of William Booth, the founder of the Salvation Army*, 2 vols. (1920) · C. Bramwell-Booth, *Bramwell Booth* (1933) · St J. G. Ervine, *God's soldier: General William Booth* (1934) · *WWW* · F. Coutts, *No discharge in this war* (1975) · personal knowledge (1959)

Archives FILM BFI NFTVA, record footage

Likenesses F. O. Salisbury, drawing, 1934, Salvation Army, London

Higgins, Ellen Charlotte (1871–1951), college head and feminist, was born at 12 Trinity Square, Brixton, London, on 14 August 1871 (she was always reticent about the date of her birth). Her parents, Henry Bell Higgins, a publisher, and his wife, Margaret Hay, who were both of Scottish descent, sent her to Scotland for her education. She attended Edinburgh Ladies' College, from which she won an entrance scholarship to Royal Holloway College (RHC) in 1890. In 1894 she gained the distinction, unprecedented at RHC, of being listed in the first class in final honours mathematics in the Oxford examinations (which were then open to women from outside Oxford), and gaining a first in BA (hons) English, with the Gilchrist prize, in London University examinations. She was a brilliant student, to whom academic success came easily, but she was also a talented musician and sportswoman. At RHC she played the violin and viola in Band, the college orchestra, and also played hockey and cricket for the college. During her years as principal of RHC she returned to Band to play the cello and the double bass. In later life she took up the clarinet, and had lessons with the great virtuoso and teacher Frederick Thurston. Her lifelong love of learning was illustrated by her beginning the study of Russian at the age of seventy.

After graduating from RHC Miss Higgins joined the staff of Cheltenham Ladies' College, where she taught mathematics from 1895 to 1907, latterly as head of department. In 1907 she was appointed principal of RHC, where she continued in office until 1935. In 1918 the post of secretary to the governors of RHC was given to Miss Ulrica Dolling, who despite her Germanic name was a native of Northern Ireland. From their first encounter Miss Higgins and Miss Dolling became inseparable companions, and lived together during their retirement, from 1935 onwards. In a more permissive age their relationship might have been acknowledged as homosexual; but in a period when lesbianism was almost unmentionable, no comment on its nature was made.

During her long principalship Miss Higgins continued to build upon the foundations laid down by her two predecessors at RHC, Matilda Bishop and Emily Penrose. She consolidated RHC's reputation for academic excellence, high moral tone, and civilized manners. Towards the end of her principalship one of her colleagues, in a eulogistic speech at a college dinner, said of her: 'More and more I seem to see that the College *is* Miss Higgins and Miss Higgins the College. ... The sense of duty, of playing the game, the lack of pose or pretentiousness, the tolerance and kindliness and hospitality, the straightforward, simple outlook of our students are I think a direct reflection of Miss Higgins' own fine attitude, they are *herself*' (Bingham, 113).

Miss Higgins held office as a senator of the University of London from 1911 to 1935, and immediately before the First World War was successful in blocking a move to expel RHC from the university on the grounds of its geographical remoteness at Egham. She employed her talents and determination in the cause of establishing the position of women in both the scholastic and administrative areas of academic life. During her principalship women were admitted to the governing body of RHC, and in 1920 the principal herself became a governor *ex officio*. Professor E. S. Waterhouse, in a memorial address for her, said:

> She fought a battle for women's education. She believed in it as a right and not as a concession or favour. She fought against men—asked no favour and gave no quarter. ... Her struggle for the rights of women perhaps made her accentuate the masculine [in herself], as though she would fight the battle on equal and level terms. (Royal Holloway College Association, *College Letters*, Dec 1952, 42–3)

Though not herself directly involved in the women's suffrage movement, she encouraged the students of RHC to be interested in the issue: early in her principalship, in 1908, the Royal Holloway College Women's Suffrage Society was founded.

Miss Higgins was also a traditionalist and an autocrat. In the later years of her principalship, after the First World War, she was reluctant to recognize the relaxation of the conventions which had governed the conduct of young unmarried women. Women's rights were not in her mind to be equated with such practical applications of women's liberation as informal mixing with the opposite sex. As a result, RHC between the two world wars gained the reputation of being a somewhat old-fashioned institution. Yet, though Miss Higgins may have seemed to her students exasperatingly reactionary, she none the less inspired their affection, and her autocratic manner won her the nickname Chief. In a verse on her retirement a colleague described her as:

> The Scottish Chief
> Of manly mien, of words directly fired
> In sentence brief,
> Whose rule was famed for steadfast
> Strength of mind,
> Resolved yet reasonable, firm but kind.
> (M. F. Richey, *Collegiate Causeries*, 1949, 33)

During her retirement Miss Higgins played no part in public affairs, but enjoyed her lifelong pleasures of literature, learning, music, walking, mountaineering, and travel. She and Miss Dolling were both members of the Ladies' Alpine Club, and they celebrated their retirement with an ascent of the Matterhorn. Miss Higgins died at their home, 8 Warrender Park Crescent, Edinburgh, on 13 December 1951. Miss Dolling, one of her executors, died in 1970.

The portrait of Miss Higgins by Sir William Orpen, which was hung in the dining hall of RHC, successfully conveys her forceful personality and her strikingly masculine appearance, which is accentuated by her closely cropped hair and the stiff-collared shirt and tie which she wears beneath her academic gown. Her obituary in *Nature* (2 February 1952, 178) referred to her 'quite famous clothes—her invariable and rather mannish day-attire and her magnificent but fashion-defying evening dresses'. These, which she wore for formal dinners in college, were always sombre in colour and rich in material, often worn with a splendid necklace of cornelians and diamonds. In her retirement she indulged a preference for a dinner jacket.

CAROLINE BINGHAM

Sources Royal Holloway College Association, *College Letters* • M. J. Powell, ed., *The Royal Holloway College, 1887–1937* (privately printed, Egham, [1937]) • M. Pick, 'Social life at Royal Holloway College, 1887–1939', typescript, Royal Holloway College, Egham, Surrey • W. E. Delp, 'Royal Holloway College, 1908–1914', Royal Holloway College, Egham, Surrey [privately printed pamphlet] • private information (2004) • C. Bingham, *The history of Royal Holloway College, 1886–1986* (1987) • b. cert. • *CCI* (1952)
Archives Royal Holloway College, Egham, Surrey, minutes of governors' meetings | Royal Holloway College, Egham, Surrey, research materials presented by Caroline Bingham • Royal Holloway College, Egham, Surrey, E. M. Blackwell MSS
Likenesses photographs, *c*.1894–1927, repro. in Bingham, *History of Royal Holloway College* • W. Orpen, oils, 1927, Royal Holloway College • photographs, Royal Holloway College
Wealth at death £1572 0s. 11d.: confirmation, 18 Jan 1952, *CCI*

Higgins, Francis (1669/70–1728), Church of Ireland clergyman and religious controversialist, was one of at least eleven children of Robert Higgins, a Limerick apothecary. Although, according to Higgins, the family's 'little fortune' was 'ruined' in the Williamite wars his brother John (also an apothecary) eventually became an alderman of the city. After education at Mr Ryland's school in Limerick Francis entered Trinity College, Dublin, aged sixteen, in May 1686, as a sizar. Ordained in 1689, while an undergraduate, the college being then under military occupation, Higgins was made curate of St Andrew's, Dublin, and was (or so he said) imprisoned by the Jacobite authorities. In February 1690 he became a reader at Christ Church Cathedral, only to be suspended shortly afterwards for dereliction of duty. He took his BA in 1691 and his MA two years later.

In 1694 Higgins was presented to the rectory of Gowran, co. Kilkenny, by the Jacobite Lord Rosse. He later claimed to have been employed as an agent by the 'lower clergy' against a bill introduced during the Irish parliamentary session of 1695–7. Otherwise he first came to public notice in the Irish convocation summoned in 1704. A proctor for the diocese of Ossory, he was one of the prominent high-churchmen who, according to Archbishop King of Dublin, 'got the management of the clergy … into their hands' (King to Archbishop Wake, 12 Sept 1717, Wake MSS). With his clerical friend William Perceval he frequented the Swan Tripe Club, a tory dining club in Dublin which was the target of a satire depicting Higgins as fat, red-faced, and loquacious: 'a son of pudding and eternal beef' (*The Swan Tripe-Club*, 1705). His former negligence forgotten, the high-flying canons of Christchurch elected Higgins to a prebend in 1705 and promptly dispatched him to England to pursue their jurisdictional dispute with Archbishop King. Higgins had already acquired a reputation as a fiery preacher, which he enhanced while in England, his partisan enthusiasm reaching a climax in a sermon preached in the Chapel Royal on Ash Wednesday (26 February) 1707, which was so strident in its denunciation of whigs as enemies of the monarchy and the established church that he was arrested for preaching sedition. Although the government entered a *nolle prosequi*, not only the offending sermon was published but also a 'postscript' (attributed to the nonjuror Charles Leslie), with an account of a prior interview with Archbishop Tenison of

Francis Higgins (1669/70–1728), by Edward Luttrell

Canterbury, in which Tenison's advice to Higgins to moderate his tone had been insolently rejected. By order of the Irish House of Lords the postscript was publicly burnt. Higgins and Perceval also ran into controversy when they testified before the convocation of Canterbury to the powers of the lower house of convocation in Dublin. Although condemned in print for acting without authority the two men were vindicated by the Irish convocation.

Higgins returned to Ireland in 1710 to spearhead the clerical reaction that accompanied the re-establishment of a tory ministry. He involved himself in a series of political disputes, in the most remarkable of which he supported fantastic allegations made by a converted Catholic priest, Dominic Langton, of an alleged republican conspiracy among provincial whigs. Unpleasant scenes followed at the Dublin quarter sessions, which Higgins attended as a JP (he had been removed in 1709 but was later restored). After he had insisted that the assembled company at the justices' dinner drink to the principle of passive obedience the grand jury presented him as 'a common disturber of her Majesty's peace'. The foreman, Lord Santry, brought this charge before the Irish privy council but was rebuffed by the tory majority there. Higgins was now the centre of attention on both sides of the Irish sea and became known as 'the Irish Sacheverell'. In 1712 he once again arrived in London: 'I believe', wrote Swift, 'he designs to make as much noise as he can in order to preferment' (Swift, *Journal to Stella*, 2.536). He was talked of for a deanery, in Ireland or England, but nothing came his way.

After the Hanoverian succession, although still a thorn

in Archbishop King's flesh, Higgins seems to have avoided political controversy. Belatedly he acquired the archdeaconry of Cashel, in 1725, in succession to Perceval, but he may have been an absentee for he retained the Christ Church prebend. He died in August 1728 and was buried in his prebendal church, St Michael and All Angels, Dublin. He is not known to have married. Besides several anonymous squibs, which may possibly be attributed to him, he published five sermons, all delivered between 1705 and 1707. D. W. HAYTON

Sources J. B. Leslie, *Ossory clergy and parishes* (1933), 268–70 · Bodl. Oxf., MS North a. 3, fols. 237–8 · H. Cotton, *Fasti ecclesiae Hibernicae*, 2 (1848), 66–8, 85 · Burtchaell & Sadleir, *Alum. Dubl.*, 397 · W. King, correspondence, TCD, Lyons collection, MSS 1995–2008 · W. King, letter-books, TCD, MSS 750(3), 2531, 2536 · Bodl. Oxf., MSS Ballard 7, 36 · *Remarks and collections of Thomas Hearne*, ed. C. E. Doble and others, 11 vols., OHS, 2, 7, 13, 34, 42–3, 48, 50, 65, 67, 72 (1885–1921), vol. 1, p. 337; vol. 2, pp. 25, 33 · Christ Church Oxf., Wake MS Arch. W. Epist. 12 · minutes of the lower house of convocation of the Church of Ireland, 1704–12, TCD, MSS 668/1–3 · *The poems of Jonathan Swift*, ed. H. Williams, 3 (1937), 1077–8, 1090–96 · J. Swift, *Journal to Stella*, ed. H. Williams, 2 (1948), 536, 540, 549 · *DNB*
Likenesses E. Luttrell, mezzotint, BM, NPG [*see illus.*]
Wealth at death c.1712 claimed family's estate 'ruined' by 1691, and that he had spent £1500 on his rectory at Gowran: Bodl. Oxf., MS North a. 3, fols. 237–8

Higgins, Francis [*called* the Sham Squire] (1746–1802), newspaper proprietor and spy, was born in Dublin, the son of Patrick Higgins, an attorney's clerk, and his wife, Mary; his parents had moved there from Downpatrick, co. Down. Higgins passed his early years in menial employments, became an attorney's clerk, by report converted to protestantism, though his name is not found in the official list of converts (and his later reconversion to Roman Catholicism is alluded to), and, through deception, married an heiress, Mary Anne Archer (d. 1767), of an eminent Dublin Catholic family, who in 1766 prosecuted him for fraud. Higgins was convicted, and was for a time imprisoned. This episode earned Higgins the sobriquet 'Sham Squire'. After his release he formed lucrative connections with lottery offices and gambling houses. In 1775 he appears as master of the Dublin guild of hosiers, which entitled him to be elected to the Dublin city commons. He was admitted an attorney at Dublin in 1780 (apparently through the influence of the attorney-general, John Scott), secured the posts of deputy coroner and undersheriff for Dublin, and in 1788 was appointed a magistrate for co. Dublin. This accumulation of offices, along with his proprietorship of the *Freeman's Journal* newspaper, meant that by the 1780s Higgins was one of the city's most influential citizens.

Founded in Dublin in 1763, the *Freeman's Journal* was an organ of radical opinion with Charles Lucas as its main contributor, and later it expressed the opinions of the 'patriots', notably Henry Grattan and Henry Flood, in their opposition to Lord Townshend. Higgins secured an editorial role from as early as 1779 and, without the knowledge of the then owners, was simultaneously in the pay of government. He skilfully maintained this equivocal role for a

period by maintaining a pretence of patriotism for the sake of the newspaper's owners but at the same time ingratiated himself with government. However, from the date of his proprietorship of the *Freeman* in 1783 (when it was purchased by government and placed under Higgins's management) until his death in 1802 it became openly subservient to Pitt's administration. Higgins continuously assailed the government's opponents in his paper, provoking Grattan's denunciation in parliament. Ironically the circulation and influence of the paper declined under Higgins's management, becoming ultimately a costly liability to its political sponsors. In 1789 Higgins's archrival, the Belfast radical John Magee, published polemical attacks in his own paper, the *Dublin Evening Post*; there he exposed Higgins's antecedents and the Archer affair and denounced Higgins as a venal journalist, a corrupt magistrate, and a profiteer from gambling. Magee also attacked associates of Higgins, including the actor and theatre manager Richard Daly. In 1790 Higgins prosecuted Magee for libel and through his alleged influence with John Scott, now Lord Earlsfort, lord chief justice, he obtained, by authority of that court, writs styled 'fiats', an obsolescent legal process under which the defendant was liable to imprisonment until he found surety for damages of £7800, which he was unable to do. Under pressure the jury returned a guilty verdict against Magee. These proceedings formed the subject of discussion in the Irish House of Commons. The case brought into focus the abuse of fiats which subsequently ceased to be used.

In 1791 Higgins was removed from the magistracy, and in 1795 he was struck off the roll of attorneys. In 1795 he warned the government of a projected attack on the new lord lieutenant, Lord Camden. Through the undersecretary of state, Edward Cooke, Higgins secretly communicated to the Irish government in 1798 information on the United Irishmen obtained through a system of spies and informers which he managed. The government account of secret service money (20 June 1798) has an entry for £1000 paid to 'F. H.' for the discovery of Lord Edward Fitzgerald. The initials are those of Higgins. Cooke recommended that Lord Castlereagh grant a yearly pension of £300 to Higgins for the same service. Although Higgins was amply rewarded by government for this and other services, he remained persistent in his demands and complaints. His role in this arrest was the subject of much historical inquiry subsequently, especially after the publication of the correspondence of Lord Cornwallis in 1859. Works by the historians R. R. Madden and W. J. Fitzpatrick appeared at a period of resurgent Irish nationalism in the 1860s, thus making Higgins's betrayal of Fitzgerald a key episode in national consciousness. It is not surprising that their assessment was coloured by that standpoint. Thus for Madden, writing in 1867: 'Higgins, in politics, in religion, in friendship, in all his pursuits, was everything by turns and nothing long. In hypocrisy and perfidy alone he was always consistent and persistent: he was always — Higgins' (Madden, *History*, 2.451). Higgins died in affluence at Dublin on 19 January 1802: his will mentions legacies worth £12,380. His heir was Francis Higgins of Philadelphia, his nephew and namesake, who was originally from Downpatrick. Higgins was buried with his parents in Kilbarrack cemetery, Dublin. THOMAS P. POWER

Sources DNB · W. J. Fitzpatrick, *The Sham Squire and the informers of 1798* (1866) · W. J. Fitzpatrick, *Ireland before the union: with revelations from the unpublished diary of Lord Clonmell* (1867) · R. R. Madden, *The United Irishmen: their lives and times*, 2nd edn, 4 vols. (1857–60) · R. R. Madden, *The history of Irish periodical literature*, 2 vols. (1867) · B. Inglis, *The freedom of the press in Ireland, 1784–1841* (1954) · E. O'Byrne, ed., *The convert rolls*, IMC (1981) · E. Keane, P. Beryl Phair, and T. U. Sadlier, eds., *King's Inns admission papers, 1607–1867*, IMC (1982) · F. J. Bigger, *The Magees of Belfast and Dublin* (1916) · NL Ire., MSS 5767, 10532
Archives NA Ire., rebellion papers, letters to Under-Secretary Edward Cooke
Likenesses engraving (*The Sham in lavender*), repro. in *Dublin Evening Post* (13 Oct 1789)
Wealth at death £12,380: Fitzpatrick, *Ireland*, 86–92

Higgins, Frederick Robert (1896–1941), poet, was born on 24 April 1896 in Foxford, co. Mayo, the eldest of the nine children of Joseph Higgins, a police constable, and his wife, Annie French. His father, a protestant unionist, was from Higginstown, Trim, co. Meath, where Higgins spent childhood holidays with relatives. After completing a national school education Higgins started work in 1912 as a junior clerk with Brooks Thomas, the main builders' providers in Dublin. Influenced by the nationalism of the literary revival, he identified with Sinn Féin, and he became estranged from his father over his refusal to enlist in the British army during the First World War, which led to his departure from the family home in Fairview, Dublin. Higgins left Brooks Thomas and, in 1918, became a secretary with the Clerical Workers' Union, where he found that his 'contact with mechanical industry intensified a passion for primitive nature' (*Evening Herald*). This passion found expression in the poetry he had begun to write. The rhythms of Irish airs and ballads are also clearly evident in his early poems, which were greatly influenced by Douglas Hyde's *Love Songs of Connaught*. He befriended Austin Clarke in 1915 and George Russell (Æ) encouraged the young poet.

Having founded a paper, the *Irish Clerk*, Higgins left the Clerical Workers' Union in 1920, edited several trade journals such as *Oil and Colour Paint Review* and the *Furniture Man's Gazetteer*, and established the first women's magazine in Ireland, *Welfare*, which ran for two issues. He also worked as a contributing editor to several literary magazines, including *The Klaxon* and *To-Morrow*.

On 3 August 1921 Higgins married a well-known harpist, Beatrice May, daughter of James Moore, a boat maker of Clontarf, Dublin. The couple set up home in Rathfarnham, co. Dublin; they had no children. Higgins won the 1924 Aonach Tailteann award for poetry for his first collection of poems, *Salt Air*, which had been published in 1923 by the Irish Bookshop. He was a pastoral poet who found inspiration in the rugged Connemara landscape, in *Island Blood* (1925), for example, and in the lush pastures of co. Meath and the Boyne valley. His work reflected a strong sense of tradition and he drew on Gaelic modes of poetry to write in the 'Celtic' manner pioneered by Austin Clarke and Padraic Colum in such poems as 'The Island Dead of Inchagoill' (in *The Dark Breed*, 1927). A major theme was the passing of the Gaelic way of life. Highly regarded by his peers, Higgins was a fastidious craftsman, working and reworking a poem until he was completely satisfied.

From 1928 to 1932 Higgins was the Aonach Tailteann adjudicator of poetry, and also served as professor of poetry at the Royal Hibernian Academy of Arts. In 1932 he was a foundation member of the Irish Academy of Letters, which was the brainchild of Yeats and had George Bernard Shaw as its first president. The academy's aim was to combat literary censorship by 'giving authority to the utterance' of Irish writers. Higgins was honorary secretary from 1936 to 1941. He was awarded the Casement medal by the academy for his collection *Arable Holdings* (1933). His poem 'The Past Generation' (1936), first published in the *Dublin Magazine*, to which Higgins regularly contributed, signalled a shift away from lyricism and showed the influence of Yeats.

Despite joining in the condemnation of Sean O'Casey's *The Plough and the Stars* in 1926, attacking both the playwright and his defender W. B. Yeats, by the mid-1930s Higgins and Yeats had become close friends. He contributed to an *Irish Times* supplement to mark Yeats's seventieth birthday in 1935, while Yeats championed Higgins and included him in the *Oxford Book of Modern Verse* (1936), and in 1937 selected poems by him for BBC and Irish radio programmes. Higgins was involved in the publication of *Broadsides*, a series of illustrated broadsheets published by the Yeats family-owned Cuala Press, of which in 1937 he became an editorial director. In April 1935 Higgins was appointed to the board of the Abbey Theatre (the national theatre of Ireland founded by Yeats), which prompted the *Irish Times* to hope that he might 'bring back to the Irish theatre something of its first poetic impulse' (*Irish Times*). In September 1935 Higgins's only play to be performed, *A Deuce of Jacks* (a one-act, low-life comedy set in early nineteenth-century Dublin), was staged at the Abbey. It was not well received by the critics; the *Dublin Evening Mail* reviewer wrote that it exhibited 'a supreme contempt for what a play should be'. Higgins enjoyed greater success in 1937 as manager of the Abbey company's tour of the United States, which took in seventy-four cities (he became managing director of the Abbey Theatre in 1938). He brought energy, vision, and a keen business sense to the job, and his policy of staging new plays revived the theatre's artistic fortunes, doing away with the need for revivals. As part of the Abbey Festival in August 1938 Higgins delivered a lecture, 'Yeats and Irish drama', in which he expounded his views on theatre. He called on dramatists to ignore box-office considerations, which he thought had a cheapening influence on a literary theatre. He argued for plays that would generate intellectual excitement, thereby making the theatre a place where the mind would be liberated as it was by the theatres of Greece, England, and France at great moments in their history. He disliked any trace of effeminacy in literature; art had to be masculine and intellectual.

Higgins was of stout build with a bespectacled, plump face and a shock of dark hair. He was a boisterous character with a taste for alcohol and malicious gossip. He fed Yeats's appetite for dirty stories with tall tales of his own sexual exploits which he later recounted for the amusement of Dublin's literati. His main recreation, according to *Who's Who*, was 'gallivanting in the country'. Higgins was an active member of the Church of Ireland. He was a member of the Boys' Brigade and, in 1932, he helped to publicize the church's celebration marking the 1500th anniversary of St Patrick's arrival in Ireland. He saw the Church of Ireland as the true successor of the early Celtic church and the home for the natural piety of a pastoral people. Higgins's last poetry collection was *A Gap of Brightness* (1940). He suffered from heart disease and died in Jervis Street Hospital, Dublin, on 8 January 1941. He was buried in Laracor, co. Meath, on 10 January 1941.

PATRICK GILLAN

Sources *Dublin Evening Mail* (8 Jan 1941) · *Evening Herald* (8 Jan 1941) · B. Macnamara, 'F. R. Higgins: the man and the poet', *Irish Times* (9 Jan 1941) · *Irish Independent* (9 Jan 1941) · *Irish Times* (10 Jan 1941) · F. R. Higgins papers, NL Ire., MS 10864 · J. Hone, *W. B. Yeats, 1865–1939* (1962) · B. Maddox, *George's ghosts* (1999) · *F. R. Higgins: the 39 poems*, ed. R. D. Clarke (1992) · P. Kavanagh, 'The gallivanting poet', *Irish Writing*, 3 (Nov 1947), 62–70 · S. O'Faolain, *Vive moi! an autobiography* (1993) · *WWW, 1961–70* · *Irish Press* (12 Aug 1938) · A. Clarke, 'A penny in the clouds', *The field day anthology of Irish writing*, ed. S. Deane, 3 (1991), 492–5
Archives NL Ire., corresp. and literary MSS | BL, corresp. with Macmillans, Add. MS 55009 · BL, corresp. with Society of Authors, Add. MS 63265
Likenesses S. O'Sullivan, oils, 1940, Abbey Theatre, Dublin

Higgins, Godfrey (1773–1833), historian of religion, only son of Godfrey Higgins of Skellow Grange, near Doncaster, and his wife, Christiana (*née* Matterson), was born on (or shortly before) 1 May 1773. He entered Emmanuel College, Cambridge, in 1790, moving to Trinity Hall in 1791, but did not take a degree. He was admitted to the Inner Temple in 1818, but was not called to the bar. On his father's death in 1794 he succeeded to a considerable estate. In 1800 he married Jane, heir of Richard Thorpe. They had three children: a son, Godfrey, a daughter, Jane, who married Lieutenant-General Matthew Sharpe of Hoddom Castle, near Dumfries, and another daughter, Charlotte, who died, unmarried, before Higgins. His London house was 20 Keppel Street, Russell Square. In 1802, during the scare of an anticipated invasion by Napoleon, Higgins became a major in the 3rd West York militia, and while in this service he was seized with a bad fever at Harwich, from the effects of which he never recovered.

After resigning his commission in 1813, Higgins devoted himself entirely to an unbiased investigation into the history of religious beliefs. He acquired a knowledge of Hebrew, and sometimes pursued his studies in foreign libraries. At the date of his death he had projected a journey to Egypt and the Near East in search of further clues to religious problems. Higgins's principal publications were in the field of comparative religion. His *Horae sabbaticae*

(1826), which received notice and criticism, contains an autobiography in the 1851 edition. In 1829 he published a work on Muhammad, and *The Celtic Druids*, which was the more critically successful of the two. His last work was *Anacalypsis: an attempt to draw aside the veil of the Saitic Isis, or, An inquiry into the origin of languages, nations, and religions*, which was printed in June 1833 but was not published until 1836. The second volume was edited by George Smallfield at the expense of Higgins's son after his father's death. Higgins claimed to be a Christian, regarding Jesus as a Nazarite, of the monastic order of Pythagorean Essenes, probably a Samaritan by birth, and leading the life of a hermit.

Higgins acted with energy as a justice of the peace, and was keenly interested in practical questions of political economy. He took part in measures for the better treatment of the insane, and provided for the erection of a house for pauper lunatics near Wakefield. He favoured the abolition of the corn laws in conjunction with the 'fund law' and game laws. He supported calls for the reform of the House of Commons and advocated the abolition of the protestant church in Ireland. His interest in social and political issues was manifested in several publications including *A Letter to Earl Fitzwilliam on the Abuses of the York Lunatic Asylum* (1814); *The Evidence of Godfrey Higgins and C. Best Taken before a Committee of the House of Commons respecting the Asylum at York* (1816); and letters and observations on the passing of the Metallic Currency Bill (1819), and on the corn laws and fund laws (1826). In 1831 several of the radical political unions of Yorkshire were anxious to elect him to parliament; he pledged himself to serve if elected, but declined to come forward as a candidate. Much of his correspondence with the political unions of Halifax, Huddersfield, Dewsbury, and Wakefield, along with some observations on the corn and fund laws and parliamentary reform, is contained in a volume published as *An Address to the Electors and Others of the West-Riding of the County of York* (1833).

Higgins attended the meeting of the British Association at Cambridge in June 1833, returned home out of health, and died at his Yorkshire residence at Skellow Grange on 9 August 1833. His wife had died eleven years earlier, on 11 May 1822 at Bath. Higgins was a freemason, and a fellow of the Society of Arts, the Royal Asiatic Society, and other learned bodies.

ALEXANDER GORDON, *rev.* MYFANWY LLOYD

Sources *GM*, 1st ser., 103/2 (1833), 371 · Venn, *Alum. Cant.* · J. Hunter, *South Yorkshire: the history and topography of the deanery of Doncaster*, 2 vols. (1828–31) · G. Higgins, *Horae sabbaticae, or, An attempt to correct certain vulgar superstitious and vulgar errors regarding the sabbath*, 3rd edn (1851) [incl. autobiography]

Higgins, Henry Bournes (1851–1929), politician and judge in Australia, was born on 30 June 1851 at Newtownards, co. Down, Ireland, the second of the nine children of John Higgins (1820–1895), a Wesleyan preacher, and his wife, Anne (1825–1917), the daughter of Henry Bournes of Crossmolina, co. Mayo. He grew up in a close-knit family in an atmosphere of evangelical piety and genteel frugality. Deemed a 'delicate' child and inhibited by a bad stammer, he was sent to the Wesleyan connexional school in Dublin at the age of ten, but ill health forced his withdrawal four years later. His mother helped him with his education at home, and he resumed his studies for a short time at a local school in Newry. His first job was in a drapery warehouse in Belfast, a city he disliked; later he found more satisfactory employment in a furniture warehouse in Dublin.

When, in 1869, Henry's elder brother, James, died from consumption, John and Anne Higgins revived earlier thoughts of emigration. A doctor recommended Victoria for its healthy climate, and in 1870 the family settled in Melbourne, where Higgins was able to combine work as a teacher with study for university matriculation. During a successful academic career at Melbourne University (LLB, 1874; MA, 1876) he continued to contribute to the support of the family, teaching and tutoring. In engaging with the great intellectual issues of the day he discarded the simple Wesleyanism of his father, and came close to agnosticism.

Having, with the help of an elocution teacher, overcome his stammer, Higgins went to the bar in 1876, though he chose equity, as it would not require him to address juries. By 1887 he had graduated to the leadership of the equity bar. On 19 December 1885 he married Mary Alice (d. 1944), the daughter of Dr George Morrison, then principal of Geelong College, and sister of George Ernest 'Chinese' Morrison. In 1887 Mary Alice gave birth to their only child, Mervyn Bournes.

With his career established, Higgins turned to public affairs. He always retained a strong interest in Irish affairs and became a supporter of home rule; in 1883 he made perhaps his first appearance on a public platform in support of the visiting nationalists John and William Redmond, and in 1887 he was prominent in a protest against the Irish Coercion Bill. In 1892 he stood unsuccessfully for Geelong for the Victorian legislative assembly, but two years later he was elected. Wishing to identify himself with the liberal interest, he found it necessary to put aside his free-trade convictions and accept the dominant policy of tariff protection which was associated with the progressive cause in Victoria.

Higgins entered parliament at a time of severe economic depression when Australia's claim to be 'a working man's paradise' was no longer plausible. It was in this context that Liberals, Higgins among them, addressed 'the social problem'. Notable among the social reforms introduced in Victoria which he supported was the Factories and Shops Act of 1896, which pioneered wage regulation in a number of sweated trades. The economic plight of the colonies, and Victoria in particular, also turned attention to proposals for federation, and in 1897 Higgins was elected as one of ten Victorian delegates to the Australasian federal convention of 1897–8. As a lawyer and political radical he made a significant contribution to the proceedings of the convention, in particular moving the amendment which was to give the commonwealth a

limited power for the conciliation and arbitration of industrial disputes. Nevertheless Higgins opposed the draft constitution when it was put before the people: he saw no justification for the senate being 'a states' house', and he feared that Australia would be saddled with a rigid constitution which would resist modernization.

In Victoria, which had strongly supported federation, Higgins's position was not a popular one. His opposition in 1899 to the sending of the Victorian contingent to the Second South African War further served to characterize him as a perverse radical. Although he was a supporter of the empire and looked forward to Ireland achieving the independence already enjoyed by the self-governing colonies, Higgins distrusted the imperial sentiment which he saw as being deployed to excuse Victoria from making its own assessment of the war. In the wake of these heresies, Higgins lost his seat in 1900 after a bitter and divisive campaign.

As a radical, however, Higgins had found favour with the labour movement, and at the first federal elections of 1901 he was elected for the predominantly working-class electorate of North Melbourne. Although generally a supporter of his colleague and friend the liberal Protectionist Alfred Deakin, Higgins continued to follow his own path, reluctantly joining with the Labor Party to defeat the Deakin government in 1904 when he considered its legislation for industrial arbitration inadequate. Higgins, although not a member of the Labor Party, served as attorney-general in the short-lived Watson Labor government which followed. While he did not see himself as a socialist, he was critical of what he called the 'bourgeois principle' and sympathetic to Labor's political ambitions. In 1905 he moved the resolution in the commonwealth parliament which urged Britain to grant Ireland home rule.

In 1906 Deakin appointed Higgins to the high court, with the added responsibility of taking over the presidency of the arbitration court from 1907. In the latter role Higgins was to become a national figure. In his first case he had to decide whether the manufacturer H. V. McKay was paying the 'fair and reasonable' wages to his employees required by the new protection legislation. In the 'Harvester judgment' (1907) Higgins ignored the dictates of the market and spelt out the rights of the worker 'as a human being in a civilized community', entitled to marry and raise a family. Popular at first with trade unions, the arbitration court had difficulty dealing with the industrial strife which erupted during and immediately after the First World War. Higgins himself was increasingly at odds with the Nationalist government led by W. M. Hughes and resigned the presidency in 1921. The following year he published his apologia, *A New Province for Law and Order*. However, the social ethos which he espoused as the justification of wage regulation played a large part in establishing the international reputation of Australia and New Zealand as 'a social laboratory for the world'. And although in the 1920s it might have seemed that industrial arbitration had lost much of Higgins's Promethean mission, the court long remained a powerful institution often seen as expressive of Australian egalitarian values, only recently challenged by the proponents of economic rationalism. Higgins remained on the high court until his death in 1929. In interpreting the constitution he sought to minimize the court's interventionist role, effectively supporting the extension of commonwealth power at the expense of the states.

Throughout his life Higgins maintained a strong attachment to the English heritage, and sent Mervyn to Balliol College, Oxford, in 1906; yet he was also interested in the development of Australian culture. In England at the time of the outbreak of the First World War, he supported the British cause, and, visiting Ireland, was encouraged by the evidence of loyalty there. He was disturbed, however, by the jingoism engendered by the imperial cause, and the war brought a personal anguish in 1916 with the death of Mervyn at Magdhaba, Egypt. Severed, as it were, from the future of Australia, Higgins's interest in Ireland intensified. Although a supporter of the Irish nationalists, he nevertheless urged John Dillon not to close the door on Sinn Féin. In 1924 he revisited Ireland, expressing particular interest in its cultural revival; his meeting with the poet 'A. E.' (George Russell) was instrumental in Higgins leaving a £20,000 bequest to the Royal Irish Academy to support the study of Irish culture.

Higgins collapsed and died on 13 January 1929 at his country house, Heronswood, Dromana. The conservative Melbourne *Argus* hailed him as 'a great Australian', while the Trades Hall flew the Australian flag at half mast. He was buried two days later in Dromana cemetery, with Anglican rites, under the Celtic cross which he had built to commemorate his son.   JOHN RICKARD

Sources J. Rickard, *H. B. Higgins: the rebel as judge* (1984) · N. Palmer, *Henry Bournes Higgins: a memoir* (1931) · J. A. La Nauze, *The making of the Australian constitution* (1972) · P. Macarthy, 'The harvester judgment: a historical assessment', PhD diss., Australian National University, 1967 · W. G. McMinn, *A constitutional history of Australia* (1979) · L. Zines, *The high court and the constitution* (1981) · *AusDB* · *The Argus* [Melbourne] (16 Feb 1929)
Archives NL Aus. | Mitchell L., NSW, E. M. Higgins MSS · NL Aus., Palmer MSS · NL Ire., Redmond MSS · TCD, Dillon MSS
Likenesses photographs, NL Aus., Higgins MSS
Wealth at death £69,187: *AusDB*

Higgins, John (b. c.1544, d. in or after 1602), poet and linguist, was a student at Christ Church, Oxford (according to Thomas Hearne), though his name does not appear in the university register. From about the age of twenty he began to 'learne the tongues' (Higgins, 130), specializing in French and Latin. He spent two years (probably 1569–70) teaching grammar, after which he began work on a new and thoroughly revised edition of Richard Huloet's *Abecedarium* (1552), published in 1572 as *Huloets Dictionarie*. His next project in the field of languages was an expanded edition of Nicholas Udall's *Flowers, or, Eloquent phrases of the Latine speach, gathered out of the sixe comoedies of Terence* (1575), which earned the praise of Thomas Newton in his *Encomia* (1589). Higgins also claimed to have: 'translated Aldus phrases fraught / With eloquence' (Higgins, 131), but

this work, if published, has not been identified. In 1585 he published another translation, *The Nomenclator, or, Remembrancer of Adrianus Junius* (1585). By 1574, when he claimed to be not yet thirty, Higgins was vicar of Winsham, Somerset, where he was still dwelling in 1585 when he wrote the dedication to *The Nomenclator*. His last published work was *An Answer to Master William Perkins Concerning Christ's Descension into Hell* (1602).

Although less accomplished as a poet than as a linguist, Higgins is today best remembered for his efforts in verse. A commendatory poem prefixed to *Huloets Dictionarie* by Thomas Churchyard suggests that by 1572 Higgins was keeping company with poets. In the same year his first published verses appeared, prefixed to John Sadler's translation entitled *The Foure Bookes of Flavius Vegetius Renatus*. His most important work, published in 1574, is *The First Parte of the 'Mirour for Magistrates'*. This was designed as a supplement to William Baldwin's *Myrroure for Magistrates* (1559), a compilation of poetic complaints by characters drawn from late medieval English history. Higgins took up Baldwin's hint that the project should be expanded backwards to cover British antiquity from the earliest beginnings. Using as his source the fabulous history of Geoffrey of Monmouth (which he claimed to have once owned in manuscript), Higgins produced sixteen complaints (or 'tragedies') by unfortunate ancient Britons *From the Comming of Brute to the Incarnation of our Saviour and Redemer Jesu Christe*. This work includes a few autobiographical stanzas following the tragedy of Mempricius which are the main source of information about Higgins's early career. A second edition followed in 1575, with additional passages and one new complaint. In 1587 Higgins's complaints were published in one volume with the original *Mirror*. For this volume Higgins wrote twenty-three new complaints by ancient Britons and Romans, as well as contributing the complaint of Sir Nicholas Burdet to the latter section of the volume.

Higgins has been sharply blamed by Lily Campbell and subsequent critics for violating the integrity of the *Mirror* project. It is true that his literary skills were barely adequate to the task he set himself, and he seems not to have fully grasped the original *Mirror*'s political aims. Intentionally or otherwise, he transformed *The Mirror* from a collection of cautionary tales into a dictionary of national (and fervently nationalist) biography. Thus, while he may have diluted the politics of the anthology, he helped ensure its enduring popularity among Elizabethan and later readers. His tragedy of Cordila is thought to have influenced both Shakespeare's *King Lear* and the description of the cave of despair in Spenser's *Faerie Queene* (book 1, canto 9).   PHILIP SCHWYZER

Sources L. B. Campbell, 'Introduction', *Parts added to the 'Mirror for magistrates'*, ed. L. B. Campbell (1946), 3–28 · Wood, *Ath. Oxon.*, new edn, 1.734–6 · J. Higgins, 'Mempricius', *Parts added to the 'Mirror for magistrates'*, ed. L. B. Campbell (1946), 130–31 · 'Subscriptions of the clergy of the see of Bath and Wells to the Thirty-Nine Articles, 1571–1583', BL, Add. MS 33973 · *DNB*
Archives BL, Higgins's translation of G. Rypley's 'Medulla Alkimiæ', Sloane 1842

Higgins, John [Jacobite Sir John Higgins, baronet] (**1676–1729**), physician, was born in Limerick, the son of Dr Patrick Higgins, physician, and his wife, Mary Loftus, daughter of John Loftus of Annacotty, co. Limerick. Both his parents were from prominent Catholic families which had suffered in the Cromwellian conquest. His paternal great-uncle, also a physician, had been hanged after the 1651 siege of Limerick, and his mother's family had been deprived of its Mungret estate in the subsequent confiscation. After the defeat of the Irish Jacobites in 1691 he went as a boy to Paris, where his mother's relative Edmund Loftus was a banker. In 1700, after a brilliant academic career, he graduated bachelor, licentiate, and doctor from the medical school at Montpellier University. The duke of Berwick, commander of the allied armies of France and Spain from 1704, persuaded him to accept the post of *médecin-major* in the medical services of the united forces during the War of the Spanish Succession. In that capacity he participated in the great military engagements in Spain over the next decade, such as the sieges of Lérida (1707) and Barcelona (1714) and the battle of Villaviciosa (1710). He was competent and efficient, but his care of the sick and wounded at Barcelona impaired his health, and having decided that his future lay in Spain he petitioned successfully to settle in Madrid. On 25 April 1712 he married Jeanne de Courtiade (1689–1764), the daughter of a Bayonne physician. They had one son, John Baptist Higgins (*b*. 1715), who subsequently became an officer in the Spanish army.

Higgins's reputation as a physician rose rapidly. From 1711 he was *medico de cámara* to King Philip V, a post in which he was confirmed in 1715. In 1717 he became chief physician to the king, gaining the appointment over the other court physicians, who were all his seniors and who strongly resented his preferment. Within months he was credited with saving the king's life from a grave illness. Thereafter he enjoyed the highest esteem at court and was in constant attendance on the king, who praised him as the finest physician in Europe. Although primarily a physician, he was also skilled in surgery. He was elected president of the Royal Academy of Medicine and Surgery at Seville in 1718 and again in 1720 at the end of his first term.

Despite having no political ambition, Higgins played some part in public affairs. In 1718 he successfully intervened with the Spanish government to secure the exclusion of Irish goods and ships from the confiscations and reprisals that followed the British sinking of the Spanish Mediterranean Fleet. In 1722 he was appointed to the council of Castile. Always a fervent Jacobite, in 1724 he was made a baronet by James III (the Old Pretender). He retained a deep love of Ireland and resented the losses suffered by the Irish Catholics, including himself and his family, emotions to which he gave strong expression when among friends. The duc de Saint-Simon, while French ambassador to Spain, was one of his patients and developed a high regard for his skill as a physician. The two men struck up a close friendship, and Saint-Simon

related in his memoirs that Higgins was excellent company, candid and frank in conversation, fluent in French, and possessed of a fine intellect and a good knowledge of literature. Full of honours and renown, and having amassed considerable wealth, he died at Seville on 11 October 1729. His widow remarried, and died on 8 May 1764.

HARMAN MURTAGH

Sources Marquis of Mashanaglass [P. MacSwiney], 'Two distinguished Irishmen in the Spanish service: Sir Toby Bourke and Dr John Higgins', *Studies*, 28 (1939), 63–84 · R. Hayes, *Biographical dictionary of Irishmen in France* (1949), 125 · R. Hayes, 'Some notable Limerick doctors', *North Munster Antiquarian Journal*, 1 (1936–9), 113–23, esp. 115–16
Wealth at death 'left widow in more than comfortable circumstances': Marquis of Mashanaglass, 'Two distinguished Irishmen'

Higgins, Sir John Frederick Andrews (**1875–1948**), air force officer, was born at Farnham, Surrey, on 1 September 1875, the son of William Higgins, chemist, and his wife, Catherine Harriette Andrews. He was educated at Charterhouse School and then attended the Royal Military Academy, Woolwich, from which he passed out third. In 1895 he was commissioned in the Royal Artillery; he saw his first active service in the Second South African War, when he was severely wounded; he was mentioned in dispatches, awarded the queen's medal, four clasps, the king's medal, two clasps, and appointed to the DSO.

Higgins was one of the original band of army officers to become interested in flying and he gained his Royal Aero Club aviator's certificate, no. 264, on 30 July 1912 in a Bristol biplane at Brooklands. He was afterwards seconded to the Royal Flying Corps (military wing) for four years as a flight commander. At that time no one in the corps had fired any sort of gun from the air, and Higgins took part in some interesting if unauthorized experiments with Robert Brooke-Popham, his commanding officer in 3 squadron. During army manoeuvres near Rugby in 1913 Higgins, acting as observer in a Blériot tandem monoplane, tried 'a revolutionary system of intercommunication' with the pilot (*Aeroplane*). This involved tying stout string to the pilot's arms, which he used as reins, indicating with a 'series of jerk signals' the course to be taken. The results were judged 'wholly satisfactory', though the procedure did not catch on.

In 1913 Higgins was given command of the newly formed 5 squadron at Farnborough, and when war was declared in 1914 his was one of the four squadrons to go overseas with the first expeditionary force. For his gallantry in these early months, when he was wounded in the air above Bailleul, he was made an officer of the Légion d'honneur. In December 1914 he was posted to Netheravon, with the rank of wing commander, to form the fourth wing. Always known as Jos or Josh in the Royal Flying Corps, Higgins proved a fine leader who instilled high morale and a culture of efficiency in his men:

> A sort of legend wove itself round him. He looked the typical Gunner officer. His eyeglass was almost his most notable feature. He had a knack of saying things which sounded almost fatuous till one awoke to their being brilliantly clever. (*Aeroplane*)

In France again in June 1915 to command the third wing,

Higgins returned to England in August to form no. 2 brigade as brigade commander, Royal Flying Corps, and temporary brigadier-general. In January 1916 he was given command of no. 3 brigade in France and commanded it throughout the battles of the Somme, when he contributed much to the solution of Royal Flying Corps's co-operation with the artillery, then in a rather sketchy state. He again proved his ability in the spring of 1917 when the Royal Flying Corps was at risk of losing local air superiority before and during the battle of Arras. The Germans were by then producing superior fighters and using them to good purpose, while the best British fighter, the Nieuport, had developed a tendency to break up in the air. By his powers of leadership and his driving energy to get technical defects corrected Higgins undoubtedly helped to save the air situation at a critical time. He was promoted to major-general in the Royal Air Force on its formation in 1918.

At the end of the war Higgins was made a CB, awarded the AFC, and given command of the air force attached to the Rhine army. On being granted a permanent commission in the Royal Air Force in 1919 as major-general, which was later converted into air vice-marshal, he resigned his army commission. That year he married Ethel Beatrice, daughter of Edward Newport Singleton, of Quinville Abbey, co. Clare; there were no children. After a year in command of the northern area he became director of personnel at the Air Ministry. From 1922 to 1924 he was commander of the newly formed Inland Area, based at Hillingdon, Middlesex, after which, in 1924, he went to succeed Sir John Salmond as air officer commanding in Iraq.

The British forces in Iraq then faced persistent local uprisings, which were contained by use of air-bombing raids. This controversial tactic secured 'control without occupation' and Salmond judged that the casualties inflicted were less than would be involved if a full military expedition were to be dispatched (*Aeroplane*). But its brutality was attacked by Labour backbenchers in parliament and Salmond's own chief staff officer resigned in protest. Higgins thus assumed his command at a difficult time, but with the full backing of Sir Hugh Trenchard, chief of air staff, to continue the bombing. When in September 1924 Turkish forces crossed the north-west border and threatened the town of Amandia, Higgins used his planes to halt the invasion, inflicting several hundred casualties. But he subsequently resisted extreme pressure from the high commissioner in Iraq to press home his advantage, confident that the Turks would retire without a further escalation of the conflict. This proved to be the case and Higgins was commended by the cabinet and the committee of imperial defence for his 'coolness and mastery' (Boyle, 512). Trenchard himself believed that Higgins was primarily responsible for averting a regional crisis and giving the League of Nations valuable time in which to address the underlying causes of the frontier dispute. Official appreciation of his conduct was marked by his creation as KBE in 1925.

Higgins probably did his most valuable work two years later, during his appointment as air member for supply

and research of the Air Council. He was a realist with a fund of common sense, a great deal of experience, and a good working technical grasp of aircraft types and their equipment. He was promoted KCB in 1928 and appointed air marshal in 1929. He retired in September 1930 and was on the board of Armstrong-Siddeley Motors Ltd from 1930 to 1935. He took a lively interest in the local affairs of the British Legion and encouraged the development of the Air Training Corps. He later worked in India for some years on the board of an aircraft company in Bangalore, but was recalled to the Royal Air Force in 1939 and served until September 1940 as air officer commanding-in-chief, India. He thus became one of a small number of high-ranking military officers to have served in the Second South African War and both world wars. He finally retired in November 1940 and died at his home West Wood, Holly Walk, Leamington Spa, Warwickshire, on 1 June 1948.

E. B. BEAUMAN, *rev.* MARK POTTLE

Sources *The Times* (4 June 1948) · personal knowledge (1959) · private information (1959) · A. Boyle, *Trenchard* (1962) · *The Aeroplane* (11 June 1948), 691 · *Flight* (10 June 1948), 643 · *CGPLA Eng. & Wales* (1948)
Archives SOUND IWM SA, oral history interview
Likenesses W. Stoneman, photograph, 1930, NPG
Wealth at death £2,610 1s. 9d.: administration, 29 July 1948, *CGPLA Eng. & Wales*

Higgins, Sir John Patrick Basil [Eoin] (1927–1993), judge, was born on 14 June 1927 at Town Parks, Magherafelt, co. Londonderry, the eldest of the eight children of John Alphonsus Higgins, town clerk of Magherafelt, and his wife, Mary Philomena Keenan. He was educated at St Columb's College, Londonderry, and at Queen's University, Belfast, where he read law and graduated with an LLB. He was called to the bar of Northern Ireland in 1948. At that time the volume of work for junior counsel was small, but he steadily began to build up a practice in the county courts throughout the province and in the High Court in Belfast. The qualities which made him an outstanding judge were apparent from his early days at the bar: his unwavering integrity, his sense of duty, and his hard work. On 29 July 1960 he married Brigid O'Neill, a medical practitioner. They had five children, and he was a devoted husband and father.

Eoin Higgins became a queen's counsel in 1967, just before the start of the troubles in Northern Ireland, which had a considerable impact on his own career. In 1969 serious rioting occurred in Belfast and in other parts of the province, and a tribunal of inquiry, chaired by Mr Justice Scarman, was appointed to inquire into the violence and civil disturbances. Higgins was appointed one of the two senior counsel to act for the tribunal, and for the next two years he was busily engaged in assisting the tribunal to carry out its task. In 1971 he was appointed a county court judge, and he served as county court judge for Armagh and Fermanagh from 1976 to 1979 and for South Antrim from 1979 to 1982, when he was appointed recorder of Belfast. He became a High Court judge in 1984. In every judicial position which he occupied he served with distinction and gained the respect of all who came before him.

After his appointment to the High Court, Higgins was for a number of years the judge of the Family Division, seeking to resolve family disputes which often related to the welfare and happiness of children. It was work for which he was eminently suited because of his human gifts of sympathy, compassion, and good sense. As well as sitting in court hearing evidence and giving judgment, he spent many hours in his chambers talking informally to children and their parents and discussing the cases with counsel, solicitors, and social workers, seeking in difficult family conflicts to find a solution which would be in the interests of the children involved. The work he did in those years was of lasting benefit to many. In addition to his work in the Family Division he took a full part in the administration of criminal justice, including the trial of defendants charged with terrorist offences in the non-jury Diplock courts, and he also sat as a judge in the Court of Appeal to hear criminal appeals in many prominent cases.

These were years when the judges in Northern Ireland were targets for terrorist attacks, and, as a Roman Catholic, Higgins was particularly singled out for assassination attempts by the IRA, all of which he survived. On one occasion an attack was made on his home in Belfast, when the police officer guarding the house was shot and wounded. On a second occasion, when he was driving home to Northern Ireland from Dublin airport with his wife and daughter, the IRA mistook the car in which he was travelling and detonated a bomb at the border between the republic and Northern Ireland, murdering a family in another car. A further attack was made on his home in Belfast when the IRA launched mortar bombs at it, again injuring two police officers on duty at the house. After this attack Higgins moved his home to a safer area outside Belfast. But these attacks in no way affected the scrupulous fairness with which he conducted criminal trials, and he continued to administer justice with unflinching courage and complete impartiality.

Higgins had wide experience of the judicial system of Northern Ireland and of its needs, and he served on many committees and tribunals dealing with legal matters. He was also a member of the committee appointed in 1974 under the chairmanship of Lord Gardiner to consider measures to deal with terrorism in the province. He was knighted in 1988.

Higgins was upright and devout. Away from his busy life as a judge, he gave much help to voluntary and charitable organizations, both in membership of committees and in personally visiting and helping those in trouble and in need. He was president of the Society of St Vincent de Paul, chairman of Voluntary Service for Belfast, and a member of the boards of management of St Joseph's College in Belfast and the Dominican College in Portstewart.

Higgins was appointed a lord justice of appeal, but he died suddenly, on 2 September 1993, from a heart attack at his home, 1 Farmhill Lane, Holywood, co. Down, the day before he was due to be sworn in as a member of the Court of Appeal of Northern Ireland. He was mourned by his judicial colleagues and by the members of the legal profession of Northern Ireland as a judge of great integrity, great courage, and great humanity. 　BRIAN HUTTON

Sources *The Independent* (6 Sept 1993) · *The Times* (8 Sept 1993) · *WWW, 1991–5* · personal knowledge (2004) · private information (2004) · b. cert. · m. cert. · d. cert.
Likenesses photograph, repro. in *The Independent*
Wealth at death £167,900: probate, 6 Dec 1993, *CGPLA NIre.*

Higgins, Matthew James [*pseud.* Jacob Omnium] (1810–1868), journalist, the youngest child and only son of Matthew Higgins and Janette, daughter of James Baillie, second son of Hugh Baillie of Dochfour, Inverness-shire, was born on 4 December 1810, at Benown Castle in co. Meath. His father died soon after his birth and he was reared by his mother. He was educated at a private school near Bath and at Eton College. On 22 May 1828 he matriculated from New College, Oxford, but never graduated. At college he preferred hunting to study. He afterwards travelled much in Spain and in Italy, where his three sisters lived in Naples, after their marriage to Italians. In 1838–9 he visited British Guiana, where he had inherited an estate, and repeated the visit in 1846–7. This experience enabled him to keep his estate in good order during the critical period which followed the abolition of slavery, and to write four effective pamphlets upon the difficulties of the sugar-producing colonies in 1847 and 1849. His first publication, however, was 'Jacob Omnium, the Merchant Prince', an amusing satire on mercantile dishonesty published in *New Monthly Magazine* (August 1845). Jacob Omnium quickly became a popular public figure and Higgins's best-known *nom de plume*. W. M. Thackeray contributed to the same number; the men met, when both enquired about the other's *nom de plume*, and became close friends. Thackeray's ballad 'Jacob Omnium's Hoss' (*Punch*, 15, 251) celebrated an episode in which Higgins was involved which led to the end of the Star Chamber; the ballad effectively caught Higgins's formidable powers as a controversialist:

> His name is Jacob Homnium, Exquire;
> And if I'd committed crimes,
> Good Lord! I wouldn't ave that mann
> Attack me in the *Times*.
> (G. N. Ray, *Thackeray: the Age of Wisdom*, 1958, 46)

In 1847 Higgins was in Ireland assisting the famine relief committee; Jacob Omnium's long letter to *The Times* (22 April 1847; reprinted in Higgins's *Essays on Social Subjects*) excoriated idle landowners, both Irish and English. Higgins followed Peel into free trade and stood as a Peelite at Westbury in 1847, being defeated by James Wilson. He never again contested a seat, but he aided the Peelites by writing for their paper, the *Morning Chronicle*, until it folded in 1854, and he often attended the Commons; with J. R. Godley he was especially active in attacking whig colonial policy.

Higgins also wrote frequently for *The Times* under a variety of pseudonyms, including Jacob Omnium, Civilian, Paterfamilias, West Londoner, Belgravian Mother, Mother

Matthew James Higgins (1810–1868), attrib. Sir Anthony Coningham Sterling, late 1840s

Social Subjects was first published privately in 1856, and published in 1875 with a memoir by Sir William Stirling Maxwell.   H. C. G. MATTHEW

Sources *DNB* · W. Stirling Maxwell, 'Memoir', in M. Higgins, *Essays on social subjects*, ed. W. Stirling Maxwell (1875) · *The letters and private papers of William Makepeace Thackeray*, ed. G. N. Ray, 4 vols. (1945–6) [with 2 vol. suppl., ed. E. F. Harden (1994)]
Archives BL, Gladstone MSS, Add. MS 44403 · Mitchell L., Glas., Glasgow City Archives, letters to Sir William Stirling Maxwell · News Int. RO, letters to John Thadeus Delane · NRA, letters to H. Jacob · Trinity Cam., letters mostly to Lord Houghton
Likenesses attrib. A. C. Sterling, two salted paper prints, 1846–49, NPG [*see illus.*] · R. J. Lane, lithograph, 1844 (after R. Fidanza), BM, NPG · R. J. Lane, lithograph, 1845 (after Count D'Orsay), BM, NPG · F. Grant, oils, exh. RA 1862, The Times Newspapers Ltd, London · R. Doyle, pen and wash caricature, BM · S. Laurence, chalk drawing, NPG · two photographs, repro. in Stirling Maxwell, 'Memoir'
Wealth at death under £70,000: probate, 17 Nov 1868, *CGPLA Eng. & Wales*

of Six, and John Barleycorn. Higgins was an amusing writer with a hard and quite radical edge. Comfortably off, he wrote because he liked to write. On 2 July 1850 his income increased when he married Emily Blanche, daughter of Sir Henry Joseph Tichborne of Tichborne and widow of the eldest son of Mr Bennett of Pythouse, Wiltshire (which house the family for a time also gained). The Higginses moved from 1 Lowndes Square to 71 Eaton Square, London. They had four children, one of whom died in infancy. Higgins was in every sense a prominent social figure (he was 6 feet 8 inches, too tall even to join the Life Guards), well known for his writing since his *noms de plume* were mostly flags rather than disguises, and a member of many metropolitan clubs and societies, including the Philobiblon Society and the Cosmopolitan Club. He bought both pictures and horses as an expert. He wrote effectively on administrative reform and on reform of the army, especially with respect to military education and the purchase of commissions, being an early champion of the abolition of that practice (1857). He also wrote for the *Edinburgh Review*, and for the *Cornhill Magazine* during Thackeray's editorship.

In 1863 Higgins quarrelled with *The Times* when the paper dropped the line of attack which, with Higgins, it had hitherto pursued against Lieutenant-Colonel Crawley during the latter's court martial for his treatment of Sergeant-Major Lilley and his wife in India; Higgins's correspondence about the rupture was published privately, as a pamphlet. Subsequently Higgins wrote for the *Pall Mall Gazette*, developing the genre of chatty titbits. His family interest also made him active in attacking the Tichborne claimant. A 'man of noble and amiable presence' (Leslie Stephen in *DNB*), Higgins was an important figure in London literary society in the 1850s and 1860s, 'the author of not a few reconciliations' (Stirling Maxwell, lxix). His health suffered some decline and he took the waters at Homburg. He was taken ill after bathing at Kingston House, near Abingdon, Berkshire, and died there six days later on 14 August 1868. Survived by his wife and three children, he was buried near his younger son in the Roman Catholic cemetery in Fulham. His *Essays on*

Higgins, Reynold Alleyne (1916–1993), archaeologist, was born on 26 November 1916 in Weybridge, Surrey, the son of Charles Alleyne Higgins (1887–1975), solicitor, and Margaret Edith, *née* Taylor (1882–1978), singer. He was educated as a foundation scholar at Sherborne School, and as an exhibitioner at Pembroke College, Cambridge. In 1937 he obtained first-class honours in the classical tripos, with special merit in the archaeological papers. His initial urge to pursue an archaeological career was temporarily postponed, at his father's wish, by employment in the civil service (the Coal Commission, later the National Coal Board), and further delayed by the Second World War, in which he served in the King's Royal Rifle Corps. During the retreat from France in 1940 he became a prisoner of war and he remained in captivity for the rest of the war. He kept up his own spirits, and raised those of his fellow prisoners, by giving lively and popular lectures on ancient Greek history; in those conditions he developed a talent for speaking to lay audiences with wit, verve, and clarity, for which he was much admired in many different contexts during his later years.

In 1947 Higgins married Patricia Williams (b. 1925), a physiotherapist at St Thomas's Hospital; they were to enjoy forty-seven years of happy marriage, raising three sons and two daughters in whom they took great pride. In the same year Higgins was appointed assistant keeper in the British Museum's department of Greek and Roman antiquities. While taking a hand in preparing the temporary displays of the first post-war years under the leadership of the keeper, Bernard Ashmole, he also undertook the major task of producing an up-to-date catalogue of the museum's vast collection of miniature Greek sculptures in clay. He received international acclaim for his magisterial study of the terracottas, published in two volumes as *Catalogue of the Terracottas in the British Museum* (1954 and 1959), which eventually earned him a DLitt degree at Cambridge (1964). His volumes were praised especially for his illuminating comments on ancient Greek dress and other aspects of daily life, made in the light of the figurines.

During the 1950s Higgins also became deeply involved in what were to be his two other main fields of research.

Reynold Alleyne Higgins (1916–1993), by unknown photographer [detail]

His early interest in the Aegean Bronze Age, fostered by the teaching of A. J. B. Wace at Cambridge, received a fresh stimulus from M. Ventris's decipherment (published in 1952) of the Minoan and Mycenaean texts in Linear B script as an early form of Greek. In his paper, *The Archaeological Background of the Furniture Tablets of Pylos* (1956), Higgins pioneered an archaeological approach to the consequences of the decipherment. The following year, turning his attention to the British Museum's Aegina treasure, a collection of prehistoric gold ornaments which had hitherto defied convincing attribution, he made an unanswerable case for their origin in Minoan Crete; his final view, for the general reader, was presented as *The Aegina Treasure: an Archaeological Mystery* (1979). Thereafter Higgins developed a broader commitment to the study of Greek and Roman jewellery from the early Bronze Age until late Roman times; his general book, *Greek and Roman Jewellery* (1961, revised 1980), was greeted as the first full coverage of the subject in English. In 1967 he also published succinct and illuminating handbooks on his two other fields of expertise: *Greek Terracottas*, and *Minoan and Mycenaean Art* (revised 1981). In recognition of wide-ranging scholarly achievement, the British Academy elected him a fellow in 1972.

Higgins was promoted deputy keeper in 1965, and became acting keeper of his department in 1967. In that year he negotiated a loan exhibition of Thracian gold from Bulgaria, the first occasion when ancient gold had been allowed to cross the Iron Curtain. In 1977 he was elected the first president of the newly constituted Society of Jewellery Historians, which in 1991 published a volume of papers in his honour. Outside the museum, his most abiding association was with the British School of Archaeology at Athens, which called in his expertise to publish important finds from its current excavations: Greek terracottas from the Sanctuary of Demeter at Knossos (1973), and early Greek gold jewellery from Lefkandi in Euboea (1980). From 1975 to 1979 he served as chairman of the school's managing committee.

After his retirement in 1977, Higgins's talent as a lively speaker continued to bring him numerous invitations to give lectures to specialist, student, and lay audiences. He delivered the prestigious series of Norton lectures in the USA and Canada in 1982–3, and was a frequent lecturer on Swan Hellenic cruises until 1991. During his last years he resumed work in the British Museum on the final volume of his terracotta *Catalogue*, devoted to the Hellenistic period. Although it was still incomplete when he died, he had prepared the way for this volume in his last published book, *Tanagra and the Figurines* (1986), a charming and humane study of the best-known aspect of Hellenistic terracottas.

Higgins possessed a rare combination of qualities: an intense striving after accurate scholarship coupled with a lively gift for communicating his expertise with wit and charm. For him, the British Museum was never an ivory tower; indeed, few museum scholars have reached such a worldwide readership and audience. The last year of his life was plagued by ill health, but cancer was diagnosed only three weeks before his death, in Dunsfold, Surrey, on 18 April 1993. He was cremated on 21 April at Guildford, and was survived by his wife and children.

J. N. COLDSTREAM

Sources E. Goring, 'Reynold Alleyne Higgins, MA, LittD, FBA, FSA', *Classical gold jewellery and the classical tradition: papers in honour of R. A. Higgins*, ed. J. Ogden, Jewellery Studies, 5 (1991), 5–6 · *The Times* (28 April 1993) · *The Independent* (22 April 1993) · private information (2004)
Likenesses photograph, repro. in *The Independent* · photograph, News International Syndication, London [*see illus.*]
Wealth at death £134,420: probate, 21 July 1993, *CGPLA Eng. & Wales*

Higgins, Terence Lionel Seymour (1945–1982), first publicly identified AIDS victim in the United Kingdom, was born on 10 June 1945 in Priory Mount Hospital, Haverfordwest, south Wales, the son of Marjorie Irene Higgins (formerly Phillips), a railway porter in Haverfordwest. His registered first forename was Terrence. Remembered through the manner of his death, and the work of the trust that bears his name, the life of Terence Higgins reflects at every turn the shifting history of the gay male community in late twentieth-century Britain.

Higgins joined the Royal Navy at the age of eighteen in 1963, and as a gay man came into conflict with the prevailing hostility towards homosexuality in the services. Consequently he decided to leave. A contemporary reports that the authorities refused to discharge him on the grounds of his homosexuality. Instead, he painted hammer and sickle motifs around his ship, was formally charged, and was asked to leave the navy.

Higgins moved to London, where the changing climate of the 1960s, the partial decriminalization of homosexuality in 1967, and the work of the Gay Liberation Front from the early 1970s had created a rapidly expanding, commercial scene of gay clubs and bars. Entering into this world he lived first in Notting Hill and Streatham, eventually settling in a flat with friends in Barons Court Road, Kensington. He worked as a telex and computer operator and as a barman in the best-known gay club, Heaven.

In the summer of 1981 Higgins began to lose weight, developing a persistent rash and gradually becoming weaker and weaker. In April 1982 he collapsed on the dance floor at Heaven and was taken to St Thomas's Hospital, discharging himself after a number of days when doctors were unable to diagnose or treat his condition. In the middle of June he collapsed again and was readmitted to the isolation unit. Diagnosed as having parasitic pneumonia, he died in St Thomas's on 4 July 1982 at the age of thirty-seven. His body was cremated. Pneumonia was given by the coroner as the cause of death on his death certificate, which was certified 'after post mortem without inquest' (d. cert.).

Higgins's death came at a time of increasing concern in the gay community over an apparently new disease affecting the immune system of a number of gay men in New York, San Francisco, and Los Angeles. In the autumn of 1982 a growing number of articles in the United Kingdom focused on what had been termed the Acquired Immune Deficiency Syndrome (AIDS) epidemic, noting the presence of cases in Britain alongside the numbers of American deaths. Although Britain's first AIDS case had been reported in *The Lancet* in 1981, it was the death of Terence Higgins that brought the disease fully into public view.

Frustrated by the absence of a medical explanation for why Higgins had contracted pneumonia, and concerned at the risk of the disease spreading further, his friends sought to use his death as a platform for further action. Meeting in mid-November 1982, Terence's former partner Rupert Whitaker, together with Martyn Butler, Tony Calvert, Len Robinson, and Chris Peel, set up the Terence Higgins Trust. Its formation was announced in the free newspaper *Capital Gay* on 26 November 1982. Under the headline 'US disease hits London', the paper identified four AIDS-related deaths in London. Terence Higgins was named as one of these men, the first person to be publicly identified as dying from an AIDS-related illness in the UK. By announcing the charity in this way his friends sought to draw some good from their loss, saying 'we have named it after Terry but we are doing it for the people who are left. He was a great inspiration to us all'. In creating this publicity they also exploited it, personalizing and humanizing AIDS in order to raise money to fund medical research into the causes of the disease and educate gay men about its potential dangers.

The Terence Higgins Trust remains the largest and best-known British AIDS organization, continuing the work of education, research, and support which started with the death and naming of Terence Higgins in 1982.

MATT HOULBROOK

Sources M. Hoskins, 'From fear to hope: the story of the Terence Higgins Trust, 1982–1997', dspace.dial.pipex.com/mhoskins/ thestory.htm, 1998 · S. Garfield, *The end of innocence: Britain in the time of AIDS* (1994) · D. Jarman, *At your own risk: a saint's testament* (1992) · b. cert. · d. cert.

Higgins, William (1763?–1825), chemist, was probably born in Collooney, co. Sligo, in 1763, the son of Thomas Higgins (c.1739–c.1790), physician. By 1784 he had gone to London, where his uncle and patron, Bryan *Higgins, was established as a doctor and chemist with a laboratory in Greek Street, Soho. Higgins matriculated on 6 February 1786 at Magdalen Hall, Oxford, and by 16 March the following year had migrated to Pembroke College. He remained there for more than a year but left without taking a degree. He was 'operator' to the professor of chemistry, William Austin; on 2 April 1787 he sent an (unpublished) analysis of a human kidney-stone to the Royal Society.

Higgins experimented in the basement laboratory of the old Ashmolean Museum in Oxford, and then in London. In 1789 he published, at a cost exceeding £100, his *Comparative View of the Phlogistic and Antiphlogistic Theories*. One of the earliest British converts to Lavoisier's view that combustion involved combination with oxygen rather than the emission of phlogiston, Higgins controverted the Irish chemist Richard Kirwan's *Essay on Phlogiston* (1784). (Kirwan subsequently converted to Lavoisier's views as, by 1800, had almost all British chemists.) Higgins's book retained an interest because of its unstated assumptions on proportions which anticipated John Dalton's atomic theory. Indeed, in 1810 and subsequently, Humphry Davy suggested that Higgins had anticipated Dalton, and in 1814 Higgins himself published *Experiments and Observations on the Atomic Theory*, urging his priority. Higgins's subsequent editors, T. S. Wheeler and J. R. Partington (1960), place his work in the context of Newtonian elective affinities; it seems that only after Dalton had published his theory could anyone see approximations to it in Higgins's writings.

In December 1791 Higgins was offered the position of chemist, on £200 per annum with coals and candles, at the newly established Apothecaries' Hall in Dublin; he returned to Ireland and was sworn in on 13 April 1792. The laboratory proved too expensive, and on 27 May 1795 Higgins lost his job. He transferred to the Royal Dublin Society at half the salary, and from 1795 to 1822 was also chemist to the Irish linen board. There he experimented and advised on bleaching with chlorine. At the Dublin Society a laboratory was equipped for Higgins, as professor, to experiment 'on Dying Materials and other Articles, wherein Chymistry may assist the Arts' (Wheeler and Partington, 17)—probably the first applied chemistry laboratory in the British Isles. He also gave courses of lectures, and supervised the collection of minerals.

In April 1817 Higgins obtained leave to visit the continent. On 1 May of the same year he was admitted as a fellow of the Royal Society, to which he had been elected in 1806. He died in Dublin in 1825, between 28 April (when he made his will) and the end of June of that year (when his death was reported to the Royal Society). His grave is unknown. He lived in rooms in Dublin, at 71 Grafton Street, but owned considerable property which he bequeathed to his nephew. He was regarded by many as a difficult person to work with, and the promise with which his career in chemistry had opened was not fulfilled.

DAVID KNIGHT

Sources T. S. Wheeler and J. R. Partington, *The life and work of William Higgins, chemist, 1763–1825* (1960) • A. Thackray, 'Higgins, William', *DSB* • *DNB*
Wealth at death £6800 in land: Wheeler and Partington, *Life and work*

Higginson, Edward (1807–1880), Unitarian minister, was born on 9 January 1807 in Heaton Norris, Lancashire, the third of six children and the eldest son of Edward Higginson (1781–1832), Unitarian minister at Stockport, and his wife, Sarah (1782?–1827), daughter of Joel Marshall, a Loughborough draper. In 1810 the elder Higginson became minister at Friar Gate Chapel, Derby, where he also kept a school, in which his children were educated; he encouraged his sons to learn woodworking, at which they became highly proficient.

Lacking the nerve to be a surgeon, as his father wanted, Higginson entered Manchester College, York, in September 1823. In 1828 he became minister to the small congregation at Bowl Alley Lane Chapel, Hull. The next year, because the stipend did not reach the promised level, he began a successful school. In 1837, when two new proprietary schools swept away his pupils, he turned to teaching girls, with the assistance of an unmarried sister, but returned to teaching boys when his competitors failed.

On 25 December 1839 Higginson married Lydia (1813/14–1856), the youngest daughter of Flower Humble, from a Newcastle mercantile family, and the adopted daughter of the banker Samuel Shore of Meersbrook (1737/8–1828), to whose wife she was collaterally related; they had a son and a daughter. In 1845, suffering from overwork and, possibly, depression, he resigned the Hull pulpit and the next year accepted an invitation from Westgate Chapel, Wakefield, where, despite a modest increase in income from his wife, he also kept a school, in time extended to girls. He delighted in the congregation and in the company of other West Riding ministers, a change from the isolation of Hull.

Lydia Higginson died on 8 February 1856, aged forty-two, and on 5 July 1857 Edward married Emily Thomas (1826–1895); the daughter of George Thomas, a Carmarthen solicitor, she had been teaching at a girls' school in Wakefield. This marriage too produced a son and a daughter. The next year he accepted an invitation to High Street Chapel, Swansea. Besides conducting a school, he was visitor and examiner at the Presbyterian college, Carmarthen, where he also lectured on English grammar and literature and on political economy. In 1875 he reluctantly accepted the presidency of the college, but, suffering from ill health, resigned both presidency and pulpit in 1876.

As a teacher Higginson was clearly ahead of his time, to judge from his call, in an essay published in *The Educator: Prize Essays* in 1839, for openness and friendliness rather than reliance on authority in the classroom, from his reservations about corporal punishment, and from the transparent pleasure he took in opening a wider world to his Welsh-speaking students at Carmarthen. He regarded teaching as a distraction from his ministerial role, though, like most of his generation, he lacked the 'popular' style increasingly taken as the guarantee of ministerial success. While noting that he 'discoursed more than he sermonized, reasoned more than he exhorted', a Wakefield correspondent in *Christian Life* (21 February 1880) also recalled his common sense, restrained eloquence, and deep religious feeling.

Higginson's strongest instinct was scholarly, though he claimed no originality: one obituarist wrote that 'he could form no conception of the perfect Christian scholar that did not define itself into the image of Mr. Wellbeloved and Mr. Kenrick', the most distinguished of his teachers at York (*Christian Life*, 21 Feb 1880). He was well-read, and his publications ranged from the usual Unitarian defences against Anglican and orthodox attacks to a distinctly Unitarian contribution (*Astro-Theology*, 1854) to the debate on the plurality of worlds launched by the confrontation of William Whewell (1794–1866) and Sir David Brewster (1781–1868). He wrote frequently for the *Christian Reformer* until its cessation in 1863, and from 1876 to his death contributed regularly to *Christian Life*. His principal concern was to reassert historically and biblically based Unitarianism against the religious intuitionism of James Martineau (1805–1900) and John James Tayler (1797–1869); ironically, one of his sisters married Martineau, while another married Martineau's redoubtable opponent Samuel Bache (1804–1876). Of his many books, only the two volumes of *The Spirit of the Bible* (1853–5) brought a modest return. *Ecce Messias* (1874) was an extended effort to trace biblical testimony to the messianic hope, which John Locke had seen as the central feature of Christianity. Its failure with the public, after which Higginson gave up writing books, suggests the end of an era in the history of Unitarian intellect. Higginson died at 2 Glanmor Terrace, Swansea, on 12 February 1880 of heart disease, and was buried in the town's Dan-y-graig cemetery on 17 February.

R. K. WEBB

Sources E. Higginson, autobiography, DWL • *The Inquirer* (21 Feb 1880) • *Christian Life* (21 Feb 1880) • M. J. Crowe, *The extraterrestrial life debate, 1750–1900* (1986) • *The Cambrian* (20 Feb 1880) • d. cert.
Archives DWL | JRL, Unitarian College MSS
Wealth at death under £10,000: probate, 12 March 1880, *CGPLA Eng. & Wales* • £1935: probate, 15 Nov 1880, resealed, Ireland

Higginson [*née* Ellis], **Eleanor Beatrice** (1881–1969), suffragette, was born on 19 April 1881 at 2 Caroline Villas, Plashet Road, Plaistow, London, the eldest of the four children of Alfred Leopold Ellis, a merchant seaman, and his wife, Elizabeth Vernon. Her family moved first to Manchester, then to Preston, Lancashire. There, Eleanor trained as a schoolteacher, working at St Mark's School until she married Arnold Higginson (1879–1938), a chemist, on 9 September 1905. The couple had five children, four of whom survived into adulthood. About 1910 Eleanor opened a health food shop in Preston, which she ran until 1920.

Eleanor Higginson's involvement in the suffrage campaign was at the instigation of another suffragette, Edith

Rigby, then honorary secretary of the Preston branch of the Women's Social and Political Union (WSPU). Preston WSPU recruited many women from the Labour Party and the Women's Labour League, and as a prominent Labour Party member Higginson was encouraged to become involved. However, she initially refused the invitation, but agreed to attend local meetings.

Higginson became actively involved in the suffrage movement relatively late in the campaign, in summer 1913. In April 1914 she became the honorary secretary of Preston WSPU, replacing another active suffragette, Elizabeth Ellen (Beth) Hesmondhalgh. Both women ran the Preston branch during late 1913 and early 1914 while its mainstay, Edith Rigby, was in hiding from the authorities.

On 21 May 1914 Higginson took part in a WSPU deputation to the king. The deputation was not received, and in the struggle of protest Higginson, like others, experienced violent treatment from the police. She later said that 'they mauled us about the shoulders and we were all of us black and blue the next day' (Raeburn, 230). She was not arrested, and so returned to the 'safe house' that had been arranged by the London membership, where she and the other women who had not been arrested were given stones and asked to go out and break windows in protest at the king's refusal to hear the deputation.

Higginson threw a brick at a pub window, and was soon arrested along with a total of sixty-five other women and two men. The scenes in court as the accused were committed for trial were chaotic, and Higginson was eventually charged, alongside two other women, with breaking a shop window in Parliament Street. Of the three charged, one pleaded guilty, while the other two were convicted by jury. All were sentenced to four months in prison.

In Holloway gaol Higginson adopted a hunger and thirst strike and was released after less than two weeks under the provisions of the 'Cat and Mouse Act'. This act allowed prisoners debilitated by hunger strikes to be released under licence, giving them time to recover before they were fit to be re-arrested and returned to prison. Higginson was released for about three weeks before being re-arrested and detained in Holloway for three days, after which she was again released on licence owing to ill health. The First World War broke out before she was required to return to prison, and thus she benefited from the amnesty that was then declared for all suffragette prisoners.

Like the WSPU leadership, the Preston branch called off its suffrage campaign during the war, and instead Higginson and her colleague Edith Rigby organized a jam-making enterprise to combat the food shortage. When the war and the campaign for the vote were over, Higginson turned to local politics. She took a keen interest in local government throughout the remainder of her life, becoming a local magistrate and from 1940 to 1945 serving as a representative on Preston town council. She took Workers' Education Association classes in Preston, was a delegate to Preston's trades and labour council and also

unsuccessfully stood as a local government candidate for Ashton ward.

Throughout her life Higginson kept in touch with Edith Rigby and a number of her suffragette colleagues. Her husband, Arnold, died on 10 June 1938, and in 1954 she moved to Bognor Regis, Sussex, where she lived for the remainder of her life with her old WSPU colleague Beth Hesmondhalgh. Eleanor Higginson died in St Richard's Hospital, Chichester, on 8 June 1969, aged eighty-eight.

HELOISE BROWN

Sources P. Hesketh, *My aunt Edith* (1966); repr. (1992) · R. Towler, typescript commentary on Preston WSPU, 1966, Lancs. RO, DDX 575/3 · G. Alderman, letter to R. Towler, 1964, Lancs. RO, DDX 575/4 · H. Brown, 'Preston lassies mun have the vote: a study of the militant suffrage movement in Preston, 1905–1914', MA diss., University of York, 1994 · A. Raeburn, *The militant suffragettes* (1973) · *The Suffragette* (25 July 1913), 710 · *The Suffragette* (3 April 1914), 577 · *The Suffragette* (29 May 1914), 122 · *The Suffragette* (5 June 1914), 136 · *The Suffragette* (7 Aug 1914), 310 · family papers of Eleanor Redshaw, descendant, priv. coll. · m. cert. · d. cert.
Likenesses Lalguette photographers, photograph, *c*.1966, Lancs. RO, DDX 575/3

Higginson, Francis (*bap.* **1586/7**, *d.* **1630**), minister in America, was baptized on 6 August 1586 (or possibly 1587) in Claybrooke, Leicestershire, the son of John Higginson, clergyman. He matriculated at St John's College, Cambridge, in 1602, and in 1609 moved to Jesus College, from which he graduated BA in 1610 and proceeded MA in 1613. In 1614 he was ordained deacon and then priest in the archdiocese of York. Tobie Mathew, archbishop of York, conferred on him the rectory of Barton in Fabis in 1615, but he was never inducted into the position. A strict conformist, Higginson resigned those posts in 1615 and obtained the living of Claybrooke. Later, he also preached at Belgrave, a neighbouring village. On 8 January 1616 at St Peter's, Nottingham, he married Anne Herbert (*d.* in or before 1640); they had nine children.

At some point between 1615 and 1627 Higginson fell under the influence of Arthur Hildersham, the suspended, and later imprisoned, nonconformist lecturer. However, he was tolerated by Bishop Williams of Lincoln until 1627, when he was deprived of his licence. Nevertheless, he was offered several other livings and was selected by the mayor of Leicester to be the city preacher, but he declined all offers. In 1628 proceedings in the court of high commission were apparently begun against Higginson, leading him in March to offer himself as minister to the Massachusetts Bay Company. In 1629 the governors of the company appointed him minister to one of their proposed settlements. With his family he sailed from Gravesend on 25 April 1629, and arrived in Salem harbour on 29 June. In early August their church was formed at Salem. Samuel Skelton was chosen minister and Higginson his assistant. Skelton and Higginson ignored the Book of Common Prayer and instituted a fairly strict discipline, leading some members of the new congregation to issue complaints against them. They denied that they were separating from the Church of England, but clearly began to lay out the principles of congregationalism.

Higginson kept a valuable journal of his voyage to New

England. The journal was sent back to London in August 1629, although it was not published until the nineteenth century, when it appeared as *A True Relation of the Last Voyage to New England*. Soon after his arrival he wrote a long letter to 'some friends' in England, which was refashioned into a pamphlet entitled *New England's plantation, or, A short and true description of the commodities and discommodities of that countrey* (1630) and went through three editions by the year's end.

Higginson contracted what contemporaneous sources refer to as 'a fever' in the summer of 1630, and died on 6 August. His widow, Anne, inherited the estate, which consisted mostly of undeveloped acreage in the Salem area. She died before 25 February 1640.

Their eldest son, **John Higginson** (1616–1708), was also a minister in America. He did not receive a formal university education (Harvard College not being founded until 1636) but nevertheless trained for the ministry under the supervision of John Cotton and others. He served as a schoolmaster and assistant pastor until, in 1659, he became the pastor of the Salem church which his father had settled. He took an active part in the discussion surrounding the 'halfway covenant' in New England in the 1660s and beyond. He died at Salem on 9 December 1708.

His younger brother **Francis Higginson** (1618–1673), Church of England clergyman, returned to England some time after 1630, was ordained, and became vicar of Kirkby Stephen, Westmorland. He was buried there on 20 May 1673. STEPHEN CARL ARCH

Sources R. C. Anderson, ed., *The great migration begins: immigrants to New England, 1620–1633*, 2 (Boston, MA, 1995), 933–7 · J. B. Felt, 'Memoir of the Rev. Francis Higginson', *New England Historical and Genealogical Register*, 6 (1852), 105–27 · [E. C. Felton], 'Samuel Skelton', *New England Historical and Genealogical Register*, 52 (1898), 347–57 · J. A. Levernier and D. R. Wilmes, eds., *American writers before 1800: a biographical and critical dictionary*, 3 vols. (1983) · F. Higginson, 'New England's plantation' with the sea journal and other writings (1908) **Wealth at death** acreage in Salem, Massachusetts area; widow died with estate valued at £250: Anderson, *Great migration*

Higginson, Francis (1618–1673). *See under* Higginson, Francis (*bap.* 1586/7, *d.* 1630).

Higginson, John (1616–1708). *See under* Higginson, Francis (*bap.* 1586/7, *d.* 1630).

Higginson, Teresa Helena (1844–1905), Roman Catholic schoolteacher and mystic, was born at Holywell in north Wales on 27 May 1844, the third child of the family of five daughters and three sons of Robert Francis Higginson (1816–1877) and his wife, Mary, *née* Bowness (*d.* 1884). Robert was a Catholic from Preston and Mary converted before their marriage in 1841.

Teresa Higginson went to school at the Convent of the Sisters of Mercy in Nottingham in 1854, where she first came across the penitential exercise known as the stations of the cross. She evidently felt her own sinfulness from an early age, and later claimed that her first trespass had been committed at the age of four, when she 'wilfully pretended not to hear' her mother calling her (O'Sullivan, 29). About 1849 her younger brother died and, according to her confessions, she began to pray that God should send

her sufferings. She kept quiet her increasingly severe self-mortifications since she 'thought that our dear Lord liked to have secrets' (O'Sullivan, 57). A nun caught her trying to burn herself, however, and told her never to do such a thing again.

Higginson's already marked desire to suffer seems to have accelerated after her first communion, which was delayed until 1857. As she did not know what name to take at confirmation, Bishop Roskell suggested Agnes to her, which she interpreted as meaning that she ought to offer herself in sacrifice as a lamb. Another chance remark by a visiting ecclesiastic made a deep impression: F. W. Faber's light admonition upon being introduced to the child, 'See that you are a Teresa' (Kerr, 36), led her to focus her ambitions on emulating her mystical namesake.

Higginson spent an unusually long time at school, leaving in 1864 or 1865, after which, by her own account, she was able to 'mortify' herself without fear of discovery. In 1871 a smallpox epidemic caused a shortage of teachers in Liverpool and she found work as a supply teacher at the school attached to St Alexander's, Bootle, run by Father Edward Powell (1837–1901). She received her teaching certificate at Orrell, near Wigan, in December 1872. In 1873 she taught at St Mary's, Wigan, under the care of Father Thomas Wells, who acted as her spiritual director for three years. It was during this period that she began to experience ecstasies including what she called wrangles with the devil. She once re-enacted the passion to horrified spectators. By Good Friday 1874 she was convinced that she had been chosen as the 'spouse of the crucified' and claimed to have developed the stigmata, or signs of Christ's wounds, on her body. Her room-mate Susan Ryland afterwards testified to the strange trances which she suffered at this time and to the mysterious appearance of articles which she prayed for: soap on one occasion, and kindling 'not like the wood we bought' (Kerr, 53–4) on another. Higginson claimed to have experienced revelations of a previously unknown devotion to the 'Sacred Head'; this was meant to complement existing devotions to the Sacred Heart, and was said to cure schoolchildren.

After a number of unexplained illnesses, Higginson left Wigan in 1876. She taught at Seacombe near Birkenhead and St Alban's, Liscard, in Cheshire, where she was soon given notice. In 1877 she went to a Jesuit mission school in Sabden, near Clitheroe, but left for Neston, Cheshire, 'on account of illness' (Kerr, 89), on 15 July 1879. On 24 July she began a series of letters to Powell which described further mystical experiences. Shortly, she joined him at Bootle, where she was to remain for eight years. An inquiry was launched by Bishop O'Reilly of Liverpool, and in 1883 Powell was ordered to stop directing her; he was replaced by Father Alfred (later Canon) Snow, who had been at St Alexander's since 1874.

In 1886 Higginson was accused of fraud and hypocrisy by local people, and was asked to leave her shared lodgings in Ariel Street; she repeatedly complained that priests in Bootle refused to bring communion to her home. When her housemates left for St Peter's, Newchurch, Higginson soon followed. There Father John

Mussely was willing to bring her communion, and his housekeeper, Margaret Murphy, thought her a saint. Father Snow, who had continued to correspond with Higginson and her circle, expected that she would soon enter the mystical state of 'espousals'. She duly claimed this experience in a letter to him dated 24 October 1887, which described revelations of the previous night. Snow arranged for her to go to Edinburgh, where his sister was superior of St Catherine's Convent. Higginson spent the next dozen years in and around Edinburgh, based at St Catherine's, but without entering the order. In 1899 she went to live with the Garnett family in Liverpool, with whom she was able to visit Rome in 1900 and Bruges in 1901. In 1904 she moved to Biddlecombe, on Lord Clifford's estate near Chudleigh, Devon, where, after a stroke, she died on 15 February 1905. She was buried at St Winefride's, Neston.

Teresa Higginson's cause began to be taken up after Snow's death in 1922. Selected letters were published in 1924 and a hagiography by Lady Cecil Kerr in 1927. Works which aimed to promote her beatification followed. Her case, which was viewed with scepticism by many, was presented to the Sacred Congregation of Rites in Rome on 7 December 1933, and refused in 1938. Thereafter, she was almost forgotten until the 1980s, when her cause began to be revived through the persistent efforts of a minority in Bootle and Neston who were convinced that she was a local saint.   MARY HEIMANN

Sources C. Kerr, *Teresa Helena Higginson, Servant of God … 1844–1905* (1927) · A. M. O'Sullivan, *Teresa Higginson, the Servant of God, school teacher, 1845–1905* (1924) · B. Honnor, *Appreciations of Teresa Helena Higginson* (1986) · B. Plumb, 'Teresa Helena Higginson, 1844–1905: a bibliography', *North West Catholic History*, 18 (1991), 40–45 · H. Thurston, 'The case of Teresa Higginson', *Catholic Medical Guardian* (July 1937), 65–70 · H. Thurston, 'Hagiography past and present', *The Tablet* (20 Nov 1937), 683–4 · M. C. Boúváaert, *Nouvelle Revue Théologique*, 63/9 (Nov 1936), 1088 [review] · *Letters of Teresa Higginson* (1937) [by a monk of Ramsgate] · *Life of Teresa Higginson, the teacher mystic* (1937) · K. O'Maola, 'Teresa Helena Higginson', *The Harvest* (May 1940) · 'Biographie succincte de Térésa Héléna Higginson', *Sagesse*, supplément A
Archives Lancs. RO, Roman Catholic Records (Liverpool Archdiocese) · priv. coll. · St Augustine's Abbey, Ramsgate, Kent | St Alexander's Roman Catholic Church, Bootle, Merseyside
Likenesses photograph, 1900, repro. in Kerr, *Teresa Helena Higginson* · photograph, 1900, repro. in Honnor, *Appreciations*
Wealth at death £99 10s.: administration, 31 March 1905, *CGPLA Eng. & Wales*

Higgons, Bevil (1670–1736), historian and poet, was, according to Venn, born at a place called Kezo, the third son of Sir Thomas *Higgons (1623/4–1691), a politician, of Greywell, Hampshire, and his second wife, Bridget Leach, *née* Granville (d. 1692), daughter of Sir Bevil Granville and widow of Sir Simon Leach, of Cadleigh, Devon. On 5 March 1686, at the age of sixteen, he matriculated as a commoner from St John's College, Oxford, but in Michaelmas he migrated to Trinity Hall, Cambridge, where he was admitted as a fellow commoner. His first production in print was a set of English verses addressed to the queen on the birth of the prince, James Francis Edward Stuart, which he wrote for inclusion in the university collection

of congratulatory poems entitled *Illustrissimi principis ducis Cornubiae … Genethliacon* (1688). He was admitted as a student of the Middle Temple on 12 November 1687, but was not called to the bar.

Higgons and his two brothers, George and Thomas *Higgons (1668/9–1733), were Jacobites and in 1689 they joined their uncle, Denis *Granville, dean of Durham, who had become Anglican chaplain to James II in exile at St Germain-en-Laye, France. Bevil kept his wit and good humour unimpaired in exile. In 1692 he and his brothers travelled in secret to England to help raise Jacobite regiments to support the abortive rising planned to coincide with a landing of James II's army in France. They were heavily involved in the Fenwick plot in 1696, another failed attempt to engineer a Jacobite rising and a French-backed Jacobite restoration. The affair was complicated by an unplanned attempt to assassinate William III and warrants were issued for the arrest of Higgons and his brothers in February 1696, but they were later released. Little is known of Bevil's movements until 1704 when he and Thomas, by then gentleman usher to James III, accompanied Mary of Modena at Dean Granville's funeral in Paris. From 1715 onwards he lived off a share of the pension that his brother Thomas had obtained from James III after he had been replaced as James's secretary of state by Lord Bolingbroke. In July of that year Bevil was ordered by James II's illegitimate son, the duke of Berwick, to go to England to find out the plans for a Jacobite rising and to consider whether James should land in England or Scotland. He never left France as the situation became too dangerous in Britain.

Higgons returned to England in 1718 and spent the rest of his life there writing in defence of the Stuarts and their cause. Of his historical works the most important was *A short view of the English history; with reflections on the reigns of the kings, their characters and manners, their succession to the throne; and all other remarkable incidents, to the Revolution, 1688*. After letting his manuscripts for this work 'lie cover'd with dust these twenty-six years', Higgons published it in London in 1723; subsequent editions were published at The Hague in 1727, and at London in 1734 and 1748. A French translation was also published at The Hague in 1729. In 1725 he published *Historical and Critical Remarks on Bishop Burnet's History of his Own Time* (2nd edn 1727). Both of these works were reissued in 1736 under the title *The Historical Works of Bevill Higgons*. A work purporting to be by Higgons, *A History of the Life and Reign of Mary, Queen of Scots and Dowager of France*, was printed in Dublin in 1753.

As a poet Higgons published several poems in Dryden's *Examen poeticum* (1693), in the first of which he applauded Dryden on his translation of Persius. He is believed to have contributed to Elijah Fenton's *Poems on Several Occasions* (1717) and published under his own name in 1731 his panegyric on the 'Glorious Peace of Utrecht'. He also wrote for the stage: in addition to a prologue and an epilogue for plays by his kinsman George Granville, first earl of Lansdowne, his own play *The Generous Conqueror, or, The Timely Discovery* was performed at the Theatre Royal in 1702. This was said to have 'illustrated the right divine and impeccability' of James II and though it met with a neutral reaction on its first night, the audience stayed away subsequently. One critic, possibly Charles Gildon, attributed the failure to the fact that the play 'was writ after an untoward manner, and above half the Town condemn'd it as Turbulent and Factious' (*A Comparison between the Two Stages, with an Examen of the Generous Conqueror*, 1702, 79–139).

Higgons died unmarried in Chiswick on 1 March 1736 and was buried in St Pancras churchyard on 6 March.

W. P. COURTNEY, *rev.* EVELINE CRUICKSHANKS

Sources Venn, *Alum. Cant.* · Wood, *Ath. Oxon.*, new edn, 4.714 · B. Botfield, *Stemmata Botevilliana: memorials of the families of de Boteville, Thynne, and Botfield* (1843), 104–5, 137 · *Le Neve's Pedigrees of the knights*, ed. G. W. Marshall, Harleian Society, 8 (1873), 172 · J. Doran, *Their majesties' servants: annals of the English stage*, ed. R. W. Rowe, 3 vols. (1888), 1.127 · E. Cruickshanks, *By force or by default? The revolution of 1688–9* (1989), 40 · E. Cruickshanks and E. Corp, eds., *The Stuart court in exile and the Jacobites* (1995), 4–11 · Marquis de Ruvigny, *The Jacobite peerage* (1904), 191, 215, 219 · *CSP dom.*, 1696, pp. 56, 73, 228; 1697, p. 288 · *State trials*, 12.1313 · Nichols, *Lit. anecdotes*, 8.169 · N. Luttrell, *A brief historical relation of state affairs from September 1678 to April 1714*, 4 (1857), 22–6, 54, 281 · G. de F. Lord and others, eds., *Poems on affairs of state: Augustan satirical verse, 1660–1714*, 7 vols. (1963–75), vol. 6, pp. 361–3 · *Calendar of the Stuart papers belonging to his majesty the king, preserved at Windsor Castle*, 7 vols., HMC, 56 (1902–23), vol. 1, pp. 362, 378, 394; vol. 7, pp. 128–9, 646 · correspondence politique, Angleterre, Sir Thomas Higgons to Cardinal Dubois, 8 Oct 1721 NS, Archives étrangères, Paris, 339, fol. 179 · T. Higgons, letter to James III, 2 Feb 1722, Royal Arch., Stuart papers, 57/126 · Bodl. Oxf., MSS Carte

Higgons, Theophilus (1578–1659), Church of England clergyman, was born in 1578 in Chilton, near Brill, Buckinghamshire, the son of Robert Higgons and his wife, Alice (*d.* 1608). He was educated partly at the free school at Thame, Oxfordshire, and in 1592, at the age of fourteen, went to Christ Church, Oxford. He graduated BA, proceeded MA in 1600, and was described as a tolerable Latin poet.

It has been said of Higgons that he was 'at first inclined to Puritanism, became a convert to Catholicism … in search of preferment: but finding none, returned to Protestantism' (Brown, 132). Thomas Ravis, the dean of Christ Church, appointed Higgons his domestic chaplain when he became bishop of Gloucester. Higgons then became a lecturer at St Dunstan-in-the-West, Fleet Street, London, where he had a following 'for his sweet and eloquent way of preaching' (Wood, *Ath. Oxon.*, 3.482). It was later alleged that he had been both overtly anti-popish and disaffected to episcopacy. Having been there some time, he married, but apparently so clandestinely that relatives and admirers were unimpressed. He subsequently left his wife and children and went to the north of England. He was rector of Little Comberton, Worcestershire, in 1605 and of Garforth, Yorkshire, in 1607. In 1608 he published *A Briefe Consideration of Man's Iniquitie and God's Justice*, a pamphlet on venial and mortal sin.

About this time Higgons was received into the Roman Catholic church by one John Fludde, probably the Jesuit John Floyd, an event which hostile commentators interpreted as motivated by ambition or through debt and want of preferment. This was a routine accusation, though it has none the less been asserted that 'Higgons had undoubtedly experienced considerable career and financial problems' (Questier, 'Crypto-Catholicism', 48). He appears to have spent two years at the English colleges at Douai and St Omer under the name Thomas Forster. His father, Robert, went over to St Omer in an unsuccessful attempt to persuade him to return to England. Instead Higgons published in 1609 *The First Motive of T.H. … to Suspect the Integrity of his Religion*, 'a conversion tract almost exclusively devoted to justification for purgatory and prayer for the dead' (ibid., 60). He also attacked protestant views on the assurance of salvation and the counsels of perfection. Sir Edward Hoby's *Letter to Mr. T.H. Late Minister, now Fugitive* was written at this time, including a letter from Robert Higgons dated Chilton, 28 May 1609, strongly criticizing his son. Higgons, then living in Rouen, wrote *The Apology of Theophilus Higgons, Lately Minister, now Catholique* (1609). Copies of this book 'were among the recently imported Catholic books seized by the English government at the house of the Venetian ambassador in July 1609' (Allison and Rogers, 1.86).

After living in Rouen for some time Higgons was reconverted to protestantism, reportedly by Thomas Morton, dean of Winchester. Again temporal motivations were alleged, Higgons being seen as not having found 'that which he expected, namely respect, preferment, and I know not what' (Wood, *Ath. Oxon.*, 484–5). He made a public recantation at Paul's Cross, as a result of which he published in 1611 *A Sermon Preached at St Paul's Crosse*. He was appointed rector of Hunton, near Maidstone, apparently secured for him by Hoby, in 1610. He would later publish *Mystical Babylon, or papall Rome … in which the miserable and wicked condition of Rome … is fully discovered* (1624). In March 1642 he was summoned by the House of Commons as a delinquent for giving his support to the recent prayer book petition from Kent. He was sequestered from his living by April 1647 and went to reside at the house of one Daniel Collins in Maidstone. He died at Maidstone in 1659 and was probably buried at the church of All Saints, Maidstone, 'in the cemetery … near to the south east door of the chancel, but hath no stone or mon. over his grave' (Wood, *Ath. Oxon.*, 3.485).

ANTONY CHARLES RYAN

Sources Wood, *Ath. Oxon.*, new edn, 3.482–6 · M. Questier, 'Crypto-Catholicism, anti-Calvinism and conversion at the Jacobean court: the enigma of Benjamin Carier', *Journal of Ecclesiastical History*, 47 (1996), 45–64 · M. C. Questier, *Conversion, politics and religion in England, 1580–1625* (1996) · J. H. Brown, *A short history of Thame School* (1927), 128, 132 · E. Hoby, *Letter to Mr. T.H. late minister, now fugitive* (1609) · Foster, *Alum. Oxon.* · A. F. Allison and D. M. Rogers, eds., *The contemporary printed literature of the English Counter-Reformation between 1558 and 1640*, 2 (1994) · H. Foley, ed., *Records of the English province of the Society of Jesus*, 7 vols. in 8 (1875–83) · *Walker rev.* · *VCH Oxfordshire*

Higgons, Sir Thomas (1623/4–1691), politician and author, was born in Shropshire, the son of Thomas Higgons (*b.* 1563/4, *d.* in or before 1640), rector of Westbury, Shropshire, and his second wife, Elizabeth (*d.* 1656), daughter of

Richard Barker of Haughmond Abbey. He matriculated from St Alban Hall, Oxford, on 27 April 1638, aged fourteen, and later resided at Merton College with his tutor, fellow Edward Corbet. On 4 February 1640 he was admitted to the Middle Temple. Subsequently he returned to Shropshire, though it is unknown whether he fought for either side during the civil war. Between about 1643 and 1646 he made a voyage to Italy; after his return to England, in 1647 or 1648 he married Elizabeth, daughter of Sir William Paulet, and widow of Robert *Devereux, third earl of Essex (1591–1646), the parliamentarian general. They lived at Greywell, and during the marriage two daughters, Elizabeth and Frances, were born. After his wife's death in 1656, Higgons delivered and later published *A Funerall Oration Spoken over the Grave* (1656) defending her against charges of adultery and other censures. In 1658 he published, as *A Prospective of the Naval Triumph of the Venetians over the Turk*, a translation of an Italian work by G. F. Busenello.

In 1659 Higgons represented Malmesbury, Wiltshire, in parliament, where he spoke in favour of recognizing Richard Cromwell as lord protector, allowing the Scottish MPs to remain in the house, and maintaining the *status quo* in general. Though he participated in this and other debates, his role was not prominent. At the Restoration he published *A Panegyrick to the King* (1660), in which he exhorted Charles II to save England's 'sinking State' and to rule like Augustus and Trajan. This work won him the praise of Edmund Waller. In the Cavalier Parliament, as MP for New Windsor, Berkshire, Higgons soon distinguished himself as a firm supporter of the king by arguing in favour of his exclusive control of the militia. He argued that the power of the king was fully compatible with the liberty of the people, and he added that the civil wars would never have happened if the king's power over the military had not been contested. In total he served on 178 committees, chairing seven, acted as teller in fifteen divisions, and made twenty-two recorded speeches, one of which, on the militia, was published (1661). For his services the crown awarded him in 1663 an annual pension of £500 and a knighthood. In November 1661 he married Bridget Leach (d. 1692), daughter of Sir Bevil *Grenville, sister of the recently created earl of Bath, who had been instrumental in the Restoration, and widow of Simon Leach of Cadleigh, Devon. Over the years they had three sons, George, Thomas *Higgons (1668/9–1733), and Bevil *Higgons (1670–1736), and three daughters, Grace, Jane, and Bridget. Sir Thomas also maintained his literary interests, publishing *Ode upon the Death of Mr Cowley* (1667) in celebration of the recently deceased poet, Abraham Cowley.

In 1665 Sir Thomas was involved in a diplomatic mission to Paris and in 1668–9 he travelled to Dresden to deliver the Order of the Garter to the elector of Saxony. From 1674 to 1677 he served as the English envoy in Venice, where he probably wrote much of his most substantial literary work, finally published in 1684 as *The History of Isuf Bassa, Captain General of the Ottoman Army at the Invasion of Candia*, which concerned a Turkish tragic hero in the war against the Venetians in the 1640s. When he returned to England during the onset of the Popish Plot, he was identified in *A*

Seasonable Argument, published at Amsterdam in 1677, as the recipient of £4000 in gifts from the crown and as one of those 'who have betrayed their country to the conspirators, and bargain'd with them to maintain a standing army in England, under the command of the bigotted popish D[uke] who … hopes to bring all back to Rome'. Though he defended the duke of York in the exclusion crisis, he also sat on parliamentary committees to protect the protestant religion. He chose not to participate in the Exclusion Parliaments but was elected MP for St Germans, Cornwall, in 1685 and served on three committees in James II's parliament. After the king's flight he maintained his loyalty, though unlike his sons Thomas and Bevil he did not become a Jacobite and follow the monarch into exile.

On 24 November 1691 Sir Thomas died from apoplexy in the court of king's bench while acting as a witness for the earl of Bath's claim to the duke of Albemarle's estate. He was laid to rest in Winchester Cathedral on 3 December, near the remains of his first wife. According to his will he had outstanding debts of £4650 but also claims to £1640 in reimbursement for his expenses on his mission to Venice. B. C. PURSELL

Sources L. Naylor and G. Jagger, 'Higgons, Thomas', HoP, *Commons, 1660–90* · *Diary of Thomas Burton*, ed. J. T. Rutt, 4 vols. (1828) · A. Marvell (?), *A seasonable argument* (1677) · CSP dom., 1664–80 · *CSP Venice, 1671–5* · Foster, *Alum. Oxon.* · H. A. C. Sturgess, ed., *Register of admissions to the Honourable Society of the Middle Temple, from the fifteenth century to the year 1944*, 1 (1949), 137 · GEC, *Peerage*

Archives BL, letters to lords Arlington and Coventry, Add. MSS 32094–32095

Wealth at death debts of £4650, but claims to £1640 in reimbursement for expenses: will

Higgons, Thomas [Jacobite Sir Thomas Higgons] (**1668/9–1733**), Jacobite court official, was the second of the three sons of Sir Thomas *Higgons (1623/4–1691), diplomat and MP, and his second wife, Bridget (d. 1692), daughter of Sir Bevil Granville. He was educated at Magdalen College, Oxford, and in 1687 was one of several Anglican scholars, the majority being Roman Catholics, whom James II nominated as a fellow of the college (Beddard, 946). After the revolution of 1688–9 Thomas and his brothers, including the historian Bevil *Higgons, remained loyal to James II, then in exile at St Germain-en-Laye. They were arrested at the time of the assassination plot in 1696, but were released soon afterwards. In 1698 they went to Paris, apparently to sell horses, but probably to visit the Jacobite court, where their uncle Denis *Granville, dean of Durham, was the Anglican chaplain. Higgons's two brothers returned to England the following year, but Thomas remained at St Germain and was soon appointed gentleman usher of the privy chamber. At about the same time he, an Anglican, married Frances Grace Mildmay (c.1678–1763), a Roman Catholic educated at the English Benedictine convent at Pontoise. The couple do not appear to have had any children.

Higgons served both James II and his son James III, with a salary of 797 livres per annum. He was not a particularly important member of the Jacobite court, which was predominantly Roman Catholic, but after the conversion to

Catholicism of Lord Middleton, the secretary of state, he became the most important among St Germain's small group of Anglican courtiers. In 1713, when the court moved to Bar-le-Duc and negotiated with the tory government in London for a possible Jacobite restoration, Lord Oxford insisted that James III send Middleton away and replace him with an Anglican. James was obliged to agree and Higgons, the only possible candidate, was given a knighthood and sworn in on 14 December, with an enormously increased salary of 5657 livres.

It was soon apparent that Higgons was not really qualified for the post. As an Anglican he was not allowed to handle the Jacobite correspondence with Rome, which was entrusted to David Nairne. Because he could not write French he was also obliged to rely on Nairne to help him with much of his own correspondence, notably with the French court at Versailles and the French diplomats in London. His influence is more difficult to assess, because none of the relevant Jacobite archives has survived. It is possible that he tried to persuade James to convert to Catholicism in order to regain his throne. He is said to have quarrelled with the king's Catholic chaplains, and in November 1714 Lord Middleton had to be temporarily recalled, though with no official position. Higgons remained Jacobite secretary of state until July 1715, when he resigned to enable James III to give the post to Lord Bolingbroke.

Higgons remained at Bar-le-Duc until the end of 1715 and then travelled to join the Jacobite rising in Scotland. He was nearly captured and escaped by sea, returning to France via Poland and Germany. He rejoined James at Avignon in 1716, but his presence was not welcome to the duke of Mar, the new Jacobite secretary of state. As his health was bad he left the court to take the waters at Bourbon and then returned to St Germain-en-Laye, where he settled permanently. He was joined there until 1718 by his elder brother, George, who betrayed him by acting as a spy for the British ambassador, Lord Stair.

Higgons and his wife had serious financial difficulties because he was not included in the list of Jacobites who received a pension from the French government after the death of Mary of Modena. James III sent him what money he could from Rome, but it was not nearly enough, and Higgons felt increasingly bitter about the way he had been treated. He eventually obtained a French pension of 3000 livres per annum, thanks to the influence of his first cousin, Lord Lansdowne, and in the summer of 1728 he briefly visited England in an unsuccessful attempt to recover some money owed him by a relative.

Higgons converted to Roman Catholicism at St Germain-en-Laye in May 1731 and died there, at the Château-Vieux, two years later, on 19 May 1733, at the age of sixty-four. He was buried the following day in the parish church of St Germain-en-Laye, his tombstone describing him as 'premier ministre de Jacques Troisième, roy d'Angleterre'. To the novelist Eliza Haywood he was 'one of the finest gentlemen that England ever bred' (Haywood, *The Fortunate Foundlings*, 1744, 125). When his wife died at St Germain in January 1763 she left her possessions to the English Benedictine convent at Pontoise, but none of his papers survived.   EDWARD CORP

Sources Royal Arch., Stuart papers · *Calendar of the Stuart papers belonging to his majesty the king, preserved at Windsor Castle*, 7 vols., HMC, 56 (1902–23) · *Calendar of the manuscripts of the marquis of Bath preserved at Longleat, Wiltshire*, 5 vols., HMC, 58 (1904–80) · Gualterio papers, BL, Add. MSS 31254, 31255 · [E. T. Corp and J. Sanson], eds., *La cour des Stuarts* (Paris, 1992) [exhibition catalogue, Musée des Antiquités Nationales de Saint-Germain-en-Laye, 13 Feb – 27 April 1992] · M. H. Massue de Ruvigny, ed., *The Jacobite peerage* (1904) · Archives départementales du Val d'Oise, Cergy-Pontoise, 68/H · E. Corp, 'An inventory of the archives of the Stuart court at Saint-Germain-en-Laye, 1689–1718', *Archives*, 23 (1998), 118–46 · Bodl. Oxf., MS Carte 212 · *The letter book of Lewis Sabran*, ed. G. Holt, Catholic RS, 62 (1971) · M. Haile, *Queen Mary of Modena* (1905) · Archives départementales des Yvelines, Versailles, A.369 · parish registers, church of Saint-Germain-en-Laye, France, 20 May 1733 [burial] · *DNB* · R. A. Beddard, 'James II and the Catholic challenge', *Hist. U. Oxf.* 4: *17th-cent. Oxf.*, 907–54

Archives Royal Arch., Stuart papers

Higgs, Eric Sidney (1908–1976), sheep farmer and archaeologist, was born on 26 November 1908 in Oldbury Wells, near Bridgnorth in Shropshire, the elder son of Sidney Higgs, carpet designer, and his wife, Florence Annie Price, whose family ran a building and haulage firm. He was educated at Bridgnorth grammar school, and took a BComm at the London School of Economics. After periods of unemployment and a spell as a professional card player, he worked in London as a specialist in the waterproofing of buildings and railway tunnels. During this period he lived in Kent and kept horses. After his first marriage, on 29 May 1936 to Marion Bett (*b.* 1900/01), daughter of William Edward Bett, a Russian jute merchant, and the birth of their only daughter, he returned to Shropshire at the outbreak of the Second World War to take up sheep farming at Clee St Margaret. His farming was largely self-taught and during the war years the government compelled him to grow food crops. He founded the Brown Clee Club, a local discussion group for politics, drama, and poetry reading, travelled with the French agronomist René Dumont throughout France and Spain, and later with his farmer friend and neighbour Michael Osler visited Yugoslavia and Greece, where he first encountered the transhumant Vlachs of the Pindus Mountains.

In 1954 Higgs moved to Cambridge to read the two-year postgraduate diploma in prehistoric archaeology under Charles McBurney and Grahame Clark. In 1956 he was appointed assistant in research in the department of archaeology and anthropology, and his new home at 35 Panton Street became the focus of undergraduate supervisions and the plotting of summer fieldwork campaigns. Shortly afterwards, in 1958, he suffered the first of a series of heart attacks. So began the longest period of his adult career at an age and in conditions of health when others would have put their feet up in early retirement. In 1963 he became senior assistant in research, and assistant director of research in 1968.

As a late entrant to the academic profession Higgs

brought fresh thinking to a discipline that he felt had become over-obsessed with studying the minutiae of artefact form, and which relied on other scientific disciplines with little interest in the human factor to supply information on the environmental background. He was convinced that the archaeological record could not be properly understood without a better understanding of the basic economy. He also believed that archaeology should address a wider public and the more general threats to human survival in the modern world. He lectured to the Workers' Educational Association, gave radio and television broadcasts, and advocated the importance of an archaeological perspective in distinguishing factors of long-term importance from the short-term noise of cultural choice.

Higgs became an expert on the study of animal bones from archaeological sites and pioneered an approach that is now a cornerstone of professional practice. Animal bones should not be thrown away or handed over to some scientific specialist but studied by archaeologists as primary data capable of yielding as much information about human activities as conventional artefacts. He founded the Cambridge 'Bone Room', and with his assistant, Don Allen, taught generations of students the rudiments of animal-bone identification.

In 1962 Higgs launched a field project in northern Greece to search for palaeolithic sites in a country where almost none were then known. Discovery of the enigmatic 'red beds' of Kokkinopilos in Epirus and subsequent excavations at the rock shelters of Asprochaliko and Kastritsa opened up a rich prehistoric record. This work stimulated new ideas about prehistoric economy, the study of site locations in relation to local landscape settings, and the importance of mobility as a primary human adaptation to regional and seasonal variations in food supply. In 1968 he was awarded the Rivers medal of the Royal Anthropological Institute, and in 1994 a square in the old part of the city of Ioannina was named after him.

From 1967 to 1976 Higgs directed the British Academy major research project on the early history of agriculture. Teams of research assistants and students were dispatched to collect animal bones and plant remains from ongoing excavations throughout Europe and the Near East and to conduct site catchment walks in the surrounding landscape. The results, published in a series of edited volumes—*Papers in Economic Prehistory* (1972), *Palaeoeconomy* (1975), and *Early European Agriculture* (1982)—documented the novel view that plant and animal domestication were not discoveries of recent millennia diffusing out from a revolutionary centre of origin in the Near East. Rather they were part of a continuing process of worldwide economic adaptation, which extended from earliest prehistory up to the modern period under the impetus of inexorable population growth and technological change.

In Higgs's archaeological years, his hunched back and balding, domed head belied a youthful approach to life allied with an impish sense of humour. He encouraged his students to challenge established orthodoxy and inspired

them with confidence to venture into new territory. Fieldwork was carried out every summer in nomadic style from an operational base in the family Land Rover with his second wife, Helen Pauline Tippett (*b*. 1936), whom he married in 1964, a chemist by training who had first analysed the red sediments of Kokkinopilos, and their children, all three of whom were brought up on the experience of fieldwork. Spartan living conditions and long hours in the field taxed those much younger and fitter than him. Students and younger colleagues alike were charmed and challenged into feats of unaccustomed accomplishment or endurance, lightened by his tales of a wider world beyond academe and by a farmer's insights into past and present land use. By 1975 his chronic heart condition worsened and after a slow decline he died at his home, 35 Panton Street, on 23 September 1976, his wife surviving him. He was buried at Clee St Margaret.

GEOFF BAILEY

Sources G. W. Barker and R. W. Dennell, *Nature*, 264 (1976), 97 · J. D. Evans, 'Prehistory in the seventies at home and abroad. Presidential address', *Proceedings of the Prehistoric Society*, 43 (1977), 1–12 · *The Times* (28 Sept 1976) · *The Times* (2 Nov 1976) · M. Osler, *Journey to Hattusas* (1957) · R. Dumont, *Types of rural economy: studies in world agriculture* (1957) · personal knowledge (2004) · private information (2004) · b. cert. · m. cert. [first marriage] · d. cert. · General Register Office for England

Archives U. Cam., bone collections · University of Sheffield, MSS

Wealth at death £37,317: administration with will, 16 March 1977, CGPLA Eng. & Wales

Higgs, Griffith [Griffin] (*bap*. 1589, *d*. 1659), dean of Lichfield and book collector, was born at Barre Place, Stoke Abbas, Oxfordshire, and baptized at St Andrew's Church, Stoke Abbas, on 28 October 1589. He was the third child and second son of Griffith Higgs (*d*. 1608), yeoman farmer, and of Sarah (*d*. 1602), daughter of Robert Paine of Caversham, near Reading. Higgs attended Reading School. William Laud, who had also been a pupil, was a fellow of St John's College, Oxford, when Higgs went there in 1606. While at St John's, Higgs gained a reputation as an orator and writer of Latin verses, including a manuscript verse biography of the college's founder, Thomas White (St John's College, Oxford, MS L11, fols. 1–25). He graduated in June 1610 and in 1611 was elected probationer fellow of Merton College, becoming MA in 1615. He was the college praelector in Greek and after his MA produced three theses ('variations') in philosophy, philology, and ancient history. In 1620 he was awarded the college's Bickley exhibition, worth £4 annually. During the period 1616 to 1625 he occupied in turn several college positions as tutor, bursar, dean, and senior proctor, 'tho' of little stature' (Wood, *Ath. Oxon.*, 3.481). In March 1625 the college offered him the living of Gamlingay in Cambridgeshire. Higgs spent some time there but had three sub-lessees; he resigned in 1630, officially because of his collation to the 'rich church' of Cliffe-at-Hoo in Kent (ibid.), but in fact he was then already in the Netherlands, as in 1627 the privy council had issued a passport to him.

In 1627 Laud was bishop of Bath and Wells but in touch

with Oxford affairs, and Merton College also had connections with the court, which probably accounts for Higgs's name being put forward as chaplain to Elizabeth of Bohemia. While at The Hague, Higgs obtained his DD from Leiden, his work for the degree being published as *Problemata theologica* (1630), and he continued to study and teach, to maintain an academic correspondence, and to keep diaries, of which those for 1630, 1632, 1637, and 1638 survive. He also continued his undergraduate interest in amateur theatricals, an interest which he shared with Elizabeth of Bohemia. During this time he collected an extensive library. The court in The Hague had little to offer financially, but Elizabeth could use her influence to obtain preferment for her chaplain; probably by that means Laud (who had been bishop of St David's until 1626) gave Higgs the precentorship of that cathedral in 1631. In 1638 the queen wrote to Laud, following which Higgs secured the deanery of Lichfield and returned to England. His Netherlands diary ends on 20 September, when he was presumably already back in England, since he had a passport to return to the Netherlands in 1639 to collect his books. On Charles I's command Higgs became a chaplain-in-extraordinary in November 1638 and a chaplain-in-ordinary in July 1639. His precise ecclesiological position is uncertain. While Laud at his trial labelled Higgs a Calvinist, John Earle the essayist described a clergyman who was probably Higgs as a 'Protestant out of judgement not faction', and Higgs probably regarded himself as among 'conformable men of learning, and good life and moderation' (Morrish, 139).

Almost all the Lichfield records were lost during the civil war and it is difficult to discover how much time Higgs spent there, but a visitation by Archbishop Laud suggests that he had been sent to put in order a very unhappy state of affairs. In 1643 there were two sieges of Lichfield, of which a Latin account by Higgs survives, implying that he was in the close at the time. With it is a tribute to Prince Rupert as liberator of the cathedral close, and a note, 'Authore D. Griff. Higgs etc. Decano'.

In 1646 Higgs was in Oxford when it surrendered to Fairfax. Later, he returned to Stoke Abbas, and died there, at Barre Place, unmarried, on 16 December 1659. He was buried in the chancel of St Andrew's Church, Stoke Abbas, on 19 December, and a mural tablet surmounted by a portrait bust and Higgs's coat of arms was erected there. The large inscription was written mostly by himself. In spite of sequestration by parliament Higgs died a rich man and in his will he gave benefactions to the church and poor of South Stoke, and £600 for the maintenance of a schoolmaster there. In addition to bequests concerning gifts from the royal family at The Hague, he left money to buy books for the Bodleian Library and the libraries of Merton and St John's, and to fund a divinity lecture at Merton. His own books, including the 'fair English Bible presented to him by the "Winter Queen"' (Morrish, 156), he left to Merton, where they became the nucleus of the college library. The books were to be collected from no fewer than eight different sources, and there proved to be more than 650 titles.   PAT BANCROFT

Sources Wood, *Ath. Oxon.*, new edn, 3.479–82 · *Fasti Angl.* (Hardy) · P. S. Morrish, 'Dr Higgs and Merton College Library', *Leeds Philosophical and Literary Society*, 21 (1988), 131–201 · W. M. Higgs, *A history of the Higges, or Higgs family* (1933) · Higgs's diaries, 1637–8, and will, Merton Oxf., MS E/2/29 · will, PRO, PROB 11/297, sig. 8 · Lichfield Cathedral, MS 13 · *Reg. Oxf.* · G. Higgs, diaries, 1630 and 1632, Bodl. Oxf., Wood almanac A · S. Shaw, *A history of Lichfield* (1828) · parish register (baptism), South Stoke, Oxfordshire, 28 Oct 1589 · parish register (burial), South Stoke, Oxfordshire, 19 Dec 1659
Archives Bodl. Oxf., diaries · Lichfield Cathedral, account of siege · Merton Oxf., diaries
Likenesses bust, St Andrew's Church, Stoke Abbas, Oxfordshire
Wealth at death approx. £2545; plus £3600 and books: Morrish, 'Dr Higgs'; will, PRO, PROB 11/297, sig. 8, printed in Higgs, *History of the Higges*

Higgs, Henry (1864–1940), civil servant and economist, was born at 17 Fore Street, Torpoint, Antony, Cornwall, on 4 March 1864, the eleventh of thirteen children of Samuel Nicholas Higgs, master butcher, and his wife, Ann Pugh. His humble origins influenced his career choice, for he had to attain sufficient financial security to sustain his parents in their old age. He took full advantage of the meritocratic opportunities offered by a newly reformed civil service. Entering as a lower-division clerk in 1881 he passed the competition for class 1 in 1884, and for the next fifteen years served in the secretary's office of the General Post Office.

When he moved to the Treasury in 1899 Higgs attracted the attention of its permanent secretary, Sir Edward Hamilton, from whom he learnt the intricacies of Britain's public finances, which he in turn communicated in a series of publications (*The Financial System of the United Kingdom*, 1914; *National Economy*, 1917; *A Primer of National Finance*, 1919; *Financial Reform*, 1924). He became private secretary to a succession of ministers, culminating with Sir Henry Campbell-Bannerman when prime minister between 1905 and 1908, when Higgs was made CB. On 16 July 1908 he married Winifred Sarah (1877/8–1939), daughter of Thomas John South, landscape gardener, of Kew, with whom he had at least one child, a son. He also served as a special commissioner to Natal in 1902–3 and as inspector-general of finance in Egypt between 1912 and 1915 before retiring from the Treasury in 1921 as principal clerk.

Upon securing his position within the established civil service in 1884 Higgs enrolled in University College, London, intending to pursue legal studies. He also studied at the University of Berlin. In 1890 he took his LLB and was called to the bar at the Middle Temple. It was none the less economics rather than the law which quickly captivated Higgs. He fell early under the influence of H. S. Foxwell, whose political economy lectures he attended in 1885–7, and thereafter his energies were increasingly devoted to economics and to the burgeoning economics profession. Quickly adept at the subject, he won a scholarship in 1886 to continue his studies at University College, and the following year began lecturing in economics at Toynbee Hall. He was a fellow of University College, and Newmarch lecturer in statistics, and was lecturer in economics at the University of Wales (Bangor), 1925–9. It was under

Foxwell's influence that he then began his lifetime interest in the physiocrats, and in particular in Richard Cantillon, who was the subject of his first economics article (*Economic Journal*, 1891) and of his most significant contribution to the history of economic thought, his translation of Cantillon's *Essai sur la nature du commerce en général* (1755; ed. H. Higgs, 1931).

Higgs is also regarded for his contribution to the British economics profession at an important early stage of its development. He was one of the founding members of the British Economic Association (later the Royal Economic Society), serving as the association's first secretary and, with F. Y. Edgeworth, as joint editor of its *Economic Journal* between 1892 and 1905. While he continued too long on the council of the Royal Economic Society, being still an active but unhelpful contributor to its meetings until his death (upon which see J. M. Keynes's bitter-sweet obituary for the *Economic Journal*), his early work for the association and its journal was invaluable in promoting the professionalization of economics. He displayed similar administrative and interpersonal skills in his re-editing of the *Palgrave Dictionary of Political Economy* (3 vols., 1923–6) under impossible conditions of minimal change. He also completed various projects, initiated but abandoned by Foxwell, most notably the publication of W. S. Jevons's *The Principles of Economics* (1905) and *A Bibliography of Economics* (1935). He stood unsuccessfully as Liberal parliamentary candidate for Putney in 1922. He died in Brighton Municipal Hospital on 21 May 1940.   ROGER MIDDLETON

Sources *The Times* (24 May 1940) · C. E. Collet, 'Obituary: Henry Higgs', *Economic Journal*, 50 (1940), 546–55 · J. M. Keynes, 'Obituary: Henry Higgs', *Economic Journal*, 50 (1940), 555–8 · E. A. G. Robinson, 'Fifty-five years on the Royal Economic Society council', *A century of economics*, ed. J. D. Hey and D. Winch (1990), 161–92 · M. Milgate, 'Higgs, Henry', *The new Palgrave: a dictionary of economics*, ed. J. Eatwell, M. Milgate, and P. Newman (1987) · b. cert. · m. cert. · d. cert.

Archives BLPES, corresp. and papers relating to Royal Economic Society | BL, corresp. with Sir Henry Campbell-Bannerman, Add. MSS 41240–41242 · BL, corresp. with Macmillans, Add. MS 55198 · BLPES, letters to Edwin Cannan · Col. U., Rare Book and Manuscript Library, letters to Edwin Seligman · Harvard U., Baker Library, letters to Herbert Foxwell · U. Cam., Marshall Library of Economics, letters to John Maynard Keynes · U. Durham L., archives and special collections, corresp. with Sir Reginald Wingate · University of Toronto Library, letters to James Mavor

Higgs [*née* Kingsland], **Mary Ann** (1854–1937), social reformer, was born on 2 February 1854 in Devizes, Wiltshire, the eldest of three children of William Kingsland (1826–1876), a Congregational minister, and his wife, Caroline Paddon (1818–1888?). In 1862 the family moved north on William's accepting the invitation to be minister at College Chapel, Bradford. Initially taught at home with her brothers, Mary went at the age of thirteen to Miss Scott's, a local private school. In 1871 she won an exhibition to the College for Women, Hitchin, which in 1873 transferred to Girton College, Cambridge. The first woman to take Cambridge's natural science tripos, she gained second-class honours in 1874, belatedly receiving an honorary MA many years later.

After eighteen months as assistant lecturer at Girton,

Mary Kingsland taught mathematics and science at the recently established grammar school for girls in Bradford, later teaching also at the Saltaire School, Shipley. Her hopes of helping her father in the church were dashed when he died of consumption in 1876. Until she married a fellow Congregationalist, Revd Thomas Kilpin Higgs (1851–1907), Mary Kingsland helped to support her family. After her marriage, which took place on 5 August 1879, Mary moved to Staffordshire, where Thomas was minister at Hanley Tabernacle; here, their first three children were born. Concern for her health prompted a move to Withington, near Manchester, in 1888, but difficulties in the church and failing health led Thomas to resign in 1890. That year a fourth child was born. After several unsettled months the family moved to Oldham, Thomas serving as minister of Greenacres Congregational Church for sixteen years until his death.

Mary Higgs's interests were wide-ranging: besides church work, she collaborated with W. T. Stead and others on a *Twentieth Century New Testament* (1898, 1900), reportedly practising Greek while making puddings in the kitchen. Subsequent religious works included poems, meditations, and a prize-winning essay, *Christ and his Miracles in the Light of Modern Psychology* (1905). This reflected her desire to reconcile her essentially mystical faith with her interest in science, particularly the new discipline of psychology to which W. T. Stead had introduced her.

Mary Higgs's pioneering social work was also inspired by her friendship with Stead—best-known for his exposé of under-age prostitution in London in the 1880s—and others, including Ebenezer Howard, originator of the garden city movement. She in turn inspired the foundation in 1902 of the much imitated Beautiful Oldham Society, and was active in its wide-ranging programme to improve the town's appearance and build a garden suburb. Her involvement led to her writing a weekly column in the *Oldham Standard* and the *Oldham Chronicle*: addressed to 'Young Oldham', it appeared from 1910 to 1937, under the pseudonym 'Mrs Minerva'. She also played a part in wider moves to improve the provision of playing fields and to cut down smoke pollution.

Higgs wrote and lectured on many social questions, notably unemployment and child development. From 1905 she collaborated with Dr John Paton, principal of the Nottingham Congregational Institute, to arrange yearly summer schools for the study of social questions: they were attended by experts from the settlement movement, temperance campaigns, and other fields of social work. She was an early advocate of family allowances, widowed mothers' pensions, and insurances for other life events. Her Oldham home, Bent House, served as a base for countless welfare organizations, many brought together in the Council of Social Welfare. Mobilizing an army of helpers, she established a paper-sorting industry to employ destitute women, pioneered mother and infant welfare centres, and founded Oldham's first evening play centre. Other initiatives included a mission and club for unemployed men, opened in 1909, and a wartime women's workroom, the model for what became known as Queen Mary's workrooms.

Mary Higgs is, however, best-known as an advocate of vagrancy reform. About 1899 she found a room where women could stay in emergencies; later, with a benefactor, she set up three women's lodging-houses in Oldham. She was, however, keen to discover for herself why women shunned existing shelters, and over many years from 1903 took the highly unusual step (for a middle-class woman) of visiting workhouse wards and common lodging-houses dressed as a tramp. Her vivid accounts of the dirt and degradation which she encountered and of the downward spiral of destitution in which homeless women found themselves helped to fuel demands for more and better regulated women's lodgings, and for lodgings geared to the needs of migrant workers. Many of her descriptions were brought together in *Glimpses into the Abyss* (1906), anticipating by over twenty years George Orwell's similar but much better known *Down and out in Paris and London* (1933). This work drew on her research into conditions in other countries and linked the need for legislation with evolutionary theories. She became an acknowledged authority, giving evidence at inquiries such as the 1906 departmental committee on vagrancy, producing practical manuals, and acting as a prime mover in founding the National Association for Women's Lodging-Homes in 1909. In 1916 opposition to conscription led Higgs to join the Society of Friends, being already sympathetic to its beliefs. She became an elder, and in later years worked through the Quakers and with the Vagrancy Reform Society on vagrancy-related issues, giving evidence to the departmental committee on the relief of the casual poor (1930). Her later work (practical and written) focused on the rising tide of homeless unemployed boys and men, and included running experimental schools for unemployed boys (1929), helping to set up training farms for Young Wayfarers, and opening a fellowship and service club and hostels in Oldham for unemployed men (1933–5). Her own spirituality found expression in her editing of *The Way to the Joyous Life* (1937), a selection of W. T. Stead's devotional writings.

Known to many as Mother Mary, Mary Higgs died on 19 March 1937 at 4 Macartney House, Chesterfield Walk, her daughter's house in Greenwich, soon after receiving an OBE for her services to Oldham. She was cremated on 23 March at Golders Green and her ashes were interred at Greenacres Congregational Church on 3 April, amid widespread tributes to her tirelessness, humour, practicality, and vision.   ROSEMARY CHADWICK

Sources M. K. H. [M. Higgs], *Mary Higgs of Oldham* [1954] · *The Times* (22 March 1937) · *Daily Herald* (20 March 1937) · *Oldham Chronicle* (20 March 1937) · *Manchester Guardian* (20 March 1937) · *Municipal Journal* (26 March 1937) · *The Friend* (26 March 1937) · M. Higgs, 'Story of a noble life: woman pioneer in many movements', *Oldham Standard* (25 Feb 1933–4 March 1993) · [M. Higgs], *Rescue work in Oldham, 1903–4* (1904?) · [M. Higgs], *History of beautiful Oldham* (1927?) · *Annual Report* [Bent House, Oldham] (1927) · *Annual Report* [Bent House, Oldham] (1929) · *Annual Report* [Bent House, Oldham] (1933) · National Association for Women's Lodging-Homes, *Report of the proceedings of the national conference on lodging-house accommodation for women … May, 1911* (1911) · *Reports and documents presented to the yearly meeting*, London Yearly Meeting of the Society of Friends (1925–37) · K. T. Butler and H. I. McMorran, eds., *Girton College register, 1869–1946* (1948) · *Congregational Year Book* (1877), 388–90 · *Congregational Year Book* (1907), 179–80 · M. Higgs, 'How fellowship hostels help those in distress', *Oldham Evening Chronicle* (21 May 1936) · *Annual report* [British Institute of Social Service], 5 (1909), 9 · d. cert. · *Oldham Chronicle* (2 Feb 1924) · *Oldham Chronicle* (22 March 1937)
Archives Oldham Local Studies and Archives, papers relating to life and works incl. newscuttings
Likenesses photograph, *c.*1930, Oldham Local Studies and Archives · two photographs, *c.*1930–1937, Oldham Local Studies and Archives
Wealth at death £221 15*s*. 1*d*.: probate, 31 May 1937, *CGPLA Eng. & Wales*

Higgs, William (1824–1883), building contractor, was born on 8 April 1824 in Ferry Street, Lambeth, London, the third son of Caleb Higgs, cooper, farmer, and dairyman, of Lambeth, and his wife, Sarah, daughter of Richard Nash, shipbuilder. As a child he had to help with his father's dairy herd. He was educated at a private school in Marshgate, Lambeth, and then to the age of thirteen at Rodney House School, New Kent Road. He was briefly employed in a printer's office, but was determined to become a builder and was apprenticed to his father's elder brother, Joshua Higgs (1793–1866), a successful builder in Bayswater and the West End of London. A fellow apprentice recorded that Higgs possessed a serene and agreeable temper—'I never met a youth so steady, and so opposed to frivolity' (Higgs, 137).

Having saved £50, Higgs set up in business on his own account at the age of twenty-one; he bought the premises of an upholsterer and undertaker in Bishop's Road, Bayswater, but devoted his whole attention to building. A love of buying and selling was, according to a member of his family, a marked feature of his character, but '"Fair play is a jewel" was a favourite proverb with him' (Higgs, 137). His perseverance and integrity 'built up a business which earned a reputation for splendid workmanship throughout London and the surrounding counties' (ibid., 139). The fifth duke of Portland, who was enlarging Welbeck Abbey, Nottinghamshire, and was a great metropolitan landlord, was a generous patron of Higgs throughout his career, often paying him cash in advance. By the age of thirty-five, 'he was carrying out as much work as any builder in London at the time' (*The Builder*, 20 Jan 1883), including the guards' barracks at Chelsea and the Royal Marine Infirmary at Woolwich. In 1873 he was able to tender for the new law courts in the Strand at a price (£900,000) which was lower than that of several of his rivals, including George Myers. Philanthropic works that he secured, such as the London Orphan Asylum, Watford, the Royal Albert Orphan Asylum, Bagshot, and St Thomas's Hospital, Lambeth (of which he became a life governor), called forth his natural generosity. In 1870 he established the 4 acre Crown Works (so named in recognition of his many government contracts) at Vauxhall near Kennington Oval, with workshops for all the principal building trades, equipped with steam-powered machinery. In the 1870s the firm seems to have been employing about five hundred men during the summers.

Private speculations formed only a small part of Higgs's business, though they included the first public (though not free) swimming baths in London at Kennington Oval and Peckham. Although his principal work was in government contracts Higgs was not averse to house building. In 1865 his tender of £52,789 won the contract for nos. 1–18 Stanhope Gardens, South Kensington (by Thomas Cundy III). His obituary in *The Builder* commented: 'It is said of him that no employer was more respected, for he was fair and honourable in all his dealings, and always had the welfare of his men at heart'.

Higgs had been brought up a Wesleyan Methodist and was a lifelong devoted nonconformist. He attended a Congregational chapel when living in Marylebone but in Lambeth he reverted to the Wesleyan chapel until he heard C. H. Spurgeon, whom he followed to New Park Street Chapel, into which he was baptized about 1858. He admitted to a cousin, 'Mr Spurgeon is the only minister who keeps bricks and mortar out of my head' during public worship (Higgs, 139). But bricks and mortar cemented his friendship with Spurgeon, for whom he built a house, a chapel in Chatham Road, Wandsworth, and the new Metropolitan Tabernacle in Newington Butts, of which he became a deacon, and to which he was a large contributor; he was also co-founder and treasurer of the Spurgeon Orphan Homes at Stockwell. He served as a guardian of the poor for Lambeth for twenty-one years, and was chairman for several years, characterized by his opposition to jobbery.

Higgs was living in the New Road, Marylebone, when on 5 April 1848 he married Letetia Ann (1825–1922), daughter of George Charlton, a prosperous master baker, also of Marylebone; they had three sons and twelve daughters. About 1852 they moved back to Lambeth and in 1858 Higgs bought Stockwell Lodge (later the site of a smallpox hospital). About 1870 he moved to nearby Kenyon House. This property he sold in building leases because of the burden its upkeep would have imposed on his widow, moving finally to Gwydyr House, Brixton Hill. In 1874 Higgs retired from business in favour of his eldest son, William, devoting himself to his charitable interests: he became president of the Builders' Benevolent Institution in 1877. However, he regarded his son as too young, at twenty-two, to conduct the firm alone, so set up a partnership with another builder, Joseph Hill of Islington; his Crown Works he rented to his successors. Throughout the twentieth century Higgs and Hill remained a major firm of contractors.

Higgs died 'somewhat suddenly' at Gwydyr House (*The Builder*, 20 Jan 1883) on 3 January 1883. For some years he had suffered from stomach ulcers, for which he had tried the waters at Karlsbad. He was buried in Norwood cemetery.   M. H. PORT

Sources W. M. Higgs, *A history of the Higges, or Higgs family* (1933) · *The Builder*, 44 (1883), 93 · E. W. Cooney, 'The building industry', *Dynamics of Victorian building*, ed. R. Church (1980) · *Souvenir of the fiftieth anniversary of the incorporation of the company of Higgs and Hill Ltd, 1898–1948* [1948] · census returns, 1871, PRO, RG 10/681, fol. 64 · *The Builder*, 23 (1865), 824 [cited in *Survey of London*, 38] · C. H. Spurgeon's autobiography: compiled from his diary, letters, and records, ed. [S. Spurgeon and J. Harrald], 4 vols. (1897–1900), vols. 2, 3 · M. H. Port, *Imperial London: civil government building in London, 1850–1915* (1995), 312 n.70 · CGPLA Eng. & Wales (1883) · m. cert. · postal directories

Likenesses photograph (in middle age), repro. in Higgs, *History of the Higges* · stained-glass window, Stockwell; repro. in *Spurgeon's autobiography*, vol. 3, p. 171

Wealth at death £51,872 9s. 7d.: resworn probate, May 1884, CGPLA Eng. & Wales (1883)

Higham, Sir Charles Frederick (1876–1938), advertising agent and publicist, was born in Walthamstow on 17 January 1876, son of Charles Higham, a lawyer. Following his father's death his family emigrated to America. He left home at thirteen and endured a pell-mell existence in the United States where, as he was wont to boast, he held as many jobs as Heinz had varieties. After returning to England he held down three more, one with W. H. Smith, newsagents. He then went on to sell space on theatre curtains and other novelties and soon found that he had effectively become manager of an agency. This became Charles F. Higham Ltd and by 1914 could claim such choice clients as Waring and Gillow, Austin Reed, and Marshall and Snelgrove, all high-class retail outlets.

Higham was a rumbustious, fiercely energetic, and indefatigable self-publicist, but though he understood the power of advertising, he failed to accept the growing trend for sophisticated market research. The aggregate of his thinking was expressed in numerous publications, including *Scientific Distribution* (1916), *Advertising: its Use and Abuse* (1931), and *Higham's Magazine*, a business and sales monthly, first issued from Imperial House, Kingsway, in March 1914.

During the First World War Higham's expertise was channelled to government use. With Thomas Russell and others, he sat on the voluntary committee on recruiting, dedicated to fostering patriotism. Posters were transformed from purely commercial art to a potent means of propaganda of unlimited stimulative possibilities, Alfred Leete's 'Lord Kitchener Needs YOU' being the best known. Higham started the 1st battalion of volunteers at the outbreak of war. 'The Optimists Corps' had little concern with advertising, but provided businessmen who, for one reason or another—age, health, or priority business—could not enlist, with the chance of learning the rudiments of soldiering. He also restored the faltering momentum of the second war loan (1915) and as director of the National War Savings Committee helped organize the victory loan campaign of 1917.

Higham's organizational capacity was boundless, embracing the War Shrine Movement for 'Remembrance Day', 4 August 1917, the Red Cross, the Star and Garter Fund, recruiting for the Royal Ulster Constabulary, and the national tribute to Lord Roberts. Having spent millions of the taxpayers' money, leading advertising men felt they had done their bit. The award of a knighthood in 1921, a vote of thanks in the House of Commons, and presentation in 1930 of the Publicity Club cup for sustained creative output seemed no more than Higham's due. A parliamentary career seemed inevitable. From 1918 to 1922 Higham sat as MP for South Islington, representing the coalition Unionists, having been chairman of the coalition publicity committee in the 1918 general election.

Certainly the finest public orator in his field and a unique force in dynamic publicity, Higham led a campaign in America in 1924 to popularize tea-drinking. It took that country by storm, and within weeks tea-shops were opening across the continent. He was an ardent believer in federations of advertising clubs, and he was president in 1920 of the Thirty Club (motto: 'For the Betterment of Advertising') when the first plans were made for the great advertising exhibition at the White City in 1921. In 1922, following up an earlier initiative in transatlantic lobbying aborted by war, he led a delegation on a barnstorming mission to the Associated Advertising Clubs of the World convention in Milwaukee, urging American media personnel to hold their 1924 meeting in London. This duly took place and from it was born in 1926 what came to be known as the Advertising Association.

Higham married twice in middle age. His first marriage in 1930 to a youthful divorcée, Josephine Janet Keuchenius, daughter of Harold Webb of Cheltenham, produced a son. This marriage was dissolved and in 1936 he married Ruth Agnes Master Dawes-Smith, with whom he had a daughter. Higham died of pneumonia and cancer of the mouth on 24 December 1938 at his home, The Mount, South Godstone, Surrey. He was survived by his second wife.   GORDON PHILLIPS

Sources *The Times* (27 Dec 1938) · T. R. Nevett, *Advertising in Britain: a history* (1982) · E. Field, *Advertising: the forgotten years* (1959) · E. S. Turner, *The shocking history of advertising!* [1952] · *WWW* · C. F. Higham, *Advertising: its use and abuse* (1931) · C. F. Higham, *Scientific distribution* (1916) · P. V. Bradshaw, *Art in advertising* (c.1930) · *The Advertising World* (Feb 1914) · m. cert. (1930) · d. cert.
Likenesses photograph, repro. in *Advertising World*, 225
Wealth at death £112,612 15s. 1d.: probate, 26 Jan 1939, *CGPLA Eng. & Wales*

Higham, Thomas (1795–1844), landscape engraver and draughtsman, was baptized on 14 February 1795 at Bramfield, Suffolk, the son of Thomas Higham, who outlived him, and his wife, Charlotte. He was apprenticed to John Greig, an antiquary and topographical engraver. His earliest engravings, which include plates for James Storer's *Antiquarian Itinerary* (1815), demonstrate the considerable skill and refinement characteristic of his mature work. He was an accomplished draughtsman; several engravings of Suffolk sites after his designs appeared in Storer's *Ancient Reliques* (1812–13), and he drew and engraved plates for the *Stationers' Almanack* from c.1826 to 1839. In the late 1820s he began using steel plates, and his 'New London Bridge' and 'Suspension Bridge over the Thames at Hammersmith' of 1828 for James Elmes's *Metropolitan Improvements* (1827–32) are some of his earliest engravings using the medium.

For the remainder of his career Higham contributed to a large number of publications, typically only producing one or two engravings for each. His engravings after

J. M. W. Turner are among his finest work; the engraver James Charles Armytage deemed his 'Rouen Cathedral' from the *Rivers of France* 'one of the plates of the century' (Huish). Higham exhibited at the Society of British Artists in 1825, 1826, and 1830, and was an auditor of the Artists' Annuity Fund. It is possible that he was the Thomas Higham who married Hannah Briers at St Luke's, Old Street, on 10 July 1825 but he was widowed and lived with his younger sister Martha at 9 Upper Brunswick Terrace, Islington, where he died on 3 January 1844.

        GILLIAN FORRESTER

Sources B. Hunnisett, *An illustrated dictionary of British steel engravers*, new edn (1989), 67–8 · B. Hunnisett, *Steel engraved book illustration in England* (1980), 99, 121 · B. Hunnisett, *Engraved on steel: the history of picture production using steel plates* (1998), 159 · J. Johnson, ed., *Works exhibited at the Royal Society of British Artists, 1824–1893, and the New English Art Club, 1888–1917*, 2 vols. (1975), 227 · J. Pye, *Patronage of British art: an historical sketch* (1845), 393 · M. Huish, *The Seine and the Loire* (1895), introduction · A. Hayden, *Chats on old prints* (1909), 39, 224 · d. cert. · census returns, 1841 · admon., PRO, PROB 6/220, fol. 267r · parish register, Bramfield, Suffolk, 14 Feb 1795 [baptism] · IGI

Highmore, Anthony (1718–1799). *See under* Highmore, Joseph (1692–1780).

Highmore, Anthony (1758/9–1829), legal writer, was born in London, the son of Anthony *Highmore (1718–1799) [see under Highmore, Joseph], draughtsman, and grandson of Joseph *Highmore, the painter. From 1766 he was educated at a school in Greenwich, and he commenced practice as a solicitor in 1783. Although he worked for over forty years as a solicitor, Highmore, a devout Christian, devoted much of his spare time to the management of charitable concerns and served as secretary to the London Lying-In Hospital. In addition he also moved in radical parliamentary circles; in particular Highmore was an intimate friend of Granville Sharp, and was active in opposition to the slave trade.

Besides contributing to the *Gentleman's Magazine*, Highmore also wrote a number of works on legal and social issues. His earliest was a digest of the law relating to the use of bail in civil and criminal cases (1783). *A Succinct View of the History of Mortmain* appeared in 1787, and explored its charitable uses. This was judged to be a pioneering work: a contemporary referred to 'his little book, but great work' (*GM*, 181). Early in the following decade Highmore published his *Reflections* (1791) on the law of libel. In this he was an ally of Charles James Fox who, the following year, gave the issue greater prominence when he persuaded the Commons to pass a bill giving juries full powers in legal actions. In 1793 Highmore brought out *Addenda to the Law of Charitable Uses*, and also an account of the laws relating to the excise.

During the alarm created by the threatened French invasion Highmore became a member of the Honourable Artillery Company, and in 1804 he wrote a history of the company, at the suggestion of its court of assistants. In 1808 a bill was brought before parliament to prevent the spreading of smallpox. This stipulated that no medical practitioner was to inoculate for the smallpox within 3 miles of any town, and provisions were made for isolating smallpox patients. Highmore, though a believer in vaccination, wrote a pamphlet opposing the terms of the bill, as amended by the Commons, in 1808.

Among Highmore's legal treatises was one on the law of lunacy (1807), a pocket book for attorneys and solicitors (1814), and a guide to the executors of wills and codicils on how to keep accounts and administer the estates of the deceased (1815). He also wrote further works about charities. *Pietas Londinensis* (1810) was a history of public charities in and near London; a second volume, *Philanthropia Metropolitana* (1822), gave an account of the charitable institutions established in London between 1810 and 1822. Highmore died at Dulwich, Surrey, on 19 July 1829, in his seventy-first year.

FRANCIS WATT, *rev.* ROBERT BROWN

Sources GM, 1st ser., 99/2 (1829), 180–83 · [J. Watkins and F. Shoberl], *A biographical dictionary of the living authors of Great Britain and Ireland* (1816)
Archives Sandon Hall, Staffordshire, Harrowby Manuscript Trust, corresp. with R. Ryder
Likenesses J. Highmore, National Gallery of Victoria, Melbourne, Australia

Highmore, Joseph (1692–1780), painter, was born on 13 June 1692 in the parish of St James Garlickhythe in the City of London, the third son of Edward Highmore, a coal merchant, and his wife, Maria, *née* Tull. From 1702 to 1704 he attended Merchant Taylors' School in London, and from 1707 trained as a lawyer, during which time, if his contemporary George Vertue is to be believed, he acquired a self-confident, perhaps even opinionated manner; 'the Natural practice of the law gives most men a good Voluable speech with a Stedfast assurance of which he has benefited in that particular. & turns it well to his advantage' (Vertue, *Note books*, 3.29). His schooling and clerkship would have provided him with a good solid education. That he was proficient in Latin, for example, is evident from his prose translation of Isaac Hawkins Browne's poem *De animi immortalitate* (1766). Highmore was, however, determined to pursue a career as an artist, no doubt in emulation of his uncle **Thomas Highmore** (1660–1720), the serjeant-painter. Thomas Highmore was born in London on 22 June 1660, one of the two sons of Abraham Highmore and the cousin of Nathaniel *Highmore, MD. He was apprenticed to Leonard Cotes for seven years in 1674, and became serjeant-painter in April 1703. In 1689 he took on as an apprentice his kinsman Sir James Thornhill, who succeeded him in the office of serjeant-painter. Thomas Highmore died in London on 8 March 1720. Curiously, Joseph was not apprenticed to his uncle Thomas (indeed he never trained directly under a master), but during his clerkship he attended the anatomical lectures of William Cheselden and Sir Godfrey Kneller's drawing academy. One of his earliest known portraits, of the ivory carver David le Marchand (*c*.1723; NPG), reveals Highmore's debt to Kneller at his most vivacious. In 1715, freed from the law, he established a portrait-painting practice, and on 28 May 1716 he married Susanna Hiller (1689/90–1750) [*see* Highmore, Susanna], with whom he

Joseph Highmore (1692–1780), self-portrait, *c*.1725

had two children, Anthony [*see below*] and Susanna. In 1724 the Highmores moved from the parish of St Swithin in the City of London to a house on the north side of the more affluent Lincoln's Inn Fields, an indication of Highmore's professional success and his social aspirations. From 1725 he is listed as a member of the masonic lodge of the Swan, Greenwich, whose master was the great English baroque artist Sir James Thornhill; this shows a certain professional canniness on Highmore's part. As he appears to have had little interest in societies or clubs, his association with the freemasons (he was junior grand warden of the grand lodge in 1727 and a regular attendee throughout the 1730s) cannot be underestimated.

Highmore made two foreign excursions, first in 1732 to the Low Countries, and second in 1734 to Paris, where he made the acquaintance of artists associated with the Académie Royale. During both journeys he made a particular study of the work of Sir Peter Paul Rubens, an artist he greatly admired and whom, in technique at least, he attempted to emulate. Highmore's clientele came predominantly from the wealthy gentry or professional middle classes. Unusually among artists of the period, he did not use students or drapery painters; as he proudly wrote: 'I do every thing my self, which I believe is not true of one painter in England besides' (letter to James Harris, 23 March 1741, Hants. RO, 9M73/G482/10). This explains why full-length portraits by Highmore are rare (a notable exception being *The Family of Sir Lancelot Lee*, 1736; Wolverhampton Art Gallery) and why he was particularly known during his lifetime for small-scale group portraits or 'conversations'. Highmore's posthumous reputation suffered until the latter half of the twentieth century due to the misattribution of his work, particularly the twelve canvasses of 1743–4 illustrating scenes from Samuel Richardson's novel *Pamela* (1740–41) (Tate collection, FM Cam., and the National Gallery of Victoria, Australia) and his group portrait *Mr Oldham and his Guests* (c.1735–45; Tate collection). The latter was from at least 1828 until 1949 ascribed to William Hogarth. The *Pamela* series was created to capitalize on the extraordinary popularity of Richardson's novel through the sale of engravings and by publicizing the display of the originals in Highmore's studio. Afterwards Highmore became an intimate of Richardson, whose portrait he painted several times and through whom he was recommended to Dr Edward Young, whose portrait he executed in 1754. *Mr Oldham* is in style and composition unique among works by Highmore's contemporaries, and should therefore be viewed as one of the most innovative portraits of the early Georgian period.

Highmore was a rather aloof figure among his professional peers, preferring instead the company of literary men such as Richardson, Hawkins Browne, James Harris, John Hawkesworth, and William Duncombe. In 1746 he presented the history painting *Hagar and Ishmael* to the Foundling Hospital in London and was subsequently made a governor. In 1761 he retired to Canterbury with his daughter and son-in-law, the Revd John Duncombe. Portraits from this period are rare, but throughout his retirement Highmore published books and articles on a variety of subjects. These include *Observations on a pamphlet entitled 'Christianity not founded on argument'* (1765), *Essays, Moral, Religious, and Miscellaneous* (1766), and a discourse on colouring published in the *Gentleman's Magazine* (1778). This last highlights what Highmore perceives as the inadequate technical training offered at the newly established Royal Academy. In other published work he provocatively defends his idol Rubens against what he describes as 'the prejudice of connoisseurship' (Highmore, 'Remarks', 353). Certainly these late publications reveal that Highmore's confidence in stating his own opinions and inclination for lively debate, attributes that Vertue had observed early in his career, remained with him throughout his life. Highmore died in Canterbury on 3 March 1780 and was buried in the cathedral.

Anthony Highmore (1718–1799), draughtsman, was born on 26 September 1718 in the parish of St Swithin, London. He was a pupil under his father, with whom he worked until about 1755. On 23 April 1740 he married at Old Brampton, Derby, Anna Maria, the daughter of the Revd Seth Ellis, with whom he had fifteen children, one of whom was the legal writer Anthony *Highmore, who was born in London. Highmore occasionally painted portraits and topographical views. His five views of Hampton Court were engraved by J. Tinney. In 1755 he painted a copy of a portrait by Sir Godfrey Kneller of William III for the Mansion House, York. After his father retired to Canterbury in 1761, Highmore gave up painting and turned his attention to the study of theology. He died in Canterbury on 3 October 1799 in his eighty-second year.

JACQUELINE RIDING

Sources J. Duncombe, 'Memoirs of the late Joseph Highmore', *GM*, 1st ser., 50 (1780), 176–9 · A. S. Lewis, 'Joseph Highmore', PhD diss., Harvard U., 1975 [3 vols.] · W. Mild, *Joseph Highmore of Holborn Row* (1990) · J. Highmore, 'Remarks on some passages in Mr Webb's "Enquiry into the beauties of 'Painting'"', *GM*, 1st ser., 36 (1766), 353–6 · J. Highmore, letter to James Harris, 23 March 1741, Hants. RO, 9M73/G482/10 · J. Highmore, 'A prose translation of Mr Browne's Latin poem, "De animi immortalitate"', *Essays, moral, religious and miscellaneous*, 2 vols. (1766), 2.109–73 · J. Highmore, 'On colouring', *GM*, 1st ser., 48 (1778), 526–7 · W. J. Songhurst, 'The minutes of the grand lodge of freemasons of England, Quator Coronati Lodge No 2076, X (1913) 1723–1739', *Transactions of the Quator Coronati Lodge no. 2076*, 10 (1913) · E. Johnstone, 'Joseph Highmore's Paris journal, 1734', *Walpole Society*, 42 (1970), 61–104 · F. Antal, 'Mr Oldham and his guests by Highmore', *Burlington Magazine*, 91 (May 1949), 128–32 · Mrs E. P. Hart, ed., *Merchant Taylors' School register, 1561–1934*, 2 vols. (1936) · C. J. Robinson, ed., *A register of the scholars admitted into Merchant Taylors' School, from AD 1562 to 1874*, 2 (1883) · *GM*, 1st ser., 69 (1799), 905 · will, PRO, PROB 11/1062, fol. 146 · *DNB* · *Waterhouse, 18c painters*
Archives Tate collection, notebook and letter · Tate collection, manuscript of Paris journal | Hants. RO, letters to James Harris, 9M73/G482/1–18
Likenesses J. Highmore, self-portrait, oils, c.1725, National Gallery of Victoria, Melbourne [*see illus.*] · J. Highmore, self-portrait, oils, c.1735–1745, Tate collection; repro. in Antal, 'Mr Oldham and his guests' · line engraving, BM, NPG
Wealth at death £550; shares in East India Company; majority of estate to son: will, PRO, PROB 11/1062/146, 5 August 1772, proved 22 March 1780

Highmore, Nathaniel (1613–1685), chemical physician and anatomist, was born on 6 February 1613 at Fordingbridge, Hampshire, the elder son of Nathaniel Highmore, rector of Purse Caundle, a village near Sherborne in Dorset. Educated at Sherborne School and Trinity College, Oxford, Highmore graduated BA (1635) and MA (1638) with the aid of a scholarship at Trinity, which he then relinquished in favour of his younger brother, Richard. On 30 December 1640 he married Elizabeth, daughter of Richard *Haydock, a prominent physician of Salisbury, with whom he probably worked as an assistant. Highmore returned to Oxford, where he was granted his BM in July 1641. Though he intended to proceed formally with medical studies for his doctorate, with the onset of civil war in 1642 Highmore became part of a scientific circle at Trinity College, Oxford, led by William Harvey, then physician to Charles I, and George Bathurst. In 1643 Highmore received his DM at Oxford under the so-called 'Caroline creations' of royal command for those who had favourably served the king at the battle of Edge Hill and its aftermath. While Highmore could indeed be described as a moderate royalist, he may have acquired the DM for attending to Prince Charles during a spell of measles in November 1642, though this remains uncertain.

The Trinity experiments on the embryonic development of chicks drew in Highmore, whose friendship and collaboration with Harvey was underlined in the dedication to him, written in 1650, of his *Corporis humani disquisitio anatomica* (1651), in which Highmore wrote: 'It is now eight years since we first had it in mind to expose our careful studies … to the judgement of the public' (A1r– v). The broad purpose of the textbook was to redesign physiology and anatomy in the direction of Harvey's theory of the circulation of the blood. The frontispiece incorporating an allegorical drawing of the new theory emphasized this. Agreeing with Harvey that the heart's sustaining relationship to the body was analogous to the sun in the wider macrocosm, Highmore explicitly defined the origin and function of circulation beyond Harvey's more circumspect treatment. Whereas Harvey, in his *Exercitationes de generatione animalium* (1651), focused on the unitary and vital nature of blood, Highmore advanced a particulate view of the blood that saw its carrying heat and nutrition and whose nature entailed constant motion. A similar shift is evident in Highmore's analysis of the pulmonary transit. Using Harvey's arguments to establish pulmonary circulation he considered the possible functions of the pulmonary vein to challenge the beliefs of those like Galen and Fernel who thought it sent air to the heart. Highmore believed that experiment showed that the pulmonary vessels contained blood and he used the techniques of Vesalius and Harvey to disprove the generation of vital spirits from the air. In describing blood as an oily substance Highmore was accepting that chemical distillation provided a surer analysis of its composition. Corpuscular philosophy also informed his understanding of respiratory functions. Believing that heat was innate in the heart and thus conveyed to the blood, respiration expelled excess heat particles residing in the blood. Moreover, the motion of the lungs helped the passage of blood from the right to the left ventricle, as experiment again proved.

In Highmore's *History of Generation* of 1651 corpuscularianism was extended to embrace atomism and it is noteworthy that the work contains the first published dedication to Robert Boyle, who was to become arguably the leading corpuscularian of his generation. Highmore had set up a practice in 1645 in Sherborne, just a short distance from Stalbridge where the young Boyle had recently returned from the continent to live on an estate purchased by his late father, the earl of Cork. A shared anatomical and medical outlook no doubt prompted Highmore to point to Boyle as 'both a pattern and wonder to our Nobility and Gentry' (N. Highmore, *History of Generation*, 1651, 3). Unlike Boyle, who was particularly reticent in using the term 'atomism' in this period because of its atheistic association with Epicurean thought, Highmore took it as 'an unquestionable law of Nature, (if, prejudice laid aside, right reason takes her place) that all actions and motions are performed by Atomes, or small bodies, moving after a different manner, proportionable to their several figures' (ibid., 115). Bearing a strong resemblance to the atomism of Gassendi, which in turn powerfully influenced Boyle, Highmore's general analysis of atoms is embedded within a broader discussion critical of supposed cure of wounds by sympathetic action at a distance, which instead points to atomic effluvia as sufficient explanation. Refuting the embryological theories of Harvey's friend Kenelm Digby, Highmore uses atoms and the circulation of the blood to explain the nature of nutrition and genetic continuity.

In any rounded assessment of Highmore's work it should be remembered that there are clear limits to Highmore's modernism. A great deal of Highmore's physiology in his *Disquisitio*, for example, understandably reflects ancient and medieval theory and practice, as it did with many of his corpuscularian contemporaries. Attempting to account for the assemblage of the dissociated atoms of the conceptus and the orderly development of the embryo in his *De generatione* led Highmore to argue for the pre-existence of embryonic parts, an idea as ancient as the atomistic concept of matter upon which his analysis was based. Highmore's 'seminal atoms' are transmuted into 'substantial formes', some of which are endowed by a directing force with an activating and vivifying principle. Also instructive is Highmore's criticism of Thomas Willis's views on hysteria and hypochondria, *Exercitationes duae … de passione hysterica … de affectionae hypochondriaca* (1660), which explained hysteria as the consequence of a disturbed pulmonary circulation. On this occasion Willis's response in *Pathologiae cerebri* (1677), that the nervous system was the arena of explanation, effectively refuted Highmore's attack.

Highmore became a JP and county treasurer in Dorset. He had a practice in Sherborne for forty years, where he was actively involved in church affairs and served for a lengthy period as a governor of Sherborne School and the town's almshouse. He died there on 21 March 1685, and was buried on the south side of the chancel of Purse Caundle church. His wife survived him. In his will Highmore endowed an exhibition to Oxford from Sherborne School, and left his tables of the muscles to the physic school at Oxford. MALCOLM OSTER

Sources R. G. Frank, *Harvey and the Oxford physiologists* (1980) · C. Webster, *The great instauration: science, medicine and reform, 1626–1660* (1975) · A. G. Debus, ed., *Medicine in seventeenth century England: a symposium held … in honor of C. D. O'Malley* [Berkeley 1974] (1974) · J. E. Gordon, 'Nathaniel Highmore, physician and anatomist: 1613–1685', *The Practitioner*, 196 (1966), 851–8 · *DSB* · *DNB*

Archives BL, corresp. and papers, Sloane MSS 534–582, 1053, *passim*

Likenesses oils, c.1660–1665, NPG · A. Blooteling, line engraving, 1677, BM, NPG

Highmore [*née* Hiller], **Susanna** (1689/90–1750), poet, was the daughter of Anthony Hiller of Effingham, Surrey (*d.* 1725), and his wife, who died in 1731. On 28 May 1716 Susanna, 'an heiress', married Joseph *Highmore (1692–1780), portrait painter. They lived in the parish of St Swithin London Stone until 1724 when, Highmore's 'reputation and business increasing', they moved to Lincoln's Inn Fields (*GM*, 1780, 177). Their friends included Isaac Watts, James Foster, James Harris, Isaac Hawkins Browne, William Duncombe, and Samuel Richardson. Susanna Highmore had two children, Anthony (1718–1799) and Susanna (1725–1812), later Susanna *Duncombe, with whom she is portrayed in a picture painted by her husband c.1727. Here she embodies elegance and domestic charm. Both children were educated at home according to Locke's principles; her daughter, imitating her mother, 'wrote verses when yet a child' (Freeman). Towards the end of Highmore's life Richardson described her as an indulgent and conscientious parent (Barbauld, 2.215); her daughter, a

Susanna Highmore (1689/90–1750), by Joseph Highmore, c.1727 [with her children, Susanna (later Susanna Duncombe) and Anthony]

poet and illustrator, wrote of theirs as a close-knit, literature-loving family (Richardson MSS).

Religious conviction led the conventionally modest Highmore to write publicly. In 1748 her obituary of Isaac Watts was published anonymously; its contents show an appreciation of Watts as an intellectual, and a respect for moderation and religious tolerance. Her sonnet 'A Calvinistical Reflection' (published in the Gentleman's Magazine, 19, 1749, 565) is a poised, pained, and ironic critique of Calvinist dogma. Two brief, witty occasional poems were later published by John Nichols: a couplet praising Hawkins Browne, 'On Reading the Essay on Satire, Occasioned by Mr Pope's Death' (June 1745); and 'On Seeing a Gate Carried by Two Men through Lincoln's Inn Fields, 1743', an extempore pastiche of Pope's 'On an Old Gate Erected in Chiswick Gardens' (which Highmore must have seen in manuscript). The control and fluency demonstrated in her small literary output suggest that she wrote much more. Her husband noted the existence of 'papers written by the deceased, at different times, and on different occasions, and left on purpose for my perusal and comfort' but these have been lost (GM, 1816, 505–6). Highmore's proficient sketch of her daughter remains in the Highmore scrapbook.

Highmore died, aged sixty, on 18 November 1750, 'after a few Days Illness', and was buried the same day at St Andrew's, Holborn. ELSPETH KNIGHTS

Sources W. Mild, Joseph Highmore of Holborn Row (Pennsylvania, 1990) · GM, 1st ser., 19 (1749), 327 · GM, 1st ser., 50 (1780), 176–9 · GM, 1st ser., 86/1 (1816), 10–11, 505–6 · J. Nichols, ed., A select collection of poems, 8 (1782), 61 · The correspondence of Samuel Richardson, ed. A. L. Barbauld, 6 vols. (1804), vol. 2, pp. 209–19, 225–37 · V&A NAL, Forster Library, Richardson papers, XV2, fol. 12 · C. R. Beard, 'Highmore scrapbook', The Connoisseur, 93 (1934), 290–96 · R. Freeman, Kentish poets: a series of writers in poetry etc. (1821), 2.342 · Read's Weekly Journal, or, British Gazetier, 1370 (24 Nov 1750), 3 · transcripts of parish registers of Effingham, Surrey, burials, 5 Feb 1725, 24 Aug 1731, Society of Genealogists, London [parents] · parish register, St Andrew's, Holborn, 18 Nov 1750 [burial] · parish register, Little Bookham, 28 May 1716 [marriage]
Likenesses J. Highmore, group portrait, oils, c.1727, Art Gallery of South Australia, Adelaide [see illus.]

Highmore, Thomas (1660–1720). *See under* Highmore, Joseph (1692–1780).

Highton, Henry (1816–1874), schoolmaster and experimenter in telegraphy, was born at Leicester on 19 January 1816, the eldest son of Henry Highton of that town. He was educated at Rugby School under Thomas Arnold, with whom he remained friendly for a number of years afterwards. He matriculated at Queen's College, Oxford, on 13 March 1834 and graduated BA, with a first class in classics, in 1837. He proceeded MA in 1840 and was Michel fellow of his college in 1840–41. In the same year he began tutoring the mathematician Henry Smith (1826–1883).

On 16 June 1841 Highton married Elizabeth, the daughter of James *Paxton (1786–1860). In the same year he was appointed assistant master at Rugby School. While at Rugby, in 1842, Highton had printed a letter addressed to Sir Moses Montefiore which offered some advice as to the recovery of the Israeli 'nationality lost for 1800 years'. In 1849 he published some sermons and, in 1851, a Catechism of the Second Advent. In 1859 he moved to Cheltenham College as principal. He served in that office until 1862, in which year he published a revised translation of the New Testament. In 1863 he published a letter to the lord bishop of London criticizing the Athanasian creed. His last theological work was Dean Stanley and Saint Socrates, the ethics of the philosopher and the philosophy of the divine (1873), an attack on Arthur Stanley (1815–1881) for his 'consistent opposition to evangelical truth'. In the same year Highton published a translation of some of Victor Hugo's poems.

In addition to his interests in education and theology Highton conducted a number of practical experiments in the application of electricity to telegraphy. In the mid-1840s he purchased the rights to exclusive use of a gold leaf instrument which he adapted for telegraphic purposes (it was used for a number of years in Baden). By the early 1870s he believed the sensitivity of the instrument would enable it to allow transatlantic communication along uninsulated underwater wires, a development which would greatly cut the cost of cable laying then being undertaken, allowing 'the poor emigrant to communicate with his family … and put an end to the necessarily almost prohibitory rates which at present prevail' (Journal of the Society of Arts, 20, 1872, 509). His 1872 paper on the subject was well received, and the Society of Arts presented him with their silver medal for it. However, Highton's experiments had been largely conducted in fresh water and by 1873 he had to concede that such a system would not work in a saline medium. He instead began campaigning for the adoption of a cheap method of insulation he had developed using vegetable tar and lead oxides.

In improving his gold leaf instrument for telegraphic purposes Highton had also done research into galvanism and the improvement of batteries. He produced several new types of battery, one of which (a type of zinc carbon battery) found much favour among electroplaters. His patents in the field were purchased about 1873 and the Highton Battery Company set up to work them. He also patented an artificial stone which for some years was popular for paving and building purposes.

Highton spent his last years in Putney, London. He died at his home there, The Cedars, on 21 December 1874; he was survived by his wife.

R. E. ANDERSON, *rev.* PETER OSBORNE

Sources Foster, *Alum. Oxon.* · *Rugby School register* · *The Times* (24 Dec 1874) · H. Highton, 'Telegraphy without insulation: a cheap means of international communication', *Journal of the Society of Arts*, 20 (1871–2), 506–10 · H. Highton, 'Galvanic batteries', *Journal of the Society of Arts*, 21 (1872–3), 62–6 · H. Highton, 'Cheap telegraphy', *Journal of the Society of Arts*, 21 (1872–3), 486 [letter] · Boase, *Mod. Eng. biog.* · *CGPLA Eng. & Wales* (1875) · GM, 2nd ser., 16 (1841), 201

Wealth at death under £4000: administration with will, 10 April 1875, *CGPLA Eng. & Wales*

Higinbotham, George (1826–1892), politician and judge in Australia, was the sixth son of Henry T. Higinbotham, a merchant of Dublin, whose family had left Holland with William III, and Sarah, the daughter of Joseph Wilson, a United States citizen of Scottish descent, formerly American consul in Dublin. He was born in Dublin on 19 April 1826, and educated at the Royal School, Dungannon, whence he went to Trinity College, Dublin, in 1844; he graduated BA in 1848 and MA in 1853. Early in 1847 he went to London, and, while reading for the bar, became a reporter on the *Morning Chronicle*; he entered Lincoln's Inn in 1848, was called to the bar in 1853, and within a few months sailed for Victoria, where the discovery of gold in 1851 had initiated rapid growth.

In Victoria, Higinbotham again combined the law and journalism; he was admitted to the local bar in March 1854, and on 30 September that year married Margaret Foreman (1835/6–1910), who was born in Kent. In August 1856 he became editor of *The Argus*, at that time the most influential newspaper in Australia. As Victorians debated the forms of the limited self-government conferred in 1855, Higinbotham pressed for enlargement of the franchise. In a debate with the proprietor, conducted in the columns of his newspaper, he championed the rapid democratization of colonial politics. In 1859 he resigned the editorship and returned to the bar.

In May 1861 Higinbotham entered political life as member for Brighton in the legislative assembly, describing himself as an independent liberal. In 1862 he lost his seat, but the following year was again elected for the same place. In June 1863 he became attorney-general in Sir James McCulloch's reform ministry, and a leading figure

George Higinbotham (1826–1892), by Batchelder & O'Neill, in or before 1863

in its contest with the legislative council, the unrepresentative upper house of the Victorian legislature. The contest began when the ministry tacked tariff measures onto an appropriation bill and the legislative council refused to pass the legislation. Higinbotham's stratagem for obtaining supply embroiled Governor Darling, who was recalled by the Colonial Office in 1866. The assembly's vote of a pension to Darling's wife in the same year, and the council's rejection of the appropriation bill containing it, extended the parliamentary deadlock until 1868, when the ministry resigned in protest against the failure of the new governor to recommend the grant to parliament.

Higinbotham's resentment of imperial interference hardened into a conviction that the colony possessed full rights of responsible government over its internal affairs, expressed in resolutions he introduced into the assembly in 1869. While critical of party organization and all other forms of collective politics that diminished the autonomy of the individual, his denunciation of what he called 'the wealthy lower orders' (*The Argus*, 24 Oct 1864) who blocked popular aspirations elevated him to heroic status in the liberal pantheon. Meanwhile in 1865 he had consolidated the statutes of Victoria, as he was to do again in 1890, and received the thanks of both houses of parliament.

Higinbotham's other principal concern at this time was educational reform. The colony had maintained a dual system of subsidies for denominational schools and limited provision of state schools. As chairman of a royal commission established in 1866, Higinbotham became convinced that the state must take full responsibility for education and withdraw aid to denominational schools, but Anglican and Roman Catholic opposition temporarily frustrated his efforts to establish a comprehensive system of state schools teaching 'common Christianity' but not sectarian doctrine. Believing that it had compromised the principles he had championed, Higinbotham resigned from the ministry in 1869 and lost his seat in parliament in 1871, though the following year it passed the act for secular education that he had advocated. He was re-elected in 1874, but in January 1876, finding himself unable to support Sir Graham Berry's ministry, which was engaged in a struggle with the legislative council on the questions of land tax and payment of members, he resigned his seat; he sympathized with the spirit which animated Berry, but disapproved his methods as subversive of parliamentary government.

Higinbotham now remained aloof from active politics, and in July 1880 was appointed a puisne judge of the supreme court of Victoria. In September 1886, on the retirement of Sir William Stawell, he became chief justice of the colony. His independence and his peculiar view of the position of a colonial government are shown by his refusal to accept a knighthood and by his intimation to the imperial government that if he were appointed to administer the government during the absence of the governor he would cease to refer any matters of local concern to the secretary of state. His minority judgment in the case Toy v. Musgrove in 1888, that the Victorian government had the right to restrict a Chinese immigrant from the British colony of Hong Kong, pressed claims for colonial sovereignty to new limits, and came to be regarded as a landmark of Australian constitutional history.

Higinbotham refused to accept the notion that a person who entered 'the kingdom of judicial heaven is bound to become a political eunuch' (Victorian parliamentary debates, 19 May 1869). His address on Science and Religion (1883), at a time of keen religious controversy, struck an anti-clerical note while it insisted on the need to 'think with fearless freedom and yet believe'. He was an early advocate of women's franchise. During 1890 he created much indignation by subscribing to the funds of the strikers in that year's great strike. He died of heart failure at his residence in Murphy Street, South Yarra, Melbourne, on 31 December 1892, and was buried privately in the Brighton cemetery on 1 January 1893.

The violence of Higinbotham's political utterances contrasted strangely with the charm and amiability of his private life; those who condemned his political views were strongly attached to him personally. His oratorical power was of a high order, and his intellectual attainments placed him in the forefront of his contemporaries in Victoria. He was independent and radical in his political views, a substantial charitable benefactor, broad-minded, and unconventional in private life. He was small in stature but strong and athletic. He left two sons and three daughters, including Edith, the wife of Professor Edward Ellis Morris, his first biographer.   STUART MACINTYRE

Sources E. E. Morris, *A memoir of George Higinbotham: an Australian politician and chief justice of Victoria* (1895) · G. M. Dow, *George Higinbotham: church and state* (1964) · S. Macintyre, *A colonial liberalism: the lost world of three Victorian visionaries* (1991) · *AusDB* · *The Australasian* (7 Jan 1893) · *The Australasian* (14 Jan 1893) · m. cert. · *The Argus* [Melbourne] (1 Jan 1893)
Archives State Library of Victoria, Melbourne
Likenesses Batchelder & O'Neill, photograph, in or before 1863, State Library of Victoria [*see illus.*] · L. B. Hall, oils, 1895, Supreme Court of Victoria, Melbourne · photographs, repro. in Morris, *Memoir of George Higinbotham* · photographs, repro. in Dow, *George Higinbotham*
Wealth at death £17,500: *Australasian* (4 Feb 1893)

Higson, John (1825–1871), topographer, was born on 25 July 1825 at Whitely Farm, Gorton, Lancashire, the son of Daniel and Letitia Higson. He lived from c.1845 to c.1865 at Droylsden, where he was employed for almost twenty years as cashier at the Victoria spinning mills and subsequently at the Springhead Cotton-spinning Company. He was an enthusiastic supporter of the Droylsden Mechanics' Institute, and an active church worker for many years. He married Elizabeth Caroline Green on 6 November 1848; they had six sons and two daughters.

To a great extent self-taught, Higson was 'a tireless inquirer' into the history of Droylsden and surrounding areas, and he spent many years gathering material for his published works, which included *The Gorton Historical Recorder* (1852) and *Historical and Descriptive Notices of Droylsden* (1852). He and John Owen rescued and preserved from destruction the first parochial register of Newton Chapel (to 1666), and Higson himself was responsible for the safeguarding for posterity of much material relating to the history of the area. With some associates he also started an unsuccessful Droylsden paper on liberal conservative lines. He was a contributor to the *Ashton Reporter* from its foundation in 1855, under the signature H. At the time of his death on 13 December 1871 at his home, Lees, Ashton under Lyne, he was working on a glossary of Lancashire idioms. He was survived by his wife.   ALAN G. CROSBY

Sources H. T. Crofton, *A history of Newton Chapelry in the ancient parish of Manchester*, Chetham Society, new ser., 52 (1904) [incl. biographical note] · R. Speake and F. R. Witty, *A history of Droylesden* (1953) · *Ashton Reporter* (16 Dec 1871), 8 · *CGPLA Eng. & Wales* (1872) · *DNB* · parish register (baptism), Manchester, Manchester collegiate church, 30 Oct 1825
Wealth at death under £800: probate, 13 Feb 1872, *CGPLA Eng. & Wales*

Hilary [Hilary of Orléans, Hilary of Le Ronceray] (*fl.* **early 12th cent.**), poet and Augustinian canon, was first suggested to have been a native of England by Jean Mabillon in the late seventeenth century. However, there is little evidence for his English nationality. His major link with England is his short (162 line) Latin poem of the life of an English recluse, Eve of Winchester. However Eve spent her latter years at the monastery of St Laurent in Angers, and as Hilary too spent part of his career in Angers and seems to have known Eve's spiritual director, Herveus, his knowledge of her life need not imply any links with England; all the more so as the lines describing (in vague and entirely conventional terms) Eve's life in England take up less than one third of the poem.

Other poems by Hilary also have English subjects: two are addressed to an English boy or boys, another to an English nun, Rose, and a fourth to William de Anfonia, whom he describes as 'the honour of England'. Nevertheless these do not provide evidence of English nationality. The English boy was probably one of Hilary's students (another student, from Angers, is the subject of another poem); the nun Rose lived at the convent of Le Ronceray, near Angers, with which Hilary was connected; and nothing is known about the otherwise unrecorded William de Anfonia, other than the fact that Anfonia is almost certainly not an English place name. Hilary's *ludi* or theatrical works on St Nicholas, Lazarus, and Daniel (all of which include refrains and other lines in correct and idiomatic Old French) contain no references at all to English subjects; his surviving correspondence is addressed exclusively to colleagues in Angers, Orléans, and Nantes. When Hilary talks of travelling to France to study under Abelard, he merely means the Île-de-France (Abelard was teaching in Paris from the second decade of the twelfth century). There is, in fact, little doubt that he was a native of Angers or (more probably) Orléans. PETER DAMIAN-GRINT

Sources Hilarius Aurelianensis [Hilary], *Versus et ludi; epistolae; ludus Danielis Belouacensis*, ed. W. Bulst and M. L. Bulst-Thiele, Mittellateinische Studien und Texte, 16 (1989) · A. G. Rigg, *A history of Anglo-Latin literature, 1066–1422* (1992) · Hilarius [Hilary], *Versus et ludi*, ed. J. B. Fuller (1929) · *DNB* · N. M. Häring, 'Hilary of Orleans and his letter collection', *Studi Medievali*, 3rd ser., 14 (1973), 1069–122 · P. Marchegay, ed., *Cartularium b. Mariae Caritatis [Le Ronceray]*, Archives d'Anjou, 3 (1854)

Hilary (c.1110–1169), bishop of Chichester, was probably of low birth, since he is baldly described by the chronicle of Battle Abbey as 'a certain man called Hilary'. The date of his birth is unknown, but it is likely to have been about 1110. He may have come from the diocese of Salisbury, for he had a brother who was a canon of that cathedral, while his closest connections with any of his episcopal contemporaries were those with Jocelin de Bohun, bishop of Salisbury (d. 1184). If this were so, it might provide the explanation for how he came by such a rare name for twelfth-century England: about 1100 the Salisbury Cathedral Library was acquiring (as Teresa Webber showed) an exceptional holding of the works of St Hilary of Poitiers. He could have received his early schooling from a Salisbury canon or priest. The Hilary recorded by the *Cartae baronum* of 1166 as holding a virgate less than half a knight's fee of Bishop Jocelin, is likely to have been a relative of Bishop Hilary, given the rarity of the name and the practice of naming after an illustrious kinsman.

Like Jocelin de Bohun, Hilary rose to prominence as a protégé of Henry de Blois (d. 1171), bishop of Winchester and brother of King Stephen. By about 1140 he held the deanery of the college of secular canons at Christchurch, Twynham, Hampshire, and before he became a bishop he had made a name for himself as an advocate at the papal curia, at just the time that St Bernard of Clairvaux was complaining to Pope Eugenius III about the rising tide of lawsuits being drawn into Rome under the burgeoning system of canon law. Certainly Hilary's character and mind were such as would be associated with a clever lawyer. David Knowles described him as 'an extremely quick-witted, efficient, self-confident, voluble, somewhat shallow man, fully acquainted with the new canon law but not prepared to abide by principles to the end. His talents were great but he used them as an opportunist' (Knowles, 27). In his early years as a bishop he was much employed by Archbishop Theobald of Canterbury (d. 1161) as a legal assessor in cases which the archbishop heard as papal judge-delegate or as metropolitan.

The evidence of Hilary's career as bishop suggests the need to question Knowles's view that he was not guided by principles and was a mere opportunist. In 1147 he was Stephen's candidate for the see of York, following the deposition of William Fitzherbert (d. 1154), and though the pope chose to appoint the Cistercian Henry Murdac (d. 1153), he shortly afterwards advanced Hilary to Chichester, vacant since 1145. But despite the circumstances of his promotion, Hilary appears consistently in politics as a king's man, often in circumstances when his actions cannot be construed as response to pressure. He is the perfect example of how canonical expertise did not at all seem to preclude political royalism or Erastianism, almost as a principle. He was an emissary of King Stephen to the Council of Rheims in 1148, where he excused the king's attempt to prevent Archbishop Theobald's attendance, which elicited from Eugenius the response, 'we thought to have turned you into a son of the Roman Church, but we have created in you a sword and an arrow' (Mayr-Harting, 'Hilary', 212). Stephen subsequently granted Hilary the chapelry of Pevensey, Sussex, and made him queen's chaplain, so that 'he might be invited to her feasts' (*Reg. RAN*, 3.184).

Hilary must early have insinuated himself into the good graces of Henry of Anjou, who in his first year as Henry II appointed him to be sheriff of Sussex, a rare case of a bishop in this position (he held it again in 1160–62). He was with the king at the siege of Bridgnorth in Shropshire in 1155, where Hugh (I) de Mortimer was in rebellion; and in 1156 he visited certain shires as a royal itinerant justice. Thus he was heavily involved in Henry II's early peace initiatives after the anarchy of Stephen's reign. To give his rule sacral mystique Henry II lent weight to the efforts of Westminster Abbey to secure the canonization of Edward the Confessor; Hilary wrote one of the letters sent to Pope Alexander III pleading for the canonization, and he was a party to its announcement in Westminster Abbey in 1161. Consequently Hilary's enmity towards Becket in the archbishop's conflict with Henry II may be seen less in the light of a canonist compromising, than of a royalist consistently pursuing, his principles. On the unimpeachable testimony of William fitz Stephen, Hilary remarked at the

Council of Northampton (1164) that he wished the archbishop would become plain Thomas again, adding bluntly with reference to Becket's period as king's chancellor, 'those who disliked you then, side with the king against you now' (J. C. Robertson and J. B. Sheppard, *Materials for the History of Thomas Becket*, 7 vols., Rolls Series, 1875–85, 3.55). As often in these fraught times, issues of principles and personalities cannot easily be disentangled, and the personality clash between Hilary and Becket clearly went back some years. It probably dated from the Council of Colchester (1157) when Hilary argued—and lost—his suit before the king that Battle Abbey ought to be subject to the bishop of Chichester's jurisdiction. He was on losing ground, because Battle claimed exemption as a royal foundation; but royalism did not mean that a bishop would fail to champion his own rights as a diocesan. It was a basic instinct of every bishop of that time to seek to protect the privileges of his see. Thus it was not against his royalism that Hilary should have opposed the king at Colchester, and his opposition was quickly pardoned. But on that occasion Becket as chancellor had gratuitously embarrassed Hilary by implying publicly that he was a hypocrite. This action was apparently not forgiven.

As with others of his episcopal contemporaries, Hilary is shown by his charters, albeit with rather sparse evidence, to have been a businesslike administrator and pastor. Early in his episcopate, in 1148, he obtained the restitution of lands belonging to the church of Chichester from a certain William Burdard, from William d'Aubigny, earl of Arundel, and from John, count of Eu. Some of these alienations may have reflected the disturbed conditions of Stephen's reign, but the problem with Bexhill and the counts of Eu went back some sixty years. As diocesan he also set an early example in trying to create vicarages, that is, to ensure that a portion of the revenues of parish churches should be set aside for the priests who would reside and do the pastoral work. There is a particularly remarkable document of Hilary's which appears to insist on this point in the case of all the parish churches belonging to Lewes Priory in Sussex. Another fragment of evidence gives a momentary glimpse of Hilary as a patron of learning, making a donation to his cathedral library of one of the earliest manuscripts in England of Peter Lombard's *Sentences*, a crucial work of Parisian theology.

Although Hilary shows himself mainly in the roles of lawyer, politician, and administrator, he can be seen as in tune with an important religious movement of his time in transforming colleges of secular canons into houses of monks or Augustinian canons, the latter being communities of pastors with a quasi-monastic way of life. He assisted in such transformations at his old college of Twynham and at St Nicholas, Arundel; and he vigorously pursued the material interests of the Augustinian canons of Lanthony, Gloucestershire, far away from his own diocese, after the death in 1148 of their great patron, Bishop Robert de Bethune of Hereford. He wrote a pleasant letter to the canons, brisk but friendly, telling them not to get excited about such things. He and other friends of the deceased bishop would look after their affairs as if these were their own; but 'you should always be intent on carrying out the divine service as you are bound' (*Acta*, 100). Hilary himself died on 13 July 1169.

HENRY MAYR-HARTING

Sources H. Mayr-Harting, 'Hilary, bishop of Chichester (1147–1169) and Henry II', *EngHR*, 78 (1963), 209–24 · H. Mayr-Harting, *The bishops of Chichester, 1075–1207: biographical notes and problems* (1963) · H. Mayr-Harting, ed., *The acta of the bishops of Chichester, 1075–1207*, CYS, 56 (1964) · D. Knowles, *The episcopal colleagues of Archbishop Thomas Becket* (1951) · *The letters of John of Salisbury*, ed. and trans. H. E. Butler and W. J. Millor, rev. C. N. L. Brooke, 2 vols., OMT (1979–86) [Lat. orig. with parallel Eng. text] · E. Searle, ed., *The chronicle of Battle Abbey*, OMT (1980) · W. fitz Stephen, *Vita Sancti Thomae Cantuariensis Archiepiscopi*, ed. J. C. Robertson, 3 (1877) · T. Webber, *Scribes and scholars at Salisbury Cathedral, c.1075–1125* (1992) · N. R. Ker, ed., *Medieval libraries of Great Britain: a list of surviving books*, 2nd edn, Royal Historical Society Guides and Handbooks, 3 (1964), 51, 247 · AM Oxf., MS 1146

Hilbery, Sir (George) Malcolm (1883–1965), judge, was born on 14 July 1883 at 30 Hilldrop Crescent, Islington, London, the fourth child in the family of five sons (one of whom died in infancy) and one daughter of Henry Hilbery and his wife, Julia Moncaster Mitcheson. His father was a City of London solicitor who soon afterwards opened offices at 4 South Square, Gray's Inn, and was the founder of the firm of Henry Hilbery & Son.

Hilbery was educated at University College School and, without passing through a university, he became a member of Gray's Inn, around which his life was principally centred thereafter. In his bar examinations he obtained a certificate of honour, and he was also granted an Arden scholarship by his inn. After his call to the bar in 1907 his first chambers were at 6 Crown Office Row in the Temple. He devilled for Patrick Rose-Innes, afterwards a county court judge, and acquired a good miscellaneous practice. He was a keen yachtsman and kept a boat at Poole harbour. During the First World War he served as a Royal Naval Volunteer Reserve lieutenant in minesweepers.

After resuming his practice at the bar Hilbery was elected a bencher of Gray's Inn in 1927 and was appointed recorder of Margate in the same year. He took silk in 1928. With chambers now at 2 King's Bench Walk he had a large civil practice and enjoyed a high reputation in running-down cases. As a student at Gray's Inn he had been an assiduous member of the Debating Society, and was a good and elegant speaker. As an advocate he had tact and discrimination in adapting himself to his tribunals, combining authority with restraint. He achieved clarity of exposition based on thorough preparation, so that his points were perfectly thought out and lucidly marshalled.

When in January 1935 Hilbery was nominated commissioner of assize on the south-eastern circuit it was evident that he was approaching the end of his career at the bar, and, in pursuance of an act of parliament of that year authorizing the appointment of two additional judges to the King's Bench Division, he was one of those. On receiving the customary honour of a knighthood he took as the motto going with his coat of arms the words 'Nosce teipsum'.

Hilbery proved a reliable judge trying cases with ability and good sense, so that he was rarely reversed on appeal. He was a firm upholder of the common law. Although his practice had been chiefly in civil litigation and he had never appeared in a murder case at the bar, he became one of the ablest criminal judges. In 1948 he tried James Camb, the liner steward who was convicted of murdering a passenger by pushing her through a porthole into the sea.

Hilbery served as treasurer of Gray's Inn in the fatal year 1941 when the inn was devastated by bombardment and the hall, chapel, and library were burnt. After the fires he saw to it that the walls of the hall should be 'capped' to prevent deterioration, so that they could form the basis of the post-war rebuilding of the hall in replica.

In the affairs of the society Hilbery exercised great authority and influence as chairman of the house committee, while his detailed knowledge of gardening made him a valuable master of the walks and chairman of the garden committee. He used his knowledge of painting to guide the society in acquiring portraits. He himself was a discriminating collector of Dutch masters. After the rebuilding of the inn he made his home at 5 Gray's Inn Square. His book Duty and Art in Advocacy (1946) was presented to every student of the inn on their call to the bar. In 1954, when the duke of Gloucester was treasurer of Gray's Inn, Hilbery acted as his deputy. He was chairman of the Berkshire quarter sessions from 1946 to 1963; in 1959, when he was senior puisne judge of the Queen's Bench Division, he was nominated a privy councillor. He retired from the bench in 1962.

Hilbery was perhaps the last of the High Court judges in the grand manner. Tall and slender with a long, grave, impressive face, he consciously upheld the image of judicial dignity and impassivity whether in or out of the court. His height lent itself to the loftiness of manner which he cultivated in speech and demeanour. He prided himself on speaking little on the bench, and wrote down and carried about with him the words of the psalmist: 'I held my tongue and kept silence, yea, even from good words, but it was pain and grief to me.' Though he gave the external impression of reserve and solemnity, in private and in congenial company he was an interesting conversationalist on a wide range of topics, well versed in English literature and with a dry ironic wit.

Hilbery was for many years chairman of the board of governors of the Royal Masonic Hospital. He was a prominent member of the Royal Thames Yacht Club, and until late in life he continued to sail.

On 14 August 1915 he married Dorothy Violet Agnes, daughter of Lieutenant-Colonel St John Christophers, who survived him. They had one adopted son, Michael Seymour, who was in the Royal Navy and died when he went below in an attempt to rescue his shipmates after his 'Q' ship was torpedoed. Hilbery died at Great Rissington Hill, Great Rissington, Gloucestershire, on 18 September 1965.   F. H. COWPER, rev.

Sources The Times (20 Sept 1965) · The Times (24 Sept 1965) · Graya, Michaelmas term (1965) [magazine of Gray's Inn] · personal knowledge (1981) · private information (1981)
Likenesses W. Dring, c.1960, priv. coll. · portrait (after W. Dring), Gray's Inn, Pension Chamber · portrait (after W. Dring), Royal Masonic Hospital
Wealth at death £101,836: probate, 8 Nov 1965, CGPLA Eng. & Wales

Hild [St Hild, Hilda] (614–680), abbess of Strensall–Whitby, was the daughter of Hereric, a Deiran prince, and his wife, Breguswith. Hereric was a nephew of Eadwine of Northumbria and the family fortunes seem to have been determined by that relationship. Hereric's exile and murder were probably a consequence of the fall of Eadwine, while the marriage of his daughter, Hild's sister Hereswith, with the East Anglian prince (later king) Æthelhere, built upon links first established by her great-uncle.

Hild was baptized with Eadwine on Easter day (12 April) 627. According to Bede, she decided to enter the religious life while staying in East Anglia, influenced by the example of Hereswith, who had already withdrawn to the Frankish monastery of Chelles. Initially Hild herself also intended to enter Chelles, but was persuaded by Bishop Áedán to return to Northumbria, where she established herself in the monastery of Hartlepool, whose founder, Heiu, another disciple of Áedán, was apparently displaced to make way for her. Bede says, with somewhat suspicious and perhaps christologically determined symmetry, that Hild was thirty-three when she became a nun, and that she lived a further thirty-three years. Presumably, therefore, her entry into religion, perhaps as a widow, is to be dated to 647 and in any case it must have been before 651, when Áedán died.

The difficulty with this narrative is that Chelles can scarcely have been founded before 648, the earliest possible date of the marriage of its founder, the Anglo-Saxon Balthild, to the Merovingian king, Clovis II; indeed it is more likely to have been established c.660. Probably, then, Bede's informants at Whitby had made a mistake, confounding Chelles with its mother house of Jouarre (founded at some time between about 620 and 630) or with Faremoutiers (founded between about 615 and 620), the earliest double monastery in the Seine basin and also home to English princesses in the mid-seventh century. At all events, the story is evidence of Hild's early contacts with the Frankish kingdom of Neustria, contacts she almost certainly maintained.

Once established in the first royal nunnery in Northumbria, Hild remained in close touch with the Northumbrian religious élite and was visited 'assiduously' by Áedán and others. In 655, in accordance with a vow made by King Oswiu before his victory over the Mercians at the battle of the Winwæd, she received custody of *Ælfflæd, his daughter and her kinswoman, whom she placed in the monastery at Hartlepool. Two years later she founded 'Streanæshalch', on one of twelve estates of ten hides given by Oswiu to the church in further fulfilment of vows made before the Winwæd. The location of this monastery is problematic. There are good reasons to link it with both

Strensall, near York, and Whitby, and it has been argued that it comprised communities in both places.

Oswiu and his queen, Hild's relative Eanflæd, probably intended *ab initio* to establish Strensall–Whitby as their family monastery and mausoleum, sending their daughter Ælfflæd thither with Hild. In 664 the monastery was the scene of the famous synod, which determined that the Northumbrian church should henceforth follow the Roman Easter. Curiously, despite her links with the Roman mission, Hild appears to have taken the part of Bishop Áedán and the Lindisfarne community. Her attitude was perhaps determined not so much by the issues as by personal considerations, in particular her friendship with Áedán and a burgeoning hostility to the young Wilfrid, in 664 the spokesman for the supporters of the Roman observance.

Strensall–Whitby's growing importance was buttressed by the school which Hild established there, five of whose pupils became bishops: Bosa (York), Ætla (Dorchester), Oftfor (Worcester), John of Beverley (Hexham and York), and Wilfrid (York). After 669 the monastery developed close links with the school established by Archbishop Theodore at Canterbury; both Oftfor and John of Beverley went on to study there. Hild's alliance with Theodore was probably strengthened by a common hostility to Wilfrid, by then bishop of York. Certainly, it was a pupil of Hild's who was intruded into York when Wilfrid was expelled from that see in 678, and she joined Theodore in sending envoys to Rome to oppose the despoiled bishop in his ensuing appeal to the Holy See. Most probably, too, hers were the English messengers responsible for inciting Ebroin, the Neustrian mayor of the palace, to such hostility towards Wilfrid that he was forced to take an indirect route to Rome through Frisia and Austrasia.

Hild was praised by Bede for her skill as a counsellor of kings, princes, and the common people; for the rule which she established at Strensall–Whitby; and for her exemplary life. Although he stresses her qualities as a spiritual mother and as a servant of the Lord, he never describes her as a virgin, and it may be that she had been married before she entered religion.

In 674 Hild was afflicted with the disease which was eventually to kill her. According to Bede, her death in 680 was accompanied by wonders, including visions (seen by nuns at Whitby itself and at the dependent community at Hackness) of her soul being taken to heaven by angels. Such visions, which also characterized the deaths of holy women at the Frankish monastery of Faremoutiers, are an indication that Hild's cult began early. Her feast day, 17 November, was observed by the early eighth century, when it was added to the calendar of St Willibrord, the Northumbrian bishop of Utrecht. She appears in the *Old English Martyrology*, and it has been suggested that the entry in this ninth-century compilation bears traces of a lost early life. She scarcely features, however, in preconquest liturgical material, and her cult was probably very local.

Hild's relics were later translated from Whitby to Glastonbury, perhaps as early as the eighth century but more probably in the reign of Edmund I (*r.* 939–46). By the twelfth century they had been placed in a monument ('pyramid') to the left of the high altar at Glastonbury. There is some evidence, however, that Whitby, which continued to commemorate both deposition and translation (25 August), never relinquished its claim to her bones. Hild became patron saint of some fourteen medieval churches, eight of them in the North Riding of Yorkshire. St Hilda's College, Oxford, founded as St Hilda's Hall in 1893, is named after her.   ALAN THACKER

Sources Bede, *Hist. eccl.* · E. Stephanus, *The life of Bishop Wilfrid*, ed. and trans. B. Colgrave (1927) · H. A. Wilson, ed., *The calendar of St Willibrord from MS Paris Lat. 10837*, HBS, 55 (1918) · *The early history of Glastonbury: an edition, translation, and study of William of Malmesbury's De antiquitate Glastonie ecclesie*, ed. J. Scott (1981) · William of Malmesbury, *Gesta regum Anglorum / The history of the English kings*, ed. and trans. R. A. B. Mynors, R. M. Thomson, and M. Winterbottom, 2 vols., OMT (1998–9) · C. E. Fell, 'Hild, abbess of Streanæshalch', *Hagiography and medieval literature: a symposium*, ed. H. Bekker-Nielsen, P. Foot, J. H. Jørgensen, and T. Nyberg (1981), 76–99 · J. E. Cross, 'A lost life of Hild of Whitby: the evidence of the *Old English Martyrology*', *The early middle ages* [Binghamton 1979], ed. W. H. Snyder (1982), 21–43 · P. S. Barnwell, L. A. S. Butler, and C. J. Dunn, 'The confusion of conversion: Streanæshalch, Strensall and Whitby and the Northumbrian church', *The cross goes north*, ed. M. Carver (2003), 311–26

Hildelith [St Hildelith, Hildilid] (*fl. c.*700), abbess of Barking, was a nun of unknown origin. Barking Abbey was founded in Essex, probably during the decade 665–75, by Earconwald, before he became bishop of London (675?–693); it was a double monastery, housing both monks and nuns, and its first abbess was Earconwald's sister, Æthelburh. Bede treats the early history of Barking in some detail (*Hist. eccl.*, 4.6–11) because he had at his disposal a *libellus* (a 'little book', now lost) on the miracles of St Æthelburh. Unfortunately, Bede does not supply a chronological framework for Barking's early history. According to John of Worcester, Æthelburh died in 675 and was succeeded by Hildelith; and Bede, drawing on the lost *libellus*, reports that she presided over the monastery for many years (ibid., 4.10). The date of her death is unknown. According to Bede, once again, Hildelith was energetic in the observance of monastic discipline, and undertook some reconstruction at Barking in order to accommodate within the church the relics of deceased members of the community. It was to Hildelith and her community of nuns that Aldhelm (*d.* 709/10) dedicated his massive prose *De virginitate*. From the structure of this work it is possible to deduce that many of these nuns were nobly born women who had divorced their husbands: one such was Cuthburh, sometime queen of Aldfrith, king of Northumbria (*d.* 705); Hildelith may have been another. Aldhelm's remarks imply that these nobly born women were remarkably well educated in the scriptures and in patristic literature. Another English scholar of the time, Wynfrith (subsequently known as Boniface), described in a letter addressed to Abbess Eadburh the details of a vision of heaven and hell seen by a monk of Much Wenlock, which had been told to him by Abbess Hildelith. Therefore, although little is known of Hildelith's life, it is clear that she enjoyed intimate contact with the outstanding scholars of the time, and may herself be presumed to have achieved a respectable degree of education.

A life of St Hildelith by John Tynemouth (which forms part of his massive *Sanctilogium*) is based principally on Bede, and adds nothing to knowledge of the saint's life. John says that she was venerated in the tenth century by Dunstan, Æthelwold, and Ælfheah, but there is no record of such veneration in pre-conquest calendars or litanies of the saints. In some post-conquest liturgical sources (principally from Barking itself) Hildelith's deposition is commemorated on 24 March; the early fifteenth-century ordinal of Barking Abbey gives instructions for the performance of daily offices on this date (as well as on the octave). MICHAEL LAPIDGE

Sources Bede, *Hist. eccl.* · John of Worcester, *Chron.* · *Aldhelmi opera*, ed. R. Ehwald, MGH Auctores Antiquissimi, 15 (Berlin, 1919) · M. Tangl, ed., *Die Briefe des heiligen Bonifatius und Lullus*, MGH Epistolae Selectae, 1 (Berlin, 1916) · J. B. L. Tolhurst, ed., *The ordinale and customary of the Benedictine nuns of Barking Abbey*, 2 vols., HBS, 65–6 (1927–8)

Hilder, Rowland Frederick (1905–1993), artist, was born at Great Neck, Long Island, New York, on 28 June 1905, the son of Roland Hilder (*b. c.*1880) and his wife, Kitty, *née* Fissenden (*b. c.*1885), both originally from Birling, Kent. The 'w' in his forename originated from a misspelling on his birth registration form. His parents had moved to America shortly after their marriage, his father working first as a butler and then as a tour organizer for Americans visiting Britain. After Hilder's birth they moved to an apartment in Manhattan, New York, off Central Park, before settling in Morristown, New Jersey, where Hilder went to school. They made annual visits home to see his grandparents at Birling, where a memorial plaque to the artist stands in the churchyard. In 1915 the family returned to England for good (his father enlisting in the Royal Horse Artillery), living above a tobacconist's shop in New Cross, London, which Hilder's father bought for his wife in case he did not return from the war.

In 1921, aged sixteen, Hilder enrolled at Goldsmiths' College, London, where he was tutored by the noted illustrator Edmund J. Sullivan, to whom he was to acknowledge a lifelong debt as his own career developed as an illustrator and draughtsman. Commissions followed, ranging from Mary Webb's *Precious Bane* (1930), to the cover wrapper for a new book by C. S. Forester, an Oxford University Press edition of *Treasure Island* (1929), and various marine subjects and boys' adventure stories. On 17 December 1929 he married Edith Elizabeth Blenkiron (1903/4–1992), a fellow student and botanical artist, and daughter of Robert Henry Blenkiron, a boot and shoe buyer. They had one son, Anthony Rowland—himself an artist, under the *nom de brosse* Anthony Fleming—and a daughter, Mary.

The popularity of Hilder's work was a testimony to the place he held in people's affections—not only in his beloved England but everywhere where 'the Englishness of English art' struck a reminiscent chord. It is hard to think of any landscape painter of his generation whose work was so widely accessible. He shared with John Constable the distinction of having seen, in his own lifetime,

an entire region of England identified with his name and art. The description 'Rowland Hilder country' (attached primarily to the weald of Kent) evokes a landscape as distinctive and personal as 'Constable's country' along the Suffolk Stour.

As an artist Hilder had two lifelong loves: the Thames, which he explored as a boy, and which prompted his early ambition to become a marine painter, and the Shoreham valley, that corner of Kent beloved of Samuel Palmer as his own 'valley of vision'. Hilder's drawings of moored sailing barges, his earliest exercises in documentary draughtsmanship, gave him a feeling for the great waterway that in those days was an artery of the empire. He immersed himself in the skills and crafts of the seaman, taught himself to sail, and worked happily amid the clatter and clamour of London's dockland, sketching scenes that few of his admirers ever set eyes on. All this gave his marine subjects the smack of authentic observation, as his exhibits at the Royal Society of Marine Artists testified. His Shoreham experience, on which his fame as a landscape painter came to be based, dated from his student days at Goldsmiths' College. As it happened, the Shoreham valley was the first stretch of undeveloped countryside, still a rich farming and hop-growing area, that Hilder and his fellow students could easily reach by train or bicycle. He himself was to return to it over and over again, walking its lanes, revisiting its farmsteads, studying its moods and the pastoral drama of the seasons. It remained a fixed point in his imaginative universe, the epicentre of his popularity as a landscape painter.

More generally, Hilder found all he needed in the familiar middle-ground of English art, a territory identified in the hugely popular exhibition at London's Hayward Gallery, 'The British landscape, 1920–1950', as 'a constant negotiation between pastoral and modernising tendencies, with the pastoral usually in the ascendant' (Jeffrey, 7). That certainly holds for Hilder, except that modernizing tendencies were seldom apparent. He remained true to the instinctively natural images of his local painting: horses, corn stooks, hay wains—not the mechanical uproar of a later age. John and Paul Nash, Eric Ravilious, Edward Bawden, and Graham Sutherland were among contemporaries of Hilder's who shared and promoted this distinctively English mood between the two world wars. Geoffrey Grigson, who supplied the text for Rowland and Edith Hilder's illustrations for *The Shell Guide to Flowers of the Countryside* (1955), wrote of the latent emotion, for the English, of words such as 'hill' and 'tree' and 'green', sensing in them origins almost beyond recall. Hilder remained close to this tradition. His images still stay in the mind, half-remembered, yet still within ken. The typical 'Hilderscape' is for the most part a land of plenty, in an untroubled heartland, most often stripped of its summer graces and clad in the naked decency of winter.

Distinguished as he was in oils, Hilder was at his most eloquent in watercolour—'the most wonderful medium of expression yet invented' (Thomas, *Rowland Hilder Sketching Country*, 8). He marvelled that he and his generation, when they started out to be artists, seemed totally unaware of the long line of creative achievement that stretches back in English art form to Cozens, Girtin, Turner, Cotman, and the Norwich men. Such names, he said, were never on his own teachers' lips, nor was he taught watercolour painting. Finding out for himself was a continuous process, both technical and artistic. One of his satisfactions was to notice how often his beloved predecessors in the English school broke away from orthodoxy, mixing media and methods, as Hilder himself liked to do in his own on-the-spot studies, whether impromptu notes or first thoughts towards more considered work to come.

Hilder was elected a member of the Royal Institute of Painters in Water Colours in 1938, becoming vice-president in 1959 and president in 1964, a post he held for ten years. He taught at Farnham School of Art, Surrey, and in London taught at Blackheath School of Art, and was professor of art at Goldsmiths' College. He was appointed OBE in 1986. In his latter years he was an active member of the Fellowship Party. He died of heart failure at the Greenwich District Hospital, Greenwich, London, on 21 April 1993, and was cremated at Sidcup crematorium. He was survived by his son and daughter, his wife having died nine months previously. The Royal Institute of Painters in Water Colours honoured him by instituting an annual Rowland Hilder award in his memory.

DENIS THOMAS

Sources personal knowledge (2004) · *WWW*, 1991–5 · *The Times* (23 April 1993) · *The Independent* (23 April 1993) · *The Independent* (12 May 1993) · *The Independent* (29 May 1993) · m. cert. · d. cert. · J. Lewis, *Rowland Hilder: painter and illustrator* (1978) · D. Thomas, *Rowland Hilder's England* (1986) · D. Thomas, ed., *Rowland Hilder country* (1987) · D. Thomas, ed., *Rowland Hilder sketching country* (1991) · I. Jeffrey, *The British landscape, 1920–1950* (1984)
Likenesses photograph, repro. in *The Times* · photograph, repro. in *The Independent* (23 April 1993)
Wealth at death £184,228: probate, 7 Sept 1993, CGPLA Eng. & Wales

Hildersam, Arthur. *See* Hildersham, Arthur (1563–1632).

Hildersam, Samuel. *See* Hildersham, Samuel (1594?–1674).

Hildersham [Hildersam], **Arthur** (1563–1632), Church of England clergyman, was born on 6 October 1563 at Stetchworth, Cambridgeshire, near Newmarket, the son of Thomas Hildersam and his second wife, Anne, daughter of Sir Geoffrey *Pole and niece of Cardinal Reginald Pole. His parents, who were both recusants, brought him up as a Roman Catholic and hoped that he would become a Catholic priest. His father sent Arthur to school at the grammar school at Saffron Walden, Essex, where the master, Desborough, 'a godly man, and a Religious Protestant', imbibed the young Hildersham with protestant principles. In 1576 he entered Christ's College, Cambridge, where like his fellow student William Perkins he almost certainly came under the influence of Laurence Chaderton, who was a proponent of the puritan wing of the church. After two years of study his father removed Hildersham to London, hoping that Catholic friends would help persuade him to go to Rome. When he

declined to do so and remained unrepentant of a protestant conviction, it seems that he was disinherited. However, with the help of John Ireton, a fellow of Christ's and later rector of Kegworth, Leicestershire, Hildersham obtained assistance from his kinsman, Henry Hastings, third earl of Huntingdon, and was able to return to Christ's and complete his studies; he graduated BA in 1581 and proceeded MA in 1584. He apparently preached in the college chapel as part of the college exercise in divinity. In 1583 he was elected a fellow at Christ's, but the master, Barwell, together with Andrew Perne and William Goad, preferred another godly candidate, Andrew Willet. Following his protest to the chancellor of the university, Lord Burleigh, Hildersham was appointed divinity reader at Trinity Hall.

Hildersham's godly training and inclinations at Christ's placed him on the edge of conformity, and fitted him for a chequered ecclesiastical career. In trouble for preaching before his ordination and licensing, he had to recant on 10 January 1588, but he had been ordained by the time he took up a lectureship at Ashby-de-la-Zouch, Leicestershire. On 5 January 1590 he married Anne Barfoot of Lamborn Hall, Essex, a county where he had kin. On the death of Thomas Wyddowes, vicar of St Helen's, Ashby, Huntingdon presented Hildersham to the living and he was instituted on 4 October 1593. His assize sermon at Leicester on 20 July 1596 on the text of 1 Kings 18:17–18 offended Judge Sir Edmund Anderson, who attempted to walk out and later threatened Hildersham with indictment by grand jury. In 1598 an attachment was sent out by the high court for his arrest, though nothing seems to have come of this. His standing as a leading godly divine is demonstrated by the fact that, with Stephen Egerton, Hildersham was one of the chief promoters of the 1603 millenary petition to James I, which requested further reforms in the liturgy, ceremonial, and structure of the church, although he was not a spokesperson at the Hampton Court conference. He distributed bequests to godly ministers, finding William Bradshaw and others employment, and supplying them with information.

But high esteem with prominent puritan clergy brought with it suspicion and opposition from those who sought no further reform of the church and desired complete obedience and conformity to its existing canons and liturgy. In 1605 William Chaderton, bishop of Lincoln, deprived Hildersham for nonconformity. However, William Overton, bishop of Coventry and Lichfield, allowed him to preach at the godly exercises which were held at Burton upon Trent and Repton, and his family enjoyed continued support from Huntingdon, who paid an annual allowance to Hildersham's son Samuel, at least between 1606 and 1611. William Barlow, who succeeded Chaderton as bishop of Lincoln, restored Hildersham's licence to Ashby in January 1609. However, when Richard Neile became bishop of Coventry and Lichfield he suppressed the exercises at Burton and Repton and James I wrote to reprimand Barlow. By 1613 Hildersham had been incorrectly accused of encouraging the heretic Edward Wightman (Whiteman), and was again suspended. In 1615 he was imprisoned in the Fleet prison, and then the king's bench prison, for refusing the 'ex officio' oath. Then he was accused of refusing to kneel for communion, and on 28 November 1616 was sentenced to imprisonment, to a fine of £2000, and to be degraded from the ministry. He eluded capture, and managed to find refuge with friends of his patron. During this time he declined an invitation to the English church at Leiden. However, following James I's death, on 20 June 1625 he was licensed by Sir Thomas Ridley, the vicar-general of Canterbury, to preach in the dioceses of London, Lincoln, and Coventry and Lichfield, and he began preaching again at Ashby on 3 August on Psalm 35: 13. On 28 September 1625 he began a series of sermons preached over a number of years on Psalm 51. He was suspended again on March 25 1630 for failure to wear surplice and hood for public worship, but was restored again on 2 August 1631.

Hildersham was one of a number of high-profile godly ministers whose nonconformity was tolerated for periods of time, and then suddenly punished. He himself did not countenance separatism, though he encouraged meetings and gatherings for more intense and private spiritual exercises, and clearly disapproved of those clergy who were unable to preach. In his *CVIII Lectures upon the Fourth of John* (1629) he remarked that:

> it were as intolerable bondage and tyranny to binde Gods people to rest upon the ministry of such as can not instruct them, as it were to compell infants to abide with such nurses as have neither sucke nor food to give them.

Like most of his godly churchmen, he advocated days of fasting and humiliation, arguing that the chief use of a religious fast is to humble, and afflict the soul with sorrow and grief, and a chief thing that makes prayer effectual with God is inward humiliation and sorrow of the soul. Many of Hildersham's sermons were preached at the communion service, and he also published *A Briefe Forme of Examination* (1619) and *The Doctine of Communicating Worthily in the Lord's Supper* (1619). His encouragement of regular communion was in contrast to the twice- or thrice-yearly practice common in most English parishes at this time. His understanding of sacraments was as 'mystical signs ordained by God, to represent and seal to the worthy receiver, salvation by Jesus Christ'. Like many of his fellow divines he emphasized their importance as ordinances of God, but also feared that they might be seen as conferring grace in themselves. Much of his homiletic material was concerned with worthy preparation and instruction, which included knowledge of the law, the gospel, and the sacrament. He stressed too the need of assurance in salvation.

Hildersham preached his last sermon on 27 August 1631. He had had bouts of illness and fever in 1614 and 1615, and again in 1624. He contracted scorbutic fever, and died at Ashby on Sunday 4 March 1632. His will asked that there should be no funeral sermon, and he was buried in the chancel of Ashby church. An epitaph in the church gives recognition to one who was 'honourably descended from Sir Richard Poole', but more honoured for his sweet disposition, wisdom, charity, and 'judgment in the Holy Scriptures' and his 'zealous preaching'. He had several children; Samuel *Hildersham (1594?–1674), by this time rector of West Felton, Shropshire, published his father's *CLII Lectures upon Psalme LI* in 1635.   BRYAN D. SPINKS

Sources S. Clarke, *The lives of thirty two English divines*, in *A general martyrologie*, 3rd edn (1677) · B. Brook, *The lives of the puritans*, 2 (1813) · Venn, *Alum. Cant.* · S. B. Babbage, *Puritanism and Richard Bancroft* (1962) · T. Cogswell, *Home divisions: aristocracy, the state and provincial conflict* (1998) · N. Tyacke, *The fortunes of English puritanism, 1603–1640* (1990), 7 · P. Lake, *Moderate puritans and the Elizabethan church* (1982), 262 · Hunt. L., HAF Box 7; HA 6758
Likenesses oils, 1619, NPG · J. Payne, line engraving, BM, NPG; repro. in A. Hildersam, *The doctrine of fasting and praier sermons delivered in sundry* (1633)

Hildersham [Hildersam], **Samuel** (1594?–1674), clergyman and ejected minister, was born at Ashby-de-la-Zouch, Leicestershire, the son of Arthur *Hildersham (1563–1632), instituted vicar there in October 1593, and his wife, Anne (*d. c.*1640), a daughter of the Barfoot family of Lambourne Hall, Essex. Admitted as pensioner to Emmanuel College, Cambridge, on 6 May 1609, he graduated BA in 1613, proceeded MA in 1616, and became a fellow of his college in 1618. Thereafter Hildersham devoted his life to the promotion of godly living. He became a BD in 1623, and may then have been ordained by an Irish bishop without subscription to the Thirty-Nine Articles. Subsequently, on 13 June 1628, he was appointed by William Cokayne, merchant of Austin Friars in London, to the impropriated rectory of West Felton, Shropshire, a place which he was to serve faithfully for over thirty years. While there he published his late father's *CLII Lectures upon Psalme LI* (1635), and also married his wife, Mary, daughter of Sir Henry *Goodere (*bap.* 1571, *d.* 1627) of Polesworth, Warwickshire.

During the civil wars Hildersham became committed to the parliamentarian cause. In 1642 and 1643 he was one of the Shropshire representatives to the Westminster assembly of divines, and in 1648 he signed a testimony of local ministers supporting the establishment of presbyterianism within the county. In the 1650s he was an assistant to the Shropshire commission, and established close friendships with two influential presbyterians, Richard Baxter and Henry Newcome; the latter remembered him as 'a very noble friend to me' (*Autobiography*, 1.56). At the same time, however, he worked alongside Baxter, Newcome, and other ministers to establish links between presbyterians and Independents. After 1656 he was a member of the Shropshire Association, although this short-lived project was eventually abandoned at the Restoration. Following the Act of Uniformity, he was ejected from his living at West Felton. He retired to Erdington in the parish of Aston, near Birmingham, a town free from the provisions of the Five Mile Act. Ultimately, though, he eschewed open nonconformity after 1662, and remained at Erdington, where he died in April 1674, 'aged eighty'. He was buried at Aston, without a funeral sermon, at his own request. His wife survived him.   S. J. GUSCOTT

Sources *Calamy rev.*, 263 · *DNB* · Venn, *Alum. Cant.* · *The autobiography of Henry Newcome*, ed. R. Parkinson, 1, Chetham Society, 26 (1852), 55–8, 61, 64; 2, Chetham Society, 27 (1852), 347–50 · *Calendar*

of the correspondence of Richard Baxter, ed. N. H. Keeble and G. F. Nuttall, 2 vols. (1991) • *VCH Warwickshire*, 7.412

Hildesley, Mark (1698–1772), bishop of Sodor and Man, was born on 9 December 1698 at Murston rectory, Kent, the oldest surviving son of the Revd Mark Hildesley (*d.* 1726), rector of Murston and vicar of Sittingbourne from 1705, and his wife, Avis. In 1710 his father moved to the living of Houghton-cum-Whitton in Huntingdonshire and Mark was sent to Charterhouse School. He was admitted to Trinity College, Cambridge, as a pensioner on 29 March 1717; he graduated BA in 1720 and was elected fellow in 1723. In the latter year he was ordained, whereupon he was appointed chaplain to Richard Temple, first Viscount Cobham; he graduated MA in 1724. Impressed by Hildesley's abilities Edmund Gibson, bishop of London, made him one of the twelve preachers at Whitehall in February 1725. Hildesley's hopes of leading the life of a don were shattered, however, when in 1726 his father died, leaving Hildesley's mother and five sisters without support.

Hildesley's search for preferment did not bear fruit until February 1731, when he accepted the college vicarage of Hitchin in Hertfordshire. In the same year he married Elizabeth Stoker (*d.* 1763). In his first twelve months at Hitchin, Hildesley buried 158 parishioners who had died of an outbreak of the plague, the average number of deaths in the parish per annum being usually less than thirty. Hildesley and his wife had only two children, Mark and Elizabeth, both of whom died in infancy, a blow from which the couple never really recovered. Hildesley's living was not rich and he was compelled to spend a great sum on renovating the vicarage. In order to recoup the money he took as boarders six gentlemen's sons. The boys caused Hildesley great embarrassment when George Whitefield came to preach in the town square; having gone into the belfry of the church they rang the bells so loudly that Whitefield's sermon could not be heard.

Hildesley, poor and childless, stayed in Hitchin for over thirty years. On 18 January 1734 he was made chaplain to Henry St John, first Viscount Bolingbroke, and on 10 May 1742 chaplain to Bolingbroke's brother John, second Viscount St John. He paid particular attention to the instruction of the young in his parish. In 1735 he was also given the neighbouring rectory of Holwell, in Bedfordshire; his kindness earned him the title Father Hildesley and he was much loved. In 1750 he was elected an honorary member of Spalding Gentlemen's Society, and on 20 February 1754 he was collated to the prebend of Marston St Lawrence, Northamptonshire. In 1755, at the age of fifty-six, he was recommended to James Murray, second duke of Atholl and sovereign lord of the Isle of Man, as successor to Thomas Wilson, bishop of Sodor and Man. Hildesley was created DD on 7 April by Thomas Herring, archbishop of Canterbury, and was consecrated bishop, by special licence, on 27 April 1755 in the Chapel Royal, Whitehall, by Matthew Hutton, archbishop of York, assisted by the bishops of Durham, Carlisle, and Chester. The following

August he was installed in the island, in the cathedral of St German, Peel.

Wilson, Hildesley's predecessor, had died at the age of ninety-two and, though he had been an excellent bishop, his vigour had waned somewhat in his later years. Hildesley immediately set about reforming his diocese. He built a court house for the transaction of church business, began Sunday schools, enlarged churches, and established parish libraries. He insisted that sermons be preached in Manx to the local people and that the catechism in Manx be used every Sunday in all churches in the island. He himself learnt a little Manx and in church always gave the final blessing in the language. His chief achievement however was to publish religious works in Manx—in particular the entire Bible. In this enterprise he was ably supported by a team of Manx-speaking clerics, most notably Philip Moore and John Kelly. The Society for Promoting Christian Knowledge (SPCK) gave financial assistance.

Under Hildesley's direction the four gospels and the Acts of the Apostles were printed in London for the SPCK in 1763. The Book of Common Prayer followed in 1765. The second part of the New Testament appeared in 1767, having been printed in Ramsey, Isle of Man, by the Whitehaven printers Sheperd. The first part of the Old Testament (Genesis to Esther) was printed by John Ware in Whitehaven in 1771 and again in 1772.

Hildesley continued to hold the rectory of Holwell *in commendam* until 1767, at which date he was presented to the mastership of Christ's Hospital at Sherburn, near Durham. The duties were slight and the income only £500 a year but the money enabled him in these, the last years of his life, not only at last to provide for the widows and orphans of the Manx clergy but also to travel more frequently to England and so alleviate the isolation that he often felt in the Isle of Man.

On Saturday 28 November 1772 Hildesley had the pleasure of receiving the final proofs of the Old Testament. This was the portion from Job to Malachi, including for some reason the two apocryphal books of the Wisdom and Ecclesiasticus. The next day was Advent Sunday and the bishop preached in his own chapel 'On the uncertainty of human life'. He suffered a stroke the following day and died at Bishop's Court, Peel, on 6 December 1772; he was buried in Kirk Michael on 10 December. Hildesley left £300 of his meagre wealth to the SPCK to finance reprints of the Manx Bible. The final portion of the Old Testament appeared after Hildesley's death in 1773. The New Testament was reprinted in 1775 and in the same year a one-volume edition of the whole Bible appeared for the first time.

N. J. A. WILLIAMS

Sources R. L. Hine, *Hitchin worthies: four centuries of English life* (1932) • R. L. Thomson, introduction, *Bible chasherick, yn lught thie / The Manx family Bible* (1979) • Venn, *Alum. Cant.* • *DNB*
Archives BL, corresp., Add. MSS 19684–19686 • Manx Museum and National Heritage, Douglas, Isle of Man, letters • Manx Museum and National Heritage, Douglas, Isle of Man, sermons • Wandsworth Local History Service Library, discourses preached in Battersea church | W. Sussex RO, letters to Miss Heywood

Likenesses Van Reyshoot, oils, *c*.1760, repro. in Hine, *Hitchin worthies*

Wealth at death under £500; left £20 to Revd P. Moore; £300 to Society for Promoting Christian Knowledge; and between £1 and £5 to the seventeen parishes of Isle of Man; £50 to Trinity College, Cambridge: Hine, *Hitchin worthies*

Hildeyard, Thomas (1690–1746), Jesuit and engineer, was born in London on 3 March 1690 into a family long established in Yorkshire and Lincolnshire. He was educated at the English College at St Omer (1702–7), entered the Society of Jesus on 7 September 1707, and was professed of the four vows on 2 February 1725. He was ordained priest about 1716. After teaching philosophy, theology, and mathematics at Liège, he was sent to the English mission, and by 1726 had become chaplain to the Bodenham family at Rotherwas, near Hereford. In September 1743 he was declared rector of the 'college' of St Francis Xavier, which included the counties of Hereford, Monmouth, Gloucester, and Somerset, and the whole of south Wales.

Hildeyard was an accomplished engineer. In 1720 he was probably the first person in continental Europe successfully to build a steam engine after the designs of Thomas Newcomen. These had been smuggled to Liège by a consortium of Irishmen involved in industrial espionage. He was also noted for devising a number of innovative clocks. One of them was described in the *Chronometrum mirabile Leodiense* (1727). This was an ingenious table clock giving time of day, information from the calendar, and all kinds of astronomical details. His 'Lectures on penance' were preserved in a manuscript at the presbytery, St George's, Worcester. Hildeyard died at Rotherwas on 10 April 1746, and was buried in the family chapel.

THOMPSON COOPER, *rev.* ROBERT BROWN

Sources Gillow, *Lit. biog. hist.* · H. Foley, ed., *Records of the English province of the Society of Jesus*, 7 vols. in 8 (1875–83) · G. Holt, *The English Jesuits, 1650–1829: a biographical dictionary*, Catholic RS, 70 (1984) · G. Oliver, *Collections towards illustrating the biography of the Scotch, English and Irish members of the Society of Jesus* (1835) · private information (2004) [M. Whitehead]

Hildilid. *See* Hildelith (*fl. c.*700).

Hilditch, Sir Edward (1805–1876), naval medical officer, was born on 13 May 1805, the son of John Frederick Hilditch, and his wife, Sarah. He studied medicine at St George's Hospital in London, took his MRCS diploma in 1826, and immediately entered the naval medical service. He was on the West Indian station from 1830 to 1855, and there gained extensive experience in dealing with outbreaks of yellow fever. For his work in several epidemics, Hilditch received successive promotions: surgeon in 1822; hospital surgeon in 1840; deputy inspector in 1844; and inspector-general in 1854. In 1855, after having met with a fearful epidemic of yellow fever in Bermuda, he was appointed to the charge of Plymouth Hospital, where he remained until he moved to Greenwich Hospital in 1861. He was placed on the retired list in 1865, receiving the honour of knighthood. In 1859 he was named honorary physician to the queen, when the distinction was first instituted. He was a warm, jovial, and unassuming man,

well liked by both patients and colleagues. He died of heart disease at his home, 18 Arundel Gardens, Bayswater, London, on 24 August 1876.

CHARLES CREIGHTON, *rev.* TIM O'NEILL

Sources *The Lancet* (2 Sept 1876), 342–3 · Boase, *Mod. Eng. biog.* · IGI

Wealth at death under £4000: probate, 4 Sept 1876, *CGPLA Eng. & Wales*

Hilditch, Thomas Percy (1886–1965), chemist, was born at Tollington Park, North Islington, London, on 22 April 1886, the eldest of the three children and the only son of Thomas Hilditch, a boot manufacturer's agent, and his wife, Priscilla, daughter of Frederick Hall, agent for a tile-manufacturing company. He was educated at Owen's School, North Islington (1901–4), and at University College, London, where he won a Tufnell scholarship (1906) before graduating with a first-class BSc degree in 1907. He became an associate of the Institute of Chemistry by examination in 1908. Between 1907 and 1911 he undertook research into organic sulphur-containing compounds, under Dr Samuel Smiles (1877–1953) in London, Professor L. Knorr at the University of Jena, and Professor P. A. Guy at the University of Geneva. For part of this period he held an 1851 Exhibition science research fellowship. In 1911 he was awarded the DSc by the University of London, was elected a fellow of the Institute of Chemistry, and published a *History of Chemistry* (2nd edn, 1922). The following year he married Elizabeth Monica Lawrence; they had three daughters before her death in 1929.

From 1911 to 1926 Hilditch worked for Joseph Crosfield & Sons, soap manufacturers, of Warrington (later part of Unilever) as a technical research chemist. There he worked under Dr E. F. Armstrong and, during the years of the First World War, was involved in the development of catalytic methods for preparing acetic acid and acetone from ethanol. After the war Hilditch studied the catalytic hydrogenation of fats, oils, and other substances, and, together with Armstrong, published a series of thirteen papers which appeared between 1919 and 1925 in the *Proceedings of the Royal Society*, series A. Through their investigations the two men realized how much still remained to be discovered about the chemical nature of animal and vegetable fats.

In 1926 Hilditch was appointed as first holder of the Campbell Brown chair of industrial chemistry at the University of Liverpool. Continuing his Crosfield interest he studied the hydrogenation and autoxidation of unsaturated fats and their constituent acids, discovering a link between the two processes. He also isolated and identified fatty acids of unknown or uncertain structure. His major contribution, however, was a study of the composition of the natural fats, which involved the development of satisfactory analytical procedures, the application of those methods to a wide range of fats, and the rationalization of data available both from the Liverpool laboratories and from other sources. The first two tasks were undertaken by Hilditch and his research students, the last by Hilditch alone. The data analysis was presented in his book *The Chemical Constitution of Natural Fats* (1940). During his early years in Liverpool (1929) his wife died. The same year he married Eva, widow of John Stephen Parsons and daughter of John Richardson, coal merchant. The union lasted until Eva's death in 1949. He married again in 1952; his third wife was Margery, daughter of George Davies, haulage contractor.

Hilditch was elected a fellow of the Royal Society in 1942 and appointed CBE in 1952. He received many other awards including the Lampitt medal from the Society of Chemical Industry, and the Chevreul medal from the French Groupement Technique des Corps Gras. He contributed in many ways to the administrative life of Liverpool University and served on the committees of various professional societies concerned with chemistry.

Hilditch's research students found he was not an easy man to know and early in their research careers regarded him with respect and awe and sought so to conduct themselves as to avoid his caustic comments on inadequate work or shoddy thinking. Slowly those first impressions gave way to respect and affection for one who was always fair, and frequently generous. Always a prodigious worker, he found his recreation in gardening, walking, and watching cricket. He was a regular worshipper and served his church, All Saints, Oxton, Birkenhead, in many capacities; he was regarded by his friends there as a shy and reserved man of great humility. He died at his home, 107 Shrewsbury Road, Oxton, on 9 August 1965, survived by his wife.   F. D. GUNSTONE, rev.

Sources R. A. Morton, *Memoirs FRS*, 12 (1966), 259–89 · private information (1981) · personal knowledge (1981) · *CGPLA Eng. & Wales* (1965)
Archives U. Lpool L., corresp. and papers
Likenesses W. Stoneman, photograph, RS
Wealth at death £41,417: probate, 20 Oct 1965, *CGPLA Eng. & Wales*

Hildrop, John (1682–1756), religious writer, born on 30 December 1682 in Petersfield, Hampshire, was the son of William Hildrop of Petersfield. He matriculated on 25 November 1698 from St John's College, Oxford, and graduated BA on 7 July 1702, MA on 8 June 1705, and BD and DD on 9 June 1743. On 14 April 1703 he was presented with the mastership of the Royal Free Grammar School at Marlborough, Wiltshire, by Thomas Bruce, third earl of Elgin and second earl of Ailesbury. He published several works on the apocalypse between 1711 and 1713, and in 1722 *Reflections upon Reason* appeared, a satire on freethinking, attributed at first to Bishop Francis Gastrell, and examined by Thomas Morgan in *Enthusiasm in Distress* (1722).

Hildrop was appointed rector of Maulden, Bedfordshire, in 1733. He resigned the school mastership on 4 December 1733 and, three months later, he resigned the rectory. On 13 April 1734 he was instituted to the rectory of Wath, near Ripon, Yorkshire, on the presentation of his patron's son Charles Bruce, Lord Bruce, later fourth earl of Elgin and third earl of Ailesbury, to whom he was chaplain. Hildrop published—alongside several less noteworthy tracts—various fugitive essays of a satirical and polemical character, chiefly directed against deists, either anonymously or under the pseudonyms of Phileleutherus

Britannicus and Timothy Hooker. Though of slight intrinsic value, they are written in an unusually nervous, yet easy and entertaining style. These include *An Essay for the Better Regulation and Improvement of Free-Thinking* (1739) and *The Contempt of the Clergy Considered* (1739); the latter argued for the liberation of the church from state control. His *Letter to a member of parliament containing a proposal … to revise, amend, or repeal … the ten commandments* is an amusing *jeu d'esprit*. On its first appearance in 1738 it was attributed to Swift, but it appears in Hildrop's *Miscellaneous Works* (1754), along with *A Modest Apology for the Ancient and Honourable Family of the Wrongheads* and *Some Memoirs of the Life of Simon Sallow*. In 1740 Hildrop became a regular contributor to the *Weekly Miscellany*. In 1741 his *An Essay on Honour* appeared and in 1742 he printed a work attempting to prove that animals' souls are degraded because of the fall of man, based on Guillaume Hyacinthe Bougeant's *Philosophical Amusement*. He also published a collection of sermons as *The Husbandman's Spiritual Companion* (1752). Hildrop died on 18 January 1756.

J. M. RIGG, rev. ADAM JACOB LEVIN

Sources Foster, *Alum. Oxon.* · Nichols, *Illustrations*, 4.323–4 · W. T. Lowndes, *The bibliographer's manual of English literature*, ed. H. G. Bohn, [new edn], 3 (1864), 1069 · F. J. G. Robinson and others, *Eighteenth-century British books: an author union catalogue*, 3 (1981), 116 · *GM*, 1st ser., 26 (1756), 43 · *GM*, 2nd ser., 2 (1834), 114 · Nichols, *Lit. anecdotes*, 2.534
Archives Bodl. Oxf., Rawl. MSS

Hildyard, Sir David Henry Thoroton [Toby] (1916–1997), diplomatist, was born on 4 May 1916 at the rectory, Limpsfield, Surrey, the youngest of three sons of Gerard Moresby Thoroton Hildyard (1874–1956), a barrister who subsequently became a county court judge and inherited a 1000-acre farm in Nottinghamshire, and his wife, Sybil Hamilton Hoare, daughter of H. W. Hamilton Hoare, a civil servant in the Board of Education. Hildyard (who was always known as Toby) was educated at Eton College (1929–34) and won a closed exhibition to Christ Church, Oxford, where he gained a second in politics, philosophy, and economics in 1938 and learned to fly with the university air squadron. He had already spent time as a student in Germany before Oxford, and on going down he studied further in Italy, Yugoslavia, and France. In France he contracted appendicitis, which led on to peritonitis, and at the outbreak of the Second World War in September 1939 he was medically unfit for service. By early 1940, however, he managed to join the RAF and he served as a pilot and navigator in Gibraltar and Malta. The following year he was posted to a flying-boat squadron in the Far East where he won the DFC in 1943 after 'an exceptionally long operational career' (*The Times*, 19 April 1997). One of his most memorable operations was the last-minute evacuation of RAF personnel from the Nicobar Islands, and the destruction of their base, on the eve of the capture of the islands by the Japanese. This operation was singled out for praise by Anthony Eden in the House of Commons. Hildyard ended the war as a wing commander in Ceylon in charge of the largest flying-boat school in the world. He subsequently attended the Nuremberg war trials as part of the intelligence staff.

After demobilization Hildyard spent some months as a management trainee with the tobacco company Carreras, and on 6 February 1947 he married Millicent Longmore, the widow of Wing Commander Richard Longmore and the daughter of Sir Edward Samson Baron, chairman of Carreras. Hildyard had met his bride not in connection with Carreras, but when he had called on her following the death in action of her first husband, who had been his close friend. It was to be a long and enduringly happy marriage, which resulted in a son and a daughter to add to the stepson and stepdaughter whom his wife brought from her previous marriage. After short periods in the tobacco industry and farming with his brothers, in January 1948 Hildyard entered the diplomatic service, which was to be his career for the next thirty years. He served mostly in Spanish speaking countries, being successively in Uruguay, Spain, and Mexico, where he was counsellor for five years from 1960, with a spell in the American department of the Foreign Office in between these postings. During this period he built a solid reputation particularly for his grasp of economic work, and it was no surprise when he returned to the Foreign Office (later the Foreign and Commonwealth Office) in 1965 as head of the economic relations department. From there he moved on promotion to be deputy head of the British mission to the United Nations in New York (he had earlier served briefly in the United Nations department) at a time when his responsibilities were complicated by the fact that his chief—Lord Caradon—was not a diplomat but a member of Harold Wilson's Labour government.

In July 1970 Hildyard was appointed ambassador to Chile in the immediate run-up to Allende's election as president—a democratic process that perversely resulted in a communist president of a largely non-communist country. Although poles apart politically, Hildyard cultivated good and close relations with Allende. This paid off in an unexpected manner when, following the kidnapping of Geoffrey Jackson (the British ambassador to Uruguay) by the left-wing Tupamaros guerrillas in that country, he was asked by the Foreign and Commonwealth Office to approach Allende with a request that the president should act as an intermediary with the guerrillas. Allende established contact and Hildyard himself attended three secret meetings in the middle of the night—blindfolded and at unknown addresses in Santiago—with Tupamaro leaders. Hildyard was instructed to reject demands for a $1 million ransom, on the grounds that to have paid up would have put other British diplomats at risk. He none the less managed to establish some measure of rapport with the kidnappers, and when some of their imprisoned collaborators escaped from gaol the Tupamaros followed Hildyard's earlier suggestion that they should release Jackson as a goodwill gesture. Hildyard was fortunate to leave Chile before the manhunt for left-wing activists that followed the Pinochet coup and placed his successors in an invidious position regarding

asylum requests. Hildyard's last post was as British permanent representative to the United Nations and other international organizations in Geneva, where his earlier United Nations experience was put to good use and where he was deeply involved with the Conference on Security and Co-operation in Europe, which led to his presence at the signing of the Final Act by Harold Wilson and the Soviet leadership in Helsinki in 1975. He was knighted (KCMG) in that year. The Turkish invasion of Cyprus also involved him in urgent negotiations in Geneva, where the foreign secretary, James Callaghan, based himself in Hildyard's house.

After retirement Hildyard lived in Onslow Square, London, and he joined the board of the Lombard Odier Bank and also helped to raise funds for the Victoria and Albert Museum. He kept up his interests in diplomacy and history and he and his wife—who had supported him as a charming and intelligent hostess—continued to entertain their friends. He died at his home, flat 6, 97 Onslow Square, of kidney failure on 5 April 1997, shortly after celebrating his golden wedding anniversary, and was survived by his wife and two children. Hildyard had to a marked degree the characteristics of openness, transparent honesty, and affability. These qualities enabled him to make friends easily, and many of the friendships he established—notably those with President Allende and with his Russian opposite numbers in New York and Geneva—were greatly to the benefit of the country he served.

JOHN URE

Sources personal knowledge (2004) · Foreign and Commonwealth Office records and reports · *The Times* (19 April 1997) · *Daily Telegraph* (14 April 1997) · *WWW* [forthcoming] · b. cert. · m. cert. · d. cert. · *FO List*
Likenesses photograph, repro. in *Daily Telegraph* · photograph, repro. in *The Times*
Wealth at death £228,298: probate, 17 Oct 1997, *CGPLA Eng. & Wales*

Hildyard, **Sir Henry John Thoroton** (1846–1916), army officer, was born on 5 July 1846, the son of Thomas Blackborne Thoroton Hildyard (1821–1888) of Flintham Hall, Newark, the Conservative MP for Nottinghamshire South (1846–52, 1866–85), and his wife, Anne Margaret, second daughter of Colonel Rochfort of Clogrenane, co. Carlow. Henry Hildyard was educated at the Royal Naval Academy, Gosport, and served as a lieutenant RN from 13 September 1859 to 28 November 1864. In 1867 he became an ensign in the 15th foot (9 March) and then the 71st foot (1 May). Promoted captain in October 1876, he graduated from the Staff College at Camberley in 1877 with special credit in German and Spanish, and he frequently contributed translations of German articles to the *Journal* of the Royal United Service Institution. He served as brigade major in Cyprus and Gibraltar from 1878 to 1882, achieving his majority on 6 May 1882. His first major campaign was the 1882 expedition to Egypt, where he served as Sir Garnet Wolseley's deputy assistant adjutant and quartermaster-general, and was at Qassasin and Tell al-Kebir. He was mentioned in dispatches and received the Osmanieh (fourth class).

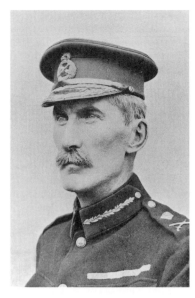

Sir Henry John Thoroton Hildyard (1846–1916), by unknown photographer

For the next nine years Hildyard, who became a brevet lieutenant-colonel on 18 November 1882, held a series of posts, including deputy assistant adjutant-general and assistant adjutant-general at headquarters, that reflected his growing reputation as a competent administrator and his status as a member of the Wolseley 'ring'. On 12 August 1893 he became commandant at the Staff College. According to *The Times*, 'The College had long been a byword for pedantry, but under his direction it became infused with a fresher and more practical spirit' (*The Times*, 27 July 1916). He aimed to combat the old evil of cramming: 'we do not want any cramming here', he declared, 'we want officers to absorb, not to cram' (Bond, 154). He vainly tried to secure abolition of all written examinations by outside examiners. He restructured the examination system, abolishing the final examination and classifying students by their work during the course, and placed greater emphasis on the practicalities of command and staff work. The timing of his reforms was important, for many of the men who were to lead the British army in the First World War—Haig, Robertson, and Allenby among them—studied at Staff College in Hildyard's day.

Hildyard left Staff College on 25 February 1898 to command 3rd brigade at Aldershot, being promoted major-general on 14 May 1899. At the outbreak of the Second South African War, on 9 October, he was appointed to command 2nd (or English) brigade in Methuen's 1st division. Hildyard handled his brigade competently in the defeat at Colenso (15 December 1899), and during the attempt to relieve Ladysmith made a successful attack at Rangeworthy Hills (20 January 1900). This was but a prelude to the disaster at nearby Spion Kop on 24 January. This defeat was rapidly followed by another at Vaal Krantz (5–7 February 1900). Again, Hildyard and 2nd brigade performed creditably but were let down by Buller's poor generalship. The capture of Monte Cristo by Hildyard's brigade on 18 February was an important preliminary to the relief of Ladysmith ten days later.

Promoted lieutenant-general on 20 April 1900, Hildyard's reward for his steady if unspectacular leadership was promotion to command 5th division. Under his command it fought a series of actions, the most important being at Alleman's Nek (June 1900), where Hildyard succeeded in moving round the flank of Boer forces strongly entrenched at Laing's Nek, 'the Gibraltar of Natal', thus handing Buller an important victory. Hildyard took on further responsibilities in October, when the Natal field force was formally disbanded; he commanded both in Natal and in part of the Transvaal. He had to hold and pacify the area as the war moved into the guerrilla phase; the Boer offensive of 1901 demonstrated the essential soundness of the arrangements.

In September 1901 Hildyard returned to Britain on leave. Mentioned in dispatches, in 1900 he had been made KCB. In 1903 he was appointed director-general of military education. In 1904 he returned to South Africa as lieutenant-general on the staff commanding troops, and from 1905 to 1908 served as general officer commanding-in-chief, South Africa.

On 20 May 1871 Hildyard had married Annette, daughter of Admiral James Charles Prevost (1810–1891). They had three sons, two of whom entered the army. A 1903 photograph depicts an alert, striking-looking man of soldierly bearing, with the obligatory military moustache; anecdotes suggest an amiable personality. Hildyard retired in 1911, living at 20 Eccleston Square, Pimlico, London, and died on 25 July 1916 at his sister's residence, Apsley Heath House, Woburn Sands, Bedfordshire. His wife survived him. At the time of Hildyard's death the British army on the Somme was undergoing its first major experience of large-scale modern industrialized warfare, led by commanders who had benefited directly or indirectly from his reforms of Staff College. Hildyard deserves a share of the credit for that army's victory in 1918.

G. D. SHEFFIELD

Sources *The Times* (27 July 1916) · *WWW, 1916–28* · *Army List* (1902) · B. Bond, *The Victorian army and the Staff College, 1854–1914* (1972) · L. S. Amery, ed., *The Times history of the war in South Africa*, 7 vols. (1900–09) · T. Pakenham, *The Boer War* (1979) · A. Carton de Wiart, *Happy odyssey* (1950) · Burke, *Gen. GB* (1937) · E. M. Spiers, *The late Victorian army, 1868–1902* (1992) · Boase, *Mod. Eng. biog.* · Burke, *Peerage* (1904)

Likenesses photograph, repro. in *Navy and Army Illustrated* (14 Feb 1903) · photograph, repro. in Bond, *The Victorian army*, facing p. 191 · photograph, NPG [*see illus.*]

Wealth at death £3672 11s. 0d.: administration with will, 11 Oct 1916, *CGPLA Eng. & Wales*

Hildyard, James (1809–1887), classical scholar, was born on 11 April 1809 at Winestead in Holderness, Yorkshire, the eighth of ten sons of the Revd William Hildyard, nine of whom became Cambridge graduates and six fellows of their colleges. He was educated under Dr Samuel Butler at Shrewsbury School from 1820 to 1829. From 1826 he was the head of the school, and in April 1829 was the chief person in a rebellion over the boys' diet known as the 'Beef Row'. In October of the same year he was entered as a pensioner of Christ's College, Cambridge, where, through the influence of the master, Dr John Kaye, he was at once elected to a Tancred divinity studentship, then worth the large sum of about £113 a year: he was ordained deacon in 1830. Hildyard won a Browne medal in 1830–33, and the members' prize in 1832. In 1833 he graduated BA as senior optime in mathematics, second in the first class of the classical tripos, and second chancellor's medallist, and was immediately elected fellow of his college. He was ordained priest in 1834. In 1840 he became Hebrew lecturer and tutor. He proceeded MA in 1836, and BD in 1846. In 1843 he was senior proctor.

During fourteen years' residence Hildyard became prominent as a university politician who relished acrimonious disagreement. Nevertheless he fought hard to improve the method of college tuition, and wrote more than one pamphlet against the system of private coaching. He wrote and spoke in favour of voluntary theological examinations for ordination candidates. He spent some time on a laborious edition of some of the plays of Plautus, with Latin notes and glossary. For two years, 1843 and 1844, he was Cambridge preacher at the Chapel Royal, Whitehall, when large congregations were present, and a printed selection from his sermons had a rapid sale. About this period he successfully fought the battle of the black gown *versus* the surplice, his opponent being the Revd Frederick Oakeley, a prominent ritualist who afterwards became a Roman Catholic priest. Hildyard's foreign travels included tours in Greece and Turkey. At Athens he caught a fever, and narrowly escaped being bled to death by King Otho's German physician. In 1846 he married Elizabeth Matilda, only daughter of George Kinderley of Lincoln's Inn, to whom he had been engaged for seven years, and in June of that year accepted the college living of Ingoldsby, Lincolnshire. He found the church and parsonage in a ruinous condition, but in the course of two or three years he restored the church, and built a new rectory at a personal cost of almost £3000. He was always a consistent advocate of the revision of the Book of Common Prayer, and his *Ingoldsby Letters* (4th edn, 1879) was an important (if characteristically intemperate) contribution to contemporary debate on the subject. He also published numerous pamphlets and sermons. He died at Ingoldsby rectory on 27 August 1887.

G. C. BOASE, *rev.* RICHARD SMAIL

Sources *Biograph and Review*, 5 (1881), 472–7 • W. Smith, ed., *Old Yorkshire*, 4 (1883), 142–6 • Venn, *Alum. Cant.*
Archives BL, letters to Samuel Butler, Add. MSS 34588–34592, *passim* • U. Edin. L., letters to James Halliwell-Phillipps
Likenesses portrait, repro. in Smith, *Old Yorkshire* • portrait, repro. in *Church Portrait Journal* (April 1877), 49–50
Wealth at death £5207 12s. 6d.: administration, 7 Oct 1887, CGPLA Eng. & Wales

Hiles, Henry (1826–1904), composer and teacher of music, was born on 31 December 1826 at Shrewsbury, the youngest of the six sons of James Hiles, a tradesman, and his wife, Sarah. He studied under his brother John Hiles (1810–1882), an organist and composer, and from the age of thirteen deputized at several churches for him. In 1845 Hiles became organist of the parish church in Bury, but moved to Bishopwearmouth in 1847. From 1852 to 1859 he travelled in Australia and elsewhere. On his return to London in 1859 he was organist of St Michael's, Wood Street, for a few months and in 1860 was appointed organist and teacher of music to the Blind Asylum, Manchester, and organist of St Thomas's, Old Trafford. From Manchester he went to the parish church of Bowden in 1861, and was at St Paul's, Hulme, from 1863 to 1867. He graduated BMus at Oxford in 1862 and DMus in 1867.

In 1876 Hiles became lecturer in harmony and composition at Owens College, Manchester, and retained his post from 1879 in the Victoria University. In 1890 he organized a faculty of music, and was installed as senior examiner and lecturer. He was also professor of harmony and counterpoint at the Royal Manchester College of Music from 1893 and took an active part in founding the Incorporated Society of Musicians in 1882. He was much in demand as a choral conductor among societies in Manchester and neighbouring towns.

Hiles was also a composer. He gained first prize for an organ composition at the College of Organists in 1864, and four others for anthems and organ music. In 1878 he also won the prize for a serious glee, offered by the Manchester Gentlemen's Glee Club, with 'Hushed in death the minstrel lies', written in 1847 on the death of Mendelssohn, and in 1882 won the Meadowcroft prize. His compositions included an oratorio, *The Patriarchs* (1872), an operetta, *War in the Household* (1885), cantatas, services, anthems, and concert overtures. He wrote many textbooks, including *Harmony of Sounds* (1871), *Grammar of Music* (1879), and *Harmony, Choral or Contrapuntal* (1894). He was editor of the *Wesley Tune Book* and the *Quarterly Musical Review* (1885–8).

A self-educated musician, Hiles had little respect for the old contrapuntalists or the 'theory' of harmony. His modern sympathies failed, however, to influence his own compositions, which as a rule contain clear-cut and beautiful melody, orthodox though rich harmony, and regular form.

Hiles was twice married: first to Fanny Lockyer, and second to Isabella Higham. There were two sons and one daughter from the second marriage. Hiles died at Worthing, Sussex, on 20 October 1904; he was survived by his second wife.

J. C. BRIDGE, *rev.* ANNE PIMLOTT BAKER

Sources *MT*, 41 (1900), 441–6 • *New Grove* • D. Baptie, *Sketches of the English glee composers: historical, biographical and critical (from about 1735–1866)* [1896], 179–80 • *IGI* • *CGPLA Eng. & Wales* (1904)
Likenesses photograph, repro. in *MT*
Wealth at death £3610 2s. 9d.: probate, 15 Nov 1904, CGPLA Eng. & Wales

Hill, Aaron (1685–1750), writer and entrepreneur, was born on 10 February 1685 in Beaufort Buildings, the Strand, the eldest son of George Hill, an attorney of Whitchurch Manor, Malmesbury, Wiltshire. Declining family fortunes forced George Hill to sell his estate in 1707. Ann Gregory, Aaron's maternal grandmother, took charge of his education, sending him first to the free grammar school at Barnstaple (where he befriended the writer John Gay), then to Westminster School (*c.*1696–1699), and finally supporting him in an ambitious trip to the East (*c*.1700–1704) to visit his distant relative Lord Paget, English ambassador to Constantinople. Hill's early adventures abroad furnished material for the lavishly illustrated subscription volume *A Full and Just Account of the Present State of the Ottoman Empire* (1709). Hill returned to Britain with Paget in April 1703, then tutored William Wentworth of Bretton Hall, Yorkshire, until Wentworth succeeded to the baronetcy in 1706.

Between 1707 and 1710 Hill acted as secretary to the maverick earl of Peterborough after defending his actions in his heroic poem *Camillus* (1707). Hill declined to follow Peterborough abroad, having, in 1710, married Margaret Morris (1694–1731), daughter of Edmund Morris, a successful grocer from Stratford, east London. The marriage proved happy: four of their nine children reached adulthood, and Hill was especially proud of the literary accomplishments of his three daughters, aptly named Urania, Astrea, and Minerva. Margaret Morris's dowry of £800 enabled Hill to relinquish his journalistic hack work for the *British Apollo* (a question and answer paper modelled on Dunton's *Athenian Mercury*, on which Gay had assisted him) to embark on a career as a theatre impresario. His period as stage manager at the troubled Theatre Royal in Drury Lane between 23 November and June 1710 ended when an actors' revolt got the better of his youth and inexperience. Later in that year he became director of opera at the Queen's Theatre in the Haymarket, achieving lasting fame for commissioning and writing the libretto for Handel's first opera for the English stage, *Rinaldo*, staged on 24 June 1711. His early tragedy *Elfrid* (premièred on 3 January 1710) met with an indifferent response not improved by its revision in 1731 as *Athelwold*. However, Hill's farce which accompanied *Elfrid*, *The Walking Statue*, quickly entered eighteenth-century repertory.

Hill's entrepreneurial energies found expression in a number of commercial ventures, the first of many he pursued during an exceptionally active life. In 1713 he took out a patent for the process of extracting oil from beechnuts and by 1716 had attracted over £12,000 from investors, but a succession of poor harvests between 1714 and 1716 ended the project. His subsequent project, the manufacture of chinaware in England, anticipated the industrial developments of Josiah Wedgwood. Another cherished plan which Hill failed to fulfil was the colonization of agricultural land in southern Carolina. Hill admired men of action as much as men of letters, as evident in his eulogistic poem to Peter the Great, *The Northern Star* (1718). Meanwhile he continued to write for the stage, his second tragedy, *The Fatal Vision, or, The Fall of Siam*, opening at Lincoln's Inn Fields on 7 February 1716. His third and best tragedy, the one-act *The Fatal Extravagance* (21 April 1721) dramatized a topical theme—ruin caused by South Sea Bubble investments. Hill permitted the play to appear under the name of his impecunious friend the Scottish poet Joseph Mitchell, signal evidence of his emerging role as a patron and friend of other writers. This play's success, coupled with the relaxing of the theatre monopolies and the growth of the unlicensed stage, encouraged Hill to attempt a return to stage management. In 1721 he

launched plans for a new resident English theatre company at the Little Theatre in the Haymarket but negotiations for this broke down late in the day. His adaptation of *King Henry the Fifth* on 5 December 1723, with a cast that included Barton Booth, Robert Wilks, and Anne Oldfield, met with moderate success.

Hill's most significant role during the 1720s was as patron and promoter of other writers. Between 1720 and 1728 he was perhaps the most important, certainly the most ubiquitous, man of letters in London literary life. His house at Petty France formed the backdrop for his friendship with many writers, members of the so-called 'Hillarian' circle (after the name Hillarius bestowed on Hill by his fervid admirer the writer Eliza Haywood). Other members of this circle were Edward Young, Richard Savage, John Dyer, Benjamin Victor, the Scottish poets Joseph Mitchell, David Mallet, James Thomson, and the poet Martha Fowke Sansom, whose autobiographical *Clio* (posthumously published in 1752) proclaimed a passionate and intense attachment to Hill. Hill's magnetic good looks (he was tall, dark-haired, and with striking blue eyes) made him the object of much female adulation. Hill helped Richard Savage promote his attempts to claim aristocratic legitimacy, publishing on his behalf *Miscellaneous Poems and Translations* (1726). Over a third of its ninety-two poems are by Hill, others by members of the Hillarian circle, documenting that group's intimate friendships. An ancillary venture was the *Plain Dealer* (1724–5), a journal inspired by Joseph Addison's *Tatler* which Hill co-edited with William Bond. This too promoted and encouraged the writings of Hill's acquaintances, with particular prominence given to religious sublime poetry. Essays by the critic John Dennis supported Hill's own enthusiasm for sublime biblical verse, first evidenced in his *The Creation* (1720) and in his epic *Gideon*, parts of which were printed in the *Plain Dealer* and *Miscellaneous Poems*.

By 1728 the Hillarian circle had begun to disperse and Hill turned once again to economic projects, his most ambitious yet, a plan funded by the York Buildings company to harvest Scottish pines on Speyside for use as mainmasts on British naval ships. Hill personally supervised the enterprise for several months during the spring of 1728, but it ultimately proved economically unsound, and by 1732 had accumulated a debit of nearly £7000. Scotland profited considerably from the company's extensive investment in the local infrastructures, but this was no consolation to shareholders.

During his absence from London, Hill achieved the dubious fame of seeing his initials featured in both Pope's *Peri Bathous* and *The Dunciad* of 1728 as a 'flying fish' and a mud-diving writer, a sly dig at Hill's inability to sustain the sublime style. The relationship between Hill and Pope was uneven, fuelled in part by Hill's envy of Pope's success and grudging admiration of his talents. He took Pope to task in a lengthy correspondence in which he maintained his dignity while Pope resorted to subterfuges denying that Hill was the intended victim of *The Dunciad*. Hill genuinely regretted Pope's incursion into 'low' satire: his *The Progress of Wit: a Caveat, for the Use of an Eminent Writer* (1730) turned the allegorical topography of *The Dunciad* against its own author, dramatizing Pope disappearing down the vortex of oblivion with his low subject matter.

Hill cared deeply about many of the issues that had motivated *The Dunciad*—namely, the decline in national cultural standards—but sought a different mode of redress. During the 1730s he lobbied Walpole's administration (notably in his 1731 *Advice to the Poets*) and members of the royal family, especially Prince Frederick in his 1737 *Tears of the Muses*, for public support for the arts, particularly the foundation of a national theatre and a dramatic academy. During the early 1730s he once again attempted to buy into the management of the Drury Lane theatre but proved unable to raise the capital. He took an active role from the sidelines, however, personally coaching actors, writing pamphlets addressing the state of the English stage (the anonymous *See and Seem Blind*, 1732) and launching *The Prompter*, which he co-edited with William Popple between 12 November 1734 and 2 July 1736, a journal which dedicated almost half its numbers to the state of the London stage. It was here that Hill formulated his theory of acting, espousing a more naturalistic mode than the rhetorical style favoured by traditional actors. His ideas were formalized in a poem called *The Art of Acting* (1746), a prose version, the *Essay on the Art of Acting*, being published in his posthumous works of 1753. Meanwhile Hill achieved his greatest success on the stage with his adaptation of Voltaire's *Zaire*. As *Zara* this first appeared during an amateur production for the benefit of the ailing William Bond at York Buildings in 1735, before being finally presented to great acclaim at the Drury Lane theatre on 12 January 1736. Voltaire's approval prompted Hill to adapt another of his plays, *Alzira*, a work with a similarly exotic setting, first staged at Lincoln's Inn Fields on 18 June 1736. Hill fell out with Voltaire in disagreement over his interpretation of the character of Brutus. His own dramatic version of the story, *Caesar*, failed to get accepted for performance, but in 1738 he published an essay on the subject, *An Enquiry into the Merit of Assassination*.

By the spring of 1737 the financial difficulties which faced Hill had become insurmountable. After several months spent in 'solitary rambles' around Britain, by August 1738 he had 'sold the best part of a too little *fortune*' (*Correspondence of Alexander Pope*, 4.111) and moved himself and his family from the house in Petty France to the rural London suburb of Plaistow. Although assailed by domestic problems (his errant son Julius Caesar, his feckless brother Gilbert, his daughter Urania's hasty marriage to the actor Warren Johnson, a nephew's suicide), he responded to his enforced 'retirement' with a flurry of activity. During his twelve years at Plaistow he planted over 100,000 French vines in hopes of creating an English wine industry and launched plans for the manufacture of potash, as well as publishing *The Fanciad* (a work designed to promote a biography of the duke of Marlborough, 1743), *The Impartial*, his 'free thoughts on the situation of our public affairs anno 1744', *Free Thoughts upon Faith* (1746), an adaptation of Voltaire's *Merope* (finished 1745, first staged in 1749), and three books of *Gideon, or, The Patriot* (1749).

Throughout the time at Plaistow (a place his friend the printer and novelist Samuel Richardson described as 'that terrible marsh-pit') Hill and his family suffered persistent poor health, but attempts to leave were thwarted by a long-standing lawsuit that was unresolved in Hill's own lifetime. The activities of these years are documented in his correspondence with Richardson (V&A, Forster MSS, fol. 13.2). Richardson and Hill enjoyed a close, even affectionate friendship. Richardson had printed both the *Plain Dealer* and *The Prompter* and went on to print all of Hill's works of the 1740s. On 8 December 1740 he sent Hill two volumes of the anonymously published *Pamela* to amuse his daughters. Hill soon guessed the author's identity and his eulogistic letters to Richardson supplemented the original preface and dedications when *Pamela* went into a second edition on 14 February 1741. Hill and his daughters were also among those readers to whom Richardson sent drafts of *Clarissa* for commentary. Richardson, anxious about the work's length, pleaded with Hill for suggestions for cuts. Hill responded with an abridged version (rejected by Richardson) which cut the novel's length by two thirds but introduced an obtrusive didacticism alien to Richardson's literary sensibility. Despite this difference of opinion, Richardson remained friends with Hill and maintained his correspondence with Urania for many years after Hill's death.

Hill was seriously ill for much of 1749 and died at his home, Hyde House in Plaistow, on 8 February 1750, the day before a benefit performance of *Merope* commanded by the prince of Wales. He was buried in Westminster Abbey alongside his wife. Many of Hill's poems and letters saw publication for the first time in a posthumous four-volume edition for the benefit of his family, *The Works of the Late Aaron Hill* (1753, second edn 1754). His plays and love letters appeared in the two-volume *Dramatic Works* (1760).

Nineteenth-century critics uniformly disparaged Hill's writings and personality. The *Dictionary of National Biography* saw him as 'absurd and a bore of the first water', an assessment only partially rectified by Brewster's biography (1913). Recent cultural historians have accorded Hill a far more interesting and pivotal role as a pioneer of developments in stage scenery and drama, as a theorist of the Longinian sublime, and particularly for his unceasing activities on behalf of writers of very different political persuasions and literary gifts. He was, in one critic's words, 'the cultural glue that holds this literary period together' (Hammond, 287).   CHRISTINE GERRARD

Sources *The works of the late Aaron Hill*, 4 vols. (1753) · D. Brewster, *Aaron Hill: poet, dramatist, projector* (1913) · R. Shiels, *The lives of the poets of Great Britain and Ireland*, ed. T. Cibber, 5 (1753), 5.252–76 · S. B. Blaydes, 'Aaron Hill', *Restoration and eighteenth-century dramatists: first series*, ed. P. R. Backscheider, DLitB, 80 (1989–), 200–18 · *Clio: the autobiography of Martha Fowke Sansom, 1689–1736*, ed. P. J. Guskin (1997) · A. D. McKillop, 'Letters [1721–1725] from Aaron Hill to Richard Savage', *N&Q*, 199 (1954), 388–91 · S. J. Barnes, 'Aaron Hill, and his father-in-law, Edmund Morris', *Essex Review*, 43 (1934), 61–8 · B. Victor, *The history of the theatres of London and Dublin*, 2 vols. (1761) · C. Gerrard, *The patriot opposition to Walpole: politics, poetry, and national myth, 1725–1742* (1994) · J. K., 'The life of Aaron Hill', in

The dramatic works of Aaron Hill, 1 (1760), i-xx • R. A. Davenport, 'The life of Aaron Hill', *The British poets* (1822), 60.7–26 • *The correspondence of Alexander Pope*, ed. G. Sherburn, 4 (1956), 94–168 • R. D. Hume, *Henry Fielding and the London theatre, 1728–1737* (1988) • T. C. D. Eaves and B. D. Kimpel, *Samuel Richardson: a biography* (1971) • B. Hammond, *Professional imaginative writing in England, 1670–1740: 'Hackney for bread'* (1997)

Archives BL, Sloane MSS, 4055, fol. 347; 4253 • BL, Stowe MS 143, fol. 128 | V&A, Forster MSS, fols. 13.2, 14.1, 15

Likenesses H. Hulsberg, line engraving, BM; repro. in Brewster, *Aaron Hill*

Hill, Abraham (*bap.* 1635, *d.* 1722), secretary of the Royal Society and cultural dilettante, baptized on 16 June 1635 at St Dionis Backchurch, London, was the eldest son of Richard Hill (*d.* 1660), a prosperous London cordwainer and alderman, and of his wife, Agnes (*d.* 1660). He seems to have had no higher education and was probably brought up as a merchant. By 1658 he had married Anne (*d.* 1661), daughter of Sir Bulstrode *Whitelocke, with whom he had a daughter, Frances (1658–1736), and a son, Richard (1660–1722). There were no children from Abraham's subsequent second marriage, to Elizabeth (1644–1672), daughter of Michael Pratt of Bromley by Bow, Middlesex.

In 1660 Hill's life took a crucial turn. He inherited a moderate fortune at his parents' death, he bought Sutton Manor at Sutton-at-Hone, Kent, and he rented chambers at Gresham College, right in the heart of the social and intellectual world of the Royal Society of London. There he was part of the discussions which preceded the society's inception. Hill's role at the centre of this institution is demonstrated by his election to its council for the sessions 1663 to 1666 and 1672 to 1721. At the same time he was treasurer (1663–6, 1677–99), and for two years he was secretary (1673–5). He attended frequently at both council and society meetings throughout his sixty-year affiliation.

Hill's role in the London intellectual scene was hardly noted by the great recorders of London life—John Evelyn, Samuel Pepys, and John Aubrey—but he played a large role in the life of Robert Hooke, whose diary provides a context for this otherwise unnoted Royal Society functionary. While in 1677 Hooke suspected that Hill backed Nehemiah Grew rather than himself for the post of secretary—'This evening Hill … plotted for Grew againste me' and 'Hill a dog for Grew. Hill and Louther slyly' (*Diary of Robert Hooke … 1672–1680*, 333, 335)—they were cronies who met at least once a week at coffee houses or taverns to discuss matters of scientific interest ('Excellent good discourse'; ibid., 245). Indeed, in 1676 they met almost every other day and sometimes up to three times in one day; and while such meetings later thinned the pattern of social life remained into the 1690s. They visited each other and for a time Hill was so central to Hooke's life that he noted the former's absences and returns to London. Apart from shared administrative tasks in the Royal Society such as the acquisition of the Arundel Library and the property and land around Chelsea College, Hooke showed Hill drafts of his papers and lectures and gave him copies of his books. They collected and shared books and occasionally collaborated on experiments. Hill was a member of the various philosophical clubs which Hooke spawned in the 1670s and 1680s and frequented all the fashionable haunts where philosophical matters were discussed.

Hill's activities within the society represent many facets of the late seventeenth-century scientific endeavour. On the council he audited accounts, pursued errant fellows' arrears, and worked on committees concerned with the society's real estate and other possessions; he registered its letters and papers and helped to index the *Philosophical Transactions*. In the society his contributions were eclectic but representative of a virtuoso's commitment to the widest definition of natural philosophy. His administrative skills came to the fore on committees such as those for the history of trades, surveying England, geological observations, and for handling correspondence and planning experiments for later meetings. He sent questionnaires to exotic places to be answered by travellers and collected curiosities brought back from such voyages; he helped to investigate water and air purity, the depth of the sea, breathing under water, hurricanes, distance travelled by shot at sea, Hooke's 'pepper mite' observations, the rate of fall of bodies, air pressure, and techniques of wine and paper making. But it is clear that Hill was not, himself, an experimenter. Many of his contributions came from his book learning—both ancient and modern authorities—and they usually displayed his eye for the exotic and strange such as Russian poisoning practices, their elk leather production, and the anatomy of whales. He used his reading for confirming or discounting what others produced at meetings. Later in life he was bequeathed money by Sir John Copley (*d.* 1709) for what was to become the Copley medal of the Royal Society.

From 1691 until the latter's death in 1694 Hill was comptroller to John Tillotson, archbishop of Canterbury. Indeed, after the accession of William and Mary his public career took off and he was a member of the Board of Trade between 1696 and 1702. In old age he retired to Sutton-at-Hone where he grew fruit for the making of perry and cider. Hill died on 5 February 1722 and was buried with his second wife in Sutton-at-Hone church. His career graphically demonstrates how multi-faceted the role of a 'man of business' and 'virtuoso' might be in the cultural life of the Royal Society and in government.   LOTTE MULLIGAN

Sources *Familiar letters which passed between Abraham Hill … and several eminent and ingenious persons* (1787) • T. Astle, *Life* [appended to *Familiar letters*] • R. E. W. Maddison, 'Abraham Hill', *Notes and Records of the Royal Society*, 15 (1960), 173–82 • T. Birch, *The history of the Royal Society of London*, 4 vols. (1756–7) • *The diary of Robert Hooke … 1672–1680*, ed. H. W. Robinson and W. Adams (1935) • 'The diary of Robert Hooke', *Early science in Oxford*, ed. R. T. Gunther, 10: *The life and work of Robert Hooke, part 4* (1935), 69–265 • M. 'Espinasse, *Robert Hooke* (1956) • M. Hunter, *The Royal Society and its fellows, 1660–1700: the morphology of an early scientific institution* (1982) • A. Hill, 'Some account of the life of Dr Isaac Barrow', in *The works of the learned Isaac Barrow … published by the Reverend Dr Tillotson*, 4 vols. (1683–7), vol. 1, pp. iv–ix • J. L. Chester, ed., *The reiester booke of Saynte De'nis Backchurch parishe … begynnynge … 1538*, Harleian Society, register section, 3 (1878)

Archives BL, corresp. and papers, Add. MSS 5488–5489 • journal book of the Royal Society; register book of the Royal Society, vol. 2 | BL, Sloane MSS 4036, 4046, 4059, 5488 · BL, commonplace books and papers, Sloane MSS 2891–2900, 2902–2903 **Likenesses** attrib. J. Hales, oils, RS

Hill, Adam (*c.*1548–1595), religious writer and Church of England clergyman, was a native of Salisbury, where he was one of the clever youths trained by Bishop John Jewel. He continued his education at Balliol College, Oxford, where he graduated on 5 April 1568 and was elected a fellow in the same year. He proceeded MA in 1572 but resigned his fellowship on 12 January 1573. He appears to have earned his living for some time as a schoolmaster, but also sought preferment in the church. In 1577 he became vicar of Westbury, and on 8 March 1578, aged about thirty, he was ordained priest by John Aylmer, bishop of London. In 1579 he was presented to the Wiltshire vicarage of Bishop's Lavington. The patron for this turn was Lord Burghley, which suggests that Hill was now regarded by the authorities as a man with a future. He resigned this second living in 1580 but in 1579 or 1580 obtained two further preferments in Dorset and Wiltshire. On 4 April 1582 he was instituted to the prebend of Gillingham Minor in Salisbury Cathedral, where on 16 January 1584 he became succentor. In the meantime he continued his studies, proceeding both BTh and DTh at Oxford on 2 July 1591.

The fruits of his learning are apparent in Hill's published writings. *The Crie of England*, a sermon denouncing the vices of the age, delivered at Paul's Cross in September 1593 and printed in 1595 at the request of the lord mayor and aldermen of London, to whom it is dedicated, is lavishly illustrated with citations from sacred and secular sources. And his learning is still more apparent in *The Defence of the Article* (1592), the article in question being the dogma of Christ's descent into hell, which Hill defended against Alexander Hume, an exiled Scottish presbyterian then employed as a schoolmaster at Bath. Here he deploys a massive array of authorities, classical, biblical, patristic, and contemporary, in a controversy which became increasingly acrimonious. When Hill complained of being traduced as 'a Bishopling and a time-server', Hume responded acidly 'Is truth a reveiling?' (Hume, 148).

The charge was an easy one for Hume to make. The *Defence* is dedicated to Archbishop Whitgift, and in it Hill stands forth as a defender of both religious orthodoxy and ecclesiastical authority. He attacks the attempt to allegorize the disputed article both because it undermines 'a most comfortable doctrine that Christ doth deliver us from hell' (Hill, *Defence*, 68v), and also because it leaves the way open to the free interpretation of all the fundamental doctrines of the church, creating a situation in which 'every man will be a head, no man a foote, every man a tung, no man a eare' (ibid., 30). Hume came back strongly, with a rejoinder (dedicated to Robert Devereux, second earl of Essex) whose title-page accuses his opponent of at least 600 'fallacies and deceits in reason', but Hill had no chance to retaliate in kind, for he died about 16 February 1595 and was buried in Salisbury Cathedral on 19 February. His exchanges with Hume reveal in passing that Hill had been an active preacher in Wiltshire, at various times

taking the pulpit in Laycock, Trowbridge, and Chippenham, and engaging in a lively dispute in Salisbury with a fellow prebendary, Abraham Conham, that had to be settled by the bishop. Such activities, combined with his evident learning and his readiness to defend the church establishment, give some support to Wood's belief that had Hill 'not been untimely snatched away by death, he would have been advanced to an high degree in the church' (Wood, *Ath. Oxon.*, 1.623).

HENRY SUMMERSON

Sources A. Hill, *The defence of the article: Christ descended into hell* (1592) · A. Hume, *A rejoynder to Doctor Hill* (1594) · A. Hill, *The crie of England* (1595) · Wood, *Ath. Oxon.*, new edn, 1.623–4 · Foster, *Alum. Oxon.*, 1500–1714, 2.709 · GL, MS 9535/1, fol. 16or · T. Phillipps, *Institutiones clericorum in comitatu Wiltoniae*, 1 (1825) · *Fasti Angl., 1541–1857*, [Salisbury], 43 · W. H. Jones, *Fasti ecclesiae Sarisberiensis, or, A calendar … of the cathedral body at Salisbury*, 2 (1881), 443

Hill, Alban (*d.* 1559), physician, was born in Wales, and studied at Oxford and at Bologna, where he took the degree of doctor of medicine. He lived in Cheapside in London for the rest of his life.

According to Wood, Hill became famous 'not only for the theoretic, but for the practical part of physic', and he was greatly respected in the parish of St Alban, Wood Street, where he lived and practised. John Caius calls him a good and learned man. Hill is mentioned in laudatory terms by Bassianus Landus of Piacenza (*Anatomia*, 1605, 2.225), with reference to a far from profound remark attributed to him about the uses of the mesentery.

Hill is said to have published a book on Galen, but no such work is known to be extant. He became a fellow of the College of Physicians on 23 March 1552, was censor each year from 1555 to 1558, and elect in 1558.

Hill died on 22 December 1559, and was buried in St Alban, Wood Street, London. His widow survived him until 31 May 1580.

CHARLES CREIGHTON, *rev.* SARAH BAKEWELL

Sources J. Cule, 'Welsh physicians in Renaissance Italy', *International congress on the history of medicine*, 21, Siena/1 (1968), 453–62 · Munk, *Roll* · Foster, *Alum. Oxon.* · J. Bale, *Illustrium Maioris Britannie scriptorum … summarium* (1548), Cert. 9, no. 38 · Wood, *Ath. Oxon.*

Hill, Albert George (1889–1969), athlete and coach, was born at 9 Bath Street, Southwark, London, on 24 March 1889, the son of William Thomas Hill, a wholesale stationer's packer, and his wife, Elizabeth Hutty. His first sporting encounters were with the local Gainsford athletic club, which he joined at the age of fifteen; he swam, cycled, and boxed, and took part in his first running race—coming second in a half mile. At this time he worked for the Brighton and South Coast Railway, at first in Brighton and then as a ticket collector at London Bridge. He continued to run with increasing success, concentrating on the longer distances; he was north London junior cross-country champion for three years in succession from 1907, and in 1910 won the Amateur Athletic Association (AAA) 4 mile championship, but did not compete in the championships in the following two years, and was not considered for the 1912 Olympic team. On 21 July 1912 he married Lily Wood (*b.* 1890), the daughter of Henry

Thomas Wood, flyman, in Tooting. They settled nearby, and subsequently moved to East Dulwich; the couple had two children.

The turning point in Hill's athletic career came in December 1912, when he joined the Polytechnic Harriers—the dominant non-university based club in metropolitan athletics before the First World War. From 1913 the club's professional coach was Scipio Africanus (Sam) Mussabini—best remembered for coaching Harold Abrahams to the Olympic title in 1924. Mussabini was a coach of considerable ability and vision, and was by far the biggest influence on Hill's career. He recognized the athlete's potential at the middle-distance events, and also the prestige that an Olympic title would bring, and set about training Hill for the 1916 Olympics.

Mussabini concentrated on three aspects of Hill's performance—his style, mental preparation, and even-paced running—and brought an innovative approach to all three. Together, Hill and Mussabini developed a distinctive style of running, known to contemporaries as the 'poly swing'. In contrast to the classical long elegant strides of the university athletes of the day, Hill held his arms low and close to the body, swinging from the elbows, while the feet and knees were carried as low as possible to achieve maximum economy of effort. Mussabini's techniques for mental preparation were well depicted in the film *Chariots of Fire*: he would gather information on other athletes, obtaining pictures and films showing them in action, and persuade his runners that their rivals had weaknesses that made them defeatable. Hill became so relaxed before major competitions that he would often sleep for several hours, and the railway-employed athlete became known as the Sleeper. Most innovative of all was Mussabini's use of the stopwatch to teach Hill how to run a race evenly. In contrast to the fashion of the day, when athletes would run races at an uneven pace, jostling for position, and then easing up before a finishing sprint, Mussabini realized that maintaining an even speed would produce better performances; he trained Hill so effectively that 'he hardly needed me standing, watch in hand, and letting him know at what rate he was covering his two or three laps' (Moon, 21).

Under Mussabini's guidance Hill made quick progress and was second in the 1914 AAA championship half-mile race. The war intervened and Hill served in France as a signalman with the Royal Flying Corps. When he returned to civilian life he was thirty years old; at that time many university-based athletes had retired by their mid-twenties. At the AAA championships in 1919 Hill showed his true potential. In one day he won the heat and final of the half-mile, the final of the mile, and ran a half-mile leg in the winning medley relay team; it was, wrote the veteran professional Walter George, 'the finest one man one day performance' he had seen (Moon, 42). It was the first time that one athlete had won both middle-distance events since 1887, and significantly Hill beat the much-fancied Swedish middle distance stars who, benefiting from Swedish neutrality, had continued to run, race, and set records during the war. Hill's performance was said to

have been influential in convincing the AAA that it was worth while to send a team to the Olympic games in Antwerp the following year.

Mussabini restricted Hill's racing in 1919 to the polytechnic and AAA championships, concentrating on training for the Olympics. At the AAA championships Hill was injured and was beaten in the half-mile by Bevil Rudd, and decided not to run in the mile. Rudd, who had previously run for England, opted instead to represent South Africa at the Olympics, and Hill was selected for the 800 metres, but only given a provisional place for the 1500 metres. The AAA honorary secretary, Sir Harry Barclay, questioned whether 'Albert wasn't over the Hill' (Moon, 46). After winning the Kinnaird mile on 17 July Hill was formally selected for the 1500 metres, along with the 1912 champion, A. N. S. Jackson—that Hill had had to prove his abilities seems nonsensical when set against the selection of the former university athlete Jackson, who had been wounded in the war and walked with a cane, and never had an intention to run.

At the Olympics Hill faced a tough heat for the 800 metres as the Belgian authorities had seeded the athletes and put all the top seeds in the same race so as to give the less able runners a chance. Hill was third in the heat to his rivals Rudd and the American Earl Elby. In the semi-final he ran the fastest time of any athlete; and on 17 August 1920 won the 800 metre final, passing Rudd in the finishing straight to record a time of 1 min. 53.4 sec., breaking the 32-year-old British record by a second. In the final of the 1500 metres, Hill ran with Philip Noel Baker, who paced him past the rest of the field, and Hill won with Baker second. Hill also ran in the 3000 metre team event, where Great Britain won a silver medal. At thirty-one, he remains the oldest athlete to have won either the 800 or 1500 metres at the Olympics.

The following year Hill prepared for an attack on the British mile record of 4 min. 16.8 sec., which had been held by Joe Binks since 1902; again he was guided by Mussabini, and also advised by Walter George, who had run 4 min. 12.75 sec. as a professional in 1887. George felt that Hill could run 4 min. 8 sec. if he kept to an even pace, but in the event he was drawn into a race with Henry Stallard, the twenty-year-old Cambridge student, and the two ran the first quarter in 59.6 seconds. They remained together stride for stride until the final bend, in a race that was considered a classic contest of inter-war athletics. As they came into the final straight Hill drew away, and the large crowd at Stamford Bridge taunted Joe Binks, by this time a journalist for the *News of the World*, with the chant 'It's going, it's going, his head is falling low. I hear those unkind voices calling, "Poor old Joe"' (Moon, 60). Hill won in a time of 4 min. 13.8 sec.

Hill retired shortly afterwards; the AAA received invitations for him to race abroad but these appear never to have been passed on. Instead Hill turned to coaching, first with Blackheath Harriers, and from November 1923 he assisted Mussabini. He spent a period of time in America from 1925 to 1926 but returned to London and took over as chief coach to Polytechnic Harriers after Mussabini's death, in 1927, continuing to train some of Mussabini's athletes, including one of the most famous sprinters of the day, Jack London. He was appointed with a salary of £40 per year, but the payment of this seems to have been irregular, and Hill always had other employment, firstly with the railways, and subsequently sorting newspapers at night for W. H. Smith. Hill's greatest achievements as a coach came with the Blackheath Harrier Sydney Wooderson, whom he began to train as a schoolboy in 1931. Hill recognized Wooderson's great potential and developed him gradually until, by the late 1930s, he was a world-record holder—Wooderson ran 4 min. 6.4 sec. for the mile in 1937 and many people believe that had the war not intervened he could have won an Olympic title and run a mile in less than 4 minutes.

Wooderson described Hill as his 'guide, philosopher and friend' (Moon, 77), and it was Wooderson who accompanied Hill to the station when he decided to emigrate to Canada with his wife and youngest daughter, in 1947. The family went to join Hill's eldest daughter, Alma, and son-in-law, who was a market gardener near Winnipeg. Wooderson and Hill never met again, and Hill's name was largely forgotten by the time of his death in Canada on 8 January 1969.   M. A. BRYANT

Sources G. Moon, *Albert Hill: a proper perspective* (1992) • P. Lovesey, *The official centenary history of the Amateur Athletics Association* (1979) • I. Buchanan, *British Olympians: a hundred years of gold medallists* (1991) • b. cert. • m. cert.
Likenesses H. F. Davis, photograph, 1925, repro. in J. Huntington-Whiteley, ed., *The book of British sporting heroes* (1998) [exhibition catalogue, NPG, 16 Oct 1998–24 Jan 1999] • photographs, repro. in Moon, *Albert Hill*, pp. 28, 80

Hill, Alexander (1785–1867), Church of Scotland minister and theologian, was born at St Andrews, Fife, on 19 July 1785, the son of George *Hill (1750–1819), principal of St Mary's College, and his wife, Harriet Scott. He studied at the university of his native city, and graduated in September 1804. He was licensed as a preacher in 1806; for nine years afterwards he travelled in England and abroad, acting as tutor to a relative and pursuing his own studies, especially in the classics. In 1815 he was ordained as minister of Colmonell in Ayrshire; in June 1816 he was translated to the neighbouring parish of Dailly, where he remained for twenty-five years. He graduated DD at St Andrews in 1828. He married Margaret (d. 1874), only daughter of Major Crawford HEICS of Newfield; they had nine children.

In 1840 Hill was appointed professor of divinity at the University of Glasgow; one of the competitors for the chair was Thomas Chalmers. Hill was an undistinguished rural clergyman, whose only significant theological publication was an edition of his father's *Lectures in Divinity* (1825); it was clear that his only real credential for the post was his descent from the impeccably moderate family which had dominated the politics of early nineteenth-century St Andrews. His victory humiliated the much better qualified Chalmers and fuelled the rivalry between the moderate and evangelical wings of the Church of Scotland.

Hill was one of several moderates whose good character helped rebuild respect for the church after the Disruption; his good judgement and kind heart made him popular with both his parishioners and his students. While his theological views remained essentially those of his father, he expressed them with greater evangelical enthusiasm. He was a hearty participant in services and a contemporary described his sermons as 'instinct with life' and breathing 'the spirit of Christianity'. His delivery was probably enhanced by his appearance: tall and thin, Hill had 'prominent and expressive' features (Smith, 368).

After an unsuccessful candidature for the moderatorship of the general assembly in 1840, Hill was elected to the post in 1845, in the wake of the Disruption of 1843. He became an important figure in the general assembly, founding an association for increasing the livings of disadvantaged clergy and assisting with other charitable schemes. He was also the author of several pastoral and devotional works, including *A Book of Family Prayers* (1837). He resigned his chair in November 1862, and died at his home, 24 Hillington Square, Ayr, on 27 January 1867.

G. W. SPROTT, rev. ROSEMARY MITCHELL

Sources *Fasti Scot.* • *Edinburgh Evening Courant* (Jan 1867) • *Dailly Parish Magazine* (July 1885) • J. Smith, *Our Scottish clergy*, 3rd ser. (1851), 364–9 • Irving, *Scots.* • J. F. Waller, ed., *The imperial dictionary of universal biography*, 3 vols. (1857–63) • S. J. Brown, *Thomas Chalmers and the godly commonwealth in Scotland* (1982), 319–20 • NA Scot., SC6/44/33/144
Wealth at death £11,575 8s. 2d.: inventory, 19 March 1867, NA Scot., SC6/44/33/144

Hill, Sir Alexander Galloway Erskine-, first baronet (1894–1947), lawyer and politician, was born Alexander Galloway Erskine Hill on 3 April 1894 at Garnreth House, Bridge of Allan, Stirlingshire, the eldest of the three children of Robert Alexander Hill (1870–1931), solicitor and broker, and his wife, Marion Clark Galloway (d. 1962), daughter of John Galloway of Kilmeny, Ardrossan, Ayrshire. In 1943 Hill formally adopted the surname Erskine-Hill. He was educated at Rugby School and at Trinity College, Cambridge, where he graduated BA with a third in the historical tripos in 1915 and went on to take his MA and LLB in 1919. In 1914 he volunteered for military service with the British expeditionary force in France and was commissioned into the 6th Cameronians, later serving with the 3rd Cameron Highlanders. He was wounded twice. From 1916 to 1918 he served as aide-de-camp to the general officer commanding-in-chief in Scotland. On 3 December 1915 Hill married Christian Hendry Colville (1887–1947), sister of (David) John Colville, the Conservative politician, and daughter of John *Colville [see under Colville family (per. 1861–1916)], a steel and iron master who had been a Liberal MP. They had two sons and two daughters.

After standing unsuccessfully as a non-coalition Liberal in North Lanarkshire at the general election of 1918, Hill returned to legal studies and in 1919 or 1920 was called to the English bar at the Inner Temple and in 1920 to the Scottish bar. As an advocate he specialized in reparation cases. In 1932 he was appointed standing junior counsel to the department of agriculture for Scotland. In the same year he was made an advocate-depute, a position he held until 1935. In August 1935 he was made a KC and shortly afterwards he was elected Unionist MP for Edinburgh North at the general election held in November of that year. As an MP he received praise for his support of small traders' interests and for sponsoring the Custody of Children (Scotland) Bill in 1939. In 1939 he was appointed parliamentary private secretary to the lord advocate.

The most significant phase of Hill's career opened with his election in December 1940 as chairman of the Conservative backbench members' 1922 committee. In this role Hill (or Erskine-Hill from 1943) played a pivotal role between the footsoldiers of the Conservative Party in the House of Commons and the coalition government led by Winston Churchill. By early 1941 there was a feeling among Conservative backbenchers that their voice was not being heard. The 1922 committee leadership was successful in defending their right to invite ministers to address the committee. In March 1941 a liaison committee of 1922 members, including Hill, was formed to work with Conservative central office and ensure, for example, that Conservative speakers were heard from ministry of information and BBC platforms.

Late in 1941 and early in 1942 Conservative MPs made clear their discontent with the government's conduct of the war. Hill reportedly approached Anthony Eden as part of the 1922 committee's attempts to limit Churchill's responsibility for running the war, but was rebuffed. These moves coincided with the long-running concern over war production on which Hill had spoken out publicly. Among Labour MPs there was pressure on this issue for taking transport, mining, and munitions manufacture into public ownership and for the extension of compulsory service for men and women. Hill, who led backbench attempts to curb 'nationalization by stealth' (*Headlam Diaries*, 16 Dec 1941, 286), spoke against both proposals in a debate on national maximum effort in December 1941. When in March 1942 Hugh Dalton, president of the Board of Trade, proposed fuel rationing with coupons, Hill impressed upon Dalton and the lord privy seal, Sir Stafford Cripps, that Conservative members did not support the government's proposal. Hill repeated this view in a letter to the *Sunday Times* of 10 May 1942, also objecting to the large number of bureaucrats such a scheme would involve. In the resulting press controversy the *Daily Herald* accused the 1922 committee of trying to intimidate the government. The official history of the war describes this controversy as an unacknowledged test of the relative strengths of the parties and interests in the coalition government.

In May 1942 Hill was responsible for tackling James Stuart, Conservative chief whip in the House of Commons, about resentment over supposed favouring of Labour MPs in debates. Another development during Erskine-Hill's chairmanship was the change, in February 1943, to the 1922 committee's rules to allow ministerial office-holders to be members, which led to more substantive discussion of parliamentary business. He retired as chairman of the 1922 committee at the end of 1944. A member of the government, R. A. Butler, who regretted Hill's election as chairman, reportedly commented that he was 'too stupid to do anything but intrigue' (*Diaries of James Chuter Ede*, 103).

Erskine-Hill was created a baronet in June 1945. At the general election in the following month he narrowly lost his Edinburgh North seat to Labour, but was adopted as prospective candidate for the next election. Ill health forced him to give up this position in the spring of 1947 and on 6 June 1947 he died at 13 Moray Place, Edinburgh, of multiple myeloma. His funeral service was held in St Giles's Cathedral, Edinburgh. Musing on his early death, a colleague, Cuthbert Headlam, reflected that although 'ambitious politically', it was unlikely that he would have much success: he was 'sound rather than showy, and not in the political or party swim' (*Headlam Diaries*, 510).

GORDON F. MILLAR

Sources *The Times* (9 June 1947) · *The Scotsman* (9 June 1947) · *WWW*, 1941–50, 361 · b. cert. · m. cert. · d. cert. · P. Goodhart, *The 1922: the story of the conservative backbenchers' parliamentary committee* (1973) · Burke, *Peerage* (1999) · J. Ramsden, *The age of Churchill and Eden, 1940–1957* (1995), 28–31 · WWBMP, vol. 3 · F. J. Grant, ed., *The Faculty of Advocates in Scotland, 1532–1943*, Scottish RS, 145 (1944), 102 · S. P. Walker, *The Faculty of Advocates, 1800–1986* (1986) · *The Times* (7 June 1947) · *The Times* (5 Dec 1941) · Kelly, *Handbk* (1947), 704–5 · R. R. James, *Anthony Eden* (1986), 261 · F. W. S. Craig, *British parliamentary election results, 1918–1949*, rev. edn (1977), 635 · F. W. S. Craig, *British parliamentary election results, 1918–1949*, 3rd edn (1983), 582 · *Parliament and politics in the age of Churchill and Attlee: the Headlam diaries, 1935–1951*, ed. S. Ball, CS, 5th ser., 14 (1999) · *Labour and the wartime coalition: from the diaries of James Chuter Ede, 1941–1945*, ed. K. Jefferys (1987)

Likenesses photograph, repro. in *The Scotsman*

Wealth at death £21,876 0s. 10d.: confirmation, 5 July 1947, *CCI*

Hill, Alexander Staveley (1825–1905), barrister and politician, was born at Dunstall Hall, Wolverhampton, Staffordshire, on 21 May 1825, the only son of Henry Hill (1789–1872), a banker, and his wife, Anne, daughter of Luke Staveley of Hunmanby, Yorkshire. Educated at King Edward's School, Birmingham, in the house of James Prince Lee, he was in the first form with Joseph Barber Lightfoot and Brooke Foss Westcott. Matriculating at Exeter College, Oxford, in 1844, he obtained fourth-class honours in classics in 1848 and graduated BA in 1852, BCL in 1854, and DCL in 1855. He held a Staffordshire fellowship at St John's College, Oxford, from 1854 until his marriage in 1864 to Katherine Crumpston Florence (d. 14 May 1868), eldest daughter of Miles Ponsonby of Hale Hall, Cumberland.

Hill was admitted to the Inner Temple on 6 November 1848 and called to the bar on 21 November 1851. He joined the Oxford circuit, and took silk in 1868. He was elected a bencher of his inn the same year, and served as treasurer in 1886. He was recorder of Banbury from 1866 to 1903 and deputy high steward of Oxford University from 1874 until his death. Meanwhile he acquired a large practice at the parliamentary bar. He had to give this up on entering the House of Commons in 1868. But until 1887 he enjoyed a good common-law practice, besides holding a leading position in the Probate, Divorce, and Admiralty Division and frequently acting as arbitrator in important rating cases. He was leader of the Oxford circuit from 1886 to 1892. He was counsel to the Admiralty and judge advocate of the fleet from 1875 until his retirement through failing health in 1904.

A staunch Conservative in politics, and an early supporter of the volunteer movement in 1859, Hill made two unsuccessful attempts to enter parliament, standing for Wolverhampton in 1861 and Coventry in March 1868. He was elected for Coventry in December 1868, retaining a seat in the house for thirty-two years—representing Coventry (1868–74), West Staffordshire (1874–85), and the Kingswinford division of Staffordshire (1885–1900). He was notable as one of the earliest supporters of the policy afterwards known as tariff reform, pressing in 1869 for an inquiry on behalf of the silk weavers of Coventry into the effect of the commercial treaty with France. In speeches delivered in 1869 and 1870 he showed the weakness of Great Britain's position in endeavouring to maintain a free-trade policy against the operation of foreign tariffs. He also represented the interests of coal owners, opposing mines legislation. In the early 1880s he became a supporter of Lord Randolph Churchill's so-called 'Fourth Party' and was disappointed when Churchill reached an accommodation with the Conservative leadership. The preferment which he sought was slow in coming; after unsuccessfully angling for the governorship of Queensland, he was placated with a privy councillorship in 1892 by the Conservative whips, fearful that he would otherwise vacate his seat.

In 1881 Hill, who was a promoter of the Imperial Federation League, went to Canada to study its suitability as a centre for emigration. He established a large cattle ranch 70 miles south of Calgary, then in the Northwest Territories, and since included in the province of Alberta. He often visited the ranch, which was called New Oxley. In 1885 he published a volume describing life among the foothills of the Rocky Mountains entitled *From Home to Home: Autumn Wanderings in the North West, 1881–1884*, illustrated by his second wife, Mary Frances (*d.* 1897), daughter of Francis Baird of St Petersburg, whom he had married in 1876. Toronto University made him an honorary LLD in 1892. Hill died at his home, Oxley Manor, Wolverhampton, on 28 June 1905. He was survived by his only child, Henry Staveley Staveley-Hill (1865–1946), a county court judge and successor to his father as Conservative MP for the Kingswinford constituency (1905–18).

C. E. A. BEDWELL, *rev.* M. C. CURTHOYS

Sources *The Times* (30 June 1905) · *Men and women of the time* (1899) · Walford, *County families* · R. Shannon, *The age of Salisbury, 1881–1902: unionism and empire* (1996)
Likenesses B. Stone, photograph, 1897, NPG · Desanges, portrait, priv. coll.; formerly in possession of family, 1912
Wealth at death £98,045 11s. 2d.: probate, 16 Aug 1905, CGPLA Eng. & Wales

Hill, Alfred Hawthorne [Benny] (1924–1992), comedian, was born in Southampton on 25 January 1924, the younger son and second of three children of Alfred Hill (*d.* 1971), a former circus performer and the manager of a surgical

Alfred Hawthorne [Benny] **Hill (1924–1992)**, by Bob Collins, *c.*1957

appliance shop in Southampton, and his wife, Helen, *née* Cave. His father's occupation caused Hill some childhood embarrassment, being taunted by shouts of 'Hillie's dad sells french letters'. His mother was by all accounts a sweet, loving person—a love reciprocated by the young Alfred. At the age of eleven he won a scholarship to the Richard Taunton School in Southampton, but he left in 1939, when he was fifteen. After a variety of menial jobs he became a milkman driving a horse-drawn cart round Southampton and fantasizing that he was Wyatt Earp, or some other Western legend. He later capitalized on this experience with the song 'Ernie—the Fastest Milkman in the West', which was a number one hit in 1971. In the early 1940s Hill became an accomplished semi-professional entertainer, specializing in broad comedy and *double entendres* that were largely lifted from Max Miller, the popular comedian of the day.

In 1943, after a mix-up in Cardiff where he had been arrested as a deserter (his call-up papers had never reached him), Hill duly joined the army as a driver/mechanic in the Royal Electrical and Mechanical Engineers. He hated it, and after the war never drove again. In 1945 he applied to and was taken on by the army entertainment unit 'Stars in battledress'. There he was spotted by Colonel Richard Stone, who liked him so much that when he returned to civilian life and started a theatrical agency he recruited Hill as one of his first clients. Before that Private Hill had become Mr Hill, his service career behind him, and after auditioning unsuccessfully at the Windmill Theatre in 1947 he considered his future; Alf Hill did not have the right ring to it and, after considering alternatives, Hill settled on Benny—the American comedian Jack Benny being one of his heroes. He then tried out his comedy material in pubs and working men's clubs—a tough but useful training ground for a would-be funny man.

Moving up-market in 1947 Hill appeared in a revue, *Spotlight*, at the Twentieth-Century Theatre in Notting Hill Gate, and after that came more appearances in pubs and clubs. It was now that Richard Stone took over and in 1948 he booked Hill into a seaside summer season in Cliftonville, Kent, in the show *Gay Time*, as 'feed' (that is, straight man) to principal comedian Reg Varney, who described Hill as 'brilliant'. Hill was indeed brilliant as a feed, but not yet as a solo comedian. However, television had erupted in the early 1950s and was to take Hill out of the also-rans and, in time, to make him an internationally known English comedian—momentarily perhaps even more famous than Chaplin—and a multi-millionaire. At a time when television was grateful for anything, Hill wrote and performed material that was well above the average for the day, and he also used the medium's technical flexibility, which enabled him to perform such tricks as impersonating the entire line-up of panel games, both male and female.

Now established on television, Hill returned to radio in 1954 with the successful series starring ventriloquist Peter Brough, *Educating Archie*, in which he played the tutor of the dummy Archie. In that role he followed in the footsteps of Tony Hancock, Max Bygraves, and Beryl Reid, among others. Then came West End theatre in the shape of *Paris by Night* (1955), which featured a number of scantily dressed showgirls. The revue, which co-starred the accident-prone comedy magician Tommy Cooper, ran for a year. Hill's next stage venture was in 1959. *Fine Fettle*, at the Palace Theatre, was a musical revue. The critic Milton Shulman, writing in the *Evening Standard* in August 1959, commented that Hill brought 'a secret lip-smacking irreverence, which gives his humour a boisterous, even bawdy, quality'. This insight summed up the whole of Hill's work. Popular as he was when he was alive, after his death he disappeared from the public consciousness very quickly, and if remembered at all it was largely for his grossness and lack of subtlety.

Hill's film career was not startling. In 1956 he starred in *Who Done It?*, written by T. E. B. Clarke and directed by Basil Dearden. According to Hill it was not a happy début. His next film was *Light up the Sky*, in 1959, in which he and Tommy Steele co-starred as partners in a music-hall double act who were called up in the Second World War and stationed on a searchlight battery. In 1965 he had a cameo role in *Those Magnificent Men in their Flying Machines*, and in 1968 another cameo role in *Chitty Chitty Bang Bang*. In 1969 came *The Italian Job*, which starred Noël Coward and Michael Caine, and in which Benny Hill played a sex-mad computer expert who lusted after large women and wound up in gaol. In 1970 he co-produced a short film, *Eddie in August*, in which he played a girl chaser (unlucky, of course). It was not a success, and Hill went back to the safer waters of television.

Apart from television shows at the BBC and at Thames Television, Hill appeared in television commercials for a popular soft drink of the day. His one essay into the classical repertory was to play Bottom in an Associated Rediffusion Television production of *A Midsummer Night's Dream* in 1964. His most popular television character was Fred Scuttle, a lisping, bespectacled buffoon, but, that said, his characters all had a certain similarity—whatever the hat or the wig he had on, it was always the same Benny Hill underneath. In 1980, in the *Los Angeles Times*, Howard Rosenberg wrote of Hill's astonishing impact on American television:

> Hill's unlikely stylistic mix of Charlie Chaplin, Ernie Kovacs and Milton Berle—the film speed-ups, blackouts, visual gags, drag queening, cheap double entendres and bawdy songs—emerges as a sort of polished drivel, a triumph of trash so revolting that unbelievably you tend to like it.

Hill was eventually sacked from Thames Television in 1988, after a ten-minute interview. He was understandably upset, but his ratings were falling, and some of his jokes and characterizations had been recycled once too often. He died, unmarried, of heart failure in his flat in Twickenham Road, Teddington, London, on Saturday 18 April 1992. He was alone and his body was not discovered until the following Tuesday—a sad end for a man who had made the world laugh.   BARRY TOOK

Sources B. Took, *Star turns* (1992) · J. Smith, *The Benny Hill story* (1988) · L. Hill, *Saucy boy*, rev. edn (1992) · M. Forwood, *The real Benny Hill* (1992) · private information (2004) · personal knowledge (2004) · *The Times* (22 April 1992) · *The Independent* (22 April 1992) · M. Lewisohn, *Funny, peculiar: the true story of Benny Hill* (2002)
Likenesses B. Collins, photograph, *c.*1957, NPG [*see illus.*] · photograph, repro. in *The Times* · photograph, repro. in *The Independent* · photographs, repro. in Took, *Star turns* · photographs, repro. in Smith, *Benny Hill story* · photographs, repro. in Hill, *Saucy boy* · photographs, repro. in Forwood, *Real Benny Hill* · photographs, Hult. Arch.
Wealth at death £7,548,192: probate, 5 June 1992, *CGPLA Eng. & Wales*

Hill, Alsager Hay (1839–1906), social reformer, born on 1 October 1839 at Gressonhall Hall, Norfolk, was the second son in a family of five sons and six daughters of John David Hay Hill, lord of the manor of Gressonhall, and his wife, Margaret, second daughter of Ebenezer John Collett of Hemel Hempsted, MP from 1814 to 1830. He was educated at Brighton College (1850–54) and at Cheltenham College (1854–7), and while a schoolboy published at Cheltenham a small volume of poems, *Footprints of Life* (1857). In 1857 he won an exhibition to Caius College, Cambridge, migrating as scholar to Trinity Hall in 1858, where he graduated LLB in 1862. At Cambridge he started the Chit Chat debating club and was treasurer of the union. A student of the Inner Temple from 3 October 1860, he was called to the bar on 26 January 1864. He joined the south-eastern circuit, but soon devoted his energies to journalism and to literature, interesting himself especially in poor-law and labour questions, and doing active work as almoner to the Society for the Relief of Distress in the east of London.

In letters to the press during 1868 Hill called attention to weaknesses in the poor law, and urged a more scientific classification of paupers (*The Times*, 9 Jan 1868). His pamphlet *Our Unemployed*, prepared as a competition essay for the National Association for the Promotion of Social Science (NAPSS) and published in 1867, was one of the first to call public attention to the problem of unemployment—and indeed to use the word—and to suggest a national system of labour registration. Other pamphlets followed, such as *Lancashire Labour and the London Poor* (1871), *Impediments to the Circulation of Labour, with a Few Suggestions for their Removal* (1873), *The Unemployed in Great Cities, with Suggestions for the Better Organisation of Labourers* (1877), and *Vagrancy* (1881), and a further important article for the NAPSS in 1875 on unemployment in large towns.

Hill was a pioneer of the system of labour exchanges in England, and in 1871 established in Greek Street, Soho, the Employment Inquiry Office and Labour Registry, which was subsequently transferred to 15 Russell Street, Covent Garden, as the Central Labour Exchange, Employment, Emigration, and Industrial Intelligence Office. There, as director, Hill gave advice to applicants for assistance. In connection with the exchange and at the same offices he founded and edited in 1871 *Labour News*, which became an organ of communication between employers and potential employees seeking work in all parts of Britain. Hill had agents and correspondents in the chief industrial centres, who sent notes on the condition of the local labour markets. Hill's venture, which was not profitable, sapped his strength and resources; on his retirement a committee of working men managed the paper and contributed from the profits to Hill's maintenance. From 1877 onwards he also edited *The Industrial Handbook*, and superintended the publication in 1881 of *The Industrial Index to London* by H. Llewelyn Williams as well as *Business Aspects of Ladies' Work*. These pamphlets were handy guides to employment, for both men and women. He also edited in 1870–71 a series of penny *Statutes for the People*, which aimed at giving the labouring class cheap legal advice. Hill likewise took a prominent part, from its foundation in 1869, in the work of the Charity Organization Society, acting as one of the honorary secretaries of the council until July 1870 and as an active member of the council until 1880, subsequently being a vice-president. Hill was distinguished in the society for being practically active as well as morally admonitory.

Through life Hill continued to write verse, collecting his poems in *Rhymes with Good Reason* (1870–71), *A Scholar's Day Dream* (1870; 2nd edn, 1881), and *A Household Queen* (1881). One of his poems, 'Mrs. Grundy's Sunday', was widely circulated to further the aims of the National Sunday League for rational Sunday recreation. He was vice-president of the league from 1876 to 1890 and lectured at its Sunday Evenings for the People. The Working Men's Club and Institute Union also found in Hill a zealous supporter. Hill fell in his last years into ill health and some poverty, living in retirement at Boston, Lincolnshire. He died there, unmarried, on 2 August 1906, and was buried at Gressonhall. He was elected a member of the Athenaeum in 1877, and was president of the Cheltonian Society (1877–8).

W. B. OWEN, *rev.* H. C. G. MATTHEW

Sources Venn, *Alum. Cant.* • A. A. Hunter, ed., *Cheltenham College register, 1841–1910* (1911) • L. G. Robinson, letter, *The Times* (4 Feb 1910) • G. S. Jones, *Outcast London* (1971) • C. L. Mowat, *The Charity Organisation Society, 1869–1913* (1961) • private information (1912) [Revd R. Hay Hill] • C. E. Collet and H. H. Collett, *The family of Collett*, 4 vols. (1935)
Wealth at death £2098 9s. 4d.: administration, 5 Nov 1906, CGPLA Eng. & Wales

Hill [*née* Paton], **Amelia Robertson** (1820–1904), sculptor, was born at Wooer's Alley, Dunfermline, Fife, the daughter of Joseph Neil Paton (1797–1874), a damask designer, and his wife, Catherine McDiarmid (*d.* 1853). The Patons were a notable Scottish artistic family; her brothers were the painters Sir Joseph Noël *Paton and Waller Hugh *Paton, both associated with Scottish Pre-Raphaelitism.

Hill began her career as a painter. An early work is her study of the novelist Dinah Mulock Craik (1844; NPG). Scant record of Hill's sculptural education survives. It is possible, however, that she trained in the studio of William Brodie (1815–1881), whose protégé D. W. Stevenson (1842–1904) developed a similar reputation to Hill's for portrait busts and imaginative subjects. Her earliest works were portraits of family and friends, including a memorial medallion of the Hon. Charles Bruce, young son of the earl of Elgin (exh. Royal Scottish Academy, 1864; priv. coll.). Her professional career took off in 1862, just before her marriage, aged forty-two, and as his second wife, to the painter and photographic pioneer David Octavius *Hill (1802–1870). It is likely that Hill's influential position as secretary of the Royal Scottish Academy for thirty years (his successor was Brodie) assisted her career as a sculptor of public monuments. D. O. Hill was eighteen years older than his wife and nearing the end of his career. Hill was thus unhindered by the conventional childbearing role of the Victorian middle-class wife. The Hills lived at Rock House, Calton Hill, and were prominent in Edinburgh artistic life. Hill shared a taste for collecting and scholarly interests with her husband. One interviewer was struck by her wide knowledge of 'literature, sociology, occultism [and] the natural sciences' (Gifford).

During the 1860s Hill's public career flourished. Her portrait subjects included Mary Louise, countess of Elgin (1863; Lord Elgin Hotel, Ottawa), R. S. Candlish, principal of New College (1865; University of Edinburgh), Thomas Carlyle (1866–7; National Trust of Scotland collection), the president of the Royal Scottish Academy, Sir George Harvey (1867), and the physicist David Brewster (1867). These portraits (all marble busts) were exhibited with success at the Royal Scottish Academy and the Royal Academy. In 1870 Hill received an important public commission for George Meikle Kemp's Scott monument (1840–46) in Edinburgh, in a scheme to mark the centenary of the birth of Sir Walter Scott. Hill contributed three figures, *Magnus Troil*, *Richard the Lionheart*, and *Minna Troil*, from Scott's novels. The other sculptors included Brodie and Stevenson. In 1875, on a similar theme, Hill produced a bronze portrait medallion for the Regent Murray memorial at Linlithgow. However, it was her bronze memorial statue of the explorer David Livingstone (1875–6; Prince's Street

Gardens, Edinburgh) that received the most public attention. It was erected by public subscription and with a donation of £50 from Edinburgh town council.

Hill's work is best represented by her portrayals of historical and literary figures such as Robert Burns and Percy Bysshe Shelley (cast exh. Royal Scottish Academy, 1882) or Arthurian legend. She declared it to be 'the dream of her life' (Gifford) to portray Shelley. A late commission was for a statue of Burns at Dumfries (1881–2; Church Place, Dumfries). Hill was also inspired by contemporary heroic figures such as Carlyle and Livingstone. Like her brother Noël, she held high moral ideals, which fired a romantically charged imagination, and both her husband and her brother were frequent subjects. Two plaster and wax medallion portraits of David Octavius Hill (c.1851) and a marble portrait bust of Noël Paton (1872) are in the Scottish National Portrait Gallery, Edinburgh.

Hill also sought out new exhibition venues, exhibiting the marble group *Goodnight Papa* at Dundee in 1877. Increased recognition came with the newly founded Edinburgh Albert Institute, which awarded her a sculpture medal in 1878. After the mid-1880s she exhibited infrequently, describing herself in the 1891 census as 'sculptor, retired'. However, Hill continued to exhibit at the Royal Scottish Academy until 1902, two years before her death at her home, Newington Lodge, 38 Mayfield Terrace, Edinburgh, on 5 July 1904 aged eighty-three. She was buried at the Dean cemetery, Edinburgh.

PATRICIA DE MONTFORT

Sources R. L. Woodward, 'Nineteenth century Scottish sculpture', PhD diss., U. Edin., 1979 · C. B. de Laperriere, ed., *The Royal Scottish Academy exhibitors, 1826–1990*, 4 vols. (1991) · Graves, *RA exhibitors* · H. Smailes, *The concise catalogue of the Scottish National Portrait Gallery* (1990) · W. Gifford, 'The Patons of Dunfermline', *Dunfermline Press* (25 July 1903) · W. Gifford, 'The Patons of Dunfermline', *Dunfermline Press* (1 Aug 1903) · S. A. Tooley, 'Notable Victorians', *Weekly Scotsman* (13 Feb 1932) · will, NA Scot., Sc 70/1/439, fol. 131 · NA Scot., GD 224 666/1–3 · C. E. C. Waters, *Women in the fine arts, from the seventh century B.C. to the twentieth century A.D.* (1900), 160 · M. H. Noel-Paton and J. P. Campbell, *Noel Paton, 1821–1901*, ed. F. Irwin (1990) · 'Art notes from the provinces', *Art Journal*, 41 (1879), 57 · Edinburgh town council minutes, 1874–9, 239; 1879–87, 305, Edinburgh City Archives · private information (2004) · D. O. Hill, correspondence, NL Scot., Macdonald–Michaelson MSS

Archives NL Scot., Macdonald–Michaelson collection

Likenesses photograph, c.1860–1869, Metropolitan Museum of Art, New York · A. Blaikley, chalk drawing, Scot. NPG

Wealth at death £541: Woodward, 'Nineteenth century Scottish sculpture'

Hill, Archibald Vivian (1886–1977), physiologist, was born on 26 September 1886 at Bristol, the only son and elder child of Jonathan Hill (d. 1924), timber merchant, and his wife, Ada Priscilla (d. 1943), daughter of Alfred Jones Rumney, wool merchant. His father left the family when his son was three. Hill was educated at Blundell's School in Tiverton, Devon, from 1900 to 1905, obtaining a foundation scholarship in 1901. In 1905 he won a scholarship to Trinity College, Cambridge, and in 1907 finished as third wrangler in the Cambridge mathematical tripos. He then decided—under the influence of Walter Morley Fletcher and Frederick Gowland Hopkins—to turn to

Archibald Vivian Hill (1886–1977), by Hubert Andrew Freeth, 1957

physiology. In 1909 Hill took a first in part two of the natural sciences tripos and started his life's work as a research worker in the Cambridge Physiological Laboratory under the direction of J. N. Langley. He had obtained a George Henry Lewes studentship and in 1910 was elected a research fellow of Trinity College, a position he held until 1916, when he accepted a fellowship at King's, Cambridge.

During the years preceding the First World War Hill's activities were of two kinds: his first published papers were concerned mainly with a theoretical and quantitative analysis of experimental results obtained by himself and his senior colleagues in the Cambridge laboratory. They included an analysis of drug action in muscle tissue, of the reaction between oxygen and haemoglobin, and of the effects of electric stimuli on nerves. Although Hill later regarded this work as being of little importance, it contained the first mathematical formulation of drug kinetics later generally known as the Michaelis–Menten or Langmuir equation. It also introduced the concept of co-operativity in complex chemical reactions, signified by a quantity which was widely referred to as the Hill coefficient.

From 1910 onwards Hill's main efforts were devoted to measurements of heat production and energy exchanges in nerve and muscle. He soon established himself as the international leader in this field and attracted pupils from many countries. He excelled in designing new thermo-electric methods for his experiments, using them to carry out very precise measurements of physical changes associated with muscular contraction and impulse conduction in nerves. He also excelled in the mathematical treatment of his results. By applying physico-chemical concepts to biological events, and by emphasizing the importance of accurate quantitative measurement, Hill greatly promoted a branch of physiology known as biophysics. Together with his famous forerunner Hermann Helmholtz in Germany, Hill is regarded as one of the founding fathers of the discipline. In 1913 Hill married Margaret Neville (d. 1970), daughter of Dr (John) Neville Keynes, registrary in the University of Cambridge and lecturer in moral science, and sister of John Maynard Keynes, the economist, and Sir Geoffrey Keynes, the surgeon and author. The couple had four children.

On the outbreak of the First World War in August 1914 Hill joined the army and his physiological research was interrupted until demobilization in March 1919. He entered the Cambridgeshire regiment as a regimental captain, but was soon asked to form and direct an anti-aircraft experimental section in the munitions inventions department. Hill assembled a distinguished group of scientists, including R. H. Fowler and E. A. Milne, who engaged in what was later called operational research. Hill was promoted to the rank of brevet major; in 1918 he was appointed OBE. The work of his anti-aircraft section was later incorporated in important textbooks (for example, *Textbook of Anti-Aircraft Gunnery*, 2 vols., 1924–5).

In 1918 Hill was elected FRS and in 1919 he returned to his researches on muscle in the Cambridge laboratory. He analysed the various phases of heat production during muscular contraction, and their relation to the development of muscle force and to the chemical changes associated with the active phase of contraction and the period of recovery thereafter.

In 1920 Hill left Cambridge to take the chair of physiology at Manchester University. He reorganized the teaching department and intensified his research on muscular movement, working with human beings as well as with isolated frog muscles. Hill's measurements of the various phases of heat production during muscle activity and recovery paralleled biochemical studies carried out at the same time by the German physiologist Otto Meyerhof. They led to the concept that the initial phase of activity and the development of muscle force did not require oxygen, but was accompanied by anaerobic breakdown of carbohydrate to lactic acid; the subsequent phase of chemical recovery and restoration, however, did depend on oxygen consumption and on the oxidative removal of a small portion of the lactic acid molecules. The impact of Hill's innovative biophysical technique and results, which converged with those of an outstanding German scientist, was considerable. It threw new light on an important biological process: the production of mechanical work by a cycle of chemical reactions in a living muscle cell. It led to early recognition by the award in 1923 of a Nobel prize to Hill and Meyerhof (the prize was dated 1922).

In 1923 Hill succeeded E. H. Starling in the chair of physiology at University College, London (UCL). Three years later he transferred from this post to the Foulerton research professorship of the Royal Society, a post he held at UCL until his retirement in December 1951. After that time, although formally retired, he continued as an active experimenter until 1966. His many scientific achievements during this period include the discovery and measurement of the heat production associated with the nerve impulse, the improved analysis of heat development which accompanies active shortening in muscle, the application of thermoelectric methods to the measurement of vapour pressure in minute fluid volumes, the analysis of physical and chemical changes associated with nerve excitation, and the formulation of electric excitation laws. Hill was also the author of several important books, some on his special scientific subjects (for example, *Adventures in Biophysics*, 1931, *Chemical Wave Transmission in Nerve*, 1932, and *Trails and Trials in Physiology*, 1965), and others on more general subjects (for example, *The Ethical Dilemma of Science*, 1960).

Hill combined his intensive personal research work in the laboratory with a remarkable life given to public service. He gave many years of service to the British Physiological Society as editor of its journal and as foreign secretary, and to the International Union of Physiology. He served as biological secretary of the Royal Society from 1935 to 1945, and as foreign secretary in 1945–6. He was also secretary-general of the International Council of Scientific Unions in 1952–6. Before the war, in 1935, Hill joined Patrick Blackett and Sir Henry Tizard on the committee which was responsible for the initiation of radar and for the early development of an effective air warning system. During the Second World War he was an independent MP for Cambridge University (1940–45), went on important missions to the United States, and in 1943–4 visited India to advise the Indian government on post-war reconstruction. He furnished a very influential report, dealing especially with the subject of medical education. But one of Hill's most important contributions was his defence of colleagues who had been persecuted by the Hitler regime. He was a founder member of the Academic Assistance Council (later the Society for the Protection of Science and Learning). Before 1939 and later, as an MP, he intervened in favour of fellow scientists in distress. For this he earned the gratitude and admiration of colleagues all over the world. He was always ready to encourage younger colleagues and imparted to them his sense of fairness. During this period, Margaret Hill was very active in social welfare work, especially in organizing sheltered housing for old people during and after the war. Hill died on 3 June 1977 in Cambridge.

BERNARD KATZ, *rev.* V. M. QUIRKE

Sources B. Katz, *Memoirs FRS*, 24 (1978), 71–149 • personal knowledge (1986) • *The Times* (4 June 1977) • *WWW*, 1971–80
Archives CAC Cam., corresp. and papers • Medical Research Council, London, corresp. and papers • Wellcome L., corresp. | CUL, corresp. with Francis John Worsley Roughton • ICL, corresp. with Herbert Dingle • IWM, corresp., mainly with Sir Henry Tizard • PRO, corresp. with Henry Dale, CAB127/218 • U. Leeds,

Brotherton L., letters to Esther Simpson • UCL, letters to Karl Pearson • University of Sheffield, corresp. with Hans Krebs • Wellcome L., corresp. with Sir Edward Sharpey-Schafer
Likenesses W. Stoneman, two photographs, 1933–42, NPG • H. A. Freeth, watercolour drawing, 1957, King's Cam. [*see illus.*] • H. A. Freeth, watercolour drawing, 1957, NPG
Wealth at death £27,994: probate, 11 Aug 1977, *CGPLA Eng. & Wales*

Hill, Arthur (1601–1663), politician, was the second son of Sir Moses (Moyses) Hill (*d.* 1630). His mother was probably Sir Moses' second wife, Anne Stafford (*née* Grogan), widow of Sir Francis Stafford, but may have been his father's first wife, Alice MacDonnell. Moses Hill, perhaps of London origins, had served as a soldier in Ireland from 1573 and secured property by grant, purchase, and lease in counties Antrim, Down, and Louth.

By 1630 Arthur Hill had married his first wife, probably Anne Bolton (1603–1636/7), daughter of Sir Richard *Bolton, future lord chancellor of Ireland; they had three sons. Hill appears to have practised law in the 1630s, secured a Dublin residence and, besides the portion of his father's lands which he inherited, set about building a landed base of his own, largely through offering mortgages to indebted Ulster landowners. Having become sheriff of co. Antrim in 1634, he was returned to the 1634 Irish parliament at a by-election, perhaps for Belfast, and was elected for Carysfort, co. Wicklow, in 1640. He was added to the commission of the peace for co. Antrim in 1640 and in that year received a command in the earl of Strafford's 'new army', raised to be used against the covenanters in Scotland. Hill's second marriage was to Mary (or Anne), daughter of Sir William *Parsons, lord justice from 1641, and they had three sons and four daughters.

With the outbreak of the Irish rising of 1641, Hill became one of the leaders of the protestant, pro-government forces in east Ulster and was given command of a cavalry regiment. In late 1642 he was one of a delegation of officers who travelled to England to plead with the two armed camps of king and parliament for aid in the Irish war lest they be forced to a truce with the confederate Catholic forces. In fact such a cessation came to pass in 1643 with royal approval, though Hill was soon persuaded of the merits of seeking supplies from the English parliament, which was committed to a policy of reopening the war. He was not, however, a supporter of parliament's solemn league and covenant and in April 1644 was one of the officers of English extraction willing to issue a proclamation, drafted by the king's government in Dublin, directed against the bond, despite its appeal in Ulster, particularly to the Scottish population there. By the early summer his commitment to renewed campaigning won out and he returned to England to seek logistical support for an Irish war to be explicitly conducted under parliament's aegis.

Hill retained his command and managed to accommodate himself to the successive Commonwealth regimes of the 1650s. He secured a number of local offices including that of a revenue commissioner for the Belfast precinct and a surveyor of confiscated lands in Ulster. In 1654 he was elected to the united protectorate parliament for the combined counties Antrim, Down, and Armagh and in 1656 he served as an auditor-general for Irish accounts. His activities endeared him neither to the Scottish nor the presbyterian populations of Ulster. In 1653 he was involved in the scheme to transplant Scottish landowners from Ulster to Tipperary. He secured the odium of presbyterian clergy as a commissioner to enforce the engagement of loyalty to the republic in 1651 and for investigating those who had failed to offer thanks for the delivery of the lord protector in 1657. Yet his own religious position was out of keeping with that favoured by English regimes. He sheltered the deposed bishop of Down and Connor, Henry Leslie, who preached and possibly ordained under his protection, while the future bishop of that diocese, Jeremy Taylor, who lived nearby, noted that Hill's home was one where the outlawed Book of Common Prayer was 'greatly valued and diligently used' (Bolton, 28). The death of Hill's elder brother, Peter, and of Peter's son Francis saw him gain the bulk of his father's pre-war properties, while the state rewarded him with further grants. In 1651 he invited Robert Child to his Ulster estate; Child remained there until his death in 1654, investigating local natural history and recording enthusiasm for agricultural improvement in the area.

With the collapse of the Commonwealth, Hill was reckoned to have 'hastened to join once more the ascendant party' (Reid, 2.255). Perhaps as early as 1659 he was associating with those who supported the return of Charles II, and by early 1660 he was noted as one who could provide armed support for an unconditional restoration. He represented County Down in the 1660 Irish convention and in the parliament elected in 1661, and secured membership of the Irish privy council. He received a pardon at Charles's return and his property was again confirmed to him. Hillsborough, where he had erected a fort, rebuilt the church and established a settlement, was made a corporate town and parliamentary borough in 1662, and he was appointed constable of the strategically located castle. He died in April 1663, his son and heir, Moyses, further uniting the Hill family properties through a marriage to his cousin Anne Hill of Hillhall.

Hill had steered close to the prevailing party in power, while retaining a commitment to the 'English interest' and to the Church of Ireland. His legacy was that of laying the 'real basis of the landed wealth of the family' (Gillespie, 140), his descendants, the marquesses of Downshire, going on to be among the most substantial and politically potent landowning families in Ireland.

R. M. ARMSTRONG

Sources B. McGrath, 'A biographical dictionary of the membership of the Irish House of Commons, 1640–1641', PhD thesis, University of Dublin, 1997 • A. Clarke, *Prelude to Restoration in Ireland* (1999) • W. A. Maguire, *The Downshire estates in Ireland, 1801–1845* (1972) • R. Gillespie, *Colonial Ulster: the settlement of east Ulster, 1600–1641* (1985) • F. R. Bolton, *The Caroline tradition of the Church of Ireland* (1958) • R. Dunlop, ed., *Ireland under the Commonwealth*, 2 vols. (1913) • T. C. Barnard, *Cromwellian Ireland* (1975) • J. S. Reid and W. D. Killen, *History of the Presbyterian church in Ireland*, new edn, 3 vols. (1867) • J. Lodge, *The peerage of Ireland*, rev. M. Archdall, rev. edn, 7 vols. (1789) • *CSP Ire., 1633–62* • R. M. Armstrong, 'Protestant Ireland

and the English parliament, 1641–1647', PhD thesis, University of Dublin, 1995

Hill, Sir Arthur William (1875–1941), botanist, was born at Herga, Watford, on 11 October 1875, the son of Daniel Hill, estate agent, and his wife, Annie Weall. He went to Marlborough College in 1890 and there acquired an interest in botany. In 1894 he entered King's College, Cambridge, as an exhibitioner studying botany; he subsequently became a foundation scholar. He was placed in the first class of both parts of the natural sciences tripos (1897, 1898) and was elected a fellow of King's in 1901 and an honorary fellow in 1932.

After graduation Hill remained at Cambridge to pursue botanical research, initially in the field of plant histology. He was appointed university demonstrator in 1899 and lecturer in 1904, soon after his return from a botanical expedition to the Andes of Bolivia and Peru. In 1907 he became assistant director of the Royal Botanic Gardens, Kew, and thereafter his life was centred on Kew, where he became director in 1922. Notwithstanding his administrative duties Hill continued his botanical research, some aspects of which were facilitated by the wealth of plants grown in the gardens. He had collected much valuable material during his travels in the Andes and for some years his investigations were concentrated on its elucidation. He was also much interested in the changes observed in some ornamental garden and glasshouse plants since their introduction from the wild. Natural plant hybrids also fascinated him, and he wrote several intriguing papers on peculiar methods of seed germination.

During Hill's career, the herbarium at Kew was perhaps the most important in the world, and Hill played a full part in maintaining its reputation. Floras of many parts of the Commonwealth and empire are compiled at Kew, and Hill himself made valuable contributions to *The Flora Capensis*, *The Flora of Tropical Africa*, and *The Flora of Trinidad and Tobago*. He was instrumental in initiating a new *Flora of West Tropical Africa*. During his directorship, Hill edited *Index Kewensis*, *Hooker's Icones plantarum*, and *Curtis's Botanical Magazine*.

Hill was most successful in obtaining additional funds to increase the activities and amenities of the Royal Botanic Gardens. During his regime a new wing was added to the herbarium, laboratory facilities were extended, land was made available for experiments, and a new banana house was erected to aid breeding new, disease-resistant varieties. Hill was much concerned about the deleterious effect of the smoky atmosphere of London on the conifers at Kew, and with the co-operation of the Forestry Commission he was largely instrumental in establishing a new national pinetum at Bedgebury, Kent.

As director of Kew, Hill was botanical adviser to the secretary of state for the colonies. He gave valuable advice to the dominions and colonies on botanical and agricultural matters, and visited most of these territories. His visits were always welcome, for he had great knowledge of the economic utilization of plants.

Hill was a keen practical gardener and the Royal Horticultural Society often sought his assistance. The society awarded him its Victoria medal of honour and also a Veitch memorial medal for his services to horticulture. He was the chief horticultural adviser to the Imperial War Graves Commission. He was elected FRS in 1920 and was appointed CMG in 1926 and KCMG in 1931. Hill was a deeply religious man and regularly read the lesson at St Luke's Church, Kew. He was widely travelled, enjoyed music and art (he painted watercolours), and had a strong sense of humour. He never married. His sister, to whom he was very close, kept house for him at Kew. Her death in 1939 was a heavy blow to him. He died on the mid-Surrey golf course in the Old Deer Park, Richmond, after a riding accident, on 3 November 1941.

F. T. BROOKS, *rev.* PETER OSBORNE

Sources F. T. Brooks, *Obits. FRS*, 4 (1942–4), 87–100 · *WWW* · private information (1959) · personal knowledge (1959) · *CGPLA Eng. & Wales* (1941)
Archives RBG Kew, diaries, notebooks, and papers | U. Glas., Archives and Business Records Centre, letters to F. O. Bower
Likenesses W. Stoneman, two photographs, 1931, NPG · photograph, repro. in Brooks, *Obits. FRS*
Wealth at death £93,379 10s. 10d.: probate, 30 Dec 1941, *CGPLA Eng. & Wales*

Hill, Benson Earle (1795–1845), soldier and writer, was born in Bristol. His parentage is unknown, but he was educated at Dr Watson's school, Shooters Hill, and at the military colleges of Marlow and Woolwich. At the age of fourteen he was commissioned second lieutenant in the Royal Regiment of Artillery. He was appointed first lieutenant on 17 March 1812, and served until 1822.

Hill was passionately stage-struck and tried to make a second career in the theatre. However, he never managed to gain more than a precarious foothold there, and the rest of his life was spent in struggle as he tried his luck with varying degrees of failure as actor, writer, journalist, and editor. He was extremely well-travelled, as the army had taken him to Ireland, North America, and Europe, and pursuit of an acting career hurried him through the length and breadth of the British Isles. Journalism finally led him to the fringe of London's literary establishment. Every experience brought adventure; none brought financial reward.

Hill's publications included an account of his military service, *Recollections of an Artillery Officer* (1836), as well as a book of anecdotes about snuff taking (1840). One of his last works, and the one for which he is remembered, was *The Epicure's Almanac*, published in London in 1841, which reflected the varied nature of his life. The title echoed that of the French *Almanach des gourmands* and its English imitators, which surveyed the restaurant scene in Paris and London in the early years of the century. Although Hill hoped to link his venture to the popularity of these forebears, his own book was addressed to a different reader, not the man who dined out, but the one who dined in, and it offered a new recipe for every day of the year 'to those who study genteel economy'. Appearing in the decade which saw the first published work by Alexis Soyer and Eliza Acton, *The Epicure's Almanac* was refreshingly original in its choice of ingredients, reflecting the cosmopolitan background and persistent insolvency of its author. The book offers many ingenious suggestions for impecunious chefs, and includes a recommendation for boiled nettles and cider with bicarbonate of soda, as a poor man's champagne.

Just as poverty forced improvisation, so military service broadened horizons: ingredients, and instructions for their preparation, were drawn from many countries. Tours of duty had placed Hill in New Orleans and Brussels, Killarney and Mons; and the inclusion of coconut, chutneys, and kebabs hint at the ripening British love affair with India and the East, as well as the service of fellow officers there. Enthusiastic recipes for punch point to the power and popularity of the West Indies sugar trade. An interest, early for England, in the cooked tomato may have been stimulated by his time in America. The French way with a caper is noted with approval.

Hill's pages are studded with British regional delicacies, from Cheshire pork pie to the north Wiltshire cheese, and tribute is paid by name to such hospitable tavern keepers as a Mr Reilly of the York-House, Bath, and a Mr Burnham of the Montague tavern, Bristol. In addition, Hill's good sense and gusto give the book a special savour: attention is paid to method and light-hearted titles add lustre to leftovers, as in the delightfully named 'Patrician bubble and squeak'. Cooking and eating are presented as serious entertainments, worthy of consideration by the enterprising.

Hill never married, but lived for many years with a sister, who died of consumption in 1842. As the *Gentleman's Magazine* sombrely reported in November 1845, Hill himself succumbed to the same illness 'in London, at an obscure abode, in penury and distress, aged 50' (*GM*, 543), after catching a cold while engaged as that most threadbare of performers, an actor on call for last-minute work, at the Lyceum Theatre. He was buried in London.

BRIDGET A. HENISCH

Sources W. P. Courtney, 'Benson Earle Hill', *N&Q*, 10th ser., 3 (1905), 162–3 · *GM*, 2nd ser., 24 (1845), 543 · A. Mathews, *Memoir of Charles Mathews, comedian*, 3 (1839), 126–42, 272–3 · G. E. Weare, 'The Epicure's almanack', *N&Q*, 10th ser., 5 (1906), 153 · B. E. Hill, *The epicure's almanac* (1841), 5, 19, 25, 97, 108 · B. E. Hill, *Recollections of an artillery officer … adventures in Ireland, America, Flanders, and France*, 2 vols. (1836) [BL]
Wealth at death died in penury: *GM*

Hill, Sir (Austin) Bradford [Tony] **(1897–1991)**, medical statistician, was born on 8 July 1897 in Hampstead, London, the third of four sons and third of six children of Sir Leonard Erskine *Hill (1866–1952), professor of physiology at the London Hospital medical college, and his wife, Janet, *née* Alexander (1867/8–1956), daughter of Frederick Alexander, bank clerk. On his father's side he was great-great-nephew of Sir Rowland Hill. When he was five years old the family moved to Loughton, a village in Epping Forest, where he acquired a lifelong love of the countryside. He was educated at Chigwell School from 1908 to 1916 and was distinguished there more by sporting than academic ability. He nevertheless became head boy, staying on for an extra year as he was not allowed to enlist

and did not want to start a long medical training during the war. On leaving school he obtained a commission in the Royal Naval Air Service and was soon posted to the Greek islands in support of the attack on the Dardanelles. While there he contracted pulmonary tuberculosis, which probably saved his life as it kept him *hors de combat*. Confined to bed, he was unable to study medicine, which he had wanted to do since boyhood, so studied economics as an external student of London University, obtaining a second-class honours degree in 1922. After a long attachment dating back to before his naval service began, on 31 July 1923 he married Florence Maud Salmon (1892/3–1980), daughter of Edward George Salmon, editor and author. They had two sons and a daughter.

An opportunity to work in the medical field occurred when the Medical Research Council (MRC) sought someone to investigate the reasons for the high mortality of young adults in rural areas and Hill obtained the appointment with the support of Major Greenwood, an old friend of his father's, who was in charge of statistical work at the Ministry of Health. This provided the opportunity to extend his knowledge of statistics (initiated in the study of economics) by attending part of the London BSc course. He was inspired by the teaching of Karl Pearson at University College, though more by his general ideas and philosophy than by his erudite mathematics, and he settled for a career in epidemiology, with a special interest in occupational medicine. A series of grants from the MRC led to a staff appointment until, in 1933, he obtained a readership in epidemiology and vital statistics under Greenwood, who had become the first professor of medical statistics at the London School of Hygiene and Tropical Medicine. In this position Hill made his first great contribution to medicine, publishing in *The Lancet* in 1937 his lectures on statistics to postgraduate medical students. The seventeen articles were subsequently brought together in a book, *The Principles of Medical Statistics* (1937), which was translated into Spanish, Korean, Indonesian, Polish, and Russian, and was repeatedly reprinted and revised: fifty years later the text was still widely read (the eleventh edition appeared in 1985), but could be considered overly simple. It was, however, its very simplicity, combined with its clarity of expression and logical development, that made it so successful and was primarily responsible for making an innumerate profession understand the need for appropriate statistical analysis and allowance for the play of chance.

With the onset of the Second World War, Hill was seconded to the research and experimental department of the Ministry of Home Security and later to the medical directorate of the Royal Air Force. With the latter he maintained a relationship as an honorary civil consultant in medical statistics until 1978. (He was also civil consultant in medical statistics to the Royal Navy, from 1958 to 1977.) Greenwood retired in 1945 and Hill was appointed to his chair and to the honorary directorship of the MRC's statistical research unit. A year later he persuaded two MRC committees to adopt a new technique for testing the value of new drugs or prophylactic regimes: namely, random allocation of subjects to treatment or control groups. He did so not for theoretical statistical reasons, but for the practical reason that it guaranteed the avoidance of bias in the allocation of treatment, something that was always possible, in one way or another, with other regimes. One of the trials (of streptomycin for the treatment of pulmonary tuberculosis) had notably clear results; the benefits of the technique were quickly appreciated and within a few years random allocation became the essential characteristic of a reliable trial.

In 1947 Hill was asked by the MRC to try to find a reason for the increased mortality attributed to lung cancer, which an MRC conference (in which Hill participated) had concluded was unlikely to be wholly an artefact of improved diagnosis. He consequently planned a study of patients with lung cancer, in which their histories would be compared with those of patients with other diseases, and he obtained the assistance of Richard Doll to undertake its day-to-day conduct. The results, published in 1950, led Doll and Hill to conclude that 'cigarette smoking is a cause, and an important cause, of bronchogenic carcinoma' (BMJ, 2, 1950, 739). This unpopular conclusion (for 80 per cent of British middle-aged men were regular smokers) was not generally accepted and Hill (with Doll) designed a different type of study to test its validity, in which 40,000 doctors were asked to describe their smoking habits and were then followed to determine their causes of death. The results soon confirmed the earlier conclusion and, with further follow-up, showed that smoking also caused many other diseases. These case-control and cohort studies, as they came to be called, broke new ground and were frequently cited as models of their type. Consideration of the evidence that had led to the conclusion that cigarette smoking was a cause of disease led Hill to review the type of evidence required to deduce causality from observational studies. His findings came to be known as 'Hill's guidelines' and they were subsequently used widely for both scientific and legal purposes.

Hill was a quiet, unassuming, private person, known to everyone as Tony, who sought to lead but not to drive. In committee he expressed his opinion firmly and cogently but never sought to impose, and was in consequence listened to with respect. He lectured brilliantly, reading texts in such a way that he was thought to be speaking spontaneously, often without the use of visual aids but always with humorous asides. His many public functions included membership of the committee on the safety of medicines (1964–75) and the MRC (1954–8), and he served as secretary (1940–50) and president (1950–52) of the Royal Statistical Society and, for two years, as dean of the School of Hygiene and Tropical Medicine (1955–7). In 1951 he was made CBE and in 1961 knighted. He was elected a fellow of the Royal Society in 1954 and received honorary degrees from Oxford and Edinburgh and many honorary fellowships and medals, including an honorary fellowship of the Royal College of Physicians of London and the gold medal of the Royal Statistical Society (1953). He retired early to devote himself to his wife, who had stayed by him

when he had pulmonary tuberculosis, and he looked after her at home when she developed Alzheimer's disease, until shortly before she died in 1980. His last years were marred by frequent transient ischaemic attacks, one of which left him with a weak left leg. He died, mentally alert to the end, in Balla Wray Nursing Home, High Wray, Ambleside, Westmorland, of bronchopneumonia, on 18 April 1991. A service of thanksgiving for his life was held at St Clement Danes on 4 October 1991.   RICHARD DOLL

Sources R. Doll, Memoirs FRS, 40 (1994), 129–40 · Statistics in Medicine, 1 (1982), 297–375 [A collection of articles in celebration of Hill's 85th birthday] · Statistics in Medicine, 12 (1990), 797–806 · The Times (22 April 1991) · The Independent (7 May 1991) · WWW, 1991–5 · Burke, Peerage · m. cert. · d. cert. · personal knowledge (2004)
Likenesses Godfrey Argent studio, photograph, repro. in Doll, Memoirs FRS, p. 128 · photograph, repro. in The Independent
Wealth at death £191,195: probate, 12 Nov 1991, CGPLA Eng. & Wales

Hill [née Smith], **Caroline Southwood** (1809–1902), writer and educationist, was born on 21 March 1809, the eldest daughter of Thomas Southwood *Smith (1788–1861), Unitarian theologian, physician, and leading sanitary reformer, and his wife, Ann, née Read, the daughter of a Bristol stoneware potter. On his wife's death in 1812, Southwood Smith left Caroline and her sister Emily with his family in Somerset while he pursued his medical studies in Edinburgh, but he later took the unconventional step of taking Caroline to live with him; a lasting emotional intimacy ensued. In 1818 Southwood Smith married Mary Christie (with whom he had one surviving child), and in 1819 or 1820 the family moved to London. Mary left Southwood Smith and emigrated to the continent in the mid-1820s.

Caroline Southwood Smith remained in Wimbledon in a private teaching post. By the 1830s she had begun to contribute articles to the Unitarian periodical the Monthly Repository, often advocating the innovative theories of the Swiss educationist Johann Heinrich Pestalozzi. She became governess to the children of James Hill (d. 1871), a former corn merchant and banker, who had requested to meet her after reading her articles. In 1835 Caroline married Hill at St Botolph without Bishopsgate in London, becoming his third wife. At their home in Wisbech, Cambridgeshire, she threw herself into the work of her Owenite husband in initiating various co-operative ventures and seeking to end local corruption. They established a Pestalozzian infant school together, and Caroline Southwood Hill was also instrumental in the running of Hill's highly radical paper, the Star in the East (1836–40). All this was in addition to caring for her six stepchildren and bearing three daughters, Miranda (b. 1836), Gertrude (b. 1837), and Octavia *Hill (1838–1912). Two more daughters, Emily (b. 1840) and Florence (b. 1843) were born after the family left Wisbech. Southwood Hill's unorthodox child-rearing methods became well known in radical circles: she shunned conventional discipline, seeking to instil in the children an ability to reason and a love of learning.

Major upheavals were to strike the Hill family: James Hill was declared bankrupt in 1840, and the children of his first marriage were taken in by members of his family. Southwood Hill and her children were greatly assisted by her father and their close friends the radical writer Mary Gillies and her sister Margaret Gillies, with whom Southwood Smith lived. They took in and brought up the young Gertrude (who later married Charles Lewes, son of the literary critic and partner of George Eliot, George Henry Lewes). The rest of the family moved from Essex to Hampstead, then to Gloucestershire, and on to Leeds, where in 1845 James Hill bought the Owenite publication the *New Moral World*. He suffered a nervous breakdown, and on medical advice decided to live apart from his family; he died alone in 1871. Caroline and her daughters moved to Finchley to be near her father.

Back in London, Southwood Hill continued to write. With the Gillies sisters, she moved in a radical circle which included such writers and reformers as William and Mary Howitt, William James Linton, and Eliza Cook. They championed progressive ideas on education, democracy, and women's emancipation. During the period from 1846 to 1851 the *People and Howitt's Journal* published much of her poetic work, and her articles on education were reissued as a book in 1845, *Memoranda of Observations and Experiments in Education*. In the early 1850s she and her daughters became involved in the Ladies' Guild, a women's craft workshop, of which Southwood Hill became manager. In 1856 she wrote an article for Charles Dickens's *Household Words* on the guild's work in training disadvantaged children in toy making. While the guild was not in itself economically successful, it became an important symbol for early feminist activists of a strategy for increasing women's employment opportunities. Southwood Hill was dismissed from the guild in 1855 after defending the right of F. D. Maurice, the Christian socialist (whose son later married her daughter Emily), to give Bible classes there.

Caroline Southwood Hill then moved to Weybridge with her daughter Emily and immersed herself in writing, but was back in London in 1859, sharing a house with Emily and Octavia, and teaching full-time once again. After sharing their house for a short, tense period with the pioneer in female medicine Sophia Jex-Blake, in 1862 Caroline, Emily, and Octavia established a school in Nottingham Place, London, which remained open until 1891, with first Octavia and later Miranda at its head. Southwood Hill acted as matron, although the school followed Octavia's more disciplinarian principals of education. Octavia Hill's burgeoning public career sometimes conflicted with her mother's ideals: for example, Octavia's volunteer cadet corps clashed with Caroline's pacifist philosophy.

A strong and influential character, Caroline Southwood Hill remained intellectually active throughout her long life. She wrote three children's books, and as late as 1895 was contributing reviews and articles to such publications as the *Nineteenth Century*. Octavia Hill published some of her mother's educational writings after her death as *Notes on Education* (1906). Southwood Hill and her family were always exceptionally close, and she continued to live with her daughters until her death at 6 Cambridge Terrace, St Pancras, London, on 31 December 1902. She was buried in Highgate cemetery.   KATHRYN GLEADLE

Sources G. Darley, *Octavia Hill* (1990) · *Life of Octavia Hill, as told in her letters*, ed. C. E. Maurice (1913) · *Life of Octavia Hill, early ideals from letters*, ed. C. E. Maurice (1928) · *Household Words* (17 May 1856), 417–20 · *Star in the East* (1836–40) [newspaper, Newspaper Library, Colindale, London] · C. S. Hill, *Memoranda of observations and experiments in education* (1865) · W. J. Linton, *Memories* (1895) · d. cert.
Likenesses photograph, repro. in Darley, *Octavia Hill*, 126–9

Hill, Charles, **Baron Hill of Luton** (1904–1989), doctor, politician, and broadcaster, was born in Islington, London, on 15 January 1904, the youngest in the family of two sons and a daughter of Charles Hill, maker of pianoforte parts, who died in 1906, and his wife, Florence Madeleine Cook, bookkeeper, the seventh of eight children of a seller of mineral water. His mother remarried in 1916, her husband being W. E. Hulme, linotype operator in the *Morning Post*.

Educated at St Olave's School, Tower Bridge, Hill was awarded a Drapers' Company scholarship and a sizarship at Trinity College, Cambridge, in 1921, and went on to read in parallel both medicine and part one of the natural sciences tripos, in which he received first-class honours in 1925. He completed his medical education at the London Hospital, obtaining his MRCS, LRCP in 1927 and MB, BChir in 1929. He then took up a hospital post in Nottingham and became deputy medical officer of health in Oxford in 1930. He obtained his DPH in 1931. Determined and ambitious and more interested in administration than in medical practice, Hill was appointed an assistant secretary of the British Medical Association (BMA) in 1932. He stayed at the BMA headquarters in Tavistock Square for the next eighteen years (gaining his MD in 1936), climbing a ladder which took him to the top rung, when in 1944 he achieved the position of secretary, the senior full-time officer post, which he held until 1950.

Convinced of the importance of winning public support to buttress the BMA's cause, Hill had by 1944 become one of the best-known figures in the country in his own right, though not under his own name, after being invited in 1941 to take part in the BBC's *Kitchen Front* programmes. In a remarkable series of wartime broadcasts, mainly given live, which came to cover a wide range of health problems, Hill, giving helpful advice as the 'radio doctor', soon won a huge audience. His rich, warm, and homely—if often booming—voice, so different from most BBC voices even in wartime, contributed to his success as a broadcaster, but did not guarantee it. His secret was careful preparation, meticulous selection of points to emphasize, and intuitive choice of exactly the right words. One of his broadcasts, which deserves the adjective classic, was delivered after the war on Boxing day in 1949. It began 'This is stomach speaking. Yes I mean it, your stomach'. This broadcast was addressed to children. Hill, who in 1931 had married Marion Spencer, daughter of Moses Wallace, a Halifax mill owner, whom he had met at Cambridge, knew a lot about children. He had two sons and three daughters, and for all his ebullience he always gave the

Charles Hill, Baron Hill of Luton (1904–1989), by Elliott & Fry, 1951

reassuring air of being a real family doctor. As secretary of the BMA, he fought hard between 1945 and 1948 to ensure that the new National Health Service would incorporate family choice of doctor and that the profession would not become a state-salaried service for general practitioners. Hill revelled in the rough and tumble of contest with Aneurin Bevan, the minister of health, whose political skills he came greatly to admire, but he could also show patience and forbearance in dealing both with politicians and professional colleagues.

It was through struggles about health policy that Hill was drawn into party politics, which had never interested him at Cambridge, and eventually in 1957 into the cabinet, although his attitude to party was as unorthodox as that of the first Lord Beaverbrook, the intermediary who arranged for him to be summoned to an interview at the Conservative Party central office in 1944. Indeed, when Hill first stood (unsuccessfully) for parliament, for Cambridge University, at the general election of 1945, it was not as a Conservative but as an independent. When he won Luton at the next general election in 1950, it was as a Conservative and Liberal. Hill used his formidable oratorical talents at that election to deliver one of the outstanding controversial political broadcasts before the age of television.

Hill did not have to wait long for governmental office, and having served from 1951 to 1955 as parliamentary secretary to the Ministry of Food—an unenviable post, for most back-benchers in his party wished to see his ministry abolished—he was made postmaster-general by Sir Anthony Eden in April 1955, being sworn of the privy council at the same time. This post greatly appealed to him and, surviving Suez, he went on under Harold Macmillan to become chancellor of the duchy of Lancaster in January 1957. His responsibilities for supervising government information services straddled these last two posts. Finally, Macmillan made him minister of housing and local government in October 1961, combined with the ministry of Welsh affairs, before removing him in his sudden, and to Hill premature, government reshuffle in July 1962. In any event Hill would have retired at the next election.

A new career now began, first in business and then in broadcasting. Hill was so successful a chairman of the Independent Television Authority, a post to which he was appointed in 1963, refurbishing its image and presiding over the recasting of the television company structure, that a Labour prime minister, Harold Wilson, moved him from Brompton Road to become chairman of the BBC in 1967. This was a highly controversial move much resented in the BBC, particularly by Sir Hugh Greene, the director-general, and Hill's first years there were difficult. But he outlasted Greene, and had his tenure extended in 1972 in order to preside over the BBC's golden jubilee. Hill was a strong, eloquent, and effective supporter of BBC autonomy.

Hill kept a diary during his years as chairman of the BBC and wrote two volumes of compact and readable memoirs, *Both Sides of the Hill* (1964) and *Behind the Screen* (1974). His only other published work, a joint one, was *What is Osteopathy?* (1937). His appearance was as memorable as his voice. Short, plump, and brimful of energy, he was a favourite of cartoonists, but he liked rather than objected to this. Hill was made a life peer in 1963 and awarded an LLD by Saskatchewan University in 1950. He died in Harpenden, Hertfordshire, on 22 August 1989. A memorial service was held in Westminster Abbey on 17 November 1989. ASA BRIGGS, *rev.*

Sources C. Hill, *Both sides of the Hill* (1964) · C. Hill, *Behind the screen* (1974) · *The Independent* (23 Aug 1989) · *The Times* (23 Aug 1989) · *The Times* (18 Nov 1989) · personal knowledge (1996) · CGPLA Eng. & Wales (1990)
Likenesses photographs, 1948–69, Hult. Arch. · Elliott & Fry, photograph, 1951, NPG [*see illus.*]
Wealth at death £88,978: administration with will, 19 March 1990, CGPLA Eng. & Wales

Hill, David Octavius (1802–1870), painter and photographer, was born on 20 May 1802 in Perth, Scotland, the eighth child (hence Octavius) of Thomas Hill, bookseller, and Emelia or Emily Murray. He was educated at Perth Academy.

Early life: landscape painter While still a teenager Hill applied the new technique of lithography to producing *Thirty Sketches of Scenery in Perthshire, Drawn from Nature and on Stone*, which was issued in six parts between 1821 and 1823 by his brother Alexander Hill, a publisher and printseller in Edinburgh. He went to study in Edinburgh at the Trustees' Academy School of Design under Andrew

David Octavius Hill (1802–1870), by David Octavius Hill and Robert Adamson, 1843–8

Wilson, a landscape painter and well-known art connoisseur. Although Hill inserted into his works depictions illustrating the manners of the Scottish peasantry, it was the subtle strength of his landscape paintings on which he rapidly built his reputation. These landscapes were admirably suited to engraving, the early nineteenth century's most influential development in the distribution of images, and many of his paintings are best-known through the engravings made from them; he had more works engraved than any other Scottish artist. Hill's great early achievement was his series of views in 1840 that were made into steel-engravings entitled *The Land of Burns*. This project was the most ambitious and expensive Scottish publication up to that time and firmly established his reputation. His painting style was delicate rather than vigorous, but exploitation of light and shade gave many of his works unexpected force. He was particularly fond of the light at sunset. An extensive assessment of his career appeared in the *Art Journal* for 1869, which asserted that:

> he is not to be classed with the school of the naturalists, applying the term to those artists who are satisfied to represent Nature as they see her, but with that of the poetists, treating his subjects in a manner that gives additional charms to whatever they may in themselves possess.

Hill was a man of tremendous good cheer and bonhomie, which served him well throughout his life. The *Edinburgh Evening Courant* (18 May 1870) recalled that 'in personal appearance he was remarkable for his striking, classical, and manly features'. Andrew Wilson had introduced him to the artistic community, in which Hill became a jovial and central figure. He joined the Association for the Promotion of Fine Arts in 1826, but was one of several artists who withdrew in a controversy. In 1829 he was a founder member of the Society of Artists, and became its secretary in the following year; from 1836 this was a paid position. In 1838 the society became the Royal Scottish Academy of Fine Arts, of which he remained secretary for the rest of his life. He undoubtedly played a part in the academy's decision to commemorate the royal charter by opening its exhibition on 10 February 1840, the day the young Queen Victoria married.

On 9 August 1837 Hill married Ann McDonald (*bap.* 1804, *d.* 1841), the musically inclined daughter of a wine merchant in Perth. Their brief life together was one active in the society of the artistic community of Edinburgh. A daughter, Charlotte, was born in 1839, but a second daughter, born in 1840, lived only a few hours. Much weakened, Ann died on 5 October 1841 and Hill and his daughter went to live with his widowed sister, Mary Watson.

Photographic pioneer: partnership with Robert Adamson
The year 1839 had seen the public announcement of the invention of photography, an art that soon brought together D. O. Hill and **Robert Adamson** (1821–1848), changing both their lives irrevocably. Adamson was born on 26 April 1821, the son of Alexander Adamson, a tenant farmer at Burnside (5 miles east of St Andrews), and his wife, Rachael Melville. He was educated at Madras School, St Andrews, where he twice took the prize for mathematics. Adamson displayed an unusual talent for mechanics, working for an engineering shop in his youth, but his fragile health prohibited this calling. His older brother, Dr John Adamson (1809–1870), practised medicine in St Andrews and associated with Sir David Brewster (1761–1868), the principal of the United Colleges of St Leonard and St Salvator, along with other members of the St Andrews Literary and Philosophical Society. Brewster also enjoyed an unusually close scientific friendship with William Henry Fox Talbot (1800–1877) of Lacock Abbey. When Talbot announced his invention of photography on paper in January 1839, Brewster took an immediate enthusiastic interest and became the conduit into Scotland for information on the new art. Dr Adamson was one of the leading figures in this fledgeling photographic circle and encouraged his younger brother in taking up the calotype. By summer 1842 Brewster had reported to Talbot that the young man was becoming well drilled in the art, and on 10 May 1843 Robert Adamson established Scotland's first calotype studio, in the small eighteenth-century Rock House, on the steps of Calton Hill in Edinburgh.

Within days after Adamson opened his studio, on 19 May 1843, there took place in Edinburgh the Disruption of the Church of Scotland, perhaps the most significant event in nineteenth-century Scottish history. Acting on deeply held principles about control of their own parishes, a substantial proportion of the ministers of the

Church of Scotland took the courageous act of signing the deed of demission, separating themselves from their livings and laying the foundations for the Free Church of Scotland. Dr Thomas Chalmers (1780–1847) presided as the first moderator of the Free Church assembly. Hill's brother-in-law, the Revd Robert MacDonald (1813–1893), one of the most fiery of the Free Church's early members, became largely responsible for their school building programme. Hill, moved by this momentous occasion, announced his intention of painting a monumental portrait of the nearly 500 ministers and lay people involved in the signing, to be engraved and published by his brother. Perhaps Hill had been inspired by the recent showing of George Hayter's *The Great Reform Bill, 1832*, a composite of 400 portraits of members of parliament painted from life. Hill's project presented immediate problems. By temperament and training a landscape painter, he had painted only one significant portrait before this. Knowing that the participants would soon scatter to all corners of Scotland, Sir David Brewster suggested Robert Adamson's new art as a means of recording their features.

Within a very short period Hill's artistic direction and Adamson's manipulatory skills merged into a partnership unlike any in the early history of photography. Even with the help of specially devised cameras, lenses, and other devices made by the ingenious Thomas Davidson of Edinburgh, the exposure times of the calotype negative forced them to move furniture and trappings out into the garden in order to take advantage of the sunlight. Mirrors and reflectors helped to direct and concentrate the light. Hill's warm and commanding personality put the sitters at ease even while locking their bodies and expressions into a form that the camera could record. Robert Adamson had mastered the intricacies of the new art, refining it in a way that led to artistically pleasing prints. When their first efforts were exhibited at the Royal Scottish Academy of Arts in 1844, they were titled as 'executed by R. Adamson under the artistic direction of D. O. Hill'. Their calotype portraits, at first seen as convenient studies for a grand painting, emerged with a power and truthfulness of their own.

Their reputation grew as rapidly as the diversity of their subject matter. Hill's extensive social contacts came into play, and their subsequent portraits recorded the society of Edinburgh and many of its famous visitors. They took their cameras to the Free Church assembly in Glasgow and to the British Association for the Advancement of Science meeting in York. The architecture of Linlithgow, Durham, York, and Edinburgh expanded their subject matter, and their panoramas of Edinburgh provide a detailed record of the city at that time. Several of these landscape views provided direct inspiration for Hill's paintings. One of their most ambitious and penetrating projects was to document the fishermen and women, principally of the village of Newhaven. Within this picturesque and self-contained society Hill and Adamson extended the vision of photography to documenting a way of life—including not only its people, but also the boats, nets, and other objects that defined their existence.

For Hill this was a return in a more sophisticated fashion to his early interest in recording the manners of the Scottish peasantry. Just as in his paintings, it was poetry and not nature that inspired Hill, and the calotype negatives were often retouched to remove distracting elements or to emphasize important features. In the end, however, they spoke with truth to the spirit of the subject.

Within the first four years of their partnership, Hill and Adamson took more than 3000 photographs, many of which remain of undeniable quality to this day. But Robert Adamson's health, the cause of his taking up photography in the first place, continued to fail. Adamson's work dropped off throughout 1847 and on 14 January 1848 his short life came to a tragic end at St Andrews. Hill was devastated, losing not only a close friend, but also the source of his success in the art of photography. He continued to live in Rock House and to distribute their photographs, but could never again achieve the artistic harmony of the works that he had produced with Adamson. He joined the Photographic Society of Scotland in 1858, even though more than a decade had passed since he had been involved in taking a photograph. A brief collaboration with the Glasgow photographer A. M'Glashon in the years 1860–62 was unproductive. The original inspiration for taking up photography, his painting of the signing of the deed of demission, was not completed until 1865, and this grand painting, now in the offices of the Free Church, is little more than a collage of the calotype photographs on which it was founded.

Later life Hill's activities as the secretary of the Royal Scottish Academy continued throughout his life and served to maintain his prominence in the artistic community. In 1830 Hill was one of the major forces in the formation of the Art Union of Edinburgh, the first institution of the kind in the nation, and one that was soon copied. In 1850 he was appointed one of the commissioners of the board of manufactures in Scotland, a body then responsible for the Government School of Art and the new National Gallery of Scotland.

Hill's only child, Charlotte (Chatty), the wife of W. Scott Dalgleish, died early in 1862. Shortly afterwards, on 18 November 1862, Hill married the sculptor Amelia Robertson Paton [see Hill, Amelia Robertson (1820–1904)], who was the sister of the Pre-Raphaelite artist Sir Noël Paton and the landscape painter Waller Hugh Paton.

In addition to his public services, Hill continued to paint and to exhibit. Some of his paintings, particularly *Old and New Edinburgh, from the Castle* and *The Braes of Ballochmyle*, were clearly inspired by the photographs he had been involved in taking. In all, Hill exhibited about 300 of his works in his lifetime. About 270 of these were shown in the annual exhibitions of the Royal Scottish Academy. Nearly all were paintings, but he exhibited seven calotypes in 1844 and ten more the following year. His reputation was grounded largely in Edinburgh—he showed only four times at the Royal Academy in London—but this was not as limiting as it might seem. The 'Athens of the north' was a powerful intellectual centre in the dual wake of the Scottish Enlightenment and the exhortations of Sir Walter Scott. It was a place where a man such as Hill could influence greatly the course of artistic development. And that he did.

Hill's marriage to Amelia was not only happy but productive. It was under her influence that Hill finally completed his Disruption painting. Although she was clearly a Scottish artist, Amelia exhibited eighteen of her sculptures at the Royal Academy in London, helping to extend her husband's reputation as well. Tragically, Hill developed rheumatic fever in 1868. They moved from the cramped but central quarters of Rock House to a more tranquil spot in Edinburgh. There—Newington Lodge, Mayfield Terrace—Hill died on 17 May 1870. Amelia Hill executed a bronze bust for his grave in the Dean cemetery.

Posthumous reputation and significance It is curious that Hill's obituaries nearly universally failed to mention his pioneering photographic work with Robert Adamson. But it is this body of work, much more than his paintings and engravings, that has lived on, inspiring successive generations of photographers and historians. The landscapes and architectural work that they accomplished are valuable records of a Scotland now changed. More significantly, however, they brought to the photograph the expressive power to record the personality of the sitters. In 1843, when Adamson started his studio, those in the know maintained a careful distinction between the daguerreotype and the photograph. Daguerreotypes, those magic little mirrors that were unique images on sheets of polished silver, had immediately taken over the province of the portrait. Photographs, which at the time meant images on paper, had lagged in this application. Perhaps part of this can be ascribed to the temperament of their inventor, William Henry Fox Talbot, for social contact was difficult for him and this shows almost inescapably in his photographs of people. Hill had no such problem and Robert Adamson ensured that the human contact he had made was expressed clearly and forcefully on a sheet of paper. The power and visual nature of Hill's and Adamson's images were likened to those of Rembrandt, and appropriately so, with their moody range of masses of light and shade. Nothing in the early history of the photograph can be compared to their body of work.

Although Hill's and Adamson's photographs fell briefly from sight within Hill's lifetime, it was not long before they regained an enduring and well-deserved reputation as beautifully symbolizing the expressive power of a radical new art. The photographer Francis Caird Inglis (1876–1940), who took over Rock House about 1900, found many negatives and prints remaining there. The Glasgow photogravure master Thomas Annan (1828–1887) had made permanent carbon prints of Hill's Disruption painting. His son, J. Craig Annan (1864–1946), had been familiar with Hill's and Adamson's photographs since he was a child, and worked with Inglis to make new prints from the negatives (a practice natural at the time but roundly discouraged today) and permanent prints in carbon. It was through Annan that Alfred Stieglitz (1864–1946) became interested in this pioneering work, introducing it not only

to the American public, but also to serious photographers worldwide. A nephew of Hill's, the bookseller Andrew Elliott, had taken over the shop and stock of Hill's brother Alexander. In addition to writing one of the early books on Hill's photographs, he commissioned Jessie Bartram to make sensitive carbon prints from the originals between 1913 and 1925. It was natural that Elliott's book should emphasize the contributions of his uncle and by the time Heinrich Schwarz had published his serious assessment in 1931 Robert Adamson was almost totally forgotten. Later historians have begun to appreciate the essentially symbiotic nature of this unique partnership, however, and it is not unusual to find their work today labelled (perhaps as it always should have been) as being by Adamson and Hill. Certainly there can be no meaningful separation of their individual contributions to their photographic masterpieces.

Robert Adamson's command of the process of making prints in silver was as unusual as it was complete, and the original prints have proven to be among the most durable of all early photographs. More than 3000 are in the collection of the Scottish National Portrait Gallery in Edinburgh and many hundreds of other originals grace the collections of museums worldwide. Nearly 1000 of their original paper calotype negatives survive, the largest group at the University of Glasgow and most of the others at the Scottish National Portrait Gallery (with smaller deposits at the Harry Ransom Humanities Research Center, University of Texas, and at the Metropolitan Museum of Art, New York). By their very nature, Hill's lithographs and engravings are scattered but survive in numerous locations. His paintings fared less well, though the Perth Museum and Art Gallery, the National Gallery of Scotland, and the Hunterian Gallery in Glasgow each hold several, and numerous others are in collections worldwide. Many were purchased by patrons, and these are still coming to market. In addition to his photographic legacy shared with Robert Adamson, Hill's greatest influence was on the development of the arts in his native Scotland. The obituary in the *Art Journal* (new ser., 9, 1870) observed that even though

> Mr. Hill's works may not rank with the highest productions of British artists, even with the best of those of Scotland, he did much to maintain the honour of the school to which he belongs … in the Art-circles of Edinburgh … his loss will undoubtedly be much deplored, and his absence from them deeply regretted.　(p. 203)

The *Edinburgh Evening Courant* (18 May 1870) stressed the character that had made it all possible, saying that Hill was 'very loveable and much beloved'.

LARRY J. SCHAAF

Sources S. Stevenson, *David Octavius Hill and Robert Adamson* (1981) · C. Ford and R. Strong, *An early Victorian album* (New York, 1976) · S. Stevenson and J. Ward, *Printed light* (1986) · D. Bruce, *Sun pictures: the Hill–Adamson calotypes* (Greenwich, CT, 1973) · S. Stevenson, *Hill and Adamson: 'The fishermen and women of the Firth of Forth'* (1991) · H. Schwarz, *David Octavius Hill: master of photography* (New York, 1931) · A. Dunbar, 'The work of David Octavius Hill, R.S.A.', *Photographic Journal*, 104 (1964), 53–65 · B. von Dewitz, *David Octavius Hill and Robert Adamson* (Cologne, 2000) · *DNB* · bap. reg. Scot [D. O. Hill, R. Adamson] · d. cert.

Archives Edinburgh Central Reference Library, letters and MSS · Royal Scot. Acad., corresp. as secretary to Royal Scottish Academy | NL Scot., Macdonald–Michaelson collection, letters and documents · NL Scot., letters to Sir Joseph Noël Paton · U. Edin. L., letters to David Laing
Likenesses R. S. Lauder, oils, 1829, NPG · R. Adamson, calotypes, 1843–7 · D. O. Hill and R. Adamson, photograph, 1843–8, NPG [*see illus.*] · A. R. Hill, plaster medallion, *c*.1851, Scot. NPG · A. R. Hill, wax medallion, *c*.1851, Scot. NPG · A. R. Hill, marble bust, 1868, Scot. NPG · R. Herdman, oils, 1870, Royal Scot. Acad. · T. Annan, carte-de-visite, NPG · T. Annan and R. Adamson, photographs, NPG, Scot. NPG · T. Annan and R. Adamson, photographs, U. Texas · J. M. Barclay, oils, Scot. NPG · C. K. Childs, woodcut (after A. R. Paton), BM; repro. in *Art Journal* (1850) · P. Park, marble bust, Scot. NPG · A. R. Paton, granite tombstone/bronze bust, Dean cemetery, Edinburgh

Hill, Sir (John) Denis Nelson (1913–1982), psychiatrist, was born on 5 October 1913 in Orleton, Herefordshire, the only child of Lieutenant-Colonel John Arthur Hill, farmer, and his wife, Doris Nelson. He was educated at Shrewsbury School and St Thomas's Hospital, where he became interested in psychiatry.

Soon after qualifying MB BS (University of London, 1936), Hill went to Maida Vale Hospital to study neurology with W. Russell (later Lord) Brain. There he met Grey Walter, who was beginning to use the new technique of electroencephalography (EEG) to investigate neurological disorders. Hill was impressed by Walter's early successes in locating cerebral tumours, and fascinated by the technical aspects of the EEG. In 1938 he married Phoebe Elizabeth Herschel, daughter of Lieutenant-Colonel H. H. Wade. They had a son and a daughter.

In 1938 Hill returned to St Thomas's as an assistant in the department of psychiatry, but this work was soon interrupted by the outbreak of war. Because of severe asthma, Hill was unfit for military service and was sent instead to the Emergency Hospital at Belmont in Surrey where he joined a talented group of psychiatrists, including Eliot Slater and William Sargant. An EEG machine was obtained from America, and Hill set up a laboratory to study the clinical applications of EEG to psychiatry and particularly to epilepsy. This led to a collaboration with Murray Falconer in the surgical treatment of temporal lobe epilepsy. He became MRCP and obtained his DPM in 1940. When the war ended Hill was the obvious person to set up an EEG laboratory as part of the new Institute of Psychiatry at the Maudsley Hospital (where he was a senior lecturer from 1948 to 1960), and to carry out similar work at the National Hospital for Nervous Diseases in London. He contributed a chapter on the treatment of epilepsies to Sargant and Slater's *An Introduction to the Physical Methods of Treatment in Psychiatry* (1948). Before long he was an acknowledged expert in his field and he edited, with Geoffrey Parr, *Electroencephalography* (1950), the first comprehensive textbook of clinical EEG. He became FRCP in 1949 and FRCPsych. in 1971. Hill served on the working party on special hospitals in 1959; the working party on the organization of prison medical services in 1962; the Aarvold committee in 1972; and the Butler committee on disturbed offenders between 1972 and 1975. His wide experience and balanced judgement led to service on other important committees. In 1956–60 he was a member of the Medical Research Council; in 1961–7 of the Central Health Services Council of the Ministry of Health; and from 1961 until his death of the General Medical Council of which he was treasurer, and chairman of the penal cases committee and the special committee to ensure that sick doctors could receive appropriate medical help while the interests of the public were safeguarded.

Despite these demanding administrative duties, Hill remained above all an outstanding clinician and teacher. First as lecturer in psychological medicine at King's College Hospital (1947–60) he worked to establish psychiatry in the medical curriculum. He became the foundation professor of psychiatry at the Middlesex Hospital medical school, where he established a department that was a model for others. He was influential in bringing about the foundation of chairs of psychiatry in other medical schools. From 1966 to 1979 he was professor of psychiatry at the Institute of Psychiatry, a postgraduate teaching school of the University of London, and influenced the workings of the institute itself and the associated Bethlem Royal and Maudsley hospitals. Under his leadership, the department of psychiatry expanded, with endowments for new chairs and a growing and wide-ranging programme of research. In all these activities he was a bridge builder—between neurology and psychiatry, between psychoanalysis and biological psychiatry, and between medicine and philosophy. His *Psychiatry in Medicine: Retrospect and Prospect* was published in 1969.

Hill's achievements led to many honours. He was knighted in 1966. He gave the most prestigious named lectures in his subject: the Maudsley lecture of the Royal College of Psychiatrists in 1972, the Adolf Meyer lecture of the American Psychiatric Association in 1968, the Vickers lecture of the Mental Health Research Fund in 1972, the Ernest Jones lecture of the Institute of Psychoanalysis in 1970, and in 1969 the Rock Carling lecture.

After Hill's first marriage was dissolved in 1960, in 1962 he married Lorna Wheelan, a consultant child psychiatrist, who was the daughter of John Fleming Wheelan, tax inspector. They had a son and a daughter. Hill was devoted to his family, and generous and loyal to his friends. In his leisure, he retained an abiding interest in the countryside and especially in the Herefordshire village in which he had grown up. In his later years he spent much time and money on the restoration of Orleton Manor, the half-timbered manor house in which his family had lived for generations. He died suddenly of a heart attack in London on 5 May 1982. His second wife survived him.   M. G. GELDER

Sources Munk, *Roll* · *The Lancet* (15 May 1982) · *BMJ* (15 May 1982), 1481 · personal knowledge (2004) · private information (2004) · *CGPLA Eng. & Wales* (1982)
Archives SOUND BL NSA
Likenesses oils, Institute of Psychiatry, London
Wealth at death £349: probate, 11 Nov 1982, *CGPLA Eng. & Wales*

Hill [*née* Dietz; *other married name* Harriott], **Diana** (*d.* 1844), miniature painter, of unknown parentage, was a pupil of the miniature painter Jeremiah Meyer. In 1775 she exhibited three miniatures at the Society of Artists and was presented with an award. At that time she lived in Angel Court, Great Windmill Street, London. Between 1777 and 1798 she exhibited miniatures, mostly of ladies, at the Royal Academy. On 1 February 1781, at St Mary's, St Marylebone, she married Haydock Hill, and in 1785 exhibited at the academy under her married name three works, of which two were flower pieces. On 21 September of that year the court of directors of the East India Company gave her permission to work in India as a portrait painter—her mother-in-law, Elizabeth Hill, and T. C. Blanchenhagen, merchant, being her approved securities.

On Diana Hill's arrival in Calcutta in 1786 the miniaturist Ozias Humphry noted that she was 'a pretty widow with two children' who possessed great merit, came with powerful recommendations, and whose brother-in-law John Hill was highly placed in the East India Company's Bengal civil service (Foster, 39). The attention and patronage that she received caused Humphry much alarm: he would 'rather have had all the male painters in England landed in Bengal than a single woman' (ibid.). An early commission came from William Larkins, accountant-general at Calcutta, whose miniature (BL OIOC, reproduced Foster, pl. 8c) is signed 'Hill, 1786'. Three of her portraits, painted in India and all signed and dated, were shown at the exhibition of miniatures held at South Kensington Museum in 1865. These included a portrait of Sarah Stackhouse (priv. coll.), wife of General Macleod, stylishly dressed in a tartan jacket and a headdress of high feathers and ribbons, of whom Mrs Hill painted another, whole-length miniature showing her seated in a landscape (priv. coll.; reproduced Foster, pl. 8d). Like the portrait of Larkins this shows, in the treatment of the hair and the large eyes, the influence of Meyer. The flattering images that her portraits—usually oval, in watercolour on ivory—display of their sitters indicate that Diana Hill's success was due not only to her social connections in India. On 7 November 1788 the painter Thomas Daniell wrote to Humphry, who had returned to England: 'Mrs. Hill is still making handsome faces, in the house you lived in last in Calcutta' (Foster, 40). In that month, however, Diana Hill gave up painting professionally when on 15 November she married Lieutenant Thomas George Harriott, of the 1st native infantry, then acting as brigade major, 3rd brigade. A miniature of her second husband (V&A) is signed 'D.H. 1791', her marriage perhaps indicating the reason for the change in her signature. Her miniature of an unknown, dark-complexioned, perhaps Indian girl in a large, almost theatrical mob cab (V&A; reproduced *British Portrait Miniatures*, pl. 77) is an intriguing portrait in which the effects of the artist's style, together with the sitter's Western dress, led to her being described as 'evidently half-caste' (Foskett, 528). In 1792 Sophia Dietz was given permission by the East India Company to join her sister in Bengal. After serving in Fatehgarh and Dinajpur, Harriott resigned in 1806 and returned to England, presumably with his wife and family, and resided at West Hall, Mortlake, Surrey, where he died in 1817, aged sixty-four. Diana Hill died at Twickenham, Middlesex, on 10 February 1844. Of her two sons with Thomas Harriott, William Henry Harriott (*d.* 1839) became a clerk in the War Office, a watercolour painter, and a friend of Cotman. Examples of his work are in the British Museum and in Bridport Art Gallery. With his wife, Sibella Mary, *née* Hunter, he had a daughter, Sibella Christina, who also became an artist.

ANNETTE PEACH

Sources W. Foster, 'British artists in India, 1760–1820', *Walpole Society*, 19 (1930–31), 1–88, esp. 39–40 • D. Foskett, *Miniatures: dictionary and guide* (1987) • *British portrait miniatures: an exhibition arranged for the period of the Edinburgh International Festival* (Arts Council of Great Britain, 1965) • Graves, *RA exhibitors* • IGI • Mallalieu, *Watercolour artists* • artist's file, archive material, NPG • will, PRO, PROB 11/1193, sig. 121 • d. cert.
Wealth at death over £10,000 to family members; plus smaller bequests to others: will, PRO, PROB 11/1193, sig. 121

Hill, Sir Dudley St Leger (1790–1851), army officer, the eldest son of Dudley Hill, of Welsh descent, and his wife, the daughter of Colonel John Clarges, was born in co. Carlow, Ireland. He was appointed ensign in the 82nd regiment on 6 September 1804, and exchanged the year after into the 95th rifles. As lieutenant he accompanied his battalion to South America in 1806, volunteered for the forlorn hope at Montevideo, and commanded the scaling party that captured the north gate of the city in February 1807. He was wounded and taken prisoner in the subsequent attack on Buenos Aires in June. He accompanied his battalion to Portugal in 1808, was present at Roliça and Vimeiro, was wounded at Benevente, and was present at Corunna. Returning to Portugal in 1809, he was present at the battle of Talavera and the operations on the Coa.

In July 1810 Hill was promoted to a company in the Royal West India rangers, but remained attached to the 95th until appointed to the Portuguese army. He commanded a wing of the Lusitanian legion at Busaco in September 1810, and a half-battalion with some British light companies at Fuentes d'Oñoro in May 1811. He commanded the 8th Portuguese *caçadores* at the storming of Badajoz in April 1812, at the battle of Salamanca in July, and in the Burgos retreat, where his battalion lost heavily at the passage of the Carrion, and where he was himself wounded and taken prisoner. After exchange he again commanded his battalion at Vitoria; at the storming of San Sebastian in September 1813 he headed the attack of the 5th division, receiving two wounds, and was present at the repulse of the sortie at Bayonne in 1814. In these campaigns he was seven times wounded.

At the peace Hill returned with the Portuguese army to Portugal, and served there; in 1820 he held a divisional command in the Portuguese service. He was made major in the newly raised 95th (Derbyshire) regiment in December 1823, from which he exchanged to half pay in January 1826. In 1834 he was appointed lieutenant-governor of the island of St Lucia, and took out with him the act of emancipation. He returned home on the occasion of his second marriage in 1838. He became major-general in 1841, and, after serving on the staff in Ireland, was appointed to a divisional command in Bengal in 1848, which post he held at the time of his death.

Hill married, first, the third daughter of Robert Hunter of Kew, Surrey, with whom he had six children, and second, on 23 June 1838, Mary, widow of Mark Davies, of Turnwood, Dorset. Hill was made CB in 1814, knighted in 1816, and made KCB in 1848. He had the Portuguese orders of the Tower and Sword, and of St Bento d'Avis, the latter conferred in 1839. He was presented with a sword and two valuable pieces of plate by his native county. He was appointed to the colonelcy of the 50th regiment in 1849. He died at Ambala, Bengal, on 21 February 1851.

H. M. CHICHESTER, *rev.* JAMES FALKNER

Sources *Army List* · *GM*, 2nd ser., 35 (1851), 552 · *Hart's Army List* · *Colburn's United Service Magazine*, 3 (1849), 137 · Boase, *Mod. Eng. biog.* · W. Cope, *The history of the rifle brigade* (1877)
Archives U. Durham L., letters to Henry George, third Earl Grey, and copies of letters from same
Likenesses J. Green, miniature, oils, 1835, princess of Wales's regiment

Hill, Edmund [*name in religion* Thomas of St Gregory] (**1564–1644**), Benedictine monk, was born in Somerset on 24 June 1564, the son of Thomas and Joan Hill. He is sometimes said to have been a Church of England clergyman but this is unlikely in the light of his own avowal that 'I was born, baptized and confirmed a Catholic' (Hill, *Quartron of Reasons*, 1600, preface). He was a servant of John Gerard, the Jesuit, who sent him to the English College of Douai, then temporarily removed to Rheims, on 21 August 1590. He left for Rome on 16 February 1593, continued his studies in the English College there, and was ordained priest on 12 March 1594 by Owen Lewis, bishop of Cassano. He was the chief troublemaker in the student uprising against the administration of the English College at Rome by the Jesuits, with their pro-Spanish sympathies. He earned sufficient notoriety in this role to receive a personal rebuke from Pope Clement VIII at the audience granted to him on his departure for the English mission.

Hill's youthful contentiousness now found a new outlet in religious controversy. On 18 January 1599 William Pole, a Devonshire justice of the peace, denounced him to Pole's grandfather, Sir John Popham, the lord chief justice, for having 'corrupted and seduced' Sir Robert Basset. Pole claimed to have written to the same effect in 1597. This accusation shows that Hill's first missionary field was his native west country. His *A Quartron of Reasons of Catholic Religion with as many Brief Reasons of Refusal* was published secretly in England in 1600, bearing the imprint 'Antwerp'. This challenge elicited two responses, the first in 1603 from Francis Dillingham, one of the translators of the Authorized Version of the Bible. A weightier response of 438 pages from George Abbot, dean of Winchester and future archbishop of Canterbury, appeared in 1604. Abbot spent a year and a half on its composition even though he dismissed Hill's work as no more than an abridgement of a similar book by Richard Bristow, usually referred to as 'Bristow's motives'. Hill wrote two other works of a devotional nature.

When Hill published his *Quartron* he was, according to his own account, 'living at Phalempyne, beyond the sea', being then a doctor of divinity. Two years later he was again labouring on the mission, and being apprehended at 'Dubscombte's house in London' was committed to Newgate prison. A Jesuit recounting his capture described him as an 'appellant priest'. On 30 April 1604 he was condemned to death for being a priest, but was reprieved at the intercession of the Spanish ambassador and banished in the following year. While in prison again in 1612 he received the Benedictine habit by commission from Leander of St Martin (John Jones). After his release he was professed a monk of St Gregory's Priory, Douai, on 8 October 1613, though he continued to work as a missioner in England where he laboured for nearly fifty years in all. In 1633 he was given the honorific title of prior of Gloucester by the English Benedictine congregation. On leaving the English mission he retired to St Gregory's at Douai, where he died on 7 August 1644.

THOMPSON COOPER, *rev.* DAVID DANIEL REES

Sources E. T. Hill, *A quartron of reasons of Catholic religion* (1600) · G. Anstruther, *The seminary priests*, 4 vols. (1969–77), vols. 1–2 · T. B. Snow, *Obit book of the English Benedictines from 1600 to 1912*, rev. H. N. Birt (privately printed, Edinburgh, 1913) · Gillow, *Lit. biog. hist.*, vol. 3 · A. Kenny, 'The inglorious revolution, 1594–1597', *The Venerabile*, 16 (1954), 240–58; 17 (1954), 7–25, 77–94, 136–55 · H. Foley, ed., *Records of the English province of the Society of Jesus*, 1 (1877), 61; 4 (1878), 654 · P. A. Welsby, *George Abbot, the unwanted archbishop* (1962) · *John Gerard: the autobiography of an Elizabethan*, trans. P. Caraman (1951) · A. F. Allison and D. M. Rogers, eds., *The contemporary printed literature of the English Counter-Reformation between 1558 and 1640*, 2 vols. (1989–94) · A. Pritchard, *Catholic loyalism in Elizabethan England* (1979) · T. G. Law, ed., *The archpriest controversy: documents relating to the dissensions of the Roman Catholic clergy, 1597–1602*, 2 vols., CS, new ser., 56, 58 (1896–8) · T. F. Knox and others, eds., *The first and second diaries of the English College, Douay* (1878)
Archives Downside Abbey, near Bath, 'Liber professionum conventus S. Gregorii M. Duacensis' · St Mary's College Library, Oscott, Birmingham, MS

Hill, Edwin (**1793–1876**), civil servant and inventor of postal machinery, was born on 25 November 1793 at Birmingham, the second of the eight children of Thomas Wright *Hill (1763–1851), schoolmaster, and his wife, Sarah Lea (1765–1842), daughter of William Lea. His elder brother was Matthew Davenport *Hill, and his younger brothers included Rowland *Hill and Frederic *Hill. Like his brothers, he was educated at his father's school and then set to teach there while still a boy. Later he took a post at the assay office in Birmingham and subsequently at a brass-rolling mill, also in Birmingham, where he rose to be manager. He was one of the signatories of the notice convening the Birmingham meeting of 22 January 1817 to petition for parliamentary reform. In 1819 he and his brother Matthew married sisters, respectively Anne (1793–1873) and Margaret Bucknall. Edwin and Anne had ten children, seven of whom survived him.

In 1827, when the family school extended to Bruce Castle, Tottenham, in addition to the existing establishment at Hazelwood, Birmingham, Edwin Hill joined the enterprise and moved to Tottenham where Rowland took charge of the teaching. Edwin was mostly concerned with the commercial management, being too much interested in his mechanical experiments to give up much of his time to teaching. In 1840, with penny postage about to commence, it was necessary to expand the stamp office. Stamps had long existed as a tax-collecting device, but now the Inland Revenue was to supply the Post Office with the new postage stamps. Rowland was appointed to the Treasury to oversee the introduction of the system, and Edwin applied for the stamp-producing appointment, asking Charles Babbage for a reference in support. Here he remained, joined later by his son Ormond, until his retirement in 1872.

Edwin's best-known invention was a machine for folding envelopes, which was shown at the Great Exhibition of 1851, though the patent had by then been bought by Warren De la Rue to whom it was there attributed. He invented many mechanical contrivances for the stamp department. At his retirement, a Treasury minute paid tribute to 'his resourcefulness and considerable mechanical ability which had contributed so much to the success of the new postage scheme'. He published pamphlets on currency (1848 and 1856) in which he was concerned with maintaining stability of monetary value while overcoming the swings of the business cycle between expansion and depression. He also published two pamphlets entitled *Criminal Capitalists* (1870 and 1872) arguing that all enterprises needed both labour and capital, while the attack on crime was directed almost entirely at the labourers; he believed that a drive against landlords who housed criminals and receivers of stolen goods would be more productive. In particular, he wished to redefine the law to make it an offence to receive goods *believing* them to be stolen. He died on 6 November 1876 at his home, 1 St Mark's Square, close to the entrance to the London Zoo, and was buried at Highgate cemetery.   I. D. HILL

Sources G. B. Hill and R. Hill, *The life of Sir Rowland Hill, and, The history of penny postage*, 2 vols. (1880) • W. E. Hill, *An account of the Julian Hill family* (privately printed, London, 1938) • E. C. Smyth, *Sir Rowland Hill, the story of a great reform, told by his daughter* (1907) • F. Hill, *Frederic Hill: an autobiography of fifty years in times of reform*, ed. C. Hill (1893) • R. Davenport-Hill and F. Davenport-Hill, *The recorder of Birmingham: a memoir of Matthew Davenport Hill* (1878) • L. B. Hill, *A range of Hills*, typescript, c.1975 • E. Hill, 'Journal or drafting book of Mr Edwin Hill of the stamping branch', PRO, IR 42, 1–10 • *DNB* • d. cert.

Archives PRO, journals, IR 42 | UCL, SDUK MSS, letters to Society for the Diffusion of Useful Knowledge

Likenesses photograph (as an old man), repro. in Hill, *Account*

Wealth at death £16,000: probate, 18 Dec 1876, *CGPLA Eng. & Wales*

Hill, Dame Elizabeth Mary (1900–1996), Russian and Slavonic scholar, was born on 24 October 1900 in St Petersburg, Russia, the fifth of the six children (and second of the three daughters) of Frederick William Hill (1860–1924), merchant, and his wife, Louisa Maria Wilhelmina Sophia, *née* Miller (1862–1929). She was baptized Bessie May and, many years later, changed her name by deed poll

Dame Elizabeth Mary Hill (1900–1996), by unknown photographer, c.1980

to Elizabeth Mary. Her father was British and her mother Russian (although of Austro-Prussian descent), and Elizabeth grew up fluent in four languages (English, French, German, and Russian). In 1917 the family left Russia and their privileged place in the British community, settled in London, and faced a life of increasing penury.

Three and a half happy years as the 'French mamzelle' at Penrhos College, north Wales, preceded Hill's studies in Russian from 1921 at University and King's colleges, London, which resulted in a first-class degree in 1924. In 1931 she completed her PhD on the early nineteenth-century Russian psychological novel, under the supervision of Prince D. S. Mirsky. During these years and subsequently, she supported herself by constant lecturing, coaching, and above all translating. With her great friend Doris Mudie (of the Mudie's Library family) she translated from French and particularly from Russian, including letters written by Dostoyevsky to his wife (1930) and by Lenin (1937), and, under the pseudonym J. Penn, produced *For Readers Only* (1936), a lively book of anecdotes (including one about an attack on Mirsky by an unsought admirer of Hill) and reminiscences of countless hours spent happily in the British Museum reading room.

It was 1936 that brought Hill's appointment at the University of Cambridge as lecturer in Slavonic, which in those years had its refuge in the department of other languages. Only in 1948, when women were awarded degrees at Cambridge for the first time, was the department of Slavonic studies established and Elizabeth Hill elected to the professorship. On her fiftieth birthday (24 October 1950) she delivered her inaugural lecture, published as *Why Need we Study the Slavs?* (1951), by which time she headed a department of ten lecturers, teaching Czech, Polish, Serbo-Croat, and Russian to growing numbers of undergraduates. Her competence in several of these languages—notably Serbo-Croat—notwithstanding, it was with the teaching of, and propaganda for, the Russian language that she was inevitably and justly linked. During the Second World War she was attached to the Ministry of Information as a Slavonic specialist, and it was largely as a result of her persuasion that the War Office agreed to set up intensive Russian-language courses at Cambridge. These were to continue during the period of national service and, in parallel with similar courses at the University of London, provided Britain with well-trained Russian linguists, many of whom pursued their studies at universities and achieved prominent positions in academe, the diplomatic service, and business.

Lisa, which is how generations of *kursanty* (participants in the services' courses) and undergraduates remembered her, was a legendary figure, black-suited, piercingly blue-eyed, and with hair swept back; and, as many Cambridge gateposts and policemen would have testified, an idiosyncratic interpreter in her black Fiat, nicknamed the Flea, of the highway code. She inspired people with a love of Russian and things Slavonic, encouraged and cajoled them, but she herself was not a publishing scholar. As one of her obituarists noted: 'she wrote almost nothing original, yet she was the direct inspirational force behind dozens of serious articles and books by other people' (*The Independent*, 6 Jan 1997). In her posthumously published memoirs, *In the Mind's Eye* (1999), she wrote of her 'creative dreams', of her work on Slavonic curses and spells in the 1920s, and of the devoted search for the 'truth' about the death of Tsar Alexander I that dominated her last years, 'but life forced me into other activities and another mould … in Cambridge it was my mission and my way to develop Slavonic Studies that obsessed me' (*In the Mind's Eye*, 218–19). Her memoirs, written with great humour, *élan*, and prejudice, but sadly unfinished, are her literary legacy, with their parade of wonderful characters, British and Slav, and endless tales, honed over the years by an accomplished raconteur. Her 'mission' she nevertheless fulfilled, with enormous dedication and energy, and not the least of her great contributions was the building up of the substantial Slavonic holdings in the Cambridge university and departmental libraries.

On her retirement from Cambridge, Hill became Andrew Mellon professor of Slavic languages and literatures at the University of Pittsburgh (1968–70). In 1976 she was made a DBE and in 1978 she received an honorary doctorate from the University of East Anglia. She was a professorial fellow of Girton College, Cambridge, a fellow of University College, London, from 1946, and on the occasion of her ninetieth birthday she was made an honorary fellow of the School of Slavonic and East European Studies, University of London.

In 1984, at the age of eighty-four, Hill married the Serbian aristocrat Stojan Veljković (1906–1998), whom she divorced three months before her death. Her account of that marriage and its end forms a sad and bitter coda to her memoirs. She had hoped to return to her home at 10 Croft Gardens, Cambridge, where she had lived since 1936, but she died of a heart attack at 77 Park Road, Chiswick, London, on 17 December 1996. After a funeral service in the Russian Orthodox cathedral in Ennismore Gardens, London, on 31 December, she was buried in Grantchester churchyard, reunited with her companion Doris Mudie (*d.* 1970).
ANTHONY CROSS

Sources *In the mind's eye: the memoirs of Dame Elizabeth Hill*, ed. J. Stafford-Smith (1999) · *Daily Telegraph* (23 Dec 1996) · *The Times* (24 Dec 1996) · *The Independent* (6 Jan 1997) · *The Guardian* (10 Jan 1997) · E. Hill, *Why need we study the Slavs? an inaugural lecture* (1951) · H. Davies, *Born 1900: a human history of the twentieth century—for everyone who was there* (1998), 92–110 · 'Professor "Lisa" Hill', *Varsity* (28 Feb 1953) · N. Kite, 'A dynamo at 90', *Cambridgeshire Pride Magazine* (Feb 1991), 7 · M. Vickers, 'From Russia with love', *Cam* (spring 1991), 4–5 · R. Eddison, 'Grateful salute to 90 years of an academic exocet', *The Observer* (28 Oct 1990) · WWW [forthcoming]
Archives CUL, MSS
Likenesses photograph, *c.*1980, Girton Cam. [*see illus.*] · photograph, repro. in *In the mind's eye*, ed. Stafford-Smith · photograph, repro. in *Daily Telegraph* · photograph, repro. in *The Times* · photograph, repro. in *The Independent*
Wealth at death under £180,000: probate, 29 July 1997, *CGPLA Eng. & Wales*

Hill, Sir Enoch (1865–1942), building society manager, was born on 10 September 1865 at Ball Haye Green, Leek, Staffordshire, the eldest of the four sons and three daughters of Henry Hill and his wife, Elizabeth Taylor, both of whom were manual workers in the silk-spinning industry. Hill joined that industry himself as a 'half-timer', aged eight, working full time when his schooling finished at the age of thirteen; he tried a number of jobs before settling as a printer. He subsequently acquired a stationery shop and became publisher of the *Leek Post*.

Hill was a devout Anglican, and his vicar helped him to remedy his lack of good schooling. In 1887 he became a lay reader in the Lichfield diocese, and married Esther Hayes (*d.* 1904) of Leek. They had two sons. His wife's uncle was secretary of the Leek United Building Society and Hill helped him part time, later becoming assistant secretary. In 1896 he was appointed secretary of the society, and in consequence handed the printing business on to his brothers. At this time he became an associate of the Chartered Secretaries' Institute, of which he was later a fellow, then treasurer, and (in 1935) president. The Leek United Building Society was in decline when Hill joined it, but by 1903 it had recovered ground, doubling its assets to over £103,000.

In 1903 the post of secretary at the Halifax Building Society became vacant; the Halifax was then Britain's fourth largest society, with assets of £1,400,000. Hill was appointed, and in that role proved a very able publicist, not least in his ability to turn public occasions to his society's advantage; in 1905 he was already setting money aside to celebrate the diamond jubilee of the Halifax in 1913. In

1906, two years after the death of his first wife, Hill married Bertha Henrietta Byrom Gee, the daughter of a musician, Samuel Gee of Leek. They lived at Willow Hall, Halifax.

From the start of his career at the Halifax, Hill strongly advocated owner occupation, then an unimportant category for large societies. In 1903 only 15% of the Halifax's mortgages were for less than £500 and 38% were for more than £5000. By 1911 these figures were reversed to 39% and 11% respectively. In the post-1918 world of rent restriction acts, with owner occupation becoming the norm, the Halifax had both the experience and the reputation to take full advantage of this change. For owner-occupiers, Hill lent a higher percentage of a house's value. Large savers were attracted by higher interest rates and a banking department. A 'penny savings' department and home safes recruited small savers. Increased staff, enlarged offices, and a rapidly increasing branch network ensured continuing good service. By 1913 the Halifax had become Britain's largest society, and a merger in 1927 with the Halifax Equitable ensured continued dominance.

Hill joined the society's board as managing director in 1916, becoming successively vice-president (1927) and president (1928). He was knighted in 1928. He served on the Yorkshire board of both Alliance Assurance and Barclays Bank. Active in the affairs of the National Association of Building Societies, he was elected to its council in 1913, and served as chairman (1921–33), deputy chairman (1933–6), and finally vice-president. He was president of the International Congress of Building Societies in 1933. When Hill retired in 1938 the Halifax had more than 16% of all building society funds, compared with 2% when he was appointed. The assets of the society had increased from £1,400,000 to £123 million.

Hill was president of the Conservative Association, successively at Leek and Halifax, and was the unsuccessful Conservative parliamentary candidate at Leek in 1922 and 1923, and also at Huddersfield in 1924 and 1929. Appointed a JP in 1913, he later chaired the lord chancellor's advisory committee for Halifax. Hill was a freemason, and his interests included golf and motoring. Hill died of heart failure at his home, Willow Hall, Halifax, on 13 May 1942. His second wife died in April 1951.   ESMOND J. CLEARY

Sources O. R. Hobson, *A hundred years of the Halifax* (1953) · R. K. Bacon, *The life of Sir Enoch Hill* (1934) · *Eighty years of home building—the Halifax plan*, Halifax Building Society (1937) · E. J. Cleary, *The building society movement* (1965) · E. J. Cleary, 'Hill, Sir Enoch', *DBB*
Archives Halifax Central Library, Halifax Building Society archives
Likenesses R. Jack, portrait, 1928, Halifax Building Society headquarters, Halifax · F. May, pen-and-ink and wash drawing, NPG · photograph, repro. in Bacon, *Life* · photographs, repro. in Hobson, *Hundred years*
Wealth at death £24,094 5s. 6d.: probate, 2 Nov 1942, *CGPLA Eng. & Wales*

Hill [née Ridyard], **Eveline** (1898–1973), politician, was born on 16 April 1898 at 133 Cross Street, Gorton, Manchester, the daughter of Richard Ridyard, an iron miller and later retail shopkeeper, and his wife, Mary Ann, née Watson. She was educated at junior and secondary schools

run by the Manchester education committee, and on leaving school entered her parents' catering business, where she continued to work until her marriage. She married, on 26 April 1922, John Stanley Hill (1894/5–1947), an oil and tallow refiner, and later company director, of Hilden Park, West Didsbury, the son of John Septimus Hill, also an oil and tallow refiner; they had one son and one daughter.

After the death of her father, Eveline Hill assumed joint control of the family business with her brother. In 1936 she was elected to Manchester city council as a Conservative for Didsbury ward. She remained on the council until 1966, and was an alderman from 1957; on her retirement she was made an honorary alderman. Hill was also a county borough organizer for the Women's Voluntary Services in Manchester (1943–50).

Hill's council work, together with her business and voluntary activities, made her well known in her region. She was adopted as the Conservative candidate for Wythenshawe, Manchester, and won the seat at the general election of 1950. She made a confident maiden speech during the debate on the address in March, criticizing the Labour government's decision to reduce its house-building programme. Hill pointed out that in her own constituency there were more than 27,000 families waiting for accommodation, and that nationally the problem was acute. Good housing, she argued, was essential to good health, and it did not make sense to increase spending on one while reducing it on the other, as the government proposed to do. Her solution was, in part, to encourage private house building and home ownership. Without being too partisan the speech ably expounded Conservative orthodoxy, and drew praise from the opposition benches. Derek Walker-Smith, who followed in the debate, suggested that Hill had shown 'by her very concise and logical marshalling of her facts what a slander it is to say that women are not logical' (*Hansard 5C*, 472, 1950, 826).

During her Commons career Hill spoke mostly on health, housing, and education. She was elected chair of the Conservative health and social services committee in 1955, later serving as vice-chair. She was also concerned with issues directly affecting women, and in May 1952 supported a motion for equal pay in the public services. In the previous year she had introduced a private member's bill designed to protect the 'deserted wife' in a broken marriage. The 'Deserted Wives Bill' would prevent the wife from being turned out of the marital home by allowing the transfer of the tenancy to her, providing that she was resident in the property concerned and there was a court order against the husband. The bill also offered greater security to the wife over her household possessions. The legislation addressed a serious problem, and one faced by many women. But it also raised complex legal questions, and these dominated discussion during the second reading on 26 January 1951. Partly as a result, the measure was lost on a closure motion by 44 votes to 51. Irene Ward, who had doggedly supported the bill during the debate, remarked ruefully that it had been 'a lawyer's day' (*Hansard 5C*, 483, 1951, 526).

It could not have escaped general notice that all six of

the women present on this occasion—three were Conservative and three Labour—supported Hill's proposal. The episode thus demonstrated the potential unity among women members, while at the same time emphasizing how few they were, and how little influence they could have. Twenty-one women were elected in 1950. This figure fell to seventeen in October 1951, only six of whom were Conservatives, a statistic that itself attracted considerable comment. In March 1952 Eveline Hill, along with Lady Davidson, Lady Tweedsmuir, and Irene Ward—the full complement of Conservative women back-benchers—wrote a joint letter to *The Times* urging action. The signatories did not blame Conservative central office, but looked instead to the constituency associations—the 'local people' who had the final say in the adoption of candidates. These were urged to select more women of merit and, equally important, to select them for winnable seats. Hill and her colleagues were concerned at the small number not just of Conservative women in parliament, but of women of all parties:

> Far too often women fight the hopeless seats over and over again. Women candidates ask no favours, only to be considered on their merits. A total of 17 women MPs is far too few in relation to the number of candidates at the last election. We write this letter, not as feminists, but because we believe there are many able and distinguished women who could serve their party and the country if given the chance. (*The Times*, 7 March 1952)

The letter probably had little effect. Though the number of Conservative women elected did increase in 1955 and 1959, to ten and twelve respectively, the number of Conservative women candidates barely changed.

Hill's own electoral position at Wythenshawe came under serious threat from Labour in 1955. At the 1959 election her majority was reduced to 1309 votes, and in 1964 she was defeated by Alfred Morris, the Labour and Co-operative candidate, who went on to represent the constituency until 1997. Hill had been one of the few women in parliament in her day with a practical knowledge of business affairs. This, combined with her experience of local government, made her specially valuable to her party in her fourteen years in the Commons. She died of heart failure on 22 September 1973 at her home, Glenavon, 115 Styal Road, Gatley, Cheshire.

MARK POTTLE

Sources WWW · P. Brookes, *Women at Westminster: an account of women in the British parliament, 1918–1966* (1967) · *The Times* (7 March 1952) · *The Times* (26 Sept 1973) · WWBMP, vol. 4 · C. Rallings and M. Thrasher, *British electoral facts, 1832–1999* (2000) · Hansard 5C (1950), vol. 472; (1951), vol. 451; (1951), vol. 500 · F. W. S. Craig, *British parliamentary election results, 1950–1970* (1971) · b. cert. · m. cert. · d. cert. · CGPLA Eng. & Wales (1973)
Wealth at death £16,315: probate, 7 Nov 1973, CGPLA Eng. & Wales

Hill, Florence Davenport (1828/9–1919). *See under* Hill, Rosamond Davenport (1825–1902).

Hill, Sir (James William) Francis (1899–1980), lawyer and historian, was born at 34 Tentercroft Street, Lincoln, on 15 September 1899, the elder of the two sons of James Hill, an immigrant to Lincolnshire from his native Scotland, and his English wife, Millicent Blinkhorn. James Hill worked in Lincolnshire as a travelling tailor.

Hill was educated at the Lincoln Technical School. In 1918 he was commissioned into the King's Royal Rifles (60th Rifles) and served in France until 1919. After demobilization he went to Trinity College, Cambridge, where he graduated in 1921. He was then articled to a Lincoln solicitor, Russell Race, and was admitted to the roll of solicitors in January 1926. He was immediately taken into partnership, and remained a partner in the firm until his death. The minutiae of provincial legal practice, however, did not satisfy him and he soon became involved in the public life of the city.

Hill was elected a city councillor in 1932, and served as councillor and later alderman until 1974, leading the independent group which controlled the council for a period after the Second World War. He was mayor in 1945–6 and was elected a freeman of the city in 1961. For many years he chaired the Lincoln education committee, and a primary school in the city is named after him. He was twice an unsuccessful parliamentary candidate: first as a Liberal, at Peterborough in 1929, and then as a Conservative and National Liberal, at Lincoln.

Over time Hill fought many local battles in Lincoln. In 1928, a threat to the twelfth-century Jews' House from a local slum clearance scheme was successfully resisted. Years later, when Lincoln corporation, backed by the Central Electricity Generating Board, planned to erect at the Lincoln power station a group of cooling towers 220 feet high which would have cut off the historic view of Lincoln from the south-west, he managed, if not to prevent their being built at all, to get their height reduced to 60 feet. His campaign in 1955 to prevent the diversion of the Roman Ermine Street north of the city to make room for a runway extension at Royal Air Force, Scampton, was finally unsuccessful, but his vigorous resistance did ensure that the decision was taken right up to cabinet level.

Frank Hill (as he was generally called) became a leading figure in local government. He was chairman of the association of municipal corporations from 1957 to 1966, and a member of the royal commission on local government (the Maud commission) from 1966 to 1969. He was chairman of the Standing Advisory Committee on Grants to Students from 1958 to 1966 and a governor of the Administrative Staff College, Henley, from 1960 to 1969. His chairmanship of the association of municipal corporations led in due course to his election as president of the European conference of local authorities, whose headquarters were at Strasbourg, a post he occupied from 1966 to 1968. He was subsequently president for three years of the International Union of Local Authorities at The Hague, an appointment that involved frequent extensive travel. From 1972 to 1978 he was chairman of Municipal Mutual Insurance plc and was regarded with affection by both senior and junior staff. In his honour the company in 1972 endowed the Francis Hill chair of local government at Nottingham University. He was made a CBE in 1954 and in

1958 received a knighthood for services to local government. He was appointed a deputy lieutenant of Lincolnshire in 1974.

Hill's service in local government and his professional work as a solicitor informed his distinguished work as a local historian of Lincoln. His four volumes of civic history, published by Cambridge University Press, *Medieval Lincoln* (1948, repr. 1965), *Tudor and Stuart Lincoln* (1956), *Georgian Lincoln* (1966), and *Victorian Lincoln* (1974) were highly regarded. He was elected a fellow of the Society of Antiquaries and an honorary vice-president of the Royal Historical Society.

Hill's work for education included serving as chairman of the governors of Lincoln School and Lincoln Girls' High School from 1935 to 1966. In 1938 he became a member of Nottingham University college council and then served as its president from 1948 and pro-chancellor in 1959. For twenty eventful years during the building of the university's splendid campus and its wide academic organization he gave the creative leadership the period required and, in recognition of this, was elected chancellor in 1972, remaining so until he retired in 1978. He received honorary degrees from the universities of Cambridge (1950), Nottingham (1961), Birmingham (1961), and Leicester (1974).

Hill leased from the dean and chapter of Lincoln a house in Minster Yard known as The Priory; he restored it substantially and in his will devised it back to the chapter. He died there, after suffering a heart attack, on 6 January 1980, and was buried at Newport cemetery, Lincoln. He was unmarried. By his will the pictures which he collected at The Priory were given to the city of Lincoln and his considerable library was bequeathed to Nottingham University. His collection of some 1400 Anglo-Saxon and Norman coins, of which nearly a thousand were minted in Lincoln or Stamford, was presented by him to the city in 1974.

PHILIP RACE

Sources WWW · Burke, *Peerage* (1967) · *The Times House of Commons* (1950) · personal knowledge (2004) · private information (2004) [Lincoln city council; U. Nott.; Municipal Mutual Insurance plc; Trinity Cam.; Andrew & Co, Solicitors, Lincoln] · b. cert. · d. cert.

Archives Lincs. Arch., antiquarian collections · Lincs. Arch., corresp. and papers relating to his proposed history of Newland incl. MS draft · Lincs. Arch., historical and official corresp., diaries, and papers · Lincs. Arch., research notes and collections rel. to history of Lincolnshire · U. Nott. L., Association of Municipal Councils and International Union of Local Authorities, papers relating to local government · U. Nott. L., papers relating to Redcliffe–Maud commission | NHM, corresp. with W. R. Dawson

Likenesses L. Boden, oils, U. Nott. · L. Boden, oils, Lincoln Guildhall · photograph, Municipal Mutual Insurance

Wealth at death £328,934: probate, 21 Feb 1980, *CGPLA Eng. & Wales*

Hill, Frank Harrison (1830–1910), journalist, was born at Boston, Lincolnshire, the younger son of George Hill, a merchant, and his wife, Betsy, daughter of Pishey Thompson. He was educated at Boston grammar school, and at the Unitarian New College, Manchester. In 1851 he completed a five-year course of study for the ministry, but never chose to preach. Meanwhile, he had registered as a

Frank Harrison Hill (1830–1910), by unknown engraver, pubd 1881

student for the BA degree at London University, and in 1851 graduated with first-class honours. He later joined Lincoln's Inn, was called to the bar in 1872, but never practised. Hill's first paid post was as a private tutor in Manchester. He owed his introduction to journalism to two very different characters: the gifted literary critic and editor of the *Spectator*, Richard Holt Hutton, and Dr Henry Dunckley, editor of the *Manchester Examiner*, who, from a desire to be in his bed before midnight, earned among his profession an undeserved reputation for indolence. Hill's fine writing and sharply independent mind clearly impressed his contemporaries for, in 1861, he was invited to succeed James Simms as editor of the *Northern Whig*, chief organ of the Ulster Liberals. It was not an easy time to take responsibility for a newspaper. In Ireland, the recently formed Republican Brotherhood, the Fenians, sought to promote armed insurrection, while in Britain uncertain political loyalties were further troubled by the American Civil War. Hill's enthusiastic support for the anti-slavery northern states made him most unpopular—not that this concerned him unduly. His natural disposition to put intellect before sentiment had been encouraged by his teacher and friend, James Martineau. It was through Martineau that Hill became acquainted with the minister's sister, Harriet, the bold and distinguished correspondent of the *Daily News*, who shared Hill's views on the American Civil War.

On 16 June 1862, at Little Portland Street Chapel, London, Hill married Jane Dalzell Finlay, daughter of the proprietor of the *Northern Whig*, Sir Francis Dalzell *Finlay. The inconclusive outcome of the 1865 election, followed by Lord Palmerston's death, offered opportunities for the progressive, liberal policies that Hill favoured. A period of political uncertainty always enhanced the political prominence and the supposed influence of the press. Hill's father-in-law encouraged him to join the *Daily News* as an assistant editor. Hill resigned his editorship of the *Northern Whig* in January 1866 and within five years had succeeded as editor of the *Daily News*. To edit the Liberal Party's chief newspaper was no sinecure, for Liberals were divided on both objectives and tactics. Hill never complained about any attempt by politicians to change or modify his editorial judgement. What annoyed him was a competing newspaper's receiving information before the *Daily News*; he expected, and generally received, favoured treatment from Liberal administrations. The relationship was advantageous to both parties.

The commercial success of the *Daily News* after 1870, when its circulation dramatically increased to 150,000, was largely due to the manager, Sir John R. Robinson. But it was Hill's personality that stamped the newspaper with its particular quality. He attracted a notable body of writers to Bouverie Street—P. W. Clayden, Justin McCarthy, John Macdonell, Andrew Lang, and Herbert Paul. Hill wrote constantly, his contributions on politics being notable for their insight. T. P. O'Connor noted Hill's brilliance, but also his cynicism. Before Gladstone chose home rule there was no more devoted Gladstonian than Hill, yet he never hesitated to upbraid the master if he thought his intention too whiggish. Gladstone sometimes complained, as to his brother in 1874, that the *Daily News* had struck him hard blows, but Hill was generally Gladstone's metropolitan mainstay. In September 1876 Gladstone described his great polemic *The Bulgarian Horrors* as 'walking as best I can in [Hill's] footsteps' (Koss, 1.210). The editor never wavered in his recognition of Gladstone's supreme claim to the Liberal leadership, avowing as much, even at the risk of offending potential candidates for that prize, like the elder Harcourt. As Hill expressed Gladstone's dominance: 'The noughts might revolt against the figure one, but cannot go on without it' (T. P. O'Connor, *Memoirs of an Old Parliamentarian*, 1929, 1.51).

Hill's particular contribution over a decade and a half to the fortunes of the Liberal Party was acknowledged by, among others, the radical Charles Dilke, the Liberal foreign secretary Lord Granville, and Edward Hamilton, Gladstone's secretary. But there were other Liberal politicians not so enamoured of Hill, particularly W. E. Forster and Joseph Chamberlain. The editor and Chamberlain had for years sparred in the pages of various reviews and there was no love lost between them. 'Stupid, ineffective … never took a hint' (Brown, 181) was Chamberlain's response to Hill's dismissal as editor of the *Daily News* in January 1886. Henry Labouchere, one of the three most influential of the *Daily News* proprietors, had long sought Hill's dismissal. He told Herbert Gladstone that Hill was 'a bad editor', 'unable to present political matters in a popular manner', and, as a consequence, the party suffered. 'Two-thirds of the Cabinet have complained to me about him' (Labouchere to Gladstone, 13 June 1885, BL, Add. MS 46015). Hill, for his part, had his own complaints. He sought a direct line of communication between his offices and Downing Street. He desired sight of certain parliamentary papers in advance. He complained that through faults of the prime minister's secretariat the directives he received were sporadic and unclear. Hill's fall was the consequence of discord within the Liberal Party hierarchy, and Labouchere's conviction that more life was needed in the leading articles, which had become too coldly critical. Hence his choice of H. W. Lucy to replace Hill, an experiment that lasted only six months and ended in failure. Hill

would accept neither financial compensation for his dismissal nor public acknowledgement by his friends for his services to the party. Within months he had become the regular political leader writer for the *World*, where his fulminations against home rule added bite to an otherwise lightweight social weekly. He also wrote regularly for the more heavyweight monthly *Nineteenth Century*.

Hill's wife died in 1904. At the time of their marriage she had been a regular contributor to the literary section of the *Northern Whig* and had continued, after their marriage, to write literary articles and reviews, chiefly for the *Saturday Review*. Hill died six years later, suddenly, at his Westminster home, 3 Morpeth Terrace, Victoria Street, on 28 June 1910.

When Hill was dismissed as editor of the *Daily News*, the *Pall Mall Gazette* suggested that for all his undoubted brilliance as a critic, he was never a journalist. Hill never chose to charm, or went out of his way to win affection. An acerbic pen and trenchant style served an uncompromising intellect that was alien to sentiment.

A. J. A. Morris

Sources *Recollections of Sir J. R. Robinson* (1904) · S. E. Koss, *The rise and fall of the political press in Britain*, 1 (1981) · L. Brown, *Victorian news and newspapers* (1985) · *DNB* · Gladstone, *Diaries* · d. cert.
Archives BL, corresp. with Sir Charles Dilke, Add. MS 43898 · BL, corresp. with W. E. Gladstone, Add. MS 44426–44787, *passim* · BL, corresp. with Sir Edward Walter Hamilton, Add. MS 48619 · Bodl. Oxf., corresp. with Sir William Harcourt · NRA, priv. coll., corresp. with Lord Fitzmaurice · PRO, corresp. with Lord Granville, PRO 30/29/426 · St Deiniol's Library, Hawarden, letters to W. E. Gladstone
Likenesses engraving, NPG; repro. in *Harper's Magazine*, 2 (1881), 668 [*see illus.*]
Wealth at death £18,902 4s. 2d.: resworn probate, 22 July 1910, *CGPLA Eng. & Wales*

Hill, Frederic (1803–1896), civil servant, was born on 29 June 1803 at Hill Top School, Gough Street, Birmingham, the sixth of the eight children of Thomas Wright *Hill (1763–1851), schoolmaster, and his wife, Sarah Lea (1765–1842). Two of his five brothers achieved professional eminence, Rowland *Hill as a postal reformer and Matthew Davenport *Hill as a criminologist and penal reformer; another brother was Edwin *Hill. Frederic was educated at his family's school which, under the name Hazelwood (from 1819), gained an international reputation for its progressive regime. At the age of thirteen he became an assistant teacher at the school. In the early 1830s he was an active Reform Bill campaigner, becoming a member, later a council member, of the Birmingham Political Union. With the passing of the Reform Act he turned his attention to educational questions and published *National Education: its Present State and Prospects* (1836). Between 1832 and 1856 he was investment manager of the Hill family fund, which was created to provide financial support to any of the siblings who encountered straitened circumstances.

When, in 1833, Hazelwood was sold, Hill's teaching career came to an end. He had long cherished the idea of entering the civil service, and his brother Matthew advised him, as a preliminary, to study the law. On 25 November 1834 Hill was admitted a student of Lincoln's

Inn. He was called to the bar on 29 January 1840, but never practised as a barrister. In 1834 he was appointed parliamentary secretary to Matthew's friend Sergeant Wilde (later Lord Truro). In the following year he obtained one of the newly created prison inspectorships. The home secretary, Lord John Russell, appointed him to the Scottish district, which also comprised Northumberland and Durham, on the grounds that 'there is most work to be done there and I know you will do it' (Hill, 116). Hill's initial salary of £600 per annum was raised to £700 in 1841. Hill was shocked by the state of the Scottish prisons: he found most of them insanitary, insecure, cold, and damp. Inadequately supervised, the prisoners were indolent, drunken, overfed, foul-mouthed gamblers. In his first report (1836) Hill proposed numerous reforms.

Hill helped prepare the Act to Improve Prisons and Prison Discipline in Scotland (2 & 3 Vict. c. 42) which created a board of directors of Scottish prisons, on which Hill served from September 1839. He was then able to influence policy and practice in the Scottish prison system. He was especially concerned to achieve the abolition of the treadmill and handcrank and the introduction of useful labour for which prisoners would be paid at market rates for the voluntary performance of work in excess of ten hours a day. He also presided over the abolition of flogging and the introduction of the 'separate system' of prison discipline. In April 1840 Hill married Martha Cowper (*b.* 1802/3), a sister of the inventor Edward Shickle *Cowper. They had three daughters.

In 1847, partly on the grounds that his work in Scotland was finished, but also because he wished to live nearer to his brothers and aged father, Hill obtained a transfer to the inspectorship of an English prison district (initially northern England and north Wales). He found the English prisons in his charge to be largely unreformed. His attempts to change them were hampered by county justices, and the resulting frustration was a factor in his resignation of the inspectorship in 1851. Although Hill's professional association with prisons ceased at this point, he remained actively interested in questions of crime and punishment, especially through his membership of such bodies as the Law Amendment Society, the Reformatory and Refuge Union, and the National Association for the Promotion of Social Science. In 1853 he published *Crime: its Amount, Causes and Remedies*, in which he set out his criminological and penological ideas. Among these were opposition to the death penalty (he thought murderers should be permanently imprisoned), support for indeterminate sentences from which prisoners could obtain their release only by giving evidence of reformation, and the imposition of charges on parents whose children were incarcerated.

In June 1851 Hill was appointed assistant secretary to the postmaster-general and, therefore, deputy to his brother Rowland. Although this position was probably inferior to that of prison inspector, Hill remained in it until its abolition in 1875. His salary on retirement was £1400 per annum, at which point he was granted a civil service pension of £1000 per annum. Hill's achievements at the Post Office included several reforms of postal practice along with the introduction of new systems of ventilation and fire precautions. It was at his suggestion, in 1854, that the postmaster-general began to submit an annual report to parliament. Hill compiled the first fourteen of these himself. Hill's last years at the Post Office were marked by policy disagreements with heads of departments. After his retirement articles in the Post Office's magazine described him as 'somewhat reserved and silent' and intensely conservative in his attitude towards personnel aspects of civil service reform (*St Martin's-le-Grand*, vols. 4 and 7).

In addition to the books already mentioned Hill wrote newspaper articles and pamphlets on a variety of subjects including punishment, local government, and civil defence. Between 1836 and 1847 he compiled annual reports as an inspector of prisons. Between 1847 and the mid-1860s he gave evidence to official inquiries on crime, punishment, and railways. He continued to lecture and write on public issues until late in life. In retirement he was also active in charitable work, being a co-founder of the Hampstead branch of the Charity Organization Society and a member of Hampstead's board of guardians. His autobiography, *Frederic Hill: an Autobiography of Fifty Years in Times of Reform* (1893), was completed and edited by his daughter Constance. Hill died on 17 November 1896 at his home, Inverleith House, 27 Thurlow Road, Hampstead. His body was cremated.   P. W. J. BARTRIP

Sources F. Hill, *Frederic Hill: an autobiography of fifty years in times of reform*, ed. C. Hill (1893) · G. B. Hill and R. Hill, *The life of Sir Rowland Hill, and, The history of penny postage*, 2 vols. (1880) · Boase, *Mod. Eng. biog.* · J. F. Waller, ed., *The imperial dictionary of universal biography*, 3 vols. (1857–63) · C. Knight, ed., *The English cyclopaedia: biography*, 6 vols. (1856–8) [suppl. (1872)] · 'The late Mr. Frederic Hill', *St Martin's-le-Grand* [Post Office magazine], 7 (1897), 95–7 · K. T. L., 'The modern spirit in the civil service', *St Martin's-le-Grand* [Post Office magazine], 4 (1894), 129ff. · Birmingham Daily Gazette (21 Nov 1896), 4 · W. P. Baildon, ed., *The records of the Honorable Society of Lincoln's Inn: the black books*, 4 (1902) · Post Office Establishment Book, 1869, Post Office Archives · Hampstead and Highgate Express (21 Nov 1896), 7 · census returns

Archives Post Office Archives and Record Centre, Mount Pleasant House, London | UCL, corresp. with E. Chadwick

Likenesses E. Hill, chalk, 1874, repro. in 'The late Mr. Frederic Hill', 96 · E. Hill, portrait, repro. in Hill, ed., *Frederic Hill* · portrait, repro. in K. T. L., 'The modern spirit in the civil service', 174

Wealth at death £11,330 19s. 1d.: probate, 30 Dec 1896, CGPLA Eng. & Wales

Hill, George (*c*.1716–1808), lawyer and eccentric, was born at Waddington, Lincolnshire, the eldest son of Nathaniel Hill MA (*d*. 1732), rector of Waddington and lord of the manor of Rothwell, Northamptonshire. As well as his father, his brother and two uncles were clergymen. Hill's father died in 1732, and George broke with family tradition by pursuing a career in the law.

Hill matriculated at Clare College, Cambridge, in 1733 and was admitted to the Middle Temple in 1734 and called to the bar in 1741. His practice seems to have been mainly 'chamber practice' of conveyancing and advice. On 6 November 1772, after thirty years of obscurity, Hill was created serjeant and king's serjeant. The explanation is possibly that Henry Bathurst, as the first tory chancellor since 1714, had difficulty in finding tory lawyers sufficiently senior for preferment. Hill held a reactionary view of recent legal development: he is quoted as saying that 'the greatest service that could be rendered the country would be to repeal all the statutes, and burn all the reports which were of later date than the Revolution' (Romilly, 72). On creation as serjeant he immediately gained an extensive practice in common pleas, as can be seen from the law reports of the period. In king's bench, however, he repeatedly clashed with the chief justice, Lord Mansfield.

Mansfield used Hill's deafness and rather ponderous advocacy to make him the butt of jokes in court, and satirized his fondness for extensive reliance on old cases in preference to general principles, so that Hill acquired the nickname of Serjeant Labyrinth. However, after Mansfield's death, as the pendulum of legal patronage and culture swung towards the tories, Hill was transmuted from an 'old fool'—his own account, to the young Eldon, of most young lawyers' view of him (Twiss, 93)—to a respected, if eccentric, elder statesman of the bar. Nineteenth-century legal memoirs preserve numerous anecdotes about Hill's eccentricity—reflecting both views; an unfriendly story tells of his accidentally producing a candlestick in court when he meant to produce a law report; a friendlier one of his ordering his servants to kill a fox which had been chased into his garden, and responding to the outraged hunt by producing a medieval case report which justified his action.

Hill married, some time before 1761, Anna Barbara, daughter and heir of Thomas Medlycote of Cottingham, Northamptonshire, and they had two daughters. One anecdote tells of his becoming so absorbed in business that he had to be called to church to attend his wedding. Any expectations which Hill might have had of the marriage were disappointed on Thomas Medlycote's death, when he was found to have left all his property on trusts which gave his daughter only a separate property for life, and that provided that she returned to using her maiden name. On his wife's death (some time between 1793 and 1799) Hill said to Eldon (then attorney-general), 'I have lost poor dear Mrs Hill', and then, after a pause, 'I don't know, though, that the loss *was* so great; for she had all her property, Mr. Attorney, to her separate use' (Twiss, 301). Hill died at his house in Bedford Square, London, on 21 February 1808, and was buried in the family vault at Rothwell, where there is an epitaph upon him by Bennett, bishop of Cloyne. An important collection of legal manuscripts was purchased from his executors by the Society of Lincoln's Inn, and is in the library there.

Mansfield's attempt to make Hill a laughing stock was transmitted by Campbell's *Lives of the Chief Justices* and has been followed by some modern authors. Hill, however, had the last laugh: for most of the nineteenth and twentieth centuries orthodox views of what made a 'sound lawyer' were closer to Hill's than to Mansfield's.

M. MACNAIR

Sources A. Polson, *Law and lawyers, or, Sketches and illustrations of legal history and biography*, 2 vols. (1840), vol. 1, pp. 76–83 • S. Romilly, *Memoirs of the life of Sir Samuel Romilly*, 1 (1840), 72 • *The public and private life of Lord Chancellor Eldon, with selections from his correspondence*, ed. H. Twiss, 1 (1844), 93, 301 • Venn, *Alum. Cant.*, 1/1 • *JHC*, 29 (1761–4), 408, 410, 441 • L.-M. Hawkins, *Memoirs, anecdotes, facts and opinions*, 2 vols. (1824), vol. 1, pp. 255–6 • John, Lord Campbell, *The lives of the chief justices of England*, 2 (1849); repr. (Freeport, NY, 1971), 571 • Baker, *Serjeants* • G. Wilson, *Reports of cases argued and adjudged in the king's courts at Westminster*, 3rd edn, 3 (1799), 391–563 [93 ER 1117] • W. Blackstone, *Reports of cases determined in … Westminster-Hall, from 1746 to 1779*, 2nd edn, 2 (1828), 859–1317 [96 ER 507–770]

Archives Lincoln's Inn, London | Inner Temple, London, Wilmott MSS

Likenesses R. Dighton, group portrait (*The coifing of serjeants Kerby and Rooke, 1781*), AM Oxf.; repro. in Baker, *Serjeants*, pl. 14 • caricature (*Singular habiliment of Geo: Hill Esq., the king's antient serjeant*), NPG; repro. in J. Oldham, *The Mansfield manuscripts and the growth of English law in the eighteenth century* (1992), p. 81 • watercolour drawing, BM

Hill, George (1750–1819), theologian and college head, was born in St Andrews on 22 May 1750, the eldest of the eight children of the Revd John Hill (*d.* 1765) and his second wife, Jean McCormick (*d.* 1796), daughter of his colleague John McCormick and a great-niece of William Carstares, the former principal of Edinburgh University. He was educated at the grammar school and university of St Andrews, graduating MA in 1765. During his second session of divinity studies at St Mary's College, Hill's scholastic ability attracted the patronage of the eighth earl of Kinnoul, then university chancellor and a key supporter of the moderate party in the Church of Scotland. Kinnoul encouraged Hill's uncle Joseph McCormick, the principal of the United College, to introduce Hill to the historian William Robertson, who subsequently recommended him as tutor to the eldest son of Pryse Campbell MP, one of the lords of the Treasury. In this capacity he travelled to London in 1767 and to Edinburgh in 1768, where he concluded his studies in divinity. During that time Hill became Robertson's protégé, and was introduced to various ecclesiastical and literary figures, including David Hume. Hill became a member of the Edinburgh Speculative Society and a frequent visitor in the home of Henry Dundas.

In 1772 Kinnoul made it possible for Hill to purchase the Greek professorship at St Andrews, a post which he held for the next sixteen years. Licensed to preach in 1775, he served as assistant at St Leonard's until he was appointed minister of the second charge of St Andrews by the town council in May 1780. On 7 June 1782 he married Harriet Scott (*d.* 1825); they had twelve children, including Alexander *Hill (1785–1867), later divinity professor at Glasgow.

Highly esteemed as a preacher and as a lecturer, Hill zealously discharged his pastoral and academic duties for the balance of his career. In 1787 he was made DD by the University of St Andrews and was appointed dean of the Order of the Thistle. He became professor of divinity at St Mary's College in 1788 and principal in 1791. Hill was elected moderator of the general assembly in 1789, and was appointed one of the king's chaplains for Scotland in 1791 and a dean of the Chapel Royal in 1799. He became minister of the first charge of St Andrews in 1808.

Hill's initial rise to national prominence was based on

his management of Scottish ecclesiastical affairs on behalf of the Dundas interest. Upon Robertson's unexpected retirement from church politics in 1780 Hill quickly assumed the leadership of the moderate party in the general assembly, a role which he earned through his ability as a speaker, his business capacity, understanding of church law, and his conciliatory spirit. These powers of oratory and persuasion, coupled with the support of Dundas, enabled the moderate party to dominate the assembly for another generation. In spite of his spirited defence of patronage, Hill was also widely respected by evangelical leaders, and disputes over the practice subsided until after his death.

While other moderate clergymen turned their abilities to 'improvements' in literature and science Hill devoted himself to the advancement of theology and theological education. *Lectures in Divinity* (1821), which he prepared for publication prior to his death, became the standard textbook in Presbyterian seminaries in Scotland and America until after the mid-nineteenth century. In addition Hill also published *The Advantages of Searching the Scriptures* (1787), *Theological Institutes* (1803), *Lectures upon Portions of the Old Testament* (1812), and a number of sermons.

Hill's theology continued in the moderate common sense tradition by emphasizing the need for a rigorous defence of traditional Christianity in the face of Enlightenment scepticism, represented by Socinianism and deism. At the same time the *Lectures* presented a concise, orderly exposition of Calvinism and endeavoured to limit the moderate tendency to rely upon natural theology by stressing the reliability and primacy of biblical revelation. In grappling with the claims of traditional orthodoxy and the priorities of the Enlightenment, Hill formulated a theology which increased the common ground between the moderate and evangelical factions and strengthened the church as a whole. This rapprochement was further enhanced by Hill's commitment to excellence in theological training and his encouragement of preaching that emphasized both doctrine and practical morality.

While in many respects Hill was responsible for the dominance of the moderates during his lifetime, other aspects of his legacy furthered the demise of his party. His rigid social conservatism, his ecclesiology, which in many ways subordinated the church to the state, and his uniting of the fortunes of his party with the Dundas interest allowed the moderates to dominate the Church of Scotland during the reactionary Napoleonic era, but did little to prepare them for the evolution in social thinking which would follow. Theologically, his resistance to the notion that only naturalistic explanations of the origins and contents of the Bible were acceptable may also help to explain why such liberal thought found little foothold in Scotland until well after 1850. It was the popularity of his *Lectures* which may in part have helped to stem criticism during the nineteenth century.

Hill died from a series of strokes on 19 December 1819 and was buried in the cemetery at St Andrews Cathedral.

DONALD P. McCALLUM

Sources D. McCallum, 'George Hill, D. D.: moderate or Erastian evangelical?', MA diss., University of Western Ontario, 1989 · G. Cook, *Life of the late George Hill* (1820) · E. Rodger, *A book of remembrance* (1913) · *Fasti Scot.*, new edn · R. Sher and A. Murdoch, 'Patronage and party in the Church of Scotland, 1750–1800', *Church politics and society: Scotland, 1408–1929*, ed. N. MacDougal (1983), 1707–1832 · R. M. Sunter, *Patronage and politics in Scotland, 1707–1832* (1986) · I. D. L. Clark, 'From protest to reaction: the moderate regime in the Church of Scotland, 1752–1805', *Scotland in the age of improvement*, ed. N. T. Phillipson and R. Mitchison (1970), 200–24 · Chambers, *Scots.* (1835) · IGI

Archives U. St Andr., letters | NL Scot., corresp. with John Lee · U. Edin. L., special collections division, letters to Alexander Carlyle · U. St Andr. L., letters to first Lord Melville and second Lord Melville

Likenesses T. Hodgetts, mezzotint (after J. Syme), BM · oils, U. St Andr.

Hill, George Alexander (1892–1968), intelligence officer, was born in Estonia, the son of a timber merchant whose business interests extended from Siberia to Persia. He was educated by French and German governesses and soon developed exceptional linguistic skills. He spoke six languages and his Russian was fluent. Hill was on a fishing trip to British Columbia when war broke out in 1914. He immediately joined a Canadian infantry regiment and was posted to Ypres in 1915. He showed exceptional daring and bravery and was seriously wounded. He was then sent to the War Office where he began his career as an intelligence officer.

Hill's first assignment was in Greece, where he flew agents behind enemy lines. In 1917 he was sent to Petrograd as a member of the Royal Flying Corps mission and arrived amid the confusion of the Bolshevik Revolution. According to Hill's own richly embroidered account of his mission he undertook the hazardous task of taking the Romanian crown jewels from the Kremlin to Iasi, helped Leon Trotsky organize a military intelligence service and the Red Air Force, ran guns to Ukrainian nationalists, and recruited a number of German agents for counter-intelligence work. When the British landed in Murmansk he was obliged to flee to Finland with the Cheka close on his heels.

Hill returned briefly to Russia and then worked for the Secret Intelligence Service (SIS) in the Middle East for the next three years, but the service was short of funds and Hill was reduced to living with his wife in a caravan in Sussex. His only recompense was appointment as an MBE and DSO, and the satisfaction of being mentioned in dispatches on three occasions. There followed a series of precarious jobs: a stint with the Royal Dutch–Shell Oil Company, manager of the Globe Theatre on Shaftesbury Avenue in London, and deputy general manager to the impresario C. B. Cochran. During this time he wrote two volumes of memoirs—*Go Spy the Land* (1933) and *The Dreaded Hour* (1936) and two unpublished plays.

When war broke out Hill was recalled to the SIS with the rank of major and worked as an instructor in section D (destruction) at Brickendonbury Hall near Hertford. His pupils included Kim Philby, who was impressed by 'Jolly George' Hill's knowledge of explosives and wryly remarked that he had actually put sand in axle boxes

(Philby, 8). In 1940 the school was taken over by the Special Operations Executive (SOE) and restructured. Hill remained on the staff until 1941 when he was selected to head an SOE mission to Moscow code-named SAM. Colonel Hill arrived in the Soviet capital in September in time for the signing of two agreements between SOE and NKVD (the Soviet security organization). The first was designed to co-ordinate sabotage and propaganda in occupied Europe and to desist from subversive activities in each other's spheres of influence. It was also agreed that they would help one another infiltrate agents into occupied Europe. The second agreement dealt with targets and priorities.

Little came of these agreements, as in the winter of 1941 all foreign missions were evacuated to Kuibyshev. Hill did much to enliven this dreary provincial town by mixing some ingenious vodka cocktails that were greatly appreciated. During this time he managed to persuade the British boffins to pass on some ingenious devices to the Soviet partisans and organized the infiltration of some Soviet agents into occupied Europe in operations code-named Pickaxe. With characteristic chutzpah Hill claims also to have written a handbook on guerrilla warfare for Soviet partisans.

There were further 'Pickaxes' in 1942 but they began to cause great concern in the Foreign Office, who were alarmed about Britain's allies finding out that they were dropping Soviet agents into their countries. This position was strongly seconded by C. SOE was appalled at the quality of some of the agents they were asked to transport and refused a number of them as totally unsuited to the task. There were only four successful drops in 1942 and Whitehall was getting very impatient with SAM. Anthony Eden, the British foreign secretary, complained that Hill did 'not know his onions' and was wasting the taxpayers' money. Hill countered that the problems resulted from 'sand in axle box tactics' in London and he was enthusiastically supported by the ambassador, Sir Archibald Clark Kerr.

In 1943 there were only six successful 'Pickaxe' missions and frustrations on both sides were mounting. In April 1944 Hill's opposite number, Colonel Chichayev, complained that SOE had done practically nothing and anyway the Soviets no longer had any need for them. SOE was frustrated by NKVD's refusal to co-operate in Soviet-occupied Europe, particularly with the Polish underground army. Hill can hardly be blamed for the failure of his mission. It was unrealistic to imagine that SOE and NKVD could ever co-operate successfully and this inevitably led to mutual accusations and recriminations.

Clark Kerr arrived in London in December 1944 and announced that there was little for Hill to do in Moscow. He was now a brigadier and it was felt that he could be replaced by a more junior officer. Hill returned to London in the summer of 1945. After the war he became a director of the British-owned German mineral water company Apollinarius. It was a strange finale for a man who was never known to have refused a drink. He died in 1968 shortly after his second marriage. MARTIN KITCHEN

Sources G. Hill, Go spy the land (1933) • G. Hill, The dreaded hour (1936) • P. Knightley, The second oldest profession (1986) • K. Philby, My silent war (1968) • P. Knightley, Philby (1988) • M. Kitchen, 'SOE's man in Moscow', Intelligence and National Security, 12/3 (1997), 95–109 • B. F. Smith, Sharing secrets with Stalin: how the allies traded intelligence, 1941–1945 (1996)
Archives Stanford University, California, MS memoirs

Hill, George Birkbeck Norman (1835–1903), writer and editor of Boswell's *Life of Johnson*, was born on 7 June 1835 at Bruce Castle, Lordship Lane, Tottenham, Middlesex, the second son of Arthur Hill (*b.* 1798), schoolmaster, and Ellen Tilt, *née* Maurice (1807–1839). Hill's mother, who died when he was four years old, was of Welsh and Huguenot descent, while his father's family were reform-minded nonconformists from the midlands. Hill was baptized with the name of his godfather, the philanthropist George *Birkbeck (1776–1841).

Hill was educated at the family school at Bruce Castle. Founded by Hill's grandfather Thomas Wright *Hill (1763–1851), this progressive school for boys was run by Hill's father and uncles on utilitarian principles. Hill later expressed regret over 'the most unscholarly education which I received' (*Letters*, 247). On 1 March 1855 he entered Pembroke College, Oxford, and there came under more literary influences. William Fulford, editor of the short-lived *Oxford and Cambridge Magazine*, introduced him to the circle of Sir Edward Burne-Jones, William Morris, Dante Gabriel Rossetti, and Charles Faulkner. He was also an original member of the Old Mortality Club, of which Algernon Swinburne, Professor Albert Venn Dicey, Professor John Nichol, and James Bryce were members. An attack of typhoid fever obliged him to give up hope of high honours and after a period of convalescence he graduated in 1858 with an 'honorary' fourth-class degree in *literae humaniores*. He proceeded BCL in 1866 and DCL in 1871.

About the time of his entrance to Oxford, Hill became engaged to Annie Scott (1837/8–1902), the intelligent seventeen-year-old daughter of Edward Scott of Wigan, Lancashire, and sister of a schoolfriend. Eager to marry on leaving university, he agreed to enter the family vocation as schoolmaster. In 1858 he became an assistant in the school at Bruce Castle and married Annie Scott on 29 December of that year. While at Bruce Castle they had five sons, including the judge Sir (Edward) Maurice *Hill (1862–1934) and the physiologist Sir Leonard Erskine *Hill (1866–1952), and two daughters, Annie Margaret who married Sir William *Ashley (1860–1927) and Lucy who married Charles George *Crump (1862–1935). In 1868 Hill succeeded to the headship on his father's retirement. He and his wife attempted reforms in the curriculum and raised the standard of scholarship, but with the contemporary development of the public schools Bruce Castle failed to prosper. Under the strain of exhaustion and overwork, Hill suffered a debilitating asthma-related illness late in 1875, which forced him to give up the school entirely the following year. Despite extended periods of convalescence in Switzerland and the Riviera, he remained a semi-invalid for the duration of his life. With the active part of his career over, he turned to scholarship to occupy his lively mind and support his family.

Hill began his writing career in 1869 as a frequent contributor to the *Saturday Review*, where he published pungent criticisms of contemporary poetry and novels. He also wrote for *The World* and *Pall Mall Gazette*. Having moved to Burghfield near Reading in 1877 to follow a more retired course of life, he continued his reviewing work, but soon developed an interest in eighteenth-century literary history, particularly the life and work of Samuel Johnson. His first publication in 1878 was *Dr. Johnson, his Friends and his Critics*, in which he evaluated the criticisms of Johnson by Thomas Macaulay, Thomas Carlyle, and others, and depicted eighteenth-century Oxford. The following year he edited a volume of James Boswell's correspondence and his *Tour to Corsica*. By this time he had formed a plan to edit Boswell's *Life of Johnson* (first published in 1791) and began accumulating information and materials for this purpose. Hill interrupted his Johnsonian studies to write a biography of his uncle Sir Rowland *Hill (1795–1879), the postal reformer (2 vols., 1880). In 1881 he published *Colonel Gordon in Central Africa, 1874–79* from original documents belonging to Gordon's sister. The death of his beloved son Walter in 1882 further delayed the progress of his work on Johnson.

In 1881 the Clarendon Press, through Benjamin Jowett's influence, accepted Hill's proposal for a new edition of Boswell's *Life*. After nearly twelve years' intermittent work, much of it done during periods of convalescence on the Riviera and Lac Leman in Switzerland, Hill's edition was published in 1887 in six volumes (with a dedication to Jowett as 'Johnsonianissimus'). Percy Fitzgerald, a rival editor of Boswell, characterized the work as 'a gigantic system of note-taking' (Fitzgerald, 6), but it was ably defended by Leslie Stephen. The edition was lauded as a masterpiece of spacious editing, and with the additions of L. F. Powell in 1934 it remains the standard scholarly edition of Boswell's book. The index, comprising nearly the entire sixth volume, is an unparalleled example of industry and completeness. Hill pursued his exegesis of Johnson's work in Johnson's *Letters* (1892, 2 vols.), *Johnsonian Miscellanies* (1897, 2 vols.), and Johnson's *Lives of the English Poets* (1905, 3 vols.), published posthumously.

While living in Berkshire, Hill, who was a committed Liberal, took an active role in local politics in Burghfield, becoming a poor-law guardian of the Bradfield Union and campaigning during the general elections of 1885 and 1886. In autumn 1887 Hill returned with his wife to live in Oxford at 3 Park Town. His literary projects prospered in this environment, and he enjoyed the social amenities of university life. The age of Johnson remained the focus of his editorial attention; he published editions of the *Letters of David Hume to William Strahan* (1888), Oliver Goldsmith's *The Traveller* (1888), a selection of Lord Chesterfield's writings (1891), *Unpublished Letters of Dean Swift* (1899), and Edward Gibbon's *Memoirs* (1900). In 1889 he retraced Boswell's and Johnson's tour of Scotland, which he described in his *Footsteps of Samuel Johnson, Scotland* (1890), illustrated by Lancelot Speed. In recognition of his work on Johnson he was elected a member of the Johnson Club of London in 1888 and was twice chosen as 'prior' of the society in

1891–2. He was especially gratified when Pembroke, his old college and Johnson's, made him an honorary fellow in November 1892.

Hill's failing health required him to quit his Oxford house in 1892, and he divided his time henceforth between his favourite winter residences, Clarens in Switzerland and Alassio in Italy, his daughter's house, 1 Holly Hill, The Wilderness, Hampstead, and a cottage at Aspley Guise, Bedfordshire. Visits in 1893 and 1896 to his daughter Annie, who was living in Cambridge, Massachusetts, resulted in Hill's publication of *Harvard College, by an Oxonian* (1894), a book warmly received in New England for its complimentary tone of comparison. Williams College in Massachusetts conferred a doctorate on him on 10 October 1893. An avid collector of autographs, Hill published a miscellaneous volume, *Talks about Autographs*, in 1896. In 1897 his *Letters of Dante Gabriel Rossetti to William Allingham* renewed memories of the Old Mortality Club at Oxford.

Hill died at Hampstead on 24 February 1903 and was buried at Aspley Guise beside his wife, who predeceased him by barely four months. He bequeathed his Johnsonian library to his old college, where his portrait is still exhibited. While the scholarly community esteemed Hill's work as an editor, his friends recalled the gentle humour and ready welcome of the prematurely balding asthmatic in the brown velvet skull-cap, seated typically in his study at the desk William Morris made for him. Hill left his final editorial project, Johnson's *Lives of the Poets*, unfinished at his death, and the work was completed by his nephew Harold Spencer Scott. The lively discursiveness and idiosyncrasy of Hill's notes belong to a previous generation of editorial practitioners, but the sound scholarship and wide-ranging erudition of his commentary contribute to the enduring usefulness of much of his work.

CATHERINE DILLE

Sources DNB · *Letters of George Birkbeck Hill*, ed. L. Crump (1906) · H. S. Scott, 'Brief memoir of Dr. Birkbeck Hill', in S. Johnson, *Lives of the English poets*, ed. G. B. Hill, [new edn], 1 (1905), ix–xxii · Boswell, *Life* · P. Fitzgerald, *A critical examination of Dr. G. Birkbeck Hill's 'Johnsonian' editions* (1898) · Foster, *Alum. Oxon.*, 1715–1886, 2.660 · G. B. Hill, *Harvard College, by an Oxonian* (1894) · G. B. Hill, *Writers and readers* (1892) · *The Times* (28 Feb 1903) · *The Times* (9 Nov 1906) · *CGPLA Eng. & Wales* (1903) · m. cert. · d. cert. · IGI

Archives Bodl. Oxf., letters · Pembroke College, Oxford, corresp. and papers, incl. autograph collection | Birkbeck College, London, letters to H. W. Gordon · BL, letters to W. Gladstone, Add. MS 44467 · BL, letters to H. W. Gordon, Add. MSS 52398, 52400 · Pembroke College, Oxford, Johnsonian Library and corresp.

Likenesses E. G. Hill, charcoal?, 1876, repro. in Crump, ed., *Letters* · W. R. Symonds, crayon, 1896, Pembroke College, Oxford; repro. in G. B. Hill, *Talks about autographs* (1896)

Wealth at death £7776 14s. 6d.: probate, 29 May 1903, *CGPLA Eng. & Wales*

Hill, Sir George Francis (1867–1948), numismatist, was born on 22 December 1867, at Berhampore, Bengal, the youngest of five children, all of notable ability, of the Revd Samuel John Hill and his wife, Leonora Josephine Müller. His father was a missionary of rigid and exemplary character who felt it his duty to live continuously in, and for, India; and it fell to his mother, although of mixed Danish and Portuguese stock rooted in India, to take the children to Britain for their education. Family means were straitened and the divided home left a deep mark on their youngest child. Hill's brother Micaiah John Muller *Hill became a distinguished mathematician and FRS.

After an unhappy period at the School for the Sons of Missionaries (later Eltham College), Hill passed into University College School, London, thence with a scholarship to University College, London, where his abilities were quickly recognized, and so in 1888 on to Oxford University, as an exhibitioner of Merton College. After an easy double first in classics (1889, 1891), it was his intention to stay on as a teacher in the university. He failed, however, to obtain a fellowship, and when in 1893 a vacancy occurred in the department of coins and medals in the British Museum he applied for the post and was selected. Already in his last year at Oxford he had been increasingly attracted by Greek art and archaeology and had been studying Greek coins under Percy Gardner.

Hill entered the museum at a moment of great activity in Greek numismatics when, largely through the work of the keeper, Barclay V. Head, scholars had begun to realize how great a contribution this science could make to the study of the ancient world. He was at once set to work on the Greek catalogue, to which he contributed successive and exemplary volumes on Lycia, Cyprus, Cilicia, Phoenicia, Palestine, and Arabia.

Meanwhile Hill's leisure produced several widely used manuals of more general scope: on Greek and Roman coins (including the revision in part of Head's *Historia numorum*), on Greek historical inscriptions, and on sources for Greek history between the Persian and Peloponnesian wars. Parallel with his classical interests, and at least equal to them in his eyes, ran his interest in the history and culture of medieval and Renaissance Italy, fostered by frequent visits to Rome and elsewhere. His work in this field was no less impressive, including, besides his careful studies of the medals and drawings of Pisanello, the monumental *Corpus of Italian Medals before Cellini* (2 vols., 1930), and the unique collections of material for Italian heraldry and iconography which he bequeathed to the British Museum and the Warburg Institute. Characteristically, his last years were devoted to producing the four volumes of what became the standard *History of Cyprus* (1940–52) from the earliest times to the present day.

In 1897 Hill married Mary (d. 1924), daughter of John Dennis Paul FGS JP, of Leicester; there were no children. In 1912 he became keeper of his department, and in 1931 director and principal librarian of the British Museum (the first archaeologist to hold an office hitherto reserved for librarians). He was made KCB in 1933, having been appointed CB in 1929. Outstanding events of his directorship were the launching of a successful national campaign to acquire the Codex Sinaiticus, and the purchase, in conjunction with the Victoria and Albert Museum, of the magnificent Eumorfopoulos collection of oriental antiquities. He retired in 1936.

Hill's departmental experience had given him a deep interest in the subject of treasure trove (characteristically, while director he found time to write the standard work on the subject) and he was able to effect a revolutionary change in its administration which now goes far to prevent concealment and clandestine disposal of finds. Indeed, in addition to his scholarship, Hill had a strongly practical side. He was secretary of the archaeological joint committee from its inception, and was thus instrumental in drafting antiquities laws for Iraq, Palestine, and Cyprus. There can be few journals touching his special interests of which he was not, at some time, editor; he was a founder of the Vasari Society, an active fellow of the British Academy, to which he was elected in 1917, and of the Society of Antiquaries, of which he was vice-president, as he was also of the Royal Numismatic, the Hellenic, and the Roman societies. He was a fellow of University College, London, and an honorary fellow of Merton College; he also received a number of honorary degrees, including the DCL of Oxford and LittD of Cambridge. He died in St Thomas's Hospital, London, on 18 October 1948.

E. S. G. ROBINSON, rev.

Sources E. S. G. Robinson, 'George Francis Hill, 1867–1948', *PBA*, 36 (1950), 241–50 • *WWW* • *The Times* (20 Oct 1948) • *A tribute to Sir George Hill on his eightieth birthday* (1948) • *CGPLA Eng. & Wales* (1949) **Archives** BL, corresp. relating to acquisition of Codex Sinaiticus by BM; heraldic collections, Add. MSS 68923–68932 *passim*; Add. MSS 46805–46821 • Bodl. Oxf., corresp. as councillor, Society for the Protection of Science & Learning | BL, corresp. with Macmillans, Add. MS 55133 • Bodl. Oxf., corresp. with J. L. Myres • Bodl. Oxf., corresp. with Sir Aurel Stein • Harvard U., Center for Italian Renaissance Studies, letters to Bernard Berenson **Likenesses** W. Stoneman, photograph, 1925, NPG • A. Lowenthal, bronze medallion, 1935?, BM • J. Gunn, oils, 1937, BM • F. C. Dodgson, drawing, BM • H. G. Riviere, oils, Merton Oxf. **Wealth at death** £60,132 11s. 2d.: probate, 28 Jan 1949, *CGPLA Eng. & Wales*

Hill, (Norman) Graham (1929–1975), racing motorist, was born at Hampstead, London, on 15 February 1929, one of the two sons of Norman Herbert Devereux Hill, stockbroker, of Belsize Park, and his wife, Constance Mary Philp. He was educated at a technical college in Hendon, where he and the property millionaire Harry Hyams were picked out as the two boys least likely to succeed. Undeterred, Hill left at sixteen for a five-year apprenticeship with Smiths, the instrument makers. In the early 1950s rowing was his main sporting interest and he would later carry the London Rowing Club's dark blue and white colours round the world on his racing helmet. He served in the Royal Navy in 1950–52.

Hill was launched on his unique motor racing career by pure chance. In 1953, with no idea what he was going to do with his life, his eye was caught by a magazine offer of laps in a racing car at the Brands Hatch circuit for 5s. a time. The most important pound he ever spent enabled him to have four laps and a chance meeting with Colin Chapman, who was starting the Lotus Car Company at Hornsey. Hill became a mechanic there for £1 a day. In 1957 Hill was taken on as a driver and the following year Lotus and Hill entered their first formula 1 grand prix at Monaco. Disappointed with two unsuccessful years, Hill told Chapman

(**Norman**) **Graham Hill** (1929–1975), by Colin Waldeck, 1964

he was joining BRM for the 1960 season. He had a little more success with the Bourne team, scoring seven points in two seasons. But 1962 was the first of his momentous years and was mainly spent duelling with Jim Clark, a rising star with the Lotus–Climax team which Hill had left. Hill won his first grand prix in the Netherlands with the BRM P57 and was also first in Germany and Italy. As Clark had won the Belgian, British, and American races, everything depended on that in South Africa. Hill won and became world champion, the first British driver to do so in an all-British car.

For the next three years Hill had to be content with being runner-up: to Jim Clark in 1963; to John Surtees (Ferrari) in 1964, by one point; and to Clark again in 1965. The 1966 formula 1 season caught most teams, apart from Brabham, unprepared for the change from 1.5 litre to 3 litre engines. BRM was no exception, and for a former world champion Hill had a mediocre year, with seventeen championship points. This included a win at Indianapolis, later to be an element in his triple crown. It was a controversial race, which began with a sixteen-car crash in the opening seconds, but eventually Hill was confirmed as the winner, the first 'rookie' in forty years. Tired of waiting for the fast but erratic H-16 BRM engine to achieve its potential, Hill rejoined Lotus for the 1967 grand prix season as equal number one driver with Jim Clark. It was a wise move because this was the year of the Lotus 49, the first car to use the Ford–Cosworth DFV V-8 engine that was to win 155 *grandes épreuves* by 1984. Hill led for the first ten laps of the Dutch grand prix but his race ended when the timing gear failed on the brand new engine. Clark went on

to win but Denis Hulme took the title that year with his Brabham–Repco. The 1968 season tested Hill's strength of character to the full following the death of Jim Clark during a formula 2 race at Hockenheim in April. By the last race in Mexico, Hill, Stewart (Matra–Ford), or Hulme (McLaren–Ford) could have become the champion. Both his rivals had mechanical misfortunes; Hill won the race and became world champion for the second time.

Hill won his last grand prix in 1969, inevitably at Monaco. His luck ran out that autumn in the American grand prix at Watkins Glen. A crash, caused by a puncture, shattered his legs so badly that surgeons feared he would never walk again without a stick. Despite intense pain, Hill finished in sixth place the following January in the South African race, driving a Rob Walker Lotus–Ford 49c. His many admirers throughout the world felt that he had made his point and should now retire, a veteran of forty. Hill scored seven points that season and although he was driving Brabham–Fords in 1971 and 1972, Shadow–Fords in 1973, and Lola–Fords in 1974 and 1975 before forming his own Embassy Hill team, his grand prix racing career was in sad decline. But in 1972 he shared the winning Matra–Simca MS670 with Henri Pescarolo at Le Mans. Hill's tenth attempt at the twenty-four hour endurance classic made him the only driver to achieve the triple crown of the formula 1 world championship, Indianapolis, and Le Mans. He retired as a driver in 1975, the most experienced in grand prix history, having competed in 176 races, of which he won fourteen; he was also second fifteen times and took thirteen pole positions. He then embarked on a second career as a team manager and elder statesman of motor racing.

Every inch the popular conception of the racing driver, with an engaging buccaneering manner, Hill was at ease in any walk of life and a superb ambassador for motor racing. As the prince of Wales wrote in the foreword to *Graham*, his zest for life was 'intoxicating and with it went a memorable sense of humour'. He was appointed OBE in 1968 and made a freeman of the City of London in 1974. An accomplished after-dinner speaker, he was given the Guild of Professional Toastmasters' award in 1971. He married in 1955 Bette Pauline, daughter of Bertie Shubrook, a compositor's assistant on *The Times*. They had two daughters and a son. Hill was killed with other members of his team on 29 November 1975 in a flying accident at Arkley, Hertfordshire, when returning to Elstree from testing in France. He was a highly experienced pilot and the cause of the crash was not established. In his memory £112,000 was raised for the National Orthopaedic Hospital at Stanmore, Middlesex, where he had been treated in 1969. His son, Damon Graham Devereux Hill (*b*. 1960), won the drivers' world championship in 1996.   COLIN DRYDEN, *rev.*

Sources G. Hill and N. Ewart, *Graham* (1976) · G. Hill, *Life at the limit* (1969) · B. Hill, *The other side of the hill* (1978) · private information (1986) · personal knowledge (1986)

Archives FILM BFI NFTVA, documentary footage · BFI NFTVA, 'Graham Hill special' · BFI NFTVA, 'Nine days in summer', 24 Aug 1997 |SOUND BL NSA, current affairs recording

Likenesses C. Waldeck, bromide print, 1964, NPG [*see illus.*] · G. Freston, photograph, 1965, Hult. Arch.

Wealth at death £47,217: probate, 9 Nov 1976, *CGPLA Eng. & Wales*

Hill, Sir Hugh (1802–1871), judge, was born at Graig, near Doneraile, co. Cork, the second son of James Hill and his wife, Mary, daughter of Hugh Norcott of Cork. He was educated at Trinity College, Dublin, where he took a BA in 1821, and kept two years' terms at the King's Inns before joining the Middle Temple in London. He practised with great success as a special pleader under the bar between 1827 and 1841, when he was called to the bar and joined the northern circuit. In 1831 he married Anoriah (*d.* 1858), daughter of Richard Holden Webb, controller of customs; they had two sons, including James Eardley Hill, who also became a barrister. It is possible that Hill may have married twice, since one source, the *Solicitors' Journal and Reporter*, gives his wife's name as Georgiana Anne Audley.

Hill became a QC in 1851 and on 29 May 1858 was appointed a judge of the court of queen's bench. He was made a serjeant-at-law and knighted at about the same time. Prolonged illness forced him to retire from the bench in December 1861. He died at the Royal Crescent Hotel, Brighton, on 12 October 1871.

W. A. J. ARCHBOLD, rev. HUGH MOONEY

Sources E. Foss, *Biographia juridica: a biographical dictionary of the judges of England … 1066–1870* (1870) · *The Times* (16 Oct 1871) · Burke, *Gen. GB* · *Solicitors' Journal*, 15 (1870–71), 904 · *CGPLA Eng. & Wales* (1871)

Wealth at death under £60,000: probate, 4 Nov 1871, *CGPLA Eng. & Wales*

Hill, Isabel (1800–1842), writer and translator, was born in Bristol on 21 August 1800, the daughter of William Hill and his wife, Isabel, *née* Savage. Her grandfather Richard Hill managed the Bristol estates of the prominent Salisbury philanthropist William Benson Earle, who stood godfather to her eldest brother, Benson Earle. He and two other older brothers were in the armed forces; their mother wrote poetry. Encouraged by her parents and Benson, Isabel began writing poetry while still at school, but regretted not being able to learn Latin or Greek. To combat the inflammation of the lungs that would recur throughout her life, she stayed with Benson at Dover from April to September 1817. From April 1820, when she joined him at Woolwich, Kent, she would live with him almost continuously for the rest of her life; he averred that they had been 'joined by mutual choice and habits' (B. E. Hill, *Playing about*, 2 vols., 1840, 2.207). In July 1822 Benson left the army for an acting career, and Isabel accompanied him for several years during his engagements in Worthing, Bath, Cheltenham, Birmingham, and Edinburgh.

Although urged by Benson's associates to gain a regular income, Hill refused to endanger her respectability by going on the stage, or to take the traditional path of governessing or teaching, but hoped instead to support herself through writing. In 1818 her first published poem had appeared in the *Pocket Magazine*. Two years later her verse drama *The Poet's Child* inaugurated a chequered career for her as a dramatist: rejected for acting by Covent Garden, the play was a sell-out when published. It deals with the calumnies afflicting writers, and celebrates their claims to genius. In 1823 she brought out a one-volume prose tale, *Constance*, and in 1824, a poem, *Zaphna, or, The Amulet*, but was cheated of the profits by W. G. Graham, her intermediary with the publisher. Soon afterwards, a verse tragedy was turned down by Covent Garden manager Charles Kemble, although praised both by him and by W. C. Macready. It was published posthumously as *Brian, the Probationer, or, The Red Hand* (1842) and while its story is psychologically compelling, its diction is somewhat gnomic.

Hill moved to London permanently in December 1827, and lived with Benson in Cecil Street, Strand. (Some time after mid-1834 they moved to Brompton.) In 1829 she brought out *Holiday Dreams, or, Light Reading in Poetry and Prose* (partly already published in periodicals such as the *Literary Museum* and *The Athenaeum*). This expressed too Hill's sense of the woman writer's dilemma—disgraced if she succeeds, and shunned if she fails—as well as her own desire to be both respected as a creative talent and rewarded financially for her work. This collection also made no profit, however, and Hill continued to contribute mostly comic material to periodicals and especially to annuals, including *Bentley's Miscellany*, *Monthly Magazine*, *Dublin University Magazine*, *Forget-me-Not*, *Juvenile Forget-me-Not*, *Amulet*, *Gem*, *Comic Offering*, and Hood's *Comic Annual*. Her work shows skill and wit, and journalist Laman Blanchard praised her intellect and her humour (B. E. Hill, 'Memoir', 98). Although welcoming a friendship with a fellow woman writer, Louisa Sheridan, editor of the *Comic Offering*, Hill found payment from the annuals unreliable. Her comedy, *The First of May*, had a short run at Covent Garden in October 1829—but in a season where playwrights offered plays *gratis* to prevent the theatre's being auctioned.

After the cold winter of 1832–3 had brought on renewed illness Hill turned to translation to support herself, producing for Bentley's Standard Novels in six weeks a new rendition of Mme de Staël's famous French novel of 1807, *Corinne, ou, L'Italie* (*Corinne, or, Italy*). Hers became the most successful nineteenth-century translation of *Corinne*, and was reprinted up to the 1880s. Her annotations are notable for their identification of ambiguities and inconsistencies on Staël's part, and especially for their criticisms of what Hill saw as Staël's ill-informed and hostile portrayal of English society. Hill also justifies her divergences from the original by invoking her desire 'to consult the taste of my own country' (I. Hill, 'Translator's preface', *Corinne*). The translation is in fact accurate and well written, although its several minor omissions weaken the emotional force of some passages. Hill's other major translation—a somewhat over-literal effort—was of Chateaubriand's *Essai sur la littérature anglaise* (*Sketches of English Literature*, 2 vols., 1836): here, adopting a male persona, she occasionally queries Chateaubriand's accuracy, notably about Milton's religious and political views. She also translated another of Chateaubriand's works as *Last of the Abencerages* (1835).

In 1834 Hill brought out a novel, *Brother Tragedians*, targeting social prejudices against actors, but again made no money; in the same year, none the less, her farce, *My Own*

Twin Brother, was produced at the English Opera House. Her monodrama for the singer Mrs Waylett, *West Country Wooing*, was also acted at the Queen's Theatre, Haymarket, and elsewhere, and she was made an honorary member of the Dramatic Authors Society. In 1839 Hill began a work on female education, a subject which had long preoccupied her, but did not live to complete it: in the spring of 1841 her tubercular problems returned. Financial difficulties had continued, but she was proud, by dint of writing while ill, to pay off a £10 debt to her friend Helena Faucit. She died at 5 Montpelier Row, Montpelier Square, Brompton, in early January 1842 and was buried in Old Brompton cemetery.   JOANNE WILKES

Sources B. E. Hill, 'Memoir', in I. Hill, *Brian the probationer, or, The red hand* (1842), 83–100 · I. Hill, 'An indefinite article', *Holiday dreams* (1829), 1–13 · B. E. Hill, *Home service, or, Scenes and characters from life, at out and head quarters*, 2 vols. (1839) · B. E. Hill, *Theatrical anecdotes and adventures, with scenes of general nature, from the life; in England, Scotland, and Ireland*, 2 vols. (1840) · N. Cross, ed., *Archives of the Royal Literary Fund, 1790–1918* (1982–3) [microfilm] · A. Nicoll, *Early nineteenth century drama, 1800–1850*, 2nd edn (1955), vol. 4 of *A history of English drama, 1660–1900* (1952–9); repr. (1967–76) · will of William Benson Earle, PRO, PROB 11/1273, sig. 194 · *BL cat.*, [CD-ROM] · *National union catalog*, Library of Congress · *Wellesley index* · *A list of the officers of the army and royal marines* (1820); (1826) · Nichols, *Illustrations*, vol. 5
Wealth at death minimal: Hill, 'Memoir'; Cross, ed., *Archives*

Hill, James (1697–1727), antiquary, was born on 7 February 1697 in the parish of St Nicholas, Hereford, the third son of John and Mary Hill. He was educated at Trinity College, Oxford, and called to the bar as a member of the Middle Temple in 1721. In 1717 he issued proposals for publishing by subscription a history of the city of Hereford in two parts, one on its ecclesiastical and the other on its secular development, with 'transcripts from original records', 'geometrical plans of the city, churches, monasteries, and chapels', and engravings of monuments, arms, ancient seals, and portraits of eminent persons. He proposed to follow this, if successful, by another volume on the county, but the work was still unfinished at his death. In 1718 he was elected FSA, and on 30 April 1719 was admitted FRS. He showed to the Society of Antiquaries in the year of his election a 'vast collection of drawings, views, inscriptions, plans, and observations in MS, the fruits of his travels in the west of England that summer' (Gough, 1.410). One of his drawings, a west view and ichnography of Tintern Abbey, Monmouthshire, was engraved by J. Harris for John Stevens's *History of Antient Abbeys* (vol. 2, 1723, 57). When at a meeting of the Society of Antiquaries on 3 January 1722 it was resolved to attempt a complete history of British coins, Hill undertook to describe the Saxon coins in Lord Oxford's possession, while his own collection was to be catalogued by George Holmes, the deputy keeper of the records in the Tower of London. During the same year he exhibited to the society an accurate survey of Ariconium (near Weston under Penyard) and of Hereford. He also composed poetry, 'a beautiful soliloquy … on hearing a parent correct his child with curses' (Gough, 1.418). A long narrative poem on Roman Britain was apparently not completed.

Hill was a friend of William Stukeley and Roger Gale, and, under the Celtic name Caradoc, a member of their Society of Roman Knights, which met to study Roman remains. By December 1725 he had acquired a house in Herefordshire, and although he told Stukeley he did not mean to leave London completely, lack of money apparently prevented him from returning. Early in 1727 he sent Stukeley his picture, in profile. He died in August that year, probably in Hereford, and was buried in Hereford Cathedral on 25 August. Verses on his death were published in John Husband's *Miscellany of Poems* (1731), from which it appears that Hill wrote some lines on 'Eternity' about ten hours before his death.

At Hill's dying request his father in March 1728 sent his Herefordshire collections to Samuel Gale, who found that, although Hill had done more than was supposed, his work was 'a mere embryo of what he had promised' (*Family Memoirs*, 1.204–5), and therefore unfit for publication. In 1752 Isaac Taylor of Ross bought the papers from Hill's brother, a schoolmaster in Herefordshire, for John Roberts MB, also of Ross, who indexed them and added a further ten volumes. After Roberts's death in 1776 the whole collection again passed to Taylor, who sold it in 1778 to Thomas Clarke FSA, principal registrar of the diocese of Hereford. On Clarke's death in March 1780 it came to the Revd James Clarke, who still owned it in 1821. Clarke offered to sell it to John Allen the younger of Hereford, who had repaired some of the volumes in 1818, but they could not agree about the price. By 1833 the collection belonged to Thomas Bird of Hereford (*d.* 1836). It passed to Robert Biddulph Phillipps (*d.* 1864), who bequeathed it to Belmont Priory, near Hereford. It was later acquired by Hereford City Library. A collection of thirty-five ancient Herefordshire deeds, most of them marked with Hill's name, was given by Joshua Blew, librarian of the Inner Temple and a native of Herefordshire, to Andrew Coltée Ducarel.   GORDON GOODWIN, rev. JANET COOPER

Sources Hereford city library, Hill MSS · Stukeley MSS, Bodl. Oxf., MS Eng. misc. c. 113, fols. 259–68 · *The family memoirs of the Rev. William Stukeley*, ed. W. C. Lukis, 1, SurtS, 73 (1882) · Foster, *Alum. Oxon.* · R. G. [R. Gough], *British topography*, [new edn], 1 (1780), 410, 417–18, 789 · R. Rawlinson, *The English topographer* (1720), 70–73 · Nichols, *Lit. anecdotes*, 4.454n.; 543n.; 6.156n. · BL, Add. MS 35057, fol. 19 · H. A. C. Sturgess, ed., *Register of admissions to the Honourable Society of the Middle Temple, from the fifteenth century to the year 1944*, 3 vols. (1949) · J. Cooper, 'Herefordshire', *English county histories: a guide*, ed. C. R. J. Currie and C. P. Lewis (1994), 176–85 · J. Allen, *Bibliotheca Herefordiensis, or, A descriptive catalogue of books, pamphlets, maps, prints, &c. relating to the county of Hereford* (1821), viii–x · IGI
Archives Herefs. RO, Herefordshire collections | BL, letters to Humfrey Wanley, Harl. MS 3781 (167, 171) · Bodl. Oxf., letters to William Stukeley, MS Eng. Misc. c113, fols. 259–68; c114 · Hunt. L., annals of the Bryde and Chandos families
Likenesses pen-and-ink drawing, 1727, BL; made for or copied by William Stukeley
Wealth at death presumably not great: Bodl. Oxf., Add. MS Eng. Misc. c.113

Hill, James (*d.* 1817), actor and singer, was believed to be a native of Kidderminster, Worcestershire. He lost his father when he was four and was adopted and educated by his maternal uncle, John Hale (*d.* 1782), rector of

Albrighton, Shropshire. On the death of that uncle, Hill was taken to another uncle in Wolverhampton, who apprenticed him to a painter when he was sixteen.

After a short visit to London, Hill went to Bristol, where he met William Dimond, the manager of the theatres there and at Bath. Although Dimond had no need for extra performers, Hill persuaded him to allow him to perform for a single night. This first performance was as Belville in the comic opera *Rosina*, by Frances Brooke, but the date and place are unclear; according to John Roach's *Authentic Memoirs* and Thomas Gilliland's *Dramatic Mirror*, it occurred at Bristol in June 1796, but John Genest's *Some Account of the English Stage* says 1 October 1796 at Bath. Hill so impressed Dimond on his début that he was awarded a five-year contract. Under the recommendation of Ann Selina Storace, Hill studied under Mr Richards, the leader of the band at the Bath theatre, and also under Xamenes, and finally with Venanzio Rauzzini.

After two years Hill was given permission to go to London and perform at Covent Garden in the 1798–9 season for £5 per week. His first performance in London was as Edwin in Leonard MacNally's comic opera *Robin Hood*, and he went on to play more than twenty-five roles at Covent Garden over the next eight years, eventually securing a salary of £12 per week. Perhaps his most successful role was as the original Sir Edward in Thomas Knight's comic opera *The Turnpike Gate*, which had twenty-seven performances in the 1799–1800 season. Hill's career in London ended at the end of the 1805–6 season, when he left Covent Garden as a result of some 'fancied' injury to his pride and is said to have gone to perform 'in the country' (Gilliland, 2.784).

Although Hill never received huge accolades as a performer, he was described in the *Authentic Memoirs* as attractive, 'with a pleasing figure' (Highfill, Burnim & Langhans, *BDA*), and Gilliland made the following observation: 'as a performer little can be said in his favour, but as a singer he is entitled to our praise; and with a due attention to his vocal studies, he might stand very high in the profession' (Gilliland, 2.784). He was apparently popular with the ladies, though his enjoyment of pleasurable pursuits was probably detrimental to his career.

It is not known when or to whom Hill was married, but a Mr and Mrs Hill performed at Edinburgh in 1810–11 and, according to the *Biographical Dictionary of Actors*, James Hill was the same man who, with his wife, joined a company headed by W. Adamson in Jamaica in 1816. According to the same source, Hill was involved with concerts there until his death at Mount Bay, Jamaica, on 27 June 1817, though his death was not registered in the *Royal Gazette* in Jamaica for 1817. Administration of his estate was granted to his brother Charles Hill, a bachelor and doctor.

VICTORIA HALLIWELL

Sources Highfill, Burnim & Langhans, *BDA* · T. Gilliland, *The dramatic mirror, containing the history of the stage from the earliest period, to the present time*, 2 vols. (1808) · [J. Roach], *Authentic memoirs of the green-room*, 2nd edn, 5 pts in 2 vols. (1806), pts 3–4 · *DNB* · C. B. Hogan, ed., *The London stage, 1660–1800*, pt 5: *1776–1800* (1968) · J. Cawthorn, *Cawthorn's minor British theatre; consisting of the most esteemed farces and operas*, 6 vols. (1806) · Venn, *Alum. Cant.*

Likenesses S. De Wilde, chalk and watercolour drawing, 1805, BM · S. De Wilde, pencil and red chalk drawing (as Leander in *The padlock*), BL · Schiavonetti, engraving, repro. in Cawthorn, *Cawthorn's minor British theatre*

Hill, James John (1811–1882), painter, was born in Birmingham, the son of Daniel Hill of Broad Street, Birmingham. He was educated at Hazlewood School and studied at John Vincent Barber's academy in Birmingham, where Thomas Creswick was a fellow student. He worked for some years in Birmingham, chiefly as a portrait painter; among his sitters were the philanthropist the Revd Dr Samuel Wilson Warneford and Mrs Glover, founder of Spring Hill College.

Hill moved to London in 1839, and in 1842 he was elected a member of the Society of British Artists. He was a frequent and popular contributor to its exhibitions until 1881, principally showing portraits, rustic scenes, and figures. He also exhibited at the British Institution (1848–55) and the Royal Academy (1845–68). He painted many portraits and several pictures of horses and dogs for Lady Burdett-Coutts, one of his most regular patrons. After some years in London, he began to concentrate on the fantasy subjects for which he is best-known. These were usually half-length figures, either singly or in small groups, studied from life, and with landscape backgrounds painted from nature. Many of the most effective were Irish studies, made on his frequent visits to Ireland from 1854. Several of his works were purchased by Herbert Ingram, founder of the *Illustrated London News*, and were published as lithographs in the weekly. He also painted figures in the works of the landscape painter Henry Bright. Later in his career Hill again changed direction and concentrated on landscapes, but these did not achieve the success of his rustic figures. He died of bronchitis at Sutton House, West Hill, Highgate, Middlesex, on 27 January 1882.   R. E. GRAVES, rev. DELIA GAZE

Sources *The Architect*, 27 (4 Feb 1882), 73 · *Birmingham Daily Post* (31 Jan 1882) · Wood, *Vic. painters*, 3rd edn · Graves, *RA exhibitors* · M. A. Wingfield, *A dictionary of sporting artists, 1650–1990* (1992) · exhibition catalogues (1842–82) [Society of British Artists]

Hill, Jenny [*real name* Elizabeth Thompson] (1848–1896), music-hall entertainer, was born in Paddington, Middlesex. Her childhood is obscured by legends spread by herself and others. Her father, Michael Thompson (1812/13–1881), was reported to be a watcher at a cab stand. Her stage début was made at the age of six or seven, when she performed as the legs of the goose in *Mother Goose* (Aquarium Theatre, Westminster), and her first appearance at a London music-hall took place about 1860 at the Dr Johnson, a pot-house in Fleet Street, at the usual fee of 3*s*. a night with refreshments. All accounts state that about 1862 she was apprenticed under articles to a Bradford tavern singsong for five or seven years, entailing drudgery and starvation which seriously jeopardized her health. Her first weekly salary was £1 at the Winchester Music-Hall, Stockwell, in 1863.

Hill may have broken her indenture by marrying John Wilson Woodley (*d.* 1890), an acrobat under the name Jean

Pasta, on 28 May 1866. The agent Maurice de Frece is credited with taking her back to London, where her first double turns took place at Deacon's and the Raglan, at a wage of 30s. per hall. By 1871 she was earning £6 a week at the London Pavilion. Another agent, Hugh J. Didcott, bestowed on her the sobriquet the 'Vital Spark', which stuck.

From 1868 to 1893 Hill was a star of the London and north-country halls. Part of her success lay in a ready wit and voluble exchanges with the audience, improvised to fit each district. Small, sharp-featured, pretty at a distance, but scarred by smallpox, she is credited with originating female low comedy in the halls. The comedian Harry Randall considered her the most versatile artist he had ever seen; she could put across racy patter, perform an energetic cellar-flap dance, yodel a ballad, and then reduce her public to tears with her pathos. Until the late 1870s she sang songs launched by others, but then introduced ''Arry', written for her by E. V. Page, in which she impersonated a bantering coster swell. In 1886 she introduced dramatic character songs, which 'made a decided change in the style of the ballads of the day' (*New York Clipper*), pathetic dramatic *scenas* like her favourite, 'The Little Stowaway', by Fred Bowyer. The most durable of these were 'The City Waif' and 'Masks and Faces', inspired by Charles Dickens and G. R. Sims. John Hollingshead speculated that 'her sense of character—low life, of course—and her dramatic power of conjuring up solid pictures of men and women who never appeared bodily on the stage, would have delighted the elder Mathews' (Hollingshead, 1.99), and a later commentator referred to her 'democratic appeal based on an intimacy with the poorest members of her audience' (Scott, 207).

At the height of her career Hill earned £30 a night per hall, often appearing at three or four locations nightly. Her forays into music-hall management were less happy. In London she was the proprietor of the Star Music Hall in June 1879, and of Springthorpe's (Mechanics' Hall), Grimston Street, for a week, and from 11 July 1882 to 1883 she kept the Albert Arms public house, Southwark. A more ambitious venture was the purchase of the Rainbow Music Hall (renamed the Gaiety Theatre) in Southampton in July 1884; opened in September of that year, it burnt to the ground two months later.

Hill entered burlesque in the 1877–8 season, in *A Frog he would a-Wooing Go* (London, Aquarium). For two seasons (1878–80) she took over Nelly Farren's principal-boy roles at the (London) Gaiety Theatre. Thereafter (until 1888) she became a favourite in pantomime in the northern provinces. In legitimate drama, she played Mrs Micawber to Joe Eldridge's Micawber and Nan in the revival of J. B. Buckstone's *Good for Nothing Nan* (Grecian Theatre, 1889), but with mediocre success.

Hill was noted for her charities and her hospitality, much of it dispensed from The Hermitage, Streatham, a bungalow on farmland whose produce she tried to hawk in London. With John Woodley she had three children: Lettie (the music-hall performer Peggy Pryde), Jenny Hill, and a boy who seems not to have survived. After Woodley's death on 8 January 1890, Hill married Edward Turnbull, a music-hall manager. By 1889 her engagements were interrupted by illness, and in December 1890 she was given a testimonial at Canterbury Hall.

The American vaudeville impresario Tony Pastor took Hill to New York for sixteen weeks from 23 February 1891. Despite extensive publicity, she was not appreciated by audiences, which had to be provided with glossaries of London slang. She became seriously ill in 1892 and was given a benefit at the Canterbury in September, but returned to the London Pavilion on 12 June 1893, when she introduced two new songs. She embarked on a tour of Birmingham, Manchester, Liverpool, and Bradford, but when her doctors recommended that she not winter in England, Hill sold off the furniture of her London house, and, at the invitation of the South African manager Luscombe Searelle, went to Johannesburg in December. She could merely be wheeled onto the stage, where she shook hands with the public. She returned to London in May 1894, and moved to Bournemouth for her health. She died at Peggy Pryde's home in Brixton, London, on 28 June 1896, of pulmonary tuberculosis, and was buried in Nunhead cemetery.   LAURENCE SENELICK

Sources *The Era* (4 July 1896) • *The Sphere* (8 July 1896) • *Illustrated Sporting and Dramatic News* (4 July 1896) • 'Some of Miss Jenny Hill's reminiscences', *The Sketch* (15 Nov 1893) • H. B. Hibbert, *Fifty years of a Londoner's life* (1916) • J. Hollingshead, *My lifetime*, 2 vols. (1895) • J. S. Bratton, 'Jenny Hill: sex and sexism in Victorian music hall', *Music hall: performance and style*, ed. J. S. Bratton (1986), 92–111 • *The Era* (1878–96) • *The Entr'acte* (1878–96) • C. D. Stuart and A. J. Park, *The variety stage* (1895) • H. Scott, *The early doors: origins of the music hall* (1946) • Boase, *Mod. Eng. biog.* • m. cert. • *The Era* (18 June 1891)
Archives Harvard TC

Hill, Joan (d. 1441). *See under* Women traders and artisans in London (act. c.1200–c.1500).

Hill, Joanna Margaret (1836/7–1901). *See under* Hill, Rosamond Davenport (1825–1902).

Hill, Sir John (c.1625–1701), army officer, declared in 1695 that he was about seventy. A native of Kent, he evidently fought for parliament in the civil wars. In 1651 he was a captain in Fitch's infantry regiment when it occupied Inverness. A strong republican, by late 1653 he was in command at Ruthven Castle in Badenoch, and three years later was made major and justice of the peace. In May 1657 he was appointed governor of the fort at Inverlochy, where he enforced justice with previously unknown impartiality. He assisted in planting presbyterian ministers and established a schoolmaster at the Inverlochy settlement, enhancing its role in spreading English culture in Lochaber. In 1660, newly promoted to lieutenant-colonel, he was as General Monck certified 'singularly active and instrumentall in his Majestie's happy restauration' (Firth and Davies, 2.519).

Monck decided that Inverlochy should be evacuated and dismantled, and Hill settled in Ireland, perhaps as a location more congenial for nonconformists. He may have married at this time: by 1690 he was a widower with daughters living near London. Sir Arthur Forbes, a royalist opponent in 1653, and later earl of Granard, was his principal Irish patron, and he was made comptroller of the household by the lord lieutenant, the earl of Essex. About 1679 he became steward at Belfast to the earl of Donegal and constable of Belfast's unfortified castle. In 1689 he persuaded Irish forces not to burn Belfast, using the support of the distant King James and a sympathetic Scottish Jacobite general, and his £300–£400 savings. The Williamite duke of Schomberg appointed him one of three temporary commissioners to manage the Ulster revenue.

In March 1690 George Mackenzie, Viscount Tarbat, another former royalist opponent, brought him to Scotland to persuade the west highland chiefs to submit to the government of King William in return for money to buy out the Argyll family's destabilizing feudal rights over them. His negotiations were sabotaged by those conducted by John Campbell, earl of Breadalbane, intended to delay the government offensive for Jacobite ends. In July 1690 Major-General Hugh Mackay built Fort William on the Cromwellian foundations at Inverlochy, and left Hill as governor of what remained a precarious outpost. At his request William granted the adjoining settlement of Maryburgh a charter on 13 November 1690, as part of renewed plans to promote a civilian settlement in Lochaber.

The garrison and Hill's prudent policies prevented the west highland clans from reassembling as a Jacobite army. He supported the presbyterian faction within the Scottish ministry, but in June 1691 the leader of the opposing faction, secretary Sir John Dalrymple (later earl of Stair), sent Breadalbane to the highlands to achieve a pacification. A cessation of arms was agreed and William proclaimed that the chiefs must take the oath of allegiance by 31 December 1691 before the privy council or sheriffs. Factional hostility and rational distrust of Breadalbane, combined with news that Breadalbane intended the destruction of Fort William (with the loss of Hill's employment and arrears), led Hill to join in unscrupulously undermining his cessation, which collapsed that autumn.

Dalrymple just survived this set-back, but Hill and the Scottish commander-in-chief, Sir Thomas Livingstone, supposed, wrongly, that their involvement in the sabotage would lead Dalrymple to seize upon any further disobedience to justify their dismissal. Hill's feelings of insecurity were increased by distrust of his deputy governor, James Hamilton, in correspondence with Dalrymple and Livingstone. Late in December 1691 the major chiefs hurried to submit ahead of the government campaign. A minor chief, Alexander Macdonald of Glencoe, arrived at Fort William on 31 December, mistakenly supposing that Hill could administer the oath. He sent him with a letter to Inveraray, where he took the oath six days late. Many Glencoe Macdonalds had submitted earlier, and Hill's obligation to the clan was increased by the formal preliminary agreement he made for Glengarry's surrender on 31 December, intended to protect Glencoe also. He ignored an order from Livingstone to attack them if they held out.

On 16 January 1692 Hill unexpectedly received William's instructions, including a conditional order to extirpate the Glencoe men as a warning, and Dalrymple's violent covering letter. Livingstone sent a still more violent letter to Hamilton emphasizing that destroying Glencoe was the way to win Dalrymple's favour. Hill considered the orders 'a nasty durty thing and was resolved rather to lay down his Comission then to have putt them in Execution' (deposition 2 July 1695, NA Scot., GD 406, bundle 633) but temporized, fearing dismissal and destitution, and hoping for a countermand. Giving the clause about Glencoe priority over William's main instructions, he let Glengarry submit on easy terms. By 12 February he had no pretext left for delay and, needing to reassert his authority over his officers, issued a brief authorization to Hamilton to march to Glencoe and execute Livingstone's orders. The massacre ensued the next morning.

Hill recovered his courage, ignored orders to hunt down survivors and solicited permission to resettle them in Glencoe. His regiment kept order in the highlands despite being undermanned, and he again worked to moderate the council's more disruptive orders. He attended the inquiries into Glencoe of 1693 and 1695; in the latter he was exonerated, the beneficiary of a bargain whereby he suppressed material incriminating Livingstone, a member of the dominant faction, in return for weight being given to his real excuses. He was knighted about 1696. Late in 1697 he blundered in accepting the insincere protestations of Simon Fraser (later Lord Lovat) just before he seized and forcibly married the marquess of Atholl's daughter. On 1 February 1698 William ordered that Brigadier-General Maitland and his regiment should replace Hill at Fort William, sparking a plot to burn the fort, which Hill quelled. Hill retired on half-pay, having made only £1000 sterling during his time as governor, and died in April 1701 at Clockmilne, a suburb of Edinburgh near Holyrood, owed £202 10s. by the government. Almost all his highland record was of disinterested and able service in a difficult borderland, but it is for his conduct during his one brief major lapse from these standards, driven by partisanship and moral cowardice, that he is chiefly remembered.

PAUL HOPKINS

Sources P. Hopkins, *Glencoe and the end of the highland war*, rev. edn (1998) · J. Gordon, ed., *Papers illustrative of the political condition of the highlands of Scotland, 1689–1696* (1845) · 1693 enquiry into massacre, Hill's 1695 deposition, NA Scot., dukes of Hamilton papers, GD 406, bundle 633 · NA Scot., Leven and Melville papers, GD 26 · W. H. L. Melville, ed., *Leven and Melville papers: letters and state papers chiefly addressed to George, earl of Melville ... 1689–1691*, Bannatyne Club, 77 (1843) · W. Fraser, ed., *The Melvilles, earls of Melville, and the Leslies, earls of Leven*, 3 vols. (1890) · W. Fraser, ed., *The earls of Cromartie: their kindred, country and correspondence*, 2 vols. (1879) · NA Scot., Cromartie papers, GD 305 · J. Prebble, *Glencoe: the story of the massacre* (1966) · NL Scot., Tweeddale MSS 7014–7019 · [H. R. Duff], ed., *Culloden papers* (1815) · D. Warrand, ed., *More Culloden papers*, 5 vols. (1923–30), vol. 1 · Worcester College, Oxford, Clarke MSS · C. H. Firth, ed., *Scotland and the Commonwealth: letters and papers relating to the military government of Scotland, from August 1651 to December 1653*, Scottish History Society, 18 (1895) · C. H. Firth, ed., *Scotland and the protectorate: letters and papers relating to the military government of Scotland from January 1654 to June 1659*, Scottish History Society, 31 (1899) · *CSP dom.*, 1689–98 · *The manuscripts of J. J. Hope Johnstone*,

HMC, 46 (1897) · C. H. Firth and G. Davies, *The regimental history of Cromwell's army*, 2 vols. (1940) · testament, NA Scot., CC 8/8/86, fols. 322v–323 · [C. Leslie], *An answer to a book, intituled, the state of the protestants of Ireland under the late King James's government* (1692) · *An abstract of three letters from Belfast to a person in London* (1690) · J. Grant, ed., *Seafield correspondence, from 1685 to 1708* (1912), 229–32 · Scottish privy council register, NA Scot., PC 1/51, 28, 107 **Archives** NA Scot., letters | NA Scot., Cromartie papers · NA Scot., Leven and Melville papers · NA Scot., Marchmont papers · NL Scot., Culloden papers · NL Scot., letters to Forbes family · NL Scot., corresp. with the first and second marquesses of Tweeddale · West Highland Museum, Fort William, letters and papers relating to Glencoe · Raehills, Dumfriesshire, Annandale papers **Wealth at death** under £1000 gained during governorship of Fort William; £202 10s. owing him from government: testament, 20 June 1717, NA Scot., CC 8/8/86, fols. 322v–323; Grant, ed., *Seafield correspondence*

Hill, John (d. 1735), army officer, was the youngest son of a London Turkey merchant, Francis Hill, and his wife, Elizabeth, the second daughter and coheir of Sir John Jenyns, of St Albans. His sister Abigail, Lady *Masham, was a favourite of Queen Anne. The collapse of Francis Hill's business ventures reduced his children to a condition of dependence upon the patronage of their cousin Sarah *Churchill, later duchess of Marlborough. The duchess clothed Jack (the name by which John was commonly known) and sent him to St Albans grammar school (1690–91), and thereafter used her influence at court as confidante to the future queen, Princess Anne, to find him a place—first in 1692 as a page to Prince George and then in 1698 as one of the grooms to the bedchamber in the duke of Gloucester's household. After the duke's death Sarah had him transferred back to Prince George's household for a brief period in 1700. Hill's elder sister Abigail was also found a position within the royal household.

Under the Marlborough influence Hill was commissioned a captain in the Grenadier Guards in November 1702 and in 1703 was appointed adjutant-general to the forces sent to Portugal. In May 1705 he was given the colonelcy of the 11th foot (the late Lord Stanhope's regiment) upon their return from Spain, having formed part of the garrison at Portalegre which capitulated in 1704. Hill's colonelcy owed as much to his sister's rising position at Queen Anne's court as to the Marlborough influence. The regiment was returned to full strength and in 1706 formed part of the expedition against the French coast under Earl Rivers, which was abandoned and sent to Lisbon. In 1707 Hill re-embarked with his regiment for Valencia and the onset of the campaign which culminated in the battle of Almanza. During the battle the 9th and 36th regiments were brigaded with the 11th under Hill's command and, although not immediately engaged, were led forward by Hill to stem the French advance and allow the remnants of the British force to make an orderly retreat. Hill, along with his regiment, was captured and taken prisoner.

Having secured his parole and returned to England, Hill re-formed the regiment, which was sent to the Netherlands in the summer of 1708 to reinforce Marlborough's command. During 1709 it took part in the siege of Mons. On 26 September Hill was ordered to take his troops and break new ground close to the enemies' palisades, and he had to beat off a determined sally from the besieged fortress, with the loss of 150 killed or maimed—including Hill himself, who was injured in the attack.

By 1710 Hill's sister, now Lady Masham, had supplanted the duchess of Marlborough in the affections of the queen, and she used her position at court, together with her alliance with Robert Harley, reputed to be a cousin, to undermine the position of Marlborough and at the same time secure her brother's continued advancement. At the behest of Harley, Queen Anne proposed Hill for the vacant colonelcy of the late earl of Essex's regiment of dragoons. Marlborough, who, according to his duchess, had never rated Hill as a soldier, refused the commission on the grounds that the imposition of a younger officer with influence, over the claims of more experienced and deserving men, would weaken his authority and undermine morale. Relations with the queen rapidly deteriorated, and the duke was unable to resist the queen's subsequent demand in April that Hill be promoted brigadier-general. In May, Hill was further recompensed with a pension of £1000 per annum, to be held during the queen's lifetime. In parliament Marlborough overreached himself. An attempt by the whigs to have Lady Masham removed from court only strengthened the queen's search for a new ministry. Marlborough's political demise can be traced to this episode.

Hill was elected a tory MP for the Cornish pocket borough of Lostwithiel in 1710, which seat he held until 1713. In the Commons he was fairly inactive, although, as the duchess of Marlborough mentioned in one of her more acerbic comments:

> when Mr Harley thought it useful to attack the Duke of Marlborough in Parliament … this honest Jack Hill, this once ragged Boy, whom I clothed, happening to be sick in bed, was nevertheless persuaded by his sister to get up, wrapped himself in warmer cloathes … to go to the House to vote against the Duke. (Green, 120–21)

Such now was the political enmity which existed between cousins.

Hill's close connections with the Harley administration brought him further promotion. In 1711 Henry St John revived the plan for an expedition to take Quebec and, to gain the queen and Abigail Masham's support, proposed Hill as the commander-in-chief. Marlborough's powers of promotion had been placed in the hands of a board under the duke of Ormond and advancement was given to those who opposed the duke. Hill was duly dispatched in April 1711 with a force of 6000 men. However, on account of poor navigation in bad weather the expedition came to grief, without a shot being fired, in the St Lawrence River with the loss of 800 men, and it returned to England. Jonathan Swift, a close social and political confidant of Hill, reported that he was 'privately blamed by his own friends for want of conduct. He called a Council of War, and therein it was determined to come back' (Swift, 9 Oct 1711). This apparent lack of leadership was doubtless a sad confirmation to Marlborough, yet the expedition's miscarriage did not prevent Hill's continued rise, socially and professionally, during the tory administration.

In June 1712 Hill was made lieutenant-general of the ordnance (having failed to win the governorship of the Tower) and was given command of the force sent to garrison Dunkirk upon the peace of Utrecht. The governorship of Dunkirk was a further favour from St John, who sought to strengthen his position through the appointment of friends. In July 1712 Hill was promoted major-general and in November he returned to London to be sworn a member of the privy council. He did not stand for election in 1713, perhaps due to talk of a peerage, never realized.

In London, Hill's conviviality, a source of some strain to his personal health, was recognized by his election to the board of brothers, or 'society', as Swift termed a small congenial club of men of wit, learning, or influence formed by himself and St John. From Dunkirk, Hill maintained his connections with Swift through the gift of a snuff-box, of which the recipient declared, '''tis allowed at court, that none in England comes near to it' (Swift, 7 Aug 1712 and 12 Aug 1712). A gathering of the club hosted by Hill at his London house in January 1713 was described by Swift as 'the greatest dinner I have ever seen' (ibid., 25 Jan 1713). In February 1714 Hill was instructed to return to Dunkirk in his capacity of commissioner to inspect the fortifications, but he was present in Whitehall in August for the accession of George I.

Upon the Hanoverian succession Hill lost all his offices, although his commission as major-general was renewed. He sold the colonelcy of his regiment in July 1715 and went into retirement. Both he and his sister retained their tory political sympathies and support for Bolingbroke, who was rumoured to be at Hill's London house for meetings with friends in 1717 (*Stuart Papers*, 56, 5.236). Hill remained unmarried, living at his seat at Egham, on the borders of Berkshire and Surrey, and his London house in Jermyn Street, where he died on 19 or 22 June 1735, some months after his sister. He left his estate to his nephew Samuel, second Baron Masham.

Hill's military career, which owed little to personal merit, offers an insight into the politics of Queen Anne's court, where first the influence of his cousin, the duchess of Marlborough, and later that of his sister propelled forward his career and social advancement. His career, moreover, played a prominent role in the downfall of the duke of Marlborough. JONATHAN SPAIN

Sources F. Harris, *A passion for government: the life of Sarah, duchess of Marlborough* (1991) · D. Green, *Sarah, duchess of Marlborough* (1967) · H. T. Dickinson, *Bolingbroke* (1970) · *The Marlborough–Godolphin correspondence*, ed. H. L. Snyder, 3 vols. (1975) · C. Dalton, ed., *English army lists and commission registers, 1661–1714*, 6 vols. (1892–1904) · R. Cannon, ed., *Historical record of the eleventh, or north Devon regiment of foot* (1845) · J. Taylor, *A history of the Devonshire regiment* (1951) · J. Swift, *Journal to Stella*, ed. H. Williams, 2 vols. (1948); repr. (1974) · *Calendar of the Stuart papers belonging to his majesty the king, preserved at Windsor Castle*, 7 vols., HMC, 56 (1902–23), vol. 5 · Fortescue, *Brit. army* · W. T. Lawrence, *The parliamentary representation of Cornwall* (1926) · HoP, *Commons, 1690–1715* [draft] · Burke, *Gen. GB*
Archives BL, Blenheim MSS, corresp. · BL, letters to Sir J. Leake, Add. MSS 5431–5443, 47968–47978

Hill, Sir John [*pseud.* the Inspector] (*bap.* 1714, *d.* 1775), physician and actor, second surviving and fourth-born son of Theophilus Hill (1680–1746) and his wife, Ann Susannah (*née* Yorke), was baptized on 17 November 1714, probably in the Peterborough-Spalding region of Lincolnshire. Hill's father, who had a Cambridge medical degree, climbed the clerical ladder at Peterborough Cathedral from prebend in 1710, to minor clerk in 1719, and canon in 1720, before resigning seven years later in favour of his first-born son, Theophilus (*b.* 1706); he later became curate of Denham parish in Buckinghamshire.

Little is known of John Hill's early years before he was apprenticed to the London apothecary Edward Angier in 1730–31. One source current until the late nineteenth century held that he was a strolling player from 1730 to 1735, but this is unsubstantiated. However, Hill's fascination with the theatre is definite, vying with his interest in botany as chief among his lifelong preoccupations. In 1738 he started collecting specimens for Lord Petre, and at some point between then and 1742 he married Susannah Travers, daughter of the steward of Richard Boyle, third earl of Burlington, though no record of the marriage survives. Hill worked as an apothecary in a shop close to the Strand, London, and during the years 1739–40 the second duke of Richmond, Lennox, and Aubigny commissioned Hill (probably as a result of an introduction from Petre) to collect specimens for him from England and Wales. This relationship continued into 1741, with Hill taking up residence at Goodwood House, the Sussex seat of the Richmonds. At Goodwood, a fashionable seat of learning, literature, and theatre (the castle boasted its own theatre), Hill met a number of the theatrical community including Owen MacSwinney, David Garrick (then at the beginning of his career), and Peg Woffington. Hill acted on the Goodwood stage, continued to collect botanical specimens, and wrote his *Orpheus, an Opera*. On 2 July 1742 Petre died, making Richmond Hill's sole employer. During his flirtation with theatricals at Goodwood, Hill became infatuated with Peg Woffington, who did not return his feelings. By 1743 Hill had finally broken away from Goodwood and settled in Westminster, retaining his interest in his original apothecary shop. Perhaps inspired by the new wave of 'natural' acting given vogue by Garrick in the 1740s, Hill went on to act in several plays, putatively at Drury Lane and Covent Garden. He studied acting with Charles Macklin and in 1744 played Lodovico in his *Othello* at the 'little theatre' in the Haymarket. Hill 'seems to have been the only person who regarded the experiment as a success' (Duerr, 241).

During this time in London, Hill began seriously to promote and expand his interest in natural science, becoming acquainted with significant naturalists and fellows of the Royal Society such as Martin Folkes, Sir Hans Sloane, Henry Baker, William Watson, and James Parsons. Hill's scientific publications consequently began to grow and multiply. In 1746 he published Theophrastus's *History of Stones* in addition to two papers in the *Philosophical Transactions*. Despite his publications and circle of friends, Hill's

Sir John Hill (*bap.* 1714, *d.* 1775), by Richard Houston (after Francis Cotes, 1757)

attempts to join the Royal Society in 1747 failed. Notwithstanding, in 1748 he published a *History of Fossils* and translated Pomet's *Complete History of Drugs*. In 1749 he assumed two editorships: of the *Monthly Review* (anonymously), and of the *British Magazine*, in which his column 'The original spectator' was carried over from the *Monthly Review*. As an editor he was responsible for reducing the use of capitals and thereby reforming the prevailing eighteenth-century style and taste in such matters.

Hill's *The Actor* appeared in 1750. It was the first English acting treatise to discuss the personal and emotional attributes of the actor rather than the rhetorical conventions of performance that had characterized earlier acting manuals. *The Actor* was a thinly disguised adaptation of a French original, *Le comédien* by Pierre Rémond de Sainte-Albine. (The second edition of *The Actor* in 1755 expanded on the first, making more extensive reference to the English stage; this version was translated back into French by Antonio Sticotti as *Garrick, ou, Les acteurs anglais* and influenced Denis Diderot's *Paradoxe sur le comédien*.) Also in 1750 Hill published two satires on the Royal Society (*Lucine sine concubitu* and *A Dissertation on Royal Societies*), sinking his hopes of ever being elected. Despite this deeply resented set-back (and perhaps because of it), Hill continued to publish prolifically in the sciences. In 1751 *A Review of the Works of the Royal Society*, *A History of the Materia medica*, and *A History of Plants* appeared. These were joined by non-scientific titles such as *The Adventures of Mr George Edwards* and *The History of a Woman of Quality*. Moreover, on 5 March of this year, his column in *The London Daily Advertiser and Literary Gazette* announced him to the world as 'the Inspector', a journalistic cognomen by which he became universally recognized, especially among the *habitués* of the Bedford Coffee House. Hill also acquired an MD degree from the University of St Andrews. In 1752 his *Essays in Natural History and Philosophy* completed the third volume of his system of the natural world, *A History of Animals*. Some time during that year Hill moved to 12 Hart Street, Bloomsbury, London.

The next year marked a departure on Hill's part away from scientific publications, perhaps because he had stopped collecting specimens. A miscellany of works materialized, including: *The Conduct of a Married Life*, *Observations on the Greek and Roman Classics*, and *The Story of Elizabeth Canning*, the last being based upon a contemporary incident concerning a servant girl (Canning) who went missing for twenty-eight days citing abduction for the purposes of prostitution. Hill gave medical evidence on Canning's behalf in this controversial and topical case, opposing the view of Henry Fielding who considered the girl's story to consist mostly of falsehoods. Hill then engaged with Fielding in a pamphlet war. Like all men of principle, Hill had a penchant for making powerful enemies, especially among the *literati* (Smollett and Richardson, for example). Hill was also satirized as an 'archdunce' in 'The Hilliad: an Epick Poem', having made an enemy of its author, Christopher Smart.

During 1753 Hill wrote his last 'Inspector' column, and married for the second time. In September 1753 Henrietta Wilhelmina Jones (*d.* 1789), the sister of Charles Jones, fourth Viscount Ranelagh, became Hill's wife at St George's Chapel, Hyde Park, London.

Despite being pursued by publishers, Hill had an unaccountably unproductive year in 1754. Garrick (at Drury Lane) and John Rich (at Covent Garden) refused Hill's *The Critical Minute: a Farce*. However, Hill managed to publish *Urania*, a dictionary of astronomy, and *The Useful Family Herbal*. His output in 1755 was more prolific, with the publication of *Thoughts Concerning God and Nature*, *The British Herbal*, and second editions of *The Actor* and *The Useful Family Herbal*. His *Naval History of Britain* (1756) made a timely appearance just before the commencement of the Seven Years' War. Hill's writing continued apace: 1757 saw his attentions turn once more to the sciences, with *Eden, or, A Compleat Body of Gardening* and *The Sleep of Plants, and Cause of Motion in the Sensitive Plant*. Hill finally secured the patronage of Lord Bute and published a long list of titles, including: *The Construction of the Nerves*, *The Virtues of Wild Valerian*, *An Idea of a Botanical Garden in England*, *The Management of the Gout*, *The History of Insects*, *A Method of Producing Double Flowers*, and *The Gardener's New Calendar*. All were published in 1758. He also made another sally at entering the theatre world with his farce *The Rout*, which proved to be prophetically titled, with Garrick breaking off for ever with Hill in 1759. In that year too, at the instigation of his patron Bute, Hill began his *magnum opus*, *The Vegetable System* (1759–75), a work which eventually ran to twenty-six volumes. The work cost Hill a considerable amount of money, some of which he recouped through the sale of herbal medicines such as 'the essence of water-dock', 'tincture of valerian', and 'pectoral balsalm of honey'. Other botanical titles of 1759 included *Virtues of Honey, Usefulness of Knowledge of Plants, Proliferous Flowers*, and *A Practice of Gardening*. In this year too he published his *Cautions Against the Immoderate Use of Snuff*, a curiously prescient tract which associates tobacco with cancerous growths. Hill also bought a property in Bayswater, London, and began to help Bute to lay out Kew Gardens. His *Flora Britanica*, published in the same year, was the first Linnaean flora of Britain. Although volumes one and two of *The Vegetable System* were published in 1761, Bute was becoming less and less involved in the project as his star rose (to prime minister in 1762) and fell (in 1763, when he was out of office). As a result of the impact of *The Vegetable System* on the continent, Hill found himself corresponding with European scientists such as Haller and Gesner. He became ill in 1764, perhaps from the effects of gout and dropsy; his *Centaury, the Great Stomachic*, a book of herbal remedies, followed in 1765, and in 1766 he published *Hypochondriasis, a Practical Treatise on the Nature and Cure of that Disorder.*

Ever-straitening financial circumstances in 1767 spurred Hill to export his herbal remedies to the American colonies. Among his publications the following year were: *A Method of Curing Jaundice, Polypody, Hortus Kewensis*, and *A New Astronomical Dictionary*. However, Hill's scientific reputation was not enhanced by suspicions at home and abroad by those who found it difficult to cope with his 'distorted mind and personality' (Rousseau, xxxii). Failing health brought Hill close to death, and he made a will on 1 January 1769. Fully recovered in the spring he researched his *Construction of Timber*; volume fourteen of *The Vegetable System* was published and he commenced work on the next volume. The *Family Practice of Physic* and *Herbarium Britannicum* followed at the end of the summer. In 1770 Hill lived almost exclusively at his house in Bayswater surrounded by his plants and herbs, quitting but not disposing of his property in St James's (Arlington Street). The *Vegetable System* grew to volumes fifteen and sixteen, and Hill continued to correspond with Carl Linnaeus and Albrecht von Haller, exciting the German's praise in particular for *The Construction of Timber*. *Cautions Against the Use of Violent Medicines in Fevers*, and *Fossils Arranged According to their Obvious Characters* also appeared in 1771. In the following year, Hill sent Linnaeus a copy of *The Vegetable System* and found himself being presented at the Swedish court (not for the first time), where he was in good standing. *Sparogenesia, or, The Origin and Nature of Spar* appeared the same year.

In 1773, despite being handicapped by a return of ill health, Hill nevertheless managed to publish volumes twenty-one to twenty-two of *The Vegetable System*, in addition to *Twenty-Five New Plants, A Decade of Curious and Elegant Trees*, and *Plain and Useful Directions for those who are Afflicted with Cancers*. In 1774 he was awarded the order of Vasa by Gustavus III of Sweden, which honour was conferred at the English court some time between 1 and 10

June. The last year of Hill's life, 1775, saw the publication of the final volumes of *The Vegetable System*, in addition to *Inquiries into the Nature of a New Mineral Acid Discover'd in Sweden* and *Circumstances which Preceded the Letters of the Earl of Mexborough*. Following further travels to the Netherlands, Hill returned to England because of continuing sickness. He died at his home in Golden Square, London, on Wednesday 22 November 1775, and was buried at Denham in Buckinghamshire; no monument remains. A will and testament of 8 November names his wife and Martha Constance Hardy as his executors. The year after Hill's death, his wife undertook to extract from Lord Bute the thousands of pounds which were allegedly promised to Hill. In 1788, after unsuccessfully pursuing litigation against Bute, she published *An address to the public, by the Honble Lady Hill; setting forth the consequences of the late Sir John Hill's acquaintance with the earl of Bute*, trying him in the court of public opinion and ascribing to him the loss of her husband's health and fortune. In 1779 *A Short Account of the Life, Writings and Character of the Late Sir John Hill, MD* was published. After the death of Hill's widow in 1789, their daughter and sole executor, Juliana, acquired Hill's medical papers and secret herbal preparations. She sold the latter to the druggist Benjamin Shaw in 1802.

Given that his knighthood was a foreign award, Hill was something of a prophet without honour in his own land. He enjoyed the company of influential people but infrequently won their favour and loyalty. Indeed he was generally reviled in his day. Hogarth included Hill in his basket of hated works in his 'Beer Street' satire. Garrick famously remarked of him: 'For Physick and Farces, his Equal there scarce is, His Farces are Physick, and his Physick a Farce is' (Little and Kahrl, 1.299). In *The Rosciad*, Charles Churchill satirized Hill as a 'Proteus'

> For who, like him, his various pow'rs could call
> Into so many shapes, and shine in all?
> Who could so nobly grace the motley list,
> Actor, Inspector, Doctor, Botanist?
> (*Rosciad*, 69)

However, behind these disparagements lie unintended compliments. In Garrick's epigram there is the admission that Hill was without equal; and in Churchill's lines there is the recognition that Hill truly had a wide-ranging, protean curiosity. According to Samuel Johnson, 'Dr Hill was … a very curious observer; and if he had been contented to tell the world no more than he knew, he might have been a very considerable man' (Boswell, 383). But Hill did not know when to temporize, nor did he suffer fools gladly. Slender, and close to 6 feet in height, Hill was a tall poppy ripe for cutting down, and the age in which he lived obliged. His reputation has been somewhat reclaimed since. At the end of the millennium, Hill was recognized as less of a quack and dilettante, and, to use George Rousseau's phrase, more 'a type of Renaissance man in the eighteenth century' (Hill, ix). BARRY O'CONNOR

Sources [J. Hill], *The letters and papers of Sir John Hill, 1714–1775*, ed. G. S. Rousseau (1982) · G. S. Rousseau, 'John Hill, universal genius manqué: remarks on his life and times, with a checklist of his works', in J. A. Leo and G. S. Rousseau, *The Renaissance man in the eighteenth century* (1978) · E. Duerr, *The length and depth of acting*

(1962) • T. Cole and H. K. Chinoy, *Actors on acting* (1970) • J. Boswell, *Life of Johnson*, ed. R. W. Chapman, rev. J. D. Fleeman, new edn (1970); repr. with introduction by P. Rogers (1980) • C. Churchill, *The Rosciad* (1769) • *The letters of David Garrick*, ed. D. M. Little and G. M. Kahrl, 3 vols. (1963) • S. Shesgreen, ed., *Engravings by Hogarth* (1973) • *DNB*

Archives priv. coll. • RBG Kew, drawings • U. Oxf., department of plant sciences, papers | BL, letters to duke of Newcastle, Add. MSS 32852–32973, *passim* • Burgerbibliothek Bern, letters to A. von Haller

Likenesses F. Cotes, ink and wash drawing, 1757, BM • R. Houston, mezzotint (after F. Cotes, 1757), NPG [*see illus.*] • Leumuth?, portrait (after line engraving by Cludy), Wellcome L. • G. Vendramini, engraving (after F. Cotes), repro. in R. Thornton, *A new illustration of the sexual system of Carolus von Linnaeus*, 2 vols. (1799), vol. 1, facing p. 17 • stipple (after F. Cotes, 1757), Wellcome L.

Hill, John (1786–1855), Church of England clergyman, was born on 23 October 1786 in the City of London, apparently in the parish of St Gregory by Paul with St Mary Magdalen, Old Fish Street, the son of John Hill. His first instructor was probably John Eden, vicar of St Nicholas, Bristol, and his early diaries show that he was also influenced in boyhood by T. T. Biddulph of St James's, Bristol. From 1803 to 1806 he boarded at a school kept by Edward Spencer, vicar of Wingfield, Wiltshire, where other notable evangelicals were educated. Hill matriculated from St Edmund Hall, Oxford, in 1806, subsequently obtaining a second class below the line in *literae humaniores* in 1809. Thereupon he was made assistant tutor, proceeding MA in 1812, when he became sole tutor and vice-principal (the principals of the Hall at this time played virtually no part in teaching or administration). During Hill's formative years at Oxford, until 1807, Isaac Crouch had been vice-principal of St Edmund Hall, followed by Daniel Wilson, afterwards bishop of Calcutta. Hill's significance in church and Oxford history can be adequately understood only in terms of his links with these two predecessors. Vice-principal from 1783, Crouch had brought into being, and Wilson continued more formally, a system of close academic teaching with constant pastoral oversight. Crouch established thus a thriving evangelical tradition at St Edmund Hall, which lasted until 1854. Hill promoted it effectively, considerably longer than Crouch, and for much longer than Wilson or his own successor, E. A. Litton, who looked back on Hill's 'pure simplicity of character and benevolence of spirit' (*The Record*, 5 March 1855, 4). The hymnologist W. H. Havergal, an early pupil, 'often spoke … of his kindness and fitness for his office' (J. M. Crane, *Records of … Wm. H. Havergal*, 1882, 6). Soon this influence extended further afield in the university: Archdeacon Phelps, scholar of Corpus from 1815 to 1822, and his undergraduate associates recalled Hill's 'friendship and counsels' long after they had all left Oxford (C. Hole, *Life of W. W. Phelps*, 1, 1871, 130).

With entire responsibility for teaching and discipline, Hill had little time to produce original works of scholarship: during the long vacation of 1818 he wrote over 1000 pages of lectures. However his 1816 version of Henry Aldrich's *Artis logicae compendium* proved an acceptable university textbook, reaching a sixth edition in 1850. Apart from this he published only a lengthy poem, *The*

Boor (1829), a scriptural analogy relating to Roman Catholic emancipation, and a few sermons. Made deacon in 1809 and ordained priest in 1810, Hill fulfilled his pastoral vocation both at the Hall and by officiating as curate of Hampton Gay, a small village near Oxford, becoming perpetual curate in 1814 and serving the parish until 1851. On 17 July 1811 at St George's, Hanover Square, London, Hill married Sophia (*c*.1788–1849), only daughter of George Warriner, linen draper of New Bond Street and of Bloxham Grove, Oxfordshire, niece of Edward Grubb, sculptor. Their house in the High Street, Oxford (latterly no. 65), a focus for evangelicals from near and far, became the centre of an affectionate family life, where between 1812 and 1824 four sons (of whom two died young) and four daughters were born.

In 1825 Hill founded a local association (still extant) of the Church Missionary Society, followed in 1827 by a similar branch of the Society for the Propagation of Christianity among the Jews. Of these he remained active secretary until he ceased to reside in the university. Among assistant secretaries, for a year in 1829–30, was J. H. Newman, then vicar of St Mary's. By this time Hill was himself a recognized evangelical leader in Oxford. Francis Newman, then an undergraduate at Worcester College, recalled that 'to young Academicians of the *Evangelical* school, whatever their College, the Revd. Mr. *Hill* was an important standard-bearer' (C. H. O. Daniel, *Our Memories*, 1893, 46). Hill's pupils included a Bampton lecturer (J. E. Riddle), a Savilian professor (W. F. Donkin), and William Jacobson, afterwards regius professor of divinity (1848–65) and bishop of Chester.

In *Gleanings of Past Years* (1879) W. E. Gladstone described Hill's men of about 1830 as ultra-Calvinistic. While this was undoubtedly true of a few contemporary Oxford evangelicals, including H. B. Bulteel (1800–1866), curate of St Ebbe's, where Gladstone sometimes worshipped, it does not seem clear how far doctrinal Calvinism at St Edmund Hall, even in Hill's time, went beyond the moderate form of article 17, if at all. But Hill did, privately at least, identify himself with Bulteel. His quieter personality and genial temperament, however, made him a more sympathetic advocate of evangelical beliefs.

In 1840–41 Hill's vice-principalship received the unusual recognition of a portrait, albeit by the minor artist John Wood, which now hangs in the old dining hall. Hill proceeded BD in 1844. During the later 1840s he felt less vigour for dealing effectively with young men. Numbers at St Edmund Hall were declining. To this period nevertheless belongs a reference of William Tuckwell, then an undergraduate of New College, recalling 'the evening parties of John Hill … where prevailed tea and coffee, pietistic Low Church talk, prayer and hymnody of portentous length' (*Reminiscences of Oxford*, 1900, 96).

The death of his wife in September 1849 was perhaps a decisive factor in Hill's decision to quit. Late in 1851 he was appointed by Charles Sumner, bishop of Winchester, as rector of Wyke Regis, Dorset. At the same time he was elected a city lecturer, requiring occasional duty in Oxford, at St Martin's, Carfax. Having made a promising start at Wyke, in 1855 serious illness intervened and he died at his rectory on 22 February. A mural tablet in Wyke church commemorates his ministry there and at Oxford, where he was buried on 2 March in his family vault in St Peter's-in-the-East churchyard. His surviving diaries were presented to St Edmund Hall by a great-grandson, the Revd A. D. du B. Hill, in 1925. Some twenty of Hill's letters, in a freer style, came to light in 1990.   J. S. REYNOLDS

Sources D. M. Lewis, ed., *The Blackwell dictionary of evangelical biography, 1730–1860*, 2 vols. (1995) · A. S. Wood, 'Spencer, Edward', *The Blackwell dictionary of evangelical biography, 1730–1860*, ed. D. M. Lewis (1995) · J. S. Reynolds, 'Crouch, Isaac', *The Blackwell dictionary of evangelical biography, 1730–1860*, ed. D. M. Lewis (1995) · J. Hill, diaries, 1805–8, Bodl. Oxf. · J. Hill, diaries, 1820–55, Bodl. Oxf. · J. Hill, letters to G. Warriner, 1814–23, Warks. CRO · J. S. Reynolds, 'Additional light on the Revd John Hill', *St Edmund Hall Magazine*, 14/1 (1990–91), 18–20 · *The Record* (5 March 1855), 4 · M. W. Warriner, *The Warriner family* (1975) [privately printed] · *Report of the Association for Oxford* [Church Missionary Society for Oxford] (1826–52) · *Report of the Association for Oxford* [Church Missionary Society for Oxford] (1855–6) · *Annual Report* [Oxford … Society for Promoting Christianity among the Jews] (1828–52) · *Annual Report* [Oxford … Society for the Promotion of Christianity among the Jews] (1855–6) · J. S. Reynolds, *The evangelicals at Oxford, 1735–1871: a record of an unchronicled movement*, [2nd edn] (1975) · J. N. D. Kelly, *St Edmund Hall: almost seven hundred years* (1989) · ordination papers, Oxon. RO · G. J. Armitage, ed., *The register book of marriages … St George, Hanover Square*, 3, Harleian Society, Register Section, 22 (1896), 33 · parish records, St Peter's-in-the-East, Oxford, 2 March 1855 [burial]
Archives Bodl. Oxf., diary | Warks. CRO, Warriner MSS
Likenesses J. Wood, oils, *c*.1840, St Edmund Hall, old dining hall · S. Bellin, engraving, 1841 (after oil painting by J. Wood), repro. in R. E. Lane Poole, *Catalogue of portraits, university, colleges, etc. of Oxford*, 3 (1926), 281
Wealth at death under £3000: PRO, PROB 8/248

Hill, John (1862–1945), trade unionist, was born on 30 July 1862 in Govan, Glasgow, the son of John Hill, a ship plater, and his wife, Matilda. He attended the local board school until the age of twelve when he began work in the local shipyards, taking on a formal apprenticeship as a ship plater when he was nineteen. He settled in his home community of Govan, then not only one of the centres of Clyde shipbuilding but also one of the liveliest areas of labour organization in Scotland. He became increasingly involved in the local affairs of the United Society of Boilermakers and Iron and Steel Shipbuilders, serving as Clyde district delegate from 1901 to 1909 and becoming well known as one of the most assertive of the area's trade unionists.

At this time Hill was also active in his local Independent Labour Party, Congregational church, and parish council, and became one of the boilermakers' first sponsored parliamentary candidates in the 1906 general election, when he stood for Govan. Both on this occasion and in the following year, when he stood in a Liverpool by-election, he campaigned on an advanced radical programme but was defeated. In 1909 he was the favoured candidate of his union's executive committee in the election for general secretary; he was successful and served in this role in Newcastle until his retirement in 1936.

The first decade of Hill's period as leader was one of prosperity and growth, so by the outbreak of war in 1914 he was able to rebuild the boilermakers' finances and industrial strength to the position they had reached under Robert Knight in 1900, having then been undermined by a period of weaker leadership. In particular Hill reasserted the control of apprentices by establishing a special section of the union, and regained the initiative in district wage bargaining by weakening and finally withdrawing from a procedural agreement which had been imposed by the employers in 1907. This assertive leadership style combined with his personal roots in Govan then made him a credible national spokesman for the grievances which erupted in the Clydeside shipbuilding industry during the First World War. He played a particularly important role both in the revision of the Munitions of War Act in the aftermath of the 'Clyde unrest' over restricted labour mobility and increased supervision in the local shipyards in 1915, and again in the reorganization of shipyard labour administration following the local strikes which arose from government mishandling of the 12½% bonus award in 1918. By the end of the war Hill was a central figure in the trade union movement and played a key role in the emergence of Labour as an independent party. He presided over the Trades Union Congress which gave the vital support to Arthur Henderson's reorientation of Labour's foreign policy in 1917, and he delivered strong craft union support for the introduction of individual membership and the development of a comprehensive political programme in the following year.

However, this was to be the high point of Hill's success. The next two decades saw an ever-deepening depression in which shipbuilding was particularly badly hit by unemployment. From the point of view of his own union, his major contribution was probably in maintaining its existence and some of its bargaining strength through this very difficult period through his intransigent resistance both to employers' wage cuts and to those among his own members who wanted higher levels of benefit and strike action than the union's financial resources could support. The level of his own commitment to this task, and that of the majority of his members' support for him, was reflected in his continuing in office until he was seventy-two years old.

Hill was of average height with dark hair, a moustache, and a penetrating gaze; he was energetic, passionate, and charismatic, but was also able to bear the daily administrative grind and emerged as the leading craft unionist of his generation. In 1887 he married Margaret McGregor (*d*. 1944); they had one daughter and four sons. Following his retirement, Hill remained active in local affairs in Newcastle; he died on 16 January 1945 at Bingley Hospital, Yorkshire, and was buried in Bingley cemetery.

ALASTAIR J. REID

Sources DLB · J. E. Mortimer, *History of the Boilermakers' Society*, 2: *1906–1939* (1982) · A. Hill, *Boilerman's Heid: a biography of the trade union leader John Hill, 1863–1945* (privately printed, Ambleside, 1996) · d. cert.
Wealth at death £1443 14*s*. 5*d*.: probate, 28 April 1945, *CGPLA Eng. & Wales*

Hill, John Cathles (1857–1915), builder and brick maker, was born in Anderson's Entry, Hawkhill, Dundee, on 12 December 1857, the eldest son of Robert Hill and his wife Eliza, *née* Cathles. There were six children, three boys (including John) and three girls, one of whom died in infancy. The elder Hill was a wheelwright and joiner, and in 1860 succeeded his father and grandfather as tollhouse keeper at Auchterhouse, living in a toll cottage there. The family was staunchly Presbyterian. An ancestor, John Hill, had been an elder of the kirk in the seventeenth century, and Robert Hill was an elder of the village church.

Hill went to the village school and, after serving an apprenticeship to his father as a joiner, attended classes at the mechanics' institute in Glasgow. At the age of twenty-one he left for London, where a relative, George Cathles Porter, was working as a speculative builder in Hornsey. This subsequently became the base of Hill's own building operations. He was initially employed as a wage-earning craftsman, but soon began to take on contracts for joinery, and from there graduated to building whole houses. On 22 June 1882 he married Matilda (*b.* 1858/9), the daughter of William Henry Mose, a grocer. She was of considerable assistance in his business career.

Over the space of some thirty years Hill built more than two thousand houses and other buildings, mainly in the district of Crouch End. In Crouch End Broadway and Tottenham Lane he built parades of shops with several storeys above crowned by elaborate gables in the Dutch style which was fashionable at the end of the nineteenth century, and he was instrumental in transforming the village of Crouch End into a fashionable shopping centre. He also built two large and spectacular public houses, the Salisbury, Green Lanes, and the Queen's Hotel, Crouch End, both outstanding examples of late nineteenth-century gin palaces, with elaborate etched and coloured glass, rich decorative plasterwork, and very high quality mahogany bar fittings and joinery from Hill's own workshops.

In 1888, when his buildings operations were at their height and he was experiencing difficulty in obtaining a regular supply of bricks, he visited the brick-producing area of Fletton near Peterborough. In the following year he purchased an ailing brickfield there and founded the London Brick Company. He rapidly expanded production in the area and built the famous 'Napoleon' kiln, the largest in the world for several years. He eventually owned some 1300 acres of brickfields, capable of producing up to 2 million bricks a week. He built 350 houses for the employees of his yards and in his obituary was described as 'a just and even generous employer' (*Peterborough and Hunts Standard*, 10 April 1915). Every year he would take his workers and their wives and families by special trains to Yarmouth for a day's outing, paying for their meals and entertainment. He was primarily responsible for the dominant position which Fletton bricks came to occupy in the construction industry. He served on several committees and organizations concerned with brick-making, including the Institute of Clayworkers, of which he was twice president.

Hill, who was described as 'the maker of modern Fletton' (*Peterborough and Hunts Standard*, 10 April 1915), took an active part in local affairs. His parents moved to Fletton in their later years, but Hill himself continued to live in London. He was elected to the Huntingdonshire county council in 1905 and the London county council in 1910.

In common with most builders, Hill financed his operations principally through mortgages, and in the 1890s, at the height of a building boom, he increased his financial commitments to purchase land in Fletton, partly to extend his brick-making business and partly for speculative building there. At the beginning of the twentieth century, however, the building cycle took a pronounced downturn and Hill's financial position deteriorated. A number of manoeuvres designed to rescue him failed, and he went bankrupt in 1912 with liabilities of over £1.2 million and assets of less than a fifth of that amount. In February 1915 an application for Hill to be discharged from bankruptcy was granted but suspended for two years. For the last four years of his life he suffered from cirrhosis of the liver. He died on 5 April 1915 at 20 Ventnor Villas, Hove, while on a visit to the resort, and was buried on 9 April in Highgate cemetery. He was survived by his wife, two sons, and a daughter. His elder son, Robert William (1884–1917), was killed in Flanders. The younger, John Edgar (1887–1937), played a prominent part in the development of the brick-making industry.

VICTOR BELCHER

Sources *Peterborough and Hunts Standard* (30 Nov 1912) · *Peterborough and Hunts Standard* (10 April 1915) · R. Hillier, *Clay that burns: a history of the Fletton brick industry* [1981] · *British Clayworker* (15 April 1915) · J. P. Bristow, 'Hill, John Cathles', *DBB* · M. Girouard, *Victorian pubs* (1984), 148–50, 192 · *Hampstead and Highgate Express* (10 April 1915) · b. cert. · m. cert. · d. cert.

Likenesses photograph, repro. in *British Clayworker*, 8 · photographs, repro. in *Peterborough and Huntingdonshire Standard* (10 April 1915)

Hill, John Harwood (1809–1886), Church of England clergyman and topographer, son of Robert Hill of Lincoln and Leamington, and his wife, Mary, was born at Louth, Lincolnshire, and baptized there on 3 October 1809. Robert Gardiner *Hill (1811–1878) was a younger brother. On 30 June 1830 he was admitted a pensioner of Peterhouse, Cambridge. His marriage on 8 December 1833 to Maria Ann Jiggins (1815–1874) brought them a large family, including John Daniel Hill, staff surgeon to the Royal Free Hospital, London.

In 1834 Hill graduated BA, was ordained deacon at Carlisle, and became curate of Glaston, Rutland. The following year he was ordained priest at Peterborough and moved to become curate of Corby, Northamptonshire, and librarian to Lord Cardigan at Deene. He compiled a black-letter catalogue of the Deene library, with etchings of his own. In 1837 he was appointed by Lord Cardigan rector of Cranoe, and by the lord chancellor in 1841 vicar of Welham, both near Market Harborough, Leicestershire. In August 1846 the church at Cranoe was badly damaged in a storm and through Hill's efforts a new church was built in 1849 by subscription. The church at Welham was also restored during his incumbency and in 1838 the rectory at Cranoe was rebuilt, largely at his expense. Hill was appointed surrogate for the diocese of Peterborough in 1852.

Hill was author of several works, of which the earliest was *The chronicle of the Christian ages, or, Record of events ecclesiastical, civil, and military to the end of 1858* (1859). His *History of the Hundred of Gartree* was published in two parts: *The History of the Parish of Langton* (1867), which was originally designed to raise funds for the rebuilding of the church at Tur Langton, and *The History of Market Harborough* (1875); both volumes included several other parishes and were illustrated with Hill's own etchings. Hill was the local secretary of the Leicestershire Architectural and Archaeological Society and contributed some seventeen articles to its *Transactions* on a wide variety of local history and genealogical subjects. He was also a corresponding member of the Royal Archaeological Institute. On 12 January 1871 he was elected FSA. He died at Cranoe rectory on 3 December 1886 and was survived by Sarah (*b. c.*1848), his second wife. He was buried in Cranoe churchyard.

GORDON GOODWIN, rev. ADAM J. N. GOODWIN

Sources *The Academy* (18 Dec 1886), 411 · Crockford (1886) · *The Guardian* (8 Dec 1886) · Venn, *Alum. Cant.* · *VCH Leicestershire*, vol. 5 · H. I. Longden, *Northamptonshire and Rutland clergy from 1500*, ed. P. I. King and others, 16 vols. in 6, Northamptonshire RS (1938–52) · Cranoe churchyard monumental inscriptions transcript, 1968, Leics. RO · census returns for Cranoe, 1851, PRO, HO 107/2079 · parish register, Louth, Lincs. Arch., 3 Oct 1809 [baptism] · G. T. Rimmington, 'The Reverend John Harwood Hill, F. S. A.', *Leicestershire Historian*, 38 (2002), 20–22
Wealth at death £3016 5s. 7d.: probate, 11 Jan 1887, CGPLA Eng. & Wales

Hill, Joseph (1625–1707), nonconformist minister, was born at Bramley, near Leeds, Yorkshire, in October 1625. His father, Joshua Hill, was minister successively at Walmsley Chapel, Lancashire, and Bramley Chapel, and died in 1632, a few hours before the arrival at his house of a citation for not wearing a surplice. Joseph Hill attended school at Pocklington, Yorkshire, and was admitted to St John's College, Cambridge, on 20 August 1646, graduating BA in 1649. He became a fellow of Magdalene College, proceeding MA there in 1651. Hill knew the young Samuel Pepys, admonishing him on 21 October 1653 for having been 'scandalously overseene in drink the night before' (Pepys, *Diary*, 1.67). Hill was a popular tutor at Magdalene and served as senior proctor in 1658. In 1660 he kept the act for the degree of BD, and when he declined to conform in 1662 the authorities 'cut his name out of their books in kindness to him' (Calamy, *Abridgement*, 2.81), preventing his formal ejection. He was a lecturer between 1660 and 1662 at All Hallows Barking. When he met Pepys again in July 1661 Hill was less censorious than he had been eight years earlier. Over glasses of wine in a tavern in Pope's Head Alley he was confident that 'the King now would be forced to favour Presbytery, or the City would leave him' (Pepys, *Diary*, 2.141). Despite the loss of his fellowship, and with the act against conventicles soon to pass the Commons, Pepys found Hill continuingly optimistic for the future of the church.

This could not be sustained for long, and Hill, 'considering the dissensions in England about Church government, etc, resolved to settle beyond sea, that I might be quiet' (*Letters of Eminent Men*, 1.254). At Leiden he stayed for two years with Matthew Newcomen, pastor of the English church there, entering Leiden University as a student on 29 March 1664. He returned in 1666, during the Second Anglo-Dutch War, landing on the Suffolk coast in a Dutch vessel, together with many other English persons. Papers in his possession were confiscated and he was pronounced 'as dangerous a person as could have been sent … to do the Dutch intelligence from England' (*CSP dom.*, 1665–6, 520). The documents found on him seem to have been quite innocuous. They included a request to procure the release of a Dutch minister held prisoner in Chelsea College, and a letter dated 3 July 1666 from Richard Mayden, minister of the English Reformed church at Amsterdam, to Peter Herringhooke, a merchant of London. This revealed that Hill wished to marry the writer's daughter Elizabeth, and had come over to settle his estate in England. He was imprisoned, but was shortly released, having undertaken not to return to the Netherlands. After the war hysteria died down, however, he did return, married Elizabeth Mayden, and following his election on 19 June 1667 was invested on 7 August as minister of the Scottish church at Middelburg, Zeeland.

There Hill remained until 1673. In that year, following the French invasion of the Dutch republic and the revolution which had brought William of Orange to power, he committed to the press of Amsterdam anonymously, under the guise of a patriotic Dutchman, 'a well-wisher to the Reformed Religion, and the welfare of these countries', *The Interest of these United Provinces, being a Defence of the Zeelanders Choice*. On the title-page he laid out his position:

I. That we ought unanimously to defend ourselves.
II. That if we cannot, it is better to be under England than France, in regard of Religion, Liberty, Estates and Trade.
III. That we are not yet come to that extremity, but we may remain a Republick, and that our Compliance with England is the onely meanes for this.

The ostensible audience for the book was Dutch; it was an exhortation to maintain the war effort against the French. Hill's book, a quite substantial work, interesting for the knowledge it displays of the diplomatic history of the century, contended that English policy had for too long been distorted by a fixation upon the danger from Spain. This had been cleverly encouraged by the dangerous and aggressive French: 'how far they have overgrown Spain in power … so great they overshadow us all' (sig. P2). Translated into English, the book can be read in the light of a second audience as part of the propaganda war being waged by William III and his agents to win over public opinion in England and so pressure Charles II into breaking his alliance with the French. Yet with its argument that it was better to be subjected to the English enemy than the French and talk of compliance rather than alliance, it was perhaps a rather more ambiguous work. Where it was unambiguous was in its warning against the

French threat, and following complaints from the French ambassador the Dutch authorities found it politic to order, on 19 August 1673, that the author be expelled until the end of the war. As he later recorded it Hill was 'banichsed, *duranto bello*, by a Frenchified party in the States' (*Letters of Eminent Men*, 1.254).

The ambiguity of Hill's position is further highlighted and perhaps explained by his reception on his return to England: Charles II rewarded him with the sinecure rectory of Llandinam, Montgomeryshire, worth £90 a year. Hill arranged that his nephew, John Spademan, later a fellow minister at Rotterdam, should be presented to the living (as he was on 18 December 1674), but should pass its profits to him. This arrangement was challenged in 1689 by the dean and chapter of Bangor on the grounds that Spademan had not taken the requisite oaths and was in the Netherlands anyway, so that the living was vacant in fact and in law. On 8 August 1696, after much dispute, the diocese agreed that Hill should be paid £70 a year. The original grant and its continuation were almost certainly a payment for Hill's activities as a government agent. In or before 1702 Hill wrote to the earl of Nottingham: complaining that 'my sine-cure was wrested from me by a punctilio by law' he offered to continue to perform the work he had done for previous secretaries of state. Obscure references in Aphra Behn's correspondence hint that he may already have been an agent by the late 1660s, though the firmest evidence comes from the 1690s.

Among Hill's most lasting achievements was his expanded version of Schrevelius's Greek–Latin lexicon, published in 1663. Another achievement was reported, though not perhaps purely out of altruism, on 25 June 1677, by William Millington, a London auctioneer, who wrote to Hill of his 'great Service done to Learning and Learned men in your first advising and effectually setting on foot that admirable and Universally approved way of selling Librarys by Auction amongst us' (*Calamy rev.*, 265). Hill left England soon afterwards. On 13 January 1678 he was instituted as a minister of the English Presbyterian church at Rotterdam. On 1 September 1681 Hill wrote to his old acquaintance Pepys explaining his emigration: 'being tired with the buss of both parties in London, I retired hither, where I live to my owne content in great peace and quietness, above the frownes of fortune and below the envy of my enemies' (ibid.). On 17 June 1687 Hill was in touch with Richard Baxter about the distribution of his *Methodus theologiae*, reporting the relief occasioned in the Netherlands by the news of the latter's release from prison. Further letters to Pepys from Rotterdam of 16 November and 7 December 1697 provided unofficial briefings on the negotiations leading to the treaty of Ryswick, and offered assistance to Pepys in the preparation of 'your great work of your Naval history' (Pepys, *Private Correspondence*, 145). In 1707 Hill found it necessary to complain to Robert Harley that he had not been paid for his services as a government agent since the late 1690s, at the same time offering to sell him his coin collection. Hill was an indefatigable student and book collector, retaining to

the last his habit of reading, though his memory had nearly gone. He died at Rotterdam on 5 November 1707.

Hill is sometimes confused with his namesake Joseph *Hill, not least because the latter also served, between 1699 and 1718, as a minister in the English Presbyterian church at Rotterdam. STEPHEN WRIGHT

Sources *Calamy rev.* · E. Calamy, ed., *An abridgement of Mr. Baxter's history of his life and times, with an account of the ministers, &c., who were ejected after the Restauration of King Charles II*, 2nd edn, 2 vols. (1713) · W. Steven, *The history of the Scottish church, Rotterdam* (1832, 1833) · G. Nuttall, 'English dissenters in the Netherlands, 1640–1689', *Nederlands Archief voor Kerkgeschiedenis*, 59 (1979), 48–9 · Pepys, *Diary* · [J. Hunter], ed., *Letters of eminent men, addressed to Ralph Thoresby*, 1 (1832) · *Private correspondence and miscellaneous papers of Samuel Pepys, 1679–1703*, ed. J. R. Tanner, 2 vols. (1926) · *CSP dom.*, 1665–6 · *Calendar of the correspondence of Richard Baxter*, ed. N. H. Keeble and G. F. Nuttall, 2 vols. (1991) · Venn, *Alum. Cant.* · *DNB*

Hill, Joseph (1667–1729), Presbyterian minister, was born at Salisbury on 11 October 1667, of godly parents. After receiving his early education from Thomas Taylor (*c*.1614–1677), an ejected minister, he entered the free school at Salisbury before he was seven, where he remained for nine years. He was then sent to Charles Morton's celebrated academy at Newington Green, until it was broken up two years later, in 1685, as a result of persecution. After studying for a year under Samuel Sprint at Andover, Hampshire, where he became proficient in Hebrew, he returned to London to complete his studies 'with such who had been Mr Moreton's pupils, who attended at this time weekly lectures, read to them by Mr Glascock' (Wood, 30). As a result he was noticed by Richard Stretton, who recommended him as chaplain and tutor to Lady Irby (*d*. 1695), with whom he lived for nearly seven years. He was ordained on 23 June 1694 with Edmund Calamy and others.

Hill was minister of the Presbyterian meeting at Swallow Street, Westminster, until 1699, when he accepted an invitation to be minister of the English Presbyterian Church at Rotterdam. He was called to the meeting at Haberdasher's Hall, Cheapside, on 16 February 1718 and remained there until his death. He was an orthodox subscriber at the Salters' Hall controversy in 1719. Shortly before his death he was chosen to preach the expository lecture on Wednesday evenings at Little St Helen's meeting-house. His only publication was a sermon preached to the society. Hill was not a popular preacher, and the congregation was left in a very declining state. It revived briefly under Stephen Ford, but the church was dissolved in 1734. Hill and his wife, Martha, had no children, and he died in London on 21 January 1729. Hill has been confused with his more celebrated namesake and fellow Presbyterian minister Joseph Hill (1625–1707). DAVID L. WYKES

Sources J. Wood, *The believer's committing of his soul to Christ considered: in a funeral sermon occasioned by the death of the late Reverend Mr. Joseph Hill who departed this life Jan. 21 1728/9, preach'd at Haberdasher's Hall, February 9th* (1729) · A. Gordon, ed., *Freedom after ejection: a review (1690–1692) of presbyterian and congregational nonconformity in England and Wales* (1917), 284, 290, 360 · W. Wilson, *The history and antiquities of the dissenting churches and meeting houses in London, Westminster and Southwark*, 4 vols. (1808–14), vol. 3, pp. 138–

9; vol. 4, p. 44 · J. Toulmin, *An historical view of the state of the protest-ant dissenters in England* (1814), 572 · E. Calamy, *An historical account of my own life, with some reflections on the times I have lived in, 1671–1731*, ed. J. T. Rutt, 2nd edn, 1 (1830), 348; 2 (1830), 522–3 · J. Evans, 'List of dissenting congregations and ministers in England and Wales, 1715–1729', DWL, MS 38.4, p. 71 · 'A view of the dissenting interest in London of the Presbyterian and Independent denominations, from the year 1695 to the 25 of December 1731, with a postscript of the present state of the Baptists', DWL, MS 38.18, pp. 49, 90 · K. L. Sprunger, *Dutch puritanism: a history of English and Scottish churches of the Netherlands in the sixteenth and seventeenth centuries* (1982), 428 · W. Steven, *The history of the Scottish church, Rotterdam* (1832, 1833), 335 · will, proved, 21 March 1729, PRO, PROB 11/628, sig. 75

Archives BL, letters to Sir William Turnbull

Wealth at death see will, PRO, PROB 11/628, sig. 75

Hill, Joseph Sidney (1851–1894), missionary and bishop in Africa, was born at Barnack, near Stamford, Northamptonshire, on 1 December 1851, son of Henry Hill, builder, who died at the age of twenty-five; his mother, a domestic servant, accepted help to send him to the Orphan Working School, Haverstock Hill, London, when he was nine. He was deeply affected by the death of a friend (whose surname, Sidney, he added to his own as a Christian name) and he determined to become a missionary. He applied to the Church Missionary Society (CMS), entered its preparatory institution at Reading in 1872, and proceeded to its college at Islington, London, in 1874. Hill was made a deacon by the bishop of London in 1876, and shortly afterwards, on 31 July 1876, he married Lucilla (d. 1894), daughter of Thomas Leachman, and proceeded to Lagos in west Africa. Within a few months he and his wife became seriously ill and they were forced to return to England.

Hill next served as a curate in Richmond, Surrey, for a year before being sent by the CMS to New Zealand. He was appointed to Wairoa, Hawke's Bay, and was ordained priest in 1879. He was to work among the Maori but had little support from his fellow missionaries and found the Maori language very difficult to master. He therefore applied to work in Auckland and resigned from the CMS in 1882. In Auckland he served mainly as a missionary and as a prison chaplain. He returned to England in 1890, again as a missionary, with the Revd W. Hay Aitken; the following year he offered to go to west Africa once again with the CMS.

The CMS's west African mission was in a state of crisis, brought on first by the actions of intolerant young European missionaries who condemned the leadership of Bishop Samuel Crowther and his fellow African clergy in the Niger delta. The missionaries had also attacked the CMS for its failure to back them in the way they thought appropriate, and the society pusillanimously conceded to many of their demands. However, Crowther then died, at the end of 1891. In this context it was inevitable that the west African church had a very strong commitment to Crowther's successor being an African, while the missionaries and their supporters in England had an equally strong conviction that he must be a European. The latter won the day, and in 1892 Hill was their choice.

Hill was widely acceptable, having many of the personal qualities required to deal with the intensity of feeling in England and in west Africa, where there was now a danger

that a church independent of Anglican structures might be created. Archbishop Benson, who was far more sympathetic to the African perspective than the CMS, insisted that Hill went to west Africa, as his commissary, prior to his consecration, to investigate the situation and to find two African assistant bishops. Hill did so in 1892, and he produced a fair-minded report which steered a middle course between the CMS (by then in effect anti-African) and the west Africans. His consecration, together with that of the two African assistant bishops he had chosen, followed on 29 June 1893. He left for west Africa in November 1893, but on 6 January 1894 he died of blackwater fever, in Lagos, where he was buried. His wife died the next day and four other missionaries died within a fortnight.

Hill's successor was another Englishman, Herbert Tugwell (1855–1936), whose nomination and consecration were pushed through with great and unusual haste in order to reduce the build-up of new pressure for the appointment of an African. This appointment was much resented in west Africa and the CMS became even more distrustful of non-European leadership. Tugwell, however, was often at variance with the CMS. Instead he came to see the need for, and the propriety of, African oversight at every level in the church.   C. Peter Williams

Sources *Register of missionaries (clerical, lay and female) and native clergy, 1840–1909*, Church Missionary Society (privately circulated, [n.d.]) · R. E. Faulkner, *Joseph Sidney Hill, first bishop in western equatorial Africa* (1895) · E. Stock, *The history of the Church Missionary Society*, 3 vols. (1899) · C. P. Williams, *The ideal of the self-governing church: a study in Victorian missionary strategy* (1990)

Archives LPL | U. Birm., Church Missionary Society archives

Hill, Sir Leonard Erskine (1866–1952), physiologist, third son of George Birkbeck Norman *Hill (1835–1903) and his wife, Annie (1837/8–1902), daughter of Edward Scott, was born at Bruce Castle, Lordship Lane, Tottenham, Middlesex, on 2 June 1866, where his father was schoolmaster. His two elder brothers were Sir Maurice *Hill, the judge, and Sir Arthur Norman Hill, an authority on shipping problems. His great-grandfather was T. W. Hill and great-uncles were Sir Rowland Hill and Matthew Davenport Hill. Hill was educated at Haileybury, where his studies were centred on the classics and general literature, with little in mathematics and nothing in experimental science, but he appears to have had some success at rugby football. Hill's own wish was to be a farmer, but he accepted his parents' choice of medicine, entering University College, London, for the preliminary science stage of its curriculum. He was stimulated by Ray Lankester's teaching of zoology, but considered that there was insufficient physics and chemistry for his later needs as a physiologist. He duly qualified in medicine in 1889, became MB (London) in 1890, and was house surgeon for a year at University College Hospital. He married, on 18 September 1891, Janet (1867/8–1956), daughter of Frederick Alexander, a bank clerk; they had four sons and two daughters.

Hill then decided in favour of an academic career in physiology, and returned with a Sharpey scholarship to University College, under Professor E. A. Schafer, where he collaborated with John Rose Bradford and William Bayliss. His own initiative led to important studies of intracranial pressure, blood flow in the brain, and the effects of gravity on the general circulation. Hill began these at University College, partly with Bayliss, and continued them with H. L. Barnard and others at the London Hospital, where he was appointed lecturer on physiology in 1895, and was to become professor when the chair was instituted, but not until 1912. With Barnard he devised several sphygmomanometers to measure, by means of an inflated cuff round the arm and a small pressure gauge, the flow of blood at the wrist. These researches on problems of the circulation provided the theme of his book *The Physiology and Pathology of the Cerebral Circulation* (1896), based on his Hunterian lectures, and in 1900 he contributed the section on the circulation of the blood to the comprehensive *Text Book of Physiology*, edited by Schafer.

In the early 1900s Hill became engaged, with J. J. R. Macleod and M. Greenwood, in an investigation of the measures required for the safe decompression of divers and others who had been exposed to high air pressures. Another study of the same problem was being undertaken for the Admiralty by J. S. Haldane, with J. G. Priestley at Oxford and A. E. Boycott at the Lister Institute. There was agreement in confirming the earlier suggestion of Paul Bert, who had attributed the dangerous symptoms of sudden or rapid decompression to the release of bubbles of nitrogen in the blood-vessels and the tissues. A rather long controversy ensued, however, concerning the best method of avoiding this—the slow, continuous decompression favoured by Hill's team, or the less tedious, stagewise procedure of Haldane and his associates. The principle of Haldane's method proved, in the end, to be the better, but its application was improved in important detail by data provided by Hill and his team.

Hill accepted in 1914 the offer of appointment as head of a department of applied physiology, in the projected National Institute for Medical Research, and he took office early in July of that year. The aims of such a department were obviously congenial to one who combined such ability in the design of simple but adequate methods for obtaining sound physiological data with so conspicuous an interest in the application of these to medical uses, and especially to the maintenance of the conditions of normal health. The almost immediate outbreak of war gave an unusual scope and direction to research enterprises of this kind. After the war, until his retirement in 1930, Hill and his department were engaged in a range of researches, largely designed to determine the significance and the modes of action of fresh air and sunshine in promoting the general health of mankind. His 'Katathermometer', exhibited at the Royal Society's conversazione of 1913, embodied a characteristically simple but effective device for measuring efficiency of ventilation. His colleague T. A. Webster made an important contribution to the discovery, then in progress at the institute, of vitamin D as a product of the ultraviolet irradiation of ergosterol. In general this final period of sixteen years gave Hill the opportunity of designing, advocating, and supervising

practical applications of knowledge which he had gathered and interpreted during the preceding twenty-two years of active experimental research, largely concerned with the physiology of the circulatory and respiratory systems.

Hill's interests and abilities extended to more than one of the arts. He wrote two story-books for children which were published and well received, and, among those who knew them, his paintings in oils, watercolour and pastel, including landscapes, portraits, and studies of animals, were highly esteemed and were shown at a private exhibition. For some reason they were specially admired by Japanese visitors, who came to know them through his friendship with a Japanese artist with the result that there were three successful exhibitions of his paintings in Japan. In Britain he became the first president of a Medical Art Society.

Hill was elected FRS in 1900 and was knighted in 1930. He was an honorary LLD of Aberdeen, a fellow of University College, London, and an honorary ARIBA. He received the gold medal of the Institution of Mining Engineers in recognition of the value of his work for the ventilation of mines, the Harben medal of the Royal Institute of Public Health and Hygiene, and the Sidey medal of the Royal Society of New Zealand for his work on the significance of solar radiation for human health and comfort. He acted as an adviser to the medical organizations of all three armed services. Hill's third son, Sir Austin Bradford *Hill FRS (1897–1991), became honorary director of the statistical research unit of the Medical Research Council and professor of medical statistics in the University of London. The younger daughter, Nannette, married Dr W. A. R. Thomson, editor of *The Practitioner*. Hill died at his home, Field Cottage, Corton, near Lowestoft, on 30 March 1952, and was buried in Corton churchyard.   H. H. DALE, *rev.*

Sources C. G. Douglas, *Obits. FRS*, 8 (1952–3), 431–43 · personal knowledge (1971) · *BMJ* (5 April 1952), 767–8 · *The Lancet* (12 April 1952), 771–2 · *ILN* (12 April 1952), 614 · *New York Times* (1 April 1952), 29 · *WWW* · A. B. Hill and B. Hill, 'The life of Sir Leonard Erskine Hill FRS, 1866–1952', *Proceedings of the Royal Society of Medicine*, 61 (1968), 307–16 · L. E. Hill, *Philosophy of a biologist* (1930) · W. J. O'Connor, *British physiologists, 1885–1914* (1991), 276–9 · *The Times* (1 April 1952), 8f · *The Times* (24 April 1952), 6f · *The Times* (3 May 1952), 8b · b. cert. · m. cert. · d. cert.
Archives Wellcome L., corresp. with Sir Edward Sharpey-Schafer
Likenesses W. Stoneman, photograph, 1933, NPG
Wealth at death £15,307 1s. 8d.: probate, 28 July 1952, *CGPLA Eng. & Wales*

Hill, Leonard Raven- (1867–1942), illustrator and cartoonist, was born at 18 New Bond Street, Bath, Somerset, on 10 March 1867, the son of William Hill, a master umbrella maker, and his wife, Anne Scott. He was educated as a day boy at the old Bristol grammar school and afterwards went to the Devon county school. He proceeded to study at the Lambeth School of Art, working side by side with C. Ricketts and C. Shannon, and later at the Académie Julian under W.-A. Bouguereau and with Aimé Morot (1885–7) in Paris. He exhibited paintings at the Salon, the Royal Academy, the New English Art Club, and the Royal

Leonard Raven-Hill (1867–1942), self-portrait

Society of Painters in Water Colours, but his own inclination led him towards pen-and-ink work. Raven-Hill served as a volunteer with the 2nd Wiltshire voluntary battalion which provided plenty of pictorial copy and which accounts for some of the insights in his drawing during the war.

Raven-Hill became a regular contributor of joke cartoons, theatrical caricatures, and illustrations to a variety of publications including *Black & White*, *The Idler*, the *Pall Mall Magazine*, and the *Windsor Magazine*—his career coincided with new methods of mechanical reproduction and the proliferation of 'light papers'. In 1890 he was appointed the art editor of *Pick-Me-Up* and was largely responsible for its success, and became a founder joint editor of the *Butterfly* (1893) which ranked high among the artistic periodicals. He was a celebrated draughtsman when his first drawing in *Punch* appeared on 28 December 1895. In 1889 Raven-Hill married Annie (d. 1922), daughter of Mark Rogers, a woodcarver. Following her death, he married in 1923 Marion Jean Lyon (d. 1940), for a number of years the able advertisement editor of *Punch*.

Raven-Hill joined the *Punch* staff and table, which he duly initialled, in 1901 on the same evening that Sir John Tenniel appeared at it for the last time, and he became a political cartoonist on the death of E. Linley Sambourne in 1910. He was second cartoonist (1910–35) to Sir Bernard Partridge, producing some notable work at a time when *Punch* was a national institution. He excelled in vitality

and energy of line, and was never so pleased as when called upon to represent a scene of violent action at the shortest possible notice. If, as sometimes happened, his design for a *Punch* cartoon proved unsatisfactory, he was willing, and even pleased, to draw an entirely different one on the same morning. He considered the political cartoon more serious, requiring careful thought, classical treatment, and considerable pains in draughtsmanship. Among the favourite subjects of his social cartoons were East End Jews, London street scenes, bridge players, deer-stalking, and motor-car incidents. He illustrated several books including *Stalky and Co.* for Kipling, and *Kipps* for H. G. Wells, to the complete satisfaction of both authors. His own publications include *The Promenaders* (1894), *Our Battalion* (1902), and *An Indian Sketch-Book* (1904). He was convivial, irascible, and often inarticulate in speech as he was eloquent with his pen. Failing eyesight and his health generally forced his retirement. Raven-Hill's earlier social cartoons, influenced by Charles Keene, evince an original sense of humour and strong powers of characterization but his reputation is inextricably linked to his long association with *Punch*. He died at Ryde, Isle of Wight, on 31 March 1942. Examples of his drawings are in the *Punch* archive and library, the British Museum and the Victoria and Albert Museum, London, and Birmingham City Art Gallery. E. V. KNOX, *rev.* SIMON TURNER

Sources *Punch*, 202 (1942), 295 • J. Pennell, *Pen drawing and pen draughtsmen* (1889), 340–41 • G. White, 'How a comic illustrator works: a chat with Mr. L. Raven-Hill', *Idler Magazine*, 8/44 (1895), 125–32 • R. G. G. Price, *A history of Punch* (1957), 217–18 • S. Appelbaum and R. Kelly, eds., *Great drawings and illustrations from 'Punch', 1841–1901* (1981) • b. cert. • M. H. Spielmann, 'Our graphic humourists: L. Raven Hill', *Magazine of Art*, 19 (1895–6), 493–7 • G. Meggy, 'Masters of black and white III: Mr. L. Raven-Hill', *Pearson's Magazine*, 22/127 (1906), 96–103 • J. A. Hamerton, *Humorists of the pencil* (1905) • *Punch* Archive, London

Archives *Punch* Archive and Library, London, letters, paper clippings, and original drawings

Likenesses M. Grieffenhagen, oils, 1927, Art Gallery and Museum, Glasgow • L. Raven-Hill, self-portrait (*I am starving*), *Punch* Archive, London • L. Raven-Hill, self-portrait, repro. in *The Year's Art* (1895) • L. Raven-Hill, self-portrait, pencil drawing, NPG [*see illus.*]

Hill, (Edward Bernard) Lewin (1834–1915), civil servant, was born on 13 January 1834 at Bruce Castle, Tottenham, the first of the four children of Arthur Hill (1798–1885), schoolmaster, and his wife, Ellen Tilt (1807–1839), daughter of Samuel Maurice and his wife, Theodosia. Two younger brothers were George Birkbeck Norman *Hill and John Edward Gray Hill. He was always known by his third name, Lewin, and was educated at his father's school, Bruce Castle. He entered the secretary's department at the Post Office as a supplementary clerk in 1855, where his uncle, Rowland *Hill, had become secretary the preceding year. There he stayed for forty-three years, becoming head of the establishments branch; at the time of his retirement in 1899 he was senior assistant secretary, the fourth most senior person in the organization, not counting the political appointment of postmaster-general. He was appointed CB in the jubilee honours of 1897.

Hill was recorded as having been 'a man with a strong personality and not afraid to champion unpopular policies … he frequently expressed his opinion with a freedom to which we are unaccustomed in officials of high position. He must often have been an embarrassing colleague.' Quite early in life he was handicapped by the loss of a limb but 'it was marvellous how little this misfortune interfered with his activities' (*St Martin's-le-Grand*, 1915, 199). Of untiring activity and possessing ripe experience, he was involved in a great variety of behind-the-scenes tasks, as a member or chairman of committees and with extensive roving commissions, yet he was little known to those outside the Post Office. It seems a pity that, as he himself recorded in print (in his preface to *Verse, Prose and Epitaphs*), when asked by a relative for a statement of what he had accomplished, all he offered was 'During my long service I have made many mistakes, all of which have been good-naturedly overlooked by my Chiefs.'

On 8 April 1863 Hill married Mary Emmeline (*b*. 1841/2), daughter of William Webb Venn, a notary public. They had two sons and two daughters, but their later life was saddened by the suicide of their younger son in 1896, following an illness that had affected his brain. Hill's *Verse, Prose and Epitaphs* (1908) consisted of a selection of entries from his commonplace book. He lived mainly in the neighbourhood of Kingston upon Thames and following retirement became a magistrate there in 1900. In 1901 he paid a visit to the United States and reported its inhabitants as 'a very remarkable people, and ahead of the English in everything but manners, in which they were sadly lacking' (*St Martin's-le-Grand*, 1901, 210). In 1905 he went to live at Maldon, Essex, where he made an effort to convince his new neighbours that their method of observing Sunday was unhistorical and irrational—'He would not be our Mr Hill if he did not speak out his mind' (*St Martin's-le-Grand* 1905, 213). He returned to the London suburbs, to live in Bromley, Kent, where aged eighty he was reported to be 'full of fun and animal spirits' (*St Martin's-le-Grand* 1914, 194). He died at 30 Applegarth Road, Hammersmith, London, on 3 March 1915. He was buried in Hammersmith cemetery.   I. D. HILL

Sources *WWW* · *St Martin's-le-Grand* [Post Office magazine], 2 (1892); 5 (1895); 7 (1897); 9 (1899); 10 (1900); 11 (1901); 15 (1905); 24 (1914); 25 (1915) · *Kingston and Surbiton News* (5 Dec 1896) · *Maldon Express* (11 March 1905) · *Maldon Express* (18 March 1905) · *Maldon Express* (25 March 1905) · *Maldon Express* (8 April 1905) · *Maldon Express* (17 June 1905) · E. B. L. Hill, *Verse, prose and epitaphs* (1908) · m. cert. · d. cert.

Likenesses portrait, repro. in *St Martin's-le-Grand* (1892) · portrait, repro. in *St Martin's-le-Grand* (1895) · portrait, repro. in *St Martin's-le-Grand* (1914)

Wealth at death £2709 15*s*. 11*d*.: probate, 17 April 1915, *CGPLA Eng. & Wales*

Hill [*née* Sandys], **Mary, marchioness of Downshire and** *suo jure* **Baroness Sandys of Ombersley** (1764–1836), landowner and politician, was born on 19 September 1764, the daughter and heir of Colonel Martin Sandys (*c*.1729–1768), and his wife, Mary (*d*. 1769), daughter and heir of William Trumbull of Easthampstead Park, Berkshire and his wife, Mary Blundell, daughter and heir of Montague,

Viscount Blundell. Following the deaths of her parents, her uncle Edwin Sandys, second Baron Sandys of Ombersley (1726–1797), was probably responsible for her upbringing, in collaboration with her maternal grandmother Mary, who in 1762 married Lord Robert Bertie. On 29 June 1786 at her grandmother's house in Mortimer Street, Cavendish Square, London, she married Arthur Hill (1753–1801), then styled Lord Kilwarlin but from 1789 earl of Hillsborough and from 1793 second marquess of Downshire, son and heir of Wills Hill, first marquess of Downshire, and his wife, Margaretta Fitzgerald, sister of James Fitzgerald, first duke of Leinster. Her father-in-law described the 21-year-old as 'a genteel, agreeable little girl, not a beauty but as nearly being so as a wise man would choose his wife to be, of a cheerful, sweet disposition' (Malcomson, 36–7). Furthermore, as contemporaries were quick to remark, Mary brought to the match 'a great accession of fortune and interest in the county of Down besides a considerable estate in this kingdom [Great Britain]' (T. Orde to the duke of Rutland, 14 June 1786, GEC, *Peerage*). This included the Trumbull estate of Easthampstead Park, Berkshire, convenient for London and Windsor, and the Blundell estates at Edenderry in King's county (14,000 acres) and Dundrum, co. Down (5000 acres) through her paternal grandmother, although until 1799 both Irish properties were in the hands of her maternal grandmother, Lady Robert Bertie. Her husband was an inferior politician to his father, but the Hill family retained their influence in London politics through her sister-in-law Mary *Cecil, marchioness of Salisbury, the Pittite hostess.

The marriage was happy and the couple had five sons and two daughters, the last son delivered three months after the marquess died (of gout of the stomach, on 7 September 1801, aged forty-eight). Lady Downshire attributed the cause of his death to the mental strain engendered by his dismissal from the post of lord lieutenant of co. Down and the division of his regiment, the Downshire militia, into two parts with a consequent diminution of his patronage and the dismissal of his friends and supporters from official posts. This was his punishment for refusing to support the Act of Union with Great Britain in 1800. Her anger was not abated by the £55,000 compensation for the family's disenfranchised boroughs which helped to pay off some of her late husband's debts. Much of her ire was focused on the Stewart family, fellow co. Down landlords who had first started to challenge the Hills for control of the county electorate in 1790. Their effective head was Robert Stewart, Viscount Castlereagh, one of the main protagonists of the Act of Union.

During her son's minority Lady Downshire administered the family estate, which in 1801 had a gross income of £30,000, and focused her energies on trouncing the Stewarts in the co. Down polls. In 1802 she agreed to an uncontested election in exchange for a United Kingdom peerage under her uncle's title, becoming Baroness Sandys of Ombersley, but in 1805, when Castlereagh was compelled to stand for re-election after he accepted the post of secretary of state for the colonies and the war department in Pitt's administration, she openly opposed him as he was an 'inveterate enemy of her family' (Lady Downshire's memorandum, 23 July 1805, Adams MSS, priv. coll.). Notices were placed in the local papers to this effect and the election became the subject of London gossip and newspaper reports. Lady Downshire made a tour of co. Down, visiting farmhouses and beseeching wives and sweethearts to exhort their menfolk to vote for Colonel John Meade, her chosen candidate. In return she received an ovation in Downpatrick during the poll. Meade's victory was considered a personal triumph for the marchioness.

From the close of the election until her son's twenty-first birthday Lady Downshire spent the greater part of each year at Hillsborough Castle, the family's co. Down seat—a marked contrast to her former husband's predilection for England. There she gained a reputation as a beneficent landlord. As well as individual acts of kindness, in 1804 she granted land and £50 towards the building of a chapel for the local Roman Catholic population. In order to forward her political influence she purchased the estate of a Miss Mauleverer at Downpatrick in 1805 for £17,450, and the Lyndon estate at Carrickfergus in 1807 for £29,000. She also instituted a practice of granting direct leases to subtenants on the estate, again to enhance the number of freeholders and potential voters. Between 1805 and 1807, 486 one-life leases were granted by her and by 1809 there were 1510 tenancies, only 880 of which were long term. This amounted to 30,000 freeholders and was famously described by T. H. B. Oldfield in his *Representative History of Great Britain and Ireland* (1816) as 'the best specimen of political agronomy to be found in Ireland' (Oldfield, 227).

In 1809 Lady Downshire's eldest son, Arthur Blundell Sandys Trumbull Hill, third marquess of Downshire (1788–1855), attained his majority. On succeeding to his property he made it his priority to clear the estate of his father's and grandfather's debts as well as the £34,000 in bond and judgement debts accrued by his mother. In order to do so he agreed in 1812 to share henceforward the county seats with the Stewart family, much to Lady Downshire's disgust. Mary retired to England where she was responsible for renovating the parish church of Ombersley in Worcestershire. She retained a two-thirds interest in the Edenderry and Dundrum estates, although her son had their entire management, and received a jointure of £5000. Her son's correspondence also suggests that she continued to take an interest in co. Down politics. She died on 1 August 1836, after a long illness, at Downshire House, Roehampton, Surrey. Her barony had been created with a special remainder in favour of her younger sons, and so she was succeeded by her second son, Arthur Moyses William Hill (1792–1860), as second Baron Sandys, and then by her third son, Arthur Marcus Cecil Hill (1798–1863). They also inherited the Ombersley estate. £500,000 in portions was also payable to her younger children in 1837. ROSEMARY RICHEY

Sources GEC, *Peerage* · W. A. Maguire, *The Downshire estates in Ireland, 1801–1845: the management of Irish landed estates in the early nineteenth century* (1972) · H. McCall, *The house of Downshire* (1880) · A. P. W. Malcomson, *The pursuit of the heiress: aristocratic marriage in Ireland, 1750–1820* (1982) · P. Jupp, 'Co. Down elections, 1783–1831', *Irish Historical Studies*, 18 (1972–3), 177–206 · W. A. Maguire, *Letters of a great Irish landlord* (1974) · T. H. B. Oldfield, *The representative history of Great Britain and Ireland*, 6 vols. (1816), vol. 6 · J. Barry, *Hillsborough: a parish in the Ulster plantation* (1962) · P. J. Jupp, 'County Down', HoP, *Commons, 1790–1820*, 2.642–4
Archives Berks. RO, family MSS, D/ED, D/EZ 88, D/EZ 91 | priv. coll., Adams MSS · PRO NIre., D607, D671, D2784/23
Wealth at death £5000 p.a. jointure on Downshire estate; Edenderry estate, King's county, Ireland, 14,000 acres; Dundrum estate, co. Down, Ireland; Easthampstead Park, Berkshire: Maguire, *Downshire estates*

Hill, Matthew Davenport (1792–1872), penal reformer, was born on 6 August 1792 at Suffolk Street, Birmingham, the eldest of the eight children of Thomas Wright *Hill (1763–1851), schoolmaster, and his wife, Sarah Lea (1765–1842). Two of his five brothers attained professional eminence: Rowland *Hill (1795–1879), postal reformer, and Frederic *Hill (1803–1896), inspector of prisons. Two other brothers had successful, if more obscure, careers: Edwin *Hill (1793–1876), civil servant, and Arthur Hill (1798–1885), schoolmaster. Hill's mother was the daughter of a factory worker. His father, a convert to Unitarianism, bought a school of his own in 1803 which, in 1819, after one earlier move, was transferred to Hazelwood in Hagley Road, on the outskirts of Birmingham.

Education, marriage, and early career Hill was educated at Wolverhampton and in his father's schools. As the eldest son of an impecunious schoolmaster, he was expected to shoulder responsibility at an early age. By 1804 he was teaching others; at the age of sixteen he was principal teacher. From about 1816 he and his brother Rowland, having become disenchanted with their father's educational ideas and methods, launched a series of reforms with the aim of making Hill Top (as it was known from 1804 to 1819) 'a thoroughly good school'. These reforms included changes in the curriculum, for which Matthew was chiefly responsible, and the creation of an entirely new disciplinary structure, the effect of which was to place real responsibility for running the school in the hands of the pupils. These reforms were described in *Plans for the Government and Liberal Instruction of Boys in Large Numbers* (1822), which was re-issued in 1825 with *Public Education* prefixed to the title. Though published anonymously, this was probably written by Hill. The book, which was widely and favourably reviewed, won Hazelwood the admiration of Jeremy Bentham, with whom Hill became friendly; Hill also acquired an international reputation, and a large influx of new pupils.

On 11 July 1814 Hill entered Lincoln's Inn, thereby becoming the first person from Birmingham to go to the bar. For several years he continued to live at Hill Top, owing to his inability to support himself in London. In 1816 he began to keep terms, but it was not until 1818 that he finally left the family home. While studying the law Hill supported himself by teaching and journalism,

Matthew Davenport Hill (1792–1872), by Charles Henry Jeens, 1878

reporting parliamentary proceedings for the *Morning Herald* and the *Sunday Review*; the latter was a weekly journal which Hill ran with two friends, John and Samuel Steer. In his teens Hill had been a regular contributor to the *Midland Chronicle*. The comparative poverty and inactivity of Hill's early years as a barrister encouraged him to continue his literary activities, and he contributed to Charles Knight's *Quarterly Magazine* under the pseudonyms of William Payne and Martin Danvers Heaviside.

On 3 November 1819 Hill married Margaret Bucknall, the elder daughter of a Kidderminster brewer. They had six children. These included Florence Davenport *Hill (1828/9–1919) [*see under* Hill, Rosamond Davenport], a poor-law reformer; Alfred Hill (1821–1907), registrar in the Birmingham court of bankruptcy; Rosamond Davenport *Hill (1825–1902), a member of the London school board and a juvenile reformatory activist; Matthew Hill (1834–1892), professor of clinical surgery at University College, London; and Joanna Margaret *Hill (1836/7–1901) [*see under* Hill, Rosamond Davenport], who was also actively involved in social issues. Until 1851, when they moved to Bristol, the Hills lived in or near London, including in Chancery Lane, Chelsea, Hampstead Heath, and Haverstock Hill.

Hill was called to the bar on 18 November 1819. He took chambers at 44 Chancery Lane and joined the midland circuit. As a young lawyer he was associated with several notable cases, including *R. v. Borron*, an action arising out of the Peterloo massacre. In 1820 he represented John Cartwright, founder of the London Corresponding Society, and Jane Carlile, when she was prosecuted for selling seditious literature. Hill won the reputation of a champion of radical political causes, representing the rioters at Nottingham during the Reform Bill crisis (1831), and the Rebecca rioters in south Wales (1843). However, while Hill

emphasized his radicalism when it suited him to do so, and was one of the early supporters of women's enfranchisement, he was no revolutionary. Later, as an MP, he described himself as being 'of Whig principles inclined to radicalism' (*Dod's Parliamentary Companion*). In line with the whigs, he advocated parliamentary reform as a means of averting revolution. He favoured universal suffrage only in the distant future, accepted without question the guilt of the Tolpuddle martyrs, and criticized trades unionism as 'the parent of unnumbered evils'. In 1848 he enrolled as a special constable to combat the Chartist threat.

Educational and political activities After severing links with his family's school, Hill's educational interests centred upon Henry Brougham's Society for the Diffusion of Useful Knowledge (SDUK). He was present at the society's inaugural meeting and remained an active member until its demise in 1846. Hill conceived the idea for the *Penny Magazine*, the SDUK's most successful publication, which at its height attained a circulation of approximately 200,000 copies per issue.

Hill was elected MP for Hull in December 1832, his candidacy having been sponsored by various leading whigs and radicals, including Lord Althorp and Thomas Attwood. Although he spoke on a range of subjects, including religious toleration, the colonization of South Australia, the abolition of 'taxes on knowledge', and electoral and criminal law reform, his political career was blighted by his injudicious allegation, subsequently retracted, that the Irish MP Richard Lalor Sheil was publicly opposing a coercion bill while privately supporting it. In the general election of January 1835, Hill finished bottom of the poll—a victim, he insisted, of tory bribery. He never stood for parliament again.

Penal and criminal law reformer In 1834 Brougham, the lord chancellor, appointed Hill a king's counsel with a patent of precedence. Hill thereupon gave up work at the criminal bar; for several years his most lucrative field of practice was the presentation and defence of election petitions before committees of the House of Commons. He also appeared in the *habeas corpus* case of the Canadian prisoners (1838–9), and for many years he represented Baron De Bode in his fruitless efforts to secure compensation for family property confiscated during the French Revolution. In May 1839, at an annual salary of £300 (increased to £400 a few years before his retirement in 1866), Hill was appointed recorder of Birmingham. He soon became embroiled in a bitter dispute with the town council over the court's conduct and management; this dispute was to continue for some sixteen years. More importantly, for more than a quarter of a century the recordership provided Hill with a public platform from which, through his addresses or charges to grand juries, he could air his views, particularly on matters of penal and criminal law reform. Many of these charges were collected and published as *Suggestions for the Repression of Crime* (1857). They, more than anything else, established Hill's reputation as a 'criminologist' and penal reformer.

Hill was not an original thinker. Rather, he was a significant adapter, synthesizer, and publicist of others' ideas. Hill's penological views were much influenced by Alexander Maconochie, whose 'mark system' was based on the notion of prisoners earning their release not by serving a pre-determined period of confinement but by gaining, through labour, a prescribed number of 'marks'. Hill was instrumental in Maconochie's appointment to the governorship of Birmingham gaol (1849–51). After Maconochie's dismissal, Hill became chief spokesman for the 'mark system'. Under the influence of Walter Crofton, chairman of the directors of the Irish convict prisons, and others, Hill modified Maconochie's ideas, which themselves were not wholly original, into a scheme for indefinite confinement, release from which, if it came at all, would be earned through reformation alone. Most prisoners would pass through various stages before release, commencing with a period of severe treatment, which might include chaining, solitary confinement, and corporal punishment, and concluding, several stages later, with release on licence and post-release assistance. Recidivists, serious offenders, and those who showed no signs of reform would be imprisoned for life in high-security gaols with no prospect of release, their morale sustained simply through the prospect of improving their conditions through good conduct.

Hill's penal and criminological ideas have been termed harsh but they were more a combination of severity and enlightenment. Although he favoured the incarceration of suspected thieves who were unable to prove legitimate means of support—a proposal which, when it was made in 1850 and again in 1851, excited a great deal of largely hostile press attention—he felt that minor offences, such as garden robbery by juveniles, should attract no punishment. He also believed some first offenders could be placed on probation, that juveniles should be neither flogged nor transported, that some prisoners should gain early release on licence, and that former prisoners should receive aftercare. As recorder he was able to put some of these ideas into practice. His practical reforms included participation in the formation of two discharged prisoners' aid societies: in Birmingham in 1856 and in Bristol in 1864.

Whether advocating leniency or severity, Hill was guided by three principles: first, that the object of criminal jurisprudence should be the reduction of crime to the lowest possible amount, the treatment of the criminal being a means to an end, not an end in itself; second, that retribution should not be a consideration in the punishment of the offender; and third, that since the deterrence of offenders was uncertain the object of punishment should be the prevention of re-offending, either through reformation or by incapacitation, including capital punishment and permanent incarceration. It followed that he sought to assist those who genuinely wished to reform, but to punish ruthlessly recidivists, those who broke faith with the trust placed in them, and those who showed no inclination to reform.

Transportation Hill played a prominent part in the controversy over the early release of convicts on so-called 'tickets-of-leave' or licences. In place of transportation to the colonies the Penal Servitude Act of 1853 provided for the initial subjection of prisoners to a harsh discipline, the severity of which would be progressively relaxed, subject to good behaviour, as the sentence proceeded. The final stage, ostensibly reserved for those who gave evidence of reformation, was early release on licence. In 1855 Hill, though a strong supporter of the ticket-of-leave principle, criticized the indiscriminate and lax way in which the licensing was administered by Joshua Jebb, chairman of the directors of convict prisons. It was revealed that Hill himself had passed excessively long sentences of penal servitude on offenders who had no chance of early release. Two years later, he criticized the Penal Servitude Act of 1857, which established definitively that those sentenced to penal servitude were entitled to early release, and which also allowed for the release on licence of some convicts after only thirty months in confinement. He accused Jebb and the home secretary, Sir George Grey, of thereby 'sapping the vitals of reformatory treatment'. The garrotting panic of the early 1860s produced a public outcry against tickets-of-leave, a backlash against reformatory treatment, and an era of harshness in penal policy. By 1862 Hill was complaining to Brougham that 'it is next to impossible to obtain a hearing on the subject of reformatory treatment' (Brougham MSS).

Juvenile reforms On the basis that 'evil courses are less painful to break through in youth than in age', Hill particularly concerned himself with the problems of juvenile crime and punishment. As recorder he witnessed a cycle of juvenile crime, conviction, confinement, release, and re-offence. He favoured two strategies as a means of breaking the cycle: probation and institutional reformatory care. As counsel at the Warwick sessions Hill had seen an embryonic probation scheme in action. It had involved the return of those who were not hardened criminals into the care of respectable and responsible parents and employers. In 1841 he introduced a refined version of the scheme in Birmingham, recruiting the assistance of the borough police to monitor its operation. Although the legality of probation was 'questioned in high quarters', Birmingham's police believed that probation was associated with encouraging rates of reformation. *The Spectator* (3 Jan 1844) described it as 'a sound principle of correctional discipline'. Encouraged, Hill urged adoption of the practice elsewhere, but when it was tried in Middlesex it failed owing to a shortage of surviving parents, co-operative employers, or responsible friends. In the 1850s, having used probation in over four hundred cases, Hill discarded it himself, preferring to send errant juveniles to reformatories.

Impressed by the results achieved by juvenile reformatories, especially at Mettray in France and Stretton-on-Dunsmoor in Warwickshire, Hill pressed for child offenders to be sent to institutions financed by a combination of public, parental, and charitable funds. To this end he campaigned on several fronts: in the press, in evidence to select committees, in correspondence with MPs, in charges to grand juries, and at conferences he had arranged with others of like mind. Above all, Hill made use of an extensive network of personal contacts to disseminate his views. One of those with whom he worked closely, especially after he moved to Bristol, was Mary Carpenter. Together they organized the influential reformatory school conferences which were held in Birmingham in 1851 and 1853. In the wake of the Birmingham gaol scandal, parliament passed the Youthful Offenders Act of 1854. This provided for Treasury and parental support for voluntary reformatory schools, to which juvenile offenders sentenced to at least fourteen days' imprisonment could be sent for periods of between two and six years. The measure did not meet all of Hill's objectives. He was particularly opposed to the preliminary punishment of offenders before transfer to a reformatory. But, as he informed Lord Brougham, he was willing to 'snatch at the present good within our reach and not indulge sickly taste for the Utopian' (Brougham MSS). Thereafter he did much to spread the reformatory ideal and press for swifter implementation of the 1854 act.

Other activities and interests, character, and death Hill was commissioner of the Bristol and district court of bankruptcy from 24 March 1851 to 31 December 1869, when the office was abolished. On accepting this post Hill withdrew from private legal practice; on relinquishing it he was granted a gratuity of £1800. An active temperance campaigner and supporter of co-operation, Hill was a co-founder of the Law Amendment Society (founded in 1844) and prominent in the National Association for the Promotion of Social Science (founded in 1857). Aside from the works already cited, Hill published numerous periodical articles and pamphlets, chiefly on legal and social questions. He edited *Remains of Thomas Wright Hill* (1859) and, with two of his daughters, *Our Exemplars Poor and Rich* (1861).

From his early twenties Hill was also a regular European traveller. On several occasions he toured Great Britain, Ireland, and the continent, including for the purpose of inspecting prisons and reformatories. In personality he appears to have been earnest, ambitious, pompous, and arrogant. In a sympathetic *Memoir* his daughters acknowledge his short temper, as did his brother Frederic. In appearance Hill was somewhat corpulent and, in later life, heavy-jowled. From early childhood he suffered poor health. He was subject to depression, which, unless he kept himself busy, brought on physical illness. In the 1860s ill health twice prevented him from giving oral evidence to select committees. His retirement in January 1866 from being recorder of Birmingham was occasioned by an attack of acute bronchitis. Hill's wife, Margaret, who had grown increasingly deaf with age, died on 31 October 1867. Hill himself died after a 'painful illness' (*The Times*), 'induced by failing strength, the result of old age' (*Law Journal*), at his home, Heath House, Stapleton, near Bristol, on 7 June 1872. He was buried next to his wife in Arnos Vale cemetery, Bristol.   P. W. J. BARTRIP

Sources R. Davenport-Hill and F. Davenport-Hill, *The recorder of Birmingham: a memoir of Matthew Davenport Hill* (1878) · P. W. J. Bartrip, 'The career of M. D. Hill with special reference to penal and educational reform movements in nineteenth-century Britain', PhD diss., U. Wales, 1975 · D. Gorham, 'Victorian reform as a family business: the Hill family', *The Victorian family: structure and stresses*, ed. A. S. Wohl (1978), 119–47 · *DNB* · F. Hill, *Frederic Hill: an autobiography of fifty years in times of reform*, ed. C. Hill (1894) · C. Knight, *Passages of a working life during half a century*, 3 vols. (1864–5) · G. B. Hill and R. Hill, *The life of Sir Rowland Hill, and, The history of penny postage*, 2 vols. (1880) · *Law Magazine*, 3rd ser., 1 (1872), 515–29 · *Law Journal* (15 June 1872), 418–20 · *Law Times* (15 June 1872), 128 · *The Times* (10 June 1872) · UCL, Brougham MSS · register of wills (1868)
Archives Bodl. Oxf., diary · UCL, SDUK MSS, letters to Society for the Diffusion of Useful Knowledge | UCL, corresp. with Lord Brougham
Likenesses woodcut, 1858, NPG · C. H. Jeens, engraving, 1878, repro. in Davenport-Hill and Davenport-Hill, *The recorder of Birmingham* [*see illus.*] · P. Hollins, bust, Birmingham council chambers · C. H. Jeens?, miniature, priv. coll. · portrait (after C. H. Jeens), repro. in Davenport-Hill and Davenport-Hill, *The recorder of Birmingham*
Wealth at death under £40,000 (in UK): probate, 24 July 1872, *CGPLA Eng. & Wales*

Hill, Sir (Edward) Maurice (1862–1934), judge, was born on 8 January 1862 at The Priory, Church Road, Tottenham, Middlesex, the eldest of the five sons of Sir George Birkbeck Norman *Hill (1835–1903), the literary scholar and editor of Johnson and Boswell, and his wife, Annie Scott (1837/8–1902). Among his younger brothers was Leonard Erskine *Hill. His great-uncle was Sir Rowland Hill, inventor of the penny post. Maurice Hill—he dropped his first forename, Edward—spent much of his childhood at Bruce Castle, Tottenham, at that time a rural suburb, where his grandfather had been and his father was headmaster of a school. Maurice himself was educated at Haileybury College. A diligent pupil, he won a classical exhibition to Balliol College, Oxford, where he graduated with first-class honours in classical moderations (1881) and *literae humaniores* (1884). In January 1888 he was called to the bar by the Inner Temple. On 27 August 1891 he married Susan Ellen Berta (1857/8–1924), fourth daughter of George Burgess Hadwen, silk mill owner, of Kebroyd, Halifax; they had two sons.

At the bar Hill built up a solid practice in commercial law. His speciality was shipping law, and particularly marine insurance, in which he had acquired the reputation of 'the greatest expert' by the time he was raised to the bench (*The Times*, 7 June 1934). In 1910 he took silk, which was granted by Lord Chancellor Loreburn. Politically, Hill was a Liberal, keenly interested in social reform and public affairs generally. He often spoke at political meetings.

Shortly before the First World War, with the help of his brother Sir (Arthur) Norman Hill (1863–1944), first baronet, a solicitor, and, like Maurice, a well-known adviser to the shipping community, Maurice Hill drafted the requisite legal forms for a scheme of state insurance designed to cover merchant shipping against war risks. Devised by a subcommittee of the committee of imperial defence, this timely scheme was implemented on 5 August 1914 and assuaged uncertainty and panic among shipowners and cargo-owners on the outbreak of war. In

November 1915 Hill, though much in demand as counsel in the prize court, gave up what was now a large practice in order to concentrate on further war work as chairman of the ship licensing committee, a body set up under the Board of Trade to regulate the flow of merchant shipping and to prevent its use for the import of non-essential goods. Under his chairmanship the committee's work 'proceeded smoothly and without friction' (Fayle, 159), but, as he repeatedly urged, its activities were palliative and quite incommensurate with the need to replace the huge amounts of tonnage lost to submarines. Its functions were subsumed, when Lloyd George became prime minister, by the newly created Ministry of Shipping. Hill received a knighthood in 1916 for his services.

On 18 January 1917 the incoming lord chancellor in the new administration, Lord Finlay, appointed Hill a judge of the Probate, Divorce, and Admiralty Division of the High Court in place of Mr Justice Bargrave Dean, who had resigned through ill health. Hill was elected a bencher of the Inner Temple. At that time Admiralty cases were handled by the president of the division and one puisne judge. The president was fully occupied by prize cases, which he alone heard, so that Hill spent nearly the whole of the first eight years of his judicial career trying the enormous volume of Admiralty cases brought on by the war. Submarine warfare, now at its height, raised a novel set of legal problems. The convoy system, involving zigzagging at full speed, without lights and often in fog, presented a constant succession of collision cases for Hill's determination. In *The Argol* (1918), where two merchant ships collided in the English Channel and one of them sank, he held that it was not unreasonable, having regard to the submarine peril, that both vessels had screened their regulation navigation lights, so that neither was to blame for the accident.

The Russian Revolution also led to Admiralty litigation. In *The Lomonosoff* (1921), the plaintiffs were allied officers detailed to serve with the white forces in northern Russia. They made off with the defendants' ship in Murmansk when that port fell to the Bolsheviks, and effected their escape under heavy fire. Hill ruled that although their first aim was to save their lives, this did not disqualify them for remuneration, for what they had done was analogous to rescuing the ship 'from pirates or mutineers, which this court has always recognised as the subject of salvage'. *The Jupiter* (1927) concerned the ownership of a ship arrested in a British port. The defendants, who claimed title as purchasers from the Soviet Union, relied on a declaration, issued by an accredited representative of the Soviet Union, that the ship had been nationalized in 1919 by virtue of a decree of the Bolshevik government. The point at issue was the legal effect of such a declaration in a case where the state concerned did not invoke sovereign immunity from jurisdiction. Hill ruled that the declaration was not conclusive of the question, and that the court was entitled to consider the evidence, a decision upheld by the Court of Appeal. He found as a fact that at the time of the decree of nationalization the ship was not

proved to have been within the jurisdiction of the Russian government, which therefore had no title to sell.

Between 1917 and 1924 Hill tried an extraordinary total of 1313 Admiralty cases, 308 of them in 1920 alone. Mindful of the consequences of delays in port while cases were heard, he strove to expedite the legal process and to get through his caseload without detriment to justice, sitting long hours and often on Saturdays. In 1924, under this heavy strain, compounded by the death of his wife, his health gave way. An additional judge was appointed to the division in 1925. By then the volume of Admiralty work had subsided, releasing into Hill's court an influx of probate, and more particularly of divorce cases, whose number rose steeply after the war and the Matrimonial Causes Act of 1923. Hill detested divorce work. Though he applied himself to it conscientiously and humanely, his sensitive nature and what Lord Wright called 'the puritan elements of his character' (*The Times*, 19 June 1934) recoiled from evidence of cruelty and from the type of sordid or intimate allegations inevitably aired in divorce proceedings. Notorious in this respect was the Ampthill succession case (*Russell* v. *Russell*, 1924), where the petitioner's proof of his wife's adultery was the birth of a child, together with his testimony that no marital intercourse had taken place. This was countered by his wife's evidence that she had conceived as a result of his 'Hunnish practices' (Graves and Hodge, 107). Hill made the heartfelt and much repeated quip that in his court he had 'one foot on sea and one in a sewer' (*The Times*, 7 June 1934), and press reporting of such details was prohibited by statute in 1926. Hill resigned from the bench in October 1930.

The most significant of Hill's judgments concerned the doctrine of sovereign immunity in relation to claims to exemption from legal liability by state-owned merchant ships. The twentieth century saw a large increase in the number of such vessels engaged in ordinary commercial trade. That a plea of sovereign immunity should relieve them from suit for loss or damage at the instance of private traders was anomalous and unfair, as Hill pointed out in *The Annette* (1919) and *The Porto Alexandre* (1920). 'A state in the mundane business of trading', he declared in *The Porto Alexandre*, 'must in fairness submit to the general rules applicable to traders: majesty cannot be asserted in the market place.' This restrictive view of sovereign immunity, though rejected by the Court of Appeal, was elaborated by Hill in a 'masterly paper' (*The Times*, 7 June 1934) published in the bulletin of the International Maritime Committee in 1923. His proposals were accepted by the committee's London conference that year and were incorporated in the Brussels convention in 1926. Another memorandum, drafted by Hill at the government's request, underlay article 379 of the treaty of Versailles, which anticipated general acceptance of the principle, subsequently embodied in the Maritime Ports Convention of 1923, that vessels of all flags should be treated in international ports 'on a footing of absolute equality'.

Hill was known for his impartiality, courtesy, and obvious desire to do justice. Though 'eminently a strong personality' and a man of high principle, whose outlook was 'infused with a Victorian seriousness' (*The Times*, 16 June 1934), he was unassuming, tolerant, and 'free from any kind of vanity or self-seeking' (*DNB*). He never strove for effect: the dignity of his court was assured by the obvious integrity of his character and 'the serenity of his temper' (*The Times*, 16 June 1934). He cited authority without show or parade, to such an extent, and no more, as was necessary to establish effectively and lucidly the determining points of law. Hill displayed great charm of manner and a quiet sense of humour. In one case a ship's captain, followed one by one in the witness-box by all of his eleven crewmen, swore solemnly to an event which was proved to be impossible. Instead of delivering himself of a homily on the evils of perjury, and a corresponding order for costs, Hill sat listening to these fabrications with 'a look of sympathetic amusement on his face'. He took the view that such collusion was 'part of a shore-going game' traditional among merchant seamen, whose first loyalty was to their skipper and their ship (*The Times*, 29 June 1934).

Hill was a particularly good judge of fact, an obvious advantage in a court of first instance. He never prejudged an issue, but gave every witness his due, though this might mean prolonging the hearing when other cases were pressing, and he made up his mind only after he had heard all the evidence. He was also known for a degree of informality on the bench unusual in those days. When he found the argument particularly interesting, he would discard his wig, flinging it on a corner of his desk. Absorbed in the intricacies of a submission, he listened, 'with his gown half-way down his back, seated sideways in his chair' (*The Times*, 29 June 1934), oblivious of the passing hours as point after point was raised for his inquisitive consideration, for 'there was no judicial problem against which he was unwilling to fairly measure his mind' (ibid.). Once he had delivered his ruling, however, it was a matter of indifference to him whether his judgment was quashed or upheld on appeal. It was regretted that Hill himself was never promoted to an appellate court from where, with his great learning in commercial law, he might have 'enriched our jurisprudence' (*The Times*, 19 June 1934).

Hill loved the countryside. He usually spent the long vacation at his holiday cottage at Llanbedr in Wales, rambling, botanizing, bird-watching, and fishing in a favourite trout stream. He was devoted to flowers both at Llanbedr and in his secluded garden at Wimbledon. As might be expected of the son of a literary man, he was steeped in English verse, especially nature poetry and Shakespeare, which, if he could be persuaded, he would recite from memory 'in his musical voice' (*The Times*, 7 June 1934). In later life he became interested in science and archaeology. Hill died at his home, 17 Hillside, Wimbledon, on 6 June 1934, of heart disease. His elder son, (Philip) Maurice Hill (1892–1952), became general manager of the chamber of shipping of the United Kingdom (1941–50).

A. LENTIN

Sources *The Times* (7 June 1934) · *DNB* · *Law reports* · *The Times* (18 Jan 1917) · *The Times* (1 Feb 1917) · *The Times* (16 June 1934) · *The Times* (19 June 1934) · *The Times* (29 June 1934) · S. Sucharitkul, *State immunities and trading activities in international law* (1959) · C. E. Fayle, *The war and the shipping industry* (1927) · R. Graves and A. Hodge, *The long week-end: a social history of Great Britain, 1918–1939* (1971) · *WWW*, 1929–40 · N. Hill, 'State insurance against war risks at sea', *War and insurance*, ed. N. Hill and others (1927), 11–53 · D. Lloyd George, *War memoirs*, new edn, 2 vols. (1938) · C. J. Colombos, *The international law of the sea*, 6th rev. edn (1967) · b. cert. · m. cert. · d. cert.
Likenesses W. Russell, oils, 1918, priv. coll.
Wealth at death £40,088 5s. 5d.: resworn probate, 25 July 1934, *CGPLA Eng. & Wales*

Hill, Micaiah John Muller (1856–1929), mathematician, was born at Berhampore, Bengal, on 22 February 1856, the eldest son of the Revd Samuel John Hill, a missionary, and his wife, Leonora Josephine Müller. Sir George Francis *Hill, numismatist, was his brother. After attending the School for the Sons of Missionaries, Blackheath, he entered University College, London, in October 1872. In 1874 he obtained his BA from the University of London, coming first in the mathematical honours list, and two years later was awarded the gold medal for his MA. In 1875 he entered Peterhouse, Cambridge, graduating as fourth wrangler and joint first Smith's prizeman in 1879. He briefly served as assistant to his old professor, Olaus Henrici, at University College before being appointed professor of mathematics at Mason College, Birmingham, in 1880. He made his final return to University College four years later when he was elected professor of pure mathematics.

Hill's research work concentrated on three main topics: hydrodynamics, differential equations, and the theory of proportion. In the first (in 1883–94) he developed the theory of cylindrical vortices of finite section moving in an infinite fluid and published the solution for the axisymmetric spherical vortex, later known as Hill's vortex, the flow of which is somewhat similar to a smoke ring. Between 1888 and 1893 he investigated the various loci connected with first order differential equations and their complete primitives, obtaining many new and important results on the more general question of loci of singular points. Further papers on differential equations were published between 1916 and 1921. It was, however, the critical reappraisal of the fifth and sixth books of Euclid's *Elements* which was to dominate Hill's mathematical research. Inspired by problems experienced when teaching students the theory of proportion, his analysis is contained in five papers in the *Transactions of the Cambridge Philosophical Society* (1897–1922), an edition of the two books in question (1900), and his book *The Theory of Proportion* (1914). In these works, by simplifying many of the proofs and deleting superfluous definitions and axioms, he was able successfully to reformulate Euclid's approach. Unfortunately, coinciding as it did with the period of Euclid's expulsion from the classroom, Hill's work was never properly appreciated.

Hill was a skilful and popular teacher. Infinitely patient, 'he possessed that rare quality, which students so keenly appreciate, of never slurring over difficulties: time spent on making a demonstration perfect was always to him time well spent' (Filon, *Journal of the London Mathematical Society*, 317). Described as 'one of the most commanding personalities' (Bellot, 390) of University College, he finally retired in 1923, although problems in finding a successor resulted in his staying on as acting professor for a further year.

A fellow of the Royal Society since 1894, Hill served on its council in 1911–13, and was vice-president of the London Mathematical Society in 1894 and 1895. He also served on the senate of the University of London in 1900–26, as vice-chancellor in 1909–11. His last honour was to be president of the Mathematical Association in 1927–8. He married Minnie Grace, *née* Tarbotton (1861–1920), on 21 December 1892, and they had two sons, the eldest of whom was the renowned air force officer Sir Roderic Maxwell *Hill, and a daughter. Illness left Hill totally blind for the last fifteen months of his life. He died at his home, 39 West Heath Drive, Golders Green, Middlesex, on 11 January 1929, and was cremated three days later at Golders Green crematorium.   ADRIAN RICE

Sources L. N. G. Filon, *Journal of the London Mathematical Society*, 4 (1929), 313–18 · L. N. G. F. [L. N. G. Filon], *PRS*, 124A (1929), i–v · L. N. G. Filon, *University College Magazine*, 3 (1923–5), 17–18 · W. P. Ker, ed., *Notes and materials for the history of University College, London: faculties of arts and science* (1898), 57 · H. H. Bellot, *University College, London, 1826–1926* (1929), 390 · *WWW*, 1929–40 · *The Times* (12 Jan 1929) · m. cert. · d. cert. [Micaiah Hill] · b. cert. [Minnie Grace Tarbotton] · d. cert. [Minnie Grace Hill] · election certificate, RS
Archives RS · UCL
Likenesses S. M. G. Johnson, cartoon, UCL, Archives · photograph, repro. in Filon, *Journal of the London Mathematical Society*, facing p. i · photograph, repro. in Filon, *University College Magazine*, facing p. 17 · photograph, Sci. Mus., Robert Tucker collection · portrait, UCL · two photographs, UCL archives
Wealth at death £8725 17s.: probate, 18 April 1929, *CGPLA Eng. & Wales*

Hill, Nicholas (1570–*c*.1610), philosopher, was born in Fleet Street, London, and was educated first at Merchant Taylors' School, then as a scholar at St John's College, Oxford, where he matriculated on 21 July 1587 as *plebei filius*. His parents are unknown. On 30 June 1590 he was admitted as a fellow of the college, but within a year he had been deprived (*amotus*), probably on account of his conversion to Roman Catholicism. Thereafter college records state that he 'went away, applied himself to the Lullian doctrine, and published certain questions in philosophy', and that he was dead by 1621 at the latest. The philosophical questions here mentioned are set out in his only published work, *Philosophia epicurea democritiana theophrastica* (Paris, 1601).

So much may be stated confidently. For the rest of his personal life there is only hearsay evidence collected sixty years after his death. This consists of two independent and incompatible accounts uncritically combined by Anthony Wood in his *Athenae Oxonienses* (1691–2). One of these, supplied to him mainly through John Aubrey, by Thomas Henshaw (who afterwards disclaimed it), rests ultimately on London gossip and statements ascribed to Edmund Sheffield, first earl of Mulgrave (1564–1646), whose qualifications as a source are unclear. It contains some demonstrable absurdities. The other account came through intermediaries at Oxford—Joseph Maynard and Obadiah Walker—from the scientist Robert Hues. Since Hues moved in the same circles as Hill and had spent his last sixteen years at Oxford, his testimony has much greater weight and, though indirectly reported, deserves respect.

From this it appears that, after leaving Oxford, Hill was for some time associated with Henry Percy, ninth earl of Northumberland, the patron of Thomas Harriot and afterwards of Hues himself, and so was to some extent involved in the 'atheist' or 'deist' circle of Northumberland and Sir Walter Ralegh, with whom Aubrey independently describes him as 'intimate'. Although a professed Catholic, Hill shared the unorthodox views of this circle. According to Hues 'he professed himself a disciple of Jordanus Brunus'. This is clearly true: the 'Lullian doctrine' to which he had applied himself was what Bruno had taught in Paris, and in his own writings Hill supports the main cosmological ideas of Bruno—a heliocentric system, atomism, the eternity of matter, the infinity of the universe, and the plurality of worlds. Hill had probably discovered Bruno's ideas in Oxford where Bruno's visit to the university in June 1583 was well remembered, especially in St John's College. Such ideas were acceptable in the Northumberland–Ralegh circle: Northumberland himself was interested in Bruno and acquired his works.

However, by the late 1590s Hill had apparently found a new patron. According to Hues, he then 'joined himself to Mr Basset, who, after Queen Elizabeth's death pretended some right for the crown; but King James being admitted, and possessed, he fled and lived in Rotterdam …'. This statement has been dismissed by C. J. Robinson in the *Dictionary of National Biography* as 'a gossiping story', but it is very specific and the episode itself is authentic. Sir Robert Basset, a restless Devon partisan of Robert Devereux, second earl of Essex, was reported in 1598–1600 to be turning to popery under the influence of 'one Hill', 'a lewd fellow Hill', and in 1600 he conceived a wild plan to seize Lundy island and declare himself heir to the throne. In 1603, on the queen's death, he actually attempted to carry out this plan, but the result was a fiasco and he fled abroad. It may be that Hill, on learning of this project in 1600, took fright and himself fled abroad—perhaps to Paris, where he published his book in 1601. The book contains some curious passages compatible with such a scenario, and Hill's eccentric dedication of it to his own infant son Laurence provided him with a pretext to denounce previous patrons who, he implied, had betrayed him. This obscure episode, never publicized at the time but confirmed by the state papers, would have been known to Hues through his then patron Ralegh, a Devon man familiar with the Basset family.

Hill's *Philosophia epicurea*, a sequence of 509 propositions in natural philosophy, is topical in another respect too. In 1600 Giordano Bruno had been burnt at the stake in Rome, and it has been suggested, by Jean Jacquot, that Hill's book was a tribute to his memory. But if so, Hill was careful to cover himself: he cites Bruno (as 'Nolanus') explicitly in a marginal note only; he states, in the title and in the dedicatory epistle, that he is offering hypotheses only ('proposita simpliciter, non edocta'); and he declares that if any of them is contrary to the Catholic faith, 'igni illud et inferis mando' ('I commit it to the flames and hell'). And if he published the book in Catholic Paris, the centre of Lullian studies, he sought safety for himself in protestant Rotterdam.

According to Hues, Hill died in Rotterdam, from taking poison because of distress at the death of his own son. Henshaw told Wood that Hill died 'in or about 1610', a detail which he may have derived, indirectly, from Hill's widow, who was living in London 'behind Bow church' about 1637. Like her husband, she was a Roman Catholic, but her identity is unknown.

Hill's book made no impact in contemporary England except as a butt for the Jacobean wits. Ben Jonson tilted at his 'atomi ridiculous' (*Epigrams*, no. 133). Reprinted in Geneva in 1619, it was violently attacked by Mersenne in his general onslaught on Bruno and the deists in 1623–5. But later, when heliocentric and atomist ideas had been made acceptable by Galileo and Gassendi, Hill was occasionally remembered as an erratic precursor, and in the 1660s he was described by Aubrey as 'one of the most learned men of his time, a great mathematician and philosopher and traveller and poet', whose unprinted works had by then unhappily been lost.

These unprinted works are said to have included a treatise—clearly Brunian—'De infinitate et aeternitate mundi' and another, 'mighty paradoxical', 'on the essence of God, etc., light, proving that there is a God, in 10 or 12 articles'. In the Bodleian Library, MS Wood F 42 fol. 174 seems to be a translation of part of the former, and MS Tanner 306 fols. 110–12—a Latin poem of eighteen lines— probably formed part of the latter. Another short Latin poem, inscribed and signed by Hill himself, is in the *album amicorum* of Sir Francis Segar in the Huntington Library (MS HM 743, fol. 82). A manuscript commonplace book now in the Brotherton Library of Leeds University (MS Lt 52), which contains a note, 'written by my cosen Mr Nicolas Hill', may be by him. If so, it is presumably an early compilation: it shows an interest in a hermit life and Catholic mysticism but no Lullian or Brunian ideas.

From his writings Hill seems to have been a crotchety, difficult, and reclusive man, with few friends, his affections being concentrated on his little son, whose 'thousand pretty tricks' enabled him to forget his personal resentments and whose death 'of a pestilential disease' in Holland precipitated his own.   HUGH TREVOR-ROPER

Sources Wood, *Ath. Oxon.* • *Aubrey's Brief lives*, ed. O. L. Dick (1949), 256 • J. Aubrey, 'Sir Walter Raleigh', *Aubrey's Brief lives*, ed. O. L. Dick (1949), 253–60 • W. H. Stevenson and H. E. Salter, *The early history of St John's College, Oxford*, OHS, new ser., 1 (1939), 367 • *Reg. Oxf.*, 2/2.160; 2/3.171 • J. Jacquot, 'Harriot, Hill, Warner and the new philosophy', *Thomas Harriot: Renaissance scientist*, ed. J. W. Shirley (1974), 107–28 • H. Trevor-Roper, 'Nicholas Hill the English atomist', *Catholics, Anglicans and puritans: seventeenth-century essays* (1987) • DNB

Hill, Nicolas [Nikolaos van den Berghe] (*d.* **1555**), printer, was a Dutch immigrant to London under Henry VIII, who went on to become one of the most active printers of protestant works during the reign of Edward VI, and later became one of the founders of the important English exile press in Emden. Hill is first recorded in London in 1542, and he took out letters of denization in 1544, though he seems to have been in England for some time before this. The letters speak of his having been in England twenty-five years, though such designations are usually very approximate; if he had been in England this long, this would have made him one of the longest established members of the English immigrant community. Little is known of Hill's time in London before he began to print. He settled outside London to the west in St John's Street, where he was assessed for subsidy at 40s. in 1549. This assessment was reduced to 20s. in 1550, though Hill must nevertheless have been a man of some substance. He employed three apprentices on his printing presses, and appeared on the membership list of the new Dutch church in 1550 as a householder and married man.

Hill's association with the printing industry began about 1542. For the first years after his printing house was established he existed on a modest diet of yearbooks and legal documents, working by and large for other, betterknown, London publishers. By the end of Henry's reign, however, he was in the position to undertake more ambitious work such as *The Bokes of Salomon* (STC, 1475–1640, 2775), a neat octavo of 340 pages printed for William Bonham. Hill was thus well placed to take advantage of the changed environment created by the accession of Edward VI, and he quickly became one of the most active printers of the new protestant ascendancy. During the six years of Edward's reign he printed at least sixty editions, almost exclusively protestant works intended for both the London Dutch and indigenous communities. Hill's presses were much in demand, and his editions during these years included projects for most of the prominent members of the protestant printing establishment: he printed books for the well-known London printers Grafton, Whitchurch, Seres, and Jugge, works which included important commissions such as an edition of the primer, the Book of Common Prayer, and Ponet's translation of Ochino. Hill's involvement in these projects underscores the English industry's dependence during these years on foreign expertise. Contemporary records list the names of some seventy French and Dutch workmen in the printing industry active in London during these years, including pivotal figures like Hill, Mierdman, and Walter Lynne. Men of this sort brought to London a sophistication and level of technical accomplishment characteristic of the major continental publishing centres such as Antwerp, and those who commissioned work from Hill would not have been disappointed. His editions are printed in a pleasing range of black letter and italic types, deployed with economy and style.

Hill seems to have functioned in London exclusively as a printer; there is no evidence that he maintained his own bookshop. Though his connections with English printers were obviously excellent, he did not forget his roots. He also undertook commissions for fellow immigrants, the Dutchman Walter Lynne and the Frenchman Thomas Gualter. Hill, as van den Berghe, also published a number of the first liturgical books of the new French and Dutch congregations in London. Hill joined the Dutch church on its foundation in 1550 and seems to have been a committed member. Between 1550 and 1553 he was promoted an elder of the church.

This commitment was put to the test when in 1553 Edward VI died, to be succeeded by the Catholic Mary. Many of the London Dutch community opted to remain in London and conform; Hill, despite his half lifetime of residence in England, chose to join the rest of the leaders of the Dutch church in seeking a new home abroad. After a perilous winter journey the church found a new home in John à Lasco's former church in Emden, East Friesland, where Hill embarked on a final but highly significant phase of his printing career. In Emden, Hill established a new partnership with his fellow former elder of the London church, Gilles van der Erve (Ctematius). Together they formed the first publishing house in Emden, which was soon—in competition with a rival venture with another London exile, Steven Mierdman—turning out a host of small tracts for the English and Dutch markets. In Emden, Hill printed under a new pseudonym—Collinus Volckwinner—an alias attributed in some of the earlier scholarship to his partner Ctematius. The correction of this tradition (the achievement of the Dutch scholar H. F. Wijnman) allows van den Berghe to take his rightful place as one of the most important publishers of English exile literature of the Marian period.

Hill's first books in Emden were fairly rudimentary in style. None of the London Dutch printers had been able to bring with them any of their types from England, and the re-equipment of the printing house was a costly business. Hill's first Emden works are printed in a fairly limited range of types, mostly German in provenance (including an unusual rounded Schwabacher type which greatly assists identification of those works published anonymously). But a steady stream of commissions from the leaders of the Emden churches—including the first edition of Micron's Dutch version of the discipline of the London church, the *Christlicken ordinancien* ('Christian ordinances')—allowed Hill and his partner to re-equip the press with a full range of good quality Gothic textura types, purchased in the Netherlands. Hill and Ctematius also benefited from the patronage of English exiles settled in Emden. Hill's mastery of the language and long experience in the English printing industry made their shop the natural choice when English protestant exiles began to turn their minds to the propaganda war with Mary's regime. Between 1554 and 1558 the Hill / Ctematius workshop turned out over twenty English works, including such important texts as Knox's *Faithful Admonition* (1554) and works by William Turner, John Olde, and John Scory. The printers indulged themselves with a full range of whimsical false addresses: 'Rome, by the Vatican church', 'Kalykow', 'Waterford'; but the typefaces used are sufficiently distinctive to permit definite attribution.

Hill did not live to see the full flourishing of this new business, since he died some time in 1555, an event which caused problems in the shop before Ctematius was able to go forward with confidence without his old partner. He

left a widow, who returned to England in 1559. Hill's achievement as a printer of English works—a total of over eighty protestant editions in two distinct phases of his career—is significant. His career spans the critical period when English printing was finally able to emancipate itself from the dependence on foreign expertise which so characterizes the first century of the English printed book.   ANDREW PETTEGREE

Sources A. Pettegree, *Foreign protestant communities in sixteenth-century London* (1986) · A. Pettegree, *Emden and the Dutch revolt: exile and the development of reformed protestantism* (1992) · E. G. Duff, *A century of the English book trade* (1905); repr. (1948) · E. J. Worman, *Alien members of the book-trade during the Tudor period* (1906) · H. F. Wijnman, 'Grepen uit de Geschiedenis van de Nederlandse emigrantendrukkerijen te Emden', *Het Boek*, 36 (1963–4), 140–68 · H. F. Wijnman, 'Grepen uit de Geschiedenis van de Nederlandse emigrantendrukkerijen te Emden', *Het Boek*, 37 (1965–6), 121–51 · F. Isaacs, 'Egidius van der Erve and his English printed books', *The Library*, 4th ser., 12 (1931–2), 336–52 · A. F. Johnson, 'English books printed abroad', *The Library*, 5th ser., 4 (1949–50), 273–6 · STC, 1475–1640

Hill, Octavia (1838–1912), housing and social reformer, was born on 3 December 1838 at 8 South Brink, Wisbech, Cambridgeshire, the eighth daughter (and ninth child) of James Hill (*c*.1800–1871), corn merchant and Owenite social utopian. Her mother was James Hill's third wife, Caroline Southwood *Hill (1809–1902), writer and educationist, daughter of Dr Thomas Southwood *Smith. The smooth course of Octavia Hill's childhood was interrupted by her father's bankruptcy in 1840, and his subsequent nervous breakdown and virtual disappearance from the family. Her mother, by now with five small daughters, turned to her own father for moral and financial support and he became in many respects a surrogate father to her children. Dr Southwood Smith was a noted health reformer, campaigning on issues from child labour in the mines to the housing conditions of the urban poor. The influence of her mother's interest in progressive educational ideas, particularly those of Pestalozzi, and her grandfather's daily experience in his work at the London Hospital in the East End gave an early impetus to Octavia Hill's urge to help the very poorest strata of society in early Victorian London.

Octavia Hill and her sisters appear to have been educated entirely at home by their mother, as the family moved around the country for some years before settling down in a small cottage in Finchley, a village to the north of London. Her grandfather lived in Highgate and gave a home to Gertrude, the second daughter, helped by the two Miss Gillies, with whom he lived. That house was a second home to all the family: it was filled with the independently minded, usually nonconformist intellectuals who were their friends, including the Leigh Smiths, the Howitts, and the Foxes, as well as interesting visitors such as Hans Christian Andersen and Charles Dickens. Gertrude later married G. H. Lewes, George Eliot's stepson.

In 1852 Caroline Southwood Hill moved into central London, to Russell Place, Holborn. She had been offered the job of manager and bookkeeper of the Ladies Guild, a

Octavia Hill (1838–1912), by John Singer Sargent, 1898

co-operative crafts workshop nearby. Aged fourteen, Octavia Hill became her mother's *de facto* assistant, with responsibility for the ragged-school girls aged between eight and seventeen who were employed there. Work at the guild brought mother and daughter into contact with the Christian socialist circle and, in particular, with F. D. Maurice. It also showed Octavia Hill the shocking reality of poverty in that area of London; the toy-maker girls whom she supervised went home to desperate conditions. Occasionally she would visit a child at home and was horrified at what she found in the hideous and insanitary 'rookeries' of Holborn, where families lived eight or ten to a room. Even in her early teens her sense of a social purpose was phenomenal. She wrote to her younger sister Emily of an enjoyable evening with friends in Romford: 'gathered round the fire … we talk of the Guild, of Ruskin, of the poor, of education, of politics and history' (C. E. Maurice, 59). Brought up a Unitarian, her mother left Octavia's religious allegiances deliberately untouched. In 1857, as a result of her friendship with F. D. Maurice and his circle, she was baptized and then confirmed into the Church of England; but she remained notably undogmatic. She regarded faith as a personal matter and never intruded upon the religious observance of the tenants she was to acquire—many of whom were Irish Catholics.

Ruskin John Ruskin came into Octavia Hill's life first through the pages of *Modern Painters* and then, in person, at the guild. She was fifteen and enthralled: 'to think that that was the man who was accused of being mad, presumptuous, conceited and prejudiced' (C. E. Maurice, 30). In 1855 he began to train her as a copyist and, as the guild

began to fail, she turned to him for advice. To replace her work with the guild, in early 1856 F. D. Maurice, head of the Working Men's College, had offered her a job as secretary to the women's classes for a salary of £26 per year. Ruskin also taught there and before long she too began to teach the young women. The college, which was in Red Lion Square, Holborn, aimed to educate women 'for occupations wherein they could be helpful to the less fortunate members of their own sex', as Maurice put it. The work reflected Octavia Hill's interests in women's education and rights; in that year she helped Barbara Leigh Smith Bodichon orchestrate a campaign for a married women's property act and collected 24,000 signatures.

By 1859 Hill's daily routine of copying in Dulwich Art Gallery or the National Gallery, followed by many more hours spent teaching, had become punishing. Even F. D. Maurice told her that trying to do without rest was very self-willed but she took no notice. A tiny woman (all the family were diminutive) with a heavy-browed head and great dark eyes, her indomitable personality was already fixed. Eventually her family forced her to go to Normandy on holiday, but a dangerous pattern of working until she collapsed was established which would periodically interrupt her work over the coming years.

The family was constantly pressed for money: repaying their father's debts and their grandfather's loans meant that the children were always shadowed by poverty. One by one, the sisters turned to teaching. Miranda Hill, the gentle eldest daughter, set up her own small establishment. In 1861 Dr Southwood Smith died, and the following year Caroline Hill and her daughters opened a school in their house in Nottingham Place. However, in 1864 John Ruskin's father died, leaving a substantial sum to his only son; Octavia Hill's long-held dream, to establish improved housing for 'my friends among the poor', was made possible by his decision to invest in her scheme, albeit for a 5 per cent return.

The Octavia Hill 'method' The first property was the unsuitably named Paradise Place, later Garbutt Place, just off Marylebone High Street, London, and a short walk from Regent's Park. A terrace of artisans' cottages, probably no more than thirty years old, it had been in the grasp of resident landlords who had packed family after family into the tiny, insanitary dwellings. Visiting the tenants, Octavia Hill found the women far beyond caring; she vowed to restore their self-respect and to help them take responsibility for the state of their lives and their homes. The new arrangement gave each family two rooms instead of one, and the premises were transformed by cleaning, ventilation, clearance of the drains, repairs, and redecoration. Bad tenants, habitual non-payers, were turned out, despite her deep misgivings. The key to her system was the weekly visit to collect rent. This allowed the ladies who performed this job—Hill herself, assisted by Emma Cons and one or two other trusted lieutenants—to check upon every detail of the premises and to broaden their contact with the tenants, especially the children. In effect they were model social workers, always available if there were personal problems to be resolved. In common with Josephine Butler and Florence Nightingale she believed that the model of the family and the ideal of the home should underlie all charitable work. Like Mary Carpenter, who argued against institutions and in favour of 'cottage homes', Hill was a passionate advocate of small-scale solutions.

Hill's tenants were people dependent on casual or seasonal work, rather than the artisan class for whom model industrial dwellings, where tenants required references from employers, were built. Often she tried to find employment for tenants in and around the houses. For the children, outings to the countryside were organized, a tenants' meeting room was established behind Nottingham Place, and each pupil at the Hills' school was assigned a child from the buildings. The space around the terrace was cleaned up as a playground. As soon as Paradise Place was transformed, she moved on; John Ruskin bought the freehold of Freshwater Place for her and the same process began again. Any surplus beyond the 5 per cent return was at the tenants' disposal (guided by the landlady); they could choose whether the money went towards a playground, sewing or singing classes, or another project.

The number of tenants and houses grew, as, exponentially, did the 'fellow-workers'—those who volunteered for rent collection or put money or property into the scheme. In the former category, some such as Henrietta Barnett, Beatrice Webb, Katherine Courtney, and Emma Cons moved on to continue their own work elsewhere. Those who provided funds or practical support ranged from royalty to City financiers, from conscientious aristocrats to leading figures in the worlds of literature and the arts. Her support snowballed year by year. As Octavia Hill developed her essentially replicable 'method', she ensured that her work was widely known through a stream of published articles and her own annual reports, privately printed and distributed, the *Letters to Fellow Workers*. Soon interest came from overseas and from cities all over the country. She tirelessly addressed meetings and interested groups to spread the word; her speaking voice, naturally musical, was one of her greatest assets.

Beginning by overhauling the physical setting of her tenants' lives, ideally by rehabilitating their existing housing rather than building new blocks, Octavia Hill then turned to the improvement of other aspects of their daily life. Holidays and festivals, such as May day, were marked, and many of her projects included the erection of halls, decorated by artist friends, in which concerts and theatre performances could be held. She made playgrounds out of the rough open spaces around the alleys and terraces, leading to campaigns for the renewal of disused central London burial-grounds as public open space and for rights of access to common land. The latter interest brought her into some of the early campaigns of the Commons Preservation Society, through which she met Robert Hunter, honorary solicitor of that body. She fought against development on precious open ground as London pushed inexorably outwards, failing to save Swiss Cottage Fields but winning her battle for Parliament Hill Fields.

Later she campaigned elsewhere in the country, including the Lake District, where she encountered the Revd Hardwicke Rawnsley, co-founder of the National Trust. The Kyrle Society, founded by Miranda Hill in 1876 as a Society for the Diffusion of Beauty, but bearing the stamp of her sister's concerns and with her support, was established to bring colour into poor lives. For a short period it expanded, setting up branches in many cities, and involved people such as William Morris and Walter Crane. Although it petered out, many of its principles were embodied in the founding articles of the National Trust, twenty years later.

Octavia Hill's firm ideas on self-respect, with their echoes of Samuel Smiles's *Self Help*, published in 1859, led to her involvement with the Charity Organization Society (COS), a contentious body which deplored dependence fostered by kindly but unrigorous philanthropy. For the COS, support to the poor had to be carefully targeted and efficiently supervised. Later in life, however, she began to think the COS line, as kept by its committee, was overharsh.

In 1877, after eleven years of immersion in the world of housing and social reform, Hill collapsed and for many months was forced to withdraw from her work. This episode, the gravest yet, finally demonstrated that she had to delegate many of her daily tasks to allow her to continue to manage her projects. There had been a number of causes for her collapse: the death of Jane Nassau Senior, a stalwart friend and experienced social worker who became the first woman poor-law inspector; her short-lived engagement to another helper, the barrister and later MP Edward Bond; and finally, an extraordinary attack on her in the pages of *Fors Clavigera* by John Ruskin. This sprang from her unwillingness to let him make over the housing schemes in which he held a financial stake to the shaky St George's Company. His own mental condition was such that he could exercise no control over his vindictiveness and spite: it was a tragic falling-out. After some months abroad and a prolonged rest, she returned to work. Her family found a companion, the redoubtable Harriot Yorke, who remained at her side until her death, relieving her of much of the petty detail and stress which had contributed to her breakdown. In the early 1880s they built a vernacular-style cottage at Crockham Hill, outside Edenbridge on the Sussex Weald: Larksfield became another source of rest and relaxation, although weekend visitors might find themselves handed secateurs and sent out to keep the local rights of way open. Octavia Hill's own taste in architecture had always tended to the ornamental, even the Tyrolean, as was evident in the two small terraces of half-timbered cottages which she built in Southwark in the late 1880s, Red and White Cross Cottages, both designed by Elijah Hoole.

The wider picture In 1884 Octavia Hill's work took on a new, and more appropriate, scale. She was asked by the ecclesiastical commissioners, embarrassed to find that the church had become a slum landlord, to take on the management of certain properties, initially in Deptford and Southwark. Gradually they handed over more and more housing to her management and, in particular, a large area of housing in Walworth, south London. Before long she was consulted on the rebuilding of the estate: she argued successfully for a domestic scale (compared to the existing model industrial dwellings) and for the involvement of the tenants in the process. The dimensions of the task meant that her women housing workers were, by the 1900s, trained and salaried. In 1889 she became actively involved with the Women's University Settlement in Nelson Square, Southwark, and addressed students at Newnham College, Cambridge, on the possibilities opening up for young working women. In housing management, as the profession became known, women soon took the lead; Hill was eager that girls should work outside the home, although she always emphasized the importance of the domestic virtues as applied to all areas of life.

Having always fought against the municipal solution to the crisis in housing, late in her life Hill had to face the setting up of the London county council and the increasing involvement of local authorities in the provision of housing for the working classes. By the 1880s she had become a key figure in policy making. In 1884 Sir Charles Dilke invited her to be a member of the royal commission on housing which he was to chair but the home secretary, Sir William Harcourt, vetoed her. There was a cabinet discussion in which Gladstone supported her candidacy 'on the principle' but not 'on the person'. She would have been the first woman member of a royal commission. In the event she was a key witness. However, in 1905 she joined the royal commission for the poor law, with Charles Booth, Beatrice Webb, and George Lansbury, as well as a number of COS stalwarts, and travelled the country for three years on commission business.

Despite the transformation of nineteenth-century philanthropy into twentieth-century social service which was taking place around her, Octavia Hill remained opposed to state or municipal action for welfare. She argued against old-age pensions; as she also opposed parliamentary votes for women, largely on the grounds that women were unfit to determine matters of international policy, defence, and national budgets. She was an enthusiastic supporter of women's involvement in politics at a local, suitably 'domestic', level. She was visionary in her attempt to bring self-respect to those who had long since lost it, and inspired in the choices and manner of campaigning to improve the lives of the impoverished. After her death from cancer on 13 August 1912 at her home, 190 Marylebone Road, London, a memorial service was held in Southwark Cathedral and the obsequies were impressive; she was buried at Crockham Hill, Kent. Her work and example lived on in a younger generation of professional housing managers and, ironically enough, in decent quality social housing largely provided in the inter-war years by local authorities. It is also at the root of the late twentieth-century change of emphasis towards smaller-scale, more personal housing management and tenant participation. Her other successful campaigns are marked by London's remarkable range of open spaces, from Hampstead Heath (incorporating Parliament Hill) to the dozens, if not hundreds, of tiny pocket parks formed from old burial-grounds, and in many of the first properties to be taken on in perpetuity by the National Trust—an organization with a membership, just over a century later, of more than 2 million.

GILLIAN DARLEY

Sources G. Darley, *Octavia Hill: a life* (1990) · C. E. Maurice, ed., *Life of Octavia Hill* (1913) · E. S. Maurice, ed., *Octavia Hill: early ideals* (1928) · E. M. Bell, *Octavia Hill* (1942) · O. Hill, *The homes of the London poor* (1875) · O. Hill, *Our common land* (1877) · O. Hill, *Letters to fellow workers* (1864–1911) · F. K. Prochaska, *Women and philanthropy in nineteenth-century England* (1980)
Archives LUL · Marylebone Reference Library, London · priv. coll. · Women's Library, London, letters | BL, letters to Sidney Cockerell, Add. MS 52722 · BLPES, letters to Canon and Mrs Barnett · BLPES, Courtney MSS · BLPES, Passfield MSS · City Westm. AC, letters to Sidney Cockerell and family · City Westm. AC, letters to Miss Schuster · HLRO, Barnett MSS · Hove Central Library, Sussex, letters to Lady Wolseley · LPL, corresp. with Davidson · LUL, corresp. with Booth family
Likenesses Barton, pencil drawing, *c.*1864, NPG · E. Clifford, pencil, 1877, Ruskin Gallery, Sheffield · J. S. Sargent, oils, 1898, NPG [*see illus.*] · Miss Abbott, effigy, 1928, Crockham Hill church, Kent
Wealth at death £20,936 2*s.* 11*d.*: resworn probate, 31 Oct 1912, CGPLA Eng. & Wales

Hill, Oliver (*b.* 1630?, *d.* after 1702), theologian and government agent, may be the son of Adam Hill of Huntingdonshire, admitted pensioner, aged eighteen, at St John's College, Cambridge, on 23 October 1648. He was an acquaintance of Robert Boyle, whose contacts extended to men of extreme religious positions, and of John Aubrey. In an account of the rise and progress of the Philadelphian Society, Hill was said to be 'intimately acquainted with' John Pordage, chief of the English followers of Jakob Boehme, whose ideas conspicuously permeate Hill's theological writings (Bodl. Oxf., MS Rawl. D833, fol. 64*r*). Hill attended meetings of the Royal Society of London in the weeks before Boyle proposed him as a member, and he was elected on 13 December 1677. However, he soon made himself unpopular by putting forward arcane views of the natural world that ran counter to the society's preference for empirical reasoning. In debates about the barometer Hill affirmed that he was master of a theory of the nature of air and mercury, and claimed to have proved by experiment that air had no gravity; but when pressed to demonstrate this, he was unable to do so. Soon afterwards his interest presumably lapsed as his name no longer occurs in the minutes.

About 1689 Hill, who may then have been residing with his wife and family at Lisbon, secured an appointment as agent for the carriage by sea of the mails to and from Spain. These had hitherto travelled the slow overland route through the Spanish Netherlands and France. Hill's ship arrived from England at Corunna on 20 March 1690, shortly before the convoy escorting Maria Anna of Neuberg, prospective second wife of Charles II of Spain. On landing, Hill immediately tried to curry favour and earn a reward by being first to announce the news at Madrid, in which he was, according to his own account, successful. His next move was to petition the king to name someone with whom he could negotiate. In this he was less successful, for in July or early August he was arrested and thrown into prison. Lord Stanhope, ambassador in Madrid, did his duty for a citizen in distress, but in reporting the event wrote:

> the station I am in obliges me to let your lordship know something of the character of the man. He is so hot headed and inconsiderate, that by his memorials and letters they look on him heer as a madman and that it is a prejudice to the service of the king to employ him in any commission whatever. (PRO, SP 94/73, fol. 12)

A letter that Hill had asked Stanhope to forward to Crispin Botello, secretary of state, was described by Stanhope as

> abusive to the whole Spanish nation, stuff'd full of Texts of Scripture and Latine verses … I know not how he is supported at home … but he can do his majestie no service heer, but will spoil any business he is imployed in. (ibid., fols. 12–13)

On 24 September John Parker, British consul at Corunna, wrote to the earl of Shrewsbury's office that Hill was talking ill of King James and the government,

> cursing the king in these words 'God dam the king suck hime to the pitt of hel and all those he hath suckled in Ireland it will but coop him up two years longer' and 'drink damnation to the bishops' very often—please advise what I should do regarding the said Hill. (PRO, SP 94/73, fols. 1–2)

By 11 October Hill's commission was revoked, after which he joined his wife and family at Lisbon. His first book, *Epistola ad Anglos, being an introduction out of a larger treatise into the mysteries of true Christian religion* (1689), was published in London, its author described as 'Oliver Hill, exile for the law and the Gospel at Lisbon in Portugal'. This was followed by *An Account of Oliver Hill's Agency in Spain* (1691?), which sought to justify his actions; it confuses the reader as both the starting and finishing dates of the year-long sequence of events are given as December 1690.

The date of Hill's return to London is unknown, but it must have preceded a sermon given at Turners' Hall that caused him to issue *Remarks of Oliver Hill, upon Mr Keith's Farewell* (1698?). He then returned to quasi-scientific battles with *The Fifth Essay of D. M. … Against the Circulation of the Blood* (1700), which was addressed to 'the learned gentlemen of the house in Warwick Lane' (meaning the Royal Society). Its title page detailed nine essays, beginning with 'Against the gravitation and pressure of the air' and interspersing four on theology with 'The motion of the earth', 'Of the first matter of metals', and 'How to increase trade and coin in any kingdom', but only the fifth essay, 'Of the non circulation of the blood', was printed. In this Hill argued that the apparent circulation was manifest only in corpses, and did not occur in living beings. The subject continued to hold his attention, for his last known book was *A rod for the back of fools: in answer to Mr John Toland's book … and to the lecture of Dr Joseph Brown against the circulation of the blood; & to the answer of one Mr John Gardiner, surgeon, to that pretended lecture* (1702). It was to be sold at the author's house in Nevil's Alley in Fetter Lane. Nothing more is heard of him; the exact date and place of his death are unknown.   ANITA McCONNELL

Sources T. Birch, *The history of the Royal Society of London*, 4 vols. (1756–7), vols. 3–4 · M. Hunter, ed., *Robert Boyle by himself and his friends* (1994), lxxi–lxxii · Bodl. Oxf., MS Rawl. D. 833, fols. 63v–64v · M. B. Hall, *Promoting experimental learning* (1991), 155–6 · *N&Q*, 4 (1851), 318 · O. Hill, *An account of Oliver Hill's agency in Spain* (1691?) · PRO, SP 94/73 · Venn, *Alum. Cant.*

Hill, Oliver Falvey (1887–1968), architect, was born on 15 June 1887 at 89 Queen's Gate, London, the third son and seventh of eight children of William Neave Hill, manufacturer, of London, and his wife, Kate Ida, daughter of Martin Franks. He was educated at Uppingham School. Having decided to become an architect, he was advised by Sir Edwin Lutyens, a family friend, to gain experience in a builder's yard. This developed his sense of texture and materials. Simultaneously, he trained his colour sense by studying Persian and Chinese ceramics in the Victoria and Albert Museum. Between 1909 and 1911 Hill attended evening classes at the Architectural Association while a pupil of William Flockhart.

Hill's first major commission was to reconstruct the house and garden at Moor Close, Binfield, Berkshire, in which his love of rich colour and baroque forms was displayed. During the First World War he served in the London Scottish regiment and attained the rank of captain. After returning to architecture, he designed Cour, Argyllshire (1921–3), a picturesque country house in local stone, and a series of houses either thatched and timbered or in neo-Georgian style, such as Cock Rock, Croyde, Devon (1926), and Woodhouse Copse, Holmbury St Mary, Surrey (1926). Hill designed furniture and paid great attention to interiors and colour schemes. He became a fashionable architect for London houses and flats, and designed two much publicized houses in Gayfere Street, Westminster, for Wilfrid Ashley (later Baron Mount Temple) in 1926 and 1931. In these, his use of mirrors and simple room arrangements indicated his developing interest in the modern movement in Europe, which became the main theme of his work in the 1930s, although never to the exclusion of other styles. Among Hill's modernist houses were Joldwynds, Holmbury St Mary (1930–32), for Wilfred (later Baron) Greene; Holthanger, Wentworth, Surrey (1935); and Landfall, Poole, Dorset (1938). He also designed the Midland Hotel, Morecambe, Lancashire, in 1933 as a pioneer modernist public building, and was involved in the attempt to build a modernist seaside resort at Frinton Park, Essex.

As designer of the exhibition of British industrial art in the home at the Dorland Hall, London, in 1933, and the exhibition of contemporary industrial art in the home in the same hall (1934), Hill promoted modernism in architecture and household objects. He was architect of the British pavilion at the Paris Exhibition of 1937, and was involved in designing displays and selecting exhibits under the chairmanship of Frank Pick. His approach to modernism was aesthetic rather than sociological or mechanistic, although he built a fine primary school at Whitwood Mere, near Castleford, Yorkshire (1939). Architects and critics with purist views were suspicious of Hill, but he helped to popularize the modern style. He was notable for commissioning works of art for buildings and displays from Eric Gill, Eric Ravilious, John Skeaping, and others.

After 1945 Hill suffered neglect, although completing some fine work, notably Newbury Park bus station in Essex (1949) and Uppingham School Library and war memorial in Leicestershire (1949). He organized the Cotswold Tradition exhibition at Cirencester in 1951 with considerable panache, and retired to Daneway House, Sapperton, Gloucestershire, where he created a new garden. He wrote several books on architecture, notably *English Country Houses: Caroline, 1625–1685* (with John Cornforth, 1966). He loved being out of doors, often without clothes, and kept many animals. He was tall and rather deaf, an unselfconscious eccentric, with a great appetite for work.

On 19 December 1953 Hill married Margaret Jeanette (Titania) Beverley (*b*. 1929/30), the musician daughter of the architect Samuel Beverley, and forty-three years his junior, who shared in the creation of a lifestyle of unworldly fantasy at Daneway; they had no children. Hill also had a long-term relationship with Helena Rosa *Wright, *née* Lowenfeld (1887–1982), family planning practitioner. He died on 29 April 1968 at home, and was survived by his wife.   ALAN POWERS, *rev.*

Sources RIBA · private information (2004) · b. cert. · m. cert. · d. cert. · A. Powers, *Oliver Hill, architect and lover of life, 1887–1968* (1989) · R. Gradidge, 'The architecture of Oliver Hill', *Architectural Design*, 49/10–11 (1979)
Archives RIBA, corresp. and papers · RIBA, sketchbooks and scrapbooks

Hill, Pascoe Grenfell (1804–1882), Church of England clergyman and author, son of Major Thomas Hill, was born at Marazion, Cornwall, on 15 May 1804. He was educated at Mill Hill School, London, and at Trinity College, Dublin, where he graduated BA in 1836. In the same year he was ordained priest, and became a chaplain in the Royal Navy. During his service at sea he saw much of the slave trade on the African coast and published two accounts of his experiences. The first, *Fifty Days on Board a Slave-Vessel in the Mozambique Channel* (1844), went to several editions in Britain and the United States and was reissued as late as 1993, being of value for its firsthand account of the shipping of slaves. In 1845 he was placed on the retired list.

On 26 January 1846 Hill married Ellen Annetta (surname unknown). They had at least two sons before her death on 18 April 1878. From 1852 to 1857 he was chaplain of the Westminster Hospital, and for some time morning reader at Westminster Abbey. On 26 January 1863 he was appointed rector of St Edmund the King with St Nicholas Acons, Lombard Street, City of London, where he continued until his death. A high-churchman, he provided a succession of preachers for his church, improved its choir, and held short services in the middle of the day. He was the first to introduce a surpliced choir into a City church.

As well as his works on slavery Hill wrote: *Poems on Several Occasions* (1845), a volume, mainly of love poems,

whose publication he later regretted; *A Journey through Palestine* (1852) and *A Visit to Cairo* (1853); and also historical works and a *Life of Napoleon* (3 vols., 1869). He died at home at the rectory house, 32 Finsbury Square, London, on 28 August 1882, and was buried in the City of London cemetery at Ilford.   G. C. BOASE, *rev.* ELIZABETH BAIGENT

Sources *City Press* (2 Sept 1882), 5 · *Citizen* (2 Sept 1882), 2 · *The Times* (30 Aug 1882), 10 · *CGPLA Eng. & Wales* (1883)
Wealth at death £3918: probate, 27 Jan 1883, *CGPLA Eng. & Wales*

Hill, Patrick (*c*.1868–1927). *See under* Knock, visionaries of (*act*. 1879).

Hill, Philip Ernest (1873–1944), property developer and financier, was born at 8 Scarborough Terrace, Torquay, on 11 April 1873, the younger son and youngest of three children of Philip Hill (1839–1922), cab proprietor, and his wife, Mary Smith (1830–1883), a lodging-house keeper. His mother died when he was ten, his only sister subsequently bringing him up. In 1886 he entered Taunton Independent college, where he received a good commercial education. At the age of sixteen he became a junior in a Newton Abbot estate agency. In 1892 he sought adventure by joining the army, but purchased his discharge two years later, just before the regiment was posted overseas. He resumed his estate agent's career, this time in Cardiff, where he married, in 1897, Katherine Keziah, daughter of Thomas Evans, a Cardiff gentleman.

After his only child—a daughter—had died, aged six, of meningitis (his wife died a little later), Hill moved to London in 1912. Aware that London agents were far better remunerated than those in the provinces, and that an exclusive locality greatly improved the chances of making good, he set up as an estate agent and valuer at 42 Albemarle Street, just off Piccadilly. He did well, but was less successful as a public works contractor during the First World War, erecting camps and portable buildings for the government. He thus emerged at the end of the war with a substantial bank overdraft, which was not fully repaid until 1922.

In 1917 he married for the second time; his second wife was Jessica Gertrude (daughter of Richard Gerrard, civil engineer), an actress and formerly the wife of Eric Spencer Wentworth Fitzwilliam (later the ninth Earl Fitzwilliam). She introduced Hill to London café society, but they were divorced in 1922. That same year he married the actress Vera Blanche Neville (daughter of Alfred Neville Snepp, cigarette manufacturer), the former wife of Henry Algernon Claude Graves (later the seventh Baron Graves), a bookmaker.

Hill entered the world of corporate finance and takeovers in 1923, as adviser to the Beecham family, whose pill-making firm had become entangled in property affairs after the purchase in 1914 by Sir Joseph Beecham (1848–1916) of the Covent Garden estate in London. By 1924 Hill had completed the buying out of the family interests and he helped to establish Beecham Estates and Pills Ltd. He carried out the first major flotation of a company on his own behalf in 1927, when he obtained control of Taylors Drug Company Ltd and other retail chemists' chains, following this up in 1928 with the acquisition of Timothy Whites Ltd. In the same year, by an adroit property deal, he divided the two not very compatible sides of the Beecham company into separate enterprises, becoming chairman of both.

Of these enterprises, the Covent Garden Properties Company Ltd concentrated entirely on general estates business. Hill's plan for the newly registered Beechams Pills Ltd was to build it up into the largest patent medicine and household goods company in Britain. Having already acquired the ailing Veno Drug Company Ltd, in 1938–9 he strengthened Beechams by purchasing on its behalf the firms which manufactured Macleans toothpaste and powders, Eno's fruit salts (which had substantial overseas assets), and the hair preparation Brylcreem. His interest in research and development for this company sprang from his friendship with the medical scientist Sir Edward Charles Dodds; and in 1936 Beechams endowed a laboratory for primary research at the Royal Northern Hospital, London. Accepting that the long-term prosperity of Beechams Pills lay in the development of ethical medicines, in 1942 Hill authorized the establishment of Beecham Research Laboratories. On these foundations his successor, Henry George Leslie Lazell (1903–1982), converted the renamed Beecham group into a major pharmaceutical company (from 1989 onwards SmithKline Beecham plc).

In 1929 Hill became a director of the Eagle Star Insurance Company which, during Britain's economic recovery in the 1930s, grew rapidly into a leading financial institution with considerable funds to invest. His reputation was such that in 1930 the chancellor of the exchequer, Philip Snowden, appointed him to a committee to assess the extent and use, and possible sale, of government property holdings. With the support of Eagle Star's chairman, Sir Edward Mountain, in 1932–3 he set up Philip Hill & Partners (which later became, through amalgamation in the 1950s and 1960s, the merchant bank Hill Samuel), and the Second Covent Garden Property Company (which eventually became part of MEPC plc), to finance industrial ventures and commercial properties respectively.

In 1933 Hill suffered the one major commercial reverse in an otherwise highly successful career: his failure to purchase Boots Pure Drug Company Ltd, which he had intended to be the core of a rationalized multiple chemists' combine in Britain. Boots, earlier controlled by the United Drug Company of America, was being sold back into British hands. Hill made an acceptable bid, only to be overruled by the Treasury, which refused to sanction the required dollars under emergency regulations introduced during the national economic crisis of 1931.

Among Hill's other property interests were those connected with the steadily growing leisure market in Britain. He secured a large stake in cinemas, most notably in Odeon Theatres Ltd, and acquired the Olympia exhibition centre in West Kensington. In 1935 he helped to form the Hawker Siddeley Aircraft Company Ltd, and thus facilitated the development of the Hurricane aircraft which fought in the battle of Britain (1940).

Hill's practice was to buy companies for cash, which he raised by issuing shares taken up mainly by financial institutions. However, he seldom subjected his acquisitions to a thoroughgoing internal restructuring, which many of them needed. He was extremely successful in selecting businesses and properties, able to make an instinctive judgement of their value, but he was less successful in his choice of managers; he behaved fairly but strictly towards employees, perhaps showing excessive loyalty to under-performing subordinates.

In the world of finance, Hill's business skills and integrity earned him wide respect. He could make bold decisions with great speed, and his word was always his bond. A strong personality reinforced his large physical presence (in later life he weighed 18 stone). His rule in life was 'start early and work late', and with so many business commitments, opportunities for recreation were necessarily limited. Latterly, however, in the pre-war years, he often spent several winter months in the West Indies or Florida, while keeping in regular touch with his businesses. He had boxed during his brief spell in the army, and in later life he was a golfer and an expert at the game of poker, thanks to his long experience of cliffhanging property deals. He also enjoyed gossiping about money matters with chosen associates, was a reader of thrillers, and a film addict. On a higher cultural level, in 1944 his initiative ensured that the Royal Opera House, Covent Garden, would return to its proper function after wartime use as a dance hall.

About 1930, after separating from his wife Vera, Hill began living with Phyllis Lytton, daughter of Reuben Partington, manufacturer's agent. A one-time dancer and in 1930 a racehorse owner twenty-five years his junior, she changed her name to Hill, married him in 1934, and gave him ten years of happiness. There were no children of the last three marriages. Hill died of prostate cancer on 15 August 1944 at his home, Windlesham Moor, Sunninghill Road, Windlesham, Surrey, survived by his fourth wife.

T. A. B. CORLEY

Sources DNB · T. A. B. Corley, 'Hill, Philip Ernest', DBB · J. M. Keyworth, *Cabbages and things: the background and story of the Covent Garden property companies to 1970* (privately published, 1990), 117–48 · H. G. Lazell, *From pills to penicillin: the Beecham story* (1975) · T. Beecham, *A mingled chime* (1944) · S. D. Chapman, *Jesse Boot of Boots the Chemists* (1974) · *Annual report of Beecham Estates and Pills Ltd* (1924–8) · *Annual report of Beechams Pills Ltd* (1928–44) · *Chemist and Druggist* (26 Aug 1944) · *The Economist* (26 Aug 1944) · *Estates Gazette* (19 Aug 1944) · A. J. Espley, 'The late Philip E. Hill', *Pharmaceutical Journal*, 99 (1944), 89 · *South Wales Echo and Gazette* (16 Aug 1944) · *The Times* (16 Aug 1944) · *The Times* (17 Aug 1944) · *The Times* (18 Aug 1944) · *The Times* (19 Aug 1944) · *The Times* (22 Aug 1944) · *Torbay Times* (25 Aug 1944) · T. A. B. Corley, *From national to multinational enterprise: the Beecham business, 1848–1945* (1983) · T. A. B. Corley, 'Beechams: from patent medicines to pharmaceuticals. I. The patent medicine era, 1848–1951' · b. cert. · m. cert. · d. cert. · CGPLA Eng. & Wales (1945)

Archives MEPC, London, minute books of Beecham Estates and Pills Ltd · SmithKline Beecham, Brentford, Middlesex, minute books of Beecham Pills Ltd

Likenesses photograph, c.1910, repro. in Keyworth, *Cabbages and things* • photograph, c.1935 • A. E. Cooper, oils, Royal Northern Hospital, London
Wealth at death £3,008,327 10s. 1d.: probate, 31 Jan 1945, CGPLA *Eng. & Wales*

Hill, Richard (*fl.* 1508–1536), merchant, was born at Hillend, in Hitchin, Hertfordshire. He was made a freeman of the Merchant Adventurers in May 1508, and from the entries in his commonplace book, appears to have travelled to markets at Antwerp and Bruges. He married Elizabeth Wyngar, daughter of a London haberdasher. Between the birth of the first son (John) in November 1518 and the second (Thomas) in May 1520, the Hill family seems to have moved from Hitchin to London, where they stayed until at least 1526 (when Hill's last and seventh child, Robert, was born).

Over the years Hill compiled a commonplace book (Balliol College, MS 354). The manuscript is a varied collection of sacred and secular poetry and prose. It combines carols and medieval poetry (e.g. selections from Lydgate, John Gower's *Confessio amantis*, and 'The Nut Brown Mayde') with extracts from the *Gesta Romanorum*, practical treatises (on breaking horses and grafting trees), recipes (for brewing, making ink, killing rats, and so on), puzzles and card tricks, and two books on courtesy (one of which doubles as an English–French conversation manual). There is also a series of ecclesiastical entries (mainly Latin), including graces, a paraphrase of the ten commandments, and a formula of questions to be asked by a confessor.

Hill's manuscript shows an interest in history and contemporary affairs. Besides a chronicle (beginning in 1413, and growing in detail in later years as Hill drew on his own experience), the book contains several historical and occasional poems, such as the lament of Eleanor Cobham, duchess of Gloucester, Thomas More's elegy on Elizabeth of York, and William Dunbar's (?) 'Praise of London', annotated in the manuscript as being 'made at Mr Shaas table when he was mayre'.

The collection reflects the life and interests of a London merchant. As well as commercial notes (on taxation, purchasing land and so on), and entries describing protocol and household stuff used at the lord mayor's banquet, the manuscript also records an extensive kin network of London merchants, compounded and celebrated through marriage and god-parenting. The last distinct entry in the chronicle is dated 1536.   CATHY SHRANK

Sources R. Dyboski, ed., *Songs, carols, and other miscellaneous poems from the Balliol MS. 354*, EETS, extra ser., 101 (1907) • E. Flügel, *Anglia*, 26 (1903), 94–285 • Balliol Oxf., MS 354 [Hill's commonplace bk] • T. Wright, ed., *Political poems and songs relating to English history*, 2 vols., Rolls Series, 14 (1859–61)
Archives Balliol Oxf., commonplace book

Hill, Richard (1655/6–1727), diplomat and public servant, was born at Hawkstone, Shropshire, and baptized at Hodnet on 23 March 1656, the second son of Rowland Hill (*bap.* 1623?) of Hawkstone and his wife, Margaret Whitehall of Doddington, Shropshire. From Shrewsbury School, Hill was admitted on 18 June 1675, aged nineteen, to St

John's College, Cambridge, where he graduated BA in 1679, proceeded MA in 1682, was ordained deacon, and was a fellow between 1679 and 1692. He served as a tutor to the Burlington family and then to that of Laurence Hyde, first earl of Rochester and lord president of the council, who advanced his career. A meeting with Richard Jones, earl of Ranelagh, paymaster-general to the army, led to his appointment as Ranelagh's deputy in Flanders. His financial skill both saved him from the disgrace that was Ranelagh's lot and helped him amass a large fortune. His father is reported to have said: 'My son Dick makes money very fast: God send that he gets it honestly' (Blakeway, 181). A moderate tory, he was distrusted by his whig employers, as the Marlboroughs' and Godolphin's correspondence displays. Speaker Richard Onslow held that his wealth 'was all acquired by himself … without any reproach as to the means of it that I ever heard of' (Burnet, 4.318).

Hill held office in England as a lord of the Treasury from 1699 to 1702 and a lord of the Admiralty from 1702 to 1708, but his most notable service was on the continent. In 1696 he was sent to Brussels as envoy, and William III, whom he admired greatly, sent him to Turin in 1699 to congratulate Victor Amadeus II, duke of Savoy, and his duchess, respectively second and first cousins of both William and Mary, on the birth of an heir. He had little taste for the envoy's life abroad, complaining that 'there is neither beef, nor veal, nor mutton which an Englishman can eat' (M. Lane, *The Nineteenth Century*, 1927, 562), but his 'clear parts, … his easy access and affable way', as well as his being 'a favourite with both parties' (*Memoirs of the Secret Services*, 145) fitted him for diplomatic life. According to a 1720 dedication to William Robinson, bishop of London, who had been lord privy seal, William III 'did often declare that he had never employed two ministers of greater vigilance, capacity and virtue than yourself, my Lord, and the Reverend Mr Hill' (Wheatly). In 1703 Queen Anne sent him again to Turin, via The Hague, where he laid his plans with the Dutch to bring the duke of Savoy into the War of the Spanish Succession against Louis XIV.

Victor Amadeus's duchy, caught between France and the empire, would be put at risk in a war, but war also presented the prospect of repossessing territory lost earlier to the French. The duke had previously proved an unreliable ally, deserting the allies in 1696, and Hill and his Dutch colleague worked hard and at last successfully to gain the full commitment of a ruler who was 'a very absolute Prince and will have everything his own way' (*Diplomatic Correspondence*, 1.315). England's subsidy to the duchy was agreed at last, and 'wee were a little out of humour, the Envoy of Holland and myself, to come so far and make so ill a bargain for so much money' (*Diplomatic Correspondence*, 1.316), but Victor Amadeus then made a further demand, forcing Hill's reluctant agreement—at a price. Nottingham, Hill's chief, and Marlborough favoured taking advantage of the diversion provided by the Camisard revolt in the Cévennes to mount an invasion of France from Piedmont, with Huguenot refugees and former

Vaudois insurgents to be recruited, and with Sir Cloudesley Shovell's fleet in support. Hill constantly argued against the scheme, as is evident from his very full correspondence, more than 600 letters copied and put in order in his retirement. Hill was his own man and risked offending even Marlborough. He said of De Miremont, the Huguenot general sent from England, that 'he knows no more of what is doing in the Cévennes than the post-man does' (*Diplomatic Correspondence*, 1.351). His scepticism was vindicated by the failure of his planned diversion on the French coast to help the Catalans, in which the four frigates at his disposal ('my little fleet') took part, the Camisard element having lost heart at rumours of their leader Cavalier's peacemaking (*Diplomatic Correspondence*, 1.343–87). When he asked later for the ambassadorship to The Hague another was appointed who, wrote Godolphin, 'will have no whimseys of his own but will be sure to follow your [Marlborough's] instructions' (Snyder, 2.146).

Hill placed the greatest importance on the lowest rated of his instructions. He was 'to give your best attention to the Vaudois … to let them know your willingness to intercede for them' and 'very earnestly to press the Duke to revoke all such edicts as have lately been made against them' (*Diplomatic Correspondence*, 1.4). The Vaudois, a medieval heretic sect, later protestants, who had suffered centuries of persecution by the dukes of Savoy, were guaranteed toleration by a secret clause of the 1690 treaty, and in 1696 by an edict which had become a dead letter by the duke's abrogation of the treaty. Hill made it his business to gain reaffirmation of this clause in the new treaty, thus making the allies guarantors for the Vaudois. After many disappointments he made the granting of the extra subsidy demanded by the duke conditional on 'the liberty of conscience of the Vaudois, which I do demand' (*Diplomatic Correspondence*, 1.389). In recognition of this and of the funds he collected in England and the benefits he gained for them the Vaudois pastors placed him 'at the head of our Nehemiahs' (*Diplomatic Correspondence*, 2.973). In retirement he continued to serve the Vaudois, conveying funds to them until the 1720s. The Vaudois link survived his death for a century or more: in 1825 by order of the House of Commons the 1690 and 1704 treaties were printed in order to hold the allies of the time to their duty to protect the Vaudois, who were again under threat.

Hill's bid for The Hague ambassadorship having failed he was given a final appointment to Brussels but withdrew. His health was bad and, as he had inscribed on his marble monument in Hodnet church, he was *militiae fessus et viarum* ('tired with war and travel'). In his three-quarter-length portrait he looks haggard, especially compared with an earlier oval study. He lived quietly as tenant at Cleveland House, St James's, and in his own house at the Old Palace, Richmond, where 'he was much resorted to by the most eminent persons of the time [and] the Royal family shewed him very particular regards' (Burnet, 4.318). He refused a bishopric in hope of that of Ely, which was not realized, and became a fellow of the Royal Society, DCL of Oxford (1708), and fellow of Eton College (1714), where he enjoyed his own chambers. Arthur Onslow, who knew

Hill, found that his letters 'proved him to have been a very considerable person, and made for higher stations than he arrived to' (Burnet, 4.318). For want of such stations he devoted his great wealth to consolidating the family's Shropshire estates and to providing from them for three nephews, especially Rowland Hill (1705–1783), later father of Richard Hill (1732–1808) and Rowland Hill (1744–1833). He rebuilt Hawkstone to his own design but Attingham Park later became the Hills' grandest seat. Hill died on 11 June 1727 at Richmond and was buried in the family vault at St Luke's Church, Hodnet. The Vaudois, who have survived and prospered, remember and honour him.

RANDOLPH VIGNE

Sources *The diplomatic correspondence of the Right Hon. Richard Hill*, ed. W. Blackley, 2 vols. (1845) • J. B. Blakeway, *The sheriffs of Shropshire with their armorial bearings and notes genealogical and biographical of their families* (1831) • Bishop Burnet's *History*, 4.36, 317–18; 6.77, 120 • N. Luttrell, *A brief historical relation of state affairs from September 1678 to April 1714*, 6 vols. (1857) • *The Marlborough–Godolphin correspondence*, ed. H. L. Snyder, 3 vols. (1975) • E. M. Jancey, 'The Hon. and Rev. Richard Hill of Hawkstone. An account of his investment in north Shropshire estates between the years 1700 and 1726', *Transactions of the Shropshire Archaeological Society*, 55 (1954–6), 143–59 • *Memoirs of the secret services of John Macky*, ed. A. R. (1733) • C. Wheatly, *A rational illustration of the Book of Common Prayer* (1720), dedication • *N&Q*, 3rd ser., 11 (1867), 456 • *N&Q*, 4th ser., 3 (1869), 161 • R. Vigne, 'Richard Hill and an eighteenth-century turning point for the Waldensians', *Bollettino della Società di Studi Valdesi*, 175 (Dec 1994), 73–9 • G. Symcox, *Victor Amadeus II and absolutism in the Savoyard state, 1675–1734* (1983) • Venn, *Alum. Cant.* • *IGI* [will, Hodnet parish register]
Archives BL, corresp., Add. MSS 37529–37530 • Bodl. Oxf., corresp. as envoy to duke of Savoy, MS Eng. Hist. D 164 • Bodl. Oxf., diplomatic corresp. • Northants. RO, corresp. • Shrops. RRC, corresp. and accounts, ledgers and estate rentals, financial papers • Yale U., Beinecke L., corresp. and papers | BL, letters to John Ellis, Add. MSS 28886–28916 • BL, letters to Sidney Godolphin, Add. MSS 28056–28057 • BL, letters to Lord Nottingham, Add. MSS 29589–29591 • BL, letters to James Vernon, Add. MS 4199 • CKS, letters to Alexander Stanhope • CUL, corresp. • Glos. RO, corresp. with William Blathwayt • JRL, corresp. with Samuel Hill • McGill University, Montreal, McLennan Library, letters to George Stepney • Yale U., Beinecke L., letters to William Blathwayt
Likenesses M. Gauci, lithograph (after G. Kneller), BM • school of Kneller, oils, Attingham Park, Shropshire • oils, Attingham Park, Shropshire • oils, St John Cam.
Wealth at death bequests totalling £63,618 16s.; plus annuities totalling £80 p.a.; South Sea and East India Company stock unspecified; a quantity of jewellery; furniture, tapestries, picture of Antwerp, library, silver, linen at Hawkstone, Cleveland Court, Richmond, and chambers at Eton College; residue of capital to be divided among three nephews; considerable landed property in Shropshire, incl. house at Hawkstone (with entail), house at Richmond, Surrey; nine rectories / benefices in Cheshire, Norfolk, Shropshire, and Suffolk; estate was 'very large, and sufficient to satisfy every public and private claim upon his generosity': will, Hodnet parish register; *Bishop Burnet's history*, vol. 4, p. 318

Hill, Sir Richard, second baronet (1733–1808), religious controversialist, was born on 6 June 1733 at the family seat—Hawkstone Park, near Shrewsbury—the eldest son in the family of ten children of Sir Rowland Hill (1705–1783), landowner, who had been created first baronet in 1727, and his first wife, Jane, the daughter of Sir Brian Broughton. The evangelical preacher Rowland *Hill (1744–1833) was his younger brother, and his great-uncle was the diplomatist Richard Hill (*d.* 1727). He was educated at Shrewsbury grammar school (1743) and at Westminster School (1744–8) before matriculating from Magdalen College, Oxford, on 8 December 1750. He was created MA on 2 July 1754. He went on the grand tour to Italy with Charles Bruce, fifth earl of Elgin, during 1756 and 1757, and from February to July recorded their travels in a notebook. Hill made a second trip to Italy in 1790–91, this time in the company of his half-brother, the Revd Brian Hill; they travelled south to Naples and spent almost two months in Sicily.

Greatly troubled by an overwhelming conviction of his own sin, Hill returned to Oxford, where he experienced an evangelical conversion on Saturday 18 February 1758; he recorded that he felt a new sense of peace and assurance and took communion 'as never before' the following day. His newly found faith strengthened by hearing the sermons of Thomas Haweis at St Mary Magdalene, he joined a small Methodist society that met regularly in Oxford. The expulsion of six students from St Edmund Hall in 1768, for having attended Methodist prayer meetings, sparked off a pamphlet war. Hill leaped to their defence with an anonymous pamphlet, *Pietas Oxoniensi* (1768), in which he scathingly denounced the college and the vice-chancellor for punishing the students for holding Calvinist beliefs that, he argued, were 'the ancient, undoubted, received tenets of the Church of *England*' (p. 57). Having acquired a taste for religious controversy, Hill vigorously participated in the often bitter debates in the Methodist movement between those who adhered to Arminian doctrines, led by John Wesley, and those who held Calvinist convictions, whose principal champion following George Whitefield's death was Augustus M. Toplady. Hill mainly sparred with Thomas Olivers and John William Fletcher but his *Review of All the Doctrines Taught by the Rev. Mr. John Wesley* (1772) drew a response from Wesley himself. He accused Wesley of teaching that a 'second justification' by works was necessary for salvation, and ruthlessly listed the contradictory doctrinal statements made by Wesley. By the end of 1773 Hill sought a reconciliation with Wesley, and the two men met for the first time and shook hands after a service conducted by Thomas Pentycross.

In May 1780 Hill was elected to parliament as MP for Shropshire; he represented his constituency, without facing a contest, for twenty-six years. He adopted an independent and moral position on political issues; characteristically his maiden speech, on 19 May 1781, was delivered on a 'bill for better regulation of the Sabbath'. Convinced that peace in America should be the primary concern of Lord North's ministry, he voted against the government in 1781–2 and in favour of the peace preliminaries presented by Lord Shelburne in February 1783. He proved a steadfast supporter of William Pitt after he had come to power, late in 1783. His speeches were lengthy, pious, and full of misguided attempts to use humour to convey his moral and political arguments; his comparison of the coalition of North and Charles James Fox to an alliance of Herod and Pontius Pilate had the house in stitches—at his expense. Despite his best efforts to bring religion into political debates his method of larding his speeches with scriptural quotations alienated rather than convinced his fellow MPs, in stark contrast to William Wilberforce, who successfully championed the evangelical cause in parliament.

Following his father's death, on 7 August 1783, Hill succeeded to the baronetcy and Shropshire estates, which brought him an income of over £15,000. He became embroiled in controversy with the high-church Anglican apologist Charles Daubeny from 1798 to 1800, after Daubeny had attacked evangelical preaching for damaging the established church. Hill replied with three pamphlets: *An Apology for Brotherly Love and for the Doctrines of the Church of England* (1798), *Reformation Truth Restored* (1800), and *Daubenism Confronted and Martin Luther Vindicated* (1800). In 1803 the controversy continued, when George Pretyman Tomline, bishop of Lincoln, severely censured evangelical preaching in his charge; Hill warmly defended the evangelical clergy from Tomline's accusations.

Hill was a keen supporter of the British and Foreign Bible Society but failing health prevented him taking a more active role in its work. Soon after the dissolution of parliament in autumn 1806 ill health forced him to give up his seat, and he retired to Hawkstone. He died there on 28 November 1808, and was buried in a vault known as the Sepulchre of the Hills in the nearby parish church of Hodnet, Shropshire, where a monument was erected to his memory. He never married, and was succeeded as third baronet by his younger brother John, the father of Rowland Hill, first Viscount Hill, and of Sir Thomas Noel Hill.   W. C. SYDNEY, rev. S. J. SKEDD

Sources E. Sidney, *The life of Sir Richard Hill* (1839) • P. E. Sangster, 'Hill, Sir Richard', *The Blackwell dictionary of evangelical biography, 1730–1860*, ed. D. M. Lewis (1995) • L. B. Namier, 'Hill, Richard', HoP, *Commons, 1754–90* • R. G. Thorne, 'Hill, Sir Richard', HoP, *Commons, 1790–1820* • Foster, *Alum. Oxon.* • J. Ingamells, ed., *A dictionary of British and Irish travellers in Italy, 1701–1800* (1997)
Archives NL Wales, letters • Shrops. RRC, family corresp. and papers | PRO, letters to William Pitt, PRO 30/8
Likenesses R. Woodman, line engraving, pubd 1839, NPG • J. Russell, chalk drawing, NPG

Hill [Hull], **Robert** (d. 1423×5), justice, was one of a west-country family that included several lawyers in the later fourteenth and early fifteenth centuries. His father was perhaps also called Robert. The relationship of the Hills to each other is not always clear, and particular care is needed to distinguish the judge from his contemporary namesake, Robert Hill of Spaxton, Somerset, who was son of Sir John Hill, justice of the king's bench from 1389 to c.1408, and who died in 1423 after a career in estate management in Somerset and Devon.

Robert Hill the future judge doubtless began his legal career by acting for west-country clients, and in 1384–5 was one of the lawyers retained for their counsel by Edward Courtenay, earl of Devon. He was described in a list of these lawyers as 'Robert Hull the son' (BL, Additional Roll 64320), to distinguish him from 'Robert Hull the father' (ibid.) who was similarly retained; Sir John Hill the future judge was a member of the earl's household at this date.

Hill was MP for various Devon towns: both Dartmouth and Tavistock in 1372; Plympton in 1373, 1377 (twice), and 1380; and Exeter in 1379. In all of the election returns save two for Plympton he is described as Robert Hill junior. He made his career as a lawyer based partly in the Westminster courts, and he joined the Inner Inn; he gained the entrée to the court of common pleas by being made a serjeant-at-law in Michaelmas term 1388.

On 14 May 1408 Hill was appointed a justice of the court of common pleas, and was reappointed on the accessions of Henry V and Henry VI. In 1421 and 1422, following the death of Richard Norton, he acted as chief justice of common pleas, though he was never formally appointed to that office. His salary was last paid at Easter 1423, although he may have lived until 1424 or 1425.

Since Hill settled at Shilston, in Modbury, Devon, he is probably to be identified as the Robert Hill who married Isabel, daughter of Sir John Wadham (justice of the common pleas, 1388–97) and Elizabeth, daughter and coheir of William Shilston of Shilston. They had several children, his heir being Robert, who according to one account was born in 1392. Isabel must have predeceased her husband, who by 1419 was married to Joan, daughter and heir of Sir Otho Bodrugan; she survived Hill, and married Sir John Trevarthyan, or Trevaygnoun, before dying in 1427 or 1428.

NIGEL RAMSAY

Sources J. L. Vivian, ed., *The visitations of the county of Devon, comprising the herald's visitations of 1531, 1564, and 1620* (privately printed, Exeter, [1895]), 486 · J. L. Vivian, ed., *The visitations of Cornwall, comprising the herald's visitations of 1530, 1573, and 1620* (1887), 227, 229 · W. Pole, *Collections towards a description of the county of Devon* (1791), 312 · Baker, *Serjeants*, 159, 518 · Sainty, *Judges*, 68 · BL, Additional Roll 64320 · HoP, *Commons* · J. J. Alexander, 'Seventh report on the parliamentary representation of Devon', *Report and Transactions of the Devonshire Association*, 71 (1939), 145–66, esp. 148, 155 · J. J. Alexander, 'Exeter members of parliament, pt 2', *Report and Transactions of the Devonshire Association*, 60 (1928), 183–214, esp. 202 · J. J. Alexander, 'Exeter members of parliament, pt 4', *Report and Transactions of the Devonshire Association*, 62 (1930), 195–223, esp. 220 · Chancery records

Hill, Robert (d. 1623), Church of England clergyman, was born in Ashbourne, Derbyshire, 'that poore and untaught towne', where he described himself as 'descended of meane but honest parentage' (R. Hill, *The Contents of Scripture*, 1596, sig A5v; PRO, PROB 11/142, fol. 87). He always remained conscious of his Derbyshire roots, and in later life dubbed a portion of his London rectory his 'Derbyshire room' (E. Freshfield, ed., *The Vestry Minute Book of St Bartholomew Exchange*, 1890, 79). He matriculated pensioner from Christ's College, Cambridge, in July 1581, graduated BA in 1585 and proceeded MA in 1588. In 1589 he was admitted a fellow of St John's College, Cambridge. Hill's subsequent activities in Cambridge reveal puritan sympathies probably acquired under the early influence of William Perkins. At St John's, Hill was among a cohort of godly young men granted fellowships in the early 1590s who later became notable puritan figures, such as William Crashawe and Abdias Ashton. While at St John's he signed petitions (organized by Henry Alvey) in favour of the imprisoned separatist Francis Johnson, and another in 1595 against the Arminian William Barrett. A disputed election for the mastership of the college in 1595 found Hill among those writing to Lord Burghley in support of candidates who included Alvey and complaining that they had been maligned as 'puritani' (Baker, 2.607). It is noteworthy that Hill's will mentions a 'Mr Henry Alvey of Cambridge' as his father-in-law, although no record has been found of this marriage. Hill was again involved in controversy about 1595–6, when he was the chief complainant to Bishop Richard Bancroft of London against a sermon given by the regius professor John Overall in his capacity as vicar of Epping, especially concerning the question of whether Christ had died for all men.

Hill's career progressed uncertainly during these years, although the feoffees of St Andrew, Norwich, appointed him as curate, a position he held from about 1591 to 1602. Nevertheless, he seems to have been based in Cambridge for much of this time and in 1596 was apparently living at Park Hall, Essex, at the house of Sir William FitzWilliam. In the dedication to his *Life-everlasting* (1601) Hill signed himself as 'your Lordships most bounden and dutifull Chaplaine', although the 'Preface to the reader' is dated from St John's College where Hill continued as a fellow until 1608–9. Hill had proceeded BD in 1595 and it was during the 1590s that he first established himself as a dedicated religious popularizer and pedagogue and a translator of continental protestant divines. In 1591 he translated William Perkins's classic, *A Golden Chaine*, into English, at the author's specific request. Hill later produced a version of the same text set out in a catechetical form, published in 1612. In 1596 he published *The Contents of Scripture*—effectively an abridgement and explication of the Bible—'wherby the yong beginner might get entrance into reading, & the old reader be readied in remembring' (sig. A7), which also contained passages from Isaac Tremelius, Francis Junius, Theodore Beza, Johannes Piscator, and John Calvin. A more scholarly work was *Life-everlasting, or, The true knowledge of one Jehovah, three Elohim, and Jesus Immanuel: collected out of the best modern divines* (1601), in which Hill espoused a hard-line position on predestination and insisted emphatically on the need for the doctrine to be fully taught to a lay audience, an insistence also reflected in his clash with Overall.

In 1602 Hill moved to the capital when he obtained a lectureship at the fashionable parish of St Martin-in-the-Fields, a position he retained until 1613. It was for this parish that he composed his most popular work, a catechism which went through eight editions and was posthumously translated into Dutch. Originally published in 1606 as *Christs Prayer Expounded, a Christian Directed, and a Communicant Prepared*, it was greatly expanded in 1609 as *The Pathway to Prayer and Pietie*. These later editions included new material such as 'A direction to Christian life' and 'An instruction to die well'. This catechism displays Hill's pastoral abilities to best advantage, and it is distinguished by its clarity of exposition, use of homely similes, and willingness to tackle difficult pastoral issues.

Although Hill obtained a living at St Margaret Moses in 1607, he continued to live in St Martin's parish, sometimes in the houses of its vestrymen, apparently lacking the means to provide himself with accommodation. During this period Hill proceeded DD, in 1609. Finally, in 1613, the support of Lord Chancellor Ellesmere gained him preferment to the prosperous City living of St Bartholomew by the Exchange, where he remained until his death in 1623. On 1 June 1614, at Canterbury Cathedral, Hill married Margaret, widow of the prebendary Adrian Saravia. She was the well-born daughter of John de Wijts, a religious refugee from Antwerp. Margaret Hill died in childbirth on 29 June 1615, aged thirty-nine, and her death was lamented in print by Hill and Joshua Sylvester in the sixth edition of *The Pathway to Prayer* (1615–16), in which it was noted that she had served in the households of the Hastings and Palavicinio families.

Hill seems always to have been a conforming puritan, and he lamented the 1607 death of Bishop Richard Vaughan of London, whom he characterized as 'an ornament to our Church in which he was a preaching Bishop' and 'a most watchfull and temperate Governour' (Hill, 1609 edn, foreword). Nevertheless, Hill's sympathy for more radical religious figures remained with him to the end. In 1620, for example, he edited the works of the nonconformist Samuel Hieron, prefacing the volume with a laudatory account which is a principal source for Hieron's life. Throughout his life Hill clearly felt dogged by the insecurity of his financial position. His will orders the sale of his library and he entreats his St Bartholomew's parishioners 'that since I was a principall meanes to builde the parsonage house they would mediate that my loving wife may not uppon a soddaine be put out of yt but have convenient tyme to provide for her selfe'. Hill also left bequests to Dr Richard Clarke 'of Canterbury', Thomas Westfield (future bishop of Bristol, whose sister, Susan, had married Hill some time after 1615) and the Vintners' Company, of which he was a member. He died in August 1623 and was buried in the chancel of St Bartholomew by the Exchange, survived by his wife.   J. F. MERRITT

Sources will, PRO, PROB 11/142, fol. 87 · Venn, *Alum. Cant.* · R. Hill, *The pathway to prayer and pietie*, 3rd edn (1609); enl. edn (1613); 6th edn (1615) · CUL, MS Gg/1/29, fols. 119a–121b · H. C. Porter, *Reformation and reaction in Tudor Cambridge* (1958), 188, 346 · T. Baker, *History of the college of St John the Evangelist, Cambridge*, ed. J. E. B. Mayor, 2 (1869), 607 · J. M. Cowper, *The memorial inscriptions of Canterbury Cathedral* (1897), 315 · *DNB* · rentals, 1575–99, 1600–19, St John Cam., fol. 214, fol. 263v
Likenesses S. de Passe, line engraving, BM, NPG
Wealth at death see will, PRO, PROB 11/142, fol. 87

Hill, Robert (1699–1777), tailor and religious writer, was born on 11 January 1699 at Miswell, Hertfordshire, the son of poor parents, Robert Hill and Phoebe, *née* Clark. His father died within a year of his birth and about five years later his mother married Thomas Robinson, a tailor in Buckingham. Robert was left to the care of his maternal grandmother, at Miswell, and on her removal in 1710 to Tring Grove he became a farmer's boy. Having proved too delicate for this occupation he was apprenticed in 1714 to his stepfather in Buckingham, where the chance acquisition of a grammar at the age of seventeen inspired him

with zeal for learning. His first studies were Latin and French, and later he studied Greek and Hebrew.

Hill married in 1721 and became a schoolmaster in 1724, on finding his increasing family hard to support. He ran his school, which had more than fifty scholars, for six or seven years. In 1728 his wife died; in 1730 he married a rich widow but she was such a spendthrift that he left her in 1732 and travelled as a tailor and stay-maker. Having heard of his second wife's death, about 1741, he returned to Buckingham in 1744 and married for the third time in 1747.

About this date Hill came to the notice of a neighbouring clergyman, who encouraged him to write. Hill was also introduced by him to Joseph Spence, who wrote an account of Hill's life in *Parallel in the manner of Plutarch, between a most celebrated man of Florence, and one, scarce ever heard of, in England* (1757). This tract compares Hill with the Florentine writer Antonio Magliabechi and was included in Robert Dodsley's *Fugitive Pieces on Various Subjects, by Several Authors* (1761). A long list of benefactors at the end of Spence's tract shows that Hill received substantial assistance, but in 1775 he was again in difficulties. In a preface to Hill's *Christianity the True Religion: an Essay in Answer to the Blasphemy of a Deist* (1775) Hill is still described as a poor but worthy man. He died at Buckingham in July 1777 after a long illness.   RONALD BAYNE, *rev.* EMMA MAJOR

Sources J. Spence, 'The life of Mr Hill', in R. Dodsley, *Fugitive pieces on various subjects, by several authors*, 2 (1761) · R. Hill, *Christianity the true religion* (1775) · J. Spence, 'Letter to the Revd Mr G. R.', in R. Hill, *Some considerations on the divinity of the Holy Ghost* (1753) · ESTC
Wealth at death poor

Hill, Robert [Robin] (1899–1991), plant biochemist, was born on 2 April 1899 at Normanhurst, Warwick New Road, New Milverton, Leamington Spa, the son of Joseph Alfred Hill, accountant in the family metalwork firm and later amateur scientist, and his wife, Clara Maud, daughter of Frank George Jackson, lecturer on principles of ornament and advanced design at the Birmingham Municipal School of Art and illustrator of J. A. Hill's *Ferns and the Microscope* (1893).

Taught botany by Elizabeth Gamble, his paternal grandmother's cousin, and watercolour drawing by his aunt Mary (Jackson), Robin Hill—as he was known—was educated at Bedales School, where A. E. Heath, later professor of philosophy at University College, Swansea, was science master. Encouraged by Heath to take an interest in natural dyes, Hill joined the Bedales dyeing club, grew dye-plants, and wrote articles on them for the school magazine. Heath also encouraged him in astronomy, and his first published paper (1917) was on sunspots.

In April 1917 Hill was admitted a scholar to Emmanuel College, Cambridge, and joined the university's Officers' Training Corps, but had time to carry out experiments on the colour reactions of the indole residue of tryptophan. In the autumn he was deemed unsuitable as an officer and was drafted to an infantry regiment—a dispiriting experience—but in February 1918 he was transferred to the anti-gas department at University College, London. In January 1919 he returned to Cambridge, where he read chemistry, physics, and botany in the natural science tripos, specializing in chemistry in part two, and gained first class in both. Because he was inquisitive about cloud formations he designed a 'fish-eye' lens to photograph them, his system giving a projection of slightly more than 180°—better than modern fish-eye cameras. Despite his shyness he was an active member of the college's Natural Science Club and was proposed a member of the university's Biological Tea Club by E. J. H. Corner and Barton Worthington.

Hill's first independent research, under F. Gowland Hopkins in the department of biochemistry, was on the relation between structure and spectra in inorganic pigments; his desire to study plant pigments had to be relegated to his spare time. His scientific reputation was built on his studies of haemoglobin's chemical and spectroscopic properties. David Keilin invited him to help with work on cytochrome in the Molteno Institute, where Hill was the first to characterize the porphyrin from cytochrome *c* and demonstrate its relation to haematoporphyrin, and thus to the porphyrin of haemoglobin.

In 1932 Hill went into deep depression, and Worthington suggested he travel to Singapore to visit Corner. They explored the forests of Johore together, and besides seeking new dye-plant sources Hill sketched plants, one of his drawings being published in Corner's *Wayside Trees of Malaya* (1940). Restored, he returned to Cambridge, where he devised a spectrocolorimeter to measure the oxygen dissociation curves of haemoglobin. On 18 March 1935 he married Amy Priscilla (*b.* 1906/7), daughter of Edgar Worthington, a railway engineer, and sister of Barton. Shortly afterwards he bought Vatches Farm, at Barton, in Cambridgeshire, where he and his wife brought up two sons and two daughters. There, also, Hill wrote his papers and conducted an extensive correspondence.

In 1936, when nothing was known about the biochemical mechanism of photosynthesis, Hill began studying oxygen production from chloroplasts freed from leaves (the 'Hill reaction'); others in the laboratory had studied oxidation-reduction reactions in cell-free extracts of animal tissues, but Hill's novel approach in plants revolutionized the study of photosynthesis. In experiments he showed that the 'light' and 'dark' reactions are linked by a redox reaction but are otherwise independent. He maintained his interest in dyes, working on the anthraquinone pigments of madder and its allies, and as part of the war effort he joined the group in the department concerned with chemical warfare, and studied vesicants, notably protoanemonin. From 1943 he was employed by the Agricultural Research Council, and although not on the university staff he gave lectures, but he was not good at it.

Hill worked with Kamala Bhagvat on the presence of cytochrome oxidase in plant tissues, the first experiments to demonstrate a particularly respiratory system in plants, but from 1950 photosynthesis was the focus of his research. From 1944 he kept notebooks concerned with thermodynamics, and in 1960, in a paper with Fay Bendall, he proposed an arrangement of the cytochromes (the Z scheme) that harmonized photosynthetic and oxidative phosphorylation, providing a framework for the whole electron transport system of the chloroplast. It made clear the thermodynamic basis of the conversion of light energy to electrical energy to chemical energy in green plants, the basis of the organic world.

Hill scorned applied science, though he went to what became Malawi, in the late 1950s, to study tea fermentation. He retired in 1966 but retained his chaotic room in the laboratory, synthesizing dyes and studying the history of work on photosynthesis; though good at devising simple equipment Hill was at a loss with modern instruments. He was elected FRS in 1946, and his honorary degrees included one at Sheffield (1990), where his impact was such that the Robert Hill Laboratories—later known as the Robert Hill Institute—were established.

Hill was a modest, unassuming person, intolerant of pomposity, but he was not easy to work with and could explode with indignation, though he had a puckish sense of humour. He died at Hope Nursing Home, Cambridge, on 15 March 1991. D. J. MABBERLEY

Sources D. S. Bendall, *Memoirs FRS*, 40 (1994), 143–70 • *The Times* (21 March 1991) • b. cert. • m. cert. • d. cert.
Archives CUL, corresp. and papers | CUL, catalogue of paintings by D. Hill • CUL, corresp. with Peter Mitchell • U. Leeds, Brotherton L., corresp. with E. C. Stoner • University of Sheffield, corresp. with Arthur Ray Clapham • Whipple Museum of the History of Science, Cambridge, fish-eye cameras, plates, and photographs
Likenesses photograph, *c.*1950, repro. in Bendall, *Memoirs FRS*
Wealth at death £374,500: probate, 25 Sept 1991, *CGPLA Eng. & Wales*

Hill, Robert Gardiner (1811–1878), surgeon specializing in the treatment of the insane, was born at Louth, Lincolnshire, on 26 February 1811, the son of Robert Hill, a tradesman, of Leamington Spa, and his wife, Mary. John Harwood *Hill was an elder brother. After being apprenticed to a local surgeon about 1825, Hill trained in London at Grainger's anatomy school and at Guy's and St Thomas's Hospitals. While a student in London, Hill became interested in the treatment of the insane, and there survives an extensive manuscript note made by him describing Philippe Pinel's liberation of the insane from their chains.

In 1834 Hill became a member of the College of Surgeons and was appointed house surgeon to the Lincoln General Dispensary. The next year he was appointed as house surgeon, or resident medical officer, to the Lincoln Asylum, where, from about 1827, Edward Parker Charlesworth, one of three physicians to the asylum, had begun to reduce the level of mechanical restraint, such as straitjackets and handcuffs, used on patients. With indefatigable energy and tremendous determination Hill took these measures further until by 1838 restraint had been abandoned altogether at Lincoln. This was the first example of what came to be known as the non-restraint system in the treatment of lunatics. Hill publicized the achievement through a lecture in Lincoln in 1838 and by a pamphlet, *Total Abolition of Personal Restraint in the Treatment of the Insane* (1839). Although Hill succeeded in abolishing mechanical restraints it was necessary for him to impose rigorous discipline on his subordinates to ensure that they did not revert to using them. As a result there was a high level of tension among the attendants and officers of the asylum. This, coupled with the animosity of the governors and physicians, led to fierce infighting at the asylum from 1839, which led to Hill's resignation in 1840. With the departure of Hill, the momentum for non-restraint was lost at Lincoln. The debate over the merits of non-restraint was transferred to the columns of *The Lancet* in 1839 to 1841 and the most prominent site for developing non-restraint methods became the Middlesex County Asylum at Hanwell, where its governors, especially John Adams, and its medical superintendent John Conolly, did most to make non-restraint an orthodox doctrine of British psychiatry.

After retiring from the Lincoln Asylum, Hill's professional career was rather unremarkable. In 1840 he applied unsuccessfully for two asylum jobs (one of them being that of medical officer at Hanwell under Conolly). After ten years of general practice partnership in Lincoln, he opened, in 1851, Eastgate House, a small private asylum for female patients. The same year Hill was presented with a testimonial by the mayor of Lincoln, and in 1852 Hill himself was elected mayor. Eastgate House closed in 1856 and Hill went to London to become a co-owner (with Dr E. Willett) of Wyke House, another small asylum. In 1860 he dissolved the partnership, returned to Lincoln, and became an owner of Shillingthorpe House at Greatford, a decaying institution with a handful of patients, which was abandoned in less than three years. In 1863 Hill again moved to London, this time to take up the position of medical superintendent and co-owner of Earl's Court House, a private asylum for about twenty-five female patients, where he spent the rest of his life. He was elected a fellow of the Society of Antiquaries in 1853.

Hill's claim to be the originator of the non-restraint system led him into conflict with his colleagues. In 1850, he responded through the correspondence columns of *The Lancet* to comments made by Conolly and Charlesworth, and reiterated his claim. The debate opened again in 1857 when Hill repeated his claim in his *Concise History of the Entire Abolition of Medical Restraint*, a work prompted by Conolly's own piece on non-restraint published the year before. The argument resurfaced again in 1870 in Hill's *Lunacy: its Past and Present*; this time he had been provoked by Sir James Clark's *Memoir of John Conolly* (1869).

Hill died on 30 May 1878 of apoplexy and chronic kidney disease at Earl's Court House, Earl's Court Road, London, and was buried in Highgate cemetery; he left a widow, Charlotte. One of his sons inherited the house, and another son also took up psychiatry.

AKIHITO SUZUKI

Sources *BMJ* (15 June 1878), 873, 879 · R. Hunter and I. Macalpine, *Three hundred years of psychiatry, 1535–1860* (1963) · A. Walk, 'Lincoln and non-restraint', *British Journal of Psychiatry*, 117 (1970), 481–96 · L. D. Smith, 'The "great experiment": the place of Lincoln in the history of psychiatry', *Lincolnshire History and Archaeology*, 30 (1995), 55–62 · d. cert. · *CGPLA Eng. & Wales* (1878) · *DNB* · parish register, Louth, Lincs. Arch., 13 Oct 1809 [baptism: John Harwood Hill, brother]
Archives Lawn Hospital, Lincoln · Wellcome L., notebook | Herts. ALS, letters to E. B. Lytton

Likenesses E. Edwards, photograph, 1868, Wellcome L. · engraving, repro. in *Medical Circular* (7 Sept 1853), 187–9 · photographs, repro. in W. T. Robertson, *Photographs of eminent medical men* (1868), 2.65–8
Wealth at death under £4000: probate, 6 July 1878, *CGPLA Eng. & Wales*

Hill, Sir Roderic Maxwell (1894–1954), air force officer, was born in Hampstead, London, on 1 March 1894, the eldest of the three children of Micaiah John Muller *Hill (1856–1929), professor of mathematics at University College, London, and his wife, Minnie (1861–1920), the daughter of Marriott Ogle *Tarbotton, borough engineer of Nottingham. Sir George Francis Hill was his uncle. His obvious scientific and artistic talent was encouraged from an early age. From Bradfield College he went in 1912 to the fine arts department of University College, London, with the intention of becoming an architect. From 1909 onwards, however, he and his younger brother Geoffrey were becoming increasingly absorbed in flying. With money earned by Roderic from drawings published in *The Sphere*, they built during 1913, and successfully flew, a glider of their own design. The following year, two months after the outbreak of war, Hill enlisted in the ranks.

Commissioned in the 12th Northumberland Fusiliers in December 1914, Hill was in France by the second half of 1915 and first saw intensive action in the battle of Loos, where he earned a mention in dispatches and suffered a wound in the side. While recovering he successfully applied to join the Royal Flying Corps. By July 1916 he had earned his wings, shown sufficient ability to be put on the tricky Moranes, and joined 60 squadron, at that time co-operating in the Somme offensive. He quickly made his mark as a skilled airman: from repeated patrols and engagements over the German lines he returned unharmed, including 'the first big air battle in history' of 9 November 1916. Shortly after this he was again mentioned in dispatches and awarded the MC.

In December 1916 Hill became flight commander of 60 squadron and was promoted captain. His growing reputation as a highly intelligent pilot capable of every aerobatic manoeuvre then led to his posting in February 1917 to take over the experimental flying department of the royal aircraft factory at Farnborough. There his energy, enthusiasm, and skill and calculated daring as a pilot made a deep impression, and his test flying contributed greatly to the eventual success of such aircraft as the SE5, the RE8, and the DH9 with Napier Lion engine. In 1918 he became a squadron leader on the formation of the Royal Air Force, and in the same year he was awarded the AFC after flying into a balloon cable to test the efficacy of a newly invented protective device.

Hill remained at Farnborough until 1923, concerned among other matters with test flying the new larger machines and the development of aids such as wireless direction finding. He was awarded a bar to his AFC and the R. M. Groves aeronautical research prize (1922), and was elected a fellow of University College, London (1924). After attending the RAF Staff College at Andover, Hill was sent

Sir Roderic Maxwell Hill (1894–1954), by Elliott & Fry

out to command 45 (bomber) squadron at Hinaidi (1924–6), where he played an important part in the running of the new Baghdad–Cairo air mail and the preservation of the internal and external security of Iraq. He went next to the technical staff of RAF Middle East headquarters at Cairo, but in 1927 he was recalled to England to join the directing staff of the RAF Staff College. In 1930–32 he was chief instructor to the Oxford University air squadron, and in 1931 received an MA degree by decree. After being posted in 1932 to the Air Ministry as head of the newly formed deputy directorate of repair and maintenance, with the rank of group captain, he did much to improve the rudimentary aircraft repair facilities of the time, although his proposal for big civil repair centres to deal with work beyond the capacity of the service depots was not adopted until later.

In 1936 Hill received his first senior command: as air officer commanding Palestine and Transjordan. His two years there were marked by the great Arab strike of 1936 and by repeated disturbances, and Hill co-operated closely and cordially in the task of maintaining order with the army under generals Dill and Wavell successively. He was twice mentioned in dispatches. Back in England by 1938, Hill was appointed to the newly formed directorate of technical development within the Air Ministry; it was typical of him that, although by 1939 he was an air vice-marshal, he soon created an opportunity to fly the new advanced fighters, the Hurricane and the Spitfire. On the outbreak of war he was sent to Canada and the United States as the RAF representative on the British purchasing

mission, but by December 1939 he was back in the Air Ministry. In May 1940 his department transferred to the newly created Ministry of Aircraft Production. Although in temperament and character he had little in common with Lord Beaverbrook, he was able to remain on terms with his exacting chief, and later in 1940 he became director-general of research and development with the acting rank of air marshal. Among other valuable decisions in this post he insisted, against his chief's opinion, on persevering with cannon as the weapon to supersede machine-guns in Spitfires, and finally saw the initial problems of mounting and jamming successfully overcome.

In 1941 Hill was selected, to his disappointment, to be controller of technical services with the British air commission in the United States. He found, however, that he greatly enjoyed his American contacts and he did much useful work in ensuring that American aircraft arrived in Britain with equipment consonant to RAF requirements. He was also an ideal vehicle for the exchange of technical information over a wide field, and among his achievements must be counted his part in persuading the Americans to make far greater provision for armament, including gun-turrets, in their heavy bombers than they had originally intended. He was appointed CB in 1941. When the problems of the commission greatly eased after America's entry into the war, Hill asked to return home. He reluctantly accepted the post of commandant of the RAF Staff College (1942–3), for which he was an ideal choice. But he was now clearly moving far away from the senior operational command he greatly desired. Retirement, indeed, was suggested to him; but such powerful personalities as Sir Guy Garrod and Sir Trafford Leigh-Mallory intervened. Although he had no direct experience of wartime operations, and was generally regarded as perhaps too quiet, too unaggressive, and too long habituated to technical posts to make an outstanding commander, Hill was given his chance with the command of 12 (fighter) group, covering the eastern counties and the midlands (July 1943).

So successful was he that only four months later Hill became air marshal commanding, air defence of Great Britain, with the main task of defending Britain from German air attack while the allied invasion of the continent was being prepared and launched. During the preparatory period he was entirely successful: the only sustained German air attack by night, the 'little blitz' on London in January–March 1944, achieved negligible results, and German reconnaissance by day was consistently restricted. Meanwhile attack by flying bombs had been foreseen for some months, and in December 1943 Hill had submitted a plan which basically envisaged defence in three successive zones: by the British fighters in the coastal areas, by the anti-aircraft guns in the folds of the north downs (where their radar would be reasonably immune from jamming), and by a balloon barrage behind the guns. There would also, however, be guns at some vital points on the coast, and the fighters could enter the gun-belt either in good weather (when they would have priority) or when in actual pursuit of a bomb.

The first flying bombs were launched on 13 June 1944,

and within a few days Hill's forces were deployed. Although results were not discreditable, far too many flying bombs were getting through. Only Hill's most modern fighters were fast enough to overtake the bombs, and misunderstandings were frequent between the guns and the fighters, with the result that the latter were sometimes coming under British fire. On 16 July Hill took a most courageous decision. Convinced by his own leading staff officers and by Sir Robert Watson-Watt, he ordered, without reference to the Air Ministry or to his superior, Leigh-Mallory, who was in France, a complete redeployment and segregation of the defences: the guns would take over the coastal belt, and the fighters operate in advance of them out to sea and behind them in the north downs area. A few hours later some 23,000 men and women were on the move, just before they had become so firmly rooted in the original dispositions as to make such a switch impracticable. The move, which gave much greater freedom of action to the guns and enabled them to take full advantage of the new proximity fuses, was of course very acceptable to Sir Frederick Pile, the commander-in-chief anti-aircraft command; but the Air Ministry disapproved and intimated to Hill that he had exceeded his powers and that his professional reputation would stand or fall by the outcome. For a few days, as the move proceeded, the casualties inflicted on the enemy declined; but thereafter they mounted steadily, with the guns beginning to claim the lion's share, and by 6 September it was clear that the main threat was defeated, even if individual flying bombs continued to get through. On that day the Air Council sent Hill their warm congratulations on the 'imaginative deployment of the defences to meet each phase of the attack as it developed'. The redeployment, one of the most dramatic and effective moves of the war, and one which saved London from a far worse bombardment than it received, was not Hill's own idea; but it was his decision, undertaken on his responsibility, and its successful outcome was accordingly his victory. He was appointed KCB in 1944.

Throughout 1944 Hill was much concerned with plans for setting up the new central fighter establishment. Towards the end of the year his command reverted to its old name of Fighter Command, and Hill remained in charge until the final surrender of Germany. In May 1945 he became Air Council member for training, and the following year he was appointed principal air aide-de-camp to the king. Meanwhile he was also acting as chairman of a committee on the future of the technical branch of the RAF. Among its recommendations, accepted in 1946, was the establishment of an expanded and distinctive technical branch as part of a three-pronged organization on the same footing as the existing operational and administrative branches. The new branch was to be headed and represented on the Air Council by an air member for technical services, and this position Hill, though he was not and never had been a technical officer, was pressed to accept so strongly that he could hardly refuse. He took up this new post in January 1947 with the rank of air chief marshal and retained it until July 1948, when he retired

from the service to become rector of the Imperial College of Science and Technology. To the last he had continued to fly—he had opened fire on a flying bomb from his Tempest—and the final entries in his pilot's logbook reveal that his appetite for flying was still as ardent as ever.

Although Hill was not a scientist and had never occupied an academic post, his links with distinguished scientists were close and he brought to his new post a determination to understand the problems of every department of the college and the desire to serve it to the full. His open-mindedness and intelligence made him an immediate success and he was able to give powerful help to the college in at least two directions—in its expansion and in a fruitful scheme to widen the interests of the students by the provision of lunch-hour concerts, illustrated lectures on the arts, and weekend study groups. In 1953 he was nominated vice-chancellor of London University, but ill health obliged him to resign in the following year before he had completed his term of office.

In 1917 Hill married Mabel Helen Catherine, the daughter of Lieutenant-Colonel Edward Ross Morton, Indian army; they had a son, killed in action in 1944, and two daughters. As a personality Hill was notable for his modesty, his rather shy and self-conscious air, and his quiet charm. He was above medium height, spare and very active. His alertness of mind, breadth of knowledge, interests and sympathy, and absence of any kind of pomposness or 'side' made an immediately favourable impression on nearly everyone who met him. He suffered a coronary thrombosis and died near St Bartholomew's Hospital, London, on 6 October 1954 and was survived by his wife.

DENIS RICHARDS, *rev.*

Sources W. Raleigh and H. A. Jones, *The war in the air*, 6 vols. (1922–37) • D. Richards and H. St G. Saunders, *Royal Air Force, 1939–1945*, 3 vols. (1953–4) • B. Collier, *History of the Second World War: the defence of the United Kingdom* (1957) • P. Hill, *To know the sky* (1962) • personal knowledge (1971) • private information (1971) • d. cert. • *CGPLA Eng. & Wales* (1955)
Archives Royal Air Force Museum, Hendon, department of research and information services, papers |FILM BFI NFTVA, news footage • IWM FVA, actuality footage • IWM FVA, news footage
Likenesses J. R. Swan, oils, 1955 (after photograph), ICL • Elliott & Fry, photograph, NPG [*see illus.*] • R. Moynihan, oils, IWM
Wealth at death £14,100 19s. 3d.: probate, 6 Jan 1955, *CGPLA Eng. & Wales*

Hill, Roger (1605–1667), lawyer, was born on 1 December 1605 at Colyton, Devon, the second of nine children and eldest son of William Hill (*d.* 1642) of Poundisford, Somerset, and Jane (*b.* 1584), daughter of John Yonge of Colyton. The family had prospered as merchants in Taunton and tenants on the bishop of Winchester's estate, showing an interest in parliament exceptional for minor gentry and contracting useful matches with several Dorset families of similar status. Hill was admitted to the Inner Temple, London, in 1624 and called to the bar in 1632. On 10 December 1635 he married Katherine, daughter of Giles Greene of Corfe Castle, Dorset. After bearing a son and a daughter, she died, and was buried on 30 November 1638.

It was probably this connection that brought Hill the

recordership of Bridport, which he represented throughout the Long Parliament. He served on more than sixty committees, showing particular interest in religious and legal issues. A zealous presbyterian, he was outspoken in his attacks on the hierarchy, especially Archbishop William Laud. On 3 August 1641 he married Abigail, daughter of Brampton Gurdon of Assington, Suffolk. Said to be of no considerable estate, he nevertheless promised £100 for the defence of parliament. He attended the second marriage of Denzil Holles, having earned 20 guineas for drafting the settlement. But he soon moved to the left in politics, though not in religion, probably under the influence of two other Dorset borough members, John Pyne, leader of the Somerset radicals, and Edmond Prideaux, in whose coach he usually commuted to Westminster. An uxorious husband, he sat up past midnight, sometimes 'after a dozen houres attending at the House' (BL, Add. 46500, fol. 24), to write letters to his wife in the country, combining assurances of affection with spiritual counsel. He was added to the Somerset committee in 1644, and at the sale of episcopal lands he bought the great manor of Taunton Dean, which he improved by enclosure. He was horrified to discover that one of his cousins was growing into strange opinions smacking of Independency and anti-nomianism, and urged Pyne to promote a petition for the establishment of presbyterianism, and for strong measures against cavaliers and malignants. But when Holles's supporters in the City invaded parliament on 22 July 1647 Hill and Prideaux were among the MPs who fled to the army for protection.

Hill was named to the high court of justice to try Charles I, but did not act, and delayed taking his seat in the Rump until 23 February 1649. On 18 May he acted as teller for the bill to establish a court for probate and marriage cases, and although he co-operated with the promoter of the conveyancing bill, he seldom attended later sessions. Hill assisted Prideaux in preparing the case against John Lilburne and the Levellers, and became a bencher in the following month. He was less of a doctrinaire republican than Pyne, with whom his relations began to deteriorate in 1650.

After the establishment of the protectorate Hill again assisted Prideaux in the trial of John Penruddock and the royalists, steering a cautiously legal course. He was rewarded with the dignity of the coif, and became baron of the exchequer in 1657, performing the usual duties of holding assizes on circuit and carrying messages to the Commons from the upper house. Hill's second wife died on 31 December 1658, and was buried with three of their four children in the Temple Church. On the fall of the protectorate he resumed his seat in the Rump, keeping a cursory diary of its proceedings. He must have welcomed the overthrow of the military junto that supplanted it, being promoted to the upper bench in January 1660. Hill lost office at the Restoration, though he insisted on retaining the style of serjeant-at-law. He had to give up Taunton Dean; but unlike Pyne he was not excluded from the Act of Indemnity.

On 1 May 1662 Hill married another Abigail, the daughter of Thomas Barnes of Alborough Hatch, Essex, coheir to her brother James and widow of John Lockey of Holmes Hill, Hertfordshire, and of the quondam radical Joshua Berners of Clerkenwell, Middlesex, over whom she is said to have exercised a moderating influence. Hill's lengthy will, which he signed on 9 March 1665, begins with an old-fashioned assurance of sharing in the resurrection of the just. He enjoyed substantial liquid assets, including £4000 advanced on mortgage to Lord Arundell of Wardour and £1424 to a Herefordshire squire. In addition he had £3000 for which he had failed to find a high-yielding investment. The sum of £200 was set aside for distribution to twenty of the industrious poor who 'truly love and feare the Lord' (PRO, PROB 11/323, fol. 347v). Hill died in London on 21 April 1667, leaving instructions for the avoidance of 'any vaine Pompe or Ceremony att all' at his funeral (ibid., 11/323, fol. 344). He was buried two days later with his second wife in the Temple Church. His widow, with whom he had no children, survived until 24 November 1713.

Hill was clearly a workaholic. To judge from the prolixity of his letters and his will, his legal opinions may have been expensive, but satisfying to those clients who wanted even the unlikeliest contingencies covered. He had laid the foundations for the social promotion of his younger son, Roger, who swiftly acquired a knighthood, a freehold estate in Buckinghamshire, and a county seat in parliament.   JOHN FERRIS

Sources J. Collinson, *The history and antiquities of the county of Somerset*, 3 (1791), 233 · Keeler, *Long Parliament* · D. Brunton and D. H. Pennington, *Members of the Long Parliament* (1954) · D. Underdown, *Pride's Purge: politics in the puritan revolution* (1971) · F. T. Colby, ed., *The visitation of the county of Somerset in the year 1623*, Harleian Society, 11 (1876), 51 · F. A. Inderwick and R. A. Roberts, eds., *A calendar of the Inner Temple records*, 2 (1898) · Foss, *Judges*, 6.442–4 · Greaves & Zaller, *BDBR*, vol. 2 · W. R. Prest, *The rise of the barristers: a social history of the English bar, 1590–1640* (1986) · G. D. Squibb, ed., *The visitation of Somerset and the city of Bristol, 1672*, Harleian Society, new ser., 11 (1992) · D. Underdown, *Somerset in the civil war and interregnum* (1973) · B. Worden, *The Rump Parliament, 1648–1653* (1974) · will, PRO, PROB, 11/323, fols. 344–347v

Archives BL, legal journal, Add. MS 61941 · BL, papers, letters to his second wife, Add. MS 46500 · Bucks. RLSS, diary

Wealth at death over £7500; also land and wife's property: will, PRO, PROB 11/323, fols. 344–347v

Hill, Rosalind Mary Theodosia

Hill, Rosalind Mary Theodosia (1908–1997), historian, was born on 14 November 1908 at Leighton House, Neston-cum-Parkgate, Chester, the youngest of the three daughters and four children of Sir (Arthur) Norman Hill (1863–1944), solicitor and notary, and his wife, Elen Mary Stratford, *née* Danson, elder daughter of John Towne Danson of Grasmere, barrister. Her father was much involved with Liverpool shipping, and acted as secretary of the Liverpool Steamship Owners' Association from 1893 to 1924. He was chairman of the Board of Trade advisory committee on shipping from 1907 to 1937 and was also British delegate to the conferences on safety of life at sea from 1913 to 1914 and in 1929. He was knighted in 1911 and created baronet in 1919. Rosalind Hill was brought up in the Wirral peninsula and in the other family home at Stockbridge in Hampshire.

Hill read history at St Hilda's College, Oxford, matriculating in 1928. After graduating with a first-class degree in modern history in 1931 she took a BLitt degree, based on research on monastic letter-books. From Oxford she went to a teaching post in medieval history at University College, Leicester, where John Plumb was among her first pupils. Some sixty years later, in a series in which academics described the people who most inspired and influenced them, Sir John Plumb chose Rosalind Hill as a young lecturer at Leicester:

> She was very young and nervous: she fluttered her papers, talked too quickly, and went pink-cheeked with terror, yet she managed to bring the medieval world alive. She knew the problems it was vital for a young historian to know about. ... I never missed a lecture. Medieval history sprang to life and I became, and remained, an addict.   (Plumb)

Her teaching influenced many generations of students who came to share and appreciate her enthusiasm for the subject. One friend and former colleague remarked: 'it is the union of this enthusiasm and the warmth and charm and kindness which all who come near her feel which explains the spell she has cast over many generations' (Baker, 12). In 1937 she left Leicester and moved to Westfield College in the University of London as a lecturer in history. She remained there until her retirement in 1976. She was appointed reader in 1955 and professor in 1971. She also acted as vice-principal of the college before her retirement.

The editing of medieval records, particularly English bishops' registers, occupied much of Hill's research activities. Her attention first turned to the diocese of Lincoln. Her monumental edition, in eight volumes, of *The Rolls and Register of Bishop Oliver Sutton, 1280–99* (1948–86) was a masterly example of editing. In later years she turned to the see of York and made annual forays to York to assist in editing the register of Archbishop William Melton (1317–40). Two volumes edited by her were published, in 1977 and 1988, and her work was continued by other scholars after her death. Another great research interest was the crusades—she regularly held a postgraduate seminar at the Institute of Historical Research in London—and in 1962 she edited the first chronicle of the first crusade, *Gesta Francorum et aliorum Hierosolimitanorum*.

Hill's knowledge of medieval texts was put at the disposal of several local and national record publishing societies and she served them well in various editorial and secretarial capacities. From 1968 to 1983 she chaired the Canterbury and York Society, which was devoted to the publishing of bishops' registers and other medieval ecclesiastical records, and she was secretary (1963–73) and then president (1973–4) of the Ecclesiastical History Society. The theme of her presidential conference, published as *The Materials, Sources and Methods of Ecclesiastical History* (1975), aptly summed up her abiding interest in the archives of the church and their interpretation.

Hill's father died in January 1944 and her brother,

Lieutenant-Colonel (Norman) Gray Hill, succeeded as second baronet but was killed on active service in Italy with the Royal Army Medical Corps in the following month. On her brother's death she inherited the title of lady of the manor of Stockbridge; she presided over her manorial court each year until her death. Her generosity to Stockbridge found tangible shape in Rosalind Hill House, a home for elderly residents of the village. At her death she made a munificent bequest to St Hilda's College, Oxford, towards the building of an accommodation block for students, to be named after her friend Christina Barratt. It was with Barratt and Gwen Chambers (both Westfield colleagues) that she shared for many years not only a large house in Radlett, Hertfordshire, but also her love of mountaineering, gardens, and animals. Her collaboration with the cartoonist Fougasse in producing *Both Small and Great Beasts* (1953) for the University Federation for Animal Welfare combined her love of animals with her love of the middle ages. She died of heart failure on 11 January 1997 at her home, 7 Loom Lane, Radlett, Hertfordshire, and was cremated at St Albans. She was unmarried.

DAVID M. SMITH

Sources *The Times* (27 Jan 1997) · *The Independent* (3 Feb 1997) · D. Baker, ed., *Medieval women: dedicated and presented to Professor Rosalind M. T. Hill on the occasion of her seventieth birthday* (1978) [on pp. 381–5 is a bibliography of her writings] · J. Plumb, 'Triumph of the good over medieval', *Times Higher Education Supplement* (8 July 1994), 17 · *St Hilda's College report and chronicle* (1997–1998), 35 · personal knowledge (2004) · private information (2004) · b. cert. · d. cert.
Likenesses Y. Sahota, photograph, *c*.1975, repro. in Baker, ed., *Medieval women* · photograph, 1975?, repro. in *The Times* · attrib. Y. Sahota, photograph, repro. in *The Independent*
Wealth at death £1,473,985: probate, 7 March 1997, *CGPLA Eng. & Wales*

Hill, Rosamond Davenport (1825–1902), social reformer and educational administrator, born in Chelsea on 4 August 1825, was the eldest of the three daughters of Matthew Davenport *Hill (1792–1872) and Margaret Bucknall (d. 1867). Her father, the first recorder of Birmingham, was the eldest child of Thomas Wright *Hill and Sarah Lea of Birmingham, whose five sons flourished as social reformers and professional civil servants in the Victorian period. Matthew's brothers included the postal reformer Sir Rowland *Hill (1795–1879), Frederic *Hill (1803–1896), one of the first inspectors of prisons, and Edwin *Hill (1793–1876).

The children of Thomas Wright and Sarah Lea Hill shared an interest in an overlapping group of social concerns, including educational reform, penal reform, and reform of the treatment of juvenile delinquents. Rosamond Davenport Hill was thus part of the third generation of social reformers in the Hill family, along with her sisters **Florence Davenport Hill** (1828/9–1919), who was also born in Chelsea, and **Joanna Margaret Hill** (1836/7–1901), who was born in Hampstead. All three were involved in prison reform and the reform of the treatment of juvenile delinquents and the children of the poor. Rosamond, the best known of the three, was also involved in educational reform. Their parents had moved from Birmingham to London after their marriage in 1819, and the family, which also included two sons, Alfred (1821–1907) and Matthew Berkeley (1834–1892), lived in Hampstead from 1831 to 1851. They were acquainted with a wide circle of reformers and writers including Charles Knight, Leigh Hunt, and William Thackeray. Contact with such individuals, as well as with their own extended family, provided Rosamond, Florence, and Joanna with a political education and fuelled in all of them a sense of social responsibility. While their parents espoused conventional Victorian notions about appropriate roles for women, the daughters were encouraged to develop independence of mind and to value their own capacities for serious work. For example, their father had a great respect for the noted Irish writer and reformer Maria Edgeworth. When she visited London in 1840 he arranged that Rosamond and Florence should pay a call on her: Rosamond's biographer, E. E. Metcalfe, relates that this visit made a deep impression on Rosamond and on Florence.

The education of the Hill sisters took place both at school and at home. Rosamond attended a day school when she was eight and later went to boarding-school, but from late adolescence she studied at home with a governess. As the eldest daughter Rosamond was especially close to her father. She acted as his private secretary, and visited prisons and reformatories with him in Great Britain and in Europe. In 1856, after a visit to Ireland, she wrote 'A lady's visit to the Irish convict prisons'. Throughout her life she continued to present and publish papers on prison reform, education, female emigration, and temperance. She and her sister Florence were co-authors, along with their father, of *Our Exemplars: Rich and Poor* (1860).

In 1851 the Hill family moved to Bristol. There Matthew Davenport Hill's involvement with prison reform brought him into close contact with the social activist Mary Carpenter, whose reform interests included educational work with society's poorest children, and with the reform of the treatment of juvenile delinquents. Rosamond, Florence, and Joanna became part of Carpenter's reforming circle. Rosamond, for example, helped to manage the St James's Back ragged school, and, with Carpenter, started an industrial school for girls. Joanna became secretary of the local workhouse visiting association, in which cause she continued to interest herself after moving to Birmingham in 1864.

Matthew died in 1872, and Rosamond and Florence 'now left Bristol and entered upon that affectionate and happy partnership which closed only with the close of life' (Metcalfe, 47). They began this new period of their lives with a trip to Australia, to visit the family of their paternal aunt, Caroline Clark, one of whose children, Emily, was, like her cousins, concerned with child welfare reform. On their return Rosamond and Florence published *What we Saw in Australia* (1875), an account of their visits to prisons, reformatories, and schools in New South Wales. In 1878 Rosamond and Florence published their life of their father, *The Recorder of Birmingham: a Memoir of Matthew Davenport Hill*.

By 1879 the two sisters had established themselves in a house in Belsize Park, where they lived until 1897, after which, in retirement, they moved to a house named Hillstow, in Headington, near Oxford. Matthew Davenport Hill and his family had been members of the Church of England, but Matthew's father, Thomas Wright Hill, had been a Unitarian, and after her father's death Rosamond left the Church of England for the Unitarians. The most public period of her life began in 1879. The Education Act of 1870 had created a network of locally elected school boards. The fact that women could serve on the boards was a significant innovation. When Rosamond Davenport Hill was elected in December 1879 as a Progressive member of the London school board for the City of London she became one of a handful of pioneer women school board members. She served until 1897. As a school board member Rosamond was noted for her activities in relation to industrial schools and also for her advocacy of the introduction of what would become known as domestic science courses for girls. In 1882 she became chair of the board's cookery committee, and published an influential article in *Macmillan's Magazine*, 'Cookery teaching under the London school board'. In 1895 she was appointed a life governor of University College, London. She died at her home on 5 August 1902.

Florence Davenport Hill continued to work in the areas of prison reform and poor law reform and took a special interest in the reform of the treatment of pauper children, especially pauper orphans. She became an advocate of the boarding-out system, rather than the workhouse, as a means of providing for such children, and published a book on the subject, *Children of the State* (1st edn, 1867; rev. and enlarged 2nd edn, ed. Fanny Fowke, 1889). In it Florence articulated her views concerning the dangers pauper children presented to the community because of the 'bad tendencies of those of evil pedigree' (p. 22) as well as the dangers they faced themselves, not only from hunger, disease, and ill treatment, but also from the workhouse, which reduced all its inmates to 'one dead level of hopeless and demoralised dependence' (p. 16). For Florence Davenport Hill the cure for the moral degradation of the workhouse included the inculcation in pauper children of the values of integrity and self-discipline. Florence believed that for boys and girls alike, but especially for girls, such positive moral values could only be instilled in a homelike environment. Florence Davenport Hill's public career also included service as a poor-law guardian for the borough of St Pancras. She died at her home in Oxford on 2 November 1919, at the age of ninety.

Joanna Hill, like Florence, was concerned with poor law reform, pauper children, and the most appropriate treatment for working-class girls in danger of becoming juvenile delinquents. She wrote *Boarding out Pauper Children* (1869), 'A plea for the extension of the boarding-out system' (1883; cited in Florence Davenport Hill, *Children of the State*, 2nd edn, 17), and *Practical suggestions for the use of associates for the department for G[irls'] F[riendly] S[ociety] candidates for workhouses and orphanages* (1884). She died at her home in Birmingham on 26 October 1901.

Of Rosamond as a woman reformer it was said: 'She conferred a boon on her own sex by demonstrating that a woman may be as capable of bearing a part in the direction of her country's affairs as her male fellow-citizens' (*Sunday Magazine*, July 1880, cited Metcalfe, 20). Rosamond and Florence were part of a wide circle of women reformers which included Octavia Hill (no relation); Helen Taylor Mill, and Frances Power Cobbe. As women reformers they took a special interest in the welfare of girls. Although they were not notably active in the women's movement, their concerns and activities did bring them into contact with such women's rights advocates as Millicent Garrett Fawcett, and they supported women's suffrage while at the same time adhering to the Victorian belief that women had special responsibilities and special gifts for maintaining moral values in both the private and the public spheres.   DEBORAH SARA GORHAM

Sources E. E. Metcalfe, *Memoir of Rosamond Davenport Hill* (1904) · D. Gorham, 'Victorian reform as a family business: the Hill family', *The Victorian family, structure and stresses*, ed. A. S. Wohl (1978), 119–47 · *The Times* (7 Aug 1902) · R. Davenport-Hill and F. Davenport-Hill, *The recorder of Birmingham: a memoir of Matthew Davenport Hill* (1878) · M. D. Hill, R. D. Hill, and F. D. Hill, *Our exemplars: rich and poor* (1860) · R. D. Hill and F. D. Hill, *What we saw in Australia* (1875) · *WW* (1899) · d. certs. [Rosamond Davenport Hill; Florence Davenport Hill; Joanna Margaret Hill] · *The Times* (5 Nov 1919) [Florence Davenport Hill] · *The Times* (29 Oct 1901) [Joanna Margaret Hill]
Likenesses portraits, repro. in Metcalfe, *Memoir*
Wealth at death £29,570 14s. 4d.: resworn probate, Feb 1903, *CGPLA Eng. & Wales* (1902) · £20,944 19s. 1d.—Florence Davenport Hill: probate, 2 Dec 1919, *CGPLA Eng. & Wales*

Hill, Sir Rowland (*c*.1495–1561), merchant and local politician, was born at Hodnet, Shropshire, the eldest son of Thomas Hill and his wife, Margaret, the daughter of Thomas Wilbraham of Woodhey, Cheshire. He was apprenticed to the London mercer Thomas Kitson, and obtained his freedom in 1519. He then became a leading merchant adventurer, exporting broadcloths to Flanders and importing linens and fustians, his growing wealth indicated by his subsidy assessments, which rose from £150 in goods in the mid-1520s to 5000 marks in goods in 1541 (only two other men in London were assessed so high). For the bulk of his civic career the centre of his business operations was the parish of St Stephen Walbrook, in which he acted as churchwarden in 1525–6 and where he owned a property fronting onto Walbrook. But he also retained an interest in the Welsh marches, and acquired extensive estates in Shropshire, Cheshire, Flintshire, and Staffordshire; between 1539 and 1547 he purchased large quantities of former monastic property. His power in his native county was reflected in his appearance on the Shropshire commission of the peace between 1543 and 1554.

The bulk of Hill's administrative energies were directed to the capital. He was prominent in the affairs of the Mercers' Company, serving as warden in 1535–6, and as master in 1543–4, in 1550–51, in 1555–6, and again in 1560–61. As sheriff in 1541–2 he endured a brief period (28–30 March 1542) of imprisonment in the Tower of London on the orders of the House of Commons for his abuse of the serjeant of parliament sent to secure the release of George Ferrers, a member of parliament imprisoned for debt in the Bread Street Counter. Although the king backed the Commons in this case of member's privilege, he showed favour to Hill shortly after the affair by knighting him, on 18 May 1542, during the prorogation of the parliament. Hill was elected to the court of aldermen on 9 November 1542, and served successively for the wards of Castle Baynard (1542–6) and Walbrook (1546–61). He took over as lord mayor for the year beginning in November 1549 in the wake of the *coup d'état* against Protector Somerset and in the midst of a period of religious uncertainty, but he oversaw some of the critical changes in the direction of godly protestantism, including the removal of altars. His mayoralty was also noted for the repurchasing by the livery companies of chantry properties seized by the crown in 1548, an initiative that was organized by the court of aldermen, and for the City's purchase in May 1550 of the former manors of Bermondsey Priory (now known as the King's Manor) and the archbishop of Canterbury (now known as the Great Liberty manor) in Southwark, together with a charter giving the aldermen extended powers over the troublesome southern suburbs. He remained an assiduous member of the court of aldermen, and attended nearly two-thirds of the meetings in the reigns of both Edward VI and Mary. He may have endured a spell of disfavour under Mary, but, although dropped from the commissions of the peace for Middlesex and Shropshire in 1554, he had recovered the regime's confidence by 1557, when he was nominated as a commissioner for the investigation of heretics.

Hill enjoyed an enviable reputation for charitable virtue. 'Grett mon was mad for ys deth, and he gayff myche to the pore' (*Diary of Henry Machyn*, 272). Although he had accumulated extensive estates, he was remembered as a paternalistic landlord who had neither raised rents nor levied entry fines. As tenant from the Mercers' Company of the precinct of the hospital of St Thomas Acre from 1542, he undertook to maintain its school, and he seems to have moved it at his own expense from the cloister into new quarters in a room on the north side of the choir or chancel. In 1555 he established a school at Market Drayton in his native Shropshire. He was also closely involved with the establishment of the London hospitals. He was the president of Bridewell and Bethlem hospitals from 1557 to 1558 and again between 1559 and 1561, and he held the post of surveyor-general of the London hospitals from 1559 until his death. But his charity had a stern edge, for he also enjoyed a reputation as 'a foe to vice and a vehement corrector' (notes on his monument at St Stephen Walbrook, London, Mercers' Hall). His mayoralty witnessed a determined campaign against moral offences, the wardmote inquests being required in April 1550 to make fresh presentments of ill rule, 'upon which indictments the lord mayor sat many times' (Hume, 167–9). The crusade was controversial because of Hill's readiness to punish wealthy offenders. Perhaps because of this determined moralism, which seems to have owed something to pressure from the protestant pulpits, and perhaps because of the coincidence of his mayoralty with a decisive turn in the English Reformation, Hill is often described as the first protestant lord mayor of London, but this tradition seems to date from no earlier than 1795, when a descendant, Sir Rowland Hill, bt, erected an obelisk to his memory in Hawkstone Park, Shropshire. Although he was one of the City's representatives in the first parliament of Mary's reign (October–December 1553), Hill is not named as one of those 'which stood for the trewe religion' (Bodl. Oxf., MS e Museo 17). His will gives little indication of fervent protestantism, and there was no celebration of godly values in either the memorial tablet in St Stephen Walbrook or in the inscription on the portrait at Mercers' Hall. His arrangement for the distribution of a dole of 12d. a house through the wards of the City as he lay dying was characteristic of his charity, but also redolent of an older type of piety. His interest in innovative charitable projects and in education may have owed more to the humanist values fashionable in London circles at this time than to protestantism.

Hill was married by 1542, but the identity of his wife, who died during his mayoralty, is unknown. There were no surviving children. He died at midnight on 28 October 1561, according to Machyn, 'of the strangwyllyon' (strangury, a disease of the urinary organs), and was buried on 5 November in the parish church of St Stephen Walbrook. The bulk of his property passed to his nieces, one of whom married the judge Sir Reginald Corbet and another Hill's fellow alderman and 'most suer and faithfull friende' Sir Thomas Leigh.   IAN W. ARCHER

Rowland Hill (1744–1833), by Samuel Mountjoy Smith, 1828

Sources will, PRO, PROB 11/44, sig. 33 · customs accounts, PRO · subsidy assessments, PRO · inquisitions post mortem, PRO · repertories of court of aldermen; journals of court of common council, CLRO · acts of court, Mercers' Hall, London · notes on funeral monument of St Stephen Walbrook, Mercers' Hall, London · H. Miller, 'Hill, Sir Rowland', HoP, *Commons, 1509–58* · A. B. Beaven, ed., *The aldermen of the City of London, temp. Henry III–*[1912], 2 vols. (1908–13) · M. Benbow, 'Index of London citizens involved in city government, 1558–1603', U. Lond., Institute of Historical Research, Centre for Metropolitan History · D. Keene and V. Harding, eds., *Historical gazetteer of London before the great fire* (1987) [microfiche] · LP Henry VIII · C. Wriothesley, *A chronicle of England during the reigns of the Tudors from AD 1485 to 1559*, ed. W. D. Hamilton, 2 vols., CS, new ser., 11, 20 (1875–7) · *The diary of Henry Machyn, citizen and merchant-taylor of London, from AD 1550 to AD 1563*, ed. J. G. Nichols, CS, 42 (1848) · M. A. S. Hume, ed. and trans., *Chronicle of King Henry VIII of England* (1889) · R. Tresswell and A. Vincent, *The visitation of Shropshire, taken in the year 1623*, ed. G. Grazebrook and J. P. Rylands, 2 vols., Harleian Society, 28–9 (1889)
Likenesses oils, 16th cent., Museum of London; version, Tatton Park, Cheshire · portrait, 16th cent., Mercers' Hall, Ironmongers' Lane, London

Hill, Rowland (1744–1833), evangelical preacher, was born at Hawkstone Park, near Wem, Shropshire, on 23 August 1744, the sixth son of the ten children of Sir Rowland Hill (1705–1783), landowner, and Mary Pole (d. 1789). He was educated at Shrewsbury School and Eton College and converted to an evangelical faith by his elder brother Richard *Hill. While at Eton, Rowland formed a short-lived religious society through which some of his friends were converted. He entered St John's College, Cambridge, as a pensioner and in 1764 formed a religious society of ten to twelve friends that included Charles de Coetlogon,

Thomas Pentycross, and David Simpson. They studied the Greek New Testament, prayed, and read evangelical literature. They also visited the sick and those in prison, and Hill preached in Cambridge and in neighbouring villages. This group was disapproved of by the university authorities, but they were not expelled, like the six students at Oxford in 1768.

After graduating BA in 1769 (he proceeded MA in 1772) Hill spent four years preaching throughout England and Wales. This angered his parents, but delighted his brother Richard and sister Jane, after whom he was most influenced by George Whitefield and John Berridge. They helped shape his Calvinistic convictions and his determination to exercise an itinerant preaching ministry. His theology meant that he was out of favour with the Methodists; his activities were regarded with suspicion by the Church of England authorities; and his temper led him to quarrel even with the countess of Huntingdon. Without this disagreement Hill might have gained her patronage and become Whitefield's successor. Another possibility was that he could have become a Presbyterian and a chaplain to Lady Glenorchy. He applied for Anglican orders but was refused by six bishops because of his irregularities. However, in June 1773 he was ordained deacon by the bishop of Bath and Wells to the curacy of Kingston, near Taunton. Though he was diligent in his parish duties, he would not be confined by the parochial system and continued to itinerate. A. M. Toplady urged him to give up his irregularities. The bishop of Carlisle promised to ordain him priest (on letters dimissory of the bishop of Bath and Wells) but the archbishop of York forbade the ordination and Hill remained in deacon's orders. In his own words, he passed through life 'wearing only one ecclesiastical boot' (*Congregational Magazine*). Hill was a unique figure in the evangelical revival and adopted a significant independent position. He was concerned with order and freedom, valued the scriptural content of the Church of England liturgy, but would not be inhibited by episcopal censure or restricted by parochial boundaries. He claimed that he was not a dissenter—'The church turned me off, and not I her' (Sidney, 138). But he could also say, 'See what a churchman I am; I must have it all correct' (ibid., 237). He accepted the authority of the Thirty-Nine Articles, but amended them to express his Calvinistic theology. He was deeply committed to the promotion of evangelical unity, and spoke of lowering the walls between denominations so 'that we may shake hands a little easier over them' (ibid., 475). For this reason he did not approve of any doctrinal restrictions being placed upon the work of the British and Foreign Bible Society.

On 23 May 1773 Hill married Mary Tudway (1747–1830), with whom he settled at Wotton under Edge, Gloucestershire. Though they had no family of their own, he deeply loved children. He preached to them, and wrote hymns, prayers, and books for them. At Wotton he built an almshouse and a modest house for himself where he tended the garden. In the adjoining chapel (rebuilt in 1851 and closed in 1973) he used the Anglican liturgy and permitted evangelicals of any denomination to preach. This practice he repeated at Surrey Chapel, Blackfriars, London (opened 1783), Cheltenham Chapel (opened 1809), and Mill Street Chapel, Leamington (opened 1828 and bought by Hill in 1831). His custom was to spend the summer months in Gloucestershire, when he made an 'episcopal visitation' to Cheltenham, and the rest of the year at Surrey Chapel. During his absence he employed Anglican clergy and nonconformist ministers. When an evangelical incumbent was appointed to Wotton, or when his biographer Edwin Sidney preached, Hill closed his chapel and encouraged his congregation to worship at the parish church. During the year Hill went on extended preaching tours throughout the United Kingdom, describing himself as the 'Rector of Surrey chapel, Vicar of Wotton-under-Edge, and curate of all the fields, commons etc. throughout England and Wales' (Burder, 127). He was deeply loved and highly regarded by evangelicals within the established church and by dissenters.

Surrey Chapel was the largest of its kind in London and could accommodate 3000 people. It was the centre of Hill's ministry and the congregation included leading evangelicals and the poor. The chapel was the focus for Hill's missionary and philanthropic work. Attached to it were thirteen Sunday schools for over 3000 children (Hill was one of the earliest supporters of the movement in London). In addition there was a Dorcas Society for the relief of poor married women, an almshouse for poor women, and a school of industry for poor girls. On the River Thames, Hill was one of the promoters of a floating chapel. He supported the London Missionary Society and raised large sums of money on his preaching tours. He was

also involved in the formation of the Religious Tract Society, supported the British and Foreign Bible Society, and was a trustee of the *Evangelical Magazine*. While living in Gloucestershire he met Dr Edward Jenner, and Hill became a keen advocate of vaccination. He wrote a tract on the subject, in 1806 opened a clinic attached to Surrey Chapel, and personally vaccinated thousands of children.

Surrey Chapel was known for its music and Hill's powerful preaching. His presence in the pulpit was arresting, his style a combination of humour, pathos, and vivid illustration. He was pre-eminent among the London preachers. Well into his eighties he still preached six or seven times a week. Though his extempory preaching was described by Isaac Milner as 'slap-dash preaching' (Sidney, 141), Richard Sheridan said that 'his ideas come red-hot from the heart' (ibid., 140). Like Whitefield, Hill could attract immense crowds—on one of his Scottish tours he preached to between 15,000 and 20,000 people. He wrote, or contributed to, a number of publications on subjects which included the debate between Calvinism and Arminianism. Hill's most popular work of fiction was his *Village Dialogues* (30 editions). He compiled a number of hymnbooks and he composed a few hymns, some of which were revised by William Cowper.

Hill was a larger-than-life character, and an aristocratic eccentric with a ready wit. He remained active almost to the end of his life. He died in Surrey Chapel House on 11 April 1833 and was buried on 19 April beneath the pulpit of Surrey Chapel. His remains were reinterred in 1881.

A. F. MUNDEN

Sources E. Sidney, *The life of the Rev Rowland Hill AM*, 5th edn (1861) · P. E. Sangster, 'The life of the Rev Rowland Hill (1744–1833) and his position in the Evangelical revival', DPhil diss., U. Oxf., 1964 · *DNB* · *Congregational Magazine*, new ser., 5 (1841), 869 · H. F. Burder, *Memoir of the Rev. George Burder* (1833) · C. Smyth, *Simeon and church order* (1940) · *Leamington Spa Courier* (22 Dec 1832) · *Leamington Spa Courier* (12 Jan 1833) · J. Julian, ed., *A dictionary of hymnology*, rev. edn (1907); repr. in 2 vols. (1915)

Archives DWL, letters and papers · Shrops. RRC, diary | SOAS, London Missionary Society archives · Westminster and Cheshunt College, Cambridge, corresp. with Selina, countess of Huntingdon

Likenesses mezzotint, pubd 1773, BM, NPG · Springforth, line engraving, pubd 1792 (after Lovelace), NPG · J. K., print, 1798, Shrops. RRC · J. Kay, etching, 1798, NPG · T. Blood, stipple, pubd 1814 (after S. Drummond), BM, NPG · T. G. Lupton, mezzotint, pubd 1828 (after S. M. Smith), NPG · S. M. Smith, oils, 1828, NPG [*see illus.*] · silhouette, 1829, Shrops. RRC · J. Russell, chalk drawing, NPG · engraving, repro. in Sidney, *Life* · oils, DWL · plaster bust, NPG

Hill, Rowland, first Viscount Hill (1772–1842), army officer, was born on 11 August 1772 at Prees Hall, near Hawkstone and Shrewsbury in Shropshire, the second son and fourth of the sixteen children of John Hill, later third baronet (1740–1824), of Hawkstone, and his wife, Mary (*d.* 1806), the daughter of Robert Chambre of Petton, Shropshire. The rising influence of the Hill family had accelerated during the career of Richard Hill (1655–1727), called 'the great Hill', lord of the Treasury and lord of the Admiralty under Queen Anne. A baronetcy was created for his

Rowland Hill, first Viscount Hill (1772–1842), by Thomas Heaphy, 1813–14

nephew Rowland in 1727, and it passed to John Hill in November 1809. Five of Rowland Hill's brothers took part in the Napoleonic wars, including his elder brother, John, of the 25th light dragoons; Clement, who long served as his aide-de-camp; Thomas Noel *Hill (1784–1832), in the Portuguese service; Francis, also in the Portuguese service; and Robert, commander of the Royal Horse Guards. George IV later told Sir John, their father: 'I am glad, indeed, to see the father of so many brave sons' (Sidney, 9). As a young child Rowland was large and somewhat awkward and reserved, but he possessed a bright mind and formed his own opinions independently, although in his younger years he much imitated John. At the age of seven or eight he went to Ightfield School for one year and then to a school in Chester, where he remained until he was seventeen, when his father wanted him to prepare to enter the legal profession. However, John had already joined the army, and Rowland told his parents that, because he did not like the study of law, he would never excel at it. Instead, he preferred a career in the army. This choice surprised his teachers—on occasion he had fainted at the sight of blood—but he stood by his choice, and his parents agreed to it.

Early army career In 1790 Sir John Hill arranged for Rowland's commission as an ensign in the 38th foot, followed by leave to study at a military academy in Strasbourg. He was promoted lieutenant early in 1791, returned briefly to England, and then received another leave of absence to resume his studies. He joined the 53rd foot in January 1792 and resumed active service that was virtually unbroken during the wars of the next twenty-three years. In 1793 he raised an independent company that carried a promotion to captain. He briefly served with Francis Drake as assistant secretary at the republic of Genoa, but when Admiral Hood landed at Toulon (28 August 1793) Hill hurried there to join his regiment. Hill energetically carried orders for Lord Mulgrave, General Charles O'Hara, and Sir David Dundas, as well as spending time in the front lines, where he received a superficial wound. When Dundas evacuated Toulon in December, Hill carried the dispatches to London. In 1794 Thomas Graham raised a regiment, the 90th foot, and Hill contributed so much in recruiting that he was promoted major and shortly afterwards lieutenant-colonel. The 90th moved about the Mediterranean and other minor venues during the next four years. The next French movement involving Bonaparte—Hill had faced his artillery at Toulon—occurred with the French landing in Egypt in July 1798, and Hill, fuming over his lack of action at Gibraltar, once more joined Drake on a mission to the continent. When he learned that the force under Sir Ralph Abercromby was preparing to sail to Egypt he raced back to take part. By then he had been promoted brevet colonel.

In March 1801 the British force anchored in Abu Qir Bay and the troops landed. On 13 March, in hard fighting, Hill, commanding the 90th, was severely wounded by a musket ball to the head; a week later Abercromby, mortally wounded, was brought into Hill's cabin and soon died. Hill rejoined the 90th after three weeks of convalescence and advanced against Cairo as French resistance weakened. By September the enemy had left Egypt. Hill was made a knight of the Crescent of Turkey. He sailed to Malta for garrison duty, an assignment that lasted for only a short time while British and French diplomats negotiated the treaty of Amiens, which seemed destined to cause a reduction of the British army and the disbanding of the 90th. Instead, after Hill had taken a short period of leave at Hawkstone, relations with France soured, and he rejoined the army at Belfast amid rumours, which seemed genuine, that the French were planning to invade Ireland. Hill meticulously reconnoitred all possible landing sites and planned for counter-measures against an invasion. Having been promoted major-general (30 October 1805), he joined a force—intended to liberate Hanover from the French—bound for the Hanoverian coast, where he was in charge of embarkation. He carried out his duties well and during this period met Sir Arthur Wellesley for the first time. After the expedition failed (1806) Hill was stationed briefly at Canterbury and served on the staff of Sir John Moore, generally recognized as the premier organizer in the army. Hill's own skills at troop management were being formed, and his reputation for being a firm disciplinarian while demonstrating humanitarian concern and equitable techniques in training and handling troops began to set him apart. Early in his career some of his men began calling him Daddy Hill, a term of appreciation for his benevolent concern for the common soldier, but it also began to create a stereotype of Hill that rather masked his ruthless combat qualities. Despite his battlefield heroism, this stereotype dogged him throughout his illustrious career.

Ireland and the Peninsula Hill spent over a year in Ireland (1807–8). In 1807 the French invaded Portugal: they seized Lisbon (1 December), and Dom João, the prince regent, and his court barely escaped and sailed with British protection to Brazil. When Bonaparte seized the Spanish throne in May 1808, and the Spanish appealed for British help, the British government decided to send an expedition to Portugal. Temporarily Wellesley was in command, and Hill was assigned to organize the embarkation. The force of about 10,000 men sailed from Cork on 12 July and arrived off Portugal on 1 August. Hill supervised the landing at Mondego Bay, about 100 miles north of Lisbon. Wellesley quickly formed his forces and engaged Delaborde at Roliça (17 August); Hill commanded the 1st brigade, which was stationed in the centre of Wellesley's position. Rifleman Harris gave a poignant account of Hill's great courage when he rallied the 29th foot after the death of its colonel. When Delaborde withdrew, Junot offered battle at Vimeiro (21 August). Hill's force occupied Wellesley's right, but the French were forced back and virtually routed. Soon afterwards the combatants signed the disgraceful convention of Cintra (22 August), following which Hill's brigade came under the command of Sir John Hope, under Sir John Moore.

Moore decided to take the offensive against the French in Spain, an unlucky decision based on poor intelligence, and Hill's men marched northwards towards the border. Bonaparte, however, poured forces into Spain, and Moore, Hill, and the other generals were forced to retreat to the coast, closely pursued by Marshal Andoche Soult's corps. They defeated Soult at Corunna on 16 January 1809, when Moore was killed, then escaped on British transports. Hill and Beresford formed the rearguard, and their men rowed to the ships as the evacuation was completed. After leave in Ireland, Hill sailed from Cork in March with about 4000 troops to reinforce Sir John Francis Cradock at Lisbon. Wellesley replaced the cautious Cradock in April, and the British force marched towards Oporto. Hill commanded the 1st division, and two other infantry divisions and a cavalry division, with Portuguese troops interspersed, brought Wellesley's meagre force to about 17,000 men. At Oporto, Soult's forces lined the northern bank of the 300-yard-wide River Douro, and on 12 May Wellesley ordered a surprise daylight crossing. Hill's troops were among the first across, and Soult was soon forced out of the city. The stunning success of the operation led to the invasion of Spain in early summer and the battle of Talavera (28 July). Hill was wounded by a musket ball during the desperate battle, and Wellesley's forces retreated towards Portugal.

Wellesley confirmed his confidence in Hill later in 1809 by appointing him to a semi-independent command in the Portuguese Alentejo based on two factors: he meticulously followed orders, and he knew how to adapt troops to unusual circumstances. With British resources so meagre, Hill was an ideal choice for such an assignment. By 1810 Soult's army of the south held Andalusia, and Marshal André Masséna had assembled a large force yet again to invade Portugal. Wellesley, now Viscount Wellington,

drew Hill's force closer to his main position at Busaco, and his men dug in on the right as the fierce battle took place on 26–7 September. After the allied troops began their retreat towards Lisbon, Hill marched to Coimbra and then southwards to the environs of Torres Vedras, where the British and Portuguese constructed strong defensive fortifications. He took a virtually impregnable position on the right of Wellington's main force, and Masséna found himself stalemated before the lines of Torres Vedras. On 14 November the French began taking positions a little to the north, and Hill's force began edging forward again. Hill contracted an infectious fever at this time, and because many men died from it he was sent to Lisbon to recuperate. When the effects of the disease persisted Hill returned home, and for six months his force came under the command of other officers. William Stewart, the ranking brigade officer, took a turn at command, but because he was prone to lead into risky engagements Wellington ordered William Carr Beresford to take command of the detached force in the south. In March 1811, when Masséna began a full retreat, Beresford began moving his corps towards Campo Mayor.

Perhaps the Albuera campaign provides a study of the clear contrasts between the executive skills of field command shown by Hill and Beresford. Beresford's clumsiness was apparent at Campo Mayor in April, but he was cleared to oppose Soult's force as it marched northwards into the vicinity of his force at Albuera (16 May 1811). In the desperate fighting Beresford's disposition was faulty, his orders were indecisive, and his losses of British troops were staggering. On 1 June, Hill resumed command of his shattered force, although Wellington told Beresford to 'write him a victory' (Vichness, 431), and Hill soon reconstructed the southern wing into a potent fighting force. He moved into the region of Portalegre, and by 1 September his corps had grown to about 16,000. Meanwhile, a worthy opponent, General Jean-Baptiste Girard, began playing cat-and-mouse games in Estremadura, near Merida. Girard's actions were designed to draw attention away from the French operations near Ciudad Rodrigo, but nevertheless Hill intermittently entertained his officers and other guests and reconnoitred the area to prepare for an opportunity against Girard. Of the former activities, Wellington once told a staff member: 'As you are a stranger, I will give you some useful information. Cole gives the best dinners in the army; Hill the next best; mine are no great things; Beresford's and Picton's are very bad indeed' (Brett-James, 69). Hill was something of an epicure and transported a handsome silver service in the Peninsula with which to serve his elegant dinners. He began extensive secret preparations to force a showdown with Girard.

Since Girard had only 6000 men around Caceres, Hill put together a larger expeditionary force to pursue Girard and attempt to bring him to action. As the October rains pounded Estremadura, Hill put his force into motion, and his own troops did not learn of his objective of relieving Caceres until the march turned eastwards. As Hill approached Caceres, Girard withdrew generally towards

Merida along a curving route that resembled a flexed elbow. By forced marches Hill moved rapidly towards the French, and by 27 October he was able to get within striking distance of Girard at Arroyo Molinos. Girard was a shrewd opponent, but, possibly on account of the torrential rain, neglected to patrol the area, affording Hill the opportunity of moving his entire force within a few hundred yards of the village occupied by the French. On the morning of 28 October he unleashed his men on the position and completely surprised Girard's units. Hill's men drove the main force into the mountains, killed 800, captured 1300, and seized all the horses, the baggage, three field pieces, and the magazine. Hill lost seven killed and sixty-four wounded. In all, the operation was a great contribution to allied morale in the dreary year of 1811 and began the steady elevation of Hill to the forefront of Wellington's generals. The earl of Aberdeen wrote to his brother in November 1811: 'I have formed a notion that he is the second best man in Portugal'; the brother replied: 'You are perfectly right' (BL, Add. MS 43224).

The later Peninsular War On 22 February 1812 Hill, on Wellington's recommendation, was made a KB. That year, as the scales began to tip towards the British in Spain, Wellington decided to move against Ciudad Rodrigo, and Hill received permission for an operation against the bridge and fortifications at Almaraz on the Tagus River. As the expedition began on 24 April, Hill selected three infantry brigades, an artillery brigade under Alexander Dickson, and two regiments of cavalry for the march, a total of 7000 men. He used elaborate ruses to conceal his intentions, because, if his movement were to be detected, strong enemy forces could intercept his retreat. He refused to let his men stage a banquet at Truxillo to celebrate the anniversary of the battle of Albuera. Instead, he ordered a march throughout the night that brought his force within 6 miles of the location of the bridge. The difficulties included strong fortifications on both sides of the river as well as a menacing castle, Mirabete, guarding the road on which Hill's men approached. A sentry detected a British soldier on the road and alerted the garrison, which began firing on the main force. Hill had no siege equipment, but his scouts located a goat trail leading down the mountain to Fort Napoleon, a stone fort with 450 men. Hill decided to surprise and storm the fort, 'a resolution', wrote William Napier:

> more hardy than it would appear … [If he failed,] every slanderous tongue would have been let loose on the rashness of attacking invulnerable forts: a military career hitherto so glorious might have been terminated in shame, but totally void of interested ambition Hill was unshaken.   (Napier, 4.163)

Hill's men crept to within 800 yards of the fort during the night of 18 May. As General Christopher Tilson-Chowne feinted against Mirabete high on the mountain, Hill's troops scaled Fort Napoleon, routed the garrison, and turned the guns there against Fort Ragusa on the opposite side of the river. The commander, Aubert, ignominiously evacuated the fort, and Hill soon controlled the

two forts and the bridge. His men destroyed the installations and large stores of food, supplies, and equipment. He retreated southwards the following day, since an attempt to besiege Mirabete would probably have brought French forces racing towards the region. But the brilliant operation permanently destroyed French communication in that area, for materials were not available for repairs. Once more, General Hill, the surpriser, had turned a difficult assignment into a great gain: 'It was', said Benjamin D'Urban, 'the most advantageous Coup of the Second Class during the war' (D'Urban, 256). George Bell called him 'the Duke's favourite and most successful General' (Bell, 63).

During the remainder of 1812 Wellington defeated Marmont at Salamanca (22 July) and advanced against Burgos, while Hill kept a force south of Madrid. When Wellington was forced to retreat westwards, Hill joined the march and went into winter quarters. Neither side could fight a winter campaign, so Hill's future assignment was that of commander of an attached wing rather than as commander of a semi-independent corps, at which he had excelled. As the advance of 1813 began, Hill commanded not only the 2nd division, the Surprisers, but the light division, the Portuguese division, and other forces, a total of 30,000 men. They moved steadily forwards towards the plains of Vitoria, where the French army formed a strong line, with Hill's corps on the right facing Gazan's army of the south. On 21 June the battle broke out near Hill's position, and he directed the movements under heavy fire. Eventually the French force broke and retreated, leaving heavy casualties on both sides, but the French lost all their artillery, stores, and baggage, together with huge sums of money and treasure. Four of the Hill brothers were reunited during the march beyond Vitoria, and the forces moved steadily towards the frontiers of France; on 9 July the brothers had their first extensive view into France.

While cantoned in the heights near Maya, Hill constantly studied the French positions. He began advancing on 8 November 1813. On 13 December his force of 14,000 was stationed at St Pierre d'Irube when Soult attacked it with a powerful force of 35,000. Because of heavy rains and swollen streams no reinforcements could reach Hill's position, but he did take advantage of a narrow front. The carnage was terrible, but at the crucial moment Hill moved the 57th foot from his right to the centre, and the French attack was repulsed. Wellington later rode up and said: 'Hill, the day's your own!' (Longford, 338). Yet Hill received only modest publicity from this great feat. In the lore of the Peninsular War, it may be better known that Hill swore at St Pierre—one of only two times, it was said, the other being at Talavera—that he won an impressive victory at worse than two-to-one odds. The allied force continued to move eastwards in 1814, and in late March Wellington's forces reached Toulouse, the taking of which appeared to be a bloody operation. Hill attacked the St Cyprien suburb, the other units began their assault, and, by 11 April, Soult's forces withdrew towards the south. At this time couriers arrived to bring official notice that Bonaparte had abdicated and peace had been declared. Wellington left Hill in command of the allied army while he travelled to Paris. Hill's accomplishments were exceeded only by those of the commander-in-chief.

At the age of forty-two Hill emerged from the Peninsular War as a proven general, but he planned to return to his estate in Shropshire. The government was preparing to expand the war in North America, and his name was mentioned as the possible commander of it, but in fact the war was giving way to negotiation. Hill had been elected an MP for Shrewsbury in 1812, on the family interest, but had never had an opportunity to be seated; he supported the government. As the Peninsular War ended, Hill and four other generals were made barons; Hill was created Baron Hill of Almaraz and of Hawkstone on 17 May 1814 and granted a pension of £2000 per annum. As he never married he wanted his title and pension to pass to his nephew, so on 16 January 1816 he was granted a special remainder to the male heirs of his brother John. On his return to Shropshire he was fêted as a hero and honoured by a memorial column in Shrewsbury costing £6000, 133 feet high and inscribed with the victories which he had gained.

Waterloo and after Following Bonaparte's escape from Elba in February 1815, the cabinet ordered Wellington to Belgium and sent Hill to join him. Hill arrived at Brussels on 2 April, and Wellington directed him to restrain the prince of Orange, commanding the Dutch-Belgian forces, from rash actions. Thousands of British troops crossed the channel, including three of Hill's brothers—Clement, Robert, and Thomas.

As Wellington formed his army, Hill received command of a corps of 25,000 to 30,000 men, which Wellington placed to the far right of his main position at Mont St Jean, south of Waterloo. Bonaparte's movements were carried out in secrecy, but Wellington could not give up his view that Bonaparte might direct his advance over good roads to Hill's position, so he kept his right wing strong, perhaps too strong. Hill's force played no appreciable part in the battle of Quatre-Bras (16 June) and was engaged only peripherally at Waterloo (18 June). As the battle progressed, when Hill saw that no threat was offered on the far right, he began leading some of his units to support the allied troops around the key position at Hougoumont. His horse was shot under him but, though bruised, he survived the desperate fighting. He accompanied the army to Paris and then went on furlough to London to consult Lord Bathurst about the succession of his peerage. He then returned to France, established headquarters at Cambrai, and served as second in command of Wellington's army of occupation. He was made GCB on 2 January 1815 and GCH in 1816, and received Portuguese, Austrian, Russian, and Dutch orders.

In 1818 Hill returned to Shropshire and undertook the renovation of his modest estate, Hardwicke Grange, which he inherited from his uncle Sir Richard Hill, second baronet (d. 1809). Sir John and his sons were not very secure financially, and Hill had to manage carefully his income from his pension, his colonelcies of various regiments, including the 53rd (1817–30), and from governorships at various times, among them that of Plymouth, the best available when he obtained it in 1830. He occasionally went to London, where he sat in the Lords, but in the early 1820s he paid only nominal attention to politics, voting tory. On 14 June 1820 he was awarded a DCL degree from Oxford University. George IV selected him to carry the royal standard at the 1821 coronation, and Hill later wrote to the College of Arms requesting it. In 1823 he declined the lieutenancy of the ordnance and in 1827 the master-generalship, offered by Wellington. However, in 1828 he replaced Wellington, then prime minister, as commander-in-chief of the army. At the request of William IV he abstained from voting on the Reform Bill.

As commander-in-chief, Hill surrounded himself with good men, such as Sir Henry Hardinge and Lord Fitzroy Somerset. He continued to be influenced by Wellington, and attempted no fundamental reforms, although he did introduce reforms to reduce drunkenness in the ranks, to provide educational and recreational outlets for troops, and to curb some of the more cruel forms of punishment, such as flogging. He approved, if reluctantly, the formation of regimental libraries. His performance at the Horse Guards became more complex when Lord Grey and the whigs came to office in 1830. Hill probably survived the political pressures because he had firm control of the army and showed skill in his policies supporting the civil power and limited military expeditions. In the late 1830s his health declined, and he resigned on 9 August 1842. On 22 September he was created Viscount Hill with remainder to his nephew Sir Rowland Hill, bt. He died at Hardwicke Grange on 10 December 1842 and was buried on 16 December in the village church of Hadnall, Shropshire. He divided his fortune of £30,000 among his family and left a fund to maintain the Shrewsbury column. He was succeeded by his nephew Sir Rowland Hill, fourth baronet (1800–1875), tory MP for Shropshire (1821–32) and for North Shropshire (1832–42).

To evaluate Hill's contributions, one should focus on his role as an army officer rather than as an administrator. He was a commander with genuine humanitarian concerns for his men. He was a loyal subordinate who never deviated from the concept that he must meticulously obey orders. He possessed sound judgement and displayed the impressive ability to be inventive when he carried out surprise operations. He showed a broad grasp of tactics and, to a degree, of strategy, although the towering Wellington dictated the course of the struggle in the Peninsula that helped to lead to the defeat of the empire. Yet Hill's battlefield performance and victories demonstrate that he had mastered the element of surprise and was one of the great commanders of the age.   GORDON L. TEFFETELLER

Sources G. L. Teffeteller, *The surpriser: the life of Rowland, Lord Hill* (1983) · GEC, *Peerage* · Burke, *Peerage* (1967) · E. Sidney, *The life of Lord Hill* (1845) · Fortescue, *Brit. army* · C. W. C. Oman, *A history of the Peninsular War*, 7 vols. (1902–30) · W. F. P. Napier, *History of the war in the Peninsula and in the south of France*, rev. edn, 6 vols. (1876) · The dispatches of … the duke of Wellington … from 1799 to 1818, ed. J. Gurwood, new edn, 13 vols. (1837–9) • Supplementary despatches (correspondence) and memoranda of Field Marshal Arthur, duke of Wellington, ed. A. R. Wellesley, second duke of Wellington, 15 vols. (1858–72) • M. Glover, Wellington as military commander (1968) • G. Bell, Soldier's story (1956) • A. Brett-James, Life in Wellington's army (1972) • Peninsular cavalry general, 1811–13: the correspondence of Lieutenant-General Robert Ballard Long, ed. T. H. McGuffie (1951) • G. M. Sherer, Recollections of the Peninsula (1823) • B. D'Urban, Peninsular journal (1930) • R. K. Porter, Letters from Portugal and Spain (1809) • A. I. Shand, Wellington's lieutenants (1902) • S. E. Vichness, Marshal of Portugal (1976) • J. W. Cole, Memoirs of British generals distinguished during the Peninsular War, 2 vols. (1856) • E. Longford [E. H. Pakenham, countess of Longford], Wellington, 1: The years of the sword (1969) • J. Philippart, ed., The royal military calendar, 3 vols. (1815–16), 197–8

Archives BL, corresp. and papers, Add. MSS 35059–35067 • Dorset RO, military corresp. • PRO, various MSS as commander in chief, War Office • Shrops. RRC, corresp. and papers | Arquivo Historico Militar, Lisbon, Portugal • BL, corresp. with Sir Robert Peel, Add. MSS 40236–40514 • Bodl. Oxf., corresp. with North family • NA Scot., corresp. with Sir Andrew Leith Hay • NAM, letters to Sir Benjamin D'Urban • NL Scot., corresp. with Sir George Brown • NL Scot., corresp. with Lord Lymedoch • NL Scot., corresp. with eighth marquess of Tweeddale • NL Wales, letters to William Lloyd • PRO NIre., letters to Lord Anglesey • U. Durham L., archives and special collections, corresp. with Henry George, third Earl Grey • U. Durham L., archives and special collections, Grey of Howick collection, corresp. with Charles, second Earl Grey • U. Southampton L., letters to first duke of Wellington • W. Sussex RO, letters to duke of Richmond

Likenesses T. Heaphy, watercolour drawing, 1813–14, NPG [see illus.] • W. Salter, oils, 1834–40 (study for Waterloo banquet), NPG • S. F. Diez, drawing, 1841, National Gallery, Berlin • J. P. Knight, oils, exh. RA 1842 (study for The heroes of Waterloo), Gov. Art Coll. • L. Clennell, watercolour over pencil drawing, BM • G. Dawe, oils, NAM • G. Hayter, group portrait, oils (The trial of Queen Caroline, 1820), NPG • J. Panzetta, statue, London Road, Shrewsbury • J. W. Pieneman, oils, Wellington Museum, Apsley House, London • G. Richmond, watercolour drawing, NPG • W. Salter, group portrait, oils (Waterloo banquet at Apsley House), Wellington Museum, Apsley House, London • C. Smith, oils; formerly United Services Club (c/o The Crown Commissioners), London

Wealth at death under £30,000: GEC, Peerage

Hill, Sir Rowland (1795–1879), postal reformer and civil servant, was born on 3 December 1795 at 96 Blackwell Street, Kidderminster, third of the eight children of Thomas Wright *Hill (1763–1851), schoolmaster, and his wife, Sarah Lea (1765–1842).

Early life The Hill family, buffeted at times by economic adversity, was exceptionally close and indeed operated as a well-ordered regiment in pursuit of the group's self-advancement and in support of its belief in liberal causes, reform, and earnest improvement. For the Hills, progressive education was one great means through which these goals might be achieved. About 1803 Rowland entered Hill Top, his father's school in a Birmingham suburb, where despite the effects of scarlet fever which permanently weakened his health he developed his skills as a budding mathematician and mechanical engineer. At the age of twelve he became an assistant to his father, and in 1819 he helped his family to establish Hazelwood, a new school in Edgbaston. There the Hills assiduously implemented an innovative educational policy based on the ideals of representative democracy and competitive capitalism, not

Sir Rowland Hill (1795–1879), by Maull & Polyblank, c.1860

unlike the approach of Jeremy Bentham's Chrestomathia. On 27 September 1827 Hill married Caroline (d. 1881), daughter of Joseph Pearson, a Wolverhampton manufacturer and county magistrate; they had one son and three daughters. In the same year as his marriage, with the aid of three of his brothers he extended the family's experiments in education by opening the Bruce Castle School in Tottenham, Middlesex.

However, Hill grew increasingly frustrated in his role as a schoolmaster. He was not, after all, the great intellectual of the family. That role was played by Matthew Davenport *Hill, the eldest brother. Furthermore, having abandoned any religious belief Hill was troubled by the fact that he had to take his pupils to church services and lead them in prayers. It is not surprising, then, that he began to look for other avenues to social progress and personal advancement. He considered an offer from the social reformer Robert Owen to manage one of his experiments in communal living, but rejected it. For a time part of his considerable energy was expended on work on a series of inventions and ideas, such as a rotary printing press, a scheme for pneumatic dispatch of messages, and road-building machinery. He also became involved in campaigns for colonizing South Australia, having produced in 1832 a paper on the subject with the characteristic title Home colonies: a plan for the gradual extinction (by education) of pauperism and the diminution of crime. By 1835 this activity bore fruit in Hill's appointment as secretary to the South Australian colonization commission, a government post which paid

£500 a year and which allowed Hill to turn over the management of the Bruce Castle School to his younger brother Arthur.

Postal reform It was another issue which was to be the great cause of Hill's life, however. In January 1837 Hill published the first edition of *Post Office Reform: its Importance and Practicability*, after submitting the gist of his proposals privately to Lord Melbourne's government. In this pamphlet Hill undertook two tasks simultaneously. The first was to attack the current postal system as overly complicated, usually requiring the recipient of a letter to pay for postage based on the number of sheets the letter contained and the distance it had been conveyed. Under this system a letter of a single sheet sent from London to Birmingham cost as much as 9*d*. Matters were made worse by the fact that London was served by three separate delivery systems. Thus a Londoner might receive mail from three different letter-carriers. Elsewhere it was usually the case that mail had to be collected from local post offices and posted not, as later, in roadside boxes, but at the same local post offices or in 'receiving' houses. Hill insisted that this unwieldy arrangement unfairly taxed the public and inhibited the expansion of trade and ideas. Hill's second goal in writing this pamphlet was to propose an alternative system of a standard prepayment for letters conveyed between principal towns and cities, regardless of the specific distance involved. Hill would later modify and improve details of this scheme, most importantly suggesting the use of stamps as one method of prepayment. However, his fundamental approach first presented in *Post Office Reform* remained unchanged for the rest of his life.

Penny post When Hill put forth these proposals in 1837 he was a relatively obscure individual approaching middle age. By 10 January 1840—the inauguration of penny post through which a letter of ½ oz might be sent anywhere in the country for 1*d*.—he had become a nationally known figure whose ideas had become government policy and who was poised for a significant career in the Victorian civil service. How had the transformation come about? Due credit should be given to Hill, who was tireless in promoting his scheme and in organizing support among the public in general and the commercial and banking community in particular. However, it should be remembered that Hill was not the lonely crusader, single-handedly opposing myopic supporters of outmoded assumptions and practices, which some accounts of his life, and indeed at times his own rhetoric, might suggest. The Post Office had already been the object of criticism from men such as Robert Wallace, MP for Greenock, who in 1833 launched an effective reform campaign. Hill's campaign also benefited from the support of like-minded individuals such as Henry Cole and Edwin Chadwick. Hence the success of Hill's attack on the Post Office is partly explained by the fact that it was only one aspect of a wider utilitarian assault on existing institutions, which characterized the post-Reform Bill generation and which called for a sweeping review of current procedures and advocated changes based on principles of rationality and political economy.

Hill was convinced that his proposals for Post Office improvement required his direct supervision and involvement if their implementation was to be successful, and from 1839 to 1842 he was attached to the Treasury at an annual salary of £1500 to carry out this assignment. Dismissed by the Peel government in September 1842 he was employed from 1843 to 1846 as first a director and then chairman of the London and Brighton Railway Company; however, he remained dedicated to the engine of reform and to driving that engine, and Peel's fall from office in 1846 was a welcome event which facilitated Hill's entry into the Post Office as secretary to the postmaster-general. In this position Hill was somewhat awkwardly inserted into the Post Office to serve as an arm of the department's political chief and a representative of the Treasury. The senior permanent official and the linchpin of the administrative structure remained the secretary to the Post Office. Nevertheless, problems and frustrations persisted. Although the penny post had stimulated a significant increase in the number of letters mailed—19 per capita in 1860 versus 3 per capita in 1839—Hill's projections of the impact of penny post on departmental finances proved inaccurate. He had predicted that gross departmental revenue would return to its pre-penny post level within five years. This prediction was not fulfilled until 1851. More seriously, during the first year the penny post net revenue fell by 69 per cent, and it was not until 1873 that the department was able to maintain consistently the £1.6 million figure earned the year before the implementation of Hill's reforms.

Economics of mail delivery Hill offered several explanations for this unexpected outcome. At times he attributed the blame to what he regarded as excessively costly railway contracts made after 1840 in the era of the decline of coaching companies. (One Post Office estimate held that railway conveyance of mail was almost four times as costly as conveyance by coach. Such estimates, of course, failed to take into consideration the improved speed of conveyance or the greater capacity of the railways to handle the weight of mails, which was three times larger after penny post.) Incensed by the situation Hill recommended that government loans to railway companies be contingent on their lowering their charges for the carriage of mail. In 1867 he carried the attack one step further by advocating nationalization of the railway industry as a way to escape from the imbroglio and to destroy the independence of the railway interest. He also attempted to account for the shortcomings of his reforms by claiming that both the efficiency of the Post Office and the effectiveness of his plans were severely diminished by the fact that a politician, the postmaster-general, headed the department. To Hill, such men—relics of the old corruption—simply lacked the necessary commitment and expertise for the task at hand. In a statement which reveals much about his view of the Post Office hierarchy and the crucial centrality of his place in that same hierarchy, he once lamented in his journal that 'The P.M.G. has ... interfered with my department' (Perry, 8). Instead Hill favoured an arrangement whereby the Post Office would be managed by a board with himself as chairman.

Hill's real wrath was reserved for a group of permanent civil servants inside the bureaucracy, who had entered the Post Office before his arrival, and who, Hill claimed, intentionally frustrated improvements. The leader of this group was Colonel William Maberly, who had been secretary to the Post Office since 1836 and who remained sceptical as to the practicality of penny post. After a bitter power struggle Hill seemingly emerged triumphant in 1854 when his old enemy Maberly resigned, and Hill succeeded him in that important position at an annual salary of £2000. Unfortunately for Hill a number of other opponents, including Anthony Trollope, John Tilley, and Frank Ives Scudamore, remained in their departmental positions. To counterbalance their influence, Hill relied on several relatives, including his brothers Edwin *Hill and Frederic *Hill and his only son, Pearson, who had been installed in Post Office jobs.

Personality and fame What Hill never realized was that the reasons for the failure of postal reform to achieve all the results he so ardently desired lay elsewhere. As Daunton has convincingly demonstrated, Hill's analysis of the economics of mail conveyance was fundamentally flawed. Hill had overestimated the elasticity of demand for mail services and underestimated the staff size required to operate the system. The irony is that some of his opponents, such as Maberly, had a much more accurate view of the complexities of postal finance than Hill did. Moreover, Hill and his family failed to recognize the reality that despite his effectiveness as an outside critic of departmental weaknesses and adherence to the status quo, Hill was not temperamentally suited to manage a complex bureaucracy from the inside. Autocratic and prone to be suspicious, he never achieved any critical detachment from his obsessive belief that postal reform constituted the great cause of modern life and that everyone should adopt that same belief. (When Hill met Garibaldi at a banquet in 1864, the only topic he wished to pursue was the state of the Italian post office.)

Hill's dogmatic approach to issues, viewing all questions according to a rigid standard of his own making, was not well suited to a department which came into more frequent contact with the public than any other government agency and which faced issues that were often less than clear-cut. For example, as a committed advocate of free trade, Hill questioned the virtue of the Post Office's monopoly of mail conveyance. Yet one result of the monopoly was that it provided a certain level of service for the entire country. Similarly, Hill was adamantly opposed to 'cross-subsidies', the practice of using profits earned in one area of the Post Office's operations to cover losses incurred elsewhere. To Hill such a practice constituted an inequitable tax on the nation at large to the benefit of smaller interest groups or particular communities. Instead every aspect of the department's operations should be self-supporting. Yet this assumption ignored the fact that there were some areas of the Post Office's responsibilities, the overseas carriage of mails being an obvious case, where simply relying on market forces to ensure low contract costs, equally low postage rates, and a healthy profit would, if adopted, not work.

These outlooks also shaped Hill's ambivalent attitude toward questions of Post Office expansion into areas beyond simply the conveyance of letters. Although in principle he supported both a parcel post and the establishment of Post Office Savings Banks, he was not an enthusiastic advocate of either idea. With regard to the former he believed that the public would regard a parcel post as unjustifiably interfering with private enterprise. The parcel post was not established until 1883, long after Hill's departure from the department. With regard to the latter Hill envisaged that Post Office Savings Banks should operate on charges based on those of the money-order system in order that a suitable surplus might be attained. If this approach had been followed by those who actively campaigned for the establishment of departmental savings banks, namely Scudamore and George Chetwynd, the system's ultimate usefulness would have been severely limited, and it is worth noting that aside from the penny post very few of the changes associated with the remarkable expansion of the nineteenth-century Post Office were advanced by Hill.

These shortcomings did not prevent Hill from becoming quite literally a Victorian icon (statues of him were erected at Kidderminster, Birmingham, and at the Royal Exchange in London). His dedication and hard work at the Post Office and an effective public relations campaign had established his reputation as a major public figure. According to W. E. Gladstone, Sir Rowland Hill's great reform 'had run like wildfire through the civilised world; never perhaps was a local invention (for such it was) and improvement applied in the lifetime of its author to the advantages of such vast multitudes of his fellow-creatures' (*DNB*). To John Stuart Mill, for example, Hill's reforms symbolized the benefits which were made possible through what Mill termed 'popular government'. Hill reaped the rewards of this fame, including fellowship of the Royal Society in 1857, a knighthood in 1860, an honorary degree of DCL from Oxford University in 1864, and the first Albert gold medal given by the Society of Arts.

Retirement and death In 1864 Hill was forced to retire as a consequence of ill health, exacerbated by stress resulting from bitter policy disagreements over salary and promotion issues with Lord Stanley of Alderley, the postmaster-general, and an unsuccessful attempt to appeal over Stanley's head to Lord Palmerston the prime minister, who perceptively described Hill as the 'spoilt child of the Post Office' (H. Parris, *Constitutional Bureaucracy*, 1969, 129). None the less, honours continued to be heaped on Hill, including a £20,000 parliamentary grant and the freedom of the City of London in 1879. After serving on the royal commission on railways in 1865–7 Hill spent much of his retirement working on a history of the penny post and his memoirs, the latter published posthumously in 1880 with the aid of G. Birkbeck Hill. Sir Rowland Hill died on 27 August 1879 at Bertram House, his home in Hampstead in north London. Venerated in death as in life, he was given a state funeral on 4 September and buried in Westminster Abbey.

C. R. PERRY

Sources M. J. Daunton, *Royal Mail: the Post Office since 1840* (1985) · C. R. Perry, *The Victorian Post Office: the growth of a bureaucracy*, Royal Historical Society Studies in History, 64 (1992) · J. Farrugia, *Sir Rowland Hill, reformer extraordinary: some notes on his life and work* (1979) · G. B. Hill and R. Hill, *The life of Sir Rowland Hill, and, The history of penny postage*, 2 vols. (1880) · D. Graham, 'Victorian reform as a family business', in A. S. Wohl, *The Victorian family* (1978) · H. Robinson, *The British Post Office: a history* (1948) · *CGPLA Eng. & Wales* (1879) · *DNB*
Archives Haringey Archive Service, London, diaries and corresp. · Royal Mail Heritage, London, journals, minutes, memoranda, and papers | Berks. RO, corresp. with Treasury relating to his dismissal and plans for postal reform · BL, corresp. with W. E. Gladstone with memoranda, Add. MSS 44380–44753, *passim* · Bristol RO, letters and papers relating to Rowland Hill Testimonial Fund · Pembroke College, Oxford, letters to A. Hill and M. D. Hill · UCL, corresp. with Edwin Chadwick · UCL, letters to the Society for the Diffusion of Useful Knowledge · W. Sussex RO, corresp. with Richard Cobden · W. Sussex RO, letters to duke of Richmond · W. Yorks. AS, Leeds, corresp. with Lord Canning
Likenesses W. O. Geller, mezzotint, pubd 1848 (after A. Wivell junior), BM, NPG · Maull & Polyblank, photograph, *c.*1860, NPG [*see illus.*] · J. A. Vinter, oils, *c.*1879 (after photograph), NPG · T. Brock, marble statue, Town Hall Square, Kidderminster, Worcestershire · E. O. Ford, bronze statue, King Edward Street, London · D. J. Pound, line engraving (after photograph by J. and C. Watkins), NPG · photograph, repro. in Daunton, *Royal mail* · statue, Birmingham · statue, Royal Exchange, London
Wealth at death under £60,000: resworn probate, Dec 1880, *CGPLA Eng. & Wales* (1879)

Hill, Sir (George) Rowland (1855–1928), rugby administrator, was born on 21 January 1855 at Queen's House, Greenwich, London, one of three children of Irish protestant parents. His father, the Revd James Hill, was headmaster of the upper school of the Royal Hospital school, Greenwich.

Hill attended Christ's Hospital school, Newgate Street, but left at the age of fifteen to take up employment with the Telegraph Construction and Maintenance Company. He worked aboard the famous *Great Eastern* steamship, helping to lay one of the Atlantic cables. He joined the civil service and became record keeper in the principal probate registry, Somerset House. He was a member of the London county council, as was his unmarried sister, and he was also a JP; for over thirty years from 1887, he was chairman of Greenwich Conservative Association and at one stage he was also the association's president. He resisted, however, the blandishments of friends who wanted him to stand for parliament.

Hill is best-known for his services to rugby football. He was involved in running the Queen's House club, founded by his brother Colonel E. Cleary Hill, which was one of the founder members, in 1871, of the Rugby Football Union (RFU). He gave up playing after the Queen's House club disbanded, but took a leading role in obtaining the Rectory Field for the Blackheath club, of which he was one of the original directors. He was elected honorary secretary of the RFU in 1881. He was the last holder of this particular office, being succeeded in 1904, after twenty-three years' service, by a paid secretary. He was elected the eighteenth

president in 1904–5 without an intervening period as vice-president, was re-elected in 1905–6, and then elected for a further year in 1906–7. He was the first person to be knighted—in 1926—for his services to the game, which covered a period of over thirty-five years. In demand as a referee, he was a member of the international rugby football board for twenty-eight years from 1890 to 1928.

Hill is remembered above all for his defence of amateurism, for he believed incipient professionalism in rugby union football to be an evil likely to lead to violent and dangerous play. His obituary in *The Times* described him as 'an amateur of amateurs and a Tory of Tories': when he resigned from the RFU secretaryship in 1904 he would accept 'neither bounty nor reward'. He opposed the Yorkshire clubs' attempts to legalize 'broken time' payments in 1893, an action which led to the breakaway in 1895 of the Northern Union, later to become the Rugby League. Hill was active in steering through changes in the RFU constitution to enshrine the amateur principle and to frame rules designed to expunge from the game all forms of monetary consideration beyond the reimbursement of travelling expenses. The years following the breakaway of the Northern Union were some of the most difficult in the history of the union game and Hill, among others, is credited with guiding the game during that period towards renewed success. In 1893, 481 clubs were affiliated to the RFU; ten years later that number had dropped to 244, but by 1911–12 membership had recovered to 319.

Hill, who never married, died at the Seamen's Hospital, Greenwich, on 25 April 1928 and was buried five days later in the Royal Hospital cemetery, Woolwich Road. On 5 October 1929, at Twickenham, the headquarters of the English game, the president of the RFU unveiled in his honour the Rowland Hill memorial gate and bronze plaque. The special commemorative game, played at Twickenham between the combined sides of England–Wales and Scotland–Ireland, and refereed by a Frenchman, attracted 25,000 spectators: the large crowds were considered the best epitaph to Hill and the other stalwarts who had fought to save the game from professionalism.

K. G. SHEARD

Sources *The Times* (26 April 1928) · U. A. Titley and R. McWhirter, *Centenary history of the Rugby Football Union* (1970) · *WWW*, 1916–28 · *CGPLA Eng. & Wales* (1928) · *The Times* (1 May 1928), 19
Likenesses etching, presented 5 Oct 1929, repro. in Titley and McWhirter, *Centenary history*, 128; copy, Twickenham rugby ground, London · Spy [L. Ward], lithograph, NPG; repro. in *VF* (1 Feb 1890)
Wealth at death £5314: probate, 11 July 1928, *CGPLA Eng. & Wales*

Hill, Rowley (1836–1887), bishop of Sodor and Man, was born at Londonderry on 22 February 1836, the third son of Sir George Hill, baronet (1804–1845), of St Columb's, co. Londonderry, and his wife, Elizabeth Sophia (*d.* 1900), eldest daughter of John and Louisa Rea of St Columb's. He was educated at Christ's Hospital, London, and Trinity College, Cambridge, where he matriculated in 1855 and graduated BA in 1859, taking his MA in 1863, and being made DD *honoris causa* in 1877. He was ordained a deacon in 1860, and served the curacy of Christ Church, Dover. In the following year he was admitted to priest's orders by the archbishop of Canterbury, and he moved to the curacy of St Marylebone, London. On 30 April 1863 he married Caroline Maud (d. 1882), second daughter of Captain Alfred Chapman RN. In 1863 he became perpetual curate of St Luke's, Edgware Road, London, and after five years' service in that parish he was presented to the rectory of Frant, in the diocese of Chichester. In 1871 he exchanged his rectory for the vicarage of St Michael's, Chester Square, London.

Hill was presented in 1873 to the vicarage of Sheffield. That large and important parish he held, with the rural deanery of Sheffield and a prebend in York Cathedral, until August 1877, when he was presented on the recommendation of the earl of Beaconsfield to the bishopric of Sodor and Man. A moderate evangelical, Hill discharged his duties with great zeal and success. But his plan of uniting the proposed bishopric of Liverpool to that of Sodor and Man was not generally approved, and was declined by the government. He published sermons, collections of Sunday school lessons, and instructions on the catechism. After the death of his first wife Hill married again, on 11 June 1884; his second wife was Alicia Eliza, daughter of Captain George Probyn. After a brief illness, Hill died at his London residence, 10 Hereford Square, Old Brompton, South Kensington, on 27 May 1887. He was survived by his second wife.   B. H. BLACKER, rev. ELLIE CLEWLOW

Sources Church Bells (15 April 1878), 215 · Annual Register (1887), 134 · ILN (4 June 1887), 628 · ILN (18 June 1887), 682 · Venn, Alum. Cant. · Men of the time (1884) · W. W. Rouse Ball and J. A. Venn, eds., Admissions to Trinity College, Cambridge, 5 (1913) · Burke, Peerage (1857) · CGPLA Eng. & Wales (1887)
Archives PRO NIre., family and estate papers, MSS of Hill family of Brook Hall, co. Londonderry
Likenesses wood-engraving (after photograph by S. A. Walker), NPG; repro. in ILN (18 June 1887)
Wealth at death £6097 18s. 3d.: administration, 14 Sept 1887, CGPLA Eng. & Wales

Hill, Samuel (1648/9–1716), Church of England clergyman and religious controversialist, was the son of William Hill of South Petherton, Somerset. He matriculated from Lincoln College, Oxford, on 10 April 1663, aged fourteen, but transferred to St Mary's Hall from where he graduated BA in 1666. Nothing is known of his activities until 18 February 1673 when he was installed in the parish of Meare, Somerset. On 21 December 1679 he married Grace Pinfold at St Augustine with St Faith, London. On 10 May 1687 he was presented to the parish of Kilmington in Somerset by Sir Stephen Fox. He was made prebendary of Buckland Dinham in Wells Cathedral on 5 September 1688, appointed master of Bruton Free School, Somerset, in 1700, installed archdeacon of Wells on 12 October 1705 (at which time he appears in the records as MA), and elected a canon residentiary of the cathedral on 25 November 1708. Anthony Wood characterized Hill as a man 'much esteemed for his learning and zeal for the Church of England' (Wood, Ath. Oxon., new edn, 1813–20, 4.564).

In his first published work, The Catholic Balance (London, 1687), the high-church Hill sets out the themes to which he would return throughout his career. He is concerned to

defend 'true doctrine', which he defines as that which is 'caught in the Scriptures, preached by the Fathers, and universally received in the Primitive Church' (p. 134), and he argues for an ecclesiastical hierarchy that is of divine and apostolic origin, and therefore independent within its own bounds. Hill followed this up in 1688 with The Necessity of Heresies Asserted and Explained (London, 1688), in which he argues that heresy is morally necessary in order to demonstrate 'right doctrine' (p. 13). De presbyteratu dissertatio quadripartita (London, 1691) was Hill's attack on the structure and doctrines of Presbyterianism.

Hill subsequently became engaged in the controversy surrounding the oath of allegiance to William and Mary imposed by parliament in 1689 upon all beneficed clergy. Six bishops and about 400 lower clergy refused to swear the oaths and were deprived of their livings in early 1690. In 1692 Hill, who was distressed at the change of bishops but had nevertheless taken the oath, published a justification of conformity entitled Solomon and Abiathar, or, The Case of the Deprived Bishops and Clergy Discussed (London, 1692). He insists that the secular deprivations are lawful because they were done for just reasons, and the church has concurred in them. Hill revisited the issue four years later in A Debate on the Justice and Piety of the Present Constitution under King William (London, 1696).

In 1694 Gilbert Burnet, bishop of Salisbury, published his Four Discourses (London, 1694). The second of these, 'Concerning the divinity and death of Christ', was challenged by Hill in his A Vindication of the Primitive Fathers (London, 1695). Burnet's exposition of the Trinity and incarnation, argues Hill, is so ambiguous that it leaves 'a latitude for various heresies in this "mystery"' (p. 7). Such latitude 'leadeth to destruction, in the service of heretical Comprehensions' (p. 53). Burnet complained to the bishop of London that his chaplain, Roger Altham, professor of Hebrew at Oxford, had licensed such a book 'full of scurrility', and Altham was obliged to make a public apology to Burnet for letting the book slip through. Although there were rumours that Hill would be suspended by the bishops for his assault on Burnet, he escaped punishment. Burnet later published an anonymous reply. Apparently Hill wrote a defence of his Vindication, and also revised his Vindication in preparation for a second edition, but neither ever appeared in print.

As early as 1693 some high-church clergy, including Hill, had been calling for a convocation of the clergy of the ecclesiastical province of Canterbury to settle the Anglican definition of the Trinity. The campaign came to a head with the publication of Francis Atterbury's Letter to a Convocation Man (London, 1696). The official response came from William Wake in his The Authority of Christian Princes over their Ecclesiastical Synods Asserted (London, 1697). Hill waded into the controversy with his Municipium ecclesiasticum, or, The Rights, Liberties, and Authorities of the Christian Church (London, 1697), the first reply to Wake. Hill declares that the church has a 'divine right' to hold synods to govern its own affairs. There are examples of synods in scripture and instances in early church history of synods running church affairs without interference from secular authorities. He later defended *Municipium ecclesiasticum* from an attack by Wake in *The Rites of the Christian Church Further Defended* (London, 1698). The subject of church power was one to which Hill returned in *A Discourse on Government* (London, 1698), *A Brief Discourse into the Grounds, Authority … of Ecclesiastical Synods* (London, 1698), and *The Rights, Liberties and Authorities of the Christian Church* (London, 1701).

After this flurry of activity nothing further appeared in print until *A thorough examination of the false principles and fallacious arguments advanced against the Christian church* (London, 1708), Hill's response to Matthew Tindal's 'pernicious' book *The Rights of the Christian Church Asserted* (London, 1708). Hill's final three works, published in 1713, were concerned with remission of sins, baptism, and the Apocrypha. He died on 7 March 1716 and is buried in Wells Cathedral.

Hill was survived by his wife, Grace, by at least two sons, William and Samuel, and by daughters. The preamble to his will, written four days before he died, conveys Hill's sense of mission as a defender of the church, thanking God for his mercies:

> transcendingly above all with the divinest of all Imployments in the Services of the Priesthood whereby I have been admitted into the knowledge of God and of his holy Oracles and enabled with a zeale to defend the faith and Church of Christ against all the Adversaries thereof these Ages.

He put himself into the hands of God, 'now the Time of my Warfare seeming to be at an end' (PRO, PROB 11/553, fol. 93*v*).

MARTIN GREIG

Sources Foster, *Alum. Oxon.* · G. Every, *The high church party, 1688–1718* (1956) · M. Greig, 'The reasonableness of Christianity? Gilbert Burnet and the trinitarian controversy of the 1690s', *Journal of Ecclesiastical History*, 44 (1993), 631–51 · *DNB* · will, PRO, PROB 11/553, sig. 144 · *Fasti Angl., 1541–1857*, [Bath and Wells] · Wood, *Ath. Oxon.*, new edn, 4.564 · *IGI*
Wealth at death £500 apportioned; plus unspecified remainder: will, PRO, PROB 11/553, sig. 144

Hill, Samuel (*bap.* 1678, *d.* 1759), textile manufacturer, was born in Soyland in the West Riding of Yorkshire and baptized on 7 September 1678 in the parish of Elland, Yorkshire, the son of James and Deborah (1657–1741) Hill of Soyland. His early life and education remain obscure though his later financial accounts and commercial correspondence demonstrate his proficiency in bookkeeping, set down in a distinctive, florid script, with long quill strokes and decorative capitals. In 1706 he purchased a remote seventeenth-century farmstead at Making Place, Soyland, at a high altitude close to the Pennine ridge, which became both his commercial base and his home for the rest of his life. On 21 April 1712 he married Elizabeth Holroyd (1691–1756) of Sowerby at Coley church in the parish of Halifax, but their family life was dogged with tragedy and disappointment. Of their six children, Sarah died on 23 July 1729, aged fifteen; her sister, Ann, on 3 April 1730 aged five; and her brothers Joseph on 14 January 1730 aged three; Samuel on 11 June 1732 aged twelve; and James on 16 January 1753, aged thirty. Moreover, their sole surviving son, Richard (*d.* 1780), who was admitted into

partnership with his father in 1746, had become estranged from his father by 1752, when he set up in business on his own account. He was declared bankrupt in February 1759, and when he was effectively disinherited by his father eight months later, he complained bitterly in his diary that his father's will, which had left him 'in a situation too deplorable to relate', was 'never formed nor invented but by the devil'. Indeed, litigation arising from the controversial will and associated deed poll, which had provided for the settlement of the major part of the estate upon his granddaughter, Betty Nuttall Hall, the sole surviving child of Richard Hill, when she came of age, continued until 1793. Lord Kenyon, the lord chief justice, was prompted to observe in 1790: 'the maker of these instruments or his advisers have certainly produced such a case as never happened before and in all probability never will happen again'.

Hill masterminded a remarkably successful international textile marketing operation, from an unpromising upland environment, accessible only to packhorse trains, and over 70 miles from the nearest port. 'We have had so much rain and snow upon these hills that we could scarce get anything dry', he explained in a letter to a Dutch customer in February 1737, expressing his frustration with the protracted Pennine winter. By 1726 he had become sufficiently well established to issue a promissory note to his brother James's creditors. He was then operating an extensive putting-out system, buying wool from all over the country and arranging for it to be spun and woven by a network of domestic outworkers, perhaps numbering as many as 250 by the 1730s. Initially, Hill traded primarily in woollen kerseys, his largest consignments destined for charitable institutions, for example Christ's Hospital, as well as military and naval requisitions and the export market. He supplied customers in most parts of Europe, especially the Low Countries, Spain, Portugal, and Russia, and indeed further afield, dispatching at least one pattern sheet to Persia, via St Petersburg and Astrakhan. He entered the worsted trade only in the 1730s, a generation after the trade had been introduced into the West Riding of Yorkshire, when worsteds were rapidly becoming fashionable for the middling and lower ranks of society, obtaining his supplies from both domestic outworkers and independent worsted manufacturers. His surviving business records reveal that the value of his annual turnover of cloth never fell below £23,000 during the period 1744–50, reaching a peak in excess of £35,527 in 1747, and confirm that he was still primarily a kersey manufacturer, selling twice as many kerseys as worsteds during the 1740s. A later pattern book, containing an impressive range of samples in both fabrics from 1750, displays the superb quality, brilliance, and diversity of colour and design achieved in the weaving and dyeing of his cloth. By this time he was one of the wealthiest entrepreneurs in the West Riding.

Hill is revealed in his correspondence as a sturdy, independent character with a shrewd business sense, determined to maintain a reputation for quality at a competitive price, insisting that his cloth, much of which carried his own name or the names of individual members of his family, was 'not to be outdone in England by any man'. Stubbornly resolute in refusing 'to deal with those who will not accept my goods at market price when ready', he displayed flexibility in his willingness to sell worsteds initially 'for small profit till they be known' and his readiness to realize 'as near as I can' the exact specifications of his customers. Moreover, his wife helped to cultivate special relationships with prized customers, by supplying them with token gifts of ham and tongue. Hill was also evidently a considerate and respected employer. He was anxious to avoid frequent changes in production so as not 'to spoil the weavers' and at least one former employee fondly recalled in a letter to his son Richard his 'good father'. He invested most of his wealth in local property, transforming Making Place and nearby Kebroyd into 'elegant places', lavishing upon the former 'at least £8000, and upon the latter £4000', as his son, Richard, observed in his diary.

Samuel Hill died at his home, Making Place, Soyland, on 22 October 1759. He was buried in the churchyard of the chapel-of-ease at Ripponden on 24 October, where, according to its curate, the antiquary John Watson, he had erected a 'handsome well-cut tombstone' over the vault containing the remains of his wife and children, and where he had planted a grove of yew trees with the help of John Collier (1708–1786), alias Tim Bobbin, the Lancashire artist and dialect poet, an erstwhile frequent visitor to Soyland. However, Watson made no reference in his parish history of 1775 to any epitaph, inscription, or monument to Hill at Ripponden. Moreover, Hill's intended public benefaction of a bridge at Soyland was apparently never realized. Nearly 200 years after his death, Hill provided the inspiration for the Halifax novelist Phyllis Bentley's character Sam Horsfall in her historical novel *Manhold*, published in New York in 1941.

JOHN A. HARGREAVES

Sources F. Atkinson, ed., *Some aspects of the eighteenth century woollen and worsted trade in Halifax* (1956) · H. P. Kendall, 'Making Place in Soyland and the Hill family', *Transactions of the Halifax Antiquarian Society* (1916), 9–70 · H. Heaton, *The Yorkshire woollen and worsted industries*, 2nd edn (1965) · J. Smail, *The origins of middle-class culture: Halifax, Yorkshire, 1660–1780* (1994) · Hill papers, 1719–1806, W. Yorks. AS, FH 434–495 · Samuel Hill, Soyland, letter-book, 1736–8, W. Yorks. AS, Calderdale, Calderdale district archives, Halifax, MISC 8/117/1 · parish register, Halifax, 1712, W. Yorks. AS, Calderdale, D53/1/9 · parish register, Ripponden, 1759, W. Yorks. AS, Calderdale, D21/2 · T. W. Hanson, *The story of old Halifax* (1920) · A. Newell, *A hillside view of industrial history* (1925) · J. Watson, *The history and antiquities of the parish of Halifax, in Yorkshire* (1775) · parish register, Elland, 1678, W. Yorks. AS, Calderdale, D79/4 · J. A. Hargreaves, *Halifax* (1999)

Archives W. Yorks. AS, Calderdale, Calderdale district archives, letter-book; business, estate, and legal records, MSS 1719–1806; pattern book, MISC 8/1171/1; FH 434–495; MISC 588/1

Wealth at death £20,000: Nov 1759, Borth. Inst.

Hill, Sir Stephen John (1809–1891), colonial governor, born on 10 June 1809, was the son of Major William Hill and his wife, Sarah. He entered the army in 1823, became lieutenant in 1825, and was promoted captain in 1842. On 30 November 1829 he married Sarah Ann, the daughter of William Vesey Munnings, chief justice of the Bahamas. In 1849 he commanded an expedition which proceeded 80 miles up the River Gambia. On 6 May he stormed and destroyed the fortified town of Bambacoo, and on the following day attacked and partially destroyed the fortified town of Keenung; he also fought a successful action on the plains of Quenella. He commanded a detachment of the 2nd and 3rd West India regiments in a successful attack by the British and French naval and land forces under Commodore Fanshawe on the pirates of the island of Basis, on the Jeba River, west Africa. For this service he received the thanks of the lords of the Admiralty and the brevet rank of major.

On 1 April 1851 Hill was appointed governor and commander-in-chief of the Gold Coast. The following year the protected chiefs consented to a poll tax on their people to defray the cost of administration, and a local force was raised for the defence of the colony under the name of the Gold Coast corps. On 6 November 1854 Hill was nominated lieutenant-governor of Sierra Leone, and on 21 November he was appointed colonel of the 2nd West India regiment. He remained there until 1859, undertaking two successful expeditions up the Great Scarcies River in January 1858 and February 1859. In July 1860, having been made CB, he returned as governor-in-chief. Ill health compelled him to return to England on 21 July 1862, when he left his son, Lieutenant-Colonel William Hill, as acting governor. His second term of administration was marked by the annexation of British Quiah in April 1861 and British Sherbro in November 1861.

On 9 February 1863 Hill assumed the office of captain-general and governor-in-chief of the Leeward and Caribbee Islands, where he remained until 1869. He was then moved to Newfoundland. The province's vote against confederation in that November was a source of annoyance to him, but he accepted the result. Acting always on the advice of his executive council, he was a trusted and popular governor. He married for the second time on 3 August 1871. His wife, who was to survive him, was Louisa Gordon, the daughter of John Sheil (d. 1847), chief justice of Antigua. In 1874 Hill was made KCMG, and he retired from active service in 1876. He died in London, at his home, 72 Sutherland Avenue, Maida Vale, on 20 October 1891.

E. I. CARLYLE, rev. LYNN MILNE

Sources *The Times* (27 Oct 1891) · J. K. Hillier, 'Hill, Sir Stephen John', *DCB*, vol. 12 · A. B. Ellis, *A history of the Gold Coast of west Africa* (1893) · A. B. C. Sibthorpe, *The history of Sierra Leone* (1881) · V. L. Oliver, *The history of the island of Antigua*, 3 vols. (1894–9) · D. W. Prowse, *A history of Newfoundland from the English, colonial, and foreign records* (1895) · CGPLA Eng. & Wales (1891)

Archives National Archives of Ghana, letters to James Bannerman and Edmund Bannerman · Provincial Archives of Newfoundland and Labrador, St John's, Newfoundland, letter-book

Wealth at death £198 2s. 3d.: administration with will, 23 Nov 1891, CGPLA Eng. & Wales

Hill, Thomas [pseud. Didymus Mountaine] (c.1528–c.1574), writer and translator, described himself as a 'Londoner', and claimed to have been 'always rudely taughte, amonge the Smythes of Vulcanus forge' (*Proffitable Arte of Gardening*, 1568, sig. dd3r). However, Hill knew Latin and

Italian and he became known as a translator of popular books on science and the supernatural. His first publication, in 1556, was a translation of a Latin compilation on physiognomy. This was dedicated to a physician, George Keble, as was its successor in 1559, a compilation on the interpretation of dreams, which ran to five editions. In 1560, the year of his first extant almanac, he was described as a leading almanac-maker, 'both lerned and honest' (Fulke, sig. B1r). Hill produced at least eight more almanacs, becoming one of the first English makers of such a series, and one of the first to produce an almanac (in 1571) with blank pages, for use as a pocket diary. About 1560 he also published *A Briefe Treatyse of Gardening*, the first book on that subject in English; this ran to nine editions.

In 1567 Hill produced three more books: another work on dreams; one on phenomena such as comets, marvellous bodies of water, fiery portents, rainbows, and earthquakes; and a collection of receipts for conjuring tricks, practical jokes, household matters, and divination, perhaps translated from Latin, and meant 'for the recreation of wittes at vacant tymes', which was reprinted as late as 1684. Hill enlarged his physiognomical translation in 1571 with a new dedication to the duke of Norfolk, an acknowledgement of help from John Dee, and liminary verses in Latin and Greek. In the same year he advertised exclusive manuscript copies of unpublished works, such as his *Guide of the Matrone*, which offered to expound 'practises purchased of manye iolly Dames, and Countesses of Italy' (*Contemplation of Mankinde*, 1571). These were attempts to raise Hill's status as an author, as may have been the elegant pseudonym Didymus Mountaine, under which a new, handsomely illustrated compilation, *The Gardners Labyrinth*, was published in 1577. Hill had died, however, before this was printed; the Latin poet Henry Dethick saw it through the press.

Hill's translations of works on chemical medicine by Conrad Gesner and Leonardo Fioravanti (*The Newe Iewell of Health*, 1576, and *A Ioyfull Iewell*, 1579) were completed by two friends of his, George Baker and John Hester. These books were instrumental in making Paracelsianism widely known in England. A mathematical and astronomical textbook, *The Schoole of Skil*, which rejects Copernicanism, was printed by William Jaggard in 1599; many of Hill's unpublished works must have been lost. Dethick, Hester, and Jaggard all commented on Hill's unornamented style and agreed that his work was nevertheless admirable. Jaggard wrote that 'It is not vnlike, but he would (if God had spared him longer life) haue held on as he began, to set forth for the common good of his and our Country diuers necessary works' (*Schoole of Skil*, sig. A4r). JOHN CONSIDINE

Sources F. R. Johnson, 'Thomas Hill: an Elizabethan Huxley', *Huntington Library Quarterly*, 7 (1943–4), 329–51 · P. H. Kocher, 'Paracelsan medicine in England: the first thirty years (ca.1570–1600)', *Journal of the History of Medicine and Allied Sciences*, 2 (1947), 451–80 · B. Henrey, *British botanical and horticultural literature before 1800*, 1 (1975) · B. S. Capp, *Astrology and the popular press: English almanacs, 1500–1800* (1979) · W. Fulke, *Anti-prognosticon* (1560) · E. G. R. Taylor, *The mathematical practitioners of Tudor and Stuart England* (1954) · P. H. Kocher, *Science and religion in Elizabethan England* (1953) · E. Southerne, *Treatise concerning the right use and ordering of bees* (1593) · J. W. Binns, *Intellectual culture in Elizabethan and Jacobean England: the Latin writings of the age* (1990)
Archives Bodl. Oxf., MS Ashmole 417, fol. 74
Likenesses engraving, c.1556, repro. in Henrey, *British botanical and horticultural literature*, 59

Hill, Thomas (d. 1653), college head, was born at Knighton-on-Teme, Worcestershire, the son of William and Mary Hill. He has been claimed as a pupil of the King's School, Worcester, but from an association based on the false identification of his birthplace as Kington in the same county. He was admitted pensioner of Emmanuel College, Cambridge, on 19 October 1618 and matriculated the same year. He advanced to a scholarship, and graduated BA in 1623. After becoming a fellow of Emmanuel he proceeded MA in 1626. He was ordained deacon in the diocese of Peterborough on 23 January 1629, and made priest the following day. While at Emmanuel he was a regular preacher at the nearby parish church of St Andrew the Great, and continued to minister to the townspeople during an outbreak of plague. He spent a period with the puritan divine John Cotton at Boston, Lincolnshire, during which time his religious convictions were sharpened. In 1633 he took his BD and four days later was instituted to the rectory of Titchmarsh, Northamptonshire, on the presentation of the earl of Manchester. He sought relief from the composition fee payable to the university by beneficed graduands, since he had paid more than his first year's income to pension the previous incumbent, and because he was not formally possessed of the living when he took his degree. The university rejected his suit, but despite this awkward beginning Hill became an energetic rural pastor. At this time he visited Lord Brooke at Warwick, through which connection he met and married Mary Willford, governess to the earl of Warwick's daughter Lady Frances Rich.

Hill was appointed to advise the Lords committee on religious reform established in March 1641. He became a member of the Westminster assembly and was a regular weekday morning preacher in Westminster Abbey; on Sundays he was heard in St Martin-in-the-Fields. Several of his sermons before parliament between 1642 and 1644 were printed, as was a fast sermon before the lord mayor and aldermen of Easter week 1644. In 1645 he was first designated master of his old college and then, because this was 'not … a sphere large enough' (Tuckney, 52), he was made master of Trinity College, Cambridge, in which post he was confirmed by parliamentary order of 17 January 1648. In 1645/6 he was vice-chancellor and in 1646 he received his DD. He obtained for the university library the reversionary interest in books bequeathed by Archbishop Richard Bancroft, and solicited from Sir John Wollaston the establishment of a mathematical lecture. Hill himself lectured every Sunday in St Michael's Church, attached to Trinity, and also preached in the parish church of All Saints opposite the Great Gate. In the pulpit he was 'plain, powerful, frequent and laborious' (Tuckney, 58). A further *Six Sermons* were published in 1649. Hill edited William

Fenner's *Wilfull Impenitency* (1648) and with Edmund Calamy edited Fenner's works, published from 1651. He also assisted Samuel Clarke with his *Lives* of puritan divines.

Hill died of a quartan ague on 18 December 1653. His friend for thirty-four years Anthony Tuckney, master of St John's, preached at the funeral in Great St Mary's on 22 December. By his will of 15 July 1650 and codicil of 7 July 1652 Hill left to his wife his house at Over Aston (Aston Court) in Knighton-on-Teme, together with other property there and at Burford, Shropshire (all which he had bought from his father) together with lands at Over, Cambridgeshire. Mary Hill subsequently became Tuckney's second wife, and died some time before 30 September 1668. When Hill made his will his parents were still alive; he also mentions sisters Jane Doughty, Margery Floyd, Anne Clarke, Mary Carbourne, and (as yet unmarried) Penelope. He made bequests to the poor of Titchmarsh, to his colleges, and to the university library. His personal effects were valued at £485 16s. 4d., including £45 in plate and £120 in books.

C. S. KNIGHTON

Sources M. Craze, *King's School, Worcester* (1972), 63 · Venn, *Alum. Cant.*, 1/2.374 · Wood, *Ath. Oxon.: Fasti* (1815), 408–9 · S. Bendall, C. Brooke, and P. Collinson, *A history of Emmanuel College, Cambridge* (1999), 28, 188, 193, 246 · *JHL*, 9 (1646–7), 664 · *CSP dom.*, 1660–61, 438 · A. Tuckney, *Thanatoktasia, or, Death disarmed* (1654) · CUL, department of manuscripts and university archives, Collect. Admin. 8, pp. 405–6 · will and inventory, 1653, CUL, department of manuscripts and university archives, vice-chancellor's court, inventories, bundle 14, Will Reg. III, fols. 310–311v · S. Clarke, *The lives of thirty two English divines*, in *A general martyrologie*, 3rd edn (1677), 230–34 · C. Sayle, *Annals of Cambridge University Library, 1278–1900* (1916), 78–9 · *JHC*, 5 (1646–8), 503
Wealth at death £485 16s. 4d.—personal effects, incl. plate £45, books £120, cash £108; houses and lands at Kington and 'Over Aston' [Aston Magna?], Worcestershire, Burford, Shropshire, and Over, Cambridgeshire: CUL, department of manuscripts and university archives, vice-chancellor's court, Will Reg. III, fols. 310–311v

Hill, Thomas (*c*.1628–1677), nonconformist minister, was born at Derby and attended Repton School. Before attending Cambridge University, according to Calamy, Hill was 'sometime a domestic to the earl' of Chesterfield (Calamy, *Continuation*, 855). He was admitted at Corpus Christi College, Cambridge, on 10 September 1645 and matriculated at Easter 1646, before graduating BA in 1650. On leaving the university he became chaplain to the countess of Chesterfield at Tamworth Castle, Warwickshire, and was then preacher at Elvaston, Derbyshire, before moving to Leicestershire. Nothing is known of Hill's marriage, except that it produced a son, Thomas *Hill, who founded and led an academy for training ministers at Findern in Derbyshire and who died in March 1720.

Refusing the engagement, the oath of loyalty to the Commonwealth in 1649, Thomas Hill acted as minister at Orton on the Hill from June 1651; the parish lay near where four counties met—Leicestershire (in which it was), Derbyshire, Staffordshire, and Warwickshire. On 16 November 1652, at the meeting of the classis of Wirksworth, Derbyshire, he 'produced two certificates, one from his neighbouring ministers concerning his ministerial abilities and godly conversation; the other from the parishioners of Orton on the Hill concerning his title there, they certifying their choice of him to be their minister'; these certificates, his 'testimony of the grace of God in him, of his inward call' and of 'his competent skill in the original tongues' were all approved by the classis (Cox, 164–5). But only after attending a second meeting on 21 December 1652, at which he preached a sermon and defended a thesis to the satisfaction of the assembled divines, was Hill accepted as fit for the ministry. He was formally ordained by the Wirksworth classis on 15 March 1653. All this, and his refusal to preach before Cromwell, may suggest that Hill was strongly of a presbyterian persuasion.

In 1660 Hill was not ejected from Orton, but the sequestered vicar was restored in that year and it seems that Hill had moved a few miles to a house at Lea Grange. He was presented by the second earl of Chesterfield to the curacy of the nearby parish of Shuttington, Warwickshire. Here he was allowed rectorial tithes belonging to the earl, and although the Five Mile Act made it impossible for him to take services he was able to engage a sympathetic Worcestershire minister for the work. Thus, 'using prudence, he had an opportunity of exercising his ministry where some others were molested' (Calamy, *Abridgement*, 2.746). It may also be that Hill's security was improved by his geographical situation. His old vicarage at Orton on the Hill was in the diocese of Lincoln, his living at Shuttington was under the jurisdiction of the bishop of Worcester, and his own residence at Lea Grange was in Staffordshire in the diocese of Lichfield.

Calamy records of Hill that 'his stature was something low, his hair black, his countenance graceful, and acceptable'; he valued the works of Richard Baxter especially, because of the 'catholic spirit' of universalism to be found in them; on admission to the university Hill was acknowledged to be already better versed in Hebrew 'than many or most of the Tutors'; an 'expert linguist' in Latin and Greek, he entertained also a lively interest in philosophy, mathematics, and history (Calamy, *Continuation*, 856, 860). It is clear that Hill shared with many of his persuasion a deeply serious and conscientious approach to his calling, preaching three times on Sunday in all weathers. His inflexibility in this seems to have brought upon him the cold which led to his death at the age of about forty-nine. He was buried at Orton on the Hill on 7 March 1677.

STEPHEN WRIGHT

Sources *Calamy rev.* · E. Calamy, ed., *An abridgement of Mr. Baxter's history of his life and times, with an account of the ministers, &c., who were ejected after the Restauration of King Charles II*, 2nd edn, 2 vols. (1713) · E. Calamy, *A continuation of the account of the ministers ... who were ejected and silenced after the Restoration in 1660*, 2 vols. (1727) · Venn, *Alum. Cant.* · J. C. Cox, ed., *Minute book of the Wirksworth classis, 1651–58* (1880)

Hill, Thomas (*d.* 1720), Presbyterian minister and tutor, was the son of Thomas *Hill (*c*.1628–1677), curate of Shuttington, Warwickshire, who refused to conform in 1662. He probably received his early education from Samuel

Shaw, master of Ashby grammar school, who had been at school with his father. He was educated for the nonconformist ministry at John Woodhouse's academy at Sheriffhales, Shropshire, but 'through want of subsistence has beene forced … to quitt' (Presbyterian Fund board minutes, fol. 79r). With a grant of £8 a year from the Presbyterian Fund (1692–3) he resumed his studies with Woodhouse. He received a gift of books under Richard Baxter's will in 1693, at which time he was living at Ashby-de-la-Zouch, probably with Shaw, whose will Hill witnessed.

Hill was ordained at Nottingham on 7 April 1703 by ten Presbyterian ministers. At the time he was minister of Findern, 4 miles south-west of Derby. He later also supplied Alvaston (c.1711–20). From about 1710 he conducted an academy in Derby preparing students for the nonconformist ministry, which some time after 1714 was removed to Hartshorne (between Ashby and Derby) and finally to Findern. In common with most other nonconformist tutors in this period he was harassed, and in August 1712 presented at the assizes for keeping a school in Derby 'for the boarding of youth' without a licence. The prosecution was initiated by the master of the free school. In his defence, Hill stated that 'I board young men; I advise them what books to read; and when they apply to me for information on anything they do not understand, I inform them' (McLachlan, 'Ebenezer Latham', 150). The case was dismissed.

From the textbooks Hill recommended, in particular the Newtonian Le Clerc's work on logic and the Cartesian Rohault on physics, he was clearly open to the latest scholarship. Nevertheless, they were the texts that John Woodhouse had employed. The use of Richard Baxter's *An End of Doctrinal Controversies* (1691) suggests Hill favoured Baxter's 'middle way'. Whether modern languages were taught is unclear, but in 1715 Hill published a collection of psalms in Latin and Greek verse which his students were expected to sing, which also indicates an unusual interest in music. The names of twenty-two students are known (there were 'many more'), of whom the most distinguished was John Taylor, the Hebraist and future principal of Warrington Academy, who migrated from Thomas Dixon's academy at Whitehaven. Hill died on 2 March 1720 at Findern, where he was buried on 5 March. After his death the academy was continued by Ebenezer Latham, who may previously have served as his assistant. Under Latham, the academy became one of the leading academies educating students on liberal theological principles.   DAVID L. WYKES

Sources H. McLachlan, 'Ebenezer Latham, MA, MD, 1688–1745, and the academy at Findern, Derbyshire', in H. McLachlan, *Essays and addresses* (1950), 149–51, 165 · 'An account of the dissenting academies from the Restoration of Charles the Second', DWL, MS 24.59, pp. 54–5 · notes on the academies of Mr Hill and Dr Latham, DWL, New College collection, L54/2/2–5, 10 · H. McLachlan, *English education under the Test Acts: being the history of the nonconformist academies, 1662–1820* (1931), 131–2 · *Calamy rev.*, 266–7 · A. Peel, 'Richard Baxter, Roger Morrice, and Matthew Sylvester', *Transactions of the Congregational Historical Society*, 5 (1911–12), 298–300, esp. 299 [list of ministerial students to receive bks under Baxter's will] · T. Hill, *Nundinae Sturbrigienses* (1709) · minute book of the Nottingham Presbyterian classis, 1654–60, U. Nott. L., records of High Pavement Unitarian Chapel, Hi 2 M/1, fol. 1v · Presbyterian Fund board minutes, vol. 1, 1 July 1690–26 June 1693, DWL, MS OD 67, fols. 79r, 99r, 116r · Presbyterian Fund cash books, 6 July 1692–5 March 1693/5 March 1694, DWL, OD114 (20 Feb 1692/3, 22/12/1693) · will, Leics. RO, 1695/48 [Samuel Shaw]

Hill, Thomas (1661?–1734?), portrait painter, is believed to have been born in 1661; but so far no clues to his birthplace or parentage have emerged. He was trained to draw by the elder William Faithorne, foremost portrait engraver of his day, whose sensitive touch was to influence Hill's own manner. Hill studied painting under the Dutch history painter Dirk Freres, whom Sir Peter Lely had encouraged to come to England. That Hill also received a liberal general education is evinced by his letters to Humfrey Wanley and the memoranda occasionally sent to George Vertue for his *Note Books*.

Hill emerged as an independent portrait painter about 1694. He had lodgings in London (in 1720, in York Buildings, off the Strand), but relished country visits to paint congenial sitters. Hill's portrait manner is graceful and unpompous. He liked to depict children out of doors, with swags of flowers or beside garden ornaments with curious antique reliefs, often with tall cypresses in the background. Waterhouse singled out *Susannah Strangways* (a young girl with a dove, c.1705; priv. coll.) as having a 'gentleness and refinement hardly to be found in any other portrait painter of the time' (Waterhouse, *Painting in Britain*, 95).

A beguiling portrait of the young actress Letitia Cross (known as 'The girl') was engraved by John Smith c.1700. Most of Hill's adult commissions were engraved; they include *Sir Henry Goodricke*, master of the ordnance (in cuirass), and *Lady Goodricke*, and several portraits of bishops, including *Philip Bisse, Bishop of Hereford* (New College, Oxford; engraved by Vertue, 1719); *George Hooper, Bishop of Bath and Wells* (1723; Wells Cathedral; engraved by G. White); and *William Wake, Archbishop of Canterbury* (NPG).

Hill's most congenial commissions came from the Strangways family (later Fox-Strangways, and from 1741 earls of Ilchester), of Melbury House, Dorset. Hill's most inventive work there was a large family group (on canvas) for the grand staircase wall. Perhaps begun towards the end of the 1690s, after the old Tudor house had been enlarged and its garden redesigned, it depicts ten members of the intermarried Hornor and Strangways families in the garden at Melbury, Erato with her lyre presiding in stone, and a complete view of the house in the background. On the right, new lovers plight their troth (his hand delicately clasping hers) and, unusually for the times, Hill introduced an additional figure of a manservant, discreetly separated by drapery, bringing them a letter of congratulation.

From Melbury, on a later visit, Hill reported to Wanley:

> I was received perfectly friendly, like a Relation, as one of the family … How shall I doe to leave a fine seat, a Coach and six to take the air in, a great deal of good Company, a table with ten or fourteen dishes of meat … to come home to my poor station in Yorke buildings, considering a cloudy, heavy,

stifled air must be my Lott? Why I shall now and then meet my friend Mr. Wanley and others such, and desire no more. (letter of 10 Sept 1720, Goulding and Adams, 449)

Hill was a long-standing friend of the eminent scholar Humfrey Wanley. In 1708 Wanley became librarian to Robert Harley, first earl of Oxford, and began to build up one of the finest collections of manuscripts ever assembled. Wanley was chiefly based at Wimpole Hall, where Hill was a welcome visitor, executing numerous commissions for the earl of Oxford; as well as copies of family portraits, these included portraits of members of Lord Oxford's circle of antiquarians, including *James Anderson* ('Mr Anderson the famous Scots antiquarian'), *Solomon Negri*, Hebrew scholar (a head, painted in 1717), and *John Daniel Schumacher*, 1722, curator of the tsar's books and antiquities, then on a visit to Wimpole. Lord Oxford also commissioned a half-length self-portrait of Hill. All these were dispersed in the late Lord Oxford's sale in 1742 (and are now untraced).

Hill painted three different portraits of Humfrey Wanley. The original of the first portrait (dated 1711, with the sitter displaying a large Greek text) is in the collection of the Society of Antiquaries of London (with a version in the Bodleian Library, Oxford). A second portrait, dated 1717, was presented to Oxford University by the second earl of Oxford in 1740 (Bodl. Oxf.); a replica is in the National Portrait Gallery. Hill's last, unique three-quarter-length portrait of his friend, painted in 1722 (and now in the British Museum), is the finest and most fully characterized of all his works. Wanley himself recognized this, writing to Schumacher that the portrait 'will be his Master-piece' (letter of 26 May 1722, P. L. Heyworth, ed., *The Letters of Humfrey Wanley*, 1966, 444–5). It depicts Wanley virtually full-face and nearly full-length, sitting at ease in a many-buttoned velvet coat, one arm held over a larger than life-size brass head of the emperor Hadrian, the latest antiquity to enter the collections which he had the honour to curate. In its reflection of a life well spent, Hill's portrait of Humfrey Wanley anticipated Hogarth's *Captain Coram* by twenty years.

Wanley died in 1726. Hill may by then have retired from painting; one of Vertue's notes in 1725 refers briefly to 'Mr Tho Hills (painter) sale of pictures drawings plaster moulds and prints' (Vertue, *Note books*, 2.8). Seemingly not recorded elsewhere, this may have been a private studio sale open only to Hill's associates. Vertue stated that Hill died at Mitcham in 1734; but his death cannot be traced there in or about that date; nor is it known whether he was married. If documentation of his life remains elusive and his self-portrait is lost, his work stands, in Ellis Waterhouse's words, as 'original and refreshing in a stereotyped age' (Waterhouse, *Painting in Britain*, 95).

JUDY EGERTON

Sources Vertue, *Note books*, 1.55, 68, 70, 71–2, 137; 2.8; 3.72; 5.17 · R. W. Goulding, *Catalogue of the pictures belonging to his grace the duke of Portland*, ed. C. K. Adams (1936), 449–50 · E. Waterhouse, *Painting in Britain, 1530–1790* (1953), 95, pl. 87(A) · Waterhouse, *18c painters*, 171–2 · J. Ingamells, *The English episcopal portrait, 1559–1835: a catalogue* (privately printed, London, 1981), 124–5, 226, 398; pls. 25, 133, 295

Hill, Thomas (1682/3–1758), Latin poet, was probably born in Southfleet, Kent, the son of Daniel Hill (*c*.1647–1729), prebendary of Rochester and headmaster of Faversham School, and his wife, Hester Wilbraham (*née* Heywood), who predeceased him. Daniel Hill's parental exactness and professional pedantry are evident from his will, which appoints Thomas as executor, contains quotations (rather unusually) in Greek, and leaves Thomas his books, repeating clock, study candlestick, snuffers, ink-box, sand-box, and little cabinet. Thomas's brothers, Frederick and Robert, and sister, Elizabeth Rogers, receive similarly detailed legacies (she gets the tea set); they share Daniel's property, as long as they reject any claim on that of their grandfather Thomas Heywood, since his own will offers 'a much better provision'.

Thomas Hill was educated at Westminster School, then a leading centre for teaching Latin verse composition. He was admitted as a pensioner at Trinity College, Cambridge, in 1701, aged eighteen. He was awarded a scholarship in 1702; he graduated BA in 1705, became a fellow in 1707, and took his MA degree in 1708. He had a public career of moderate distinction, being elected a fellow of the Royal Society in 1725, and serving as secretary to the lords commissioners of trade from 1737 to his death in 1758.

Hill was chiefly remembered, however, as a poet rather than as a public servant. His reputation rested on a single Latin poem, *Nundinae Sturbrigienses*, describing a visit to Stourbridge Fair, just outside Cambridge, in 1702. The poem was probably composed shortly afterwards, during Hill's undergraduate career at Trinity; it achieved considerable success when it was published a few years later, in 1709 (perhaps related to the similar success of Edward Holdsworth's *Muscipula* in the same year). We hear brawling coachmen; 'There nauseous Fish offend my curious Nose' (in the version by R. S. in 1709); and a historical pageant celebrates Anne's triumphs, giving (perhaps significantly) rather more prominence to Eugene than Marlborough. Hill's Latin reference to Churchill's new Crécy is also omitted in R. S.'s translation. Students (and dons) face temptation, which R. S. translates effectively:

Some in curst Dice their wanton fancies Pride,
And love to see the Iv'ry Traytors glide.

The tired author retreats to Cambridge: 'Hic Auriga suos, hic sistit Musa caballos' ('here stops the coachman, here the Muse, their nags').

An indication of Hill's success is the publication of *Nundinae* and two other poems at the opening of *Musae Britannicae* (1711), a collection put together by the highly commercial publisher Edmund Curll. 'Non dantur ideae innatae' ('There are no innate ideas') is an alcaic ode in ten stanzas, 'Rationes boni et mali sunt eternae et immutabiles' ('The reasons of good and evil are eternal and unchanging') a hexameter poem: both titles indicate philosophical poems of the sort popular for tripos verses or other academic exercises (such as Milton's 'De idea Platonica'). They are good examples of the type; the ending of 'Rationes' has some powerful rhetoric:

Nequicquam: namque haud virtus mutabilis aurae
Arbitrio popularis.

('In vain! For virtue changes not at the whim of popular opinion.')

An English poem by Hill, 'On the Death of Vulcan, of Sordid Memory, an Old Servant at Trinity-College, Cambridge', appears in another of Curll's collections, *Original Poems and Translations by Mr Hill, Mr Eusden, Mr Broome, Dr King etc.* (1714):

> But far be banish'd those, if such there be,
> Who dread a Quart of Ale, and tipple Tea,
> The sole Disgrace and Scandal of your Year,
> Sworn foes to Pipes, and Enemies to Beer.
> (p. 8)

Alas, the blue-gowned lads of Trinity can no longer hold 3 quarts a man; the old college servant dies in disgust.

Thomas Hill himself died on 20 September 1758. Unlike his father's elaborate will, his own was simple, drawn up in 1745, leaving everything to 'my dearly beloved wife Catharine Hill', apart from a legacy of £100 to a servant. It mentions an annuity of £21 from the exchequer.

D. K. MONEY

Sources Venn, *Alum. Cant.* · R. S., *A translation of Mr Hill's Nundinae Sturbrigienses* (1709) · will, PRO, PROB 11/840, sig. 268 · D. K. Money, *The English Horace: Anthony Alsop and the tradition of British Latin verse* (1998) · L. Bradner, *Musae Anglicanae: a history of Anglo-Latin poetry, 1500–1925* (1940) · will, PRO, PROB 11/633 [Daniel Hill, father], fols. 168–9

Hill, Thomas (1760–1840), book-collector, was born in Lancaster in May 1760 and went at an early age to London, where for many years he carried on an extensive business as a drysalter at Queenhithe. He patronized Robert Bloomfield (1766–1823), whose *Farmer's Boy* he read in manuscript and recommended to a publisher. Hill was part proprietor of the *Monthly Mirror*, and befriended Henry Kirke White when a contributor to that periodical. Robert Southey felt that Hill's was probably 'the best existing collection of English poetry' (Knight, 2.27).

Hill occupied a house in Henrietta Street, Covent Garden, London, and a cottage at Sydenham, Kent. There, in his celebrated 'Sydenham Sundays', he used to entertain 'literati, artists, wits and actors' (*New Monthly Magazine*, 43), including John and Charles Kemble, Theodore Hook, Campbell, Edward Dubois, the Hunts, James and Horace Smith, and the comedian Charles Mathews. These hospitable parties are vividly recalled in a number of memoirs, including those of Mrs Mathews, who celebrates 'days of unmixed pleasure' (Mathews, 626).

A lifelike picture of Hill is rendered in Hook's novel *Gilbert Gurney*, where he figures as Hull. The scenes in which he appears were read over to him before publication. He was always thought to be the original of John Poole's comedy *Paul Pry*, immortalized at the Haymarket in 1825 by Liston, although Poole himself insisted that the character was never intended 'as the representative of any one individual' (*New Monthly Magazine*, 31/1, 1831, 280). His familiar peculiarities are also represented in the person of Jack Hobbleday of Poole's *Little Pedlington*. Lockhart called him 'the most innocent and ignorant of all the bibliomaniacs'. 'He had no literary tastes and acquirements; his manners were those of his business' (C. Redding, *Fifty Years' Recollections*, 1858, 2.212). But the 'jovial bachelor, plump and rosy as an abbot' (Hunt, 181), 'a fat florid, round little man like a retired elderly Cupid' (*New Monthly Magazine*, 80/1, 45), with his famous 'Pooh! pooh! I happen to know', his ceaseless questionings in a harsh, guttural voice, his boastings, his insatiable curiosity, his extensive and distorted knowledge of all the gossip of the day, was spoken of by everyone as a very kind-hearted and hospitable man. Even at an advanced age he was unusually young-looking; hence the joke of Samuel Rogers, that he was one of the little Hills spoken of as skipping in the Psalms, and the assertion of James Smith that the record of his birth had been destroyed in the fire of London.

About 1810, after losing heavily through an unsuccessful speculation in indigo, Hill retired to second-floor chambers at 2 James Street, Adelphi, London, where he lived until his death, varying his strict economy with occasional binges. Longmans gave between £3000 and £4000 for his books, which formed the basis for their *Bibliotheca Anglo-poetica* (1815). He caught a severe cold at Rouen in the autumn of 1840 and died in the Adelphi on 20 December in his eighty-first year, leaving to Edward Dubois most of his remaining fortune. His furniture and plate were sold by auction on 23 April 1841.

H. R. TEDDER, rev. JOHN D. HAIGH

Sources W. Maginn and D. Maclise, *A gallery of illustrious literary characters, 1830–1838*, ed. W. Bates (1873), p. 137, no. 51 · *Bentley's Miscellany*, 9 (1841), 86–90 · Mrs Mathews, *Memoirs of Charles Mathews, comedian*, 3 (1839), 624–7 · *New Monthly Magazine*, new ser., 80 (1847), 43–8, 137–43 · R. H. D. Barham, *The life and remains of Theodore Edward Hook*, 1 (1849), 64–70, 173–8 · *Annual Register* (1841), 176–7 · L. Hunt, *The autobiography of Leigh Hunt*, ed. J. E. Morpurgo (1949), 180–92, 482 · *The poetical and prose works of Henry Kirke White, with life by Robert Southey*, ed. R. Southey (1855), 1.xiv · W. Knight, ed., *Memorials of Coleorton: being letters from Coleridge, Wordsworth and his sister, Southey and Sir Walter Scott to Sir George and Lady Beaumont of Coleorton, 1803–1834* (1887) · *N&Q*, 2nd ser., 12 (1861), 222–3
Archives BL, corresp., Add. MSS 20081–20083
Likenesses J. Brown, stipple, pubd 1838 (after Linnell), NPG · Linnell, portrait, repro. in *Bentley's Miscellany* · D. Maclise, lithograph, BM, NPG; repro. in W. Maginn, *A gallery of illustrious literary characters* (1873) · C. Moon, lithograph, NPG

Hill, Thomas (1808–1865), topographer, elder son of the Revd Isaac Hill (1773–1856), headmaster of Mercers' School, London, 1804–1840, was born in London. He matriculated in 1825 and entered Clare College, Cambridge, in 1828; he graduated BA in 1830 and proceeded MA in 1832. Hill was admitted at the Inner Temple on 26 May 1831. On 22 December 1833, however, he was ordained deacon in London, and the next year, on 21 December, was ordained priest. He was assistant classical master at Mercers' School from 1832 to 1850, and was presented to the living of Holy Trinity Minories, Queenhithe, London, in 1850. He was author of *The Harmony of the Greek and Latin Languages* (1841) and *The History of the Nunnery of St Clare and the Parish of Holy Trinity* (1851). Hill died at his home, 30 Little Trinity Lane, Queenhithe, on 13 February 1865.

H. M. CHICHESTER, rev. JOANNE POTIER

Sources Venn, *Alum. Cant.* · *GM*, 3rd ser., 18 (1865), 385 · Boase, *Mod. Eng. biog.* · *CGPLA Eng. & Wales* (1865)
Wealth at death under £12,000: administration, 27 March 1865, *CGPLA Eng. & Wales*

Hill, Thomas Ford (*d.* 1795), antiquary, was the son of a glove manufacturer of Worcester. He was a Quaker, and intended for a commercial life in the linen trade. After serving an apprenticeship at Pontefract, he was taken into the house of Messrs Dawson and Walker in Cornhill, London, probably securing the position because Walker, also a Quaker, was his brother-in-law. During this period Hill seems to have lived with his mother at Ely Place in London, where she had moved from Worcester after her husband's death.

Hill soon abandoned business for literature and antiquities, and in 1780 he made an antiquarian tour through Scotland. On this tour he collected Erse songs, which he published together with a description of his journeys in the *Gentleman's Magazine* of 1782 and 1783. These were held to be a valuable contribution to the 'Ossian' debate, on which Hill maintained a largely neutral stance. The songs he collected were privately printed as *Antient Erse poems, collected among the Scottish highlands, in order to illustrate the Ossian of Macpherson* in 1784. In 1784 he visited the continent, residing at Geneva to learn French, and afterwards exploring the mountainous district of Savoy. In 1787 he went on to Italy to pursue antiquarian studies and was in Rome by February that year. His portrait was painted in Rome by Gavin Hamilton. During his five years abroad he became acquainted with eminent scholars and with Cardinal Borgia and Prince Kaunitz; he travelled to Ravenna, Venice, Prague, the Netherlands, and various places in Germany. In 1790 he was back in London, where he rented a house in Charlotte Street, Portland Place. He made two other journeys to the continent in 1791 and 1792, when he travelled through a greater part of Germany, and also visited Paris. He published in 1792 a work on current events in France, which a reviewer in the *Gentleman's Magazine* found too favourable to the Revolution. In the same year he was elected a fellow of the Society of Antiquaries. He returned to Italy in 1794, and died on 16 July 1795 at Ariano in Apulia, worn out by the difficulties he had encountered on his journey to Calabria earlier that year.   T. E. JACOB, *rev.* ALEXANDER DU TOIT

Sources *GM*, 1st ser., 66 (1796), 126–31 · Nichols, *Lit. anecdotes*, 8.154–5 · *GM*, 1st ser., 52 (1782), 570–71 · *GM*, 1st ser., 53 (1783), 33–6, 140–45, 398–400, 489–94, 590–92 · *GM*, 1st ser., 62 (1792), 361 · *GM*, 1st ser., 65 (1795), 704
Likenesses G. Hamilton, oils, 1787

Hill, Thomas George (1876–1954), botanist, was born on 13 February 1876 at 32 Colls Road, Peckham, London, the son of Henry William Hill, a paper maker's clerk, and his wife, Sarah Ann, *née* Sands. He was educated in London at St Olave's Grammar School and the Royal College of Science before becoming demonstrator in biology at St Thomas's Hospital. He subsequently held various lectureships in botany and biology in the University of London before being appointed in 1912 to a readership in vegetable physiology at University College, London (UCL).

This appointment signalled Hill's establishment in the then rapidly evolving botanical profession. Before the 1870s the principal concerns of British botanists had been taxonomical, expanding with the empire from descriptions of native species to surveys of flora throughout the world. Continental European botanists, especially those working in Germany, had specialized to a greater extent on the internal workings of the plant and by 1900 the importance of their work was increasingly recognized. Hill was one of the first generation of British botanists to incorporate this expanding knowledge of plant physiology into their teaching and research, and a little later he was closely involved with the beginnings of another challenge to traditional botany: the study of plant ecology.

Hill's early work was devoted to the anatomy of plants: with Ethel De Fraine, a London University colleague, he published a series of articles in *Annals of Botany* and *New Phytologist* on seedling structure. Even here it was apparent that by the end of the series in 1913 he had moved towards a physiological explanation for variations in the structure of seedlings. F. W. Oliver, the head of the department at UCL, was one of the British pioneers of ecological studies, and Hill took part in the expeditions that Oliver led to Blakeney Point in Norfolk and to France, subsequently publishing papers on the water content of shingle beaches and the osmotic properties of the root hairs of salt marsh plants. When the first meeting of the British Ecological Society was held at UCL in 1913 Hill was a member of its council. At the same time he was also writing about microscopic and biochemical techniques. In 1913 he collaborated with P. Haas on *An Introduction to the Chemistry of Plant Products*, later editions of which (the last was published in 1928) included a second volume which covered physiological topics. By this time his research interests also included the metabolism of marine algae. Earlier, in 1915, he had published *Essentials of Illustration*, a short guide based on his interest in book illustration and his experience of botanical publishing.

Hill succeeded Oliver as head of the department of botany at UCL in 1929, becoming at the same time professor of plant physiology. Familiarly known to his contemporaries as TG, he was said to hide his essential kindliness under an exterior which was variously described as breezy, awe-inspiring, and gruff; when chairing committees he could be short with those who were verbose. His lectures were remembered as logically constructed and vivid, and those who worked under him found him an effective head of department, in which role he continued until the end of the Second World War, when he was nearly seventy. He lived at Hambledon in Surrey, where he painted, cultivated his garden, and, for many years, helped to run the cricket club. There he was known as Major Hill, a rank to which he was promoted when adjutant to the University of London Officers' Training Corps during the First World War. He remained unmarried and died at St Thomas Hospital, Hambledon, following an operation, on 25 June 1954. He was buried in Hambledon on 29 June.   PAUL BRASSLEY

Sources *Nature*, 174 (1954), 159–60 · *The Times* (26 June 1954) · *The Times* (30 June 1954) · J. Sheail, *Seventy-five years in ecology: the British*

Ecological Society (1987) · Desmond, *Botanists*, rev. edn · private information (2004) · b. cert. · d. cert. · *CGPLA Eng. & Wales* (1954)
Likenesses group portrait, photograph, 1911 (includes T. G. Hill), repro. in Sheail, *Seventy-five years in ecology*, pl. 4
Wealth at death £16,401 12s. 7d.: probate, 17 Sept 1954, *CGPLA Eng. & Wales*

Hill, Thomas Henry Weist- (1828–1891), violinist and conductor, son of Thomas Hill, goldsmith and freeman of the City, was born in Islington, London, on 3 January 1828. He showed an aptitude for the violin at an early age and appeared at Gravesend as an infant prodigy. In 1844 he entered the Royal Academy of Music, where he studied with Prosper Sainton and in 1845 was awarded the king's scholarship. He was subsequently a professor of the violin at the Royal Academy and conducted its choir and orchestra. He then joined the orchestra of the Princess Theatre, but he soon became known as a concert violinist, and was taken up first by Edward Loder and then by Louis Jullien. With the latter he toured in the United States of America, where he gave the first American performance of Mendelssohn's violin concerto, and later visited several European cities. On his return to London he was engaged as first violin in the Royal Italian Opera orchestra by Michael Costa.

When the Alexandra Palace opened in 1873 Weist-Hill was appointed music director, and until 1876 he performed works by British composers and held a symphony competition for them; he also revived forgotten works, such as Handel's *Esther* and *Susanna*. In 1878 he conducted the orchestral concerts of Madame Viard-Louis at St James's Hall, at which several works by French composers were heard for the first time in England, including Bizet's suite *L'Arlésienne* and pieces by Massenet, Gounod, and Berlioz. He conducted the first performance in London of Brahms's second symphony. In 1880 he was appointed first principal of the Guildhall School of Music, where he also taught the violin.

In 1885 the journal *Musical Opinion* regarded Weist-Hill as the greatest living English conductor. He wrote a few compositions, mostly for violin and cello, of which the *Pompadour Gavotte* became popular. He died of cancer at South Kensington, London, on 25 December 1891. His two sons also became musicians; one of them, Ferdinand Weist-Hill, was a well-known violinist.

J. C. HADDEN, *rev.* ANNE PIMLOTT BAKER

Sources *The Lute* (March 1891) · H. Barty-King, *GSMD: a hundred years' performance* (1980) · *Musical Herald* (Feb 1892) · *New Grove* · Boase, *Mod. Eng. biog.* · *CGPLA Eng. & Wales* (1892)
Likenesses photograph, repro. in Barty-King, *GSMD* (1980)
Wealth at death £224: administration with will, 4 April 1892, *CGPLA Eng. & Wales*

Hill, Sir Thomas Noel (1784–1832), army officer, seventh son of Sir John Hill, third baronet (1740–1824), of Hawkstone, Shropshire, and his wife, Mary, née Chambre (d. 8 March 1806), and younger brother of Rowland *Hill, Viscount Hill, was born on 14 February 1784. He entered the army on 25 September 1801 as cornet in the 10th light dragoons, becoming lieutenant in 1803 and captain in 1805. He exchanged to the 53rd regiment the year after,

and on 16 February 1809 was appointed major in the Portuguese army under Marshal Beresford. He commanded the 1st Portuguese regiment with distinction at the battle of Busaco, the capture of Ciudad Rodrigo, the battles of Salamanca and Vitoria, and the capture of San Sebastian. He was appointed captain and lieutenant-colonel 1st foot guards (Grenadier Guards) on 25 July, and was knighted on 28 July 1814. He served as assistant adjutant-general in the Waterloo campaign. He retired from the guards on half pay on 27 May 1824. He was deputy adjutant-general in Canada in 1827–30, and was afterwards appointed commandant of the cavalry depot, Maidstone.

Hill married, on 27 July 1821, Anna Maria Shore (d. 25 Feb 1886), second daughter of John *Shore, the first Lord Teignmouth; they had six surviving children.

Hill was a KCB (January 1815), and had the orders of the Tower and Sword of Portugal and of Maximilian Joseph of Bavaria. He died at Maidstone, Kent, on 8 January 1832, and was buried in Maidstone churchyard.

H. M. CHICHESTER, *rev.* JAMES FALKNER

Sources *Army List* · *GM*, 1st ser., 102/1 (1832), 84, 650 · F. W. Hamilton, *The origin and history of the first or grenadier guards*, 3 (1874) · J. Philippart, ed., *The royal military calendar*, 3rd edn, 5 vols. (1820), vol. 4 · Burke, *Peerage*

Hill, Thomas Wright (1763–1851), schoolmaster, was born in Kidderminster on 24 April 1763. He was the son of James Hill, a baker and dealer in horse-corn, and his second wife, Sarah, who was the daughter of a Kidderminster apothecary named John Symonds. His forefathers for three generations had been freeholders and tradesmen of Kidderminster, descended from Walter Hill, a landowner of Abberley, Worcestershire (d. 1693). They claimed relationship with Samuel Butler, author of *Hudibras*. Both of his parents were strict dissenters and Hill received part of his education at a school kept by Stephen Addington, a dissenting minister, at Market Harborough, Leicestershire. He was afterwards moved to Kidderminster grammar school. In early childhood he developed a taste for literature, and interested himself in mathematics, astronomy, and natural philosophy. When nine years old he attended several of the philosophical lectures of James Ferguson, of which he gives an interesting account in his autobiography.

When fourteen years of age Hill was apprenticed to a brass-founder in Birmingham, but he found the business uncongenial, and his voluntary efforts as a Sunday school teacher at the chapel of Joseph Priestley led him ultimately to devote his special attention to teaching. He joined Priestley's congregation, and was much influenced by his pastor, whose scientific interests he shared.

On 29 July 1791 Hill married Sarah Lea (1765–1842), the daughter of a Birmingham working man. They had six surviving children: Matthew Davenport *Hill; Edwin *Hill; Sir Rowland *Hill, the postal reformer; Arthur Hill, headmaster of Bruce Castle School; Frederic *Hill, inspector of prisons; and Caroline Hill, who became the wife of Francis Clark of Birmingham. Honest, guileless, and unconventional, Hill was said to have been endowed

Thomas Wright Hill (1763–1851), by unknown engraver

with every sense but common sense. That deficiency his wife, a woman of strong character, tried to supply.

A manufacture of woollen stuffs in which Hill had engaged was ruined in 1795 by the French war. The family moved to Wolverhampton, where Hill became a works superintendent. Reduced to great straits, at the suggestion of his wife he opened a school in order that his children might be properly educated. The school was first opened in 1803 at Hill Top, then on the outskirts of Birmingham. His simple love of truth and courtesy made him a fair teacher, but he lacked mental perspective, and treated all kinds of knowledge as of equal importance. His private pupils in mathematics in the town included Edwin Guest, afterwards master of Gonville and Caius College, Cambridge, and Benjamin Hall Kennedy, afterwards professor of Greek at Cambridge. Hill never freed himself from debt, but his buoyant optimism never allowed his poverty to trouble him, although his wife felt it keenly. Their son Rowland soon took charge of their money affairs, with admirable effect.

The school remained at Hill Top until 1819. Rowland had then become its chief director, and it was moved to Hazelwood. Although Hill did not retire from teaching until 1835 it is thought that his sons Rowland and Matthew were largely responsible for the modernization of Hazelwood School in accordance with the principles of utilitarian and radical educational thought. The school attracted a great deal of attention from Jeremy Bentham and other members of the Chrestomathic group and in 1827 a new branch was opened at Bruce Castle in Tottenham. This eventually superseded Hazelwood School, which closed in 1833. Hill died at his home in Bruce Terrace, Tottenham, on 13 June 1851, aged eighty-eight.

Hill's *Remains*, containing an autobiographical fragment and some notices of his life, were privately printed in London in 1859. A volume of selections from his papers appeared in London in 1860. It includes a brief account of his system of shorthand. He originally devised this ingenious system about 1802, and by various changes at length reduced it to a complete philosophical alphabet, on a strictly phonetic basis, without depriving it of its stenographic character. His hope that it might come into general use was not realized. The volume also includes 'A system of numerical nomenclature and notation, grounded on the principles of abstract utility' (1845); in this new system the names of the numbers are made, by virtue of arithmetical significance given to the vowels and diphthongs, to indicate their precise meaning by their structure.

Among his other activities Hill made a close study of letter sounds. Dr Guest, his former pupil, attributed to him the discovery of 'the distinction between vocal and whisper letters' (*A History of English Rhythms*, 1838, 1.9). Perhaps the most significant product of his inventiveness was his scheme for proportional representation, to ensure the representation of minorities in elections. The idea, apparently the result of Hill's mathematical interests, was adopted for committee elections in a scientific society founded by his son, Rowland, and was recommended by Rowland Hill in 1839 for adoption in municipal elections in South Australia. Hill has been accounted the first Englishman to propound the idea of a single transferable vote as the basis for proportional representation (Hart, 7–9).

THOMPSON COOPER, *rev.* C. A. CREFFIELD

Sources T. W. Hill and M. D. Hill, *Remains of … Thomas Wright Hill, together with notices of his life* (1859) • G. B. Hill and R. Hill, *The life of Sir Rowland Hill, and, The history of penny postage*, 2 vols. (1880) • J. L. Dobson, 'The Hill family and educational change', *Durham Research Review*, 2 (1959) • J. L. Dobson, 'The Hill family and educational change', *Durham Research Review*, 3 (1960) • *GM*, 2nd ser., 36 (1851), 326 • F. L. Colvile, *The worthies of Warwickshire who lived between 1500 and 1800* [1870] • J. Hart, *Proportional representation* (1992)
Likenesses Mrs C. Pearson, photograph, Birmingham Museums and Art Gallery • engraving, repro. in Hill and Hill, *Life of Sir Rowland Hill*, 8 • engraving, NPG [*see illus.*]

Hill, William (1618–1667), classical scholar, was the son of Blackleech Hill, an attorney of Hemlingford hundred in Warwickshire. He was born at Cudworth, Warwickshire, and matriculated at Merton College, Oxford, on 21 November 1634. By December 1638 he had received his BA degree, and he became a fellow of the college in 1639 owing to his proficiency in Greek, Latin, and physics. Shortly after his election as fellow he moved to Sutton Coldfield, to take the post of master of the free school there, where he proved to be as successful a schoolmaster as he had been a scholar. His marriage to a rich wife (Wood, *Ath. Oxon.*, vol. 3, col. 800) proved short-lived, his wife dying by 1641, the year when Hill received his MA degree from Oxford. Perhaps the death of his wife, to whom he was very much attached, was the reason why he decided to leave Warwickshire and travel to London to start a career as a physician.

Having made his name there Hill married again, this time to the daughter of another physician who had links to Sutton Coldfield. This latter marriage did not prove as happy as his first one, as a result of the scandal caused by the birth of a son seven months after the marriage. Hill tried in vain to convince his medical colleagues that the boy was conceived within the marriage, even going so far as to write a manuscript treatise on the subject. In the later 1640s he may have been at Oxford, where his name is included in the lists of those who submitted to the parliamentary visitation. Certainly he had leave to graduate BM and DM from Oxford on 8 June 1649. His dedication of his popular *Dionysion oikoumenēs periēgēsis: Dionysii orbis descriptio commentario critico et geographico … ac tabulis illustrata a Guilielmo Hill* (1658) to Henry Cromwell may account for his subsequent move to Ireland, where he became chief master of the cathedral school of St Patrick's, Dublin. However, on the Restoration he was forced out of this position and moved to Finglas, where he tutored privately. His only other work was an (unpublished) epitome of the physician Lazarus Riverius. Before his death he is reputed to have been given an honorary doctorate by Trinity College, Dublin. Hill died at Finglas as a result of a fever and was buried on 29 November 1667 in Finglas church. Little is known of his family save that the fever which killed him also killed 'most of his family' (Wood, *Ath. Oxon.*, vol. 3, col. 801).

This William Hill is often confused with another **William Hill** (*fl.* 1647–1662), who likewise was a student of Merton College. The latter Hill was the son of a nonconformist of Herefordshire and followed his father's tendencies in this regard. He attended Merton from 1647 onwards. While it is unclear whether it was he or the former William who submitted to the parliamentary visitation on 12 May 1648, it seems more likely that it was the younger Hill. Wood's description of him as 'a tale-bearer to the parliamentarian visitors' and 'a factious person' substantiates this view (Wood, *Ath. Oxon.*, vol. 3, col. 801). On his departure from the university he became a parson, but because of his parliamentary sympathies lost his benefice on the Restoration. However, two years later, in 1662, he received 'a considerable benefice' in Gloucestershire (ibid., col. 802). The reason for this lies in the murky Tong plot. Hill seemingly heard of a plot among his former associates against the king. Whether Hill turned state's evidence or was a double agent is unclear, but his own relation of his role in his *Narrative of the Said Plot*, attached to the 1662 publication *A brief narrative of that stupendious tragedy, late intended to be acted by the satanical saints of these reforming times, humbly presented to the king's majesty*, depicts his involvement in a favourable light. He did not live to enjoy his benefice, dying a few years later.

ELIZABETHANNE BORAN

Sources Wood, *Ath. Oxon.*, new edn, 3.800–02 · *The whole works of Sir James Ware concerning Ireland*, ed. and trans. W. Harris, 3 (1746), 347 · Foster, *Alum. Oxon.*, 1500–1714, 2.714 · A. Chalmers, ed., *The general biographical dictionary*, new edn, 17 (1814), 498–9 · M. Burrows, ed., *The register of the visitors of the University of Oxford, from AD 1647 to AD 1658*, CS, new ser., 29 (1881), 521 · B. S. Capp, *The Fifth Monarchy Men: a study in seventeenth-century English millenarianism* (1972), 209 · W. Hill, *A brief narrative of that stupendious tragedie* (1662) · *British Museum general catalogue of printed books … to 1955*, BM, 263 vols. (1959–66), vol. 12, p. 224 · Burtchaell & Sadleir, *Alum. Dubl.*, 2nd edn, 400

Hill, William (*fl.* 1647–1662). *See under* Hill, William (1618–1667).

Hill, William. *See* Bennet, John (*d.* 1690).

Hill, William (1903–1971), bookmaker, was born in Birmingham on 16 July 1903, the second son and fourth of the eleven children (there were also a twin son and daughter who died at birth) of William Hill, journeyman coach-painter, and his wife, Lavinia Knight, the daughter of a farmer who also kept an inn on the border of Warwickshire and Leicestershire.

Hill ran away from school at the age of twelve to work on an uncle's farm. After a short time working for his father he moved to a tool-making factory in Birmingham, where he took up bookmaking in a small way, by collecting bets on his motor bicycle. Shortly afterwards he became a more serious bookmaker, but plunged too heavily at first and lost all his capital. However, he started again in the cheaper rings, and after five years moved to London in 1929.

Hill started betting at greyhound stadiums, then extended to pony-racing at Northolt Park, and in 1934 opened a one-room office in Jermyn Street. He soon moved to much larger premises in Park Lane (and later to even larger offices at Piccadilly Circus in 1947). By 1939 he

William Hill (1903–1971), by unknown photographer, 1951

had given up the dogs and the main business was credit betting, though he was still operating at Northolt Park.

In 1944 Hill produced the first fixed-odds football coupon, and set up a separate football company in 1944. In 1955 he gave up on-course bookmaking. In 1960 his great rivals, Ladbrokes, went into the football business, and Hill sued them for infringement of the copyright in his coupon. The case went to the House of Lords, where Hill won the £1 damages for which he had asked, with costs. In 1954 with Lionel Barber he bought 75 per cent of Holder's Investment Trust, to which he sold his interests between 1955 and 1961 for over £5 million. So successful was the business that Holder's shares rose from 2s. 10d. in 1956 to £18 10s. in 1960. This purchase of a 'shell' company was the first time that the manoeuvre had been executed and the first time that a bookmaking company had been floated on the stock exchange.

Hill loathed the idea of betting shops, which were legalized in 1960, but rivals moved in and he followed in 1966. In the same year he reluctantly began to take bets on elections. He did not, as he said on 9 December 1958, when as owner of Be Careful he spoke at the Gimcrack dinner, object to bookmakers paying something towards the racing industry's expenses. However, as he wrote in the following May, it galled him to be expected to do so and still to be refused admission to the members' enclosures at smart meetings.

Hill's first stud was Whitsbury in Hampshire, which he bought in 1943. Nimbus was foaled there in 1946, and, having been sold for 5000 guineas at the yearling sales, won the 1949 Two Thousand Guineas and Derby. In 1945 Hill bought Sezincote stud in Gloucestershire, where he stood his stallion Chanteur II, sire of Pinza, winner of the 1953 Derby.

William Hill was a great bookmaker, who had the courage to take enormous bets. He was an ebullient, sometimes irascible, charming man. In his latter years he took little day-to-day interest in racing, but was seen as an elder statesman of the turf. He had become accustomed to great wealth, but he had a social conscience and may even have considered himself a socialist.

In 1923 Hill married Ivy Burley, a ladies' hairdresser of Smallheath, Birmingham, who survived him. They had one daughter. Hill died in Newmarket on 15 October 1971.

C. R. HILL, *rev.*

Sources *The Hill story* (1955) · R. Kaye, *The Ladbrokes Story* (1969) · *The Times* (16 Oct 1971) · C. R. Hill, *Horse power: the politics of the turf* (1988) · William Hill Organisation Press Release, 4 Feb 1988 · private information (1993)
Likenesses photograph, 1951, Popperfoto, Northampton [*see illus.*]
Wealth at death £1,014,803: probate, 23 Feb 1972, *CGPLA Eng. & Wales*

Hill, William Noel-, third Baron Berwick (1773–1842), diplomatist, was the second son of Noel Hill, first Baron Berwick, great-nephew of Richard *Hill (1655/6–1727), and his wife, Anne, daughter of Henry Vernon of Hilton, Staffordshire. Born on 21 October 1773, he was educated at

William Noel-Hill, third Baron Berwick (1773–1842), attrib. Richard Cosway

Rugby School and Jesus College, Cambridge (1791–3), and was MP for Shrewsbury (1796–1812) and Marlborough (1814–18), sitting as a silent Pittite. He courted Lady Hester Stanhope, ultimately unsuccessfully, though he was briefly engaged to her. He was appointed envoy to Regensburg in 1805—'a little bit of a job', Lady Bessborough thought (HoP, *Commons*)—but war prevented him from going there. He was envoy to Sardinia from 1807 to 1824. In 1822, he rejected Canning's offer of the undersecretaryship of foreign affairs. In 1824 he assumed the additional name of Noel; in the same year he was created a privy councillor, and went as envoy to Naples, where he served until 1833. There he was, Harold Acton thought, 'a middle-aged sybarite who loved good cheer though some thought him heartless. His reputation for wit was not justified by his despatches' (Acton, 6). In 1832 he succeeded his elder brother, Lord Thomas Noel, as third Baron Berwick. He was an FSA. He died unmarried at Redrice, near Andover, on 4 August 1842. His large library was dispersed by sale.

H. C. G. MATTHEW

Sources *GM*, 2nd ser., 18 (1842), 423 · HoP, *Commons* · H. M. M. Acton, *The last Bourbons of Naples, 1825–1861* (1961)
Archives Shrops. RRC, corresp. and papers | BL, letters to Butler, Add. MSS 34583–34592, *passim* · BL OIOC, letters to William Pitt

Amherst, MS Eur. F 140 · U. Nott. L., letters to Lord William Bentinck, etc.
Likenesses attrib. R. Cosway, portrait, Attingham Park, Shropshire [*see illus.*]

Hill, Wills, first marquess of Downshire (1718–1793), politician, was born on 30 May 1718 at Fairford, Gloucestershire, the third but only surviving son of Trevor Hill, first Viscount Hillsborough (1693–1742), landowner, and Mary (1684–1742), daughter of Anthony Rowe of North Aston, Oxford, and widow of Sir Edmund Denton, first baronet, of Hillesden, Buckinghamshire. His first name was received from General Sir Charles Wills, one of the sponsors at his baptism.

Family background and political beginnings The family's fortunes had been linked with Ulster since 1573, when Moyses Hill joined Walter Devereux, first earl of Essex, on his expedition to colonize Antrim. The connection with co. Down was established in 1607. A series of judicious marriages saw estates and titles grow, so that in 1742 Wills Hill inherited, at twenty-four, an Irish viscountcy, control of five seats in the Irish parliament, and estates that enabled him to succeed his father as lord lieutenant of co. Down, a dignity he held for the rest of his life. Moreover, in the previous year he had been elected member of parliament for Warwick. Entry into the Irish House of Lords in November 1743 completed formal proof of his Anglo-Irish political standing.

Thereafter, Hillsborough demonstrated an unwavering ambition to advance himself. His first success was to be created, on 3 October 1751, Viscount Kilwarlin and earl of Hillsborough in the Irish peerage. Five years later, on 17 November 1756, he acquired the British title of Baron Harwich of Harwich and so left the House of Commons. Continuing to be known as Hillsborough, he became, on 28 August 1772, Viscount Fairford and earl of Hillsborough in the British peerage. A final promotion occurred on 26 August 1789 when he was styled marquess of Downshire, though this he was obliged to accept as an Irish title. He never succeeded in becoming lord lieutenant of Ireland nor secured an Irish dukedom. This unremitting pursuit of advancement did not escape notice. It has been pointed out (GEC, *Peerage*, 4.458n.) that he secured a barony, two viscountcies, two earldoms, and a marquessate, making him, by this reckoning, the equal of Wellington and twice as honoured as Nelson.

Despite being involved in politics for almost half a century, Hillsborough attracted only fitful attention. He has no biographer and is barely mentioned in many scholarly studies. Only between 1763 and 1774 was his role in English politics of sufficient prominence to gain much notice.

Hillsborough was returned as MP for Warwick in May 1741; an absence of private correspondence and an equal lack of commentary—nothing is known of his education or upbringing—obscure his connection with the Greville family through whom he secured an unopposed election. He quickly became a regular, if hardly significant, contributor to the proceedings of the house. He first made his mark as an opposition whig, connected with Bubb

Wills Hill, first marquess of Downshire (1718–1793), by Pompeo Batoni, 1766

Dodington and Viscount Barrington, and his speeches won the approval, not to be immutably sustained, of Horace Walpole, who noted in March 1751, when Hillsborough moved the address of condolence on the death of the prince of Wales, that:

> Lord Hillsborough was a young man of great honour and merit, remarkably nice in weighing whatever cause he was to vote in, and excellent at setting off his reasons, if the affair was at all tragic, by a solemnity in his voice and manner that made much impression on his hearers. (Walpole, *Memoirs of … George II*, 1.56)

Contemporaries noted his love of opera.

By now, Hillsborough had abandoned opposition and become a supporter of government, a shift matched by that of William Greville, seventh Lord Brooke, the proprietor of his seat at Warwick. A reward was his becoming, in October 1751, earl of Hillsborough in the Irish peerage. Winning the approval of the duke of Newcastle he was appointed, in May 1754, comptroller of the household and an English privy councillor. This began his identification with the monarchy: he has been judged 'of all George III's ministers, the most convinced "King's Friend"' (Pares, 171n.).

A further advance was not long delayed: in December 1755 Hillsborough became, at Newcastle's instance and with Henry Fox's support, treasurer of the chamber, a position he gave up in November 1756 when the Pitt–Devonshire ministry was formed. His consolation was to receive the English title of Lord Harwich and thus a place in the House of Lords. This was too high a price to be acceptable to George II but Devonshire insisted that it had to be met. Hillsborough could claim Fox, George Grenville, and Halifax as friends and he also had not incurred the hostility of William Pitt. Even so, it was a promotion that recognized the needs of ministerial reconstruction, not his political merit.

Marriage on 1 March 1748 to Lady Margaret Fitzgerald (1729–1766), daughter of the nineteenth earl of Kildare and Mary O'Brien and sister of James, first duke of Leinster, rendered Hillsborough's connections with Fox as much family as political: the wives of Leinster and Fox were sisters, daughters of the second duke of Richmond. Their eldest daughter, Mary Amelia *Cecil, became a renowned political hostess. Assisted initially by a £20,000 dowry, Hillsborough acquired further estates. In 1749 he bought lands at Bainbridge and developed a centre for the linen trade. He also undertook the rebuilding of Hillsborough. Additional estates were inherited in 1751 on the death of a distant relative, Marcus Trevor, second Viscount Dungannon. Absence from office and the House of Commons after 1756 made possible an increased attention to Ireland. On a visit to Ulster in September 1758 Mrs Delany was invited to Hillsborough, which she found set in 'a very fine cultivated country, little inferior to some parts of Gloucestershire'. An intention to build a new house and bestow the present residence on the bishop of Down was announced. Despite this activity, Hillsborough still came no more than 'once a year for a month or two, to set forward his works' (Autobiography … Mrs Delany, 3.512–14). Great landlord of co. Down he might be, but that did not make him its leading resident.

The years of American policy, 1763–1772 Hillsborough returned to government in September 1763, one of the ministerial changes occasioned by the departure of Bute, the death of Egremont, and the elevation of his friend George Grenville. He replaced Shelburne as president of the Board of Trade, an office he would hold until dismissed by Rockingham in July 1765. Exceptionally conscientious as an administrator, he was absent from only three of the 262 meetings of the board convened during his presidency. Against this, no influence on ministerial policy can be discerned. Even if his statement in parliament, after the event, is accepted, that 'he thought the Stamp Act was inexpedient, had advised against it when first proposed' (Basye, 142–3), the act had been passed and Hillsborough never threatened to resign. Accounts of this major political crisis hardly mention him.

During Hillsborough's presidency the Board of Trade's principal task was to acquire and assess details and views relating to imperial policy and possessions. The aftermath of the Seven Years' War and the territorial gains secured at the peace of Paris in 1763 provided an abundance of referred topics, ranging from American Indian relations and colonial land grants to the administrative incorporation of new American and Caribbean possessions and the collection of reports on tensions in the colonies. But the board, while it could formulate, did not initiate policy. That was the function of members of the cabinet.

The significance of American events was all too evident to an Irish peer long hostile to any growth of parliamentary powers in Dublin. In 1751 a pamphlet was published entitled A Proposal for Uniting the Kingdoms of Great Britain and Ireland; it was believed by contemporaries and is accepted by historians to have been Hillsborough's work. The author argued that a union would bring new members to Westminster willing to support the interests of prince and people, not those of 'an unnecessary malignant opposition to his measures' (Sedgwick, 2.141). A meeting of the Irish parliament in 1759 showed that Hillsborough was still thought to hold these views. Fears that a French invasion might occur during a Commons recess had brought proposals that emergency meetings should then be called. Opponents declared that not only would this give undue control to the administration but that Hillsborough, who was present, was leading a plot to bring about union and abolish parliament. On 5 December several thousand demonstrators engaged in an anti-union riot without and within the Dublin parliament. Although Hillsborough always gave precedence to his English ambitions, Irish mistrust remained constant.

In July 1765 Rockingham replaced Grenville and Hillsborough was forced from office. A year later in August 1766, on the return of Chatham, he was restored to his post. Rather curiously, he accepted on conditions of exclusion from the cabinet and the power of the board being reduced to the provision of reports. His connections with Fox and an unwillingness to encounter Chatham at close quarters may have curbed an inveterate pursuit of position. He wished, he explained to Grenville, 'that I might do the business in an easy manner to myself' (Thomas, British Politics, 288–9). If this was his hope, it would not be fulfilled: the business of the board continued much as before. A further reduction of his labours was achieved at the end of 1766 when he was appointed joint postmaster-general—'laid up in lavender … till he shall be wanted elsewhere', as Barrington put it (ibid., 289). It was a position that ranked two steps below cabinet level but which, in exchange for occasional light duties, provided an annual income of about £2900. Thus rewarded, Hillsborough could remain, in a truly 'easy manner', present on the political scene.

It was a well-timed break from ministerial responsibilities. Had he remained at the Board of Trade, Hillsborough would inevitably have been involved in Charles Townshend's attempt, by raising an American revenue, to resolve the financial problems of an administration from which its leader, Chatham, had dissociated himself. A faltering ministry, faced with collapse after Townshend's sudden death in September 1767, required reconstruction by the duke of Grafton. Major concern with American problems warranted the creation of a new, third secretaryship of state. But who should fill it? A process of elimination by age, experience, and factional commitments left Grafton with Hillsborough. Availability, rather than merit, earned him this promotion in January 1768.

As the new secretary Hillsborough faced three major issues: the fate of the Townshend duties, the extent and form of western settlement, and the provision of government for Quebec. All held particular significance for an Anglo-Irish landlord, involving as they did the raising of revenues from reluctant local bodies, economic and social development in areas which resisted control, and the consequences of admitting an overwhelmingly Catholic population into a governmental system hitherto confined to protestants. Their consideration confirmed Hillsborough's conservative fears.

Learning of Hillsborough's appointment, American colonial agents in London offered a guarded welcome. William Samuel Johnson reported home to Connecticut that the new secretary 'is esteemed a nobleman of good nature, abilities, and integrity; is a man of business, alert, lively, ready, but too fond of his own opinions and systems, and too apt to be inflexibly attached to them' (*Trumbull Papers*, 252). On the other hand, it might prove the case that, as a native of Ireland possessing 'vast property' there, he would have 'formed reasonable notions of the rights and liberties of the distant branches of this empire' (ibid.). Of this hope, Johnson would soon be disabused.

Since Hillsborough had declared that he was urging North, the new chancellor of the exchequer, to repeal the Townshend duties, Benjamin Franklin's first impressions were not unfavourable. Whatever view Hillsborough may have held, his belief in colonial subordination took priority and was challenged by American responses. In February 1768 the Massachusetts house of representatives dispatched a circular letter to the other continental colonies, urging agreement that only their assemblies should impose taxes. Informed of this by Governor Francis Bernard, the secretary issued his own circular letter, in which he announced that all American governors must combat this 'open opposition to and denial of the authority of Parliament', if necessary by the prorogation or dissolution of assemblies (Thomas, *Townshend Duties Crisis*, 81).

It was of no avail. Eight colonies had responded positively to Massachusetts before Hillsborough's letter reached their governors, and the other four did so by the end of the year. In Massachusetts his demand for the rescinding of the circular letter was rejected on 30 June by ninety-two votes to seventeen, numbers that in the struggle became synonymous with patriots and tories. Colonial resistance, expressed through non-importation agreements, intensified after Hillsborough in June 1768 instructed General Gage to send troops to Boston. During the next four years, though the repeal of the Townshend Acts in March 1770, whereby only the duty on tea was retained to assert parliamentary authority, reduced popular disorder, Hillsborough devised no solutions. The long-standing difficulties created by the needs of Quebec, disputes with the colonial assemblies, the absence of effective support for governors and officials, remained unresolved. Bostonian opposition was marked by the daubing of properties of suspected tories with 'Hillsborough paint'—compounded of faeces and urine.

The problems of western expansion and Indian relations persisted. Decisions were needed on the territorial extent and direction of settlement and on the maintaining of frontier peace, issues that brought Hillsborough's resignation as secretary of state in August 1772. The immediate cause was a proposal to create a colony on the Ohio. To be called Vandalia, as a compliment to the queen, it would have been the first established in North America beyond the Atlantic seaboard. Hillsborough's opposition was unwavering but had led to his encouraging the project's supporters to apply for an even larger grant. Intended to ensure its rejection, this did not work. Much to the dismay of North, who resisted to the end the loss of 'one of the best and firmest friends I have in the Cabinet' (Marshall, 731), Hillsborough's enemies, led by Rochford and supported by Gower and Suffolk, refused to accept his indefinite avoidance of a decision. The king deplored the conflict, but admitted that it was due in part to 'suspicion in Lord Hillsborough' (ibid.). The secretary of state's resignation did not weaken North's position, since Dartmouth, an old friend and member of his family, agreed to accept the office. But by mid-August 1772 the case for the new colony appeared to be won, its opponent having been defeated and driven from office.

Out of office, 1772–1779   As consolation, Hillsborough received a constantly coveted prize—advancement in the peerage. On 28 August 1772 his Irish became a British earldom. He did not join the opposition, though he had lost authority: his attempt in May 1774 to block Dartmouth's proposal for the westward extension of the boundary of Quebec was flatly rejected. The rapidly growing resistance of the American colonies reinforced Hillsborough's opinions. When the new parliament met on 30 November 1774, he moved the Lords' address 'in a very long and severe speech on the colonies' (*Last Journals of Horace Walpole*, 1.410). At no time during the years of the American war did he express any sympathy for the rebels or support moves towards peace.

Having resigned, Hillsborough turned his attention to co. Down. Although he admitted, a month later when back at Hillsborough, to his undersecretary, William Knox, that 'I did not, you know, wish to resign', he claimed that he was 'not now at all sorry'. He continued:

> I have totally forgotten that I was ever concerned in public business, and am so employed in church-building, road-making, farming and every rural occupation that belongs to an estate and a country gentleman that I go to bed every night very much tired, and find little time for anything else. (*Various Collections*, 6.108)

By then he had remarried, following the death of his first wife on 25 January 1766. Mary Stawell, Baroness Stawell of Somerton (1726–1780), whom he married on 11 November 1768, the only daughter and heir of Edward, fourth Baron Stawell, and the widow of Henry Bilson-Legge, brought Hillsborough another substantial dowry.

Hillsborough's resignation certainly did not serve to extinguish an ambition to become lord lieutenant of Ireland, even though this met continual rejection. When in October 1776 an appointment was giving much trouble to

North, the king declared that only Hillsborough must be excluded. With landed estate solely in Ireland an unacceptable precedent would be established. Further, as the entire cabinet was aware, 'I am sorry to say, I do not know a man of less judgment than Lord Hillsborough, and consequently less qualified to fill that office with dignity or propriety' (George III to John Robinson, 15 Oct 1776, *Abergavenny MSS*). Departure from government did not lead to longer stays in Ulster. Although he watched zealously over the economic and political interests of his estates and dependants, visits took place in the summer months. Any political prospect, including the hope of becoming lord lieutenant, derived from London. If that hope persisted, so did his reputation for duplicity.

Return to office, 1779–1782 In September 1779 Hillsborough returned to office, replacing Weymouth as secretary of state for the southern department. Typically, this represented a last political resort of an increasingly beleaguered North, not a strengthening of the ministry. It may have revived Hillsborough's Irish ambitions since the southern secretary acted as the ministerial link with the lord lieutenant and, theoretically, could thus exercise a crucial influence. There is no indication, however, that Hillsborough did so. On entering office he had declared to the lord lieutenant that he was 'very little acquainted with the Politics & Intrigues of Dublin' (Johnston, 86). Certainly, officials dominated, even directed, the ensuing correspondence between Whitehall and Dublin. Hillsborough's presence in government attracted little attention in respect of either Irish or foreign affairs. That is not to say that Irish issues, especially demands for trade equality and the formation of the volunteers, could be overlooked. Hillsborough's opening remarks, as was his custom, sought to please. He declared that he had accepted office on the understanding that Ireland and England would be put on an equal commercial footing. He thus yielded as a matter of expediency to a popular demand whose consequences he feared more than welcomed.

In London during June 1780 Hillsborough's apprehensions of mob activities were renewed as the Gordon riots threatened property and his security. The continued growth in Ulster of a movement whose Dungannon convention of February 1782 gave prominence to what Hillsborough had initially applauded but now called 'Your cursed Volunteers and Patriots' (Bardon, 215) left him in a state of alarm. He experienced this even in Hillsborough when the visit of the lord lieutenant was greeted at a corporation dinner by a toast to the Volunteers. 'Ld H cried "Fy, fy, fy," and each time knocked his hand on the table— Do you know, Sir, there is not a toast could be more disagreeable to G'ment' (Young, 170).

Hillsborough's vehement reactions to challenges to authority never changed: as late in the American war as November 1781, he declared in the Lords that 'he hoped that the independence of America would never be admitted in that House, nor that a majority of their lordships would consent to a measure which, if it should be adopted, must prove the ruin of this country' (Cobbett, *Parl. hist.*, 22, 1781, 661). But with the failure of the war and

the downfall of North's ministry, loss of office was inevitable. If he did not, others knew the price he would pay. As the duke of Rutland, lord lieutenant in 1786, remarked: 'Lord Hillsborough's uniform principle is *perseverance* in anything once adopted—in spite of the changes which time and events may have produced' (duke of Rutland to Lord Sydney, 29 Jan 1786, *Rutland MSS*, 3.279). His last speech in the Lords, on 24 January 1786, had provided confirmation as he once again 'recommended a union with Ireland as the best method of connecting and consolidating the interests of both kingdoms' (Cobbett, *Parl. hist.*, 25, 1786, 996).

Later years This did not mark Hillsborough's final involvement in politics. That followed closely upon his securing in 1789 the Irish marquessate of Downshire. His son and heir, Lord Kilwarlin, now became earl of Hillsborough but continued, as he had since 1776, to represent County Down in the Irish House of Commons. His last election in 1783 had cost about £3000, but this bore no comparison to that of 1790 which saw the family's claim to both county seats challenged by the young Robert Stewart, the later Lord Castlereagh. His family mounted an 'independent' campaign to break the Downshire hold on both seats. A bitter, extended, and costly election ensued: polling the 6000 electors occupied sixty-nine days until Stewart won a seat.

The contest was sufficiently expensive to prevent Stewart from completing his Mount Stewart mansion house and to generate additional Downshire debts. If the family fortunes had benefited from advantageous marriages, settlement charges had subsequently diminished them: at Downshire's death in 1793 the estate was £69,600 in debt. His end was not unexpected. There were frequent references to 'old age' during his later years. After suffering a stroke in the autumn of 1790, he died at Hillsborough Castle on 7 October 1793, having 'wholly retired for some years' from public and political affairs (*GM*, 1st ser., 63/1, 1793, 962). He was buried at Hillsborough.

Both contemporaries and historians have judged Hillsborough adversely: by the time of the Falklands crisis in 1770 he had become to Horace Walpole 'a pompous composition of ignorance and want of judgment' (Walpole, *Memoirs of … George III*, 3.133), while Wraxall, noting his attention to public business, thought 'his natural endowments, however solid, did not rise above mediocrity' (*Historical and Posthumous Memoirs*, 1.381). George III did not withhold criticism of however faithful a servant: 'Lord Hillsborough', he complained, 'always puts things off to the last minute, and though an amiable man, the least a man of business I ever knew' (*Correspondence*, ed. Fortescue, 5.418). A modern historian has commented that 'No historian has had a good word to say for Hillsborough' (Shy, 292), although his commitment, as distinct from his achievements, while secretary of state for America has won some recognition. Even so, the failure of British policy in the American colonies between 1768 and 1772 must be related to its direction by Hillsborough.

Found charming on occasion, particularly by women, to whom he was known affectionately as the Black Earl,

Hillsborough sustained a political presence through persistence, not talent. He possessed no parliamentary following at Westminster and was insufficiently skilful as either minister or politician to prevail in his own right. That he should have been one of the leading Irish magnates to participate in English politics in the second half of the eighteenth century provides some indication of the comparative political talent of the peers of the two kingdoms.   PETER MARSHALL

Sources P. D. G. Thomas, *British politics and the Stamp Act crisis: the first phase of the American revolution, 1763–1767* (1975) · P. D. G. Thomas, *The Townshend duties crisis* (1987) · P. D. G. Thomas, *Tea party to independence: the third phase of the American Revolution, 1773–1776* (1991) · E. M. Johnston, *Great Britain and Ireland, 1760–1800* (1963) · J. Shy, *Toward Lexington* (1965) · J. Brooke, *The Chatham administration, 1766–1768* (1956) · W. A. Maguire, *The Downshire estates in Ireland, 1801–1845: the management of Irish landed estates in the early nineteenth century* (1972) · H. M. Hyde, *The rise of Castlereagh* (1933) · *The correspondence of King George the Third from 1760 to December 1783*, ed. J. Fortescue, 6 vols. (1927–8) · *The autobiography and correspondence of Mary Granville, Mrs Delany*, ed. Lady Llanover, 1st ser., 3 vols. (1861) · J. Bardon, *A history of Ulster* (1992) · *Correspondence of Emily, duchess of Leinster (1731–1814)*, ed. B. Fitzgerald, 3 vols., IMC (1949–57) · *Collections of the Massachusetts Historical Society*, 5th ser., 9 (1885) [*The Trumbull papers*, vol. 1] · *The political journal of George Bubb Dodington*, ed. J. Carswell and L. A. Dralle (1965) · J. C. D. Clark, *The dynamics of change: the crisis of the 1750s and English party systems* (1982) · P. Marshall, 'Lord Hillsborough, Samuel Wharton and the Ohio grant, 1769–1775', *EngHR*, 80 (1965), 717–39 · *The historical and the posthumous memoirs of Sir Nathaniel William Wraxall, 1772–1784*, ed. H. B. Wheatley, 5 vols. (1884) · H. Grattan, *Memoirs of the life and times of the Rt Hon. Henry Grattan*, 5 vols. (1839–46) · *The correspondence of the Right Hon. John Beresford, illustrative of the last thirty years of the Irish parliament*, ed. W. Beresford, 2 vols. (1854) · R. M. Young, ed., *Historical notices of old Belfast and its vicinity* (1896) · A. H. Basye, *The lords commissioners of trade and plantations* (1925) · S. E. Rees, 'The political career of Wills Hill, earl of Hillsborough (1718–1793), with particular reference to his American policy', PhD diss., U. Wales, 1976 · H. Walpole, *Memoirs of King George II*, ed. J. Brooke, 3 vols. (1985) · H. Walpole, *Memoirs of the reign of King George the Third*, ed. G. F. R. Barker, 4 vols. (1894) · *The last journals of Horace Walpole*, ed. Dr Doran, rev. A. F. Steuart, 2 vols. (1910) · M. R. O'Connell, *Irish politics and social conflict in the age of the American revolution* (1965) · R. Pares, *King George III and the politicians* (1953) · K. Ellis, *The Post Office in the eighteenth century: a study in administrative history* (1958) · *Report on manuscripts in various collections*, 8 vols., HMC, 55 (1901–14), vol. 6 · *The manuscripts of his grace the duke of Rutland*, 4 vols., HMC, 24 (1888–1905), vol. 3 · *DNB* · GEC, *Peerage* · R. R. Sedgwick, 'Hill, Hon. Wills', HoP, *Commons, 1715–54* · J. Brooke, 'Hill, Wills', HoP, *Commons, 1754–90*
Archives BL OIOC, corresp. and papers relating to India · PRO NIre., corresp. and papers | BL, corresp. with William Eden and Lord Carlisle, Add. MSS 34417–34418 · BL, corresp. with George Grenville, Add. MS 57812 · BL, letters to Sir William Hamilton, Add. MS 41198 · BL, corresp. with Lord Holland, Add. MS 51386 · BL, letters to Sir H. Moore, Add. MS 12440 · BL, letters to Lord Mountstuart, Add. MS 36801 · NMM, letters to Lord Sandwich · Norfolk RO, corresp. with earl of Buckinghamshire · NRA Scotland, priv. coll., letters to Lady Mary Coke · U. Mich., Clements L., corresp. with William Knox
Likenesses A. Devis, group portrait, oils, *c.*1760 (*1st marquess of Downshire and family*), NPG · P. Batoni, oils, 1766, Ulster Museum, Belfast [*see illus.*] · J. Downman, watercolour drawing, 1786, Hatfield House, Hertfordshire · J. Rising, oils (after G. Romney), Hatfield House, Hertfordshire · portrait (with his family), NPG
Wealth at death approx. 100,000 acres in Irish estates; also left debts of £69,660: Maguire, *The Downshire estates*

Hillary, Richard Hope (1919–1943), air force officer and author, was born on 20 April 1919 in Sydney, Australia, the only child of Michael Hillary (1886–1976), DSO, OBE, an Australian government official, and his wife, Edwyna Mary Hope (d. 1966). He arrived in England at the age of three, when his father received a London posting. From Shrewsbury School he went in 1937 to Trinity College, Oxford, where he started to read philosophy, politics, and economics and then moved to modern history. He stroked the Trinity boat to head of the river, and as a notably good-looking but somewhat challenging undergraduate enjoyed to the full the leisured life of his college. He also joined the university air squadron, with the motive, he later asserted, not of patriotism but self-realization. The Second World War began before he took his degree.

After enlistment and commissioning in the RAF and completion of his service flying training Hillary was posted on 6 July 1940 to 603 (City of Edinburgh) fighter squadron in Dyce. The battle of Britain was beginning, and on 10 August no. 603 was ordered south to Hornchurch. Hillary's valiant combat career lasted three weeks, during which he was credited with five enemy aircraft. On 3 September 1940, over the North Sea, he was himself shot down. He fell from his Spitfire, but was sustained in the water by his buoyancy jacket and parachute. Horribly burned about the face and hands, he was rescued after three hours by the Margate lifeboat. There followed months in hospital and repeated operations, mostly by Archibald McIndoe. His face was miraculously mended—he was given new upper eyelids and a new upper lip—but he was left with very wasted and weakened hands.

During 1941 Hillary persuaded the Air Ministry to send him to the United States on a speaking tour. But when he arrived there the British embassy expressed fears that his scarred features would only reinforce anti-involvement sentiments among American parents. His talks were confined to broadcasts, where he could not be seen. In America, Hillary met many prominent people and enjoyed the affection of the film star Merle Oberon. He also finished a book and secured its publication there (in February 1942) under the title *Falling through Space*.

The book was retitled *The Last Enemy* and published in England the following June. It begins with a vivid account of Hillary's final flight. The narrative switches back to Oxford and the RAF, and then forward again to his hospital and surgical experiences. But it is concerned less with the facts of his life than with his feelings and motivation. The self-analysis is sustained and unflattering. Hillary presents himself as an individualist, who only later and almost reluctantly becomes aware of the wider aspects of the war as a battle for civilization and humanity. The success of *The Last Enemy* was immediate. The author was acclaimed not only as a born writer but also as a representative of the doomed youth of his generation, although in his constant self-analysis he was in fact a most untypical British fighter pilot of 1940.

After returning from the United States in October 1941 Hillary had gone through Staff College and thence to the headquarters of Fighter Command. But he became

Richard Hope Hillary (1919–1943), by Eric Kennington, 1942

obsessed with a desire to return to operations—as he saw it, to keep faith with his dead comrades. After repeated pleas he secured a medical board to consider his case. Surprisingly, it passed him fit for operations. On 24 November 1942 Hillary joined 54 operational training unit at Charter Hall in Berwickshire for training as a night fighter pilot. On 8 January 1943, in a night of poor weather, he was circling a beacon on an exercise when his Blenheim lost height and crashed nearby, at Crunklaw Farm, Edrom, killing both Hillary and his radio operator. The subsequent inquiry, unable to determine a specific cause for the accident, concluded that the pilot had lost control of his aircraft. Later a Richard Hillary Trust was instituted and a Hillary archive was accumulated at Trinity College, Oxford.

After Hillary's death a considerable literature developed. Arthur Koestler, Eric Linklater, and John Middleton Murry all wrote about him, the last-named falsely hypothesizing a death wish and suicide. Lovat Dickson, his publisher, wrote a biography. Much later, in 1988, Michael Burn, in *Mary and Richard*, published a selection of the love letters which had passed in 1942 between Hillary and Mary Booker, an understanding and beautiful woman twenty-two years Hillary's senior, whom Burn later married. A fully detailed biography by David Ross appeared in 2000. Hillary's own letters, remorselessly self-analytical as ever, confirm the writing talent of this brave, charming, self-assertive, mocking, and rather uncomfortable young man.   DENIS RICHARDS, *rev.*

Sources R. Hillary, *The last enemy* (1942) · A. Koestler, 'The birth of a myth', *Horizon* (April 1943) · E. Linklater, 'Richard Hillary', *The art of adventure* (1947), 73–98 · R. L. Dickson, *Richard Hillary: a biography* (1950) · M. Burn, *Mary and Richard* (1988) · S. Faulks, *The fatal Englishman: three short lives* (1996) · D. Ross and others, *Richard Hillary* (2000) · *WWW*, 1971–80 [Michael Hillary] · d. cert. · *CGPLA Eng. & Wales* (1943)

Archives Trinity College, Oxford, corresp. and papers; biographical material |SOUND BL NSA, documentary footage · IWM SA, 'British RAF fighter pilot shot down over sea, September 1940', BBC, 14 July 1941, 2270 · IWM SA, 'Experiences in battle of Britain', BBC, 2 Oct 1941, 2271 · IWM SA, oral history interview

Likenesses E. H. Kennington, pastel drawing, 1942, NPG [*see illus.*] · E. H. Kennington, portrait, Trinity College, Oxford

Wealth at death £2076 14s. 4d.: administration, 16 April 1943, *CGPLA Eng. & Wales*

Hillary, William (1697–1763), physician, was born at Birkrigg, an isolated farmhouse near Hawes in Upper Wensleydale, Yorkshire, on 17 March 1697. He was the second son of John Hillary and his wife, Mary Robinson, Quakers who belonged to an influential group of Friends in Wensleydale that included the Robinson, Fothergill, and Hillary families. The Hillarys moved in 1699 to a substantial farmhouse in the nearby village of Burtersett which to this day is known as Hillary Hall. Nothing is known of Hillary's schooling but in 1715 he was apprenticed to a Quaker apothecary in Bradford, Benjamin Bartlett. After seven years he went to the University of Leiden, where he was a student of Hermann Boerhaave, and where he graduated MD in 1722 with a thesis entitled *Dissertatio medicas inauguralis practica de febribus intermittentibus*. Hillary then settled as a physician in Ripon where he stayed until 1734. During this time he recorded the changes in the weather and the epidemics he encountered in an attempt to correlate weather and disease. His observations were published in the second edition of his *A Practical Essay on the Smallpox* (1740). He had by then moved to Bath where he practised from 1734 until 1746.

At Bath, Hillary's attention was drawn in 1737 to a spring in Lyncombe, to the south of Bath, which he was to dignify with the name of a spa. His *An Enquiry into the Contents and Medicinal Virtues of Lincomb Spa Water Near Bath* (1742) extolled the manifold virtues of the spa water, which had been taken by, among many others, the fourth earl of Chesterfield, to whom Hillary dedicated his book. By 1746, however, his position in Bath had become, for obscure reasons, unsatisfactory. Then, through the good offices of John Fothergill, a family friend, also formerly apprenticed to Benjamin Bartlett, Hillary moved to the island of Barbados, arriving there in early 1747. He sought to continue the work on weather and disease that he had begun in Ripon but an unfortunate accident to his barometer prevented him from starting his observations until 1752. In 1751 he had an important consultation. Lawrence Washington, in the company of his brother George, and in search of relief from the mortal tuberculosis from which he suffered, sought Hillary's opinion on his disorder. The event was recorded by George Washington in his diary.

On All Saints' day 1755 Hillary witnessed the remarkable ebbing and flowing of the tide in Barbados which suggested to him that there must have been a cataclysmic earthquake far out at sea. Only two months later did he hear of the Lisbon earthquake which had occurred that same day. From a knowledge of the time difference Hillary was able to calculate that the shock wave had travelled across the Atlantic at over 400 miles an hour, a remarkable speed, he commented, for anything to be transmitted through water. His work in Barbados was recorded after he returned to England in his *Observations on the changes of the air, and the concomitant epidemical diseases in the island of Barbados, to which is added a treatise on the putrid bilious fever, commonly called the yellow fever; and such other diseases as are indigenous or endemial, in the West India islands or in the torrid zone* (1759). This was one of the first books in English to deal specifically with tropical disease. It contains an early description of the disorder known as tropical sprue, a form of intestinal malabsorption causing nutritional deficiency that occurs particularly in islands such as Puerto Rico and in countries of the Far East. Hillary did not confine his comments to medical matters. He was forthright in condemning local sartorial fashions. For the hot climate of the West Indies he advised a 'loose gown or Banjan', the dress of the mandarins, immensely more comfortable than 'a thick rich Coat and Waistcoat, daubed and loaded with Gold', under which he had seen men melting, 'preferring the Character of a Fop' to that of a 'Man of Sense and Honour'.

Hillary returned to London in 1759 after seeming to have had a financially successful stay in Barbados. A contemporary stated that Hillary had made £6000 during his twelve years in the island. He lived at first in East Street, off Red Lion Square in Bloomsbury. After seeing his *Observations* through the press he was occupied with other literary ventures, first *The Nature, Properties, and Laws of Motion of Fire* (1760). He then embarked on one of his most ambitious and idealistic ventures, *An inquiry into the means of improving medical knowledge, by examining all those methods which have hindered, or increased its improvement in all past ages* (1761). It was in fact an eighteenth-century history of medicine.

Hillary died, a lifelong bachelor, on 25 April 1763. He was described in the records of the Friends as of 'St Dunstan in the West' and had been a member of Peel Meeting, which met at St John Street, Clerkenwell. He was buried on 1 May in the Quaker burial-ground at Bunhill Fields. The cause of his death was said to be 'fever'. He left no will but an administration was granted to his younger brother, Richard, merchant of Liverpool. Richard Hillary's second son, named for his doctor uncle, was Sir William Hillary, founder in 1824 of the Royal National Lifeboat Institution. CHRISTOPHER C. BOOTH

Sources C. C. Booth, 'William Hillary: a pupil of Boerhaave', *Medical History*, 7 (1963), 297–316 · *Chain of friendship: selected letters of Dr. John Fothergill of London, 1735–1780*, ed. B. C. Corner and C. C. Booth (1971) · W. Hillary, *Observations on the changes of the air … in the island of Barbados* (1759) · E. M. Shilstone, 'The Washingtons and their doctors in Barbados', *Journal of the Barbados Museum and Historical Society*, 20 (1953), 71 · *GM*, 1st ser., 33 (1763), 35, 202 · RS Friends, Lond.

Wealth at death possibly £6000 in 1759: Shilstone, 'Washingtons'

Hillary, Sir William, first baronet (1771–1847), founder of the Royal National Lifeboat Institution, was born in Wensleydale, the second son of Richard Hillary and his wife, Hannah, *née* Wynne, of whom little is known. His elder

brother, Richard, was a member of the house of assembly in Jamaica, where he died unmarried in 1803. Mary *Rolls, a poet, was his sister.

Hillary was appointed equerry to the duke of Sussex, with whom he spent two years in Italy, returning home in 1800. On his return to England he married Elizabeth Disney Fytche, on 21 February 1800. They had twins, a son and a daughter. He came into property both by marriage and inheritance during that year. He used part of his fortune (£20,000) to raise the first Essex legion of infantry and cavalry. He commanded the legion of 1400 men against the French upon the renewal of the war with France in 1803. The legion constituted the largest force then offered by any private individual for the defence of his country. In recognition of his services he was created a baronet on 8 November 1805. Three years later, owing to a heavy loss of property in the West Indies, Sir William left his estate in Danbury Place in Essex and settled at Fort Anne, near Douglas, in the Isle of Man, where on 30 August 1813 he married Emma Tobin, his first wife having died.

Hillary witnessed a large number of shipwrecks off the coast of the Isle of Man and, after the destruction of *Vigilance* (the government cutter) and *Racehorse* (the naval brig) in 1822, he became involved in the question of safety and life-saving at sea. In February 1823 he issued *An appeal to the British nation on the humanity and policy of forming a national institution for the preservation of lives and property from shipwreck*, which he dedicated to George IV. The proposal was supported by George Hibbert and by Thomas Wilson, an influential city member, and on 4 March 1824 a public meeting was held at the London tavern under the chairmanship of the archbishop of Canterbury (Manners-Sutton). The Royal National Institution for the Preservation of Life from Shipwreck (from 1854 the Royal National Lifeboat Institution) was then founded and established upon a permanent basis, with the earl of Liverpool as first president. The movement attracted the approval of the king, the royal dukes, and William Wilberforce, the archbishop of York.

On his return to the Isle of Man, Hillary established in 1826 a district association, of which he became president. He provided the four chief harbours of the island with lifeboats and Manby and Trengrouse safety apparatuses. Hillary frequently went out in the boats himself, and was instrumental in saving many lives. In December 1827, assisted by his son, he helped to save seventeen men from the Swedish barque *Fortroindet*, and in the same year he helped to rescue the crew of the *St George*. He suffered six fractured ribs as a result. In November 1830 he set out with a crew of fourteen volunteers and helped to save sixty-two people. Again he put his own life at risk and was washed overboard. However, he survived to be awarded the Shipwreck Institution's gold medal, as he was on two other occasions. In 1832 he planned the tower of refuge on St Mary's, or Conister Rock, in Douglas Bay. He established a sailors' home at Douglas, and was strongly behind a proposal that the government should build a breakwater and make a harbour of refuge in Douglas Bay. His last public act was to preside at a meeting held at Douglas to lobby the government on this subject in March 1845, when he had to be carried from his residence at Fort Anne to the court house in a chair. He died at Woodville, near Douglas, on 5 January 1847, and was buried in Douglas churchyard; many people attended the funeral. He was succeeded in the baronetcy by his son, Augustus William (1800–1854). His daughter, Elizabeth Mary, was married in 1818 to Christopher Richard of Blackmore Priory, Essex.

At the time of Hillary's death the institution which he had been instrumental in founding owned some twenty lifeboats and had an annual income of £350. It was reorganized in 1849. In addition to his central work, Hillary also promoted other public schemes, publishing pamphlets entitled *Suggestions for the Improvement and Embellishment of the Metropolis* (1824), *A Sketch of Ireland in 1824: the Sources of her Evils and their Remedies Suggested* (1825), and *Suggestions for the Occupation of the Holy Land by the Knights of St John of Jerusalem* (1841), as well as *The National Importance of a Great Central Harbour of Refuge for the Irish Sea at Douglas* (1842; based on a tract of 1826) and a lifeboat *Appeal*, which went through several editions.

THOMAS SECCOMBE, *rev.* SINÉAD AGNEW

Sources R. Kelly, 'For those in peril': the life and times of Sir William Hillary, the founder of the RNLI (1979) · E. Lodge, ed., The genealogy of the existing British peerage and baronetage, new edn (1859), 715 · GM, 2nd ser., 27 (1847), 423 · The Lifeboat, or, Journal of the National Shipwreck Association (July 1852), 75–6 · Book of the lifeboat (1909), 26–33 · G. B. Gattie, Memorials of the Goodwin sands (1890), 220–21 · The Times (5 March 1825) · Bibliotheca Monensis, rev. edn, 24, rev. W. Harrison, Manx Society (1876), 132, 137, 147, 149, 158, 164 · Debrett's Peerage (1855) · F. Mundell, Stories of the lifeboat (1895), 15

Archives BM, pamphlets · Manx National Heritage Library, Douglas, Isle of Man, corresp. relating to Isle of Man customs agitation · Royal National Lifeboat Institution, Poole, letters relating to lifeboat stations on the Isle of Man

Hilles, Richard (*c.*1514–1587), religious activist, was the son of another Richard Hilles, who was master of the Merchant Taylors in 1504, and his wife, Elizabeth. In 1535 he was himself admitted to the freedom of the company, which was customarily awarded at the age of twenty-one. By his own testimony he was apprenticed to one Nicholas Cosyn on London Bridge. As an apprentice he seems to have embraced protestant views, and in 1532 fell out with his master for expressing forthright opinions on justification. In January 1533 he appealed for assistance to Thomas Cromwell from the refuge which he had sought at Rouen in Normandy; his mother, too, begged Cromwell to help her son. Hilles must have been reconciled with Cosyn in order to secure his freedom, but it is not known how that came about. His religious views seem to have become increasingly radical, and in 1536 he had a brush with John Stokesley, bishop of London, from which he was rescued by his mother.

Following the Act of Six Articles in 1539 Hilles felt his position to be increasingly dangerous, and in 1540 he used his business as an excuse to migrate to Strasbourg. In August of that year he initiated a correspondence with the Zürich reformer Heinrich Bullinger, to whom he wrote 'I have determined not to return thither [England], unless it

please God to effect such a change as that we may serve him there without hindrance' (Robinson, *Original Letters*, 1.198), and in June 1541 secured a residence permit in Strasbourg, describing himself as a cloth merchant. He did not apply for citizenship, for fear of losing his status as a merchant tailor, but travelled extensively up and down the Rhine on business, visiting Bullinger at Zürich in 1542. He also became well known to other protestant Englishmen in the area and to the local leaders of reform, usually through his friendship with Bullinger. The letters which he wrote at this time represent his chief claim to fame and to evangelical credentials. In August 1548, having had time to assess the religious climate in England, he moved his family back to London.

Hilles's former master, Nicholas Cosyn, was master of the Merchant Taylors in 1549–50, and this may help to explain why Hilles was called to the livery in 1549. By 1553 he seems to have been a member of the common council of London, and his children, born abroad, were naturalized by statute in March of that year. In June he was one of four merchant tailors who signed the letters patent in favour of Queen Jane. From this point on, Hilles gave his career precedence over his religious opinions, although he does not appear to have changed the latter. By November 1554 he was attending mass, a fact which he later made no pretence of denying. In 1555 he was a warden of the company, and probably senior warden the following year. Throughout Mary's reign the London livery companies conspired to defeat the vigilance of the ecclesiastical authorities, and Hilles's degree of conformity was quite sufficient to enable him to continue providing money and surreptitious support for protestants both at home and abroad. In 1561 he became master of the company and co-founder of the Merchant Taylors' School, London, donating £500 towards the purchase of the site. His active involvement with the company continued after his mastership, and he became auditor in 1569, a position which he retained until shortly before his death. After 1559 his protestant convictions could safely reappear, and he resumed his correspondence with Bullinger as though nothing had happened. He also became active in supporting godly ministers when the opportunity arose. He had resumed (or continued) his overseas business connections after 1548, but moved the focus from Strasbourg to Antwerp. He received a grant of arms in 1568, and about 1582 was listed as one of the hundred or so wealthiest and most 'substantial' citizens of London.

At some point before 1538 Hilles had married Agnes, daughter of Christopher Lacey of Yorkshire, gentleman. His eldest son, John, was born in that year, and three others, Gerson, Barnabas, and Daniel, followed between 1540 and 1548. It is probable that Agnes, John, and Barnabas predeceased him, because when he came to make his will in June 1586 he referred only to Daniel, Gerson, and Barnabas's daughter Elizabeth. His major bequests were charitable, particularly land and tenements on Tower Hill, to be developed and used as almshouses for widowed and impoverished company members. Perhaps it was for that reason that after his father's death in the following January Daniel questioned the will, and was given a copy by the court of the Merchant Taylors on 3 February 1587.

DAVID LOADES

Sources O. C. Hilles, *Richard Hilles, citizen and merchant taylor* (1927) · C. M. Clode, ed., *Memorials of the Guild of Merchant Taylors of the fraternity of St John the Baptist* (1875) · H. Robinson, ed. and trans., *Original letters relative to the English Reformation*, 1 vol. in 2, Parker Society, [26] (1846–7) · E. F. M. Hildebrandt, 'A study of the English protestant exiles … 1539–47', PhD diss., U. Durham, 1982 · R. R. Sharpe, ed., *Calendar of wills proved and enrolled in the court of husting, London, AD 1258 – AD 1688*, 2 (1890), 712–13 · *LP Henry VIII*, 6, nos. 99–100

Archives Merchant Taylors' Hall, London | Municipal Archive, Zürich

Wealth at death substantial: Sharpe, ed., *Calendar of wills*, 2.712–13

Hillgarth, Alan Hugh (1899–1978), intelligence officer and author, was born on 7 June 1899 at 121 Harley Street, London, the second son and third of five children of Willmott Henderson Hillgarth Evans, a general surgeon with a special interest in dermatology, and his wife, Ann Frances, also a doctor, the daughter of the Revd George Piercy, of Canton (Guangzhou), China. Alan assumed the surname of Hillgarth by deed poll in 1928. Alan Hillgarth's father imbued his children with a respect for tradition, as was evident in his second son's choice of career. When Alan entered the navy he was the representative of the eighth generation of his family to become naval officers. However, his own tastes for travel and adventure were expressed in a preference for the career of ordinary naval officer over that of naval surgeon, which had been the customary familial role in the senior service. Having entered the Royal Naval College, Osborne, in 1911, at the age of twelve, he proceeded to the Royal Naval College, Dartmouth, in 1913, but his education was interrupted the following year with the outbreak of the First World War. He soon saw active service as a midshipman, particularly in the Dardanelles, where he was seriously wounded when still only sixteen years old. However, he recovered and was sent to King's College, Cambridge, at the end of the war to make good his formal education. There he consolidated his interest in international affairs, cultivated his love for English literature, and developed his mastery of foreign languages, including German. He was promoted to the rank of lieutenant in 1919, returned to active service and pursued his naval career with distinction until his retirement on 15 December 1927, with the rank of lieutenant-commander.

By then Hillgarth had already embarked upon a second career as a writer of adventure novels. He was an author who understood that the best research for his literary genre was personal experience. Thus, a prospecting trip to Bolivia in 1928 yielded not gold but literary treasure—*The Black Mountain* (1933), his fifth and penultimate novel, which was favourably reviewed by Graham Greene and translated into Spanish. In 1929 Hillgarth married Mary Sidney Katharine Almina (*b.* 1896), third daughter of Herbert Coulstoun Gardner, Baron Burghclere, and former wife of Geoffrey Hope Hope-Morley, later Baron Hollenden. They had two daughters, and a son who became professor of history at the University of Toronto. They lived on the island of Majorca where Hillgarth was appointed British vice-consul at Palma in 1932. He was therefore strategically located at the outbreak of the Spanish Civil War in 1936.

Throughout that conflict Hillgarth was busily engaged in humanitarian work, a disinterested labour which culminated in February 1939 in his arranging the peaceful surrender of republican-held Minorca. Hillgarth's civil wartime role in Majorca not only earned him promotion to consul and appointment as OBE in 1937, but also won the admiration of Captain J. H. Godfrey, whose ship, the *Repulse*, was able to visit Barcelona in 1938, free from fear of fascist air attack, thanks to Hillgarth's influence with the Francoist camp. When Franco won the civil war in 1939 Godfrey, then director of naval intelligence, secured the appointment of Hillgarth, who was fluent in Spanish, as naval attaché in Madrid (with promotion to the rank of commander, and in 1940, captain) where his many contacts with the new regime could be exploited in the British interest.

Godfrey never regretted his choice, coming to regard Hillgarth as a 'super-attaché' (Beesly, 143) in view of the latter's varied and valuable services to the British cause in Spain during the Second World War. These included the deterrence of the Francoist authorities from all but desultory collaboration in the Nazi logistical effort to refuel and resupply their U-boats in Spanish ports. The vigilant team of agents which Hillgarth organized throughout the Spanish ports limited incidents of submarine reprovisioning to about twenty-six and also cut short a campaign conducted by Italian human torpedoes against royal naval ships in Gibraltar harbour. However, the naval attaché also moderated British policy towards Spain. Hillgarth, and under his influence Britain's wartime ambassador to Spain, Sir Samuel Hoare, succeeded in dissuading London from applying so rigorous an economic blockade of Franco's Spain as to push that country into the war, at the very time, 1940–41, that the odds were already so heavily stacked against British survival. Again, Hillgarth's role in alerting the British government to the dangers of precipitate, preventive military action against Iberian territory was crucial in averting an unnecessary provocation of hostilities with Franco, at this most delicate juncture in the war. Winston Churchill was ready to listen to Hillgarth's counsels of prudence on Spain because he knew the attaché personally, had real affection for him, and regarded him as a 'very good' man, 'equipped with a profound knowledge of Spanish affairs' (Churchill's handwritten comment on A. H. Hillgarth to W. S. Churchill, 27 July 1940, PRO, PREM 4/21/2A).

With such powerful support it was no wonder that Hillgarth was afforded an unusual authority over, and autonomy within, the sphere of British intelligence operations in Spain. Much to the professional envy of MI6's Kim Philby, Hillgarth was granted substantial funds to maintain his own network of information and influence in

Franco's Spain. However, his clandestine activities were not confined to espionage. He won London's approval for a large-scale effort to bribe leading Spanish generals (half in cash down and half in a blocked account in Argentina) to exert themselves in favour of upholding their country's non-belligerency. Using the good offices of the financier Juan March, Hillgarth was able to disburse large sums among members of the Spanish military to secure Spain's neutrality. The scale and significance of this affair may be deduced from the fact that the British were trying in the autumn of 1941 to free from US government control 10 million dollars which had been paid to Spaniards 'for a consideration', an effort being made at Churchill's prompting: 'We must not lose them now after all we have spent—and gained. Vital strategic issues depend on Spain keeping out or resisting [German invasion]' (A. H. Hillgarth's 'most secret' note, not dated, for W. S. Churchill, and Churchill's comment dated 25 Sept 1941 on Sir Kingsley Wood's minute of 23 Sept 1941, PRO, PREM 4/32/7).

By 1943 the battle for Spanish neutrality was won. In 1943 Hillgarth was transferred to Asia to become chief of intelligence, Eastern Fleet. The following year he was appointed chief of British naval intelligence, eastern theatre. In these positions he developed an intelligence organization whose high-grade product, particularly that emanating from the cryptanalytical establishment, HMS *Anderson*, materially aided the allied war effort at sea against Japan and eased US naval resentment at the belated participation of a British Pacific Fleet in that struggle. Ian Fleming, a future spy novelist, but then a colleague of Hillgarth in naval intelligence, was sufficiently impressed by his performance in the Pacific theatre of the war, to describe him to a friend as 'a useful petard and a good war-winner' (Lycett, 158).

In 1943 Hillgarth was appointed CMG. His first marriage having been dissolved in 1946, in 1947 he married Jean Mary (*d.* 1975), daughter of Frank Cobb, who owned and ran a silverware manufacturing firm in Sheffield; they had two sons and a daughter. He retired to an estate in co. Tipperary, Ireland, where he devoted much time to his passion for forestry. He walked several miles a day, inspecting his trees. He also joined the Rio Tinto Company and acted as Juan March's representative in the UK. Of medium height, he had dark brown hair and eyes, with pronouncedly bushy eyebrows. He had a slight figure, which gave the impression of immense energy, and he was always well dressed. Later in life, he became a Roman Catholic. Despite his literary inclinations, he refrained from writing memoirs, believing that an intelligence operative has a lifelong responsibility under the Official Secrets Act. However, an internal history of the Far East and Pacific War, which he wrote with R. T. Barrett, can now be freely consulted in the Public Record Office. Nevertheless, much remained secret. He died on 28 February 1978 at his home, Illannanagh House, Ballinderry, co. Tipperary, Ireland. DENIS SMYTH, rev.

Sources W. S. Churchill, *The Second World War*, 2–3 (1949–50) · P. Elphick, *Far Eastern file: the intelligence war in the Far East, 1930–1945* (1997) · P. Beesly, *Very special admiral: the life of Admiral J. H. Godfrey* (1980) · M. Gilbert, *Winston S. Churchill*, 6: *Finest hour, 1939–1941* (1983) · D. McLachlan, *Room 39: naval intelligence in action, 1939–1945* (1968) · K. Philby, *My secret war* (1968) · N. West, *MI6: British secret intelligence operations, 1909–45* (1983) · private information (1986) · CUL, Templewood MSS · *WWW* · D. Smyth, *Diplomacy and strategy of survival: British policy and Franco's Spain, 1940–41* (1986) · A. H. Hillgarth to W. S. Churchill, 27 July 1940, PRO, PREM 4/21/2A · Sir Kingsley Wood, minute, 23 Sept 1941, PRO, PREM 4/32/7 · A. Lycett, *Ian Fleming* (1995), 158 · b. cert. · Burke, *Peerage* (1921) · *CGPLA Éire* (1978)

Archives CUL, Templewood MSS

Wealth at death £18,395: probate, 31 Aug 1978, *CGPLA Éire*

Hilliard, Laurence (1582–1648), miniature painter, was born probably at the London tenement where his parents lived in Gutter Lane, adjoining Goldsmiths' Hall, and was baptized at St Vedast-alias-Foster, Foster Lane, Cheapside, on 5 March 1582, the fourth of the seven children of Nicholas *Hilliard (1547?–1619), miniature painter, and his first wife, Alice Brandon (*bap.* 1556); she was a daughter of Nicholas's former master, Robert Brandon, goldsmith, of London, and his first wife, Katherine Barber. Laurence was named after his maternal grandmother, daughter of an Exeter goldsmith, John Wall, to whom his grandfather Richard had been apprenticed. His surname appears in his signature on his will as Hillyard.

Throughout his career Nicholas Hilliard had been plagued by money troubles, and in a letter to his loyal patron Sir Robert Cecil, dated 28 July 1601, he said that he could not have afforded to have remained in London in Queen Elizabeth's service if he had not also done 'common' but better-paid works for other people (Hatfield House, Nicholas Hilliard MS, CP 87/25). Hoping to train more limners for the queen's service, he had taken various foreign and English pupils and had been unable to give enough instruction to his son. On 7 June 1605 Laurence Hilliard became a freeman of the Goldsmiths' Company, not by a completed apprenticeship but by virtue of his father's freedom. In his letter of 1601 Nicholas Hilliard had urged Cecil to take Laurence into his service: he had 'an enterance into well wryting and drawing [miniature painting]' (ibid.). The predictable response was that Nicholas should provide more art training; and in a letter dated 6 May 1606—a year after Cecil had become first earl of Salisbury—he reported that Laurence was now giving good service to James I (who had acceded to the English throne in 1603) in making miniatures and gold medals (Hatfield House, Nicholas Hilliard MS, CP 115/130). In 1599 Nicholas Hilliard had (belatedly) been granted an annuity of £40 as the sovereign's limner, and on 13 October 1608— probably thanks to Lord Salisbury—Laurence was granted the office in reversion after his father's death. This was confirmed by patent dated 13 October 1619. Laurence continued in office under Charles I, who acquired some of his father's works from him. Laurence's annuity stopped at the outbreak of the civil war in 1642, but the office remained nominally in being, and after the restoration of Charles II the portrait painter Sir Peter Lely succeeded him.

Some of the stock miniatures of James I, Queen Anne of

Denmark, and their family done before 1619 can probably be attributed to Laurence Hilliard rather than Nicholas, but the son inherited none of the brilliance or versatility of the father. Only a few signed miniatures by him are now known; these bear a Roman monogram LH or HL. An example of his work, a lady wearing a wide-brimmed hat, is in the Victoria and Albert Museum, London, and an unknown man (1640) is in the Fitzwilliam Museum, Cambridge. On 4 December 1611, at St Saviour's, Southwark, Laurence married Jane Farmer (*bap.* 1579), the daughter of a well-to-do merchant family called Cullymore, his near neighbours in the Cheapside parish of St Mary-le-Bow; she was the widow of George Farmer, haberdasher, who had died earlier that year. The couple settled in the parish of St Bride, Fleet Street, where they had three sons and one daughter. In 1648 Laurence Hilliard died in that parish and was buried in St Bride's on 23 February. His will, made seven years earlier, includes information about then intended bequests of works of art. His eldest son, Brandon Hilliard (1612–1672), was forced to flee to France and the West Indies during the Commonwealth, and at the restoration of Charles II in 1660 he was among many petitioners seeking recompense for past unpaid royal service and subsequent hardships. Brandon said that his father and grandfather had served Charles II's father, grandfather, and ancestors as limners for eighty years, and that £600 was owing of Laurence's annuity. Brandon was buried at St Clement Danes in the Strand on 2 March 1672. It seems that there were no male descendants of Nicholas Hilliard after this generation.   MARY EDMOND

Sources Nicholas Hilliard MS, 28 July 1601, Hatfield House, Hertfordshire, CP 87/25 · Nicholas Hilliard MS, 6 May 1606, Hatfield House, Hertfordshire, CP 115/130 · *The visitation of London, anno Domini 1633, 1634, and 1635, made by Sir Henry St George*, 1, ed. J. J. Howard and J. L. Chester, Harleian Society, 15 (1880), 386 [Hilliard pedigree (supplied by Laurence 1634)] · Laurence Hilliard's will, PRO, PROB 11/203/45 · Laurence Hilliard's patent as sovereign's limner, PRO, E 403/2699/9 · M. Edmond, *Hilliard and Oliver: the lives and works of two great miniaturists* (1983) · E. Auerbach, *Nicholas Hilliard* (1961), 224–32 · M. Edmond, 'Limners and picturemakers', *Walpole Society*, 47 (1978–80), 60–242, esp. 68–72 · J. Murdoch and others, *The English miniature* (1981), 61–2, 84 · G. Reynolds, *English portrait miniatures* (1952); rev. edn (1988), 34–5 · C. Lloyd and V. Remington, *Masterpieces in little* (1996), 14–15, 64, 68, 74 [exhibition catalogue, Queen's Gallery, Buckingham Palace, 23 July – 5 Oct 1997] · records, Goldsmiths' Company
Archives Goldsmith's Hall, London, MSS | Hatfield House, Hertfordshire, corresp. with Nicholas Hilliard

Hilliard, Nicholas (1547?–1619), miniature painter, was the eldest of the four sons and four daughters of Richard Hilliard (*d.* 1594), leading citizen and goldsmith of Exeter in Devon, and his wife, Laurence, daughter of Richard's former master, John Wall. Nicholas was probably born in 1547, the year of the death of Henry VIII and the accession of his son, Edward VI.

Early years Richard Hilliard and the 'princely merchant' John Bodley were zealous supporters of the Reformed religion and in 1549 became involved in the siege of Exeter by west-country Roman Catholics—then in the majority—

Nicholas Hilliard (1547?–1619), self-portrait, 1577

who were violently opposed to the young king's protestant prayer book. At Edward's death in 1553, and the accession of his Roman Catholic half-sister, Mary I, many English protestants fled to the continent to escape persecution. Among them was John Bodley, who went first to Wesel and Frankfurt in Germany and then to Switzerland. At some point Bodley summoned his entire household to join him, and on 7 June 1557 they were admitted to the English congregation in the Calvinist stronghold of Geneva, of which John Knox was a minister. In the party was Nicholas Hilliard, then aged about ten, a little younger than Bodley's son Thomas (later founder of the great Bodleian Library at Oxford). Richard Hilliard no doubt allowed his eldest son to go abroad for his own safety, perhaps paying for the privilege. This gave the boy an unexpectedly early chance to learn French and to get his first look at the works of continental artists.

Large numbers of goldsmiths were arriving in Geneva at this time, most of them Huguenot refugees from Paris and Rouen. Among a group admitted on 15 October 1557 was Pierre Olivyer from Rouen, presumed to be the father of Isaac Oliver, future pupil and then rival of Nicholas Hilliard. Elizabeth I acceded to the English throne at the death of her half-sister, Mary, on 17 November 1558, and this, together with the church settlement of 1559, allowed the protestant exiles to return home. John Bodley received permission to leave Geneva on 5 September 1559; he settled in London and young Hilliard probably remained in the household. He was now able to study the miniatures of Hans Holbein the younger, who had fallen victim to an outbreak of plague in London at the end of 1543. Later he was to express profound admiration for the German master: 'the most excellent [easel] painter and limner … after the life that ever was' (Hilliard, *Arte of Limning*, 69).

Apprenticeship, 1562–1569 Nicholas Hilliard and his younger brother John were both apprenticed to, and lodged with, leading goldsmiths in Cheapside, the most famous street in the city of London. (The third and fourth brothers, who remained in Devon, were Jeremy, who died in 1631/2, an Exeter goldsmith with their father, and Ezekiel, a clergyman). Goldsmiths' Hall was, and the present one still is, on the north side of Westcheap, near St Paul's and in the parish of St Vedast, Foster Lane, and Goldsmiths' Row was the particular glory of the south side. John Stow, in his *Survey of London* (1598), describes the row, built in 1491, as 'the most beautiful frame of fayre houses and shoppes … within the Walles of London, or else where in England'—ten houses and fourteen shops within the frame, all four storeys high (1.345). Hilliard's master, Robert Brandon, a wealthy man who had become a freeman of the Goldsmiths' Company by redemption (purchase) in 1548, had his establishment at the sign of the Gilt Lion, and from 1583 until his death in 1591 he was chamberlain of London—in effect chief executive. John Hilliard's master, Edward Gylbert, at the sign of The Ship, was an alderman in the early 1560s.

Robert Brandon had married his first wife, Katherine Barber, on 13 June 1548 at the church of St Mary Woolnoth in Lombard Street, so it was she who kept a motherly eye on young Hilliard when he joined the household on 13 November 1562. Of the couple's seven children who survived to adulthood the third, Alice, was baptized at St Peter Westcheap (adjoining St Vedast to the east) on 11 May 1556. At the age of twenty she became Hilliard's wife and, subsequently, the mother of his children. Brandon played an important part in Hilliard's career: he was a leading goldsmith and jeweller to Queen Elizabeth, and taught those arts—so closely allied to limning—to his apprentice.

Most of the artists in London at the time were foreigners, as Hilliard notes in his treatise: 'generally they are the best, and most in number' (Hilliard, *Arte of Limning*, 69). Henry VIII had secured the services of members of two of the leading Ghent–Bruges families, the Horneboltes and the Bennincks, to enhance the lustre of the Tudor dynasty. Gerard Hornebolte of Ghent, court painter to Margaret of Austria, regent of the Netherlands, and renowned for his miniatures in illuminated manuscripts, travelled to London with his family about 1525. He probably returned to the continent later, but his son Lucas and daughter Susanna stayed on, and Lucas appears in the royal household accounts as king's painter, and was granted a property in the parish of St Margaret's, Westminster, where he would have had his home and studio. He is said to have taught Holbein the techniques of limning, and he died very shortly after him, in the spring of 1544. Susanna, also a painter, died while Hilliard was still a boy but he would have seen work by her when he eventually reached London. Simon Benninck, born in Ghent but buried in Bruges, was regarded as the best illuminator in Europe. His eldest daughter, Levina, who certainly became a miniaturist, married George Teerlinc of Blankenbergh, and was appointed 'paintrix' to the Tudor court, with an annuity of £40, in 1546. Although a rather shadowy figure, of modest talent, she remained in office until her death thirty years later. She and/or others may have given Hilliard some

advice, and he probably had her partly in mind when he wrote in the treatise of 'an excellent white … made of quicksilver which draweth a very fine line; this white the women painters use' (ibid., 91). It was a subject of particular interest to him; exquisite renderings of the Elizabethan ruff are a feature of many of his limnings.

No doubt Robert Brandon often took his apprentice to help when he was working at court, and presumably he presented Hilliard to the queen when his skill in limning became apparent. Hilliard himself does not disclose who may have given him instruction in any art: inscriptions in gold are a feature of some of his finest miniatures, and he would presumably have sought some instruction from a master calligrapher. Hilliard states, more than once, his conviction that in painting or drawing from the life the most important part is 'the truth of the line' (Hilliard, *Arte of Limning*, 85), and that in limning the face should usually be done without shadowing. If shadowing really is required it must be done 'with the point of the pencil [tip of the brush] by little light touches' (ibid., 101). He strongly advises the aspiring limner to begin by repeatedly copying the hatching (shadowing) in Dürer's small engraved pieces with the pen until the print is so accurately copied that 'one shall not know the one from the other'; then, when the tip of the brush can be used in the same way, he may begin to limn. 'This is the true order and principal secret in limning' (ibid.).

Most of the artists mentioned in the treatise were, like Albrecht Dürer (1471–1528), the sons of master goldsmiths and were better known at the time of writing as engravers rather than painters. Hilliard considers Dürer the most perfect engraver on copper 'since the world began', although his rules for painting and engraving are for the most part hard to remember and tedious to follow (Hilliard, *Arte of Limning*, 69). There were plenty of works of all kinds by the 'strangers' in London for Hilliard to study, and Graham Reynolds takes the view that in limning Hilliard was largely self-taught.

The treatise This exists, so far as is known, only as the first part of a manuscript now in Edinburgh University Library. It is dated 'the 18 of March 1624 Londres' (Hilliard, *Arte of Limning*, 115) and is in the hand of an unknown copyist. It was not published in full, as a book on its own, until 1981, and the editors, R. K. R. Thornton and T. G. S. Cain, gave it the short title *The Arte of Limning*. A long title preceding the text at Edinburgh is in the hand not of Hilliard but of the eighteenth-century antiquary George Vertue, who owned the manuscript for a time. They do not consider the copyist to have been very intelligent or careful (ibid., 33–4) and provide an exact transcript with a facing text (quoted in this article) with modernized spelling and several emendations. In 1598 Dr Richard Haydocke of New College, Oxford, had published a translation of Paolo Lomazzo's treatise on the arts (Milan, 1584), of which the first part is on easel painting. He then, by his own account, persuaded Hilliard—so famous at home and abroad—to write something similar on limning. The result is thought to date to about 1600 and sets out the author's beliefs, experiences, and accumulated knowledge at the end of the greatest period of his career. It seems to be an early draft, which perhaps partly accounts for its freshness and spontaneity. It is one of the most important documents in the history of English art and, unusually, includes insights into the mind and character of the author.

Hilliard emphatically declares that limning is the highest form of art, and the perfection of it 'to imitate the face of mankind' (Hilliard, *Arte of Limning*, 75). It is most properly practised by gentlemen and 'for the service of noble persons very meet', since it requires the presence of the sitter for most of the time: the limner must be a gentleman 'of good parts and ingenuity', able to provide 'seemly attendance' (ibid., 65). Hilliard has sometimes been derided for making unjustified claims to gentility but this charge is not borne out by the evidence. He spent his whole professional life at the higher levels of society; he is nearly always referred to in contemporary records as Master Hilliard; and it is an undoubted gentleman who appears in the celebrated self-portrait miniature of 1577 (V&A), dressed in black with an elegant ruff and a black bonnet—embellished with ornaments no doubt fashioned by himself—set on the curly hair inherited from his father. In a declaration signed by his son Laurence *Hilliard, provided in 1634 in response to an official inquiry into arms and pedigrees, the head of the family (and grandfather of Nicholas) is entered as John Hylliard, a gentleman of Cornwall the south-western tip of England adjoining Devon.

Hilliard writes as a perfectionist in love with his art: it breeds delight, removes melancholy, avoids 'evil occasions' and cures rage (Hilliard, *Arte of Limning*, 67). Near the start there is an outburst against 'botchers' and 'bunglers' who increase so fast that good artists tend to abandon their best skill, 'for all men carry one price' (ibid., 63). His indignation erupts again later on, sandwiched between *The Sapphire* and *The Emerald*, in a long passage about colours and precious stones (ibid., 107). The best practitioners—of whatever art—are usually poorer than the bunglers, because their work takes them longer. They prefer to demonstrate their art in a single piece, while the others turn out six or seven, pleasing most people, since time is of the essence and a lower price all-important. This time the main target is the bungling jeweller, who often spoils a precious stone, while the expert improves on nature in the cutting, polishing, and setting, thereby doubling its value.

The treatise sets out strict rules for the conduct of the limner: moderation in eating and sleeping, and no 'violent exercise in sports', although a little dancing or a game of bowls is permissible; everything must be scrupulously clean, with no dust, smoke, noise, or stench (Hilliard, *Arte of Limning*, 73, 75). This must have been difficult when Hilliard was working at home in one of the small alleys off Westcheap. The aspect of the workplace should be 'northward, somewhat toward the east, commonly without sun shining in'. 'Discreet talk or reading, quiet mirth or music, offend not'—they 'quicken the spirit' in limner and sitter. In an apparent tribute to his father Hilliard says that a wise man finds out the natural inclinations of his children

early and sets them on the right course. But natural ability is not enough and he urges the limner to be 'diligent, yea ever diligent … to excel all others' (ibid., 65).

The limner must use only the finest vellum (parchment), 'from young things found in the dam's belly' (Hilliard, *Arte of Limning*, 97), 'dressed as smooth as any satin' (ibid., 99), and stuck onto card. Hilliard was extremely innovative technically and, with the specialized knowledge of a jeweller, he writes much of the importance of 'giving the true lustre to pearl and precious stone' and 'working gold and silver with themselves' (ibid., 63). He ground leaves of the metals to powder, mixed them with a little gum water, and burnished them with 'a pretty little tooth of some ferret or stoat or other wild little beast' (ibid., 99). Of the sitters he writes with delight of 'those lovely graces, witty smilings, and those stolen glances which suddenly like lightning pass' (ibid., 77); and with disgust of know-all sitters and studio visitors who try to instruct the limner. He has no space to recount all the 'ridiculous, absurd speeches' he has had to endure. His advice to the limner is to keep his temper, proceed with his work, and 'pity their ignorance' (ibid., 97, 99).

Instant renown, 1570–1576 Nicholas Hilliard completed his apprenticeship, and became a freeman of the Goldsmiths' Company, on 29 July 1569. He entered the new decade a complete and versatile artist, at the age of about twenty-two—goldsmith, limner, jeweller, calligrapher, and designer for engravings. (The editors of *The Arte of Limning* use a woodcut border dating to the 1570s, with an NH monogram centre top and probably designed by Hilliard, for the title-page of their book; the border was used for several different titles in the sixteenth century.) Queen Elizabeth had been alarmed in the early years of her reign by the poor quality of royal representations, and she was no doubt much relieved that an artist of distinction was now free to serve her. She was just as much aware of the importance of 'the image' as any public figure in our own times.

Hilliard's first known adult miniature is dated 1571, when his sitter was *A Man Aged 35* (priv. coll.); the next, dated 1572, is of *A Man Aged 24* (V&A) and shows the full excellence of Hilliard's developed style. Sadly both have to be described as 'Unknown'. All researchers would echo the words of John Aubrey (1626–1697), author of *Brief Lives*, who once lamented, ''Tis pity that in noblemen's galleries [and elsewhere] the names are not writ on or behind the pictures'.

Hilliard took a number of apprentices, both English and foreign, during his career; the first was John Cobbold, who was transferred to him in 1570 by the widow of Cobbold's former master on payment by Hilliard of 40s. for her goodwill, with the promise of a further 20s. in a year's time. In 1571 a foreign goldsmith called Gualter Reynolds (born in Brunswick and attending the Dutch church), who had come to England to increase his knowledge of his art, was probably being supervised by Hilliard, on his company's orders, to ensure that Reynolds did not try to usurp any privileges enjoyed by native-born goldsmiths. On 13 March 1573 William Smythe was apprenticed to Hilliard;

on the following 20 July, William Franke (probably a German), who had begun an apprenticeship with Edward Gylbert, former master of Hilliard's brother John, was transferred to Hilliard and entered his household, replacing Cobbold, who had been freed the month before. John Pickering was apprenticed to Hilliard on 21 March 1575.

Years later, in a letter dated 28 July 1601 to his loyal patron Sir Robert Cecil (then the queen's chief secretary), Hilliard recalled that the original intention in taking apprentices had been 'to provide for the Queen's better service' (Hilliard, MS letter, Hatfield House, CP 87/25). The apprentices—it is possible to find clues to about nine in all—had 'pleased the common sorte exceding well' (by 'common' he means people of good but not noble birth: 'commoners', as we would say); but he too had been forced to do 'common woorkes for other persons' in addition to his royal duties, since they were 'more proffitable' (ibid., 69). In the treatise he pointedly refers to Henry VIII's 'royal bounty' to his artists, implicitly criticizing the parsimony of his daughter (Hilliard, *Arte of Limning*, 69). In other countries, he maintains, artists are by 'pension or reward of princes ... competently maintained', but not in England, 'the more is the pity' (ibid., 109). In defence of Queen Elizabeth, she had acceded to the throne of a country encumbered by debts, inflation, and a debased currency, and was determined to practise extreme thrift and caution in the manner of her grandfather Henry VII. But although in private she was a woman of frugal habits, no expense was spared on her public appearances, which were designed for the greater glory of her realm.

The first of Hilliard's many limnings of the queen (NPG) is dated 1572. He had met members of the Knollys family during the period of English protestant exile in Geneva, and it is likely that Sir Francis, the queen's first cousin by marriage, who had become treasurer of the royal household on 13 July 1572, actually commissioned the artist. During the first sitting, by his account, Elizabeth asked about shadowing, and Hilliard replied that while 'great pictures', displayed high up or far off, required 'hard shadows', these were not necessary for small ones, which had to be 'viewed ... in hand near unto the eye' (ibid., 85, 87). Shakespeare mentions the art of limning several times; both *Hamlet* and the treatise are supposed to have been written about 1600, and in the former the prince, confronting his mother in her bedchamber, invites her to:

> Look here upon this picture, and on this,
> The counterfeit presentment of two brothers.
> (*Hamlet*, III. iv)

Hilliard, in his advice to the queen, advocated 'open light' for a limning and he reports that it was she who 'chose ... to sit in the open alley of a goodly garden, where no tree was near' (Hilliard, *Arte of Limning*, 87). The artist, in his mid-twenties, was about 6 feet (his recommended distance for a portrait miniature) from the queen, in her late thirties, and they may well have sat in the privy garden of the palace of Whitehall. Hilliard concludes that it would take 'some better clerk' to speak or write about later conversations with the queen, which probably were spread over the years.

At some time in the 1570s Hilliard became involved in a typical Elizabethan 'adventure'—one of his frequent over-optimistic attempts to make some money. This one was to promote goldmining in Scotland. A Dutch fellow artist and lapidary, Cornelius Devosse, persuaded Hilliard to take part in the scheme, no doubt believing that his powerful connections would be helpful. Another friend, Arthur Van Brounckhorst, acting as their agent, would 'set sundry workmen to work' at Crawford Moor in Lanarkshire, as Stephen Atkinson, in *The Discoverie and Historie of the Gold Mynes in Scotland* (written 1619; ed. G. L. Meason, 1825), recorded. Not surprisingly, 'Mr Hilliard and Cornelius Devosse lost all their charges, and never since got any recompense' (Atkinson, 35).

Hilliard notes that artists are 'generally given to travel, and to confer with wise men' (Hilliard, *Arte of Limning*, 109). By 1576 he must have decided that he would do well to follow suit. In that year he painted a limning of the queen's favourite Robert Dudley, earl of Leicester, then aged forty-four (NPG). On 25 June he may have ridden out to the then fashionable village of Stepney for the funeral of Levina Teerlinc—if indeed she had helped him during his youth. Three weeks later, on 15 July, he married Alice Brandon at the church of St Vedast, Foster Lane, and in the following month they sailed for France.

In France, 1576–1578 The newly appointed English ambassador to France was Sir Amyas Paulet, a prominent puritan and a faithful servant to the queen who, like so many Elizabethan Englishmen, incurred much personal expense in the performance of public duties. He landed at Calais on 25 September 1576, *en route* for Paris. By December, sending his latest expense account to the exchequer in London, he complained that his train had been greatly enlarged by 'divers gentlemen' recommended by the queen, including 'Mr Helyer' (Edmond, 61). Elizabeth had presumably instructed her limner to provide likenesses (which he did) of François, duc d'Alençon, the subject of her last and longest matrimonial ploy (examples in the Musée de Condé, Chantilly; Kunsthistorisches Museum, Vienna; and BM). Alençon was the third son of Catherine de' Medici and brother of Henri III of France, and for a time both women had wanted an alliance. In 1577 the words 'Nicolas Béliart, peintre anglois' appear in Alençon's household accounts.

Hilliard's fluent French, acquired during his time in Geneva as a boy, allowed him to fit easily into French society, and there is considerable evidence of his friendship with leading artists and others. One of his greatest admirers was Blaise de Vigenère, philosopher and man of letters, who negotiated with him to provide wood-engravings of the duc and duchesse de Nevers. Hilliard seems to have stayed with the goldsmith and medallist Germain Pilon and to have met Jacques Gaultier the painter and Léonard Gaultier the engraver, and the poet Ronsard.

Queen Elizabeth became restive at the continuing absence of her gifted limner, and on 19 February 1578 Ambassador Paulet wrote to Sir Francis Walsingham to give an assurance that 'Helyar' had no intention of leaving her service. He had gone to France simply 'to increase his knowledge … and upon hope [apparently unfulfilled] to get a piece of money of the lords and ladies here for his better maintenance in England at his return' (Edmond, 65). He intended to return 'very shortly', bringing his wife with him; he was understandably anxious to do so since Alice was in the later stages of her first pregnancy. But on 16 June the ambassador wrote from Paris to tell the earl of Hertford that Hilliard had been ill. He now hoped to finish a promised jewel 'within three weeks' and would then send or deliver it. It had been supposed that Richard Hilliard went over to France to collect his daughter-in-law in 1577, since that is the date on his son's miniature of him (V&A), but recent rigorous re-examination, using the most advanced techniques, suggests that the last figure had flaked away and been repainted at some stage, so perhaps the date should read 1578, for Alice's baby was baptized (Daniel) at St Vedast, Foster Lane, on 16 May of that year.

In London, on 22 August, Hilliard's apprentice William Franke sought to be admitted to the Goldsmiths' Company, but his master was still 'beyond the seas', and he was told to wait for six weeks, while Master Warden Robert Brandon wrote to his son-in-law. A master was required to present his young man to the company's court in person, and in fact Franke had to wait more than six weeks. He finally became a freeman on 3 November 1578.

Back home: supremacy Shortly after Hilliard's return from France the family settled into a tenement at the sign of The Maidenhead, owned by the Goldsmiths' Company and close to their hall. The exact date of the move is not known. The Maidenhead was on the west side of Gutter Lane and just within the parish of St Vedast, Foster Lane, where the rest of the Hilliard children were baptized: Elizabeth (1579), Francis (1580), Laurence (1582), Lettice (1583), Penelope (1586), and Robert (1588). The queen herself may have been godmother to Elizabeth; it was not unknown for a Tudor monarch to oblige when a baby was born to a member of the household or, like Hilliard, a close servant. The godfather of Francis was probably Sir Francis Knollys; Laurence took his name from his paternal grandmother; the names of the last three powerfully suggest godparents from the circle of the queen's principal favourite, Lord Leicester, and his successor, the second earl of Essex. Lettice was the name of the eldest daughter of Knollys, wife of the first earl of Essex and mother of their eldest daughter, Penelope (b. 1562?), and a brother, Robert (b. 1566). Leicester had become stepfather to the pair by secretly marrying Lettice in 1578, and he did much to promote the advancement at court of the young earl. No likeness is known to survive of the formidable Penelope, but in 1581 she was married off to Robert, third Baron Rich, and about eight years later the poet Henry Constable wrote a sonnet addressed to 'Mr Hilliard, upon occasion of

a picture he made of the Ladie Rich'. This includes a reference to Hilliard's universally admired method of portraying jewels. Before him:

> no man knew aright,
> To give to stones and pearls true dye and light.
> (*The Poems and Sonnets of Henry Constable*, ed. J. Gray, 1897, cited in Edmond, 94)

The original employment of limners had been to provide small, private portraits for 'noble persons', as Hilliard explains—for themselves and their peers (Hilliard, *Arte of Limning*, 65)—but inevitably, as time went on, the range of sitters widened to include men of achievement, such as Hilliard's fellow Devonians Ralegh (NPG) and Drake, and indeed anyone who could pay. In addition to the men Hilliard limned a number of beautiful but often sadly 'Unknown' ladies. He was convinced that 'rare beauties are … more commonly found in this isle of England than elsewhere' (ibid., 73).

In the 1580s and earlier part of the 1590s Hilliard continued to paint many of his finest miniatures. A draft warrant dated 1584 states his monopoly right to paint limnings of the queen but it has sometimes been misinterpreted to mean a diminution of his duties in relation to those of the then serjeant-painter, George Gower. In fact the serjeant-painter's court office was in the realm of painters and decorators rather than of art: the holder of the office headed a department responsible for the maintenance and embellishment of the royal palaces and other residences. The activities of successive serjeant-painters are more often than not to be found in the works accounts (Exchequer E 351 series, PRO).

In 1584 Hilliard's responsibilities increased: he secured the important, but costly and time-consuming, commission to design the second great seal of the realm, the first being more or less worn out. This probably caused some resentment among engravers. The actual engraving, or most of it, seems to have been done by Derick Anthony, of an immigrant family originally from Germany, and the seal came into use in 1586. On 8 November of that year Hilliard delivered a letter from Sir Francis Walsingham to the chancellor of the exchequer, saying that the queen 'was pleased to bestow' on her limner 'a lease in reversion' of £40 a year for his work on the seal and 'divers other services', for which he had received no recompense or allowance (Blakiston, 103). This was but one of a number of dubious royal promises, several involving small properties, leases, and tithes, which did not benefit Hilliard in any way; they were a device for avoiding spending real money. 'In reversion' usually meant 'after someone else'—in practice, 'never'. The main benefit of the office of royal limner was undoubtedly the prestige it conferred—the value of being 'spoken of', as Hilliard once said (Hilliard, *Arte of Limning*, 109).

A rival emerges: late 1580s From the 1580s, for a short period from about 1587 to 1595, Hilliard began to produce a few limnings, larger than his customary small oval ones, known as cabinet miniatures, all full-lengths of men, and all but one rectangular. (The word miniature did not necessarily mean something very small; like limning and illumination it derived from the Latin *minium*, the red lead used by medieval illuminators to embellish their manuscripts.) It is surely more than mere chance that Hilliard's decision to do something different coincided with the emergence of his former pupil Isaac *Oliver as a serious rival. Oliver's first known miniature, dated 1587, is of a young, middle-class woman (priv. coll.), three-quarter length—perhaps an experiment—but it is immediately followed, in 1588, by assured and accomplished limnings of a youth of nineteen (priv. coll.) and a bearded man of seventy-one, both unidentified, and of a fifty-nine-year-old Dutchman (Dutch royal collection, The Hague). Their sober, naturalistic style is in complete contrast to Hilliard's enigmatic man raising his right hand to clasp one emerging from a cloud—also dated 1588 (V&A)—but reverting to the small oval shape. The significance of the Latin inscription 'Attici amoris ergo' defeats all scholars.

Of Hilliard's larger miniatures the *Young Man among Roses* (V&A), perhaps the first of the new-look group, is without doubt the most famous of all his works, and probably of all English miniatures of any period. It is a unique elongated oval and a supreme example of the miniature as a kind of emblem, device, or *impresa*. The classic definition of the *impresa*, 'as the Italians call it', is by the historian and herald William Camden: ('a device in picture with his motto ... borne by noble and learned personages, to notify some particular conceit [conception, notion] of their own' W. Camden, *Remaines of a Greater Worke Concerning Britain*, 1605, 158). The motto should be in 'some different language'. Hilliard's theme is fidelity—but to whom? The roses with their sharp thorns perhaps symbolize pleasure and pain, fidelity enduring through good times and bad. The inscription, 'Dat poenas laudata fides', is taken from a passage by Lucan—known in translation at the time—saying that fidelity, though praised, can carry penalties when given to people in trouble. Even at the time the significance of this privately commissioned and obviously costly work would have been known only to a small number of people; the meaning of the motto, required by Camden to be 'neither too obscure, nor too plain', is now—four centuries and more later—surely irretrievable. It was David Piper who suggested that the young man might be the earl of Essex (Edmond, 202, n. 16) and this has been strongly argued by Roy Strong in *The English Renaissance Miniature* (1983) and elsewhere. According to Strong, Hilliard must have visited Fontainebleau during his time in France; in his view the *Young Man among Roses* is much influenced by Italian works there.

The subjects of Hilliard's other cabinet miniatures are all well known and include *George Clifford, 3rd Earl of Cumberland* (NMM), *Robert Devereux, 2nd Earl of Essex* (priv. coll.), and *Henry Percy, 9th Earl of Northumberland* (Rijksmuseum, Amsterdam). There are links with the accession day tilts, popular public shows held on 17 November, the date on which Elizabeth became queen.

End of the Elizabethan age Hilliard's duties as royal limner continued. He must have known the famous face better than anyone but, as the years passed, he had the delicate task of combining something of a likeness with the need to promote the legend of the Virgin Queen. No sittings would have been required and the royal tirewomen would have produced the necessary robes and adornments. The queen's jeweller, Robert Brandon, died on 30 May 1591 and was buried at St Vedast, Foster Lane, on 8 June. His long will lists his surviving son, Edward; Alice Hilliard's four married sisters and their husbands, and a young unmarried half-sister by Brandon's second wife; also seventeen grandchildren, not including the Hilliards. Alice's sisters had all 'married well', as Brandon would have seen it. For Alice there was a £50 annuity, to be paid quarterly by way of the Goldsmiths' Company, towards her maintenance. Of Hilliard there is no mention. In 1579 Brandon had lent him the large sum of £70, to be repaid one year later. He wrote in the treatise of artists being 'commonly no misers, but liberal above their little degree'; of sometimes not being in the mood ('in humour') to concentrate on the main work in hand; and of sometimes giving away a rare work 'for very affection' (Hilliard, *Arte of Limning*, 109). He attacked the 'common slander' that such men are 'ever unthrifts', which may hint at resentment over criticisms by an exasperated father-in-law (ibid.).

Hilliard's father, Richard, had made his will on 2 November 1586 but he did not die until the summer of 1594. He bequeathed to Nicholas property in Exeter, and his best gown and gold ring with a cornelian stone in it. In the manner of the day he lists the sons first (John was unnamed, which perhaps confirms that he had died), and then the four daughters—two married and two unmarried. Dates and order of births are unknown. Francis, son of Nicholas Hilliard, is named; his brother, Robert, had not been born when the will was made. Bequests fulfilled, the remainder of the estate went to Richard's widow and executrix, Laurence, who proved the will on 9 August.

Troubles accumulated for Hilliard towards the end of Elizabeth's reign, and his miniatures of this period lack some of his earlier assurance. One deserves mention for literary rather than artistic reasons, that of *Henry Wriothesley, 3rd Earl of Southampton* (FM Cam.)—Shakespeare's patron—who came of age in 1594, the date of the miniature, which had presumably been specially commissioned. If the earl was indeed the 'lovely boy' of the sonnets, as is widely supposed, sonnet 16 would be highly significant. The poet writes of the sitter's 'painted counterfeit' (presumably that of 1594) and in line 10 he refers to 'this times pencil [limner's brush] and my pupil pen'. 'This time's pencil' can surely mean no other than the famous portrayer of the age.

In 1591 Hilliard had been commissioned to design a third great seal; work went on for years in fruitless attempts to satisfy the queen, and in the end the second seal remained in use until her death. This time Hilliard's colleague was Charles Anthony, probably a son of Derick, and it seems that his appointment may again have caused some resentment. On 2 June 1599 Anthony delivered to Sir Robert Cecil a letter in which Hilliard denied that he was competing for Anthony's office, graver of the mint. He had indeed spoken about it at one stage to a member of the household but had learned that Anthony had a written promise from Cecil's late father, Lord Burghley. This incident serves as a reminder of how much lobbying court servants had to do on their own behalf. Hilliard went on to claim that he had missed many commissions because of the work on the projected seal, and he reported that—predictably—he had received only one instalment of the £40 annuity 'in reversion' promised by the queen in 1591. He was now 'brought into great extremes'.

Probably it was thanks to Cecil that an unconditional warrant followed, on 17 August, granting a £40 annuity to her majesty's 'goldsmith and our limner' and making Hilliard a member of the household (warrant, letters patent, PRO). The sum represented no advance on the one granted to the royal 'paintrix' Levina Teerlinc more than half a century earlier. Three years later Hilliard was forced to mortgage the annuity and hand over the patent to meet debts, although the patent was restored in 1611. His father-in-law may well have feared something of the sort when he omitted Hilliard from his will; he was trying to block money intended for his daughter from being diverted to her husband's creditors. On 28 July 1601 Hilliard wrote to Cecil, seeking the queen's permission—which was of course refused—to go abroad again for a year or two. He was sure he could earn enough to pay off his debts 'very easeilye'.

The Goldsmiths' Company were having difficulty during these years in extracting Hilliard's annual rent of £3 for The Maidenhead, and were refusing to renew his lease. Their minutes show that on 19 March 1599 he offered £20 for the lease plus 'a picture' (presumably a miniature, subject unspecified) worth 20 nobles (£6 13s. 4d.); the queen intervened on her servant's behalf by way of the privy council; on 4 July 1600 the company insisted on £30 for the lease, and the 'picture' had become 'a faire picture in greate' of the queen. A minute dated 28 November 1600 notes that Hilliard had promised to pay the money on receipt of the lease; as for the picture the winter was a 'verie unseasonable tyme to worke' (Goldsmiths' Company records). He would do it in the summer. There the matter seems to rest; the company probably stopped pressing for the picture at the queen's death. In any case the entries do not constitute hard evidence that Hilliard ever painted easel pictures, although it is sometimes argued that they do. Various portraits of Elizabeth, in particular the 'Phoenix' (NPG) and the 'Pelican' (Walker Art Gallery, Liverpool), are now often attributed to him on stylistic grounds. The queen died on 24 March 1603, and Hilliard attended the funeral in Westminster Abbey on 28 April, having received the customary allowance of 4 yards of black cloth for his livery. The lord chamberlain's book names the hundreds of people who had been serving the last of the Tudors at the end of Elizabeth's reign; Hilliard is listed as 'picturedrawer' (LC 2/4 (4), PRO).

Last years Hilliard continued as limner to James I, with the £40 annuity. For the first time in fifty-six years England had a married monarch, and James's queen, Anne of Denmark, soon had her own household. Unlike her husband the queen was genuinely interested in art—as their sons,

the princes Henry and Charles, would be—and in 1605 she appointed Isaac Oliver as her limner, again at £40 a year. Hilliard was kept busy for almost the whole of his remaining years, turning out presentation miniatures and gold medals of King James and members of the royal family. The lugubrious Scottish face clearly did not interest him, and he sometimes seems to devote more attention to the clothes and accessories than to the man. Occasionally Hilliard painted a more attractive and characteristic work if the sitter was to his liking. On 7 June 1605 he presented his son Laurence to the Goldsmiths' court to become a freeman of the company, and a week later his last apprentice, Richard Osbaldeston. He was assisted in his work by Laurence, by the painter Rowland Lockey, who had served an eight-year apprenticeship with him from 1581, and perhaps by others. Lockey died in 1616.

Robert Cecil was created earl of Salisbury in 1605. In an undated letter to him, endorsed '1606' by a secretary, Hilliard reports that—true to form—he had sought to 'trim' the late queen's tomb but had been told by the serjeant-painter that that was *his* responsibility. If he had known, Hilliard writes, he would not have been so bold for he had once had 'envy inoughe about a great seale, for … dooing well in other mens offices' (Hilliard, MS letter, Hatfield House, 119/8). In his last surviving letter, dated 26 March 1610, he extols goldsmiths' skills in repairing the highways, which the 'playne Cuntree folke and common laboring men' cannot manage on their own (Hilliard, MS letter, PRO, SP 14/53/43).

At some unknown date Hilliard moved from London to Westminster, presumably to be nearer the court; rent and lease books of this period are notoriously misleading, and no conclusions can be drawn from the Goldsmiths' records. The present frame of Alice Hilliard's miniature (1578; V&A) bears the words 'UXOR PRIMA', and an Alice Hillyard, who could be the miniaturist's wife, was buried at St Margaret's, Westminster, on 16 May 1611. The loss of a homemaker usually prompted a widower and/or son to seek another quickly, and it may be significant that the bachelor Laurence Hilliard married on 4 December 1611 and settled in the parish of St Bride, Fleet Street. The date of Alice Hilliard's burial, if she is correctly identified, would rule out a Susan Gysard, married to a Nicholas Hilliard in 1608, as the supposed second wife. There were a number of Hilliards (variant spellings) in London and Westminster at the time, and more than one Nicholas.

Hilliard and Francis Bacon—now Baron Verulam and lord chancellor—had known each other since their time in France in the 1570s, and it may be that Bacon heard about Hilliard's last illness; a small account book covering 'gifts' and 'rewards' in the autumn of 1618 includes a note about £11 for 'old Mr Hillyard' (PRO, SP 14/99, no. 86). Hilliard died shortly afterwards and was buried at his parish church of St Martin-in-the-Fields on 7 January 1619. He bequeathed 20s. (not then a negligible sum) to the poor of the parish, money for his sister Mrs Anne Avery, and bedding and his best household stuff to his servant Elizabeth Deacon. His estate passed to Laurence Hilliard, who laid out 52s.—much more than for any other parishioner at the time—for the funeral. The estate included what must have been a handsome gold creation, which incorporated miniatures—copied from earlier portraits—of Henry VII, Henry VIII, Edward VI, and his mother, Jane Seymour. It was called the Bosworth jewel and commemorated the battle of 1485, which resulted in the death of Richard III and the start of the Tudor dynasty, and it was eventually conveyed by Laurence to Charles I. The jewel was presumably broken up and sold during the Commonwealth but the miniatures are now back in the Royal Collection.

Reputation Nicholas Hilliard has rarely been out of favour, and his reputation has never been higher than in the twentieth century. A major exhibition, entitled *Nicholas Hilliard & Isaac Oliver*, was mounted in London in 1947, marking the quatercentenary of Hilliard's supposed birth. A second exhibition, of miniatures from 1520 to 1620, followed in 1983. £3 or £4 was the standard rate for a Hilliard miniature without an elaborate setting in his day. A limning of twenty-one-year-old *Jane Coningsby, Mrs Boughton* (priv. coll.), which he did in 1574, sold for £75,000 at Sothebys in 1980, then an auction record for any portrait miniature. The development of colour photography and printing, and television, have enhanced Hilliard's renown. He writes in the *Treatise* of artists in England being mostly immigrants, although he recalls Ronsard saying that when 'the islands' do occasionally produce one, it is often 'in high perfection' (Hilliard, *Arte of Limning*, 69). Hilliard, never one for false modesty, continues: 'I hope there may come out of this our land such a one, this being the greatest and most famous island of Europe' (ibid.). It is not difficult to deduce whom he has in mind. He is one of the outstanding English artists in any medium. It is a happy accident that he was born in time to portray the leading figures of a notable period of English history. MARY EDMOND

Sources N. Hilliard, MS letter to Cecil, 16 March 1594, Hatfield House, Hertfordshire, CP 22/74 • N. Hilliard, MS letter to Cecil, 2 June 1599, Hatfield House, Hertfordshire, CP 70/76 • N. Hilliard, MS letter to Cecil, 28 July 1601, Hatfield House, Hertfordshire, CP 87/25 • N. Hilliard, MS letter to Cecil, 6 May 1606, Hatfield House, Hertfordshire, CP 115/130 • N. Hilliard, MS letter to Cecil, [n.d.], Hatfield House, Hertfordshire, CP 119/8 [endorsed 1606] • N. Hilliard, MS letter to Cecil, 1610, PRO, state papers, SP 14/53/43, 26 March 1610 • warrant, letters patent, 17 Aug 1599, PRO, E 403/2453/316 • N. Hilliard, 'A treatise concerning the arte of limning', U. Edin. L., MS La 3.174 • N. Hilliard, *A treatise concerning the arte of limning*, ed. R. K. R. Thornton and T. G. S. Cain (1981) • Goldsmiths' Company MS records and property plans, Goldsmiths' Hall Library, London • Huguenot Society publications (quarto series): aliens' returns and denizations • *The visitation of London, anno Domini 1633, 1634, and 1635, made by Sir Henry St George*, 1, ed. J. J. Howard and J. L. Chester, Harleian Society, 15 (1880), 386 [Hilliard pedigree supplied by son Laurence, 1634] • Nicholas Hilliard, will, 1619, PRO, PROB 11/133/2 • Richard Helliard, will, 1594, PRO, PROB 11/84/58 • Jeremy Hilliard, will, 1632, PRO, PROB 11/161/2 • Robert Brandon, will, 1591, PRO, PROB 11/77/43 • W. A. Littledale, ed., *The registers of St Vedast, Foster Lane, and of St Michael le Quern, London*, 2 vols., Harleian Society, register section, 29–30 (1902–3) • parish register, St Peter Westcheap, GL, Guildhall MS 6502 • St Martin-in-the-Fields churchwardens' accounts, City Westm. AC, F.2, vol. 2 [amount spent on funeral] • G. Reynolds, *Nicholas Hilliard and Isaac Oliver: an exhibition to commemorate the 400th anniversary of the birth of*

Nicholas Hilliard (1947) [exhibition catalogue, V&A, 1947] • G. Reynolds, *Nicholas Hilliard and Isaac Oliver: an exhibition to commemorate the 400th anniversary of the birth of Nicholas Hilliard*, 2nd edn (1971) [exhibition catalogue, V&A, 1947] • G. Reynolds, *English portrait miniatures* (1952); rev. edn (1988), 11, 17 • G. Reynolds, 'Hilliard, Nicholas', *The dictionary of art*, ed. J. Turner, 14 (1996), 545–8 • E. Auerbach, *Tudor artists* (1954) • E. Auerbach, *Nicholas Hilliard* (1961) • M. Edmond, *Hilliard & Oliver* (1983) • J. Murdoch and others, *The English miniature* (1981) • R. Strong and V. J. Murrell, *Artists of the Tudor court: the portrait miniature rediscovered, 1520–1620* (1983) [exhibition catalogue, V&A, 9 July – 6 Nov 1983] • R. Strong, *The English Renaissance miniature*, rev. edn, 1984 (1983) • J. Murrell, *The way howe to lymne: Tudor miniatures observed* (1983) • K. Hearn, ed., *Dynasties: painting in Tudor and Jacobean England, 1530–1630* (1995) [exhibition catalogue, Tate Gallery, London, 12 Oct 1995 – 7 Jan 1996] • C. Lloyd and V. Remington, *Masterpieces in little* (1996) [exhibition catalogue, Queen's Gallery, Buckingham Palace, 23 July – 5 Oct 1997] • N. Blakiston, 'Queen Elizabeth's third great seal', *Burlington Magazine*, 90 (1948), 103; n. 14 • G. Reynolds, *The sixteenth- and seventeenth-century miniatures in the collection of her majesty the queen* (1999)

Likenesses N. Hilliard, self-portrait, miniature, 1560, priv. coll. • N. Hilliard, self-portrait, miniature, 1577, V&A [*see illus.*]

Hillier, Edward Guy (1857–1924), banker, was born on 11 March 1857 in Cambridge, the posthumous son of Charles Batten Hillier (d. 1856), British consul in Bangkok and sometime chief magistrate of Hong Kong, and his wife, Eliza Mary, the daughter of the Revd Dr W. H. *Medhurst (1796–1857) of the London Missionary Society. He was the youngest son in a family of three sons and one daughter. He was educated at Blundell's School, Tiverton, Devon, and Trinity College, Cambridge, where he gained a BA in Chinese studies. Fluent in the language, he was first employed as tutor to Robert W. Buchanan-Jardine and went to the East as private secretary to the governor of British North Borneo. He briefly joined Jardine Matheson in Hong Kong, but in 1883 was recruited by Ewen Cameron, then Shanghai manager, for the Hongkong and Shanghai Banking Corporation. In 1885, after training in Shanghai, he was sent north to the Tientsin (Tianjin) office and from there to Peking (Beijing), where Cameron foresaw China's future sovereign-risk loans would be negotiated.

When Hillier first entered Peking it was as a resident representative with no right, as defined by the treaties, to undertake business. Local bankers objected, and the Hongkong Bank for a period lay low. Hillier went on leave in 1886, but the banking activities of the 'sub-agency' were tentatively re-established by Charles Addis. After a period in Tientsin, where he was a successful amateur jockey, Hillier returned to Peking in 1891, at which time the existence of the agency was announced formally. In 1894, in Peking, he married his first wife, Ada (d. 1917), the daughter of Frederick William Everett, a stockbroker; they had two daughters and two sons, including the painter Tristram Paul *Hillier.

Hillier undertook routine banking while establishing an intelligence network through the compradores. He supervised young bank staff assigned to Peking for language study. He was the intimate of the legations in part helped by his brother Walter Caine Hillier, who was for a time Chinese secretary of the British legation. Hillier was also friendly with Sir Robert Hart, the inspector-general of the Chinese maritime customs. All sought his advice, but Hillier's main negotiations were connected with China's major borrowing—first for the finance of the Sino-Japanese War, then for the 1896 and 1898 indemnity loans, for railway construction, and, finally, for the 1913 reorganization loan.

By 1896 Hillier had lost the sight of one eye; the other was threatened with glaucoma. He left China temporarily for what proved to be an unsuccessful operation in Vienna, and was on leave when the Boxers laid siege to the Peking legations in 1900. The uprising was, however, virtually confined to the north of China; Hillier accordingly negotiated and signed on behalf of the bank, then acting for the British government, a loan with the co-operative Hukuang (Huguang) viceroy, Zhang Zhidang, enabling him to pay his troops. In 1901 Hillier became the British representative on the Shanghai-based International Commission of Bankers dealing with the technical aspects of the Boxer indemnity. For this he was created CMG in 1904.

In Peking loan negotiations had become increasingly politicized. Indeed, of all the foreign bank managers in the capital Hillier was the only qualified banker, the others having been seconded from their respective diplomatic services. By 1907, however, he was virtually blind and offered to resign; instead, the bank provided him with a private secretary, Eleanor Isabella, the daughter of the China missionary Dr Timothy Richard. They were married in 1919.

Hillier continued to represent the Hongkong Bank in Peking until his death. The bank had become the British member of a multinational consortium, popularly known as the 'China consortium'. In the early post-Boxer years Hillier had expected to work closely with the British and Chinese Corporation, of which the Hongkong Bank was joint manager in China (with Jardine Matheson), and with the Chinese Central Railways, a combination of British, French, and Belgian interests. The early railway loan negotiations assumed the lender would retain control of each project through the associated companies, but this ran counter to 'Young China' sentiment typified by the Rights Recovery Movement. Hillier began reluctantly to negotiate purely financial loans. This brought him into conflict with the outspoken publicist J. O. P. Bland, the British and Chinese Corporation's representative in China; Bland was dismissed. As a principal negotiator for the consortium, in 1911 Hillier successfully concluded the £6 million Hukuang Railways loan, but, fearing that any official recognition would aggravate international rivalries, Sir Charles Addis, then the bank's London manager, advised the Foreign Office against a proposed knighthood for Hillier.

In the intrigues that accompanied the eventually successful negotiations for the £25 million reorganization loan (1913), Hillier underestimated China's ability to find alternative sources of finance. In consequence, China for a time circumvented consortium controls by accepting the Birch Crisp loan (1912), masterminded by Charles Birch Crisp.

During the First World War, European finance for Chinese development was impractical. Hillier, moreover, suffered personal losses; his eldest son was killed and his first wife died, although he was able to return briefly to England in 1917 to be at her deathbed. Political critics of his policies attempted unsuccessfully to brand him 'pro-German', a charge lent credibility because of his official and personal relations with Heinrich Cordes, the manager of the Deutsch-Asiatische Bank and an alleged German agent.

After the war the New China consortium was established by a formal government-to-government agreement, which the experienced Hillier deplored as impractical. He nevertheless remained as representative of a more broadly based British group, his work frustrated by petty arguments and, more importantly, by China's lack of creditworthiness. In his final years in Peking, Hillier, the great banker–diplomat, had become a mere intermediary, with policy decided in London by Sir Charles Addis. Yet he remained a symbol to contemporaries of that unique era—the last days of imperial China. His long experience with the language enabled him to develop a system of Braille for Chinese; in 1917 he founded Peking's first public school for the blind. A Roman Catholic, he played the organ at the French Catholic Cathedral to the last.

In late 1923 Hillier's health deteriorated further, and he died in the German Hospital in Peking on 12 April 1924. His pallbearers included the doyen of the diplomatic corps, the British and French ministers, and representatives of the foreign-managed customs, salt, and postal administrations. Other heads of diplomatic missions followed the cortège on foot through the legation quarter. Hillier was buried on 13 April in the cathedral cemetery. Had he lived but a few more months, he would have received a knighthood: his name was intended for inclusion in the king's birthday honours list.

As the representative of the Hongkong and Shanghai Banking Corporation in Peking 1885–6 and from 1891 to his death in 1924, Hillier tested the very limits of the 'treaty system', establishing close relations both with modernizing compradores and with imperial officials. It was Hillier's genius to understand the politics of the foreign diplomatic community, to learn what was possible in the London market, to determine what was acceptable politically in China, and to match all three—on terms to the benefit of the Hongkong Bank, its associate companies, and, indeed, the general British position in China.   FRANK H. H. KING

Sources D. J. S. King, 'China's early loans, 1874–95, and the role of the Hongkong and Shanghai Banking Corporation', HSBC Group Archives, London • D. J. S. King, 'On the relations of the Hongkong Bank with Germany', 2 vols., 1981, HSBC Group Archives, London, BBME Archive • F. H. H. King, ed., *Eastern banking: essays in the history of the Hongkong and Shanghai Banking Corporation* (1983) • F. H. H. King and others, *The history of the Hongkong and Shanghai Banking Corporation*, 4 vols. (1987–91) • *The Times* (15 April 1924) • b. cert. • consular d. cert.

Archives HSBC Group Archives, London, Hongkong Bank group archives · Matheson and Co., London, Chinese Central Railways archives, British and Chinese Corporation · PRO, FO 678/1863 · SOAS, Addis MSS · Toronto University Library, Bland MSS
Likenesses photograph, HSBC Group Archives, London, Hongkong Bank Group archives; repro. in F. H. H. King, *The history of the Hongkong and Shanghai Banking Corporation: The Hongkong Bank between the wars and the bank interned, 1919–1945: return from grandeur*, 3 (1988), following p. 26
Wealth at death £56,523 11s. 8d.: probate, 3 July 1924, *CGPLA Eng. & Wales*

Hillier, George Alexander (1815–1866), antiquary and publisher, was born in Kennington, Surrey, the son of William Hillier, commander RN, and his wife, Ann (d. 1862). He was educated at Place Street House Academy, Ryde, Isle of Wight (*DNB*), and it is known that he lived afterwards at 3 Crescent Place, Mornington Crescent, London, and Sedley Lodge, Ryde, Isle of Wight. In 1847 he was granted permission to make drawings from manuscripts in the British Museum and collected material relating to the Isle of Wight. He was commissioned to research into the history of a number of aristocratic families both in the British Museum and in their own archives. From 1853 he sold manuscripts to the British Museum but their quantity and quality aroused the suspicions of Sir Frederic Madden, keeper of manuscripts. Hillier could not demonstrate title, and some may indeed have been forgeries. In 1854 he was suspended, and despite threats it was felt expedient to keep the affair out of the gaze of the law courts and the public (Hockey).

Despite such setbacks Hillier was actively publishing. *The Topography of the Isle of Wight* appeared in 1850 and ran to several editions over the next few years. He published four historical works, *A Narrative of the Attempted Escapes of Charles the First from Carisbrook Castle* (1852), *The Sieges of Arundel Castle* (1854), *A Memorial of the Castle at Carisbrook* (1855), and *The Stranger's Guide to the Town of Reading, with a History of the Abbey* (1859).

Hillier also carried out archaeological investigations which he published as *Result of the Excavations on Brighstone and Bowcombe Downs, Isle of Wight, August 1854* (1854) and subsequently in the *Journal of the British Archaeological Association* (vol. 9, 1855, pp. 34–40). In 1855 he excavated an early Anglo-Saxon cemetery at Chessell Down (Arnold, *The Anglo-Saxon Cemeteries of the Isle of Wight*), which attracted considerable antiquarian attention and acclaim. Further controversy ensued after he sold the artefacts to Lord Londesborough, but subsequently pledged them to a Dorset pawnbroker. In 1867 they were acquired by the British Museum, some from Charles Warne, another Dorset antiquary who had employed Hillier as an illustrator.

One obituarist implies that throughout this period Hillier suffered financial problems and a breakdown (*GM*); his difficulties were exacerbated by the lack of subscribers to his projected 'History and antiquities of the Isle of Wight', which was never completed. The only finished section surveyed the archaeology and history of the Isle of Wight to the medieval period and was illustrated with his own hand-coloured engravings, notably of his discoveries at Chessell Down. The second section, a study of the borough of Newport, finished in mid-sentence after only thirty-two pages.

Hillier died on 1 April 1866 in Ryde and was buried at Binstead church, Isle of Wight. The lease of their property was transferred to his wife, Marie, as he died 'without leaving any property for her maintenance' (Isle of Wight RO, uncatalogued draft leases).

For his time Hillier was an accomplished excavator whose detailed records have fortunately survived. In his latter years he had enjoyed considerable support from noted antiquaries—hence his glowing entry in the *Dictionary of National Biography*—but they were probably unaware of the questionable side of Hillier's life, about which equally influential individuals preferred to remain silent.

CHRISTOPHER J. ARNOLD

Sources C. J. Arnold, 'George Hillier: an Isle of Wight antiquary', *Proceedings of the Hampshire Field Club and Archaeological Society*, 34 (1977), 59–63 · F. Hockey, 'Stolen manuscripts: the case of George Hillier and the British Museum', *Archives*, 13 (1977–8), 20–28 · C. J. Arnold, *The Anglo-Saxon cemeteries of the Isle of Wight* (1982), 15–17 · *DNB* · uncatalogued draft leases, Isle of Wight RO, Newport · *GM*, 4th ser., 2 (1866), 262
Archives BL, corresp., Add. MSS 39984, 46616; Egerton MS 2845 · Bodl. Oxf., corresp. and papers, MS Eng. misc. c. 96, fols. 526–610 · Isle of Wight RO, Newport, notebook, M41

Hillier, Sir Harold George (1905–1985), horticulturist, was born at Culross, Romsey Road, Winchester, on 2 January 1905, the second son in a family of three sons and two daughters of Edwin Lawrence Hillier, nurseryman and head of the family firm, Hillier Nurseries, and his wife, Ethel Marion, *née* Gifford. He was educated at Peter Symonds School in Winchester and King Edward VI Grammar School in Southampton.

In 1921 Hillier joined Hillier Nurseries, where he spent a number of valuable years assisting his father to rebuild the firm's collection of plants and its stocks which had been sadly depleted by the First World War. He accompanied his father to estates and gardens throughout the country, collecting plants. New plant material was also acquired from abroad. His experiences established his deep appreciation and love of plants, as a result of which he initiated a correspondence with horticulturists and estate owners which he continued for the rest of his life. He was appointed a partner in 1930 and became head of the firm in 1944 on the death of his father. Then began a period of expansion, with a large increase in the staff and nursery land. Hillier assembled a vast collection of trees and shrubs from the northern temperate region, larger than that of any other nursery.

In the early 1950s Hillier made his first visit to the United States. This was followed by visits to in particular Europe, Asia, Australasia, and the Americas, where he gathered seeds and new plants for his collection. Hillier acknowledged that he put plants before money. His dedication was equalled by his generosity and he distributed a great many rare and endangered species. He gave a collection of tender plants to Ventnor Botanic Gardens in the Isle of Wight, where they could grow more satisfactorily than in Hampshire, and in recognition of this he was the

From 1947 onwards the family firm received a gold medal at every Chelsea Flower Show. Hillier also served for many years on the Westonbirt arboretum advisory committee.

In 1954 Hillier was elected a fellow of the Linnean Society of London and in 1965 he was awarded the Thomas Roland medal of the Massachusetts Horticultural Society. In 1976 he was made an honorary member of the Garden Society and he was also an honorary fellow of the Japanese Horticultural Society. He was appointed CBE in 1971 and knighted in 1983 for services to horticulture.

Hillier was a dedicated Christian, being a deacon (later a life deacon) of the Congregational church, Winchester. When this church became part of the United Reformed Church he was appointed an elder. He was a man of infinite courtesy and modesty, with a delightful sense of humour and complete integrity. He was warm and sincere in his affections.

In 1934 Hillier married Barbara Mary, daughter of Arthur Philip Trant, flour miller. He had two sons, who succeeded their father in the family firm, and two daughters. It was a close and united family. Hillier died on 8 January 1985 in the Durban Private Nursing Home at Romsey in Hampshire.　　　　J. G. S. Harris, rev. John Martin

Sources H. Hillier, *Hillier's manual of trees and shrubs* (1972) · H. R. Fletcher, *The story of the Royal Horticultural Society, 1804–1968* (1969) · *WWW* · *CGPLA Eng. & Wales* (1985) · b. cert. · m. cert. · d. cert.
Likenesses Salmon, photograph, Royal Horticultural Society, Lindley Library [*see illus.*] · photographs, repro. in Hillier, *Hillier's manual*
Wealth at death £82,861: probate, 21 Feb 1985, *CGPLA Eng. & Wales*

Sir Harold George Hillier (1905–1985), by Salmon

first recipient of the Hillier trophy presented by the South Wight borough council. He donated many plants to the Royal Horticultural Society for the collection at its Wisley Gardens. Westonbirt arboretum was the recipient of a collection of ornamental cherries (*Prunus* species).

Hillier's greatest contribution to the field of conservation was the creation of the Hillier arboretum at Ampfield near Romsey, as a national and international asset. To secure the future of this unique collection of many thousands of different species and varieties of plants Hillier presented the arboretum as a gift to Hampshire county council in 1977. Unfortunately he rarely put pen to paper. Apart from his correspondence he left little record either of his work in the family firm or of the people he met, though he had a story for every plant. His main achievement as an author was the preparation and publication of *Hillier's Manual of Trees and Shrubs*, which was first published in 1972.

Hillier showed a dedicated commitment to the Royal Horticultural Society, with which he had a close relationship and of which he was made an honorary fellow in 1972. He served with distinction on its council for twenty-five years and was elected a vice-president in 1974. He continued to attend the society's shows and to contribute to its committees. He was awarded the Victoria medal of honour in 1957 and the Veitch memorial medal in 1962.

Hillier, Tristram Paul (1905–1983), painter, was born in Beijing, China, on 11 April 1905, the youngest in the family of two daughters and two sons of Edward Guy *Hillier (1857–1924), banker and diplomat, and his first wife, Ada Everett (d. 1917). His brother was killed in the First World War. Hillier came to England at an early age but, after schooling at Downside School, returned to China in 1922–3 to study its language before continuing his education at Christ's College, Cambridge. In due course his father's death released him from any obligation to study there.

Hillier began his training as an artist, first in London, at the Slade School of Fine Art, in 1926, where he studied under Henry Tonks, and then for two further years as a pupil of André Lhôte in Paris. Here he came to know most of the surrealist painters, and this strand of influence thereafter substantially moulded his art. He was particularly influenced by Max Ernst and the early de Chirico, although his brand of surrealism had none of the histrionics of Salvador Dalí or the ferocity of André Masson. He brought to the exposition of his personal surrealist vision a quality of pure, dreamlike serenity which was wholly English in spirit. Very much a part of the British surrealist avant-garde in the 1930s, Hillier was a member of the Unit One Group led by Paul Nash. Hillier was twice married, first in 1931 to Irene Rose, daughter of Horace Hodgkins, an off-course bookmaker. They had twin sons, Jonathan and Benjamin. The marriage was dissolved in 1935. In 1937 he married Leda Millicent, daughter of Sydney Hardcastle, a captain in the Royal Navy, who invented the Hardcastle torpedo used in the First World War. They had two daughters, Mary and Anna-Clare. Hillier always remained a surrealist, as was made clear in the exhibition 'A Timeless Journey', presented at the Bradford Art Gallery immediately after his death in 1983. As Nicholas Usherwood wrote in the introduction to the exhibition catalogue:

> The gradual drift of his style in the late 1930s towards an apparently more traditional figurative manner, based on Flemish fifteenth-century art, was taken by its protagonists as 'a fall from grace'. It was seen as a sell-out to academic conservatism for which he has to this day not been fully forgiven. (Usherwood)

Hillier's stature as a painter rests on the magical way in which he invests inanimate objects, and his subjects in general—harnesses, still lifes, boats, harbours, and especially anchors—with an ambiguous, dream-like presence, creating a world of images, symbols, and metaphors peculiar to himself.

During the Second World War, Hillier served with the Royal Navy, and with the free French naval forces in the rank of lieutenant in the Royal Naval Volunteer Reserve. In 1945, after a spell of living in France and Spain, Hillier settled permanently in Somerset, near Castle Cary. He was not by nature a countryman, although he enjoyed riding. The depths of the country provided him with the peace and isolation that were so important to the realization of his art. He was elected an associate of the Royal Academy in 1957 and Royal Academician in 1967. He exhibited mainly at Arthur Tooth & Sons, but also at the Lefevre Gallery, London. He is represented in the Tate collection, and in many private and public collections.

Hillier was handsome, elegant, and something of a dandy, fastidious to a fault. His family tell how he insisted on the immaculate, virtually mathematical placing of the cutlery on the dining-table, this insistence growing more intense and demanding if his mood blackened, as it frequently did. This sense of precision relates perfectly to the character of his aesthetic vision and technical style. As a father he was strict and aloof, forbidding his daughters to enter his studio except by his express invitation. Born into the Catholic faith, he lapsed, but returned to the Roman church in 1945. After the conversion of the Tridentine mass from Latin into English and other vernaculars in 1964, he reacted passionately to the change, and in later years increasingly set himself against the Vatican and the papacy. Hillier died in hospital at Bristol on 18 January 1983.   MERVYN LEVY, rev.

Sources [N. Usherwood], *A timeless journey: Tristram Hillier, R.A., 1905–1983* (1983) [exhibition catalogue, Cartwright Hall, Lister Park, Bradford, 11 June – 31 July 1983] · T. Hillier, *Leda and the goose* (1954) · private information (1990) · *CGPLA Eng. & Wales* (1983) · G. Popp and H. Valentine, *Royal Academy of Arts directory of membership: from the foundation in 1768 to 1995, including honorary members* (1996)

Wealth at death £245,369: probate, 27 May 1983, *CGPLA Eng. & Wales*

Hillingdon. For this title name *see under* Mills family (*per.* 1773–1939) [Mills, Charles Henry, first Baron Hillingdon (1830–1898); Mills, Charles William, second Baron Hillingdon (1855–1919)].

Hillman, Edward Henry (1889–1934), transport entrepreneur, was born on 19 March 1889 in Croydon, Surrey, the son of Edward Hillman and his wife, Annie. He left school at the age of nine, and worked as a brush maker. He joined the army as a drummer boy at the age of twelve. The First World War saw him rise to the rank of sergeant-major in a cavalry regiment, and also provided him with a gratuity on demobilization, which he used to buy a taxi. Success in this venture led to the sale of the cab and the purchase of a cycle shop in Romford with the proceeds. Suburban Essex remained his base, from which he built up a deserved reputation as a thorn in the side of the existing transport establishment.

It is said that Hillman's entry into the motor coach business arose from his taking a booking agency for a local firm, the commission showing him the profits that could be made from running his own service. In December 1928 he started to run a service between Stratford Broadway and Brentwood, with a garage and office at 52B Romford Road, Stratford. This was an immediate success, being faster and cheaper than the existing bus services. By the summer of 1931 he had extended the route to serve Clacton, Ipswich, Norwich, Southwold, and Yarmouth, offering short-stage fares between all points, to the irritation of local bus operators.

Hillman had entered the industry relatively late in its period of expansion, and when route licensing began in 1931 he faced considerable opposition in the new traffic courts. This, and the establishment of the London Passenger Transport Board in 1934 (which had been foreseen for some years), may have influenced his diversion into air transport. The compulsory acquisition of sixty-five of his ninety-three coaches on 10 January 1934 would have provided an input of capital, but it was on 1 April 1932 that he started an air service between Maylands airfield, near Romford, and Clacton-on-Sea, with a three-seater Puss Moth aircraft. In the following season he reinstated the Clacton service, and started to fly to Margate, and to Paris. In 1934, with all-year operation developing, he moved his base to what was later to become RAF Stapleford Tawney, at Abridge, near Chigwell, and obtained a Post Office mail contract for a service to Belfast, later extended to Glasgow. On the Paris service he undercut the fares charged by Imperial Airways and Air France, but his operating standards were high, and his airline had only one fatal accident.

The de Havilland DH-84 Dragon airliner was Hillman's favoured machine, and he claimed that it had been designed to his specifications. He was also closely associated with the manufacturers of Gilford coaches, and his home in Romford was called Gilford Lodge. He was exceptional among airline operators in his practice of managing aircraft in the same way that he managed his coaches. There is a telling anecdote of Hillman on a bank holiday, standing in his shirtsleeves on the tarmac, pushing a mug of tea into the hand of one of his pilots, and telling him to 'get back to Paris and do another relief' (private information). Not only was he ready to drive his own coaches, he also learned to fly, so that he knew what he was expecting of his staff.

Late in 1934 Hillman's Airways was floated, with an authorized capital of £150,000. Hillman intended to be managing director and deputy chairman for at least seven years. With this injection of new capital, further ventures were to be expected, but the promise was cut off by his untimely death. His interest in the company was acquired by the bankers, D'Erlanger, and subsequently Whitehall Securities merged the company with other independents to form British Airways, the government's second 'chosen instrument' (the first having been Imperial Airways). The coach services, which he had continued to operate, were sold to the Eastern National and Eastern Counties Omnibus companies, who removed the local fare stages, thus increasing fares for short-distance travellers.

Hillman was always a rough diamond, who could at times be moody and intolerant. What sets him off against the general run of entrepreneurs in the transport business is the combination of hands-on management and strategic insight, which might have changed the nature of air transport by offering frequent, low-cost services over domestic routes. He died at his home, Gilford Lodge, Hare Street, Gidea Park, Romford, Essex, on 31 December 1934, of a heart attack and stroke. He was survived by his wife, Annie, née White, and their son Edward.   JOHN HIBBS

Sources *The Omnibus Magazine* (Feb 1934) · *Flight* (3 Jan 1935) · D. Spurgeon, 'Edward Hillman, portrait of a pioneer', *BEA Magazine* (May 1952) · *BEA Magazine* (June 1952) [comments in letters] · R. D. S. Higham, 'British Airways Ltd, 1935–40', *Journal of Transport History*, 4 (1959–60), 113–23 · P. W. Brooks, 'A short history of London's airports', *Journal of Transport History*, 3 (1957–8), 12–22 · J. Pudney, *The seven skies: a study of BOAC and its forerunners since 1919* (1959) · R. E. G. Davies, *A history of the world's airlines* (1964) · R. Higham, *Britain's imperial air routes, 1918 to 1939* (1960) · W. Lambden, *The Manx transport systems: road, rail, tram, sea and air* (1964) · G. de Havilland, *Sky fever: the autobiography of Sir Geoffrey de Havilland* (1961) · J. Lock and J. Creasey, *The log of a merchant airman* (1943) · private information (2004)
Wealth at death £18,217 4s. 9d.: probate, 3 May 1935, *CGPLA Eng. & Wales*

Hillman, William (1848–1921), bicycle and motor vehicle manufacturer, was born on 13 November 1848 in Chapel Street, Stratford, Essex, the son of William Hillman, a shoemaker in Stratford, and his wife, Sarah Stichbury. He trained in the engineering works of John Penn & Co. at Greenwich together with James Starley, who was later to be known as 'the father of the cycle industry'. Skilled engineers were being sucked into the expanding midlands industries and Hillman followed his friend there to the Coventry Sewing Machine Company, which, in an attempt to compensate for a slump in sewing machine sales, had become the first British manufacturer of bicycles, based on French designs. When the Franco-Prussian War of 1870 halted French production, Coventry manufacture boomed and Hillman helped Starley to establish the Coventry Machinists Company and build the Ariel, the first practical penny-farthing cycle. In 1875 he founded his own enterprise, Auto Machinery, with capital

put up by William Henry Herbert, the son of a Leicester builder and brother of Alfred Herbert who established a machine tool business which became the largest in Britain.

Alongside bicycles, the company also made roller-skates and sewing machines; it pioneered the mass production in Britain of ball and roller bearings, and the energetic Hillman established a variety of valuable patents. He was so successful that four plants were established in Coventry and the firm expanded to Nuremberg in Germany in 1896.

By then the cycle boom was at its peak, with improved road surfaces and the introduction of the pneumatic tyre. Employment in the industry almost quadrupled, to 30,000, and it was reported that 'agents hurried from factory to factory, cash in hand, pleased if they could secure even a couple of makes'. Hillman became known as the world's largest manufacturer of cycles, with patent innovations swelling his revenues. In 1896 he hived off the bicycle interests into the New Precision Cycle Company, which employed 600 people and produced cycles at the rate of over 100 a day.

It made him a millionaire. He moved from his home at 7 The Quadrant, Coventry, to a mansion outside the city, Abingdon House, at Stoke Aldermoor. Like many other cycle manufacturers he became increasingly interested in the motor car, for which the first factory in Britain was set up in Coventry in 1896. But he was later than many of his neighbours in the cycle-making trade to turn to motor manufacture: Sunbeam, Rover, Standard, and (very much earlier) Humber had all preceded him when in 1905 his enthusiasm for the motor races staged to promote and celebrate the new industry led him to build his own car, with the intention of winning the Isle of Man tourist trophy.

Hillman poached the young French designer Louis Coatalen from the Humber works a stone's throw from his house and set up a factory in his grounds, founding the Hillman–Coatalen Company in 1907. Coatalen married one of Hillman's six daughters and enhanced his reputation as one of the most gifted designers of the day with the production of a small number of large, well-engineered vehicles with 6.4 and 9.7 litre engines—which, however, failed to win the coveted tourist trophy. He also produced a smaller 2.3 litre car before joining the rival Sunbeam company, selling his shares back to Hillman in 1909.

Although the larger cars continued in limited production until the First World War, following the departure of Coatalen, Hillman concentrated on smaller models. In spite of the blow to his racing ambitions, Hillman maintained a competition department and continued to seek performance records on the basis that racing was the best means of developing design. Like many of its rivals, the company pottered before the war, had no strong sense of purpose, and met with limited success. Attempts to market a small taxi failed and although a 9 hp car kept the company afloat and found a market niche separate from the all-conquering Model T Ford, records suggest that in 1913 Hillman produced only sixty-three cars. The size of the company was limited by Hillman's refusal to go outside for funds. All but £1000 of its capital was put up by him as debentures which amounted to £20,400.

The company continued after the war with an improved 9 hp version and greatly increased sales, but Hillman died at his home, Keresley Hall, Coventry, on 4 February 1921, only a few days after one of his light cars had set a new speed and endurance record for its class of 78 m.p.h. The company was taken over by Humber in 1925 and merged into the business empire being created by the Rootes brothers, the car dealers who amalgamated many of the early midlands marques. The Hillman name, particularly associated with the Minx, carried on into the 1960s, while the family connection with the industry continued with the marriage of a second daughter to John Black, who ran both Hillman and the larger Standard, and a third to Spencer Wilks, joint managing director of Hillman with Black, who was to lead Rover. MARTIN ADENEY

Sources S. B. Saul, 'The motor industry in Britain to 1914', *Business History*, 5 (1962–3), 22–44 · K. Richardson and C. N. O'Gallagher, *The British motor industry, 1896–1939* (1977) · F. Alderson, *Bicycling: a history* (1972) · J. R. Woodforde, *The story of the bicycle* (1970) · B. Long, *The marques of Coventry* (1990) · d. cert. · b. cert. · *Coventry Herald* (12 Feb 1921)

Likenesses photographs, National Motor Museum, Beaulieu · photographs, Peugeot-Talbot Motor Company, Coventry

Wealth at death £184,422 16s. 10d.: probate, 21 May 1921, CGPLA Eng. & Wales

Hills, Arnold Frank (1857–1927), shipbuilder and philanthropist, was born at Denmark Hill, London, on 12 March 1857, the youngest son of Frank Clarke Hills and his wife, Ann Ellen, daughter of James Rawlings. His father had made a fortune as a manufacturing chemist and acquired a large interest in the Thames Ironworks and Shipbuilding Company at Blackwall. Hills was educated at Harrow School (1871–6) and at University College, Oxford (1876–9). Starting in classics, Hills took his final degree in modern history, but at both school and university he was better known as a football player and a long-distance runner than as a scholar. In 1886 he married Mary Elizabeth, daughter of Alfred Lafone of Hanworth Park, Middlesex, and they had one son and four daughters.

In 1880, at the age of twenty-three, Hills became a director of Thames Ironworks. The company had been set up in 1856 when the earlier shipyard of C. J. Mare was reorganized. It occupied sites on both banks of the River Lea at the point where it joins the Thames, with 30 acres in West Ham and 5 acres in Blackwall. In 1860 the yard launched HMS *Warrior*, Britain's first ironclad battleship. After 1865 Thames Ironworks concentrated mainly on warship building, for the Royal Navy and foreign governments, and its merchant ship output was largely restricted to cross-channel packets, Thames river steamers, and tugs. In 1872 the firm became a limited liability company, the Thames Ironworks and Shipbuilding Company Ltd. It was one of the largest and most productive shipyards on the Thames, but by the 1880s all the Thames shipyards were facing increased competition from the cheaper products of the shipyards on the Clyde and in north-east England.

Hills was a student of social problems and from the first sought to improve the lives of his workforce. For five years (1880–85) he lived in Canning Town, devoting his days to the shipyard and his evenings to the improvement and recreation of his workers. Clubs were set up, lectures given, and concerts and other entertainments were organized, all at the expense of the firm. However, such philanthropy did not prevent growing industrial unrest in the shipyard. Hills clashed with the trade unions, especially about the employment of non-union labour, and this led to costly strikes.

The nationwide engineers' strike of 1897–8 proved a turning point for Hills. The workers were defeated and returned to work in a bitter and hostile mood. Hills decided to try and forge a new relationship between the firm and its workforce. He took Thames Ironworks out of the Federation of Shipbuilders and in future negotiated only with his own men. He introduced a forty-eight hour week, being one of the first employers to do so, and he also set up a profit-sharing scheme. These measures, together with Hills's honesty and force of personality, won over his workers, and industrial relations improved. Hills's deep personal commitment to keeping shipbuilding alive on the Thames was in marked contrast to other shipyards, such as Yarrows and Thornycroft, which in the early 1900s left the Thames and found new shipbuilding sites and cheaper labour elsewhere in Britain.

The year 1898 was also a turning point for the firm's organization. It was reconstituted as the Thames Ironworks, Shipbuilding, and Engineering Company Ltd to take over the engine builders John Penn & Sons of Blackheath and Deptford. The new firm had a total capital of £600,000 in ordinary shares and £200,000 in preference shares. Thames Ironworks became increasingly diversified. The six departments included a shipbuilding section as well as one devoted to boatbuilding: the latter produced 206 lifeboats for the Royal National Lifeboat Institution, including 11 motor lifeboats from 1908 onwards. A civil engineering department carried out construction projects such as the Barry Dock gates, Hammersmith Bridge, and the roof of Alexandra Palace. Cranes were manufactured, as also were switches, drills, and marine engines. When demand for the last began to decline, Hills started building motor vehicles under the trade name Thames at the Blackheath engine works. The shipyard reached its apogee at the end of the 1890s, when four first-class battleships, totalling 56,000 displacement tons, were being built there at the same time. These were the *Albion*, *Cornwallis*, and *Duncan* for the Royal Navy and the Japanese battleship *Shikishima*; and they were launched between 1898 and 1901.

Thames Ironworks appeared to enter the new century at the height of its productive powers. However, Hills's commitment to shipbuilding on the Thames soon began to look misplaced. The shipyards on the Clyde and in north-east England could now turn out warships much more cheaply than Thames Ironworks. Hills claimed that firms such as Vickers and Armstrong Whitworth could only do so because of the monopoly profits they made on their armour and gun production, but the Admiralty was not impressed by this argument. After 1901 Thames Iron-works only received three Admiralty contracts and government fears about unemployment in the East End of London seem to have been an important factor in granting them. Thus Thames Ironworks was allowed to build the cruiser HMS *Black Prince*, launched in 1904, even though the firm's tender was £20,000 above those from shipyards in north-east England.

As well as having high labour costs, Thames Ironworks found construction hampered by the cramped nature of the shipyard's site, but Hills would not even consider moving the yard to a new site further down the Thames estuary, such as Dagenham or Tilbury. Given these problems of space it was a little surprising that Thames Ironworks should receive a contract to build the dreadnought battleship HMS *Thunderer* (22,500 displacement tons), the last and largest ship constructed by the firm. The ship was produced efficiently and on time, being launched in 1911, but a special wharf had to be hired at Dagenham to fit her out as there was no room in the shipyard. Despite considerable agitation, led by Hills, no further orders were forthcoming, and the shipyard closed down at the end of 1912.

Hills fought to save his shipyard at the same time as he was struggling against his own physical decline. Growing ill health left him completely disabled by 1906: his mind was still vigorous, but he was unable to move hand or foot. At the launch of the *Thunderer* he spoke from a wheelchair and in 1912 his workers carried him on a stretcher at a demonstration in Trafalgar Square.

An ardent advocate of total abstinence as well as of vegetarianism, Hills had many philanthropic activities, which were not solely restricted to his own workers. The most lasting, if unintended, legacy of his career was West Ham United Football Club. Originally established by him in 1895 as the Thames Ironworks Football Club, it soon became highly successful, and in 1897 Hills provided the club with its own ground (Memorial Ground). The club became increasingly professional, rather than amateur, and its links with the works diminished. In July 1900 the club became the West Ham United Football Club Ltd. Hills was still associated with the club, but relations became increasingly strained as West Ham moved further away from his ideal of amateur sport. In 1904 Hills refused to rent Memorial Ground to the club any longer. West Ham moved to the Boleyn Ground and soon severed its last links with Hills and Thames Ironworks.

Hills died on 7 March 1927 at his home, Hammerfield, Penshurst, Kent.   ALAN G. JAMIESON

Sources P. Banbury, *Shipbuilders of the Thames and Medway* (1971) · A. F. Hills, *Cause of the Thames Ironworks collapse* (1911) · F. C. Bowen, 'Thames Ironworks', *Shipbuilding and Shipping Record*, 66 (1945) · C. P. Korr, 'West Ham United Football Club and the beginnings of professional football in East London, 1895–1914', *Journal of Contemporary History*, 13 (1978), 211–32 · b. cert. · d. cert.
Archives GL, Thames Ironworks archives · LMA, Thames Ironworks archives
Wealth at death £60,496 14s. 9d.: probate, 20 Sept 1927, *CGPLA Eng. & Wales*

Hills, Edmond Herbert Grove- [*pseud.* Colonel Rivers] (1864–1922), astronomer, was born on 1 August 1864 at High Head Castle, Cumberland, one of the three sons of Herbert Augustus Hills (1837–1907), a judge serving in Egypt, and his wife, Anna, the daughter of Sir William Robert *Grove (1811–1896), natural philosopher and judge, and his wife, Mary Emma Diston Powles (d. 1879). Educated at Winchester College, then for two years at the Royal Military Academy, Woolwich, Hills passed out as senior cadet in 1884 and was commissioned into the Royal Engineers. On 7 April 1892 he married Juliet, the daughter of James Spencer-Bell MP. They had two sons and a daughter.

Astronomy was one of Hills's early interests, and in 1893 he was elected a fellow of the Royal Astronomical Society (RAS), where he presented a paper on optics and (in 1894) a simple method for using photography of the moon to determine terrestrial longitude. Also in 1894, to the Royal Society, he presented photographs of the spectrum of solar prominences and corona taken during the eclipse of the sun in 1893 from Senegal; his spectra registered hydrogen lines further into the ultra-violet than any before. Hills's main astronomical interest was solar physics, and his expertise in combining slit spectroscopy and photography on eclipse expeditions cemented friendships with the leading astronomers W. H. M. Christie and H. H. Turner in 1896 in Japan, and with H. F. Newall (1857–1944) in 1898 in India, where his observations complemented that of J. Norman Lockyer in confirming that the chromosphere's 'flash' spectrum was not merely a reversal of the solar spectrum. For many years Hills was secretary of the RAS and the Royal Society's joint permanent eclipse committee.

Hills's scientific abilities were recognized by his appointment in 1896 as instructor in chemistry and photography at the School of Military Engineering, Chatham, then from 1899 to 1905 as director of the general staff's geographical section during the Second South African War. He addressed the theoretical and practical geodetic problems of extending surveys from South Africa towards the thirtieth meridian, preparing and supplying the great demand for maps and co-operating with Sir David Gill's measurement of much of the long meridian arc to Cairo. In 1902 he received a CGM for his expert service as secretary to the Holdrich commission's delimitation of the boundary between Chile and Argentina. He retired as a major in 1905, but was employed organizing and improving surveys for several states of the empire. While travelling to Kiev in 1914 to observe an eclipse, he was recalled as assistant chief engineer of the eastern command; he was later promoted colonel, and in 1918 was made temporary brigadier-general. For war work he was made CBE in 1919.

Hills was keenly interested in the variation of latitude due to movement of the earth's axis of rotation; his collaboration with Sir Joseph Larmor resulted in an important paper to the RAS in 1906 on the geodynamical movement of the pole. Having been asked to provide expert honorary directorship of the Durham University observatory from June 1911, he first proved that their novel almucantar telescope of 1900 was unreliable in its performance. He then designed a suspended zenith telescope (believing it would eliminate all temperature and reduce other sources of errors) in which the vertical was determined by the suspension of the telescope and the variation in its position among the stars found photographically. At the time of his death Hills was rigorously testing this instrument which might determine variation in the earth's axis. His friendship with Larmor and Newall made Newall's Cambridge observatory the natural beneficiary in 1909 of his valuable spectroscopes, heliostat, and 12 inch mirror, worth some £700. It was one of the contributions which consolidated Cambridge's domination of British observational astrophysics.

Hills was elected a fellow of the Royal Society in 1911, in 1908 was president of the British Association's geographical section, and became secretary and vice-president of the Royal Institution in 1915. He served the RAS as treasurer from 1905 to 1913 and president in 1913–15. Both his sons were killed during the war. Hills identified the actual extent of a post-war crisis in the RAS finances, and even before his nomination for a second term as treasurer in February 1922 had instituted a special fund which saved the society from being potentially crippled.

Hills was of distinguished appearance, and his quick analytical mind and wonderful memory enabled him to achieve as man of science, scholar, and administrator; he excelled at shooting and fishing. Many amusing stories, especially from his eclipse expeditions, contributed to the 'Oxford note book' in *The Observatory* are attributed to 'Colonel Rivers'. In 1920 he assumed the additional surname Grove on becoming heir to his uncle. He was overtaken that June by a serious illness, and died at his home, 1 Campden Hill, Kensington, London, on 2 October 1922 of cancer of the pancreas, 'to the great grief of a large circle of friends' (Dyson, *PRS*, xxii). He was survived by his wife, and was buried at St Mary Abbots, Kensington, on 5 October. His published papers cannot reflect the high regard contemporaries had for his abilities and advice, and for the fact that he put the finances of the RAS onto a sound basis. He bequeathed to the RAS an 'invaluable collection' (Tayler, 10) of mathematical and astronomical books published before 1700.   ROGER HUTCHINS

Sources F. W. D. [F. W. Dyson], *PRS*, 102A (1922–3), xx–xxii • H. G. Lyons, *The Observatory*, 45 (1922), 352–3 • [F. W. Dyson], *Monthly Notices of the Royal Astronomical Society*, 83 (1922–3), 241–3 • F. W. Dyson, *The Times* (26 Oct 1922) • E. H. Hills, 'On the suspended zenith telescope of Durham University', *Monthly Notices of the Royal Astronomical Society*, 80 (1919–20), 564–74 • *History of the Royal Astronomical Society*, 2: 1920–1980, ed. R. J. Tayler (1987) • *The Times* (4 Oct 1922), 7d • *The Times* (6 Oct 1922), 13b • *The Times* (26 Oct 1922), 18c • *The Times* (4 Jan 1923), 13c • E. H. Hills, correspondence with Messrs Cooke & Son of York, and with curators of the observatory, U. Durham, observatory MSS 828, 842, 852(i), 865/4 and 865/5 • J. Foster, *Men-at-the-bar: a biographical hand-list of the members of the various inns of court*, 2nd edn (1885), 192 • *WWW* • *Catalogue of scientific papers*, Royal Society, 15 (1916) • *GJ*, 60 (1922), 384 • d. cert.

Archives RAS, corresp. and papers • U. Durham, observatory MSS
Likenesses photograph, RAS
Wealth at death £127,483 2s. 1d.: probate, 29 Dec 1922, *CGPLA Eng. & Wales*

Hills, Henry, senior (*c*.1625–1688/9), printer, was, according to a broadside of 1684, the son of a ropemaker in Maidstone, Kent; the *Dictionary of National Biography* characterized both this work and a similar tract of 1688 as 'scurrilous' but Muddiman argued that 'nearly all their statements can be corroborated' (Muddiman, 5). It is possible that Hills was indeed from Kent as one of his apprentices was the son of a Henry Hills from Sevenoaks, although equally Hills may also have had links with Wales, from where no fewer than five other of his apprentices came. According to the 1684 broadside, just before the outbreak of the civil war Hills served under the future regicide Thomas Harrison, who 'put him out an Apprentice to a Printer for his better qualification to serve the *Cause*' (*A View*). A marginal note named the 'printer' in question as the London partnership of Matthew Simmons and Thomas Paine but, if this was the case, neither man formally bound Hills as his apprentice. Either way, Hills did not remain long with them but 'Lifted himself in the *Rebel-Army* under *Essex*', fighting 'fiercely' at Edgehill (ibid.).

According to the broadside, it was in the late 1640s that Hills began the series of political and religious tergiversations that made him one of the most notorious printers of the seventeenth century: 'He ever made it his business to be of the rising side, let what Card would turn up Trump, he would still follow the Suit, his Heart and Hand were also so well furnish'd' (*A View*). In summer 1647 he was printing for the New Model Army at Oxford with the printer John Harris. By the following year he was based in London at Southwark, where he had his first brush with the authorities, who ordered the seizure of a 'very dangerous book' being printed by Hills (*CSP dom.*, 1648–9, 7). In 1649 he was printing again for the army and also appears to have been made printer to the council of state; however, this did not prevent him from printing in the same year at least two editions of *Eikon basilike* as well as a number of Leveller tracts.

Hills joined the Particular Baptist church of William Kiffin and in 1650 he was living openly with the wife of a Blackfriars tailor, Thomas Hams, although he was apparently already married. His conduct led to a fine and imprisonment in the Fleet, from where he wrote *The Prodigal Returned to his Fathers House*, recanting his crime and asking to be readmitted to the congregation; this work survives only in a reprinted form in *The Life of H. H.* (1688). The broadside of 1684 claimed that Hills went on to become both a printer and a preacher for the Baptist movement before misappropriating their funds, and he did indeed sign a letter from the London Baptists in 1653, as well as publishing many Particular Baptist works between 1652 and 1661.

According to the broadside Hills participated in the battle of Worcester of September 1651 and was seen in

Lieutenant-General Charles Fleetwood's tent the day after the battle. If this is true, it was evidently not the first time that Hills had come to Fleetwood's attention: a month earlier the Stationers' Company of London received letters from Fleetwood, recommending Hills for the freedom of the company. Hills was accordingly freed by redemption (that is, by payment rather than apprenticeship) on 7 October. His imprints of this time do not often specify a location of his business but in 1652 he was at the sign of Sir John Oldcastle in Fleet Yard, while in the following year he appears to have moved his business to Pie Corner, just to the north-east of the city walls. When he bound his first apprentice in April 1654, he had moved further west, as he described himself as a printer in Aldersgate Street; he was probably already married to Dorothy (d. 1666) as the first of at least four sons, Henry Hills junior [see below], was born to them about this time.

Hills's close relationship with Cromwell as both printer to the council of state and to the lord protector evidently aided him in his attempt, with John Field, in 1655 to secure a monopoly in printing English bibles and psalms, privileges that belonged to the king's printers (whose office had been in legal limbo since the civil wars) and the Stationers' Company respectively. In March 1656, despite protests from members of the trade, the company acceded to an order from Cromwell ordering it to register the rights of the Bible with the two men. In July the two men also secured the right to print bibles for the university press at Oxford and in October they were elected to the company's livery. Their intimacy with Cromwell was such that they walked in his funeral cortège, while their long-standing position as printers to the government was evidently financially beneficial—in April 1659, for example, the two men received almost £2800 from the treasury.

The Restoration presented obvious new challenges for Hills. He seems to have been briefly imprisoned and was a suspected plotter against the king in 1662, but when the rights of Christopher Barker and John Bill to the king's printing office were reaffirmed, Barker almost immediately assigned his share to a group of stationers including, perhaps pragmatically, Hills. The history of the privileges related to the office of king's printer is particularly complicated in this period as shares were reassigned and subdivided, patents expired, and new reversions were granted. Nevertheless Hills not only remained as an assign for the rest of his life but in 1672 he bought a one-sixth share of the thirty-year reversion in the king's printing office that would come into effect with the expiry of the original patent in January 1680, while in December 1675 he and the manager of the printing house, Thomas Newcombe, received a thirty-year patent to begin following the termination of this reversion in 1710. In 1677 Hills and Newcombe were formally recognized as the king's printers. A year later Hills was elected to the governing body of the Stationers' Company.

Hills served as the company's under-warden for two successive terms between 1682 and 1684 and was in office when the company, along with most of the other chartered London livery companies, was forced to surrender its original charter in March 1684 as part of Charles II's policy of remodelling England's corporations. Hills was one of the few not to resign his position and his name was included on the fresh charter issued to the company in May 1684. He served as upper-warden for 1684–5, a position he used to initiate a series of legal challenges against Oxford University Press regarding its printing privileges, which led to a new agreement between the company and the university in September 1685. It was also during his term of office and shortly after the accession of James II in February 1685 that Hills formally converted to Catholicism. However, despite his earlier professed conformity to the Church of England especially at the time of the new charter, it seems likely that Hills's Catholic sympathies dated as far back as 1666. On 14 April of that year, less than two months after the burial of his first wife, Hills married Elizabeth Versing, alias Knoff (d. in or after 1707), a widow of St Margaret's, Westminster, who later described herself as 'being born beyond [the] sea and bred a papist' (CSP dom., 1694–5, 206). Together they had two further sons who, according to their step-brother Henry, were 'brought up that [Catholic] way' (CSP dom., 1690–91, 485). Significantly, three of Hills's children by his first marriage, including Henry, were baptized on 23 August 1681 at St Martin Outwich, Threadneedle Street, London, when they were all in their twenties, suggesting that they too had been brought up outside the Church of England, although probably as Baptists rather than Catholics.

The purges and counter-purges of London's liverymen by James II in 1687 had its impact on the Stationers' Company and as a result Hills became master of the company in October. He was re-elected unanimously the following June and remained in post until 27 November when a final purge restored the pre-1684 *status quo* and Hills was ousted. With William of Orange already landed in England, Hills evidently believed he would not be able to survive another change in national government. On 10 December 1688 he drew up his will and fled to St Omer; on the night of 11–12 December an anti-Catholic mob 'destroy'd Mr. *Henry Hills* Printing-House; spoil'd his Forms, Letters, &c and burnt 2 or 300 Reams of Paper, printed and unprinted' (*English Currant*, 2). Hills died at St Omer before 24 December 1689. His widow, Elizabeth, was convicted of recusancy in 1691; the Stationers' Company charitably turned a blind eye to the news, allowing her to retain her share, inherited from her husband, in the company's joint-stock venture. She surrendered this share only in December 1707 when she was noted as recently remarried.

The career of Hills's son **Henry Hills junior** (c.1654–1710x12) was almost as notorious as his father's. Following a request by the East India Company in January 1670 to 'send out an able Printer' to Bombay to print 'some of the Ancient Braminy Writings', Hills was offered the post in April 1674. However, on his arrival in India, Hills's English types were not sufficient for the proposed printing so new types were cut locally by Indian metalworks; as a result, several sheets had been printed in 'the Banian character' by January 1677, probably in Surat (Primrose, 102). Hills evidently proved a disappointment: a letter from India to London dated 21 January 1679 described Hills as:

> not being found here anyways usefull in his profession … he hath given soe little content that it was thought convenient to discharge him … especially being at soe high a sallary as £50 per annum and to doe nothing for it.   (ibid., 102–3)

Hills was back in London by 7 July 1679 when he was freed by patrimony into the Stationers' Company and elected to the company's livery; he bound his first apprentice the following June.

On 13 July 1680 Hills, described as a bachelor of St Anne's, Blackfriars, and aged about twenty-six, married Mrs Ann Buckstone (c.1657–1700x12), a widow of about twenty-three from St Mary's, Surrey, at the Charterhouse chapel. They baptized their first child, Henry, on 17 April 1681 at St Anne's and in 1695 they were noted as living in Holland Street in the same parish with three children; they were still in the parish in 1700. Hills seems to have begun printing books from about 1680. In November 1682 he borrowed £100 from the Stationers' Company (in 1686 he was ordered to pay it back or find new sureties). He fined for the office of renter warden in 1687 and this seems to have been the highest company office he held; however, in August 1688 he successfully petitioned for the company to acknowledge his service as the messenger (that is, inspector) of the press and to receive an annual wage of £10.

The events of 1688–9 changed Hills's fortunes. His support of the new regime apparently estranged him from his father, whose will, although describing him as 'my welbeloved son', left him only a relatively small legacy as he had 'been by me advanced already' (PRO, PROB 11/398, fol. 45r). In April 1689 the crown ordered the arrest of Henry Hills for high treason but whether this referred to father or son is unclear; the son was definitely back in favour with the authorities later in the year, as he was reconfirmed as the messenger of the press. Henry senior's will was proved on 21 January 1690 but the conviction of Henry senior's widow as a recusant and the bankruptcy of the other executor led to Henry junior's younger brother, Gilham, being granted both the administration of the estate on 18 September 1691 and his mother's share of his father's interest in the king's printing house. Effectively disinherited, Henry Hills petitioned the crown in 1691 and 1694 claiming that his father had forfeited his rights in the printing house because of his Catholicism; a further petition in 1698 went further, claiming that Gilham was supporting the Catholic side of the family with the profits from the king's printing house.

Hills's notoriety stemmed from his activities during 1708–9 when he pirated a multitude of short literary works (including pieces by Dryden, Rochester, Congreve, Defoe, and Swift) and sermons—all sold very cheaply and claiming to be published for the benefit of the poor. He even reprinted a run of The Tatler. The bookseller John Dunton described him as 'that ARCH-PIRATE and hard'ned Wretch' (Bond, 264). However, the Copyright Act of 1710 seems to have curbed his activities, although he did reprint his father's 1649 edition of John Lilburne's trial in

that year. He died at some point before 29 March 1712, when his son Peter was granted administration of his estate; his stock was sold off in November 1713.

I. GADD

Sources DNB · private information (2004) [M. Treadwell, Trent University, Canada, and M. Turner, Bodleian Library, Oxford] · D. F. McKenzie, ed., Stationers' Company apprentices, [1]: 1605–1640 (1961) · Wing, STC · H. R. Plomer and others, A dictionary of the booksellers and printers who were at work in England, Scotland, and Ireland from 1641 to 1667 (1907) · H. R. Plomer and others, A dictionary of the printers and booksellers who were at work in England, Scotland, and Ireland from 1668 to 1725 (1922) · D. McKitterick, A history of Cambridge University Press, 1 (1992) · will, PRO, PROB 11/398, sig. 6 · will, PRO, PROB 11/401, sig. 168 [H. Hills sen.] · J. G. Muddiman, 'Henry Hills, sen., printer to Cromwell and to James II', N&Q, 163 (1932), 5–7 · J. B. Primrose, 'A London printer's visit to India in the seventeenth century', The Library, 4th ser., 20 (1939–40), 100–04 · H. R. Plomer, 'The king's printing house under the Stuarts', The Library, new ser., 2 (1901), 353–75 · A. F. Johnson, 'The king's printers, 1660–1742', The Library, 5th ser., 3 (1949), 33–8 · R. L. Haig, 'New light on the king's printing office, 1680–1730', Studies in Bibliography, 8 (1956), 157–67 · court books, Stationers' Hall, London · A view of the part of the many traiterous, disloyal, and turn-about actions of H. H. senior (1684) · The life of H. H. (1688) · C. Blagden, 'Charter trouble', Book Collector, 6 (1957), 369–77 · administration, PRO, PROB 6/88/46 [H. Hills jun.] · W. J. Cameron, 'Henry Hills—pirate', Turnbull Library Record, 14 (March 1960), 6–11 · F. F. Madan, A new bibliography of the 'Eikon basilike of King Charles the First' (1950) · H. Carter, A history of the Oxford University Press, 1: To the year 1780 (1975) · CSP dom., 1648–9; 1689–91; 1694–5; 1698 · English Currant, 2 (12–14 Dec 1688) · Greaves & Zaller, BDBR, 2.91–2 · R. P. Bond, 'The pirate and the Tatler', The Library, 5th ser., 18 (1963), 257–74 · J. M. Velz, '"Pirate Hills" and the quartos of Julius Caesar', Papers of the Bibliographical Society of America, 63 (1969), 177–93

Hills, Henry, junior (c.1654–1710x12). See under Hills, Henry, senior (c.1625–1688/9).

Hills, Sir John (1834–1902), army officer, was born at Nishchintpur, Bengal, on 19 August 1834, the third son in a family of six sons and four daughters of James Hills of Nishchintpur, one of the largest landowners and indigo planters in Bengal, and his wife, Charlotte Mary, daughter of John Angelo Savi of Elba and Moisgunge, Bengal, and granddaughter of General Corderan, commander of the French forces at Pondicherry.

Educated at the Edinburgh Academy and at Edinburgh University, where he won the Straton gold medal, Hills entered Addiscombe College on 6 August 1852, and was commissioned second-lieutenant in the Bombay Engineers on 8 June 1854. After instruction at Chatham, Hills arrived at Bombay in August 1856, was posted to the Bombay sappers and miners, and having passed in Hindustani was appointed, on 14 January 1857, assistant field engineer with the 2nd division of the Persian expeditionary force under Major-General Sir James Outram. He was present at the capture of Muhammarah, and was promoted lieutenant on 5 November 1857. While at home on leave he was elected fellow of the Royal Society of Edinburgh, on 21 March 1859.

After returning to India, Hills was for a time garrison engineer at Fort William, Calcutta, and in January 1862 became assistant to the chief engineer in Oudh in the public works department at Lucknow. Promoted captain on 1

September 1863, he was appointed executive engineer in Rajputana in 1865. In 1867 he joined the Abyssinian expedition under Major-General Sir Robert Napier. He was at first employed as field engineer at Koomayli camp, where he was mainly occupied in sinking wells for water supply. Later he helped to construct the road from the railhead at Koomayli to Senafe, a distance of over 50 miles, with elevations rising to over 7000 feet.

After the campaign Hills resumed work at Lucknow. From 1871 to 1883 he was commandant of the Bombay sappers and miners at Kirkee, near Poona. Meanwhile he was promoted major on 5 July 1872 and lieutenant-colonel on 1 October 1877. He was commanding royal engineer of a division of the Kandahar field force during the Second Anglo-Afghan War of 1879–80, as well as the south Afghanistan field force in 1881. He took part in the defence of Kandahar and distinguished himself on several occasions. He was mentioned in dispatches for his services, was created CB on 22 February 1881, and made brevet colonel on 1 October 1881.

After a furlough Hills served as commanding royal engineer of the expeditionary force to Burma in 1886–7. He retired on 31 December 1887 with the honorary rank of major-general. He was created KCB in May 1900. In his prime Hills had been an all-round sportsman, a first-rate cricketer, a powerful swimmer, a fine swordsman, and an excellent shot, as well as a keen follower of horse-racing. He died unmarried at 50 Weymouth Street, London, on 18 June 1902, and was buried in the family vault at Kensal Green.

Sir John Hills's elder brother **Sir James Hills-Johnes** (1833–1919), army officer, was born at Nishchintpur on 20 August 1833, the second son of James Hills. The younger James Hills went to Scotland in 1837, where he spent his early life, and was educated at the Edinburgh Academy, the Royal Naval and Military Academy, Edinburgh—a private institution which from about 1833 to 1863 trained many officers—and Addiscombe College (1851–3). There he became the lifelong friend of Frederick Sleigh Roberts, whom he much resembled and with whom he served on a succession of campaigns. Hills, known to his friends as Jemmy, was commissioned second-lieutenant in June 1853.

Hills, a horse-artillery officer, served throughout the mutiny, including the siege and storming of Delhi, the siege and capture of Lucknow, and the Rohilkhand campaign, and was wounded and mentioned in dispatches. He was awarded the Victoria Cross for gallantry in defence of his guns on 19 July 1857, and a brevet majority (lieutenant, September 1857). He was aide-de-camp to the viceroy, Lord Canning (1859–62), and assistant resident in Nepal (1862–3). He was promoted captain in November 1862 and major in January 1864. In the Abyssinian campaign (1867–8) he commanded the 8 inch mortar battery; he was promoted brevet lieutenant-colonel (lieutenant-colonel, August 1868). He commanded the Peshawar mountain battery in the Lushai expedition (Assam, 1871–2), and was made a CB.

Promoted colonel in February 1876 and major-general in

July 1879, Hills served in the Second Anglo-Afghan War. He was assistant adjutant-general of the Kandahar field force under Major-General Sir Donald Stewart; subsequently he joined Roberts's column in the Kurram valley—Roberts later wrote, 'I was delighted to have so good a soldier with me' (Roberts, 394)—and accompanied it to Kabul, where, in October, Roberts appointed him military governor of the city. In 1880 he commanded the 3rd division of the northern Afghanistan field force; he was present at Sherpur, Charasia, and the defence of Kandahar. He was mentioned in dispatches and in May 1881 made KCB (GCB 1893). On 16 September 1882 he married, at Westminster Abbey, Elizabeth, youngest daughter and coheir of John Johnes of Dolau Cothi (near Lampeter), Carmarthenshire; she survived her husband. In September 1883 he assumed by royal licence the additional name and arms of Johnes. Promoted lieutenant-general in December 1883, he retired in 1888.

Hills-Johnes resided at his seat, Dolau Cothi, and was JP, deputy lieutenant, and chairman of the county Territorial Force Association. As a private friend, in 1900 he accompanied Roberts in South Africa, until the occupation of Pretoria. On 3 January 1919, reportedly the oldest VC and the last of the mutiny VCs, Hills-Johnes died at Dolau Cothi of influenza, during the post-war pandemic.

R. H. VETCH, rev. ROGER T. STEARN

Sources Army List · Indian Army List · The Times (20 June 1902) · The Times (4 Jan 1919) · E. W. C. Sandes, The Indian sappers and miners (1948) · private information (1912) · T. J. Holland and H. Hozier, Record of the expedition to Abyssinia, 2 vols. (1870) · D. G. Chandler, 'The expedition to Abyssinia, 1867–8', Victorian military campaigns, ed. B. Bond (1967), 107–55 · H. B. Hanna, The Second Afghan War, 3 vols. (1899–1910) · B. Robson, The road to Kabul: the Second Afghan War, 1878–1881 (1986) · J. Hills, The Bombay field force, 1880 (1900) · H. M. Vibart, Addiscombe: its heroes and men of note (1894) · WWW · C. Hibbert, The great mutiny, India, 1857 (1978) · D. James, The life of Lord Roberts (1954) · Lord Roberts [F. S. Roberts], Forty-one years in India, 31st edn (1900) · Burke, Peerage · CGPLA Eng. & Wales (1902)
Archives NL Wales, letters to James Hills-Johnes
Wealth at death £585 8s. 6d.: probate, 19 July 1902, CGPLA Eng. & Wales · £14,935 9s. 4d.—Sir James Hills-Johnes: probate, 26 April 1919, CGPLA Eng. & Wales

Hills, John Waller (1867–1938), politician and angler, was born at 68 Belgrave Road, Pimlico, London on 2 January 1867, the second son of Herbert Augustus Hills (1837–1907) of Highhead Castle, Cumberland, a barrister who was a judge of the International Court of Appeal, Cairo, until 1903, and his wife, Anna (d. 1909), daughter of William Robert *Grove, the scientist and judge. He was educated at Eton College and, like his father, at Balliol College, Oxford, where he rowed in the college boats and took seconds in classical moderations (1887) and Greats (1889). He read for the bar, but was admitted a solicitor in 1897, when he became a partner in the firm Hills and Halsey. On 10 April 1897 he married Stella (1869–1897), the eldest daughter of Herbert Duckworth of Orchardleigh Park, Somerset; after her father's death her mother, Julia Prinsep, married Leslie Stephen, as his second wife, and Stella was brought up in the Stephen household as the elder half-sister to Vanessa Bell, Virginia Woolf, and Adrian Stephen. Shortly after the marriage Stella was taken ill with peritonitis, and she died in July 1897. Hills made over the income on her marriage settlement to Vanessa and Virginia. With Vanessa he developed a close relationship, though marriage was ruled out by her position as his deceased wife's sister, while to Virginia he was the subject of tart comment and an object of humour.

Hills gave up legal practice in 1912, having entered parliament at the general election of 1906 as Conservative MP for Durham City. The beginning of his political career was unconventional, in that he stood as an independent tariff-reform Conservative against the sitting Liberal Unionist (and free-trader) A. R. D. Elliot. From 1906 to 1914 he was an active back-bencher, and his main areas of interest and expertise were tariff reform and social reform. He was an architect of the radical Conservative 'unauthorized programme' of 1908, which supported old-age pensions and called for the introduction of national insurance, land reform, housing reform, and regulation of wages and conditions in the 'sweated' trades. Hills was also a leading figure in the National Anti-Sweating League, and in 1908 brought forward a private member's bill on 'sweating' which anticipated the Liberal government's Trade Boards Act of 1909. He was re-elected in both the January and December elections of 1910. His interest in social reform was confirmed when he became a member of the Unionist Social Reform Committee in 1911. In 1913 he wrote a report for the committee on the reform of the poor law, and in 1914 he was the chief author of the committee's pamphlet *Industrial Unrest*.

On the outbreak of the First World War Hills immediately volunteered, and was made a captain in the Durham light infantry in October 1914. In October 1915 he was promoted to the rank of major and in July 1916 during the Somme offensive was made acting lieutenant-colonel. He was badly wounded in September 1916, and mentioned in dispatches. From 1917 to 1918 he was a member of the Munitions Council. In 1918 he resumed his political career, though by then, as he confided to Virginia Woolf, he had few prospects of advancement: 'I'm not in the hierarchy. I shall never be in the government' (Woolf to Vanessa Bell, 1 July 1918, *Letters of Virginia Woolf*, 257). He was returned as MP for Durham, although his old seat had been absorbed into a much larger constituency as part of the boundary changes that had preceded the 1918 general election. In 1922 he very briefly held a ministerial post as financial secretary to the Treasury in Bonar Law's 'caretaker' administration, between the fall of the coalition in October and the general election of November. Hills lost his seat at the general election, but remained financial secretary until the following March, when he lost a by-election at Liverpool Edge Hill, a fate identical to that which befell Patrick Gordon Walker in 1964.

For reasons which are not clear Hills was not a candidate at the general elections of 1923 and 1924, and he did not return to parliament until December 1925, when he won a by-election at Ripon following Edward Wood's appointment as viceroy of India. But he was not appointed to office under Baldwin, and although he retained his seat in

1929, and also in the general elections of 1931 and 1935, he never held office again.

Hills did not enjoy a high-flying political career, and it is for his ideas rather than for any achievements in office that he deserves recognition. Before the First World War he was among the most energetic and innovative Conservative thinkers on social reform, and both his speeches and published contributions on this subject repay serious study. Between the wars he continued to develop some of the themes he had developed in *Industrial Unrest* by co-operating with the young Harold Macmillan in advocating schemes of government arbitration of industrial disputes and pressing for British ratification of the Washington convention on hours of labour. In 1924 he published *The Finance of Government*, which appeared in a second edition in 1932. This was a thorough and dull description of the administrative processes of the Treasury and revenue raising. His second book on economic questions, *Managed Money*, published in 1937, was very different, and was one of the most emphatic endorsements of Keynesian economics produced by a Conservative.

Hills is, however, best remembered for his non-political interests. He was a devotee of fly-fishing, as was made clear in his book *My Sporting Life*, published in 1936. In 1921 he wrote *A History of Fly Fishing for Trout*, but it is his book *A Summer on the Test* for which he is most revered. First published in 1924, it went into five editions (in 1930, 1941, 1946, and 1972) and is generally regarded by anglers as one of the finest books on dry fly-fishing ever written, evoking a time when the great trout river of England, the Test, was unspoiled and commercially unexploited.

Hills was 'red-copper coloured', with brown eyes, and his appearance reminded Woolf of 'an excellent highly polished well seasoned brown boot' (*Diary of Virginia Woolf*, 1.170); she found his 'Wallerish' conversation opinionated and sententious (ibid., 3.33). On 13 June 1931 he married his second wife, Mary Grace Ashton, daughter of Leon Albert Ashton. They had a son, Andrew Ashton Waller Hills (1933–1955). Hills died at his home, 2 Palace Gardens Terrace, Bayswater, London, on 24 December 1938. He was to have been nominated to a baronetcy in the new year's honours list of 1939, but as a result of his death the baronetcy was created in favour of his son. E. H. H. GREEN

Sources WWW · WWBMP · Walford, *County families* (1919) · I. Elliott, ed., *The Balliol College register, 1833–1933*, 2nd edn (privately printed, Oxford, 1934) · H. Macmillan, *Winds of change, 1914–1939* (1966) [vol. 1 of autobiography] · E. H. H. Green, *The crisis of conservatism: the politics, economics and ideology of the Conservative Party, 1880–1914* (1995) · *Parliament and politics in the age of Baldwin and MacDonald: the Headlam diaries, 1923–1935*, ed. S. Ball (1992) · J. Ramsden, *The age of Balfour and Baldwin, 1902–1940* (1978) · HLRO, Bonar Law papers · Q. Bell, *Virginia Woolf: a biography*, 2 vols. (1972) · NA Scot., Steel-Maitland papers · *The letters of Virginia Woolf*, ed. N. Nicolson, [another edn], 2 (1994) · *The diary of Virginia Woolf*, ed. A. O. Bell and A. McNeillie, 1 (1977) · *The diary of Virginia Woolf*, ed. A. O. Bell and A. McNeillie, 3 (1980) · b. cert. · m. cert. [Mary Grace Ashton] · d. cert.

Archives Bodl. Oxf., corresp. with Gilbert Murray · HLRO, Bonar Law papers · NA Scot., Steel-Maitland papers

Wealth at death £3378 2s. 9d.: probate, 13 March 1939, *CGPLA Eng. & Wales*

Hills, Lawrence Donegan (1911–1990), horticulturist, was born on 2 July 1911 at 4 Valetta Terrace, Dartmouth, Devon, the second son of William Donegan Hills (*d.* 1962), science teacher, and his wife, Mabel Anne, *née* Saunders (*d.* 1967). As an undiagnosed coeliac he spent much of his childhood in a wheelchair, and was educated at home. On medical advice he began to pursue a career in horticulture in 1927, when he took up a series of jobs for leading nurseries in which he gained considerable experience of growing alpines. By the start of the Second World War he was writing articles for a number of leading gardening magazines. During his period of war service with the RAF he was in charge of landscaping campsites, including the provision of sanitation for the servicemen, an experience which encouraged him to think about organic methods. He wrote his first book, *Miniature Alpine Gardening* (1944), in hospital before being invalided out of the RAF, on D-day.

Following his military service, Hills's publishers Faber and Faber invited him to become their horticulture and agriculture editor. The success of his first book led to a succession of publications, including *Rapid Tomato Ripening* (1946) and his seminal work *Propagation of Alpines* (1950). In conjunction with his parents he also ran a successful business selling gardening sundries in addition to growing a variety of plants for sale, among them comfrey. In 1951, following the breakdown of his health from high-gluten cookery, the family sold the business and Hills moved to Blackheath, where he eked out a living as a full-time horticultural writer, publishing, among others, *Alpines without a Garden* (1953) and *Alpine Gardening* (1955).

In between the bouts of ill health that dogged him for most of his life, Hills continued to study alternative methods of production, recognizing the environmental consequences of intensive, chemical-based farming methods. This led to the publication of his book *Russian Comfrey* (1953), which chronicled the life of the nineteenth-century pioneer of organic gardening Henry Doubleday and his interest in comfrey. In the following year he decided to establish, in Essex, the Henry Doubleday Research Association (HDRA), with himself as managing director, a position he retained until his retirement in 1986. He continued writing articles while running the trial grounds, and was gardening correspondent of *The Observer* from 1958 to 1966. In the 1950s he became an ardent critic of plant mutations caused by atom bomb tests. In 1960 he published *Down to Earth Fruit and Vegetable Growing*.

On 26 September 1964 Hills married Hilda Cecilia (Cherry) Brooke, *née* Fea (1896–1989), physiotherapist, and daughter of Herbert Reginald Fea, farmer. She was a member of the Soil Association and co-founder of the Brookdale Garden Community Association. She was the first person to recognize the cause of his illness and put him on a gluten-free diet. This enabled him to enjoy prolonged periods of good health for the rest of his life. She was also very supportive in editing his letters and prolific output of text. The improvement in his health led to the most productive phase of his life, and enabled him to embark on a number of overseas lecture tours and to write even more

extensively than before. He was gardening correspondent of *Punch* (1966–70), *The Countryman* (1970), and *Gardening News* (1981–90), an associate editor of *The Ecologist* (1973), and contributing editor of *Organic Gardening* (1988–90). Among his publications were *Down to Earth Gardening* (1967), *Grow your Own Fruit and Vegetables* (1971), *Comfrey: its Past, Present and Future* (1976), *Organic Gardening* (1977), *Fertility Gardening* (1981), *Month by Month Organic Gardening* (1983), and an autobiography, *Fighting Like the Flowers* (1989). The royalties from many of these books were donated to the HDRA.

In the 1970s Hills became very concerned about the way in which a combination of EEC legislation and commercial pressure was leading to the wholesale loss of traditional vegetable varieties. He observed that while art-lovers could go to America to see lost masterpieces, 'once we lose the Goyas and Rembrandts of the kitchen garden they are lost for ever' (*The Guardian*, 27 Sept 1990). In order to ensure their survival, he persuaded Oxfam to fund the national vegetable gene bank at Wellesbourne, Warwickshire. He also established the HDRA's seed library scheme, which facilitated the exchange of rare vegetable seeds that could not legally be sold because of EEC regulations. This led eventually to the HDRA establishing Heritage seeds, dedicated to the survival of these heirloom varieties and ensuring genetic diversity.

Hills was a leading advocate of the organic movement at a time when such ideas were unfashionable. His pioneering views were formally vindicated with the establishment of the HDRA, which became the principal organization in Britain for upholding and disseminating the benefits of organic cultivation. Within his own lifetime he also had the satisfaction of knowing that his once highly unfashionable ideas had become widely accepted by the community at large, including the prince of Wales, who began farming organically. He established the Drought Defeaters project in the developing world. This encompassed an extensive programme of research to produce suitable strains of drought-tolerant, fast-growing trees which could be planted in arid areas to re-afforest the land, to prevent desertification, and to supply a renewable fuel crop.

In 1986, when his wife's health was beginning to fail, Hills retired as managing director of the HDRA, but remained as president. In the same year he moved along with the organization to the 22 acre site of an old riding school on green belt land at Ryton upon Dunsmore, near Rugby, Warwickshire, where he lived in a bungalow, still actively involved in a variety of projects, including building a scented garden for the blind and partially sighted. His wife died in 1989, and his last book, *The Good Potato Guide* (1990), was published shortly before his own death. He died of cancer at his home, Ryton Court Bungalow, Wolston Lane, Ryton upon Dunsmore, on 20 September 1990. His main regret was that he had still not completely solved the problem of slugs, the *bête noire* of most gardeners.

JOHN MARTIN

Sources L. D. Hills, *Fighting like the flowers* (1989) · *Annual Obituary* (1991), 538–9 · D. Hodges, 'Lawrence D. Hills and his work', *The*

Friend (7 Dec 1990) • *The Independent* (24 Sept 1990) • *Daily Telegraph* (25 Sept 1990) • *The Guardian* (27 Sept 1990) • *The Times* (29 Sept 1990) • *WWW, 1981–90* • b. cert. • m. cert. • d. cert.
Archives Henry Doubleday Research Association, Ryton upon Dunsmore, Coventry, archives | FILM BFI NFTVA | SOUND BL NSA
Likenesses photograph, repro. in *The Times* • photographs, repro. in Hills, *Fighting like the flowers* • photographs, Henry Doubleday Research Association, Ryton upon Dunsmore, Coventry
Wealth at death under £115,000: probate, 15 Nov 1990, *CGPLA Eng. & Wales*

Hills, Robert (1769–1844), landscape and animal painter, was born at Islington, Middlesex, on 26 June 1769. He received lessons from the drawing master John Alexander Gresse, possibly at Mrs Broadbelt's school in Queen Square, Bloomsbury, and he entered the Royal Academy Schools in 1788. The artist made his début at the academy in 1791, showing a *Wood Scene with Gypsey Fortune Tellers*, but he exhibited few works in the following decade, concentrating, instead, on producing and publishing an extensive set of *Etchings of Quadropeds* (1798–1815). This eventually comprised 780 images of domestic, farm, and wild animals, and, according to the title-page, was aimed at amateur and student artists 'for the embellishment of landscape'. The etchings, covering a wide range of characteristic poses, were the outcome of a vast number of studies made from nature, as well as close anatomical study. The print room at the British Museum holds a collection of over 1200 of the finest impressions and proofs.

Hills's animal and landscape studies from the 1790s show a fluent draughtsmanship, but his use of watercolour—his favourite medium—was rather old-fashioned. From around 1800, however, he had begun to move in more advanced watercolour circles. Along with his friend James Ward, and neighbours Samuel Shelley and William Henry Pyne, Hills took a leading role in a sketching society which met from 1800 to 1806 in the winter months to sketch and talk about art, as well as undertaking expeditions to study from nature in the summer. The society encouraged the ambitions of watercolourists and the members, including Hills, Shelley, and Pyne, were prime movers in the foundation of the Society of Painters in Water Colours in 1804 as an independent exhibition. Hills was the society's first secretary and, during the period from 1805 to 1812, one of its staunchest supporters, showing 203 works. He resigned in 1812 when it was decided to allow oils into the exhibitions, though he continued to exhibit until 1818. Resuming his connection with the society in 1823, he acted as treasurer from 1827 to 1831, and as secretary again from 1832 until his death in 1844. In all, Hills showed almost 600 works at the society, including collaborations with artists such as George Fennel Robson, George Barret the younger, David Cox, and William Andrews Nesfield.

Hills's exhibited works ranged in scale and price. The simplest comprised small animal groups and were often described as sketches in exhibition catalogues. The artist also produced more complex farm scenes which featured picturesque buildings and rural activities. Hills's most ambitious works, however, were larger in scale, typically combining a highly detailed landscape setting, based on careful topographical studies, with skilfully composed animal groups. Hills was perhaps at his best in works such as *A Village Snow Scene* (1819; Yale U. CBA), which shows his characteristic stipple technique and an inventive use of blank areas of paper. However, many of his later finished works were spoilt by an overheated palette, and today it is the more immediate colour sketches made on the spot, often accompanied with notes in shorthand, that maintain his reputation as both a sensitive observer of the natural world and an accurate recorder of the early nineteenth-century agricultural landscape. The most important group of sketches is to be found in Birmingham Museum and Art Gallery. Hills occasionally produced oil paintings, and a number were among the forty-four works he showed at the Royal Academy from 1791 to 1824; he also modelled a number of animals in clay.

Hills's travels in Britain were primarily confined to the Lake District and to the south-eastern counties, particularly in Kent near the home of his main patron, John Garle. There is some evidence of a link with the group of artists surrounding Samuel Palmer at Shoreham known as the Ancients. In addition, Hills made a number of visits to the continent: in 1814 he went to Paris, and in July 1815 he travelled through Holland and Flanders to visit the battlefield of Waterloo, where he made a series of sketches. These formed the basis of fifty-three aquatints etched by himself which were published as *Sketches in Flanders and Holland with some account of a tour shortly after the battle of Waterloo* (1816). Although Hills emerges as a curiously dispassionate observer of the aftermath of war, the images also provide a compelling record of Flemish topography and its people. The artist also visited Jersey twice, the second time with G. F. Robson in 1833.

Hills died unmarried at 17 Golden Square, London, on 14 May 1844. He was buried at Kensal Green cemetery, Middlesex. The long list of bequests left in his will reinforces the impression of a man dedicated to the art of the watercolour who had a wide circle of friends. Among the benefactors was Isaac Mendez Belisario of Kingston, Jamaica, an exhibitor at the Society of Painters in Water Colours from 1815 to 1831 whose works were in a style close to that of Hills, his friend and teacher.

GREG SMITH

Sources J. L. Roget, *A history of the 'Old Water-Colour' Society*, 1 (1891), 136–8, 309–11, 446–7; 2 (1891), 278 • B. S. Long, 'Robert Hills', *Walker's Quarterly* [whole issue], 12 (1923) • L. Herrmann, 'Robert Hills at Waterloo', *The Connoisseur*, 150 (1962), 174–7 • M. Lambourne, 'A watercolourist's countryside: the art of Robert Hills', *Country Life*, 144 (1968), 235–8 • M. Hardie, *Water-colour painting in Britain*, ed. D. Snelgrove, J. Mayne, and B. Taylor, 2: *The Romantic period* (1967), 139–41 • *Watercolours by Robert Hills* (1968) [exhibition catalogue, Albany Gallery, London, 2–26 July 1968] • *The Royal Watercolour Society: the first fifty years, 1805–1855* (1992) • C. Payne, *Toil and plenty: images of the agricultural landscape in England, 1780–1890* (1993) [exhibition catalogue, U. Nott. Art Gallery, 7 Oct – 14 Nov 1993; Yale U. CBA, 15 Jan – 13 March 1994] • d. cert. • *DNB*
Likenesses J. Jackson, watercolour drawing, 1820, BM • R. Owen, pencil drawing, 1835, BM • W. T. Fry, engraving (after J. Jackson), Albany Gallery, London
Wealth at death over £4500: Long, 'Robert Hills', 20

Hillyar, Sir James (1769–1843), naval officer, eldest son of James Hillyar, surgeon in the navy, was born on 29 October 1769 at Portsea, Hampshire. He entered the navy in 1779, on the *Chatham*, under Captain John Orde, and was in her at the capture of the *Magicienne* off Boston on 2 September 1781. The *Chatham* was paid off at the peace in 1783, but Hillyar, continuing actively employed on the North American and home stations, was in 1793 appointed to the *Britannia*, flagship of Admiral Hotham. From there he was removed to the *Victory*, flagship of Lord Hood, who rewarded his conduct at Toulon, and afterwards in Corsica, with a commission, on 8 March 1794, as lieutenant of the *Aquilon* with Captain Robert Stopford. In her he was at the action of 1 June 1794; he was shortly afterwards moved, with Stopford, into the *Phaeton*, one of the frigates with Cornwallis in his retreat of 17 June 1794, and remained attached to the Channel Fleet until June 1799. Hillyar, again following Stopford, was then moved into the *Excellent*, from which in April 1800 he was promoted to command the *Niger*, armed *en flûte*, and sent out to the Mediterranean with troops. On 3 September 1800 he commanded the boats of the *Minotaur* and *Niger* in the cutting out of two Spanish corvettes at Barcelona; and in the following year, while on the coast of Egypt, served under Sir Sidney Smith in command of the armed boats on the lakes and the Nile.

Throughout 1803 Hillyar continued in active service, cruising under the orders of Nelson, who wrote to Lord St Vincent, on 20 January 1804, specially recommending him for promotion and immediate employment.

> At twenty-four years of age he maintained his mother and sisters and a brother, … he declined the *Ambuscade* which was offered him, because although he would get his rank, yet if he were put upon half-pay his family would be the sufferers. (*GM*, 651)

The armament of the *Niger* was increased, and she was made a post ship, Hillyar being continued (29 February 1804) in the command, which he held, attached to the Mediterranean Fleet, until the end of 1807. In 1809 he commanded the *St George* (98 guns) as flag captain to Rear-Admiral Sir Eliab Harvey, and afterwards to Rear-Admiral Pickmore in the Baltic, where Sir James Saumarez appointed him to the *Phoebe*, a 36-gun frigate. In her, in the following spring, he went out to the East Indies, where he assisted in the capture of Mauritius (December 1810) and of Java (August 1811).

After returning to England, Hillyar was early in 1813 sent out to the Pacific to destroy the American fur establishments in the north. At Juan Fernandez, where he was joined by the sloops *Racoon* and *Cherub*, he heard that the United States frigate *Essex* (46 guns) was taking British merchantmen on that station. Having gone as far north as the Galápagos Islands, he sent the *Racoon* to execute his former orders; and, with the *Cherub* in company, ranged down the coast looking for the *Essex*. After five months' search he found her, at the beginning of February 1814, at Valparaiso, Chile, where she was lying with three prizes, one of which she had armed as a tender, renamed *Essex*

Sir James Hillyar (1769–1843), by unknown artist, 1807–12

Junior. David Porter, the captain of the *Essex*, expected an immediate attack; and, if Hillyar had found her, as he had been informed, with half her men on shore and quite unprepared, he might perhaps have closed with her. But as she was ready for action, he gave up any such intention and, allegedly, meeting Porter on shore assured him that he would respect the neutrality of the port. The story, however, rests on Porter's uncorroborated assertion, and is intrinsically improbable, for the *Essex's* armament of 32-pounder carronades was, at short range, enormously superior to the *Phoebe's* long 18-pounders.

Nevertheless, the *Phoebe* and the *Cherub* maintained a blockade for six weeks; and after several vain attempts to elude it, Porter resolved on 27 March to force his way through, but he had scarcely got outside before, in a sudden squall, the *Essex* lost her main topmast. He tried to regain the anchorage but failing ran into a small bay about 3 miles from the town, and anchored within a few hundred yards of the shore. Under heavy fire and after sustaining significant damage, Porter surrendered. Hillyar was accused of a breach of faith, and of making an unfair attack on the *Essex*, though he had merely pressed home his advantage. The *Essex Junior* surrendered without resistance, and the *Essex*, having been sufficiently repaired, sailed in company with the *Phoebe* for England, where they arrived in the following November. Hillyar was made a CB in June 1815.

In 1830–31 Hillyar commanded the *Revenge* (74 guns) in the experimental squadron under Sir Edward Codrington, and for a short time as senior officer in the North sea during the siege of Antwerp. He was then appointed to the *Caledonia* (120 guns) and employed on the coast of Portugal during 1832 and the beginning of the following year. On 10 January 1837 he became rear-admiral. He was made KCH in January 1834, and KCB on 4 July 1840.

Hillyar married on 14 July 1805 Mary (1787/8–1884), a daughter of Nathaniel Taylor, naval storekeeper at Malta. They had three daughters and three sons, among whom were Admiral Sir Charles Farrell Hillyar (*d.* 1888) and Admiral Henry Shank Hillyar. Hillyar died at his home,

Tor House, Torpoint, Cornwall, on 10 July 1843, and was buried on 15 July in the parish churchyard, Anthony, near Torpoint.   J. K. LAUGHTON, *rev.* ROGER MORRISS

Sources J. Marshall, *Royal naval biography*, 2/2 (1825) · *Colburn's United Service Magazine*, 3 (1843), 271 · W. James, *The naval history of Great Britain, from the declaration of war by France in 1793, to the accession of George IV*, [5th edn], 6 vols. (1859–60), vol. 6 · T. Roosevelt, *The naval war of 1812* (1882) · D. Porter, *Journal of a cruise made to the Pacific ocean*, 2 (1815) · O'Byrne, *Naval biog. dict.* · D. D. Porter, *The life of Commodore Porter* (1875) · L. Farragut, *The life of D. G. Farragut* (1879) · *The dispatches and letters of Vice-Admiral Lord Viscount Nelson*, ed. N. H. Nicolas, 7 vols. (1844–6), vol. 5 · P. Mackesy, *The war in the Mediterranean, 1803–1810* (1957) · R. Muir, *Britain and the defeat of Napoleon, 1807–1815* (1996) · *GM*, 2nd ser., 20 (1843), 650–53
Archives NMM, papers of and relating to him and his sons; papers relating to capture of USS *Essex*
Likenesses portrait, 1807–12, NMM [*see illus.*]

Hillyard [*née* Bingley], **Blanche** (1863–1946), tennis player, was born on 3 November 1863 at Stanhope Lodge, Greenford, Middlesex, the daughter of Charles Bentley Bingley, 'gentleman', formerly proprietor of a tailoring business in Great Marlborough Street, London, and his wife, Elizabeth Harrison. In Greenford, on 13 July 1887, she married Commander George Whiteside Hillyard RN (1864–1943), with whom she had a son, Jack, and a daughter, Marjorie.

Blanche Hillyard's remarkable career in competitive tennis spanned three decades. In 1884, aged twenty, as Blanche Bingley, she burst upon the tennis scene when she was among the field of thirteen in the first ladies' singles championship at Wimbledon. After winning two matches, she lost to the eventual champion, Maud Watson, in the semi-final. In 1912, aged forty-eight, after twenty-eight years of first-class tennis playing and six singles titles, she was again a semi-finalist at Wimbledon but lost to Edith Larcombe, who went on to win the title. Her twenty-fourth and last Wimbledon followed the next year, when she went out early on to Ethel Hannam (Little and Tingay, 9). She first won the Wimbledon championship in 1886, when she defeated Maud Watson, who had repeated as champion in 1885. She won again in 1889 against Helene Rice, in 1894 against Lucy Austin, and in 1897, 1899, and 1900 against Charlotte Cooper. Her only superior in the early days was Lottie Dod, five-time champion and the greatest sportswoman of the age. Between 1885 and 1901, except on the four occasions when she did not compete, she was either Wimbledon champion or runner-up. The fourteen-year span between her first and last Wimbledon titles is the longest in history, while her last title at the age of thirty-six distinguished her as the second oldest women's singles champion up to 1996.

In addition to her Wimbledon successes, Hillyard won an amazing number of other singles, doubles, and mixed doubles championships, including the Irish, Welsh, north of England, south of England (eleven times between 1885 and 1905), London, Cheltenham, Middlesex, Buxton, Exmouth, English covered court, 'All England' doubles, mixed doubles, and married couples, Wimbledon non-championship doubles, German, south of France, and Monte Carlo titles. A tireless tennis enthusiast, she continued to play in public long after her skills had waned,

Blanche Hillyard (1863–1946), by unknown photographer, 1894

rather than allowing protection of her reputation to interfere with a pastime that gave her immense pleasure.

Blanche Hillyard was the first woman player whose standard of performance could be described as formidable. Her style was not particularly varied and like most of her contemporaries, she played a baseline rather than a volleying game; her backhand was defensive and relatively weak, and her overhand serve, although an unusual stroke for women in her day, was not especially strong. What gave her play distinction was a remarkable natural forehand that had topspin and was much more powerful and accurate than those of her contemporaries, her follow-through going so far that the impact of her right hand and wrist badly bruised the upper part of her left arm and shoulder (Hillyard, 131). Excellent footwork and great agility and speed, along with clever tactics, good judgement, and intense concentration were also major assets, as were her fierce competitiveness, tremendous determination, dogged persistence, and unfailing self-control. Hillyard never knew when she was beaten or what it was to be too tired to play on. By her own description, her most memorable match was the 1889 Wimbledon final against Helene Rice. Rice won the first set 6 games to 4 and led in the second set 5 games to 3 and 40–15 in the ninth game, before Hillyard staged an extraordinary rally to take the set 8 games to 6 and went on to win a well-fought third set 6 to 4 (Chambers, 113–15).

Unlike many sportswomen, Hillyard did not give up serious competition with marriage and motherhood, although she never allowed her love of tennis to interfere with domestic duties and her championship record is marked by breaks that coincided with periods of family building. To a large extent her social life revolved around tennis. Her courtship with George Hillyard was frequently conducted on the tennis court, and both played competitive tennis on their honeymoon. Commander Hillyard, a fine cricketer and tennis player (especially at doubles), also competed at Wimbledon, although with less success than his wife. More than that, he was one of the founders of the Lawn Tennis Association (1888), and from 1907 to 1924, as secretary of the All England Lawn Tennis Club, he was a great power in the tennis world. The Hillyards' estate at Thorpe Satchville, near Melton Mowbray in Leicestershire, included a private golf course and tennis court and exuded an uninhibited sporting atmosphere. The Hillyards adored dogs and allowed their pack of pocket beagles and other terriers to wander in and out of the house at will. Hunting and tennis parties, including most of the leading tennis players of the day, were common. Indeed, according to Dame Mabel Brookes, the wife of Norman Brookes, the first Australian to win Wimbledon, Thorpe Satchville was 'an institution rather than a house' (Brookes, 72).

Blanche Hillyard was a tall, plain, athletic-looking woman with a bold, clear signature that reflected her definite, businesslike manner on and off the court. A sports all-rounder who was an excellent horse- and huntswoman (she hunted with the Quorn for thirty years) as well as tennis player, she was known for her exceptional sportsmanship and pleasantness to opponents weak and strong: the frowns that characterized her tennis play resulted from concentration rather than annoyance. She was known also for a minor sartorial eccentricity in that she always played in soft white leather gloves, evidently to assure a firm grip on the racket.

As one of the pre-eminent woman tennis players of her age, Hillyard was asked to contribute articles on tennis to various journals and books, including H. W. W. Wilberforce's *Lawn Tennis* (1890) and Lady Greville's edition of *The Gentlewoman's Book of Sports* (1892). These reveal that, although far from advocating 'women's rights', she believed in dress reform in sport and that participation in sport advanced the position of women. 'In tennis', she wrote, 'our sex can compete with a certain amount of equality with the "lords of creation"', for playing 'promotes … that coolness of head and judgment which we are so often taunted with lacking' (Mrs G. Hillyard, 'Lawn tennis', *Young Woman*, 2, 1893–4, 370).

Blanche Hillyard's full life and 'direct approach kept her bravely active, until at a great age and crippled with arthritis, she cried "enough" and passed on' (Brookes, 73) at her home, Greenford, Mare Hill, Pulborough, Sussex, on 6 August 1946.   KATHLEEN E. MCCRONE

Sources A. Little and L. Tingay, *Wimbledon ladies: a centenary record, 1884–1984, the Single champions* (1984) · L. Tingay, *100 years of Wimbledon* (1977) · K. E. McCrone, *Sport and the physical emancipation of English women, 1870–1914* (1988) · A. W. Myers, ed., *Lawn tennis at home and abroad* (1903) · G. W. Hillyard, *Forty years of first class lawn tennis* (1924) · E. C. Potter jun., *Kings of the court: the story of lawn tennis* (1963) · V. Wade and J. Rafferty, *Ladies of the court: a century of women at Wimbledon* (1984) · M. Brookes, *Crowded galleries* (1956) · D. L. Chambers, *Lawn tennis for ladies* (1910) · F. R. Burrow, *The centre court and others* (1937) · b. cert.

Likenesses photograph, 1894, Hult. Arch. [*see illus.*] · portrait, repro. in M. Robertson, *Wimbledon, 1877–1977* (1977), facing p. 16 · portrait, repro. in Potter, *Kings of the court*, facing p. 232 · portrait, repro. in Lady Greville, *The gentlewoman's book of sports* (1892), 147 · portrait, repro. in Chambers, *Lawn tennis for ladies*, facing pp. 82, 116 · portraits, repro. in Myers, ed., *Lawn tennis*, pp. 37–9, 50, 118, 146, 167, 198 · portraits, repro. in Hillyard, *Forty years*, facing pp. 194, 178

Wealth at death £11,645 13s. 10d.: probate, 12 Dec 1946, CGPLA Eng. & Wales

Hilsey, John (d. 1539), bishop of Rochester, may have originated at Hildsley in Berkshire. He is said to have been educated at the Dominican house in Bristol, before becoming a friar there, and subsequently transferred to the Oxford convent, where he became BTh in 1527 and DTh in 1532. Of his religious inclinations at this time little is known, but having become prior of the Bristol Dominicans, he preached against the sermons of Hugh Latimer; in May 1532 he wrote to Thomas Cromwell in apologetic terms explaining why he did so. A little later Cromwell saw his potential value to the crown and the penitent Hilsey, no doubt eager to reassure the king of his loyalty, was appointed provincial of the English Dominicans on 13 April 1534, and at the same time was commissioned with the Augustinian friar George Browne to visit all the friaries in England; they soon secured acceptance of the royal supremacy. In 1535 Hilsey requested the Charterhouse monks to attend at Paul's Cross every week to lighten their hearts by knowledge and save their souls—that is, by assenting to the supremacy. Such was his impact that in May of that year the conservative bishop John Stokesley of London stopped Hilsey from preaching at Paul's Cross, fearing that like George Browne he might have 'some pernicious doctrine' (*LP Henry VIII*, 8, no. 1054).

Nevertheless, Hilsey's diligent and effective advocacy of the supremacy quickly brought him rewards, though of a modest sort, when on 7 August 1535 he was elected bishop of Rochester, the poorest and smallest English diocese, in succession to John Fisher, who had been deprived and executed for treason. Royal assent was granted on 12 August, he was consecrated by Cranmer on 18 September, and the temporalities were restored on 4 October. Hilsey's own background, when set against his predecessor's indefatigable stand against the royal supremacy and exemplary record as diocesan, was bound to make his appointment controversial among conservatives, but for the crown and reformers like Cranmer it was a perfectly logical one—the diocese was often held by men with a theological training and its proximity to London could ensure that Hilsey's energy and talents were fully employed.

Hilsey immediately encountered problems with the administration of his temporalities (and consequently saw the royal supremacy from a rather different angle)—he reported to Cromwell that crown agents in his woodland seemed to be taking everything, and asked him for Fisher's mitre, staff, and seal, pleading poverty. This was genuine as Hilsey also pleaded for livings *in commendam* to supplement his meagre £200 per annum. Cromwell finally licensed him to hold two additional benefices, though at the expense of losing Frekenham manor to Edward North, chancellor of augmentations. During his episcopate the London residence of the bishops of Rochester, Lambeth Marsh, was also lost. It is unlikely that he ever had surplus income, and while it is as well to be cautious about Bishop Griffith's statement in 1558 that the £100 that *he* had spent on repairs was more than anybody had spent in the last twenty-four years at Rochester, the claim does seem plausible. On the whole Hilsey seems to have been competent at managing his leases and finances, in contrast to some other bishops who had once been monks.

Following his consecration Hilsey appointed Maurice Griffith his chancellor to carry out his primary visitation of the cathedral and diocese. Almost immediately, however, Hilsey's authority was suspended during a royal visitation and he seems to have encountered some hostility from Richard Layton, the king's visitor, late in October telling Cromwell that Layton wanted the advowson of a benefice which Rochester Cathedral priory hoped to give to Hilsey's chaplain. The same letter provides evidence for Hilsey preaching in favour of the royal supremacy, and shows him eager to demonstrate his conformity and reliability. He was installed in person in his cathedral on 30 November 1536 before a large congregation. During his short episcopate he showed himself concerned to appoint those favoured by Cromwell to religious houses. Two clergy were deprived of benefices for reasons unknown, and a mariner named Foster of Greenwich abjured heretical opinions before the bishop at Lambeth Marsh palace on 6 April 1538. Hilsey did not ordain any clergy during his episcopate, but diocesan administration appears to have been efficient, the detailed list of church incomes hinting at thoroughness for taxation purposes at least.

It was preaching the supremacy which brought Hilsey to prominence, and preaching which maintained his high profile. He was appointed by Cromwell to certify preachers for Paul's Cross and himself twice preached there early in 1536. But his most notable appearances there were on 24 February 1538, when he exposed the rood of Boxley to ridicule, and on 24 November following, when he did the same with the blood of Hailes. Hilsey found appointing preachers difficult, partly because of clashes with the conservative Stokesley, but also because of the hostile reception reformers often had from listeners. In 1539 Hilsey suggested that the bishop of London was in a better position to certify preachers, as only Hilsey himself or his chaplain John Bird were willing to take a reforming line. Bird preached at the cross on 20 July 1538 and clearly followed Hilsey's reformist thinking, as Stokesley complained, although Bird's subsequent career as bishop of Chester suggests pragmatism rather than thoroughgoing protestantism, which might raise questions about Hilsey's own theological radicalism. Hilsey's devotion to the pulpit is nevertheless clear—his last sermon at Paul's Cross was delivered only eight days before he died—and

his preaching aroused much opposition; in 1539 he claimed to go in fear of his life. His strong views, and perhaps his earlier performance as visitor of the friaries, prompted demands for his removal during the Pilgrimage of Grace, and though he does not seem to have been as radical as fellow bishops like Latimer and Shaxton, in 1537 he was described as 'Knave bishop and heretic' and as 'heretic and Loller' (*LP Henry VIII*, 12/1, no. 530; 13/1 no. 715).

As far as monks and friars were concerned, Hilsey continued to demonstrate reforming zeal. He criticized one Harcocke of Norwich for seditious preaching and moral laxity, so showing that he maintained his broader role of provincial of his order with some diligence. But he clearly felt no automatic hostility towards the regulars, for in 1535 he defended the patronage rights of Langley Priory, and in 1538 he wrote to commend a friar to Cromwell for his learning. There is no record of disharmony with his own cathedral priory, notwithstanding his enthusiasm for preaching in favour of the royal supremacy.

Hilsey has been described as one of the 'more pliable' bishops who helped the royal cause in the last session of the Reformation Parliament (Lehmberg, 39). He may have assisted in the compilation of the ten articles of 1536. This, and his staunch defence of the royal supremacy, would account for his unpopularity with the Pilgrimage of Grace, but does not reveal much more about his theology than that he was a reformer who supported the king. In 1539 he published *The manuall of prayers, or the prymer in Englyshe, most necessary for the educacyon of chyldren*, at Cromwell's instigation, a mildly protestant work which reduced the number of saints invoked in the litany from fifty-eight to thirty-eight but upheld the doctrine of the real presence. He initially opposed the more conservative six articles of 1539, but even at this stage he was probably less doctrinally radical than Cranmer, Latimer, Shaxton, or Fox. Overall he can perhaps best be characterized as pragmatic, conformist, and eager to please his royal master, but none the less sincere and diligent as a diocesan bishop. Hilsey died in Rochester on 4 August 1539, his last letters complaining of 'cyatica' and of being sick and asleep, although he preached as late as 27 July, and was still discussing the publication of his manual and the management of leases in his diocese two days later. He was buried in Rochester Cathedral on 8 August, leaving no will.

S. THOMPSON

Sources diocesan records, CKS, C/127 · *LP Henry VIII* · *Fasti Angl.*, *1300–1541*, [Monastic cathedrals] · Wood, *Ath. Oxon.*, 1st edn · Emden, *Oxf.*, 4.289–90 · J. Caley and J. Hunter, eds., *Valor ecclesiasticus temp. Henrici VIII*, 6 vols., RC (1810–34) · M. Maclure, *The Paul's Cross sermons, 1534–1642* (1958) · F. Heal, *Of prelates and princes: a study of the economic and social position of the Tudor episcopate* (1980) · C. Haigh, *English reformations: religion, politics, and society under the Tudors* (1993) · J. Ridley, *Thomas Cranmer* (1962) · S. Thompson, 'The pastoral work of the English and Welsh bishops, 1500–58', DPhil diss., U. Oxf., 1984 · S. E. Lehmberg, *The Reformation Parliament, 1529–1536* (1970)

Archives CKS, diocesan records, episcopal records of bishops Fisher, Hilsey, Heath, and Holbeach, C/127

Hilton, George (*fl.* 1682–1686). *See under* Hilton, John (*fl.* 1679–1688).

Hilton, Harold Horsfall (1869–1942), golfer and journalist, was born on 14 January 1869 at West Kirby, Cheshire, the son of Benjamin Holden Hilton, manager of the Crown Assurance Company, and his wife, Eliza Eleanor Pugh. As a child Harold was good at most sports but rapidly excelled at golf. Educated at Norfolk county school, Elmham, he did not go on to university and was for a while employed by his father. He concentrated, though, on his golf, and had the great good fortune to learn the game on one of the finest and most demanding courses in the world, the links of the Royal Liverpool Golf Club, Hoylake. At that time the Royal Liverpool club could have challenged any national side anywhere with reasonable confidence, with the great John Ball and any number of distinguished champions among the members. But Hilton himself probably owed most to Willie More, a former Hoylake member, subsequently a professional, who taught him the value of a serious, scientific approach to both the golf swing and the game as a whole.

Hilton remained a top amateur golfer for almost a quarter of a century, from the early 1890s to the First World War. Only three amateurs have won the open championship and Hilton did it twice—in 1892 at Muirfield, the first championship to be played over seventy-two holes, and five years later on his home links at Hoylake. He lost three amateur championship finals in the 1890s, but at last carried off the title at Royal St George's in 1900, when he convincingly beat James Robb by eight and seven. He repeated this feat the following year, this time by defeating John Low by the much narrower margin of one hole. Hilton also won the Irish open amateur championship in three consecutive years from 1900, as well as the Irish open in the first two of those years. In 1911, perhaps his greatest year, Hilton's putt to tie for the open championship shaved the hole, but he went on to complete what was then a unique double of victories in the amateur championship and in the United States amateur championship. At Prestwick, Hilton defeated E. A. Lassen comfortably, four and three, but in the American championship at Apawasis, north of New York, he defeated his opponent Fred Herreshoff only at the thirty-seventh hole, having been at one time six up with fifteen to play. Hilton remains the only British golfer ever to win the United States amateur championship. He won his fourth and final amateur championship in 1913 at St Andrews.

Only 5 feet 7 inches, Hilton used an unusually short-shafted putter to compensate for his height, but he was well built, with an energetic swing that often caused him to lose the cap that he habitually wore. His long game, with fairway woods and punched irons, was the strongest feature of his game, but he was a shotmaker with most clubs. Not only could he hit the ball a long way in a straight line but he could also fade and draw the ball when necessary, an unusual skill for an amateur player. Hilton was an inveterate smoker, who could consume fifty cigarettes during a round of golf.

A prolific writer on outdoor sports, particularly on golf but also extensively on cricket and tennis, Hilton became in 1911 the first editor of *Golf Monthly*, a post he held until 1914. He also edited *Golf Illustrated* after the death of Garden Smith in 1913. As well as *My Golfing Reminiscences* (published in 1907, when his fortunes as a player were at a low ebb), he edited with Garden Smith *The Royal and Ancient Game of Golf* (1912) and contributed instructional and historical chapters to a number of golfing books, including Horace Hutchinson's *The Book of Golf and Golfers* (1899) and George Beldam's *Great Golfers: their Methods at a Glance* (1904). He played a significant role in establishing the Professional Golfers' Association when a conversation with J. H. Taylor at a sporting function early in 1901 prompted a leading article in *Golf Illustrated* on 'The professional's lot' that appealed for better treatment of their professional by golf clubs. The ensuing correspondence signalled to Taylor that his fellow professionals wanted him to take the lead in building an organization to protect their interests. Hilton used the journals to air his views on golfing issues, and, in the opinion of Bernard Darwin, was the most interesting and stimulating talker of golfing 'shop' that ever lived, with a truly encyclopaedic knowledge of the game. In 1902 Hilton joined the debate on the new rubber-cored Haskell ball versus the traditional one made from gutta-percha, suggesting that only the shorter drivers would gain much yardage from the Haskell, and that putting was more difficult because it would not run uniformly. The average club golfer did not care: the Haskell ball may have been twice as expensive as the 'gutty'; they may have been harder to control on the greens; but, as Hilton put it in the *Golf Illustrated* on 4 July 1902, 'no power on earth, except perhaps the police, will deter men from using a ball that will add to the length of their drive'. In 1904 a discussion arose about whether the open championship should include an element of match play: Hilton noted tellingly that those who wished to change the format of the championship were those who had never won it.

Hilton represented the gentlemen in a match against the players in 1894, an event which was dominated by the professionals and despite his own triumphs in the open championship, he believed that professionals would generally be better golfers than the leading amateurs. Writing in 1909, Hilton considered that economic dependence upon success on the links meant that the professional had constantly 'to think everything out, particularly in relation to his own game. He knows his own game, its strengths and its weaknesses, and had invariably some antidote for his shortcomings'. Essentially the professional puts in more practice than the amateur, who is 'content to obtain as much amusement and pleasure as he can out of the game and leave the hard labour alone' (Lewis, 37). This was not the case with Hilton himself, whose constant practice and experimentation enabled him to make shots with any club. His weakness was an occasional unwillingness to play the simple stroke, and instead to invent a shot for the challenge of the situation. An extrovert, Hilton loved playing before large crowds. In October 1910 he played a seventy-two hole match, arranged by the *Ladies' Field*, against the nineteen-year-old Cecil Leitch, subsequently a ladies' champion, whose victory (two and one) against her older, male opponent was much publicized in the context of the campaign for women's suffrage.

Hilton was for a time secretary of the West Lancashire and the Ashford Manor golf clubs. His later years were not easy, and he died on 5 May 1942 at his home, Bethlehem Westcote, near Kingham, Stow on the Wold, Gloucestershire, of cardiac failure and paralysis agitans, survived by his widow, Frances Cooper Hilton.   WRAY VAMPLEW

Sources J. L. B. Garcia, *Harold Hilton: his golfing life and times* (1992) · H. H. Hilton, *My golfing reminiscences* (1907) · b. cert. · d. cert. · D. Stirk, *Golf history and tradition* (1998) · P. N. Lewis, *The dawn of professional golf* (1995) · B. Ferrier and G. Hart, eds., *The Johnnie Walker encyclopedia of golf* (1994) · *WWW* · *Golf Illustrated* · T. Barrett, *The Daily Telegraph golf chronicle* (1994)
Likenesses J. J. Inglis, oils, repro. in Garcia, *Harold Hilton*, frontispiece · R. Jack, oils, Royal Liverpool Golf Club · bronze statuette, Ashford Manor Golf Club, Middlesex · photograph (after sculpture by Cassidy), repro. in Barrett, *Daily Telegraph golf chronicle* · photographs, repro. in Garcia, *Harold Hilton*
Wealth at death £204 2s. 5d.: probate, 24 Sept 1942, *CGPLA Eng. & Wales*

Hilton, James (1900–1954), author and screenwriter, was born on 9 September 1900 at 26 Wilkinson Street, Leigh, Lancashire, the home of his maternal grandparents. He was the only son of John Hilton (1872–1955) and Elizabeth, *née* Burch (*b.* 1870), who died in America during the Second World War. John Hilton spent his working life as an elementary schoolteacher in Walthamstow, north-east London. He married Elizabeth in the Wesley Chapel at Leigh in 1898, and the couple lived in Walthamstow for twenty years, moving to Woodford Green in 1920. He was one of several models for Mr Chips.

James Hilton was sent to a local elementary school in Walthamstow—not his father's—and vividly recalled its 'prevalent smell of ink, strong soap, and wet clothes' (Hilton, 16). He 'probably learned more in the street' than at grammar school, though he maintained that 'I have certainly never worked so hard in my life since' (ibid., 27).

In June 1914 Hilton won a scholarship to a public school, but since his father, a lifelong pacifist, objected to its Officers' Training Corps (OTC), James spent that autumn learning Russian, before applying unsuccessfully for employment with a Russian bank. Eventually his father suggested that he should search for a suitable school by himself. On this 'eccentric but interesting quest' (Hilton, 33), he was welcomed by most headmasters. After falling in love with Cambridge he entered himself for The Leys, and this nonconformist foundation probably appealed to John, who never tackled him about its OTC. On the whole James enjoyed his schooldays: he edited the school magazine, and wrote short stories and poems on topical themes.

Hilton was called up, but never saw active service, and from 1918 to 1922 read English and history at Christ's College, Cambridge, graduating in 1921 and being awarded a college scholarship for a further year. His first novel, *Catherine herself*, appeared in 1920. At Cambridge he wrote twice weekly for the *Irish Independent* and contributed to the *Manchester Guardian*. He apparently lived for a time in Vienna, then settled in Wanstead, subsisting for some ten years on journalism, reviewing, and a regular output of creditable journeyman novels, including *Terry* (1927), in which the germ of *Lost Horizon* can be found. His first public recognition came with *And Now Goodbye* (1931), followed in May 1933 by *Knight without Armour*. In September 1933 *Lost Horizon* was published. In this romantic adventure story three men and a woman find themselves transported to a utopian paradise in the Himalayas where peace reigns and time stands still. The novel coined the term 'Shangri-la' and won the Hawthornden prize in 1934.

After this prolonged apprenticeship Hilton wrote, in only four days in November 1933, the short novel that established his reputation. *Goodbye, Mr Chips* (1934) spans over sixty years in the life of a schoolmaster, recalling his career at Brookfields, his brief, idyllic marriage and his influence on the generations of boys he has taught. Its extraordinary success—particularly in America—catapulted Hilton into the second half of his career. On 19 October 1935 he married his first wife, Alice Helen Brown (1903–1962). That year he made a reconnaissance trip to America, and acquired a literary agent in New York. By March 1936 he was already settled in Hollywood, which Hilton described in a letter to Cecil Roberts as 'full of charming and interesting people' (30 March 1936), and was adapting *Camille* for Greta Garbo. He was well equipped to take advantage of the burgeoning world of the talkies. Even his early novels employed flashback techniques easily adaptable to screen and radio. *Lost Horizon* was filmed in 1937 by Frank Capra and starred Ronald Colman. On 14 April 1937 he obtained a Mexican divorce from Alice and on 20 April 1937 he married an actress, Galina Kopernak, whose real name was Galina Rabinowitsch.

The film version of *Goodbye, Mr Chips* (1939), starring Robert Donat, was, like that of *Lost Horizon*, irredeemably sentimental after radical adaptation by other hands, but both were enormously successful. Hilton spent the rest of his life in America, becoming one of Hollywood's highest paid screenwriters and a vice-president of the Screenwriters' Guild. Throughout his career he wrote systematically, with enviable fluency. Walter Reisch, a fellow writer at Metro-Goldwyn-Mayer, recalled 'an endless procession of great names, and … with the exception of James Hilton, they did not know how to write an original story for a motion picture star' (McGilligan, 224). He continued to produce novels regularly, but lost favour with the critics despite the 'undeniably readable' *Random Harvest* (1941), filmed in 1942. He was also one of the Oscarwinning scriptwriters for *Mrs Miniver* (1942), whose propaganda value to Britain was praised by Churchill. Galina Kopernak divorced Hilton in 1945 and he never remarried.

Hilton was a professional middlebrow novelist, and often economically recycled his own plots and characters. In his later years he frustrated some critics by devoting his undeniable skill and versatility to producing 'near-masterpieces'. However, *Morning Journey* (1951) gives a riveting glimpse of Tinseltown through Hilton's increasingly disillusioned eyes. If he believed, with his character Paul Saffron, that Hollywood was 'swarming with craftsmen who might have been artists if only they'd stayed away' (*Morning Journey*, 330), he was realistic enough to enjoy the privileges that his particular talents had brought him, and to mid-twentieth-century readers and audiences the benevolent authority of Mr Chips, and the civilized serenity of Shangri-La, offered escape, comforting entertainment, and a fleeting reassurance of stability.

Hilton's relations with Alice remained close. She and his long-time secretary Adèle Barricklow were with him when he died of liver cancer on 20 December 1954 at Long Beach, California. Alice was evidently associated with Robert Porterfield's Barter Theater in Abingdon, Virginia: after her death in 1962 he arranged for the removal of Hilton's remains from Long Beach to Knollkreg Memorial Park, Abingdon, where the couple are buried together.

FELICITY EHRLICH

Sources J. Hilton, *To you, Mr Chips* (1938) · *WWW*, 1951–60 · *New York Times* (21 Dec 1954) · *New York Times* (22 Dec 1954) · *The Times* (22 Dec 1954) · C. Roberts, *Sunshine and shadow* (1972) · P. McGilligan, ed., *Backstory 2: interviews with screenwriters of the 1940s and 1950s* (c.1991) · L. Coffee, *Storyline* (1973) · private information (2004)
Archives BBC WAC · CAC Cam. · NYPL for the Performing Arts, Lawrence and Lee collection
Likenesses photograph, 1934, Hult. Arch. · photograph, repro. in *WWW* · photograph, repro. in *New York Times*
Wealth at death £14,090 2s. 3d.: probate, 1955, *CGPLA Eng. & Wales*

Hilton, John (1599–1657), organist and composer, was probably born in Cambridge, the son of John Hilton, composer and organist of Trinity College, Cambridge, from 1594 to 1607. Having according to his own account studied music for ten years, he graduated MusB from Trinity on 1 July 1626 and published *Ayres or Fa Las for Three Voyces* the following year. On 15 June 1627 he married Frances Trapp at St Margaret's, Westminster, and in 1628 was appointed organist and parish clerk there, receiving for the former office a salary of £6 13s. 4d., or 10 marks a year.

In addition to the *Ayres or Fa Las* Hilton's works include songs, dialogues, and catches, as well as a certain amount of church music which is hard to disentangle from his father's. There is also an elegy on the death of his friend William Lawes ('Bound by the near conjunction of our souls'), published in Henry Lawes's *Choice Psalmes* (1648), and some consort music, including fourteen three-part fantasias. Hilton is best known as the compiler of *Catch that Catch Can*, a collection of rounds and catches published by John Playford in 1652 and subsequently enlarged in 1658 and 1663. It contains twelve canons and thirty catches by him together with similar compositions by numerous other composers. Among those by Hilton which have remained popular over the years are 'Come follow, follow' and 'Turn Amaryllis to thy swain'. Most of his songs and dialogues survive in manuscript: the dialogues, especially those on the judgment of Paris ('Rise princely shepherd'), the judgment of Solomon ('When Israel's sweet singer slept'), and the temptation of Job

('Amongst my children dares the fiend appear'), are among the most interesting manifestations of this musico-dramatic form in England. The solo songs, which include settings of Donne's 'Hymne to God the Father' ('Wilt thou forgive the sin where I begun?') and Wotton's 'On his Mistress the Empress of Bohemia' ('You meaner beauties of the night'), are, for the time, somewhat old-fashioned in style but none the less attractive. In contrast to the seriousness of the songs, the consort music shows a lightness of style that has more in common with the *Ayres and Fa Las*. Hilton died in 1657 and was buried in St Margaret's, Westminster, on 21 March.

IAN SPINK

Sources P. Le Huray, 'Hilton, John (ii)', *New Grove* · Venn, *Alum. Cant.* · *DNB*
Likenesses J. Caldwell, oils, 1649, U. Oxf., faculty of music · J. Caldwell, line engraving, BM, NPG; repro. in J. Hawkins, *A general history of the science and practice of music*, 5 vols. (1776)

Hilton, John (*fl.* 1679–1688), informer, was of unknown parents. Little is known of him prior to his notoriety in the 1680s as an informer against nonconformists. The Quakers tried to discover his origins in order to expose his misdeeds. Apparently his roots were among the Roman Catholic minor gentry of Westmorland, where he was a crony of Sir Richard Sandford, cavalier baronet of Howgill Castle. After a career of barratry and unpaid debts he moved to London during the 1670s. There he kept an ale house in Fetter Lane and was said to have seduced into marriage and then deserted the under-age daughter of a man whom he defrauded. He was possibly at some stage a soldier, and called himself Captain Hilton.

Hilton's moment came in May 1682, when he and his inseparable brother, **George Hilton** (*fl.* 1682–1686), informer, secured the king's verbal commission to put the laws against protestant dissenters into execution. For the next four years the Hilton gang terrorized London dissent, monopolizing prosecutions for nonconformity, and securing the closure of meeting-houses of every denomination. Around forty gang members are identifiable, fifteen of them women, who secured warrants and arrests, and served as witnesses, bailiffs, and bouncers. Several members were especially prominent in these activities: Gabriel Shadd, Christopher Smith, John and Hester Collingwood, and Eleanor Shafto. Collingwood and Shafto were illiterate; Shafto was Hilton's mistress. They operated chiefly under the Conventicle Act of 1670, which allowed informers one third of the fine levied upon attenders at illegal worship. The gang raised tens of thousands of pounds in fines. On Sundays they tracked down conventicles (the women sometimes feigning religious conversion); on weekdays they distrained victims' goods for non-payment of fines. No denomination was spared, and the principal leaders of dissent were their victims, including William Penn, Richard Baxter, George Fox, and Stephen Lobb. Once, in 1684, Hilton played for the highest stakes, when his female spies were crown witnesses in a treason charge against Thomas Rosewall for words spoken in a sermon. Rosewall was convicted, but the king was persuaded that it would be impolitic to execute a man on the evidence of Hilton's gang.

Hilton's campaign belonged to secular politics too, for it was part of the tory purge of whigs in the wake of Charles II's dismissal of parliament in 1681 and the royal coup against the whig governors of the City of London in 1682. Hilton carried the purge to the level of parish officers, prosecuting constables who connived at dissent. He also brought a charge against the whig plutocrat Sir Robert Clayton but the case fell through when Clayton undermined Hilton's credentials as a witness.

It is probably unique for an informer such as Hilton to produce a newspaper advertising his exploits. Thirty issues of the *Conventicle Courant* appeared between July 1682 and February 1683. As propaganda it was a junior partner to Sir Roger L'Estrange's *Observator* and Nathaniel Thompson's *True Domestic Intelligence*. Hilton had the backing of tories in high places: Sir George Jeffreys (lord chancellor from 1685), and particularly Sir Thomas Jenner, recorder of London. The shady ecclesiastical lawyer Sir Thomas Pinfold, 'the spiritual dragoon', connects Hilton with the Anglican hierarchy, which valued the gang's services but took care to avoid public avowals. Archbishop Sancroft is reported to have 'excused' Hilton, for 'there must be some crooked timber used in building a ship' (Whitehead, 500).

The dissenters played an adept game of cat and mouse with Hilton. They exposed and vilified him in *A Letter to Hilton, the Grand Informer* (1683) and *The English Guzman, or, Captain Hilton's Memoirs* (1683). They brought cases for debt and blackmail. They instructed constables how to evade the law's requirements—notably in Thomas Ellwood's *Caution to Constables* (1683). Starting up the cry in the streets, 'Informer, Informer', they summoned up belligerent crowds of apprentices, sending the Hiltons scurrying for the city militia. But his reign of intimidation was not broken until James II adopted a policy of religious toleration. In 1686 Hilton met his nemesis in the Quaker shopkeeper George Whitehead, who secured the king's commission for a public inquiry, held in June. Whitehead's case notes are in the Friends' (Quaker) archives. Gang members were then prosecuted for perjury and peculation; several were pilloried and flogged. Hilton was reduced to penury and obscurity. In 1688 Henry Care's tolerationist newspaper *Public Occurrences* reported him to be living incognito. Hilton then disappears from the record, though he haunted City tories in the election of 1690, when whig pamphlets urged voters to reject candidates who had provided him with warrants. His date of death is unknown, as is that of his brother George.

During the final attempt in English history to coerce the nation into religious uniformity, Hilton was at the sharp end. An odious thug, a liar, drunk, blackmailer, and rapacious fraudster, he suited the tory magnates of the 1680s. His campaign reveals the extent and the limits of law enforcement at the height of Stuart authority.

MARK GOLDIE

Sources M. Goldie, 'The Hilton gang and the purge of London in the 1680s', *Politics and the political imagination in later Stuart Britain*, ed. H. Nenner (1998), 43–73 · *Conventicle Courant* (1682–3) · *The English Guzman, or, Captain Hilton's memoirs* (1683) · 'Original record of sufferings', RS Friends, Lond. · G. Whitehead, *Christian progress* (1725) · BL, Stowe MS 305 · *The arraignment and tryal of the late Revd Mr Thomas Rosewall for high treason* (1718) · C. Horle, *The Quakers and the English legal system, 1660–1688* (1988)
Archives CLRO, conventicles box 2.2

Hilton, John (1805–1878), anatomist and surgeon, eldest son of John and Hannah Hilton, was born in Sible Hedingham, Essex, on 22 September 1805. He was the uncle of the physician Charles Hilton Fagge (1838–1883). Hilton's father, originally of humble circumstances, subsequently engaged in the straw-plaiting industry, purchased brickfields, and built Hilton House in Swan Street, later a general-practice surgery. After attending King Edward VI Grammar School, Chelmsford, Hilton studied in Boulogne, becoming fluent in French, before entering Guy's Hospital, London, as a student in 1824. He became MRCS in 1827 and was appointed anatomy demonstrator in 1828. Many of his meticulous dissections were copied in wax by Joseph Towne at Guy's Hospital, and these copies remained preserved in its Gordon Museum. Hilton's mastery of anatomy enabled him to deduce that the same nerve trunks supplied articulations, their controlling muscles, and overlying skin, to ensure harmonious interaction and, in response to pain, physiological rest for inflamed or injured joints, a concept since known as Hilton's law. For this and research on the superior laryngeal nerve, Hilton was elected FRS in 1839.

One of the original fellows of the Royal College of Surgeons in 1843, Hilton became assistant surgeon to Guy's Hospital in 1844. He was in effect starting his surgical apprenticeship, as until this point he had not been exposed to surgical practice, his work previously being restricted to anatomical dissection and teaching. Hilton became anatomy lecturer at Guy's in 1845 and full surgeon in 1849; he also consulted privately from his home at 10 New Broad Street, City of London. At the Royal College of Surgeons he was elected a council member in 1854, Hunterian professor from 1859 to 1862, and president in 1867, when he gave the Hunterian oration. Hilton's lectures at the college between 1860 and 1862 were published individually in *The Lancet*, and reprinted in 1863 in a collected edition entitled *On the influence of mechanical and physiological rest in the treatment of accidents and surgical disease, and the diagnostic value of pain*. This was edited with comments by W. H. A. Jacobson, as *Rest and Pain*, in 1876, 1880, 1887, and 1892, and by E. W. Walls and E. E. Philipp in 1950. Hilton wrote: 'Rest is the necessary antecedent to the healthy accomplishment of both repair and growth' (J. Hilton, *Rest and Pain*, ed. E. W. Walls and E. E. Philipp, 1950, 6). Reflecting a pivotal interest in nerves, he commented: 'I have striven, by agency of a more precise nervous anatomy, to unravel and render patent the meaning of pains which have so often been described as anomalous or obscure.' He concluded: 'Pain the monitor, and Rest the cure, are starting-points for contemplation which should ever be present in the mind of the surgeon' (ibid., 477).

After retirement from Guy's in 1870, Hilton continued in private practice, being appointed surgeon-extraordinary to Queen Victoria and becoming president of the Pathological Society. Hilton, who was twice married, died at Hedingham House, Clapham, London, from a carcinoma of the stomach, on 14 September 1878. He was survived by his second wife, Elizabeth Mary Ann, formerly Clarke, by his stepson Fielding Clarke, and by the children from his first marriage.

In the biographical introduction to the sixth edition of *Rest and Pain*, H. J. B. Atkins observed that Hilton's obituary notice in *Guy's Hospital Reports* had appeared only in 1892, with an apology for the delay by Jacobson. Further *The Lancet*, which had published Hilton's lectures, and the *British Medical Journal*, printed unduly terse factual obituaries. In explanation Atkins suggested that Hilton may not have had a socially endearing character. None the less his unrivalled knowledge made him a fascinating lecturer and teacher. To be Hilton's dresser at Guy's was considered a 'blue riband' of attainment, even if he was no easy master, being rough in speech and prone to sarcasm, with a particular dislike of eponymous terminology. In 1892 S. Wilks and G. T. Bettany reported: 'It was his misfortune to say disagreeable things, for he was really a kindhearted man' (Wilks and Bettany).

Hilton made many contributions to *The Lancet*, *Guy's Hospital Reports*, and *Proceedings of the Medical and Chirurgical Society* but his name is perpetuated in *Rest and Pain*, a classic of medical literature, influencing among others the anatomist F. Wood Jones who encouraged all medical students and practitioners to read it.   JOHN KIRKUP

Sources DNB · W. H. A. Jacobson, 'In memoriam: John Hilton FRS', *Guy's Hospital Reports*, 3rd ser., 34 (1892), xxxvii–xcii · V. G. Plarr, *Plarr's Lives of the fellows of the Royal College of Surgeons of England*, rev. D'A. Power, 1 (1930), 540–42 · S. Wilks and G. T. Bettany, *A biographical history of Guy's Hospital* (1892), 347–51 · H. J. B. Atkins, 'Introduction', in J. Hilton, *Rest and pain*, ed. E. W. Walls and E. E. Philipp (1950), xiii–xxvii · 'John Hilton, 1805–1878', *British Journal of Surgery*, 7 (1919–20), 435–7 · C. H. Fagge, 'The Hunterian oration, 1936: John Hunter to John Hilton', *The Lancet* (22 Feb 1936), 409–14 · *Guy's Hospital Gazette*, new ser., 3 (1878), 135–7 · *Proceedings of the Royal Medical and Chirurgical Society*, 8 (1875–80), 388–90 · *BMJ* (21 Sept 1878), 456 · *The Lancet* (28 Sept 1878), 460 · private information (2004) · CGPLA Eng. & Wales (1878)
Likenesses Barraud & Jerrard, photograph, 1873, Wellcome L. · H. Barraud, oils (in middle age), RCS Eng. · London Stereoscopic and Photographic Co., photograph, Wellcome L. · J. L. Tupper, plaster relief medallion (as a young man), RCS Eng. · photograph, Wellcome L.
Wealth at death under £40,000: probate, 4 Dec 1878, CGPLA Eng. & Wales

Hilton [*née* Case], **Marie** (1821–1896), promoter of child welfare, was born on 11 July 1821 in London. Deprived of early parental care, she was brought up near Richmond, Surrey, by her grandmother, a rigid Anglican who forbade her to repeat a visit she had made to the village nonconformist chapel. She persisted, however, and when, after her grandmother's death, she moved to London in her twentieth year, she joined Westminster Congregational Church, and was active in church, Sunday school, and temperance work there. Subsequently she was briefly at East Retford, Nottinghamshire, and from 1843 in Brighton. At Brighton she became uneasy about the ordinance of the Lord's supper and for some years absented herself from it, subsequently attending Quaker meetings. In 1853 she married a Quaker, John Hilton (1820–1908); they had five children. In the early 1860s they moved from Brighton to London, where he was private secretary to the proprietor of a large manufacturing establishment: in connection with it was a non-sectarian mission church which claimed their active support. Marie Hilton was received into the Society of Friends in 1866. In 1868, following the 1867 cholera epidemic and the distress in east London consequent on the great strike in the shipping trade, she began to take part in mission and social work at Ratcliff Friends' meeting-house and the family moved to nearby Burdett Road. Impressed with the needs of mothers who had to be out at work, often leaving small babies with inadequate care, in the summer of 1870 she visited the crèche at Brussels, which then catered for some 500–600 children. Fired by this experience she opened her crèche in Stepney Causeway on 22 February 1871, with 10 infants and 15 young children. By the time of her death it catered for 120 children.

Social work all too often went hand in hand with insensitive and sometimes aggressive sectarian teaching. Marie Hilton would have none of it and campaigned against 'the battle of creeds over the cradle', insisting that the confidence of the mothers could be won only by an appeal to their (sometimes hidden) love for the helpless and suffering. Her strong personality and intrepid courage enabled her to go into alleys where the police dared not venture and to enter, undaunted, the homes even of violent criminals if she felt she were needed. Her practical common sense, determination, and courage enabled her to overcome the mothers' fears and her opponents' accusations of pampering. She secured the patronage of Queen Victoria's daughter Princess Christian and the interest of the earl of Shaftesbury. Various auxiliary institutions were added to the crèche, including an infirmary and a country home at Feltham, Middlesex. Marie Hilton, having a powerful intellect and considerable administrative ability, remained manager and fund-raiser, eschewing any supporting committee. On her death responsibility for 'Mrs Hilton's Crèche' devolved upon her husband, who was treasurer, until 1899 when it was transferred to Dr Barnardos.

About 1892 the Hiltons moved to Shore House, 19 Shore Road, South Hackney. Marie Hilton began to be troubled by acute gout and, after being bedridden for three months, died at home on 10 April 1896; her body was interred in the Quaker burial-ground at Wanstead.

EDWARD H. MILLIGAN

Sources J. D. Hilton, *Marie Hilton: her life and work, 1821–1896* (1897) · *Annual Monitor* (1897), 68–78 · *The Friend*, new ser., 36 (1896), 294 · *The crèche at Ratcliff, being particulars of its formation and incidents of its first year* (1872) · *The [Second–Sixth] Year of the Crèche* [journal of Marie Hilton's crèche at Ratcliff, London] (1873–7) · *The Crèche Annual* [journal of Marie Hilton's crèche at Ratcliff, London] (1878–99) · 'Dictionary of Quaker biography', RS Friends, Lond. [card index]
Likenesses photograph, c.1885, RS Friends, Lond.

Hilton, Ralph (1923–1981), road transport entrepreneur, was born on 8 August 1923 at Lewisham, the son of Ralph Hilton, fruiterer and greengrocer, and his wife, Ruby, *née* Williams. On leaving school at fourteen, he became a hotel page-boy. He joined the army in the Second World War, his military experience in vehicle servicing providing some preparation for his eventual career. He did not, however, enter road haulage until 1954 (in Vauxhall), having worked in his father's public house after demobilization in 1948. Indeed, he took over the licence on his father's retirement, and retained it until 1959, so that his first venture in road haulage was part-time only. The acquisition of a filling station in 1956, with useful facilities for his lorries, was a significant move towards his full-time career in transport; his fleet reached sixteen in 1957 and more than tripled to forty-nine by 1959.

On Hilton's auditor's advice, Hilton Transport Services Ltd (HTS) was formed in July 1959. Hilton remained sole proprietor, with his wife, Pearl Ivy Hilton, as the only other director, and she assisted with administration (a common feature of small road haulage concerns). The business grew in the 1960s, largely by the acquisition of similar businesses for their 'A' licences (which permitted the unrestricted carriage of goods for hire or reward). The report of the eventual Companies Act investigation characterized Hilton as a hard worker, with initiative and drive and a 'robust attitude to business affairs' (Hytner and Irvine, 15). In assessing him, it is important to give due weight to these positive characteristics, and to his personal qualities of warmth, loyalty, generosity, and humour. He epitomized the 'rough diamond' element so often encountered in the road haulage industry, and it is a reasonable hypothesis that his conduct as a businessman crossed the boundaries of what is acceptable only with the growth of his undertaking beyond its optimum size for a man of Hilton's talents, background, and characteristics (ibid., 17–18).

This excessive growth was particularly associated with a move into storage and distribution, in addition to transport, areas in which Hilton was out of his depth. In 1961 HTS had acquired a small grocery distributor, but the two crucial developments were the acquisition of 6 acres of warehousing at Charlton, London, in 1967, and the nearby Harvey's warehouse in 1970, which proved unsuitable for HTS and expensive to convert. At the same time HTS was acquiring larger companies than previously, such as the Joy Group with 155 vehicles, when HTS already had a fleet of over 400, making it one of a small minority of public hauliers operating several hundred vehicles. The flotation of HTS as a public company in November 1970 by the Industrial and Commercial Finance Corporation was criticized in the report, on the grounds that the concern had probably exceeded Hilton's competence as a manager, especially with its new directions in warehousing, whereas his successful experience had been in transport. Moreover, the growing rumours about him, and the nature of the HTS management structure were points of weakness, which should have been addressed at that stage.

Between May 1970 and January 1972 nine companies were taken over by Hilton's company, and turnover increased to £8.64 million, thus creating, in a very short period, a national network of transport and distribution. The acquisition of the J. and H. Transport Group Ltd in May 1971 tested the management resources of HTS beyond their limit: the report considered that its management structure virtually collapsed from the autumn of that year. Despite this, three further haulage companies were acquired from British Oxygen. Some indication of the true state of affairs at HTS led Gallaher to drop a takeover bid in March 1972 and in June the accountants Peat Marwick Mitchell & Co. were called in to investigate HTS. Profit forecasts proved to have been seriously overestimated. The appointment of an independent businessman as chief administrator could not prevent a worsening of its financial position, and in March 1973, Cork Gully, liquidation specialists, were called in. Pressure from his fellow directors led to Hilton's resignation the following month.

However, Hilton still owned 35 per cent of the equity of HTS (until February 1974), and attempted to influence its affairs by forcing the holding of an extraordinary general meeting in October 1973 and issuing a 'programme for recovery' in January 1974, three days before his arrest. He had also acquired two firms in the Surrey docks, and attracted some HTS staff away to them. At his trial in June 1975 he was acquitted of conspiracy, but found guilty of falsifying accounts. He went on to develop Hilton Amalgamated Transport, which had several trading subsidiaries, including WBS Transport. These were put up for sale in September 1985 when trading losses, in part due to the effect of dock strikes, resulted in the appointment of a receiver. Hilton's son, Ralph John Hilton, also followed an entrepreneurial career in road transport, and became head of Hilton Amalgamated Transport. A freemason, Hilton's principal hobby was power boat sailing, which also served to provide some publicity for his firm. He died on 28 August 1981 at his home, Magnolia, Cricket Ground Road, Chislehurst, and was survived by his wife.

RICHARD A. STOREY

Sources B. A. Hytner and I. A. N. Irvine, *Roadships Limited: report of an investigation under section 165(b) of the Companies Act* (1976) · R. Storey, 'Hilton, Ralph', *DBB* · R. Hilton, 'Hilton Transport Services', *The entrepreneur: eight case studies*, ed. R. Lynn (1974) · 'The battle to drive Ralph Hilton Transport', *Sunday Times* (13 Jan 1974) · *Roadway* (Oct 1981) · *Motor Transport* (26 Oct 1983), 30 · *Motor Transport* (26 Sept 1985), 10 · d. cert. · *CGPLA Eng. & Wales* (1982)
Wealth at death £788,397: probate, 12 March 1982, *CGPLA Eng. & Wales*

Hilton, Sir Reynald (*fl. c.*1380). *See under* Lollard knights (*act. c.*1380–*c.*1414).

Hilton, Roger (1911–1975), painter, was born at Northwood, Middlesex, on 23 March 1911, the second son and second child in the family of three sons and a daughter of Oscar Hildesheim MD, a general medical practitioner, a cousin of the founder of the Warburg Institute, and his

Roger Hilton (1911–1975), by Snowdon, 1963

wife, Louisa Holdsworth Sampson, who before her marriage had trained as a painter at the Slade School of Fine Art. Because of anti-German feeling during the First World War, the family name of Hildesheim was changed to Hilton in 1916. He was educated at Bishop's Stortford College, Hertfordshire, and then at the Slade (1929–31 and 1935–6), where he was awarded the Orpen prize in 1930 and the Slade scholarship, which was not taken up, in 1931.

Between 1931 and 1939, Hilton spent a total of about two and a half years in Paris, partly attending the Académie Ranson, where Roger Bissière taught. Hilton had his first one-man exhibition at the Bloomsbury Gallery, London, in 1936. He joined the army in December 1939, transferring to the newly formed commandos in August 1940. He took part in the Dieppe raid in 1942 and was taken prisoner of war. He taught art at Bryanston School, Dorset, in 1947–8.

In 1947 Hilton married the violinist Ruth Catherine David, daughter of the Revd James Frederick Paul David, teacher of classics at a public school. They had a son and a daughter. This marriage ended in divorce and in 1965 he married the painter Rosemary Julia Phipps, daughter of Robert Charles Phipps, a master baker: they had two sons.

It was not until he was more than forty years old that Hilton became prominent as a painter. He was one of the

tiny band of British artists inspired by E. J. Victor Pasmore's conversion to abstract painting in 1947–8. Hilton's first abstract was executed in 1950. His paintings of 1950–52, in which forms are located in shallow pictorial space, reflected Paris abstraction of the time. In 1953, after meeting the Dutch artist Constant in London and visiting Amsterdam and Paris with him, Hilton simplified his painting, limiting his palette to the primaries, black and white, and a few earth colours, applying them in a few ragged shaped areas; some works suggest landscape or the human female figure but some are among the most uncompromisingly abstract paintings of their time executed in Britain. In works of 1953–4 the forms appear to move out into the real space in front of the picture plane, not into illusory pictorial space behind. This could have led to making three-dimensional constructions, but this possibility was rejected by Hilton, who was committed to painting on a flat surface.

From 1955 Hilton's paintings show a return to using shallow pictorial space. He made visits to St Ives in Cornwall from 1956 onwards and from that year there are increased suggestions of rocks, boats, beaches, and bodies floating in water in his pictures. An allusive abstraction (neither completely abstract nor representational) characterizes much of his work. In 1961, however, he surprised many of his admirers and perhaps dismayed not a few when he painted the first of a few large-scale female nudes which were overtly figurative. In 1965 Hilton and his family moved from London to St Just in west Cornwall, where he lived for the rest of his life. When confined to bed through ill health for more than two years before his death, he was able to paint only in gouache; his themes included abstracts, animals wild and domestic as well as imaginary, boats, carts, and the female nude, executed in colours which seem to have become brighter as death approached.

Making art involves taking risks and that is something Hilton was always doing. A courageous painter whose work was frequently well ahead of the taste of even the informed public, often he was not fully appreciated at the time. Hilton thought deeply about painting; acutely perceptive and outspoken about art and people, he was often discomfiting company, particularly when inflamed by alcohol, when he often became verbally aggressive, though he had a deep streak of tenderness. Like his art, he could be both abrasive and life-enhancing. Hilton was a painter and draughtsman of authority and a subtle colourist, almost unable to make marks on paper not charged with energy, used to produce images of great vitality, many with suggestions of the sensual and sexual, some both erotic and absurd. Hilton's paintings hint at some of the essential qualities of life: slightly messy, awkward, unpredictable, comic, and transient.

Hilton was appointed CBE in 1968. He won the first prize at the John Moores Exhibition at Liverpool in 1963 and represented Britain at the Venice Biennale in 1964 when he was awarded the UNESCO prize. He exhibited at Gimpel Fils, London, between 1952 and 1956 and at Waddington

Galleries, London, from 1960. Hilton's work is represented in the Tate collections and about twenty other public collections in Britain, as well as the Stedelijk Museum, Amsterdam, the Gulbenkian Foundation, Lisbon, the National Gallery, Ottawa, and the Museum des 20 Jahrhunderts, Vienna. Hilton died at his home, Botallack Moor, St Just, on 23 February 1975.

DAVID BROWN, rev.

Sources R. Hilton, ed., *Roger Hilton: night letters and selected drawings* (1980) [introduction by Michael Canney] • personal knowledge (1986) • private information (1986) • *Roger Hilton, schilderjen; Gwyther Irwin, collages; Bernard Meadows, plastiek; Joe Titson, constructies* (Stedelijk Museum, Amsterdam, 1965) [exhibition catalogue] • *Roger Hilton* (South Bank Centre, London, 1993) [exhibition catalogue] • P. Moorhouse, *Roger Hilton* (Hayward Gallery, London, 1994) [exhibition catalogue] • *CGPLA Eng. & Wales* (1975) • *The Times* (28 Feb 1975)
Likenesses Snowdon, photograph, 1963, NPG [*see illus.*] • R. Hilton, self-portrait, pencil on paper, NPG
Wealth at death £41,564: probate, 30 July 1975, *CGPLA Eng. & Wales*

Hilton, Walter (*c.*1343–1396), religious writer, was born about 1343, a date deducible from his academic career. Neither his birthplace nor the date of his ordination is known. It is presumed that he studied at Cambridge University, on the assumption that he is identical with the Walter Hilton, bachelor of civil law, a clerk of Lincoln diocese, who was granted the reservation of a canonry and prebend of Abergwili, Carmarthen, in January 1371, and with the Walter Hilton, bachelor of civil law, recorded at the Ely consistory court in 1375. He is described in two fifteenth-century manuscripts as inceptor in canon law— that is, as one who qualified for the doctorate but did not take it. Given the exigencies of the academic curriculum, he could have been a bachelor of canon law in 1376, and ready to incept as doctor in 1381–2.

Links have been established between Hilton and various northern clerks employed by Thomas Arundel, bishop of Ely from 1374 to 1388. Some were given preferment at Peterhouse, a college with a strong bias towards canon law. Arundel and his circle at Ely were active in responding to incipient Lollardy; after Arundel's translation to York in 1388, Hilton and others would have been instrumental in the policy of imposing rule and order upon an 'enthusiastic' piety that was influenced by the tradition of the hermit Richard Rolle (*d.* 1349), as well as in the conflict with Lollardy.

Hilton's letters reveal that, having renounced a promising legal career, he spent some time as a solitary, but they show him unfulfilled in this condition; he was at heart a pastor and a 'community' man. He joined the priory of Augustinian canons at Thurgarton, Nottinghamshire, presumably *c.*1386, the year when a correspondent, Adam Horsley, joined the Beauvale Charterhouse, and he remained there until his death on 24 March 1396. In 1388 the prior of Thurgarton was authorized, with others, to examine heretics. But while Hilton's writings are severely critical of 'heresy' and of 'enthusiastic' piety, his fame as a spiritual writer rests rather on his positive statement of

orthodox ascetic and mystical theology, to which contemporary controversy has added precision.

Hilton's greatest work is *The Scale of Perfection* (the title is editorial), in two books. The first book, datable to his early years at Thurgarton, is addressed ostensibly to an anchoress, and speaks of the renewal of God's image in man as the prelude to contemplation, with practical counsel on meditation and prayer, on humility and charity, and on the conquest of the capital sins. The second, which can only have been completed shortly before his death, is addressed to a wider readership, and views contemplation as an integral aspect of the fulfilment of the baptismal life, to which all Christians are called. His account of the journey towards contemplation through the 'luminous darkness', the way of the Cross, develops further the teaching of the first book. There are indications of mutual influence between Hilton and the unknown author of *The Cloud of Unknowing*, who may have been a monk of Beauvale, but Hilton firmly eschews the element of negative, or 'apophatic', theology to be found in the *Cloud*.

Closely associated with the first book of *The Scale of Perfection*, is *Mixed Life*, addressed to a devout layman with temporal responsibilities; this prescribes a rule of life appropriate to such men living in the world. The *Scale* was translated from English into Latin, probably before 1400, by the Carmelite Thomas Fyslake, who had become BD at Cambridge *c.*1375. The *Scale* (in English) and *Mixed Life* were printed in London in 1494 by Wynkyn de Worde (*d.* 1534), and continued to be reprinted until the Reformation changed the pattern of English religion. Augustine Baker (1575–1641), an English Benedictine, used the *Scale*, among other authorities, for the nuns under his direction at Cambrai. A fresh edition of the *Scale* and *Mixed Life*, probably prepared by Serenus Cressy, also a Benedictine, was printed in 1659 for sale in London. Since the nineteenth century there has been renewed interest in Hilton, with fresh editions and studies, first among Roman Catholics and then among Anglicans.

Hilton's Latin letters to individuals contain material which is taken up in the *Scale* within a broader framework. He is also credited with *Conclusiones de ymaginibus*, defending the veneration of images, and with *Of Angels' Song*, a response to the enthusiasm of Rolle's followers for this phenomenon. An English commentary on the psalm 'Qui habitat' may well be his. He was also responsible for 'Eight chapters on perfection', a translation of a work by Luis de Fontibus, an Aragonese Franciscan whose regency in theology at Cambridge may be dated to either 1391–3 or 1392–4. The *Prickynge of Love*, an expanded English version of the popular *Stimulus amoris*, compiled by the thirteenth-century Franciscan Giacomo da Milano and later writers, is also attributed quite plausibly to Hilton in some manuscripts.

While Hilton's Latin letters provide some personal details, his English writings are an authoritative statement of doctrine, and partly, though not wholly, veil his own personality. They reflect his clear legal mind and interest in moral theology, as well as his wide grasp of spiritual theology, especially in the tradition of Augustine, Gregory the Great, and the Cistercians. He avoids the appearance of innovation, but can still give fresh applications to old principles. He emerges as a firm yet compassionate pastor, with a sense of moderation in ascetic practices. His openness to people in varying states of life goes beyond the more strictly monastic bias of *The Cloud of Unknowing*. J. P. H. CLARK

Sources Emden, *Cam.* · J. Russell-Smith, 'Walter Hilton and a tract in defence of veneration of images', *Dominican Studies*, 7 (1954), 180–214 · J. P. H. Clark, 'Walter Hilton in defence of the religious life and of the veneration of images', *Downside Review*, 103 (1985), 1–25 · *Walter Hilton's Latin writings*, ed. J. P. H. Clark and C. Taylor, 2 vols. (1987) · R. Dorward, *The scale of perfection*, ed. and trans. W. Hilton and J. P. H. Clark (1991) [trans. from middle Eng., with an introduction and notes] · J. P. H. Clark, 'Walter Hilton and the psalm commentary *Qui habitat*', *Downside Review*, 100 (1982), 235–62 · J. P. H. Clark, 'The problems of Walter Hilton's authorship: *Bonum est*, *Benedictus* and *Of angels' song*', *Downside Review*, 101 (1983), 15–29 · J. P. H. Clark, 'Walter Hilton and the *Stimulus amoris*', *Downside Review*, 102 (1984), 79–118 · M. G. Sargent, *James Grenehalgh as textual critic*, 2 vols., Analecta Cartusiana, 85 (1984) · J. Hughes, *Pastors and visionaries: religion and secular life in late medieval Yorkshire* (1988)
Archives BL, Harley MS 6579 · CUL, Add. MS 6686 · LPL, MS 472

Hilton, William (1786–1839), painter, was born in Lincoln on 3 June 1786, the son of the japanner and scenery and portrait painter William Hilton (1752–1822) and his wife, Mary (1755–1835). He was renowned as a painter of history and like Benjamin Robert Haydon attempted to turn the taste of English collectors away from portraiture and landscape in the interests of establishing the school of grand manner painting as advocated by Sir Joshua Reynolds. He retained close connections with Lincoln and is commemorated in the cathedral alongside his close friend Peter DeWint, with whom he had studied under the engraver John Raphael Smith (*c*.1801) and who became his brother-in-law. A visit to Paris in 1814 was followed by his tour of Italy with Thomas Phillips in 1825 when they met David Wilkie, Dawson Turner, and Seymour Stocker Kirkup. Hilton entered the Royal Academy Schools on 4 January 1806, was elected associate of the Royal Academy in 1813, Royal Academician in 1819 (*The Theft of Ganymede*, RA Diploma Gallery), and became keeper in 1827. His friends included John Taylor, John Keats, Charles Lamb, and John Clare, who described him as 'the most unlike Londoner I saw' (Clare to J. A. Hessey, 2 April 1820, *Letters*). His uncompromising stance towards portraiture (fine portraits survive of his family—for example *Mrs. Harriet de Wint and her Daughter*, Usher Art Gallery, Lincoln)—and the production of large-scale oil paintings necessitating great investment of time and materials resulted in hardship. But recognition came in limited but, for the period, significant ways. In 1814 the British Institution purchased his *Mary Anointing the Feet of Jesus* for £525 and presented it to St Michael, Cornhill (des.; version Usher Art Gallery). Sir John Fleming Leicester commissioned two works: in 1818 *The Rape of Europa* (250 guineas; sold de Tabley sale, 7 July 1827, 300 guineas to the earl of Egremont; still at Petworth House, Sussex) and in 1820 *The Mermaid* (100 guineas, still at Tabley House, Cheshire). Both were hung at his purpose-designed gallery in Hill Street, London, alongside works by Gainsborough, Reynolds, and West. Robert Vernon, another pioneer patron of contemporary British art, bought his *Rebecca at the Well* (exh. RA, 1833; Tate collection). In 1827 Hilton was commissioned to design an east window for St George's Church, Liverpool (rebuilt 1819–25). Hilton was paid 1000 guineas for his triptych *The Crucifixion* (painted window dem. with church, *c*.1902; design in Walker Art Gallery, Liverpool). The city of Lincoln granted Hilton its freedom on 28 January 1828. In 1834 Sir John Soane commissioned *Marc Antony Reading Caesar's Will* for his house in Lincoln's Inn Fields (100 guineas, Sir John Soane's Museum, London). *The Crucifixion* was engraved by W. Finden for the Art Union in 1847. Other works by Hilton deemed sufficiently popular to be engraved were *The Rape of Europa* and *Sir Calepine Rescuing Serena*, purchased by subscription after his death and presented to the National Gallery, London. By 1839 commissions from churches had dwindled, domestic accommodation seldom permitted canvases measuring 8 feet by 6, and interest in mythological and biblical subjects had given way to contemporary genre painting. Hilton died at Peter DeWint's house at 40 Upper Gower Street, London, on 30 December 1839, two years after his wife Justina (*née* Kent) and just before the scheme to decorate the houses of parliament brought both employment and frustration to a new generation of artists. He was buried in the chapel of the Savoy, Strand, London. At a studio sale on 4 June 1841 organized by his executor, DeWint, the efforts of a lifetime went for what Hilton's sister saw as lamentably low sums. Hilton employed bitumen in his work and as a result many of his paintings are now in poor condition. At best it is still possible to see why the *Art Journal* in 1855 thought his poetical compositions distinguished by the highest qualities and why a German connoisseur, Waagen, found his 'an unusual talent for historical painting, being intellectual in invention' while the 'slender encouragement he received' showed 'how little the taste for historical painting prevails in England' (Waagen, 1.372).

MARCIA POINTON

Sources 'British artists, their style and character: no. VIII, William Hilton', *Art Journal*, 17 (1855), 253–5 · *Art Union*, 9 (1847), 109 · W. Carey, *Some memoirs of the patronage and progress of the fine arts in England and Ireland* (1826), 21 · *The letters of John Clare*, ed. J. W. Tibble and A. Tibble (1951) · Farington, *Diary* · D. Hall, 'The Tabley House papers', *Walpole Society*, 38 (1960–62), 59–122, esp. 76 · *The diary of Benjamin Robert Haydon*, ed. W. B. Pope, 5 vols. (1960–63) · J. A. Picton, *Memoirs* (1873), 2.12 · M. Pointon, 'The Italian tour of William Hilton, RA, in 1825', *Journal of the Warburg and Courtauld Institutes*, 35 (1972), 339–58 · M. Pointon, 'Keats, Joseph Severn and William Hilton: notes on a dispute', *N&Q*, 218 (1973), 49–54 · G. F. Waagen, *Treasures of art in Great Britain*, 1 (1854), 372 · J. E. Hodgson and F. Eaton, *The RA and its members* (1905)
Archives priv. coll. · Usher Art Gallery, Lincoln, papers | Usher Art Gallery, Lincoln, Harmsworth MSS
Likenesses C. H. Lear, pencil drawing, *c*.1839, NPG · C. H. Lear, pencil drawing, *c*.1845, NPG · W. Hilton, self-portrait, Usher Art Gallery, Lincoln

Himmelweit [*née* Litthauer], **Hildegard Therese** (1918–1989), university teacher and social psychologist, was born on 20 February 1918 in Berlin, Germany, the younger child and only daughter of Dr Siegfried Litthauer (d. 1935), chemist and industrialist, and his wife, Feodore Remak. Culturally and materially this Jewish family was of high standing. Hilde was proud of her great-grandfather, the first Jew to become a professor at a German university, though he had refused to be baptized. Her lifelong identification with Jewishness was based on the family's origin, not on Judaism as a religion; it was only strengthened by the advent of Adolf Hitler. A few days before her death she reminded a non-Jewish friend to bring a hat to her Jewish funeral. It was the custom in well-to-do German families to send children abroad to finish their secondary education. Hers began in Berlin and continued from 1934 at the Hayes Court School, Kent; she returned to Germany during the holidays. Following her father's death, her mother emigrated to England in 1938. At Newnham College, Cambridge, she obtained a second class (division II) in part one of the economics tripos (1938) and a first in part two of the medieval and modern languages tripos (1940). Two years later she earned another first-class degree in psychology at Cambridge. She qualified as an educational and clinical psychologist in 1943 and in 1945 she obtained a PhD degree in psychology from the University of London. In 1940 she married Dr Freddy Himmelweit (d. 1977), virologist. He came from a South African family, his father, Felix Himmelweit, being a businessman. They had one daughter.

Hilde Himmelweit's first job was at the Maudsley Hospital, in London (1945–8). During these years her professional identity as a social psychologist began to emerge. The transition from one culture to another, the experience of the war years and their aftermath, the fate of the Jews, and the fate of Germany predisposed her to emphasize in her professional work the impact of social conditions and political events on psychological phenomena. In 1949 she was appointed a lecturer at the London School of Economics, becoming a reader in 1954 and a professor in 1964.

Her first major contribution to the understanding of the contemporary world came when Hilde Himmelweit was director of the Nuffield television inquiry (1954–8). Her resulting book (with A. N. Oppenheim and P. Vince), *Television and the Child* (1958), established her reputation in Europe and the United States; it also led to some heated discussions between her and some television personalities, who regarded empirical evidence as superfluous. That she exposed herself to such encounters was typical of her style of work: her studies were invariably meant for two audiences, the research community and policy makers, even recalcitrant ones. Accordingly she spent much time and energy in giving research-based advice in formal and informal settings. From 1969 to 1974 she chaired the academic advisory committee of the Open University and from 1974 to 1977 she was a member of the committee on the future of broadcasting chaired by Lord Annan.

The second major aspect of Hilde Himmelweit's work was political psychology. With a team of gifted collaborators she followed a sample of young people for fifteen years, during which there were six general elections, to illuminate the process of decision making by voters. Here again the resulting publications were intended for both researchers and politicians. Hitting two targets with one stone was, she realized, a difficult task. She agonized about how to combine her meticulous attention to the technical aspects of her work with readability. Her greatest satisfaction came not from writing the reports but from presenting the results personally and directly to potential users, and here she excelled.

As her international reputation grew Hilde Himmelweit was invited to be a visiting professor and fellow at universities and institutes abroad. In 1981 she was given the Nevitt Sanford award for achievements in social psychology. She was also vice-president of the International Society for Political Psychology (1978–81). The distinction that pleased her most was an honorary doctorate from the Open University (1976). She was active in the British Psychological Society and on a committee of the Social Science Research Council.

Hilde Himmelweit's friends enjoyed in equal measure her engaging personality, her mind, and her beauty, which she retained to the end of her life. Early in her career she may have had to prove to herself and others that there was more to her than met the eye. In her maturity she carried her beauty unselfconsciously, with grace and dignity, and had an unobtrusive elegance in dress. Hilde Himmelweit died of cancer on 15 March 1989 at her home, 4 Downshire Hill, Hampstead, London.

MARIE JAHODA, *rev.*

Sources *The Times* (17 March 1989) · personal knowledge (1996) · private information (1996) · *CGPLA Eng. & Wales* (1989)
Wealth at death £786,262: probate, 25 Oct 1989, *CGPLA Eng. & Wales*

Himsworth, Sir Harold Percival (1905–1993), physician, was born on 19 May 1905 in Huddersfield, the son of (Joseph) Arnold Himsworth (d. c.1959), a businessman, and his wife, Amy Eliza, née Barraclough (c.1880–1962). Harry, as he was always called, had a struggle to get a good education, but from Huddersfield board school he won a scholarship to King James's Grammar School, Almondbury, in 1916. From there his parents removed him, at the age of sixteen and a half, to work in a worsted mill. A year later they reluctantly agreed to allow him to continue his education. As an external student he matriculated at the University of London and obtained a first MB with distinction. In January 1924 he entered the medical sciences faculty of University College, London. After moving on to University College Hospital medical school he qualified, gaining the university medal, and in 1930 obtained his MD, again with a gold medal. On 3 August 1932 he married Charlotte (1907–1988), daughter of William Gray of Walmer, Kent. Theirs was a very happy marriage. There were two sons, John Ross (b. 1934) and Richard Lawrence (b. 1937). Himsworth joined the medical unit at University College Hospital in 1930, became its deputy director in 1936, and director and professor of medicine in 1939. He became a member of the Medical Research Council (MRC) in 1948 and its secretary in 1949. He became deputy chairman in 1967 and retired in 1968. He was appointed KCB in 1952

Sir Harold Percival Himsworth (1905–1993), by Elliott & Fry, 1953

and elected FRS in 1955. From 1969 to 1976 he was chairman of the board of management of the London School of Hygiene and Tropical Medicine. In 1974–6 he was prime warden of the Goldsmiths' Company.

During his career Himsworth made major contributions in two fields. The first was research in clinical medicine, leading to sixty-one publications, in particular in relation to diabetes and liver disease. This work was done in the 1930s and 1940s at a time when there was a great deal of enthusiasm for such research, when the application of physiology and chemistry to clinical medicine was developing fast, when there was not an emotional distrust of science, and when professors were not plagued by a constant search for funding. He worked in an institution with a particularly strong background for such research. In his work on diabetes he gave one of the earliest and clearest descriptions of two types of diabetes and he developed a test to distinguish between them, one type being due to lack of insulin and controllable by the administration of insulin, the other not associated with lack of insulin and not responsive to its administration. The other major field in which he worked was that of experimental liver damage, whether due to malnutrition, to poisons such as trinitrotoluene or carbon tetrachloride, or to viral infections. The pattern of damage was not specific to particular causes: the severity of damage was related to the magnitude of the insult and whether it was repeated. Himsworth's work was important in understanding human disease, for example the massive necrosis of acute yellow atrophy or the diffuse fibrosis of cirrhosis of the liver sometimes seen as a sequel to the fatty infiltration of kwashiorkor.

Himsworth's second major contribution was as secretary of the MRC. He held this post at a time when there was a great demand for money for medical research and the government was willing to provide it without any interference with the scientific policies of the council. For most of his time as secretary he reported to the lord president of the council, a minister of high standing without departmental responsibilities. Himsworth was a man with a strong personality, very able, very energetic, always bubbling with enthusiasm, and an immensely hard worker. He was able to grasp the importance of all kinds of research from fundamental areas such as molecular biology to the interface between medicine and the social sciences, and had a fair understanding of every field. He thus had a remarkable grasp of the work of the MRC and came to dominate the council as well as being respected and trusted in Whitehall, where he gained a reputation for using public money effectively and insisting on high standards of work. It is worth noting that twelve of those who were on the staff of the MRC during his period of office managed to win thirteen Nobel prizes at some stage in their careers. This was the result of his belief that the most important role of an organization such as the MRC was to choose the right people as leaders of research teams. He did use his influence to encourage certain areas of research. The National Health Service (NHS) had been established shortly before he was appointed as secretary. Shortly after that it was agreed with the Ministry of Health that the major part of the funding of clinical research should be by a clinical research board run by the MRC and consisting of nominees of both the MRC and the ministry. He was convinced of the need for clinical research units where clinicians could work in collaboration with laboratory scientists in a way not easy in conventional university departments, and the number of such units rose rapidly.

Somewhat similar changes took place in regard to tropical medicine. When Himsworth became secretary he also became chairman of the colonial medical research committee. Before the end of the 1950s the arrangements were changed and the MRC took over the responsibility, establishing a tropical medicine research board with Himsworth as chairman and half the members nominated by the Colonial Office and its successors. He was very interested in this field, and during his time as secretary all the main centres of the MRC's research in the tropics were established. He visited them in the Gambia, in Uganda, and in the West Indies regularly. He made a special contribution to radiation medicine by chairing the MRC committee (1956), which, at the request of government, established levels at which individuals did not need to feel undue concern about developing any of the delayed effects. He made a major contribution to the development of the MRC Laboratory of Molecular Biology at Cambridge.

After retirement Himsworth had more time for fishing

and walking, but was often called on for advice. He was invited to inquire into the use of CS gas in Northern Ireland, and with colleagues he recruited he came to the conclusion that while it was a potent respiratory irritant it was not a systemic poison. He also wrote several books about research with a philosophical bias. The death of his wife in 1988 was a great blow to him. He died in London of a stroke on 1 November 1993, and was cremated. He was survived by his two sons and several grandchildren.

JOHN GRAY

Sources D. Black and J. Gray, *Memoirs FRS*, 41 (1995), 201–18 • personal knowledge (2004) • private information (2004) [family] • *The Times* (12 Nov 1993) • *The Independent* (9 Nov 1993) • WWW
Archives Wellcome L., notebooks, reports, and research files | Wellcome L., letters to Sir Edward Mellanby
Likenesses Elliott & Fry, photograph, 1953, NPG [*see illus.*] • J. Ward, 1969, Medical Research Council, head office; repro. in Black and Gray, *Memoirs FRS*, 200 • J. Ward, 1969, priv. coll. • L. Durbin, medal, 1990, Goldsmiths' Hall
Wealth at death £921,679: probate, 23 Dec 1993, *CGPLA Eng. & Wales*

Hinchley, John William (1871–1931), chemical engineer, was born on 21 January 1871 in Grantham, the fourth in the family of nine children of John Hinchley (*d.* 1913), plough fitter and Methodist lay preacher, and his wife, Eliza Holland (*d.* 1932), a worker in a lace factory. His education was hampered by lack of money but, following the family's move to Lincoln in 1872, he attended John Holton's school until 1881, when he won a scholarship to Lincoln grammar school. Between school hours he earned money cleaning and mending clocks and watches for a local clockmaker. After leaving school, he became an engineering apprentice with Ruston Proctor & Co. Ltd of Lincoln (1887–90), also attending evening classes at Lincoln School of Science. For one year, 1891–2, he taught science at a boys' school in Eastbourne, Sussex. In 1892 he moved to London and graduated in mining in 1896 at the Royal School of Mines. In 1903 he married Edith Mary, daughter of John Mason, whom he had met while she was at the Royal College of Art.

Graduation was followed by a difficult period in consulting, and Hinchley's appointment as assayist to the royal mint of Bangkok in 1903 was a welcome relief; his wife joined him there in 1904. They returned from Siam in 1907 and Hinchley started consulting again, covering topics as diverse as sherardizing and the manufacture of composition billiard balls. Another consulting activity which lasted until his death concerned the manufacture of pencils, which took him to various parts of Europe.

It was later that Hinchley became a teacher of chemical engineering, starting in 1909 with an evening course of twenty-five lectures and practical work at Battersea Polytechnic. He moved to Imperial College in 1911, was appointed assistant professor of chemical engineering in 1917, and was elevated to the chair in 1926. Hinchley's courses included a practical element: his earliest students learned to erect experimental plant and do pipe fitting. His methods trained men to work well in the chemical industry of the day.

Parallel with his teaching was Hinchley's concern with professional bodies. His work led to the formation in 1919 of the chemical engineering group of the Society of Chemical Industry. This was not enough: he pursued with renewed vigour his ideal of a qualifying body and, following many meetings of kindred enthusiasts, the Institution of Chemical Engineers was incorporated on 21 December 1922 with Hinchley as its first honorary secretary. One who attended these meetings described Hinchley as an enthusiast, 'obviously highly strung, quick in thought and rapid in speech, as though his overfilled brain could scarcely get rid of the thoughts and ideas quickly enough—sensitive to a hostile audience but quick to respond to a friendly one'.

Hinchley was a balanced man who never allowed the professor or the scientist to take over his life. His leisure was as full and useful as his working hours. In later life he became a devoted freemason. After a short illness, Hinchley was taken to the Freemasons' Hospital in Chelsea where, following an operation, he died on 13 August 1931; he was cremated at Golders Green crematorium, where his ashes were scattered. He was survived by his wife.

E. H. T. HOBLYN, *rev.*

Sources E. M. Hinchley, *John William Hinchley, chemical engineer* (1935) • *Professor Hinchley: memorial bulletin*, Institution of Chemical Engineers (1931) • personal knowledge (1993) • E. Hoblyn, 'Famous men remembered', *Chemical Engineer*, 423 (Feb 1986), 52–3 • *CGPLA Eng. & Wales* (1931)
Likenesses E. M. Hinchley, pencil sketch, Institution of Chemical Engineers, Rugby; repro. in Hoblyn, 'Famous men remembered' • photograph, repro. in Hinchley, *John William Hinchley*, frontispiece
Wealth at death £4546 5s. 11d.: resworn probate, 27 Oct 1931, *CGPLA Eng. & Wales*

Hinchliff, John Ely (1777–1867), sculptor, was baptized on 29 April 1777 at St Martin-in-the-Fields, Westminster, London, the son of William Hinchliff and his wife, Mary. At an early age Hinchliff was apprenticed as a mason to John Hinchliff the elder, who may have been his grandfather. In 1806 the quality of Hinchliff's carving brought him to the attention of the sculptor John Flaxman, whose chief assistant he became for the next twenty years. In January 1808 he entered the Royal Academy Schools, when his age was given as thirty.

During that time Hinchliff established himself as a neoclassical sculptor in the style of Flaxman. In 1814 he exhibited at the Royal Academy a group, *Christian and Apollyon*. The following year he exhibited another group, *Leonidas at Thermopylae*. These were followed over the next thirty years by six further works at the British Institution and some thirty-six groups at the Royal Academy. Of these *Venus and Aurora as the Morning and Evening Star* was described by M. H. Grant as 'of first rate excellence, recalling the triumphs of Flaxman' (Grant, 126).

After Flaxman's death in 1826, Hinchliff completed many of Flaxman's unfinished civic and imperial commissions, including the statues *The Marquis of Hastings* (Calcutta), and *John Philip Kemble* (Westminster Abbey). He also executed a few busts, including one of his former master, which he exhibited at the British Institution in 1849. Hinchliff is best-known for his monumental work. His bas-reliefs and mural tablets can be found in Chichester and Canterbury cathedrals, York Minster, and Bermondsey and Marylebone parish churches. He died on 23 November 1867, aged ninety, at his home of many years at Mornington Place, 185 Hampstead Road, London. His obituarist noted that he 'enjoyed the sincere regard of a large number of friends' (*Art Journal*, 48). In the 1950s M. H. Grant noted his 'real talent' in subjects of a 'classical and poetical nature' (Grant, 126). But Gunnis described his 'neo-hellenic' work as neither 'exacting' nor 'very inspired' (Gunnis, 202).

Hinchliff's son, **John James Hinchliff** (1805–1875), landscape engraver, engraved after topographical and architectural works by T. H. Shepherd (1829–31), and for J. Brittan and E. W. Brayley's *Devonshire and Cornwall Illustrated* (1832). He contributed illustrations to S. C. Hall's *Book of Gems* (1838). In 1847 he engraved a portrait of Benvenuto Cellini after Vasari for Cellini's *Memoirs* (1847). He provided illustrations to W. Beattie's *Castles and Abbeys of England* (1848) and H. Gastineau's *Picturesque Scenery of Wales* (1860), and several portraits for the 1872 edition of John Evelyn's *Diary and Correspondence*. He retired to Clifton, Bristol, and later moved to Walton by Clevedon, Somerset, where he died on 16 December 1875.

L. H. CUST, rev. JASON EDWARDS

Sources *Art Journal*, 30 (1868), 48 · Redgrave, *Artists* · *The exhibition of the Royal Academy* [exhibition catalogues] · C. E. Clement and L. Hutton, *Artists of the nineteenth century and their works: a handbook containing two thousand and fifty biographical sketches*, 2 vols. (1879) · Boase, *Mod. Eng. biog.* · M. H. Grant, *A dictionary of British sculptors from the XIIIth century to the XXth century* (1953) · R. Gunnis, *Dictionary of British sculptors, 1660–1851* (1953); new edn (1968) · *CGPLA Eng. & Wales* (1867) [John Ely Hinchliff] · S. C. Hutchison, 'The Royal Academy Schools, 1768–1830', *Walpole Society*, 38 (1960–62), 123–91, esp. 164 · IGI · B. Hunnisett, *An illustrated dictionary of British steel engravers*, new edn (1989)
Wealth at death under £1000: probate, 9 Dec 1867, *CGPLA Eng. & Wales*

Hinchliff, John James (1805–1875). *See under* Hinchliff, John Ely (1777–1867).

Hinchliff, Thomas Woodbine (1825–1882), mountaineer and writer, was born on 5 December 1825 at 25 Park Street, Southwark, London, the eldest son of Chamberlain Hinchliff of Lee, Kent, and his wife, Sarah Parish, sister of Sir Woodbine Parish. The spelling of the family name changed from Hinchliffe to Hinchliff between 1849 and 1852. After attending the grammar school at West Ham and then the Blackheath proprietary school, he went to Trinity College, Cambridge, where he graduated BA in 1849, and MA in 1852. He was admitted to Lincoln's Inn in 1849 and was called to the bar in 1852, but did not practise.

Hinchliff did much to bring mountain climbing into vogue. He was an active mountaineer in the 1850s and a prominent figure in the Alpine Club, which he helped to found in 1857. That year, after numerous alpine ascents over the preceding three summers, he published *Summer Months among the Alps*, a work that was well regarded by other mountaineers. From 1858 to 1860 he climbed in the Alps with Leslie Stephen, who remembered him for his good humour, boyish enthusiasm, and lack of ambition: 'He was not tormented by the feverish ambition of us youngsters, who were for winning glory as well as pleasure' (*Alpine Journal*, 41–3). Early meetings of the Alpine Club were held in Hinchliff's rooms at Lincoln's Inn, and he served as the club's first honorary secretary, and its president from 1874 to 1877.

In 1862, when he lost part of his right hand in a gun accident, Hinchliff stopped climbing. He nevertheless continued to travel in the Alps and outside Europe. In 1861 he toured Argentina, Uruguay, and Brazil, a journey later described in *South American Sketches* (1863), and in 1871 he returned to South America. In 1873–4 he went around the world, a trip later described in *Over the Sea and Far Away* (1876). He was also an amateur botanist, and wrote articles (1876–81) on the Italian lakes and Lake Geneva for *Picturesque Europe*. While on his way to the Italian lakes, Hinchliff was taken ill. He died a few hours later, on 8 May 1882, at Aix-les-Bains, France, where he was buried. He never married. A memorial obelisk was erected by his friends on the flanks of the Gorner Grat, near the Riffelalp Hotel.

T. G. BONNEY, rev. PETER H. HANSEN

Sources *Alpine Journal*, 11 (1882–4), 39–44 · A. L. Mumm, *The Alpine Club register*, 1 (1923) · *Proceedings* [Royal Geographical Society], new ser., 4 (1882), 424–5 · Venn, *Alum. Cant.*
Archives Alpine Club, London, archives, corresp. relating to founding of Alpine Club
Likenesses medallion, Alpine Club, London · photograph, repro. in *Alpine Journal*, 32, 227
Wealth at death £10,554 4s. 4d.: resworn probate, March 1883, *CGPLA Eng. & Wales* (1882)

Hinchliffe, John (1731–1794), bishop of Peterborough, was born in Westminster, London, the son of Joseph Hinchliffe, a livery stable-keeper in Swallow Street. Despite his origins Hinchliffe was appointed on the foundation of Westminster School in 1746. One contemporary argued: '[h]is promotion afforded a strong instance of what may be done by merit alone' (*GM*, 93) and Hinchliffe in a speech in 1779 would pronounce himself 'raised … to a situation in life far above my expectations' (Cobbett, *Parl. hist.*, 20.1055). In 1750 he was chosen one of the Westminster scholars to Trinity College, Cambridge, where he matriculated as pensioner in 1751. His academic career thereafter revolved around Trinity: scholar in 1751, BA in 1754, fellow in 1755, MA in 1757, and DD in 1764. He took clerical orders as deacon in 1756 and priest in 1757.

Hinchliffe served from 1757 to 1764 as assistant master (usher) at Westminster School. One of his pupils and friends was John Crewe of Crewe Hall, Cheshire. In 1763, while travelling with Crewe, he met the duke of Grafton; most of Hinchliffe's ecclesiastical and political patronage was thereafter tied up with the rise and fall of Grafton and his allies. He married Elizabeth Crewe, sister of John Crewe; they had two sons and three daughters. Hinchliffe was chosen headmaster of Westminster School in 1764. 'Our new Master, Dr. Hinchliffe', wrote one senior, 'is, I believe, very good natured: he did not flog anyone the first week, but he has gone on at a good rate since', though he was apparently careful 'never to beat a boy of rank' (Tanner, 31). Unfortunately Hinchliffe resigned the post only three months later on account of ill health. From 1764 to 1766 he tutored the duke of Devonshire. Through Grafton's patronage Hinchliffe received the valuable living of Greenwich in 1766.

Grafton's administration, although brief, brought a rapid series of promotions to Hinchliffe: he was chaplain-in-ordinary to George III in 1768–9; appointed and installed master of Trinity College, Cambridge, from 1768 to 1788; vice-chancellor of the university in 1768–9. One professor complained of the last-mentioned sinecure: 'our Vice-Chancellor, Dr Hinchliffe, is not here and is not expected for some months. To say the truth, we have not had much … of his company this year'. Although often an absentee from Cambridge, Hinchliffe did play a role in university electoral politics into the 1780s. His disapproval of the 1786 memorial of the 'ten junior fellows' led by George Waddington, and their ensuing legal appeal, demonstrated that he was not interested in increasing the academic rigour of the procedure for examining and electing fellows. When at the end of 1769 he was consecrated bishop of Peterborough he resigned the vicarage of Greenwich, though he was able to retain the mastership of Trinity.

Hinchliffe was a fairly vocal and outspoken bishop in the Lords, and his worry in 1776 that he would be seen as 'a busy meddler in political matters' was not unfounded. In early 1775 he defended the luxury duty on tea and the related Massachusetts enforcement acts ('a necessity of adopting coercive measures … condescension would defeat its very purpose'), although wishing for 'the middle way' of 'reconciliation upon the very easiest terms … consistently with the just authority' (Simmons and Thomas, 5.398–400). Yet by the end of 1775 his view was that coercion had already failed to bring about the desired cowing of faction, 'reconciliation', and 'lasting re-union with the colonies'. Arguing 'we now certainly know that they can and will fight … if [not for] liberty itself, … at least [for] the opinion of liberty', he proposed acceptance of the congressional petition for conciliation (ibid., 6.80–82). He was a vocal supporter of the duke of Grafton's 1776 motion for conciliatory measures on grounds that coercion had already proven unworkable (ibid., 482–4). He was one of the few bishops who opposed the Anglo-American War, referring to it in 1778 as an attempt to 'establish desolation upon system' by use of 'savage fierceness', and arguing in 1779 that it had led to a general 'spirit of dissention, animosity, and resentment' of lower orders in Britain as well as rebelliousness and threats of loss in its possessions (Cobbett, *Parl. hist.*, 20.9–11, 1054–6).

In the debate in 1778 on the Bill for the Security of the Protestant Religion, Hinchliffe supported Catholic relief on grounds of 'reason, justice, and Christian benevolence', but worried that it might be a time 'peculiarly unfavourable for such an experiment', since any change during the crisis might provoke 'the phrenzy of religious zeal'. He also objected that relief did not forbid 'Popery' from making converts of protestants through schools or bribery, did not reiterate strongly enough forbidding papists from civil or military power, and did not favour potential protestant heirs to Catholic estates. He maintained until the 1790s his opposition to any form of Catholic relief that might allow Catholic seminary-keepers to convert children of protestant parents. His moderated anti-Catholicism won him the support of the Gordon agitators, who conducted his carriage 'with great respect and honour' to the house, although they attacked other politicians (W. S. Lewis and A. D. Wallace, *Horace Walpole's Correspondence with the Countess of Upper Ossory*, 2, 1965, series volume 33.175, n. 8).

The remainder of Hinchliffe's parliamentary career included support for the commutation of tithes for outright grants of lands to clergy in cases of bills of enclosure (1781) and advocacy of excluding crown revenue officers from the right to vote for MPs (1782; Cobbett, *Parl. hist.*, 22.47–67; 23.99–100). His association with 'reforming bills' rather than the high-church clerical interest meant that he was one of only two bishops who attended the first levee of Lord Rockingham's ministry, one of his last brief connections with the 'ins' before his final decade of renewed oppositionism. Although Walpole thought that Hinchliffe was one of the two likeliest choices to be the new bishop of Salisbury in June 1782, he was not chosen.

Hinchliffe's political career in university and parliamentary life seemed dedicated to the principle which he had articulated in 1780, 'that so long as prejudices and passions form a part of human nature, there is no preserving any government whatever in peace and security without attending to them' (Cobbett, *Parl. hist.*, 21.754). His opposition to university reform, his sympathy with the prejudices of the American rebels, and his fears about consequences of a more general Catholic emancipation all pointed to a belief in *quieta non movenda* that was far more akin to earlier old whiggism than the nineteenth-century 'Liberalism' of which he has been seen as a progenitor. By 1788 Hinchliffe had so offended George III that Pitt wrote to the king of a 'means of preventing any application for his farther advancement on the Bench' (Aspinall, 394–5), while at the same time placating Grafton. Pitt's stratagem was to offer the rich deanery of Durham to Hinchliffe on condition of his resigning the mastership of Trinity. Hinchliffe was appointed dean of Durham on 24 September 1788.

Hinchliffe died at his palace in Peterborough on 11 January 1794 of paralysis, after a long illness, and was buried in the cathedral there. He was survived by his wife. His literary career was marked by 'very fond' friendship with Horace Walpole, who admired him for his 'patriotism', and who 'sent him his Chatterton, and invited him to dine at Strawberry Hill' in 1779. Unfortunately '[n]either side of the HW–Hinchliffe correspondence has been found' (Cole's MS note at the end of To Cole, 12 April 1779, Lewis and Wallace, *Horace Walpole's Correspondence with the Rev. William Cole*, 2, 1937, series volume 2.155–6, n. 1). His 1763 travels had introduced him to Sir Horace Mann and George Montagu. He also attended meetings of the Antiquary Society about 1773.

Hinchliffe was famous in his day as a speaker and preacher, being noted for his 'remarkable mellow voice' (*GM*, 94) and fine delivery. His speeches in the Lords as reported are good specimens of polished oratory. His only pamphlet publications were single sermons. A volume of thirteen collected sermons on apologetic and practical devotional theology was published in 1796. These sermons favoured 'the rational belief and steady practice of religion' and refuted 'scepticism and infidelity' by giving rationalistic arguments for biblical miracles and religion's value to the 'happiness of society' (Hinchliffe, *Sermons*, 1796). They were thus solidly in the latitudinarian tradition, written 'with correctness and simplicity … to promote virtuous manners' (*Monthly Review*, Sept–Dec 1796, second series, 21.71–3). He was also the translator of *A sermon preached by order of her imperial majesty on the tomb of Peter the Great in the cathedral church of St. Petersbourg* (1770).

J. J. CAUDLE

Sources *Fasti Angl., 1541–1857*, [Bristol] · *GM*, 1st ser., 64 (1794), 93–4, 99–100 · Venn, *Alum. Cant.* · L. E. Tanner, *Westminster School* (1934) · D. A. Winstanley, *Unreformed Cambridge: a study of certain aspects of the university in the eighteenth century* (1935) · R. C. Simmons and P. D. G. Thomas, eds., *Proceedings and debates of the British parliaments respecting North America, 1754–1783*, 6 vols. (1982–7) · Cobbett, *Parl. hist.*, vols. 20–23 · *The later correspondence of George III*, ed. A. Aspinall, 5 vols. (1962–70) · Walpole, *Corr.*, vols. 1, 33 · *Old Westminsters*, vol. 1

Archives PRO NIre., letters to Mrs Walsingham · Suffolk RO, Bury St Edmunds, letters to third duke of Grafton · U. Nott. L., letters to third duke of Portland

Likenesses J. S. Copley, chalk drawing, Metropolitan Museum of Art, New York · W. Grainger, line engraving (after W. H. Brown), NPG; repro. in *The Senator* (1791) · J. Greenwood, pencil drawing, BM · W. Peters, oils, Trinity Cam.

Hinchliffe, William (1691–1742), poet and bookseller, was born on 12 May 1691 and baptized on 24 May at St Olave, Southwark, the son of Edward Hinchliffe, a tradesman, and Elizabeth, *née* Hurt. He was educated at a private grammar school in Reigate, Surrey, alongside his friend Henry Needler. He then served an apprenticeship to Arthur Bettesworth, a bookseller on London Bridge, 'and afterwards followed that business himself near thirty years' (Cibber, 5.24). In 1718 he married Jane Leigh, daughter of a prominent London citizen.

Hinchliffe's first poems were complimentary addresses to Harley on the peace (1713) and to George I on his arrival at Greenwich (1714): the latter is also the earliest traced work of which he was the publisher. He also wrote and published a *History* (1716) of the 1715 rising, dedicated to the duke of Argyll. Most occurrences of his name in later imprints are as one of a 'conger' (an alliance of booksellers) for joint publication of substantial (often scholarly) works, such as Joseph Trapp's *Virgil* (1731–5) or the Royal Society's *Philosophical Transactions Abridged* (1734). His last traced publication is *The Turkish Spy*, eleventh edition, eight volumes (1741), in a conger of twenty-two booksellers. His business address was at Dryden's Head, under the Royal Exchange.

In 1718 Hinchliffe published his own *Poems, Amorous, Moral, and Divine*, a collection of imitations and translations from Latin, pastorals, complimentary poems, and so

on, dedicated to his friend Henry Needler. Some modern scholars think that 'The Seasons' in this volume gave hints to James Thomson. Hinchliffe later mastered French and published in 1734 his translation of *La vie de Mahomet* (1730) by the freethinker Henri de Boulainviller. The translation was dedicated to his 'old Companion' William Duncombe, and carried a preface in which Hinchliffe expresses admiration for Muhammad and denounces popish corruption. At his death he left in manuscript a translation of the first nine books of Fénelon's *Télémaque*. Hinchliffe died on 29 September 1742 and was buried in the parish church of St Margaret Lothbury. His wife, three daughters, and a son were already dead; he was survived only by his son William.

JAMES SAMBROOK

Sources R. Shiels, *The lives of the poets of Great Britain and Ireland*, ed. T. Cibber, 5 vols. (1753), 5.24–6 · *IGI* · H. R. Plomer and others, *A dictionary of the printers and booksellers who were at work in England, Scotland, and Ireland from 1726 to 1775* (1932) · D. Foxon, *English poetry, 1701–1750: a catalogue* (1975) · letters of administration, PRO, PROB 6/118

Hinckley, John (1617/18–1695), Church of England clergyman and religious controversialist, was born in Coughton (or possibly Chilvers Coton), Warwickshire, the son of Robert Hinckley. Hinckley states that 'I was borne of, and educated by religious parents' (*Two Sermons*, sig. t7). Influenced by his schoolmaster, Josiah Packwood, Hinckley was persuaded early on to prepare for the ministry. He later wrote 'I came [to Oxford] … well principled in … Religion towards God. My dearest friends were accounted Puritanes, in those days' (*Fasciculus literarum*, 243). He matriculated at St Alban Hall on 4 July 1634, aged sixteen. He graduated BA on 11 April 1638 and MA on 22 March 1641. A sermon by Peter Wentworth of Balliol College in St Mary's challenged several of his own political and religious assumptions, propelling him into a convinced conformity within the Church of England.

Hinckley was invited by George Purefoy of Wadley, near Faringdon, Berkshire, to serve in his household, perhaps as a teacher. Subscription records indicate Hinckley was ordained priest on 28 May 1643. He was presented as vicar of the nearby parish of Coleshill, Berkshire. On 14 January, probably in 1647, he married Susannah Shelley (*c.*1621–1671) of Sussex. They had nine children, three of whom—Walter (1648–1699), John (1654–1705), and Henry (1660–1732)—followed their father into the ministry. After the death of his wife on 24 July 1671, Hinckley married Frances Tracy (*c.*1625–1701) in 1675, their twenty-year marriage ending at his death.

In 1660 Hinckley accepted the rectory of Northfield, Warwickshire. He experienced early success in attracting local nonconformists to his preaching ministry. But after publishing his *Piqanalogia, or, A Persuasive to Conformity by Way of a Letter to the Dissenting Brethren* (1670) he became involved in an increasingly rancorous dispute with nonconformists in general and Richard Baxter in particular. Baxter took offence at published remarks which he considered unfair and responded by letter in a series of four private exchanges with Hinckley from August 1670 to February 1672. In 1680 Hinckley undertook to publish the entire correspondence, as well as another letter in which he dismissed Baxter's own published defences of non-conformity as 'Canting Gibberish' (*Fasciculus literarum*, 269). Charging Hinckley with a breach of faith, Baxter published his own defensive response in 1681, *A Third Defense of the Cause of Peace*. Both parties claimed victimization by the other, and neither accepted responsibility for the increasingly shrill tone. It was a conflict which served mainly to diminish both men. During the course of this controversy Hinckley was honoured by his colleagues among the clergy and at Oxford. On 15 October 1673 he was made a prebendary of Lichfield Cathedral, and on 9 July 1679 the degrees of BD and DD were conferred on him by Oxford University.

Hinckley's last years at Northfield were marred by a bitter conflict with Thomas Jolliffe, lord of the manor at Cofton Hackett. According to Hinckley, in 1690 Jolliffe broke an agreement made twenty years earlier which exempted him from having to pay Jolliffe an annual pension of £7 from the living. Hinckley's indignant account, 'The tru stating of something concerning the parsonage of Northfield', is written on the back pages of the second volume of Northfield parish register. In it Hinckley claims that, following the death of the one witness to their agreement, Jolliffe instigated legal proceedings and unfairly used his influence to procure a judgment against Hinckley in which he was forced to pay £600. Hinckley died at Northfield on 13 April 1695 and was buried on 17 April in the chancel of St Laurence's Church, Northfield.

J. WILLIAM BLACK

Sources Oxford County Archives Office, Oxford diocesan MS, e.13 • Coleshill parish register transcripts, Oxford County Archives Office • J. Hinckley, *Fasciculus literarum, or, Letters on several occasions* (1680) • [J. Hinckley], *Piqanalogia, or, A persuasive to conformity by way of a letter to the dissenting brethren* (1670) • J. Hinckley, *Two sermons preached before the judges of assize* (1657) • R. Baxter, *A third defense of the cause of peace* (1681) • L. G. Day, 'Notes on a passage from a monumental inscription in the chancel of Northfield Church', Northfield Conservation Group occasional paper, no. 2, 1978 • Foster, *Alum. Oxon.*, 1500–1714, vol. 2 • L. G. Day, ed., *Registers of the parish of Northfield in the county of Worcester, part one, 1560–1757*, 2 vols. (1978–9), vol. 2 • Wood, *Ath. Oxon.*, new edn, vol. 4 • bishop's transcripts, Coughton, Herefs. RO, BA 2006 14/1–52, b736

Hincks, Edward (1792–1866), orientalist, eldest of the seven children of Thomas Dix *Hincks (1767–1857) and his wife, Anne Boult (1767–1835), was born at Princess Street, Cork, on 19 August 1792. His younger brothers included William *Hincks and Francis *Hincks. The family moved to Windmill Hill (later St Patrick's Hill) about 1797. After education by his father and some time at Midleton School from 1800, he proceeded on 2 November 1807 to Trinity College, Dublin, where he was elected a scholar on 18 June 1810 and graduated BA with the gold medal on 11 February 1812. He was elected a junior fellow on 14 June 1813. He was ordained deacon in 1815 and priest in 1817, taking his MA in the same year. After acting for various periods as deputy librarian, he later published a *Catalogue of the Egyptian Manuscripts in the Library of Trinity College, Dublin* (1843). In

September 1819 Hincks was named rector of Ardtrea, leaving Dublin possibly because of differences with the provost. On 6 February 1823 in Lurgan church he married Jane Dorothea Boyd (1792–1870); they had four daughters. Hincks became BD in July 1823 and DD in 1829. In October 1825 he was appointed rector of Killyleagh, co. Down, where he lived until his death. His hopes of advancement in the church remained unfulfilled, probably because of his liberal views.

Despite the seclusion of his country rectory, Hincks established a reputation of the first order among the pioneers of decipherment, with articles published mainly in the *Transactions of the Royal Irish Academy*. His earlier contributions were chiefly on the subject of Egyptian hieroglyphs, and Hincks was the first to employ the true method for their transliteration. From 1846 his studies were directed to cuneiform, as was shown by his papers on Babylonian, Assyrian, old Persian, and Elamite inscriptions, and the Urartian inscriptions from Van. The analytical powers displayed in these essays were very considerable. Hincks enjoyed the distinction of the discovery of the true nature of the Babylonian cuneiform syllabic system, showing greater perception than Sir Henry Creswicke Rawlinson (1810–1895) in his work on the same subject at Baghdad. Many other discoveries may be noted among his numerous articles. He was one of those chosen in 1857 in a public demonstration of the accuracy of cuneiform decipherment and was awarded the Prussian order of merit in 1863. But Hincks was disappointed at the lack of public recognition of his achievements in Britain, and his failure to obtain a more financially secure position to allow him to devote more time to his studies. He died suddenly at Killyleagh rectory on 3 December 1866 while reading in bed, possibly from a heart attack or stroke, and was buried in the old parish graveyard there.

M. L. BIERBRIER

Sources E. F Davidson, *Edward Hincks: a selection from his correspondence, with a memoir* (1933) • K. J. Cathcart and P. Donlon, 'Edward Hincks (1792–1866): a bibliography of his publications', *Orientalia*, 52 (1983), 325–51 • K. J. Cathcart, ed., *The Edward Hincks bicentenary lectures* (1994) • *Annual report of the Royal Asiatic Society of Great Britain and Ireland* (1867), xix–xxiii • private information (2004)
Archives BL, readings of inscriptions on the Nineveh Marbles (1 vol.), Add. MS 22907 • TCD, notebooks on Assyrian • U. Oxf., Oxford, Griffith Institute, corresp. and papers | BL, letters to Sir Austen Layard, Add. MSS 38978–38988 • Pembroke College, Oxford, letters to Peter Renouf
Likenesses portrait, *c*.1830, TCD • X. Barthe, bust, *c*.1905, Cairo Museum
Wealth at death under £3000: probate, 23 Jan 1867, *CGPLA Eng. & Wales* • £550 p.a. plus house: Davidson, *Edward Hincks*

Hincks, Sir Francis (1807–1885), politician and journalist in Canada, was born on 14 December 1807 at Cork, Ireland, the youngest of the seven children of the Revd Thomas Dix *Hincks (1767–1857) and his wife, Anne Boult (1767–1835). Edward *Hincks was his elder brother. Hincks's father left the Presbyterian ministry for a teaching career, and in 1821 joined the Royal Academical Institute at Belfast, where Hincks received his early education. Two of his brothers became prominent academics and a third, William *Hincks, became a Unitarian minister; Hincks was also a Unitarian for most of his life, though about 1871 he became a member of the Church of England. After a year at the University of Belfast, Hincks worked for five years at John Martin & Co., a Belfast shipping firm. Restless, he visited the Canadas in 1830–31, and in September 1832 he returned there with his new bride and settled in York (renamed Toronto in 1834), Upper Canada. Martha Anne Stewart (d. 1874), whom he married on 29 July 1832, came from Legoniel in northern Ireland; they had five children. In premises rented from some protestants from Cork, William Warren Baldwin and his son Robert, he started a mercantile business.

A rising bourgeois politician Despite the growth of Upper Canada's population from 75,000 people in 1812 to 450,000 by 1842, Hincks failed in his business and moved into banking and insurance. Although he managed businesses only of the second rank, he acquired a lasting reputation as a top-class financial manager. The 1830s were formative in other ways, too. Given his father's reformist political views, Hincks's close relationship with Robert Baldwin, the colony's leading moderate reformer, was predictable. The Baldwins were well-off lawyers, members of Upper Canada's patrician élite. Hincks, while hardly poor—his mother enjoyed a substantial inheritance—was more the respectable man on the make with an eye for the main chance, but he was, like the Baldwins, an Irish protestant. In the increasingly bitter political conflicts that beset the colony in the 1830s, Hincks became a prominent political tactician and controversialist.

In 1836 Hincks was appointed secretary of Toronto's Reform Constitutional Society, which protested against the 'unconstitutional proceedings' (Read and Stagg, 48) of the lieutenant-governor, Sir Francis Bond Head, an avid supporter of the tory family compact. Increasingly frustrated, some reformers followed William Lyon Mackenzie in an unsuccessful armed rebellion in 1837. Although Hincks opposed rebellion and favoured a form of responsible government which would render the executive council answerable to the assembly, some of the directors of the Bank of the People, which he managed, were implicated in the affair. Hincks went into hiding until tempers cooled. Discouraged, he considered moving to Iowa, but a land deal collapsed. When the British government appointed Lord Durham (the earl of Lambton) to determine the reasons for the Canadian uprisings, reformers rallied. Hincks resigned from the bank and became owner and editor of *The Examiner*, a Toronto paper dedicated, as its masthead proclaimed, to 'responsible government and the voluntary principle'. Leading tories soon branded Hincks as the most effective reform leader: his writings, one tory lamented, are 'of a character to unhinge the public mind—and are leading to much and serious mischief' (Sanderson, 2.283). Hincks's editorials helped move Durham towards the moderate reform camp.

When Durham's recommendations for closer links between the executive council and the assembly and for uniting the two Canadas reached Upper Canada in April

1839, reformers rejoiced. Realizing the importance of reform unity under the proposed union, Hincks quietly encouraged an alliance between the leading French-Canadian reformer, Louis-Hippolyte LaFontaine, and Robert Baldwin, and by acting as political broker helped construct the framework within which union politics would unfold.

The union's first governor, the ex-businessman Charles Poulett Thomson (Lord Sydenham), had an important influence on Hincks. Thomson opposed party development and wished to govern in harmony with the assembly. Hincks initially feared that this would mean tory one-party rule and strongly opposed Sydenham's position. But after being elected as a member of the assembly for Oxford, a rural Upper Canadian community, he gradually re-evaluated his stance. In fact Hincks and Sydenham had much in common: both were pragmatists; both wished, as Sydenham put it, to 'take the moderates from both sides' (Mills, 117), or, as Hincks later advised Baldwin, 'to select [for patronage] Tories from the same class that we select our friends' (Mills, 120), and both looked to the politics of economic development as the ultimate means of effecting political and social stability. Hincks supported many of Sydenham's economic policies: a proposed Bank of Issue, the creation of district councils and a board of works, and the use of a British loan of £1.5 million for canal construction. His support of Sydenham led to a temporary break with Baldwin and other Reformers and, more lasting, to his being labelled a political opportunist.

In 1842 Hincks sold *The Examiner* and became inspector-general (finance minister) under Sydenham's successor, Sir Charles Bagot. Baldwin and LaFontaine soon joined him in the ministry. Before conflict could emerge over whether responsible government was in operation (whether the governor or the executive council answerable to the assembly controlled patronage), Bagot, severely ill, resigned. Hincks saw responsible government as an opportunity to play an important role on an expanding colonial stage. He visualized himself fighting the 'battle of the middle classes against the aristocracy' (Mills, 117), and through control of the executive he hoped to effect a social revolution, putting in place a society run by respectable men of business. The imperial government had to provide sufficient scope for the realization of these ambitions. Bagot's successor, Sir Charles Metcalfe, refused to provide such scope: Baldwin, LaFontaine, and Hincks resigned in November 1843 in protest at his refusal to allow them control of patronage.

Hincks then moved to Montreal and founded a Reform paper, *The Pilot*, and helped unite Irish and French-Canadian workers for the Reform cause. After being defeated in the ensuing election he spent much of his own money in a struggle to keep *The Pilot* afloat. In 1848, when LaFontaine and Baldwin, victors in the 1847 election, were asked to form a ministry, Hincks sold *The Pilot* and joined them as inspector-general.

The political ascendancy of the middle class Arguably Hincks was the ministry's most important member. He stabilized the government's chaotic financial affairs.

When the Rebellion Losses Bill, which indemnified rebels for property losses in 1837, excited tory riots in Montreal, Hincks kept London investors on side. He argued for strict punitive measures against public officials who signed the annexation manifesto circulated as a response to England's repeal of the Navigation Acts and the apparent end to protected trade with Britain. He worked for a reciprocity trade agreement with the United States, and signed one in 1855. Following Sydenham's ideas, he promoted the immigration of Britain's surplus population, who would work on public projects financed by imperial loans. The loans would be paid off by the sale of public lands to the immigrants. But a major weakness in the programme, overlooked by Hincks, was the fact that the most valuable crown land had long since been sold.

Between 1848 and 1851 as inspector-general, and from 1851 to 1855 as co-leader (with A. N. Morin) of the Reform government, Hincks followed this programme. When the imperial government refused financial support, Hincks attracted leading British capitalists and railway builders by providing loan guarantees for several large railways, such as the Grand Trunk, the Great Western, and the Northern. He passed legislation which allowed Upper Canada's municipal governments to borrow money for local improvements. Unlike the government's more cautious London financial agents, Glyn Mills & Co. and the Baring Brothers, Hincks correctly believed that British investors would pour capital into the colony. By 1851 Baldwin and LaFontaine, finding this speculation somewhat distasteful, retired, leaving Hincks at the helm.

Hincks occupied the shifting centre, opposed by Clear Grits, led by George Brown, the editor of the influential Toronto *Globe*, on the left and tories on the right. To make matters worse, he became tainted by scandal. He used his position as a public representative to further his private profit. He argued that in no case did the public lose out by such activity and that private speculation by public officials, even in areas of public policy, was in accord with much past and present practice. So it was, but Hincks, in this era of rapid change, failed to keep pace with changing perceptions of public morality, leaving his ministry open to fatal attacks.

Colonial governorships and later career Hincks resigned in 1855, but his public career continued. The Colonial Office wished to reward colonial statesmen with imperial appointments and offered Hincks the governorship of Barbados and the Windward Islands in 1856. During his five years there he worked to better the educational and living standards of the islands' native populations. While he instituted a programme of non-sectarian education, his attempts to improve living conditions were defeated by an entrenched planter class who desired cheap labour. None the less, in 1861 England rewarded him with the governorship of British Guiana (later Guyana) and a CB. For the next eight years Hincks bickered with the colony's chief justice and with colonial businessmen known as the Bermuda clique. He did not receive a new appointment, although he did acquire a knighthood in 1869.

That same year Hincks became Canada's finance minister in Sir John A. Macdonald's Conservative government. The appointment angered many Conservatives, but Hincks applied his skills as a broker and financial expert to good effect. He resolved an impasse between bankers and government concerning government involvement in issuing public currency, and he allowed small banks to commence operations with a lower amount of paid-up capital. In 1874 he quit formal politics and returned to his old careers in banking, insurance, and journalism. His banking business ended in a scandal: he did not pay sufficient attention to the activities of an underling who embezzled funds, and the courts censured him for his negligence.

On 14 July 1875 Hincks married Emily Louisa Delatre (d. 1880), the widow of Robert Baldwin Sullivan. He published several partisan defences of his past politics: *The Political History of Canada between 1840 and 1855* (1877) and *Reminiscences of his Public Life* (1884). He died of smallpox in Montreal on 18 August 1885 and was buried at St Jude's Church on 19 August. After the payment of debts, he warned his executor, there would be 'little if any surplus' (Careless, 196) left for his heirs. He bequeathed Canada a similarly mixed legacy: railways were built, including the world's longest, the Grand Trunk, but they were not profitable. Government guarantees came due and money for such unanticipated debts proved extremely hard to find. Hincks's focus on economic development over religious and ethnic strife, however, provided a common ground on which politicians from both the Canadas could unite.

PETER A. BASKERVILLE

Sources G. A. Davison, 'Francis Hincks and the politics of interest, 1831–54', PhD diss., University of Alberta, 1989 · G. A. Davison, 'The Hincks–Brown rivalry and the politics of scandal', *Ontario History*, 81 (1989), 129–51 · R. S. Longley, *Sir Francis Hincks* (1943) · M. J. Piva, 'Continuity and crisis: Francis Hincks and Canadian economic policy', *Canadian Historical Review*, 66 (1985), 185–210 · M. J. Piva, *The public borrowing process: public finance in the province of Canada, 1840–67* (1992) · W. G. Ormsby, 'Sir Francis Hincks', *The pre-confederation premiers: Ontario government leaders*, ed. J. M. S. Careless (1980), 148–96 · D. Mills, *The idea of loyalty in Upper Canada, 1784–1850* (1988) · S. J. R. Noel, *Patrons, clients, brokers: Ontario society and politics, 1791–1896* (1990) · J. M. S. Careless, *The union of the Canadas: the growth of Canadian institutions, 1841–1857* (1967) · G. E. Boyce, *Hutton of Hastings: the life and letters of W. Hutton, 1801–61* (1972) · C. Read and R. J. Stagg, eds., *The rebellion of 1837 in Upper Canada* (1985) · *The Arthur papers*, ed. C. R. Sanderson, 2 (1957) · W. G. Ormsby, 'Hincks, Sir Francis', *DCB*, vol. 11

Archives NA Canada, corresp. · PRO NIre., corresp. | Bodl. Oxf., corresp. with Sir John Crampton · Bodl. RH, letters to Henry Labouchère · Lpool RO, letters to fourteenth earl of Derby · Metropolitan Toronto Reference Library, Robert Baldwin MSS · NA Canada, La Fontaine MSS · NA Canada, T. S. Shenston MSS

Likenesses portrait, 1855, repro. in Longley, *Sir Francis Hincks*, following p. 256

Wealth at death 'very little': own assessments

Hincks, Thomas (1818–1899), Unitarian minister and naturalist, was born on 15 July 1818 at Exeter, one of the eight children of William *Hincks (1793?–1871), Unitarian minister and naturalist, and his wife, Maria Ann Yandell (1788/9–1849). His grandfather, Thomas Dix *Hincks, was a Presbyterian minister in Ireland, his uncle Sir Francis

Hincks was prime minister of Canada, and another uncle, Edward Hincks, was an orientalist. From 1833 to 1839 he attended the Unitarian Manchester New College at York (where his father was on the staff), where he trained to be a minister; his first post was in Cork, Ireland, from 1839. In 1840 he gained a BA from London University. His rise in the Unitarian church was rapid. He held ministries at Eustace Street Chapel, Dublin; Warrington; Exeter; Upper Chapel, Sheffield; and, from 1855, at Mill Hill Chapel, Leeds, one of the most noted Unitarian congregations.

In 1846 Hincks married Elizabeth, daughter of John Allen of Warrington. In Leeds he was an active minister, from 1862 organizing an Old Scholars Society which met regularly for tea followed by a lecture. He also presided over the Leeds Literary and Philosophical Society for three years, and was responsible for arranging its museum. His bi-monthly *Mill Hill Chapel Record* ran for 102 issues, from January 1858. Many of his sermons were published. He also published a collection of fifty-two hymns (including three of his own) in 1868, the year in which he permanently lost his voice. He retired from the ministry in 1869, and moved first to Taunton and then to Stokeleigh, Leigh Woods, near Bristol.

As a zoologist Hincks specialized in two marine animal groups, the Hydrozoa and the Bryozoa. In retirement he continued with the biological research he had begun while serving as a minister, and he was elected FRS in 1872. Between 1851 and 1893 he published about fifty papers on Hydrozoa and Bryozoa, much of his research based on his own dredging off the coast of south-west England from Swanage to Devon, and especially around Salcombe. His *History of British Hydroid Zoophytes* (1868) and his *History of Marine Polyzoa* (1880) both remained standard works for more than a century. His *Collected Papers* (2 vols., 1894–5) brought together the articles which he wrote over many years for the *Annals and Magazine of Natural History*. His work was marked by precise observation, was prepared lucidly for publication, and was accompanied by highly accurate illustrations.

In later life Hincks continued with voluntary work for the Unitarian church, serving as honorary secretary of the Lewin's Mead Domestic Mission between 1886 and 1889. He also helped plan the 1898 Bristol meeting of the British Association for the Advancement of Science but was unable to attend due to failing health. He died at Stokeleigh on 25 January 1899 and was buried, at his own request, near Leeds. He was survived by his wife and his two daughters.   PAUL F. S. CORNELIUS

Sources C. Hargrove, *The Inquirer* (4 Feb 1899), 69–71 · L. C. Miall, 'Rev. Thomas Hincks, 1818–1899', *Obituary notices of fellows of the Royal Society reprinted from the year-book of the society, 1900, 1901* (1901), 39–40 · S. F. Harmer, *Nature*, 59 (1898–9), 374 · *The Times* (26 Jan 1899), 7 · *DNB*
Archives Marine Biological Association of the United Kingdom, Plymouth, catalogue of his library | NHM, letters to Joshua Alder and Alfred Merle Norman
Likenesses W. J. Edwards, stipple and line print, NPG
Wealth at death £11,315 7s. 6d.: probate, 14 March 1899, *CGPLA Eng. & Wales*

Hincks, Thomas Dix (1767–1857), non-subscribing Presbyterian minister and academic, was born at Bachelor's Quay, Dublin, on 24 June 1767. His father, Edward Hincks (*d.* 1772), had moved in that year to Dublin from Chester. Dix was his mother's maiden name. On her husband's early death she retained his post in the Dublin customs. Hincks went to school in Nantwich, Cheshire, and Dublin. Originally intended for medicine, he was apprenticed in 1782 to a Dublin apothecary, but after two years he entered Trinity College, Dublin. He did not finish his course, but in September 1788 entered Hackney New College, under Drs Price, Kippis, and Rees. Kippis recommended him as assistant to Samuel Perrott at Cork. He began his ministry there in 1790, but was not ordained until 1792 by the southern presbytery. In September 1791 he married Anne (1767–1835), eldest daughter of William Boult of Chester, the grandfather of Swinton Boult, director of the London, Liverpool, and Globe insurance company. They had seven children.

Meanwhile in 1791 Hincks opened a school, which he continued until 1803, when he became a member of the Royal Irish Academy, and a salaried officer of the Royal Cork Institution, of which he was the planner. He lectured on chemistry and natural philosophy (1810–13). He left his church and the institution and moved to Fermoy, co. Cork, in 1815, succeeding Dr Adair as tutor of the Fermoy Academy. There in 1818 he formed a small Presbyterian congregation which met in the court house. He resigned his positions and from 1821 to 1836 he was classical headmaster in the Royal Belfast Academical Institution, filling also the chair of Hebrew in the collegiate department of the institution until the establishment of the Queen's College in 1849.

Hincks was a member of most of the scientific societies of Ireland. His published works include several school textbooks and while in Cork he edited the *Munster Agricultural Magazine*. After settling in Belfast he was admitted a member of the Antrim presbytery and attended the church of William Bruce, who was a friend and colleague. His theology was Arian, but he avoided polemics, and got on well with clergy from all denominations. In 1834 he was made LLD of Glasgow. He died on 24 February 1857 in Murray's Terrace, Belfast, and was buried in the churchyard of Killyleagh, co. Down, his eldest son's parish. There is a memorial window to him in the First Presbyterian Church, Belfast. Three of his sons, Edward *Hincks, Francis *Hincks, and William *Hincks, attained distinction. Thomas (1796–1882) was archdeacon of Connor from 1865. John (1804–1831) was minister at Renshaw Street, Liverpool (1827–31). A daughter, Anne, died unmarried in 1877 at Montreal.

      ALEXANDER GORDON, rev. DAVID HUDDLESTON

Sources W. B. [W. Bruce], 'Biographical memoir of the Rev. Thomas Dix Hincks', *Christian Reformer, or, Unitarian Magazine and Review*, new ser., 13 (1857), 228–34 · *Bible Christian* (1835), 144 · G. E. Evans, *A history of Renshaw Street Chapel* (1887), 21–32 · *Belfast News-Letter* (30 March 1882) · *A history of congregations in the Presbyterian Church in Ireland, 1610–1982*, Presbyterian Church in Ireland (1982),

341, 479 · J. Jamieson, *The history of the Royal Belfast Academical Institution, 1810–1960* (1959, [1960]), 82 · A. Gordon and G. K. Smith, *Historic memorials of the First Presbyterian Church of Belfast* (1887), 113
Archives PRO NIre., papers · U. Lpool, Sydney Jones Library, corresp.
Likenesses portrait, repro. in Jamieson, *History of the Royal Belfast Academical Institution*

Hincks, William (1793?–1871), Unitarian minister and naturalist, was born on 16 April, about 1793, in Cork, the second of five sons and two daughters born to Thomas Dix *Hincks (1767–1857), Irish Presbyterian minister, and his wife, Anne (1767–1835), daughter of William Boult of Chester. His brothers included Edward *Hincks and Francis *Hincks. He was educated in his father's school and in 1809–14 was a student at Manchester College, York.

In 1814 Hincks was ordained in his father's chapel in Prince's Street, Cork; the next year, after a ministry of more than two decades, the elder Hincks moved to Fermoy Academy, and in 1816 William Hincks was appointed to George's Chapel, Exeter, following Lant Carpenter (1780–1840) as junior colleague to the Revd James Manning (1754–1831); his yearly stipend averaged £205. In 1817 he married Maria Ann Yandell (1788/9–1849), who had been adopted by the wife of William Jillard Hort (1764–1849), minister at Cork from 1817 to 1849; the eldest of the Hinckses' eight children, Thomas *Hincks (1818–1899), became a reputable zoologist and a Unitarian minister whose theological views diverged sharply from his father's.

In 1822 William Hincks moved to an even more prestigious congregation, Renshaw Street, Liverpool, where he was active in the intellectual life of the town. In 1827, with reluctance, he was persuaded to accept the tutorship in mathematics and philosophy at Manchester College, York, along with management of student residence, fees from which supplemented his salary; to these posts he brought abundant energy and a buoyant personality. One student noted occasions when Hincks was less than fully in command of mathematics, but to his mind it was a pursuit inferior to metaphysics, to which he brought full command of the natural religion and necessitarian philosophy then dominant among the Unitarians. Throughout his life an active botanist, a subject that meshed well with his religious convictions, he also lectured on botany at the York medical school.

A serious dispute in 1838 with the college committee—itself preoccupied with the declining state of the college and the imminent retirement of the principal, Charles Wellbeloved (1769–1858)—about income and outlay on the student residence led to Hincks's resignation in 1839. He accepted the ministry at Stamford Street Chapel in London, taking students at University College, London, as boarders and doing private tutoring as well. In 1842 he added the editorship of a newly founded Unitarian newspaper, *The Inquirer*. The perils of the paper's early days were considerable, with uncertain readership and rapid turnover in ownership, but by 1843 Hincks had established it firmly, with a readership of about 900, and had become proprietor as well. Doing much of the work himself, he had scope to indulge his passion for politics—which his pupil W. R. Wood thought more important to him than science or philosophy—and he confidently defended the Unitarian tradition descended from Joseph Priestley (1733–1804) and Thomas Belsham (1750–1829) against the rising revisionism associated with James Martineau (1805–1900). A general, not merely a denominational paper, *The Inquirer* may never have been livelier than it was in those early years.

In 1847 Hincks stepped down. Ownership of *The Inquirer* was transferred to the printer Richard Kinder (1814–1884), and the editorship, after a brief period in committee, passed to John Lalor (d. 1856). At loose ends and suffering financially—Stamford Street at best paid £60 a year—Hincks undertook an unsuccessful lecture tour of the United States and in 1849 returned to native soil as professor of natural history at the newly founded Queen's College, Cork. His wife died that year, and on 6 October 1852 he married Sarah Maria Hodges (b. 1806/7), the widowed daughter of George Lucas, a farmer.

In 1853 Hincks was made professor of natural history at University College, Toronto, despite powerful support for another candidate, Thomas Henry Huxley (1825–1895). Hincks's experience and scientific conservatism must have influenced the decision, but one cannot overlook Huxley's wry observation that testimonials, however strong, could hardly prevail against the superior qualification of having a younger brother, Francis Hincks, as Canadian premier.

Hincks's books, papers, specimens, and apparatus were all lost in the sinking of the ship carrying them to Canada, but his teaching may have been more seriously hampered by outdated methods—reliance on rote memory and adherence to the 'quinarian' system of biological classification associated with William Swainson (1789–1855) and William Sharp Macleay (1792–1865), a fashionably persuasive innovation when Hincks was at Manchester College. Recollections of Toronto students depict a large, florid man with perfect manners who was accorded the indulgence owing to a 'character'.

As he had done at Cork, Hincks built up the natural history collections of the University Museum, a forerunner of the Royal Ontario Museum. In 1869–71 he served as president of the Canadian Institute, whose journal he edited, and to which he contributed twenty-five articles, among them efforts to revise the quinarian system and to reassert the divine plan of creation against the rising doctrine of evolution by natural selection. He was also acting minister of the Unitarian church in Toronto from 1853 to 1857 and officiated from time to time thereafter. He died in Toronto of kidney disease on 10 September 1871 and was buried in the necropolis there on 13 September.

R. K. Webb

Sources *The Inquirer* (30 Sept 1871) · *The Globe* [Toronto] (12 Sept 1871) · *The Globe* [Toronto] (14 Sept 1871) · minute books, Manchester College, York, Harris Man. Oxf. · J. Kenrick, letter to G. W. Wood, 23 April 1827, Harris Man. Oxf., Wood MSS · W. R. Wood, letter to G. W. Wood, 30 Oct 1830, Harris Man. Oxf., Wood MSS ·

W. R. Wood, letter to G. W. Wood, 7 Nov 1830, Harris Man. Oxf., Wood MSS · W. R. Wood, letter to G. W. Wood, 20 March 1831, Harris Man. Oxf., Wood MSS · L. Huxley, *Life and letters of Thomas Henry Huxley*, 1 (New York, 1901), 108 · E. H. Craigie, *A history of the department of zoology of the University of Toronto up to 1962* (1966) · *University of Toronto Monthly*, 35 (1935), 152 · private information (2004) [A. Smith, J. Coggon] · d. cert. · d. cert. [Maria Ann Hincks] · J. R. Dymond, *History of the Royal Ontario Museum of Zoology* (1940) · *The Report of the President, Queen's College, Cork* (1851–2), 6–7 · K. Gilley, ed., 'The Inquirer': a history and other reflections (1993) · J. Raymond and J. V. Pickstone, 'The natural sciences and the learning of the English Unitarians', *Truth, liberty, religion: essays celebrating two hundred years of Manchester College*, ed. B. Smith (1986), 127–64 · J. Patterson, ed., *General index to publications, 1852–912* (1914) · George's Meeting, Exeter, minute books, Devon RO · W. Hincks, letter to R. Tayler, 3 April 1848, DWL · J. Coggon, 'Quinarianism after Darwin's *Origin*: the circular system of William Hincks', *Journal of the History of Biology*, 35 (2002), 5–42

Archives Leics. RO, lecture notes · PRO NIre., corresp. with parents [copies] · PRO NIre., corresp. | DWL, corresp. with Richard Tayler

Likenesses photograph, University of Toronto Archives · photographs, repro. in Dymond, *History of the Royal Ontario Museum of Zoology* · photographs, repro. in Craigie, *A history of the department*

Wealth at death under £1000 (in England): administration with will, 15 Feb 1872, *CGPLA Eng. & Wales* · £634: inventory appended to will probated 28 Sept 1871, Archives of Ontario, microfilm reel G.S. 1-969, grant number 1287

Hind, Arthur Mayger (1880–1957), art historian, was born at Waterloo Street, Horninglow, Burton upon Trent, on 26 August 1880, the second son of Henry Robert Hind, schoolmaster, and his wife, Sarah Mayger. He was educated at the City of London School and at Emmanuel College, Cambridge, where he obtained first-class honours in part one of the classical tripos of 1902. In the following year, after studying at Dresden under Max Lehrs, the distinguished authority on early German engraving, he entered the department of prints and drawings of the British Museum as an assistant, the equivalent of the later assistant keeper. His first important employment there was to help Sidney Colvin in the preparation of a volume on native and foreign line engravers in England from the time of Henry VIII to the Commonwealth, to which he contributed the lists of the works of the engravers. This was published by the trustees of the British Museum in 1905. Of greater intrinsic importance was the *Catalogue of Early Italian Engravings in the British Museum*, issued in 1910 under the editorship of Colvin, but virtually all the work of Hind. Many years later he returned to this subject to compile a complete illustrated corpus of all existing Italian engravings of the fifteenth century, which became the standard work in this field. The first part appeared in 1938 in four massive and finely produced volumes, but the publication of the second part (3 vols., 1948) was delayed by the Second World War.

Although this corpus of Italian engraving was Hind's most impressive contribution to the material for the study of art, it was by no means the only one. Already by 1908 he had produced the useful *Short History of Engraving and Etching*, 'perhaps the most influential guide ever written to the history of print making' (Griffiths, 236); it went into a third edition in 1923. He also compiled what on the whole remains the most satisfactory catalogue of Rembrandt's etchings; this first appeared in 1912 and was revised and reissued in 1923. His *Introduction to a History of Woodcut*, originally intended as a companion volume to the *History of Engraving and Etching*, did not appear until 1935 and then its two bulky volumes covered only the fifteenth century.

In the meantime Hind had turned his attention to the study of drawings and had projected a complete catalogue of the extensive series of those by Dutch and Flemish artists in the British Museum. The first volume dealt with the drawings of Rembrandt and his school and appeared in 1915. There followed a second on Rubens and his school in 1923, and finally, in 1926 and 1931, two volumes of the Dutch drawings of the seventeenth century arranged in an alphabetical sequence. Although many of the conclusions reached in these volumes have been modified, they formed the basis for all scholarship in this area. Indeed, it was characteristic of Hind that he was content to provide the material for further research and welcomed the rectification of any errors he might have committed. He was also a pioneer in the study of the drawings of Claude Lorrain, producing an admirable official handlist of the incomparable series of his drawings in the British Museum (1926) and a book of plates a year earlier.

In 1933 Hind succeeded Laurence Binyon as keeper of the department of prints and drawings and retired in 1945. Realizing after his retirement that opportunities for travel and research would be lacking, he decided to devote his time to a more elaborate study of early English engraving. With undiminished energy he accordingly embarked on *Engraving in England in the Sixteenth and Seventeenth Centuries*, the first volume of which appeared in 1952 and the second in 1955; the third, which had not been completed at his death, was published posthumously, in 1964. This laborious undertaking is valuable rather to the historian and bibliographer than to the student of art history.

Hind served from 1915 to 1918 in the Army Service Corps, being three times mentioned in dispatches, reaching the rank of major, and being appointed OBE in 1918. He was made an honorary LLD of Glasgow in 1945, Slade professor of fine art at Oxford (1921–7), Charles Eliot Norton professor at Harvard (1930–31), and a Leverhulme research fellow (1945). His Harvard lectures on landscape design with special reference to Rembrandt, expanded into a book under the title of *Rembrandt*, were published in 1932, and contained in the final chapter a statement of his own artistic beliefs. In spite of his numerous accomplishments Hind was always conscious of his own limitations. He never professed to be infallible, even on the subject of early Italian engraving, and was always ready—perhaps too ready—to rely on the judgement of other experts which may have been less sound than his own.

On 28 June 1912 Hind married Dorothy Alice Pakington (*b.* 1881/2), third daughter of the third Lord Hampton, with whom he had three daughters, all of whom became professional musicians. Two enthusiasms engrossed Hind's leisure, drawing and music. It was in fact uncertain at the beginning of his career whether he should devote himself professionally to the latter, and he liked to describe himself as a landscape painter rather than as a museum official. Competent, delicate, and sensitive as was much of his œuvre as a landscape draughtsman, it remained the work of a gifted amateur. As a musician he was an extremely accomplished performer on the viola and violin, and he and his wife and daughters gave concerts at home for their friends. Hind died at St Andrew's Nursing Home, Henley-on-Thames, on 22 May 1957.   A. E. POPHAM, *rev.*

Sources A. E. Popham, *Burlington Magazine*, 99 (1957), 242 · *The Times* (23 May 1957) · personal knowledge (1971) · private information (1971) · A. Griffiths, ed., *Landmarks in print collecting: connoisseurs and donors at the British Museum since 1753* (British Museum Press, 1996) [exhibition catalogue, Museum of Fine Arts, Houston, TX, 1996, and elsewhere] · *CGPLA Eng. & Wales* (1957) · b. cert. · m. cert.
Archives U. Glas. L., letters to D. S. MacColl
Likenesses F. Dodd, charcoal drawing, *c*.1953, BM · L. Pasternak, drawing, priv. coll.; in possession of the family, 1971
Wealth at death £1951 5*s*. 7*d*.: probate, 16 July 1957, *CGPLA Eng. & Wales*

Hind, Henry Youle (1823–1908), geologist and explorer in Canada, was born on 1 June 1823 at Nottingham, the third of five sons of Thomas Hind (*d*. 1845), a lace manufacturer, and his wife, Sarah Youle (*d*. 1885). As a youth Hind attended the Nottingham Free Grammar School and then spent the two years 1837–9 in the Leipzig Handelslehranstalt. Between 1839 and 1843 he was tutored privately by William Butler in Nottingham. During 1843–4 he studied at Queens' College, Cambridge, and the following year found him in France. After some months in the United States, Hind moved to Toronto, Canada, during the winter of 1846–7. Although essentially self-taught in the sciences, he obtained an assistant mastership in the Upper Canada normal school in October 1847, teaching mathematics, natural philosophy, and agricultural chemistry. In 1849 he suggested a curriculum for a proposed technical school and published his lectures on agricultural chemistry in the following year. On 7 February 1850 he married Katherine Cameron, second daughter of Lieutenant-Colonel Duncan Cameron, in York Mills. They had seven children.

Hind joined the new Canadian Institute in 1849 and became the first editor of its official publication, the *Canadian Journal*, from 1850 to 1855, honing his skills as a science journalist. Beginning in 1851 he moonlighted as professor of chemistry in the new Anglican Trinity University's medical school. Two years later he resigned from the normal school to devote himself to full-time teaching of chemistry and geology at Trinity, a poorly paid post which he held until 1864. The university awarded him an MA in 1853.

In 1857, through political connections, Hind managed to obtain appointment as geologist to the provincial exploring party to the Red River district of what is now Manitoba—despite his lack of scientific credentials. The following summer found him as leader of another government expedition to the Assiniboine and Saskatchewan river valleys. His geological work for both expeditions was mediocre, but he had an excellent eye for detail and a colourful turn of phrase. He reworked his official reports into a popular *Narrative*, published in 1860, which brought him to realize that exploration and popular writing were more fulfilling than teaching. In the summer of 1861 he led a small expedition, along with his artist brother, William, up the Moisie River in Labrador; of little value scientifically, the expedition did provide the basis for another popular work. During the late 1850s Hind contributed to a number of popular journals, advocating Canadian western expansionism. He later became a strong advocate of Canadian confederation.

In 1861 the Upper Canada board of arts and manufactures retained Hind to edit its new journal, which advocated industrial expansion and technical education. While thus engaged, he edited and partly wrote his best-known work, *Eighty Years' Progress in British North America* (1863). Thanks to further political connections, Hind left for New Brunswick in 1864 to undertake a geological survey of the northern half of the province. Despite competent work he ran afoul of the surveyor of the southern counties, University of New Brunswick professor Loring Bailey, and the resulting controversy spelled an end to government-supported geology in that province until after confederation. With no position or prospects, Hind moved his family to Windsor, Nova Scotia, in the autumn of 1866. There he obtained government contracts for geological surveys and worked for private mining companies.

By 1876 Hind was back in his element, exploring the coast of Labrador and examining the fisheries. In the following year, when an international commission on Atlantic fisheries convened in Halifax, Hind appeared as the Newfoundland representative. His journalistic reputation brought him the task of editing the commission's papers. However, by 1878, Hind, who had never been accepted by official scientific circles in Canada, began attacking the Canadian government, businessmen, corporations, and the geological survey of Canada for presumed fraud in the fisheries discussions and, later, for Canadian immigration and agricultural policies in the north-west. By 1883 his publications gave the impression of near insanity. Then, for reasons unknown, he suddenly ceased combat and lapsed into quiet retirement.

During the 1880s Hind was a governor of King's College, Windsor, Nova Scotia, and published a history of it. The college, in turn, awarded him an honorary DCL in 1890. That same year he became a trustee of the Edgehill School for Girls in Windsor. Hind died on 8 August 1908 in Windsor and was buried in Maplewood cemetery, Windsor. His wife survived him.   RICHARD A. JARRELL

Sources W. L. Morton, *Henry Youle Hind, 1823–1908* (1980) · M. Zaslow, *Reading the rocks: the story of the geological survey of Canada* (1975) · W. O. Kupsch and W. G. E. Caldwell, 'Mid-nineteenth century Cretaceous studies in the Canadian interior plains', *History of Canadian Sciences, Technology and Medicine Bulletin*, 6 (1982), 59–84 · *DNB* · R. A. Jarrell, 'Hind, Henry Youle', *DCB*, vol. 13
Archives Public Archives of Nova Scotia, Halifax · RGS, corresp. relating to Northwest Territories · Trinity College, Toronto, letters | McGill University, Montreal, William Edmond Logan MSS · Metropolitan Toronto Reference Library, Toronto Mechanics'

Institute MSS · NA Canada, Sir Edward William Watkin MSS · Public Archives of New Brunswick, Samuel Tilley MSS
Likenesses W. Notman, photograph, *c.*1883, McCord Museum, Montreal

Hind, James (*bap.* 1616, *d.* 1652), highwayman and royalist soldier, was baptized at Chipping Norton, Oxfordshire, on 15 July 1616, the tenth of thirteen children of Edward Hind (*d.* 1656), a saddler, and his wife, Anne Smythe. His father was evidently a man of some position in the parish, three times serving as churchwarden. On 24 February 1638 Hind married Margaret Rowland at Chipping Norton, where they baptized four children between 1640 and 1648. According to the Oxford antiquary Anthony Wood, who knew men who had been Hind's accomplices, 'the great robber' was 'a little dapper desperat fellow' (*Life and Times*, 1.155–6).

The chapbook hero A legend grew up around Hind as highwayman and royalist during his lifetime and thirteen pamphlets published in the last year of his life or shortly afterwards have survived. Wood dismissed the fullest of these, George Fidge's *The English Gusman* (1652), as 'very weakly performed. Many things are true in it, but most are false, and many material things are omitted' (*Life and Times*, 1.156): an apt comment on most of Hind's lives. According to chapbook accounts Hind was sent to Chipping Norton grammar school for a couple of years, but 'profited little or nothing' from the experience; later evidence as to whether he could read is contradictory (Fidge, *English Gusman*, sig. B1v). His father tried to teach him his trade but, failing, bound him apprentice to a butcher. At the age of seventeen Hind ran away to London where he joined Thomas Allen's band of highwaymen and gained a reputation for committing robberies which were hallmarked by polite, gentlemanly behaviour and by wit. An ardent royalist, he served in the garrison of Sir William Compton at Banbury during the first civil war; he was present at the siege of Colchester in 1648 in Compton's regiment but escaped when the town fell to Sir Thomas Fairfax.

Hind himself provided an account of his services in the royalist cause from May 1649 onwards. After spending three days in the Netherlands in meetings with the king's council, he spent nine months in Ireland where he served under the marquess of Ormond and was wounded at Youghal. To avoid the plague he spent eight months on the Scilly Isles and then a further three months on the Isle of Man before leaving for Scotland. Granted an audience with Charles II at Stirling, Hind pledged his services in the imminent invasion of England and was recommended by the king to serve as a trooper in the life guard of George Villiers, second duke of Buckingham. Hind seems never to have been an officer in the king's army: his acquired epithet of 'captain' was an ironic reference to his leadership of his gang. He fought at the battle of Worcester where the royalists were decisively defeated. After making his way to London and spending five weeks in hiding he was captured at a barber's shop in Fleet Street on 9 November.

James Hind (*bap.* 1616, *d.* 1652), by unknown engraver, pubd 1651

Hind's Ramble was published a fortnight before his capture (the London bookseller George Thomason dated his copy 27 October). Hind's royalism was always a part of the persona created around him. Indeed the earliest chapbooks were blatantly cashing in on a rumour current in the weeks following Worcester—when the whereabouts of the king were still unknown—that Hind was helping the fugitive Charles II. On 15 September a broadside had appeared, *Another victory in Lancashire obtained against the Scots … also the Scots king going with Hind the great robber*, though on the latter subject all it could say was that 'its thought he [Charles II] lies sculking about in some private corners with Hind his guide' (Ollard, 95–6). A pamphlet recounting the earl of Derby's scaffold speech promised, but failed to deliver, an account of 'the manner how the King of Scots took shipping at Graves-end on the fourth of this instant October, with Captain Hind, disguised in seamens Apparel and safely arrived at the Hague in Holland'.

Hind's Ramble duly played on the same hunger for news of Charles II's whereabouts, claiming on the title page to recount Hind's 'going to the Scotch King, where he was made scoutmaster general, and afterwards (as 'tis generally reported) was the onely man that conveyed the Scotch King to London, who since is shipt away far beyond seas'. However, again this was hardly spoken of in the pamphlet; the 'many flying Speeches' that he had brought the king safely from Worcester to London and thence to the Netherlands providing a peg to sell a collection of picaresque anecdotes, mainly fanciful stories of Hind's career as a highwayman. If his part in the escape were true, it concluded, 'he hath done things unparallelled, but if not true, he hath the name of it' (Fidge, *Hind's Ramble*, 41).

However, Hind's royalism forms only a small part of an unstructured set of anecdotes, and seems mainly to have added a couple of parliamentarian figures to the cast of social types—gentlemen, lawyers, clergymen, usurers, and the like. Thus one of Hind's victim's was a county committee man, one of those figures whose financial demands for the parliamentarian regime could make him appear a bigger thief than any highwayman. On another occasion he set upon a troop of young soldiers fit enough for collecting taxes but not up to facing determined highwaymen. However, Fidge (in a section dropped from his later life of Hind) presented Hind's royalism sardonically, describing how Hind had used the opportunities provided by service at Banbury to run a protection racket and harry local carriers. When the closing in of the parliamentarian forces on Banbury made his 'trade' there no longer profitable, he stole the governor's best horse to return to the life of a highwayman. Other pamphlets in similar picaresque vein followed: *An excellent comedy, called the prince of priggs revels, or, The practices of that grand thief Captain James Hind, relating divers of his pranks and exploits, never heretofore published by any* (11 November; a play which concluded its stories of cozenage and disguise with a short scene in which Hind leads the king from the field of Worcester) and the two volumes of *Hind's Exploits* (of which only the second, dated by Thomason 19 November, survives).

Prisoner in Newgate Hind was committed to Newgate prison on 11 November. From there he actively promoted himself—or was promoted—as a soldier, a royalist, and honest rogue rather than as a highwayman in two pamphlets: *The True and Perfect Relation of the Taking of Captain James Hind* (14 November) and *The Declaration of Captain James Hind* (18 November). Although strict orders were given that he should be put in isolation, he was able to play to the crowd of curious visitors and fellow prisoners while his irons were being put on and his cell prepared, offering a toast to the king's health as he was being shackled; *The True and Perfect Relation* was a journalist's first-hand account of his words on this occasion. *The Declaration*, evidently by the same writer, claimed that it had been authorized by Hind himself:

> Whereas there hath been sundry and various Relations of the proceedings of Capt. James Hind, fraught with impertinent fictions; I am (in order thereunto) desired by the said Mr Hind, to publish this ensuing Declaration, for satisfaction, and true information, of the People. (*Declaration*, 1)

The account it presented of Hind's royalist service over the previous two years appears in its essentials to be Hind's own: if not (as the pamphlet implied) smuggled out of Newgate, then probably a version of the testimony that he had given before the council of state. The hostile *Weekly Intelligencer* confirms that these pamphlets were at most elaborating rather than imposing on Hind a stance of defiant royalism: it also recorded Hind's toast, while sourly

noting as evidence of the calibre of the king's supporters only Hind's fellow convicts joined him in it.

Hind truthfully denied any part in the king's escape. *The True and Perfect Relation* described an exchange between Hind and a gentleman from Chipping Norton in Newgate. When the visitor commiserated with his plight Hind replied 'That imprisonment was a comfort to him, in suffering for so good and just a Cause, as adhering to the KING', and when the gentleman refused to join in the toast, Hind angrily cried, 'The Devill take all Traytors: Had I a thousand lives, and at liberty, I would adventure them all for King Charles; and pox take all Turn-coats' (*True and Perfect Relation*, 4). Hind also at once distanced himself from, while appealing to, the picaresque myth. The stories about him in *Hind's Ramble* and *Hind's Exploits* were 'fictions' but, he added, 'some merry Pranks and Revels I have plaid, that I deny not' (ibid., 6). He was happy to portray himself both as a loyal subject of the king and an administrator of rough-and-ready social justice.

> Neither did I ever wrong any poor man of the worth of a penny: but I must confess, I have (when I have been necessitated thereto) made bold with a rich Bompkin, or a lying Lawyer, whose full-fed fees from the rich Farmer, doth too too much impoverish the poor cottage-keeper. (ibid., 5)

When he met a poor man he would challenge him whether he was for king or parliament: if the former, he would give him 20s., if the latter he would leave him alone. In both these pamphlets Hind denied ever shedding any innocent blood.

Trials and execution Hind appeared briefly at the Old Bailey on 12 December 1651, accused of treason in accompanying Charles Stuart to Worcester, but no indictment was drawn up against him. Because there was evidently no wish to make a martyr of him, the political charges were dropped and the council of state chose to pursue another course, sending him to stand trial at the next assizes for Berkshire, where there were outstanding indictments against him. He was taken from Newgate to Reading where he was tried at the beginning of March for the murder of one Poole, whom he was accused of having killed in a row over a bet. Found guilty of manslaughter, Hind was qualified to receive benefit of clergy—the commutation of the death penalty to a branding on the thumb on condition of reading a passage from the Bible. He was unable to read the 'neck-verse' but his luck held: the judge reprieved him and he came within the terms of the recently passed Act of Oblivion, which offered a general pardon for all crimes except high treason.

However, the positive image of Hind as a royalist hero meant that the authorities could not release him, fearing that he would remain 'a rallying point for royalist sentiment' (Faller, 13). The account of Hind's trial at the Old Bailey, published on 15 December, had recycled material from the earlier Newgate pamphlets while presenting him as a figure accepting his likely fate for his loyalty with humour and nobility. The pamphlets which continued to appear about Hind followed the fanciful and anecdotal tone of the earliest chapbooks, adding new material:

Fidge's *The English Gusman* introduced the tale that a cunning woman had given Hind a charm which had kept him free from capture for three years. Most had absorbed material from the Newgate pamphlets and continued to contain elements of anti-parliamentarian satire, some more explicit than others. *A pill to purge melancholy, or, Merry newes from Newgate: wherein is set forth the pleasant jests, witty conceits, and excellent couzenages, of Captain James Hind* (26 January 1652) deployed a carnivalesque Hind to criticize the new regime. 'It hath bin a constant custom observed among the people of this Nation, to spend the time of Christmas in mirth and jollity, using to have maskings, mummings, wasselings, &c.', it opened (recalling a whole set of customs which the new regime was bent on suppressing), before describing a Christmas-time lark in a brothel in Chancery Lane which had culminated in Hind, dressed as a woman, robbing a lecherous old lawyer (*Pill*, 3). *We have Brought our Hogs to a Fair Market, or, Strange Newes from New-Gate* (14 January 1652) purported to print Hind's instructions to 'Our Royal Gang and Fraternity' urging them 'to be in charity with all men, except the Caterpillars of the Times, viz., Long-gown men, Committee-men, Excize-men, Sequestrators, and other Sacrilegious persons' (p. 1). It also told how, in Newgate, Hind had received a vision of Charles I, with his crown upon his head, urging him to 'Repent, repent, and the King of Kings will have mercy on a Thief' (p. 5), and how Hind had once conjured up a vision of a lion rampant (the Scottish symbol no doubt an allusion to Charles II) to scare away his pursuers.

So Hind stayed a prisoner and the council of state fell back on the charge of treason: in July 1652 it sent down the examinations which it had collected against Hind the previous winter to the assize judges, heavy-handedly advising them that it left it to them to proceed against him according to law. At the beginning of September he was convicted at the Worcester assizes of treason. Reportedly, as the sentence was delivered

> he lookt very austerely, and said, 'Gentlemen, I thank you; this is no more but what I ever expected, since the time of my captivity in Iron; and this I am assured of, that as envy must cease in the grave, so will my bloud be requir'd at your hands'. (*The Faithful Scout*, 85, 27 Aug–3 Sept 1652, 665)

The council of state rejected his wife's appeal for a reprieve, claiming that it could not interfere in the matter. Hind went to the gallows at Worcester on 24 September 1652. A letter published in a newsbook recorded how he knelt at the foot of the gallows and read over a little book for a while, before taking leave of his son and giving money to a butcher in the town. His last words presented himself both as penitent thief and loyal subject, interrupted by a burst of anger against the men whom he blamed for his death:

> after he had fetcht two or three very deep sighs, he said, He was sorry that he had not been ruled by his Wife, who had upon her knees many times begged of him to give over his unlawful course of living, for it would at last bring him to an untimely death. Then he railed against one Mr Moor, and Mr Wall, saying, that they were the cause of his death … For which he was checked by … the Gaoler … [He said that] he

had taken the Oath of Allegiance, to be true to his King *and prayed God to bless his King, and all that wished him well.* (*A Perfect Account*, 91, 22–9 Sept 1652, 728)

Hind was spared the full horrors of a traitor's death: he was apparently not drawn on a hurdle to his execution; his body was mutilated and dismembered only after he was completely dead; and his body (or at least his torso) was allowed a proper burial. His fate is a striking testament to the power of his reputation: only a handful of English royalists were executed for their part in the war of 1651, and they in its immediate aftermath, not a full year later.

Hind was remembered as a royalist, the first in a literary tradition where highway robbery was combined with loyalty to the crown. However, in much of the literature in his lifetime and afterwards, the individuality of the man and his convictions was lost in favour of a generic type of rogue to which he himself had been willing to appeal. *No jest like a true jest being a compendious record of the merry life and mad exploits of Capt James Hind the great robber of England* was the characteristic title of a chapbook first published in 1657 and republished several times up to 1800. This was the version of Hind's life elaborated in early eighteenth-century criminal biographies: the jovial rogue whose exploits cocked a snook at England's puritan rulers. According to Alexander Smith the Allen gang had tried to hold up Oliver Cromwell at Huntingdon; heavily outnumbered, most of the gang were taken and later hanged, though Hind managed to escape. Later Hind ambushed notorious regicides; according to Smith these were John Bradshaw and the puritan preacher Hugh Peters, while Charles Johnson added the Fifth Monarchist Thomas Harrison.   BARBARA WHITE

Sources L. B. Faller, *Turned to account: the forms and functions of criminal biography in late seventeenth- and early eighteenth-century England* (1987) • G. Spraggs, *Outlaws and highwaymen: the cult of the robber in England from the middle ages to the nineteenth century* (2001) • O. M. Meades, *The adventures of Captain James Hind of Chipping Norton: the Oxfordshire highwayman* (1985) • *CSP dom.*, 1651–2, 12, 63–4, 146, 340, 397 • G. F. [G. Fidge], *Hind's ramble, or, The description of his manner and course of life* (1651) • G. F. [G. Fidge], *The English Gusman, or, The history of that unparallel'd thief James Hind* (1652) • *The true and perfect relation of the taking of Captain James Hind* (1651) • *A declaration of Captain James Hind (close prisoner in Newgate)* (1651) • *The trial of Captain James Hind* (1651) • *Weekly Intelligencer* (11–18 Nov 1651), 346 • *A Perfect Account*, 62 (3–10 March 1652), 496 • *A Perfect Account*, 87 (25 Aug–1 Sept 1652), 696 • *A Perfect Account*, 91 (22–9 Sept 1652), 728 • *The Faithful Scout*, 35 (12–19 Sept 1651), 271 • *The Faithful Scout*, 85 (27 Aug–3 Sept 1652), 665 • *The life and times of Anthony Wood*, ed. A. Clark, 1, OHS, 19 (1891), 155–7 • *An excellent comedy, called, the prince of priggs revels, or, The practices of that grand thief Captain James Hind* (1651) • *A pill to purge melancholy, or, Merry newes from Newgate: wherein is set forth the pleasant jests, witty conceits, and excellent couzenages, of Captain James Hind and his associates* (1651/2) • *We have brought our hogs to a fair market, or, Strange newes from New-Gate* (1651/2) • *The humble petition of James Hind to the … councell of state* (1651) • *Wit for mony. Being a full relation of the life, actions, merry conceits and pretty pranks of Captain James Hind* (1652) • *No jest like a true jest being a compendious record of the merry life and mad exploits of Capt James Hind the great robber of England* (1657) • *The pleasant and delightful history of Captain James Hind* (1651) • *The last will and testament of James Hynd, high-way lawyer* (1651) • R. L. Ollard, *The escape of Charles II* (1966) • *The true speech delivered on the scaffold by James earl of Derby* (1651) • C. Johnson, *A history of the lives and adventures of the most famous highwaymen* (1734), 88–90 •

A. Smith, *The history of the lives and robberies of the most noted highway-men, foot-pads, shop-lifts and cheats*, 2 vols. (1714), 1.271–80
Likenesses woodcut, 1652 (*The true portraiture of Capt James Hind*), Mary Evans Picture Library; repro. in H. Evans and M. Evans, *Hero on a stolen horse* (1977) • portrait, repro. in A. Smith, *History of the lives and robberies of … highwaymen* • woodcut, BM, NPG • woodcut, BM, NPG; repro. in *Declaration* [*see illus.*]

Hind, John (1796–1866), mathematician, was born in Cumberland. He entered St John's College, Cambridge, as a sizar, on 2 February 1813 and was elected to a scholarship in 1815. He completed his BA in 1818 as second wrangler and second Smith's prizeman, and the following year was chosen Taylor mathematical lecturer and fellow-commoner (BA) of Sidney Sussex College. In 1821 he obtained his MA and was ordained; he was elected a fellow of Sidney Sussex College in 1823 and served as tutor, but resigned his lectureship and his fellowship on his marriage in 1824. His wife's name was Elizabeth. Of his family, one son, John Norman Parker Hind (*b.* 1831) and two daughters, Mary Georgina and Elizabeth Stoddont, are known. Hind acted as moderator of the tripos in 1822, 1823, and 1826, and as examiner in 1824 and 1827. He was a fellow of the Cambridge Philosophical Society and of the Royal Astronomical Society. In 1829 he was given the care of the parish of Madingley in Cambridgeshire.

Hind published seven mathematics textbooks and one book of solutions to exercises in the period 1827–56. Most of these books were reissued in anything up to eight editions, and were highly regarded at the time. He died at 22 Trumpington Street, Cambridge, on 17 December 1866.

JULIA TOMPSON

Sources *Light Blue: a Cambridge University Magazine*, 2 (1867), 120 • Venn, *Alum. Cant.* • calendars, U. Cam. • *GM*, 4th ser., 3 (1867), 254
Wealth at death under £1000: probate, 6 Feb 1867, *CGPLA Eng. & Wales*

Hind, John Russell (1823–1895), astronomer, was born on 12 May 1823 in Nottingham, the son of John Hind, a lace manufacturer. He was educated privately, then at Nottingham grammar school, and when aged seventeen was placed as assistant to a civil engineer in London. He had been devoted to astronomy since the age of twelve, and in late 1840 he obtained a junior assistantship in the magnetic division at the Royal Observatory, Greenwich. He relieved tedious night duties by calculating orbits, and in his leisure time he used the Sheepshanks equatorial to search for comets. Having been elected a fellow of the Royal Astronomical Society (RAS) in 1844, he was recommended by the astronomer royal, George Airy, as observer to George Bishop (1785–1861). On 10 July 1846 he married Fanny (*b. c.*1828), the daughter of Matthew Fuller, a gentleman, at St Pancras Old Church, and in 1849 the first of their six children was born.

Bishop's observatory, built in 1836 at his home, South Villa, Regent's Park, had a Dollond refracting telescope of 7 inches aperture, then a powerful instrument. Aspiring to make the observatory useful, he first employed from 1839 to May 1844 William Rutter Dawes, who measured double stars. When Hind arrived at South Villa in October 1844, the solar system comprised the seven major planets

and four minor planets (asteroids) discovered between 1800 and 1807 orbiting between Mars and Jupiter. In December 1845, after a fifteen-year search, Karl Hencke, a German amateur, discovered the fifth asteroid, Astraea. In September 1846 came the sensational discovery of Neptune. Bishop decided to devote his resources to searching for planets. From November 1846 Hind began a systematic search using the newly available Berlin charts. He discovered two comets in 1846 and 1847. In July 1847 Hencke found the sixth asteroid, and by October Hind had discovered the seventh and eighth. These were considered of such interest and importance that John Couch Adams, ignoring thoughts of a medal for Neptune, recommended that Hind and Hencke each have the RAS medal in 1848. Instead, they, Adams, and nine other nominees received testimonials.

The Berlin charts were incomplete. Bishop undertook to produce better charts to fainter limits. The consequent night-time exposure and overwork led to the first breakdowns in Hind's health, in 1848 and 1849. He borrowed £15 from John Lee to fund his recuperation, and a year later lodged his testimonial as security. In September 1850 he discovered his third asteroid, Victoria. Hind's financial stress was relieved in 1851 when he received £100 from the Royal Bounty Fund and in 1852 by the scarce award of a civil-list pension of £200 for important astronomical discoveries.

In 1850 Bishop engaged Norman R. Pogson (trained by Hind) as second assistant, then from 1852 Eduard Vogel, from 1853 to 1855 Albert Marth, and in 1860 George Talmage. In July 1851 Hind travelled to Sweden and successfully observed the total eclipse. In 1852 Hind found four asteroids and in 1854 two more, the last, aptly named Urania, being his tenth. He then gave up regular observing but continued supervision. Great interest in minor planets waned only after 1860, when powerful telescopes indicated they might exist in infinite numbers. After Bishop's death in 1861 his son removed the observatory to Twickenham. Talmage rejoined; Hind moved there and supervised the publication of seventeen of the twenty-four charts before the observatory closed in 1877.

The variety of Hind's discoveries demonstrated the skill and perseverance which underlay his achievements. In 1848 he discovered the second 'temporary star' or nova of the nineteenth century, and only the seventh ever recognized in the West; N Oph 2 suddenly appeared in the constellation Ophiuchus at fifth magnitude, then faded to tenth. Comets remained mysterious; when Biela's comet returned in December 1848 Hind reported its pear shape, and ten days later it divided in two. In October 1852 Hind discovered a small nebula adjacent to the star T Tauri; 'Hind's nebula' became famous for displaying unmistakable yet inexplicable changes. In 1855 Hind made his first discovery of many variable stars, U Geminorum.

In 1853 the superintendence of the *Nautical Almanac* office at Gray's Inn became vacant. Against stiff competition the Admiralty chose Hind, who superintended the *Nautical Almanac* until 1891 and introduced important changes. After making a comparison, in the early 1860s he dropped Buckhardt's lunar tables and adopted those of Hansen, later modified by Newcomb; similarly, Le Verrier's uniform solar and planetary tables were adopted. Hind ensured the *Almanac*'s punctuality and accuracy.

Hind was never a theorist. His enduring reputation is as a first-rate practical astronomer. He was an able and tireless computer, calculating for everything he discovered or observed, including one comet so precisely that he observed it at midday when close to the sun. Beyond writing seven popular books and booklets (1841–63), he made a considerable contribution to current practical astronomy by correspondence and more than 130 papers and notices to the international journals of four nations; the astronomer William Plummer said: 'few men have made fewer mistakes' (Plummer, *Nature*, 202). Hind was foreign secretary of the RAS (1847–57, 1878–80) and served on its council (1846–59, 1864–7). In deference to Airy, who was seeking a fourth term, he withdrew from the presidential nomination for 1864. Popular and respected, he was again proposed by Adams in 1879. When Airy, aged seventy-eight and nearly deaf, intimated he would stand again, Adams with unusual speed procured unanimous nomination of Hind, who was duly elected for 1880–82. Hind was elected FRS in 1863. His many distinctions included in 1851 corresponding membership of the Académie Royale des Sciences, associateships of the Russian academy and the Swedish academy, and in 1882 an honorary LLD from Glasgow University. He received the gold medals of the Royal Society (1855), the RAS (1853), and the king of Denmark (1847), and was awarded the Lalande medal three times.

Hind retired in 1891. Of a kindly disposition, he was generous with information, but of a very shy nature. Behind a strong appearance, he suffered repeated attacks of nervous exhaustion throughout his career. His recreation was learning 'much curious information' on old comets from ancient records, and recalculating their orbits (Plummer, *Nature*, 202). He continued his contributions until a chill precipitated his death from heart disease at his home, 3 Cambridge Park Gardens, Twickenham, on 23 December 1895. He was buried in the churchyard of St Mary the Virgin, Twickenham.   ROGER HUTCHINS

Sources *Monthly Notices of the Royal Astronomical Society*, 56 (1895–6), 200–05 · I. Howard-Duff, 'George Bishop (1785–1861) and his South Villa observatory in Regent's Park', *Journal of the British Astronomical Association*, 96 (1985–6), 20–26 · W. E. Plummer, 'Dr John Russell Hind, F.R.S.', *Astronomische Nachrichten*, 139 (1896), 255 · *History of the Royal Astronomical Society*, [1]: *1820–1920*, ed. J. L. E. Dreyer and H. H. Turner (1923); repr. (1987), 99, 115–16, 216 · *DNB* · A. J. Meadows, *Greenwich observatory: the story of Britain's oldest scientific institution*, 2: *Recent history (1836–1975)* (1975), 77–8 · J. Ashbrook, *The astronomical scrapbook: skywatchers, pioneers, and seekers in astronomy*, ed. L. J. Robinson (1984), 34, 300 · J. C. Adams, 'Address delivered by the president on presenting the gold medal of the society to Mr Hind', *Monthly Notices of the Royal Astronomical Society*, 13 (1852–3), 141–5 · W. E. Plummer, 'Dr John Russell Hind', *Nature*, 53 (1895–6), 201–2 · *The Observatory*, 19 (1896), 66–7 · G. B. Airy, *Autobiography of Sir George Biddell Airy*, ed. W. Airy (1896), 142, 180, 201, 210, 216 · F. R. Hind, 'Galactic nebulae', *Astronomy of the 20th century*, ed. O. Struve and V. Zebergs (1962), 381–407, esp. 402–3 (Variable nebulae) · H. S. Hogg, 'Variable stars', *The general history of astronomy*, ed. O. Gingerich, 4A, pt A (1984), 82 · *Catalogue of scientific papers*, Royal Society, 19 vols. (1867–1925) · *Men and women of the time* (1891), 452–3 · J. F. Tennant, 'On the *Nautical Almanac*', *Monthly Notices of the Royal Astronomical Society*, 50 (1889–90), 349–57 · *CGPLA Eng. & Wales* (1896) · parish register, 10/7/1846, St Pancras Old Church, London

Archives Birr Castle, Offaly, archives, letters to earl of Rosse · LPL, corresp. with John Lee, 1843–52 · RAS, corresp. and papers, incl. notebook on cometary astronomy; letters to RAS; letters relating to 1870 eclipse · RAS, letters to Richard Sheepshanks · RS, corresp. with Sir John Herschel

Likenesses ink, *c.*1852, repro. in *ILN* (28 Aug 1852), 168 · H. J. Whitlock, carte-de-visite, NPG · wood-engraving (after a daguerreotype by Claudel), NPG; repro. in *ILN* (28 Aug 1852)

Wealth at death £831 19s. 3d.: administration, 10 Jan 1896, *CGPLA Eng. & Wales*

Hind, Richard Dacre Archer- [*formerly* Richard Dacre Hodgson] (1849–1910), classical scholar, was born at Morris Hall, near Norham, Northumberland, on 18 September 1849 and came of an ancient Northumbrian family. He was the third and youngest son of Thomas Hodgson (1814–1911), a learned horticulturist and graduate of Trinity College, Cambridge, and his wife, Mary Ann, his first cousin and second daughter of John Thomas Huntley, vicar of Kimbolton. On the death of a brother in 1869, his father succeeded to the estates of Stelling and Ovington and assumed the surname of Archer-Hind. Richard Hodgson received his early teaching in Latin and Greek from his father, and even when he was at Shrewsbury School (1862–8), where he was the pupil of Dr B. H. Kennedy and Dr H. W. Moss, his father continued to assist his studies. In 1868 he went into residence at Trinity College, Cambridge, living with his parents, who established themselves at Cambridge, as they had at Shrewsbury, so that he could enjoy the comforts of a home life while pursuing his education. He was elected to a college foundation scholarship in 1869 and to a Craven university scholarship in 1871. In 1872 he was placed third in the first class of the classical tripos and won the first chancellor's medal for classical learning. He was elected to a fellowship in his college in October 1873 and was appointed assistant lecturer in April 1877 and assistant tutor in December 1878. On 17 March 1888 he married Laura, youngest daughter of Lewis *Pocock. At Easter 1899 he was made a senior lecturer, and in December 1903 he retired from the staff. During the last two years of his life Archer-Hind was an invalid. He died at his home, 2 Gonville Place, Cambridge, on 6 April 1910. He was cremated at Golders Green, and his ashes were buried at Cambridge. He was survived by his widow and one son, Laurence, born in 1895.

Both in Latin and in Greek the exceptional quality of Archer-Hind's scholarship was recognized from the beginning of his Cambridge career. But Greek came to interest him more than Latin. At a later time, while his love of Pindar, Aeschylus, and Sophocles never diminished, his admiration for Plato grew. In 1883 he published an edition of the *Phaedo*, in which he investigated the argument of the dialogue and traced its relations to the rest of Plato's writings. A second edition appeared in 1894. In 1888 he brought out his *magnum opus*, an original and complete edition of the difficult, important, and at that time still neglected *Timaeus*, which gave a new impetus to Platonic studies. The translation is exact and scholarly; the commentary is helpful, learned, many-sided; and in the introduction Archer-Hind sets out the results of his profound study of Plato's metaphysic. After a century his views on difficult passages in the Greek text are still taken seriously. Papers in the *Journal of Philology* (especially 24, 1896, 49; 29, 1904, 266; 31, 1910, 84) supplemented the editions of the *Phaedo* and the *Timaeus*.

An industrious teacher and a singularly efficient examiner, Archer-Hind took no prominent part in the affairs of the university; but his occasional allocutions at university discussions and college meetings were incisive and epigrammatic. He was always an earnest supporter of the movement for the education of women, and gave much time to the affairs of Newnham College and the instruction of its students. He loved his garden, and kept an exact record of the rare plants which it contained. He took a passionate interest in music; his knowledge of certain favourite composers was intimate and minute. He had made a careful study of Greek music. Like many of his academic generation he was a member of the Alpine Club. His quiet, retiring manner covered strong convictions tenaciously held. HENRY JACKSON, *rev.* M. C. CURTHOYS

Sources private information (1912) · personal knowledge (1912) · *Cambridge Review* (28 April 1910) · *The Times* (8 April 1910) · Venn, *Alum. Cant.* · *CGPLA Eng. & Wales* (1910)
Wealth at death £1919 13s. 9d.: probate, 8 June 1910, *CGPLA Eng. & Wales*

Hinde, William (1568/9–1629), Church of England clergyman and author, was almost certainly born at Kendal, Westmorland. He was probably educated at Kendal, and on 9 December 1586, aged seventeen, was admitted as a 'plebeian' to Queen's College, Oxford. He graduated BA on 2 July 1591 and proceeded MA on 2 July 1594. Subsequently elected a fellow of Queen's, he was ordained some time after 1595. While at Oxford he acquired the godly values that were to dominate his life.

About 1603 Hinde was appointed curate in the parish of Bunbury, Cheshire. In or before 1605 he was married, probably to Margaret, the wife mentioned in his will; a son, Joseph (himself admitted to Queen's in 1623), was born by early 1606. William and Margaret had nine surviving children. He soon became an active and outspoken puritan minister, participating regularly in teaching exercises within the county and speaking vigorously against popery and recreations on the sabbath. At the same time he maintained contacts with puritans in other areas. In 1614 he published, with John Dod, *Bathshebaes Instructions to her Sonne Lemuel*, the work of 'a godly and learned man, now with God' sometimes mistakenly attributed to Robert Cleaver. In his editions of two works by John Rainolds, *The Prophecies of Obadiah Opened* (1613) and *The Discovery of the Man of Sinne* (1614), Hinde held church ceremonies to be matters indifferent and attacked the wealth of the richest clergy.

Increasingly such behaviour brought Hinde into conflict with Bishop Thomas Morton of Chester, and in 1617, following several discussions about church government,

he was presented and fined. When in 1618 Morton's relations with his nonconformist clergy were further undermined by the publication of the bishop's Book of Sports, Hinde became disillusioned with the episcopate. He devoted the rest of his life to his family and scholarship, although he continued to be presented for nonconformity. His *A Path to Pietie* (1613) was followed up by *A Brief and Plaine Catechisme* (1623). *The Office and Use of the Moral Law of God* (1622), reissued a year later, revealed that he had not lost a taste for controversy. He also completed *A Faithfull Remonstrance of the Holy Life and Happy Death of John Bruen*, finally published posthumously by his son Samuel in 1641, but became exhausted by a life of self-sacrifice. Following a short illness, he died at Bunbury in June 1629 and was buried in Bunbury churchyard.

S. J. GUSCOTT

Sources *DNB* · Foster, *Alum. Oxon.* · will and inventory, Ches. & Chester ALSS, Wills Supra (WS) [William Hinde of Bunbury, clerk], 9 March 1629 · W. Urwick, ed., *Historical sketches of nonconformity in the county palatine of Cheshire, by various ministers and laymen* (1864), vii, ix, xi, 145 · R. C. Richardson, *Puritanism in north-west England: a regional study of the diocese of Chester to 1642* (1972), 3, 9, 22, 34 · *VCH Cheshire*, 3.29 · R. Halley, *Lancashire, its puritanism and nonconformity*, 2nd edn (1872), 104–5; 278 · *ESTC*
Wealth at death £230 15s. 1d.: will and inventory, Ches. & Chester ALSS, 9 March 1629

Hinden [*née* Gesundheit], **Rita** (1909–1971), journalist and campaigner on colonial issues, was born on 16 December 1909 in Cape Town, Cape Colony, and given the name Rebecca, which she never used. She was the second of the four children of Jacob or Jacov Gesundheit (1880–1955), an ostrich farmer originally from Warsaw, Poland, and his wife, Bella Harris (1881–1950), who was born in Łódź. After the farm failed in 1912 the family moved into the city, where Jacob prospered sufficiently in the textile industry to emigrate with them to Palestine in 1927—the first South African family to do so—and to establish himself in the citrus industry in Tel Aviv. At home Rita received a traditional Jewish preparation for marriage and family life, and she became fluent in Hebrew. Wanting to pursue her studies further, after matriculating in December 1925 from the Seminary of Good Hope, she attended the University of Cape Town for a year. In Tel Aviv she could find no equivalent higher education and so practised journalism until she could prevail upon her father to allow her to continue her education in England. In 1928 she entered the London School of Economics and Political Science (LSE), where she joined some socialist and Jewish societies. On gaining a second-class degree in economics in 1931 she returned to journalism in Palestine. The previous year, on a Young Zionists walking holiday, she had met, and soon became engaged to, Elchon Hinden (1907–1977), a graduate of Cambridge University and a medical student at St George's Hospital, London. His father, a Latvian, had started as a barrow-boy and became a moneylender in Liverpool. The couple married in Tel Aviv on 14 February 1933 and returned to London for Elchon to complete specialist training in paediatrics, though as ardent Zionists they intended to settle in Palestine. Meanwhile they joined the Willesden branch of the Independent Labour Party.

Their return to Palestine in 1935 was a disappointment. Possibly because her family were settled there, Rita easily found work as a freelance journalist. In addition, under the auspices of the Jewish Agency for Palestine Economic Research Institute, supervised by David Horowitz, she undertook research into the Palestinian economy. While there Rita developed osteosclerosis, a condition of the inner ear, aggravated by pregnancy, in which the bones fuse to the ear-drum, resulting in deafness. The only remedy at that time was a hearing aid; however, shortly before her death an operation restored her hearing, to her great delight. At the same time, Elchon encountered difficulty in obtaining a permanent hospital post because of local medical ethics and practices, and both Elchon and Rita were troubled by the aggressive nationalism and dogmatism developing in Palestine in reaction to Hitler's activities in Europe. They became agnostics, and in 1938, while on holiday in England, decided after great heart searching that they should bring up their children, Judith and Jonathan, in London.

Although a proud and devoted mother, Rita could not settle into the housewifely role envisaged by her parents. With the help of a nanny she was able to return to the LSE to complete her research and in 1939 was awarded a doctorate for her thesis 'Palestine: an experiment in colonialism'. Spin-offs from that research were four papers written in collaboration with Horowitz and her husband on Palestinian industry, economy, demography, and food. Following advice from R. R. Kuczinski, a reader at the LSE, to specialize in colonial economic studies, she sought openings in that field. Early in 1939 she had joined both the Labour Party and the Fabian Society. A few days before the Hindens had departed for Tel Aviv, at an Independent Labour Party reception, Rita had greatly impressed Arthur Creech Jones by her interest in colonial issues. He kept in touch with her activities and in 1939 contrived her appointment as assistant to Leonard Woolf in drawing up a colonial version of the society's series Facts and Figures. When the Second World War broke out, G. D. H. Cole and Margaret Cole formed a Fabian war aims committee. Rita was made joint secretary with Margaret Cole, principally to liaise with the Labour Party and other political groups embarking on similar investigations to prevent duplication of work. The Fabians chose to study the League of Nations, the colonies, and post-war reconstruction. Advised by a working party of Margery Perham, Creech Jones, Leonard Barnes, and Julian Huxley, Rita produced *Plan for Africa* (1942), which defined most of the principles of Fabian colonial policy developed and expounded during the war years.

Rita Hinden always claimed that she knew nothing about the colonies as a whole before 1938. At the outset of this new work she had great difficulty in gathering reliable facts. Discussion of this problem with Woolf and Margaret Cole led to the creation of the Fabian Colonial Bureau, to act as a 'clearing-house' for information of all kinds on the colonies, to provide the Labour Party with a sound basis for the formation of colonial policy, to supply MPs with reliable facts for parliamentary debates on colonial affairs, and to organize their questions in the house. Creech Jones, who had long pressed for such a body within the labour movement, was nominated chairman and Rita its unsalaried secretary. Thus began a powerful partnership and a deep friendship which lasted far longer than their running of the bureau. This exacting work filled the painful gap caused by the necessary evacuation of her children to the country and Elchon's departure for India in the Royal Army Medical Corps. To elicit information, Rita consulted Creech Jones's contacts in the Colonial Office, and thereby gained the trust and friendship of colonial officials and servants. She devised conferences of Fabians, academics, and colonial experts, and edited and wrote much of the journal *Empire* (later *Venture*) as well as a continuous stream of Tracts, Research series, and Colonial Controversy series pamphlets on specific colonial subjects. These helped shape opinion in Britain and throughout the empire on political, social, and economic colonial development; her edition of *Fabian Colonial Essays* (1945) co-ordinated and lent further authority to those statements. Rita and Creech Jones became recognized as experts on colonial affairs and respected advisers to and friends of many of the emerging political leaders in the colonies. Her office was an essential port of call for colonial officers on leave. To her delight, she was an official guest of the Ghanaian government at its independence celebration.

Before 1945 Rita and Creech Jones jointly led delegations on topical issues to the colonial and dominions offices. After 1945 her clear-thinking, creative criticism was recognized by appointment to the Colonial Office's Economic and Development Council and its labour advisory committee, the Labour Party's advisory committee on imperial affairs, and the TUC's colonial affairs committee. After serving very critically on the 1951 Waddington commission of inquiry into the constitution of British Guiana, she became a founding member of the Africa Bureau in protest against the federation of Central Africa.

By 1950 opinion on development as an essential prerequisite for independence was becoming less generous because of the perceived cost. Rita Hinden, hurt by the current trend, resigned from the bureau, which she thought had become less of a research body and too much of a pressure group. She moved to the Labour Party research department before taking on the editorship of the monthly publication *Socialist Commentary*. In editorials and articles in this journal, and in her choice of contributors, Hinden was again able to give voice to her ardent and essentially ethical form of socialism, which made her an influential revisionist and the ideal presenter of *The Radical Tradition* (1964), the memorial volume of R. H. Tawney's essays. *Socialist Commentary* presented the views of the Gaitskellite section of the Labour Party as opposed to those of Harold Wilson's adherents and *Tribune*; nevertheless, Rita herself staunchly opposed Hugh Gaitskell's anti-Common Market stance at the 1962 Labour Party conference. In *Socialist Commentary* and in many articles for other journals and newspapers she expounded the fundamental principles of socialism, whether writing about trade unionism, higher education, or political developments in the newly independent states.

In her youth Rita Hinden was good-looking, with dark eyes and hair, a thoughtful, listening expression, and a sensitive mouth. In her early sixties one was struck less by her appearance—the grey hair escaping from a bun, lines on her face, bird-like posture of her head, and slight limp (the relic of a mild stroke suffered in her fifties)—than by her benign, gentle authority, that of the Jewish matriarch, which coaxed others to accede to her wishes. She died of a second stroke on 18 November 1971, at Whipps Cross Hospital, London, and was cremated at Golders Green crematorium. Memorial lectures were given in her honour until 1974.   PATRICIA M. PUGH

Sources Bodl. RH, Fabian Colonial Bureau MSS, MS Brit. Emp.s.365 · Bodl. RH, Creech Jones MSS, MS Brit. Emp.s.332 · BLPES, Fabian Society MSS · Bodl. RH, Africa Bureau MSS, MS Afr.s.1681 · P. Pugh, *Educate, agitate, organize: 100 years of Fabian socialism* (1984) · A. Flanders, 'Rita Hinden', in K. O. Morgan, *Labour people: leaders and lieutenants, Hardie to Kinnock*, rev. edn (1992), 179–82 · A. Flanders, 'Hinden, Rita', *DLB*, vol. 2 · K. Jones, 'A quiet fame', diss., Ruskin College, Oxford, 1985 · 'Special section in appreciation of Rita Hinden', *Socialist Commentary* (Jan 1972) · *The Times* (20 Nov 1971) · private information (2004) [J. Hinden]

Archives Bodl. RH, papers · U. Warwick Mod. RC, papers as editor of *Socialist Commentary* | Bodl. RH, corresp. with Margery Perham and related papers

Likenesses photograph, repro. in *Socialist Commentary* · photographs, Bodl. RH

Wealth at death £17,340: probate, 18 Aug 1972, *CGPLA Eng. & Wales*

Hinderer [*née* Martin], **Anna** (1827–1870), missionary, was born on 19 March 1827 at Hempnall, Norfolk, the daughter of William Martin, merchant; her mother died when she was five and she was brought up by her aunt and grandfather. For several years she lived with the Revd Francis and Mrs Richenda Cunningham (*née* Gurney) in the vicarage at Lowestoft, where she acted as Sunday school teacher and secretary. The vicarage was a centre of East Anglian evangelical connections—Richenda Cunningham was the sister of Elizabeth Fry—and from an early age Anna Martin had an ambition to become a missionary overseas. On 14 October 1852 she married David Hinderer (1820–1890) of Weisbuch near Schorndorf, Württemberg, a Church Missionary Society (CMS) missionary in west Africa. At the end of 1852 she accompanied him to Ibadan, one of the major states of Yoruba; they arrived in April 1853. With the exception of two short breaks in Britain and Germany, this was to be the centre of her and her husband's work for the next seventeen years.

Although the CMS Yoruba mission had been established since 1845, Ibadan was a new station and the mission there was to be the Hinderers' creation. Its foundation was part of a broader expansion of CMS work in this part of west Africa in the early 1850s. Initially the intention was for the Hinderers to press further inland to the Hausa states of the interior but the warm welcome they received on arrival led them to concentrate on consolidating the CMS mission within Ibadan itself. While her husband

turned to proselytism and to translating the Old Testament, Anna Hinderer's main work lay in the field of education. She established the mission Sunday school and a day school and taught in both. For long periods while her husband was working away from Ibadan, she was left to run the mission on her own. The survival of the Ibadan mission particularly through the difficult years of the early 1860s owed much to her determination and courage, together with the support of the group of Yoruba converts she gathered around her household.

Conditions in Ibadan in this period were difficult. The work of the mission was disrupted by the Yoruba wars and more particularly the struggle between Ibadan and its neighbours, Ijaiye, Abeokuta and Ijebu, after 1860. The wars left the Hinderers cut off from the coast and from the other stations of the CMS for five years, until 1865; the severe privations of this period undoubtedly contributed to Anna Hinderer's later ill health. Yet the mission in Ibadan flourished: the first converts were received in 1855 and by the 1860s new churches were being opened in the area; Ibadan continued to be a pillar of the CMS long after the Hinderers had left.

Anna Hinderer experienced repeated ill health during her time in Ibadan, particularly in the late 1860s, and in 1869 she was forced to return permanently to England, her husband following shortly afterwards. She lost the sight of her right eye. In 1870 David Hinderer took up the curacy of Martham in Norfolk and Anna began work with the mothers of the parish, but she died from nervous exhaustion at Martham vicarage on 6 June 1870.

Anna Hinderer's reputation was made by the posthumous publication of her memoirs, *Seventeen Years in the Yoruba Country* (1872). Her career and privations in Ibadan, together with her relatively early death, struck a chord with sections of the British public. If her reputation depends to a degree on the image the book created of the lone missionary abandoned among warring peoples, the survival of the CMS mission in Ibadan remains a lasting testimony to her life's work.   MARTIN LYNN

Sources A. Hinderer, *Seventeen years in the Yoruba country: memorials of Anna Hinderer, wife of Rev. David Hinderer* (1872) · E. Stock, *The history of the Church Missionary Society: its environment, its men and its work*, 1–3 (1899) · A. J. C. Hare, *The Gurneys of Earlham*, 2 vols. (1895) · J. F. A. Ajayi, *Christian missions in Nigeria, 1841–1891* (1965) · C. P. Groves, *The planting of Christianity in Africa*, vol. 2 (1954) · E. Thorp, *The swelling of Jordan* (1950) · m. cert. · d. cert.

Archives U. Birm. L., CMS archives, David Hinderer MSS

Likenesses engraving, repro. in Hinderer, *Seventeen years*, frontispiece

Hinderwell, Thomas (1744–1825), philanthropist and antiquary, was born on 17 November 1744 at St Nicholas Cliff, Scarborough, the elder son of the four children of Thomas Hinderwell (*bap.* 1705, *d.* 1798), master mariner and shipowner, and his wife, Rebekah (1716/17–1797). At Coxwold grammar school, as a boarder, he studied classics and then, at the age of eleven, he was apprenticed to Robert Burn, a Scarborough master mariner. As ship's boy, master, and eventually owner he spent the next twenty years at sea. By 1775 he was rich enough to retire and settle ashore permanently at Scarborough. Three years later he was elected to the Common Hall, the corporation's ruling body, and in 1781–2, 1784–5, 1790–91, and 1799–1800 he served as one of the two bailiffs, the town's most senior officers. He finally stepped down as 'father of the Hall' in 1816.

Unmarried and with more than sufficient income from his shipping interests Hinderwell devoted himself to many charitable causes: 'feeding the hungry, clothing the naked, instructing the ignorant, visiting the afflicted [and] saving the drowning' (Bottomley, 9). He was president of Scarborough's Trinity House and its Merchant Seamen's Society, both of which had local hospitals for 'broken seafarers', widows, and orphans. He was trustee and president of the Amicable Society, an Anglican charity that clothed and schooled the town's poorest children. Both the Lancasterian School and the School of Industry, which gave moral and practical instruction to poor girls, received gifts in his will. In 1812 he was founder and became first president of Scarborough's Auxiliary Bible Society. One of his most beneficial and lasting achievements was his campaign to provide Scarborough with a lifeboat, the second in Britain. He launched a public appeal for the lifeboat fund, chaired the lifeboat committee, and supported Henry Greathead's design. During its first year Scarborough's lifeboat saved the lives of at least five crews. Later he was responsible for founding Scarborough's Humane Society, which gave food, clothing, and accommodation to shipwrecked seamen. After his death his private collection of fossils and minerals formed the basis of Scarborough's Rotunda Museum when it opened in 1828.

Though he published many essays on subjects as varied as shipwrecks and Sunday observance, Hinderwell is most valued today for his *History and Antiquities of Scarborough and the Vicinity*, first published at York in 1798. A second, improved edition, dedicated to his friend and fellow campaigner against slavery, William Wilberforce, appeared in 1811; a third, posthumous revision, which included a tribute to the original author, was published in 1832. Hinderwell's was the earliest history of Scarborough, yet two centuries later it remains indispensable—the mature fruit of wide reading, extensive travel, unrivalled local knowledge, privileged access to the corporation's rich archive, the expert research of his many professional assistants, and his own humanitarian wisdom. For his pioneer work Hinderwell engaged the services of Dr Belcombe, Scarborough's resident physician, Dr William Travis, surgeon and local antiquarian, the Revd Daniel Lysons, who devilled for him in the Tower of London and the British Museum, and the Revd Francis Wrangham, a formidable scholar and bibliophile, who gave him 'many interesting favours' (T. Hinderwell, *The History and Antiquities of Scarborough*, 2nd edn, 1811, vi).

Hinderwell died at his home in Newborough, Scarborough, on 22 October 1825 and was buried three days later in St Mary's parish churchyard, under the same plain gravestone as his father, mother, sister Ann, and brother-in-law. The executors of his will were directed to distribute £50 worth of bread to the town's poor and 'to avoid the ostentation of a public funeral' (Cole, 39).

JACK BINNS

Sources J. Cole, *Thomas Hinderwell: memoirs of his life, writings and character* (1826) · B. Evans, memoir, in T. Hinderwell, *The history and antiquities of Scarborough*, 3rd edn (1832) · S. Bottomley, *A sermon on the death of Hinderwell* (1825) · parish register, Scarborough, St Mary, 14 Dec 1744 [baptism; Scarborough Central Library (typescript copies)] · parish register, Scarborough, St Mary, 25 Oct 1825 [burial; Scarborough Central Library (typescript copies)] · will, 1825, PRO, PROB 11/1705, sig. 578 · *DNB*
Archives priv. coll., letters [copies, Scarborough Library] · Rotunda Museum, Scarborough, collection of fossils, minerals, and other specimens of natural history
Likenesses J. R. Smith, 1797 (Sothebys) · M. Baynes junior, oils, Art Gallery store, The Crescent, Scarborough · J. Greenwood of Hull, engraving, repro. in Hinderwell, *History and antiquities of Scarborough* · J. Posselwhite, stipple (after J. Jackson), BM, NPG · oils, Town Hall, St Nicholas Street, Scarborough
Wealth at death £15,850; incl. £15,600 left to nephews, nieces, and sister; £10 to servant; remainder to local charities: will, 1825, PRO, PROB 11/1705 · left £50 for bread for the poor: Cole, *Thomas Hinderwell*, 39

Hindle, John (1761–1796), singer and composer, was the son of Bartholomew and Mary Hindle of Westminster. He was a student of Benjamin Cooke, and by 1783 he was described as a harpsichordist and teacher of music. A countertenor, Hindle is recorded as singing at the Worcester festival in August 1780, at the Handel commemoration concerts at Westminster Abbey and the Pantheon in May and June 1784, at the Tottenham Street concerts in 1786, and at the Covent Garden oratorios in March 1792. He was a lay vicar of Westminster Abbey. On 16 November 1791 he matriculated from Magdalen College, Oxford, and was apparently awarded a BMus. He published a collection of songs and one of glees. His best-known composition was the glee 'Queen of the Silver Bow', published in the *Professional Collection of Glees* (c.1790). Hindle died in London, apparently unmarried, in 1796; his mother was granted the administration of his estate.

K. D. REYNOLDS

Sources *DNB* · Highfill, Burnim & Langhans, *BDA* · W. H. Husk, 'Hindle, John', Grove, *Dict. mus.* (1927) · Foster, *Alum. Oxon.*

Hindley, Charles (1796–1857), politician and factory reformer, was born on 25 June 1796 at the Fairfield Moravian Settlement, Droylsden, near Manchester. He was the third son of Ignatius Hindley (1756–1803), a muslin manufacturer in Dukinfield, Cheshire, and his wife, Mary, *née* Ambler (1762–1801).

Hindley was educated within the Moravian community, first at the academy at Fairfield, then at Fulneck, near Leeds. He went on to study with the Revd C. A. Pohlman at Haverfordwest in Wales before becoming classical and mathematical tutor at the Moravian settlement at Gracehill, Ireland. He was intended for the Moravian ministry and had started to preach locally when the death of his elder brother in 1819 led to his return to manage the family's two cotton mills. The Hindleys were among the earliest mill owners in Dukinfield and Charles obviously inherited their entrepreneurial spirit as the business expanded in the 1820s.

Hindley married Hannah Buckley (1801–1837), a Mossley mill owner's daughter, in September 1822. They had six children, but only two daughters, Hannah (1830–1857) and Susan (1835–1846), survived infancy. These girls were brought up by Hindley's second wife, Ann (1805–1854), whom he married in 1839. She was the daughter of Richard Fort of Read Hall, Lancashire. Ann became a Moravian and was involved in many of her husband's interests, including the Ashton under Lyne Mechanics' Institute. She predeceased him on 16 December 1854. Hindley's daughter Hannah was the author of two locally published books which describe the family's travels in the Holy Land. She married Henry Woods, who became MP for Wigan, and she died on 12 July 1857.

Hindley was involved in social concerns from the 1820s, when he helped set up the Ashton Mechanics' Institute (1825), of which he was president until his death. By the early 1830s he had made his fortune and had begun to devote his mind and wealth to social and political concerns, adopting the cause of factory reform. His speeches show humanitarian concern for the health and educational welfare of children working in the mills. After an agitation in which he was involved, Ashton became a parliamentary constituency and he unsuccessfully contested the seat in December 1832, but was elected in January 1835 and remained Liberal MP until his death.

Althorp's Factory Act had become law in 1833, but was proving ineffective and Hindley's entrance to parliament was seen by the factory reformers as a chance to remedy this. He introduced a new bill designed gradually to introduce a ten-hour day for workers under the age of twenty-one, but this was felt to be too cautious by many in the factory movement, especially Richard Oastler. They were further disillusioned when Hindley dropped the bill in return for a government promise to enforce the 1833 act more rigorously. In 1834 and 1836 legal proceedings were taken against Hindley's own mill (the day-to-day running of which was in the hands of his nephew) for breaches of the Factory Act and long hours were still being worked there in 1848. As a result Hindley became an ambivalent figure, and he never regained the trust of some factory reformers, in particular Joseph Rayner Stephens, whose denunciations of him as untrustworthy coloured Hindley's subsequent reputation.

Hindley continued to support factory reform and in 1843 served on a select committee inquiring into the operation of the Factory Acts. He had Chartist sympathies and has been credited with helping to draw up the People's Charter, but, although he was one of several MPs involved in the early stages, he was not connected with the final draft. He voted for the ballot in 1853. He was also president of the Universal Peace Society in the 1840s and presided over the first International Peace Congress in London.

Hindley died of heart disease on 1 December 1857 at his home, Dartmouth House, Queen Street, Westminster, and was buried four days later in the Moravian cemetery, Chelsea. His final illness and its treatment were the subject of a pamphlet by the physician Augustus Bozzi Granville, *Dr Todd and the Late Member for Ashton: Fatal Effect of the stimulating Treatment of Disease* (1860).   ALICE LOCK

Sources M. Nevell, *People who made Tameside* (1994), 31–6, 77 · J. W. Follows, *Antecedents of the International Labour Organization* (1951), 10–21 · *Ashton Weekly Reporter* (5 Dec 1857), 3 · S. Martin, *Address delivered at the burial of Mrs Hindley, wife of Charles Hindley Esq. MP by Samuel Martin, to which is affixed a brief biographical sketch* (1855) · I. Haynes, *Dukinfield cotton mills* (1993) · M. Tylecote, *The mechanics' institutes of Lancashire and Yorkshire before 1851* (1957) · M. S. Edwards, *Purge this realm: a life of Joseph Rayner Stephens* (1994) · J. Evans, *Lancashire authors and orators* (1850), 132–5 · C. E. Sutcliffe, *The lot of the righteous: a sermon preached in the Moravian chapel, Dukinfield, December 13th 1857 … on the occasion of the decease of the late Charles Hindley Esq. MP* (1857) · W. Glover, *History of Ashton-u-Lyne and the surrounding district* (1884) · PRO, records of the Fairfield and Dukinfield Moravian chapels [and on microfilm at Tameside Local Studies Library]
Archives UCL, letters to Henry Brougham, incl. letters from Charles Hindley
Likenesses S. W. Reynolds, engraving, pubd 1837 (after painting by B. Garside) · oils, Tameside Local Studies Library, Stalybridge, Cheshire
Wealth at death under £30,000: administration, 1858

Hindley, Sir Clement Daniel Maggs (1874–1944), railway engineer, was born in Dulwich, London, on 19 December 1874, the son of Charles Hugh Hindley, carpet warehouseman, and his wife, Mary Ann Miller. He was educated at Dulwich College and entered Trinity College, Cambridge, in 1893, where he graduated BA in mechanical sciences in 1896. In the following year he was appointed assistant engineer on the East Indian Railway. He married, in 1899, Anne, daughter of Henry Rait, of Murshidabad, Bengal; they had three sons.

After a visit in 1904 to America and Canada as member of an official delegation from the Institution of Civil Engineers, he returned to India to become in 1905 personal assistant to the chief engineer of the East Indian Railway. He took charge in 1906 of the technical section of the agent's office, with responsibility for the scrutiny of all plans and estimates for engineering works. Later he assumed charge of the Delhi district and the completion of other sections of the region. He became secretary of the East Indian Railway in 1914, deputy general manager in 1918, and general manager in 1920.

In 1921 Hindley was appointed chairman of the commissioners of the Port of Calcutta, and in the following year became the first chief commissioner of railways for India, with responsibility for decisions on technical matters. He was the sole adviser to the government of India on railway policy and oversaw many important changes, including the reorganization of the railway department, the separation of railway finance from the general budget, the transfer of the East Indian and Great Indian Peninsula Railways to state management, and the opening of the first railway staff college. He did much to restore the Indian railways to a state of efficiency after the effects of the First World War and initiated a programme of new construction which added 4000 miles to the railways. He was knighted in 1925 and, retiring in 1928, was appointed KCIE in 1929. He was also a commander of the Belgian order of Leopold.

On his return to England, Hindley was appointed first chairman of the Racecourse Betting Control Board and although his task was difficult, and entirely new to him, his wisdom, tact, and great administrative ability soon made themselves felt. Hindley was a man of imposing personality and great charm of manner, and he was much in demand for committee work, for he was a master of procedure and his memoranda were remarkable for their clarity: his attention was thus turned to matters which included the channel tunnel, forest products, inland water, building research, and fuel efficiency. He was a member of the Advisory Council for Scientific and Industrial Research, of the board of the National Physical Laboratory, and chairman of the steel structures research committee. From 1939 to 1942 he was regional works adviser for the London civil defence region. At the time of his death he was chairman of the codes of practice committee for civil engineering and building under the minister of works, and of the building and civil engineering industries holidays with pay scheme. He was a valued member of the Institution of Civil Engineers of which he was president, 1939–40, and had much to do with the initiation of its journal and its research committee. He died at his home, High Elms, Hampton Court Road, Hampton, Middlesex, on 3 May 1944. He was survived by his wife.

W. T. HALCROW, *rev.* ANITA McCONNELL

Sources G. Huddleston, *History of the East Indian railway* (1906) · *The Times* (6 May 1944) · J. N. Sahni, *Indian railways: one hundred years, 1853 to 1953* (1953) · *WWW* · *Journal of the Institution of Civil Engineers*, 22 (1943–4), 357–9 · Venn, *Alum. Cant.* · d. cert. · *CGPLA Eng. & Wales* (1945)
Likenesses W. Stoneman, photograph, 1931, NPG · A. Devas, portrait, 1940, Inst. CE
Wealth at death £21,408 8s. 10d.: probate, 25 Jan 1945, *CGPLA Eng. & Wales*

Hindley, Henry (1700?–1771), clockmaker and mechanician, was probably born in or near Manchester, but his early life is obscure. Already married to his wife, Sarah, he had moved to York by 1731 and was admitted to the freedom of the city on the presentation of two clocks, now in the Mansion House and the Guildhall at York. He soon established himself as a maker of domestic and turret clocks, all his early pieces having dead-beat escapements. His Roman Catholicism probably helped secure patrons among the wealthy local Catholic families; however, during the Jacobite rising of 1745 he was required to pay a surety of £100 and to obtain a licence before travelling any distance.

Hindley's son, Joseph, having been apprenticed to his father in 1742 at the age of twenty, was made free by patrimony in 1754 and continued active in the family business. In 1750 Henry received an order for a new turret clock for York Minster, at a cost of £300; he gave it a 52 foot, 4 second pendulum. Thereafter, he continued to make ingenious and complex domestic clocks and fine turret clocks,

the most distant going to the Orphan Hospital, Edinburgh. These later pieces used recoil escapements. Hindley also sold conventional watches, but these were not by his hand. He occasionally supplied machine tools; Alexander Aubert had a Hindley lathe, while Joseph held discussions with Matthew Boulton, though the outcome is unknown. Henry was credited with the design of wheel and fusee cutting engines illustrated in Rees's *Cyclopaedia* but these were made by his younger brother Roger, who had been apprenticed to Henry, probably before the move to York, and became a watch cap maker in London.

Henry's friend John Smeaton considered that 'especially in his latter days he got into many schemes which appear to me to be much more cost to him than worship' (Law, 696). These days were overshadowed by the deaths of Hindley's daughter Elizabeth in 1762 and his wife, Sarah, in 1763, while he himself died at York on 23 March 1771, and was buried two days later in St Michael le Belfry. Joseph then took on the business but died suddenly on 4 March 1774, after which his father's tools were sold at auction.

Henry Hindley is important in the history of mechanics because of the machine tools which were already complete when he first befriended the young Smeaton in 1741. Smeaton was shown an engine for both cutting the teeth of clock wheels and dividing angular scales. In the second role, it established the general arrangement used in all subsequent circular dividing engines, a horizontal wheel rotated through precise angles by an endless screw engaging with teeth cut in the edge of the wheel. However, Hindley's wheel, about 13 inches in diameter, had only 360 teeth, while the endless screw was globoidal: that is, its sides were curved so that all 15 turns of the thread were fully meshed with the teeth. This type of screw is still sometimes called a Hindley worm. To control the cutting of the teeth of the wheel, Hindley devised his own method of circular dividing. He drilled a sequence of equally spaced holes in a brass strip about 8 feet in length, then joined the ends to form a circular hoop, which was fitted onto a wooden block turned in the form of 'a short piece of a cone of a large diameter' (Smeaton, 187).

Smeaton's description establishes that, as early as 1741, Hindley's workshop contained not only the wheel-cutting and dividing engine but a great lathe capable of turning pieces over 2½ feet in diameter and a chock (chuck) lathe with (in later terminology) a lead-screw and change-wheels. Hindley was then using his engine to construct one of the earliest examples of a telescope mount 'of the equatorial kind' (Smeaton, 183), although he later advertised it as 'a portable Instrument of universal use in the Mensuration of Angles in Coelestial or Terrestrial Observations' (Setchell, 'Hindley & Son', 55). It was eventually sold in 1761. Soon afterwards, Hindley completed another improved instrument for the duke of Norfolk, which has been identified with an equatorial in the Science Museum. Apart from a pyrometer (also in the Science Museum), Hindley is not known to have made any other scientific instruments.

In 1785 Smeaton published a description of Hindley's

engines and his method of dividing, but the latter was not taken up. However, knowledge of the engines had already reached the instrument maker most capable of appreciating their importance. A journeyman of Hindley's named John Stancliffe moved to London, where, before setting up on his own by 1773, he worked as foreman to Jesse Ramsden. These were the years when Ramsden constructed his two circular dividing engines. Ramsden adopted Hindley's layout, though with a much larger wheel, and cut the cylindrical endless screw with a machine based on principles exactly similar to those of Hindley's lathe. The bed of Ramsden's version was a triangular bar, a feature which William Ludlam stated had also been introduced by Hindley. Finally, Ramsden and many others used Hindley's design for the cutter which inscribed the angular divisions of the scale; Edward Troughton called it a 'beautiful contrivance' (Troughton, 128). Thus, through the publications of Smeaton and Ramsden, Hindley's most important innovations became readily accessible at a critical period in the evolution of precision machine tools. They established Hindley's reputation as 'a man of the most communicative disposition, a great lover of mechanics and a most fertile genius' (John Holmes in Law, 206).

JOHN BROOKS

Sources J. Smeaton, 'Observations on the graduation of astronomical instruments ...', *Miscellaneous ... Communications to the Royal Society* (1814), 182–90 · J. R. M. Setchell, 'Henry Hindley & Son: clock and instrument makers and engineers of York', *Annual Report* [Yorkshire Philosophical Society] (1972), 39–67 · J. R. M. Setchell, 'Henry Hindley: his age, his clocks and the Lancashire link', *Antiquarian Horology and the Proceedings of the Antiquarian Horological Society*, 9 (1974–6), 409–11 · R. J. Law, 'Henry Hindley of York', *Antiquarian Horology and the Proceedings of the Antiquarian Horological Society*, 7 (1970–72), 205–21, 682–99 · J. Brooks, 'The circular dividing engine: development in England, 1739–1843', *Annals of Science*, 49 (1992), 101–35 · E. Troughton, 'An account of a method of dividing astronomical and other instruments', *PTRS*, 99 (1809), 105–45 · H. Murray, *Directory of York goldsmiths, silversmiths and associated craftsmen* (1998), 76 · 'Cutting engine', A. Rees and others, *The cyclopaedia, or, Universal dictionary of arts, sciences, and literature*, 45 vols. (1819–20) · 'Fusee', A. Rees and others, *The cyclopaedia, or, Universal dictionary of arts, sciences, and literature*, 45 vols. (1819–20) · private information (2004) [A. McConnell, extract from Marylebone rate book] · J. R. M. Setchell, 'The friendship of John Smeaton, FRS, with Henry Hindley ... and the development of the equatorial mounting telescope', *Notes and Records of the Royal Society*, 25 (1970), 79–85 · J. R. M. Setchell, 'Further information on the telescopes of Hindley of York', *Notes and Records of the Royal Society*, 25 (1970), 189–91 · W. Steeds, *A history of machine tools, 1700–1910* (1969), 15, 152 · G. Goodship, 'Henry Hindley, York', *Antiquarian Horology and the Proceedings of the Antiquarian Horological Society*, 8 (1972–4), 647 · D. F. Nettell, 'Henry Hindley of York', *Antiquarian Horology and the Proceedings of the Antiquarian Horological Society*, 8 (1972–4), 915 · T. Reid, *Treatise on clock and watch making, theoretical and practical* (1826), 137, 285, 289

Hindley, John Haddon (1765–1827), orientalist, was born in Manchester, the son of Charles Hindley, a cloth merchant there. He was educated at Manchester grammar school before matriculating on 21 April 1784 at Brasenose College, Oxford, where he was elected a Hulme exhibitioner in 1788 and graduated BA in 1788 and MA in 1790. In 1792 he became chaplain of Manchester collegiate church and librarian of Chetham's Library, resigning the latter position in 1804. In his later years his mind gave way. He died unmarried at Clapham on 17 June 1827.

The many valuable oriental manuscripts at Chetham's Library led Hindley to the study of Persian. He translated several books from Persian including works by Hafiz, Attar, and Jami. His versions from Hafiz are in both prose and verse. His verse is very pleasant and at times quite elegant.

C. W. SUTTON, rev. PARVIN LOLOI

Sources J. F. Smith, ed., *The admission register of the Manchester School, with some notices of the more distinguished scholars*, 1, Chetham Society, 69 (1866), 205 · *Miscellanies: being a selection from the poems and correspondence of the Rev. Thomas Wilson, with memoirs of his life*, ed. F. R. Raines, Chetham Society, 45 (1857) · *Palatine Note-Book*, 4 (1884), 168 · Foster, *Alum. Oxon.* · Allibone, *Dict.* · C. E. Buckland, *Dictionary of Indian biography* (1906) · Watt, *Bibl. Brit.*
Archives Chetham's Library, Manchester, corresp.

Hindley, John Scott, Viscount Hyndley (1883–1963), businessman and coal industry administrator, was born in Margate on 24 October 1883, the son of the Revd William Talbot Hindley (1845–1906), vicar of Holy Trinity, Margate, and his wife, Caroline, daughter of John Scott. He was educated from 1899 to 1901 at Weymouth College, where he was president of the debating society. He decided not to go to Oxford, which he considered too sports-orientated. As he had already decided to enter industry, he became an engineering apprentice at Murton colliery in co. Durham. On 1 July 1909 he married Vera (b. 1887/8), daughter of James Westoll, shipowner, of Coniscliffe Hall, Darlington, for whom he had worked at Murton colliery; they had two daughters.

Hindley did not complete his apprenticeship, as he had soon changed over to the commercial side of the business; and it was in the large-scale distribution of coal at home and abroad that he first made his name as a capable and energetic businessman. In 1938 he became chairman of the large and then well-known coal merchanting and coal exporting concern, Stephenson, Clarke Ltd. He was also associated with one of the most conspicuous colliery groups in south Wales, the Powell Duffryn Steam Coal Company Ltd, of which he was a managing director from 1931 to 1946. He was on the board of a considerable number of other companies and as early as 1931 he had become a director of the Bank of England. Hindley's success in business sprang from his genial manner and sense of humour, a capacity for working with many sorts of people, his high executive ability in the day-to-day conduct of business, and an extremely shrewd judgement. He was knighted in 1921, and created a baronet in 1927 and Baron Hyndley in 1931.

Hyndley became associated with coal business at a time when the coalmining industry had reached and passed the peak of its nineteenth-century development. Coal had enjoyed something like a monopoly of the market for energy during the first great phase of European industrial expansion. It lost that position in Britain after 1913. The coal industry had to find its way through a period of painful contraction, through disturbed, often bitter, industrial relations, and two world wars. These were the conditions in which Hyndley, as a prominent man of business, became associated with national politics and administration.

Hindley first entered government service during the war as a member of the coal controller's export advisory committee in 1917. Between the wars, he was commercial adviser to what was then the mines department, a small department with inferior personnel and limited powers, which was the only existing medium of communication between government and the coal industry at that time. When the Second World War began, the coal industry ran into grave difficulties which arose partly out of the decline of the industry in the previous twenty years and partly out of the demand for recruits for the forces when France fell in 1940. This latter emergency stripped the mines of workers just when the munitions drive, with its need for coal, was getting into its stride.

The mines department did not survive the fuel crisis of 1941–2; it was replaced in 1942 by the much larger, wider, and better-staffed Ministry of Fuel and Power. Hyndley became the ministry's controller-general and carried the main responsibility for coal output and distribution under the first minister of fuel and power, Major Gwilym Lloyd-George (later Viscount Tenby). Hyndley was thus associated with the fuel effort during the most critical years of the war. But his position was awkward, for the ministry also possessed a secretary directly responsible to the minister. The personal resolve of the two men concerned was needed to avoid trouble, which on the whole they managed successfully. However, although Hyndley had an undoubted capacity for business, and especially for marketing, he was not ideally suited to the strategic role he was called upon to play in the ministry, and he resigned at the end of 1943 to be succeeded by Sir Hubert Houldsworth. During his time at the ministry Hyndley nevertheless made an important contribution to the debate about the future of the coal industry, advocating that it should ultimately be run 'on public corporation lines' (Supple, 612).

For the next three years, until 1946, Hyndley devoted himself largely to his business interests. But the coal industry was towards the centre of the political stage after the war and Hyndley with his intimate knowledge of its problems seemed too valuable a man to lose. When the mines were nationalized in 1946 it was Hyndley who was asked by the Attlee government to take on the heavy and thankless post of first chairman of the National Coal Board. This he held until 1951, when he was again succeeded by Houldsworth. Hyndley brought loyalty, hard work, and fortitude to his five years at the board. He established excellent personal relations with, and earned the liking of, a deeply divided industry. According to the official history of the coal industry, Hyndley's colleagues recognized that 'he was first-rate in the conduct of business at meetings and he was skilled in reaching satisfactory arrangements with politicians' (Ashworth, 122). A colleague compared him favourably with his successor: 'whereas Hyndley conducted cabinet government, Houldsworth's style was presidential' (ibid., 192).

How far the organization Hyndley helped to set up was wholly effective for the long-term requirements of fuel and power policy is another question. It could not be answered out of an examination of his efforts alone, for the establishment of the board was much influenced by contemporary political and economic conditions. Hyndley was shrewd rather than adventurous. But he certainly assisted to close one chapter in the history of British coalmining and to open another. To that extent he left his personal mark on the economic development of Britain at the time. He was appointed GBE in 1939 and advanced to a viscountcy in 1948. Hyndley died at his London home, 59 Cadogan Place, Chelsea, on 5 January 1963. His titles became extinct at his death.

W. H. B. COURT, *rev.* ROBERT BROWN

Sources B. Supple, *The history of the British coal industry, vol. 4, 1913–1946: the political economy of decline* (1987) · W. Ashworth, *The history of the British coal industry, vol. 5, 1946–1982: the nationalized industry* (1986) · N. Chester, *The nationalization of British industry, 1945–51* (1975) · *The Times* (7 Jan 1963) · *DBB* · probate
Likenesses W. Stoneman, two photographs, 1942, NPG
Wealth at death £241,320 19s.: probate, 29 March 1963, CGPLA Eng. & Wales

Hindlip. For this title name *see* Allsopp, Henry, first Baron Hindlip (1811–1887).

Hindmarsh, Sir John (*bap.* **1785**, *d.* **1860**), naval officer and colonial governor, was baptized on 22 May 1785, the son of John Hindmarsh, gunner on the *Bellerophon*, and his wife, Mary, *née* Roxburgh. He entered the navy in March 1793 as a volunteer on the *Bellerophon*, in which he remained for seven years, and was present at the battle in the north Atlantic on 1 June 1794, in Cornwallis's retreat (17 June 1795), at the battle of the Nile (1 August 1798), and at the capture of the forts at Gaeta in 1799. In the battle of the Nile the *Bellerophon*, while accidentally anchored, was exposed to the full weight of *L'Orient's* broadside, was dismasted and sustained exceptional loss. The captain, Darby, went below wounded, and for a few minutes Hindmarsh was the only officer on deck, just as *L'Orient* burst into flames. He ordered the cable to be cut, and, setting the spritsail, got the ship clear of the imminent danger in a manner that elicited the warm approval of Captain Darby, who afterwards personally introduced him to Nelson and Lord St Vincent as having saved the ship. He lost the sight of an eye. In May 1800 he followed Captain Darby to the *Spencer* (74 guns), and in her was present in the actions at Algeciras on 6 July and in the Strait of Gibraltar on 12 July 1801.

In 1803 Hindmarsh went out to the Mediterranean in the *Victory* (100 guns), and in August was promoted by Nelson to lieutenant of the *Phoebe* (36 guns), in which he was present at Trafalgar on 21 October 1805. In November he was moved into the sloop *Beagle* (18 guns) for four years' cruising against the French coasting privateers. In April 1809 the *Beagle* convoyed the fireships to the Basque Roads, and took part in the subsequent operations. On 4 November 1809 Hindmarsh married Susannah Wilson Edmeades: they had three daughters and a son.

Hindmarsh was appointed first lieutenant of the *Nisus* (38 guns) with Captain Philip Beaver, and in her took part in the capture of Mauritius and Java. In May 1813 he returned to England invalided, and was promoted commander on 15 June 1815. In March 1830 he was appointed to command the *Scylla* (18 guns), in the Mediterranean, and was posted from her on 3 September 1831. He went out to Alexandria in September 1834 in the hope (in the event unfulfilled) of assuming command of the Egyptian navy.

At his own request, and through influence, in February 1836 Hindmarsh was appointed first governor of South Australia (at a salary of £800), and in May was made KH. He sailed in the *Buffalo* (6 guns) for Australia in June. On 28 December he and his party landed at Holdfast Bay, where the orders in council creating South Australia a British colony and Hindmarsh's commission as governor were read. With its new capital, Adelaide, the settlement grew, and Hindmarsh made a large profit from selling land. Hindmarsh was associated with John Fisher, as commissioner for the sale of crown lands, but the dual government did not work well, and after disputes and controversy Hindmarsh was recalled in February 1838, and sailed for England on 14 July, hoping to be reinstated. In the event, although Fisher was removed, the new governor, George Gawler, was vested with sole authority.

From September 1840 until 1856 Hindmarsh was lieutenant-governor of Heligoland. On 31 January 1856 he was advanced to flag rank. Hindmarsh's wife died at Brighton on 2 April 1859, and he died at 11 Denbigh Terrace, Belgrave Road, London, on 29 July 1860. They had one son, John, a barrister, and three daughters, one of whom, Mary, married G. M. Stephen, brother of Sir Alfred Stephen, chief justice of New South Wales; another, Jane, married A. M. Mundy, colonial secretary for South Australia, and nephew of Admiral Sir George Mundy.

J. K. LAUGHTON, *rev.* ROGER MORRISS

Sources O'Byrne, *Naval biog. dict.* · *Annual Register* (1860), 448 · *GM*, 3rd ser., 9 (1860), 327 · J. Marshall, *Royal naval biography*, 4/2 (1835), 474 · *AusDB* · P. Mackesy, *The war in the Mediterranean, 1803–1810* (1957) · C. N. Parkinson, *War in the eastern seas, 1793–1815* (1954) · R. Muir, *Britain and the defeat of Napoleon, 1807–1815* (1996) · Boase, *Mod. Eng. biog.* · *CGPLA Eng. & Wales* (1860)

Wealth at death under £4000: probate, 25 Sept 1860, *CGPLA Eng. & Wales*

Hindmarsh, Robert (1759–1835), Swedenborgian preacher, was born in Alnwick, Northumberland, on 8 November 1759, the son of James Hindmarsh (1732–1812) and his wife, Elizabeth (d. 1775). His father was one of the schoolmasters at Wesley's school at Kingswood in the 1760s, and subsequently an itinerant preacher for Wesley. Hindmarsh was a student at this school and was converted during a revival in the school in 1768. Apprenticed to a Quaker printer in London, he was introduced to 'mystical' literature and became a devotee of the writings of Emanuel Swedenborg, which he published when he became a printer in his own right. If his cheerful and purposeful character appears somewhat at odds with the image of the early Swedenborgians, his rational distaste for the Trinity attracted him to the new doctrines; his efficiency

Robert Hindmarsh (1759–1835), by Samuel William Reynolds senior and Samuel Cousins, pubd 1824 (after Joseph Allen)

and his gift for languages made him very valuable to the 'new church'. In 1783 he was appointed the secretary of two of the early Swedenborgian societies and he sat as an equal alongside an intellectual élite in a society of talents. As former Methodists, he and his father wanted a chapel where they could worship God according to Swedenborgian theology, and his father became the first preacher when the New Jerusalem church was established. On 7 May 1782 Hindmarsh married Sarah Paramor (d. 1833) of Monckton, Thanet; they had five children.

Hindmarsh was certainly a high-profile figure in the early Swedenborgian group, promoting the doctrines even to Joseph Priestley in 1791, but he was also not frightened to follow the bolder ideas of some Swedenborgians about spiritual marriage and was expelled from membership of the chapel, although he was later encouraged to produce its magazine. He further soured of the society by 1793 when they rejected the episcopalian status sought by his father in favour of the more usual nonconformist congregational system of church government, at a time when such views were politically charged. He did little for the cause apart from attempting to found a new London congregation of the 'new church' in 1799 and publishing translations of Swedenborg's works until 1810. During this period he was an active member of the stock exchange, but was then invited to serve as minister of a proprietary chapel of the New Jerusalem church in Salford, Lancashire. He withdrew again from active involvement in the denomination in 1824, spending his retirement in writing his history of the sect, a highly partisan interpretation which was not published until 1861, but has influenced all subsequent interpretations of the sect, despite his curious bias. He then caused an abiding controversy in that sect through his claim that he did not need ordination when he commenced his ministerial career in 1810 because he had been ordained 'by the divine auspices of heaven' at the time of the first ordinations of the church in 1788. Hindmarsh died in his daughter's house in Gravesend on 2 January 1835, two years after his wife, and was buried in Milton-next-Gravesend. He is a striking blend of the sectarianism on the fringes of the evangelical revival. His career is controversial even to the church he founded, and his biographer pictures him 'with the sword in one hand and the trowel in the other' (Odhner).

PETER J. LINEHAM

Sources R. Hindmarsh, *Rise and progress of the New Jerusalem church*, ed. E. Madeley (1861) · C. T. Odhner, *Robert Hindmarsh: a biography* (1895) · P. J. Lineham, 'The origins of the New Jerusalem church in the 1780s', *Bulletin of the John Rylands University Library*, 70 (1988), 109–22 [*Sects and new religious movements*] · *DNB* · D. M. Lewis, ed., *The Blackwell dictionary of evangelical biography, 1730–1860*, 2 vols. (1995) · J. Hyde, *New Church Magazine*, 24 (1905), 65–72, 114–23 · *Intellectual Repository* (1833), 437–8 · S. Noble, *A sermon occasioned by the death of R. H.* (1835), 13

Likenesses S. W. Reynolds senior and S. Cousins, mezzotint, pubd 1824 (after J. Allen), BM, NPG [*see illus.*]

Hinds, John (1862–1928), politician and businessman, was born at Cwnin Farm, Carmarthen, Carmarthenshire, on 26 July 1862. He was the eldest son of William Hinds and his wife, Mary, *née* Jones, had four brothers and one sister, and was brought up in a Welsh-speaking environment. His father was a freehold farmer, and the family were nonconformists who worshipped at Penuel Welsh Baptist Church, Carmarthen. His mother was the daughter of David Jones, a farmer of Penronnw, Llanpumsaint, near Carmarthen. Educated at the Lancastrian School, Carmarthen, Hinds then worked on the land until he was apprenticed to an uncle, Charles Jones, in the town. He moved to London in June 1881 and, having been employed by several firms, set up his own drapery business at Blackheath in 1887. In 1893 he married Elizabeth (Lizzie), daughter of R. Powell of Cefntrefra, Llandovery, Carmarthenshire. The marriage produced a son, William, and a daughter, Gwladys.

In 1908, around the time Hinds retired from direct involvement in the drapery business on a day-to-day basis, it became a limited company, trading as Hinds & Co. He retained a connection with the trade and later served as president of the Drapers' Chamber of Trade for Great Britain. An active freemason, he chaired five lodges in London and held many other masonic offices in both London and Carmarthen. He was also active in London Welsh circles and served as a deacon at Castle Street Welsh Baptist Church and as president of the Welsh Baptist Union.

Hinds was drawn into Liberal Party politics through his connection with David Lloyd George, a fellow member at Castle Street. In January 1910 he unsuccessfully sought the Liberal nomination at Merthyr Tudful in succession to D. A. Thomas. A better opportunity arose when John Lloyd Morgan, Liberal MP for West Carmarthenshire, became a judge late in 1910. Although opposed by a number of strong contenders, including Sir Owen Philipps, MP for Pembroke Boroughs, Hinds narrowly captured the nomination by a mere two votes at the expense of Henry Jones-Davies, brother-in-law of the late Liberal chief whip, Tom Ellis. Hinds comfortably won the seat in December 1910 and held it for the next thirteen years. In 1914 he built a new home, Neuadd Deg, close to his birthplace on the outskirts of Carmarthen. His London home was at 14 Clarendon Court, Paddington.

In many ways Hinds was an orthodox Liberal MP whose local appeal was based upon his effective use of the Welsh language at public meetings, and his personal, family, and religious connections within the community. He emphasized the traditional Welsh issues of church disestablishment (opposing any compromise settlement) and agricultural matters, which reflected the concerns of many of his constituents. He was also a supporter of Welsh home rule, and an ally of E. T. John, its main advocate in the Commons. A loyal follower of Lloyd George during the First World War, he fully supported government policy, although he was absent from the first reading of the Conscription Bill in January 1916. In February 1916 his son, Lieutenant William Pugh Hinds, was killed at the age of eighteen while on active service in France with the London Welsh battalion. John Hinds's association with Lloyd George was a key factor in his appointment as lord lieutenant of Carmarthenshire in 1917, a post he held until his death. At the general election of 1918, Hinds was awarded the 'coupon' and returned unopposed for a redrawn Carmarthen division, even though a minority within the local National Farmers' Union sought to oppose him with an agriculturist candidate. He spent much of the campaign supporting coalition candidates in neighbouring constituencies.

Hinds played little part in the bitter infighting in west Wales between Asquithian and Coalition Liberals, which reached a climax in the Cardiganshire by-election of 1921. However, his allegiance to Lloyd George led to his being opposed at the general election of 1922 by an Asquithian Liberal, as well as an agriculturist, Daniel Johns. Even so, Hinds held the seat by a 3741 majority over the Conservatives. In 1923 he served as chairman of the Welsh Liberal Party but retired from parliament at the general election of that year, ostensibly on health grounds. Hinds continued his involvement with Liberal politics and remained chairman of the Welsh National Liberal Federation until his death. In Carmarthenshire he played a leading role in the United Counties Agricultural Society, served as president of the Carmarthenshire chamber of agriculture, and was a founder member of the Carmarthenshire Antiquarian Society. In 1925, although not an elected member of the town council, he served as mayor of Carmarthen and was later made a freeman of the borough.

To many in his native county, Hinds was an archetypal London Welshman who 'went to London years ago as a simple country youth, armed with nothing but what his parents gave him. He made himself a great gentleman and returned as such to his native town' (*Carmarthen Journal*, 27 July 1928). He died at 7 Mandeville Place, London, on 23 July 1928. After a service at Penuel, Carmarthen, he was buried at Carmarthen public cemetery on 26 July 1928. In his native Carmarthen a field, Parc Hinds, which he donated to the town, commemorates him. Hinds did not make a great impact at Westminster, and was essentially a loyal Liberal back-bencher, deeply rooted in Welsh nonconformist radicalism. IOAN MATTHEWS

Sources *Carmarthen Journal* (25 Nov 1910) · *Carmarthen Journal* (27 July 1928) · *Carmarthen Journal* (3 Aug 1928) · *The Welshman* [Carmarthen] · *Western Mail* · K. O. Morgan, *Wales in British politics, 1868–1922*, 3rd edn · b. cert. · d. cert. · WWW · CGPLA Eng. & Wales (1928)
Archives NL Wales, corresp. with E. T. John
Wealth at death £104,696 17s. 6d.: resworn probate, 1928, CGPLA Eng. & Wales

Hinds, Samuel (1793–1872), bishop of Norwich, son of Abel Hinds of Barbados, was born in Barbados, some members of his family having been among the earlier settlers and chief landed proprietors. He was educated at Charterhouse and then entered Queen's College, Oxford, in November 1811, and graduated BA 1815 (2nd class), MA 1818, and BD and DD 1831. In 1818 he won the chancellor's prize for a Latin essay, and in 1822 he was ordained.

Early in life Hinds was connected as a missionary with the Society for the Conversion of Negroes. He was for some time principal of Codrington College, Barbados. In 1827 he became vice-principal of St Alban Hall, Oxford, under Richard Whately DD, who had been his private tutor; on Whately's elevation to the archbishopric of Dublin in 1831, Hinds was appointed his domestic chaplain. This office, however, he was obliged to resign owing to ill health, in 1833, when he returned to England. In 1834 he was presented to the vicarage of Yardley, Hertfordshire, which benefice he held with the rural deanery of the district until January 1843, when he was appointed to the vicarage of the united parishes of Castleknock, Clonsilla, and Mullahidart, with the prebend of Castleknock in St Patrick's Cathedral, in the diocese of Dublin. At the same time he again became one of Archbishop Whately's chaplains. In 1846 he was appointed first chaplain to the earl of Bessborough, lord lieutenant of Ireland, and in the following year to the earl of Clarendon, who had succeeded to the lord lieutenancy. He resigned the benefice of Castleknock in September 1848, when he was presented by the crown to the deanery of Carlisle. In October 1849 he was raised to the bishopric of Norwich, on the death of Bishop Stanley, and he held it until 1857, when ill health required him to resign.

In 1850 Hinds chaired the royal commission on Oxford University, being appointed by Lord John Russell (who had considered him for the regius chair of divinity in 1847). His chairmanship reflected both his liberal credentials and his competence. His commission's report, in 1852, provided an opportunity of a turning point in the history of the university, of which the latter only partially took advantage.

Hinds married, first, a daughter of Abel Clinkett of Barbados, who died in 1834. About 1856 he married his second wife, Sarah Emily, who survived him. He published many sermons, pamphlets, and books of a broad-church character on a variety of subjects, including *History of the Rise and Early Progress of Christianity* (2 vols., 1828), *The Three Temples of the one True God Contrasted* (1830), *Sonnets and other Short Poems, Chiefly on Sacred Subjects* (1834), and *On the Colonisation of New Zealand* (1838). His *Introduction to Logic* (1827) was taken from Whately's *Elements*. Several of his works were originally articles in the *Encyclopaedia metropolitana*.

Hinds was a man of learning, ability, and engaging character. In politics he was a moderate Liberal, while he represented one of the most 'advanced' schools of thought on religious questions, especially during the last few years of his life. He died at 40 Clarendon Road, London, on 7 February 1872. B. H. BLACKER, *rev.* H. C. G. MATTHEW

Sources Boase, *Mod. Eng. biog.* · W. R. Ward, *Victorian Oxford* (1965) · I. Ellis, *Seven against Christ: a study of 'Essays and reviews'* (1980) · CGPLA Eng. & Wales (1872)
Archives Norfolk RO, letter-book | BL, W. E. Gladstone MSS, Add. MSS 44369, 44414–44419 · LPL, letters to bishop of Meath · PRO, Russell MSS
Likenesses T. H. Maguire, lithograph, 1851, BM, NPG · portrait, repro. in *ILN*, 60 (1872), 60
Wealth at death under £60,000: probate, 14 March 1872, CGPLA Eng. & Wales

Hine, Henry George (1811–1895), comic artist and landscape painter, born at Brighton, Sussex, on 15 August 1811, was the son of a coachman, William Hine, and his wife, Mary Roffey. He was entirely self-taught as an artist, though he was encouraged in his study of nature by a vicar of a neighbouring Sussex village, who had a collection of watercolours by Copley Fielding, whose style strongly influenced Hine's own. Hine made his name in Sussex with seapieces and scenes of the coast near Brighton before moving to London, where he was apprenticed as a draughtsman to the engraver Henry Meyer. He then spent two years in France, at Rouen, developing his skills in oil painting, before returning again to Brighton. On 13 November 1840 he married Mary Ann Eliza (*b.* 1818/19), daughter of James Egerton, a coach maker; they had ten daughters and four sons.

Not finding the commissions he desired, Hine moved once more to London, where he became a professional wood-engraver. In 1841 he was discovered by Ebenezer Landells, who at that time was projecting the publication of a landscape periodical called *The Cosmorama*. Pleased with a little comic sketch by Hine of a dustman and his dog, Landells recommended that he become a contributor to *Punch*, the first number of which had appeared on 17 July 1841. Hine's first contribution appeared in September and he continued to work for *Punch* until 1844, supplying 'blackies' (black comic sketches) and cartoons. Thereafter, he contributed to several short-lived rival publications, such as *Puck*, *Joe Miller the Younger*, and the *Man in the Moon*, as well as to the *Illustrated London News*, before returning to landscape painting. His favourite subject remained the

Sussex countryside of his youth (which he depicted, according to the *Magazine of Art* in 1893, with 'something of a geologist's knowledge of the land'), though he did paint many scenes of Northumberland and London, as well.

Between 1830 and 1851 Hine had sent six pictures to the Royal Academy; he also sent twelve to the Suffolk Street Gallery, including, in 1856, *Picts Wall in Carrfield Crags, Northumberland*. By 1861 he had sent eight works to the Royal Academy, the most successful of which was *Wrecks on the Beach at Brighton* (exh. 1861). In 1863 Hine was elected as associate of the Institute of Painters in Water Colours, and exhibited there *St. Paul's from Fleet Street*. He was elected a full member in 1864, and became a regular contributor to the Institute (from 1885 Royal Institute) of Painters in Water Colours, even serving as vice-president from 1884 to 1895. Hine died at his home, 4 Gayton Crescent, Hampstead, London, on 16 March 1895.

EMILY M. WEEKS

Sources F. Wedmore, 'Henry G. Hine', *Magazine of Art*, 16 (1892–3), 87–91 · *DNB* · M. H. Spielmann, *The history of 'Punch'* (1895), 414–17 · *The Athenaeum* (23 March 1895), 384 · Wood, *Vic. painters*, 3rd edn · Mallalieu, *Watercolour artists* · Bénézit, *Dict.* · Thieme & Becker, *Allgemeines Lexikon* · Bryan, *Painters* (1964), 3.47 · Graves, *RA exhibitors* · m. cert. · *CGPLA Eng. & Wales* (1895)
Likenesses W. Hodgson, chalk and wash drawing, 1891, NPG · E. Wheeler, photograph, repro. in Wedmore, 'Henry G. Hine', 87 · wood-engraving, NPG; repro. in *ILN* (14 May 1892)
Wealth at death £1004 17s. 7d.: probate, 9 May 1895, *CGPLA Eng. & Wales*

Hine, Reginald Leslie (1883–1949), lawyer and author, was born on 25 September 1883 at Newnham Hall, Newnham, near Baldock, Hertfordshire, the second son of Joseph Neville Hine (1849–1931), a farmer, and his wife, Eliza (1843–1892). He was educated at Grove House, Baldock, was tutored by the Revd George Todd of Baldock, and attended Kent College, Canterbury, and the Leys School, Cambridge. Slender of frame, he stood 6 feet 1 inch tall, and was a keen amateur in tennis and cricket. He enjoyed walking and cycling, but was an unwilling motorist. In 1901 he was articled pupil to W. O. Times, solicitor with Hawkins & Co., of Portmill Lane, Hitchin, where he remained until 1936. The quaint old-worldliness of the venerable firm rubbed off onto its willing pupil.

Those who availed themselves of Hine's professional skills were startled by the visual richness of his office, with its roaring fire in winter, illuminating the spines of his substantial book collection, and the Bukhara prayer mat which adorned the floor. Those who corresponded with him were enraged by his execrable handwriting, which Hine valued for the ambiguities which might arise from its interpretation. The fruits of his study, his old-world courtesy, and his shrewd perception endeared him to Hitchin at large, where he gave many talks and lectures to local societies, on topics such as nonconformity in Hitchin, the highways and byways of Hitchin, and Celtic poetry, as well as on the history of Hitchin. Many of these lectures were expanded and subsequently published—at his own expense and always at a loss, he wryly commented—in bindings of more than average quality, including

The History of Hitchin (1927, 1929), *Hitchin Worthies* (1932), and *The Natural History of the Hitchin Region* (1934). A further collection was published posthumously by his friend Richenda Scott as *Relics of an Un-common Attorney* (1951).

On 11 April 1912, at New College chapel, Hampstead, Hine married Florence Lee Pyman (*b*. 1888/9), the daughter of a shipowner, and their daughter, Felicity, the only offspring of the marriage, was born in 1915. Repeatedly deemed unfit for military service, Hine moved to Hitchin in 1917, and lived twelve years in 52 Wymondley Road, a house built by the local architect Geoffrey Lucas. In 1929 the family moved to Old Hall, Willian; that year Hine was elected FSA, and the following year a fellow of the Royal Historical Society. He was a vigorous proponent of the foundation of Hitchin's museum, which houses much historical material collected by him. In 1936 he entered into partnership with Reginald Hartley in Hitchin, from which he retired suddenly on 31 March 1949. On 14 April that year, after an unexceptional conversation with a fellow traveller at Hitchin Station, he threw himself before an arriving Cambridge train. His ashes were scattered at Minsden Chapel on 19 April. His wife survived him.

Widely read, Hine's aim was to elevate the writing of history from discussion of political minutiae (*de minimis non curat lex*) to the resurrection of past souls whose actions, opinions, and feelings were revealed by the documents which outlived them. Attempting to write local history as a *speculum mundi*, he succeeded best in his highly readable two-volume *History of Hitchin*, which was widely praised on publication, although it is now treated warily by some for a want of intellectual rigour and bibliographical accuracy. Blessed with a need for less sleep than most, his study of the documentary records of Hitchin took place from 5.30 a.m. until the beginning of the working day, and from its close until late at night. Much of his eccentric personality is revealed in the pages, and sometimes unwittingly between the lines, of *Dreams and the Way of Dreams* (1913), a curious compendium of his own recollected dreams and nightmares. *Confessions of an Un-common Attorney* (1945) reveals Hine's attitudes to clients and life in general: in retrospect it is probably too easy to overemphasize the importance there of the frequent references to suicide and disturbed mental conditions, but it is clear from the inquest that he was subject to periodic fits of depression.

ALAN L. FLECK

Sources R. L. Hine, *Confessions of an un-common attorney* [1945] · *Hertfordshire Pictorial* (20 April 1949) · *Hertfordshire Pictorial* (3 Oct 1952) · *The Citizen* (2 Feb 1945) · *CGPLA Eng. & Wales* (1949) · m. cert. · *Hitchin Pictorial* (20 April 1949)
Archives Bodl. Oxf., corresp. · Herts. ALS, MS notes, collections, documents, etc. · Hitchin Museum, Hertfordshire · S. Antiquaries, Lond., corresp. and papers relating to graffiti in English churches | Herts. ALS, letters mostly to J. R. Currie · Herts. ALS, notes and bibliography relating to John Carrington sen.
Likenesses G. Ceunis, oils, 1930–40, Hitchin Museum, Hertfordshire · E. Lee, bronze, 1949, Hitchin Museum, Hertfordshire
Wealth at death £9516 13s. 2d.: probate, 28 May 1949, *CGPLA Eng. & Wales*

Hine, William (1687–1730), organist and composer, was born at Brightwell, Oxfordshire. He was a chorister of

Magdalen College, Oxford, in 1694, and clerk in 1705. He studied music with Jeremiah Clarke in London, and in 1707 was appointed deputy to the organist of Gloucester Cathedral. He succeeded as organist in 1713, and shortly afterwards married Alicia, daughter of Abraham *Rudhall (1657–1736), the famous bell-founder. The dean and chapter were so appreciative of his services that they voluntarily increased his annual salary, and recorded their generosity on the tablet over his grave. He died on 28 August 1730 at the age of forty-three; his widow survived until 28 June 1735. Both were buried in the cloisters of the cathedral. His chief pupils were Richard Church and William Hayes. After Hine's death, his widow published by subscription *Harmonia sacra Glocestriensis*, containing anthems for one, two, and three voices, and a Te Deum and Jubilate; all were by Hine except the Te Deum, which was by Henry Hall.   L. M. MIDDLETON, *rev.* K. D. REYNOLDS

Sources W. H. Husk, 'Hine, William', *New Grove* • 'Hine, William', Grove, *Dict. mus.* (1927) • J. E. West, *Cathedral organists past and present* (1899) • J. R. Bloxam, *A register of the presidents, fellows … of Saint Mary Magdalen College*, 8 vols. (1853–85), vol. 1, p. 124; vol. 2, pp. 85, 211

Likenesses portrait, Examinations Schools, Oxford

Hingeston, John (*c.*1606–1683), instrumentalist and composer, was born in the parish of St Lawrence, York, the son and one of at least seven children of Thomas Hingeston (*d.* 1619/20), vicar-choral at York Minster and rector of St Lawrence in the city, and his wife, Dorothy. Through his father he secured a place in the choir at York Minster. The date on which Hingeston became a chorister is unknown, but his name is included among two lists of singing boys recorded in a medius decani partbook in the years 1618 and 1619. On 17 March 1620 he played 'upon the organs' (Chatsworth, Bolton MSS, book 98, fol. 142) in an entertainment given for Emanuel Scrope, lord president of the council in north, by the Yorkshire nobleman Francis Clifford, fourth earl of Cumberland, a 'worthy lover and patron of that facultie music' (W. Byrd, *Psalmes, Songes and Sonnets*, 1611). Hingeston joined the Clifford household in 1621 and was formally apprenticed to the earl in August of that year. He was sent to London the following month to study with the organist and composer Orlando Gibbons, whom he later described as 'my ever hono'rd Master' (PRO, PROB 11/375, q. 134). Some time before February 1625 Hingeston returned to the Clifford estates at Skipton and Londesborough in Yorkshire, where, in addition to his musical duties, he served as butler and yeoman of the wine cellar. He remained in the family's employment until 1645 when the household was dispersed following the capture of Skipton Castle by parliamentary forces.

Hingeston's career blossomed during the interregnum. In 1651 he was listed in John Playford's *Musicall Banquet* as one of nine 'excellent and able masters' for the organ and virginal. Shortly after the establishment of the protectorate household in April 1654, he was appointed organist to Oliver Cromwell at a fee of £100 per annum, and was placed in charge of 'his Highness Musique', a band of eight musicians and two apprentices. According to Anthony Wood, Hingeston 'breed up two Boyes to sing

John Hingeston (*c.*1606–1683), by unknown artist, late 1650s? [detail]

with himselfe Mr. Dearings printed latine songes for 3 voices [Richard Dering's *Cantica sacra*, 1662]; which Oliver was most taken with' (Bodl. Oxf., MS Wood D19/4). Hingeston's concern for the plight of his fellow musicians led him to petition the Council for the Advancement of Musick on 19 February 1657. He sought the incorporation of a college with powers to regulate the practice of music and instrument making, and funding to maintain and encourage professors of the art. His final act as master of Cromwell's music was to head the band of musicians who marched in the protector's funeral procession on 23 November 1658.

Hingeston joined the royal household at the Restoration and was appointed as a violist in the Private Musick and the Chapel Royal, and as keeper of his majesty's wind instruments. He became a member of the Corporation of Musick, holding office as warden (1662–4 and 1674–5) and deputy marshal (February–June 1672). In his will Hingeston mentions two apprentices—his nephew Peter Hingeston, who later became organist of St Mary-le-Tower in Ipswich, and Henry Purcell—and a scholar named John Blagrave. Hingeston died, unmarried, at his home in Great St Anne's Lane, Westminster, between 12 and 17 December 1683, and was buried on 17 December in St Margaret's New Chapel yard beside Stretton Ground. His bequests amounted to about £600 in money, excluding arrears of pay from the royal household, six portraits, including one of Orlando Gibbons which he gave to the music school at Oxford, several stringed instruments, an organ, music books, and various properties.

Hingeston was a prolific composer. His consort music for viols and violins with continuo is mainly preserved in a set of partbooks which he presented to the music school at Oxford between 1661 and 1682 (Bodl. Oxf., MSS Mus. Sch. D.205–11), and in a related autograph organ book acquired by the university some time after the composer's death (Bodl. Oxf., MS Mus. Sch. E.382). The fantasias and airs for three bass viols (BL, Add. MS 31436), which probably date from Hingeston's employment in the Private Musick, are unusual in their scoring for three equal instruments. His suites for cornets and sackbuts written for the protectorate court survive in an incomplete set of part-books bound with the personal coat of arms of Oliver Cromwell (V&A, Clements TT14–15).   LYNN HULSE

Sources Bodl. Oxf., MSS Mus. Sch. D.205–11, E.382 • BL, Add. MS 31436 • V&A, Clements TT14–15 • Bedfordshire County RO, MS DDTW 1172 • Royal College of Music, London, Pr. Book II.F.10 • Christ Church Oxf., MS 47 • Magd. Cam., Pepys Library, Pepys MS 2803, fols. 108v–11 • L. Hulse, *Chelys*, 12 (1983), 23–42 • L. Hulse, 'The musical patronage of the English aristocracy, c.1590–1640', PhD diss., U. Lond., 1993 • A. Ashbee, ed., *Records of English court music*, 1 (1986) • A. Ashbee, ed., *Records of English court music*, 5 (1991) • A. Ashbee, ed., *Records of English court music*, 8 (1995) • A. Ashbee and D. Lasocki, eds., *A biographical dictionary of English court musicians, 1485–1714*, 1 (1998), 574–6 • E. W. Bock, 'The string fantasies of John Hingeston, c.1610–1683', PhD diss., University of Iowa, 1956 • J. Richards, 'A study of music for bass viol written in England in the seventeenth century', BLitt diss., U. Oxf., 1961 • C. D. S. Field, 'The English consort suite of the seventeenth century', DPhil diss., U. Oxf., 1971

Archives Beds. & Luton ARS • BL, Add. MS 31436 • Christ Church Oxf. • Magd. Cam., Pepys Library, Pepys MS 2803, fols. 108v–11 • Royal College of Music, London | V&A, Clements TT14–15

Likenesses oils, 1656?–1659, U. Oxf., faculty of music [*see illus.*]

Wealth at death owed money by the crown; bequests in excess of £590; he owned six portraits, eleven stringed instruments, an organ, various books, and at least four houses, a public house, and various tenements: will, 12 Dec 1683

Hingley, Sir Benjamin, first baronet (1830–1905), chain and anchor manufacturer, was born on 11 September 1830 at Cradley, Worcestershire, a younger son among at least four sons and one daughter of Noah *Hingley (1796–1877), chain manufacturer, of Cradley, and his first wife, Sarah (1794–1832), daughter of Noah Willett of Kingswinford, Worcestershire.

After leaving Halesowen grammar school at the age of fifteen, Hingley entered his father's business, Noah Hingley & Sons. Noah Hingley, son of a small chain maker making mainly chains for agricultural use, had built up a large chain making business in the Netherton district of Dudley, Worcestershire, making ships' cables and heavy chains, despite being so far from the sea, because of the high quality of Black Country wrought iron. In 1838 Noah Hingley started to manufacture anchors, and this became successful a decade later. To ensure a supply of local raw materials he built his own ironworks at Netherton, and acquired collieries nearby, in the 1850s.

After his brother Hezekiah's death in 1865, Benjamin Hingley took over management of the firm, and became head of the business after the death of his father in 1877. He continued to expand the business, buying more ironworks at Old Hill and Harts Hill and new coal mines, and he survived the depression in the shipbuilding industry between 1876 and 1886 to take advantage of the huge expansion in demand for heavy cables and anchors at the end of the nineteenth century, which meant that by the beginning of the First World War the Black Country chain makers had a virtual monopoly of the world market in ships' cables. In 1890, when the firm became a limited company, with Hingley holding over half the shares and his nephews most of the rest, it employed 3000 men and produced 40,000 tons of chains and anchors a year.

Hingley entered parliament in 1885 as Liberal MP for North Worcestershire. Opposition to home rule led him to join the Unionists in 1886, though by 1892 he had rejoined the Liberals. Gladstone rewarded him with a baronetcy in 1893, and he did not stand in the 1895 election. As an MP he served on committees concerned with commercial questions, and was a member of a committee of inquiry into Admiralty contracts. He was also involved in local government, and served two terms as mayor of Dudley, in 1887 and 1890. He was high sheriff of Worcestershire in 1900.

Active also in employers' organizations, Hingley was chairman of the South Staffordshire and East Worcestershire Ironmasters Association from 1881 until his death. He was president of the midland iron and steel wages board, and a member of the South Staffordshire coal trade wages board. He was elected president of the Mining Association of Great Britain and vice-president of the Iron and Steel Institute in 1903.

Unlike many other Black Country industrialists, such as Sir Alfred Hickman, Hingley did not build himself a grand country residence, or buy a London house, but lived in the house his father had owned, Hatherton Lodge, in Cradley. He died at home on 13 May 1905, and was buried at Halesowen. He was unmarried, and the baronetcy passed to his nephew, George Benjamin Hingley, son of his eldest brother, Hezekiah.   ANNE PIMLOTT BAKER

Sources R. Trainor, 'Hingley, Sir Benjamin', *DBB* • G. C. Allen, *The industrial development of Birmingham and the Black Country, 1860–1927* (1929) • R. H. Trainor, *Black Country élites: the exercise of authority in an industrialised area, 1830–1900* (1993) • *The Times* (15 May 1905) • *Journal of the Iron and Steel Institute*, 67 (1905), 508–10

Likenesses A. S. Hope, portrait, 1901, Dudley Art Gallery; repro. in Trainor, 'Hingley, Sir Benjamin'

Wealth at death £158,696 16s. 6d.: probate, 3 July 1905, *CGPLA Eng. & Wales*

Hingley, Noah (1796–1877), ironmaster and manufacturer of chain cables, was born at Rowley, Staffordshire, on 7 March 1796, the son of Isaac Hingley and his wife, Esther, *née* Willetts. The surname of Hingley, largely confined to the Black Country, was reputed to be derived from Huguenot antecedents. Following his father's trade, Hingley entered the small-chain business already well established in the area and about 1820 set up a chain shop on the banks of the Mousesweet brook, a tributary of the Stour.

The idea of supplying iron chain cables for ships to replace hempen ones arose from one of Hingley's visits to Liverpool about 1820 when he agreed to supply a chain made from 1½ inch iron bar, a very large size at that time. The first chain cables had been made at North Shields in 1808. After many difficulties this was achieved and people are said to have come from miles around to see the largest

Noah Hingley (1796–1877), by unknown engraver

chain ever made in the district. Hingley married for the first time on 25 December 1814; his wife was Sarah Willett (1794–1832), daughter of Noah Willett of Kingswinford; of the several children of this marriage at least Hezekiah, Joseph, Samuel, and Sir Benjamin *Hingley later took part in the management of the firm. There were no children from Hingley's second marriage, to Anne Linton Whittingham (1798–1871).

In 1838, with his sons, Hingley established a works at Netherton, on the southern outskirts of Dudley. This was always known as Noah Hingley & Sons and made wrought iron, chain, and anchors. The site was bounded by the Cradley Road, Halesowen Road, Chapel Street, and the Dudley Canal. As the business grew other blast furnaces, iron puddling furnaces and rolling mills, and collieries were opened or absorbed. The making of anchors is said to have started in 1848 and Hingley bought the first steam hammer in the Black Country from the inventor James Nasmyth in 1850 for the purpose; many others were later added for 'shingling' the iron.

Hingley's genius lay in his insistence on controlling all stages of the manufacture himself and thus being able to guarantee the quality of iron and chains. This and geological and geographical advantages, and the high skill of his workmen, led to his rise from workshop to riches. The firm at its peak employed 3000 men, supplied wrought iron all over the world for mines, railways, and shoeing horses, and became one of the three Admiralty-approved contractors for chain and anchors, supplying ground tackle for many great ships.

Hingley was mayor of Dudley in 1870–71 and stood for parliament for the borough in 1874, after the result of the general election of that year was set aside due to violence and intimidation locally. Although unsuccessful he fought a very game campaign which was unusual in that almost none of his speeches mentioned politics, the theme always being the improvement of trade. He is said to have been much liked and respected locally and was noted for his generosity to many good causes. Like many self-made men, however, he seems to have had an authoritarian streak; his son Samuel was not allowed to enter the church as he wished, while a daughter is reputed to have been 'cut off with a shilling' for marrying a labouring man against her father's wishes.

Noah Hingley died at his home, Hatherton Lodge, Cradley, on 21 October 1877, and was buried five days later with public ceremony at Halesowen parish churchyard on the 26th. The funeral was attended by seven coachloads of Dudley council, and the cortège was followed by 2000 of his workmen. A stained glass window in the church was erected in his memory.   P. D. HINGLEY

Sources T. W. Traill, *Chain cables and chains* (1885) · R. Godden, *A time to dance, no time to weep* (1987) · *Dudley Herald* (28 Feb 1891) · 'Hingley, Sir Benjamin', *DNB* · Burke, *Peerage* [Sir Benjamin Hingley] · M. H. W. Fletcher, *Netherton: Edward I to Edward VIII* (1969) · R. Moss, 'William Bannister & Co., chainmakers', *The Blackcountryman*, 26/1 (winter 1993), 18–24 · *Dudley Guardian* (13 March 1869) · typescript list of Nasmyth Hammers, 1845–1919, Salford Public Library · R. Trainor, 'Hingley, Sir Benjamin', *DBB* · *CGPLA Eng. & Wales* (1877) · private information (2004) · census returns · Hezekiah Hingley's funeral inscription · *Dudley Herald* (27 Oct 1877)
Archives Dudley Archives Office, Coseley, Staffordshire, Hingley MSS · Dudley Archives Office, Coseley, Staffordshire, Wright MSS
Likenesses I. B. York, engraving, Dudley Archives, Coseley, Staffordshire · engraving, Dudley Archives, Coseley, Staffordshire [see illus.] · oils, priv. coll.
Wealth at death under £2000: probate, 29 Nov 1877, *CGPLA Eng. & Wales*

Hingston, John. *See* Hingeston, John (c.1606–1683).

Hingston, Thomas (bap. 1799, d. 1837), antiquary, third son of John Hingston, a clerk in the custom house, and Margaret, his wife, was baptized at St Ives, Cornwall, on 9 May 1799, and educated there. His medical studies began in the house of a general practitioner, and in 1821 he moved to Edinburgh. In 1822 he won the medal offered by George IV to Edinburgh University for a Latin ode on the occasion of the king's visit to Scotland. The original poem is lost, but a translation made by Hingston's brother is preserved in *The Poems of Francis Hingeston* [sic] (1857). In 1824 he was admitted to the degree of MD at Edinburgh, after publishing an inaugural dissertation, 'De morbo comitiali', and in the same year he brought out a new edition of William Harvey's *De motu cordis et sanguinis*. He was admitted to Queens' College, Cambridge, in December 1823 and matriculated in 1824, but took no degree.

Hingston practised as a physician first at Penzance from 1828 to 1832 and subsequently at Truro. He contributed to the *Transactions of the Geological Society of Cornwall* and to volume 4 of Davies Gilbert's *Parochial History of Cornwall* (1838). He died at Falmouth, where he had moved for the benefit of the sea air, on 13 July 1837.

G. C. BOASE, *rev.* CHRISTINE NORTH

Sources R. Polwhite, *Reminiscences in prose and verse*, 2 (1836), 153 · *GM*, 2nd ser., 8 (1837), 318 · Boase & Courtney, *Bibl. Corn.*, 1.242 · G. C. Boase, *Collectanea Cornubiensia: a collection of biographical and topographical notes relating to the county of Cornwall* (1890) · Venn, *Alum. Cant.* · parish register (baptism), St Ives, 9 May 1799

Hingston, Sir William Hales (1829–1907), surgeon, was born at Hinchbrook, Huntingdon, in the province of Quebec, Lower Canada, on 29 June 1829, the eldest son in a family of two sons and two daughters of Lieutenant-Colonel Samuel James Hingston (*d.* 1831), of the Canadian militia, and his second wife, Eleanor McGrath of Montreal. William was educated at a grammar school in Huntingdon and then at the Collège St Sulpice, Montreal (1842–3) and the Petit Seminaire (1843–4). In 1844 Hingston became apprentice to a Montreal chemist, R. W. Rexford, and managed to save enough from his earnings as a clerk to train in medicine. In 1847 he entered the medical faculty at McGill University. He graduated in pharmacy at the College of Physicians and Surgeons of Lower Canada in 1849, and took a degree at the university in 1851.

That same year Hingston travelled to Edinburgh and studied under James Young Simpson and James Syme. Simpson paid Hingston the rare compliment of taking his pupil with him on his visits to private patients. Hingston was made LRCS (Edin.) in 1852, and afterwards he worked at St Bartholomew's Hospital, London. He then worked in Dublin for a few months under William Stokes, Dominic Corrigan, and Robert Graves. Having acquired a fair knowledge of German he next proceeded to the continent, where during the following two years he studied in Paris, Berlin, Heidelberg, and Vienna. Although Simpson urged him to remain at Edinburgh as his personal assistant, Hingston returned to Canada to begin practice in Montreal in 1854.

During the second year of his practice Hingston performed valuable work during a cholera epidemic. In 1860 he was nominated to the staff of the Hôtel Dieu. With a few colleagues, in 1865 he was instrumental in reviving the Montreal Medico-Chirurgical Society, of which he became president. He founded the Women's Hospital in Montreal in 1870 and the Samaritan Hospital for Women in 1895. He remained on the active staff of the Women's Hospital until its amalgamation with the new Western Hospital, of which he was a charter member, consulting surgeon, and chairman of the medical board. In 1867 he revisited Edinburgh, where he worked with Sir James Simpson. After returning to Canada, in 1873 Hingston was made dean of the medical faculty at Bishop's College, Lennoxville, and in 1878 he became professor of clinical surgery at Laval University. He was president of the College of Physicians and Surgeons of Quebec in 1886.

Hingston failed to master the meticulous routine of modern asepsis, preferring to keep faith with the old system. His surgical ability was, however, widely acknowledged. In 1892, when the British Medical Association held its annual meeting in Nottingham, he delivered the address on surgery. In 1900 he received the honorary fellowship of the Royal College of Surgeons of England. He was knighted on 15 July 1895.

On 16 September 1875 Hingston married Margaret Josephine Macdonald, daughter of Donald Alexander Macdonald, lieutenant-governor of Ontario. They had four sons and one daughter. Hingston, who was an uncompromising Catholic, died in Montreal on 19 February 1907, survived by his wife. He was buried two days later in Notre-Dame-des-Neiges cemetery.

ANDREW MACPHAIL, *rev.* JEFFREY S. REZNICK

Sources D. Goulet and O. Keel, 'Hingston, Sir William Hales', *DCB*, vol. 13 · *The Times* (20 Feb 1907) · 'Sir William Hingston', *Montreal Medical Journal*, 36, 194–202 · H. J. Morgan, ed., *The Canadian men and women of the time* (1898) · private information (1912)
Likenesses J. Colin Forbes, portrait; in possession of the family, 1912 · G. Delfosse, portrait, City and District Savings Bank, Montreal

Hinkler, Herbert John Louis [Bert] (1892–1933), aviator, was born on 8 December 1892 at Woodbine Cottage, Gavan Street, Bundaberg, Queensland, the eldest of the five children of John William Hinkler (*d.* 1927), a stockman originally from Germany, and his wife, Frances Atkins, *née* Bonney. He was educated at north Bundaberg state school, 1898–1906, and at the age of fourteen went to work at Bundaberg foundry. From an early age he showed a passion for aviation and design and he travelled to Brisbane in search of other aviation enthusiasts, joining there the Queensland Aero Club and the Aerial League of Australia. He later used his savings from work in a sugar mill to pay for a correspondence course in mechanics and in 1911–12 built two gliders, one to his own design, which he flew on Mon Repos Beach near his home.

Hinkler gained valuable practical experience while working as the ground mechanic to the American airman Arthur Burr Stone, who visited Bundaberg in his Blériot monoplane in May 1912, and subsequently employed Hinkler during a tour of southern Australia and New Zealand. In 1913 he went to Sydney and then worked his way to England aboard ship. Upon arrival, during Easter 1914, he obtained a job with the Sopwith aviation company. After the outbreak of war he enlisted, on 7 September 1914, in the Royal Naval Air Service and underwent training at Upavon. He saw active service as an observer and air gunner with 3 wing in France and Belgium, and was awarded the DSM in November 1917. He was subsequently recommended for a commission and pilot training, which he began at the Royal Naval College, Greenwich, on 30 December. In July 1918 he was posted to 28 squadron, RAF, stationed in Italy, where he flew a Sopwith Pup in operations against the Austrians.

After his demobilization in 1919 Hinkler hoped to enter that year's air race to Australia, but his plans foundered and he went to work instead with A. V. Roe & Co. at Hamble, near Southampton, where he test-flew the 35 hp

Avro Baby. He subsequently bought his own model and on 31 May 1920 he left Croydon intending to fly to Australia. Nine-and-a-half hours later he landed at Turin, having covered 650 miles non-stop. It was a remarkable achievement and although mechanical troubles forced him to end his journey at Rome, the Turin leg won him the Britannia challenge trophy. Then, as later, he shied away from the publicity that the flight generated. He returned to Hamble, where he resumed his test-flying duties. An expert aviator, he could fly an aeroplane 'to the very edge of disaster without crashing it' and his training as a mechanic made him an especially valuable test pilot (*Aeroplane*, 165). At 5ft 4in. he sometimes sat on cushions to gain the necessary height in the cockpit. Always known as Bert he wore 'crumpled, double-breasted suits and a pleasant grin', and often a bowler hat, a 'pardonable affectation' for a civilian in a profession dominated by service pilots (Mackenzie, viii).

In 1921 Hinkler shipped his Avro to Australia and on 11 April flew from Sydney to Bundaberg, covering 800 miles in nine hours. The flight enhanced Hinkler's growing reputation for long-distance solo flying. He returned to England and again to Avro, where he was chief test pilot from November 1921 until March 1927. He began his work with two remarkable first flights, in the Avro 549 Aldershot heavy bomber and Avro 555 Bison fleet spotter. Like many inter-war pilots he was an air racer and he entered competitions, usually with Avro backing. He won the Lympne light aeroplane competition in 1923 and the Grosvenor challenge cup in 1924, and in 1925 he was reserve pilot for the British Schneider trophy team in Baltimore. In 1927 he tested early autogiros for the Spanish designer Juan de la Cierva. An extraordinarily clever inventor, he contributed to the design of the new Avro Avian, and in August 1927 flew his own Avian, G-EBOV, 1200 miles nonstop from Croydon to Riga, Latvia. After a failed attempt at a record non-stop London–India flight in November 1927, with Captain R. H. McIntosh, Hinkler concentrated on fund-raising for the Australia flight that remained his dream. He later recalled: 'My agent and I went round London, and the response was as good as if I had been trying to sell rotten fruit' (*The Times*, 29 Feb 1928, 18d).

Forced to rely on his own scant funds, he left Croydon at 6.50 a.m. on 7 February 1928, and the stages of his rapid progress were noted daily in the press. He arrived at Darwin, Northern Territory, at 5.55 p.m. local time on 22 February, a little over fifteen days after his departure. With a minimum of expense and organization he had become the first man to fly solo to Australia. He had also beaten the record of twenty-eight days established by the Smith brothers, Sir Ross and Sir Keith, in November–December 1919. In the press and in parliament his flight was hailed as a landmark in aviation. The very ordinariness of his Avian, powered by a single Cirrus engine of modest horsepower, demonstrated the potential of air travel within the British empire. He was honoured at a series of civic receptions in Brisbane and Sydney, awarded the Air Force cross, made an honorary squadron leader in the Royal Australian Air Force, and later awarded a second Britannia challenge

trophy. He declined, though, to capitalize on his fame and passed up the opportunity of a potentially lucrative lecture tour in Australia. Donations from well-wishers and a cash award from the Australian government nevertheless ensured that he left the country around £10,000 richer.

He invested this money in the design and construction of his own aircraft, the Ibis, a high-winged light amphibian monoplane aimed at the private owner. In January 1930 he registered the Ibis Aircraft Co., with Rowland Bound, an Avro engineer, as his co-director. Construction went on at Hinkler's home, Mon Repos, at Thornhill, near Southampton, and a prototype, G-AAIS, was flown. The project however stalled for lack of funds and in September 1930 Hinkler travelled to Canada to promote the plane. Against the background of world economic depression this proved impossible and in April 1931 he bought a Canadian-assembled de Havilland Puss Moth, with a view to beginning an aerial taxi business. After this venture also failed Hinkler decided to fly the plane back to Britain. Without publicizing his intentions he left New York for Jamaica on 27 October 1931 making the first non-stop flight on that route. He then flew in stages to Brazil, and from there crossed the south Atlantic to west Africa. This flight would prove to be the most difficult of his career, and in many respects the greatest. Low cloud forced him to fly at wave height until darkness fell. He then climbed to 12,000 feet, but still found himself in cloud, and later a fierce thunderstorm. At dawn on 25 November he descended into clear weather and landed at Bathurst in British Gambia; in 22 hours and 40 minutes of blind flight he had drifted only 100 miles from his course. It was a remarkable feat of navigation and endurance which was recognized with the Segrave trophy, the Johnston memorial air navigation trophy, the gold medal of the Royal Aero Club, and a third Britannia challenge trophy.

The flight brought Hinkler acclaim, but not financial gain, and on his return to England in December 1931 he faced an uncertain future. He travelled to America in 1932 contemplating a global circumnavigation, but returned to London to prepare for a new attempt on the record to Australia. He left Feltham aerodrome in his Puss Moth on 7 January 1933 and after negotiating storms over the Alps headed towards Florence. Soon afterwards his plane crashed on the northern slopes of Pratomagno, in the Apennines between Florence and Arezzo, and was covered by snow. It is possible that he was attempting an emergency landing after losing a propeller in flight. His body was eventually found by a group of charcoal burners, on 27 April, a short distance from the wreckage of the plane. On Mussolini's orders he was buried with full military honours in Florence on 1 May. Hinkler was one of the outstanding pilots of his day and his death was lamented as a particular waste. Unable to find the employment that, by common consent, his talents deserved, he was driven to undertake risky solo flights on meagre resources. A forthright and honest man, he was also highly individual, and could be outspoken and difficult to use. One of the staff of *Flight* magazine recalled speaking to him in advance of the Turin flight in 1920: 'As usual, he insisted on no publicity before he started. His maxim always was "Do the thing first and talk about it afterwards"—but he usually forgot to do the subsequent talking' (*Flight*, 16 Feb 1933, 151).

Sources disagree over Hinkler's marital status. During the 1920s he appears to have lived with an Englishwoman, Nancy (or Nance), whom he may have married some time before 1923. At the time of his arrival in Australia in 1928 *The Times* made a number of references to a 'Mrs Bert Hinkler' who travelled to Fremantle 'to join her husband' (*The Times*, 4 April 1928, 13g). He is known to have married one Katherine Rome in Connecticut, on 21 May 1932; there were no children by this marriage.   ROBIN HIGHAM

Sources *AusDB* · R. D. Mackenzie, *Solo: the Bert Hinkler story* (1963) · *The Aeroplane* (1 Feb 1933) · *Flight* (16 Feb 1933), 151 · *Flight* (4 May 1933), 416 · *The Times* (8 Feb 1928), 11d · *The Times* (23 Feb 1928), 14a, 15b–c · *The Times* (28 Feb 1928), 8c · *The Times* (29 Feb 1928), 18d · *The Times* (20 March 1928), 15g · *The Times* (4 April 1928), 13g · *The Times* (29 April 1933) · J. A. Mollison, ed., *The book of famous flyers* (1934) · H. Penrose, *British aviation: the ominous skies, 1935–1939* (1980)
Archives Hinkler House Museum, Bundaberg, Queensland, Australia, MSS
Likenesses photographs, 1928–31, Hult. Arch. · portrait, Hinkler House Museum, Bundaberg, Queensland · portrait, repro. in *The Times* · portrait, repro. in *ILN*
Wealth at death £906 10s. 10d.: administration, 23 June 1933, CGPLA Eng. & Wales

Hinks, Arthur Robert (1873–1945), astronomer and geographer, was born in Stoke Newington, London, on 26 May 1873, the eldest of the five sons and three daughters of Robert Hinks, a civil servant and later university lecturer, of Croydon, Surrey, and his wife, Mary, *née* Hayward. From 1882 to 1892 he was educated at Whitgift Grammar School, Croydon, where he secured exhibitions to Trinity College, Cambridge, to read for the mathematical tripos. In 1895 he graduated BA and was appointed second assistant at the Cambridge observatory under Sir Robert Ball and demonstrator in practical astronomy in the university. He married on 11 April 1899 Lily Mary (*d.* 1928), the daughter of Jonathan Packman, a civil engineer, of Croydon; they had two sons, of whom the elder, Roger Packman, became an art critic, and the younger, David Arthur Gilbert (*d.* 1948), junior bursar of Trinity College, Cambridge. As chief assistant from 1903 to 1913, Hinks was actively concerned in the design and the installation of apparatus, notably the Sheepshanks telescope of the unusual coudé form, built by Howard Grubb, with optics by Cooke. He also worked with Horace Darwin of the Cambridge Scientific Instrument Company on apparatus for the new science of photographic astrometry. He determined the solar parallax and the mass of the moon from observations of Eros at the time of its closest approach to the earth in 1900. For this he was awarded the gold medal of the Royal Astronomical Society in 1912 and elected FRS in 1913. He was secretary of the Royal Astronomical Society from 1909 to 1912 and a vice-president from 1912 to 1913.

In 1903 Hinks had studied the surveying methods taught at the School of Military Engineering at Chatham.

This led to his appointment in 1908 as lecturer in surveying and cartography in the Cambridge school of geography and an association with the Royal Geographical Society, which had co-operated with the university in the establishment of the school. As assistant secretary of the society from 1912, and as secretary and editor of the *Geographical Journal* from 1915, Hinks found that geography came to dominate his interests, though from 1913 to 1941 he gave the annual Gresham lectures in astronomy at the University of London. He was one of the four British delegates to the International Map Congress at Paris in 1913 which defined formats for the international 1:1,000,000 map.

Hinks was involved with the society's move from Savile Row to Lowther Lodge, Kensington Gore, before the First World War, and later in the planning of the extensions opened at the centenary in 1930. He also widened the scope of the *Journal* to include cartography and the newer aspects of human geography, a subject, however, which, with his precise mind, he seemed to regard with a little misgiving. During the First World War he did valuable geographical and map preparation work for the general staff; during the Second World War the society's drawing office under his guidance compiled a map of Europe and the Middle East, including an Arabic edition, for the British Council. In addition to numerous papers Hinks wrote *Map Projections* (1912) and *Maps and Survey* (1913), both of which went into several editions. He appreciated the value of survey by oblique air photographs, and he brought stereo-photogrammetry within the range of the society's work. His interest in maps was not limited to their scientific accuracy: he wanted his maps to be things of beauty in colour and lettering, as expressed in his presidential address to the geography section of the British Association in 1925, 'The science and art of map-making'. Among his other works was the eleventh edition of *Hints to Travellers* and his recasting, in collaboration with many explorers, of the second volume (1938) of that work. He was also a leading figure of the Mount Everest committee of the Alpine Club and the Royal Geographical Society.

In 1920 Hinks was appointed CBE and chevalier of the Belgian order of the Crown; in 1938 he received the Victoria medal of the Royal Geographical Society and in 1943 the Cullum medal of the American Geographical Society. He died at his home, White Cottage, Heathfields, Bassingbourn, near Royston, Hertfordshire, on 18 April 1945.

R. N. RUDMOSE BROWN, *rev.* ANITA MCCONNELL

Sources H. S. Jones and H. J. Fleure, *Obits. FRS*, 5 (1945–8), 717–32 · *The Times* (19 April 1945) · *GJ*, 105 (1945), 146–51 · private information (1959) · H. R. Mill, *The record of the Royal Geographical Society, 1830–1930* (1930) · m. cert. · d. cert. · Venn, *Alum. Cant.*
Archives NL Scot., corresp. with Sir J. M. Wordie and relating to Discovery Committee · RAS, letters to Royal Astronomical Society · RGS, corresp. and papers relating to map projections and surveys · U. Cam., Institute of Astronomy Library, corresp. and papers | Bodl. Oxf., corresp. with J. L. Myres · Bodl. Oxf., corresp. with Sir Aurel Stein
Likenesses H. Ruttledge, two photographs, 1939, RGS · photograph, repro. in Jones and Fleure, *Obits. FRS* · two portraits, RGS
Wealth at death £4805 15s. 1d.: probate, 12 June 1945, CGPLA Eng. & Wales

Hinkson, Katharine. *See* Tynan, Katharine (1859–1931).

Hinshelwood, Sir Cyril Norman (1897–1967), physical chemist, was born on 19 June 1897 in London, the only child of Norman Macmillan Hinshelwood, chartered accountant, and his wife, Ethel Frances Smith (*d.* 1959). As a child he was taken by his parents to Canada, and received some schooling in Montreal and Toronto. When his father died in 1904 his mother returned with him to a small flat, 13 Holbein House, Pimlico Road, Chelsea, which was their London home until her death and which he continued to use all his life. He never married.

Hinshelwood attended the Westminster City School, and won a Brackenbury scholarship to Balliol College, Oxford, in 1916. Because of the First World War he deferred his university entrance and was employed as a chemist at the explosives supply factory at Queensferry. There he displayed remarkable ability and was known as 'the boy wonder'. He was appointed deputy chief chemist at the age of twenty-one.

Chemical research from 1919 Hinshelwood went up to Oxford in January 1919, and while still an undergraduate, tutored by Sir Harold Hartley, published three papers in the *Journal of the Chemical Society* on the decomposition of solid explosives. After five terms of residence he won distinction in the shortened war degree course, and was elected to a research fellowship at Balliol in 1920. In the following year he was elected a tutorial fellow of Trinity College, which shared with Balliol a number of rather primitive and ill-equipped teaching and research laboratories. Here for the next twenty years Hinshelwood lectured and carried out research with his students. Nearly all of his work was on the kinetics and mechanisms of chemical reactions (including those occurring in biological systems).

From 1921 to 1928 Hinshelwood and his students carried out a comprehensive study of the kinetics of chemical reactions catalysed by surfaces. He took as his starting point the realization by the American chemist Irving Langmuir (1881–1957) that molecules are often strongly attached to surfaces by what is called chemisorption, and that the chemical interaction occurs between the chemisorbed molecules. Hinshelwood carried out carefully designed experimental studies of a number of chemical reactions occurring on various surfaces, and explained the kinetic behaviour in terms of the extent of binding of the reactant molecules at the surface. This work laid a firm foundation for the much more detailed studies that were later carried out with the use of more refined experimental techniques.

In 1926 Hinshelwood began a comprehensive series of investigations of chemical reactions that occur entirely in the gas phase. He made pioneering contributions of particular importance on so-called unimolecular reactions, in which individual molecules split into smaller molecules or change (isomerize) into molecules having a different structure. If collisions between molecules supplied the energy, the rate would be expected to be proportional to the frequency of collisions and therefore to the square

Sir Cyril Norman Hinshelwood (1897–1967), by Sir Gerald Kelly, exh. RA 1960

of the pressure of the gas; there was some evidence, however, that this was not the case. A solution to the dilemma was suggested in 1921 by F. A. Lindemann in terms of the formation by collisions of an energized molecule with a long enough life that it could be deactivated by collisions before undergoing reactions. Hinshelwood saw that the mathematical equation resulting from this hypothesis was capable of experimental test, and in 1926 and 1927 he and several of his students confirmed the general idea by studying several organic decompositions. Also, in 1927, Hinshelwood made an important theoretical extension to Lindemann's hypothesis by treating, in terms of statistical theory, how the energy randomly distributed in a complicated molecule can become organized in such a way that reaction can occur. The Lindemann–Hinshelwood ideas were used in subsequent theories of unimolecular reactions, and remained valid despite the fact that it was later found that all of the 'unimolecular' reactions studied experimentally by Hinshelwood and his students are not really unimolecular, but occur in a much more complicated way.

In 1927 Hinshelwood, with his student H. W. Thompson, began to investigate the kinetics and mechanisms of explosions in gases. They made careful experimental studies of the reaction between hydrogen and oxygen, and in 1929 showed that there is a pressure range within which explosion occurs, and above and below which there is slower reaction. They explained these results in terms of chain reactions involving active intermediates. It had previously been suggested that there may be so-called branching reactions which give rise to a great increase in the number of active species, and therefore to explosion. Hinshelwood explained the upper and lower explosion limits in terms of the way in which the active species are destroyed, either at the surface of the vessel or by collisions with gas molecules. In 1927 the Russian chemist N. N. Semyonov had provided evidence for a lower explosion limit, but Hinshelwood was the first, in 1929, to discover both lower and upper limits, and to provide the general explanation accepted by chemists.

In 1930 Hinshelwood began a series of investigations, also continued for several decades, on reactions of organic substances in solution. At first there was little understanding of the details of how such reactions occur, but his work soon brought about a considerable clarification. By comparing the behaviour in different solvents, Hinshelwood and his students were able to gain understanding of the role of the solvent. Important conclusions were also drawn from comparisons between the reactions of series of organic compounds in which minor structural changes had been made ('substituent effects'). Many of the results were later of great value to physical–organic chemists, especially in the study of 'correlation analysis' which continued to be under active investigation for many years.

The new physical chemistry laboratory In 1937, following the retirement of Frederick Soddy, Hinshelwood was elected as Dr Lee's professor of chemistry at Oxford, with responsibility for both physical and inorganic chemistry. This involved a change of residence from Trinity College to Exeter College, but Hinshelwood delayed the move for a few years, continuing to carry out his research in the Trinity laboratories until 1941. In that year, through the generosity of Lord Nuffield, a physical chemistry laboratory was opened on South Parks Road. Although his professorship included responsibility for the inorganic laboratory, Hinshelwood left the running of it entirely to its senior member; by contrast, he took his administrative responsibilities at the physical chemistry laboratory rather more seriously than was necessary, with little delegation. As a result he was at times overstrained, irritable, and unapproachable. His own research work suffered to some extent, but with the help of capable senior assistants he was able to direct much research.

In the new laboratories Hinshelwood directed an important series of studies on charcoal and other materials for use in respirators; as a result, on D-day in 1944 the army had much improved equipment. Hinshelwood also continued his work on reactions in solution. More of his effort was devoted to the kinetics and mechanisms of reactions of organic substances in the gas phase. Certain evidence had convinced Hinshelwood that such reactions occur partly by a molecular mechanism (involving no intermediates), and partly by a chain mechanism. (In the 1950s most organic reactions occurring in the gas phase were shown convincingly to occur entirely by chain mechanisms, but Hinshelwood was slow to accept this conclusion.)

In 1945 C. J. Danby was appointed as Hinshelwood's assistant and gave much support with research and teaching. In particular he took charge of the mass spectrometers used for the analysis of reaction products in Hinshelwood's research in gas kinetics.

Hinshelwood's main interest in the new laboratories was the chemical kinetics of bacterial growth, which he had begun to investigate in 1937. He was particularly concerned with the adaptation shown by bacteria in accommodating themselves to their environment when their supply of foodstuff is changed. They even gradually adapt to substances initially poisonous to them; this is of crucial importance in the adaptability of hostile organisms to substances that could destroy them. Hinshelwood and his students explained their results in terms of changes in chemical equilibria brought about by the environment, changes that are carried into future generations when the bacterial cells divide. In 1949 Hinshelwood was joined in his bacterial work by Alastair C. R. Dean, who collaborated closely with him until 1967 and helped to direct the work of many students.

During the earlier years of Hinshelwood's investigations of bacteria, his conclusions were strongly criticized by some biologists, who mistakenly thought that he was ignoring the well-established conclusion that mutation and natural selection are important factors in the transmission of characteristics from one generation to another. Remarkable developments in molecular genetics were taking place at that time, and to some biologists Hinshelwood's contributions seemed unsound. Some went so far as to say that he was coming dangerously close to 'Lamarckism', the belief in the inheritance of acquired characteristics. In several of his publications, however, Hinshelwood emphasized that he had never denied the importance of mutation and natural selection. Some of his experiments indeed provided evidence for mutation. In some cases his results could not be explained entirely in terms of mutation and natural selection, and this led to his conclusion that the adjustment of chemical equilibria in the bacteria must be an additional factor. Subsequent work by biologists has confirmed the importance of the adaptive changes proposed by Hinshelwood and his associates, and has shown that (for example, in some cases of neoplastic transformation—abnormal tissue growth) they may be the predominant factor. Some later biologists have recognized his bacterial work to have been of pioneering importance.

Writing and teaching Hinshelwood exerted a great influence on physical chemistry through his books. In 1926 he published his *Kinetics of Chemical Change in Gaseous Systems*, which lucidly expounded the new ideas about gas reactions. It appeared in two more editions, to be superseded in 1940 by his *Kinetics of Chemical Change*, which although shorter than the third edition also included his work on reactions in solution. His monograph *The Structure of Physical Chemistry* appeared in 1951 and explained his personal point of view about the unity and continuity of the subject. This book, of great interest to experts in the field, was criticized by some for including no references to sources and for presenting the subject in the form of theoretical ideas for which no experimental basis was given. Hinshelwood's bacterial work was expounded in two influential books, *The Chemical Kinetics of the Bacterial Cell* (1946) and *Growth, Function and Regulation in Bacterial Cells* (1966), the latter in collaboration with Dean.

Hinshelwood was an outstanding college tutor, lecturer, and research supervisor. He was tolerant of his students, gently guiding them toward the important responsibilities that many were to assume later. His meticulously prepared lectures were, like his writings, models of precision and clarity. Particularly in his earlier years—before he became harassed by too much administration—he was able to keep in close and friendly contact with his research students, and was always readily available for consultation.

Humanities and the philosophy of science Hinshelwood was unusual for the breadth of his interests. He was a painter from his boyhood, and continued to use the small palette he had bought at the age of nine. An exhibition of more than a hundred of his paintings at Goldsmiths' Hall after his death showed his skill with a wide range of subjects, including portraits of colleagues, interiors, a racing eight, and his cat. His fine draughtsmanship, colouring, and sense of composition were all used to striking effect.

Hinshelwood was also a remarkable linguist. He was highly proficient in French, German, Italian, and Spanish, and was able to carry out conversations in Russian and Chinese. With the aid of gramophone records he perfected his pronunciation of some languages; he could pass for a Frenchman. He was well versed in Latin, less well in Greek, and had the unique distinction of serving as president of the Royal Society and of the Classical Association at the same time. In his presidential address to the Classical Association in 1959 he expounded his philosophy of languages, and illustrated their individuality with examples of German genders, Arabic plurals, and the difficulties of translating classical Chinese. One of his more remarkable contributions was a paper on Dante's imagery, in which he quoted many passages from the *Divina commedia*.

As president of many important societies, Hinshelwood gave a number of memorable addresses, always presented with great style and eloquence. In them he revealed his personal philosophy, his reflections on the place of science in society, and his sound appreciation of the connection between the theoretical and the practical.

Hinshelwood was energetic, and sometimes combative, in his efforts to promote science at Oxford. He was often extremely suspicious of the higher officials of the university, who generally did not have a science background. According to his student Sir Harold Thompson, he 'hated bureaucracy, and developed a distrust in the University Establishment. ... He was ever watchful of the Gazette to see what the Registrar was up to' (*Memoirs FRS*, 381). His administrative relationships were, however, less abrasive in his capacity as a delegate to the Oxford University Press,

and the steady growth of its publications, particularly in science, owed much to his advice and initiative. In 1967 the delegates described him as 'the most eminent scientist ever to be a member of the board' (ibid., 386).

Honours and awards Hinshelwood received many honours, including the Faraday and Longstaff medals of the Chemical Society, and the Copley medal of the Royal Society of which he was elected a fellow in 1929 at the early age of thirty-two. He received many honorary degrees, and was an honorary fellow of Trinity, Balliol, Exeter, and St Catherine's colleges, Oxford. He was an honorary member of many foreign academies, including the US Academy of Sciences and the Academy of Sciences of the USSR. He was president of the Chemical Society (1946–8) for its delayed centenary celebrations in 1947, and of the Royal Society (1955–60) for its tercentenary in 1960, having been its foreign secretary since 1950. In 1964–5 he was president of the British Association. He was knighted in 1948, and was admitted to the Order of Merit in 1960.

In 1956 Hinshelwood shared a Nobel prize in chemistry with N. N. Semyonov. To the surprise of his many admirers, this award was criticized in some quarters. The explanation is twofold. The award was given to him at a time when the mistaken criticism of his bacterial work was at its peak. Also, at the time of the award, Hinshelwood's work was not at its most original. He pointed out in 1957 that there are three stages in the study of a branch of science. The first is one of 'gross oversimplification, reflecting ... a too enthusiastic aspiration after elegance of form'. The second stage involves more detailed studies in which 'recalcitrant facts increasingly rebel against conformity'. In the third stage 'a new order emerges, more intricately contrived' (*PRS*, 243A, 1957, v–xvi). There is no doubt that Hinshelwood excelled in the first of these stages, and was less effective in the others. His earlier work, on reactions on surfaces, unimolecular reactions, and explosions, belonged to the first stage, and merited a Nobel prize; if it had been awarded fifteen years earlier, there would have been few complaints. Chemists who were unaware of the history of their subject and knew only of Hinshelwood's later contributions might well have been critical of his failure to adopt some of the latest experimental techniques such as gas chromatography, and of his tendency to ignore the latest theoretical developments in his field.

In 1964 Hinshelwood retired from his professorship and returned to his Chelsea flat. He became a senior research fellow of Imperial College, London, and continued his studies on bacterial growth; he retained this appointment until his death. Free of administrative duties he became noticeably happier and more relaxed. His help and advice were quickly in demand as a consultant. He entered into fruitful associations with the Arts Council, the British Museum, Queen Elizabeth College, London, the National Gallery, and the Goldsmiths' Company, of which he had become an honorary member in 1952. His connection with the company was one of his great pleasures, and he left a large legacy in support of their charitable work. Hinshelwood died suddenly and unexpectedly of a heart attack, alone at home, on 9 October 1967.

KEITH J. LAIDLER

Sources *DNB* · H. Thompson, *Memoirs FRS*, 19 (1973), 375–431 · E. J. Bowen, 'Sir Cyril Hinshelwood, 1897–1967', *Chemistry in Britain*, 3 (1967), 534–6 · K. J. Laidler, 'Chemical kinetics and the Oxford college laboratories', *Archive for History of Exact Sciences*, 38 (1988), 197–283 · K. Hutchison, *High speed gas: an autobiography* (1987) · R. F. Barrow and C. J. Danby, *The Physical Chemistry Laboratory: the first fifty years* (privately printed, Oxford, 1991)
Archives RS, papers | CAC Cam., corresp. with A. V. Hill · Rice University, Houston, Texas, corresp. with Sir Julian Huxley
Likenesses photograph, 1956 (with Nobel prize winners), Hult. Arch. · D. H. Anderson, oils, 1958, Physical Chemistry Laboratory, Oxford · G. Kelly, oils, exh. RA 1960, RS [*see illus.*] · E. I. Halliday, oils, *c.*1965, Exeter College, Oxford · C. N. Hinshelwood, self-portrait, Goldsmiths' Hall · G. Kelly, oils, Chemical Society · portraits, RS, library
Wealth at death £149,047: probate, 1 Feb 1968, *CGPLA Eng. & Wales*

Hinsley, Arthur (1865–1943), Roman Catholic archbishop of Westminster, was born at Carlton, near Selby, Yorkshire, on 25 August 1865, the second son of Thomas Hinsley, carpenter, and his wife, Bridget (or Brigid) Ryan. At the age of eleven he went to St Cuthbert's College at Ushaw, near Durham, with a view to entering the priesthood. He later obtained an external degree in classics from London University. In 1890 he went on to the English College in Rome where he won a doctorate in divinity. He was ordained priest for the diocese of Leeds on 23 December 1893. Hinsley returned to Ushaw to teach classics and later philosophy. However his impatience with the traditions of the college led to his being transferred to St Anne's, Keighley, as curate in 1897.

Hinsley was so convinced of the importance of Catholic education that by 1900 he had founded the small Catholic grammar school of St Bede in Bradford. Hinsley threw himself wholeheartedly into the task of building it up, and won the unwilling agreement of the governors to buy a house for boarders, to which was soon added a large mansion. 'He scoured the countryside on his bicycle looking for new scholars, organised schemes for providing finances, presided over the boarders, directed the studies and himself took many classes' (Heenan, 28). The governors, under the chairmanship of his bishop, William Gordon, took fright at his enthusiasm and blocked his plans for future expansion. In the friction which ensued they agreed to part company and in 1905 he transferred to the diocese of Southwark where he was appointed chaplain to a convent and then resident priest at a small church.

In 1911 Hinsley became parish priest of Our Lady and St Philip Neri, a typical suburban parish with a large debt, which housed many Catholic Belgian refugees during the war years. To the surprise of some of the English bishops he was appointed rector of the English College in Rome when that post became vacant in 1917. He introduced a new style into college life, consulting students before making decisions but demanding that they be accepted once made. While setting great store by the personal piety

Arthur Hinsley (1865–1943), by Simon Elwes, 1940

of the students, he at the same time insisted that this be balanced by serious academic study. He put much effort into repairing and improving the college buildings, and acquired a large villa at Palazzola on the slopes of Lake Albano where the students spent their summer vacations.

In 1926 Hinsley was appointed part-time visitor apostolic to east Africa, and was consecrated titular bishop of Sebastopolis. Most of the schooling there was provided by Catholic missionary congregations of different nationalities, without any local financial assistance. Hinsley's terms of reference were to co-ordinate their work with the latest educational thinking coming through the British Colonial Office. His tact and administrative abilities won the co-operation of all the parties involved. Typically he was insistent on consulting the consumers as well as the providers. He is reputed to have travelled some 50,000 miles in two years sometimes using primitive forms of transport. So successful was his mission that he was made delegate apostolic for Africa with his base at Nairobi and titular archbishop of Sardis in 1930. This meant his ceasing formally to be rector of the English College in Rome.

An attack of paratyphoid fever forced Hinsley to retire in 1934, and he was given a sinecure canonry at St Peter's basilica in Rome. Pius XI, who had affectionately known him as Romanus, now called him Africanus. To Hinsley's dismay and to the surprise of many Pius XI ordered him to become archbishop of Westminster when the see became vacant on the death of Cardinal Bourne. He was enthroned in Westminster Cathedral on 29 April 1935, and created cardinal priest of the title of St Susanna on 13 December 1937.

It was a difficult role to undertake at the age of seventy, especially as he had been out of England for so long and knew virtually none of the Westminster clergy. He faced it with his customary vigour. In addition to the usual administrative and ceremonial duties of the post he found time to pay informal visits to most of the priests in those early years. With his strong belief in consultation he soon inaugurated various advisory groups including a diocesan council, a finance board, and a schools commission on which laymen sat alongside priests. Perhaps his most striking decision was to hand over ownership of *The Tablet*, the most influential Catholic weekly, which had been bought by Cardinal Vaughan to ensure its control, to a group of independent lay people.

Cardinal Hinsley quickly won the affection of the nation. This was due largely to his distinctively English character: a Yorkshire bluntness; an innate dignity without any desire for pomp and circumstance. He hated injustice, but had a strong belief in the justice of British administration whether it was in the colonies or at home. He argued the case of equal financial support for voluntary schools alongside local authority ones, holding that the British public would support the Catholic case if its justice could be clearly demonstrated. Hinsley supported the 1936 Education Act which allowed local authorities to pay up to 75 per cent of the cost of new voluntary schools and improvements to existing ones. However, he feared 'the craze for monotype education' which was to become central to the 1944 Education Act.

Hinsley was a great exponent of Christian social teaching especially when it became clear that its principles were being attacked in totalitarian countries. With the outbreak of war in 1939 he used the media to defend the allied cause as a confrontation with forces of evil. He did all he could to support the morale of both civilians and the armed forces in ways much appreciated by Churchill and other members of the government. Perhaps his greatest achievement in the eyes of his fellow Christians was the establishment of the Sword of the Spirit movement on 1 August 1940 to work out the principles of a just peace, and how a Christian social order might emerge from the chaos of war. He invited the co-operation of the other church leaders in this exercise and the excitement of its ideals swept the country. They published a joint statement in *The Times* that December. Unfortunately his fellow bishops, notably Downey of Liverpool and Godfrey, recently appointed apostolic delegate, did not share his enthusiasm for this early form of ecumenism. When he led the shared recital of the Lord's prayer on a public platform they employed the service of moral theologians and canonists from the Westminster seminary to prove that this was against Vatican rules. He was eventually forced to accept that the Sword of the Spirit was a Roman Catholic organization under the control of the bishop of each diocese, and that other Christians could not be full members

of its executive. In this as in other matters he proved, even at his age, to be before his time.

After a short illness he died on 17 March 1943 at Hare Street House, Buntingford, Hertfordshire, from angina. The following day the *Daily Telegraph* wrote that: 'no English Cardinal since Cardinal Manning has made a deeper impression on his own community and on the national life', and the *Daily Mail* that he was 'probably the best loved Cardinal that England has ever had'. His funeral mass at Westminster Cathedral was attended by most members of the government. He was buried in the cathedral crypt.

MICHAEL GAINE

Sources J. C. Heenan, *Cardinal Hinsley* (1944) · G. Wheeler, 'The archdiocese of Westminster', *The English Catholics, 1850–1950*, ed. G. A. Beck (1950), 151–86, esp. 181–6 · A. Hastings, *A history of English Christianity, 1920–1990*, 3rd edn (1991) · *DNB* · *The Tablet* (20 March 1943) · private information (2004) · *Daily Telegraph* (18 March 1943) · *Daily Mail* (18 March 1943)
Archives Venerable English College, Rome, papers · Westm. DA, corresp. and papers; corresp. on Noyes's *Voltaire* | FILM BFI NFTVA, 'Archbishop enthroned', *Gaumont British news*, 2 May 1935 · BFI NFTVA, news footage · BFI NFTVA, propaganda film footage (ministry of information)
Likenesses S. Elwes, oils, 1940, Archbishop's House, Westminster [*see illus.*] · N. Lytton, oils, 1942, St Edmund's College, Ware · H. Coster, photographs, NPG · oils, English College, Rome
Wealth at death £1338 11s. 2d.: probate, 29 May 1943, *CGPLA Eng. & Wales*

Hinsley, Sir (Francis) Harry (1918–1998), cryptanalyst and historian, was born on 26 November 1918 at 28 Rowland Street, Walsall, the son of Thomas Henry Hinsley, ironworks waggoner, and his wife, Emma, *née* Adey. He went to the local elementary school and then to Queen Mary's Grammar School, Walsall, and in 1937 won a scholarship to St John's College, Cambridge, to read history. Although he obtained a first in part one of the historical tripos in 1939, he never completed a first or any subsequent degree. When the Second World War broke out he was recruited to the naval section at the Government Code and Cipher School at Bletchley Park. Congregated there was a group of young, highly accomplished men and women, living a completely secret life in conditions somewhat resembling a physically uncomfortable university senior common room. Young as he was, Hinsley became the leading expert on the decryption and analysis of German wireless traffic, and, particularly after the capture of German Enigma code machines and materials, which allowed their settings to be broken, played a vital role in supplying the Admiralty with crucial intelligence analysis derived from Admiral Doenitz's signals. This information helped to win the battle against U-boats in the Atlantic. His powers as an interpreter of decrypts were unrivalled and were based on an ability to sense that something unusual was afoot from the tiniest clues. He was not always believed, particularly in early days. His warning, for example, that something was happening in the Baltic just before the German invasion of Norway went unheeded.

Only after 1979, with the publication of the first of his five monumental volumes of *British Intelligence in the Second*

World War, was it possible for Hinsley to discuss the significance of what he and others had achieved at Bletchley Park during the war. He said that the long period of enforced silence was made easier because he could at least discuss it with his wife, Hilary Brett Brett-Smith (1914/15–1998), the daughter of Herbert Francis Brett Brett-Smith, Goldsmiths' reader in English at Oxford from 1939 to 1947, whom he married on 6 April 1946, and who had been there too. The official history dealt with both successes and failures and set out to be dispassionate in every way. It was thought to be heavy-going and dry, but Hinsley, who had wrestled with every kind of sensitivity during its writing—internal and those of foreign governments, occasionally to the point of threatening to give up the whole project—simply responded that 'it was meant to be bloodless' (personal knowledge). When all was over, however, he supplied a highly entertaining edited version of Bletchley Park memoirs under the title *Codebreakers: the Inside Story of Bletchley Park* (1993), which served to add the flesh and blood excluded from the official account. Perhaps most interesting of all was his personal assessment of the ultimate result of the intelligence effort. It had not been a 'war winner' but was a 'war-shortener'. He thought that the war might have been as much as two years longer without it, certainly one year. 'Without it', he often said, 'Rommel would have got to Alexandria. The U-boats would not have done us in. But they would have got us into serious shortages and put another year on the war' (personal knowledge).

Following his wartime service Hinsley returned to St John's College, Cambridge, where he had been elected a research fellow in 1944. He became a university lecturer in history in 1949, reader in the history of international relations in 1965, and professor of the history of international relations in 1969. He also served as president (1975–9), then master (1979–89), of St John's College, and as vice-chancellor of Cambridge University (1981–3). He was a great teacher, an important writer, and a notably competent administrator. Countless generations of undergraduate historians at Cambridge remembered the extraordinarily vivid way in which he taught them, but the research school in the history of international relations that he established in the 1960s and 1970s was one of his greatest achievements. The combination of the books he himself was writing, particularly *Power and the Pursuit of Peace* (1963) and *Sovereignty* (1966), and the work that his PhD students did and subsequently published, showed interconnections between the evolution of the philosophy of international relations and the realities as they unfolded. This changed the way in which both international relations and their history were studied, and the result was an alteration in the intellectual basis of discussion. Few scholars achieve such turning points but Hinsley was one. It was particularly remarkable because, partly as a result of the war, he did not have any research training, nor did his own books proceed from empirical work: in his case, information was supplied to support an argument, not the other way round.

Hinsley's work demonstrated two preoccupations: the first was the evolution and function of the state, the relationships that develop between states, and the effect of this on the actions of politicians and rulers. The second was the wish to show how, taking the long view, an essentially rational interpretation of history revealed a record of progress in the conduct of affairs. His near-passion for evaluating the significance of the existence of the state did not, however, leave him able only to conceive of a state-centric world either in the past or the future. The tools he used to describe how his own world worked were equally useful in analysing the pre-state world and in predicting a very different world system in the future. Late in life he would explain with some glee that the evident transfer of power from weak states to international humanitarian institutions in some parts of the world was wholly explicable in the terms he had developed to discuss the idea of sovereignty. It is a tribute to the depth of his approach to international relations that idealists could claim him for his optimism while entirely rejecting the basis for it, and realists could feel comfortable with his techniques while being entirely unable to accept his conclusions. This was not a case of being all things to all men—he was completely his own man; what he created was a quarry sufficient to supply stone for many different structures.

For many of his students, it was Hinsley's analytical skill so honed at Bletchley Park that affected them most. Whether in private—and always unstinting—discussion or at the famous weekly seminar he ran for all interested parties at every level, from behind a thick pall of pipe smoke, he reacted to the wider implications of what had been discovered or reassessed; and he would comment rapidly, almost electrically, on the true significance of what he had just heard or read. He never forgot any student he had taught or been tutor to, and his students never forgot their exposure to how he thought about things and the often striking language he used to describe what he thought. They also never forgot the risk of personal annihilation which visiting him entailed. The threat came from showers of books which could and did fall from hopelessly overstressed and ancient shelves. He had the gift of total concentration on the person he was dealing with, whatever the circumstances, and was perfectly capable of forgetting that there were often other people waiting in his room during tutorial consultations. Both the skills and the gratitude of his students were laid out in two books: *British Foreign Policy under Sir Edward Grey* (1977), which he edited, and *Diplomacy and Intelligence during the Second World War* (1985), edited by Richard Langhorne.

Hinsley was a strikingly rich character, almost a phenomenon of nature, in contrast to his bespectacled and physically slight appearance. He took his turn at the tasks of university administration, perhaps more as a duty than as a pleasure. He reached the peak both at college and university level, and, apart from a mild tendency to be testy with people who failed to take a common-sense view of hard realities, he was gently conservative and even sometimes parsimonious as an administrator but always as patient and persistent in this role as he was in academic life. He was made OBE for his work at Bletchley in 1946 and knighted in 1985. He died at Addenbrooke's Hospital, Cambridge, on 16 February 1998, of lung cancer, and was survived by his wife, Hilary (who died shortly after him), and by their three children, Clarissa, Hugh, and Charles.

RICHARD LANGHORNE

Sources R. Langhorne, introduction, *Diplomacy and intelligence during the Second World War*, ed. R. Langhorne (1985) · R. Langhorne, 'In memoriam: Professor Sir Harry Hinsley: an appreciation', *Diplomacy and Statecraft*, 9/2 (1998) · F. H. Hinsley and A. Stripp, eds., *Codebreakers: the inside story of Bletchley Park* (1993) · *The Times* (18 Feb 1998) · *Daily Telegraph* (18 Feb 1998) · *The Guardian* (18 Feb 1998) · *The Independent* (19 Feb 1998) · *WWW* · personal knowledge (2004) · private information (2004) · b. cert. · m. cert. · d. cert.
Likenesses photograph, *c*.1979, repro. in *The Independent* · photograph, 1993, repro. in *Daily Telegraph* · photograph, repro. in *The Times* · photograph, repro. in *The Guardian*

Hinton, Christopher, Baron Hinton of Bankside (1901–1983), civil engineer, was born on 12 May 1901 at Tisbury, Wiltshire, the third of the four children (the eldest of whom died at the age of two) and elder son of Frederick Henry Hinton, the village schoolmaster, and his wife, Kate, formerly a children's nurse, and daughter of Samuel Charles Christopher, of Ware, Hertfordshire. All four grandparents had been teachers. Hinton attended his father's next, larger, school in Chippenham before entering Chippenham secondary (later grammar) school; he performed precociously at elementary school, but not at secondary school until his last year.

In 1917 Hinton became a premium engineering apprentice with, first, a small firm and then the Great Western Railway at Swindon. His foreman's tribute—'you're the best craft apprentice I've ever had'—gave him as much pleasure as his later first-class degree. After evening study at Swindon Technical College—on top of a working week of fifty-four hours (later forty-seven hours)—he won in 1923 an Institution of Mechanical Engineers scholarship at Trinity College, Cambridge, gained a first-class degree in the mechanical sciences tripos (1925) in two years, and spent his third year in research, winning university and college awards. Trinity made him an honorary fellow in 1957.

With this perfect blend of practical and theoretical training Hinton joined Brunner, Mond, soon to become the alkali group of the new Imperial Chemical Industries (ICI), and at the age of twenty-nine became chief engineer. Engineers were then second-class citizens, but he achieved equal status with management and research, and great authority. Here he met and married in 1931 Lillian (*d.* 1973), head of the tracing office, and daughter of a power-house operator, Thomas Boyer, of Winnington, Northwich, Cheshire. They had one daughter, who married the son of Sir Charles Mole, director-general of the Ministry of Works.

In 1940 Hinton became director of ordnance factory construction at the Ministry of Supply, and in 1941 of the explosive filling factories, where he replaced chaos, and

Christopher Hinton, Baron Hinton of Bankside (1901–1983), by Godfrey Argent, 1970

fear of an ammunition shortage scandal, with great efficiency; in 1942 he became their deputy director-general. Exhaustion, aggravated by sleeping in ministry air-raid shelters, led him to the verge of breakdown.

When the war ended Hinton returned briefly to ICI, but thereafter worked exclusively in the public sector. The government had decided to establish a native atomic project, and ICI, refusing to be a main contractor for the factories, urged that they should be a government undertaking under Hinton. He accepted, and arrived with six of his former colleagues, including William Leonard Owen as his assistant controller, at his Risley headquarters near Warrington, in February 1946.

From this nucleus grew the industrial group of the British atomic project, collaborating with Harwell's research establishment and the establishment for weapons research (later at Aldermaston). The government regarded production of fissile material as supremely urgent for atomic bombs and industrial power. This meant four very different types of plant: nuclear reactors—two experimental reactors at Harwell and two plutonium producers at Windscale in Cumberland; a plant near Preston to produce fuel rods from uranium ore; a chemical plant to separate plutonium, and associated plants at Windscale; and a gaseous diffusion plant at Capenhurst, Cheshire, to enrich uranium. United States law permitted no transfer of information to Britain. Hinton relied on teamwork, but played a crucial part in all phases and parts of the enterprise. All plants were built to programmed times and cost and fulfilled their task, although in 1957 the two Windscale reactors were closed after a fire.

After the first British bomb test in 1952, it was decided to meet increased demands for plutonium from reactors that would also produce power. In 1956 Calder Hall's nuclear reactors were the first in the world to feed power into a national grid. Hinton's organization built them faultlessly to time and cost and they had an excellent operating record. Even before Calder 'went critical', Britain had announced a modest civil nuclear power programme based upon its reactors, but with an open mind about future types to be built by consortia of private firms. Hinton's staff were also designing and building an experimental fast breeder reactor at Dounreay in Scotland.

In 1954 atomic energy had been transferred from the Ministry of Supply to the quasi-independent Atomic Energy Authority with Hinton as member for engineering and production. In 1956, during his absence (on a triumphant visit to Japan, which ordered a British reactor), a new, greatly enlarged, nuclear power programme was produced, but Hinton feared the effects of this general nuclear euphoria. Nervous strain affected relations with some of his staff.

In 1956 the government appointed Hinton chairman of the new Central Electricity Generating Board (CEGB), established to supply electricity in bulk to the retailing area boards. He regretted that as chairman (rather than board member for engineering) he could not build the strong engineering design and construction department necessary to ensure prompt commissioning and high plant availability. Transmission engineering was, however, excellent, and Hinton developed both CEGB's research and its concern for the environment. He questioned the size of the enlarged nuclear power programme and insisted on basing atomic, like other, judgements on engineering and economic criteria, rather than prestige.

Knighted in 1951, appointed KBE in 1957, he retired with a life peerage as Baron Hinton of Bankside in 1965. He called himself the 'odd job man'—chairing the world energy conference, advising the World Bank, serving vigorously as president of the Institution of Mechanical Engineers, the Council of Engineering Institutions, and the new Fellowship of Engineering. He was active in the House of Lords and as the first chancellor of Bath University. An excellent lecturer, he also wrote five short lucid books. He especially enjoyed his deputy chairmanship, from retirement to his death, of the generating industry's research council. A fall shortly after the council's party for his eighty-second birthday led to his death, at King's College Hospital, Denmark Hill, London, on 22 June 1983.

Hinton's deeply probing mind encompassed country churches, history, and Jane Austen, as well as engineering. He was proud, uncompromising in his standards, incapable of dissimulation, and neither gave, nor expected, soft answers. With his commanding presence, intellect, creativity, and managerial skills he was considered by his colleagues at the time, and in retrospect, to be one of Britain's relatively few truly great engineers. In 1976 he was admitted to the Order of Merit, crowning his many fellowships (FRS in 1954) and honorary degrees, which included an Oxford DSc (1957) and a Cambridge ScD (1960). He also received medals from five British societies and honours from Austria, Japan, Sweden, and the United States.

MARGARET GOWING, *rev.*

Sources M. Gowing and L. Arnold, *Independence and deterrence: Britain and atomic energy, 1945–1952*, 2 vols. (1974) · M. Gowing, 'Hinton, Christopher Lord Hinton of Bankside', *DBB* · L. Hannah, *Engineers, managers, and politicians: the first fifteen years of nationalised electricity supply in Britain* (1982) · papers, Institution of Mechanical Engineers, London, archives · personal knowledge (1990) · *The Times* (23 June 1983), 16g · *The Times* (29 June 1983), 12g · d. cert.

Archives CAC Cam., papers, mainly relating to nuclear power · Institution of Mechanical Engineers, London, corresp. and papers · PRO, papers relating to UK Atomic Energy Authority, AB19 | University of Bath Library, corresp. with Leonard Rotherham

Likenesses G. Argent, photograph, 1970, NPG [*see illus.*] · J. Mendoza, crayon, *c*.1979, NPG

Wealth at death £346,250: probate, 5 Sept 1983, *CGPLA Eng. & Wales*

Hinton, Henry (*bap.* 1749, *d.* 1816), ironmonger and antiquary, was baptized on 28 May 1749 at Kingston Bagpuize, Berkshire, the fourth child and first surviving son of John Hinton (*d.* 1756) and his wife, Rebecca. He was apprenticed to an Oxford ironmonger, and took over his late master's shop in Cornmarket in 1777. From his retirement in 1803 he was 'indefatigable in his researches to illustrate the history and topography of the counties of Oxford and Berks' according to his obituary in the *Gentleman's Magazine* (*GM*). His collections survive in the Bodleian Library. He visited most of the parishes in both counties, recording in a series of notebooks details of the antiquities and of local events, accompanying them with sketches, particularly of the parish churches, monuments, and coats of arms. He revised his notes, added extracts from the manuscripts of the seventeenth-century antiquaries Anthony Wood and Matthew Hutton, and drafted several prefaces in preparation for publication. Hinton's inspiration was the need to record the evidence of the past at a time of rapid change

> when ancient families are become extinct; when manorial records are lost or dispersed, and parochial or ecclesiastical monuments are mouldering by decay. … Every day will cut off some source of information … and as agriculture is rapidly increasing all remains of Roman roads, barrows, entrenchments etc. are levelling by the plough (Bodl. Oxf., MS Don. d. 143, fol. 1)

Hinton was destined to share the fate of the many local antiquaries who had preceded him—'the same ambition to collect and the same misfortune never to methodise or publish' (ibid.). His collections for Oxford city and university are enlivened by anecdotes and engravings, illustrating 'an excellent taste for biography and a well-cultivated and experienced admiration and fondness for engraved portraits' to which the obituary in the *Gentleman's Magazine* drew attention. The interest of his topographical collections is enhanced by a remarkable series of rubbings of brasses in Oxfordshire and Berkshire, the earliest dated 1795.

During the last seven years of his life Hinton acquired a protégé, a young druggist and chemist named James Hunt (1795–1857), who accompanied him on his tours and began to compile similar topographical notes. Having bought Hinton's collections from his sister in 1816 after Hinton's death, Hunt added to them until the demands of business and a growing family persuaded him to abandon his researches and to sell his own and Hinton's manuscripts to Sir Thomas Phillipps—those for Oxfordshire in 1818 and the remainder for Berkshire in 1820. Together they fill a significant gap in the record of Oxfordshire and Berkshire topography, in particular providing information about monumental inscriptions and church interiors that disappeared or were substantially altered in the restorations of the late nineteenth century.

Hinton, who did not marry, was a religious and retiring man, in Hunt's opinion 'averse to company almost to a fault' (Bodl. Oxf., MS Phillipps-Robinson c. 406, fol. 192). He died on 5 April 1816 and was buried on 14 April in his father's grave at Kingston Bagpuize.

MARY CLAPINSON

Sources M. Clapinson, 'The topographical collections of Henry Hinton (1749–1816) and James Hunt (1795–1857)', *Oxoniensia*, 37 (1972), 215–20 · *GM*, 1st ser., 86/1 (1816), 381 · *Jackson's Oxford Journal* (16 Aug 1777) · *Jackson's Oxford Journal* (13 April 1816) · parish register, Kingston Bagpuize, 28 May 1749 [baptism] · parish register, Kingston Bagpuize, 14 April 1816 [burial] · J. Hunt, letters to Sir Thomas Phillipps, Bodl. Oxf., MSS Phillipps-Robinson c. 405, fols. 150–55; c. 406, fols. 182–96; b. 106, fols. 174–95 · *Oxford University and City Herald* (13 April 1816) · Bodl. Oxf., MS Don. d. 143, fol. 1

Archives Bodl. Oxf., Berkshire (church) collections · Bodl. Oxf., brass rubbings from churches in Oxfordshire and Berkshire with additional notes and papers · Bodl. Oxf., drawings, engravings, notes, and papers relating to brass rubbings and other subjects · Bodl. Oxf., MS, notes and additions to books by Anthony Wood · Bodl. Oxf., notes on Oxford University, churches, and the city

Hinton, James (1822–1875), otologist and writer on philosophy, second son of John Howard *Hinton (1791–1873), Baptist minister, was born at Reading, Berkshire. He was educated by his uncle at a school in Old Butcher Row, Oxford, which was founded by his grandfather, and afterwards at a school for nonconformists at Harpenden, Hertfordshire. He was a strictly religious and somewhat meditative boy. Following a family move, in 1838 he worked as cashier in a wholesale woollen-drapery shop in Whitechapel. The degradation of Whitechapel life made an indelible impression on his mind. Afterwards he obtained a clerkship in an insurance office and devoted his nights to the study of languages, history, mathematics, and philosophy. At nineteen Hinton fell in love with Margaret Haddon (b. 1825/6), daughter of John Haddon, a printer; he proposed, and was rejected. He could not have been a very prepossessing suitor, as he had no social graces and no small talk, and was very solemn. After an illness caused by work and anxiety, on the recommendation of his family doctor he became a medical student at St Bartholomew's Hospital, London; during his studies he made a voyage to China as the surgeon of a passenger ship, the *City of Derry*. On his return in 1847 he gained the MRCS. Meanwhile, at the cost of prolonged mental suffering, he had lost his

James Hinton (1822–1875), by Charles Henry Jeens, 1876

belief in Christianity; Miss Haddon rejected a second proposal from him on this account, and later in 1847 he became medical officer on board a ship chartered by the government to carry free black people from Sierra Leone to Jamaica.

Returning home in the spring of 1850 Hinton was oppressed by a sense of sin, read the Bible, David Nelson on *The Cause and Cure of Infidelity*, and other apologetic books, and was almost persuaded to be a Christian. Miss Haddon now consented to an engagement, and Hinton began general practice in London at Bartholomew Close. They subsequently married on 17 June 1852; the writer Charles Howard Hinton was their son, and their daughter Ada married the painter John Trivett *Nettleship (1841–1902). After his marriage Hinton went into otological practice on his own.

Hinton's first few years as a specialist were strenuous but not altogether happy. He ardently wished to devote his time to philosophy and was somewhat repelled by the necessary commercial side of medicine. Writing to his wife he said:

> I fully perceive and understand that the part I have to act by my profession is not to do my best for it but for myself. I must make it yield me, in the first place, tables and chairs and a house, butcher-meat and bread, a good coat and a gold watch, and then I may seek from it scientific and philosophical pleasure, moral elevation, the happiness of doing good, etc.. I perceive and assent. (Hopkins, 105)

Much of his spare time was occupied in arranging and classifying the Toynbee collection. Thus started his close association with Joseph Toynbee (1815–1866), with whom he spent time on the wards, in the consulting room, and in the laboratory.

Hinton became interested in the theory of sound and gave a course of lectures in 1854–5. About this time he was befriended by William Gull, physician at Guy's Hospital, who gave him the use of the dissecting rooms and later was influential in his appointment in 1863 as the first aural surgeon to Guy's. Gull and Hinton were in the habit of walking together in the early morning before work. Hinton would talk unceasingly, mostly of his philosophical ideas. After they had parted one day Gull was asked the whereabouts of Hinton. He replied: 'The last I saw of him he was up there,' pointing to the clouds (Reading, 465).

Hinton began his literary career in 1856 with the publication, in the *Christian Spectator*, of some papers on physiology and ethics. In October 1858 he contributed to the *Medico-Chirurgical Review* an article entitled 'Physical morphology, or, The law of organic forms', in which he maintained that organic form is the result of motion in the direction of least resistance. In 1859 he published a little book on the relations of religion and science, *Man and his Dwelling-Place*, which was so favourably received that he gave up surgical practice to devote himself entirely to philosophical meditations and writing. Two years later he published *Life in Nature*, which was not financially profitable, and with the pressure of an increasing family he returned to practice. He wrote the treatise on diseases of the ear for Timothy Holmes's *System of Surgery* (1862), and was one of the editors of the *Year-Book of Medicine* (New Sydenham Society) in 1863. In 1866 he published a little essay entitled *The Mystery of Pain*, which is probably the best-known of his writings. He then joined the newly established Metaphysical Society. In the autumn of 1870 he visited the island of St Michael in the Azores, where he had bought a small estate. On his way there he considered asceticism, which shortly led to such a thorough change in his ethical views that he was accustomed to describe it as a 'moral revolution'. The change consisted in the substitution of altruism for individualism as the basis of morals. To resolve this idea he determined to retire from practice, and, to be the better able to do so, threw himself with redoubled energy into otology. Initially in practice in Hanover Square, on Toynbee's tragic death in 1866 Hinton took over his extensive practice in Savile Row. He had extraordinary powers of observation and with an otoscope which reflected daylight into the external meatus he was able to view the tympanic membrane. His wife, Margaret, was a skilled watercolourist and on his instruction faithfully reproduced his observations: these were later published in the *Atlas of the membrana tympani, with descriptive text, being illustrations of the diseases of the ear* (1874). He noted that an aural polyp was not a disease of the external meatus alone but 'might grow through a perforation in the membrana tympani'. He showed how 'molluscous tumours' (cholesteatoma) might lead to death by eroding bone and causing intercranial spread. He recommended 'early puncture of the membrane in acute suppuration within the tympanum' and observed that 'an important sign of disease of the mastoid process is a red

swelling of the posterior wall, which might be confounded with a boil if the symptoms did not indicate a more serious affection.' Hinton was the first in Britain to perform a mastoid operation, hitherto practised only in Europe. He urged prompt surgery, employing a drill with a moveable guard, 'enabling the bone to be penetrated to the desired extent'.

Hinton was a prolific writer. In 1874, besides editing a manual of physiology entitled *Physiology for Practical Use, by Various Writers*, he published *The Place of the Physician, being the Introductory Lecture at Guy's Hospital, October 1873*; *Essays on the Law of Human Life and on the Relations between the Organic and Inorganic Worlds*; and translations of works by A. F. van Tröltsch on the surgical diseases of the ear, and by H. Helmholtz on the mechanisms of the ossicles and the membrana tympani, both for the New Sydenham Society. In his book *The Questions of Aural Surgery*, also published in 1874, he describes otitis media with effusion (glue ear) and the attempt to insert ventilation tubes (grommets).

By 1873 Hinton's behaviour and speech had become erratic and he grew more and more absent-minded. His disabilities forced him to retire in 1875 to his estate in the Azores, and he died the same year, on 16 December, in hospital on Ponta Delgada of 'inflammation of the brain'. He was buried in the English church on Ponta Delgada. Sadly, Hinton never lived to enjoy the pursuit of abstract thinking which had been his goal and the reason why he reluctantly worked so hard as a brilliant otologist. Dr (later Sir) Samuel Wilks in his *Lancet* obituary of Hinton wrote:

> When I say he was one of the most remarkable men in our profession, I feel astonished that he was ever in it but being *in it*, was never *of it*. I believe accident alone must have made him a medical student, just as a kind of chance gave him his speciality. … It was certainly not his forte to deal with his fellow creatures, and treat their various complaints in a commonplace way, any more than it was his inclination to devote himself to medicine with a purely scientific spirit. So far from his being able to pursue a special department of science in the chemical or physiological laboratory, I believe he was totally unfitted for such work. It was the ideal, speculative, philosophic and metaphysical, which occupied his mind. Whatever chance it might have been which led him to his professional speciality, he could not but bring a great force of intellect to bear upon it, and it necessarily grew in his hands. … I feel that I have not a full conception of his views, and am not sure that I have ever grasped them, for all his doctrines are very visionary, and his writings 'mystic, wonderful'. (Wilks, 72–3)

Hinton's fugitive essays were edited by his son, C. H. Hinton, with an introduction by Shadworth Hodgson, under the title *Chapters on the Art of Thinking, and other Essays* (1873). Two volumes of selections from his commonplace book (printed for his own convenience in 1874) were published: one entitled *Philosophy and Religion*, edited by his sister-in-law Caroline Haddon (1881), and the other *The Law Breaker and the Coming of the Law* (1884), edited by his widow with considerable help from his young disciple Havelock Ellis, who at an impressionable age had read Hinton's *Life in Nature* and had undergone a 'conversion' to Hinton's conviction that all life was one and that he and nature were not separate and apart but each flowing into the other. Ellis, while in Australia, had also read Ellice Hopkins's *Life and Letters of James Hinton* and had experienced a similar awakening to Hinton's, namely that he should follow a career in medicine. With very little personal funds his medical education at St Thomas's was supported by Caroline Haddon who ran a girls' boarding-school at Dover. Ellis always felt a great sense of obligation both to her and to the Hintons. This was later borne out in his wife Edith's book *James Hinton: a Sketch* (1918).

As a thinker Hinton, whatever his faults, lacked neither originality nor comprehensiveness. Accepting from idealism the doctrine that existence is limited by consciousness, he sought in the activity exhibited in volition, which he identified with spirit, the key to the interpretation of the noumenal, or, as he preferred to say, the 'actual' world, and the reconciliation of religion and science. Ideas of matter and force, and also the ordinary theological idea of God, must give place to that of universal spirit as the 'actuality' of things. Accordingly Hinton named his system 'actualism' as opposed to idealism and materialism.

In the moral sphere Hinton believed that as an individual self, man is a negation, a limitation of the divine spirit, and can thus only attain his true life through unselfishness, whereby he transcends himself and becomes one with God. Man has in fact done just the opposite, making himself the centre of the universe, his own supposed interest, mundane or spiritual, being his principal concern. Hinton therefore advocated that the moral centre of gravity should be shifted from self-regard to regard for others, from egoism to altruism or mutual service. This was perhaps a seductive argument for doing as one likes as long as one persuades oneself that the main object is to give pleasure to others. Caroline Haddon was later forced to reveal the true sexual side of Hinton who was involved with all sorts of women and whose justification for his behaviour was that he was 'serving' them as an artist in love. At that time (1885) there were rumours of Hinton's madness possibly due to syphilis and even of his suicide. Caroline Haddon confirmed that Hinton was in a disturbed sexual state shortly before his death: 'What upset his morals was not his own morbid sexual desire, but the conviction that was forced upon him of the needs of women' (Grosskurth, 99). This championship of women and indignation about the fetters that marriage frequently placed on them proved to have a major influence on Havelock Ellis. Hinton supported polygamy as did Caroline Haddon, and even his son Howard was arrested in 1885 for bigamy. This last revelation caused a strong opponent of Hinton's beliefs, Karl Pearson, to react, as Grosskurth puts it, with the wrath of an Old Testament prophet in the face of this 'most dramatic proof of Hintonian immorality!' (Grosskurth, 102).

NEIL WEIR

Sources N. Weir, *Otolaryngology: an illustrated history* (1990) · E. Hopkins, ed., *Life and letters of James Hinton* (1879) · Mrs H. Ellis [E. M. O. Ellis], *James Hinton: a sketch* (1918) · P. Reading, 'James Hinton', *Proceedings of the Royal Society of Medicine*, 62 (1969), 464–70 · S. Wilks, 'The late Mr James Hinton', *The Lancet* (8 Jan 1876), 72–3 · *DNB* · m. cert. · P. Grosskurth, *Havelock-Ellis: a biography* (1981)
Likenesses C. H. Jeens, engraving, 1876, NPG [*see illus.*] · Beynon & Co., group portrait, colour lithograph (*The past surgeons and physicians of Guy's Hospital, Southwark, London*; after M. Hanhart), Wellcome L. · C. H. Jeens, engraving, repro. in Hopkins, ed., *Life and letters* · half-tone, repro. in Ellis, *James Hinton* · photograph, Wellcome L. · photogravure, repro. in Ellis, *James Hinton*, frontispiece · stipple, NPG
Wealth at death under £3000: probate, 20 Jan 1876, *CGPLA Eng. & Wales*

Hinton, Sir John (1603?–1682), physician, was born in London. He had at least three brothers, all of whom supported the crown during the civil war. On 10 April 1633, aged thirty, he entered Leiden University, where he probably proceeded MD. He presented himself as a practitioner of midwifery at the censor's board of the College of Physicians, London, on 6 February 1634; but as he had not been engaged in practice for the statutable period of four years, was not examined. On 7 November 1640 Hinton again appeared at the college, and presented letters from the earl of Dorchester, testifying that he had been appointed physician to the queen. After the outbreak of the civil war Hinton busied himself in promoting a petition to the Long Parliament styled 'The inns of court peticion for peace', for which he was repeatedly examined, as he alleges, by the House of Commons, and before long 'was forced to fly from my house and family, whereupon they immediatly plundered mee to the losse of above one thousand pound, and my wife and children were left in very bad condition …' (Hinton, 7). There is no mention of any such examination in the *Journals* of the House of Commons. Hinton joined the king at York, marched with the army to Beverley, Hull, and Nottingham, and was present at the battle of Edgehill (1642). After accompanying the king to Oxford, he was there created MD on 1 November 1642, and was appointed physician-in-ordinary to Prince Charles. By the king's command he attended the queen to Exeter, where she gave birth in 1644 to the Princess Henrietta; afterwards he saw the queen into Cornwall and safely embarked for France.

In 1646 Hinton was living at Fulwood's Rents, London, having been in Exeter when it was taken by Sir Thomas Fairfax. Hinton was examined before the council of state on 27 August 1649. He appears to have lived for some time at The Hague in the suite of Charles II. On his return to London he was arrested and frequently examined. He claimed that he was on one occasion interrogated by Cromwell, who, he said, 'swore by the liveing God, hee would wrack every veine in my heart if I did not discover the designes against him' (Hinton, 27–8). Fortunately for Hinton, 'by the means and intercession of some zealous women, my patients', he was freed. According to his own account, a close watch was, however, kept on him until the Restoration.

Hinton was certainly in London in July 1655, and, although under suspicion, was allowed to remain there on account of his patients. After the Restoration he was appointed physician-in-ordinary to the king and queen, a position he held until 1673, and in December 1664 was admitted an honorary fellow of the College of Physicians. 'At the latter end of the plague' (1665) he was knighted, in recognition of his having procured a private advance of money for the duke of Albemarle to pay the army. In 1672 he purchased fee farms from the crown. In 1679 he presented a memorial to the king in which he set out, in the form of an autobiography, the losses he had incurred during the civil war and afterwards, and praying that such might be made good either to him or his children. One hundred copies of these *Memoires* were printed from the original manuscript in 1814. Hinton lived in the parish of St Bride, London, but before his death moved to the parish of St Martin-in-the-Fields. He must have died in poverty during the autumn of 1682, for on 14 November of that year administration of his estate was granted to Humphrey Weld (1612–1685), a principal creditor.

GORDON GOODWIN, rev. MICHAEL BEVAN

Sources J. Hinton, *Memoires* (1679) · Munk, *Roll* · Wood, *Ath. Oxon.* · W. A. Shaw, ed., *Calendar of treasury books*, [33 vols. in 64], PRO (1904–69) · M. A. E. Green, ed., *Calendar of the proceedings of the committee for advance of money, 1642–1656*, 3 vols., PRO (1888) · *CSP dom.*, 1649–50; 1655 · administration act book, 1682, PRO, PROB 6/57, fol. 154 · E. Peacock, *Index to English speaking students who have graduated at Leyden University* (1883), 49

Hinton, John Howard (1791–1873), Baptist minister and theologian, was born on 24 March 1791 in Oxford, where his schoolmaster father was the minister for thirty years. James Hinton (1761–1823) was one of those Baptist leaders who, at the end of the eighteenth century, secured the revival of Baptist life in Britain. His wife, Ann (1765–1832), was the daughter of Isaac Taylor, the engraver, a member of an important Congregational family. John Howard was so named by his mother at the request of John Howard, the prison reformer, after the loss of his own son.

After secondary education in his father's school, Hinton studied medicine with an Oxford surgeon. Influenced by John Sutcliffe and Andrew Fuller, his father's close friends in the work of the infant Baptist Missionary Society, and called by the church in Oxford to ministry, Hinton entered Bristol Baptist college in 1811 for training, but in 1813 proceeded to Edinburgh University, where he graduated MA in April 1816. He married, in 1818, Eliza, only daughter of the Revd Isaiah Birt, then minister of Cannon Street Chapel, Birmingham. They had two sons; the younger was James *Hinton, ontologist and writer on philosophy.

Following a first pastorate at Haverfordwest, Pembrokeshire (1816–20), Hinton moved to Reading (1820), where he led his congregation into more prestigious premises in the King's Road, which established Hinton's reputation as a denominational leader. In 1837 he succeeded Thomas Price, the editor of the *Eclectic Review*, as minister of the historic Devonshire Square Chapel in the City of London, where he remained until 1863. He was both a formidable writer on theological topics (which he undertook in the context of a busy London pastorate, rather than with the support of any academic community) and an activist in a large number of important religious societies.

A keen campaigner against slavery, it was Hinton who proposed a divisive motion seeking to exclude slave

holders from membership of the infant Evangelical Alliance in 1846. He was a lecturer for Joseph Sturge's Complete Suffrage Union and was also active in the Christian Instruction Society, using its platform to argue against Owenism. He helped found the Liberation Society, or the Anti-State Church Society as it was first called, and earned a reputation as the most distinguished of the society's lecturers; for it he wrote *The Test of Experience, or, The Voluntary Principle in the United States* (1851). With other Baptists, however, he withdrew from the work of the society after 1855, troubled by the increasing aggressiveness of Edward Miall. His voluntary church principles led him to attack in print the education clauses of Graham's Factory Bill of 1843. Temperance, with its built-in tendency towards intervention once education into temperance was shown to be an unrealistic hope, led him in later life to become critical of absolute voluntarism in all aspects of life: he defended government initiatives in social legislation and underlined the need for Christian ministers to combat class distinctions, arguing that labour and capital were properly to be seen as joint partners in the creation of wealth. An evangelicalism shared with many Anglicans made him an enthusiastic supporter of the Evangelical Alliance, though he was bitterly critical of new ritualistic developments within the established church.

In 1841 Hinton became secretary of the Baptist Union, a post then vacant because of the resignation of Joseph Belcher who was unhappy with having to communicate the British union's censure of American Baptists who owned slaves. Hinton, who edited *The History and Topography of the United States* (2 vols., 1830, 1832), was, by contrast, clear in his hostility to slavery. In his new position, which he held for a quarter of a century, Hinton found himself in the ironic position of being a complete individualist seeking to engineer the unity of a group of independent churches, but his obituarist was fair in his judgement that the Baptist Union 'owed its preservation in times of comparative feebleness to his perseverance' (*Baptist Hand-Book*).

Hinton sat on the committee of the Baptist Missionary Society, for which he wrote *A Vindication of Christian Missions in India* (1826) and a *Memoir of William Knibb* (1847), but he was uncertain whether the missionaries or the London committee should determine mission strategy and action. He came to believe that missionaries should not create dependent churches but should move on swiftly to open up new areas of work, always remembering that much missionary work remained to be done in Europe. Hinton himself visited Holland, Germany, and Sweden in support of the newly planted Baptist Missions in these countries. In 1840 one of the leaders of the Baptists in Germany, G. W. Lehmann of Berlin, travelled to London to be ordained by him.

Full of enthusiasm for Jonathan Edwards and the New Divinity revivalism which Edwards stimulated, Hinton saw the development of church life in the USA as abundant corroboration of free-church principles. Hinton was sometimes regarded as the successor to Andrew Fuller as the leading moderate Calvinist among the Baptists, but his attempts to secure a new synthesis in the Calvinist–Arminian debate were less than satisfying, leading him into unsatisfactory teaching on human responsibility and original sin, for which the rationalism of his Edinburgh education may be in part to blame. In his *The Work of the Holy Spirit in Conversion* (1829) he sought to provide a theology of revivalism, but in its endeavour to release human capacity from the old shackles of a theology of inability it went too far, fatally limiting the work of the Spirit in maintaining that 'a sinner has power to repent without the Spirit.' Such a controversial affirmation, enunciated by the occupant of one of the Particular Baptists' historic London pulpits, was one reason for the establishment of the London and East Anglian associations of Strict Baptist churches outside the Baptist Union. A strenuous advocate of personal evangelism, however, Hinton became seriously worried by the drift from historic orthodoxy among the Congregationalists. In 1860 he joined with Charles Haddon Spurgeon in opposing Baldwin Brown's *Divine Life in Man*, upon which he published strictures, characterizing Brown's thinking as 'the first inroad into English Nonconformist churches of a theology totally deficient in the truth and power of the gospel' (C. H. Spurgeon, *Autobiography of C. H. Spurgeon*, 1899, 2.269).

Hinton retired from Devonshire Square in 1863 and the Baptist Union in 1866, and returned to Reading, where he founded the new Carey Chapel. He twice occupied the chair of the Baptist Union, in 1837 and 1863. In 1868 he moved to 1 Redland Terrace, Bristol, where he died on 17 December 1873, having the previous year represented the Baptist Union at a service in St Paul's Cathedral to give thanks for the recovery of the prince of Wales. He was buried on 22 December in Arnos Vale cemetery, Bristol.

J. H. Y. BRIGGS

Sources B., 'Memoirs of Baptist ministers deceased', *Baptist Hand-Book* (1875), 277–80 · I. Sellers, 'John Howard Hinton', *Baptist Quarterly*, 33 (1989–90), 119–32 · J. H. Y. Briggs, *The English Baptists of the 19th century* (1994) · E. A. Payne, *The Baptist Union: a short history* (1959) · *The Times* (22 Dec 1873) · *ILN* (10 Jan 1874) · S. A. Swaine, *Faithful men* (1884) · R. Carwardine, *Transatlantic revivalism: popular evangelicalism in Britain and America, 1790–1865* (1978) · d. cert.
Archives Regent's Park College, Oxford, Baptist Union MSS
Likenesses B. R. Haydon, group portrait, oils (*The Anti-Slavery Society Convention, 1840*), NPG · portrait, repro. in *ILN*, 35–6
Wealth at death under £3000: double probate, Oct 1876, CGPLA Eng. & Wales (1873)

Hinton, Nicholas John (1942–1997), charity administrator, was born at the vicarage, Westbury, Wiltshire, on 15 March 1942. He was the son of a west-country clergyman, Canon John Percy Hinton, and his wife, Josephine Eleanor Calcutt. He was educated at Salisbury Cathedral choir school, where he was head chorister, and then at Marlborough College. He won a choral exhibition to Selwyn College, Cambridge, although his broken voice did not live up to the promise of his treble. He read history and law, though music remained a personal passion all his life, especially church and choral music. He directed the Edington Music Festival between 1965 and 1970; he met Deborah Mary Vivian (*b.* 1944), book restorer, there, and they married on 18 December 1971. She was the eldest of the five daughters of the Hon. Douglas David Edward Vivian, only son of George Crespigny Brabazon Vivian, fourth Baron Vivian, and his second wife, Nancy Lycett, *née* Green. They had one daughter.

After leaving Cambridge, Hinton began work with the Northorpe Hall Trust, near Leeds, which helped young offenders, and trained there as a psychiatric social worker. His experiences there and enthusiasm for the work directed his whole career. He soon moved as training officer to the newly formed National Association for the Care and Resettlement of Offenders (NACRO), quickly making his name and becoming its director in 1973. In 1977 he was appointed director of the National Council for Voluntary Organizations. As at NACRO, he was an inspirational leader, pushing voluntary bodies into more activity than many had experienced in the years of state domination that followed the Second World War.

Hinton then had a brief flirtation with politics, standing unsuccessfully as the candidate for the Social Democrat–Liberal alliance in the 1983 general election for Somerton and Frome. But thereafter he returned to the voluntary sector, as director-general of the Save the Children Fund, a post he held from 1985 to 1994. He transformed that organization, raising its income from £16 million a year before he joined to over £100 million a year by 1993. He worked well with the princess royal, the organization's patron, and deployed her presence and presentational skills to great effect.

So far Hinton's career had been one of continued success. He was, in many ways, an establishment figure: his friends and contacts were people in authority in government and society. Unlike many in the voluntary sector, he never played the role of the rebel, in appearance or behaviour. He once said that to change things in Britain you should wear a dark suit and think radical thoughts. That was very much what he did, albeit with sartorial style. Some regarded him as an *enfant terrible*, but in reality he was that great combination of an able administrator and a fearless activist. He was appointed CBE in 1985.

In 1994 Hinton was appointed chief executive of the Millennium Commission. Perhaps the different nature of this job, answering to close ministerial control instead of carrying with him the boards of worthies of the voluntary sector, was too great a change in style for him. Hinton must have thought that he could exercise, as chief executive, the same independence that his charisma had guaranteed him in the voluntary sector. He appointed a former colleague as his deputy without clearing the appointment with the commissioners, and in the clash of personalities that ensued, he was dismissed before ever formally taking up the job. He returned to the voluntary sector, to Save the Children, and in 1995 became president and chief executive of the international crisis group working in the overseas aid sector in both the Balkans and particularly Africa. He brought his usual energy to getting things done and galvanizing governments to positive action. He was on his way to meet his staff in Sarajevo (they had been given a budget to monitor the implementation of the Dayton peace accord) when he died of a heart attack at Split, Croatia, at fifty-four on 20 January 1997. His ashes were interred in the churchyard at Edington, Wiltshire.

Hinton was a member of the Central Council for Education and Training in Social Work from 1974 to 1979, a board member of Stonham Housing Association (1976–9), a member of the committee of inquiry into UK prison services (1978–9), member of the executive committee of Business in the Community (1982–8), and of the parole system review (1987–8). He was on the council of the Royal Society of Arts and a trustee of the Charities Aid Foundation. In a sense he was, for the voluntary sector in Britain, the right man at the right time. The establishment of the welfare state in the years following the Second World War saw the voluntary sector in decline. But that was to change, particularly after 1979. His efforts to inspire the voluntary sector, working from a position of acceptance by governments of both parties and the establishment generally, did much to pave the way for the revival of voluntary activity in the later years of the twentieth century. In his last years he had moved more on to the international scene, but still essentially remained outside formal government activity. His early death was a great loss to the many causes he had both espoused and inspired.

TOM CAULCOTT

Sources *The Times* (23 Jan 1997) · *The Independent* (22 Jan 1997) · *Daily Telegraph* (23 Jan 1997) · *WW* (1997) · personal knowledge (2004) · private information (2004) · b. cert. · m. cert. · d. cert. **Wealth at death** £82,865: probate, 11 March 1997, *CGPLA Eng. & Wales*

Hinton, Paula Doris (1924–1996), ballerina, was born at 132 Cranbrook Road, Ilford, Essex, on 1 June 1924, the elder child of (Alfred) Ernest Hinton (1895–1962) and his wife, Doris Clara Miriam, *née* Hurley (d. 1972). They were travelling players, appearing in operas and other entertainments, so their daughters' early lives were peripatetic. The family settled in Liverpool; Paula Hinton was already in her mid-teens when, acting in a pantomime and liking the ballets in it, she decided she wanted to become a dancer. After studying locally, she made her ballet début in 1943 as Helen of Troy in an Old Vic *Dr Faustus* at the Playhouse, Liverpool. Her late start did not prevent her from being accepted into Ballet Rambert the next year. Small roles came quickly, some in the classics calling for a neat technique, others for a sense of humour in ballets by Frederick Ashton, Frank Staff, and Antony Tudor. There was no one Hinton 'look' on stage; she soon learned to transform herself with each role. Her lively qualities were noted by the resident choreographer, Walter Gore [*see below*], and one of her first leading parts was in his ballet *Plaisance*.

Walter Gore [*real name* Frederick Robert Taylor] (1910–1979), dancer, choreographer, and ballet director, was born on 8 October 1910 at Waterside, Ayrshire, to John William Taylor and his wife, Margaret Anne, *née* Snape; both parents were actors. Gore went to London in 1924 to study drama at the Italia Conti School of Drama and Dance; he appeared in plays, and a revue by C. B. Cochran starring the dancer Leonide Massine, whose example

Paula Doris Hinton (1924–1996), by Roger Wood, 1949 [with Walter Gore]

inspired Gore to take up ballet. He studied with Marie Rambert and appeared with her company from its first season in 1930, also taking roles with the Vic-Wells Ballet, most intensively during 1934–5 when he partnered Ninette de Valois in *Coppélia* and created the title role in *The Rake's Progress*. A flair for characterization, through both movement and his expressively lively, sharply angled face, quickly marked him out to create roles for Ashton (in *Façade*, *Les masques*, etc.), de Valois (*Job*), and Tudor (*Dark Elegies*). In such parts he was unequalled, but he succeeded also in the virtuoso display of *Bluebird*, or even in romanticism as Albrecht in *Giselle*, thanks to his intensity and sense of style. During the mid-1930s he took time off to appear in musicals, where he also did his first choreography, besides meeting the dancer Aase Lavendt Nissen (*b.* 1915/16), whom he married on 16 September 1938. That year also saw his first ballet for Rambert, *Valse finale* to music by Ravel, soon followed by further pieces among which the short, tense *Confessional* (based on a poem by Browning) in 1940 was the most notable and durable. This revealed Gore's flair for dance drama and also that of its soloist, Sally Gilmour, who became the choreographer's off-stage partner (his wife had returned to her native Scandinavia). During the Second World War Gore was called up into the navy (1942–4) but was discharged on medical grounds after being twice torpedoed. On returning to dance he had a particular success with *Simple Symphony*, a lively interpretation of Britten's youthful music, and with the comic *Mr Punch*. Ballet Rambert's long Australian tour in 1947–9 brought a change in his private life. This was mirrored in a new ballet, *Winter Night*, where he played a man torn between his old and new loves, Gilmour and Paula Hinton. From then on, Hinton and Gore worked as a team; they married on 9 January 1950 following the dissolution of his first marriage. They shared a serious sense of purpose, enthusiasm for hard work, and a flair for theatrical effect.

Gore's *Antonia* in 1949, showing an irresistibly fascinating slut murdered by her lover, was an emphatic manifesto of Hinton's and his dramatic force. Then in 1950 Gore and Hinton left Rambert, and Hinton made guest appearances with the Original Ballet Russe, giving a glittering account of the title role in *Le coq d'or*, with Festival Ballet (she was outstanding as Giselle among other roles), and with Les Ballets des Champs-Elysées in Paris, where Gore created *La damnée* showing her burnt as a witch. Thereafter the couple spent much time abroad, he becoming director and she leading dancer with companies in Germany, Norway, and Portugal. They formed companies of their own, too, in Australia and twice in Britain: the Walter Gore Ballet (1953–5) and the London Ballet (1961–3). A stubborn refusal to compromise on artistic standards and perhaps a certain impracticality in business matters precluded more permanent operations. But they also worked with many small companies in Britain and Europe, where Gore created ballets, most of them starring Hinton. Through all these peregrinations Hinton, believing that communication with the audience was more important than the occasion, never gave less than her absolute best, whether in heavy drama or light comedy. Even when in 1965, to help Western Theatre Ballet out of an emergency caused by injuries, she learned one of its major roles in Peter Darrell's *The Prisoners* at only a few days' notice, she danced it as convincingly as it had ever been done.

The couple's range was demonstrated in 1958 when within twelve months Gore made three contrasting dramas for Hinton: in *Eaters of Darkness* as a woman wrongly confined to an asylum who goes mad in consequence; in *The Magical Being*, where she played a creature like the fierce firebirds of Russian tradition; and in a powerful though reticent duet about jealousy, *Night and Silence*. But they enjoyed equal success in ballets with a comic touch, such as *Peepshow* or *Light Fantastic*, with no story but a lively and individual animation. Unfortunately, their constant travels prevented their great talents from being as fully recognized as they deserved.

Gore died on 15 April 1979 in Pamplona, Spain, where he and Hinton were working for a time. Hinton subsequently attempted to arrange revivals of his ballets, but with limited success because continuing links with established companies were lacking. She retired to Birkenhead, where she died in Arrowe Park Hospital on 5 November 1996 and was cremated. Hinton and Gore had no children.　JOHN PERCIVAL

Sources Rambert Dance Company archives, London · P. Noble, *British ballet* (1948) · C. W. Beaumont, *Ballets of today* (1954) · H. Koegler, *Concise Oxford dictionary of ballet* · L. J. H. Bradley, *Sixteen years of Ballet Rambert* (1946) · *The Times* (16 Nov 1979) [obit. of Walter Gore] · J. Pritchard, ed., *Rambert, a celebration* (1996) · M. Clarke, *Dancers of Mercury* (1962) · b. cert. · d. cert.

Likenesses R. Wood, photograph, 1949, repro. in *The Independent* (13 Dec 1996) [*see illus.*] · photographs, Theatre Museum, London

Hinton [Henton], **Simon of** (*fl. c.*1248–1262), Dominican theologian, is of unknown parentage and origins. The possibility that he took his name from Hainton in Lincolnshire is no more than that. The only certain facts in his career are that he was provincial of the English Dominicans from 1254 until 1261, when he was removed from office by the general chapter, meeting at Barcelona, because the English provincial chapter was refusing to implement the order's decision to have a *studium generale* at Oxford; as a penance he was sent to teach in Germany, but in 1262 he was allowed to return to England. Since the possibility of his teaching in Cologne was specifically mentioned, it is probable that he had already graduated in theology. Presumably he became DTh about 1248, and served as regent master in Oxford in succession to Richard Fishacre, who died in that year. This would suggest that he became a bachelor not later than the mid-1240s (the claim that he was already a bachelor before 1240 is groundless). Together with Walter de Cantilupe, bishop of Worcester, and Adam Marsh, Hinton was commissioned by Alexander IV on 22 June 1256 to investigate the sanctity of Richard of Wyche, who was canonized in 1262.

Only part of Simon's considerable corpus of writings survives, including an incomplete text of his *quaestiones* (*c.*1240–50), some biblical commentaries, and a *summa iuniorum*. This last was by far his most successful work; it was designed to provide a handy compendium of essential Christian doctrine and morality and to supplement the resources of local libraries. Since, most unusually for an Oxford theologian, it includes citations from Albert the Great (*d.* 1280), it was probably composed after Hinton's stay in Germany. Although not an outstanding theologian, he is an interesting representative of the early Dominican school in Oxford. Strongly Augustinian, he nevertheless displays a willingness to differ from his authorities, and a particular interest in the material reality and appearance of things, rather than in high-flown speculation. His successive writings show that he continued to study and to absorb new material. One of his sermons has been identified (Bodl. Oxf., MS Laud misc. 511), but the ascription to him of the collation which follows it is unfounded. His alleged connection with Cambridge rests on a probably false identification of Hinton with a Simon of Hunton who was granted long-term use of two manuscripts. He may also be the author of the sermon attributed to Henton in Oxford, New College MS 88, fols. 111–114*v*.　SIMON TUGWELL

Sources T. Kaeppeli, *Scriptores ordinis praedicatorum medii aevi*, 3 (Rome, 1980), 345–7 · Emden, *Oxf.* · W. A. Hinnebusch, *The early English Friars Preachers* (1951), 369–74 · A. Walz, 'The "Exceptions" from the "Summa" of Simon of Hinton', *Angelicum*, 13 (1936), 283–368 [author, OP] · A. Dondaine, 'La somme de Simon de Hinton', *Recherches de Théologie Ancienne et Médiévale*, 9 (1937), 5–22, 205–18 · B. Smalley, 'Two biblical commentaries of Simon of Hinton', *Recherches de Théologie Ancienne et Médiévale*, 13 (1946), 57–85 · B. Smalley, 'Some more exegetical works of Simon of Hinton', *Recherches de Théologie Ancienne et Médiévale*, 15 (1948), 97–106 · B. Smalley, 'The *quaestiones* of Simon of Hinton', *Studies in medieval* history presented to Frederick Maurice Powicke, ed. R. W. Hunt and others (1948), 209–22 • N. R. Ker, 'Cardinal Cervini's manuscripts', *Xenia medii aevi historiam illustrantia oblata Thomae Kaeppeli O. P.*, ed. R. Creytens and P. Künzle (1978), 64–5 • M. E. O'Carroll, *A thirteenth-century preacher's handbook: studies in MS Laud Misc. 511* (1998), 386–400 • S. Wenzel, 'A Dominican preacher's book from Oxford', *Archivum Fratrum Praedicatorum*, 68 (1998), 187 • B. M. Reichert, ed., *Acta capitulorum generalium ordinis praedicatorum*, 1 (Rome, 1898)

Hiorne, Edmund (d. 1669),

local government official, was the son of Edmund Hiorne (d. 1629), yeoman, of Great Tew and Woodstock, Oxfordshire, and his wife, Elizabeth. Precise details of his education are lacking but it is evident that he was educated in the law, perhaps as an attorney, and that he had an excellent knowledge of accounting in the new style being adopted. In 1605 he became a freeman of Woodstock and in December 1607 he was appointed town clerk in succession to Thomas Rawlins, whose daughter Ann was Hiorne's wife. His duties were to act as deputy steward and clerk of the manor court. The borough court, known as the portmoot, met fortnightly and dealt with a wide range of business, being one of the three courts of record in the county. Hiorne recorded all its business, mostly in Latin but with some of the depositions in English, and was responsible for the proper keeping of the borough accounts and, with the mayor, for the guardianship of all the borough records. He also became a borough JP. By 1618 he held three freehold properties in the town and leased another property belonging to New College; in the deeds of the latter he is described as 'gentleman'.

When the civil war began in 1642 Hiorne worked so actively for the king that he ran foul of the House of Commons. He gave Woodstock's town armoury, which included muskets, to the royalists in Oxford, and then caused a proclamation to be posted in the town denouncing the earl of Essex as a traitor; a man was paid 4d. to guard it from defacement. On 4 October 1642 Hiorne was called to acknowledge his faults on his knees at the bar of the Commons before the speaker, William Lenthall, recorder of and MP for Woodstock. On his expression of contrition Hiorne was discharged but, in circumstances which are not clear, he was dismissed from his post in 1645, and succeeded by John Williams. Hiorne remained in Woodstock and showed his opposition to the new regime in 1652 by voting against a known parliamentarian sympathizer, Richard Croke of Marston and Oxford, as a freeman. He also withheld his rents to the town.

The Restoration brought Hiorne back as town clerk in 1662 but he retired the following year and was replaced by George Ryves, the husband of his granddaughter Ann Fleetwood. By the time Hiorne made his will in 1665 he had two sons and four daughters living. He died in 1669, clearly aged over eighty, and was buried in Woodstock on 27 June; his wife died in 1673. He typified the new style of town government emerging at that time: efficient, punctilious in record keeping (many of his official papers survive), and providing a route from highly respected citizen to gentry status.   MARY HODGES

Sources *VCH Oxfordshire*, vol. 12 • M. Maslen, ed., *Woodstock chamberlains' accounts, 1609–50*, Oxfordshire RS, 58 (1993) • R. F. Taylor,

ed., *Calendar of the court book of the borough of New Woodstock, 1607–1614* (1996) [privately printed] • A. Ballard, *Chronicles of the royal borough of Woodstock* (1896) • will, Oxon. RO, MS wills Oxon 33/2/28 • Bodl. Oxf., MS Top. Oxon. d. 885, fol. 94 • *JHC*, 2 (1640–42), 279 [4 Oct 1642] • borough muniments, Town Hall, Woodstock, B76–B83 • deeds of properties leased by Hiorne, Bodl. Oxf., MSS ch. Oxon nos. 2398, 2399, 2400

Archives Town Hall, Woodstock Borough Archives, accounts • Town Hall, Woodstock Borough Archives, Woodstock, court minute books

Hiorne, Francis (1744–1789),

architect, was the elder son of William Hiorne (c.1712–1776), mason and architect of Warwick, and his first wife, Mary Duncalfe. William Hiorne and his younger brother David (1715–1758) had established themselves as leading practitioners of their trade in the midlands area, and Francis Hiorne succeeded to the family business on the death of his father. By then he was already active as an architect and his subsequent practice, mainly in the midlands but also on occasion further afield, developed immediately; however, his career was cut short by his early death at the age of forty-five and the total number of his executed works was not large.

Hiorne's work in a classical idiom included two buildings of some individuality, the churches of St Anne's, Belfast (1776; dem.), which showed the influence of the baroque St Philip's, Birmingham, and Tardebigge, Worcestershire (1777), with its striking needle spire. But it was as an architect specializing in the Gothic style that he gained a particular reputation. His best-known work, Tetbury church, Gloucestershire (1777–81), is one of the most elegant examples of late eighteenth-century Gothic and was widely admired at the time: the poet William Mason, for example, commented that it gave him 'the very highest opinion' of Hiorne's 'Gothic taste'. Hiorne's approach to Gothic design appears to have embraced at least the rudiments of scholarship as well as its decorative appeal: his preparations for carrying out work at Arundel Castle, Sussex—a project curtailed by his death—were reported by a correspondent of the antiquary Richard Gough in 1787:

> At Greystoke Castle I found Mr. Hiorne the gothic architect, whom the Duke of Norfolk had invited there to consult with relative to his intended repairs at Arundel Castle; and we made a party to see Alnwick Castle, etc. in Northumberland, for Mr. Hiorne's information.   (Nichols, 423)

Hiorne's antiquarian leanings are reflected in his election as a fellow of the Society of Antiquaries in 1784; and like his father, who had been an alderman of Warwick and served as mayor in 1765–6, he was also a prominent figure in the public life of his home town. He was elected an alderman in October 1773, held office as mayor in 1773–4, 1782–3, and 1787–8, served as treasurer to the corporation from 1781 to 1789, and as the Warwickshire county bridgemaster during the same period. He died in Warwick on 9 December 1789, in his will leaving to his wife, Elizabeth, a newly built house at Beausale, near Warwick.   PETER LEACH

Sources Colvin, *Archs.* • J. Gwilt, *The encyclopaedia of architecture*, rev. edn, rev. W. Papworth (1867), 223 • *GM*, 1st ser., 59 (1789) • *GM*, 1st ser., 70 (1800) • A. Gomme, 'William and David Hiorn', *The architectural outsiders*, ed. R. Brown (1985), 45–62 • Nichols, *Illustrations*, vol. 6

Hipkins, Alfred James (1826–1903), writer on musical instruments, was born on 17 June 1826 at 22 Medway Street, Westminster, London, the only son in the family of two children of James Hipkins (1800–1882), a cabinet and piano maker, and his wife, Jane Mary Grant (1802–1865). As a boy he wanted to become a painter, but in 1840 he was apprenticed as a piano-tuner with Broadwood's, and worked there for the rest of his life. He began working on equal temperament and the standardization of pitch in the 1840s, and gained the distinction of tuning instruments for Chopin, who always used Broadwood pianos when he was in England. On 2 October 1850 Hipkins married Jane Souter Black, a Scot. Their daughter, Edith (b. 1854), became a portrait painter, and their son, John (1851–1933), who was deaf and mute, became a distinguished wood-engraver.

Apart from a few piano and organ lessons in the early 1840s, Hipkins had no musical training, but he became an excellent pianist, and gave more than forty recitals on Broadwood pianos at the Great Exhibition of 1851; he also became an authority on the history of keyboard instruments. In 1881 he was invited to Berlin and Potsdam by the crown princess of Prussia to examine the pianos which had belonged to Frederick the Great. From 1883 he performed and lectured on early keyboard instruments, and played Bach's 'Chromatic' fantasia and fugue on the clavichord and the 'Goldberg' variations on the harpsichord before the Musical Association in 1886. In 1896 he published *A Description and History of the Pianoforte*.

Hipkins did not confine himself to keyboard instruments, and became interested in non-Western music. His *Musical Instruments, Historic, Rare, and Unique* (1888) included instruments from India, China, and Japan, and his preface to C. R. Day's *The Music and Musical Instruments of Southern India and the Deccan* (1891) came to be seen as a landmark in ethnomusicology. In it he argued that the music of non-European cultures should be understood on its own terms, and not in terms of the experience of the European musician. He also helped A. J. Ellis, who was tone deaf, in his study of non-European scales, *On the Musical Scales of Various Nations* (1885), using a series of tuning-forks to determine the pitch of notes produced by non-European instruments and then calculating the distance between them. Hipkins also wrote 134 articles for the first edition of Grove's *Dictionary of Music and Musicians* (1879), and contributed articles on pitch and the piano to the ninth edition of the *Encyclopaedia Britannica*. Parry relied on his advice for his chapter on scales in *The Evolution of the Art of Music* (1896).

Hipkins helped in the preparation of many exhibitions, including the music section of the Inventions Exhibition in 1885. He left his collection of tuning-forks to the Royal Institution and his collection of musical instruments, which included a spinet which had belonged to Handel, to the Royal College of Music. He was elected FSA in 1886, and was a member of the council and honorary curator of the Royal College of Music. He died at home in Kensington on 3 June 1903, and was buried at Kensington Hanwell cemetery, Ealing.   ANNE PIMLOTT BAKER

Sources Grove, *Dict. mus.* • *New Grove* • K. Wachsmann, 'Spencer to Hood: a changing view of north European music', *Proceedings of the Royal Anthropological Institute of Great Britain and Ireland for 1973* (1974), 8 • M. Hood, *The ethnomusicologist* (1971), 90–91 • *MT*, 39 (1898), 581–6 • Brown & Stratton, *Brit. mus.* • *MT*, 44 (1903), 459–60 • *DNB* • *CGPLA Eng. & Wales* (1903)
Archives BL, corresp. and papers, Add. MSS 41636–41639 • LUL, papers • Royal College of Music, London, Instrument collection | Bodl. Oxf., letters to Lord Lovelace
Likenesses E. Hipkins, oils, exh. RA 1898 • photograph (after E. Hipkins), repro. in *MT*
Wealth at death £2512 6s. 4d.: probate, 7 July 1903, *CGPLA Eng. & Wales*

Hippisley, Elizabeth (*fl.* 1742–1769). See under Hippisley, John (1696–1748).

Hippisley, Jane (1719–1791). See under Hippisley, John (1696–1748).

Hippisley, John (1696–1748), actor and theatre manager, was born on 14 January 1696 near Wookey Hole in Somerset. He made his theatrical début as Fondlewife in William Congreve's *The Old Bachelor* at Lincoln's Inn Fields on 7 November 1722. Although he was then billed as having appeared on the stage previously, there is no account of his having done so elsewhere. Later in the same season he played Scrub in George Farquhar's *The Stratagem*, Sir Hugh Evans in *The Merry Wives of Windsor*, Gomez in John Dryden's *The Spanish Fryar*, and various other comic parts, including Polonius and Pandarus, and these certainly indicate that he may have had some experience in such roles. He remained with John Rich at Lincoln's Inn Fields until the 1732–3 season, when he began working at Covent Garden, first appearing there on the theatre's opening night, 6 December 1732, as Sir Wilful Witwould in Congreve's *The Way of the World*. Over the previous decade his repertory of characters had grown impressively and now included Scapin in Thomas Otway's *The Cheats of Scapin*, Sir Francis Gripe in Susannah Centlivre's *The Busy Body*, Barnaby Brittle in Thomas Betterton's *The Amorous Widow*, Sir William Wisewood in Colley Cibber's *Love's Last Shift*, Scruple in Charles Shadwell's *The Fair Quaker*, and Sancho in Aphra Behn's *The Rover*.

Hippisley was popular for his portrayal of fools and scoundrels, for his provincial accents, and for his portrayal of female roles. He was equally renowned for his comic presentation of the aged—Corbaccio in Ben Jonson's *Volpone* being a notable success. For his benefit on 3 May 1723 he played Pandarus in *Troilus and Cressida* and for that of 23 April 1731 he took the part of the Welshman David Shenkin in his own farce *The Journey to Bristol, or, The Honest Welshman*. This production may well have first been presented the previous year at Bristol, where Hippisley had built a playhouse.

Hippisley's connection with Bristol had begun in 1728, when he travelled there to perform his play *The English Thief, or, The Welsh Lawyer* on 14 August. Towards the end of that year he leased land adjacent to the Horse and Groom in Jacob's Wells, where the city's first permanent theatre was later erected; it opened on 23 June 1729 with Congreve's *Love for Love*. The building was only modest in size and required actors exiting on one side of the stage to walk round the exterior of the building if they had then to enter from the other wing. The first decade of his management incurred great debts, however, and by 1736 Hippisley had to mortgage his Covent Garden salary in order to sustain the venture. Between 1741 and 1747 he regularly occupied the theatre over the summer seasons, and he performed a series of roles there, including Scapin, Permain, Day in Sir Robert Howard's *The Committee*, and Dogberry in *Much Ado about Nothing*. In November 1747 he proposed to build a larger playhouse in Bath, though he did not live to see the project completed. Despite commitments in the west country, Hippisley also managed to participate in the summer fairs, and appeared on 22 August 1730 at Bartholomew fair. In July 1731 he played with the Richmond troupe to offer a collection of performances and in August he joined in the co-management of a booth at Bartholomew fair, where he performed Shallow in *The Emperor of China*; the production transferred to Southwark fair that September.

From 1732 until his death Hippisley remained at Covent Garden. New parts performed over the years included Shallow in *2 Henry IV*, Scaramouch in Behn's *The Emperor of the Moon*, Phaeax in Dryden's version of *The Tempest*, Muckworm in Henry Carey's *The Honest Yorkshireman*, Ananias in Jonson's *The Alchemist*, Clown in *The Winter's Tale*, Drudge in the pantomime *Orpheus and Eurydice*, and Gardiner in *King Henry VIII*. On 17 January 1747 he was also the original Sir Simon Loveit in Garrick's *Miss in her Teens*.

In the epilogue to his own work *Journey to Bristol*, Hippisley declared that 'his ugly face is farce', and according to Samuel Foote in *Roman and English Comedy* 'the left corner of his Mouth, and the Extremity of his Chin, became very near Neighbours' (Foote, 33). This was the result of a burn sustained as a youth, and Hippisley fully exploited his unconventional appearance for its on-stage comic potential. Davies refers to him as a 'comedian of lively humour and droll pleasantry' (*Life of Garrick*, 1.356), and informs us that, although it was customary to compare his performances negatively with those of Benjamin Johnson, Hippisley's Corbaccio was considered the superior of the two. His Fondlewife matched Cibber's own portrayal of the character and his performance of Fumble in Thomas D'Urfey's *Plotting Sisters* was considered to have saved the play.

Hippisley was not a prolific dramatist. After the apparently unpublished *The English Thief* (1728) he adapted Thomas Doggett's *Hob, or, The Country Wake* as the ballad opera *Flora*, performed and published in 1729. His other two ballad operas, *Journey to Bristol* and *A Sequel to the Opera of Flora*, were published in 1731 and 1732 respectively. His monologue *The Drunken Man*, published posthumously in 1776, remained popular with public and performers for the remainder of the century.

Hippisley died in Bristol on 12 February 1748, having been ill for several months, and was even reported as dead in October 1747 (provoking a witty denial in response from the actor). He had drawn up a will on 1 February in which he had properly provided for his partner, Mary Charley, and two of his children (Elizabeth Hippisley [*see below*] was left out of the testament) as well as for his legal wife, Elizabeth. It is not known when he married and separated from his wife, nor whether he had more than three children. The Hippisley family's association with the theatre and circus continued into the twentieth century.

The three of Hippisley's children of whom something is known all appeared on the stage. **Elizabeth Hippisley** (*fl.* 1742–1769) first took to the stage as Angelina in Colley Cibber's *Love Makes a Man* on 25 January 1742 at Giffard's playhouse in Goodman's Fields. In her first season she adopted the role of Rose in Farquhar's *The Recruiting Officer*, which she was to play numerous times in her career. She established herself at Lincoln's Inn Fields and Covent Garden and spent summer seasons performing at her father's theatre in Bristol. In the 1750s and 1760s she played numerous secondary roles at Drury Lane, her last recorded appearance being on 8 April 1769 as Myrtilla in Cibber's *The Provoked Husband*. As Mrs Fitzmaurice, she apparently played in York and Bath, though she ended her career as a dresser in Bath.

Jane Hippisley (1719–1791) made her first appearance at her father's benefit at Covent Garden on 18 March 1735 as Cherry in Farquhar's *The Stratagem*. She had considerable success in her stage career, and played Ophelia to Garrick's Hamlet in her first season at Goodman's Fields, Kitty Pry in Garrick's *The Lying Valet*, and Biddy in his *Miss in her Teens*. She was said to have had a liaison with Garrick in 1746–7, and it is possible that she called herself Mrs Green after 1747 to cover the birth of a child: Samuel *Cautherley was rumoured to be the product of her relationship with Garrick, but neither parent can be confirmed. Mrs Green performed in Dublin in 1751–2, was the first Mrs Hardcastle in Oliver Goldsmith's *She Stoops to Conquer* (1773), and was the first Mrs Malaprop in 1775. She acted in Garrick's *The Irish Widow* in Bristol as late as 4 July 1781. She made her last appearance on the London stage, as Mrs Hardcastle, on 26 May 1780 and died in her house at Jacob's Wells, Bristol, in the winter of 1791. Hippisley's son, John *Hippisley, began his career as a child actor, but is better remembered as a writer on African economics.

MARK BATTY

Sources T. Davies, *Dramatic miscellanies*, 3 vols. (1784) · T. Davies, *Memoirs of the life of David Garrick*, 2 vols. (1808) · S. Foote, *The Roman and English comedy consider'd and compar'd* (1747) · Genest, *Eng. stage* · D. E. Baker, *Biographia dramatica, or, A companion to the playhouse*, rev. I. Reed, new edn, rev. S. Jones, 3 vols. in 4 (1812) · Highfill, Burnim & Langhans, *BDA* · R. M. Prothero, 'John Hippisley on the populousness of Africa: a comment', *Population and Development Review*, 24 (1998), 609–12 · D. P. Henige, *Colonial governors from the fifteenth century to the present* (1970) · *GM*, 1st ser., 37 (1767), 47 · *DNB*
Likenesses W. Hippisley-Green, engraving, 1801 (as Scapin in *The cheats of Scapin*) · Hogarth, oils (as Peachum in *The beggar's opera*), Tate collection; repro. in Highfill, Burnim & Langhans, *BDA* · Sykes, engraving (as Sir Francis Gripe in *The busy body*; after Hogarth), repro. in Highfill, Burnim & Langhans, *BDA*

Hippisley, John (*bap.* **1729**, *d.* **1766**), writer on trade and administrator in west Africa, was baptized on 21 June 1729 at St Andrew's, Holborn, London, the son of John *Hippisley (1696–1748), an actor and theatre manager, and his partner, Mary Charley. Little is known of his early life and education. He played Tom Thumb in Henry Fielding's *Tragedy of Tragedies* at Covent Garden in 1740 but otherwise seems not to have followed the theatrical life of his father and two sisters, Elizabeth *Hippisley (*fl.* 1742–1769) and Jane *Hippisley (1719–1791) [*see under* Hippisley, John (1696–1748)]. His later writing indicates an education that complemented an above-average intellect.

By the mid-century, probably through his family's Bristol connections, he was in the employ of the Committee of Merchants Trading with Africa, which had taken over the functions of the chartered Royal African Company in 1750. The committee was responsible for the forts in west Africa which (with the help of the Royal Navy) protected British interests in the slave trade. Its officers were few in number, mainly stationed in forts on the Gold Coast, and these Hippisley joined in a junior capacity at a salary of £80 a year. The committee employed men of good education, from the middle class, and with respectable connections. Promotion was rapid, largely because of high mortality, and in 1751 he was in charge of the fort at Succondee. His record was not without blemish and in the following year he was reported for a misdemeanour and warned that he might be dismissed for further misconduct. He later served in Tantumquerry, Anamaboe and Winneba, but in mid-1760 he left the service, possibly dismissed for the sale of slaves, in which officers of the committee were forbidden to participate.

The next four years Hippisley probably spent as a merchant in Bristol, for he described himself as such in his will of 1764, though his name does not appear in the records of the city's Society of Merchant Venturers. Certainly he spent time preparing a slim volume of *Essays* which appeared in 1764, one among many publications in the eighteenth century on various matters relating to the slave trade. The first essay, 'On the populousness of Africa', is the most interesting and original, and one of the earliest extant discussions of this theme. It defended the need for the slave trade and the capacity of Africa to continue to supply this need, but it was no crude defence and displayed a level of knowledge and understanding of contemporary thinking, for example in references to Montesquieu's *Esprit des lois* and to certain medical matters. Hippisley was certainly influenced by the Enlightenment and, notwithstanding his activities, displayed a remarkable degree of humanity. The other essays are more polemical and less well written. 'On the trade at the forts on the Gold Coast' argued that officers of the committee should be permitted to participate in the trade in slaves, and probably reflected his experience of dismissal from the service. 'On the necessity of erecting a fort at Cape Appolonia' stressed the need for further protection of English interests against the Dutch and the French. The *Essays* have been frequently referred to by historians but remain to be examined in detail.

How he came to regain favour with the Committee of Merchants is not known, but in his will he stated that he was 'bound for the coast of Africa'. His preferment was

rapid and in March 1766 he became governor of Cape Coast Castle, the senior appointment on the Gold Coast, but his time in office was brief and he died there in August the same year. His death was recorded by Philip Quaque, then chaplain at the castle, in a letter dated 28 September, thus correcting a later announcement in the *Gentleman's Magazine* that it took place in January 1767. Hippisley, he wrote, 'proved to us in all points a worthy friend … very humane and hospitable … a great observant of the public worship of Almighty God' (Priestley, 113–14). Even with allowance for some overstatement (and Quaque was later suspended) these words match a view of Hippisley to be gained from his writing.

His estate, of which there are no details, went to his wife, Mary, whom he married in Bristol in 1764 and with whom he had a son. However, the Cape Coast Castle chaplain recorded that he christened in June 1766 a son of Hippisley, then twelve, borne presumably by his west African 'wench', as was common among Europeans on the Gold Coast at the time. Both sons carried their father's name.

R. MANSELL PROTHERO

Sources R. M. Prothero, 'John Hippisley on the populousness of Africa: essay and comment', *Population and Development Review*, 24 (1998), 601–12 · PRO, T 70, CO 391 · J. Hippisley, *Essays* (1764) · F. Jones, *The Hippisley family* (1952) · M. Priestley, 'Philip Quaque of Cape Coast', *Africa remembered: narratives by west Africans from the era of the slave trade*, ed. P. D. Curtin (1967), 99–139 · E. Donnan, ed., *Documents illustrative of the history of the slave trade to America*, 2 (1931) · E. C. Martin, *The British west African settlements* (1927) · A. W. Lawrence, *Trade castles and forts of west Africa* (1962) · H. S. Klein, *The Atlantic slave trade* (1999) · H. Thomas, *The slave trade: the history of the Atlantic slave trade, 1440–1870* (1997)

Hippisley, Sir John Coxe, first baronet (1745/6–1825), politician, was born in Bristol and baptized (a little belatedly) John Cox Hipsley at Christchurch, Bristol, on 17 February 1747. He was the elder and only surviving son of William Hipsley (*bap.* 1718, *d.* 1800), haberdasher, and his wife, Anne (*d.* 1776), daughter of Robert Webb of Cromhall, Gloucestershire. He was educated at Bristol grammar school and Hertford College, Oxford, whence he matriculated in 1764. He proceeded to the Inner Temple in 1766 and was called to the bar in 1771; he later held the offices of master of the bench (1803), reader (1812), and treasurer (1813–14). He was awarded an honorary DCL from Oxford in 1776, and MA from Cambridge in 1811.

An ambitious barrister, Hippisley became the lover of the Countess Percy, with the hope of becoming Lord Bute's son-in-law. When she eventually left him he pursued her ineffectively to Germany, whence, in dire straits, he hitched a ride to Rome in 1779. There he acted as *cicerone* to visiting grandees, but also sent confidential information to the government. He married in Rome on 1 February 1780 his first wife, Margaret (1754/5–1799), second daughter of Sir John Stewart, third baronet (*d.* 1796), of Allanbank, Berwickshire, and Margaret Agnes Smith (*d.* 1807). They had three daughters and one son. He returned home in 1781, but soon departed to Madras to take up a position in the East India Company that had been secured for him through the influence of Lord Bute, and of William Windham, whom he had met in Rome. He served as company writer (1782), factor (1783), and paymaster at Tanjore (1786–7) and returned to England in 1789 with a fortune of over £100,000, having bought up company bills at discount. He now aspired to parliament and, assisted by Windham, he became recorder (1789), then member (1790) for Sudbury. The election contest cost £6000: ironically he had rejected Bristol to avoid expense. In the 1790s he bought a country estate at Warfield Grove in Berkshire.

In parliament Hippisley acted as an opposition spokesman on India but illness forced him to relinquish this role to others in February 1791. On his recovery in April he denounced belligerent expansion, and pressed for payment of arrears to the native army, which was secured in June. In 1792 his complaints about Cornwallis's wartime recruitment of native allies stung the viceroy into characterizing Hippisley's fortune as ill-gotten. His bronchitis prevented his voice being heard at Westminster from 5 April 1792, but he none the less distanced himself from his more radical whig colleagues by instigating a Sudbury address against sedition, and urging government to prosecute radical publications. He returned to Rome in the hope of restoring his health, stopping *en route* at Paris for Louis XVI's trial in December 1792. His enthusiasm for Pope Pius VI's projected Holy Alliance against France spurred him to bring about Cardinal Erskine's mission to London, and to pester friends at home for official recognition of his role in 1793. He purveyed supplies for the British fleet from the Romagna and, following Windham into supporting Pitt's administration, he proceeded to lobby the new government. In August 1794 he petitioned for a baronetcy. He returned home the following summer endowed with the Roman senate's insignia, and reappeared at Westminster on 3 December to support anti-radical measures. Despite his efforts to secure new Italian markets for the depressed Sudbury wool trade, his prolonged absence from his constituency counted against him, and his erstwhile patron, Sir James Marriott, stood himself as a candidate and so, facing a contest at the approaching election, Hippisley withdrew. He received his baronetcy, through the duke of Portland's influence, on 30 April 1796.

Hippisley next busied himself by successfully negotiating the princess royal's marriage to the duke of Württemberg's heir, which attracted the king's notice. In 1799 he espoused the cause of Henry, Cardinal York, last of the royal Stuarts, and procured him a pension from George III. In 1800 he was sheriff of Berkshire, and was later vice-president of the West of England Agricultural Society. He was a founder member of the Royal Institution, a fellow of the Royal Society and of the Society of Antiquaries, and vice-president of the Literary Fund. He also promoted literary institutions in Bristol and Bath. As a governor of the Levantine Company he warned government about Napoleon's designs on India. In September 1799 his wife had died and he married, on 16 February 1801, Elizabeth Anne (1762/3–1843), widow of Henry Hippisley Coxe MP, of Ston Easton, and only daughter of Thomas Horner of Mells Park and Elizabeth Paget. They had no children. Through his marriage he acquired enough property to consider standing for Somerset. A vacancy at Sudbury, however, obviated this and he was elected unopposed at his old constituency in 1802.

Although Hippisley joined Windham in opposition in 1804 he was neither reliable nor loquacious, except in championing the Irish petition for Catholic relief in 1805. He had first championed the Irish Catholic cause in 1799–1800, which earned him the gratitude of the Irish Roman Catholic hierarchy, and led him to petition for an Irish peerage. In 1806 he published his plan for Catholic relief in his *Observations on the Roman Catholics of Ireland*, which was followed by *Additional Observations* (1806), and, until 1818, by a stream of speeches and correspondence on the question. Windham, in office under Grenville in 1806, could not achieve Hippisley's wish for an Irish peerage although Hippisley's annual income was then £8000. Hippisley failed in his attempt to win office as governor of the Cape, as privy councillor, as a member of the Board of Trade, or even any appointment in India under the new viceroy, Lord Minto, in 1807. His only real gesture of support was his vote against Grenville's dismissal on the Catholic question on 9 April 1807. He afterwards voted with the opposition spasmodically. His annual speeches in favour of Irish Catholic relief were overlong and over-elaborate; fearing popular prejudice he insisted on securities to guard against interference from Rome and to ensure a royal veto on Irish episcopal appointments. The whigs' failure to regain office dashed his hopes of entering the privy council and, after his re-election in 1812, a party agent advised Lord Grey that he surrender his seat, since Catholic relief monopolized his attention. On 11 May 1813 he exasperated its supporters by trying to halt the Catholic Relief Bill and substitute a committee on securities; he abstained at the division on 24 May, when the bill was defeated. Thereafter he obstructed all measures for Catholic relief that were not on his exact terms, which greatly perturbed Catholic opinion. In 1816 and 1817 he voted against Grattan's motions for Catholic relief on the grounds that there should be scrutiny of securities that existed elsewhere in Europe, a matter on which he claimed expertise. He deserted the opposition more generally, for example he supported the government's proposed penalties against seditious meetings on 10 March 1817.

Weary of politics, and having failed to persuade the regent to send him as emissary to Württemberg, Hippisley returned to Rome in 1818, whence he sent his dimittis to Sudbury before the 1818 election. In his final years he turned to the question of prison discipline, and publicly advocated the handcrank instead of the treadmill in a pamphlet of 1823; he was also an active magistrate in Somerset. He died in Grosvenor Street, London, on 3 May 1825 in his eightieth year and was buried in the crypt of the Inner Temple Church on 12 May. Monuments were erected to him in both Ston Easton and Inner Temple churches. He was survived by his wife and was succeeded by his son, John. Hippisley's unflagging, though wholly unsuccessful, quest for office led Joseph Jekyll to describe him in 1811 as 'Sir John Coxe Hippisley MP FRS SAS XYZ etc.' (Stokes and Thorne, 206).   ROLAND THORNE

Sources I. F. Jones, *Some notes on the Hippisley family* (1952), 134–6 · W. Stokes and R. G. Thorne, 'Hippisley, Sir John Coxe', HoP, *Commons, 1790–1820*, 4.202–6 · GM, 1st ser., 95/1 (1825), 643 · *BL cat.* · Farington, *Diary*, 3.865 · J. E. Martin, ed., *Masters of the bench of the Hon. Society of the Inner Temple, 1450–1883, and masters of the Temple, 1540–1883* (1883), 90 · F. G. Stephens and M. D. George, eds., *Catalogue of political and personal satires preserved … in the British Museum*, 8 (1947), 112–14, nos. 9923–9923a · GM, 1st ser., 93/1 (1823), 502 · *DNB* · L. S. Benjamin, *The Windham papers*, 2 vols. (1913), 1.52, 159; 2.255, 261, 306, 343 · death duty registers, PRO, IR 26/1045, fol. 343 · J. Ingamells, ed., *A dictionary of British and Irish travellers in Italy, 1701–1800* (1997), 501–2 · GEC, *Baronetage* · *Register of burials at the Temple Church, 1628–1853* (1905) [with introduction by H. G. Woods]
Archives Biblioteca Apostolica Vaticana, Vatican City, corresp. · BL, corresp. and papers, Egerton MS 2401 · BL, corresp. relating to India, Add. MS 41622 · BL, letters and papers relating to Irish and Roman Catholic affairs · NL Scot., corresp. and papers · Suffolk RO, Bury St Edmunds, corresp. and papers | BL, corresp. with Lord Grenville, Add. MSS 58975–58976 · BL, letters to Lord Hardwicke, Add. MSS 35650–35763, *passim* · BL, corresp. with Lord Liverpool, Add. MSS 38233–38323, 38572, *passim* · BL, corresp. with Sir Robert Peel, Add. MSS 40221–40376, *passim* · BL, letters to second Earl Spencer · BL, corresp. with William Windham, Add. MSS 37848, 37849 · Devon RO, corresp. with Lord Sidmouth · Hunt. L., corresp. with Charles O'Conor · NL Scot., corresp. with Cardinal York · PRO NIre., corresp. with Lord Castlereagh · U. Durham L., letters to second Earl Grey · U. Nott. L., letters to third duke of Portland · Wilts. & Swindon RO, corresp. with earl of Pembroke
Likenesses J. Plura, bust, 1779 · H. Thresham, portrait, 1779 · Pars, portrait, *c*.1780, priv. coll. · G. Head, portrait, after 1795, priv. coll.; repro. in Jones, *Some notes*, 134–6 · effigy on monument, 1825, Ston Easton church, Somerset
Wealth at death under £35,000: PRO, death duty registers, IR 26/1045, fol. 343

Hiraethog, Gruffydd. *See* Gruffudd Hiraethog (d. 1564).

Hiraethog, Gwilym. *See* Rees, William (1802–1883).

Hirsch, Clara de [*née* Clara Bischoffsheim], **Baroness de Hirsch** (1833–1899), philanthropist, was born in Brussels on 18 June 1833, the daughter of the Jewish banker Raphael Jonathan Bischoffsheim (1808–1883) and his wife, Henrietta Goldschmidt. In 1855 Clara married Baron Maurice de *Hirsch (otherwise Moritz von Hirsch) (1831–1896), a distant relative whose family were bankers to the Bavarian royal court, and who in 1850 had entered the Brussels office of her father's business, Bischoffsheim and Goldschmidt, where she acted as secretary and adviser. Her father was deeply immersed in Jewish affairs, becoming in time a member of the central committee of the Alliance Israélite Universelle, formed in Paris in 1860 as an international agency to protect Jewish interests worldwide. Clara de Hirsch was thus able to engage her husband in Jewish philanthropic work while he proceeded to amass a vast fortune as a banker on his own account. In time this wealth secured for him an entrée into the circle of Edward, prince of Wales, of whom he became a very close friend and racing companion.

Maurice de Hirsch was antipathetic to territorial Zionism, regarding the notion of the re-establishment of a Jewish state as fantastic. But he was prepared to believe that the Jews had a future as an agricultural people, and, under Clara's influence, became increasingly drawn to the financing of schemes of agricultural resettlement. He made regular large donations to the Alliance in support of its work in the Middle East, and invested heavily in Jewish educational and welfare schemes in Austria. His donations to London hospitals were prodigious. In 1888 the Baron de Hirsch Foundation was established to further educational reforms among Jews living in Galicia and the Bukovina, and in 1891 the Baron de Hirsch Fund was established in New York to facilitate the settlement of immigrants in the USA and later Canada. But these benefactions were dwarfed by his establishment, in 1891, through a donation of £2.4 million, of the Jewish Colonization Association; based in London, the mission of the association was to relieve the plight of oppressed Russian Jewry by promoting the movement of Jews from Russia first to Argentina, but later to Canada, Brazil, Cyprus, Turkey, and—ultimately—Palestine.

Contemporary observers all agreed that it was Clara who provided the stimulus for these charitable works, many of which were her brainchildren, though executed in the name of her husband. But the couple had a tragic domestic life. Their only daughter died in infancy and their only son, Lucien, born in 1856, died of pneumonia in 1887. Clara and Maurice de Hirsch seemed to have turned instinctively to ever greater acts of philanthropy as a way of filling the void thus created in their lives. Clara de Hirsch made many charitable donations in her own right, notably to the Pasteur Institute and Paris University. On Maurice's death in 1896 she became the sole administrator of his estate, making charitable disbursements totalling £3 million; by the terms of her will a further £2 million were donated for the endowment of a variety of philanthropic causes, including the Jewish Board of Guardians in London.

In 1898, by order of the Emperor Franz Joseph of Austria, Clara de Hirsch was appointed to the order of Elizabeth. As her death approached, she adopted Maurice's two illegitimate male offspring as her own children, successfully petitioning the emperor to confer Maurice's barony upon the elder of the bastard sons, the Oxford-educated Maurice; on his death in 1912 the title passed to his younger brother, Raymond (d. 1968), a close friend of Winston Churchill and Liberal MP for West Ham North from 1911 to 1918.

Clara died of cancer at her Paris home on 1 April 1899 and was buried, two days later, beside her husband in the family vault in the Montmartre cemetery. The presence of the British, Austrian, Belgian, and Italian ambassadors to France at her funeral reflected the esteem in which she was held in these countries. In London the chief rabbi, Hermann Adler, conducted (at the Jewish convalescent home she had endowed in Hampstead) a special memorial service, a remarkable act of homage to a lady who was never, in fact, a British citizen.

GEOFFREY ALDERMAN

Sources T. Norman, *An outstretched arm: a history of the Jewish Colonization Association* (1985) • A. Allfrey, *Edward VII and his Jewish court* (1991) • *Jewish Chronicle* (7 April 1899) • C. Bermant, *The cousinhood: the Anglo-Jewish gentry* (1971) • C. Roth, ed., *Encyclopaedia Judaica*, 16 vols. (Jerusalem, 1971–2)

Hirsch, Maurice de [*formerly* Moritz von Hirsch], **Baron de Hirsch in the Bavarian nobility (1831–1896)**, businessman and philanthropist, was born on 9 December 1831 in Munich, the third child and oldest son of Joseph von Hirsch (1805–1885) and his wife, Karoline Wertheimer. His grandfather Jacob had established the family as one of the first Jewish families to acquire great wealth and social acceptability in Bavaria, and had become a court banker and substantial landowner. He received patents of hereditary nobility in 1818. Moritz's father Joseph carried on these business activities which became centred in Munich. His mother came from an Orthodox Frankfurt family and ensured that the children were properly instructed in Jewish matters.

After attending school in Munich, at the age of thirteen Moritz was sent to Brussels for schooling, receiving, according to his obituary in the *Jewish Chronicle*, a 'plain but sound education'. Though bright he was disinclined to undertake prolonged formal education. At seventeen he joined the banking house of Bischoffsheim and Goldschmidt in Brussels. He was soon regarded as a financial genius with a special interest in railway promotion. Speculation in sugar and cotton shares also brought him rapidly accumulated wealth and promotion. In 1855 he married Clara Bischoffsheim (1833–1899) [see Hirsch, Clara de], daughter of the senior partner, Senator Jonathan Bischoffsheim. After his marriage he moved to Paris to join the board of the branch of Bischoffsheim and Goldschmidt there. The heads of the firm followed his speculations with a certain amount of trepidation, and refrained from making him a partner, though they allowed him to use the firm's facilities for making transactions. The main foundation of his vast fortune came when he purchased the bankrupt firm of Langrand Demonceau. This possessed valuable assets including the rights to construct railways in Turkey and the land upon which to do so. Hirsch then focused his energies upon constructing railways through the Balkans and Turkey, and in particular that linking Vienna and Constantinople—the Orient Express line, as it came to be known—which he eventually completed despite much opposition in Austria.

Hirsch's methods of raising finance were often daring and imaginative and gave rise to accusations of dubious practice, though this was never proved. For example, a section of the Orient Express line was financed by floating a popular loan of 792 million francs in the form of 3 per cent Turkish lottery bonds, for which 1,980,000 tickets at 400 francs each were issued in 1870. There was to be a draw every two months enabling small investors to make quick gains. They were popular in France and Germany.

The bankruptcy of the Turkish state, following the international financial crisis of 1873, led to suspension of payment in 1875 and many of the gamblers lost their stakes. Hirsch was rumoured to have made a fortune from the transaction, though he denied it.

Despite occasional setbacks, by 1890, besides his huge railway interests, banking houses, and a number of industrial firms, Hirsch owned vast estates in Austria–Hungary and France, and was one of the wealthiest men of his day with assets whose worth was estimated at between £16 million and £30 million. That estimates were so much at variance indicates the scale and complexity of his operations, which probably no one but himself could fully comprehend. He worked sometimes in association with other financiers, including, in Britain, Sir Ernest Cassel, whose early career he appears to have nurtured, but the details of such associations remain mysterious. His personal financial activities in Britain appear to have been few and no information is known about them. He attributed his success to mastery of detail, economy in small things, and close personal watch over his transactions, which he combined with undeniable financial flair, and inexhaustible energy and industry. His working day typically began at 5 a.m. and lasted far into the night.

Hirsch was a good-looking man, slim in his younger days, later described by Wolf as 'portly and robust' (Wolf). He was a well-known and ubiquitous member of the smart set in Paris, the south of France, and London. Although a lavish host, he and his wife were frugal in their domestic life. His London address was Bath House, Piccadilly. In France he owned what his obituary in the *Jewish Chronicle* described as a 'princely house' in the rue de l'Élysée palace in Paris and the Château de Beauregard near Chesnay; in Moravia he owned a picturesque castle near Brünn (Brno) and 'enormous property' (*Jewish Chronicle*, 24 April 1896) in Hungary. He supervised the most minute household details of each residence, directing them personally as he did his businesses.

His *Times* obituary commented that 'he carried the same coolness and system [of his business dealings] into his amusements'. Every year he went to London for the season. He belonged to the circle of the prince of Wales (later Edward VII) and shared his interest in horse-racing. His racing-stables, Grafton House at Newmarket, were famous, and his colours were often successful. He just missed winning the Grand Prix with Matchbox in 1894 but with La Flèche won the One Thousand Guineas, the Oaks, and the St Leger, all in 1892, and the Ascot Cup in 1894. It was a source of great disappointment and surprise to him that La Flèche did not win the Derby. He was elected as a foreign member of the Turf Club. This followed his rejection by the Jockey Club in Paris, and he thereafter lived more in London than in Paris. It was not well known that his winnings on the English turf were always donated to London hospitals, but his *Jewish Chronicle* obituary retailed that he liked to tell friends that his horses 'raced for charity'. Substantial sums were involved, amounting to £7000 in 1891, and £35,000 in 1892. When in 1893 his horses won only £7500 he doubled the amount before giving to the hospitals, saying that they should not suffer for the poor performance of his stable. Over the years he gave some £100,000 in total. He loved hunting and was a good shot, and he frequently entertained the prince of Wales, the duke of Devonshire, Lord Curzon, Earl Grey, and other members of the English nobility in Hungary during the hunting season.

Hirsch's wife, Clara de Hirsch, took little pleasure in the social scene, though she often travelled with him. She had more interest in philanthropic activity, especially after the death of their only son Lucien (*b.* 1856) in 1887, of pneumonia. They had previously lost their only other child, a daughter, in infancy. Lucien had been studious and little interested in finance though he appears to have been popular in London society. The parents were inconsolable. Shortly thereafter Hirsch retired from business and both he and his wife devoted themselves to humanitarian causes. He later wrote in response to a letter of condolence: 'My son I have lost, but not my heir, humanity is my heir' (Adler-Rudel, 39).

Hirsch had become active in humane causes even before his son's death, however, probably because of his wife's influence and also as a result of observing the poverty of the Jews of Turkey and the Balkans as he travelled in connection with his railway transactions. He primarily exerted himself to relieve the poverty and persecution suffered by Jews in Turkey and the Balkans, and later in Russia and Galicia. Clara had been secretary to her father when he was a member of the general committee of the Alliance Israélite Universelle, which was the major channel for assistance from rich Jews of prosperous parts of the world to the poor and persecuted. Hirsch also became a committee member, in 1876. In December 1873 he donated a million francs to the Alliance for the furtherance of education in Turkey. From 1879 he contributed an annual 50,000 francs to the training scheme of the Alliance for artisans. From 1882 he underwrote its large annual deficit, keeping it in independent existence. In 1882 he contributed a million francs to an emergency fund for refugees from the Russian pogroms. By the time of his death he had donated at least 12 million francs to the Alliance. An equivalent amount went primarily for the education and training of Jews in Austria against resistance from the government of Austria. In 1889 he opened welfare agencies in towns in central and eastern Europe dispensing aid to those in need, and he supervised these agencies closely. His policy was to give relief only in such a way as positively to assist people to become self-supporting, for example through acquiring training or the tools of a trade. He refused also to give to communities which had other substantial sources of relief, such as the poor of London and Paris.

Hirsch sought to introduce similar schemes in Russia, but faced with the resolute opposition of the government sought instead to assist mass emigration of Jews. He gave large sums to poor Jews arriving in America through the Baron de Hirsch Fund, established in 1891. His agent in Russia from 1890, enquiring about the condition of the Jews and the most effective ways to assist, was the British campaigner against Jewish immigration Arnold White. White believed that immigration of poor Jews was exacerbating poverty in Britain and that Russian Jews should be supported in their native country or in colonies elsewhere, where they could be self-sufficient. Hirsch did not find this objectionable. Above all he wished to establish and endow a safe Jewish colony. He initially expected this to be located somewhere in the Americas, through the instrument of the Jewish Colonization Society which he established in 1891 with headquarters in London to raise money for this enterprise and make it a reality. It was floated with a capital of £2 million issued in shares of £100 each. He held 19,993 of these, the others being taken up by prominent London Jews. He distributed his shares around prominent European Jewish organizations, and invested at least £38 million in this enterprise before his death. He had high hopes of establishing a colony in Argentina, where a large amount of land was purchased and where Jews settled. Smaller colonies were funded elsewhere including, after Hirsch's death, Palestine.

Jewish colonization had become the centre of Hirsch's life and of his incessant work (though his financial dealings never ceased) by the time of his sudden death on 21 April 1896, on the estate of his friend Anton Ehrenfeld in the small village of Ogyalla near Komorn in Hungary. He was having a hunting lodge built nearby. According to his *Jewish Chronicle* obituary an autopsy led to the pronouncement that the cause of death was apoplexy; according to *The Times* he died of heart disease. He was interred in the family vault at the Montmartre cemetery, amid, according to the *Jewish Chronicle*, 'demonstrations of sympathy from all classes of society, from the Head of State and the bearers of the proudest names in the old French aristocracy, down to the meanest Christian ouvrier and the poorest Polish Jewish immigrant'. His wife was his main heir and she carried on the philanthropic and colonizing work on which they had previously worked jointly until her death in 1899. He also left a million francs for various charities, and a million to his adopted daughter (probably the illegitimate daughter of his son) Luciena Premelie. The Hirsches had adopted two boys who were still under age at his death. In his later years he signed himself Maurice de Hirsch, baron, by which time his father, a baron in the Bavarian nobility, had died. He was a citizen of Austria–Hungary at his death.

Arnold White wrote in the *English Illustrated Magazine* (reprinted in the *Jewish Chronicle*, 29 May 1896) after Hirsch's death:

> the roses and raptures with which his wealth and hospitality surrounded him always seemed to me to cover a deep and sterling character of which the gay world knew very little. If he was a little too fond of playing the young man it was only in the hours of relaxation. How many of his censors and traducers, who sneer at what they do not understand, have devoted several hours a day, all the year round over a series of years to remedy the wrongs and lightening the burdens of men, women and children whom they have never seen.

With regard to the allegations then current as to Hirsch's being an 'upstart', White noted that he was born rich:

Except that he became richer as his life developed and expanded, there was no sudden leap from poverty to riches which could turn his head. In his youth there was a theological tutor who presented to the future millionaire so vivid a contrast between precept and practice that for ever after the dogmas of creed ceased to exercise any effect on his mind. He told me that he had never entered a synagogue for worship.

Like his contemporaries historians have barely grasped the many-sidedness of Hirsch's character and career.

PAT THANE

Sources *Jewish Chronicle* (24 April 1896) · *The Times* (22 April 1896) · *Jewish Chronicle* (1 May 1896) · *Jewish Chronicle* (15 May 1896) · A. White, *Jewish Chronicle* (24 April 1896) · L. Wolf, 'Glimpses of Baron De Hirsch', *Jewish Chronicle* (6 May 1896) · S. Adler-Rudel, 'Moritz Baron Hirsch: profile of a great philanthropist', *Leo Baeck Yearbook* (1971), 29–69 · *Jewish Chronicle* (7 April 1899) · C. Roth, ed., *Encyclopaedia Judaica*, 16 vols. (Jerusalem, 1971–2)
Archives Archive of the Jewish Colonization Society
Likenesses photograph, *c.*1875, priv. coll.; repro. in Roth, ed., *Encyclopaedia Judaica*
Wealth at death £1,372,163 10s. 10d.: administration with will, 7 Aug 1896, *CGPLA Eng. & Wales*

Hirschell [Hirschel, Herschell], **Solomon** (1762–1842), chief rabbi, was born in London on 12 February 1762 (not 1761 as often cited). He was the third and youngest son (there were also three daughters) of Polish-born Zevi Hirsch Lewin (1721–1800), who as rabbi of the Great Synagogue, Duke's Place, London, from 1754 to 1764 was generally known as Hart Lyon, and his wife, Golda (d. 1794), daughter of David Tevele Cohen, a leader of the Jewish community of Glogau, Silesia. On his father's side Solomon Hirschell (as he spelled his name, which also appears as Hirschel or Herschell) came of a long line of continental rabbis, some extremely eminent. In early life he was known as Solomon Hart. His formative years were spent in the German states, for in 1764 his father became rabbi of Halberstadt, accepting a call to Mannheim in 1770 and in 1773 to Berlin. Sent to Poland for a traditional Jewish education, and becoming an able Talmudic scholar, Solomon Hirschell toyed with the idea of becoming a wine merchant before embarking on a rabbinic career and taking up a position at Prenzlau, Prussia. In 1791 he offered himself for the vacancy at the Great Synagogue occasioned by the death of his father's successor there, Rabbi David Tevele Schiff, but for economic reasons the congregation made no appointment until 1802, when Hirschell was comfortably elected to the post from a shortlist of three. His British birth helped his case, yet he never mastered the English language, relying on certain congregants when he needed to communicate with the secular authorities. His habitual vehicle was Yiddish. A few of his sermons, notably one giving thanks for the British victory at Trafalgar, were translated into English and appeared in print.

Hirschell married, about 1778, a distant cousin, Rebecca Königsberger (d. 1832). The couple had four sons, David Tevele, Saul, Ephraim, and Hirsch, and four daughters, Golda, Rosa, Feiga (known as Fanny), and Shayndel (known as Jeanette). Apparently despairing of the comparatively lax Jewish observance in London, he sent his

Solomon Hirschell (1762–1842), by Frederick Benjamin Barlin, c.1802

children to live in Poland as soon as they reached marriageable age, and consequently left no descendants in Britain. Two of his sons eventually settled in Jerusalem, where the eldest, Rabbi David Tevele Hirschell (or Berliner), was murdered in 1851.

By the time of Hirschell's appointment the Ashkenazi Jews of Britain significantly outnumbered their Sephardi counterparts, and their three synagogues in London had begun to co-operate with each other on such matters as charitable relief. This trend led to Hirschell, as rabbi of the senior and largest Ashkenazi congregation, being regarded as their natural spokesman, and his authority steadily increased in range. All queries regarding Jewish law and procedure, from Ashkenazi congregations and individuals in Britain as well as in the colonies, came to be directed to him, and he thus became the first chief rabbi of the British empire. He was widely dubbed, in the general press, the 'high priest' of Anglo-Jewry. The designation Doctor, which was used by him from the outset of his career in Britain, was an honorific, presumably adopted to enhance the dignity of his office.

Hirschell's incumbency coincided with several noteworthy developments. There was an upsurge in millenarianism and consequently in missionary activity, with Hirschell vigorously condemning the activities of the London Society for Promoting Christianity Amongst the Jews, founded in 1809. There was, too, a burgeoning genuine philosemitism on the part of influential Britons; a highlight of Hirschell's ministry was a visit to a service at the Great Synagogue that same year by three pro-Jewish sons of George III. In 1827 the Post Office demonstrated its goodwill by quite extraordinarily waiving all postage due on unstamped letters to impecunious Jews in England from friends and relatives in Russia and Poland which were arriving care of Hirschell in ever-increasing numbers and whose cost he would otherwise have continued to bear. The closing years of his life were marked by failing health and by crisis and controversy, such as the trumped-up ritual murder accusation against Damascus Jewry in 1840, about which he issued a public statement, and the formation that same year of a Reform congregation in London, which aggravated him and made him weary of the rabbinate. As a single-minded, inflexible rabbi of the old eastern European type, he could not accommodate demands for change and found himself out of his depth; his successor in office was the moderate and sophisticated Nathan Marcus Adler, who had enjoyed a secular university education.

In 1840 Hirschell fell and broke his thigh, a mishap which sapped his spirit. Two years later he fell again, breaking his collarbone. He died shortly afterwards, on 31 October 1842, at his long-time residence, 5 Bury Court, St Mary Axe, in the City of London. He was buried on 2 November at Mile End, many non-Jewish as well as Jewish shops in the area closing as a mark of respect. A frugal lifestyle and prudent investments enabled him to leave £14,000 in addition to a library of Hebraica, which was acquired by the London Bet Hamidrash ('house of study'), and a Judaica collection which was auctioned. In accordance with his wishes, his personal papers were destroyed at his death.

Hirschell penned no significant writings and made no pastoral visits to congregations outside London except Portsmouth's. Yet he had loyal admirers both within and without the Jewish community; the latter included the eminent Dublin Hebraist James Henthorn Dodd (1805–1869) and Henry Hawkes, a staunchly philosemitic Unitarian minister in Portsmouth, both of whom paid public tribute to Hirschell on his death. Hawkes's address was subsequently published as a pamphlet advocating Jewish emancipation. A medal in Hirschell's memory, bearing his likeness on one side, was commissioned in 1844 from City of London jeweller Henry Hyams; forty were struck, symbolizing the number of years he held office.

HILARY L. RUBINSTEIN

Sources C. Duschinsky, *The rabbinate of the Great Synagogue, London, from 1756–1842* (1921) · C. Roth, *The Great Synagogue, London, 1690–1940* (1950) · H. A. Simon, *Forty years a chief rabbi: the life and times of Solomon Hirschell* (1980) · *Voice of Jacob* [London] (11 Nov 1842) · J. Picciotto, *Sketches of Anglo-Jewish history*, rev. edn, rev. I. Finestein (1956) · H. S. Morais, *Eminent Israelites of the nineteenth century* (1880) · *Jewish World* (16 Jan 1888) [family tree] · *European Magazine and London Review*, 59 (1811), 163–5 · private information (2004) [office of the chief rabbi, London] · H. Rabinowicz, 'Selling the heritage', *TLS* (27 Aug 1999)
Archives Jewish Theological Seminary, New York, Adler MSS · office of the chief rabbis, London, minutes of the London Beth Din; Beth Din corresp. · U. Leeds
Likenesses F. B. Barlin, oils, *c*.1802, NPG [*see illus.*] · S. Drummond, engraving, 1808, NPG · W. Holl, stipple, pubd 1808 (after J. Slater), BM, NPG · W. Ridley, stipple, 1811 (after S. Drummond), BM, NPG;

repro. in *European Magazine and London Review* · H. Hyams, medal, 1844 · G. Abbott, wax bust, N. M. Rothschild & Sons · F. B. Barlin, engraving, NPG · S. Drummond, oils
Wealth at death £14,000; excl. important library of Hebraica: Simon, *Forty years a chief rabbi*

Hirst, Sir Edmund Langley (1898–1975), chemist, was born on 21 July 1898 in Preston, Lancashire, the elder son (there were no daughters) of the Revd Sim Hirst (1856–1923), a Baptist minister, and his wife, Elizabeth (1869–1955), daughter of Joseph Langley, flour merchant and baker, of Liverpool. Owing to the frequent ministries of his father, Edmund Hirst had a mixed schooling. He attended kindergarten in Burnley, had lessons privately, and studied at schools in Burnley and Ipswich, and finally at Madras College, St Andrews. He gained a £40 bursary and a Carnegie scholarship to the University of St Andrews.

In 1917 Hirst was called up for military service and then seconded back to the university for the urgent study of mustard gas. In 1918 he joined the special brigade of the Royal Engineers and saw service in northern France. He returned in February 1919 to study classics, mathematics, and chemistry. Hirst gained his BSc that year with special distinction in chemistry. He was also awarded first-class honours in mathematics and natural philosophy in the MA degree. He then gained a Carnegie research scholarship and studied carbohydrate chemistry under W. N. Haworth, graduating PhD in 1921. In 1923 he secured a lectureship in chemistry at Manchester University and a year later rejoined Haworth who was then at Armstrong College at Newcastle upon Tyne. Thus began a fruitful collaboration which lasted for over twelve years.

In 1925 Hirst married Beda Winifred Phoebe, daughter of Frank Ramsay, solicitor, of Glasgow. However, Beda was soon diagnosed as suffering from an incurable progressive mental illness, which ultimately (1937) led to her hospitalization. In the year of Hirst's marriage, Haworth moved to the Mason chair of chemistry at Birmingham University, and two years later in 1927 appointed Hirst as a lecturer and his assistant director of research. Together they led a talented team of research students which unravelled the molecular structures of simple sugars and complex polysaccharides, and whose work culminated in determining the structure and synthesis of vitamin C.

Hirst obtained his DSc (Birmingham) in 1929 and his readership and fellowship of the Royal Society in 1934. In 1936 he was appointed to the Alfred Capper Pass chair of organic chemistry at Bristol University and began research into starch, plant gums, and mucilages. However, during 1939–44 Hirst was heavily involved in the Bristol laboratories' research on explosives. He served on numerous committees and travelled widely to inspect ordnance factories for the Ministry of Supply. He also served as Home Office senior gas adviser for the southwest region.

In 1944 Hirst was appointed to the Samuel Hall chair of organic chemistry at Manchester University, where he built up a strong research group, planned new laboratories, and served as chairman of the research section of the working party set up by Sir R. Stafford Cripps to report on the cotton industry.

In 1947 Hirst was invited to occupy the newly established Forbes chair of organic chemistry of the University of Edinburgh. Here with a large group of staff and students he spent twenty-one happy years. The move to Edinburgh also marked the beginning of a happier phase in Hirst's private life. Following the dissolution of his first marriage in 1948, Hirst married Kathleen Jenny (Kay), an inspector of schools and daughter of Charles Lyall Harrison, headmaster, in 1949. This marriage was an ideally happy one. Hirst's research work at Edinburgh was devoted to carbohydrate chemistry. His early work established the ring structures of monosaccharides and laid the foundations of his later work on vitamin C and complex polysaccharides. With his colleagues and students he published about 300 papers which made him known worldwide.

Hirst's work was recognized by the award of a Coronation Medal in 1953, appointment as CBE in 1957, and a knighthood in 1964. He received honorary doctorates from the universities of Aberdeen, Birmingham, St Andrews, and Trinity College, Dublin, and the fellowship of Heriot-Watt College. He served twice on the council of the Royal Society, was awarded the Davy medal (1948), and gave the Bakerian lecture (1959). He was president of the Chemical Society (1956–8), and was awarded the Longstaff medal. He was elected to the Royal Society of Edinburgh in 1948 and later served as president (1959–64). He was an honorary member of the Royal Irish Academy (1967) and an honorary fellow of the Royal Scottish Society of Arts (1964). He was also chairman of the chemistry research board of the Department of Scientific and Industrial Research (1950–55).

Hirst's hobbies were hill climbing, gardening, and studies of railways (of which he had an encyclopaedic knowledge). He was of distinguished appearance and of quiet and humorous disposition. He died in Edinburgh on 29 October 1975, survived by his wife, Kay. There were no children from either marriage.

MAURICE STACEY, rev.

Sources M. Stacey and E. Percival, *Memoirs FRS*, 22 (1976), 137–68 · personal knowledge (1986)
Archives RS, corresp. with Sir Robert Robinson · Trinity Cam., corresp. with R. L. M. Synge
Likenesses W. Stoneman, photograph, 1946, RS · W. Bird, photograph, before 1959, RS

Hirst, Francis Wrigley (1873–1953), journalist and writer, was born on 10 June 1873 at Dalton Lodge, near Huddersfield, the third of the five children of Alfred Hirst (*d.* 1913), woolstapler, and his wife, Mary Wrigley (*d.* 1932) of Huddersfield. Brought up within a strong tradition of nonconformity and Liberalism, he was educated at Clifton College (where Asquith's brother, a maternal relative, was a master), and Wadham College, Oxford, one of a remarkable cohort that included C. B. Fry, F. E. Smith, and John Simon. He took a double first in classics (1894, 1896) in which he always found pleasure, and latterly, consolation,

Francis Wrigley Hirst (1873–1953), by Lafayette, 1929

and in 1899 was awarded the Cobden essay prize for political economy. He was also a member of the Russell Club (a Liberal club), president of the Oxford Union, and author with his friends of the influential *Essays in Liberalism by Six Oxford Men* (1897).

In 1896 Hirst gained the first Russell scholarship at the fledgeling London School of Economics, where he was also lecturer in political science from 1897 to 1900. His fruitful co-operation with Josef Redlich led in 1903 to the publication of the latter's classic *Local Government in England*. Hirst also read for the bar at the Inner Temple and was called in 1899, but far more influential for his future was the time he spent during the Second South African War devilling for John Morley's *Life of Gladstone*. For he fully shared Morley's distaste for the war, and played a significant part in the pro-Boer movement, particularly the League against Armaments and Militarism. In *Liberalism and Empire* (1900), written with his friends J. L. Hammond and Gilbert Murray, he expressed a traditional radical dislike of excessive public expenditure on armaments, but with the progressive rider that this might also crowd out potential social expenditures. He now became wholeheartedly attached to the Cobdenite creed of free trade, peace, and goodwill among nations, to which the rest of his life was fervidly devoted. His views were well summarized in his important collection *Free Trade and other Fundamental Doctrines of the Manchester School* (1903), while doctrinal attachments took a more personal form with his marriage on 25 July 1903 to Helena Mary Carroll Cobden (*d.* 1965), the great-niece of Richard. They had no children.

Hirst was not a success at the bar, and increasingly devoted himself to writing and journalism. His early works included *Adam Smith* (1904) and *Monopolies, Trusts and Kartels* (1905). In 1899 he helped Hammond set up *The Speaker*, for which he wrote regularly as well as for the *Manchester Guardian*, *The Tribune* (as its City editor), and *The Nation*. Although one of the band of influential radical journalists who did so much to revivify the post-Gladstonian Liberal Party, Hirst's own bent was less towards social reform than towards reasserting the permanent value of free trade and a pacific foreign policy. He thus played a key literary part, especially through the publications of the Cobden Club, in the Edwardian campaign against tariff reform, and even more so in the crusade against armaments expenditure. In *The Arbiter in Council* (1905), commissioned by the radical John Pennington Thomasson, he mused in Socratic style on war and peace, but in a more practical vein he worked with Sir Robert Reid for the reform of international maritime law.

Having made a reputation for his lucid writing and sprightly intelligence, in February 1907 Hirst was appointed the editor of *The Economist*, which he succeeded in returning to the weight it had enjoyed under Bagehot as a journal both for the City financier and for the Liberal public. At Oxford, Hirst had studied economics with F. Y. Edgeworth and combined an interest in the statistical and technical with broader political interests, which he sustained by writing his own pungent leaders. He also recruited a string of talented journalists, including its first woman journalist, Mary Hamilton, despite his own strong anti-feminism (the source of a temporary separation from his wife in 1912). He continued to write specialist works (for example, *The Stock Exchange* in 1911) as well as polemical brochures promoting continuity between the Gladstonian past and the more fashionable tenets of the Edwardian new Liberalism. He was also an influential 'Trouble Maker', seeking the support of Liberals such as Sir John Brunner in his attempts to foster Anglo-German friendship and to reduce armaments expenditure. In 1913 he published *The Six Panics* (1913), updating Cobden's classic dissection of war-scaremongering. Although defeated at Sudbury in the general election of January 1910, Hirst, with the circulation of *The Economist* rising, was one of the most powerful Liberal voices of Edwardian Britain, dogmatically arguing that permanent progress depended on free trade, retrenchment, and peace.

The outbreak of the First World War—'perhaps the greatest tragedy of human history' (*The Economist*, 8 Aug 1914)—tested Hirst's creed to the full. While not strictly a principled pacifist, he—like his close friend and mentor, Morley—abhorred Britain's decision to enter the war. The self-conscious guardian of the 'old Liberal' principles in wartime, he campaigned trenchantly against conscription, irresponsible war finance, the threat of protection, and the threat the war posed to civil liberties. He even returned to the bar of the House of Lords to defend the case of Arthur Zadig, prosecuted under the Defence of the Realm Act. Given his outspoken position, it was surprising that it was not until July 1916 that he was forced to resign from *The Economist*. He now set up his own paper, *Common Sense* (financed by anti-Lloyd George Liberals), devoted to a negotiated peace, retrenchment, and economy. In 1917 he acted as the linchpin of Lord Lansdowne's negotiated peace initiative, and was among the leading British radicals consulted by Colonel House before the formulation of Woodrow Wilson's Fourteen Points. After the war Hirst took part in a series of public economy movements, and was also involved in bodies such as the Carnegie Endowment for International Peace and the Cobden Club. He remained a thorough and persistent analyst of budgetary policy, publishing a string of works preaching with fearless but unfashionable rectitude the moral necessity of retrenchment. But with the folding of *Common Sense* in June 1921 his real influence within Liberalism greatly diminished.

In the 1920s Hirst's pen was prolifically deployed not only in journalism but in correspondence with a vast range of politicians and publicists around the world. He lectured in South Africa, Austria, and extensively in the United States, where he numbered Hoover and Roosevelt among his friends. His more permanent writings—on the history of free trade, Jefferson, and Morley—reflected the beliefs he strove to keep alive in the Liberal Party. The last of these testified to a friend whose 'life had consoled me more than anything else for the horror, cruelties and perversities of this hateful age' (Hirst to J. L. Hammond, 27 Sept 1923, Hirst papers). In more optimistic vein Hirst hoped his friend Simon might seize the political initiative from Lloyd George, while he himself vainly fought Shipley in the general election of 1929. Having come to appreciate the Labour government's anti-protectionist policies, Hirst came briefly to prominence during the political crisis of 1931 when he orchestrated the opposition to the introduction of tariffs by the National Government. His unchanged message of public economy and balanced budgets was reinforced by the timely publication of *Gladstone as Financier and Economist* (1931), while as chairman of the Liberal Free Trade Committee he sought energetically to keep the Liberal Party loyal to its past principles. In the early 1930s he became the literal as well as ideological custodian of the Cobdenite legacy, taking charge of the Dunford House Cobden Memorial Association and organizing lectures and conferences on familiar themes. The pure milk of the 'Cobdenian faith' strongly informed his substantial study *The Consequences of the War to Britain* (1934), and in *Liberty and Tyranny* (1935) he powerfully restated his belief in individual and economic liberty in the face of the distasteful contemporary trends towards totalitarianism and socialism.

As the Second World War approached, Hirst supported the League of Nations Union (chairing its economic committee) and the Munich agreement. During the war he was still 'a convinced Lansdownian', as he told Liddell Hart (20 Aug 1940, King's, Lond., Liddell Hart MSS), in whom he found perhaps an unlikely fellow spirit in his crusade against conscription and total war. He signed the Society of Individualists' manifesto on British liberty in 1942 and issued from the seclusion of Dunford House his Cassandra-like warnings about the perils of huge increases in expenditure and bureaucratic servitude. After the war he emerged as a critic of Keynesian finance and the welfare state (the 'Beveridge Hoax') but he welcomed the Atlantic charter and what he saw, with characteristic wishful thinking, as its potential for the rebuilding of the world according to Cobden's teaching. In 1946 he helped organize in elegiac vein the centenary celebrations of the repeal of the Corn Laws. While still the epitome of the 'stern and unbending Cobdenite', Hirst's affability and witty conversation continued late into his life to charm the young, including the dons of his old college, where he had been elected an honorary fellow. He was also governor of the London School of Economics for almost forty years.

Hirst was a keen fisherman and chess player. He retained into old age his youthful appearance, while A. F. Thompson recalled him as 'intellectually tough, morally hard … courteous and lovable, kindly and gay' (*F. W. Hirst by his Friends*, 39). In 1948 he published a first volume of memoirs, *In the Golden Days* (which ended pointedly in 1906). He died, following long illness and influenza, at the Drove Hotel, Singleton, Sussex, on 22 February 1953. His stalwart liberal political economy, antiquated in his day, has not been without parallels in the more recent revival of libertarian and free-market ideas.   A. C. HOWE

Sources Bodl. Oxf., MSS Hirst · DNB · F. W. Hirst, *In the golden days* (1948) · *F. W. Hirst by his friends* (1958) · A. Howe, *Free trade and liberal England, 1846–1946* (1997) · R. Dudley Edwards, *The pursuit of reason: The Economist, 1843–1993* (1993) · *The Economist* (1907–16) · *Common Sense* (1916–21) · F. W. Hirst, *The formation, history and aims of the Liberal Free Trade Committee, 1931–1946* (1947) · P. F. Clarke, *Liberals and social democrats* (1978) · W. Sussex RO, Cobden papers [incl. Cobden Club and Dunford House papers] · Bodl. Oxf., MSS Gilbert Murray · Bodl. Oxf., MSS Simon

Archives BL OIOC, corresp. and papers, MS Eur. D 573 · BLPES, papers relating to local government · Bodl. Oxf., papers · priv. coll., Hirst budget papers | BLPES, Beveridge papers · BLPES, Courtney papers · BLPES, League of Nations Union papers · BLPES, letters to Edwin Cannan · Bodl. Oxf., Hammond papers · Bodl. Oxf., Ensor papers · Bodl. Oxf., corresp. with Gilbert Murray · Bodl. Oxf., corresp. with Lord Simon · Col. U., James Truslow Adams papers · Col. U., J. B. Clark papers · Harvard U., Houghton L., corresp. with Oswald Garrison Villard · JRL, letters to *Manchester Guardian* · JRL, corresp. with James Ramsay MacDonald · King's Cam., Keynes papers · King's Lond., Liddell Hart C., corresp. with Sir B. H. Liddell Hart · NRA, letters to John Stewart Bryan · TCD, corresp. with John Dillon · U. Cam., Marshall Library of Economics, letters to John Maynard Keynes · U. Lpool L., letters to Sir John Brunner · U. Newcastle, Robinson L., corresp. with Walter Runciman · Virginia State Library, Richmond, John Stewart Bryan papers · W. Sussex RO, Cobden (incl. Cobden Club and Dunford House) papers

Likenesses Lafayette, photograph, 1929, NPG [*see illus.*] · G. C. Beresford, photograph, NPG · photograph, repro. in Hirst, *In the golden days*, facing p. 32 · photograph, repro. in *F. W. Hirst by his friends*, frontispiece

Wealth at death £11,013 9s. 5d.: probate, 29 April 1953, CGPLA Eng. & Wales

Hirst, George Herbert (1871–1954), cricketer, was born at Kirkheaton, near Huddersfield, on 7 September 1871, the son of Mary Elizabeth Woolhouse. He left school at ten and worked first as a hand-loom weaver and then at a neighbouring dye works. By the time he was fifteen he was in the village eleven, winning prizes both for batting and bowling offered by a local newspaper. Subsequently he played for stronger clubs such as Elland, Mirfield, and Huddersfield, and made his first-class début for Yorkshire against Somerset in 1891. Two years later he had established himself in the Yorkshire side, taking ninety-nine wickets in all first-class matches in the season at an average of 14.39. In 1894 he made his first century—against Gloucestershire—while taking ninety-eight wickets. The bowler's century of wickets came in 1895, followed in

1896 by the 'double' of over 1000 runs and 100 wickets during the season. This feat he performed on fourteen different occasions, eleven of them consecutively. On 1 January 1896 Hirst married Emma (*b.* 1873/4), daughter of George Kilner, a miner; they had one son and two daughters.

A stocky, powerfully built man, Hirst bowled left-arm at above medium pace. He could make the ball swing late and dip sharply into the batsman. The cricket historian H. S. Altham wrote that his bowling had 'a resiliency, vigour and optimism which from the very outset claimed from the batsman the moral supremacy' (Altham, 254). He batted right-handed and his quickness of eye and foot presented difficulties to those who bowled to him. His favourite strokes were the hook and the pull. His great value, as a batsman, was to rescue a team in crisis, frequently from a lower-order position.

For one who would prove so remarkable a county cricketer—Lord Hawke, his county captain, called him 'the greatest of all time' (*Wisden*, 1955, 931)—Hirst did not have a distinguished record as a test cricketer. He played his first test at Sydney in 1897. Both on that Australian tour (1897–8) and that of 1903–4 he achieved little as a bowler or batsman. Hard Australian wickets did not suit his bowling nor large grounds his hooking. He appeared in every home England series between 1899 and 1909. At Edgbaston in 1902 he took three for 15 in the dismissal of Australia for 36. Bowling at the other end—with seven for 17—was his Yorkshire colleague Wilfred Rhodes. The two men dominated Yorkshire cricket, as all-rounders, for almost a quarter of a century. Hirst took five for 9 against the same Australians, though not in a test match, at Headingley four days later. In the fifth test of that series, at the Oval, he made two notable batting contributions. His 43 (batting at number eight) saved England from following-on and his 58 not out (after a century by G. L. Jessop) gave England a one-wicket victory. He and Rhodes came together with 15 needed. Hirst allegedly said 'We'll get them in ones.' Save for a single two they did so in forty-five minutes. His best bowling performance in test matches was against the Australians in the first test at Edgbaston in 1909, when he took nine for 86. He bowled, except for two overs, throughout the match. Yet he was not an automatic choice for England and the fourth test, at Old Trafford, proved to be his last. In twenty-four tests (1897–1909) he secured fifty-nine wickets (average 30.00) and scored 790 runs (average 22.57).

It was as a Yorkshire bowler that Hirst performed the majority of his feats. In 1901 he had figures of seven for 12 against Leicestershire. The latter county lost seven for 18 against him in 1906, while he took five for 15 against Worcestershire. In that season he achieved a feat which will probably never be matched in the context of first-class cricket, the double 'double', by scoring 2385 runs (average 45.86) and taking 208 wickets (average 16.50). It drew no comment from the editor of *Wisden*, but Yorkshire recognized that the figures, remarkable as they were, did 'not give anything like an adequate idea of what his presence meant to the eleven' (*Wisden*, 1907, 23). A bank holiday crowd at Bath saw him make 111 and 117 not out, and take eleven for 115. 'It was quite Hirst's match' (ibid., 198). Hirst's highest score came in 1905, when he made 341 against Leicestershire. Yorkshire's reply to Leicestershire's 419 stood at 22 for three when Hirst began an innings which lasted for seven hours and included fifty-four boundaries. Not surprisingly, he did not bowl in the Leicestershire innings as Yorkshire just failed to dismiss their opponents twice. His triple century remained the highest score ever made for Yorkshire beyond the end of the twentieth century. In the remaining years until the outbreak of the First World War he performed the 'double' in all but one season.

In 1914 Hirst was forty-three, and his war work lay in a munitions factory while playing on Saturday afternoons in the Bradford league. When first-class cricket resumed in 1919 he achieved his customary 1000 runs, though the county largely rested on him as a bowler. During the summer of 1920 he was appointed coach at Eton College, where he remained until 1938. During this time Eton was undefeated by Harrow at Lord's. Both as coach to the young men of aristocratic mould at Eton and to the Yorkshire lads whom he saw in the school holidays he was successful, impressive, respected, and 'frankly adored' (Thomson, 84). When he retired from Eton he was chief guest at a dinner at which the flower of Eton cricket was present.

Hirst had played for Yorkshire in the Eton holidays of 1921 and, on his fiftieth birthday, he led the Players to victory against the Gentlemen at Scarborough. He was a modest man, gentle in character, courteous in manner, and blessed with a smiling countenance. He was genuinely overcome by the warmth of the farewell that the Scarborough crowd gave him. Yet humour lurked. 'When you're both a batsman and a bowler, you enjoy yourself twice as much' (Thomson, 90). The enjoyment continued, with a last appearance at the Scarborough festival in 1929 and with club appearances until his seventies. In first-class cricket he made 36,356 runs (average 34.13) with sixty centuries and took 2742 wickets (average 18.73), while 604 catches were some measure of his outstanding ability as a mid-off.

Yorkshire awarded Hirst a benefit in 1904, which raised £3703 after deductions. No other pre-1914 benefit was comparable. Within the context of his day Hirst made a competent living from the game of cricket. Cricket rewarded him, on other terms, with honorary membership of MCC in 1949—deservedly one of twenty-six former professionals so recognized. He died at his home, 33 Glebe Street, Marsh, Huddersfield, on 10 May 1954.

M. M. REESE, rev. GERALD M. D. HOWAT

Sources Wisden (1955) · A. A. Thomson, Hirst and Rhodes (1959) · R. Webber, Cricket records (1961) · H. S. Altham, A history of cricket (1926), pt 1 · CGPLA Eng. & Wales (1954)
Likenesses Spy [L. Ward], caricature, lithograph, NPG; repro. in VF (20 Aug 1903)
Wealth at death £5844 10s. 10d.: probate, 9 Aug 1954, CGPLA Eng. & Wales

Hirst [formerly Hirsch], **Hugo**, **Baron Hirst** (1863–1943), electrical engineer and company manager, was born in Munich on 26 November 1863, the son of Emanuel Hirsch, a distiller. Educated in Munich, he at first studied chemistry, intending to go into his father's business, but instead moved to Britain and entered the electrical industry. He took the name Hirst on naturalization in 1883 and three years later joined Gustav Byng, who had founded a firm for the sale of electrical appliances. He married in 1892 his cousin, Leontine Hirsch (d. 1938).

Hirst had the vision to see the possibilities which lay in the manufacture of electrical appliances, and the determination necessary to carry the project through to success. In 1889 friends put up the capital which enabled the formation of the General Electric Company (GEC), of which Hirst became managing director in 1900 and chairman in 1910; he held both appointments until his death. By that time, the company had some forty factories in Great Britain, as well as subsidiary organizations in Commonwealth and other countries, and GEC was known the world over for the manufacture and supply of every kind of electrical equipment.

The leading position which the company attained was due in no small measure to the creative energy with which Hirst matched the opportunities offered by a new and expanding industry. He was among the first to realize the importance of research, and before long the company had its own laboratories doing valuable work at Wembley. He had, moreover, the wisdom—and the humility—to rely upon his staff, giving them responsibility, a full share of credit, and his unfailing support. He believed strongly in the advantages of attracting university and public-school recruits into industry, and himself employed them wherever possible. In staff relations the company was ahead of its time, for Hirst, a sincere and kindly man, of simple and unaffected manner, never forgot that, however vast it might become, his organization comprised human beings. He himself enjoyed a game of billiards or golf, kept a good racing stable, was one of the earliest motorists, and took a keen personal interest in providing for the welfare and recreation of his employees.

Hirst was generous in his benefactions, which included a gift of £20,000 to the benevolent fund of the Institution of Electrical Engineers, of which he became an associate in 1888, a member ten years later, and an honorary member in 1935. Prominent, as was natural, in all that concerned his own industry, he was active also in a wider field, for he always felt himself deeply indebted to the country which had given him his chance and he rarely missed an opportunity to forward the cause of British industry or empire. From the days of Joseph Chamberlain, he was a convinced protectionist and for nearly twenty years was treasurer of the Empire Industries Association. He was also chairman of the empire committee of the Federation of British Industries, and he presided over the federation itself in 1936 and 1937. He came to be recognized by the government as an expert in international trading and he served at various times as a member of the advisory council of the Board of Trade, as economic adviser to the cabinet research committee, as a member of the cabinet trade and employment panel, and on the committee on industrial research. He was also a member of the Blanesburgh committee of inquiry into unemployment insurance (1925–7) and of the committee of inquiry into the possibilities of co-operative selling in the coal industry (1926). He took part in the Mond–Turner discussions in 1928, and later in the year went with three others on a prolonged economic mission to Australia, which would have proved more fruitful had not the world economic crisis supervened.

For his services, Hirst was created a baronet in 1925, and in 1934 was raised to the peerage as Baron Hirst of Witton, Warwickshire. The Hirsts had two daughters and one son, Harold, who died in 1919 of an illness resulting from four years' active service on various fronts. Four months after the latter's death, a son, Hugh, was born, who was killed on operational duties as a pilot officer in 1941. The peerage therefore became extinct when Hirst died, of heart failure, at his home, Foxhill, White Knights Park, near Reading, on 22 January 1943. His body was cremated at Golders Green on 26 January 1943. H. M. PALMER, *rev.*

Sources *The Times* (25 Jan 1943), 6f · *The Times* (26 Jan 1943), 6f · *The Electrician* (29 Jan 1943), 102–4 · C. C. Paterson, 'Lord Hirst', *Nature*, 151 (1943), 218 · *Journal of the Institute of Electrical Engineers*, 90 (Dec 1943), 537 · d. cert. · *CGPLA Eng. & Wales* (1943)
Archives Marconi archives, Chelmsford, corresp. of and relating to articles, speeches | BL OIOC, letters to Lord Reading · BLPES, letters to tariff commission
Likenesses photographs, GEC–Marconi, Hugo Hirst MSS
Wealth at death £498,650: probate, 4 June 1943, *CGPLA Eng. & Wales*

Olive Mirzl Hirst (1912–1994), by Baron Studios, 1964

Hirst, Olive Mirzl (1912–1994), advertising agent, was born in Mortlake, Surrey, on 20 June 1912. Little is known of her early life. She was educated at the Abbey School, Mill Hill, north London, which she left in 1930 to work in the overseas department of Sells, an advertising agency founded in 1869, as secretary to H. G. Wood. She remained with Wood, who in 1935 became chairman and managing director, helping him to run Sells and its accounts, which included Brylcreem and Timothy Whites. With experience of all the departments, she was responsible for setting up the film and screen advertising department. Sells was given the Post Office contract during the Second World War, and it was Olive Hirst who had the idea of selling advertising space in books of stamps, a scheme which brought in extra revenue for the Post Office.

In 1950 Hirst was appointed a director of Sells, and on the death of Wood later that year she became managing director, the first woman to become managing director of a British advertising agency. She was also elected, in 1950, the first woman vice-chair of the Publicity Club of London, having served on the council and as secretary to the finance committee since 1946. She chaired the membership committee from 1946 to 1951, a period in which more than 900 new members joined. Sells was awarded the Publicity Club's prestigious Layton trophy in 1959. Hirst was the first woman fellow of the Institute of Practitioners in Advertising, and the first woman to be elected to its council.

Hirst was also an influential member of the Women's Advertising Club of London (WACL), of which she was president from 1959 to 1960. The WACL, founded in 1924 to act as hostesses to the overseas delegates to the International Advertising Convention, developed into a group of fifty women holding senior positions in advertising, including chairwomen and directors of advertising agencies. Membership was by invitation only, and the club held monthly dinner meetings with speakers and maintained close contact with similar clubs abroad, especially in the United States. Hirst was one of the main instigators of a project which led to the publication of Patricia Mann's *150 Careers in Advertising, with Equal Opportunity for Men and Women* (1971), with cartoons by Ralph Steadman, sponsored by the WACL. Aimed at school leavers, graduates, and those who came to advertising from another career, the book explained career opportunities in advertising for women and men, but, recognizing that advertising was a business where women could more easily find a good job, it included information especially for women, written by women.

After she retired from Sells, Hirst worked for several years for an international oil equipment company. A Roman Catholic, she was involved in the advertising for the Catholic Information Centre. In her leisure time she liked to paint. She died of lung cancer at the Hospital of St John and St Elizabeth, Westminster, on 26 February 1994. Unmarried, she was survived by two brothers and a sister. ANNE PIMLOTT BAKER

Sources P. Mann, *150 careers in advertising, with equal opportunity for men and women* (1971) · *The Times* (4 March 1994) · d. cert. · *CGPLA Eng. & Wales* (1994)

Hirst, Thomas Archer (1830–1892), mathematician, was
born on 22 April 1830 in Heckmondwike, West Riding of
Yorkshire, the youngest son of Thomas Hirst (1797–1842),
wool-stapler, and his wife, Hannah, daughter of John
Oates, wool merchant and shipowner. In 1828 his father
retired from business and moved to Wakefield to educate
his three surviving sons, and in 1840 Hirst entered the
West Riding proprietary school where 'Mathematics was
my favourite study' (Hirst, 799). In 1845 he was articled for
five years to an engineering surveyor in Halifax, surveying
for the West Yorkshire Railway, and meeting and working
with John Tyndall, a close friend whom he greatly
admired and who would have a major influence on his
life.

On arriving in Halifax, Hirst began to record his experiences in a journal, which became a major chronicle of
scientific life in the Victorian era. Covering over forty-five
years and amounting to almost two million words, his
diaries describe with clarity and perceptiveness the scientific circles in which he lived and the people he met—both
in England and on the continent. Inspired by Tyndall, he
embarked on a programme of self-improvement, enrolling at the Halifax Mechanics' Institute and reading widely
in literature and the sciences. Meanwhile, in 1848, Tyndall
had left Halifax with Edward Frankland to study for a doctorate in Marburg, Germany. Hirst visited them, and on
completing his apprenticeship in 1850 returned there to
study chemistry with Robert Bunsen, physics with Christian Gerling, and mathematics with Friedrich Stegmann.
He was particularly interested in geometry, which
became a lifelong passion, and within two years wrote a
PhD dissertation on conjugate diameters of the triaxial
ellipsoid.

With the successful completion of his dissertation in
July 1852, Hirst decided to travel, first to Göttingen, where
he conducted magnetic experiments with Wilhelm
Weber and met Carl Friedrich Gauss, and then to Berlin,
where he spent the winter semester attending the lectures of Lejeune Dirichlet, the analyst and number theorist, and the geometer Jakob Steiner. On returning to England in mid-1853 he secured a teaching job at Queenwood
College in Hampshire, where practical work was encouraged, and he presented geometry in the context of surveying, rather than through rote learning of Euclid's *Elements*.
Whenever he could he visited London to see Tyndall and
attend the lectures of Michael Faraday and others at the
Royal Institution.

In Marburg, Hirst had struck up an acquaintance with
Anna Martin, the sister of the Irish naturalist John Martin
(1812–1875), and he married her on 28 December 1854.
Shortly after their wedding Anna began to exhibit signs of
advancing tuberculosis. Hirst gave up his post to look after
her, and they visited the spas of southern France vainly
seeking a cure. In July 1857 Anna died. Hirst never fully
recovered from the tragedy of her death, and did not

Thomas Archer Hirst (1830–1892), by Maull & Co., *c*.1866

marry again. He decided to devote his life to research
rather than returning to teaching, and settled in Paris
where he befriended some of the foremost French mathematicians of the day—Michel Chasles, Joseph Liouville,
and Louis Poinsot. He read widely, translated many mathematical and scientific works into English, and investigated problems in geometry. In August 1858 he left for
Italy to work with mathematicians in Rome, Naples, and
Milan. He was able to live on his own resources, having
inherited a substantial sum from his mother in 1849. In
mid-1859 he returned to England, obtaining lodgings near
Tyndall, who introduced him to the London scientific
scene. He became acquainted with the mathematicians
James Joseph Sylvester and Arthur Cayley, and attended
lectures by Thomas Huxley and others. From 1860 to 1864
he taught mathematics at University College School.

Hirst quickly became a key figure in the London scientific establishment. In April 1861 he became a fellow of the
Royal Society, and he was elected to its council in November 1864. He was a founder member of the X-club, a group
that met monthly to debate the scientific issues of the day,
untrammelled by religious dogmas; this club was to influence the organization and image of English science for
the next twenty years. He was active in the formation of
the London Mathematical Society in 1865, becoming its
first vice-president and later (in 1872–4) its president. In
1866 he was admitted a fellow of the Royal Astronomical

Society, and became general secretary of the British Association for the Advancement of Science, an onerous post which he held for four years. Meanwhile, he continued to travel widely throughout Europe, meeting mathematicians and attending meetings.

On 18 August 1865 Hirst was appointed professor of mathematical physics at University College, London, one of only seven physics professors in the country. Two years later he became professor of mathematics, replacing Augustus De Morgan who had resigned. However, his duties took up much time, and in 1870 he resigned his chair and became assistant registrar in the University of London in order to gain more time for his researches. One of his lasting contributions was to mathematics education. Long convinced that Euclid's *Elements* should be supplanted as the main geometry textbook in English schools, he helped to establish the Association for the Improvement of Geometrical Teaching (later, the Mathematical Association), and was its first president, for eight years.

In 1873 Hirst embarked on his final role when he became the first director of studies at the Royal Naval College in Greenwich. This position enabled him to stay in touch with the international mathematical community, entertaining such major figures as Felix Klein and Pafnuty Chebyshev. In 1878 he was elected to membership of the Cambridge Philosophical Society, and in 1883 the Royal Society awarded him its prestigious royal medal. He resigned his Greenwich post in 1883, due to ill health. As the 1880s continued, he increasingly withdrew from his various activities. In the winter of 1891–2 London was hit by one of the worst influenza epidemics of the century, and Hirst quickly succumbed. He died at his home, 7 Oxford and Cambridge Mansions, Marylebone, on 16 February 1892 and was buried in Highgate cemetery four days later.

Hirst's geometrical researches are largely forgotten today. Although his twenty papers were published in major journals, his work on such topics as equally attracting surfaces, the inversion of curves, and the correlation of planes, quickly went out of fashion as mathematics developed in other directions. ROBIN J. WILSON

Sources T. A. Hirst, journals, Royal Institution of Great Britain, London • W. H. Brock and R. M. MacLeod, *Natural knowledge in social context, the journals of Thomas Archer Hirst FRS* (1980) [booklet and microfiche] • H. J. Gardner and R. J. Wilson, 'Thomas Archer Hirst—mathematician Xtravagant', *American Mathematical Monthly*, 100 (1993), 435–41, 531–8, 619–25, 723–31, 827–34, 907–15 • *DNB* • *The Times* (18 Feb 1892) • *Men and women of the time* (1891) • d. cert.
Archives Royal Institution of Great Britain, London, journals | BL, letters from John Tyndall, Add. MS 63092 • RAS, letters to RAS • UCL, corresp. relating to London Mathematical Society
Likenesses Maull & Co., photograph, c.1866, UCL [*see illus.*] • photograph, c.1866, London Mathematical Society • photograph, c.1866, RS • portrait, Royal Naval College, Greenwich; repro. in *Journal of the London Mathematical Society* (1966)
Wealth at death £14,640 15s. 5d.: resworn probate, July 1892, CGPLA Eng. & Wales

Hirst, William (d. 1770?), astronomer, was the eldest son of William Hirst DD (d. 1760), master of Hertford Free School, vicar of Bengeo, and rector of Sacomb, Hertfordshire. He was educated at Peterhouse, Cambridge, where he obtained his BA in 1750–51 as fifteenth junior optime and proceeded MA in 1754. He became a naval chaplain. In April 1754, being then resident at Hornsey, Middlesex, he sent the Royal Society an account of a fire-ball seen there, which led to his election as fellow on 20 February 1755. That year he sailed in the *Hampton Court* (64 guns) to Lisbon after the earthquake, and made a drawing of the city in its ruins. In 1759 he was chaplain of the *Lenox* (74 guns) and secretary to Rear-Admiral Samuel Cornish on the East India station, where he was present at the sieges of Pondicherry and Vellore. On 6 June 1761 he observed the transit of Venus across the sun at Government House, Madras, in company with the governor, afterwards Lord Pigot.

In March 1762, Hirst left the Royal Navy and joined the East India Company, to be appointed chaplain to the factory of Calcutta by the favour of Henry Vansittart, then governor of Bengal, and in November of that year he sent to the Royal Society an account of a severe earthquake in Bengal and of two eclipses of the sun and moon observed at Calcutta. His astronomical observations were used in the compilation of Dunn's map of Bengal. Among the surveys taken home by Vansittart was a 'map of the River Samelpore, laid down by Mr Hirst' (BL OIOC, Orme MSS, 134). In December 1764 Hirst returned to England with Vansittart in HMS *Medway*. On the voyage he took a view of the Cape of Good Hope, which was engraved in 1766 by Peter Charles Canot. At the invitation of the astronomer royal, Hirst observed the second transit of Venus on 3 June 1769 at the Royal Observatory, Greenwich, with Vansittart recording the times for him.

Hirst then took chambers in Fig Tree Court, Inner Temple, London. Though in comfortable circumstances, his old friendship induced him to accompany Vansittart, sent out as one of three commissioners by the East India Company in 1769 to investigate alleged corruption in company affairs in India. Hirst was chaplain to the commission, and his friend William Falconer was purser of the *Aurora*, the frigate in which they sailed. A Latin ode, 'Ad amicum navigaturum', addressed to Hirst on the occasion by James Kirkpatrick MD, was printed in the *Gentleman's Magazine* (39, 1769, 550). The *Aurora* sailed for Bengal from the Cape of Good Hope on 27 December 1769, but was never heard of again. Some of Hirst's letters to John Duncombe and William Fazakerley were printed in Duncombe's *Letters by Several Eminent Persons Deceased* (Duncombe, 3.84, 94, 142, 154, 159). GORDON GOODWIN, *rev.* DEREK HOWSE

Sources *GM*, 1st ser., 39 (1769), 550 • *GM*, 1st ser., 41 (1771), 190 • W. Hirst, 'An account of a fire-ball, seen at Hornsey', *PTRS*, 48 (1753–4), 773–6 • W. Hirst, 'An account of an observation of the transit of Venus over the sun', *PTRS*, 52 (1761–2), 396–8 • E. Gulston, 'An account of an earthquake at Chattigaon', *PTRS*, 53 (1763), 251–6 • W. Hirst, 'An account of an earthquake in the East Indies', *PTRS*, 53 (1763), 256–62 • W. Hirst, 'Account of several phaenomena observed during the ingress of Venus into the solar disc', *PTRS*, 59 (1769), 228–35 • Revd A. G. Kealy's MS list of Royal Navy chaplains, 1887, PRO • R. H. Phillimore, ed., *Historical records of the survey of India*, 1 (1945), 339 • D. Hepper, *British warship losses in the age of sail, 1650–1859* (1994), 47 • J. Duncombe, *Letters by several eminent persons* *deceased ... with notes explanatory and historical*, 2nd edn, 3 vols. (1773)

Hislop, Joseph Dewar (1884–1977), singer and singing teacher, was born at 16 Bowmont Place, Edinburgh, on 5 April 1884, the second child in the family of two sons and two daughters of Joseph Dewar Hislop (1849–1915), painter and decorator, and his wife, Mary White Lunn (d. c.1935). He was educated in the choir school of St Mary's Episcopal Cathedral, Edinburgh. He left school, trained as a photo-process engraver in Edinburgh and London, and then took up the post of demonstrator in a firm at Göteborg, Sweden, in 1907. In his spare time he sang in a male voice choir, Till Sång. His potential was recognized in 1910 by a visiting soloist who introduced him to Dr Gillis Bratt in Stockholm. Hislop trained with Bratt. After attending the Royal Opera School and making a test recording for the Gramophone Company at Hayes, Middlesex, in June 1914, he made his début as a principal singer at the Royal Swedish Opera, Stockholm, as Faust in C. F. Gounod's opera on 12 September 1914.

Hislop sang for a season at the San Carlo Opera in Naples, Italy, in the spring of 1920, sharing the role of Mario Cavaradossi with Gigli. He made his Covent Garden début on 14 May 1920 as Rodolfo in Puccini's *La Bohème*. In 1920 and 1921 he appeared in Chicago and New York, touring America three times. A return to Italy in 1923 saw him in Venice, Turin, and at La Scala, Milan, where his was the first appearance by a British male singer in a leading role (Edgardo in Donizetti's *Lucia di Lammermoor*). Hislop sang regularly in most of the major European houses, but also appeared frequently in the Baltic states as well as in the Colon, Buenos Aires (1925). He made a farewell British tour in 1934. He became a Swedish citizen in 1937 in order to take up the offer of teaching posts in the Royal Opera School and the Music High School (later renamed the Royal Academy of Music), Stockholm, where he had great influence on a generation of singers, including Birgit Nilsson and Jussi Björling, whom he taught (the latter privately). In 1949 he became professor of singing at that academy. From 1948 to 1954 he was an artistic adviser to the Royal Opera House, Covent Garden, and at Sadler's Wells. In 1952 he became a professor of singing at the Guildhall School of Music. There, he taught a succession of fine singers—Peter Glossop, Elizabeth Fretwell, and William McAlpine as well as (privately) Alberto Remedios and Donald Pilley. He retired to Fife in 1964, where he continued to teach for many years, his most celebrated pupil at this time being the baritone Donald Maxwell.

Hislop was awarded the gold medal Litteris et Artibus in 1922 by Sweden for achievement in the arts. In 1926 he was made a knight of Dannebrog (Denmark) and in 1929 made a knight of the Vasa (Sweden).

On 26 May 1915 he married Karin, daughter of Olof Asklund, owner of a large Göteborg bakery firm. They had one son and two daughters, one of whom, Geraldine, trained as an actress and singer and appeared with some success before her death in 1984. Divorced in 1940, in the same year Hislop married Agnes (Nancy) Fraser (1911–1987), daughter of Walter Passmore, character comedian in the Savoy Opera Company. There were no children of the second marriage. Hislop died on 6 May 1977 at his home, Berryside, near New Gilston, Fife, and he was cremated at Kirkcaldy crematorium on 10 May.

Hislop had a relatively small repertory of 29 spinto tenor roles, giving some 921 performances in total between 1914 and 1934. He made 180 recordings, 4 for Pathé Frères in Stockholm, the remainder for the Gramophone Company (later EMI).

MICHAEL T. R. B. TURNBULL

Sources M. T. R. B. Turnbull, *Joseph Hislop: gran tenore* (1992) • M. F. Bott, 'Joseph Hislop', *Record Collector*, 23/9–10 (June 1977) • M. F. Bott, 'Joseph Hislop', *Record Collector*, 25/1–2 (March 1979) • M. F. Bott, 'Joseph Hislop—a centenary tribute', *Opera*, 35 (1984), 730–34 • R. Hay, 'Talking with Joseph Hislop', *Scots Magazine*, 99 (1973), 173–8 • M. T. R. B. Turnbull, 'Joseph Hislop (1884–1977): a cultural ambassador', *Review of Scottish Culture*, 6 (1990), 21–6 • private information (2004) [G. Donald]

Archives NL Scot., papers • priv. coll. | FILM BFI NFTVA • Scottish Screen Archive, Glasgow | SOUND BL NSA, 'My ideal Rodolfo', B4582/01 • BL NSA, performance recordings

Likenesses G. Loring, bust, c.1930, Usher Hall, Edinburgh • J. D. Hislop, two self-portraits, oils, priv. coll. • G. Loring, bust, Scot. NPG

Wealth at death approx. £20,000: private information (2004) [G. Donald]

Hislop, Stephen (1817–1863), missionary and geologist, was born at Duns, Berwickshire, on 8 September 1817, the youngest of the six children of Stephen Hislop, mason and an elder in the Relief church, and his wife, Margaret Thompson. Even as a boy he was a keen observer of nature and interested in geology, and after local schooling he went to Edinburgh University, in 1834. He then tutored for a year before beginning the study of divinity at Glasgow University. He returned to Edinburgh for the remainder of his course and was completing his preparations for the ministry when the Church of Scotland was split by the Disruption of 1843. He joined the Free Church and while waiting for his licence became secretary of the Ladies' Society for Female Education in India. In January 1844 Hislop volunteered as a missionary to the Foreign Missions Committee. On 16 July he married Erasma Hull, daughter of William Hull, plumber, of Olney, Buckinghamshire, and granddaughter of Erasmus Middleton. He was then ordained by the Free Presbytery of Edinburgh, in September, and he and his wife reached Bombay in December of the same year. During their time overseas they had three daughters and a son.

The Free Church's main problem in India was that although it had secured the services of all its missionaries stationed there, it had lost a great deal of property. A substantial legacy was available for the establishment of a new mission at Nagpur, however, and Hislop was charged with its foundation. After a long and arduous journey, mostly on horseback, he arrived at Nagpur on 22 February 1845. Based at first at the British camp just outside the town he equipped himself for the task ahead by learning Marathi. In May 1846 he founded the school which eventually became Hislop College. In March 1847 he was joined by Robert Hunter, a man of similar interests but of very different character. The two men were particularly absorbed by the geology of central India. They collected fossils which they sent to the Geological Society of London and Hislop published a joint memoir in their own *Quarterly Journal*, as well as contributing to the *Journal of the Royal Asiatic Society*. Hunter left India in 1855 but Hislop continued to pursue his interests; a greenish mineral which he discovered was called 'hislopite' after him.

The aboriginal inhabitants of the region, the Gonds, were considered to be a promising and unprejudiced audience for missionary effort and Hislop also studied and preached in Gondi. The people were the subject of a paper to the British Association in 1859, and after Hislop's death his manuscript of *Papers Relating to the Aboriginal Tribes of the Central Provinces* (1866) was prepared for publication by Sir Richard Temple. In 1850 Hislop acted as deputy in Madras for John Anderson, but he resisted attempts to abandon Nagpur as a mission station and make his attachment there permanent. He survived the upheaval of the Indian mutiny unscathed, having received a timely warning by which the Europeans in Nagpur were saved. He reluctantly returned home on two years' sick leave in 1858 and ministered for a while in the fishing community of Ferryden in Forfarshire, then in the grip of a religious revival. He returned to India at the end of 1860.

Hislop's last years at Nagpur were his most influential. He had long objected to the presence of British officials at Hindu festivals and, once the area was annexed to British rule, he continued to criticize the civil administration through letters to the *Friend of India*. After Temple became chief commissioner of the central provinces in 1862, the two men worked closely together and it was while they were on a joint tour of inspection that Hislop met his end. While returning to Bori from the study of some archaeological remains at Takalghat on 4 September 1863, in falling darkness Hislop's horse plunged into a swollen backwater and he was unseated and drowned. The turf clutched in his hands when he was found spoke of his desperate misfortune. Hislop had already cheated death several times, having survived a shipwreck, a bite from a mad dog, and a beating from a vengeful mob. He was buried in the Nagpur cemetery at Sitabaldi. Over £4000 was subscribed for the care of his family.

Hislop was thought distinctively Scottish: tall, wiry, and rugged, with a 'full roundish face—broader than common across the somewhat high cheek bones … prominent eyebrows, partially-sunk eyes, and deep lines slanting from the outer edges of the nostrils to the corners of the mouth' (Smith, 9); a contemporary described him as 'just fit for a missionary pioneer, a man full of bodily and mental energy, practical sense, and indomitable determination' (Mackenzie, 298). His words, which were few but weighty, were delivered slowly and earnestly; yet those who pierced his initial reserve found also the warmest friendship. The range of his scientific and scholarly interests was substantial, but it never interfered with his missionary ambitions. The fact that his efforts were cut short served only to emphasize the extent of his achievements.

C. L. KINGSFORD, *rev.* LIONEL ALEXANDER RITCHIE

Sources G. Smith, *Stephen Hislop* (1888) · R. Hunter, *History of the missions of the Free Church of Scotland in India and Africa* (1873) · J. Wilson, *Memorial discourse on the death of the Rev. Stephen Hislop of Nagpur* (1864) · *Free Church of Scotland Monthly Record*, 17 (1 Dec 1863), 385–8 · A. C. Ramsay, *Quarterly Journal of the Geological Society*, 20 (1864), xxxix–xl · *The Geologist*, 6 (1863), 428–9 · R. Temple, *Men and events of my time in India* (1882), 241–2 · H. Mackenzie, *Life in the mission, the camp, and the Zenana, or, Six years in India*, 3 (1853), 298 · W. Ewing, ed., *Annals of the Free Church of Scotland, 1843–1900*, 1 (1914), 186 · Duns, Berwickshire, parish register (births and baptisms) [8, 21/9/1817] · St Cuthbert's, Edinburgh, parish register (marriage) [16/7/1844]
Archives NL Scot., corresp. and papers
Likenesses portrait (aged twenty-seven; after calotype by D. O. Hill), repro. in Smith, *Stephen Hislop*, frontispiece

Hislop, Sir Thomas, first baronet (1764–1843), army officer, was born on 5 July 1764, the third and youngest son of Lieutenant-Colonel William Hislop (*d.* 1779), Royal Artillery. His two elder brothers were killed in India, James at the battle of Polillur in 1781, when aide-de-camp to Sir Eyre Coote, and William, captain Royal Artillery, at Cundapore in 1783.

Hislop entered the Royal Military Academy, Woolwich, on 31 March 1778, and on 28 December the same year was appointed ensign in the 39th (East Middlesex) foot, with which he served throughout the siege of Gibraltar (1779–83) and was promoted lieutenant on 28 January 1783. He became captain by purchase in the 100th foot on 28 January 1785, exchanged back to the 39th on 4 February 1785, and in December 1792 was appointed aide-de-camp to Major-General David Dundas, on whose staff he served in Ireland, at Toulon, and in the expedition to Corsica. He brought home the dispatches announcing the capture, on 19 February 1794, of San Fiorenzo, for which he was promoted major on 16 August 1794. In May the same year he was appointed aide-de-camp to Lord Amherst, then commander-in-chief. He was employed by the prince of Wales on a special mission in Germany, and on his return was appointed, on 25 March 1795, lieutenant-colonel of the 115th foot, from which he exchanged once more to the 39th on 1 September 1795. He accompanied the 39th to the West Indies, and commanded it at the capture of Demerara, Berbice, and Essiquibo in 1796. He remained in military command of those settlements until their restoration to the Dutch at the peace of Amiens in May 1802. On 6 September 1798 he became lieutenant-colonel of the 11th West India regiment, which he raised. He was promoted colonel on 29 April 1802, joined the 8th West India regiment in 1803, and became lieutenant-governor of Trinidad. He joined the army under Sir George Beckwith at Martinique in 1809, and commanded the 1st division at the capture of Guadeloupe in 1810. He was promoted major-general on 25 October 1809. He left Trinidad in ill health in 1811.

On 28 March 1812 Hislop was appointed commander-in-chief at Bombay with the local rank of lieutenant-general, and sailed in the frigate *Java*, which in December 1812 was captured by the United States frigate *Constitution* off the coast of Brazil. Hislop, whose bravery was conspicuous during the action, was put on shore at San Salvador, and returned home. On 27 May 1813 he was appointed commander-in-chief at Madras (Fort St George). He was given the full rank of lieutenant-general on 4 June the same year, and on 2 November was created a baronet. He was made KCB in 1814.

Hislop arrived at Madras late in 1814. During the Third Anglo-Maratha War, of 1817–18, he was commander-in-chief of the army of the Deccan. After a delay from illness he assumed the command at Hyderabad on 10 November 1817. At Mehidpur on 21 December, with a force of 5500 men, Hislop signally defeated the Maratha army of Indore, consisting of 30,000 light cavalry, 5000 infantry, and 100 guns, under the command of the youthful Malhar Rao Holkar. The surrender by the Marathas of certain border fortresses followed. The division under Hislop's personal command arrived before the fort of Talnar, the governor of which, after a parley, refused to obey the order to surrender. By Hislop's order he was hanged as a rebel, and the garrison of 300 men killed. When the chief objects of the campaign had been accomplished, the army of the Deccan was broken up at Aurangabad in March 1818, and Hislop returned to his command at Fort St George, which he held until 1820. He was made GCB in 1818.

Explanations of Hislop's severities at Talnar had been called for by Lord Moira, the governor-general [see Hastings, Francis Rawdon], and the home government; the House of Commons, in voting thanks to the army of the Deccan, specifically excepted Hislop in consequence. Wellington defended Hislop in the House of Lords on the ground of his previous high character. The explanations eventually sent home were never made public, and the subject dropped. Another controversy arose from the conflicting claims of the Bengal and Madras armies to the spoils known as the Deccan prize. The privy council, after hearing counsel, decided that the Bengal army under the marquess of Hastings, though at a great distance from the scene of capture, were co-operating by their presence in the field, and entitled to share equally with the troops under Hislop's command. Wellington remarked that the sole satisfaction he felt at the decision was that, had the sum thus put into the pockets of the army fallen to Sir Thomas Hislop, it would have vanished in Mexican bonds or Columbian securities, like Hislop's private fortune.

In 1822 Hislop received an 'honourable augmentation' to his arms in recognition of his distinguished services in India. On 30 October 1823 he married Emma, daughter of the Rt Hon. Hugh Elliot, governor of Madras, and they had one daughter. He was appointed colonel of the 51st foot on 4 June 1822 and of the 48th foot on 25 December 1829, and served for many years as equerry to the duke of Cambridge. He died at Charlton, Kent, on 3 May 1843.

H. M. CHICHESTER, rev. ALEX MAY

Sources Army List · private information (2004) · R. N. Buckley, 'Brigadier-General Hislop's remarks on the establishment of the West India regiments, 1801', *Journal of the Society for Army Historical Research*, 58 (1980), 209–22 · R. N. Buckley, *Slaves in red coats: the British West India regiments, 1795–1815* (1979) · Fortescue, *Brit. army*, vol. 4 · M. Duffy, *Soldiers, sugar, and sea power: the British expeditions to the West Indies and the war against revolutionary France* (1987) · J. G. Duff, *A history of the Mahrattas*, 3 vols. (1826) · M. Edwardes, *Glorious sahibs: the romantic as empire-builder* (1968) · GM, 2nd ser., 20 (1843), 317–19

Archives NL Scot., corresp. and papers | Mount Stuart Trust, Isle of Bute, archive, letters to Lord Hastings

Hitch, Samuel (1800–1881), physician and specialist in the treatment of the insane, was born on 1 April 1800 at Stonehouse in Gloucestershire, the son of John Hitch (1762–1818), clothier, and Betty Smith (1761/2–1823). He was educated at Magdalen Hall, Oxford, where he matriculated on 11 December 1830, and attended medical schools in France and Italy as well as in England. He qualified initially as a surgeon and became a licentiate of the Royal College of Physicians in 1840. Hitch married three times. His first wife was Anne Scammell Prosser (1796/7–1858), daughter of the Revd William Prosser, rector of Walton, Cardiff. On 21 October 1858 he married Elizabeth Shute, *née* Stratford (1809/10–1869), a widow, at Tewkesbury. On 23 September 1874 he married Letitia Anne Willes (1828/9–1909), daughter of Thomas Gibson Willes, surgeon.

The prominent asylum physician J. C. Bucknill later recalled Hitch as 'an able, busy, bustling intelligent man' (Walk and Walker, 607). He was small in stature, with red hair. According to family legend he was not blessed with good looks, but considered that he could make up for this with charm.

Hitch was appointed in 1828 as house surgeon and superintendent of the Gloucestershire County Lunatic Asylum. Under his management Gloucester Asylum achieved recognition for its unusually high proportion of recoveries. The Belgian Dr C. Crommelinck in 1842 described it as 'one of the most agreeable, best kept and most important establishments in England' (Crommelinck, 108). Hitch was a diligent superintendent, energetically pursuing what he considered the interests of the house and its patients. His power and influence were consolidated in July 1839 when he replaced the elderly matron with his wife, Anne.

Hitch's approach to treatment was based on the premise that mental disorders had a physical basis. He wrote in 1844 that the insane were 'under the influence of physical disease, masked and hidden, it is true, but occasionally shewing itself and becoming susceptible of amelioration or of cure' ('Report of the insane poor confined in the workhouse Birmingham'). The treatment process therefore began by seeking the organic lesion in order to remove or neutralize it. Hitch was also, however, strongly influenced by the principles of moral management. The emphasis of the therapeutic regime at Gloucester was on promoting employment and occupation, similar to the model developed by William Ellis at the West Riding Asylum. Patients were employed indoors on a range of domestic tasks and clothing manufacture, and outside in the extensive grounds, as well as in construction and maintenance work on the building. There was also a range of recreational activities, including games, music-making, dancing, and concerts.

Hitch became an early adherent of the movement to abolish mechanical restraint in treatment of the insane after visiting the Middlesex Asylum in April 1840. He quickly reduced restraint at Gloucester, and had virtually eliminated it by late 1842. Other innovations followed, including the introduction of training for medical students, unescorted outings of patients to church, and trial leave for those who were recovering. He maintained that the degree of confidence he placed in his patients was 'a point of treatment, on which I flatter myself that I leave all the other doctors far behind me' (Crommelinck, 112). Some of his liberal policies were criticized by the commissioners in lunacy, who even questioned their legality.

Hitch's desire to disseminate new ideas and promote good practice led him in 1841 to initiate the Association of Medical Officers of Asylums and Hospitals for the Insane (AMOAHI). He was its driving force, serving as secretary until 1851, and then treasurer until 1854. The association later became the Royal Medico-Psychological Association and ultimately the Royal College of Psychiatrists. Hitch's wider concerns included a particular interest in the problems of Welsh lunatics, and he lent his active support to the campaign to develop the North Wales Lunatic Asylum at Denbigh. His prestige brought appointment in September 1844 as a temporary assistant poor law commissioner to enquire into the treatment of pauper lunatics in the Leicester and Birmingham workhouses. His influential report condemned many of their practices and strongly advocated public asylum care for all insane people, however unlikely their prospects of recovery. He contended strongly that the order and discipline of an asylum could transform behaviour.

In the summer of 1845 Hitch resigned as superintendent of Gloucester Asylum with ill health given as the reason. However, he and his wife had become increasingly discontented about aspects of conditions there which they felt unable to influence. The committee of visitors, reluctant to lose his services, prevailed upon him to continue as consulting physician, maintaining an overall direction while giving up many of the day-to-day responsibilities. Relations with the visitors became increasingly uneasy over the next two years, with Hitch seeking to develop a private practice, and becoming resentful of limitations on his sphere of responsibilities. He finally left in October 1847, opening a private asylum at Sandywell Park, a mansion near Cheltenham.

Hitch continued to be active in the AMOAHI until he withdrew in 1854. The remaining years of his life were characterized by frustration and disappointment. He maintained the asylum at Sandywell Park, with the help of his daughter and son-in-law, until about 1865, when his extravagance forced him to sell it to pay his debts. During much of the remainder of his life financial difficulties were a source of embarrassment to his family as well as himself. Widowed twice, his third marriage was an unhappy and acrimonious one. His death on 29 September 1881 at his home, Barnwood House, Upperton Road, Eastbourne, may have followed a self-administered overdose of laudanum. By then his earlier work had been largely forgotten. His passing went largely unnoticed in the medical press, with no obituary in either *The Lancet* or the *Journal of Mental Science*. He was survived by his third wife.   LEONARD D. SMITH

Sources A. Walk and D. L. Walker, 'Gloucester and the beginnings of the R. M. P. A.', *Journal of Mental Science*, 107 (1961), 603–32 · annual reports, Glos. RO, Gloucester, Horton Road Hospital and Coney Hill Hospital, HO 22/8/1 · minutes of visitors, Glos. RO, Gloucester, Horton Road Hospital and Coney Hill Hospital, HO 22/1/1 · house committee minutes, Glos. RO, Gloucester, Horton Road Hospital and Coney Hill Hospital, HO 22/3/1–3 · letters to Samuel Hitch, Glos. RO, D 3848/1 · C. Crommelinck, *Rapport sur les hospices d'aliénés de l'Angleterre, de la France et d'Allemagne* (1842) · 'Report of the insane poor confined in the union workhouse at Leicester', 23 Oct 1844, PRO, MH 12/6470/18259 · 'Report of the insane poor confined in the workhouse Birmingham', 31 Oct 1844, PRO, MH 12/13288/18261 · J. C. Prichard, *A treatise on insanity* (1835) · T. O. Wood, 'The early history of the Medico-Psychological Association', *Journal of Mental Science*, 42 (1896), 241–60 · Foster, *Alum. Oxon.* · private information (2004) [Sir Crispin Tickell] · CGPLA Eng. & Wales (1882)

Archives Glos. RO, material relating to Gloucester Asylum, D 3848/1; HO 22/1/1; HO 22/3/1–3: HO 22/8/1 · PRO, reports as an assistant poor law commissioner, MH 12/6470/18259; MH 12/13288/18261

Likenesses portrait, repro. in Walk and Walker, 'Gloucester and the beginnings of the R.M.P.A.'

Wealth at death £996 11s. 1d.: probate, 7 March 1882, CGPLA Eng. & Wales

Hitcham, Sir Robert (*bap.* 1573, *d.* 1636), barrister and politician, was born at Levington, Suffolk, the only son of Robert Hitcham, yeoman, of Nacton, Suffolk, and his wife, Joan Gillet; he was baptized at Nacton on 8 March 1573. After attending Ipswich's free grammar school he went on to Pembroke College, Cambridge, in 1587, and entered Gray's Inn, as from Barnard's Inn, in November 1589. Hitcham was called utter-barrister in 1595 at the reading of Richard Barker, a Cecil protégé. The same connection probably underlies his return for West Looe in the parliament of 1597 and his appointment by September 1603 as Queen Anne's attorney-general. In June 1604 Hitcham was knighted and again returned to parliament, this time for the borough of King's Lynn. His colourful report to the Commons in March 1606 following a rumoured attempt on the king's life was almost immediately contradicted by other testimony, whereby 'Sir R [H]Itchams credit in the opinion of divers was much impaired' (*Diary of Robert Bowyer*, 89). Neither this reverse nor his relatively infrequent subsequent contributions to debate curtailed Hitcham's parliamentary career. In 1614 he represented the borough of Cambridge, where he had been retained as fee'd counsellor since at least 1609–10, as he was also at Ipswich, while in the three parliaments from 1624 to 1626 he succeeded Sir Edward Coke as member for Orford, where he had earlier replaced Coke as recorder. His 1624 speech defending the legality of impositions aroused so much resentment that Sir Thomas Wentworth moved successfully for it to be struck from the clerk's record.

Called ancient and permitted to sit at the Gray's Inn readers' table from January 1604 in respect of his royal office, Hitcham was chosen reader towards the end of the following year. The 1606 Lent readings at all four inns incurred the judges' displeasure, but Hitcham's bad example was particularly censured. His temporary suspension from commons for providing over-lavish entertainment and an abbreviated reading may have been a symbolic punishment, but cannot have enhanced his professional reputation. This perhaps explains why he was sarcastically termed 'a great learned man' (*Letters of John Chamberlain*, 1.541) on the news of his call as serjeant in 1614. Having given up his attorney-generalship, Hitcham's legal practice thereafter appears to have been confined largely to the court of common pleas and local East Anglian jurisdictions. Although promoted king's serjeant in 1616, he never rose above the rank of chief serjeant, except as a commissioned assize judge. His stalled career may have reflected a lack of effective patronage after Buckingham's rise to power; a 'writhen face and sneering look' (BL, Harley MS 6395, fol. 53) possibly also told against him, though his contemporary likeness displays no such traits.

Yet if there were doubts about Hitcham's legal learning and professional morality, his overall ability was unquestionable. Indeed he was possibly no more anxious for promotion to the judicial bench than to end his jealously guarded bachelorhood. In material terms his career was outstandingly successful: 'not born to £200 … not to £20 or £2' a year (HoP, *Commons, 1558–1603*, 2.319), his land purchases culminated with a payment of £14,000 for the earl of Suffolk's castle and manor of Framlingham. He died at Ipswich on 15 August 1636 and was buried at Framlingham.

Hitcham's will made passing allusion to the 'glorious and incomprehensible Trinity' but only a cursory statement of personal faith (PRO, PROB 11/173, fol. 249r). Most of his fortune went to his old Cambridge college, on condition that it should erect and maintain almshouses and a school for the poor at Framlingham. The wording of this bequest occasioned disputes and litigation which continued into Charles II's reign. WILFRID PREST

Sources W. J. Jones, 'Hitcham, Robert', HoP, *Commons, 1558–1603*, 2.319 · W. R. Prest, *The rise of the barristers: a social history of the English bar, 1590–1640*, 2nd edn (1991) · Baker, *Serjeants* · will, PRO, PROB 11/173, sig. 33 · *DNB* · *The parliamentary diary of Robert Bowyer, 1606–1607*, ed. D. H. Willson (1931) · R. J. Fletcher, ed., *The pension book of Gray's Inn*, 1 (1901) · *The diary of Sir Richard Hutton, 1614–1639*, ed. W. R. Prest, SeldS, suppl. ser., 9 (1991) · *The letters of John Chamberlain*, ed. N. E. McClure, 2 vols. (1939) · R. Loder, *History of Framlingham* (1798) · *IGI* · parish register, Nacton, Suffolk RO · BL, Harley MS 6935, fol. 53 [printed H. F. Lippincott, '*Mery passages and jeasts': a manuscript jestbook of Sir Nicholas Le Strange (1603–1655)* (1974)] · R. Green, *The history, topography, and antiquities of Framlingham and Saxsted* (1834) · Fuller, *Worthies* (1840), 3.89 · J. P. Ferris, 'Hitcham, Robert', HoP, *Commons, 1604–29* [draft]
Likenesses oils, type of c.1620, NPG · engraving, repro. in Loder, *History of Framlingham*
Wealth at death £1500 p.a.: Green, *History*, 106–7

Hitchcock, Alfred Joseph (1899–1980), film director, was born on 13 August 1899 in Leytonstone, Essex, the youngest of the three children of William Hitchcock (1862–1914), a greengrocer and poulterer, and his wife, Emma Jane Whelan (1863–1942). In childhood he was an isolated, tubby little boy, with few schoolfriends. The Hitchcock household appears to have been characterized by an

Alfred Joseph Hitchcock (1899–1980), by Yousuf Karsh, 1960

atmosphere of discipline, something that perhaps later helped inspire the portrayal of authoritarian fathers (as in *Strangers on a Train*, 1951) and claustrophobic, sometimes emotionally disturbed mothers (as in *Marnie*, 1964). A painful memory, which he often cited

> as having shaped his attitude towards authority, fear and guilt, was being sent by his father at the age of five with a note addressed to the superintendent of the local police station, where he was locked in a cell for ten minutes and then released with the words, 'That is what we do to naughty boys.' (*DNB*)

Hitchcock was educated at various schools in London, including St Ignatius College, Stamford Hill, a Jesuit school which, along with his own family's religious background, may have been to some extent responsible for the 'Catholic' themes of his films. Obliged to leave school at the age of fourteen, after his father's death, he found work as a draughtsman and advertising designer with the Henley Telegraph and Cable Company. However, he was able to extend his artistic talents by attending night school courses in art and art history. The stories of Edgar Allan Poe intrigued him from an early age, and he was keen on American films, and in particular those of D. W. Griffith and Buster Keaton. Hearing that a film studio was to be opened in London by the Famous Players-Lasky Company, Hitchcock approached it with a portfolio of his artistic work. In 1920 he was appointed to design and illustrate silent movie titles; and he soon made himself indispensable at the Islington studios, where he came under the influence of the director George Fitzmaurice, whose meticulous preparation, eye for detail, and storyboard planning clearly left their mark. In 1924 the studio was taken over by a British company, Gaumont Pictures; but Hitchcock's talent was soon recognized by the head of Gainsborough at Islington, Michael Balcon, who subsequently offered him the chance to direct his first feature film, *The Pleasure Garden* (1925).

By this time two important events had taken place in Hitchcock's life: he had met the film editor Alma Reville (1900–1982), and visited Germany. He married Alma on 2 December 1926 at the Brompton Oratory in Knightsbridge. They lived at 153 Cromwell Road, where their daughter Patricia was born on 7 July 1928, and later acquired a house in the country, in Surrey. An editor who had also been working at Islington, Alma was to remain an important collaborator and adviser throughout Hitchcock's career, often mentioned in the credits of films made well into his career (for example, *The Paradine Case*, 1947). Patricia trained as an actress and appeared in three of Hitchcock's films (*Stage Fright*, 1950; *Strangers on a Train*, 1951; *Psycho*, 1960).

Early films Not long after meeting Alma, Hitchcock spent time in Germany in the mid-1920s as an assistant director. In 1924 he assisted Graham Cutts on *The Blackguard*, an Anglo-German production filmed at UFA Studios, and then worked in 1925 at Emelka Studios in Munich, where he made *The Pleasure Garden* and the now lost *The Mountain Eagle* (1926). The dominant characteristics of German expressionist cinema—above all, chiaroscuro lighting, visual distortions, and theatricality—left their mark on Hitchcock's early work, perhaps most notably in *The Lodger* (1926). But even later films such as *Suspicion* (1940), *Psycho*, and *Marnie* mix mainstream studio house styles of deep shadows and sumptuous sets with traces of an aesthetic mode with which Hitchcock became familiar by watching F. W. Murnau and others at work on the sound stages next door to where *The Blackguard* was being filmed. Expressionism, though, was not alone responsible for shaping Hitchcock's art. Hollywood pace (for example, in *The Lady Vanishes*, 1938), Soviet montage (*The Thirty-Nine Steps*, 1935), and the dream landscapes of surrealism (*Number 17*, 1932) reveal early on the extent of Hitchcock's indebtedness to other film styles.

After returning to Britain to resume his career, Hitchcock directed *The Lodger*, based on the novel by Marie Belloc Lowndes. But as Ivor Novello, a romantic star of the stage at that time, was cast in the lead role, the script had to remove the ambiguity surrounding the main character's innocence. Drawing on Hitchcock's lifelong fascination with classic English murders, the film was about a man suspected of being Jack the Ripper. At a cost of £12,000, a considerable sum for the time, the film seemed doomed at first, since the financial executive at the studio, C. M. Woolf, disliked its 'Germanic' and 'unAmerican' style. But after Ivor Montagu, an editor, had worked on the titles and various scenes, a slightly modified version of the film was finally shown to the press, to great acclaim. On the back of this success *The Pleasure Garden* and *The Mountain Eagle* (which had been shelved) were also released. Hitchcock made two further films at Gainsborough, both

adaptations: *Downhill* (1927), based on a play by David Le Strange (a pseudonym for Ivor Novello), and *Easy Virtue* (1927), by Noël Coward, neither of which reached the heights of *The Lodger*.

From Gainsborough, Hitchcock moved to British International Pictures. Here he made *The Ring* (1927), scripted for the first time by Hitchcock himself, *The Farmer's Wife* (1928), a comedy, *Champagne* (1928), a melodramatic comedy, and *The Manxman* (1929), his last silent film. Apart from the odd flourish, none of these is particularly striking, but they prepared the way for his next brilliant success, *Blackmail* (1929), his first sound film, and one that helped substantially to establish his reputation as a British director with a common touch who was also aware of international trends. The plot of *Blackmail* involved a police officer in love with an accidental murderess. The script was quarried from a play by Charles Bennett, who was to become a regular collaborator of Hitchcock's over the next few years. Among the most remarkable features of the film is the use of sound montage. Dialogue here is used creatively, sometimes to emphasize the state of mind of a character rather than serve merely as a simple tool of communication. The scene at breakfast, where the cinema audience and the girl who has just killed a man hear only the word 'knife' in the monologue delivered by a woman at the breakfast table, is a masterly example of this technique. *Blackmail* was also the film in which Hitchcock first made what was to become his trademark appearance, an early indication of a lifelong passion for self-publicity that also resulted at this time in the setting up of Hitchcock Baker Productions to promote his work. But as with *The Lodger*, so too with *Blackmail*: the film was followed by disappointing work, not always of Hitchcock's own choosing: *Juno and the Paycock* (1930), based on the play by Sean O'Casey; *Murder!* (1930), a reworking of *Enter Sir John*, a play by Clemence Dane and Helen Simpson; and *The Skin Game* (1931) by John Galsworthy. As ever, the films are redeemed by characteristic touches, and their theatricality served at the very least to develop Hitchcock's enduring interest in the theme of artifice.

With the completion of *The Skin Game* Hitchcock and family went in 1931 on a world cruise. This gave him the idea for a film about a couple who spend an unexpected legacy on a sea voyage. The result was *Rich and Strange*, an underrated bitter-sweet comedy with a trademark interest in faded desire. But shooting the film, eventually reworking a story by Dale Collins, had to be postponed. When Hitchcock returned to British International Pictures he was under instruction to make *Number 17* (1932), a rather stiff, melodramatic play by Jefferson Farjeon. These were Hitchcock's last two films at the studio. Before he teamed up again with Michael Balcon at Gaumont-British he made one film for Tom Arnold: *Waltzes from Vienna* (1933), a musical play that had earlier had great success on the stage. Jessie Matthews, a famous musical star, who was given the lead, enjoyed a poor relationship with Hitchcock, who, she claimed, perhaps not unreasonably, seemed uncomfortable directing a musical.

This deviation from his usual interests was soon forgotten as Hitchcock went on at Gaumont-British to make some of the most interesting sound films of his British period: *The Man Who Knew Too Much* (1934), *The Thirty-Nine Steps* (1935), *Secret Agent* (1936), *Sabotage* (1936), *Young and Innocent* (1937), and *The Lady Vanishes* (1938). With one or two minor blemishes, such as the rather mannered theatricality of John Gielgud in *Secret Agent*, these are the masterly achievements of a director in full command of his creative talent, working more or less according to his own tastes and instincts, making films that began increasingly to attract the attention of Hollywood.

In 1937 Hitchcock duly set sail for America, where he met for the first time David O. Selznick, an important figure in his early Hollywood career. A deal with Selznick was still a couple of years away, and in the interim Hitchcock made two films: the first, the brilliant *The Lady Vanishes*, on which he worked for the first time with Launder and Gilliat, and the second, *Jamaica Inn* (1939), one of his least convincing, in no small measure the result of Charles Laughton's overblown acting. In March 1939 the Hitchcocks returned to America, this time permanently, considering Britain too burdened by class-consciousness, a country where film was dismissed as a form of entertainment fit only for the uncultured. Perceived attitudes like these contributed to Hitchcock's eventual decision to become an American citizen (20 April 1955).

Hollywood The success of *The Thirty-Nine Steps*, *Young and Innocent*, and *The Lady Vanishes*, and the extremely enthusiastic notices his films had been receiving in the American press, alerted Hollywood to Hitchcock. New York film critics had even voted him the best director of 1938. He agreed to work for David Selznick, hoping that at a smaller studio he would be a favoured director, allowed to get on with his own projects uninterruptedly. The original intention was to make a film based on the *Titanic*, but this project was soon dropped, and Hitchcock started work instead on *Rebecca* (1940), a critical success and his only film to be awarded an Oscar for best picture. He remained contracted to Selznick for several tension-filled years, during which he was loaned out to various studios from time to time.

Like *Jamaica Inn* (and *The Birds*), *Rebecca* was based on a Daphne du Maurier novel. Its atmosphere of suspense and entrapment allowed Hitchcock to explore the familiar psychological territory of the pale and vulnerable, 'gothic' heroine searching for authenticity in a labyrinth of social pressure and expectation. Although he himself had reservations about the film, largely because he felt it remained too faithful to the original source, it clearly belongs both formally and thematically to his mainstream obsessions. But once Hitchcock started work on *Rebecca* he began to resent the interference of Selznick, who felt that the script Hitchcock had mined from Daphne du Maurier's novel was too free. Other sources of tension between the two men included Hitchcock's method of cutting in the camera, a technique that meant

Selznick could not tamper with the film in the later editing stage. These disagreements encouraged Selznick to loan Hitchcock out to other studios. At first he worked with Walter Wanger on a film that was to become *Foreign Correspondent* (1940). The relationship with Wanger was altogether more agreeable to Hitchcock, especially as he was left to his own devices. Gary Cooper was his first choice for the lead role but, after he declined, Joel McCrea was cast in the role of the American correspondent who becomes embroiled in European espionage at the outbreak of the war. Denounced as a deserter by many, including Michael Balcon, Hitchcock saw this film as a contribution to the war effort of his native country, and he mixed fiction with up-to-date information about actual events taking place at that time in Norway, the Netherlands, and elsewhere. Other patriotic gestures of this type included making in 1944 for the British Library of Information two short films about the war: *Bon Voyage* and *Aventure Malgache*. Still contracted to Selznick, Hitchcock was next loaned out to RKO for two films, *Mr and Mrs Smith* (1941) and *Suspicion* (1941); the latter marked the first of four appearances in a Hitchcock film by Cary Grant, who, along with James Stewart (who also appeared four times), played some of the most complex and significant of the male characters in Hitchcock's repertory of screen heroes.

Hitchcock next made two films at Universal Studios: the first, *Saboteur* (1942), continued the war theme but the second marked Hitchcock's return to familiar territory in one of his undoubted masterpieces, *Shadow of a Doubt* (1943). A film that characteristically celebrates America, *Shadow of a Doubt* sees Hitchcock in the darkest of moods. Based on an original story by Gordon McDonell, it is a melodrama, scripted by Sally Benson, Alma Reville, and Thornton Wilder. The continuing influence of Alma is apparent here, while Thornton Wilder's awareness of the nuances of small-town America, most famously associated with his play *Our Town*, adds the necessary authenticity to a narrative about the camouflage of murderous desires by provincial manners.

In 1942, too, Hitchcock's mother and brother died. Increasingly worried about his own health, especially his weight, he nevertheless continued to work vigorously and entered one of the most productive periods of his career, making films that even when slight were never less than fascinating in their formal experimentation. The challenge of *Lifeboat* (1943), for instance, was to grip the audience's attention in a film where the action was entirely restricted to one setting, the inside of a lifeboat of an American merchant ship that has been torpedoed by a German U-boat. This film, again on a Second World War theme, aroused controversy for its refusal to treat the Nazi character as a cardboard cut-out stereotype of villainy. The film that followed, *Spellbound* (1945), made once more at Selznick's studios, was his greatest commercial hit after *Rebecca*. Reprising Hitchcock's interest in psychoanalysis and surrealism, and chiming in with America's obsession in the 1940s with psychoanalysis, *Spellbound* highlights the aggressive drives of individuals disorientated by changing notions of gender, further confusing men already uncomfortable with the demands of socialized forms of masculinity and troubled by newer attitudes to femininity, as women began in the post-war period increasingly to challenge male ascendancy. The film was again characterized by heavy interference from Selznick, who had himself been in analysis. Selznick placed his own therapist on the film, and used her as a consultant throughout shooting, a decision that infuriated Hitchcock, especially as she often questioned his judgement about character motivation. Although it was Hitchcock's idea to rework Francis Beedings's novel *The House of Dr Edwards*, as well as to use Salvador Dalí for the dream sequence, *Spellbound* was very much a Selznick production. For Hitchcock, though, the film is additionally significant in its use for the first time of Ingrid Bergman, who was to appear in two other Hitchcock films, *Notorious* (1946) and *Under Capricorn* (1949); the latter was a somewhat disappointing effort, but the former was one of his most compelling films where, working at last as his own producer, he was able to experiment brilliantly in a film characterized by inventive use of montage, crane shots, long shots, and much else besides.

In their exploration of the relations between weak men and strong women these films seem in some ways confessional, the stylized screen versions of their author's own domestic dramas. *The Paradine Case* (1947) continues this theme in its story about a lawyer (Gregory Peck) who is infatuated with a *femme fatale* (Alida Valli). This was Hitchcock's last film for Selznick and attracted the attention of the Hays office, which was unhappy with some aspects of the script, such as the inclusion of a lavatory in the woman's prison cell. The censors also insisted on the removal of such supposedly blasphemous expressions as 'Good God!'

Independent film-making After *The Paradine Case*, Hitchcock teamed up with Sidney Bernstein to launch an independent company, Transatlantic Pictures. This led to *Rope* (1948) and *Under Capricorn* (1949), neither of which, though interestingly experimental in form, was well received either critically or commercially. Hitchcock followed this excursion into independent film-making with a return to studio work: at Warner Brothers (1949–53 and 1957); Paramount (1954–8 and 1960); MGM (1959); and Universal (1963–9). Although contracted to these studios, he worked steadily towards gaining control over his productions, skilfully manoeuvring himself within the changing studio system to gain true independence, and thereby becoming the first of a new breed of film-maker–investors. His independence was truly established after the enormous commercial and critical success of *Psycho* (1960), made on a budget of $800,000, but which grossed $42 million within only six months of its release.

Hitchcock's first independent American film, *Rope*, was also his first film in Technicolor and offered him the opportunity to experiment with long takes, which sometimes lasted as much as ten minutes. This was followed by *Under Capricorn*, *Stage Fright* (1950), and *Strangers on a Train* (1951), a psychological thriller. For the last of these Raymond Chandler was hired to turn Patricia Highsmith's

novel into a screenplay, but this proved to be another fraught relationship between two strong-willed men. Chandler was eventually replaced by Czenzi Ormonde, Barbara Keon, and, significantly again, Alma Reville. *Strangers on a Train* is one of Hitchcock's greatest achievements, and focuses on questions of guilt and shared responsibility. The divisions and conflicts of human desire are here split and projected onto two characters. But what initially seems like a simple contrast between a clean-cut all-American hero (Guy Haines, played by the boyishly handsome Farley Granger) and a decadent, Oedipal villain (Bruno Anthony, played with captivating devilry by Robert Walker) becomes a complex pattern of shared instincts and responsibilities. As Hitchcock himself put it to Truffaut: 'Though Bruno has killed Guy's wife, for Guy it's just as if he had committed the murder himself' (Truffaut, 166). This tangle of interrelated desires does not spare the viewer, who, through a whole series of formal and thematic strategies, above all in the use of the subjective shot, becomes identified with a character's point of view, forced into complicity with the behaviour of guilty as well as of innocent men and women.

The difficulties with Chandler on this film were to some extent mirrored a year later by tensions on *I Confess* (1952), involving Montgomery Clift, whose 'method' style of acting was not to Hitchcock's taste. More problems arose with the casting of the lead female; however, once the decision had been made to jettison Anita Bjork for fear of antagonizing the American public on account of her illegitimate child, Hitchcock turned to Anne Baxter, one of several glacial blondes by whom he became obsessed, both on and off screen. She was, however, soon superseded in his affections by Grace Kelly, who began the first of her three collaborations with Hitchcock on *Dial M for Murder* (1953). Her other films were *Rear Window* (1954) and *To Catch a Thief* (1955), all made in quick succession.

Rear Window was also the first of six films made by Hitchcock in the mid- to late 1950s at Paramount Studios, a period during which he was in full creative flow: *Rear Window*, *To Catch a Thief*, *The Trouble with Harry* (1955), *The Man Who Knew Too Much* (1956), *Vertigo* (1958), *North by Northwest* (1959), and *Psycho* (1960) were all made at Paramount. All demonstrate Hitchcock's imaginative use of cinematic resources: *Rear Window*, for instance, required the building of thirty-one apartments to face the one from which James Stewart's L. B. Jefferies could voyeuristically spy on his neighbours; in addition to its brilliant interplay between the Cary Grant and Grace Kelly characters, *To Catch a Thief* was remarkable for its glossy colour photography, a feature which earned Robert Burks an Academy award for cinematography. This film was followed by *The Trouble with Harry* (1955) and *The Man Who Knew Too Much* (1956); the former, among other things, marked the first of Bernard Herrmann's neo-romantic musical scores crossed with Bartók and Wagner, while the latter offered Hitchcock the opportunity for reworking a film he had made twenty-one years previously in Britain.

At this time, too, Hitchcock was encouraged by his agent, Lou Wasserman, to consider launching a television series. Accordingly, in 1955, Hitchcock agreed to become involved with CBS in a weekly half-hour series, entitled *Alfred Hitchcock Presents* (it later became *The Alfred Hitchcock Hour*), on a salary of $129,000 per episode. The Hitchcock team included Joan Harrison and Norman Lloyd as co-producers. Although Hitchcock himself had only a marginal role, he did introduce all the programmes, with a signature tune taken from Gounod's 'Funeral March of a Marionette'. All in all he directed twenty programmes, and the series lasted—although it moved studios on a couple of occasions—until 1964. With his portly shape and chubby face Hitchcock became 'the only director in the history of the cinema to be instantly recognizable to the general public' (*DNB*). An actress who appeared in the first television show, Vera Miles, was next in line for the special Hitchcock blonde-fantasy treatment. She was promoted to the lead female role in *The Wrong Man* (1957), but clearly had no romantic interest in Hitchcock and soon married Gordon Scott, a 1950s Tarzan. Grace Kelly's supposed replacement became a temporary outcast as Hitchcock embarked on his next project and left for Britain to prepare for the remake of *The Man Who Knew Too Much*.

In 1957 Hitchcock had an operation on his hernia, gallstones, and gall-bladder, but lost none of his creative energy. While hoping to film *The Wreck of the Mary Deare*, a project which was never realized, he began work on another film based on a French novel by Pierre Boileau and Thomas Narcejac, translated as *From Among the Dead*. When the script by Alec Coppel was considered unsatisfactory, Sam Taylor took over. On the advice of Lou Wasserman the lead female role was to be offered to Kim Novak, a part originally intended for Vera Miles. *Vertigo*, the title given to one of Hitchcock's greatest, most elegiac, films, was eventually completed in 1958, the year in which he won the Golden Globe award for best television series.

Hitchcock began to prepare *North by Northwest* (1959), working on the script with Ernest Lehman, to whom he had been introduced by Bernard Herrmann. A comedy thriller, this remains one of Hitchcock's most stylish films, full of witty dialogue and narrative pace; in its settings (the UN building, Plaza Hotel, and Grand Central Station in New York, and Mount Rushmore) it celebrates some of the visual splendours of urban and rural America. Elegant lightness of touch was followed by one of Hitchcock's darker moods, in *Psycho* (1960), based on the novel by Robert Bloch, some of whose short stories had already been used by Hitchcock in his television series. The screenplay was written by Joe Stefano, and made as cheaply as possible at Hitchcock's television studio, where he used the series's technical crew. At this time Hitchcock moved his operations from Paramount to Universal Studios, as MCA, his agents, had taken over Universal. He traded the rights for *Psycho* and the television series for stock in MCA and became one of the company's major shareholders.

Psycho remains one of Hitchcock's most disturbing and perhaps most widely discussed films. At first a critical failure, it was an immediate commercial success. The publicity surrounding the film—Hitchcock insisted that no one be allowed into the cinema after the film had started—perhaps in no small measure added to its mystery.

Hitchcock's involvement with MCA, a move which made him a phenomenally rich man and earned him the independence he craved, did not, however, lead to prolific creativity in the last phase of his career. He directed six more feature films but of these only two are now regarded as undisputed masterpieces: *The Birds* (1963) and *Marnie* (1964). In 1961 Hitchcock had read about a bird invasion of California. This event reminded him of a story by Daphne du Maurier, and he eventually signed up Evan Hunter to write the screenplay after Joe Stefano had turned down the offer. For the lead female role Hitchcock cast Tippi Hedren, a model whom he had first seen on television advertising soft drinks, appointed Robert Burks as director of cinematography, and as art director chose Robert Boyle, who claimed that he had been inspired for his sets by Edvard Munch's painting *The Scream*. Once again Hitchcock's knack for publicity did not desert him. He announced everywhere in the film's promotional material, in a deliberate solecism, that '*The Birds* is coming' (a ploy later borrowed for the publicity of the Mary Millington British soft-porn classic *The Playbirds*, 1978).

In a gesture now regarded by biographers as a further sign of his desire to control the latest female object of his desire, Hitchcock turned Tippi into 'Tippi'; it was as though the single inverted commas rechristened her as a Galatea clone, a creature given life only by her Pygmalion of a film-making master. The mixture of love and hate felt by Hitchcock towards Tippi Hedren, which was to reach its most awkward levels in *Marnie*, was in evidence in his treatment of her during the shooting of some of the scenes, especially those involving the attack by the birds at the end of the film. In this sequence the lower lid of one of her eyes was gashed by a bird, the final straw that almost led to her nervous breakdown. She was not at first considered for the role of the frigid thief in *Marnie*, but was assigned the part after Claire Griswold turned it down.

After *Marnie* Hitchcock received many awards, such as the Milestone award from the Screen Producers' Guild (1965) and the New York cultural medal of honor (1966), and in Britain he lectured at the Cambridge University film society (1966), as well as attending an evening in his honour organized by the Association of Cinematograph, Television and Allied Technicians. The last films, *Torn Curtain* (1966), *Topaz* (1969), *Frenzy* (1972), and *Family Plot* (1976), all of them distinguished by wonderful moments, were generally substandard by comparison with some of his earlier work. *Torn Curtain*, written by Brian Moore and loosely based on the Burgess–Maclean spy scandal, included one or two inspired moments, especially the scene where the hero (Paul Newman) struggles to kill the East German agent detailed to follow him. This film marked the end of the collaboration between Bernard Herrmann and Hitchcock, who was angered by the former's refusal to produce a pop-tune score, a fashionable money-spinning tendency in contemporary films such as *From Russia with Love* (1963). *Topaz* was equally uneven, a film once again with odd moments of brilliance, such as when the Cuban revolutionary leader kills his treacherous lover, allowing her purple cloak to fall from her body in a way that suggests a spreading pool of blood.

Of the last films only *Frenzy*, shot at Pinewood, reaches perhaps more consistently some of the heights of Hitchcock's earlier achievements. Vladimir Nabokov was first approached to write the screenplay, but after he declined the offer, Anthony Shaffer, whose play *Sleuth* had just been a hit in London, took on the challenge. Shaffer's dialogue was constantly sabotaged by Hitchcock's linguistic archaisms. On this film outdated memories of a bygone Britain were oddly matched by Hitchcock's desire to take advantage of some of the more daring liberties the cinema was enjoying through relaxation of the codes of film censorship. Accordingly, the film includes for the first time in a Hitchcock film two scenes showing naked women, the first in a particularly brutal moment when the Barbara Leigh-Hunt character is being raped and strangled to death by a serial killer, the second when the Anna Massey character has spent the night with her lover in a London hotel. While the film was commercially successful (it cost $2 million and grossed $16 million), it was a critical failure; regarded as in many ways anachronistic, its grisly theme was not treated with Hitchcock's customary wit or humanity. The last film, *Family Plot*, which reverted to an American narrative setting, recovered some of the wit, but seemed strangely lightweight, even though it was marked, as ever in Hitchcock, by elegant features.

Anglo-American themes Hitchcock was enchanted by America: the small town ambience of *Shadow of a Doubt*, political grandeur in *Strangers on a Train*, historic national landmarks in *Saboteur* and *North by Northwest*, Hollywood history and the screwball tradition in *Mr and Mrs Smith*, for instance, all reflect this fascination; of the latter he remarked: 'I want to direct a typical American comedy, about typical Americans' (Spoto, *Life*, 237). Even American slang captivated him, as when the East German agent keeping an eye on the Paul Newman character in *Torn Curtain* wonders whether the expression 'strictly for the birds' is still in common usage. Yet for all their dependence on some of the most iconic of American stars—James Stewart, Grace Kelly, and so on—many of Hitchcock's films also rely on British actors and actresses. Cary Grant, that most recognizable of Hitchcock heroes, was British (as were, for instance, James Mason, Ray Milland, Ann Todd, Richard Todd, and a host of minor regulars, such as Leo G. Carroll). Despite a reluctance ever to return to live in Britain (prompted by impatience with British bureaucracy, lax timekeeping, and perhaps even guilt over seeming betrayal of his native country in its hour of need), Hitchcock's love of America never shook off his earlier allegiance to a culture and artistic heritage that remained a source of fascination throughout his life. Britishness was often used by him, as if in self-imposed exile seeing more clearly the essence of his own disowned roots of national identity, as a kind of measure of American achievement.

In common with some of Hollywood's other European émigrés, Hitchcock remains to some extent a victim of memory, his films often embroidered by a pattern of contrasts between America and Britain. Besides the use of British actors, the British settings of *The Paradine Case*, *Stage Fright*, *Dial M for Murder*, and *The Man Who Knew Too Much* testify to this continuing engagement with the lingering memories and distant perspectives of his native culture. The lure of Britain is clear in all of these. Even in *Marnie*, a film whose original British setting in Winston Graham's novel is replaced by Baltimore and other American locations, Hitchcock uses Sean Connery and Alan Napier (Mr Rutland Sr), both British actors, in ways that underline the equivocal force of Britishness, especially in relation to the constraining influence over the American way of life of the somewhat stiff and archaic values of the upper classes. As Mark Rutland, Sean Connery—fresh from his success as James Bond in *Dr No* (1962)—is used, like Cary Grant before him, ambivalently: the perverse, self-appointed saviour of his frigid object of desire, played by Tippi Hedren. The perversity of the role is to some extent developed from the Bond-like qualities of Connery's action-man physique and manner. But it also emerges from the un-Americanness, or Britishness, of Connery himself, a British (Scottish) actor, whose idiosyncratic British-Scottish-English accent plays, together with Alan Napier's, against the American sounds of Marnie. Her flight from Mark Rutland is thus not simply a psychological escape from her own inner demons but also, culturally, for Hitchcock as well as for Marnie, release from the oppression of a supremacist masculinity identified with the prejudices of his British upbringing.

Hitchcock's penultimate film, *Frenzy*, exemplifies these preoccupations most brutally. Here an early contrast is made between an idealized vision of England—conveyed through a politician's quotation of Wordsworth's *The Prelude*—and the reality of a crime-ridden city terrorized by the 'necktie' murderer, one of whose victims is washed up by the Thames at the very moment he pompously invokes England's glorious heritage. The film recalls Kipling's phrase about the 'foreignness of England', and offers no eulogy of London landmarks, but prefers instead, in its concentration above all on Covent Garden (then in its last throes as the capital's foremost fruit and vegetable market), to view it as a site of rottenness, decay, and brutality. Another food-obsessed film (a natural consequence, perhaps, of its obese director's famously inexhaustible appetite for food and drink), it endows the setting with almost scriptural significance as a place of God-given harmony converted into an Edenic 'garden' made in the image of fallen mortals inspired not by love but by base and fatal desires. London becomes the target for a self-exiled Londoner's critique of English culture as a whole. In the circumstances, it seems appropriate that the script (even though written by another Englishman, Anthony Shaffer) uses a British-English archaism, that had long since become standard American usage, further to underline the tensions between the two cultures: 'necktie', no longer used in British English, becomes a minor linguistic example of the triumph of America over England. What is obviously at one level deference to American audiences, more familiar with 'necktie' than 'tie' for this article of clothing, becomes at another a mark of reverse colonization. It is the equivalent of the scene in *Foreign Correspondent*, where the intervention of the American Johnny Jones (Joel McCrea) in the European war in 1940 leads to his solution of various mysteries as soon as his European bowler is blown off his head in the Dutch countryside, an act of nature that enables him to think clearly as an American unhampered by the Old World formality and rigidity symbolized by the hat.

Sin and guilt The 'Edenic' allusions of *Frenzy* belong to a sustained network of references to biblical motifs and concepts. Generally speaking, the church itself (Catholic or protestant), both as an institution and as a projection of patriarchal tendencies in Western notions of family life, is such an essential component of an alienating culture that no reflection on the life of the mind, of social institutions, of history itself, can adequately be made without acknowledgement of its centrality. In Hitchcock's fallen paradise the religious affiliations of characters are often discreetly acknowledged, as when Manny in *The Wrong Man* is seen carrying a rosary with him throughout his ordeal as the innocent victim of mistaken identity. Sometimes the reference is playful, as when Julie Andrews overhears a remark about the mess the religious section is in when she makes contact with a pro-Western spy in a Scandinavian bookshop in *Torn Curtain* (1966). Elsewhere, though, the cruelty and capriciousness of human behaviour is allowed a more developed religious *mise-en-scène*, as in *Vertigo*, where scenes in a church bell-tower or at a cemetery provide fitting backgrounds for a film about mortality and a man's frustrated redemption through love.

But, as many commentators have remarked, guilt is the 'Catholic' theme to which Hitchcock returns with greatest regularity. The blurred boundaries between guilt and innocence provide some of the most striking moments in films such as *The Wrong Man*, *I Confess*, and *Strangers on a Train*. The themes of all of these films are, additionally, threaded around the motif of the double, sinner/saint narratives exemplifying an aleatory law regulating human destiny. An acknowledgement of guilt is an important element in the struggle against immorality, but it is additionally, for the Catholic Hitchcock, confirmation of the sinful nature of human beings whose redemption depends on renunciation of desire. Moving beyond a strictly Catholic notion of post-lapsarian sinfulness, these films also rely on a Poe-like pattern of doubles, a motif underlining the conviction that no human being is spared the torments of dark desires. Hitchcock's admiration of Poe goes beyond a fascination with horror (traces of which may be found, for instance, in *Psycho*), to those stories such as *William Wilson* that hinge on the doubles motif, narratives that in their exploration of questions of identity through patterns of symmetry and reversal also recall G. K. Chesterton's fascination with equivocal personality in such stories as *The Man Who Was Thursday*. There is never really a 'wrong man' or 'wrong woman' in Hitchcock's films, even though his characters are often legally innocent or 'wrongfully' suspected of villainy. The most seemingly innocent of individuals—as, say, John Robie (Cary Grant), who, in *To Catch a Thief*, turns out not to be a cat burglar—is cursed by a shared human destiny of complicity or guilt, unable to shake off the original sin of earlier misdemeanours. The reverse is also true, for example in *Suspicion*, where Johnny Aysgarth (Cary Grant) has all the appearance of a murderer only to be found no more guilty of criminality than his virtuous wife, Lina (Joan Fontaine).

Human dynamics Although many Hitchcock films often concentrate on the loneliness and vulnerability of the individual, the vast majority additionally explore the dynamics of human relationships. *Vertigo*, *North by Northwest*, and *To Catch a Thief* are films that condemn their heroes to moments of isolation, insisting on their confrontation with an ultimately inescapable inner solitude. In *Vertigo* Scottie is a 'wanderer', roaming the streets of San Francisco in search not only of the illusory Madeleine, but also of his own authenticity. The scene in *North by Northwest* where Roger Thornhill is left to fend for himself against an implacable enemy in the shape of the crop-duster offers the viewer a poignant metaphysical image of human isolation. Even in a lighter narrative such as *To Catch a Thief*, the hero's pursuit of the real cat burglar's identity carries the weightier significance of the unavoidable solitariness of the human condition. But loneliness is also a feature of human relationships. Hitchcock combines affirmation with scepticism: acknowledgement of the emotional fulfilments of romantic love is balanced by cynicism towards marriage. The disillusionment of such early films as *Rich and Strange*, which concentrates on the break-up and eventual fragile reconstitution of a marriage during a sea voyage, is preserved throughout Hitchcock's Hollywood period. The shared attraction to romantic love is paralleled by feelings of dread prompted by fears of the entrapments of marriage. L. B. Jefferies (James Stewart) is clearly drawn to Lisa (Grace Kelly) in *Rear Window*, but he is also petrified by the thought of marriage to her, or to any woman. Lisa may be a radiant Fifth Avenue goddess, but to L. B. Jefferies she is also a suffocating source of darkness, her feared powers given visual expression when her shadow spreads over Jefferies' immobilized body, itself a sign of the male's psychological paralysis, during her first appearance in the film. The pattern is reversed in a film like *Marnie*, where Hitchcock concentrates instead on the marital anxieties of the female who strives—here ultimately in failure—to maintain her independence in a world that demands her submission.

Films such as *Suspicion* or *Topaz*, focusing on relationships within marriage, sooner or later expose the compromises and frustrations and, sometimes, the destructive urges to which the institution gives rise. In both these films, as elsewhere, the optimism that initially drew the partners together has quickly given way to feelings of mutual suspicion and unease. In *Suspicion* Lina lives in fear of her very life; in *Topaz* the married couple, Nicole and André, have long-standing extramarital relationships to add spice to lives growing stale through familiarity or indifference. The discontents of the married couple are also reflected onto their offspring. In *Strangers on a Train* Bruno is the perverse child of monstrous parents; *Psycho*, *Marnie*, and *Frenzy* are all films that deal with individuals whose lives have been twisted by disturbed parents. The autobiographical resonances of the generational motif in Hitchcock's films acquire further significance in *Shadow of a Doubt*, where the somewhat stifling mother (Patricia Collinge) has the same name as Hitchcock's own mother, Emma. Norman Bates and Bob Rusk have become killers, Marnie a thief and frigid man-hater. The claustrophobia of family life and the overpowering presence of controlling parents are nowhere more brilliantly expressed than in *Marnie*, where, additionally, the negative influence of a stern form of Christianity has helped deform the mind of an impressionable child.

Hitchcock's male characters are often damaged, rootless, ill at ease with the demands of a changing world: Scottie suffers from vertigo, L. B. Jefferies is immobilized by a broken leg, John Ballantyne suffers from amnesia—all conditions that beyond their literal meanings figuratively attest to male psychological damage or confusion. To stress even further the identification between his screen heroes and their tormented creator, Hitchcock often turns his male characters into voyeurs. The memoir of the scriptwriter Evan Hunter, concerning his differences with Hitchcock over the characterization of Marnie's husband, Mark Rutland, reveals in Hitchcock's insistence on the scene of marital rape during the first night of the honeymoon cruise more than artistic conviction. Hitchcock was here being true to the original, where in Winston Graham's novel Marnie is indeed raped early on in her marriage by her husband, but his complex attitudes towards women cannot be overlooked as reasons behind Hunter's dismissal from the film and the appointment of a writer, Jay Presson Allen, who agreed to preserve the controversial scene.

Women, by contrast, for all their trials as the objects of male victimization, or outright mental or physical torture (for example, Lina in *Suspicion*, Marion Crane in *Psycho*, or Melanie Daniels in *The Birds*), often take the initiative, displaying greater self-confidence and determination. Dr Petersen helps solve the mystery of John Ballantyne's illness in *Spellbound*; Teresa Wright's young Charlie frees herself from the pernicious influence of her misogynistic, widow-preying uncle, and helps bring about his fatal end; and Ingrid Bergman's Alicia Huberman in *Notorious* and Doris Day's Jo McKenna in *The Man Who Knew Too Much* are female characters through whose actions evil is defeated. Even Julie Andrews's Sarah Sherman in *Torn Curtain* refuses to obey Paul Newman's Michael Armstrong when he tells her to stay out of his important mission to infiltrate East Berlin, and insists on accompanying him on his dangerous journey. Many of these characters are played by blonde actresses, famously seen by Hitchcock himself as icy sirens whose impassive exteriors conceal wild and furious passions. Of these, Tippi Hedren (*The Birds*, *Marnie*) is

Hitchcock's most Poe-like beauty: her 'lofty and pale forehead' recalls Ligeia's strange and dream-like appearance, accentuated perhaps by her stiff, untrained method of acting. The former model was forced to endure Hitchcock's offscreen attentions, an obsession that according to her turned to victimization when her refusals of his sexual overtures led for many years after *Marnie*, through his intervention, to an embargo on her acting career.

Significance Hitchcock's themes—perversion, identity, love, violence, sadism, masochism, isolation, mortality—are relayed through popular narratives: comedy thrillers, melodramas of espionage or family life, horror stories, even the odd screwball comedy (*Mr and Mrs Smith*) and musical (*Waltzes from Vienna*). The films often rely for narrative mechanisms on what Hitchcock called the 'MacGuffin', which he defined through a story about two travellers to Scotland. One asks the other about the contents of his suitcase; the other replies that it contains a contraption for trapping lions. The first traveller answers the second's objection that there are no lions in Scotland by remarking that there are no MacGuffins either. The wit of the exchange exemplifies Hitchcock's impatience with literalist readings of his films. His art, like the painter's, asks the viewer not to agonize over degrees of realism but to approach it with a mixture of emotional involvement and cool detachment, a response that demands as much attention to the artifice of the film (something highlighted by, among other things, his preference for so many theatrical settings) as to its commentary on the human condition. The film's truths emerge from its formal construction and inventiveness, especially its visual qualities, in which Hitchcock delighted even to the very end of his career, where the MacGuffin in *Family Plot* (1976) uses the pursuit of diamonds as a mechanism for unlocking questions related to human desire. *Family Plot* also displays Hitchcock's enduring interest in film form, and sees him experimenting with narrative structure. These experiments often rely in his great sound films on lessons learned in his silent film days. Some of the opening shots—for instance, of *Psycho*, *Marnie*, and *Rear Window*—work all the more powerfully for being silent, allowing the viewer to concentrate on visual patterns, the effects of the camera, of lighting and framing. In *Frenzy* one of the film's most disturbing moments arises when the camera withdraws from the room where the 'necktie' murderer will kill his latest victim, leaving the viewer's mind to imagine without sound effects the ordeal soon to be undergone by the unfortunate woman. Through their delicate balance of narrative, camera-work, editing, dialogue (or silence), music, *mise-en-scène*, and actors' performance Hitchcock's films simultaneously delight and instruct, at their best pleasing the senses as well as involving the spectator in the moral and existential dilemmas faced by his characters and the audiences they represent.

Showman, self-publicist, control-freak perfectionist, a mass of contradictions, an English American, Alfred Hitchcock is also probably the most important director in the history of the British cinema. His work has appealed to mass audiences and film historians alike. In numerous interviews with the press Hitchcock schooled his audience on what to expect in his films: 'After a certain amount of suspense', said Hitchcock, the audience must find relief in the catharsis of laughter. However, towards the end of his career he increasingly craved the attention and approval of serious critics, concerned that his work should be accorded the status of art. Young, but highly influential French film critics writing in *Cahiers du Cinéma*, and elsewhere, especially François Truffaut and Claude Chabrol, proclaimed that 'Hitchcock was a cinematic genius who had a distinctive moral vision of the human condition' (Kapsis, *ANB*, 864). To his delight, in 1963 the Museum of Modern Art, New York, screened *The Birds* and launched a retrospective of his films in his honour. His work was further recognized in 1968 when he was honoured both by the Academy of Motion Picture Arts and Sciences, and by the Directors' Guild of America. In 1972 an honorary doctorate was conferred on him by Columbia University. That award, his biographer Donald Spoto has written, was 'only the beginning of the greatest outpouring of adulation America gave Hitchcock in over a decade'. Since the late 1960s his films have become to film studies what Shakespeare is to English literature courses, an almost obligatory focus of discussion not just on thrillers or spy narratives but on film language and the history of film in general.

Beyond the academy, Hitchcock's films inspired other film-makers, both directly and indirectly, both playfully and respectfully: hugely influential through their books in making him even more central to serious discussion of film, Claude Chabrol (in *Le boucher*) and François Truffaut (in *La mariée était en noir*) were enormously indebted in their own films to Hitchcock; Mel Brooks's *High Anxiety* (1977) gestures comically to films such as *Spellbound* and *Vertigo*; Brian de Palma in *Carrie* (1976) and *Dressed to Kill* (1980) glosses Hitchcock's themes of violence and perverse desires; Gus van Sant remade *Psycho* (1998), in colour and with different actors but in other ways almost identically, shot by shot. But beyond these direct influences, Hitchcock's work has become a source of reference for countless film-makers everywhere. His films continue to be at the centre of critical and theoretical debate in influential books and articles on film written all over the world, and the regular showing of his films on television has ensured their popularity with successive generations of film enthusiasts everywhere.

Hitchcock was made an honorary KBE in the new year's honours list for 1980. He died at home in Los Angeles on 29 April 1980. His ashes were scattered in the Pacific Ocean.

PETER WILLIAM EVANS

Sources D. Spoto, *The life of Alfred Hitchcock: the dark side of genius* (1983) · J. R. Taylor, *Hitch: the life and work of Alfred Hitchcock* (1978) · F. Truffaut, *Le cinéma selon Hitchcock* (Paris, 1966) · C. Barr, *English Hitchcock* (1999) · R. E. Kapsis, 'Hitchcock, Alfred', *ANB* · R. E. Kapsis, *Hitchcock: the making of a reputation* (1992) · E. Rohmer and C. Chabrol, *Hitchcock* (Paris, 1957) · S. Gottlieb, *Hitchcock on Hitchcock* (1995) · R. Wood, *Hitchcock's films revisited* (New York, 1989) · J. Freedman and R. Millington, eds., *Hitchcock's America* (New York, 1999) · L. Brill, *The Hitchcock romance: love and irony in Hitchcock's films* (Princeton, 1988) · E. Hunter, *Me and Hitch* (1997) · T. Modleski, *The women who knew too much: Hitchcock and feminist theory* (1988) · D. Spoto, *The art of Alfred Hitchcock: fifty years of his motion pictures* (1977) · P. Condon and J. Sangster, *The complete Hitchcock* (1999) · *DNB*

Archives FILM BFI NFTVA, 'Alfred Hitchcock', 20 May 1966 · BFI NFTVA, 'Hitchcock at the NFT', 19 June 1970 · BFI NFTVA, 'Alfred the great', 5 Aug 1972 · BFI NFTVA, 'The men who made the movies', 1973 · BFI NFTVA, 'Alfred Hitchcock, 1899–1980', 1980 · BFI NFTVA, 'The art of film', 1980 · BFI NFTVA, 'Hitchcock', 22 Sept 1982 · BFI NFTVA, 'Hitchcock, il brivido del genio', 1985 · BFI NFTVA, *Omnibus*, 26 Sept 1986 · BFI NFTVA, *Omnibus*, 3 Oct 1986 · BFI NFTVA, 'Alfred Hitchcock', 15 Sept 1989 · BFI NFTVA, 'Alfred Hitchcock's gun', 1997 · BFI NFTVA, 'Close up on Hitchcock', BBC2, 27 April 1997 · BFI NFTVA, *Reputations*, BBC2, 3 May 1999 · BFI NFTVA, 'Hitchcock on Hitchcock', BBC2, 1 June 1999 · BFI NFTVA, 'Hitchcock, Selznick and the end of Hollywood', Channel 4, 1 Jan 2000 · BFI NFTVA, current affairs footage · BFI NFTVA, documentary footage | SOUND BL NSA, 'Alfred Hitchcock, a radio portrait', 29 March 1955, NP10726W · BL NSA, 'Hitch: a tribute to Alfred Hitchcock', BBC Radio 4, 1980, T3614 R TR1 · BL NSA, 'Time of my life', T132W BD1 · BL NSA, documentary footage · BL NSA, performance footage

Likenesses photographs, 1926–80, Hult. Arch. · H. Coster, photographs, c.1936, NPG · I. Penn, gelatin silver print, 1947, NPG · Y. Karsh, photographs, bromide print, 1960, NPG [*see illus.*] · B. Willoughby, photograph, bromide print, 1964, NPG · J. Fraser, wax head, 1967, Madame Tussaud's, London

Hitchcock, Sir **Eldred Frederick** (1887–1959), businessman, was born on 9 December 1887 in Islington, London, the eldest, with his twin sister, Effie, of the seven children of Eldred Hitchcock, superintendent of Dr Barnardo's Home, Epsom, and his wife, Louisa Naomi Orchard. He was educated at Burford grammar school and in 1910 obtained a diploma in economics from the University of Oxford. In September 1912, attracted to Fabian socialism, he became a resident at Toynbee Hall, also serving there as secretary and, from 1915 to 1924, as a member of the council of the Universities' Settlement Association. When the warden instigated a move to Poplar in 1915 Hitchcock remained at Whitechapel, where he supervised educational and institutional activities, placing particular emphasis upon courses of Jewish interest. When the Poplar project failed, Hitchcock assumed the role of acting warden in 1917. He oversaw the reinvigoration of Toynbee Hall, reopening the residential quarters, attracting new residents, and appealing for funds to enable the settlement to participate in the task of post-war reconstruction. In these activities Hitchcock was supported by Ethel May (Patricia) Cooper (d. 1956), daughter of New Zealand sheep farmer Adolphus Frederick William Lorie and widow of a Ceylon tea planter, whose journalistic ambitions had led her to London and thence to the East End, whom he married in 1915. They had two children: Hilary Mary and Eldred Arnold.

Hitchcock's other, and principal, wartime employment was as a War Office statistician (he later became a life fellow of the Royal Statistical Society); he became assistant director of raw materials and finally deputy director of wool textile production. He travelled widely, and served in the war trade department, the Comité International de Ravitaillement (1915–19), the Wool Control Board, and as

Sir Eldred Frederick Hitchcock (1887–1959), by Harold Knight, exh. RA 1950

chairman of the standard clothing committee. He was made a CBE in 1920, received the order of St Stanislas (second class) from the tsarist government, and became a chevalier of the Belgian order of Crown.

Hitchcock's experience steered him towards a business career after his resignation from Toynbee Hall in 1919. His involvement in a travel agency proved nearly ruinous; the establishment late in life of a tea estate in the Tanganyikan Usambara Mountains was unsuccessful. However, an investment in 1926 in the sisal firm which became Bird & Co. (Africa) Ltd, followed by election to the company board, led to distinguished employment in the east African sisal industry. In 1937 he settled in Tanganyika, becoming in 1939 managing director of the company's sisal estates there and, in 1950, chairman. Hitchcock was the leading figure during a period of great expansion in Tanganyikan sisal production. From 1946 onwards he was continuously either chairman or vice-chairman of the Tanganyika Sisal Growers' Association. He secured favourable terms for growers from the wartime British bulk purchase of east African sisal and strengthened their position in relation to London-run estates and merchants. A confrontation between Hitchcock and the London Sisal Growers' Association, who accused him of peculation while chairman, ended in the replacement of the association by a London committee chosen by east African growers (Westcott, 456). When bulk purchasing ceased in 1948, Hitchcock organized a Tanganyika Sisal Marketing Association, which accounted for approximately half of the colony's sisal output. The robust style which won him

acclaim as a brilliant negotiator sometimes had its drawbacks: the probability that growers would elect him chairman of the sisal board, reformed at the end of the war, was regarded by the authorities as 'very unwelcome … if not a calamity' and deterred them from allowing growers to select their own chair (Westcott, 457).

Hitchcock's 'barbed tongue' (Bates, 226) also enlivened his relations with some British governors of Tanganyika. He opposed the east African groundnut scheme, regarding it as agriculturally unsound and as presenting unfair competition to the sisal industry. Although Hitchcock, a leading representative of those Europeans advocating multiracialism, was one of thirty 'unofficials' nominated by Sir Edward Twining to the legislative council in 1955, he was 'neither happy nor effective' (*DNB*), and resigned at the first opportunity. He was also, in February 1956, a founder member of the unsuccessful United Tanganyika Party, which aimed at keeping race out of politics. He served on the east African commission's transport committee. Hitchcock's youthful progressivism was still manifest on economic as well as racial issues: he was instrumental in the effective organization of trade unionism in the sisal industry and sought to improve labour conditions.

Hitchcock's style challenged contemporaries' stereotype of a colonial capitalist. Situated in the same building as his offices, his flat evidenced his 'remarkable and deep instinctive feeling for all the visual arts and for history' (Freeman-Grenville, 3). His collection of medieval Islamic pottery was sufficiently important to be catalogued as *Islamic Pottery from the Ninth to the Fourteenth Centuries A. D.* (1956), with an introduction by Arthur Lane, keeper of ceramics at the Victoria and Albert Museum. Other interests included Chinese porcelain and African art and archaeology. He instigated the visit of Sir Mortimer Wheeler and Gervase Mathew to Tanganyika and the establishment of a Tanganyikan department of antiquities, and sought to secure a proposed British school of archaeology and history in east Africa for Tanganyika. He derived immense pleasure from his election as fellow of the Society of Antiquaries in 1957. In Britain he formed a business called Sculptures and Memorials intended not only to raise the standard of churchyard memorials—partly by substituting English stones for Italian marble and by improving the lettering—but also to secure more commissions for friends including Eric Gill and Gilbert Ledward.

Hitchcock was knighted in 1955. In the same year he published *The Sisal Industry of Tanganyika*; other publications included articles and encyclopaedia entries on sisal and economics. Short and 'pugnacious', Hitchcock could when angry be 'outrageously rude' (*DNB*). He was nevertheless valued for his dynamism, generosity, and loyalty. Resident in Tanganyika for much of his adult life, he retained an attachment to youthful haunts, being a great friend and benefactor of Burford grammar school, his old school, and undertaking the restoration of the fifteenth-century St Peter's Chapel, Burford church. His failing wife lived just long enough to see its completion and to unveil their joint memorial; she died on 21 November 1956.

Hitchcock himself died in Tanga, Tanganyika, of a heart attack, on 6 April 1959, and his ashes were strewn in Burford churchyard. SARAH STOCKWELL

Sources *The Times* (7 April 1959) · G. S. P. Freeman-Grenville, *Tanganyika Notes and Records*, 52 (March 1959) [with additional information from G. S. P. Freeman-Grenville, p. 3] · J. E. R., letter, *The Times* (14 April 1959) · B. Nihill, letter, *The Times* (22 April 1959) · C. W. Guillebaud, letter, *The Times* (13 April 1959) · *The Times* (28 Nov 1956) [obit. of Lady Hitchcock] · *DNB* · J. A. R. Pimlott, *Toynbee Hall: fifty years of social progress, 1884–1934* (1935), 190–207 · N. Westcott, 'The East African sisal industry, 1929–1949: the marketing of a colonial commodity during depression and war', *Journal of African History*, 25 (1984), 445–61 · A. Briggs and A. Macartney, *Toynbee Hall: the first hundred years* (1984), 88–91 · *CGPLA Eng. & Wales* (1960) · Kelly, *Handbk* (1956) · J. Iliffe, *A modern history of Tanganyika* (1979) · D. Bates, *A gust of plumes: a biography of Lord Twining of Godalming and Tanganyika* (1972), 226–7 · *Burford grammar school, 1571–1971* (1971), 119–21

Archives Bodl. RH, notes for East African commission on labour problems, MSS Afr. S.960 | GL, London Sisal Association MSS

Likenesses H. Knight, oils, exh. RA 1950; formerly in Tanganyika, copyprint, NPG [*see illus.*] · photograph, repro. in Pimlott, *Toynbee Hall*, facing p. 192

Wealth at death £39,504 10s. 4d.—in England: probate, 28 Nov 1960, *CGPLA Eng. & Wales*

Hitchcock, Richard (1825–1856), antiquary, was the son of Rodney Hitchcock (*d.* 1853), a farmer, of Spring Vale, co. Cork, Ireland. He was born at Blennerville, near Tralee, co. Kerry, in March 1825. He spent much of his early life studying the antiquities of his native county, which he examined enthusiastically, writing accurate descriptions of them illustrated with his own minute drawings. His work soon brought him to the notice of Dr Charles Graves, later bishop of Limerick, Ardfert, and Aghadoe, who had him appointed an assistant librarian at Trinity College, Dublin. He made good use of his position as librarian and contributed many papers to the *Journal of the Kilkenny and South-East of Ireland Archaeological Society*. These were invariably characterized by accuracy. Ogham writing was his favourite study; two manuscript volumes of his notes on ogham inscriptions are in the Royal Irish Academy. Hitchcock died at Roundwood, co. Wicklow, on 3 December 1856, leaving a widow.

WILLIAM REYNELL, *rev.* MICHAEL HERITY

Sources private information (1888) · *Journal of the Royal Historical and Archaeological Association of Ireland*, 4th ser., 10 (1889) [index to vols. 1–19, 81] · *Journal of the Kilkenny and South-East of Ireland Archaeological Society*, new ser., 1 (1856–7), 242 · Boase, *Mod. Eng. biog.*

Archives Royal Irish Acad.

Hitchcock, Robert (*fl.* 1573–1591), soldier and writer, described himself as a gentleman of Caverfield, Buckinghamshire, and the family is known to have had property in the county in the late fifteenth century. His right to Caverfield was disputed by two other claimants, but in March 1573 judgment was given in Star Chamber, apparently in his favour. Hitchcock's vocation was war. In the early 1580s, as England prepared for war with Spain, he was selected among the 'Marshall men & captaines ... to be presently imployd' (BL, Lansdowne MS 113, fol. 148r), and other sources also testify to considerable experience. In 1586 he raised nearly 200 'voluntarie men' from Buckinghamshire for a company in Dutch service, though it was

among several 'cassed' (disbanded) by the states general in spring 1587. Hitchcock received the last £145 owed him by the Dutch only on 29 June 1588, and since he collected the arrears due to three other English captains, he was probably liked and certainly trusted by his fellow officers. Between July and October 1587 he commanded a 150-strong band from Buckinghamshire in the royal army that unsuccessfully attempted to relieve Sluys. This was his last active service.

Hitchcock was also a writer. His early works were on military strategy and circulated only in manuscript, though they attracted attention. John Foxe kept a copy of Hitchcock's 'A discourse for defence against the threatened invasion of the Holy League' (BL, Lansdowne MS 389, fols. 339r–350v), which Strype praised in his *Annals of the Reformation*. Written in 1571, it was submitted to the queen in 1580; her grant to Hitchcock a year later of lands worth £133 6s. 8d. a year suggests she approved of it. In January 1581 Hitchcock published his first book, *A politique platt for the honour of the prince, the greate profite of the publique states, reliefe of the poore, preservation of the rich, reformation of roges and idle persons, and the wealthe of thousands*, with a preface by his brother Francis. It detailed a scheme for developing the Newfoundland herring fisheries that had come before parliament in 1576. Hitchcock had invited virtually all the MPs for seaport boroughs to a lavish dinner in an attempt to win their support. Thomas Digges, another soldier interested in technical matters, introduced the proposal into the Commons, but an early prorogation of parliament prevented further progress. In 1590 Hitchcock published *The Quintessence of Wit*, a translation from the Italian of a miscellany of Francisco Sansovino's work. Finally, in 1591 he published *The Arte of Warre*, written by William Garrard, another veteran of the Dutch wars, who had died in 1587. Hitchcock 'corrected, finished and published Garrard's MS' (Webb, 48), but appended an original work on logistics, *A Generall Proportion and Order for Provision*.

The soldier–writers in late sixteenth-century England formed a close circle. Robert Hitchcock, unlike Thomas Churchyard, Barnaby Rich, Barnaby Googe, Roger Williams, or George Gascoigne (all of whom he must have known), wrote neither prose narratives nor verse. Nor does he compare to them in literary quality: as he admitted, others wrote with 'pleasanter wordes and [more] sugred stile then I' (*A Politique Platt*, preface). Nevertheless, he was a member, albeit a marginal one, of a group that was of great importance in the English literary renaissance. The date of his death is unknown.

D. J. B. TRIM

Sources *DNB* · *APC*, 1571–5; 1586–8 · Nationaal Archief, The Hague, Archief van de staten-generaal, no. 12536 · Nationaal Archief, The Hague, Archief van de raad van state, no. 1524 · Nationaal Archief, The Hague, Archief van Johan van Oldenbarnevelt, no. 2943 · BL, Add. MS 48084, fols. 84r, 86r · BL, Lansdowne MS 113, fols. 148r, 339r–350v · BL, Lansdowne MS 389 · M. J. D. Cockle, *A bibliography of military books up to 1642*, 2nd edn (1957); repr. (1978) · H. J. Webb, *Elizabethan military science: the books and the practice* (1965) · PRO, E 351/240; SP 9/93, fol. 53r · J. Strype, *Annals of the Reformation and establishment of religion ... during Queen Elizabeth's happy reign*, new edn, 2/2 (1824), 368–70 · Bodl. Oxf., MS Tanner 79, fols. 69v–70r • *CPR*, 1580–82 • W. H. Rylands, ed., *The visitation of the county of Buckingham made in 1634*, Harleian Society, 58 (1909)

Hitchcock, Robert (*d.* 1809), actor and playwright, was a member, with his wife, Sarah, of the company of the Theatre Royal, Norwich, from 1769 to 1771 when they both joined Tate Wilkinson's travelling company, based in York. Here they remained until 1777. Hitchcock's comedy *The Macaroni* was produced in York in 1773, and at the Haymarket Theatre later that year. It was published first by subscription in York, and then in London, Belfast, Dublin, and Philadelphia. *The Coquette, or, The Mistakes of the Heart*, his adaptation for the stage of Eliza Haywood's novel *The History of Miss Betsy Thoughtless*, was first performed in Hull in 1775, and two years later was produced at the Haymarket Theatre and published in Bath.

The Hitchcocks performed with their son Robert (then aged only eight or nine) in Bristol and Bath in the summer of 1776, and joined the company at the Haymarket the next year. Sarah Hitchcock performed a large number of roles here, but her husband appeared much less frequently on the stage, taking up duties as prompter. His son and his daughter Mary Anne also made débuts at the Haymarket in 1777, in Garrick's *Lilliput*. Both she and her brother Robert would be actors in their youth, but later leave the stage: Robert became a member of the Irish bar; Mary Anne married a Dublin barrister, Jonas Greene.

Hitchcock was the model for the character of the prompter in *The Manager in Distress* (1780) by George Colman the elder, the manager of the Haymarket. In the winter seasons, Hitchcock and his wife continued to act for Wilkinson's York company. In 1781 the family moved to Dublin to work for Richard Daly at Smock Alley, Hitchcock as prompter, his wife and daughter as actresses. In 1788 Hitchcock published *An Historical View of the Irish Stage; from the Earliest Period Down to 1788* (vol. 2 published 1794). In this year he moved with Daly to Crow Street, where he worked until his death, at 5 Clarendon Street, Dublin, in 1809 (*European Magazine*, 54, 478). His wife continued to be a successful actress, and was still performing in 1810, but the date of her death is unknown. The Hitchcocks had at least seven children, the seventh, Sarah, being born in 1781. Hitchcock's character is described in Tate Wilkinson's memoir, *The Wandering Patentee* (1795).

JOHN MULLAN

Sources Highfill, Burnim & Langhans, *BDA* • C. B. Hogan, ed., *The London stage, 1660–1800*, pt 5: 1776–1800 (1968) • *ESTC*

Hitchen, Charles (*c.*1675–1727?), thief-taker and marshal of the City of London, is of unknown parentage and background. He was apprenticed as a cabinet-maker and practised that trade for some years. In 1703 he married Elizabeth, the daughter of John Wells of King's Walden, Hertfordshire, and they subsequently came to live in a house on the north side of St Paul's Churchyard in the City of London. Hitchen was fortunate in his marriage, for Elizabeth inherited property from her father when he died in 1711 and that property (which Hitchen persuaded his wife to sell) enabled him to purchase the office of under-marshal of the City for £700 in the following year (CLRO,

repertories of the court of aldermen 116.60; journals of the common council, 57.207).

Hitchen wanted the office for a purpose. The two City marshals, with their small force of six men, carried out policing duties that centred principally on keeping the streets clear of vagrants, prostitutes, and illegal traders. Fees accruing for this and other work carried out at the behest of the lord mayor, as well as an annual salary and allowances of about £100, repaid the purchase price of the office over time. But Hitchen was clearly interested in the more corrupt possibilities that the authority of the marshal's office provided. Soon after assuming office he began to extort protection money from brothel- and tavern-keepers. But he particularly used his powers of arrest to threaten young pickpockets with prosecution, not to discourage them from thieving but to coerce them into bringing him the goods that they stole so that he could negotiate with their victims for the return of their belongings for a fee.

Thief-takers of this kind, acting as middlemen between thieves and their victims, were well known in Anne's reign; indeed, their activities may have been increasing then because of efforts made by parliament and the magistrates of the City to seek out and punish receivers of stolen goods. It was safer in those circumstances, and perhaps more profitable, for thieves to return the items they stole for a portion of their value. On the other side many of their victims were willing to pay to recover their goods— particularly merchants and tradesmen who lost pocket-books and valuable commercial papers to pickpockets and other thieves. Hitchen may well have been involved in arranging such transactions before he invested his wife's money in the office of under-marshal. But he became more active with the authority of the office behind him. He openly bragged about controlling dozens of young pickpockets and sought out their victims to pressure them to use his services as a middleman. His tactics were so aggressive and crude, and so many respectable men in the City complained about him, that in September 1712— barely ten months after taking up the post—the court of aldermen investigated his activities, interviewed his accusers and several of the young pickpockets he had dealt with, and in June 1713 suspended him from office (CLRO, Misc MS 105.8; papers of the court of aldermen, 1712–13; repertories 117–18).

Hitchen survived as under-marshal. The aldermen were clearly reluctant to discharge him from an office that he had so recently purchased, fearing perhaps to devalue the post, since the City treasury benefited from a portion of the sale price. He was reinstated in April 1714 (CLRO, repertories, 118.219), in part because he claimed to be developing a plan to diminish crime in the City, and at that moment—in the months after the end of the War of the Spanish Succession and the demobilization of Marlborough's continental army, and the discharge of large numbers of sailors—violent street crime was a pressing issue for the government of the City. Hitchen's dealings as a middleman almost certainly continued but in the meantime he had inadvertently encouraged a powerful rival by engaging Jonathan Wild as his assistant during his suspension from office. They were soon to fall out when Wild—seizing the opportunities to profit from the increase in serious offences in the post-war years—set out to construct a more ambitious system of thief-taking than Hitchen had operated, a system that combined the return of stolen goods with the prosecution of street robbers and other offenders whose conviction brought handsome rewards. Their rivalry became public knowledge when Hitchen sought to enlarge his own reputation and win the support of the court of aldermen for his plan to eliminate crime by publishing in 1718 an attack on Wild as the 'regulator' of the criminal world—charging him with manipulating evidence to convict and hang minor offenders while protecting greater villains and profiting from the return of stolen valuables (C. Hitchen, *A True Discovery of the Conduct of Receivers and Thief-Takers in and about the City of London*). Wild replied with an account of his work as Hitchen's assistant and of the marshal's conniving at, and profiting from, the thefts carried out by numerous young pickpockets in the City. Even more damagingly, perhaps, he included evidence of Hitchen's homosexuality by telling how the marshal had taken him to a molly house, one of several such clubs for homosexual men established in London in the early decades of the eighteenth century (J. Wild, *An Answer to a Late Insolent Libel*, 1718, 30–31).

Hitchen made a feeble attempt to turn these charges aside by reissuing his condemnation of Wild, in a slightly enlarged version, under a new title (*The Regulator, or, A Discovery of the Thieves, Thief-Takers and Locks*, 1718), but he appears to have been very largely silenced by this exchange. He no doubt continued to profit corruptly from his office, but he only came to public attention again a decade later because of his alleged homosexuality, when he was caught up in a campaign conducted against 'sodomitical practices' by the Societies for the Reformation of Manners. Hitchen was tried at the Old Bailey in April 1727 for the capital offence of sodomy, and although acquitted of that charge he was convicted on a second indictment of attempted sodomy (Old Bailey sessions papers, April 1727, 5–6). He had been saved from the gallows but, along with a fine of £20 and six months' imprisonment, his sentence included an hour on the pillory—a frightening prospect for men convicted of homosexual offences, particularly in his case, for, as the newspapers revealed, he had particularly targeted young men. He was to be pilloried, it was reported, 'at Katherine-Street End in the Strand, near the Place where he made his vicious Attacks upon young Youths' (*Parker's Penny Post*, 26 April 1727). In the event he was badly mauled by the large crowd that came well prepared to torment him—pelted with missiles, stripped of his shirt and breeches, and 'cruelly beaten'. The under-sheriff took him down long before his appointed hour had passed (*London Journal*, 6 May 1727; *Evening Post*, 29 April–2 May 1727). He was taken back to Newgate prison to serve out his term. In September, as his six-month sentence was coming to an end, Hitchen was dismissed as under-marshal by the court of aldermen for his 'notorious and wicked practices' and—as though that

would not be sufficient justification—for neglecting the duty of the office for the previous six months (CLRO, repertories 131.408, 421–2). He died shortly thereafter in poverty, leaving his long-suffering wife to petition the common council of the City for help; she was granted an annuity of £20 for her support (CLRO, journals 57, 207).

J. M. BEATTIE

Sources G. Howson, *Thief-taker general: the rise and fall of Jonathan Wild* (1970) · J. M. Beattie, *Policing and punishment in London, 1660–1750: urban crime and the limits of terror* (2001) · T. Wales, 'Thief-takers and their clients in later Stuart London', *Londinopolis: essays in the culture and social history of early modern London*, ed. P. Griffiths and M. R. S. Jenner (2000), 67–85 · R. Norton, *Mother Clap's molly house: the gay subculture in England, 1700–1830* (1992) · *The proceedings on the king's commission of the peace* [Old Bailey sessions papers] · CLRO, Misc. MS 105.8

Hitchens, (Sydney) Ivon (1893–1979), painter, was born on 3 March 1893 at 35 Kensington Square, London, the only child of Alfred Hitchens (*b.* 1861), a painter, and his wife, Ethel Margaret Seth-Smith. Alfred Hitchens was a modestly successful, conventional artist who won gold medals in national competitions for painting and drawing and exhibited several times at the Royal Academy. His wife, who came from a reasonably prosperous family, was herself a gifted amateur artist, and consequently Ivon inherited natural gifts and spent much of his infancy in his father's studio, posing, aged one, as the infant Jesus for one of his father's works.

In 1900, at the age of seven, Hitchens was sent away to Conamur School at Sandgate, near Folkestone, Kent. There he was reasonably happy and had the dubious distinction of acting as a go-between for one of his schoolmistresses and the sexually indefatigable H. G. Wells. In 1903 he went as one of the early pupils to Bedales School, Hampshire, founded in 1893 by J. H. Badley. It was there that he had his first experience of the Sussex and Hampshire downlands which were to influence his work so profoundly. His skills in painting and drawing were encouraged by G. H. Cooper, his art master, but his school career was abruptly ended by his contracting acute appendicitis. His parents sent him on a recuperative voyage to New Zealand, via Ceylon and Australia, to stay with an aunt of his mother's who had married a sheep farmer there. In 1911 he began his formal art education at the St John's Wood Art Schools, while living with his parents in London. From 1912 to 1916 and in 1918–19 he studied at the Royal Academy Schools, where his instructors included Sir William Orpen, John Singer Sargent, and George Clausen.

Deemed unfit for active service in 1914 because he had—despite his year in the Antipodes—never fully recovered robust health, Hitchens's studies at the RA Schools were interrupted by two years' war service working in hospital supply. When both the war and his interrupted studies ended he moved, in 1919, into his own studio at 169 Adelaide Road in Hampstead, London, where he stayed until 1940. In that year, driven out by wartime bombs, he moved with his wife and infant son to a caravan in Sussex. He had married, on 27 June 1935, Mary Cranford (Mollie) Coates (1909–1993), daughter of the Revd Matthew Francis Coates of Hove, Sussex. Their only son, John Hitchens (*b.* 1940), also became a successful painter. Greenleaves, Lavington Common, near Petworth, began as a caravan and a small studio and gradually grew, with Hitchens's increasing success, to become, with numerous additions, a delightful, sprawling, and spacious one-storey home, with the caravan eventually functioning as a modest guest house. The house and its extensive wilderness-like grounds with massive rhododendrons and a small lake, complete with wooden boat, totally secluded (by a virtually concealed drive) from the outside world, enabled the artist to live like a recluse when he so chose. Visitors came by invitation only and could not find the house without careful directions from its owner. Yet, while he lived like a recluse, he and his wife were in fact selectively gregarious and both generous and hospitable. Greenleaves was both protection and inspiration for the gently ruthless pursuit of his painting. It kept outsiders at bay and it provided, with its vast, wild garden, endless raw material for landscapes, flower pieces, and, in the case of the caravan, a temporary home for the occasional models he used for his figure paintings.

The move to Greenleaves was the watershed of Hitchens's life and career, forming the base for nearly four decades of entirely individualistic and largely unfashionable activity. But before his move, he had been very much a part of the mainstream of the modern movement in Britain. In 1921 he had exhibited at the second Seven and Five show and, in 1922, was elected a member of the Seven and Five Society, one of the most influential groups of British modern artists, including as it did David Jones, Barbara Hepworth, Frances Hodgkins, Henry Moore, Ben Nicholson, Winifred Nicholson, John Piper, and Christopher Wood.

In 1925, aged thirty-two, Hitchens had his first one-man exhibition at the Mayor Gallery, London. One picture was bought by the influential civil servant and patron of young artists Sir Edward Marsh. His second show was at Tooth's in 1928, and his reputation burgeoned both at home and abroad (he exhibited at the 1937 and 1938 Pittsburgh International Exhibitions) until the outbreak of war in 1939 resulted in the confinement of his reputation to the United Kingdom.

Hitchens's art before 1939 was heterogeneous and to a considerable extent influenced, particularly in his landscapes, by Cézanne, as in *Curved Barn* (1922). In his experiments with abstraction he was inevitably influenced by Ben Nicholson, as in *Control* (1935), or the superb *Coronation* (1937) which was bought by the Chantrey bequest for the Tate Gallery. Yet, significantly, by 1934 he had taken part in an exhibition at the Zwemmer Gallery entitled 'Objective abstractions' which represented a move away from the Seven and Five Society and teamed him with, among others, Victor Pasmore, Rodrigo Moynihan, and Ceri Richards.

After 1940 Hitchens moved to the Leicester Galleries and showed regularly there until 1960, when the Waddington Galleries became his dealer and ensured for him a quiet and highly organized prosperity. In the 1940s, having found his true home in Sussex, he also found his mature style and developed the paintings for which he is principally known—the subtle, quasi-abstract landscapes, invariably 'cinemascope' in shape, also sometimes referred to as 'double-square format[s] … in which the sweep of a broad full brush can connote seasonal moods, a stretch of sky or water or the movement of wind' (F. Spalding, *20th Century Painters and Sculptors*, 1990, 240). These were painted in a restricted number of sizes and always meticulously framed, under his own supervision, in considerable depth. Although abstract in appearance and often divided into three carefully, almost architecturally organized sections, these paintings are in fact supremely sophisticated landscapes inspired by the Sussex downlands in general or his own estate in particular. They are often analogous to musical compositions, reflecting his wife's early career as a pianist and his own abiding passion for music which was often playing on the gramophone while he painted. He was a sumptuous colourist and these landscapes are among the glories of English painting in the second half of the twentieth century.

Hitchens was also a figure painter of much distinction and his nudes are probably second in quality and appeal in England in the twentieth century only to those of Matthew Smith and Stanley Spencer. Hitchens excelled in the difficult and now rare art of mural painting, and his huge (16 ft x 82 ft) mural for the English Folk Song and Dance Society at Cecil Sharp House in Regent's Park, London, is, apart from its great size, a major work of the intellect and the visual imagination. In 1955–6 he designed a set for the Royal Opera House production of Sir Frederick Ashton's ballet *La Péri*, starring Margot Fonteyn and Michael Somes.

Hitchens exhibited at the 1956 Venice Biennale, was appointed CBE in 1958, and had a major Arts Council retrospective exhibition at the Tate Gallery in 1963 and a Royal Academy retrospective in 1979. For his friends and serious admirers he was a remarkably lucid, discursive, and critically gifted correspondent. To those who knew him well he was a man of paradox—a prolific artist who worked rapidly, yet frequently modified and improved canvases for up to ten years before considering them finished. A frail figure, he was something of a valetudinarian, wearing multiple layers of warm clothing even in summer. Yet he was a hardy and ceaseless worker into his eighties. A ruthlessly dedicated artist for whom the act of painting came before everything else, he was nevertheless a man of great human warmth and much grace, both internal and external, and possessed a genuinely gentle disposition and true sweetness of spirit. He was a prodigious correspondent and his letters almost invariably contain examples of his constant theorizing about art in general and his own painting in particular. He also published a notable essay, 'Notes on painting', in *Ark* (18, Nov 1956, 51–2), the journal of the Royal College of Art. In both his art and his life he was quintessentially English and of true distinction. Hitchens died at Greenleaves on 29 August 1979 and was buried at Petworth, Sussex.

T. G. ROSENTHAL

Sources P. Heron, *Ivon Hitchens*, Penguin Modern Painters (1955) • A. Bowness, ed., *Ivon Hitchens* (1973) [with an introductory essay by T. G. Rosenthal] • P. Khoroche, *Ivon Hitchens* (1990) • personal knowledge (2004) • private information (2004)
Archives Tate collection, letters to Michael Ayrton • Tate collection, letters to Kit Barker • Tate collection, notes for and letters to Alan Bowness • Tate collection, letters to Adrian Hill • University of East Anglia Library, Norwich, corresp. with J. C. Pritchard
Likenesses J. S. Murray, photograph, 1933, NPG • I. Hitchens, self-portrait, 1950, Tate collection • J. S. Lewinski, photograph, 1964, NPG • photograph, repro. in Khoroche, *Ivon Hitchens*, frontispiece
Wealth at death £73,315: probate, 11 Feb 1980, *CGPLA Eng. & Wales*

Hitchins, Fortescue (1784–1814). *See under* Hitchins, Malachy (*bap.* 1741, *d.* 1809).

Hitchins, Malachy (*bap.* **1741**, *d.* **1809**), astronomer, the son of Thomas Hitchins, was born at Little Trevince, Gwennap, Cornwall, where he was baptized on 18 May 1741. His mother was a sister of Thomas Martyn, the compiler of a map of Cornwall, and the missionary Henry Martyn (1781–1812) was his cousin. The topographical writer Richard Polwhele, a friend of Hitchins, says that he worked first as a miner, but went to Exeter to assist Benjamin Donn in the creation of his map of Devon, which was published in 1765. Hitchins had previously contributed mathematical replies to the *Ladies' Diary* for 1761. In December 1762 he was residing at Bideford. On 10 October 1763 he matriculated at Exeter College, Oxford. Polwhele says that the expenses of his university education were met by his wife, Joanna Hawkin, whom he married on 10 January 1764 at Buckland Brewer, Devon. Hitchins did not, however, graduate BA until 27 February 1781; in 1785 he was incorporated at St John's College, Cambridge, where he graduated MA in the same year.

The first British *Nautical Almanac* was that for the year 1767. It was edited by the astronomer royal, Nevil Maskelyne, who devised a 'cottage industry' system of computation whereby all important calculations were done twice, by two 'computers' working quite separately in their own homes; these two sent their results to Maskelyne at Greenwich, and he would forward them to the 'comparer' for checking the one against the other. Late in 1767 Hitchins was recommended to Maskelyne by Thomas Hornsby as a possible computer, which he became in 1768. In 1769 he became the comparer, a post he retained, working in Cornwall, until his death forty years later.

From April to August 1769 Hitchins was at the Royal Observatory, Greenwich, temporarily acting as Maskelyne's assistant in the place of William Bayly, who went to Norway in order to observe the transit of Venus on 3 June. Hitchins himself successfully observed the transit in the eastern summer house at Greenwich with the Revd William Hirst. While at Greenwich he entered holy orders, and after moving to Exeter was for a short time vicar of Hennock. On 6 November 1775 Bishop Keppel presented him to the vicarage of St Hilary, Cornwall, and on 23 May 1785 to that of Gwinear. Hitchins retained both livings until his death.

In 1793 there occurred a crisis in the affairs of the computers of the *Nautical Almanac* when the board of longitude

decided that, because much improved astronomical tables were about to be produced in France, the *Nautical Almanac* should in future be published five, rather than ten, years in advance. (That for 1804 was already published.) Hitchins petitioned the board:

> Having been employed for 26 years past by the Hon. Board of Longitude in computing and revising the Nautical Almanac ... he is sorry to find that he is now suddenly and unexpectedly to lose his Appointment for 7 or 8 years to come, and perhaps for ever. (CUL, RGO MS 14/22, fol. 221)

In the event, work was found for the computers, but their income was much reduced.

Hitchins assisted Polwhele with his *History of Cornwall*, published between 1803 and 1808. He was a friend of Davies Gilbert, a fellow Cornishman who became president of the Royal Society. Hitchins died at St Hilary on 28 March 1809 and was buried in the church there.

Hitchins and his wife had four sons. The eldest, Richard Hawkin Hitchins (1764–1827), was a fellow of Exeter College, Oxford, and rector of Baverstock in Wiltshire. The youngest, **Fortescue Hitchins** (1784–1814), born at St Hilary on 22 February 1784, became a solicitor at St Ives. He published a number of poems and other slight works, admired in their day, and compiled material for a history of Cornwall, which after his death was edited by Samuel Drew and published in 1824. He died at Marazion on 1 April 1814. C. L. KINGSFORD, *rev.* DEREK HOWSE

Sources E. Dunkin, 'Notes on some points connected with the early history of the Nautical Almanac', *Journal of the Royal Institution of Cornwall*, 9 (1886–9), 7–18 • D. Howse, *Nevil Maskelyne: the seaman's astronomer* (1989) • Maskelyne to Hornsby, 31 Dec 1767, RAS • J. Winthrop, W. Heberden, and J. Lind, 'Observations of the transit of Venus over the sun, June 3, 1769', *PTRS*, 59 (1769), 351–65 • M. Hitchins, 'Account of the discovery of silver in Herland copper mine', *PTRS*, 91 (1801), 159–64 • R. Polwhele, *Biographical sketches in Cornwall*, 3 vols. (1831) • CUL, RGO, MS 14

Hives, Ernest Walter, first Baron Hives (1886–1965), aero-engine designer and industrialist, was born on 21 April 1886 at 20 Cholmeley Road, Earley, Reading, the twelfth child of John William Hives, a factory clerk, of Reading, and his wife, Mary Washbourne. He was educated at Redlands School, Reading. After working in a Reading garage, in 1903 Hives got a job in the garage of C. S. Rolls's car sales company. After a brief period with another sales firm, he joined the Napier company where he spent three years, probably as both a mechanic and a driver. In 1908 he joined Rolls-Royce, the company he was to serve for nearly fifty years. He was originally engaged at Derby to supervise experimental work. A great deal of this was road testing and he became one of the firm's outstanding drivers in the major automobile trials which were a feature of the European scene before the First World War. He was one of the first men to achieve 100 m.p.h. on the racing track. He married, on 29 January 1913, Gertrude Ethel (1891/2–1961), daughter of John Alfred Warwick, a merchant navy captain, and his wife, Caroline Drusilla. They had four sons and three daughters.

The outstanding reputation of the Rolls-Royce company rested on the work of many gifted people, among whom four stood out above the rest. Of these, C. S. Rolls died in

1910 before his work for the motor car company he helped to create was complete, but the other two founders, Henry Royce and Claude Johnson, built an organization based on talented and meticulous engineering which gained and kept worldwide admiration. The fourth of the great Rolls-Royce characters, whose reign began in 1936 and lasted for twenty years, was Hives.

The First World War brought great changes. Royce designed his first aero-engine, the twelve-cylinder Eagle (220–360 hp), in 1915 and in that year Hives began its development. In 1919 it powered the twin-engined Vickers Vimy bomber on the first direct flight across the Atlantic. Other notable engines followed, all of which were developed under Hives's direction. Of these the Kestrel marked perhaps the greatest single advance and from it sprang both the 'R' series, which powered the winning Schneider Trophy racers of 1929 and 1931, and later the Merlin, which powered the Hurricanes and Spitfires which won the battle of Britain in 1940. Hives, who had been responsible for the Merlin's development, became responsible also for its production, for in 1936 he succeeded to the general works management of the factory and a year later was elected to the board. He became managing director in 1946 and chairman of the Rolls-Royce company in 1950. In 1957 he retired.

It was in May 1941 that the first British jet-propelled aeroplane, powered by the Whittle W1 gas turbine engine, flew. Frank Whittle's company, Power Jets Ltd, was collaborating with other companies and, by 1942, particularly with the Rover company. In that year Hives decided 'to go all out for the gas turbine' and arranged with the Ministry of Aircraft Production to take over the Rover gas turbine establishment while Rover took over from Rolls-Royce the production of the Meteor tank in which a variant of the Merlin engine was installed. This was perhaps the most important policy decision in Rolls-Royce history and, under Hives's direction, the company rapidly moved into a commanding world lead in the design development and manufacture of gas turbine aircraft engines, both jet and turbo-prop.

Hives was a leader of men, especially engineers, whom he trained to detect and solve development problems in new engines as early as possible so as not to blot Rolls-Royce's reputation for reliability. He seemed rarely, if ever, to seek advice but he never resented criticism from subordinates. He carried responsibility with supreme self-confidence, was delighted by success, and undismayed by delay in achieving it: there was never in his philosophy room for failure. He was sparing with praise, but all his life he took pride in being able to use any tool on the shop floor. Hives, through his relationships with ministers, service chiefs, and senior civil servants, had an undoubted influence on government policy, including the establishment of the wartime 'shadow' factories.

Hives was a sturdy man of medium height. Outside his domestic life, he lived for Rolls-Royce, and recreations played only a small part in his activities: golf occasionally, fishing sometimes, and snooker (a game for which he had a predilection comparable only with his liking for the songs of Ethel Merman).

Hives was appointed MBE in 1920, a Companion of Honour in 1943, and a baron in 1950. He was an honorary DSc of Nottingham (1949), an honorary LLD of Cambridge (1951), and an honorary DSc (Eng.) of London (1958). He was awarded the gold medal of the Royal Aeronautical Society (1935). Hives died on 24 April 1965 in the National Hospital for Nervous Diseases, Queen Square, Holborn, London. He was succeeded in the barony by his eldest son, John Warwick Hives (b. 1913).

KINGS NORTON, rev. ROBIN HIGHAM

Sources DBB · DNB · H. Nockolds, *The magic of a name*, 2nd edn (1957) · S. Hooker, *Not much of an engineer: an autobiography* (1984) · H. Smith, *Aircraft piston engines* (1986); repr. (1988) · I. Lloyd, *Rolls-Royce: the years of endeavour* (1978) · I. Lloyd, *Rolls-Royce: the growth of a firm* (1978) · I. Lloyd, *Rolls-Royce: the Merlin story* (1978) · R. W. Harker, *Rolls-Royce from the wings, 1925–1971* (1976) · WW (1950); (1960) · *The aeroplane directory* (1961) · R. Schlaifer and S. D. Heron, *The development of aircraft engines and fuels* (1950) · b. cert. · m. cert. · d. cert. · A. Harvey-Bailey, *Rolls-Royce: Hives, the quiet tiger* (1985) · A. Harvey-Bailey, *Rolls-Royce: Hives' turbulent barons* (1992)
Archives Rolls Royce Enthusiasts' club, Northamptonshire, corresp. and papers · Rolls Royce Heritage Trust, Derby, papers
Likenesses J. Gunn, portrait, 1954; known to be at The Bendalls, Milton, Derby, 1981; copy, Rolls Royce, London · portrait, Royal Aeronautical Society, London · portrait, Flight International, Sutton, Surrey, photo archives · portrait, repro. in Harvey-Bailey, 'Rolls-Royce' · portrait, repro. in DBB
Wealth at death £111,934: probate, 10 June 1965, CGPLA Eng. & Wales

Hlathir, Erik of. *See* Erik of Hlathir (*fl.* 995–1023).

Hlothhere (d. 685), king of Kent, was the son of *Eorcenberht (d. 664), king of Kent, and *Seaxburh (d. c.700), daughter of Anna, king of the East Angles, and later abbess of Ely. He succeeded to the kingship after the death of his brother *Ecgberht I [*see under* Eorcenberht] in July 673. It has been argued that there was an interregnum of several months before Hlothhere managed to establish himself as king; but this hypothesis is based on the testimony of an unreliable charter (AS chart., S 7), and it seems best to follow Bede, who dates the period of Hlothhere's rule from July 673 to February 685. Hlothhere does, however, appear to have experienced difficulties at the beginning of his reign. His brother Ecgberht had had some degree of control in Surrey (AS chart., S 1165), but overlordship of that area had passed to Wulfhere, king of the Mercians, at some point before 674; even more indicative of a new Kentish weakness was the devastating invasion of the kingdom in 676 by Wulfhere's successor, Æthelred, during which the city of Rochester was sacked and destroyed. It is possible that the instability of the kingdom in this period was the result of dynastic conflict. King Ecgberht's two sons, Eadric [*see below*] and *Wihtred, had been passed over on his death. Eventually Eadric enlisted the help of the South Saxons to oust his uncle from the kingship; Hlothhere was fatally wounded in the ensuing battle and died on 6 February 685. He was buried in the monastery of St Peter and St Paul (later St Augustine's Abbey) in Canterbury.

Before this encounter Eadric may at some stage have ruled jointly with his uncle: his consent is referred to in the record of a land grant which Hlothhere made in 679 (*AS chart.*, S 8), and a law-code has survived which is said to represent 'the decrees which Hlothhere and Eadric, kings of Kent, established' (*English Historical Documents*, 1.360). The lawgivers declare explicitly that their new laws are additional to the existing law of the Kentish people (which may be a reference to the law-code of Æthelberht I), and for the most part the decrees simply give supplementary detail about the fines for criminal activity and about legal procedure. However, some extra interest attaches to a series of provisions regarding the purchase of land in London by a Kentishman, which seem to indicate that the Kentish kings maintained a hall and a reeve in that city; it is not clear whether this means that Hlothhere and Eadric enjoyed some degree of political control over London, or whether these arrangements were simply a reflection of the city's importance as a trading centre, an 'emporium of many peoples' (Bede, *Hist. eccl.*, 2.3).

Eadric (*d.* 686), king of Kent, ruled for a year and a half. His violent bid for the kingship appears to have formed a precedent, for after his death, in Bede's words, 'various usurpers or foreign kings plundered the kingdom for a certain space of time until the rightful king, Wihtred, son of Ecgberht, established himself on the throne and freed the nation from foreign invasion' (Bede, *Hist. eccl.*, 4.26). The first of these incursions came from Wessex. The Anglo-Saxon Chronicle notes that in 686 King Cædwalla and his brother Mul ravaged Kent; in the following year Mul and twelve companions were 'burnt' in Kent, prompting another West Saxon ravaging of the kingdom. There is some evidence that Mul was installed for a short time as king of Kent, and that he was buried in the monastery of St Peter and St Paul, Canterbury, at that time the principal Kentish royal burial church. During the West Saxon occupation of the kingdom Cædwalla appears to have founded a monastery at Hoo.

The next 'usurper' was Swæfheard, who came to power in Kent at some point in the year before 29 February 688. He was the son of Sæbbi, king of the East Saxons, and his success in Kent was probably due at least initially to an invasion by an East Saxon army; at some stage he also came to rely on Mercian support, acknowledging the overlordship of Æthelred, king of the Mercians. Another Mercian candidate, a certain Oswine, also emerged as king in Kent in the course of 688, or perhaps in very early 689; about 690 he was reigning jointly with Swæfheard, but he quickly disappears from the record. One very difficult charter in the archive of Minster in Thanet (*AS chart.*, S 11) suggests that there may have been a King Swæfberht in Kent at this time, also ruling jointly with Oswine (although there is a good chance that the name in the charter is a corruption of Swæfheard's).

In the early 690s Eadric's brother Wihtred was able to gather enough support to make a bid for the kingdom. In July 692 he was ruling jointly with Swæfheard in Kent; by 694 Swæfheard had disappeared and Wihtred was the sole ruler of the kingdom.

S. E. KELLY

Sources Bede, *Hist. eccl.*, 2, 4–5 · *AS chart.*, S 7–15, 233, 1165 · *ASC*, s.a. 687, 688, 694 · *English historical documents*, 1, ed. D. Whitelock (1955), 360–61 · S. E. Kelly, ed., *Charters of St Augustine's Abbey, Canterbury, and Minster-in-Thanet*, Anglo-Saxon Charters, 4 (1995), at appx 3, 'The kings of Kent' · D. P. Kirby, 'Bede and Northumbrian chronology', *EngHR*, 78 (1963), 514–27, esp. 517 · N. Brooks, *The early history of the church of Canterbury: Christ Church from 597 to 1066* (1984), 77–8; 343, n. 3 · K. H. Krüger, *Königsgrabkirchen der Franken, Angelsachsen, und Langobarden* (Munich, 1971), 264–87 · R. U. Potts, 'The tombs of the kings and archbishops in St Austin's Abbey', *Archaeologia Cantiana*, 38 (1926), 97–112

Hoadly, Benjamin (1676–1761), bishop of Winchester, was born on 14 November 1676 at Westerham in Kent, the sixth of the nine children of the Revd Samuel *Hoadly (1643–1705), schoolmaster at Westerham, and his second wife, Martha (1639–1703), the daughter of Benjamin Pickering. He came from a strongly puritan and clerical family. His paternal grandfather, John Hoadly, had emigrated to New England in Charles I's reign before returning to Scotland in the 1650s to become chaplain of Edinburgh Castle, while his maternal grandfather had been a member of the Westminster assembly. His uncle John was rector of Halsted, Kent, and his younger brother John *Hoadly (1678–1746) also pursued a clerical career, rising to become archbishop of Armagh.

Early life In 1678 the family moved to Tottenham High Cross, Middlesex, and thence in 1686 to Brook House school in Hackney. Benjamin was educated at home by his father and acquired a reputation as an excellent musician. On 18 February 1692 he entered St Catharine's College, Cambridge, as a pensioner. It was at this time, according to his son, that he contracted smallpox and the intervention of an unskilful surgeon left him crippled (*Biographia Britannica*, 99). For the rest of his life he used crutches to walk at home and sticks in public, kneeling on a stool in order to preach. He was indulged seven terms on account of his serious illness, before graduating BA in 1695 and MA in 1699. Hoadly was ordained deacon by Henry Compton, bishop of London, in December 1698 and priest on 22 December 1700, almost certainly on the title of the fellowship of St Catharine's, to which he had been elected in 1697. In 1699 he became tutor and praelector, but two years later he resigned his fellowship, probably on the occasion of his marriage, on 30 May 1701, to Sarah Curtis (1676?–1743), a portrait painter of some reputation who had trained under Mary Beale [see Hoadly, Sarah]. Together they had five sons: Samuel (*b.* 1703), Benjamin *Hoadly (1706–1757), John *Hoadly (1711–1776), and two who were stillborn.

In 1701 Hoadly was appointed to the lectureship of St Mildred Poultry, serving at the same time as curate to William Hodges at St Swithin's. His first published work was a sermon preached at St Swithin's on 2 September 1702, the anniversary of the great fire, warning in conventional providential language that London was once again threatened by the wrath of God. In the following year Hoadly identified himself much more clearly with whig and low-

Benjamin Hoadly (1676–1761), by William Hogarth, 1741

church opinions. First, in a sermon delivered on 30 January, he not only omitted any direct reference to the execution of Charles I but also implied his support for the comprehension of moderate dissenters within the Church of England by yielding 'Things of little Importance ... for the sake of a greater Union' (*Works*, 3.661). Then, in November, he wrote a tract defending the bishops who had voted against the Occasional Conformity Bill, arguing again for a comprehension and defending the practice of occasional conformity as a support of protestant unity.

Between the publication of these two tracts Hoadly produced a far more substantial work, *The Reasonableness of Conformity to the Church of England* (1703), an answer to the defence of dissenting separation by the eminent Presbyterian Edmund Calamy in his *Abridgment* (1702) of Richard Baxter's *History of his Life*. The ensuing controversy lasted until 1707 and included four further tracts from Hoadly, most notably *A Persuasive to Lay-Conformity* (1704) and *A Brief Defense of Episcopal Ordination* (1707). At first sight this pamphlet might appear to sit uneasily alongside the rest of Hoadly's œuvre; Archbishop Thomas Herring certainly found it hard to reconcile with his famous sermon on the kingdom of Christ. It condemned the dissenters' separation as leading unavoidably to 'Confusion and Disorder, Indecency in the Worship of God, Irregularity, Strife, and Emulation, Heat, and Passion, Ill-will, and Malice' (*Works*, 1.264). Its arguments were powerful enough to be instrumental in convincing the leading New England high-churchman Samuel Johnson to abandon Congregationalism.

In fact Hoadly's position was based on sound low-church principles. His tract was aimed at the moderate nonconformists, who supported the ideal of a national church, and he argued that it was 'unaccountable, and inconsistent, to *separate* from an *imperfect* Church, in order *to press a farther Reformation*' (*Works*, 1.262). He accepted that the constitution of the Church of England was imperfect and declared that he favoured some reform himself. Crucially, however, he provided a strong defence of the church on one of the major issues in dispute with the Presbyterians: the government of the church by bishops. He denied that episcopacy was *jure divino* and thus 'essential to a *Christian Church*'. However, he did argue that the practice was of apostolical origin, that it was supported by tradition, and that it was binding on the church unless 'Imitation is unpracticable' (ibid., 477). Thus he refused to condemn the foreign reformed churches and, unlike most high-churchmen, he accepted the validity of Presbyterian ordination during the interregnum.

Rector of St Peter-le-Poer, 1704–1716 In March 1704 Hoadly was appointed to the rectory of St Peter-le-Poer by the dean and chapter of St Paul's, apparently on the recommendation of the dean, William Sherlock, whose son Thomas had been Hoadly's contemporary at St Catharine's. In later life there was considerable rivalry between Hoadly and Thomas Sherlock, who were widely regarded as the leaders of rival parties in the church. At this time, however, there was no hint of any animosity, and William Sherlock had assisted Hoadly in the composition of his *Letter to the Reverend Mr Fleetwood, Occasioned by his Late Essay on Miracles* (1702). In this pamphlet Hoadly took issue with Fleetwood's claim that only God could work miracles, but at the same time he strongly defended their importance as one among a number of the evidences of true religion, concluding that it was clear that Christ was sent from God because of the 'long uninterrupted Series of great Miracles' that he performed (*Works*, 1.14). Far from alienating Fleetwood, who was himself a rising star among whig low-churchmen, the *Letter* secured his admiration, and his recommendation also played a part in Hoadly's preferment.

As the new rector of St Peter-le-Poer one of Hoadly's first acts was to preach a sermon on 8 March, the anniversary of Queen Anne's accession. Published at the request of his parishioners, this was a rallying cry to the whigs directed against 'the Abuses of that Day' (*Works*, 3.620). Praising the achievements of William III, he reminded his audience that Anne's title was dependent on the revolution settlement, as William's had been, and called on her subjects to 'pursue the Paths of Peace, and Union' and 'to entertain ... a true Christian *Moderation*' (ibid., 2.108). This sermon brought Hoadly to the attention of Sarah Churchill, duchess of Marlborough, who pressed the queen to give him a prebend at Canterbury. Her efforts were unsuccessful, foundering on the opposition of Archbishop John Sharp, Anne's ecclesiastical confidant, but the episode marked the beginning of a friendship that was to play a significant part in Hoadly's life. By the 1730s the two had fallen out and the duchess condemned Hoadly for ingratitude, but for many years he was an intimate in the Marlborough household, he was supported financially by the duchess, and he wrote an early version of her justification of her conduct during the reign of Queen Anne. Meanwhile he continued his defence of the revolution in a sermon preached before the lord mayor of London at St Lawrence Jewry on 29 September 1705. Selecting as his text Romans 13: 1, a passage often used by high-churchmen to expound the duties of non-resistance and passive obedience, Hoadly glossed it in whig fashion, developing a doctrine of conditional obedience. While admitting that government was 'ordained of God', he argued that it was ordained for 'the Good of the Public'. Thus it would be 'the highest profaneness' to treat rulers who abused their power as the 'Vice-gerents' of God; 'a *Passive Non-Resistance*' would be a greater sin than resistance (ibid., 20–21).

The appearance of this sermon pushed Hoadly to the forefront of political debate. As he noted in 1754, it brought down upon him 'a Torrent of *angry Zeal*' (*Works*, 3.621). The lower house of convocation complained that it contained 'positions contrary to the doctrine of the church' and demanded synodical censure, and in the Lords, Bishop Compton accused Hoadly of encouraging rebellion and resistance (Cardwell, 2.723). Hoadly's major contribution to the ensuing controversy was *The Measures of Submission to the Civil Magistrate Considered* (1706), an extended defence of his sermon in which he argued that the doctrine of 'absolute *Passive-Obedience*' (*Works*, 2.93) was a recent innovation for which no justification could be found in scripture, the homilies, or the works of the most esteemed Anglican divines. While all high-churchmen were infuriated by these views the exchanges between Hoadly and Francis Atterbury developed into a more personal feud, spilling over into other issues. As the debate between the two continued through 1708, Hoadly seized on expressions dropped by Atterbury in a funeral sermon and a charity sermon to criticize his notions of virtue and morality, even accusing his adversary of arguing that vice was preferable to virtue.

It was, however, the related issues of obedience and allegiance that lay at the heart of Hoadly's polemical endeavours in this period. He further developed his ideas in two assize sermons preached at Hertford in 1708, in which he attacked the scriptural foundations of divine-right theories by arguing that strict lineal succession had not even prevailed among the Israelites and that the behaviour of St Paul supported his case that oppression could be lawfully resisted. Equally controversially he stated unequivocally the view, not universally shared even among fellow whigs, that the crown and the two houses of parliament shared a co-ordinate power. In the following year Hoadly took on another prominent tory, Offspring Blackall, who had recently been promoted to the bishopric of Exeter and had preached a sermon on the anniversary of the queen's accession advancing an unequivocally high-tory interpretation of 'the divine institution of magistracy'. Hoadly attacked Blackall for abandoning his earlier, more moderate views, and in the course of two pamphlets he restated the twin argument that government was instituted for the good of the people and that civil authority was vested in the magistrate by their agreement. He concluded by pointing out that Blackall's doctrine of non-resistance led inevitably to Jacobitism.

One of Hoadly's most effective adversaries was Charles Leslie, whose journal, *The Rehearsal* (1704–9), was a vehicle for attacking Locke, Hoadly, and other whigs and for expounding high-flying notions of patriarchalism, non-resistance, and passive obedience. In the eyes of the whigs Leslie was the more dangerous because, as a nonjuror, he was freed from the need to reconcile high-church principles with the events of 1688–9. Consequently when he published *The Constitution, Laws and Government of England, Vindicated* (1709), itself a contribution to the controversy between Hoadly and Blackall, it was inevitable that it would provoke an answer from Hoadly. Thus when his *Original and Institution of Civil Government* appeared in December 1709 it was first and foremost a polemical response to Leslie. But, as Frederic Ward points out, it was also 'the most extensive political treatise published in this period' (Ward, 90), an important contribution to whig thought that was crucial in reintroducing Lockean political theory to the debates of the early eighteenth century. There were important differences between the *Original and Institution* and Locke's *Two Treatises*, if only because Hoadly was combating Leslie rather than Filmer. None the less Hoadly's contractarianism was deeply Lockean. The basic structure of the *Original and Institution* owed a great deal to Locke. Like the *Two Treatises* it was divided into two halves, the first examining patriarchalism and the second developing Hoadly's views. Like Locke, moreover, Hoadly adopted the pretence of defending Richard Hooker's views on civil government, even quoting the same passages as a way of legitimating their own more radical ideas.

Leslie Stephen may have been right to claim that Hoadly said nothing new (Stephen, 2.153), but in the context of the political debates of the middle of Anne's reign it is difficult to overestimate the tract's significance. Appearing at a time when the attention of the public had been gripped by Henry Sacheverell's incendiary sermon *The Perils of False Brethren*, which was widely seen as an overt attack on revolution principles, the whigs seized gratefully on Hoadly's tract. On 13 December 1709, the same day that the whig majority in the Commons agreed to impeach Sacheverell, it also passed a resolution recommending Hoadly to the queen for preferment 'for having often strenuously justified the principles, on which her Majesty, and the Nation proceeded, in the late happy Revolution' (*JHC*, 16.242). Hoadly became a national figure, widely seen as the low-church counterpart to Sacheverell. With his high-flying antagonist he was one of the first clergy to be the subject of satirical prints; throughout 1710 he was portrayed as the representative of 'moderation', latitudinarianism, and heterodoxy, and he was depicted in one print with 'Asses Ears and two Horns, with a Couple of Wings' (*Remarks*, 2.20). In the tory celebrations following the Sacheverell trial and at the elections later in 1710 he was burned in effigy at Oxford, and his books were consigned to the flames in places such as Exeter, Hereford, and Sherborne.

The Commons' resolution in favour of Hoadly was a calculated criticism of the queen's religious policy; Blackall's sermon, against which Hoadly had written, had after all been preached before the queen and published at her request. Unsurprisingly the Commons' request was ignored, but on 13 February 1710 Elizabeth Howland, 'unasked, unapplied to' (*Works*, 3.622), presented Hoadly to the rectory of Streatham, and at the same time her grandson the duke of Bedford made him a domestic chaplain, qualifying him to hold the living in plurality with St Peter-le-Poer. Hoadly then threw himself into the 1710 election campaign, writing a series of pamphlets in support of the whig cause. In the aftermath of defeat he attacked high-church attempts to use convocation to condemn the heterodox views of William Whiston but in general he was less active as a pamphleteer, contributing only the occasional sermon to the struggle against the principles of toryism in Anne's last years.

It is important, however, not to see Hoadly merely as a political clergyman. Little is known of his pastoral work within his parishes, although he admitted 'many Imperfections in the discharge of … my Office' due to his disability. None the less he did preach a series of sermons at St Peter-le-Poer, *The Terms of Acceptance with God*, which in their published form were intended as a manual for piety to be 'read, either in the Family, or the Closet' (*Works*, 3.495). Hoadly considered the duties of a Christian and how to achieve salvation. He emphasized the practical duties of Christianity—the practice of virtue and the renunciation of sin—but he explained those duties in strongly biblical language and stressed the role of Christ as redeemer. He argued against the errors both of 'relying upon Faith' and of 'relying upon External Performances'—works were the fruit of true faith, yet without 'Holiness of Life' (ibid., 562) the performance of external duties was worthless. Like many low-churchmen Hoadly also emphasized that Christianity was, if not an 'easy' religion, then one suited to man's condition. God did not expect 'absolute Perfection' as a condition of salvation. Indeed 'absolute Perfection' was unattainable; rather God demanded 'a daily Progress, and sincere Endeavour, after Perfection' (ibid., 536).

Hoadly's theology was therefore firmly grounded in both scripture and the English protestant anti-Calvinist tradition. He was no deist, despite the claims of some contemporaries and later commentators. In 1713 he preached a series of sermons, not printed until they appeared as *Four Sermons* in 1715, in which he answered 'the many writings … which seemed on the one hand to attack the *Christian religion* itself, and on the other to discourage a free *examination* of it' (*Biographia Britannica*, 102). Later that year his *Queries Recommended to the Authors of a Late Discourse of Free-Thinking* was one of a number of responses to Anthony Collins's manifesto. Hoadly again sought to defend free enquiry by Christians, relying on scripture and the reason given to them by God. But he vigorously condemned the methodology and epistemology of the deists, who latched onto trivial, man-made inconsistencies in the gospels and who used wit, ridicule, and banter rather than reason to undermine faith.

Bishop of Bangor, 1716–1721 It was to be expected that, as one of the leading whig clergymen and propagandists from Anne's reign, Hoadly would receive some reward on the Hanoverian succession. In fact it was some time before he was taken notice of by the new administration. As the royal chaplaincies were filled during 1715, Hoadly's name was conspicuously absent, perhaps because he did not frequent the court and perhaps because the princess of Wales suspected that he 'was not a Churchman' (Beinecke Library, Osborn MS f.c. 110, fol. 20). By the end of the year, however, his name was being canvassed at Whitehall. His friends believed that 'a good Deanry, or Residentiaryship of St Pauls' would be most 'proper' for him, but he preferred a bishopric and, having failed of Lincoln, was nominated to Bangor in December 1715 (Bodl. Oxf., MS Add. A. 269, p. 52). He was created DD by Archbishop William Wake on 26 January 1716 and only then was he appointed to a royal chaplaincy, on 14 February. In later years the duchess of Marlborough claimed the credit for Hoadly's promotion, and over the next few years he was one of the most prominent episcopal allies of the earl of Sunderland, the duchess's son-in-law. Another strong supporter was Charlotte Clayton, one of the ladies of the bedchamber to the princess of Wales, who persuaded Caroline to adopt a more favourable opinion of Hoadly. The acquiescence, at least, of Lord Townshend, the secretary of state, would have been essential, and he may well have played a more active role. According to one radical whig report Hoadly's appointment was 'a lay triumph' pushed through in the face of the opposition of a united episcopal bench (Surrey HC, Somers MSS, letter, 29 Dec 1715). It was certainly controversial: when he visited his diocese in 1718 he was attacked by a mob at Brecon.

William Whiston's claim that Hoadly never set foot in Bangor has long been demonstrated to be false. There is clear evidence that he was there in both 1718 and 1719, although the disappearance of the records for his episcopate makes any assessment of his pastoral work very difficult. His disability undoubtedly restricted him; Edmund Gibson was concerned that he might find regular attendance in the House of Lords difficult, noting that 'at first *Crutches* will look a little ungainly there!' (Bodl. Oxf., MS Add. A. 269, p. 52). But other bishops were willing to provide assistance, and Bishop John Wynne performed an ordination tour in the summer of 1720.

Hoadly's pastoral efforts, however, continued to be overshadowed by his controversial work. He preached against the Jacobite rising in 1715, and one of his first acts after his consecration in 1716 was to deliver the Restoration day sermon before the king. Both were strongly whig in tone, the latter arguing that the Restoration had only been made a 'blessing' to the nation by the securing of the succession in the protestant line in 1688. But his most significant work during the early months of George I's reign appeared anonymously in May 1715: his *Dedication to Pope Clement XI*, prefixed to Richard Steele's *Account of the*

State of the Roman Catholic Religion. In this tract he high-lighted what he saw as the similarities between the Church of England and the Church of Rome, arguing that the former had inherited the intolerant and persecuting practices of the latter. Both asserted an infallible author-ity and both denied the individual the right to interpret the scriptures, though the Church of England claimed to do the opposite. The only difference between the two churches was 'That You *cannot* Err in any Thing You deter-mine, and We never *do*: That is … You are Infallible, and We always in the Right' (*Works*, 1.535). The Church of Eng-land indeed was becoming more and more like the Church of Rome. In time, Hoadly told the pope, 'no Man of Sense will be able to see any Difference between *Your Popery*, and *that* of many amongst *Us*, but that *Ours* is *Prot-estant Popery*, and *Yours* is *Popish Popery*' (ibid., 544).

This tract marked a change in tone in Hoadly's work. In common with many whigs and low-churchmen he was worried by the increasing stridency and extremism of the nonjurors both politically, in their support for Jacobitism, and theologically, in their adoption of more 'Catholic' rites and practices. Even more worrying, at a time when the protestant succession appeared very precarious, was the creeping sacerdotalism of many high-flying clergy and their apparent sympathy for the nonjuring position. Hoadly's response was to focus, more explicitly than ever before, on the threat from within the Church of England. He highlighted the issue of authority and made the right of private judgement *the* distinguishing characteristic of protestantism. Over the next two years these themes were developed in two further pamphlets, *A Preservative Against the Principles and Practices of the Nonjurors* (1716) and *The Nature of the Kingdom or Church of Christ* (1717), provoking the most famous politico-religious controversy of the eighteenth century, the Bangorian controversy.

The *Preservative* was occasioned by the posthumous pub-lication of *The Constitution of the Catholick Church* (1716), in which the leading nonjuror George Hickes argued that the Church of England was a schismatic church teaching a heretical doctrine of obedience, and that the state had no rights over the church, rendering the deprivation of non-jurors invalid. Hoadly sought first to defend the revolu-tion settlement and the exclusion of all Catholics from the line of succession. He went on to demonstrate that the civil power was 'endowed with every *Power* necessary to its *Defense* as a *Civil Power*' (*Works*, 1.582) and thus had the right to deprive bishops who, in 'the Exercise of the *Episcopal Office*' (ibid., 581), were threatening the state with destruc-tion. Finally he ridiculed the claim of the nonjurors to confine salvation to the 'Communion of your particular, little, *Body*, or *Church*' (ibid., 592), asserting instead that the essence of true religion lay in 'sincerity':

> Your *Title* to God's favour … cannot depend Simply upon your adhering to this Communion; because the very adhering to this *Communion*, if it were against your Conscience, would entitle you to His Anger: But must depend upon it, considered as a Conduct honestly entered into, by the Dictate of your Conscience. The favour of God … follows *Sincerity* … And consequently, equally follows every *Equal Degree* of *Sincerity*. (ibid., 593)

This doctrine was an important development in latitudin-arian theology and was recognized as such even by Hoad-ly's more conservative whig colleagues. Bishop Nicolson, for example, was content to endorse Hoadly's justification of the deprivation of the nonjurors and was reluctant to take issue with his denial of the apostolical succession, but he bridled at the idea that 'our people be taught that they are *not to expect any of God's Graces Benedictions or Absolutions, from any hands but his own*' (Christ Church, Oxford, Arch.W.Epist. 20, fols. 277–8). He believed that Hoadly's doctrines deprived the clergy of the spiritual authority conferred on them at their ordination and were irreconcilable with those of the Church of England.

If the *Preservative* was, ostensibly at least, directed at the nonjurors, the doctrines advanced by Hoadly in his ser-mon *The Nature of the Kingdom, or Church, of Christ*, preached on 31 March 1717, were of more general application. Developing themes explored in the *Preservative*, Hoadly argued that Christ was the 'Sole *Law-giver* to his Subjects, and Sole *Judge*, in matters relating to Salvation' (*Works*, 2.409). Consequently:

> in the Affairs of *Eternal Conscience* and *Salvation* … He hath … left behind Him, no visible, humane *Authority*; no *Vicegerents*, who can be said properly to supply his Place; no *Interpreters*, upon whom his Subjects are absolutely to depend; no *Judges* over the Consciences or Religion of his People. (ibid., 404)

From this he went on to demonstrate that the rewards and punishments of Christianity occurred in a future state, and that to apply temporal rewards and punishments was 'to act contrary to the Interests of True Religion' (ibid., 406–7). It has been pointed out that Hoadly's words echoed those preached by Arthur Ashley Sykes in an archi-diaconal sermon at Cambridge the previous December, but Sykes was at this time a relatively obscure country clergyman. Moreover Hoadly's sermon acquired far greater significance from its context. The bishop was close to the new Sunderland–Stanhope ministry, which was for-mulating a more radical religious policy that included sig-nificant concessions to the dissenters, and he was known to be in high favour at court. The sermon indeed was deliv-ered before the king and printed at his command. It was evident to many that it provided a timely ideological justi-fication for the repeal of the Test Act—the statute restrict-ing civil office to members of the Church of England—which was beginning to be canvassed by the administra-tion.

The response was both immediate and prolonged, the exchange of pamphlets dragging on into 1720. Leslie Stephen comments that 'There is a bewildering variety of theological, ecclesiastical, political, historical, exegetical, and purely personal discussions' (Stephen, 2.156). Much of it was trivial, such as the exchange involving Hoadly, Bishop William Nicolson, and White Kennett over whether the sermon had been altered between preaching and publication. But major issues were at stake. In particu-lar many churchmen believed that Hoadly's doctrines denied any authority to the visible church and thus under-mined the position of the Church of England. This was made clear in the report of the committee of the lower house of convocation, which condemned Hoadly for having subverted 'all government and discipline in the Church of Christ' and also for having impugned the king's 'supremacy in causes ecclesiastical, and the authority of the legislature to enforce obedience in matters of religion by civil sanctions' (Cardwell, 2.829). The committee also highlighted the doctrine of sincerity, which, it claimed in an argument developed by William Law, made the truth or falsehood of belief irrelevant and placed all religions on the same level with respect to salvation. The representation was received *nemine contradicente* by the lower house on 10 May 1717. On the same day the ministry, fearing synodical censure of its episcopal champion, ordered the prorogation of convocation to 8 November 1717. Apart from a brief session in 1741 it did not meet again to do business until 1852.

There is no denying that the Bangorian controversy was of enormous significance in the politico-religious history of the early eighteenth century. It is important to recognize that it not only reinforced divisions between high- and low-churchmen. Some of Hoadly's most prominent critics were indeed high-churchmen; Andrew Snape and Thomas Sherlock were particularly effective, while the *Three Letters*, written by the young nonjuror William Law, were much admired by nineteenth-century commentators. But the controversy also saw a fracturing of the low-church alliance that had been so powerful during the reign of Queen Anne. Leading whig churchmen like Archbishop Wake and Bishop Gibson, who had championed the low-church cause during the convocation controversy, were privately horrified by Hoadly's writings. Others, including John Potter, bishop of Oxford, and Francis Hare, a former chaplain to the duke of Marlborough, went into print, while Robert Cannon played a leading role in the deliberations in convocation. Hoadly had his supporters, but they formed only a section of whig low-church opinion.

What is much less clear is whether the controversy marked an important shift in Hoadly's own views. At the time it was commonly believed that his writings at the beginning of George I's reign represented an abandonment of the positions that he had advanced at the outset of his career, particularly in his pamphlets against nonconformity. One country clergyman commented of his sermon in 1717 that 'he gives up Episcopacy entirely' (BL, Add. MS 22560, fol. 48), a view echoed in the twentieth century by Norman Sykes. Part of the problem is that *The Nature of the Kingdom … of Christ* lacked clarity and could easily be interpreted, or misinterpreted, in many ways. But Hoadly did something to clarify his position in the twelve further pamphlets that he contributed to the Bangorian controversy and other later writings. By emphasizing that the right to judge men's consciences belonged to Christ alone, by asserting that the fundamentals of Christianity were simply the 'Practice of all the Duties we owe to Ourselves, and to our Neighbour' (*Works*, 2.509), and by stressing the importance of sincerity, Hoadly certainly diminished the role of visible churches in the economy of salvation. By repeating the Lockean

argument that the office of the civil magistrate was confined to the well-being of civil society and had no part in 'the Care of *True Religion*' (ibid., 536), he was striking at the justification for the Test Act. But he stopped short of questioning the utility of the church establishment, making clear his belief that 'all *Visible Churches* ought to be *orderly Societies*' (ibid., 898). He also reiterated his adherence to the Church of England, acknowledging that it was not 'all perfection, and uncapable of Amendment', but insisting that he was convinced 'of its Excellency above any Other' that he knew of (ibid., 3.42). Significantly *The Reasonableness of Conformity* was reprinted in 1720; Hoadly may not have approved of excluding dissenters from state office but he still believed that they could not justify their separation from the Church of England. His writings in the period 1715–20 are thus best seen in terms of a change of tone rather than substance, a response to what he saw as the growing threat to protestantism and to civil and religious liberty from within the church.

Bishop of Hereford, Salisbury, and Winchester, 1721–1761 Having resigned the rectory of St Peter-le-Poer in 1720 Hoadly was nominated to the bishopric of Hereford on 21 September 1721 and confirmed on 7 November. Rumours circulated that this was a reward for his support of the ministry during the South Sea crisis yet in many ways it was an odd promotion. Hereford was worth little, if any, more than Bangor, and the suspicion must remain that the translation was a favour intended to relieve Hoadly of the pastoral care of the large, distant, and mountainous diocese of Bangor. In any event his tenure of the see was short, and on 29 October 1723 he was translated to the bishopric of Salisbury, whereupon he resigned the rectory of Streatham. This was a move to which Hoadly's seniority among the whig bishops entitled him, but he had further recommended himself to the favour of the ministry by his vigorous pamphleteering on its behalf. While Hoadly had been closely identified with the liberal religious programme of the Sunderland–Stanhope administration, he remained a strong supporter of Walpole and Townshend. In September 1722 Walpole took over the leading opposition newspaper, the *London Journal*, and immediately Hoadly started contributing regular articles to it under the pseudonym Britannicus. In the collected edition of Hoadly's works his son included 110 letters for the period from 1722 until 9 January 1725, although not all of these are generally accepted to be by the bishop.

The Britannicus letters defended the revolution settlement on Lockean principles, much as *The Original and Institution of Civil Government* had done. But first and foremost they were pieces of journalism focusing on the issues of the moment, such as the plight of the German protestants being persecuted by Catholics in Thorn, or the ministry's case for an excise duty on tea, coffee, and cocoa. No issue of this period attracted more attention, however, than the trials of the bishop of Rochester and other conspirators in the Atterbury plot. Hoadly vigorously defended the sometimes dubious manipulations of the law by the administration from the suspension of habeas corpus onwards and devoted letter after letter to a meticulous dissection of

Atterbury's defence of his conduct in the House of Lords. Even after he stopped writing for the *London Journal* Hoadly continued to support the government's policies and record. In 1727 he even turned to foreign affairs, publishing *An Enquiry into the Causes of the Conduct of Great Britain*, which provided a detailed defence of whig foreign policy and the 1725 alliance of Hanover, emphasizing the crucial role of Britain in the defence of protestantism and liberty. It was followed two years later with *A Defence of the Enquiry*.

In 1729 the leading latitudinarian theologian Samuel Clarke died. He had been a close and long-standing friend of Hoadly, who wrote a life of him that was prefaced to his published sermons (1732) and works (1737), laying 'hold on *His* Fame, to prop and support *My own*' (*Works of Samuel Clarke*, 1.xiv). Clarke was widely viewed in the early eighteenth century as the leading advocate of an Arian doctrine of the Trinity, and Hoadly revealingly declined to offer an opinion on 'so difficult a Question' (ibid., vii). But however much Hoadly admired Clarke as a man and a Christian, and however much he may have sympathized with his desire to see parts of the church's doctrine and liturgy reformed, there were important differences between them. In his later career Clarke had been unwilling to accept any preferment that would require further subscription to the Thirty-Nine Articles. Hoadly, by contrast, felt no scruples about the terms of conformity imposed by the church and stressed that, while 'a parish-minister', he had always 'observed the rules prescribed; and, amongst other injunctions, that he had never omitted the Athanasian creed, when ordered to be read in the church' (*GM*, 53.1029).

Hoadly was never an uncritical supporter of the Walpole administration or its predecessors. He confided to Lady Sundon, for example, his disapproval of attacks on the liberty of the press through the prosecution of printers. He had never been trusted by Walpole on ecclesiastical policy; the rise of Edmund Gibson, bishop of London, in the 1720s demonstrated the ministry's determination to reassure the clergy that Hoadleian principles would not be applied in the church. It may have been Gibson's influence that determined that the bishopric of Durham was given to Edward Chandler in October 1730—a bitter disappointment for Hoadly, though by this time his friendship with Queen Caroline, the other important influence over the disposal of church preferments, also had cooled. Hoadly continued to be a loyal supporter of the ministry in the House of Lords, but the episode contributed to a tension between him and Walpole. Thus in 1732, when Walpole was seeking Hoadly's assistance in discouraging the dissenters from pressing for a repeal of the Test and Corporation Acts, the approach was made through the queen. Hoadly agreed to intercede with his friends among the dissenters, advising them that the attempt was likely to fail and at the same time would damage the whig interest. But he could not resist reiterating his opposition to those laws on account of their 'unreasonableness … in a social light, and the profaneness of them theologically considered', and he declared that if the matter were to come before the House of Lords he would be obliged both to speak and to vote for repeal (Hervey, 1.126–7). He even wrote a tract, developing his views, in answer to Edmund Gibson's *The Dispute Adjusted*, although it was not published until 1736, and even then anonymously, by the Presbyterian Benjamin Avery under the title *The Objections Against the Repeal of the Corporation and Test Acts Considered*. It would be misleading, however, to see Hoadly's nomination to the bishopric of Winchester on 3 September 1734 as the reward of a grateful court. It was rather, if Lord Hervey's account is to be believed, the performance of a promise extracted from a reluctant Caroline and George II by Hoadly himself, supported by Hervey and Lady Sundon (ibid., 2.395–9).

The dissenting campaign for the repeal of the Test and Corporation Acts also provided the context for Hoadly's last major new publication, *A Plain Account of the Nature and End of the Sacrament of the Lord's Supper*, which appeared anonymously in 1735. The political meaning was made explicit by his emphasis that the sacrament was a purely religious duty and that the only obligation to it derived from Christ's institution. More generally his intention was to remove all 'Superstition', or mystery, from the understanding of the sacrament, believing that the best defence of Christianity against 'Unbelievers … is to remove from it whatever hinders it from being seen as it really is in itself' (*Works*, 3.845). Adopting a resolutely scriptural approach, he attacked both the Catholic and protestant eucharistic doctrines, arguing that the bread and wine were merely symbols and that the rite was simply a remembrance of Christ's sacrifice. *A Plain Account* was widely condemned, many commentators, including Daniel Waterland, believing that it tended towards Socinianism. Waterland also accused Hoadly of 'novelty', but in this he was certainly mistaken (*Works of the Rev. Daniel Waterland*, 4.465). As some twentieth-century historians have noted, Hoadly's eucharistic beliefs were based on the memorialism of the sixteenth-century Swiss reformer Huldreich Zwingli, although the bishop had probably become acquainted with them through John Hales's *Tract on the Sacrament of the Lord's Supper*, which had first appeared in 1635.

In pastoral terms Hoadly was not a model bishop and it is futile to attempt to portray him as such. However, he was far more conscientious than many commentators have been prepared to admit. It has been claimed that he never went to Hereford but, as at Bangor, this claim is untrue. He performed an ordination in the cathedral there on 1 July 1722 and then carried out a visitation of the diocese. While at Salisbury he visited the diocese twice, in 1726 and 1729, and he also conducted a personal visitation of Winchester in 1736. In both dioceses he also ordained regularly, conducting as many as eighty-one ordination services between 1743 and 1761, the only period for which his act book at Winchester survives, and there is evidence that he examined candidates rigorously. It is true that he could be a divisive presence in his dioceses—at Hereford the predominantly tory country gentry refused to wait on him—and he was widely distrusted by his clergy. On his translation to Winchester the chapter pointedly omitted from the return of the election the conventional formula that he had been chosen '*by the Aid and immediate Direction of the Holy Ghost*' (Lewis Walpole Library, Clarke–Sundon correspondence). Hoadly was well aware of their suspicions and assured them that he would never consent 'to any thing, that may hurt either [the church's] Establishment, or legal Revenues', adding that where his judgement differed from theirs he hoped that they would believe that 'I as truly … and as sincerely intend their Service, as any One of Themselves can do' (*Works*, 3.492). But many of them were hardly likely to have been reassured by his patronage of advanced low-churchmen such as Arthur Ashley Sykes, Jonathan Shipley, and Edmund Pyle.

Hoadly's first wife, Sarah, died on 11 January 1743. Two years later, on 23 July 1745, at the age of sixty-eight, he married Mary Newey, the daughter of the dean of Chichester, at Farnham Castle. By this time he was becoming noticeably less active in the discharge of his episcopal functions. Despite his reputation as a political bishop he had never frequented the House of Lords regularly, and after the fall of Walpole in 1742, he gave up attendance in parliament altogether. By the end of the decade he was relying upon Bishop Matthias Mawson to undertake a confirmation tour for him in the Isle of Wight, and in the 1750s it became usual for him to turn to his colleagues to perform ordinations and confirmations. Hoadly's decline, however, was physical rather than mental. He oversaw the publication of two volumes of his collected sermons, in 1754 and 1755, and in 1757 he was even persuaded to take up his pen again to defend his reputation against the forgeries of Bernard Fournier. He died, after an illness of less than twenty-four hours, at Winchester House, Chelsea, in the evening of 17 April 1761, leaving an estate of £17,000, barely enough, according to Edmund Pyle, to 'pay two annuities, & one legacy, and his funeral charges, & dilapidations of 3 vast houses' (Pyle, 357–8). He was buried in Winchester Cathedral, where 'but a decent monument' was erected, contrary to his own wishes, by his son John.

Reputation Hoadly was arguably the most famous churchman of his generation. As a young and relatively obscure London preacher in the early years of Anne's reign he was able to establish himself as one of the leading whig and low-church propagandists of the period, and as a junior bishop at the beginning of George I's reign he was at the centre of the most famous politico-religious controversy of the century. William Warburton was merely stating the obvious when in 1765 he identified Hoadly as the leader of the low-church party in the early Hanoverian church (*Works*, 4.7). Predictably a figure of such prominence attracted praise and condemnation in equal measure. High-churchmen and tories routinely denounced him as heterodox—'an infamous and Scandalous Advocate for Rebellion', according to Thomas Hearne (*Remarks*, 3.87), a 'true Jeroboam' priest, according to Browne Willis (NL Wales, Ottley correspondence, 1825). For many whigs and low-churchmen, on the other hand, he was 'an exemplary divine', as Henry Fielding described him (Thomas, 75), a

leading advocate of the principles of religious and political liberty. Some attempted more balanced assessments. Thus Daniel Waterland, who wrote against Hoadly's doctrine of the sacrament, was none the less prepared to recommend his sermons to undergraduates as 'exact and judicious' models of the preacher's art. It was remarked after his death that he had 'lived to see the Nation become his converts' (Nichols, *Lit. anecdotes*, 3.141), but in reality his reputation was contested as much in the second half of the eighteenth century as it had been in the first half. He continued to have his admirers, both Richard Price and William Paley invoking the authority of 'the excellent Hoadly' (Thomas, 74; Gascoigne, 241), while detractors like Lewis Bagot and Samuel Horsley denounced his Socinianism and republicanism.

In the nineteenth century, however, under the impact of tractarianism and evangelicalism, attitudes became more uniformly critical. The tone of most nineteenth- and even twentieth-century portraits of Hoadly was set by S. H. Cassan in his biographies of the bishops of Winchester. Cassan admitted that Hoadly's private life was 'exemplary and praiseworthy', but he found fault with the 'low-Church principles' of 'this anti-prelatical Prelate', marvelling at 'how so great a Dissenter could have retained, I will not say the episcopal, but even the priestly character' (Cassan, 2.403–5). Like many churchmen Cassan found it particularly hard to forgive Hoadly his role in the destruction of convocation, which was attributed to his 'weakness and time-serving compliance' (ibid., 403). To these attacks on Hoadly's heterodoxy was added a new critique of his pastoral failings, his record, according to C. J. Abbey, being 'glaring even above others' in a century characterized by 'disgraceful absenteeism' (Abbey, 2.2). Even more liberal churchmen, who might be supposed to have been more sympathetic to Hoadly's low-churchmanship, contributed to the tide of condemnation. Thus W. J. Conybeare lamented how the 'comprehensive Christianity of Tillotson and Burnet too soon degenerated into the worldliness of the Sadducean Hoadly' (Conybeare, 350). Leslie Stephen may have praised Hoadly's stand against 'bigotry' but he also dismissed him as a 'bore' who had nothing original to say and who was often 'evasive', refusing to recognize the deist implications of his arguments (Stephen, 2.153, 155).

Remarkably, perhaps, Hoadly benefited little from the powerful assault launched against nineteenth-century orthodoxies by Norman Sykes. Sykes accepted much of Stephen's interpretation, talking of the 'essentially Deist basis of his thought' and agreeing that a great deal of what Hoadly wrote 'may well be swept to the dustheaps' (Sykes, 'Benjamin Hoadly', 137, 150). Indeed for many historians he still remains the leading example of whig opportunism and 'blatant clerical' careerism (Young, 33). In the last decades of the twentieth century, however, a more positive assessment of Hoadly has emerged. While there has been a reappraisal of his pastoral work it is clear that he still fell some way short of the best standards of the eighteenth-century church. But he was a crucial figure in the propaganda wars of the post-revolutionary years, articulating a powerful rebuttal to the revival of patriarchalism and divine-right ideology during the reign of Queen Anne. In so doing he played a leading role in the transmission of Lockean contractarianism into the mainstream of eighteenth-century political thought in both England and North America. Moreover it is becoming increasingly clear that, despite the allegations of Socinianism and deism, Hoadly stood firmly in a protestant tradition that can be traced back through Hales, Chillingworth, and Hooker. Through his development of the concept of sincerity and through his 'memorialist' eucharistic thought he contributed significantly to the development of an Anglican latitudinarian tradition that minimized the role of the priesthood in the church and of mystery in its doctrines. While not particularly innovative Hoadly none the less exercised a profound influence over political and religious thought in eighteenth-century England.

STEPHEN TAYLOR

Sources *Biographia Britannica, or, The lives of the most eminent persons who have flourished in Great Britain and Ireland*, 7 vols. (1747–66), vol. 6, pt 2, suppl. · *The works of Benjamin Hoadly, D.D.*, ed. J. Hoadly, 3 vols. (1773) · E. Cardwell, *Synodalia: a collection of articles of religion, canons, and proceedings of convocation in the province of Canterbury from the year 1547 to the year 1717*, 2 vols. (1842) · Cobbett, *Parl. hist.* · *JHC* · Lady Sundon, correspondence, Yale U., Beinecke L., Osborn MS f. c. 110 · Gibson–Nicolson correspondence, Bodl. Oxf., MS Add. A. 269 · M., Margaret Cocks to Mary Cocks, 29 Dec 1715, Surrey HC, Somers papers, 317/14/O/2/84 · W. Wake, correspondence, Christ Church Oxf., Arch. W. Epist. · L. Stephen, *History of English thought in the eighteenth century*, 3rd edn, 2 vols. (1902) · diary of John Tomlinson, BL, Add. MS 22560 · *The works of Samuel Clarke, D.D.*, 4 vols. (1738) · *GM*, 1st ser., 36 (1766), 51–3 · *GM*, 1st ser., 53 (1783) · John, Lord Hervey, *Some materials towards memoirs of the reign of King George II*, ed. R. Sedgwick, 3 vols. (1931) · Clarke–Sundon correspondence, Yale U., Lewis Walpole Library · *The works of the Rev. Daniel Waterland*, ed. W. van Mildert, 2nd edn, 6 vols. (1843) · [E. Pyle], *Memoirs of a royal chaplain, 1729–1763*, ed. A. Hartshorne (1905) · *The works of the Right Reverend William Warburton, D.D. lord bishop of Gloucester*, new edn, 12 vols. (1811) · *Remarks and collections of Thomas Hearne*, ed. C. E. Doble and others, 11 vols., OHS, 2, 7, 13, 34, 42–3, 48, 50, 65, 67, 72 (1885–1921) · Nichols, *Lit. anecdotes* · Ottley correspondence, 1825, NL Wales · D. O. Thomas, 'Benjamin Hoadly: the ethics of sincerity', *Enlightenment and Dissent*, 15 (1996), 71–88 · J. Gascoigne, *Cambridge in the age of the Enlightenment* (1989) · S. H. Cassan, *The lives of the bishops of Winchester*, 2 vols. (1827) · C. J. Abbey, *The English church and its bishops, 1700–1800*, 2 vols. (1887) · S. Taylor, 'Bishop Edmund Gibson's proposals for church reform', *From Cranmer to Davidson: a Church of England miscellany*, ed. S. Taylor (1999), 169–202 · N. Sykes, 'Benjamin Hoadly, bishop of Bangor', *The social and political ideas of some English thinkers of the Augustan age, 1650–1750*, ed. F. Hearnshaw (1928), 112–55 · B. W. Young, *Religion and Enlightenment in eighteenth-century England* (1998) · S. L. Rutherford, 'Reformation principles: the religious and political ideas of Benjamin Hoadly (1676–1761)', PhD diss., University of Northumbria, Newcastle, 2000 · F. R. Ward, 'The early influence of John Locke's political thought in England, 1689–1720', PhD diss., U. Cal., Riverside, 1995 · R. L. Warner, 'Early eighteenth-century low churchmanship: the glorious revolution to the Bangorian controversy', PhD diss., U. Reading, 1999 · CUR Liber Gratiarum θ, CUL · faculty office muniment book, 1708–22, LPL, FI/F, fols. 103v–104 · lord chamberlain's books, PRO, LC 3/63, p. 129 · Archbishop Herring to William Herring, 27 Dec 1754, U. Nott. L., PWV 121/113 · H. Schneider and S. Schneider, eds., *Samuel Johnson, president of King's College: his career and writings*, 4 vols. (New York, 1929), 1.13 · R. M. Burns, *The great debate on miracles from Joseph Glanvill to David Hume* (1981) · G. J. Schochet, *Patriarchalism in political thought: the authoritarian family and political speculation and attitudes especially in seventeenth-century England* (1975) · G. V. Bennett, *The tory crisis in church and state, 1688–1730: the career of Francis Atterbury, bishop of Rochester* (1975) · J. A. W. Gunn, *Beyond liberty and property: the process of self-recognition in eighteenth-century political thought* (1983) · M. A. Goldie, 'Tory political thought, 1689–1714', PhD diss., U. Cam., 1977 · G. Holmes, *The trial of Dr Sacheverell* (1973) · J. Miller, *Religion in the popular prints, 1660–1832* (1986) · P. Monod, *Jacobitism and the English people* (1989) · N. Sykes, *Church and state in England in the XVIII century* (1934) · G. Rupp, *Religion in England, 1688–1791* (1986) · R. Browning, *Political and constitutional ideas of the court whigs* (1982) · C. B. Realey, *The London Journal and its authors, 1720–1723* (1935) · S. L. Rutherford, 'Benjamin Hoadly: the sacrament of the Lord's supper and eucharistic thought in early eighteenth-century England', *Anglican and Episcopal History* [forthcoming] · act book, 1743–67, Hants. RO, Winchester diocesan records, 21M65 A2/1 · W. M. Marshall, 'Episcopal activity in the Hereford and Oxford dioceses, 1660–1760', *Midland History*, 8 (1983), 106–20 · Herefs. RO, Brydges papers, A81/IV/Francis Brydges, 1721–3 · Westminster Abbey Library and Muniment Room, Zachary Pearce papers · Archbishop Herring to the earl of Hardwicke, 28 Aug 1749, BL, Add. MS 35598, fols. 421–4 · H. Walpole, *Memoirs of King George II*, ed. J. Brooke, 3 vols. (1985) · W. B. Gardner, 'George Hickes and the origins of the Bangorian controversy', *Studies in Philology*, 39 (1942), 65–78 · *Both sides pleas'd, or, A dialogue between a Sacheverelite parson, and a Hoadlean gentleman* (1710) · F. Harris, 'Accounts of the conduct of Sarah, duchess of Marlborough, 1704–1742', *British Library Journal*, 8 (1982), 7–35 · M. Goldie, ed., *The reception of Locke's politics*, 6 vols. (1999) · Venn, *Alum. Cant.*

Archives BL, corresp. and other papers, Add. MSS 5791, 5831, 5841, 6116–6117, 6210, 32556, 35637, 36183, 37222, 37684, 39311; Add. Ch 5975; Egerton MS 1954; Egerton Ch 7842, 8076, 8084, 8088; Sloane MS 4054; Stowe MS 750 · LPL, papers relating to election · U. Nott. L., MS of a prologue spoken by Lady Anne Spencer to *Anthony and Cleopatra* | BL, Blenheim papers, Add. MS 61464, fols. 161–85 · BL, Blenheim papers, account of the duchess of Marlborough, Add. MS 61426 · BL, corresp. with first Lord Hardwicke, Add. MSS 35586, 35588–35589, 35598 · BL, letters to duke of Newcastle, Add. MSS 5831, 32689, 32695, 32891, 32901 · BL, corresp. with earl of Sunderland, Add. MSS 61496, 61604, 61612, 61650 · Suffolk RO, Bury St Edmunds, Hervey papers, Ac.941/47/4 · Winchester College, letters to Thomas Cheyney relating to Winchester College · Yale U., Beinecke L., corresp. with Lady Sundon, Osborn MS f. c. 110

Likenesses attrib. W. Hogarth, oils, c.1704, Hunt. L. · satirical print, copper-plate, 1709, BM · satirical print, copper-plate?, 1709, BM · oils, c.1710–1715, St Catharine's College, Cambridge · attrib. N. Ferrers, oils, c.1715, St Catharine's College, Cambridge · S. Hoadly, oils, c.1730, NPG · attrib. J. Ellis, oils, c.1732–1734, Winchester · W. Hogarth, oils, 1741, Tate collection [*see illus.*] · B. Baron, copper-plate print, 1743 (after W. Hogarth, 1741), Tate collection · I. Gosset, medallion, 1756 · J. Basire, line engraving, 1773 (after I. Gosset), BM, NPG; repro. in *Works*, ed. Hoadly (1773) · S. Hoadly, oils; formerly at LPL · J. Simon, mezzotint (when rector; after unknown artist), BM, NPG · G. Vertue, line engraving, BM, NPG · J. Wilton, relief bust on monument, Winchester Cathedral

Wealth at death £17,000: Edmund Pyle, cited in *Memoirs of a royal chaplain*, ed. Hartshorne, 357–8

Hoadly, Benjamin (1706–1757), physician and playwright, was born on 10 February 1706 in Broad Street, London, the elder surviving son of the Revd Benjamin *Hoadly (1676–1761), who became bishop of Winchester, and his first wife, Sarah Curtis (1676?–1743) [*see* Hoadly, Sarah]. His father was musical, and his mother a trained portrait painter. He was educated at Dr Newcome's academy, Hackney, Middlesex, and from 1722 at Corpus Christi College, Cambridge. He read humanities and mathematics, and attended the lectures of the blind professor Nicholas Saunderson. He graduated MB in 1727, and MD in April 1728, having been elected a fellow of the Royal Society in 1726. He was made registrar of Hereford by his father, who was bishop there from 1721 to 1723.

Hoadly was married twice: first, on 6 November 1733 to Elizabeth, daughter of Henry Betts, of Suffolk; they had one son, Benjamin, who died young. On 4 June 1747 he married Ann, daughter of General Armstrong; they had no children.

Settling in London, Hoadly was elected a fellow of the Royal College of Physicians in 1736 (censor, 1739); in 1737 he delivered uninteresting Goulstonian lectures on respiration, and in 1742 a commonplace Harveian oration, all of which were published. He was physician to St George's Hospital (1736–46); in 1736 he also became physician to the Westminster Hospital. In 1742 he became physician to the king's household, and in 1746 physician to the household of the prince of Wales.

Hoadly was fond of the stage, as was his brother John *Hoadly, and wrote a popular comedy, *The Suspicious Husband*, which was first acted at Covent Garden on 12 February 1747 and often repeated. There were at least twenty-four different printings and editions between 1747 and 1829. It is a comedy of lovers, muddles, escapes, ladders, and bedrooms, with a happy ending. Garrick wrote both the prologue and the epilogue, and acted the part of Ranger. Johnson said that Ranger was 'just a rake, and a mere rake, and a lively young fellow, but no *character*' (Boswell, *Life*, quoted in *Medical Bookman*, 25). The play was dedicated to George II, who sent Hoadly £100. The plot and style were widely, though not universally, praised. Hoadly's father the bishop did not go. A satire by Charles Macklin, *The Suspicious Husband Criticized, or, The Plague of Envy*, was acted in March 1747, but was a failure and not printed.

Hoadly wrote another comedy, *The Tatlers*, which was acted at Covent Garden on 29 April 1797, but was never printed, and also published *Observations on a Series of Electrical Experiments* (1756) with Benjamin Wilson FRS. He died on 10 August 1757 at his house at Chelsea, which he had built ten years before.

NORMAN MOORE, *rev.* JEAN LOUDON

Sources J. Hoadly, 'Introductory account', *The works of Benjamin Hoadly*, ed. J. Hoadly, 1 (1773), vi–xii • Munk, *Roll* • *GM*, 1st ser., 27 (1757), 386 • *GM*, 1st ser., 31 (1761), 189 • *GM*, 1st ser., 36 (1766), 51–3 • *GM*, 1st ser., 44 (1774), 212–14 • Venn, *Alum. Cant.* • S. C. Lawrence, *Charitable knowledge: hospital pupils and practitioners in eighteenth-century London* (1996) • 'Benjamin Hoadly, 1706–57', *Medical Bookman*, 1/10 (1947), 25–6 • J. Doran and R. W. Lowe, *'Their majesties' servants': annals of the English stage*, rev. edn, 2 (1888), 111 • D. E. Baker, *Biographia dramatica, or, A companion to the playhouse*, rev. I. Reed, new edn, 1 (1782), 236–8 • A. Nicholl, *A history of early eighteenth century drama, 1700–1750* (1925), 206–8, 337 • T. Davies, *Memoirs of the life of David Garrick*, 2 vols. (1780), vol. 1, p. 102 • M. Drabble, ed., *The Oxford companion to English literature*, rev. edn (1995), 961 • *The record of the Royal Society of London*, 4th edn (1940)

Likenesses W. Hogarth, oils, 1740, NG Ire. • F. Hayman, double portrait, oils (with his wife), Wellcome L. • W. Hogarth, oils, FM Cam.

Hoadly, John (1678–1746), Church of Ireland archbishop of Armagh, was born at Tottenham, Middlesex, on 27 September 1678, son of the Revd Samuel *Hoadly (1643–1705) and his second wife, Martha, *née* Pickering (1639–1703); his elder brother was Benjamin *Hoadly (1676–1761). He was educated at St Catharine's College, Cambridge, where he graduated BA in 1697. In September 1700 he was appointed deputy headmaster of Norwich grammar school, of which his father was headmaster. Having passed some years there he became chaplain to Bishop Gilbert Burnet, who preferred him to the rectory of St Edmund's, Salisbury, and made him successively prebendary (21 February 1706), archdeacon (6 November 1710), and chancellor (16 April 1713) of that diocese. In 1717 Lord King, then chief justice of the common pleas, presented him to the rectory of Ockham in Surrey. He was also appointed chaplain-in-ordinary to George II.

On 3 September 1727 Hoadly was consecrated bishop of Ferns and Leighlin. William Whiston violently objected to this appointment on account of Hoadly's standard of learning. Others were more complimentary about his accomplishments: 'I know', wrote the primate, Archbishop Hugh Boulter, 'his affection for his majesty, and that he has spirit to help to keep up the English interest here.' In July 1729, when the archbishopric of Dublin fell vacant, Boulter again wrote of Hoadly's loyalty to the crown, this time to Sir Robert Walpole. Hoadly was accordingly translated to Dublin on 13 January 1730. When Boulter died, Hoadly was chosen to succeed him as primate and was appointed on 7 October 1742.

As primate Hoadly displayed a tolerant spirit by consenting to the abolition of restrictions on Roman Catholic services. As archbishop of Dublin he built the residence of Tallaght, co. Dublin, at a cost of £2500. Unlike his brother, Hoadly was not a prolific theological writer. His few publications included several sermons, a pastoral letter on the Jacobite rising of 1745, a defence of Gilbert Burnet, and a commentary on the work of Bishop William Beveridge of St Asaph. Details of Hoadly's marriage are unknown but his only daughter, Sarah, married Bellingham Boyle, MP for Bandon Bridge (1731–60) and for Youghal (1761–8).

Hoadly was for many years influential in managing the Irish privy council and the House of Lords, especially after his appointment as a lord justice on 25 November 1742. He died at Rathfarnham on 16 July 1746, of a fever caught while superintending workmen, and was buried at Tallaght. 'He gave universal content and satisfaction', said a writer in the *Dublin Courant* (22 July 1746) 'by his easiness of access, his knowledge of affairs, and capacity for business.'   RICHARD GARNETT, *rev.* J. FALVEY

Sources B. Bradshaw and others, 'Bishops of the Church of Ireland from 1534', *A new history of Ireland*, ed. T. W. Moody and others, 9: *Maps, genealogies, lists* (1984), 392–438 • H. Cotton, *Fasti ecclesiae Hibernicae*, 6 vols. (1845–78) • R. Mant, *History of the Church of Ireland*, 2 vols. (1840) • Burtchaell & Sadleir, *Alum. Dubl.* • J. J. Falvey, 'The Church of Ireland episcopate in the eighteenth century', MA diss., University College, Cork, 1995 • Venn, *Alum. Cant.*

Likenesses T. Beard, print, *c*.1729 • J. Faber junior, mezzotint, 1733 (after I. Whood), BM, NPG • S. Slaughter, oils, 1744, NG Ire. •

M. Slaughter, wax sculpture, 1745, V&A · I. Whood, portrait, NL Ire.

Hoadly, John (1711–1776), poet and playwright, born in Broad Street, London, on 8 October 1711, was the youngest son of the Revd Benjamin *Hoadly (1676–1761), subsequently bishop of Winchester, and his first wife, Sarah Curtis (1676?–1743) [see Hoadly, Sarah], a portrait painter. He attended Dr Newcome's school at Hackney where he distinguished himself by his performance as Phocyas in John Hughes's *Siege of Damascus*. Hoadly's love of the theatre proved to be lifelong. He assisted his brother, the physician Benjamin *Hoadly (1706–1757), in writing *The Contrast, or, A Tragical Comic Rehearsal of Two Modern Plays*, which was brought out at Lincoln's Inn Fields theatre on 30 April 1731, and performed several times. With its ridicule of living authors such as James Thomson, the wits and the critics were both intrigued and offended in equal measure. The play was quickly suppressed at Bishop Hoadly's request.

Hoadly matriculated from Corpus Christi College, Cambridge, in 1731 and graduated LLB in 1736. Though originally admitted at the Middle Temple on 1 November 1726, he opted to pursue a career in the church, if only because of the patronage his father, newly translated to the wealthy see of Winchester, could confer on him. He was ordained deacon on 7 December 1735 and priest on the 21st. On 26 December he was named chaplain to Frederick, prince of Wales, having been appointed as chancellor of the Winchester diocese (29 November 1735) even before taking holy orders. On 10 February 1736 Hoadly married Elizabeth, daughter of James Ashe, of Salisbury. There were no children. Over the next two years Hoadly received further ample patronage: the rectory of Mitchelmersh, Hampshire, on 8 March 1737; that of Wroughton, Wiltshire, on 8 September; that of Old Alresford, Hampshire (with the chapelries of New Alresford and Medstead), on 29 November. The same day he was collated canon of the second prebend in Winchester Cathedral. This was far from the end of his accumulations. Hoadly was rector of Wield, Hampshire, from 1737 to 1776; on 9 June 1743 he was instituted to the rectory of St Mary's, Southampton, and on 16 December 1746 to the vicarage of Overton, Hampshire. On 4 January 1748 the LLD degree was awarded to him by Thomas Herring, archbishop of Canterbury. Hoadly was appointed a chaplain in the household of Augusta, the princess dowager of Wales, on 6 May 1751. In May 1760 he was awarded the mastership of St Cross, Winchester. He was a valued assistant to his father in the latter's declining years, on whose behalf he held a visitation in the Winchester diocese in 1759.

Hoadly spent his summers in alternate years at his houses in Old Alresford and Southampton. He told William Hogarth jestingly that he visited Alresford occasionally as the shepherd should always be seen among his flock even if only to fleece them. A regular visitor to David Garrick at Hampton (who dubbed him the 'Rev'd Rigdum Funnidos'), he persuaded his friends to take part in amateur theatricals at every opportunity. Hoadly wrote a variety of texts for performance. They included *Florimel, or,*

Love's Revenge (1734), a dramatic pastoral, after an anonymous original, set to music by Maurice Greene; *Jephtha* (1737), an oratorio (anonymous), music by Greene; *Phoebe* (1748), a pastoral opera (anonymous), music by Greene; *The Force of Truth* (1744), an oratorio (anonymous original, taken from the book of Esdras). Hoadly composed the fifth act of James Miller's tragedy adapted from Voltaire, *Mahomet the Imposter* (1744), and completed and revised George Lillo's *Arden of Feversham* (1764). He may have assisted his brother Benjamin in the writing of *The Suspicious Husband*. Hoadly left several dramas in manuscript, including 'The Housekeeper, a Farce', on the plan of James Townley's *High Life Below Stairs*; 'The Beggar's Garland', a one-act burlesque opera; and a tragedy on the life of Thomas Cromwell. He also dabbled in humorous versifying; some of his poems are in Dodsley's *Collection*, with the best a translation of Edward Holdsworth's 'Muscipula' in volume 5 (1737). Ever protective of Bishop Hoadly's reputation, John Hoadly edited his father's works in three volumes in 1773, to which he prefixed a short life originally contributed to the supplement to the *Biographia Britannica*. He also wrote for Greene's academy at the Apollo, and composed the verses for Hogarth which were placed under the prints of *The Rake's Progress*. A friend of the novelist Sarah Fielding, Hoadly erected a monument in her memory.

After many years suffering from acute gout, Hoadly died on 16 March 1776 at St Mary's rectory, Southampton, and was buried in Winchester Cathedral. He had retained all his preferments except the rectory of Wroughton and the prebend of Winchester which he had resigned on 12 June 1760. Hoadly's talents may not have run to serious theology, but there was a charitable side to his life which became apparent to all when his will set aside money for apprenticing the poorer children of the diocese. There was also a generous bequest to the widows of clergymen lodged at Bishop Morley's Wolvesey College in Winchester. John Hoadly had gifts of loyalty, good humour, friendship, and personal modesty which were not spoilt by his rich accumulation of church livings. NIGEL ASTON

Sources GM, 1st ser., 46 (1776), 164–6 · GM, 1st ser., 50 (1780), 123, 141, 173–4 · 'Memoirs of the late Dr John Hoadley', *Annual Register* (1776), 39–40 · Venn, *Alum. Cant.* · *Fasti Angl., 1541–1857*, [Canterbury] · W. R. Ward, *Parson and parish in eighteenth-century Hampshire: replies to Bishops' visitations* (1995), xx–xxi, 203, 208, 211, 221, 234 · A. J. Robertson, *A history of Alresford derived from manuscript notes by Robert Boyes* (1938) · VCH Hampshire and the Isle of Wight, 2.197; 3.306; 4.218; 5.218 · Nichols, *Illustrations*, 3.295–8; 5.730 · Nichols, *Lit. anecdotes*, 3.127, 138–43, 385 · F. Busby, *Winchester Cathedral, 1079–1979* (1979), 169 · *The letters of David Garrick*, ed. D. M. Little and G. M. Kahrl, 3 vols. (1963) · R. Paulson, *Hogarth: his life, art and times*, 2 vols. (1971) · DNB · IGI · will, BL, Add. MS 37682, fol. 252 · admissions to house and chambers, 1695–1737, Middle Temple, London, vol. G

Archives BL, letters to Lord Hardwicke, Add. MSS 35605–35612, *passim* · Hants. RO, letters to Richard Warner · V&A NAL, letters to David Garrick

Likenesses F. Hayman, double portrait, oils, 1746 (with Maurice Greene), NPG

Wealth at death see will, BL, Add. MS 37682, fol. 252

Hoadly, Samuel (1643–1705), schoolmaster, was the son of John Hoadly (1617–1668), a clergyman, and his wife, Sarah (*bap.* 1625, *d.* 1693), widow of one Bushnel; the couple had met aboard the ship which was taking them to New England in April 1639, refugees both from the Laudian persecution. Samuel, their first child, was born at Guilford, Connecticut, on 30 September 1643. The family returned to Britain in October 1653, and in the following June, John Hoadly went to Edinburgh as chaplain to the castle garrison. Samuel had his schooling in the city, and at Michaelmas 1659 entered King James's College there. In July 1662 the Hoadlys moved to Rolveden, Kent. In January 1663 Samuel began teaching at the neighbouring school of Cranbrook. On 19 June 1666 he married Mary Wood, a widow, who died giving birth to a stillborn child on 25 November 1668. Hoadly married again on 29 September 1669; his second wife was Martha (*b.* 1639), daughter of the puritan divine Benjamin Pickering, with whom he had nine children.

Hoadly set up a private school at Westerham, Kent, where his brother John helped him. In 1678 he moved to Tottenham High Cross, Middlesex, and in May 1686 to Brooke House, Hackney. In April 1700 he was appointed headmaster of Norwich School, where he is now remembered only as father of Bishop Benjamin *Hoadly, although in his day he was celebrated as an educationist and writer of textbooks. His *Natural Method of Teaching* (1688) went through many editions, and he also produced an edition of Phaedrus and worked on a Latin dictionary. Several of his letters to the eminent Dutch Latinist Johann Georg Graevius are printed in Bishop Hoadly's *Works*. Hoadly was in orders, but never beneficed. He died on 17 April 1705 and was buried in St Luke's Chapel, Norwich Cathedral, alongside his second wife (who had died on 13 January 1703). Of their children besides Benjamin, John *Hoadly (1678–1746) also attained eminence in the church, Frances married one Hawkins, a dancing-master at the Hackney School, and Sarah married the well-known London bookseller Timothy Childe.   C. S. KNIGHTON

Sources *The works of Benjamin Hoadly*, ed. J. Hoadly, 1 (1773), vi–vii • R. H. Harries, ed., *A history of Norwich School* (1991), 66

Hoadly [*née* Curtis], **Sarah** (1676?–1743), portrait painter, is of obscure origins. Little is known of her life or of her work before her marriage on 30 May 1701 to Benjamin *Hoadly (1676–1761), who, having given up a Cambridge fellowship to marry her, then took holy orders. Their younger son, John *Hoadly, includes a brief account of his mother in his biographical preface to the *Works* of Bishop Benjamin Hoadly (3 vols., 1773). He states that his mother was 'born at Pontefract, in Yorkshire, about six months before his lordship' (Hoadly, xi), who was born on 14 November 1676; but her birth is not recorded in the Pontefract parish register for or about 1676, and nothing is known of her parentage or of the circumstances that took her to London and secured her a place in Mary Beale's studio.

Vertue, in his *Note Books* (3.113), states that Sarah Hoadly 'learnt to paint of Mrs Beal' presumably having started as a teenaged apprentice or assistant in Mary Beale's studio in Pall Mall, and that 'she had been for her self set up in

business near 7 years before Mrs Beal dyd [October 1699]' (ibid.), which suggests that she was probably fifteen when she began to work on her own. Vertue adds that 'her first beginnings. was with some difficulties to Subsit'. No works predating her marriage at the age of about twenty-five are now known. The circumstances in which she encountered her future husband throw some light on ways in which young women who had to earn a living in London might group themselves together. Vertue relates that Sarah Curtis had lodgings in a house near Covent Garden with two stairways. She lived up one stairway, while two of Benjamin Hoadly's sisters ('mantua makers') lived up the other; 'by this means came their first acquaintance, and afterwards Marriage' (Vertue, *Note books*, 5.14).

Vertue asserts that marriage left Sarah Hoadly 'at Liberty to practice the Art or leave it just as her affections inclind her. therefore after that good Fortune. she painted the pictures only of Intimates & friends' (Vertue, *Note books*, 3.113). Her 'Liberty to practice the Art' was inevitably curtailed by childbearing—stillborn twins (*c.*1702); Samuel (*b. c.*1704), who died young; Benjamin *Hoadly (*b.* 1706); John (*b.* 1711)—followed by successive household moves—to Bangor (1716), Hereford (1721), Salisbury (1723), and Winchester (1734)—as her husband moved rapidly up the episcopal ladder; probably his physical disability (he was crippled) threw extra work upon her. Portraits painted (in oils) during the twenty-five years or so after her marriage indicate that she certainly did not choose to 'leave' her art. Those of Bishop Hoadly include an early portrait recorded in George Scharf's sketchbooks as being at Lambeth Palace (but now untraced) and another, as chancellor of the Order of the Garter, of about 1726–30 (NPG). In 1713 she painted Richard Ducane, a director of the Bank of England and governor of Christ's Hospital (priv. coll.); otherwise her known sitters were all clergymen. Her portrait of Gilbert Burnet, historian and bishop of Salisbury (*d.* 1715), now untraced, was engraved in 1723 by Vertue, who also engraved (in 1720) perhaps her most characterful portrait, of William Whiston, theologian and mathematician (priv. coll.; anonymous copy, NPG).

Sarah Hoadly's portraiture is direct and unaffected, deriving little from Mary Beale's more fully rounded, Lely-inspired style. Though Vertue considered her skill 'remarkable' her competence (on present evidence) was no higher than that of the average portraitist of her day. Sarah Hoadly died on 11 January 1743.

JUDY EGERTON

Sources Vertue, *Note books*, 3.88, 113; 5.1, 14 • J. Hoadly, 'preface', *Biographia Britannica, or, The lives of the most eminent persons who have flourished in Great Britain and Ireland*, suppl. (1766); rev. and republished as preface, B. Hoadly, *Works*, ed. J. Hoadly, 3 vols. (1773), vol. 1, esp. pp. xi, lxiv; repr. in *GM*, 1st ser., 44 (1774), 212–14 • H. Walpole, *Anecdotes of painting in England*, ed. R. Wornum, new edn, 3 vols. (1849); repr. (1876), vol. 2, p. 300 • D. Piper, *Seventeenth-century portraits in the National Portrait Gallery* (1963), 374–5 • J. Kerslake, *National Portrait Gallery: early Georgian portraits*, 2 vols. (1977), vol. 1, pp. 141–2; vol. 2, pl. 386 • E. Walsh, R. Jeffree, and R. Sword, *The excellent Mrs Mary Beale* (1975), pp. 43–4, cat. nos. 45 (*William Whiston DD*, repr.), 46 [exhibition catalogue, Geffrye Museum, London, and Towner Art Gallery, Eastbourne, 13 Oct 1975 – 21 Feb 1976] •

T. Barber, *Mary Beale: portrait of a seventeenth-century painter, her family and her studio* (1999), 87 [cat. no. 45, Sarah Hoadly, *Benjamin Hoadly* (not repr.); exhibition catalogue, Geffrye Museum, London, 21 Sept 1999 – 30 Jan 2000] • T. Murdoch, ed., *The quiet conquest: the Huguenots, 1685–1985* (1985) [no. 431, *Richard Ducane*; exhibition catalogue, Museum of London, 15 May – 31 Oct 1985]
Likenesses W. Hogarth, oils, Hunt. L.

Hoar, Leonard (1630–1675), college head, was the son of Charles Hoare (d. 1638), a brewer, alderman, and sheriff in Gloucester, and Joanna Hinksman (d. 1664). His father's will provided for Leonard to matriculate at Oxford, but following the elder Hoare's death in 1638 and the deprivation of the Revd John Workman, whose ministry the Hoares had followed, Joanna and her children migrated to New England, settling in Braintree, Massachusetts. Hoar thus attended Harvard College rather than Oxford, receiving his AB in 1650 and his MA three years later.

Like many Harvard graduates of this period, Leonard journeyed to England following his studies in order to pursue a career in the ministry of the reforming English church. He was incorporated MA at Cambridge in 1654. After preaching in various places, in 1656 he was presented by the protector to the post of rector at Wanstead, Essex, which he held until he was ejected following the Restoration. He married Bridget Lisle (d. 1723), the daughter of the regicide judge John *Lisle and his wife, Lady Alice *Lisle, and was active in the dissenting community during the 1660s. During this period he pursued interests in botany and medicine, which brought him into contact with Robert Boyle and other members of the Royal Society. Such connections were instrumental in obtaining a royal order to the University of Cambridge that led to his being granted the degree of doctor of physic in 1671. The university subscription book shows that he signed his name to the three articles despite his puritan religious convictions. During this time Hoar also continued his theological studies and published *Index Biblicus* (1668), a guide to the historical books of the Bible.

In 1672 Hoar returned to New England, ostensibly to accept a ministerial post with the Third Church of Boston. The previous year, however, Massachusetts leaders had written to John Owen, John Collins, and other English dissenters seeking aid for Harvard and soliciting advice regarding a successor to the ageing Charles Chauncy as president of Harvard College. When he arrived in the colony, Hoar carried with him a recommendation from Owen and the others that he be the new president. From his installation in December 1672 his tenure was not very successful. Some colonists questioned the fact that Hoar did not bring with him a letter of dismissal from his English congregation, and further criticism concerned the fact that in accepting the Harvard post he had broken an implicit promise to minister to the Third Church. In addition, he was probably the victim of disaffection sowed by unsuccessful candidates for the post. The fellows and students turned against Hoar, and a number of them left the college. Though the authorities gave him lukewarm support, his position became untenable and he resigned the post in March 1675. Yet his vision for the college was a

forward-looking one. He had sought to introduce experimental science into the curriculum and provided equipment to do so. He secured a new charter that gave more power to the college fellows and less to the overseers. He had also used his English connections to raise funds to replace some of the older college buildings.

Hoar's health declined dramatically after he left Harvard. He died in Boston on 28 November 1675, and was buried on 6 December in Braintree, Massachusetts.

FRANCIS J. BREMER

Sources S. E. Morison, *Harvard College in the seventeenth century* (Cambridge, Mass., 1935) • M. A. Peterson, 'Hoar, Leonard', *ANB* • F. J. Bremer, *Congregational communion: clerical friendship in the Anglo-American puritan community, 1610–1692* (1994) • J. L. Sibley, *Biographical sketches of graduates of Harvard University*, 1 (1873) • J. Savage, *A genealogical dictionary of the first settlers of New England*, 4 vols. (1860–62) • *Calamy rev.*
Archives Harvard U.

Hoard, Samuel (1599–1658/9), Church of England clergyman and religious writer, was born in London. In 1614, aged fifteen, he became a clerk or chorister at All Souls College, Oxford, where he matriculated aged eighteen on 10 October 1617. After migrating to St Mary Hall he graduated BA on 20 April 1618, and proceeded MA on 25 January 1621, being incorporated at Cambridge the following year. By 1622 Hoard was curate and lecturer at St Christopher-le-Stocks, London, for on 22 August that year he and John Blackwell were cited before the London consistory court and ordered to produce documents empowering them to officiate in that church; there is no evidence of subsequent action in their case. As a chaplain of Robert Rich, earl of Warwick, Hoard was presented to the rectory of Moreton, Essex, in 1625. By 1628 he had married Mary (d. 1645/6), whose other name is unknown. A son, Samuel, baptized on 2 December 1628, died young, as did his sister, Mary, baptized on 12 July 1631, but Grace, baptized on 31 October 1632, survived; ten other children were born between 1633 and 1645 or 1646.

With other ministers patronized by Warwick, Hoard supported Thomas Hooker when the latter's conformity was questioned in 1629, and he proceeded BD on 15 June 1630. By 1633 Hoard had forsaken his Calvinist principles and embraced Arminian tenets, a decision he explained in *Gods Love to Man-Kinde* (1633). Repudiating the reformed doctrine of predestination as a novelty with little or no acceptance in antiquity and citing its alleged affinity with Manichaean fatalism, he asserted that it dishonoured God by making him the author of sin and responsible for the eternal torment of sinners. By abdicating human responsibility the doctrine undermined government, he asserted. It was contrary to such divine attributes as holiness, mercy, and justice as well as antithetical to the purpose of the word and sacraments, and it hindered efforts to pursue a holy life while encouraging despair. John Davenant, bishop of Salisbury, responded in *Animadversions ... upon a Treatise Intitled 'Gods Love to Mankind'* (1641), accusing Hoard of promiscuously extending the scope of God's love and thereby obscuring his special mercy to the elect. Another refutation came from William Twisse in *The Riches of Gods*

Love (1653), which included a critical examination of material apparently appended to Hoard's book by the London minister Henry Mason. Subsequent editions of *Gods Love to Man-Kinde* were published in 1635, 1656, and 1673, and the book's thesis was incorporated in a debate between Edward Reynolds and Thomas Pierce of Magdalen College, Oxford.

Dedicated to Warwick, Hoard's second book, *The Soules Misery and Recoverie* (1636; 2nd edn, 1658), was a lengthy disquisition on Ephesians 4: 30 in which he explained how Christians could avoid offending God by presumptuous, deliberate sins. He followed this with *The Churches Authority Asserted* (1637), a sermon preached at Chelmsford, Essex, on the occasion of Archbishop William Laud's visitation on 1 March 1637. Seeking to diminish confusion and disorder in the church, which he deemed the root of heresy and schism, he defended the church's right to impose 'a compleate and cheerfull *conformity*' (p. 65) even though ceremonies were not part of the substance of religion. Ministers, he insisted, must conform in doctrine and practice and teach their parishioners to do so as well. An accomplished debater, he was well read in the patristics and scholastics. On 29 March 1637 Hoard was collated to the prebend of Wilsden at St Paul's, London.

In the 1640s Hoard lost his prebend but was not sequestrated from his living. Following his death on 15 February 1658 or 1659, he was buried in the chancel at Moreton. In his will, dated 8 March 1657 and proved on 20 April 1659, he anticipated bequests from the sale of his property totalling £868. By this time his eldest daughter, Grace, had married Nathaniel Eyre. His eldest surviving son, William (*bap.* 9 Aug 1637), after studying at Eton College, had been admitted to King's College, Cambridge, in 1656. He graduated BA in 1660, was ordained on 20 September 1662, and proceeded MA in 1663. He was a fellow at King's from 1659 to 1669, and served as vicar of Sturminster, Dorset, from 8 January 1666 until his death some time before 12 October 1670.   RICHARD L. GREAVES

Sources Wood, *Ath. Oxon.*, new edn, 3.449–50 · Foster, *Alum. Oxon.* · Venn, *Alum. Cant.* · *Fasti Angl., 1541–1857*, [St Paul's, London], 65 · P. S. Seaver, *The puritan lectureships: the politics of religious dissent, 1560–1662* (1970) · Wood, *Ath. Oxon.: Fasti* (1815), 379, 393, 456 · D. D. Wallace, jun., *Puritans and predestination: grace in English protestant theology, 1525–1695* (1982) · N. Tyacke, *Anti-Calvinists: the rise of English Arminianism, c.1590–1640* (1987) · J. Davenant, *Animadversions ... upon a treatise intitled 'Gods love to mankind'* (1641) · W. Twisse, *The riches of Gods love unto the vessells of mercy* (1653) · *Walker rev.*, 154 · will, PRO, PROB 11/290, fols. 284v–285v · *IGI* [parish register of Moreton, Essex]
Archives BL, Add. MS 5872, fol. 67 · GL, MS 9531/15, fols. 94v, 127v
Wealth at death approx. £868: will, PRO, PROB 11/290, fols. 284v–285v

Hoare, Angelina Margaret (1843–1892), missionary, was born on 17 May 1843 at 13 New Street, Spring Gardens, London, the sixth of the twelve children of Henry Hoare (d. 1866), banker, and his wife, Lady Mary *née* Marsham (1811–1871), third daughter of the second earl of Romney. Her parents were active members of the Church of England, and her father campaigned vigorously for the revival of convocation. She was educated at home, but as a young woman she developed a weak heart; nevertheless she led an active life, and was strongly attracted to missionary work.

Angelina's brother Walter Hoare became curate to Robert Milman at Great Marlow, Buckinghamshire; Milman became bishop of Calcutta in 1867 and in 1874 his sister Maria invited Henry Hoare's daughters to Calcutta to help in the zenana missions for Indian women. Angelina Hoare arrived in Calcutta in January 1876. Within weeks Milman died, but his successor was supportive. Hoare soon realized that schools were more effective as specifically missionary agencies than the zenana houses, which were closely supervised by husbands who objected to the Christian teaching being given to their wives. In 1878 she started village schools south of Calcutta in the extensive rice-growing area called the Sunderbunds. There were no roads and the only means of communication was by flat-bottomed boats. About thirty schools were established, funded by money raised in England principally among Angelina Hoare's banking family connections. In 1882 she bought a large house in Calcutta with 9 acres of land, to serve as her mission house, and began a number of schools for Indians, some of whom became teachers in the Sunderbunds. Hoare adopted Indian dress and learnt Bengali: in return she won widespread admiration and support.

Failing health hastened Hoare's decision to retire from the mission house, and the sisters from the community of St John Baptist, at Clewer, who had been working in Calcutta, were invited to run the mission house while she agreed to retain the schools. Soon after returning from a visit to England she became ill and died from a brain haemorrhage, on 10 January 1892. She was buried in the English cemetery in Calcutta and a memorial was placed in the cathedral. Following her death the Clewer sisters also took over the village schools.   VALERIE BONHAM

Sources Mrs W. M. Hoare, *Life of Angelina Margaret Hoare, by her sisters and Mrs Walter M. Hoare*, 2nd edn (1897) [with introduction by H. Whitehead] · V. Bonham, *A joyous service: the Clewer sisters and their work* (1989) · V. Bonham, *Sisters of the raj* (1997)
Archives C. Hoare & Co., London, letters and MSS · Community of St John Baptist, Clewer, Berkshire
Likenesses photograph, C. Hoare & Co., London · photograph, repro. in Hoare, *Life of Angelina Margaret Hoare* · photographs, Community of St John Baptist, Clewer
Wealth at death £13,859 10s. 3d.: resworn probate, Sept 1892, *CGPLA Eng. & Wales*

Hoare, Charles James (1781–1865), Church of England clergyman, was born in London on 14 July 1781, the third son of Henry Hoare (1750–1828), banker, of Fleet Street, London, one of the founders of the Church Missionary Society, and his wife, Lydia Henrietta (d. 1816), daughter and coheir of Isaac Malortie of Hanover and London, merchant. He was educated privately under the Revd John Simons of Paul's Cray, Kent, before matriculating as a pensioner at St John's College, Cambridge, in 1802. Here among his friends were Henry Martyn, Charles and Robert Grant, William Dealtry, and J. W. Cunningham. In 1803 he passed as second wrangler, second Smith's prizeman, and second classical medallist, graduated BA in the same year and MA in 1806, and was Seatonian prizeman in 1807. On 24 March 1806 he was chosen Lady Margaret fellow of his college, and was ordained in 1804 as curate to Thomas Rennell, dean of Winchester and vicar of Alton, Hampshire. He was ordained priest in 1806. In 1807 he was presented by the dean and chapter of Winchester to the living of Blandford Forum, Dorset. Hoare married, on 4 July 1811, Jane Isabella (d. 1874), only daughter of Richard Holden of Moorgate, Yorkshire, with whom he had seven children.

In March 1821 Hoare moved to the family living of Godstone, near Reigate, Surrey, which he held for the remainder of his life. In 1829 he became rural dean of South-East Ewell, and on 10 November in the same year the archdeacon of Winchester. On 2 December 1831 he was made a canon residentiary of Winchester Cathedral. He published on the defence of the Irish church, the maintenance of cathedral establishments, and the cause of education. He was a great supporter of religious societies, and held a yearly missionary gathering at Godstone vicarage.

On 14 November 1847 Hoare was transferred to the archdeaconry of Surrey, where he took an interest in the church extension movement in south London. A committed, but not narrow, evangelical, Hoare was on close terms with Hannah More, Wilberforce, the Thorntons, Venn, Macaulay, and Simeon. He had also been one of Sumner's appointments. He resigned his archdeaconry in 1860. Hoare died at Godstone vicarage on 15 January 1865, and was buried in a vault in the churchyard on 21 January.

G. C. BOASE, rev. ELLIE CLEWLOW

Sources GM, 3rd ser., 18 (1865), 249–50 · Sussex Agricultural Express (28 Jan 1865), 6 · Venn, Alum. Cant. · D. M. Lewis, ed., The Blackwell dictionary of evangelical biography, 1730–1860, 2 vols. (1995) · D. Rosman, Evangelicals and culture (1984); repr. (1992)
Archives Dorset RO, letters to J. W. Cunningham · Hagley Hall, Hagley, letters to fourth Baron Lyttelton
Wealth at death under £30,000: probate, 30 March 1865, CGPLA Eng. & Wales

Hoare, Christopher [Kit] **Gurney** (1882–1973), stockbroker, was born on 29 May 1882 at Mill Field House, Heaton, Newcastle upon Tyne, the second son of Robert Gurney Hoare (1844–1899), banker, and his wife, Anne Hoare. The Gurney Hoares combined two Quaker families, the greater being the Gurneys of Keswick (Norfolk) and Norwich; they had headed the London bank Barnett, Hoare & Co. since the eighteenth century. Samuel Hoare, second Viscount Templewood, was a first cousin to Kit. In 1884, the family merged its City interests with Lloyds Bank. Well before then, Hoare's father, a younger son, had left Norfolk to become a partner in Hodgkin Barnett Pease Spence & Co., a private bank in Newcastle, which itself merged with Lloyds in 1903.

Hoare was educated at Harrow School and at King's College, Cambridge. At King's, he gained a second class in the first part of the classical tripos and took his BA in 1904. After leaving the university, he worked for a few months in Lloyds' recently acquired Northumberland branches, but soon took the bank's advice and moved to London. In

the City he was first employed as a clerk by the stockbroker D. A. Bevan & Co., but in 1910 he joined Cohen Laming & Co., whose senior partners' practice of working alternate halves of the year offered him greater scope to build his own connection. The firm then specialized in option business and by the end of the year he was a partner. On 25 October 1907 he married Eveline Hamilton Lucas (1888/9–1960), the daughter of Colonel Alfred George Lucas. They had a son and a daughter.

On the outbreak of war, Hoare joined the 2nd line Essex yeomanry, but served through most of the conflict with the Royal Horse Guards, earning the Military Cross in 1918. Thereafter he gradually became well known and respected in the City. In 1929 his firm, along with many others, was caught out by the collapse of the Hatry group of companies, and Hoare himself was one of the first brokers interviewed by the subsequent stock exchange inquiry. More importantly, however, the then Cohen Laming Hoare was among a small number of broking houses in the inter-war years that operated in the new issue market for industrial companies. Capital-raising for corporations, collieries, and electricity and gas companies predominated, but a £500,000 rights issue for British Burmah Petroleum in 1936 was a pointer to the future. More generally, Hoare was also building a reputation as a company broker, acquiring ICI, Vickers, Distillers, and P. & O. as major clients. He became senior partner in 1930. Belatedly, in 1940, the style of the firm was changed to Hoare & Co.

After the Second World War, and despite advancing age, Hoare came into his own as one of the most powerful and forceful brokers in the City. In the next fifteen years his firm was employed by virtually every merchant bank in the City, but developed particularly close relationships with Robert Fleming, Morgan Grenfell, and Lazards, co-operating with them in major issues for companies like Canadian Eagle Oil, Rootes Motors, Anglo-Iranian, Dunlop, P. & O., and Esso. From 1953, the firm also participated in the denationalization of the steel industry. Whenever possible, however, Hoare preferred to operate without the backing of a merchant bank or finance house, drawing on his network of banking, institutional, and industrial contacts to act alone or in association with a select group of City and provincial brokers. Thus considerable sums were raised for some of Britain's most prominent companies, including ICI, Vickers, Distillers, P. & O., Harrods, Associated Portland Cement, and Lloyds Bank. Hoare's fierce competitiveness, however, upset the gentlemanly conventions of the City and stirred resentment. At the end of 1957, he excluded his major rival, Cazenove & Co., from a giant £41 million debenture issue for BP. Cazenove returned in kind, blocking Hoare's participation in a Shell issue shortly after.

Hoare remained nominally senior partner throughout the 1960s, but spent most of his final years at Gateley Hall, near East Dereham in Norfolk, enjoying a small collection of old masters—including work by Veneziano, Tiepolo, Rubens, Gainsborough, Fragonard, Rembrandt, and Tintoretto—which he had acquired since the 1920s. Field sports were also an enduring love; in Cambridge he was master of the Trinity beagles in the 1904–5 season, and he later chose his Exford home so that he could ride with the Devon and Somerset staghounds.

Somewhat rough in character early in his career, Hoare was high-spirited and single-minded in the pursuit of his many interests. In business he made decisions quickly, without consulting partners and, as the *Times* business diarist recalled, 'was very much the master of his own company' (23 Nov 1973, 23). Once described as a man who 'actually thought angrily' (*The Times*, 28 Nov 1973, 22), his propensity to scold staff made him appear irascible and formidable, but he was also remembered for his kindliness, twinkling eye, and keen sense of fun. His success as a businessman had been built upon his vast web of contacts, his courage and self-confidence, attention to detail, and finely tuned judgement of the market. To these qualities were added a Quaker standard of values and sense of duty. According to one younger contemporary: 'He prayed for a right judgement in all things and set his standards accordingly' (*The Times*, 28 Nov 1973, 22).

Ripe in years, and recalled affectionately as one of the London stock exchange's greatest members, Hoare died at 20 Orchard Court, Portman Square, London, of cerebral arteriosclerosis on 22 November 1973.

BERNARD ATTARD

Sources private information (2004) · *The Times* (23 Nov 1973) · *Annual Report of the Council* [King's College, Cambridge] (1974) · *The Times* (23 May 1899) · *The Times* (29 July 1970) · 'Business diary', *The Times* (23 Nov 1973) · *The Times* (28 Nov 1973) · D. Kynaston, *Cazenove & Co.: a history* (1991), 152–4, 160, 197–9, 209, 230–31 · R. S. Sayers, *Lloyds Bank in the history of English banking* (1957), 43–5, 343 · GL, manuscripts section, MS 14600, vols. 82, 86, 87, 101, 124, 137 · GL, MS 14609, vol. 9 · *Members and firms of the Stock Exchange* [List of Members to 1955] (1910/11–1970/71) · *Issuing House Yearbook* (1935–47) · *Times Issuing House Yearbook* (1948–64) · J. Kinross, *Fifty years in the City: financing small business* (1982), 184 · *WW* · b. cert. · d. cert. · m. cert.

Likenesses photograph, repro. in *The Times* (23 Nov 1973), 23

Wealth at death £412,169: probate, 21 Feb 1974, CGPLA Eng. & Wales

Hoare, Clement (1788/9–1849), vine grower, cultivated a vineyard at Sidlesham, near Chichester, from where he moved in 1841 to Shirley vineyard, near Southampton. He was the author of several works on the practicalities of vine growing, including, in 1844, *A Descriptive Account of an Improved Method of Planting and Managing the Roots of Grape Vines*. This proposed growing vines in hollow pillars, a method which 'at once met with the condemnation it merited' (*Cottage Gardener*, 1849). Soon after the publication of this work, which he financed himself, Hoare became insolvent, his vineyard was broken up, and 'heart-subdued, he was sunk before his time into the grave' (ibid.). He died on 18 August 1849, at Vauxhall, Surrey, aged sixty.

GILES HUDSON

Sources *Cottage Gardener*, 2 (1849), 306 · *GM*, 2nd ser., 32 (1849), 437 · *DNB*

Hoare, Sir (Richard) Colt, second baronet (1758–1838), landowner and antiquary, was born on 9 December 1758

Sir (Richard) Colt Hoare, second baronet (1758–1838), by Samuel Woodforde, 1795 [left, with his son]

at Barn Elms, Barnes, Surrey, the eldest son of Sir Richard Hoare, first baronet (1735–1787), banker, and Anne Hoare (1737–1759), known as Nanny, daughter of Henry *Hoare (1705–1785), banker, of Stourhead, and his wife, Susan Colt (d. 1743). Colt Hoare's parents were first cousins. His mother died when he was six months old and his father married, second, Frances Ann Acland (1736–1800), with whom he had four sons and two daughters. Colt Hoare grew up with his half-brothers and sisters 'in a delightful and extensive villa on the Thames between Putney and Mortlake' (Woodbridge, 71); he was particularly close to the eldest, Henry Hugh (1762–1841). He attended a preparatory school in Wandsworth run by Mr Davis and later studied at Dr Samuel Glasse's seminary in Greenford, Middlesex. He continued his classical studies with a private tutor, the Revd Joseph Eyre, while learning the profession of banker at the family bank in Fleet Street. Henry Hoare favoured his grandson by giving him a house in Lincoln's Inn Fields and an annual allowance of £2000 on his coming of age. His marriage on 18 August 1783, at Barnes, to Hester Lyttelton (1762–1785), daughter of William Henry *Lyttelton of Hagley, Lord Westcote, later Lord Lyttelton, and his first wife, Mary Macartney (d. 1765), was short-lived. The couple's only surviving child, Henry, was born on 17 September 1784; Hester did not live to see his first birthday for she died on 22 August 1785. Colt Hoare never remarried. In the same year, under the terms of his grandfather's will, he inherited Stourhead, with its estates in Wiltshire, Somerset, and Dorset, and severed all connection with the bank except as a customer.

Deprived of both wife and career, and needing 'new scenes and new occupations ... to detach my mind from melancholy reflections', Colt Hoare turned his back on England and his young son and began his extensive travels abroad, equipped with an annual income of about £10,000 ('Memoirs', Colt Hoare MSS). He was away for an almost continuous period of six years. His copious notes and journals, which chronicle his travels, were written up later in 'Recollections abroad: journals of tours on the continent, 1785–1791' (1815–18), but little is revealed in them of his private life. His focus was on Italy, Rome and Naples in particular, but he travelled as well in France, Switzerland, and Spain, writing home regularly to his steward Thomas Charlton at Stourhead and to his half-brother Henry Hugh Hoare. He visited all the classical sites and immersed himself in the landscape, all the time drawing, recording, and collecting for his house and portfolio. In Rome he discovered the work of the Swiss watercolourist Louis Ducros (1748–1810), whose revolutionary style of painting he believed would have a profound influence on the English school. He brought back large-scale Italian views by Ducros for Stourhead.

After a brief return home Colt Hoare resumed his travels in 1788, 'no longer as a tourist but as a systematic antiquarian ... quitting ... the road for the path, the capital for the provinces' (R. C. Hoare, *A Classical Tour through Italy and Sicily*, 1819, x). He passed through the Netherlands, Germany, Venice, and Florence and finally settled in Siena. He sought to locate the major sites of the Etruscan civilization, then explored the Appian way with his sketchbook and returned south in order to visit the recently publicized Greek ruins at Paestum and those in Sicily. His romantic response to Italy was at once tempered and inflamed by a close interest in the classical authors, who turned his attraction into a passion; virtually nothing he saw was without resonance from a documented source: 'every scene bears a classic character and every district acquires double interest from the recollections it calls forth' (R. C. Hoare, *Recollections Abroad*, 2.130).

The French Revolutionary War closed the continent to travellers, and Colt Hoare arrived in Britain in the summer of 1791 at a time when travel through France was still possible, if not comfortable. He never went abroad again. He carried on the habit of keeping meticulous diaries detailing his visits and journeys until his death. Each spring he would travel in the British Isles and in 1806 he went to Ireland. He had a particular fondness for Wales, as did many of his fellow antiquaries, and he made a significant contribution to its travel literature with his translation of Gerald of Wales, published as *Giraldus de Barri, Itinerary of Archbishop Baldwin through Wales AD 1188* (1806). He provided the illustrations for William Coxe's *Historical Tour of Monmouthshire* (1801) and did the same for his friend Roger Fenton in his *Historical Tour through Pembrokeshire* (1811). He bought a fishing-lodge at Bala in 1796; throughout his life Colt Hoare was an enthusiast for all field sports. He spent some winter months at his London house in St

James's Square and in 1805 served as high sheriff for Wiltshire.

Apart from time spent touring, Colt Hoare's energies were fully occupied with developing his inheritance at Stourhead and with his ambitious publishing projects on the ancient and modern histories of his own county. He embarked on grand tree-planting schemes in the gardens, and his election as a fellow of the Linnean Society (1812) recognized his particular contribution to the cultivation of exotic plants; according to one expert, 'his collection of Geraniaceae exceeds every other in this country' (R. Sweet, *Geraniaceae*, 5 vols., 1820–22, 1.18). He had been elected as a fellow of the Society of Antiquaries and admitted to the Society of Dilettanti in 1792. Building work at Stourhead began in 1792 and continued after the outbreak of war with France. After 'finding in the mansion house, as it was, not sufficient room for either his collection of paintings or library of books he made in the year 1800 a considerable addition ... by adding two wings' (A. Hoare, introduction). In the picture gallery Colt Hoare gave pride of place over the chimney-piece to his most important Italian purchase, *The Adoration of the Magi* by Ludovico Cardi (Cigoli) (1605), but it was the library which was his most 'significant contribution to culture' (Woodbridge, 251). He gave his collection of Italian topographical and historical works to the British Museum in 1825 but in its place he collected nearly every book on the history and topography of the British Isles. He created in his house the scholarly atmosphere of a medieval monastery, without any of the discomforts, and provided most of the documentary sources required by himself and his collaborators for their work on the history and archaeology of Wiltshire. This unique collection of books and drawings was dispersed in the Stourhead heirloom sales (Sotheby, Wilkinson, and Hodge, 1883 and 1887). The library was handsomely furnished by Thomas Chippendale the younger, whose ailing business, after he was made bankrupt in 1804, relied heavily on Colt Hoare for survival.

Colt Hoare's ambition, however, was to be an author, not just a collector of books. In this he had the invaluable assistance of William Cunnington of Heytesbury, a tradesman turned antiquary, who was excavating the prehistoric barrows in his neighbourhood. He was the moving spirit behind the team that produced the first volume (in three parts) of *The Ancient History of South Wiltshire* in 1812. Colt Hoare was the financier and author. As a survey of Wiltshire barrows it is incomplete but Colt Hoare was commended: 'No antiquary had ever the same means or opportunities before Sir Richard Hoare and no-one ever availed himself more entirely of the advantages which he possesses' (*Quarterly Review*, 5, 1811, 118). The second volume, *The Ancient History of North Wiltshire*, appeared in 1819. Cunnington had died in 1812 but Colt Hoare gave him the final word: 'to him alone the discovery of the numerous settlements of the Britons, dispersed over our hills, must be justly attributed' (*Ancient Wiltshire*, 2.126).

Colt Hoare's characteristic desire to promote British artists established him as a significant patron. He continued his grandfather's close association with the watercolourist Francis Nicholson, who recorded the now maturing landscape at Stourhead, and with Samuel Woodforde, who painted the full-length double portrait of Colt Hoare and his son for the collection of family portraits in the hall at Stourhead. Sir John Leicester of Tabley introduced him to the young Turner, who painted a series of watercolour views of Salisbury Cathedral between 1794 and 1806 for Colt Hoare. Furthermore, Turner copied one of Colt Hoare's own drawings for his oil of *Lake Avernus with Aeneas and the Cumaean Sybil* in 1815. These works were sold in 1883.

Colt Hoare's son, Henry, showed little interest in anything more serious than the life of pleasure available to a well-born young man of means. He married Charlotte Dering and they had one daughter, Ann, born in 1808. Relations between Colt Hoare and his daughter-in-law were not warm and, following his son's nervous breakdown in 1811, there ensued a bitter period of disharmony between father and son. Henry's instability and propensity for debt led to further unhappiness. He and Charlotte separated, and Colt Hoare was plagued by demands to settle his son's debts at a time when the country was in the grip of an economic crisis. Henry died at Hastings in 1836.

Colt Hoare was reserved in his manner and intellectual in his tastes but his evident enjoyment of society leads one to suspect that he would have embraced family life. He faced the breakdown in his relationship with his only child while struggling with gout, rheumatism, and increasing deafness, ailments that were to plague him for the rest of his life. Increasingly confined to Stourhead, he went to Bath for relief and assiduously worked on his county history of Wiltshire, taking as his immediate model John Nichols's *History and Antiquities of the County of Leicester*. The first part, 'The hundred of Mere', appeared in 1822; it described most of Colt Hoare's own possessions. In all, fourteen parts were published on the hundreds of south Wiltshire, under the title *The History of Modern Wiltshire* (1822–44), usually bound in six volumes. The last two hundreds were written after Colt Hoare's death in order to complete the project. His last fieldwork was to see the Roman Pitney pavement uncovered at Somerton. He published a report on this excavation in 1831, which has proved invaluable as the pavement was destroyed five years later.

Colt Hoare died on 19 May 1838 at Stourhead and was buried in the family mausoleum in the churchyard of St Peter's, Stourton. His memorial, a marble statue by R. C. Lucas, is in Salisbury Cathedral. The estate passed to his half-brother Henry Hugh Hoare. In due course Stourhead passed to the National Trust and became one of its finest properties.   VICTORIA HUTCHINGS

Sources K. Woodbridge, *Landscape and antiquity: aspects of English culture at Stourhead, 1718 to 1838* (1970) · Hoare's Bank Archive, London, Colt Hoare MSS · R. C. Hoare, *The journeys of Sir Richard Colt Hoare through Wales and England, 1793–1810*, ed. M. W. Thompson (1983) · *Stourhead, Wiltshire*, National Trust, rev. edn (1990) · R. C. Hoare, *Recollections abroad during the years 1790, 1791*, 2 vols. (1815–18) · R. C. Hoare, 'Memoirs', c.1815, Stourhead, Colt Hoare MSS ·
A. Hoare, 'Catalogue of Pictures at Stourhead', 1898, Stourhead · *DNB*

Archives BL, Modern English and Reader Services, Humanities and Social Sciences, authorial copy with annotations of his pedigrees and memorials of the family of Hore · BL, corresp. relating to antiquities at Camerton, Add. MS 33665 · BL, journal of Elba tour, Add. MS 41761 · Brighton and Hove Library Service, Brighton, wash drawings · Cardiff Central Library, tour journals · CUL, notes on works of art and journal of tours in Italy · Devizes Museum, Wiltshire, Wiltshire Archaeological and Natural History Society, travel notebooks and journals, accounts, drawings, and papers · Devon RO, collections relating to Bruton Abbey, etc. · Hagley Hall, Hagley, genealogical account of Lyttelton family · Hoare's Bank Archive, London · NL Wales, Welsh tour journals · NMG Wales, drawings · S. Antiquaries, Lond., archaeological papers relating to Wiltshire · Stourhead, Wiltshire · Wilts. & Swindon RO, diaries, journals, corresp. and papers; notebook as a justice of the peace · Yale U., Beinecke L., drawings | Bath Central Library, corresp. with John Skinner · BL, letters to Aylmer Lambert, Add. MS 28545 · Bodl. Oxf., letters to W. P. Carey · Bodl. Oxf., corresp. with Sir Thomas Phillipps · Devizes Museum, Wiltshire Archaeological and Natural History Society, letters to John Britton · Devizes Museum, Wiltshire Archaeological and Natural History Society, letters to William Cunnington · priv. coll., letters to second earl of Radnor · Som. ARS, letters to Samuel Hazell relating to excavations at Littleton · Tabley House, Cheshire, de Tabley MSS · Wilts. & Swindon RO, letters to Lord Bruce

Likenesses W. Hoare, oils, c.1780, Stourhead, Wiltshire · S. Woodforde, oils, 1795, Stourhead, Wiltshire [*see illus.*] · S. Woodforde, oils, exh. RA 1802, Stourhead, Wiltshire · S. C. Smith, oils, c.1831, Stourhead, Wiltshire · H. Edridge, pencil and watercolour drawing, Stourhead, Wiltshire · W. Hoare, pastel drawing, Stourhead, Wiltshire · R. C. Lucas, statue on monument, Salisbury Cathedral · R. C. Lucas, wax bust, Stourhead, Wiltshire · F. Nicholson, watercolour, Stourhead, Wiltshire · attrib. S. Woodforde, oils, Stourhead, Wiltshire

Wealth at death owned 11,000 acres in 1791; estate intact at death; mansion house and contents; also London house: 1827, schedule of lands, Stourhead archive, Wilts. & Swindon RO · est. income £9000–£10,000 p.a.; was 'high in the group of 300 wealthy men below the great landed nobility': Woodbridge, *Landscape*, 145

Hoare, Henry (1677–1725), banker and philanthropist, familiarly known as Good Henry by reason of his philanthropy, was born on 21 July 1677 in the parish of St Vedast-alias-Foster in the City of London, and baptized there. He was the second surviving son of Sir Richard *Hoare (1648–1719) and his wife, Susanna Austen (1658–1720). His elder brother, Richard (1673–1720), pursued an independent and unsuccessful mercantile career; Henry, therefore, became the natural heir to his father's banking business. He married his first cousin Jane (d. 1741), daughter of Sir William Benson of Bromley, knight, on 19 May 1702, having been taken into partnership with his father at the sign of the Golden Bottle in Fleet Street in 1699; they had eleven children. His two surviving sons, Henry *Hoare (1705–1785) and Richard *Hoare (1709–1754) [*see under* Hoare, Sir Richard], succeeded him in business and three of his daughters—Jane (b. 1702), Susanna (b. 1704), and Martha (b. 1708)—lived to adulthood and married. Good Henry and his family lived with his parents in the banking house as a condition of partnership.

On his father's death Henry Hoare's younger brother Benjamin (1693–1750) was made a partner in the business. The terms of the agreement allocated a three-quarters

Henry Hoare (1677–1725), by Michael Dahl

share of the profits and assets of the bank to the elder brother and a quarter share to the younger. From a secure financial base Hoare further enriched himself by highly successful speculation, especially in South Sea Company stock. Between 1718 and 1725 his profits from the bank exceeded £115,000.

Hoare's purchase of the Stourton estate in Wiltshire from Sir John Meres for £14,000 was made in 1717, prior to his sudden increase in fortune. To this he added other country properties, notably Stourton Caundle, Dorset, and Quarley, Hampshire, for a sum totalling £37,150. Landed estates were a good investment and an attractive one for wealthy businessmen with political and social aspirations. Hoare's customers at Fleet Street would have been reassured to have their deposits so well secured but, in any case, he was personally obliged and financially enabled to invest in such a way by the terms of his marriage settlement.

Hoare dismantled the ruinous old Stourton Castle, for centuries the seat of the Stourton family, and built a neo-Palladian villa nearby, which he called Stourhead. His choice of Colen Campbell as architect was a fashionable one, no doubt influenced by his brother-in-law William Benson, surveyor-general, who chose Campbell as his deputy. Benson's own designs for his Wiltshire house, Wilbury, at Newton Toney, and Campbell's designs for Stourhead were published in Campbell's *Vitruvius Britannicus* (1715–25). Hoare appointed Nathaniel Ireson, a Wincanton pottery owner, to supervise the building works at Stourhead, which began in 1721, and the improvements to St Peter's Church, Stourton. Hoare died just as his house was completed. He never lived there. Hoare left it to his son

Henry, directing that his mother should live there for the rest of her life.

Good Henry was known in his lifetime and remembered after his death for his staunch Anglican faith and his compassion for the poor. He was a friend of the religious writer Robert Nelson (1656–1716). The most enduring testimony to his piety is the still extant Henry Hoare Bible Fund, set up under the terms of his will with £2000 for the purchase and free provision of bibles, books of common prayer, and other religious works in 'the English Tongue as are entirely agreeable to the principles and doctrine of the Church of England' (codicil to will of Henry Hoare). The same amount was to be spent on erecting and encouraging charity schools and workhouses. Hoare was one of a small band of philanthropists 'in an age remarkable for its apathy' who were conspicuous among a public that 'had not yet been educated up to a realization of its duty towards poorer brethren' (*The Hospital*, 1914). On 14 January 1716 Hoare and three others met at St Dunstan's Coffee House and founded the Westminster Charitable Society, the first faltering step towards the foundation of Westminster Hospital in 1724. This was a remarkable innovation, being the first hospital in England sustained entirely by voluntary subscriptions to provide free medical care and accommodation for the poor of the parish.

Hoare died in the banking house on 12 March 1725 and was buried at St Peter's Church, Stourton, Wiltshire. His monument is in the church with an encomium of his excellent character written by his widow, who died on 25 June 1741 and was buried beside him. He left his house and his good works unfinished but his legacies of £30,000 were generous to his family, servants, and charities.

VICTORIA HUTCHINGS

Sources private accounts, C. Hoare & Co., London · Bible Fund papers, C. Hoare & Co., London · details of estate and legacies, C. Hoare & Co., London · K. Woodbridge, *Landscape and antiquity: aspects of English culture at Stourhead, 1718 to 1838* (1970) · C. G. A. Clay, 'Henry Hoare, banker, his family and the Stourhead estate', *Landowners, capitalists, and entrepreneurs: essays for Sir John Habakkuk*, ed. F. M. L. Thompson (1994), 113–38 · *Hoare's Bank, a record: the story of a private bank* (1955) · R. C. Hoare, *Pedigrees and memoirs of the families of Hore and Hoare* (1879) · *Stourhead, Wiltshire*, National Trust, rev. edn (1990) · *The Hospital* (Dec 1913–March 1914) · R. C. Hoare, *The history of modern Wiltshire*, 1/1: *Hundred of Mere* (1822)
Archives C. Hoare & Co., London, papers
Likenesses attrib. M. Dahl, oils, c.1720–1724, C. Hoare & Co., London · M. Dahl, oils, Stourhead, Wiltshire [*see illus.*]
Wealth at death £50,000: archives, C. Hoare & Co., London

Hoare, Henry (1705–1785), banker and patron of art, was born on 7 July 1705, the eldest son of Henry *Hoare (1677–1725), banker, and his wife, Jane (d. 1741), daughter of Sir William Benson of Bromley. His grandfather, Sir Richard *Hoare (1648–1719), was the founder of Hoare's Bank. The elder Henry Hoare bought the manor of Stourton in Wiltshire in 1717 and employed Colen Campbell to build a new house, Stourhead, which was completed in 1724, just before his death, and which he bequeathed to his son. The younger Henry (known in the family as Henry the Magnificent) moved to Stourhead on his mother's death in 1741, but succeeded his father immediately as a partner of embellishment of the house through collecting and patronage. He transformed the Stourhead landscape into a Claudian idyll, damming the River Stour to create a lake and engaging Henry Flitcroft, who designed the classical temples of Flora (1745) and Apollo (1765), and the Pantheon (1753–4), which is regarded as an outstanding example of his work, recalling Claude Lorrain's *Coast View of Delos with Aeneas*. The gardens at Stourhead are historically important as an early example of 'le jardin anglais'.

It was Hoare who started the picture collection at Stourhead: he patronized John Wootton, Samuel Woodforde, and his namesake, William Hoare of Bath (no relation, but whose daughter Mary married Hoare's nephew Henry, known as 'Fat Harry' (1744–1785) in 1765). Among his old masters were two pictures by Nicolas Poussin, a double portrait by Carlo Maratta (*Marchese Pallavicini and the Artist*), and pictures by Rembrandt, Gaspard Dughet, and Claude-Joseph Vernet. He commissioned *Caesar and Cleopatra* from Anton Raffael Mengs in 1758 as a companion to the Maratta. Both pictures remained in the house, though many were sold at the Stourhead heirlooms sale at Christies in 1883. The sculptor John Michael Rysbrack was associated with Stourhead from 1744 to his death in 1770. His *Hercules* (1756) is in the Pantheon at Stourhead, together with his *Flora* (1761).

Not only was Stourhead an attractive and dependable asset for the bank's customers, but also, Hoare's profits exceeding £10,000 p.a., it enabled him to make generous provision for his daughters, and to increase his country estates in addition to spending well on them. He was troubled in his old age by the threat to the country and his beloved Stourhead, by Lord North's weak wartime government, leading to 'public calamity' and 'our ruin'. Accordingly, on Colt Hoare's betrothal to Hester Lyttelton in 1783, he settled his estate on his grandson, provided all connection with the bank was severed. He left his share of the bank, and his house in Lincoln's Inn Fields, to Colt's father, his nephew (and son-in-law) Richard, who felt deprived of his full inheritance. Hoare moved to his house, The Wilderness, Clapham, designed for him by Flitcroft thirty years before, where he died on 8 September 1785, his children having predeceased him. He was buried in Stourton churchyard.

VICTORIA HUTCHINGS

Sources K. Woodbridge, *Landscape and antiquity* (1970) · Henry Hoare's private accounts, family letters, 1752 and 1755, C. Hoare & Co. Archives, London · K. Woodbridge, 'Henry Hoare's paradise', *Art Bulletin*, 47 (1965), 83–116 · C. G. A. Clay, 'Henry Hoare, banker, his family, and the Stourhead estate', *Landowners, capitalists and entrepreneurs*, ed. F. M. L. Thompson (1994), 113–38 · E. H. Hoare, *Early history and genealogy of the families of Hore & Hoare* (1883) · *Stourhead, Wiltshire*, National Trust, rev. edn (1990) · *List of pictures* (The National Trust, 1989)
Archives C. Hoare & Co., London, archives · Stourhead, Wiltshire · Sturmy House, Savernake, Wiltshire · Wilts. & Swindon RO, corresp. | Wilts. & Swindon RO, letters to Lord Bruce · Wilts. & Swindon RO, Stourhead and Tottenham House (Savernake) archives
Likenesses M. Dahl and J. Wootton, equestrian portrait, oils, 1726, Stourhead, Wiltshire · J. Wootton, equestrian portrait, oils, 1729 · W. Hoare, pastel drawing, Stourhead, Wiltshire [*see illus.*] ·

Henry Hoare (1705–1785), by William Hoare

Hoare's Bank in 1726, abandoning his previous life, which he had led largely at Quarley in Hampshire 'hunting and drinking with other young men of his age', and applied himself to serious study of the classical writers. In 1734 he bought the Palladian mansion Wilbury House in Wiltshire, and was elected MP for Salisbury. Later he went abroad to pursue his study of painting and began collecting works of art. The death of his uncle Benjamin (1693–1750) made him undisputed senior partner of the bank and the steady rise in deposits and profits reflected his constant attendance to bank affairs. He was keenly aware that the success of his plans for Stourhead depended entirely on the careful management of the business.

Hoare married first in 1726 Anne, daughter of Samuel *Masham, first Baron Masham [*see under* Masham, Abigail, Lady Masham]. She died in 1727, leaving one daughter, Anne (*d.* 1735). He married second, in 1728, Susan, daughter and heir of Stephen Colt (*d.* 1708), and from this marriage had three sons (two died in infancy, and his surviving son, Henry, died in 1752) and two daughters. His elder daughter, Susanna (1732–1783), married first in 1753, Charles Boyle, Viscount Dungarvan (*d.* 1759), and second, in 1761, Thomas, Baron Bruce, of Tottenham Park, Wiltshire, created earl of Ailesbury in 1776. His younger daughter, Anne (1737–1759), married in 1756 her first cousin, Richard Hoare (1735–1787), created baronet in 1786; their son, Richard Colt *Hoare, second baronet (1758–1838), inherited his grandfather's estate. He recalled Henry thus: 'tall, comely in his person, elegant in his manners and address and well versed in literature'.

Hoare's second wife died in 1743, and as a widower, he began in earnest the creation of the gardens and the

W. Hoare, portrait, pencil, C. Hoare & Co. • oils (after pastel by W. Hoare), C. Hoare & Co.

Wealth at death approx. £50,000; incl. Stourhead House and contents; legacies; cash to executors; annual income from bank and London rents; excl. value of country estates, rents, London properties: C. Hoare & Co., London; wills and ledgers

Hoare, Jane (1646–1694). *See under* Pinney, Hester (1658–1740).

Hoare, Joseph Charles (1851–1906), bishop of Victoria (Hong Kong), born at Ramsgate on 15 November 1851, was the fourth son of Edward Hoare, vicar of Holy Trinity, Tunbridge Wells, and honorary canon of Canterbury. His mother was Maria Eliza (*d.* 1863), daughter of Sir Benjamin Collins *Brodie, surgeon. Educated first at Brighton, then (1863–70) at Tonbridge School, he passed with a scholarship to Trinity College, Cambridge, graduating BA in 1874 with a second class in the classical tripos, and proceeding MA in 1878 and DD in 1898. In December 1874 he was ordained deacon by the bishop of London for missionary work, and, after acting for some months as his father's curate, sailed in October 1875 to join the Church Missionary Society's mid-China mission at Ningpo (Ningbo). He was ordained priest by the bishop of north China in 1876. His chief work at Ningpo was the founding and successful conduct of a training college for Chinese evangelists. Hoare rapidly acquired a knowledge of the Ningpo colloquial language, and in it produced versions of 'Pearson on the creed', 'Trench on the parables', and 'Ryle on St Matthew'. By 1891 he had sent out 164 students, of whom 61 were then either evangelists or schoolteachers.

In 1882 Hoare married Alice Juliana, daughter of Canon John Patteson of Norwich; she died in 1883. He later married Ellen Tunnicliffe, daughter of the Revd F. F. Gough, who survived him; they had two sons and three daughters.

In 1898 Frederick Temple, archbishop of Canterbury, invited Hoare to succeed John Shaw Burdon as bishop of Victoria, Hong Kong, and he was consecrated at St Paul's Cathedral on 11 June 1898. The change from mid-China to south China entailed the learning of two new dialects, and, as a bishop, Hoare had the oversight of a colony, as well as of missionary work in several provinces. He won the respect of all classes in the colony, worked among the sailors of the port, and continued his policy of fostering a spirit of self-reliance among the Chinese Christians. Unswervingly loyal to the Church Missionary Society, he was not always at one with the home authorities. On 14 September 1906 he set out from Hong Kong in his houseboat on a preaching tour along the coast. Caught in the typhoon of 16 September, he headed back to Hong Kong, but the boat capsized in Castle Peak Bay, 12 miles from Hong Kong, and two Chinese sailors alone escaped. Hoare's body was not recovered. Both at Ningpo and at Hong Kong Hoare left a permanent mark on the work of his mission by the influence of a fine personality and by his contributions to vernacular literature.

A. R. BUCKLAND, *rev.* H. C. G. MATTHEW

Sources *The Record* (28 Sept 1906) • *Church Missionary Intelligencer*, 57 (Nov–Dec 1906) • private information (1912) • E. Stock, *The history of the Church Missionary Society: its environment, its men and its work*, 4 vols. (1899–1916)

Wealth at death £3694 6*s.* 4*d.*: probate, sealed, London, 20 Dec 1906, CGPLA Eng. & Wales

Hoare, Louisa Gurney (1784–1836), educationist and author, was born in Norwich on 25 September 1784, the seventh of the eleven children of the Quaker John Gurney (1749–1809) of Earlham and Catherine Bell (1754–1792). Among her siblings were the prison reformer Elizabeth *Fry, the philanthropists Joseph John *Gurney and Samuel *Gurney (1786–1856), and the banker and antiquary Daniel *Gurney. Catherine Bell Gurney was by all accounts a remarkable mother, and when she died, her youngest child being only three, her place was taken by the eldest daughter, also Catherine (Kitty), guided by a memorandum concerning the education of children and their daily routine which the elder Catherine had prepared in 1788. Aided by governesses, whom the children generally disliked, Kitty (whom they loved) superintended a growing-up that was rich in play, adult converse, and a variety of experiences sometimes frowned upon by the Quaker elders of Norwich. The children had the freedom of the Earlham library, which included Rousseau, Voltaire, and Paine. They were permitted to explore other religious traditions, and had both Unitarian and Roman Catholic friends. The eldest son studied at Dr Enfield's school in Norwich, and his sisters were permitted to attend select lectures with him. All the children were encouraged in diary writing for the sake of self-examination and correction: Louisa was a particularly avid writer, recording her adolescent passions and enthusiasms for nature, music (especially dancing), and politics, as well as her aversion to the more tedious aspects of Quaker observance, her detestation of injustice in the treatment of herself and her siblings, and her distaste when her twelve-year-old cousin kissed her. She later married this same cousin, the banker Samuel Hoare (1783–1847) of Hampstead, on 24 December 1806, and was baptized into the Church of England with him in 1812.

Louisa's intellect and energy were acknowledged by her family, who considered her the most talented of them all. She shared more quietly in the concerns and campaigns which occupied her more famous relatives—the antislavery campaign of her brother-in-law Sir Thomas Fowell Buxton, and the prison reform movement of her sister Elizabeth Fry and her own husband. She was, for example, one of the founders of the Ladies' Society for Promoting Education in the West Indies (1825), an organization supported by Hoares, Gurneys, Buxtons, and Ricardos, the work of which continued for more than a half-century.

Education was Louisa's chief concern, particularly the education of parents to raise their own children. Her first book on the subject, *Hints for the Improvement of Early Education and Nursery Discipline* (1819), claimed to be the 'simple result of experience', an expanded version of the rules she had written down for the nursemaid she employed for her first-born, as her mother had done. Her experience, however, was shaped by family tradition and influenced by

Louisa Gurney Hoare (1784–1836), by unknown engraver (after Andrew Robertson, exh. RA 1830)

such eighteenth- and early nineteenth-century authorities as Locke, Fénelon, John Foster, Thomas Babington, and Philip Doddridge, with a list of contemporary recommended reading such as Sarah Trimmer and Hannah More. Her second book, *Friendly advice on the management and education of children, addressed to parents of the middle and labouring classes of society* (1824), was intended to supplement schooling, treating parenthood as a Christian discipline for both child and parent. Her insistence that discipline should 'preserve children from evil, not from childishness' anticipates the Victorian celebration of childhood. In the call for parents to respect their children, to deal justly with them, not to 'infringe upon [their] rights', and to help children learn through doing, the books express a view not unlike the child-centred educational theory of the second half of the twentieth century.

Hints was a particularly successful book, editions appearing both in Britain and in the United States for more than eighty years after its first publication. A third book, *Letters from a Work-House Boy* (1826), concluded Louisa's literary career, though she continued a literary and artistic acquaintance. She died in Hampstead on 6 September 1836. Of her six children, her son Edward left an account of his upbringing that confirms his mother's excellence in practice as well as precept.

SUSAN DRAIN

Sources L. G. Hoare, *Letters from a work-house boy, with a short account of the writer* (1826) · V. Anderson, *Friends and relations: three* centuries of Quaker families (1980) · V. Anderson, *The Northrepps grandchildren* (1968) · *Edward Hoare … a record of his life based on a brief autobiography*, ed. J. H. Townsend (1896) · E. Hoare, *Some account of the early history and genealogy … of the families of Hore and Hoare* (1883) · A. J. C. Hare, *The Gurneys of Earlham*, 2 vols. (1895) · *Memoir of the life of Elizabeth Fry, with extracts from her letters and journal*, ed. [K. Fry and R. E. Cresswell], 2 vols. (1847) · Mrs T. Geldart, *Memorials of Samuel Gurney* (1857) · *Biographical catalogue: being an account of the lives of Friends and others whose portraits are in the London Friends' Institute*, Society of Friends (1888) · C. E. Sargeant, *A book for mothers; or, Biographical sketches of the mothers of great and good men* (1850) [inc. Catherine Bell Gurney] · Register of births, Norwich, PRO, RE6-981, 25 Sept 1784

Archives NRA 15293, Journal of Louisa Gurney, 1797–1806 | Friends' House Library, Gurney MSS

Likenesses G. Richmond, portrait, repro. in Anderson, *The Northrepps grandchildren* · engraving (after A. Robertson, exh. RA 1830), NPG [*see illus.*]

Hoare, Michael. *See* Halfpenny, William (d. 1755).

Hoare, Prince (1755–1834), playwright and artist, was born at Bath, the younger son and fourth of the five children of William *Hoare RA (1707/8–1792) and his wife, Elizabeth, *née* Barker (d. 1793). He was educated by Mr Hele, first master of the grammar school at Bath, and instructed in art by his father. In 1772 he gained a Society of Arts premium, and in that year moved to London to study at the Royal Academy. In 1776 he visited Rome, and there studied under Mengs, together with Fuseli and Northcote. On his return to England in 1780 he painted for some time, exhibiting at the Royal Academy in 1781 and 1782. His exhibited work included a classical picture called *Alceste*, and a portrait of Sir T. Lawrence when a child. He ceased to exhibit after 1785.

In 1788 Hoare took a voyage for his health to Lisbon, returning in June to London. During his absence his first play, a tragedy, *Such Things Were*, was acted at Bath on 1 January 1788, and afterwards (as *Julia, or, Such Things Were*) at Drury Lane on 2 May 1796, for the benefit of Sarah Siddons. His best-known production, *No Song, No Supper*, a farce, with music by Storace, was first acted at Drury Lane on 16 April 1790, and often subsequently. Hoare's other productions include: *The Cave of Trophonius*, a musical farce performed at Drury Lane on 3 May 1791; *Dido*, an opera staged at the Haymarket, on 23 May 1792; *The Prize*, a musical farce first performed at the Haymarket on 11 March 1793, and often subsequently; *The Three and the Deuce*, a comic drama played at the Haymarket on 2 September 1795; *Mahmoud*, an opera performed at Drury Lane on 30 April 1796; and *The Italian Villagers*, staged at Covent Garden on 25 April 1797.

In 1799 Hoare was appointed honorary foreign secretary to the Royal Academy, and in this capacity he published *Extracts from a Correspondence with the Academies of Vienna and St Petersbourg* (1802), *Academic Correspondence* (1804), and *Academic Annals of Painting* (1805; 2nd edn, 1809). He was a fellow of the Society of Antiquaries, and of the Royal Society of Literature, to which he bequeathed his library. He also produced several other volumes, including *An Inquiry into the … Art of Design in England* (1806), *Epochs of the Arts* (1813), and *Memoirs of Granville Sharp* (1820). He edited a collection of essays (some his own work) entitled *The Artist* (2 vols., 1809–10). Prince Hoare died at Brighton on 22 December 1834.

W. W. WROTH, rev. M. CLARE LOUGHLIN-CHOW

Sources Redgrave, *Artists*, 2nd edn · *GM*, 2nd ser., 3 (1835), 661–2 · D. E. Baker, *Biographia dramatica, or, A companion to the playhouse*, rev. I. Reed, new edn, rev. S. Jones, 1 (1812), 353 · *The thespian dictionary, or, Dramatic biography of the present age*, 2nd edn (1805)
Archives Bodl. Oxf., letters | BL, letters to Bellamy and Thomas Hill, Add. MS 20081, fols. 150–253 · Bodl. Oxf., corresp. with Francis Chantrey · Bodl. Oxf., letters to Isaac D'Israeli · CUL, letters to Ignatius Bononi · V&A, letters to James Northcote
Likenesses P. Hoare, self-portrait, 1779, Uffizi Gallery, Florence · P. Hoare, self-portrait, 1780, Uffizi Gallery, Florence · W. Ridley, stipple, 1796 (after J. Northcote), BM, NPG; repro. in *Monthly Mirror* (1796) · J. Hopwood, stipple, 1807 (after J. Opie), BM, NPG; repro. in *The Cabinet* (1807) · W. Brockedon, pencil and chalk drawing, 1831, NPG · C. Turner, mezzotint, pubd 1831 (after T. Lawrence), BM, NPG · G. Dance, pencil drawing, BM · J. Jackson, drawing, Victoria Art Gallery, Bath

Hoare, Sir Reginald Hervey (1882–1954), diplomatist, was born on 19 July 1882 at Minley Manor, Hawley, Hampshire, the fourth son in the family of four sons and three daughters of Charles Hoare (1844–1898), a senior partner of Hoare's Bank, and his wife, Katharine Patience Georgiana (d. 1915), third daughter of the Rt Revd Lord Arthur Charles *Hervey, bishop of Bath and Wells. His maternal grandfather was Frederick William Hervey, first marquess and fifth earl of Bristol (1769–1859). From 1895 to 1901 he was educated at Eton College, where he was in the cricket eleven in his last term. He entered the diplomatic service as an attaché in December 1905, and passed the competitive examination in March 1906. Appointed to Constantinople in August 1906, he was promoted third secretary in March 1908 and transferred to Rome in March 1909. There he was promoted second secretary in November 1913. In June 1914 he was transferred to Peking, and in May 1917 to Petrograd, where he witnessed the Bolshevik revolution. He left Petrograd in February 1918 but returned to Russia that August as secretary to the special mission to Archangel headed by Francis Lindley. Promoted first secretary in April 1919, he acted as chargé d'affaires at Archangel from May to August that year. After a brief spell at the Foreign Office he was again posted abroad, to Warsaw in January 1921. He acted as chargé d'affaires there from May to August 1922. While on leave, on 9 November 1922 he married Lucy Joan Cavendish Bentinck (d. 1971), elder daughter of William George Frederick Cavendish Bentinck, barrister and public servant. They had one son, Joseph (b. 1925).

Hoare returned to Peking as counsellor in July 1923, but in December 1924 he was transferred to Turkey, where he remained for four years. The period was one of turmoil and crisis in Turkish interior affairs as Mustapha Kemal consolidated his authority in the opening years of the republic, but in foreign relations the years 1924–8 were ones of relative calm, with the exception of the Mosul crisis. Following the Kurdish revolt of 1925, the Turkish government asserted its claim to this former Ottoman possession. The dispute was referred to the League of Nations, which in December 1925 upheld the British contention

that the Mosul province should form part of Iraq, a decision in which Mustapha Kemal acquiesced in June 1926. To Hoare, who frequently acted as chargé d'affaires, some of the credit for this was due; he was appointed CMG in the same year. After leaving Turkey in February 1928, he spent three and a half years in Cairo, where he served under Lord Lloyd and Sir Percy Loraine, and was promoted minister in October 1929.

In October 1931 Hoare was appointed envoy-extraordinary and minister-plenipotentiary at Tehran. He came to a difficult task. During the First World War and especially after the Russian Revolution British influence in Persia had increased, by force of circumstances, to an extent which was resented by the Persians and unwelcome to successive British governments. The British aim was to be in treaty relations with a self-reliant and friendly Persia which would safeguard the rapidly expanding interests of the Anglo-Persian Oil Company and guarantee the right of ships of the Royal Navy to call at the Gulf port of Bushehr. Hoare's predecessors had already abdicated the major part of the quasi-imperial British position, but in spite of the strong British support given at the time of his rise to power to Reza Shah Pahlavi, the latter and his government remained suspicious of British intentions. No treaty had been signed when Hoare arrived in Tehran and he made it quite plain that he was in no hurry. His aim was to restore calm to a situation which had grown feverish. In 1932 the Persian government attempted a final showdown with the British and cancelled the oil concession granted to William Knox D'Arcy in 1901. Hoare, influenced perhaps by his Turkish experiences, advised his government to refer the matter immediately to the League of Nations. Nevertheless he also made clear that 'our interests would be best served by helping to build a bridge' (Bamberg, 36). The result was a new contract between the company and the Persian government, signed the next year. To the chagrin of the extremists the showdown ended quietly, without a breach in relations or serious loss. The treaty, however, remained unsigned. In 1933 Hoare was promoted KCMG.

In February 1935 Hoare was transferred to Bucharest, again with the rank of minister-plenipotentiary. There his task was to encourage the 'little entente' interest, but after the defeat of all Romania's continental allies between 1938 and 1940, pro-German elements inevitably gained control. The German army began to move in during early 1941. In this period and often on his own initiative, Hoare maintained protest against the atrocities of the Nazi-style regime which followed King Carol's abdication in September 1940. In February 1941 the British government decided to extend economic warfare to Romania, and Hoare's mission was withdrawn on the 10th. The evacuation of the British community, consulates, and legation was supervised by Hoare with his accustomed calm, earning him much personal gratitude. In July 1942 he retired from the service, with great reluctance, but remained in government employment until 1944. He then joined the family bank in Fleet Street as a managing partner. He died on 12 August 1954 at his home, 80 Harley

House, Marylebone Road, London, after a short illness, and was survived by his wife and son.

Hoare was a remarkably talented diplomat whose abilities were easily underestimated because at the height of his career they were used in holding operations and not in posts where their effects could be positive and spectacular. He was aware of misfortune in this respect but was incapable of embitterment. He was of genial temper, with a strong and somewhat fantastical sense of humour, enjoying wide private interests from sport to economics, of which he was a gifted student.   C. H. SYKES, rev.

Sources *The Times* (13 Aug 1954) · Burke, *Peerage* · *FO List* (–1942) · *WWW* · J. H. Bamberg, *The history of the British Petroleum Company*, 2: *The Anglo-Iranian years, 1928–1954* (1994) · private information (1971) · personal knowledge (1971) · *CGPLA Eng. & Wales* (1954)
Archives Bodl. Oxf., corresp. with Sir Auriel Stein
Likenesses W. Stoneman, photograph, 1933, NPG · S. Elwes, portrait, priv. coll.
Wealth at death £53,524 12s. 4d.: probate, 24 Sept 1954, *CGPLA Eng. & Wales*

Hoare, Sir Richard (1648–1719), banker, was the only child of Henry Hoare (d. 1699), a horse-dealer of Smithfield, and his wife, Cicely (d. 1679). His parents were resident in the City of London parish of St Botolph, Aldersgate. Nothing is known of Hoare's childhood until 9 June 1665 when he was apprenticed for seven years to the goldsmith Richard Moore, who died before the end of Hoare's term. Hoare was then 'turned over' to Robert Tempest at the sign of the Golden Bottle in Cheapside. He was admitted to the freedom of the Goldsmiths' Company on 5 July 1672, the date considered to mark the foundation of Hoare's Bank. Tempest's death in November 1673 gave Hoare the opportunity to buy his business and operate on his own account in earnest.

Hoare married Susanna, daughter of John Austen (d. 1670) of Brittens, Essex, on 27 July 1672 in the chapel of Lincoln's Inn. They lived in the parish of St Mary Woolnoth, where their first child, also Richard, was born on 24 May 1673. Hoare and his wife had seventeen children, ten of whom died in infancy.

The early goldsmiths' books reveal that Hoare contracted out much of the plate and jewellery trade, and from the start acted as banker to his customers. He kept 'running cashes' and opened named accounts, honouring drawn notes and issuing receipts. He took money on deposit, and lent at interest. In the autumn of 1690, he moved his business to Fleet Street, to premises formerly called the Golden Hinde, which he renamed the Golden Bottle. He acquired the goodwill of a goldsmith's shop already on the site and added to its customers a list of established clients he had brought from Cheapside.

Hoare was in an excellent position to attract good customers in London and the country. Many were distinguished in their own fields, and all were looked after assiduously by Hoare, as Lord Ashburnham testified: 'Upon all occasions [you] have so eminently showed your affection, care and diligence in promoting the wellfare and interest of mee and myne … I shall never be wanting nor shall those that belong to mee' (Ashburnham to

Hoare, 12 May 1698, Hoare's Bank Archives). Until 1702, when he was joined by his son Henry *Hoare (1677–1725), Hoare worked alone, except for the assistance of three clerks. He was a good judge of investments and his standing among City financiers was high, which no doubt assisted his progress in his career as public servant. He was appointed a receiver for the Salt Duty Act (1694) and for the Malt Duty Act (1697), and began his political career in the tory interest by his election to the aldermanic bench for Bread Street ward in 1703. He was elected sheriff in 1708 and attained the office of lord mayor, by seniority, in 1712. In that year he also became one of the founding directors of the South Sea Company.

Queen Anne conferred on him a knighthood on her visit to the Guildhall on 29 October 1702; and Hoare secured her privy purse account through the offices of her lady-in-waiting, his friend Lady Abigail Masham (d. 1734), whose daughter Anne was to be the first wife of Hoare's grandson, Henry *Hoare (1705–1785). Interested in the development of his native city, Hoare presided over Christ's Hospital from 1713 to 1719 and over the London workhouse, and served as prime warden of the Goldsmiths' Company (1703–4), and as one of the committee for building fifty new churches in London. He finally succeeded in gaining a seat in parliament in 1710, representing the City of London until 1715. Hoare provided Robert Harley's administration with advice and financial aid, but his support waned over the issue of protecting British trade interests during the War of the Spanish Succession. He joined Sir Francis Child (1642–1713) and other goldsmith bankers in opposition to the whig-sponsored Bank of England, and published his objections to its foundation (1694) and to the renewal of its charter (1707) (*The Anatomy of Exchequer Alley*, 16 March 1707). Never allowing politics to be an obstacle to good business, however, he welcomed two of the directors as bank customers. A high-church Anglican, he privately supported the tory preacher and pamphleteer Dr Sacheverell, but while serving as sheriff Hoare was instrumental in the suppression of the published text of the sermon Sacheverell had delivered at St Paul's Cathedral on 5 November 1709.

Hoare succeeded in establishing an enduring private banking dynasty, but in his lifetime his ambition for four of his sons was that they should be established abroad in the merchant service with a special interest in the diamond trade. He was a conscientious father and a diligent correspondent, offering encouragement as well as strict advice; but his entreaties to his sons abroad to acquire good business habits were doomed to fail, and their incapacity, allied with a wartime depression in the trade, laid waste his plans. His eldest son Richard was perpetually in debt to his father, and so his second surviving son, Henry, became his heir, inheriting the business with his brother Benjamin (1693–1750).

Seldom at leisure, Hoare nevertheless enjoyed his country house at Hendon and took an interest in its furnishing and garden. By the terms of his marriage settlement he bought an estate in Staplehurst, Kent, where subsequent generations of his family were to settle. From his father he inherited a lifelong interest in horses, and hunted into middle age. Early in 1718 Hoare was taken ill, and he died at Hendon on 6 January 1719. His funeral, on 13 January, at St Dunstan-in-the-West, opposite his banking house, was attended by a great number of people of all ranks. He was buried there, and a monument, designed by Thomas Stayner, was subsequently erected by his heir. His wife, Susanna, survived him.

Sir Richard's bank at the sign of the Golden Bottle acquired a reputation as one of the most conservative and solid of the West End banking houses. Although he was himself unequivocally a mercantile figure, his son Henry and grandson Henry became landed proprietors as well as bankers, and were responsible for the creation of the gardens at Stourhead. Another grandson, **Sir Richard Hoare** (1709–1754), banker, was lord mayor of London at the time of the Jacobite rebellion in 1745, and was knighted on 31 October 1745. He married Sarah Tully (d. 1736) in 1732, and, after her death, Elizabeth Rust (d. 1752) in 1737; he had two sons and two daughters. The younger Sir Richard died on 12 October 1754, and was buried in the family vault in St Dunstan-in-the-West. VICTORIA HUTCHINGS

Sources H. P. R. H., 'Hoare's Bank: portrait of a family and their business', unpublished typescript, Hoare's Bank archives • E. Hoare, *Some account of the early history and genealogy ... of the families of Hore and Hoare* (1883) • 'Hoare, Sir Richard', HoP, *Commons* [draft] • letters and letter books, Hoare's Bank archives • ledgers, 1672–1720, Hoare's Bank archives • *DNB* • K. Woodbridge, 'Accounts rendered, 1700–1714', *History Today*, 19 (1969), 783–91 • papers and documents relating to shrievalty and mayoralty, Hoare's Bank archives • other MSS deposits, Hoare's Bank archives • [H. P. R. Hoare], *Hoare's Bank, a record, 1672–1955: the story of a private bank*, rev. edn (1955) • C. G. A. Clay, 'Henry Hoare, banker, his family and the Stourhead estate', *Landowners, capitalists, and entrepreneurs: essays for Sir John Habakkuk*, ed. F. M. L. Thompson (1994), 113–38 • IGI • will, 1718 • J. Wilford, *Memorials and characters ... of divers eminent and worthy persons* (1741)

Archives Hoare's Bank, London • Stourhead House, Wiltshire

Likenesses J. Richardson, oils, 1712–13, Hoare's Bank, London • J. Worthington, engraving, 1819, repro. in R. C. Hoare, *Pedigrees and memoirs of the families of Hore* (1819) • J. Richardson, oils, Stourhead, Wiltshire

Wealth at death Henry inherited father's estates and co-partnership of the business with Benjamin who received £6000; wife was left £400 p.a. annuity and use of house in country, plus £2000 on signing release of all claims to real and personal estate to Henry; debts of £6000 written off: will, 1718

Hoare, Sir Richard (1709–1754). *See under* Hoare, Sir Richard (1648–1719).

Hoare, Samuel John Gurney, Viscount Templewood (1880–1959), politician, was born in London on 24 February 1880, the elder son of Sir Samuel Hoare, first baronet (1841–1915), Conservative and Unionist MP for Norwich (1886–1906), of Sidestrand Hall, near Cromer, Norfolk, and his wife, Katharin Louisa Hart (d. 1931), the daughter of Richard Vaughan Davis, commissioner of audit. He was a classical scholar at Harrow School and went on to New College, Oxford, where he received firsts in classical moderations (1901) and modern history (1903) and found time to earn a blue in rackets and to join the Bullingdon and Gridiron clubs. He came of the Anglo-Irish branch of an

Samuel John Gurney Hoare, Viscount Templewood (1880–1959), by Walter Stoneman, 1921

old Quaker family long established in banking. His ancestors relocated to England in the mid-eighteenth century and eventually abandoned Quakerism for the Anglo-Catholicism to which Samuel Hoare was deeply dedicated. He was the ambitious son of a family equally ambitious for him, and on 17 October 1909 he married the youngest daughter of Frederick *Lygon, sixth Earl Beauchamp, Lady Maud Lygon (1882–1962), whose aspirations for her husband were at least as great. The couple came to make their home in London at 18 Cadogan Gardens and at Sidestrand Hall, which Hoare inherited (with his baronetcy) upon his father's death in 1915. Though the marriage was not from the first a love match and produced no children, they came to form a devoted partnership for almost fifty years.

Hoare was short and slight, even delicate, of frame. His health was never robust, and he turned to games and athletics to bolster his physique as well as to satisfy an inherent competitiveness. He became an excellent figure skater and was a tournament-level shot and tennis player throughout his life. He was fastidious about his appearance and much enjoyed wearing the symbols and uniforms related to the honours he loved receiving. He lacked charisma and, not surprisingly, he was not a compelling platform speaker. His career reflected his natural talent as an administrator and his keen ambition to achieve an important place in public life, rather than an abundance of sheer brilliance or personal charm.

Early career, 1905–1922 In 1905 Hoare's father arranged for him to serve as secretary to Alfred Lyttelton, the Conservative colonial secretary. After a failed bid for a parliamentary seat at Ipswich in the 1906 election, Hoare's first political success came when he was elected to the London county council (1907–10). In January 1910 he became MP for the London constituency of Chelsea, the seat that he was to hold for thirty-four years. Hoare was little interested in his fellow Conservatives' battles to stave off Irish home rule or preserve the powers of the House of Lords. He gravitated toward the progressive wing of the party, joining the Unionist Social Reform Committee and supporting tariff reform, women's suffrage, and public education. A committed Anglican, he also fought hard against the disestablishment of the Church in Wales. From this point, perhaps to mitigate his stiff manner, he adapted to being addressed by the shortened version of his Christian name (a style he never cared for), and thereafter he became universally known as Sam.

When the First World War began in 1914, Hoare was initially disappointed to secure only a commission as a recruiting officer in the Norfolk yeomanry. He was a talented linguist, however, and in 1916 his knowledge of Russian earned him assignment to the British intelligence mission with the Russian general staff. He soon became head of mission and in due course was promoted lieutenant-colonel. When an experienced intelligence officer was needed to head a similar mission in Rome, Hoare was entrusted with the assignment in March 1917. His primary responsibility was to encourage the Italian government to resist calls to drop out of the war. He remained at his Rome headquarters until the close of the war and his return to civilian life. For his efforts he was appointed CMG and received several foreign honours, including the order of St Stanislaus, awarded him by Tsar Nicholas II.

Re-elected to parliament in 1918 as a supporter of the Lloyd George coalition, Hoare returned to full-time political work after the armistice. His enthusiasm for the prime minister diminished quickly, however, after the 'honours scandal' of the summer of 1922 and the so-called Chanak crisis, which almost brought war with Turkey in October. He played a significant role in organizing Conservative back-benchers to abandon Lloyd George and their pro-coalition leader, Austen Chamberlain, and return direction of the party to the former leader Andrew Bonar Law. The majority of the parliamentary party agreed: Conservative MPs voted at the celebrated Carlton Club meeting of 19 October 1922 to withdraw from the coalition, and Lloyd George and Chamberlain resigned. Bonar Law abandoned his retirement to become leader and, immediately thereafter, prime minister of a Conservative government. Hoare was rewarded with a privy councillorship and became secretary of state for air (outside the cabinet), an office he was destined to hold in four different administrations. In May 1923 Bonar Law's declining health caused his resignation and supersession by Stanley Baldwin. Hoare retained his office and entered the cabinet, where he

remained, save for the brief intervals of the two Labour governments, almost continually until 1940.

Air Ministry and India Office, 1922–1935 In his new office Hoare found himself in the midst of the struggle over control of military air power between the new Royal Air Force and the older services; and in partnership with the chief of the air staff, Air Marshal Sir Hugh Trenchard, he ensured the existence of an independent RAF. He also created air squadrons at Oxford and Cambridge universities and re-established on a permanent basis the air cadet college at Cranwell. Hoare strove to make civilian air transport more accessible to the public, and presided in 1923 over the amalgamation (with a £1 million state subsidy) of the four principal private air carriers into Imperial Airways. He and Lady Maud travelled by air whenever possible and created something of a sensation when, in December 1926, they embarked on the first civilian flight to India. By the time the government gave way to the second Labour administration in 1929, this had become a regularly scheduled route, as did the air link between London and Cape Town. Between 1924 and 1929 the number of miles flown by British civil aviation increased from 700,000 to more than 1 million, and the number of passengers from 10,000 to more than 28,000, much of this owing to the championing of air transport by Hoare himself. For his efforts he was appointed GBE in June 1927, his wife having been appointed DBE in February 1927.

During the period 1929 to 1931, when the Conservatives were in opposition, Hoare solidified his credentials as a party stalwart by taking on the difficult job of party treasurer. His status as a national and party figure was also enhanced by his service as a delegate to the first India round-table conference of 1930–31, and in the difficult role as mediator in the struggle between the former premier, Baldwin, and the newspaper proprietors lords Beaverbrook and Rothermere, who wished to force him to embrace a policy of empire-wide tariffs. Hoare also represented his party in the August 1931 inter-party talks that led to the creation of a new coalition or National Government which included the Conservatives. Ramsay MacDonald remained prime minister and Hoare became secretary of state for India (26 August 1931).

With the government ostensibly committed to eventual Indian self-governance, a second Indian round-table conference began soon after the creation of the new government. Though Hoare got on well with another celebrated delegate, Mohandas K. Gandhi, the Indian leader and his Congress movement rejected the British policy of moving India gradually toward dominion status. By the standards of his time and party, Hoare (like Baldwin) supported a liberal position on Indian autonomy, and he held firmly to it throughout the round table and the extended hearings of the select committee of both houses which, between April 1933 and November 1934, was appointed to consider the government's proposals. Hoare's cautious vision of an India progressing eventually to autonomy within the empire was embodied in one of the most complicated pieces of legislation in British parliamentary history, the

1935 Government of India Bill. The draining and ultimately successful effort to pass his bill was to prove fruitless, however, for it could not be fully implemented before the nation again found itself at war. When that conflict ended, conditions were so changed that the government of the day acceded rapidly to the Indian demand for independence.

Hoare's most energetic opponents in the debate over the India Bill were to be found on the right wing of his own party; and none struggled so hard against it as Winston Churchill, who became thoroughly estranged from the Conservative leadership over the India issue. The two clashed regularly during the extended debate; the ill feeling between the two reached its peak in April 1934, when Churchill accused Hoare of improperly influencing the Manchester chamber of commerce to reverse its policy of opposition to the Indian government's retaining the authority to levy tariffs against British textiles. Churchill insisted that Hoare (aided by the earl of Derby) had committed a breach of parliamentary privilege, and the matter passed before the committee on privileges. Churchill's accusation was rejected by the committee and Hoare was completely exonerated, but the affair left behind a deep division between the two men which was never healed. The episode did provide the occasion for a notable parliamentary exchange when on 13 June 1934, after Churchill's powerful speech in the House of Commons criticizing the committee's finding, L. S. Amery counter-attacked and asserted that the ex-minister's real goal was to destroy the government. Churchill remained, Amery asserted, true to his 'chosen motto'—'Fiat justitia ruat coelum'. When the angry Churchill snarled 'translate it', Amery replied to peals of laughter: 'If I can trip up Sam, the Government's bust' (Gilbert, 545).

In June 1935 Baldwin succeeded MacDonald as prime minister in the National Government. Hoare's tenure at the India Office was much praised, and he was delighted to be made GCSI in the new year's honours list of January 1934. The four-year struggle to bring his India Bill to completion, however, had left him close to exhaustion, and he was much in need of an extended rest. This was not to be, however, as apparently Baldwin encouraged him to choose between two offices in a reshuffled administration: Indian viceroy or foreign secretary. Hoare chose service and advancement over his concern for his health. His commitment to his India policy as well as the grandeur of the viceroyalty appealed to him, but, with an eye toward the premiership which was his eventual goal, he accepted the Foreign Office (7 June 1935). It was a decision which almost destroyed his career.

Foreign Office, 1935 In the years following the First World War the European powers spoke forcefully of their commitment to the League of Nations and the pursuit of what was then called 'mutual security'—international co-operation to suppress armed aggression and prevent the spread of war. This was the thinking behind both the peace of Paris and the celebrated Locarno treaty of 1925. By the end of the 1920s, however, it was clear that the democracies were unprepared to bear the human or financial cost of military action to prevent a greater war. When Hoare became foreign secretary, both Italy and Germany were in the hands of fascist regimes, and the German Führer, Adolf Hitler, had recently announced that he would not abide by the clauses of the treaty of Versailles which limited his armed forces. In March 1935 MacDonald reluctantly announced in a famous white paper that Britain would initiate her own programme of limited rearmament. Then, in one of his final acts as prime minister, he and his foreign secretary, Sir John Simon, met their French and Italian counterparts at the Italian city of Stresa in April 1935 to reiterate their commitment to peace and pledge their co-operation to restrain Hitler. This so-called 'Stresa Front' came to nothing as Britain almost immediately and without consultation with her Stresa partners accepted Hitler's offer to limit the size of the German surface fleet to 35 per cent and her submarine force to 45 per cent of the British navy. This Anglo-German naval agreement upset the French, who at almost the same time (and equally unilaterally) signed a mutual defence pact with the Soviet Union, a nation much distrusted by the British government.

Despite his protestations of peace at Stresa, the Italian dictator, Benito Mussolini, already planned to re-establish an Italian empire at the expense of the small independent African kingdom of Abyssinia. By mid-1935 undeclared hostilities had already taken place between Italian and Abyssinian forces, and Hoare was charged to make known British disapproval. In the greatest speech of his career, before the league assembly in Geneva on 12 September 1935, he reminded the world that peace depended upon international commitment, and that Britain stood firmly 'for steady and collective resistance to all acts of unprovoked aggression' (Hoare, Nine Troubled Years, 170).

Though widely praised in the world press, these words did not deter Mussolini, and on 3 October a full-scale Italian invasion began. The league imposed limited economic sanctions against Rome, though this action stopped short of an embargo on the sale of petroleum. There the crisis rested when on 14 November the National Government, led now by Baldwin, went to the voters with their programme of limited rearmament and commitment to the league. In the end it was a bluffer's hand, for the government (with the agreement of the league council) authorized Hoare to find a way short of war to satisfy Mussolini and convince him to rein in his armies.

Hoare's solution was to send the head of the Foreign Office Abyssinian department, Sir Maurice Peterson, to Paris to fashion a compromise offer to be presented to Mussolini: in effect to offer him enough of the helpless Abyssinia to convince him that further hostilities were unnecessary. By the end of November an Anglo-French plan was agreed upon which included the cession to Italy of substantial territories in the north and the conversion of the south of Abyssinia into an Italian economic development sphere. The Abyssinian army was to be replaced by a legion under Italian control. Hoare and the government (without, of course, consulting the Abyssinians) were prepared to accept the plan as the price of peace. In early December the foreign secretary was in poor health, as the demands of dealing with this crisis were layered upon those of the long struggle over the India Bill. Suffering from a serious infection and periodic fainting spells, he planned a brief skating holiday in Switzerland and was persuaded to stop briefly in Paris to consult with the French premier, Pierre Laval, to finalize the offer to Mussolini. The result of these conversations became infamous as the 'Hoare–Laval pact', to which the British cabinet unanimously agreed on 9–10 December.

As Hoare proceeded on to Switzerland, the details of the proposed arrangement were leaked to the French press and, immediately thereafter, appeared in the London dailies. The British public had re-elected a government pledged to the league covenant, to collective security, and to limited rearmament, and the popular reaction to what appeared to be a capitulation to armed aggression against a small nation was uniformly hostile. Parliament reflected the public mood, and a badly shaken prime minister and cabinet backed away from the plan. Hoare (who, to add to his troubles, had been injured in a skating accident) returned to Britain on 16 December, only to find that government support for his plan had evaporated. Remembered for both the promises of the brave Geneva speech and the disgraced 'Hoare–Laval' pact, Hoare became the focus of public and parliamentary ire, and he resigned two days later.

Admiralty and Home Office, 1935–1939 Despite this humiliating episode, Hoare retained powerful friends in Baldwin and his acknowledged heir, the chancellor of the exchequer, Neville Chamberlain. Hence, in June 1936, he was recompensed for stoically playing the part of scapegoat for the government by being ushered back into the cabinet as first lord of the Admiralty. Despite the aspersions heaped on him the previous December, the appointment received remarkable approbation in the press and in parliament. His stay at the Admiralty was not a long one, however. Baldwin retired in May 1937, and Chamberlain succeeded him and offered Hoare any office except the exchequer, which was to go to Simon. Hoare had wanted the Treasury but settled for the Home Office (28 May 1937), and it turned out to be an office that suited him. Judicial and prison reform were long-time family concerns—Hoare's great-great-aunt was Elizabeth Fry, the pioneering penal reformer—and he embraced this family legacy. He came close in 1939 to carrying the most comprehensive criminal justice reform bill in the nation's history and failed only when the coming of the Second World War intervened. He managed, however, to bring to life the new air raid precautions department and founded the related Women's Voluntary Service organization, both of which were to play important roles in the war to come.

Much of Hoare's energy in the years 1938–9 was invested outside his department, as Britain was caught up in an almost constant foreign policy crisis. In September 1938 Chamberlain established an informal inner cabinet of his most trusted advisers, including Hoare, Simon, and the foreign secretary, Lord Halifax. The policy known as appeasement, warmly supported by this inner cabinet, was carried out to Chamberlain's design, but it also had the approval of the majority of the electorate, parliament, and the press. Its small band of critics, led in parliament by Churchill, represented a very modest constituency until the Chamberlain programme had proven its bankruptcy.

Czechoslovakia was the issue over which the Führer threatened war in 1938, and Hoare stoutly supported Chamberlain in his efforts to convince the German dictator to accept an arrangement under which his territorial demands would be met without war. Hoare was among the few consulted by the prime minister about his unprecedented 'Plan Z', to fly to the Reich to meet privately with Hitler—which Chamberlain did twice in September 1938. Finally Chamberlain and the Führer met with Mussolini and the French premier, Edouard Daladier, on the 29th in the famous Munich conference, at which all the German demands on Czechoslovakia were met. Their foreign policy failed, despite the best efforts of Chamberlain, Hoare, and the other appeasers, because Hitler remained unsatisfiable by peaceful means. On 1 September 1939 what soon became a Second World War began.

Exile and retirement, 1940–1959 Chamberlain continued as premier for eight months, and during this period Hoare served in the nine-man war cabinet, first as lord privy seal (3 September 1939) and briefly (5 April 1940) once again as air minister. In May 1940 Churchill became prime minister and refused to give Hoare (unlike Chamberlain, Halifax, and Simon) a place in the new government. It was the end of his ministerial career. Desperate for activity, Hoare accepted Churchill's only offer, the Madrid embassy, and thus he was the only one of the major appeasers sent immediately into exile. In the end his mission was widely praised, even by Churchill, and he was credited with preventing any Spanish hazard to the allied invasion of north Africa in November 1942 and also in securing the release of thousands of allied prisoners of war interned in Spanish prisons. His greatest contribution was perhaps in striving to convince the pro-German regime of General Francisco Franco to remain out of the war. His mission came to a close in December 1944, not long after he agreed to accept a peerage and bring to a close his long connection with the House of Commons. He chose the title Viscount Templewood of Chelsea (14 July 1944), thus coupling his long-time constituency with the name of the country house he built on the grounds of the Sidestrand estate.

Hoare retired completely from party politics but not entirely from public life, as he energetically supported penal reform and particularly the 1947 Criminal Justice Bill and the movement to abolish capital punishment. He accepted a number of company directorships but gave most of his time to other long-term interests. He continued his presidency of the Lawn Tennis Association (1932–56) and the chancellorship of the University of Reading (1937–59), and to these added the chairmanship of the council of the Howard League for Penal Reform (1947–59) and the presidencies of the Magistrates' Association (1947–52), the Air League of the British Empire (1953–6), and the National Skating Association (1945–57).

In 1950 he became a member of the political honours scrutiny committee and he was its chairman from 1954 until his death. He was an elder brother of Trinity House (1936–59) and held honorary degrees from Oxford, Cambridge, Nottingham, and Reading universities and was an honorary fellow of New College, Oxford.

Though never a compelling speaker, Templewood was a gifted writer. During his political career he had published several successful books, including *India by Air* (1927), an account of the first civilian flight from England to India, and *The Fourth Seal* (1930), relating his Russian experiences in the First World War. In retirement he published frequently and with great success: his books included *Ambassador on Special Mission* (1946), about his Spanish ambassadorship, *The Unbroken Thread* (1949), a family memoir, and *The Shadow of the Gallows* (1951), his case against capital punishment. His best-known volume remains his memoir of the years of the National Governments, 1931–40, *Nine Troubled Years* (1954).

Viscount Templewood died at his London home, 12a Eaton Mansions, Chelsea, on 7 May 1959 after suffering a heart attack. Predeceased by his brother, his titles became extinct with his death. He is buried in Sidestrand parish church, Northrepps, Norfolk. Samuel Hoare was talented and immensely hard-working; in office he was a tireless and efficient administrator, but his competence did not in public or private life make up for his lack of warmth. He had appreciative colleagues but few real friends, and his keen ambition earned him too many enemies. Sir Robert Vansittart, who knew him well, recalled him as prim and precise but not resilient in the rough and tumble world of high politics. Vansittart's successor at the Foreign Office, Sir Alexander Cadogan, was harsher in the dark days of 1940, and saw in Hoare's ambition the stuff from which a British quisling could be fashioned. Even his warmest admirers, Amery or Lord Beaverbrook for example, were prepared to defend him until the end but were unlikely to describe him as lovable.   R. J. Q. ADAMS

Sources J. A. Cross, *Sir Samuel Hoare: a political biography* (1977) · U. Cam., Templewood MSS · S. Hoare, *Nine troubled years* (1954) · S. Hoare, *Ambassador on special mission* (1946) · S. Hoare, *The unbroken thread* (1949) · S. Hoare, *The fourth seal* (1930) · S. Hoare, *India by air* (1927) · J. Ramsden, *The age of Balfour and Baldwin, 1902–1940* (1978) · R. J. Q. Adams, *British politics and foreign policy in the age of appeasement, 1935–39* (1993) · R. A. C. Parker, *Chamberlain and appeasement: British policy and the coming of the Second World War* (1993) · K. Middlemas and J. Barnes, *Baldwin: a biography* (1969) · A. J. P. Taylor, *Beaverbrook* (1972) · M. Gilbert, *Winston S. Churchill*, 5: *1922–1939* (1976) · D. Dilks, *Neville Chamberlain: pioneering and reform, 1869–1929* (1984) · *The diaries of Sir Alexander Cadogan*, ed. D. Dilks (American edn, [1972]) · Lord Vansittart [R. G. Vansittart], *The mist procession: the autobiography of Lord Vansittart* (1958) · R. Blake, *The Conservative Party from Peel to Thatcher* (1985) · WW

Archives BL OIOC, corresp. and papers relating to India, MS Eur. E 240 · CUL, corresp. and papers · PRO, corresp., FO 800/295 | BL, corresp. with Lord Cecil, Add. MS 51083 · BL, corresp. with Albert Mansbridge, Add. MS 65253 · BL OIOC, corresp. with Sir John Anderson, MS Eur. F 207 · BL OIOC, corresp. with Lord Brabourne, MS Eur. F 97 · BL OIOC, corresp. with Lord Erskine, MS Eur. D 596 · BL OIOC, corresp. with Lord Linlithgow, MS Eur. F 125, file 159 · BL OIOC, corresp. with Sir Frederick Sykes, MS Eur. F 150 · Bodl. Oxf., corresp. with Lord Monckton · Bodl. Oxf., corresp. with Lord Sankey · Bodl. Oxf., corresp. with Lord Simon · CAC Cam., corresp. with Lord Croft · CAC Cam., corresp. with Sir Eric Phipps · CUL, Baldwin MSS · HLRO, corresp. with Lord Beaverbrook · HLRO, letters to R. D. Blumenfeld · HLRO, corresp. with J. C. C. Davidson · HLRO, letters to David Lloyd George · HLRO, corresp. with Lord Samuel · King's Lond., Liddell Hart C., corresp. with Sir B. H. Liddell Hart · Lpool RO, corresp. with Lord Derby · NA Scot., corresp. with Lord Elibank, GD32 · NA Scot., corresp. with Lord Lothian · PRO NIre., corresp. with Lord Dufferin · U. Birm., Chamberlain MSS · Women's Library, London, corresp. with Eleanor Rathbone | FILM BFI NFTVA, news footage · IWM FVA, actuality footage · IWM FVA, documentary footage · IWM FVA, news footage | SOUND BL NSA, news recordings

Likenesses W. Stoneman, photograph, 1921, NPG [see illus.] · photograph, 1924 (with wife), Hult. Arch. · E. Kapp, drawings, 1934–5, Barber Institute of Fine Arts, Birmingham · group portrait, photograph, 1935, Hult. Arch. · Allen, photograph, 1936, Hult. Arch. · group portrait, photograph, 1937, Hult. Arch. · photograph, 1937 (with royalty), Hult. Arch. · Bellamy, group portrait, photograph, 1939 (with war cabinet), Hult. Arch. · Ray, group portrait, photograph, 1939 (with war cabinet), Hult. Arch. · G. Anthony, photographs, 1946, Hult. Arch. · P. Phillips, oils, c.1953, U. Reading · A. C. Davidson-Houston, oils, 1956, Templewood, Sidestrand, near Cromer, Norfolk

Wealth at death £186,944 3s. 6d.: probate, 22 Sept 1959, CGPLA Eng. & Wales

Hoare, William (1707/8–1792), portrait painter, was born near Eye, Suffolk, the eldest of the three children of John Hoare, a prosperous farmer and land agent. The family soon moved to Berkshire and William was sent to school in Faringdon where he showed an early talent for drawing. His father was persuaded to send him to London in the early 1720s, where he joined the studio of Giuseppe Grisoni, an Italian who had come to England in 1718. When Grisoni returned to Italy in 1728, he took Hoare with him. Once in Rome, Hoare shared lodgings in via Gregoriana with Peter Angillis, Laurent Delvaux, and Peter Scheemakers. He joined the studio of Francesco Imperiali, a history painter, and also frequented the studios of the French Academy nearby in the Corso. Personable and well educated, he formed lasting friendships with many young grand tourists who became his patrons: Henry Bathurst, the future third and fourth dukes of Beaufort, Robert Dingley, Henry Hoare (1705–1785) (no relation), George Lyttelton, Charles Hanbury Williams, and Joseph Spence, tutor to the future second duke of Dorset and later to the earl of Lincoln.

Hoare returned to England in 1737 or 1738. He had connections with the entourage of Frederick, prince of Wales, and drew the *Prince's Portrait* in pastel (ex Sothebys, 11 April 1991, lot 28), but he did not prosper and decided to move to Bath, where his brother Prince (d. 1769) was a sculptor and where the Bath seasons were to furnish him with a constant stream of sitters. He quickly came to the notice of Beau Nash and Ralph Allen, whose portraits he painted in oil (1749, Bath corporation; 1758, Exeter Health Authority). In 1742 Hoare was elected a visitor to the Mineral Water Hospital, the duty of which he performed regularly until 1779. This appointment brought him many commissions and the hospital itself still contains a fine collection of Hoare's works, including *Self Portrait* (pastel, 1742) and *Dr Oliver & Mr Peirce Examining Patients* (oil; exh.

William Hoare (1707/8–1792), self-portrait

Society of Artists, 1761). He obtained a major commission for an altarpiece for the Octagon Chapel in Bath, *The Pool of Bethesda* (1765; Bath Masonic Hall Association). An habitué of Stourhead, he furnished the younger Henry Hoare with many family portraits still *in situ*. On 4 October 1742 Hoare married at Lincoln's Inn chapel, London, Elizabeth Barker (*d.* 1793); they had five children: Mary (1744–1820), who was also an artist, mainly in crayon, Anne (1751–1821), William jun. (1752–1809), the playwright and painter Prince *Hoare (1755–1834), and Georgiana (*b.* 1759), who died in infancy.

Many of Hoare's old Rome acquaintances had become his patrons, and a very substantial part of his income came from politicians' portraits (for example, *William Pitt the Elder*, *c.*1754; NPG), their replicas, and the fine mezzotints by Richard Houston commissioned after them. Hoare remained in close touch with the London art milieu. He was connected to the Foundling Hospital and to the Magdalen Hospital, to which he presented a *Portrait of Robert Dingley*, its founder, in 1762. In 1755 he joined others in signing a request for the founding of an academy. He first exhibited publicly at the Society of Artists in 1761 and in 1769 became a founder member of the Royal Academy at the king's special request, exhibiting intermittently. Hoare died in Edgar Buildings, Bath, on 10 December 1792, and his wife on 30 November 1793. There is a wall tablet to both in Walcot church, near Bath, and a wall monument to Hoare by Chantrey (1828) in Bath Abbey.

EVELYN NEWBY

Sources Vertue, *Note books*, vols. 3, 6 · E. Edwards, *Anecdotes of painters* (1808); facs. edn (1970) [BM print room, grangerized edn] ·
R. Wright, MS notes on Bath artists, Victoria Art Gallery, Bath · R. Wright, typescript of lecture, Bath Public Library · Bath Mineral Water Hospital minutes, 1742– · stato delle anime, San Giovanni in Laterano, Rome [religious census] · Wilts. & Swindon RO, Stourhead papers · land documents, Berkshire County Archives, Faringdon, Oxfordshire · E. Newby, *William Hoare of Bath* (1990) [exhibition catalogue, Victoria Art Gallery, Bath] · *IGI* · J. Ingamells, ed., *A dictionary of British and Irish travellers in Italy, 1701–1800* (1997) · monument inscription, Bath Abbey
Archives Wilts. & Swindon RO, account books, Stourhead archives, letters, etc.
Likenesses W. Hoare, self-portrait, pastel, 1742, RA · J. Zoffany, group portrait, 1772 (*Royal academicians, 1772*), Royal Collection · S. W. Reynolds, mezzotint, *c.*1794 (after P. Hoare) · F. Chantrey, medallion on monument, 1828, Bath Abbey · P. Hoare, oils (in old age), Stourhead, Wiltshire · W. Hoare, self-portrait, oils, Victoria Art Gallery, Bath · W. Hoare, self-portrait, pastel drawing, Royal National Hospital for Rheumatic Diseases, Bath [*see illus.*]

Hoare, William Henry (1809–1888), divine, born at Penzance, Cornwall, on 31 October 1809, was the second son of William Henry Hoare (1776–1819), a banker, of Broomfield House, Battersea, Surrey, and his wife, Louisa Elizabeth (1784/5–1816), daughter of Sir Gerard Noel Noel, bt, of Exton, Rutland. He held a scholarship at St John's College, Cambridge, from 1827 to 1831, when he graduated BA as thirty-first wrangler and seventh classic, and was bracketed with Dean Blakesley for the chancellor's medals. In 1833 he was elected fellow of his college, and proceeded MA in 1834, but vacated his fellowship following his marriage on 17 July 1834 to Araminta Anne, third daughter of Lieutenant-General Sir John *Hamilton, bt (1755–1835). They had three sons and one daughter.

In 1841 Hoare became curate of All Saints, Southampton, but ill health prevented him from accepting any of the livings which were offered to him. He concentrated on theological study, became a good Hebrew scholar, and produced several works affirming the literal truth of the Bible, including *Harmony of the Apocalypse with the Prophecies of Holy Scripture* (1848) and *The Veracity of the Book of Genesis* (1860). In 1863 he wrote two treatises attacking Bishop Colenso's view that the Pentateuch was unhistorical. He acted for some time as commissary to the bishop of Newcastle, New South Wales, was diocesan inspector of the diocese of Chichester, and the founder and secretary of the Worth Clerical Association. Hoare died on 22 February 1888 at Oakfield, Crawley, Sussex, which he had purchased, and where he lived after 1848, and was buried on 29 February in Worth churchyard.

GORDON GOODWIN, *rev.* M. C. CURTHOYS

Sources *The Times* (25 Feb 1888), 7 · Boase, *Mod. Eng. biog.* · E. Hoare, *Some account of the early history and genealogy … of the families of Hore and Hoare* (1883)
Wealth at death £19,001 7*s.* 1*d.*: probate, 26 April 1888, *CGPLA Eng. & Wales*

Hoban, James (1762–1831), architect and designer, was born in Callan, co. Kilkenny, Ireland, the son of Edward Hoban and his wife, Martha *née* Bayne. Details of his early life are not known, but he studied drawing under Thomas Ivory in one of the schools of the Dublin Society, and in 1780 was awarded a premium for drawings of architectural details. He was then employed, probably as a joiner, in the construction of several Dublin buildings, including the royal exchange (now the city hall) and the custom house. Seeking more opportunity for advancement, he emigrated to the United States after the American War of Independence and settled first in Philadelphia, where in May 1785 he advertised his services as a joiner and carpenter.

Two years later Hoban moved to South Carolina, where he met George Washington, who was then on a tour of the southern states. This led to his selection as one of the nine architects who took part in the competition of 1792 to design the proposed federal public buildings. He won the competition for the design of the President's House, later called the White House, and was appointed to supervise its construction at a salary of 300 guineas a year. He thereupon moved to Washington, where he stayed for the rest of his life. The principal elevation was originally based on plate 51 in James Gibbs's *Book of Architecture* (1728), and bore a distinct resemblance to Leinster House (1751) in Dublin. Subsequent changes, including some suggested by Washington and Thomas Jefferson, and later additions by Benjamin Latrobe which were executed by Hoban in 1824 and 1829, resulted in the present well-known façade. The corner-stone of the building was laid by President Washington on 13 September 1793, and Hoban assisted at the ceremony as master of the federal masonic lodge, which he had helped to organize a few days before. The building, still unfinished at the time, was first occupied by President Adams in 1800, and Hoban continued in charge until its initial completion in 1803.

At the same time Hoban was employed at intervals to superintend the construction of the Capitol, until Latrobe became the surveyor of public buildings in 1803; he also engaged in the construction of other public and private buildings, and the purchase of numerous plots of land, in and around the federal capital. By 1799 he was captain of the Washington artillery, and in January of the same year he married Susannah Sewell, with whom he had ten children, one of whom, James (*c.*1808–1846), became the district attorney in Washington. During the presidency of Jefferson (1801–9), who was himself an accomplished architect, Hoban got few government commissions, but by that time he was no longer dependent on them as a major source of income. On the incorporation of the city of Washington in 1802 he was elected to the city council and remained a member until his death.

Towards the end of the Anglo-American War a detachment of British forces under General Robert Ross marched on Washington and burnt some of the principal buildings, including the Capitol and the White House. The interior of the White House was destroyed but the stonework survived, and Hoban supervised the work of rebuilding from 1815 to 1829. During the same period he was responsible for the design and construction of the state department and war department buildings, commenced in 1818. The *Dictionary of American Biography* describes him as 'quiet and conciliatory, but self-respecting and capable of firmness when occasion demanded' and refers to his 'knowledge, abilities and probity' as a 'solid citizen and patriarch of the city'. He died in Washington on 8 December 1831, leaving an estate valued at $60,000 (*DAB*). His grave was later moved to Mount Olivet cemetery in the city of Washington after it was founded as a Roman Catholic cemetery in 1858. RONALD M. BIRSE

Sources *DAB* [incl. comprehensive bibliography] · P. Scott and A. J. Lee, *Buildings of the District of Columbia* (1993) · H. Boylan, *A dictionary of Irish biography*, 2nd edn (1988) · P. Scott, 'Hoban, James', *ANB* · *IGI*

Archives Maryland Historical Society, Baltimore · Office of Public Buildings and Grounds, Washington, D.C. | Mass. Hist. Soc., Coolidge collection

Likenesses portrait, repro. in *Infopedia UK 96* (1996)

Wealth at death $60,000: *DAB*

Hobart Pasha. *See* Hampden, Augustus Charles Hobart- (1822–1886).

Hobart, Albinia, countess of Buckinghamshire (1737/8–1816). *See under* Hobart, George, third earl of Buckinghamshire (1731–1804).

Hobart [*née* Egerton], **Lady Frances** (1603–1664), religious patron and benefactor, was born in London, the eldest child of Sir John *Egerton (1579–1649), from 1617 first earl of Bridgewater, and Lady Frances *Egerton, *née* Stanley (1583–1636). Put under the charge of a Huguenot governess before she could talk, she acquired a lifelong fluency in French, and Reformed views on church discipline and doctrine. The latter were reinforced by her beloved father, who admonished her against Arminianism. She received religious instruction from the family chaplain, besides learning reading, writing, and accounting, sewing, and household management. She also learned to sing, play the lute, and dance, to fit her for court. There she was high in favour with Queen Anne and Prince Charles, and used to participate in masques and pastimes, even on Sundays, to her later regret.

Regarded as beautiful, and a potential heiress, Lady Frances was sought in marriage by the earl of Oxford and others. Early in 1622 she married a widower, Sir John Hobart (1593–1647), second son and heir of Sir Henry *Hobart, first baronet (*d.* 1625), chief justice of common pleas, and Dorothy (*d.* 1641), daughter of Sir Robert Bell. By December they had had a son, but he, like seven other children, died in infancy, leaving one daughter, Philippa (*bap.* 1635, *d.* 1655), who eventually married her cousin and her father's heir, Sir John *Hobart (*bap.* 1628, *d.* 1683). Lady Frances and her husband were temperamentally well suited and mutually devoted; he referred to his 'dear saint', and she cared tenderly for him in twenty years of illness. They lived mainly at Blickling Hall, Norfolk, where Sir John incurred large debts completing the magnificent building begun by his father. Lady Frances managed all the family estates and audited the accounts, succeeding in reducing the debt by £6000 in six years. Nevertheless in 1644 she wrote an eloquent letter to the earl of Leicester, the brother of Sir John's first wife, pleading for the remission of 'so great a sum' to avoid ruining the family, since the financial difficulties caused by war made payment impossible (Bodl. Oxf., MS Tanner 286, fol. 167). Lady Frances was deeply religious, and came to a life-changing faith through Mr John Carter of St Peter Mancroft, Norwich. She then became solicitous for her husband, and he too was converted.

Lady Frances supported Sir John in politics, first, in 1626, as MP for Brackley, Northamptonshire, where her father was the leading influence, and as member for Norfolk in the Short Parliament of 1640. He opposed arbitrary government and prelacy and after the outbreak of civil war was a leading member of the county committees, which often met at Blickling Hall because it was dangerous to go elsewhere. When in 1646, despite deteriorating health, he was elected to parliament as knight of the shire, most of the household, including Lady Frances, moved to London to be with him. There the couple encountered John Collinges, a young presbyterian-inclined minister, who was invited to become their chaplain. Collinges established a lasting pattern of prayers thrice daily, with exposition of scripture twice, as well as catechizing and sermon repetition. At the summer's end illness forced Sir John to return home with his family. Lady Frances assiduously kept him company by day and watched by night. On his death in April 1647 she determined never to remarry.

As Blickling Hall passed to her nephew, Lady Frances moved to a house at Chapelfield in Norwich, still accompanied by Collinges as chaplain. There she used to rise for her private devotions soon after four until she became infirm, reading the psalms monthly, the New Testament thrice each year, and the Old once. In addition to many prayer books she bought £100 worth of theological books to increase her understanding of scripture, and was an inveterate sermon-goer, hearing three or four on weekdays, and three on Sundays. After visiting fellow believers, spinning or sewing with the maids, and supping, she would read and pray in her closet until midnight or after, leading what Collinges described as a most mortified life. Not content with this, she set up a lecture in her house. She also ate and clothed herself simply, expending a quarter of her outgoings on godly ministers and on poor Christians, to whom she sent her physician, and sometimes Collinges, when they were sick.

Lady Frances shared Collinges's presbyterianism, and during the Commonwealth, apparently fearing that the New Model Army's backing for Independency, which was strong in Norwich, would prevent presbyterian sympathizers from meeting publicly, she converted some of her lower rooms to make a chapel seating 200. Collinges preached a lecture there each week, and repeated his sermons each night after public ones in the town were finished. This continued for sixteen years to a full chapel. Latterly Collinges began preaching a morning sermon on Sundays as well, probably on his ejection in 1662 from nearby St Stephen's Church. It is clear that Lady Frances continued to allow presbyterian services there because, in April 1664, before the Conventicle Act forbade more than five people to meet thus, Sir Joseph Paine and other officers of the city had, as Lady Frances put it, 'affronted her in her own house, thus doing Injury … both in relation to my duty towards God in his service as a Christian: [and] to my owne Hon[ou]r [and] Priviledge as the daughter of a Peere

of the realme' (Bodl. Oxf., MS Tanner 115, fol. 50). She not only protested to Lord Townsend, but also appealed to her nephew, the earl of Exeter, for assistance, and received profuse apologies and assurances from Townsend that she would not be disturbed again—apparently in spite of the legislation which was passed in May. Lady Frances's wholehearted patronage, as well as Collinges's preaching gifts, help to account for the existence in 1669 of two Norwich congregations described as presbyterians and Independents, one pastored by Collinges, and the other near Chapelfield House; together they numbered about 500 members.

Lady Frances became ill from dropsy about March 1664. On 27 November that year she died at home in Norwich; she was buried beside Sir John in the family vault at Blickling church on 1 December. Having written her will on the New Testament principles of doing good and providing for her household and fellow believers, she accordingly left money for the poor of Wymondham, Norwich, and villages including Blickling, specifying that the recipients should be as near as possible to 'the household of faith', widows, orphans, and 'those lately in communion with us' (will). Six ejected ministers received £45, including presbyterians such as Benjamin Snowden and at least one Independent, William Sparrowe. Other beneficiaries included Collinges, John Hawes, her physician, godly women friends, all members of her household, and her sister, the dowager countess of Exeter. Her beloved niece and executor, Lady Katherine Courten, wife of William *Courten (d. 1655) [see under Courten, Sir William (c.1568–1636)], inherited her movables and landed property, including Chapelfield House, the latter probably because services could then continue there. Lady Frances's memory lingered: Mrs Mitchell, wife of a presbyterian dissenter, valued a lock of her hair so much that she bequeathed it to a friend in 1698.   ELIZABETH ALLEN

Sources J. C. [J. Collinges], 'The excellent woman', Par nobile (1669), 2–10, 12–22, 24–5, 29–32, 34, 36–9 • GEC, Peerage • J. Collinges, A memorial for posteritie (1647), title-page, A2, 15, 18–20 • A. W. Hughes Clarke and A. Campling, eds., The visitation of Norfolk … 1664, made by Sir Edward Bysshe, 1, Harleian Society, 85 (1933), 97, 101 • The letters of John Chamberlain, ed. N. E. McClure, 2 vols. (1939), vol. 1, pp. 111, 190; vol. 2, pp. 264, 379, 424, 468, 492, 506 • F. Blomefield and C. Parkin, An essay towards a topographical history of the county of Norfolk, [2nd edn], 11 vols. (1805–10), vol. 4, p. 183; vol. 6, p. 399 • will, Norfolk RO, NRS 20738 4103 • Calamy rev., 77, 128, 351, 453 • Bodl. Oxf., MSS Tanner 115, fol. 50; 286, fol. 167 • C. B. Jewson, The return of conventicles in Norwich diocese, 1669, Norfolk Archaeological Society (1965), 12, 15–16 • Blickling Hall, National Trust, new edn (1987), 15–16, 25 • W. B. Bidwell and M. Jansson, eds., Proceedings in parliament, 1626, 2: House of Commons (1992), 73 • J. C. [J. Collinges], The spouses hidden glory (1646), A, A3 • J. Browne, A history of Congregationalism and memorials of the churches in Norfolk and Suffolk (1877), 252, 254–5 • G. B. Jay, The first parish register of St George, Tombland, Norwich (1891), 192, 195 • Norfolk: Norwich and north-east, Pevsner (1997), 400 • Report on the manuscripts of the marquess of Lothian, HMC, 62 (1905), 143

Likenesses double portrait, oils? (with Sir John Hobart), repro. in Report on the MSS of the marquess of Lothian; formerly at Blickling Hall, 1703

Wealth at death approx. £550 in specific legacies; also jewels; gold clock; silver watch; Chapelfield House; another good house let to Dr Hawes; household goods: will, 1664, Norfolk RO, Norwich, NRS 20738 4103

Hobart, George, third earl of Buckinghamshire (1731–1804), theatre manager and politician, was born in London on 8 September 1731, the eldest of the two sons (there were no daughters) of John *Hobart, later first earl of Buckinghamshire (1693–1756), and his second wife, Elizabeth Bristow (*bap.* 1694, *d.* 1762). He entered Westminster School in 1739 and was elected king's scholar in 1746. He does not seem to have attended university. In 1754 he was elected to one of the parliamentary seats in St Ives, Cornwall. On 16 May 1757 he married Albinia [**Albinia Hobart**, countess of Buckinghamshire (1737/8–1816)], the eldest of the two daughters of Lord Vere Bertie, the third son of Robert, first duke of Ancaster and Kesteven, and his wife, Ann Casey, the illegitimate daughter of Sir Cecil Wray, bt, and, through her, heir to estates in Ireland.

With the influence of the Hobart family diminishing in St Ives, Hobart was not returned there in 1761 but was instead elected for Bere Alston, Devon. His ambitions, however, lay in diplomatic service. He had applied for the position of British resident in Hamburg in 1756, and in August 1762 he accompanied his half-brother, John *Hobart, second earl of Buckinghamshire, to Russia as secretary to the embassy. The posting was unsuccessful: on 21 October 1762 Buckinghamshire wrote to his aunt Henrietta, countess of Suffolk, that the comfort-loving Hobart was 'a good deal out of spirits' (Buckinghamshire, 1.76) in the bleak surroundings of Moscow, and on 27 December he reported that Hobart was 'determin'd to ask leave to return to England' (*Lothian MSS*, 171) and on 13 April 1763 that he was on the point of departure. He arrived in London in July 1763.

Hobart's diplomatic career was over, but a few years later he found a new direction as manager of the opera at the King's Theatre in the Haymarket. The opera had had aristocratic managers before, such as Charles Sackville, earl of Middlesex (later second duke of Dorset), for several years after 1741, but Hobart showed more application in running the opera as a viable business. He bought a controlling share in the opera patent between July and September 1769 and ran a programme containing both serious and comic operas. The main challenge of his tenure came at the beginning of 1771, when Theresa Cornelys added 'harmonic meetings' to her assemblies at Carlisle House. The leading performer was a countertenor castrato, Gaetano Guadagni, who had been the leading countertenor at the King's Theatre until his resignation, prompted, according to Horace Walpole, by Hobart's promotion of Anna Maria Zamperini—believed to be Hobart's mistress—over Guadagni's sister. Hobart employed spies to gather evidence; Cornelys and Guadagni were brought to trial and both were fined. Hobart continued to work to vary the offerings at the King's Theatre, and at the beginning of the 1771–2 season brought the dancer Anne-Frédérique Heinel over from Paris to help raise the profile of dance. At the beginning of 1773 he retired from the opera, perhaps through financial strain, and sold at least some of his shares to the actor James Brooke.

Thereafter Hobart seems to have lived as a gentleman, having inherited the hall and estate at Nocton in Lincolnshire from a distant relative, Sir Richard Ellys, third baronet, when it was relinquished by Ellys's widow in 1766. He visited Paris in 1776 and 1779. It may have been during this period that he met Mary Ann Joseph Delibossart of Paris, possibly his mistress; she and her daughters Augusta Joseph Bezos and Seraphina Delibossart are mentioned in his will, as is Ann Barker, the wife of John Barker of Belgrave Square. He remained MP for Bere Alston until 1780, by which time his half-brother had sold his interest in Bere Alston to Hugh Percy, first duke of Northumberland. He does not seem to have sought another seat, and was probably content to leave the family's political affairs to his eldest son, Robert *Hobart, later fourth earl of Buckinghamshire. He maintained connections with the theatrical world; his daughter Albinia (1759–1853) married Richard Cumberland, son of the playwright, in 1784, and he probably retained a financial interest in the King's Theatre. He was a member of the committee of mortgagees and creditors who petitioned the lord chamberlain in 1791 to allow a rebuilt King's Theatre to continue as an opera house when the patent, following the fire of 1789, had been allowed to migrate to the Pantheon.

However, by this time Hobart had been eclipsed as a public figure by his wife, Albinia. Leading a separate life from her husband, she became well known for her lavish assemblies and for her dramatic performances, which usually featured herself and her daughters, and were often staged at Nocton Hall or at the Hobarts' house on Ham Common. This was modelled on Frederick the Great's villa and named Sans-Souci after it. In 1784 she joined the campaign of her relative Sir Cecil Wray in the notorious Westminster election. She was not the highest in rank of the ladies who supported Wray, the ministerial candidate, nor even the most active, but her obese figure—her appearance was likened to a beefsteak—made her a target for satirists seeking a subject who could be contrasted with the Foxite whig campaigner and renowned beauty Georgiana Cavendish, duchess of Devonshire. She could also, like Wray, be charged with apostasy, as most of her social circle were supporters of Fox.

Hobart succeeded his half-brother as earl of Buckinghamshire on 3 September 1793, but did not inherit the family estates, which the second earl had divided among his daughters. The new countess, already infamous as a gambler, was reported as opening her house for faro games twice a week in order to raise the funds to maintain her new dignity. Charles Pigott, in *The Female Jockey Club*, attacked her as someone who, if she were not of a noble family, 'would in all probability have passed much of her time in the house of correction' (Pigott, 106), and affected to praise her theatrical productions on the grounds that they could cure the most intractable cases of insomnia. In March 1797, alongside Lady Elizabeth Luttrell, she was fined £50 for illicit gambling.

Buckinghamshire, meanwhile, was happy to accept the additional honours and duties that became his rank. In

1797 he became colonel of the 3rd regiment of Lincolnshire militia, and on 12 January 1799 he was awarded the rank of colonel in the army for as long as his regiment should remain embodied for active service. He died on 14 November 1804 at Nocton, Lincolnshire, and was buried there. He was survived by his wife and by two of his five sons—Robert, fourth earl of Buckinghamshire, and Henry Lewis (*bap.* 1774, *d.* 1845), dean of Windsor from 1816. Three other sons—George (*bap.* 1758), George Vere (*bap.* 1764, *d.* 1802), governor of Grenada, and Charles (*bap.* 1766, *d.* 1782), a naval officer killed in action—predeceased him. His eldest daughter, Albinia, was lady of the bedchamber to the daughters of George III from 1796 to 1812 and was the mother of the army officer Richard Francis George Cumberland; his twin daughters, Henrietta Anne Barbara (*bap.* 1762, *d.* 1828) and Maria Frances Mary (*bap.* 1762, *d.* 1794), married, respectively, the politician John Sullivan and George Augustus *North, third earl of Guilford [*see under* North, Frederick, second earl of Guilford]; and his youngest daughter, Charlotte (*d.* 1798), married Edward Disbrowe, an army officer, and was the mother of the diplomatist Sir Edward Disbrowe. Albinia, dowager countess of Buckinghamshire, died on 11 March 1816 at Nocton, Lincolnshire, and was buried there like her husband.   Matthew Kilburn

Sources D. Nalbach, *The King's Theatre, 1704–1867* (1972) · C. Price, J. Milhous, and R. D. Hume, *Italian opera in late eighteenth-century London*, 1: *The King's Theatre, Haymarket, 1778–1791* (1995) · *The history of the Westminster election* (1784) · Walpole, *Corr.* · earl of Buckinghamshire [J. Hobart], *The despatches and correspondence of John, second earl of Buckinghamshire, ambassador to the court of Catherine II of Russia, 1762–1765*, ed. A. D. Collyer, 2 vols. (1900–02) · *Report on the manuscripts of the marquess of Lothian*, HMC, 62 (1905) · J. Brooke, 'Hobart, Hon. George', HoP, *Commons, 1754–90* · C. Pigott, *The Female Jockey Club* (1794) · GEC, *Peerage*, new edn · *GM*, 1st ser., 63 (1793), 868 · *GM*, 1st ser., 69 (1799), 536 · *GM*, 1st ser., 74 (1804), 1170 · *GM*, 1st ser., 86/1 (1816), 374 · *Old Westminsters* · will, PRO, PROB 11/1419, sig. 3 · D. Donald, *The age of caricature: satirical prints in the reign of George III* (1996) · A. Stott, '"Female patriotism": Georgiana, duchess of Devonshire, and the Westminster election of 1784', *Eighteenth-Century Life*, 17 (1993), 60–84 · C. Bennett, 'E. J. Willson and the architectural history of Nocton Old Hall', *Lincolnshire people and places: essays in memory of Terence R. Leach*, ed. C. Sturman (1996), 26–42
Archives BL, letters · Norfolk RO, estate and family papers
Likenesses T. Rowlandson, caricature, 1784 (Albinia Hobart), repro. in Donald, *Age of caricature* · caricature, 1787 (Albinia Hobart), repro. in Walpole, *Corr.*
Wealth at death see will, PRO, PROB 11/1419, sig. 3; PRO, C 107/91

Hobart, Henrietta. *See* Howard, Henrietta (*c.*1688–1767).

Hobart, Sir Henry, first baronet (*c.*1554–1625), lawyer and judge, was the second son of Thomas Hobart (1522/3–1560) of Plumstead, Norfolk, and his wife, Audrey (*d.* 1580), daughter of William Hare of Beeston, Norfolk. He was the great-grandson of Sir James Hobart, attorney-general to Henry VII. Hobart was admitted to Peterhouse, Cambridge, in 1570, and after studying at Furnival's Inn he entered Lincoln's Inn on 30 July 1575, and was called to the bar on 24 June 1584. Hobart was appointed counsel for Great Yarmouth in October 1586, and by 1590 he was made under-steward to Lord Burghley. It was probably Burghley

who secured his return to parliament in 1589 for the Cornish borough of St Ives.

On 20 April 1590 Hobart made a settlement on his marriage (the actual marriage was variously reported as on 21, 22, or 29 April) to Dorothy (*bap.* 1572, *d.* 1641), daughter of Robert *Bell of Beaupré Hall, Norfolk, the chief baron of the exchequer. They had twelve sons and four daughters, eight sons and two daughters surviving him. By the early 1590s, when he became a Norfolk JP, Hobart was becoming established in local county society. In 1592 he became a freeman of Norwich; he was appointed counsel for King's Lynn in 1594, and became steward of Norwich in 1595. He was made a bencher of Lincoln's Inn in 1596, the same year that he purchased Intwood in Norfolk. In 1597 he was returned to parliament for Great Yarmouth, sitting on the committee of privileges and returns, and successfully defending the port's interests against those of its rival, Lowestoft. He was again elected for Great Yarmouth in 1601, again sitting on the committee of privileges and returns and on the parliament's main business committee. He was made a serjeant-at-law in May 1603, his patrons being the earl of Kent and the judges Francis Gawdy and George Kingswell, and gave the reading at Lincoln's Inn on 27 Eliz. I c.4 (fraudulent conveyance). He was knighted on 23 July 1603. In 1604 he was returned to parliament for Norwich, being appointed to many committees and playing a role in the attack on Bishop Thornborough of Bristol for discussing in a book the debate of the House of Commons on union with Scotland. He was a union commissioner in 1604–6.

On 2 November 1605 Hobart was discharged from the coif upon his appointment as attorney of the court of wards and liveries, an office he owed to Robert Cecil, earl of Salisbury. In 1606, as a government spokesman in the Commons, he responded to the Gunpowder Plot, supported the king's prerogative in the controversy over purveyance, and supported a grant of supply to pay Queen Elizabeth's debts and to improve the state of the coinage. On 4 July 1606 he was appointed attorney-general, much to the chagrin of Sir Francis Bacon. Controversy attended his continuance as an MP, as in his capacity as attorney-general he had been summoned as an assistant to the House of Lords, and there were no precedents for an attorney-general to continue to sit in the lower house. The matter was debated inconclusively on 22 November 1606, and eventually settled when Hobart accompanied the speaker into the chamber and took his seat on 24 November. He then became heavily involved in the legislative business of the Commons. In his capacity as attorney-general in 1608 he appeared for the plaintiff, Robert Calvin, in the case of the post-nati. He was named a commissioner of ecclesiastical causes in 1608, and appointed to the committee of the Virginia Company in 1609. In the 1610 session of parliament he was the principal government spokesman on the great contract and supply, supporting the king's right to impositions. He also led the attack on Dr Cowell's book *The Interpreter*, speaking at a conference with the Lords in May 1610. On 11 May 1611 Hobart was created a baronet, one of the first to receive that honour. In the summer of 1611 he was reported to be seriously ill, but subsequently recovered. In 1612 Hobart became chancellor to Henry, prince of Wales. Following the death of Salisbury in May 1612, he was one of the few mourners at the earl's funeral. Also in 1612 he became a commissioner on the enfranchisement of copyholders and a member of the North West Passage Company. On 26 November 1613 he was appointed chief justice of common pleas, but he was not always regarded as amenable to the court. In 1615, when James I wished to secure the conviction of Edmund Pearson on the western circuit, Hobart was dispatched on the home circuit instead. In November 1616 Hobart purchased the manor of Blickling, Norfolk. On 1 September 1617 he leased part of his house at Blickling, plus the outbuildings and 201 acres, for six years at £110 p.a., presumably to provide some income from the estate while he embarked upon an extensive building programme. Between February 1618 and April 1622 Hobart spent over £6500 on Blickling, and work still continued after his death. Another outlet for Hobart's surplus cash was the East India Company, of which he became a member in 1617.

Hobart's appointment as chief justice was revoked on 1 April 1617, with a fresh appointment dated 2 April to make allowance for the fact that he was now also chancellor to Charles, prince of Wales. On the bench Hobart opposed the draconian fine which Sir Edward Coke wished to impose on the earl of Suffolk in 1619, following his dismissal as lord treasurer. In 1619 he was named to a commission on the relief of the poor. In 1621 Hobart was one of the commissioners who found in favour of Archbishop Abbot following the accidental death of a gamekeeper who had been killed by a cross-bow shot from Abbot during a hunt. Hobart was reappointed a judge on 29 March 1625, following the accession of Charles I. Hobart's death was variously reported to have taken place on 26, 28, or 29 December 1625, the latter date appearing to be the most likely.

According to Judge Jenkins: 'in Hobart were many noble things, an excellent eloquence, the éclat of ancestry, the most engaging sweetness animated with a singular gravity' (*Lothian MSS*, viii). Hobart was buried on 4 January 1626 at Blickling. He left houses at Highgate and St Bartholomew's in London, and Chapel in the Fields, Norwich. He was succeeded by his son John, the second baronet. Hobart's widow was buried at Blickling on 30 April 1641. In 1641 a volume of his law reports was published, with subsequent editions in 1650, 1671, 1678, and 1724.

STUART HANDLEY

Sources C. Kyle, HoP, *Commons, 1604–29* [draft] · G. M. Coles, 'Hobart, Henry', HoP, *Commons, 1558–1603* · GEC, *Baronetage* · Sainty, *Judges* · Baker, *Serjeants* · Sainty, *King's counsel* · W. Harvey, *The visitation of Norfolk in the year 1563*, ed. G. H. Dashwood and others, 2 vols. (1878–95), 98–139 · Foss, *Judges*, 6.328–31 · C. Stanley-Millson and J. Newman, 'Blickling Hall: the building of a Jacobean mansion', *Architectural History*, 29 (1986), 1–42 · *Report on the manuscripts of the marquess of Lothian*, HMC, 62 (1905) · *State trials*, vols. 2–3 · PRO, PROB 11/148, fol. 438r–v · *Report on the manuscripts of the family of Gawdy, formerly of Norfolk*, HMC, 11 (1885) · W. R. Prest, *The rise of the barristers: a social history of the English bar, 1590–1640*, 2nd edn (1991)
Archives Norfolk RO, papers
Likenesses D. Mytens, oils, *c*.1620, Blickling Hall, Garden & Park, Norfolk · C. Jansen, portrait, NPG · S. de Passe, line engraving, BM; NPG · oils (after type of *c*.1615–1620), NPG

Hobart, Sir James (*d.* 1517), judge, was born at Monks Eleigh in Suffolk, the son of Thomas Hobart. He trained at Lincoln's Inn, and gave his second law reading in Lent 1479. Between Michaelmas 1486 and Michaelmas 1506 he was elected annually as the senior governor, and lent the inn significant sums of money to rebuild its hall. Hobart seems initially to have lived at Bacton in Suffolk; appointed a JP for the county in 1466, he sat for Ipswich in the parliaments of 1467–8, 1478, and January 1483. In 1482 he switched to the Norfolk commission of the peace, probably as a result of moving his major residence to Hales Hall, Loddon.

Hobart's principal early clients were the Mowbray dukes of Norfolk and he continued to serve Elizabeth, the dowager duchess, until her death in 1506. By 1463, however, he was also being employed by Sir John Howard, the future first Howard duke. Hobart appears in the Paston letters as the servant of both families (as well as a personal friend of John (III) Paston). Steward for Howard's Suffolk estates, Hobart was also his principal legal adviser, and one of the retinue. In 1484 he promised to supply at his own expense three armed men for the force that the newly elevated duke was raising for Richard III, and in addition 'to gete hym as many men as he can gete' (Collier, 2.481). Hobart was also feed by Richard himself.

Given this history it is surprising that James Hobart was not dropped as a JP after Bosworth with other Howard supporters, and even more that on 3 November 1486 Henry VII appointed him as attorney-general, the law officer closest to the monarch. Influence must be presumed—either the earl of Oxford (another client), or more probably Thomas Lovell, also of Norfolk and Lincoln's Inn, and a professional colleague.

Hobart rapidly became one of Henry VII's principal courtiers and counsellors. As attorney-general he oversaw all the courts of law, and was a major agent of the king's policy 'to keep all Englishmen obedient through fear' (*Anglica historia*, 127). Promoting all and any litigation from which the king could profit, his methods were none too principled. Particularly important were cases where royal rights could be elaborated by judicial construction, such as *Stonor's case* (1495–6). Perkin Warbeck certainly had some grounds for stigmatizing Hobart in 1496 as one of 'the catiffs and villains of simple birth whom the king alone trusted' and whose 'subtle inventions and pilling of the people' were the 'principal occasions of misrule and mischief now in England' (Pollard, 2.153). From 1500 Hobart joined with a handful of the king's other leading advisers on a special board, known as 'the council learned in the law', which maximized royal profit by every device of law and pressure, and assisted the king in manipulating the bonds and recognizances through which Henry sought to ensnare individuals and families in a web of indebtedness to the crown.

Hobart was an equally vigorous agent of the royal council on the local scene—which explains Norwich's selecting him in 1496 as its recorder! In Suffolk Sir James (as he became on 18 February 1503) sat as a JP more often than anyone else (he was probably *custos rotulorum*), and returned a disproportionate number of cases involving royal rights. Hobart also had the common lawyer's suspicion of the church and its courts. He encouraged defendants to bring charges against clerical judges under the Statute of *Praemunire* (1393), and construed the promise of costs to informers under a Riotous Assembly Act of 1495 as applying to the act of 1393. In 1505 the attorney-general even brought a charge of *praemunire* against the bishop of Norwich, Richard Nix, who urged William Warham, archbishop of Canterbury and lord chancellor, to excommunicate Hobart as 'the enemy of God and his churche' (Gunn, 16).

It has been suggested that the high-profile Nix prosecution led to Hobart's resignation or dismissal in 1507. John Erneley, his successor as attorney-general, was appointed on 12 July. The change, however, signalled no relaxation of royal pressure on the church, and it is more probable that Hobart left in the normal way and on account of age. He had ceased to ride the assizes in 1503. By 1507 he was in his middle or late sixties, and four days before Erneley's appointment he had sued out a replacement copy of his own patent—a step typical of a royal servant about to hand over office. The crown continued to summon him to the Lords (as it had when he was attorney-general).

It is possibly another sign of a desire to withdraw from active life that about 1500 Hobart and his third wife put in hand major works of charity. He assisted—probably completed—Bishop Goldwell's choir in Norwich Cathedral, and constructed at his own expense a parish church for Loddon. Lady Hobart built the bridge over the Waveney at St Olave's with an adjacent causeway. She was Margaret, daughter of Piers Naunton of Letheringham, widow of John Dorward, and the mother of the sons Walter and Miles and daughter Katherine who survived Sir James. The estates he purchased, principally in Norfolk, were substantial—sufficient to endow both sons. Hobart's first wife, whom he had married before 1470, had been Margery, the sister of John Lyhert and niece of Walter Lyhert, bishop of Norwich. Hobart named his son and heir after Lyhert, for whom he was an executor (as also for Bishop Goldwell, Lyhert's successor). His second wife was Dorothy, daughter of Sir John Glemham. Sir James died on 24 February 1517 and was buried in a chapel he built on the north side of the nave of Norwich Cathedral but the chapel has not survived, nor have his tomb and military brass. A number of painted panels exist, showing Sir James in armour with a heraldic tabard, and his wife in a heraldic mantle (for instance at Blickling Hall, Loddon church, and Lincoln's Inn).   E. W. IVES

Sources E. W. Ives, *The common lawyers of pre-Reformation England* (1983) · N. Davis, ed., *Paston letters and papers of the fifteenth century*, 2 vols. (1971–6) · *Household books of John, duke of Norfolk, and Thomas, earl of Surrey*, ed. J. P. Collier, Roxburghe Club, 61 (1844) · *The reports of Sir John Spelman*, ed. J. H. Baker, 2 vols., SeldS, 93–4 (1977–8) · M. M. Condon, 'Ruling elites in the reign of Henry VII', *Patronage, pedigree and power in later medieval England*, ed. C. D. Ross (1979), 109–42 · R. Virgoe, 'The recovery of the Howards in East Anglia, 1485–1529', *Wealth and power in Tudor England: essays presented to S. T. Bindoff*, ed. E. W. Ives, R. J. Knecht, and J. J. Scarisbrick (1978), 1–20 · will, PRO, PROB 11/19, sig. 33 · R. L. Storey, *Diocesan administration in fifteenth-century England*, 2nd edn (1972) · F. Blomefield and C. Parkin, *An essay towards a topographical history of the county of Norfolk*, [2nd edn], 11 vols. (1805–10) · R. Somerville, 'Henry VII's "council learned in the law"', *EngHR*, 54 (1939), 427–42 · J. C. Wedgwood and A. D. Holt, *History of parliament … 1439–1509*, 2 vols. (1936–8) · C. Haigh, *English reformations: religion, politics, and society under the Tudors* (1993) · J. Weever, *Ancient funerall monuments* (1631) · R. Somerville, *History of the duchy of Lancaster, 1265–1603* (1953) · W. Hudson and J. C. Tingey, eds., *The records of the city of Norwich*, 2 vols. (1906–10) · *The Anglica historia of Polydore Vergil, AD 1485–1537*, ed. and trans. D. Hay, CS, 3rd ser., 74 (1950) · A. F. Pollard, ed., *The reign of Henry VII from contemporary sources*, 3 vols. (1913–14) · PRO, Chancery, inquisitions post mortem, C142/32/15 · S. J. Gunn, *Early Tudor government, 1485–1558* (1995)

Likenesses painted panel, 17th/18th cent., Lincoln's Inn, London · painted panel, 17th/18th cent., Blickling Hall, Garden, & Park, Norfolk · painted panel, 17th/18th cent., Loddon church, Norfolk

Wealth at death lands: will, PRO, PROB 11/19, sig. 33; PRO, C 142/32/15

Hobart, Sir John, third baronet (*bap.* 1628, *d.* 1683), politician, was baptized at Ditchingham, Norfolk, on 20 March 1628, the second but first surviving son of Miles Hobart (1595–1639) of Intwood, Norfolk, and his first wife, Frances (*bap.* 1595, *d.* 1631), daughter of Sir John Peyton, first baronet, of Isleham, Cambridgeshire. He entered Emmanuel College, Cambridge, on 5 March 1644, and was admitted to Lincoln's Inn on 20 May 1645. He succeeded his uncle, Sir John Hobart, second baronet, to the baronetcy and to Blickling Hall, Norfolk, on 20 April 1647, and the same year he married his cousin, Philippa (*bap.* 1635, *d.* 1655), daughter of his predecessor and of Lady Frances *Hobart. They had one son, who died an infant.

The second baronet had been a strong parliamentarian and Hobart appears to have been involved in local administration from about 1650. He sat in the protectorate parliaments of 1654 and 1656. After the death of his first wife in 1655, on 3 June 1656 he married Mary (*bap.* 1630, *d.* 1689?), daughter of John Hampden of Great Hampden, Buckinghamshire, and the widow of Colonel Robert Hammond (*d.* 1654) of Chertsey, Surrey. They had four sons (one of whom died young), and three daughters (one of whom died young). On 11 December 1657 he was made a member of Cromwell's 'other house'. Hobart joined Lord Richardson and Sir Horatio Townshend, third baronet, on 28 January 1660 in presenting the Rump with an address from Norfolk asking for the return of the secluded members and for filling up vacancies without 'oath or engagement'; this address was subsequently presented to General Monck at St Albans in February. Hobart was named to the Norfolk commission in the Militia Act of March 1660, and was active in promoting the Restoration. He was defeated in the Norfolk election to the Convention on 2 April 1660, and sought fit to take out a pardon for his activity during the interregnum, although he was proposed for the abortive order of the Royal Oak (with an income of £1000 p.a.).

Although Hobart served as a JP following the Restoration he clearly had to work his way back into favour. He served as sheriff of Norfolk in 1666–7 and became a deputy lieutenant in 1668. Thereafter he was a key figure in Restoration Norfolk's local government, serving as a JP, militia captain, and deputy lieutenant. Indeed, between 1668 and 1675 he rarely missed a meeting of the Norfolk lieutenancy. Hobart's rehabilitation was completed when he entertained the king at Blickling in 1671, the occasion being marked by the knighthood bestowed upon his son Henry.

Despite protestations of loyalty and conformity many old cavaliers were disappointed when, on 17 February 1673, Hobart was returned unopposed in a by-election as knight of the shire for Norfolk. In the House of Commons he supported the bill for the ease of protestant dissenters in 1673. In Norfolk politics in 1675 he opposed the attempt by the earl of Danby to obtain a seat for his son-in-law, Robert Coke, at King's Lynn, and supported Sir Robert Kemp, an opponent of the court, for the county in a by-election. The divisions appearing in Norfolk politics provided Danby with the excuse to have Lord Townshend removed from the lord lieutenancy in 1676, and Hobart resigned as a deputy lieutenant as a consequence, and was left out of the commission of the peace. In 1677 the earl of Shaftesbury noted Hobart as 'thrice worthy'.

Hobart was defeated for Norfolk at the general election held on 10 February 1679, but whig party strength in the Commons ensured that the election was declared void on 21 April, and Hobart duly won the seat at the by-election held on 5 May 1679. However, the writ was delayed and he missed the division on the first Exclusion Bill, a measure which he supported even though it was 'so sharp and hazardous a remedy' (Knights, 31). The temporary whig ascendancy in central government saw Hobart restored to the bench in May 1679, only to be removed again in July on the orders of the king, for whom Hobart was a man 'who will never be obliged and any countenance I give them is only used against myself and government' (Finch MSS, 2.42). In Norfolk he was under attack as a nonconformist, which was perhaps not surprising given the high visibility of some of his dissenting supporters. However, on 3 June 1679 he wrote that he attended 'the public service of God Almighty according to the establishment of our church' (Cruickshanks, 2.553). He was duly elected for the county at the general election held on 25 August 1679. In July 1680 Paul Barillon, the French ambassador, described him as one of the most considerable MPs opposing the court, and also as a republican. The election on 7 February 1681 saw Hobart returned with a much reduced majority, and he duly attended the third Exclusion Parliament.

Hobart was now clearly held in a great deal of suspicion by the court. One report in February 1682 had Hobart as the head of the 'disaffected' party, who 'having been one of Oliver's lords, retains a respectful memory for his master and his cause' (CSP dom., 1682, 54–5). Following the discovery of the Rye House plot his house was searched, on 13 July 1683, and a small number of arms seized. Hobart must have been ill for he died on 22 August 1683 and was buried at Blickling on the 30th. His widow probably survived until 1689, when her will was proved. Hobart was succeeded by his son, Sir Henry, who took over his mantle as leader of the Norfolk whigs.　　　　STUART HANDLEY

Sources E. Cruickshanks, 'Hobart, Sir John', HoP, Commons, 1660–90, 2.552–3 • W. Harvey, The visitation of Norfolk in the year 1563, ed. G. H. Dashwood and others, 2 (1895), 76–80, 100, 140–41 • Venn, Alum. Cant. • J. M. Rosenheim, The Townshends of Raynham (1989), 37–60 • J. Miller, 'A moderate in the first age of party: the dilemmas of Sir John Holland, 1675–85', EngHR, 114 (1999), 844–74, esp. 848–71 • CSP dom., 1659–60, 332; 1682, 54–5 • Norfolk lieutenancy journal, 1660–1676, ed. R. M. Dunn, Norfolk RS, 45 (1977), 7–8, 152, 155 • L. K. J. Glassey, Politics and the appointment of justices of the peace, 1675–1720 (1979), 34, 43–4 • Report on the manuscripts of Allan George Finch, 5 vols., HMC, 71 (1913–2003), vol. 2, p. 42 • M. Knights, Politics and opinion in crisis, 1678–1681 (1994), 31, 124, 137, 203, 286 • Norfolk quarter sessions order book, 1650–1657, ed. D. E. H. James, Norfolk RS, 26 (1955), 25 • R. H. Mason, The history of Norfolk (1884), 327 • Report on the manuscripts of the marquess of Lothian, HMC, 62 (1905), 87

Archives Bodl. Oxf., letters • Norfolk RO, accounts kept as county treasurer for Norfolk | Norfolk RO, letters to William Windham, Wkc

Hobart, John, first earl of Buckinghamshire (1693–1756), politician and courtier, was born on 11 October 1693, the only son of Sir Henry Hobart, fourth baronet (1657/8–1698), of Blickling, Norfolk, and his wife, Elizabeth (d. 1701), the daughter and coheir of Joseph Maynard of Clifton Reynes, Buckinghamshire. He was educated at Westminster School and at Clare College, Cambridge, where he matriculated on 20 May 1710, but did not take a degree. He probably left there in 1713 or 1714, when he presented the college with a silver punchbowl. At the 1715 election he was returned to the Commons for St Ives, Cornwall, where he controlled one of the two parliamentary seats. On 8 November 1717, at Thorpe Market, Norfolk, he married Judith (d. 1727), the daughter of Robert Britiffe, MP for Norwich and legal adviser to Hobart's Norfolk neighbours the Townshends and the Walpoles, and his first wife, Judith Edgar. They had three sons, only one of whom, John *Hobart, later second earl of Buckinghamshire, survived infancy, and five daughters, of whom again only one, Dorothy (d. 1798), who married Sir Charles Hotham-Thompson, eighth baronet, survived. Hobart was appointed vice-admiral of Norfolk in 1719, and in 1720 he inherited the Maynard family estate at Bere Alston in Devon, with an influence in that parliamentary seat.

Hobart gained his first ministerial appointment in 1721, as a commissioner of the Board of Trade and Plantations; although he never held high office he remained a holder of government or court positions for the rest of his life. His security was often attributed to the influence that his sister Henrietta *Howard, countess of Suffolk, was said to have over George II, but he survived her eclipse at court in the 1730s. He was made KB on 27 May 1725 and was invested on 17 June. In 1727 he became treasurer of the chamber to George II; his influence in Cornwall was also recognized by his appointment as assay master of the stannaries, a post he held until 1738. In the general election of 1727 he was elected for Norfolk, but on 28 May 1728 he was created Baron Hobart of Blickling. Following the death of his first wife on 7 February 1727, he had married, on 10 February 1728, at St Paul's Cathedral, London, Elizabeth (d. 1762), the daughter of Robert Bristow (d. 1706), who had been heir to estates in Virginia and Hampshire, and the sister of Robert Bristow, MP for Winchelsea and clerk of the green cloth. They had two sons, George *Hobart, later third earl of Buckinghamshire (1731–1804), and Henry (1738–1799), MP for Norwich from 1786.

In December 1739 Hobart was appointed lord lieutenant of Norfolk. In this capacity he raised a regiment to counter the Jacobite rising of 1745, and it was perhaps in recognition of this action that he was created earl of Buckinghamshire on 5 September 1746. The promotion may also have been belated compensation for having to exchange the position of treasurer of the chamber for that of captain of the gentleman pensioners on the formation of the broad-bottom ministry in 1744. At some point he bought an estate in Buckinghamshire, costing approximately £35,000.

Buckinghamshire died at his home in St James's Square, Westminster, on 22 September 1756, and was buried at Blickling. He left his Norfolk and personal estate to his widow, who died on 12 September 1762 and was buried on 25 September at Richmond, Surrey.

MATTHEW KILBURN

Sources E. Cruickshanks, 'Hobart, Sir John', HoP, *Commons, 1715–54* · A. Collins, *The peerage of England: containing a genealogical and historical account of all the peers of England*, 4th edn (1768) · GEC, *Peerage*, new edn · Burke, *Peerage* (1999) · GM, 1st ser., 26 (1756), 451 · GM, 1st ser., 9 (1739), 661 · Venn, *Alum. Cant.* · *Old Westminsters* · *Report on the manuscripts of the marquess of Lothian*, HMC, 62 (1905), 145, 147, 170 · John, Lord Hervey, *Some materials towards memoirs of the reign of King George II*, ed. R. Sedgwick, 1 (1931), 40, 66; 3 (1931), 383 · will, PRO, PROB 11/824, sig. 239

Archives BL, letters · Norfolk RO, estate and family papers
Wealth at death see will, PRO, PROB 11/824, sig. 239

Hobart, John, second earl of Buckinghamshire (1723–1793), politician, second, and first surviving, son of John *Hobart, first earl of Buckinghamshire (1693–1756), politician, and his first wife, Judith Britiffe (d. 1727), was born in Greenwich, Kent, on 17 August 1723. He was educated at Westminster School (1732–9) and at Christ's College, Cambridge, where he was admitted in October 1739, but did not take any degree. On 4 October 1745 he was appointed a deputy lieutenant for the county of Norfolk, and at the general election in June 1747 was returned as a whig to parliament for the city of Norwich and the borough of St Ives, Cornwall, on his family's interest. He elected to sit for Norwich and was again returned for that city at the general election in April 1754. In December 1755 he was appointed comptroller of the household to George II, and on 27 January 1756 was sworn of the privy council. He succeeded his father as second earl of Buckinghamshire on 22 September 1756 and took his seat in the House of Lords on 14 December. Resigning the comptrollership he was appointed a lord of the bedchamber on 15 November 1756.

John Hobart, second earl of Buckinghamshire (1723–1793), by Thomas Gainsborough

He held the post until dismissed in November 1767 for having supported the duke of Bedford's motion of April 1767 for a Lords' address to the king to take into consideration a Massachusetts Bay act pardoning rioters in the Stamp Act disturbances.

By this date Buckinghamshire, who on 14 July 1761 had married Mary Anne Drury (1740–1769), daughter and heir of Sir Thomas Drury, baronet, of Overstone, Northamptonshire, had served as ambassador and minister-plenipotentiary to Russia. He accepted the responsibility of concluding a new treaty with Russia on 17 July 1762. The difficulty was that the Russians' priority was a political treaty, whereas Britain desired a treaty of commerce. He commenced negotiating in Moscow in December 1762 but the draft treaty proposed by the Russians in August 1763, which committed Britain to support Russia's interests in Sweden, Poland, and, in the event of war, Turkey, was unacceptable. By his own account Buckinghamshire was made very welcome at the Russian court, but his high social profile did not compensate for the lack of initiative and imagination he displayed in negotiation, and it was clear by August 1764, when Lord Sandwich effectively directed him to get the stalled negotiations moving or return to Britain, that he was not the man to bring a treaty into being. He left Russia in January 1765, having handed over the negotiating responsibility to Sir George Macartney. In October 1766, shortly after the establishment of the Chatham administration, Buckinghamshire refused Lord Shelburne's request for him to become ambassador to Spain. Despite this, he remained eager for governmental employment, but he was neither sufficiently well liked nor sufficiently able to command notice, and this dovetailed with his alienation of the king to ensure a wait of ten years for his next appointment. Indeed, it was only because Lord Dartmouth and Lord Rochford could not be prevailed upon to accept the lord lieutenancy of Ireland that Lord North and George III agreed to grant him the 'very important charge' (*Correspondence of George III*, 3.363) that was Ireland. He was appointed lord lieutenant of Ireland on 18 December 1776 and arrived in Dublin on 25 January 1777.

As a consequence of the augmented role carved out for the lord lieutenant by Lord Townshend (1767–72), sympathy for the cause of the American colonists, and the higher profile of the patriots in the Irish House of Commons, Buckinghamshire took charge of Ireland at a difficult moment. He began badly by choosing a family friend, Richard Heron, who 'was totally unacquainted with politics and parliament' (Rosse MS C/12/1), for the crucial position of chief secretary. He compounded matters by accepting the advice of the duke of Leinster and Thomas Conolly that he should abandon those upon whom his predecessor had relied. One consequence of this was that experienced figures like John Hely-Hutchinson, John Beresford, and Henry Flood were passed over in favour of Philip Tisdall, Hussey Burgh, John Scott, and John Foster. These were not without skill or experience, but they did not possess the same authority as those they replaced in the House of Commons and were not always reliable. Despite this and the problems engendered by the unexpected death of Tisdall in September 1777, Buckinghamshire was able to negotiate the vigorous challenge offered by the patriots during the 1777–8 session with reasonable comfort. Furthermore, the ratification of a measure of Catholic relief and the vote of a record amount of taxes permitted him to put a more positive gloss on the session than a close analysis of proceedings sustains.

One of the factors that helped the lord lieutenant in early 1778 was the conclusion of a treaty between France and the American colonies. However, privateer activity off the Irish coast and rumours of a planned French invasion in the summer of 1778 prompted the anxious protestant population to found volunteer corps to aid with the defence of the kingdom. The volunteers, as these corps were known, were entirely independent of government, and Buckinghamshire's attempt to establish a modicum of control over them by granting temporary commissions to the officers was repulsed. Irish resentment at the modest trade concessions agreed at Westminster in 1778 combined with the downturn in economic activity due to war gave rise to a non-importation campaign aimed at British goods and a powerful demand for the removal of restrictions on Ireland's right to trade with Britain and the

empire in 1779. Buckinghamshire appealed to London to be allowed to respond with commercial concessions when the Irish parliament met again in October 1779, but Lord North, whose preference was for a union, tergiversated, with the result that when MPs reassembled the lord lieutenant found he could not carry the House of Commons. His most difficult moments were the spectacular volunteer protest at College Green on 4 November and the Commons' refusal to sanction other than a six months' money bill. Compelled to agree with Buckinghamshire that the only option was concession, Lord North yielded 'free trade' and it was given legislative effect in 1780. Buckinghamshire was able only then to achieve a measure of control over the House of Commons and to defeat a number of motions on constitutional points in 1780, but his earlier failures and the general frailty of English government in Ireland under his leadership ensured that he was not to be allowed to remain in his Irish posting. He felt so 'slighted and insulted' (J. Hobart to Lord G. Germain, 2 Nov 1780, *Lothian MSS*, 375) by what he regarded as Lord North's mistreatment when news of his replacement was announced that he prepared a lengthy 'vindication' of his conduct during his time in Ireland (*Lothian MSS*). He had grounds in that North was both inattentive and inconsistent with his advice to him. At the same time it is clear that Buckinghamshire was ill-equipped personally and politically to cope with the difficulties he faced in Ireland. Subsequently he had to be content with a minor political role. He supported the Fox–North coalition in 1783 and opposed Pitt's Regency Bill in 1788–9. He was elected FSA on 1 April 1784.

Following the death of his first wife on 30 December 1769 Buckinghamshire married on 24 September 1770 Caroline Conolly (*c*.1755–1817), third daughter of William Conolly of Stratton Hall, Staffordshire, and Anne Wentworth. They had four children: three sons, all of whom died in infancy, and one daughter, Lady Amelia Anne, who survived together with the four daughters from his first marriage. Buckinghamshire died at his home, Blickling Hall, Norfolk, on 3 September 1793, aged seventy, and was buried in 1794 under the pyramidal mausoleum on the Blickling estate. He was succeeded by his brother George *Hobart, third earl of Buckinghamshire (1731–1804), politician. His youngest daughter, Lady Amelia Anne Hobart (*d.* 1829), married on 9 June 1794 Robert *Stewart, later second marquess of Londonderry, but better known as Viscount Castlereagh (1769–1822), politician.

JAMES KELLY

Sources NL Scot., Lothian MSS · *Report on the manuscripts of the marquess of Lothian*, HMC, 62 (1905) · BL, Mackintosh collection, Add. MS 34523 · NL Ire., Heron MSS · GEC, *Peerage* · A. Valentine, *Lord North*, 2 vols. (1967) · H. Butterfield, *George III, Lord North, and the people, 1779–80* (1949) · R. B. McDowell, *Ireland in the age of imperialism and revolution, 1760–1801* (1979) · Birr Castle, Birr, Offaly, Ireland, Rosse MSS · H. Grattan, *Memoirs of the life and times of the Rt Hon. Henry Grattan*, 5 vols. (1839–46) · *The correspondence of King George the Third from 1760 to December 1783*, ed. J. Fortescue, 6 vols. (1927–8) · *The correspondence of the Right Hon. John Beresford, illustrative of the last thirty years of the Irish parliament*, ed. W. Beresford, 2 vols. (1854) · Venn, *Alum. Cant.* · *Old Westminsters*, 1.465

Archives BL, account of Catherine the Great and her court, Add. MS 69091 · BL, corresp. and papers, Add. MSS 22358–22359 · Durham RO, executors' papers · NL Scot., corresp. and papers relating to Ireland · Norfolk RO, corresp. and papers | BL, corresp. with George Grenville, Add. MS 57812 · BL, letters to Lord Hardwicke, Add. MSS 35611–35615 · BL, corresp. with Lord Liverpool, Add. MSS 38216–38223, 38306–38310, *passim* · BL, corresp. with duke of Newcastle, etc., Add. MSS 32867–32960, *passim* · BL, corresp. with Lord Sandwich and R. Phelps, Stowe MSS 253–260, *passim* · BL, corresp. with Lady Suffolk, Add. MS 22629 · Hunt. L., letters to Lord Pery · NL Ire., Heron MSS · NMM, letters to Lord Sandwich · PRO NIre., letters to marquess of Downshire · U. Hull, Brynmor Jones L., Hotham MSS · U. Hull, Brynmor Jones L., letters to Sir Charles Hotham-Thompson
Likenesses F. Cotes, oils, 1766, Melbourne Hall, Derbyshire · Guericiffinoff, line engraving, 1766, BM, NPG · engraving, 1777, repro. in *Hibernian Magazine* (May 1777) · T. Gainsborough, oils, Blickling Hall, Norfolk [*see illus.*] · T. Gainsborough, oils, second version, North Carolina Museum of Art, Raleigh · line engraving, BM

Hobart, Sir Miles (1598/9–1632), politician, was the son of Miles Hobart of London and his third wife, Elizabeth. He was descended from William Hobart, brother of Henry VII's attorney-general Sir James Hobart. He matriculated from Queen's College, Oxford, on 30 June 1615, aged sixteen, and was admitted to Gray's Inn the following year. Knighted at Salisbury on 8 September 1623, when he was described as of Halford, Buckinghamshire, he sat for Marlow in the same county in the parliament of 1628–9.

There is no history of Hobart's having refused to pay the forced loan in 1626–8, but by 1629 he had become one of the group of activists led by Sir John Eliot and John Selden who staged a demonstration in the House of Commons on 2 March 1629. Their aim was to condemn religious change and unparliamentary taxation while preventing the dissolution or adjournment of parliament. During the tumultuous proceedings, as Eliot attempted to read a declaration stating their position while John Holles and Benjamin Valentine held the speaker down in his chair, Hobart locked the door of the house (the serjeant-at-arms having refused to do so) and pocketed the key. This was a significant act which committed Hobart visibly to the protest. It prevented the speaker or indeed any other member from leaving the chamber and the usher of the black rod from entering. The pretension of the house to adjourn itself at the conclusion of the protest was predicated on Hobart's action.

Hobart was one of nine members of the Commons arrested and interrogated after the session and whose recalcitrance encouraged the king's decision to dissolve the parliament. Hobart refused to give an account of his actions but did not deny having locked the door of the house. On 2 April he was sent close prisoner to the king's bench prison, and on 6 May he and five other of the prisoners sued for writs of habeas corpus, seeking bail. The petition of right (1628) could bear on the case and the cause of imprisonment notified by the crown was contempt and sedition. Hobart was also subject to the Star Chamber information filed by Sir Robert Heath, the attorney-general, which proceedings, answered by an appeal to parliamentary privilege, were later allowed to lapse. In May and June 1629 the habeas corpus arguments were heard in court and Hobart sensibly relied on Sir Edward Littleton's brief for Selden. On 23 June the prisoners were due to appear in court to be bailed, but the king subverted the authority of the law by placing them in the Tower of London where they languished throughout the summer. King Charles, in confronting a significant political and constitutional threat, sought to have the prisoners submit to his authority and legitimize his use of arbitrary imprisonment against them. The prisoners took out further writs for the first day of the Michaelmas term, and most refused a bond of good behaviour when brought before the judges in camera. In court on 5 October they again refused the bond—which would have amounted to an admission of guilt—and were remanded to prison. Hobart applied in vain for an alleviation of the conditions of his imprisonment. He was not tried with Eliot, Holles, and Valentine, the ringleaders in the parliamentary demonstration, but nevertheless chose to remain in prison for a further two years.

In 1631, at a time of plague, Hobart eventually gave the required sureties and was released. He died in a coaching accident in London on 29 June 1632 and was buried at Great Marlow on 4 July. On 18 January 1647 parliament voted £500 to erect a monument to him there. Hobart was not a prominent parliamentary speaker and is famed for his actions more than his words. He leaves the impression of a practical and principled individual who showed solidarity with his parliamentary associates in the face of royal wrath. The events in which Hobart participated in 1629–30 give him an enduring place in English history: they influenced Charles I in his eventual rejection of parliament and European war as well as revealing his inclination to arbitrary rule.

L. J. REEVE

Sources DNB · Foster, *Alum. Oxon.* · king's bench controlment roll, Hilary term, 1629, PRO, KB 29/278, mem. 33 · W. A. Shaw, *The knights of England*, 2 (1906), 182 · L. J. Reeve, *Charles I and the road to personal rule* (1989) · L. J. Reeve, 'The arguments in king's bench in 1629 concerning the imprisonment of John Selden and other members of the House of Commons', *Journal of British Studies*, 25 (1986), 264–87 · L. J. Reeve, 'The legal status of the petition of right', *HJ*, 29 (1986), 257–77 · J. Forster, *Sir John Eliot: a biography*, 2 vols. (1864) · S. R. Gardiner, *History of England from the accession of James I to the outbreak of the civil war*, 10 vols. (1883–4) · State trials · C. Russell, *Parliaments and English politics, 1621–1629* (1979) · R. P. Cust, *The forced loan and English politics, 1626–1628* (1987) · will, PRO, PROB 11/164, fol. 81
Likenesses marble bust on monument, c.1646–1647, All Saints' Church, Marlow, Buckinghamshire
Wealth at death see will, PRO, PROB 11/164, fol. 81

Hobart, Sir Percy Cleghorn Stanley (1885–1957), army officer and military reformer, was born in India, at Naini Tal, on 14 June 1885, the third son of Robert Thomson Hobart, of Dungannon, co. Tyrone, Ireland, a civil servant in India, and his wife, Janette (née Stanley), of Roughan Park, co. Tyrone. His sister Elizabeth (Betty) was married to Field Marshal Lord Montgomery. Hobart (pronounced Hubbert) was educated at Clifton College and the Royal Military Academy, Woolwich, and in 1904 he was commissioned into the Royal Engineers. He returned to India in 1906, having been posted to the 1st (later George V's own)

Sir Percy Cleghorn Stanley Hobart (1885–1957), by Elliott & Fry, 1952

sappers and miners. Hobart's regiment subscribed to a strict code of bachelorhood, and any officer who had the temerity to become engaged was required to resign. Hobart threw himself into regimental life with gusto: he played polo, and went pigsticking and big game hunting. He also pursued intellectual activities (which was not unusual in the engineers), dabbling in philosophy, art, and oriental mysticism. His first confidential report in 1906 declared, 'This officer is addicted to the reading of poetry' (Macksey, *Armoured Crusader*, 12). Hobart was an energetic and self-confident officer. He had first shown his initiative while serving as a staff captain on the Delhi durbar military staff (1911–12) when he promptly put out a fire, an action which gained him the personal thanks of King George V and the official thanks of the government of India.

After the outbreak of the First World War Hobart was posted to France in January 1915. He was awarded the MC at Neuve Chapelle in March, and on 1 September was appointed general staff officer, grade 3 (GSO3) on the staff of the 3rd (Lahore) division. This formation was transferred to Mesopotamia in January 1916, where Hobart served in aerial reconnaissance. His main duty was to sit in the observer's seat of a BE2C aircraft and sketch the enemy's positions, as at this time Mesopotamia completely lacked aerial cameras. In April 1916 he was awarded the DSO for his exploits after being wounded. On recovering, he was appointed brigade major of the 8th brigade on 12 December 1916. It was from this date that he

first began to display a streak of that reckless, self-righteous belief in his own rectitude that was to be his undoing. That Hobart was sometimes vindicated tended to increase rather than decrease his masterful zeal when ignoring the views of others. Nobody could deny Hobart's abilities or courage as a staff officer, however, and in October 1918 he was appointed GSO2 to the 53rd division, Egyptian expeditionary force. The end of the war meant that he had no job to do, and he became depressed, and briefly contemplated leaving the army, though this mood passed quickly. In 1919 he was appointed OBE.

From April to December 1919 Hobart passed through the Staff College, Camberley, on the first post-war staff course, and in 1921 he proceeded to active service on the north-west frontier. In 1922 he was posted, as GSO2 headquarters eastern command, to Naini Tal. The following year he joined the Royal Tank Corps (RTC). Although he had enjoyed no previous experience on the western front with armour, he showed all the zeal of a fairly late convert. In 1923–7 he was an instructor at the Staff College, Quetta, as a lieutenant-colonel, and received the brevet of colonel in 1928. He was second-in-command of 4th battalion RTC at Catterick (1927–30) where he quarrelled bitterly with his commanding officer, Lieutenant-Colonel M. C. Festing, whom he briefly outranked. His track record, despite his readiness to pick quarrels, was good but not brilliant. During these years, Hobart also threw down the gauntlet by challenging convention. Although the pre-1914 regimental strictures against marriage had been relaxed somewhat, Hobart became involved in an affair with the wife not only of a brother officer, but also one who had been a student in his syndicate (or seminar of officers, the assessment of whom was Hobart's prime responsibility) at Quetta. Without a moment's hesitation Hobart flouted these taboos. Dorothea Chater (*née* Dorothy Florence, daughter of Colonel Cyril Field, Royal Marines) was divorced by her husband in the summer of 1928, and she and Hobart were married on 21 November 1928. Affairs with other officers' wives were forbidden; to pursue the wife of an officer whom Hobart was teaching (and whose future promotion was in his hands) was considered a gross abuse of his authority.

After Hobart's successful tour of command of the 2nd battalion RTC at Farnborough (1931–3), the highest ranks of the army seemed open to him, despite his imprudent marriage. By the early 1930s he had become a close friend of the journalist and military reformer, Captain B. H. Liddell Hart, who used his not inconsiderable influence to advance Hobart's career. In 1933 he became inspector, the head of the RTC, and the following year he commanded the 1st tank brigade, his performance receiving glowing praise in Liddell Hart's columns in the *Daily Telegraph*. Hobart's abilities as a trainer of troops were acknowledged by all. But there was another side to Hobart's personality that Liddell Hart did not see, and failed to acknowledge. Hobart's zeal tended to become obsessive, his intolerance tyrannical, and his self-confidence degenerated into foul bad-temper when confronted or frustrated. It is ironic that this intellectually sophisticated officer and fascinating conversationalist, tended, when placed in a strictly hierarchical organization like the army, towards monomania and uncontrolled rages. Hobart had become on occasion a savage bully, and it took a very brave officer to stand up to him.

The 'advanced' thinking attributed to Hobart by earlier historians had been formulated and developed by more vital and original intellects than his, not least that of Major-General J. F. C. Fuller, as well as Liddell Hart. Hobart put their ideas into practice with unswerving faith. He was highly critical of the Cardwell system, which encouraged a rapid turn-over of poorly trained and inexperienced replacements for infantry battalions stationed in India; future armoured warfare, he argued, would demand highly trained and proficient soldiers. Moreover, the Cardwell system fixed officers' eyes on the horizons of regimental soldiering, making a shift in conceptual thinking difficult to achieve. Hobart believed in a responsive and centralized command system, and he deployed a small, advanced headquarters, which simultaneously communicated with the front line and the rear headquarters, by radio. His tactical prescriptions, however, are more controversial. He overrated the importance of mobility, neglected firepower, and exaggerated the importance of the resemblance of future armoured actions to naval battles. Some of the criticisms advanced by revisionist historians on his tactical views are justified, but not all.

Despite his radicalism Hobart gained the support of the conservative chief of the Imperial General Staff, Sir Archibald Montgomery-Massingberd. In 1937 Hobart became deputy director of staff duties (armoured fighting vehicles) at the War Office. Shortly afterwards he was appointed director of military training in the rank of major-general. The following year Hobart was posted to Egypt to command the mobile division being formed. This posting came as a relief to Hobart as he detested the bureaucratic routines of the War Office and the subtle demands of interregimental and corps politics for which he was temperamentally unsuited; the spirit of compromise was not his strong suit.

Hobart's dynamism made a favourable impression on his new subordinates, many of whom probably awaited his arrival with trepidation. He was determined to impose a professional ethos on his new division, and ensure that it would fight as a division, and not as a collection of units. Hobart succeeded in imposing his standards on what became the 7th armoured division, and that imprint was so firm that it lingered on long after he was no longer there to burnish it. Yet Hobart quarrelled over tactics with the commander of British troops in Egypt, Lieutenant-General Sir Robert Gordon-Finlayson. Hobart was intolerant and automatically dismissed any headquarters not under his command as incompetent, and invariably said so. Matters were made worse by Lady Gordon-Finlayson's refusal to invite Mrs Hobart to any social occasions. Gordon-Finlayson wrote an adverse confidential report on Hobart, claiming that he would be unsuitable for field

command in war. Such a claim was ridiculous, considering how many far less capable generals commanded divisions in the Second World War. Hobart's disagreements became especially acerbic with Gordon-Finlayson's successor, Henry Maitland Wilson, who objected to his 'all-tank' ideas and the 'excessive centralization of his command' (Harris, 99). Criticism of the former was probably sound; the latter was not. There was also a personal element to these disputes. Both of Hobart's bosses had been divisional colonels at Quetta's sister staff college at Camberley, and knew about his affair with Dorothea. Their criticisms of his professional conduct also reflected deep-seated distrust of his character and integrity. In November 1939 Wilson asked Wavell, the commander-in-chief, Middle East, for Hobart's removal, and he returned to England. He was retired on 9 March 1940.

Hobart's sacking should have been fatal to his career. He served as a corporal in the Home Guard in 1940, but he was plucked from obscurity by the prime minister, Winston Churchill. He was appointed to command the 11th armoured division (1941–2), and then in March 1943 the 79th armoured division. Hobart was ordered to develop specialized armour to facilitate the crossing of beaches, rivers, and other obstacles, based on the lessons of the ill-fated Dieppe raid of 1942. Hobart was also involved in other schemes concerning specialized armour, such as the canal defence light, designed to support night attacks with dazzling light. 79th armoured division made a vital contribution to the D-day landings and the campaigns in north-west Europe, though it provided units to support other attacking formations, and did not itself fight as a division.

Hobart was appointed CB in 1939 and KBE in 1943, and was finally retired in 1946. From 1947 to 1951 he was colonel commandant of the RTR (representative colonel commandant 1948–51), and from 1948 to 1953 lieutenant-governor of the Royal Hospital, Chelsea. He died at Farnham, Surrey, on 19 February 1957. He was survived by his wife and one daughter.   BRIAN HOLDEN REID

Sources K. Macksey, *Armoured crusader* (1967) · K. Macksey, 'Hobart', *Churchill's generals*, ed. J. Keegan (1991), 243–55 · J. P. Harris, 'Eclipse and revival of an armoured commander', *Fallen stars*, ed. B. Bond (1991), 86–106 · B. H. Liddell Hart, *The tanks: the history of the royal tank regiment and its predecessors*, 2 vols. (1959) · K. Macksey, *The tank pioneers* (1981) · private information (2004) · Burke, *Peerage* (1959) · *Army List* (1923) · CGPLA Eng. & Wales (1957)
Archives King's Lond., Liddell Hart C., corresp. with Sir B. H. Liddell Hart and papers | SOUND IWM SA, oral history interview
Likenesses E. Kennington, pastel drawings, *c.*1944, Tank Museum, Wareham, Dorset · Elliott & Fry, photograph, 1952, NPG [*see illus.*] · W. Stoneman, photograph, 1952, NPG
Wealth at death £10,165 12s. 0d.: probate, 17 June 1957, CGPLA Eng. & Wales

Hobart, Robert, fourth earl of Buckinghamshire (1760–1816), politician, was born on 6 May 1760, second but first surviving son among the four sons and four daughters of George *Hobart, third earl of Buckinghamshire (1731–1804), politician, of Nocton, Lincolnshire, and his wife, Albinia Bertie (1737/8–1816), elder daughter and coheir of Lord Vere Bertie [see Hobart, Albinia, under Hobart,

Robert Hobart, fourth earl of Buckinghamshire (1760–1816), by John Hoppner, c.1800

George]. His parents resided at Nocton from 1766. His surname was then pronounced 'Hubberd'. As a boy he performed in plays produced for select audiences by his mother and, like his father, he became a patron of opera and theatre in his adult life. He entered Westminster School in 1770 and after enlisting as ensign in the 59th foot proceeded in 1776 to Strasbourg military academy for a year. He subsequently served in North America, becoming a captain in the 30th foot in 1778, and major in the 18th light dragoons in 1783. He returned from service in 1784 on becoming aide-de-camp to the lord lieutenant of Ireland; subsequently he was made inspector-general of recruits in Ireland. He was a supporter of the ministry, as he assured Pitt in 1788 when aspiring to a lieutenant-colonelcy, though his father leaned to opposition. He sat in the Dublin parliament for Portarlington from 1784 to 1790 and Armagh from 1790 to 1797, where he was mocked for his affected lisp. He was also by-elected to Westminster as member of parliament for Bramber on 15 December 1788 and was returned, after a contest, in 1790 for Lincoln, a seat for which he had been recommended four years before. His parliamentary career, however, was confined largely to Dublin, especially when in 1789 he was appointed chief secretary to the lord lieutenant and sworn on 21 April an Irish privy councillor. Lord Buckingham valued him for having 'quickness, parts and the most intimate knowledge of every man in Ireland' (Fortescue MSS, 1.428). On 4 or 5 January 1792 he married Margaretta Adderley (d. 1796), daughter of Edmund Burke of Corry and widow of Thomas Adderley of Inishannon, co. Cork,

an Irish member of parliament. Lady Holland, in reporting his honourable conduct in so doing, described him as 'pleasing, sensible and well-looking, the finest teeth imaginable' (Holland, 1.236). The couple had a son, who died young, and a daughter, Sarah, the future countess of Ripon.

Although Hobart acquired a reputation for a convivial personality in Irish government circles, his parliamentary performance in Dublin was less convincing. In the 1790–91 session he failed to answer the oppositionist Henry Grattan's charge that over a third of the 300 members were in the pay of the government. He refused to accept a petition for enfranchisement from the Catholic Committee at the end of the session; however, no member was willing to present it either. He had nevertheless to come to terms with the British government's wishes, as expressed by Pitt and Henry Dundas, for concessions to be made to the Irish Catholics. During visits to London in November 1791 and April 1792, as well as in correspondence in the interim, he defended the protestant ascendancy in Ireland and, supported in 1792 by Sir John Parnell, persuaded ministers temporarily that, if withstood, the Catholics would back down. Richard Burke, Hobart's former schoolfellow, tried to dissuade him from this role, which caused his father, Edmund Burke, to write off Hobart as a stooge of the ascendancy establishment. A cosmetic Relief Bill, affecting just a few of the Catholic disabilities, was substituted.

On 27 April 1792 Hobart spoke at Westminster in favour of abolition of the slave trade, but three days later disparaged parliamentary reform, particularly in Ireland. Despite his warnings that the Irish administration would be undermined by such a measure, and the lord lieutenant the earl of Westmorland's attempts to dissuade the British ministers, Hobart was by them compelled to introduce a comprehensive Catholic Relief Bill in the Dublin parliament, on 4 February 1793. London insisted on this as a concomitant to the Irish Militia Bill intended to raise Catholic as well as protestant recruits to replace the British regiments being withdrawn from Ireland now that war against revolutionary France had started. Hobart consoled himself with the reflection that, at least on the continent, Catholicism was a crippled creed, but the thrust of the debate on the principle of concession lay rather with the argument that protestants and Catholics, as property owners, should unite against the threat presented by the French Revolution. The bill, though mauled in detail, was carried in five weeks, and so was the Militia Bill. Hobart, sworn of the British privy council on 1 May, was cock-a-hoop, and proposed at the end of the session to induce leading Irish oppositionists to coalesce with government. In October he was named governor of Madras, and dismissed a vengeful letter from Richard Burke on his dereliction of Ireland as downright insanity. When he left Dublin in December he was assured that he might eventually become governor-general of Bengal, and obtained the reversionary grant of the Irish clerkship of the common pleas in exchequer. At Westminster he defended the Irish administration on 8 April 1794, before leaving for India.

He did not vacate his seat before the dissolution, and later maintained an interest in Lincoln elections.

Hobart took over at Fort St George on 7 September 1794. His government began with a personally conducted expedition to Malacca which destroyed the Dutch settlements, but subsequent developments were less favourable to him. The death of Mohammed Ali, nawab of the Carnatic, soon after his arrival prompted Hobart to propose fiscal reforms there conducive to the relief of the oppressed peasantry. The new nawab opposed this policy by reference to a treaty of 1792 which had the assent of the former governor-general, Cornwallis. Recognizing this agreement as his chief obstacle, Hobart proposed, without consulting Sir John Shore, the current governor-general, to seize Tinnevelly as compensation for the nawab's debts to the East India Company. Shore objected to this as being contrary to treaty. After an appeal to the company's court of directors in London, the eventual decision went in favour of Shore, and Hobart's recall was ordered. Meanwhile Hobart had placed himself in similar jeopardy by extracting a surrender of territory from the raja of Tanjore in satisfaction of his debts to the company. Shore objected to this treaty as an exercise of *force majeure*, but this time the court of directors sided with Hobart. Shore was by his own admission better advised by Hobart when the latter refused to back Shore's projected expedition against Spanish Manila, and he ceased to regard Hobart as an unsuitable successor. This prospect, however, was marred by the arrival of the court of directors' order on the Carnatic appeal. Hobart, whose wife had died in Madras on 7 August 1796, left in August 1798, complimented on his services. Later he was credited with having laid the ground for the campaign against Tipu in Mysore. The company awarded him a pension of £1500 a year in view of his disappointed expectation of the governor-generalship; he might have received more, but in May 1798, he had succeeded to his sinecure Irish clerkship for life. He also had hopes of a peerage, but failing this was summoned to the Lords in his father's barony of Hobart on 30 November 1798. In the Lords he supported Pitt's proposals for Irish union, assisting William *Eden, first Baron Auckland, in drawing up details. He remained hostile to an accompanying measure of Catholic relief, though he accepted a state subsidy for the Catholic clergy. On 1 June 1799 he married the daughter of Auckland and his wife, Eleanor Eliot, Eleanor Agnes Eden (1777–1851), whom her father had intended to become Pitt's wife. They had no children, but Hobart's illegitimate son, Sir Henry *Ellis, was brought up in their household.

Suitable employment for Hobart had become problematic. He was considered as a possible envoy to Russia, but preferred domestic office, especially as neither the governor-general nor the East India Company board were prepared to reinstate him in India. In March 1801 Pitt's successor, Addington, gratified him by appointing him (as second choice) secretary for war, adding to his duties in July by transferring charge of the colonies to him from the Home Office. In August 1803 his circular curbing the proliferating volunteer militias was not well received, and

when Pitt, whose consent to his accession to the cabinet in 1801 he had sought, returned to power in 1804 he lost his office and declined the compensatory captaincy of the yeomen of the guard. He was, however, immortalized in the naming of the new town of Hobart in Van Diemen's Land.

On 14 November 1804 Hobart succeeded his father in the earldom. In January 1805 he returned to office as chancellor of the duchy of Lancaster, as part of Addington's uneasy reconciliation with the premier; this gave him a cabinet seat again. In July, however, he resigned with his chief over Lord Melville's naval administration: he had hoped to succeed Melville to the Admiralty. He nevertheless visited Pitt on his deathbed. It was he who induced Addington, by then Lord Sidmouth, to adhere to the Grenville administration in January 1806, and he himself became joint postmaster-general, though without a seat in the cabinet, to his disappointment. Resident at this time at Derby House, St James's Square, of which his father had been a tenant, he was a member of White's Club from 1805. On the dismissal of Grenville in 1807 he was left without office until April 1812 when the new premier, Lord Liverpool, made him president of the Board of Control for India and, for two months only, chancellor of the duchy of Lancaster. On 9 April 1813 he vindicated the renewal of the East India Company charter in the Lords. He retained his presidency until his death on 4 February 1816 in Hamilton Place, London, which followed a fall from his horse in St James's Park some time before. He was buried at Nocton and succeeded in the title by his nephew George Robert Hobart, fifth earl of Buckinghamshire.   ROLAND THORNE

Sources DNB · GEC, *Peerage* · HoP, *Commons* · Bucks. RLSS · *Collins peerage of England: genealogical, biographical and historical*, ed. E. Brydges, 9 vols. (1812), vol. 4, p. 372 · *The manuscripts of J. B. Fortescue*, 10 vols., HMC, 30 (1892–1927), vol. 1, p. 428 · *The journal of Elizabeth, Lady Holland, 1791–1811*, ed. earl of Ilchester [G. S. Holland Fox-Strangways], 2 vols. (1908), vol. 1, p. 236 · T. Bartlett, *The fall and rise of the Irish nation: the Catholic question, 1690–1830* (1992) · K. K. Datta and others, eds., *Fort William–India House correspondence*, 13 (1959) · J. Ehrman, *The younger Pitt*, 3: *The consuming struggle* (1996) · F. Hill, *Georgian Lincoln* (1966), 10–11, 96 · GM, 1st ser., 86/1 (1816), 279–80 · *Old Westminsters*, 1.465

Archives BL OIOC, Home misc. series, corresp. and papers relating to India · Bucks. RLSS, corresp. and papers; papers as governor of Madras · University of Minnesota, Ames Library of South Asia, papers relating to India | BL, letters to Lord Hardwicke, Add. MSS 35644–35673, *passim* · BL, corresp. with Lord Wellesley, Add. MSS 37282–37310, *passim* · BL OIOC, letters to Sir Evan Nepean, MS Eur B 25 · Bucks. RLSS, corresp. with Scrope Bernard · Hunt. L., letters to Grenville family · Mount Stuart Trust, archives, letters to Lord Hastings · NAM, corresp. with Sir George Nugent · NL Scot., letters to Lord Melville · NL Scot., corresp. with first earl of Minto · priv. coll., letters to Lord Hastings · PRO, corresp. with Lord Cornwallis · PRO NIre., corresp. with Lord Castlereagh · PRO NIre., letters to Lord Hillsborough · Royal Arch., letters to George III · U. Southampton L., corresp. with Arthur Wellesley · Worcs. RO, letters to Lord Coventry

Likenesses T. Lawrence, oils, *c*.1795, Marlborough House, London · J. Grozer, mezzotint, 1796 (after T. Lawrence, 1795), BM, Marlborough House, London · J. Hoppner, oils, *c*.1800, priv. coll. [see illus.] · J. Gillray, caricature, 1801, BM · W. W. Barney, mezzotint, pubd 1806 (after W. Beechey), BM, NPG · W. Richardson, engraving, 1808 (after T. Lawrence, 1795) · R. Dunkarton, mezzotint (after T. Lawrence, 1795), BM · T. Lawrence, oils, National Gallery of Victoria, Melbourne, Australia

Hobart, Vere Henry, Lord Hobart (1818–1875), administrator in India, was born on 8 December 1818 at Welbourne, Lincolnshire, the eldest son of Augustus Edward Hobart, from 1878 Hobart-Hampden, sixth earl of Buckinghamshire (1793–1885), and his first wife, Mary (d. 1825), daughter of John Williams, serjeant-at-law; his brother, Augustus Charles Hobart-*Hampden, was a naval officer and adviser to the Turkish fleet. Vere studied under Dr Mayo at Cheam School, Surrey, and in 1836 won an open scholarship to Trinity College, Oxford, where he graduated in 1840 with a second in classics.

In March 1842 Hobart took up a clerkship procured for him in the Board of Trade by Lord Ripon and later the same year accompanied Sir Henry Ellis as secretary on a diplomatic mission to Brazil. In 1849, on his father's accession to the earldom, he took the courtesy title of Lord Hobart. In 1853 he married Mary Catherine (d. 1914), daughter of Thomas Carr, a former bishop of Bombay. They were a close couple and throughout their married life Hobart rehearsed his many political theories and proposals with his wife prior to placing them before the public.

Hobart took a keen interest in the anti-cornlaw movement and, although from a protectionist background, by 1845 he had swung round to an unflinching belief in free trade and minimal government. In 1850, frustrated in his parliamentary ambitions by a lack of money, he began to publish political articles, initially on Irish topics. He bemoaned the expenditure on public works during the famine as a criminal waste of capital and argued that Ireland's problems lay in under-development, not overpopulation. Much of his writing was designed to show how a proper application of the laws of political economy could ease pauperism. For example, in 1853 he published a pamphlet urging the introduction of limited liability for companies, arguing that such legislation would aid the productive deployment of capital and nurture co-operative societies. A collection of these writings appeared in 1866 under the title *Political Essays*.

In 1854 Hobart became private secretary to Sir George Grey, then colonial secretary, but resigned the post early the next year in order to be able to protest against the Crimean War. In a striking letter to *The Times* of 22 February 1855 he called upon the government to resist the humbug of public opinion and pull back from its over-proud and un-Christian attempt to humiliate Russia.

In 1861–2 Hobart was dispatched on a Foreign Office mission to investigate the condition of Turkish finances, a labyrinthine undertaking in which he himself had little faith. In 1863 he resigned his Board of Trade clerkship and shortly thereafter returned to Constantinople as director-general of the Ottoman Bank. In 1872 the Gladstone government appointed him governor of Madras.

Inevitably Hobart was too radical for the Madras civil service and his term in office was marked by controversy.

A devout Protestant, he had nevertheless long advocated religious tolerance and the abolition of the established church. In Madras his tolerance manifested itself as a desire to treat all religions even-handedly and in particular to counteract the under-representation of Muslims in government employment, a policy which led to accusations in the civil service and press that he was naïvely pro-Muslim. He was determined to expand elementary education but without increasing taxation and therefore proposed reallocating the government's existing income to give more weight to education. The government of India, however, refused to sanction any tampering with established heads of expenditure. Hobart was similarly defeated in his attempts to raise funds for major sanitary works, but he did win India Office approval for the construction of a harbour at Madras, and on this score even his critics were loud in their praise.

Hobart died suddenly, at Government House, Madras, of typhoid fever on 27 April 1875 and was buried in St Mary's Church, Fort St George. In 1885 Lady Hobart, who was created CI for her charitable work in India, published her late husband's *Essays and Miscellaneous Writings*, prefacing them with a biographical sketch. They had had no surviving children and in 1879 she married, secondly, Charles Coates of Bath. She died in 1914.

N. D. F. PEARCE, *rev.* KATHERINE PRIOR

Sources *Essays and miscellaneous writings by Vere Henry, Lord Hobart*, ed. M. Hobart, 2 vols. (1885) · *Charivari's album* (1875) · *The Times* (29 April 1875), 5 · Burke, *Peerage* (1959) · J. C. Sainty, ed., *Officials of the board of trade, 1660–1870* (1974) · J. J. Cotton, *List of inscriptions on tombs or monuments in Madras possessing historical or archaeological interest* (1905) · *List of statues, monuments and busts erected in Madras in honour of distinguished servants of the state* (1898) · GEC, *Peerage* · *CGPLA Eng. & Wales* (1875)
Archives Bucks. RLSS, corresp. and papers | BL, Gladstone MSS · Hatfield House, Hertfordshire, Salisbury MSS [a microfilm of these is available at BL OIOC] · NRA Scotland, priv. coll., letters to duke of Argyll
Likenesses group portrait, photograph, c.1872, BL OIOC · group portrait, photograph, c.1874, BL OIOC · M. Noble, bust, c.1875, St Mary's Church, Fort St George, Madras; replica Chepank Park, Senate Hall, Madras: now probably removed · photograph, repro. in Hobart, ed., *Essays and miscellaneous writings*, 1, frontispiece
Wealth at death £40,000: administration with will, 25 June 1875, *CGPLA Eng. & Wales*

Hobbes, John Oliver. *See* Craigie, Pearl (1867–1906).

Hobbes, Robert (d. 1538), abbot of Woburn, is of unknown origins, and nothing can be said of his life before he became abbot of the Cistercian abbey of Woburn in 1524. On 27 January 1530 he obtained a royal licence for the abbey to hold two annual fairs in the town, and on 5 April 1532 he was one of the 'general reformers' commissioned by the king to hold a visitation of the whole Cistercian order; in that capacity he was present at the investigation into the misconduct of John Chascombe, abbot of Bruern, Oxfordshire.

In 1534 Hobbes acknowledged the royal supremacy and persuaded the more reluctant members of his abbey to do likewise. Soon, however, influenced by the martyrdom of the London Carthusians and by the suppression of the lesser monasteries in 1536, Hobbes significantly altered his position, declaring in January 1538 that 'The Bysshop of Rome's Auctorite is good and lawful within this Realme accordyng to the old trade, and that is the true waye. And the contrary of the kynges parte but usurpacion disceyved by flattery and adulacion' (Scott Thompson, 137). He may also have been encouraged by the appointment of James Prestwich, a staunch conservative in religion, to be schoolmaster to the small group of royal wards then boarding in the abbey. Although several monks sympathized with Hobbes's stance, notably the sub-prior, Ralph Barnes, and the sexton, Laurence Blunham, others were opposed to his views, and in the spring of 1538 he was reported to Cromwell by William Sherburne, curate of the parish chapel and a former friar with whom Hobbes had had various disagreements. Cromwell acted quickly, dispatching William Petre and John Williams in May to take depositions, and on 14 June Hobbes, the sub-prior, and the sexton were tried at Woburn. Barnes and Blunham recanted but it appears that Hobbes held firm, although in some places it is difficult to establish an exact meaning from the long and rambling depositions of a man physically ill from strangury, and to disentangle apologies for bluntness of speech from repentance on points of principle. It is certain, however, that to the very end he remained opposed to the suppression of the monasteries, the distribution of 'wretched heretic books' by Cromwell, and the royal divorce, all sufficient to make his conviction a formality. Indeed, he confessed his offences and offered no defence. Along with his two colleagues Hobbes was shortly afterwards hanged, drawn, and quartered and the abbey confiscated by attainder. According to local tradition an oak tree in the abbey grounds served as the gallows.

Despite the account by John Stow and the much later versions by James Froude and Francis Gasquet of the events leading to his execution, it is clear that Hobbes was no political radical and took no part in the northern rising of 1536, as Stow mistakenly believed. On the contrary he was simply a conservative in religion and an able administrator of his abbey (it is significant that no charge of mismanagement or misconduct was brought against him) who opposed the destruction of the monasteries.

NICHOLAS DOGGETT

Sources D. Knowles [M. C. Knowles], *The religious orders in England*, 3 (1959), 72, 373–6 · *VCH Bedfordshire*, 1.367–70 · G. Scott Thompson, 'Woburn Abbey and the dissolution of the monasteries', *TRHS*, 4th ser., 16 (1933), 129–60 · *LP Henry VIII*, 4, no. 6047; 10, no. 1239; 13/1, nos. 955–6, 981 · A. H. Thompson, ed., *Visitations in the diocese of Lincoln, 1517–1531*, 2, Lincoln RS, 35 (1944), 215–17 · Dugdale, *Monasticon*, new edn, 5.478 · S. Dodd, *An historical and topographical account of the town of Woburn, its abbey and vicinity* (1818), 38 · F. A. Gasquet, *Henry VIII and the English monasteries* (1906), 283–90 · J. A. Froude, *Short studies on great subjects*, 1 (1878), 430–41 · J. Stow and E. Howes, *The annales, or, Generall chronicle of England … unto the ende of the present yeere, 1614* (1615), 573 · S. Brigden and N. Wilson, 'New learning and broken friendship', *EngHR*, 112 (1997), 396–411

Hobbes, Thomas (1588–1679), philosopher, was born on 5 April 1588 in Westport, a parish of the town of Malmesbury, Wiltshire, the second of the three children of

Thomas Hobbes (1588–1679), by John Michael Wright, c.1669–70

Thomas Hobbes, curate, and his wife, Catherine, *née* Middleton.

Family and childhood Hobbes's father belonged to a prosperous family of Malmesbury clothiers. An Edmund Hobbes, probably the philosopher's great-uncle, became 'alderman' (mayor) of the town in 1600; a William Hobbes, possibly Edmund's brother, was also a prominent clothier. Francis Hobbes, the elder brother of Hobbes's father, was a successful glover and, being childless himself, took a special interest in his brother's children, supporting Hobbes's education at Oxford and entering Hobbes's elder brother, Edmund, in his own trade. Of Hobbes's mother's family nothing is known, except that John Aubrey described it as 'a yeomanly family' of Brokenborough—the parish, just to the north-west of Malmesbury, of which Hobbes's father was curate (*Brief Lives*, 1.323).

Hobbes's father may well have depended financially on his relatives, as his own career in the Church of England was a peculiarly inglorious one. His curacy, Brokenborough, was one of the poorest livings in the district; he appears not to have had a university education, which must have limited his prospects; and in December 1602 he was brought before the archdeacon's court 'for want of quarter sermons and for not catechisinge the younge' (Wilts. & Swindon RO, archdeaconry of Wiltshire act books, office, 1, fol. 132v). In the following year he was accused of slandering Richard Jeane, the vicar of a nearby parish, and required to make a public act of penitence in Jeane's church; he failed to do this, and also failed to pay the fine of 33s. 3d. which was subsequently levied on him.

As a result he was formally excommunicated. One Saturday morning in February 1604 he came across Richard Jeane in the churchyard of Malmesbury Abbey, shouted abuse, and then physically assaulted him (Wilts. & Swindon RO, episcopal deposition book, instance, 22b, fols. 48v–49r). Violence against a clergyman was a serious offence, liable to corporal punishment. According to Aubrey, who knew several members of Hobbes's family, Thomas Hobbes senior 'was forcd to fly for it' and died 'in obscurity beyound London' (*Brief Lives*, 1.387). His date of death is unknown, and, indeed, after his assault on Jeane he disappears from the records entirely.

By this time Hobbes was already at Oxford. His early education had taken place in Westport and Malmesbury; particularly influential was the teaching of a young clergyman, Robert Latimer, who had just graduated from Magdalen Hall, Oxford. Latimer (who was vicar of Westport, and took over the curacy of Brokenborough after the departure of Hobbes's father) was a fine classicist, and gave Hobbes a good grounding in Latin and Greek. He later also taught the young John Aubrey; this connection was one reason for Aubrey's special interest in Hobbes, which would eventually bear fruit in his valuable compilation of biographical information about him, on which all modern accounts of Hobbes's life depend.

Oxford Probably because of Latimer's advice or connections, Hobbes was entered at Magdalen Hall, Oxford. His precise date of matriculation is not known; in his autobiography he wrote that it was in his fourteenth year (that is, between April 1601 and April 1602) but Aubrey dated it to 'the beginning of an. 1603' (*Brief Lives*, 1.330). The latter date seems plausible, as Hobbes himself recorded that he stayed at Oxford for five years, and it is known that he was admitted BA in February 1608. In the late sixteenth and early seventeenth centuries Magdalen Hall had a reputation as a stronghold of puritanism—a reputation enhanced by the appointment of John Wilkinson, a strict Calvinist divine, as principal in 1605. Hobbes's familiarity with Calvinist theology (evident in his later controversies with John Bramhall) may well have been acquired during his Oxford years.

In his autobiographical writings Hobbes gave a very jaundiced account of his Oxford education, complaining that it consisted mainly of learning the barbarisms of scholastic Aristotelianism. There was some justice in this charge: there had been a definite revival of Aristotelianism at Oxford in the final decades of the sixteenth century, and modern anti-Aristotelian movements, such as Ramism in logic, had made only limited progress there. But Aristotelity, as Hobbes later called it, did not loom as large in the Oxford curriculum as it did in his retrospective complaints. Undergraduate studies were fundamentally humanist, involving wide reading among classical authors on rhetoric, moral philosophy, and history—an accomplishment clearly discernible in Hobbes's later writings. Many fellows of Oxford colleges also took an active interest in new developments in mathematics and the physical sciences. When Hobbes states in his verse autobiography that, instead of studying the prescribed texts, he preferred to look at maps of the earth and the heavens, he gives the impression that geography and astronomy were excluded from university studies; this is not correct. Unfortunately it is not known whether he had any contact with established Oxford scientists. All that can be deduced from the surviving evidence is that astronomy was one of Hobbes's earliest intellectual enthusiasms—a point confirmed by his own account, in his manuscript refutation of Thomas White, of his careful observation of a comet that appeared in 1618.

Early employment and first European tour After being admitted BA in February 1608 and completing the requirements for 'determination' in arts during the following term, Hobbes was recommended for the post of tutor to William Cavendish. William's father, Baron Cavendish of Hardwick, was one of the major landowners of Derbyshire, with estates centred on Hardwick Hall and (from 1616) Chatsworth. The choice of such a young graduate as a tutor—Hobbes was only two years older than his pupil—was unusual; the idea, apparently, was to provide intellectual companionship as much as formal pedagogy. At the same time, the fact that Hobbes was recommended by the Magdalen Hall authorities suggests that he was regarded as both morally and theologically sound. His pupil had real intellectual abilities, but was little interested in academic studies; he spent some time at St John's College, Cambridge (where Hobbes joined him in the summer of 1608 and incorporated as a Cambridge BA), but left the university in November 1608.

In his verse autobiography Hobbes described his time with William Cavendish—who was knighted in 1609, became Lord Cavendish on his father's elevation to the earldom of Devonshire in 1618, and succeeded him as second earl in 1626—as 'by far the sweetest period of my life'; he noted that his pupil became not so much a master as a friend, allowing Hobbes both leisure and whatever sorts of books he needed for his studies (*Opera philosophica*, 1.lxxxvii–lxxxviii). These comments probably relate more to the latter part of his service to Cavendish, who came to treat him as a secretary and companion. The early years of his employment may sometimes have tried the patience of this young graduate, who, according to Aubrey, was treated as 'his lordship's page, and rode a hunting and hawking with him, and kept his privy purse' (*Brief Lives*, 1.330–31). As Cavendish was a notorious spendthrift, the responsibility for his purse was onerous, involving frequent meetings with creditors. At the same time, however, Hobbes's page-like duties would have brought him into contact with the Anglo-Scottish courtier society of Jacobean London. (Cavendish married the daughter of a prominent Scot and royal political agent, Lord Bruce of Kinross.) But Cavendish also had literary interests, including an evident passion for Bacon's *Essayes*, and in 1611 he published an extended essay of his own, *A Discourse Against Flatterie*; it can be assumed that Hobbes was involved (at the very least secretarially) in the preparation of this work.

The household accounts of Cavendish's father mention a number of books purchased during the period 1609–13, presumably for Cavendish's studies with Hobbes: these included works by Plutarch, Cicero, Ramus, Montaigne, Huarte, Bacon, Keckermann, and Botero, as well as 'iii of the kinges bookes in defence of the othe of allegiance' (Hardwick MS 29, pp. 91, 219b, 303, 316, 355). The same source also reveals that Hobbes co-operated with the surveyor William Senior in his mapping of the Cavendish estates—which suggests that Hobbes had, or acquired, at least some practical knowledge of geometry at this early stage (ibid., p. 128, entry for April 1610).

Also listed among the books purchased were several primers and dictionaries of French and Italian, evidently in preparation for a continental tour. The traditional dating of this tour, 1610–15, given in most biographies of Hobbes, is incorrect; the household accounts show that Hobbes and Cavendish left in June 1614 and returned by October 1615 (Hardwick MS 29, pp. 371, 453). Their main destination was Venice; from there they made a trip to Rome in October 1614, returning to stay in Venice until the summer of 1615. Here Cavendish worked hard on his Italian, translating Bacon's *Essayes* into that language—once again, presumably, with Hobbes at his side. He also met the most influential intellectual in Venice, Paolo Sarpi, a man of wide scientific interests, suspected of protestant sympathies or even atheistic tendencies, who as 'state theologian' had defended Venice during its great dispute with the papacy in 1606. Cavendish (and, it may be assumed, Hobbes) cultivated the acquaintance of Sarpi's assistant Fulgenzio Micanzio, and Cavendish began corresponding with him during their return journey, via Paris, to England.

Secretarial employment (to 1628) The correspondence with Micanzio continued for thirteen years, being ended only by Cavendish's death. Only Micanzio's letters have survived, in English translations by Hobbes. These were made, evidently, not for Cavendish (who knew Italian well) but for circulation to other readers, who might be interested not only in Micanzio's detailed political news but also in his thinking about foreign policy (which aimed at a strategic anti-papal and anti-Spanish alliance). Micanzio took a special interest in the Croatian-Venetian churchman Marc' Antonio de Dominis, archbishop of Split, who fled to England in 1616, joined the Anglican church, supervised the publication in London of Sarpi's *Historia del concilio tridentino*, and published a major anti-papal treatise of his own, *De republica ecclesiastica*. In 1617–18 de Dominis helped to revise Cavendish's Italian translation of Bacon's *Essayes* for publication, and therefore probably came into direct contact with Hobbes. Admiration for Bacon united Cavendish, Micanzio, and de Dominis; Micanzio's letters show that Cavendish was in personal contact with Bacon from 1616 onwards, and Hobbes is known to have visited Bacon on the legal business of the Cavendish family in 1619 and 1620. Aubrey records that Hobbes also did secretarial work for Bacon, taking dictation from him and translating some of his essays into Latin; biographers have traditionally assumed that this work took place after Bacon's fall from office in 1621, but it

is now clear that Hobbes's connections with Bacon predated that event by several years.

Another sign of Cavendish's admiration for Bacon was his composition of a collection of essays of his own, published (anonymously) in 1620, under the title *Horae subsecivae*. The volume also contained his *Discourse Against Flatterie* and three other discourses: a description of Rome (arising from Cavendish's visit there with Hobbes in 1614), 'Discourse upon the beginning of Tacitus', and 'Discourse of lawes'. A fair copy manuscript of the essays (but not the discourses) in Hobbes's hand survives at Chatsworth; this demonstrates that he was not the author of the essays, as his occasional misreadings of the text he was copying are corrected in manuscript by another hand. However, a recent 'wordprint' analysis has suggested that the three new discourses printed in 1620 have the characteristics of Hobbes's own prose, and can therefore be attributed to him (*Three Discourses*, esp. 10–19). This claim has not been universally accepted by Hobbes scholars. Nevertheless, even if Hobbes's role in the preparation of these texts was little more than that of a sounding board, secretary, or stylistic improver, they must constitute important evidence of the cultural and political attitudes to which he was most directly exposed at this time. Particularly striking are the coolly political analysis of religion, the Tacitean emphasis on the role of interest and the value of dissimulation in political affairs, and the stress laid on the special evil of anarchy and civil war.

Cavendish himself had some experience of politics: he was a member of the parliaments of 1610, 1614, 1621, and 1624, and it can be assumed that Hobbes would have followed the debates in which he took part. More importantly, Hobbes was also associated with his master's activities in two trading and colonizing companies, the Virginia Company and the Somers Islands Company. Hobbes was granted a share in the former in 1622; the precise date at which he joined the latter (which dealt with the Bermudas) is not known. Between 1622 and 1624 Hobbes attended thirty-seven meetings of the governing body of the Virginia Company; there he must have encountered prominent politicians and writers such as Sir Edwin Sandys, Sir Dudley Digges, and John Selden. Both as an assistant to Cavendish and in his own right, Hobbes was thus involved in public or quasi-public affairs; it is significant that in the first surviving item of his own correspondence, a letter to him from a Cambridge don, Robert Mason, in 1622, he is treated as a well-placed source of social and political gossip.

In 1626 Cavendish succeeded his father as second earl of Devonshire. His tendency to lavish spending was now unchecked, and, given his literary interests, it is likely that he was an active and generous patron of other writers. These may have included Ben Jonson, with whom, according to Aubrey, Hobbes was well acquainted by 1628. Cavendish's patronage certainly extended to the physician and minor poet Dr Richard Andrews, a friend of Donne (and of Jonson), who visited him in Derbyshire; in August 1627 Cavendish, Andrews, and Hobbes went on a tour of the Derbyshire Peak District, visiting the so-called 'wonders of the Peak'. Travelogue poems celebrating this tour were written by Andrews (in English) and Hobbes (in Latin), and Hobbes's work later received a small, undated printing (probably in 1636), under the title *De mirabilibus pecci*.

Before the composition of that poem Hobbes had probably already completed a much more significant work: a complete translation of Thucydides, taken (unlike the only existing English version at the time) directly from the Greek. In his verse autobiography Hobbes explained that Thucydides was his favourite ancient historian; what apparently attracted him was the cool dissection of political motivation and the 'realist' approach to power, together with the peculiarly Thucydidean analysis of the role of rhetoric in political debate. This translation was an important achievement, establishing Hobbes at a stroke as one of the leading Grecianists of his day. Hobbes also drew the elaborate map of ancient Greece which accompanied the text. Possibly he had planned to add further materials of his own; otherwise it is not clear why he did not hasten to publish the work, eventually remarking in the preface: 'After I had finished it, it lay long by me' (*English Works*, 8.ix). In the end, the catalyst for its publication was the sudden death of his pupil–patron in summer 1628. By November Hobbes had prepared the dedication (a eulogy of the late second earl, addressed to his young son), and was nervously clearing it with the dowager countess: no doubt he hoped that such a public monument to his former employer would earn her approval and guarantee his re-employment. The book was published in early 1629; Hobbes was not, however, re-employed.

Second European tour; tuition of the third earl Hobbes spent much of 1629 and 1630 in the service of a Nottinghamshire landowner, Sir Gervase Clifton, escorting his son Gervase on a European tour. The reason for this temporary departure from the Cavendish family is not clear; the dowager countess was making what savings she could, but she still needed a tutor for her two sons (aged twelve and nine in 1629), and did indeed employ one. Possibly Hobbes had hoped to carry on working as secretary and librarian, and was reluctant to teach at such an elementary level; his new pupil, Gervase Clifton, was aged seventeen or eighteen. On the other hand, although a later memorandum drawn up by Hobbes stated that he was 'discharged' after the death of the second earl (Hobbes MS D.6, fol. 2r), he was still receiving a half-yearly payment from the dowager countess as late as June 1630. So perhaps his service to the Cliftons might better be described in terms of being 'on loan' from the Cavendishes.

Hobbes and his new pupil travelled to France in October 1629 and spent the winter in Paris; in March–April 1630 they moved to Geneva, where they lodged with a Reformed minister. A planned visit to Italy was aborted because of the warfare raging there, and by late June they were in France again, at Orléans. At this stage they were intending to spend the coming winter in Paris; but the trip was curtailed, and Hobbes was back in England by the beginning of November 1630. He returned to the countess of Devonshire's house, Hardwick Hall, and wrote from there to Sir Gervase Clifton on 2 November: 'That I am welcome home, I must attribute to yor favorable letter, by wch my lady understandes yor good acceptance of my service to Mr Clifton' (*Correspondence*, 1.17).

Hobbes now re-entered the service of the countess, replacing the tutor who had been teaching her elder son—'wch imployment', as he put it in his later memorandum, 'he [Hobbes] nevertheless undertooke, amongst other causes cheifly for this, that the same did not much divert him from his studyes' (Hobbes MS D.6, fol. 2r). In his verse autobiography Hobbes recorded that he gave the young third earl tuition in Latin, rhetoric, 'the precepts of demonstration' (meaning either logic or mathematics, or both), geography, and law (*Opera philosophica*, 1.lxxxviii–lxxxix). Some traces of this teaching survive among the manuscripts at Chatsworth: exercise books with geometrical problems and passages from the ancient historians Livy and Valerius Maximus. Of special interest is a dictation book in which the young earl took down Hobbes's Latin translation of Aristotle's *Rhetoric*—a text concerned as much with psychological analysis as with the rhetorical art. An English translation of this Latin 'digest' was later published as *A Briefe of the Art of Rhetorique* (1637).

Early philosophical interests Biographers of Hobbes have traditionally dated the emergence of his serious philosophical interests to the early 1630s. The neat dichotomy between his 'humanist' period (up to the 1630s) and his 'philosophical' one (thereafter) is perhaps too neat, as his earlier interests had evidently not been confined to classical literature. His early passion for astronomy has already been noted; his connection with Bacon must have prompted some interest in that author's scientific and philosophical writings; and, whether or not Hobbes was himself the author of the three *Discourses*, it seems likely that he had shared the interest displayed in those texts in the analysis of religion, politics, and law. The earliest library catalogue at Chatsworth (Hobbes MS E.1.A) was drawn up by Hobbes, about 1629 (with a few items inserted as later additions); given Hobbes's later recollection, cited above, that the second earl had supplied him with all sorts of books for his studies, it can be assumed that many of the items in this list were bought by and for Hobbes. It includes numerous items by Calvin, many works of Catholic and protestant controversial theology, especially ones relating to the political issues disputed by Bellarmine, Suárez, and King James, and works by Machiavelli, Guiccardini, Botero, Bodin, Charron, Grotius (his *De jure belli ac pacis* is a late addition), and Selden. Scientific writings are less well represented, but the list includes the works of the geometrician Clavius, Napier and Briggs on logarithms, and textbooks by Case and Keckermann on physics. It may be significant that scientific works feature more prominently among the later additions (made, it seems, soon after Hobbes's return in 1630): these include Clavius's edition of Euclid, the works of Robert Fludd, Gilbert on magnetism, Vieta's algebra, and two volumes of the astronomer Tycho Brahe.

In his prose autobiography Hobbes stated that it was during his European trip with Clifton that he acquired his special interest in geometry, when he happened to look at a copy of Euclid's *Elements*. (Aubrey, telling this story, gives the place where this happened as '. . . . . a', with the number of dots corresponding to the missing letters of Geneva; Bodl. Oxf., MS Aubrey 9, fol. 36*r*.) What Hobbes emphasized in his account, however, was that Euclid impressed him 'not so much because of the theorems, as because of the method of reasoning': in other words, he may well have known some geometry before this, but he had not previously thought about the power of a deductive method based on definitions and axioms (*Opera philosophica*, 1.xiv). This suggests that he was already thinking about some philosophical problems to which Euclidean method seemed to supply a solution.

The only surviving clues as to the nature of those problems are a comment made by Hobbes in 1641, when he wrote that he had explained his 'doctrine of the nature and production of light, sound, and all phantasms and ideas' to the earl of Newcastle and his brother in 1630 (*Correspondence*, 1.108), and a similar claim addressed to Newcastle himself in 1646, referring to 'that wch about 16 yeares since I affirmed to your Lo^{pp} at Welbeck, that Light is a fancy in the minde, caused by motion in the braine' (BL, Harley MS 3360, fol. 3*r*). William Cavendish, earl of Newcastle, was a cousin of the earl of Devonshire, and had houses close to Hardwick (at Bolsover in Derbyshire and Welbeck Abbey in north Nottinghamshire); Hobbes would certainly have had contact with him during the second earl of Devonshire's lifetime, and his friends Jonson and Andrews both benefited from Newcastle's patronage. Newcastle had scientific as well as literary interests, and his brother Sir Charles Cavendish had a passion for mathematics and physics. The Newcastle Cavendishes played a key role in awakening Hobbes's scientific interests: thanks to them, he was put in touch during the early 1630s with the scientists Walter Warner (a survivor of the circle of Thomas Hariot) and Robert Payne (Newcastle's chaplain), with whom he discussed problems of optics and epistemology.

The central principle of the new epistemology explored by Hobbes was that developed by Galileo (and Beeckman and Descartes), the subjectivity of secondary qualities—meaning that 'redness' or 'heat' were not qualities or forms inhering in nature, but features of the human experience of external bodies whose motions impinged on the brain in certain ways. Hobbes made a special effort to find a copy of Galileo's *Dialogo* in London in 1634, at Newcastle's request; and it is possible that he actually met Galileo in Italy at the end of the following year.

Whether Hobbes wrote up his own theories in any systematic form during the early 1630s is very uncertain. A manuscript on the principles of physics and psychology, known as the 'Short tract', has commonly been attributed to Hobbes and assigned to this period; it has sometimes been dated to 1630 on the strength of the remarks by Hobbes quoted above. However, those remarks referred to claims made in conversation, not to any written work, and in his verse autobiography he emphasized that he began to write up his theories only after his return from his third

European tour in 1636. Recent studies of the 'Short tract' have shown on the one hand that it contains phrases that reappear in Hobbes's later works, and on the other hand that it is not in his handwriting (as previously thought) but in Payne's, and that its theory of light is closer to Payne's views than to Hobbes's. The attribution of this text remains uncertain, therefore, and it is possible that Payne may have composed it (perhaps in the mid- to late 1630s) while making use of some Hobbesian ideas or materials.

Third European tour In April 1634 Hobbes and the third earl of Devonshire were planning to travel to France within a few weeks; instead they reverted to a previous plan, which involved spending the summer months in Oxford (from where Hobbes visited his family and old friends in north Wiltshire). But by October they were in Paris, where they stayed until the end of August 1635. Then they travelled via Lyons to Italy: their destination was Venice, but it is not clear whether they reached it, or whether the military situation forced them to change their route. If they did stay in Venice, it seems likely that Hobbes would have renewed his acquaintance with Fulgenzio Micanzio. In November or December Hobbes and Devonshire travelled to Rome; on 26 December they dined at the Jesuit English College there.

It is during their journey to Rome that the meeting of Hobbes and Devonshire with Galileo (in his villa outside Florence) is traditionally supposed to have taken place. Tantalizingly, there is a reference in a letter written by Galileo on 1 December 1635 NS to a recent visit by an English lord, who told him that his *Dialogo* was translated into English: this probably alluded to a manuscript translation commissioned by the earl of Newcastle, a fact which strengthens the possibility that his informants were Devonshire and Hobbes. Yet Galileo's letter was addressed to Micanzio, and he obviously had no inkling that he was referring to mutual friends. An element of mystery still surrounds this episode, though Aubrey's definite statement that 'When he [Hobbes] was at Florence … he contracted a friendship with the famous *Galileo*' must carry considerable weight (*Brief Lives*, 1.366). Aubrey's reference may in fact be to the period of several weeks in April 1636 when Hobbes and Devonshire stayed in Florence on their way back from Rome.

In May they moved to Turin, and then to Geneva and Lyons; they reached Paris on 1/11 June. Hobbes had kept up a correspondence with the earl of Newcastle during this tour; Sir Charles Cavendish put him in touch with the French mathematician Claude Mydorge, and it was probably thanks to Sir Charles's contacts that Hobbes made the acquaintance of the Minim friar, scholar, scientist, and intellectual impresario Marin Mersenne. In his verse autobiography Hobbes wrote that it was during this stay in Paris that he discussed his ideas about matter and motion with Mersenne, proudly adding that 'from that time, I too was counted among the philosophers' (*Opera philosophica*, 1.xc).

Philosophy and politics, 1636–1640 When Hobbes returned with Devonshire to England in October 1636 he was in the grip of a *furor philosophicus*: 'the extreme pleasure I take in study', he wrote to Newcastle, 'overcomes in me all other appetites' (*Correspondence*, 1.37). Physics, optics, epistemology, psychology, metaphysics, and logic seem to have been his main concerns. In a letter to Newcastle in 1635 he had expressed a wish to be the first person to explain 'the facultyes & passions of the soule'; by late 1636 he had informed Sir Kenelm Digby (who had been with him in Paris) of his plans to write a 'Logike' (ibid., 1.29, 42). His interest in optics received a special stimulus in October 1637 when Digby sent him a copy of Descartes's *Discours de la méthode*, the work which also contained an essay on refraction, the 'Dioptrique'. Hobbes made a careful study of this essay, and sent a lengthy criticism of it to Mersenne (a 56-page letter, now lost) in November 1640, shortly before returning to Paris himself. He also wrote a treatise on optics in Latin, containing several criticisms of Descartes; this work may have been substantially completed before his move to Paris in late 1640, though the surviving manuscript is a fair copy made by a Parisian scribe, probably in 1641 or 1642.

According to his verse autobiography, it was in the period 1637–40 that Hobbes began to organize his ideas in a tripartite scheme, dealing with 'body' (metaphysics and physics), 'man' (epistemology—including optics—and psychology), and 'citizen' (politics). The works eventually published under the titles *De corpore*, *De homine*, and *De cive* would be described as the three 'sections' of his 'elements of philosophy'. How fully worked out this scheme was during the late 1630s is not clear, though it may be significant that the Latin optical treatise contains a reference to the preceding section ('sectione Antecedente'; Harley MS 6796, fol. 193v). Some manuscript notes on early chapters of *De corpore* do survive, but their dating is uncertain.

In view of the predominantly scientific interests of the people who had stimulated this philosophical awakening (Mersenne, Sir Charles Cavendish, Payne, and Warner), it may seem odd that Hobbes should have included politics as the culminating part of his philosophical programme. The personal interests of the earl of Newcastle—who was now playing an increasingly important role as a courtier-politician—were probably important here. But Hobbes's own experience must also have stimulated his interest in political theory. In 1627 he helped to collect money for Charles I's unpopular 'forced loan' in Derbyshire, which may have prompted some thoughts about the relation between political authority and property; and in January 1640 he was put forward by the earl of Devonshire—unsuccessfully—as a possible parliamentary candidate. Hobbes had also had some contacts in the 1630s (the precise chronology is again uncertain) with the so-called Great Tew circle, a group of literary men, divines, and lawyers who gathered round Lord Falkland at his country house near Oxford: the topics discussed by members of this circle, such as Edward Hyde and William Chillingworth, included the nature of religious authority and the relation between church and state.

It was at Newcastle's bidding that Hobbes first put his political theory down on paper, in an English treatise which may have been based, to some extent, on draft materials for his Latin work 'on the citizen'. This treatise, *The Elements of Law*, was completed on 9 May 1640 (just after the dissolution of the Short Parliament), and distributed in manuscript copies produced by a production line of scribes. Starting with an account of human psychology and a powerful analysis of the origins (and the necessity) of the state, it mounted a strong defence of royal authority in such matters as the imposition of taxation. Hobbes's name was now in circulation as a hardline theorist of royal absolutism. When the Long Parliament began to debate these issues in November 1640 such views came under fierce attack. Hobbes, who was staying in London at the time, hurriedly packed his bags and travelled to Paris.

Hobbes's own account of the reasons for this move (given in a letter from Paris five months later) emphasized the parliamentary debates, but also added that 'I thought if I went not then, there was nevertelesse a disorder comming on that would make it worse being there then here' (*Correspondence*, 1.115). His fear of being hauled before parliament may only have hastened a move which he had already planned for other reasons, both political and personal. One sign of such planning is the fact that in September 1640 he had withdrawn a sum of £100 which the steward of Chatsworth had invested for him; he also withdrew the £400 which he had banked with the Cavendish family, and thus had the financial security for a long stay abroad. His tutorial duties had ended in 1637, and the earl of Devonshire (who attained his majority in late 1638) may have used him thereafter only for minor secretarial services. With Newcastle distracted by politics, the prospects of a period of quiet study in Newcastle's household had receded; Mersenne's Paris thus became the most natural and alluring alternative. Hobbes would remain there for eleven years.

Paris, 1640–1648 Friendship with Mersenne provided an ideal entrée to Parisian intellectual life. The friar held regular meetings of scholars and scientists in his convent; thanks to him Hobbes became acquainted during the early 1640s with the anti-Aristotelian philosopher Pierre Gassendi, the mathematician Gilles Personne de Roberval, and young Huguenot intellectuals such as Thomas de Martel and Samuel Sorbière. Visitors to Paris who also frequented Mersenne's meetings included Sir Kenelm Digby and the Catholic philosopher Thomas White. Mersenne was a close friend of Descartes; he circulated Descartes's *Meditationes* to various writers, including Hobbes, soliciting their critical comments, which he published, with Descartes's replies, in 1641. In the case of Hobbes's criticisms, Descartes's responses were acerbic to the point of open contempt—an attitude expressed also in his correspondence with Hobbes (conducted via Mersenne) during the early months of that year. In November 1642 Mersenne performed another service for Hobbes when he organized the private printing and distribution of *De cive*, the third 'section' of his intended 'elements of philosophy'. This treatise presented (in Latin) the key political arguments of *The Elements of Law*, omitting the earlier text's material on psychology and developing further

Hobbes's arguments about religion (which, probably, were the reason for Mersenne's cautious method of publication). *De cive* established Hobbes's reputation among select intellectual circles; later editions printed in the Netherlands by Elsevier in 1647 (at Sorbière's behest) spread it among a much wider public.

It was probably at Mersenne's invitation that, in 1642–3, Hobbes composed a huge manuscript refutation of a recently published work, Thomas White's *De mundo dialogi tres*. White's philosophical position was an amalgam of scholastic Aristotelianism and elements of the new mechanistic science; Hobbes's criticisms were directed particularly at White's scholasticism, and at the metaphysical and theological assumptions that underlay it. (This manuscript was read by Mersenne, but seems to have become unknown thereafter, being rediscovered only in the twentieth century.) Mersenne also published some short pieces by Hobbes, on physics and optics, in two scientific compilations which he edited in 1644. These pieces (some of them extracted from the critique of White) were evidently intended as samples of Hobbes's work in progress. His own efforts were now mainly directed at composing the first section of his philosophical elements, *De corpore*—a huge task, which involved setting out in a proper 'method' all the principles of logic, metaphysics, and physics. Sir Charles Cavendish, who was corresponding with Hobbes, wrote to his friend John Pell in December 1644: 'Mr Hobbes puts me in hope of his Philosophie, which he writes he is nowe putting in order, but I feare that will take a long time' (BL, Add. MS 4278, fol. 190r).

Sir Charles and his brother arrived in Paris in April 1645; from Hobbes's point of view their renewed patronage was a mixed blessing, since they caused several interruptions to his work. In the summer of 1645 Newcastle set up a philosophical disputation between Hobbes and an exiled Anglican bishop, John Bramhall, on free will and necessity; the short text Hobbes wrote on this subject was later published, without his authorization, as *Of Libertie and Necessitie* (1654). In late 1645 and early 1646 it was also at Newcastle's bidding that Hobbes wrote a treatise on optics in English. (The fair copy was written out by William Petty, who had contacted Hobbes in Paris in 1645 at the behest of the mathematician John Pell, to solicit a demonstration from Hobbes for a work eventually published by Pell in 1647.) And a further diversion came in the summer of 1646: when Hobbes was just about to travel to Montauban in the south of France (home of his friend Martel) to work intensively on *De corpore*, he was required to stay in Paris to give lessons in mathematics to the young Prince Charles, who arrived there in July. While this appointment further delayed the completion of *De corpore*, however, it did give Hobbes a personal acquaintance with the future king which stood him in good stead in Restoration England: the prince adopted an attitude of bemused affection towards his tutor, commenting, reportedly, that he was the oddest fellow he ever met.

In the second half of 1647 Hobbes's work suffered a much graver interruption, an illness which nearly killed him: according to his later recollections he was in bed for six months, and went for six weeks without eating. Recovering at last, he soldiered on with his work on *De corpore*. Prince Charles left Paris in the summer of 1648; so too did Newcastle, and his brother, who reported just after their departure that 'M^r: Hobbes hath nowe leasure to studie & I hope wee shall have his [philosophy] within a twelve moneth' (BL, Add. MS 4278, fol. 273r). Sure enough, in June 1649 Hobbes informed Sorbière that he hoped to complete *De corpore* by the end of that summer. So confident was he that the work was in its final form that he was already having the figures engraved, to facilitate speedy publication. And yet the book was not published for another six long years.

Paris, 1649–1651: *Leviathan* The main interruption to the completion of *De corpore* was a self-inflicted one: the writing of Hobbes's major treatise on psychology, politics, and religion, *Leviathan*. The precise date at which he began it is not known; the evidence of his pattern of work on *De corpore*, described above, suggests that he may have started it only in 1649, but his verse autobiography implies that he had been working on it since 1646. In May 1650 Robert Payne (who was corresponding with Hobbes from England) learned that he had completed thirty-seven chapters; and in April 1651 Edward Hyde, on a visit to Paris, was told that the book 'was then Printing in England, and that he receiv'd every week a Sheet to correct' (E. Hyde, *A Brief View and Survey of the Dangerous Errors … in … Leviathan*, 1676, 7). It was published in the following month, by the London bookseller Andrew Crooke. The fact that this work was written in English and published in England strongly suggests that it was intended as a contribution to the internal political debate in that country. According to Hyde, when Hobbes was asked why he was publishing the work, he replied: 'The truth is, I have a mind to go home' (ibid., 8). Certainly the final section of the book, entitled 'A review and conclusion', contained a strong justification of submission to the new regime in England. It summarized Hobbes's general argument about the rational basis of political authority, pointing out that there was a reciprocal relationship between protection and obedience: Hobbes's point was that since the king (now Charles II) could not protect people in England, they were impelled by the dictates of self-preservation to transfer their obedience to the power that now ruled there. Whether this argument had any direct relevance to someone who, like Hobbes, was no longer living in England, is much less clear.

There were, nevertheless, some personal reasons why life in Paris may have seemed no longer so attractive to Hobbes. Mersenne had died in 1648; Gassendi had left for the south of France soon thereafter; Sorbière was permanently away from Paris during these years; Martel was absent for most of the time between 1646 and 1654. Hobbes did have some old friends there, and also acquired some new ones—notably the Huguenot physician Abraham du Prat and a young amateur mathematician from the Bordeaux region, François du Verdus, who became a fervent admirer. But Mersenne had been the linchpin of Hobbes's intellectual life in Paris, and his loss was keenly felt. In August 1651, when Hobbes had another severe illness, he was treated by the famous physician and philosophical sceptic Guy Patin: according to Patin, the pain that he was suffering, combined with his natural melancholy, had inclined Hobbes's thoughts to suicide. Significantly, however, he also recorded that Hobbes was so grateful for his treatment that he promised that he would send Patin a present when he was back in England: the move was definitely planned by this stage.

During his years in Paris, Hobbes had kept in touch with the earl of Devonshire, who returned to England in 1645 and made his peace with the parliamentary authorities. For most royalists living in England, 'compounding' for their estates was a practical necessity to which, by the end of the 1640s, no stigma applied. Some of the more flamboyant exiled royalists of Hobbes's acquaintance could not return, for reasons of personal safety: Newcastle was in this category, and so was the poet Sir William Davenant, whose epic *Gondibert* Hobbes praised in a letter published with Davenant's preface to the poem in 1650. But even friends such as these do not seem to have objected to Hobbes's own decision to go back.

More problematic was the political theory of *Leviathan*, which implied that the submission of former royalists to the new authority in England was not a provisional measure, pending the return of the rightful king, but rather a recognition of a new authority just as valid as the previous, royal, one. Few of the politicians in exile could be happy with this view. Hobbes's arguments about religion also caused offence, though in different ways. The Anglican 'old royalists' in exile, such as Hyde, disliked Hobbes's rejection of the intrinsic authority of the church and his total subordination of religious activity to state power; the other main faction among the exiled courtiers and politicians, the so-called Louvre group, which clustered around the widowed Henrietta Maria, was offended by Hobbes's outspoken attack on Catholicism. One of the most important features of *Leviathan*, indeed, is its constant attention to the role of belief (especially religious doctrine) in subverting political authority. Hobbes's advice here may have been directed, at least implicitly, at the new powers in England, who had the opportunity to create a new, rational settlement of religion there. But it was also directed at the young Charles II, to whom, after his return to Paris in October 1651, Hobbes gave a fair copy manuscript of the work. Within two months Hobbes's enemies at the court-in-exile succeeded in having him banned from the court; there were also rumours that the French clergy intended to arrest him. He left Paris in mid-December, and sailed to England.

England, 1652–1660 In his verse autobiography Hobbes suggests that on his arrival in England he was fearful that he might be taken for a royalist spy—he was, he emphasizes, a prominent defender of the rights of the crown—and says that he therefore presented himself to the council of state to regularize his position. This sounds retrospectively disingenuous. Although some royalists (such as the young Charles Cotton, whose translation of *De cive* was published in 1651) did see Hobbes as a defender of their cause, the ideologists of the parliamentary regime, such as Marchamont Nedham and John Hall of Durham, were well aware that Hobbes's theories could be used to support the new political settlement. His reconciliation with the council of state seems, unfortunately, to have left no trace in the written records of that body; but it was probably assisted by the young William Brereton (cousin of a parliamentary commander), who had studied mathematics under John Pell and was a friend of Sir Charles Cavendish.

Hobbes soon returned to the service of the earl of Devonshire, who stayed frequently at Latimers, a country house in Buckinghamshire. But it seems that his duties were slight, and that he spent much of his time during the 1650s in London, pursuing his own studies. *De corpore* was finally published there in 1655 (an English translation, supervised by Hobbes, appeared in the following year); *De homine* followed in 1658. Hobbes was able to renew some old friendships—with, for example, the physician William Harvey—and make some new ones. John Aubrey, a friend of Harvey's, became personally acquainted with Hobbes at some time in the early 1650s. Having sent John Selden a copy of *Leviathan* on its publication, Hobbes struck up a somewhat quarrelsome friendship with him; Selden's epigone, the lawyer John Vaughan, became a more unqualified admirer of Hobbes's work.

Sir Kenelm Digby and Thomas White returned to London in late 1653 or early 1654; Hobbes continued his philosophical disputes with White, but may have been sympathetic to White's main political aim, which was to win a settlement for English Catholicism by renouncing the authority of the pope in temporal affairs. This was a quasi-Erastian version of Catholicism; while Hobbes was not Erastian in the narrowest sense of the term (meaning that each state should have a single state church), Erastianism in its broadest sense (the subordination of religion to state control) was an attitude shared by him and many of his friends at this time.

Equally, Hobbes's views on religion, and on the relations of church and state, gained him many new enemies. Particularly offended were believers in the jurisdictional powers of the church, whether Laudian, presbyterian, or Catholic. Even the leaders of the Independents, such as John Owen at Oxford, who had least reason to reject Hobbes's ecclesiology, were scandalized by the scoffing, anti-theological tone of the last part of *Leviathan*. Critical responses to that book began to appear within a year of its publication, and the easiest targets for the critics were Hobbes's views on theological questions—his materialism, his 'mortalist' doctrine about the soul, and his apparent identification of Moses as the first person of the Trinity. One particularly tenacious critic was the Anglican bishop John Bramhall, who, offended by the publication (albeit unauthorized by Hobbes) of Hobbes's 1645 critique of his views on free will, issued two refutations of Hobbes, eliciting two further responses (*The Questions Concerning Liberty, Necessity and Chance*, 1656, and *An Answer to a Book Published by Dr Bramhall*, written in 1668 but not published until 1682). The desire for theological rectitude, however, was not the only motive of Hobbes's critics. Some, such as Seth Ward at Oxford, felt threatened by Hobbes's call for a reform of the universities; others, such as Ward's colleague John Wallis, were keen to discredit such an outspoken opponent of presbyterianism.

The publication of *De corpore*, with its incompetent geometrical demonstrations, provided an ideal opportunity for Wallis, who was one of the leading mathematicians of the age. His disdainful work of refutation, *Elenchus geometriae Hobbianae* (1655), set off a long-running dispute, in which Hobbes's philosophically acute remarks about the conceptual basis of mathematics were unfortunately quite overshadowed by his frequent mathematical blunders. Other mathematicians and scientists, such as John Wilkins and Robert Boyle, also joined the anti-Hobbesian campaign, and Hobbes would (to his irritation) never be invited to become a member of the Royal Society. In general intellectual terms, Hobbes was on the same side as these leading scientists—a proponent of the mechanistic 'new science' against the old scholasticism. But the more widely Hobbes was denounced for his dangerous theological and political errors, the more reason his fellow scientists had to dissociate themselves from him by attacking him as well. He could console himself with the thought that his works were—as his loyal French correspondents assured him—highly prized in French philosophical circles: François du Verdus even learned English in order to translate *Leviathan* into French, though his version was never in fact published. In England there were some equally fervent admirers, such as the maverick scholar Henry Stubbe, who began translating *Leviathan* into Latin; but as Stubbe's correspondence with Hobbes shows, admiration for the philosopher had to be a somewhat covert affair in 1650s Oxford.

After the Restoration, 1660–1679 In some ways the Restoration was beneficial to Hobbes: Aubrey cleverly arranged a meeting between him and his former pupil, the king, at the studio of the painter Samuel Cooper, whereupon the king ordered that Hobbes 'should have free access to his majestie' (*Brief Lives*, 1.340). Within a few years Hobbes was receiving a royal pension of roughly 100 guineas per annum. But the Restoration settlement also involved the return to power of an Anglican establishment that strongly disapproved of Hobbes's religious views. In 1662 a Printing Act was passed which required books to be licensed by episcopal authority; thereafter, nothing that Hobbes wrote in the controversial fields of politics, law, history, or religion could be published in his lifetime. (The last such contentious work, *Mr Hobbes Considered*, a short apologia replying to Wallis's accusations about his political record, was published in the summer of 1662, having apparently gone to press before the act was passed.)

Although the publication of *Leviathan* in 1651 was covered by the Act of Oblivion, Hobbes appears to have been genuinely afraid that he might be prosecuted for heresy: there was a rumour in the early 1660s that some of the bishops were planning such a move, and in 1666 a committee of the House of Commons called for an examination of the theological contents of *Leviathan*. Hobbes responded to the first of these threats by writing a treatise on the law of heresy, arguing that no one could be burnt for that offence; the second may have prompted his composition of a long appendix to the Latin edition of *Leviathan* (1668), in which he also defended himself from the charge of heresy. His fears seem to have been exaggerated; and he enjoyed, in any case, the protection of the earl of Devonshire, in whose household he remained, spending his summers in Derbyshire and the winter months in the Devonshires' town house in London.

Hobbes may have been fearful and old (he was aged seventy-two at the Restoration), but he continued to display a remarkable vigour as an author—all the more remarkable given that since the mid-1650s he had suffered so badly from the 'shaking palsy' (probably Parkinson's disease) that he was obliged to dictate to an amanuensis. In the fields in which publication was permitted he kept up a stream of new works: a treatise on physics in dialogue form, *Problemata physica* (1662), a sequence of responses to his mathematical critics, *De principiis et ratiocinatione geometrarum* (1666), *Rosetum geometricum* (1671) and *Lux mathematica* (1672), and a scattering of pamphlets on physics and geometry.

More significant were the things he was unable to publish, at least in England. His Latin translation of *Leviathan*, with its important appendix, was made for an edition of his Latin philosophical works produced by Johan Blaeu in Amsterdam (1668). At some time in the late 1660s Hobbes wrote (in English) a history of the civil war in dialogue form, in which he paid special attention to the interplay of religion and human ambition: this eventually appeared in an unauthorized edition in 1679, and was later reprinted under the title *Behemoth*. His last reply to Bramhall (mentioned above) was written in 1668. Shortly thereafter (perhaps in 1670, but by 1673 at the latest) he wrote a treatise on law, *A Dialogue between a Phylosopher and a Student, of the Common-Laws of England*, in which he defended his theory of legislative sovereignty against what he regarded as the excessive claims of the common lawyers. Also significant for the study of his political thought is a long Latin poem about the encroachments of priestcraft down the ages, *Historia ecclesiastica*, completed in 1671 and eventually published in 1688. His Latin verse autobiography, written in 1672, was also published posthumously.

In 1674 Hobbes was permitted one small exception to the ban on his controversial publications: after John Fell, dean of Christ Church, Oxford, had inserted some abusive comments about him into an entry on Hobbes in a work by Anthony Wood, he wrote a letter of complaint and self-defence, and obtained the king's permission to print it, having approached him in person in St James's Park. This was the last year in which Hobbes was in London; thereafter, he resided only at Hardwick Hall and Chatsworth. Though his strength was failing, his intellectual energy was unabated: he published translations of Homer (books 9–12 of the *Odyssey* in 1673, the rest of that work in 1675, and the whole of the *Iliad* in 1676), as well as another treatise on physics in dialogue form, *Decameron physiologicum*, in 1678. In March 1678, just before his ninetieth birthday, he commented in a letter to Aubrey: ''Tis a long time since I have been able to write my selfe, and am now so weake that it is a paine to me to dictate'; yet his last dated letter (18 August 1679), addressed to his publisher, William Crooke, contained the tantalizing phrase, 'I am writing somewhat for you to print in English' (*Correspondence*, 2.767, 774).

Illness and death Hobbes had enjoyed good health for most of his adult life, the only known exceptions being his two bouts of serious illness in France, another in London about 1668, and his 'shaking palsy'. When Aubrey first saw him (in 1634) he was struck by his 'briske' deportment; he would later describe him as a tall man (over 6 feet), with a 'fresh, ruddy complexion' and 'a good eie … which was full of life and spirit, even to the last'. This last observation is confirmed by three of the best portraits of Hobbes: by Samuel Cooper (1660s; Cleveland Museum of Art, Cleveland, Ohio), John Baptist Gaspars (1663; Royal Society, London), and John Michael Wright (c.1669–1670; NPG). Aubrey also recorded that he was 'temperate, both as to wine and women', and that he kept to a simple daily routine, going for a morning walk to compose his thoughts, taking an early lunch, and writing in the afternoon. His health may also have benefited from his sceptical attitude towards contemporary medical science: he said he preferred 'to take physique from an experienced old woman … then from the learnedst but unexperienced physician' (*Brief Lives*, 1.332, 347–51).

In October 1679 Hobbes suffered from strangury (pain when urinating); on 27 November he had a severe stroke, which left him paralysed and unable to speak. He died on 4 December, at Hardwick Hall. His amanuensis, James Wheldon (the earl of Devonshire's baker), reported that he seemed 'to dye rather for want of the fuell of life … and meer weaknesse and decay' (*Brief Lives*, 1.383). He was buried two days later in the local church of Ault Hucknall, Derbyshire.

Hobbes's will Hobbes had made three versions of his will. The earliest, in July 1674, included bequests to two nieces (daughters of his brother), five smaller bequests to members of the Devonshire household, and a legacy of £100 to Elizabeth Alaby, described as 'an Orphan and remitted by me to the Tuition of my Executor'; the residue was to go to his executor, James Wheldon. In the second version (December 1675) the five smaller bequests were omitted, and money left instead to 'the poore' and the minister of the parish where he was buried; Hobbes also stated his wish that Elizabeth Alaby be married off to Wheldon's son Jack, 'provided they liked one another, and that he was not a Spendthrift'. At this stage Wheldon calculated that Hobbes had £787 (Hardwick MS 19, final page). The final version (September 1677) added bequests to his brother's grandchildren, and doubled the legacy to Miss Alaby. Hobbes's estate, in the end, was worth nearly £1000 (*Brief Lives*, 1.346). The special attention paid to Elizabeth Alaby

in his will seems to have given rise to the popular belief that Hobbes had an illegitimate daughter. In fact she was an orphan child, possibly the daughter of a travelling musician, who had turned up at Rowthorn (Wheldon's village, near Hardwick) in May 1674, 'supposed about 5 yeares old', and whose plight had evidently touched the heart of the elderly philosopher (Hardwick MS 19, final page).

Reputation Hobbes's enemies, of whom there were many, portrayed him as a disagreeable character: bullying, dogmatic, and irascible. Seth Ward's biographer claimed that 'if any one objected to his Dictates, he would leave the Company in a passion, saying, his business was to Teach, not Dispute' (W. Pope, *The Life of … Seth, Lord Bishop of Salisbury*, 1697, 118). His friends, on the other hand, took a different view: Aubrey commented on 'His goodness of nature and willingnes to instruct any one that was willing to be informed and modestly desired it' (*Brief Lives*, 1.352), and Sorbière exclaimed, in a letter to Hobbes, that he admired 'your goodness, your courtesy, and all those fine qualities which make you a perfect gentleman as well as a great philosopher' (*Correspondence*, 2.619). The truth may be that Hobbes was affable and generous towards his friends, and intolerant only in company which he felt was predisposed to hostility towards him.

The negative stereotype of Hobbes which developed during and after his lifetime was based, however, more on his teachings than on his personal character. There were three main charges: that he was an atheist (or, at least, guilty of gross heresies), that his political theory glorified despotism, and that he overturned traditional morality. The third charge connected the first and second: he was accused of deriving morality not from God or reason but from the will of the sovereign.

Whether, in his heart, Hobbes believed in God is a question no biographer can answer with certainty; the fact that he attended Anglican services and took holy communion does not settle the matter. In his writings he displayed not only a fierce anti-clericalism but also a type of negative theology in which the possibility of human knowledge of God's intentions was virtually eliminated; but neither of these is necessarily the same as atheism. As for despotism, his political theory did propose that sovereignty, to be real, must be absolute, and he observed that 'tyranny' was merely a term used for monarchy by those who disliked it. Yet at the same time he tried to demonstrate that it was in the interests of rulers to promote the well-being of their people, and his entire theory supposed that the authority of the ruler rested on nothing other than the will of the ruled. His moral theory was indeed unorthodox, but neither relativist nor arbitrarist: he believed that certain moral rules (the 'laws of nature') followed necessarily from the human condition, and his position might best be described as a naturalistic adaptation of the natural law tradition.

The many denunciations of Hobbes by theological writers (including Henry More, Ralph Cudworth, Thomas Tenison, and Richard Cumberland) helped to reinforce a popular notion of 'Hobbism' in Restoration England as a concentrate of libertinism and irreligion. Some of the rare open admirers of Hobbes (such as the early deist Charles Blount) idolized him precisely because they thought he had undermined traditional religion; his name would continue to be invoked in this way by the radical Enlightenment. But his writings also had a more positive influence on some European thinkers, especially in the Netherlands (Velthuysen, de la Court, Spinoza), Germany (Leibniz), and France (Merlat, Bossuet); and the frequent reprintings of *De cive* on the continent guaranteed that writers such as Rousseau and Kant would give serious consideration to his ideas. In the nineteenth century a more sympathetic view of him emerged among utilitarians (who recognized an affinity with his moral theory) and legal positivists (who admired his theory of sovereignty). Some twentieth-century writers portrayed Hobbes as an ancestor of totalitarianism; but the tendency of modern scholarship has been to see his political theory as both authoritarian and individualist, embodying an unusual and intriguing mixture of illiberal and liberal elements. Increasingly, too, he is recognized as a philosopher whose importance extends far beyond the realm of political theory—someone whose work in theology, metaphysics, science, history, and psychology entitles him to be described as one of the true founders of modernity in Western culture.   NOEL MALCOLM

Sources The English works of Thomas Hobbes of Malmesbury, ed. W. Molesworth, 11 vols. (1839–45) · Thomae Hobbes Malmesburiensis opera philosophica quae Latine scripsit omnia, ed. W. Molesworth, 5 vols. (1839–45) · The correspondence of Thomas Hobbes, ed. N. Malcolm, 2 vols. (1994) · Brief lives, chiefly of contemporaries, set down by John Aubrey, between the years 1669 and 1696, ed. A. Clark, 2 vols. (1898) · H. Macdonald and M. Hargreaves, Thomas Hobbes: a bibliography (1952) · T. Hobbes, Critique du De mundo de Thomas White, ed. J. Jacquot and H. W. Jones (1973) · T. Hobbes, The elements of law, natural and politic, ed. F. Tönnies (1889) · F. Micanzio, Lettere a William Cavendish (1615–1628) nella versione inglese di Thomas Hobbes, ed. R. Ferrini (1987) · [W. Cavendish], Horae subsecivae (1620) · Three discourses: a critical modern edition of newly identified work of the young Hobbes, ed. N. B. Reynolds and A. W. Saxonhouse (1995) · book of accounts, beginning 1608, ending 1623, Chatsworth House, Derbyshire, Hardwick MS 29 · library catalogue, c.1629 (with later additions), Chatsworth House, Derbyshire, Hobbes MS E.1.A · W. Cavendish, 'Essayes', Chatsworth House, Derbyshire, Hobbes MS D.3 · 'A narration of the proceedings both publique and private, concerning the inheritance of the earl of Devonshire', Chatsworth House, Derbyshire, Hobbes MS D.6 · J. Wheldon's personal account book, Chatsworth House, Derbyshire, Hardwick MS 19 · T. Hobbes, Latin optical treatise, c.1640–41, BL, Harley MS 6796, fols. 193–266 · T. Hobbes, 'A minute or first draught of the Optiques', 1646, BL, Harley MS 3360 · letters from Sir Charles Cavendish to John Pell, 1641–51, BL, Add. MS 4278, fols. 161–322 · will, PRO, PROB 11/362, fol. 294 · K. Schuhmann, Hobbes: une chronique (Paris, 1998) · T. Sorrell, ed., The Cambridge companion to Hobbes (1996) · A. A. Rogow, Thomas Hobbes: radical in the service of reaction (1986) · S. Schaffer and S. Shapin, Leviathan and the air-pump: Hobbes, Boyle, and the experimental life (1985) · A. Pacchi, Convenzione e ipotesi nella formazione della filosofia naturale di Thomas Hobbes (1965) · S. I. Mintz, The hunting of Leviathan: seventeenth-century reactions to the materialism and moral philosophy of Thomas Hobbes (1962) · N. Malcolm, 'Hobbes, Sandys, and the Virginia Company', HJ, 24 (1981), 297–321 · L. L. Peck, 'Constructing a new context for Hobbes studies', Politics and the political imagination in later Stuart Britain: essays presented to Lois Green Schwoerer (1997), 161–79 · R. Tuck, 'Hobbes and

Descartes', Perspectives on Thomas Hobbes, ed. G. A. J. Rogers and A. Ryan (1988), 11–41 · N. Malcolm, 'Hobbes and the Royal Society', Perspectives on Thomas Hobbes, ed. G. A. J. Rogers and A. Ryan (1988), 43–66 · A. Pritchard, 'The last days of Hobbes: evidence of the Wood manuscripts', Bodleian Library Record, 10 (1980), 178–87 · D. M. Jesseph, Squaring the circle: the war between Hobbes and Wallis (1999) · P. Milton, 'Hobbes, heresy and Lord Arlington', History of Political Thought, 14 (1993), 501–46 · Q. Skinner, Reason and rhetoric in the philosophy of Hobbes (1996), esp. 215–56 · K. Schuhmann, 'Le "Short tract", première œuvre philosophique de Hobbes', Hobbes Studies, 8 (1995), 3–36 · T. Raylor, 'Hobbes, Payne, and A short tract on first principles', HJ, 44 (2001), 29–58 · J. Collins, 'Thomas Hobbes and the English revolution', PhD diss., Harvard U., 1999 · J. M. Lewis, 'Hobbes and the Blackloists: a study in the eschatology of the English revolution', PhD diss., Harvard U., 1976 · N. Malcolm, 'Charles Cotton, translator of Hobbes's De cive', Huntington Library Quarterly, 61 (1999–2000), 259–87 · J. J. Hamilton, 'Hobbes's study and the Hardwick library', Journal of the History of Philosophy, 16 (1978), 445–53 · N. Malcolm, De Dominis (1560–1624): Venetian, Anglican, ecumenist and relapsed heretic (1984), esp. 47–54

Archives Bibliothèque Nationale, Paris, Fonds français · Bibliothèque Nationale, Paris, Fonds latin · BL, corresp., Add. MS 32553 · Chatsworth House, Derbyshire, papers and literary MSS | Bodl. Oxf., letters to John Aubrey · U. Nott. L., Clifton MSS

Likenesses line engraving, 1646, BM, NPG · attrib. D. Beck, oils, c.1650, Scot. NPG · oils, 1650–59, RS · R. Vaughan, line engraving, 1651?, BM, NPG; repro. in T. Hobbes, Philosophicall rudiments (1651) · S. Cooper, watercolour miniature, 1660–69, Cleveland Museum of Art, Cleveland, Ohio · J. B. Gaspar, oils, 1663, RS · W. Hollar, line engraving, 1665 (after J. B. Gaspar), BM, NPG · W. Faithorne, line engraving, 1667–8, BM, NPG; repro. in T. Hobbes, Opera philosophica (1668), frontispiece · J. M. Wright, oils, c.1669–1670, NPG [see illus.] · oils, 1676, Hardwick Hall, Derbyshire · W. Faithorne, line engraving, BM, NPG

Wealth at death under £1000: Aubrey, Brief lives, vol. 1, p. 346

Hobbes, William (d. 1488), physician and surgeon, was the son and heir of John Hobbes (d. 1462), surgeon, of Fetter Lane, London; his mother was probably John's widow, Juliana. As a member of the mystery of surgeons of London, who himself owned many books, it is not surprising that John Hobbes should have sent his son to read medicine at Oxford University. In January 1459, after three years of study and twelve of practice, William Hobbes was awarded the degree of bachelor of medicine and permitted to lecture on the Aphorisms of Hippocrates. He then moved to Cambridge, where he incepted as doctor of medicine three years later.

Unlike most English physicians, Hobbes did not enter the priesthood and consequently remained free to practise as a surgeon (clergy in higher orders had, in 1215, been forbidden to use a lancet or a cautery). His dual expertise made him especially useful to patrons such as Richard, duke of York (d. 1460), who retained him as his medicus et sirurgicus. On York's death Hobbes entered the household of his son, Edward IV, and was thus assured a position at the pinnacle of his profession. The rewards proved considerable, although his training had been expensive and he still owed his father £12 in June 1462. The investment paid off; thanks to royal patronage, Hobbes was destined to become one of the wealthiest practitioners of his day.

Already, in April 1462, Hobbes had received 'a place, wharf, crane and diverse houses' (CPR, 1461–7, 183) worth £14 a year in London from Edward; and in 1469 he obtained the confiscated goods of a city merchant. As 'principal surgeon of the royal body' (*CPR*, 1467–77, 211), an annual fee of 40 marks (£26 13*s*. 4*d*.) was assigned to him for life soon afterwards. When parliament sought to revoke several such grants as an economy measure, in 1473, 'our trusty and well-beloved servant, William Hobbys, cirurgion for oure body' (*RotP*, 6.83) was formally exempted. In 1478 he was given custody of a lesser piece of the seal used for registering debts in Norwich, along with all the fees accruing from its use; and in the following year he became the first lay master of St Mary of Bethlehem, the London hospital for the insane.

Hobbes was required to advise, attend, and treat the king on a regular basis. He accompanied him on his expedition to France in 1475, and was sent, at the head of a contingent of eight surgeons, to serve under Edward's younger brother, Richard of Gloucester, in Scotland seven years later. This connection assured him of continued preferment when Richard seized the throne in 1483. Indeed, he assumed the more prestigious post of royal physician, with an increase in salary to £40 a year. Hobbes's success undoubtedly attracted many other wealthy patients. His will of 1488 shows him to have accumulated a fine collection of plate and tapestry, which may have been given in return for treatment. But despite his evident skill as a practitioner, he was as vulnerable as any other courtier to the vagaries of political fortune, and the death of Richard III at Bosworth brought his profitable association with the crown to an end.

Hobbes remained proud of his long attachment to Richard of York and his two sons, and requested that his tombstone, in Holy Trinity Priory, Aldgate, London, should record his years in their service. He died on 27 September 1488, leaving a daughter named Agnes. A bequest of an ornate silver cup and £5 to the barbers of London suggests that he continued to identify with the craftsmen among whom he had spent his youth. CAROLE RAWCLIFFE

Sources C. H. Talbot and E. A. Hammond, *The medical practitioners in medieval England: a biographical register* (1965) · R. T. Beck, *The cutting edge: early history of the surgeons of London* (1974) · Chancery records · R. R. Sharpe, ed., *Calendar of wills proved and enrolled in the court of husting, London, AD 1258 – AD 1688*, 2 vols. (1889–90) · Emden, *Oxf.*, 2.938 · Emden, *Cam.* · C. Rawcliffe, 'The profits of practice: the wealth and status of medical men in later medieval England', *Social History of Medicine*, 1 (1988), 61–78 · C. Rawcliffe, *Medicine and society in later medieval England* (1995) · *CPR, 1461–7*, 183; *1467–77*, 211 · *RotP*, 6.83
Wealth at death £5 cash; land valued at £3 p.a.; plate: will, Sharpe, ed., *Calendar of wills*, vol. 2, pp. 590–91

Hobbs, Sir John Berry [Jack] (1882–1963), cricketer, was born on 16 December 1882 at 8 Brewhouse Lane, Cambridge, the eldest of twelve children (six boys and six girls) of John Cooper Hobbs (*d.* 1901), a slater's labourer, and his wife, Flora Matilda Berry. He had a childhood deprived of material benefits and often close to poverty but enriched by family warmth and an upbringing on the fringes of first-class cricket. His father became a net bowler at Fenner's, the university cricket ground, and proudly styled himself in *Kelly's Directory* as 'J. Hobbs, cricketer'. When

Sir John Berry [Jack] Hobbs (1882–1963), by W. Smithson Broadhead, 1920s

John Hobbs senior went on to be groundsman at Jesus College, Jack—as his son was universally known throughout his life—played in his first proper match. The choirboys of Jesus College were one short and the twelve-year-old was called upon. Nevertheless, he was already aware of the distinction between town and gown. John Hobbs knew better than to let his son play in the college nets except in vacation. Town, for the Hobbses, meant cricket on Parker's Piece, a public playing ground. Gown meant watching Ranjitsinhji batting for the university.

Surrey début After leaving St Matthew's church school, which he attended from 1888 to 1896 (and where he had played in the cricket team), Jack helped his father at Jesus College for 7*s*. 6*d*. a week and played on Parker's Piece at a match fee of a penny. There he was noticed by Tom Hayward, against whom he batted for Cambridge town against the Surrey player's own eleven in 1901. Hayward became the most important influence on Hobbs's early career. A century for Ainsworth brought him two appearances for Cambridgeshire and his début in *Wisden* as 'Mr J. Hobbs, junr' (*Wisden*, 1902, 377). Sadly, when that *Wisden* was published, he was no longer 'junr'. His father had died, leaving the family more impoverished than ever. Hayward organized a benefit match for Mrs Hobbs and, of more significance, secured a trial for Jack with Surrey. Its successful outcome brought him a Surrey contract, 30*s*. a week, with £1 in winter, and the need to qualify by residence over two years. He played for Surrey club and ground and for Cambridgeshire before his first-class début in 1905. Against the Gentlemen of England, captained by W. G. Grace, he opened the batting with Hayward, scoring 88 and proving 'an emphatic success' (*Wisden*, 1906, 139). In his second match he made 155 and was awarded his county cap on the steps of the pavilion. Essex, who had declined to give him a trial two years earlier, were Surrey's opponents. W. G. Grace had witnessed his most accomplished successor. Not even Donald Bradman, against whom Hobbs would play in the 1930s, would eclipse him as a batsman for all conditions.

For Surrey, over ten seasons, Hobbs and Hayward would share forty opening partnerships of over a century, four of them in five days in 1907. Hayward was the only one of the four great players with whom he opened the batting in his career to whom Hobbs played the junior role. He remained in awe of the older man, learned much from him in the art of looking for runs and in mutual understanding, but, as a 'modern', evolved his own technique. Not for Hobbs the classical front-foot, off-side style of Hayward. He was quick-footed, able to make a very late decision on whether to play forward or back. He had the full range of strokes and could control the pace with which he dispatched the ball. To all this was added a mental awareness of the position of fielders and the state of a game. After three seasons in first-class cricket Hobbs was selected to go to Australia in 1907–8 with MCC: a shade lucky in that others, such as Hayward, had rejected the terms offered, but well earned in a period of strong batting.

In 1906 Hobbs married Ada Ellen Gates of Cambridge. They would have three sons and a daughter. In the years before 1914 his overseas tours were clouded both by the absence of his wife and by his own unrelenting seasickness. After 1919 she often accompanied him and he travelled overland through Europe as far as he could.

Test cricketer in the 'golden age' It was on new year's day 1908 that Hobbs made his test début at Melbourne, scoring 83, and he remained an England player (never 'dropped') when available until his retirement from test cricket. He and Hayward opened the batting for England only once—at Lord's in 1909—and it would be Wilfred Rhodes who would be his partner in eighteen test matches up to 1914. The two players came together on MCC's 1909–10 tour of South Africa. Rhodes was already an established all-rounder and Hobbs momentarily bade fair to become one as well, opening the bowling in three of the tests and securing his only wicket at that level in his career. As a batsman, he alone mastered the South African googly bowlers on their matting wickets and his average of 67.37 was more than twice that of anyone else. Two years later, in Australia, it was his domination of the spinners which helped England to a 4–1 victory. He and Rhodes established a new first-wicket record when they put on 323 at Melbourne.

There were no visitors in 1914 and Hobbs played in every Surrey match to help the county win the championship for the only time in his association with them. His 2499 runs included ten centuries. 'Among all those brilliant innings, it would be difficult to pick out any better than the rest' (*Wisden*, 1915, 4). But his double-century against Yorkshire in August—with a partnership of 290 with Hayward—conferred a valedictory benediction upon the 'golden age' of cricket. In the twenty-five days after war had broken out, Hobbs scored 585 runs at an average of 73.25 as if buying time from Armageddon. Those who saw him play either side of the First World War believed he was at his peak in 1914. 'He can make strokes off balls that anyone but a genius would be content to play', recorded *World of Cricket*, and declared that a worldwide poll would make him 'first among the batsmen of the day' (ibid.).

Hobbs at first worked in a munitions factory during the war before joining the Royal Flying Corps in 1916. He played some cricket in the Bradford league and, as Air-Mechanic Hobbs, made 86 at Lord's in a charity match in 1918. In the following year Surrey gave him a benefit against Kent—rearranged from one in 1914. He was rewarded with £1671 and the spectators with a swift 47 runs in 32 minutes in bad light to give Surrey victory. With the proceeds he bought a shop at 59 Fleet Street, London. Jack Hobbs Ltd prospered through his own business acumen and his courtesy and personal presence. There he worked to within weeks of his death and the firm, which transferred to Islington in 1974, continued to flourish. The years which followed brought him financial independence beyond the dreams of the average county cricketer. Together with the shop, his income from Surrey (with another benefit of £2670 in 1926), bonuses, overseas tours, several books, and advertising brought him probably £1500 a year. His books were all 'ghosted' and included three autobiographies, two instructional manuals, and two novels. After he retired he did some reporting for the press in a style more descriptive than analytical. He allowed his heart to rule his head in judging players. In the field of advertising he was in the forefront of cricketers being identified with products, and gave his name to Waterman's pens and to cricket equipment. The prosperity which came his way was reflected in such modest displays of wealth as buying an Austin 12 car and financing his wife's passage on overseas tours. In achieving affluence he retained a concern for his family's security denied in his own childhood.

Post-war records Hobbs, in 1919, was 'just as great as ever' (*Wisden*, 1920, 84), scoring a century in all three matches for the Players against the Gentlemen and making 700 runs more than anyone else in the season. In 1921, however, he was taken ill during the test match at Leeds and his life was saved by an emergency operation for an ulcerated appendix. In 1923 he became only the third player to make a century of centuries. Two years later, against Somerset at Taunton, he both equalled and beat W. G. Grace's record of 126 centuries. For three weeks previously he had been pursued by the press and the motion-picture crews while billboards carried the heading 'Hobbs fails again' (after a mere half-century). He ended the season of 1925 by making 266 not out for the Players against the Gentlemen, the highest score in that historic fixture. In all, he made sixteen centuries that year and he headed the English averages with 3024 runs (average 70.32). Throughout these years his regular Surrey opening partner was Andy Sandham, the pair sharing sixty-six opening stands of over 100. Against Oxford University in 1926 they put on 428, with Hobbs making 261. Later in the season he scored 316 not out against Middlesex at Lord's. This proved to be his own personal highest score and remained a ground record until 1990. An earlier 176 not out against Middlesex brought him an undefeated aggregate against that county of 492 runs. He topped the national batting averages (77.60), with Herbert Sutcliffe coming second.

In the twelve years after the war, it was Sutcliffe, replacing Rhodes, who was Hobbs's greatest test partner. 'Hobbs and Sutcliffe' became almost a synonym for English stability. The two came together against South Africa in 1924 with successive stands of 136 and 268, a performance even bettered when their initial partnerships against Australia in 1924–5 were ones of 157, 110, and 283. In all they achieved fifteen century opening stands. Two of them instance the ability of both men to bat in difficult conditions on a turning or 'sticky' wicket. At the Oval in 1926 England regained the Ashes after fourteen years, with Hobbs making exactly 100. In Melbourne in 1929 their batting made possible an England three-wicket victory against all the odds. Hobbs's 49, with only one four, was to be measured not by figures but by footwork. Eight weeks later, on the same ground, he became the oldest player to score a century in an England–Australia test match. Indeed, apart from two tests in 1928 (when he averaged 106.00) against the West Indies, all his runs in test cricket were made against Australia or South Africa. His final test appearance, at the Oval in 1930, saw him go quietly from the scene. After fielding out 695 runs, he batted in the evening light and was dismissed for 9. He had played in sixty-one test matches (1908–30), making fifteen centuries and scoring 5410 runs (average 56.94).

Hobbs continued to play for Surrey. Not a man who pursued records, he would nevertheless have liked to have made 200 centuries. But by 1934 he was limiting his appearances and in that season his solitary 100 was made against Lancashire in George Duckworth's benefit match at Old Trafford. He was content with his 197 centuries in first-class cricket and he would have no truck with those who set store by some he had made in India on a private tour. *Wisden* has enshrined both his number of centuries (at 197) and his career figures of 61,237 runs (average 50.65). Neither will ever be eclipsed. Hobbs was a good enough medium-pace bowler to take over 100 wickets. In 1920 he had been second in the English batting averages and top of the bowling. As a cover point, he had few equals and an affected lethargy lured many a victim (fifteen in Australia in 1911–12) to his doom.

Honoured retirement In 1934 Surrey named their gates at the Oval after Hobbs and in the following year made him a life member. In 1949 he was among the first band of professionals to be made life members of MCC and four years later he became the first professional cricketer to be knighted, an honour he accepted with surprise and even embarrassment. There had been earlier 'firsts'. In 1926 he had become the first professional to serve on a test match selection committee and, during that season, he captained England in the fourth test after A. W. Carr became ill. His playing career had effectively ended with his retirement but there would be a century in the fathers' match (he was a grandfather) at Kimbolton School in 1941. The statisticians credited him with 244 centuries at all levels.

Hobbs's biographers and obituarists could strike no discordant note. He was a man of moral probity, religious conviction, and personal commitment. And he was humble enough to see himself as an ordinary person blessed with one extraordinary talent, which he put into its proper perspective. It was an attitude of mind which tempered the sternness of his approach with an engaging humour and a delight in playing practical jokes. He ended his days at Hove, occasionally watching cricket and devotedly caring for his ailing wife, who predeceased him by nine months. Jack Hobbs died at his home, 23 Furze Croft, Furze Hill, Hove, Sussex, in his sleep on 21 December 1963. He was buried in Hove cemetery. He belonged, said *The Times*, to the golden age of cricket. He 'was the gold standard itself'.   GERALD M. D. HOWAT

Sources R. Mason, *Jack Hobbs* (1960) · J. Arlott, *Jack Hobbs* (1981) · P. Landsberg, *Jack Hobbs* (1953) · J. Hobbs, *My life story* (1935) · *Wisden* (1964) · *The Times* (23 Dec 1963) · *The Cricketer*, 45 (1 Feb 1964) · W. A. Bettesworth, 'Surrey batsman', *Cricket*, 25 (1906), 54 · *World of Cricket*, 1/18 (1 Aug 1914), 385 · J. Hobbs, *Playing for England* (1931) · J. Hobbs, *My cricketing memories* (1924) · *Wisden* (1902–35) · P. Bailey, P. Thorn, and P. Wynne-Thomas, *Who's who of cricketers*, rev. edn (1993) · C. Martin-Jenkins, *World cricketers: a biographical dictionary* (1996)

Archives Surrey HC, letters to F. S. P. L. Gridlestone, 3035/11 |FILM BFI NFTVA, 'Hobbs scores his 124th century', Topical Budget, 20 July 1925 · BFI NFTVA, 'Life of Jack Hobbs', 1925 · BFI NFTVA, advertising film footage · BFI NFTVA, documentary footage · BFI NFTVA, news footage · BFI NFTVA, sports footage

Likenesses photograph, 1906, repro. in Bettesworth, 'Surrey batsman', 54 · Hawkins of Brighton, photograph, 1914, repro. in *World of Cricket* · W. S. Broadhead, oils, 1920–29, Surrey County Cricket Club, Oval, Kennington, London [*see illus.*] · photographs, 1922–39, Hult. Arch. · Central News Agency, photograph, 1925, repro. in *Wisden* (1926) · cigarette card, colour, 1934, Lord's, MCC collection · R. S. Sherriffs, ink caricature, 1936, NPG · W. Stoneman, photograph, 1953, NPG · H. L. Oakley, silhouette, NPG · photographs, repro. in W. A. Powell, ed., *Surrey CCC (archive photographs)* (1996), 41–65 · photographs, Lord's, MCC collection · photographs, repro. in *World of Cricket*

Wealth at death £19,445: probate, 24 Feb 1964, *CGPLA Eng. & Wales*

Hobbs, Thomas (1648–1698), surgeon and physician, son of Moses Hobbs (d. 1655), gentleman, of Winchester, and his wife, Emma, was born at 6 a.m. on 11 May 1648, according to a horoscope by Charles Bernard. Apprenticed to James Molins (1631–1687) in May 1667, he was free of the Barber–Surgeons' Company in July 1674. By 1678 he was a rising surgeon living in Fleet Street with his first wife, Hellinor Hachet, who was of St Bride's when they married on St Thomas's day 1676. Bernard recorded her birth as at 4 p.m. on 16 December 1653 in Copenhagen. Sir Thomas Browne called her 'my cosen Hobbes' in letters to his son Edward and in one of 10 May 1679 thought her pregnancy must have reached term (*Letters*, 123). The burial of a Hester Hobbs at St Bride's that day may explain her fate.

Hobbs succeeded Thomas Hollier as a lithotomist at St Bartholomew's in December 1680, alternately with Molins until his death, then alone. He was surgeon to the King's troop of horse guards from July 1683 to 1690, and was brought in to bleed Charles II from the jugular vein in his final illness and signed the necropsy report. Sworn surgeon to the household of James II in April 1685, he followed Molins as surgeon-in-ordinary in February 1687. The following June he was granted a crest and confirmation of his paternal arms, and in August became master of his company, although he had in December 1684 been licensed to practise medicine by the Royal College of Physicians. A book on lithotomy in 1683 and Nahum Tate's translation of Fracastoro's *Syphilis* in 1686 were dedicated to him as a surgeon, as which he performed the necropsy on Queen Mary in December 1694. He was sometimes identified as the venereologist Guiacum in Garth's *The Dispensary* of 1699.

It was probably in late 1687 that Hobbs married Katharine (*bap.* 1666, *d.* 1738), eldest surviving daughter of John Stanyan (1624?–1714) of Harefield, Middlesex, and his wife, Susanna (1640–1707), daughter of John Pritchet, bishop of Gloucester. Daughters, Catherine and Susannah, baptized at St Clement Danes in November 1688 and September 1689, were followed by a son, Thomas (1690?–1707). They moved in 1693 from Essex Street to a house he bought in Lincoln's Inn Fields. He had also bought the manor of Ashley, close to a house called Rookley that he may have inherited, and leased the rectory of Barton Stacy, besides other property in Hampshire. Hobbs is also known to have been an investor in a street lighting scheme in the City of London.

Having received a Lambeth doctorate in medicine in July 1691 from Archbishop Tillotson, Hobbs resigned from St Bartholomew's in June 1693, paid arrears to the college, and completed the rare transformation into a formally qualified physician. As such he earned the gratitude of Dryden in a postscript to *The Works of Virgil* of 1697, in which one plate was dedicated to Hobbs, who had the whole set at his country house. Inventories of Rookley and the London house were made when his surviving children, Thomas and Susannah, sued their mother, as executrix, for greater maintenance from their father's will, dated 13 October 1697. Hobbs had died at Lincoln's Inn Fields on 12 July 1698 and been buried at Barton Stacy. His wife had over £400 a year for life, but most of his estate was to descend in tail male through his son or, as happened, through the four sons of his sister Elizabeth Weekes. His considerable library was sold in 1712. Portraits of Hobbs, his wife, and their two children, in the London house at his death, have disappeared. His widow had that house until her marriage in October 1700 to Richard Chaundeler, whom she survived. The daughter Susannah had £5000 at twenty-one; she married in January 1721 Temple Stanyan, her mother's first cousin, and died childless in March 1725.   G. C. R. MORRIS

Sources C. Bernard, 'Astrological schemes', BL, Sloane MS 1684, 28 • PRO, PROB 6/31 [Moses Hobbs, 1655], fol. 246 • G. C. R. Morris, 'The household goods of Thomas Hobbs, 1647?–1698, surgeon to James II, physician to Dryden', *Transactions of the London and Middlesex Archaeological Society*, 23 (1972), 204–8 • G. C. R. Morris, 'Dryden, Hobbs, Tonson and the death of Charles II', *N&Q*, 220 (1975), 558–9 • PRO, PROB 11/447, fol. 215 • J. Dryden, *The works of Virgil* (1697), 595, 623 • K. Gilbert, *Life in a Hampshire village: the history of Ashley* (1992), 98–100 • E. B. Krumbhaar, 'Two contemporary manuscripts bearing on the death of Charles II of England', *Transactions of the College of Physicians of Philadelphia*, 4th ser., 6 (1938), 51–9 • *The letters of Sir Thomas Browne*, ed. G. Keynes (1946) • *A catalogue of part of the library of that late eminent surgeon Thomas Hobbes, MD* (1712) • PRO, T 53/12, 524 • Barber-Surgeons' Company, freedoms, court minutes, apprentices, GL • BL, Stowe MS 677, fol. 69 • E. S. de Beer, 'Collections for the history of London street lighting', *N&Q*, 181 (1941), 4–8 • *The manuscripts of the House of Lords*, new ser., 12 vols. (1900–77), vol. 1, pp. 541–4 • private information (2004)
Likenesses portrait, *c.*1698
Wealth at death approx. £1400 p.a. freehold and leasehold property; £1133 15*s.* 6*d.* household goods; approximately £4500 owing to him: Morris, 'The household goods'

Hobday, Sir Frederick Thomas George (1870–1939), veterinary surgeon, was born at Burton upon Trent, Staffordshire, on 3 November 1870, the eldest son of Thomas Hobday, a brewer's manager for Messrs Bass, and Mary Newbold, his wife. Educated at Burton grammar school, he left to work for his uncle's coal business. After a short time he moved to Hanley, where he stayed for two years as an articled apprentice to Alfred Hodgkins, a veterinary surgeon. He then entered the Royal Veterinary College, London, in 1888, and graduated MRCVS on 18 May 1892. He was appointed resident hospital surgeon at the Royal Veterinary College after his graduation, and served there for six months before entering private practice with Arthur Blake, of Redhill. It was while he was in practice that he began to explore different ways of administering hydrocyanic acid to animals to cause death, thus relieving them, in the shortest possible time, of any suffering.

In October 1893 Hobday returned to the Royal Veterinary College as a junior professor, in charge of the outpatients' department and the teaching of materia medica and later hygiene. In 1895 he married Elizabeth, daughter of Thomas Evans and widow of William Chambers, a veterinary surgeon of Bromyard, Herefordshire; they had a son and a daughter. Hobday became FRCVS on 14 May 1897 and was awarded the John Henry Steel medal in 1899. In the same year he resigned his professorship and joined Frank Ridler in private practice in Kensington. The seven years he worked at the college 'marked an epoch in veterinary science. His work on anaesthesia, and small animal surgery, was monumental and destined to light a flame which has never diminished' (McCunn, 250).

Hobday became a skilful surgeon, the craftsman rather than the reasoning diagnostician. Hardworking and ambitious, he spared neither himself nor his assistants. He was urbane with clients and courteous to students; he was a Bohemian, a member of the Savage Club, and a great socialite, who possessed boundless energy. He entered fully and generously into schemes for the advancement of his profession, and developed surgical techniques of the animal reproductive system and for small animals and horses. He was pre-eminent as a surgeon and his practice at 'Church Street, Kensington became a veritable Mecca

Sir Frederick Thomas George Hobday (1870–1939), by unknown photographer

Hobday was in command of no. 22 Veterinary Hospital at Abbeville in France, with the rank of major; it was the 'largest reception hospital for horses and mules on the western front' (Cotchin, 141). At the end of 1916 he took his hospital to Italy. For his services he was twice mentioned in dispatches and appointed CMG (1918); he also received French and Italian decorations. Hobday retired from the army with the esteem of many influential veterinary surgeons of allied countries; he was an honorary member of the veterinary associations of Paris, Belgium, Norway, Sweden, and the United States of America. By maintaining his friendships abroad he became the best-known and most widely travelled British veterinary surgeon. In appreciation of his work for the profession the Central Veterinary Society presented him with the Victory medal (1921). Later he received the honorary doctorate of veterinary medicine from Zürich University (1933), the foreign associateship of the Veterinary Academy of France, and corresponding membership of the Academy of Medicine of Romania (1936).

After the war Hobday had turned to his practice in Kensington—where he lived, at 31 Argyll Road, for the rest of his life—and his numerous public activities. For example, he served on the council of the Royal College of Veterinary Surgeons from 1925 to 1939, and he was a member of its examining committee. He was also a council member of the National Veterinary Medical Association. Between 1924 and 1926 he was president of the section of comparative medicine of the Royal Society of Medicine. He was elected an honorary fellow of the Royal Society in 1937. Hobday was prominent, too, in the work of several animal welfare organizations, including the Universities Federation for Animal Welfare, of which he was president (1927–39). He played a significant part in the Metropolitan Water Trough Association, Our Dumb Friends League, and the Council of Justice to Animals. He served on parliamentary committees dealing with the export of horses 'and was largely responsible for the introduction of humane methods in the slaughter house' (McCunn, 253), and he conducted very important initiatives to promote research on canine distemper. He was also made an honorary fellow of the Hunterian Society.

In 1927 Hobday gave up his practice in Kensington to return to the Royal Veterinary College as principal in succession to Sir John McFadyean. He thereby became responsible for the administration of the college, the professorship of surgery, and the appeal and planning for reconstruction—a burden too great for any one man. He began the job with enthusiasm and remarkable energy; in his inaugural address he declared the governors' scheme inadequate and called for £250,000. By 1936 he had succeeded: he had managed to tap the soul of the animal-loving British population, and many people from the king to small children made contributions to the college rebuilding fund. Also, the income and student entry had been more than doubled, the college staff had been enlarged, and the debt of 1927 had been cleared. In 1933 he was knighted, in recognition of his work for the college.

However, in 1936 defects in the college administration

for veterinarians from all parts of the world' (McCunn, 250). Hobday also perfected Karl Adolf Günther's and Professor Williams's operation for the relief of 'roaring' in horses, introduced by W. L. Williams, and he became so successful at performing the operation that the technique became known as 'Hobdaying'. He also found time to develop, commercially, two thermometers for domestic animals and fowl, and for the dog and cat, and apparatus for administering anaesthetic.

Hobday published more than 250 articles for the veterinary press during his lifetime: for the *Veterinary Journal*, of which he was editor from 1906 to 1939; for the *Journal of Comparative Pathology and Therapeutics*, and for the *Veterinary Record*. He also published several useful textbooks, of which *Surgical Diseases of the Dog and Cat* (1901) was 'a milestone in small animal surgery' (Formston, 5). However, Hobday lacked the disposition for reflection and critical study, and he acquired the habit of seeking ideas from more informed minds, especially from Henry Gray, his neighbour and friend of more than forty years.

In 1912 Hobday was gazetted honorary veterinary surgeon to Queen Alexandra, an appointment he held for the rest of his life. On the outbreak of the First World War he joined the army veterinary corps and was posted as veterinary officer to King Edward's Horse. From 1915 to 1916 were alleged. The governors appointed a committee of inquiry and called upon Hobday to resign. It was not a popular decision; two college governors resigned in protest, and a question about Hobday's retirement was asked in the House of Commons by the MP for Doncaster, Richard Short. Denied an opportunity of defending himself, Hobday refused to resign, whereupon the governors announced his resignation on the grounds of his having passed the age limit. When reminded at a subsequent meeting that no age limit had been specified in the appointment of the principal, the governors ruled that Hobday's salary would cease at the opening of the new buildings, until which date he would remain absent on leave. Professor Formston, who was at the college during this time, has revealed that it is possible that Hobday was forced to resign because of the administrative shortcomings of the college secretary who had not exercised sufficient control over his immediate subordinate, whose office was found 'in some disarray. The accounts were in a state of chaos, bills had not been passed for payment, the cash book had not been written up and no posting had been done in the ledgers for six months' (Cotchin, 152). Hobday was invited to the opening of the new buildings by the king and queen in November 1937, but he was a broken man. Disillusionment embittered his forced retirement, and resentment sapped his strength.

Hobday nevertheless returned to practice as a consultant and took up the cause to establish a chair of comparative medicine at the Royal Veterinary College. He wrote his autobiography in 1938, but became ill later that year. He died at St Andrew's House, Droitwich, Worcestershire, on 24 June 1939, while staying with a friend. Professor McCunn, writing a memoir of 'Freddie', as everyone knew him, said, 'no man has ever done more for his profession. His name will live in our hearts forever and we will never see his like again' (McCunn, 255). Hobday's ashes were scattered in Putney Vale cemetery following a funeral service at St Mary Abbots Church, Kensington.

LINDA WARDEN

Sources E. Cotchin, *The Royal Veterinary College, London: a bicentenary history* (1990) · C. Formston, 'Major Sir Frederick Thomas George Hobday … the first Sir Frederick Hobday memorial lecture', *Equine Veterinary Journal*, 4/2 (1972), i–xiv · J. McCunn, 'Sir Frederick Hobday, 1870–1939: a memoir', *Veterinary Journal*, 95 (1939), 249–70 · minute book, 1876–1906, Royal Veterinary College, London · minutes of the General Purposes Committee, Royal Veterinary College, London, 2 Nov 1936, 312–14; 30 March 1936, 283–4 · F. Hobday, *Fifty years a veterinary surgeon* (1938) · *Veterinary Record* (1 July 1939), 816–19 · *Veterinary Record* (27 Nov 1937), 1524–6 · *Veterinary Record* (15 Aug 1936), 990–92 · *Veterinary Record* (7 Jan 1933), 1–3 · *Veterinary Record* (1895), 642 · *The Incisor*, 2/1 (1937), 4–7 · J. Y. Bogue, 'Sir Frederick Hobday', *Nature*, 144 (1939), 184 · R. H. Dunlop, *Veterinary medicine: an illustrated history* (1996) · b. cert. · d. cert. · DNB
Archives Royal Veterinary College, London, historical collections | FILM Royal Veterinary College, London, historical collections
Likenesses Hassall, oils, 1937, Royal Veterinary College, London · photograph, Royal Veterinary College, London [*see illus.*]
Wealth at death £11,676 12s. 8d.: probate, 24 Aug 1939, CGPLA Eng. & Wales

Hobday, William Armfield (1771–1831), portrait and miniature painter, was born in St Mary's Square, Birmingham, and baptized there in St Martin's Church, the second son of Samuel Hobday (1745/6–1816), a wealthy manufacturer of spoons, and Elisabeth Armfield. A talented draughtsman, Hobday was sent to London in 1786, and was apprenticed for six years to the engraver W. J. Barney. In 1790 he was admitted to the Royal Academy Schools, where he studied alongside Martin Archer Shee, and made rapid progress. Without completing his academic studies, however, he established himself at 9 Charles Street, London, as a painter of portraits in miniature and watercolour. From 1794 he became a regular exhibitor at the Royal Academy, and soon secured a fashionable clientele including Lord Howard de Walden and Lady Wilson of Charlton. His friends included the painters George Morland, Charles Landseer, James Northcote, and George Chinnery. About 1800 Hobday married Elizabeth Dorothy Ivory and moved to 9 Holles Street, where, supported mainly by his father, he lived extravagantly.

In 1804 Hobday moved to Bristol, where he painted chiefly portraits, including miniatures, of officers embarking for the theatre of war in the Peninsula. His work, in the manner of Sir Joshua Reynolds, included large oil portraits and subject pictures. However, he never achieved Reynolds's skill as a draughtsman, or his eye for colour. Despite the good income he generated by his work, Hobday's lavish lifestyle created increasing financial difficulties. In 1817 he returned to London, where he took Winchester House, Old Broad Street, hoping (but failing) to renew former artistic and social connections, although he painted a small family group portrait, *The family of W. N. Rothschild, esq., consul general of his Austrian majesty at the British court* (exh. RA, 1821; priv. coll.) for 1000 guineas. His work became increasingly mannered, his oils lacking the delicacy and compositional grace he attained in his small watercolours. In 1821 or 1822 Hobday moved to 54 Pall Mall, to which large galleries were attached. After a disastrous speculation in a panoramic exhibition 'Poecilorama' at the Egyptian Hall, he opened these galleries, which he called Hobday's Gallery of Modern Art, in order to sell pictures on commission. The venture failed, although supported by leading English and French artists including Delacroix and Horace Vernet, and in 1829 Hobday went bankrupt. Following his wife's death that year, on 31 October 1830 he married Maria Ustonson (d. 1859), a fishing tackle maker, of 205 Fleet Street. Hobday died of inflammation of the lungs on 17 February 1831 and was buried on 23 February at St Bride's, Fleet Street, London. He was survived by his sons Alfred Hobday (1824–1884), lithographer, and George Smith Armfield Hobday (1811–1893), animal painter, and a daughter, Harriet Eliza.

At the height of his career Hobday was generally well patronized: at one time he averaged six sitters per day, charging 10 guineas per miniature and 20 guineas for a three-quarter length portrait. From 1794 to 1830 he exhibited seventy works at the Royal Academy; the most acclaimed was his portrait of Charles Evans entitled *Portrait of Carolus (lately Deceased, Distinguished as the Hermit of*

Tong Castle, Shropshire) (1823; exh. RA, 1823, British Institution, 1824, Hobday's Gallery of Modern Art, London, 1829). His full-length portrait *Miss Biggs in the Character of Cora (a Print, from the Tragedy, 'Pizarro'*) (exh. RA, 1801; V&A) was engraved by W. Bond in 1804, and *The Late R[ichard] Reynolds, Esq., the Bristol Philanthropist* (exh. RA, 1817; Bristol Art Gallery and Museum) was engraved by William Sharp. Hobday died virtually unknown and has since remained in obscurity, although his *Lady in a White Dress with a White Sash, Pink Cloak Lined with Fur* (sold at Christies in 1911 for 1350 guineas) briefly raised his profile.

F. M. O'DONOGHUE, *rev.* LIZ MELLINGS

Sources 'Memoir of William Armfield Hobday', *Arnold's Library of Fine Arts*, 11/2 (1831), 384 · Graves, *RA exhibitors* · 'Early English pictures: high prices at Christies', *The Times* (13 Feb 1911) · 'British portrait miniatures', www.portrait-miniatures.com/british.htm, 16 Sept 2000 · Bryan, *Painters* · H. H. Hobday-Horsley, *Birmingham Weekly Post* (23 Feb 1884) · Graves, *Artists* · S. Edwards, *Miniatures at Kenwood: the Draper gift* (1997), 182–3 · B. S. Long, *British miniaturists* (1929) · W. A. Hobday, *Accessory after the fact* (Boston, MA, 1911) · *Revue de l'Art Ancien et Moderne*, 30 (1911), 256 [O. C. 1500] · parish register, Birmingham, St Martin, July 1771 [baptism] · *London Directory* (1820–29) · private information (2004) [R. A. Hobday, great-great-grandson; Stuart Hobday, cousin of R. A. Hobday]
Archives priv. coll., archives
Likenesses W. A. Hobday, self-portrait, 1793, V&A · W. A. Hobday, self-portrait, miniature, 1793, V&A · W. A. Hobday, self-portrait, oils, 1814 (*Portrait of an artist*), Birmingham Museums and Art Gallery
Wealth at death bankrupt: private information (2004) [R. A. Hobday]; 'Memoir', *Arnold's Library*, 384

Hobhouse, Arthur, Baron Hobhouse (1819–1904), judge, was born on 10 November 1819 at Hadspen House, Hadspen, Somerset, the fourth and youngest son of Henry *Hobhouse (1776–1854), barrister and archivist, and his wife, Harriett (*d.* 1858), sixth daughter of John Turton of Sugnall Hall, Staffordshire. Edmund *Hobhouse, bishop of Nelson, New Zealand, and Reginald Hobhouse (1818–1895), archdeacon of Bodmin, were elder brothers. Hobhouse could read at the age of two and learned Latin from the age of four. He attended a private school and Eton College (1830–37). In 1837 he went to Balliol College, Oxford, where he graduated BA in 1840 with a first class in classics and proceeded MA in 1844. Entering Lincoln's Inn on 22 April 1841, he was called to the bar on 6 May 1845, and soon acquired a large chancery practice. On 10 August 1848 he married Mary (*d.* 1905), daughter of Thomas Farrer, solicitor, and sister of Thomas Henry *Farrer, the civil servant. Her sister, Cecilia Frances (*d.* 1910), was the wife of Stafford Henry *Northcote, the tory politician.

In 1862 Hobhouse became a QC and a bencher of his inn, serving as treasurer in 1880–1. A severe illness in 1866 led him to retire from practice and accept the appointment of charity commissioner. Hobhouse threw himself into the work with energy. He was not only active in administration but advocated a reform of the law governing charitable endowments. The Endowed Schools Act, 1869, was a first step in that direction, and under that act George Lyttelton, Hobhouse, and Canon H. G. Robinson were appointed commissioners with large powers of reorganizing endowed schools. Much was accomplished in regard to endowed schools, but the efforts of Hobhouse and his fellow commissioners received a check in 1871, when the House of Lords rejected their scheme for remodelling the Emanuel Hospital, Westminster. Hobhouse disliked the ensuing controversy and with little regret he retired in 1872 in order to succeed Sir James Fitzjames Stephen as law member of the council of the viceroy of India. Hobhouse had meanwhile served on the royal commission on the operation of the Land Transfer Act in 1869.

Hobhouse 'on his departure for India received strong hints that it would be desirable for him to slacken the pace of the legislative machine', which had been quickened by the consolidating and codifying activities of Fitzjames Stephen and of Stephen's immediate predecessor, Sir Henry Sumner Maine (Ilbert, 138). That suggestion he approved. Whitley Stokes, secretary in the legislative department, was mainly responsible for the measures passed during Hobhouse's term of office, with the important exception of the Specific Relief Act, 1877, in which Hobhouse as an equity lawyer took an especial interest, and a revision of the law relating to the transfer of property, which became a statute after he left India. A strong Liberal, Hobhouse found himself strongly opposed to several aspects of Disraeli's government's policy toward India, especially with respect to legal changes and Afghanistan. He signed the dispatch of 7 June 1875 replying to Lord Salisbury's dispatch of 22 January 1875 on Afghanistan and was consequently involved in the prolonged dispute which followed.

On the conclusion of his term of office in 1877 Hobhouse was made a KCSI, and on his return to England soon engaged in party politics as a thoroughgoing opponent of the Afghan policy of the Conservative government. In 1880 he and John (afterwards Viscount) Morley unsuccessfully contested Westminster in the Liberal interest against Sir Charles Russell, third baronet, of Swallowfield, and W. H. Smith. Hobhouse was at the bottom of the poll.

In 1878 Hobhouse was made arbitrator under the Epping Forest Act (41 & 42 Vict. c. 213) and in 1881 he succeeded Sir Joseph Napier on the judicial committee of the privy council. There without salary he did useful judicial work for twenty years. He delivered the decision of the committee in 200 appeals, of which 120 were from India. Several cases were of grave moment. In *Merriman v. Williams*, an action between the bishop and dean of Grahamstown, Hobhouse set forth fully the history of the relationship of the Church of South Africa with the Church of England, and decided that the South African church was independent of it. In the consolidated appeals in 1887 by several Canadian banks against the decisions of the court of queen's bench for Quebec, which involved the respective limits of the power of the dominion and provincial legislatures to regulate banks, Hobhouse's judgment upheld the right of the province to tax banks and insurance companies constituted by act of the dominion legislature. In a case from India in 1899 (26 Indian Appeals, Law Reports 113) which necessitated the review of a number of conflicting decisions of the Indian courts, Hobhouse settled a long disputed point in Hindu law and decided, contrary to much tradition, that when an individual person was adopted as an only son, the fact of adoption should be legally recognized and the parents' plenary powers admitted.

In 1885 Hobhouse accepted a peerage from the outgoing Liberal government with a view to assisting in the judicial work of the House of Lords, but a statutory qualification by which only judges of the high courts of the United Kingdom could sit to hear appeals had been overlooked. In 1887 the disqualification was removed by act of parliament in regard to members of the judicial committee; but Hobhouse did not take up the work of a judge in the House of Lords. He only sat there to try three cases, in two of which, *Russell v. Countess of Russell* (1897) and the *Kempton Park case* (1899), he was in a dissenting minority. As a judge Hobhouse, who was always careful and painstaking, invariably stated the various arguments fully and fairly, but he was tenacious of his deliberately formed opinion.

While engaged on the judicial committee, Hobhouse devoted much energy to local government of London. From 1877 to 1899 he was a vestryman of St George's, Hanover Square. In 1880 he assisted to form and long worked for the London Municipal Reform League, which aimed at securing a single government for the metropolis. From 1882 to 1884 he was a member of the London school board. On the creation of the London county council in 1888 Hobhouse was one of the first aldermen. Advancing years and increasing deafness led him to retire from the judicial committee in 1901.

Hobhouse was to the last an advanced Liberal. In his heyday he influentially advocated (to the meeting of the Social Science Congress in Birmingham in 1868) changes in the law on married women's property, published in a pamphlet in 1869, and changes to the law of endowments and property settlement, the latter published in *The Dead Hand* (1880). At the end of his life he strongly opposed imperialism, believing, as he wrote to Sir Charles Hobhouse on 14 April 1902, 'we have chosen *Imperium* and rejected *Libertas*. We are fast becoming a military empire' (Hobhouse and Hammond, 223). He assisted his niece, Emily *Hobhouse, with her campaign exposing conditions in the concentration camps in South Africa, and he became an important link between Victorian Liberalism and the 'New Liberalism' of the early 1900s, exemplified by the admiring memoir of him by his nephew Leonard *Hobhouse, on whom he was a significant influence.

Hobhouse died at his London house, 15 Bruton Street, Berkeley Square, on 6 December 1904, and was cremated at Golders Green crematorium; his wife survived until 2 May 1905. The couple were childless and the peerage became extinct on Hobhouse's death.

C. E. A. BEDWELL, *rev.* H. C. G. MATTHEW

Sources L. T. Hobhouse and J. L. Hammond, *Lord Hobhouse: a memoir* (1905) · J. Foster, *Men-at-the-bar: a biographical hand-list of the members of the various inns of court*, 2nd edn (1885), 220 · J. Haydn, *The book of dignities: containing rolls of the official personages of the British empire* (1851) · *The Times* (7 Dec 1904) · *The Times* (10 Dec 1904) · *The Times* (18 April 1854), 9 · *GM*, 2nd ser., 42 (1854), 78–80 · Foster, *Alum. Oxon.* · *Dod's Peerage* (1854), 301–2 · C. Ilbert, *Legislative methods and forms* (1901)

Archives National Archives of India, New Delhi, notes and minutes | BL, corresp. with W. E. Gladstone, Add. MSS 44481–44789, *passim* · Co-operative Union, Holyoake House, Manchester, archives, letters to George Holyoake · ICL, corresp. with Thomas Huxley · LPL, letters to Lord Selborne

Likenesses G. Richmond, chalk drawing, 1854, Lincoln's Inn, London · print, NPG

Wealth at death £96,037 16s. 9d.: resworn probate, 3 Jan 1905, *CGPLA Eng. & Wales*

Hobhouse, Sir Benjamin, first baronet (1757–1831), politician, was born in Bristol on 29 March 1757, the second son of John Hobhouse (1712–1787), a Bristol merchant, of The College, Westbury-on-Trym, Gloucestershire, and his first wife, Mary Smith, *née* Medley (d. 1759), of Hereford. He was educated at Bristol grammar school where the local MP, Edmund Burke, presented him with a copy of *Paradise Lost* following his delivery of an oration. He entered Brasenose College, Oxford, in 1774, graduating BA in 1778 and MA in 1781, and in 1776 entered the Middle Temple, from where he was called to the bar in 1781. He practised on the western circuit until 1783, when he travelled to France and Italy for his health; he later published *Remarks* on his travels (1796). After his return he married on 12 September 1785 Charlotte (*c.*1760–1791), daughter of Samuel Cam of Bradford, Wiltshire, clothier and partner in a Bath bank; they had three sons and two daughters. He married second on 18 April 1793 Amelia (1767–1846), daughter of Dr Joshua *Parry (1719–1776), Presbyterian minister of Cirencester, and Sarah Hillier; they had four sons and ten daughters. Both marriages drew the Anglican Hobhouse into dissenting circles. He became interested in unitarianism, wrote several pamphlets, notably against the Test Acts, but also on heresy, dogma, unrest, and intentional regicide, and described his creed as humanitarianism.

Politics also attracted Hobhouse. In 1780 he had canvassed for the ministerial candidates at Bristol, following his father's politics. By 1792, however, his sympathies were whig and reformist, on which platform, also championing peace, he was defeated at Bristol in 1796. On 20 February 1797 he entered parliament for Bletchingley, his seat purchased from Sir Robert Clayton for £4000. In his first session he persistently criticized the bank stoppage of cash payments, and went on to oppose Pitt's administration on most major questions, displaying ethical concerns in advocating abolition of the slave trade and religious toleration. He joined the Whig Club on 5 June 1798. In 1800 he invested £33,000 in Whitbread's brewery. When his college friend Addington succeeded Pitt in 1801 he remained in opposition, but was gradually won over, especially when peace was negotiated. As a committee chairman he was soon neutralized. In 1802 he declined candidature for Bristol or Chippenham in favour of a bought seat for Grampound. Addington converted him to support the resumption of war, and he defended territorial army measures, himself accepting a Wiltshire commission. Addington, who had wished to make him chairman of committees, appointed him secretary to the India Board of Control in November 1803. He followed Addington into opposition in May 1804 and was thought of for office when Addington (now Sidmouth) and Pitt were reconciled, but approved of Sidmouth's rift with government over Melville's conduct at the Admiralty in 1805.

When Sidmouth regained office in 1806 Hobhouse was appointed first commissioner for settling the Carnatic nawabs' debts (so remaining until 1829), and subsequently chairman of committees, both without salary. From 1806 he sat for Hindon on the Calthorpe interest, paying his expenses. He went into opposition with Sidmouth in 1807, and gave up his chairmanship for health reasons after the first session of that parliament. Ill health and differences from Sidmouth ensured that he abjured office, and he often voted with the opposition until 1812, when Sidmouth rejoined the government. He was appointed a commissioner of inquiry into Lincoln gaol in June, and created a baronet on 22 December 1812. He supported the government when present, albeit seldom vocally, in his last parliament. Retiring in 1818 when his eldest son, John Cam *Hobhouse, espoused radical politics, he was disappointed in his wish for a peerage. He was FRS, FSA, a vice-president of the Royal Society of Literature, and president in 1805–17 of the West of England Agricultural Society, which commissioned his bust by Chantrey for their Bath premises. He died on 14 August 1831 at his Berkeley Square house in London.   ROLAND THORNE

Sources B. Murphy and R. G. Thorne, 'Hobhouse, Sir Benjamin', HoP, *Commons, 1790–1820* · Baron Broughton [J. C. Hobhouse], *Recollections of a long life*, ed. Lady Dorchester [C. Carleton], 6 vols. (1909–11), vol. 1, pp. 1–3; vol. 4, p. 129 · *GM*, 1st ser., 101/2 (1831), 653 · *DNB* · *Public characters of 1805* (1805) · letters to John Cam Hobhouse, BL, Broughton MSS · letters to Henry Addington, Devon RO, Sidmouth papers · T. Green, *Extracts from a diary of a lover of literature* (1810), 235 · death duty registers, 1831, PRO, IR 26/1261 · Burke, *Peerage* (1949)
Archives BL, corresp., Add. MSS 27823, fol. 362, 29184, fol. 87, 32166, fol. 25 · BL OIOC, reports on Indian politics and finance, MS Eur. E261 | BL, corresp. with J. C. Hobhouse, Add. MSS 36456–36466, *passim* · Devon RO, Sidmouth MSS, letters to H. Addington
Likenesses F. Chantrey, bust, 1818, Victoria Art Gallery, Bath · F. Chantrey, pencil drawing, 1818, NPG · P. Audinet, line engraving, pubd 1825 (after T. Phillips), BM, NPG · J. Cochrane, stipple (after J. Jackson), BM, NPG; repro. in W. Jerdan, *National portrait gallery of illustrious and eminent personages* (1832)
Wealth at death under £250,000: PRO, death duty registers, IR 26/1261; will, 1831, PRO

Hobhouse, Sir Charles Edward Henry, fourth baronet (1862–1941), politician and diarist, was born on 30 June 1862 at Dormansland, near Lingfield, Surrey, the only son and third of six children of Sir Charles Parry Hobhouse, third baronet (1825–1916), Wiltshire landowner and former judge in the high court of Calcutta, and his wife, Edith Lucy, daughter of Sir Thomas Turton, second baronet, of Felcourt. His mother died in 1867 and his father soon remarried, having a further son and four daughters. Hobhouse was educated at Eton College (1875–9) and at Christ Church, Oxford (1880–81), and seemed destined for a military career, attending the Royal Military College,

Sandhurst. He joined the King's Royal Rifle Corps in 1884. He was diverted into politics both by his upbringing in a Liberal tradition and by his marriage on 24 April 1890 to Georgina Fleetwood (d. 1927), daughter of George Pargiter Fuller, of Neston Park, a neighbouring squire and Liberal MP.

In 1892 Hobhouse narrowly won Wiltshire East for the Liberals against a formidable Conservative opponent. In the ensuing parliament he served as a private secretary at the Colonial Office. The Liberal set-back in 1895 cost him his seat, and his chronic hay fever directed him to an urban constituency. He won East Bristol in 1900 and retained it in the general elections of 1906 and 1910.

The Liberals returned to office in 1905, and in 1907 Hobhouse became under-secretary of state for India. He headed a royal commission into decentralization whose report influenced subsequent Indian legislation. In April 1908 he became financial secretary to the Treasury, and in October 1911 gained a place in the cabinet as chancellor of the duchy of Lancaster. His career reached its peak in February 1914 when he became postmaster-general, an office then involved in the early developments of wireless telegraphy and the controversies concerning rival telegraphic systems. He succeeded his father in the baronetcy in 1916.

Hobhouse commanded confidence as a hard-working administrator and straightforward spokesman for his department. He did not make a great impact beyond his own office, nor was he in sympathy with some trends in Liberal affairs. He stood by traditional causes, such as free trade and Irish home rule, but he believed that David Lloyd George, as chancellor of the exchequer, should restrain spending and not encourage it. He deplored Sir Winston Churchill's big-navy policy, and he opposed quite provocatively the campaign for women's suffrage.

The First World War ended Hobhouse's career. He lost office when the first coalition was formed in May 1915, suffered discredit by opposing, and then capitulating to, the campaign for military conscription and, as a supporter of H. H. Asquith (later first earl of Oxford and Asquith), was crushed in the 1918 election by a Lloyd George Liberal and a Labour candidate. (He even suffered the indignity of losing his deposit, a provision but recently instituted to discourage 'freak' candidates.) Hobhouse remained active in Liberal affairs after 1918. Only as the party faded did he turn his attention from politics to his estates.

Hobhouse began keeping a diary during his round-the-world honeymoon in 1893, and continued to do so for five years. He returned to the practice in 1904 and did not cease until he lost office in 1915. These documents are of particular interest for a succession of dramatic episodes. Notwithstanding personal predilections and occasional misunderstanding of events, his diaries provide incisive sketches of key individuals and insights into the course of events. Their value is enhanced by the fact that at the time no official records were kept of cabinet meetings (apart from the prime minister's low-key letter to the king), and few diaries by leading politicians have survived from this period. Extracts from Hobhouse's diaries were published in 1977.

Of medium height and strong build, Hobhouse (despite his hay fever) was much given to outdoor activities, undertaking long expeditions on his bicycle and riding to hounds with a recklessness that sometimes resulted in personal injury. His first wife died in 1927. On 18 June 1931 he married Aimée Gladys (d. 1965), widow of Benjamin Adams Brendon, of the Indian Civil Service, and daughter of David Charles Ballinger Griffith, of Huntworth, Bedford. Both marriages were childless. Hobhouse died at his home, Monkton Farleigh Manor, Bradford-on-Avon, Wiltshire, on 26 June 1941. He was succeeded in the baronetcy by his half-brother, Reginald Arthur (1878–1947).

TREVOR WILSON, rev.

Sources *Inside Asquith's cabinet: from the diaries of Charles Hobhouse*, ed. E. David (1977) · *The Times* (27 June 1941) · *Manchester Guardian* (27 June 1941) · *The political diaries of C. P. Scott, 1911–1928*, ed. T. Wilson (1970) · Burke, *Peerage*
Archives BL, journals, Add. MSS 60504–60507 | U. Newcastle, Robinson L., corresp. with Walter Runciman
Likenesses G. Swaish, oils, 1915, priv. coll.; repro. in *Inside Asquith's cabinet*, ed. David, facing p. 70 · photograph (in later life), repro. in *Inside Asquith's cabinet*, ed. David, facing p. 247
Wealth at death £29,951 11s. 3d.: probate, 6 May 1942, CGPLA Eng. & Wales

Hobhouse, Edmund (1817–1904), bishop of Nelson, New Zealand, born in London on 17 April 1817, was elder brother of Arthur *Hobhouse, first Baron Hobhouse of Hadspen, and was second son of Henry *Hobhouse (1776–1854), under-secretary of state for the Home department, and his wife, Harriett Turton (1784/5–1858). He entered Eton College in 1824, but left it in 1830 because of ill health caused by overwork, and studied privately with tutors. He matriculated at Balliol College, Oxford, on 16 December 1834, and graduated BA in 1838, proceeding MA in 1842, BD in 1851, and DD in 1858. He rowed in the Balliol boat for four years (1835–8), and was stroke in 1836–7. He then studied theology at Durham University, where he graduated LTh in 1840. At his father's wish, he entered for a fellowship at Merton, and was elected at his third attempt in 1841. He was ordained deacon in the same year and priest in 1842. In 1843 he became vicar of the college living of St Peter-in-the-East, Oxford, which he held with his fellowship until 1858.

Hobhouse worked his parish with zeal and declined offers of better preferment. Bishop Samuel Wilberforce made him rural dean, and as secretary of the diocesan board of education he did much for the church schools and helped to found the Culham Training College for schoolmasters. On his father's death in 1854 he devoted part of his patrimony to providing at St Edmund Hall and St Alban Hall, Oxford, help for needy students. On 1 January 1858 he married Mary Elizabeth Brodrick; they had two sons.

On the subdivision of the diocese of New Zealand, Bishop G. A. Selwyn obtained the appointment of Hobhouse to the new see of Nelson, for which he was consecrated in September 1858. He arrived in New Zealand in January 1859, participating in the first general synod. Hobhouse organized the diocesan and parochial structure of his 20,000 square mile diocese, subsidizing diocesan expenditure from his own funds. His attempts to open Maori schools bore little fruit, but he founded Bishop's School in Nelson. Despite his obvious dedication, his episcopacy was controversial. He was sometimes regarded as intolerant and he was also seen, unjustly, as a Tractarian by local evangelicals. His cousin and one of his staff, the Revd H. M. Turton, was accused (and acquitted) of sodomy; the case increased the burdens on Hobhouse, and his always delicate health broke down. Moreover, in October 1864 his wife died. His resignation took effect in 1866 and he returned to England in June of that year. In 1867 he became incumbent of Beech Hill, near Reading. He married on 14 January 1866 Anna Maria, daughter of David Williams, warden of New College, Oxford.

On Bishop Selwyn's translation to Lichfield he made Hobhouse, in 1869, his assistant bishop, and in 1871 gave him the rectory of Edlaston, Derbyshire. During 1874–5 he was chancellor of the diocese, though he had no legal training. On the death of Selwyn in 1878, the new bishop, W. D. Maclagan, retained him as assistant, but ill health led him to resign in 1881. He retired to Wells; the Somerset Archaeological Society gained in him an active member, and he helped to found the Somerset Record Society, for which he edited several medieval texts. He died at Wells on 20 April 1904, his wife surviving him.

A. R. BUCKLAND, rev. H. C. G. MATTHEW

Sources *The Times* (22 April 1904) · *The Guardian* (27 April 1904) · *The Athenaeum* (30 April 1904), 562 · H. F. Ault, *The Nelson narrative* (1958) · W. P. Morrell, *The Anglican church in New Zealand* (1973) · *DNZB*, vol. 1 · W. Hobhouse, 'Memoir', in E. Hobhouse, *Sermons and addresses, with a short memoir by his son*, ed. W. Hobhouse (1905)
Archives Bodl. Oxf., letters · LPL, corresp. · NL Aus. · NRA, priv. coll., corresp. and journals
Likenesses photographs, NPG · wood-engraving (after photograph by Maull & Polyblank), NPG; repro. in *ILN* (26 Feb 1859)
Wealth at death £8586 3s. 4d.: probate, 31 May 1904, CGPLA Eng. & Wales

Hobhouse, Emily (1860–1926), social activist and charity worker, was born on 9 April 1860 at St Ive, in Cornwall, the fifth of the six surviving children of Reginald Hobhouse (d. 1895), archdeacon of Bodmin, Cornwall, and his wife, Caroline (d. 1880), daughter of Sir William Salusbury-Trelawny, eighth baronet. Her youngest brother was Leonard Trelawny *Hobhouse (1864–1929), and they maintained their childhood companionship in later life. Her uncle was Arthur *Hobhouse, Baron Hobhouse (1819–1904); he and his wife, Margaret or Mary, provided for her materially and supported her campaigning work. Emily was educated at home by her mother and governesses, with one term at school in London in 1876. She remained at home, living in a way that was typical for unmarried women of her class, caring for her parents and doing parish work, but after her father's death she broke away from that life and went to the USA and Mexico to do philanthropic work for Cornish miners who had emigrated. She

Emily Hobhouse (1860–1926), by H. Walter Barnett, c.1902

went to the mining town of Virginia, Minnesota, and although she found that the few Cornish miners there had little need of her help, being set apart by their 'sobriety, energy, skill and work' (Fry, 47), she undertook various mission welfare and temperance projects. After a broken engagement to an American businessman, John Carr Jackson, and the loss of much of her money, she returned to England in 1898.

Hobhouse became interested in the struggle for women's emancipation, and in November 1898 was elected to the executive of the Women's Industrial Council (founded in 1894). She worked as an investigator for the council, producing reports on child labour, and in 1900 was involved in a scheme to set up a company providing housing for 'educated working women' in London (*Women's Industrial News*, Dec 1900). She was also a supporter of the women's suffrage movement, although she did not endorse the militancy of the suffragettes.

Following the outbreak of the Second South African War (11 October 1899) Hobhouse became a member of the South African Conciliation Committee, launched on 1 November 1899 with Leonard Courtney as its president, one of a number of organizations formed to combat the often violent 'jingoism' of the war's supporters. She was the honorary secretary of its women's branch, formed early in 1900, and organized a number of protests against the war. Anger and concern about the effects of the war increased during 1900, after reports reached Britain of the British army's scorched-earth policy, which drove Boer

women and children from their farms to be housed in refugee camps (subsequently described as concentration camps).

Emily Hobhouse set up a philanthropic committee, the South African Women and Children Distress Fund, to collect money to help the women and children, and, despite the reservations of her friends and family, travelled to South Africa in December 1900 to investigate conditions and to distribute funds. She obtained military permission to visit some of the camps and spent several months travelling between different camps in the Orange River and Cape colonies. She saw at first hand the disease and death, especially of children, that had resulted from overcrowding and lack of food and medical facilities. She worked with local women to improve conditions in those camps to which she was given access, and returned to Britain in May 1901. She travelled back on the same ship as Sir Alfred Milner, the British high commissioner, from whom she was surprised to learn that he had been sent more than sixty reports of her activities in South Africa.

Hobhouse and other members of her committees campaigned extensively to publicize the conditions in the camps, often against officially orchestrated hostility. She had some correspondence with members of the British government, including St John Brodrick and Joseph Chamberlain, and her report to the South African Distress Fund was published in June 1901. Influenced by Hobhouse, with whom he had had an interview, the Liberal leader, Sir Henry Campbell-Bannerman, asked in a speech on 14 June: 'When is a war not a war? When it is carried on by methods of barbarism in South Africa' (Wilson, 349). Hobhouse's report had become a famous indictment. The government responded by appointing six women as a committee of inquiry into the camps, headed by Millicent Fawcett. Although conditions in many camps had been improved since Hobhouse's visits, the Fawcett committee shared her opinion about the lack of suitable accommodation and the poor organization of the camps, and their report, published in February 1902 (*Parl. papers*, 1902, 67), made many of the same recommendations that she had made almost a year earlier.

Emily Hobhouse was refused membership of the committee, and when she tried to re-enter South Africa in November 1901 was not allowed to land, and was forcibly transferred to another ship and deported. She returned to South Africa in 1903 and set up various resettlement and rehabilitation projects, including the establishment of industrial schools for lace-making, spinning, and weaving, and in 1907 was appointed an adviser to manage public funds for the schools. Her co-worker and the honorary treasurer of the Boer Home Industries was the Quaker Anna Ruth Fry (1878–1962), who compiled the first of the three memoirs of Hobhouse's life (1929).

In 1907–8 the organization of the schools was taken over by the new governments in Transvaal and the Orange River Colony and Hobhouse resigned her post, returning to Europe in October 1908. In honour of her work for South Africa, Hugo Naudé was commissioned to paint her portrait, which was hung in the Pretoria Museum of Cultural History. She maintained friendships with many of the Boer leaders and others in South Africa, including Olive Schreiner and Mahatma Gandhi.

Emily Hobhouse lived mainly in Italy until the outbreak of the First World War, when her commitment to pacifism found practical expression in her work for the international women's movement for peace, and she worked at its secretariat in Amsterdam for three months in 1915. In 1916 she travelled through Germany and Belgium to investigate conditions for refugees, interned civilians, and prisoners of war, and met the German foreign minister, Gottlieb von Jagow (1863–1935), who, she claimed, gave her the impression that he wanted her to suggest peace talks to the British authorities. She returned to England and helped to promote schemes for the exchange of prisoners of war.

After the armistice Hobhouse helped to set up a relief fund for enemy children—the Fund to Aid Swiss Relief—whose work was incorporated with that of the Save the Children Fund in April 1919, and she was also chairwoman of the Russian Babies' Fund. In September 1919 she visited Austria as a representative of the Save the Children Fund and compiled a report on conditions in Vienna and Leipzig; she set up a relief fund and oversaw its administration locally. For that work she was honoured by the city of Leipzig, and the German Red Cross gave her its decoration of second class. A marble bust of her was placed in the Rathaus of Leipzig, a copy of which was also sent to the war museum in Bloemfontein.

Hobhouse maintained her connections with South Africa, where subscriptions were raised to enable her to buy a house at St Ives, in Cornwall, in 1921, although she remained there only for two years, moving to London in 1923. She spent the last few years of her life working on an autobiography and a memoir of her work in South Africa, neither of which she was able to complete, although much of it has been published. A draft of the autobiography is held by the state archives in Bloemfontein. She published three accounts of the Second South African War: *War without Glamour, or, Women's War Experiences Written by Themselves, 1899–1902* (1924); *The Brunt of the War and where it Fell* (1902); and a translation of the diary of Alida M. Badenhorst, *Tant'Alie of Transvaal (A.M. Badenhorst): her Diary, 1880–1902* (1923).

Emily Hobhouse contracted pleurisy after a long illness and died in London on 8 June 1926. A memorial service was held for her at St Mary Abbots Church, Kensington, and on 26 October 1926 her ashes were buried at the Bloemfontein war memorial, South Africa, where only she, President Steyn, and General de Wet are buried. The ceremony testified to her status as a heroine among the Boer people and is recorded in a number of photographs, some of which are in Hobhouse family collections and others in the war museum at Bloemfontein. Her reputation remained strong in South Africa, where many tributes were published. J. C. Smuts wrote of her 'great spirit of human service' and 'the strong and vivid personality which at times made her difficult to work with', concluding that 'She lies buried in the hearts of a grateful people' (Fry, 10–11).

ELAINE HARRISON

Sources A. R. Fry, *Emily Hobhouse: a memoir* (1929) · *Emily Hobhouse: Boer War letters*, ed. R. van Reenen (1984) · J. H. Balme, *To love one's enemies: the work and life of Emily Hobhouse* (1994) · J. O. H. Fisher, *That Miss Hobhouse* (1971) · S. B. Spies, 'Hobhouse, Emily', *DSAB* · J. A. Hobson and M. Ginsberg, *L. T. Hobhouse, his life and work* (1931) · A. Davey, *The British pro-Boers, 1877–1902* (1978) · J. Wilson, *C. B.: a life of Sir Henry Campbell-Bannerman* (1973)

Archives National Archives of South Africa, Bloemfontein, first draft of autobiography, corresp., and documents · National Archives of South Africa, Bloemfontein, material for *War without glamour* · NRA, priv. coll., corresp. and papers · University of Cape Town, MSS · University of Cape Town Library, papers | BL, corresp. with Lord Ripon, Add. MSS 43638–43640 · Sheff. Arch., letters to Henry Joseph Wilson

Likenesses H. W. Barnett, photograph, *c*.1902, NPG [*see illus.*] · A. van Welie, 1903, War Museum of the Boer Republics, Bloemfontein · H. Naudé, portrait, 1908, Pretoria Museum of Cultural History · L. Rautenbach, bronze bust, 1965, University of Orange Free State · M. Molitor, bronze bust, War Museum of the Boer Republics, Bloemfontein · M. Molitor, marble bust, Rathaus, Leipzig · photographs, War Museum of the Boer Republics, Bloemfontein · photographs, priv. coll.

Wealth at death £5621 1*s*. 9*d*.: probate, 6 July 1926, *CGPLA Eng. & Wales*

Hobhouse, Henry (1776–1854), archivist, was born at home at Hadspen House, near Castle Cary, on 12 April 1776, only son of Henry Hobhouse (1742–1792), barrister, and Sarah (*d*. 1777), daughter of Richard Jenkyns, canon residentiary of Wells. He went to Eton College in 1791 and matriculated from Brasenose College, Oxford, on 10 April 1793. He graduated BA in 1797, proceeded MA in 1799, and was created DCL on 27 June 1827. On 23 January 1801 he was called to the bar at the Middle Temple. He married, on 7 April 1806, Harriett, sixth daughter of John Turton of Sugnall Hall, Staffordshire; she died at Bournemouth on 7 May 1858, aged seventy-three, having had eight children. Their sons included Arthur *Hobhouse, lord of appeal, and Edmund *Hobhouse, bishop and antiquary.

Hobhouse was solicitor to HM customs from 1806 to 1812, and then became solicitor to the Treasury. He was appointed permanent under-secretary of state for the Home department on 28 June 1817, and therefore directed the office through the whole period of Peel's reforms. He held that office until July 1827, when he retired on a pension of £1000 per annum. He was sworn of the privy council on 28 June 1828. He was one of the ecclesiastical commissioners for England, and chairman of the Somerset quarter sessions until 1845.

In the meantime Hobhouse had begun a second career. He advised Sir Robert Peel, then home secretary, on the appointment of a commission to supervise the publication of the state papers, and succeeded John Bruce as keeper of the state papers in 1826. He himself became a commissioner on 10 June 1852. The commission published *The State Papers of Henry VIII*, in eleven volumes, the last appearing in 1852. Hobhouse superintended the editing, and took great pains to produce an accurate text. He also supervised the systematic arrangement and listing of the papers. The office was absorbed by the Public Record

Office in 1854, when the publication of the records was continued by the series of *Calendars of the State Papers*, extending to more than 200 volumes. Hobhouse died at home at Hadspen House on 13 April 1854.

G. C. Boase, rev. G. H. Martin

Sources GM, 2nd ser., 42 (1854), 79–80 · Dod's Peerage (1854), 301–2 · The Times (18 April 1854), 9 · J. D. Cantwell, The Public Record Office, 1838–1958 (1991) · H. Hobhouse, Hobhouse memoirs (1927)
Archives Balliol Oxf., letters to Henry Jenkyns · BL, corresp. with Sir Robert Peel, Add. MSS 40276–40600, passim · Bodl. Oxf., letters to Richard Heber · Derbys. RO, letters to Sir R. S. Wilmot-Horton
Likenesses engraving, Hadspen House, Somerset · watercolour, Hadspen House, Somerset

Hobhouse, Henry (1854–1937), politician, was born at Hadspen House, near Castle Cary, Somerset, on 1 March 1854, the only son of Henry Hobhouse and his first wife, Charlotte Etruria, youngest daughter of James Talbot, third Baron Talbot de Malahide. On his father's death in 1862 he became head of the younger branch of the Hobhouse family, which had been located at Hadspen House since 1785. He was a country squire with an inherited estate of about 2500 acres. His father and grandfather before him had set conspicuous examples of duty and public spirit in the unpaid work of petty and quarter sessions; and although he was not quite eight years old when his father died, the tradition was handed on to him by his uncle and guardian, Arthur *Hobhouse (afterwards Lord Hobhouse), the well-known judge. He was also first cousin to Leonard Trelawny *Hobhouse, the philosopher and journalist. Educated at Eton College and at Balliol College, Oxford, of which he was a scholar, he was awarded a second class in classical moderations (1873) and a first class in *literae humaniores* (1875). In 1880 he was called to the bar by Lincoln's Inn, and in the same year was appointed a county magistrate: he practised as a parliamentary draftsman and counsel until 1885. In 1884 he collaborated with Sir Robert Wright on *An Outline of Local Government and Local Taxation in England and Wales*, which remained a standard legal textbook for over half a century; its eighth main edition appeared in the year of his death.

In 1885 Hobhouse entered parliament for East Somerset as a Liberal, and in 1886 he retained the seat as a Liberal Unionist. In the debates in 1888 on the County Councils Bill he was very influential. No member excelled him in direct knowledge of county administration, and the bill's policy—to transfer administrative authority from quarter sessions to elected county councils—was one of which he, unlike some rival specialists, entirely approved. When Lord Salisbury formed a coalition ministry with the Liberal Unionists in 1895, Hobhouse's standing was high enough to warrant his inclusion; but his party's eminent front-benchers were so disproportionate to its total membership that no relative newcomer stood a chance. Repeatedly passed over in favour of Conservatives, he evinced no sourness, but concentrated increasingly on county questions. In 1902 he gave weighty support to the Balfour Education Bill, which he helped to shape. Its passage perhaps partly determined his acceptance in 1904 of the chairmanship of the Somerset county council, a post which he filled

Henry Hobhouse (1854–1937), by Walter Stoneman, 1917

with great distinction for twenty years. He took a leading part in forming in 1889 the County Councils Association, of which he was an original member and from 1914 to 1920 chairman. He retired from parliament in 1906, having been sworn of the privy council in 1902.

Hobhouse was, in his day, the archetypal public-spirited country gentleman. No aspect of local welfare escaped him, but his favourite subjects were education and agriculture. He started three secondary schools and after 1902 was keenly interested in the foundation of others by his county council. He was a member of the Bryce royal commission on secondary education (1894–5), a notable governor and benefactor of the King's School, Bruton, and very influential in the conversion of University College, Bristol, into Bristol University, of which he was pro-chancellor (1909–37) and which conferred upon him the honorary degree of LLD. His interest in farming had many sides. He was chairman of the Cider Institute at Long Ashton, and raised a fund for it. At one time he was much concerned to combat the urban bias in rural education, but had only moderate success. He cared much for painting, architecture, scenery, and literature, and took to learning foreign languages in order to study their masterpieces in the original. A devoted churchman, he was an ecclesiastical commissioner from 1890 and a member of the church assembly from 1920. He shot regularly, but not very well; he rode a good deal about his estate, but never hunted.

Hobhouse was twice married. His first wife, whom he

married in 1880, was Margaret Heyworth (d. 1921), seventh daughter of Richard Potter of Standish House, Gloucestershire; she was one of the well-known sisters who included (Martha) Beatrice *Webb and Lady Courtney of Penwith [see Courtney, Catherine]. In 1923 he married Anne Mackessack, elder daughter of William Grant of Forres, Morayshire. By his first marriage he had four sons and three daughters; the youngest son was killed in the First World War and the youngest daughter died in infancy. The third son was the shipowner Sir John *Hobhouse (1893–1961). Hobhouse died at Hadspen House on 25 June 1937.

R. C. K. ENSOR, rev. H. C. G. MATTHEW

Sources *The Times* (28 June 1937) · private information (1949)
Archives JRL, corresp. · Meteorological Office, London, meteorological notes · Som. ARS, collections for a history of Somerset
Likenesses W. Stoneman, photograph, 1917, NPG [see illus.] · H. Neile, portrait, c.1924; at Hadspen House, 1949
Wealth at death £55,700 4s. 10d.: probate, 6 Aug 1937, CGPLA Eng. & Wales

Hobhouse, John Cam, Baron Broughton (1786–1869), politician, was born at Redland, Bristol, on 27 June 1786, the eldest child of Sir Benjamin *Hobhouse, first baronet (1757–1831), politician and financier, and his first wife, Charlotte (d. 1791), daughter and heir of Samuel Cam of Chantry House, Bradford-on-Avon, Wiltshire. He had two brothers and two sisters, one of whom died in infancy. His background was one of unenfranchised nonconformity and commercial wealth—important factors in understanding the way in which his politics developed. His father was a noted Unitarian who campaigned for the repeal of the Test and Corporation Acts; his mother was also a dissenter. He went to Lewin's Mead, John Prior Estlin's Unitarian school at Bristol, then to Westminster School, and then to Trinity College, Cambridge. There he obtained the Hulsean prize in 1808 (for an essay entitled 'On the origin and intention of sacrifices'), graduating BA in 1808 and MA in 1811. His mother died in 1791, and from his father's second marriage, to Amelia Parry, he acquired fourteen half-siblings.

Travels in Europe and relations with Byron At Cambridge Hobhouse founded a whig club and became the close friend of Byron, with whom in 1809 he travelled across Portugal and Spain to Gibraltar. From Malta he and Byron were encouraged by English naval and diplomatic intelligence to travel into Albania, where they stayed with Ali Pasha from 19 to 23 October 1809; an English naval force meanwhile took over most of the Ionian Islands, a fact on which Ali congratulated them. They then went into Greece, where they were surprised to discover considerable anti-Turkish feeling among the inhabitants. They based themselves in Athens, visiting Marathon on 24 January, and then went via Smyrna to Constantinople, where they attended an audience with Sultan Mahmoud II on 10 July. On 31 October 1809 Hobhouse recorded in his diary, 'Byron is writing a long poem in the Spenserian stanza'— the first reference to *Childe Harold's Pilgrimage* (BL, Add. MS 56527, fol. 65r). Prior to its publication Hobhouse had regarded Byron as his poetic equal. Lines 247–62 in the first edition of *English Bards and Scotch Reviewers* (1809) are

John Cam Hobhouse, Baron Broughton (1786–1869), by Sir William John Newton, 1843

by him. In their absence from England, Hobhouse's anthology *Imitations and Translations* was published, containing several poems by Byron. On returning Hobhouse published a comic poem, *The Wonders of a Week at Bath*, and his account of their eastern tour, *A Journey through Albania, and other Provinces of Turkey*, went through two printings. It is notable for its final section, about the aspirations and failures of Sultan Selim III. The book brought him a fellowship of the Royal Society in 1814.

From May 1813 to February 1814 Hobhouse made a long tour through wartime Europe, visiting Stralsund, Berlin, Vienna, Leipzig, Prague, Fiume, Weimar, and Amsterdam. The suffering he witnessed affected him. When in April 1814 the news broke of the abdication of the greatest of his heroes, Napoleon, he hurried to Paris, accompanied by Henry Grattan—Byron had at first agreed to go, then changed his mind. On 3 May Hobhouse witnessed Louis XVIII entering the capital. Throughout this period he was a member of the Holland House whig circle, and considered, but rejected, the idea of standing as MP for Cambridge University. He heard of Byron's engagement to Annabella Milbanke via a third party. However, on 2 January 1815 he acted as best man at the wedding, having made an attempt—probably with Byron's encouragement—to dissuade the minister from performing the ceremony. Annabella learned about this, and it increased her dislike of him (Lovelace MSS, Bodl. Oxf. 88. 25).

On Napoleon's escape from Elba, Hobhouse again went

to Paris, where he met Benjamin Constant and witnessed Napoleon's attempt to become a constitutional ruler. He saw Bonaparte on several occasions. Waterloo—the news of which reached him as he was trying to cross the Swiss border with Michael Bruce—depressed him, and he was disgusted by the second reinstatement of Louis XVIII, 'this king of shreds and patches' (Berg collection, 4.101). In the following year he published an account of the 'hundred days', *The substance of some letters written by an Englishman resident in Paris during the last reign of the Emperor Napoleon*, in which he displayed his hatred of the Bourbon dynasty and his sympathy with Bonaparte—despite the death of his brother Benjamin at Quatre Bras. The book—the third edition of which was dedicated to Byron—was reviewed ironically in *The Quarterly*. Its French translation was seized by the government, and both printer and translator were fined and imprisoned. He also wrote the prologue to Charles Maturin's play *Bertram* which opened at Drury Lane on 9 May 1816.

Hobhouse was loyal to Byron throughout the separation from Annabella, drawing up 'a full and scrupulously accurate account' of the events. This was printed privately in 1870 in the wake of the Beecher Stowe controversy, and reprinted in *Recollections of a Long Life* (2.191–366). He had seen Byron off at Dover on 25 April, and in the autumn of 1816, with Scrope Davies, visited the poet at the Villa Diodati near Geneva, arriving on the day Shelley left. He and Byron dined often with Madame De Staël at Coppet, and made two alpine tours. Passing the Simplon in October, they visited Milan, where they were entertained by Ludovico di Brême, and met Vincenzo Monti, Stendhal, and Silvio Pellico, whose tragedy *Francesca da Rimini* Hobhouse translated, assisted at first by Byron. In Austrian-occupied Milan, Byron and Hobhouse found that their politics created an appreciative audience for them such as they had never experienced in England. They then visited Venice and Rome together. During late 1817 and early 1818 Hobhouse wrote some of the notes for canto iv of *Childe Harold*; the poem was afterwards dedicated to him by Byron. The section on Italian literature in his book *Historical Illustrations to the Fourth Canto of Childe Harold's Pilgrimage* was written for him, in uneasy collaboration, by Ugo Foscolo. In 1823 he was outraged when Foscolo proposed to his stepsister Matilda.

Westminster radical Hobhouse became a member of The Rota, a dinner club for the promotion of political reforms. In 1819 he contested the parliamentary seat of Westminster, which had become vacant after the suicide of Sir Samuel Romilly. He stood as a radical, supported by his father and by Sir Francis Burdett, but was defeated on 3 March by the whig George Lamb, Lord Melbourne's brother. Riots followed, and a breach opened between him and the Holland House whigs. About this time he wrote several political pamphlets, and his anonymous reply to a sarcastic speech of Canning's, *A Letter to the Right Honourable George Canning, M. P.* (1818), attracted much attention. In 1819 he published an anonymous pamphlet entitled *A Trifling Mistake*, in which to the question 'What prevents the people from walking down to the House, and

pulling out the members by the ears, locking up their doors, and flinging the key into the Thames?' he answered that 'their true practical protectors ... are to be found at the Horse Guards, and the Knightsbridge barracks' (pp. 49–50). The House of Commons analysis of this passage, ignoring the answer, read the question as rhetorical, and found Hobhouse guilty of breach of privilege. Arrested on 14 December 1819, he remained in Newgate (in rooms next to the governor's) until the dissolution of parliament on 29 February 1820. On 5 February 1820 the court of king's bench had refused to interfere with the speaker's warrant, and Hobhouse could only respond with a protest in *The Times*. Prior to his release he issued his address *To the Independent Electors of Westminster*.

While Hobhouse was in Newgate the Cato Street conspiracy occurred. Mrs Arbuthnot records in her diary Wellington's conviction that if it had succeeded, and the conspirators had offered Hobhouse the headship of their provisional government, he would have accepted. (In later years Hobhouse and Wellington were on excellent terms.) With Francis Place as his campaign manager Hobhouse succeeded in beating Lamb at Westminster at the general election of 1820 (25 March), and was returned to parliament as Burdett's colleague. Hobhouse's radicalism was qualified, and his statements of principle were vague. The exact nature of the franchise extension he envisaged was unclear. He never spoke out for universal suffrage, annual parliaments, or even the ballot. He was much clearer when attacking corrupt privilege. When in Newgate he rebuffed overtures made to him by William Cobbett, who thought of him as playing Sancho Panza to Sir Francis Burdett's Quixote.

Hobhouse was a supporter of Queen Caroline throughout her trial in 1820. He made his maiden speech in the House of Commons on 9 May, and thenceforth was an active debater, supporting many liberal measures, including prison reform and libel law reform. He became the leading parliamentary spokesman for the state regulation of factory labour—though by the 1840s his ardour against child labour had abated. His Select Vestries Bill of 1831 was an important step towards the establishment of fair and representative local government. He assisted in the foundation of London University.

Byron's executor Hobhouse had advised against the publication of *Don Juan* i and ii in 1819—but he did correct the poem's proofs, which show, in their margins, his amusing altercations with Byron. Canto i, stanza 15, on Romilly's suicide, was suppressed on his initiative. The circulation of Byron's lampoon on his imprisonment, which he discovered on 16 April 1820, caused him severe disillusionment, which was stoically borne (the poem mocks him from an élitist whig viewpoint). He visited Byron for the last time at Pisa in September 1822, where he met Teresa Guiccioli. When they parted, on 22 September, Byron said, 'Hobhouse, you should never have come, or you should never go' (*Recollections*, 3.8).

On 14 May 1824 Hobhouse received the news of Byron's death. In July, as one of the executors, he proved Byron's will, and superintended the funeral at Hucknall Torkard on 16 July. He went on censoring Byron to the end: had he desired the preservation of the memoirs, which Byron had given to Thomas Moore, to Hobhouse's fury, and which had been sold by Moore to John Murray, they would probably not have been destroyed on 17 May (fearful, perhaps, of their contents, Hobhouse does not seem to have read them). He was one of the most active members of the London Greek committee and after Byron's death he at first resolved to go to Greece himself in order to manage the Greek loan, although ultimately Henry Lytton Bulwer went in his place.

An admirer of *The Corsair* and *Childe Harold*, iv, Hobhouse was out of sympathy with Byron's later works. He loathed *Cain*, and confessed in a diary entry for 1 June 1828 to having just read *Don Juan* x, xi, and xii for the first time, and to have discovered Byron to have been 'a great humourist' (BL, Add. MS 56552, fol. 105r). The possibility that *Don Juan* contains numerous references and jokes, only detectable to a close friend of Byron such as Hobhouse, is strong. Hobhouse refused to give Moore any help in the writing of his life of Byron. Having campaigned twice without success for the placement of Thorwaldsen's statue of Byron in Westminster Abbey, he saw it in 1844 put in the Wren Library at Trinity, where he admitted it went very well.

Hobhouse's need for more than casual female company seems to have been in abeyance throughout Byron's life, although in 1821 he did express a fondness for Susannah Burdett. In 1827 he fell in love with another of Burdett's daughters, Sophia, and proposed, but was refused. After an affair with the wife of a Wiltshire friend he married, on 28 July 1828, Lady Julia Tomlinson Hay (d. 1835), sister of the eighth marquess of Tweeddale, and niece to both Lord Lauderdale and 'King Tom' Maitland. Not a robust person, she collapsed after the ceremony, but bore him three daughters, Julia, born in 1829, Charlotte in 1831, and Sophia in 1832, before dying of tuberculosis on 3 April 1835. The well-connected marriage gave Hobhouse entry to Almack's. His daughters survived a smallpox attack in 1840, but Julia died of cholera on 5 September 1849. Hobhouse's friend Peacock composed a moving elegy.

Office in whig administrations The 1832 Reform Bill brought forward by Grey's whig-led ministry corrected, in Hobhouse's view, the inequities of the old system, and his radicalism cooled. He thought the Chartists foolish dupes, and the Tolpuddle martyrs misguided. By 1836 Francis Place was describing him as 'live lumber' (Joyce, 283). He succeeded his father as second baronet on Sir Benjamin's death on 14 August 1831, and on 1 February 1832 was appointed secretary-at-war, being sworn of the privy council on 6 February. He tried to reform his chaotic department, and in the teeth of much opposition succeeded in abolishing several sinecures, and in restricting flogging in the army to certain defined misdemeanours— although he was regarded by many as having failed in not having abolished it completely. His attempt at reducing the size of the army was not successful and, discouraged, he exchanged the post for that of chief secretary for Ireland on 28 March 1833. His tenure of this office, one more difficult even than the previous, was short-lived.

In April 1833 Hobhouse refused to vote with the government against the abolition of the house and window tax, on the grounds that he had urged its abolition while independent. He resigned both his office and—to the incomprehension of many—his seat for Westminster. However, though he offered himself for re-election, he found that his conservatism had lost him popularity. He was pelted on the hustings, and on 10 May was defeated by the radical Colonel George de Lacy Evans, though tory collusion was suspected.

On Melbourne's coming to power in July 1834 Hobhouse accepted the post of first commissioner of woods and forests. Melbourne's confidence in Hobhouse's loyalty may have been strengthened by his knowledge of the part he had played in discouraging Byron's elopement with Melbourne's late wife, Lady Caroline Lamb, on 29 July 1812. Melbourne and Hobhouse were often the sole guests at Buckingham Palace dinners. Hobhouse was returned for Nottingham at a by-election, also in July 1834. In 1841 he was accused of having won the by-election by bribery and intimidation (traditional approaches, without which campaigning in Nottingham would have been difficult) but was exonerated twice by select committee. He stood again for Nottingham in 1847, bribed no-one, and lost to a Chartist—the economic depression in the town was an important contributory factor in his defeat. However, he was returned as member for Harwich (one of the country's most corrupt constituencies) at a by-election in April 1848, without even making a personal canvass.

On the dismissal of Melbourne in November 1834, Hobhouse resigned with the rest of his colleagues. When Melbourne formed his second administration he was pressed to resume his old post at the War Office, but refused, and was appointed president of the Board of Control for India, with a seat in the cabinet, on 29 April 1835. He was present at Queen Victoria's first council at Kensington Palace on 20 June 1837. He was one of Palmerston's strongest supporters on the question of the Russian threat in central Asia, and was in part responsible for the English occupation of Afghanistan in 1838, the installation of the unpopular puppet ruler Shah Shuja, and the subsequent death-march from Kabul of January 1842—in which his nephew John Byron Hobhouse was killed. The retreat, plus his acquiescence (at least) in what looked like Foreign Office editing of certain dispatches from India, represented a low-water mark in his reputation. He had resigned, with Melbourne, in September 1841.

Peerage and retirement On 10 July 1846 Hobhouse resumed the India post, with a seat in Lord John Russell's first cabinet—of which, it was noted, he seemed one of the most conservative members. An unabashed imperialist, he promoted railway development in India, and approved of Dalhousie's annexation of the Punjab in 1849. Though he was delighted by the fall of Metternich, the 1848 continental revolutions worried him, and he anticipated a Chartist equivalent in England. He was created Baron Broughton of Broughton de Gyfford on 26 February 1851 and, on his final retirement from office, on the resignation of Russell on 21 February 1852, was made KCB (22 April 1852). From this time he withdrew from public life. He debated for the last time during the discussion of the Government of India Bill in July 1858. He spent his retirement at Tedworth House, Wiltshire, and at his London house, 42 Berkeley Square, revising his books and enjoying the society of his friends.

Hobhouse died after a short illness at 42 Berkeley Square on 3 June 1869, aged eighty-two, and was buried at Kensal Green cemetery. He had been a vigorous debater, an excellent classical scholar, a competent versifier, an entertaining companion (though he was shy at unfamiliar social gatherings), and a staunch friend. On 10 April 1826, while speaking in the Commons, he invented the phrase 'His Majesty's Opposition', a phrase which gained instant currency. The barony became extinct on his death, but the baronetcy descended to his nephew Sir Charles Parry Hobhouse.

Hobhouse was short and of pugnacious appearance, having inherited a hooked nose from his mother. He was fond of shooting and fishing. A sceptic when young, he became a comfortable churchgoer when older. His writings are best approached as useful but only partial repositories of information. A collection of his diaries and correspondence is mostly in the British Library, although four volumes of his diary are in the Berg collection in New York. His privately printed *Some Account of a Long Life* (1865) was augmented by his daughter Lady Dorchester with edited entries from his diary and extracts from his other books, and published by Murray as *Recollections of a Long Life* between 1909 and 1911.   PETER COCHRAN

Sources J. C. Hobhouse, MS diary, BL · J. C. Hobhouse, diary, NYPL, Humanities and Social Sciences Library, Berg collection · M. Joyce, *My friend H* (1948) · R. M. Zegger, *John Cam Hobhouse: a political life* (1973) · C. P. Hobhouse, *Some account of the family of Hobhouse* (1909?) · E. R. Vincent, *Byron, Hobhouse and Foscolo* (1949) · *Byron's bulldog: the letters of John Cam Hobhouse to Lord Byron*, ed. P. W. Graham (1984) · Baron Broughton [J. C. Hobhouse], *Recollections of a long life*, ed. Lady Dorchester [C. Carleton], 6 vols. (1909–11) · J. C. Hobhouse, *A journey through Albania* (1813) · Lord Broughton [J. C. Hobhouse], *Travels in Albania and other provinces of Turkey in 1809 and 1810*, new edn, 2 vols. (1855) · J. C. Hobhouse, *The substance of some letters written … in Paris* (1816) · Lord Broughton [J. C. Hobhouse], *Italy: remarks made in several visits, from the year 1816 to 1854*, 2 vols. (1859) · J. C. Hobhouse, *A trifling mistake …*, ed. M. Kelsall (1984)
Archives BL, corresp. and MSS, Add. MSS 36455–36483, 43744–43765, 46914–46915, 47222–47235, 56527–56571, 61826–61829 · BL, diary · BL OIOC, letter-books and papers, MS Eur. F 213 · NYPL, diary | BL, Broughton MSS · BL, corresp. with Lord Byron, Add. MS 42093 · BL, corresp. with Francis Place, Add. MSS 35148–35154, 37949–37950 · BL OIOC, corresp. with Sir Bartle Frere, MS Eur. F 81 · BL OIOC, corresp. with marquess of Tweeddale, MS Eur. F 96 · Bodl. Oxf., corresp. with Sir Francis Burdett · Bodl. Oxf., corresp. with Lord Byron · Bodl. Oxf., letters to Benjamin Disraeli · Bodl. Oxf., Lovelace MSS · Hunt. L., letters · Lambton Park, Chester-le-Street, letters to earl of Durham · Lpool RO, letters to Lord Stanley · PRO, corresp. with Charles Napier, PRO 30/64 · PRO, corresp. with Lord John Russell, PRO 30/22 · PRO NIre., corresp. with Lord Anglesey, D619/31 · U. Durham, corresp. with third Earl Grey · U. Southampton L., corresp. with Lord Palmerston · U. Southampton L., letters to first duke of Wellington · W. Sussex RO, letters to duke of Richmond · Wilts. & Swindon RO, family corresp.
Likenesses R. Dighton, caricature, coloured etching, pubd 1819, NPG · H. Meyer, stipple, pubd 1819 (after A. Buck), NPG · C. Turner, mezzotint, pubd 1826 (after J. Lonsdale), BM, NPG · G. Hayter, group portrait, oils, 1833 (*The House of Commons*), NPG · W. J. Newton, miniature, 1843, NPG [*see illus.*] · H. Graves, oils, 1866 (*The Society of Dilettanti*), Brooks's Club, London · G. Cruikshank, pencil drawing, BM · J. Doyle, caricatures, BM · F. Grant, portrait · J. Hopwood, stipple (after A. Wivell), BM, NPG; repro. in Finden, *Byron* · D. Maclise, drawing, V&A · W. Newby, miniature
Wealth at death under £250,000: probate, 16 July 1869, *CGPLA Eng. & Wales*

Hobhouse, Sir John Richard (1893–1961), shipowner, was born on 27 February 1893 at Hadspen House, Castle Cary, Somerset, the third son of Henry *Hobhouse (1854–1937), Liberal member of parliament for East Somerset, and his first wife, Margaret Heyworth Potter (d. 1921), sister of (Martha) Beatrice *Webb. She was one of the nine Potter sisters, one of whom married Robert Holt (brother of Alfred, founder of the Ocean Steamship Company). This relationship doubtless helped to direct his career towards the shipping industry.

Hobhouse was educated at Eton College (1906–11), where he was a King's scholar, and at New College, Oxford (1911–12), where he studied botany and zoology for a year; he later became an ardent and knowledgeable gardener. He joined the Ocean Steamship Company in 1912. In the First World War he served as a captain in the Royal Garrison Artillery, and was awarded the MC in 1917. From 1920 he was a manager of the Ocean Steam Ship Company of Liverpool, with his cousins, Richard and Lawrence Holt, Leonard Cripps, and Roland Thornton, the last two being also related to the Holts by the Potter connection; and was chairman from 1953 until he retired in 1957. He was also a director of the Royal Insurance Company from 1933 to 1961 and chairman in 1954–7. In 1926 Hobhouse married Catherine, daughter of Henry Stewart Brown, of Allerton, Liverpool, produce broker; they had three sons and two daughters.

Throughout his working life Hobhouse was an outstanding and dedicated professional shipowner. He derived his standards and strategy very much from the Holt family predecessors, who set exemplary standards of operation and management for deep sea cargo trades. He, like them, believed in 'doing one thing and doing it well'. On the other hand, the tradition embraced the principle that managers should be able to combine a high level of public work with their business commitments. He made important contributions to the progress of British liner trade between Europe and the Far East, where his companies were the principal operators. In an era when shipowners were regarded, with some justice, as remote and unapproachable, he travelled extensively in Asia, and established easy formal relations with a wide range of eastern traders. His early scientific training gave him a ready understanding of the commercial aspects of marine technology. He rationalized many traditional methods of carrying tropical produce, and, in particular, he pioneered the bulk movement of vegetable oils and also of liquid latex, which brought immense wealth to Malaya and revolutionized modern upholstery. It also provided major cargoes at a time of world depression.

Hobhouse was for a long time one of the government's principal advisers on the shipment of explosives and other dangerous goods in peace and war. His responsibilities included the Mecca pilgrim traffic, in respect of which he introduced important changes in the international regulation of this trade. In 1936, against the personal philosophy of Sir Richard Holt, the senior partner, he established a company pension scheme. He was additionally well trusted by the trade unions, and displayed notable determination, patience, and foresight in the affairs of the National Maritime Board, the National Dock Labour Board, and the port industry generally, all of which he served effectively for long periods.

Hobhouse's suggestion in 1930 that the Liverpool Trades Council should employ an industrial economist full time to investigate ways of reducing the costs of industry without detriment to wages or conditions of work, and to make Merseyside 'the place where industrial peace always reigns', was positively visionary. He did as much as any man to determine the conditions which kept the large and essential element of Chinese ratings in service on British merchant ships throughout the Second World War. He brought about co-operative policies with the Chinese government in 1942, after the fall of Hong Kong and Singapore, which maintained their morale in the face of these crushing disasters.

In that war Hobhouse was initially deputy regional commissioner and later the government's chief shipping representative in the north-west. As chairman of the Liverpool Steam Ship Owners' Association, for the years 1941 and 1942, he played a leading and constructive part in establishing the General Council of British Shipping, which thereafter represented the interests of all British shipowners; he was chairman in 1942–3. He was knighted in 1946 for his war services, and later received the Order of Orange Nassau for his help to Dutch shipping based in Britain. In 1948–50 he was chairman of the National Association of Port Employers. He was also chairman of the British chamber of commerce for the Netherlands East Indies (1945–51).

A member of the council of the University of Liverpool for many years until 1957, Hobhouse was treasurer in 1942–8, and president of the council in 1948–54. He was a pro-chancellor in 1948–57. He gave much time to the university's business and carried a large responsibility for planning its post-war development. He received the honorary degree of LLD in 1958. He was a member of the council of the Liverpool School of Tropical Medicine from 1932 to 1961 and its chairman from 1949 to 1955 and took an intense and beneficial interest in the school's affairs.

Hobhouse served on the Liverpool city council for only one year, 1924, but was a magistrate from 1929 to 1957. He became an imaginative member of the juvenile panel and was for several years a highly successful chairman of the chancellor of the duchy of Lancaster's advisory committee in Liverpool. He was deeply concerned with many Liverpool charities and causes including the Liverpool Improved Houses Movement, and especially its Personal Service Society, an organization for the discreet assistance of those in financial difficulty, which, under his guidance, did much valuable and original work. He was a member of the royal commission on population, 1944–9.

Hobhouse inherited, from his Somerset forebears, a compelling sense of obligation and a profound belief in the worth of individuals. Although not politically active, he was an avowed Liberal. A man of courage and decision, he was equipped with a penetrating and practical intellect coupled with exceptional vigour, which gave a forceful, and even aggressive, slant to an essentially kindly and unselfish character. These attributes flourished in Liverpool, which in his time retained much of its Victorian pride and independence, while subject to acute social problems because of its vulnerability to world trade fluctuations.

Hobhouse's clear and direct approach, his exacting standards, and his power of logical analysis were widely respected, but he was generally regarded as a formidable and somewhat uncompromising personality. Yet his substantial achievements owed much more to quite other characteristics, not least his absolute integrity and broad wisdom.

Hobhouse's advice continued to be sought after his retirement in 1957. His term as senior partner from 1953 to 1957 did not reflect the dynamism of leadership that might have been expected. His work in the Second World War had been highly demanding and this, coupled with the tragic early death of a son soon after the war, doubtless contributed to a weariness of spirit. He also saw dark clouds on the horizon as the spread of communism threatened south-east Asia. None the less, his report on the Singapore situation in March 1956 showed an almost Churchillian fighting spirit. He was chosen to sit on the Chandos committee which advised the government about the replacement for the 'Queens' (the great Cunard cruise liners) in 1959, and in the same year he was elected chairman of the South-West Regional Museums Service, a tribute to his broad cultural interests.

Hobhouse died at Musgrave Park Hospital, Taunton, Somerset, on 9 May 1961 and was buried on 12 May in West Monkton parish church. He was survived by his wife.

John Nicholson, *rev.* J. Gordon Read

Sources M. Falkus, *The Blue Funnel legend: a history of the Ocean Steam Ship Company, 1865–1973* (1990) · *The Times* (10 May 1961) · *The Times* (13 May 1961) · *The Times* (30 May 1961) · *Eton College School List* (1909) · private information (1981) · personal knowledge (1981) · *CGPLA Eng. & Wales* (1961) · *DNB*

Archives Merseyside Maritime Museum, Liverpool, Ocean Archives · U. Lpool, school of tropical medicine · U. Lpool

Likenesses photograph, repro. in *The Times* (10 May 1961)

Wealth at death £133,680 18s. 4d.: probate, 15 June 1961, *CGPLA Eng. & Wales*

Hobhouse, Leonard Trelawny (1864–1929), social philosopher and journalist, was born on 8 September 1864 at St Ive, near Liskeard, Cornwall, the youngest of the seven children of the Revd Reginald Hobhouse (1818–1895), rector of St Ive for fifty years and archdeacon of Bodmin from

Leonard Trelawny Hobhouse (1864–1929), by Elliott & Fry

1877 to 1892, and his wife, Caroline (1820–1880), daughter of Sir William Lewis Salusbury-Trelawny, eighth baronet, of Trelawny, Cornwall.

Early life Hobhouse's parents influenced him in very different ways. His vivacious and witty mother treated him as a 'first-rate companion' and introduced him to Latin and literature. His father was a more distant figure, 'an incarnation of justice and iron rectitude' (Hobson and Ginsberg, 15–16). The death of two siblings cast a morbid shadow over the family. As a child Hobhouse was sent to a preparatory school at Exmouth and then proceeded in January 1877 to Marlborough College, where he remained until 1883. When Hobhouse's mother died in 1880, the ensuing affectionate relationship he then forged with his father was undoubtedly abetted by the boy's long absences. His sister Emily *Hobhouse, who was to make her name as a reformer on South African issues, painted a far more depressing picture of home life with a narrow-minded and taciturn valetudinarian. The setting in which Hobhouse grew up was further complicated not only by his father's religious orthodoxy but by his political Conservatism, against a backdrop of a highly politicized family. Hobhouse's grandfather Henry Hobhouse was for many years keeper of the state papers, and his uncle Sir Arthur Hobhouse was a lawyer and moderate Liberal reformer who managed at times to convey the impression of a dangerous radical. While Hobhouse struck out politically on his own innovative path, and could have pursued a political career in his own right, he did not contemplate such a role seriously. The blend of warm emotion and cold reason he experienced in his youth had a profound impact

on shaping his approach both to politics and to philosophy, and it was also indicated in a continual nervous disposition, in which physical ailments merged with psychological mood swings, insomnia, and breakdowns, throughout most of his life.

At Marlborough, Hobhouse initially made little impression but began to blossom in the sixth form, as he used its library to strike an acquaintance with the works of Herbert Spencer, Mazzini's *Essays*, and in particular J. S. Mill, who remained a steady source of inspiration. Encouraged by liberal masters and a tradition of public debate, especially on current politics, he demonstrated early signs of his future radicalism on questions of democracy and even republicanism, while also displaying a propensity to fit badly into institutional frameworks. He was judged rather childish and immature for his years, and his headmaster prevailed in 1882 upon Hobhouse's father to keep the youth another year at Marlborough before entering him for an Oxford scholarship.

Oxford: the synthesis of theory and practice In 1883 Hobhouse went up to Corpus Christi College, Oxford, with a classical scholarship. As an undergraduate he continued to engage in radical activities, attempting to organize agricultural labourers, and touring nearby towns and villages in a temperance campaign (close to the heart of T. H. Green, one of Hobhouse's scholarly inspirations) together with Gilbert Murray and Charles Roberts, the future Liberal MP. He joined societies in which practical matters of economic and social reform were firmly on the agenda. By then an agnostic, he was drawn towards the study of philosophy, developing the curious compound of holism and empiricism that was to characterize his more technical scholarship. He obtained a first in classical moderations in 1884 and a first in *literae humaniores* in 1887, and in the same year won a prize fellowship at Merton College. Hobhouse was an active university society debater and was elected president of the radical Russell Club. In 1890 he was appointed assistant tutor in Corpus, before being elected a fellow in 1894. As a tutor he was conscientious and demanding, occasionally stimulating and even brilliant, cultivating the originality and enthusiasm of his students, yet often keeping his distance through asperity and sarcasm. With his colleagues he could be argumentative and sometimes quick-tempered, though immediately placable. Hobhouse was uncomfortable in the senior common rooms of Oxford, and hostile to their reactionary atmosphere. Among the few close friends he made there were Hubert Llewellyn Smith, the future senior civil servant, Arthur Sidgwick, fellow of Corpus, and Sidney Ball, fellow of St John's and magnet for aspiring social reformers. With the last he shared not only political views as a member of Ball's social science club but also amateur dramatics: he played Hastings to Ball's Hardcastle in *She Stoops to Conquer*. Hobhouse had a strong comic streak, verging on buffoonery, and frequently entertained family and friends with Cornish songs. Graham Wallas was later to recall his special gift for mimicry.

Invitations from Lady Rosalind Howard to vacation parties at Castle Howard issued in new friendships, including one with her daughter Mary—the future wife of Gilbert Murray—with whom Hobhouse corresponded frequently. The letters adumbrated the two linchpins of the young Hobhouse's academic method, which were to change but little in the years to come. On the one hand was a belief in evolution as the scientific validation of a teleological development of human consciousness and interaction. That, however, required also philosophical support which Hobhouse now pledged to seek. On the other was a reading of Mazzini that discovered in the Italian patriot a unity of thought and action, and the notion of synthesis reflected in a deft blending of rights and duties as an ethical principle, and of individual and social life as a political principle.

In 1891 Hobhouse married Nora Hadwen (1862–1924), daughter of George Burgess Hadwen, a mill owner of Sowerby Bridge who lived at Kelroyde; they had a son, Oliver (1892–1963), and two daughters, Leonora (1896–1944) and Marjorie Berta (1898–1951). A strongly supportive family life had far more to offer than institutional Oxford. Nora was a spirited companion, who shared in her husband's political activities and served as unpaid secretary. Hobhouse's son recalled scientifically fought military battles on the drawing-room floor and a shared passion for railway trains. Outside his small circle of friends, however, Hobhouse showed limited interest in people, while remaining passionate about humanity.

From the late 1880s Hobhouse had developed a keen interest in trade union affairs. He supported the cause of the dock strike in 1889, and came into contact with labour leaders such as Tom Mann and Ben Tillett. He also visited Toynbee Hall, and exchanged views with Sidney Webb and other Fabians. These concerns culminated in a book, *The Labour Movement*, first published in 1893, in which Hobhouse presented the aims of trade unionism, the co-operative movement, and state socialism as directed towards a common organic good, based on a recognition of mutual dependence. He adopted the claim of a minimum wage as a first charge on industry from current Fabian arguments, and employed Alfred Marshall's *Principles of Economics* for demanding that the surplus—after accounting for labour, rent, and interest—should go not to employers' pockets but to its real creators, the community.

Hobhouse's first major scholarly work was *A Theory of Knowledge* (1896). In it he attempted to redirect the idealism still dominant in Oxford philosophy towards a more empirical and realist foundation. He saw knowledge as a mutually interdependent structure, in that truth reflected the orderly coherence and harmony of its components, and reality was an interconnected whole. Nevertheless, he rejected the unity of knowledge as universal spiritual consciousness; instead he raised the possibility of mind developing empirically on an evolutionary curve, and the consistency of its components as subject to experiential testing. The book attested to the ambivalent position Hobhouse occupied between the idealist holism of T. H. Green and the scientific lessons to be learned from biology and evolution. Significantly, Hobhouse had also studied physiology and biochemistry under the direction of J. S. Haldane in the late 1880s. Hobhouse's social philosophy has frequently been interpreted as an offshoot of Green's early form of social liberalism, but his intellectual development was far more diverse and wide-ranging, and his scientific organicism—broadly shared with his future colleague and intellectual comrade-in-arms J. A. Hobson—became the hallmark of the new liberal thinking. Hobhouse was satisfied neither by Green's metaphysics, which he believed had to be tempered by the questioning explorations of science, nor by Green's fledgeling theory of the relationship between liberty and communitarianism. *A Theory of Knowledge* may have been written before its time; certainly, it met with little success—Hobhouse's friend F. W. Hirst later described it as 'caviare to the general' (F. W. Hirst, *In the Golden Days*, 1947, 142)—and was disappointingly dismissed by F. H. Bradley, whose approval Hobhouse was eager to secure.

Journalism: the *Manchester Guardian* and radical Liberalism Hobhouse's disillusionment with Oxford was now complete. Sidgwick recommended him as a strong progressive Liberal to C. P. Scott, the formidable editor of the *Manchester Guardian*, and in 1897 Hobhouse moved to Manchester as a part-time journalist, working in the evenings, with the leisure to pursue his academic studies in the mornings. The empirical and the practical intermingled with the speculative and philosophical, setting an occupational pattern for the rest of his life. His family joined him later that year, and they lived in Manchester until 1902. During this phase of his life Hobhouse proved to be a prodigious writer of long and short leaders and of book reviews, and through the latter activity became acquainted with most of the major British works on political and social theory written at the time. Scott described him as 'writing very rapidly … In less than half the time that most men would take, his tall figure would stalk into the room and deliver the goods' (Hobson and Ginsberg, 7). Hobson estimated that in his final year in Manchester Hobhouse wrote 322 articles for the *Guardian*. This extraordinary gift, combined with an ability to clarify the most abstruse issues, served him well throughout his journalistic career and provided him with a podium for political influence though, unsurprisingly, such facility laid him open to the criticism that his academic work was diffuse and at times impetuous, mirroring its author's temperament. But among the staff of the newspaper, as J. L. Hammond recalled, Hobhouse 'was unrivalled when the hour demanded close and exact argument' (J. L. Hammond, *C. P. Scott*, 1934, 81).

Hobhouse's initial employment by the *Manchester Guardian* coincided with the Second South African War, and he became an outspoken, even crusading, castigator of the government's imperialist policy, condemning the use of concentration camps and the suspension of the Cape constitution. He was also an opinion-former on other foreign affairs—an arena which in those years provided him with the most pronounced instances for gauging moral principle. Concurrently he intensified his involvement in questions of social reform, education, free trade, and taxation. On the 1897 engineering dispute for shorter hours he wrote forty-five articles. He was a close confidant of Scott on most political as well as managerial issues, and engaged with him in frequent correspondence, though Scott insisted on toning down the criticism Hobhouse occasionally reserved for the Liberal Party. The culmination of many of Hobhouse's views at the time, based on articles published in the Liberal weekly *The Speaker*, was a trenchant book entitled *Democracy and Reaction* (1904). In it he argued for a reorganization, on which advanced Liberals and moderate socialists could agree, of the modern democratic state not as a military concern but as an enterprise directed at the moralization of industrial life and the development of human faculty. In line with other theorists of human welfare such as D. G. Ritchie and Hobson, Hobhouse effected a reconciliation between utility and rights by contending that though social welfare was the supreme end, it always had to include the upholding of those rights without which both individual and community could not develop, and which could be advanced through selected collective measures. The crucial role he was to play in the formulation of the new liberalism was already taking shape. In those years he also moved in Liberal Party circles, in particular making the acquaintance of John Morley, no new liberal himself, but like Hobhouse a staunch anti-imperialist.

Professional sociologist In 1902 Hobhouse resigned his *Guardian* post and moved to Wimbledon in London, intending to find more time for his academic work, while continuing to write occasionally for the paper. In 1901 he had published *Mind in Evolution*, the first of a trilogy which began to establish his name as a synthesizer of philosophical and empirical sociology. The distance he had travelled from Oxford idealism was signalled in his reliance on animal psychology, and some of the study's conclusions were based on observations in Manchester's Belle Vue Zoological Gardens. Hobhouse's work began to attract interest from new directions. He became involved in the establishing of the new Sociological Society in 1903 and was an active member of the committee to formulate its aims and to draft its constitution. In that year Hobhouse gave a course of lectures at Birmingham University, and in 1904 he lectured at the University of London on comparative ethics. In 1905 he was approached by the University of Wisconsin about the possibility of a professorship. But two factors temporarily intervened to postpone this potential re-entry into academic life. Financial difficulties experienced by his family induced him to accept in 1903 the paid post of secretary of the Free Trade Union, formed to counter the protectionism of Joseph Chamberlain, which he held until early 1905. And in late 1905 he embarked upon a new journalistic venture, becoming political editor of *Tribune* under the proprietorship of Franklin Thomasson, an old liberal of the Manchester school. Predictably, it was an enterprise doomed to failure, and Hobhouse soon clashed with his employer and the managing director, S. J. Pryor, both over policy and presentation, resisting pressures to play to the popular gallery.

By January 1907 Hobhouse had left *Tribune*, which soon after folded up. Scott then attempted to lure him back to Manchester, but Hobhouse preferred to restore a looser relationship with the *Guardian*, pursuing his journalistic work from London, and becoming a director of the company in 1911. Concurrently, Hobhouse joined H. W. Massingham's team on *The Nation*, writing frequently and participating in the famous *Nation* lunches, though H. W. Nevinson, his colleague in that radical discussion forum, felt Hobhouse was by then prey to too many conflicting interests. On the political front, Hobhouse supported women's suffrage after the Liberals came to power in 1906, and in his academic writings there are intermittent references to women's emancipation and to a reassessment of the structure of the family.

Meanwhile Hobhouse had published part two of his trilogy, entitled *Morals in Evolution*, in 1906. The book secured his academic reputation and marked his growing detachment from Spencer's individualistic evolutionism and Auguste Comte's crude positivist historicism. Hobhouse offered a comparative cultural investigation of the progress of morality, reflected in the social institutions of developing and developed societies, as a historical unfolding of social co-operation and individual freedom. This process was also one towards increasing universalism, as obligations were directed at humanity as a whole; indeed, the double meaning of humanity played here a crucial role. The breadth of Hobhouse's scholarship caught the attention of Victor Branford, who put forward Hobhouse's name as a candidate for the first chair in sociology, newly endowed by Martin White, at the London School of Economics. Hobhouse was duly elected in 1907 and occupied the chair until his death. In 1908 he became the editor of the relaunched journal of the Sociological Society, the *Sociological Review*, but he stepped down in 1910 owing to a combination of overwork and disagreements over the strong editorial path the journal was pursuing within the fragmented field of sociology. He was always loath to yield to pressures to change his position.

With the final volume of his trilogy, *Development and Purpose* (1913), in which the organic view of social life was more clearly revealed as the product of a purposive rational evolution, Hobhouse completed his most substantial work of scholarship, but not the one which has had the most extensive impact. His interpretation of sociology constituted an epilogue to a grand nineteenth-century intellectual movement, but it was already being replaced by a plethora of empirical, functional, and specialized approaches, increasingly severed from philosophy. The central message of Hobhouse's sociological work, one taken up also by his specific brand of liberalism, was the affirmation of orthogenic evolution: progress was a corollary of the development of mind and reason, it was teleological in its nature, and the measure of its success was ethical. Evolution had produced one species capable of controlling through consciousness the evolutionary process itself, replacing struggle and competition with co-operation. Though the terminology changed over time, the guiding principle of interpreting evolution as the improvement of the human mind had already been formed during Hobhouse's Oxford days. Both his sociology and philosophy served that end; both were intended—through the master concept of purposive evolution—to bridge the gap between science and ethics or, more specifically in the light of Hobhouse's earlier intellectual origins, between positivism and idealism. A book co-authored in 1915 with G. C. Wheeler and Hobhouse's pupil and successor Morris Ginsberg, *The Material Culture and Social Institutions of the Simpler Peoples*, transposed that enterprise to the domain of comparative anthropology.

Liberalism before and during the war In 1910 Hobhouse was commissioned by the Home University Library to write what became his most enduring work, *Liberalism* (1911). In conjunction with Hobson, he emerged in this brilliant and lucid book as the prime theorist and standard-bearer of the new liberalism, combining the traditional allure of mutual forbearance with the newer ethical imperative of mutual aid under the aegis of a guiding social intelligence, co-ordinated by the democratic state. Because mind evolved in the direction of increased rationality and ethicality, and these in turn revealed the unity of purpose and the organic interdependence of social life, a collectivist liberalism was emerging out of its earlier individualist manifestations. Consequently, the community, as well as its members, had rights that required protection, in the form of common property for the common good. Yet the community was never more than the sum of its parts, and could thrive only when individual personality was allowed optimal expression; hence Hobhouse's rejection of stronger versions of socialism and his espousal of an over-optimistic harmony between individual and social ends. Nevertheless, a full civil efficiency was central to individual responsibility and to the full conception of inclusionary citizenship that Hobhouse upheld. State compulsion was thus permitted to constrain coercive conduct—physical, economic, and ethical—that violated individual or social rights, in order to secure a radical reinterpretation of liberty as human growth. Liberalism was a vital, animating principle that encompassed the flowering of civilization itself.

Though the greater vision was naïve in its ironing out of conflict, in practical terms Hobhouse was at the cutting edge of social reform thinking, advocating the right to work and to a living wage, the redistribution of resources, unemployment and health insurance, and taxation that would identify socially created wealth and put it at the disposal of the community. He was also an early enthusiast for universal old-age pensions. In 1911 he helped to form the short-lived Foreign Policy Committee, whose role was to raise parliamentary awareness, and foster parliamentary control, of foreign affairs, and served as its chairman. An invitation to lecture at Columbia University in April 1911 resulted in the publication of the talks under the title *Social Evolution and Political Theory*, notable among others for the critical stance it adopted *vis-à-vis* eugenics, versions of which were attracting progressive thinkers.

When the First World War broke out Hobhouse initially joined the British Neutrality Committee, but the growing

German threat made him change his mind, causing a clash with his pacifist sister Emily. His association of Prussianism and Hegelianism as a menace to liberal civilization was famously expressed in his preface to *The Metaphysical Theory of the State* (1918), dedicated to his son, then serving in the RAF. An air raid had interrupted Hobhouse's examination of Hegel's theory of freedom: 'In the bombing of London I had just witnessed the visible and tangible outcome of a false and wicked doctrine, the foundation of which lay, as I believe, in the book before me' (p. 6). This also signalled Hobhouse's final break with idealism, which he had increasingly seen as a vehicle for the pernicious infiltration of an alien statist mysticism into British universities. The book, a mirror-image attack on Bernard Bosanquet's *The Philosophical Theory of the State* (1899) and its confounding of state with society, reiterated the new liberal discovery of self-determination as a developmental liberty, but proclaimed also the war-induced cautiousness of new liberals, now wedded to the absence of unjustifiable constraints on individuals and resistant to the notion of state compulsion, even with regard to conscription. Hobhouse's anti-Germanism was not a retreat to a cultural Little Englandism. He praised the democratic humanitarianism of the French and Dutch, as well as the English, traditions, and hailed the March 1917 Russian revolution in a *Guardian* editorial as an example to Britain of how freedom and democracy should be promoted.

Post-war years: consolidation and decline In parallel with his theoretical interest in labour relations, Hobhouse became involved in trade boards, which engaged among others in establishing minimum wage rates. This involvement offered a forum for the application of his social theories. Immediately after the war he chaired nine boards on their establishment at the invitation of the Ministry of Labour and defended trade boards when they came under ministerial and public attack. As a chairman, he was a commanding personality: eager to get at the facts, purposive and impartial, discouraging verbosity, and insistent on uncovering the underlying moral principles of each settlement. Hobhouse also served as chairman of the subcommittee on wages and hours of the national industrial conference in 1919. In that year he received an honorary degree from the University of St Andrews, having already collected one from the University of Durham in 1913.

The post-war years were marked both by a continued prolificity in writing and by an increase in the bouts of pessimism with which Hobhouse had contended for most of his life. A search for a conception of common humanity was now stimulated by the awareness that 'history forbids the cheap optimism which assumes that everything will always go forward' (*The World in Conflict*, 1915, 96). The result was another trilogy of books: *The Rational Good* (1921), *The Elements of Social Justice* (1922), and *Social Development* (1924). In them he developed a theory of rights based on the reciprocal claims of individual personality, differentiated from socialism by protecting private interests, yet—in tandem with R. H. Tawney—also insisting on the importance of social service as the basis of economic reward, while reiterating the ultimate harmony between the individual and the communal. He employed a psychological account of the growth of sociability and rationality from impulse, but disparagingly dismissed the newer psychoanalytical thinking of Freud as a passing fashion. In these last major works Hobhouse was involved in reworking and honing the project he had pursued throughout the last twenty-five years of his life, and whose intellectual conception now seemed increasingly out of touch with post-war culture. Though his sharpness and lucidity continued unabated, his creativity had become muted. A student observed that Hobhouse's 'very intellectual honesty stood in his way … for he could remain so long with suspended judgment that he was regarded as unable to make up his own mind' (*Manchester Guardian*, 26 June 1929).

By 1924 Hobhouse's health had seriously deteriorated as a consequence of phlebitis, causing him to abandon the second part of a two-year Muirhead lectureship at Birmingham University begun in 1923. Notwithstanding, his London duties intensified from 1925, when the Martin White chair was converted from a part-time to a full-time basis. Other activities continued. He became chairman of the council of the British Institute of Philosophical Studies, formed in 1925, and in the same year was elected a fellow of the British Academy. Hobhouse continued to follow politics, but from a distance. He collaborated with Gilbert Murray and others in advocating internationalism. The plight of the Liberal Party depressed him, but like his friend Hobson, he remained ill at ease with the rising Labour Party. He played a small role in the Liberal industrial inquiry which produced the famous 'Yellow book' of 1928, but mainly sat on the sidelines of Liberalism. Instead, he hoped for a break-up of the British party system so that an ideological realignment between 'ordinary labour' and 'good liberals' would emerge which would reduce the impact of trade unionism.

Hobhouse was a tall, bulky, and shaggy man. He was gentle and courteous, yet could be 'blastingly frigid' in curtailing useless discussion. He lectured without notes, possessed an astonishing memory, and commanded great respect from his occasionally intimidated students. Yet his intellectual *gravitas* was punctuated by a childlike sense of humour, often involving the exploits of a jackdaw apparently encouraged to disperse his papers at his home. Both his private and public persona were forever blowing hot and cold. In his declining years Hobhouse's students were often transfixed by his trembling hand as he relit his pipe. In search of medical treatment, he spent a part of his last summers in Bagnôles de l'Orne in Normandy under the care of a specialist. He was due to retire from the London School of Economics in 1929 but had accepted a year's extension at the request of the director, William Beveridge. That was not to be. Hobhouse died suddenly in hospital in Alençon, France, on 21 June 1929 as a consequence of a duodenal ulcer and was buried a week later at St Mary's churchyard in Wimbledon.

MICHAEL FREEDEN

Sources J. A. Hobson and M. Ginsberg, *L. T. Hobhouse: his life and work* (1931) • S. Collini, *Liberalism and sociology: L. T. Hobhouse and political argument in England, 1880–1914* (1979) • *Manchester Guardian* (24 June 1929) • *The Nation* (29 June 1929) • *Nation and the Athenaeum* (29 June 1929) • V. Branford, 'The sociological work of Leonard Hobhouse', *Sociological Review*, 21 (1929), 273–80 • *The Times* (24 June 1929) • J. Owen, *L. T. Hobhouse, sociologist* (1974) • M. Freeden, *The new liberalism* (1978) • M. Freeden, *Liberalism divided* (1986) • E. Barker, 'Leonard Trelawny Hobhouse, 1864–1929', *PBA*, 15 (1931), 536–54 • P. Clarke, *Liberals and social democrats* (1978) • *DNB* • A. R. Fry, *Emily Hobhouse: a memoir* (1929) • *CGPLA Eng. & Wales* (1929)
Archives BLPES, corresp. and MSS • priv. coll., MSS | BL, C. P. Scott MSS • Bodl. Oxf., letters to Francis Marvin • Bodl. Oxf., letters to Gilbert Murray • Castle Howard, Yorkshire, letters to Rosalind, countess of Carlisle • JRL, corresp. with C. P. Scott • Keele University Library, LePlay collection, corresp. and minute book entries as member of Sociological Society committees
Likenesses Elliott & Fry, photograph, BLPES [*see illus.*] • photograph, repro. in Hobson and Ginsberg, *L. T. Hobhouse*, frontispiece
Wealth at death £19,422 15s. 4d.: resworn probate, 27 July 1929, *CGPLA Eng. & Wales*

Hoblyn, Richard Dennis (1803–1886), educational writer, was the eldest son of Richard Hoblyn (1771–1827), rector of All Saints, Colchester, and his wife, who was the daughter of James Blatch. He was born at Colchester on 9 April 1803, and educated in his native town, and at Blundell's School, Tiverton. Thence he went as a scholar to Balliol College, Oxford, where he took second-class honours in classics and graduated BA in 1824, proceeding MA in 1828. He took orders four years later, but he resigned the clerical life, and devoted himself to teaching and educational writing in London. His chief work was *A Dictionary of Terms used in Medicine and the Collateral Sciences* (1832; rev. 14th edn, 1909). In conjunction with an American writer, John Lee Comstock (1789–1858), he produced a number of elementary science textbooks, including *A Manual of Chemistry* (1841), *A Manual of the Steam Engine* (1842), and *First Book of Natural Philosophy* (1846). He married, on 4 April 1843, Fanny, daughter of the Revd W. A. Armstrong. They had a son, Richard Armstrong Hoblyn. Hoblyn was well-known in the borough of Marylebone, where he lived for fifty-nine years at 2 Sussex Place, Regent's Park. He died there on 22 August 1886.   FRANCIS WATT, rev. M. C. CURTHOYS

Sources Foster, *Alum. Oxon.* • *Marylebone Mercury* (4 Sept 1886) • *GM*, 2nd ser., 19 (1843), 528 • private information (1888) • Boase, *Mod. Eng. biog.* • *CGPLA Eng. & Wales* (1887)
Wealth at death £8029 17s.: resworn probate, Dec 1887, *CGPLA Eng. & Wales* (1886)

Hoblyn, Robert (*bap.* 1710, *d.* 1756), politician and book collector, was born at Nanswhyden House, St Columb Major, and baptized at St Columb Major in Cornwall on 5 May 1710. He was the only son of Francis Hoblyn (1687–1711), a justice of the peace for Cornwall and a member of the stannary parliament, and Penelope, daughter of Colonel Sidney Godolphin of Shropshire. Following his father's death, his mother married secondly, on 5 September 1714, Sir William Pendarves of Pendarves.

Robert Hoblyn attended Eton College. He matriculated from Corpus Christi College, Oxford, on 18 December

1727, took a BCL degree in 1734, and in the same year contributed verses to the *Epithalamia Oxoniensia*. His translation of the first book of *The Georgics* of Virgil was published, posthumously, in 1825. He sat as one of the members of parliament for the city of Bristol from 24 November 1742 to 8 April 1754, voting generally with the opposition, and was appointed speaker of two convocations of the stannary parliament in Cornwall. He was elected a fellow of the Royal Society on 13 June 1745, and admitted on 24 October. He married Jane Coster, the only daughter of Thomas Coster, a Bristol merchant.

Early in life Hoblyn had travelled in Italy, where he collected many scarce books. He inherited an ample fortune, which was greatly increased by the profits from his successful investment in the Cornish tin mining industry. With his wealth he restored his ancestral home, Nanswhyden House, about 1740, employing Thomas Edwards and John Potter as his architects. This building is described in William Borlase's *Natural History of Cornwall* (1758), with a plate engraved at the expense of Jane Hoblyn. Hoblyn also delighted in collecting books, and he destroyed all the documents relating to their cost. His library was divided into the classes of natural and moral philosophy, and he made a manuscript catalogue in which he marked with an asterisk those works which were not in the Bodleian Library. All clergymen and persons of literary tastes had free access to the library.

Hoblyn died at Nanswhyden House on 17 November 1756. His monument in St Columb church, where he was buried on 29 November, bears a very long inscription which is printed by Polwhele. His widow married John Quicke of Exeter in 1759. Hoblyn's estates went to the male descendants of Thomas Hoblyn of Tresaddern, while his library remained with his widow.

In 1768 John Quicke printed Hoblyn's catalogue in two volumes, entitled *Bibliotheca Hobliniana, sive, Catalogus librorum juxta exemplar quod manu sua maxima ex parte descriptum reliquit Robertus Hoblyn, armiger de Nanswhyden in comitatu Cornubiae*. An edition in one volume was published by J. Murray in 1769. Dibdin says in referring to it: 'I know not who was the author of the arrangement of this collection, but the judicious observer will find it greatly superior to everything of its kind, with hardly even the exception of the "Bibliotheca Croftsiana"' (Dibdin, 374). Hoblyn's books were sold in London in 1778, and produced about £2500. Nanswhyden House was destroyed by fire on 30 November 1803, with its collections of ancient documents, the records relating to the stannary parliament, and a valuable cabinet of minerals.

G. C. BOASE, rev. IAN MAXTED

Sources R. Polwhele, *The history of Cornwall*, 7 vols. (1803–8), vol. 5, pp. 94–6 • J. Polsue, *A complete parochial history of the county of Cornwall*, 1 (1867), 233–4 • Nichols, *Illustrations*, 5.863 • Nichols, *Lit. anecdotes*, 3.730; 7.449, 481, 709; 9.709–10 • Boase & Courtney, *Bibl. Corn.*, 1.246 • T. F. Dibdin, *Bibliomania, or, Book madness: a bibliographical romance*, new edn (1876), 374 • W. Borlase, *Natural history of Cornwall* (1758), 90, pl. 8 • *GM*, 1st ser., 73 (1803), 1179 • Colvin, *Archs.*, 335 • HoP, *Commons*

Archives BL, letter, Add. MS 11759, p. 230

Hobry [Aubry; *other married name* Defermeau], **Mary** (*d.* **1688**), murderer, was a French Catholic midwife of the parish of St Martin-in-the-Fields who emerged into prominence in late January 1688 when the head, torso, and limbs of her husband, Denis Hobry, were discovered one by one around London. His trunk was behind a dunghill in Parker's Lane, his limbs in one privy in the Savoy, his head in another. Much speculation centred on these body parts. The case became one site of rumour and debate over the Catholic menace in the months prior to the fall of James II. That three illustrations of Mary Hobry's crime and punishment are included in a deck of playing cards about the Revolution suggests the significance of the crime as a portent of the social and political disorder which could flourish under a Catholic king.

The reassembled body was displayed in the St Giles bone house in the hope of determining the victim's identity. Once the victim was identified as Denis, Mary Hobry was apprehended on 2 February at the house of one of her clients. At the time of the murder she had been married to Denis for four years. Confusion as to the couple's last name seems to have been a consequence of the fact that they did not speak English, and that their English neighbours had a hard time grasping their name. Mary Hobry also seems to have been known by the name of her first husband, Defermeau. She had two children from her earlier marriage, a married daughter and a thirteen-year-old son who was a weaver's apprentice. Although both were living in London, neither lived with Hobry and her husband in Castle Street. A coroner's inquest was held on 8 February. A true bill was found against Mary at the Old Bailey on 22 February; she was arraigned the same day for petty treason and murder. She pleaded guilty.

The fullest account of the events of 27 January appears in Roger L'Estrange, *A Hellish Murder Committed by a French Midwife, on the Body of her Husband, Jan. 27, 1687/8* (London, 1688); other printed versions seem to have been based on this lengthy pamphlet. Since Hobry had confessed to her crime, and there was no trial, the tory journalist Sir Roger L'Estrange was concerned that there would be no published account to counter the many rumours circulating about the case, especially those attaching political significance to the murder: 'The late Barbarous Murder of Denis Hobry, (what with Malice, Prejudice, Credulity and Mistake) has put more Freaks and Crotchets into the Hearts and Minds of the Common People, than any Story of that size perhaps ever did in this World before' (L'Estrange, sig. A2*r*). Therefore L'Estrange assembled and published what he viewed as the case against Hobry: the sworn testimony of numerous witnesses, taken before him as investigating magistrate, as well as her own detailed 'confession', which he secured in a private interrogation with the help of a translator. L'Estrange emphasized the domestic nature of the murder. He explicitly pressed Mary on why she had disposed of parts of the body in privies at the Savoy, thereby incriminating the religion she professed. She replied that her only thoughts had been 'to part the Limbs and the Body, and hoped the Water might carry them away' (L'Estrange, sig. F3*r*). Similarly Henry Care, a journalist who was a whig ally of the king's, was concerned to refute 'the Croakings of the Faction' (*Publick Occurrences*, 3, 6 March 1688), who had been busily turning the murder 'to the disadvantage of the Government, and scaring people, as it must needs be acted on some Religious score, and but the Bloody Prologue to some greater Tragedy' (ibid., 1, 21 Feb 1688). Care emphasized that the murder was the result of '*private Malice* or *Revenge*' (ibid.).

All accounts of the murder suggest that the marriage had been contentious and violent. The couple fought about Denis's extravagance, especially his seizure and waste of what Mary Hobry earned through her 'industrious Care' as a midwife (*Warning-Piece*, 2), his drunkenness and dissolute life, which Mary claimed had infected her with a sexually transmitted disease, and his insistence that she 'submit to a compliance with him in Villanies contrary to Nature' (L'Estrange, sig. E3v). The couple alternated between separations, when Denis returned to France, and brief reconciliations, during which he would promise to amend his ways, with spells of open hostility.

A Hellish Murder presents not only the fullest account of the murder itself, but also the one most sympathetic to Mary Hobry, since it so vividly details her provocation. On the night of the murder, by this account, Denis 'attempted the Forcing of this Examinate to the most Unnatural of Villanies, and acted such a Violence upon her Body in despite of all the Opposition that she could make, as forc'd from her a great deal of Blood' (L'Estrange, sig. Fr). He also beat Mary, threatened her, and 'bit her like a Dog' (ibid., sig. Fv). After he fell asleep she contemplated her limited options and decided to deliver herself from misery by killing him. She strangled him with a piece of packthread he used as a garter. Mary then spent several days deciding how to dispose of the body; at last, on 30 January, she dismembered him.

Presenting the murder as the culmination of marital conflict did not render it less threatening, as L'Estrange seemed to hope. After all, murdering one's husband was distinguished from other murders as petty treason, and was associated by analogy with high treason, that is, any threat to or assault on the monarch and his or her government. For women, the punishments for petty and high treason were the same: burning at the stake. On 23 February Hobry was sentenced to be burnt; the sentence was carried out at Leicester Fields on 2 March. While the timing of the murder and Mary Hobry's status as a French Catholic made her crime even more controversial, her gruesome death links her to other murderous wives, whose murder of their husbands was also understood as treason.   FRANCES E. DOLAN

Sources [R. L'Estrange], *A hellish murder committed by a French midwife, on the body of her husband, Jan. 27, 1687/8* (1688) · *A cabinet of grief, or, The French midwife's miserable moan for the barbarous murder committed upon the body of her husband* (1688) · *Publick Occurrences Truely Stated*, 1 (21 Feb 1687/8); 2 (28 Feb 1887/8); 3 (6 March 1687/8) · *Publick Occurrences Truely Stated*, 2 (28 Feb 1688) · *Publick Occurrences Truely Stated*, 3 (6 March 1688) · *A warning-piece to all married men and women, being the full confession of Mary Hobry, the French midwife, who murdered her husband on the 27th. of January 1687/8* (1688) · E. Settle, *Epilogue to the French midwifes tragedy who was burnt in Leicesterfields March 2 1687/8 for the barbarous murder of her husband Denis Hobry* (1688)

Likenesses portrait (queen of clubs, and one and two of spades, from playing cards depicting 'The Revolution'), BM, Schreiber collection · portrait, repro. in [L'Estrange], *A hellish murder*

Hobson, Edward (1782–1830), botanist and weaver, was born on 23 May 1782 in Ancoats Lane, Manchester. When he was three he was taken in by an uncle in Ashton under Lyne following his father's death and the subsequent alcoholism of his mother, while a younger brother remained in Manchester with his grandfather. Hobson attended schools in Ashton and Manchester, having swapped guardians with his brother after a few years. In 1794 he began to weave, producing muslins until some time after 1812 when, despite engaging in political activity to protect hand-loom weavers, he left the craft. By 1815 he was a warehouseman in Manchester.

Hobson's early enthusiasm for astrological herbalism may have inspired his interest in botany. About 1809 he began to attend botanical meetings held by working men in various pubs in and around Manchester at which participants would bring freshly gathered plants to be named aloud by the most expert botanist present, who acted as president of the meeting. Hobson established a strong friendship with John Dewhurst, who was president of Sunday pub meetings attended by working-men botanists from a wider region. Soon Hobson was assisting Dewhurst as namer of plants, eventually becoming president in the 1820s, as well as encouraging John Horsefield, who would later succeed Hobson as president. James Crowther was a good friend who possibly introduced Hobson to George Caley, who returned to Lancashire for the period 1811–16. During this time Hobson and Caley were extremely close and they maintained a correspondence after Caley's departure for St Vincent.

From 1811 Hobson took up the difficult study of mosses and liverworts, soon becoming expert in this area. By 1815 his discoveries led William Jackson Hooker to seek a meeting with him in Manchester. Impressed by Hobson's abilities in finding and distinguishing these little-studied cryptogamic plants, Hooker gave him a microscope and began a correspondence with him in order to receive further information and specimens. With Hooker's encouragement, Hobson produced and sold about twenty-five sets of *A Collection of Specimens of British Mosses and Hepaticae*, known as *Musci Britannici* (2 vols., 1818–22). These dried specimens were designed to accompany Hooker and Thomas Taylor's *Muscologia Britannica: Containing the Mosses of Great Britain and Ireland* (1818), in which they were advertised. In preparing *Musci Britannici*, Hobson exchanged letters and specimens with a wide range of naturalists from different social classes.

Hobson longed to travel like Caley as a botanical collector but, despite interest from Hooker and Robert Brown in 1819, was unable to do so because of responsibilities to his wife, Bridget (d. 1848), two sons, and seven daughters. Instead he was active in various scientific circles in 1820s Manchester, ranging from working-men's botanical meetings in pubs to involvement with the museum of the élite and exclusive Natural History Society. By this time Hobson was primarily interested in entomology; the beetle *Chrysomela hobsoni*, discovered by Hobson, is described in James Francis Stephens's *Illustrations of British Entomology* (4, 1831, 343). Despite an offer of well-paid curatorial work of £100 a year from the Manchester Natural History Society in 1829, Hobson remained a warehouseman.

In 1829, together with other artisans, Hobson founded and presided over the Banksian Society for the study of natural history, in which he encouraged a socially mixed membership. This society did not meet in a pub and, in contrast to the oral nature of pub meetings, deliberately emphasized a more literate culture in its organizational structure. One of the committee members, the radical Rowland Detrosier, gave the opening address, which was published under the title of *The Benefits of General Knowledge: more especially, the sciences of mineralogy, geology, botany, and entomology*, in which he stressed the right of all to enter the 'temple of science'.

Possibly because of his mother's alcoholism, Hobson was extremely abstemious. He possessed an immense capacity for fieldwork, disregarding bad weather and climbing trees and onto roofs searching for mosses. When his health began to fail in the summer of 1830, well-to-do friends moved him to Bowdon, Cheshire, away from the smoky air of Manchester. Aware of the potential value of his specimens, Hobson wrote a will requesting they be sold for the support of his family. Over 11,000 dried plants were purchased by the Manchester Horticultural and Botanical Society for £90 and his insect cabinet was sold to the Banksian Society (eventually passing to the Manchester Mechanics' Institution) for £65.

Hobson died of consumption at Bowdon on 7 September 1830 and was buried at St George's Church, Hulme, Manchester. A memorial tablet inside the church commemorates his scientific achievements as well as his 'natural simplicity of manners'. Hobson was a source of inspiration not only to artisan naturalists but also to gentlemen. James Aspinall Turner, Liberal MP for Manchester from 1857, began his extensive collection of coleopterous insects following the gift of two beetles from Hobson; Joseph Dalton Hooker maintained that his love of bryology was stimulated by Hobson's *Musci Britannici* in his father's library; and William Jackson Hooker himself declared to Dawson Turner in a letter of 14 October 1815, just after his only meeting with Hobson: 'I hardly ever saw a man possessed of more enthusiasm than this poor fellow'.   ANNE SECORD

Sources J. Moore, 'A memoir of Mr. Edward Hobson', *Memoirs of the Literary and Philosophical Society of Manchester*, 2nd ser., 6 (1842), 297–324 · J. Horsefield, 'John Horsefield, the botanist [pt 2]', *Manchester Guardian* (24 April 1850) · J. Horsefield, 'John Horsefield, the botanist [pt 3]', *Manchester Guardian* (21 Dec 1850) · Edward Hobson's 'Pattern book, 1794', Middleton Library, Archives cupboard 1 · J. Cash, 'The early botanical work of the late William Wilson', *The Naturalist* (1887), 181–90 · L. H. Grindon, *Manchester walks and wild-flowers: an introduction to the botany and rural beauty of the district* [1859], 133–4 · W. J. Hooker and T. Taylor, *Muscologia Britannica* (1818), x · letter from William Willis, *Manchester Times* (20 Dec

1834) · Banksian Society minutes, Man. CL, Manchester Archives and Local Studies, MS 590. 6. B3 · W. Wilson, letter to W. J. Hooker, 7 Feb 1831, Royal Collection, Directors' correspondence, vol. 2, letter 198 · will, 31 Aug 1830, Middleton Library, Archives cupboard 1 · *Account of the formation of the Manchester Field-Naturalists' Society … and report of the first meeting* (1860), 20 · 'Sir Joseph Hooker's reminiscences of Manchester', *Lancashire Naturalist*, 1 (1907–8), 118–20 · W. J. Hooker, letter to D. Turner, 14 Oct 1815, Royal Collection, W. J. Hooker letters, vol. 1, fols. 200–201 · *Gardener's Magazine*, 6 (1830), 749 · *Manchester Guardian* (11 Sept 1830)

Archives Bolton Museum and Art Gallery, Lancashire, specimens · Chetham's Library, Manchester, specimens · Liverpool Museum, specimens · Man. CL, specimens · Manchester Museum, botany department, corresp. and specimens · NHM, specimens · NL Wales, specimens · Whipple Museum, Cambridge, specimens | RBG Kew, directors' corresp. · W. Yorks. AS, Halifax, Calderdale district archives, Roberts Leyland corresp.

Wealth at death plant specimens valued at £90; plus insect specimens valued at £65: letter from W. Wilson to W. J. Hooker, 7 Feb 1831, directors' correspondence, vol. 2, letter 198; Banksian Society minutes, Man. CL; RBG Kew, archives, MS 590.6 B3

Hobson, Ernest William (1856–1933), mathematician, was born on 27 October 1856, at Duffield Road, Derby, the eldest son of William Hobson, founder, editor, and part proprietor of the *Derbyshire Advertiser* and a prominent figure in municipal affairs, and his wife, Josephine Atkinson. John Atkinson *Hobson, the economist and publicist, was one of his brothers. His early education was obtained at Derby School. In 1871 he was elected to a scholarship at what became the Imperial College of Science, South Kensington, and studied physics for a time in London under Frederick Guthrie. Although a versatile student he was always primarily a mathematician, and in 1874 he obtained a scholarship at Christ's College, Cambridge, where he remained for the rest of his life.

Hobson was senior wrangler in January 1878 and was elected a fellow of his college in the autumn of the same year. In 1883 he was chosen as one of the first university lecturers in mathematics, and in 1903 as Stokes lecturer, a position of particular distinction. From 1910 to 1931 he was Sadleirian professor of pure mathematics. He was a conspicuous figure in international science, and received many honours including a royal medal (1907) of the Royal Society, of which he had been elected a fellow in 1893, the De Morgan medal (1920) of the London Mathematical Society, honorary degrees, and memberships of foreign academies.

Hobson's early career was not particularly distinguished. It was not until he was nearly forty that he published his first important work, an elaborate memoir on 'spherical harmonic' in the *Philosophical Transactions of the Royal Society* for 1896. A classic in its field, its preparation may well have occupied him for several years. None the less his development as a mathematician seems to have been strangely slow, and this was partly due to the Cambridge traditions of the time, namely the extravagant importance attached to position in the tripos and the general indifference to research. It was one of Hobson's greatest services to Cambridge later to help to break down these traditions.

As was then customary, Hobson served many years as a

private coach for the tripos, at which he was good and successful. Although less notorious than E. J. Routh or Robert Rumsey Webb, he had one famous triumph. In 1890 one of his pupils, Philippa Fawcett, was placed above the senior wrangler in the university examinations, though as a female she could not formally contend for wrangler status. John Maynard Keynes was another of his pupils.

It was not until 1903 that Hobson abandoned coaching to do more research, and not until he was fifty that he developed fully the dominant interests of his life. The modern theory of real functions, as understood in Europe since the days of Riemann and Weierstrass, was hardly known in England before 1890. A. R. Forsyth's *Theory of Functions of a Complex Variable* (1893) raised the first interest in the subject, but Forsyth cared only for the 'complex' theory, and the more fundamental 'real' theory remained neglected; it was in work on the latter that Hobson found the great opportunity of his life. His *Theory of Functions of a Real Variable* was published in 1907. The modern theories of measure and integration, initiated in France by Bore and Lebesgue, were then still unfamiliar, and Hobson and William Henry Young (who never held a regular position in the university) were the first Cambridge mathematicians to grasp the significance of the new ideas. The subject expanded rapidly, and Hobson's book, in its various editions, occupied him for twenty years. It is a fine book, written with full mastery of a vast subject and with many important contributions of his own. Despite this, the establishment of real analysis as a research subject at Cambridge was left to his successors to accomplish.

Hobson wrote four other books. The most important is *Spherical and Ellipsoidal Harmonics* (1931): this contains much of his early work, and in particular his memoir of 1896. His earliest book, *A Treatise on Plane Trigonometry* (1891), is an important if rather elementary textbook which ran through many editions. This was the first English book, apart from the *Algebra* of George Chrystal, to give any serious account of the elements of 'algebraical analysis'. *Squaring the Circle* (1913), a reprint of six lectures given in that year, was a successful 'popular' book. In *The Domain of Natural Science* (1923), the Gifford lectures delivered at Aberdeen in 1921–2, Hobson reveals his interest in philosophy. His selection as lecturer was quite appropriate, but the book, although competent and scholarly, is slightly disappointing, the position which he defends, a rather extreme and abstract form of the 'descriptive' view of natural science, being much more reasonable than exciting.

On 1 July 1882 Hobson married Selina Rosa, daughter of Rudolf Knüsli, a merchant, of Glarus, Switzerland; they had four sons, of whom one predeceased him. Apart from his position as a leading British mathematician, Hobson was also a conspicuous and influential figure in Cambridge. He was proctor twice, served on the council of the senate and on important syndicates, and was a frequent speaker in Senate House discussions. He was regarded as a 'radical', as radicalism was understood in university circles in the early twentieth century, and he usually voted with the reformers on the university senate, the controversy over women's degrees being an exception. He was one of the leaders in the movement for the reform of the mathematical tripos which resulted in 1910 in the abolition of the Order of Merit.

Hobson died at the Evelyn Nursing Home, Cambridge, after an operation, on 18 April 1933.

G. H. HARDY, rev. J. J. GRAY

Sources *Obits. FRS*, 1 (1932–5), 237–49 · *Journal of the London Mathematical Society*, 9 (1934) · private information (1949) · personal knowledge (1949) · b. cert. · m. cert. · d. cert.

Archives RS

Likenesses K. Green, oils, 1925, Christ's College, Cambridge · W. Stoneman, photograph, 1926, NPG · Elliott & Fry, photograph, Christ's College, Cambridge · Maull & Fox, photograph, RS

Wealth at death £28,219 7s. 4d.: probate, 25 May 1933, *CGPLA Eng. & Wales*

Hobson, Geoffrey Dudley (1882–1949), historian of bookbindings, was born on 17 March 1882 at Bromborough, Cheshire, the fourth son of Richard Hobson DL, of The Marfords, Bromborough, cotton broker and company director, and his wife, Mary Eleanor, daughter of John Chadwick DL, of Stockport.

Hobson was educated at Harrow School (1896–1900) and at University College, Oxford, where he was placed in the first class of the honours list in modern history in 1903. He passed the Foreign Office examination but his severe loss of hearing meant he was unable to pursue a legal career. In 1908 he was part of a group led by Montague Barlow which purchased the old-established auctioneering firm of Sotheby, Wilkinson, and Hodge. Here, too, his deafness handicapped him, and he never conducted sales on the rostrum. But he contributed shrewd business skills to the firm, while the work there also allowed him to develop his appreciation of, and expertise in, the wide variety of items handled by the auction house. His interest turned particularly to early books, and especially bookbindings, and on the latter he became the greatest authority of the day. For Sothebys, it has been said, the 'respect he gained over the years as a bibliophile provided the firm with a scholarly respectability unprecedented in auctioneering history' (Faith, 40). Hobson made Sothebys the centre of the world's rare book business, and the scholarly standards he attempted to impose across all areas of the business improved the standing of the firm significantly.

Hobson was described as the art of bookbinding's 'finest historian' (*TLS*). While most writers on bindings in all countries had concentrated upon the work of their own lands, and usually that of a single period, Hobson developed a wide knowledge of western European bindings, although it was strongest on the Romanesque period, on English sixteenth-century panel-stamps, and on the gold-tooled bindings of France in the sixteenth century and of England in the seventeenth and eighteenth centuries.

In 1920 Hobson married Gertrude Adelaide (d. 1938), daughter of the Revd Thomas Walter Vaughan, and widow of Henry Dyson Taylor. They had one son. In 1922 Hobson was appointed MVO.

In *Maioli, Canevari and Others* (1926) Hobson demonstrated his critical scholarly approach by comprehensively disproving some long accepted myths which had dominated some aspects of the field. The same year he was appointed Sandars reader in bibliography at Cambridge. In 1927 he produced an elaborate study of Romanesque work, published as *English Binding before 1500* (1929), although he subsequently modified his views as to the nationality of much of the material studied. He produced the extensive *Bindings in Cambridge Libraries* in 1929, and *English Bindings 1490–1940 in the Library of J. R. Abbey* in 1940. Hobson was innovative in his discussions of bindings, often using parallels, particularly in iconography, drawn from other forms of art, to illuminate his points. By his output and newly scientific approach Hobson perhaps did more than anyone else to promote the serious study of bindings as a feature in bibliography.

Although remembered by contemporaries as a pleasant companion in a social setting, Hobson could be at times autocratic in his relations with his staff, and could bring this manner on occasions even to scholarly discussions with his peers. His involvement with Sothebys gave him the benefit for his study of access to the many works handled by the firm, and his skill and effort in research enabled him to take the fullest advantage of this. He died at his residence at 11 Chelsea Park Gardens, Chelsea, London, on 5 January 1949, and was cremated at Golders Green on 8 January.   J. B. OLDHAM, *rev.* MARC BRODIE

Sources N. Faith, *Sold*, 2nd edn (1987) · *The Times* (6 Jan 1949) · *TLS* (22 Jan 1949), 64 · J. W. Moir, ed., *The Harrow School register, 1885–1949*, 5th edn (1951) · *WWW* · *CGPLA Eng. & Wales* (1949) · personal knowledge (1959) · private information (1959)
Wealth at death £90,904 2s. 10d.: probate, 25 March 1949, *CGPLA Eng. & Wales*

Hobson, Sir Harold (1904–1992), theatre critic, was born on 4 August 1904 in Thorpe Hesley, near Rotherham, Yorkshire, the only son of Jacob Hobson, miner, and later insurance agent, and his wife, Minnie, *née* McKegg. Although left disabled by polio in his eighth year and largely educated at home by his working-class parents, who brought him large quantities of books from the public library, he recovered sufficiently to attend Sheffield grammar school, from where he gained a scholarship to Oriel College, Oxford; he graduated with a second-class degree in modern history in 1928. While at Oxford he met and developed a close friendship with Erwin Canham, later editor of the *Christian Science Monitor*. Hobson began to write London theatre reviews for the paper in 1931, and in 1935 he was placed on its permanent staff. He remained its London drama critic until 1974. Regular employment enabled him to marry, on 13 July 1935, a radiantly cheerful schoolteacher, (Gladys) Elizabeth Johns (1899/1900–1979), eldest daughter of James Johns. The marriage was the cornerstone of Hobson's private and professional life. They had one daughter, Margaret.

As Hobson made clear in his autobiography, *Indirect Journey* (1978), his critical attitudes were shaped by his experiences of life. His crusading moral zeal was a legacy of his parents' faith (which he inherited) in Christian Science

and its belief in the unreality of disease. His catholicity of taste was formed by his omnivorous early reading, which embraced everything from the Authorized Version to the entire works of Sir Walter Scott. And his emphasis in acting on the import of a single gesture, or even a vocal inflection, was a consequence of his own severe physical restrictions. His subjective approach to theatre was complemented by formidable scholarship but he was, essentially, a romantic critic who believed in the passionate communication of a highly individual response.

Hobson's romanticism was fuelled by his boyhood experiences of theatregoing in Sheffield: seeing Sir John Martin-Harvey in the Dickensian adaptation, *The Only Way*, he was haunted by the heart-rending desolation with which the actor expressed his failure to arouse affection or esteem. But Hobson's impressionable temperament was accompanied by a shrewd intellect: as an Oxford history student he was overwhelmed by Thucydides' account of the disastrous Athenian expedition against Syracuse which, with its famous reversal of fortune, affected his view both of drama and of the structure of theatrical criticism.

It was through a mixture of enterprise and good fortune that Hobson became drama critic of the *Sunday Times*. In 1939 he provided the newspaper with a front-page scoop about the evacuation of schools in the event of war. That led to regular book-reviewing throughout the war, his appointment as assistant literary editor in 1942, and from 1945 his acting as deputy to the paper's legendary drama critic, James Agate. The belated discovery by the *Sunday Times*'s proprietor, Lord Kemsley, of Agate's homosexuality led to Hobson, an approved family man, being appointed his successor in 1947. He remained as theatre critic of the paper until 1976.

In his early years Hobson championed the work of T. S. Eliot, Christopher Fry, and John Whiting, who, like himself, were all committed Christians. But two significant events elevated him into a critic of enormous influence. One, paradoxically, was the appointment of Kenneth Tynan as his opposite number at *The Observer* in 1954: Tynan's voluptuous stylishness was seen as the antithesis of Hobson's puritan zeal, but it gave Sunday theatre-reviewing the heady air of a keenly fought intellectual duel. Even more crucial was the emergence in the 1950s of a new style of drama to which Hobson responded with intuitive understanding. He carried on a weekly campaign on behalf of Samuel Beckett's *Waiting for Godot* (1954), helping it to become a commercial success. He recognized, though less vehemently than Tynan, the romantic individualism of John Osborne's *Look Back in Anger* (1956) and, alone of all critics, he saw the merits of Harold Pinter's *The Birthday Party* (1958), describing its author as 'the most original, disturbing and arresting talent in theatrical London' (Elsom, 85) and encouraging him, after the play's box-office failure, to go on writing.

Not all Hobson's enthusiasms were widely shared: few others believed as steadfastly as he in the dramatic genius of William Douglas-Home. However, his love of French theatre was enormously influential in breaching English isolationism. His adoration for Edwige Feuillère and Jean-Louis Barrault was well known, but it was his endorsement of dramatists such as Jean Genet, in whom he heard echoes of the Catholic mass, and Marguerite Duras, that led to their gradual acceptance in Britain. In recognition of his pioneering enthusiasm, which included such books as *The French Theatre of Today* (1953) and *French Theatre since 1830* (1978), he was created a chevalier of the Légion d'honneur in 1960. He returned the decoration eight years later in protest at the French government's dismissal of Jean-Louis Barrault from his tenure at the Odéon. In 1971 he was created CBE for his services to theatre and he was knighted in 1977. The honour he most prized, since his adolescent ambition had been to become an Oxford academic, was being elected honorary fellow of Oriel College in 1974.

Hobson was often regarded as a wayward, mercurial critic. His lasting achievement lay in his constant championship of avant-garde writers. His most distinctive quality was his ability to discover an epiphanic experience in a single moment, such as Olivier's rising inflection on the phrase 'troops of friends' in the course of Macbeth's downfall. Penelope Gilliatt once wrote that 'the characteristic sound of an English Sunday was that of Harold Hobson barking up the wrong tree' (Hobson, *Indirect Journey*, 107). Posterity has shown that, more often than not, he barked up the right tree.

Hobson's life was an astonishing triumph over disability. His kindness to young critics was a constant inspiration. However, his greatest happiness came from his marriage to Elizabeth. Following her death in 1979 he wrote (in his 1981 *Who's Who* entry, under 'recreations') of 'her incomparable charm and wisdom, and the unquenchable radiance of her personality'. On 7 April 1981 he married their friend Nancy Penhale (*b.* 1909/10), who remained his companion during his final days in Westhampnett Nursing Home, Westhampnett, Chichester, Sussex. He died there on 12 March 1992. He was survived by his wife and the daughter of his first marriage. A memorial service was held at St Paul's, Covent Garden, on 24 November 1992. MICHAEL BILLINGTON

Sources H. Hobson, *Indirect journey* (1978) · H. Hobson, *Theatre in Britain: a personal view* (1984) · J. Elsom, ed., *Post-war British theatre criticism* (1981) · *The Times* (14–19 March 1992) · *The Times* (25 Nov 1992) · *The Independent* (14–18 March 1992) · *WWW*, 1991–5 · personal knowledge (2004) · private information (2004) · m. certs. · d. cert.

Archives Bodl. Oxf., letters to Jack Lambert

Likenesses photograph, repro. in *The Times* (14 March 1992) · photograph, repro. in *The Times* (17 March 1992) · photograph, repro. in *The Independent* (14 March 1992)

Wealth at death under £125,000: probate, 7 Aug 1992, *CGPLA Eng. & Wales*

Hobson, John Atkinson (1858–1940), social theorist and economist, was born on 6 July 1858 at Iron Gate, Derby, the second son of William Hobson (1825–1897), founder, editor, and part proprietor of the *Derbyshire Advertiser* and twice mayor of Derby, and his wife, Josephine Atkinson. The mathematician Ernest William *Hobson was his elder brother.

John Atkinson Hobson (1858–1940), by unknown photographer

Early life and influences, and marriage Hobson was educated as a day boy at Derby School (1868–76), which had been converted by a snobbish headmaster from a grammar school into a dull and antiquated public school. He grew up in a wealthy middle-class environment that prepared him, as he wrote in his autobiography, *Confessions of an Economic Heretic* (1938), 'for a complacent acceptance of the existing social order' (Hobson, 15). As a teenager, though, a budding rationalist streak caused him to question the moderate puritanism of his family's church connections, and he later wryly recalled the irony of receiving in 1873 a school prize for divinity from the prince of Wales. By the time he went up to Lincoln College, Oxford, in 1876, having won an open scholarship, he felt the need to obtain remission in his second year from attending chapel. That was as far as his revolt against the smugness of middle England would go at the time.

A further teenage experience planted the seeds for Hobson's future activities both as an economist and as an enthusiast for university extension teaching. At the age of sixteen he attended a Cambridge University extension board course in economics taught by the Revd William Moore Ede (1849–1935), who emphasized the moral underpinnings of political economy. Hobson's preferred subject at Oxford would hence have been a version of the future modern Greats; instead, he had to settle for classics and *literae humaniores*. His college career was chiefly marked by an aptitude for sprinting and the high jump, which secured him a place in the university athletic team, though the longer-term effect of his studies was to endow him with an enhanced humanist disposition. When he duly obtained, respectively, a second (moderations) and a third in *literae humaniores*, he regarded himself as a failure. Consequently, he seemed destined for a conventional and intellectually timid career, and took up two posts as classics master, first at Faversham School in 1880 for two years and then as assistant master at Exeter grammar school.

Exeter, however, was the location of two fortunate encounters which ruffled Hobson's burgeoning provincialism. The first one was with Florence Edgar (*b.* 1858/9), daughter of Jonathan Edgar, an attorney from New Jersey. Florence was a vivacious American with an enquiring bent of mind, a poet, writer, occasional pamphleteer, and campaigner for women's rights whom Hobson married on 12 August 1885, and who complemented and energized his social concerns. They had a daughter, Mabel Josephine (1886–1969), and a son, Harold (1891–1973). The other encounter, which changed the course of Hobson's professional life, was with the businessman and mountaineer A. F. Mummery. Mummery, who was to disappear on Nanga Parbat in the Himalayas in 1895, first introduced Hobson to the theory of over-saving, which Hobson adopted and expanded in his later work on underconsumption.

Intellectual life in London In 1887 Hobson made a decisive move. Abandoning his school career, he moved to London. Initially, he became involved in university extension (extramural) lecturing, displaying a lucidity and a personal touch which brought him into friendly contact with students. He lectured on literature for the Oxford University extension and for the London Society for the Extension of University Teaching. He later branched out into political economy and practical reform issues for the Oxford extension, for which he taught until 1896. London was an eye-opener for the still impressionable young man and he soon developed a cosmopolitan outlook which he eagerly imparted to his former townspeople through the pages of his father's newspaper from 1887 to 1897. His 'London Letter' conveyed some of the pace and excitement of living in the capital. His intellectual curiosity stimulated, all was grist to his mill. He became a fervent reader of the press, including some of the major literary and political monthlies, and a formidable and often ironic witness to London political and cultural life. He read voraciously, delved into biography, and extended his purview to cover continental and American politics. He visited art galleries as well as settlement houses; his wife had opened a soup kitchen in a London slum in 1888. Evenings were frequently spent at the theatre or opera. In sharp contradistinction to the impression gained from the high-minded prose of Hobson's *œuvre*, there emerged another side to him, not above relishing tittle-tattle and trivia.

Instead of admiring luminaries such as Herbert Spencer from afar, as Hobson had done in Derby, he now began to rub shoulders with members of the London intelligentsia. This was another facet of Hobson's newly found dynamism, actively sampling the intellectual wares of the metropolis and increasingly associating with key discussion groups. His arrival in London coincided with a period of great ideological ferment among the progressive left of centre, which included Fabians, new liberals, and socialists of every variety. He was hence fortunate enough to live through a decade when ideas were acknowledged to matter in Britain, and when small but dedicated radical groups were vying with each other in producing innovative social theories. In casting around for a profession he was inadvertently shaping the course of his life: free thinking expressed through journalism and freelance writing, lecturing, and essays, radical political activism, and frequent trips abroad—a lifestyle supported embarrassingly by the inherited income he reviled in principle—became the pattern of his calling. Early on he attended a meeting of the Fabian Society but was unimpressed. He reported that 'some clever speeches were made, but all seemed tainted by the assumption that capital did not work, and that consequently "interest" was an extortion' (*Derbyshire Advertiser*, 28 Oct 1887). Likewise he contemptuously dismissed the 'most appalling Germanity' of the first volume of Marx's *Das Kapital* (*Derbyshire Advertiser*, 18 Nov 1887), just published in an English translation, though his views on Marx softened in later years. His developing radicalism was to seek alternative outlets.

Political economy: underconsumption In 1889 Hobson's friendship with Mummery bore fruit in a collaborative book, *The Physiology of Industry*, an enterprise in which Mummery was the senior partner. Rejecting the classical doctrine expressed in Say's law, that production created its own demand, as well as standard Victorian exhortations to thrift, they argued that the wealthy, who benefited from unearned income which they could not wholly consume, were led into over-saving which translated into over-investment. The consequence was a series of crises of capitalism characterized by widespread underconsumption of capital goods, production gluts, trade depression, and increasing unemployment. The solution lay initially in encouraging the well-to-do to consume more or in bolstering new forms of national expenditure. In later years Hobson modified this view by contending that underconsumption resulted from a maldistribution of wealth across society, and sought cures in augmenting the incomes of the poor, through tax and welfare measures. This pattern of a growing coalescence of economic and ethical arguments became noticeable in his thought. Markets could both be inefficient and intrinsically unfair.

The immediate reaction of the mainstream economists who dominated the academic establishment to the Mummery and Hobson volume was almost uniformly unfavourable. F. Y. Edgeworth, Drummond professor of political economy at Oxford, belittled its claims in a review. The leading organ edited by Edgeworth, the *Economic Journal*, retained many of those reservations when reviewing some of Hobson's later works. H. S. Foxwell, of Cambridge and later London University, repeatedly blocked Hobson's attempts to teach political economy for the London Extension Society, though the society's ban was lifted in 1894 and he taught for it sporadically until 1910, as well as lecturing occasionally at the London School of Economics. However, his self-confidence had been further rattled and he believed to the end of his life that his detractors worked behind the scenes to destroy any hope he might have entertained for a university appointment or academic recognition. Only in his old age did Manchester University decide to confer upon him an honorary degree; by then he was too frail to accept. It is characteristic of his fortunes that, while a street in Chamonix commemorates Mummery (albeit for his alpine achievements), Hobson's native land has not celebrated his life's work in similar fashion.

The ethical movement Though political economy as a vocation was effectively shut off, Hobson continued to explore the practical costs and mechanics of capitalism in *Problems of Poverty* (1891), *The Problem of the Unemployed* (1896), and his highly successful *The Evolution of Modern Capitalism* (1894). However, his new social and intellectual milieux spurred him on to explore further his particular brand of qualitative economics and took him into hitherto unexplored terrain. He found his own niches of congeniality, which offered safe havens from the menace of establishment orthodoxy, and podiums on which to test his ideas in the making, amid generally sympathetic support. Within that confined, but ultimately creative and influential, world Hobson's star quickly rose. The two groups which contributed most significantly to the process of his maturing, and which he in turn helped to shape, were the South Place Ethical Society and the Rainbow Circle.

Hobson's initial contact with the ethical movement, a loose set of organizations devoted to developing a rational secular ethics and to furthering social and moral reform, was through his membership of the London Ethical Society, then under the leadership of J. H. Muirhead and Bernard Bosanquet, which he joined in 1890. However, he soon took objection to its 'moral individualism' (Hobson, 56) and to the retrograde views on social progress which were voiced through its close association with the Charity Organization Society—where Bosanquet was also a leading light—and he resigned in 1896. In 1895 he joined the South Place Ethical Society, to whose members he had delivered his first lecture in 1892. In 1899 he became an appointed lecturer of the society, a post he held until 1934, sharing the Sunday podiums alternately with J. M. Robertson and Herbert Burrows, and later with C. Delisle Burns and S. K. Ratcliffe. These wide-ranging secular sermons were a sounding board for many of Hobson's theories and critiques.

The Rainbow Circle, which began convening monthly in 1894, joined together some of the leading new liberal and socialist thinkers, activists, journalists, and reformers, including Ramsay MacDonald, Herbert Samuel, and J. M. Robertson. It was thus well placed to serve as a crucible for the welfare-oriented liberal–social ideas which inspired both the Liberal and the Labour parties in the early twentieth century, and as an incubator for ethical foreign policy views which were to be heard during the First World War. Hobson was a member from its inception and played a pivotal role in the circle's debates, delivering twenty-two lectures between 1894 and 1923, on topics ranging across the economic deficiencies of the Manchester

school, a progressive party, imperialism, capitalism in the USA, the referendum, collectivism, causes of social unrest, and the newspaper. One of the circle's ventures was the founding in 1896 of a monthly, the *Progressive Review*, on which many hopes were pinned. Hobson became second editor under the Fabian journalist William Clarke. The review failed, however, to achieve commercial viability and suffered from discord over attitudes towards Liberal Imperialism and the Jameson raid in South Africa—Hobson having begun to develop his critical ideas on the subject. It closed a year later, but the circle survived and flourished, and returned eight members to Westminster in the 1906 general election. At the time Hobson could not have known how quietly influential the circle would be, nor realized how important his contribution would be to fashioning the climate of opinion it promoted.

Social philosophy of the new liberalism From the early 1890s Hobson had begun the long exploration of social thought that would inform his entire opus. A favourable mention of *The Physiology of Industry* in J. S. Mackenzie's *An Introduction to Social Philosophy* alerted him to Mackenzie's work. Mackenzie's book not only reinforced Hobson's search for a qualitative economics but also linked that search with John Ruskin's notions of the illth and wealth of human life as measures of welfare. This was bound together by the holism so characteristic of idealist thought, though Hobson did not adopt the metaphysical and methodological position of idealism. Instead, he developed three fundamental and mutually sustaining themes: a conception of the social, a qualitative reformulation of utilitarianism, and a psychological account of social conduct. Undoubtedly, he lacked the conceptual sophistication, though not the intelligence, to elaborate theories which would have passed muster among professional social philosophers. But he brought an inventiveness and freshness, nourished by his psychologically driven iconoclastic disposition, which more than made up for his technical deficiencies. In a series of works—from 'Rights of property', published in the *Free Review* (1893), edited by Robertson, through to his lectures for the Christian Social Union in London, which resulted in the ground-breaking *The Social Problem* (1901), and his most important work of political theory, *The Crisis of Liberalism* (1909)—he explored the idea of society as an organism. It was a system of interdependent individuals, whose free individuality was essential to the health of the whole, yet who could also develop rational and collective aims embodied in an impartial, benevolent, and democratically accountable state. These ideas of Hobson were central to the formulation of the new liberal ideology.

The balance between the individual and the social nature of human beings was a problem with which Hobson grappled throughout his life, and it included a recognition that society too was a maker of values, a worker, and a consumer. This supplemented the distinction he drew between, on the one hand, the creative and individualistic artistic aspect of work, and, on the other, routine labour that could be socialized. On another dimension, his holism postulated a view of human welfare resting on a combination of physical, psychological, and mental factors that were also mutually interconnected. Within such a framework no subject area, economics included, could be perceived as a separate discipline. Thus there emerged a central feature of Hobson's writings, in which the study of economics, politics, sociology, international relations, and, to some extent, psychology, were intermeshed.

Hobson's *Work and Wealth: a Human Valuation* (1914), followed by *Wealth and Life: a Study in Values* (1929), were the most mature expression of his social welfare theory. In those books he combined his organic view with an exposition of the art of the qualitative consumption of social and economic goods which had become a corner-stone of his thinking. The blending of ethics and economics continued his earlier Ruskinian line of argument, but his theories were always grounded in the collation of facts and empirical observation. At a time of an increasing specialization of learning, he ran the risk of amateurish overstretching; yet his insights into social and cultural interlinkages were ahead of, as well as behind, their times, and his views on the complexity of social knowledge can once again be appreciated from more recent vantage points. Although well schooled in economic tools, his heresy lay not so much in a dissenting economics as in the subsuming of economics under broader social ends and in its evaluation in terms of such 'externalities'. He would have done better to adopt the identity of a social theorist rather than persevere in directing his arguments at economists.

Hobson's new utilitarianism became much in evidence in the thinking behind the British welfare state. Like J. S. Mill, he recognized the importance of qualitative rather than quantitative criteria of utility as the measure of human welfare. But he distanced himself even further from the atomistic individualism of the Benthamite school by insisting that it had to be replaced by the test of social utility. The potentially illiberal conclusions were kept at bay by his liberal organicism, which firmly promoted the harmony between public and private goods. Nevertheless, he occasionally skirted near social authoritarianism—as did many progressive thinkers—when emphasizing the guiding role of experts in a democracy, or when experimenting with eugenic ideas. His social analyses gained additional depth from his study of Gustave Le Bon's work, which contributed to his growing awareness of the irrational aspects of human behaviour, on which he wrote in *The Psychology of Jingoism* (1901) and in 'The ethical movement and the natural man' (*Hibbert Journal*, 1922).

The three facets of human behaviour which fascinated Hobson most were crowd psychology, which fed into his conceptions of an organic group mind and character, the relationship between action and motivation, which distanced his economic thinking from solidly socialist theories through an emphasis on incentives to productivity, and the importance of leisure and play, which imported an amateur Freudianism into his later thought through an acknowledgement of the wholesomeness of the 'animalistic' foundations of rational conduct. His experience of the early rejection of his own economic ideas combined with his sociological insights into the bases of knowledge to produce a sensitivity to the human factor in supporting or repudiating theories. This was spelt out in *Free-Thought in the Social Sciences* (1926), an innovative study of the biases of scholarship.

Imperialism In the course of his journalistic career Hobson frequently travelled abroad—including lengthy trips to the USA, Canada, and Switzerland, where he studied the referendum—and produced numerous investigative articles and pamphlets. In the USA he gleaned a sharp insight into the workings of capitalism and also gathered a respectful following. But the journey that established his radical reputation in the wider world was a visit in 1899 to South Africa, on L. T. Hobhouse's recommendation, as the special correspondent of C. P. Scott's *Manchester Guardian*, to report on the Second South African War. As Hobson himself realized, that was 'both a turning-point in my career and an illumination to my understanding of the real relation between economics and politics' (Hobson, 59). The immediate result was his *The War in South Africa: its Causes and Effects* (1900), which presented the war as fought in the interests of a confederacy of international financiers and capitalists, who also controlled the press. That book also gave voice to prevalent antisemitic stereotypes directed against foreign and immigrant Jews, already evident in Hobson's 'London Letter'. His ties with the *Manchester Guardian* were later strengthened when his daughter married Scott's son Edward in 1907.

Hobson returned to Britain to campaign against the Second South African War, but the main impact of the war was to crystallize his views on imperialism, elaborated in the book by that name (1902), and later to be applauded by Lenin. Though his work on imperialism was often regarded as an independent theory and frequently overshadowed his larger opus, it extended his previous economic and social analysis to the relationships between a mother country and its colonies. He understood imperialism as driven by its underconsumptionist economic taproot—a dimension of activity additional to its more obviously political forms of control, and specifically fashioned by private and sectional interests. He had already identified a major form of 'improperty' on the domestic scene: an unearned and unproductive surplus, or rent, over and above legitimate production costs, which was expropriated by private individuals, and which could be applied to any factor of production, to capital even more than land or labour. This was a significant departure from current theories of marginalism as the basis of prices.

Hobson insisted that those surpluses were due to concerted social effort and could, in the domestic field, be reclaimed by society through redistributive graduated taxation on income and inheritance, without their being shifted onto the consumer. However, as measures to reduce underconsumption had not been in place during the growth of empire, the colonies provided an important outlet for the investment of that illegitimately owned surplus and the taking of private profits, in particular by financial capitalists and manufacturers. Imperialism was hence damaging not only to the exploited colonies but also to the mother country in its furtherance of economic greed, aggression, and militarism. Much of the drive towards imperialism could therefore be assuaged through addressing the maldistribution of domestic consuming power. Significantly, it could also be shown that trade did not follow the flag and that there was therefore no economic advantage in imperialism. In *The Industrial System* (1909) and its much reprinted popularization through the Home University Library, *The Science of Wealth* (1911), he gave a full account of his underconsumptionist and redistributive theories.

New liberal journalist, the war, and after Although Hobson had moved from west London to the predominantly Fabian community of Limpsfield, Surrey, in 1899, his London activities were thriving. For many years he had hoped for an editorship of a radical newspaper or periodical, but apart from a short term as co-editor of the *Ethical World* in 1899–1900 he was unable to secure such a post. After a spell writing for the short-lived daily *Tribune* in 1906, he joined in 1907 the staff of *The Nation*, which became the leading new liberal weekly under H. W. Massingham's inspiring editorship. His contribution to the face of the new liberalism through its pages is incalculable, but he also returned to his literary and cultural interests via occasional 'middles', some of which are gathered in *A Modern Outlook* (1910). Usually carrying with him a thriller to the *Nation* office for light reading, he participated in the famous *Nation* lunches, together with Hobhouse, J. L. Hammond, H. N. Brailsford, F. W. Hirst, H. W. Nevinson, and C. F. G. Masterman. Colleagues later commented on the brilliance and 'sudden glory' of his wit around the table (Nevinson, 214) and on his 'formidable gift for irony and satire' (Brailsford, 4), a feature more in evidence in conversation than on the written page. His spare prose reflected his concern that passion and eloquence could be hindrances to scientific acceptance, not the least his own. Sarcasm rather than effusiveness was his occasional refuge from the mechanistic, material, and hypocritical world he condemned.

Hobson was also a founder member of the Sociological Society and served on its council, as well as holding office as its chairman (1913–22) and vice-president (1922–32); and he was a member of the national birth-rate commission from 1913 to 1916. With the outbreak of the First World War the internationalist outlook of his thought became pronounced. Just before the war broke out, he was among the founders of the British neutrality committee, soon to develop into the Bryce committee, as well as being an active member of the International Arbitration League. He joined the Union of Democratic Control, served on its executive committee, and actively participated in formulating its policy, favouring a negotiated peace settlement and open diplomacy while censuring the government's

position. He later became its chairman and held that office until his death—the only remaining political activity of his old age. In the early stages of the war he warned against the spirit of Prussianism which he perceived behind assaults on civil liberties in Britain. He became alarmed at the domestic operations of a 'military-bureaucratic state', which were far removed from his interpretation of beneficial state activity. The state, he now emphasized, was only one aspect of the network of individuals and groups that constituted society.

International relations, too, were subject to Hobson's organic perspective. Initially they were adjunct to the domestic problems on which he had concentrated, but by the time of the First World War he had modified his views. Although he subscribed to aspects of Cobdenite free trade, he regarded the international system as a holistic entity, through which the parts—the nation state and other organizations—interacted in complex but potentially rational relationships. He foresaw nationalities co-operating, overcoming the narrow limits of nationalism, and subject to democratic procedures. He recommended their engagement in structured federative collaboration through international organizations such as a league of nations, and even in forms of international government buttressed by arbitration and conciliation as well as force. The actual League of Nations, however, attracted his criticism. In international relations he was less tolerant of irrational manifestations of conduct, circumscribed aspects of which he had allowed on the individual level.

For the 1918 'coupon' general election Hobson stood for parliament for the combined universities seat for Liverpool, Birmingham, Bristol, Leeds, Sheffield, Durham, and Manchester universities. He had broken with the Liberal Party during the war, when the government abandoned free trade. Though sympathetic towards the Labour Party, he ran as an independent and was defeated. Although he finally joined the Labour Party in 1924, he did not feel 'quite at home in a body governed by trade union members and their finance, and intellectually led by full-blooded Socialists' (Hobson, 126). In 1926 he was a member of a small committee that drew up the Independent Labour Party's report entitled *The Living Wage*, but throughout the 1920s and 1930s he continued to seek a progressive middle course, signing the Next Five Years group manifesto in 1935, which voiced predominantly centrist–liberalist opinions. He kept up his ceaselessly prolific journalistic output in the inter-war years, and extended it also to the New York *Nation*. He continued to put his expertise at the disposal of public policy-making, among others as a member of the Whitley committee on the creation of joint industrial councils of workers and employers in 1917–18, of the Ministry of Reconstruction committee on trusts in 1918–19, and as a witness to the Sankey commission on the coal industry of 1919 and to the Colwyn committee on national debt and taxation of 1924–6. He also derived pleasure from Keynes's acknowledgement of his pioneering work on underconsumption in the

General Theory, although that was qualified by a criticism of Hobson's failure to distinguish appropriately between saving and investment.

Hobson's tall, gaunt figure could frequently be seen walking across Hampstead Heath, in conversation with colleagues such as Ramsay MacDonald. He had a slight hitch in his speech and struck his contemporaries as frail and in poor health, although these may have been the outward signs of a nervous disposition and bouts of insomnia, exacerbated by the emotional strain occasioned by his 'heresies'. Nevertheless, he was an indefatigable writer, and produced over fifty books and pamphlets and over 600 articles and reviews. Hobson's humanism, kindliness, and wit were occasionally accompanied by a blunt violence of expression, reflecting an unwillingness to compromise on matters of intellectual integrity and, as his South Place colleague C. E. M. Joad observed, by 'a touch of malice, the iron hand behind the velvet glove' (*South Place Monthly Record*, May 1940). His modesty and honesty alerted him to the defects even of his own economic humanism, but his influence as a unique public intellectual and as a moulder of the social liberalism at the root of British welfare thought and policy has been profound.

In his final years Hobson bemoaned the renewed slippage of civilization into a brutal irrationality through the rival ideologies of communism and Fascism, which cast a shadow over his optimistic internationalism. Yet he placed his faith in the triumph of liberal democracy, bolstered by an increase in equitable home consumption, and inspired by the new liberalism he had himself so centrally, albeit unwittingly, shaped. Hobson did not live to see the victory he had confidently predicted. He died on 1 April 1940 at his home, 3 Gayton Crescent, Hampstead, and was cremated two days later in a private ceremony at Golders Green crematorium.　　Michael Freeden

Sources J. A. Hobson, *Confessions of an economic heretic* (1938) · J. A. Lee, 'The social and economic thought of J. A. Hobson', PhD diss., U. Lond., 1970 · *Derbyshire Advertiser* (5 April 1940) · *Manchester Guardian* (2 April 1940) · *TLS* (6 April 1940) · *South Place Monthly Record* (May 1940) · *New Statesman and Nation* (6 April 1940) · H. N. Brailsford, *The life-work of J. A. Hobson* (1948) · H. W. Nevinson, *Fire of life* (1935) · J. Allett, *New liberalism: the political economy of J. A. Hobson* (1981) · M. Freeden, ed., *Reappraising J. A. Hobson: humanism and welfare* (1990) · J. Townshend, *J. A. Hobson* (1990) · J. Pheby, ed., *J. A. Hobson after fifty years* (1994) [incl. comprehensive bibliography] · D. Long, *Towards a new liberal internationalism: the international theory of J. A. Hobson* (1996) · M. Schneider, *J. A. Hobson* (1996) · M. Freeden, ed., *J. A. Hobson: a reader* (1988) · *CGPLA Eng. & Wales* (1940) · m. cert.
Archives BLPES, corresp. with the Fabian Society · JRL, letters to the *Manchester Guardian* · U. Hull, Brynmor Jones L., corresp. and papers | BL, corresp. with Macmillans, Add. MS 55209 · Bodl. Oxf., corresp. with Gilbert Murray · JRL, corresp. with C. P. Scott · Keele University Library, LePlay collection, corresp. and minute book entries as member of Sociological Society committees · U. Cam., Marshall Library of Economics, corresp. with John Maynard Keynes
Likenesses photograph, BL PES [*see illus.*] · photographs, London School of Economics, Rainbow Circle album
Wealth at death £2704 6s. 10d.: probate, 27 May 1940, *CGPLA Eng. & Wales*

Hobson, Sir John Gardiner Sumner (1912–1967), barrister and politician, was born on 18 April 1912 at Long Clawson Hall, Melton Mowbray, the son of Major Gerald Walton Hobson, of the 12th lancers, and his wife, Winifred Hilda, daughter of John Gardiner Muir JP DL, of Farmingwoods Hall, Northamptonshire. He was educated at Harrow School and at Brasenose College, Oxford, where he was a scholar and obtained second-class honours in history in 1934. He was called to the bar by the Inner Temple in 1938. In 1939 he married Beryl Marjorie, daughter of A. Stuart Johnson, of Henshall Hall, Congleton, Cheshire; they had three daughters.

Hobson's background, like his bearing and his inclination, tended towards the military. He was a keen territorial. In the Second World War he joined the Northamptonshire yeomanry, rising to the rank of lieutenant-colonel, as his father had done in the First World War, and served with the British expeditionary force in France in 1940 and with the First Army in north Africa. In 1944–5 he was at the headquarters of the Twenty-First Army group, with special responsibilities for tracked and armoured vehicles. He was mentioned in dispatches, and was appointed OBE in 1945.

Hobson's virtues and abilities, particularly in the field of organization, were those of a soldier, although he used to say that he learned more as head boy of Harrow than at any subsequent period of his life. His capacity for leadership was enhanced by a deep love and knowledge of country matters. He was a skilled horseman, an enthusiastic rider to hounds, and a first-class shot; every year he holidayed in Scotland in order to stalk. His practice at the bar reflected this provenance. Questions under the Agricultural Holdings Acts or local Water Acts were his speciality on the midland circuit. He was at his most characteristic when prosecuting a poacher. As chairman of Rutland and of Bedfordshire quarter-sessions, and as recorder of Northampton (1958–62), he played a full part in the public life of the shires. He took silk in 1957.

It was Anthony Eden's chance resignation in 1957 that brought Hobson into the House of Commons as Conservative member for the former prime minister's constituency, Warwick and Leamington. Although his arrival was accidental his capacity for hard work and clear expression became immediately apparent; he was soon elected to the powerful back-bench 'one nation' group. In February 1962 he was made solicitor-general and in July attorney-general. He was knighted in that year and sworn of the privy council in 1963.

Some disagreeable duties fell to Hobson during the last few years of the long and stale Conservative administration. Inevitably the disgrace in 1963 of his old school and regimental friend John Profumo involved him in painful labour. He prosecuted the spy Vassall in 1962 and played the leading role before the Radcliffe tribunal that followed the revelations in Vassall's trial. In the course of the inquiry Hobson felt obliged to press two journalists (Reginald Foster and Brendan Mulholland) to disclose the sources of their information. When they refused to answer Hobson procured their committal to prison early in 1963 for contempt of court, a course of duty that he fully realized would bring down upon himself, his government, and his profession the full weight of a displeased press—as indeed it did.

Hobson had a leading part to play in the crop of extradition and deportation cases that plagued the home secretary at this period. The most famous of these, the Enahoro case (1963), led to Hobson being reported to the benchers of his inn by a fellow bencher, Reginald Paget, an old hunting companion, for unprofessional conduct on two counts. The masters of the bench held that the charges were unfounded.

When the Conservatives went into opposition in 1964 Hobson became even more valuable to them. The front bench relied increasingly on his advice and particularly on his uncanny power of drafting; he could produce perfect clauses, and amendments to clauses, absolutely on the spot. From his short period in office he had acquired an unrivalled knowledge of the art of the parliamentary draftsman. He was not exciting, but many of his colleagues considered him the best law officer that the Conservative Party had produced since the first Viscount Hailsham.

Hobson's return to private practice at the bar was less successful. He was never a showy advocate and never courted publicity; his previous connections had been provincial rather than metropolitan. Financially the years after 1964 were lean. In the autumn of 1967 it was strongly rumoured that his circumstances had compelled him to seek a judicial appointment, for which he was excellently suited: he was clear, firm, compassionate, hard-working, and the soul of honour. But he complained one evening of a crippling pain in the leg, and by the next evening (4 December 1967) he was dead, killed by an entirely unsuspected tumour of the brain.

CHARLES FLETCHER-COOKE, rev.

Sources private information (1981, 2004) · personal knowledge (1981, 2004) · *The Times* (5 Dec 1967) · *CGPLA Eng. & Wales* (1968)
Wealth at death £52,366: probate, 18 Jan 1968, *CGPLA Eng. & Wales*

Hobson, Paul (d. 1666), Particular Baptist preacher, was a tailor from Buckinghamshire according to the heresiographer Thomas Edwards. An opponent of the solemn league and covenant in 1643, Hobson had probably by this time joined the London separatist church founded by John Spencer and John Green in 1639. By 1644 Hobson had organized a Particular Baptist church; in 1644 and 1646 he and Thomas Gower, on behalf of their congregation, signed the Particular Baptists' confession of faith articulating their Calvinist and separatist tenets and their belief in believers' baptism by immersion. Hobson's tenets prompted the presbyterian Sion College to condemn him along with Milton, Roger Williams, John Biddle, and other radicals in December 1644. Hobson was now serving as a captain in Charles Fleetwood's regiment in the eastern association army. When Lawrence Clarkson heard him preach, Hobson 'brake forth with such expressions of the in-comes and out-goes of God, that my soul much desired such a gift of preaching' (L. Clarkson, *The Lost Sheep Found*, 1660, 10). In 1645 Hobson published three works, a collection of sermons entitled *Christ the Effect not the Cause of the Love of God*, *A Discoverie of Truth*, and *The Fallacy of Infants Baptisme Discovered*, which had been written for a debate, subsequently banned by the lord mayor, between various Baptists and the presbyterian Edmund Calamy. Opponents such as Edwards and Richard Baxter denounced Hobson as an antinomian. In June 1645 Sir Samuel Luke had captains Hobson and Richard Beaumont, who were travelling on a pass from Fleetwood, arrested at Newport Pagnell, Buckinghamshire, for preaching contrary to the Westminster assembly regulations. Luke sent them to Sir Thomas Fairfax in Leicester, where they complained that Luke's officers had maltreated them. Praising Hobson's and Beaumont's military service, Fairfax had Luke's officers cashiered. Fleetwood too defended the captains and protested about their uncivil treatment. Infuriated by their return to Newport, Luke complained to the MP Richard Knightley, but a parliamentary committee released Hobson after examining him in London. Until he received orders in August to go to Leicester, Hobson preached in London. Thereafter he was ordered to Bristol, which Fleetwood's troops helped capture and garrison. Here too Hobson preached. After a farewell sermon to the army in June 1646, he went to Exeter to raise support for the godly cause. He published *Practicall Divinity* (1646), an exposition about the Christian life, and *A Garden Inclosed* (1647), articulating an almost mystical experience.

Hobson returned to the army in 1647 as a major in Robert Lilburne's infantry regiment. As an army agent he met the royalist Sir Lewis Dyve, who gave him an introduction to Charles in search of a negotiated settlement. In the autumn Dyve told Charles that John Lilburne deemed Hobson 'the fittest man to be employed' by the king to strike an agreement with army dissidents such as Edward Sexby ('Letter-book', 92), but when troops in Robert Lilburne's regiment mutinied at Ware in November, Hobson joined other officers in denouncing the rebels. By July 1648 Hobson was in Newcastle upon Tyne, where his troops were quartered on the residents, raising fears of an uprising. At Newcastle he served as deputy governor to Sir Arthur Hesilrige. After signing a letter supporting the Leveller petition of 11 September condemning negotiations with Charles, on 9 October he endorsed *The Declaration of the Armie* to Fairfax, denouncing the Newport talks with the king. Promoted lieutenant-colonel by October 1648, he was appointed an assessment commissioner for Durham and Newcastle in December 1649, November 1650, and (for Durham only) December 1652. His prominence prompted a conservative attack in 1649 entitled *Newes from Powles*, alleging his troops had baptized a colt in St Paul's Cathedral, London. At Newcastle he became embroiled in controversy when he exposed a Scottish witchpricker commissioned by the common council as a fraud. In January 1650 he quashed a minor rebellion by cavaliers and moss-troopers. During the spring he lamented the distrust between the 'honest' parties in England and Scotland, which may explain the council of state's suspicion in July that he was prepared to serve Scottish interests and was thus unfit to be deputy governor. Nevertheless, during the ensuing Scottish campaign Cromwell put him in charge of four garrisons at Leith, and he was responsible for conveying Scottish prisoners from Dunbar to Durham. An estimated 1600 died *en route*, and comparable numbers perished in Durham owing to inadequate food. Some time after this, Hobson resigned from the army.

Hobson now focused on religious activities, especially in Newcastle, where he and Gower had founded a Baptist church about 1649. In February 1653 he was appointed a commissioner for propagating the gospel in the north. He welcomed the nominated assembly as an indication of the imminence of Christ's earthly kingdom, signing a congratulatory address to Cromwell from the people of co. Durham on 28 April 1653. After the assembly's dissolution, he called for the excommunication of church members who signed addresses of loyalty to Cromwell. He was involved in religious controversies, including one with Hexham Baptists in 1653 over the belief that ministers should not be wholly dependent on their churches for financial support; the following year Thomas Tillam and the Hexham Baptists accused Hobson of fomenting dissension. The General Baptist Henry Haggar accused Hobson of being out of communion with other Baptists. Hobson's attack on the Arminian doctrine of a limited atonement, *Fourteen Queries and Ten Absurdities* (1655), provoked a response from William Pedelsden, *Sound Doctrine* (1657), and Tillam's *The Fourth Principle of Christian Religion* (1655) criticized Hobson's opposition to the laying on of hands. Hobson also battled with the Quakers, who converted six of his followers. On a preaching foray in Wiltshire about 1655 he denounced Quaker tenets, prompting John Story and John Wilkinson to complain that he said 'many filthye things to render the truth odyouse' (Swarthmore papers, 1, fol. 35r). In *The Quaker's Jesus* (1658) William Grigge unconvincingly associated Hobson with Socinians. From 1654 until his ejection in 1660 Hobson served as chaplain of Eton College, and about 1657 he was a visitor of Durham College. Appointed a militia commissioner for Durham in July 1659, he subsequently supported Lambert's efforts to prevent the restoration of monarchy.

On settling in London in 1660, Hobson joined William Kiffin's church. With Tillam and Christopher Pooley he established a godly community for several hundred families from the Durham area on former monastic lands in the palatinate, and while abroad he preached to congregationalists in Rotterdam. On his return to London, he apparently associated with Nathaniel Strange, but he was in Durham by August 1661, when Bishop Cosin arrested and briefly imprisoned him owing to suspicions about his German project. To avoid interrogation by deputy lieutenants in November Hobson fled to London, where he was briefly detained in the spring. Suspected of complicity with the Tong plotters, he was rearrested in November 1662, but released on a £1000 bond. By this time he was practising medicine at Bishopsgate, London. The following year, Hobson, alias Dr Love, participated in the conspiracy that culminated in the northern rebellion in October. Hobson was arrested on 20 August. According to a fellow conspirator, Robert Atkinson, Hobson informed on his compatriots, though continuing to urge them to act, partly by ambushing Buckingham's troops as they marched north in August (a plan the conspirators were unable to implement). Accused of treason, Hobson was incarcerated in the Tower, moved to Chepstow Castle in March 1664, and then back again in January 1665. Suffering from ill health, he repeatedly sought permission to go to Jamaica. He was finally released on 28 April 1665 on condition that he move to Carolina, though he never went. His final work, *Innocency, though under a Cloud, Cleared* (1664), was an apologia. After his release he was accused of sexual misconduct with two female members of the Devonshire Square Baptist Church. His will, in which he described himself as a barber–surgeon, was dated on 12 March 1664 and proved on 13 June 1666. He expected his wife, Hester, and his children, Paul, Lydia, Sara, and Reubenah, to settle on his property at Sacriston, Durham; a fourth daughter, Hester, was married to Henry Woolfe. One of the leading Baptists in the north-east, Hobson was a tireless promoter of godly government and society.

RICHARD L. GREAVES

Sources CSP dom., 1645–50; 1657–65; 1667–8 · R. L. Greaves, *Saints and rebels: seven nonconformists in Stuart England* (1985), chap. 5 · *The letter books of Sir Samuel Luke, 1644–45*, ed. H. G. Tibbutt, Bedfordshire Historical RS, 42 (1963) · 'The Tower of London letter-book of Sir Lewis Dyve, 1646–47', ed. H. G. Tibbutt, *Bedfordshire Historical Record Society*, 38 (1958), 49–96 · *Calamy rev.* · R. L. Greaves, *Deliver us from evil: the radical underground in Britain, 1660–1663* (1986) · T. Edwards, *Gangraena, or, A catalogue and discovery of many of the errours, heresies, blasphemies and pernicious practices of the sectaries of this time*, 3 vols. in 1 (1646) · B. Whitelocke, *Memorials of English affairs*, new edn, 4 vols. (1853) · *Report on the manuscripts of F. W. Leyborne-Popham*, HMC, 51 (1899), 73–4 · *The writings and speeches of Oliver Cromwell*, ed. W. C. Abbott and C. D. Crane, 2 (1939), 334 · C. H. Firth and G. Davies, *The regimental history of Cromwell's army*, 2 vols. (1940) · C. H. Firth and R. S. Rait, eds., *Acts and ordinances of the interregnum, 1642–1660*, 3 vols. (1911) · E. B. Underhill, ed., *Records of the Churches of Christ, gathered at Fenstanton, Warboys, and Hexham, 1644–1720*, Hanserd Knollys Society (1854) · R. Howell, 'Conflict and controversy in the early Baptist movement in Northumberland: Thomas Tillam, Paul Hobson and the false Jew of Hexham', *Archaeologia Aeliana*, 5th ser., 14 (1986), 81–97 · PRO, PROB 11/319, fols. 58r–59v · RS Friends, Lond., Swarthmore papers

Archives BL, Add. MSS 4159, fols. 195ff.; 33770, fol. 35 · PRO, state papers, 29/63/34.1; 29/70/58 | BL, Egerton MS 786, fols. 25, 45, 47 · RS Friends, Lond., Swarthmore papers, 1, fol. 35

Hobson, Richard (1795–1868), physician, was born at Whitehaven, Cumberland, the second son of Christopher Hobson, a barrister, of Bootle, Cumberland, and Anna Dixon. After school at St Bees and at Wakefield, he was sent to study medicine at St George's Hospital, London. He became a member of the Royal College of Surgeons, and having finally decided to become a physician, went to Magdalene College, Cambridge, in 1820, before migrating to Sidney Sussex College, and finally to Queens' College, where he graduated MB in 1825 and MD in 1830.

In 1826 Hobson settled in Leeds, where he rapidly

acquired a large practice, and on 30 September 1833 he was elected physician to the infirmary there, a post which he resigned in June 1843. During this period he published in the *Medical Gazette* some notes on diabetes and on the external use of croton oil. He was consulting physician to the Hospital for Women and Children from 1853 to his death.

Hobson was devoted to field sports from his youth, and while in Leeds he belonged to the Harewood coursing club, bred racehorses, and hunted with the Bramham hunt. For a short time he kept a pack of harriers. He had some knowledge of natural history, and built up excellent collections of stuffed birds, mosses, and lichens. In 1836 he became acquainted with the naturalist Charles Waterton, who lived at Walton Hall, about 12 miles from Leeds. Hobson became physician to the family and a frequent visitor, and Waterton often wrote to him. Their friendship ended a few years before Waterton's death. Hobson had written a memoir of Waterton and claimed he had received the naturalist's approval for the work, *Charles Waterton: his Home, Habits, and Handiwork*, which was published in 1866. However, abundant internal evidence shows that the statement about Waterton's approval of the manuscript is untrue. Many of the stories in the book appear to be false, and the letters given were altered.

After being injured in a fall from his carriage, Hobson was confined to his house, where he broke his thigh bone, and died unexpectedly on 29 November 1868 at 10 Park Place, Leeds. His wife, a daughter of Peter Rhodes of Leeds, had died some years before. There were no children. Hobson was accounted 'one of the oldest and most respected medical men in Leeds' by his contemporaries (Mayhall, 3.224).   NORMAN MOORE, *rev.* PATRICK WALLIS

Sources Venn, *Alum. Cant.* · *The Lancet* (5 Dec 1868) · *BMJ* (5 Dec 1868), 604 · J. Mayhall, *The annals of Yorkshire*, 3 vols. (1866–74) · S. T. Anning, *The General Infirmary at Leeds*, 2 vols. (1966) · private information (1891) · Boase, *Mod. Eng. biog.*
Wealth at death under £4000: probate, 12 Jan 1869, *CGPLA Eng. & Wales*

Hobson, Samuel George (1870–1940), political activist and journalist, was born on 4 February 1870 in Bessbrook, near Newry, Northern Ireland, one of nine children of William Hobson, a Quaker minister, and his wife, Elizabeth, a teacher. Hobson's parents were both strict observers of their religion and they moved to England when Samuel was a child partly to ensure that their children could be educated at a Quaker school in Saffron Walden, which Samuel attended from 1880 to 1883. After the completion of his secondary education at the Friends' school, Sidcot, Somerset (1883–8), and having failed to win a university scholarship, Hobson moved to Cardiff and became involved in socialist circles. He joined the Fabian Society in 1891 and the Independent Labour Party in 1893. He engaged in propaganda work and travelled widely. His early political career was not always successful. He missed the first Independent Labour Party conference in Bradford after a traffic accident, an event which, at least to Hobson himself, symbolized his status as something of an outsider. None the less, throughout the 1890s Hobson was a regular contributor to the *Labour Leader* and stood for parliament as an Independent Labour Party candidate for East Bristol in 1895. He was elected to the Fabian Society's executive in 1900.

Hobson's major impact on British politics came when he resigned from the Fabian Society in 1910. Increasingly irritated at the timidity of parliamentary Labour politics, he drifted away from mainstream socialism. In 1912 he became a columnist for A. R. Orage's weekly *New Age*, and in 1914 Hobson's series of articles on industrial policy emerged as a book, *National Guilds: an Inquiry into the Wage System and a Way Out*, published under Orage's editorship. Here, Hobson espoused an ideal of an industrial system composed of self-governing guilds, where neither the state nor capitalists would control industry but where the pay and conditions of work would be decided democratically by workers themselves. His theory became, for a while, the most influential statement of what became known as guild socialism.

Hobson's prominence did not last long. The arrival of the precocious Oxford academic George Douglas Howard Cole in guild socialist circles during the First World War threatened Hobson's supremacy. Their theoretical disagreements became a staple point of debate in the intellectual world of early twentieth-century socialism. The central contention often appeared to concern the role of the state in a prospective guild utopia, but in reality that issue was only testament to a far wider set of disagreements as to the nature of the underlying ideology, especially concerning the rights of the individual in relation to the authority of the guilds (see G. D. H. Cole, 'The guilds, the state, the consumer, Mr. S. G. Hobson and others', *New Age*, 6 Dec 1917). In 1915 Hobson joined with Cole as a founder member of the National Guilds League, but Cole's domination of the organization unsettled the less educated man, and Hobson never played a particularly large role in the movement, the focus of his attentions remaining with the *New Age*.

Even that was not to last. After Orage committed the *New Age* to support of the proposals of the maverick economist C. H. Douglas in 1919, Hobson became disillusioned with the journal. In its place, he moved to practical action and attempted to create a co-operative guild in the building trade in the early 1920s. Economic downturn, however, ensured that these were unsuitable years for industrial innovation and the guild soon collapsed. In its wake, he continued to work in the labour movement but never again achieved his earlier level of recognition.

Away from politics, Hobson appears to have lived a full life. He was never as emotionally committed to political activism as his more successful contemporaries and, as a result, he was able to pursue a series of other careers. These included the management of a banana plantation in British Honduras and the editorship of an investment journal, *The Mint*. Many of his experiences are retold in his engaging autobiography, *Pilgrim to the Left: Memoirs of a Modern Revolutionist*, which was published to some acclaim in 1938. He died at his home, 6 Albion Street, in Dunstable, Bedfordshire, on 4 January 1940.   MARC STEARS

Sources S. G. Hobson, *Pilgrim to the left: memoirs of a modern revolutionist* (1938) • J. Vowles, 'Hobson, S. G.', *BDMBR*, vol. 3, pt 1 • M. Cole, 'Guild socialism and the labour research department', *Essays in labour history, 1886–1923*, ed. A. Briggs and J. Saville (1971), 260–83 • F. Mathews, 'The building guilds', *Essays in labour history, 1886–1923*, ed. A. Briggs and J. Saville (1971), 284–331 • G. Field, *Guild socialism* (1920) • S. T. Glass, *The responsible society: the ideas of guild socialism* (1966) • D. Howell, *British workers and the independent labour party, 1888–1906* (1983) • d. cert.
Archives Nuffield Oxf., National Guilds League collection | U. Hull, F. W. Dalley MSS

Hobson, Thomas (1545–1631), carrier, was the elder son of Thomas Hobson and his wife, Elinor. His birthplace has been stated as Buntingford, Hertfordshire, on the strength of his father's having been born there, but a note on the back of a contemporary petition relating to Hobson states that he was born at Holbeach, Lincolnshire, near which (at Moulton, and elsewhere) Hobson owned land in 1630, and at which his brother resided.

His father, also a carrier, had settled in Cambridge by 1561, and was at the time of his death, in 1568, one of the treasurers of the corporation. He devised his copyhold lands in Grantchester to his son Thomas, to whom he bequeathed 'the teame wayre that he now goeth with that is to say the carte & eighte horses & all the harneyes and other things thereunto belonginge with the nagge' (Cooper, 231). After his father's death Thomas continued the business with great success. The business was conducted by carts, and later by wagons drawn by teams of six or seven horses; there is no evidence that Hobson ever used packhorses. Both goods and passengers were carried, as well as 'a certayne greate tunn or vessell' containing live fish for the royal household. All the extant references show that the actual driving was done by servants, rather than by Hobson himself. Hobson was also active in hiring out horses, and his refusal to allow any horse to be taken except in its proper turn is said to have given rise to the saying, 'Hobson's choice', that is 'this or none'. Hobson used to tell the Cambridge scholars that they would get to London early enough 'if they did not ride too fast' (Clarke, 111). His fame extended far beyond the university, as in 1617 a tract appeared entitled *Hobson's Horse Load of Letters, or, Precedents for Epistles of Business.*

Hobson married his first wife, Agnes Humbrestone, at Ware on 2 December 1577. They had three sons (none of whom survived him) and five daughters. His will refers to the large portions provided on the marriage of two of his daughters, one to a baronet and the other to a gentleman, 'whereby my estate is much lesse then heretofore it was' (PRO, PROB 11/159, q. 17). Agnes died in 1615. His second wife was named Mary; she also predeceased him.

In 1626 Hobson presented a large Bible to the church of St Benedict, in which parish he resided. In 1627 he acquired the site of the priory of Anglesey, with the manor of Anglesey-cum-Bottisham, Cambridgeshire. He was also owner of the manors of Crowlands, Lisles, and Sames in Cottenham and, as lessee of the crown, held the Denny Abbey estate, with the manors of Waterbeach and Denny. His will mentions other property in Cambridge, Chesterton, Tidd St Giles, and Moulton. On 30 July 1628 he

Thomas Hobson (1545–1631), by unknown artist [original, 1629]

conveyed to the university and town of Cambridge the ground on which was erected the structure commonly known as the Spinning House, but more correctly called 'Hobson's Workhouse'. In spite of his advanced age he continued his journeys to London until 1630, when they were suspended on account of the plague. During this cessation of business he died at Cambridge on 1 January 1631. He was buried in the church of St Benedict on 12 January. Milton wrote two humorous epitaphs on Hobson.

A street in Cambridge is named after Hobson. In his will he provided for the maintenance of the existing conduit on Market Hill, and for making it 'halfe a yard higher or more (if with conveniencye it may be done)'; on the strength of this it became known as Hobson's Conduit, and it still survives (in the late twentieth century) on a different site (PRO, PROB 11/159, q. 17).

THOMPSON COOPER, *rev.* DORIAN GERHOLD

Sources C. H. Cooper, *Annals of Cambridge*, 3 (1845), 159, 179, 204–5, 230–7 • PRO, PROB 11/159, q. 17, Thomas Hobson • CUL, Archdeaconry of Ely, WR 3:84 • BL, Add. MSS 15828, fol. 25; 5813, fol. 52 • PRO, STAC 8/1/19, 8/1/26, 8/3/8, 8/30/10 • S. Clarke, *The lives of thirty two English divines*, in *A general martyrologie*, 3rd edn (1677), 111 • W. Stukeley, *Itinerarium curiosum, or, An account of the antiquities and remarkable curiosities in nature or art*, 2nd edn, 1 (1776), 18
Likenesses oils, 1620, Guildhall, Cambridge • J. Payne, line engraving, BM, NPG • oils (after original, 1629), NPG [*see illus.*]

Hobson [*married names* Havelock-Allan, Profumo], (**Babette Louisa**) **Valerie** (1917–1998), actress, was born on 14 April 1917 at Sandy Bay, Larne, Ireland, the daughter of Commander Robert Gordon Hobson (1877–1940), naval

(Babette Louisa) **Valerie Hobson** (1917–1998), by Bassano, 1949

officer, and his wife, Violette, *née* Hamilton-Willoughby (*fl. c.*1890–1955). She was stage-struck, it seemed, almost from birth, enjoying wrapping a towel around herself at the age of two and pretending to be the queen of Sheba. Ballet was her first love. She began dancing lessons at the age of three, appearing at concerts dressed as Cupid in pink tulle and carrying a silver bow and arrow. The ballet teacher Espinosa gave her instruction twice weekly from the age of five, for which she would be brought up to London from the country by her nanny. Her academic education was at St Augustine's Priory, London. She later remarked that she went on stage to find an audience because 'I was a very plain, wishy-washy child. Large wistful eyes. A real gum drop. Awful … everybody called me Monkey' (*The Guardian*, 16 Nov 1998); this was very different from her later screen image as the epitome of aristocratic English beauty, with big eyes, sculpted cheekbones, and long auburn hair.

As a child, Valerie Hobson was immensely ambitious. She grew too tall to be a ballerina, so acting became her potential career. The impresario Charles B. Cochran was so charmed by her when she was aged nine that he offered her a part in *White Birds*. Her parents refused to allow her to take up the offer, but were persuaded by Cochran to let her attend the Royal Academy of Dramatic Art for a year. On leaving the academy in 1932 she made her professional début, aged fifteen, in Basil Foster's *Orders are Orders*. Oscar Hammerstein II noted her in this and, spotting her lunching with her mother at Claridge's, offered her a part in his

play *Ball at the Savoy* at Drury Lane. In it she played a Lancashire lass in the mode of Gracie Fields. She demonstrated fine comic talents and a gift for mimicry that would seldom be given full rein in her later career.

Hobson's success on stage led to minor roles in a string of British 'B' movies and 'quota quickies', which, being still under age, she made while chaperoned by her nanny. An offer then came from Hollywood. Watched over now by her mother, she made six films under contract for Universal Studios, most notably *The Bride of Frankenstein* (1935) and *The Werewolf of London* (1935). She was earmarked for the role of Estella in *Great Expectations*, but was considered too young, so lost the part to another actress: twelve years later she played it in the David Lean film of Dickens's novel. She became frustrated by the colourless parts she was offered by Universal, commenting that 'I was getting tired of horror pictures and doing nothing but scream and faint' (*The Independent*, 16 Nov 1998). She screamed so well that Universal kept a tape of her in their sound library for use in films that featured actresses with more limited abilities.

A financial crisis at Universal led to Hobson's returning in 1936 to England, where her Hollywood experience made her highly attractive to producers. Her first film after her return was *Jump for Glory* (1937), in which she starred with Douglas Fairbanks jun. She regarded this film as a turning point in her career. The producer Alexander Korda admired her part in it, and cast her as leading lady in *The Drum* (1938). In this she became the first British star actress to be filmed in Technicolor; Korda had wanted her for the part because her pale skin would show up so well on the print. She played to great acclaim in *This Man is News* (1938), a wisecracking high comedy compared by critics to the Hollywood Thin Man films, and a substantial box-office success. Other notable starring roles followed, including those in *Q Planes* (1939) with Ralph Richardson and Laurence Olivier, *The Spy in Black* (1939), and *Contraband* (1940), all thrillers that extended her range as an actress.

At Pinewood Studios, Valerie Hobson renewed a professional acquaintance with the producer Anthony James Allan Havelock-Allan (b. 1904) (the son of Allan Havelock-Allan, of independent means). Havelock-Allan had produced *This Man is News* and its equally well-regarded sequel, *This Man in Paris* (1939). They married on 12 April 1939. They had two sons, one of whom had Down's syndrome. Although her disabled child later lived in a specialist home, Hobson devoted much of her time to him and to her family generally. As a consequence, she worked relatively little during the war years. Refusing to leave her husband behind in London, in 1942 she turned down the offer of a second Hollywood contract from David O. Selznick. By her own choice she made no films between 1943 and 1946, during which time her reputation was eclipsed by those of a new generation of earthier, less patrician female stars, such as Margaret Lockwood and Phyllis Calvert.

The immediate post-war period was a golden age for British films, and also for Hobson. She was quickly re-established as one of the British cinema's biggest stars and most stylish leading ladies. This was partly thanks to Cineguild, the production company founded by Havelock-Allan, David Lean, and Ronald Neame, devising big film projects that included ideal roles for her. She played Estella in Lean's *Great Expectations* (1946), and followed this with several other striking period performances. She had the title role opposite Stewart Granger in *Blanche Fury* (1947), a Victorian bodice-ripper in which she was cast against type as a racy, wilful *femme fatale*. This film was her favourite, but it never quite resonated with the public, perhaps because Hobson's innate ladylike (to use a word she abhorred in reference to herself) qualities prevented her from being a sufficiently ruthless Blanche.

To most eyes Hobson's performance as Edith d'Ascoyne in *Kind Hearts and Coronets* (1949) represented the summit of her screen career. The film, with its literate script and imaginative casting, was claimed by many to be the greatest made at Ealing Studios, and was a landmark of British cinematic culture. It was most remarked upon for Alec Guinness's *tour de force* in playing eight different roles, but Hobson's exquisite timing and clipped Edwardian manner made her perfect for the part of the beautiful, but priggish, Edith. 'I have always thought', she later observed, 'that the main reason for the success of *Kind Hearts* was that it was played dead straight' (*The Independent*, 16 Nov 1998). She and Guinness played opposite each other again in *The Card* (1952), based on Arnold Bennett's novel of the same name, where once again she was an Edwardian aristocrat.

Hobson's crowning success as an actress came, however, not on film, but on the stage. In 1953 Rodgers and Hammerstein offered her the part of the Governess in the first London production of *The King and I*, in which Herbert Lom played the King. Despite not being a trained singer she received great acclaim for her interpretation of the role, and played it for over a year: but it was her swansong. She said she could not imagine being offered a better part, so it was an appropriate moment to retire from acting. In a screen career lasting twenty-two years she had appeared in forty-five films, the last of which was *Knave of Hearts* (1954).

Valerie Hobson's retirement also coincided with her wedding on 31 December 1954 to a Conservative MP, John Dennis Profumo (*b.* 1915) (eldest son of Baron Albert Peter Anthony Profumo KC), her marriage to Havelock-Allan having been dissolved in 1952. They had a son, and for the next nine years Hobson was the model wife of an MP and minister, giving unstinting support to her husband in his successful political career. In June 1963 Profumo, by then minister for war, had to resign from his post and from the Commons after it was feared he had compromised security during a brief affair with Christine Keeler. Hobson unflinchingly stood by her husband, then and in his subsequent years of work for the poor at Toynbee Hall in London's east end. She won huge admiration for her dignity and bearing at a traumatic time, and was central to the rebuilding of Profumo's life as a popular and highly respected worker for charity.

Hobson was herself a tireless supporter of good causes. Her and Havelock-Allan's disabled son led to her close involvement with the Down's Syndrome Association over many years. She also raised money for Lepra, a charity for those with leprosy, and for blind people in India. She 'adopted' two Indian children, helping to pay for their upbringing and education, and was frequently by her husband's side at functions for Toynbee Hall. Although she was often invited to return to acting, she declined; she preferred the absorbing and for her entirely fulfilling role of wife, mother, grandmother, and charity worker. She much enjoyed an active social life. A woman of great charm and good humour, she was always modest about, and unaffected by, the conspicuous success of her early years and her significant place in the history of the British cinema. She died in London of a heart attack on 13 November 1998 and was cremated after a funeral service at St Paul's, Knightsbridge, on 23 November 1998. She was survived by her husband, John Profumo, by her former husband, Sir Anthony Havelock-Allan, and by her sons Mark Havelock-Allan and David Profumo. A memorial service was held at St Paul's, Covent Garden, London, on 23 September 1999.   SIMON HEFFER

Sources *The Times* (16 Nov 1998) · *Daily Telegraph* (21 Nov 1998) · *Daily Telegraph* (24 Sept 1999) · *The Guardian* (16 Nov 1998) · *The Independent* (16 Nov 1998) · WWW · www.uk.imdb.com, 1 March 2001 · B. McFarlane, ed., *An autobiography of British cinema* (1997) · personal knowledge (2004) · private information (2004) · b. cert. · m. certs. · d. cert.

Archives priv. coll., papers | FILM BBC News Library · Independent Television News Archive

Likenesses M. Smith, oils, *c.*1945–1955, priv. coll. · Bassano, photograph, 1949, NPG [*see illus.*] · photographs, BFI

Hobson, William (1792–1842), naval officer and colonial governor, was born in Waterford, Ireland, on 25 September 1792, the third of the five sons of Samuel Hobson, a barrister, and his wife, Martha Jones. In 1803 he entered the Royal Navy as a gentleman volunteer. He was first involved in North Sea action during the Napoleonic wars, in 1806 was made a midshipman while in the West Indies, and by 1814 had risen to lieutenant. From August 1816 he was unemployed for eighteen months, then had a brief posting in the Mediterranean before commencing a career of service against pirates and slavers in the West Indies. He was captured in 1821 and again in 1823, when commanding an attack on pirate strongholds on the Cuban coast. Promotion to commander in 1824 and captain in 1828 was fitting recognition of a distinguished record, but years of exhausting service and illness—three bouts of yellow fever—left the slightly built Hobson in indifferent health. From mid-1828 he was without a command.

At Nassau, in the Bahamas, on 17 December 1827, Hobson had married Eliza Ann (1811–1876), the only daughter of Robert Wear Elliott, a Scottish West India merchant. The Hobsons lived at Plymouth for six years until, in December 1834, through the patronage of Lord Auckland, Hobson was appointed commander of the frigate *Rattle-snake*. Dispatched to serve in the East Indies and in Australian waters, the ship arrived at Port Jackson (Sydney) in

August 1836 and helped with the foundation of Port Phillip settlement (Melbourne).

When Maori warfare in early 1837 led to an appeal from James Busby, British resident in New Zealand, Hobson left for the Bay of Islands, charged with drawing up a report on the country. The fighting subsided without need of mediation and Hobson made brief visits to several other locations. His report proposed limited British intervention in New Zealand—a system of trading factories similar to those in India and a treaty with the Maori to confirm purchase of land and secure jurisdiction.

Hobson arrived in England in early 1838 and in February 1839 accepted appointment as British consul to New Zealand; a second commission as lieutenant-governor followed, with instructions provided by the Colonial Office. Prefaced by an apology for intervention, which acknowledged an 1835 declaration of the country's independence signed by northern Maori, these instructions were essentially guidelines for establishing a British colony. Land, purchased from Maori, would be sold to settlers at a profit to fund government business.

At Port Jackson Hobson conferred with his immediate superior, Governor George Gipps of New South Wales, and selected his staff. He arrived at the Bay of Islands in the *Herald* on 29 January 1840. The following day he read the queen's commission appointing him lieutenant-governor, cautiously adding that it was over the British settlements 'in progress'.

With Busby's assistance a treaty was drafted and translated by Henry Williams, a member of the Church Missionary Society. Local Maori leaders met on 5 February 1840 at Busby's Waitangi residence, where Williams interpreted. Hobson wanted a cession of sovereignty but, aware that Maori suspected British motives, he presented the treaty as a limited intrusion on Maori rights; the treaty was needed so that he could better control unruly settlers and protect the Maori. Long-term implications were not raised. Heated debate followed, but the next day Hobson received assent from more than forty chiefs, twenty-six of whom had signed the 1835 declaration of independence. However, shortcomings of translation and lack of explanation left Maori leaders with inadequate understanding of the agreement.

Anxious to press forward treaty negotiations elsewhere, Hobson sailed for Waitemata harbour, but on 1 March 1840 a stroke left him partially paralysed. Willoughby Shortland, colonial secretary, began to organize the collection of treaty signatures by sending copies of the treaty to various parts of the country. Hobson, soon resuming most duties, expanded these missions by deploying Major Thomas Bunbury, who arrived in April with the Hobson family and a detachment of troops.

While treaty copies were circulating, Hobson became concerned about asserting British authority. Faced with an independent stance adopted by New Zealand Company settlers at Port Nicholson (Wellington), he proclaimed British sovereignty over the whole country on 21 May. Two months later, faced with a French attempt to found a settlement in the South Island, he responded with a show of occupation. Meanwhile he decided to relocate his government, and founded a new capital at Auckland on Waitemata harbour. Officials moved there in February 1841, and on 3 May Hobson took the oath as governor; by royal charter New Zealand became a crown colony. Now he was able to deal directly with the home government, rather than dealing via New South Wales as had been the case when he was lieutenant-governor, Hobson nevertheless had to rely on his own judgement: his staff, boosted by local recruits, lacked ability, and responses to dispatches took nine months to reach him.

Aware that his administration was closely scrutinized by a Maori population that vastly outnumbered settlers, Hobson depended on missionary support to influence Maori leaders. In April 1840 he appointed the missionary George Clarke as protector of aborigines, but, since Clarke was required to be government land purchaser as well as protector, this was less than reassuring to the Maori. When revenue failed to meet official expenditure, Hobson handled the crisis poorly. Sensitive to opposition, he was overly irritated when settler unrest over land and other policies was fomented by journalists. He had been unwell since his first stroke, and he suffered another stroke and died, at Government House, Auckland, on 10 September 1842. He was given a military funeral on 13 September and interred in a vault in Grafton cemetery, Auckland. Eliza Hobson, with their four daughters and a son, returned to live at Stoke, Devon; she died in 1876.

Hobson had enjoyed a warm family circle and was an entertaining host and speaker. A member of the Church of England, he was tolerant of other denominations. For his public office he was not well prepared, however. By training and disposition he was accustomed to exercising authority and commanding respect. The skills needed to control a constantly changing frontier situation within the parameters of unrealistic Colonial Office expectations were altogether different. The effort required of a new colonial governor strained his weakened constitution and hastened Hobson's end.   CLAUDIA ORANGE

Sources G. H. Scholefield, *Captain William Hobson* (1934) · A. H. McLintock, *Crown colony government in New Zealand* (1958) · NL NZ, Turnbull L., William Hobson MSS, paper 46 · *Correspondence and other papers relating to New Zealand*, 3–4 (1970) [repr. from *Parl. papers* (1835–47)] · C. Orange, *The treaty of Waitangi* (1987) · P. Adams, *Fatal necessity: British intervention in New Zealand, 1830–1847* (1977) · parish register (baptism), St Patrick's, Waterford, Ireland, 9 Jan 1793 · *Government Gazette* [New Zealand] (10 Sept 1842) · *Nelson Examiner* (29 Oct 1842)
Archives NL NZ, Turnbull L., journals and papers
Likenesses J. E. Collins, portrait, *c*.1835, priv. coll.; copy, NL NZ, Turnbull L.
Wealth at death £3000 in 3½ per cent stock; property in Nassau; land in Auckland: NL NZ, Turnbull L., William Hobson MSS

Hoby. For this title name *see* individual entries under Hoby; *see also* Russell, Elizabeth, Lady Russell [Elizabeth Hoby, Lady Hoby] (1528–1609).

Hoby, Sir Edward (1560–1617), politician and diplomat, was born at Bisham, Berkshire, on 20 March 1560, the eldest son of Sir Thomas *Hoby (1530–1566) and his wife, Elizabeth (1528–1609), third daughter of Sir Anthony

Sir Edward Hoby (1560–1617), by unknown artist, 1583

*Cooke of Gidea Hall, Essex, and later wife of John, Lord Russell [see Russell, Elizabeth, Lady Russell]. The puritan magistrate and MP Sir Thomas Posthumous Hoby was a younger brother. From 1571 Edward attended Eton College, where he struck up a lasting friendship with Sir John Harington, the courtier and translator. He matriculated from Trinity College, Oxford, as a gentleman-commoner on 11 November 1574, aged fourteen. He was allowed to graduate BA on 19 February 1576, after only eight terms, and proceeded MA on 3 July of the same year. Thomas Lodge the dramatist was a 'scholar' under him at Trinity. In June 1576 Hoby obtained a dispensation to travel on the continent, which he did until 1579. Subsequently, as he stated in his *Counter-Snarle* (pp. 61, 72), he entered the Middle Temple, but he does not appear in its surviving records.

Hoby had the means to provide for an independent lifestyle. He succeeded his father upon the latter's death in 1566, and when his mother purchased his wardship, his lands in Berkshire and Worcestershire were valued at £220 a year. One of the most highly educated women of her time, Hoby's mother prepared him for his career at the royal court. Through her he was related to the Cecils and Cookes, and his access to the court was increased by his marriage to Margaret (d. 1605), daughter of Henry *Carey, first Baron Hunsdon, on 21 May 1582. He was knighted by the queen at Somerset House on the day after the wedding. Local offices came quickly afterwards. He was appointed JP for Berkshire, Kent, and Worcestershire from 1583, Middlesex from 1593, and Surrey from 1601.

Under the auspices of his uncle, William *Cecil, Lord Burghley, Hoby rose into high favour at court, and was frequently employed on confidential missions. In August 1584 he accompanied his father-in-law on a special mission to Scotland. His affability and learning greatly impressed James VI. After attending the Scottish ambassador as far as Durham, Hoby received from James a flattering letter in which the king intimated his longing for his company, and how he had 'commanded his ambassador to sue for it'. James Hamilton, third earl of Arran, also wrote to the same effect, enclosing a 'small token' which he begged Hoby 'to wear in testimony of their brotherhood' (*CSP Scot. ser., 1509–89*, 489). The queen disliked these signs of favour, and Hoby found it convenient for a time to plead the ague as an excuse for not attending the court. Domestic troubles also harassed him.

Hoby was returned MP for Queenborough, Kent, in 1584 and 1586, gaining distinction as a spokesman in the Commons. On 31 October 1586 he complained that he had been 'not only bitten but overpassed by the hard hand of' Sir Francis Walsingham, and appealed to Secretary William Davison to use his influence with the queen on his behalf (*CSP dom., 1581–90*, 365). Argumentative, he quarrelled with Lord Burghley, Sir John Conway, Sir Humphrey Gilbert, and Sir Thomas Heneage. Ultimately restored to favour through his mother's interventions, in July 1588 Hoby was chosen to report to the queen on the progress of preparations against the Spanish Armada in the Isle of Sheppey, where he also served as grain commissioner.

Elected MP for Berkshire in 1589, Hoby introduced a bill on 14 February against the extortions of exchequer officials, and spoke out against royal purveyance. He was reproached by Burghley but the house cleared his name of breaching its privileges, although his plan for reforming the exchequer was defeated by the queen, who regarded him as one of those 'busy' against her prerogative; none the less in 1592 she visited him at Bisham. In the parliaments of 1589 and 1593 Hoby was an active member of committees for harbour repairs, parliamentary privilege, purveyance, poor relief, and subsidies. In 1593 he was publicly rebuked by the queen and briefly placed under house arrest for insulting a fellow committee member, the privy councillor Sir Thomas Heneage.

Hoby's career moved more fully to Kent when he was chosen MP for the county in February 1593. Having served as vice-admiral of Milton hundred since 1585, he was appointed *custos rotulorum* of the county in 1594. He took an active role as judge in the Milton hundredal court. Royal favours included in 1594 letters patent for buying and providing wool for sale in England for ten years, which were ratified in the succeeding reign. Hoby's only military endeavour was accompanying the expedition to Cadiz in 1596. Appointed constable of Queenborough Castle on the Isle of Sheppey, on 9 July 1597, he kept detailed records of his work there. On the following 28 October he received a commission to search out and prosecute all offences against the statute prohibiting the export of iron from England, his reward being half the forfeitures. He continued to serve the queen in diplomatic ventures, and had established a correspondence with the Russian diplomat Grigori Ivanovich Mikulin by 1602.

Elected MP for Rochester in 1597 and 1601, Hoby was particularly active in those parliaments. He sat on at least fourteen committees and most of his work was on economic, legal, and religious issues. In 1601 he chaired the privileges and returns committee, and distinguished himself in urging the house to protect its privileges in individual cases, and to make precedents in issuing election writs. He had several confrontations with Sir Robert Cecil, but in the debate on monopolies he stood for not challenging the royal prerogative no matter how 'foul' its practices (Henderson and Philips, 2.322). Hoby's favour at court enabled him to act as a knight of the canopy at the queen's funeral in 1603. He continued to be elected for Rochester in the succeeding parliaments of 1604–10 and 1614.

Hoby's career at court was solidified at the accession of James I. The king made him a gentleman of the privy chamber in 1605, and forgave him by warrant the arrears of rent of the royal manor of Shirland, Derbyshire, amounting to over £500. Earlier Hoby had defaulted on the rent of properties in Kent leased from Brasenose College, Oxford, and was sued successfully in 1593 for £500 in arrears. Hoby, blessed with wealth, had little acumen to preserve it. He turned again to the royal court and James granted him an exclusive licence on 21 August 1607 to buy wool in Warwickshire and Staffordshire. Hoby frequently entertained the king at Bisham, but his social relationship did not include the king's political agenda.

While most is known about his career as a parliamentarian in the later parliaments of Elizabeth I, Hoby was perhaps a more important figure in the early parliaments of James I. According to contemporary MPs in the parliaments of 1604–14, his appearances were impressive, his manner affable, his head clear, and his knowledge of parliamentary history and usage unparalleled (Notestein, 61). An independent figure, often at odds with court policies, he was listened to attentively. A candidate for speaker in 1604, he was quite effective in promoting the house's position on privileges, precedents, and impositions, and using delaying tactics to stymie Anglo-Scottish union. Sitting as a commissioner for the bill on union, he refused to subscribe his name to the engrossed document (Inner Temple MS 537, 8.123). He was often appointed as the Commons' representative on joint committees of the Lords, and the record shows that he stood up to the Lords strongly and effectively, pushing the independence of his house. When his own personal interests were at issue in attacks on the wool monopoly, accusations of his 'jobbing and brogging' were quietly dismissed in the Commons (*Parliamentary Diary of Robert Bowyer*, 141).

Hoby was a keen theologian, collector, and scholar. He spoke out for tough laws against recusants in Elizabeth's reign. In James's reign he contested with the Catholic convert Theophilus Higgons and the Jesuit John Floyd, publishing his exchanges with them between 1609 and 1615 in such works as *A Counter-Snarle for Ishmael Rabshacheh, a Cecropidan Lycaonite* (1613) and *A curry-combe for a coxe-combe*

... *in answer to a lewd libell lately fornicated by Jabal Rachil against Sir Edward Hobies 'Counter-Snarle'* (1615). His religious views were of a moderate Calvinist conformist to the Church of England. He was an inveterate collector, and manuscripts that he is known to have owned include medieval English poetry, fifteenth-century herbal and medicinal remedies, and Dutch medical treatises (BL, Add. MSS 8151, 4897–4899). He collected and placed in Queenborough Castle portraits of many of its constables. Hoby was also a copious letter-writer, copyist, and—like his father—translator. His published works included a translation from Latin of Matthieu Coignet as *Politique Discourse upon Trueth and Lying* (1586), and from the Castilian of Bernardino de Mendoza as *Theorique and Practise of Warr* (1597). Hoby cultivated the friendship of learned men, especially William Camden, who eulogized his bounty and accomplishments in *Britannia* (under 'Bisham' and 'Queenborough'). Camden also dedicated his *Hibernia* (1587) to him. In 1612 Hoby presented to the library of Trinity College, Oxford, Sir Henry Savile's sumptuous edition of *St Chrysostom*.

Hoby's first wife died in 1605; about 1613 he married Cecily, daughter of Sir Edward Unton and widow of Sir John Wentworth of Gosfield Hall, Essex, who survived him. Hoby died in Queenborough Castle on 1 March 1617 and was buried at All Saints' Church, Bisham: his will asked that he be buried without pomp or ceremony in the family chapel there.

Hoby had no children from his marriages. He was succeeded by his illegitimate son with Katharine Pinckney, **Peregrine Hoby** (1602–1679), politician, born on 1 September 1602. Hoby recognized the boy as his heir, brought him up, and at his death committed him to the care of Archbishop George Abbot. Peregrine attended Eton College between 1612 and 1616. He may have served on the expeditions to Cadiz in 1625 and to La Rochelle in 1627. He initially resisted compounding for knighthood in 1630 but eventually promised to pay £30. On 14 April 1631 he married Katherine (d. 1687), daughter of Sir William Doddington of Breamore, Hampshire. In 1640 Hoby was elected to the Long Parliament as MP for Great Marlow, Buckinghamshire (which lay just across the Thames from Bisham), in a pair of controversial elections on 21 October, and, after the Commons ordered a new election, on 23 November. Hoby was elected by the corporation in the first election, though the householders who challenged such a restricted franchise apparently would also have voted for him but not the other MP then elected. His second election, on a broader franchise, was challenged in the committee of privileges on the grounds that the franchise, which included the bargemen and almsmen of the town, was now too wide: 'Mr Maynard mooved that the poore should not have a voice' (Hirst, 78). His election was confirmed, but the situation was further complicated because just before the second election he had been pricked as sheriff, which precluded him from leaving the county and sitting as MP. Indeed, though Hoby's election was confirmed in January 1641, he was apparently required to serve out his term as sheriff and was absent from the Commons for most of the year. He was present by June 1642 and was an active member from 1643 to 1648. In the same period he sat on the parliamentarian county committee for Berkshire. He was secluded from the Commons at Pride's Purge, returning to the Commons in 1659 when the representation of Great Marlow was restored. He sat for the borough in the Convention Parliament (1660) and in the Cavalier Parliaments (1661–78), where he was very much a second- or third-rank figure. He was moderately active on committees and showed some concern with the danger of popery: in 1667 he brought before the Commons a complaint (unfounded, as it turned out) about the Jesuits seducing a young heir. The earl of Shaftesbury in 1677 considered Hoby politically sympathetic, noting him as 'worthy'. Peregrine Hoby was buried at Bisham on 6 May 1679.   LOUIS A. KNAFLA

Sources *Reg. Oxf.*, 2/1.69; 2/2.57; 2/3.55 · Wood, *Ath. Oxon.*, new edn, 2.194–7, 382 · J. C. Henderson and M. A. Philips, 'Hoby, Sir Edward', HoP, *Commons, 1558–1603* · J. Hutchinson, ed., *Notable Middle Templars* (1902), 123 · W. Camden, *Britannia*, trans. (1610) [under 'Bisham' and 'Queenborough'] · *The diary of Lady Margaret Hoby, 1599–1605*, ed. D. M. Meads (1930) · F. Heal, 'Reputation and honour in court and country: Lady Elizabeth Russell and Sir Thomas Hoby', *TRHS*, 6th ser., 6 (1996), 161–78 · '"Moi Chestneishii I Dorogoi Drug Grigorii Ivanovich Mikulin": Pis'mo Angliiskogo Gosudarstvennogo Deiateliak Russkomu Diplomatu Nachala XVII', *Otechestvennye Arkhivy*, 6 (1995), 86–90 · will, PRO, PROB 11/129, sig. 131 · P. J. Begent, *The heraldry of the Hoby memorials in the parish church of All Saints, Bisham, in the royal county of Berkshire* (1979) · J. Nichols, *The progresses and public processions of Queen Elizabeth*, 3 (1821), 130–36 · S. D'Ewes, *The journals of all the parliaments during the reign of Queen Elizabeth* (1682) · J. E. Neale, *Elizabeth I and her parliaments, 1584–1601* (1953) · H. Townshend, *Historical collections: or, An exact account of the proceedings of the four last parliaments of Queen Elizabeth of famous memory* (1680) · W. Notestein, *The House of Commons, 1604–1610* (1971) · *The parliamentary diary of Robert Bowyer, 1606–1607*, ed. D. H. Willson (1971) · M. Jansson, ed., *Proceedings in parliament, 1614 (House of Commons)* (1988) · *CSP dom.*, 1581–90; 1595–7; 1603–10 · parliamentary speeches, 1593–1603, Inner Temple, London, Misc. MS 537, vols. 8, 12, 20 · Sir Edward Hoby's commonplace book, 1582–96, BL, Add. MS 38823 · Sir Edward Hoby's parliamentary correspondence as MP for Rochester, 1605–6, BL, Stowe MSS 168, 178 · Sir Edward Hoby's epitaph and family notes, BL, Stowe MS 748, fol. 212 · *The works of Francis Bacon*, ed. J. Spedding, R. L. Ellis, and D. D. Heath, 14 vols. (1857–74); repr. (Stuttgart–Bad Cannstatt, 1961–3), vol. 10, pp. 200, 215, 245, 261; vol. 12, pp. 61–4 · 'Wills of the Hoby family', ed. J. W. Walker, Yorkshire Archaeological Society, record ser. 95 (1938) · *CSP Scot. ser., 1509–1603* · J. Nichols, *The progresses, processions, and magnificent festivities of King James I, his royal consort, family and court*, 4 vols. (1828) · T. Birch, *The court and times of James the First*, 2 vols. (1848) · *Report on the manuscripts of his grace the duke of Buccleuch and Queensberry … preserved at Montagu House*, 3 vols. in 4, HMC, 45 (1899–1926) · *The letters of John Chamberlain*, ed. N. E. McClure, 2 vols. (1939) · Caesar papers, BL, Lansdowne MSS 33, fol. 203; 42, fol. 21; 43, fol. 34; 48, fol. 136ff.; 51, fol. 47; 68, fol. 230; 69, fols. 19–23; 72, fol. 222; 75, fols. 20–30; 78, fol. 38 · Keeler, *Long Parliament* · M. W. Helms, L. Naylor, and G. Jagger, 'Hoby, Peregrine', HoP, *Commons, 1660–90* · M. R. Frear, 'The election at Great Marlow in 1640', *Journal of Modern History*, 14 (1942), 433–48 [Peregrine Hoby] · D. Hirst, *The representative of the people? Voters and voting in England under the early Stuarts* (1975) [Peregrine Hoby] · Foster, *Alum. Oxon.* · W. Sterry, ed., *The Eton College register, 1441–1698* (1943) · *The travels and life of Sir Thomas Hoby, kt. of Bisham Abbey, written by himself, 1547–1564*, ed. E. Powell (1902)
Archives BL, commonplace book, Add. MS 38823 · LPL, book of prayers
Likenesses oils, 1578, Bisham Abbey, Berkshire · oils, 1583, NPG [*see illus.*]

Hoby [*née* Dakins], **Margaret**, Lady Hoby (*bap.* **1571**, *d.* **1633**), diarist, was baptized on 10 February 1571, the only child of Arthur Dakins (*b. c.*1517, *d.* 1592), gentleman and JP of Linton in the East Riding of Yorkshire, and his wife, Thomasine Gye (*d.* 1613). She was educated in the household of Henry Hastings, third earl of Huntingdon, president of the council in the north, and she learned there the puritan habits of self-examination and regular religious exercises which she later practised in her own household. As an heiress she was a valuable commodity in the Elizabethan marriage market, and she was married three times, to well-connected younger sons approved by the Hastings family.

In 1588 or 1589 she married Walter (*b. c.*1569), son of Walter *Devereux, first earl of Essex, the Irish adventurer. The younger Walter was the brother of Robert, second earl of Essex, and stepson of the countess of Huntingdon's brother, Robert Dudley, earl of Leicester. The manor and parsonage of Hackness in the North Riding were purchased for the couple, and remained Margaret's property after the death of Devereux at the siege of Rouen in 1591. Before the end of the year she had been married again, to Thomas Sidney, brother of Sir Philip Sidney, the poet, and nephew of the countess of Huntingdon. When Sidney died in 1595, Margaret agreed to Huntingdon's deathbed request that she marry another suitor of 1591, Sir Thomas Posthumous Hoby (1566–1644), second son of Sir Thomas *Hoby, of Bisham, Berkshire, and his wife, Elizabeth [*see* Russell, Elizabeth, Lady Russell]. They were married on 9 August 1596 and lived at Hackness, where Hoby established a political powerbase (he was JP and MP) and a reputation as a humourless puritan and cantankerous opponent of rival, especially Catholic, gentry.

Margaret Hoby's diary—the earliest known by an Englishwoman—is notable for its depiction of the domestic disciplines of Elizabethan puritanism. Written between 1599 and 1605, it describes the religious exercises and prayers for the whole household as well as the private prayers and readings which occupied a large part of each day, and in which Lady Hoby was guided by her chaplain, Richard Rhodes. The diary also shows other aspects of the household routine of a gentlewoman: managing the estate in her husband's frequent absences, supervising and paying servants, sorting linen, playing music, gardening, giving medical advice and treatment to neighbours and tenants. It tells little about the writer's private feelings. It is a document written as a pious exercise, and its discipline and restraint spring from that. References to Sir Thomas Hoby are perhaps deceptively formal, though Margaret was strong-minded enough to resist until 1632 his request that she make over her Hackness and other properties to him and his heirs. She had no children herself. Puritanism, the household, and property dominate the diary, as perhaps her whole life.

Lady Hoby died in 1633 and was buried on 6 September

in the chancel of Hackness church, where her husband erected an alabaster monument to her. It still survives, but St Margaret's Chapel in Harwood Dale, which Hoby also built to her memory, is in ruins.   PAUL SLACK, *rev.*

Sources *Diary of Lady Margaret Hoby*, ed. D. M. Meads (1930) · C. Cross, *The puritan earl: the life of Henry Hastings, third earl of Huntingdon* (1966), 55–60, 172 · J. T. Cliffe, *The Yorkshire gentry from the Reformation to the civil war* (1969)
Archives BL, diary and memoranda, Egerton MS 2614 | BL, Harley MSS, Hastings corresp. · HMC, Salisbury (Cecil) MSS, Hastings corresp., HMC 9 · Hunt. L., Hastings corresp.
Wealth at death manor of Hackness and related property worth £1500 p.a.: *Diary*, ed. Meads, 43

Hoby, Peregrine (1602–1679). *See under* Hoby, Sir Edward (1560–1617).

Hoby, Sir Philip (1504/5–1558), diplomat and administrator, was the first son of William Hoby (*d.* after 1532), landowner, of Leominster, Herefordshire, and his first wife, Katherine Foster. Sir Thomas *Hoby (1530–1566), the courtier and translator, was his half-brother. He came from a Welsh family that settled in Leominster during his father's time. Nothing is known of his education but he was proficient in several foreign languages and was clearly well educated, having probably travelled through Europe as a young man.

Hoby was by 1538 identified as one of the grooms of the privy chamber and probably had a strong connection with Sir Thomas Cromwell, who identified him as a friend sharing the same interest in religious reform. His career was advanced through service to Cromwell, probably going back to the early 1530s. He served Dr Nicholas Hawkins, resident ambassador to Charles V, between 1532 and 1534, learning his craft as a diplomat. His first formal overseas assignment came as a special mission for Cromwell. Between about 28 February and about 1 April 1538 he accompanied Hans Holbein the younger to obtain portraits of potential marriage partners for Henry VIII. He seems to have received a total diet of £46 13s. 4d. Hoby was instructed by Cromwell to visit the household of Claude de Lorraine, first duc de Guise, to examine his two daughters. Before this Hoby and Holbein went to the Low Countries, where they had an audience with the regent about 11 March, the artist making the drawing for his famous portrait of Christina of Denmark the following day. While not a diplomatic mission, it certainly added to Hoby's qualifications to undertake royal business abroad.

Hoby had experience in a working embassy, had the advantage of skill in languages and foreign travel, and enjoyed Henry VIII's confidence and Cromwell's patronage. He was the quintessential Tudor lay diplomatic representative, when his first formal assignment came on 10 October. His instructions were to join the resident ambassador, Sir Thomas Wyatt the elder, to advise Charles V, with whom he had an audience on 1 November, on various foreign policy matters as Henry saw them, all intended to promote peace in Europe. His mission, one of no great consequence, was concluded by 17 December. He was appointed woodward of Ashwood, Leominster, from 25 March 1538 to 28 April 1546 in reward.

Sir Philip Hoby (1504/5–1558), by Hans Holbein the younger

Hoby continued as a leading courtier, who was often entrusted with military duties, until the end of the reign. He was part of the reception for Anne of Cleves in 1540, an understandable assignment since he had been special ambassador to the Cleves court in a poorly documented mission between about 8 and 25 November 1539, when he probably negotiated her marriage to Henry and apparently obtained a painting of her. No disadvantage seemed to attach to him in the Cleves divorce and the fall of Cromwell. Instead, he was given a more prominent role in government. By 1540 he had married well, to Elizabeth (*c.*1500–1560), daughter of Sir Walter Stoner of Stoner, Oxfordshire. Holbein probably produced the drawings of the couple about this time. They had no children. Elizabeth Hoby was part of the protestant court circle surrounding Katherine Parr and this connection reinforced her husband's position. On 4 February 1542 Philip Hoby submitted to the privy council the books containing examinations and inventories of the goods of Jews who had been arrested under his commission. He was in trouble himself over his own religious beliefs, being committed to the Fleet prison on 18 March 1543 for having maintained the cleric Thomas Parson, whose 'evill opinions' regarding the sacrament of the altar were well known (*APC*, 1542–7, 101). Hoby was released six days later and appointed gentleman usher of the black rod and to the Order of the Garter on 3 November, as well as being a member of Katherine's council between 1543 and 1548. It took military service at Boulogne to secure his knighthood on 30 September 1544. He subsequently served in the invasion of Scotland led by Edward Seymour, earl of Hertford, in September 1545, in which he was master of the ordnance northward. He was appointed on 12 May Katherine's steward for foreign receipts and steward for her husband, Thomas Seymour, Lord Seymour, in 1548. Hoby was remembered in Henry VIII's will with a bequest of £133 6s. 8d. and benefited from royal land grants, acquiring former monastic property in Worcestershire in 1541 and in Lincolnshire in 1544.

Edward VI's reign was the high point of Hoby's diplomatic career. He served in the parliament of 1547 as an MP for Cardiff Boroughs, having probably been advanced by Sir William Herbert, Katherine's brother-in-law, but seemingly missed the majority of the sessions due to service abroad. He was also appointed JP for Middlesex and for Worcestershire in May 1547 (of the quorum from 1554). He was resident ambassador to the emperor from about 15 April 1548, with specific instructions to secure military assistance in countering a presumably impending French invasion. His secretary was John Bernardino. Charles's peripatetic court moved between the Low Countries and parts of Germany, with Hoby dutifully following. His residency was punctuated with a brief return home in autumn 1549 to pursue private patronage objectives, during which Hoby earned some notoriety. He apparently played a key role in the capitulation of Hertford, now duke of Somerset, to the privy council and John Dudley, earl of Warwick. Hoby, trusted by both sides, and previously a strong supporter of Somerset, served as a skilled negotiator between 6 and 13 October as both factions manoeuvred to avoid civil war. He was well aware that the London councillors intended to strip Somerset of his power. It is notable that Hoby guaranteed the duke's life, being instrumental in gaining his surrender on 11 October through his careful diplomacy, and his thoughts at the ultimate dénouement may be imagined. Hoby's resumption of resident responsibilities in Brussels, this time accompanied by Sir Thomas Cheyne, included an explanation to the emperor of recent events in London and a repeated request for imperial troops to assist the English at Boulogne. This residency formally ended on 20 November 1550. Charles praised his diplomatic skills upon Hoby's return.

Hoby was a member of the entourage of William Parr, marquess of Northampton, when he was sent to France from 25 April to 12 August 1551. This was a major embassy that was designed to impress and even overawe the French court, leaving England with a large train that included Thomas Goodrich, the bishop of Ely, Henry Manners, second earl of Rutland, William Somerset, third earl of Worcester, Thomas Butler, eleventh earl of Ormond, and several barons, among a great many others. Hoby alone provided for thirty retainers and servants in his retinue, with a diet of £3 6s. 8d. per day to support this. The purpose of the embassy was to convey the Garter to Henri II, to negotiate the marriage of Edward to a French princess, and to cement the Anglo-French amity. In this mission Hoby was presumably a strategic negotiator, for he carried unusual status—the third-ranking envoy among a group of luminaries—but his specific role remains obscure. He was rewarded with appointment to the privy council on 16 August. His importance as a privy councillor and master of the ordnance (26 March 1547 to 11 May 1554) was such that, when the court departed London for the country in autumn 1552, he was required to remain at the Tower of London with half the privy council to continue the business of royal government. Shortly thereafter he secured the former abbey at Bisham, Berkshire. This site is closely identified with him, his half-brother Thomas Hoby, and his highly literate sister-in-law, Elizabeth *Russell, née Cooke (1528–1609), who constructed a magnificent monument there to both Philip and Thomas Hoby.

Yet another diplomatic assignment came between 13 February and about 5 March 1552. Sent to the regent in the Low Countries in company with Sir Thomas Gresham, it was Hoby's responsibility to secure a renegotiation of English loans from the Fuggers, and also to protest various imperial infringements on English naval and commercial rights in the area. A final, formal diplomatic duty was carried out from 2 April 1553, when Thomas Thirlby, bishop of Norwich, and he went to the emperor. Thirlby remained as the resident ambassador, while Hoby assumed a similar role with the regent in the Low Countries, receiving an audience on 18 May. He remained until 1 September, when he was recalled by Mary I. Hoby's sojourn in the Low Countries allowed him to avoid more direct involvement in the attempt to alter the succession, although he continued to comply with orders from the privy council after being informed of Edward's death. The source of Professor A. F. Pollard's speculation about whether Lord Guildford Dudley would receive the crown matrimonial or not is a letter from Hoby and Sir Richard Morison to the privy council of 15 July in which they informed them that rumours to that effect were current in the Low Countries. Although he supported Mary's marriage to Philip of Spain and was named capital burgess of Leominster on 28 March 1554, Hoby's importance diminished sharply, especially in the paranoid atmosphere in the wake of the rebellion of Sir Thomas Wyatt the younger.

Simon Renard, the imperial ambassador, identified Hoby as one of the craftiest heretics in England but no other indictment is known. Philip and Thomas Hoby nevertheless felt it prudent to go into exile, although the queen was willing to appoint the elder brother as resident ambassador to the regent in the Low Countries at the outset of his travels. Sir Philip Hoby's announced specific purpose for going abroad was to take the waters at Liège and Aix-la-Chapelle in order to try to gain some relief from recurrent illness. He visited the regent in July 1554, and then continued on to Italy. There he consorted with various exiles, some of whose activities were actually treasonous. In fact, Renard voiced the suspicion that Hoby was abroad only to plot against the regime with various dissidents. Both Hobys are noted as spending considerable time with Sir John Cheke at Padua in 1555. It may also be at this time that Hoby began a friendship with the artists Titian and Pietro Aretino.

The Hobys made their way back to England in January 1556, but not before securing assurances of safety from Philip in the Low Countries. Philip pursued a policy of currying favour with important Englishmen whose future usefulness might prove valuable. Sir Philip Hoby's next two years at Bisham were ones of declining health, culminating in his death at his London home in Blackfriars on 9 May 1558, aged fifty-three. His will was written on 1 May and proved on 2 July. In it, his ties to Sir William Cecil, Sir John Mason, and Sir Henry Paget are clear. The bulk of his property went to his half-brother. His body was later moved to Bisham, where a magnificent monument is still to be found, the inscription on which gives his date of death as 31 May. GARY M. BELL

Sources APC, 1542–54 · B. L. Beer, Northumberland: the political career of John Dudley, earl of Warwick and duke of Northumberland (Kent, Ohio, 1973) · BL, Add. MSS 5498, 5828, 5935, 46367, 48123, 48126 · BL, Cotton MSS Caligula B.xii; Galba B.xii; Titus B.ii; Titus B.v · BL, Harley MSS 284, 295, 353, 523 · M. L. Bush, The government policy of Protector Somerset (1976) · CPR, 1547–8; 1550–58 · CSP dom., 1547–58 · CSP for., 1547–58 · CSP Spain, 1547–8 · CSP Venice, 1555–6 · The acts and monuments of John Foxe, ed. S. R. Cattley, 8 vols. (1837–41) · C. H. Garrett, The Marian exiles: a study in the origins of Elizabethan puritanism (1938) · HoP, Commons, 1509–58, 2.366–8 · D. E. Hoak, The king's council in the reign of Edward VI (1976) · W. K. Jordan, Edward VI, 1: The young king (1968) · W. K. Jordan, Edward VI, 2: The threshold of power (1970) · LP Henry VIII, vols. 7–10, 12–17, 20 · J. K. McConica, English humanists and Reformation politics under Henry VIII and Edward VI (1965) · A. J. A. Malkiewicz, 'An eye-witness's account of the coup d'état of October 1549', EngHR, 70 (1955), 600–09 · DNB · will, PRO, PROB 11/40, sig. 34 · PRO, SP 68 · VCH Berkshire · private information (2004)

Archives BL, Add. MS 5498 | BL, Harley MSS, corresp. with council, esp. Somerset and Cobham · BL, Cotton MSS, corresp. with Somerset and council, etc. · NL Scot., corresp. with Richard Scudamore

Likenesses H. Holbein the younger, chalk drawing, c.1538, Royal Collection · H. Holbein the younger, portrait, Royal Collection [see illus.] · alabaster tomb effigy, All Saints' Church, Bisham, Berkshire; see illus. in Hoby, Sir Thomas (1530–1566)

Wealth at death see will, PRO, PROB 11/40, sig. 34; PRO, C 142/115/74; both cited in HoP, Commons

Hoby, Sir Thomas (1530–1566), courtier and translator, was born at Leominster, Herefordshire, the second son of William Hoby, of Radnor, and his second wife, Katherine, daughter of John Forden. He matriculated pensioner from St John's College, Cambridge, on 20 May 1545 and studied for the next two years under John Cheke. In August 1547 he left without taking a degree, spending almost a year in Strasbourg as a guest of Martin Bucer, studying classics and theology. His first translation was The Gratulation of M. Martin Bucer unto the Church of England (1549). After returning to Britain he was introduced at court at Christmas 1550. The following May he went to France in the train of William Parr, marquess of Northampton, who invested the French king with the Order of the Garter. A convinced protestant, Hoby remained overseas for much of Queen Mary's reign. His 'Travels and Life' (1551–64) shows him to be an interested and perceptive participant in aristocratic life abroad. Out of that experience came his translation of Castiglione's Il cortegiano, done in Paris in 1552–3 and published in 1561. Besides setting the standards of social behaviour for the English cultivated public, The Courtier left a profound mark on Elizabethan literary and stylistic practice, and Hoby's elegantly sober style was to influence Royal Society prose.

On the death of his half-brother, Sir Philip *Hoby, in May 1558 Hoby inherited Bisham Abbey, Berkshire, and on 27 June married Elizabeth (1528–1609) [see Russell, Elizabeth], daughter of Sir Anthony *Cooke (1505/6–1576). They took up residence at Bisham on 8 July 1559, and spent the next six years extending the buildings. His first son, Edward *Hoby, was born on 20 March 1560, and on 27 May 1562, 'was my wief delivered of a wenche (Elizabeth)' ('Travels', 129). Their second daughter, Anne, was born on 16 November 1564. Both girls died in February 1571. Hoby was knighted at Greenwich on 9 March 1566, and was appointed ambassador to France at the end of the month. When he landed at Calais on 9 April, a soldier at the town

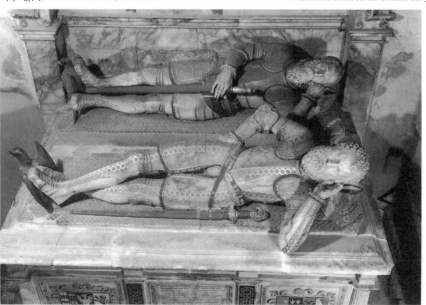

Sir Thomas Hoby (1530–1566), attrib. Cornelius Cure, in or after 1566 [the tomb of Sir Philip Hoby and Sir Thomas Hoby (foreground)]

gate put two shots through the English flag. Hoby demanded an apology, which was grudgingly given, but he was not permitted to inspect the fortifications built after the French had recaptured the town in 1558. He died in Paris on 13 July 1566, and was buried on 2 September in Bisham parish church, where a monument was erected to his memory. His second son, Thomas Posthumous Hoby, was born after his death.   L. G. KELLY

Sources B. Castiglione, *The book of the courtier*, ed. V. Cox, trans. T. Hoby, new edn (1994) · T. Hoby, 'The travels and life of Sir Thomas Hoby', ed. E. Powell, *Camden miscellany, X*, CS, 3rd ser., 4 (1902) · P. J. Begent, *The heraldry of the Hoby memorials in the parish church of All Saints, Bisham* (privately printed, 1980) · W. Raleigh, introduction, in B. Castiglione, *The book of the courtier*, trans. T. Hoby (1561); repr. (1900) · J. Burke and J. B. Burke, *A genealogical and heraldic history of the extinct and dormant baronetcies of England, Ireland and Scotland*, 2nd edn (1841); repr. (1844), 265–6 · Venn, *Alum. Cant.* · L. G. Kelly, *The true interpreter: a history of translation theory and practice in the West* (1979)
Archives BL, travel journals and memoirs, Egerton MS 2148 · Staffs. RO, instructions as ambassador to France
Likenesses attrib. C. Cure, alabaster sculpture, in or after 1566, All Saints' Church, Bisham, Berkshire [*see illus.*]
Wealth at death Bisham Abbey £61 19s. 8d., London house(?); legacies £2500 in toto?: will, Hoby, 'Travels and life'

Hocart, Arthur Maurice (1883–1939), anthropologist and archaeologist, was born at Etterbeck, near Brussels, on 26 April 1883, son of James Hocart (1843–1923), Unitarian minister, and his wife, Mary Doulton. He had his early education at the Athénée d'Ixelles, Brussels, and Elizabeth College, Guernsey. His paternal ancestors, originally French, had lived on Guernsey for many generations. At Elizabeth College Hocart showed early signs of his gift for languages. He won prizes for Greek, Latin, French, and German. An open classical scholarship took him to Exeter College, Oxford, in 1902. He received second classes in both classical moderations (1904) and *literae humaniores* (1906).

In Hocart's student days new fields of study, like psychology and anthropology, were just beginning to gain academic recognition. There were classicists at Exeter (L. R. Farnell, R. R. Marett) who had extended their interests into anthropology. Hocart's own transition, however, took place more indirectly. He had read psychology as an optional special subject. His teacher, William McDougall, had a small but enthusiastic group of students. Three of them (Cyril Burt, J. C. Flugel, May Smith) went on to become professional psychologists. Initially Hocart too headed in the same direction. Soon after graduation he proceeded to Berlin University, where he followed courses in philosophy and psychology and did research at the psychological institute. The turning point came in 1908 when he joined McDougall's polymathic teacher, W. H. R. Rivers, on an expedition to Melanesia. With Rivers's guidance and collaboration Hocart learned anthropology in the field, mainly on Eddystone Island (Simbo) in the western Solomons. In Pat Barker's historical novel, *The Ghost Road* (1995), there are flashbacks to their field experiences.

Having served his apprenticeship, Hocart began his own research in Fiji in 1909. The opportunity to do so was provided by the governor of Fiji, Everard im Thurn, an enthusiast for anthropology, who appointed him headmaster of a newly opened school. As headmaster Hocart was in touch with Fijians of varying age and rank. Among them was his assistant master and a future public figure, J. L. V. Sukuna.

The headmastership was followed by a senior studentship from Exeter College (1912–14), which helped Hocart to travel widely in the Fijian archipelago and in neighbouring groups of islands (Rotuma, Samoa, Tonga, Wallis Island). His method of operation was the one advocated by Rivers: rapid surveys of larger areas combined with intensive studies of smaller communities. The results of these explorations were recorded in some 6000 pages of field notes and 400 photographs. With that baggage he returned to England in the first half of 1914.

There was a good deal of work ahead of him. In addition to the analysis of his own materials, there was a projected joint sequel to Rivers's *History of Melanesian Society* (1914). Neither project could proceed smoothly, however, because of the outbreak of war in August 1914. In the first year of the war Hocart did some temporary teaching at Oxford. He deputized for McDougall in psychology, and also gave courses in anthropology. But by the second year he was in France with the Oxfordshire and Buckinghamshire light infantry. He reached the rank of captain and was mentioned in dispatches.

In post-war England careers in anthropology were almost as scarce as before. Hocart had to settle for one in archaeology, not at home but overseas. The position of archaeological commissioner of Ceylon (now Sri Lanka) was offered to him by the Colonial Office through A. A. Macdonell, professor of Sanskrit and keeper of the Indian Institute at Oxford. Hocart's training for the position began under Macdonell's own supervision; it was continued with the ancient monuments branch of the office of works, and concluded with the Indian archaeological survey. Hocart took charge of his department in Ceylon in January 1921.

The department, begun in 1890, had been in abeyance since the sudden death of the previous commissioner in 1914. The new commissioner, therefore, had to reorganize it, and much of his time and energy went into urgent tasks of conservation. Ancient monuments in Ceylon were not relics of a forgotten past but part of a continuing tradition. Hence Hocart was able to combine his interests in archaeology and anthropology. In these years he compiled a monograph on a historic Buddhist temple (*The Temple of the Tooth in Kandy*, 1931), his first book on Fiji (*Lau Islands*, 1929), and his first comparative treatise (*Kingship*, 1927). On the more strictly archaeological front he worked towards a chronology of Ceylonese material culture. To that end he did three seasons' digging at the ancient port site of Mantai. This work, however, was brought to an abrupt end in late 1928 by illness, which compelled him to retire prematurely a year later. The presence of his gifted local assistant, Senarat Paranavitana, allowed the department a degree of continuity and helped to avert the sort of disruption that had occurred in 1914.

Back in England, Hocart married Elizabeth Graham Hearn (1884–1947), daughter of Charles Henry Hearn and his wife, Florence Maria Perry, of Surrey, on 6 October 1930. They set up house in London. While residing there Hocart took a closer interest in the affairs of the Royal Anthropological Institute (of which he had been a fellow since 1909) as its librarian from 1930 to 1932, and as a member of its council from 1932 to 1934. The institute, in turn, awarded him the Rivers memorial medal in 1935 for his fieldwork in Melanesia, Polynesia, and Ceylon.

In an era of increasing specialization, the institute still aspired to the old ideal of the unity of anthropology. Hocart shared this aspiration and expressed it in his introductory text *The Progress of Man* (1933). His personal contacts and sympathies, too, were largely with those in interdisciplinary research. As an honorary lecturer in ethnology at University College, London, he was in contact with Grafton Elliot Smith, W. J. Perry, and their associates. He supported the efforts of S. H. Hooke (of King's College, London) to build bridges between anthropology, archaeology, and biblical studies. It was also in these years that he developed his friendship with fellow council member of the anthropological institute Lord Raglan. Out of the new generation of social anthropologists trained at the London School of Economics, E. E. Evans-Pritchard was more appreciative of Hocart's wide-ranging interests than were others. It was Evans-Pritchard who recommended Hocart for the chair of sociology which he had vacated at the Fuad I University of Cairo. Hocart and his wife moved to Cairo in the latter half of 1934.

In Egypt, as previously in Ceylon, Hocart pursued a combined interest in the past and the present. His findings were summarized in a chapter in the collective volume *The Legacy of Egypt* (1942). References to Egypt also became more numerous in his comparative studies: *Kings and Councillors* (1936) and *Les castes* (1938), which resumed explorations begun in *Kingship*. The central theme in this comparative trilogy was kingship. With its ubiquitous presence in the pre-modern world, kingship, Hocart believed, held vital clues for understanding a surprising variety of human beliefs and practices. A parallel trilogy on Fiji was also in preparation: following his earlier publication on eastern Fiji (*Lau Islands*), he drafted new volumes on northern and central parts. This project was advanced but incomplete at the time of his death. Following a brief illness, contracted on a tour of the Fayum, Hocart died at the Anglo-American Hospital, Cairo, on 9 March 1939. His remains were buried in the British military cemetery at Cairo.

Hocart's widow, who died in 1947 (there were no children), bequeathed funds to the Royal Anthropological Institute for the publication of her husband's manuscript on northern Fiji and also for an essay prize in his name, which was established the following year. The unfinished book was edited by Hocart's literary executor, Raglan, who brought out other of his works as well: the English original of *Caste* (1950), *The Life-Giving Myth and other Essays* (1952), and *Social Origins* (1954). Following Raglan's death in 1964, the task of introducing Hocart to a new generation of students was taken over by Rodney Needham, who compiled *A Bibliography of A. M. Hocart* (1967); reissued *Kings and Councillors*, and *The Life-Giving Myth* (both in 1970); and edited a new selection of essays, *Imagination and Proof* (1987).

Given that Hocart wrote on a wide range of subjects, it is not unusual for readers of some parts of his *œuvre* to know little about its other parts. Likewise, those who knew him personally in some contexts did not always know much about him in others. In England, where he never secured gainful employment, Hocart was generally seen as shy and retiring. In varying capacities elsewhere (as a headmaster in Fiji, head of a government department in Ceylon, professor in Egypt, fieldworker in all three places), he appeared more outgoing. The pains he took to learn the languages of all three places showed a sustained openness to other cultures—an openness that was unusual even for an anthropologist.   KITSIRI MALALGODA

Sources A. M. Hocart, 'Curriculum vitae', *c*.1938, NL NZ, Turnbull L., MS papers 60 · R. Needham, 'Introduction', in A. M. Hocart, *Kings and councillors* (1970) · K. Malalgoda, *A. M. Hocart: anthropologist and archaeologist* [forthcoming] · *The Times* (13 March 1939) · *The Times* (17 June 1939) · m. cert.
Archives NL NZ, Turnbull L., papers, MS 60
Likenesses P. Jenkins, photograph, 1930, Tunbridge Wells, Kent; repro. in Hocart, *Kings and councillors*, frontispiece · N. Labouchère, sketch, 1939, repro. in A. M. Hocart, *Imagination and proof*, ed. R. Needham (1987), frontispiece · photograph, NL NZ, Turnbull L.
Wealth at death £9950: *The Times* (17 June 1939)

Hoccleve [Occleve], **Thomas** (*c*.1367–1426), poet and clerk, may have derived his name from Hockliffe, Bedfordshire, but nothing is known of his family. The date of his birth can be inferred from his *Dialogue with a Friend* (*c*.1420), where he speaks of himself as then aged 'fifty wyntir and three' (Hoccleve, *Dialogue*, 1.246). Hoccleve's early years are unrecorded, but his education evidently included instruction in French and Latin, then the official languages used at the privy seal. He joined that office at the age of about twenty, probably at Easter 1387, since he says in the *Regiment of Princes* (*c*.1411) that he has been writing for the seal 'xxti year and iiij, come Estren' ('for twenty-four years, come Easter'; Hoccleve, *Regiment*, 11.804–5). His career there continued until shortly before his death, for some thirty-eight years. He started as an under-clerk: in a will of 1392 Guy Rouclif left 5 marks and a 'book called the War of Troy' to Thomas Hoccleve 'my clerk'. Later he became one of the five or six senior clerks of the office, and his career there can be traced in a long series of chancery and exchequer records of grants and payments. On 12 November 1399 the new king, Henry IV, granted him an annuity of £10 for life, a grant raised to 20 marks (£13 6*s.* 8*d.*) in 1409; and half-yearly payments continued until the last on 11 February 1426. He also enjoyed other benefits, among them board and lodging in the privy seal hostel,

Th'errour which sones of iniquitee

Thomas Hoccleve (*c*.1367–1426), workshop of Hermann Scheerre, *c*.1412 [kneeling, right]

money for robes at Christmas, two corrodies, and occasional bonuses, as well as fees and favours from privy seal clients. Towards the end of his career he compiled a volume of more than a thousand model privy seal documents, in French and Latin, for the benefit of other clerks. This formulary is now BL, Add. MS 24062.

Further information about Hoccleve's life is to be found in his poems, which contain an unusual amount of autobiographical material. *La male regle de T. Hoccleve* (1405–6) describes his early years in London and Westminster as a period of youthful dissipation, of eating and drinking to excess and staying up too late. It must have been during this period, however, that he made the acquaintance of Geoffrey Chaucer (*d.* 1400), whom he celebrates in the *Regiment of Princes* as his master in the art of English poetry, and whose portrait he caused to be preserved there. Hoccleve's earliest datable poem is the *Letter of Cupid* (1402), a rendering into very Chaucerian rhyme-royal stanzas of a poem by the French poetess Christine de Pisan, then fashionable at the court of Henry IV. This *Letter* and the *Male regle* are chief among his poems surviving from before the *Regiment*. Other short petitionary pieces throw light on his financial difficulties, complaining, as he commonly does, of 'coynes scarsetee'. It was at some

time during this period that he abandoned thought of taking holy orders and married a wife, as he says, 'only for love' (Hoccleve, *Regiment*, 1.1561); he was married by 1410.

The Regiment of Princes, addressed to the future Henry V, was by far the most successful of Hoccleve's writings. It survives in no fewer than forty-three manuscripts. In a long prologue, the poet describes how, after a sleepless night in his privy seal hostel 'at Chestre Ynne, right fast be the Stronde' (Hoccleve, *Regiment*, 1.5), he walks out in the fields and meets an old beadsman, from whom he receives words of consolation for his worries about poverty and advancing age. The old man advises that he should seek the good lordship of Prince Henry by addressing a poem to him. The second half of the *Regiment* accordingly offers the prince advice on the virtues necessary in a good ruler, drawing on such sources as the *De regimine principum* of Giles of Rome and the pseudo-Aristotelian *Secreta secretorum*. An early copy of the *Regiment* made for John Mowbray (BL, Arundel MS 38) preserves a picture, probably from the workshop of Hermann Scheerre, which shows the poet as a somewhat idealized 45-year-old in the act of presenting his book to Henry. Once Henry became king in 1413, Hoccleve continued to write for and about him, celebrating public occasions such as a gathering of the Garter knights and the king's triumphal return from France in 1421. He lays stress upon Henry's role as champion of religious orthodoxy against Lollard heretics, notably in a poem addressing the Lollard insurrection under Sir John Oldcastle in January 1414. The poet had no time for:

> Th'errour which sones of iniquitee
> Han sowe ageyn the feith.
> (*Works: Minor Poems*, 40)

Hoccleve's major work during the reign of Henry V, however, was a sequence of linked poems now known as the Series. This consists of a *Complaint* and *Dialogue with a Friend*, which together form a prologue to two stories translated from the *Gesta Romanorum* and a piece on the art of dying from the *Horologium sapientiae* of Heinrich Suso. The *Complaint* and *Dialogue* were written, for the most part, in 1420. In them the poet recalls an earlier 'wylde infirmitee' when he temporarily lost his 'wit' and 'memorie' (Hoccleve, *Complaint*, 11.40ff.). He recovered from this illness, he says, 'five years ago last All Saints', that is, on 1 November 1414 (ibid., 11.55–6); but people have continued ever since to doubt his mental stability. This suspicion is shared even by the poet's friend, who advises him in the ensuing *Dialogue* against risking his precarious health by undertaking further literary labours; but by the end of the *Dialogue*, having convinced the friend of his full recovery, Hoccleve stands ready to embark on the first of the *Gesta* stories. The Series claims a part in the poet's personal rehabilitation after his illness; but it also addresses itself, like much of Hoccleve's verse, to a great man from whom patronage may be expected—in this case, Humphrey, duke of Gloucester, whose praises are sung in the *Dialogue*. Of the six surviving manuscripts, one was written by Hoccleve himself (Durham University Library, Cosin MS V.iii.9); but this copy is directed in a final stanza, not to Humphrey, but to Humphrey's aunt, Joan Neville, countess of Westmorland.

Hoccleve's annuity was confirmed under the new king, Henry VI, on 24 January 1423, and the poet continued to work in the privy seal, probably until some time in 1425. None of his datable poems can be assigned to these last years; but it was during this period that he produced not only his formulary, but also the three holograph manuscripts which between them contain all his surviving poetic output apart from the *Regiment*. These are the Durham Series and two manuscripts now in the Huntington Library, California (MSS HM 111 and HM 744). On 4 March 1426 the exchequer issue rolls recorded the last of a series of payments to Hoccleve reimbursing him for red wax and ink bought earlier for office use; but he died soon after. On 8 May 1426 his corrody in Southwick Priory was granted to Alice Penfold to be held 'in manner and form like Thomas Hoccleve now deceased' (Brown, 270 n.1).

J. A. Burrow

Sources exchequer, exchequer of receipt, issue rolls, PRO, E403 · patent rolls, PRO, C 66 · *Hoccleve's works*, ed. F. J. Furnivall, 3: *The regement of princes*, EETS, extra ser. 72 (1897) · *Hoccleve's works: the minor poems*, ed. F. J. Furnivall and I. Gollancz, rev edn, rev. J. Mitchell and A. I. Doyle, EETS, extra ser., 61, 73 (1970) · J. A. Burrow, *Thomas Hoccleve* (1994) · A. L. Brown, 'The privy seal clerks in the early fifteenth century', *The study of medieval records: essays in honour of Kathleen Major*, ed. D. A. Bullough and R. L. Storey (1971), 260–81
Archives BL, Arundel MS 38 · BL, Add. MS 24062 · Bodl. Oxf., poems and treatises · Hunt. L., MSS HM 111, HM 744 · U. Durham L., Cosin MS V.iii.9
Likenesses workshop of H. Scheerre, manuscript illumination, *c*.1412, BL, Arundel MS 38, fol. 37r [*see illus.*]

Hochepied, de. For this title name *see* Larpent, Sir George Gerard, first baronet, and Baron de Hochepied in the Hungarian nobility (1786–1855).

Hock, Susanne. *See* Jeans, Susanne, Lady Jeans (1911–1993).

Hocking, Joseph (1860–1937). *See under* Hocking, Silas Kitto (1850–1935).

Hocking, Silas Kitto (1850–1935), novelist and United Methodist minister, was born at St Stephen in Brannel, Cornwall, on 24 March 1850. He was the third son of James Hocking, part owner of a tin mine, and his wife, Elizabeth Kitto, who was related to John Kitto, author of *The Pictorial Bible*, and who came of one of the oldest Cornish families. Educated at local grammar schools and later privately, he initially intended to be a mine surveyor. In 1869, however, he was accepted as a candidate for the ministry of the United Methodist Free Church, and was ordained in 1870. He held pastorates at Pontypool, Spalding, Liverpool, and Manchester. In Liverpool in 1876 he married Esther Mary (*d.* 1940), daughter of Richard Lloyd; he had with her one son and two daughters. It was there also that he wrote his first novel, *Alec Green* (1878), but he achieved fame with his second book, *Her Benny*, a story of street children in Liverpool, the copyright of which he sold for £20. This 'street arab' tale sold over a million copies, and was translated into many languages. In 1879 he was made a fellow of the Royal Historical Society. In 1883 he went to Duke Street, Southport, where during the next thirteen years he preached to crowded congregations. In 1884 he went on a lecture tour of Canada in association with the British Association of Methodist Churches.

Hocking resigned from the ministry in 1896 in order to devote himself to writing, Liberal politics (he unsuccessfully contested the Aylesbury division of Buckinghamshire in 1906 and Coventry in January 1910), lecturing, and journalism. In all he wrote fifty books, including his reminiscences, *My Book of Memory* (1923), and at one time was said to be the best-selling English novelist. Some of his best books are for children, and most have a didactic slant. Among his most popular works were: *For Light and Liberty* (1890); *Where Duty Lies* (1891); *A Son of Reuben* (1894); and *For such is Life* (1896). In 1894 he became editor of the *Family Circle*, and two years later established, with Frederick Anthony Atkins, the *Temple Magazine*, a sixpenny illustrated monthly journal for Sunday reading. Hocking died at Heatherlow, Avenue Road, Highgate, Middlesex, on 15 September 1935. His wife survived him.

His brother **Joseph Hocking** (1860–1937), novelist and Methodist minister, the youngest son of James Hocking, and his wife, Elizabeth Kitto, was born at St Stephen in Brannel, Cornwall, on 7 November 1860. He was first educated privately and later at Crescent Range Theological College, Manchester, where he was first in his year, winning the Cuthbertson prize, and at Owens College, Manchester. He was an avid reader of Scott and the classics. At the age of thirteen he wrote his first novel, which, he said, 'was not a success'. At sixteen he began to study land surveying, but after four years entered the ministry of the United Methodist Free Church, and was ordained in 1884. In 1887 he travelled extensively in the Middle East, and on his return became minister of Woodford Green Union Church in Essex. In 1887 he married Annie, eldest daughter of Joseph Brown JP FCS. They had a son who was killed on active service in 1918, and four daughters.

Jabez Easterbrook, the first of Hocking's fifty-three published books, appeared in 1891. It was about the encounter of a young Wesleyan minister with a woman who was an agnostic. It displayed his regard for fiction as an effective medium for conveying religious ideas to a popular public, and his works generally have a very strong theological bias. Some of his novels appeared serially in the *British Weekly* and other journals. They describe the middle-class life of the day and dramatize the conflicts of Catholics and protestants. Some, like *The Romance of Michael Trevail* (1909) and *Felicity Trevenbyn*, draw on the Cornwall of his childhood; his theological training is evident in *The Trampled Cross* (1907) and *The Jesuit* (1911), while *The Woman of Babylon* (1906) is influenced by his travels in the Holy Land. He resigned from the ministry in 1910. Joseph Hocking died at Perranporth, Cornwall, on 4 March 1937.

R. G. Burnett, rev. Sayoni Basu

Sources *The Times* (16 Sept 1935) · S. Hocking, *My book of memory* (1923) · *Men and women of the time* (1899) · E. Picasso, 'Hocking, Silas K.', *The 1890s: an encyclopedia of British literature, art, and culture*, ed. G. A. Cevasco (1993), 278–9 · *Methodist Recorder* (19 Sept 1935) · *Tit-Bits* (5 Jan 1909) · E. Picasso, 'Hocking, Joseph', *The 1890s: an encyclopedia of British literature, art, and culture*, ed. G. A. Cevasco (1993) · *The Times* (5 March 1937)

Archives U. Warwick Mod. RC, papers and sermons
Likenesses O. Edis, print, NPG · J. Russell & Sons, photograph, NPG · Spy [L. Ward], caricature, chromolithograph, repro. in *VF* (14 Nov 1906) · W. & C. Yates, stipple (after photograph by Allen & Co.), NPG

Hodder, James (*fl.* 1659–1673), arithmetician, also taught writing, shorthand, and accounting at his school 'next dore to the Sunne' in Tokenhouse Yard, Lothbury, City of London. He is first known as author of *The Penman's Recreation*, published about 1660 (2nd edn, 1673), which has a preface by him dated 1659. It was 'invented and written' by Hodder, and the thirty plates, each bearing his name, were 'engraven' by Edward Cocker. The dedication is to Sir Walter Earle.

In 1661 Hodder issued his more successful work, *Arithmetick, or, That Necessary Art Made most Easie*. The publisher was Thomas Rooks, who published for Cocker also, and it seems likely that the two teachers were friends. In the ninth edition (1671) Rooks inserted a preface, saying 'in this bad time of trade in Books, in less than ten months, I sold of them 1550'. After the tenth edition, of 1672, the next known is the twelfth (1678), edited by Henry Mose (or Moss), described as 'late servant and successor to' Hodder. A page of verse signed 'S. Hodder', presumably a close relation, heaps praise on Mose, concluding remarkably 'Posterity shall make Account, It owes to Hodder's Memory, but Much more, to Mose'. Mose's editions ended with the twenty-sixth, of 1720, followed by a final one edited by W. Hume (1739).

The *Arithmetick* has been described as 'the most general book of the kind ever published' (Granger, 377). Cocker's more famous *Arithmetick* (1678) was very similar; De Morgan suggested that if Hodder's work 'had given the new mode of division [without crossings-out], it must have stood in the place of Cocker' (De Morgan, 46).

The great fire of 1666 forced Hodder to move to Bromley by Bow, where he set up a boarding-school. While there, in 1668, he published *Hodder's Decimal Arithmetick*, with a third and final edition in 1672. In 1671 he was able to return to Lothbury, apparently to the same address, and was still there in 1673. S. Hodder's verse demonstrates that Hodder was dead by 1678. Another apprentice of his, besides Mose, might have been the penman and arithmetician Eleazar Wigan, whom Samuel Pepys described as 'pupil to Mr. Hodder' (Heal, 115).   RUTH WALLIS

Sources A. Heal, *The English writing-masters and their copy-books, 1570–1800* (1931) · A. De Morgan, *Arithmetical books from the invention of printing to the present time* (1847), 46 · J. Granger, *A biographical history of England, from Egbert the Great to the revolution*, 2 (1769), 377, 414
Likenesses R. Gaywood, engraving, 1659, BM; repro. in J. Hodder, *The Pen-mans recreation*, 2nd edn (1673), frontispiece · R. Gaywood, engraving, 1661, BM, NPG; repro. in J. Hodder, *Hodder's Arithmetick* (1661), frontispiece · F. H. Van Hove, engraving, repro. in J. Hodder, *Hodder's Arithmetick*, rev. H. Mose, 26th edn (1720), frontispiece

Hodder, Matthew Henry (1830?–1911), publisher, was baptized on 5 January 1831 at Providence Independent Chapel, Uxbridge, Middlesex, the fourth among the ten children of Thomas Henry Hodder (*b.* 1803), a chemist and druggist, and Jane Elizabeth Rayner (*bap.* 1809). His

younger brother, Edwin, became an author. Matthew Hodder's schooling was elementary, and on 5 August 1844 he arrived in London to be apprenticed to Jackson and Walford, publishers to the Congregational Union. At sixteen he experienced religious conversion at the King's Weigh House Chapel, and there he met his future wife, Frances Ann Biddulph (*bap.* 1830, *d.* 1917). Hodder married Frances on 5 July 1855 at Denmark Place Baptist Chapel, Camberwell, London. Before marriage he lived near Tower Hill and Frances lodged at Rotherhithe. Their only child, Mary Frances, was born on 22 April 1856 at Camberwell, where the family lived until 1869.

In 1861 with savings of £6335 Hodder bought a third share in the Jackson and Walford business, which traded as Jackson, Walford, and Hodder until 1868. To buy out his ageing partners Hodder sought a congenial partner with funds. He found him in Thomas Wilberforce *Stoughton. Various occasions have been suggested for Hodder's acquaintance with Stoughton: both were in the orbit of the Congregationalist Dr Thomas Binney; both had fathers who had lived in Windsor; Jackson, Walford, and Hodder were publishers to Thomas's father, Dr John *Stoughton. Hodder and Stoughton established their publishing partnership on 16 June 1868 at 27 Paternoster Row, London. In June 1869 Hodder sailed to the USA and Canada, promoting his publishing business and speaking at religious meetings as delegate for the YMCA. According to his diary of this journey he never lost an opportunity to convert a soul to Christianity. He returned in September to a new house, Gothic Lodge, on Bromley Common, Kent. Hodder's frequent profitable journeys to North America, the last in 1899, kept the firm solvent; he also travelled the north of England and London. In 1871 G. A. Sala was awarded £500 damages in a libel action against the firm, based on its publication of a work by J. H. Friswell (1870).

Publishing was an aspect of Hodder's evangelism. He was a connoisseur of sermons, and this devotion resulted in many titles: Joseph Parker's *Ecce Deus* (1868), his series The City Temple Pulpit, and Paxton Hood's *Life of Dr Binney* (1874). In its second year the firm published J. J. van Oosterzee's *Theology of the New Testament* (1870), the first of several of his works translated from the Dutch. The scientific theology of Henry Drummond's *Natural Law in the Spiritual World* (1883) challenged traditional belief and was published only on commission. In 1887 the first of forty-eight volumes of *The Expositor's Bible* was published. Theology and devotional works dominated the list, and secular titles had to meet a strict evangelical morality. Hodder's salesmanship and his luck, as in his purchase of the text of William Thayer's *From Log Cabin to White House* (1881) just before the murder of President Garfield, supported publication of expensive theological works in English and Greek.

Hodder conducted a mission on Bromley Common, was chairman of the General Committee of the YMCA, and led its £160,000 building appeal. In maturity he had the appearance of a benevolent patriarch with a long white beard and soft voice. He was active in publishing until a few weeks before his death at Carisbrooke, his home on

Bromley Common, on 18 October 1911. After a funeral service at St Luke's Church, Bromley Common, he was buried in St Luke's cemetery on 21 October.

Sir (John) Ernest Hodder-Williams (1876–1927), publisher, was born on 16 September 1876 at Bromley, Kent, the eldest of seven children of John T. Williams (1844–1931) and Mary Frances (1856–1931), only child of Matthew Henry and Frances Hodder. His father, nephew of Sir George Williams, founder of the YMCA, came from Dorset. John Ernest was given the third baptismal name Hodder and was known as Ernest. Williams attended Quernmore School, Bromley, and from 1889 to 1891 the City of London School. He spent a year in Paris and Berlin and attended the English course at University College, London, for one year before joining Hodder and Stoughton in 1894 under the tutelage of W. R. Nicoll. In 1901 he toured North America and studied its book trade. On 4 October 1902 he was made a partner of Hodder and Stoughton, and on 9 October he married Ethel (1872–1918), publisher's reader and younger daughter of John George Oddy JP, in Holt United Free Methodist Church, Norfolk; Matthew Hodder and John Williams provided a special train to carry guests from London. They had no children.

In 1906 Ernest Williams negotiated a joint venture with Oxford University Press, and in 1908 the firm bought into George Doran Company, New York, designating Williams vice-chairman. He became a best-selling author with *Where's Master?* (1910), written on the death of Edward VII about the royal dog. After Hodder's death in 1911 Williams led the firm until the death in 1917 of the surviving founding partner, Thomas W. Stoughton, when he became senior partner. He was unfit to enlist in the 1914–18 war but was close to its political conduct. He wrote, edited, and published propaganda for the government and produced fund-raising books such as *Princess Mary's Gift Book* (1914) and *King Albert's Book* (1914). In 1915 Williams was made liveryman of the Stationers' Company and co-opted to the City of London corporation; in 1918 he was elected chairman of its county purposes committee.

Ethel Williams died of cancer on 15 June 1918, and Ernest sold their home at Bickley, Kent, where they had entertained wounded soldiers, and took a flat in town. On 6 June 1919 he adopted by deed poll the surname Hodder-Williams. That month he went to Paris for the signing of the peace treaty, and in December he registered the firm as a limited company, with Cecil Stoughton and Percy Hodder Williams as the other two directors. Under Hodder-Williams's direction the firm launched cheap fiction reprints known as 'Yellow Jackets' (price 2s.), entered a joint venture as University of London Press Ltd (1920), acquired Wakley & Son, publishers of *The Lancet* (1920), and joined with Liverpool University Press. He was chairman of the Royal Female Orphanage at Beddington, Surrey, and introduced reforms consistent with his support for female suffrage. On 4 August 1920 he married Lilian (d. 1959), daughter of John R. Pakeman, at St George's, Hanover Square, London. They had no children. Knighted in 1919, he received other British and European honours for his war efforts: he was appointed CVO (1921) and a knight of grace of the order of St John of Jerusalem (1921), was awarded the Médaille du roi (Albert I of Belgium) (1920), and was made ufficiale della corona d'Italia (1920) and commendatore (1921).

Hodder-Williams's leadership of the firm was enterprising though not unfailingly meticulous or successful; he took life intensely and sometimes suffered physically; his personality was magnetic, inspiring loyalty in family and employees. In January 1927 he suffered an internal haemorrhage and died of heart failure on 8 April 1927 at his home, 23 Cadogan Place, London SW1. On 12 April a City memorial service was held at Christ Church, Greyfriars, followed by the funeral at Westminster Chapel, Buckingham Gate, and burial in St Luke's cemetery, Bromley Common. His widow gave £1000 to St Thomas's Hospital to endow a bed.   DOROTHY WINDUS COLLIN

Sources J. Attenborough, *A living memory: Hodder and Stoughton publishers, 1868–1975* (1975) · notes, correspondence, cuttings, and photographs, GL, MS 16355/1–6 · S. Hine, 'Three crowded years: John Ernest Hodder-Williams, Kt., C. V. O., 1917–1920' (bound typescript), GL, MS 16367 · M. H. Hodder, diary, 1869–73, GL, MS 16364 · bound volume of receipts (1823) and advertisements, GL, MS 16262 [Henry Hodder] · J. Stoughton, *Recollections of a long life* (1894) · G. H. Doran, *Chronicles of Barabbas, 1884–1934* (1935) · T. H. Darlow, *William Robertson Nicoll: life and letters* (1925) · *WWW, 1916–28* [John Ernest Hodder-Williams] · J. H. Friswell, *Modern men of letters honestly criticised* (1870), 159–68
Archives GL, journal of visits to North America selling books
Likenesses photographs, repro. in Attenborough, *Living memory*
Wealth at death £43,408 0s. 3d.: probate, 6 Dec 1911, CGPLA Eng. & Wales · £280,291—J. E. Hodder-Williams: probate, 19 May 1927, CGPLA Eng. & Wales

Hoddesdon, Sir Christopher (1533/4–1611), merchant, was the second son of Simon Hoddesdon (c.1500–c.1560), a landowner of Edgware, Middlesex, and his second wife, Joan (c.1505–c.1560), the daughter of John Etheridge. The spur to his future career came in 1544, when, at the age of only ten, he 'came from Dantzic by land, through all the marine towns except Stade and Emden, and found no Englishman trading nor cloth to be sold but by the stillyard men' (namely the Hanse; *CSP dom., 1601–8*, 160). His most active years were spent developing English trade in north-eastern Europe, especially Russia.

Hoddesdon was apprenticed to Sir George Barne, a merchant and haberdasher, and in 1552 lord mayor of London. In 1553 Chancellor's curtailed China expedition revealed the trade potential in Muscovy. Interested merchants, Barne among them, began forming a new joint-stock enterprise, the Russia Company, and Hoddesdon entered its service, initially in London. Having joined Chancellor's second voyage to Russia, Hoddesdon was at Vologda in September 1555 and Yaroslavl in November, and afterwards in Moscow and Nizhniy Novgorod, where he struck good bargains. After a five-month spell in temporary charge of company affairs in Moscow he spent two further years at Nizhniy Novgorod, and finally headed the English factory at Moscow, where he was in September 1559. The Russia trade proved very profitable for the company: Hoddesdon claimed that in Moscow he obtained £13,644 for English goods which cost only £6608.

Eight years 'in Russeland' did not, however, make Hoddesdon's own fortune. Unsettled after the deaths of his patron Barne in 1558 and both his parents about 1560, he returned home in 'meane estate' in 1562. After raising capital from inherited land he set about establishing a 'good trade' of his own. In 1565 he sued his brother Nicholas (who plainly had not expected him to return from Muscovy) for further land in Edgware—early evidence of a lifelong taste for litigation. Although he was nominally a haberdasher, his merchant activities in fact ranged widely. By 1568 he was married to his master's granddaughter, Alice (c.1535–1602); she was the daughter of Alexander Carleill, the sister of Christopher Carleill, and the stepdaughter of Francis *Walsingham. Hoddesdon's new relatives included several important members of the Russia Company—'a useful background in an age of kinship and patronage' (Willan, 34).

Having been recalled by the company in 1567, Hoddesdon was posted to Narva to build English commerce in the Baltic; Queen Elizabeth wrote recommending him to the protection of the kings of Denmark and Sweden. Seven ships carried £11,000 worth of cloth, kerseys, and salt, on which he realized a 40 per cent profit. In 1568 Hoddesdon was accused of having traded on his own account at Narva instead of looking exclusively after the company's interest. He petitioned Leicester and Cecil, and, with his reputation intact, returned to Narva, where he remained for some years as chief of the English factory. In 1570 he asked the company to send out armed ships, which in July defeated six Polish privateers off Tüter in the Gulf of Finland. Hoddesdon himself wrote announcing this victory to Ivan IV.

Since he was rising in stature in the Company of Merchant Adventurers, Hoddesdon began to be employed by Elizabeth as a financial agent in Germany: in July 1575 he was to receive at Heidelberg 50,000 crowns due to the queen from Condé, and in June 1576 he was again in Germany, to raise a loan of £200,000. In 1577 he went to Hamburg with £20,000 for Duke John Casimir, to pay for cavalry destined for France and then the Low Countries. By 1578 he was master of the Merchant Adventurers at Hamburg, where he was free to trade for himself: in August 1579 he was licensed to bring saltpetre and gunpowder from Hamburg. He also had a venture in Frobisher's search for a north-west passage, and in 1580 he was one of the commissioners who assayed Frobisher's supposed gold ore. In the same year he invested in a voyage to Brazil. From 1580 to 1582, representing the Adventurers but also receiving some official allowance, he sent regular political intelligence from Emden and Antwerp to Walsingham and Leicester. Hoddesdon was now wealthy: he had a house in Bishopsgate, London, and in 1582 he acquired a country property, when he bought from the Barne family the manor of Leighton Buzzard in Bedfordshire. Like other new proprietors, he sought to improve his estates by enclosures. This and his stance on customary rights brought lengthy disputes with his tenants, but he had the respect of his peers, and in 1591–2 he served as sheriff of Bedfordshire. The suggestion in the *Dictionary of National Biography* that he was an alderman and MP for Cambridge in 1593 rests on a mistaken identity.

By 1600 Hoddesdon had become master of the Company of Merchant Adventurers. He staunchly defended their privileges—to the point of fearing he would 'bring his grey hairs untimely to the ground' (*CSP dom.*, 1601–8, 164)—against licences and monopolies granted to courtiers. This was his last position of note; he was knighted by James I at Whitehall on 23 July 1603, just before the coronation. In semi-retirement at Leighton Buzzard, he maintained interests in merchant affairs, and in 1605 became a charter member of the revived Spanish Company. He also occupied himself with further lawsuits (against debtors of his wife; against his late daughter's relatives by marriage; against a factor in Muscovy). He died at Leighton Buzzard on 8 February 1611; armigerous, he was buried there with full heraldic ceremony on 14 February. In the parish church is a crude tablet, perhaps a vault cover, to 'Sur Chritover Hodsin', and outside are two stone cists, now empty, said to be those of Hoddesdon and his first wife, Alice.

Hoddesdon's sole child, Ursula, born about 1572–3, married in 1588 Sir John Leigh of Stoneleigh, Warwickshire. She died about 1597. Their son, Sir Thomas Leigh, married Mary, the granddaughter of Lord Chancellor Ellesmere. Hoddesdon's first wife died in 1602, and about 1604 he married Elizabeth (d. 1638), the daughter of William Blount of Osbaston, Leicestershire, and the widow of Richard Saunders of Dinton, Buckinghamshire. She was his sole executor. In a letter of 1577, written on his departure for Hamburg, Hoddesdon commended a 'son', Francis, to Walsingham's care; this seemingly refers to a ward or apprentice, there being no other evidence of his having had any children besides Ursula. The suggestion in the *Dictionary of National Biography* of another son, Christopher, a Roman Catholic, is entirely undocumented.

JAMES HODSDON

Sources *CSP for.*, 1575–80 · *CSP dom.*, 1547–1611; addenda, 1580–1625 · *CSP col.*, vol. 2, 1577–80 · R. Hakluyt, *The principal navigations, voyages, traffiques and discoveries of the English nation*, 2nd edn, 3 vols. (1598–1600); repr. 12 vols., Hakluyt Society, extra ser., 1–12 (1903–5) · T. S. Willan, *The early history of the Russia Company, 1553–1603* (1956) · F. A. Blaydes, ed., *The visitations of Bedfordshire, annis Domini 1566, 1582, and 1634*, Harleian Society, 19 (1884), 175 · Magd. Cam., Pepys Library, Pepys MS 2503, fols. 745–7 · PRO, REQ2/219/57 · PRO, SP12/185/74 · PRO, STAC 5/H7/38 · PRO, PROB 11/117, fols. 133r–135 · BL, Add. MS 14417, fol. 42 · *DNB* · W. A. Shaw, *The knights of England*, 2 (1906); repr. (1971), 125 · *Camden miscellany, VI*, CS, 104 (1871) · *VCH Bedfordshire* · deeds, Bedfordshire County RO, DDKK 1–27 · BL, Cotton MSS, Galba, B. xi. 425; C. vii. 81, 86, 127, 142 · *APC*, 1578–80 · *The visitation of Buckinghamshire*

Wealth at death approx. £1500 bequests; properties in Bedfordshire and Warwickshire: will, PRO, PROB 11/117, fols. 133r–135

Hoddesdon, John (c.1632–1659), writer, was the second son of John Hoddesdon (bap. 1594) and Isabel Rymell, daughter of Anthony Rymell. Probably born in London, he was descended from Nicholas, elder brother of Sir Christopher Hoddesdon, merchant adventurer. His father died young and a lawyer great-uncle, Christopher Hoddesdon of the Inner Temple, befriended him and was the dedicatee of his first two books. Hoddesdon's first publication,

"Though, in this darker Shade, there somthing lyes,
Might bee the Loadstone of all learned eyes;
There's ne'r a leafe in which I cannot ſ
Th'Author in's more true Anatomie—
Yet All's too little: Hee is but made leſs
By th'Painters Pencil, or the Printers Preſs.

John Hoddesdon (c.1632–1659), attrib. John Fillian, pubd 1650

religious epigrams entitled *Sion and Parnassus* (1650), contains as frontispiece a lively engraved portrait, once keenly collected, of Hoddesdon aged eighteen, but is now mainly noteworthy for the young Dryden's prefatory verses commending the author. The future poet laureate here credited 'my friend' Hoddesdon with having 'inspired' in him some poetic proficiency. Dryden had then only recently left Westminster School for Cambridge, and it is reasonably inferred that Hoddesdon too had attended Westminster (his father had certainly been there, and at Oxford in 1612 had contributed to verses lamenting the death of Prince Henry). No later association between Hoddesdon and Dryden is known. Hoddesdon's own verse sits within a broadly puritan tradition but is infected by a relentless punning, even on sacred subjects, that grated on successive commentators. In 1652 he compiled a life of Thomas More. It was later compared unfavourably with other early lives—typically, Hoddesdon devotes a section to More's 'Wit and Wisdome'—and a previous owner has annotated the copy in the London Guildhall Library 'a ridiculous author'. His last literary endeavour, the rare *Holy Lives of God's Prophets* (1654), attracted little notice.

Hoddesdon turned to trade, becoming in 1658 the East India Company's third-ranking factor in Persia, with an annual salary of £30. He soon moved to the company's base at Surat, north of Bombay, and explored trading opportunities along the coast southwards to Ceylon. He died suddenly at Surat on 28 January 1659, leaving privately contracted debts of 62,775 mahmudis. A year later contention persisted between creditors in India and consignees of his goods in England. Letters of administration were granted to his elder brother, Christopher, on 28 March 1660. The 1662 reissue of Hoddesdon's life of More (essentially unaltered, though the dedicatee had died in 1660) was perhaps to help clear remaining debt. He was unmarried. JAMES HODSDON

Sources J. Hoddesdon, *Sion and Parnassus, or, Epigrams on severall texts of the Old and New Testament* (1650) · *The works of John Dryden*, ed. E. N. Hooker, H. T. Swedenberg, and V. A. Dearing, 20 vols. (1956–2000) · W. Foster, ed., *The English factories in India*, 10 (1921) · court minutes of the East India Company, BL OIOC · T. Corser, *Collectanea Anglo-poetica, or, A ... catalogue of a ... collection of early English poetry*, 8, Chetham Society, 102 (1878) · J. Granger, *A biographical history of England from Egbert the Great to the revolution*, 5th edn, 6 vols. (1824) · E. Phillips, *Theatrum poetarum, or, A compleat collection of the poets, especially the most eminent of all ages* (1675) · J. D. Hodson, one name study of the surname Hodsdon and variants, MS [priv. coll.] · W. B. Bannerman, ed., *The registers of St Helen's, Bishopsgate, London*, Harleian Society, register section, 31 (1904) · A. M. B. Bannerman, ed., *The register of St Matthew, Friday Street, London, 1538–1812, and the united parishes of St Matthew and St Peter Cheap*, Harleian Society, register section, 63 (1933)

Likenesses attrib. J. Fillian, line engraving (aged eighteen), BM, NPG; repro. in Hoddesdon, *Sion and Parnassus*, frontispiece [see illus.]

Wealth at death died in debt; value assumed negligible: East India Company records, 1659

Hodge, Arthur (d. 1811), planter in the West Indies and murderer, is of unknown parentage. About 1792 he inherited the Belle Vue estate in Tortola, one of the Virgin Islands then within the British colony of the Leeward Islands. He married Ann (d. c.1805), further details of whom are unknown. A prominent figure and a member of the island's council (with the title Honourable), he was also notoriously brutal to his slaves. In 1811, after quarrelling with another council member, he was accused of having murdered at least twelve of them four or five years earlier. Affidavits were sworn by a 'free woman of colour' (black people were not allowed to give evidence), Pereen Georges, who had worked in Hodge's household, and by one of his former overseers, Stephen McKeogh; these testified to the murders, mostly by floggings inflicted at Hodge's orders and including two women slaves, one of whom had had boiling water poured down her throat. Hodge was charged with murder and arrested.

The case aroused great public interest in the island. A Leeward Islands statute, the so-called Melioration Act of 1798, declared the killing of a slave to be murder, and one Tortola planter had already been tried for murdering a slave, but acquitted. It was believed that Hodge's enemies had brought the charges maliciously for personal reasons, particularly as they were all cases that had happened several years earlier and had not been brought up before. Governor Hugh Elliot, a former diplomat who had disgraced his diplomatic career in Europe and had been sent out to govern the Leeward Islands, constituted a special commission to hear the case promptly (the regular sessions being over) and hastened to Tortola himself for the trial. Hodge was charged with the murder of his slave Prosper by flogging. Eight more indictments were drawn up to charge him with other murders, should this charge fail, and the manacled skeleton of one of the victims was dug up to be used in evidence, if necessary. The case for the defence consisted chiefly of attempts to defame the two chief witnesses. The case began at 10 a.m. and went on until 8 a.m. the following morning, when, after an hour and a half of deliberation, the jury found Hodge guilty. Seven of the twelve jurors recommended him for mercy but he was sentenced to death.

During the week that followed Elliot, fearing public disturbance, declared martial law, called out the militia, and asked the captain of the naval ship that had brought him to Tortola to have sailors and marines ready to land and restore order if need be, since he feared that the members of the militia, composed of white men and 'free persons of colour', once they had arms in their hands, might be provoked by this controversial case to turn them against one another. Hodge was hanged on 8 May 1811 and buried the same day at Road Town, Tortola. There was no public disturbance, martial law was ended, and the militia disbanded. Hodge's execution, the first of its kind in the British West Indies, was a public warning to slave owners that murdering a slave could be a capital crime.

G. P. MORIARTY, rev. CHRISTOPHER FYFE

Sources DNB · Leeward Islands, 1811, vol. 1, PRO, CO/152/97 · A. M. Belisario, *The trial of Arthur Hodge* (1811) · *GM*, 1st ser., 81/2 (1811), 79 **Archives** PRO, CO/152/97, Leeward Islands, 1811, vol. 1

Hodge, John (1855–1937), trade unionist and politician, was born on 29 October 1855, at Linkeyburn, Muirkirk, Ayrshire, the son of William Hodge, a puddler at a local ironworks, and his wife, Marion (née Henderson). As a child Hodge moved to Motherwell and then to Glasgow. He was educated at the Motherwell ironworks school, and at Hutcheson's Boys' Grammar School in Glasgow. His early employment included periods as a solicitor's clerk and in a grocer's shop, but he finally settled down in the iron trade. After working at Coatbridge, he moved to the Colville works in Motherwell, as a third hand in the melting shop. In 1885 he married Mary Lambie (d. 1931); they had four daughters.

Hodge became a trade unionist as the result of a dispute at Colville's in 1885. This conflict led to the formation of the British Steel Smelters' Association in January 1886 with Hodge as secretary. From its initial base in Scotland the association expanded southwards and by 1888 was a TUC affiliate with twenty branches and 750 members. The Smelters rapidly became identified with industrial conciliation and collaboration. This style reflected Hodge's own values; his control over the union was often thorough.

Hodge's industrial achievements placed him in the second rank of trade union leaders, the dominant figure in a medium-sized organization but not a leader of the big battalions. His presidency of the Glasgow Trades Council led to him chairing the Glasgow TUC of 1892; he served on the TUC's parliamentary committee in 1892–3 and in 1895. Alongside his trade union career, however, he began to achieve some political prominence.

Hodge's roots were in Scottish radicalism and in the 1890s he was active in the Liberal Party. In 1891 he was a Glasgow city councillor. Following the shift of the Smelters' head office to Manchester in 1892, he was active in that city's Liberal organization and was a councillor from 1898 to 1901. Yet he was affected by the trade union debates about political independence, a position he endorsed for the trade union movement in his 1892 TUC Address. The Smelters became interested in financing a parliamentary candidate and were represented at the foundation conference of the Labour Representation Committee (LRC) in February 1900. Hodge was elected to the LRC's first executive; the Smelters were the first trade union to affiliate formally to the LRC.

The general election of 1900 saw fifteen LRC candidates. Hodge was sponsored by his union and contested the Gower constituency in south Wales. Many of the voters were miners; there were also tin-plate workers. In a straight fight, Hodge lost to the Liberal by 423 votes. In May 1903 Hodge fought a by-election in Preston with its strong tradition of working-class Conservatism, its employment dominated by 'King Cotton'. In a straight fight with a Conservative employer, he lost by just over 2000 votes. Eventually in the 1906 general election Hodge won Gorton, an industrial constituency to the east of Manchester. He enjoyed a straight fight with a Conservative and achieved a majority of over 4000. He was also successful, albeit with much smaller majorities, at the two elections of 1910.

With his election to the Commons, Hodge became a London-based labour leader, his union headquarters moving with him. In the pre-1914 Parliamentary Labour Party (PLP) Hodge was a solid contributor, speaking on his own industry and on broader questions of employment and welfare. But with the outbreak of war he became an exponent of the extreme patriotic tendency within the Labour Party, arguing for the suspension of traditional union practices and vehemently opposing strikes.

Hodge's patriotism initially strengthened his position in the PLP. In November 1914 he was elected vice-chairman and, when Arthur Henderson (1863–1935) joined the Asquith coalition in May 1915, Hodge became acting chairman. He also participated in initiatives to advance the claims of 'patriotic Labour'. In May 1915 he was active in the formation of the Socialist National Defence Committee. This was transformed into the British Workers' National League (later the British Workers' League or BWL) in the spring of 1916. Hodge became president, backed by other Labour trade union MPs. The league was nationalist, imperialist, and opposed to liberal economics; it became linked with Lord Milner's attempts to construct an instrument for his social imperialist agenda.

Hodge's political career reached its peak in December 1916 when, following the formation of the Lloyd George coalition, he became the first minister of labour. He was a second choice, the post having been turned down by the railwaymens' leader, Jimmy Thomas. Hodge brought to the post an uncomplicated distaste for industrial stoppages which earned him the plaudits of Conservatives, but his experience of the steel industry with its conciliatory traditions offered little guidance to the broader industrial field. Moreover, by 1917 there was a widening rift between some trade union officials and sections of industry where radical shop stewards' movements were powerful. In August 1917 Hodge was moved to the Ministry of Pensions where he devoted himself to publicity rather than to detailed administration.

Hodge's ultra-patriotism and immersion in the affairs of the Lloyd George coalition meant that he was increasingly isolated in a Labour Party which was responding to industrial pressures and to franchise reform with a more assertive independence. The position of the Labour ministers became more difficult, while from early 1918 a more hostile position was taken towards Labour members' participation in the British Workers' League. Hodge had problems with the Gorton Trades Council over his candidacy. A compromise was reached, but required Henderson's intervention and resulted in Hodge's resignation from the BWL.

Hodge's commitment to the Lloyd George government ended only in late November when his union's executive instructed him not to join a post-election coalition. He fought the 1918 election successfully as a straight Labour candidate opposed by an unofficial Conservative and by the shop stewards' leader, J. T. Murphy. He formally left the pensions ministry in January 1919. He won Gorton again in November 1922, but did not stand in December 1923. His post-war political involvement was limited; unlike some wartime ministers he remained with the Labour Party, but his influential years as a politician were over.

Hodge's main concern as a trade unionist had been to promote an amalgamation of unions in the steel trade, an ambition which for many years met with the resistance of other trade unions. However, the changed industrial environment of the First World War produced more favourable conditions for amalgamation. The scheme agreed in 1916 and implemented in 1917 was complex. All newly recruited members would join the British Iron Steel and Kindred Trades Association; all constituent unions would join the Iron and Steel Trades Confederation (ISTC). The latter body would affiliate to the TUC and carry out industrial functions. Political work would be carried out by the trade association which would continue the Smelters' affiliation to the Labour Party.

Hodge became president of the ISTC in 1917 with Arthur Pugh (1870–1955) as general secretary. The depression in the steel industry throughout the 1920s did not produce a change in the industry's industrial relations. Hodge's role became less central; he vainly attempted to persuade the ISTC executive committee not to participate in the 1926 general strike. He appealed to the union's industrial traditions, but was unable to overcome a feeling of loyalty to

the wider movement. This was perhaps deepened by the fact that Pugh was that year's TUC chairman. In 1931 Hodge had a vigorous disagreement with colleagues over the powers of the union executive. Not for the first time, he offered his resignation; but for the first time it was accepted immediately.

Hodge was a physically large, puritanical, and authoritarian figure with a reputation for tactlessness. His religious background was Scottish Presbyterian, which later transmuted into Wesleyanism. His career offers insights into two complex issues—trade union shifts from radical Liberalism to Labour and the impact of the First World War on the labour movement. He retired to Bexhill and died there at 50 Wilton Road on 10 August 1937, his wife having predeceased him.   DAVID HOWELL

Sources J. Hodge, *Workman's cottage to Windsor Castle* (1931) · D. Howell and J. Saville, 'Hodge, John', *DLB*, vol. 3 · A. Pugh, *Men of steel, by one of them: a chronicle of eighty-eight years of trade unionism in the British iron and steel industry* (1952) · R. Lowe, *Adjusting to democracy: the role of the ministry of labour in British politics, 1916–1939* (1986) · R. Douglas, 'The national democratic party and the British Workers' League', *HJ*, 15 (1972), 533–52 · J. O. Stubbs, 'Lord Milner and patriotic labour, 1914–18', *EngHR*, 87 (1972), 717–54 · F. Bealey and H. Pelling, *Labour and politics, 1900–1906: a history of the Labour Representation Committee* (1958) · H. A. Clegg, A. Fox, and A. F. Thompson, *A history of British trade unions since 1889*, 1 (1964) · A. S. T. Griffith-Boscawen, *Memories* (1925) · *The modernisation of conservative politics: the diaries and letters of William Bridgeman, 1904–1935*, ed. P. Williamson (1988) · P. F. Clarke, *Lancashire and the new liberalism* (1971) · d. cert. · *CGPLA Eng. & Wales* (1937)

Archives Labour History Archive and Study Centre, Manchester, papers | HLRO, corresp. with Lloyd George · U. Warwick Mod. RC, Trades Confederation MSS |FILM BFI NFTVA, propaganda footage (Hepworth Manufacturing Company)

Likenesses W. Stoneman, photograph, 1917, NPG

Wealth at death £3194 18s. 7d.: resworn probate, 25 Oct 1937, *CGPLA Eng. & Wales*

Hodge, Samuel (*c.*1840–1868). *See under* Gordon, William James (1864–1922).

Hodge, Sir William Vallance Douglas (1903–1975), mathematician, was born in Edinburgh on 17 June 1903, the younger son and second of three children of Archibald James Hodge, a searcher of property records, and his wife, Janet, daughter of William Vallance, proprietor of an Edinburgh confectionary business. He was educated from the age of six at George Watson's School, Edinburgh, proceeding in 1920 on a mathematical bursary to Edinburgh University where he graduated with first-class honours in mathematics in 1923. With a van Dunlop scholarship from Edinburgh and an exhibition from St John's College he then went to Cambridge and took part two of the mathematical tripos, as a wrangler with distinction, in 1925. He spent a further year in Cambridge supported by a Ferguson scholarship.

In 1926 Hodge went as an assistant lecturer to Bristol, where, with a helpful head of department in Professor H. R. Hasse and a stimulating and learned colleague in Peter Fraser, the next few years were very profitable. In 1929 he married Kathleen Anne, daughter of Robert Stevenson Cameron, publishing manager of the Edinburgh

Hodge's work extended to higher dimensions the basic relation between the topology and analysis of algebraic functions of one variable which had been established in the nineteenth century. The passage of time has served to justify Weyl's assessment, and the theory of harmonic integrals has continued to occupy a central place in mathematics.

During the Second World War the shortage of staff in Cambridge led to Hodge's taking on the additional post of steward (or bursar) of Pembroke. This further involvement in college affairs no doubt played its part in his appointment in 1958 as master of the college, a post he held until his simultaneous retirement from the Lowndean chair in 1970.

On the national scene Hodge was, for several decades, one of the dominating mathematical figures. He was one of the founders of the British Mathematical Colloquium and was chairman of the International Congress of Mathematicians in Edinburgh in 1958. He also played an important part in the International Mathematical Union, helping to revive it after the war. Elected FRS in 1938, Hodge was the Royal Society's physical secretary from 1957 to 1965 and was involved in the move from Burlington House to Carlton House Terrace. He was awarded the royal medal of the Royal Society in 1957 and the Copley medal in 1974. He was knighted in 1959.

Hodge's standing in mathematics is indicated by the many honours he received. He held honorary degrees from the universities of Bristol (1957), Edinburgh (1958), Leicester (1959), Sheffield (1960), Exeter (1961), Wales (1961), and Liverpool (1961). He was an honorary member of several foreign academies including the USA National Academy of Sciences, and was an honorary fellow of both St John's (1964) and Pembroke (1970) colleges in Cambridge.

Despite his high offices and honours Hodge was modest and unassuming. Genial in manner and temperament, endowed with sturdy Scottish common sense, he got on well with colleagues and students. He thrived on hard work and responsibility. Hodge died on 7 July 1975 in Cambridge.   M. F. ATIYAH, rev.

Sources M. F. Atiyah, *Memoirs FRS*, 22 (1976), 169–92 · personal knowledge (1986) · *The Times* (9 July 1975), 16g · *The Times* (2 Aug 1975), 14h · *CGPLA Eng. & Wales* (1975)
Likenesses Elliott & Fry, photograph, 1959, NPG [*see illus.*] · photographs, RS
Wealth at death £52,320: probate, 28 Sept 1975, *CGPLA Eng. & Wales*

Sir William Vallance Douglas Hodge (1903–1975), by Elliott & Fry, 1959

branch of the Oxford University Press. They had a son and a daughter.

By 1930 Hodge had taken the first steps in the direction which would rapidly establish his international reputation. In November of that year he was elected to a research fellowship at St John's College, and the following year he was awarded an 1851 Exhibition studentship. Supported in this way he was able to take up an invitation from Solomon Lefschetz, the foremost geometer and topologist of that time, to spend a year at Princeton University, accompanied by his wife. Hodge was already a firm follower of Lefschetz's mathematics and his stay at Princeton, under the influence of Lefschetz's dominant personality, propelled him further along his already chosen path. While in America Hodge also spent a couple of months at the Johns Hopkins University, Baltimore, where Oscar Zariski was the leading light in algebraic geometry.

Hodge returned to Cambridge in 1932 and was appointed to a university lectureship (1933) and fellowship (1935) at Pembroke College. In 1936, by a stroke of good fortune, H. F. Baker retired from the Lowndean chair of astronomy and geometry and Hodge, although only thirty-two, was elected as his successor.

Hodge's major achievement in mathematics was his development of the theory of harmonic integrals. This work, for which he was awarded the Adams prize in 1937, was published in definitive form in 1941. It was described by Hermann Weyl as 'one of the great landmarks in the history of science in the present century'. Essentially

Hodges, Charles Howard (1764–1837), portrait painter and mezzotint engraver, was born in London on 23 July 1764, the son of the miniature painter of the same name. He learned the rudiments of drawing from his father and at the age of fifteen he went to work in the studio of a family friend, the engraver, art dealer, and printseller William Humphrey. Hodges enrolled in the Royal Academy Schools as a student of etching and engraving in 1782. Later he worked in the studios of Sir Joshua Reynolds and John Raphael Smith. On 12 August 1784 Hodges married

Charles Howard Hodges (1764–1837), self-portrait

Margaret Harmar (1759–1819) at St George's Church, Hanover Square, London. They had three children, James Newman, Mary, and Emma Jane. James Newman later worked in his father's studio, but few prints by him are now known.

Hodges published his first mezzotint—a portrait of Lady Dashwood with a child, after Reynolds—in 1784. He rapidly gained renown for his skill in the mezzotint medium and was much in demand to make prints after portraits of important personages of the time by painters including Reynolds, George Romney, and John Hoppner. Among his pupils was Samuel William Reynolds (1773–1835), who served a seven-year apprenticeship with him.

After a business visit to the Netherlands with William Humphrey, Hodges decided to settle there and in 1792 moved his family to The Hague. In the Netherlands, Hodges worked initially as a mezzotint printmaker, although he also began to produce portraits in pastel. From about 1790 these pastel portraits were very successful, and he carried out numerous commissions for portraits from persons of standing at court and in the magistracy and the church. Hodges's family moved to Amsterdam in 1797 and eventually settled at 206 Prinsengracht, where the artist remained until his death.

Hodges also painted portraits in oil, receiving his first commissions from about 1800. His reputation in the Netherlands continued to grow, and he portrayed vast numbers of bankers, merchants, shipowners, and members of the aristocracy. Among his sitters were such eminent political figures as Louis Napoleon (1809; Frans Halsmuseum, Haarlem), William I (1816; Rijksmuseum, Amsterdam) and Rutger Jan Schimmelpenninck (1806;

priv. coll.). Hodges also continued to engrave in mezzotint from the portraits painted by himself.

While in the Netherlands, Hodges worked as an art dealer in association with William Humphrey, chiefly in selling prints, many to English collectors. When the kingdom of the Netherlands was formed, Hodges was appointed one of the commissioners sent to Paris in 1815 to identify and recover the pictures looted by Napoleon in 1795 (now in the Mauritshuis, The Hague). He died in Amsterdam on 24 July 1837 and was buried at the English church in the Begijnhof. His works are frequently found in collections in the Netherlands.

L. H. CUST, rev. RUTH COHEN

Sources A. C. A. W. van der Feltz, *Charles Howard Hodges, 1764–1837* (1982) · *DNB* · Thieme & Becker, *Allgemeines Lexikon*, 17.170 · J. C. Smith, *British mezzotinto portraits*, 2 (1879), 625–40
Likenesses C. H. Hodges, self-portrait, oils, Rijksmuseum, Amsterdam [*see illus.*]
Wealth at death house contents and art collection fetched over 15,500 Dutch guilders in 1820: van der Feltz, *Charles Howard Hodges*, 374

Hodges, Edward (1796–1867), organist and composer, was born at Bristol on 20 July 1796. He became organist at Clifton church, Bristol, and then of St James's Church (1819) and St Nicholas's Church (1821), both also at Bristol. Around this time he began composing services and anthems. In 1825 he took the degree of doctor of music from Sidney Sussex College, Cambridge. His academic interests were reflected in his literary essays and writings on music, such as *An Apology for Church Music and Music Festivals* (1834) and contributions to the *Quarterly Musical Magazine* and *Musical World*, some of which were reprinted in *Essays on the Objects of Musical Study* (1838).

In 1838 Hodges went with his family to America. In New York he was appointed organist to St John's Episcopal Chapel, and in 1846 to the newly opened Trinity Church, whose organ was built from his specifications. Besides composing psalms, hymn tunes, and several more services, some of which were published in New York between 1858 and 1865, notably as part of *The Trinity Collection of Church Music* (1864), Hodges continued with his literary endeavours, publishing *An Essay on the Cultivation of Church Music* (1841).

In 1863, prostrated by illness, Hodges resigned his appointments and returned to England. He died at Beaufort Buildings, Clifton, Bristol, on 1 September 1867. He was survived by his daughter Faustina Hasse Hodges (*b.* near Malmesbury, 7 August 1823, *d.* Philadelphia, 4 February 1895) and his son John Sebastian Bach Hodges (*b.* Bristol, 1830, *d.* Baltimore, 1 May 1915), both of whom became organists and composers. Faustina Hodges edited much of her father's music and published a memoir of him, *Edward Hodges, Doctor in Music of Sydney Sussex College* (1896). L. M. MIDDLETON, rev. NILANJANA BANERJI

Sources *New Grove* · Venn, *Alum. Cant.* · Brown & Stratton, *Brit. mus.* · J. D. Brown, *Biographical dictionary of musicians: with a bibliography of English writings on music* (1886) · *Clifton Chronicle* (4 Sept 1867) · D. Baptie, *A handbook of musical biography* (1883)

Hodges, Edward Richmond [Edward Richard] (1825?–1881), orientalist, was probably the person of that name baptized on 2 October 1825 at St Mary Magdalen, Bermondsey, London, the son of Edward and Ann Hodges. While a London apprentice, he became a student of Hebrew, and, after being for a short time a scripture reader, was sent as a missionary by the Society for Promoting Christianity among the Jews, first to Palestine, and afterwards to Algeria (until 1856). A few years later he left the society, and for some time he acted as a minister of the Reformed Episcopal church.

Hodges was best-known as a scholar and teacher of oriental languages, and assisted George Smith (1840–1876) in his cuneiform researches. He wrote numerous magazine articles, and ten entries on Middle Eastern and Indian languages in the 1873 supplement to the arts and sciences division of Charles Knight's *English Cyclopædia*. He was also a competent editor; he thoroughly revised, annotated, and updated Henry Craik's *Principia Hebraica* (2nd edn, 1863) and Isaac Cory's *Ancient Fragments of Phœnician … and other Authors* (new [3rd] edn, 1876), as well as W. J. Mickle's translation, *The Lusiad*, of Camões's Portuguese epic poem for Bohn's Standard Library (5th edn, 1877). At the time of his death he was preparing a translation of the Armenian history by Moses of Khorene and a study of the cult of Mithras.

Hodges died of chronic bronchitis and asthma at his home, 43 Regina Road, Finsbury Park, Middlesex, on 9 May 1881, aged fifty-five, leaving a widow and six children.   W. A. J. ARCHBOLD, *rev.* R. S. SIMPSON

Sources *Morning Post* (9 June 1881), 6 · *The Academy* (18 June 1881), 454 · Boase, *Mod. Eng. biog.*, 1.1491 · IGI · d. cert.

Hodges, Frank (1887–1947), labour leader and politician, was born at Woolaston, Gloucestershire, on 30 April 1887, the son of Thomas and Louisa Hodges. Hodges' family moved to south Wales during the pre-1914 boom years when annual production in the coal industry reached its peak. After attending Queen Street elementary school, Abertillery, Hodges started work as an ordinary collier, but his leadership qualities were quickly realized. He obtained a union-sponsored scholarship to Ruskin College, Oxford, in 1909 and was involved in the establishment of the breakaway Central Labour College. He became miners' agent for the Garw valley in 1912, shortly after his marriage to Henrietta Carter of Abertillery, which was to produce one daughter, Väninna. At this time Hodges was associated with that group of worker intellectuals, notably including Noah Ablett, who were challenging the conciliatory policies of the South Wales Miners' Federation (SWMF), and advocating syndicalism and workers' control. Hodges, however, was never so radically minded, preferring the more moderate approach of guild socialism.

Hodges quickly gained local and national recognition, including election as a fellow of the Royal Statistical Society. In 1918 the Miners' Federation of Great Britain (MFGB), to which the SWMF was affiliated, decided to appoint a full-time president and secretary. Hodges was nominated for the latter post by south Wales, defeating Ablett in the process, and was elected to the office itself on the fifth round of the national ballot. The MFGB's goal at this time was nationalization, following government assumption of control of the industry during the war. Despite recommendations in favour of this course by the Sankey commission (1919), of which Hodges was a member, the mines were returned to private ownership on 1 April 1921. Immediate attempts at wage cuts brought a three-month lock-out. At the outset, the miners' partners in the triple alliance—the railway and transport workers—failed to honour commitments to strike in support. Hodges' role in that decision was a controversial one. His apparent willingness, at an informal meeting of MPs on 14 April 1921, to consider waiving the miners' twin demands for a national wages board and a national pool in the interests of achieving a temporary agreement enabled the miners' allies to urge further negotiations; and, on the following day, 'black Friday', to forsake their promise of support. Hodges' action was disavowed by the miners' executive but the damage had been done, not least to his reputation.

The legacy of resentment over 'black Friday' was revealed at the annual conference of the MFGB in 1923, when a suggestion that the rule stating that the secretary must step down on becoming an MP might be set aside in Hodges' case was easily defeated. Notwithstanding, he stood at the general election that year, being elected as member for Lichfield, Staffordshire. After the election, despite attempts by the executive council of the MFGB to overturn the conference decision, Hodges was forced, with some bitterness, to resign as secretary. He was at Westminster only for a brief time, as he was defeated at the general election of 1924; during this time he served as civil lord of the Admiralty in the first Labour government. On leaving parliament, Hodges became secretary of the International Federation of Miners (1925–7). Here he again antagonized former colleagues when co-ordinating opposition to proposals emanating from Britain for the creation of an all-embracing trade union international. His estrangement was complete when he gave evidence to the Samuel commission in 1925 indicating that British miners should be prepared to work longer hours.

Hodges' final break with the labour movement came with the launching of a successful business career. He was a director of a number of companies, including Securities Management Trust, a subsidiary of the Bank of England established to finance inter-war industrial reconstruction, and he also served as chairman of the Glasgow Iron and Steel Company. Hodges died on 3 June 1947 at Ruthin Castle, Denbighshire. Wales's premier newspaper, the *Western Mail*, described him as one of the foremost leaders in industry. To many of his erstwhile colleagues in the labour movement, however, he remained someone who, through self-seeking opportunism, betrayed his early promise and 'passed to the other side of the barricade'.
KEITH DAVIES

Sources R. P. Arnot, *South Wales miners / Glowyr de Cymru: a history of the South Wales Miners' Federation*, [2] (1975) · R. P. Arnot, *The miners: a*

history of the Miners' Federation of Great Britain, 2: ... *from 1910 onwards* (1953) • H. Tracy, ed., *The book of the labour party: its history, growth, policy, and leaders*, 3 (1925) • F. Hodges, *My adventures as a labour leader* (1925) • WWBMP • *The Times* (5 June 1947) • *Western Mail* [Cardiff] (4 June 1947) • d. cert.

Archives Bank of England Archive, London, papers as a director of Securities Management Trust Ltd • U. Warwick Mod. RC, corresp. with International Federation of Miners

Wealth at death £132,959 12s. 4d.: probate, 22 Oct 1947, *CGPLA Eng. & Wales*

Hodges, Nathaniel (1629–1688), physician, was born on 14 September 1629 in Kensington, the son of Dr Thomas Hodges, the vicar of Kensington. He was a king's scholar at Westminster School, and in 1646 was awarded a scholarship at Trinity College, Cambridge. He transferred to Oxford in 1648, and was appointed by the parliamentary visitors to a studentship at Christ Church (BA 1651, MA 1654, MD 1659). In 1654 Hodges contributed to the Oxford volume of verse issued to celebrate the peace with the Dutch. He practised medicine from his house in Walbrook, London, where he was admitted as a candidate for fellowship of the College of Physicians in 1659; he was not admitted to fellowship until 1672, an unusually long delay.

When the plague broke out in London in 1665, Hodges remained in the City. The College of Physicians and the Society of Chemical Physicians disagreed on the causes and best treatment of the plague; while at Christ Church, Hodges had belonged to the Oxford Experimental Philosophy Club, and his own understanding of the plague set it within a largely Galenic framework of humoral medicine, but also showed the influence of Paracelsian ideas. It is significant that in 1656 he and his father translated from the Latin Michael Maier's *Themis aurea* (1618), dedicating it to Elias Ashmole. This work recommends the prudent use of chemical methods in drug preparation, so that the 'occult property' of a substance may be extracted in its pure form. In 1666 Hodges published *Vindiciae medicinae et medicorum: an Apology for the Profession and Professors of Physic*, where he attacked both those who rejected all of chemistry and those who embraced chemical ideas at the expense of Galenism; a good physician, Hodges argued, was one who did not 'stiffly adhere to one or the other party'. By 1666, having seen the lack of success of chemical remedies for the plague, Hodges reviled Paracelsians as 'these scandalous opposers of the college'. A contagionist, he believed that the plague was spread by 'pestilential effluxes' from person to person, but he considered that the availability of very cheap cherries and grapes had contributed to making bodies more open to such effluxes.

As medical adviser to the City, directing a group of physicians serving London during the outbreak, Hodges recommended the isolation of the sick and also, in separate accommodation, of those who had been in contact with them. He did not consider there was any benefit in shutting up the sick with the well, while isolation in one's own home could be fatal, as the healthy would shun the sick and normal neighbourly help would be withdrawn. Hodges believed that collective action by the City should

be supported by personal responsibility for the maintenance of health. To prevent the plague, he recommended drinking sack, on the basis that it encouraged breathing through the pores and thus drew out any early infection. Twice during the epidemic Hodges felt as if he had been infected, despite his precautions of taking an anti-pestilential electuary before seeing patients in the morning, and burning a disinfectant on hot coals when entering a house where there was a plague sufferer, but after increasing his intake of sack he felt better. Drugs to bring on sweating were also prescribed for sufferers, as were open blisters and 'issues' in the left arm and right leg, through which impurities could pass out of the body. Hodges criticized the prophylactic and curative use of amulets and tobacco, and also attacked old nurses who used human excrement as an antidote to plague. In 1671 he completed his account of the plague, which was published in 1672 as *Loimologia, sive, Pestis nuperae apud populum Londinensem grassantis narratio historica*. This was translated into English in 1720, but was edited by John Quincy to remove 'the most affected peculiarities and luxuriances' from the prose style. There also survives, in a collection of pieces on the plague published in 1721, 'An account of the first rise, progress, symptoms and cure of the plague: being the substance of a letter from Dr Hodges to a person of quality' (it is dated 6 May 1666).

Hodges was elected a fellow of the College of Physicians on 2 April 1672; he was censor in 1682 and delivered the Harveian oration in 1683. As censor he presented the college with a fire engine, for which he received a £15 deduction in his subscription. This is the first hint of the financial difficulties which led to Hodges's imprisonment in Ludgate for debt; he died there on 10 June 1688. He was buried at St Stephen Walbrook, where his bust and inscription are still to be seen. Hodges's medical commonplace book survives in the British Library (Sloane MS 810); it contains over 1000 pages, most of them blank, apart from the headings. In addition to organizing material under such headings according to the pattern definition, signs, prognosis, and treatment, and including recipes and case histories from his practice dating from the 1650s, Hodges pasted in letters, including one from Thomas Willis. The book includes a chart of diseases (fol. 434).

Hodges's insistence on staying in London during the plague is an action for which he has been all but canonized by medical historians; his account of his practice in this period, cautiously used, remains one of the best sources of information on the medical and social effects of this disease. HELEN KING

Sources N. Hodges, commonplace book, BL, Sloane MS 810 • N. Hodges, *Vindiciae medicinae et medicorum: an apology for the profession and professors of physic* (1666) • N. Hodges, *Loimologia, sive, Pestis nuperae apud populum Londinensem grassantis narratio historica* (1672) • *Munk, Roll* • C. Webster, *The great instauration: science, medicine and reform, 1626–1660* (1975), 167 • Wood, *Ath. Oxon.* • DNB

Hodges, Richard (d. 1657), schoolmaster and author, lived and worked for most of his professional life in Southwark, London, 'near the midle-gate in Montague Close' adjacent to St Saviour's Church, Southwark. Although virtually nothing is known of his early life—his parentage, place and year of birth, extent and locations of his education—his writings reveal a man who was well lettered in the classical subjects, a keen observer of the history, phonology, and orthography of vernacular English, an able practitioner of arithmetic and accounting, and a staunch protestant.

Hodges' first known publication, *A Childes Counting-Book* (1624), printed and sold in the Cornhill area of London, presented 'an entrance into arithmetic [and] how to set down a bill of accounts' as well as the names of the books of the Old and New testaments, short scriptural passages, and several daily prayers for young scholars. A decade later he produced a second book, *Enchiridion arithmeticon, or, A Manuel of Millions* (1634), intended for the use of accountants, merchants, paymasters, and others engaged in bookkeeping and commerce. Being among the first examples of a 'ready reckoner' his manual apparently found wide acceptance, with a second edition in 1651 and further reprints.

For English language scholars, however, Hodges' most noted contributions were in early literacy instruction and in his sage observations on written English, especially concerning orthography and pronunciation. An advocate of vernacular literacy as a means of attaining personal salvation, Hodges produced his first publication for this purpose, *A Special Help to Orthographie* (1643/4), a 38-page pamphlet that comprised illustrative sentences that distinguished the spellings of common homonyms of the time ('There was no *signe*, either of a *sine* or tangent'), some basic orthographic rules (*ch* pronounced in English words as in *church*, but in Hebrew and Greek words as in *Christ*), and several recommendations for orthographic reform ('It is … needles(se) to put a double consonant in the middle of such words'). Next Hodges produced *The English Primrose* (1644), a creative approach to teaching reading and writing that used diacritical marks to indicate the customary pronunciations of vowel and consonant spellings of seventeenth-century English orthography. Later, in 1649 and 1653 respectively, he published *The Plainest Directions for the True-Writing of English* and *Most Plain Directions for True-Writing*, printed by William Dugard (headmaster of Merchant Taylors' School), which were mainly combined and amended editions of his 1643 and 1644 books.

The significance of Hodges' productivity is attested to both by contemporaries and by later scholars. Samuel Hartlib, Hezekiah Woodward, and others of his era called attention to his work. Allibone (1859) described him as 'the Noah Webster of his time, and anticipated the modern spelling of many words' (Allibone, *Dict.*, 1.857). Wheatley brought Hodges to the attention of a wider audience of nineteenth-century philologists. Among numerous twentieth-century scholars of early modern English phonology and spelling who have cited Hodges, E. J. Dobson, in his monumental study *English Pronunciation* (1968), described him as 'one of the most important sources of our evidence' (Dobson, 1.165).

A paucity of public records leaves important gaps concerning Hodges' personal life—it is known that he married Elizabeth Phillips on 2 October 1638, possibly a second marriage—but his published works reveal his editorial goals. He sought to hasten and ease the task of learning to read, write, and 'cast up accounts' so that, in the context of seventeenth-century protestantism, the Bible and other sacred materials would be readily accessible to all. Both in purpose and in practice he was, as the burial register of St Saviour's parish noted for 31 March 1657, 'Richard Hodges—a schoolmaster for the church'.

RICHARD E. HODGES

Sources E. J. Dobson, *English pronunciation, 1500–1700*, 2nd edn (1968) · H. B. Wheatley, 'Notes on some English heterographers', *Transactions of the Philological Society*, 7 (1865), 13–59 · Allibone, *Dict.* · D. G. Scragg, *A history of English spelling* (1974) · R. Hodges, *A special help to orthographie, or, The true-writing of English* (1643/4), Ao #145 [Thomason tract E 35(9)] · R. Hodges, *The English primrose* (1644); repr. (1969) · R. Hodges, *The plainest directions for the true-writing of English* (1649) · R. Hodges, *Most plain directions for true-writing* (1653); repr. (1968) · R. Hodges, *Enchiridion arithmeticon, or, A manuel of millions* (1634) · G. H. Turnbull, *Hartlib, Dury and Comenius: gleanings from Hartlib's papers* (1947) · parish register, Southwark, St Saviour, 2/10/1638 [marriage] · parish register, Southwark, St Saviour, 31 March 1657, LMA, P92/SAV/3003, X 39/b [burial]

Hodges, Thomas (*c*.1600–1672), dean of Hereford, was of unknown parentage. He matriculated at Jesus College, Cambridge, in 1620, graduating BA in 1624 and proceeding MA in 1627. He was curate of Ilford, Essex, in 1625, and was probably the Mr Hodges who was lecturer of St Edmund, King and Martyr, Lombard Street, London, in 1628 and 1629. By about 1625 he had married his first wife; several of their children were baptized between 1626 and 1632. By 1630 he was probably curate or lecturer at Highgate Chapel in Hornsey, Middlesex, and he was still there on 25 July 1633, when, as a widower, he married Elizabeth Turner (*b*. 1606/7) of St Martin-in-the-Fields, widow of Henry Turner, at St Peter Cornhill. From 1631 to 1634 he was lecturer at St Olave Jewry in London, and by 1636 he was one of the lecturers at St Bartholomew by the Exchange, London. In June 1641 Hodges, who was then said to be lecturer at St Mary Abbots, Kensington, was appointed vicar there through the interest of the earls of Holland (to whom he may have been distantly related) and Mulgrave; he retained the living until his death.

Hodges was often in demand as a preacher, preaching before the House of Commons in September 1642, June 1645, and March 1647, and before the Lords in July 1645 and March 1647. He was also an active member of the Westminster assembly. In March 1649 he was Holland's chaplain at the earl's execution. From April 1660 to July 1661 he was chaplain to the House of Lords, conducting the opening prayers each day, and in August 1660 the Lords recommended Hodges to the king for preferment; he was granted his Cambridge DD by the king's letters but his suit for the deanery of Lichfield failed. The Lords repeated their request in July 1661 and again in December 1661, and after the last Hodges was finally advanced, being installed dean of Hereford on 18 February 1662; that October he was also made rector of St Peter Cornhill, London.

During his time at Hereford the major achievement was the restoration of cathedral, organ, and the houses in the close. He died on 22 August 1672, 'aged seventy-two or thereabouts' (BL, Lansdowne MS 986, fol. 103r), and was buried in Kensington church. He was survived by his third wife, Margaret (1622/3–1696).

On one level Hodges's career is the pattern of a time-serving and self-interested cleric who remained a member of the established church all his life. There are hints, however, of altogether more unorthodox leanings. In 1638 Sir John Lambe, dean of the arches, annotated the deposition of a former member of the Family of Love that 'Mr Hodges is lecturer just behind the Exchange, he hath all these books Theol: Germanic: or the rule of perfection etc', and he named one alleged heretic as a 'Hodgekin' (PRO, SP 16/520, fols. 126v, 127r). Thomas Hodges would seem to be the lecturer Lambe had in mind, and his implication both that Hodges had a collection of perfectionist and mystical books including the anonymous *Theologia Germanica* and Benet of Canfield's *The Rule of Perfection*, and that he was a member of an underground antinomian circle. The suggestion is strengthened by further circumstantial evidence. There were links between Hodges and John Everard, Hodges's predecessor as lecturer at Kensington, who was charged in 1636 with various heresies including antinomianism: Hodges shared his pulpits at Highgate and St Olave Jewry on a number of occasions in the 1630s with Everard, who was also linked to the earl of Holland. Robert Towne, another antinomian, later mentioned a sermon preached at St Bartholomew by the Exchange to which many ministers took offence and which may have been preached by Hodges or by his allowance. Moreover, the 'Mr Hodges' who was one of the addressees of John Eachard's antinomian epistle in 1631 may have been this Thomas Hodges (Foster, 633).

Nevertheless, by 1642 Hodges was an early and prominent critic of antinomianism, and his later career and advancement betray no signs of unorthodox views. He preached against libertinism before the Commons in September 1642 (Hodges, *Glimpse of Gods Glory*, 16–17), returning to the theme when chosen to preach to the Commons at a special humiliation against the growth of heresy in March 1647; that sermon was published as *The Growth and Spreading of Haeresie* (1647). The common bond between Hodges and the others might have been mysticism, alchemy and Rosicrucianism, and not antinomianism or other heretical beliefs. Everard had translated the *Theologia Germanica* for the earl of Holland and was influenced by hermeticism and alchemy, while it was probably two of Hodges's sons, Nathaniel *Hodges the physician and Thomas, who in the 1650s translated a Rosicrucian work, Michael Maier's *Themis Aurea* (1656) (*Ashmole*, ed. Josten, 2.680–1). The matter is unproven, and Hodges's beliefs and career remain an enigma.

IAN ATHERTON

Sources private information (2004) [D. R. Como] · W. Kennett, biographical notice of Thomas Hodges, BL, Lansdowne MS 986, fol. 103r · deposition concerning sectaries in London, c.1638, PRO, SP16/520, fols. 126–27 · *JHL*, 11 (1660–66) · T. Hodges, *The growth and spreading of haeresie* (1647) · T. Hodges, *A glimpse of Gods glory* (1642) · Nathaniel Hodges's notes on his family, BL, Sloane MS 810, fols. 1–2 · J. F. Wilson, *Pulpit in parliament: puritanism during the English civil wars, 1640–1648* (1969) · S. Foster, 'New England and the challenge of heresy, 1630 to 1660: the puritan crisis in transatlantic perspective', *William and Mary Quarterly*, 38 (1981), 624–60 · N. Smith, *Perfection proclaimed: language and literature in English radical religion, 1640–1660* (1989), 107–43 · Venn, *Alum. Cant.* · *The several speeches of Duke Hamilton … Henry earl of Holland … upon the scaffold* (1649) · T. Faulkner, *History and antiquities of Kensington* (1820), 201–9, 232–3 · *Elias Ashmole (1617–1692): his autobiographical and historical notes*, ed. C. H. Josten, 5 vols. (1966 [i.e. 1967]), vol. 2, pp. 680–81 · M. Maier, *Themis Aurea: the laws of the Fraternity of the Rosie Crosse* (1656) · E. Freshfield, ed., *The vestry minute books of the parish of St. Bartholomew Exchange in the City of London, 1567–1676* (privately printed, London, 1890), 127, 133, 141 · P. S. Seaver, *The puritan lectureships: the politics of religious dissent, 1560–1662* (1970), 142 · G. Hennessy, *Novum repertorium ecclesiasticum parochiale Londinense, or, London diocesan clergy succession from the earliest time to the year 1898* (1898) · S. W. Carruthers, *The everyday work of the Westminster assembly* (1943) · PRO, SP29/25, fol. 3

Hodges, Sir William, first baronet (*c*.1645–1714), merchant and politician, was born about 1645, the son of John Hodges of Cotherstock, or Cotterstock, in Northamptonshire. Little is known of his family background beyond the information supplied when he received a grant of arms in 1698, and it seems likely that his origins were humble. He married in 1681 (by licence granted on 25 April) Sarah (*d.* 1717), the daughter and coheir of Joseph Hall, a merchant of London and Balasore in India. He may have begun his career in the service of the East India Company—his wife was the daughter of a Bengal factor, and he himself was to act as the company's agent in Spain—but by 1683 he was established in Cadiz, where the hospitality he afforded the visiting Samuel Pepys formed the basis of an enduring friendship.

Hodges first came to prominence in the mid-1690s, when his firm provided cash advances for the victualling of Admiral Edward Russell's Mediterranean Fleet. For this and other important services in support of the war effort, and also to compensate him for the Treasury's slowness in settling his account, he was granted a baronetcy in 1697. Three years later he decided to return to England, perhaps because his only child, a twelve-year-old son, who had hitherto been educated privately at home (as Hodges himself told Pepys, 'for reasons you may imagine'), was fast approaching adolescence. Hodges's great wealth and his close associations with prominent City of London families, such as the Houblons (his own close friends) and the Hernes (his wife's relations), made him a natural recruit to the board of the Bank of England, to which he was chosen a director in 1703. At the general election of 1705 he took a further step towards eminence in public life when his money bought a parliamentary seat for the corrupt Cornish borough of Mitchell. Like many another representative of the 'moneyed interest', which to its critics was growing fat on the profits of continental warfare, he took his place in the ranks of the whig party in the House of Commons, but he was always a pragmatist in politics and displayed moderation rather than party zeal. He was also, it would appear, a staunch churchman and no particular friend to protestant dissenters. After standing down at the

Sir William Hodges, first baronet (*c*.1645–1714), by John Smith, 1715 (after Sir Godfrey Kneller, 1713)

1710 election he maintained good relations with the predominantly tory administration established by Robert Harley. Each needed the other: Hodges's many commercial interests could derive considerable benefit from the favour of government, while Harley, for his part, was looking to recruit moderate whigs in the bank and East India Company (to which Hodges was elected as a director, for one year, in 1712) to help him construct his own 'party' in the City and maintain public credit. Thus Hodges' son Joseph was given employment in the lottery office in 1712, while Sir William himself advised the ministry on the settlement of the Spanish trade after the peace of Utrecht.

Hodges died in London between 14 and 29 July 1714, and was buried in his parish church of St Stephen, Coleman Street, on 31 July, after a funeral of unusual magnificence, even for one of the great merchant princes of London. His son, Joseph Hodges, after inheriting a great fortune in money and stocks, went to live abroad, first in France and then in Spain, where he entirely wasted his inheritance and died, unmarried, in 1722. The baronetcy was thereby extinguished.

Hodges has been identified erroneously with the 'William Hodges, mariner', who between 1693 and 1699 published at least five pamphlets as part of a one-man campaign to improve the methods of paying naval wages and thus ameliorate the miserable conditions suffered by English sailors. However, Sir William's prolonged residence in Spain at this time, and the failure of the last pamphlet in the series to reflect the acquisition of his title, renders this identification impossible.   D. W. HAYTON

Sources GEC, *Baronetage* · J. Foster and W. H. Rylands, eds., *Grantees of arms named in docquets and patents to the end of the seventeenth*

century, Harleian Society, 66 (1915), 110, 126 · G. J. Armytage, ed., *Allegations for marriage licences issued by the vicar-general of the archbishop of Canterbury, July 1679 to June 1687*, Harleian Society, 30 (1890), 60 · W. M. Acres, 'Directors of the Bank of England', *N&Q*, 179 (1940), 57–62, esp. 60 · will, 14–29 July 1714, PRO, PROB 11/541, sig. 139 · J. P. Malcolm, *Londinium redivivum, or, An antient history and modern description of London*, 4 vols. (1802–7), vol. 4, p. 603 · W. A. Shaw, ed., *Calendar of treasury books*, [33 vols. in 64], PRO (1904–69), vols. 19–20, 24–6, 29 · *Calendars of treasury papers, 1697–1707* · *Private correspondence and miscellaneous papers of Samuel Pepys, 1679–1703*, ed. J. R. Tanner, 2 vols. (1926) · HoP, *Commons* [draft]

Likenesses J. Smith, mezzotint, 1715 (after G. Kneller, 1713), BM, NPG [*see illus.*]

Wealth at death see will, 14–29 July 1714, PRO, PROB 11/541, sig. 139, fol. 66

Hodges, William (1744–1797), painter, was born in London on 28 October 1744, the only child of Charles Hodges, a blacksmith who owned a shop in St James's Market, and his wife, Ann, *née* Richards, sister of the curate of St Sepulchre at Newgate. His parents placed him in William Shipley's school in 1755, where he learned to draw. While there he was brought to the attention of Richard Wilson, the landscape painter, and at the age of fourteen was articled to him for seven years as an assistant, making rapid progress.

Leaving Wilson's studio in 1765, Hodges joined the Incorporated Society of Artists of Great Britain where he exhibited his work including in 1766 *A View of London Bridge from Botolph Wharf* and *A View of Speldhurst, Kent*. He lived for a while in Derby where he worked as a scene-painter, returning to London in 1771. In 1772, through the intervention of Lord Palmerston, he obtained the post of draughtsman on Captain James Cook's second voyage to the south Pacific (1772–5), during which he made sketches and paintings of the islands and native people. On his return he supervised the engraving (by William Woollet and others) of plates from his work as illustrations for Cook's official account, *A voyage towards the south pole, and round the world: performed in his majesty's ships the Resolution and Adventure in the years 1772, 1773, 1774 and 1775*, 2 vols. (1779). The Admiralty employed him for a further two years to make large finished oil paintings, several of which he exhibited at the Royal Academy, including *The War Boats of Otaheite* (National Maritime Museum, London) in 1777. On 11 May 1776 Hodges married Martha Nesbit at St George's, Hanover Square, London, and settled in Pimlico. However, within a year his wife died in childbirth. In 1779 Hodges travelled to India where he came under the patronage of Warren Hastings. He remained in India some six years, recording scenes of interest and architectural landmarks. Between 1785 and 1788 he published *Select Views in India in the Years 1780–1783*, which included a series of forty-eight aquatints adapted from sketches drawn on the spot and engraved by him. In 1793 his *Travels in India, 1780–1783* was published and illustrated with fifteen plates from his drawings. In addition Indian scenes engraved by Thomas Morris were published in the *European Magazine* and *London Review*. In his *Cosmos: a Sketch of a Physical Description of the Universe*, Alexander von Humboldt says that the sight of Hodges' Indian views was one of the inducements which led him to travel (A. von Humboldt, trans. E. C. Otte,

1849, 2.371–2). Through his work Hodges made a substantial contribution to the British perception of India's past.

Having made a considerable fortune abroad, in 1784 Hodges settled in London at Queen Street, Mayfair, where he built himself a studio. On 16 October in the same year he married Lydia Wright, who died soon afterwards. In December 1785 he married Ann Mary Carr (d. 1797), a talented pianist; they had five children who survived. Hodges also had a natural son born in India who had been brought to England. His family, lifestyle, and ambitious publications soon led to a drain on his resources. In his *Diary* Farington noted on 27 September 1806 that 'he had many good qualities' but was prone to 'extravagant notions caused by pride and ostentatious liberality' (Farington, *Diary*, 8.2863).

Hodges was elected an associate of the Royal Academy in 1786 and Royal Academician in 1789, continuing to exhibit at the Royal Academy until 1794, including in 1788 his Diploma work, *The Ghats at Benares* (RA). He is included in a group portrait of Royal Academicians (1793) by Henry Singleton. Hodges' ability was highly regarded among his fellow artists. However, during the Cook voyage he developed an individual response to the problems of representing light and meteorological conditions which brought criticism from a society not yet ready for a departure from recognized traditions.

In his later work Hodges showed an interest in painting in the 'grand manner' literary subjects, including Shakespeare, in landscape settings, some inspired by the work of Salvatore Rosa, into which figures were introduced by George Romney and William Gilpin. *Jaques and the Wounded Stag in the Forest of Arden* (1789; Yale U. CBA, Paul Mellon collection), from Shakespeare's *As You Like It*, was exhibited at Boydell's Shakspeare Gallery, as was *Portia's Garden* (1790) from *The Merchant of Venice*, said in a contemporary review to be 'eminently brilliant' (Press Cuttings, 1790, 2.558, V&A.). This was engraved together with other work from the period including *The Belisarius* (1794), dedicated to Warren Hastings (now known only from the engraving by J. Ogborne). About 1790 he travelled on the continent and visited St Petersburg, of which he painted a view. Hodges' attempt to elevate landscape painting as a method of expressing moral values resulted in two large canvases entitled *The Effects of Peace* and *The Consequences of War* exhibited in Mr Orme's room, 14 Old Bond Street, London in December 1794. The political nature of the paintings brought condemnation from the duke of York, who felt they showed 'sentiments not suited to the public tranquillity' and ordered the exhibition closed (Edwards, 251). Discouraged, Hodges gave up his profession and left London with his family in July 1795 to settle in Brixham, near Dartmouth, Devon, where he opened a bank. Contemporary financial problems proved the ruin of his small firm, however. His sudden death in Brixham on 6 March 1797 was precipitated by a fever and gout in the stomach. His wife survived him by a few months. Examples of his drawings are in the British Museum and the Victoria and Albert Museum, London; the National Archives of Canada,

Ottawa; the Mitchell Library, Sydney, and the Commonwealth National Library, Canberra, Australia. His paintings are in many collections in the USA, India, and Great Britain including the Yale Center for British Art, New Haven, Connecticut, the National Gallery of Modern Art, New Delhi, and the India Office and the Tate collections.

L. H. Cust, rev. Lindsey Macfarlane

Sources I. C. Stuebe, *The life and work of William Hodges* (1979) · R. Joppien and B. Smith, *The art of Captain Cook's voyages*, 3 vols. (1985–8), vols. 1–2 · Farington, *Diary* · W. Foster, 'British artists in India, 1760–1820', *Walpole Society*, 19 (1930–31), 1–88, esp. 40–42 · E. Edwards, *Anecdotes of painters* (1808); facs. edn (1970) · G. Tillotson, *The artificial empire: the Indian landscapes of William Hodges* (2000)
Archives BM, drawings and papers
Likenesses G. Dance, drawing, 1793, RA · W. Daniell, engraving (after G. Dance, 1793) · H. Singleton, oils (*Royal Academicians, 1793*), RA · Thornthwaite, line engraving (after R. Westall), BM, NPG; repro. in *Literary Magazine* (1792)

Hodges, Sir William (1808–1868), legal writer and judge, eldest son of William Hodges of Weymouth, and Sarah, second daughter of William Isaac of Weymouth, was born at Melcombe Regis, Dorset, on 29 September 1808, and educated at a private school at Salisbury and at the University of London. Lectured by John Austin (1790–1859) and Andrew Amos (1791–1860) on jurisprudence and law, he was called to the bar at the Inner Temple on 3 May 1833. He married in 1835 Mary Schollar, daughter of James Sanders of Weymouth, and they had four sons and four daughters.

Hodges went the western circuit, and in 1835 he began to report cases in the court of common pleas (published 1835–7), presided over by Sir Nicholas Tindal, who in 1837 appointed him revising barrister for Devon and Cornwall. In 1838 he began to report in the queen's bench. In 1839 he published *Report of the case of the Queen v. Lumsdaine, with observations on the Parochial Assessment Act* and, in 1840, jointly with Graham Willmore and F. L. Wollaston, *Reports of Cases Argued and Determined in the Court of Queen's Bench … Hilary Term to Michaelmas Term, 1838*. In 1842 he published a small treatise entitled *The Law Relating to the Assessment of Railways* and, in 1845, *The Statute Law Relating to Railways in England and Ireland*. In 1846 he was appointed recorder of Poole, Dorset. *The Law Relating to Railways and Railway Companies*, which he published in 1847, reached a seventh edition, edited by J. M. Lely, in 1888, and became a standard work on the subject. He also drafted the Public Health Act of 1848, and acquired some parliamentary and general practice at Westminster.

In 1857 Hodges was appointed to the chief justiceship of the supreme court of the Cape of Good Hope, and to the presidency of the legislative council and of the court of admiralty. He was made KCMG in 1858. He discharged his official duties with energy and efficiency until his death at his residence, Sea Point House, Cape Town, on 17 August 1868. He was honoured with a public funeral.

J. M. Rigg, rev. Lynn Milne

Sources A. F. Hattersley, 'Hodges, Sir William', *DSAB* · *GM*, 5th ser., 2 (1869), 256 · *Law Times* (26 Sept 1868), 394 · *Law Magazine*, new ser., 26 (1868–9), 186 · private information (1891)

Likenesses portrait, repro. in *South African Law Journal* (1934)
Wealth at death under £450: administration, 12 Oct 1869, *CGPLA Eng. & Wales*

Hodgetts, James Frederick (1828–1906), children's writer and naval officer, son of James Hodgetts (*d.* 1830) and his wife, Judith, daughter of Richard May, portrait painter, was born in London on 18 January 1828. After his father's death his mother married the writer on science Edward William Brayley. Hodgetts did not get on with his stepfather, who educated him for a scientific career. As a boy he assisted Sir Samuel Rush Meyrick in the arrangement of the Tower armoury. At an early age he went to sea, was in the East India Company's service in the Second Burmese War (1851–3), became commander in the Indian navy, was shipwrecked, and had a narrow escape from drowning off the coast of Australia.

When Hodgetts' health gave way under the tropical climate, he volunteered for service in the Crimean War, but was refused. He then became professor of seamanship at the Prussian naval cadets' school in Berlin until the school closed in 1866. Having studied Russian in India, he transferred to St Petersburg and Moscow at the suggestion of a friend of his stepfather's, Sir Roderick Impey Murchison. In Russia he lectured as professor in the Imperial College of Practical Science.

On his retirement in 1881, Hodgetts returned to London, where he patented a design for ships' hulls, and wrote adventure stories for boys based on his own wide experience. They were initially published in the *Boy's Own Paper*, and later separately. The first, *Harold the Boy Earl*, appeared in 1883. He also published lectures given at the British Museum, including *Older England* (1884) and *The English in the Middle Ages* (1885), and contributed to the *Journal of the British Archaeological Association* and *The Antiquary*.

Hodgetts was married twice: in 1858 to Isabella Gough (*d.* 1862), with whom he had a son, Edward Arthur Brayley Hodgetts; and in 1867 to Augusta Louisa von Dreger, with whom he had one daughter. He was engaged on an unfinished life of Alfred the Great when he died at his home, 24 Cheniston Gardens, Kensington, London, on 24 April 1906. Alexander Gordon, *rev.* Victoria Millar

Sources *The Athenaeum* (5 May 1906), 546 · *The Times* (26 April 1906), 8 · *Annual Register* (1906) · Allibone, *Dict.*, suppl. · W. D. G. Lofts and D. J. Adley, eds., *The men behind boys' fiction* (1970) · private information (1912)

Hodgkin, Sir Alan Lloyd (1914–1998), physiologist, was born on 5 February 1914 at 61 Broughton Road, Banbury, Oxfordshire, the eldest of the three sons of George Lloyd Hodgkin (1880–1918), banker, and his wife, Mary Fletcher, *née* Wilson (1891–1978), daughter of Henry Wilson and his wife, Theodora.

Family, early years, and education Hodgkin's forebears on both sides were Quakers. The historian Thomas Hodgkin (1831–1913) was his grandfather; Thomas Hodgkin of Hodgkin's disease (1798–1866) was his great-great-uncle; and the meteorologist Luke Howard (1772–1864) was his great-great-grandfather. The crystallographer and Nobel

Sir Alan Lloyd Hodgkin (1914–1998), by Derek Hill, 1975

prize-winner Dorothy Hodgkin (1910–1994) was the wife of a first cousin. His father was at first a civil engineer but from the time of his marriage in 1913 he worked in a bank in Banbury. During the First World War he incurred much local animosity by refusing, on Quaker principles, to undertake any work that would help the war effort. He took part in relief work in Armenia, and in 1918 died of dysentery on a second journey to that country. Hodgkin's mother married, in 1932, Lionel Smith, rector of Edinburgh Academy and son of A. L. Smith, master of Balliol College, Oxford.

Hodgkin's main boyhood interests were in natural history, which he was able to pursue during visits to relatives in many parts of the country and at his two schools: the Downs School at Colwall, Herefordshire (1923–7), and Gresham's at Holt in Norfolk (1927–32). In December 1931 he won an open scholarship to Trinity College, Cambridge, and in the interval between school and college he had his first taste of research, at the Freshwater Biological Station in the Lake District. He also spent a few months with a family in Germany where a first-hand view of Nazism destroyed the pacifist principles of his upbringing. He remained an agnostic throughout his adult life.

Hodgkin's original intention at Cambridge was to specialize in zoology, aiming for a career in applied biology, probably overseas. For the first two years of the degree course he took zoology, chemistry, and physiology, obtaining a first class; he became more interested in physiology and chose this as his final year subject, again obtaining a first class. A factor that stimulated his interest in physiology was the close friendship between his father and Keith Lucas, a physiologist of great distinction who established the 'all-or-none' nature of the impulse in individual nerve or muscle fibres.

Research up to 1939 Hodgkin began research during his final undergraduate year, and in the following year he obtained the first experimental evidence for a theory of the mechanism of conduction in nerve fibres that had been widely accepted since the 1880s (the local-circuit theory). On the strength of this he was elected to one of the junior research fellowships at Trinity College, an unusual distinction so soon after graduating. He then went on to work with large nerve fibres which, by a lucky chance, he had found he could dissect from the leg nerves of crabs and lobsters. With these he showed that a local electrical change was generated by a fibre in response to a stimulus that was nearly but not quite strong enough to give rise to the propagated 'all-or-none' impulse.

Hodgkin spent 1937–8 at the Rockefeller Institute in New York, where he encountered a more professional style of research than existed at that time in Cambridge. A contact that strongly influenced his later work was with K. S. Cole, who with H. J. Curtis had recently performed a remarkable experiment that showed a great decrease in the electrical resistance of the surface membrane of a nerve fibre during the impulse. This experiment was made possible by using the giant nerve fibre of the squid (about 0.5 mm in diameter), discovered a few years before by J. Z. Young. Jointly with Cole, Hodgkin used this nerve fibre in measuring the resistance of the resting membrane, and it was the preparation that he used in most of his nerve experiments after the war. He also used it in another experiment performed while in the USA in which he showed that the speed of conduction was increased by reducing the longitudinal electrical resistance outside the fibre. This gave final proof that the local circuits are an essential part of the propagation mechanism, a matter that was still controversial at the time, particularly in the USA.

At the Rockefeller Institute Hodgkin also made the acquaintance of the pathologist Peyton Rous, who was later also a Nobel prize-winner (1966). Hodgkin married Rous's eldest daughter, Marion de Kay (Marni; b. 1917), on 30 March 1944 when on a short visit to the USA in connection with his war work. The marriage was outstandingly happy and successful. They had three daughters and a son. Marni wrote two detective novels and worked as children's book editor for the publishers Rupert Hart-Davis and, later, Macmillan.

Hodgkin returned in September 1938 to Cambridge, where he had been appointed to a lectureship in Trinity College and a university demonstratorship in the department of physiology. He continued his experimental work on nerve, partly in collaboration with W. A. H. Rushton. Jointly with A. F. Rawdon-Smith of the psychology department he built new recording apparatus with cathode-follower input and direct-coupled valve amplifiers; four sets were made and remained in service for many years.

In the summer vacation of 1939 Hodgkin went to the laboratory of the Marine Biological Association at Plymouth in order to do experiments on the squid fibre. He was joined by A. F. Huxley, who had just completed undergraduate work in Trinity College, and they recorded the resting potential of the fibre and the action potential (the change of electrical potential accompanying the impulse) directly with an electrode inserted inside the fibre. On the theory current at that time the internal potential should have risen during the impulse from its negative resting value nearly to equality with the external potential, but they found that it actually overshot and went substantially positive. They did not have time to investigate the origin of this positivity, leaving Plymouth a few days before the outbreak of the Second World War.

War work, 1939–1945 For the first few months of the war Hodgkin held an unpaid post at the Royal Aircraft Establishment at Farnborough, Hampshire, working under B. H. C. Matthews on the physiological problems of high altitude flying in unpressurized aircraft. In February 1940 he was transferred to the establishment later known as TRE (Telecommunications Research Establishment), where airborne radar was being further developed, and stayed with it until the end of the war. After occupying various sites in south Wales and on the south coast of England it was moved into the buildings of Malvern College, a boys' school in Worcestershire.

Airborne radar working on a wavelength of 1.5 metres was already in service, mainly for ship detection, but versions for aircraft interception were just coming into service. Their usefulness was limited by the breadth of the beam, unavoidable because narrowing the beam would require an aerial system with dimensions several times the wavelength. The chief disadvantage of the broad beam was that it extended downwards and gave echoes from objects on the ground at all distances greater than the height of the aircraft, and these obscured the echo from a target. Hodgkin joined the team of A. C. B. Lovell aiming to develop radar on shorter wavelengths. After experiments at 50 cm they moved to the ambitious project of using 5 or 10 cm, which became practicable through the invention of the cavity magnetron by J. T. Randall and H. A. H. Boot at Birmingham University. This gave greatly increased power at the required very high frequencies. A paraboloid reflector of about 70 cm diameter gave a suitably narrow beam but this needed to be scanned through a range of angles in order to pick up a target aircraft. A design by Hodgkin was adopted; it used a spiral scan and gave an easily interpretable display. Hodgkin and several of his colleagues took part in many flights with experimental and prototype versions of this equipment in order to cure teething troubles and to test their usefulness. The risks were considerable: one of his colleagues lost his life when the aircraft in which he was flying was misidentified and shot down; Hodgkin himself had a narrow escape when the same thing nearly happened to the aircraft in which he was flying; and four others of the group were killed when their aircraft crashed.

In the autumn of 1942 Hodgkin was transferred to work on the defence of night bombers against fighter attack. The initial requirement was to provide only the range of the target when the gun turret could be aimed visually; later he worked on a system for blind firing. When attacks with the pilotless aircraft V1 began in 1944, an attempt was made to adapt this system for shooting down the V1s, but before it was ready for operational use the launching sites were overrun by allied land forces. Hodgkin was then put in charge of development of a radar to be fitted in a steerable rocket that was under development for launching from a fighter aircraft, but the war came to an end before any such development could be completed.

Post-war research Hodgkin moved back to Cambridge with his wife and first child in August 1945. He resumed his teaching duties in Trinity and in the department of physiology. He was promoted to university lecturer in 1946 and to assistant director of research in 1947. In 1952 he was appointed to the Foulerton research professorship of the Royal Society, which freed him from teaching duties, and in Trinity he moved to a senior research fellowship. In January 1970 he moved to a university research chair, the John Humphrey Plummer professorship of biophysics, and to a professorial fellowship at Trinity. He relinquished the professorship on reaching the university retiring age in 1981, though he continued his experimental research for some years. His active scientific work was brought to an end by the early death of his last collaborator, B. J. Nunn, in 1987. From 1946 until then he was leader of a well-defined group in the physiological laboratory of Cambridge University.

Much of Hodgkin's research until 1951 was done in collaboration with Huxley, who returned to Cambridge in January 1946 after his war work. The main question facing them at first was the cause of the overshoot that they had observed in 1939, that is, the fact that the interior of the nerve fibre became strongly positive at the peak of an impulse. They were already discussing the idea that turned out to be correct, that the decrease in membrane resistance shown by Cole and Curtis was due to a large and specific increase in the permeability of the membrane to sodium ions: since their concentration is much higher in the surrounding fluid than inside the fibre, sodium ions are thereby enabled to diffuse inwards carrying their positive charge. On this theory the membrane potential would be restored by the outward diffusion of an equivalent amount of potassium ions (present in relatively high concentration inside each fibre), and in 1946 Hodgkin, with Huxley, used an indirect method to estimate the amount of potassium leaving a nerve fibre per impulse transmitted. They showed that this was sufficient to restore the membrane potential, and in their publication they suggested that the initial rise of potential, overshooting the zero level, was probably due to sodium entry.

Firm evidence for or against the sodium theory required experiments on the squid giant fibre; these were possible only at the laboratory at Plymouth, which had been severely bombed during the war and was not available until the summer of 1947. Hodgkin then obtained evidence for the sodium theory by showing that the potential reached at the peak of the impulse, and also its rate of rise,

varied with external sodium concentration in the way required by the theory. He presented these results verbally at the International Congress of Physiology in Oxford in late July that year. In September he was joined at Plymouth by Bernard Katz, who had independently realized that the overshoot might be due to sodium entry. Together they extended the observations made by Hodgkin, providing conclusive evidence for the sodium theory. Owing to delays in publication this work did not appear in print until 1949.

It remained uncertain whether the sodium mechanism was used by excitable tissues of vertebrates as well as by the nerves of molluscs such as the squid. During a visit to the USA in early 1948 Hodgkin met Gilbert Ling, who was measuring the resting potential of muscle fibres of frogs by means of a microelectrode consisting of a saline-filled glass pipette with a very fine tip which was pushed through the surface membrane of the fibre. However, the response of the equipment was not fast enough for recording the potential change during the impulse. Later that year Hodgkin, with W. L. Nastuk from the USA, improved the technique so that faithful records of the impulse could be obtained, and they showed that it responded to external sodium concentration in the same way as in the squid nerve fibre. Their technique quickly became a standard one for experiments on a wide variety of cells.

It was generally supposed at that time that the 'all-or-none' character of the impulse was due to the membrane permeability increasing instantaneously when the internal potential reached a critical value. On the basis of experiments before the war, however, Hodgkin suspected that the current–voltage relation was continuous but included a region with negative slope. This would cause instability since any increase of inward current in this range would cause a further rise of internal potential, in turn causing a further increase in inward current. This would result in an explosive 'all-or-none' change of membrane potential.

An unstable current–voltage relation of this kind would be difficult to investigate experimentally, but both Hodgkin and Cole had the idea of using electronic feedback to an internal electrode to control the internal potential, which could thereby be raised suddenly and held at the new level. The electrode had to extend over a considerable length of the fibre in order to keep the internal potential uniform. Cole with George Marmont had a system of this type (the voltage clamp) operating in the summer of 1947. They showed that there is indeed a continuous relation between membrane potential and current, but did not take the analysis further. During his visit to the USA in the spring of 1948 Hodgkin met Cole, who told him about these experiments; in turn Hodgkin told Cole of his observations with Katz on the effects of sodium concentration.

Together with Katz and Huxley, Hodgkin did his first voltage clamp experiments in the summer of 1948, and his final series of experiments (with Huxley) in 1949. They analysed the origins of the measured current by altering the external sodium concentration and by imposing a second step of potential change. They thus separated the current into components carried by sodium and by potassium ions, and they fitted equations to the time courses of the permeabilities of the membrane to these two ions following a step change of membrane potential. They used these equations to calculate the time course of the potential change that would result if the membrane potential were not controlled by feedback. This agreed well with the time course of a normal action potential recorded after a short electrical stimulus; and the calculated amounts of sodium and potassium entering and leaving the fibre agreed well with the values found by the use of radioactive tracers by R. D. Keynes, for whom Hodgkin had been the PhD supervisor shortly after the war.

These results were published in 1952 and led to the award in 1963 of the Nobel prize for physiology or medicine to Hodgkin and Huxley, together with John Eccles. The award was 'for their discoveries concerning the ionic mechanisms involved in excitation and inhibition in the peripheral and central portions of the nerve cell membrane'. Eccles's contribution was on transmission from a nerve terminal to a cell body in the spinal cord, and was quite independent of Hodgkin's and Huxley's work.

These 'Hodgkin–Huxley equations' were plausible on the assumption that sodium and potassium ions crossed the nerve membrane through 'gates' in the membrane that were opened or closed in response to changes in the potential difference across the membrane. It would have been natural to investigate further the identity and nature of these gates, but in 1952 it was impossible to see how this could be done. There was later enormous progress in this direction, beginning about 1970, but it depended on advances in other fields, notably in molecular genetics, which was begun by the 1953 paper of J. D. Watson and F. H. C. Crick, and in electronics, which made possible the detection of the small amounts of charge carried across the membrane when gates opened or closed, and later (1976) the recording by Erwin Neher and Bert Sakmann of the minute currents passing through individual gates. Hodgkin therefore changed his field of research, first to other aspects of the movements of ions in nerve and muscle and finally to the mechanism by which the rods and cones of the vertebrate retina are excited by light.

Hodgkin collaborated with R. D. Keynes, P. C. Caldwell, and T. I. Shaw in investigating the mechanisms by which the entry of sodium and loss of potassium during activity are reversed during subsequent resting periods, showing that they are driven by the utilization of adenosine triphosphate (ATP). In some of these experiments they injected ATP and other substances into the interior of the giant fibre of the squid using a device designed by Hodgkin and Keynes.

With Bernhard Frankenhaeuser from Sweden, Hodgkin investigated the effects of changed calcium concentration on the voltage dependence of the permeabilities to sodium and potassium ions. With Shaw, P. F. Baker, and Hans Meves from Germany, he replaced the contents of the giant fibre with artificial solutions, showing that the

effects of wide alterations in the internal concentrations of sodium and potassium ions on the resting and action potentials agreed well with what was to be expected from the voltage clamp experiments, in which only the external sodium concentration had been altered. With Paul Horowicz from the USA he investigated the effects of altered ion concentrations in the external fluid on both the membrane potential and the contraction of frog muscle. In the middle 1960s he pursued this line of research in collaboration with R. H. Adrian and W. K. Chandler from the USA, using feedback between microelectrodes of the type devised by Hodgkin and Nastuk, to achieve a voltage clamp of individual muscle fibres. With Shigehiro Nakajima he measured the membrane capacity of muscle fibres of different diameters, thus distinguishing clearly between the components due to the surface membrane and to the system of tubules that extend inwards from the surface of muscle fibres but not of nerve fibres. With Baker, M. P. Blaustein, and E. B. Ridgway he measured the movements of calcium into and out of the squid giant nerve fibre.

Hodgkin's work on vision began with a short period of collaboration with M. G. F. Fuortes, an Italian physiologist who had moved to the USA, during a visit in 1962 to the Marine Biological Laboratory at Woods Hole, Massachusetts. Hodgkin joined Fuortes in his experiments recording the changes of membrane potential in visual cells of the horseshoe crab *Limulus*. It was known that there was a long delay between exposure to a flash of light and the resulting change of membrane potential, indicating that there were several steps intervening between the two events; Fuortes and Hodgkin showed that this delay was reduced when the sensitivity of the eye was reduced by adaptation to bright light, and they gave a straightforward explanation for the connection between these two effects. Hodgkin's change to full-time work on vision began in 1970 when he collaborated with D. A. Baylor from the USA doing on the eyes of vertebrates experiments similar to those which he and Fuortes had done on the eye of *Limulus*. He continued these experiments in collaboration with T. D. Lamb, P. A. McNaughton, P. M. O'Bryan, P. D. Detwiler, K.- W. Yau and B. J. Nunn.

President of the Royal Society, 1970–1975 Hodgkin succeeded Lord Blackett as president of the Royal Society in November 1970, serving until December 1975. The society was then already in financial difficulties owing to the rapid inflation that had begun a few years before. This was primarily the responsibility of the treasurer of the society, but Hodgkin was active in pressing for the necessary reforms, which included increasing the fellows' annual subscriptions, reducing their entitlement to free copies of the society's journals, requesting an increase in the government grant to the society, and launching an appeal. By these means financial stability was restored without loss of the society's independence through excessive dependence on government funds.

The main support of scientific research in Britain was provided through the research councils, which received grants directly from the government and provided funding for research both in their institutes and in the universities. Shortly before Hodgkin became president of the Royal Society, however, the Ministry of Agriculture, Fisheries and Food had proposed that it should take over the Agricultural Research Council. Most scientists, including Hodgkin and the council of the Royal Society, were opposed to this proposal, on the ground that it would stifle initiative in basic research, and a letter to this effect was sent to the secretary of state for education and science, Margaret Thatcher. Hodgkin had an interview with her, with the outcome that the head of the Central Policy Review Staff, Lord Rothschild, produced a consultative document, *A Framework for Government Research and Development*, which recommended that the research councils should be financed mainly by contracts for specific pieces of research, placed by the relevant ministries. The Royal Society sent a memorandum strongly opposing this scheme, which nevertheless was adopted, though the extent of the transfer of funds was somewhat reduced. Sadly, this affair clouded the long-standing friendship between Hodgkin and Rothschild.

On the international front the Royal Society re-established contacts with both Japan and China. Hodgkin was a member of a delegation that visited Japan shortly before he became president, as Blackett was ill. An exchange agreement was established, similar to those with many other countries, and it was during Hodgkin's presidency that Emperor Hirohito of Japan was elected to the equivalent of what was later designated as honorary fellowship. Hodgkin also visited China but the outcome was little more than the re-establishment of occasional contacts, since the cultural revolution was still in progress and the only research allowed was of the most applied kind. Hodgkin also visited India, the USA, Canada, and Australia during his presidency; he had visited the USSR in 1967, and later he visited Kenya and Iran. As chairman of the council, which met monthly for most of the year, Hodgkin, although holding strong views, did not impose them on the other members. He generally asked another member to start a discussion.

Master of Trinity College, Cambridge, 1978–1984 In nearly all the Oxford and Cambridge colleges the head is elected by the fellows, but in Trinity College, Cambridge, the master is appointed by the crown. Since the fellows do not control the appointment they give the master less power and fewer duties than in other colleges, though he is chairman of the weekly meetings of the college council and of the occasional meetings of all the fellows, and he has considerable personal influence. Hodgkin served as master of Trinity College from October 1978 to June 1984. Under his guidance the courts known as Whewell's courts were renovated, and much of the fellows' garden was replanned. Women students were admitted from the start of Hodgkin's mastership, the decision having been taken previously; Hodgkin wholeheartedly approved of the change. The master's lodge gave him and his wife, Marni, scope for their talent as hosts, to students as well as to

Cambridge academics and visitors. They restored the custom by which the visiting High Court judge occupied part of the lodge during his tours of duty in Cambridge.

Last years Hodgkin suffered from a series of illnesses that began soon after he retired as master of Trinity. An operation in 1989 to relieve pressure on the spinal cord from an intervertebral disc in his neck left him without the ability to sense the position of his legs and he was therefore unable to walk without support. Thereafter his condition deteriorated steadily. He was nevertheless able to continue research until 1987, and after that to write with the help of a word processor. He wrote his autobiography, *Chance and Design: Reminiscences of Science in Peace and War* (1992), during this period. He started this as an account of his wartime work, partly because this was not adequately covered in any of the war histories and partly in memory of colleagues who had lost their lives while testing new radar equipment. He then added a very full account of his boyhood, his time as an undergraduate, and his research up to 1963, with only short accounts of his later work and his times as president of the Royal Society and master of Trinity. His only other book, *The Conduction of the Nervous Impulse* (1964), was an expanded version of the Sherrington lectures that he gave at Liverpool University in 1961; it presented his own work on nerve in the context of other research.

Hodgkin became KBE in 1972 and was appointed OM in 1973. He had been elected a fellow of the Royal Society in 1948, and received its royal medal in 1958 and its top award, the Copley medal, in 1965. He was elected an honorary or foreign member of eleven overseas academies. As well as his ScD from Cambridge University he received fifteen honorary doctorates from other universities. He was president of the Marine Biological Association from 1966 to 1976, and chancellor of the University of Leicester from 1971 to 1984.

Personal characteristics and influence Hodgkin had a remarkable ability to recognize important problems in his areas of interest and at the same time to see ways of tackling them experimentally. This was combined with skills in dissection and in electronics, and with his exceptional fluency in the necessary mathematics; together these characteristics enabled him to succeed in projects of exceptional difficulty. As a result he was usually ahead of the field and could afford to proceed at his own pace without worrying about being overtaken by other laboratories. He was always ready to discuss his current work with others. Apart from three or four early pieces of research carried out alone he did his experimental work with one, two, or occasionally three collaborators; he had no wish to build up a large group. As well as his own collaborators he usually had in his section of the physiological laboratory one or two visitors doing their own research and publishing independently; he was free with advice and help to them.

Hodgkin remained a very modest man despite his achievements and his distinctions. He had many interests outside science, notably literature, art, and travel, which were shared by his wife. He got much pleasure from fly-fishing and bird-watching during their holidays in the western highlands of Scotland.

Hodgkin's analysis of the mechanism of the nerve impulse is universally recognized as the foundation of later understanding of all excitable tissues. It was greatly extended by others, both in its application to other tissues (notably heart muscle) and in finding the molecular basis of the permeability changes. Similarly his electrical recordings from the light-sensitive elements in the retina led to the recognition that there are many intermediate steps of amplification between the initial absorption of a quantum of light and the production of a nerve impulse, but the identification of these as a cascade of chemical reactions was outside the range of Hodgkin's skills and was achieved by others. Probably the most important practical application so far of Hodgkin's work has been in the improved understanding of irregularities of the heart beat.

Hodgkin died on 20 December 1998 at his home, 18 Panton Street, Cambridge. He was cremated on 30 December at Cambridge crematorium and buried there. He was survived by his wife, Marni, and their four children.

ANDREW HUXLEY

Sources personal knowledge (2004) · private information (2004) [Lady Hodgkin] · A. L. Hodgkin, *Chance and design: reminiscences of science in peace and war* (1992) · B. Lovell, *Echoes of war: the story of H2S radar* (1991) · A. F. Huxley, *Memoirs FRS*, 46 (2000), 219–41 · Royal Society, minutes of the council · *WWW* · b. cert. · d. cert. · *CGPLA Eng. & Wales* (1999)

Archives Trinity Cam., professional papers | CAC Cam., corresp. with A. V. Hill | FILM Dr Heinrich Walter, International Media Productions, Luxembourg (interview for German-language educational series 'The Stars')

Likenesses J. Ward, pen and ink, and wash, 1962, Trinity Cam. · D. Miller, photograph, 1972, Hult. Arch. · D. Hill, oils, 1975, RS [*see illus.*] · M. Noakes, oils, 1980, Trinity Cam. · B. Organ, oils, 1983, University of Leicester · M. Yeoman, pen and ink, 1988, Royal Collection · N. Sinclair, bromide print, 1993, NPG · photographs, priv. coll.

Wealth at death £470,159: probate, 1999, *CGPLA Eng. & Wales*

Hodgkin, Dorothy Mary Crowfoot (1910–1994), chemist and crystallographer, was born on 12 May 1910 in Guizeh, near Cairo, Egypt, the eldest of four daughters of John Winter Crowfoot (1873–1958) and his wife, Grace Mary (Molly) Hood (1877–1957). Her father was an inspector with the ministry of public instruction for Egypt and the Sudan, but he also developed considerable expertise as an archaeologist, and later became director of the British School of Archaeology in Jerusalem. Her mother, although largely self-educated, shared her husband's interest and became an authority on ancient textiles in her own right. Both were descended from moderately prosperous East Anglian families. The Crowfoots came from Beccles in Suffolk, where many of John Crowfoot's relatives entered the medical profession, although his own father had taken holy orders and eventually became chancellor of Lincoln Cathedral. The Hoods owned the small estate of Nettleham Hall, near Lincoln.

Early years and education Until the outbreak of the First World War Dorothy and her next two sisters, Joan and

Dorothy Mary Crowfoot Hodgkin (1910–1994), by Maggi Hambling, 1985

Elisabeth, lived in Cairo with their parents, returning to England for three months each year to escape the summer heat. In 1914 their mother left the girls in the care of their nurse at a house near to their Crowfoot grandparents, who had retired to Worthing in Sussex. She and her husband stayed in Cairo and Khartoum throughout the war; John Crowfoot was appointed director of education for the Sudan in 1916. After the armistice Molly Hood arrived back in England bearing a fourth baby daughter, Diana, and soon afterwards took the family to live at her parents' home, Nettleham Hall in Norfolk. Dorothy had attended school in Worthing, but her mother decided that for the next year she would educate her daughters and some of their cousins herself, developing a curriculum that strongly featured her own interests in history, nature study, and poetry.

In 1920 the Crowfoots took a lease on the Old House in Geldeston, near Beccles. Here the four daughters spent the rest of their childhood, cared for largely by friends and relatives while their parents continued to spend most of the year in Khartoum, and subsequently Jerusalem. As the eldest daughter, Dorothy assumed a degree of responsibility for her sisters from an early age. She attended a small class in Geldeston run by the Parents' National Educational Union. Here for the first time she encountered chemistry, growing crystals of alum and copper sulphate. 'I was captured for life', she wrote in her memoirs, 'by chemistry and by crystals' (Ferry, 8). She at once set up her own laboratory in one of the attics at home, and carried out experiments with materials bought from the local pharmacist. At the age of eleven she was enrolled in a mixed, state-run secondary school, the Sir John Leman School in Beccles. She successfully fought to be allowed to continue her studies in chemistry, then regarded as exclusively a subject for boys even though the chemistry teacher at the school, Criss Deeley, was a woman. When she was thirteen Dorothy and her sister Joan made a three-month visit to their parents in Khartoum, during which she received further encouragement from the government chemist, Dr A. F. Joseph. After helping her to identify a sample of ilmenite she had 'panned' from a stream in the garden, he presented her with a surveyor's box containing forty-eight tubes of chemicals and tools for mineralogical analysis which she took home to add to her attic laboratory. Dorothy's mother also encouraged her interest in chemistry, presenting her with the published volumes of the Royal Institution Christmas lectures given by Sir William Bragg in 1923 and 1925. Here Dorothy read for the first time of the use of X-ray diffraction to 'see' the arrangement of atoms in crystals, the technique demonstrated by Bragg and his son Lawrence in 1912.

After leaving school with an outstanding result in school certificate, she entered Somerville College, Oxford, in 1928 to read chemistry, with the intention of specializing in crystallography. There were only three other scientists among that year's intake at Somerville, and in the university's honour school of chemistry as a whole men outnumbered women by at least twelve to one. Dorothy quickly established a reputation as an exceptional student whose enthusiasm for laboratory work extended to analysing samples of ancient coloured glass sent by her parents from excavations in Palestine. She also found time to develop her own interest in archaeology through completing a detailed illustration of a Byzantine mosaic for one of her father's publications, and joining in local digs at weekends. She was an active member of the Labour Club; her interest in left-wing politics was also sparked by her mother, who had encouraged her to stand as a Labour candidate in a mock election at school.

Early research After the first three years of her course Dorothy undertook research for part two of the honours degree under the supervision of H. M. 'Tiny' Powell, the university demonstrator in the department of mineralogy. Powell had just acquired Oxford's first X-ray set for crystallographic work, which was installed in the University Museum. They worked on the structures of a class of organometallic compounds, the thallium dimethyl halides. Dorothy grew the crystals and took the X-ray photographs, calculating from the diffraction patterns she obtained that the compounds had a face-centred lattice similar to that of common salt but more elongated. A short report of the work was published in *Nature* in 1932 (H. M. Powell and D. Crowfoot, 'Layer-chain structures of thallium di-alkyl halides', *Nature*, 130, pp. 131–2).

On graduating from Oxford with first-class honours, Dorothy went to Cambridge as a research student in the laboratory of John Desmond Bernal. Bernal had trained with Sir William Bragg at the Royal Institution in London, and now headed the X-ray crystallography laboratory in the mineralogy department at Cambridge. There he was

pioneering the use of the technique to study biological molecules. Before Dorothy's arrival he had resolved a dispute between two rival groups of organic chemists over the three-dimensional structure of the sterols. As a result his laboratory was in great demand to analyse crystals of compounds whose structure was unknown. As Bernal was frequently abroad pursuing his political interests (he was a fervent admirer of the Soviet Union, and a prolific writer on the social function of science), much of this work fell to Dorothy. Most significantly, she assisted Bernal in the first description of a diffraction pattern taken from a protein, the digestive enzyme pepsin. Neither the data collection apparatus nor the methods available for mathematical analysis were sufficiently advanced at the time to solve the structure of this complex molecule, but the experiment established for the first time that proteins had regular structures and therefore were potentially amenable to crystallographic analysis (J. D. Bernal and D. Crowfoot, 'X-ray photographs of crystalline pepsin', *Nature*, 133, 1934, 794–5). Bernal also showed that in order to obtain good data from protein crystals it was necessary to keep them wet, photographing them inside a fine glass tube containing the mother liquor.

Soon after she left for Cambridge, Dorothy was offered a temporary fellowship at Somerville College. She hesitated, not wishing to leave the stimulating environment of Bernal's laboratory, but accepted when Somerville agreed that she could remain in Cambridge for the first year of the fellowship. She therefore returned to Oxford in 1934, completing her Cambridge PhD on the sterols two years later. With funds obtained from ICI on her behalf by Sir Robert Robinson, the professor of organic chemistry, she set up her own X-ray equipment in a new laboratory she shared with Powell in a basement corner of the University Museum. Almost at once Robinson presented her with crystals of another protein, insulin. Her successful attempt to obtain an X-ray diffraction pattern from the crystal (despite having dried it) was published in *Nature* the following year, the first paper on which she was sole author (D. Crowfoot, 'X-ray single crystal photographs of insulin', *Nature*, 135, 1935, 591–2). She remained in close touch with Bernal, whom she regarded as a mentor on both scientific and political matters until the end of his life, but at the same time was recognized as a member in her own right of the élite circle of protein crystallographers then being established in Britain.

Marriage and family In 1937 Sir William Bragg invited Dorothy to use the superior X-ray equipment at the Royal Institution to try to get better photographs of her insulin crystals. While in London she stayed with Margery Fry, the former principal of Somerville, who had befriended Dorothy when she was a student there. Staying in the house at the same time was Thomas Lionel *Hodgkin (1910–1982), son of Robert Howard Hodgkin, provost of Queen's College, Oxford. He was Fry's cousin, a graduate in history who had been Dorothy's exact contemporary at Oxford. He had recently lost his job as personal secretary to the British high commissioner in Palestine through his vociferous support of the Arabs, had become a communist, and was now reluctantly being trained as a school-teacher.

Dorothy's beauty had an other-worldly quality, with her slight figure, wavy fair hair, startlingly blue eyes, and preference for handmade clothes that made few concessions to fashion. She appears not to have noticed men at all until she went as a research student to Cambridge, where relationships frequently developed among the men and women who were represented more or less equally in the crystallography and biochemistry laboratories. When she first met Thomas Hodgkin, Dorothy was in love with Bernal, who was not only married but involved in at least one other serious alliance. But after only one or two further meetings, she and Thomas agreed to marry. By the time of their wedding on 16 December 1937, Thomas had discovered a vocation in adult education and was teaching history to unemployed miners in Cumberland. Dorothy, with the support of both families, retained her fellowship at Somerville, which had by this time been made permanent, and continued her research. She published under the name Dorothy Crowfoot until 1949, when she bowed to social pressure and gave her name as Dorothy Crowfoot Hodgkin on the first major publication on the penicillin structure.

The couple's first child, Luke, was born in December 1938. Soon afterwards, following a breast infection, Dorothy suffered an attack of acute rheumatoid arthritis. She was treated both with gold injections and by spa baths at Buxton and made a good recovery. But her hands were left permanently distorted, and the arthritis recurred as she grew older, often causing her intense pain. She had two further children, Elizabeth in 1941 and Toby in 1946. The family set up home in a flat in Bradmore Road, north Oxford, that belonged to Dorothy's parents-in-law. For the first eight years of their marriage Thomas lived mostly in lodgings where he was teaching, first in Cumberland and later in Stoke-on-Trent, returning to Oxford only for weekends and holidays. The Hodgkins' almost daily correspondence during this period provides a very full record of their activities and concerns. Dorothy meanwhile employed nursemaids and cooks to enable her to keep working.

In 1945 Thomas at last settled in Oxford when he was appointed secretary to the university's delegacy for extramural studies. Three years later he was invited to visit the Gold Coast, Nigeria, and the Sudan to advise on the establishment of adult education programmes in countries working towards independence from British rule. Thereafter he devoted himself to chronicling the progress of African nationalism. He resigned his post at Oxford and throughout the 1950s made extensive trips to Africa. From 1957 the Hodgkin family shared a large house in the Woodstock Road with Dorothy's sister Joan, whose marriage had broken down, and her five children. A constant stream of visitors—eminent scientists, African politicians, schoolfriends—mingled over convivial dinners: Thomas was a great *bon viveur* and liked to cook for whomever happened to be passing through when he was at home.

In 1961 Thomas was personally appointed by Kwame Nkrumah as director of the Institute for African Studies in Accra, Ghana. Thereafter Dorothy visited him in Ghana for a month or two each year, until with Nkrumah's fall from power in 1966 Thomas returned to England. With his health in a precarious state—he was a lifelong smoker and suffered from emphysema—he and Dorothy eventually moved into Crab Mill, the rambling stone house in Ilmington, Warwickshire, that had been bought by Thomas's parents before the Second World War. They both received frequent invitations to visit other countries and often travelled together—as far afield as Vietnam, India, Africa, and the US.

Thomas died in March 1982 in Tolon, Greece, while returning with Dorothy from a winter sojourn in the Sudan. He was buried in a nearby graveyard overlooking the sea. Dorothy was grief-stricken at his death. With his frequent absences (and several acknowledged infidelities), he could not be classed as a wholly supportive husband to a woman with a busy research career; however, at the time of their marriage he was unusual in accepting that his wife might have a career at all. And there seems little doubt that despite the outwardly unconventional course of their marriage, Dorothy and Thomas were bound by a strong mutual affection, admiration for each other's work, and passionately held political views.

Later research   In 1940 Dorothy received a large grant from the Rockefeller Foundation to continue her work on the structure of insulin. At the same time she took over equipment evacuated from Bernal's lab (he had moved from Cambridge to Birkbeck College in London), and two of his research assistants, Harry Carlisle and Käthe Schiff. With Carlisle she solved the complete three-dimensional structure of cholesterol iodide, including all the bond lengths and angles. This was the first crystallographic study she had pursued to its conclusion, and the first anywhere of such a complex organic molecule (C. H. Carlisle and D. Crowfoot, 'The crystal structure of cholesterol iodide', *PRS*, 184A, 1945, 64–83).

At the same time Dorothy was beginning to collaborate with other Oxford scientists on the study of penicillin. Howard Florey and Ernst Chain demonstrated its efficacy against bacterial infections in animals and humans during 1940 and 1941, but its chemical formula was unknown. The chemists suggested two opposing theories, the thiazolidine-oxazolone formula championed by Sir Robert Robinson, and the beta-lactam formula, which included an unusual four-membered ring, favoured by Edward Abraham and Ernst Chain. A successful X-ray crystallographic study could resolve the question, but penicillin proved extremely difficult to crystallize. Dorothy did not obtain suitable crystals until 1944, when samples of benzylpenicillin were shipped from America and brought to her by Kathleen Lonsdale, then a senior crystallographic researcher at the Royal Institution. With her assistant Barbara Low, one of her students from Somerville, Dorothy embarked on studies of three different salts of benzylpenicillin, each with a different heavy atom, trusting that the structure would emerge from comparisons between the three.

In collaboration with Charles Bunn and Anne Turner-Jones at ICI's Northwich laboratories, who analysed the sodium salt using the 'fly's eye' method of modelling diffraction patterns, they solved the penicillin structure by 1945. With the help of the scientific computing service run by L. J. Comrie, they calculated the complete three-dimensional structure on a Hollerith punched card calculator, one of the earliest examples of crystallographic computing. News of the success gradually leaked out into the crystallographic community: what had begun as wartime secrecy continued after VE-day as commercial secrecy to protect the interests of the US firms who had undertaken the mass production of the drug, and the penicillin structure was not formally published until 1949 (D. Crowfoot, B. W. Rogers-Low, and A. Turner-Jones, 'The X-ray crystallographic investigation of the structure of penicillin', *The Chemistry of Penicillin*, ed. H. T. Clarke, J. R. Johnson, and R. Robinson, 1949, 310–67).

Oxford University was slow to recognize Dorothy's scientific distinction. She was shortlisted for the readership in chemical crystallography in 1944, but the post went to Powell, her former supervisor. In 1946 she was appointed to the lesser post of university demonstrator, which nevertheless doubled her income; she had previously kept her family on only her college fellowship. The following year she was elected a fellow of the Royal Society at the relatively early age of thirty-six.

Through her work on penicillin Dorothy had made many industrial contacts, and in 1948 Lester Smith of Glaxo gave her some dark red crystals of the anti-pernicious anaemia factor, vitamin B12. Soon afterwards the Glaxo chemists told her that the factor contained cobalt, which was heavy enough to show up on the Patterson maps that were Dorothy's preferred approach to structure analysis and could therefore help to solve the problem of phase determination. With a series of assistants, principally her student Jenny Pickworth (later Jenny Glusker), she embarked on a solution of the structure. At the same time Alexander Todd and his colleagues in Cambridge were working on a chemical analysis of the vitamin, whose formula was unknown. From Todd's laboratory Dorothy obtained a crystal of a cobalt-containing fragment of B12, the hexacarboxylic acid, that made it possible to elucidate the inner core of this complex molecule.

While actively encouraging the establishment of the first computing facilities in Oxford, Dorothy took advantage of an offer from Kenneth Trueblood of the University of California at Los Angeles to calculate atomic positions on one of the first electronic computers, the National Bureau of Standards western automatic computer, at no cost. Between 1953 and 1955 data and results went back and forth across the Atlantic, until the structure of the fragment was solved (D. C. Hodgkin and others, 'The crystal structure of the hexacarboxylic acid derived from B12 and the molecular structure of the vitamin', *Nature*, 176, 1955, 325–8). It proved to include an unusual set of rings known as the corrin nucleus. Working out from this nucleus, Dorothy and her colleagues solved the full structure of vitamin B12 by 1957. The fact that she had succeeded with a molecule of 100 atoms of unknown chemical formula moved Lawrence Bragg to describe her achievement as 'breaking the sound barrier'.

As Dorothy established her pre-eminence in the field, honours quickly followed. Oxford University promoted Dorothy to a readership in 1955. In 1956 the Royal Society awarded her its royal medal, and four years later appointed her its first Wolfson research professor, a post she could hold at any university and which came with funds both for her personal salary and for research assistance and expenses.

In 1964 (having been proposed at least twice previously) she was awarded the Nobel prize for chemistry, only the third woman to be so distinguished after Marie Curie and her daughter Irène Joliot-Curie, and the fifth woman to win any science Nobel. To date (2001) she remains the only British woman scientist to win a Nobel prize. When the prize was announced she was visiting Thomas in Ghana, and she heard the news from two young Ghanaian reporters who had been sent to cover the story. The telegram from Stockholm arrived three months later, forwarded by sea mail from Woodstock Road by a niece brought up to be careful with money, along with all the other telegrams of congratulation.

In the following year Dorothy received a black-bordered envelope from Buckingham Palace, containing an invitation to join the Order of Merit. She and Benjamin Britten were admitted to the order to fill the vacancies left by the deaths of Sir Winston Churchill and T. S. Eliot. Although she disliked titles and had frequently declared to Thomas that she would refuse a DBE if it were offered, she saw the OM as 'rather different really' (Ferry, 294), and accepted—just as she accepted the first freedom of Beccles, an honour hastily invented for her by the town in which she spent her schooldays.

Dorothy's greatest scientific achievement was still to come. She had never given up hope of solving a protein structure, and specifically the structure of insulin which she had photographed in 1935. From the end of the 1950s onwards insulin was the primary focus of the research in her group. In 1958 and 1959 John Kendrew and Max Perutz at the Medical Research Council's laboratory of molecular biology in Cambridge had solved the structures of myoglobin and haemoglobin, showing for the first time that protein molecules were indeed amenable to crystallographic analysis. They used the heavy atom method, in which the diffraction patterns of derivatives containing different heavy atoms at the same sites were compared. Insulin was more difficult because its threefold symmetry complicated the ever-present problem of calculating the phases. It also proved difficult to prepare suitable heavy atom derivatives—either the crystal would not take up the heavy atoms at all, or they might attach themselves to so many sites that it was impossible to compare one derivative with another, or the crystal might simply fall apart.

Dorothy acted as a source of inspiration and encouragement to an evolving population of researchers working on insulin in her lab, principal among whom was Guy Dodson who joined her in 1962 having just gained his PhD in New Zealand. Dodson soon afterwards married Eleanor Coller, an Australian with a degree in mathematics whom Dorothy had recruited as a technician. Eleanor Dodson undertook the task of analysing the vast amount of data generated by the insulin project with the limited computing resources available at the time, and subsequently played an important role in developing new mathematical approaches to solving the structure. Over the course of a decade a series of advances steadily improved both the quality of the data and the resources that could be deployed to analyse it. First, Dorothy learned from two Swedish chemists that it was possible to remove the zinc atoms that sat at the centre of each insulin molecule, and replace them with other metal atoms. Using this method members of the group successfully made lead and cadmium insulin crystals as well as zinc-free crystals. With the uranyl derivatives produced by Tom Blundell, who joined the department of chemical crystallography in 1964 as a part two student and stayed on to work with Dorothy's group, they at last had a series of suitable crystals that could in principle yield adequate data for a solution. But the data collection called for great accuracy and precision, comparing minute differences in the intensity of the X-ray reflections. Only in 1968, when Dorothy purchased an early model of the automatic four-circle diffractometer developed by David Phillips and Uli Arndt, did they finally obtain data of high enough quality.

Late in July of the following year it finally became clear that the electron density maps based on analysis of these measurements could be interpreted to show the positions of the atoms in the molecule. Over a single weekend, working almost non-stop, Dorothy, with Guy Dodson and M. Vijayan, a visiting scientist from Bangalore, built the first model of the molecule, an occasion which Dodson remembers vividly. 'It was a triumphant occasion in which Dorothy, though suffering from swelling ankles and forced into wearing slippers, worked with concentration and wonderful spirits' (Dodson). In a characteristic gesture she gave the honour of presenting the structure a few weeks later at the 1969 meeting of the International Union of Crystallography to Tom Blundell, the youngest member of the group, who had been abroad and so missed the excitement of the model-building weekend (M. J. Adams and others, 'Structure of rhombohedral 2-zinc insulin crystals', *Nature*, 224, 1969, 491–5).

In the case of each of the three projects for which she is best known—penicillin, vitamin B12, and insulin—Dorothy pushed the boundaries of what was possible with the techniques available. Her distinction lay not in developing new approaches, but in a remarkable ability to envisage possibilities in three-dimensional structures, grounded in a profound understanding of the underlying chemistry. She kept an open mind, not committing herself to a structure until it was supported by the unequivocal evidence of a successfully completed crystallographic study. She was exceptionally determined, persisting with apparently unpromising projects long after others would have given up in despair. While she did not consider it part of her role to explore the function of the molecules she studied, her results made it possible for others to increase their understanding of their biosynthesis and chemical interactions, and hence to develop improved therapies for disease.

Laboratory life Despite her increasing eminence, Dorothy retained a gentleness of manner, quietness of speech, and egalitarian outlook that inspired loyalty and devotion among most of her younger colleagues. She drew her research team partly from among the Somerville chemistry students she supervised (these briefly included Margaret Roberts, later the British prime minister Margaret Thatcher), and partly from a steady stream of mostly international post-doctoral workers who wrote asking if they could join. She insisted that everyone in her lab, from the most junior technician to the most distinguished academic visitor, simply call her Dorothy.

Partly, though not entirely, as a result of the Somerville connection the lab contained approximately equal numbers of male and female research workers, exceptional among chemistry laboratories at Oxford. Dorothy herself denied that her gender had ever hindered her progress, but when she encountered instances of discrimination against her own junior female colleagues she resisted them vigorously. For example, she was incensed to discover that female graduate students routinely had their grants reduced on marriage. However, it took a stint on a committee investigating the administration of Birmingham University in 1970 to bring home to her the insecurity of many women workers with families, including those in her own lab. After this she ensured that they had proper contracts with paid maternity leave, rather than simply paying them for the hours they worked.

She directed the laboratory with a very light touch, taking it as read that everyone was as committed as she was to the task in hand. To outside observers the lab could appear chaotic, with the younger members as likely to be engaged in games of indoor cricket or political arguments as scientific experiments. Dorothy herself avoided administrative tasks as far as possible, unless they were directly related to advancing her research. The officers of funding bodies (particularly the Rockefeller Foundation, which continued to support her until the 1960s) often had to remind her to ask for grants. Yet against all appearances the lab was immensely productive.

For all its success, her group was entirely dependent on Dorothy for its continued existence; not one of her assistants held a permanent post. As an interdisciplinary science, the crystallography of biological molecules did not fit into any of the established departments at Oxford. Over the years it was moved from mineralogy to inorganic chemistry, thence to zoology, and ultimately (well after Dorothy's retirement) to biochemistry. It was always a challenge to find enough space to accommodate her research assistants and the equipment that she had no difficulty in funding through outside grants: her appointment to the Wolfson chair was greeted privately by the university authorities as a 'new and confusing problem' (Ferry, 284). But although at different times Dorothy received offers to move elsewhere that included attractive research facilities, she chose to stay in Oxford because of her family circumstances.

With a view to strengthening the position of crystallography in Oxford, and recruiting someone to deputize for her during her increasingly frequent absences abroad, in the early 1960s Dorothy encouraged David Phillips, then at the Royal Institution, to think of moving to Oxford. He eventually did so in 1966, having negotiated with the university authorities a personal chair, permanent posts for several members of his group, and space for a laboratory of molecular biophysics within the new department of zoology. But Dorothy's own group remained separate from Phillips's, belatedly accommodated in the adjacent department of experimental psychology, and by the time she retired all of its members had found jobs elsewhere. As long as she had been present in Oxford, Dorothy had been able to keep her show on the road by virtue of her great distinction and her powers of persuasion. But she had never undertaken the political negotiations that would have been necessary to establish her group on a more permanent footing.

International and political activities In 1925 Dorothy's mother, who had lost all four of her brothers as a result of the First World War, took her to observe the sixth assembly of the League of Nations in Geneva. Dorothy retained a lifelong conviction that the problems of the world could be resolved through dialogue, and that armed conflict should be avoided at all costs. Under the influence first of her mother, and later of Bernal and Thomas Hodgkin, she also developed an unshakeable faith in socialism and an admiration for communist regimes that often blinded her to the abuses of human rights perpetrated by their leaders.

However, she was no party hack: she exercised her political consciousness on the level of personal contacts with individuals, being particularly concerned to keep channels of scientific communication open despite antagonism between East and West. As a result her politics never prevented her from interacting comfortably with those who held more conventional views, whether in the scientific or the political sphere. The only serious opposition she encountered was from the US government during the McCarthy era. Her membership of an organization called Science for Peace (and possibly her links with Bernal and Thomas Hodgkin) resulted in her being declared 'statutorily inadmissible' by the state department in 1953, and she was unable to obtain a waiver of this ruling until 1957, despite numerous appeals on her behalf by members of the American crystallographic community. For the rest of her life every visit to the US necessitated a trip to the embassy in London to have the waiver renewed. Her exclusion from that country in 1953 provided an opportunity for her to make the first of many visits to the Soviet Union. Her

support for its scientists and for East–West *détente* was recognized by the Mikhail Lomonosov gold medal in 1982, and by the Lenin peace prize in 1987.

In 1959 Dorothy was one of a delegation of British academics who visited China to mark the tenth anniversary of the founding of the People's Republic of China. On discovering that Chinese scientists were working on insulin, she gave them every support and encouragement, and made several return visits right through the period of the cultural revolution, when China was virtually closed to the outside world. In her capacity as president of the International Union of Crystallography from 1972 to 1975 she was the first to report the success of the Chinese team in arriving at an independent solution of the insulin structure, and she worked tirelessly for the readmission of China to that body (finally achieved in 1978). She developed equally warm relationships with India through a succession of visitors to her lab, who came mostly from the Indian Institute of Sciences in Bangalore during the 1960s and 1970s.

In addition to promoting international scientific contacts, she realized that her Nobel prize put her in a position to campaign on behalf of other causes in which she believed strongly. She was a member of the Campaign for Nuclear Disarmament, and vehemently opposed America's intervention in Vietnam and Cambodia. She accepted an invitation to become president of the Medical Aid Foundation for Vietnam, and later sat on an international commission into US war crimes in Vietnam. She and Thomas visited North Vietnam in 1971, and again in 1974 when their daughter Elizabeth was teaching English and editing English-language publications in Hanoi.

In the early 1960s Dorothy had attended a meeting in London of the Pugwash Conferences on Science and World Affairs, an organization founded by Bertrand Russell, Albert Einstein, and others in 1955 to bring together scientists from East and West to discuss disarmament. She attended a few further meetings, but did not become actively involved until 1975, when she was invited to become its president. Accepting with some misgivings at the commitment involved, she thereafter travelled tirelessly on behalf of the organization, working in particular on a goal dear to her heart, the participation of Chinese representatives in the Pugwash meetings. After her former student Margaret Thatcher was elected prime minister in 1979, she took the opportunity to approach her personally to argue for a rapprochement with the Soviet Union, and corresponded with her on detailed questions such as the verification of chemical test bans.

Another cause in which she believed strongly was that of support for higher education. In 1970 she was elected chancellor of the University of Bristol, normally a purely honorary position. However, she made a point of visiting the students and hearing their concerns, and used the role to protest about the swingeing cuts in university budgets introduced by the government in 1981, which resulted in reduced student numbers and the closure of Bristol's school of architecture. She also helped to establish Hodgkin House, a hostel for international students at Bristol, in memory of Thomas, and encouraged the students to raise funds to support a Hodgkin scholarship for students from South Africa.

Last years Dorothy retired from her university post in 1977, but retained a room in the chemical crystallography department where she could work. She continued to refine the structure of insulin with Guy Dodson, who had moved to the University of York, until 1988. In that year they published a solution of the structure at such high resolution that the position of every intervening water molecule could be discerned (E. N. Baker and others, 'The structure of 2Zn pig insulin crystals at 1.5Å resolution', *PTRS*, 319A, 1988, 369–456).

In the same year Dorothy gave up her other commitments, to Pugwash, the University of Bristol and other organizations, and began to turn down more of the invitations to travel and speak that she still received in great numbers. Her arthritis was making walking increasingly difficult, and she had begun to use a wheelchair. In 1990, a few months after friends and colleagues from all over the world had gathered in Oxford and at Crab Mill to celebrate her eightieth birthday, she fell at home and broke her hip. Despite her great frailty she recovered, although she never walked again and she ceased to give lectures. However, she continued to delight in the company of her children, grandchildren, and great-grandchildren, and of former colleagues who visited whenever they could. She retained an intense interest in world affairs and scientific progress.

In September 1993 the International Congress of Crystallography was to be held in Beijing. After watching a television programme critical of China, Dorothy suddenly announced that she intended to go to the congress, and no one could dissuade her. Both the Royal Society, which was to fund her trip, and her Chinese hosts expressed their anxiety that she would not survive the journey. Her doctor refused to certify her fit to travel. But accompanied by Elizabeth and with the support of the Dodsons she successfully made the journey to Beijing and back. While there she attended several of the lectures, and back in her room each evening she would 'whisper shrewd observations about them' (Ferry, 401). But her obvious frailty was a shock to many of her international colleagues who had known her previously.

In the following July Dorothy suffered another fall, and two weeks later, on 29 July 1994, she died at home at Crab Mill with her family and friends around her. She was buried in the churchyard of the parish church of St Mary the Virgin in Ilmington. A service was held in her memory on 4 March 1995 at the university church of St Mary the Virgin in Oxford, attended by all of her family, many of her scientific colleagues, and a large crowd of well-wishers including Sir Isaiah Berlin, Baroness Thatcher, and Lord Jenkins. The address was read by Max Perutz, who had been a close friend since he came to Cambridge from Vienna as a young researcher in 1936. His summing up of Dorothy's character has not been bettered:

> There was a magic about her person. She had no enemies, not even among those whose scientific theories she

demolished or whose political views she opposed … It was marvellous to have her drop in on you in the lab, like the Spring. Dorothy will be remembered as a great chemist, a saintly, tolerant and gentle lover of people and a devoted protagonist of peace. (Ferry, 402)

Many of the bodies with which Dorothy was associated took steps to ensure that she would remain permanently in the public eye. The Royal Society commissioned portraits from Graham Sutherland and Bryan Organ, together with an exquisite pen-and-ink drawing of her hands by Henry Moore. Somerville College has a bronze bust of Dorothy modelled from life by Anthony Stones in 1983. The best-known and most controversial portrait is the 1985 painting by Maggi Hambling that hangs in the National Portrait Gallery. It shows Dorothy in severe, black-framed spectacles, wisps of hair rising unrestrained from her head, hard at work in her room at Crab Mill. To indicate the rapidity with which Dorothy worked through the electron density maps on her cluttered desk, the artist has given her an extra pair of hands. Dorothy is also commemorated through the Dorothy Hodgkin fellowships awarded by the Royal Society to young researchers, many of them women, and by a plaque placed on the wall of the inorganic chemistry laboratory at Oxford University as part of the Royal Society of Chemistry's national chemical landmarks scheme.   GEORGINA FERRY

Sources G. Ferry, *Dorothy Hodgkin: a life* (1998) · *The collected works of Dorothy Crowfoot Hodgkin*, ed. G. Dodson and others (1994) · *Memoirs FRS* (Nov 2002) · *WWW* · *The Times* (30 July 1994) · *The Independent* (1 Aug 1994) · b. cert. · m. cert. · d. cert. · O. Wojtas, 'A sparkling career', *Times Higher Education Supplement* (17 March 1995), 23 · *CGPLA Eng. & Wales* (1995)
Archives Bodl. Oxf., corresp. and MSS | Bodl. Oxf., Lord Phillips MSS · Bodl. Oxf., corresp. with Sir Rex Richards · CUL, Bernal MSS · RS, corresp. with Sir Robert Robinson relating to his memoirs · Trinity Cam., corresp. with R. L. M. Synge · Wellcome L., corresp. with Ernst Chain | FILM Biochemical Society, London, archives · RCP Lond., Medical Sciences Video-Archive | SOUND BL NSA, 'Finding what's there', NP8534/01 TR1 · BL NSA, oral history interview
Likenesses Ramsey & Muspratt, bromide print, *c.*1937, NPG · photograph, 1937, NPG; repro. in *The Independent* · photograph, 1964, Hult. Arch. · G. Sutherland, watercolour, 1979, RS · B. Organ, oils, 1982, RS · A. Stones, bronze bust, 1983, Somerville College, Oxford · M. Hambling, oils, 1985, NPG [*see illus.*] · bronze bust, University of Bristol · photograph, repro. in *The Times* · portrait, Royal Society of Chemistry, London
Wealth at death £71,229: probate, 31 Jan 1995, *CGPLA Eng. & Wales*

Hodgkin, John (*d.* 1560), Dominican friar and bishop-suffragan of Bedford, is of unknown origins, and nothing is known of his family. He is first recorded in 1512, as a member of the Dominican convent at Cambridge, when he was ordained successively subdeacon and deacon. By July 1521 he was at Oxford, supplicating for the degree of BTh; in 1525 he was recorded as DTh at Cambridge. By 1527 he was provincial of the English Dominicans. In 1531 he was one of the friars who tried to persuade Thomas Bilney to recant before his execution for heresy. In 1536 he was deprived of his office as provincial, but later reinstated. On 2 December in the following year he was nominated suffragan bishop of Bedford by John Stokesley, bishop of

London, and consecrated a week later. When Stokesley died, Hodgkin preached movingly at his funeral, held in St Paul's on 14 September 1539, causing 'weeping eyes' among his hearers (Wriothesley, 1.107). Made rector of Layham, Suffolk, in 1537, he had resigned this benefice by the end of 1539. On 12 February 1541 he was admitted vicar of Saffron Walden, but in 1544 exchanged it for the rectory of Laingdon-cum-Basildon. On 26 November 1548 he was admitted to the prebend of Harleston in St Paul's Cathedral.

Under Edward VI Hodgkin took part in the consecrations of Nicholas Ridley (1547) and Miles Coverdale (1551) as bishops, and in 1553 he may have been a supporter of Lady Jane Grey; as the young king lay dying, Hodgkin, probably acting on orders from Ridley as bishop of London, omitted to pray for the princesses Mary and Elizabeth. But when in 1554 he was deprived of all his preferments it was for having married, allegedly on the advice of Thomas Cranmer. Soon afterwards, however, he repudiated his wife, whose identity is unknown, and on 2 April 1555 was admitted rector of St Peter Cornhill in London. He lost this benefice on the accession of Elizabeth I, but probably in 1559 was reinstated in his prebend of Harleston and rectory of Laingdon. On 17 December 1559 he assisted in the consecration of Matthew Parker as archbishop of Canterbury. Hodgkin died in 1560, some time before 7 July.   ANDREW A. CHIBI

Sources C. Wriothesley, *A chronicle of England during the reigns of the Tudors from* AD *1485 to 1559*, ed. W. D. Hamilton, 2 vols., CS, new ser., 11, 20 (1875–7) · Emden, *Oxf.*, 4.291 · *LP Henry VIII* · *Calendar of the manuscripts of the dean and chapter of Wells*, 2 vols., HMC, 12 (1907–14) · *N&Q*, 2nd ser., 2 (1856), 2 · Cooper, *Ath. Cantab.*, 1.206–7 · Rymer, *Foedera*, 1st edn, 613 · Wood, *Ath. Oxon.*, new edn · R. Newcourt, *An ecclesiastical parochial history of the diocese of London*, 2 vols. (1708–10) · J. Strype, *Memorials of the most reverend father in God Thomas Cranmer*, new edn, 2 vols. (1812) · Venn, *Alum. Cant.* · *Fasti Angl., 1541–1857*, [St Paul's, London]
Archives Episcopal Register Stokesley, MSS 9531/11 · Episcopal Register Bonner, MSS 9531/12

Hodgkin, John (1766–1845), grammarian and calligrapher, was born at Shipston-on-Stour, Worcestershire, on 11 February 1766, the son of John Hodgkin, shopkeeper and wool stapler, and his wife, Elizabeth, *née* Gibbs. He was educated partly at a Quakers' school at Worcester, and partly by his uncle, Thomas Hodgkin, a successful private tutor in London, who invited his nephew to enter his own profession. In 1787 he joined the physicist and Egyptologist Thomas Young in superintending the education of the antiquary Hudson Gurney. The two tutors seem to have given each other mutual instruction for four years, and all remained warm friends. He was briefly a master at Ackworth Friends' school, Yorkshire, before leaving for France.

In 1792 Hodgkin spent some months at Vincennes in order to improve his knowledge of French. His recollections of the royal family are recorded in his manuscript autobiography (Wellcome Institute, London). When Louis XVI took the oath to the constitution, Hodgkin, as a Quaker, had a conscientious objection to raise his hand with the multitude swearing fidelity to the compact between king and people, while his plain dress caused him to be continually taken for a priest. He managed, however, to escape real danger. He describes in graphic language the consternation at Vincennes on 10 August 1792, the day of the massacre of the Swiss guard.

Upon his return to England Hodgkin married on 1 May 1793 at Lewes, Sussex, Elizabeth Rickman, a cousin of Thomas Rickman the architect. Their sons Thomas *Hodgkin (1798–1866) and John *Hodgkin (1800–1875) are noticed separately. Hodgkin soon became well known as a private tutor, chiefly to ladies belonging to the families of wealthy citizens in the environs of London. He resided for some years at Pentonville, London, and then moved to Tottenham. He instructed his pupils in the classics and mathematics, but especially in the art of handwriting, in which he greatly excelled.

Hodgkin has left a remarkable record of his skill in handwriting in his *Calligraphia Græca* (1794), dedicated to Hodgkin's friend Thomas Young, at whose suggestion it was composed. Young also furnished the gnomic sentences from various authors, which Hodgkin wrote in beautiful Greek characters, and his friend Henry Ashby engraved. A translation by Young of Lear's curse into Greek iambics, undertaken 'rogatu viri omnium disertissimi Edmundi Burke', was also added. The work was not published until 1807, when it appeared together with *Pœcilographia Græca*, in which nineteen Greek alphabets of various periods are figured, and some seven hundred contractions used in Greek manuscripts are given. Some of the latter were brought to Hodgkin's notice by the Greek scholar Richard Porson, with whom he had a slight acquaintance. Hodgkin also published, besides school and exercise books: *Definitions of some of the Terms Made Use of in Geography and Astronomy* (1804; 2nd edn, 1812); *Specimens of Greek Penmanship* (1804); *An Introduction to Writing* (4th edn, 1811); and *A Sketch of the Greek Accidence* (1812). He contributed to *Excerpta ex J. F. Bastii commentatione cum tabulis lithographicis a J. Hodgkin transcripta* (1835). He died in August 1845 at Tottenham, Middlesex, and was survived by his wife.

THOMAS HODGKIN, *rev.* HELEN CAROLINE JONES

Sources Wellcome L., WMS/PP/HO [incl. MS autobiography] · Watt, *Bibl. Brit.* · *IGI* · K. Hodgkin, 'The uncertainties, mistakes, dilemmas and other contributions to a happy family life', 1992–4, priv. coll.
Archives Durham RO, papers · Wellcome L., autobiography, corresp., and papers
Likenesses portrait, priv. coll.; repro. in Hodgkin, 'Uncertainties, mistakes, dilemmas'

Hodgkin, John (1800–1875), barrister and Quaker minister, was born on 11 March 1800 in Penton Street, Pentonville, London, and grew up in Pentonville and in Tottenham. He was the youngest child of John *Hodgkin (1766–1845), tutor and calligrapher, and Elizabeth Hodgkin, *née* Rickman (1768–1833). Both parents belonged to long-standing Quaker families. Their only other child to survive infancy was the medical writer Thomas *Hodgkin (1798–1866). Both boys (who were close friends all their lives) were educated at home, chiefly by their father. They received a thorough classical training and some knowledge of science. It was a sheltered upbringing, which John Hodgkin felt was responsible for his painful sensitivity as a young man. In his childhood and for the rest of his life periods of intense intellectual work alternated with ill health.

Advised by his family and by Joseph John Gurney (1788–1847), Hodgkin chose to become a barrister rather than follow his father into teaching. In 1819 he was admitted to Lincoln's Inn (where his Quaker principles made it necessary to ensure that his dues would not subsidize the chaplain and thus the established church) and from 1821 to 1824 he trained in the chambers of George Harrison, the first Quaker to be called to the bar. Hodgkin rarely appeared in court but had a large practice and was in considerable demand as a teacher. His specialism was conveyancing, and his chief concerns were clarity and concision: in an 1829 pamphlet he proposed simplifying the conveyancing process by setting up a general register of titles to property.

In 1829 Hodgkin married Elizabeth Howard (1803–1836), daughter of Luke *Howard (1772–1864), Quaker chemical manufacturer and meteorologist. Hodgkin credited her with vivifying his previously austere life, bringing him a conception of religion based on love rather than law. They lived in Tottenham and had four surviving children, including the historian Thomas *Hodgkin (1831–1913). In 1836 Elizabeth Hodgkin died in childbirth.

The 1830s brought the Beaconite controversy: the Society of Friends divided over the perceived aridity of Quaker orthodoxy. Dissidents called for greater appeal to the emotions and less stress upon law. Hodgkin's marriage had connected him with Friends who left the society, but he remained a member and sought to synthesize the two approaches. Shortly after his first wife's death he urged reconciliation at his local meeting—his first 'offering'— and in 1840 he was officially recorded as a minister.

The 1840s were a pivotal period for Hodgkin. In 1843 he married Anne Backhouse (1815–1845); they had one child before her death of Bright's disease. Also in 1843 he retired from legal practice after a breakdown in his health, although he continued to advise Friends on legal matters and retained an interest in legal reform. Conversely, he poured energy into his activities as a minister, travelling frequently in this capacity. In 1850 and 1851 he was clerk to the yearly meeting in London. By the end of his life he had visited almost all the Friends' meetings of the United Kingdom and many abroad, always preaching strictly extempore and being noted for his empathy with the particular circumstances of his listeners.

In 1847 and 1849 Hodgkin visited the Friends' meetings in Ireland and in 1850 married Elizabeth Haughton (1818–1904), an Irish Quaker. They had six children. Participation in Irish famine relief efforts (he took a particular interest in the fishing settlement of the Claddagh, near Galway) involved him in drafting the Encumbered Estates Act (1849) which aimed to encourage Irish landlords to invest in their properties, but he turned down a position administering the act.

In 1857 Hodgkin left Tottenham for Lewes in Sussex, his mother's home town. He remained energetic in the Friends' cause. A visit to the United States in 1861 coincided with the outbreak of civil war, in which Friends found themselves caught between the conflicting principles of anti-slavery and pacifism. In 1863 he went to Spain as one of a delegation to plead for imprisoned protestants. In November 1874 he suffered a stroke which left him paralysed. He died at Durley Dean in Bournemouth on 3 July 1875 and was buried at Winchmore Hill, Middlesex. CHRISTOPHER HILTON

Sources Wellcome L., Hodgkin family MSS, WMS/PP/HO · J. Hodgkin, autobiography, c.1863–1869, Wellcome L., WMS/PP/HO/E/C5 · 'Dictionary of Quaker biography', RS Friends, Lond. [card index] · Durham RO, Hodgkin MSS, D/HO · A. M. Kass and E. H. Kass, *Perfecting the world, the life and times of Dr. Thomas Hodgkin, 1798–1866* (1988) · 'John Hodgkin', *Friends of a half century*, ed. W. Robinson (1891) · L. von Glehn Creighton, *Life and letters of Thomas Hodgkin* (1917) · *DNB* · M. Rose, *Curator of the dead: Thomas Hodgkin, 1798–1866* (1981) · L. Rosenfeld, *Thomas Hodgkin: morbid anatomist and social activist* (1993)

Archives Durham RO, corresp. and papers · E. Sussex RO · RS Friends, Lond., letters · Wellcome L., corresp. and papers | LMA, Howard family MSS

Likenesses photograph, c.1860, repro. in Kass and Kass, *Perfecting the world* · Meisenbach, engraving, c.1865–1869 (after photograph by Elliott & Fry), repro. in 'John Hodgkin' · Elliott & Fry, photograph, 1867, Wellcome L. · J. Sperling, group portrait, oils (with family), repro. in Creighton, *Life and letters*

Wealth at death under £80,000: probate, 29 July 1875, CGPLA Eng. & Wales

Hodgkin, Thomas (1798–1866), physician and social reformer, was born on 17 August 1798 in Pentonville, London, the third of the four sons (two died young) of John *Hodgkin (1766–1845), calligrapher and teacher, and his wife, Elizabeth (1768–1833), daughter of Richard Peters Rickman and his wife, Mary (Verrall) and a cousin of the architect Thomas Rickman. Both families had been Quakers since the mid-seventeenth century. Hodgkin was educated at home along with his younger brother, John *Hodgkin (1800–1875), until 1816, when he became private secretary to William Allen, apothecary, scientist, and social activist. Allen introduced him to medicine and also reinforced his Quaker concerns for social reform. When an apprenticeship with Allen could not be arranged, Hodgkin was articled to an apothecary firm in Brighton.

Hodgkin quickly recognized that medicine better suited his interests, and spent a year walking the wards at Guy's Hospital, London. In 1820 he enrolled at the University of Edinburgh, where he received the MD in 1823. His thesis, *De absorbendi functione*, received praise for the excellence of the Latin prose. Hodgkin interrupted his Edinburgh studies with a year in Paris, where he gave particular attention to morbid anatomy (pathology) and learned to use the stethoscope from R. T. H. Laennec. On his return from Paris, he introduced the stethoscope to the Physical Society of Guy's Hospital.

Following his graduation, Hodgkin spent two more years on the continent, initially as physician and travelling companion to Abraham Montefiore, afterwards in

Thomas Hodgkin (1798–1866), by unknown photographer

additional medical studies in Paris. Returning to London in 1825, he became a licentiate of the Royal College of Physicians and was appointed lecturer in morbid anatomy and curator of the anatomical museum of Guy's Hospital medical school. There he gave the first systematic lectures on morbid anatomy in England, conducted numerous autopsies, prepared many exhibits, and published a catalogue for the museum (1829). His significant medical papers included those on the discovery of the striated appearance of voluntary muscles, and a description of the shape of erythrocytes (1827); studies of carcinoma (1829); a description, before Sir Dominic Corrigan, of retroversion of aortic valves (1829); and discussion of the 1832 cholera epidemic. The paper that gained him eponymous fame, 'On some morbid appearances of the absorbent glands and spleen' (*Medico-Chirurgical Transactions*, 17, 1832, 68–114), described seven cases with an unusual appearance of the lymph glands and spleen. Sir Samuel Wilks made similar observations more than thirty years later, and recalling Hodgkin's earlier paper, it was he who named the disorder Hodgkin's disease. Two of Hodgkin's cases, and possibly one other, have since been verified as meeting histological criteria for Hodgkin's disease. Hodgkin's books included *Lectures on the Means of Promoting and Preserving Health* (1835), based on lectures delivered at the Spitalfields Mechanics' Institute, and *Lectures on the Morbid Anatomy of the Serous and Mucous Membranes* (vol. 1, 1836; vol. 2, 1840).

Simultaneously, Hodgkin was active in reform, publishing *An Essay on Medical Education* in 1828, and serving on the general committee of the British and Foreign School Society. He advocated the colonization of Africa by freed American black people as a solution to slavery, supported the American Colonization Society, and created the British African Colonization Society for the further promotion of colonization in Liberia. His youthful concern for the plight of North American Indians became a lifelong defence of all indigenous groups threatened by the advance of Western civilization. He was one of the founders of the Aborigines' Protection Society, and its foremost spokesman. In 1836 he was appointed to the senate of the newly organized University of London and remained active in its oversight of medical education.

Hodgkin expected to be promoted assistant physician at Guy's in 1837 and was bitterly disappointed when he did not receive the post. The rejection was due to the animosity of Benjamin Harrison, treasurer of the hospital, who disliked Hodgkin's Quaker practices and his reformist activities, particularly those relating to the treatment of Indians by the Hudson's Bay Company, of which Harrison was deputy chairman. None the less, Hodgkin is remembered as one of the 'great triumvirate of Guy's' (Cameron, 127).

Following his rejection, Hodgkin resigned from Guy's and developed a small private practice. He often treated poor patients gratis and was known to undercharge rather than take advantage of anyone's pocket. He spent 1842–3 teaching at St Thomas's Hospital medical school.

Hodgkin wanted to marry his first cousin, Sarah Godlee, but Quaker practice forbade it. He remained a bachelor until 3 January 1850, when at the age of fifty-one he married Sarah Frances Callow Scaife (1804–1875), a widow, whose husband had been Hodgkin's patient. The couple lived at 35 Bedford Square, London. Hodgkin had no children of his own but was devoted to his brother, John, and to his eleven children, from whom the distinguished Hodgkin family is descended. This includes the historian Thomas Hodgkin (1831–1913), Sir Alan Hodgkin, winner of the Nobel prize for medicine, and Robin Hodgkin, mountaineer.

Hodgkin adhered loyally to Quaker tenets. He dressed in Quaker garb and used Quaker speech patterns. In 1837 he refused fellowship in the Royal Society of Physicians: non-Anglicans were not customarily admitted to the fellowship, and Hodgkin, who regarded his nomination as something which would place him in an invidious position, did not want exemption from a discriminatory rule.

Hodgkin increasingly devoted his time to non-professional activities. He continued to support Liberia and other schemes for African colonization. He was a founder of the Ethnological Society of London and active in the British Association for the Advancement of Science, especially the section dealing with ethnology. He was honorary secretary of the Royal Geographical Society for fourteen years and then honorary foreign secretary. He also worked for the Syrian Medical Aid Society which sent physicians to Beirut and Damascus. Hodgkin's persistence, often in the face of public indifference to or disapproval of some of the causes he espoused, was one of his more remarkable characteristics.

As a result of his travels with Abraham Montefiore, Hodgkin became a good friend of Sir Moses Montefiore, the Anglo-Jewish leader and philanthropist. He accompanied Montefiore as personal physician on five overseas missions for the relief of oppressed Jews, to places including the Holy Land, Morocco, and Constantinople. Hodgkin died of dysentery, or possibly cholera, in Jaffa, Palestine, on 4 April 1866, while travelling with Montefiore, and was buried there on 5 April in the protestant cemetery. Montefiore, heart-stricken at the loss of his friend, had a granite obelisk placed over the grave, to mark their friendship and commemorate Hodgkin as 'a man distinguished alike for scientific attainments, medical skill, and self-sacrificing philanthropy'.　　　AMALIE M. KASS

Sources A. M. Kass and E. H. Kass, *Perfecting the world, the life and times of Dr. Thomas Hodgkin, 1798–1866* (1988) · E. H. Kass and A. H. Bartlett, 'Thomas Hodgkin, MD, 1798–1866: an annotated bibliography', *Bulletin of the History of Medicine*, 43 (1969), 138–75 · C. Hilton, 'The Hodgkin family papers', *Medical History*, 40 (1996), 90–104 · A. M. Kass, 'Friends and philanthropists: Montefiore and Dr Hodgkin', *The century of Moses Montefiore*, ed. S. Lipman and V. D. Lipman (1985) · H. C. Cameron, *Mr Guy's Hospital, 1726–1948* (1954) · S. Wilks and G. T. Bettany, *A biographical history of Guy's Hospital* (1892) · private information (1947) · *CGPLA Eng. & Wales* (1866)
Archives American Colonization Society, Washington, DC · Bodl. RH, corresp. as secretary of the Aborigines' Protection Society · Durham RO, family and personal papers · RGS, letters to the RGS · Royal Anthropological Institute, London · RS · RS Friends, Lond. · University of Toronto, notes on the geology of Morocco · Wellcome L., corresp. and papers | BL, corresp. with his nephew J. E. Hodgkin, Add. MS 42502a · RS, corresp. with Sir J. F. W. Herschel
Likenesses R. Cruikshank?, lithograph, c.1830, Wellcome L. · P. Levin, oils, c.1854, Guy's Hospital medical school, London · T. Sully, oils, 1858, Hist. Soc. Penn. · photograph, unknown collection; copyprint, NPG [*see illus.*]
Wealth at death under £10,000: probate, 28 May 1866, *CGPLA Eng. & Wales*

Hodgkin, Thomas (1831–1913), historian, was born on 29 July 1831 at Bruce Grove, Tottenham, the second son of John *Hodgkin (1800–1875), barrister of Lincoln's Inn, and his first wife, Elizabeth (d. 1836), daughter of the meteorologist Luke *Howard. The Hodgkins were Quakers, and Thomas, debarred from Oxford and Cambridge by the university tests, was educated at Grove House, Tottenham, and University College, London, where he graduated BA with honours in classics in 1851. He had entered Lincoln's Inn in 1850 to read for the bar, but found life in London deleterious to his health.

Hodgkin's connections readily opened a career in banking to him, and he moved first to Pontefract, and then to Whitehaven. In 1857 the failure of the Northumberland and District Bank in Newcastle upon Tyne created an opening for a new enterprise there, and the firm of Hodgkin, Barnett, Pease and Spence took up the opportunity in 1859. Hodgkin was the longest-lived of the partners, but

Thomas Hodgkin (1831–1913), by John Worsnop, 1911

he retired from business well before the bank was absorbed into Lloyds Bank in 1902, and from 1874 devoted his time to literary work.

On 7 August 1861 Hodgkin married Lucy Ann (1841–1934), daughter of Alfred and Sarah Ann Fox (*née* Lloyd) of Falmouth. They had six children: three sons and three daughters. Though he had added the care of a family to his daily business, and was involved in a variety of civic activities, Hodgkin found time and energy for intellectual pursuits, and they became an absorbing interest. As an undergraduate he had written a prize essay on the classical historians, and in Northumberland he readily immersed himself not only in Roman archaeology but also in topography and general antiquities. He was not active in national politics, but as a liberal he supported the cause of Italian unification, and his first visit to Italy in 1868 fired him with a desire to write a major history of that country. There was, however, more than democratic enthusiasm in his resolution. Under the Italian sky and sun he understood, he said, why medieval emperors and princes had readily ventured from their northern territories for the prizes that the peninsula offered.

The vigorous commerce and culture of Newcastle were a decisive influence in Hodgkin's life. On his return he gave a series of lectures in Newcastle on Renaissance Italy. His first thoughts were of a general history that would come down to his own day, but he soon turned to a more specialized though no less ambitious project. He proved well matched to the task, and the first edition of *Italy and* her *Invaders* (4 vols.) came out in 1870. The second edition (8 vols.) appeared between 1892 and 1899. The theme of the work, the end of the Roman hegemony and the emergence of the culture and institutions of medieval Italy, derives plainly enough from Hodgkin's early studies. His interest in historiography was matched by literary scholarship. His book on Claudian (1875), an accomplished author and observer of the late empire who first wrote in Greek, has lasted well. Hodgkin's enthusiasm for the light and landscape of Italy speaks for itself, but his eventual decision to concentrate upon the collapse and the complex legacy of Roman power also owes something to the landscape of northern England. He saw that country not only as an imperial frontier but also as the setting of the Anglian kingdom of Northumbria, a perception which enabled him to break new ground in the *History of England from the Earliest Times to the Norman Conquest*, which he contributed in 1906 to the series edited for Longmans by R. L. Poole and T. F. Tout.

Italy and her Invaders, despite an intricate publishing history, did not completely fill Hodgkin's time. He contributed more than fifty articles and notes to *Archaeologia Aeliana*, the journal of the Society of Antiquaries of Newcastle upon Tyne, and many occasional pieces to Quaker and other publications besides pamphlets and reviews. He translated the letters of Cassiodorus (1886), wrote a life of Theodoric (1891), and was instrumental in establishing the monumental *History of the County of Northumberland*, published in fifteen volumes between 1893 and 1940. He was a founder fellow of the British Academy, and received honorary doctorates from the universities of Durham and Oxford.

From 1864 to 1894 the Hodgkins lived at Benwell Dene, Newcastle, a house designed by Alfred Waterhouse, a fellow pupil at Grove House, who had married Thomas's sister Elizabeth. They later moved to rural Northumberland, first to Bamburgh, and in 1899 to Barmoor Castle, at Beal. Hodgkin died on 2 March 1913, while on holiday at Treworgan, Mawnan, near Falmouth, and was buried in the Quaker burial-ground at Budock, Cornwall.

In an age of nascent professionalism Hodgkin made himself a professional. His work was based upon an extensive knowledge of literary and narrative sources, Italian topography, and the continental scholarship of his day. He bears comparison with Gibbon, on his own terms, and with Grote, a fellow banker, and his history of Italy held its own until the middle of the twentieth century. Though it is no longer of commanding authority, its humane and balanced narrative can still be read with pleasure and some advantage. G. H. MARTIN

Sources F. W. Dendy, 'Thomas Hodgkin', *Archaeologia Aeliana*, 3rd ser., 9 (1913), 75–88 • L. von Glehn Creighton, *Life and letters of Thomas Hodgkin* (1917) • D. A. Bullough, *Italy and her invaders* (1968) • *DNB* • *CGPLA Eng. & Wales* (1913)
Archives U. Durham L., archives and special collections, translation MS of letters to Cassiodorus • U. Newcastle, Robinson L., travel journals and historical papers • Wellcome L., corresp. and papers | BLPES, corresp. with E. D. Morel

Likenesses J. Worsnop, photograph, 1911, NPG [*see illus.*] • H. S. Mendelssohn, carte-de-visite, NPG • photograph, repro. in *Archaeologia Aeliana*, 9 (1913), frontispiece
Wealth at death £150,281 5s. 3d.: probate, 1 May 1913, *CGPLA Eng. & Wales*

Hodgkin, Thomas Lionel (1910–1982), historian, was born on 3 April 1910 at Mendip House, Headington Hill, near Oxford, the elder son of Robert Howard (Robin) Hodgkin (1877–1951), historian of Anglo-Saxon England, and his wife, Dorothy Forster (1886–1979), fourth child of the historian Arthur Lionel *Smith (1850–1924) and his wife, Mary Florence Baird. Hodgkin's childhood was disrupted by the First World War as his father, despite a Quaker upbringing, served in the army on the home front. The family returned to Oxford in 1919 and Hodgkin began an accomplished progress through the Dragon School, Winchester College, and Balliol College, Oxford, to a first in Greats in 1932. As an undergraduate he indulged in social escapades, wrote and acted in plays, contributed to university journals, and spoke at the union. He was believed to fall in love easily, and out of love painfully. A student contemporary, Diana Hopkinson, recalled that the striking colour of his fair hair 'gave him the appearance of a magnificent golden mole' (Hopkinson, 78). Hodgkin, in the hope of going to Palestine, went for Colonial Office interview in his final year and was offered instead an appointment in Gold Coast Colony. Friends, tutors, and family urged him not to lose himself in what was then regarded as darkest Africa. Hodgkin succumbed and rejected the post. In a letter to F. F. Urquhart of Balliol College, on 13 September 1932, he described the Gold Coast as 'a country with no past and no history—and no present either—only perhaps a promising future—and that at a Kindergarten level' (priv. coll.).

Hodgkin went to Palestine to an archaeological dig at Jericho for the first half of 1933. After spells of teaching in Cumberland and Manchester, when he began to encounter Marxist ideas, in April 1934 he was offered the cadetship he wanted in the Palestine civil service. Two years in this post gave him a disturbing awareness of the nature of Western imperialism in general, and of British imperialism in particular. In a time of Arab nationalist awakening Hodgkin, on prison visits, was impressed that the Palestine Communist Party had members of all religions. He resigned from the colonial service and hoped to remain in Palestine to observe the aftermath of the Arab uprising of April 1936. However, the British administration in May ordered him to leave Palestine within twenty-four hours. He sent an anonymous article to *Labour Monthly* for July 1936 criticizing Britain for holding the Arabs down by force.

Hodgkin subsequently travelled for three months in Syria and Lebanon before returning to Britain in September 1936 to take digs with no bathroom in Holford Square, London, and join the London Library and the Communist Party. He became a committed user of the library but an intermittent and fringe member of the party. He went on to stay in west London with his father's cousin Margery

Thomas Lionel Hodgkin (1910–1982), by David Jones, 1929–30

Fry, penal reformer and former principal of Somerville College, Oxford. A fellow guest in March 1937 was the Somerville scientist Dorothy Mary Crowfoot (1910–1994) [see Hodgkin, Dorothy Mary], who was in London to photograph insulin at the Royal Institute. Undertaking a teacher training course, Hodgkin had an uncomfortable experience of teaching schoolboys. He therefore abandoned the training and left London at the end of March 1937 for more congenial adult education in Cumberland. Margery Fry had encouraged him to go for medical examination in which narcolepsy was diagnosed and benzedrine treatment prescribed. Hodgkin and Dorothy Crowfoot were married on 16 December 1937. They were to have a son in 1938, a daughter in 1941, and a second son in 1946. Dorothy Hodgkin became one of the most eminent scientists of her time.

Hodgkin was rejected on medical grounds for military service in the Second World War. In September 1939 he became a Workers' Educational Association tutor in north Staffordshire, where the future Labour politician George Wigg was district secretary. Hodgkin spent the war years conducting classes with civilians and armed forces personnel, and in September 1945 became secretary of the Oxford University delegacy for extra-mural studies. With the stimulus of George Wigg and Colonial Office interest, he began in 1947 to initiate extramural work in Gold Coast Colony and Nigeria. Hodgkin's first journey to the Gold Coast in February 1947 brought him into contact with many Africans, including the senior history master at Achimota College, Miguel Ribeiro. It was a turning point in Hodgkin's life as he first learned of the kingdoms of

western Sudan and recanted his error of fifteen years earlier that the Gold Coast had no history. After further journeys to Africa, Hodgkin wrote for the periodical *West Africa* in 1950 (and again in 1951) a long series of topical and scholarly articles on the background to African nationalism. He and Basil Davidson, the general secretary of the Union of Democratic Control (UDC), organized a pioneering conference at Haywards Heath on 22 and 23 October 1950 for Europeans and Africans to discuss the 'crisis in Africa'. An enduring friendship followed Hodgkin's meeting in Accra in March 1951 with Kwame Nkrumah, then recently released from colonial imprisonment to lead the Gold Coast government (and eventually independent Ghana). The UDC in August 1951 published a pamphlet by Hodgkin supporting freedom for the Gold Coast. Hodgkin's political views had by now raised alarm both in the Colonial Office and in Oxford.

Hodgkin left his delegacy post in May 1952 and spent his gratuity on independent travel in Africa, including France's colonies. Under close watch by French intelligence, he found pre-colonial history a less sensitive theme than his keen interest in contemporary politics, but soon became devoted to history. He published a seminal book entitled *Nationalism in Colonial Africa* (1956), then in the late 1950s turned to the considerable role of Islam in African history and the recovery of Arabic manuscript sources for that history. He took part-time appointments in American and Canadian universities and produced an important anthology of historical writings, *Nigerian Perspectives* (1960), and a contemporary comparative study, *African Political Parties* (1961). The former study was revised and republished in 1975. He served as joint secretary of a commission on reform of the Ghana university system, and in 1962 returned to Ghana for three years as director of a new Institute of African Studies in the University of Ghana.

For Hodgkin the decolonization of history and the rediscovery of the African past was implicit in the political decolonization. The changed perception was filtering into the university mainstream. Oxford University created an appointment for him in October 1965 as lecturer in the government of new states and he was elected to a senior research fellowship at Balliol. He supervised graduate students from many countries in academic fields he had helped originate. When he took early retirement in 1970 thirty scholars contributed papers to a Festschrift and a selection was published as *African Perspectives* (1970). He intended to write stories for children but was diverted into an unpublished satirical novel entitled 'Qwert'. Journeys to Vietnam in 1971 and 1974 led to a history of Vietnam over 4000 years, *Vietnam: the Revolutionary Path* (1981).

Hodgkin was increasingly debilitated by emphysema. He was the Antonius memorial lecturer at St Antony's College, Oxford, in June 1981, and attended, but his paper was read on his behalf. He went to Sudan to escape the harshness of the English winter and spent from November 1981 to mid-March 1982 in Omdurman. However, on the return journey to England he paused in the Greek Peloponnese in the resort village of Tolon, near Nafplion. There he suffered a heart attack and died at the Hotel Minoa, Tolon, on

25 March 1982. His obituary in *The Times* said he did more than anyone to establish the serious study of African history in Britain. Hodgkin was buried on 27 March in the Tolon cemetery overlooking the Aegean Sea.

MICHAEL WOLFERS

Sources *Thomas Hodgkin: letters from Palestine, 1932–36*, ed. E. C. Hodgkin (1986), vii–xx · *The Times* (26 March 1982) · *The Guardian* (26 March 1982) · *West Africa* (12 April 1982) · *History Workshop Journal*, 14 (1982), 180–82 · T. Hodgkin, 'Where the paths began', *African studies since 1945*, ed. C. Fyfe (1976), 6–16 · C. Allen and R. W. Johnson, eds., *African perspectives: papers in the history, politics and economics of Africa presented to Thomas Hodgkin* (1970) [incl. sel. bibliography of works] · T. L. Hodgkin, *Don Tomas: fragment of an autobiographical epic* (privately printed, Wellingborough, 1983) · T. L. Hodgkin, 'George Antonius, Palestine and the 1930s', Antonius memorial lecture, 17 June 1981 [typescript] · [T. L. Hodgkin], 'The events in Palestine', *Labour Monthly*, 18 (1936), 409–17 [repr. as appx II in E. C. Hodgkin, ed., *Thomas Hodgkin: letters from Palestine, 1932–36* (1986), 191–201] · 'The crisis in Africa: a report of a conference organised by the Union of Democratic Control', mimeograph, Oct 1950 · T. Hodgkin, *Freedom for the Gold Coast* (1951) · T. L. Hodgkin to F. F. Urquhart, 13 Sept 1932, priv. coll. · W. A. Hislop, medical report, 20 July 1937, priv. coll. · D. Hopkinson, *The incense tree* (1968), 78 · b. cert. · m. cert. · d. cert. · private information (2004) [E. Hodgkin; D. Hopkinson]
Archives Bodl. Oxf. · Bodl. RH, corresp. and papers relating to higher education in Ghana · priv. coll., corresp., MSS, and papers · PRO · Rewley House, Oxford
Likenesses D. Jones, watercolour and pencil on paper, 1929–30, priv. coll. [*see illus.*]
Wealth at death £246,850: probate, 8 Dec 1982, *CGPLA Eng. & Wales*

Hodgkins, Frances Mary (1869–1947), painter, was born on 28 April 1869 at Royal Terrace, Dunedin, New Zealand, and baptized at St Paul's Anglican Church, Dunedin. She was the third child and second daughter of Rachel Owen, *née* Parker (d. 1926), whose family settled first in New South Wales, Australia, in 1822, and an English immigrant who had arrived in New Zealand in 1860, William Mathew Hodgkins (d. 1898), solicitor, landscape painter, and president of the Otago Art Society. While it was in the context of British art of the 1930s and 1940s that Hodgkins forged a central place, this positioning was not achieved until the artist was in her sixties and seventies. Her career had its beginnings in the colonial context of Dunedin in the 1890s, where Hodgkins received her early training from her father, from the Dunedin School of Art, and, in 1893 (the year women gained the vote in New Zealand), from the visiting Italian painter Girolamo Pieri Nerli. She was one of a number of colonial artists who furthered their artistic practice by travelling and training in Europe: in 1901 and later she studied with Norman Garstin in France; in 1903 she worked in north Africa—whence her ecstatic, orientalist letters describe how she is 'revelling in this place—such sumptuous color' (12 Jan 1903, *Letters*, 152); and before the First World War she went to France, Holland, Italy, and England. In 1908 she studied with Pierre Marcel-Beronneau in Paris. She exhibited from 1890 with art societies in New Zealand, producing watercolour works, mainly portraits and domestic genre scenes, such as *Maori Woman and Child* (1900; Te Papa Tongarewa, Museum of New Zealand); she was based there from 1904

to 1905 and again in 1913. Late in 1912 she held successful exhibitions in Melbourne and in 1913 in Adelaide and Sydney. The years from mid-1908 to the end of 1912 were spent in France, mainly in Paris, where in 1910 Hodgkins taught a watercolour painting class at the Académie Colarossi and had her own school in 1911. Over this period she developed a vibrant, fluid version of the impressionist style she had begun to form in New Zealand, focusing on figure subjects, often of women, as in *The Hill Top* (watercolour, *c*.1908; Te Papa Tongarewa), and her work attracted some favourable notices in the Parisian press. Exhibiting venues over the years 1902–13 included galleries in New Zealand, in London (Dore Gallery, 1902; Fine Art Society, 1904), as well as the Royal Academy (1903–5), and, in Paris, the Société Internationale d'Aquarellistes (1906, 1910). In 1913 she travelled from New Zealand to Europe, spending time in Italy, but with the outbreak of war in 1914 settled in St Ives at Porthmeor Studios, where she stayed throughout the war years. She adopted an *intimiste*-related style—a more modernist approach than that of her associates— began experimenting with oil and tempera, and concentrated largely on figure subjects, as in the expressively painted, evocative *Loveday and Anne* (oil, 1916; Tate collection). Over this period she exhibited with the Royal Academy, the National Portrait Society, and the International Society of Sculptors, Painters, and Gravers. She continued teaching both local and foreign students.

Frances Hodgkins's long, productive career spanned six decades. Her shift into the mainstream of modernist practice in Britain *c*.1930 took place after lengthy periods in France in the 1920s, a period of experimentation with cubism exemplified in *The Red Cockerel*, (oil, 1924; Dunedin Public Art Gallery), and six months in 1925 working for the Calico Printers' Association in Manchester. Among the factors contributing to this shift were (besides withdrawing from teaching), her election, with the support of Cedric Morris, to the Seven and Five Society, which provided her with an important exhibiting context from 1929 until 1934, and, in 1930, the signing of a contract with Arthur Howell of the St George's Gallery. Her successful 1930 solo exhibition there marked a watershed in her practice. She wrote presciently, after describing herself at last 'pleasantly anchored', as feeling as if 'something is really happening at last—and yet this, I feel, is only a half-way stage' (19 Oct 1930, *Letters*, 435). She was then sixty. The support at this crucial time—which as in earlier years involved financial hardship—of artists and friends such as Morris and Lett Haines, of the collector and gallery director Lucy Wertheim, and of close women friends such as Dorothy Selby was critical, and the same applied later in the 1930s when those championing and collecting her work included Myfanwy and John Piper, Katharine Church and Anthony West, the collectors Rée Gorer and her son Geoffrey, and Eardley Knollys. While figure studies continued, among them *The Bridesmaids* (oil, 1930; Auckland Art Gallery) and the outstanding large-scale drawing *Seated Woman* (940 × 600mm, late 1920s; Tate collection), Hodgkins's forte at this time was combining genres: she produced many particularly experimental and subtle variations of the 'still-life landscape', especially over the Seven and Five years, but also a number later in her career. Among these are *Wings over Water* (oil, 1931–2; Tate collection), and *Walled Garden with Convolvulus* (watercolour and gouache, 1942–3; priv. coll., New Zealand). The former has a central, emblematic arrangement of large shells fronting a lusciously painted green and silver-mauve seascape, which is enlivened by a faux-naïf boat in the style of Alfred Wallis and the striking colours of a parrot. In the latter, the foreground still life of pots and urns is reduced to a few spectral, calligraphic outlines among the lively, gestural strokes of the enveloping setting. With her sensuous application of paint and superbly subtle colouring, critics frequently remarked on the 'French' qualities of her work, which differentiated her approach from British colleagues including Ben Nicholson, John Piper, and Paul Nash. The 1930s also saw Hodgkins experiment highly inventively with another combination of genres: that of still life and self-portraiture, and she adopted the strategy of metaphor to construct identity in *Self-Portrait: Still Life* (oil, c.1935; Auckland Art Gallery) and *Still Life: Self-Portrait* (oil, c.1935; Te Papa Tongarewa). In both, brightly patterned scarves and a pink slipper speak of the 'self', while the latter work includes a mirror, whose blankness amusingly thwarts the viewer's expectation of the reflection of appearance. These two works constitute a highly individual and major intervention in the context of self-representation in Britain—and Europe—at the time.

Two visits to Spain, first in 1933 to Ibiza (when she withdrew from the avant-garde artists' group Unit One), and in 1935–6 to Tossa de Mar, when she produced the singing reds and pinks of *In Perspective* (*En perspective*) (gouache and watercolour, 1936; V&A), saw Hodgkins experiment further in her use of colour and merging of abstraction and representation. From 1934, although continuing to travel, and spending time at Bradford-on-Tone in Somerset, she was based mainly in Dorset, at Corfe Castle.

The late 1930s and the 1940s saw Hodgkins's work associated with neo-Romanticism, as in *Broken Tractor* (gouache, 1942; Tate collection) and *The Courtyard in Wartime* (oil, 1944; University of Auckland art collection). In works such as these, and in her remarkable late gouaches (*Church and Castle, Corfe*, gouache, 1942; Ferens Art Gallery, Hull) she uniquely synthesized neo-Romantic concerns with her 'French' painterliness. Exhibiting frequently with such artists as Piper, Henry Moore, and Graham Sutherland, for example in the 'Recent Paintings by Francis Bacon, Frances Hodgkins, Henry Moore, Matthew Smith, Graham Sutherland' exhibition held at the Lefevre Gallery, London, in 1945, and also with younger neo-Romantics like John Minton, she also held a number of solo exhibitions at the Lefevre and the Leicester galleries, and importantly, in 1946, a retrospective exhibition at the Lefevre Gallery, which included seventy-nine works and a catalogue essay by Eric Newton. She also exhibited in Paris at the British Council exhibition 'Quelques Contemporains Anglais', in 1945; in New York at the world fair exhibition 'Contemporary British Art', in 1939, and in 'British

Contemporary Painters', Albright Art Gallery, Buffalo, in 1946, and was one of the artists selected to represent Britain at the 1940 Venice Biennale. John Piper negotiated a civil-list pension for her in 1942, and Hodgkins exhibited frequently until 1946. After an illness of several months she died at Herrison House, a hospital near Dorchester, on 13 May 1947 and was cremated on 17 May at Weymouth.

Frances Hodgkins was regarded as a major artist in the context of British art over the 1930s and 1940s. In the first monograph on Hodgkins, in the Penguin Modern Painters series (1948), Myfanwy Evans's poetic essay describes her as 'luxuriating in calligraphy' (Evans, 16), while 'within each folded space [is] a life of colour' (ibid., 17). Certainly her strengths as a colourist were frequently noted, as in John Piper's 1940 *Spectator* review which held that 'probably no living painter has such extraordinary powers of arranging colours in original and telling ways.' (*Letters*, 501 n. 18). While she was alert to surrealist tendencies, to the French 'school', to abstraction, neo-Romanticism, and child art, Frances Hodgkins's achievement was to produce, over the last two decades of her life, a constantly evolving personal language of form and colour. As she put it, 'Myself, I would say that I, my medium and my subject act & react to produce new & vital creations &, if possible, achieve a perfect balance' (19 Oct 1941, *Letters*, 519). Her status in the context of New Zealand art and social history is high, while in the context of the British arts scene it is currently undervalued. There have been some small solo exhibitions celebrating her achievement such as 'Frances Hodgkins: The Late Work', held at the Minories Art Gallery, Colchester (1990), and she has been included in recent reassessments of British art such as Frances Spalding's *British Art since 1900* (2nd edn, 1989). But she has been omitted from the re-evaluation of other contexts in which she was a prominent figure at the time, as in *A Paradise Lost: the neo-Romantic Imagination in Britain, 1935–55*, the exhibition held at the Barbican Art Gallery, London, in 1987. Her works are held largely in British and New Zealand public and private collections, with a number of important drawings, textile designs, and paintings such as *Methodist Chapel* (selected for the 1940 Venice Biennale) reappearing in recent years.   ELIZABETH EASTMOND

Sources I. Buchanan, M. Dunn, and E. Eastmond, *Frances Hodgkins: paintings and drawings* (Auckland, 1994); rev. edn (2001) · *Letters of Frances Hodgkins*, ed. L. Gill (1993) · E. H. McCormick, *Portrait of Frances Hodgkins* (Auckland, 1981) · M. Evans, *Frances Hodgkins*, Penguin Modern Painters (1948) · A. R. Howell, *Frances Hodgkins: four vital years* (1951) · E. H. McCormick, *The expatriate: a study of Frances Hodgkins* (Wellington, 1954) · E. H. McCormick, *Works of Frances Hodgkins in New Zealand* (Auckland, 1954) · CGPLA Eng. & Wales (1947) · R. D. J. Collins, ed., 'Hodgkins '97', *Bulletin of New Zealand Art History*, special ser., 4 (1998) · E. Eastmond, 'Landscape / painting, landscape / writing: Frances Hodgkins's late landscapes', *Manufacturing meaning: the Victoria University of Wellington art collection in context* [exhibition catalogue, Adam Art Gallery, Victoria University of Wellington, 22 Sept 1999–31 Jan 2000] · E. Eastmond, 'Metaphor and the self-portrait: Frances Hodgkins's *Self-portrait: still life*, and *Still life: self-portrait*', *Art History*, 22 (1999), 656–75 · I. Buchanan and R. Collins, 'Frances Hodgkins on display: galleries, dealers and exhibitions, 1890–1950', *Bulletin of New Zealand Art History*, special ser., 5 (2000)

Archives Auckland Art Gallery Research Library, letters [transcripts] · Auckland Art Gallery Research Library, papers · NL NZ, Turnbull L., corresp., MS 85 · NL NZ, Turnbull L., papers · Tate collection, papers | Tate collection, letters to Arthur R. Howell, art dealer · Tate collection, Cedric Morris papers · Tate collection, Paul Nash archive · Tate collection, corresp. with Jane Saunders · Tate collection, Seven and Five Society records · Tate collection, Unit One archive, press cuttings book | SOUND BL NSA, 'Portrait of an artist', 1969 · Radio New Zealand, Sound Archives, documentary recording, 19 April 1961
Likenesses C. Morris, gouache, 1917, Tate collection · A. L. Haines, drawing, 1919, repro. in *Frances Hodgkins, 1869–1947: a centenary exhibition* (Auckland City Art Gallery, 1969), cover [exh. cat.?]; priv. coll. · A. L. Haines, drawing, 1919, repro. in McCormick, *Portrait*, p. 92 · C. Morris, watercolour, 1919, priv. coll. · C. Morris, oils, 1928, Auckland City Art Gallery · photographs, NL NZ, Turnbull L.
Wealth at death £2863 6s. 10d.: probate, 18 June 1948, CGPLA Eng. & Wales

Hodgkinson, Eaton (1789–1861), structural engineer, was born on 26 February 1789 at Anderton, near Northwich, Cheshire, the son of James Hodgkinson (1756–1794), a farmer, and his wife, Mary (1767–1835). He had two sisters. Originally intended for the church, he was enrolled at John Dean's Grammar School at Witton, near Northwich, but it proved uncongenial so he was transferred to a Mr Shaw's private school, which also better suited his growing interest in mathematics. In 1811 the family gave up their farm and his mother bought a pawnbroker's shop in Salford. Little is known about Hodgkinson's activities during the next ten years, but it is known that he was tutored by John Dalton. In 1820 he joined the Manchester Literary and Philosophical Society. He read his first paper, 'On the transverse strain and strength of materials', to a meeting of that society in 1822. It was of major importance for a new technology.

The construction of the huge textile mills that were features of the industrial revolution raised serious design problems for builders using cast iron, which was then a new material. A beam, loaded in the middle, will undergo compression in the upper part and tension in the lower part, the forces of compression and of tension being equal; in between there will be a neutral line. This had been shown by Parent, Coulomb, and, later, the elder John Robison. However, the builders of the first iron-framed mills overlooked their works and evaded the complications by using comparative method, or scaling up, from a small sample that could be broken under load, to full size. In his first paper Hodgkinson, following Robison, showed how to locate the neutral line and how to estimate the transverse strain in a beam. With Dalton's help, he experimentally determined the neutral line in different beams.

In this paper Hodgkinson had used old-fashioned mathematics—proportions and fluxions; in his next papers to the society, on the catenary in suspension bridges and on the strength of iron beams, he used, probably thanks to Dalton, modern mathematics. More importantly these papers set the strength of materials on a firm basis. He showed in the last paper that cast iron was much stronger in compression than in tension, so that the top flange of a beam could be thinner than the bottom flange. In this way the most economical beam for a given strength could be designed. At the same time, through the good offices of Peter Ewart, he began a long scientific partnership with William Fairbairn, who possessed facilities for testing large beams at his works.

Hodgkinson's studies of materials under tension or compression below the breaking point led him to consider what was called the set, or the permanent deformation left after the load is removed. Thomas Tredgold had argued that set takes place at one-third breaking load. Hodgkinson, in his report to the British Association in 1843, showed that permanent deformation takes place under the smallest load. No material, he said, is perfectly elastic. He also studied the behaviour of pillars under load. Euler's theory of struts was too abstract to be of use, and he resolved to repair the deficiency. The result was his paper in the *Philosophical Transactions* of 1840 that earned him fellowship of the Royal Society and its royal medal in 1841. On 2 June of that year, at Cross Street Chapel, Manchester, Hodgkinson married Catherine Sparke Johns, daughter of the Revd William Johns (with whom John Dalton had lodged). The witnesses included Dalton and Fairbairn. Catherine died a year later. On 15 October 1853 he married Eliza Holditch (d. 1882), daughter of Captain Henry Holditch, at the parish church, Kensington. One of the witnesses was Robert Stephenson. There were no children of either marriage.

By the 1840s Hodgkinson was much concerned with the British Association for the Advancement of Science, of whose council he was a member three times, and as railway engineering became increasingly important his interest changed from mills to railways. He was a member of the royal commission on the use of iron in railway structures (1847–9) and he collaborated with Robert Stephenson and William Fairbairn in the design and construction of the revolutionary Conwy and Britannia tubular bridges (1850).

Hodgkinson occasionally engaged in researches outside his chosen field of the strength of materials. On behalf of the British Association he investigated the increase in temperature with the depth of deep mines (1837–8), and he also measured the air resistance to moving objects (1842). In 1832 he was appointed a director of the Manchester Mechanics' Institute. In 1847 he was appointed to the chair of the mechanical principles of engineering at University College, London. From 1848 to 1850 he was president of the Manchester Literary and Philosophical Society and he was an honorary member of the Institution of Civil Engineers.

Hodgkinson suffered from a nervous affliction and was a retiring man. He died on 18 June 1861 at his home, Eaglesfield House, Higher Broughton, Manchester, and was buried in the family plot at Anderton. He was survived by his wife. DONALD CARDWELL

Sources B. Warburton, 'Eaton Hodgkinson (1789–1861) and the science of strength of materials', PhD diss., University of Manchester Institute of Science and Technology, 1971 · R. Rawson, 'Memoir of the late Eaton Hodgkinson, FRS', *Memoirs of the Literary and Philosophical Society of Manchester*, 3rd ser., 2 (1865), 145–204 · I. Todhunter, *A history of the theory of elasticity and of the strength of materials from Galilei to the present time*, ed. K. Pearson, 2 vols. (1886–93) ·

S. Timoshenko, *History of strength of materials* (1953) · J. Robison, 'Strength of materials', *Encyclopaedia Britannica*, 3rd edn (1797), vol. 18 · N. Rosenberg and W. G. Vincenti, *The Britannia Bridge: the generation and diffusion of technological knowledge* (1978) · 'Royal commission to inquire into the application of iron to railway structures', *Parl. papers* (1849), vol. 29, no. 1123 · H. Dorn, 'Hodgkinson, Eaton', *DSB · PICE*, 21 (1861–2), 542–5 · *Catalogue of scientific papers*, Royal Society, 3 (1869), 374 · d. cert.
Archives UCL, letters
Likenesses photograph, North Western Museums and Art Galleries Service, Manchester
Wealth at death £4000: probate, 14 Aug 1861, *CGPLA Eng. & Wales*

Hodgkinson, George Christopher (1816–1880), schoolmaster and meteorologist, was born at Newark, the son of George Hodgkinson, attorney, and his wife, Julia Beevor. From King Edward VI School, Louth, he went in 1833 as a pensioner to Trinity College, Cambridge, graduating BA (fourteenth wrangler) in 1837 and MA in 1842. His first posts were as master at the King Edward VI Free School, Bury St Edmunds, Suffolk, then as principal of Hull College. He was ordained deacon in 1842, and priest in 1843. About 1845 he married Isabella Lydia Spencer, niece of Sir James Clark Ross; of the twelve children born to them, not all survived infancy. In January 1846 he was appointed principal of the Royal Agricultural College, Cirencester, an unlikely choice, for despite having glowing references as a teacher Hodgkinson knew nothing of agriculture. His emphasis on theory caused friction and his demands for more staff took the college to the brink of financial ruin. He was dismissed in June 1847, after which he became principal of the Diocesan Training College, York, and, from 1864 to 1876, headmaster of his former school at Louth. Besides sermons and tracts Hodgkinson published in 1854, in reply to the archbishop of York and bishop of Ripon, his defence of the teaching of the diocesan college, and some pamphlets on the examinations for the Indian Civil Service, approving open competition.

An enthusiastic alpine climber, Hodgkinson was among those seeking to improve the mountain aneroid barometer so that it would function as an altimeter, but although he offered a reward through the Alpine Club, none of the London makers took this up. The Royal Society contributed towards the cost of apparatus with which Hodgkinson made a series of actinometrical observations on the summit of Mont Blanc in 1866. Using a lighter, less costly version of the Herschel actinometer, he corresponded with the astronomer royal as to the most effective mode of registering the amount and intensity of sunshine. He died at his home at Car Colston, Nottinghamshire, on 25 April 1880. He was survived by his wife.

R. E. ANDERSON, rev. ANITA MCCONNELL

Sources G. C. Hodgkinson, 'Actinometrical observations among the Alps, with the description of a new actinometer', *London, Edinburgh, and Dublin Philosophical Magazine*, 4th ser., 33 (1867), 304–14 · *The Times* (12 May 1880), 13b · *Louth Advertiser* (1 May 1880), 3e · A. McConnell, *King of the clinicals: the life and times of J. J. Hicks* (1998) · W. W. Rouse Ball and J. A. Venn, eds., *Admissions to Trinity College, Cambridge*, 4 (1911), 382 · R. Sayce, *The history of the Royal Agricultural College, Cirencester* (1992) · private information (2004)
Archives CUL, letters to Sir George Stokes

Wealth at death under £5000: probate, 11 June 1880, *CGPLA Eng. & Wales*

Hodgkinson, George Edward (1893–1986), local politician, was born on 9 August 1893 at 21 Villa Street, Beeston, the eldest of four sons born to Walter Hodgkinson (1872–c.1943), a lace-making-machine minder, and his wife, Charlotte Wormell (1876–1907). He attended Nether Street elementary school in Beeston until he was thirteen. After several jobs with engineering firms he enrolled for evening classes at Nottingham University and completed his engineering education at the Harris Institute in Preston. He was much influenced by the harsh working conditions he witnessed, and in 1913 he joined the Independent Labour Party and the Amalgamated Society of Engineers on the same day.

In September 1914 Hodgkinson moved to Coventry, where he worked as a turner. On 26 December that year he married (Victoria) May Smith (1892/3–1925), daughter of Herbert Smith, waggon examiner. By 1915 he had become the leading shop steward at the Radford Daimler factory. In 1919 he was nominated for a place at Ruskin College, Oxford. His experiences there are vividly recorded in his surviving correspondence with his first wife. He returned to Coventry in 1920 to find his reputation as a shop steward had preceded him. He was often victimized, and, with a young family to support, he was driven to seeking poor relief before regaining employment with Daimler in January 1923.

In October 1923 Hodgkinson began work as the full-time Coventry Labour Party agent. His dynamism helped transform the local party: the debt of £240 was cleared, women's sections were established, and the membership increased significantly. In 1936 Richard Crossman became the local Labour candidate. Crossman and Hodgkinson became close friends: Hodgkinson admired Crossman's intellect and energy, while Crossman learned much from Hodgkinson's expertise in party management. After the death of his first wife in 1925, Hodgkinson married, on 7 May 1927, Carrie Wilson (1895/6–1997), a tailor, daughter of Thomas Arthur Wilson, iron polisher.

Hodgkinson's career in local government began in 1928 when he won the Radford ward. Nine years later, the Labour Party won control of Coventry council for the first time. He led the council for a year before making way for Sidney Stringer; between them, they dominated the Labour group. Hodgkinson played a pivotal role in co-ordinating the local response to the devastation caused by the German air raid on Coventry in November 1940. He was instrumental in restoring gas supplies and in establishing communal restaurants. After the war his enthusiasm for the bold changes envisaged by the city architect, Donald Gibson, helped persuade his fellow councillors to accept them. He was mayor of Coventry in 1944–5 and, as his membership of strategic committees continued unabated throughout the 1940s and 1950s, he played a major role in Coventry's post-war development. His hopes of a parliamentary seat were, however, dashed in 1945 when the Labour Party vetoed his nomination on the grounds that he was a paid official. In 1949 he was appointed OBE.

Though Coventry council achieved much in the post-war period, there was a feeling that the local Labour Party was increasingly out of touch with the social trends of the 1950s. Hodgkinson's public pronouncements sometimes betrayed a hint of puritanism which sat uneasily with the prevailing mood of an age of increasing affluence. Although his ability to express his political views was circumscribed by his being a party agent, a position he finally relinquished in 1958, there is no doubt that his sympathies were with the left.

Hodgkinson was a frequent visitor to eastern Europe after the war and deplored what he considered to be the crude distinctions made between the eastern bloc and western Europe. In 1967 he lost his council seat when Labour was swept from power in Coventry. His autobiography, written at Crossman's insistence, was published in 1970 and he continued to live an active life thereafter, particularly as a campaigner for international understanding. He was a genial, sincere man: a near teetotaller, he lived in a council house on principle until his death. He was an accomplished fisherman, who competed in the 1936 All England championships. His life was an epitome of dedication to the labour movement and its ideals. He died on arrival at Coventry and Warwickshire Hospital on 19 August 1986 as a result of a heart attack while at the wheel of his car; his body was cremated at Canley crematorium. He was survived by his wife, a daughter from his first marriage, and a son from his second.

RICHARD TEMPLE

Sources G. Hodgkinson, *Sent to Coventry* (1970) • N. Tiratsoo, *Reconstruction, affluence and labour politics: Coventry, 1945–60* (1990) • R. Storey, *A shop steward in Oxford* (1980) • F. Carr, 'Engineering workers and the rise of labour', PhD diss., University of Warwick, 1978 • 'Biographical notes of George Edward Hodgkinson', *c.*1976, Coventry Central Library, Local Studies section, JN 920 H 689 • U. Warwick Mod. RC, Coventry borough labour party MSS, MSS 11 • F. Carr, 'Municipal socialism: Labour's rise to power', *Life and labour in a twentieth century city: the experience of Coventry*, ed. B. Lancaster and T. Mason [n.d., *c.*1987], 172–203 • U. Warwick Mod. RC, George Hodgkinson MSS, MSS 23 • U. Warwick Mod. RC, Richard Crossman MSS, MSS 154 • *Coventry Evening Telegraph year book and who's who* (1986) • private information (2004) • m. certs. • d. cert.

Archives Coventry Central Library, MSS, 702, 980, 1134 • U. Warwick Mod. RC, corresp. and papers; Coventry borough labour party MSS | U. Warwick Mod. RC, Richard Crossman MSS, MSS 154 • U. Warwick Mod. RC, David Sutton MSS, MSS 252 | SOUND IWM SA, 'British civilian worked as engines machinist for Daimler … conscientious objector', IWM, May 1976, 764 • IWM SA, oral history interview

Hodgkinson, Grosvenor (*bap.* 1818, *d.* 1881), politician and lawyer, was baptized at Newark-on-Trent parish church on 12 February 1818, the second son of George Hodgkinson (*d.* 1856), a solicitor in Newark, and his wife, Julia (*d.* 1844). Hodgkinson entered his father's practice in the Northgate in Newark in 1839 and soon became an important figure in the town. On 21 October 1845 he married Alice (*d.* 20 May 1900, aged eighty), the only daughter of Robert Harvey, gentleman; they had five children. As his residence, Hodgkinson rented Winthorpe Hall from

Lord Middleton, moving back to the Northgate after his father's death, at which time he expanded the practice by amalgamation with John Pratt, another solicitor in Newark. In April 1859 he was elected for Newark, standing as a Liberal, and held the seat until the general election of 1874, when he retired. A conscientious but not prominent back-bencher, Hodgkinson became famous on 17 May 1867 when he successfully moved what became known as 'Hodgkinson's amendment' to the Conservative government's Representation of the People Bill. Hodgkinson had proved something of a maverick on political reform and was regarded as a political freebooter on the question (Smith, 197). He had voted against Gladstone's amendment on 12 April, thus contributing to the humiliation of his party leader in the Commons. Disraeli's bill was intended to enfranchise every householder who paid rates, but the existence of the 'compound householder' (the householder whose rates were paid by the landlord) greatly complicated the question, for it implied substantial disfranchisement. Various ways were proposed to get round this difficulty without significantly increasing the extension of the franchise. It was therefore to general astonishment that Disraeli, in a small house, and without prior consultation with his colleagues, accepted Hodgkinson's amendment, which then passed without a division. The amendment enabled more than 400,000 compounders to register, effectively removed ratepaying as a restriction to the urban suffrage, and, after various inconsistencies of drafting had been tidied up, allowed household suffrage to become a reality: about four times as many electors as expected when the bill was first introduced came into the register in 1868 as a result of Hodgkinson's initiative.

Hodgkinson ceased to practise as a solicitor in 1870. He was a director of the Midland Railway and for a time chairman of the London, Chatham, and Dover Railway. He was also a director of the Law Life Assurance Society and a magistrate for Newark and Nottinghamshire. In January 1881 he suffered a stroke, and died at his house in the Northgate, Newark, on 14 February 1881. The town of Newark closed on 18 February, the day of his funeral at Balderton parish church.

H. C. G. MATTHEW

Sources *Newark Advertiser* (16 Feb 1881) • *Newark Advertiser* (23 Feb 1881) • *Newark Advertiser* (16 Jan 1981) • G. Y. Hemingway, 1982, Newark Library • F. B. Smith, *The making of the second Reform Bill* (1966) • Gladstone, *Diaries* • Boase, *Mod. Eng. biog.*

Likenesses photograph, Newark Library

Hodgkinson, Terence William Ivan (1913–1999), art historian and museum director, was born on 7 October 1913 at Glencot, Wells, Somerset, the only son of Ivan Tattersall Hodgkinson and Kathryn Van Vleck Townsend, daughter of the vicar of All Angels, Manhattan, who later (1929) married the civil servant Sir Gilbert Upcott KCB. Hodgkinson was brought up by his paternal grandmother in Somerset, where the family had run a long-established papermaking business. After Oundle School he went to Magdalen College, Oxford, in 1932 to read politics, philosophy, and economics. His interest in the history of art had already been kindled and in 1935, as a volunteer in the

Fitzwilliam Museum, Cambridge, he worked on the catalogue of prints in the Pepysian Library at Magdalene College. During this period he also helped Rudolf Wittkower with translations from the German at the newly arrived Warburg Institute and his contact with outstanding émigré scholars provided Hodgkinson with the scholarly standards that he maintained in his later work. At the outbreak of war he was called up and soon transferred to military intelligence, becoming a major in 1943. By this date he had already met Hans Schneider (d. 1995), a Jewish refugee from Vienna and later head of design and technology at Marks and Spencer, who remained his partner for over fifty years—a partnership in which Hodgkinson's English restraint was well matched by Schneider's central European ebullience.

In 1946 Hodgkinson became an assistant keeper in the department of architecture and sculpture at the Victoria and Albert Museum, where his first task was to organize the display of the large collection of English medieval alabasters recently given by one of the museum's major donors, Dr W. L. Hildburgh. It was on this somewhat unlikely subject that he wrote his first article in the Burlington Magazine in 1946. Hodgkinson's organizational abilities were soon recognized and he was made assistant to the director, Leigh Ashton. This gave him great responsibility at a crucial point in the museum's history. The collection was being returned to the museum from wartime storage in Wales and he played a key role in realizing Ashton's bold scheme to organize some of the displays according to periods and styles rather than by material. As the director became steadily more debilitated, by the early 1950s Hodgkinson was effectively running the museum. Although extremely able as an administrator, he was successful not least because he worked so well with staff at all levels; in an institutional culture where patrician hauteur was the norm among curators, he genuinely liked his colleagues and they liked him.

Hodgkinson maintained his interest in sculpture and was pleased to return to that department in 1962. There, as assistant keeper and from 1967 as keeper, he took on responsibility for post-medieval English sculpture—a subject that had only begun to be studied seriously in the 1930s—and, with characteristic discrimination, began to acquire a series of outstanding works, culminating in the purchase of Louis François Roubiliac's statue of Handel. One of the strengths he brought to this area was an ability to link English sculpture with continental traditions, above all French, where his knowledge was unrivalled in this country and much respected by colleagues in France. Although his proposals were often thwarted by John Pope-Hennessy (as keeper and later director), with whom he had a difficult relationship throughout his career at the Victoria and Albert Museum, he succeeded in buying superb pieces by J.-A. Houdon, J.-B. Pigalle, and A. Pajou as well as two spectacular groups by Antonio Corradini carved for the gardens in Dresden. Writing did not come easily to him, though a reader would not have realized this from publications written with great clarity in a prose

style that was as immaculate as his appearance. The articles he wrote on sculptors such as Christopher Hewetson (1958), Joseph Wilton (1967), and on Roubiliac's Handel at Vauxhall (1969) were for the most part modest in scale, but in their thoroughness of documentation and cogency of argument they set a new standard for writing about English sculpture. The same rigour was apparent in his catalogues of sculpture in the Frick and Waddesdon collections (1968 and 1970) where his economically brief entries rest on, but scarcely reveal, much original research involving the judicious weighing of evidence. The clearest register of his qualities as a scholar lies in the meticulous notes he wrote in his distinctive angular hand on the catalogue cards in the sculpture department. As well as being a model of clarity these are informed throughout by a tough scepticism that made him disinclined to engage in what he would have regarded as unjustified speculation. While he would make a careful note of another scholar's publication in this vein, he would add simply: 'No new information'. Despite his distaste for scholarly sloppiness Hodgkinson was far from unsympathetic to other art-historical approaches and nobody could have been more encouraging to younger researchers. He made the collection and his own knowledge accessible to numerous foreign scholars and prompted his colleagues to explore areas which they were to make their own, most notably Michael Baxandall, whose Limewood Sculptors of Renaissance Germany (1980) resulted from Hodgkinson's suggestion that he should work on German wood sculpture in the collection.

Hodgkinson continued to combine these scholarly activities—he would himself deny being a scholar of any consequence—with administrative duties that ranged from reorganizing the department's record and storage systems and serving between 1951 and 1967 as secretary to the museum's advisory council. For the latter he was appointed CBE in 1958. On Pope-Hennessy's departure for the British Museum in 1974, many staff at the Victoria and Albert Museum hoped that Hodgkinson would succeed him. This did not happen and instead he embarked upon a 'retirement' that involved reorganizing several institutions that greatly benefited from his remarkable combination of abilities. The first was the Wallace Collection where as director from 1974 to 1978 he initiated a refurbishment programme that turned it into a modern museum. Then in 1978, after the unexpected death of Benedict Nicholson, he took on for three years the editorship of the Burlington Magazine. Here he applied not only his precision as a scholar but also his practical sense by setting the magazine on a firm financial footing. Then followed a period as, first a member, and then vice-chairman of the museums and galleries commission. His judgement and knowledge were much valued and he played an influential part in the appointment of several major figures within the art world in Britain. He was also a long-standing committee member of bodies such as the National Art-Collections Fund, the Walpole Society, and the Samuel Courtauld Trust. Here, as in his many acts of personal kindness and generosity, he acted with integrity and without fuss. He and Hans Schneider lived in Highgate with a garden overlooking Hampstead Heath. Walking on the heath was one of their pleasures in later life, as was an annual visit to the Schubertiade in Salzburg, followed by a stay at the celebrated Elephant Hotel in Brixen—a town for which Hodgkinson's father had written the first English guidebook in 1923. An exemplary museum official and an underestimated art historian, Hodgkinson played a key but quiet role in the development of museums and public art collections in Britain from the late 1940s until the 1980s. He died at Cheverton Lodge Nursing Home in London on 4 October 1999.

MALCOLM BAKER

Sources *The Times* (13 Oct 1999) · *The Independent* (13 Oct 1999) · *The Guardian* (14 Oct 1999) · *Daily Telegraph* (22 Oct 1999) · *WWW* · personal knowledge (2004) · private information (2004) · b. cert. · d. cert.
Likenesses group portrait, photograph, repro. in *The Independent*
Wealth at death £1,087,327—gross; £1,053,355—net: probate, 9 May 2000, *CGPLA Eng. & Wales*

Hodgkinson, William (1661/2–1731), merchant and landowner, was probably born at Overton in the parish of Ashover, Derbyshire, where he was baptized on 2 April 1662; he was the second son of George Hodgkinson (d. 1692) of Overton and his wife, Anne. George Hodgkinson's ancestor Richard Hodgkinson had acquired Overton in 1556, although it was later sold, and George himself repurchased the estate in 1641. From at least the mid-sixteenth century, the Hodgkinsons had established themselves in Ashover as parish gentry. Like virtually every north Derbyshire family of the same class in this period, they were involved in the lead trade, sending shipments from Hull (where George Hodgkinson lived for a time) both to London and directly overseas, chiefly to Amsterdam. In common with most Hull merchants, the Hodgkinsons also engaged in trade with Baltic countries, importing iron and, to a lesser extent, tar, flax, timber, and hemp from Sweden, to which they exported small quantities of woollen goods.

William Hodgkinson is unusual in that, alone of provincial Baltic merchants of his generation, a large proportion of his accounts survive, making it possible to amplify through a case study what is known in general about Hull's overseas trade. Fragmentary records exist from 1678, when George Hodgkinson was living in Hull, but the bulk of the material begins in 1684, when William, aged twenty-two, was in Stockholm, working as his father's factor, a conventional training for merchants' sons. He was to remain there until 1689, and in 1687, the year for which his Swedish accounts are best preserved, he shipped approximately 570 tons of bar iron to Hull on behalf of some twenty merchants, including his father and younger brother Obadiah (1666–1732). He also dealt on a smaller scale in other Baltic goods.

On his return to England, William Hodgkinson lived at Hull for about a year but he moved to Overton at the start of 1691. His father, whose heir he became on the death of his elder brother, George, in 1687, died in June 1692.

Shortly afterwards William almost completely rebuilt Overton, which remained his home for the rest of his life. His accounts show that he continued to trade through Hull, exporting lead and importing iron and other commodities from Sweden. Most of the iron was consigned to Hull merchants for distribution throughout the adjoining region, but Hodgkinson sold small quantities direct to blacksmiths and nailers in Ashover and the surrounding district. Like most Derbyshire lead merchants, he also had interests in the mining and smelting of lead in several local parishes. Although it cannot be demonstrated from his accounts, William evidently continued his father's practice of acquiring land adjoining Overton and by the beginning of the eighteenth century the Hodgkinsons were probably the most substantial of the various minor gentry families resident in Ashover. They did not appear at Sir William Dugdale's visitation of Derbyshire in 1662, but they were using arms by 1687, if not before. In 1704 William Hodgkinson built and endowed a school at Ashover.

Hodgkinson was married to Elizabeth (d. 1732), the daughter of Robert Ferne of Bonsall, Derbyshire. They had been married for more than thirty (possibly forty) years when he died on 6 December 1731, probably at Overton, his wife surviving him. Although in his will he asked merely to be buried in the churchyard at Ashover, he was interred on 9 December in the church itself, where a monument describes him as one who was 'bred a merchant and added considerably to his paternal estate by his industry and frugality, virtues which he practised himself and greatly encouraged in others'. Subject to his wife's life interest, he left his whole estate, including lead mines as well as land, to his grandson William (1719–1761), the second son of his daughter and sole heir, Ann (d. 1730). In 1714 Ann had married Joseph Banks (d. 1741) of Revesby Abbey, Lincolnshire. Under the terms of the bequest, William Banks took the additional surname Hodgkinson, but he gave up both surname and Overton on inheriting Revesby Abbey in 1741. Overton then passed to his younger brother Robert (d. 1792), who also took the Hodgkinson name. On Robert's death Overton was inherited by William's son, the explorer and naturalist Sir Joseph *Banks (1743–1820).

PHILIP RIDEN

Sources P. Riden, 'An English factor at Stockholm in the 1680s', *Scandinavian Economic History Review*, 35 (1987), 191–207 · T. N. Ince, 'The family of Hodgkinson, of Overton Hall, in Ashover', *The Reliquary*, 12 (1871), 254–5 · D. Lysons and S. Lysons, *Magna Britannia: being a concise topographical account of the several counties of Great Britain*, 5 (1817) · 'The autobiography of Leonard Wheatcroft of Ashover, 1627–1706', ed. D. Riden, *A seventeenth-century Scarsdale miscellany*, ed. [J. V. Beckett and others], Derbyshire RS, 20 (1993), 71–117 · M. Craven, *A Derbyshire armory*, Derbyshire RS, 17 (1991) · monument, Ashover church · Derbys. RO, D. 253A PI 1/1 · will, PRO, PROB 11/648, fol. 204 · H. B. Carter, *Sir Joseph Banks, 1743–1820* (1988)
Archives Derbys. RO, account books, D.2806 [microfilm]
Wealth at death see will, 29 Oct 1726, PRO, PROB 11/648, fol. 204

Hodgskin, Thomas (1787–1869), economist, political theorist, and journalist, was born on 12 December 1787 in Chatham, the son of a keeper of stores at the Admiralty docks. He described his childhood as impoverished and joyless. When he reached twelve his father cut short his education and procured him a naval cadetship in March 1800. For the next twelve years he cruised in the North Sea and Mediterranean and along the coasts of Africa. Although he distinguished himself in action Hodgskin found naval discipline irksome and his comrades' company desultory. While at sea he began to read widely, but necessarily unsystematically. Conflicts with his superiors deprived him of the prospect of promotion, and at the age of twenty-five he found himself on the retired list, reduced to half pay in 1812. In his first published work, *An Essay on Naval Discipline* (1813), he contrasted the arbitrary brutality of naval life with the good government with which Britain was reputedly blessed. Publication of the *Essay* brought Hodgskin to the attention of the London radicals, notably Francis Place, who was to offer Hodgskin intellectual companionship and patronage.

In July 1815 Hodgskin embarked on a walking tour which took him first to Paris and later to Germany, where he made a detailed study of the political and economic institutions of Hanover. Although his investigations were shaped by a questionnaire devised by Jeremy Bentham, his suggestion, in *Travels in the North of Germany* (2 vols., 1820), that 'many evils are in Germany, occasioned by governing too much' was far from Benthamite. Hodgskin expounded a minimalist conception of the state, insisting that government tended to shackle the energies and liberties of individuals. The guarantor of good government was the influence of public opinion. He concluded that if Britain was better governed than the states of Germany this was principally because of the greater freedom of expression in Britain and because the political education of the working classes had progressed further in Britain than in Germany. By 1819 Hodgskin was in Edinburgh, married to Elisabeth, a young German woman whose surname is unknown. The next few years were marked by excruciating poverty. He failed to break into the charmed circle of the Edinburgh reviewers, and was constantly held back by his painful self-abnegation and the growing radicalism of his opinions. Late in 1822 he arrived back in London and Place secured him a position as a correspondent for the *Morning Chronicle*.

Respectable journalism gave Hodgskin a regular income, but no outlet for his real opinions. In 1823 he was instrumental in establishing the *Mechanics' Magazine* and the mechanics' institute, where in 1825 he delivered a course of lectures later published as *Popular Political Economy* (1827). His reputation as an economist rests on these lectures, the trenchant *Labour Defended Against the Claims of Capital* (1825), and *The Natural and Artificial Right of Property Contrasted* (1832). He has frequently been described as a 'Ricardian socialist', but the description is more ironic than accurate. Certainly Hodgskin used elements from Ricardian economics, but only as tools with which to undermine the Ricardian edifice. At the same time he pressed the labour theory of value to far more radical ends than David Ricardo, seeing skilled labour as both the measure and producer of all value. Fixed capital was no

more than accumulated labour. Hodgskin saw a shameless deception at the centre of Ricardian economics and British capitalism: both pretended that capital was productive and the essential spring to greater prosperity, but, Hodgskin argued, capitalists were always parasitic, holding wages close to subsistence levels and diverting the fruits of labour's productivity to unproductive and anti-social consumption. Although Karl Marx's formulation of the theory of surplus value was more sophisticated, his debt to Hodgskin is unmistakable.

Hodgskin fathered seven children, and the need to provide for his family may explain his failure to produce any major work after 1832. He intended to complete a critical study of law, 'The absurdity of legislation demonstrated', but this never appeared. Instead he became a prolific journalist, contributing to at least four daily newspapers, as well as several provincial weeklies; and for a time he assisted Thomas Hansard in publishing parliamentary reports. In the early 1840s he published pamphlets for the Anti-Corn Law League, and in 1846 he joined the staff of *The Economist*. In the same year the navy awarded him the rank of retired commander. Hodgskin's enthusiasm for free trade was rooted in a belief that the power of governments would wither as the relationships within society became subject to economic laws rather than arbitrary legal systems. In two lectures in 1857 he attributed crime not to personal depravity but the corrupting tendencies of the law. He died in Feltham, Middlesex, on 21 August 1869 after a short illness. No London newspaper published a notice of his life and work. DAVID EASTWOOD, *rev.*

Sources E. Halévy, *Thomas Hodgskin*, trans. A. J. Taylor (1956) • W. Stafford, *Socialism, radicalism and nostalgia* (1987) • S. Hollander, 'The post-Ricardian dissension', *Oxford Economic Papers*, 32 (1980), 370–410 • M. B. Levin, 'Thomas Hodgskin', PhD diss., Columbia University, 1955 • J. Sokolow, 'Hodgskin, Thomas', *BDMBR*, vol. 1 • *DLB* • d. cert.

Archives UCL, letters to Society for the Diffusion of Useful Knowledge • UCL, letters to University College London • Yale U., Sterling Memorial Library, corresp., literary MSS, and papers | BL, corresp. with Francis Place, Add. MSS 35152–35153

Hodgson, Bernard (*bap.* 1743, *d.* 1805), college head, was baptized on 5 November 1743 at St Martin-in-the-Fields, Westminster, the third son of Mark and Eleanor Hodgson of that parish. He was educated at Westminster School from 1754, where in May 1759 he was elected a king's scholar. In May 1764, as captain of the school, he was elected to a studentship of Christ Church, Oxford, whence he matriculated on 20 June 1765 and graduated BA (1768) and MA (1771). On 30 October 1775 he became principal of Hertford College, and proceeded DCL on 24 January 1776. He was presented by the dean and chapter of Christ Church to the vicarage of Tolpuddle, Dorset, in December 1775. On 1 May 1783 at Chippenham, Wiltshire, he married Harriet Sainsbury; they had one son.

Hodgson's published works comprise *Solomon's Song Translated from the Hebrew* (1786), *The Proverbs of Solomon Translated from the Hebrew* (1788), and *Ecclesiastes: a New Translation from the Original Hebrew* (1790). In addition, he probably wrote the blank verse *The Monastery: a Poem on the Building of a Monastery in Dorsetshire* (1795). The author, alarmed by the success of a recent Trappist foundation at Lulworth, aimed 'to discourage indulgence to the papists, till they have renounced the supremacy of the pope' (*GM*, 1796).

Hodgson died on 28 May 1805 after a painful illness. On his death the college was dissolved, and was not refounded until 1874. His wife had predeceased him; his son, Charles (*d.* 1846), was also educated at Christ Church, Oxford, and became vicar of St Tudye in Cornwall in 1817.

G. F. R. BARKER, *rev.* JOHN D. HAIGH

Sources *GM*, 1st ser., 75 (1805), 586 · *GM*, 1st ser., 66 (1796), 317 · J. Hutchins, *The history and antiquities of the county of Dorset*, 3rd edn, ed. W. Shipp and J. W. Hodson, 2 (1863), 634 · Foster, *Alum. Oxon.* · A. Wood, *The history and antiquities of the colleges and halls in the University of Oxford*, ed. J. Gutch (1786), 647–8 · *IGI* · will, PRO, PROB 11/1427, fols. 152v–155r · *Old Westminsters*

Hodgson, Brian Houghton

Hodgson, Brian Houghton (1801?–1894), diplomatist and Nepalese scholar, was born on 1 February 1801, or (less probably) 1800, at Lower Beech, Prestbury, Cheshire, the second of the seven children of Brian Hodgson (1766–1858), country gentleman, and his wife, Catherine (1775/6–1851), daughter of William Houghton of Manchester and Newton Park, Lancashire. The name Brian had also been borne by his grandfather and great-grandfather, landowners in the midlands and north-west England. Following failure in a banking venture, his father sold their home at Lower Beech but family connections, including a great-aunt married to Beilby Porteus, bishop of London, helped to offset financial difficulties. He remained in Cheshire until 1814 when he moved to Clacton, Essex, on appointment as warden of the Martello towers. In 1820 he became barrack-master at Canterbury.

Hodgson was educated at Macclesfield grammar school until 1814 and from 1814 to 1816 under Daniel Delafosse at Richmond, Surrey. In 1816 he was nominated for the Bengal civil service by James Pattison, a director of the East India Company. From February 1816 to December 1817 he attended the company's training college at Haileybury, where the influence of Thomas R. Malthus, professor of history and political economy, turned him into 'an advanced liberal' (Hunter, 23). He excelled in economics, classics, and Bengali and graduated head of his year.

After arriving in Calcutta early in 1818, Hodgson led a full social life while continuing the study of Sanskrit and Persian at Fort William College. He was particularly successful with Persian, then still an official language within British India and the medium of formal communication with independent Indian states; but a near-fatal attack of fever interrupted his course, making an immediate hill posting essential. In late 1819 he was appointed assistant commissioner of Kumaon, a territory annexed from Nepal in 1815 during the war which ended the country's expansion and deprived it of a third of its pre-war territory. Hodgson worked on the revenue settlement under the commissioner, George Traill, a strong believer in a paternalist administrative style and in detailed study of the land and its people. In 1820 he was promoted to the assistant residentship at the Nepalese capital, Katmandu,

but he moved to Calcutta in 1822 as acting deputy secretary in the Persian department of the Foreign Office. Renewed ill health necessitated his return to Katmandu in early 1824 as residency postmaster until his reappointment as assistant resident in 1825. He was to be plagued by illness throughout his time in Nepal and India. He gave up meat and alcohol after recurrence of a liver complaint in 1837.

Continuing studies begun in 1820–21, he investigated Nepalese institutions and commerce and became proficient in Nepali and Newari, the language of the Katmandu valley's indigenous inhabitants. Despite family obligations which kept him in debt until 1837, he retained at his own expense a group of local research assistants, training himself and some of his staff as naturalists, specializing particularly in ornithology. He described 39 new mammalian and 150 bird species and published 127 zoological papers. He was also an avid collector of Buddhist scriptures in Sanskrit and Tibetan and was the first to reveal to the West the Sanskrit literature of northern, or Mahayana, Buddhism, which had been preserved only in Nepal. Texts he sent to Paris enabled the Sanskritist Eugène Burnouf to produce his seminal studies. In his own interpretation of his Buddhist Sanskrit materials, guided by his Nepalese friend and pandit Amritananda, Hodgson adopted a misconceived division of Buddhist doctrine into four 'schools' and, as he later admitted, wrongly argued that his Sanskrit texts were older than the Pali scriptures of Hinyana Buddhism. Nevertheless, much of his analysis still holds good.

Hodgson finally became resident in his own right on 21 January 1833, having been acting resident between 1829 and 1831. He was already convinced that Nepal's continuing resentment of defeat, her isolationist policy, and the maintenance of a large standing army were a threat to peace which could be removed by encouraging the growth of commerce with British India and Tibet and by employing the country's military manpower in the East India Company's forces. Like previous residents he initially favoured co-operation with Bhimsen Thapa, the minister who had long dominated Nepalese politics but relied heavily on the support of the army. However, he soon decided that relations with the British would improve if managed directly by the young King Rajendra. He began pressing for direct access to the king and for concessions on trade but was restrained by the Indian government.

Hodgson sympathized with Bhimsen's prominent opponent, Ranjang Pande, and was particularly influenced by Ranjang's Brahman ally, Krishna Ram Mishra. When Bhimsen sought British support for his weakening position, Hodgson strengthened the opposition by ensuring no substantive negotiations took place during a visit to Calcutta in 1835–6 by Bhimsen's nephew. In July 1837 Bhimsen was arrested on suspicion of involvement in the death of King Rajendra's infant son, and when the king asked for his advice Hodgson recommended that Bhimsen be kept in custody during investigations. The following summer, finding that both the king and Ranjang's faction were in fact ready to capitalize on anti-British feeling both at home and among other independent Indian states, Hodgson transferred his sympathies to the Poudyal brothers. This Brahman family had long been rivals with the Mishras for influence with the royal family. He formed a particularly close relationship with the second brother, Krishna Ram Poudyal, frequently reporting and seconding his opinions in letters to the governor-general.

During 1839 much of the nobility felt threatened by Ranjang's faction and began looking to the residency for political support. In July Bhimsen Thapa committed suicide in prison. According to the Nepalese officials who brought Hodgson the news, he wept on hearing it; he had at first refused Bhimsen's smuggled plea to intervene on his behalf and his later request to the governor-general for permission to speak out was sent too late. Instability continued into 1840 with an armed Nepalese incursion into British territory and a brief army mutiny that seemed at one point to threaten the residency itself. As well as successfully demanding a Nepalese withdrawal, the governor-general, Lord Auckland, now authorized Hodgson to press the king to appoint new advisers friendly to the British. With an army embroiled in Afghanistan, Auckland was not ready for a full-scale campaign against Nepal, but Hodgson's negotiations and the movement of troops closer to the border secured the appointment at the beginning of 1841 of a 'British ministry' including both Krishna Ram Poudyal and his more prominent brother, Ranganath.

In April 1842 Hodgson was involved in a public clash with King Rajendra over an Indian merchant who had taken refuge at the residency. He subsequently decided not to deliver to the king a letter concerning the incident from the new governor-general, Lord Ellenborough, believing it would weaken the position of the pro-British ministers. Ellenborough ordered his instant dismissal but subsequently relented and left him in post with instructions to disengage gradually from internal politics. He complied, but still sought to influence events through policy advice. Hodgson wanted to remain in Nepal until 1844, ostensibly to complete a general study of the country but, according to oral tradition in Katmandu, also because of the birth of a third child to his Nepalese Muslim lover, Begum Meharunnisha. Despite an appeal from King Rajendra for his retention, Ellenborough insisted on his departure from Katmandu in December 1843. Offered only a minor post at Simla, he resigned from the civil service and returned to England in 1844.

The portrait of Hodgson as the complete master of events in Katmandu presented by his friend and biographer, William Hunter, is no longer accepted, and even Lord Auckland, who allowed him a free hand in late 1840, sensed that his sudden enthusiasms could leave him open to manipulation. Nevertheless, Hodgson did succeed in keeping the peace, and the war with Nepal which Auckland had thought likely to come was avoided. The regret expressed in Katmandu at his departure reflected a belief that he had prevented a clash with British India which would have ended Nepalese independence.

After time with his parents in Canterbury and with his sister Fanny, who was educating his two elder children in Holland, Hodgson returned to India in 1845. Barred by the British authorities from returning in a private capacity to Katmandu, he settled at Darjeeling, a hill station just east of the Nepal border. He kept somewhat aloof from the local European community and his correspondence shows unhappiness at his countrymen's increasing racism towards Indians. The botanist Joseph Hooker stayed with him from 1848 to 1850 and he was also joined by his own son Henry, who died at Darjeeling in 1856. He was for a time entrusted with the education of a son-in-law of Jang Bahadur Rana, who had become master of Nepal in 1846. In October 1857 he helped persuade the governor-general, Lord Canning, to accept Jang Bahadur's offer of Nepalese help in suppressing the mutiny.

Hodgson continued work on zoology and the physical geology of the Himalayas, but concentrated in particular on the ethnology of the peoples of northern India, relying extensively on linguistic comparisons. Though taking the part of aboriginal peoples against later, Hindu settlers, he also advocated mass European settlement in the hills. His belief that all the 'non-Aryan' peoples of India belonged to one great 'Tamulian' family was misconceived, but he successfully demonstrated the relationship of many languages of Nepal and north-east India to Tibetan and Chinese. He had opposed William Bentinck's 1835 decision to accept Macaulay's arguments and make English the medium of both education and administration in India. He now continued his advocacy of mother-tongue education, arguing from analogy with the replacement of Latin for scholarly purposes by the modern languages of Europe. In 1854 he saw the principle of mass vernacular education accepted by the Indian government.

During a visit to Europe in 1853 Hodgson met and married Anne Scott (1815/16–1868), daughter of General Henry Alexander Scott, probably shortly after the death of his Nepalese partner, who had remained throughout in Katmandu. His wife returned with him to Darjeeling, but because of her ill health and that of his father, Hodgson left India in 1858. He retired to Gloucestershire, living first at Dursley and then at Alderley Grange, near Wotton under Edge, and, after 1883, wintering at Menton on the French riviera. His wife died in January 1868 and in 1869 he married Susan Townshend, daughter of the Revd Chambré Townshend of Derry, co. Cork. His children born in Nepal all died early and there were none from either of his marriages. He himself enjoyed a vigorous old age, riding to hounds until the age of sixty-eight, keeping up his academic interests, and holding a candle for Gladstone and Irish home rule among the largely tory local gentry. He died peacefully at 48 Dover Street, London, on 23 May 1894 and was buried in Alderley churchyard; his second wife survived him.

The most important of Hodgson's non-zoological writings were reissued as *Essays on the languages, literature and religion of Nepal and Tibet together with further papers on the geography, ethnology and commerce of those countries* (1874) and *Miscellaneous Essays Relating to Indian Subjects* (2 vols.,

1880), which are regularly reprinted in India and Nepal. He donated some 400 Sanskrit manuscripts, two sets of the Tibetan Kahgyur and Stangyur encyclopaedias (the Tibetan Buddhist canon, and commentaries on the scriptures and other treatises, respectively), 10,000 zoological specimens, and 1800 drawings to libraries and museums. Materials that he gave to the India Office Library in 1864 remain a key source for Nepalese history. Recognition in his lifetime included his being made a member of the Royal Asiatic Society (1828), elected a fellow of the Linnean Society (1835) and of the Royal Society (1877), made a chevalier of the Légion d'honneur (1838), and awarded the honorary degree of DCL at Oxford University (1889).

Surviving photographs and the bust by T. E. Thornycroft confirm references to Hodgson's finely cut features and dignified bearing. Brought up in the Church of England he remained a theist but was unwilling to discuss his religious beliefs. He could show rash judgement and oversensitivity to affronts. To a modern reader his writings sometimes show signs of pomposity and, less frequently, of a patronizing attitude towards Indians and Nepalese. His virtues included a marked ability to inspire affection and loyalty, prodigious intellectual energy and enthusiasm, and a strong belief in the human potential of all races.   JOHN WHELPTON

Sources W. W. Hunter, *Life of Brian Houghton Hodgson, British resident at the court of Nepal* (1896) [incl. work list] · J. Whelpton, *Kings, soldiers and priests: Nepalese politics and the rise of Jang Bahadur Rana, 1830–1857* (1991) · D. N. Gellner, 'Hodgson's blind alley? On the so-called schools of Nepalese Buddhism', *Journal of the International Association for Buddhist Studies*, 12 (1985), 7–19 · H. R. Joshi, 'Brian Houghton Hodgson: the untold tale' [in forthcoming vol. on Hodgson, ed. D. Waterhouse] · *DNB* · P. Pels, 'The politics of aboriginality: Brian Houghton Hodgson and the making of an ethnology of India', *International Institute for Asian Studies Yearbook*, ed. P. van de Velde (1994), 147–68 · P. Denwood, 'Introduction', in B. H. Hodgson, *Miscellaneous essays relating to Indian subjects* (1972) · K. Mojumdar, *Anglo-Nepalese relations in the nineteenth century* (1973) · D. L. Snellgrove, *Indo-Tibetan Buddhism: Indian Buddhists and their Tibetan successors* (1987) · B. S. Cohn, 'The recruitment and training of British civil servants in India', *An anthropologist among the historians, and other essays* (1987), 500–53 [details of Haileybury and Fort William College] · private information (2004) [F. Pinn]
Archives BL OIOC, corresp. and papers; foreign political proceedings; foreign secret proceedings; Nepal residency records · Bodl. Oxf., corresp. and papers · Linn. Soc., catalogue of Nepalese mammals · NHM, corresp. and papers · RCS Eng., catalogue of Nepalese birds · Royal Asiatic Society, London, corresp. and papers · Zoological Society of London, corresp. and papers | BL, Auckland MSS · Bodl. Oxf., corresp. with Lord Ellenborough · Cleveland Library, Ohio, John Hopkins MSS · NHM, letters to A. C. L. G. Gunther · RBG Kew, letters to Sir William Hooker
Likenesses M. Carpenter, oils, 1817, Haileybury College, Hertfordshire; repro. in Hunter, *Life of Brian Houghton Hodgson* · T. E. Thornycroft, marble bust, 1844, Asiatic Society, Calcutta; repro. in Hunter, *Life of Brian Houghton Hodgson*; copy, Royal Asiatic Society, London · Kampf, photograph, 1871, repro. in Hunter, *Life of Brian Houghton Hodgson* · L. S. Canziani, oils, 1872, NPG; repro. in Hunter, *Life of Brian Houghton Hodgson* · S. Hodgson, photograph, 1891, repro. in Hunter, *Life of Brian Houghton Hodgson* · C. Alexander, oils, Indian Institute, Oxford
Wealth at death £5070 4s. 5d.: probate, 2 July 1894, CGPLA Eng. & Wales

Hodgson, Christopher Pemberton (1821–1865), traveller, was the son of the Revd Edward Hodgson (1793–1853), vicar of Rickmansworth, and Charlotte, his third wife, daughter of Francis William Pemberton of Trumpington Hall, Cambridge. He is known to have had a stepbrother and two brothers. Unlike many male members of his family, he was not educated at Cambridge but emigrated to New South Wales in 1840, remained in Australia (where his elder brother Arthur had earlier settled) for five years, and accompanied several expeditions into the interior. On his return to England he published *Reminiscences of Australia, with Hints on the Squatters' Life* (1846). After a short stay in England he travelled through Egypt and Abyssinia, made two journeys to Arabia, and visited Ceylon. He described these travels in *El Ydaivur* (1849). From 15 October 1851 to 17 March 1855 Hodgson was honorary vice-consul at Pau, where he was popular, and interested himself in local history and antiquities. In 1855 he published *Pyrenaica; a history of the viscounts of Béarn to the death of Henry IV, with a life of that monarch*. He subsequently was appointed vice-consul at Caen, where he remained for two years, and on 18 June 1859 became officiating consul at Nagasaki, Japan. In October 1860 he moved to Hakodate, to take charge of French as well as English interests. He remained in Japan until March 1861, and on his return to England published *A Residence at Nagasaki and Hakodate* (1861) to which his wife, of whom no more is known, contributed a series of letters on Japan. Hodgson thenceforth lived chiefly at Pau, but had a London address at 53 Pall Mall. He died at Lescar, near Pau on 11 October 1865.

G. P. MORIARTY, *rev.* ELIZABETH BAIGENT

Sources Burke, *Gen. GB · CGPLA Eng. & Wales* (1865) · Boase, *Mod. Eng. biog.* · *FO List* (1865) · *GM*, 3rd ser., 19 (1865), 797 · Venn, *Alum. Cant.* · *BL cat.*
Archives RBG Kew, letters to Sir William Jackson Hooker
Wealth at death under £1500: probate, 30 Dec 1865, *CGPLA Eng. & Wales*

Hodgson, Edward (b. c.1719), flower painter, was born in Dublin. Of his parents, nothing is known. He practised as a drawing-master in Ireland before 1765, when he was living in Mitre Court, London, and contributed chalk and watercolour drawings to an exhibition in Maiden Lane for the relief of distressed artists and their families. By 1767 he had moved to Oxenden Street, possibly as a drawing-master. He moved out within two years. He exhibited two flower paintings at the Royal Academy in both 1780 and 1781, and one piece in 1782, and one piece again in 1787 and 1788; he also exhibited at the Free Society of Artists in 1782 and 1783. During this time he lived at 123 Jermyn Street, London. He became treasurer of the Associated Artists in Water Colours. Earlier biographers record that Hodgson died in Great Newport Street in 1794, but he is not recorded as owning a house there. It is possible that Hodgson was the same Edward Hodgson who married Anne Oates in Chelsea on 25 September 1744. Mallalieu noted that his daughter exhibited flower pieces with the Free Society from 1770 to 1775.

L. H. CUST, *rev.* NICHOLAS GRINDLE

Sources W. G. Strickland, *A dictionary of Irish artists*, 2 vols. (1913); repr. with introduction by T. J. Snoddy (1989) • Graves, *RA exhibitors* • poor rate books, City Westm. AC, F.550 • Desmond, *Botanists* • Mallalieu, *Watercolour artists*

Hodgson, Francis (1781–1852), college head and poet, second son of James Hodgson, rector of Humber, Herefordshire, and Jane, daughter of the Revd Richard Coke, was born at Croydon, Surrey, on 16 November 1781. In 1794 he entered Eton College as a pupil of John Keate, and in 1799 he was elected scholar of King's College, Cambridge, where he became acquainted with Thomas Denman, J. H. Merivale, and Henry Drury. He graduated BA in 1804, MA in 1807, and BD in 1840. He obtained a fellowship at King's College in 1802, was private tutor for three years to the sons of Lady Ann Lambton, and in 1806 held a mastership for one year at Eton. He then contemplated the bar as a profession, but, being dissuaded by Denman, turned his attention to literature. During the next ten years he wrote many reviews, verses, translations, and rhyming letters, of which the most important was his translation of Juvenal (1807). He was a frequent contributor in 1811 to the *Critical Review* and *Monthly Review* on classical and literary subjects. In 1807 he was appointed to a resident tutorship at King's, which he held until his marriage.

Hodgson became best known for his literary friendship with Byron, dating from 1806, when he contributed to the *Anthologia Graeca*, which Byron later eulogized. Byron mediated after Hodgson had seduced the mistress of the Revd Robert Bland, who was one of the editors of the *Anthologia* and a master at Harrow School. For his part, Hodgson, alarmed at Byron's religious scepticism, strove to impress upon the poet the truth of Christian teaching during a long correspondence in 1810–11 when Byron was abroad. The death of Hodgson's father in 1810 left him encumbered with debts, which Byron helped him to meet. A gift of £1000 by Byron in 1813 enabled him to marry, on 5 August 1815, Matilda, the daughter of Archdale Wilson Tayler, her mother having at first objected to his suit on the grounds of his lack of means. Frederick and William Tayler were his brothers-in-law. During the separation of Lord and Lady Byron in 1816 Hodgson corresponded with Byron and Mrs Leigh, and made an unsuccessful appeal to Lady Byron. His poetic works in this period included *Lady Jane Grey* (1809) and *Leaves of Laurel* (1812), and a translation, undertaken with the classical scholar Samuel Butler, of Lucien Bonaparte's poem *Charlemagne* (1815).

Hodgson was ordained in 1814, serving a curacy at Bradden, Northamptonshire, in 1815 before being presented in 1816 to the living of Bakewell, Derbyshire. There he enhanced his reputation as an accomplished classical scholar by producing a number of works on Latin versification, specially adapted for use at Eton. He contributed Latin verses to *Arundines Cami* (ed. H. Drury, 1841), an influential early anthology. His first wife died, childless, in 1833 and he married, on 3 May 1838, Elizabeth, second daughter of Lord Denman, his Cambridge friend. His whig connections brought him further ecclesiastical preferment: Melbourne had appointed him to the archdeaconry of Derby, in succession to Samuel Butler in 1836, and in 1838 the duke of Devonshire presented him to the living of Edensor, Derbyshire.

Hodgson was nominated by the queen, on Melbourne's recommendation, provost of Eton College in April 1840, the fellows having shown a preference first for Dr Keate and then for John Lonsdale of King's College, London. He graduated BD at Cambridge to qualify himself for the office, which he held in conjunction with the rectory of Cottesford, Oxfordshire. The reputation he had gained in Derbyshire as a conscientious and efficient administrator was maintained at Eton, where it was said that no provost had 'more thoroughly realized the duties and responsibilities' attaching to that office (Lyte, 476). He encouraged the headmaster, E. C. Hawtrey, in carrying through a number of reforms, taking a particular interest in improving the accommodation of the collegers and in the restoration of the chapel. Much of his effectiveness was due to a combination of energy with tact and courtesy. After suffering from influenza, he died at The Lodge, Eton College, on 29 December 1852, leaving a widow and five children. He was buried on 4 January 1853 in the college chapel.

N. D. F. PEARCE, *rev.* M. C. CURTHOYS

Sources [J. T. Hodgson], *Memoir of the Rev. Francis Hodgson BD scholar, poet and divine*, 2 vols. (1878) • Venn, *Alum. Cant.* • L. A. Marchand, *Byron: a biography*, 3 vols. (1957) • H. C. Maxwell Lyte, *A history of Eton College, 1440–1910*, 4th edn (1911) • Boase, *Mod. Eng. biog.* • GM, 2nd ser., 39 (1853), 442–3 • *Benjamin Robert Haydon: correspondence and table-talk*, ed. F. W. Haydon, 2 vols. (1876) • J. Arnould, *Memoir of Thomas, first Lord Denman*, 2 vols. (1873)
Archives Bodl. Oxf., corresp. | BL, corresp. with Bishop S. Butler
Likenesses engraving, 1818, repro. in Hodgson, *Memoir*, frontispiece • W. Walker, mezzotint, pubd 1850 (after F. Grant), BM, NPG • oils, Eton

Hodgson, Geraldine Emma (1865–1937), promoter of teacher training, was born on 19 May 1865 at 52 Montpelier Road, Brighton, Sussex, the youngest daughter of George Frederick Hodgson, surgeon, and his wife, Elizabeth Chamney. She was educated privately, and from 1886 at Newnham College, Cambridge, where she was Cobden scholar and gained a first class in the moral sciences tripos in 1889. She was an assistant mistress at Blackburne House School, Liverpool, in 1889–90, was briefly secretary to Rosalind, Lady Carlisle in 1890, and was mistress in charge of Newcastle upon Tyne preparatory school from 1891 to 1894. For three years (1894–7) she was deputy head of Leamington High School for Girls (later the Kingsley School) until becoming a lecturer in English literature at University College, Aberystwyth, in 1897.

After leaving Aberystwyth in 1899 Geraldine Hodgson was briefly a member of the factory inspectorate, and published the first of her four novels, *Antony Delaval LLD* (1900), usually regarded as the best. In 1902 she was appointed head of the women's secondary teacher training department at University College, Bristol. A distinguished figure in the training of women teachers, she became one of the leading women academics of her generation until her university career was cut short by the 'Hodgson affair'. During her time at Bristol she published more than a dozen books and numerous papers and reviews, including valuable studies of early Christian education (1906), an analysis of the ideas of rationalist English educators (1912) critical of the utilitarian tradition, and a pioneering history of French educational thought from Rabelais to Rousseau (1908), which contained a sharp attack on Rousseau's writings on the education of women. In 1909 she received the degree of DLitt from Trinity College, Dublin, having taken her BA degree there in 1904.

In 1916 Geraldine Hodgson was dismissed from her post at Bristol for reasons which remain unclear, though there was a long-running dispute about the lack of tenure of academic staff. Her position had been a rather uneasy one, and was exacerbated by the removal of the secondary training department from the faculty of arts. Because there was no statutory requirement for teachers in secondary schools to be trained teachers, her department at Bristol never had more than ten students. Her relationships with colleagues, both in teacher training and in the university generally, appear to have been strained. Jealousy of her scholarship or hostility to her political activities (she had produced pamphlets for the National Union of Women's Suffrage Societies) may have played a part. Newspaper reports indicated prolonged disputes with Isambard Owen, the vice-chancellor: 'a lady lecturer intimated that certain unnamed persons in the University have endeavoured to undermine her position and make it impossible' (*Bristol Times and Mirror*, 19 May 1913).

In January 1917 Geraldine Hodgson was appointed vice-principal of the Ripon and Wakefield and Bradford Diocesan Training College at Ripon, Yorkshire, remaining there until her retirement in 1922. An active churchwoman, from 1920 to 1929 she was a member of the house of laity for the Ripon diocese in the church assembly. Latterly her published work concentrated on religious themes, and particularly mysticism. Her study *English Mystics* appeared in 1922 followed by a definitive study of the life of Richard Rolle (1926), the fourteenth-century hermit and poet. She was also a literary historian and critic, producing a comparative study of Henry Vaughan, William Wordsworth, Robert Browning, and Francis Thompson (1914), and a biography of the poet James Elroy Flecker (1925). After retirement from Ripon, Geraldine Hodgson returned to live in Bristol, where she died at her home, 17 Sion Hill, Clifton, on 3 December 1937.

JOHN B. THOMAS

Sources *The Times* (7 Dec 1937), 18c · *WWW* · J. E. Roscoe, *The dictionary of educationists* (1914) · J. B. Thomas, 'University College, Bristol: pioneering teacher training for women', *History of Education*, 17 (1988), 55–70 · D. W. Humphreys, *The University of Bristol and the education and training of teachers* (1976) · C. Dyhouse, *No distinction of sex? Women in British universities, 1870–1939* (1995) · b. cert. · d. cert. · *CGPLA Eng. & Wales* (1938)

Wealth at death £1325 6s. 4d.: probate, 3 Feb 1938, *CGPLA Eng. & Wales*

Hodgson, James (*bap.* 1678?, *d.* 1755), mathematician, is probably identifiable with the son of James Hodgson (or Hodson) and his wife, Elizabeth, who was baptized at St

James Hodgson (*bap.* 1678?, *d.* 1755), by George White (after Thomas Gibson)

James's, Clerkenwell, on 25 February 1678. From 1 April 1695 he was assistant to John *Flamsteed, the first astronomer royal, at the Royal Observatory, Greenwich; he later claimed that this was the main source of his education. Flamsteed states that he arrived because 'Sir Christopher Wren would needs put a relation of his, an ingenious youth, … into my service' (Baily, 64); the relationship is confirmed by letters in which Wren's son addressed Hodgson as cousin.

Hodgson was evidently employed by Flamsteed under a seven-year indenture, as on 6 February 1702 he was 'nearly out of his time' (RS, MS 798.1). His handwriting appears frequently among Flamsteed's surviving papers from the intervening period, in observation notes, calculations, tables, copies of letters, and other documents. In 1701 Flamsteed evaluated him in the following words:

> a Sober Young man about 22 Years of Age. A very good Geometrician and Algebraist [who] Understands the Series and fluxions tho I have not Suffered him to Spend much time in them because I could not Spare him from the calculation work he understands the Latin Tongue indifferently, haveing got [it] since he became my Servant he knows my method and is acquainted with all my Labors and will easily finish and print them If God should call me hence before I shall have perfected them my Self. (Royal Greenwich Observatory papers, RGO 1/33, fol. 173)

On 31 October 1702 Hodgson married Ann Heming, Flamsteed's niece (in effect adopted daughter), without first seeking Flamsteed's approval; she continued to live at the observatory (after her husband had left Flamsteed's employment) until October 1706, then moved to London to join her husband. Among their children were Katharine (b. 1706), John (b. 1708), and James (b. 1710), who were baptized at St Peter-le-Poer, St Botolph (Aldersgate) and Christ Church Greyfriars respectively, all in the City of London. On 20 February 1703 Flamsteed wrote of Hodgson 'my Elder servant has left me about 4 moneths agone to teach Mathematicks in London' (BL, Add. MS 36452, fol. 134r); the following August Hodgson could be contacted at Jones's coffee house in Finch Lane, Cornhill. He was elected as a fellow of the Royal Society on 30 November 1703 and admitted on 15 December following, leading Flamsteed to comment: 'they have a limbe of me ... but he is honest and discreet and ... will not serve some mens small designs as they expect he should' (RS, MS 798.14).

Hodgson not only taught privately but also participated in the growing fashion for coffee-house lecturing. In October 1704 he launched a course 'For the Advancement of Natural Philosophy and Astronomy', held at the Hand and Pen, formerly Ayers' Writing School, in St Paul's Churchyard. A printed advertisement at the end of the first edition of Halley's *Miscellanea curiosa* (1705) gives details and states that much of the necessary apparatus was supplied by the elder Francis Hauksbee. The venture seems to have been a success: by December 1705 Flamsteed said Hodgson was 'full of business with a book of Navigation in the press. Pretty store of pupills and some business in my Concernes' (RS, MS 798.40). The book was *The Theory of Navigation Demonstrated* (1706), dedicated to Prince George of Denmark. In the following year Hodgson succeeded John Harris as lecturer on mechanics at the Marine Coffee House, near the Royal Exchange.

On 12 January 1709 Hodgson was appointed to run the Royal Mathematical School at Christ's Hospital, at an annual salary of £100. As one of the most competent of the school's early masters, he had no difficulty retaining the post until his death, and from 1748 he was permitted to employ a deputy on the grounds of old age. He published material designed for his pupils' use as *A System of the Mathematics* (1723).

Hodgson's other mathematical publications include *The Doctrine of Fluxions* (1736) and several shorter treatises on practical subjects. He also produced *A Theory of Jupiter's Satellites* (1750) and papers in the *Philosophical Transactions* on astronomical topics. He remained in close touch with Flamsteed, who relied on him as an intermediary in his dealings with the Royal Society and with the 'referees' overseeing publication of the *Historia coelestis* (1712); he later acted jointly with Flamsteed's widow to ensure that the 'authorized' version of this work (1725) and the *Atlas coelestis* (1729) were completed. After Mrs Flamsteed's death, Hodgson had custody of Flamsteed's papers and relics from the Royal Observatory; in 1736 and 1737 he gave the Royal Society a clock and object-glass from this source. He died on 25 June 1755, probably at Christ's Hospital, London. His place of burial is likely to have been Christ Church Greyfriars, London, but this has not been confirmed.   FRANCES WILLMOTH

Sources CUL, Royal Greenwich Observatory papers, RGO 1/6, fols. 24r, 39r, 176r; RGO 1/33, fols. 126v, 128r, 173, 210v • J. Flamsteed, letters to A. Sharp, RS, Flamsteed papers, MSG 798 • journal books, RS, vol. 10, pp. 53, 55 • F. Baily, *An account of the Revd John Flamsteed, the first astronomer-royal* (1835) • Christ's Hospital records, GL, MSS 12,806/9–12,806/11 • letters from Christopher Wren jun., BL, Add. MS 6209, fols. 203r–205r • R. Hovenden, ed., *A true register of all the christenings, mariages, and burialles in the parish of St James, Clarkenwell, from ... 1551 (to 1754)*, 1, Harleian Society, register section, 9 (1884) [christenings, 1551–1700] • W. A. Littledale, ed., *The registers of Christ Church, Newgate, 1538 to 1754*, Harleian Society, 21 (1895) • E. Halley, ed., *Miscellanea curiosa* (1705) • L. R. Stewart, *The rise of public science: rhetoric, technology, and natural philosophy in Newtonian Britain, 1660–1750* (1992), 114–17, 173, 331n • C. R. Weld, *A history of the Royal Society*, 2 vols. (1848), vol. 1, p. 255n • *GM*, 1st ser., 25 (1755), 284 • R. V. Wallis and P. J. Wallis, eds., *Biobibliography of British mathematics and its applications*, 2 (1986), 14–15

Archives BL, Add. MS 6209 • BL, Sloane MSS, Add. MSS 4038, 4050 • CUL, Royal Greenwich Observatory papers, notes and papers

Likenesses G. White, mezzotint (after T. Gibson), BM, NPG [see illus.] • portrait, Christ's Hospital, Horsham, Sussex

Hodgson, John (1617/18–1684?), army officer and autobiographer, was a native of Yorkshire. He took up arms for parliament in late 1642 and began his military service as ensign in the regiment of Colonel Forbes. He fought under Sir Thomas Fairfax and was badly wounded in the defeat at Sancroft Moor. When the marquess of Newcastle captured Bradford (July 1643) he was made prisoner and stripped, but, being released, made his way to Rochdale, where he suffered a fever. He rejoined Fairfax at Knutsford Heath, to undertake the attack on Lord Byron at Nantwich (January 1644). His company then entered Colonel John Bright's regiment, and he took part in the 1645 siege of Pontefract.

On 17 April 1646 he married a woman surnamed Stancliffe; they had two sons, Timothy and Eleazer, and three daughters, Sarah, Martha, and Lydia. In the summer of 1647, as tension mounted between parliament and its armies, Hodgson was prominent in securing the alignment of the northern association army with the New Model. With Major Henry Lilburne he led troops through Leeds to a rendezvous on the moors. Papers were read concerning the New Model's desire to co-operate with their northern comrades, agitators were chosen, including Hodgson, a general rendezvous was demanded, and Poyntz, the commander of the northern forces, was arrested. Hodgson feared dismissal because of his actions, and appears to have remained in the army due to the protection of John Lambert, the future major-general.

Hodgson fought in the battle of Preston (August 1648) as a lieutenant in Captain Spencer's company, leading the 'forlorn of foot' with Major Pownall. When Cromwell invaded Scotland in 1650, Hodgson, whose regiment was now commanded by Lambert, took part in the campaign. His description of the battle of Dunbar is perhaps the most valuable part of his autobiography. After Dunbar he was given command of a company in Cromwell's regiment of foot, sent into Lancashire to assist Colonel Lilburne against the earl of Derby. Though he did not arrive until after Derby's defeat, his regiment helped to intercept the Scots after Worcester, and took part in the capture of the Isle of Man (1651).

When Lambert was appointed lord deputy of Ireland, Hodgson wrote of his desire to follow his commander. After Cromwell became protector, Hodgson wished to leave the army 'to live quietly in the practice of my calling' (BL, Add. MS 21422, fol. 374) but was appointed lieutenant in Lambert's regiment of horse, quartered in Yorkshire, to enable him to be near his family. On 11 April 1657 he acquired Coley Hall, near Halifax, by lease for fifteen years. He acted as an army surgeon, although he lacked official medical qualifications; he would later be indicted for practising medicine without a medical degree despite his eleven years as an army doctor.

On Saturday 28 May 1659, when the restored Rump Parliament agreed the officer list for Lambert's regiment, Hodgson was 'excepted' and appears to have lost his place until he received a new commission from the speaker on 3 August. In October 1659, following the army coup, he was assigned to the regiment of Colonel Saunders, and ordered to join George Monck's army in Scotland. Monck declared against the army regime, but Hodgson would not fight against Lambert and with Captain Roger Coates sought to raise money for his old commander. By now he had given evidence of Quaker opinions. In response to the crisis of 1659 he appears to have written two Quaker pamphlets, *A Letter from a Member of the Army* and *Love, Kindness, and due Respect*, warning of men turning away from the Lord and serving themselves. A John Hodgson also signed *A Declaration of the People of God in Scorn called Quakers* (1659) protesting against the expulsion of Friends from civil and military positions. He was on close terms with the Quaker officers captains William Siddall, Amor Stoddard, and John Leavens.

When Monck marched into England, Hodgson's prospects of further employment ended and, after the Restoration, he was the object of government suspicion. He was listed among those from the West Riding imprisoned in 1660 for not taking the oath of allegiance, and a meeting of 'a hundred fanatics, ministers, and others' was reported as held on 3 July 1660 at Coley Hall. Hodgson, referred to as a 'great Phanatique', spent five months in York Castle for treasonable words spoken against Charles II. In July 1661 he narrowly escaped arrest at Adderton fair, but suffered arrest again, being suspected of involvement in radical plots. In 1663 he was found guilty of misprision of treason, for not revealing knowledge of the northern rising, but seems to have eventually secured a pardon by bribery. He was rearrested, on suspicion of continued involvement in planned disturbances, in August 1665.

By now Hodgson had moved from Coley Hall to Cromwell Bottom, moving thence to Ripon in 1680. He is probably the John Hodgson mentioned by Oliver Heywood as dying impoverished at Ripon on 24 January 1684 aged sixty-six. The last date in his diary is 11 January 1684. His 'Memoirs', first published with Sir Henry Slingsby's 'Original memoirs' in 1806, appear in part to have been written in response to the persecution he received after the

Restoration, although they contain much of interest with regard to his military experiences. He avoids commenting on his political and religious views, though it seems clear that he was not as innocent after 1660 as he makes out.

THOMPSON COOPER, *rev.* D. N. FARR

Sources *Autobiography of Captain John Hodgson*, ed. J. H. Turner (1882) · *Original memoirs written during the great civil war: being the life of Sir Henry Slingsby and memoirs of Capt. Hodgson*, ed. W. Scott (1806) · D. N. Farr, 'John Hodgson: soldier, surgeon, agitator and Quaker?', *Journal of the Friends' Historical Society*, 58 (1997–9), 220–34 · *The Rev. Oliver Heywood … his autobiography, diaries, anecdote and event books*, ed. J. H. Turner, 4 vols. (1881–5) · J. Raine, ed., *Depositions from the castle of York relating to offences committed in the northern counties in the seventeenth century*, SurtS, 40 (1861), 86–7, 157–8 · PRO, Assi. 45 6/1 no. 75 · PRO, C5/500/47, C10/492/83 · BL, Add. MSS 21417–21427 · A. Cole, 'The peace testimony in 1659: more light on John Hodgson', *Journal of the Friends' Historical Society*, 46 (1954), 48–52 · 'Addition to the library', *Journal of the Friends' Historical Society*, 42 (1950), 80–82 · *The Clarke papers*, ed. C. H. Firth, [new edn], 2 vols. in 1 (1992), vol. 1, pp. 142–3, 169 · *A Continuation of Certaine Speciall and Remarkable Passages* (July 1647) [Thomason tract E 399(4)] · *Perfect Weekly Account*, 25 (14–21 July 1647) [Thomason tract E 399(12)] · *Kingdomes Weekly Intelligencer*, 218 (13–20 July 1647), 600 [Thomason tract E 399(13)] · *Moderate Intelligencer*, 2 (19–26 Aug 1647), 16 [Thomason tract E 404(28)] · J. Morrill, 'Mutiny and discontent in English provincial armies, 1645–1647', *Past and Present*, 56 (1972), 49–74, esp. 70 · *A further proposal from his excellency Sir Thomas Fairfax*, 24 July 1647, BL, E399(32) · *A declaration and representation from the forces of the northern association to Fairfax*, 13 July 1647, BL, E398(5) · C. H. Firth and G. Davies, *The regimental history of Cromwell's army*, 1 (1940), 257 · *JHC*, 7 (1651–9), 668, 680, 712 · D. Hirst, 'The fracturing of the Cromwellian alliance: Leeds and Adam Baynes', *EngHR*, 108 (1993), 868–94 · PRO, SP 29/8/180 · R. L. Greaves, *Deliver us from evil: the radical underground in Britain, 1660–1663* (1986) · A. Marshall, *Intelligence and espionage in the reign of Charles II, 1660–1685* (1994) · 'Extracts from the A. R. Barclay MSS', *Journal of the Friends' Historical Society*, 28 (1931), 53 · *A declaration of the people of God in scorn called Quakers, to all magistrates and people*, 1659 [Wing C7201]

Archives BL, mainly financial and personal affairs, Add. MSS 21417, fols. 297, 316, 318, 328; 21418, fols. 8, 112, 121, 130, 141, 155, 162, 274, 314, 320, 355; 21419, fols. 19, 42, 55, 81, 120, 129; 21421, fols. 92, 110, 163, 176, 242; 21422, fols. 165, 176, 190, 374, 471, 487, 517; 21423, fols. 58, 114, 122, 144; 21424, fol. 70; 21426, fols. 149–54; 21427, fol. 315

Wealth at death thought to be impoverished: Turner, ed., *Rev. Oliver Heywood*

Hodgson, John (1757–1846), army officer, was the son and heir of Studholme *Hodgson (1707/8–1798), an army officer, and his wife, Catherine (1734–1798), the second daughter of Lieutenant-General Sir Thomas Howard. He was educated at Harrow School and in 1779 obtained an ensigncy in his father's regiment, the 4th King's Own; he served very many years with it in North America and was wounded in command of it in the Netherlands in 1799. He was later governor of Bermuda and of Curaçao, which latter appointment he held until the settlement was restored to the Dutch in 1815. His handling of the governorship earned Hodgson repeated thanks from the British government. In addition he served as colonel in succession of the 3rd garrison battalion, the 83rd, and his old corps, the 4th King's Own, and became a full general in 1830. He married Catherine Krempion of St Petersburg, a sister of the countess of Terrol, and had a large family, including John Studholme *Hodgson, the eldest son, and Studholme

John Hodgson [see below]. Like his father, John Hodgson attained a great age, and died at his home in Welbeck Street, London, on 14 January 1846 from the effects of a cold caught while out shooting.

Hodgson's second son, **Studholme John Hodgson** (b. after 1805, d. 1890), army officer, entered the army in 1819 as an ensign in the 50th foot and served for many years in Ceylon, India, and Burma in the 45th, 39th, and 19th regiments. For some time he commanded the forces in Ceylon and the Straits Settlements, and in Ceylon also administered the civil government. In 1856 he became colonel of the 54th, and in 1876, like his father and grandfather, colonel of the Royal Lancaster regiment. He died at Torquay on 31 August 1890.

H. M. CHICHESTER, rev. PHILIP CARTER

Sources R. Cannon, ed., *Historical record of the fourth, or the king's own, regiment of foot* (1839) · *Army List* · *The Times* (3 Sept 1890) · V. C. P. Hodson, *List of officers of the Bengal army, 1758–1834*, 4 vols. (1927–47)

Archives NAM, corresp. relating to colonelcy of 3rd garrison battalion

Hodgson, John [pseud. Archaeus] (1779–1845), antiquary, son of Isaac Hodgson, stonemason and slater, and Elizabeth (bap. 1755), daughter of William Rawes, was born at Swindale, in the parish of Shap, Westmorland, on 4 November 1779. He studied at Bampton grammar school from the age of seven to nineteen. As his parents were too poor to make a university education possible, from the age of twenty he had to earn his own livelihood, first as the master of the village school at Matterdale, near Ullswater, then at Stainton, near Penrith. Early in 1801 he was appointed to the school of Sedgefield, co. Durham. The rector of Sedgefield, George Barrington, a nephew of the bishop of Durham, and his curates showed much kindness to Hodgson, and helped him by the loan of books. He was offered an appointment as director of Lemmington ironworks near Newcastle, with a salary of £300 a year; but he refused this tempting offer on the ground that he wished 'to pursue a literary rather than a mercantile life'. In 1802 he failed in an examination for holy orders, which disappointment, combined with ill health, led him to leave Sedgefield in 1803 for the mastership of the school at Lanchester, near Durham. There in 1804 he succeeded in passing his ordination examination, and became curate of the chapelries of Esh and Satley, two hamlets in the parish of Lanchester, where he still kept his school.

The vestiges of a fine Roman camp at Lanchester attracted Hodgson's attention, and led him to study Roman antiquities. In 1807 he published a little volume, *Poems Written at Lanchester*, including 'Langovicum, a Vision', a poetical account of the Roman camp. In 1806 he left Lanchester for the curacy of Gateshead, then in 1808 he was presented by the patron, Cuthbert Ellison, with the living of Jarrow-with-Heworth. The income barely amounted to £100 a year, but it was very congenial to a man of Hodgson's tastes to serve the church where Bede had been a monk. On 11 January 1810 he married Jane Bridget (1786–1853), daughter of Richard Kell, a local stone merchant, and in the same year was commissioned to write the

account of Northumberland for Brayley and Britton's *Beauties of England and Wales*. This gave him an opportunity for exploring the county, where he made many friends. The following year he did the same for Westmorland. Of this series Hodgson's volumes were widely regarded as the best. In 1812 he rewrote for a Newcastle publisher *The Picture of Newcastle-on-Tyne*, a guidebook to the town, incorporating much research about the Roman wall and the early history of the coal trade. That May a colliery explosion at the Felling pit in Hodgson's parish caused the death of ninety-two people. Hodgson appealed for help for the widows and orphans, and published his funeral sermon, to which he prefixed an account of the accident. This book, *An Account of the Explosion at Felling* (1813), is valuable for its accurate account of the colliery, accompanied by a plan of the workings, and is one of the very few trustworthy records of the old system of coalmining. For the next few years Hodgson was employed in making experiments and attending meetings of the Society for the Prevention of Accidents in Coal Mines. In 1815 he visited the Dudley coalfield, to examine means of preventing colliery accidents, and later that year Sir Humphry Davy met Hodgson on his visit to Newcastle, so beginning an acquaintance acknowledged as enabling him to complete his invention of the safety lamp ('New researches on flame', *Philosophical Transactions of the Royal Society*, 1817). Meanwhile Hodgson was instrumental in the foundation of a society of antiquaries in Newcastle, which came into existence in 1813, and served with John Adamson as co-secretary (1813–34). The first three volumes of the society's *Transactions* contain many papers by him.

In 1817 Hodgson began work on his *History of Northumberland*. In 1819 he visited London to work in the various archive repositories, and on his return announced his book to appear in six volumes, published by subscription, limited to 300 copies. The first to appear, in 1820, was the fifth volume, which contained records and papers relating to border history. In 1821 Hodgson again visited London, with an expedition to Oxford for the purposes of his researches. He was also engaged in raising money for a new church at Heworth, which he designed himself. This simple building did much to revive a taste for ecclesiastical architecture in the north of England. It was consecrated in May 1822.

In 1823 Bishop Barrington presented Hodgson to the vicarage of Kirkwhelpington, a country parish in the centre of Northumberland. His obligations in regard to the new church at Heworth, which was not yet paid for, made it desirable that he should continue to hold the living of Jarrow until the parish of Heworth had been separated from it. This he continued to do until 1833, appointing two curates, and had many financial troubles in consequence. Two gentleman antiquarians, Sir John Edward Swinburne of Capheaton and Walter C. Trevelyan of Wallington, resident near Kirkwhelpington, gave him much help and encouragement. It was not until 1827 that he was able to publish the first volume of his parochial history of Northumberland, dealing with Redesdale, largely helped by a subscription of £200 from Bishop Barrington. In 1828 the sixth volume was published, containing fresh documents and records, and in 1832 followed the second volume of the parochial history. But in spite of its remarkable thoroughness the book met with little immediate success, and Hodgson suffered considerable loss on each volume. His health was failing, and the loss of three children gave Kirkwhelpington melancholy associations. In 1833 he was appointed to the vicarage of the neighbouring parish of Hartburn, where he enjoyed a larger income. This enabled him in 1835 to publish an extra volume of his history, containing the pipe rolls for Northumberland. In 1839 the third volume of the parochial history appeared, containing an account of the Roman wall; in it Hodgson first clearly established the claim of Hadrian to be considered as its builder. His health, however, gave way while this volume was passing through the press, and he was unable to carry his work any further. After much suffering from many infirmities, including a stroke, he died at Hartburn vicarage on 12 June 1845, and was buried in Hartburn churchyard on 17 June.

Besides the works already mentioned Hodgson contributed papers to the *Gentleman's Magazine* from 1821 onwards, under the pseudonym Archaeus. His great work, however, was his *History of Northumberland*, which for excellence of design and completeness of execution is still a model of what a county history might be. The 100 volumes of manuscript collectanea for the completion of his work are now preserved in the Northumberland Record Office. Because of the thoroughness of his research for the date of publication, Hodgson's *History* has effectively prevented publication of a comprehensive modern history of the county. The *History of the County of Northumberland* in fifteen volumes, published between 1893 and 1940, covers areas omitted from his work. Raine, his biographer, recalled Hodgson as 'thin and spare, of a thoughtful countenance and a composed garb', but blessed with a 'singularly captivating' smile.

MANDELL CREIGHTON, rev. C. M. FRASER

Sources J. Raine, *A memoir of the Rev. John Hodgson* (1857) · C. M. Fraser, 'John Hodgson: county historian', *Archaeologia Aeliana*, 5th ser., 24 (1996), 171–85 · personal information (1891)
Archives Northumbd RO, Newcastle upon Tyne, corresp. and papers incl. antiquarian collections; letters and papers | U. Newcastle, Robinson L., letters to Sir Walter Trevelyan
Likenesses T. Mogford, drawing, pencil, 1829 (after miniature), V&A · E. Scriven, engraving (after miniature by H. F. S. Mackreth), repro. in J. Hodgson, *A history of Northumberland*, 2/2 (1832)

Hodgson, John Evan (1831–1895), genre painter, was born in London on 1 March 1831, the eldest son of John Hodgson (*d.* 1856), a merchant trading with Russia. In 1835 his father and mother emigrated to St Petersburg. Initially he lived with them there, but about 1843 he returned to England to live with his uncle James Hodgson, the editor of the *Newcastle Chronicle*, in Newcastle upon Tyne. He was enrolled at Rugby School in 1846, and on completing his education there he went to work in his father's counting-house at St Petersburg. His study of old masters in the Hermitage collection and of Ruskin's *Modern Painters* persuaded him to abandon commerce for art, and in 1853 he

returned to London and enrolled at the Royal Academy Schools. During the next few years he combined study there with extensive travel on the continent. Hodgson exhibited his first painting at the Royal Academy in 1856, the year his father died, and this was followed over the next ten years by further historical pictures. On 29 December 1857 he married Helen Elizabeth Todd, the daughter of another merchant.

Hodgson's early works were of two sorts: scenes of contemporary British and continental European life and depictions of colourful episodes from history. *The Arrest of the Poacher* (exh. RA, 1857) is an example of his contemporary genre painting, and *The Return of Francis Drake [from Cadiz], 1587* (exh. RA, 1862; Wolverhampton Art Gallery) is one of his historical scenes. In 1858 Hodgson and his wife settled at 5 Hill Road, St John's Wood, where they remained for the next thirty years. His depiction of scenes from Tudor and Stuart times, combined with residence in St John's Wood, led him to join the St John's Wood Clique, a group of young artists, of whom David Wynfield and W. F. Yeames were the early leaders, who shared an interest in historical genre painting. They met regularly both for recreation and to criticize each other's works. One winter, members of the clique decorated the walls of the painting-room at Hodgson's house with frescoes. The figures included portraits by P. H. Calderon of Hodgson and his wife in Elizabethan costume. Hodgson is also depicted in Elizabethan dress in Frederick Walker's cartoon *A Vision of the Clique* (1865; reproduced Marks, 1.90), indicating that he was then best known for his Elizabethan scenes.

Following his visit to north Africa in 1868, most of Hodgson's paintings in the following decade comprised scenes of north African life. J. F. Lewis had not, he argued, exhausted this subject. *The Arab Story-Teller* (exh. RA, 1869) and *The Snake Charmer* (exh. RA, 1872) are two of a long series of oriental pictures of life in Morocco, Algeria, and Tunis. Sometimes he depicted encounters between Europeans and north Africans: *East and West* (1883; Aberdeen Art Gallery and Museums) shows a meeting between Arabs and British sailors.

In the early 1870s Hodgson experimented with marine painting and in 1873 was elected an associate of the Royal Academy. On his election as Royal Academician in 1879 he submitted as his diploma work to the academy *A Shipwrecked Sailor Waiting for a Sail* (RA). After 1880 he returned to painting domestic scenes and also produced a number of portraits. *The Queen, God Bless her* (exh. RA, 1885; reproduced Wood, 245) depicts two soldiers drinking Queen Victoria's health in the middle of a desert landscape, combining the unswerving patriotism of Hodgson's early historical works with an exotic setting. A good scholar and linguist, Hodgson was appointed librarian and professor of painting at the Royal Academy in 1882. He gave the library a more varied character by purchasing for it the works of prominent poets and men of letters. With Fred Eaton, secretary of the Royal Academy, Hodgson wrote a history of the first sixty years of the academy, contributing biographies of its early members. This work first appeared in article form in the *Art Journal* and was published as a book after his death. His *Fifty Years of British Art* was published to coincide with the Manchester exhibition in 1887.

Unlike his history of the Royal Academy, Hodgson's paintings were little valued during his later years. In particular critics regarded his north African scenes as well executed but lacking in originality. In 1890 he moved to the village of Coleshill, near Amersham, Buckinghamshire, where he died at his home, The Larches, on 19 June 1895; his wife survived him.   A. R. PENNIE

Sources Bryan, *Painters* (1903–5) · Graves, *RA exhibitors* · H. S. Marks, *Pen and pencil sketches*, 2 vols. (1894) · C. Wood, *Victorian panorama* (1976) · DNB · B. Hillier, 'The St John's Wood clique', *Apollo*, 79 (1964), 490–95 · Thieme & Becker, *Allgemeines Lexikon*, vol. 17 · Bénézit, *Dict.* · J. E. Hodgson, 'Forty years ago', *Newcastle Daily Chronicle* (17 May 1887) · J. E. Hodgson, *Fifty years of British art* (1887) · S. C. Hutchison, *The history of the Royal Academy, 1768–1968* (1968) · Wood, *Vic. painters*, 3rd edn · m. cert. · d. cert. · *CGPLA Eng. & Wales* (1895)
Likenesses D. W. Wynfield, photograph, c.1862–1864, NPG · F. Walker, pen-and-ink drawing, 1865, repro. in Marks, *Pen and pencil sketches*, vol. 1, p. 90 · J. E. Hodgson, self-portrait, oils, 1882, Aberdeen Art Gallery · W. W. Ouless, oils, exh. RA 1884, RA · H. J. Brooks, group portrait, oils (*Private view of the Old Masters Exhibition, Royal Academy, 1888*), NPG · R. W. Robinson, photograph, NPG
Wealth at death £428 17s. 2d.: probate, 29 Aug 1895, *CGPLA Eng. & Wales*

Hodgson, John Studholme (1805–1870), army officer, was born at Blake Street, York, on 24 April 1805, the second son of General John *Hodgson (1757–1846) and his wife, Catherine Krempion of St Petersburg. Hodgson entered the Royal Military Academy, Woolwich, in 1821, was commissioned ensign in the 23rd Bengal native infantry on 3 February 1822, and arrived in India on 12 July the same year. On 1 May 1824 he became lieutenant in the 12th regiment, and was promoted captain on 21 June 1834.

Hodgson was on sick leave from the effects of numerous tiger wounds when the First Anglo-Sikh War broke out in December 1845, but he was determined to join his regiment. Finding the communications interrupted, he walked 30 miles, narrowly escaping attack from the enemy. He served throughout the campaign of 1845–6, and was present at the battle of Sobraon, where he was wounded. He was made brevet major on 9 November 1846, and was selected to raise the first Sikh regiment embodied in the British service. On 14 December 1846 he was made commandant of the 1st Sikh infantry, and commanded it in the Second Anglo-Sikh War (1848–9), a task of peculiar difficulty, which he performed with notable success. Among other conspicuous services he led the attack upon the raja of Juswan Dun on the night of 2 December 1848, and took and destroyed the fort of Ukrot. For this action he was specially commended, and received the brevet rank of lieutenant-colonel on 7 June 1849.

On 29 October 1850 Hodgson was selected as commandant of the Punjab irregular force, in which post he served until July 1854. In 1853 he successfully directed military operations against the hill peoples west of the Derajat. While in command of the Derajat frontier he was chosen to succeed Sir Colin Campbell in command of the Peshawar frontier. He was promoted major on 28 August 1853,

brevet colonel on 28 November 1854, lieutenant-colonel on 25 April 1858, colonel of the 12th native infantry on 24 July 1858, and major-general on 23 July 1861. He published his *Musing on Military Matters* in 1851 and his *Opinions on the Indian Army* in 1857. In 1865 Hodgson retired from active service, and settled in London. He died at his home, 10 Stanhope Terrace, Hyde Park, London, on 14 January 1870.   GEORGE CLINCH, *rev.* ALEX MAY

Sources *Indian Army List* · private information (1891) · V. C. P. Hodson, *List of officers of the Bengal army, 1758–1834*, 4 vols. (1927–47) · *The Times* (18 Jan 1870) · H. C. B. Cook, *The Sikh wars: the British army in the Punjab, 1845–1849* (1975) · E. J. Thackwell, *Narrative of the Second Seikh War, in 1848–49* (1851) · *CGPLA Eng. & Wales* (1870)
Archives BL, letter-book, Add. MS 47438 | BL, letters to Lieutenant-Colonel H. Bruce, Add. MS 43996
Wealth at death under £7000: resworn probate, Feb 1870, *CGPLA Eng. & Wales*

Hodgson, Joseph (1756–1821), Roman Catholic priest, son of George Hodgson and his wife, Mary Hurd, of London, was born on 14 August 1756. He was educated at Sedgley Park School, Staffordshire, from 1766 to 1769 and at the English College of Douai, which he entered on 18 December 1769. He was retained in the college as professor, first of philosophy, and then of divinity. He was appointed vice-president to John Daniel in 1792. French revolutionary forces seized the college in February 1793 and he was imprisoned, later in the year, with the rest of the professors and students, first at Arras and afterwards at Doullens.

On their liberation in 1795 Hodgson went to London, and was appointed one of the priests at St George-in-the-Fields, Southwark. In 1803 he was appointed vicar-general to Bishop Douglass, and moved to the bishop's residence at 4 Castle Street, Holborn. He was later vicar-general to Bishop Poynter and secretary to the chapter. He also had the spiritual care of the ladies' school at Brook Green, Hammersmith, where he died on 30 November 1821. He was buried in Hammersmith parish churchyard.

Hodgson's account of the last days of Douai, *Narrative of the seizure of Douay College, and of the deportation of the seniors, professors, and students to Doullens*, was printed in volumes one and two of the *Catholic Magazine and Review* (1831–2); a later edited version was printed in the *Ushaw Magazine* (1929–32). The original manuscript is in the archives of the archbishop of Westminster.

                    THOMPSON COOPER, *rev.* G. BRADLEY

Sources G. Anstruther, *The seminary priests*, 4 (1977), 139 · Gillow, *Lit. biog. hist.*, 3.319 · J. Kirk, *Biographies of English Catholics in the eighteenth century*, ed. J. H. Pollen and E. Burton (1909), 120 · B. Ward, *History of St Edmund's College, Old Hall* (1893) · B. Ward, *Catholic London a century ago* (1905) · D. Milburn, *A history of Ushaw College* (1964)
Archives Archive of the Archbishop of Westminster, London, MS, 'A narrative of the seizure of Douay College and the deportation of seniors, professors and students to Doullens'
Wealth at death £200: Anstruther, *Seminary priests*, 140

Hodgson, Joseph (1788–1869), surgeon, son of a Birmingham merchant, was born at Penrith, Cumberland, and was educated at King Edward VI Grammar School, Birmingham. After serving an apprenticeship to George

Freer, a surgeon at Birmingham General Hospital, Hodgson, whose father had lost money heavily, was enabled by an uncle's generosity to commence study at St Bartholomew's Hospital, London. He obtained the diploma of the Royal College of Surgeons in 1811, and gained in the same year the Jacksonian prize for his essay, 'On wounds and diseases of the arteries and veins'. He began practice in London at King Street, Cheapside, and also served for a short time at the York Military Hospital, Chelsea. He eked out his income by taking pupils and by writing for, and acting for some years as editor of, the *London Medical Review*; he also produced other works, including helping with the pioneering book on congenital heart disease by John Richard Farre, and his *Treatise on the Diseases of Arteries and Veins* (1815) was translated into French and German and won him an international reputation.

In 1818 Hodgson moved to Birmingham, and on 23 January married Mary Ann Marston Ledsam, daughter of a wealthy clergyman. Hodgson was quickly elected surgeon to the General Dispensary and, in 1822, to Birmingham General Hospital. He held the latter appointment until 1848. He took a prominent part in founding the Birmingham Eye Infirmary in 1824, and was at first the only surgeon there. He had a large practice in Birmingham, numbering among his patients, and friends, Sir Robert Peel and several members of his family. Hodgson was particularly successful at lithotomy, for which his mortality rate was strikingly low. In 1831 he was elected to the fellowship of the Royal Society, and in 1843 he became one of the original fellows of the Royal College of Surgeons. In 1832 he was present at the meeting at Worcester at which the Provincial Medical and Surgical Association, later the British Medical Association, was founded. In 1842 he performed the post-mortem examination on Thomas Arnold, the reforming headmaster of Rugby, whose premature death from coronary artery disease has been much discussed by medical historians. Such was Hodgson's reputation that, at different times, he was invited to London to join the staff of the Middlesex Hospital or to accept the chair of surgery at King's College Hospital. He declined these invitations.

Hodgson had lost the sight of an eye in 1841, and in 1849, because of deteriorating health, he retired to London with a considerable fortune. He was elected a member of the council of the Royal College of Surgeons, and examiner in surgery to the college and to London University. In 1851 he was president of the Medico-Chirurgical Society, and in 1864 he was president of the Royal College of Surgeons. He died at his home, 60 Westbourne Terrace, London, on 7 February 1869, aged eighty-one. His wife had died twenty-four hours earlier. He was buried in Highgate cemetery on 13 February.

Hodgson was an able surgeon and an accurate diagnostician but he was cautious in treatment and pessimistic in prognosis. He is said to have been a born conservative, averse to innovations, and he certainly opposed the foundation of the Birmingham medical school in 1828. Nevertheless, while declining to lecture there, he wrote wishing

the school success. He also included a plea for the furtherance of physiological research in his Hunterian lecture at the Royal College of Surgeons in 1855. In later years he was remarkable for his suavity and kindness of manner.

G. T. BETTANY, *rev.* PETER R. FLEMING

Sources V. G. Plarr, *Plarr's Lives of the fellows of the Royal College of Surgeons of England*, rev. D'A. Power, 1 (1930), 549–50 · B. T. Davis, 'Joseph Hodgson, first provincial president of the Royal College of Surgeons of England', *Queen's Medical Magazine*, 53 (1961), 4–7 · D. E. Bedford, 'The surgeon cardiologists of the 19th century', *British Heart Journal*, 29 (1967), 461–8 · J. O. Leibowitz, *The history of coronary heart disease* (1970), 119–22 · *BMJ* (13 Feb 1869), 154–5 · *The Lancet* (13 Feb 1869) · CGPLA Eng. & Wales (1869)

Likenesses S. Cousins, mezzotint (after J. Partridge), BM, Wellcome L. · J. Partridge, portrait, Queen Elizabeth Hospital, Birmingham; repro. in Bedford, 'Surgeon cardiologists'

Wealth at death under £140,000: probate, 19 March 1869, CGPLA Eng. & Wales

Hodgson, Kirkman Daniel (1814–1879), financier, was born in London, the first son of John Hodgson (*d*. 1857), of Hampstead, and his wife, Caroline (*d*. 1884), daughter of Jean Delamain. His ancestors had been sugar refiners in eighteenth-century London. He was educated at Charterhouse School, and became a partner in the firm of Hodgson, general and commission merchants. Under its articles of partnership, dated 1859, he and his brother, and sole partner, James Stewart Hodgson each provided capital of £80,000. In 1865 their firm merged with Kay, Finlay & Co. of London, and Thomson, Finlay & Co. of Liverpool, to form the new firm of Finlay Hodgson, with capital of £360,000 divided into seventy-two shares, of which Kirkman Hodgson held fourteen. Finlay Hodgson acted as general and commission merchants until 1867, when it was absorbed by the merchant bank of Barings.

Thomas Baring (1799–1873) was Hodgson's colleague on the board of the Grand Trunk Railway of Canada, and knowing him as a careful, clever, discreet man, Baring hoped that he would steady the bank's impulsive younger partners, E. C. Baring and Russell Sturgis. As Hodgson made only a limited impact at Barings, and is not associated with any particular achievement or responsibility, there was possibly an internal alliance to negate his influence. He was a partner from 1 July 1867 until his retirement, in consequence of illness, on 31 December 1878.

Hodgson was elected to the Political Economy Club in 1853, and gave evidence to House of Commons committees, such as those investigating commercial distress (1848) and the commercial crisis (1857–8). It was at the suggestion in 1863 of Hodgson and Robert Crawford that G. J. Goschen (1831–1907) stood for the City of London constituency, and forty years later Goschen described his two political sponsors as 'splendid specimens of the British Merchant, cultivated, versed in all the higher questions both of commercial and banking finance, and wielding an exceptional influence in the City' (Elliot, 47).

Hodgson was a director of the Bank of England from 1840 until 1878. He served as deputy governor in 1861–3, and by rotation was governor in 1863–5 during a difficult period in the American Civil War. His place in the bank's history is unostentatious. He was one of three financial experts who examined the accounts of the joint-stock bankers Overend and Gurney after its failure in 1866, and advised against attempting a rescue. As a result of his family's investments, Hodgson was a director from 1841 until his death of the Pelican Life Office, the life assurance company associated with the Phoenix Fire Insurance Office. Hodgson joined Phoenix's board in 1846, serving until his death. No particular policy or success is associated with him at Pelican or Phoenix, which in the mid-nineteenth century were both characterized by cautious and even stultified enterprise.

In politics he was an advanced Liberal whose judgement was respected by Gladstone. He was elected without contest as MP for Bridport, Dorset, in March 1857, and held the seat until November 1868, when he stood unsuccessfully at Penryn in Cornwall. He was elected for Bristol in June 1870, and was returned again at the head of the poll there in 1874. His health began to fail in the autumn of 1877, and in the winter session of 1878 he retired from parliament.

For many years Hodgson had a house near Watford, and was a magistrate, deputy lieutenant, and in 1845 high sheriff, of Hertfordshire. In London he lived at 67 Brook Street. He married, in 1843, Frances (d. 1851), daughter of John Laforey Butler, of Southgate, Middlesex, and had a son and daughter. In later life he acquired a seat at Ash Grove, Sevenoaks, Kent, where he died on 11 September 1879.   RICHARD DAVENPORT-HINES

Sources A. D. Elliot, *The life of George Joachim Goschen, first Viscount Goschen, 1831–1907*, 1 (1911), 44, 47 · ING Barings, London, Barings archives · Phoenix MSS, CUL · C. Trebilcock, *Phoenix Assurance and the development of British insurance*, 2 vols. (1985–98) · P. Ziegler, *The sixth great power: Barings, 1762–1929* (1988) · D. Kynaston, *The City of London*, 1 (1994) · Gladstone, *Diaries* · d. cert.
Archives Bishopsgate Institute, London, Baring MSS · CUL, Phoenix MSS
Likenesses portrait, Bishopsgate, London, Baring MSS
Wealth at death under £500,000: resworn probate, Feb 1880, *CGPLA Eng. & Wales*

Hodgson, Leonard (1889–1969), theologian, was born on 24 October 1889, at Fulham, the son of Walter Hodgson (1853–1934), official shorthand writer to the House of Commons, and Lillias Emma (b. 1859), daughter of William Shaw of Wolsingham, co. Durham. He was a scholar at St Paul's School, London, winning a scholarship to Hertford College, Oxford, where he gained firsts in both Greats and theology. He was ordained deacon in 1913 after a year at St Michael's College, Llandaff, which began a long association with Wales. He later served on the council of St David's College, Lampeter, and declined the offer of the bishopric of Monmouth. After a curacy at St Mark's, Portsmouth, he became vice-principal of St Edmund Hall, Oxford, in 1914 through the influence of his former tutor, H. H. Williams, who had become principal. He was awarded honorary fellowships there and at Selwyn College, Cambridge, in 1957. He was examining chaplain to the bishop of Lichfield from 1917 to 1925, and to the bishop of Winchester from 1932 to 1939.

In 1919 Hodgson became dean of divinity and tutor in theology at Magdalen College, Oxford, and on 7 April 1920 married Ethel Margaret du Plat (1888–1960), daughter of

Charles Frederick Archer, rector of Moy, co. Tyrone. They had one son and one daughter. In 1917 he had proposed in vain to the novelist Dorothy L. Sayers, who, although calling him 'a perfectly delightful padre' (*Letters*, 1.130), spurned what soon became an infatuation. In 1925 he published *The Place of Reason in Christian Apologetic*, which provided the basis for his future work. The creeds, he held, were 'a rational construction' which tried to say 'something about the universe without ignoring the problem presented by the appearance of Jesus Christ upon the pages of this world's history' (p. 41). This book was based on lectures given at the General Theological Seminary, New York, where he was appointed professor of Christian apologetics in 1925, and which later made him an honorary STD in 1931. In 1928 he published *And Was Made Man* on the relationship between the gospels and Christology, and in 1929 his first collection, *Essays in Christian Philosophy*, where, against both Hegelianism and positivism, he elaborated his philosophical position which emphasized both the rational character of revelation and the importance of experience: it was 'God's will' that man 'should think' (p. 168). He returned to New York in 1936 to give the Paddock lectures, published as *The Grace of God in Faith and Philosophy*, his most developed account of the relationship between the critical synthesis of philosophy and the rational insight of theology: Christian philosophy was 'the attempt to interpret the meaning of all things in the light of God's self-revelation in Christ' (p. 20). He was a canon of Winchester from 1931 until his election as regius professor of moral and pastoral theology and canon of Christ Church, Oxford, in 1938. At Christ Church he gave lectures beyond the theology faculty (published in 1952 as *Christian Faith and Practice*) that attracted large numbers of undergraduates. During the 1930s he became a keen ecumenist, serving on the Anglican Council on Foreign Relations and as theological and general secretary of the Edinburgh world conference on faith and order in 1937, editing the proceedings (*The Second World Conference on Faith and Order*). The conference took an ambiguous stand on the situation in Germany, refusing to condemn the German government which had deprived delegates from the evangelical churches of their passports. Hodgson also wrote a number of pamphlets on ecclesiology and Anglicanism, criticizing what he regarded as the authoritarian theology of Karl Barth and Emil Brunner. His theology developed in more systematic directions with the publication of his Edinburgh Croall lectures, *The Doctrine of the Trinity* (1944): although mysterious, the Trinity was 'not an irrational mystery' (p. 95).

In 1944 Hodgson succeeded Oliver Chase Quick (who had been a significant influence on him) as regius professor of divinity; he retained this position until his retirement in 1958, declining the offer of the bishopric of Carlisle soon after the Second World War. Despite his severe appearance and staccato speech, he was an inspiring and popular lecturer on the international scene. He was made an Oxford BD and DD in 1938, an honorary DCL of Bishop's University, Lennoxville, Canada, in 1929, and an honorary DD of Edinburgh in 1938 and Glasgow in 1956. It was in

Glasgow that he delivered his Gifford lectures, *For Faith and Freedom*, from 1955 to 1957, which again investigated the relationship between faith and philosophy. From 1954 until 1966 he was warden of William Temple College, Rugby; there representatives of industry, psychiatrists, sociologists, and theologians were brought together. His book *Sex and Christian Freedom* (1967) was the fruit of such conversations, in which he sought to 'talk twentieth-century common sense without being disloyal to our ordination vows' (p. 8). He died on 15 July 1969 at his home, 34 Newbold Terrace, Leamington Spa, and was buried in Epwell churchyard, Oxfordshire.

Although Hodgson was original neither as a philosopher nor as a theologian, he stressed the fundamental agreement of philosophy and theology, retaining a great sense of the intelligibility and purposiveness of the universe. He communicated a dynamic, rational and attractive theology to a wide audience both at home and abroad. His focus on the interaction between the material and the spiritual, between grace and freedom, as 'the obverse and reverse sides of a single process' (Hodgson, *Essays*, 48), helped shape English theology's continuing concern with the reconciliation of modern science and the claims of religion. MARK D. CHAPMAN

Sources L. Hodgson, introduction, in L. Hodgson, *Essays in Christian philosophy* (1930) · L. Hodgson, introduction, in L. Hodgson, *The grace of God in faith and philosophy: Bishop Paddock lectures, 1936* (1936) · L. Hodgson, introduction, *The doctrine of the Trinity* (1944) · L. Hodgson, introduction, *Sex and Christian freedom* (1967) · private information (2004) [Christopher Hodgson] · *The Times* (16 July 1969) · *The Times* (19 July 1969) · *Church Times* (18 July 1969) · Crockford · *WWW* · T. C. Platts, 'A comparative study of the theologies of Leonard Hodgson and John Baillie', DPhil diss., U. Oxf., 1987 · *The letters of Dorothy L. Sayers*, ed. B. Reynolds, 1 (1995) · B. Reynolds, *Dorothy L. Sayers: her life and soul* (1993) · D. Coomes, *Dorothy L. Sayers: a careless rage for life* (1992) · L. Hodgson, *The place of reason in Christian apologetic* (1925)
Likenesses H. A. Freeth, drawing, Christ Church Oxf. · portrait, priv. coll.
Wealth at death £4618: probate, July 1969, *CGPLA Eng. & Wales*

Hodgson, Sir Mark (1880–1967), trade unionist, was born on 19 November 1880 in Newington, Hull, the son of Joshua Hodgson, a boilersmith, and his wife, Lydia. His mother died when he was eight years old and his father left home when he was young, so he was brought up by relatives in Sunderland, where he attended Diamond Hall School before taking on an apprenticeship as a plater and continuing his education in evening classes at the local technical college. He became increasingly involved in the local affairs of the United Society of Boilermakers and Iron and Steel Shipbuilders, being appointed in 1913 as the Tyne and Wear representative on the executive council, and serving as chairman of the council from 1923 to 1936, and then as general secretary until 1948.

In contrast to his distinguished predecessors, Robert Knight and John Hill, Hodgson had a relatively short and straightforward period as leader of the boilermakers. He nursed the union's recovery from the inter-war depression, and represented its interests effectively during the Second World War. He was involved in complex negotiations on overtime, relaxation of working practices during the war, dilution, and the development of a pioneering pay-as-you-earn income tax. He played the role in local affairs which had come to be associated with his office, as a magistrate, chairman of the Newcastle Co-operative Printing Society, and a leading light of Methodism. However, this was also a period of increasing state intervention, with expanding opportunities for union leaders to play a role in public administration at both local and national levels. Hodgson began in a relatively modest way as a member of the National Arbitration Tribunal and the North-East Industrial Development Association. Then in his so-called retirement he went on to play a major role in the development of post-war regional policy, through the North-East Housing Association and as chairman of the Northern Regional Board for Industry from 1949 to 1965. Moreover, he participated in the administration of the newly nationalized industries, through membership of an inquiry into the organization of the National Coal Board in 1948 and as chairman of the Railway Users' Consultative Committee from 1951 to 1955.

Hodgson was a man of average height with dark hair and a moustache. In 1900 he married Elizabeth Jane Davis from Sunderland; they had a son and two daughters. No doubt affected by the loss of his own parents early in life, he had close and warm relationships with his family: his younger daughter worked as his secretary, and his son was the boilermakers' solicitor. However, beneath a modest, establishment appearance on the right wing of the Labour Party, Hodgson was highly energetic and independent. Following a long life of public service, for which he was appointed OBE in 1938 and a knighthood in 1945, Hodgson died on 17 October 1967 at his home, 31 Kenton Road, Kenton, in Newcastle, and was cremated in Newcastle. He was survived by his wife. ALASTAIR J. REID

Sources DLB · J. E. Mortimer, *History of the Boilermakers' Society*, 2: *1906–1939* (1982) · J. E. Mortimer, *History of the Boilermakers' Society*, 3: *1940–1989* (1994) · d. cert.
Wealth at death £9140: probate, 1 Dec 1967, *CGPLA Eng. & Wales*

Hodgson [Hudson; *née* Dyer], **Mary** (*bap.* 1673?, *d.* 1719?), singer, was most probably the daughter of the dancing-master Benjamin Dyer and his wife, Mary, baptized at St Andrew's, Holborn, London, on 26 December 1673. As Mrs Dyer she performed in Henry Purcell's opera *The Fairy Queen* at Dorset Garden Theatre in May 1692, when she sang the role of Mystery and the song 'If love's a sweet passion'. On 16 May 1692, two weeks after the première, Mary Dyer married the actor John Hodgson or Hudson (*fl.* 1689–1721) at St Dunstan and All Saints, Stepney. From song headings and play texts we know that she sang Purcell's music in the revival of the opera *Dioclesian* in 1693 and at least five plays, as well as incidental songs by John Eccles. She remained a singer in the United Theatre Company in London until December 1694, when she and her husband joined Thomas Betterton's breakaway group at Lincoln's Inn Fields Theatre. There Eccles and Gottfried Finger were the house composers, and she sang in numerous plays and in the musical entertainment *The Loves of Mars and Venus*

(November 1696). William Congreve praised her performance as Juno in the setting by Eccles of his *The Judgment of Paris* (1701). Mrs Hodgson was also a leading singer in concerts at York Buildings in the early 1700s and sang at court in performances for royal birthdays in 1697, 1704, and 1706. John Hodgson was sued for debt three times in the early 1690s, and in June 1699, when bailiffs trying to arrest him at the playhouse were beaten off by the players, his servant was 'cowardly run through the back by a baylif, and immediately dyed, having nothing but a stick in his hand' (Luttrell, 529). John Hodgson appears to have left the stage in 1701, but his wife remained a leading singer until shortly after the company's move to the Queen's Theatre in 1706. The mistaken statement that she was an oboist (Highfill, Burnim & Langhans, *BDA*) seems to arise from a mistranscription of an advertisement in the *Daily Courant* for 11 December 1703. After 1706, we know only of benefit performances for her in 1710, in 1718, and finally on 18 May 1719. It seems likely that she was the Mary Hudson of Cross Street, Holborn, buried at St Andrew's, Holborn, on 28 June 1719.

OLIVE BALDWIN and THELMA WILSON

Sources W. Van Lennep and others, eds., *The London stage, 1660–1800*, pt 1: *1660–1700* (1965) · E. L. Avery, ed., *The London stage, 1660–1800*, pt 2: *1700–1729* (1960) · *Daily Courant* (17 March 1703) · *Daily Courant* (11 Dec 1703) · *Daily Courant* (29 March 1704) · *Daily Courant* (6 March 1705) · *Post Boy* (27 June 1702) · *Post Boy* (15 Dec 1702) · *Post Man* (23 April 1698) · *Post Man* (19 March 1700) · *Post Man* (22 March 1701) · wordbook for the performance at court for Queen Anne's birthday in 1704, CUL, Brett-Smith a.15 · C. L. Day and E. B. Murrie, *English song-books, 1651–1702: a bibliography with a first-line index of songs* (1940) · D. Hunter, *Opera and song books published in England, 1703–1726* (1997) · O. Baldwin and T. Wilson, 'Purcell's stage singers: a documentary list', *Performing the music of Henry Purcell* [Oxford 1993], ed. M. Burden (1996), 275–81 · J. Milhous and R. D. Hume, eds., *A register of English theatrical documents, 1660–1737*, 2 vols. (1991) · N. Luttrell, *A brief historical relation of state affairs from September 1678 to April 1714*, 4 (1857) · T. Colyer-Fergusson, ed., *The marriage registers of St Dunstan's, Stepney* (1899) · parish register, Holborn, St Andrew's, 26 Dec 1673 [baptism] · parish register, Holborn, St Andrew's, 28 June 1719 [burial]

Hodgson, Ralph Edwin (1871–1962), poet and cartoonist, born at 2 Garden Street, Darlington, co. Durham, on 9 September 1871, the sixth son in the family of seven sons and three daughters of Ralph Hodgson (1834–1884), coal and coke merchant, and Mary Hodgson, *née* Graham (1838–1918). The painter William Bewick was his grandfather's cousin. Little is known of Hodgson's childhood and youth. His father died in 1884, and Mary Hodgson supported the family by opening a private school in Darlington (which later moved to Newcastle upon Tyne and then London) for the education of young ladies. His own formal education did not progress beyond elementary school and he is thought to have spent much of his teenage years working with travelling fairs performing in boxing booths. He claimed to have travelled to the United States in 1888 and worked as a scene-painter in a New York theatre, though there is no evidence to support this.

Hodgson's principal talent was certainly artistic, however, and in 1889 he found work as a cartoonist on an early children's comic, *Funny Cuts*, produced in London in Fleet Street by the Dalziel Brothers and edited by a pioneer of the genre, Alfred Gray. In 1893 he was employed by Alfred Harmsworth as the lead cartoonist on Harmsworth's pioneering *Evening News*. Hodgson claimed a close friendship with the newspaper proprietor, who attended his marriage to Janet (Dolly) Chatteris (1874–1920) on 6 February 1896. By then Hodgson had left the *Evening News* and, after working on journals such as Jerome K. Jerome's *The Idler*, and *The Minster* (on which he collaborated with cartoonists such as Alfred Sime and Phil May), he returned to children's comics on Arthur Pearson's seminal *Big Budget* boys' paper. Here he worked alongside Tom Browne (succeeding him as art editor in 1900) and Jack B. Yeats, producing comic strips such as 'Airey Alf' and 'Bouncing Billy'. It was while working on *Big Budget* that he was persuaded by the playwright Rudolph Besier to submit certain poems to the *Saturday Review*. In November 1904 'The Storm Thrush' appeared, the first of many to be featured in the *Review* in the years before the First World War.

Poetry now became Hodgson's principal preoccupation, though his output would always be sparse, his subsequent reputation resting on just two collections: *The Last Blackbird* (1907) and *Poems* (1917). The latter contained poetic standards such as 'Time you Old Gypsy Man', 'Stupidity Street', 'Eve', 'The Bull', and 'The Song of Honour', the last two winning him the Polignac prize in 1914. He was also invited by the editor Edward Marsh to submit these and other pieces to the famous *Georgian Anthology*. His work appeared in volumes 2 and 3 of these.

Although Hodgson was classified as a Georgian, and was the friend of poets such as Edward Thomas, W. H. Davies, and John Freeman, and later Siegfried Sassoon, he mistrusted literary cliques and preferred to remain cloistered within a personal world of Fleet Street colleagues and dog-breeding experts. (He was a fine judge of bull terriers, and even judged them at Cruft's on occasion.) He also kept a close hold on anything he wrote, being obsessed with copyright. In 1913 he founded, along with the artist Claude Lovat Fraser, and writer Holbrook Jackson, the publishing house Sign of the Flying Fame and produced a series of chapbooks and broadsides featuring his own work as well as pieces by James Stephens and Walter de la Mare. The *Fames* were extremely influential, being both striking and innovative in their juxtaposition of visual decoration and verse.

During the First World War Hodgson served with various navy and army anti-aircraft batteries up and down the east coast of England and rose to the rank of lieutenant. After the death of his first wife he married the journalist Muriel Fraser (1885–1961), on 1 June 1921, but this marriage ended in divorce in September 1933. On 24 October of the same year, in Yokohama, Japan, he married his third wife, Lydia Aurelia Bolliger (d. 1984). He had ceased writing poetry altogether during the war years, and it would not be until the mid-1930s that he commenced work on anything substantial. By then he was guest lecturer in English literature at the Japanese University of Sendai. He had accepted the post in 1923 on condition that Edmund Blunden also accept a similar post in Tokyo.

Hodgson remained in Japan until 1938, latterly working on translations of the ancient *Mannyoshui* poems for the Japanese ministry of education. It was for this that he received the award of the insignia (fifth class) of the order of the Rising Sun.

Hodgson returned to England in 1938, and although pressed by T. S. Eliot to illustrate the latter's *Old Possum's Book of Practical Cats* (the two men had met in 1932 and had become good friends), he travelled on to the USA where he settled with his third wife on a farm in Minerva, Ohio, and set about producing his final long poem, 'The Muse and the Mastiff'. He never finished it, though sections of it appeared regularly, along with various shorter pieces, in the form of *Flying Scrolls*—successors to the *Flying Fame* broadsheets of before the First World War. In 1946 he received the annual award of the National Institute of Art and Letters (USA) and, in 1954, the queen's gold medal for poetry. A selection of Hodgson's work was collected in 1958 in *The Skylark and other Poems*, edited by Colin Fenton. His *Collected Poems* appeared in 1961, the year before his death of a stroke on 3 November 1962 at his farm, Owlacres, in Minerva. He was buried on 6 November at Pleasant Grove cemetery, Minerva, Carroll county, Ohio. His third wife survived him.

Hodgson's main inspirations were the enchantment of nature and man's idiotic abuse of it, as well as a passionate love of animals, particularly birds. He also possessed a unique vision of man and history, set in a commanding sweep of historical imagination. His most praised poem, 'The Song of Honour', is a rapturous recital of the world's harmonious hymn of being and was a huge influence on a generation of writers which followed him. His last poem, 'The Muse and the Mastiff', taking off from a single line of Coleridge's 'Christabel', is, to quote Mick Imlah, 'as vigorous and strangely charming as it is cranky and incoherent' (Imlah, 230).   JOHN HARDING

Sources *DNB* · private information (2004) · W. D. Sweetser, *Ralph Hodgson: a bibliography* (1974) · A. G. Kershner jun., 'Ralph Hodgson: a biographical and critical study', PhD diss., University of Pennsylvania, 1952 · M. Imlah, 'Hodgson, Ralph Edwin (1871–1962)', *The Oxford companion to twentieth-century poetry in English*, ed. I. Hamilton (1994) · b. cert. · m. cert. [R. E. Hodgson and J. Chatteris]

Archives BL, poems and corresp., Add. MSS 56348–56350 · Bodl. Oxf., corresp. and papers · Bodl. Oxf., Fenton/Hodgson uncatalogued MSS · Bryn Mawr College Library, Pennsylvania, corresp. and papers · Yale U., Gen MS 245 | BL, letters to S.S. Koteliansky, Add. MS 48973 · NYPL, Berg collection

Likenesses T. Spicer-Simson, plaster medallion, 1922, NPG · W. Rothenstein, portrait, 1923, repro. in W. Rothenstein, *Men and memories*, 3 vols. (1931) · T. Spicer-Simson, bronze cast, 1970, NPG · W. Rothenstein, portrait, repro. in W. Rothenstein, *Twenty-four portraits*, 2nd ser. (1923)

Hodgson, Sir Robert MacLeod (1874–1956), diplomatist, was born in West Bromwich on 25 February 1874, the eldest son of the Revd Robert Hodgson (1844–1917), founder of the West Bromwich Albion Football Club and later prebendary of Lichfield and archdeacon of Stafford, and his first wife, Katharine, daughter of Robert Gauler of Hornsey. He was educated at Radley College, and Trinity College, Oxford, where he gained a third in classical moderations (1895), captained the university hockey team (1896), and graduated in the pass school in 1897. He began his connection with the Foreign Office by working in a subordinate position in the consulate-general at Algiers and later (1901–6) at Marseilles where he became a paid vice-consul in 1904. He had always taken a great interest in the commercial work of these posts and in 1906 he was sent by the Foreign Office to Vladivostok as commercial agent, being given the rank of vice-consul in 1908 and of consul in 1911. He remained there until 1919, acquiring that knowledge of the Russian language and character which was to determine the course of so much of his future career. During the period of allied intervention in Russia, he was moved as acting high commissioner to Omsk where an anti-Bolshevik government had been set up. When Omsk was evacuated by the allies in November 1919 he was appointed commercial counsellor in Russia. In 1920 he married a Russian, Olga, daughter of Paul Bellavin; they had one son. In the same year he was appointed CMG.

After the signature of the Anglo-Russian trade agreement in 1921 Hodgson was appointed official agent on the British commercial mission to Russia, which was intended to promote economic and political links between the two countries. His position was a difficult one, in view of the two governments' attitude of mutual suspicion and the constant surveillance of his mission, but Hodgson was a man of transparent integrity, and, so far as it was possible for any British representative at that time to do so, he gained the goodwill of the Russians with whom he carried out a succession of prolonged negotiations. His reports provided the British government with an understanding of the motives underlying the workings of the official Russian mind. Following the diplomatic recognition of Russia by the Labour government in 1924 Hodgson became chargé d'affaires; he remained in Moscow until 1927 when the diplomatic mission was recalled and the trade agreement ended. He was appointed KBE in 1925.

Despite his achievements in Russia, Hodgson's abilities were not always recognized at the Foreign Office, and his appointment as minister to Albania in 1928 came as a disappointment, especially as he had been led to expect a more important post. He eventually retired in August 1936, having been kept on for more than two years beyond the normal age. In December 1937 he was brought back as British agent to General Franco's administration in Burgos. In February 1939 he was accredited as chargé d'affaires to the Spanish government, and it was a surprise to many that he was not chosen as ambassador in April on the establishment of full diplomatic relations with General Franco. Nevertheless his services to the British government were recognized by his advancement to KCMG in 1939. In 1944–5 he again emerged from retirement to serve in the Foreign Office as adviser to the censors.

Hodgson was a man of dynamic energy. His speech matched his mental processes in speed, and his powerful frame, like his mind, rebelled against inactivity. Retirement was for him an irksome experience. For some years he was chairman of the council of the School of Slavonic Studies. In 1953 he published *Spain Resurgent*, an account of the Spanish Civil War and its aftermath. Carpentry, which had always been one of his hobbies, occupied much of his spare time, but he always wanted more to do. Lovable and of strong sensibilities, he had a multitude of friends and was deeply affected by the purges in Russia when so many of the people he had known were liquidated, often apparently for no other reason than having been his visitors at the embassy. His skill in negotiation was considerable and he might ordinarily have been expected to have been chosen to fill posts of greater responsibility, but he inevitably suffered from not having started his career in the regular diplomatic service. He died at St Stephen's Hospital, Chelsea, London, on 18 October 1956.

DAVID SCOTT, *rev.* MICHAEL HUGHES

Sources PRO, Foreign Office MSS · R. Hodgson, *Spain resurgent* (1953) · R. Hodgson, 'Memoirs of an official agent [pts 1–2]', *History Today*, 4 (1954), 522–8, 613–17 · M. Hughes, *Inside the enigma* (1997) · private information (1971) · personal knowledge (1971) · *The Times* (19 Oct 1956) · R. Hodgson, 'Britain and Russia', *Journal of the Royal Central Asian Society*, 30 (1943), 102–13 · CGPLA Eng. & Wales (1957) · WW
Archives PRO, Foreign Office records
Likenesses W. Stoneman, photograph, 1931, NPG
Wealth at death £1998: probate, 3 Jan 1957, CGPLA Eng. & Wales

Hodgson, Sarah (*bap.* 1760, *d.* 1822). *See under* Hodgson, Solomon (*bap.* 1760, *d.* 1800).

Hodgson, Shadworth Hollway (1832–1912), philosopher, was born at Boston, Lincolnshire, on 25 December 1832, the eldest son of Shadworth Hodgson, of Boston, and his wife, Anne, daughter of John Palmer Hollway, also of Boston. He was educated at Rugby School, and Corpus Christi College, Oxford (1850–54). He married Ann, daughter of the Revd Edward Browne Everard, rector of Burnham Thorpe, Norfolk, in 1855. His wife and only child died in 1858. He withdrew entirely from general society after their death to devote himself to philosophy.

Noted for the breadth of his reading and for the ease with which he read the classical authors, and Italian, German, and French literature in the original, Hodgson had a passion for the poetry of Swinburne and Coleridge. Painstakingly, with fixity of purpose, he nurtured the study of philosophy in London. He was a member of the Metaphysical Society from its foundation until its dissolution. Under his tenure as president of the Aristotelian Society (1880–94), it became the premier forum for philosophical discussion in London. After each meeting of the Aristotelian Society, Hodgson entertained a small circle of friends at his chambers on Conduit Street, where philosophical debate was pursued well into the night. The rapid increase in the society's membership was tribute to his energetic leadership. While some contemporaries found him unyielding in his adherence to his own philosophical premises, it was never his intention to found his own school, and he encouraged all strands of enquiry. He presided over several generations of philosophical debate, and bequeathed an imposing legacy of service to his chosen field.

In *Time and Space: a Metaphysical Essay* (1865) Hodgson distinguished psychology from philosophy, and contributed to the movement that led to the separation of the two disciplines as fields for study. He defined psychology as the empirical science that investigates the causal relations between mind or consciousness on the one hand and the bodily organs or neuro-cerebral system on the other. He equated philosophy with metaphysics, inclusive of epistemology, and identified its subject matter as the facts or phenomena or objects of consciousness. He introduced the distinction between three orders of consciousness: the order *existendi*, the order *essendi*, and the order *cognoscendi*. The first order is the existence of consciousness, and in the explanation of the fact *that* consciousness is, Hodgson found its causes to be exclusively physical. Moreover, since he foreclosed on the possibility of consciousness causally affecting the physical system, he introduced a psycho-physical dualism that came to be known as epiphenomenalism. The orders *essendi* and *cognoscendi* comprise the subject for philosophy. The order *essendi* concerns *what* is; it requires the metaphysical analysis of the elements, data, or phenomena presented in consciousness. The order *cognoscendi* concerns knowledge; it involves the epistemological investigation of the relation between what is presented in consciousness and its objects as known. Hodgson's tripartite distinction in his first book guided his later philosophical investigations.

Hodgson's *Theory of Practice* (1870) presents his ethical theory. Striving to overcome utilitarianism and deontology, Hodgson analysed feelings, which he deemed to be the material content of all phenomena, and focused on emotions as a distinct kind of feelings, which differ from sensations in that they involve intentionality. Hodgson contrived an elaborate table of emotions, and stressed the role of emotions in voluntary action. While his epiphenomenalism entailed determinism, he later qualified it as 'free will determinism', to separate it from 'compulsory determinism'.

In *The Philosophy of Reflection* (1878) Hodgson defined reflection as consciousness of consciousness, distinguishable from prereflective or primary consciousness at the lower level and from postreflective or direct consciousness at the higher. He established reflection as the cardinal point of his metaphysics. Pressing his analysis of temporal consciousness, he pronounced the mere empirical present to be unreal or 'specious', and discovered the real present to be a fusion of the past and the future. Before William James he held that consciousness is like a stream, that the dualism of subject and object is added to prereflective consciousness by reflection, and that things as objects of consciousness in the order *cognoscendi* are what they are known as.

Hodgson regarded his four-volume work *The Metaphysic of Experience* (1898), the result of twenty years' labour, as the supersession of all his earlier work, and the final statement of his philosophy. The work did not attract the favourable attention that he had hoped it would. His metaphysical method prescribed the laborious analysis of experience to detect its ultimate elements and aspects, and the dismissal of all assumptions in respect to concepts or objects that cannot be based in experience. Although he perpetuated the appeal to experience sounded by Hume and Kant, he broke new ground, undercutting both the mechanical tenets of psychological associationism and the generalities of German idealism that were fashionable in his time. William James explicitly acknowledged his influence, and echoes of his thinking are audible in Henri Bergson, in George Santayana and critical realism, in the theories of the logical construction of objects associated with Bertrand Russell and C. D. Broad, and in Edmund Husserl and phenomenology.

Hodgson was a founding member of the British Academy, to which he was elected in 1901. He was elected an honorary fellow of Corpus Christi College in 1882, and was awarded an honorary LLD from the University of Edinburgh. He died at his home, 45 Conduit Street, Regent Street, London, on 13 June 1912, after a short illness.

ANDREW J. RECK

Sources DNB · G. E. Davie, 'Hodgson, Shadworth Hollway', *The encyclopaedia of philosophy*, ed. P. Edwards (1967), 47–8 · A. J. Reck, 'The ethics of Shadworth H. Hodgson', *Agora: A Journal in the Humanities and Social Sciences*, 4 (1979–80), 32–44 · A. J. Reck, 'Hodgson's metaphysic of experience', *Philosophy and archaic experience: essays in honour of Edward G. Ballard*, ed. J. Sallis (1982), 30–47 · S. F. Spicker, 'Shadworth Hodgson's reduction as an anticipation of Husserl's phenomenological psychology', *Journal of the British Society for Phenomenology*, 2 (1972), 57–73 · K. Schumann, 'Husserl and Hodgson: some historical remarks', *Journal of the British Society for Phenomenology*, 3 (1973), 63–5 · *The Times* (18 June 1912) · *Proceedings of the Aristotelian Society*, new ser., 12 (1911–12), 326–33 · T. F. Tout, 'Thomas Hodgkin, 1831–1913', *PBA*, [6] (1913–14), 503–7 · H. Wildon Carr, *Mind*, new ser., 21 (1912), 473–85 · *CGPLA Eng. & Wales* (1912)
Likenesses photograph, repro. in R. B. Perry, *The thought and character of William James* (1935), vol. 1, p. 596
Wealth at death £41,728 4s. 3d.: probate, 26 Aug 1912, CGPLA Eng. & Wales

Hodgson, Solomon (bap. 1760, d. 1800), printer and newspaper proprietor, was baptized in Long Marton, Westmorland, on 29 September 1760, the son of Solomon Hodgson (1715/16–1779) of Knock, in that parish and his wife, Sarah Lothian (1718/19–1806), of Kirkoswald. He married in St John's Church, Newcastle upon Tyne, on 15 February 1785, Sarah [**Sarah Hodgson** (bap. 1760, d. 1822)], printer and newspaper proprietor, fifth daughter of Thomas Slack (1723?–1784) and Anne Fisher (1719–1778), who after Solomon Hodgson's death in 1800 continued and expanded the printing, bookselling, and newspaper businesses, in which she was always actively concerned.

It is supposed that Hodgson was apprenticed to Thomas Slack, assisting him in the work of his printing shop and in the publication of the *Newcastle Chronicle*, a weekly newspaper launched by Slack in March 1764. On 21 February 1785 the executors of Thomas Slack's estate transferred to Solomon Hodgson the *Newcastle Chronicle*, together with the printing, bookselling, and stationery business. It is probable that Hodgson also offered binding for, according to Thomas Bewick, he employed Gilbert Gray, a bookbinder who had served his time under Allan Ramsay, the Edinburgh poet and bookseller. Solomon, and later his widow, like Slack, also sold by retail and

wholesale many nostrums, advertisements for them appearing regularly in their newspaper. The imprint 'S. Hodgson' appears in 1784 on an edition of *The History of All Nations*, printed for G. Robinson in London; he must, therefore, have assumed responsibility for the business immediately on the death of Thomas Slack, who bequeathed it, in a poorly drawn will, to his daughter Sarah. In 1794 Hodgson sold his bookselling and stationery business at his shop in Union Street to John (I) Bell (1755–1816), his former manager who had married Hodgson's sister-in-law, Anne Slack. In June 1800 Sarah Hodgson made clear her intention to buy back this business at the end of Bell's lease; this was completed by 1803 and thereafter she infused new life into the whole concern.

Solomon Hodgson continued to develop the *Newcastle Chronicle*, acting as reporter, editor, and publisher, as well as advertising agent. His retentive memory allowed him to report political and other speeches without recourse to notes taken at the time. Richard Welford writes that Hodgson

> uniformly advanced the genuine sentiments of his mind, uninfluenced by party, or any political society … and so long as he could do it consistently with personal safety, he exercised the privilege of declaring his sentiments on every important subject with a boldness and freedom becoming a Briton …   (Welford, *Men of Mark*, 2.544–5)

Hodgson's efforts 'raised the *Chronicle* to the position of the leading organ of Whig politics in the North of England' (Welford, 'Early Newcastle typography', 46). Following Hodgson's death the *Chronicle* of 11 April 1800 carried an advertisement from his widow in which she stated that she had taken over the paper from her late husband, adding 'She trusts that, in Consequence of the Arrangements which she has it in her Power to make, that Paper will be found not unworthy of the Patronage from a generous Public which it has hitherto experienced'. From 1784 the newspaper had been composed by William Preston, who assisted Sarah Hodgson with the editing and publishing of the *Newcastle Chronicle* after the death of her husband. Preston left in May 1808 to set up in business as a printer with William Heaton, another former Hodgson employee. Sarah was later assisted in the production of the newspaper by her sons Thomas (1785–1850) and James (1798–1867), later an alderman who became mayor of Newcastle upon Tyne in 1841. In 1850 the *Chronicle* was sold to Mark William Lambert (1812–1893), who, in turn, sold it to Joseph Cowen (1831–1900), industrialist and MP, when it became a radical campaigning journal; it ceased publication in 1953.

The Hodgsons continued the successful publications started by Thomas and Anne Slack, in particular the *Newcastle Memorandum-Book*, an annual which ceased publication only in 1893, and Mrs Slack's *Ladies' Own Memorandum-Book*, which he, followed by Sarah Hodgson, published jointly with the London publishers George Robinson & Co.; until the latter failed in 1805. Hodgson also issued editions of two more works by Mrs Slack, published under her maiden name, Anne Fisher: *A Practical New Grammar*, which appeared in 1785, 1787, 1788, 1789 (with a London-printed edition in the same year), 1795, and 1800; and *The New English Tutor* (undated, but probably after 1786). Sarah published an edition of her mother's *Young Scholar's Delight* in 1802. Solomon also issued editions of S. Thomas's (supposedly Thomas Slack's pseudonym) *The Banker's Sure Guide* in 1791 and 1798, with an issue by Sarah in 1803; *The British Negociator* in 1791, with one by Sarah in 1814; and *The Ready Calculator* in 1786.

Many of the works listed for Solomon Hodgson in the *English Short-Title Catalogue* are slight items such as sermons and advertisements for subscription concerts, but it was not long after taking charge of the business that he became concerned with more substantial new material. In 1785 he printed the first volume of William Hutchinson's *History and Antiquities of the County Palatine of Durham*, a large illustrated quarto. The second volume appeared in 1787, but, having fallen out with the author, Hodgson was not responsible for the third.

In 1786 Hodgson printed and published Mary Smith's *The Complete House-Keeper* (always a popular subject), and in the same year three works by Claude Fleury, *A Larger Historical Catechism*, *The Manners of the Israelites*, and *The Manners of the Christians* (the latter two translated by Charles Cordell, a Catholic priest living in Newcastle). Each year thereafter saw substantial works for which he was responsible, among them John Bailey's *General View of the Agriculture of the County of Northumberland* (1797) for Sir John Sinclair's board of agriculture.

The Hodgsons were also innovative in their choice of titles. Edward Moises' *The Persian Interpreter* (1792) was the first book to be printed in an Arabic typeface in England outside London and the university towns of Oxford and Cambridge. At the end of this volume Moises presented proposals for the publication by subscription of an edition in six volumes of *The Persian Poets, Historians, and Moralists*, and of a large, one-volume Persian, Arabic, and English dictionary; nothing seems to have come of these proposals.

About 1803 Sarah Hodgson started printing an Arabic version of the Old Testament, prepared by Joseph Dacre Carlyle (1759–1806), vicar of Newcastle upon Tyne, chancellor of Carlisle, and professor of Arabic at the University of Cambridge. Charles Wilkins, in the advertisement for his edition of John Richardson's *Dictionary, Persian, Arabic and English* (1806), wrote of the Arabic typeface used in that work:

> The punches were gratuitously designed by myself, and executed, under my superintendence, by that ingenious mechanic, Mr William Martin [employed by George Nicol as type designer and typefounder for the Shakspeare Press of William Bulmer], expressly for the purpose of printing a portable edition of the Old Testament in the Arabic language … [by] … that celebrated Arabic scholar … the Reverend Mr. Carlisle …

This work, with the New Testament in Arabic, was finally published in 1811 as *The Holy Bible Containing the Old and New Testaments in the Arabic Language*; it was produced under the patronage of Shute Barrington (1734–1826), bishop of Durham. After Carlyle's death it was seen through the press by

Henry Ford, lord almoner's reader in Arabic at Oxford. This work should have been the first showing of Martin's Arabic type, which actually appeared first in William Jones's *Grammar of the Persian Language* (1804). The Society for the Propagation of the Gospel in Foreign Parts contributed £250 for 1000 copies of the Arabic Bible to be distributed in Africa and Asia, and the British and Foreign Bible Society also gave £250, purchasing or receiving over 1000 copies. Sarah Hodgson also used Martin's Arabic typeface in 1809 in *The Arabick Alphabet*, a slim octavo booklet by Thomas Burgess, bishop of St David's.

Solomon Hodgson was friendly with the wood-engraver Thomas Bewick, and when the latter and his business partner, Ralph Beilby, were considering publishing *A General History of Quadrupeds* they consulted the printer 'as to the probability of such a publication paying us for our labours', and were 'most warmly encouraged … to proceed', adding the footnote 'In this we were greatly mistaken, for Solomon's dissipated life prevented him attending to it' (*Memoir*, 105–6). Hodgson printed (and published) the first four editions of the *General History* in 1790, 1791, 1792, and 1800, and printed the first two editions of *Land Birds*, volume 1 of the *History of British Birds*, in 1797 and 1800, and *Figures of British Land Birds* in 1800. The name Hodgson does not appear in the imprint of these works after 1800.

After the death of Solomon Hodgson, Bewick quarrelled bitterly with his widow over a small discrepancy in the account for the printing of the first volume of the *History of British Birds*. The engraver found he 'could not go on pleasantly with Mrs Hodgson in the Printing of the Quadrupeds' (*Memoir*, 125), and offered to buy her share in the work; she refused to sell and later sold it to the London publisher Longman. Nevertheless, in 1805 the engraver had recovered from his ill feeling sufficiently to withdraw the charge that he had made for a memorial cut to Samuel Hodgson, reproduced in John Sykes's *Local Records*, (1866, 2.2).

In 1799 Hodgson printed and published *The Hive of Ancient & Modern Literature*, a selection by himself of short pieces of prose and verse 'to inculcate in the minds of youth strong impressions of their moral obligations'. It is 'embellished with a number of engravings on wood by T. Bewick and L. Clennell, both of Newcastle' and was reprinted several times, Sarah publishing the third edition in 1806 and the fourth in 1812.

In 1788 Hodgson printed for the Newcastle Dispensary (founded in 1777) a report on inoculation, and in the following year one on the resuscitation of drowned persons. He started printing the dispensary's annual reports in 1796, and was followed until 1821 by Sarah Hodgson when she transferred the work to her sons. Sarah also took over the printing of the annual reports of the Newcastle Literary and Philosophical Society in 1800, continuing until the year of her death, when her sons again took over. The society had been founded in 1793 by William Turner, the Unitarian minister of Hanover Square Chapel, Newcastle, and it may be that Sarah changed her religious affiliation about this time. The first of Turner's sermons to be printed by her appeared in 1800, and she and her sons were reported to have been members of Turner's Unitarian congregation (Welford, *Men of mark*, 2.548). Sarah printed several more of Turner's sermons and other works for the Unitarian chapel. It appears that Solomon had remained an Anglican. He died on 4 April 1800 and was buried under a table monument in the churchyard of St John's Church, Newcastle.

Sarah Hodgson died on 10 September 1822 at Newcastle upon Tyne after a short illness, reported by the *Tyne Mercury* as cholera morbus (presumably European cholera). The Revd William Turner preached the sermon, afterwards published, at her funeral at the Hanover Square Chapel on 15 September.   PETER ISAAC

Sources R. Welford, *Men of mark 'twixt Tyne and Tweed*, 3 vols. (1895) · R. Welford, 'Early Newcastle typography', *Archaeologia Aeliana*, 3rd ser., 3 (1907), 1–134, esp. 45–8 · C. J. Hunt, *The book trade in Northumberland and Durham to 1860: a biographical dictionary* (1975) · P. J. Wallis, *The book trade in Northumberland and Durham to 1860: a supplement to C. J. Hunt's biographical dictionary* (1981) · *Local catalogue of material … in the central public library, Newcastle upon Tyne*, Newcastle upon Tyne Public Libraries (1932) · *A memoir of Thomas Bewick, written by himself*, ed. I. Bain (1975) · S. Roscoe, *Thomas Bewick: a bibliography raisonée* (1953) · 'The "Newcastle Chronicle"', *Monthly Chronicle of North-Country Lore and Legend* (1890), 223–6 · J. Sykes, *Local records, or, Historical register of remarkable events, which have occured in Northumberland and Durham … from the earliest period to the present time*, ed. T. Fordyce, rev. edn (1866) · U. Newcastle, Robinson L., Bell MSS · *IGI*

Archives Tyne and Wear Archive Service, Newcastle upon Tyne, personal and family papers | BL, letters to T. Bewick, Add. MSS 50240–50242 · U. Newcastle, Robinson L., Bell MSS · V&A, letters to T. Bewick

Wealth at death sold bookselling business; known to 'hit the bottle', so business perhaps run down

Hodgson, Studholme (1707/8–1798), army officer, was the son of John Hodgson, a Carlisle merchant whose family originated from Wormanby, Burgh by Sands. After attending Carlisle grammar school and, in 1727, being made free of his father's guild by patrimony, he entered the army as an ensign in the 1st foot guards on 22 January 1728. He became lieutenant and captain in the same regiment on 25 April 1740 and captain and lieutenant-colonel on 22 February 1747. A shooting companion of General Oglethorpe, he was aide-de-camp to the earl of Albemarle at Dettingen and Fontenoy and to the duke of Cumberland at Culloden. Henry Conway and others of the staff nicknamed him the Old Boy, on account of his long-standing seniority; the Dutch, however, complained of his rudeness towards them at Laffelt.

Hodgson married Catherine Howard (1734–1798), the sister of Field Marshal Sir George *Howard, on 22 July 1756. The same year he was appointed colonel of the recently raised 52nd, later 50th foot. In 1757 he commanded a brigade in the Rochefort expedition and was among those who voted for withdrawal before a landing had been attempted. Two years later he was promoted major-general and transferred to the colonelcy of the 5th foot. In 1761, with the return to favour of the duke of Cumberland at court, Hodgson was given command of the expedition against Belle Île. The calibre of many of his

troops left him unimpressed and the first attempt to effect a landing on the island failed. With the arrival of reinforcements, however, a lodgement was secured, the French were driven back to the citadel of Palais, and, after a siege of six weeks, on 7 June 1761 the fortress surrendered. Throughout the siege Hodgson was critical of the quantity and quality of the stores provided for him by the Board of Ordnance. In response, Lord Ligonier, master-general of the ordnance, wrote and accused Hodgson of wasting ammunition. Hodgson took umbrage at the letter: 'Surely Lady Betty Germain is at the head of the Army and has the impertinence to sign herself Ligonier' (Albemarle MSS, HA 67, 894/B/B10). None the less, Hodgson received high compliments from the king and Pitt for a service which had a decided influence upon the peace negotiations.

Hodgson was master of the horse to the duke of Cumberland, and he remained his trusted friend until the duke's death in 1765. The same year Hodgson was appointed governor of Fort George and Fort Augustus. He became colonel of the 4th King's Own foot in 1768, was promoted general in 1778, and was in succession colonel of the 4th Irish horse and the 11th dragoons. On 30 July 1796 he was created field marshal. Hodgson died, aged ninety, at his home in Old Burlington Street, London, on 20 October 1798 and was buried six days later within the parish of St James's, Piccadilly. His heir was John *Hodgson (1757–1846), the only one of three sons and two daughters to survive him.

H. M. CHICHESTER, *rev.* ALASTAIR W. MASSIE

Sources Suffolk RO, Ipswich, Albemarle MSS, HA 67 894/B/B1–22 · BL, Hodgson MSS, Add. MS 36995 · Cumbria AS, Carlisle, Merchants' guild papers, DGC4/1 and 2 · grammar school register, 1699–1798, Cumbria AS, Carlisle, Dean and Chapter Archive · *GM*, 1st ser., 68 (1798), 914 · *Army List* · T. R. Keppel, *The life of Augustus, Viscount Keppel*, 1 (1842), 1.298–325 · H. Howard, *Indication of memorials, monuments, paintings and engravings of persons of the Howard family* (1834) · Royal Arch., Cumberland papers, Box 24/159, 169 · J. S. Corbett, *England in the Seven Years' War; a study in combined strategy*, 2 (1907), vol. 2 · parish register, St James's, Piccadilly, City Westm. AC [burial] · will, PRO, PROB 11/1315 · BL, Newcastle MSS, Add. MSS 32944, 32954–32955, 32962, 32966 · R. Cannon, ed., *Historical record of the fourth, or the king's own, regiment of foot* (1839)

Archives BL, corresp., Add. MS 36995 · Lancaster City Museum, order books | Suffolk RO, Ipswich, letters to second earl of Albemarle

Likenesses W. Bond, stipple, pubd 1796 (after G. Romney), BM, NPG

Hodgson, Studholme John (b. after **1805**, d. **1890**). *See under* Hodgson, John (1757–1846).

Hodgson, William (**1745–1851**), politician and author, was descended from an 'ancient border family' (*GM*), and in early life studied medicine in the Netherlands, where he developed an interest in botany. On his return to England he attended with success, through a severe illness, a member of Lord Holland's family, but he declined Lord Holland's offer of an appointment. He adopted extreme political views, chiefly derived from the French philosophers, and Benjamin Franklin and Simón Bolívar were among his warmest friends. On 9 December 1793 he was tried at the Old Bailey on charges of having proposed as a toast 'the French republic', and of having 'compared the king to a German hog butcher'. He was found guilty and was sentenced to be confined in Newgate for two years, to pay a fine of £200, and to find securities of £400 for a further two years. While incarcerated he wrote his best-known work, *The Commonwealth of Reason* (1795). After regaining his liberty Hodgson relinquished politics for literature and science, becoming an independent printer-publisher and publishing numerous works on topics such as French and English grammar, chemistry, and the life of Napoleon Bonaparte, in addition to a pamphlet on his own conviction for sedition, *The Case of W. Hodgson* (1796). He appears to have been a member of the Freethinking Christian congregation in 1810. He wrote for William Sherwin's *Political Register* in 1817. Hodgson died of bronchitis in Hemmington Terrace, Islington, London, on 2 March 1851, at the age of 106. He had been married three times and was 'survived but by one son' (*GM*).

THOMPSON COOPER, *rev.* STEPHEN M. LEE

Sources *Annual Register* (1851), pt 2, p. 268 • *GM*, 2nd ser., 35 (1851), 560 • [J. Watkins and F. Shoberl], *A biographical dictionary of the living authors of Great Britain and Ireland* (1816) • *N&Q*, 6th ser., 9 (1884), 475–6 • I. McCalman, *Radical underworld: prophets, revolutionaries, and pornographers in London, 1795–1840* (1988); pbk edn (1993)

Hodgson, William Ballantyne (1815–1880), educationist and economist, the elder son of William Hodgson, printer, friend, and works manager of James Ballantyne (1772–1833), was born at 23 Gardner's Crescent, Edinburgh, on 6 October 1815. He had a brother and a half-sister on his mother's side. His father intended him for the law and, after attending Edinburgh high school from 1823, he worked for a short time in a lawyer's office. But he loathed legal study, preferring to pursue the literary interests he had developed as an omnivorous reader since early childhood. In 1829, when just turned fourteen, he entered Edinburgh University, but did not graduate. Breaking away from the strict Calvinism of his upbringing, he became strongly influenced by the phrenological writings of George Combe, which offered a more hopeful message of human perfectibility and opened up possibilities of rational progress. With Combe and others he helped to found, in 1832, the Edinburgh Ethical Society for the Practical Application of Phrenology, which later became the Edinburgh Philosophical Association, and published articles in the *Phrenological Journal* between 1836 and 1841. He lectured in literature, education, and phrenology in the towns of Fife, publishing in 1837 an address on education delivered to the Edinburgh Association of the Working Classes.

On 1 June 1839 Hodgson was appointed secretary to the mechanics' institute in Liverpool. As well as providing popular evening lectures, the Liverpool institute had a library, sculpture gallery, and two non-sectarian schools (catering mainly for middle-class pupils), to which Hodgson added a third, for girls, in 1844. Under him the institute, which was one of the most innovative educational institutions of its time, flourished. On 11 March 1846 he received the degree of LLD from Glasgow University. From 1847 to 1851 he was principal of Chorlton high school. In 1849 (and again in 1864–6) he was a vice-president of the College of Preceptors. Shortly after his appointment at Liverpool he met and married (1841) Jane, third daughter of George Lissant Cox, of Liverpool, who lapsed into invalidity within a month of their marriage.

Hodgson was a strong Liberal in politics. He declined the editorship of two newspapers in Liverpool and Manchester, not wishing to abandon teaching, but was an active supporter of the Anti-Corn Law League and became associated with Cobden and Bright. He later belonged to the Financial Reform Association and the Liberation Society (which advocated church disestablishment). He mixed in Unitarian circles, admiring in particular the views of William Johnson Fox, whose works he edited (1865), and making the acquaintance of George Eliot, upon whom he practised mesmerism when she visited James Martineau's home in the Lake District in 1844. She found him a congenial companion on subsequent meetings at the home of John Chapman, the owner of the *Westminster Review*, to which he contributed an article on languages in the school curriculum (October 1853). In 1854 he was party to James Martineau's unsuccessful move to wrest control of the *Review* from Chapman, which led to the establishment of the rival *National Review*.

In 1851 Hodgson travelled abroad, partly for the sake of his wife's health, remaining in Paris from October 1851 to July 1852 before moving on to Germany and Italy. After returning to Edinburgh in 1853, he attended classes at the College of Surgeons to qualify himself for teaching physiology. He strongly believed that the laws of health, 'sanitary science', should be taught as part of the school curriculum; emphasizing their importance to women, he included ladies' classes in his popular lectures on the subject. Like his friend William Ellis, the promoter of secular schools, he also stressed the importance of teaching political economy, 'social science', insisting that all classes (and both genders) should understand the laws regulating the production and distribution of wealth. His lecture at the Royal Institution, London, was published as *On the Importance of the Study of Economic Science as a Branch of Education for All Classes* (1855) and went through three editions. He also prompted the establishment of the Edinburgh Phrenological Association in 1855. In 1858 he was appointed an assistant commissioner of inquiry into popular education, for the commission chaired by the duke of Newcastle, and produced a report on elementary schools in the south and west of London.

Hodgson's wife died, childless, on 1 July 1860, and he married, on 14 January 1863, Emily, second daughter of Sir Joshua *Walmsley, the radical MP, with whom he had two sons and two daughters. From 1863 to 1868 he was examiner in political economy to London University, and was a member of the council of University College, resigning on 19 January 1867 in support of James Martineau, who had been rejected for the vacant chair of mental philosophy. Believing in the educability of the whole population, he was a strong supporter of the campaign for the higher education of women, publishing his views in *The Education of Girls and the Employment of Women and the Upper Classes: Two Lectures* (2nd edn, 1869). As early as 1848 he had pressed for the Royal Institution of Manchester to admit women to its classes. He backed Emily Davies's campaign to admit girls to Cambridge local examinations (1864), and subsequently he delivered lectures on economics to the North London Collegiate School for Ladies (whose headmistress, Frances Mary Buss, was a close associate), the Ladies' Institute at Belfast, and to ladies' classes at the Birmingham and Midland Institute. He gave evidence on women's education to the schools' inquiry commission in November 1865. He looked forward to a time when men and women students would be taught together in the same classes, and was not enthusiastic about Emily Davies's proposed college for women at Hitchin. Hodgson and his wife were members of the Married Women's Property Committee, and he belonged to the Women's Suffrage Association and the National Anti-Contagious Diseases Acts Association.

During the 1860s the Social Science Association provided a platform for Hodgson's views on the importance of teaching economics to schoolchildren. His 1867 critique of the narrowness of the elementary school curriculum laid down by the revised code, *Exaggerated Estimates of Reading and Writing as Means of Education*, continues to interest historians of literacy (see *History of Education Quarterly*, 26, 1986, 377–93). Under the auspices of the Social Science Association he published papers under the title *The True Scope of Economic Science and Competition* (1870). By then his reproofs against strikers and trade unions rather overshadowed his original, equally important objective, to warn capitalists against the folly of speculation and 'panics'. Although a popularizer of orthodox economics, he was not a rigid Ricardian, and his lectures were enlivened by numerous and sometimes humorous examples drawn from his vast reading. His influence was largely the result of his wide circle of friends: he produced no significant work of economic theory. In politics he remained a Liberal, though he had broken with John Bright over the American Civil War—Hodgson, who feared the Americanization of British institutions, supported the Confederates—and was alarmed by the 1867 Reform Act.

On 17 July 1871 the Merchant Company of Edinburgh elected him as the first holder of the newly founded chair of commercial and political economy and mercantile law at Edinburgh University. Though his lecture delivery was somewhat monotonous, he was regarded with affection by his students: they recalled his 'long dark hair, slight figure, and face indicating keen intellect, sensibility and humour', and his habit of wearing a black silk skull cap in classes (*Life and Letters*, 244). On returning to Edinburgh he bought Bonaly Tower, Midlothian, a fortified tower partly rebuilt by Henry Cockburn, Lord Cockburn (1779–1854), in 1838, where he liberally entertained his students (see J. Small, *The Castles and Mansions of the Lothians*, 1883). At his death his friend Professor John Stuart Blackie (1809–1895) wrote *The Burn o'Bonaly*.

Hodgson's strong opposition to vivisection led him into controversy when a new medical school was established in the university in 1875. Education was his life's work, and much of his later activity was directed to improving the standing of teachers. He belonged to several educational associations, favoured teacher training, and advocated the founding of professorships of education. In 1875 he was made president of the Educational Institute of Scotland, and in 1880 president of the Edinburgh chamber of commerce. Hodgson, who had suffered from heart disease for many years, died of angina pectoris on 24 August 1880 while attending an educational congress in Belgium. He was buried at the Grange cemetery, Edinburgh, survived by his wife. A posthumous work, *Errors in the Use of English* (1881) arose from the project of his later years to compile an English dictionary.

M. C. CURTHOYS

Sources *Life and letters of William Ballantyne Hodgson*, ed. J. M. D. Meiklejohn (1883) • Boase, *Mod. Eng. biog.* • *Men of the time* (1875) • R. H. I. Palgrave, ed., *Dictionary of political economy*, 3 vols. (1894–9) • *Testimonials in favour of W. B. Hodgson … candidate for the professorship of political and commercial economy and mercantile law in the University of Edinburgh* (1870) • R. Cooter, *Phrenology in the British Isles: an annotated historical biobibliography and index* (1989) • W. A. C. Stewart and W. P. McCann, *The educational innovators*, 2 vols. (1967–8) • *The George Eliot letters*, ed. G. S. Haight, 9 vols. (1954–78) • L. Holcombe, *Wives and property: reform of married women's property law in nineteenth-century England* (1983) • D. I. Allsobrook, *Schools for the shires: the reform of middle-class education in mid-Victorian England* (1986) • *DNB* • Burke, *Gen. GB* (1972)
Archives NL Scot., letters to J. S. Blackie • NL Scot., corresp. with George Combe
Likenesses engraving (after photograph), repro. in Meiklejohn, ed., *Life and letters*, frontispiece; priv. coll.
Wealth at death under £12,000: probate, 22 Sept 1880, *CGPLA Eng. & Wales* • £3918 12s. 3d.: confirmation, 5 Oct 1880, *CCI*

Hodgson, William Hope (1877–1918), author, was born on 15 November 1877 at Blackmore End, Essex, the second of the twelve children of Samuel Hodgson (1846–1892), an Anglican clergyman, and Lissie Sarah (1852–1933), daughter of Burdett Lambton Brown, an engineer. He attended St Margaret's, a boarding-school in Margate, but ran away at thirteen with the intention of going to sea. An apprenticeship in the mercantile marine was obtained for him in 1891; he was eventually certificated as third mate and rose to the rank of lieutenant. Although short in stature, he took a keen interest in body-building and in 1899 left the sea to found his own school of physical culture in Blackburn, Lancashire. He was also an enthusiastic photographer; he used pictures taken during his travels to illustrate lectures which he gave for commercial reasons and to assist his assiduous campaigning for better conditions for seamen.

When Hodgson's school was forced to close in 1902 he began writing articles for popular magazines, soon branching out into fiction. His first published story was 'The Goddess of Death' in the April 1904 issue of the *Royal Magazine*. He found his métier with weird tales of the sea featuring various kinds of monstrous creatures. His most famous story of this kind was 'The Voice in the Night' (1907), and his first published novel, *The Boats of the 'Glen*

Carrig' (1907), featured eighteenth-century castaways menaced by a whole series of exotic life forms.

Hodgson's second novel, *The House on the Borderland* (1908), uses an account of a house 'haunted' by swinish invaders from another dimension as a bracketing device for a series of visions, which include a remarkable account of the cosmos revealed by contemporary astronomy and the future evolution of the solar system. *The Ghost Pirates* (1909) replaces the house with a ship which slips into the borderland between this world and another and is eventually invaded by its horrid inhabitants. Similarly swinish creatures continued to crop up in Hodgson's work; one is glimpsed in 'The Hog', the final (posthumously published) adventure of the occult detective whose early adventures were collected as *Carnacki the Ghost-Finder* (1910), and another such creature assumes command of an experimenter trying to make spiritual contact with the absolute in 'Eloi, Eloi, sabachthani' (first published in abridged form as 'The Baumoff Explosion' in 1919).

The last novel Hodgson published—though it may have been the first he wrote—was *The Night Land* (1912), in which a medieval visionary embarks on a hallucinatory odyssey in a far future when mankind is on the brink of extinction. An inhabitant of the 'Last Redoubt' must cross an eternally dark landscape inhabited by exceedingly strange and menacing life forms in order to rescue the woman who is the reincarnation of the dreamer's dead lover.

Hodgson always struggled to make a living as a writer, although his less exotic tales of life at sea, collected in *Men of the Deep Waters* (1914), *The Luck of the Strong* (1916), and *Captain Gault* (1917), were better received in his own day than his fantasies. On 26 February 1913 he married Bessie Gertrude Farnsworth (1877–1943) in London. The couple initially settled in the south of France but returned to Britain in 1914 when the First World War broke out. Hodgson joined the University of London Officers' Training Corps and was commissioned in the Royal Field Artillery in 1915. He was discharged from active service in 1916 after a head injury sustained when he was thrown from a horse, but persuaded the RFA to recommission him a year later, and was posted to France in October 1917. He was killed by a shellburst near Ypres on 19 April 1918, while reporting from a forward position on the accuracy of his battery's fire, and was buried at the foot of Mont Kemmel.

Hodgson was eventually recognized as an important pioneer of modern imaginative fiction. He was one of a handful of writers—the others included H. G. Wells, M. P. Shiel, and J. D. Beresford—who produced visionary scientific romances extrapolating from ideas in contemporary science as far as the literary imagination could take them. The figures of menace in his short horror stories are always rationalized by reference to biology or metaphysical speculation; in his longer works he attempted to cultivate a sense of the sublime which recognized the awesome magnitude of the universe revealed by contemporary science.   BRIAN STABLEFORD

Sources S. Moskowitz, 'William Hope Hodgson', in *Out of the storm: uncollected fantasies by William Hope Hodgson*, ed. S. Moskowitz (1975) · R. A. Everts, 'Some facts in the case of William Hope Hodgson', *The Shadow* (April 1973), 4–11; (Oct 1973), 7–13 · I. Bell, ed., *William Hope Hodgson: voyages and visions* (1987) [incl. biographical material] · P. Tremayne, 'W. Hope Hodgson: his life and work', *William Hope Hodgson: a centenary tribute, 1877–1977* (1977)
Likenesses photographs, repro. in Everts, 'Some facts in the case of William Hope Hodgson', *Shadow* (April 1973)

Hodgson, William Noel [*pseud.* Edward Melbourne] (1893–1916), soldier and poet, was born at the vicarage, Thornbury, near Bristol, Gloucestershire, on 3 January 1893, the fourth and youngest child of Henry Bernard Hodgson (1856–1921), vicar of Thornbury and later the first bishop of St Edmundsbury and Ipswich, and his wife, Penelope Maria Warren. At the age of four, Hodgson moved with his family to Berwick upon Tweed when his father became vicar there. The family had roots in the north of England and both Durham and the Lake District feature in much of his poetry.

In September 1905 Hodgson entered Durham School as a king's scholar. He was a gifted student and a talented athlete, achieving several sporting prizes. In 1911 he won an exhibition to his father's college, Christ Church, Oxford, where in 1913 he took a first in classical moderations before going on to read Greats. He developed his poetic style during his time at Oxford, though he does not appear to have been part of any particular literary clique. His early poetry was written in a Georgian style and idealizes nature and youth.

The outbreak of the First World War prevented Hodgson from completing his degree, and in September 1914 he was commissioned in the 9th Devonshire regiment as a second lieutenant. He trained in Borden near Aldershot before sailing to France on 28 July 1915 and joining the front line near Festubert, where the 9th Devons were incorporated in the 7th (Immortal) division. Frustrated by their long period of training in England, the 9th Devons were eager to see action. However, they were quickly made aware of the realities of war; their first important experience of battle, at Loos on 25 September 1915, resulted in the deaths of fifteen officers and 461 men. During the conflict Hodgson, with three other officers and a hundred men, defended a trench for thirty-six hours before reinforcements arrived. His poem 'Back to Rest', describing the exhilaration of war, was written soon after this experience. For his actions during the engagement Hodgson was awarded the Military Cross in October 1915.

In February 1916, while the battalion was stationed at front-line trenches in Fricourt, Hodgson began to contribute articles to *The Spectator*, *Yorkshire Post*, and *Saturday Review* under the pseudonym Edward Melbourne. These pieces are markedly different in tone to his poetry. Vivid and unflinchingly realistic, they reveal a precocious talent. Their grim subject matter is offset by a wry sense of humour. He does not pass judgement on the wisdom of his commanders—to do so would have been unpatriotic. Instead he gives honest reports of the day-to-day trials of life in the trenches, restraining from comment on the morality of either side and leaving the reader to draw their own conclusions. Although the pieces were intended for readers keen to hear what life was like for their husbands and sons, he did not conceal the hardships of battle.

In April 1916 the 9th Devons moved to Mametz. After a brief period of leave, Hodgson returned to his regiment to make preparations for the Somme offensive, otherwise known as the 'big push': the battle that Haig hoped would end the war. Possibly with the future offensive in mind, Hodgson wrote his most famous poem, 'Before Action', on 29 June 1916. This touching and beautiful poem reads like a prayer, imploring God to give him strength. Like his university poetry, 'Before Action' is written in a Georgian style, but the pastoral images are subverted into metaphors of wartime bloodletting. The poem is also full of regret for the instances of beauty he never fully appreciated. Two days later, on 1 July 1916, the first day of the Somme offensive, he was killed near Mansel Copse outside Mametz while bringing forward the supply of grenades. He was one of the 60,000 men from the British army who were killed or wounded on this one day. He was buried in the Devonshire cemetery near Mametz Wood.

Hodgson was tall and athletic with light-coloured hair and a pleasant face. He was known as Smiler to the regiment. His poetry and writings show him as sensitive, especially to the concerns of his fellow soldiers—qualities acknowledged in his regiment's official history: 'Lieutenant Hodgson, the Bombing Officer, was a particularly fine officer, a most inspiring personality with a great hold on his men, and nearly as much liked and respected by the 8th as by his own battalion' (Atkinson, *The Devonshire Regiment, 1914–1918*, 151). A memorial was placed in the chapel in Durham School, where there is also a stained glass window inscribed in his memory.

Hodgson's work was popular during the war, possibly because it seems so resilient in tone; his verse, like that of Rupert Brooke, focuses resolutely on higher ideals and refuses to be demoralized by the wretchedness of trench life. His volume *Verse and Prose in Peace and War*, published posthumously in 1916, was reprinted four times, and individual poems have subsequently been included in anthologies.   CATRIONA HAIG

Sources W. N. Hodgson, *Verse and prose in peace and war* (1916) [including a memoir] · J. Medomsley, *William Noel Hodgson: the gentle poet* (1989) · A. Powell, ed., *A deep cry: First World War soldier–poets killed in France* (1998) · P. Fussell, *The Great War and modern memory* (1975) · C. T. Atkinson, *The Devonshire regiment, 1914–1918* (1926) · C. T. Atkinson, *The Seventh Division, 1914–1918* (1927) · b. cert. · Commonwealth War Graves Commission, www.cwgc.org [debt of honour register] · *CGPLA Eng. & Wales* (1916) · will · A. B. Thompson and E. W. Moses, eds., *The war record of old Dunelmians, 1914–1919* (1919)
Likenesses Langfier, photograph, 1915–16, repro. in Hodgson, *Verse and prose*
Wealth at death £190 0s. 5d.: probate, 9 Nov 1916, *CGPLA Eng. & Wales*

Hodsoll, Sir (Eric) John (1894–1971), civil servant, was born in Marylebone, London, on 11 October 1894, the only child of Commander John French Hodsoll RNR and his wife, Wilhelmina Ann White. He was educated at Christ's Hospital (1904–11). He then hoped to take up engineering and went to the Great Western Railway's works at Swindon as an apprentice. On the outbreak of the First World War he joined the Royal Naval Air Service. With the rank of temporary sub-lieutenant he first served at Calshot in the Solent. In June 1918 he became squadron commander in command of the seaplane base at Alexandria. He had transferred to the Royal Air Force when it was formed in April 1918, and a month later was mentioned in dispatches. After the end of the war (having been mentioned in dispatches on two further occasions) he was given a permanent commission as captain in the RAF. Promotion to the rank of squadron leader and three years at the Air Ministry (1919–22) were followed by a year's course at the Staff College, Camberley (1923–4).

In 1925 Hodsoll was again posted overseas, to the imperial secretariat at Delhi, New Delhi, and Simla. After his return home in 1929 he was made assistant secretary (air) to the committee of imperial defence, whose secretary, Sir Maurice Hankey, chose him to act as one of Britain's two secretaries at the London naval conference in 1930. Two years later, when Hankey was attending the Lausanne conference, he left Hodsoll as one of two British secretaries acting in his place. By then air attack on Britain was regarded as more likely and the government's planning of air-raid precautions (ARP—the precursor of civil defence) became more urgent. Hodsoll was appointed secretary of the ARP (policy) and ARP (official) committees. In 1934 he was put in charge of a newly formed ARP department in the Home Office. In May 1935, now on the RAF retired list, he was appointed assistant under-secretary, thus becoming senior to some Home Office officials. Inevitably this caused friction: it was almost unknown to appoint, without open competition, an outsider with no previous experience of a department.

Hodsoll's function was to make ARP widely known. In July 1935 the department issued to all local authorities (and sold to the public for 2d.) a 'first circular' or statement on civil defence. It asked local authorities and private employers to co-operate with Whitehall in creating machinery for this purpose. Hodsoll's RAF background enabled him fully to comprehend the threat the Germans presented and the probable scale, intensity, and effects of bombing. With 'a hide like a rhinoceros', and determined to achieve his aims, he tirelessly toured Britain lecturing in the hope of getting local officials, industry, and the public to co-operate effectively. The formation of an air raid wardens service, for which members of the public were encouraged to volunteer, was announced in March 1937. In 1938, the year of 'Munich', more was done at the centre with the aim, as the home secretary told parliament, of 'greatly strengthening' ARP organization. In that year Hodsoll was appointed to another new post: inspector-general of ARP services, and stayed in it until the end of the war. After the allied landings in north Africa in 1943 he went to allied headquarters in Algiers to help French authorities to plan civil defence.

In the first half of 1945 British civil defence services were stood down by a progressive release of members. However, the dropping of an atomic bomb on Hiroshima in August opened the possibility of the spread of atomic warfare. A full review of civil defence was necessary and Hodsoll, who had been confined to supervising a small training organization, now became director-general of civil defence training, a post he held until he retired from the civil service in 1954. He then became chief civil defence adviser to NATO (then based in Paris), in charge of civil emergency planning. He retired in 1961.

Hodsoll was appointed CB in 1934 and was knighted in 1944. In his last years he was awarded the first gold medal of the (British) Institute of Civil Defence, and similar honours in Denmark, the USA, and India, and honorary chieftainship of the Scancee tribe of Alberta, Canada. On 22 November 1919 he married Winifred Joyce, daughter of Colonel Morton Tomlin OBE, deputy lieutenant. She died in 1935, and in 1937 he married her sister Elizabeth Morton. With his first wife he had one daughter, and with his second twin daughters. He died on 14 March 1971 at Tarrant Rushton, near Blandford Forum, Dorset, where he lived; he was survived by his second wife.

T. H. O'BRIEN, *rev.*

Sources *The Times* (17 March 1971) • S. W. Roskill, *Hankey, man of secrets*, 2 (1972) • S. W. Roskill, *Hankey, man of secrets*, 3 (1974) • private information (1986) • *CGPLA Eng. & Wales* (1971)
Archives CAC Cam., corresp. and MSS | FILM BFI NFTVA, propaganda film footage
Likenesses W. Stoneman, photograph, 1948, NPG
Wealth at death £10,376: probate, 4 June 1971, *CGPLA Eng. & Wales*

Hodson, (Francis Lord) Charlton [Charles], **Baron Hodson** (1895–1984), judge, was born on 17 September 1895 at Charlton Kings' vicarage, Cheltenham, the seventh son and seventh of eight children of the Revd Thomas Hodson (1850–1915), rector of Oddington in Gloucestershire, and his wife, Catherine Anne (*d.* 1932), daughter of Thomas Maskew, headmaster of Dorchester grammar school. He was educated at Cheltenham College, where he won a classical scholarship to Wadham, his father's college at Oxford. Always known as Charles, he was a keen oarsman and stroked the Cheltenham boat in 1914.

The outbreak of the First World War (in which his sixth brother was killed in 1915) interrupted his studies and settled his immediate future. He joined the 7th battalion of the Gloucestershire regiment and fought in Gallipoli and Mesopotamia where he was wounded several times. In the fighting for the relief of Kut he won the MC. He was demobilized in 1919 with the rank of captain. He decided to read for the bar, but beforehand took the shortened course in jurisprudence at Oxford (1920). By then he was a married man. On 19 August 1918 he had married Susan Mary (*d.* 1965), daughter of Major William Greaves Blake DL of Eccleshall, Sheffield. They had a daughter and two sons, the elder of whom was killed in 1943 during the Second World War. The daughter, Anthea *Joseph, died in 1981.

Reading for the bar was shortened for those who had served in the forces and Hodson was called by the Inner Temple in 1921. Earning a livelihood could not be so swift. He began to practise in common-law chambers and would

have stayed on there if he could have afforded to wait five years and upwards for an income. As a married man he could not. Progress was much faster at the divorce bar. The consequence of an easy start is proverbially a dead end. So it was thought to be in divorce, a jurisdiction which in the great amalgamation of 1873 had been bundled into the new High Court with Probate and Admiralty as its companions. The few at the divorce bar who took silk earned less than busy juniors. They could not even dream of the bench since on the reasonable assumption that ignorance of adultery could be more swiftly dispelled than ignorance of navigation, the judges were promoted from the Admiralty bar.

Until 1936 the basis of divorce law was that the bond could be dissolved only by adultery. In that year A. P. Herbert persuaded parliament to add cruelty and desertion as grounds for divorce. It was rightly anticipated that the number of petitions would greatly increase; indeed, ten years later they had multiplied tenfold. The appointment of a judge from the divorce bar could not be evaded. None of the silks was found worthy. Hodson was by then recognized as the most capable of the juniors; in 1935 he had been made Treasury counsel in probate matters. So when Herbert's bill was about to become law the lord chancellor sent for Hodson and advised him to apply for silk. He was of course given it (1937) and a few months later he was appointed a justice of the High Court, at forty-two the youngest ever to hold that office, and duly knighted (1937). Thus was the proverb dishonoured. In 1938 he became a bencher of the Inner Temple.

In 1951 the increase in the number of lords justices of appeal from six to nine made it imperative that one should come from divorce. Hodson was obviously the man and at the same time he was admitted to the privy council. Nine years later seniority made him the natural choice for the succession as a lord of appeal in ordinary, with a life peerage (1 October 1960). He retired in 1971 and lived quietly at Rotherfield Greys. Though he was a reserved man, he had the gift of making friends and made many among his colleagues.

Hodson's thirty-four years of judicial service left little or no mark on the law. He took the law as he found it, whether he liked it or not. He did not like the treatment of unhappiness in married life as a reason for the dissolution of marriage. His memorandum to the royal commission on marriage and divorce (1951–5) summarized his opposition to any extension of the grounds for divorce; he returned to the theme in his presidential address to the Holdsworth Club in 1962. As a churchman he was an active member of the laity.

In appellate work Hodson was at ease with the common law. But it was at first instance that he won his high reputation. He was a man of strong moral principle and with a clear perception of what was just and fair. These virtues flowed evenly within the banks of the law into his judgments. His judicial demeanour was near to perfection. He talked little and listened attentively. He was quiet, courteous, and firm. In his court justice proceeded *de die in diem* with the strength and serenity of a Bach mass. His quality was much admired in his one excursion outside the field of English law. This was in the British branch of the International Law Association where he presided in 1955. He became an honorary fellow of Wadham College in 1939. Hodson died at Thames Bank Nursing Home, Goring-on-Thames, on 11 March 1984, having lived latterly at Fishers, Rotherfield Greys, Henley-on-Thames.   DEVLIN, *rev.*

Sources personal knowledge (2004) · Burke, *Peerage* (1969) · *WWW* · *The Times* (14 March 1984) · E. S. Skirving, ed., *Cheltenham College register, 1841–1927* (1928) · b. cert. · d. cert.
Wealth at death £243,959: probate, 13 July 1984, *CGPLA Eng. & Wales*

Hodson, Frodsham (1770–1822), college head and Church of England clergyman, the son of the Revd George Hodson, was born at Liverpool on 7 June 1770. He entered Manchester grammar school in January 1784, and left it in 1787 to proceed to Brasenose College, Oxford, where he graduated BA in 1791, MA in 1793, BD in 1808, and DD in 1809. In 1791 he succeeded to a Hulmean exhibition, and in 1794 was elected a fellow of his college. In 1793 he gained the university prize for an essay in English prose on 'The influence of education and government on national character' (*Oxford English Prize Essays*, 1836, 1). In 1795 he was chosen lecturer at St George's Church, Liverpool, and subsequently became chaplain of the same church. His persistence in holding the chaplaincy, although he rarely in later years visited Liverpool, gave offence in the town. In 1803–4, and again in 1808–10, he filled the office of public examiner at Oxford. In 1808 he was appointed rector of St Mary's, Stratford-le-Bow, London, and vacated his fellowship. He married, on 30 June 1808, Anne (*d.* 23 April 1848), daughter of John Dawson, of Mossley Hill, Liverpool. They had four daughters and one son.

In 1809 Hodson was elected principal of Brasenose College. He presided over the college with great distinction for thirteen years, during which admissions to the college markedly increased. He took a leading part in the affairs of the university. He was one of the most energetic managers of Lord Grenville's election in 1809 as chancellor. The Revd W. Agutter retracted a libel on his character in the *Anti-Jacobin Review* (1811). He served the office of vice-chancellor in 1818, and was appointed regius professor of divinity, with the appurtenant canonry of Christ Church and rectory of Ewelme, in 1820. It was believed that Lord Liverpool intended him for a bishopric, but he died in Oxford, after a short illness, on 18 January 1822, aged fifty-one. He was buried in the ante-chapel of his college, where he is commemorated in a Latin inscription by Dr E. Cardwell.

In the university Hodson was long remembered for his success as a college tutor and administrator, and for the dignity of his personal appearance and address. He edited Thomas Falconer's *Chronological Tables* (1796). His probationary exercise as a fellow of Brasenose was published in the same year, entitled *The Eternal Filiation of the Son of God*

Asserted on the Evidence of the Sacred Scriptures. His only other works were three occasional sermons preached at Liverpool, and printed in 1797, 1799, and 1804.

C. W. SUTTON, *rev.* M. C. CURTHOYS

Sources J. F. Smith, ed., *The admission register of the Manchester School, with some notes of the more distinguished scholars*, 2, Chetham Society, 73 (1868), 125 · [C. B. Heberden], ed., *Brasenose College register, 1509–1909*, 1, OHS, 55 (1909), 388 · G. V. Cox, *Recollections of Oxford* (1868), 193 · W. R. Ward, *Victorian Oxford* (1965) · R. Brooke, *Liverpool as it was during the last quarter of the eighteenth century* (1853), 52 · D. Thom, *Liverpool churches and chapels* (1854), 27 · M. Pattison, *Memoirs*, ed. Mrs Pattison (1885), 3 · *GM*, 1st ser., 92/1 (1822), 189
Archives Bodl. Oxf., commonplace book · Bodl. Oxf., diary as vice-chancellor · Lancs. RO, papers | BL, corresp. with Lord Grenville, Add. MSS 59412–59413, 69105–69107, 69110 · Bodl. Oxf., letters to Richard Heber · Brasenose College, Oxford, corresp. with bishop of Lincoln
Likenesses Fittler, engraving (after Phillips) · T. Phillips, oils, Brasenose College, Oxford

Hodson [*married names* Pigeon, Labouchere], **Henrietta** (1841–1910), actress, born at Upper Marsh in St Mary's parish, Westminster, on 26 March 1841, came from a theatrical family, her grandfather being George Hodson, the manager of the Bower Saloon, a prosperous little theatre in Stansgate, Westminster. She was the eldest daughter of his son George Alfred Hodson (1822–1869), an Irish comedian and singer, and his wife, Henrietta Elizabeth Noel. Her father also kept the Duke's Arms inn in Westminster. Her two sisters, Kate (afterwards Mrs Charles Fenton but known professionally as Kate Gordon) and Sylvia, were also on the stage. Henrietta was a pupil of Edmund Glover of the Theatre Royal, Glasgow, where she made her first appearance as a mute 'super' in 1858, and later played small parts.

Early in 1860 Henrietta Hodson was acting in Greenock and there met Henry Irving, with whom she travelled to Manchester. They were engaged there by Knowles for his Theatre Royal stock company, and both made their first appearance on 29 September in *The Spy, or, A Government Appointment*. In the autumn of 1861 she became a member of J. H. Chute's Bath and Bristol companies, and in both cities soon acquired popularity as a soubrette and burlesque actress. On 4 March 1863, at the opening of the Theatre Royal, Bath (newly built after destruction by fire), she played Oberon in *A Midsummer Night's Dream*. The cast included Madge Robertson (later Mrs Kendal), who was also the manager, and Ellen Terry, who recalled that Hodson was 'a brilliant burlesque actress, a good singer, and a capital dancer with great personal charm' (Terry, 43). Shortly afterwards (on 2 July 1864) she married Richard Walter Pigeon, a widowed Bristol solicitor, and retired from the theatre; on the early death of her husband, however, she returned to the stage under her maiden name, which she continued to use throughout her career.

On 26 December 1866 Hodson made an auspicious début in London at the Prince of Wales's Theatre, during the second season of the management of Marie Wilton (later Lady Bancroft) and H. J. Byron, as Prometheus in Byron's grand new Christmas show, *Pandora's Box, or, The Young Spark and the Old Flame*. In 1867 the Queen's Theatre, Long

Henrietta Hodson (1841–1910), by unknown photographer

Acre, was built by Samuel Lamon and opened by a syndicate which included Henry *Labouchere (1831–1912), then a member of parliament and later also a well-known journalist. The original company included Charles Wyndham, Irving, J. L. Toole, Lionel Brough, Hodson, and Terry, and opened with Charles Reade's *The Double Marriage* on 24 October 1867. Here she played several parts over a three-year period. In 1868 she married Labouchere, but continued on the stage, where she maintained her reputation. On 3 September 1870 she opened the Royalty for a season under her own management, when it was said that the style of entertainment was the most ambitious the tiny theatre had yet seen. She herself appeared in Reece's *Whittington Junior and his Sensation Cat* and other burlesques. Labouchere had bought out the other lessees and the proprietor of the Queen's, and Hodson's experience of management proved invaluable to her husband. She returned there to play Ariel in a spectacular revival of *The Tempest*, followed by Imogen in *Cymbeline*. Her sister Kate joined the company as the principal soubrette. In October 1871 she entered a second period of management at the Royalty with several well-cast comedies, notably a revival of *The Honeymoon*, with herself as Juliana. There she inaugurated the system of using an unseen orchestra below the stage. In December 1871 came a popular revival of John O'Keefe's *Wild Oats*, in which she played Lady Amaranth to Wyndham's Rover. She won lavish praise as Jane Theobald

in the new comedy *Ought we to visit her?* in January 1874, although the conduct at rehearsals of one of the authors, W. S. Gilbert, was highly distasteful to her. She concluded her management in July 1874 as Peg Woffington to the Triplet of the veteran Benjamin Webster. On 29 November 1875, in Liverpool, she was the first Clytie in Joseph Hatton's dramatization of his novel of that title; she also played the part at the Olympic in 1876. She again fell out with W. S. Gilbert when, in January 1877, she played in a revival of his *Pygmalion and Galatea* at the Haymarket and she attacked his dictatorial control in a pamphlet-letter addressed to the profession. On 3 January 1878 she appeared successfully at the Queen's as Dolores, Countess Rysoor, in *Fatherland*, her husband's adaptation of Sardou's *Patrie*. Shortly afterwards she retired from the stage and from that time was known chiefly as her husband's hostess at Pope's Villa, Twickenham, and Old Palace Yard, Westminster. She was a charming and intelligent ingénue actress of individuality and high technical accomplishments, seen at her best in humorous or even farcical parts. In 1881 she was instrumental in introducing Lillie Langtry to the stage, and in 1882 she accompanied her to America; however, she made a quick return to London owing to a violent dispute with her protégée.

In 1903 Labouchere acquired Villa Christina, near Florence, to which the couple retired. Hodson died there suddenly of apoplexy on 30 October 1910. She was survived by her husband and a daughter, Mary Dorothea (Dora), who had married in 1903 the Marquess Carlo di Rudini and whose second husband was the Prince Gyalma Odescalchi. W. J. LAWRENCE, rev. J. GILLILAND

Sources H. B. Baker, *The London stage: its history and traditions from 1576 to 1888*, 2 vols. (1889) • E. Terry, *The story of my life* (1907) • *Daily Telegraph* (1 Nov 1910) • F. C. Burnand, ed., *The Catholic who's who and yearbook* (1908) • C. Scott, *The drama of yesterday and today*, 2 vols. (1899) • D. Cook, *Nights at the play* (1883) • A. L. Thorold, *Life of Henry Labouchere* (1913) • A. Davies and E. Kilmurray, *Dictionary of British portraiture*, 4 vols. (1979–81) • Hall, *Dramatic ports.* • C. E. Pascoe, ed., *The dramatic list*, 2nd edn (1880) • J. Hollingshead, *Gaiety chronicles* (1898) • J. Knight, *Theatrical notices* (1893) • m. cert. [1st marriage]
Archives Theatre Museum, London, corresp.
Likenesses London Stereoscopic Co., carte-de-visite, 1873, NPG • F. G. Netherclift, print (after photograph), Harvard TC • double portrait, photograph (with E. V. K. Terry), repro. in Terry, *Story of my life* • double portrait, photograph (with Jack Sheppard), NPG • photograph, repro. in Terry, *Story of my life* • photograph, Harvard TC • photograph, NPG [see illus.]

Hodson, Henry Vincent [Harry] (**1906–1999**), journalist, was born on 12 May 1906 at 10 Linzee Road, Hornsey, Middlesex, the elder son in the family of two sons and two daughters of Thomas Callan Hodson (d. 1953), Indian civil servant, academic administrator, and anthropologist, and his wife, Kathleen Elfrida, fourth daughter of Henry Manly, a leading London actuary. His father had entered the Indian Civil Service in 1894, served in Bengal and Assam, and retired in 1901; was registrar of East London College, University of London, from 1903 to 1914; served in France during the First World War, retiring with the rank of colonel; and thereafter pursued a career in anthropology at Cambridge, where he was reader in ethnology from

1926 to 1932 and William Wyse professor of social anthropology from 1932 to 1937.

Hodson owed his excellent education—at Gresham's School in Norfolk and at Balliol College, Oxford—to his determined ability to win scholarships even after initial failure in both cases. At Oxford he achieved in 1928 not only a first in philosophy, politics, and economics, but also a prize fellowship at All Souls, the first awarded in economics. It was his tutor Kenneth Bell who suggested he apply for All Souls, a fellowship which was, as he later recalled, 'an elevation for me, something that drew me up' ('Recollections', 1 Nov 1991).

Hodson fell instantly in love with All Souls. It was, to him, a magic garden, where young and old, scholars and men of action, the eminent and the obscure, could mingle on terms of equality, and he remained devoted to the college thereafter. His election allowed him to choose between an academic career and a non-academic one. He decided against academia in 1929, when he turned down a suggestion from his economics tutor, Lionel Robbins, to succeed him as a fellow of New College. Despite his family connections he also declined to sit for the Indian Civil Service, on the grounds—far-sighted then—that British rule in India had not long to last. He did sit for the home civil service examination and was in process of passing it when he decided to withdraw to pursue a freer, if riskier, career as a writer and journalist.

With All Souls as his weekend base (until his marriage in 1933), Hodson worked in London on *The Economist* under Walter Layton, and in the Cabinet Office on Ramsay MacDonald's Economic Advisory Council, before settling down as assistant editor (from 1931) and then editor (from 1934) of the *Round Table*. This quarterly journal, devoted to the affairs of the British empire, was sponsored (and largely written) by a remarkable group of Liberal imperialists who had been members of—or associated with—Lord Milner's 'kindergarten' in South Africa. Several of them—Lionel Curtis, Robert Brand, Geoffrey Dawson, Dougal Malcolm—were senior fellows of All Souls and thus well known to Hodson. Other members of the Round Table 'Moot' included Philip Kerr, who became Lord Lothian (the first editor), and Lionel Hichens. Some, led by Curtis, were proponents of imperial federation. Others, including Hodson, could see that the empire was already evolving in quite other directions, with the statute of Westminster as the great landmark of that process. Hodson many years later recalled Curtis as 'a great seducer' ('Recollections', 1 Nov 1991) who flattered people into taking on the jobs he wanted done. Hodson remained editor of the *Round Table* until the outbreak of the Second World War. He returned briefly to cover an interregnum in 1946. But in a sense he never left. He remained for the rest of his life a contributor of articles (over sixty in all) and an active member of the Moot. Widely read, courteous in debate, yet firm and often challenging in his opinions, he was a much-respected member of that society.

One consideration which drew Hodson to work for the Round Table in the 1930s was the requirement to travel widely in the empire and the provision of splendid introductions to many of those whom it was interesting to meet there. He travelled slowly, with leisure to digest his experiences and write thoughtfully about them. His visits to Canada, India, and Australia were the highlights; and it was in Sydney that he met his Australian wife, Margaret Elizabeth Honey (1913–2002), whom he married in Brisbane in 1933 after a whirlwind courtship. They had four sons. In India his insights, more clear-sighted than most of his peer group's, must have owed something to two unusually progressive viceroys, Lord Chelmsford and Lord Irwin, whom he knew as colleagues at All Souls.

These insights were a factor in the next major chapter in Hodson's public life: his work in (and on) the Indian subcontinent. In 1939 his age and his Cabinet Office experience pointed him towards war work as a temporary civil servant; and he served with distinction at the ministries of Information (1939–41) and Supply (1942–5). But the most important event of his war years was his period of eighteen months in India, as 'reforms commissioner' or constitutional adviser to the viceroy, in 1941–2. He was appointed by the secretary of state for India, Leo Amery, whom he knew as an All Souls colleague. Amery's views on imperial evolution were well to the right of Hodson's, but he saw the need for someone with Hodson's expertise on how other components of the empire had moved towards self-government. It turned out to be a frustrating job. Amery had wanted Hodson to have a private reporting line direct to himself. But the viceroy, Lord Linlithgow, frustrated this. Even reporting to the viceroy was hampered by bad relations with Linlithgow's masterful private secretary, Gilbert Laithwaite. The middle-level bureaucracy distrusted him as an outsider, and upset him by going back on what he regarded as promises made to him in London about his salary and housing. He was also appalled at the lack of understanding between the Delhi government and the India Office in London, which he blamed for the initial mishandling of the Cripps mission in early 1942. That mission offered the one big opportunity for constitutional advance. Hodson played an important and constructive role throughout it. But its ultimate failure, which he blamed on Stafford Cripps's deviousness as a negotiator, led rapidly to the deep-freezing of all constitutional issues for the duration of the war. Hodson's post and department were left in limbo. He wisely resigned, returning to London. Nevertheless two victories emerged unexpectedly from this defeat. First, he was able to ensure that his successor would be his deputy, V. P. Menon, who played such a crucial part in the final independence negotiations after the war. Second, his experiences in 1941–2 were a major factor in Lord Mountbatten's decision to ask him in 1963 to write a history of the transfer of power in the subcontinent and to offer him unfettered access to the enormous Mountbatten archive. *The Great Divide* was published six years later. It was an impressive book: lapidary, perceptive, dispassionate, and scrupulously fair.

Hodson was thirty-nine in 1945 when the war ended. He had no wish to stay on at the Ministry of Production. But his wide range of friends, and his diligence in keeping his friendships in good repair, meant he was not short of other possibilities. From lack of party conviction he declined to run the Conservatives' new policy research department. Other friends suggested the City. But it was to his first love, journalism, that he chose to turn. His brother-in-law, Norman Crump, who had been a colleague at *The Economist* in 1929, was now financial editor of the *Sunday Times*. Hodson's credentials were enhanced by his already being the author of several books on international economics and on the British empire and Commonwealth: *The Economics of a Changing World* (1933), *Slump and Recovery* (1938), and *The British Commonwealth and the Future* (1939). (These were followed by *Twentieth Century Empire* in 1948, *Problems in Anglo-American Relations* in 1963, and *The Diseconomics of Growth* in 1972.) He became assistant editor of the *Sunday Times* in 1946 and was editor from 1950 to 1961.

The editor's role in a great national newspaper is many-sided. Hodson brought to it great strengths and some weaknesses. With the end of wartime restrictions it was an era of opportunity but also of competition. Hodson's temperament was analytic rather than commercial. In the early 1950s the *Sunday Times*'s circulation was overtaken by *The Observer*'s. But this was reversed in 1956 when *The Observer* lost readers by opposing the Suez adventure. Hodson's own attitude to Suez was characteristic: privately he doubted the wisdom and feasibility of Sir Anthony Eden's policy, but in public he believed that the paper's duty was to support the government when the country was in effect at war.

Hodson was also criticized for his patrician detachment. His reluctance to stay for the final weekly convulsions on Saturday evening was logically correct, since there was little more an editor could do by that stage. But it was thought psychologically wrong for the captain to be seen leaving the bridge. He also had to endure many passages of arms with Lord Kemsley, the proprietor of the newspaper, whose political views were far to the right of Hodson's. Hodson won some of these battles and lost others. He blocked a demand that the paper should call for an American nuclear strike during the Korean War; and he refused to withdraw a call for the liberalization of the then draconian laws on homosexuality. On the other side, Fleet Street relished the perhaps apocryphal story of a landowner who sued the paper for printing on the front page a photograph of his prize bull with vital parts of its anatomy air-brushed out because they outraged Lady Kemsley's modesty.

Kemsley sold his papers, including the *Sunday Times*, to Roy Thomson in 1959. The contrast was total. Hodson stayed on for two years, grateful for Thomson's complete indifference to editorial policy but never comfortable with his earthy style. Thomson was equally uncomfortable with a man he found too donnish, too literary, and above all too uncommercial, and he eventually found a minor issue over which Hodson felt bound to resign. Hodson's reputation as an editor was never comparable to the brilliance of David Astor at *The Observer*. But he performed

well at the most important aspects of the job: the high-level contacts in London and across the globe, the shrewd political judgements, the elegant editorials, and above all the building up and retaining of a staff of high intellectual quality and cosmopolitan sophistication. By the time he left the *Sunday Times* its pre-eminence was established and its circulation had doubled to over 1 million.

Hodson was by then ready for a change and soon agreed to become the first director of the Ditchley Foundation (with the title 'provost of Ditchley', though that was discarded by his successors). This Anglo-American conference centre, with its superb James Gibbs house near Woodstock, had recently been founded by David Wills's generous gift of the house and money to restore it. Hodson's attention was drawn to it when Lord Sherfield, at dinner in All Souls, asked him to suggest someone who could be its first provost. The Hodsons presided at Ditchley for ten highly successful years. The foundation was built up and the prestige of its conferences established. Hodson's way of operating was simple: 'go for the best'. Conference participants included the leading figures in the relevant fields, which ranged from major international issues to culture and trade unionism. To get them to come, the charm of the great house was matched by impeccable comfort, service, food, and drink. And to make the conferences memorable, the host and hostess took infinite pains to make everyone feel welcome and to ensure that the chemistry between them was right. It was not an easy job. An average of two conferences a month meant over 700 guests a year to be persuaded to come, welcomed, and kept in touch with afterwards. Fund-raising was a constant worry and relations with the governing council were not always easy. But the magic of Ditchley was established as part of Britain's national life.

In his limited spare time from Ditchley, Hodson was able for the first time to play a major part in running the Mercers' Company, the most prominent of the City's ancient guilds, of which he was a hereditary member. He served as its master in 1965. Thereafter as a 'past-master' he had much to do with its charitable work and resurrected its affiliate, Gresham College in London, as a respected part of the new City University.

After reappointment for a second five-year term at Ditchley in 1966 (despite a heart attack the previous year), Hodson was looking forward to a third term, which would have taken him to the age of seventy. So it was a bad shock when the then council chairman, Lord Caccia, who made no secret of disliking him, told him in 1970 that his successor had already been selected and would take over the following year. But Hodson's resilience was once again demonstrated when in 1973 he embarked on his final career achievement: his twenty years as editor and later consultant editor of the *Annual Register*, the indispensable reference book and record of world events started by Edmund Burke in 1758. Hodson enlarged and modernized it, adding an editorial and sections on arms control, the environment, technology, and sport, as well as economic statistics. For several years he followed Burke's example in writing a substantial part of the work himself. He finally retired in 1993, though he remained active in the Round Table and other causes until his death, on 27 March 1999 at the Chelsea and Westminster Hospital, London. He was survived by his wife and four sons. A memorial service was held at St Mary-le-Bow, Cheapside, where he had regularly worshipped, on 12 May 1999.

The length, vigour, and variety of Hodson's life were remarkable. But it was full of disappointments as well as of success. He loved and in many ways epitomized the British establishment of his day. But he never felt securely part of it. He would have liked to have had a classical education, to have attended one of the great public schools, to have independent wealth, above all to receive public recognition. His failure to appear on any honours list was a sadness, and not easy to explain. His achievements were manifest. On social and professional occasions his charm and courtesy were legendary. His circle of friends was vast and far-flung. But he also had plenty of enemies, who thought him a snob and found him cantankerous in business dealings. He quarrelled over the terms of his employment in India, at the *Sunday Times*, and at Ditchley. But the real explanation for the lack of recognition probably lay deeper. In two respects, Hodson did not fit into the categories with which British public life was familiar. Temperamentally, he was a scholar who led mainly a life of action. Pure scholars thought him a worldling, men of the world thought him too academic. He also upset his contemporaries' notions of political faith: he was too radical for conservative tastes and too conservative for radicals. He was probably happiest as provost of Ditchley, where he saw his role as requiring him to play, for a time, the *grand seigneur* he would have liked to have been; or as a young man at Balliol and All Souls, with no doubts about his title to a small share in the Garden of Eden.

ROBERT WADE-GERY

Sources *The Times* (29 March 1999) · *The Independent* (31 March 1999) · *Daily Telegraph* (15 April 1999) · *WWW* · H. Hobson, P. Knightley, and L. Russell, *The pearl of days: an intimate memoir of the Sunday Times, 1822–1972* (1972) · personal knowledge (2004) · private information (2004) · b. cert. · d. cert. · 'Recollections', 1 Nov 1991 [talk at All Souls College, Oxford]
Archives SOAS, corresp. relating to partition of India | BL, letters to Albert Mansbridge, Add. MS 65259 · Bodl. Oxf., corresp. with L. G. Curtis · NA Scot., corresp. with Philip Kerr, eleventh marquess of Lothian
Likenesses photograph, *c*.1950, repro. in *The Independent* · J. Teesdale, portrait, 1962, repro. in *Daily Telegraph* · photograph, *c*.1990–1999, repro. in *The Times* · photograph, repro. in Hobson, Knightley, and Russell, *Pearl of days*, 274
Wealth at death £132,468: probate, 26 Jan 2000, *CGPLA Eng. & Wales*

Hodson, Margaret. *See* Holford, Margaret (*bap.* 1778, *d.* 1852).

Hodson, Septimus (1768–1833). *See under* Holford, Margaret (*bap.* 1778, *d.* 1852).

Hodson, William (*fl.* 1617–1640), poet and religious writer, was born in London, the son of John Hodson (*d.* 1628), citizen. He followed his lawyer brother John up to Peterhouse, Cambridge, as a pensioner, matriculating a decade after his elder sibling on 3 May 1617. He graduated BA in 1621 and MA in 1624. Thereafter he seems to have lived at Tottenham in Middlesex; he was resident there in 1628 when he acted as executor for his father's will. The only known portrait of Hodson is an engraving by the royalist William Marshall (published as the frontispiece to his *Credo resurrectionem carnis* of 1636), in which he appears as a blond-haired cavalier gentleman in a fine satin suit with a wide lace collar. Marshall illustrated all three of Hodson's theological tracts.

At the death of James VI and I, when 'each poetaster blubbers forth a verse', Hodson joined them, producing a ninety-five-line poem, printed between heavy mourning bands, entitled *The plurisie of sorrow, let blood in the eye-veine, or, The muses teares for the death of our late soveraigne* (1625; quotation at sig. A*3r, line 50). In this unlikely classical poem he drew on Pliny's *Natural History* for a conceit based on the death of the queen bee. To this poem the young graduate appended twelve lines commending the late king's scholarship and a thirty-six-line verse welcoming Charles as monarch, 'Illustrissimo regi'. The little volume closes with three pages of distichs on the mottoes engraved on the new coinage.

As a gentleman scholar Hodson wrote a tract on the eleventh article of the Nicene creed, *Credo resurrectionem carnis*, which ran to a second, expanded, edition in 1636, after the first, which had been entered for publication on 20 April 1633, was destroyed 'by some deficiencie, suffred in the printer's stocks' (*Credo*, sig. A3v). Two other theological tracts from his pen—*The Holy Sinner* (1639), based on Luke 7, and *The Divine Cosmographer* (1640), a tract on Psalm 8— are the serious writing of a pious layman living in the environs of London, grounded in the theology of James VI and I whom he saluted as 'of our nobles the most skilful in Divinitie' (*Divine Cosmographer*, 9), who kept some contact with his Cambridge contemporaries; John Cosin, Thomas Bainbridge, and Ralph Brownrigg are among those who licensed both works for publication.

It is not known when after 1640 Hodson died.

NICHOLAS W. S. CRANFIELD

Sources Venn, *Alum. Cant.* · T. A. Walker, ed., *Admissions to Peterhouse or St Peter's College in the University of Cambridge* (1912)
Likenesses W. Marshall, line engraving, BM, NPG; repro. in W. Hodson, *Credo resurrectionem carnis* (1636), frontispiece

Hodson, William Stephen Raikes (1821–1858), army officer in the East India Company, was born on 19 March 1821 at Maisemore Court, near Gloucester, third son of the Revd George Hodson, chaplain to the bishop of Gloucester and later archdeacon of Stafford and canon of Lichfield, and his wife, Mary, daughter of John Stephen, a master of chancery. Hodson was educated at home, and from 1834 to 1840 at Rugby School, where he was head of his house. According to his former fag, 'Hodson was never really an Arnold man' (Cork, 11). He entered Trinity College, Cambridge in 1840, gaining his BA in 1844.

Hodson began his military career in Guernsey with a militia commission, but in 1845 entered the East India Company's service. He landed at Calcutta on 13 September 1845, went to Agra, and joined the 2nd Bengal grenadiers, then part of the governor-general's escort. He served in

William Stephen Raikes Hodson (1821–1858), by unknown engraver, pubd 1859

the First Anglo-Sikh War, at the battles of Mudki, Ferozeshahr, and Sobraon. He formed a poor opinion of the Bengal sepoy but was to develop a remarkable empathy with the Sikhs. He was soon after transferred to the 1st Bengal European fusiliers. In 1847 he was appointed adjutant of the corps of guides, and with them he gained the experience and displayed the powers which afterwards made him an outstanding leader of irregular cavalry and exceptional intelligence officer. For his services he received the thanks of the governor-general. When in 1849 the Punjab was annexed, he was transferred to the civil department as assistant commissioner, and was stationed for some time at Amritsar. After a spell in the hills establishing a school at Sanawar, Kasauli, for the children of British private soldiers, for which task he had been specially selected by Henry Lawrence, Hodson accompanied Lawrence on an expedition to Kashmir, newly taken from the Sikhs.

On 5 January 1852 at Calcutta, Hodson married Susan, widow of John Mitford of Exbury, Hampshire; their daughter, Olivia, was born in 1853 but died in infancy. Susan died in 1884. By the first week in March 1852 Hodson had resumed his duties at Kasauli as assistant commissioner; in September 1852 he was delighted to be given command of the guides. It was his success in dealing with incursions along the north-west frontier that brought Hodson to such prominent notice.

Hodson's career to this time had been successful; but his rapid rise, apparent arrogance, and outspoken criticism of others had made him enemies. There was confusion in the regimental accounts, and charges of dishonesty as well as of harsh treatment of his Indian soldiers were brought against him. An inquiry was held by a special military court, which ended its sittings in January 1855. Its report was unfavourable, and he was removed from command. Hodson appealed, and a second inquiry, under Major Reynell Taylor, after a long investigation, reported on 13 February 1856 exonerating Hodson. The second report was only sent in May 1857 to Sir Henry Daly, commandant of the guides, with a minute from Lord Canning expressing dissatisfaction and directing explanations. Daly was soon afterwards wounded, and Hodson, who temporarily took over command, obtained the report, which was found in his trunk after his death. Hodson also allegedly embezzled the funds of the Lawrence Asylum at Kasauli and the pay of another officer. Sir George Lawrence, Lord Lawrence, and apparently Lord Canning believed him guilty of embezzlement.

Hodson had rejoined the 1st fusiliers at Dagshai, practically beginning his military career again, but gaining the favourable attention of the commander-in-chief, General Anson. On 10 May 1857 occurred the outbreak of mutiny at Meerut, followed by the massacre of Delhi. Hodson rose to the opportunity, and, after going with the 1st fusiliers to Ambala and then to Karnal, the commander-in-chief ordered him to raise and command a new regiment of irregular horse, which became known as Hodson's Horse. He was also put in charge of the intelligence department, and operated a network of spies among the mutineers. In June 1857 he was at Delhi, and there met his old corps of guides, who received him with great enthusiasm. Hodson was one of the junior officers who unsuccessfully urged an early assault on the city. He killed an Indian officer, Bisharat Ali, allegedly because he owed Ali money. Delhi was captured on 20 September 1857, and on the following day Hodson obtained, with some difficulty, General Archdale Wilson's permission to capture the king of Delhi, Bahadur Shah. He went with only fifty of his own men to Humayun's tomb, where the king had taken refuge. The king surrendered and Hodson brought him to the commander-in-chief, in spite of the thousands following them, any one of whom could have shot Hodson. This seizure of the king was considered to be perhaps the most striking blow the rebellion had received.

Next day, 22 September, with a hundred picked men, Hodson again went to Humayun's tomb, where the three *shahzadahs*, princes of Delhi, had taken refuge. Hodson demanded their surrender; they came out and were sent away towards the city under a guard, travelling in *tufhs* (covered bullock carts). The tomb was crowded with thousands of the servants and hangers-on of the palace and city. Hodson demanded instant surrender of their arms. Despite the paucity of his force, they obeyed, and, after leaving the arms with a guard, he followed after the prisoners. A large mob had collected, and were threatening the guard. After appealing to the crowd, saying that these were the butchers who had murdered helpless women and children, Hodson took a carbine from one of his men and shot the princes. He afterwards wrote that he had destroyed 'the villains who ordered the massacre of our women and children, and stood by and witnessed the foul barbarity' (Hodson, 297). The critical situation in India, the belief that the princes had been involved in the massacre of Europeans at Delhi, and the need for immediate action for his and his soldiers' safety gained for Hodson's action the approval of most Europeans then in India, but he was criticized, then and long after.

After the fall of Delhi, Hodson's Horse went towards Cawnpore with a convoy of supplies for the commander-in-chief's army, and had much hard fighting. One of Hodson's most brilliant exploits was his ride from Mainpuri to the commander-in-chief's camp at Miran-ki-sarai to open communications between the two forces: he rode 94 miles on one horse in a day, through a country swarming with enemies.

On 6 March Hodson was before Lucknow. On 11 March he went as a volunteer with his friend Brigadier Napier, who was directing an attack on the begum's palace in the *kaisarbagh*. British soldiers were clearing the buildings of rebels. Though warned to await the arrival of gunpowder bags, impulsively Hodson alone entered a room in which were rebels, and was shot through the liver. He died next day, 12 March 1858, at Banks' House, and was buried at La Martinière College, Lucknow, on the same day. Sir Colin Campbell and others praised his military brilliance and his bravery. Yet, apparently indicative of his reputation, it was soon said that he died while looting. This was untrue, though he may have intended looting. While looting—by British, Sikhs, and Gurkhas, officers and other ranks—was widespread, Hodson was allegedly 'the most notorious looter in the whole army' (Hibbert, 361). General Pelham Burn, Sir Henry Daly, and Sir Henry Norman all alleged his looting. That loot was not officially found among his possessions after his death and that his wife left under £400 in 1884 were hardly conclusive evidence of his innocence. The case against him was apparently strong, if unproven. Long after his death the controversy over his moral character, including his alleged looting, continued, with accusers, notably R. Bosworth Smith in his *Life of Lord Lawrence* (1885 edn), and defenders, notably Hodson's brother, the Revd G. H. Hodson, in his *Hodson of Hodson's Horse* (1883 and later editions), presenting Hodson as an English Christian hero.

Hodson was described as 'A tallish man with yellow hair, a pale, smooth face, heavy moustache, and large, restless, rather unforgiving eyes' (Hibbert, 289). His favoured weapon was a hog-spear. Apparently more the barbarian warrior than the Arnoldian ideal of the Victorian gentleman, he was an exceptional soldier, horseman, swordsman, and leader of Indian irregular cavalry. Lord Roberts called him 'a brilliant soldier' (Roberts, 137). He was brave, hard, reckless, impatient, and impulsive, and he enjoyed battle. He despised most other officers, including many of his seniors. He was also ruthless, and may have been unscrupulous and dishonest.

H. R. LUARD, rev. JAMES LUNT

Sources B. J. Cork, *Rider on a grey horse: a life of Hodson of Hodson's horse* (1958) · W. S. R. Hodson, *Hodson of Hodson's horse*, ed. G. H. Hodson, 5th edn (1889) [pre-1883 edns entitled *Twelve years of a soldier's life in India*] · L. J. Trotter, *Hodson* (1901) · F. G. Cardew, *Hodson's horse* (1928) · Lord Roberts [F. S. Roberts], *Forty-one years in India*, 1 (1897) · C. Hibbert, *The great mutiny, India, 1857* (1978); repr. (1980)
Archives NAM, corresp., diaries, and papers
Likenesses black and white photograph, repro. in Cork, *Rider on a grey horse*, frontispiece · engraving, repro. in W. S. R. Hodson, *Twelve years of a soldier's life in India* (1859), frontispiece [*see illus.*]
Wealth at death £170: *DNB*

Hody, Humphrey (1659–1707), Church of England clergyman and classical scholar, was born on 1 January 1659 at Odcombe, Somerset, the son of Richard Hody (*b.* 1621/2), rector of Odcombe, and his wife, Jane. He matriculated at Wadham College, Oxford, on 10 March 1676, at the same time as two elder brothers, and was admitted scholar on 28 September 1677. He graduated BA in 1679, proceeded MA in 1682, BD in 1689, and DD in 1693. He was admitted fellow of Wadham College in July 1685, and was elected subdean of Wadham in 1682, humanity lecturer in 1685, catechist in 1686, dean in 1688, sub-warden in 1689, and bursar in 1691 and 1692. In 1690 Edward Stillingfleet, bishop of Worcester, made him his chaplain. John Tillotson, archbishop of Canterbury, appointed him his chaplain in May 1694, and he continued in this office under Tillotson's successor, Thomas Tenison. Tenison presented Hody to the living of Chartham, Kent, in 1695, which he quickly exchanged for the united parishes of St Michael Royal and St Martin Vintry, London (from which he resigned in 1702). On 15 March 1698 Hody was appointed regius professor of Greek at the University of Oxford. In November 1701 he became rector of Monks Risborough, Buckinghamshire, and on 1 August 1704 was made archdeacon of Oxford. He married Edith Daniel (*d.* 1736), but they had no children.

Hody was praised, even by critics such as Thomas Hearne, for his industry, memory, and zeal for learning. These characteristics are apparent in his writings. In his earliest publication, *Contra historiam Aristeae de LXX interpretibus dissertatio* (Oxford, 1684), Hody demonstrates that the letter of Aristeas containing an account of the production of the Septuagint was a late forgery. Subsequently, along with Henry Aldrich and Edward Bernard, he issued an edition of Aristeas's *History* (Oxford, 1692). He also wrote the 'Prolegomena' to the Greek chronicle of John Malada (Oxford, 1691).

Following the revolution of 1688 Hody became engaged in the controversy surrounding the oath of allegiance to William and Mary imposed by parliament in 1689 upon all beneficed clergy. Six bishops and about 400 lower clergy refused to swear the oaths and were deprived of their livings in early 1690. These nonjurors refused to accept the validity of the new bishops. About April 1691, the time that the first appointments to the vacant sees were made by King William, Hody and Richard Bentley found in the Bodleian Library at Oxford a Greek manuscript of the late thirteenth century which could be used to bolster the case of the new bishops. Ascribed to the Constantinopolitan historian Nicepherus Callistus, this treatise contained a list of patriarchs of Constantinople who had been unjustly deposed and replaced by uncanonical appointees, and yet neither the people nor the ejected patriarchs refused communion with them unless they were heretics. To Hody the parallel seemed obvious, and he and Bentley proceeded to translate the treatise into English and publish it, with a dedication to Tillotson, under the title *The Unreasonableness of a Separation from the New Bishops* (London, 1691). Hody also published a Latin version at Oxford in 1691.

Hody's friend, the nonjuror Henry Dodwell, replied with *A Vindication of the Deprived Bishops* (London, 1692), in which he demonstrates that the manuscript was not by Nicepherus and had been inaccurately translated. Furthermore, he argues that the treatise was written to explain a special case, and that in nearly all the instances in the manuscript the deprived bishops had either been pressured to resign or some synodical proceedings had been taken against them. Attached to the *Vindication* is a page entitled 'The canons in the Baroccian manuscript, omitted by Mr. Hody'. These canons, clearly belonging to the manuscript, show that only synodical deprivations are valid.

Hody answered with two works. In *A Letter ... to a Friend Concerning a Collection of Canons Said to be Deceitfully Omitted* (Oxford, 1692) he lamely argues from circumstantial and textual evidence that the canons are unconnected with the treatise. In *The Case of Sees Vacant by an Unjust or Uncanonical Deprivation Stated* (London, 1693), he concedes in the preface that 'all Lay Deprivations are invalid', but insists that the civil power is irresistible, and challenges his opponents to produce historical examples to the contrary. Dodwell retorted with *A Defence of the Vindication* (London, 1697) in which he sets forth an argument for the complete independence of the church from the state. This remained unanswered until 1699.

In the meantime Hody published two more works. The first was *The Resurrection of the (same) Body Asserted* (London, 1694) in which he sets out to prove that the resurrection of the corporeal body is the doctrine of the gospel. In addition, 'and designed only for the more Curious', he attempts to demonstrate that this was also the belief of 'the heathens and the Jews' (H. Hody, *Resurrection Asserted*, 1694, preface). The second was *Animadversions on Two Pamphlets Lately Published by Mr. Collier* (London, 1696). Tenison had asked Hody to respond to Jeremy Collier, who had written two pamphlets in defence of himself and two other nonjuring ministers who had pronounced absolution on the Jacobite conspirator Sir William Parkyns on the scaffold prior to his execution for treason for his part in the assassination plot. Such an act, says Hody, was an offence to both the church and the state.

In 1699 Hody returned to his feud with Dodwell over authority in the church. This time the issue was the rights of the convocation of Canterbury. In his *Some Thoughts on a Convocation, and the Notion of its Divine Right* (London, 1699) Hody produces his answer both to Dodwell's *Defence* and Samuel Hill's *Municipium Ecclesiasticum* (London, 1697). Quoting copiously from 'that Great Man' (H. Hody, *Some Thoughts*, 1699, 30) Richard Hooker and 'the great [Hugo] Grotius' (ibid., 19) Hody argues that, according to the English constitution, English kings have the power to summon convocations and that such convocations cannot make any canon or constitution without the king's approval. Furthermore, there is nothing in scripture, natural law, or early church history, after the emperor was Christian, which suggests that the clergy have a divine right to independence that would override the constitution. Hody followed this up two years later with a more substantial study of the English constitution entitled *A History of English Councils and Convocations* (London, 1701).

In 1705 Hody published his last work, *De bibliorum textibus originalibus* (Oxford, 1705), in which he revisits his earlier studies on the Septuagint.

Hody died on 20 January 1707 while travelling to Bath, and was buried in Wadham College chapel. In his will, made in November 1706, he wished that all copies of his last book unsold at the time of his death should be 'disposed of beyond Sea and let none be sold in England besides those perhaps of the larger paper' (PRO, PROB 11/493, sig. 85). He gave first choice of his library to the university, and what it did not want was to go to the fellows' library at Wadham (under conditions for their security which suggest that Hody did not entirely trust the fellows). He left £100 each to his parish of birth and to his old London and present Buckinghamshire livings for binding out poor children as apprentices on condition that they had attended catechism. But the bulk of his property—in Somerset and Oxford—was to go to the maintenance of his wife during her life (unless she remarried), and then to pass to Wadham College for the establishment of six exhibitions in Greek and four in Hebrew. Edith Hody died on 28 November 1736 and the first Hody exhibitioners were elected in June 1738. Among the papers Hody left behind at his death was a manuscript entitled 'An account of those learned Grecians, who retired into Italy', which was published posthumously by Samuel Jebb as *De Graecis illustribus* (London, 1742). Prefixed to this is a short biography of Hody in Latin. His portrait by Thomas Forster was presented to Wadham College by his widow.

MARTIN GREIG

Sources R. B. Gardiner, ed., *The registers of Wadham College, Oxford*, 2 vols. (1889–95) · M. Goldie, 'The nonjurors, episcopacy, and the origins of the convocation controversy', *Ideology and conspiracy: aspects of Jacobitism, 1689–1759*, ed. E. Cruickshanks (1982), 15–35 · *DNB* · muniments, Wadham College, Oxford, 10/2/4/3, 10/2/4/5 · will, PRO, PROB 11/493, sig. 85 · G. Every, *The high church party, 1688–1718* (1956) · Foster, *Alum. Oxon.*
Archives Bodl. Oxf., collections and papers | Bodl. Oxf., Rawl. MS d. 1221; Add. MS A 65 · Wadham College, Oxford, muniments
Likenesses T. Forster, oils, before 1708, Wadham College, Oxford · attrib. W. Sonmans, oils, before 1708, Bodl. Oxf. · portrait, before 1708, Wadham College, Oxford · Kraus, line engraving, BM, NPG · M. Vandergucht, engraving (after T. Forster), repro. in H. Hody, *De bibliorum textibus originalibus* (1705) · M. Vandergucht, line engraving (after T. Forster), BM, NPG
Wealth at death an estate in parish of Merriott, Somerset, and property in the parish of St Mary Magdalen, Oxford; provided for the foundation of ten exhibitions at Wadham; books donated to Wadham College, Oxford, and the Bodleian; bequeathed £100 each to the parishes of Odcombe in Somerset, St Michael Royal

and St Martin Vintry in London, and Monks Risborough in Buckinghamshire: will, PRO, PROB 11/493, sig. 85

Hody, Sir John (d. 1441/2), justice, was the son of Thomas Hody, lord of the manor of Kington Magna in Dorset, and of Margaret, daughter of John Cole of Nethway in Devon. His grandfather was Adam Hody, who may have been born a serf. John Hody held estates at Stowell in Somerset (purchased in the 1420s) and at Pilsdon in Dorset, the latter through his wife, Elizabeth (d. 1473), daughter of John Jewe of Whitfield, near Wiveliscombe, Somerset. They had several daughters and five sons, one of whom, William *Hody, became attorney-general in 1485 and chief baron of the exchequer in 1486.

Hody was a member of parliament for Shaftesbury (1421–7), Devon (1431), and Somerset (1433–7). Retained by the dean and chapter of Wells, 1414–17, he appears in the year-books from 1425. He argued in the exchequer chamber in 1426, was described as an apprentice in 1429, and became a serjeant-at-law in 1438, acting as serjeant of the avenary and clerk of the market of the royal household in 1441. From 1428 onwards he held commissions in the west country and the home counties, mainly of inquiry (the inquiries included concealed crown income and piracy), gaol delivery, and oyer and terminer (Cornwall and Devon in 1440, Oxfordshire and Berkshire in 1441), and was also a justice of assize on the western circuit (1439) and on the eastern circuit (1440). At the same time he was an escheator in Somerset and Dorset (1431–2), recorder of Bristol (c.1438), and a justice of the peace in Somerset (1430), Berkshire (1439), Staffordshire, Shropshire, and Gloucestershire (1439–40), Kent, Surrey, and Sussex (1440), and Essex (1441).

Although never a puisne justice of the king's bench, Hody became its chief justice in 1440, the year in which he was knighted. In 1441 he was appointed umpire in arbitration involving Joan Dogge, later a celebrated litigant in *Shipton* v. *Dogge* (1442), an action debated by all the judges in the exchequer chamber and a landmark in the development of contract law. Retained by Peterborough Abbey (1433/4), by the earl of Stafford (1437), and by the duchy of Lancaster (1438/9), he was by Henry VI's order summoned to Sheen in August 1440 to discuss threatened riots. In 1441 he condemned to execution Roger Bolingbroke, the priest implicated in the witchcraft trials involving Eleanor Cobham, duchess of Gloucester. In December 1441 he was summoned to parliament, but was prevented by death from attending. His will, stating his wish to be buried in Woolavington church, Somerset, is dated 17 December 1441, and the keepers of goods for the church of Tintinhull in Somerset recorded thereafter as an expenditure of 6s. 8d. 'a legacy from Sir John Hody, Kt.' His widow, Elizabeth, afterwards married Robert Cappes, who was sheriff of Somerset and Dorset in 1444/5. NORMAN DOE

Sources Sainty, *Judges* · Baker, *Serjeants* · R. A. Griffiths, *King and country: England and Wales in the fifteenth century* (1991) · C. Rawcliffe, *The Staffords, earls of Stafford and dukes of Buckingham, 1394–1521*, Cambridge Studies in Medieval Life and Thought, 3rd ser., 11 (1978) · S. E. Thorne and J. H. Baker, eds., *Readings and moots at the inns of court in the fifteenth century*, 1, SeldS, 71 (1954) · R. Somerville, *History*

of the duchy of Lancaster, 1265–1603 (1953) · *Chancery records* · HoP, *Commons, 1386–1421* · J. B. Hyson, 'The history of a medieval village, gathered from ancient sources', *Somerset Archaeological and Natural History Society*, 32 (1886) · E. F. Jacob, ed., *The register of Henry Chichele, archbishop of Canterbury, 1414–1443*, 2, CYS, 42 (1937), 605–6

Hody, Sir William (d. 1524), judge, was the second son of Sir John *Hody (d. 1441/2), lord chief justice, and his wife, Elizabeth (d. 1473), daughter and heir of John Jewe of Pilsdon, Dorset. He was almost certainly a member of the Middle Temple by the later years of Henry VI, and is mentioned as counsel in the year books for 1475. He was seated at Gothelney in Somerset at the time when he became a justice of the peace for that county in 1470. He also had property at West Bower in the same county, and part of his mother's inheritance at Pilsdon. He married Eleanor, daughter of Baldwin Malet of Corypool, Somerset.

In 1472–5 Hody served as member of parliament for Totnes, and in 1483 for Bridgwater. At the beginning of Henry VII's reign Hody was appointed attorney-general, but served only until 29 October 1486, when he was made chief baron of the exchequer. He was knighted in January 1487. Though not a serjeant-at-law he was qualified as chief baron to act as an assize judge, and went on the Oxford circuit until 1507. After a very long tenure of the office of chief baron, and at what must have been a considerable age, he retired on 10 February 1522. He died on 18 June 1524. Although he had two sons, his heirs were his two granddaughters. J. H. BAKER

Sources Foss, *Judges*, 5.187–8 · J. C. Wedgwood and A. D. Holt, *History of parliament*, 1: *Biographies of the members of the Commons house, 1439–1509* (1936), 461 · *The reports of Sir John Spelman*, ed. J. H. Baker, 2, SeldS, 94 (1978), 2.382, 390 · J. L. Vivian, ed., *The visitations of the county of Devon, comprising the herald's visitations of 1531, 1564, and 1620* (privately printed, Exeter, [1895]), 490 · Sainty, *Judges*, 94 · *Les reports des cases* (1680), Hilary 15, Edward IV, fol. 19, plea 8 [Year Books] · PRO, C 142/41/42 · PRO, C 67/48, m. 33 · PRO, C 67/52, m. 12

Hoechstetter, Daniel (1525–1581), mining promoter, was born in Augsburg, Germany, the second son of the twenty-year-old Joachim Hoechstetter and his wife, Anna, daughter of Eitelhans Langenmantel, patrician and Anabaptist. Joachim died, probably in Denmark, in 1535. At some time before 1541 his relatives placed Daniel Hoechstetter with a branch of his grandmother's Wieland family, who trained him at their lead, copper, and silver mines and smelting works in the Rauris and Gastein valleys in the Tyrol, part of the archbishopric of Salzburg. He was apparently fully trained by 1549 and began to operate independently. On 16 July 1553 he married, in Augsburg, the twenty-year-old Radagunda, daughter of the prominent Augsburg merchant Leonhard Stammler. They had five sons and five daughters, of whom three sons and four daughters survived infancy. Between December 1555 and January 1557 he returned to live in Augsburg with his growing family.

Nothing is known about Hoechstetter's activities until he was authorized, by Elizabeth I's signet of 8 July 1563, to prospect for minerals in England, which he did during that summer. For reasons which can only be guessed at, he decided to establish himself near Keswick in Cumberland

and returned in the following year with Hans Loner, a relative by marriage, and twelve German workers, to set up works and to prospect more fully. In 1564 he also concluded an agreement with the Augsburg firm of Haug, Langnauer & Co. to finance the enterprise with himself as manager, and to invite English participation. By 1568 they were incorporated as one of the first two English joint-stock companies, the Society of the Mines Royal, with some important royal servants and London merchants as members. The English partners became increasingly reluctant to supplement their original investment of £1200 per share and finally refused in 1580, and agreed to lease the works and mines to Hoechstetter and 'customer' Thomas Smith, one of the wealthiest London merchants.

Hoechstetter had meanwhile built up the works, from a large smelter in three storeys to coal-sheds, workshops, a stamp mill, and housing in Brigham, almost a mile east of Keswick on the River Greta. They produced fair quantities of copper and a little silver but, with a declining market for copper, could not cover the costs of installations and the travelling expenses of almost 150 Austrian and German craftsmen, a total which amounted to about £50,000. The lease from 1580 worked well enough to provide some regular rent for the society, even after Hoechstetter's death just before 14 May 1581, when he was buried in Crosthwaite church. Radagunda was buried next to her husband in 1610.

On fragmentary evidence, Hoechstetter impresses as a reasonable and well-educated man, with a typical prospector's irrepressible enthusiasms. At first two of his sons, Emanuel (who died on 22 August 1614) with Daniel Hechstetter (as the English descendants called themselves), and then Daniel with Emanuel's son Joseph, continued, more modestly and successfully, to operate the works and mines until about 1634, when they went bankrupt. GEORGE HAMMERSLEY, rev.

Sources G. Hammersley, Daniel Hechstetter the younger, memorabilia and letters, 1600–1639 (1988) · F. Blendinger, 'Hoechstetter', Neue Deutsche Biographie, 11 (1972), 302–5 · W. Hoechstetter, Stammtafel der Hoechstetter (1976)

Hoellering, George Michael (1897–1980), film-maker and exhibitor, was born on 20 July 1897 in Baden, near Vienna, Austria, the third of four children of Georg Höllering, musician and impresario, and his wife, Maria Magdalene. Watching his father at work in the theatre was an early inspiration, but on the outbreak of war in 1914 he joined the Austrian army and fought on the eastern front, where he narrowly avoided serious injury. After the war he took over rehearsals at the Wiener Komödienhaus when his father fell ill, but his real enthusiasm was now film and, with his father's support, he entered the profession that would later bring him distinction by becoming a cinema-owner at the age of twenty.

Hoellering moved to Berlin in the early 1920s and, like many, sought an opportunity to enter film production, while acquiring photographic and editing skills. His first chance came through meeting a surgeon who wanted to film complex operations with an overhead camera, which Hoellering helped him do. This led to work as a producer and director with the Association of German Documentary Producers, but his aim was dramatic production and this remained elusive until, in 1931, the collapsing left-wing film company Prometheus, which had previously triumphed with Battleship Potemkin, hired him to co-produce a film about the workers' self-help movement, directed by Slatan Dudow and written by the rising poet and playwright Bertolt Brecht. Despite Prometheus's bankruptcy, he managed to steer Kuhle Wampe to completion, with the help of the communist entrepreneur Willi Münzenberg and a Swiss company, Praesens-Film. The film's success in 1932 was short-lived: when the Nazis came to power a year later, it and all its makers were black-listed.

Hoellering returned to Austria, but found no work and went on to Hungary, where in 1935 he made a stirring semi-documentary account of the herdsmen of the Great Plain, Hortobágy, with the involvement of the famous writer Zsigsmond Móricz and the composer Laszlo Lajtha. Although this caught the mood of the time, matching other epics of rural survival being made by Robert Flaherty in Ireland and Pare Lorentz in the United States, its portrayal of 'backwardness' was unpopular with the Hungarian authorities. The menace of Hitler determined Hoellering's final move, to Britain, in 1936. Elsie *Cohen (d. 1972) showed Hortobágy at the Academy Cinema on Oxford Street, London, where Hoellering became a partner and, from 1944 until his death, managing director.

Hoellering was planning another feature, about a typical factory worker and his girl, when war broke out and he was interned on the Isle of Man. Here, he learned how to cook endless turnip dishes, read T. S. Eliot's Murder in the Cathedral, and met the artist Peter Strausfeld, whose distinctive linocut posters would help establish the Academy's unique image. He was released to make Ministry of Information films and an inspirational documentary, Message from Canterbury (1944). Another documentary about the history of art, Shapes and Forms, followed in 1949; but Hoellering's main ambition was now to film Murder in the Cathedral, for which he gained Eliot's enthusiastic support and the film won awards for best costume design and art direction at the Venice Film Festival of 1951. Though somewhat stiff and severe in style, this belonged to a widespread desire to link cinema with contemporary art, but despite its prestige no other productions followed.

Hoellering married twice. His first wife, Dora Constance Lehmann, was previously married and had a son, Ivo, before she married Hoellering in 1929 in Baden, Austria. Their only child, Andrew, was born in Vienna in 1932, and Dora died in England in 1955. Hoellering subsequently married on 24 November 1956 Anne Allnatt (b. 1925/6), daughter of Alfred Ernest Allnatt, a building contractor.

After 1951 Hoellering devoted his energies to distribution and exhibition, first with his own company, Film Traders, then in partnership with Bill Pallanca's Connoisseur Films, which had offices in the Academy block, exercising his famously exacting judgement in selecting films and film-makers often far ahead of public taste. Alongside such Academy mainstays as Michel Carné's Les enfants du

Paradis (1945) and Akira Kurosawa's *Seven Samurai* (1954), he showed the first fruits of the Soviet 'thaw', from Grigori Chukrai's *Ballad of a Soldier* (1959) to Andrey Tarkovsky's début, *Ivan's Childhood* (1964). The Czech new wave of Jiri Menzel, Milos Forman, and their contemporaries was equally associated with the Academy; as was the lyrical formalism of the Hungarian Miklos Jancso, for whom Hoellering understandably felt a special affinity. Potential scandal was apparently defused by the Academy's reputation for high seriousness, which allowed Joseph Strick's *Ulysses* (1967), an adaptation of James Joyce's novel, and Dusan Makavejev's *WR: Mysteries of the Organism* (1971) to show at length, and highly profitably. In 1964 the surrealist Angus McBean redecorated the Academy cinemas in crimson *trompe l'oeil* drapery, and a third screen was later added, while office rents subsidized films that lost money at the box office.

Above all, Hoellering will be remembered for his fierce championing of original film-makers, from whatever quarter. He showed Nagisa Oshima, initially to empty houses, and he helped launch the reputations of Ingmar Bergman, Satyajit Ray, and Roman Polanski, as well as that of Ken Loach, when he ran *Kes*, and Bill Douglas, whose uncompromising *Trilogy* he staunchly supported. But the Academy was not only devoted to 'art cinema' from Europe or the Third World. Hoellering was proud of having rescued the liberal western *The Ox-Bow Incident* (1943) and Nicholas Ray's *They Live by Night* (1948) from their American distributors' indifference; and three decades later he would enthusiastically promote Martin Scorsese's *Mean Streets* (1973). For years the Academy ran a regular Buster Keaton festival and thus helped to create a new audience for this neglected comic genius. Hoellering died on 10 February 1980 in the West Suffolk Hospital, Bury St Edmunds, Suffolk. He was survived by his second wife, Anne.

At the time of Hoellering's death, specialized film distribution and exhibition were already changing rapidly, and his uncompromising principles no longer held sway. New competitors had appeared, and compromises with television and video were imminent. Hoellering's high standards of programming ('not really an Academy film', he would say), of technical quality, and of publicity, with impeccable press notes and posters that were eagerly collected, all belonged to a disappearing era of cinema. His stepson and publicist Ivo Jarosy, also his closest aide, continued to run the cinemas until 1987, when the premises were sold to a department store chain.   IAN CHRISTIE

Sources I. Nemeskürty, *A pictorial guide to the Hungarian cinema* (1983) · D. Powell, 'George Hoellering, 1898–1980', *Sight and Sound*, 49 (1979–80), 122–3 · private information (2004) [Andrew Hoellering, son] · B. Brewster and C. MacCabe, 'Making *Kuhle Wampe*: an interview with George Hoellering', *Screen*, 15/4 (1975), 71–9 · *The Times* (14 Feb 1980) · m. cert. [Anne Allnatt] · d. cert.

Hoey, Frances Sarah Cashel [*née* Frances Sarah Johnston] (1830–1908), novelist, was born at Bushy Park, near Dublin, on 15 February 1830, one of eight children of Charles Bolton Johnston, secretary and registrar of the protestant cemetery at Mount Jerome, and Charlotte Jane Shaw, a half-sister of George Bernard Shaw's mother. Frances Sarah had two daughters with her first husband, Adam Murray Stewart, whom she married on her sixteenth birthday, 15 February 1846. Just after her marriage she met Daniel O'Connell and became and remained a fervent Irish nationalist for the rest of her life. Her first published articles appeared in the Young Ireland papers the *Freeman's Journal* and *The Nation*.

Following her husband's death on 6 November 1855, Frances Stewart moved to London. On 9 February 1858 she married John Baptist Cashel Hoey (1828–1892) [*see below*], and she converted to Roman Catholicism at the time of their marriage and became a zealous churchwoman. Her faith is often evident in her novels, notably *Out of Court* (1874), which exposes the evils of divorce and applauds Ireland for rejecting it, and *The Question of Cain* (1882) and *The Lover's Creed* (1884), both of which feature providential conversions on the brink of death. Hoey's correspondence with Edmund Downey, a fellow Catholic, shows that her Christian charity made serious inroads on her modest income, especially in her final years when she was widowed and largely dependent on a civil-list pension of £50 granted her on 15 August 1892. Earlier, when her literary earnings were at their peak, Bentley twice had to write off advance payments made to her and Chambers had to threaten legal action against her for recovery of a debt.

Frances Hoey's eleven novels, published between 1868 and 1886, abound in sensational crises and exemplary tragedies of misplaced love. But although her relative Bernard Shaw ridiculed them, they are not entirely conventional or devoid of wit and moral sense. *A Golden Sorrow* (1872) and *Griffith's Double* (1876) are perhaps the best. About 1870 the rumour began to circulate that Hoey had secretly collaborated with Edmund Yates on several of his novels and had even written the whole of one of them, *A Righted Wrong* (1870). After Yates's death, the allegation was endorsed by William Tinsley, the publisher of some of the novels, in his *Random Recollections* (1900). Hoey privately confirmed that the collaboration had occurred, though rejecting Tinsley's assertion that he had been unaware of it at the time. But Tinsley apparently had not preserved the manuscripts partly or wholly in her hand, and in their absence, and that of any discernible signs of composite authorship in the novels as published, the story remains barely credible.

Between the 1860s and the 1890s Frances Hoey regularly contributed sub-leaders and reviews (particularly of travel books) to *The Spectator*, whose joint editor, Richard Holt Hutton, was a close friend of her husband's. Between 1865 and 1875 she was a prolific contributor of both fiction and 'digests' of travel books to *Chambers's Journal*. For the last thirty-four years of her life she wrote notices of books and probably paragraphs of gossip for Edmund Yates's weekly, *The World*, and an unsigned column, 'A lady's letter from London', for *The Australasian* (Melbourne). She translated thirty-five or more books from the French, seven of them in collaboration with John Lillie.

Frances Hoey died at Beccles, Suffolk, on 9 July 1908, and was buried in the grounds of the Benedictine church at

Little Malvern, which had for many years been one of her favourite retreats.

John Baptist Cashel Hoey [*pseuds.* C. H., D. F. B., Cu-Ulad] (1828–1892), journalist, was born on 25 October 1828 at Dundalk, Louth, Ireland, the only son of Cashel Fitzsimmons Hoey. He was educated at St Patrick's College, Armagh, and remained a devout Roman Catholic throughout his life. A member of the Young Ireland party, he assisted Sir Charles Gavan Duffy when he revived *The Nation* in 1849, and edited the journal from August 1855 to 1858, after Duffy's departure for Australia. He wrote verse for *The Nation* under the signatures C. H., D. F. B., and Cu-Ulad, and also contributed many articles to the *Irish Quarterly Review*, the *Dublin Review*, and *The Spectator*.

On 9 February 1858 Hoey married Frances Sarah Stewart (*née* Johnston); he was called to the bar of the Middle Temple on 18 November 1861. He sub-edited the *Dublin Review* from 1865 to 1879, while also writing many essays for it, and producing an edition of W. C. Plunket's *Speeches at the Bar and in the Senate* (1865). Through Duffy's patronage, Hoey secured the post of secretary to the agent-general for Victoria in London (1872–3 and 1879–92), and that of secretary to the agent-general for New Zealand (1874–9). On 19 October 1881 he was made CMG for his service in these positions.

Hoey was made a knight of the orders of Malt, Este, Pius IX, Francis I, and El Caridad. He was a fellow of the Roman Academy of the Catholic Religion. Hoey died on 6 January 1892 at 17 Campden Hill Road, Kensington, London, and was buried in Malvern, Worcestershire.

P. D. EDWARDS

Sources P. D. Edwards, *Frances Cashel Hoey: a bibliography* (1982) · *Collected letters: Bernard Shaw*, ed. D. H. Laurence, 4 vols. (1965–88), vol. 1 · W. Tinsley, *Random recollections of an old publisher*, 2 vols. (1900) · F. C. Hoey, letters to E. Downey, NL Ire., Downey MSS, MSS 10028, 1–2 · *The archives of Richard Bentley & Son, 1829–1898* (1976) [microfilm, pt 1, reels 1, 2, 41, 48] · NL Scot., W. and R. Chambers MSS, TD 1709 · Boase, *Mod. Eng. biog.* · *ILN* (16 Jan 1892), 70, 86 · C. G. Duffy, *My life in two hemispheres*, 2 vols. (1898) · C. A. Read, *The cabinet of Irish literature: selections from the works of the chief poets, orators and prose writers of Ireland*, new edn, 3 (1909), 274–81 · d. cert. · *DNB* · m. cert.

Archives BL, Richard Bentley MSS · NL Ire., Downey MSS · NL Scot., W. Chambers and R. Chambers MSS

Wealth at death £160 7s. 7d.: administration, 27 Nov 1908, *CGPLA Eng. & Wales*

Hoey, John Baptist Cashel (1828–1892). *See under* Hoey, Frances Sarah Cashel (1830–1908).

Hoffman, William (1867–1941), traveller and rogue, the son of William Hoffman, a surgical maker, was born in Magdeburg, Saxony, on 10 October 1867 but brought up in England from very early childhood. The explorer Henry Stanley met him in London in 1884 and employed him, despite his total inexperience, as his servant or valet. Hoffman made a career from his association with the internationally famous author, obtaining money from Stanley and then from his widow. Dorothy Stanley remarked, 'I mistrust Hoffman through and through', calling him 'thriftless' and 'a weak, untruthful man' (Dorothy Stanley to Henry Wellcome, 15 Aug 1905, RGS).

Hoffman's command of German was needed by Stanley in 1884–5 when he attended the Berlin conference which divided the map of Africa among white nations. They then went together to the USA, where Stanley lectured. A second tour was curtailed when Stanley was requested to return to Africa. He took Hoffman with him, and their trans-Africa journey was the best-documented account of European travellers in Africa. Stanley's *In Darkest Africa, or, The Quest, Rescue and Retreat of Emin, Governor of Equatoria* (1890) sold hundreds of thousands of copies in several languages and editions. From Egypt in early 1887, via Cape Town to the River Congo and into the heart of equatorial Africa, Hoffman attended on Stanley. In Uganda, Emin rescued Stanley's sick and starving expedition; they reached the Indian Ocean in December 1889, a 6000 mile journey that had taken three years. Hoffman had been accused of theft from Stanley and his officers, and dismissed for stealing and lying, and for 'being filthy in his person'. This has been variously interpreted as hinting at cannibalism or sexual practices. He was court-martialled by the officers, and whipped on Stanley's orders.

Hoffman found work as an interpreter at the customs in Mombasa. His white colleagues returned to Europe, fame, and authorship (six further books in 1890, four in 1892). Hoffman worked at Basoko in the Congo Free State for three years and in 1897 was Stanley's valet on a trip to Rhodesia.

On 9 June 1902 Hoffman married Elizabeth Kezia Jane Blanch (1872–1941), in Acton, Middlesex. She was the daughter of John Blanch (who was of German descent) and Elizabeth, *née* Brooks, both of whom were caretakers for R. A. Everett, publishers, at 42 Essex Street, London. Hoffman stole proofs of Guy Burrows's *The Curse of Central Africa*, which later reached Belgium. In 1903 Everett and Burrows were accused of libel against three Belgian officials; an injunction prevented the book being published until it was modified, 'unprecedented in the modern annals of British publishing' (G. Burrows, *The Curse of Central Africa*, 1903, vii). The book had to be re-edited; Belgian supporters of the rapacious regime in the Congo Free State viewed the Burrows affair as proof that all British accusations were slanderous. The report of the trial was published and circulated by the Congo authorities in 1904.

Stanley died in 1904, leaving Hoffman £300. But Hoffman had no employment and he now obtained money from Dorothy Stanley. From mid-1905 to September 1906, after Dorothy Stanley recommended him, Hoffman and his wife accompanied six Congo pygmies whom James Jonathan Harrison had brought to tour Britain and Germany. He then proposed selling film negatives and prints to Lady Stanley, who passed the problem to her millionaire businessman friend Henry Wellcome. All three were aware that Stanley's already waning reputation could be damaged.

On 1 July 1907 Hoffman, one of two white survivors of the 1887–9 expedition, was described in the *Evening News* as 'in desperate need'. Wellcome sent him clothes, paid his rent, lent him money against negatives and Africana, and recommended him as a London club servant. Cheques continued to be squeezed 'month after month' from Lady Stanley.

In 1910 Hoffman, described by Lady Stanley as 'wonderful at African languages' (Dorothy Stanley to Major Darwin, 15 July 1910, RGS), sought work in Africa and found it with Lever Brothers in the French Congo (1911–13). He next worked as a bread delivery man in London (his wife had a steady income from tailoring), then pushing a barrow. The couple lived at 42 Essex Street from 1922, eventually becoming the caretakers. Dorothy Stanley's death in 1926 forced Hoffman to turn his attention to Wellcome, and items were sold to the millionaire, who observed Hoffman's veiled threats to publish his version of the African journey. Wellcome's purchases were stored in his company's strongroom, the action of a protector, not of a collector. After Wellcome's death in 1936 Hoffman had his *With Stanley in Africa* published in 1938. It was ghost-written and his name was spelt Hoffmann. Hoffman stated that Stanley 'knew I would never betray the trust he placed in me' (*With Stanley in Africa*, 247), but for decades he had obtained money through threatening to expose Stanley's weaknesses and lies.

Tropical diseases and old age took their toll, but Hoffman still went carousing with fellow members of the Royal Antediluvian Order of Buffaloes until the last months. Being a German national, Hoffman had his radio confiscated when war broke out in 1939; he fell ill and was housed at the Old Windsor Emergency Hospital in Windsor, Berkshire, where a German bombing raid killed him on 26 February 1941. Essex Street was also almost destroyed but his wife's brother found his Congo medal in the rubble and sold it on his way home. Hoffman's wife died very shortly afterwards.

The ginger-haired man whose life had been changed by his meeting with Stanley had amused the idle and curious with his tales. Yet he had seen horrors and wonders in Africa. Had Hoffman understood Stanley's weaknesses and failings, in his private tent every evening, after the stresses of leadership as their expedition stumbled across tropical Africa? No one else had such access. The two men's lives were intertwined. JEFFREY GREEN

Sources RGS, Stanley and Hoffman files · Wellcome L., Western papers, 6010, 6011 · private information (2004) [family] · m. cert. · d. cert.

Archives RGS, Stanley and Hoffman files | Wellcome L., Western papers, 6010, 6011

Likenesses W. & D. Downey, photograph, 1905, repro. in *History Today* (Aug 1995), 38; priv. coll. · B. Stone, photograph, 1905, NPG; repro. in *History Today* (Aug 1995), 33 · photograph, repro. in J. Green, *Black Edwardians* (1998), 124

Wealth at death £100 14s. 6d.: administration, 23 May 1941, *CGPLA Eng. & Wales*

Hoffmann, Professor. *See* Lewis, Angelo John (1839–1919).

Hoffnung, Gerard [*formerly* Gerhardt] (1925–1959), cartoonist and musical humorist, was born in Grünewald, Berlin, on 22 March 1925, the only child of German-Jewish parents, Ludwig Hoffnung, a wealthy grain merchant, and his wife, Hilde, a widow, whose first husband, Schnabel,

Gerard Hoffnung (1925–1959), by Peter Keen, late 1950s

was killed in the First World War. His mother was a keen amateur musician and artist who encouraged his artistic talents. From his earliest years he was interested in the macabre—fairy tales, practical jokes, and the comic drawings of the famous German illustrators and caricaturists.

In the wake of the Nazi persecutions the Hoffnungs left Germany in 1938. Ludwig Hoffnung settled permanently in Israel. Gerard and his mother went to London, renting a house in Hampstead Garden Suburb which was to be Hoffnung's home for the rest of his life. In 1939 he became a pupil at Highgate School, where he was remembered for his anarchic spirit. His first cartoon was published in *Lilliput* while he was still at school. He studied at Hornsey College of Art but was expelled and became art-master at Stamford School, Lincolnshire, in 1945 and later at Harrow School. He was already working as a freelance cartoonist and his work appeared in the London *Evening News* (1947) and a number of British, continental, and American magazines including *Punch*, *Strand Magazine*, and *The Tatler*. He also produced advertising work for Kia-Ora, Guinness, and other companies. He held several one-man exhibitions of his work, including those at the Little Gallery, Piccadilly (1949), and the Royal Festival Hall, London, in 1951 and 1956.

Hoffnung developed a distinctive style which owed something to the German illustrator Wilhelm Busch. He mainly drew with a mapping pen and Indian ink, and also used watercolours and wax crayons. His illustrations in colour for Colette's libretto for Ravel's opera *L'enfant et les sortilèges* were outstanding. Much of his humour centred on the world of music, particularly the various instruments of the orchestra with which he was fascinated. (He taught himself to play the tuba.) In 1953 he published *The*

Maestro, the first of a series of six little books of cartoons on musical themes which had a worldwide success. They were animated by Halas-Batchelor with music by Francis Chagrin in the television series *Tales from Hoffnung* (1965), and were available on gramophone records, as were several of his humorous speeches and broadcasts. He broke new ground in musical humour when in 1956 he organized the first of a series of concerts of symphonic caricature at which new music, some of it by respected composers such as Malcolm Arnold, was played on ludicrous instruments or to the accompaniment of vacuum cleaners or road rammers. These 'April Fools Concerts' in Liverpool and Hoffnung Music Festivals in London became more and more elaborate and proved highly popular with the public.

In 1950 Hoffnung began a career as a broadcaster, during the course of which he made many appearances on the radio as both raconteur and panel member. He was a brilliant improviser with a dry wit and a masterly sense of timing. An Oxford Union speech in 1958 in which he told 'The story of the bricklayer' became a classic recording. The story, involving a bricklayer's misfortunes as he attempted to lower some bricks in a barrel from the top of a building, was not especially funny, but his manner and delivery reduced his audience to hysterics. Other publications include *Ho Ho Hoffnung* and *Hoffnung's Acoustics* (both 1959) and a number of posthumous collections of his drawings and cartoons. He also provided illustrations for works by other writers, including J. Broughton's *The Right Playmate* (1951).

In appearance Hoffnung was stocky, bald, and benign. Nicolas Bentley described him as looking like a 'Teutonic Pickwick'. His manner, voice, and looks were those of a much older man and his wife was sometimes mistaken for his daughter. A man of conscience, he was a Quaker and a prison visitor. In 1952 he married Annetta Perceval, daughter of Percy Alfred Bennett, electrical contractor, of Folkestone, Kent. They had one son and one daughter. Hoffnung was only thirty-four when he died of a cerebral haemorrhage in New End Hospital, London, on 28 September 1959. He was survived by his wife. Posthumous exhibitions of his work include those at the Berlin festival (1964); the Brighton and Edinburgh festivals (1968); the Lincoln Center for the Performing Arts, New York (1970); and Orleans House Gallery, Twickenham, London (1992).

RICHARD INGRAMS, rev.

Sources *The Times* (29 Sept 1959) · A. Hoffnung, *Gerard Hoffnung* (1988) · *CGPLA Eng. & Wales* (1960) · R. Malbert, *Independent Magazine* (5 Dec 1992) · M. Bryant and S. Heneage, eds., *Dictionary of British cartoonists and caricaturists, 1730–1980* (1994) · F. Spiegel, 'Hoffnung, Gerard', *New Grove* · *WWW* · private information (2004)
Likenesses P. Keen, photograph, 1956–9, NPG [*see illus.*]
Wealth at death £20,257 7s. 6d.: probate, 8 Jan 1960, *CGPLA Eng. & Wales*

Hofland [*née* Wreaks], **Barbara** (*bap.* 1770, *d.* 1844), children's writer and novelist, was probably born in Sheffield, Yorkshire, the daughter of Robert Wreaks (*d.* 1773), ironmonger. She was baptized in Sheffield on 16 February 1770. After her father's death and her mother's remarriage, Barbara was brought up by a maiden aunt. From July 1794 she began contributing poems to the Sheffield newspaper *The Iris*, edited by Robert Montgomery. She married a local businessman, Thomas Bradshawe Hoole (1766–1799), in June 1796, but he died three years later and his business collapsed, leaving her virtually penniless and with a baby son, Frederic, to raise. She continued writing verse and her *Poems* of 1805 sold over 2000 copies. She also began writing children's stories, *The History of an Officer's Widow* being published in 1809, the year she opened a girls' school in Harrogate. Running the school proved difficult, but consolation was at hand, and on 28 January 1810 Barbara married Thomas Christopher *Hofland (1777–1843), a talented landscape artist.

The couple moved to London in 1811 and Hofland exhibited at the Royal Academy. Barbara Hofland's literary career developed. Her tale *The Daughter-in-Law* (1812) so impressed Queen Charlotte that she gave permission for the author to dedicate a later book to her. In 1812 Barbara Hofland also published an adult novel, *Says she to her Neighbour what?*, as well as her most popular children's book, *The Son of a Genius*, the story of an impulsive artist whose erratic behaviour brings poverty to his wife and son, a tale which may contain autobiographical elements. *The Son of a Genius* was frequently reprinted in England, reaching a fourteenth edition by 1841, and was reprinted at least nine times in America, as well as being translated into French and other European languages. Barbara Hofland made friends with many celebrities, including the architect John Soane and the writers Maria Edgeworth and Mary Russell Mitford.

But her literary efforts did not make Barbara Hofland rich. She was paid only £10 for *The Son of a Genius*, and though her husband exhibited six pictures at the Royal Academy in 1815, his earnings were erratic, often affected by lack of self-discipline and poor health. In 1816, for example, he produced an illegitimate son, Thomas Richard Hofland, whom his wife took in and treated as her own. Financial difficulties continued. In 1819 the Hoflands finished a book commissioned by the marquess of Blandford about his estate at Whiteknights, Reading, but were paid nothing for their labours. In 1822 an exhibition of Hofland's paintings failed. But children's books, novels, textbooks, and verse continued to flow from Barbara Hofland's pen. By the 1830s, however, she found writing painful because of a shoulder injury, and in 1833 she suffered a severe blow with the death of her son Frederic, a much-loved parish priest. After her husband's death in 1843, Barbara Hofland finished her last children's book, *Emily's Reward, or, The Holiday Trip to Paris* in August 1844. She died of erysipelas at her home, The Hollies, Richmond-on-Thames, on 4 November 1844, and was buried in the parish churchyard, Richmond-on-Thames, Surrey. Barbara Hofland was a prolific author whose bibliography lists sixty-six titles, not including contributions to periodicals, such as the 'Letters to kinfolk', articles of literary gossip printed in regional papers. Her most popular books, however, were her didactic moral tales for children, often depicting the struggles of a Christian family in adverse circumstances. Though characteristic of the period, these often contain realistic details about hardship, work, and ordinary family life, seen particularly in such books as *Ellen, the Teacher* (1814) and *Elizabeth and her Three Beggar Boys* (1833), which some scholars think may have influenced Charlotte Brontë's *Jane Eyre* and Dickens's *Oliver Twist*. Although Barbara Hofland's adult novels were not successful, some of her adventure stories, such as *The Young Crusoe* (1829), achieved popularity. Her portraits of brave and resourceful heroines in such tales as *Decision* (1824) are also noteworthy. Her books were frequently reprinted in Britain and America throughout the nineteenth century and often translated. She seems to have been a loving and attractive person—an engraving of 1818 reveals a friendly, humorous face with dark eyes and amused mouth—and it is the strength and resource behind her arduous and ultimately heroic life that her books best convey.

DENNIS BUTTS

Sources T. Ramsay, *The life and literary remains of Barbara Hofland* (1849) · D. Butts, *Mistress of our tears: a literary and bibliographical study of Barbara Hofland* (1992) · D. Butts, 'Mrs Barbara Hofland (1770–1844): a bibliographical and literary study', MPhil diss., Sheffield University, 1980 · A. G. L'Estrange, ed., *The friendships of Mary Russell Mitford: as recorded in letters from her literary correspondents*, 2 vols. (1882) · *Letters of Mary Russell Mitford*, ed. H. Chorley, [2nd edn], 2 vols. (1872) · *Memoirs of the life and writings of James Montgomery*, ed. J. Holland and J. Everett, 7 vols. (1854–6) · Sheffield parish register, no. 9
Archives Sheff. Arch., letters to James Montgomery · Sir John Soane's Museum, letters to Mr Soane and Mrs Soane · U. Reading L., Longman archives
Likenesses Dean and Monday, engraving, 1818, Bodl. Oxf. · E. Finden, stipple, pubd 1849, BM, NPG; repro. in Ramsay, *Life and literary remains* · stipple, BM, NPG; repro. in *La Belle Assemblée*, no. 180 (1 Oct 1823) · stipple, NPG
Wealth at death left property to husband's son

Hofland, Thomas Christopher (1777–1843), landscape painter, was born on 25 December 1777 in Worksop, Nottinghamshire, the only child of a wealthy manufacturer of cotton-mill machinery. Hofland was brought up in the expectation of leading a life of leisure and his youth was spent indulging a passion for field sports, especially angling. The family moved to London in 1790 but in 1796–7 his father was ruined by imprudent speculation. Hofland, already practised as an amateur painter, took lessons for a short period from the landscape painter John Rathbone. He first exhibited at the Royal Academy in 1798, and made a living by teaching in Kew, supporting both himself and his parents. Through his position as captain in the local volunteers he attracted the attention of George III, who commissioned some botanical drawings and offered to send him as draughtsman on a naval survey, but this was declined. Hofland moved to Derby in 1805, where he was a popular teacher, then in 1808 to Leeds. There he was one of the most prolific exhibitors in what were Britain's first regular provincial exhibitions, showing sixteen works in the inaugural exhibition of the Northern Society at Leeds, 1809, twenty-four the following year from a Harrogate address, and sixteen in the third exhibition in 1811. He married the writer Barbara Hoole, *née* Wreaks, (*bap.* 1770,

d. 1844) at Knaresborough [*see* Hofland, Barbara] on 28 January 1810.

In 1811 Hofland returned to London and in 1814 carried off the first prize for landscape at the British Institution with *A Storm off the Coast of Scarborough*, which was purchased by the marquess of Stafford. Other landscapes were bought by Sir George Beaumont and Lord Coventry. In 1816, according to Farington, Hofland was employed to copy works by Claude for Hart Davies, though Hofland reserved his greatest personal admiration for Wilson.

In 1816 Hofland was commissioned by the marquess of Blandford to make paintings of his house at Whiteknights near Reading. They were engraved by T. Medland and L. Byrne and published in *A descriptive account of the mansion and gardens of Whiteknights a seat of his grace the duke of Marlborough* with text by Mrs Hofland in 1819. Hofland was never paid for this work, his only recompense being the profits from the sale of the twenty-three engravings, a fact which still rankled nearly ten years later, after the marquess had succeeded to the title of duke of Marlborough.

When his most ambitious landscape, a view on the Thames at Richmond, was rejected by the Royal Academy in 1821, Hofland held his own exhibition at 106 New Bond Street (the work was probably the canvas measuring approximately 1.5 x 2.5 m sold at Christies on 10 December 1971, of which there is a photograph at the Paul Mellon Centre for British Art, London). The praise heaped on his work by certain sections of the press attracted accusations of favouritism and failed to help his efforts to secure election to the Royal Academy. As a candidate at the election for associates in 1822 he excited a vitriolic attack from Constable: 'Hofland has sold his shadow of Gaspar Poussin—for 80 gns—it is nothing more like Gaspar than the shadow of the man like himself on a muddy road. It is a beastly [thing]' (*Constable's Correspondence*, 101). Hofland's lack of official recognition must have been one of his reasons for taking a leading role in the creation of the Society of British Artists in 1823 and serving both as trustee and its first vice-president. From the first exhibition in 1824 until his death Hofland showed no fewer than 119 works there. Despite adverse comment on the quality of the work, the society succeeded in finding a market among the middle classes, though Hofland's own reputation was left exposed. In the following year, 1825, C. W. Westmacott made a point of supporting Hofland in his review of the Royal Academy exhibition, but suggested that the artist had not helped his own cause: '[Hofland] ought long ago to have been honoured with some academical distinction; but "kissing goes by favour" and this artist, we hear, is not of a very compromising spirit' (Westmacott, 237). His income remained so low that he was reputedly reliant on his wife's writing of school textbooks and children's fiction.

Jerusalem at the Time of the Crucifixion commissioned by Lord de Tabley in 1823–4 was a rare excursion by Hofland into historic landscape, perhaps in emulation of the huge success of John Martin. Hofland could not finish it in time for the opening show of the Society of British Artists but exhibited an earlier version (first shown in 1821) in 1827. In

1829 he exhibited with the newly founded Hull and East Riding Institution for the Promotion of the Fine Arts. Otherwise, Hofland's subjects were exclusively British, with a preponderance of Lake District views and a number of country house portraits, the Whiteknights incident notwithstanding. In 1839 Hofland published *The British Angler's Manual*, a work he illustrated himself; some of the original paintings of scenes in England, Scotland, and Wales were exhibited at the Society of British Artists in 1838. Only in 1840 did Hofland make his first—and only—journey to the continent, with a commission from Lord Egremont for a series of views of Italy. He spent nine months in the vicinity of Rome and Naples. On his return he completed five of an anticipated series of twelve subjects but illness prevented further progress. He went in 1842 to Leamington Spa in search of medical assistance, and it was there that he succumbed to the stomach cancer from which he died on 3 January 1843.

TIMOTHY WILCOX

Sources T. C. Hofland, *The British angler's manual*, 2nd edn (1848) · *DNB* · H. Hubbard, *An outline history of the Royal Society of British Artists* (1937) · Farington, *Diary*, 13.4593; 14.4906 [10 Oct 1814; 8 Oct 1816] · D. Hall, 'The Tabley House papers', *Walpole Society*, 38 (1960–62), 59–122, esp. 76–7 · J. Gage, *A decade of English naturalism, 1810–1820* [1969] [exhibition catalogue, Norwich Castle Museum, 15 Nov – 15 Dec 1969, and V&A, 15 Jan – 28 Feb 1970] · L. Parris, *Landscape in Britain, c.1750–1850* (1973) [Tate catalogue no. 252] · C. W. Westmacott, *The annual descriptive and critical catalogue of the exhibition at the Royal Academy* (1825), 237 · *John Constable's correspondence*, ed. R. B. Beckett, 6, Suffolk RS, 12 (1968) · W. T. Whitley, *Art in England, 1800–1820* (1928); *Art in England, 1821–1837* (1930) · T. Fawcett, *The rise of English provincial art: artist, patron and institution outside London, 1800–1830* (1974) · C. Davidson, *The world of Mary Ellen Best* (1985), 14 · [B. Hofland], *GM*, 2nd ser., 19 (1843), 540–41 · m. cert.
Archives Ches. & Chester ALSS, corresp. concerning Hofland's pictures | Federation of British Artists, Carlton Terrace, London, MSS of the Royal Society of British Artists
Likenesses J. Lonsdale, oils, exh. RA 1823; sold Bonhams, 7 December 1989, lot 124 · photograph, NPG

Hofmann, August Wilhelm [*formerly* Georg Christian Wilhelm August Hofmann], **Baron von Hofmann in the Prussian nobility** (1818–1892), chemist, was born in Giessen (in the state of Hesse) on 8 April 1818, the youngest of the six children of Johann Philipp Hofmann (1776–1843), a government architect, and (Friederike) Wilhelmine Badenius (1780–1854). After attending local schools and studying while living with an uncle, in 1836 he matriculated at Giessen, but was uncertain whether to study law, philology, or architecture. The most celebrated member of the Giessen faculty at this time was the chemist Justus Liebig, whose revolutionary scientific work and innovative educational methods were making him world famous. Liebig's success was such that repeated expansions of his laboratory were necessary, the crucial one of 1839 having been designed and directed by Hofmann's father. Hofmann studied with Liebig, earned the doctorate in 1841, then continued in Giessen with his research. Hofmann's first scientific paper (1843) was the earliest competent investigation of coal tar; this work provided the foundation of much of his future career. Concentrating on the organic bases, Hofmann isolated and identified aniline

(phenylamine, a centrally important aromatic substance), and took the first steps towards an understanding of its constitution and chemical relationships. In the same year Liebig made Hofmann his private assistant, and the young chemist began planning a scholarly career. Since a chemical professorship was unlikely to become available to him in Giessen, in the spring of 1845 Hofmann transferred to the University of Bonn. He was anxious to achieve the financial means to marry his intended, Helene Moldenhauer (1824–1852), Liebig's niece.

Meanwhile, in London, plans were being laid for a new private college of chemistry. The impetus for this development came from Liebig himself, who visited England in 1837 and again in 1842, effectively publicizing the usefulness of chemistry to technology. A group of technically knowledgeable investors in London sought the advice of Liebig and the help of the British government for this plan; Prince Albert played an instrumental role. Liebig recommended Hofmann to lead the new enterprise. Hofmann wanted assurance from the Prussian authorities that he could return to Bonn if the new school were to collapse. To ensure this, Prince Albert used his German connections to arrange that Hofmann be promoted to *extraordinarius* (associate professor) in order to be eligible for a two-year leave of absence from the university. Thus Hofmann became sole professor and director of the Royal College of Chemistry, established in October 1845 in rented rooms in a house on George Street, Hanover Square. Twenty-six students enrolled for the first session, among them several who later achieved recognition in the science, such as Warren De la Rue, Frederick Abel, and Edward Nicholson. The following summer a new building for the college was erected nearby, in Oxford Street, the cornerstone being laid by the prince consort. In the same year, on 12 August, Hofmann married Helene Moldenhauer.

The two guiding ideas behind the Royal College of Chemistry were the transplantation of the highly acclaimed Liebigian science pedagogy into Great Britain, and the establishment of an institution where students could be trained for practical careers in agriculture, pharmacy, and chemical industry. There was tension between these goals, for the former, strongly favoured by Hofmann, stressed the value of basic research, while the latter, preferred by the shareholders and members of the council, emphasized practical applications. The pecuniary arrangements with Hofmann were generous, but a shortage of student customers meant that the council had increasing difficulty meeting its contractual obligations. Consequently, the college gradually sank into insolvency.

Meanwhile, Hofmann's boundless energy, captivating teaching talent, and scientific brilliance began to lay the foundation of his future fame. After a pause in his research while establishing the college, he continued his investigations of organic compounds containing nitrogen. Hofmann's phenomenal burst of creative work from 1848 to 1851 has few parallels in the history of chemistry. This is all the more remarkable when it is considered—as all witnesses uniformly testify—that he was unskilled in manual laboratory operations. However, he had an uncanny knack for selecting outstandingly talented experimentalists among his students and junior colleagues, and was always careful publicly to acknowledge their important assistance.

In compensation for his own lack of manual dexterity Hofmann held his laboratory to rigorous working standards, and he possessed superb scientific skills, including remarkable chemical intuition. If it was often the hands of students and junior colleagues doing the manipulating in Hofmann's lab, they were usually being guided by the ideas of their leader. This is not to suggest that Hofmann was a high theorist—indeed, he was more inclined towards a conventionalist or instrumentalist stance toward scientific theories—but he was exquisitely responsive to leading ideas in the science, and he developed a nearly unerring sense of fruitful directions to explore.

This was, indeed, a labile period in chemical theory. In the 1830s and 1840s the French chemists Auguste Laurent and Charles Gerhardt pointed to emergent weaknesses in the prevailing dualistic theory of organic compounds, in which molecules were depicted as held together by polar electrochemical forces. Laurent and Gerhardt sought to build a more holistic, non-electrochemical theory, based upon the substitutability of atoms and emphasizing the presumed arrangements of atoms within molecules. In the period of Hofmann's education and early career, these ideas were largely ignored by the leaders of French, English, and German chemistry—including Hofmann's mentor, Liebig.

Hofmann's conversion to the ideas of Laurent and Gerhardt dates from 1848, when he encountered a chemical phenomenon that could be explained only by the French theory: the inability of aniline to form a nitrile (organic cyanide). Hofmann's new substitutionist viewpoint, together with the nearly simultaneous and similarly inspired work of his collegial friends Adolphe Wurtz (of the Paris Faculté de Médecine) and Alexander Williamson (of University College, London), provided the starting point for Hofmann's masterwork. The theories of Laurent and Gerhardt had been largely schematic; Hofmann's studies substantiated them through experimental evidence. In papers published in 1849, 1850, and 1851, Hofmann described the preparation and studied the properties of dozens of new substituted ammonias, including mono-, di-, tri-, and tetra-methyl, ethyl, and amyl amines and anilines. Just as Williamson succeeded in outlining a new 'water type' based on what soon would be referred to as the divalence of oxygen atoms, so Wurtz and especially Hofmann created the 'ammonia type', which was based on the ability of nitrogen atoms to create connections to three different atoms or groups. These developments utterly transformed the science of chemistry during the 1850s, leading to the formulation of the theory of atomic valence (with the participation of Edward Frankland and others) and the theory of chemical structure (proposed formally by August Kekulé and Archibald Couper in 1858).

Hofmann's novel nitrogenous aromatic compounds proved as momentous for industrial research as they had for theoretical chemistry. After Hofmann's young student William Henry Perkin dropped out of the college (against Hofmann's advice) and made a fortune on his newly discovered aniline purple (mauve), the first successful dye derived from coal tar, Hofmann himself became interested in similar substances. From 1862 he studied reactions connected with rosaniline (magenta), the second major synthetic organic dye; in 1863 he created two new hues in collaboration with his former student Nicholson, who like Perkin had become a chemical industrialist. These colours, called 'Hofmann violets', were the first commercially successful fine chemicals developed with the aid of specific knowledge derived from basic research, and their licensed production made both Nicholson and Hofmann a great deal of money. The age of synthetic chemicals, behind which lay Hofmann's pedagogy and research, had begun. However, although he ever after derived significant income from his work with coal-tar dyes, he never became an entrepreneur or an industrialist himself, always preferring the roles of the pure scientist and the consultant.

In his London years Hofmann became a central player in British chemistry, indeed in British science. His growing international fame led to several offers from German universities. In the early 1860s, Hofmann found himself negotiating simultaneously with two major universities, Berlin and Bonn; in their efforts to attract Hofmann both institutions built magnificent new chemical institutes. These were the first of a new generation of academic laboratory buildings, representing a quantum leap in scale and outfitting. It was Berlin that Hofmann chose, partly because of his attraction to the Prussian capital. Although he began teaching there in April 1865, his international prestige and negotiating power was such that he held exclusive options on all three positions (including London) from late 1863 until the end of 1866. England had lost Hofmann to his homeland, but his two decades in London had had a decisive impact on the teaching and practice of British laboratory science, as well as on British chemical technology.

Just as he had succeeded in transplanting effective Liebig-style group research to Great Britain, Hofmann's Berlin laboratory served as the rallying point for a rejuvenation of the chemical sciences in Prussia. The research productivity was enormous, indeed unprecedented in scope. Hofmann supervised more than 150 doctoral dissertations, and a total of about 900 papers emerged from the laboratory during his time there—about 150 by Hofmann himself. In addition to these contributions, Hofmann wrote an elementary textbook, a number of occasional pieces, and over fifty important biographies of his colleagues. In April 1888 he was raised to the Prussian hereditary nobility; he was thereafter called von Hofmann.

Hofmann became the unofficial (but universally acknowledged) leader of German chemistry. His scientific success contrasts with his private misfortunes, for his first wife's early death in 1852 was followed by those of his second, Rosamund Wilson (1838–1860), an Englishwoman, whom he married 13 December 1856, and third, Elise Moldenhauer (1845–1871), whom he married on 19 May 1866, both of whom died before the age of thirty. His fourth wife, however, Bertha Tiemann (1854–1922), whom he married on 11 August 1873, outlived him by thirty years. Possessed of outstanding health himself, Hofmann was hardly ill until suddenly struck down on 5 May 1892 with a heart attack. He was buried, amid great splendour, in the Dorotheenstädtischer cemetery in Berlin.

A. J. ROCKE

Sources J. Volhard and E. Fischer, *August Wilhelm von Hofmann: ein Lebensbild* (1902) · H. Armstrong and others, 'Hofmann memorial lecture', *JCS*, 69 (1896), 575–732 · C. Meinel and H. Scholz, eds., *Die Allianz von Wissenschaft und Industrie: A. W. Hofmann, 1818–1892* (1992) · G. Ronge, 'A. W. Hofmann', *Neue deutsche Biographie*, ed. Otto, Graf zu Stolberg-Wernigerode (Berlin, 1953–) · W. H. Brock, 'Hofmann, August Wilhelm von', *DSB* · M. N. Keas, 'The structure and philosophy of group research: August Wilhelm Hofmann's research program in London', PhD diss., University of Oklahoma, 1992 · B. Lepsius, *Festschrift zum Feier des 50jährigen Bestehens der Deutschen Chemischen Gesellschaft und des 100. Geburtstag ihres Begründers August Wilhelm von Hofmann* (1918) · M. Müller, 'Die Lehrtätigkeit des Chemikers A. W. von Hofmann in Zusammenhang mit seinen Leistungen als Forscher und Wissenschaftsorganisator', PhD diss., Humboldt University, Berlin, 1978 · A. S. Travis, 'Science's powerful companion: A. W. Hofmann's investigation of aniline red and its derivatives', *British Journal for the History of Science*, 25 (1992), 27–44 · J. R. Partington, *A history of chemistry*, 4 (1964), 432–44 · W. H. Brock, ed., *Justus von Liebig und August Wilhelm Hofmann in ihren Briefen, 1841–1873* (1984) · A. J. Rocke, *The quiet revolution: Herman Kolbe and the science of organic chemistry* (1993) · *Vossische Zeitung* (9 May 1892)
Archives Bayerische Staatsbibliothek, Munich · Berlin-Brandenburgische Akademie der Wissenschaften, Berlin, Chemiker-Briefe · Deutsches Museum, Munich, Sondersammlungen · ICL, Royal College of Chemistry collection · ICL, Royal School of Mines collection · Royal Society of Chemistry, London · RS · Staatsbibliothek zu Berlin, Haus 2, Darmstädter Sammlung, incl. an autobiographical fragment · Vieweg Verlag, Braunschweig, Germany, archives · Wellcome L. | ICL, Lyon Playfair collection · Liebig-Museum, Giessen, Germany, Liebig MSS · Niedersächsische Staats- und Universitätsbibliothek, Göttingen, Germany, Wöhler collection · Open University, Milton Keynes, Edward Frankland archives
Likenesses group portrait, daguerreotype, c.1841, repro. in Lepsius, *Festschrift zum Feier* (1918), following p. 8 · heliogravure, 1846 (after drawing), repro. in Volhard and Fischer, *August Wilhelm von Hofmann*, following p. 32 · J. W. Cook, engraving, 1853, repro. in J. S. Muspratt, *Chemistry: theoretical, practical, and analytical* (1853) · photograph, c.1865, repro. in Armstrong and others, 'Hofmann memorial lecture', frontispiece · photograph, 1870, repro. in Lepsius, *Festschrift zum Feier*, following p. 16 · C. Günther, photograph, c.1871, Staatsbibliothek Preussischer Kulturbesitz, Berlin, Darmstädter Sammlung G2 1858 (5), fol. 162; repro. in Meinel and Scholz, eds., *Die Allianz*, 54 · C. Günther, photograph, 1881, repro. in Meinel and Scholz, eds., *Die Allianz*, 226; priv. coll. · H. von Angeli, oils, 1890, Liebig-Museum, Giessen; repro. in Lepsius, *Festschrift zum Feier*, frontispiece · photograph, c.1890, repro. in Armstrong and others, 'Hofmann memorial lecture', frontispiece

Hofmeyr, Jan Frederik Hendrik (1894–1948), classical scholar and politician in South Africa, was born in Cape Town on 20 March 1894, the younger son of Andries Brink Hofmeyr (1851–1897), a newspaper manager, and the imperious Deborah Catherina Beyers (1863–1959). His mother developed a neurotic fear of her son dying young and became over-possessive of a boy who soon revealed

his genius. Almost eight when sent to the South African College School in Cape Town, Hofmeyr matriculated at twelve and three years later obtained a degree in classics with honours at the South African College itself. He also won a Rhodes scholarship in 1910, but was deemed too young to go to Oxford, so wrote a massive biography of the Cape politician Jan Hendrik Hofmeyr. By the time this was published in Cape Town in 1913 Hofmeyr was at Balliol, where he obtained a double first in Greats and was active in the Oxford and Bermondsey Mission, the Student Christian Movement, and the Balliol Boys Club. His strong Christian faith was to underpin his political liberalism; a key statement of where he stood was his Hoernlé memorial lecture of 1945, entitled 'Christian principles and race problems'.

On his return to South Africa in 1916 Hofmeyr first lectured in classics at the South African College, while there winning a prize for an essay subsequently published as *History and Control of National Debts* (1918). In 1917 he went to Johannesburg as the first professor of classics at the South African School of Mines and Technology. He became that school's principal in 1919, at the age of twenty-five, and transformed it into the University of the Witwatersrand. But though an able administrator, he was disliked by staff and students for his lack of human understanding, and in a notorious case he insisted that the dean of medicine resign because of an extramarital romantic attachment. Hofmeyr was rescued by being appointed administrator of Transvaal by J. C. Smuts in 1924. In his five years in that post he proved himself to be exceptionally efficient in administration.

Hofmeyr's highest political goal at this time was unity between English- and Afrikaans-speaking white people, and he worked to bring together the South African and National parties, as a preliminary to any solution of the problem of ensuring the future of what he called 'European civilisation' in a country with a black majority. He put forward his ideas on reconciliation of the two white 'races' in a series of publications, including *Coming of Age* (1930) and the general history of his country which he wrote at this time, *South Africa* (1931).

From 1929 Hofmeyr served in parliament, where he soon became one of Smuts's chief advisers and his protégé. He gave Smuts his complete loyalty. It was J. B. M. Hertzog, however, who after coalition was achieved—in part as a result of Hofmeyr's efforts—gave him his first cabinet post (education, the interior, and public health) in 1933. After fusion, and the birth of the United Party, it was again Hertzog who allowed him to speak and vote—one of only eleven members of parliament to do so—against the Representation of Natives Bill, which removed the Cape African franchise, in April 1936. In an outstanding speech—Hofmeyr was known as one of the finest orators ever heard in the South African parliament—he charged that the bill was wrong in principle and based on fear. He rejected the idea of communal representation for Africans and the implication in the legislation that the country should remain divided. He was to urge, instead, the importance of promoting the development of the

African population of the towns. But while his speech on the Cape African franchise led some to hope that he would break with the United Party and establish a separate liberal party, this was not to happen. How conservative and limited his liberalism was became evident in 1937, when he agreed to support the Native Laws Amendment Bill. He feared uncontrolled African migration to the towns, and did not perhaps anticipate how repressive the consequences of the measure would be. Though he was more liberal than the rest of the cabinet, especially on matters concerning the Indian community, his liberalism had distinct limits: his biographer Alan Paton, seeking a liberal hero in the past, exaggerated his liberal sympathies.

From 1936 Hofmeyr was minister of mines, education and labour, and social welfare, but soon after retaining his Johannesburg North seat in the 1938 general election, he resigned from the cabinet because he opposed the appointment to the senate of a man who was supposed to be especially qualified to speak for Africans, but clearly was not. Smuts accused him of 'running away', but Hofmeyr saw this 'prostitution of the constitution' as a matter of principle. Some now again hoped that the articles he then published in *Forum* would herald the birth of a liberal party, but he was too timid to take any initiative in that regard. Though so strongly opposed to the Asiatics (Transvaal Land and Trading) Bill of 1939 that he resigned from the United Party caucus on the issue, he would not break with Smuts, his mentor, and he continued to argue that more could be achieved by trying to influence policy in a liberal direction within the United Party than by breaking away. In the Second World War he had an opportunity to show how far he could go within that party.

Fully supporting Smuts over entry into the war in September 1939, Hofmeyr was given the ministries of finance and education. Throughout the war he worked very hard in support of the war effort, frequently acting as prime minister when Smuts was abroad, and for other colleagues when they were not available. Again he proved himself an outstanding administrator, and the honours he received after the war included the honorary degree of DCL from Oxford and being sworn of the privy council. But he did relatively little for Africans beyond providing more money for education, and he failed to understand the problems of the Natives Representative Council. He offered his resignation over anti-Indian legislation in 1943, but was persuaded by Smuts to withdraw it in the interests of the war effort; he grudgingly voted for the Asiatic Land Tenure and Indian Representation Bill of 1946. During the debate on that bill, he said that he stood for 'the ultimate removal of the colour bar from our constitution' (*DSAB*, 2.313), and on another occasion argued that it was inevitable that black people would elect representatives to parliament one day. Such statements played into the hands of the Nationalists, who focused on his alleged liberalism in their attacks on the United Party. Though health problems led him to give up the finance portfolio in January 1948, he was officially appointed deputy prime minister at that time, and remained Smuts's heir apparent. When the United Party was defeated in the May general election, people within and outside the party blamed Hofmeyr.

How nebulous his views remained was revealed in the articles Hofmeyr published in *The Star* in late 1948. He called for 'White Christian trusteeship over the Bantu' (*DSAB*, 2.313), in the interests of the ward. He raised the question of what was likely to happen when the ward grew up, but provided no answer. And he expressed the hope that economic forces would prove stronger than the ideological drive of Nationalist politicians toward a *Herrenvolk* republic. His health deteriorated at about this time, and on 3 December 1948 he died in Pretoria, following a heart attack; he was buried in Pretoria on 5 December. His mother, with whom he lived throughout his life, blamed Smuts for his early death. Speaking at Hofmeyr's funeral, Smuts said that now that he was dead 'South Africa will not have a conscience. I felt his death more keenly than that of my son' (Paton, 530).

For all his brilliance of mind, his efficiency as an administrator, his capacity for enormous work, and his gift of public speaking, Hofmeyr never overcame the problems associated with being a 'mother's boy'. He never married, and never showed much creativity. He was not a success as a political tactician. He lacked the common touch, and was too insecure to try to steer the country in a new direction or to take decisive action. It was fitting that the American edition of Alan Paton's great biography of him should be entitled *A South African Tragedy*.

CHRISTOPHER SAUNDERS

Sources A. Paton, *Hofmeyr* (1964) · A. Harington, 'Hofmeyr, Jan (Frederik) Hendrik', *DSAB* · C. Driver, 'Alan Paton's *Hofmeyr*', *Race*, 6 (1964–5), 269 · W. K. Hancock, *Smuts*, 2: *The fields of force, 1919–1950* (1968) · E. Arndt, 'In memoriam: Jan Hendrik Hofmeyr', *Tydskrif vir Wetenskap en Kuns*, new ser., 9/2 (1949), 18–24 · *DNB* · B. K. Murray, *WITS, the early years: a history of the University of the Witwatersrand, Johannesburg, and its precursors, 1896–1939* (1982) · M. Ballinger, *From union to apartheid* (1969) · J. H. Hofmeyr, *South Africa*, ed. J. P. Cope, 2nd edn (1952) · K. Ingham, *Jan Christian Smuts: the conscience of a South African* (1986) · P. Rich, *Hope and despair* (1993)
Archives JRL, letters to the *Manchester Guardian* · University of the Witwatersrand, Johannesburg, Cullen Library | Bodl. Oxf., letters to A. E. King · CUL, Smuts MSS · University of Cape Town Library, Cape Town, corresp. with C. J. Sibbett | FILM BFI NFTVA, news footage
Likenesses K. Lloyd, portrait, Bodl. RH · photographs, repro. in Paton, *Hofmeyr* · portrait, University of the Witwatersrand, Johannesburg, Senate Room · portrait, University of Cape Town

Hofmeyr, Jan Hendrik (1845–1909), politician in Cape Colony and newspaper editor, was born at Welgemeend, Camp Street, Cape Town, on 3 or 4 July 1845, the eldest of twelve children (seven of whom survived into adulthood) who were born to a farmer near Somerset West—another Jan Hendrik Hofmeyr (1818–1893), descendant of an eighteenth-century German immigrant—and his wife, Rykje Hester, *née* Roos (1823–1897).

Early career Educated in Cape Town at Tot Nut van 't Algemeen and the South African College, Jan became fully bilingual in Dutch and English. He entered public life through journalism, as editor, from 1862 to 1871, of the *Volksvriend*, a newspaper devoted to the defence of middle-

Jan Hendrik Hofmeyr (1845–1909), by Rees, pubd 1908

of-the-road reformed religion against the dominant liberal values. He later brought together the *Volksvriend* and the *Zuid Afrikaan*, absorbing in his own venture a newspaper which had first appeared in 1830. The *Zuid Afrikaan*, as the amalgamated paper came to be known, remained under Hofmeyr's editorship until 1883, but he maintained an active relationship with it until the appearance of *Ons Land* in 1892—on Hofmeyr's initiative, it seems, with perhaps some help from Cecil Rhodes, following a policy disagreement between Hofmeyr and the editor of the *Zuid Afrikaan*, J. F. van Oordt, over the Bond's relationship with Rhodes. The *Zuid Afrikaan* succumbed to its rival's pressure in 1894.

Hofmeyr had also revived an earlier literary periodical, the *Zuid Afrikaansche Tijdschrift*, in 1878, to stimulate public concern for the Dutch language among Afrikaners. Since the reforms of Lord Charles Somerset in the 1820s, the use of Dutch in public life had gradually receded at the Cape, though without disappearing altogether, and reached a low point in the 1860s. Though an admirer of English culture, Onze Jan, as Hofmeyr was nicknamed, worked successfully to revive the waning Dutch culture of the Cape, more especially the Dutch language, which he always preferred to spoken Afrikaans, although he did campaign for a simplified form of spelling. He was to campaign energetically and successfully for equal rights for the Dutch and English languages, including the use of Dutch in debate in the Cape parliament, which was granted on a motion introduced by him in 1882. Later, in 1905, he was to engage in a further public debate over the relative merits of Dutch and Afrikaans in which D. F. Malan, Gustav Preller, and other notable figures were involved—a prelude, first, to the recognition of parity for English and Dutch in the

South Africa Act of 1909, but ultimately to the recognition of Afrikaans in 1925. These efforts, combined with his involvement in religious and political journalism, made Hofmeyr the foremost Afrikaner editor of the century, rivalling in influence the editors of *Die Afrikaanse Patriot*, an Afrikaans-language politico-cultural weekly founded in 1876 to promote a radical form of Afrikaner nationalism.

In parliament Although Hofmeyr had spent most of his early years in Cape Town, as the son of a wine farmer he led a protest in 1878 against the threatened imposition of an excise on colonial brandy by the Sprigg government whose main support lay in the eastern Cape. He also established a Boeren Beschermings Vereeniging ('farmers' protection union') with the long-term object of making the Afrikaner Boers of the west as politically conscious as the English-speaking farmers of the eastern Cape had become. With the backing which resulted, he entered parliament as a member for Stellenbosch in 1879, at the head of a small, loosely knit farmers' party.

The effective establishment of a rival Afrikaner Bond led by the Revd S. J. Du Toit of Paarl, in 1880, faced Hofmeyr with a difficult problem, for he did not share either Du Toit's anger at English cultural colonization, or the fundamentalist Calvinism which this rival political movement then professed. He objected to Du Toit's plan to set up the Afrikaner Bond as an umbrella body for all anti-imperial Afrikaner nationalist movements, with a united Afrikaner republic as an ultimate objective. By astute manoeuvring, however, he set up a branch of the Bond in Cape Town in terms of the Bond's own constitutional rules, and managed from within this branch to moderate the movement's radical policies, eventually securing the amalgamation of the Bond and his own farmers' union in 1883. He retained the parliamentary leadership of the united body, and further strengthened his hold in 1889, when he became chairman of its new disciplinary committee, the Commissie van Toezicht op Elekties. Du Toit's departure for the Transvaal in 1883, to a post in Kruger's government, had left Onze Jan in uncontested possession of the field.

As leader of the only organized party in the Cape parliament, Hofmeyr commanded enough votes to make and unmake ministries, and to secure the passage of measures agreeable to the Bondsmen; but the Bond was never, until 1908, able to obtain a clear majority in the Cape lower house. Hofmeyr's refusal to form a government was a constant theme of attack by his opponents, though—given the predictable reaction among non-Bond opponents to a Bond dominated government—it may be doubted whether it would ever have been possible for him to maintain a stable administration. He held cabinet rank only for a few unhappy months in 1881, as minister without portfolio, resigning after a tiff with John X. Merriman, a cabinet colleague. He retired from parliament in 1895 in order to avoid opprobrium within his party over a bill to deal with the scab disease on sheep—an issue which split the Bond from top to bottom. In this way Hofmeyr managed to maintain his political influence unscathed.

To some extent Hofmeyr was affected by the anti-imperial spirit of the late 1870s and early 1880s. He was full-blooded enough an Afrikaner to oppose the British policy of confederation except on the basis of an independent Transvaal, and to commend passive resistance to the Transvalers after 1877 as a way of undermining the British annexation of that year. With political crises on the highveld and in the coastal areas highlighted by the Transkei War (1877–81), the Anglo-Zulu War (1878–9), the First South African War (1880–81), the Sotho gun war (1880–83), and fresh tensions on the 'road to the north' (1882–5), Hofmeyr opposed the restoration of British rule in Basutoland and its establishment in the Transkei and the Transvaal's western border. These were problems to be handled by southern African governments working together, Hofmeyr thought; but the British protectorates of Basutoland and Bechuanaland were created despite his opposition.

Yet Hofmeyr began with, and never lost, a sense of the Cape's dependence on the British government as the ultimate guarantee of the colony's security. That was mainly why he rejected Du Toit's republicanism. This led him, as a Cape delegate to the Colonial Conference in London in 1887 (after which he was offered but declined a knighthood), to urge the construction of a deep-sea west coast cable from London to Cape Town as a means of improving communications for defensive purposes. He was slow at first to encourage the strengthening of economic ties across the frontiers of southern Africa, but quick to change his mind when the discovery of gold on the Rand in 1886 produced an isolationist mood in the governments of the Boer republics which might have ended with the coastal colonies being left out in the cold. He initially accepted the right of the Boer republics to promote their own railway schemes north of the Orange, even against the interests of Cape promoters; but when it became apparent that Kruger's republic was bent on channelling its economic ties with the outside world via Delagoa Bay, he was not only persuaded of the need to extend the Cape railway system and the colony's economic influence northwards, but took active steps from 1888 to promote them. By this time the Afrikaner Bond was on the way to becoming less an Afrikaner political movement than a Cape Colonial farmers' party, composed more and more of rural landowners conscious that their growing economic interests needed protection. Some of them were already beginning to set their sights on prospects in the far north.

Alliance with Rhodes It was the Transvaal's rejection in 1890 of Hofmeyr's advice to extend the Port Elizabeth–Colesberg railway via Bloemfontein through Pretoria to the Limpopo that threw him, willy-nilly, into the arms of Cecil Rhodes, who became premier of the Cape in that year. An alliance between the Bond and Rhodes during the latter's premiership (1890–95) was of advantage to both

parties. Rhodes obtained a secure basis of power in the colony from which to consolidate and expand his development plans in Griqualand West, the Transvaal, and north of the Limpopo. The Bondsmen obtained agricultural, labour, and railway policies to their liking, for Rhodes (through Du Toit, who had by then returned to the Cape) was able to offer farms in the new Rhodesia, a ready means of obtaining farm labour through his 'bill for Africa', the Glen Grey Act of 1894, and a railway extension plan which brought many inland farming areas within easier reach of the ports. On the strength of this, Bond membership rose markedly, with the help of a revitalized newspaper press in the creation of which Rhodes's hand can almost certainly be seen, as well as tempting offers of De Beers and British South Africa Company shares to key Bond leaders on favourable terms. The ties between Hofmeyr and Rhodes snapped, however, as a result of the Jameson raid in December 1895. Hofmeyr worked hard to discover who was to blame, wrongly suspecting Graham Bower, the imperial secretary, and failing to attach any responsibility to the governor, Sir Hercules Robinson; but he realized that Rhodes's self-defence lacked candour, and would have nothing more to do with him. The Bond formally broke with Rhodes at its Malmesbury congress in 1897, despite efforts by Du Toit, who had fallen captive to the great tycoon's favours, to patch things up. So what had started as a promising experiment in regional Anglo-Afrikaner co-operation was undermined, on the eve of a war which was soon to produce far greater ethnic bitterness, so that in the era of contrived reconciliation which followed that war it proved impossible to keep a new brand of injured Afrikaner nationalism off the political stage for nearly a hundred years.

This marked the beginning of the dark night of Hofmeyr's political career. His masterly statesmanship during the raid crisis, designed not only to expose the guilty but also to reconcile the imperial and Transvaal authorities, was matched by his responsible handling of the 1899 crisis, when he walked a tightrope by cautioning Kruger and Smuts on the one hand, and his own Bondsmen on the other, to avoid precipitate action without letting go of their principles. His efforts to maintain peace were ineffective, however, because although he persuaded Kruger to give ground, he was not able to prevail upon Milner to do the same. As a result, when Kruger declared war and invaded the colony, many Afrikaners (but very few Bond leaders) went into rebellion.

Hofmeyr organized a campaign for the relief of Boer widows and orphans when the Second South African War broke out, as he had done during the First South African War in 1881; but in September 1900 he retreated to Bad Nauheim in Germany, a sick and disillusioned man, having declined to respond to Merriman's plea for help with a remonstrance to be delivered at the bar of the House of Commons in support of the independence of the defeated republics. Meanwhile a campaign to suspend the Cape constitution, together with the disfranchisement—in the first instance for life—of some 10,000 Cape rebels—threatened the power base of his own party. This was enough to bring Hofmeyr politically alive again when he returned to the Cape late in 1902, in time to work on Joseph Chamberlain during the latter's visit and persuade him with some success that the Bond was less of an evil presence than hostile propaganda had made it out to be. On his return Hofmeyr resumed effective leadership of the Bond, from his position as chair of both the Cape Town branch and the Commissie van Toezicht which he held until death. The Bond, together with its English-speaking allies, now collectively known in parliament as the South African Party, campaigned for conciliation between Boer and Briton. It returned to active politics at its congress in 1903, and found in L. S. Jameson (premier 1904–8) an amenable opponent who was prepared to restore the votes of disfranchised Bondsmen, thus enabling them to gain control of both houses of the Cape parliament in the general election of 1908.

Though Hofmeyr never returned to parliament, he remained active in politics, devoting much of his energy to the restoration of Dutch language rights. He also supported the Cape colour-blind franchise, as he had frequently done in congress debates and in parliament, and endorsed the argument during the campaign for the unification of South Africa, though the Bond had previously shown little support for black political rights where these looked like being effective. Not even Hofmeyr wanted black members of parliament. In the run-up to the national convention of 1908–9—of which he was not a member, though Merriman, the new premier, had offered him a seat—Hofmeyr devoted most of his energy to advocating a federal rather than a unitary constitution, in harmony with the views of one South African Party leader, W. P. Schreiner (who could not attend the convention), but in opposition to those of Merriman, the Bond's chosen premier, whose unitary preference ultimately triumphed, largely owing to the influence of Smuts. Hofmeyr was persuaded, however, though a sick man, to join the delegation which took the draft South Africa Bill to London in July 1909. He died there, after the British parliament had enacted the legislation, on 16 October. He was buried at the Dutch Reformed church in Somerset West on 18 November.

Personal life and beliefs Hofmeyr was a private person who, perhaps for accidental reasons, never became a family man. His successive marriages to the two Hendriksz sisters of Somerset West—to Alida Brink from 17 August 1880 until her death in 1883, and to Johanna from 1 September 1900—were both childless. His instincts were conservative and conventional, as reflected in his attitudes to religion and race. He abhorred both Methodist and Calvinist tendencies in religion. His attitudes to race shrank from personal intimacy across the colour line, but abhorred personal disrespect, as was shown in his relationship with John Tengo Jabavu, the Xhosa editor of *Imvo Zabantsundu*, when he and his liberal white allies broke with Rhodes. Despite his posture as editor of the *Volksvriend*, Hofmeyr stands in the tradition of the liberal Afrikaners who advocated a colour-blind franchise in 1853. The key to his

liberalism was respect for others whose traditions differed from his own—a quality which he shared, despite their periodic personal differences, with Merriman. It was ironic that Merriman should have been the one to mock his subterranean manipulative king-making skills by dubbing him the 'Mole', for the respect which this short man with a large head on his shoulders still enjoyed among his followers, after acting as their arbitrator-in-chief for thirty years, suggests a figure who could as easily have dignified the bench as the hustings, had he gone for tertiary training instead of embarking on a journalistic career at the age of sixteen. T. R. H. DAVENPORT

Sources J. H. Hofmeyr and F. W. Reitz, *The life of Jan Hendrik Hofmeyr (Onze Jan)* (1913) · M. Tamarkin, *Cecil Rhodes and the Cape Afrikaners* (1996) · T. R. H. Davenport, *The Afrikaner Bond* (1966) · H. Giliomee, 'Western Cape farmers and the beginning of Afrikaner nationalism', *Journal of Southern African Studies*, 14 (1987), 38–63 · R. I. Rotberg, *The founder: Cecil Rhodes and the pursuit of power* (1988) · P. Lewsen, *John X. Merriman: paradoxical South African statesman* (1982) · *Selections from the correspondence of J. X. Merriman*, ed. P. Lewsen, 4 vols. (1960–69) · J. S. Marais, *The fall of Kruger's republic* (1961) · E. A. Walker, *W. P. Schreiner: a South African* (1937) · L. M. Thompson, *The unification of South Africa, 1902–1910* (1960) · *Selections from the Smuts papers*, ed. W. K. Hancock and J. van der Poel, 7 vols. (1966–73), vols. 1–4 · J. A. I. Agar-Hamilton, *The road to the north: South Africa, 1852–1886* (1937) · P. Van Breda, 'Die Geskiedenis van die Zuid-Afrikaansche Boeren beschermingsvereeniging in die Kaapkolonie, 1878–1883', MA diss., University of Stellenbosch, 1981

Archives National Library of South Africa, Cape Town, files of the *Volksvriend*, *Zuid Afrikaan*, *Ons Land*, *De Goede Hoop* and *Zuid Afrikaansche Tijdschrift* | Bodl. Oxf., letters to A. E. King · Cape Archives Depot, F. S. Malan MSS · Cape Archives Depot, T. N. G. te Water MSS · JRL, letters to the *Manchester Guardian* · National Library of South Africa, Cape Town, J. X. Merriman MSS · National Library of South Africa, Cape Town, J. Rose Innes MSS · National Library of South Africa, Cape Town, W. P. Schreiner MSS · University of Cape Town Library, corresp. with C. S. Sibbett

Likenesses W. H. Schröder, 1883, repro. in Davenport, *The Afrikaner Bond* · F. Wolf, portrait, 1895, repro. in Hofmeyr and Reitz, *Life of Jan Hendrik Hofmeyr* · Mac, portrait, 1908, repro. in Davenport, *The Afrikaner Bond* · Rees, photograph, pubd 1908, NPG [*see illus.*] · Grip [C. Edwards], caricature cartoon, University of Cape Town, Cape Town, South Africa · C. Penstone, caricature cartoon, University of Cape Town, Cape Town, South Africa · C. Penstone, caricature wood carving in bas-relief, University of Cape Town, Cape Town, South Africa · E. Roworth, oils, parliament, Cape Town, South Africa · A. Van Wouw, statue, Church Square, Cape Town, South Africa · bronze bust, parliament, Cape Town, South Africa · cartoon, University of Cape Town, Cape Town, South Africa · photograph, repro. in Hofmeyr and Reitz, *Life of Jan Hendrik Hofmeyr*, frontispiece · photographs, repro. in B. L. W. Brett, *Makers of South Africa* (1944)

Hog, James (*d.* 1736?), Church of Scotland minister and religious controversialist, was the son of Thomas Hog (1625–1680/81), minister of Larbert, Stirlingshire, and Marjory Murray of Philiphaugh (*d.* in or before 1693). Distinguished as a pious and thoughtful youth, with a particular gift for languages, philosophy, and theology, he graduated MA from Edinburgh University in 1677. However, the persecution suffered by his father (deprived in 1662 and outlawed in 1675), and by other covenanter ministers who refused to accept the declarations of indulgence, compelled him to cut short his studies and to seek refuge in the Netherlands. Once there he enrolled in Utrecht University to study divinity, and supported himself by offering private tuition to two young noblemen from The Hague. Although pressed by his friends to take up a ministry in the Reformed church there he declined on account of his inability to accept the doctrines of that church in their entirety. At the request of his mother he returned to Scotland after the revolution of 1688–9, and was licensed by the presbytery of Edinburgh before being ordained as the minister of Dalserf, Lanarkshire, on 20 January 1691.

Hog soon became disillusioned with the course charted by the Scottish church, particularly in its willing acceptance of interference from temporal powers, and came to believe passionately that it had squandered the golden opportunities offered to it by the revolution. Consequently, even though he continued to support the person and the political legitimacy of William III, his conscience would not permit him to take the oath of allegiance in 1693. Elected as a member of the assembly of the Church of Scotland in 1695 he again refused to take the necessary oaths and returned home, having secured a certificate of attendance from that body even though he had never actually been permitted to take his seat. His criticisms of Erastian encroachments, the role of curates, and the failure of the church sufficiently to acknowledge the centrality of the covenant led to a rapid deterioration in his relationship with his parishioners and the elders of the presbytery of Hamilton. As a result he pleaded ill health and chose to demit his office on 30 March 1697.

Hog did, however, respond to a timely call from Carnock parish, in Dunfermline, and was admitted as minister there on 23 August 1699. In 1711 he stood as an unsuccessful candidate for the chair of divinity at Marischal College, Aberdeen. The rest of his career was devoted to writing and publishing tracts in order to defend and propagate his personal vision of a church loyal to the covenanter traditions of the previous generation. In particular he attacked the terms of the Act of Union, the implementation of the abjuration oath, and the attempts to restore lay patronage to the church during the reign of Queen Anne. However, it was his discovery—'by a merciful and most unexpected disclosure of providence'—of Edward Fisher's *Marrow of Modern Divinity* (1645) that reignited doctrinal controversy within the kirk and sparked fresh calls for separation from it (Fisher, 1789, xii). In 1718 Hog played an instrumental role in the republication of the work, which had 'been traversing the World since the Days of Oliver Cromwell', and contributed a fresh preface to it (*Snake in the Grass*, iii; Fisher, 1789, xii–xiii). This new edition of the *Marrow* was intended to refute the general assembly's decision, in 1717, that it was no longer sound 'to teach that men must forsake sin in order to come to Christ' (*Correspondence of the Rev. Robert Wodrow*, 1.24), and also in order to combat the perceived growth of Arminian practices within the Church of Scotland. Its impact was immediate and its growing popularity, among the laity, came to be seen as a threat to the authority of the hierarchy of the church. As a consequence, the *Marrow* was condemned, on 20 May 1720, by an act of the assembly of the Church of Scotland,

which ordered ministers to forbid members of their congregations from reading it, on account of its reputed antinomian errors. Enraged, Hog was one of the twelve clergymen—subsequently dubbed the 'Marrow men' by their detractors—who launched a vigorous protest against the decision. As an extremely prolific writer and polemicist he poured forth a stream of books and pamphlets that sought to explain passages in that work and to vindicate its leading tenets (*A Letter to a Gentleman*, 1719; *Cromwellian Ghost Conjur'd*, 1720; *A letter wherein the scriptural grounds … for the reformation of the churches … are succinctly considered*, 1717; *Twelve Queries*, 1812). As a result he not only rendered himself 'most obnoxious to the ecclesiastical leaders of the day', but also contributed indirectly to the secession of several ministers from the church in 1733 (Fraser, 125). His health failed in 1729, and he probably died in Edinburgh in 1736. He had married, and had two daughters, Alison and Janet, both of whom married ministers in the Church of Scotland. Powerful and solemn in his manner of speech and preaching, his Scottish accent was roughly overlaid with Dutch as the result of his early years spent in exile. He was eulogized in verse by his friend the Revd Ralph Erskine as a

> venerable sage
> the humble witness 'gainst the haughty age

—on account of his thorough opposition to deism.

JOHN CALLOW

Sources J. Hog, *Otia Christiana, or, Christian recreations* (1708) • *Memoirs of the public life of Mr. James Hogg* (1798) • E. Fisher, *The marrow of modern divinity: in two parts* (1718); 8th edn (1789) • *Fasti Scot.*, new edn, vols. 3–5 • D. Fraser, *The life and diary of the Reverend Ralph Erskine* (1834) • *The correspondence of the Rev. Robert Wodrow*, ed. T. M'Crie, 3 vols., Wodrow Society, [3] (1842–3) • J. Brown, *Gospel truth accurately stated and illustrated by the Rev. … James Hog … occasioned by the republication of the 'Marrow of modern divinity'* (1831) • *The twelve queries, proposed by the commission of the general assembly of the Church of Scotland, 1721, to the Rev. James Hog* (1812) • *The snake in the grass, or, Remarks upon a book, entituled, 'The marrow of modern divinity' … lately revised, corrected and published by the Rev. Mr. James Hog* (1719) • J. Hog, preface, in T. Halyburton, *National religion insufficient and revealed necessary to man's happiness in his present state* (1748) • [A. Stevenson], *Memoirs of the life of Mr. Thomas Hog, minister of the gospel at Kiltearn, in Ross* (1756) • [A. Stevenson], *An abridgement of the memoirs of the life of the Rev. Mr. Thomas Hog*, ed. W. A. Clarke (1779)
Archives NL Scot., copies of autobiography, Add. MSS 22710, 32, 38 | NL Scot., Wodrow MSS, Lett, Adv MS. 27 6 2

Hog [Hogg], **Sir Roger, of Harcarse**, **Lord Harcarse** (1634/5–1700), judge, was born in Berwickshire, the eldest son and heir of William Hog of Bogend, advocate. He was admitted advocate on 25 June 1661, and was knighted and appointed an ordinary lord of session as Lord Harcarse on 16 November 1677. He represented Berwickshire in the convention of estates held at Edinburgh in June and July 1678, and succeeded Sir John Lockhart of Castlehill as a lord of justiciary in November of that year. On 13 February 1688 he was removed from the bench by James VII and II, having voted against the wishes of the ministry regarding the tutors of the young marquess of Montrose. Following the revolution of 1688 Harcarse was appointed a commissioner of supply for Berwick on 7 June 1690, but subsequently lived the remainder of his life in retirement.

Harcarse left a work entitled *Decisions of the court of session collected by Sir Roger Hog of Harcarse, one of the senators of the college of justice from 1681 to 1691*, published in 1757. This volume also contains a brief account of the life of Harcarse, who is described as 'in high esteem with all the great lawyers of his time, for his judgement and industry ... Both in his public and private capacity' (Walker, 178). However, Robert Pittilloch, solicitor-general in 1655, published a pamphlet in 1689 entitled *Oppression under the Colour of Law*, attacking Harcarse for improper judicial interference in favour of his son-in-law Aytoun of Inchdairnie.

Harcarse married, first, Catherine, daughter of John Paterson, parson of Oldhamstocks; she died before September 1681. On 13 June 1682 he married Barbara, daughter of Laurence Scott of Bavelaw and widow of Laurence Charteris, advocate; his third wife, whom he married on 24 February 1685, was Jean Don, Lady Greenhead. He died in March 1700, aged sixty-five, and was succeeded by his eldest son, William Hog of Harcarse.

J. A. HAMILTON, *rev.* DEREK JOHN PATRICK

Sources G. Brunton and D. Haig, *An historical account of the senators of the college of justice, from its institution in MDXXXII* (1832) · M. D. Young, ed., *The parliaments of Scotland: burgh and shire commissioners*, 1 (1992) · D. M. Walker, *The Scottish jurists* (1985) · Anderson, *Scot. nat.* · *APS*, 1670–86; 1689–95 · J. Lauder, ed., *The decisions of the lords of council and session*, 2 vols. (1759–61) · *Reg. PCS*, 3rd ser., vol. 8

Hog, Thomas (1628–1692), Church of Scotland minister, was born at Tain, Ross-shire. His parents are unknown, though his biographer describes them as 'honest ... native Highlanders, somewhat above the vulgar rank' (Stevenson, 9). He was educated at Tain grammar school and Marischal College, Aberdeen, from where he graduated MA in 1650. He was licensed in 1654 and became chaplain to John Gordon, earl of Sutherland. On 24 October that year he was ordained minister of Kiltearn, a parish 6 miles from Dingwall, on the shore of the Cromarty Firth, and soon gained a reputation for his ministerial abilities. Some time after 12 April 1656 he married a sister of John Hay of Inshock and Park.

Hog sided with the more extreme protesters during the 1650s religious controversy with the resolutioners, and on refusing to disown the protestation, was deposed in 1661 by the synod of Ross. He was forced to leave his charge in 1662 and retired to Knockoudie in Auldearn, Nairnshire, at the invitation of his brother-in-law John Hay. In July 1668 he was delated by the bishop of Moray for preaching in his own house and keeping conventicles. For these offences he was imprisoned in Forres, but was eventually released on the intercession of the earl of Tweeddale, upon giving bail to appear when called on. Nevertheless, Hog continued to preach: in 1674 he was delated again for seditious practices, and in August 1675 letters of intercommuning were issued against him, forbidding all persons to harbour or help him in any way. He was arrested in January 1677, and the following month was committed to the Tolbooth of Edinburgh, from where he was taken to the Bass Rock.

Hog's health deteriorated while he was in prison and a petition was made to the privy council to have him released. Archbishop James Sharp refused this plea, and is said to have removed Hog instead to a worse dungeon on the Bass. In October 1677, owing to some influence asserted on his behalf, he was brought back to the Edinburgh Tolbooth, and shortly afterwards the privy council ordered his release, provided he confined himself to Kintyre. It is unclear whether he was in fact released, for he was on the Bass in July 1679, when he was freed with other ministers under caution of 10,000 merks.

Hog seems to have continued in his former ways, and in November 1683 he was charged before the Scottish privy council with keeping house conventicles. As he refused to answer the charge it was held that he had confessed, and he was fined. In January 1684 he was banished from Scotland and given one month to leave; however, the redoubtable minister refused to bind himself not to preach during that month, and was in consequence given forty-eight hours to pack his bags. He travelled first to Berwick and then to London, perhaps intending to join those Scots who planned to emigrate to Carolina. However, he arrived in the capital at an inopportune moment and was arrested on suspicion of complicity with the duke of Monmouth's plot. He was subsequently released and in November 1685 fled to the Netherlands, where he met the prince of Orange and preached in The Hague.

Hog was one of the ministers who, on the announcement of James VII's indulgence to presbyterians, returned to Scotland in 1688, though he does not seem to have preached at this time. He was a member of the Church of Scotland general assembly in 1690, and in 1691 was appointed domestic chaplain to King William, though by then he was too ill to take up the appointment. The same year saw him restored to the parish of Kiltearn, as he is said to have predicted thirty years before would be the case. He died on 4 January 1692 and at his own request was buried beneath the threshold of his church door, with this inscription over the remains: 'This stone shall bear witness against the parishioners of Kiltearn if they bring an ungodly minister here' (*Fasti Scot.*, 7.42). Memoirs of his life were published by Andrew Stevenson in 1756, and transcripts of his sermons survive (NL Scot.). A memorial church in his name was erected in Evanton village, Ross-shire.

THOMAS HAMILTON, *rev.* GINNY GARDNER

Sources T. McCrie, ed., *The Bass Rock* (1848), 174–97 · *Fasti Scot.*, new edn, 7.41–2 · [A. Stevenson], *Memoirs of the life of Mr. Thomas Hog, minister of the gospel at Kiltearn, in Ross* (1756) · W. G. Scott-Moncrieff, ed., *Narrative of Mr James Nimmo*, Scottish History Society, 6 (1889)

Hogan, John (1800–1858), sculptor, was born on 14 October 1800 in Tallow, co. Waterford, the son of John Hogan, a building contractor, and his wife, Frances Cox (*d.* 1823), who came from a landowning gentry family in Cork. When he was a child his family moved to Cork. He was apprenticed to Michael Foote, a Cork solicitor, and in 1818 joined the architectural firm of Thomas Deane where his father was foreman. At the Academy of Casts in Cork, which he attended from 1820 to 1822, he drew from casts of the Vatican marbles, made under the supervision of Canova and presented by Pope Pius VII to the prince regent who sent them in 1818 to the Cork Society for the Promotion of the Fine Arts. He began to exhibit in Cork in 1821 and was commissioned by the Roman Catholic bishop of Cork, John Murphy, to carve twenty-seven small wooden figures of saints for St Mary's Cathedral. His work was seen by William Paulet Carey, an engraver and publicist, who successfully induced Sir John Fleming-Leicester, Lord De Tabley, and others, to subscribe to send Hogan to Rome. He thus left Cork in January 1824, stopping in London where he met Francis Chantrey and Sir Thomas Lawrence, and arrived in Rome at Easter. There he studied at the English Academy and at the Vatican and Capitoline museums. In 1825 he set up his studio at vicolo degli Incurabili 8, near the Corso, and in 1827 he visited Naples. During the late 1820s he established himself in the wake of Canova and Bertel Thorvaldsen with a series of ideal subjects: *The Italian Shepherd Boy* (1825, formerly Powerscourt, co. Wicklow), *The Dancing Faun* (1826, Crawford Municipal Art Gallery, Cork), *Eve Startled at the Sight of Death* (1827, formerly Lord De Tabley collection), and *The Dead Christ* (1829, St Teresa, Dublin), which was shown at the Royal Academy in London in 1832. He married Cornelia Bevignani on 11 November 1837. They had seven daughters and four sons, of whom one, John Valentine Hogan, became a sculptor in Rome.

Hogan revisited Ireland in 1829, 1833, 1840, 1842, 1843, and 1846 to deal with clients and receive commissions. Most of his work was commissioned by Irish middle-class patrons who had need for commemorative and religious sculpture following Catholic emancipation in 1829. He produced a series of religious works, one of which was a *pietà* (1843) for Loreto Abbey at Rathfarnham, south of Dublin. In 1837 he won the competition for a memorial to Bishop James Doyle (1840) for Carlow Cathedral, which led to commissions for statues of Irish national heroes—notably Daniel O'Connell (1846, City Hall, Dublin; 1856, Limerick) and Thomas Davis (1852, City Hall, Dublin). The finest of these was the marble group *Hibernia with a Bust of Lord Cloncurry* (1844, National Gallery of Ireland, Dublin). He made a large number of funerary reliefs, notably those for Jeanette Farrell (1843, St Andrew's, Dublin), Bishop John Brinkley (1845, Trinity College, Dublin), and Bishop Fleming (1853, St John's, Newfoundland), and received commissions for busts of numerous Roman Catholic clergy such as Bishop Murphy (1834, Cork), Father Theobald Matthew (1844, Capuchin friary, Church Street, Dublin), and Archbishop Daniel Murray (1844, National Gallery of Ireland, Dublin).

Hogan was recognized in Rome, where a reproduction of his *pietà* was published in *L'Ape italiana* (1837) and praised by Thorvaldsen. He was honoured by being made a member of the Virtuosi of the Pantheon in 1839 and from 1840 he began to receive critical notices in Ireland. After the Roman revolution of 1848–9 he returned to Ireland and settled at 14 Wentworth Place, Dublin. His final work, completed by Giovanni Benzoni after his death, was the gigantic bronze relief of Civil and Religious Liberty (Wellington Testimonial, Dublin).

Hogan's style was based on Roman neo-classicism, which he used for Irish national and religious imagery, reflecting the political and social changes of the period. He died at his home in Wentworth Place on 27 March 1858; his funeral took place on 30 March, followed by burial at Glasnevin cemetery in Dublin. A civil-list pension was granted to his widow.   JOHN TURPIN

Sources J. Turpin, *John Hogan: Irish neoclassical sculptor in Rome* (1982) · S. Atkinson, 'John Hogan', *Irish Monthly Magazine*, 2 (1874), 383 ff. · W. G. Strickland, *A dictionary of Irish artists*, 1 (1913), 489–96 · J. Turpin, 'John Hogan, Irish sculptor, 1800–58', *Apollo*, 115 (1982), 98–103 · *CGPLA Ire.* (1858) · *Dublin directory* (1849–58)
Archives PRO NIre., letter-book | NL Ire., J. J. Bouch MSS, account book, MS 8726
Likenesses C. Grey, pencil drawing, NG Ire.; repro. in *Dublin University Magazine*, 35 (1850) · B. Mulrenin, charcoal and wash drawing, NG Ire. · B. Mulrenin, Indian ink drawing, NG Ire. · J. B. Mulrenin, drawing, NG Ire. · woodcut, BM, NPG; repro. in *Art Journal*, 12 (1850)
Wealth at death under £800: administration, 1 June 1858, *CGPLA Ire.*

Hogarth, Ann [*real name* Margaret Ann Gildart Jackson; *married name* Margaret Ann Gildart Bussell] (**1910–1993**), puppet-master, was born on 19 July 1910 at Hazelgrove, Shottermill, Frensham, Surrey, the fourth of the five children of William Gildart Jackson (*d.* 1937/8), a retired schoolmaster, and his wife, Olive Mary Howle. Her mother died when she was two, and she was brought up mainly by her stepmother. Encouraged by winning prizes for public speaking at St Catherine's School, Bramley, she resolved to become an actress and, after ensuring her future by obtaining secretarial qualifications, she studied at the Royal Academy of Dramatic Art. She then became stage manager at the experimental Players' Theatre, London. The producer there was **John Garrett** [Jan] **Bussell** (1909–1985). Born at 239 Woodstock Road, Oxford, on 20 July 1909, he was the eldest of the three children of John Garrett Bussell (1883–1915), clergyman and schoolmaster, and his wife, Dorothea Bickerton (1885–1962). His father was killed in action at Ypres when Jan was six. His mother encouraged his early passion for model theatre productions and was amused rather than annoyed by his defection from Brasenose College, Oxford, to join Edward Stirling's English Players in France. On his return to London he met Waldo Lanchester and Harry W. Whanslaw, then running the London Marionette Theatre, and there he served his apprenticeship as a puppeteer. He was instrumental in securing a booking for the London Marionette Theatre with John Logie Baird, who was experimenting with television. Their performance of Pirandello's *The Man with the Flower in his Mouth* was in 1931 one of the first puppet productions to be transmitted. At the Players' Theatre he met Ann Hogarth, and in 1932 they set up their own puppet company, the Hogarth Puppets. The couple married on 23 March 1933 and spent their honeymoon camping and touring the Cotswolds with the Hogarth Puppets. They did everything themselves, booking the church halls, advertising, carrying scenery and puppets, selling tickets, showing people to their seats, and finally performing their puppet circus show, billed as 'One and a half hours of scintillating entertainment!' There followed

Ann Hogarth (1910–1993), by unknown photographer, 1954 [standing, centre, with her daughter, Sally, her husband, Jan Bussell, and Muffin the Mule]

more and more complex productions, and fifty years of touring both in Britain and around the world.

The Bussells felt that it was the excellence of the acting that was unique to British puppetry; so having begun with circus and variety, they widened their repertory to include scenes from *Macbeth*, poetry, and operetta. They wrote and commissioned plays and ballets especially for puppets. A ballet based on the life of a rose was an early success. There were many musical items, including a whole burlesque orchestra, and shadow puppets were also introduced. Oscar Wilde's *Happy Prince*, cut in silhouette by their friend Lotte Reiniger, was particularly outstanding. Abstract figures were made and shown successfully, but it was the versatile voices of their puppets and their dramatic ability that made for a close rapport with their audiences. The shows always had panache, pace, and professionalism.

At first puppets were just a 'paying hobby'. Jan was employed as the director of Sheffield Repertory Theatre and then joined the BBC in Manchester as a regional producer of radio programmes. He transferred to television at Alexandra Palace as a drama producer in 1936—pioneering times—until the war came and he joined the navy. This was when he started to write; he eventually published three autobiographical books—*The Puppets and I* (1950), *Puppet's Progress* (1953), and *Through Wooden Eyes* (1956)—as well as books about puppet theatre production and plays.

On 4 August 1946 Muffin the Mule made his début on *For the Children* and became the first star made by British television. The fifteen-minute programmes, in black and white, were transmitted 'live' from Alexandra Palace and later from Lime Grove Studios at 5 p.m. on alternate Sundays for eight years. The marionette characters and their charming human partner, Annette *Mills, delighted young and old. Muffin received an enormous fan mail and more carrots than anyone could eat. Ann worked all the puppets, devised the shows, and wrote the scripts and many of the books that spread his fame. Annette Mills, sister of Sir John Mills, was Muffin's presenter. She interpreted the puppets' mime and composed the special songs to which they danced while she sang and played the piano. The lid of her grand piano made their stage. Jan made Muffin's first friends: intelligent but cross Peregrine the Penguin, coy Louise the Lamb, and sweet, stupid Oswald the Ostrich. Eventually more friends were added. Tours in Australia, New Zealand, and South Africa brought Katy the Kangaroo, Kirri the Kiwi, and Zebbie the Zebra, all made by Stanley Maile, a brilliant puppet designer first met at the London Marionette Theatre. Muffin was originally commissioned from Fred Tickner (a famous carver of Punch puppets) to be part of a circus act, but after Annette picked him and christened him, Ann invented a whole new life for him as a naughty schoolboy, and children, new to 'the magic of television', thought he was alive. Replicas of Muffin can be found in London, Moscow, and New York, and a Royal Mail stamp was issued in 1996. A new fan club, the Muffin the Mule Collectors' Club, was set up in 2000. Muffin himself passed to Sally, the Bussells' only child, who grew up with Muffin and must always have influenced his career more than she knew. When Annette Mills died in 1955, the BBC said goodbye to Muffin, but he continued his career in theatre, films, and books. His last appearance was as compère to a BBC documentary *The Lime Grove Story* in 1991. Ann was then over eighty, but had lost none of her skills, and Muffin was as young and cheeky as ever.

The Hogarth Puppets toured the world, playing West End theatres, the outback of Australia, and the ice caps of Canada. Jan served for two terms as president of the Union Internationale de la Marionnette, which unites the puppet companies of over eighty countries, and the Bussells welcomed many foreign puppeteers to their home. They taught two apprentices and gave generously of their time to help other puppeteers. In summer they toured the many parks of London with their caravan and tent theatres, giving pleasure to countless children. But their versatility was such that they could also provide the puppets and puppetry for Falla's opera *Master Peter's Puppet Show* for festival audiences and gain excellent reviews. It was with the Glyndebourne production team that they produced a large-scale marionette version of *The Water Babies*, which was later restaged by the National Puppet Theatre of Australia. This was the show which inspired larger productions in Britain during the 1960s and 1970s, but only after annual grant aid was made available for other puppet theatres to follow in the pioneering footsteps of the Hogarth Puppets.

When the Bussells retired from performing to Devon

they set up an international exhibition of puppets, showing all the figures they had collected and been given during their travels. This is now owned by the Puppet Centre Trust in London and is regularly on display. Jan Bussell died on 23 April 1985, and Ann moved to Budleigh Salterton to be near her daughter and family. She found old age and living alone very frustrating, but was much loved and respected for her sensible criticisms of the next generation's puppet shows. She died at a nursing home, Links Pinewood House, Victoria Place, Budleigh Salterton, on 9 April 1993 and was cremated in Exeter on 17 April.

Ann Hogarth and Jan Bussell were leaders of their profession. Their talent and friendship influenced puppeteers and audiences worldwide, and Muffin the Mule, just one of their many delightful puppets, became a national institution.   JANE PHILLIPS

Sources personal knowledge (2004) · private information (2004) [Sally McNally, daughter] · J. Bussell, *The puppets and I* (1950) · J. Bussell, *Puppet's progress* (1953) · J. Bussell, *Through wooden eyes* (1956) · A. R. Philpott, *A dictionary of puppetry* (1969) · *The Hogarth Puppets*, Deutschen Institut für Puppenspiele, Meister des Puppenspiele · H. Jurkowski and P. Francis, *A history of European puppetry*, pt 2: *The twentieth century* (1998) · *Illustrated Magazine* (19 Dec 1953) · theatre programmes and newspaper cuttings, Battersea Arts Centre, London, Puppet Centre Trust · *The Times* (24 April 1993) · b. cert. · b. cert. [John Garrett Bussell, husband] · m. cert. · d. cert. · d. cert. [John Garrett Bussell, husband]
Archives Battersea Arts Centre, London, Puppet Centre Trust, Hogarth International Collection of Puppets · Museum of the Moving Image, London, replica Muffin · priv. coll., Muffin the Mule | FILM BBC Enterprises, BBC video of Muffin the Mule programmes, incl. Muffin and Sooty together · BBC Film Archive
Likenesses group photograph, 1954, Hult. Arch. [*see illus.*] · photographs, NPG · photographs, Museum of the Moving Image, London · photographs, Battersea Arts Centre, London, Puppet Centre Trust · photographs, repro. in Bussell, *The puppets and I* · photographs, priv. coll. · photographs, Hult. Arch.
Wealth at death £118,000: probate, 16 June 1993, CGPLA Eng. & Wales

Hogarth, David George (1862–1927), archaeologist and traveller, was born at Barton upon Humber, Lincolnshire, on 23 May 1862, the eldest son of the Revd George Hogarth (1827–1902), vicar of that parish for over thirty years (1858–89), and his wife, Jane Elizabeth (1834–1921), daughter of John Uppleby, town clerk of Scarborough. The family was descended from the Hogarths of Berwickshire, Scotland, who claimed to be cousins of the painter William Hogarth.

Education Hogarth was educated at Winchester College, where he was a commoner from 1876 to 1881. He gained distinction as a runner (in his last year he won the mile, half-mile, and quarter-mile) and acquired a reputation for greater ability than he cared to show. Although he claimed to have had 'no feeling for the grey Gothic austerities' of the college (Hogarth, 2), he observed, when his own son was a pupil there, that 'At Winchester I learned how to learn things, and that was a great deal' (*DNB*).

In October 1881 he went up to Oxford as a demy of Magdalen College. Ostensibly more interested in horse-racing and athletics, he obtained first classes in both classical moderations (1882) and *literae humaniores* (1885). He was

the president of junior common room, and was generally recognized as a man of outstanding ability. After taking his degree in 1885, a year of uncertainty followed, when he contemplated the possibilities of fellowships, of the bar, and of the British Museum without much enthusiasm. In the following year, 1886, he was elected to both a fellowship (and tutorship) at Magdalen College and a Craven university fellowship. This allowed him to travel to Greece, where in January 1887 he was admitted as a student at the newly established British School at Athens directed by Francis Penrose. His fellow student was the Cambridge-educated Ernest Gardner.

Early travels in Asia Minor and Cyprus Hogarth hoped to follow in the footsteps of Alexander the Great, whose conquests 'fired my imagination and stirred a lust for discovery' (Hogarth, 2). A short study on the deification of Alexander appeared in the *English Historical Review* (1887), followed by a full study: *Philip and Alexander of Macedon* (1897), a work dedicated to his old Oxford college. His first taste of travel in the Ottoman empire was in spring 1887, when he took a boat to Salonika to study Macedonian inscriptions (*Journal of Hellenic Studies*, 1887). In May he joined William Mitchell Ramsay at Smyrna for a journey through Asia Minor, and in Hogarth's own words 'entered on an arduous apprenticeship to the best epigraphist in Europe' (Hogarth, 6). They travelled up the Lycus valley, visiting Hierapolis and Pamukkale, then up the Maeander valley into Phrygia, and crossed the Taurus Mountains into Cilicia.

Hogarth gained his first experience of excavation in Cyprus at Old Paphos (Palaeopaphos) in 1888. Ernest Gardner, now director of the British School at Athens, was in charge of the work under the auspices of the Cyprus Exploration Fund, set up with the support of the Hellenic Society. Though Gardner had gained practical experience of excavating with Flinders Petrie in Egypt, Hogarth and his fellow diggers (including Montague Rhodes James) 'were so raw as not to know if there were any science of the spade at all' (Hogarth, 11). The results appeared in the *Journal of Hellenic Studies* (1888) with shorter notices in the *Classical Review* (1888). It was during this excavation that Hogarth came to know the tomb robber turned digger Gregorios Antoniou of Larnaca, who later became the foreman of the excavations at Knossos under Arthur Evans. Antoniou claimed in later life that he had saved Hogarth's life at Salamis in Cyprus when he was allegedly attacked by a two-headed snake. Hogarth's travels through the island that summer were recorded in *Devia Cypria* (1889), a work which he drily commented 'has deceived more than once … sanguine buyers of Erotica' (ibid.).

A second trip with Ramsay through Asia Minor was made in 1890 in the company of Arthur Cayley Headlam. This time they made their way through Pisidia, and later in the journey Hogarth was introduced to the Hittites and their epigraphy at Gürün. The Hittites became a major interest in his later career. A third trip with Ramsay had been planned for summer 1891, but illness prevented Hogarth from meeting him in Mersin. Instead Hogarth travelled with John Arthur Ruskin Munro and Gregorios Antoniou, making a study of the Roman roads and milestones. The results appeared as *Modern and Ancient Roads in Eastern Asia Minor* (1893). The group had hoped to see some Hittite inscriptions at Marash in Commagene, but these had been looted and moved to a North American museum.

Hogarth was involved in the Oxford University Dramatic Society production of Aristophanes' *Frogs* (1892), helping Hubert Parry to prepare suitable music. One of the Magdalen students he influenced was John Linton Myers, who travelled to Greece in 1893 and worked with William Roger Paton on the survey of the Bodrum peninsula. In 1893 Hogarth's fellowship and tutorship at Magdalen College came to an end, and he was forced to look for suitable employment.

Excavations in Egypt In the following year Hogarth's career took an Egyptian turn which, in his view, taught him how to excavate. In January he visited Flinders Petrie's excavations of Koptos (Quft) to the north of Luxor. Because Hogarth had epigraphic experience in Asia Minor, Petrie invited him to prepare the Greek and Latin texts for publication in *Koptos* (1896). Hogarth's main task, however, was to join the Egypt Exploration Fund's excavations at Deir-el-Bahari, the location of Queen Hatshepsut's temple cut into the rock face, ostensibly to assist Édouard Naville, the Swiss archaeologist employed by the fund, but in reality to investigate Flinders Petrie's complaints about the conduct of the excavations. Egypt also offered Hogarth the opportunity to develop his long-standing interests in Alexander the Great. The Graeco-Roman Museum had been established in Alexandria in 1892, and Hogarth saw the opportunity for exploring the ancient city. He conducted a short survey after the Deir-el-Bahari excavations; limited excavations were conducted from February to April 1895 at Kom al-Dikka. The report,

co-authored with Edward Frederic Benson, appeared as *Report of Prospects of Research in Alexandria* (1895).

In the mean time Hogarth returned to Britain, via the upper Euphrates, and on 7 November 1894 he married Laura Violet (*d*. 1952), daughter of Major George Charles Uppleby (1819–1891), of Barrow Hall, Ulceby, Lincolnshire, who was a distant relative of his mother; the Upplebys were patrons of the living at Barton upon Humber, though the Revd George Hogarth was now rector of Harston in Leicestershire. They had one son, William David, born in 1901.

Egypt was perceived as a potential source for new ancient classical texts written on papyri and preserved in the dry conditions. Hogarth's expectation for this type of archaeology is revealed in *Philip and Alexander of Macedon* (1897), where he looked forward to 'some Egyptian grave giv[ing] up the *Philippica* of Theopompos, or the *Macedonica* of Anaximenes' (p. 2). From December 1895 to February 1896 he worked with the classical scholar Bernard Pyne Grenfell, a former holder of a Craven studentship, in El Faiyûm. They concentrated on the sites of the Ptolemaic temples at Kom Aushim and Kom el-Atl. The disappointing results were published (with Arthur Surridge Hunt) as *Fayum Towns and their Papyri* (1900). Hogarth found that Egypt was not to his liking, and indicated that he wished to resign from his work with the Egypt Exploration Fund. However, he encouraged the fund to continue to search for classical papyri, the result of which was the creation, in summer 1897, of the Graeco-Roman Research Account. Grenfell and Hunt subsequently turned their attention to Oxyrhynchus, where they were rewarded with the types of find for which Hogarth had longed.

The British School at Athens Hogarth was now invited to be director of the British School at Athens as successor to Cecil Harcourt-Smith, whose two-year secondment from the British Museum ended in summer 1897. However,

David George Hogarth (1862–1927), by unknown photographer, *c*.1911

Hogarth's reputation as a traveller seems to have influenced Valentine Chirol's choice to ask him to report on the Cretan revolt for *The Times*; for Hogarth the decision was not difficult: 'I had never been in Crete, and a scholar may rarely watch war' (Hogarth, 21). Hogarth arrived at Canea in early March to the sight of burning houses. In spite of intervention by the international powers, the Muslim population was removed. At the end of March attention was focused on Thessaly and Hogarth made a short visit to the frontier before joining a pre-arranged expedition to Lycia with John George Clark Anderson to study the cities of Xanthus, Patara, and Myra. In early April the Sublime Porte declared war on Greece, and Hogarth headed for Crete, travelling into the interior accompanied by 'an Italian bugler and a stalwart Highlander of our Seaforths, whose native brae was Wapping' (ibid., 39).

Hogarth took up residence in Athens in October 1897, giving him the security of a £200 salary. He was expected to instruct the students of the school, as well as to guide British visitors round some of the key sites and museums in Athens. Hogarth's solution was to employ George Chatterton Richards as assistant director for four months with responsibility for lecturing to the students, paid from his own salary. Robert Carr Bosanquet, who was appointed assistant director in 1899, made the arrangement clear in a letter to his father: 'Hogarth to be responsible for excavations, the other man for teaching and running the School in Athens' (5 May 1899). Hogarth as director was nominally in charge of the British School's excavations at Phylakopi on the island of Melos which had been started under Cecil Smith in 1896; in practice, it was Duncan Mackenzie, Evans's future assistant at Knossos, who took charge of the day-to-day aspects of the work, though they collaborated in spring 1898. Hogarth held Mackenzie's skill as a field archaeologist in high regard, and was prepared to write strong references in his favour. The report on the season's excavations appeared in the *Annual of the British School at Athens* (1897–8). From February to May 1899 Hogarth directed the excavations, supported by the Society of Dilettanti, at the Greek settlement at Naukratis in the Nile delta, a site first explored by Petrie and Ernest Gardner. The results appeared in the *Annual of the British School at Athens* (1898–9). Hogarth returned to the site in 1903 for further excavations which were published in the *Journal of Hellenic Studies* (1905).

Excavations in Crete Crete, now under the control of the international powers, was ready for excavations. In spring 1899 Hogarth accompanied Evans to Knossos. They then toured the island prospecting for potential sites to excavate. The Cretan Exploration Fund was launched subsequently with Hogarth as one of the directors. The Cretan Exploration Fund provided Hogarth with a steady income, so he resigned as director of the British School where he was succeeded by Bosanquet. Hogarth remained a member of the managing committee of the British School at Athens. To this period belongs the collection of essays *Authority and archaeology: sacred and profane. Essays on the relation of monuments to biblical and classical literature* (1899),

brought together under his editorship. Apart from Hogarth's own chapter, 'Prehistoric Greece', other contributors included Ernest Gardner, Francis Llewellyn Griffith, and Francis Haverfield. Hogarth conducted three major excavations in Crete. In 1900 he directed an excavation near Knossos—separate from Evans's work on the site of the 'Palace of Minos'—published in the *Annual of the British School at Athens* (1899–1900). Hogarth made the reason for this separate dig clear in a letter to Evans:

> I have made digging so much my trade that I have various ways and methods (largely of course learnt from Petrie) which I consider essential and must apply for myself, under no more than very general direction from home. (Momigliano, 39)

It was Hogarth's suggestion that Mackenzie, then in Rome, should be appointed to help Evans with the excavation of the palace.

Hogarth's second excavation at the Dictaean Cave near Psychro on the Lassithi plateau is memorable for the use of dynamite to remove the thick layers of stalagmites and stalactites which covered the archaeological layers (a technique later used at Carchemish to break through the Roman levels). The third set of excavations was conducted at Kato Zakro in spring and early summer 1901, assisted by John Hubert Marshall, who was shortly to be appointed director-general of antiquities for India. During the excavations the campsite was swept away by the exceptional flood waters surging down the 'Gorge of the Dead'. Hogarth's failure to locate the palace (excavated in 1961) was in contrast to the success of Evans's high-profile excavations at Knossos. While excavating on Crete, Hogarth was responsible for encouraging the American Harriet Boyd to excavate in the east of the island. Hogarth's expertise as an archaeologist is reflected in his essay on archaeology in the Royal Geographical Society's *Hints to Travellers* (1901).

Travels and excavations in the Near East, and keeper of the Ashmolean Museum Hogarth remained interested in the Near East. His book *A Wandering Scholar in the Levant* (1896) had already earned him a reputation; T. E. Lawrence commented in 1910 that it was 'one of the best travel books ever written' (*Selected Letters of T. E. Lawrence*, 87). It was later combined with *Accidents of an Antiquary's Life* (1910) and reissued as *The Wandering Scholar* (1926). Hogarth's interest in the Near East, of vital importance to the British government in the First World War, was consolidated with two regional studies, *The Nearer East* (1902) and *The penetration of Arabia: a record of the development of Western knowledge concerning the Arabian peninsula* (1904). He was one of the discoverers and champions of the traveller Charles Montagu Doughty (1843–1926), whose life he subsequently wrote (1928). Although these works reflect Hogarth's detailed knowledge of the published material on the region, it is significant that his first visit to Arabia was not made until 1916, when he visited Jiddah during the Arab uprising.

After a visit to Cyrene in spring 1904, Hogarth's experience of working in the Ottoman empire brought him the opportunity to dig on behalf of the British Museum on the site of the temple of Artemis at Ephesus (1904–5). Flooding on the site was eased through the loan of a pump from the Ottoman Railway Company. This work was published as *Excavations at Ephesus: the Archaic Artemisia* (1908). Hogarth was elected a fellow of the British Academy in 1905. His interest in the Greeks in western Anatolia was presented in a series of lectures to the University of London and appeared as *Ionia and the East* (1909).

Archaeology in Egypt began to attract Hogarth again, perhaps with talk of the establishment of a British School of Archaeology in Egypt which was being mooted by Petrie. During winter 1906–7 Hogarth excavated, on behalf of the British Museum, in the Bronze Age cemeteries cut into the cliffs near Asyut in Middle Egypt; perhaps significantly, Petrie was working only 6 miles away at Rifa. Most of the tombs had been robbed in antiquity, and Hogarth's experiences appeared in *Accidents of an Antiquary's Life*.

Hogarth was now a celebrated archaeologist known through his prolific writing. In November 1907 he made the first of his lecture-tours to the United States of America. In 1908 he was awarded the Lucy Wharton Drexel medal (first awarded in 1902) by the University of Pennsylvania for 'his important archaeological work in Greece, Crete, Asia Minor and Egypt'; he followed other British archaeologists including Arthur Evans and Flinders Petrie. Further tours to North America were made in 1909 and in 1921.

One of Hogarth's last major travels was undertaken in spring 1908. He made a further reconnaissance of the Euphrates valley, visiting the sites of Carchemish and Tell Bashar. For domestic reasons he wanted a more settled life with a regular income, and so in November 1908 he succeeded Arthur Evans as keeper of the Ashmolean Museum in Oxford. This period saw the marked development of the holdings in Cretan and Hittite antiquities. 'The routine details of his office he conducted efficiently and without fuss', Frederic Kenyon recalled, 'and he combined with his museum duties other work for the university, particularly as delegate of the Clarendon Press, where his knowledge and his practical sense were of great value' (*DNB*). A. H. Sayce recognized that Hogarth had two key qualities for the Ashmolean, 'tact and conciliatory temper' (Sayce, 302).

In autumn 1910 Hogarth was granted permission by the Ottoman government to excavate at Carchemish on behalf of the British Museum; the *firman* described him as 'a specialist in the science of archaeology' (BM, Central Archives, Carchemish file, 53). The site of Carchemish was adjacent to the proposed bridge for the Berlin to Baghdad railway, then under construction by German engineers. Hogarth reputedly persuaded the Kaiser to ensure that the mound should not be damaged. Hogarth's relationship with the German engineers is reflected by the donation of a pot to the Ashmolean Museum in 1914 by a Herr Hoffmann of the Baghdad railway staff. Late in February 1911 Hogarth travelled out to start the excavation of Carchemish in the company of Reginald Campbell Thompson, T. E. Lawrence, and Gregori, who had assisted with Hogarth's

Cretan investigations. Lawrence, a recent graduate in history, had been awarded a demyship at Magdalen College, Oxford, on Hogarth's recommendation; Lawrence recalled Hogarth's friendship as 'perhaps the most important of his life' (*Selected Letters of T. E. Lawrence*, 40). It was Hogarth who encouraged Lawrence to learn Arabic. Although Hogarth visited Carchemish again in 1912 and 1914, the excavations were continued under the direction of C. L. Woolley (formerly of the Ashmolean Museum) and Lawrence. The results were published as *Carchemish: Report on the Excavations, Part I: Introduction* (1914). The survey of the Sinai peninsula ('The wilderness of Zin') by Lawrence and Woolley under Captain Stewart Francis Newcombe RE during winter 1913–14 was at the prompting of Hogarth through the Palestine Exploration Fund.

The Arab Bureau With the outbreak of the First World War, Hogarth's knowledge of the Arab world and the Ottoman empire was invaluable. Working for the geographical division of naval intelligence in London, he made frequent trips to Cairo from late in 1914 as part of a group operating under the auspices of Gilbert Falkingham Clayton, the director of civil and military intelligence in Cairo. The campaign against the Turks was not going well, with the siege of Kut-al-Amara and the disaster at Gallipoli. Mesopotamia technically came under the auspices of the India Office, but moves were afoot to place Arab affairs under the control of Cairo. In 1915 William Reginald (Blinker) Hall, director of the intelligence division, decided to develop operations in the Middle East through the formation of the Arab Bureau. Hogarth and Hall, whose grandfather the Revd Henry Thomas Arnfield of Leeds had been a close friend of Hogarth's father, discussed matters. Hogarth travelled to Athens, meeting Compton Mackenzie at the British School (in July 1915), and then to Cairo. In a letter home to his mother (9 August 1915) from Cairo he indicated that his role was that of an expert on Turkey, and that part of his function was to interrogate Turkish prisoners. Hogarth returned to London, and then, holding (from October 1915) the rank of lieutenant-commander in the Royal Naval Volunteer Reserve, travelled back for November and December to Cairo, where he joined C. L. Woolley and Lawrence. The team was supplemented in late November 1915 by the Arabist, and close friend of Hogarth's sister Janet, Gertrude Bell, who was personally briefed by Hall.

Cairo became Hogarth's permanent base from March 1916 where he worked as part of the Arab Bureau under Clayton. The Arab Bureau, which included a major library on the Middle East paid for by Hogarth, was located in the Savoy Hotel next to the Grand Continental, where its members lodged. This group was mainly responsible for the development of the British–Egyptian (as opposed to the British–Mesopotamian) point of view concerning the aims and policy of operations in Arabia, Palestine, and Syria. It was for the home government to decide how far such aims should be adopted and carried out. The Arab Bureau prepared the *Arab Bulletin*, which appeared from spring 1916. Hogarth was involved with the writing of several reports published by the Arab Bureau: *Handbook of*

Hejaz (1916), *Position and Prospects of King Husein* (1918), (with Major Kinahan Cornwallis) *Handbook of Yemen* (1917), and (with T. E. Lawrence and Lieutenant-Colonel Cyril Edward Wilson) *Tribal Politics in Feisal's Area: 'King of the Arabs'* (1918).

The war was not going well in Mesopotamia and at the end of April 1916 the British force at Kut surrendered. French interests in Syria were also threatening to undermine the British efforts to bring the Arab world into a revolt against the Ottoman empire. Moreover the agreement between Mark Sykes and F. Georges Picot for dividing up the Arab lands after the cessation of hostilities was contrary to promises already made by British officials to Husain ibn Ali, the sharif of Mecca. The Arab Bureau now started to play a more prominent role in Arab affairs. Late in May 1916 Sir Henry McMahon sent a telegram to the foreign secretary recommending that substantial payments should be made to the sharif of Mecca: 'Will send Storrs as required accompanied by member of Arab Bureau' (24 May 1916, political and secret records, BL OIoC). So in early June 1916 Hogarth, along with Ronald Storrs and Kinahan Cornwallis, travelled to Jiddah on HMS *Dufferin* along with £10,000 worth of gold for the sharif of Mecca; the Arab uprising had begun.

Alfred Parker, the former military governor of Sinai (1906–12), had been expected to be the first director of the Arab Bureau, but his services were required on the ground as a political officer at the port of Rabegh in the Hejaz. Cornwallis was now in Jiddah, and Gertrude Bell had left for Basrah, and so Hogarth was left in charge of the bureau at Cairo. Cornwallis was recalled to Cairo in autumn 1916 to be the acting director to relieve the demands made on Hogarth. However, as Hogarth was to confide to his wife, 'in a sense I am the A.B., though Cornwallis is its official chief' (5 May 1917). Hogarth was largely responsible for the difficult and delicate diplomacy which underlay the Arab campaign so brilliantly conducted in the field by his former archaeological disciple, T. E. Lawrence. F. Reginald Wingate was to note at the time:

> I cannot speak too highly of Hogarth's work in the Arab Bureau. His detailed knowledge of Arabic, sound judgment and general scholarship, have been of the greatest assistance to us and if … you require expert local advice you cannot do better than send for him. (Wingate to Harding, 16 June 1917, Sudan Archive, University of Durham; Westrate, 45)

The situation in the Arab world became complicated in May 1917 when Sykes and Picot travelled to Jiddah to meet the sharif of Mecca. Fearing that the revolt would be undermined if Arab aspirations were not met, Hogarth returned to London in July 1917 to counter Sykes's manoeuvring in favour of France.

Allenby's Palestine campaign was gathering momentum. Hogarth was present during the British attack on Gaza in November 1917, although he found time to investigate a mosaic between the coast and Beersheva. In December 1917 Jerusalem was captured and Hogarth was busy negotiating with the sharif of Mecca about the future of the Arab lands. It is probably at this point that he was

aboard a Japanese gunboat, memorable for the experience of eating Japanese food. In February 1918 Hogarth was at Allenby's general headquarters at Umm al Kaleb near Arish when Lawrence, then attached to Feisal's army as a political officer and disillusioned by what he perceived as broken promises to the Arabs, arrived to 'come to beg Allenby to find me some smaller part elsewhere' (*Seven Pillars of Wisdom*, 1935, chap. 90, p. 502, 21 Feb 1918).

At about the same time Hogarth interviewed the Syrian Dr Faris Nimr to explore the possibility of an independent Syria, a development contrary to the Sykes–Picot agreement. In June Hogarth was asked by a Syrian delegation to clarify British policy towards the Arabs, the so-called Declaration to the Seven. Hogarth reinforced this declaration during his visit to London in August, where he was warned that if separate Arab states were not created, it would be 'considered a breach of faith and damaging to British prestige' (memo, 9 Aug 1918, PRO, FO 371/3381, fol. 146; Westrate, 166). His frustration was vented on Robert Cecil at the Foreign Office:

> As for my supposed anti-French sentiment, it is confined to colonial matters. Three years have taught me that in these, without trace or exception, the French work against us, their interests being contrary to ours everywhere except in Europe, and ready to offer active opposition as soon as the War is over. (18 Aug 1918, PRO, FO 371/3381, fol. 146; Westrate, 167–8)

The capture of Damascus in October brought the realization that the French would control Lebanon and Syria, and that the Arabs, under Feisal, would have control of the territory to the east of Jordan. The policy advocated by Hogarth and the Arab Bureau had been thwarted. For his wartime services, Hogarth was appointed CMG (1918) and was awarded the order of the Nile (second class) and the Sherifican order (second class); he was also mentioned in dispatches three times.

At Gertrude Bell's prompting, Hogarth was recalled from Cairo in March 1919 to join the British delegation at the peace conference at Versailles and Sèvres. His disappointment at the way the negotiations were going was revealed to Clayton:

> I must resign and go back to Oxford sick at heart at all this fiasco and the melancholy consummation of four years work. To think that we are to hand over Faisal and Syria to Senegalese troops … I won't blame the Arabs … if they get out their rifles. (19 March 1919, St Antony's College, Oxford, Hogarth papers, F4; Westrate, 171–2)

There was a proposal that he should join the American commission's visit to Syria, but France was hostile to the suggestion.

Post-war: return to the Ashmolean Hogarth returned to his former Oxford position at the Ashmolean Museum early in June 1919, though he did not formally resign his commission until July. Although he had a 'contempt for the party system, for canvassing, and for votes' (Fletcher, 322), he was persuaded to accept the nomination for the burgess-ship of Oxford University in parliament following the death of Mark Sykes from influenza in February 1919; to his relief, this came to nothing. In Oxford he served on the hebdomadal council, and was an active member of the statutory commission on Oxford University to implement the recommendations of the royal commission of 1920. Hogarth did, however, return to Egypt. In spring 1921 Winston Churchill, now in charge of the Colonial Office and Middle East affairs, convened a Cairo conference; Hogarth, Clayton, and Lawrence were among his party. It was agreed to uphold the earlier commitments to the sharif of Mecca, in part through the creation of Transjordan.

In the post-war period the colourful character of Lawrence had captured the public imagination, and in 1920 Hogarth prepared an anonymous short biographical essay on him for William Rothenstein's *Twenty-Four Portraits* (1920). A portrait of Hogarth in charcoal was made by Augustus John for the subscription edition of Lawrence's *Seven Pillars of Wisdom* (1923), for which Hogarth was the literary executor. Lawrence wrote to Hogarth after seeing the portrait in the Alpine Gallery: 'John's thing of you is wonderful. Might have been drawn by a drunken giant, after eating a mammoth. … Mrs. Hogarth won't like it' (letter of Easter day, 1 April 1923; *Selected Letters of T. E. Lawrence*, 407). Although Lawrence wrote to R. B. Buxton, 'It's good news that the Ashmolean has taken the John drawing of D. G. H. That's the first breach in their wall against modernism' (23 June 1927; *Selected Letters of T. E. Lawrence*, 525), the portrait was finally accepted by the Ashmolean Museum as a gift from Lawrence only in 1935.

In 1917 Hogarth was awarded the gold medal of the Royal Geographical Society; he had been a fellow since 1896. He became an Oxford DLitt in 1918 and a Cambridge LittD in 1924. His post-war work took him back to the world of the Hittites, first in his study *Hittite Seals with Particular Reference to the Ashmolean Collection* (1920), and second in his Schweich lectures of 1924 which appeared as *Kings of the Hittites* (1926). He prepared several chapters on the Hittites for volumes of the *Cambridge Ancient History* (1924, 1925). In 1925 he became president of the Royal Geographical Society, and his presidential address of 1927 dealt with Gertrude Bell's journey to Hayil in 1913–14. He also served as chairman of the Palestine Exploration Society.

The man: last years and reputation Sir Frederic Kenyon described Hogarth as:

> somewhat above middle height, well set-up, dark in colouring, with a rather sardonic expression which suited a cynicism of phrase characteristic of him. It was only a superficial and good-natured cynicism, quite compatible with readiness to serve and help others. The outstanding impression given by him was that of mastery of his work. Indeed, except during the War, he never seemed to have a task which called out his full powers. He disliked routine and a fixed employment; hence he passed from one piece of work to another, and settled down to nothing till past middle life. He was a wise adviser, because he was full of knowledge and experience without being led astray by unbalanced enthusiasm, and because he was quite free of envy or jealousy. He was not a fighter or self-assertive, but he generally succeeded in attaining his end, for he knew his own mind and was trusted. (*DNB*)

In 1926 Hogarth's health started to deteriorate, and in October 1927 he applied for special leave from the Ashmolean as he was suffering from a heart condition. He died suddenly in his sleep on 6 November 1927 at his home, 20 St Giles', Oxford. T. E. Lawrence, then in Karachi, received Hogarth's obituary from *The Times*; he replied to Lionel Curtis, commenting that 'nobody could value Hogarth without knowing him' and that Hogarth 'never struck me as a scholar, but as primarily a civilised person' (letter of 22 Dec 1927; *Selected Letters of T. E. Lawrence*, 557–8). On reflection, he noted to David Garnett that 'Hogarth was the last archaeologist to marry humanity and science in that fashion' (letter of 14 Feb 1930; ibid., 680). Hogarth left unfinished *The Life of Charles M. Doughty* (1928), which was to be completed by his son. DAVID GILL

Sources *The Times* (7 Nov 1927), 19 • *DNB* • A. H. Sayce, 'David George Hogarth, 1862–1927', *PBA*, 13 (1927), 379–83 • P. Lock, 'D. G. Hogarth (1862–1927): " … a specialist in the science of archaeology"', *Annual of the British School at Athens*, 85 (1990), 175–200 • J. H. Breasted, 'Obituary: David George Hogarth', *Geographical Review*, 18 (1928), 159–61 • H. R. Hall, 'David George Hogarth', *Journal of Egyptian Archaeology*, 14 (1928), 128–30 • C. R. L. Fletcher, 'David George Hogarth, president RGS, 1925–1927', *GJ*, 71 (1928), 321–44 • J. E. Courtney, 'David George Hogarth, *in memoriam fratris*', *Fortnightly Review*, 129 (1928), 23–33 [Hogarth's sister] • *Selected letters of T. E. Lawrence*, ed. D. Garnett (1938) • D. G. Hogarth, *Accidents of an antiquary's life* (1910) • N. Momigliano, 'Duncan Mackenzie: a cautious canny highlander & the palace of Minos at Knossos', *Bulletin of the Institute of Classical Studies*, suppl. 72 (1999) • A. Brown, *Before Knossos: … Arthur Evans's travels in the Balkans and Crete* (1993) • H. V. F. Winstone, *The illicit adventure: the story of political and military intelligence in the Middle East from 1898 to 1926* (1982) • B. Westrate, *The Arab Bureau: British policy in the Middle East, 1916–1920* (University Park, Pennsylvania, 1992) • J. A. Perry, 'Rediscovering D. G. Hogarth: a biographical study of Oxford's Near Eastern archaeologist and World War I diplomat', MA diss., State University of New York at Buffalo, 2000 • D. P. Ryan, 'David George Hogarth at Asyut, Egypt, 1906–7: the history of a "lost" excavation', *Bulletin of the History of Archaeology*, 5/2 (1995), 3–16 • Venn, *Alum. Cant.* • British School at Athens, list of members • private information (2004) [C. Barron] • A. Brown and K. Bennett, eds., *Arthur Evans's travels in Crete, 1894–1899*, BAR International Series, 1000 (2001) • D. Huxley, ed., *Cretan quests: British explorers, excavators and historians* (2000)

Archives BM, notebooks • Egypt Exploration Society, London, corresp. and MSS • priv. coll., diaries • St Ant. Oxf., corresp. and notes | BL, corresp. with Sydney Cockerell, Add. MS 52722 • BL, corresp. with Macmillans, Add. MS 55133

Likenesses photograph, *c*.1911, priv. coll. [*see illus.*] • W. Stoneman, photograph, 1917, NPG • A. John, charcoal, *c*.1920, AM Oxf. • group portrait, photograph, IWM; repro. in *Selected letters*, ed. Garnett, frontispiece • photograph, repro. in *GJ*, 71 (1928), facing p. 321

Wealth at death £6790 2*s*. 2*d*.: probate, 20 Dec 1927, *CGPLA Eng. & Wales*

Hogarth, George (1783–1870), music critic, was born at Carfrae Mill, near Oxton, Berwickshire, on 6 September 1783, the son of Robert Hogarth, a farmer, and his wife, Mary, *née* Scott. He studied law in Edinburgh, becoming a writer to the signet, and practising between 1810 and 1830. He also studied the cello and composition, and acted as joint secretary to the Edinburgh music festival in 1815. His literary friends included Walter Scott and John Lockhart, and he was himself one of the most brilliant writers on the *Edinburgh Courant*. In 1817, with Scott and his own brother-in-law James Ballantyne, he bought the *Edinburgh Weekly Journal*.

On 30 May 1814 Hogarth married Georgina (1793–1863), daughter of the Edinburgh music publisher and editor George *Thomson (1757–1851); they had ten children. Giving up the law and moving to London in 1830 (at least partly for financial reasons), he wrote for *The Harmonicon*, but was disappointed of the editorship of *The Courier*. In 1831 he went to Exeter to edit the tory *Western Luminary*, and in the following year he moved to Halifax as the first editor of the *Halifax Guardian*; the pressures of his growing family led him to offer his services as a teacher in this town. In 1834 he returned to London and was engaged by the *Morning Chronicle* as a writer on political and musical subjects. A large share of the management of this paper devolved onto him, and it was here that he first encountered Charles *Dickens, who was writing for the paper under the pseudonym 'Boz'. In 1835 Hogarth, as co-editor, commissioned Dickens to write a series of 'Sketches' for the *Evening Chronicle*, an offshoot of the *Morning Chronicle*. In 1836 Dickens married Hogarth's daughter Catherine, and Hogarth actively promoted his son-in-law's career. The cordial relationship between the two men deteriorated with Dickens's marriage, and by 1854 the author was remarking, 'I think my constitution is already undermined by the sight of Hogarth at breakfast' (cited in Carlton, 87). The eventual breakup of the marriage caused a further rift with the Hogarths, not least because Catherine's sister Georgina *Hogarth chose to remain with Dickens.

Hogarth was editor of the *Musical Herald* in 1846–7, and on the foundation of the *Daily News* in 1846 (with Dickens as editor) he was appointed music critic, a post he held until 1866 when ill health caused his resignation. Between 1850 and 1864 he acted as secretary of the Philharmonic Society. He was also for many years music critic at the *Illustrated London News*, and contributed to many periodicals and edited various musical and literary works. A man of liberal sympathies and considerable learning, Hogarth was a just, outspoken, and generous critic. His most important publications are *Musical History, Biography and Criticism* (1835) and *Memoirs of the Musical Drama* (1838, rev. 1851 as *Memoirs of the Opera*). *The Philharmonic Society of London, 1813–1862* (1862) was valuable for introducing music to a wide public, and Hogarth's writings remain interesting for their frank and lively account of Victorian music-making. He also composed songs and piano pieces. In January 1870 he fell down the stairs at the office of the *Illustrated London News*, breaking an arm and a leg; he never recovered from the effect of these injuries, and died at the house of his daughter Helen Roney, 10 Gloucester Crescent, Regent's Park, on 12 February 1870.

JOHN WARRACK

Sources Grove, *Dict. mus.* • *New Grove* • *ILN* (19 Feb 1870) • J. Forster, *The life of Charles Dickens*, 3 vols. (1872–4) • A. A. Adrian, *Georgina Hogarth and the Dickens circle* (1957) • *The letters of Charles Dickens*, ed. M. House, G. Storey, and others, 1 (1965) • W. J. Carlton, 'George Hogarth: a link with Scott and Dickens', *The Dickensian*, 59 (1963), 78–89 • *DNB*
Archives NA Scot., corresp. with George Combe
Likenesses photograph, Dickens House, London

Hogarth, Georgina (1827–1917), companion and confidante of Charles Dickens, was born on 22 January 1827 at 2 Nelson Street, Edinburgh, the eighth of ten children of George *Hogarth (1783–1870), friend and legal adviser of Sir Walter Scott and subsequently professional music critic and journalist, and his wife, Georgina (1793–1863), daughter of the musician and publisher George *Thomson, a friend of Robert Burns. Georgina's eldest sister, Catherine, married Dickens in 1836. Her next eldest, Mary Scott Hogarth, was a much loved visitor in the couple's home and her sudden death there in 1837, at the age of seventeen, was a source of great anguish to both Catherine and Dickens. Five years later Georgina went to live with them and began making herself useful to her sister in running the household and coping with the busy social life that centred on Catherine's celebrated husband. She helped especially with the ever increasing number of children, and taught the younger boys to read before they went to school. She deputized for her sister on social occasions when Catherine was unwell and looked after the family during Catherine's pregnancies.

Dickens came increasingly to value Georgina's companionship (she was one of the few people who could keep pace with him on his long daily walks). He admired her intelligence, enjoyed her gift for mimicry, and thought her 'one of the most amiable and affectionate of girls' (*Letters of Charles Dickens*, 7.172). She acted in the private theatricals Dickens organized in his home at Tavistock House and was his amanuensis when he was writing *A Child's History of England* for *Household Words* (1851–3). She declined to marry Augustus Egg, even though Dickens favoured the idea, and when Dickens's own marriage came under strain she strove hard to keep it afloat. When the break finally came she elected to remain with Dickens, out-facing scandal and her mother's angry opposition: Dickens, she declared, was 'a man of genius' and 'ought not to be judged with the common herd of men' (Fielding, 'Dickens and his wife', 212–22). For the remainder of Dickens's life she ran his home at Gad's Hill, nominally in consort with his elder daughter Mary (Mamie), and supported him in dealing with family problems such as the frequent financial embarrassments and failures of various of his sons.

Georgina was alone with Dickens at Gad's Hill on the evening of 8 June 1870 when he collapsed, and his last conscious words were to her. He had appointed her and John Forster as his executors; in his will he described her as 'the best and truest friend man ever had' and bequeathed to her £8000, many personal items, and all his private papers. After the sale of Gad's Hill, Georgina returned to London and set up house with Mamie. She was reconciled to Catherine and kept up a regular, anxious correspondence with Dickens's expatriate sons; she also kept in close and friendly touch with many members of the Dickens circle, including Nelly Ternan (Adrian, 205), and maintained a voluminous and intimate correspondence with Dickens's much loved friend Annie Fields, the wife of his American publisher, with whom she had herself formed a close friendship.

In March 1878 Georgina began work, assisted by Mamie, on a selected edition of Dickens's letters, intended, she told Mrs Fields, as a 'sort of supplement' to Forster's *Life of Dickens* (*Letters of Charles Dickens*, 1.ix). The first two volumes appeared in 1880, followed by a third in 1882 and a one-volume edition in 1893. The letters chosen for inclusion were, Georgina wrote, 'cut and condensed *remorselessly*' (ibid.) and ones touching on private and personal matters were excluded altogether. In 1879 she destroyed many family letters of this kind, including some showing 'most discreditable and dishonest dealings' towards Dickens on the part of his father (ibid., xx). From 1886 Georgina lived alone in a succession of London flats or with Dickens's most successful son, Henry, and his family. As 'high priestess of the Dickens cult' (Adrian, 256) she was venerated by the Dickens Fellowship (founded in 1902) and continued into extreme old age as vigilant guardian of the 'Beloved Memory'. She died of natural causes at 72 Church Street, Chelsea, on 19 April 1917 and was buried at Mortlake old cemetery. MICHAEL SLATER

Sources A. A. Adrian, *Georgina Hogarth and the Dickens circle* (1957) • G. Curry, *Charles Dickens and Annie Fields* (1988) [repr. from *Huntington Library Quarterly*, 51 (w/1988)] • K. J. Fielding, 'Charles Dickens and Colin Rae Brown', *Nineteenth-Century Fiction*, 7 (1952–3), 103–10 • K. J. Fielding, 'Charles Dickens and his wife: fact or forgery ?', *Études Anglaises*, 8 (1955) • K. J. Fielding, 'Dickens and the Hogarth scandal', *Nineteenth-Century Fiction*, 10 (1955–6), 66–74 • *The letters of Charles Dickens*, ed. M. House, G. Storey, and others, 1–10 (1965–98) • *CGPLA Eng. & Wales* (1917)
Archives Dickens House Museum, London • Hunt. L.
Likenesses F. Stone, photograph, *c*.1850 (after oils), Dickens House; repro. in Adrian, *Georgina Hogarth* • photographs, 1870–1912, Dickens House • O. M. Jones, drawing, 1904; copy, Dickens House • A. Egg, photograph, Dickens House; repro. in Adrian, *Georgina Hogarth* • D. Maclise, group portrait, pencil sketch, V&A • D. Maclise, oils (*The girl at the waterfall*), V&A
Wealth at death £317 6s. 3d.: probate, 5 May 1917, *CGPLA Eng. & Wales*

Hogarth [*married name* Courtney], **Janet Elizabeth** (1865–1954), writer and encyclopaedia editor, was born on 27 November 1865 at Barton upon Humber, Lincolnshire, the second daughter and fifth child of the Revd George Hogarth (1827–1902), rector of Barton, and Jane Elizabeth (1834–1921), daughter of John Uppleby of Scarborough. One of fourteen children, of whom nine survived into adulthood, she was largely educated at home with her sisters by a series of governesses. Despite both parents' fears that a university education would foster religious doubt as well as rendering her unfit for 'home life', she was permitted to attend the recently founded Lady Margaret Hall at Oxford from 1885 to 1888. She graduated with the equivalent of a BA first class in philosophy (official degrees not being awarded to women in her day). Although the Oxford of the 1880s was unreceptive to women, Janet Hogarth evidently regarded her time as a student as one of personal and intellectual expansion. She formed several lasting friendships, notably with Gertrude Bell, and proved herself an outstanding student. In *An Oxford Portrait Gallery* (1931) she affectionately recalls this period of her life, as well as the Oxford experiences of her older brother David

*Hogarth, and of the editor of the *Encyclopaedia Britannica*, Hugh Chisholm.

Few employment possibilities were open for women with her educational qualifications, and after coming down from Oxford, Hogarth was able to obtain only a part-time teaching position at Cheltenham Ladies' College. She moved to London in 1891 and the following year found a clerical post with the royal commission on labour. In 1894 she became the first superintendent of women clerks at the Bank of England, a position she held until 1905. Throughout this period she wrote numerous articles and reviews for literary periodicals and acted as reader and sub-editor for William Leonard *Courtney, formerly her Oxford tutor, at the *Fortnightly Review*. She described this period of her life as one of living 'in a backwater' (Courtney, 167), and wrote that, for women, clerical work, 'was a soul-destroying avocation, from which any woman, let alone a woman of higher education, might well pray to be delivered' (ibid., 139). In 1906 she took a position at *The Times* Book Club, which soon became a vortex of disputes about book pricing and controversies about censorship. There she encountered the American businessman Horace Hooper, who had recently acquired the rights to the *Encyclopaedia Britannica*. At the end of 1909 she agreed to join the editorial staff of the landmark eleventh edition of the *Britannica*. Hogarth's task was to organize the work's immense index, and to supervise a large group of women indexers and sub-editors; she was also responsible for updating or rewriting some 700 of the shorter biographies, while acting as chief confidante to the editor-in-chief, Chisholm. In July 1911 she married W. L. Courtney and continued to work at the *Britannica* until the First World War, when she was employed at the Ministry of Munitions. She returned to work on the twelfth edition of the *Britannica* after the war and made a promotional tour of the United States with Chisholm. In her sixties, and in the years after her husband's death in 1928, she wrote several volumes of memoirs which give considerable insight into the experiences of educated women of the period. She died in London on 24 September 1954.

As a young woman under the influence of Mrs Humphry Ward and her fellow student, Gertrude Bell, and wishing to dissociate herself from militant suffragists, Hogarth took an anti-suffrage position and even served on the executive of the Women's National Anti-Suffrage League. Like many others, she later reversed her position, claiming that she was particularly affronted, after her marriage, by the social and legal assumption that one who had been 'for years a self-respecting and tax-paying citizen, at once becomes incapable of paying her own taxes'. It was this, she asserted, that served to 'finally topple me off the fence into the suffragist camp' (Courtney, 250).
GILLIAN THOMAS

Sources J. E. Courtney, *Recollected in tranquillity* (1926) • G. Thomas, *A position to command respect: women and the eleventh Britannica* (1992) • H. Kogan, *The story of the Encyclopaedia Britannica* (1958) • *The Times* (25 Sept 1954) • *Brown Book* (1954)
Likenesses photograph, Lady Margaret Hall, archives, photo album 9

Hogarth, William (1697–1764), painter and engraver, was born in Bartholomew Close, Smithfield, London, on 10 November 1697 and baptized in St Bartholomew-the-Great on 28 November 1697, though his birth and baptism were entered in the nonconformist register. He was the eldest of the three children of a schoolmaster and author, Richard Hogarth (*d.* 1718), and his wife, whose maiden name was Anne Gibbons (*d.* 1735). The two other children were Mary, born on 23 November 1699 and baptized on 10 December at St Bartholomew's, and Ann, born in October 1701 and baptized at St Sepulchre on 6 November 1701. Richard, by tradition the son of a farmer or shepherd from the Vale of Bampton, Westmorland, became a schoolmaster, and went to London in the late 1680s. Richard, also by tradition, had a brother Thomas, known as Ald Hogart, who was, according to the Cumberland historian Adam Walker, celebrated as a ploughman playwright and poet, organizing villagers in dramatic performances (Nichols, 1–4). Despite the importance attached to him by John Nichols and John Ireland, his connection to Hogarth is shadowy, and his known poems are not especially rustic.

Richard Hogarth's main enterprise in London was to publish Latin and Greek textbooks, the first appearing in May 1689, but he also ran a Latin-speaking coffee house in Clerkenwell from 1703 to 1707/8, and on its failure was confined for debt in the Fleet prison and then allowed to live nearby within the rules of the Fleet, from which he was freed in 1712. He managed to publish another Latin textbook in the same year, but his great aim was to compile a Latin dictionary, for which he failed to find a publisher, and his son remembered until late in life 'the cruel treatment he [Richard] met with from Bookseller and Printers particularly in the affairs of a lattin Dictionary' (Hogarth, 'Autobiographical notes', 204–5). Richard died on 11 May 1718 and was buried at St Bartholomew's. This sad career effectively denied his son all hopes of university or professional training, 'putting him in a way to shift for himself' (ibid., 201), and obliging him to take the route of a modest apprenticeship. He ended up in the undistinguished silver workshop of Ellis Gamble in Cranbourne Street, Leicester Fields, London, where he remained from February 1714 probably until early 1720. Hogarth's determination to rise in the world and his later cantankerousness may have had their origins in the family's early misfortunes.

Early career: the 1720s The passion for collecting rare Hogarth prints in the late eighteenth century led to the attribution to him of numerous silver designs from the period of his apprenticeship. In fact, only the *Walpole Salver* (Bindman, *Hogarth and his Times*, no. 87; V&A), made long after in 1728, is at all convincing. He was able to set up as a copper-engraver soon after his apprenticeship, producing his own shop-card dated 23 April 1720 (Paulson, *Graphic Works*, no. 3), and over the next five or six years establishing himself as a jobbing engraver. He took on shop-cards, funeral tickets, and book illustrations, but it was elaborate satires on contemporary themes that brought him to wider notice. *The South Sea Scheme* of *c.*1721 (ibid., no. 43), attacked the familiar target of the South Sea

William Hogarth (1697–1764), self-portrait, 1745 [*The Painter and his Pug*]

Bubble, and *Masquerades and Operas* of 1723–4 (ibid., no. 44), the taste of the 'Town'. Each employs numerous figures and a minute handling in the Dutch manner to present, in the former, crowds in the pursuit of greed, and, in the latter, the popularity of meretricious foreign entertainment, like masquerades, harlequin plays, and Italian operas, while English classics are carted away as waste paper. His small illustrations to Samuel Butler's mock-heroic *Hudibras*, published in 1726 but executed earlier (ibid., nos. 5–21), led to an ambitious project to publish by subscription, through the publisher Philip Overton, twelve large plates, also in illustration of *Hudibras* (ibid., nos. 82–93), unequivocally of his own invention, with monumental figures and learned allusions to Italian art.

The large *Hudibras* series was a work of high ambition, and it reflects an awareness of the wider artistic world. Hogarth claimed later that even as an apprentice 'the painting of St Pauls and gree[n]wich hospital … were during this time runing in my head' (Hogarth, 'Autobiographical notes', 205), referring here to the enormous schemes for the decoration of the dome of St Paul's and for the Greenwich Hospital by the English-born painter Sir James Thornhill, who held the office of sergeant-painter to the king. Hogarth had enrolled at the St Martin's Lane Academy, London, in 1720, and at the drawing school run by Thornhill in Covent Garden probably shortly after its opening in November 1724. It is possible that *Masquerades and Operas* was already an attempt to side with Thornhill in his struggles with the leaders of the new taste for Palladian architecture, the earl of Burlington and the painter William Kent, for the latter is lampooned by being placed on top of a pediment with figures of Michelangelo and Raphael in adoration beneath.

Beginnings as a painter Hogarth must have received some kind of instruction from Thornhill in the mechanics of painting; his broad handling of the brush and use of colour make his debt clear. Very few works can be attributed confidently to Hogarth before 1728, when he made the first versions of his painting of John Gay's *The Beggar's Opera*, first performed that year. The first three versions, probably all finished before the end of 1729 (Birmingham City Art Gallery; priv. coll.; National Gallery of Art, Washington), reveal him as a painter of much ingenuity, but the final two, of 1729–31 (Yale U. CBA; Tate collection) are of real accomplishment. They exhibit a satirical resonance and topicality beyond Gay's opera by incorporating into the composition recognizable members of the fashionable audience. On the basis of this success he moved into the demanding genre of the conversation piece, which required delicacy of touch, a mastery of elegant gesture, and an ability to set figures in a convincing space. It is scarcely credible that an artist could have mastered such a specialized field so quickly, but Hogarth's ability was immediately noted by the astute chronicler George Vertue, who remarked on the painting of the Wollaston family (1730; priv. coll., on loan to Leicester Art Gallery) that 'this is really a most excellent work containing the true likeness of the persons, shape, aire & dress—well disposd, genteel, agreeable—& freely painted & the composition great variety & Nature' (Vertue, *Note books*, 3.46). Hogarth added to his skills an entrée into a wider world by marrying Thornhill's daughter, Jane (*c*.1709–1789), on 23 March 1729, reputedly after an elopement. Thornhill as well as a painter was member of parliament for Weymouth and Melcombe Regis, and a supporter of the Walpole government.

Hogarth quickly exploited his new family connections, and it was probably through Thornhill that he obtained a commission in 1729 for a painting of the parliamentary inquiry, led by James Oglethorpe, into conditions in the Fleet and other prisons (NPG). Hogarth and Thornhill were friendly with John Huggins, who had sold the patent of the Fleet as late as August 1728 to his deputy, Thomas Bambridge. It is possible that the bestial characterization of Bambridge, also evident in the oil sketch in the Fitzwilliam Museum, Cambridge, is evidence of an attempt by Hogarth to exonerate Huggins. Several of those depicted in the painting became patrons of Hogarth; Viscount Malpas, later earl of Cholmondeley, Sir Robert Walpole's son-in-law, commissioned a family conversation (1732; Houghton Hall, Norfolk), and the large painting of a performance of Dryden's *The Indian Emperor, or, The Conquest of Mexico* (priv. coll.) is evidence of the artist's connections, for it takes place in the house of John Conduitt, the master of the Royal Mint in succession to Isaac Newton, in the presence of younger members of the royal family.

Hogarth's circle of patrons was largely, though not exclusively, within the court or government; he was conspicuously ignored by landowning families influenced by the Burlington circle. Vertue reports that the earl of Burlington used his influence to deprive Thornhill of commissions, and his son-in-law of the privilege of painting the royal family:

> he had some time ago begun a picture of all the Royal family in one peice by order the Sketch being made. & the P. William the Duke had sat to him for one. This also has been stopt. So that he can't proceed. (Vertue, *Note books*, 3.68)

The first 'modern moral subjects': *A Harlot's Progress* and *A Rake's Progress* By the early 1730s Hogarth had none the less achieved a solid position in the world. In addition to a thriving practice as a painter of portrait groups he had some success with humorous satirical paintings, such as *The Denunciation* (National Gallery of Ireland, Dublin) and *The Christening* (priv. coll.), both *c*.1729, and amorous scenes, such as the two versions of *Before and After* (Fitzwilliam Museum, Cambridge, and Getty Museum, Malibu). His studio was in Covent Garden before he moved to Leicester Fields in 1733; it was something of a meeting-place for men about town, and he clearly used them as an audience to try out different kinds of painting. He was tiring of conversation pictures, for 'that manner of Painting was not sufficiently paid to do every thing my family requird' (Hogarth, 'Autobiographical notes', 216). Vertue tells us that he 'began a small picture of a common harlot, supposd to dwell in drewry lane. Just riseing about noon out of bed … this whore's desabillé careless and a pretty Countenance & air' (Vertue, *Note books*, 3.58). In discussion with visitors to the studio

> some advisd him to make another. to it as a pair. which he did. then other thoughts encreas'd, & multiplyd by his fruitfull invention. till he made six. different subjects which he painted so naturally … that it drew every body to see them. (ibid.)

Hogarth's high-minded version in retrospect of this momentous change in direction was that he 'turn[ed] my thoughts to still a more new way of proceeding, viz painting and Engraving moder[n] moral Subject[s] a Field unbroke up in any Country or any age' (Hogarth, 'Autobiographical notes', 216).

By 'modern moral subjects' Hogarth meant pictorial narratives of contemporary-life subjects in series. The first, *A Harlot's Progress*, was made up of six paintings (des. in a fire at Fonthill Abbey in 1755), and the engravings (Paulson, *Graphic Works*, nos. 121–6) were published initially by subscription in April 1732. *A Harlot's Progress* tells the sordid story of a country girl, M. (for Mary or Moll) Hackabout, who arrives in Cheapside in London on the York stage and is procured for the notorious Colonel Charteris (scene 1), becomes the mistress of a Jew (scene 2), then a Drury Lane prostitute (scene 3), and after a spell in Bridewell (scene 4), dies of syphilis in a miserable hovel (scene 5), and is mourned insincerely by her fellow harlots

(scene 6). The horror and squalor of the story are mitigated by a fascinating profusion of incident, topical references, and satirical humour directed towards clergymen,
moral crusaders like Sir John Gonson, doctors, and prostitutes themselves, heedless of their fate. The story is told as
if each painting or engraving is the act of a play or chapter
in a novel. No verbal narrative is given even on the engravings, though verbal signs in the form of notices and discarded letters and wrappers clarify the action in most
scenes. Almost every scene has a precise location so that
one could plot the episodes of the harlot's rise and fall on a
map of London. The success of the engravings was extraordinary, and it can be measured as much in the piracies
and adaptations, in the form of plays, pamphlets, fans,
and china, as in the number of impressions sold. According to Vertue:

> daily Subscriptions came in, in fifty or a hundred pounds in a
> Week—there being no day but persons of fashion and Artists
> came to see these pictures … before a twelve month came
> about whilst these plates were engraving he had in his
> Subscription. between *14 or fifteen hundred*.   (Vertue, *Note
> books*, 3.58)

Hogarth, now a celebrity, published in March 1733 an
engraving that was imitated more than any other of his
prints: *Midnight Modern Conversation* (Paulson, *Graphic
Works*, no. 128), a rowdy drinking scene whose moralizing
caption did nothing to discourage its use on tankards and
punchbowls as a celebration of male conviviality. At the
same time he was working on a second series, *A Rake's Progress* (ibid., nos. 132–9), that surpassed even the success of
its predecessor. The series of eight paintings (Sir John
Soane's Museum, London) was probably completed by the
middle of 1734, but the artist delayed publication of the
engravings, for which he was assisted by the French
engraver Louis Gerard Scotin, to allow for an act of parliament to protect his copyright, that he had initiated
through well-placed friends, to become law on 25 June
1735. This was the Act for the Encouragement of the Arts
of Designing, Engraving, Etching &c., usually known as
Hogarth's Act, which vested the copyright of engravings
in their artists rather than their publishers, forbidding
unauthorized copies for a period of fourteen years.
Because of the delay piracies actually came out before the
publication of *A Rake's Progress*, and the effect of the act
was to deter slavish copies, but not in the end to prevent
imitations, of which there were a great many.

The rake, Tom Rakewell, is a male counterpart of the
harlot, but as the son of a miserly financier he is a member
of the middling orders, pursuing social advancement
with as much vigour as he pursues sensual pleasure. His
career is a vehicle for satirizing the mores of the 'great' he
seeks to emulate. These are not the men of virtue who live
up to the ideals of their station in life, but those who use
wealth and social position for selfish ends. In the first
scene, on the basis of the fortune he inherits, he repudi-
ates his pregnant fiancée, Sarah Young, to set himself up
in a grand house in the West End of London. He then
receives petitioners at a levee, ranging from an opera composer and a dancing-master to a jockey and bodyguard, as

a line of others queue for an audience (scene 2). He spends
a riotous evening in a sordid brothel in Drury Lane, where
he is deftly deprived of his watch by a prostitute (scene 3).
While being carried in a sedan chair towards a royal reception at St James's Palace he is arrested for debt, only saved
by the fortuitous arrival of Sarah Young, who offers her
savings (scene 4). The remaining four scenes show the
rake's downward descent. He attempts vainly to regain his
fortune by marrying a rich, deformed heiress (scene 5),
and by gambling at table (scene 6), but he is confined to
the Fleet prison, now losing his sanity (scene 7), ending his
days in Bedlam among richly characterized lunatics,
lamented only by Sarah Young (scene 8).

After the *Rake*: new challenges   The richness of content and
wit of *A Rake's Progress* surpassed even *A Harlot's Progress*,
confirming Hogarth's fame, and increasing his fortune.
He was now virtually independent of the market place he
had so astutely exploited, in a position to take on other
challenges. His first concern seems to have been to take on
the mantle of Sir James Thornhill, who had died on 4 May
1734. By a masterly stroke he was granted a large-scale
wall-painting commission at St Bartholomew's Hospital,
becoming a governor, by offering to paint free of charge
two walls in the entrance hall. These had already been
assigned to the gifted Venetian painter Jacopo Amigoni, a
painter who had taken away a major commission from
Thornhill at Moor Park, Hertfordshire. Hogarth thus
gained a major public place for his first attempt at history
painting, avenged his late father-in-law, and established
himself as a gentleman of public spirit. This manoeuvre
gave rise to Vertue's famous remark of Hogarth, 'a good
Front and a Scheemist' (Vertue, *Note books*, 3.78), but it also
left him with having to paint two immense surfaces with
biblical scenes, *The Good Samaritan* and *The Pool of Bethesda*
(still *in situ*), in a genre in which he was virtually untrained.
The result is wonderful and absurd in equal measure; the
figure of Christ in *The Pool of Bethesda* is inept, but the
painting is redeemed by the varied group of the sick and
the lame waiting to be cured. Though Vertue tells us that
'as to this great work of painting it is by every one judged
to be more than coud be expected of him' (ibid.), it left him
exposed to ridicule in later life, providing evidence that he
was ignorant of painting's capacity to elevate the mind.

Two projects of the late 1730s built as much on the painting *Southwark Fair* (1733; priv. coll.) and its engraving (Paulson, *Graphic Works*, no. 131) as on the 'modern moral subjects'. *Southwark Fair* presents a dense panorama of London street life, contrasting the insubstantial, precarious,
and idealized life of the theatre with the equally theatrical
life of the streets. This concern with illusion and reality
led towards two projects, both published at the same time
in May 1738: the *Times of Day* series of four paintings (*Morning* and *Night*, Upton House, Warwickshire; and *Noon* and
Evening, priv. coll.) and engravings (ibid., nos. 146–9), for
which Hogarth had the help of the French engraver Bernard Baron, and the painting (des. in a fire, 1874) and
engraving *Strolling Actresses Dressing in a Barn* (ibid., no. 150).
As a meditation on the street life of London, *The Times of
Day* can be related to such precedents as John Gay's *Trivia*,

or, The Art of Walking the Streets of London (1716). The four scenes *Morning, Noon, Evening,* and *Night* are governed neither by a narrative nor common characters; nor are they set in one part of London. The action takes place respectively in Covent Garden, the vicinity of St Giles-in-the-Fields, Sadler's Wells, and Charing Cross. Nor are they confined to one season; *Morning* takes place on a winter's day, *Evening* on a warm summer's evening. They are unified by the contrast of order and disorder in urban life, carefully staged by the artist through visual anecdotes. Each scene is animated by accidental conjunctions, some setting off a change of consequences, comic and pathetic. *Strolling Actresses Dressing in a Barn* plays humorously upon the discomforts of a group of female players forced to prepare for a rural performance in a barn strewn with stage machinery and props. It offers a profound meditation upon the disjunction between the mundanity of real life and the mythological subject of the play, *The Devil to Pay in Heaven,* which requires the actresses to play Olympian gods and goddesses.

Portrait painting: an English grand manner Hogarth entered the field of individual portraiture in the late 1730s and early 1740s. His portraits of this period deliberately challenge the French grand-manner portrait and those of Thomas Hudson, but he never became a professional in the sense of developing a large studio and using drapery painters. Hogarth's decision to take up grand-manner portraiture was provoked by the success of the French painter J. B. Van Loo, who arrived in London in late 1737. According to Vertue 'the English painters have great uneasines[s] it has much blemishd their reputation—and business' (Vertue, *Note books*, 3.84). Hogarth's reply in effect was the magnificent portrait of Captain Coram, painted in 1740 for the Foundling Hospital (Foundling Hospital, London). Though often seen as essentially English, it derives from French examples, combining a composition derived from Hyacinthe Rigaud's portrait of Samuel Bernard (Bindman, *Hogarth,* fig. 102) which Hogarth would have known from the 1729 engraving, with the surface vitality of Van Loo. The success of the portrait seems to have inspired Hogarth to take on more such commissions, mainly from friends. He applied the grand manner unusually to a female sitter, in the three-quarter length of Mary Edwards (1742; Frick collection, New York). She is shown as a great chatelaine, the speech at her right elbow by Queen Elizabeth I, the busts of the latter and King Alfred in the background, the faithful dog and her direct gaze emphasizing her regal stout-heartedness. Other portraits of this period combine the monumental with the genial, and some have a distinctively demotic rather than aristocratic character, as if Hogarth were developing an alternative mode from Van Dyck and French portrait painters. The portraits of George Arnold (*c*.1740; Fitzwilliam Museum, Cambridge) and, curiously, the portrait of William Cavendish, fourth duke of Devonshire (1741; Yale U. CBA), among a number of others, are notable for their direct gaze and vivid expression. He was also capable of bestowing a papal dignity on two prominent ecclesiastics: Benjamin Hoadly,

bishop of Winchester (1741), and Thomas Herring, archbishop of Canterbury (1744–7) (both Tate collection). Hogarth made a number of portraits of children in this period, most notably the large group of the Graham children (1742; National Gallery, London). It is a conversation piece on a grand scale, the fleetingness of childhood suggested by the precarious stability of the composition, the distinctive behaviour of each child according to age, and the rich fabric of allusion to the passing of time.

Other portraits of note are the very large *David Garrick as Richard III* (1745; Walker Art Gallery, Liverpool), a history painting with the actor in a famous role, and the later portrait of Frank Matthew Schutz (*c*.1755–1760; Castle Museum, Norwich), in which the sitter is shown in bed vomiting into a chamber pot, a sign of the life he has given up for marriage. This portrait belongs to a period of return to portraiture, announced in February 1757, as a relief from the rigours of the *Election* series and dealing with engravers. Though some portraits of this period, like *David Garrick and his Wife* (1757; Royal Collection), are highly finished, Hogarth aimed also to produce a simplified type of portrait, based on few sittings and minimal trappings, like those of such friends and associates as Samuel Martin (*c*.1759; Koriyama City Museum of Art, Japan), James Caulfeild, first earl of Charlemont (*c*.1759; Smith College Museum of Art, Northampton, Massachusetts), and Henry Fox (1761; priv. coll.). Also probably of this period is the densely painted and firmly characterized group of six heads known, on early but not conclusive authority, as *Hogarth's Servants* (*c*.1750–1755; Tate collection). They are 'character heads' made from observation, illustrating different ages, probably intended as studies, of a similar date and purpose to the brilliantly free sketch *The Shrimp Girl* (National Gallery, London).

'Comic history painting' and *Marriage a-la-mode* In the late 1730s and early 1740s Hogarth began to present himself as the leader of a national school of painting, speaking out for British artists against the assumption of connoisseurs whose taste had been formed on the grand tour that only paintings by the great Italian masters were worthy of serious consideration. Under the name Britophil, Hogarth wrote to the *St James's Evening Post* of 7–9 June 1737 defending Thornhill and attacking the importing of 'shiploads of dead Christs, Holy Families, Madona's, and other dismal dark subjects, neither entertaining nor ornamental'. His claims to a national role were indirectly bolstered by the playwright and novelist Henry Fielding, who in the preface to *Joseph Andrews* of 1742 paid Hogarth the singular compliment of claiming his art to be the basis of his own theory of the novel and its purposes, arguing that his moral engravings were 'calculated more to serve the Cause of Virtue, and for the preservation of Mankind, than all the Folios of Morality which have ever been written'. This endorsement was important in providing a theoretical underpinning for Hogarth's enterprise. Fielding's further claim that Hogarth was a 'Comic History Painter', rather than a practitioner of 'Caricatura' or burlesque, defined his art as socially useful, distinctively English, and with a wide popular appeal.

In 1743 Hogarth completed a new and more accomplished series of 'modern moral subjects', *Marriage a-la-mode*, consisting of six paintings (National Gallery, London), engraved entirely by French engravers, whom Hogarth had recruited after his first visit to Paris in 1743, and published on 1 April 1745 (Paulson, *Graphic Works*, nos. 158–63). Hogarth claimed in a newspaper advertisement that the theme was 'a Variety of Modern Occurrences in High-Life', and that he had taken pains to avoid 'the least Objection to the Decency or elegancy of the whole work' (ibid., 114). The paintings are indeed elegant in composition, painterly in handling and in the interaction of the figures, but this elegance is rendered superficial by the moral hypocrisy of those who pursue the high life for its own sake, and their heedlessness towards those who fall victim to it, like the earl's son and merchant's daughter, the subject of the original marriage agreement. This takes place in the old master-bedecked house in the West End of the elderly earl of Squander, himself the very picture of aristocratic arrogance and fecklessness, in debt from building a preposterous double-porticoed Palladian town house (probably a stroke at the earl of Burlington) (scene 1). The merchant is equally culpable, seeking to gain social advancement by buying it rather than earning it by admirable conduct. Their children, the young viscount and the merchant's daughter, studiously ignore each other, the former an overdressed, self-admiring fop, the latter, weeping and weak-willed, open to the covert courtship of the lawyer Silvertongue. The story is of the mutual alienation of the couple, predetermined by the circumstances of their marriage, and their separate paths to destruction, as they each pursue the characteristic vices of their social class. The young viscount, who becomes an earl on the death of his father, pursues sexual dissipation (scenes 2 and 3), while the new countess acts out the role of a great lady, holding a levee in the French manner (scene 4), entertaining an even more grotesque company of hangers-on than the rake, and arranging an assignation with Silvertongue. The earl dies in a duel after surprising the lovers in a private room in a *bagnio* in Covent Garden, but the countess, surprisingly but movingly, stays with her dying husband rather than fleeing with her lover out of the window (scene 5). Her own end is depicted in the last scene (scene 6), where she dies in her father's house in the City, within sight of London Bridge. This house, by contrast with the opulence of the earl's West End mansion, is a bare, miserly dwelling with vulgar Dutch paintings on the wall, of the kind Hogarth despised as much as the earl's Italian pictures.

Contrasting directions: history painting and 'the lower Class of People' It is perhaps not surprising that the posthumous revival of interest in Hogarth as a painter rather than an engraver should date from William Hazlitt's first opportunity to study the *Marriage a-la-mode* paintings at the British Institution exhibition in 1814. They are astonishing in the fluid confidence of their brushwork; they were clearly intended to stand in their own right as paintings, and not just act as vehicles for engraving. A similarly confident handling of paint can be found in *Moses Brought*

before Pharaoh's Daughter (1746; Foundling Hospital), one of a set of four paintings for the Council Room of the Foundling Hospital, the others being by Francis Hayman, Joseph Highmore, and James Wills. The Foundling Hospital was founded by Captain Thomas Coram to rescue and train for military and domestic service, and manufacturing, children abandoned on the streets of London. Hogarth was involved in the hospital from the beginning, painting Captain Coram (see above), and, realizing the hospital's potential as a public exhibiting space, he involved other artists in the venture. By the end of the decade it was filled with portraits, landscape paintings, and sculpture by most of the best artists of the time: Thomas Gainsborough, Thomas Hudson, Allan Ramsay, Joshua Reynolds, John Michael Rysbrack, and Richard Wilson.

The success of *Moses Brought before Pharaoh's Daughter* may have emboldened Hogarth to take on a more ambitious biblical subject in *Paul before Felix* (1748), for Lincoln's Inn. Such a subject invited comparison not with Thornhill or visiting Italian painters but with Raphael, whose cartoons, then at Hampton Court, especially *St Paul Preaching at Athens*, provided the ultimate challenge to Hogarth's prowess in the elevated style. In the event the monumental forms of Hogarth's painting are laboured and the faces approach caricature, but the drama and the overall colour harmony make it a convincing performance. Unfortunately Hogarth left himself open to ridicule by issuing in May 1751 a ticket for the engraving illustrated by a coarse and amusing etched parody of the subject, entitled *Paul before Felix Burlesqued* (Paulson, *Graphic Works*, no. 191), with the caption 'Design'd and scratch'd in the true Dutch taste', and in the third state, 'in the rediculous manner of Rembrandt'. His intention was to contrast the nobility of his own painting with what a Dutch artist might have made of the subject, but it left satirists an opening to suggest that the parody represented the 'real' Hogarth.

In 1747 Hogarth published a series of twelve engravings, *Industry and Idleness* (Paulson, *Graphic Works*, nos. 168–79), based not on paintings but on drawings (all are in the British Museum), in a deliberately simplified style to appeal to apprentices and the poor in general. The series tells the parallel stories of two apprentices, one insufferably virtuous and ambitious called Francis Goodchild, who works hard, marries his master's daughter, and rises to be lord mayor of London. The other, the dissolute Tom Idle, gambles, blasphemes, and steals his way to the hangman's noose at Tyburn. *Industry and Idleness* was the first set of prints directed not primarily towards amateur collectors (to whom he also made them available), but towards the direct improvement of those contemplating them. In February 1751 Hogarth issued *Beer Street* and *Gin Lane* (ibid., nos. 185–6) and *The Four Stages of Cruelty* (ibid., nos. 187–90), his ambitions for which are clearly stated in the *General Advertiser*: 'As the Subjects of those Prints are calculated to reform some reigning Vices peculiar to the lower Class of People in hopes to render them of more extensive Use, the Author has published them in the cheapest Manner possible.' *Beer Street* and *Gin Lane* were a response to Henry Fielding's *An Enquiry into the Causes of the Late Increase of Robbers*, published in January 1751, and were probably issued in support of the campaign for the imposition of the Gin Act, which came into force in the summer of 1751. *The Four Stages of Cruelty* were, in Hogarth's words, 'done in hopes of preventing in some degree that cruel treatment of poor Animals which makes the streets of London more disagreeable to the human mind, than any thing what ever' (Hogarth, 'Autobiographical notes', 226). The earnestness of his desire that this series should reach a public beyond even the engravings, which in any case cost 1s., and an extra 6d. if they were on fine paper, is confirmed by his attempt to produce larger woodcut versions, cut by J. Bell. In the end only the final two of the series, *Cruelty in Perfection* and *The Reward of Cruelty* appeared in that form, and it is probable that the scheme was abandoned perhaps because of technical difficulties.

The state of the nation: *The March to Finchley* and the *Election* series In 1750 Hogarth arranged for the Foundling Hospital to receive his painting *The March to Finchley* (Foundling Hospital, London), by giving it the unsold tickets from a lottery he had set up with the painting as a prize, probably to stimulate interest in the engraving, published in December 1750 (Paulson, *Graphic Works*, no. 184). *The March to Finchley*, probably painted 1749–50, is a historical picture looking back to the events of the Scottish invasion of 1745–6, when the Pretender's (James Stuart's) army was feared to be in danger of threatening London, probably stimulated by debates on proposals to reform the army at the end of the decade. The relentlessly dissolute behaviour of the soldiery in the foreground, by contrast with a disciplined troop in the middle distance, suggests a degraded and directionless population beyond rational control. The central figure, perhaps meant to represent the nation, is the hapless grenadier in the foreground, beset by two women each demanding his commitment, as has often been pointed out, like Hercules between Vice and Virtue. The woman on the viewer's left, in both painting and engraving, represents nature (she is pregnant), patriotism (she holds a broadside, 'God save our king'), and support for the duke of Cumberland's reforms (she holds a print of him). The older woman to the right threatens him with newspapers, mainly of the opposition; she represents faction or 'party'. The sordidness of much of the activity, and the underlying political message, sit oddly with the sensuousness of the painterly handling, first evident in *Marriage a-la-mode*, but here applied to the uniforms of the grenadiers, and to the wittily variegated group of prostitutes leaning out of the windows of the brothel on the right. Hogarth's painting *O the Roast Beef of Old England* ('The Gate of Calais', 1748; Tate collection) and the engraving from it published in March 1749 (Paulson, *Graphic Works*, no. 180) also reconstruct a recent event, but this time one in Hogarth's own life. In 1748 Hogarth had visited France for a second time and was arrested as a spy while drawing the famous English Gate. He was brought before the commandant but soon released; in the words of his autobiography 'it was Judged necessary only to confine me to my lodging till the wind changed for our coming away to England where I no

sooner arrived but set about the Picture' (Hogarth, 'Autobiographical notes', 228). The painting dramatizes the event by playing with gross humour on contemptuous English assumptions about the French and Jacobites, from the ignorant *poissardes* on the left, the starving soldiers on either side, the corpulent monk tasting the fat on the enormous joint being carried to the English hostelry by a skinny servant, the priests through the gate carrying out superstitious rites, to the miserable Scottish soldier freezing in his kilt. Hogarth is seen before the gate drawing, as a disembodied hand appears on his shoulder. He later summed up his perception of France as 'A farcical pomp of war, parade of riligion and Bustle with little with very little bussiness in short poverty slavery and Insolence with an affectation of politeness' (Hogarth, 'Autobiographical notes', 227).

Despite references to the notorious Oxfordshire election of 1754, Hogarth's paintings are more than a conventional exposure of current corruption. The *Election* series of four paintings (Sir John Soane's Museum), begun in 1753–4 and engraved in 1754–8 (Paulson, *Graphic Works*, nos. 198–201), like *The March to Finchley*, also comments on the state of the nation. The first scene, *An Election Entertainment*, the most traditional in content, shows the two candidates involved in bribing the rapacious and violent electorate. Again the brilliant handling of paint and the radiant colour effects sit oddly with the rumbustious goings-on. The second scene, *Canvassing for Votes*, is set in a village with a tory inn, the Royal Oak, in the foreground, and a whig tavern, The Crown, in the background. In front of the Royal Oak a bemused farmer is faced with a choice between two offers of money for his vote by the hosts of the two rival taverns, while two old seamen, true patriots, relive the naval victory of Portobello in 1739. The third scene, *The Polling*, centres on the vote itself, with a varied collection of derelicts, led by an old soldier taking the oath with his hook, waiting to cast their doubtful votes. The fourth scene, *Chairing the Member*, shows the successful candidate carried aloft, a goose flying over his head, but far from being a real triumph, the human edifice supporting him is about to topple over, as a family of pigs runs through the procession. The series betrays a deep cynicism about the electoral process, and the choices available to the voters, but not about government itself; three of the engravings are dedicated to leading 'old corps' whigs, associated with the late prime minister Sir Robert Walpole: Henry Fox, Sir Charles Hanbury Williams, and Sir Edward Walpole, and the fourth to George Hay, a commissioner of the Admiralty, the last a close friend.

While working on the *Election* prints Hogarth received in May 1755 his largest commission for a religious painting, the altarpiece for the church of St Mary Redcliffe in Bristol, for which he was paid a fee of £525. The final work, painted in 1756, is an astonishing feat, consisting of a triptych 17 feet in height, with a central panel, *The Ascension*, and side panels, *The Sealing of the Sepulchre* and *The Three Marys Visiting the Sepulchre*. The grandeur of the figures matches the scale, and there are brilliant and surprising light effects in the central panel that suggest that Hogarth had learned much from Venetian artists resident in England.

Reflecting on art: *The Analysis of Beauty* Fielding's characterization in 1742 of Hogarth as a comic history painter had encouraged the artist to reflect on the nature of his own art and art in general. These reflections, aided by discussion with philosophical friends like Dr Thomas Morell, were to culminate in the treatise *The Analysis of Beauty*, published in 1753, but in gestation at least from the mid-1740s. The print *Characters and Caricaturas*, published in April 1743 (Paulson, *Graphic Works*, no. 156), claimed, with reference to Fielding's preface to *Joseph Andrews*, that the figures in his paintings and engravings represented human character in its fullness, rather than the comic exaggeration of a single feature in caricature, now a fashionable pursuit among those who had travelled in Italy. The self-portrait painting *The Painter and his Pug* (1745; Tate collection), engraved in 1749 as *Gulielmus Hogarth* (Paulson, *Graphic Works*, no. 181), attempts to create an air of paradox and mystery around Hogarth's increasingly complex ambitions. He presents himself with pugnacious directness, his own pug reinforcing his challenge to French elegance and artificiality. But the directness is undermined by the fact that the portrait is itself a painting within the painting. As a still life the canvas forms part of an allegory of Hogarth's own intellectual ancestry, for the portrait rests (in the painting not in the engraving where the books are not identified) on three books, by Shakespeare, Milton, and Swift. On the left-hand side the palette labelled 'The Line of Beauty and of Grace' has a curved line that is given physical substance by a shadow. According to the preface to *The Analysis of Beauty* this line was there to excite curiosity:

> The bait soon took; and no Egyptian hieroglyphic ever amused more than it did for a time, painters and sculptors came to me to know the meaning of it, being as much puzzled with it as other people, till it came to have some explanation. (p. x)

The explanation was finally given in *The Analysis of Beauty*, a volume of 153 pages, published in 1753, accompanied by two large engraved plates of illustrations (Paulson, *Graphic Works*, nos. 195–6), that Hogarth wrote with the help of Dr Morell and other friends. The book deliberately eschews the 'more beaten path of moral beauty' (p. iv), concerning itself with what the eye sees and how this can be reduced to methodical principles. It applies empirical study to issues that have been 'over-born by pompous terms of art' (p. 3), and is best understood as an investigation into what 'seem[s] most to *please and entertain the eye*' (p. 12). It is a deliberate challenge to the idealism of academic theory, opposing nature against art as the true standard of beauty, present experience against antiquity, and variety against symmetry. Much of the criticism that the volume attracted, along with much admiration, centred on Hogarth's claim at the beginning that the 'Line of Beauty' was an underlying and invariable form that defined beauty, but it can be argued in his defence that it is essentially an exemplification of the qualities of visual beauty: fitness, variety, intricacy, and

quantity. Though claiming philosophical and scientific authority, the volume none the less manages to retain, especially in the two plates of illustrations, the droll humour and unexpected observations of Hogarth's visual work. The 'Line of Beauty' is illustrated by the forms of chair legs, corsets, the figure of Antinous contrasted with a stiff-backed dancing-master, and, in its absence, in the inelegant dancers at a country ball.

Hogarth under attack: Sandby and Reynolds The quality of Hogarth's argument, recognized by Edmund Burke and others, did not prevent scurrilous attacks on *The Analysis*. There was no organized campaign, but Hogarth and *The Analysis* became the target of a series of eight little-known but brilliant and intricate caricatures by the young landscape painter Paul Sandby, produced between December 1753 and April 1754 (Bindman, *Hogarth and his Times*, nos. 103–9). Sandby's vehemence was focused on Hogarth's rejection of the idea of an artists' academy, the alleged pretentiousness and absurdity of *The Analysis*, and the artist's hubris in attempting the grand manner in such paintings as *Paul before Felix*. Despite Hogarth's persistent attempts to dissociate his art from 'low' Dutch painting, Sandby makes claims of Hogarth's essential Dutchness, exemplified by the unfortunate subscription ticket for *Paul before Felix*, which appears, itself parodied, in more than one of the satires. Though a household name whose images were frequently cited approvingly by novelists and poets, Hogarth now found himself increasingly in a world in which satire was no longer a dominant literary form, yet he himself was frequently the object of satire. With the return of Joshua Reynolds from Italy in 1748 a new generation of artists was emerging who looked forward to an academy on continental lines, saw Italy as an English artist's true university, and England itself as artistically provincial, though few artists were without some admiration and gratitude for Hogarth's achievement. Reynolds's three articles in Samuel Johnson's *The Idler* for the months of September to November 1759 reasserted 'the invariable, the great and general ideas which are fixed and inherent in universal nature' against 'a servile attention to minute exactness' (Reynolds, *The Idler*, 79, 20 Oct 1759). The latter phrase was hardly a fair account of Hogarth's style, but Reynolds was no more inclined than Sandby to absolve Hogarth from 'Dutchness'.

If Hogarth's critical position was under threat in the later 1750s, his standing at court was consolidated by his appointment on 6 July 1757, shortly before the death of his brother-in-law John Thornhill, to the post of sergeant-painter to the king. Hogarth received this office through the favour of the lord chamberlain, the duke of Devonshire, whose portrait he had painted (see above), and it was worth about £200 per annum. He commemorated this event by an engraving, captioned *Wm. Hogarth Serjeant Painter to his Majesty* (Paulson, *Graphic Works*, no. 204), taken from a small painting (NPG). This shows him painting the comic muse on a canvas, a copy of *The Analysis of Beauty* leaning casually against a leg of the easel. The apparent self-satisfaction of the portrait is belied by the X-ray of the painting, which has in the foreground a pug cocking his leg over a pile of framed old master paintings. Hogarth painted this out, but it is indicative of his sensitivity in the face of criticism. By the late 1750s he appeared to be associated with an older political and religious order; the governmental oligarchy rather than the emergent populism of the City, and latitudinarian bishops rather than the Methodist-inspired clergy, whom he satirized with ferocity in what is perhaps his most elaborate satire, *Credulity, Superstition, and Fanaticism*, published in April 1762 (Paulson, *Graphic Works*, no. 210 2), a reworking of *Enthusiasm Delineated* of *c*.1760 (ibid., no. 210 1), known in only two impressions (BM and Achenbach Foundation, San Francisco).

The artist embattled: the Sigismunda affair Hogarth's last years from the late 1750s until his death in 1764 were dominated by a series of self-generated mishaps, followed by painful self-justification, in which he rehearsed his sense of frustration at the ascendancy of his opponents. Yet his increasing paranoia did not affect adversely the quality of imagination and execution in his paintings. Perhaps the defining incident of his last years was the affair of the paintings of *The Lady's Last Stake* (Albright-Knox Art Gallery, Buffalo) and *Sigismunda Mourning over the Heart of Guiscardo* (Tate collection). James Caulfeild, first earl of Charlemont, commissioned from him in 1758–9 a painting in the comic history mode, the subject being, in Hogarth's words, 'a virtuous married lady that had lost all at cards to a young officer, wavering at his suit whether she should part with her Honr. or no to regain the Loss which was offerd to her' (Hogarth, 'Autobiographical notes', 219). The painting shows the officer's moment of triumph, but leaves her choice unresolved, though she appears to lean slightly in the direction of the eager young officer. It is painted with all the solidity and warmth of colouring of Hogarth's late manner, and its sophisticated wit understandably delighted its patron. Charlemont then showed it proudly to Sir Richard Grosvenor, who asked Hogarth for a similar work. Hogarth, though reluctant, agreed because Grosvenor being 'infinitely Rich Prest me with more vehemence to do what subject I would, upon the same terms much against my inclination' (ibid., 220). However, Hogarth perversely produced not a comic but a tragic history painting, *Sigismunda Mourning over the Heart of Guiscardo*, based upon a story in Boccaccio, translated by Dryden, of a king's daughter who falls in love with a family retainer. The king showed his disapproval by having the retainer killed and his heart sent to his daughter, who is seen in the painting holding the object in a goblet. The subject referred to a painting, then attributed to Correggio but now to Francesco Furini (Birmingham Museums and Art Gallery), that had sold at the Sir Luke Schaub sale on 26 April 1758, for what Hogarth believed to be an absurdly high price of £404. *Sigismunda* was rejected by Grosvenor, and the picture, partly because of Hogarth's fierce defensiveness, was subjected to much ridicule at the time. Horace Walpole described it as 'a maudlin whore tearing off the trinkets that her keeper had given her, to fling at his head' (Paulson, *Hogarth*, 3.325). It remained notorious long after Hogarth's death, but, despite elements of bathos and the unfortunate presence of the heart, it is a serious attempt to stimulate the spectator's empathetic response; the artist claimed that on seeing it 'Peoples heart[s] were as easily touchd as I have seen them at a Tragedy' (Hogarth, 'Autobiographical notes', 220).

For Hogarth 'the anxiety ... which attended this affair coming at a time when perhaps nature rather wants a more quiet life ... brought on an Illness which continued a year' (Hogarth, 'Autobiographical notes', 220–21). Horace Walpole visited the artist in his studio in May 1761 and finding him 'too wild', cast doubts on his sanity. Hogarth was particularly worried that Walpole, working on *Anecdotes of Painting in England*, might 'say anything against' Sir James Thornhill. Hogarth revealed to Walpole that he was working on a book himself, which he describes as 'a critical work ... an apology for painters', intended as 'a Supplement to my Analysis' (Paulson, *Hogarth*, 3.326). The text of the 'apology for painters' has been pieced together from Hogarth's manuscripts in the British Library (Kitson), but it was in a far from publishable state when Hogarth left it. Among other things it states the case against the idea of an academy, on the grounds that it would inevitably base its teaching on sterile copying. The neglect of contemporary artists is now blamed more on trading interests than aristocratic connoisseurs, but he continues to assert the authority of the artist over the amateur as a judge of art.

The wrong politics: Hogarth on the defensive The opposition to trading interests was probably connected with Hogarth's association with the Society of Artists, in opposition to the Society for the Encouragement of Arts, Manufactures, and Commerce (the Society of Arts), which hosted art exhibitions in April 1760 and 1761. The latter exhibition was followed by the Society of Artists exhibition on 9 May, the catalogue of which was adorned by two designs by Hogarth, engraved by Grignion (Paulson, *Graphic Works*, nos. 236–7). One shows a monkey dressed as a connoisseur watering the stumps of dead trees, signifying the old masters; the other shows healthy plants watered by Britannia from a fountain presided over by the new king, George III. Hogarth's vigorous defence of English art had brought him allies as well as opponents, and he could count on the support at this time of the actor David Garrick, the playwright George Colman, and the journalist Bonnell Thornton. Thornton's efforts in particular, and his interest in popular culture as a distinctive manifestation of English culture, led to the opening on 22 April 1762 of the Sign Painters' Exhibition, partly 'designed as a ridicule on the Exhibitions of the Society for the Encouragement of the Arts, &c. and of other Artists' (Paulson, *Hogarth*, 3.353). Hogarth was assumed by satirists to have been a prime mover, and many works in the exhibition make specific reference to motifs in his prints, but it is not certain that he was directly involved, or that any of his own work was exhibited.

Hogarth, unlike many of his peers, was unmoved by the 'new politics' of William Pitt and later of John Wilkes, which were expansionist, warlike, populist, and anti-court. Instead he drew closer to the court and to the king's unpopular adviser, the earl of Bute, even making an unexpected return to party political satire by issuing 'The Times', pl. I (Paulson, Graphic Works, no. 211) in September 1762, followed by 'The Times', pl. 2, which was not issued in Hogarth's lifetime (ibid., no. 212). Hogarth had made a number of overtly political satires in the 1720s, but he seems pointedly to avoid them in the next decade, refusing, for example, to produce a 'Robin's progress' to satirize Sir Robert Walpole. There are undeniable political and national allusions in The March to Finchley and the Election series, but 'The Times', pl. I adopts specific party positions and alludes to immediate events and personalities. Hogarth claimed that he made the print to

> stop a gap in my income this produce[d] the Print call the Times the subject of which tended to Peace and unanimity and so put the opposers of this humane purpose in a light which gave offence to the Fomenters of distruction in the minds of the people.   (Hogarth, 'Autobiographical notes', 221)

It was an answer to an anonymous print, John Bull's House Sett in Flames (impression in the British Museum), and it shows Pitt fanning the flames of the war, and the government trying to put out the fire. Pitt is shown as a figure on stilts with bellows, in the first two states as Henry VIII, adored by the aldermen and mob of the City of London. Revealing his political colours in that way was extremely rash; it led to a breach with John Wilkes, who had been a friend, as well as with the poet Charles Churchill. Wilkes had established the anti-government periodical, the ironically titled North Briton, with the particular intention of targeting Bute. On hearing of Hogarth's intention to publish 'The Times', pl. I, he remonstrated unsuccessfully with the artist, whose allegiance to the court evidently surprised him.

'A feeling mind': retaliation, despair, and death Taking on Wilkes and Churchill was bound to invite retaliation, and David Garrick pleaded with Churchill not to reply for fear of Hogarth's fragile state of mind (Paulson, Hogarth, 3.384). Wilkes's retaliation took the form of a long essay, published on 25 December 1762, which took up the whole of no. 17 of the North Briton. It was a devastating attack, all the more effective for its cool tone and pretended air of solicitude. It makes the point, by then commonplace, that Hogarth's gifts were only in treating of vice, or what Wilkes calls 'gibbeting in colours', because he is incapable of depicting virtue. Wilkes sneers at his vanity, and his acceptance of a place at court, dwelling at length on the pretentiousness of Sigismunda and his dismissal of the old masters. Hogarth is above all self-centred and greedy: 'Gain and vanity have steered his light bark quite thro' life. He has never been consistent, but to those two principles.' He has behaved disgracefully to his fellow artists, claiming that 'There is at this hour scarcely a single man of any degree of merit in his own profession, with whom he does not hold a professed enmity.' Hogarth was by now seriously ill, indeed widely believed to be dying, and his account of the affair in his 'Autobiographical notes', written shortly afterwards, could not be more poignant:

'being at that time at my worst in a kind of slow feaver, it could not but hurt … a feeling mind' (p. 221). However, he recovered sufficiently to take revenge. After Wilkes published no. 45 of the North Briton in April 1763, he was arrested for attacking the king's speech. Hogarth went to Westminster Hall and drew him during the hearing that culminated in acquittal; in Wilkes's words 'the painter was wholly employed in caricaturing the person of the man, while all the rest of his fellow citizens were animated in his cause' (Paulson, Hogarth, 3.395). Hogarth's drawing, indented for transfer to the plate, still survives (BM), and the etching he made from it (Paulson, Graphic Works, no. 214) is a masterpiece of restrained caricature, 'as like as I could as to feature at the same time some indication of his mind' (Hogarth, 'Autobiographical notes', 221), suggesting by slight exaggeration Wilkes's leering cynicism. It is also deliberately paired with Hogarth's portrait etching of Lord Lovat, the Jacobite beheaded for treason in 1747 (Paulson, Graphic Works, no. 166).

Hogarth's quarrel with Wilkes provoked a flood of hostile caricatures playing on the painter's supposed closeness to the earl of Bute (Bindman, Hogarth and his Times, nos. 119–21). A further blow was the publication at the end of June 1763 of Charles Churchill's Epistle to William Hogarth, though it had nothing like the effect on the artist of Wilkes's attack, and its description of Hogarth's decrepitude excited more sympathy than contempt. Hogarth responded to it by producing a satire of Churchill as a bear, published in August 1763 (Paulson, Graphic Works, no. 215), captioned 'The Bruiser, C. Churchill (once the Rev.d!) In the Character of a Modern Hercules, Regaling himself after having Kill'd the Monster Caricatura that so Sorely Gall'd his Virtuos friend the Heaven born Wilkes'. Hogarth made the print by rubbing down the portrait image of the self-portrait plate of 1748, Gulielmus Hogarth (see above), a literal self-effacement that anticipates the alterations he made in 1764 to the other self-portrait print of 1758, Wm. Hogarth Serjeant Painter to his Majesty. He removed the title, replacing it with 'William Hogarth, 1764', and altered the face, replacing the smile with a grave expression.

Hogarth's last print, The bathos, or, Manner of sinking in sublime paintings, inscribed to the dealers in dark pictures (Paulson, Graphic Works, no. 216), designed to 'serve as a Tail-Piece to all the Author's Engraved Works', is a bleak and apocalyptic summation of his sense of personal failure and the failure of human aspirations. In a parody of the language of elevated paintings and grandiose church monuments, an expiring Father Time lies among broken symbols of nature, church, and state, every element referring, often punningly, to the end of all things. A collapsing inn sign for the World's End is adorned with the world in flames, and even Apollo in his chariot falls from the sky. Hogarth's principal concern in his last months was to refresh his copperplates, to bolster his posthumous reputation and produce a continuing income for his widow, and he continued to work on his autobiography. He died in his house in Leicester Fields, during the night of 25–6 October 1764, and was buried in Chiswick churchyard on 2 November.

According to Horace Walpole he died of 'a dropsy of his breast' (Walpole, 4.80), but Nichols claimed in later editions of *Biographical Anecdotes* that he died of 'an aneurism' (Paulson, *Hogarth*, 3.532). He left his copperplates and properties to his widow, Jane, and she made her living by reprinting from them until her own death in 1789.

Posthumous reputation and afterlife Hogarth has often been described as the father of British painting, but he was not the first English-born painter of note; William Dobson and his own father-in-law, Sir James Thornhill, could also claim that honour. But his impact on his own time and upon subsequent generations has been overwhelming. His 'modern moral subjects', especially *A Rake's Progress*, have seen numerous adaptations over the last two centuries, in the form of plays, operas, novels, and painted and printed series. He has been frequently celebrated, rightly or wrongly, as archetypally English in the literariness of his imagination, and the coarseness and directness of his imagery. His paintings have been, since the early nineteenth century, among the most admired of the British school, but his wider fame before recent times was based on the ubiquity of his engravings, usually in late printings and other debased forms. Even so, from his own lifetime his reputation was international. He was an important figure in later eighteenth-century Germany, largely through the brilliant commentaries on the prints by Georg Christoph Lichtenberg (1742–1799), which first appeared between 1784 and 1796 in the *Göttinger Taschenkalender*. It is noteworthy that *The Analysis of Beauty* appeared in two German editions in 1754: in Hanover, published by J. W. Schmidt, and in Berlin and Potsdam, published by C. F. Voss; an Italian edition was published in Leghorn in 1761, and a French edition was published in Paris in 1805.

Hogarth was a posthumous victim, even in his wife's lifetime, of what Edmund Malone called in 1781 'Hogarthomania', the fanatical desire to collect rare impressions and states of his prints (Bindman, *Hogarth and his Times*, 58). This was stimulated by the publication of Walpole's *Anecdotes of Painting in England* and John Nichols's *Biographical Anecdotes of William Hogarth*, also in 1781. Several collectors, most notably George Steevens, sought complete collections in the best impressions, and competed furiously against other collectors for rarities (Steevens's collection is in the Lewis Walpole Library, Farmington, Connecticut). The result was to add a large number of dubious prints to Hogarth's *œuvre*, especially juvenilia, and Samuel Ireland, though he bought a number of genuine works from Mrs Hogarth, had a great many doubtful works and some outright forgeries. The other early collection to remain intact is the Royal Collection started by George III, with many rarities added by George IV. Meanwhile the copperplates inherited by Mrs Hogarth continued to be printed off on demand, and were then bought after her death by John and Josiah Boydell and printed in an edition of 103 plates. In 1818 they were acquired by Baldwin, Cradock, and Joy, and restored by James Heath; in 1835 they passed to Henry G. Bohn, in 1864 to Chatto and Windus, and some time later to Bernard Quaritch. They were printed from almost incessantly until the end of the nineteenth century, and those that have survived are completely worn out.

Many commentators on Hogarth's work from his own time to the present, including Horace Walpole, Charles Lamb, and William Hazlitt, all of whom wrote extended accounts of Hogarth's engravings, have remarked upon their contradictory nature; pathos coexists with ribald humour and subtlety with coarseness. In the years after his death two barely reconcilable versions of Hogarth emerged, championed by opposing parties. For Horace Walpole, in the fourth volume of *Anecdotes of Painting in England*, printed privately in 1771 and published in October 1780, Hogarth was a highly sophisticated practitioner of social comedy like Molière, catching 'the manners and follies of an age *living as they rise*' (p. 357); for John Ireland, in *Hogarth Illustrated* (1785), on the other hand, he is an outsider, a countryman in touch with his north country background, 'the pupil,—the disciple,—the worshipper of nature!' appalled at the corruptions of the 'town' (1884 edn, 53). Hazlitt countered this view by pointing out: 'I know no one who had a less pastoral imagination than Hogarth. He delights in the thick of St Giles's or St James's. His pictures breathe a certain close, greasy, tavern air' (W. Hazlitt, *Lectures on the English Comic Writers*, 3rd edn, 1841, 292). Though both versions of Hogarth have had passionate supporters, the notion of Hogarth as an unsophisticated man of the people, implacably opposed to those in power, has tended to remain alive, though there is little basis for it in his life. It can be seen in George Augustus Sala's *William Hogarth: Painter, Engraver, and Philosopher* (1866), where his rural ancestry as 'descendent of a long line of north country yeomen' with 'Saxon' forebears, made him a 'healthy' example to modern urban youth. Marxist authors, like Francis David Klingender in *Hogarth and English Caricature* (1944), have seen him as part of a popular stream, alienated from power, while Frederick Antal in *Hogarth and his Place in European Art* (1962) identified him plausibly as a member of the progressive bourgeoisie of his time.

For subsequent artists Hogarth has been the touchstone for a morally inflected realist art, an art of social utility. Wherever such art has emerged in strength, in the Victorian period, in the aftermath of the First World War, in the United States in the 1930s, and in recent years in the aftermath of modernism, Hogarth has always been strongly invoked. Yet even self-proclaimed modernists have found merit in Hogarth's vigorous independence and apparent alienation from conventional society. Perhaps his greatest single contribution has been through the idea of the 'Progress' as a narrative life-history in a series of satirical episodes, allowing for pathos, indignation, and wit. Of the many artists who have made explicitly Hogarthian series the following may be noted: in the eighteenth century, Thomas Rowlandson, James Gillray, John Collet, James Northcote, and Daniel Chodowiecki; in the nineteenth century, Johann Heinrich Ramberg, George Cruikshank, Augustus Egg, and William Powell Frith; in the twentieth century, Otto Dix, George Grosz, Peter Howson, Jörg

Immendorf, David Low, and Ronald Searle. The two best-known twentieth-century interpretations are associated with the painter David Hockney (*b.* 1937): the series of sixteen etchings (1961–3) entitled *A Rake's Progress* (Bindman, *Hogarth and his Times*, no. 1), in which the story of the rake is used as a frame for a narrative of the artist's first visit to New York, and the opera by Igor Stravinsky, with libretto by W. H. Auden and Chester Kallman, *The Rake's Progress* of 1951, for which Hockney designed sets for Glyndebourne in 1975, using Hogarth's designs and a cross-hatching technique based on his engravings. There will be many more Hogarthian progresses in the twenty-first century.

DAVID BINDMAN

Sources W. Hogarth, 'Autobiographical notes', *'The analysis of beauty', with the rejected passages from the manuscript drafts, and autobiographical notes*, ed. J. Burke (1955) [compilation of Hogarth MSS in BL] · M. Kitson, ed., 'Hogarth's "Apology for painters"', *Walpole Society*, 41 (1966–8), 46–111 · W. Hogarth, *The analysis of beauty* (1753) · R. Paulson, *Hogarth*, 1 (1991) · R. Paulson, *Hogarth*, 2 (1992) · R. Paulson, *Hogarth*, 3 (1993) · R. Paulson, *Hogarth: his life, art and times*, 2 vols. (1971) · R. Paulson, *Hogarth's graphic works*, 3rd edn (1989) · Vertue, *Note books*, vol. 3 · R. B. Beckett, *Hogarth* (1948) [catalogue of paintings] · A. P. Oppé, *The drawings of William Hogarth* (1948) [catalogue] · E. Einberg and J. Egerton, *The age of Hogarth: British painters born 1675–1709* (1988) · J. Egerton, *The British school* (1998) · F. G. Stephens and M. D. George, eds., *Catalogue of prints and drawings in the British Museum, division 1: political and personal satires*, 3 (1877) · H. Walpole, *Anecdotes of painting in England … collected by the late George Vertue, and now digested and published*, 4 (1771, [1780]) · J. Nichols, *Biographical anecdotes of William Hogarth, and a catalogue of his works chronologically arranged with occasional remarks*, 3rd edn (1785) · J. Nichols and G. Steevens, *The genuine works of William Hogarth* (1817) · D. Bindman, *Hogarth* (1981) · D. Bindman, *Hogarth and his times: serious comedy* (1997) [exhibition catalogue, BM, Sept 1997 – Jan 1998] · D. Kunzle, 'Plagiaries-by-memory of the *Rake's progress* and the genesis of Hogarth's second picture story', *Journal of the Warburg and Courtauld Institutes*, 29 (1966), 311–48 · R. Simon and C. Woodward, eds., *A rake's progress: from Hogarth to Hockney* (1997) [exhibition catalogue, Sir John Soane's Museum, London, 26 March – 31 Aug 1997] · W. Busch, *Das sentimentalische Bild: Die Krise der Kunst im 18. Jahrhundert und die Geburt der Moderne* (1993) · L. Gowing, *Hogarth* (1971) [exhibition catalogue, Tate Gallery, London] · *Lichtenberg's commentaries on Hogarth's engravings*, trans. I. Herdan and G. Herdan (1966) · B. W. Krysmanski, *Hogarth's enthusiasm delineated: Nachahmung als Kritik am Kennertum* (1996) [incl. bibliography] · A. Dobson, *William Hogarth* (1907) · family bible, BL, C.45.3.15

Archives BL, drafts of *The analysis of beauty*, Add. MS 27992, Egerton MSS 3011–3016 · BL, fragments of autobiography, corresp., and notes, Add. MS 23394, 27991, 27993, 27995

Likenesses W. Hogarth, self-portrait, oils, 1745, Tate collection [*see illus.*] · self-portrait, group, oils, 1748 (*O the roast beef of old England*; 'The Gate of Calais'), Tate collection · engraving, pubd 1749 (after self-portrait, group, oils by W. Hogarth, 1748), repro. in Paulson, *Graphic works*, no. 180 · W. Hogarth, self-portrait, oils, *c.*1758, NPG · L. F. Roubiliac, terracotta bust, NPG

Wealth at death see will, Paulson, *Hogarth: his life*, vol. 2, p. 508

Hogarth, William (1786–1866), vicar apostolic of the northern district and Roman Catholic bishop of Hexham and Newcastle, was born on 25 March 1786 at Dodding Green, near Kendal, Westmorland, where his family had retained their faith and their lands through penal times. William and his elder brother Robert (1785–1868) were educated from 1796 as church students at Crook Hall, co. Durham, where students from the English secular college at Douai had settled in 1794 and which was removed to Ushaw in 1808. They both survived an outbreak of typhus at the college in the winter of 1808–9 (during which five fellow students died) and were among the first to be ordained priests at Ushaw—Robert in March 1809 and William in the following December.

Robert was engaged in pastoral work for most of his life but William remained at Ushaw as professor, prefect-general, and procurator from 1811 to 1816, during which time Charles Newsham and Nicholas Wiseman were among his pupils. In 1816 he was appointed chaplain to the Lawson family at Cliffe Hall, and when the Cliffe and Darlington missions were united in 1824 he transferred to Darlington, where he passed the rest of his life. From 1838 he was vicar general successively to bishops Briggs, Mostyn, and Riddell, vicars apostolic of the northern district. In 1848 he succeeded Riddell as vicar apostolic and was consecrated bishop of Samosata *in partibus infidelium* at Ushaw on 24 August. When the hierarchy was restored by Pius IX, he was translated, on 29 September 1850, to the new see of Hexham, renamed Hexham and Newcastle in 1861.

Throughout his life Hogarth retained a close interest in the affairs of Ushaw College. He supported his friend Charles Newsham, fifth president, in his plans for its major expansion between 1848 and 1858 and advocated its independence from episcopal control. He was older than most of his episcopal colleagues and, while not aloof from ecclesiastical politics, he preferred to concentrate his energies on promoting the interests of his diocese, rather in the spirit of the former vicars apostolic. It is said that every church or chapel was either built or enlarged under his management. He was well respected by his fellow bishops, and was a friend and confidant of Nicholas Wiseman. Although somewhat rough in manner, he was well known for his personal kindness, and he generously supported all good causes in Darlington, irrespective of religious denomination. He built St Augustine's Church in 1827 and was popular with his own congregation, which he increased from 200 in 1824 to 3000 in 1866. He was, above all, an energetic and capable administrator who established his new diocese on a sound footing. He died at Darlington on 29 January 1866, aged seventy-nine years, and was buried at Ushaw College.

ROBIN M. GARD

Sources *Weekly Register* (3 Feb 1886) · *Weekly Register* (10 Feb 1886) · *Newcastle Daily Chronicle* (30 Jan 1866), 4 · *Newcastle Daily Chronicle* (7 Feb 1866), 4 · *The Times* (31 Jan 1866) · W. M. Brady, *The episcopal succession in England, Scotland, and Ireland, AD 1400 to 1875*, 3 (1877), 346–7, 357, 410–13 · *Records and recollections of St Cuthbert's College, Ushaw … by an old alumnus* (1889), 127–31 · Gillow, *Lit. biog. hist.* · G. A. Beck, ed., *The English Catholics, 1850–1950* (1950), 71–2 · D. Milburn, *A history of Ushaw College* (1964) · *The Northern Catholic Calendar for the use of the Diocese of Hexham and Newcastle*, 1 (1869)

Archives Hexham and Newcastle Diocesan Archives, Newcastle upon Tyne, corresp. and papers; papers · Ushaw College, Durham, Ushaw Archives, corresp. and papers

Likenesses J. Ramsay, portrait, *c.*1850–1860, Ushaw College, Durham; repro. in Milburn, *History of Ushaw College*, pl. 15 · photographs, Ushaw College, Durham, Ushaw archives · portrait, repro. in Beck, ed., *English Catholics*, 6

Wealth at death under £1500: resworn probate, March 1869, *CGPLA Eng. & Wales* (1866)

Hogben, Lancelot Thomas (1895–1975), biologist, was born in Southsea, Hampshire, on 9 December 1895, the eldest of three surviving sons of Thomas Hogben and Margaret Alice Prescott. He had three elder sisters (an elder brother died in infancy). His father was a dry-salter and a Methodist who devoted himself to evangelism. His mother was the daughter of a successful building contractor in Stoke Newington who retired to Southsea. When her father died the family returned to Stoke Newington in 1907.

At the age of eleven Hogben was sent to Middlesex county secondary school, Tottenham, where he developed a keen interest in biology. In 1912 he won a scholarship to Trinity College, Cambridge, where he studied natural science from 1913. He graduated in 1916, having discovered the socialist politics of William Morris, and joined the Society of Friends. Before graduating he had also entered non-combatant service as an ambulanceman. This position would have exempted him from conscription for military service but, characteristically, once conscription was introduced he chose to give up the post and to declare himself a conscientious objector (for which he was imprisoned for several months). Indeed, throughout his life, Hogben displayed a brilliance whose rewards were undermined with 'a sheer genius for making enemies'. His professional ambition in a new field and a wish to reach out to wider audiences were combined with an inborn awkwardness of character. Difficulties in personal relations were aggravated both by a thyroid disorder and by the social and cultural distance between the narrow worlds of his upbringing and of his subsequent academic career.

Towards the end of the First World War Hogben made a precarious living lecturing to workers at Birkbeck College, the centre of part-time education, and at the Plebs League. On 21 June 1918 he married (Dorothy) Enid Charles (*b.* 1894/5), an economist and mathematician with strong socialist views and a pioneering feminist. The couple later had two sons and two daughters. In 1919 Hogben moved to the Royal College of Science, where he conducted original research on chromosome cytology and also worked to improve his mathematics. The combination of mathematics with biology was to be a lifelong fascination.

In 1922 Hogben moved to Edinburgh as deputy to F. A. E. Crew, director of the Institute of Animal Genetics, continuing research on colour changes and metamorphosis in amphibians. In 1925 he moved again, to take up an appointment as assistant professor of medical zoology in McGill University, Montreal. In his two years there he published important papers on the blood of invertebrates. Seeking academic preferment in 1927 he became the professor of zoology in the University of Cape Town. There, in addition to radically revising the teaching curriculum, he investigated the endocrine physiology of *Xenopus*, a local clawed frog. Intellectually, professionally, and financially this was a rewarding appointment, but his antipathy to the race relations of South Africa ultimately drove him to leave.

In 1930 Hogben was appointed to the new professorship of social biology at the London School of Economics, which had been founded with the support of the Rockefeller Foundation. The school's left-wing political ambience was to his taste though Hogben was too iconoclastic to be a communist. He joined the group of biological thinkers known as the 'Tots and Quots' which included also, among others, Solly Zuckerman, J. D. Bernal, and Julian Huxley. His position seemed to give him an opportunity to promote the wider significance of his science. In his inaugural lecture he pointed to the, by now, well-established fear of depopulation and linked it to the idea of the biological invention popularized by J. B. S. Haldane. At a nearby laboratory he could pursue his research on amphibians. His continuing study of *Xenopus* led to the Hogben pregnancy test developed in the late 1930s. In his *Political Arithmetic* of 1937, which summarized the work of the department, Hogben called for applications of biology as practical as the applications of chemistry. Unlike many of his contemporaries, however, he never flirted with eugenics, believing it methodologically unsustained and socially undesirable.

Priding himself on his hard-headedness, Hogben despised such 'idealist' philosophies as the holism propounded by Smuts to the 1929 meeting of the British Association in South Africa. In opposition he called himself a 'publicist', by which he meant to emphasize the distinction between materially grounded public knowledge and the intuitions of the private citizen. His philosophy was articulated in *Nature of Living Matter*, published in 1930. His reputation as a scientist was confirmed by election to the Royal Society in 1936.

Hogben disliked the chemical and physical reductionism associated with his friend Bernal and promoted a biological view of life. His own family settled in Devon to be distant from London pollution. He reverted to the socialism of Robert Owen and William Morris, and the biological idealism of Patrick Geddes, believing in the possibility of a citizenship living in equality and harmony with the land. In popular lectures and essays Hogben promoted the concept of a 'bio-aesthetic' utopia and the benevolence of biotechnology (a word he popularized but did not coin) which would draw upon biological raw materials rather than coal and oil.

In 1933, during a period of convalescence from septicaemia, Hogben had written up lectures originally given in South Africa as a primer to elementary mathematics for the public, *Mathematics for the Million*. Fearing the adverse effect of such popularization on his professional reputation he did not permit publication until 1936. It proved enormously successful and was followed, in 1938, with the scarcely less successful *Science for the Citizen*, which he preferred, and which had been written while Hogben commuted between London and the family home in Devon. These two books combined a formal approach to mathematics and science, and questions at the end of each chapter for the studious reader, with a highly personal style and a materialist historical approach. They constituted the first of what Hogben called his primers for the age of plenty. Later he published such children's versions of these books as *Man must Measure* (1955).

After the Rockefeller Foundation ended its support for social biology Hogben had once more to find a new position. In 1937 he was back in Scotland as regius professor of natural history in Aberdeen. There he developed a lasting interest in comparative linguistics and edited *The Loom of Language* by his friend Frederick Bodmer, published as the third of his primers. To improve the access of ordinary people around the world to science, while fire-watching during the Second World War, he compiled his international language, Interglossa, published in 1943 as 'a draft of an auxillary for a democratic world order'.

In January 1942 Hogben moved to Birmingham University, initially as Mason professor of zoology. Wartime work took him to London as acting director of medical statistics (1944) and when he returned to Birmingham he was given the professorship of medical statistics and human genetics (1947), a new chair created with him in mind. With his old mentor, Crew, he was the first editor of the British Medical Association's *British Journal of Social Medicine* (1947).

In 1942 Hogben had bowed to necessity and undergone a thyroidectomy. A second was necessary in 1951. At this time he sought to revive a breaking marriage by buying a cottage at Glyn Ceiriog in Wales as a retreat, but it made no appeal to Enid, with whom he agreed finally to part in 1953. After his divorce he married, on 12 October 1957, a local (retired) headmistress, (Sarah) Jane Roberts (*née* Evans), a widow seven years his junior. The following year he withdrew from the Society of Friends, considering himself ultimately as a scientific humanist. He retired in 1961, though he had a brief spell (1963–5) as vice-chancellor of the newly founded University of Guyana. In 1963 he received two honorary degrees: DSc (Wales) and LLD (Birmingham). His health and that of his wife deteriorated in the late 1960s; Jane died in 1974 and he himself died in the War Memorial Hospital in Wrexham on 22 August 1975.   ROBERT BUD

Sources DNB · A. Hogben and A. Hogben, eds., *Lancelot Hogben: scientific humanist* (1998) · G. P. Wells, *Memoirs FRS*, 24 (1978), 183–221 · G. Werskey, *The visible college* (1978) · L. Hogben, *Author in transit* (1940) · R. Bud, *The uses of life* (1993) · L. Hogben, 'The foundations of social biology', *Economica*, 11 (1931), 4–24 · L. Hogben, ed., *Political arithmetic: a symposium of population studies* (1938) · m. certs. · d. cert.

Archives CUL, corresp. · LUL, corresp. · RS, professional reminiscences · U. Birm. L., corresp. and papers | BLPES, corresp. with Lord Beveridge · CAC Cam., corresp. with A. U. Hill · CUL, Needham MSS · Rice University, Houston, Texas, Woodson Research Center, corresp. with Sir Julian Huxley · U. Sussex Library, letters to J. G. Crowther

Likenesses H. Meyerowitz, bust, 1928, U. Birm., school of medicine · W. Stoneman, photograph, 1936, NPG

Wealth at death £21,962: probate, 10 Nov 1975, *CGPLA Eng. & Wales*

Hogbin, Herbert Ian Priestley (1904–1989), anthropologist, was born Herbert William Hogbin on 17 December 1904 in Bawtry, Yorkshire, the first son and eldest of three children of Herbert Hogbin (1880–1940), landscape gardener, and his wife, Edith Fanny Smart (*b.* 1882). The family emigrated to Australia in 1914, where Hogbin was educated at Fort Street Boys' High School, Sydney, and at the University of Sydney, where he graduated BA in English and geography in 1926 and proceeded MA with first-class honours in anthropology in 1929.

In 1926 Hogbin changed his middle name by deed poll and, abandoning his intention of being a schoolteacher, became one of the first in a remarkable set of anthropologists gathered by A. R. Radcliffe-Brown, foundation professor of anthropology at the University of Sydney, who sent him to the Solomon Islands in 1927 for fieldwork after twelve months' study of the discipline. When Rennell Island proved unsuitable (he later learned that the Rennellese planned to kill him as they had two missionaries some years before) he moved to Ontong Java, another Polynesian outlier in the Solomons. His findings, presented for a PhD under Bronislaw Malinowski at the London School of Economics in 1931, were published as *Law and Order in Polynesia* (1934). Thus began Hogbin's lifelong love of Melanesia and fascination with the challenge it presented to ethnographers. He was to carry out fieldwork in Guadalcanal, Malaita, Wogeo, Busama, and other places (some of which he was still revisiting in the 1970s), but rejected an opportunity for research in Africa and was never tempted by the New Guinea highlands. In 1943 he joined the British Solomon Islands defence force, and later the Australian army's directorate of research and civil affairs as a lieutenant-colonel advising on such topics as native labour and local courts and government. With hindsight he regretted having advocated reliance on customary instead of Australian law, having come to believe that the former was irrelevant to modern needs.

Apart from fieldwork and a number of overseas visits, mainly to Britain, Hogbin spent his career at Sydney University (lecturer 1931–3, 1936–48; reader 1948–69). After retiring he took a position at Macquarie University (professorial fellow 1969–79). His lectures were noted for their style and ironic humour. A stickler for plain English, he once suggested that his principal contribution to anthropology was that his postgraduate students wrote clearly and well. Hogbin had an eye for telling detail and believed in giving rounded accounts of the societies he studied. His publications included nine books and many articles (twenty-eight in *Oceania*, 1930–70) as well as several edited or co-authored collections, most notably the anthropology section of the *Encyclopaedia of New Guinea*. Their range is unsurpassed and their quality places him among the foremost contributors to the literature of Melanesia.

Hogbin took particular interest in kinship, social and political organization, and religion, both pagan and Christian, but was deeply interested also in social change and applied anthropology. He was not an original thinker and was temperamentally averse to grand theories, regarding them as remote from ordinary life, the study of which he viewed as the nub of anthropology. After his initial embrace of Radcliffe-Brown and Malinowski, whom he always admired (while deprecating their vanity and conceit and disliking Malinowski as a person), he showed little taste for further theoretical innovation but remained broadly in sympathy with their views, particularly with the former's insistence on relating economic, political, and other institutions to social structure. Hogbin was sceptical of the French structuralism which began sweeping through anthropology in the 1960s, but it gave him a stimulus to revisit his field data on the traditional religion of Wogeo. The result was *The Island of Menstruating Men* (1970), the first full-length study of a Melanesian religion since Reo Fortune's *Manus Religion* (1935). In it he presented myths and rituals against the sober background of social and economic life and of the differentiation of the sexes, but with judicious attention to the theories of Malinowski, Radcliffe-Brown, and Mary Douglas. It was typical of him that he made no attempt to exploit the lurid possibilities suggested by the title. An exception to his usual practice of concentrating on one society at a time was *Social Change* (1958), based on his Josiah Mason lectures at the University of Birmingham in 1953, a comparative study ranging far beyond Melanesia in which he stressed the role of values in determining which new opportunities would be seized and the chain reactions triggered by these choices.

A confirmed bachelor of dapper appearance and fastidious taste who prided himself on never having played sport, Hogbin took part in student politics and theatre in his younger days when he suffered the sobriquet Percy Pigbucket. His enthusiasm for the arts and music led him to travel extensively to inspect paintings and architecture, and to attend innumerable concerts and opera performances, but he never attempted to integrate this passion with anthropology. Brought up in the Church of England, he had lost all religious faith by the time he became an undergraduate.

A fascinating picture of Hogbin's life and opinions is given in *Conversations with Ian Hogbin* (1989), recorded when Hogbin was in his eighties by Jeremy Beckett. He died in a nursing home at Potts Point, Sydney, on 1 August 1989, leaving his body for scientific research. His estate was valued at A$401,871. KENNETH MADDOCK

Sources J. Beckett, *Conversations with Ian Hogbin* (1989) · L. R. Hiatt and C. Jayawardena, eds., *Anthropology in Oceania* (1971) [contains comprehensive bibliography] · *Oceania*, 60 (1989–90), 158–60
Archives University of Sydney, biographical file and personal archives
Likenesses photographs, 1927–67, repro. in Hiatt and Jayawardena, *Anthropology* · photograph, 1928, repro. in Beckett, *Conversations*
Wealth at death A$401,871: probate office, supreme court of New South Wales, Sydney

Hogenberg, Frans [Franz] (*c*.1540–*c*.1590), engraver, and his brother **Remigius Hogenberg** (*c*.1536–*c*.1588), also an engraver, were born in Malines, just south of Antwerp, the sons of Nicolas Hogenberg (also Nikolaus, and sometimes called Hans, Johann, or Johannes in apparent confusion with his nephew of that name; *b*. *c*.1500, *d*. in or before 1539), an engraver, etcher, and woodcutter who was probably born in Germany but worked for most of his life in the Netherlands. The two brothers, their father, and Frans's sons Abraham and Johannes formed a notable Netherlandish family of artists who moved between Germany, France, England, and the Netherlands and, though not among the first artists and engravers of their day, were industrious, capable, and adaptable.

Frans Hogenberg may have trained as an engraver in Malines but was from the 1550s in Antwerp, where he worked with Abraham Ortelius. It has been suggested that he moved to England from Antwerp. Such suggestions rest on his engraved portraits of William Cecil, Robert Dudley, and Elizabeth (all published in Matthew Parker's *Bishops' Bible* of 1568) and on his engraving of two views of London. By 1570, however, he is known to have been in Cologne.

Hogenberg is best-known for his close involvement in two of the most important cartographic enterprises of his day. The first was *Theatrum orbis terrarum*, compiled by Abraham Ortelius and first printed in Antwerp in 1570. This is considered the first atlas—that is the first collection of maps which aimed uniformly and systematically to depict the world. Its fifty-three maps were engraved by Hogenberg with the assistance of Johannes van Doetecum and later of Ambrosius and Ferdinand Arsenius. Hogenberg may also have engraved the title-page. Ortelius was a friend and travelling companion as well as a collaborator, and he took a keen interest in Hogenberg's later work on the *Civitates orbis terrarum*. This latter work was edited by Georg Braun and largely engraved by Hogenberg, being published in six volumes between 1572 and 1617 in Cologne. Hogenberg may indeed have initiated the project, which Braun referred to as 'Master Frans's Book of Cities' (Elliot, 26), and he was certainly responsible for engraving the majority of its 546 prospects, bird's-eye views, and map views of cities throughout the world and for shaping its content—for example by including place names in native tongues rather than Latin alone, to increase the work's popular appeal.

Hogenberg died in Cologne about 1590, and was survived by his two sons.

Remigius Hogenberg is less well known than his brother but had stronger ties to Britain. His first known work is his large view of the city of Münster in Westphalia (1570, now in the British Library), after a drawing by Hermann tom Ring, Münster's most distinguished sixteenth-century artist. He moved to England and by 1573 was in the service of the archbishop of Canterbury, Matthew Parker, and was living in Lambeth Palace. For Parker, Hogenberg and another artist and engraver, Richard Lyne, constructed genealogies. Hogenberg also engraved portraits. Between 1575 and 1578 he engraved several county maps and the famous title-page showing Elizabeth as patron of geography and astronomy for Christopher Saxton's *Atlas of England and Wales* (1579). The last view on which his name appears is the bird's-eye view of Exeter of 1587 (BL, maps C5.a.3), surveyed by John Hooker, chamberlain of the city of Exeter, which was copied by John Speed for his *Theatre of the Empire of Great Britain* (1611–12). Hogenberg painted and engraved portraits of several French sitters, and this has led to suggestions that he may have visited that country, but he was probably in England about 1588 when he died, probably unmarried.

ELIZABETH BAIGENT

Sources C. van Mulders, 'Hogenberg family', *The dictionary of art*, ed. J. Turner (1996) · *Biografisch woordenboek der Nederlanden* (1867), vol. 8 · *Biographie nationale* [*de Belgique*] (1886–7), vol. 9 · *Neue deutscher Biografie* (1971), vol. 9 · *DNB* · J. Elliot, *The city in maps: urban mapping to 1900* (1987) · C. Delano-Smith and R. J. P. Kain, *English maps: a history* (1999) · J. Werner, *Abraham Ortelius (1572–1598): aartsvader van onze atlas* (Amsterdam, 1998) [exhibition catalogue, Universiteitsbibliotheek, Amsterdam, 12 June – 12 Aug 1998] · M. van den Broecke, P. van der Krogt, and P. Meurer, eds., *Abraham Ortelius and the first atlas: essays commemorating the quadricentennial of his death, 1598–1998* (1998) · J. Keuning, 'The *Civitates* of Braun and Hogenberg', *Imago Mundi*, 17 (1963), 41–4

Hogenberg, Remigius (*c*.1536–*c*.1588). *See under* Hogenberg, Frans (*c*.1540–*c*.1590).

Hogg, Alfred George (1875–1954), theologian and missionary, was born on 23 July 1875 in Ramlah, Egypt, the fourth surviving child of John Hogg (1833–1886), missionary, and his wife, Bessie Kay (*b*. 1841). His father hailed from East Lothian, and his mother was the niece of Hope Waddell, a pioneer Scottish missionary in Jamaica and west Africa. John Hogg died at the age of only fifty-two in 1886, and the family returned to Scotland. Alfred attended George Watson's College (1882–93) and Edinburgh University, where he read philosophy in preparation for ordination. His most influential teacher at Edinburgh was the Hegelian Andrew Seth (after 1898 Andrew Seth Pringle-Pattison). Hogg graduated in 1897 and went on at once to the Theological Hall of the United Presbyterian church to train for the ministry, but discontinued after a crisis of faith.

Thanks chiefly to the influence of David S. Cairns (1862–1946), who had earlier been helped in similar circumstances by John Hogg, in 1901 Alfred Hogg resumed and completed his theological training, although he was not ordained until 1915. In 1902 he was approached with a view to taking a temporary teaching post in Madras Christian College. Being a layman, he had far more freedom to speculate than did his missionary contemporaries, and the *Madras Christian College Magazine*, an outstanding publication of its kind, provided him with ample opportunity to write. He arrived in India early in 1903 and remained there apart from the usual furloughs—as principal from 1928—until his retirement in 1938. On 14 May 1907 he married Mary Maclaine Patterson (*d. c*.1964), a missionary teacher hailing from the island of Mull, but there were no children of the marriage.

Hogg's missionary career was outwardly unspectacular. He was never at the forefront of controversy, and had little to say in public on the political issues of the time. He was however an original and creative thinker. He wrote extensively in journals, but his books numbered only four in all: *Karma and Redemption* (1909), which first appeared as a series of articles in the *Madras Christian College Magazine*; *Christ's Message of the Kingdom* (1911), a course of Bible studies on the question of the kingdom of God, and by far the most widely read of Hogg's writings; *Redemption from this World* (1922), his weightiest theological work, delivered originally as lectures in Edinburgh; and after his retirement, *The Christian Message to the Hindu* (1947). Hogg was no orientalist, and made little or no use of Indian languages (he taught and wrote only in English). Both philosophically and theologically he was an ethicist, and was concerned with questions of fundamental principle, especially where the encounter between Christian and Hindu forms of belief were concerned. He always drew a clear distinction between faith and beliefs in matters of religion: faith is immediate trust in God, however conceived; beliefs are the intellectually and culturally conditioned formulations to which people resort in attempting to delimit and explain faith. Faith is absolute; beliefs are relative and subject to constant revision, although frequently taken in error to be themselves absolute. Hogg was prepared to affirm that 'the innermost faith of all religions which are still, at any time, worthy of the name must be one and the same' (*Karma and Redemption*, 1923 edn, 5), while allowing that differences in beliefs are immensely important nevertheless. In his own work he paid particular attention to the contrast between the Hindu doctrine of *karma*—a judicial system without a judge—and the moral principles implicit in Christian notions of forgiveness and redemption.

An early Hindu response came from a young college student, a member of Hogg's philosophy class, Sarvepalli Radhakrishnan (1888–1975), ultimately president of the Indian republic and the most distinguished Hindu apologist of his day, whose first book, *Ethics of the Vedanta* (1907), was prompted by Hogg's original karma and redemption articles. Otherwise Hogg was perhaps not an outstanding teacher. The best of his students he inspired; to the majority he was, one imagines, barely comprehensible, though always regarded with the utmost respect.

As principal, Hogg's main achievement was to preside in 1937 over the removal of the Madras Christian College from its central site to its new campus at Tambaram, south of the city. He had dreamed of a Christian university in India, but the politics of the time did not permit it. In 1938 the Tambaram campus became the venue of an important conference of the International Missionary Council at which Hogg himself, who had just retired from the principalship and had never before attended such a gathering, made a deep impression. He left India shortly afterwards. Despite many invitations he was never able to return. The war years he spent as an obscure parish minister in obscure corners of Scotland, afterwards publishing *The Christian Message to the Hindu*, and much in demand as a devotional leader at conferences, but otherwise never in the public eye. Ultimately he was able to retire with his wife to the village of Elie on the coast of Fife. His last years were much troubled by rheumatoid arthritis, and at the age of seventy-nine he died at Elie on the last day of 1954. His wife survived him by a decade.

ERIC J. SHARPE

Sources E. J. Sharpe, *Alfred George Hogg, 1875–1954: an intellectual biography* (1999) • E. J. Sharpe, *The theology of A. G. Hogg* (1971) • R. L. Hogg, *A master-builder on the Nile: being a record of the life and aims of John Hogg, D. D., Christian missionary* (1914)
Archives U. Edin., New Coll.
Likenesses photographs, U. Edin., New Coll., Hogg collection • portrait, Madras Christian College, Tambaram
Wealth at death £1307 14s. 1d.: confirmation, 2 March 1955, *CCI*

Hogg, Douglas McGarel, first Viscount Hailsham (1872–1950), lawyer and politician, was born at 10 Chesham Place, Belgravia, London, on 28 February 1872, the eldest son of Quintin *Hogg (1845–1903), merchant and philanthropist, and his wife, Alice Anna, *née* Graham (d. 1918). He was a grandson of Sir James Hogg and of William Graham, both of whom were members of parliament. Educated at Cheam School and Eton College, he spent eight years with the family firm of sugar merchants, partly in the West Indies and British Guiana, a commercial education that provided a valuable background to his later careers in both politics and the law. He served in the Second South African War in the 19th (Berwick and Lothian) yeomanry, and was wounded and decorated—useful experience and good standing for a future secretary of state for war. After returning from South Africa he was called to the bar by Lincoln's Inn in January 1902; he took silk as a king's counsel in 1917 and became a bencher of Lincoln's Inn in 1920.

Hogg married, on 14 August 1905, Elizabeth (d. 1925), daughter of James Trimble Brown, an American judge from Tennessee and widow of Hogg's cousin the Hon. Archibald John Marjoribanks, son of Dudley Coutts Marjoribanks, first Baron Tweedmouth. She had two children from her previous marriage, to whom Hogg became stepfather, including Edward Marjoribanks (1900–1932), whose brilliant early career as a writer and MP ended in suicide. She and Hogg had two sons, the elder of whom was Quintin McGarel Hogg, Baron Hailsham of St Marylebone (1907–2001). After her death in 1925 he married on 3 January 1929 Mildred Margaret (d. 1964), daughter of the Revd Edward Parker Dew and widow of the Hon. Alfred Clive Lawrence, son of Alfred Tristram Lawrence, first Baron Trevethin. There were no children of the second marriage.

Though after his father's death in 1903 he committed much time to developing Quintin Hogg's foundation, the Polytechnic Institution, Hogg mainly devoted the next two decades to the law. Despite starting in the profession late, he rapidly built up a reputation, and a practice in both the common law and the commercial sectors. Viscount Simon, who knew him well as their legal and political careers developed, recalled that:

> Hogg had all the qualities that go to make a leader at the bar: an accurate grasp of complicated facts, a clear view of the principles of law which had to be applied to them, a sturdy attitude in the face of the situation with which he had to deal, and a manner which was genial and conciliatory with a persuasive force behind it well calculated to win assent from the tribunal he was addressing. He was never at a loss, and no counsel was more adept at preparing the way to meet the difficulties of the case. (*DNB*)

All these attributes were also assets in his subsequent career in politics, especially when he was appointed to ministerial office.

Conservative MP and attorney-general Hogg had strong Conservative opinions, tempered with respect for his party's interests. Hence, though approached to become the candidate for Marylebone, he stood down before the general election of 1918 rather than challenge the sitting member. He was, however, already known to the Conservative Party leadership as a coming man, and had for example assisted in their legal harrying of the Liberals during the Marconi scandal in 1913. When, after the Carlton Club meeting of October 1922, Bonar Law found himself prime minister but with former coalitionists refusing to serve under him and hence short of law officers, he made Hogg attorney-general and only then ensured his unopposed entry into the Commons as MP for the safely Conservative Marylebone, which he represented until he went to the House of Lords in 1928. But if Bonar Law knew of Hogg, others in the party were bemused by his sudden appearance among its leaders. Harold Macmillan later recalled Lord Derby trying to reassure the duke of Devonshire with the news that 'They have found a wonderful little man. One of those attorney fellows, you know. He will do all the work.' Asked to identify this political maid of all work, Derby announced, so completing what Macmillan thought 'a truly Trollopian scene', that the party's saviour was called 'Pig' (Macmillan, 129).

Hogg therefore started in the Commons on the front bench, and within days had to help pilot through the house the controversial bill which established the Irish Free State constitution after the treaty of 1921. Within four weeks of entering office he was also being deputed, along with Lord Chancellor Cave and Neville Chamberlain, to draft a politically sensitive reply from Baldwin to a delegation of the unemployed. Though not yet in the cabinet, he was sworn of the privy council and knighted (in December 1922). From this point Hogg was predominantly a politician, remaining in the same office when Baldwin became prime minister six months later. He maintained an active Commons role even when his party went into opposition in January 1924, and made indeed some of the best speeches during Conservative attacks on Ramsay MacDonald's Labour government. Describing the debate that installed MacDonald, Neville Chamberlain thought that Hogg's speech 'made a great impression and heartened up our party immensely'. This quality was most notable in the debate on the Campbell case in October 1924. This time Chamberlain declared that

> Hogg's summing up was a real tour-de-force. Until then I confess to having been rattled by the special pleading on the other side and only when I heard Hogg did I realise how strong the case against the Govt still remained. (*Diary Letters*, 204, 251)

When Baldwin then began his second term as prime minister later in October 1924, Hogg was again made attorney-general, but now with a seat in the cabinet.

Already he was being talked about for higher things, canvassed as a possible future home secretary, and, as his career developed, even mentioned from time to time as a possible future prime minister. He played a full part in cabinet debates after 1924, but gave advice in particular on legal matters, for example over the general strike in 1926, and it seems likely that other members still thought of him mainly as a lawyer–politician rather than an all-rounder. He was for example the minister responsible for the arrest and prosecution of a number of British communists on charges of subversion in October 1925, though responsibility for this was generally attributed to the more flamboyant home secretary, Joynson-Hicks.

Lord chancellor, opposition, and secretary of state for war
Hence, when a vacancy for the lord chancellorship arose after the resignation of Lord Cave in March 1928, Hogg was offered the post. He hesitated though, aware that the hereditary peerage which went with it could inhibit both his own chances of the premiership and his son's political career—as indeed it did. The demands of party loyalty and the opportunity to become the political head of his original profession won out in the end. He became lord chancellor on 29 March 1928, was created a peer as Baron Hailsham on 5 April, and was promoted to a viscountcy in 1929. As it turned out, he had little over a year in the post before the Conservatives' loss of the general election in 1929 removed him to the opposition side of the Lords, where he again took a more broadly political role.

Hailsham acted as Conservative leader in the Lords from 1930, but was not prominent in support of Baldwin when attacked by party critics, and was indeed being widely talked about as a possible successor if Baldwin were to fall—speculation that he did not apparently seek to stifle. The former party whip Lord Bayford thought in March 1931 that 'the only possible suggestion made at present is that Hailsham should lead the party and Neville [Chamberlain] be leader in the Commons' (*Real Old Tory Politics*, 245). All this explains why he was not given a cabinet seat when the National Government was formed in August 1931, and why he refused the honorific post of lord privy seal when not offered the more senior lord chancellorship. He was, however, made secretary of state for war and rejoined the cabinet after the general election held in November 1931. He soon revealed his political skills once again by suggesting the formula of an 'agreement to differ' by which the parties in the cabinet stayed together even though they could not agree on the core economic policy issue of free trade or protection.

Hailsham's formula enabled the Conservatives to press on with plans for tariffs, while remaining in alliance with Liberals and National Labour, and then quickly to dispense with the free traders among their allies once tariff plans had been agreed internationally. He was one of the ministers chosen to represent the National Government at the Ottawa Imperial Economic Conference in 1932, which brought protection about after a thirty-year struggle by its supporters—among whom he was one of the keenest. At Ottawa, as Baldwin told his friend Tom Jones, 'the bulk of the negotiations have been done by Neville

[Chamberlain], "ably assisted" (as the papers would say) by Hailsham', but Baldwin also wryly admitted that he had let those two do the work 'because if they failed the Die-Hards at home would know it was not from half-hearted trying' (Jones, 49–50). Hailsham was also leader of the House of Lords from 1931 to 1935, and hence obliged to maintain a wider political role, one that was rather exposed in 1934–5 when Lord Salisbury was harrying the government over its Indian policy. Hailsham was not as highly regarded in his party in the mid-1930s as ten years earlier.

At the War Office Hailsham proved a popular minister with the senior army men with whom he had to deal, though in times of stringent economy there were few opportunities to shine in any defence post. Even when the government began to prepare for rearmament in 1934–5, the priority was the Royal Air Force, and to a lesser extent the Royal Navy, so that although he presided over the first serious plans for rearmament of the army, it fell to his successors to carry them out.

Lord chancellor again Hailsham seems therefore to have taken great satisfaction from his switch to lord chancellor, on 7 June 1935, when Baldwin returned to the premiership, and this time he had a term of three years, for he continued in office when Neville Chamberlain succeeded Baldwin in May 1937. Hailsham was thought to have presided over the Lords with due dignity, and to have led the House of Lords as a court with judicial authority. Lord Simon, who was lord chancellor himself from 1940, identified a number of cases of significance in the Lords in which his judgments 'illustrated his power of lucid reasoning and his command of appropriate language': *Addie* v. *Dumbreck* (injury to child trespasser, 1929); *Tolley* v. *Fry* (defamation, 1931); *Swadling* v. *Cooper* (contributory negligence, 1931) (*DNB*). In December 1935 Hailsham had to preside, again with great dignity, over the last trial of a peer 'by his peers', when the lord chancellor was also made lord high steward to facilitate the trial of Lord de Clifford in the House of Lords for manslaughter. He ruled that there was no case for Lord de Clifford to answer, but also suggested that this ancient procedure might be inappropriate for modern conditions, a view which may well have contributed to the abolition of the procedure in the Criminal Justice Act of 1948. His standing in the legal profession and in public affairs more generally was indicated by the honorary doctorates of letters or civil law variously conferred on him by the universities of Belfast, Birmingham, Cambridge, Oxford, and Reading.

Hailsham was not thought to enjoy good enough health to make his second term on the woolsack as fulfilling as might have been expected, given that he was only sixty-three when appointed. Ill health was already a serious problem in 1936 and forced his transfer to the post of lord president of the council, with fewer departmental duties, in March 1938, but he had to leave the government altogether in the following October. This was just four days after his elder son Quintin had been elected to the Commons at a by-election, so beginning a career which led him, too, close to the highest office and in which he was also twice lord chancellor. Shortly afterwards, Hailsham, partially paralysed by a stroke, had the misfortune to be in the Carlton Club when it was bombed, and observers 'saw through the fog the figure of Quintin Hogg escorting old Lord Hailsham from the ruins, like Aeneas and Achises' (*Harold Nicolson's Diaries and Letters*, 121).

Last years and reputation Hailsham's final years were characterized by continuing poor health which precluded his playing much of a role in the House of Lords as a private member, though he continued to be as active as he could in such outside bodies as the Inns of Court regiment (honorary colonel, 1935–48) and the British Empire Cancer Campaign (chairman, 1936–50). He spent much of this time at his country home in Sussex, where he had become a prominent county figure, a justice of the peace for the county from 1923, and president of Sussex County cricket club in 1931. His presidency of the MCC in 1933 happily united an interest in cricket with his earlier constituency connection with Marylebone. Lord Hailsham died at his home, Carter's Corner Place, Hailsham, Sussex, on 16 August 1950, and was buried in the churchyard of All Saints', Herstmonceux. The title passed to his son Quintin.

Hailsham was a popular man among his party colleagues, and though he could be their scourge in debate he seems not to have been much hated by opponents. He was certainly a man hugely admired by colleagues. Neville Chamberlain thought in 1926 that he was 'one of the best, straight and loyal and possessed of a wonderful brain. Moreover he is a first-class fighting man' (*Diary Letters*, 338). Two years later, Chamberlain's half-brother Austen was telling a sister of knotty legal issues that he faced at the Foreign Office, over which Hailsham 'was unable to help me to a decision, which if you knew him would alone be sufficient to show you how extremely difficult of solution these problems are'. As the parliament ended in May 1929, Austen decided that Hailsham's judgement was 'I think as good as that of any member of the Cabinet' (*Diary Letters*, 322, 330). Perhaps such success, coming quickly to a man who had started political life only when he was already fifty, made him overplay his hand in the events of 1929–31, though his acceptance of the lord chancellorship had by then already removed him from the Commons, whence all future national leaders were now to come. William Bridgeman thought that all this had not impaired

> his great ability in debate, though it did I think interfere with his political judgement … He never suffered a reverse until the defeat of the party in 1929, an experience which would have been beneficial if he had had it. (*Modernisation*, 232)

In appearance, Hailsham had a cherubic face a little like Winston Churchill's, and was more often to be seen smiling than frowning. Chips Channon thought that as lord chancellor he looked like Gilbert and Sullivan's lord chancellor in his robes, but, as Lord Denning later recalled, if he 'looked like Pickwick', he also 'spoke like Demosthenes' (*Chips*, ed. James, 125; Lewis, 1).

JOHN RAMSDEN

Sources DNB · R. F. V. Heuston, *Lives of the lord chancellors, 1940–1970* (1987) · Burke, *Peerage* (2000) · Lord Hailsham, *The door wherein I went* (1975) · Lord Hailsham, *A sparrow's flight: memoirs* (1990) · T. Jones, *A diary with letters, 1931–1950* (1954) · G. Lewis, *Lord Hailsham* (1997) · S. Ball, *Baldwin and the conservative party: the crisis of 1929–1931* (1988) · H. Macmillan, *Winds of change, 1914–1939* (1966) [vol. 1 of autobiography] · Harold Nicolson's diaries and letters, 2: *The war years, 1939–1945*, ed. N. Nicolson (1967) · J. Ramsden, *The age of Balfour and Baldwin, 1902–1940* (1978) · *Real old tory politics: the political diaries of Sir Robert Sanders, Lord Bayford, 1910–40*, ed. J. Ramsden (1984) · *Chips: the diaries of Sir Henry Channon*, ed. R. Rhodes James (1967) · *The Austen Chamberlain diary letters: the correspondence of Sir Austen Chamberlain with his sisters Hilda and Ida, 1916–1937*, ed. R. C. Self, CS, 5th ser., 5 (1995) · *The Neville Chamberlain diary letters*, ed. R. Self, 2: *The reform years, 1921–1927* (2000) · *The modernisation of conservative politics: the diaries and letters of William Bridgeman, 1904–1935*, ed. P. Williamson (1988)

Archives CAC Cam., papers | Bodl. Oxf., corresp. with L. G. Curtis · Bodl. Oxf., corresp. with Lord Ponsonby · Bodl. Oxf., corresp. with Lord Sankey · CUL, corresp. with Sir Samuel Hoare · HLRO, corresp. with Lord Beaverbrook · NA Scot., corresp. with Lord Elibank | FILM BFI NFTVA, news footage

Likenesses W. Stoneman, photographs, 1922–33, NPG · W. Nicholson, oils, 1930, Lincoln's Inn, London · J. A. A. Berrie, oils, 1945–9, Abbey National Building Society · T. Cottrell, cigarette card, NPG · Lady Kennet, bust, priv. coll. · oils, University of Westminster, London · photograph, NPG

Wealth at death £225,032 18s. 2d.: probate, 16 Sept 1950, CGPLA Eng. & Wales

Hogg, Henry (*bap.* 1831, *d.* 1874), poet, was baptized on 6 November 1831 in Radford, Nottingham, the son of Joseph Hogg, who was in the hosiery trade, and his wife, Elizabeth. Hogg was raised and educated in Nottingham, and practised as a solicitor there. In addition to his legal work, however, he also composed much poetry; his first poem, 'Mournful Recollections', was in blank verse, and appeared in 1849. In 1852 he published a collection of poetry, described by a contemporary critic as 'an unpretending … volume of poems … inheriting many of the blemishes, as well as beauties, of his model Tennyson' (Wylie, 247). Hogg also contributed a number of short poems to the *Christian Miscellany*, and wrote hymns and carols, which were popular in the district; he himself set some of them to music. A later volume of poems was issued, but was subsequently withdrawn from publication. Hogg died of lung disease on 19 June 1874 at his Elm Avenue home in Nottingham. He was survived by his wife, Sarah, *née* Anderson, and at least one son, Joseph T. Hogg, who was present at his father's death.

W. E. DOUBLEDAY, rev. MEGAN A. STEPHAN

Sources W. H. Wylie, *Old and new Nottingham* (1853), 247–8 · Boase, *Mod. Eng. biog.*, 1.1501 · R. Mellors, *Men of Nottingham and Nottinghamshire* (1924), 61–2 · Allibone, *Dict.* · IGI · d. cert. · CGPLA Eng. & Wales (1874)

Wealth at death under £5000: probate, 28 Sept 1874, CGPLA Eng. & Wales

Hogg, Jabez (1817–1899), ophthalmic surgeon, the youngest son of John Hogg and Martha, his wife, was born on 4 April 1817 at Chatham, where his father was employed in the royal dockyard. He was educated at Rochester grammar school, and in 1832 was apprenticed for five years to a medical practitioner. On 25 August 1841 he married Mary Ann, a daughter of Captain Robert Davis of the Indian navy. After her death he married Jessie Terraneau, youngest daughter of Captain James Read, of the Indian army on 16 June 1859; she survived him.

In 1843 Hogg published *A Manual of Photography*, which brought him to the notice of the proprietors of the *Illustrated London News*. He joined the staff of this periodical, and from 1850 to 1866 he acted as editor of a series of illustrated educational works published by Herbert Ingram. In 1846 he was sub-editor of the *Illuminated Magazine*, to which the illustrators Hablot Knight Browne and John Leech contributed, and he edited the *Illustrated London Almanack* from 1845 to 1895.

Hogg entered as a student in London at the Great Windmill Street school of medicine and at Charing Cross Hospital in 1845, though he was not admitted a member of the Royal College of Surgeons until 1850. From 1855 he was the personal assistant to George James Guthrie, founder of the Royal Westminster Ophthalmic Hospital, and he was appointed surgeon there from 1871 to 1877. He was also ophthalmic surgeon to the Hospital for Women and Children, Waterloo Bridge Road, London, and to the masonic charities.

Hogg devoted himself to the study of diseases of the eye, and he soon became proficient in the use of the ophthalmoscope, then newly introduced. He was a vice-president of the Medical Society of London in 1851–2, and he was elected a fellow of the Linnean Society in 1866. He served as honorary secretary of the Royal Microscopical Society from 1867 to 1872, and retired in order to become president of the new Medical Microscopical Society, inaugurated in January 1873. He was a prominent freemason, in both the craft and arch degrees. Hogg died at his home, 102 Palace Gardens Terrace, Kensington, London, on 23 April 1899, and was buried in Kensal Green cemetery.

Hogg was an extremely prolific writer; besides works on ophthalmology he authored treatises on the microscope, the elements of physics, and pathology. His book in 1858 on the ophthalmoscope, the first in English, was, however, mediocre. The third edition of 1863 was devastatingly criticized as loaded with dedications to excessively illustrious personages, and 'so utterly and unutterably bad ... from beginning to end such an incoherent mass of errors and mis-statements about every subject with which it deals' (*Ophthalmic Review*, 1, 1865, 96–109). Hogg's own comments at this time admit to his uncertainty about the difference between direct and indirect ophthalmoscopy.

D'A. POWER, *rev.* ANITA MCCONNELL

Sources J. Hirschberg, *The history of ophthalmology*, trans. F. C. Blodi, 8a (1987), 319–21 • G. L'E. Turner, *God bless the microscope!* (1989) • *The Times* (26 April 1899), 8b • *American Monthly Microscopical Journal*, 20 (1899), 259 • *Nature*, 59 (1898–9), 612 • *The Lancet* (6 May 1899), 1263 • *Men and women of the time* (1895), 425 • *ILN* (29 April 1899), 604 • Boase, *Mod. Eng. biog.* • *CGPLA Eng. & Wales* (1899)
Likenesses portrait, repro. in *ILN*, p. 604
Wealth at death £243 2s. 4d.: probate, 2 June 1899, *CGPLA Eng. & Wales*

Hogg, James (*bap.* 1770, *d.* 1835), poet and novelist, was the second among the four children of Robert Hogg (*c.*1729–1820), shepherd and farmer, and Margaret Laidlaw (1730–

James Hogg (*bap.* 1770, *d.* 1835), by Sir John Watson-Gordon, 1830

1813). He was born in Selkirkshire at the farm of Ettrick Hall (also known as Ettrickhill). The farm lay in the valley of the River Ettrick, at the heart of Ettrick Forest, one of the ancient Scottish royal hunting grounds. By Hogg's time, however, the Scottish court had long since departed to London and the royal forest had dwindled to a remote, backward sheep-farming district. Nevertheless Ettrick remained a rich storehouse of oral tradition in story and song, and Hogg's mother's family were noted tradition-bearers.

Childhood and education For much of his life Hogg believed that he was born on 25 January 1772. He took great pride in sharing the birthday of Robert Burns; indeed there is much evidence that he saw his life's work in terms of being Burns's successor. However, the parish register of Ettrick records Hogg's baptism at Ettrick church on 9 December 1770, a fact that he discovered with disappointment during his later years.

In his *Memoir of the Author's Life* Hogg gives an account of his childhood and family background. His father 'was bred to the occupation of a shepherd' but by the time of his marriage in May 1765 he had saved enough money to take the lease of the farms at Ettrick House and Ettrick Hall. He began to deal in sheep, buying large numbers and driving them to English and Scottish markets. However:

> owing to a great fall in the price of sheep, and the absconding of his principal debtor, he was ruined, became bankrupt, every thing was sold by auction, and my parents were turned out of doors without a farthing in the world.

Hogg was six at the time, and the 'distressed and destitute condition' of his parents remained vivid in his memory.

The 'late worthy Mr. Brydon, of Crosslee', came to the family's rescue, temporarily at least, when he took 'a short lease of the farm of Ettrick House' and employed Robert Hogg as his shepherd there (*Memoir of the Author's Life*, 4–5). A monument dating from 1898 now marks the site of Hogg's birthplace at Ettrick Hall.

Robert Hogg's bankruptcy cut short the formal schooling of his children, and the young James for the remainder of his childhood had to earn his keep by doing menial work (herding cows and the like) on various local farms. The *Memoir of the Author's Life* gives a brief and understated account of the hardships involved. Being 'exceedingly bare of shirts' Hogg after a time gave up 'wearing them altogether'. He recalled that he 'certainly made a very grotesque figure', particularly as he 'could never induce my trews, or lower vestments, to keep up to their proper sphere, there being no braces in those days' (*Memoir of the Author's Life*, 7). At fourteen he bought a violin with money he had saved from his wages. In the evenings, after work, he would spend 'an hour or two … sawing over my favourite old Scottish tunes' (ibid.). When he reached his late teens he graduated to the responsible work of shepherding; this increase in his status ensured that he had the time to begin to master once again the long-neglected skill of reading.

Jamie the Poeter, 1790–1810 In 1790 Hogg found work as a shepherd at Blackhouse Farm in the Yarrow valley in Ettrick Forest. He remained there for ten years, during which time he began a lifelong friendship with his employer's son William Laidlaw (later the manager of Sir Walter Scott's Abbotsford estate). At Blackhouse, Hogg had free access to a wide selection of books, and he read voraciously. He also began to write poems, plays, and songs. These found a ready audience in Ettrick, earning him the local nickname Jamie the Poeter. Hogg became a published writer in 1794, when 'The Mistakes of a Night', a vigorous, hilarious, and uninhibited poem of rural courtship, appeared in the October number of the *Scots Magazine*.

The happy years at Blackhouse came to an end in 1800, when, following his brother's marriage, Hogg moved to Ettrick House to assist his father, who was now just over seventy. About the beginning of the nineteenth century sheep-farming was expanding rapidly in the Scottish highlands in the wake of the clearances. With a view to turning his sheep-farming skills to good account Hogg gave serious consideration to moving to the highlands with his elderly parents, and about this time he made a series of summer journeys to the area. In 1804 he made arrangements for a move to Harris, to take over a large sheep farm. His plans reached an advanced stage but did not come to fruition, and involved him in considerable financial loss. However, Hogg published accounts of his various highland journeys of the early 1800s, and he retained a lively and well-informed interest in highland culture throughout the remainder of his life.

Hogg's first book, *Scottish Pastorals* (a short collection of poems), was published in Edinburgh in 1801 but attracted little attention. Nevertheless from this time onwards

Hogg regularly had material accepted for publication in magazines. Through William Laidlaw he was also helping to provide assistance in collecting traditional ballads for the third volume of Walter Scott's *Minstrelsy of the Scottish Border* (1803), and in 1802 Laidlaw was instrumental in setting up a meeting in Ettrick between Hogg and Scott. A friendship developed that was to last until Scott's death in 1832.

After the failure of the projected move to Harris in 1804, Hogg obtained work as a shepherd in Dumfriesshire, in south-west Scotland, an area in which Burns had spent the final years of his life. Indeed, while living in Dumfriesshire, Hogg made the acquaintance of Jean Armour, Burns's widow. With Scott's encouragement two books by Hogg appeared in 1807. One was *The Mountain Bard*, a collection of poems in the manner of the ballads of *Minstrelsy of the Scottish Border*, and the other was *The Shepherd's Guide: being a Practical Treatise on the Diseases of Sheep*. Both were well received, and Hogg used the substantial proceeds to set himself up as a sheep-farmer in Dumfriesshire.

Hogg's letters indicate that he fathered at least one illegitimate child at this stage in his life. His Dumfriesshire years were spent in an area that had been part of the heartland of the covenanters in the religious wars of the seventeenth century, and as a result Dumfriesshire scenes often surface in his stories of the covenanters and of the supernatural. This period of his life produced lasting friendships, for example, with the poet Allan Cunningham, but his Dumfriesshire farming ventures did not prosper. Bankruptcy followed, and in 1810 he set out for Edinburgh in an attempt to establish himself as a professional writer. He was by then forty years old.

An Edinburgh poet, 1810–1817 Having arrived in Edinburgh with no writings to hand but some of his old songs, Hogg duly prepared *The Forest Minstrel* (a collection of songs) for publication. This book appeared in 1810, but sold badly. The aspiring professional writer found that while periodicals were perfectly willing to publish his writings payment was sparse. Profits seemed to go to the proprietors of the periodicals rather than the authors, so Hogg took the bold but logical step of setting up his own weekly paper. Named *The Spy*, it was produced on a shoestring and was largely written by Hogg himself. A variety of material, including essays, prose fiction, and poetry, was published during its run, from 1 September 1810 to 24 August 1811. *The Spy* foundered, however, because of a perception among its readers that it lacked what was called 'delicacy'; that is to say it did not exhibit enough discretion and restraint in dealing with subjects such as extra-marital sex.

The Spy nevertheless had various supporters, including James Gray of the Edinburgh high school, with whom Hogg shared Dumfriesshire links. Through Gray, Hogg established contacts with radical whig political circles in Edinburgh. In the early 1810s he also became actively involved in 'the Forum', a public debating club that attracted large paying audiences, often several hundred strong; indeed, Hogg for a time received a small salary as secretary of the Forum. He also got to know Dr Andrew

Duncan, who was active at this period in improving the treatment of the mentally ill in Edinburgh. Shocked by conditions in Edinburgh's city bedlam, after the death of his patient the poet Robert Fergusson in 1774, Duncan managed to ensure that it was replaced by a new Edinburgh lunatic asylum, which opened in 1813. From the 1810s onwards penetrating studies of madness begin to feature in Hogg's writings, and it seems likely that his friendship with Duncan helped to deepen his insights into such matters.

The Forest Minstrel, *The Spy*, and the Forum were not enough to sustain Hogg financially in his early Edinburgh years; his situation would have been dire indeed had it not been for the financial assistance of John Grieve, an old Ettrick friend who was now a prosperous hatter in Edinburgh. Hogg's situation changed radically for the better, however, with the publication in January 1813 of *The Queen's Wake*. This book-length narrative poem tells of the return of Mary, queen of Scots, to Scotland after her long sojourn in France. To welcome the young queen a poetic competition—described by Hogg as a 'wake'—is held at Holyrood Palace among the minstrels of Scotland. The poem tells the story of this event, interspersed with the songs sung by the minstrels. *The Queen's Wake* was immediately recognized as a major achievement, with spice added by the circumstances of Hogg's background and upbringing. Indeed, George Goldie, the publisher of the poem, assured readers in the second edition (1813) that the work was 'really and truly the production of *James Hogg*, a common shepherd, bred among the mountains of Ettrick Forest, who went to service when only seven years of age; and since that period has never received any education whatever' (p. vi).

Hogg's reputation as one of the leading poets of his generation was now established. As a rival of Scott and Byron among the fashionable poets of the 1810s he produced a formidable output in the years following the publication of *The Queen's Wake*. The third edition of that poem (1814) contains important revisions and was followed in 1815 by *Pilgrims of the Sun*, dedicated to Byron. Two new volumes followed in 1816: *Mador of the Moor*, which echoes and interrogates Scott's *Lady of the Lake*; and *The Poetic Mirror*, a volume of Hogg's brilliant and well-received poetic parodies (of Wordsworth, Coleridge, Byron, Scott, Hogg, and others). *Dramatic Tales*, a two-volume collection that reflects Hogg's long-standing interest in the theatre, followed in 1817. His status was confirmed with the publication by Archibald Constable in 1822 of his four-volume *Poetical Works*.

Hogg's new-found fame was accompanied by other improvements in his fortunes. For example, in 1815 the duke of Buccleuch gave him the farm of Altrive Lake, in Yarrow, rent-free, for life. This provided Hogg with a much-valued base in his native Ettrick Forest, and for the remainder of his life he divided his time between Ettrick and Edinburgh. Likewise his new acceptance as an established literary figure helped him to play a significant part in the founding of *Blackwood's Edinburgh Magazine* in 1817.

The new magazine's fortunes were secured by the publication of the notorious 'Chaldee manuscript' in the number for October 1817. This satirical article was drafted by Hogg and revised and expanded by John Wilson and John Gibson Lockhart. Hogg already had contacts with tory circles through his friendship with Scott, and from 1817 onwards the tory group of writers associated with *Blackwood's* were to play an important part in his life. Hogg's dealings with the tory wits were never comfortable or easy (although he shared their interest in the traditions and customs of the old Scottish peasantry). Nevertheless *Blackwood's* was liberal in its payment of authors, and Hogg's frequent contributions to its pages provided him with a useful source of income.

Hogg's poems of 1815–17 did not emulate the great popular success of *The Queen's Wake*. As people got used to the idea that 'a common shepherd' could 'really and truly' be the author of first-rate poems the delightful sense of novelty began to wear off. Furthermore Hogg's middle-class audience began to feel increasingly uncomfortable about a subversive strand discernible in the writings of this uncouth farmworker. Hogg, like Burns before him, really believed that:

> The rank is but the guinea's stamp,
> The Man's the gowd for a' that
> (R. Burns, 'For a' that and a' that')

and his middle-class audience came to have reservations about the way in which this uppity peasant demanded that his social superiors treat him as an equal. Hogg's raw talent was recognized, but increasingly his talent was felt to be deeply flawed by vanity, by lack of discretion, by 'indelicacy', and by a lack of knowledge of cultivated society and cultivated manners. In short for many middle-class readers of the late 1810s and the 1820s the fellow simply did not know his place, and showed himself to be incapable of properly recognizing and paying due deference to the many virtues of his social superiors. For example, the heroine of Hogg's *Mador of the Moor* is a peasant girl. This was bad enough, but she becomes pregnant out of wedlock, which was worse; worst of all she is not only presented as a character worthy of the reader's admiring sympathy but she eventually marries her seducer, who turns out to be no less a person than the king of Scots. Middle-class readers of the late 1810s could and did recognize that *Mador of the Moor* is a highly readable and skilfully written poem but many of them found it hard to accept a story that was willing to take seriously and reward a peasant girl who indulges in pre-marital sex.

At all events the comparative lack of success of the poems that followed *The Queen's Wake* seems to have generated, about 1817, something of a crisis in Hogg's self-confidence. In that year he abandoned an epic poem, *Queen Hynde*, of which he had already written more than two books, and for the next few years his creative energy was mainly directed towards the writing of prose fiction.

Hogg the novelist, 1818–1824 Hogg had already published prose fiction in *The Spy*, and from the early 1810s he had planned a collection of 'rural and traditionary tales' of the kind told round the cottage fire during the long dark evenings of a Scottish winter. His first book of prose fiction, however, was *The Brownie of Bodsbeck and other Tales* (2 vols., 1818), which consists of three tales by Hogg, each dealing with Ettrick society at a different stage of its development. Thus 'The Hunt of Eildon' is a tale of the supernatural set in the time when Ettrick was a royal hunting forest; 'The Brownie of Bodsbeck' focuses on the experiences of the people of Ettrick during the terrible civil wars of the late seventeenth century; and 'The Wool-Gatherer' is a love story set in the Ettrick of Hogg's own lifetime.

For his next major literary project Hogg set out to collect the songs of the Jacobite risings of the eighteenth century. In this he was encouraged by the Highland Society of London, and the project, which is akin to Scott's ballad-collecting for *Minstrelsy of the Scottish Border* and Burns's efforts to collect and preserve traditional Scottish songs, bore fruit in the two volumes that make up Hogg's *Jacobite Relics* (1819; 'second series', 1821). In these volumes Hogg prints the music as well as the lyrics and provides extensive notes.

Hogg's comparative prosperity in the years after *The Queen's Wake* enabled him to marry Margaret Phillips (1790–1870), daughter of a prosperous Dumfriesshire farmer, in April 1820. Margaret was the younger sister of the first wife of Hogg's friend James Gray, of the Edinburgh high school. Hogg got to know her at Gray's house in Edinburgh during the 1810s, when she was in her twenties. Though there was an age gap of some twenty years the marriage proved to be a very happy one, and the couple had four daughters and a son.

Other events of 1820 included the death of Hogg's father, at Altrive in October, at the age of ninety-one and the publication in Altrive of Hogg's well-received *Winter Evening Tales* (2 vols.). Encouraged by the fact that his financial position had been further improved by his marriage settlement, Hogg in 1821 took on a nine-year lease of Mount Benger, a farm adjacent to Altrive Lake. He was still far from affluent, however, and it was necessary for him to gather together as much capital as possible in order to stock the farm. This was the context in which he made arrangements for the publication of a new and revised edition of *The Mountain Bard* (1821) and for the publication of his four-volume *Poetical Works* (1822).

In 1822 a tight financial situation was transformed into a potentially disastrous one when a relative of Margaret's mother absconded to America, leaving the Phillips family responsible for his debts. Instead of receiving the expected help from his parents-in-law with regard to the stocking of Mount Benger, Hogg had to provide them with support and a home for their few remaining years. The 1820s proved a period of agricultural recession, in the aftermath of the Napoleonic wars, and Hogg had to cope with the high rent of Mount Benger without having the capital to run the farm to best advantage.

Nevertheless the early 1820s were a particularly fruitful time for Hogg the writer. His three-volume novel *The Three Perils of Man* appeared in 1822. This 'Border romance' set in the middle ages is in effect what Hollywood would call a

'prequel' to Scott's narrative poem *The Lay of the Last Minstrel* (1805); in it Hogg both celebrates and questions the account of medieval chivalry in Scott's recent novel *Ivanhoe* (1820). *The Three Perils of Man* tells the story of a siege in the manner of a Waverley novel, but it is also a tale of the supernatural, typical of what late twentieth-century critics would call Hogg's magic realism.

Hogg's next novel, *The Three Perils of Woman* (1823), also employs a dual narrative; here a tale of lowland Scotland set in Hogg's own period mirrors and interacts with a tale of highland Scotland set around the time of the battle of Culloden, in 1746. Yet another dual narrative, *The Private Memoirs and Confessions of a Justified Sinner*, followed in June 1824. It offers competing attempts to tell the story of the life of Robert Wringhim; first a fictional 'Editor' produces a narrative constructed after the manner of one of Scott's Waverley novels, then the 'Editor' prints Robert's own private memoirs and confessions. Later in 1824 Hogg completed *Queen Hynde*, which he had laid aside in 1817; this idiosyncratic alternative version of the Ossianic epics of James Macpherson was published in December 1824. These major works of the early 1820s have come to be much admired but they were not particularly well received at the time of their first publication.

Later years, 1824–1835 From the early 1820s onwards Hogg's considerable fame derived not only from his own writings but also from his portrayal as 'the Ettrick Shepherd' in the 'Noctes Ambrosianae' of *Blackwood's Edinburgh Magazine*. The 'Noctes' articles were chiefly written by John Wilson and John Gibson Lockhart, and they purport to record the table talk of the *Blackwood's* group of writers as they dine in Ambrose's Tavern. Much of the popularity of *Blackwood's* derived from the 'Noctes'—and much of the attraction of the 'Noctes' derived from the figure of the Ettrick Shepherd. From the 'Noctes' the shepherd emerges as a vain, boastful, and bibulous oaf who nevertheless has the poetic inspiration of a genuine child of nature; the Noctean shepherd may be a boor but his unsophisticated simplicity can often enable him to get to the heart of the matter. Hogg's attitude to the 'Noctes' fluctuated; sometimes he was infuriated and sometimes he enjoyed the joke. Partly as a result serious quarrels between Hogg and William Blackwood occurred from time to time.

Blackwood's was also an important outlet for Hogg's own shorter writings. *The Shepherd's Calendar* (2 vols., 1829) consists in the main of short stories that he had contributed to the magazine during the 1820s. Likewise *A Queer Book* (1832) consists of poems by Hogg, most of which had already appeared in *Blackwood's*. Other volumes from his later years include *Songs, by the Ettrick Shepherd* (1831), *Familiar Anecdotes of Sir Walter Scott* (1834), and *A Series of Lay Sermons* (1834). The three-volume *Tales of the Wars of Montrose* (1835), a collection of interconnecting short stories and novellas, is one of Hogg's most daring and most innovative works.

By the 1820s periodicals had become much more generous in paying authors than when Hogg founded *The Spy* in 1810. In his later years Hogg often contributed to various periodicals (including, from 1830, *Fraser's Magazine* in London), and this source of income helped him to struggle on with Mount Benger until the end of his lease, in 1830. At that point he became bankrupt. The rent-free farm of Altrive Lake remained to him, and on returning there with his family he was able to regain financial stability. However, he was by then sixty, and he was anxious to provide if possible for his young wife and younger family. Hogg therefore began to hatch plans for a collected edition of his writings along the lines of Sir Walter Scott's hugely successful *Magnum opus* collected edition, publication of which had commenced in 1829.

Plans for the collected edition took Hogg to London in the early months of 1832. He was rapturously received there, not only as the author of *The Queen's Wake* but also as the famous shepherd of the 'Noctes Ambrosianae'. The collected edition promised well, and the first volume (*Altrive Tales*) appeared in 1832, after Hogg's return to Scotland. His hopes for it were destroyed, however, when its publisher, James Cochrane, became bankrupt shortly afterwards.

In the autumn of 1835 Hogg fell ill. Jaundice was diagnosed, and as the illness progressed it became clear that there was little hope of his recovery. Friends came to Altrive to try to help: Hogg was a much liked man. One lifelong Ettrick friend was Alexander Laidlaw, of Bowerhope farm, who in a letter describes how:

> I visited him on the 22nd October, and almost daily till the 19th November. After this I was in the room in which he died, never took off my clothes, but rested occasionally on a sofa—never got home till the Saturday after the funeral. (Garden, 326)

In its way Laidlaw's account is as moving as William Wordsworth's well-known 'Extempore Effusion on the Death of James Hogg'.

Hogg died at his home, Altrive Lake farm, on 21 November 1835. He was buried in Ettrick churchyard, a stone's throw from his birthplace at Ettrick Hall.

Hogg's reputation and significance James Hogg's status as a major writer was not fully recognized in his own lifetime because his social origins led to his being smothered in genteel condescension. The collected editions of his works published after his death did further damage; some major texts (for example, *The Three Perils of Woman*) are omitted entirely, while others (such as *The Private Memoirs and Confessions of a Justified Sinner*) are heavily bowdlerized. In short the nineteenth-century collected editions offer a bland and lifeless version of Hogg's writings. It was in this version that he was read by the Victorians, and unsurprisingly he came to be regarded as a minor figure, of no great importance or interest. However, the second half of the twentieth century saw a spectacular revival in Hogg's reputation as reliable texts of his writings increasingly became available. In 1995 Edinburgh University Press began to publish the multi-volume Stirling–South Carolina research edition of the collected works.

Like Burns, Hogg questioned and subverted aspects of the Scottish Enlightenment, and created a space in which the allegedly 'marginal' and 'primitive' culture of the old Scottish peasantry could speak with eloquence and power. Like Burns, Macpherson, and Scott, Hogg made a distinctive Scottish contribution to European Romanticism.   DOUGLAS S. MACK

Sources J. Hogg, *Memoir of the author's life and familiar anecdotes of Sir Walter Scott* (1972) • N. Parr, *James Hogg at home* (1980) • M. G. Garden, *Memorials of James Hogg* [1884] • J. Hogg, letters, NL Scot. • G. Hughes, 'James Hogg and the Forum', *Studies in Hogg and his World*, 1 (1990), 57–70 • A. Beveridge, 'James Hogg and abnormal psychology', *Studies in Hogg and his World*, 2 (1991), 91–4 • J. Hogg, *Memoir of Burns*, vol. 5 of *The works of Robert Burns*, ed. J. Hogg and W. Motherwell (1838–41) • E. C. Batho, *The Ettrick Shepherd* (1927) • A. L. Strout, *Life and letters of James Hogg* (1946) • parish register, Ettrick, Selkirkshire, 9 Dec 1770 [baptism] • *Collected letters*, ed. G. Hughes, 3 vols. [forthcoming]
Archives Hunt. L. • LUL, notebook and letters • NL NZ, Turnbull L. • NL Scot., corresp. and papers • NL Scot., corresp., papers, poems, engraved portrait, and material for a biography • NL Scot., poems and letters • NRA, priv. coll., corresp. and papers • Yale U., Beinecke L., corresp. and papers | BL, letters to George Thomson, Add. MSS 35264–35265 • NL Scot., letters to Oliver & Boyd
Likenesses W. Nicholson, oils, *c*.1817, Scot. NPG • W. Bewick, chalk drawing, *c*.1823, Scot. NPG • J. Watson-Gordon, portrait, 1830, Scot. NPG [*see illus.*] • W. Brockedon, pen and chalk drawing, *c*.1832, NPG • W. Archibald, line engraving (after J. W. Gordon), BM • S. P. Denning, watercolour drawing, NPG • W. C. Edwards, line engraving (aged sixty; after C. Fox), repro. in J. Hogg, *Altrive tales* (1832) • C. Fox, watercolour, NPG • D. Maclise, caricature, BM, NPG; repro. in *Fraser's Magazine*, 11 (Jan 1835) • W. Nicholson, oils, Aikwood Tower, Scottish Borders • W. & D. Lizars, etching (after 'P. M.'), BM, NPG; repro. in Lockhart, *Peter's letters to his kinsfolk* (1819)
Wealth at death very little: Garden, *Memorials*

Hogg, James (1806–1888), publisher, was born near Edinburgh on 26 March 1806, the son of James Hogg. He was educated by the Revd Thomas Sheriff (*d*. 1836). On 24 August 1818 he was apprenticed to James Muirhead, printer, in Edinburgh. He subsequently entered the printing house attached to the *Caledonian Mercury*, where the printing of the seventh edition of the *Encyclopaedia Britannica* had commenced in 1827, and became reader on the *Caledonian Mercury*. On 13 November 1832 he married Helen Hutchison (1803–1890), of Hutchiestown Farm, near Dunblane.

In 1837 Hogg set up business on his own account as a printer and publisher in Edinburgh. The first publication which bears his imprint is *The Honest Waterman*, a small tract brought out in 1837. On 1 March 1845 the first number of *Hogg's Weekly Instructor* appeared, a non-sectarian periodical. In 1849 the title was changed to *The Instructor* and later to *Titan*. The last number is dated December 1859, and the entire work comprises twenty-nine volumes. Hogg did his own editing, latterly with the assistance of his eldest son, James. He also published the principal works of George Gilfillan.

In 1849 he made the acquaintance of Thomas De Quincey, who contributed his *Autobiographic Sketches* and other papers to the *Weekly Instructor*. He then agreed with Hogg to bring out his *Collected Works*, and Hogg later contributed his reminiscences of De Quincey to H. A. Page's (A. H. Japp) *Thomas de Quincey: his Life and Writings* (1877). In 1858 Hogg's printing office was discontinued, and in the autumn of that year his sons John and James, who had been taken into partnership, set up a branch publishing office in London, where Hogg later re-established the whole business. Besides the *Churchman's Family Magazine*, the firm then published several series of successful books for young people. The periodical entitled *London Society*, which was projected by James Hogg jun. in February 1862, attained at one time a circulation of twenty-five thousand monthly. The firm of James Hogg & Sons was dissolved in July 1867. Hogg died at The Acacia, 7 Crescent Road, St John's, Kent, the home of his son John, where he had been living, on 14 March 1888.   G. C. BOASE, rev. DOUGLAS BROWN

Sources *The Bookseller* (7 April 1888), 363 · H. A. Page [A. H. Japp], *Thomas De Quincey: his life and writings* (1877)
Wealth at death £275: probate, Oct 1888, *CGPLA Eng. & Wales*

Hogg, James Macnaghten McGarel, first Baron Magheramorne (1823–1890), civic administrator, eldest son of Sir James Weir *Hogg, first baronet (1790–1876), chairman of the East India Company, and his wife, Mary Claudine Swinton (*d*. 1874), was born at Calcutta on 3 May 1823. The merchant and philanthropist Quintin *Hogg was his younger brother. He was educated at Eton College and Christ Church, Oxford, where he matriculated in May 1842. Considered 'a very good boy, if not a particularly brilliant scholar' (Owen, 158), he left Oxford in 1843 to join the 1st Life Guards. He became major and lieutenant-colonel in 1855, retiring from the army in August 1859. On 31 August 1857 he married Caroline Elizabeth Emma (1834–1924), eldest daughter of Edward Gordon Douglas-Pennant, later first Lord Penrhyn. The couple had five sons and one daughter.

Son of a Peelite Conservative, Hogg remained loyal to the Conservative Party after the corn-law split, representing Bath as MP from 1865 to 1868 and Truro from 1871 to 1885. From 1885 until his accession to the peerage in 1887 he sat for the Hornsey division of Middlesex. In May 1876 he succeeded his father as second baronet, and in February 1877 he assumed the additional surname of McGarel by royal licence on succeeding to the estates of his brother-in-law, Charles McGarel of Magheramorne, Antrim. McGarel Hogg was raised to the peerage as Baron Magheramorne in July 1887.

In 1867 Hogg became a member of the Metropolitan Board of Works, the authority elected by members of the capital's secondary authorities to handle London-wide functions such as main drainage and street improvements, representing St George's, Hanover Square. In November 1870 he was elected chairman of the board. He expected to serve only one year as chairman, the Home Office having indicated that reform of metropolitan government was imminent; in the event he remained chairman until the board's eventual abolition in 1889. The chairmanship brought him the KCB on the completion of the Chelsea Embankment in 1874, but it also ensured that his reputation was permanently stained by the scandals which engulfed the board in its final years. Speculation by board members and officers in land acquired for street improvements prompted the appointment of a royal commission into the board in 1888. Though the commission heard that the board's balances were kept at a bank of which he was a director (Davis, 109), Magheramorne (as Hogg had by then become) was not under suspicion for the failings of his subordinates, but his appearance before the commission, when his explanation of the board's functions required frequent prompting from the board's counsel, was unimpressive. If the board was divided, as W. T. Stead claimed, into 'clever knaves who jobbed and virtuous nobodies who winked' (Owen, 207), Magheramorne belonged to the second group, but the commission's report was unquestionably a condemnation of his light-handed chairmanship. Deteriorating health during the 1880s, his duties as an MP, and his frequent trips to Ireland left him dangerously unaware of the board's day-to-day operations, and made his tenaciously protective defence of the board from valid criticism hard to excuse.

Though described in 1887 as a 'fine-looking, soldierly man, with clear-cut features, and snow-white hair' (Owen, 159), Magheramorne's final years were darkened by ill health, intensified by the Metropolitan Board of Works scandal, and he died on 27 June 1890 at his home in 17 Grosvenor Gardens, London. He was buried at Brompton cemetery. Only the first of his five sons married, producing no heir, and his Irish barony passed to his first three sons in succession, becoming extinct with the death of Ronald, the fourth Baron Magheramorne, in 1957.

                                                                    JOHN DAVIS

Sources GEC, *Peerage* · *The Times* (28 June 1890) · *Men of the time* (1887) · Boase, *Mod. Eng. biog.* · J. Davis, *Reforming London* (1988) · D. Owen, *The government of metropolitan London, 1855–1889* (1982) · G. C. Clifton, *Professionalism, patronage and public service in Victorian London* (1992) · *Saturday Review*, 70 (1890), 2
Archives BL OIOC, business, estate, and legal papers, MS Eur. E 342
Likenesses Lock & Whitfield, woodburytype photograph, 1876, NPG; repro. in T. Cooper, *Men of mark: a gallery of contemporary portraits*, 7 vols. (1876–83) · Spy [L. Ward], chromolithograph, NPG; repro. in VF (15 Nov 1873) · portrait, repro. in *St Stephen's Review* (5 July 1890) · portrait, repro. in *Pictorial World* (3 July 1890), 26 · wood-engraving, NPG; repro. in ILN (7 Dec 1867) · wood-engraving, NPG; repro. in ILN (10 Dec 1870)
Wealth at death £200,405 9s. 5d.: resworn probate, Jan 1892, *CGPLA Eng. & Wales* (1890)

Hogg, Sir James Weir, first baronet (1790–1876), director and chairman of the East India Company, was born at Stoneyford, near Lisburn, co. Antrim, on 7 September 1790, the elder son of William Hogg (1754–1824), of Belmont, co. Antrim, and his wife, Mary, daughter of James Dickey of Dunmore, co. Antrim. He received his early education at Dr Bruce's academy in Belfast and in 1808 was elected a scholar of Trinity College, Dublin. There he gained the gold medal for oratory and graduated BA in 1810. In 1811 he entered Gray's Inn, London, in order to qualify for the Irish bar.

In 1814, upon being admitted as a barrister at the King's Inns in Dublin, Hogg sailed for Calcutta and over the next eight years built up an exceptionally lucrative law practice. On 26 July 1822 he married Mary Claudine (*d*. 1874), second daughter of Samuel Swinton of Swinton, Berwickshire, a Bengal civil servant. Also in 1822 he accepted the office of registrar of the supreme court of Calcutta, which post he held until 1833, when he returned to Britain with a large fortune.

In 1835 Hogg was elected for Beverley as a Conservative. He continued to represent Beverley until 1847, when he was returned unopposed for Honiton, a seat which he held until narrowly defeated in the general election of March 1857. Throughout his parliamentary career Hogg resolutely supported Sir Robert Peel and his free-trade policies and in June 1846, shortly before leaving office, Peel repaid his loyalty with a baronetcy.

In September 1839 Hogg was elected a director of the East India Company and thereafter functioned as the *de facto* representative of Leadenhall Street in the House of Commons. Indeed, although he enjoyed a reputation as an excellent orator, he rarely spoke in the house except on Indian matters. He so valued his connection with the company that in 1845 he turned down Peel's offer of the post of judge-advocate-general rather than surrender his position as deputy chairman. In all he was deputy chairman of the company in 1845–6, 1850–51, and 1851–2, and chairman in 1846–7 and 1852–3. In these roles he robustly defended the much criticized system of the dual government of India and, in his insistence on the independence and political integrity of the court of directors, generated considerable friction with the Board of Control, especially during the second presidency (1846–52) of John Cam Hobhouse.

As both a prominent director and an MP, Hogg was subject to frequent attacks by the company's critics, most notably Sir Charles Napier. Unlike many Conservatives, Hogg was not averse to all acquisitions of new territory in India (for example, he approved of Dalhousie's annexation of Nagpur in 1854), but he deplored Napier's self-propelled conquest of Sind and was further outraged by Napier's publicly expressed scorn for the directors and their servants in India. For his part, Napier freely criticized Hogg in the press, especially in a savage letter published in *The Standard* and *The Times* in October 1848, to which Hogg responded in turn by encouraging the court to resist parliamentary pressure to install Napier as commander-in-chief in India.

In 1853 Hogg declined the governorship of Bombay. After his defeat in 1857 he made no attempt to re-enter parliament, but in 1858 under the Government of India Act he took a seat as one of seven former directors on the new Council of India. He remained on the council (serving as vice-president in 1860) until his retirement in early 1872, the year also in which he was sworn a member of the privy council.

Hogg died at his home, 11 Grosvenor Crescent, London, on 27 May 1876, and was buried in Kensal Green cemetery. His wife, mother to their seven sons and seven daughters, had died two years earlier. Their eldest son, Lieutenant-Colonel Sir James Macnaghten McGarel *Hogg, afterwards first Lord Magheramorne (1823–1890), succeeded Hogg in the baronetcy. Their seventh son, Quintin *Hogg, became a successful merchant and philanthropist.

G. F. R. BARKER, *rev.* KATHERINE PRIOR

Sources BL OIOC, Hogg MSS · M. E. Yapp, *Strategies of British India: Britain, Iran and Afghanistan, 1798–1850* (1980) · *Dod's Parliamentary Companion* · B. Gardner, *The East India Company* (1971) · Burke, *Peerage* (1954) · *DNB* · E. Keane, P. Beryl Phair, and T. U. Sadlier, eds., *King's Inns admission papers, 1607–1867*, IMC (1982) · [J. H. Todd], ed., *A catalogue of graduates who have proceeded to degrees in the University of Dublin, from the earliest recorded commencements to … December 16, 1868* (1869) · *The Times* (21 Oct 1848), 3 · *The Times* (24 Oct 1848), 5 · *CGPLA Eng. & Wales* (1876)

Archives BL OIOC, corresp. and papers, MSS Eur E 342 | BL, letter to John Charles Herries · BL, corresp. with Sir John Cam Hobhouse, Add. MSS 36479–36480 · BL OIOC, corresp. with Sir John Cam Hobhouse, MSS Eur F 213

Likenesses R. J. Lane, lithograph, 1856 (after E. U. Eddis), BM, NPG · Smyth, engraving, repro. in *ILN* (9 Oct 1858), 331

Wealth at death under £350,000: probate, 20 June 1876, *CGPLA Eng. & Wales*

Hogg, John (1800–1869), classical scholar and naturalist, was born on 21 March 1800 at Norton near Durham, the second of four sons (there were also two daughters) of John Hogg (1761–1823), barrister, and his wife, Prudentia Jones (c.1767–1838). His brother Thomas Jefferson *Hogg was a close friend of the poet Shelley. Hogg was educated at Durham grammar school and entered Peterhouse, Cambridge, in 1818, where he was selected Ramsay scholar in 1820. He graduated BA in 1822, and proceeded MA in 1827, when he was also elected a bye-fellow at Peterhouse. He became an MA at Oxford in 1844. In 1828 he was admitted to the Inner Temple, and was called to the bar in 1832. He practised on the northern circuit and was a justice of the peace and deputy lieutenant for co. Durham. He married Anne Louisa Sarah (d. 1864), second daughter of Major Goldfinch of The Priory, Chewton Mendip, Somerset. They had one son and two daughters.

Hogg was a learned classicist with wide interests, a capable antiquary and geographer, well read in modern languages, and knowledgeable in natural history. His books include texts on ancient and biblical history, hagiography, archaeology, and philology, as well as on the botany, geology, and geography of Sicily, and the natural history of Stockton-on-Tees and surrounding areas. He wrote articles on the natural history of his home county for botanical journals and contributed plant records to Winch's *Flora of Northumberland* (1831). In 1838 a paper of his on the action of light on the colour of the river sponge (Royal Society Archives) was read before the Royal Society, who elected him a fellow in the following year. He was also a fellow of the Linnean Society, and a member of the Royal Society of Literature, which he served as foreign secretary and vice-president in 1866. He belonged to the Cambridge Philosophical Society, and to the Royal Geographical Society (secretary in 1849–50). He was a member of the Royal Society of Northern Antiquaries of Copenhagen, president of the Tyneside Naturalists' Field Club, and an active contributor to meetings of the British Association.

Hogg was kind-hearted and popular, though said to lack practical common sense. In many of his studies he was assisted by his brother Thomas Jefferson Hogg, about whom he wrote a memoir for the *Gentleman's Magazine* in 1862. He died at his home, Norton House, co. Durham, on 16 September 1869.

GORDON GOODWIN, *rev.* ALEXANDER GOLDBLOOM

Sources Desmond, *Botanists*, rev. edn, 347, col. 1 · *Cambridge University Calendar* (1796) · *Inner Temple registry* · *Stockton Herald* (24 Sept 1869) · *GM*, 3rd ser., 17 (1864), 802 [obit. of Anne Louisa Sarah Hogg] · Walford, *County families* · *Royal Society of Literature: annual report of the proceedings* (1859) · *Royal Society of Literature: annual report of the proceedings* (1870) · *Proceedings of the Royal Geological Society*, 14, 298–9 · *Durham County Advertiser* (24 Sept 1869) · private information (1891) · Venn, *Alum. Cant.*
Archives RBG Kew, letters · U. Durham, commonplace books | CUL, letters to Thomas Jefferson Hogg · Linn. Soc., Winch MSS
Likenesses Maull & Co., sepia photograph, RS · Maull & Polyblank, sepia photograph, RS
Wealth at death under £16,000: probate, 2 Nov 1869, *CGPLA Eng. & Wales*

Hogg, Quintin (1845–1903), merchant and philanthropist, of Scottish descent, fourteenth child and seventh son of Sir James Weir *Hogg, first baronet (1790–1876), East India Company chairman and MP, and his wife, Mary Claudine (*d.* 26 June 1874), daughter of Samuel Swinton, HEIC Bengal civil service, was born on 14 February 1845 in Grosvenor Street, London. James Macnaghten McGarel *Hogg, first Baron Magheramorne (1823–1890), was his eldest brother; four other brothers were in Indian government service.

Hogg, known to his family as Markee, was sent aged seven to a private school in Berkshire, where he was bullied and acquired bad language that shocked his father. He was then sent to Lee's, a fashionable school at Brighton. In 1858 he entered the Revd J. L. Joynes's house at Eton College. Known as Piggy Hogg, he joined the rifle volunteers and in 1863 shot for Eton at Wimbledon. He was active in games, especially association football, which he continued to play until he had 'fifty years of footer' (Wood, *The polytechnic and its Founder*, 25). He was seven years captain of the Old Etonian FC, when they were undefeated, and from 1864 to 1870 he captained Scottish teams against English. At Eton he showed strong religious convictions and held prayer meetings. As his grandson, the second Lord Hailsham, wrote, Hogg was 'inspired and driven on from first to last by his Christian faith' (Wood, *A History of the Polytechnic*, 15), and he wrote in 1885, 'Christian profession without Christian work is an anomaly' (Wood, *The polytechnic and its Founder*, 106).

In 1863 Hogg left Eton for the office of Messrs Thompson, tea merchants, in the City of London; eighteen months later, by the influence of his brother-in-law Charles McGarel, he entered the firm of Bosanquet, Curtis & Co., sugar merchants. He soon became a senior partner of the house, which was renamed Hogg, Curtis, and Campbell, and under his direction greatly prospered. The firm's factories were concentrated in Demerara, British Guiana, which Hogg frequently visited. In 1869 he went to Trinidad, caught yellow fever, and, returning ill, inadvertently drank excessive amounts of medicine containing mercury. He almost died of mercury poisoning, and permanently impaired his health. Innovative, he modernized sugar production in Demerara, gave generously in the colony, and endowed the Coolie Mission. Following press criticism and polytechnic members' concern, he refused to take any of his firm's profits derived from rum. He was

Quintin Hogg (1845–1903), by unknown photographer

also a director and subsequently chairman of the North British and Mercantile Insurance Company, and a director of the San Paolo Coffee Estates, the National Discount Company, the London and Paris Securities Corporation, and the Baker Street and Waterloo Railway. After 1882 competition from sugar beet from continental protectionist states, subsidized by export bounties, injured the trade, and Hogg's income suffered. He retired from the firm in 1898, but continued other commercial interests until his death. A successful businessman, he became rich, and his wealth enabled his philanthropic achievement.

Hogg was of medium height and sturdy build, with broad shoulders, a large head, and penetrating blue eyes. Committed, dynamic, and hard-working, he suffered from ill health, insomnia, and depression, and, according to his daughter's description, may have been manic-depressive. From 1872 he and his wife assisted—with facilities, organization, and finance—the British missions of D. L. Moody, the American evangelist. In 1885 Hogg was briefly a Liberal parliamentary candidate, then withdrew.

Christian-motivated philanthropy was the main concern of Hogg's life. In the winter of 1864–5, with the help of his Eton friend Arthur (later eleventh Baron) Kinnaird, he started in Of Alley (later York Place), Charing Cross, a ragged school for boys. Larger premises were taken in Castle Street, off Hanover Street. In the building Hogg soon also started for 'better'-class boys a Youths' Christian Institute. In 1878 the institute was transferred to Long

Acre, and the ragged school was dissociated from it and soon superseded by board schools. In the new premises, accommodating 500 members, Hogg offered technical courses, which proved almost as attractive as the recreation schemes, for which in 1880 he provided a ground at Mortlake. He also paid for boys' emigration to North America.

The Royal Polytechnic Institution in Regent Street, London, had been founded by Sir George Cayley, sixth baronet, the aeronautical pioneer, and others, and opened in 1838. It held scientific and technical exhibitions and classes, but by 1882 had failed financially and was for sale. Hogg purchased the lease for £15,000 and spent larger sums on alterations. He retained the name Polytechnic, but made it an institution under public management which provided artisan and lower-middle-class young men and women with instruction, recreation, and social opportunities, so contributing to the increased educational opportunities for women.

Though no religious tests were imposed, his polytechnic was a Christian institution, and the first class held there was a Bible class. He held services there, and stated that if necessary he would refuse external funding rather than end religious classes, which he believed the most important. The new polytechnic was opened on 25 September 1882, with 2000 members. During the first winter the numbers rose, under Hogg's energetic direction, to 6800. He greatly increased and improved the technical classes. Activities included sports, athletics, a mock parliament, savings bank, Christian workers' union, and volunteer unit (attached to the 4th Middlesex rifle volunteer corps). Partly to utilize the polytechnic facilities during the daytime, in 1886 he founded there a day school for boys, and in 1888 another for girls; both flourished. He became especially fond of the boys' school, and its old boys called themselves Old Quintinians. From 1886 the polytechnic organized low-priced overseas holiday tours for members. In 1891 an employment bureau was added, and on Hogg's suggestion, after a conference at the polytechnic in 1902, an act of parliament authorized metropolitan borough councils to establish publicly funded labour bureaux.

Under Hogg as president and chairman of the governing body, the polytechnic, the largest adult education provider in London, continued to grow, flourish, and achieve examination and sporting success. Hogg spent much on it—in 1888 his aggregate contributions reached a total of £100,000—but it was also financed by his friends and supporters, by fees, and by grants from London parochial charities and from local and central government, including 'whisky money' for technical education. The polytechnic enriched the lives and furthered the careers of many, and engendered great affection and loyalty.

By his success at the Regent Street Polytechnic, Hogg initiated the polytechnic movement in London. In February 1889 he was elected an alderman of the first London county council, holding office until 1895. He served on the housing and technical education committees, and

encouraged the formation by the LCC of other polytechnics. In 1880 Hogg started and edited *Home Tidings of the Young Men's Christian Institute*, from 1887 the *Polytechnic Magazine*. Later he appointed a paid editor, but continued a frequent contributor. In 1900 he published *The Story of Peter*, religious addresses delivered at his Sunday afternoon class at the polytechnic during 1896–7.

Hogg's activities told on his health, and he often sought recuperation in foreign travel or in yachting. On 16 May 1871 he married Alice Anna (*d.* 5 Aug 1918), eldest daughter of William Graham (1817–1885), merchant and Liberal MP for Glasgow, 1865–74. They had three sons and two daughters. Their eldest son, Douglas McGarel *Hogg (1872–1950), became first Viscount Hailsham, and their second son, Ian Graham Hogg (1875–1914), lieutenant-colonel 4th hussars, died of wounds in September 1914 in France. Their younger daughter, Ethel Mary (Mrs Herbert Frederick Wood), wrote Hogg's biography and a history of the polytechnic.

Hogg had accommodation at the polytechnic. On the morning of 17 January 1903 he died there in his bath, killed by fumes from a gas heater in the inadequately ventilated room. After cremation, his ashes were buried on the 21st in the Marylebone cemetery at Finchley, Middlesex. In his memory a Quintin Hogg recreation ground and boathouse at Grove Park, Chiswick, were provided in 1904, costing £25,000, and a bronze group statue by Sir George Frampton was erected in 1906 in Langham Place, opposite the polytechnic. The sum of £90,000 was also raised in 1910 by Hogg's friends and admirers for rebuilding the old premises.

Hogg self-sacrificingly achieved great good for others, ironically by means of a substance, sugar, now considered by some harmful to health. Long after his death his great adult education and community centre, the polytechnic, became Westminster University, and his beloved day school a London comprehensive.

G. S. WOODS, *rev.* ROGER T. STEARN

Sources E. M. Wood, *The polytechnic and its founder Quintin Hogg* (1932) • E. M. Wood, *A history of the polytechnic* (1965) • *WWW, 1897–1915* • GEC, *Peerage* • Burke, *Peerage* (1924) • *The Times* (19 Jan 1903) • private information (1912) • G. Gibbon and R. W. Bell, *History of the London county council, 1889–1939* (1939) • P. W. Musgrave, *Society and education in England since 1800* (1968) • H. J. Dyos and M. Wolff, eds., *The Victorian city: images and realities*, 2 vols. (1976) • G. Crossick, ed., *The lower middle class in Britain, 1870–1914* (1977) • J. Kamm, *Hope deferred: girls' education in English history* (1965)
Archives University of Westminster, London, corresp.
Likenesses G. Frampton, group portrait, bronze statue, 1906, Langham Place, London • E. W. Appleby, oils, University of Westminster, London • E. W. Appleby, oils, Polytechnic of Central London • L. Dickinson, portrait, Regent Street Polytechnic • photograph, repro. in Wood, *The polytechnic and its founder*, frontispiece • photographs, University of Westminster, London • photogravure, repro. in E. M. Hogg, *Quintin Hogg* (1904) [*see illus.*]
Wealth at death £161,253 8*s.* 9*d.*: probate, 21 Feb 1903, *CGPLA Eng. & Wales*

Hogg, Thomas Jefferson (1792–1862), biographer of Percy Bysshe Shelley, was born on 24 May 1792 at Norton near Stockton-on-Tees, co. Durham, the eldest of six children of John Hogg (1761–1823), a non-practising barrister

Thomas Jefferson Hogg (1792–1862), by R. Easton, 1857

and country gentleman, and his wife, Prudentia (c.1767–1838), daughter of the Revd Watkin Jones. The classical scholar and naturalist John *Hogg was his brother. A reserved boy acutely conscious of his status as a gentleman, Jefferson attended Durham grammar school from the age of twelve until 1810 before matriculating at Oxford in February 1810. In October he met another first-year student, Percy Bysshe Shelley, whose friendship transformed his life.

Although Hogg's articles of 1832 on Shelley at Oxford, reprinted in The Life of Percy Bysshe Shelley (2 vols., 1858), depict him as Shelley's mentor, Hogg at eighteen was as flighty and unconventional as his friend. As the unaltered versions of Shelley's letters prove, Hogg joined Shelley in writing provocative letters to clergymen, declared his 'love' for Shelley's sister Elizabeth even before his sole glimpse of her (through a church window on a clandestine visit to Field Place), and wrote an anti-religious novel, 'Leonora', which Shelley encouraged him to publish. In March 1811 he was expelled along with Shelley for refusing to reveal who wrote The Necessity of Atheism. Though Shelley wrote the final version and arranged the printing and distribution, Hogg had garnered philosophical arguments for the essay and probably wrote an early draft. Consequently, his decision to share Shelley's expulsion was partly a matter of loyalty and partly of pride—he could not allow his friend to accept full credit (or blame) for their joint production.

Sent to York to serve a legal apprenticeship, the nineteen-year-old Hogg not only corresponded with Shelley but followed him to Edinburgh, returning to York along with Shelley and his sixteen-year-old bride, Harriet Westbrook. When Shelley, barely nineteen himself, left Harriet under Hogg's 'protection' while he journeyed to Field Place to beg money from his father, Hogg declared his 'love' for Harriet, who did not reciprocate his feelings. After Shelley's return, Hogg confessed his indiscretion. Soon afterwards the young couple left York for Keswick. After a frenzied correspondence in which Hogg threatened suicide and Shelley grappled with the loss of 'the brother of his soul', Shelley stopped trying to counter his friend's sophistry and ended the correspondence.

Despite having lost Shelley, apparently forever, Hogg retained his unorthodox views, making anti-religious jokes and later becoming a vegetarian. His novel The Memoirs of Prince Alexy Haimatoff (1813) reveals his view of love (in contrast to Shelley's) as being primarily a matter of sexual attraction. Even his political views, contrary to his self-depiction in the Life, remained liberal until about 1836, as his voluminous correspondence makes clear.

Hogg was admitted to the Middle Temple in November 1812. When Shelley arrived unannounced at his door a month later, their friendship was resumed but on a less intimate level than at Oxford or York. Shelley introduced Hogg to his London circle, which included the eccentric vegetarian J. F. Newton, Newton's sister-in-law Harriet Boinville, and somewhat later, Thomas Love Peacock and Leigh Hunt. Shelley's elopement with Mary Godwin in July 1814 temporarily strained the friendship, but the satirical hook-nosed Hogg could not resist Shelley's charm—or, it appears, the women associated with him. By January 1815 Hogg was writing love letters to Mary, giving her presents, and requesting a lock of her hair, all with Shelley's full knowledge and approval.

In 1816 Hogg took a brief European tour before resuming his legal studies in the north. Called to the bar in October 1817, he began the monotonous circuit of Northumberland and Durham, from which he found relief by hunting partridges and reading Greek. The next few years were marked chiefly by loss: the suicide of Harriet Shelley in December 1816, Shelley's departure from England in 1818, and the deaths of two young brothers, Robert in 1817 and William in 1821. Though Hogg's few letters to Shelley hide his feelings under a dry satirical wit, his affection for the poet was still strong; the news of Shelley's death in July 1822 resulted in 'sudden mental anguish' which '[threw] him off his guard' (Shelley's Friends, ed. Jones, 92).

Hogg soon found consolation by falling in love with Jane Williams (1798–1884), to whom Shelley had addressed such famous lyrics as 'To Jane with a Guitar' and 'The keen stars were twinkling'. Hogg's attraction to the last of Shelley's women is hardly surprising, but her attraction to the crotchety young lawyer seems to have resulted chiefly from Hogg's willingness to provide a home for her two fatherless children and the appearance at least of respectability. Neither a divorce nor a legal marriage to Hogg was possible for Jane, who had lived with Edward Williams as his wife but was legally married to a Captain John Edward Johnson. Not only did Hogg condone her past, he grudgingly embarked on a second European tour, memorialized in *209 Days*, at her request. In any case, her decision to live as Mrs Hogg was necessitated by pregnancy: Mary Prudentia Hogg was born in November 1827 (*d.* May 1829). A second daughter, Prudentia Sarah, was born in 1838.

Outwardly respectable but still opinionated and satirical, the middle-aged Hogg bore little resemblance to the Oxford student expelled with Shelley. Perhaps to compensate for his unorthodox 'marriage'—his family refused to see either his 'mistress' or their children—he became increasingly conventional, even attending church on occasion as a social rather than a religious obligation. His success as a lawyer was limited, but he supplemented his income by writing articles for the *Encyclopaedia Britannica* and various periodicals. In 1832 he was appointed to the royal commission on municipal corporations and in 1838 he became revising barrister for Northumberland and Berwick, a post which he held for twenty years.

In 1857 Sir Percy and Lady Jane Shelley invited the 64-year-old Hogg to write a biography of the long dead poet using the letters and journals in their possession. With these materials and his own collection of letters from Shelley, Hogg ought to have produced a valuable book. But his intention, expressed in an unpublished letter to Lady Shelley, to allow no one to see his manuscript must have warned the Shelleys that neither the tone nor the content would meet their expectations. Disturbed by Hogg's caricature of Shelley and his 'indiscreet use' of their materials (Thoma, 616) and correctly suspecting from his treatment of Shelley's letters to Thomas Hookham that Hogg had altered his own correspondence with Shelley as well, Sir Percy requested the return of his documents and placed an injunction on Hogg to prevent publication of subsequent volumes. The book was in fact even more distorted than the Shelleys realized. Hogg barely mentions and never analyses Shelley's poetry and he denies the poet's strongly held political and intellectual convictions. In addition, he conceals information, including the identity of Shelley's correspondents other than himself and Godwin, and even suppresses a letter from Shelley announcing his new attachment to Mary Godwin. He invents anecdotes to support his depiction of 'poor Shelley' as a bumbling eccentric and of himself as the rational 'prop' on whom 'poor Shelley' leaned. The story of the newly vegetarian Shelley, the son of a Sussex farmer, greedily devouring bacon for the first time ('So this is bacon!'), or the tale of Hogg removing the balls from Shelley's duelling pistols to prevent a shooting accident fully justify Lady Shelley's charge that the Shelley depicted by Hogg is a mere caricature.

This flawed biography, which protected Hogg's reputation at Shelley's expense, strained Hogg's friendships with Peacock and the dying Hunt. Unhappy, gout-stricken, and overweight, Hogg died at his home, 33 Clifton Road, Carlton Hill, St John's Wood, on 27 August 1862, aged seventy. He was buried on 2 September in Kensal Green cemetery. CAROL L. THOMA

Sources C. L. Thoma, 'Hogg's "Life of Shelley": a pseudo-biography', PhD diss., University of Arizona, 1993 · W. Scott, *Jefferson Hogg* (1951) · J. Rees, *Shelley's Jane Williams* (1985) · *The letters of Percy Bysshe Shelley*, ed. F. L. Jones, 2 vols. (1964) · F. L. Jones, 'Hogg and the "Necessity of atheism"', *Publications of the Modern Language Association of America*, 52 (1937), 1423–6 · *Maria Gisborne and Edward E. Williams, Shelley's friends: their journals and letters*, ed. F. L. Jones (1951) · *After Shelley: the letters of Thomas Jefferson Hogg to Jane Williams*, ed. S. Norman (1934) · T. J. Hogg, *The life of Percy Bysshe Shelley*, 2 vols. (1858) · K. N. Cameron, D. H. Reiman, and D. D. Fischer, eds., *Shelley and his circle, 1773–1822*, 10 vols. (1961–2002) · W. S. Scott, *The Athenians: being correspondence between Thomas Jefferson Hogg and his friends Thomas Love Peacock, Leigh Hunt, Percy Bysshe Shelley and others* (1943); repr. (1974) · F. L. Jones, 'Hogg's peep at Elizabeth Shelley', *Philological Quarterly*, 29 (1950), 422–6 · d. cert. · *The letters of Mary Wollstonecraft Shelley*, ed. B. T. Bennett, 3 vols. (1980–88)
Archives BL, letters, Ashley 5730 · BL, MS of his life of Shelley and papers, Add. MS 43803–43805 · NYPL, corresp. | BL, letters to Jane Williams, Add. MS 41686 · Bodl. Oxf., Abinger MSS · Bodl. Oxf., Shelley adds., MS · Bodl. Oxf., letters to his father relating to his relationship with Shelley · Bodl. Oxf., corresp. with Mary Wollstonecraft Shelley · NYPL, Carl H. Pforzheimer Collection of Shelley and His Circle, corresp. · Trinity Cam., letters to Lord Houghton · UCL, letters to Lord Brougham and Henry Brougham
Likenesses silhouette, *c.*1810, repro. in Scott, *Jefferson Hogg* · R. Easton, ink drawing, 1857, Bodl. Oxf. [*see illus.*]
Wealth at death under £18,000: probate, 7 Nov 1862, *CGPLA Eng. & Wales*

Hogg, William (*fl.* 1682–1702), Latin poet, was Scottish, and, according to Anderson, a native of Gowrie, Perthshire. The details of his life are uncertain. He may be one of several graduates of Edinburgh University of the name Gulielmus Hog—MA in 1670, 1686, or 1692. The 1670 graduate seems most likely.

Although he appears to have made little impact on literary historians, or compilers of Scottish biography, Hogg is notable as one of the most prolific Latin writers of his age. His output was remarkable, consisting of biblical paraphrase, complimentary poems, and translations of long English works into Latin. Throughout he was motivated by the search for patronage, presumably hoping to make a career for himself on the London literary scene. He succeeded in having many works printed, but his obscurity suggests that he was otherwise unsuccessful: the commercial viability of his work is also unclear.

Hogg began with *Paraphrasis in Jobum poetica* (1682), continuing the popular seventeenth-century tradition of turning parts of the Bible into elegant Latin (or sometimes Greek) verse, as practised by such distinguished figures as George Buchanan and Arthur Johnston in Scotland, or the Englishmen James Duport and Joshua Barnes in Cambridge, or John Ailmer of New College, Oxford. Hogg published his paraphrase of Ecclesiastes (*Satyra sacra*) about 1686.

Hogg's most important work is probably his *Paraphrasis poetica* of Milton's *Paradise Lost*, *Paradise Regained*, and *Samson Agonistes* (1690). Hogg had no patron, and therefore no fulsome dedication, for Job and Ecclesiastes, but now he has found a 'Maecenas' in the physician Daniel Cox, who has encouraged him to undertake this massive task of translation, supported the labour, and paid for its publication. As for the critics: 'omnes Zoilorum contumelias flocci facio, et insulsos superciliosae arrogantiae criticismos contemno. Nam haec aetas Zoilorum est feracissima' ('I give but a straw for all the insults of Zoiluses [critics], and scorn the absurd criticisms of supercilious arrogance. For this age has a fruitful crop of Zoiluses'; p. ix). He tells the reader bluntly that his motivation is 'Non amor famae, sed timor famis' ('not love of fame, but fear of hunger'; p. xxii). Foreign ignorance of Milton's verse is a reason for offering him in an international language: but, as with William Dobson's later Latin version of *Paradise Lost* (in 1750), a domestic audience could also be entertained by the translator's elegant Latinity.

In 1695 Hogg turned to the first book of Sir Richard Blackmore's *Prince Arthur*, not at Blackmore's instigation, but by the wish of Hogg's new, aristocratic patron Thomas, earl of Pembroke, and the bishop of Salisbury (who had admired Hogg's Milton). Hogg's Latin can deal cleverly with Blackmore: 'This Molehill Earth has lost its former Charms' becomes 'Haec Terra, exiguo, quae mole simillima colli est' (p. 61)—the noun *moles*, literally 'mass', puns on 'mole'. Hogg's Blackmore translation emphasizes the patriotic allegory of William III; his whiggish support for William is even clearer in his poem on the fall of Namur: 'rumoribus … Jacobitae falsis fremuere' ('Jacobites raged with false rumours'; Money, 141). As well as native royalty, Hogg writes of Christian V of Denmark (Princess Anne's brother-in-law).

Hogg is of particular interest as one of relatively few whig Latin poets (besides Joseph Addison). He congratulates Robert Harley on becoming speaker (1701): 'qui me saepe, dum paene fame peribam, … sublevasti' ('you have often saved me from near-starvation'). Harley, though a moderate tory, was then reconciled with William: 'rex Gulielmus amat' ('King William loves you'); the people await Harley's voice 'velut aridus imbrem / optat ager' ('as a parched field desires rain'); his eloquence is like Orpheus's. Hogg is over the top (in a slightly absurd echo of Lucretius), but full of vigour.

The earl of Pembroke received another biblical paraphrase, *Cato divinus, sive, Proverbia Solomonis* (1699). The title probably refers to the proverbial *Disticha de moribus* attributed to the obscure Dionysius Cato (usually printed with Publilius Syrus's *Sententiae*), but it inevitably suggests the great Stoic moralists, Cato the elder and younger, and thus may be considered a precursor of whig use of the name, in Addison's *Cato* or John Trenchard's and Thomas Gordon's *Cato's Letters* (1724). Hogg produced a number of other Latin works, mostly commemorative or panegyric, by 1702; he is easily the most productive Latin poet of the 1690s, and deserves further study. Apart from William Lauder's interest in 1739 (he used Hogg's version for his attack on Milton as a plagiarist), he appears to have been decidedly and undeservedly ignored. According to Thomas Birch he was reduced to poverty in London and died on the streets (Anderson, *Scot. nat.*).

D. K. MONEY

Sources L. Bradner, *Musae Anglicanae: a history of Anglo-Latin poetry, 1500–1925* (1940) • D. K. Money, *The English Horace* (1998) • D. Laing, ed., *A catalogue of the graduates … of the University of Edinburgh*, Bannatyne Club, 106 (1858) • Anderson, *Scot. nat.*

Hoggan [*née* Morgan], **Frances Elizabeth** (1843–1927), physician and social reformer, was born on 20 December 1843 at the vicarage, Brecon, the eldest of the five children of Richard Morgan (*d.* 1851) and his wife, Georgiana Catherina Philipps. Her early childhood was spent mainly in Aberafan, where her father was vicar from 1845 until his death in 1851. Thereafter her family home continued to be in Wales although she attended a girls' school in Windsor from the age of ten. She was then allowed to study in Paris in 1858 and in Düsseldorf in 1861, where she formed the ambition to become a doctor.

By 1866 Morgan was receiving private medical tuition in London intending to follow the precedent set by Elizabeth Garrett (later Garrett Anderson), who in 1863 had obtained the licence of the Society of Apothecaries, so becoming the first woman trained in Britain to appear on the General Medical Council's register. Garrett provided clinical instruction for Morgan at the St Mary's Dispensary for Women and Children in Marylebone, London. Morgan passed the Society of Apothecaries' preliminary examination in arts with honours in January 1867. But soon afterwards the society revised its licence regulations so as to exclude would-be candidates who had had only private, rather than regular, medical school instruction. This effectively excluded women from the medical register as all British medical schools (and all other British medical qualifications) appeared firmly closed to them.

In the autumn of 1867 Morgan went to Zürich University where the Russian Nadezhda Suslova was about to become the first female medical graduate. Morgan's academic achievements in Zürich were to become legendary. She completed the medical course in three years rather than the expected five. Staff and fellow students were impressed with the 'seriousness, the aristocratic calm and the royal superiority of this remarkable girl' (Bonner, 38). In March 1870, she was only the second woman to defend an MD thesis (on progressive muscular atrophy) before the entire medical faculty of Zürich University. More than 400 spectators watched her do so with consummate skill and become the first British woman to obtain a European MD degree.

After graduating Morgan travelled to Vienna, Prague, and then Paris to further her clinical training and then set up in practice at 13 Granville Place, London, as a qualified but unregistered medical practitioner. In March 1871 she was appointed by Elizabeth Garrett as the first assistant physician to St Mary's Dispensary and then to its successor, the New Hospital for Women, when it opened in 1872.

On 1 April 1874, Morgan married George Hoggan (1837–1891), a former engineer with the Indian navy, who had graduated in medicine from Edinburgh University in 1872. For the next decade Frances and George Hoggan practised together from different rooms in the same building and jointly published several scientific papers—for example, 'Notes of a case of transfusion by Aveling's apparatus'

(*British Medical Journal*, 31 March 1877). They had no children.

Frances Hoggan's irregular position as a practising but unregistered medical practitioner was resolved in 1877 when the King and Queen's College of Physicians in Ireland opened its licentiate examinations to women. In the meantime the British Medical Association had declared her election to the association as void on the grounds of her unregistered status when elected. In 1878 she resigned as assistant physician at the New Hospital for Women, apparently unhappy at the extent of high risk abdominal surgery, including ovariotomy, being undertaken by Garrett Anderson. A conservative stance towards abdominal surgery would have been in accord with Hoggan's active support for preventive health measures and moral and sanitary reform in preference to heroic curative interventions. In 1871 Hoggan, with her close friend Elizabeth Blackwell, the first woman on the medical register, was co-founder and also honorary secretary of the National Health Society, which aimed to promote sanitary education under the motto 'prevention is better than cure'. Between 1875 and 1885 Hoggan published pamphlets and read papers at many conferences on such topics as the physical education of girls and the benefits of swimming to women's health. Her 1883 pamphlet *On the Advantages of a Vegetarian Diet in Workhouses and Prisons* advocated the withdrawal of meat from inmates' diets on grounds of economy and the moral benefits ensuing from restricting habitual criminals' and paupers' sensual gratification.

In the mid-1870s Hoggan and her husband's championing of the anti-vivisectionist cause kept her name in the public eye. A letter from George Hoggan, published in the *Morning Post* on 2 February 1875, described in emotive terms his experiences during four months working in Claude Bernard's Paris laboratories. The letter fuelled the developing campaign against animal experiments being orchestrated in particular by Frances Power Cobbe. The Hoggans were founder members of Cobbe's Victoria Street Society for the Protection of Animals Liable to Vivisection from 1875. As qualified doctors with some first-hand experience of animal experimentation their support was particularly valued by anti-vivisectionists. However, they resigned in 1878 when, under Cobbe's leadership, the Victoria Street Society adopted a policy committed to total abolition of all animal experiments whereas the Hoggans' opposition appears to have been only to painful experiments.

Frances Hoggan was also publicly active in the women's movement. She promoted better education for girls, for example, in *Education for Girls in Wales* (1882) and, particularly, the case for medical women. Here too she was not afraid to court public controversy. While at Edinburgh University, George Hoggan had been an ardent supporter of the rights of his fellow female medical students, the so-called 'Edinburgh Seven', to obtain a full medical education. But in an essay on 'Women in medicine' published in T. Stanton, ed., *The Woman Question in Europe* (1884), Frances Hoggan and her husband were highly critical of Sophia Jex-Blake's confrontational tactics in the later

stages of the Edinburgh campaign, alleging they had been counter-productive compared to the uneventful but real progress made by those such as Frances Hoggan herself, who had studied in London and abroad.

Between 1881 and 1885 Hoggan campaigned actively for medical women in India, where religious proscriptions precluded many women from seeking medical advice from male doctors. Through articles in the *Contemporary Review* (August 1881) and on 'Medical work for women in India' in the *Englishwoman's Review* (15 April and 15 May 1885), and in many speeches, she argued that priority should be given to opening medical schools for Indian women rather than training British women to go to India. This position created some tension between her and medical women at the London School of Medicine for Women, who were actively raising funds for scholarships for women planning to work in India to train at the school.

In 1885 George Hoggan's health broke down and the couple moved to the French riviera. Frances Hoggan returned to London after his death in May 1891. Although she did not resume medical practice she continued to take an active interest in a range of contemporary social issues including the women's suffrage campaign and racial inequalities in the United States and southern Africa. She spent her last years in Brighton, where she died in a nursing home at 13 Clarence Square, on 5 February 1927. Her body was cremated at Woking on 9 February.

M. A. ELSTON

Sources O. Thomas, *Frances Elizabeth Hoggan, 1843–1927* (privately printed, Brecon, 1970) · T. N. Bonner, *To the ends of the earth: women's search for education in medicine* (1992) · J. Manton, *Elizabeth Garrett Anderson* (1965) · M. A. Elston, 'Women doctors in the British health service: a sociological study of their careers and opportunities', PhD diss., U. Leeds, 1986 · *BMJ* (27 June 1891), 1411 · *BMJ* (19 Feb 1927), 357 · *The Lancet* (19 Feb 1927) · *The Times* (7 Feb 1927) · M. A. Elston, 'Women and anti-vivisection in Victorian England, 1870–1900', *Vivisection in historical perspective*, ed. N. Rupke (1987), 259–94 · E. A. Impey, 'Notes on Frances Elizabeth Hoggan', 1948, Wellcome L., Medical Women's Federation Archives, SA/MWF.C.3 · N. A. Sahli, 'Elizabeth Blackwell MD (1821–1910): a biography', PhD diss., University of Pennsylvania, 1974 · d. cert. · *CGPLA Eng. & Wales* (1927)

Likenesses photograph, *c.*1867–1870, University of Zürich, Switzerland, Medizinhistorisches Institut; repro. in Bonner, *To the ends of the earth*

Wealth at death £2987 10s.: probate, 12 April 1927, *CGPLA Eng. & Wales*

Hogge, James Myles [*formerly* James-Miles] (1873–1928), social researcher and politician, was born on 19 April 1873 at 4 St Cuthbert's Lane, Edinburgh, the son of Robert Hogg, a journeyman tailor, and his wife, Mary-Ann-Grameleslay Miles. He later changed the spelling of his middle name and surname. He was educated at the Edinburgh Normal School and thereafter was a pupil–teacher with the Edinburgh school board. After attending Moray House Training College, he went on to Edinburgh University where he graduated MA in 1897. His time at university coincided with developments which were giving the student body a more marked corporate identity. As a joint editor of the *Scottish Students' Song Book* and of the *British*

Students' Song Book he helped give expression to this movement. Hogge was also an editor of the *Student*. He was senior president of the Edinburgh students' representative council and was president of the Edinburgh University Liberal Association.

Hogge gave up his intention to be a teacher and after attending New College, Edinburgh, he qualified as a preacher in the United Free Church of Scotland. After a short period as an assistant minister and some anxiety about whether the church was the best way of leading a life of service, Hogge again changed direction and began to concentrate on social work. Initially he participated in settlement work in Edinburgh and then went on to York. There he joined in social investigation work with Joseph Rowntree, B. Seebohm Rowntree, and the temperance advocate and later Liberal MP Arthur Sherwell, was for a time with the labour bureau, and was secretary of the York distress committee. This work also involved extensive travel in continental Europe, Scandinavia, and Russia for investigative and comparative purposes and led him to publish in the interests of the anti-gambling and temperance movements. As his choice of careers showed, Hogge would appear to have been an intense person. His later *Who's Who* entry gave his recreation as 'work'.

Hogge's interest in social issues also found expression in the development of his political career. He was an early office bearer in the Young Scots' Society, founded after the Liberal election defeat of 1900 to educate young men in the principles of Liberalism and in the study of social science and economics. He first stood as a Progressive candidate in the Castlegate ward in York in 1905 and was a member of the York city council for this ward from 1907 until 1913. Here he made his mark as a champion of municipalization and as an opponent of private provision of local services. He was president of the York City and County Liberal Club and secretary of the Thirsk and Malton Liberal Association.

On 4 February 1905 Hogge married, in a Society of Friends ceremony, Florence Rebecca Metcalfe (*b.* 1868/9), of Malton, a widow, the daughter of Thomas Hopkins, gentleman. They had one son and two daughters.

Hogge's radical father had encouraged him to attend public meetings. In one of a series of articles which Hogge wrote about his youth, he described refusing to sell a ticket his father had given him for a meeting to be addressed by W. E. Gladstone. In December 1910 Hogge attempted to carry his own political career further by standing as a Liberal in the Camlachie division of Glasgow. He narrowly lost to a Liberal Unionist, but his advanced new Liberal policies were credited with greatly reducing the Labour vote. At a by-election in February 1912 he was elected Liberal MP for Edinburgh East. In this position he continued his interest in anti-gambling and temperance matters as well as pensions, national insurance, and Scottish home rule. Together with advanced radicals such as William Mather Rutherford Pringle, Hogge tried to force the issue of Scottish self-government onto the political agenda. He published work on all these subjects, including *Licensing in Scandinavia*, which drew on his travelling research experience. He enjoyed the reputation of being a vigorous platform speaker and a witty, if at times tactless, contributor in parliament. Noted for his mastery of the rules and customs of the House of Commons, he was regarded by the pre- and wartime Liberal leadership as a rebellious and generally troublesome back-bencher.

Hogge was also a critic of the Lloyd George coalition, accusing the Ministry of Information, for example, in a parliamentary debate of November 1918 of making a film aimed at presenting the prime minister in a heroic light. As a non-coupon Liberal he substantially increased his majority in Edinburgh East at the 1918 election. In the new parliament he continued to align himself with the independent Liberal MPs, the Asquithians or 'Wee Frees', as they were also known. Hogge belonged to the radical wing of this group and personally held strong reservations about Asquith's leadership. In early 1919 Hogge was elected chief whip of this small group of MPs in a reaction to Asquith's appointment of George Rennie Thorne. This dispute was resolved by Hogge and Thorne serving as joint chief whips, and notably together with the interim Asquithian leader Sir Donald Maclean they ran a vigorous and, in proportion to their numbers, extraordinarily influential opposition to the government, especially in the period before Asquith's return to parliament in February 1920. This did not mean the group itself was coherent. On the provisions of the Versailles treaty, for example, Hogge was opposed and Thorne supportive. Despite being a chief whip, Hogge was also largely excluded from work, such as candidate selection and control of the wider party and its finances, that had been carried out by his predecessors. When Thorne resigned in February 1923 the relatively inexperienced Vivian Phillipps was preferred to Hogge, the obvious successor to the position of sole whip Asquith then wanted. Hogge refused to accept the offer of the position of Scottish whip under Phillipps.

Hogge's departure may have been a relief to the Asquithians for both personal and political reasons. Unlike his former colleague Pringle, he had not made his peace with the inner circle of Asquithians and their reservations about his character increased as he became more active in promoting reunion with Lloyd George Liberals. Already in 1920 Maclean was describing Hogge as 'born crooked and a natural wrecker' (Douglas, 137). C. F. G. Masterman concurred, describing Hogge in 1923 as 'corrupt', particularly as he suspected that he had already been in the pay of Lloyd George when he was independent Liberal whip (*Political Diaries of C. P. Scott*, 439). Lord (Herbert) Gladstone gave a lurid account (ibid., 441) of Hogge's frequent inebriation and a near scandal during the general election campaign of 1922 when he was supposed to have run off to Scotland with a House of Commons waitress known as 'the Fairy'. Politically Hogge does not appear to have been incapacitated, however. In the immediate postwar period he had been identified with those left-wing 'Wee Frees' who wished to maintain a distance from Labour, but were thought to favour an alliance with it and to support a capital levy and some form of nationalization. This was not incompatible with the unsuccessful approaches Hogge made in 1922 to Lloyd George on behalf of a group of left-wing 'Wee Frees' on the subject of Liberal reunion. The Asquithians believed Hogge to be close to Sir William Sutherland, who was particularly associated with Lloyd George's journalistic activities. During the first half of 1923 Hogge was again associated with a series of back-bench moves aimed at Liberal unity and, with his reported acceptance of a salary of £1000 from Lloyd George, £400 more than he had been offered as Scottish independent Liberal whip, was regarded by the Asquithians as having defected. Twice in this turbulent period, at the general elections of 1922 and 1923, Hogge continued to be returned by strong majorities in Edinburgh East. His parliamentary career ended at the general election of 1924, however, when he came bottom of the poll on the first occasion since his election in 1912 that a Labour candidate had stood.

Hogge was president of the National Federation of Discharged and Demobilized Sailors and Soldiers from 1919 to 1920. He was a parliamentary adviser to the National Association of Schoolmasters and to the Association of Ex-Service Civil Servants. Shortly before his death he was appointed a research assistant in the office of the Liberal chief whip, Sir Robert Hutchinson, and director of investigations in connection with the safeguarding of industries under the Liberal campaign committee.

Dogged by ill health, Hogge died at his home, 63 The Grove, Hammersmith, London, on 27 October 1928. He was buried at the Hammersmith cemetery, Mortlake, Surrey, on 31 October 1928 at a ceremony attended by representatives of all sections of the Liberal Party.

GORDON F. MILLAR

Sources The Scotsman (29 Oct 1928) · The Times (29 Oct 1928) · WWW, 1916–28, vol. 2 (1992), 389 · WWBMP, 3.168 · Yorkshire Gazette (14 Oct 1905) · Yorkshire Gazette (5 Oct 1907) · Yorkshire Gazette (9 Nov 1907) · Yorkshire Gazette (19 June 1909) · Yorkshire Gazette (5 Nov 1910) · Yorkshire Gazette (27 Jan 1912) · Yorkshire Gazette (10 Feb 1912) · Yorkshire Gazette (3 Nov 1928) · b. cert. · m. cert. · d. cert. · I. G. C. Hutchison, A political history of Scotland, 1832–1924 (1986) · The Scotsman (30 Oct 1928) · The Scotsman (31 Oct 1928) · The Times (1 Nov 1928) · The Times (30 Nov 1928) · The political diaries of C. P. Scott, 1911–1928, ed. T. Wilson (1970) · R. Douglas, History of the liberal party, 1895–1970 (1971) · G. R. Searle, Corruption in British politics, 1895–1930 (1987) · K. O. Morgan, Consensus and disunity: the Lloyd George coalition government, 1918–1922 (1979) · M. Bentley, The liberal mind, 1914–1929 (1977) · R. D. Anderson, Education and opportunity in Victorian Scotland (1985) · F. W. S. Craig, British parliamentary election results, 1885–1918 (1974) · F. W. S. Craig, British parliamentary election results, 1918–1949, 3rd edn (1983)
Likenesses drawing, repro. in Yorkshire Gazette (5 Oct 1907) · photograph, repro. in The Times (29 Oct 1928) · photograph, repro. in Yorkshire Gazette (3 Nov 1928)
Wealth at death £251 3s. 4d.: probate, 24 Nov 1928, CGPLA Eng. & Wales; The Times (30 Nov 1928)

Hogge, Ralph (d. 1585), gun-founder, was a leading figure in the expansion of the iron industry in the Sussex Weald. Nothing is known of his parentage or place of birth, though he was probably born in Sussex. He had business connections with Brian Hogge, a brother or close relative,

who worked in the ordnance office for fifty years. Holinshed gave to Hogge and Peter Baude the credit of being, in 1543, the first to cast iron guns in England, at a furnace in Buxted, Sussex. This achievement is more likely to have been the first successful casting of an iron gun in one piece, breach and barrel together. Hogge's part, though important, was probably that of the skilled furnace master. He and Baude, then the leading bronze gun-founder, would have worked under the direction of William Levett, the king's 'gunstonemaker', who went on to supply cast-iron ordnance until his death in 1554. In his will Levett left Hogge, his 'servant', £10 and a quantity of iron (PRO, PROB/11/37/5).

Hogge may at first have worked Levett's furnaces, for on 14 November 1559 he was appointed to Levett's post of 'gunstonemaker'. Then on 13 May 1560 he was married at Maresfield, Sussex, to Margaret Henslowe, from a well-to-do family; her father, Edmund, was master of the game in Ashdown Forest. Hogge being of humbler origins, the marriage would have been a significant upward step in his career. He opened two new furnaces near Maresfield and his production began to be reflected in contemporary records: the lease of woodlands in Fletching, where he lived, and the delivery of guns, shot, and iron materials to the ordnance. The navy however preferred bronze to cast-iron guns.

Nevertheless, before the end of the 1560s as many as eight furnaces within a few miles of Buxted were casting iron guns; and this over-production was to characterize the industry for the rest of the century. To the alarm of the privy council and the merchant community, guns surplus to local needs were finding eager purchasers abroad: they were bought by privateers, pirates, and even the Spanish. The council's response was, on 5 March 1568, to vest in Ralph Hogge an exclusive right to the export of guns and shot. This should have bolstered Hogge's business while ensuring for the state an immediate supply of ordnance in time of danger. But Hogge's monopoly was soon challenged. By 1574 he was complaining bitterly to the council of the ease with which iron guns were sold across the channel. He appears to have reduced his own capacity to one furnace.

The threat to national security and trade caused sharp alarm in the council; and vigorous efforts were made, without in the end much success, to eliminate these clandestine sales. Hogge, however, believed that at last his concession would be protected and that increased production was justified. Within two years he was managing four furnaces capable of turning out guns, all conveniently close together in the Maresfield and Buxted area.

Hogge is the only sixteenth-century founder of iron guns of whose transactions some record has survived. Between 1576 and 1578 he used his brother-in-law John Henslowe as an agent. Henslowe recorded regular payments to woodcutters, colliers, miners, and carriers; and he also accounted to Hogge for occasional sales of guns and shot. The accounts cover a short period only and Henslowe was not the only agent used. Despite this it is possible to construct a picture of the likely surplus Hogge earned.

From one furnace with a mixed output of guns, shot, and pig iron Hogge might have shown an annual surplus of £300. Working three or four furnaces should have given him, for those days, a very good income. However, there is no evidence that Hogge was in fact making vast amounts of money, or was sharing it with partners or investors. The only sign of affluence was his construction in 1581 of a house of modest size in Buxted (subsequently known as Hogge House), perhaps for his retirement.

About this time, however, Hogge took a case against another agent, accusing him of embezzling £6000. In the course of this dispute (which was never settled) Hogge claimed that he himself could neither read nor write and was so disabled he could not physically supervise his furnaces. If true, this suggests that towards the end of his career Hogge's affairs were in disarray due to a combination of factors: rapid expansion; lack of education and managerial ability; physical handicaps; and the need to rely on agents who may have been both inefficient and dishonest.

Hogge died in 1585 and was buried at St Margaret the Queen, Buxted, on 14 December. Although the leading sixteenth-century producer of cast-iron guns, he died by no means a rich man. His will made no mention of ironworks or equipment (PRO, PROB/11/69). All he had was his house, which he left to his widow for her lifetime and then, since they had no children, to his nephew Thomas, who quickly sold the reversion. John Henslowe moved in with his sister, claiming that Hogge had mortgaged the property to him for £120. This claim eventually failed after many years of dispute.   EDMUND TEESDALE

Sources E. B. Teesdale, *Gunfounding in the Weald in the sixteenth century* (1991) · APC, 1542–99 · PRO, C66/940 m22 · Dulwich MS (Henslowe's diary), Dulwich College · PRO, C66/1040 · PRO, SP12/95/16, 79 · PRO, C3/K5/30 · will, PRO, PROB 11/69 · R. Holinshed and others, eds., *The chronicles of England, Scotland and Ireland*, 2nd edn, ed. J. Hooker, 3 vols. in 2 (1586–7) · will of William Levett, PRO, PROB 11/37/5 · C. Little, ed., *Maresfield parish registers*, 1 (1980) · VCH Sussex
Wealth at death left property to wife during her lifetime and thereafter to nephew; legacies of £10 each to niece, sister-in-law, and brother-in-law: will, PRO, PROB 11/69

Hoghton, Daniel (1770–1811), army officer, born on 28 August 1770, was the second son of Sir Henry Hoghton, sixth baronet (1728–1795), of Hoghton Tower, near Blackburn and Walton Hall, near Preston, Lancashire, MP for Preston, and his second wife, Fanny (d. April 1803), eldest daughter of Daniel Booth, of Hutton Hall, Essex, a director of the Bank of England. Without passing through the lower ranks, he obtained a majority in the 97th (Strathspey Highlanders) on its formation on 8 February 1794. After serving as marines in the Channel Fleet, the regiment was disbanded in 1795, and Hoghton was transferred to the 67th foot on 12 August 1795. The 67th went to San Domingo in 1796, and to Jamaica in 1798. On 31 January 1799 Hoghton was transferred to the 88th foot (Connaught Rangers), and joined them in India. They served in the expedition to Egypt in 1801, but Hoghton seems to

have remained in India, and to have been sent home with dispatches from Lord Wellesley in the spring of 1804.

Hoghton had become lieutenant-colonel in the army on 3 May 1796, and on 22 November 1804 he was appointed lieutenant-colonel of the newly raised 2nd battalion of the 8th foot. On 1 January 1805 he was promoted colonel. He remained at home with his battalion until April 1810, when he was appointed to the staff of the British force at Cadiz as brigadier. He was promoted major-general on 25 July, and in September he left Cadiz to join Wellington's army in Portugal. He was given the command of the 3rd brigade of the 2nd division under Sir William Stewart, with whom he had served at Cadiz, and who had been his lieutenant-colonel in the 67th.

In the battle of Albuera on 16 May 1811, when the Spaniards gave way on the right, Stewart's division was hurried up to take their place. Its leading brigade (Colborne's) was nearly destroyed by a flank attack of cavalry, and Hoghton's brigade was deployed and moved up to the crest of the hill, which had become the key of the position. There it stood for some time against the 11,000 strong French 5th corps, its three regiments (29th, 57th, and 1st battalion 48th) losing three quarters of their men. Hoghton himself was killed by gunshot as he led forward the 29th. He was buried on 17 May. Wellington wrote to Lord Wellesley: 'I understand that it was impossible for anybody to behave better than he did … he actually fell waving his hat and cheering his brigade on to the charge' (*Supplementary Despatches*, 7.134). A public monument, voted by parliament, was placed in the north transept of St Paul's Cathedral.

E. M. LLOYD, *rev.* DAVID GATES

Sources GM, 1st ser., 81/1 (1811), 679 · *Supplementary despatches (correspondence) and memoranda of Field Marshal Arthur, duke of Wellington*, ed. A. R. Wellesley, second duke of Wellington, 15 vols. (1858–72), vol. 6, p. 574; vol. 7, p. 134 · C. W. C. Oman, *A history of the Peninsular War*, 4 (1911), 385–8 · H. E. E. Everard, *History of … the 29th, Worcestershire foot, 1694–1891* (1891) · Burke, *Peerage* (1959) · D. Gates, *The Spanish ulcer: a history of the Peninsular War* (1986) · A. B. Rodger, *The war of the second coalition: 1798–1801, a strategic commentary* (1964)
Archives Lancs. RO, letters, diaries, and journals
Likenesses F. Chantrey, monument, St Paul's Cathedral, London

Hoghton, Sir Henry, fifth baronet (1676x9–1768). *See under* Hoghton, Sir Henry, sixth baronet (1728–1795).

Hoghton, Sir Henry, sixth baronet (1728–1795), politician, was born on 22 October 1728 at Lancaster, the only son of Philip Hoghton and his first wife, Elizabeth (d. 1731), daughter of Thomas Slater of Denham, Lancashire. His was a very old county family, who had acquired the property of Hoghton Tower, near Blackburn, in the early fourteenth century and first represented Lancashire in parliament in 1322. Richard Hoghton (1570–1630), MP for Lancashire in 1601 and 1603–4, was created a baronet in 1611. A staunch presbyterian, he established the family's vigorous tradition of practising and promoting active dissent.

Henry Hoghton was educated at Northampton Academy. On 23 June 1760 he married Elizabeth, daughter and heir of William Ashurst of Hedingham Castle, Essex; she died on 19 May 1761 after giving birth to a daughter, Elizabeth. Hoghton married on 8 July 1766 Fanny (d. 1803), daughter and coheir of Daniel Booth of Hutton Hall, Essex, a director of the Bank of England. They had two sons, Henry Philip (1768–1835) and Daniel *Hoghton (d. 1811). Hoghton succeeded to the baronetcy and Lancashire estates on the death of his paternal uncle, **Sir Henry Hoghton**, fifth baronet (1676x9–1768), landowner and politician, on 23 February 1768.

The fifth baronet was the eldest surviving son of Sir Charles Hoghton, fourth baronet (c.1644–1710), politician, and his wife, Mary (1655/6–1732), daughter of John Skeffington, second Viscount Masserene. He was educated at the Middle Temple and was three times married: in October 1710 to Mary Boughton (c.1687–1720); on 14 April 1721 to Elizabeth, née Lloyd (d. 1736), the widow of Lord James Russell; and on 21 July 1737 to Susanna Butterworth. He was MP for Preston in 1710–13, 1715–22, and 1727–41, and for East Looe in 1724–7. He unsuccessfully contested Lancashire in 1722 and Kingston upon Hull in 1724. He was active in organizing Lancashire resistance to the Jacobite rising of 1715 and was rewarded with a lucrative commissionership for the sale of forfeited estates. He was Walpole's judge-advocate-general from 1734 until his defeat at the general election of 1741. During the 1745 rising he and his family took refuge in Yorkshire. His subsequent rigorous proceedings as a magistrate against Catholics were quashed by the government. He died at Walton Hall on 23 February 1768 aged between eighty-nine and ninety-one.

Six weeks after he succeeded his uncle as the sixth baronet, Hoghton stood for Preston with Lord Derby's candidate at the general election and, after defeat at the polls in a violent contest, was seated on petition. He retained the seat at the next four general elections, two of them contested. In parliament he gave general but not slavish support to the Grafton and North administrations. He spoke frequently, particularly on issues relating to Lancashire. He supported the Shelburne and Portland ministries, was one of the St Alban's tavern group which tried to reconcile Pitt and Fox in 1784, and thereafter steadily supported Pitt's government. As the representative of essentially moderate dissent, who had no truck with Manchester radicals or Unitarians, he was a member of the 1787 committee formed to agitate for repeal of the Test and Corporation Acts. He briefly and unimpressively seconded motions for that object on 28 March 1787, 8 May 1789, and 2 March 1790. He voted to abolish the slave trade in 1791, supported war with revolutionary France in 1793, and sat on the secret committee of inquiry into treason and sedition in 1794. Wraxall described him as 'a rigid Presbyterian, of ample fortune, adorned with the mildest manners' (*Historical and Posthumous Memoirs*, 4.437). In 1804 Lord Wellesley recalled him as 'worthy' but 'stiff-necked' (Fisher, 4.213). He continued the practice of employing a private chaplain for the Presbyterian congregation at Hoghton, but was probably the last head of his family to espouse active dissent; his elder son and successor was educated at Charterhouse and Cambridge. Hoghton died at his home

at Walton Hall, near Preston, on 9 March 1795, and was buried at Walton. His elder son replaced him as MP for Preston. An anonymous obituarist wrote of his 'highly respectable and exemplary' conduct as an MP and his 'marked gentleness and sweetness of disposition' in private life (*GM*, 216).   D. R. FISHER

Sources J. Brooke, 'Hoghton, Sir Henry, 6th bt', HoP, *Commons, 1754–90* · D. R. Fisher, 'Hoghton, Sir Henry, 6th bt', HoP, *Commons, 1790–1820* · E. Cruickshanks, 'Hoghton, Sir Henry, 5th bt', HoP, *Commons, 1715–54* · I. Cassidy, 'Hoghton (Houghton), Sir Charles, 4th bt', HoP, *Commons, 1660–90* · *GM*, 1st ser., 65 (1795), 260–61 · G. C. Miller, *Hoghton Tower* (1948) · G. M. Ditchfield, 'The campaign in Lancashire and Cheshire for the repeal of the Test and Corporation Acts, 1787–1790', *Transactions of the Historic Society of Lancashire and Cheshire*, 126 (1977), 109–38, esp. 111, 114, 116, 128–30 · B. Nightingale, *Lancashire nonconformity*, 6 vols. [1890–93], vol. 1, pp. 20, 66–7 · H. McLachlan, *Warrington Academy: its history and influence*, Chetham Society, 107, new ser. (1943), 14, 73, 112 · *The historical and the posthumous memoirs of Sir Nathaniel William Wraxall, 1772–1784*, ed. H. B. Wheatley, 5 vols. (1884), vol. 4, p. 437 · Cobbett, *Parl. hist.*, 21.556 · GEC, *Baronetage* · Burke, *Peerage* · IGI

Archives BL, corresp. with earl of Liverpool, Add. MSS 38221–38222, 38307–38310

Likenesses T. Rowlandson, engraving, 1784 (*The apostate Jack R—*), BM · J. Sayer, print, 1790 (*The repeal of the Test Act*), BM

Hohenthal, Countess Walpurga Ehrengarde Helena de (d. 1929). *See under* Paget, Sir Augustus Berkeley (1823–1896).

Hoker [Hooker], **John** (*fl.* 1525–1543), author, was a member of the Hoker family from the region of Maidstone, Kent. Hoker became a demy of Magdalen College, Oxford, in 1525. He graduated as BA in 1527, and proceeded to MA in 1535 and bachelor of theology in 1540. Hoker was praised by John Leland, in his *Cygnea cantio* (1545), where he includes a line of praise for 'Hocherus nitor artium bonarum' (sig. E1v). He lectured at his college in many subjects, including natural philosophy, moral philosophy, and, between 1541 and 1543, theology. Several literary works are attributed to Hoker, although many have not survived. These include 'Piscator' (or 'The Fisher Caught'), which Thomas Warton believed to have been a comedy acted by the students of Magdalen College, as well as an introduction to rhetoric and various poems and epigrams.

A letter from Hoker, apparently to Bullinger and dating from approximately 1538, was published along with an edition of *S. Clementis epistolae duae ad Corinthios* (1687), and printed in an English translation by Gorham. In this letter Hoker describes the recent exposure and destruction of a 'wooden god' in Kent, a mechanical idol apparently able to 'nod with his head, to scowl with his eyes, to wag his beard, to curve his body, to reject and receive the prayers of pilgrims'. Hoker writes that the idol was taken from its place in a Kentish church by the brother of a certain Nicholas Partridge, who opened it up in front of the local parishioners to show its internal mechanical workings; from there it was taken to London, denounced, and thrown to an indignant audience who smashed it into pieces. The *Life of Sir Peter Carew* occasionally attributed to Hoker was in fact written by his namesake, John Hooker, alias Vowell, of Exeter. CHRISTOPHER BURLINSON

Sources J. R. Bloxam, *A register of the presidents, fellows … of Saint Mary Magdalen College*, 8 vols. (1853–85) • W. D. Macray, *A register of the members of St Mary Magdalen College, Oxford*, 8 vols. (1894–1915) • G. C. Gorham, *Gleanings of a few scattered ears, during the period of the Reformation in England* (1857) • T. Warton, *The history of English poetry*, 4 vols. (1774–81) • Wood, *Ath. Oxon.*, new edn • Foster, *Alum. Oxon.*

Holbeach [*formerly* Rands], **Henry** (d. 1551), bishop of Lincoln, is of obscure birth but certainly took his name in religion from his Lincolnshire place of origin. His family name was Rands. He became a Benedictine monk of Crowland and subsequently proceeded to Cambridge, where he became BTh in 1527 and DTh in 1534. He was made prior of Buckingham College, the Benedictine house for students in Cambridge which for a time provided hospitality for Thomas Cranmer. It also offered Holbeach the opportunity to undertake reformed biblical and patristic studies. It is uncertain whether he stayed on in Cambridge following his doctorate, but the deep impression he made on Cranmer, by then archbishop of Canterbury, as one of only two 'of that habit, that be of better learning, judgement, conversation and all qualities meet for an head and master of an house' (*Writings and Disputations*, 2.310) resulted in his election as prior of Worcester on 13 March 1536, the king's assent being granted on the 22nd. He took the customary oaths of succession and supremacy, and was probably delighted that one of his first acts as prior was to receive the visitation of Hugh Latimer, the newly appointed bishop of Worcester. Among the new bishop's injunctions was a requirement of the prior to provide a whole Bible in English for the convent, and to have a chapter of it read each day at dinner. The friendship between prior and bishop, which may have begun at Cambridge, resulted in the consecration of the former as suffragan bishop of Bristol in 1538. Two years later, however, the priory was surrendered to the king, and on 24 January 1542 Holbeach was appointed dean of the new foundation of Worcester, with prebendaries, minor canons, lay clerks, organists, choristers, and schoolmasters, to say nothing of forty king's scholars under his charge—a rather more numerous required foundation than the monastery had boasted at its dissolution. He did not preserve the collegiate character of Worcester, and it was not long before dean and canons dined apart, while in the year of his appointment the dean supervised the demolition of the images of St Oswald and St Wulfstan. He also acquired the reputation with contemporaries for so exploiting the lands of the cathedral church that by 1559 neither he nor his successors left 'a patch of land sufficient for a horse to graze upon' (Wilson, 371).

Holbeach's reputation at Worcester did not prevent his translation to the see of Rochester in 1544, his election on 3 May receiving royal assent on the 26th, and he was made king's almoner in the same year. His growing reputation was recognized in his selection to preside at the funeral of Charles Brandon, duke of Suffolk, in 1545, and in his attendance at Henry VIII's funeral. He was appointed preacher at the commemoration of the death of François I of France in June 1547. Holbeach commended François 'for setting forth of the Bible and the New Testament in the French tongue to be read of all his subjects' (Wriothesley, 1.184). He also preached to celebrate the victory at Pinkie, fought on 10 September against the Scots, which suggests that he had the favour of the duke of Somerset. This resulted in his confirmation as bishop of Lincoln on 20 August 1547, but not without the gift of thirty manors and the episcopal palace at Holborn in London to the protector. On the latter's fall Holbeach received thirty-six rectories, formerly appropriated to monastic houses, which had already been leased out by the court of augmentations, together with the return of the manor of Buckden and such buildings as remained of Thornton Abbey. So inequitable was the exchange that the see of Lincoln from being one of the richest in England became one of the poorest.

Holbeach was in demand, however, to advance a protestant order in England and especially to support Thomas Cranmer in forwarding the preparation and defence of a vernacular liturgy. He assisted in the framing of the offices and in the very famous discussions on the drafts of the 1549 prayer book that came before the bishops in 1548 and were debated in the House of Lords in November. His was a reformist position in recognizing the elements as 'mystically' the body and blood of Christ (Tomlinson, 44). His cathedral received him late; he was not installed at Lincoln until 20 March 1548, more than six months after his election and confirmation as bishop. It saw some of the first experiments with the liturgy in English. Virtually nothing survives of Holbeach's activities as a diocesan, but at a national level he fought critics of the prayer book, such as Stephen Gardiner, as well as the Anabaptists who saw no point in it at all. He was a reliable supporter of Cranmer, whether on a commission to dissolve an unfortunate royal marriage of William Parr (brother of the dowager queen) in 1547, or to make sure that the University of Oxford was brought in line with the new order in 1549. Like the archbishop, Holbeach probably married in 1544 if not earlier; his wife was Joan Manett. His was a radicalism based on scripture and it is possible that his extravagance in parting with the temporalities of the see was prompted by a monastic experience of thrift as much as by his desire to promote the cause of reform on the bench of bishops. He seems to have spent his last years at Nettleham and died there on either 5 or 6 August 1551.

MARGARET BOWKER

Sources R. E. G. Cole, ed., *Chapter acts of the cathedral church of St Mary of Lincoln*, 2–3, Lincoln RS, 13, 15 (1917–20) • J. Noake, *The monastery and cathedral of Worcester* (1866) • D. MacCulloch, *Thomas Cranmer: a life* (1996) • *DNB* • Venn, *Alum. Cant.*, 1/3.419 • J. T. Tomlinson, *The first prayer book of Edward VI: the great parliamentary debate in 1548 from the original MS now in the British Museum* (1892) • *Writings and disputations of Thomas Cranmer*, ed. J. E. Cox, Parker Society, [17] (1844) • J. M. Wilson, 'Visitation injunctions of Cardinal Wolsey and Archbishop Cranmer to the priory of Worcester in 1526 and 1534', *Associated Architectural Societies*, 36, pt 2 (1922), 356–71 • C. Wriothesley, *A chronicle of England during the reigns of the Tudors from AD 1485 to 1559*, ed. W. D. Hamilton, 1, CS, new ser., 11 (1875) • Lincs. Arch., Register

XXVII, fols. 275–290v • will, PRO, PROB 11/34, sig. 28 • A. R. Maddison, ed., *Lincolnshire pedigrees*, 3, Harleian Society, 52 (1904) **Wealth at death** see will, PRO, PROB 11/34, sig. 28

Holbeach [Holbech], **Martin** (*bap.* **1597**, *d.* **1670**), schoolmaster and ejected minister, was baptized at Fillongley, Warwickshire, on 28 August 1597, the second of at least three sons of George Holbech and Millicent, daughter of John Poultney, probably of Exhall, near Coventry. The Holbechs or Holbeechs were a prominent local family whose many branches are difficult to disentangle. Martin was admitted pensioner at Queens' College, Cambridge, on 24 September 1617, to be joined later by a younger brother, Gabriel. His tutor was the controversial fellow John *Preston, whose will he witnessed in July 1618 and through whom he probably first made the acquaintance of the future East Anglian ministers John Cotton and Thomas Hooker. Having matriculated in 1621, Holbeach graduated BA early in 1622. Ordained deacon in London on 23 May 1624, he proceeded MA in 1625 and was at some point curate of Black Chapel, Essex, a county to which his university circle had given him access. However, after teaching at schools at Braintree in 1626–7 and Halstead in 1627, on the recommendation of Preston (by this time dean of Emmanuel College, Cambridge, and preacher at Lincoln's Inn, London) in 1627 Holbeach was appointed master of Felsted School by Robert Rich, second earl of Warwick.

Although now launched on a distinguished teaching career, Holbeach, like his early assistant John Seaton, seems to have been a member of Hooker's local fraternal of godly ministers, many of whom were at odds with the ecclesiastical hierarchy. When Thomas Shepard, later minister in New England, rashly sought a confrontation with William Laud, then bishop of London, during his visitation of December 1631, it was Holbeach who plucked him out of the protesting crowd and spirited him away on horseback, saving him from William Weld's fate of being detained and hauled before the high commission. The same year Holbeach visited the eminent local minister Daniel Rogers while he was under suspension. Like Warwick and others in the 'ministerial network' (Webster, 260), in the early 1630s Holbeach contributed to John Durie's ecumenical schemes. The network and the godly reputation of Felsted, which Holbeach maintained in tandem with the vicar, Samuel Wharton, ensured that numbers at the school rose to between 100 and 120 and that, contrary to the founder's intention, students also came from outside the county. Notable pupils included the four sons of Oliver Cromwell and Henry Mildmay (1619–1692), later MP for Essex. Samuel Rogers, son of Daniel, praised the 'diligent labours of my godly master' (ibid., 136); others who felt the benefit of Holbeach's generous personal attention were John Wallis, the future mathematician and cryptographer, and Isaac *Barrow, the future mathematician and theologian. When in 1642 Barrow's father proved unable to continue paying for his son's education, Barrow was taken into Holbeach's house and made

tutor to another boy, William Fairfax, third Viscount Fairfax of Emley; later Holbeach offered to make Barrow his heir.

Holbeach had prospered. On 6 December 1632 he bought Lawsells, the largest house in Felsted; in 1638 the earl of Essex raised his salary to £50 a year. The coming of civil war initially left Holbeach relatively untouched, though his kinsman Thomas Holbeach (*bap.* 1606, *d.* 1680), a graduate of Emmanuel College with whom he has been confused, was sequestered from his vicarage at Epping, Essex, in 1643. After the Restoration John Bramston claimed that Holbeach 'scarce bred any man that was loyall to his prince' (*The Autobiography of Sir John Bramston*, CS, 32, 1845, 124). He exaggerated, but Holbeach had a reputation in godly quarters such that on 17 June 1643 the House of Commons resolved to place in his charge two sons of the Roman Catholic third Lord Arundell of Wardour, who were parliament's prisoners; in May 1644 the boys were exchanged for grandsons of the earl of Warwick who had been captured by the king's forces. On the other hand, he was probably not the Martin Holbeach who challenged two Coventry men in July 1647 to comply with parliament's order to surrender land belonging to the earl of Leicester: this was more likely to have been a near kinsman, possibly the brother of the lawyer and Warwickshire county committee man Matthew Holbeach.

In the later 1640s Martin Holbeach's developing Independent convictions led to a rift with his patron the earl of Essex. In the aftermath of the siege of Colchester in 1648, Essex's presbyterian steward, the historian Arthur Wilson, informed Holbeach that he was 'generally heere censured to bee the fomenter of the disvinous that are amongst us'. Wilson, who expressed 'a better opinion' of him, urged him to use his considerable influence, to 'rise up like a Neptune and calme theise troubled waves' (Craze, *A History*, 63). However, at Christmas 1649 he left Felsted School, where he was succeeded as master by a former pupil, Christopher Glascock. He took up residence a few miles away at his recently acquired vicarage of High Easter. A parochial inquisition of September 1650 found that he had served the cure 'for the space of two yeares last past', but had received 'very little proffitts' (H. Smith, 282–3) from a living worth £34; a lease on some of the tithes was held by the Glascock family. Its value was augmented by the committee for plundered ministers, but Holbeach's income seems to have dropped again later. Within the next few years the manor of High Easter was bought by the earl of Essex's kinsman the radical army officer Nathaniel Rich, but no details are known of the two men's association, if any. In 1654 Holbeach was appointed an assistant to the county commission of triers and ejectors.

According to Bramston, by 1661 Holbeach's dissatisfaction with the restored Church of England was apparent. The following year he was ejected from his living; his successor was instituted at High Easter on 20 January 1663. Holbeach moved back to Felsted, where 'his antiritualistic preaching' was said by some to have 'stirred up strife in the village' (C. F. Smith, 203). His business interests there and his ownership of property at High Easter is revealed in a letter of 31 May 1664 to Mr Kendall, a friend at Hatfield. Mary Rich, countess of Warwick, noted in her diary on 30 September 1670 the report that Holbeach had died at Dunmow. He was buried at Felsted. An inventory taken on 21 October valued his goods at £268 15s. His widow and legatee Lydia, about whom nothing else is known, was still living in Felsted when she made her will on 7 February 1679; it was proved on 12 February 1682.

VIVIENNE LARMINIE

Sources T. Webster, *Godly clergy in early Stuart England: the Caroline puritan movement, c.1620–1643* (1997) · Venn, *Alum. Cant.* · *Calamy rev.*, 270–71 · *IGI* [transcripts of Fillongley parish register, 1538–1653] · W. Camden, *The visitation of the county of Warwick in the year 1619*, ed. J. Fetherston, Harleian Society, 12 (1877), 351 · *VCH Warwickshire*, 4.71–5 · G. J. H. Wright, *Alumni Felstedienses* (1903) · M. Craze, *A history of Felsted School, 1564–1947* (1955) · M. Craze, *A short history of Felsted School* [1965] · H. Smith, *The ecclesiastical history of Essex under the Long Parliament and the Commonwealth* [1932] · C. Fell Smith, *Mary Rich, countess of Warwick (1625–1678): her family and friends* (1901) · J. T. Cliffe, *The puritan gentry: the great puritan families of early Stuart England* (1984) · *Walker rev.*, 154–5 · *JHC* · A. Hughes, *Politics, society and civil war in Warwickshire, 1620–1660* (1987) · C. Thompson, 'Martin Holbeach', *Essex Archaeological Society Newsletter* (2001)

Archives BL, letter, 1664, Egerton MS 2649, fol. 100r · GL, subscription book, MS 9539A, vol. 1 | CUL, letters of Arthur Wilson, Add. MS 33, fols. 81r–83r · Essex RO, Chelmsford, conveyances to him, D/DHE T 108/1, 13, 18

Wealth at death approx. £268 15s.: *Calamy rev.*, 271

Holbein, Hans, the younger (1497/8–1543), artist, was born in Augsburg in southern Germany, the second son of the artist Hans Holbein the elder (1465–1524) and his wife, Anna Mair. He was the younger brother of the painter Ambrosius Holbein, and his age is given as fourteen in a metalpoint drawing of the two brothers by their father dated 1511 (Staatliche Museen, Berlin). However, copies of a lost self-portrait bear an inscription giving the date 1543 and indicating that Holbein was then in his forty-fifth year. Hans Holbein the elder arrived in Augsburg in 1494 after working in Ulm. Presumably Ambrosius and the slightly younger Hans took their places in his workshop, which produced many large altarpieces, often in collaboration with sculptors, but there is no record of their training. There is no documentation at all of the younger Holbein in Augsburg.

Basel, 1515–1526 By 1515 both Hans and his brother appear to have migrated to Basel in Switzerland, where they worked on a variety of projects, largely separately. The date 1515 is established by the survival of a copy of Erasmus's *Praise of Folly* (Kunstmuseum, Basel), in which the margins are illustrated in pen and ink by Holbein and his brother. From this point onwards there are a number of documentary references to Holbein in Basel, and also a number of paintings and other works signed or documented as his work. He was active there not only as a painter of portraits, religious pictures, and wall paintings, but also as a designer of woodcuts, engravings, and stained glass.

Holbein's earliest surviving dated paintings are the portraits of Jacob Meyer, burgomeister or mayor of Basel, and his second wife, Dorothea Kannengiesser, painted in 1516,

Hans Holbein the younger (1497/8–1543), by unknown artist, *c.*1542–3 [possibly a self-portrait]

and originally joined together to form a diptych (Kunstmuseum, Basel). These vivid but sober and carefully designed images, taken from still surviving drawings carefully recording the sitters' likenesses (Kunstmuseum, Basel), and set within ambitious architectural space made sumptuous by Renaissance ornament, established the artistic foundations for the making of Holbein's reputation in Basel, as well as his later career. In 1517, however, he went to work at Lucerne, where the elder Holbein had a commission to decorate the house of Jacob von Hertenstein (1460–1527), chief magistrate and merchant. Holbein there produced the *Portrait of Benedict von Hertenstein* (Metropolitan Museum of Art, New York), which includes a frieze in the manner of Mantegna's *Triumphs*. He had returned to Basel by 25 September, when he was admitted as a master in the town's painters' guild. On 3 July 1520 he became a citizen of Basel. Before this date it is likely he had married Elsbeth Schmid, the widow of a tanner, shown with their two elder children, Philip and Catherine (the third, Jacob, not yet born), in the monumental and moving portrait painted on paper of about 1529 (Kunstmuseum, Basel).

Much of the success of Holbein's art in the decade before he left Basel for England depended on extending the possibilities of the depiction of depth and movement in space. His reputation in Basel, where he was appointed town painter in 1518/19, was made as a house painter of a most spectacular kind: in his decorative painting for the Haus zum Tanz (destroyed, but recorded in drawings) peasants danced along narrow ledges, musicians leant over balconies, and a rider on a rearing horse was poised to jump from on high out into the street below. Holbein, with his knowledge of the Renaissance architectural repertory and, above all, his extraordinary facility in the representation of moving figures from all angles, took the convention of illusionistic wall painting to its limits. His work for the town hall, for which he was paid between 1521 and 1522 and again in 1530, is also lost, but according to surviving drawings consisted of interior wall paintings on classical and Old Testament themes.

It is a remarkable aspect of Holbein's art that his designs for the façades of buildings are as convincing as the smallest of his woodcuts, just as, later on in England, his portrait miniatures, when enlarged to the scale of the full-size portraits, maintain an entirely convincing solidity and sense of design. His designs for Basel printers, notably the two famous series the *Dance of Death* and the *Old Testament*, designed in the 1520s but not published for another decade, show in abundance his mastery of composition which here happens to be on a miniature scale. Above all, the figures in these woodcuts display a characteristic sense of movement which played an increasingly pivotal role in all Holbein's artistic production.

That many of his Basel paintings survive and can be identified as Holbein's work is the result of the patronage of the Amerbach family of that city: they collected his work and listed it in the inventory of their art collections made in 1586. These works passed into the public collections of the city of Basel. They include not only Holbein's head-and-shoulders portrait of the young Bonifacius Amerbach in 1519, with Latin verses composed by the sitter (Kunstmuseum, Basel), but a number of religious works, including the *Dead Christ* of 1522 (Kunstmuseum, Basel). The precise function and original location of this work is unknown, its power to disturb the viewer with its graphic depiction of the corpse of Christ undisputed: the body is shown stiffened, the flesh around the wounds and in the face becoming green. Yet this is no straightforward realism: Holbein has constructed the composition with immense care, manipulating space and lighting to create the most dramatic effects, and employing a surprisingly free technique.

Holbein is usually thought of as a supremely realistic painter, yet drama, artifice, and a love of rich colour, allied to his father's exceptional ability as a colourist, played an equally significant part in his work. This is evident in the boldness with which he approaches the composition of the other religious works painted at Basel, which include the *Passion* altarpiece doors, the *Last Supper* (both Kunstmuseum, Basel), and the *Meyer Madonna* (priv. coll.). In all three, usually dated to the middle years of the 1520s, Holbein demonstrates the combination of controlled arrangement of figures in shallow space with the depiction of sumptuous colour and texture. Secular works such as the *Venus and Cupid* and *Lais Corinthiaca* (1526; Kunstmuseum, Basel), similarly show an increased richness and a subtle use of shadow sometimes associated with the visit to France Holbein made about 1524, when drawings of

tomb sculpture show he had visited Bourges. He may also have had the opportunity to see works by Leonardo at the French court, though this is uncertain, as is the proposition that he journeyed to Italy during his years in Switzerland.

Holbein's Basel work foreshadows the imagination, the inventiveness, the richness of technique, and the ability to concentrate meaning into gestures of significance with great economy that is reflected in his English portraits. Yet he painted relatively few portraits while working there. The most important are undoubtedly those he produced of the humanist Erasmus in 1523: two profile portraits (Musée du Louvre, Paris; Kunstmuseum, Basel), and a more elaborate half-length (priv. coll., on loan to the National Gallery, London), in which Erasmus is shown against an interior evoking a scholar's study, with his hands resting on a book designated as the fruits of his 'Labours of Hercules', his classical studies in the service of Christianity. In a letter of 3 June 1524 Erasmus mentioned he had sent one version of his portrait to England, almost certainly the latter type. On 29 August 1526 Erasmus wrote to his friend Pieter Gillis (Petrus Aegidius) in Antwerp. He told him that 'the arts in Basel were freezing' and Holbein was on his way to England to 'pick up some angels [a pun on the English coins]' (*Opus epistolarum*, 6.392, no. 1740).

First visit to England, 1526–1528 It was presumably the lure of the possible rewards of royal service that tempted Holbein to leave Basel for England in 1526 (and may also have taken him to France earlier). It appears his quest was successful almost immediately, for, if the identification of Holbein as 'Master Hans' is accepted as valid, he was within a few months employed as a decorative painter at court, for the festivities at Greenwich in 1527. He was paid the large sum of £4 10*s*. for a 'plat' showing the defeat of the French in battle, and the highest daily wage of any artist, 4*s*., for creating a ceiling painting of the heavens in collaboration with the king's astronomer, Nikolaus Kratzer. No doubt he was assisted by the powerful connections that the patronage of Erasmus could have provided for him: Sir Thomas More's brother-in-law John Rastell was one of the creators of the Greenwich revels, and Sir Henry Guildford, one of the humanist's English correspondents, and comptroller of the royal household, was in charge of the whole project.

Holbein's portrait of Erasmus seems to have spawned a group of half-length paintings which took the juxtapositions of figure and background in the work of 1523 as their starting point, and varied and elaborated them. The portrait of Warham, patron of Erasmus (Musée du Louvre, Paris), flatters both artist and scholar by imitating the 1523 portrait most closely, substituting the mitre and crozier of the archbishop for the classical column, flask, and books used in the earlier work. In the portrait of the royal astronomer and fellow German Nikolaus Kratzer of 1528 (Musée du Louvre, Paris) the subject faces the opposite direction and his instruments are introduced as the accessories. The portraits of Sir Henry and Lady Guildford (in the Royal Collection and the Museum of Art, St Louis, Missouri) of 1527 abandon the convention of tables or parapets at the lower edges of the compositions, and, while a lively and elegant variant on the classical pilaster of the portrait of Erasmus balances the smaller figure of Lady Guildford, the green curtain seen in the scholar's portrait reappears behind the massive figure of Sir Henry, its rail reappearing in the pendant uniting the pair. The portrait of Sir Thomas More (1527; Frick Collection, New York), defines him as statesman rather than scholar: his gilded collar of Tudor SSs lies over his deep fur collar, and Holbein draws a brilliant contrast between the dark green of the curtain looped behind him and the rich red velvet folds of his sleeve.

For More, Holbein also painted a remarkable group portrait on linen cloth (lost, known only through copies and a series of original drawings). One drawing (Kunstmuseum, Basel), shows the whole composition, with annotations by Holbein recording changes which More had presumably requested. The composition is modelled on contemporary depictions of the holy kindred, adapted to include a Tudor interior and the likenesses of More's own immediate kin, who were identified on the drawing by Nikolaus Kratzer, so that the sketch could be sent to their friend Erasmus in Basel; the latter recorded his delight on receiving it. The portrait drawings for the heads in this group and for those of most of the other portraits mentioned from this period are still preserved (in the Royal Collection; that of Lady Guildford is at Basel). Both portrait drawings and the corresponding painted heads are notable for Holbein's sensitivity to characterization and to details such as the light glinting on the stubble of More's beard in the painted portrait or the wrinkles of Warham's face. Yet Holbein would not be averse to some adaptation of such realities if the results required it: the faces of both Sir Henry and Lady Guildford were altered between drawing and painting—the latter radically, a smile being changed to a stern countenance. The portrait of the still unidentified *Lady with a Squirrel and a Starling* (National Gallery, London), underwent a transformation during painting: the pet squirrel on a chain was added, presumably at the lady's request. The brilliant blue background with its pattern of leaves and branches is typically ambiguous, hovering between convincing as sky and outdoor vegetation and deluding as background decoration.

Return to Basel, 1528–1531/2 Holbein's first visit to England lasted only two years, and he was probably concerned at this stage to retain his links with Basel. He also had work to complete there, but the advent of the Reformation, with the violent destruction of many religious works in 1529, must have done considerable damage to the livelihood of artists and encouraged Holbein's swift return to England; the last record of his presence in Basel is a payment for painting a clock face on 7 October 1531. He appears to have returned a protestant, although initially a reluctant convert: records of the attendance of Basel citizens at the new protestant service show that he had asked for a better explanation of it before agreeing to join the congregation; shortly afterwards his attendance is recorded. It is possible that Erasmus's outburst against him in a letter of 1533, in which he claims that 'Olpeius', probably to be identified with Holbein, has 'deceived

those to whom he was recommended' in England (*Opus epistolarum*, 10.193, no. 2788), relates to this conversion to protestantism.

Holbein may not have intended to settle in England permanently. He retained his membership of the painters' guild in Basel and seems not to have wanted to sever his links with the town. Two years was the normal maximum period of absence allowed to a Basel citizen, and the town council ruled in 1521 that no citizen could enter the service of a foreign prince. However, the council made an exception for Holbein, in the constant expectation of his imminent return; his presence in Basel is documented in 1538, and it is possible he went back on other occasions. This arrangement no doubt suited Holbein well, for the council maintained his family in his absence, while his will reveals that by the time of his death in 1543 he was keeping a second family in London.

England, 1531/2–1543: painter to Henry VIII A letter with the date 26 July 1532 in a portrait called *Hans of Antwerp*, a royal jeweller, but probably representing a German merchant (Royal Collection), gives the earliest indication of Holbein's return to England in that year, though he may have travelled back the previous year. The 'Master Hans' paid in 1533 for painting a gilded statue of Adam and Eve made by the royal goldsmith Cornelis Hayes, listed in an account immediately after references to a cradle for Princess Elizabeth, is likely to have been Holbein, and Holbein was certainly the designer of a table fountain, the drawing for which (Kunstmuseum, Basel), accords with a description of a new year's gift from Anne Boleyn to Henry VIII. The latter confirms Holbein's presence at court soon after his return from Basel in 1532, even if the evidence of his work as a court portrait painter is uncertain until Jane Seymour became queen in 1536.

In 1536 the *Paidagogeion* of the French humanist poet Nicholas Bourbon was published, with a woodcut of the poet after a drawing by Holbein. Bourbon had been exiled in England from France on account of his protestant sympathies. In a prefatory letter he addresses the friends he had made at the English court, including Holbein, the king's painter: 'D. Hansi pictori Regio, huius aevi Apelli'. This is the first known reference to Holbein as the king's painter, and suggests that the artist's appointment dates from 1535, when Bourbon was in England, or even earlier. The royal accounts in which payments to Holbein are recorded do not survive as a complete sequence, and the first accounts which mention his salary are those of 1537; for this reason it is even conceivable that he was also engaged as a salaried painter during the period of his first visit to England, in 1526–8. In the royal accounts of the 1530s and 1540s Holbein is not consistently called king's painter, but this title is used when special payments and advances of salary are made to him concerning his trips abroad. In his will Holbein calls himself 'the Kinges Majesties servaunte'.

Holbein is assumed to have been employed by Henry VIII principally as a portrait painter. Certainly his most important documented function was to supply vital pictorial information on the appearance of the king's prospective brides. In March he was sent to Brussels to paint the portrait of Christina of Denmark, duchess of Milan, with whom Henry was contemplating marriage. After a three-hour sitting he arrived back in London with an image which contemporaries record delighted the king. This was presumably a drawing or series of drawings, the basis for the surviving full-length painted portrait (National Gallery, London), in which Christina, dressed in the black satin of mourning for her husband, seems to advance seductively towards the viewer; the portrait was kept in Henry's collection even though he did not proceed with the marriage. In June 1538 Holbein was sent to Le Havre in France to depict two further potential brides, and in August to Burgundy for three further candidates, two of whom were portrayed; after this he travelled on to Basel. None of these portraits survives. In 1539 the artist was sent abroad again to take the portraits of Anne and Amelia of Cleves. Two portraits of Anne survive, a three-quarter-length one on parchment (Musée du Louvre, Paris) and a miniature head and shoulders (V&A). Both were presumably based on a lost drawing, and made for Henry's inspection; disenchantment came with Anne's arrival in person, but Holbein's record of her appearance is not known to have been put in question.

Holbein appears to have painted few other portraits for Henry VIII. It is not certain that an individual likeness of the king such as the exquisite small portrait in the Museo Thyssen-Bornemisza, Madrid, was painted for Henry himself. The list of portraits of Henry VIII's immediate family in the inventory of his collection is surprisingly small, but it is possible that Holbein made some portraits of Henry to be sent abroad of which there is no record. The portrait of Edward, prince of Wales, with its Latin verses by a Tudor propagandist, Richard Morison (National Gallery of Art, Washington), is almost certainly that given to the king by Holbein himself as a new year's gift in 1539.

Holbein's great dynastic portrait of Henry VIII, his third wife, Jane Seymour, and his parents, Henry VII and Elizabeth of York, was painted on the wall of the Palace of Whitehall in 1537, probably in the privy chamber (destroyed in the fire of 1698). Its appearance can be reconstructed from the survival of the cartoon for the left half (NPG), showing the life-size figure of Henry with his father, and from the copy by Remigius van Leemput made for Charles II in 1667 (Royal Collection); the veracity of the Latin inscription celebrating the two heroes of the dynasty on a stone altar between the kings is confirmed by a record of it made by a foreign visitor to Whitehall in 1600. Between the cartoon—where the head is close to the image of the Thyssen portrait—and the finished portrait Holbein reorientated the face of the king so that it looks directly at the viewer, an imposing confrontation with the monarch which was to be reiterated in numerous painted copies of the full-length image. None of these individual portraits of Henry is indubitably Holbein's work; however, a portrait of Jane Seymour (Kunsthistorisches Museum, Vienna) by Holbein, showing the queen against a plain blue background and wearing slightly less elaborate dress and jewellery, relates to the image of the queen in the wall painting and to a preparatory drawing connected to both. It is not known for whom this portrait was produced.

Sixteenth-century court painters were also on occasion required to provide designs for goldsmiths' work, and there is some evidence that Holbein might have done so. The payment to a Master Hans for painting a statue of Adam and Eve made by the royal goldsmith Cornelis Hayes, the design for a table fountain given to the king by Anne Boleyn, both referred to above, as well as the designs for a cup for Jane Seymour (AM Oxf. and BM), suggest royal requirements in this area, though other work, such as another elaborate design, for a clocksalt, commissioned by Sir Anthony Denny to give to the king in 1544, was given by courtiers rather than the king. Of a number of surviving designs for jewellery and other decorative items (BM and Kunstmuseum, Basel), a few might be associable with royal requirements; others were probably for courtiers.

Court ceremony often required decorative paintings to be produced at speed, and Holbein's work at Greenwich in 1527, for which he was well paid, is one such instance. There were fewer and less elaborate revels of this kind in the next decade. However, an undated entry in an account connected with the office of revels survives, but is difficult to interpret. This is a payment for a 'peynted boke of Mr. Hansse holby makyng', perhaps a book of designs, or conceivably a stage property (Losely MS 1891, Guildford Muniment Room).

Holbein's position as a court artist must have established his position in London, contributed considerably to his prosperity, and resulted in his decision to further his career there, rather than in Basel. At £7 10s. a quarter, amounting to £30 a year, Holbein's salary fell a little short of Lucas Horenbout's remuneration of £33 6s., but was higher than that of any other court painter during Holbein's own lifetime. He seems to have achieved some degree of prosperity, or at least the show of it, to judge from records of his return to Basel in 1538, monied and wearing fine clothes. Like other court artists he was granted a licence to export 600 tuns of beer in May 1538. However, despite this, his will mentions no assets such as property or even the tools of his trade, and there were debts of £16 13s. to be paid. He appears never to have become a denizen, unlike Lucas Horenbout, even though this meant paying higher taxes.

It is unlikely that Holbein ever lived at court. The so-called Holbein Gate at Whitehall Palace was not connected with the painter until many years after his lifetime. Holbein is known to have been living in the parish of St Andrew Undershaft in Aldgate ward in the city of London in 1541, but there are no records which might indicate his occupancy before this date. Holbein would have been affected by the regulations forbidding foreigners to have workshops in the city. Those who were not denizens were not entitled to take on apprentices and journeymen. However, there is no evidence to suggest that he worked at

Whitehall Palace. Conceivably Holbein was given facilities near the palace, outside the city but within Westminster, which was to become increasingly favoured by painters, but there is no proof of this. It is likely that his position as king's painter allowed him some degree of freedom and protection from the tightly drawn laws otherwise applying to foreigners without denizenship. Presumably Holbein's royal position both permitted him to take on commissions from those who were not themselves royal, and ensured that other painters were unable to prevent him, as a foreigner, from doing so. The regular payment of a salary meant that the king could call on the painter when he was needed, and that he would not return to Basel. The high daily wages paid to 'Master Hans' in 1527, and the responsibility of the tasks given by Henry VIII, including bringing him vital pictorial information on the appearance of his prospective brides, suggests that Holbein's capabilities were highly valued by the king or his advisers.

England, 1531/2–1543: portraits for courtiers and others In addition to his role as painter to Henry VIII, Holbein took the portraits of many of his courtiers, as well as those of others living in London, among them several German Hanseatic merchants. A number of painted portraits survive, mostly unsigned, but there are a far greater number of preparatory drawings for them, the vast majority of which (more than eighty) are today in the Royal Collection at Windsor Castle. These drawings include examples which can be matched to surviving painted portraits, and demonstrate that Holbein rarely departed from the method of working established early in his career in Basel—that of taking a head and shoulders likeness during a sitting, and embellishing this at the painting stage by adding background details and sometimes altering clothing. Nevertheless, the drawing, using coloured chalks and sometimes Holbein's own notations as well, was crucial in establishing the details of likeness. The faces in Holbein's painted portraits are usually identical in dimensions to those surviving corresponding drawings—for instance the painted portraits of Sir Richard Southwell (1536; Galleria degli Uffizi, Florence) and Simon George (Städelsches Kunstinstitut, Frankfurt) compared to their respective drawings (both Royal Collection): this fact has helped to establish the method Holbein almost certainly used for creating his painted likenesses, one that involved tracing the outlines of the drawn portrait onto the panels he used for painting. Earlier in his career Holbein used mixtures of metalpoint and coloured chalks to make his portrait drawings, but by the 1530s he seems to have settled on the practice of drawing with chalks onto flesh-tinted paper and reinforcing the likenesses with extensive use of ink and brush, often employed at the same time in handwritten annotations recording the colour or simply the material of the costume to be painted.

The existence of inscriptions naming the sitters in many of the surviving drawings has assisted in identifying a number of those in the painted portraits, as well as testifying to the range of courtiers Holbein depicted. According to the inventory of the Lumley collection, made at the end of the sixteenth century, and in which the drawings, then bound as a book, are recorded, the identifications were made by Sir John Cheke, tutor to Edward VI. Although the current inscriptions date from a considerably later period, the assertion of the Lumley inventory is a plausible one (not at odds with the few identifications known to be inaccurate).

The drawings, considered with those painted portraits which bear inscriptions identifying their subjects, testify to Holbein's immense success at court. Early in his career he secured the patronage of Sir Thomas More, but he followed this before 1534 with that of Thomas Cromwell (the inscription on the letter he holds in his portrait in the Frick Collection, New York, gives his title as master of the jewel house, the position he held before he became king's secretary in that year), producing a half-length portrait showing Cromwell seated beside a table bearing books and papers. His three-quarter-length portrait of the third duke of Norfolk (Royal Collection) shows the duke full-face, as Henry VIII himself had been depicted, bearing his two staffs of office, while in a group of exceptionally subtle and beautiful studies for which no corresponding painted versions survive Holbein portrayed the duke's son, the earl of Surrey, his wife, and his sister (all Royal Collection). A number of sitters commissioned pairs of portraits: the humanist Sir Thomas Elyot and his wife, Margaret, were shown in this way (only drawings survive; Royal Collection), as were the royal physician Sir William Butts and his wife, Margaret (both Isabella Stewart Gardner Museum, Boston).

In addition to these full-scale portraits Holbein painted several portrait miniatures in a technique using colours mixed with gum on vellum, an illuminator's technique which his biographer Carel van Mander states he learned in England from Lucas Horenbout. His earliest known essay in this technique appears not to have been in portraiture, but in the manuscript known as the 'Canones horoptri', a manual for an astronomical instrument which the royal astronomer Nikolaus Kratzer presented to Henry VIII in 1528 (Bodl. Oxf.). His portrait of Lady Audley is dependent on a large-scale drawing (both are in the Royal Collection), but it is not known whether Holbein also made a large-scale painted portrait, or whether he invariably made drawings to prepare for the painting of the miniatures. The portrait of Mrs Small (V&A; formerly known as Mrs Pemberton) shows the sitter at half-length and is remarkable for the confident placing of the sitter within the small circle of vellum and for the degree of detailed characterization achieved on this scale, which can withstand a considerable degree of magnification with no loss of effect whatsoever. This portrait is also of interest for the fact that the sitter was from a merchant rather than a courtier family, though she had court connections. Similarly, of two small portraits on panel of a man and woman of 1534 (Kunsthistorisches Museum, Vienna), one shows the man in the livery of Henry VIII's servants; they were perhaps court officials of a rank similar or only a little above that occupied by Holbein himself.

The painted portraits of Holbein's English sitters from his second visit to England differ from those of the first brief visit of 1526–8 in the simplicity of their compositions: curtains and tables are largely absent and few sitters are framed by accessories or architecture in background or foreground. A dark blue background sometimes broken by the gilt letters of an inscription giving the year and age of the sitter (not in most cases the identity) was the most common adjunct to the figures. While some were posed with the noble accessory of a falcon (such as Robert Cheseman in the portrait of 1533 in the Mauritshuis, The Hague, or the unidentified man of 1541 in the same collection) or with the lute, less commonly the attribute of a courtier (for example, the unidentified man in the Gemäldegalerie, Berlin), most sitters were shown at half-length or in a head-and-shoulders composition completely alone, looking out of the picture away from the viewer, and without gesture to draw attention to them. The presence of shadows against the blue backgrounds, as well as the presence of inscriptions, however, acted as a subtle reminder of the illusionism that Holbein purveyed: the shadowed blue could not be the sky, and the inscriptions proclaimed that the likenesses were art, not reality.

The number of portraits painted by Holbein which are certainly of Hanseatic merchants is small. Merchant marks and various inscriptions in these portraits, often on letters giving the address of the sitter as the merchants' steelyard beside the Thames, identify them; records show some did business with courtiers. These portraits are distinctive in format: half-lengths, often with inscriptions of a type not found on surviving portraits of English sitters, they were almost certainly painted to be sent home. The portrait of Derich Born of 1533 (Royal Collection) includes a Latin inscription on a parapet which challenges the viewer to say whether the real Derich or a painted version is present. In the portrait of Derick Tybis the sitter holds a piece of paper with a pious reference to his age, thirty-three, the age at which Christ was crucified.

The portrait of Georg Gisze of 1532 (Gemäldegalerie, Berlin), is more elaborate than that of any other single individual painted by Holbein. It includes virtuoso representations of a glass vase with water, of pink satin seen through it, and of the coarse stitches of the Turkey carpet. Gisze's portrait is inscribed not only with the sitter's age and the date, but also, in Latin, 'No joy without sorrow', and further lines in Latin, headed in Greek, which draw attention to the veracity of the portrait as a representation of Gisze. The idea of the world's mutability is perhaps also evoked by the fragility of the glass vase, which stands on the edge of the table, by scales seeming to fall, and by the presence of the clock.

Holbein's largest and most elaborate surviving portrait is the painting of 1533 known as *The Ambassadors* (National Gallery, London). Its exceptional qualities derive in large part from the fact that it depicts two Frenchmen—on the left, Jean de Dinteville, French ambassador to England, who commissioned the portrait, resplendent in pink satin and a black silk gown trimmed with fur, and on the right, in a long clerical gown, Georges de Selves, bishop of Lavaur, who visited Dinteville in England in the late spring of that year. Between the two men are shelves full of objects: globes of heaven and earth, other astronomical instruments, books, and musical instruments. Behind is a green damask curtain, which in the top left-hand corner has been drawn aside just sufficiently to reveal a silver crucifix. The two men stand on an inlaid pavement of elaborate geometrical design. Between them, at a diagonal, is a long greyish shape, the distorted image of a skull, which resolves into the correct perspective if the viewer stands parallel to the picture on the right-hand side or views it through a glass cylinder from the front. Holbein signed the picture with an unusually full signature, and if seen by English courtiers Holbein's talent must have astounded. However, the details of the composition were idiosyncratic and personal to Dinteville, and the painting itself was taken back to France to adorn his château of Polisy in Champagne.

While the precise meanings of the objects on the shelves in *The Ambassadors* have been much debated, it seems clear that collectively, ranging across the arts and sciences from astronomy to music to mathematics, they express a *vanitas* theme, perhaps a particular preoccupation for Dinteville, who wears a hat badge with a tiny skull, and expressed much melancholy in letters written from the English court. Such a theme may be echoed in the broken string of the lute, but the presence of a Lutheran hymnbook has been linked to the bishop's concern for the divisions caused by the Reformation and with the exacerbation of such divisions caused by Henry VIII's marriage to Anne Boleyn while Dinteville himself was in London. Whether or not such specific events inspired the detail of the painting, there is little evidence to support theories that the astronomical instruments in it show dates and times of significance.

One more large-scale portrait, *Henry VIII and the Barber–Surgeons' Company* (Barber–Surgeons' Hall, London), is recorded in van Mander's biography of 1604 and survives today, along with the overpainted cartoon used to create it (Royal College of Surgeons, London). The portrait records the granting of a charter by the king in 1541 to combine the hitherto separate organizations of the Barbers and Surgeons, and includes portraits of the royal physicians William Butts and John Chambers which are similar to individual portraits by Holbein. The seated, frontal image of the king bears some relation to the image of the Whitehall painting, but the hieratic composition with its rows of heads is unexpectedly formal, closer to the woodcut on the title-page of the Coverdale Bible. Parts of the painting have been embellished at a later date, and its condition makes it difficult to ascertain today the precise extent of Holbein's contribution to the painted surface, but other painters were certainly involved.

England, 1531/2–1543: non-portrait commissions The German Hanseatic merchant community in London did not only commission portraits from Holbein. In 1533 the city of London staged a series of nine pageants to celebrate Anne Boleyn's entry to the city on 31 May, the day before her coronation. According to Hall's *Chronicle*, the London

Hanseatic merchants were responsible for the second pageant, which showed Apollo and the muses on Parnassus. A drawing by Holbein (Kupferstichkabinett, Berlin), shows just such a Parnassus scene, set on top of a triumphal arch of classical design. The drawing must certainly be connected with this occasion, but it is less clear whether it was made as a record or should be interpreted as evidence that Holbein was the designer of the pageant of Parnassus. It is conceivable that the commission was not a Hanseatic one, and that the English humanists John Leland and his collaborator Nicholas Udall may have involved Holbein in the plans for this or even the whole series of pageants.

It is certain, however, that Holbein painted two large canvases for the Hanseatic merchants, *The Triumph of Riches* and *The Triumph of Poverty*, both now lost. According to van Mander both paintings hung in the *eet sael*, or dining-room. Several copies survive, as well as Holbein's own drawing for *The Triumph of Riches*. Copies of the two works made by Lucas Vorsterman in the seventeenth century show a semi-grisaille colour scheme with a frieze-like arrangement of allegorical figures in shades of brown processing with horse-drawn chariots against a blue sky, both decorous and elegant. The two works differed in length and composition, suggesting they were designed for specific positions, *Riches* (AM Oxf.) occupying a long wall and *Poverty* (BM) a short. *Poverty* showed an old woman in a farm cart drawn by oxen and asses, while *Riches* depicted an old man seated in a chariot accompanied by figures drawn from antiquity. On one copy of *Poverty* are verses which refer to the turning of the wheel of fortune, and the cares brought by riches as well as poverty; there is no evidence to support the legend that these verses were composed by Sir Thomas More.

Similar in style is the exquisite miniature painting on vellum in a grisaille technique of *Solomon and Sheba* (Royal Collection). It would have been well suited to presentation to the king as a new year's gift, but it is not recorded in any of the surviving lists of such. It includes a biblical inscription also used by writers asserting Henry's supremacy over the English church, and is likely to have been devised as an allegory of the English Reformation, one of a small number of such images which Holbein appears to have produced in England, probably through his association with Thomas Cromwell.

Holbein's *Allegory of the Old and New Testaments* (NG Scot.) appears to be the only picture that he painted in England using protestant imagery. Elements of its composition are echoed in the artist's design for the title-page of the Coverdale Bible, published in 1535, and its painterly, colourful style is close to paintings of the early 1530s, such as *The Ambassadors*. Holbein's painting is divided into two halves by the presence of a tree, which is bare of leaves on the left-hand side and in full leaf on the right. Underneath the tree sits a naked man with the prophet Isaiah and John the Baptist. On the left are Old Testament scenes: Moses receiving the tablets, Adam and Eve, the brazen serpent, and manna being showered from heaven, as well as a decayed tomb with a skeleton. On the right are the annunciation to the Virgin, the annunciation to the shepherds, the crucifixion, Christ and the apostles, and the resurrected Christ trampling a skeleton and the devil. The composition has a close relationship with one of the key images of the protestant Reformation, which was produced in several versions by Lucas Cranach the elder.

Holbein's title-page for the Coverdale Bible, although based on the opposition between the law and grace displayed in other contemporary bibles, is tailored specifically to English circumstances: the lower part of the design here is occupied by the king enthroned, distributing the Bible to the bishops in the presence of the laity. The image of Henry VIII is placed directly underneath the tetragrammagon, in apparent acknowledgement of his position as the direct representative of God on earth, without the mediation of the pope. Holbein's design also includes a clear emphasis on the propagation of the word of God, placing Moses receiving the tablets opposite Christ and the apostles, and Esdras opposite the apostles preaching. The clarity and economy of the title-page show his mature powers of illustration and design to the full.

In addition to the Bible title-page, Holbein produced a New Testament title-page and a design for Melanchthon's *Loci communes*, all of which were possibly intended to be produced as a gift for the king in 1535. Three small woodcuts by Holbein were used in later books, but seem not to appear in publications during his lifetime—perhaps because the political climate made texts and images alike seem too radical: all three images show monks in the role of the biblical pharisees in scenes from Christ's ministry in the New Testament. Had Holbein lived into the reign of Edward VI he might perhaps have made a greater contribution to the development of a specifically English protestant iconography. His sudden death in November 1543, probably from the plague, prevented this.

Holbein's achievement, influence, and reputation Holbein's surviving portrait paintings and drawings, their likenesses remarkably unaffected by the conventions and fashions of their time, provide a unique and unparalleled depiction of the men and women of the Tudor court, including an image of Henry VIII so powerful that its influence in shaping our vision of Henry has endured to the present day. The loss of several of Holbein's largest and most spectacular paintings in both Basel and London distorts the degree of his achievement, more readily appreciated today in the design of book illustrations, portraits large and small, and altarpieces than in large-scale decorative designs. The range of his abilities in a number of media and artistic forms was remarkable: one of the greatest of European portraitists, Holbein was also instrumental in introducing the decorative styles of the Renaissance to England through his wall paintings and goldsmiths' designs, and he set a standard of extraordinary technical and artistic skill for the new form of the portrait miniature.

Holbein was one of the very few early northern European artists to achieve lasting fame. His name endured from the sixteenth century through to the nineteenth, although it was frequently misapplied, particularly to English portraits of Tudor appearance and especially to images of Henry VIII. Holbein himself appears to have left no lasting stylistic legacy in England as a portrait painter, and his foreign status may have precluded the establishment of a workshop, but many copies of the portraits were produced, and his work appears to have continued to be well known to artists and collectors. Nicholas Hilliard wrote in the reign of Elizabeth I: 'Holbein's manner of limning I have ever imitated and hold it for the best' (Hilliard, 68–9). In the following century the fourteenth earl of Arundel, much preoccupied with collecting antiquities and the works of artists such as Rubens, confessed his particular 'weakness' for the work of Holbein, many of which he collected. Holbein's first biographer was Carel van Mander, whose life appeared with those of other artists in his *Schilderboek* of 1604; it includes much information on Holbein's work in London, although van Mander himself appears never to have visited England. In 1676 a detailed list of Holbein's *œuvre* was published by Charles Patin and Sebastian Faesch. One hundred years later in England Horace Walpole created his own tribute to Holbein in the Holbein Chamber at Strawberry Hill, adorned with tracings of the Holbein drawings in the Royal Collection made by his compatriot George Vertue. In the nineteenth century the first art historical studies of his work were published, including the first in German by Alfred Woltmann and the first in English by Ralph Wornum. It was for long erroneously believed that Holbein lived through the reign of Edward, dying in 1554, permitting a number of later portraits to be wrongly ascribed to him; the publication of his will in 1861 revealing the date of his death as 1543 led inevitably to a reassessment of the documentary and pictorial sources for the study of his work, culminating in the comprehensive study of life and work by A. B. Chamberlain published in 1913.

A number of portraits depicting Holbein survive, some showing him holding a paintbrush, possibly based on a self-portrait (such as the miniature version attributed to Lucas Horenbout, Wallace Collection, London). A drawing held to be a self-portrait is in the Uffizi. All show a bearded face and features which can plausibly be related to the portrait drawing of 1511 by his father.

SUSAN FOISTER

Sources BL, accounts of Henry VIII, accounts of the treasurer of the chamber, Arundel MS 97, Stowe MS 554 · *LP Henry VIII* · A. B. Chamberlain, *Hans Holbein the younger*, 2 vols. (1913) · J. Rowlands, *The paintings of Hans Holbein the younger* (1985) · C. van Mander, *Het schilderboek* (1604) · N. Bourbon, *Paidagogeion* (Lyons, 1536) · *Opus epistolarum des. Erasmi Roterodami*, ed. P. S. Allen, 12 vols. (1906–58) · will, GL, MS 9171, vol. 11, fols. 116r, 116v, 121r · Guildford Muniment Room, Guildford, Losely MS 1891 · 'Treasury of the receipt, miscellaneous books', PRO, E 36/227 (LP 1V (2) 3104) [Greenwich revels accounts] · Folger, MS Zd 11 (LP XIII (2) 1280, pp. 538–9) · K. T. Parker, *The drawings of Hans Holbein in the collection of his majesty the king at Windsor Castle* (1945) · S. Foister, *Drawings by Holbein from the Royal Library, Windsor Castle* (1983) · J. Rowlands and G. Bartrum, *Drawings by German artists in the department of prints and drawings in the British Museum: the fifteenth century, and the sixteenth century by artists born before 1530*, 2 vols. (1993) · 'Canones horoptri', Bodl. Oxf., MS Bodley 504 · S. Foister, *Holbein and the court of Henry VIII* (1978) [exhibition catalogue, Queen's Gallery, Buckingham Palace, 1978] · *Hans Holbein der Älterer und die Kunst der Spätgotik* (1965) [exhibition catalogue, Augsburg Rathaus, 1965] · E. Foucart-Walter, *Les peintures de Hans Holbein le jeune au Louvre* (1985) [exhibition catalogue, Musée du Louvre, Paris, 1985] · L. Campbell, 'Holbein's miniature of "Mrs Pemberton": the identity of the sitter', *Burlington Magazine*, 129 (1987), 366–71 · L. Campbell, 'Holbein's miniature of Jane Pemberton: a footnote', *Burlington Magazine*, 132 (1987), 213–14 · S. Foister, A. Roy, and M. Wyld, *Holbein's Ambassadors: making and meaning* (1997) · C. Müller, ed., *Die Zeichnungen von Hans Holbein dem jüngeren und Ambrosius Holbein: Katalog der Zeichnungen des Kupferstichkabinetts Basel* (1996) · S. Foister, A. Roy, and M. Wyld, 'Hans Holbein's *Lady with a squirrel and a starling*', *National Gallery Technical Bulletin*, 15 (1994), 6–19 · S. Foister, 'Holbein and the English Reformation', MA diss., Courtauld Inst., 1977 · N. Hilliard, *A treatise concerning the art of limning*, ed. R. K. R. Thornton and T. G. S. Cain (1981) · S. Foister, '"My foolish curiosity": Holbein in the collection of the earl of Arundel', *Apollo*, 144 (1996), 51–6
Likenesses H. Holbein the younger, self-portrait, drawing, chalks, *c.*1523–1524, Öffentliche Kunstsammlung, Basel, Switzerland · chalk drawing, *c.*1542–1543 (self-portrait?), Uffizi, Florence [*see illus.*] · attrib. L. Horenbout, miniature, Wallace Collection, London
Wealth at death will mentions no assets; debts of £6 13s. to be paid: will, GL, MS 9171, vol. 11

Holberry, Samuel (1814–1842), Chartist, was born on 18 November 1814 at Gamston in Nottinghamshire, the youngest of nine children of John and Martha Holberry, who were agricultural labourers on the duke of Newcastle's estate. Samuel did a child's work on the land, and sometimes cleaned spinning machinery at Gamston. He learned basic skills at a Sunday school and at a day school. In his early teens he was sent to board as a farm servant to earn his keep, and graduated to labourer status. At the age of seventeen, in March 1832 he followed his brother and enlisted. During three years in the 33rd regiment he served in Ireland and in Northampton, where he may have been used to harass and suppress English reformers and trade unionists. There he attended night school, and was influenced by the radical shoemakers. Disgusted with army life, he bought himself out in April 1835. He worked for a year as a cooper, then as a rectifying distiller in Sheffield until late 1837, when he was laid off, and sought work in London. In 1835 he had met Mary (*b.* 1816), a daughter of John and Ann Cooper, labourers of Oakes Green, Attercliffe, Sheffield. After Holberry's return in 1838 from London, where he had made his first contact with Chartists, they married on 22 October and lived at several addresses in Sheffield.

Holberry's conspiracy was not just part of the Chartist movement, which he had joined in 1838, but the culmination of fifty years of struggle for parliamentary reform in Sheffield, beginning with the Constitutional Society, formed in 1791. There were demonstrations in 1802 and 1812, and petitions to parliament for reform in 1816 and 1830. The discovery at the first general election after the Reform Act of 1832 that, thanks to its property qualification, only one in eight Sheffield men had been given the vote led to the formation of the Sheffield Political Union of the Working Classes. In 1837 the union changed its name to the Sheffield Workingmen's Association, and in

Samuel Holberry (1814–1842), by C. Demain, 1842

1838 it joined the emerging Chartist movement, whose six-point Charter demanded universal suffrage. With police and dragoons harassing their meetings, the Chartists who advocated moral force failed in 1839, when their great petition was rejected, and their divided leadership was suppressed. Local initiatives for direct physical action then prevailed, but were unco-ordinated; a first rising at Newport in Wales was crushed in November 1839.

The testimony of Samuel Thompson, a Chartist who confessed during his trial, established that at secret meetings in a room in Fig Tree Lane, Sheffield, Holberry tried to organize an armed rising of the whole of the West Riding, to seize the centres of Sheffield, Barnsley, Dewsbury, and Bradford on the same night, as Chartist 'forts'. For this his military training was important, and he made and tested grenades and firebombs. Having been laid off work in November, and with his wife pregnant, in December and January he communicated with London and Birmingham, and as a delegate of the Sheffield Chartist committee visited a number of Yorkshire towns, where he necessarily relied on the assurances of local groups. The first rising of 1840 was to be at 2 a.m. on Sunday 12 January in Sheffield. Holberry's plan was to capture the town hall and Tontine Hotel, and to barricade and defend them; setting fire to the cavalry barracks and houses of the wealthy would divert the troops, while Holberry led eighty-three picked men against them. Soldiers and watchmen were to be assassinated; if the plan failed they would 'Moscow' (that is, set fire to) the town, in the hope that even temporary success might win political concessions. But James

Allen, a Rotherham man, betrayed the plans. Holberry was arrested at midnight on the 11th, just as he was about to leave home to lead a fire party, a dagger in his pocket, arms and grenades in his house. He admitted that he was ready to take life 'in obtaining the Charter … and in defence of liberty' (*Northern Star*, 21 March 1840).

The rising was reported in the moral-force Chartists' newspaper the *Northern Star* of 15 January 1840 as 'the stark staring mad proceedings of a small knot of fools at Sheffield!', and at the Yorkshire assizes on 16 March Holberry and others were indicted for seditious conspiracy and riot. Holberry admitted intent to upset the government, and professed willingness to die for the Charter. In a court crowded with defendants, lawyers, and spectators, thirty were found guilty and six acquitted. Mary Holberry had been arrested and was interrogated, but kept her secrets and was released. The National Charter Association cared for Mary when she had a breakdown after their baby son died later that year.

Holberry and John Clayton received the exemplary sentence of four years. At first the conspirators were in Northallerton gaol, where, besides the 'silent system', the notorious diet and five weeks on the treadmill before months of solitary confinement broke their health. Yet the Major Williams who interviewed Holberry in prison found him to be 'a man of considerable resolution and talent' (Thompson, *The Chartists*, 281). After the death of Clayton in 1841, even the prison inspectors were critical of the conditions under which Holberry was confined. Removal in September 1841 to the hospital of York Castle was delayed too long. Ravaged by tuberculosis, he died there of inflammation of the liver on 21 June 1842.

The news that 'Poor, brave Holberry is dead' at the age of twenty-seven reached a city angry at the May rejection of the latest Chartist petition, and made desperate by poverty (Thompson, *The Chartists*, 281). On 27 June 1842 the hearse from Attercliffe was followed through Sheffield by a great procession with bands and banners. Between 20,000 and 50,000 people paid respects to their 'martyr to the cause of Democracy', as his coffin plate was inscribed. At the graveside the hymn 'Great God! Is this the patriot's doom!' composed especially for the occasion by John Henry Bramwich, a stockinger, was sung; the address by George Harney, a National Charter Association leader, exhorted all 'to labour with heart and soul for the destruction of the horrible system under which Holberry has perished' (Gammage, 214–15). Holberry's death was marked by Chartist group meetings in many towns and cities.

Mary Holberry had joined the female Chartists (who had a section in Holberry's cortège) in 1839, and campaigned alongside the men until the National Charter Association was disbanded in the 1850s. In 1845 she married Charles Pearson, a widower publican; they named their first son Holberry, and two more after Chartists. In 1842 Charles Demain, an artist and Chartist, apparently took a death mask and made a bust of Holberry, which latter was placed with the portraits of Cobbett, Paine, Henry Hunt, Robert Emmett, John Frost, and Feargus O'Connor in the meeting room at Fig Tree Lane, where the Chartists' weekly discussions and family meetings were held. The family later retrieved the bust, which is now in the Kelham Island Museum, Sheffield. Holberry's grave in the Sheffield general cemetery was found in 1978, and the headstone cleaned. In 1998 eight new cascades in Sheffield city centre were dedicated with a plaque to him. The citizens of Sheffield have honoured him as a martyr not only because he led their insurrection but because he declared his willingness to fight for, and then died for, the Charter. His significance was in leading a rising that was not a response to economic slump, but part of a political struggle to obtain for working people the vote, the right to organize, and decent living conditions.

ROGER HUTCHINS

Sources J. Baxter, *Samuel Holberry (1814–1842): Sheffield's revolutionary democrat*, 3rd edn, Holberry Society (1986) • B. Moore, *Samuel Holberry and the chartist movement in Sheffield*, Holberry Society (1987) • D. Thompson, ed., *The early Chartists* (1971), 18, 40, 250, 264–9, 271–2, 273–9 • 'The riots', *Northern Star* (15 Jan 1840) • 'Sheffield, trial of Samuel Holberry', *Northern Star* (21 March 1840) • R. G. Gammage, *History of the Chartist movement, 1837–1854*, new edn (1894), 173, 175, 213–16 • D. Thompson, *The Chartists: popular politics in the industrial revolution* (1984), 141, 281 • A. Briggs, ed., *Chartist studies* (1959); repr. (1962), 145, 204 • J. Taylor, 'The chartist conspiracy in Sheffield: how it was detected', *Sheffield Daily Telegraph* (Feb 1864) • S. P. Thompson, 'Deposition regarding the Sheffield rising', *Thompson* (1971), 270–79 • B. Moore, 'Samuel Holberry and Sir Stuart Goodwin', speech to Sheffield council committee, 16 Feb 1998, 1 • E. Royle, *Chartism*, 3rd edn (1996) • private information (2004) [B. Moore, Holberry Society] • d. cert.
Likenesses C. Demain of York, bust, 1842 (after death mask), Kelham Island Museum, Sheffield [*see illus.*]

Holborne, Antony (*d.* 1602?), lutenist and composer, may have been the man admitted in May 1562, possibly after attendance at Merchant Taylors' School, 'pensioner' of Christ's College, Cambridge, and in November 1565 to the Inner Temple. On 14 June 1584 at St Margaret's, Westminster, he married Elizabeth Marten; they had three daughters, Anne, Honor, and Dorothy, and an unnamed son known only from a letter of his mother, written in 1606. The family lived in that parish from 1584 to 1585 and from 1594 to 1596, but possibly elsewhere in between. Holborne styled himself gentleman and servant to the queen and was described by Robert Dowland in 1610 as gentleman usher to Queen Elizabeth, but no such appointment is recorded. He was probably a gentleman usher 'extraordinary', receiving no wages (and thus with no entry in the privy chamber accounts) and with no specific duties, but enjoying the status of gentleman and the protection conferred by nominal membership of the royal household. This honorary position would enable him to perform musical services to the queen under the guise of occasional attendance at court. A close parallel would be the place of gentleman-extraordinary of the Chapel Royal.

Holborne's earliest surviving compositions seem to be 'The Countess of Pembrokes funeralls', probably commemorating the deaths in 1586 of Mary Herbert's father, mother, and brother, Sir Philip Sidney, and 'The Countess of Ormond's Galliard', given as the tune for a song in Anthony Munday's *Banquet of Daintie Conceits* (1588). A letter of 1594 requests some of his lessons for the bandora

and there are two such by 'AH' in William Barley's *New Booke of Tabliture* (1596). Holborne's own first publication was *The Cittharn Schoole* (1597), containing graded pieces, some with separate bass parts, but without instructions. His brother William contributed 'sixe short Aers Neapolitan like to three voices'. Holborne himself was the most prolific composer for these wire-strung instruments; many pieces appear, besides his works for lute and for string ensembles, in English and foreign manuscripts. He provided commendatory verses in English to Thomas Morley's *A Plaine and Easie Introduction* (1597), and in Latin to Giles Farnaby's *Canzonets* (1598). Holborne's *Pavans, galliards, almains and other short aiers both grave and light, in five parts, for viols, violins, or other[wise] musicall winde instruments* (1599) was the first English publication comparable with the continental collections, in several of which his music appears. Only two of his songs survive: 'O Lord whose grace' in the 'Swarland' manuscript, and 'My Heavy Sprite' in Robert Dowland's *A Musicall Banquet* (1610).

The Cittharn Schoole was dedicated to Thomas, Lord Burgh, who died in the year of publication (1597). In *Pavans, Galliards, Almains* Holborne addresses Sir Richard Champernowne 'from the experience of many years', suggesting patronage over a period, perhaps in Champernowne's household at Modbury, Devon. There may have been a connection between Holborne and the countess of Pembroke's literary circle; their intense interest in emblematic literature could explain some of his esoteric titles, which have, for example, biblical and Ovidian links.

Holborne is the only Elizabethan composer from whom there are several different versions of the same music, all apparently from his own pen. Certain pieces exist for solo lute, bandora, and cittern, as well as for five-part instrumental ensemble and for mixed consort (though the last may have been arranged by others). This may be no more than an accident of survival, but is in marked contrast to the works of most of his contemporaries. The key of a piece is often adjusted to suit the particular instrumental medium, but the tune and bass usually remain the same. Holborne excels in melodic and rhythmic invention, and he was clearly an accomplished player of the lute and other plucked instruments. His five-part ensemble collection is conceived as functional dance-music, with correct if unimaginative inner parts. There is little of the wayward part-writing of a Dowland nor the sustained interest of individual lines demanded by amateur string players.

In January 1599 Holborne was sent by the queen with letters to the states of the United Provinces. On 29 November 1602 Elizabeth Holborne wrote to Cecil of her husband's taking cold on his business, fearing that it would cost him his life and that she would be unable to give him a suitable burial. The letter is endorsed 'primo December 1602 Widow Olborne' (Cecil MS 96, fol. 86), suggesting Holborne had probably died in London in the interim. The burial is unrecorded, but in 1606 Elizabeth described herself as a widow.

IAN HARWOOD

Sources B. Jeffery, 'Antony Holborne', *Musica Disciplina*, 22 (1968), 129–205 • M. Kanazawa, ed., *Music for lute and bandora: The complete* works of Antony Holborne, 1 (1967) • New Grove • Hatfield House, Cecil MS, 96, fol. 86

Holborne, Sir Robert (1598–1648), barrister and politician, was born to a gentry background on 15 November 1598, the eldest son of Nicholas Holborne (fl. c.1570–1620) of Chichester, Sussex. His mother was possibly Anne (fl. c.1570–1620), sister of John Lane. Holborne began his legal education at Furnival's Inn before entering Lincoln's Inn on 9 November 1615 and was called to the bar in 1623. He married Anne (d. 1663), daughter of Sir Robert Dudley, the illegitimate heir of the Elizabethan courtier Robert Dudley, earl of Leicester. Holborne was steward for a Sussex manor in 1622 and was involved in further land transactions in that county in 1628 and 1636. Through his marriage Holborne acquired an interest in his wife's Warwickshire lands valued at £80 a year.

During the 1630s Holborne emerged as a critic of the fiscal policies of Charles I's personal rule (1629–40) during which the king governed without parliament or aid of parliamentary subsidy. Along with Oliver St John he served as counsel for John Hampden in the ship money case, making an elaborate four-day argument from 2 to 5 December 1637. His distaste for the fiscal measures of the personal rule persisted and in 1639 he attacked tonnage and poundage on behalf of a merchant's widow. In 1640 he became a bencher of his inn and sat in the Short Parliament for Southwark speaking occasionally on issues relating to parliamentary subsidies and the legality of ship money. In the Long Parliament he sat for the borough of St Michael, Cornwall, which he may have procured through his association with members of the Arundell family with whom he had been familiar at Lincoln's Inn. In parliament he emerged as a leading royalist, changing sides probably for reasons of religion. Holborne championed both episcopacy and the legislative autonomy of the clerical estate against a rising tide of Erastian sentiment in the early Long Parliament. On 15 December 1640 he confronted his former ally and co-counsel Oliver St John and John Pym over the legality of the 1640 canons passed by convocation after the dissolution of the Short Parliament. Holborne argued that not only could convocation make canons by royal assent alone without parliamentary confirmation but also that these canons could bind the laity provided that they 'weere not against law' (D'Ewes, 152). Holborne argued further that the king was within his right to continue convocation by separate commission after the dissolution of parliament, citing numerous precedents that his opponent Sir Simonds D'Ewes described as 'being very dangerous examples' (ibid., 153). In the spring of 1641 Holborne both opposed in the house and ultimately voted against the attainder of the earl of Strafford. In November of that year he spoke in defence of the impeached twelve bishops on charges of high crimes and misdemeanours. His last committee appointment in the House of Commons was 29 March 1642 and he appears to have absented himself soon afterwards.

Later in the same year Holborne reappeared, having joined the king at Oxford, where he published The reading in Lincolnes-Inne, Feb. 28. 1641: vpon the stat. of 25.E.3. cap. 2., being the Statute of Treasons. At Oxford the king made him attorney-general to the prince of Wales, knighting him on 19 January 1643. He also received the degrees of MA and DCL from the University of Oxford on 1 November 1642 and 7 February 1643. Also about this time the Long Parliament sequestrated his estates. He was probably not, as the Dictionary of National Biography recorded, the author of The Freeholders Grand Inquest (1648), a tract that more recent scholarship has convincingly reattributed to Sir Robert Filmer. However, it is possible that Holborne was among those whom Filmer consulted in the composition of the tract. He was an avid follower of astrology, being a devotee of William Lilly, at one point paying £100 to Nicholas Fiske for the calculation of his nativity. He died childless, in London or Middlesex, and was buried under Lincoln's Inn chapel on 16 February 1648.   D. A. ORR

Sources DNB • Keeler, Long Parliament, 134–5 • Foster, Alum. Oxon., 1500–1714 [Sir Robert Holbourne] • R. Filmer, Patriarcha and other writings, ed. J. Sommerville (1991), xxxiv–xxxvii • E. S. Cope and W. H. Coates, eds., Proceedings of the Short Parliament of 1640, CS, 4th ser., 19 (1977), 179, 194, 208 • J. Bruce, ed., Verney papers: notes of proceedings in the Long Parliament, CS, 31 (1845), 55, 58, 136 • The journal of Sir Simonds D'Ewes from the beginning of the Long Parliament to the opening of the trial of the earl of Strafford, ed. W. Notestein (1923), 152–7 • Elias Ashmole (1617–1692): his autobiographical and historical notes, ed. C. H. Josten, 5 vols. (1966 [i.e. 1967]), vol. 2, p. 471 • W. R. Prest, The rise of the barristers: a social history of the English bar, 1590–1640 (1986), 370 • VCH Warwickshire, 4.88; 6.126 • C. Russell, The fall of the British monarchies, 1637–1642 (1991), 232–3, 290, 438

Holbroke [Holbrook], **John** (d. 1437), mathematician and astronomer, was a native of Suffolk. He is first recorded in August 1393, when he was admitted to a fellowship at Peterhouse, Cambridge; he became master about June 1421 and held that position for the rest of his life. He was ordained priest in 1413 and was styled DTh by 1418; no doubt he had been awarded the degree of MA several years before. Holbroke endowed the Barnard Castle loan chest at Peterhouse with 10 marks in 1426 and 20 marks in 1436. Borrowers from the chest were to pray for the souls of Holbroke and their other benefactors. He served as proctor of Cambridge University in 1398–9 and as chancellor of the university in November 1429 and in 1430. During his chancellorship a memorable dispute, the 'Barnwell Process', arose with the bishop of Ely concerning ecclesiastical jurisdiction over university scholars. Pope Martin V (r. 1417–31) delegated the adjudication to the prior of Barnwell, who ruled in favour of the university's autonomy from diocesan control. Holbroke was a chaplain to Henry V and Henry VI. According to the astrological treatise, Cum rerum motu (a work of uncertain authorship, preserved only in CUL, MS Ee.3.61, fols. 159–75), Henry V, detained by the siege of Meaux, dispatched Holbroke to Windsor to be present at the birth of the king's son. Holbroke is said to have been the first man to set eyes on the infant prince, the future Henry VI. Apparently he twice calculated Henry VI's natal horoscope: Cum rerum motu cites the royal nativity 'secundum Mag.J.Holbroke'. However, an amended version appears in a manuscript owned by Holbroke (BL, Egerton MS 889, fol. 5r; an additional copy in Bodl. Oxf.,

MS Ashmole 369, fol. 182v). There is no record of his interpretation of these bare natal horoscopes, that is, of the astrological portents for Henry VI's reign.

Holbroke's reputation as a mathematician derived from his compilation of astronomical tables for the Cambridge meridian. His *Opus primum* is a set of tables which allow the calculation of the true and mean positions of the sun, moon, and planets. Striving for greater accuracy, Holbroke extended the calculation of planetary locations to ten sexagesimal places in his *Opus secundum*. The tremendous, if vain, effort of drafting the *Opus secundum* impressed users of the tables well into the next century. One sixteenth-century scholar remarked: 'This man was the mathematical glory of Cambridge for ther was nower any one good in this knowledge before Holbrooke who was *satis profundus*' (Gloucester, Cathedral Library, MS 21, fol. 163). Holbroke died in Cambridge in or before July 1437 and was buried in the chancel of St Mary-the-Less, Cambridge, where a monumental brass remains (although it has been severely damaged). He presented three books to Peterhouse in 1426: a copy of Haly Abenragel's *De judiciis stellarum* (now Oxford, Corpus Christi College, MS 151), John Ashenden's *Summa judicialis de accidentibus mundi* (London, Royal College of Physicians, MS 390), and Holbroke's astronomical tables, written partly in his own hand (BL, Egerton MS 889, also known as the Codex Holbrookensis). Another manuscript owned by Holbroke entered the Peterhouse Library at a later date (Cambridge, Peterhouse, MS 267). To the university he gave a copy of Gregory's *Super Ezechielem*, and two knives with ivory handles. Holbroke's will also provided for the construction of the lower choir stalls for the chapel of Peterhouse.

KEITH SNEDEGAR

Sources Emden, *Cam.*, 309 · H. M. Carey, *Courting disaster: astrology at the English court and university in the later middle ages* (1992) · R. Lovatt, 'Two collegiate loan chests in late medieval Cambridge', *Medieval Cambridge: essays on the pre-Reformation university*, ed. P. Zutshi (1993), 129–65
Archives Bodl. Oxf., MS Ashmole 369, fol. 182v · Gloucester Cathedral, MS 21, fol. 163 | BL, Egerton MS 889 · CUL, MS Ee.3.61
Likenesses monumental brass, St Mary-the-Less, Cambridge · oils, Peterhouse, Cambridge
Wealth at death executors used part of estate for construction of lower choir stalls in St Mary-the-Less: Emden, *Cam.*

Holbrook [*née* Jackson], **Ann Catherine** (1780–1837), actress and author, was probably born in London. Her father, Thomas Jackson, was an actor, and she was brought up to that profession. Before she was eighteen she played with success such characters as Juliet, Roxana, and Alicia. Her mother died in 1794 and her father at Norwich in 1798. On his deathbed he commended her to his own manager, John Brunton, of the Colchester theatre, who failed to fulfil this last request. She then went to London to seek work on the stage through a theatrical 'register-office' in Russell Court, which referred her to a provincial company at Lewes in Sussex. Three months later, in Battle, Sussex, she married a man named Holbrook who was an actor with the same company. They acted together with various provincial companies in such towns as Taunton, Preston, and Lancaster, where 'the noble ladies' made her a liberal present. They then tried engagements in Cheltenham, where the countess of Kenmare attended their benefit, in Windsor, and in Daventry, where there was a fire in the theatre. An engagement with W. C. Macready in the midlands followed during which they hoped to earn more for the support of their children, but they soon left the stage, disillusioned with the 'nine years of misery' produced by the general conditions they had encountered in the theatre and with management in particular. Ann Holbrook then turned to writing, and produced in 1809 *The Dramatist, or, Memoirs of the Stage, with the Life of the Authoress*. A large part of this small book, subscribed to by nine members of the aristocracy among numerous others, is devoted to the financial difficulties of life as an actor and the insensitive treatment by management, which she hoped might prove a deterrent to others wishing to enter the profession. She did not hesitate to recount anecdotes against herself, such as a description of a time when she lost her wig on the stage, to the embarrassment of cast and audience. She continued to write, producing *Tales, Serious and Instructive* in 1821, *Constantine Castriot, an Historical Tale* in 1829, and *Realities and Reflections: a Series of Original Tales* in 1834. She died in London in January 1837.

J. GILLILAND

Sources A. C. Holbrook, *The dramatist, or, Memoirs of the stage, with the life of the authoress* (1809) · *GM*, 2nd ser., 7 (1837)

Holbrook, John. See Holbroke, John (d. 1437).

Holbrooke, Joseph Charles [Josef] (1878–1958), composer and pianist, was born on 5 July 1878 at Waddon, Croydon, one of the five children (two sons and three daughters) of Joseph Charles Holbrooke (*fl.* 1860–1900), a music-hall musician and piano teacher from Bristol, and his wife, Alice Scotland (d. 1880), of Newport, Paisley, Fife. Holbrooke studied at the Royal Academy of Music (1893–5), winning various prizes. During 1896–9 he eked out a living as pantomime band conductor, music teacher, and composer of many salon pieces. He subsequently adopted the forename Josef professionally, to avoid confusion with his father. In June 1896 Holbrooke made his début as a solo pianist at St James's Hall, London; his repertory included piano concertos by Rakhmaninov and Tchaikovsky. He married Dorothy Elizabeth, daughter of T. Hadfield of Morthen. They had two sons and three daughters.

In 1900 Holbrooke began to achieve success and recognition as a composer. In that year his tone-poem *The Raven* was accepted by Sir August Manns for première at a Crystal Palace concert on 3 March. His Proms première came later that year when his variations for orchestra, *Three Blind Mice*, was played at a Prom on 3 November; it was later a great favourite with audiences at the Proms. Holbrooke briefly taught at the Birmingham and Midland Institute, but the popularity of his works at chamber and orchestral concerts in London encouraged him to concentrate on composing; and commissions from the major music festivals began to arrive. His orchestral piece *Queen Mab* was given at the Leeds festival in 1904, and *Ulalume* at the Queen's Hall, London, under Sir Henry Wood later the same year. Other festival premières of his works took place at Norwich, Bristol, and Birmingham.

A significant event of these years was Holbrooke's introduction to the poet Herbert Trench. The latter commissioned a setting of his poem 'Apollo and the Seaman' from Holbrooke, who produced a seventy-minute symphony, premièred at the Queen's Hall in 1908. This featured a large orchestra and chorus behind a screen on which a magic lantern projected text and images. The slides were unfortunately out of sequence with the music, and the event became the quarry from which a number of writers on music subsequently extracted humorous anecdotes.

An important boost to Holbrooke's career followed from a meeting with the wealthy Lord Howard de Walden, who became his benefactor. He transformed Holbrooke's existence with major commissions, as well as other kinds of subsidy: gifts, a cottage in Harlech, holidays (he went on de Walden's honeymoon cruise of the Mediterranean in 1912). Unfortunately, all this largesse came to an end with de Walden's death in 1946. However, de Walden wrote a triptych of three poetic plays, collectively known as *The Cauldron of Annwn* and based on the Mabinogion; and Holbrooke was commissioned to set all three. He conceived them as Wagnerian music dramas, rather than operas; they appeared as *Dylan* (1910), *The Children of Don* (1912), and *Bronwen* (1920). The first two were performed under Artur Nikisch and Thomas Beecham respectively. Because of the First World War *Bronwen* did not receive its première until 1929. By that time, the first two works had been put on in Vienna and Salzburg, 'which indicates the wide performance that Holbrooke's music received in the first quarter of the century' (Pirie, 642).

Already by the end of the First World War, however, there were signs that Holbrooke's reputation was beginning to wane. There were still occasional BBC broadcasts of his works, as well as chamber concerts and performances by provincial orchestras; but it was clear that musical tastes had moved on. His chances of performance were not helped by the fact that 'Many of his works are scored for a very large orchestra and are of long duration—for a composer of less than first rank this makes a formidable barrier' (Pirie, 642). Although he attempted to write foxtrots, and was associated with the dance band music of the 1920s, he made little impression. Holbrooke was handicapped, from the late 1920s, by profound deafness.

A vigorous and articulate advocate of British music, Holbrooke included not only his own works but the music of many others in the chamber music concerts he organized (1903–35). His book *Contemporary British Composers* was published in 1925. As late as 1946, the year of his benefactor's death, the London Symphony Orchestra played his works at two concerts in the Kingsway Hall, London.

Holbrooke's reputation is that of a composer of large, outdated works in a sub-Wagnerian idiom; not just overblown, but musically uninspired. 'His enormous oeuvre is very uneven, and his music is sometimes clumsy and tasteless' (Pirie, 642). Yet the *New Grove* article goes on to add that 'there is much that is lively and original, and his

scoring was always vivid' (ibid.). Indeed, although the music dramas are large-scale, the effects and imagination at work are often fresh and challenging. In addition, many of the orchestral pieces are quite short and are scored for orchestras of standard proportions. The music is always tonal, and in the chamber music (of which there are two sextets, six string quartets, three violin sonatas, and much else) a distinctly French exoticism, intriguingly tangled with music-hall vulgarity and vigour, is to the fore. Works which are still praised include his second clarinet quintet, the sextet for piano and wind op. 33a, and the piano quintet op. 44. Holbrooke also wrote eight symphonies, although a number of the later scores seem to be lost. The material for the early orchestral tone-poems is accessible, and during the 1990s several commercial recordings were made. A number of tone-poems were inspired by the prose and poetry of Edgar Allan Poe, including *The Raven*.

Holbrooke died at his home, 55 Alexandra Road, St John's Wood, London, on 5 August 1958, survived by his wife. The bassoonist Gwydion Brooke (*b.* 1912) was his son. Although his reputation is clearly ripe for reassessment, the judgement of Holbrooke's *Times* obituarist is unlikely to be wide of the mark: 'Holbrooke's was an exuberant, versatile talent, and his output, particularly of chamber music, was large. Though widely performed, his music has never become widely familiar.'

ROBERT BARNETT

Sources G. Lowe, *Josef Holbrooke and his work* (1920) · J. Holbrooke: *various appreciations by many authors* (1937) · R. Barnett, *Joseph Charles Holbrooke: an annotated list of his works* (1999) · P. J. Pirie, 'Holbrooke, Joseph', *New Grove* · *The Times* (7 Aug 1958) · L. Foreman, ed., *From Parry to Britten: British music in letters, 1900–1945*, pbk edn (1987) · W. Waterhouse, 'Brooke, Gwydion', *New Grove* · *WWW* · *CGPLA Eng. & Wales* (1958) · Barber Institute of Fine Arts, Birmingham, Bantock letters archive · J. Holbrooke, pamphlet, BBC WAC · d. cert.
Archives CUL, corresp. | Barber Institute of Fine Arts, Birmingham, letters to Granville Bantock · University of Melbourne, Grainger Museum, letters to Percy Grainger |SOUND BL NSA, performance recordings
Likenesses H. Lambert, photogravure, *c.*1922, NPG · photograph, *c.*1953, University of Melbourne, Grainger Museum · photograph, repro. in *The Times*
Wealth at death £472 4s. 4d.: probate, 11 Sept 1958, *CGPLA Eng. & Wales*

Holburne, Francis (1704–1771), naval officer, was the second son of Sir James Holburne, first baronet, of Menstrie, Edinburghshire. He entered the navy in 1720 as a volunteer in the *St Albans*, and passed his examination on 28 January 1726; he was promoted lieutenant on 12 December 1727 and captain on 14 July 1739. In 1740 he commanded the frigate *Dolphin* in the channel and North Sea. In 1745–6 he commanded the *Argyle* in the West Indies, and in December 1747 he was appointed to the *Kent* as Rear-Admiral Edward Hawke's flag-captain in the channel and the Bay of Biscay. In September 1748 he exchanged into the *Bristol*, but was almost immediately afterwards moved into the *Tavistock* (50 guns), a worn-out ship, in which he was sent to the Leeward Islands as commodore and commander-in-chief. His principal work was diplomatic rather than naval. By the terms of the treaty of 1684 Tobago was neutralized; but early in 1749 it came to

Holburne's knowledge that M. De Caylus, the governor of Martinique, had established a fortified post there. As Holburne's squadron consisted of one rotten ship of 50 guns and two equally rotten 20 gun frigates, it was impossible for him to prevent this by force. He knew that De Caylus, who was a naval officer, was aware of this; but upon Holburne's remonstrances the fortifications were dismantled and the garrison withdrawn. Holburne returned to England in 1752. On 5 February 1755 he was promoted rear-admiral of the blue, and in the following May, with his flag in the *Terrible*, he sailed with a strong squadron to reinforce Vice-Admiral Edward Boscawen, whom he met off Louisbourg on 21 June, and with whom he returned to England in November. In 1756, with his flag still in the *Terrible*, he commanded in the third post in the fleet under Hawke or Boscawen off Brest and in the Bay of Biscay, and in the following January he sat as a member of the court martial on Admiral John Byng. On 24 February 1757 Holburne was promoted vice-admiral of the blue and on 7 May, after many delays, he sailed from Cork with a fleet of ships of war and transports intended for the reduction of Louisbourg, which had been restored to the French by the treaty of Aix-la-Chapelle. It was not, however, until 9 July that the expedition reached Halifax, Nova Scotia. By this date the French had taken advantage of the delay to strengthen the garrison and to collect a numerous fleet. Holburne, in consultation with the general, the earl of Loudoun, decided that nothing could be done without more force. As the season wore on, he determined to parade his fleet before Louisbourg, possibly in the hope that the French would accept his challenge. However, the French fleet, its crews weakened by disease, remained in port. While Holburne waited on the coast his fleet was caught on the night of 24 September by a violent storm, which drove some of the ships on shore, and wholly or in part dismasted almost all. After such refit as was possible Holburne returned to England, where he arrived in the beginning of December. A few days later he was appointed to the command in chief at 'that villainous' Portsmouth (Rodger, 32) a charge which he held either continuously or more probably with a break for the very unusual term of eight years, the latter part of the time being enlivened by a curious inquiry into an alleged plot in November 1764 to set fire to all the dockyards. The several commanders-in-chief and resident commissioners were ordered to investigate the matter; but this was done with the utmost secrecy, and the report cannot now be found.

During the Seven Years' War Holburne continued to have good relations with Admiral Hawke. These persisted well into Hawke's term as first lord of the Admiralty (1766–71). Boscawen's earlier view of Holburne was less favourable: 'I don't like him, nor ever did' (Mackay, 138); and in 1758 Lord Anson thought him subversive, an opinion that probably drew something from Holburne's Scottish origins and his failure to adopt English 'manners' as befitted a naval officer. On 5 August 1767 Holburne attained the rank of admiral of the blue, and on 28 October 1770 admiral of the white; about the same time he was appointed rear-admiral of Great Britain. He was one of the lords of the Admiralty from February 1770 to January 1771, when he accepted the post of governor of Greenwich Hospital. He died at the hospital on 15 July 1771.

Holburne had married at Barbados the widow of Edward Lascelles, collector of customs for the island; they had one son, Francis, who in 1772 succeeded to the baronetcy on the death of his cousin, Sir Alexander, third baronet. J. K. LAUGHTON, *rev.* RUDDOCK MACKAY

Sources R. F. Mackay, *Admiral Hawke* (1965) · N. A. M. Rodger, *The wooden world: an anatomy of the Georgian navy* (1986) · W. L. Clowes, *The Royal Navy: a history from the earliest times to the present*, 7 vols. (1897–1903) · C. C. Lloyd, ed., *The naval miscellany*, 4, Navy RS, 92 (1952)
Archives BL, letters · NMM, corresp. and letter-books · PRO, Adm MSS | NA Scot., corresp. with Sir John Clerk · priv. coll., letters to James Oswald
Likenesses J. Reynolds, oils, 1756–7, NMM

Holcombe, Henry (*fl.* 1707–1748), composer, was, according to Charles Burney, a chorister at Salisbury (not Shrewsbury, as the *Dictionary of National Biography* stated). As a youth he joined the Anglo-Italian opera at Drury Lane, billed as 'the boy' in Purcell's masque *Timon* (1 January 1707) and in the masque attributed to the same composer *The Tempest, or, The Inchanted Island* (5 March 1706). Under his own name he sang between the acts of *The Recruiting Officer* at Dorset Gardens (24 October and 1 November 1706), and of *Rosamond* (4 March 1707) at Drury Lane. He sang at the Queen's Theatre in the 1709–10 season, but appeared no more on the stage until 26 February 1729 when he sang six songs at his own benefit concert at Drury Lane. His voice broken, and unable to compete with the vogue for Italian singers, Holcombe became a successful teacher of singing and the harpsichord. He published two collections of songs, *The Musical Medley* and *The Garland*, and *Six Solos for Violin*, all in 1745. Two of his songs, 'Happy Hour' and 'Arno's Vale', were very popular in their day. He was one of the original subscribers to the Society of Musicians in 1739, and was living in Russell Street, Covent Garden, in 1748. He has been tentatively identified with the Henry Holcombe whose wife, Martha, was buried on 16 August 1752 at St Paul's, Covent Garden, in which case he was living at that date. If this identification is correct, it seems further likely that his wife was Martha Haynes, who married Henry Holcomb on 12 May 1716 at St Giles Cripplegate. R. F. SHARP, *rev.* K. D. REYNOLDS

Sources Highfill, Burnim & Langhans, *BDA* · M. Sands, 'Holcombe, Henry', *New Grove* · 'Holcombe, Henry', Grove, *Dict. mus.* (1927) · Burney, *Hist. mus.* · IGI

Holcot, Robert (*c.*1290–1349), Dominican friar and theologian, was born about 1290, on the evidence of his later career. His surname, and his later association with the Dominican priory at Northampton, suggest he was born in or near the village of Holcot in Northamptonshire. He probably joined the Dominicans in Northampton, before moving to Oxford, where he remained from *c.*1326 to *c.*1334, attending the Dominican school there. In March 1332 he was granted licence to hear confession in the diocese of Lincoln, which included Oxford. He held the Dominican chair of theology in Oxford for a year, ending probably in early 1334—his final sermon for this period refers to the riots between northern and southern students, but not to the subsequent migration to Stamford in spring 1334. Holcot looked back on his regency as arduous, describing problems that included strong competition for the post and difficulties with his lecture room; for some unknown reason he had to lecture in hired rooms, rather than at Blackfriars.

From Oxford, Holcot was sent to Cambridge and held a second regency c.1334–c.1336. During this time he wrote his famous and popular *Commentary on Wisdom*, which represents a two-year lecture course. At some period after this Holcot was one of the scholars who worked as assistants to the book-collecting bishop of Durham, Richard Bury. Holcot may have had some involvement in the production of the *Philobiblon*, a book written in Bury's name. This stage in his life was probably over before the next definite date for Holcot, who during 1342 was granted licence to hear confessions in the diocese of Salisbury. Licences also show that from 10 February 1343 until 21 October 1348, he was at Northampton. He died at Northampton in 1349, reputedly of plague, and was buried there, at the church of Northampton Blackfriars. A will made as late as 1536 left vestments and plate to the church and asked that the deceased, Mary Middleton, should be buried next to Holcot.

Robert Holcot was a prolific scholar who produced a large number and range of works, mainly but not exclusively theological. Many of these were very popular and survive not only in manuscript, but also in printed editions. Holcot is interesting in a number of ways beyond his undoubted role as a theologian. He was a humanist and a moralist, with a lively sense of humour described as the strongest of any medieval moralist by Beryl Smalley, who considered him the most celebrated and the most diversely gifted of all the friars of her famous 'classicizing group'—those English friars dedicated to integrating classical tales and knowledge into their religious works, in order to increase the interest and appeal for the reader or listener. The notable success of works of this type indicates the shrewdness of their authors. However, their decision to use this method was no cynical marketing ploy, but rather a reflection of these writers' own personal fascination with, and delight in, such classical culture as they were able to obtain access to. Holcot's enjoyment of, and enthusiasm for, such classical material shows clearly in his writings. In his case, classical lore and theological learning were allied to vivid descriptions of the political and social issues of his day: the student riots of the 1330s, the deposition of Edward II, the Scottish wars, and many other topical subjects are referred to in his theological works.

The diversity of Holcot's interests is further shown by the fact that he also played a part in the history of science, and in the development of English calculation, through his *Tractatus de stellis*, a text on astronomy, geography, and astrology which is in effect a commentary on Aristotle's *De coelo*.

Holcot was an important figure in the development of English scholasticism which followed upon the work of William Ockham. Ockham and Thomas Aquinas were his two chief mentors, although he was capable of disagreeing with both, as he did, for instance, on the nature of the Trinity. In the earlier part of the twentieth century Holcot was thought to be an intellectual sceptic, but later close study of his works by Fritz Hoffman and others has suggested that the reverse is true.

In his *Commentary on 'Sentences'*, Holcot famously disagreed with Ockham on the nature of logic, concluding that there must be two systems of logic: Aristotelian logic, appropriate to the natural order; and a logic of faith, differing in its rules from Aristotle and more appropriate to the supernatural order. Later in his career he changed his views, and his *quodlibeta* show a return to the belief that Aristotelian logic was universally applicable. Holcot's theological views attracted attention both during his lifetime and long afterwards. He was one of the Pelagians attacked in Thomas Bradwardine's defence of predestination; throughout his career Holcot argued that each individual had the free will to make confession of his or her sins, and subsequently receive God's grace. His views on predestination were studied by a number of medieval scholars, and were still discussed in works as late as those of the Reformation theologian Johann Eck.

Holcot's works typically show a great range and number of quotations in illustration of his themes. The sources he used were astonishingly numerous and varied, ranging from the common *exempla* collections of the period to the rarer of Seneca's letters and the *Noctes Atticae* of Aulus Gellius, said to be a scarce book in England. This is particularly true in his *Commentary on Wisdom*. The earliest surviving manuscript, Oxford, Balliol College, MS 27, dates to the middle of the fourteenth century or earlier, and if not an actual autograph copy is close to it. Many editions were later printed, at least five before the end of the fifteenth century.

Holcot's *Commentary on Wisdom* was one of the most popular commentaries of the late middle ages. It made his name famous throughout medieval Europe, and surviving catalogues show that every well-stocked library came to have a copy. It is a vast work, and although it follows most of the conventions of its genre, in many ways it resembles one of the pastoral handbooks popularized in the late thirteenth century. It could certainly have functioned as such: indeed it seems probable that this quality was one of the main reasons why it was such an outstanding and lasting success. Alongside its many chapters on youth, education, and the family, lie lengthy discussions of married life, society, and its structure, theories on the republic, the duties of kings and judges, and many other topics. A late fourteenth-century *explicit* attributes its success to the fact that it addresses and informs rulers. This would have appealed in an age of growing interest in political science, and was certainly a factor in the success of the *Communiloquium* of John of Wales. The contents of this earlier pastoral handbook have much in common with Holcot's the Wisdom of Solomon commentary: Holcot owed John of Wales a substantial debt, which he himself only partly acknowledged.

While the *Commentary on Wisdom* was probably Holcot's most famous work, he wrote many others. At least ten survive today, and careful study has established the order in which some of them were written. This makes it possible to trace the development of Holcot's views on theology, politics, and logic, to an extent that was not previously possible.

One of his earliest works must have been his *Quaestiones super libros Sententiarum*, completed before 1332, when Holcot took up his Oxford regency. More than thirty complete manuscripts survive, and several partial manuscripts. The text was studied by many medieval scholars, and was printed three times (Lyons 1497, 1505, 1518). The Parisian master Jacques Almain wrote a treatise upon it.

Another early work was the *Commentary on the Twelve Lesser Prophets*. Only four manuscripts of this survive, and it is in a very rough and unfinished form. It tells stories about Oxford that suggest it was written there, and it refers to Holcot's own *Quaestiones super libros Sententiarum*. It probably dates to Holcot's Oxford regency in 1333–4, immediately before the Wisdom of Solomon commentary of 1334–6. The latter was followed not long afterwards by the *Moralitates*, which survives in many manuscripts, and also three printed editions (Venice 1505, Paris 1510, Basel 1586). The *Moralitates* must have been completed before 1342, as it was a major source for the famous *Gesta Romanorum*, a collection of classical tales whose earliest manuscript dates to this year.

Holcot's *Commentary on Ecclesiasticus*, although incomplete, was also popular and was printed at least six times (including Venice 1509). It appears to have formed part of a lecture course, and its nature, and the sources used, which include Pierre Auriol's *Compendium litteralis* and works by Nicholas de Lyre, indicate that it belongs to the last few years of his life, the late 1340s, when he was teaching at Blackfriars in Northampton. This supports the medieval tradition that Holcot was still working on it when he fell victim to plague in 1349.

Holcot's other published works were long believed to include a commentary on Proverbs (Paris 1510), now attributed to the Dominican Thomas Ringstead, and possibly one on the Song of Songs (Venice 1509). He also left a number of works which were never published and survive in only a very few manuscripts. These include his *Sermons*, a lifetime's collection surviving only in Cambridge, Peterhouse, MS 210, and his *Quodlibeta*, found in a few manuscripts including BL, Royal MS 10 C.vi, fols. 141–174. The sermon collection covers a wide range of subjects, and contains sermons from many stages of his career. It is therefore an important source for those wishing to trace the development of Holcot's views. The *quodlibeta* are an essential source for their author's late conversion to the general applicability of Aristotelian logic.

Other lesser works by Holcot include a fragmentary commentary on Ecclesiastes (BL, Royal MS 2 D.iv, fols. 90–159); the *Principium* for an unfinished lecture series on St Matthew (probably dating from February 1334—see BL, Royal MS 10 C.vi, fol. 136vb), and a preaching aid, the *Convertimini*, dated by Smalley to the period 1337–41.

JENNY SWANSON

Sources B. Smalley, 'Robert Holcot O.P.', *Archivum Fratrum Praedicatorum*, 26 (1956), 5–97 · B. Smalley, *English friars and antiquity in the early fourteenth century* (1960) · A. B. Emden, 'Dominican confessors and preachers licensed by medieval English bishops', *Archivum Fratrum Praedicatorum*, 32 (1962), 180–210 · F. Stegmüller, ed., *Repertorium biblicum medii aevi*, 3–6 (Madrid, 1951–8), nos. 7411–25 · F. Hoffman, *Die theologische Methode des Oxforder Dominikanerlehrers Robert Holcot* (1971) · *Exploring the boundaries of reason: three questions on the nature of God by Robert Holcot*, ed. H. G. Gelber, Pontifical Institute of Mediaeval Studies: Texts and Studies, 62 (1983) · R. E. Gillespie, 'Robert Holcot's *Quodlibeta*', *Traditio*, 27 (1971) · J. C. Wey, 'The *Sermo finalis* of Robert Holcot', *Mediaeval Studies*, 11 (1949), 219–24 · Emden, *Oxf.*

Archives Balliol Oxf., MS 27 · BL, Royal MS 2 D.iv, fols. 90–159 · BL, Royal MS 10 C.vi, fols. 141–174 · BL, Royal MS 10 C.vi, fol. 136vb · Peterhouse, Cambridge, MS 210

Holcroft, Fanny Margaretta (*bap.* 1785, *d.* 1844). *See under* Holcroft, Thomas (1745–1809).

Holcroft, Francis (1628/9?–1692), clergyman and ejected minister, was a younger son of Sir Henry Holcroft (*c.*1580–1650), of Green Street, East Ham, Essex, and his wife, Lettice, daughter of Francis Aungier, first Baron Aungier of Longford in Ireland. He was admitted as a pensioner at Clare College, Cambridge, on 24 June 1647, and had as his 'chamber-fellow' John Tillotson, later archbishop of Canterbury. Holcroft graduated BA in 1650, became a fellow in 1651, and proceeded MA in 1654. While at Cambridge he embraced puritan principles, and became a communicant with the congregation of Jonathan Jephcot, vicar of St Mary, Swaffham Prior, acting for a time as an unpaid minister at Littlington, Cambridgeshire. On 8 January 1656 he accepted the living of Bassingbourn, and also in that year joined the voluntary Cambridgeshire association of ministers. On 10 December 1657 he was appointed an assistant to commission for the ministry in the counties of Cambridge and Huntingdon.

In 1660 Holcroft was ejected from both his fellowship and his living. He stayed in London for a time and preached at Croydon with Thomas Taylor, the former pastor at Bury St Edmunds. In 1663 it was reported that he 'lyes at Widdow Hawkes att Barly in Harfordshire who hath meetings of 300 at a time … meets with many hundreds at Cambridge' (*Calamy rev.*, 271). Holcroft formed a gathered church on congregational principles; the wide geographical spread of his people led, after a meeting at Eversden, to the recruitment as elders of Joseph Oddy and two others. A government agent reported that these rode 'by turns … into Hertfordshire, Cambridgeshire and Bedfordshire to gather a concourse of people to their meetings' (Davids, 621).

In August 1663 Holcroft was imprisoned in Cambridge gaol for illegal preaching, and was said to have been sentenced 'either to take the oath of abjuration of the kingdom, never to return, or be hanged … if theyl transport him and sell him for a slave it will be worse than death'

(*Heywood ... Autobiography*, 3.83). In August 1664 he petitioned for a pardon, protesting that he had taken the oaths of allegiance and supremacy, and asked to be able to travel overseas for a time. A reprieve was granted following the intervention of the earl of Anglesey, but travel plans were disrupted first by plague, and then by war with France, and he was still in prison in July 1666. In 1669 Holcroft was reported as preaching at the city of Cambridge, in Histon, Over, Stoke-cum-Quy, and Haddenham (all in Cambridgeshire), and also at Hugglescote, Leicestershire. The episcopal returns report meetings of about a hundred in four of these parishes. On 8 May he was licensed to teach as a congregationalist in Bridge Street, Cambridge, and he was released on 17 May, but the licence did not discourage the authorities from rearresting him on 6 April the following year. Renewed imprisonment resulted in insolvency and committal to the Fleet prison, where it was reported that he frequently preached to large crowds of people. He was helped through these difficulties, Edmund Calamy reports, by his old room-mate, John Tillotson.

Holcroft's troubles, however, continued. He appears to have moved to Chesterton, Cambridgeshire, for on 1 September 1676 he was presented for absence from church for a month as of that place. Also in that year he and Oddy debated at Triplow with the Quaker Samuel Cater. In a bad-tempered series of exchanges, Holcroft described Cater's view that every man is enlightened by Christ as 'cursed idolatry' and Cater said Holcroft was 'in knowledge more brutish than a beast'; the two congregationalists are said to have 'hastened away with railing words' (Whiting, 123). Holcroft is known to have preached in Hitchin on 24 May 1678. It is not known how long he actually spent in Cambridge gaol—the few months following the indulgence are the only certain extended period of freedom during the years from 1662 to 1680. Whether his preaching activities in other periods stemmed from the sympathies of his gaoler or from official discharges is unclear. In his *A Word from the Watch Tower*, dated from Cambridge Castle, 27 December 1679, he states that he had been there for seven years. The work was directed to 'the faithful brethren in Christ in London'; this reflected his connection with the congregational churches whose leaders were John Owen and John Griffith.

On 7 October 1680 at the quarter sessions, Holcroft 'late of Chesterton' was imprisoned for having failed to appear in church for a month; recently 'in the mansion house of one Robert Stainsmore, in Chesterton aforesaid' he had been 'voluntarily present at an unlawfull assembly' (*The Case of many Protestants in the County of Cambridge*). His efforts were regarded with suspicion on the respectable wing of dissent, and not only because of his opposition to communion with members of the established church. Edward Pearse wrote to Richard Baxter on 23 December 1687 complaining that at Holcroft's house 'Anabaptists have exercised there, and young raw fellows have exercised upon scripture their own conceits' (Keeble and Nuttall, 2.293). Holcroft himself seems to have come to regret his own liberalism, for after 1689 he became prone to deep depression 'promoted by grief for the headiness of some

of his people, who turned preachers, or encouraged such as did so' (Calamy, *Abridgement*, 2.86); reference was later made to 'God's dark and severe dispensation towards him in his latter days' (Milway, 21). According to Thomas Milway's *A Funeral Sermon* (1692), Holcroft died at Triplow, Cambridgeshire, on 6 January 1692 aged sixty-three, and was buried in the dissenters' graveyard at Oakington, although his memorial there gives his age at death as fifty-nine.

STEPHEN WRIGHT

Sources Calamy rev. • E. Calamy, ed., *An abridgement of Mr. Baxter's history of his life and times, with an account of the ministers, &c., who were ejected after the Restoration of King Charles II*, 2nd edn, 2 vols. (1713) • W. Urwick, *Nonconformity in Hertfordshire* (1884) • C. Whiting, *Studies in English puritanism* (1931) • A. Gordon, ed., *Freedom after ejection: a review (1690–1692) of presbyterian and congregational nonconformity in England and Wales* (1917) • *Calendar of the correspondence of Richard Baxter*, ed. N. H. Keeble and G. F. Nuttall, 2 vols. (1991) • G. Nuttall, *Visible saints: the congregational way, 1640–1660* (1957) • T. Milway, *Funeral sermon preached upon the death of the reverend and godly divine, Mr Francis Holcroft* (1692) • J. Rylands, *On the families of Holcroft* (1877) • *The case of many protestants in the county of Cambridge* (1680) • [F. Holcroft], *A word from the watch tower by a faithful embassador in bonds for the gospel divers years* (1680) • *The Rev. Oliver Heywood ... his autobiography, diaries, anecdote and event books*, ed. J. H. Turner, 3 (1883) • T. W. Davids, *Annals of evangelical nonconformity in Essex* (1863)

Holcroft, Thomas (1745–1809), writer, was born in Orange Court, Leicester Fields, London, on 10 December 1745, the son of Thomas Holcroft (d. 1797), a shoemaker, and his wife, Sarah, an occasional costermonger. He was baptized at St Martin-in-the-Fields on 25 December. Detailed knowledge of Holcroft's life comes mainly from his autobiography. The elder Thomas Holcroft was probably from Martin Mere near Stockport and was the son of a 'white cooper' or maker of pails and tubs for domestic and dairy use. He kept a shoemaker's shop in Orange Court specializing in the unique boots worn by sedan-chair carriers, and later hired out horses.

Early years When the family encountered financial difficulties they settled in Berkshire, beyond Ascot Heath. Here Holcroft's father taught him to read; he went through eleven chapters of the Old Testament a day and read chapbooks such as *Parismus and Parismenes* and *The Seven Champions of Christendom*. Holcroft's parents then became itinerant pedlars throughout East Anglia and the midlands. Holcroft later wrote of his father, 'I believe few men in the kingdom had in the course of their lives been the hucksters of so many small wares; or more enterprising dealers in articles of a half-penny value' (Holcroft, 1.26). They kept a run-down house at Rugeley, Staffordshire, and attended markets and fairs. The young Holcroft was put to many tasks to augment the family income, and at times the family had to sleep rough, permanently impairing Holcroft's health. Holcroft's father was a sober man and proud of his son's intellectual superiority to other boys, but he had a short temper and often beat Thomas for minor faults.

For a while Holcroft was apprenticed to a stocking weaver at Nottingham, but having a passion for horses he became a stable boy at Newmarket in 1757 and worked for various grooms of noblemen horse-breeders over two and

Thomas Holcroft (1745–1809), by John Opie, c.1804

a half years. Here he lived relatively well, though he was occasionally thrown by horses and was called upon to defend himself with his fists against bullying. At Newmarket he continued his informal education, learning arithmetic and singing from occasional teachers and reading whatever he could find, including ballads and broadsheets pasted on alehouse and cottage walls. His father's friend gave him *The Spectator* and *Gulliver's Travels*; he loved the latter, and tales of the marvellous, though he disbelieved in spirits and ghosts. He also enjoyed pious books such as *The Whole Duty of Man* and Horneck's *Crucified Jesus*, and he ranked Bunyan 'among the most divine authors I had ever read' (Holcroft, 1.93). He caught betting fever at Newmarket, and was chagrined to find that boys he thought intellectually inferior were cleverer at placing wagers. Unpopular with most of his workmates, he eventually left Newmarket to work at his father's cobbling stall in South Audley Street, London, continuing to spend any spare money on books. When he was nineteen he accompanied his father to Liverpool and taught reading at a school before returning to London and the cobbling trade.

In 1765 Holcroft married and had a daughter, Ann, but nothing more is known of this union, and his wife appears to have died prematurely. He had some essays published in the *Whitehall Evening Post*, but an attempt to start a school in the country failed. He then entered the household of Granville Sharpe as part servant, part secretary, but was dismissed for persistently attending a spouting club for amateur dramatic recitation. Holcroft considered joining the East India Company army, but instead turned to the theatre; he played small parts with Samuel Foote's

Haymarket Theatre in summer 1770 and then, with Charles Macklin's introduction, became a prompter and bit-part actor at William Dawson's Capel Street Theatre in Dublin. He quarrelled with Dawson and joined Henry Mossop's Smock Alley company briefly, then a company at Leeds, and then Roger Kemble's company at Hereford. After another quarrel he joined Samuel Stanton's company at Birmingham. In 1774 he married Matilda Tipler from Nottingham; in the autumn of that year the couple joined Booth's company at Carlisle, where Holcroft remained for a year and a half. A son, William, was born in 1773 and a daughter, Sophy, at Cockermouth in 1775; their mother died soon afterwards, apparently from complications of childbirth. Aiming to better himself in London, Holcroft, like many others, wrote to David Garrick, stating that he specialized in low comedy and old men, knew music well, had some French, and could fence; he enclosed a poem, 'Hope, or, The Delusion', but received no response. He met the composer William Shield and knew Muzio Clementi, the pianist and composer; he sang in concerts and continued to play the violin. He carried on acting in the provinces, from Edinburgh to Canterbury, and, conscious of his haphazard education, he read such books as Lowth's grammar and Pope's translation of Homer, preferring moral to descriptive and sentimental poets. Wherever he was, he cultivated men of enquiring mind and literary bent, such as the antiquary and promoter of vegetarianism Joseph Ritson at Stockton upon Tees.

Stage career and early writings Holcroft still longed for a career in London, however, and went there in 1777. Soon afterwards, on 14 June 1778, he married for the third time. With his new wife, Dinah Robinson, he had a fourth child, Fanny [*see below*], who later became a novelist, playwright, and translator. He and his wife kept a house in Southampton Buildings and took lodgers to make ends meet. While with Booth he had written dramatic sketches, and he now sent an afterpiece, 'The Crisis, or, Love and Fear', to the wife of R. B. Sheridan, with a long list of the roles he played and his other theatrical skills. He landed a place in the Drury Lane company at 20s. a week, and began in small singing parts in January 1777. 'The Crisis', with music by Shield, lasted only one night, 1 May 1778, but Sheridan raised his wage. In summer 1778 Holcroft joined W. W. Dimond's company at Canterbury for the London off-season, during which he acquired many new parts and staged his comedy 'Rosamond, or, The Dutiful Daughter'. Back at Drury Lane in the autumn, still with only minor parts, he tried any kind of writing possible to earn more money. A small volume of poems entitled *Elegies* (1777) received little attention. He completed two afterpieces, 'The Shepherdess of the Alps' and 'The Maid of the Vale' (a translation of Goldoni's opera *La buona figliuola*, then being performed in London). His series of essays entitled 'The philosopher' and a serial novella, *Manthorn, the Enthusiast*, were published in the *Town and Country Magazine* (1777–8, 1778–9). He also wrote some pieces for Thomas King, manager of Sadler's Wells Theatre, and songs with music by Shield for performance at the Vauxhall pleasure gardens, some of which achieved popularity. His column entitled 'The actor', which dealt with theatrical issues, ran in the *Westminster Magazine*. He fictionalized his experiences as a strolling player, including his aspirations for upward mobility, in an epistolary picaresque novel, *Alwyn, or, The Gentleman Comedian* (1780), that followed in the tradition of Le Sage, Fielding, and Smollett. Holcroft also wrote two books about the infamous Gordon riots of 1780, more as a journalist for money than out of any political leanings: *A Plain and Succinct Narrative* was described in the *Town and Country Magazine* as 'one of the best productions of the kind' in pamphlet form (vol. 12, July 1780, 351), and was followed the next year by Holcroft's account of Gordon's trial. Holcroft financially helped his mother and father, now living in or near Bath, and continued to do so for many years. He took minor roles at Drury Lane through the season of 1781–2 and parts in provincial companies at Portsmouth, Nottingham, and elsewhere in the summers. His comedy *Duplicity*, whose plot resembles the story of Edward Moore's popular tragedy *The Gamester*, was staged at Covent Garden on 13 October 1781 and was performed six more times, but was postponed on several occasions because of a leading actor's illness.

Although Holcroft felt the play was not allowed an appropriate run, this modest success encouraged him. He also widened his artistic and intellectual circle with friends such as Richard Fulke Greville and William Nicholson. Still aiming to rise socially and professionally, he wrote to Lord Shelburne seeking a place in the British embassy at Paris and identifying himself as a well-wisher to the government. In 1783 he went to Paris, as a correspondent for a newspaper, the *Morning Herald*, at a guinea and a half a week, a little more than he had been getting as an actor. The printer John Rivington engaged him to scout for French publications suitable for translating; some of these translations Holcroft later made himself, though the extent of his published translation has been questioned. At Paris he wrote a tragedy, 'Ellen, or, The Fatal Cave', and met the children's writer Arnaud Berquin, some literary aristocrats including the marquis de Dampierre, later a general in the French revolutionary army, and L. S. Mercier and Nicholas de Bonneville, who became his close friends. He had left another play, 'The Noble Peasant' (music by Shield), with Colman, manager of the Haymarket summer season theatre, and it had a successful run of ten performances in 1784. Rivington's payments were irregular, and Holcroft returned to London, where he edited and wrote much of the *Wit's Magazine* in 1783–4. He published *Tales of the Castle*, translated from the popular French writer Mme de Genlis, who produced works in the genre usually called the 'novel of education'. Beaumarchais's *Le mariage de Figaro* was the rage in Paris, and Holcroft and Bonneville transcribed it from performances there in autumn 1784; Holcroft's adaptation as *Follies of a Day* (Covent Garden, 14 December) was performed twenty-eight times in the season and brought him £600 plus sale of the copyright. It was performed during every season through the 1790s and into the next century. Another comic opera, *The Choleric Fathers* (Covent Garden,

10 November 1785), had seven performances and brought him £140; *Seduction: a Comedy* (Drury Lane, 12 March 1787) had nine performances and made him £250. By now critics were distinguishing Holcroft's work from others' for its somewhat more careful construction and more serious moral and social criticism. He was also making significant income from translation, receiving £1200 for the works of the king of Prussia.

Turn to reformist politics By now, too, Holcroft's political views had changed, and he acquired a considerable library in preparation for a 'history of *bad* governments' (Holcroft, 1.281), based on the career of Frederick II of Prussia and attacking the effects of war and despotism. With friends such as Shield, Nicholson, and Samson Perry, the journalist and editor, Holcroft attended clubs debating both broad philosophical questions and issues of the day. In 1786 he met William Godwin, who later termed Holcroft one of his 'four principal oral instructors, to whom I feel my mind indebted for improvement' (Kegan Paul, 1.17). By 1788 they were close friends, meeting almost daily. Both followed the materialist argument that society and the individual are products of the political and economic order, and they developed a philosophical anarchism that advocated the elimination of government with the aim of freeing humanity to exercise its innate benevolence and sense of justice. Godwin, Holcroft, and their friends advocated open discussion and press freedom to effect the spread of truth that would emancipate all people. As a self-conscious vanguard who believed they had, through superior talents, discipline, and study, escaped indoctrination by the prevailing and unjust order, they practised an idealized, philosophical, and classical republican moderation, abstemiousness, and public virtue, and aimed in their writings to set an example as public intellectuals, while still making a living. Holcroft's philosophical stoicism was severely tested in 1789, however. His son William committed suicide on a ship at Deal rather than face his father, from whom he had taken some money in a plan to flee to the West Indies. Though supported by Godwin's friendship, Holcroft took more than a year to recover from the loss. His wife died in 1790.

Meanwhile Holcroft had to support himself, and the theatre was his mainstay. A play entitled *The German Hotel* (adapted from Johann Christian Brandes's *Trau, Schau, Wem!*; Covent Garden, 11 November 1790; eleven performances) is usually ascribed to him but was probably by James Marshall (Hogan). In the early 1790s Holcroft did have further theatrical successes. *The School for Arrogance* (based on P. N. Destouches's *Le glorieux*; Covent Garden, 4 February 1791; nine performances) was restaged into the late 1790s. *The Road to Ruin* (Covent Garden, 18 February 1792; thirty-seven performances) was his major hit; it made him £900 from performances plus several hundred from publication, and ran every season into the next century. These plays advanced reformist social criticism in the comic and genially satirical form that was fairly common at the time. One result was an account of Holcroft in the *European Magazine*, representing him as 'an instance of the great effects of persevering fortitude' who had by his own efforts 'rendered himself one among the first of writers in a nation abounding with men whose talents have been cultivated under every advantage' (vol. 22, December 1792, 405).

Sympathizer with the French Revolution Holcroft and his friends, with many others like them throughout Britain and Europe, were electrified by the French Revolution, which in its early stages effected many of the reforms they advocated, and which seemed but the beginning of a process that would bring about an earthly paradise where even disease and death would be eradicated. The French Revolution debate was conducted largely through the press, especially after publication in November 1790 of Edmund Burke's anti-revolutionary *Reflections on the Revolution in France*. Many replies were rushed into print, and Holcroft joined the committee to publish part 1 of Tom Paine's *Rights of Man* early in 1791, when it became clear that most publishers were unwilling to risk it. By autumn 1791 Holcroft was working on his own intervention in the revolution debate, which, characteristically, addressed a wider readership than polemical disputations or philosophical treatises. Holcroft understood that dramatic writing had to be highly conventionalized to suit the repertory theatre company system and the expectations of audiences drawn from all social classes and interests. The novel, though widely disparaged at the time as inartistic, commercialized, and intellectually and morally corrupting, would enable him to reach a large reading public while expressing more radical social criticism than drama could accommodate. As he later put it in his review of Robert Bage's *Man as he is*:

> When we consider the influence that novels have over the manners, sentiments, and passions, of the rising generation,—instead of holding them in the contempt which, as reviewers, we are without exception said to do,— we may esteem them, on the contrary, as forming a very essential branch of literature. (*Monthly Review*, 10, March 1793, 297)

Holcroft's *Anna St Ives* (7 vols., 1792) revises the plot and characters of Richardson's *Clarissa* and *Sir Charles Grandison* for the French Revolution debate. In epistolary form, it also contains numerous extended dialogues expounding republican and pro-revolutionary views, but, as in the romantic comedy that was Holcroft's literary mainstay, the plot enacts reform rather than overthrow of the social order, through replacement of the weak and vicious by the virtuous and public-spirited. The work was well received, and was enjoyed as a lively novel despite the fact that its utopian politics were treated with scepticism or ridicule in some reviews. Holcroft was also engaging directly in political organization. The success of the French revolutionary government in defeating the armies of the European monarchist forces in September 1792 inspired new sympathy for the revolution in Britain, especially among artisans and middle-class people. In October Holcroft began attending meetings of the predominantly middle-class Society for Constitutional Information, which aimed to create an informed and politically conscious public, largely through public discussion and print.

In November he joined the society, but he remained on its more cautious wing. According to Elbridge Colby, editor of Holcroft's memoirs, in two years Holcroft missed only half a dozen of the society's fortnightly meetings and belonged to the joint committee of correspondence and co-operation formed with similar groups, but, 'fearful that partisan sentiment might hurt his literary and dramatic reputation', he avoided a conspicuous role (Holcroft, 2.27n.). At meetings he spoke seldom, counselled caution, and felt that decisions should be made by reasoning rather than majority vote.

Trial for treason and public notoriety In 1793 Godwin published his *Political Justice*, enunciating positions worked out with Holcroft and other friends, and the work caused a sensation, partly because of its comprehensiveness, partly because it transformed the particulars of the French Revolution debate into abstract and general arguments, and partly because of its detached yet energetic style. Holcroft, too, preferred to respond to the debate with general principles and dispassionate argument. Others opted in favour of practical action and counteraction. After the 'British convention' of reformists held in 1793 at Edinburgh and modelled on the French revolutionary conventions of the early 1790s, the government reacted by successfully trying several participants, whom Godwin and Holcroft knew, for treason in the Scottish court. Such so-called English Jacobins as Godwin, Holcroft, and their friends expected a similar move in England. Holcroft continued to write, working on another novel and staging two dramatic pieces, *Love's Frailties, or, Precept Against Practice* (based on O. H. Gemmingen's *Der deutsche Hausvater*; Covent Garden, 5 February 1794) and a prelude, *The Rival Queens, or, Drury-Lane and Covent-Garden* (based on Fielding's *Covent Garden Tragedy*; Covent Garden, 15 September 1794). In *Love's Frailties* the hero, Charles Seymour, attacks fashionable society, insincerity, corruption, social snobbery, and other social vices. Lady Fancourt, as her name indicates, follows fashion, but is converted to the cause of virtue by the example of the direct and sincere Paulina. According to the *Monthly Review* (vol. 13, April 1794, 449), the play's liberal reviews evoked a politically motivated campaign to disrupt performance and the work was withdrawn after six representations. *The Rival Queens* was performed only once. Loyalist organizations were energetically harassing prominent reformists, and the government suspended habeas corpus and banned seditious meetings and publications in May 1794. When a carefully selected group, including Holcroft, the artisan Thomas Hardy, and the scholar John Horne Tooke, was indicted for treason, Holcroft's friends and his father urged him to flee the country, but he had already decided to face the situation directly. He turned himself in and was confined in Newgate. He was mocked in the loyalist press, but friends such as Godwin, Elizabeth Inchbald, and the publisher Robinson visited him in gaol. The prominent lawyer Thomas Erskine defended Holcroft without fee. At the trial Horne Tooke made the government's charges seem ridiculous, and he and Hardy were acquitted. The prosecution then abandoned the case against the others, including Holcroft, and they were released, to widespread public rejoicing. Deprived of his say in court, and smeared after release as an 'acquitted felon' (Holcroft, 2.78), Holcroft vindicated himself and impugned government and loyalist persecution in *A Narrative of Facts, Relating to a Prosecution for High Treason* (1795), in which he included letters to various participants in the trial and the defence he would have read to the jury. He addressed the heightened level of political confrontation in *A Letter to the Right Honourable William Windham* (1795), deploring the intemperate rhetoric and conduct of the government and its supporters.

Holcroft's courage in facing arrest and trial and the high-minded tone and public-spirited arguments of his two pamphlets made him a model for reform-minded intellectuals such as Robert Lovell, Thomas Dermody, and the New York Theatre manager William Dunlap, and he became an adviser to Godwin's ward Thomas Cooper. When the young Tom Wedgwood planned an academy to educate a vanguard for social change, he envisaged Holcroft among the presiding committee. Others shunned Holcroft because of his political associations. He published the first part of a picaresque novel of education, *The Adventures of Hugh Trevor* (3 vols., 1794; second part, 3 vols., 1797), which recounts the vicissitudes of a well-meaning young man in the face of systemic social corruption and in pursuit of a profession that will permit him to retain his moral integrity and ethical values.

Holcroft devoted time to his family; his daughter Sophy had married a Mr Cole, and in 1796 his eldest daughter, Ann, married Colonel Harwood, who too was a member of the Society for Constitutional Information. Holcroft continued to support his father, providing £20 a year, and visiting him occasionally, until his death in 1797. He enjoyed riding, and belonged to a musical club that included Shield, Clementi, Crompton, and Villeneux, but withdrew when membership proved too expensive. He collected books, including a number in languages he could not read, and some pornography. He bought rare musical instruments, invested in a device for copying handwriting, and speculated in buying and selling paintings; these endeavours lost money. His health was impaired, too; he suffered some kind of stroke in 1792, apparently from overwork, and fell from a tree in 1794 during a visit to his daughter Sophy. He may have sought another partner about this time; after Mary Wollstonecraft returned from France and Scandinavia and was abandoned by Gilbert Imlay she received in January 1796 an impassioned proposal that may have come from Holcroft. While contributing regularly to the *Monthly Review* from 1792 to 1796, Holcroft continued to turn out plays, though with little success. *The Deserted Daughter* (Covent Garden, 2 May 1795), based on Richard Cumberland's *The Fashionable Lover*, had twelve performances and was restaged into the late 1790s. Then there was a series of flops, including *The Man of Ten Thousand* (Drury Lane, 23 January 1796, seven performances); *Duplicity* restaged as *The Mask'd Friend* (Covent Garden, 6 May 1796, one performance; 1 June 1797, two performances); *The Force of Ridicule* (Drury Lane, 6 December

1796, one performance); and *Knave or not* (based on Goldoni's *La serva amorosa* and *Il padre di famiglia*; Drury Lane, 25 January 1798, six performances). In the preface to the published version of *Knave or not* Holcroft attributed these failures to political persecution, and in August 1798 a satirical engraving in the magazine *Anti-Jacobin* included Holcroft in a crowd of so-called 'English Jacobins'. Only *He's much to Blame* (adapted from Pont-de-Veyle's *Le complaisant* and Goethe's *Clavigo*; Covent Garden, 13 February 1798), with twenty-one performances, interrupted the series of failures. These continued with *The Inquisitor* (from Unzer's *Diego und Leonore*; Haymarket, 23 June 1798, three performances) and *The Old Cloathsman*, an afterpiece with music by Thomas Attwood (Covent Garden, 2 April 1799, two performances).

Holcroft nevertheless maintained an active social life with intellectual and artistic friends and fellow reformists such as George Dyer and Benjamin Flower. Every second Sunday he dined with Godwin and other friends. He married as his fourth wife Louisa, daughter of his friend L. S. Mercier, on 4 March 1799 but, facing insolvency, had already planned moving to the continent to live more cheaply, to pursue translating work, to deal in paintings, to familiarize his daughters with foreign languages, and to absent himself from England 'till certain prejudices in the public mind, respecting me, should subside' (Holcroft, 2.222). As he wrote to the commissioners for the Income Bill:

> My income has always been the produce of my labour; and that produce has been so reduced, by the animosity of party spirit, that I find myself obliged to sell my effects for the payment of my debts, that I may leave the kingdom till party spirit shall subside.   (ibid., 2.248)

Later years The Holcrofts left England in May 1799 and settled in Hamburg for a year with the Coles, who were in trade there. Holcroft wrote some 'Letters concerning emigration' addressed to the public, but they remained unpublished. He met literary figures such as Klopstock, Voss, Sander, and Stolberg and set up a periodical, the *European Repository*, but it soon failed, and he lost money through dealing in paintings. He then lived in Paris for two years and there visited the likes of the Mountcashells and Mme de Staël, arranging for a friend to translate her recent novel. When *The Times* on 26 January 1802 reported that he was employed by the French secret service, some of the Holcrofts' acquaintance dropped them. They returned to England in October 1802. The experiment of living abroad was a qualified success, and Holcroft's literary career and income revived. He enjoyed a run of success with *Deaf and Dumb* (Drury Lane, 24 February 1801, nine performances) and *A Tale of Mystery* (1802), which Thomas Dibdin claimed was 'the first entertainment acted on the English stage under the description of melodrama' (*Reminiscences*, 1827, 336–7). Holcroft made £1500 from the copyright of *Travels from Hamburg, through Westphalia, Holland, and the Netherlands, to Paris* (2 vols., 1804). It belongs to a form of philosophical travel writing begun by Dr John Moore, Helen Maria Williams, and others, and it capitalizes on the British public's fascination with the political and social condition of the European states amid the prolonged Revolutionary and Napoleonic wars. *Travels* is an essay in social, cultural, and political analysis of the revolutionized European countries, and especially of France and Paris, after more than a decade of internal and international struggle, and insists that, despite a long catalogue of errors and crimes in the name of progress, application of education and reason would effect gradual enlightenment, resolve present conflicts, and ameliorate the human condition. Still trying to establish himself through business, Holcroft, with Mercier, set up a printing house, but it failed. In the theatre he had two more successes with the comedy *Hear both Sides* (1803) and the melodrama *The Lady of the Rock* (1805). He published another novel, *Memoirs of Bryan Perdue* (3 vols., 1805), picaresque in form and partly following Sterne's reflexive style. With its plebeian anti-hero, scenes of low life, and comprehensive range of social criticism and satire it sustains the impulse of the political novel of the 1790s and foreshadows the later 'Newgate novel' and the fiction of Dickens. *Tales in Verse* (1806) attempted to cash in on the emerging vogue for narrative poetry. Neither novel nor poems did anything for Holcroft, and the failure of his play *The Vindictive Man* (Drury Lane, 20 November 1806, two performances) left him and his family in straitened circumstances, according to Charles Lamb (letter to T. Manning, 5 Dec 1806, *Letters of Charles Lamb*). He continued working on a number of plays and other works, but he suffered increasingly from asthma and his health began to deteriorate.

Holcroft began dictating his autobiography, intended:

to excite an ardent emulation in the breasts of the youthful readers; by shewing them how difficulties may be endured, how they may be overcome, and how they may at last contribute, as a school of instruction, to bring forth hidden talent.   (Holcroft, 1.38)

He had a reconciliation with Godwin, from whom he had been estranged since his return to England in 1802. Thomas Holcroft died on 23 March 1809 and was buried in Marylebone greater cemetery. He was survived by his fourth wife.

The Romantic liberal William Hazlitt completed what Holcroft had begun and, using Holcroft's letters, diaries, and other papers, published *Memoirs of the Late Thomas Holcroft* in 1816. This helped found the nineteenth-century genre of working-class autobiography. Republished and annotated several times until 1925, it established Holcroft in liberal literary and political culture as an 'author sprung from the people' (Mitford, vol. 1, chap. 7), exemplifying the liberal ideology of the sovereign subject and public-spirited citizen. As H. N. Brailsford wrote in 1915, 'The true monument to such a man is not his Opera Omnia, but his biography' (quoted in Holcroft, 1.xvi). Apart from the *Memoirs*, Holcroft's 'opera omnia' were forgotten. The renewed interest, from the 1960s on, in social history, especially of the lower classes, brought new attention to the political and cultural context of Holcroft and his works, including particularly his novels and also some of his comedies and melodramas.

Fanny Margaretta Holcroft (*bap.* 1785, *d.* 1844) followed her father in making a career in writing. She was the daughter of Holcroft's third wife, Dinah, and was baptized on 11 June 1785 at St Andrew's, Holborn, London. Fanny Holcroft seems to have been very devoted to her father, and to have received a broad and liberal education in modern languages and the arts; she shared her father's liberal political opinions and assisted him in his literary work. In 1802, on the recommendation of William Godwin, she was engaged by Lady Mountcashell as governess for her daughters—a post previously held by Mary Wollstonecraft—but she was quickly dismissed when *The Times* reported that Thomas Holcroft was a French spy. Fanny Holcroft provided the incidental music for her father's successful melodrama *The Lady of the Rock* (1805). She also provided translations of politically liberal plays by Alfieri, Weisse, Lessing, Calderón, and Moratin for her father's periodical the *Theatrical Recorder* (1805–6). She published *Memoirs of the Life of the Great Condé* (1807), a translation of a biography of the French prince and military leader during the seventeenth-century French civil wars. After her father's death Fanny Holcroft published two novels, *The Wife and the Lover: a Novel* (3 vols., 1813) and *Fortitude and Frailty: a Novel* (4 vols., 1817), dedicated to her father's memory. These adapt his reformist politics to the post-Napoleonic era of emergent liberalism with stories of vicissitudes in private life, recommending personal virtue and social conciliation.

GARY KELLY

Sources 'Account of Mr. Thomas Holcroft', *European Magazine*, 22 (Dec 1792), 403 · Highfill, Burnim & Langhans, *BDA*, vol. 7 · E. Colby, 'A bibliography of Thomas Holcroft', *Bulletin of the New York Public Library*, 26 (1922), 455, 664, 765 · E. Colby, 'Financial accounts of Holcroft's plays', *N&Q*, 146 (1924), 42–5, 60–63 · C. B. Hogan, ed., *The London stage, 1660–1800*, pt 5: *1776–1800* (1968) · T. Holcroft, *The life of Thomas Holcroft*, continued by W. Hazlitt, ed. E. Colby, 2 vols. (1925) · *The letters of Charles Lamb: to which are added those of his sister, Mary Lamb*, ed. E. V. Lucas, 3 vols. (1935) · M. R. Mitford, *Recollections of a literary life*, 3 vols. (1852) · C. Kegan Paul, *William Godwin: his friends and contemporaries*, 2 vols. (1876) · W. St Clair, *The Godwins and the Shelleys* (1990) · *IGI*

Archives Bodl. Oxf., Shelley MSS, corresp. with William and (Mary Jane?) Godwin

Likenesses J. Opie, oils, c.1782, NPG · T. Hodgetts, mezzotint, c.1804 (after J. Opie), BM, NPG · J. Opie, oils, c.1804, NPG [*see illus.*] · J. Condé, stipple, BM, NPG; repro. in *European Magazine*, 403 · G. Dance, pencil drawing, BM · W. Ridley, stipple (after S. Drummond), BM, NPG; repro. in *Monthly Mirror* (1799)

Holden, Charles Henry (1875–1960), architect, was born on 12 May 1875 at Great Lever, Bolton, Lancashire, the youngest of five children of Joseph Holden, draper and milliner, and his wife, Ellen Bolton. His childhood was unsettled by the bankruptcy of his father, and then by the death of his mother in 1883. He went to school in St Helens where his father, trained as a fitter and turner, had found work. In April 1892 Charles Holden was articled to Everard W. Leeson, a Manchester architect, and during his articles he attended Manchester School of Art (1893–4) and Manchester Technical School (1894–6), where he was an outstanding student. These were formative years. He made lasting friendships, especially with the artist Muirhead Bone, and he found inspiration in the writings of Walt

Whitman. Holden's domestic life was always simple, even austere, and he approached his architectural work in an unaesthetic, increasingly impersonal way, anxious to get into it the stuff and strength of the streets. Much of this goes back to Whitman.

With his articles completed, Holden worked for Jonathan Simpson in Bolton from 1896 to 1897. He then went to London, where he worked for about a year for the arts and crafts architect C. R. Ashbee. Ashbee's architectural office in Chelsea was perhaps too aesthetic for him, but he lived at this time in the eighteenth-century house in the East End of London that housed Ashbee's workshops, and which he recalled as 'a rare experience' (RIBA Journal, June 1942, 134). About 1898 Holden began living with Margaret Steadman (1865–1954), daughter of J. C. Macdonald. She had married a Scottish schoolteacher, James Morrison Steadman, in 1888 and they had a son aged by this time about eight. But Steadman was alcoholic and abusive, and she had moved to Liverpool with her son to escape him. They were never divorced, and it seems unlikely that she and Holden were ever legally married. With Holden she enjoyed a long and loving relationship, though they had no children. They lived at first in Norbiton in south London. About 1902 they moved to Codicote in Hertfordshire, where Ashbee's wife, Janet, visited them in 1906 and found 'bananas and brown bread on the table; no hot water; plain living and high thinking and strenuous activity for the betterment of the world' (Ashbee journals, 24 June 1906). Shortly after this they moved a few miles to Harmer Green, just outside the village of Welwyn, where Holden designed their house. Their way of life combined spirituality, ruralism, and social responsibility in a way that is characteristic of Hertfordshire. Holden attended the Quaker meeting-house in Hertford (though born an Anglican), tended a much-loved garden, and commuted daily to London.

Now that he was living with Margaret Macdonald, Holden needed a larger income, and in October 1899 he joined the practice of H. Percy Adams as chief assistant. A brilliant planner with a competitive spirit, Adams specialized in hospital design. He gave his young assistant scope, and a series of buildings justifying this confidence followed in rapid succession, among them Belgrave Hospital for Children, Kennington, London (1899–1901), the British Seamen's Hospital, Constantinople (1901–2), additions to the Incorporated Law Society in Chancery Lane, London (1903–4), and the King Edward VII Sanatorium at Midhurst, Sussex (1903–6). Holden won the competition for the Central Reference Library, Bristol (1903–6), with drawings done in his spare time. Its happy relationship with the cathedral and the adjoining eleventh-century gateway, its dramatically simple rear elevation, and its long freedom from structural defects were remarkable achievements for one so young. In 1907 he entered into partnership with Adams, and works of this time include the British Medical Association at 429 Strand, London (1906–8; now Zimbabwe House), and the Bristol Royal Infirmary (1909–12).

Before and during the First World War, Holden was not committed to any particular style. At the Law Society he was influenced by Alfred Stevens. King's College for Women, Campden Hill (1914–16), shows his love for Wren. Belgrave Hospital, Sutton Valence School, Kent (1910–12), and Midhurst Sanatorium might be personal tributes to Philip Webb and C. R. Ashbee. This was not façadism, but its opposite: generating a building from its plan and function, and then creating appropriate elevations. When he thought of the exterior of buildings, he thought principally of massing, and he simplified his work until it achieved the clearest expression of purpose.

During the First World War, Holden served with the London ambulance column, and then with the directorate of graves registration and enquiries in France. In 1920 he was appointed one of the Imperial War Graves Commission's principal architects for France and Belgium, alongside Reginald Blomfield, Herbert Baker, and Edwin Lutyens. Over the next eight years he and his assistant architects, notably W. C. von Berg and W. H. Cowlishaw, were responsible for the layout and buildings of sixty-seven cemeteries. Holden's cemetery buildings demonstrate his love of Portland stone and the growing simplification of his work: they are on the whole more severe than those of his colleagues, and their reticence is moving.

Between the wars Holden's practice was known as Adams, Holden, and Pearson—Lionel Pearson had become a partner in 1913. 'C. H.', as Holden was known in the office, was a shy, meticulous, kindly employer, and he had the loyalty of his staff. But he stood rather apart from his partners because so much of his time went on two large but very different projects: for the London Underground and for the University of London. By this time his designing was no longer eclectic. For both clients he designed austerely detailed, geometrical masses, in a style which aimed not to be a style.

The work for the London Underground was done in the name of the coherent system of public transport which the chairman, Lord Ashfield, aimed to create out of a tangle of existing networks—and in the name of modernity, the special concern of Ashfield's assistant Frank Pick. In the mid-1920s Holden designed façades for stations on the Northern Line extension from Clapham South to Morden: spare, Portland-stone frames that could be bent, like a screen, to suit different sites. This did not take matters far. But in the 1930s, following a short study tour of transport architecture in northern Europe, he designed complete stations at either end of the Piccadilly Line: flat-roofed structures in brick and concrete, quiet, rational, and distinctly modern. Arnos Grove (1932) is the best-known. He also designed equipment and furniture, working towards a coherent visual identity for the underground. When he was elected a royal designer for industry in 1943, it was for transport equipment. Between these two phases came the headquarters of the London Underground, 55 Broadway (1926–9), also part of Ashfield's campaign for unification. A tall, steel-framed building with the upper storeys stepped back in the American manner, 55 Broadway rose with easier grace and to a greater height than any of its contemporaries, and earned Holden the London architecture medal in 1929.

In 1931 Holden was commissioned to design the University of London's central building in Bloomsbury. The university wanted a tower, partly to give a sense of identity to the many departments scattered over Bloomsbury. Holden designed an immense building facing onto Malet Street between Montague Place and Torrington Place, with a long spine on the axis of the British Museum, towers at either end, and lower wings between the spine and the street. The university could not afford to build this scheme, and in 1932 Holden reduced it to its southern part, which forms the present Senate House, plus individual buildings placed around the edge of the site to the north. It was still ambitious, a tower 215 feet high with space for 950,000 books on an internal steel frame. The rest of the building was of traditional masonry because Holden could not trust steel to last the centuries he and his clients planned for the building. He wanted to temper its nakedness with sculpture, but the university authorities would not allow this. Parts of his scheme to the north were completed after the Second World War, with buildings for Birkbeck College, the students' union, the School of Oriental and African Studies, and the Warburg Institute.

Holden's buildings display the work of many notable sculptors, including Eric Gill and Henry Moore, but he is chiefly associated with the controversial figure of Jacob Epstein, whose unidealized, partly clothed figures on the British Medical Association building caused a public uproar. This only confirmed Holden in his view that Epstein was a raw, Whitmanic genius, and he employed him again at 55 Broadway, with more uproar. He wished that Epstein's work could have graced the sides of Senate House.

During the last decade of his working life Holden was mainly concerned with town planning and reconstruction. Between 1944 and 1946 he reported on the reconstruction of Canterbury with H. M. Enderby, and of the City of London with William Holford. In 1947 he was commissioned by the London county council to prepare a scheme for the layout of buildings on the South Bank between County Hall and Waterloo Bridge, to supersede the planning sketch of the area included in the wartime county of London plan. His experience of large and varied urban projects fitted him for these tasks. Although none of these late schemes of post-war construction was carried through faithfully, this modest and retiring man had already, through 55 Broadway, Senate House, and the tube stations, left a more enduring mark on London than any architect of his generation.

Holden would have been happy with such an epitaph. He was gentle and unassuming, and spoke softly with a faint northern accent. But for all his non-smoking, scarcely drinking Hertfordshire quietism, he was strong, even passionate, when it came to the principles of his work. In 1942 his friend Hope Bagenal read Eric Gill's *Autobiography* and was fired by Gill's hatred of industrialism. He wrote to Holden, who took a quite different stand:

It comes simply to this: that I was born in an industrial age; that I was urged by a passion for building and for service; and that I have an invincible belief in the power of the human soul, the God in man, to rise above and master ugliness and desolating conditions. I had to exercise this passion even in the industrial age into which I was born. (Adams, Holden, and Pearson archive, RIBA BAL, AHP/28/23/1)

For many years Margaret Macdonald was a partial invalid, and blind in her last years. After her death in 1954 Holden gradually withdrew from active practice to live quietly at his home at 87 Harmer Green Lane, near Welwyn. He died there on 1 May 1960.

CHARLES HUTTON, *rev.* ALAN CRAWFORD

Sources E. Karol and F. Allibone, *Charles Holden: architect, 1875–1960* (1988) · A. Forty, *Objects of desire: design and society, 1750–1980* (1986) · G. Stamp, *Silent cities: an exhibition of the memorial and cemetery architecture of the Great War* (1977) · RIBA BAL, Adams, Holden, and Pearson MSS · biography file, RIBA BAL · C. Barman, *The man who built London Transport: a biography of Frank Pick* (1979) · C. Hutton, 'Dr Charles Holden', *Artifex*, 3 (1969), 35–53 · T. Ruddock, 'Charles Holden and the issue of high buildings in London, 1927–1947', *Construction History*, 12 (1996), 83–99 · N. Harte, *The University of London, 1836–1986: an illustrated history* (1986) · R. Cork, *Art beyond the gallery* (1985) · M. T. Saler, *The avant-garde in interwar England: medieval modernism and the London Underground* (1999) · *RIBA Journal*, 67 (1959–60), 383–4 · Ashbee journals, King's Cam. · CGPLA Eng. & Wales (1960) · b. cert. · *The Times* (2 May 1960), 21 · *London: north*, Pevsner (1998)

Archives RIBA BAL, drawings and papers · RIBA BAL, drawings, family photographs, and ephemera · RIBA BAL, papers and architectural drawings of H. P. Adams, Adams and Holden, and Adams, Holden, and Pearson | Transport for London, group archive, Frank Pick papers, corresp.

Likenesses F. Dodd, oils, c.1907, Art Workers' Guild, London · F. Dodd, chalk drawing, 1915, NPG; related etching, NPG · photograph, c.1945, RIBA BAL · P. Vincze, portrait medallion, c.1951, Bristol Public Library · D. Whiting, bronze head, c.1960, RIBA · L. Tarling, bust, LUL, Senate House Library

Wealth at death £60,184 4s. 9d.: 16 Aug 1960, *CGPLA Eng. & Wales*

Holden, Sir David Charles Beresford (1915–1998), civil servant, was born on 26 July 1915 in Wolverhampton, the third son of Oswald Addenbrooke Holden (1874–1917), Church of England clergyman, and his wife, Ella Mary, *née* Beresford (1877–1959). He was educated at Pilgrims School, Westerham, Kent, and at Rossall School in Lancashire before entering King's College, Cambridge, as a scholar reading classics. There he distinguished himself by achieving a double first, while also captaining the college's rugby fifteen.

Because of concern for his widowed mother, Holden declined an offer of an appointment to the Indian Civil Service, accepting instead an appointment to the Northern Ireland civil service, where in 1937 he joined the ministry of finance as an assistant principal. However, as a member of the Territorial Army he was mobilized in 1939 to serve with the 8th (Belfast) heavy anti-aircraft regiment, Royal Artillery, an all-volunteer unit which shortly afterwards embarked for France with the British expeditionary force. The regiment returned to Britain before Dunkirk and, after re-training, left in May 1942 to serve in the Arakan and Burma campaign. It was in India, while on leave at Kalimpong, that Holden met his future wife, (Elizabeth) Jean Odling (b. 1923). He left India (where he had served as brigade major to the 1st Indian anti-aircraft

Sir David Charles Beresford Holden (1915–1998), by unknown photographer

brigade) in 1945, and after demobilization and a brief secondment to the Treasury in London, resumed his career with the Northern Ireland ministry of finance. He married Jean Odling on 9 April 1948. They had a son and a daughter.

In the Northern Ireland ministry of finance Holden's quiet charm and meticulous intellect carried him steadily forward through the most senior posts. Major Holden, as he was generally known by his colleagues in those days, was the complete master of the arcane financial relationships between the government of Northern Ireland and the Treasury, where (as in the City) he commanded real respect. His military and civilian services were recognized by the award of the Emergency Reserve decoration in 1954, and by his appointment as CB in 1963.

In July 1970 Holden succeeded Sir Cecil Bateman as permanent secretary at the ministry of finance, which was at that time coupled with the headship of the Northern Ireland civil service. He assumed these responsibilities at a time of deepening crisis in Northern Ireland. Widespread disorder had already brought about the extensive deployment of the army in support of the beleaguered police, and the Northern Ireland government's authority and credibility were being rapidly eroded. In the civil service the heaviest burden of the deepening political crisis fell initially to be borne by the cabinet secretary, Sir Harold Black. However, with the introduction of direct rule in 1972 (the year that Holden was appointed KBE) and the appointment of William Whitelaw as the first secretary of state for Northern Ireland, there came about a fundamental change in Holden's role.

Whitelaw, with characteristic political shrewdness, decided to build a Northern Ireland civil service element into his strategic team at Stormont Castle alongside the new arrivals from Whitehall. Leaving the day-to-day supervision of the ministry of finance to his able deputy Robert Kidd, Holden joined the senior members of the old cabinet office, Sir Harold Black and Kenneth Bloomfield, in a central secretariat which not only served to give Whitelaw the benefit of local knowledge, experience, and sensitivity, but worked with other senior members of the Northern Ireland civil service on contingency planning for constitutional development. In this new role Holden joined the United Kingdom delegation at the Sunningdale conference in December 1973 and acted as co-chairman, with an able Irish civil servant, Noel Whelan, of a steering group to clarify the role and functions of a council of Ireland. These efforts were, however, overtaken by the Ulster Workers' Council strike of May 1974 which brought down the 'power-sharing executive' and destroyed the Sunningdale settlement. Thereafter Holden returned to his duties at the ministry of finance until he retired in June 1976.

After a twelve-month interregnum as director of the Ulster office (Northern Ireland's 'shop window' in London), Holden retired with his wife, Jean, and lived quietly near Salisbury at Wilsford-cum-Lake in Wiltshire, involving himself contentedly in his local church until he died from bronchopneumonia in Salisbury District Hospital on 31 August 1998. He was buried at St Michael's, Wilsford-cum-Lake, Amesbury, on 11 September 1998. His most happy marriage to Jean, who survived him, had lasted more than fifty years. He was survived also by their two children.

Holden's appearance and personality recalled C. P. Snow's fictional mandarin Douglas Osbaldiston. With his slim build and light, athletic tread, he also reminded many of the great cricketer Peter May. Never a man for the limelight, he was at his happiest and most comfortable in courteous and lucid dealing with his colleagues. He had a passion for P. G. Wodehouse, from whose works he could quote copiously. KENNETH BLOOMFIELD

Sources *The Guardian* (5 Sept 1998) · *The Times* (8 Sept 1998) · *WWW* · personal knowledge (2004) · private information (2004) [Jean Holden, widow]
Likenesses photograph, repro. in *The Guardian* · photograph, News International Syndication, London [*see illus.*]
Wealth at death under £200,000: probate, 26 Oct 1998, *CGPLA Eng. & Wales*

Holden [*married name* Smith], **Edith Blackwell** (1871–1920), artist and illustrator, was born on 26 September 1871 at Holly Green, Church Road, Moseley, Birmingham, the fourth of seven children of Arthur Holden (1836–1913), a paint and varnish manufacturer, and his wife, Emma

Edith Blackwell Holden (1871–1920), by unknown photographer

flowers in their sketchbooks and select suitable verses to write alongside. Privately she compiled her own notebook, which she called 'Nature notes for 1906'. This was not her first venture; a similar, less developed version for 1905 was discovered in 1988. In 'Nature notes for 1906' she recorded the countryside around the family's new home at Gowan Bank, Kineton Green Road, Olton, Warwickshire. On completion she kept the nature diaries as useful source material for her developing career as a book illustrator. Between 1907 and 1910 Edith's concern about the treatment of animals led her to contribute about forty illustrations to the *Animals' Friend*, the magazine of the National Council for Animal Welfare. Some of these illustrations were also sold as calendars and postcards by the charity. Between 1907 and 1914 she illustrated at least seven children's books, such as M. M. Rankin's *Woodland Whisperings* (1911), and *Animals Around Us* (1912), by Martin Merrythought (A. J. Maas).

On 1 June 1911 Edith married the sculptor (Alfred) Ernest Smith (1879–1938) by special licence at Chelsea register office. The couple lived in a small attic flat at 2 Oakley Crescent, Chelsea. Ernest was principal assistant to the sculptor Lady Feodora Gleichen at her studio at St James's Palace. Edith's marriage did not meet with her family's approval and relations with them deteriorated. Little is known about her marriage and there were no children. On 15 March 1920 Edith drowned in a tributary of the River Thames at Kew Gardens Walk, London, and her body was not discovered until the following day. An inquest at Richmond coroner's court heard that she had probably lost her balance while collecting chestnut buds to paint from a tree at the water's edge. The coroner recorded the verdict 'found drowned'. On 19 March 1920 Edith Holden Smith was cremated at Golders Green.

When Edith Holden's personal 'Nature notes for 1906' was published by Webb and Bower in association with Michael Joseph as *The Country Diary of an Edwardian Lady* in June 1977, it was an instant and exceptional best-seller. Translations of the book appeared in thirteen languages, making Edith's nature diary one of the great international publishing success stories of the twentieth century. The book was also influential in creating a fashion for rural nostalgia when merchandise appeared bearing designs from the book, a nostalgia unimpeded by the fact that its author was by background a suburban socialist, and not the leisured country-dweller conjured up by its title.

INA TAYLOR

Sources I. Taylor, *The Edwardian lady: the story of Edith Holden*, rev. edn (1990) · R. Samuel, *Theatres of memory* (1994) · coroner's report, Richmond coroner's court, Middlesex, 18 March 1920 · *Richmond and Twickenham Times* (20 March 1920)
Likenesses photograph, priv. coll. [*see illus.*] · photographs, repro. in Taylor, *The Edwardian lady*, pp. 55, 61, 140, 203, 205, and frontispiece; priv. coll.
Wealth at death £1084 13s. 1d.: administration, 17 May 1920, CGPLA Eng. & Wales

Wearing (1836–1904), formerly a governess. She was brought up a Unitarian. The family believed they had psychic powers and participated in séances where Edith was encouraged to demonstrate her powers of automatic writing. She received no formal elementary education but was taught by her mother. From 1884 to 1890 Edith studied part-time at the Birmingham Municipal School of Art. In 1891 she spent a year studying animal painting at an art school run by Joseph Denovan Adam at Craigmill, Stirling, and returned for a six-week painting holiday most summers for the next sixteen years.

In 1890 Edith exhibited her first painting at the Royal Birmingham Society of Artists and continued to exhibit there annually until 1907. She also exhibited at the Royal Academy (1907 and 1917), the Walker Gallery in Liverpool, and the Society of Women Artists. The subjects of these oil paintings were usually animals in a landscape frequently inspired by Scotland. From 1906 to 1910 she taught art one afternoon a week at a private girls' school in Solihull, Warwickshire. In 1906 she encouraged the girls to paint wild

Holden, Sir Edward Hopkinson, first baronet (1848–1919), banker, was born on 11 May 1848 at the Bull's Head, Tottington, Lancashire, the elder son of Henry Holden

(1823–1876), calico bleacher, and later beer seller, and his wife, Ann, *née* Hopkinson (1826–1891). He was educated locally at the Wesleyan elementary school in Summerseat, and on leaving school became a clerk in local shops and warehouses. His banking career started in 1866, when he began an apprenticeship at the Bolton branch of the Manchester and County Bank. After seven years he was promoted to a clerkship at the Manchester head office and remained there for another seven years. This seemingly slow progress belied an obviously determined young man, who attended evening classes in political economy, law, and logic at Owens College, Manchester, in a rigorous programme of self-education.

In 1881 Holden answered an advertisement in *The Economist* for the post of accountant at the Birmingham and Midland Bank at a salary of £300. Asked about his ambitions at his interview, he is reputed to have said, 'I want to be the manager of a big bank.' At that time Midland was still a small Birmingham company with only a scattering of branches in the region. However, the appointment of John Dent Goodman as chairman in 1881 heralded a policy of expansion within the bank, in which Holden was to be deeply involved.

As accountant Holden proved his worth in a managerial role, overseeing bank premises and the recruitment of staff. In 1883 he was on the verge of leaving the bank; its lack of commercial progress did not fit his ambitions. The bank directors retained him by promoting him to secretary, and later in that year Holden jointly supervised the acquisition of the Union Bank of Birmingham. This venture was to be the first of many amalgamations over the next thirty years. The targets selected were usually joint stock banks from the north or the midlands which had strong industrial links. Among those banks which amalgamated with Midland under Holden's firm hand were the Preston Banking Company in 1894, the Leicestershire Banking Company in 1900, and the Yorkshire Banking Company in 1901.

Holden was heavily involved in the process of amalgamation, both in picking suitable banks, and as a negotiator. His rise through the bank (sub-manager in 1887, general manager in 1890, and joint general manager in 1891) mirrored the success of the bank as it became an organization of national importance. In 1891 Midland entered London with its purchase of the Central Bank of London, giving the bank a seat in the London Clearing House for the first time. In 1895 the Midland's directors voted Holden 2000 guineas for his 'conspicuous ability in conducting and completing the recent amalgamations' (HSBC Group Archives, board minutes, 19 Feb 1895). In these negotiations, mostly held in railway hotels up and down the country, Holden was a formidable presence, meticulous in his scrutiny of bad and doubtful debts, and merciless with those bankers whose knowledge of their own balance sheets did not match his own. A director of the City Bank, on joining the board of Midland, stated: 'how glad I am to have him on the same side of the table as myself, for I know what it is to have a table between us' (HSBC Group

Archives, report of the general meeting of shareholders, January 1899). This amalgamation with the City Bank in 1898 was the most risky of all Holden's acquisitions—he conducted the negotiations alone, and for the first and last time he had to win over opposition from a section of his directors and shareholders regarding the price to be paid. This amalgamation brought Midland to a prestigious new headquarters in Threadneedle Street, and to its position as the fourth largest clearing bank in the UK.

Promotion to managing director followed later in 1898, and Holden was to hold this position until 1919 at a salary of £5000. In the next ten years he concentrated on centralizing and unifying the structure of the bank; a necessary task, given that it was composed of different provincial businesses, each with its own traditions and methods. Uniformity in accounting was introduced throughout the branches, and all lending decisions were made in London. Holden's diaries show his meticulous attention to detail, even over the minutiae of decisions relating to staff and premises. A series of visits to North America in the early years of the twentieth century inspired him to modernize the bank's office systems—a large internal telephone network was introduced, office machinery was more widely used, and printing and stationery was standardized. During one of these visits, one journalist described him thus: 'no dreamer,—he moves quickly, thinks rapidly. Grey moustached and ruddy, he had a pair of decidedly electric eyes. He talks political economy as easily as some men talk horses' (*Toronto News*, 24 Sept 1904).

In the early years of the twentieth century, with the bank strongly placed in its home markets, Holden began to look further afield for new business. He used his American visits as an opportunity to extend the bank's correspondent network, and in 1905 the bank established a foreign exchange department in London, the first of the clearers to take such a step. The bank also became involved in loans and new issues for foreign governments and major international companies. Holden was especially interested in the opportunities in Russia; Midland issued bonds for a Russian railway loan in 1909, and in 1917 opened a branch office in St Petersburg.

Holden became chairman of Midland in 1908. Although less involved in the day to day running of the bank, in amalgamations he continued to select targets and conduct preliminary negotiations. Important amalgamations during these years included the North and South Wales Bank in 1908, the Metropolitan Bank in 1914, and the London Joint Stock Bank in 1918. The last brought the Midland's total deposits to £349 million, making it the largest bank in the world. This amalgamation was opposed by some in the press and in parliament, on the grounds that such mergers would reduce competition between the banks. A parliamentary committee, the Colwyn committee, was appointed to investigate the issue. Holden replied characteristically that Britain should be mindful of the international banking world. If British banks were to compete in a world arena then they would need to be able to match the capitalization and deposits of their rivals.

The amalgamation proceeded as planned and the government rejected the committee's proposal to legislate against further amalgamations.

In his role as Midland's chairman, Holden was also a spokesman and leader of the banking community. His annual speeches to his shareholders were used to expound his views on financial policy and were eagerly awaited, both in England and on the other side of the Atlantic. He argued, against the Bank of England, that the clearing banks needed to hold their own gold reserves; he also argued that the country should maintain its own gold-based war chest. These views, backed by Holden's Liberalism and support of free trade, recommended him to Asquith. Holden had been MP for Heywood, Manchester, since 1906, but had kept a low profile, fearing that to seek success in politics would open the bank to criticism. However, in 1910 Asquith recommended him for chancellor of the exchequer. Lloyd George's threat to resign ensured the withdrawal of this recommendation, and later that year Holden did not seek re-election at the polls. Thereafter he remained an informal adviser to the government on financial matters. In the period prior to the outbreak of the First World War he returned to the issue of gold reserves, requesting that a royal commission be appointed to investigate the matter. On the outbreak of war, Holden recommended to Lloyd George the declaration of a moratorium on lending, and was credited with the idea of issuing currency notes. In September 1915 he joined Lord Reading in a special commission to New York to negotiate the stabilization of exchange rates. Following this, he helped to raise the Anglo-French loan of £100 million, for which the United States government agreed to waive collateral.

Holden's influence had helped him to mobilize the support of the clearing banks for the Yorkshire Penny Bank in 1911, when it faced a crisis due to the depreciation of its securities. In 1916 he persuaded the Treasury to join the banks in guaranteeing the Penny Bank's reserves when they faced another crisis. Holden also campaigned for reforms in the Institute of Bankers, and was successful in his attempts to bring increased democracy and a greater range of activities for the ordinary members.

By habit and by inclination, Holden was a hard worker who found it difficult to take holidays. Despite his sometimes autocratic style of management, his staff often found him to be a considerate and forgiving employer. Outside the bank, Holden had few interests. He established a freemasons' lodge in 1902, the Holden Lodge; membership was restricted to the bank's directors and staff. He was an omnivorous reader of books concerning finance, and a keen golfer and cyclist.

Holden married Annie (*d.* 1905), daughter of William Cassie of Aberdeen, on 6 January 1877; they had known each other since their youth at Summerseat. Their family home was The Grange, at Thorpe, Chertsey, in Surrey, where Holden was a church steward. They had two sons and a daughter. Their elder son, Cassie, continued the family influence in the bank, becoming a director and deputy chairman after a career as a barrister. Holden was created a baronet in 1909, and twice declined a peerage. He died suddenly, on 23 July 1919, at Duff House Sanatorium in Banff, of cerebral thrombosis and heart failure, after a week's illness. His will was sworn at under £100,000, and included an endowment fund for education in the principles and practice of international banking. He was buried in the Wesleyan chapel in Summerseat, Lancashire, with his wife.   EDWIN GREEN

Sources E. Green, 'Holden, Sir Edward Hopkinson', *DBB* • A. R. Holmes and E. Green, *Midland: 150 years of banking business* (1986) • W. F. Crick and J. E. Wadsworth, *A hundred years of joint stock banking* (1936) • private information (2004) • *The Times* (24 July 1919) • *Morning Post* (24 July 1919) • *Financial News* (24 July 1919) • *Toronto News* (24 Sept 1904) • HSBC Group Archives, London, Midland Bank archives • M. Cecco, *Money and empire* (1974)
Archives HSBC Group Archives, London, corresp. and diaries
Likenesses photograph, 1881, HSBC Group Archives, London, Midland Bank archives • W. W. Ouless, oils, 1909, HSBC Group Archives, London, Midland Bank archives • G. Leward, bust, 1943, HSBC Group Archives, London, Midland Bank archives
Wealth at death under £100,000: administration, 5 Sept 1919, *CGPLA Eng. & Wales*

Holden, George (1783–1865), Church of England clergyman and biblical scholar, only son of the Revd George Holden LLD, headmaster of the free grammar school at Horton in Ribblesdale, Yorkshire, was born there in 1783. He was educated at Glasgow University, where he graduated. In 1811 he was presented to the perpetual curacy of the village of Maghull, near Liverpool; living there in seclusion he read and wrote much. He succeeded his father as vicar of Horton in 1821, but resigned that living in 1825, preferring to devote himself to Maghull. He died suddenly at Maghull on 19 March 1865, aged eighty-one. He was not married, and his large library and more than half of his property were left for the benefit of clergy of the diocese of Ripon.

Holden's fifteen works show him to have been a competent Hebraist and an able Christian apologist. His early works include *An Attempt towards an Improved Version of the Proverbs of Solomon* (1819), *The Scripture Testimonies to the Divinity of our Lord Jesus Christ* (1820), *An Attempt to Illustrate the Book of Ecclesiastes* (1822), and *A Dissertation on the Fall of Man* (1823). In the 1830s he published several expositions of scripture, and *The Authority of Tradition in Matters of Religion* (1838). His later works include *The Anglican Catechist* (1855) and *An Essay on the Angels of the Church* (1862).

For many years Holden compiled the *Liverpool Tide Tables*, which were begun by his grandfather and continued by his father.   C. W. SUTTON, *rev.* H. C. G. MATTHEW

Sources *GM*, 3rd ser., 18 (1865), 657 • *Clergy List* (1865) • H. Fishwick, *The history of the parish of Garstang* (1878)
Archives U. Leeds, Brotherton L., library catalogue and registers
Wealth at death under £6000: resworn probate, 13 Oct 1865, *CGPLA Eng. & Wales*

Holden, Henry (1596/7–1662), Roman Catholic priest, was born in 1596 or early 1597 into a long-established Lancashire gentry family. He was the second son of Richard

Holden of Chaigley Manor, near Clitheroe, and Eleanor Gerard from near Wigan. His family was strongly recusant on both sides. Nothing is known of his early education, but he entered the English College, Douai, to study for the priesthood in September 1617, using the alias of Johnson for several years. His philosophy teacher was the controversial Thomas White (alias Blacklo), of whom he remained an enduring and important ally as well as an occasional but mild critic thereafter. Following ordination at Cambrai in March 1622 he joined the community of English ecclesiastics and scholars at the college of Arras, Paris, in late 1623, and resumed his studies at Paris University, where he was an MA in October 1625. The next year he interrupted them as he obtained the position of almoner in the household of Michel de Marillac, keeper of the seals, which brought him into contact with prominent *dévot* circles, including the reformed Carmelites of Pontoise. In 1627 he obtained *lettres de naturalité* enabling him to hold benefices in France. He remained with Marillac after his disgrace and exile to Châteaudun in late 1630, attending him on his deathbed in August 1632. He then rejoined Arras College, and resumed his theology studies, taking twenty-third place in the 1636 licentiate and the doctorate in October 1636. He defended Richard Smith and the English hierarchy against perceived Jesuit efforts to undermine it in the seculars–regulars controversy of the early 1630s. He was briefly agent of the English Catholic clergy in Rome (from 1638 to early 1639), failing to obtain papal recognition of the English chapter established by William Bishop to administer the English Catholic church in the absence of episcopal hierarchy. The low opinion he formed of the papacy's handling of English questions owed something to Gallican attitudes he had already developed in France, and doubtless reinforced them.

Made a canon of the English chapter (1638) with Blacklo and others by Smith, Holden was directly involved in the affairs of the English church, visiting London in 1639–40, 1641–2, and later. In 1647 he participated in short-lived attempts to win toleration of Catholics from Independent army leaders who had rejected both Anglican and presbyterian church settlements, but he, White, and a few others, later to be nicknamed Blacklo's cabal, were ready to make some controversial concessons in order to achieve that goal. Holden's Gallicanism enabled him to support an oath of allegiance from Catholics, the expulsion of the Jesuits, and a frank rejection of the pope's deposing power. His own daring plan for a restored episcopate, if necessary without papal approval and largely independent of papal authority, was typical of the Blackloist approach, ever eager for an agreement with Cromwell, but predictably it alienated the moderate and conservative forces in English Catholicism. Although condemned by the Holy Office, Holden escaped punishment, possibly because of French protection.

In Paris, Holden taught theology at the university and was penitentiary of St Nicolas-du-Chardonnet, one of the city's most reform minded parishes, but he was never a vicar-general of the diocese (his name was probably confused with that of Cardinal de Retz's vicar-general, Hodencq). His Gallican and anti-Jesuit views facilitated accusations of unorthodox sympathies during the Jansenist crisis of the mid-1650s. Although initially willing to defend Antoine Arnauld, whose apologia of the church fathers he had previously approved, he was one of many doctors who withdrew from the faculty assemblies rather than condemn and expel Arnauld (1655–6). He subsequently signed the condemnation to clear his name and defend his own orthodoxy, though his embarrassment appears in letters to Féret, curé of St Nicolas, and to Arnauld, in which he pleaded for Arnauld to take his own Thomist position on divine grace and related questions. Apart from publishing a defence of the anti-Jansenist formulary (1661), he largely avoided the Jansenist controversy in later years. His attention turned again to English Catholic ecclesiastical politics after Smith's death (1655) reopened older controversies over episcopacy, in which he showed his customary anti-Jesuit and Blackloist views, especially in 1661 when a House of Lords committee held discussions about the conditions for repealing the penal laws.

Holden's published output dates largely from the final decade of his life, but probably gestated over many years. The *Divinae fidei analysis* (1652) is his most systematic work of theological scholarship, and adopted an approach to its subject matter that was unusual for its time. He aimed to distinguish the certain from the uncertain in Christian teaching, fundamental truths from theological speculation, and to establish the degree of assent required for each kind of truth. But as the object of one's belief could not be known directly, everything depended upon the means by which it was transmitted to believers, and Holden stoutly defended unbroken tradition within an institutional church as superior to scripture or individual inspiration. He showed his Gallican convictions by insisting that only a general council could define truth, leaving the pope the lesser role of judge of theological controversies. The logical rigour and intellectual solidity of this work was admired by scholars like Richard Simon or Ellies du Pin, and even J. H. Newman, but on publication its novelty and boldness struck contemporaries, leading to suggestions of unorthodoxy. Other items of Holden's *œuvre*— on usury, on schism, his exchanges with Arnauld and others, several defences of Blacklo—figured in later editions of the *Analysis*, which first appeared in English in 1658. A treatise on the truth of Christianity was apparently lost in England during the civil wars.

Having helped Richard Smith and Thomas Carre to establish the English convent of Our Lady of Syon, in Paris, in 1634, Holden acted in his final years as superior to newly settled English blue nuns in Paris, using his connections to smooth the way to their installation there. He also persuaded them to exchange their original Franciscan rule for that of the immaculate conception of the Blessed Virgin, essentially because the archbishop of Paris insisted on the nuns' subjection to episcopal authority. He visited England for the last time in June–September 1661, falling ill on his return of a quartan fever, of which he died in March 1662. He left much of his estate to the blue nuns but only with great difficulty was the crown dissuaded from seizing it under French laws governing property owned by foreigners resident in France.

JOSEPH BERGIN

Sources J. Gillow and R. Trappes-Lomax, eds., *The diary of the 'blue nuns' or order of the Immaculate Conception of Our Lady, at Paris, 1658–1810*, Catholic RS, 8 (1910) • R. Pugh, *Blacklo's cabal*, ed. T. A. Birrell (1970) • A. F. Allison, 'An English Gallican: Henry Holden (to 1648)', *Recusant History*, 22 (1994–5), 319–49 • T. A. Birrell, 'English Catholics without a bishop, 1655–1672', *Recusant History*, 4 (1957–8), 142–78 • J. Bossy, *The English Catholic community, 1570–1850* (1975) • G. Garavaglia, *Società e religione in Inghilterra* (1983) • J. M. Grès-Gayer, *En Sorbonne, autour des Provinciales* (1997) • J. M. Grès-Gayer, *Le Jansénisme en Sorbonne* (1996) • J. Le Brun, ''L'Institution dans la théo-logie de Henry Holden', *Recherche de Sciences Religieuses*, 71 (1983), 191–202 • G. H. Tavard, *The seventeenth-century tradition* (1978) • R. Clark, *Strangers and sojourners at Port Royal* (1932) • G. Anstruther, *The seminary priests*, 2 (1975), 158–9 • *VCH Lancashire*, vol. 7 • Biblio-thèque Nationale, Paris, MS Lat. 15440 • Bibliothèque Saint-Geneviève, Paris, MS 826; MS 941, fol. 42v

Holden, Henry (1814–1909). *See under* Holden, Hubert Ash-ton (1822–1896).

Holden, Henry Smith (1887–1963), botanist and forensic scientist, was born at Castleton, near Rochdale, Lanca-shire, on 30 November 1887, the elder of the two sons of Henry Carlton Holden, a clerk and cotton merchant, and his wife, Betsy Cockcroft. He was educated at Manchester grammar school and, on a scholarship, at the University of Manchester, where he graduated in 1909 with second-class honours in botany. His father, who seems to have been a less than ideal husband and parent, died while he was still at school, and his mother had to go to work to sup-port him and his brother Ernest during their education. Holden helped to support Ernest through university as soon as he was able to do so.

Immediately after graduating, Holden joined the staff of University College, Nottingham, as an assistant lec-turer in botany, and in 1911 gained his Manchester MSc. He remained at Nottingham until 1936, becoming senior lec-turer in botany and head of the subdepartment of indus-trial bacteriology in 1927. In the following year he was appointed head of the department of biology; in 1932 he became professor of botany and later (1934) head of the botany department. His career at Nottingham was inter-rupted only by a wartime post (1916–19) as a bacteriologist in the Royal Naval Hospital, Plymouth. He was an effective academic teacher, able to enliven his lectures with an impressive display of ambidexterity on the blackboard.

Holden published twenty-five papers on botanical sub-jects, mainly in the *Annals of Botany* and the *Journal of the Linnean Society*, between 1911 and 1962. Many are notable for the photographs and superb draughtsmanship dis-played, as they dealt largely with plant anatomy. Later he specialized in palaeobotany, especially that of the coal measures. In 1921 he was awarded the degree of DSc from Manchester University for his work on seedling structure. Holden was elected a fellow of the Linnean Society in 1910, and of the Royal Society of Edinburgh in 1927. In 1917 he

married Annie Janet, daughter of Richard Hamer, a civil engineer from Oswestry, Shropshire; they had a son and a daughter.

Holden had two careers, and his reputation rests mainly on the second. During the latter part of his academic period he began to be consulted by the local police on scientific problems which they encountered (primarily cases of water pollution and food contamination), and on the uses of science in crime detection; this work grew rap-idly into his main interest. (According to one source, the association started by his being consulted by the local CID superintendent, who was a keen cricketer, about the care of the grass on his cricket pitches.) Thus, when the East Midland Forensic Science Laboratory, the first of the Home Office regional forensic science laboratories in Eng-land and Wales, was established in Nottingham in 1936, Holden was appointed its first director, with a scientific staff of two graduates and two technicians. His staff found his enthusiasm, his forceful personality, and the drily witty encouragement which he gave them memorable. As he said to one of them: 'Forensic science is a practical job, and all you have to do is to get in ten years' experience as quickly as you can.'

Holden soon became one of Britain's foremost forensic scientists, and was both tireless and effective in educating the police about the ways in which science could help them. His advice was frequently sought by the Home Office during the late 1930s, when its forensic science ser-vice was taking shape. In 1946 he was appointed director of the larger and more prestigious Metropolitan Police Laboratory, where he provided the scientific evidence in several of the most notorious criminal cases of the post-war years (for example, the Haigh, Heath, Hume, and Raven murder trials). Holden was a member of the Medico-Legal Society from 1947 to 1958, and served as a member of council during that time. He published three papers on the subject in the early 1950s, but his health began to deteriorate, and he suffered a stroke in 1951. On his recovery in 1952, he moved to the less arduous post of forensic science adviser to the Home Office, from which he retired in 1958 to work in the British Museum (Natural History) on palaeobotanical research, 'before I go com-pletely ga ga'. He was appointed CBE (1958).

Professionally Holden was a considerable 'character', with a blunt, down-to-earth manner of expression which made him popular with the police officers who consulted him, but which, with its sardonic side, could also make him a little intimidating. He sought at all times to elimin-ate the risk of a miscarriage of justice, and insisted that his scientific findings should be available to the defence. Privately he was a man of simple conventional tastes—his home and garden, cricket, fell-walking, and the country-side. He held no particular religious beliefs, and was inactively Conservative in politics. He was undoubtedly proud of the status and deference which his position in the world of forensic science and his CBE brought him. Holden died, after a brief illness, on 16 May 1963 in Dene Hospital, Caterham, near his Surrey home, at Kenley. He was survived by his wife. In 1974 the University of Nottingham established the H. S. Holden botanical lectures, to be given annually to a public audience.

H. J. WALLS, rev. K. D. WATSON

Sources F. M. Wonnacott, 'Henry Smith Holden (1887–1963)', *Journal of the Society of the Bibliography of Natural History*, 4 (1962–8), 230–34 · C. G. C. Chesters, 'Dr H. S. Holden, CBE', *Nature*, 199 (1963), 330–31 · T. M. Harris, 'Henry Smith Holden', *Year Book of the Royal Society of Edinburgh* (1962–3), 24–5 · *WWW* · *The Times* (18 May 1963) · *Medico-Legal Journal*, 31 (1963), 203 · *CGPLA Eng. & Wales* (1963) · personal knowledge (1981) · private information (1981)
Archives Linn. Soc. · NHM
Likenesses Elliott & Fry, photograph, repro. in Wonnacott, 'Henry Smith Holden (1887–1963)'
Wealth at death £12,505 5s. 0d.: probate, 12 July 1963, *CGPLA Eng. & Wales*

Holden, Hubert Ashton (1822–1896), classical scholar, was born in Birmingham, the son of the Revd Hyla Holden, incumbent of Erdington, Warwickshire. He was educated at King Edward's School, Birmingham, first under Francis Jeune, and then under James Prince Lee. He proceeded to Trinity College, Cambridge, and in his first year of residence in 1842 gained the first Bell university scholarship. He graduated BA in 1845, being senior classic and junior optime in the mathematical tripos. He was fellow of Trinity College from 1847 to 1854, when he vacated his fellowship by his marriage on 18 July to Laetitia, elder daughter of R. E. Lofft of Troston Hall, Suffolk.

Holden was ordained deacon in 1848 and took priest's orders in 1858. He was assistant tutor and classical lecturer of his college from 1848 until 1853, when he was appointed vice-principal of Cheltenham College, continuing in that post until 1858. From 1858 to 1883 he was headmaster of Queen Elizabeth's School, Ipswich. In 1890 he was appointed by the crown to a fellowship of the University of London, where he was classical examiner from 1869 until 1874, and examiner in Greek from 1886 until 1890. In 1892 the degree of LittD was conferred on him by Dublin University. He was a vice-president of the Hellenic Society from 1893. He died on 1 December 1896 at 20 Redcliffe Square, London, in his seventy-fifth year, and was buried on 5 December at Highgate cemetery.

Holden, who was a classical scholar of fine taste and full knowledge, was best known for his collections of English passages for translation into Latin and Greek, *Foliorum silvula* and *Foliorum centuriae* (1852), and for a selection of Latin and Greek versions of these published as *Folia silvulae* (1865 and 1870). He also produced useful editions of various classical texts, including several of Plutarch's *Lives* and Xenophon's *Hiero* (1883) and *Cyropaedeia* (1887–90).

A cousin, **Henry Holden** (1814–1909), classical scholar and Church of England clergyman, was born at Birmingham, the second son of Henry Augustus Holden (d. 1870), a clergyman. He was the elder brother of Luther *Holden, surgeon and anatomist. Educated at Shrewsbury School under Samuel Butler, he matriculated at Balliol College, Oxford, in 1832, the holder of one of the earliest scholarships at that college to be awarded by open competition. Gaining first-class honours in *literae humaniores*, he graduated BA in 1837 and MA in 1839, and was ordained in the

latter year. He was incumbent of Upminster from 1839 to 1845. As headmaster of Uppingham School from 1845 to 1853 (and predecessor to Edward Thring), with Richard Dacre Archer Hind he edited *Sabrinae corolla in hortulis regiae scholae Salopiensis continuerunt tres viri floribus legendis* (1850), a collection of poetical extracts with translations into Latin or Greek, which was highly influential on the practice of versification in schools and universities. Holden was headmaster of Durham Cathedral school from 1853 until 1882, then vicar of South Luffenham, Rutland, from 1881 until 1898. He was married: first, on 19 January 1847, to Elizabeth Margaret Anne, daughter of the Revd Richard Edmonds, and second, on 19 December 1857, to Georgiana, daughter of Byron Aldham, a merchant. He retired to Boscobel, Streatham Common, London, where he died on 30 March 1909.

C. E. HUGHES, rev. RICHARD SMAIL

Sources Venn, *Alum. Cant.* · *The Times* (4 Dec 1896) · m. certs. [Henry Holden] · *CGPLA Eng. & Wales* (1898)
Wealth at death £16,493 6s. 5d.: resworn probate, March 1898, *CGPLA Eng. & Wales* (1896) · £41,787 0s. 5d.—Henry Holden: probate, 29 April 1909, *CGPLA Eng. & Wales*

Holden, Sir Isaac, first baronet (1807–1897), inventor of a wool-combing machine, entrepreneur, and politician, was born on 7 May 1807 at Hurlet, near Paisley, the seventh child of Isaac Holden (d. 1826) and his wife, Alice, née Forrest. His father, a native of Cumberland, combined small-scale farming with leadmining there before moving in 1801 with his Scottish-born wife to Nitshill, between Glasgow and Paisley, where he worked as a coalmine foreman developing local educational facilities in his spare time. The family moved several times during Isaac's youth: to Kilbarchan, where a brief spell at grammar school was followed at the age of eleven by employment as a draw boy and attendance at night school, where he became interested in mechanical matters; to Johnstone, where Isaac combined cotton-factory work with part-time schooling; and when he was fifteen to Paisley, where a year later he became a full-time student, and then teaching assistant, at James Kennedy's school, where the curriculum included maths, physics, Latin, and Greek. Isaac thus received a well-rounded education despite his early acquaintance with the world of work, and his enthusiasm for study, allied to a weak constitution, indicated a cerebral rather than a physical career.

During his early twenties, to support his mother after the death of his father in 1826, Isaac held a succession of teaching posts in Yorkshire and Reading, where he allegedly discovered the Lucifer match. At the same time a deep commitment to Wesleyanism and extensive preaching engagements suggested the possibility of a life of ministry. In 1828 he returned to Glasgow but two years later, poised to establish his own school specializing in commercial subjects, he accepted a bookkeeping position at the worsted manufacturing firm of Townend at Cullingworth, near Keighley in Yorkshire. He achieved semi-managerial status during his sixteen years there and developed, through his own efforts, an expertise in mechanical engineering. Although his employers recognized his value they failed to offer Holden the partnership he frequently requested. At the age of forty he left the firm to form his own small and short-lived worsted factory in Bradford. In 1832 he had married Marion Love, daughter of Angus Love of Paisley, with whom he had four children, Angus (*b*. 1833), Edward (*b*. 1835), Mary (*b*. 1839), and Margaret (*b*. 1842); Marion died in 1847 following a period of ill health and on 5 April 1850 Holden married his second wife, Sarah Sugden (*d*. 1890), daughter of John Sugden of Keighley and sister of the Sugden brothers, worsted manufacturers of Oakworth. Her family was known for Wesleyan piety. Sarah was an important force in his life, particularly in religious matters. They had no children.

It was while he was employed at Townends that Holden became fascinated by the problem of mechanizing the combing of wool, which, for several decades since Edmund Cartwright's first patent for the process in 1789, had proved intractable. Holden was determined to produce a commercially viable machine comb and upon leaving Townend he sought to make the acquaintance of Samuel Cunliffe *Lister, a wealthy and influential Bradford worsted manufacturer, who not only shared his intense interest in wool-combing technology, but owned the patents of the main elements of the machine he hoped to bring to perfection. Pooling their knowledge, but making particular use of Holden's efforts, a patent was filed in 1848—significantly in Lister's name only—on which the 'square-motion' comb was based. The next step was to exploit the machine commercially, by establishing a wool-combing enterprise. A partnership agreement was reached in 1848 (signed 1 January 1849) whereby Lister was to provide the necessary capital and machinery (and was to be free to develop other interests) while Holden was to manage the business and perfect the machine. The enterprise was to be located in France because the square motion was particularly suited to conditions in the industry there, and because the partners wished to dominate French wool-combing by impeding the diffusion of competing technology and filling the market with combed wool produced on their own machine. Accordingly a factory, previously owned by John Collier, also an inventor of a significant machine comb, was rented at St Denis and business began in 1849. As planned, Holden perfected his machine, and developed an enterprise that was organizationally and technically unique. The square motion was one of 169 combing techniques patented in the peak of the 1840s and 1850s, yet it was one of only a handful that achieved long-term commercial success. It possessed special features and was unique in its ability to comb all grades and thicknesses of wool, but its position among the leaders was also the result of Lister's manipulation of the patent system. Through the practice of purchasing patents on inventions which competed with their own designs, the partners achieved a technical near-monopoly, and Holden created a machine that removed potential competitors by producing the finest combed wool. Once the square-motion comb was fully protected he set his mind on manufacturing and on the problems of conducting business in a foreign country.

Operations at St Denis were immediately successful, returning profits of £2000–£3000 per month by the early 1850s. Expansion into the mainstream of the French industry quickly followed; in 1853 production began at purpose-built factories at Croix and Rheims, which became the focus of the Holden family empire. In 1858 Holden bought Lister's share of the business, thus ending ten turbulent years of partnership, and in 1860 the St Denis plant ceased production. Upon Lister's departure, Holden's sons, Edward and Angus, became partners, while the active management of the French factories was undertaken by his nephews, Jonathan Holden and Isaac Holden Crothers, who each received a 10 per cent share in the firm. Holden's activities took the French industry by storm: between 1865 and 1895 his two factories produced 25 per cent of the industry's requirement of combed wool. Production was on the basis of commission combing, and although Holden could not take credit for introducing it into France, he was responsible for maximizing its potential and extending its practice. His factories, which expanded rapidly, were revered as the marvel of the period and in time were copied and became the standard for the wool-combing industry. On the basis of immense profits (over £1 million at Rheims alone in 1863–80, £4000 per week at the two factories during the 1870s), Holden became a wealthy man. While he was not completely self-made, he did practise the well-rehearsed Smilesean values (to the extent of embarrassing his children with his extreme thrift) and his approach to people and business typified the French paternalist entrepreneur. Such was his influence that he became a respected authority on French textile matters and the town of Croix became known as Holden City.

Upon Holden's return to Yorkshire in 1860, Penny Oak Mills in Bradford were acquired for Angus and Edward, and what was to be his own main wool-combing concern in Yorkshire, Alston Works, Bradford, was opened in 1864. He settled at Oakworth House, constructed to his own specification, and became a central figure in the West Riding textile community, a position strengthened by the marriage of three of his children to members of the Illingworth family [*see* Illingworth, Alfred]. He retained a close interest in his French factories, which continued to be managed by his sons and nephews, and although business and mechanical issues remained important to him—legal wrangles with Lister over the invention of the square motion preoccupied his later years—political and religious interests absorbed more of his time. He was sustained in his religious life by his exceedingly devout second wife. While in France he built Wesleyan chapels and ran Bible classes at the sites of each of his enterprises. He gave generously to further the cause of British Wesleyanism, and in 1871 donated £5000 for fifty chapels in the London area. He entered parliamentary politics following the advice of his doctor to find a less onerous occupation after a period of ill health. He sat as Liberal MP for Knaresborough in 1865–8 and remained involved in political activity, offering policy advice on economic matters to the Liberal cause, until he located a replacement seat. In 1882 he became MP for the north-west division of the West Riding and in 1885–6 sat as member for Keighley. In recognition of his contribution to the nation's political life, Holden received a baronetcy in 1893. He died at his home, Oakworth House, Oakworth, on 13 August 1897.

KATRINA HONEYMAN

Sources F. Byles and A. J. Best, *The Holden–Illingworth letters* (1927) • K. Honeyman and J. Goodman, *Technology and enterprise: Isaac Holden and the mechanisation of woolcombing in France, 1848–1914* (1986) • E. M. Sigsworth, 'Sir Isaac Holden, Bt: the first comber in Europe', *Textile history and economic history: essays in honour of Miss Julia de Lacy Mann*, ed. N. B. Harte and K. G. Ponting (1973) • E. Jennings, 'Sir Isaac Holden (1807–1897): "The first comber in Europe"', PhD diss., University of Bradford, 1982 • D. J. Bird, 'The Holden comb', BTech diss., University of Bradford, 1971 • J. M. Tricket, 'A technological appraisal of the Isaac Holden papers', MSc diss., University of Bradford, 1977 • private information (2004) • *CGPLA Eng. & Wales* (1898) • m. cert. [Sarah Sugden] • d. cert.
Archives U. Leeds, Brotherton L., diaries; political, family, and business corresp. and papers • University of Bradford, J. B. Priestley Library, political, business, and family corresp. and papers
Likenesses H. Furniss, pen-and-ink drawing, NPG • I. S. Sidley, oils, City of Bradford Art Gallery
Wealth at death £315,883 16s. 3d.: probate, 18 Feb 1898, *CGPLA Eng. & Wales*

Holden, Lawrence (1710–1778), Presbyterian minister and author, was born at Bolton-le-Moors, Lancashire, probably the son of John Holden, and might have been baptized at Bolton-le-Moors on 14 January 1711. He was educated for the ministry at Warrington under Charles Owen and commenced his ministerial career about 1732 at Whitworth, Lancashire, moving to Doncaster in 1735 and finally to Maldon, Essex, in 1740, where he remained until his death.

Holden was a rational dissenter whose beliefs evolved through Arianism into the adoption of unitarian principles, and 'he had not the smallest tincture of Calvinistic divinity about him' (*Monthly Repository*, 1806, 561–3). His theological views were considered advanced in Maldon, and there was opposition from the parish church to the school which he ran. 'He was possessed of learning but his style was remarkably diffuse … he appears to have been a very amiable man though not a popular preacher' (Burls, 22). His amiability did not prevent a split in the congregation arising over his theology, the seceders opening a separate place of worship in 1765. At his death the original congregation disappeared, and the seceders moved back into the old building the following year. Holden's chief works were paraphrases of books of the Old Testament. *A Paraphrase of the Books of Job, Psalms, Proverbs and Ecclesiastes*, published in 1763, was widely quoted among dissenters, with *A Paraphrase on Isaiah* following in 1776.

Holden married, first, a daughter of Mr A. Whitworth in the 1720s and, second, between 1736 and 1740, a daughter of John Slack of Long Elmsel, West Riding; she died on 7 January 1808 aged eighty-five. He died on 5 August 1778 at Maldon of a bladder disorder. His son by his second marriage, **Lawrence Holden** (1752–1844), also a Presbyterian minister but later a Unitarian minister, was born at Maldon on 17 December 1752. He took over his father's theological position and developed it over a long life. In 1766 he entered Hoxton Academy, which while orthodox in foundation provided the basis for his future thinking: 'almost all the students were against me' (*Christian Reformer*, 780–83). He was much influenced while at the academy by Caleb Fleming, whose biography he later edited.

Holden was appointed assistant minister at the Presbyterian meeting-house at Tenterden, Kent, in July 1772 at the age of nineteen ('the laying on of hands I considered an absurdity'; *Christian Reformer*, 782), and was still the nominal minister when he died aged ninety-one. A ministry of nearly seventy-two years is a remarkable feat of endurance, though he played only a very limited part in preaching after the appointment of Edward Talbot as a co-minister in 1827. In January 1777 he married Mary, a daughter of James Blackmore; she died in 1809. Longevity and his strong views made him a well-known figure among dissenters, and he was rightly considered by Edward Talbot as 'the father and apostle of Unitarianism in Kent' (ibid., 780). He died at Tenterden on 19 March 1844 and was buried in the burial-ground of the meeting-house he had served for so long on 26 March.

ALAN RUSTON

Sources *Monthly Repository*, 1 (1806), 561–3 • *Christian Reformer, or, Unitarian Magazine and Review*, 11 (1844), 263–4 • 'A brief memoir of the Rev. Lawrence Holden', *Christian Reformer, or, Unitarian Magazine and Review*, 11 (1844), 780–86 • *IGI* • A. Sparke, *Bibliographia Boltoniensis* (1913), 83 • R. Burls, *A discourse on early nonconformity in Maldon* (1840); repr. (1926), 22 • *DNB* • Bolton Metropolitan Archives, MSS ZZ 6/22 • T. W. Davids, *Annals of evangelical nonconformity in Essex* (1863), 426 • *Monthly Repository*, 3 (1808), 50 • W. Stevens, *Funeral sermon* (1844) • R. Stott, *Hallfold Congregational Chapel, 1698–1948* (1948), 20 • C. E. Surman, index to dissenting ministers, DWL • will, PRO, PROB 11/2000, sig. 466 [Lawrence Holden (1752–1844)] • J. van den Berg and G. F. Nuttall, *Philip Doddridge* (1987), 76, n. 35
Likenesses engraving (Lawrence Holden (1752–1844)), repro. in B. A. Packer, *The Unitarian heritage in Kent* (1991), 19 • silhouette (Lawrence Holden (1752–1844)), repro. in B. A. Packer, *The Unitarian heritage in Kent* (1991), 19
Wealth at death Lawrence Holden (1752–1844): will, PRO, PROB 11/2000, fol. 123

Holden, Lawrence (1752–1844). *See under* Holden, Lawrence (1710–1778).

Holden, Luther (1815–1905), surgeon and anatomist, was born on 11 December 1815 in his grandfather's house at Birmingham. He was the second son of the Revd Henry Augustus Holden (1785–1870), who married his cousin Mary Willetts, daughter of Hyla Holden of Wednesbury in Staffordshire. The classical scholar Henry *Holden [see under Holden, Hubert Ashton] was his brother. His father, on retiring from the army with the rank of lieutenant, matriculated at Worcester College, Oxford, in 1814 (BA 1817), and held the curacies of Wolstanton in Shropshire and of Warmington near Banbury. Here he took pupils, but on being left a small fortune gave up his curacy and lived at Brighton and afterwards in London. His eldest son was Henry *Holden (1814–1909) [see under Holden, Hubert Ashton]. His fourth son, Philip Melanchthon Holden (1823–1904), was for forty-two years rector of Upminster in Essex.

Luther Holden, after successive education at home with

his father's pupils, at a private school in Birmingham, and at Le Havre in 1827, where he made rapid progress in French, entered St Bartholomew's Hospital, London, in 1831. Apprenticed for five years at the age of seventeen to Edward Stanley, he was admitted MRCS in 1838, and then studied for one year in Berlin and another in Paris, where an Italian student taught him to speak and to read Italian. He was surgeon to the Metropolitan Dispensary, Fore Street, from 1843, living in the Old Jewry and teaching anatomy to private pupils, among whom was William Palmer, the poisoner. Holden was one of the twenty-four successful candidates at the first examination for the newly established order of fellows of the Royal College of Surgeons (24 December 1843).

Appointed in 1846 with A. M. McWhinnie superintendent of dissections (or demonstrator) at St Bartholomew's Hospital, Holden was elected in 1859 jointly with Frederic Skey to lecture upon descriptive and surgical anatomy. This office he resigned in June 1871. Elected assistant surgeon to the hospital in July 1860, and full surgeon in August 1865, he became consulting surgeon in 1881. He resigned his hospital appointments on reaching the age of sixty-five, and, moving from his house at 54 Gower Street to Pinetoft, Rushmere, near Ipswich, he then spent much of his time travelling, visiting Egypt, Australia, India, and Japan. In 1898 he visited Johannesburg. He remained surgeon to the Foundling Hospital from 1864 until his death. At the Royal College of Surgeons Holden was a member of the council (1868–84), an examiner in anatomy and physiology (1875–6), and a member of the board of dental examiners (1879–82). He was vice-president (1877–8), president in 1879, and Hunterian orator in 1881. Holden was married twice (both wives bore the same name and were of the same family): first, in July 1851 he married Frances, daughter of Benjamin Wasey Sterry of Upminster, Essex; second, in 1868, he married Frances, daughter of Wasey Sterry, who survived him. He had no children.

Holden, one of the last members of the anatomical school of surgery of the mid-nineteenth century, was primarily interested in anatomical, and only in a subordinate degree in surgical, study, and then in its clinical rather than in its operative aspect. He believed that anatomy could be learned only by personal dissection and examination of the dissected subject, and not by lectures, books, or pictures. 'One thing he abhorred with all his might, and that was the modern specialist. He believed in the good general surgeon who knew his anatomy and physiology and their applications to surgery' (Plarr, 552). An unpublished paper by him, 'On the mechanism of the hip joint', read at the Abernethian Society at St Bartholomew's Hospital (24 November 1850), proved to be influential. It dealt with the effect of atmospheric pressure in retaining the ball-shaped head of the femur within the socket of the acetabulum, and with the importance of keeping the anterior part of the capsular ligament in the erect attitude.

Holden's publications include a *Manual of the Dissection of the Human Body* (1850), a book which proved popular, and *Human Osteology* (2 vols., 1855), which is his most important

work. The illustrations by Holden and etched on stone by Thomas Godart, librarian of the medical school of St Bartholomew's Hospital, are of the highest order; they formed at the time a new feature in the teaching of anatomy, for the origins and insertions of the muscles were shown upon the figures of the bones in red and blue lines. His 'Landmarks medical and surgical', first published in *St Bartholomew's Hospital Reports*, 2 (1866), and 6 (1870), was separately issued in an enlarged and revised form in 1876; and was translated into Spanish by D. Servendo Talón y Calva (Madrid, 1894). It was a study of the application of anatomy to surgery, proving how much anatomy could be learned on the surface of the living body while the skin was yet unbroken.

A fluent linguist and a good classicist, as well as a keen sportsman, Holden was a conspicuously handsome member of a handsome family, and was seen at his best in the hunting field, 'for though physically bold he was mentally timid! He far preferred clearing a five-barred gate in the hunting field to doing a major operation' (*BMJ*, 338). Holden died at Walcot Lodge, Putney, on 6 February 1905, and was buried in the cemetery of the parish church at Upminster. By his will he bequeathed £3000 to the medical school of St Bartholomew's Hospital to endow a scholarship in surgery. He also made generous bequests to St Bartholomew's Hospital and to the Foundling Hospital.

D'A. POWER, *rev.* MICHAEL BEVAN

Sources *The Lancet* (18 Feb 1905), 405–53 · *BMJ* (11 Feb 1905), 337–8 · V. G. Plarr, *Plarr's Lives of the fellows of the Royal College of Surgeons of England*, rev. D'A. Power, 2 vols. (1930) · personal knowledge (1912) · private information (1912) · *CGPLA Eng. & Wales* (1905) · *St Bartholomew's Hospital Reports*, 41 (1905), xxxi–xxxviii · J. N. Bagnall, *A history of Wednesbury* (1854)
Archives St Bartholomew's Hospital, London
Likenesses T. H. Maguire, lithograph, 1858, Wellcome L. · J. E. Millais, oils, 1880, St Bartholomew's Hospital, London · J. Linnel, etching, 1890 (after J. E. Millais), Wellcome L. · J. E. Millais, portrait, 1912, St Bartholomew's Hospital, London · T. Godart, oils, St Bartholomew's Hospital, London · photograph, repro. in *The Lancet* · photograph, repro. in *BMJ*
Wealth at death £110,289 1s. 1d.: probate, 10 April 1905, *CGPLA Eng. & Wales*

Holden, Moses (1777–1864), astronomer, was born on 21 November 1777 at Black Horse Street, Bolton, Lancashire, the youngest of the three children of Thomas Holden, a hand-loom weaver, and his wife, Joyce. His parents moved some five years later to Preston, where Holden first worked as a hand-loom weaver. On their return to Bolton he laboured in a foundry there until disabled by an accident, after which he found employment as a landscape gardener near Preston. His love of astronomy developed at an early age, leading him to acquire an extensive library of books to guide his studies of this and other sciences. He gave talks on astronomy, and found patrons among the rising manufacturers of Preston, including Samuel Horrocks MP, to whose daughters he gave lessons in astronomy.

In 1814 Holden began to design his celebrated grand orrery, manufacturing its castings and gear wheels with the assistance of several local mechanics and a watch-maker. He learned to paint on glass the pictures of the planets and the various diagrams which, projected by a magic lantern, accompanied his demonstrations. His first public lecture with the orrery and lantern slides was given at the Theatre Royal in Preston in April 1815. A tour through the northern towns which followed proved so successful and profitable that for the next eleven years Holden toured continually throughout England. In 1826 he devoted the proceeds of one of his lectures to the erection of a memorial tablet in St Michael's Church, Toxteth, near Liverpool, dedicated to the astronomer Jeremiah Horrocks (1618–1641), who was born and died at Toxteth. Holden published a small atlas of fixed stars in 1818 which ran through several editions, and issued a yearly almanac from 1835 until the repeal of stamp duty flooded the market with cheap almanacs. He made the acquaintance of many scientists and astronomers, including William Rogerson of the Royal Greenwich Observatory; Rogerson's letter praising the educational value of Holden's orrery and a testimonial signed by the worthies of Preston were useful advertisements. The date of Holden's marriage to Isabelle is not known. She, and their daughter, Ann Leonora (b. 1829), survived him; their son, William Archimedes Holden (b. 1818), predeceased him, leaving a young family. Holden settled again in Preston from 1828, giving courses on astronomy there until 1852 and occasionally lecturing in nearby towns. In 1834 he was presented with the freedom of the borough of Preston.

Holden was a skilful mechanic and made several microscopes and at least one telescope, the latter for the Revd William Carus Wilson, who declared it superior to the more expensive one he had purchased from the noted London maker Dollond. He helped to establish the Institution for the Diffusion of Knowledge in Preston, and from 1837 was an enthusiastic member of the British Association for the Advancement of Science, attending their yearly meetings until 1855. Holden frequently officiated as a Methodist preacher and, though he attended services in the established church, he took part in Wesleyan Bible and prayer meetings throughout his life. Despite the theatrical nature of his own lectures, he refused to attend stage plays, nor could his friends persuade him otherwise even when his son played the ghost in a local performance of Hamlet. Holden was none the less known for his ability to tell humorous stories, in a rich Lancashire accent which he never lost. In his later years he suffered from poor health, and he died at his home, one of two houses he owned in Jordan Street, Preston, on 3 June 1864.

ANITA McCONNELL

Sources Preston Guardian (11 June 1864), 6 · d. cert. · will, 1864
Archives Lancs. RO
Wealth at death under £3000: probate, 13 Aug 1864, CGPLA Eng. & Wales

Holden, Samuel (1674/5–1740), merchant, was baptized at Christ Church, Southwark, Surrey, in August 1675, the son of the merchant Joseph Holden, citizen and haberdasher of London (originally from the East Riding of Yorkshire), and his second wife, Priscilla Watt. His father died in 1683,

when Samuel was only eight, but the boy inherited useful connections in the City. In 1692, at seventeen, he was apprenticed, in the Drapers' Company, to the great Baltic merchant, Nathaniel Gould, later treasurer of the Eastland Company, governor of the Russia Company, director and governor of the Bank of England, and director of the new East India Company, a major collaborator of Sir Gilbert Heathcote in the creative whig financial activity of 1694–1710. Gould sent young Holden to Riga to learn his trade. At the conclusion of his apprenticeship, he continued in business in Russia, but had returned to London as an independent merchant by 1709, when on 1 March he was elected assistant (director) of the Russia Company, and on 4 April married, at St Michael, Wood Street, Jane (1679/80–1766), daughter of John Whitehall (or Whitehaulgh), citizen of London. They raised one son, who died in 1736, and three daughters.

During his Riga years, Holden became friendly with Matthew Shiffner (d. 1756), with whom he later participated in major commercial undertakings. Shiffner, a native of Russia, had resided long enough in England to become naturalized on 8 October 1711. On his subsequent return to Russia, Shiffner married in 1720 Hedwig Agnata Bruiningk (1704–1793) of Riga, later gouvernante to Anna, duchess of Courland, niece of Peter the Great, and future Russian empress (1730–40). Such court connections must have appeared most useful to his allies trading to Russia, where firms with which Shiffner was connected—particularly Shiffner and Wolff—had enough influence to obtain valuable export privileges and army supply contracts.

In London, Holden was at various times active in the trades to Lisbon, Leghorn, Smyrna, the West Indies, and New England, but he played a major part in trade to Russia. He collaborated with John Gore in importing Russian iron, and with Shiffner and Wolff in cloth shipments to the Russian army and in hemp exports from Russia. Some of this hemp was sent directly to Leghorn, and olive oil returned to Russia. Peter the Great showed confidence by entrusting Holden with the care of Russian apprentices sent to England for training. The British government also entrusted him with the transportation of horses to Russia as gifts for the tsar, as well as with remittances to British diplomatic representatives there. In London, his growing standing was marked by his selection as assistant, consul, and ultimately (1728–40) governor of the Russia Company, and by his long service during 1720–40 on the court of directors of the Bank of England, of which he became deputy governor in 1727–9 and then governor in 1729–31. In 1737 he was also one of the City trustees for the loan of £370,000 to the holy Roman emperor, secured on the copper mines of Hungary. Holden, close to the Walpole administration, was regularly consulted by the Board of Trade on the negotiations leading to the British–Russian commercial treaty of 1734, and in 1735 was elected member of parliament for East Looe, a Treasury-controlled borough. He was also named one of the directors of the Royal Hospital at Greenwich.

By the 1730s Samuel Holden was a leading figure among dissenters. In 1735 he was asked by the Massachusetts house of representatives to serve as their agent in London, but he declined the honour as inconsistent with his other commitments. Nevertheless, in 1732, when the dissenting communities were seriously excited by the possibility of obtaining the repeal of the Test and Corporation Acts, he agreed to serve as chairman of a committee set up that year by the deputies from the three principal dissenting confessions to work for repeal. His personal opinions were, however, expressed in his presidential address to a 'general assembly' of dissenters on 29 November 1732. He warned his listeners that, with a parliamentary election in the offing, this was not a propitious time to bring the issue before parliament. Yet he made his own unqualified dissenting sympathies clear by referring in the speech to the 'bigotry' and 'interest' of those who opposed repeal. The printing of his address in the London press evoked a pamphlet reply (*A Letter to Samuel Holden*, 1732) from a proministerial author more sympathetic to the established church. Holden's rejoinder (*An Answer to a Letter to Samuel Holden*, 1732) was his only known avowed publication. Several other pro-repeal pamphlets published about the same time were addressed to Holden, by implication recognized as the lay leader of dissent. One of these (*An inquiry into the Propriety of Applying to Parliament for the Repeal of the Corporation and Test-Acts*, 1732) referred to the divisions among the dissenters 'heightened by a secret management, under ministerial direction, by representing the most dismal consequences to some of them, at private conferences, which by these few were to be sent among the rest of the people'. This can be interpreted as criticism both of Holden's closeness to the ministry, and of his style of leadership, but had little immediate effect. Holden kept his committee quiet during the excise crisis of 1733 and the election of 1734, but, when the repeal question was finally brought before the Commons in 1736, Walpole disappointed his dissenter friends by continuing inactive and neutral. Holden, obviously embarrassed, spoke for the repeal bill during that session, but, on its defeat, felt obliged to resign as chairman of the dissenting deputies' special committee.

Holden was particularly interested in the Congregational colonies in New England. His correspondents there included the prominent Boston clergyman Benjamin Colman, who, on a visit to London in the 1690s, had lodged with Holden's mother, Mrs Thomas Parkhurst. In the 1730s, Holden sent Colman books and cash worth nearly £1000 sterling, for distribution to the deserving. At Holden's death Colman published in Boston a memorial sermon of tribute (1740), and in London a selection of Holden's letters to him on spiritual topics (1741). Samuel Mather, another eminent Massachusetts divine, dedicated to Holden his *An Apology for the Liberties of the Churches in New England* (1738).

At the time of his death, Samuel Holden resided in Roehampton House, Surrey, an impressive leased villa, and kept a counting house in Bishopsgate Street in the City. He also owned property in Lincoln's Inn Fields, as well as landholdings in Derbyshire, which secured his wife's dower rights. At his death on 12 June 1740, he left a personal estate of over £80,000. Of this, £60,000 was left to his wife and two surviving daughters, with the balance to be used for charitable purposes selected by his widow. Part of this benefaction went to Harvard College, and was used there for the construction of Holden Chapel. Holden was buried in St Bride's Church, Fleet Street on 20 August 1740. In 1744 Samuel Holden's daughter Mary became the second wife of John Jolliffe MP. In 1866 their greatgrandson, W. G. H. Jolliffe, was created Baron Hylton.

JACOB M. PRICE

Sources S. Holden, estate papers, Som. ARS, Lord Hylton's deposit, DD/HY boxes 12–13, 42, 45 · London Port Book, 1718–19, Leeds Central Library, Archive Department, NH 2440 · will of Joseph Holden, 1681, proved, 1683, PRO, PROB 11/374, sig. 125 · GL, Russia Company Minutes, MS 11741 · IGI · 'Boyd's Inhabitants of London', Society of Genealogists, London, nos. 35, 141 · Lord Hylton, 'A city man two hundred years ago', *National Review*, 78 (1921–2), 539–47 · E. Cruickshanks, 'Holden, Samuel', HoP, *Commons, 1715–54*, 2.144–5; L. B. Namier, 'Shiffner, Henry', HoP, *Commons, 1754–90*, 3.434–6 · *GM*, 1st ser., 10 (1740), 317 · W. M. Acres, 'Directors of the Bank of England', *N&Q*, 179 (1940), 80–83, esp. 81 · N. C. Hunt, *Two early political associations: the Quakers and the dissenting deputies in the age of Sir Robert Walpole* (1961) · N. C. Hunt, 'The Russia Company and the government, 1730–42', *Oxford Slavonic Papers*, 7 (1957), 27–65 · D. Reading, *The Anglo-Russian commercial treaty of 1734* (1938) · P. Boyd, ed., *Roll of the Drapers' Company of London* (1934) · F. W. Steer, ed., *The Shiffner archives: a catalogue* (1959) · Lord Hylton [H. G. H. Jolliffe], *The Jolliffes of Staffordshire* (1892) · J. T. Adams, 'Colman, Benjamin', *DAB* · B. Colman, *A funeral sermon on the death of the Honourable Samuel Holden, esq., of London …* (1740) · H. F. Waters, 'Genealogical gleanings in England', *New England Historical and Genealogical Register*, 45 (1891), 163–4 · 'Index to London marriage licenses, 1705–9', GL · BL, Add. MS 23800, fols. 325–8 [re Hungarian copper loan] · *An inquiry into the propriety of applying to parliament for the repeal of the Corporation and Test Acts: in a letter to S. H.* (1732); 2nd edn (1732) · *A letter to Samuel Holden, esq.: occasioned by his speech delivered from the chair, at a general assembly of dissenters, on the 29th of November, 1732* (1732) · S. H. [S. Holden], *An answer to a letter to Samuel Holden* (1732) · *Letters of Samuel Holden, esquire, to Dr Benjamin Coleman of Boston, New England* (1741), 16 · parish register (burial), Fleet Street, St Bride's · H. von Bruiningk, *Das Geschlecht von Bruiningk in Livland* (Riga, 1913), 33–7

Archives E. Sussex RO, Shiffner MSS · Som. ARS, Hylton MSS

Wealth at death £82,000—book value of personal estate: S. Holden estate MSS, Taunton; *GM*

Holden, Thomas (*d.* 1441), founder of St Mary's College, Oxford, was the son of John Holden, and grandson of Robert Holden, of the village of that name near Whalley, Lancashire. Having probably met Thomas Langley (*d.* 1437) when the latter was heavily involved in the administration of the duchy of Lancaster during the late 1390s, Holden had entered Langley's employ by 1401, and five years later followed his lifelong lord and patron to Durham. During Thomas Langley's thirty-one years as bishop there (1406–37) Holden was always his most important lay servant and councillor, holding office as his chamberlain throughout that period and as episcopal steward after 1422. He also served on various occasions as the bishop's receiver-general and as one of his justices, and was handsomely rewarded for his labours. Married to the wealthy and three times widowed Elizabeth Davis (she had married successively Sir Robert Monboucher, Sir William

Whitchester, and Roger Fulthorp), Holden acquired estates not only in the town and county of Durham but also in Yorkshire, Lancashire, Essex, and the suburbs of London. His most important residence in the north was the manor of Ludworth, 6 miles east of Durham, which he leased for life from his bishop in 1411 and proceeded to fortify during the following decade. Even more generous was Langley's gift to him of the Durham episcopal manor house of the Old Ford, situated on the River Lea 3 miles east of London.

A parliamentary knight of the shire for Northumberland in 1423, even before Langley's death in 1437 Holden was moving in highly influential national circles. Among his fellow executors of the bishop's will were Richard Neville, earl of Salisbury (d. 1460), Richard Beauchamp, earl of Warwick (d. 1439), and William Alnwick, then bishop of Lincoln (d. 1449). It has been conjectured that Alnwick, recently involved himself in a project to establish the first academic college of Benedictine monks at Cambridge, may have helped to persuade Holden to devote part of his considerable fortune to the establishment of a college of Augustinian canons at Oxford. However, the knowledge that the general chapter meetings of the English black canons were urgently seeking the resources to create a common residence at the university must have been very widespread ever since their objective had formed the basis of a petition to parliament in 1421. Three years later Sir Peter Bessels, a Berkshire knight, had indeed agreed to grant Frewin Hall, a large private house within the western circuit of the walls of Oxford, for such a purpose. However, it was only after Bessels's death in 1426 that Thomas Holden acquired the site and subsequently delivered it to the Augustinian canons—in 1435 Holden and his wife received royal licence to transfer Frewin Hall and its large garden to Prior John Sevenokes and his fellow Augustinian canons studying at Oxford. Although the construction of buildings on the site proceeded very slowly, by the time he died between 1 and 13 August 1441, Thomas Holden could be certain that his intervention in the sphere of monastic university education had proved decisive and successful. Within his extremely long will he bequeathed £103 6s. 8d. towards the expenses of building the chapel and library of the new St Mary's College; and he also requested burial, together with his wife (who after his death married Sir Robert Hilton), under a marble tomb in the chapel. His wishes must have been fulfilled, for by the summer of 1443 that chapel was already in use, and the Augustinian general chapter, then meeting at Osney Abbey, solemnly processed to their new college to receive seisin from Elizabeth Holden in the presence of the Oxford town bailiffs. With the dissolution of St Mary's College less than a century later, in 1540, its not undistinguished history was cut abruptly short, and Thomas Holden's tomb—like his prospects of perpetual commemoration—disappeared into undeserved oblivion.

R. B. DOBSON

Sources E. F. Jacob, ed., *The register of Henry Chichele, archbishop of Canterbury, 1414–1443*, 2, CYS, 42 (1937), 579–84, 658–9 · *The register of Thomas Langley, bishop of Durham, 1406–1437*, ed. R. L. Storey, 6 vols., SurtS, 164, 166, 169–70, 177, 182 (1956–70) · R. L. Storey, *Thomas Langley and the bishopric of Durham, 1406–1437* (1961) · E. Evans, 'St Mary's College in Oxford for Austin canons', *Oxfordshire Archaeological Society Report* (1931), 367–91 · Bodl. Oxf., MS Rawl. statutes 34 · J. Blair, 'Frewin Hall, Oxford: a Norman mansion and a monastic college', *Oxoniensia*, 43 (1978), 48–99, esp. 65 · A. Wood, *Survey of the antiquities of the city of Oxford*, ed. A. Clark, 2, OHS, 17 (1890) · R. B. Dobson, 'The religious orders, 1370–1540', *Hist. U. Oxf.* 2: *Late med. Oxf.*, 539–79 · H. E. Salter, ed., *Chapters of the Augustinian canons*, OHS, 74 (1922)

Archives Durham Cath. CL, Durham palatinate records, Bishop Thomas Langley

Wealth at death considerable

Holder, Sir Frederick William (1850–1909), politician in Australia, was born at Happy Valley, near Adelaide, on 12 May 1850, the eldest son of James Morecott Holder, a freeman of the City of London, who had migrated to South Australia shortly after marrying Martha Breakspear Roby, the daughter of a London tailor. He was educated first by his schoolteacher father, and then at St Peter's College, Adelaide. He became a teacher himself and in 1875 was headmaster of the Kooringa public school at Burra Burra, a small township 100 miles north of Adelaide. On 29 March 1877 he married Julia Maria, the daughter of John Ricardo Stephens, a Cornish doctor, farmer, and teacher. Both were staunch and active Wesleyans, and Julia Holder later became president of the Women's Christian Temperance Association and vice-president of the National Council of Women.

Holder's career soon blossomed. He became manager of a local store, town clerk, and managing editor of the *Burra Record*, was elected to the Burra council (mayor in 1885–6), and served on the council of the South Australian School of Mines and Industries. In 1887 he was elected to the house of assembly as member for Burra as a Free-Trader who also favoured the reform of the land laws and payment of members.

Holder sat on several committees and commissions of inquiry, including those on pastoral lands and intercolonial free trade, and in June 1889 became treasurer of the colony in John Cockburn's ministry; when it fell in August 1890 he became leader of the opposition. Briefly premier in 1892, he then succeeded in rallying the disunited liberal forces in the South Australian parliament to form a powerful progressive combination. On 16 June 1893 he joined C. C. Kingston's government as commissioner of public works, and the following April became treasurer and minister in charge of the Northern Territory. Here he promoted settlement, and as treasurer he introduced progressive land and income taxes which enabled him to balance the budget despite the prevailing economic depression. The government also sponsored the enactment of votes for women and Aborigines (the first Australian colony to do so), a conciliation and arbitration act for industrial disputes, a workers' compensation act, and liquor licensing with local option. In December 1899 Holder formed his second administration, becoming treasurer and minister of industry in a ministry which established rural public libraries, sponsored legislation for the early closing of shops and the restriction of coloured immigration, significantly extended the factories and workers' compensation acts, and completed two major water schemes.

A strong supporter of federation, Holder was a member of the convention which framed the commonwealth constitution in 1897–8, and helped secure its acceptance by the South Australian electorate at the referendums in 1898 and 1899. In May 1901 he was elected to the commonwealth parliament for Wakefield, which included his former seat of Burra, and, though a misunderstanding denied him the treasurership in the first federal ministry, he was unanimously elected speaker of the lower house. There he helped establish its procedures and conventions. He was created KCMG in 1902. His report of 1903 laid the foundations for the national library. He was re-elected speaker in 1904 and 1907, but in 1909, after a turbulent all-night sitting, he had a cerebral haemorrhage and died within a few hours in the parliament house at Melbourne on 23 July 1909. He was survived by his widow and eight children. Following a state funeral at Adelaide on 26 July he was buried at West Terrace cemetery. Described by the Adelaide *Advertiser* (24 July 1909) as 'one of the pillars of Australian Liberalism', he had 'stood consistently for the democratic cause', and he made notable contributions to Burra Burra and South Australia.

CHEWTON ATCHLEY, rev. ELIZABETH BAIGENT

Sources *AusDB* · *The Times* (27 July 1909) · A. Deakin, *The federal story: the inner history of the federal cause*, ed. H. Brookes (1944) · D. Jaensch, ed., *The Flinders history of South Australia*, 2: *Political history* (1986) · *The Advertiser* [Adelaide] (24 July 1909) · T. A. Coghlan, *Labour and industry in Australia, from the first settlement in 1788 to the establishment of the commonwealth in 1901*, 4 vols. (1918); repr. (1969)
Archives National Archives of Australia, Canberra · NL Aus.
Likenesses R. Holder, portrait, NL Aus. · E. A. J. Webb, portrait, South Australian House of Assembly, Adelaide, Australia · E. A. J. Webb, portrait, House of Representatives, Canberra, Australia
Wealth at death £5819 17s. 1d.: probate, Australia

Holder, William (1615/16–1698), Church of England clergyman and natural philosopher, was born in Southwell, Nottinghamshire, the elder son of Clement Holder (d. 1638), prebendary of Southwell and rector of Kilvington and South Wheatley. William matriculated pensioner from Pembroke College, Cambridge, in 1633, aged seventeen; he graduated BA in 1637 and proceeded MA in 1640. He was a fellow of his college from 1640 to 1642. He was rector of Barnoldby-le-Beck in Lincolnshire in 1641–2.

About the time war broke out Holder resigned his fellowship and moved to royalist Oxfordshire, becoming rector of Bletchingdon and tutor to the young Christopher Wren, the future architect. In 1643 he married Christopher's elder sister, Susanna Wren (1626/7–1688). Their union was long and happy, but childless. Susanna had (says Aubrey) a 'strange sagacity as to curing wounds', ministering to rich and poor alike, and at one stage incurring the enmity of the court physicians by curing Charles II of a swollen hand (*Brief Lives*, 1.405). Susanna's father, Dean

Christopher Wren, joined them after the war at Bletchingdon, where he died in 1658. At Oxford Holder was incorporated MA in 1644, watched over the undergraduate Christopher Wren, helped obtain the Savilian chair of astronomy for Seth Ward in 1649 after the parliamentary visitation, and became a member of the circle of natural philosophers surrounding Ward and John Wilkins.

At the Restoration Holder was incorporated DD at Oxford in 1661, and was among the first institution of ordinary members of the Royal Society. Through the patronage of Susanna's uncle, the nepotistic Bishop Matthew Wren of Ely, he became prebendary of Ely (installed in 1660), rector of Northwold, Norfolk (1662–87) and, in plurality, rector of Tydd St Giles in the Isle of Ely (1663). He was also a prebendary of Southwell from 1660 to 1664. In 1672 he succeeded to Bishop Stillingfleet's prebendal stall at St Paul's, and from 1674 to 1689 was subdean at the Chapel Royal, where for his haughty discipline and exacting musical standards he was called 'Mr Snub-dean' (Hawkins, 541–4). In 1687 he took up the living of Therfield in Hertfordshire, where he retreated after the death of his wife in 1688. Latterly he overwintered at Alderman Keynton's home in Hertford, where, growing 'old and crazy' (BL, Add. MS 4275, fol. 294), he died on 24 January 1698. He left £455 in his will, in addition to property, much of it in the form of gifts and legacies to his servants and the poor. He was buried, with his wife, in the undercroft of St Paul's Cathedral, their monument standing near to that of its architect.

Holder was, according to his friend and correspondent John Aubrey, 'a handsome, gracefull person, and of a delicate constitution, and of an even and smooth temper … a perfect good man' (*Brief Lives*, 1.404–5). Wood acclaimed him 'a great virtuoso' (Wood, *Ath. Oxon.: Fasti*, 2.59). In 1660 at Bletchingdon he achieved considerable fame by teaching a deaf mute, Alexander Popham, to speak 'plainly and distinctly, and with a good and graceful tone'. Afterwards regressing, Popham was retaught by the eminent mathematician John Wallis, author of a theoretical treatise on speech, who ostentatiously claimed the credit. In 1668 Holder presented a paper to the Royal Society on the workings of the ear, and followed it in 1669 with a treatise, *Elements of Speech*, in which he deplored the 'faulty alphabets' of grammarians and named and analysed the physical parts of speech in pursuit of a basis for a universal language. Wilkins's treatise of 1668 on universal language had owed much to discussions with Holder. Holder's account in the *Elements* of his work with Popham provoked an exhaustive and unconvincing rebuttal from the disputatious Wallis (in his *A Defence of the Royal Society*, 1670, and in the *Philosophical Transactions* of July 1670). In a long-delayed reply Holder accused Wallis of 'rifling his Neighbours, and adorning himself with their spoyls' (Holder, *Supplement*, 10), supplying extensive details to support his charge. Senior fellows, including Hooke and Oldenburg, supported Holder; Wallis's eminence sheltered him. Holder was a moderately active member of the Royal Society, mainly between 1663 and 1683, although his practical contributions were disappointing, and also a member of

Robert Hooke's informal 'clubb for Natural Philosophy and mechanicks' ('Espinasse, 109, 114–15).

A competent composer of services and anthems, Holder in retirement wrote an influential and well-received treatise, *Principles of Harmony* (1694), the surviving correspondence concerning which illustrates the complexities of contemporary music publishing. It was still regarded as a standard work for long afterwards, both in England and abroad, and remains of interest for its account of meantone tuning.

Holder's subsequent *Discourse Concerning Time* (1694), written to explain the issue of calendar reform and reissued in 1701 after the renewed English rejection of the Gregorian calendar, was an elegant exposition of the concept of harmony on a cosmic scale. In it he developed the idea that rational human perception was required to give meaning to creation, for 'Time is always Transient, in a continual Flux, neither to be seen, nor felt, nor reserved; but only measured by an Act of the Mind' (Holder, *Discourse Concerning Time*, 1–2, 13).

Holder's reputation was probably hampered in his day by his lack of intellectual competitiveness. His work was none the less of enduring value, memorable for his declaration of the value of the written word: 'Written language … is permanent, and it reacheth the absent, and posterity, and by it we speak after we are dead' (Holder, *Elements*, 8–9).   ROBERT POOLE

Sources *Brief lives, chiefly of contemporaries, set down by John Aubrey, between the years 1669 and 1696*, ed. A. Clark, 1 (1898) • Wood, *Ath. Oxon.: Fasti* (1820) • T. Birch, *The history of the Royal Society of London*, 4 vols. (1756–7) • J. Wallis, *A defence of the Royal Society* (1678) • J. Hawkins, *A general history of the science and practice of music*, 5 vols. (1776) • H. E. Poole, 'The printing of William Holder's *Principles of harmony*', *Proceedings of the Royal Musical Association*, 101 (1974–5), 31–43 • B. J. Shapiro, *John Wilkins, 1614–1672: an intellectual biography* (1969) • M. 'Espinasse, *Robert Hooke* (1956) • M. Hunter, *The Royal Society and its fellows, 1660–1700: the morphology of an early scientific institution*, 2nd edn (1994) • M. Hunter, *Establishing the new science: the experience of the early Royal Society* (1989) • M. Hunter, *John Aubrey and the realm of learning* (1975) • M. Tilmouth, 'Holder, William', *New Grove* • will, PRO, PROB 11/443, sig. 39 • Venn, *Alum. Cant.* • Foster, *Alum. Oxon.* • *New view of London*, 2 (1708) • J. A. Bennett, *The mathematical science of Christopher Wren* (1982) • J. Bentham, *The history and antiquities of the conventual and cathedral church of Ely*, ed. J. Bentham, 2nd edn (1812) • F. Blomefield and C. Parkin, *An essay towards a topographical history of the county of Norfolk*, [2nd edn], 11 vols. (1805–10), vol. 2 • Burney, *Hist. mus.*, vol. 3 • E. Carter, *The history of the University of Cambridge* (1753) • R. Clutterbuck, *History and antiquities of the county of Hertford* (1728) • F.-J. Fétis, *Biographie universelle des musiciens, et bibliographie générale de la musique*, 8 vols. (Brussels, 1835–44), vol. 5 • J. Granger, *A biographical history of England, from Egbert the Great to the revolution*, 2 vols. (1769); suppl. (1774) • W. Kennet, *Register and chronicle of the history of England* (1728) • *Peter Langtoft's chronicle (as illustrated and improv'd by Robert of Brunne) from the death of Cadwalader to the end of K. Edward the First's reign*, ed. T. Hearne, 2 vols. (1725) • *Fasti Angl., 1541–1857*, [Ely] • *Fasti Angl.* (Hardy) • N. Luttrell, *A brief historical relation of state affairs from September 1678 to April 1714*, 6 vols. (1857) • R. Newchurch, *Repertorium: … history of the diocese of Lincoln* (1708) • *The correspondence of Henry Oldenburg*, ed. and trans. A. R. Hall and M. B. Hall, 6 (1969) • E. F. Rimbault, ed., *The old cheque-book, or book of remembrance, of the Chapel Royal, from 1561 to 1744*, CS, new ser., 3 (1872) • W. Holder, 'Of an experiment, concerning deafness', *PTRS*, 3 (1668), 665–8 • review, *PTRS*, 4 (1669), 958–9 • J. E. Stephens, *Aubrey on education* (1972) • T. Thomson, *History of the Royal Society from its institution to the end of the eighteenth century* (1812) • J. Ward, *The lives of the professors of Gresham College* (1740) • T. Warton, *Life and literary remains of Ralph Bathurst* (1761) • J. Wilson, *Roger North on music* (1959) • C. Wren, *Parentalia, or, Memoirs of the family of the Wrens* (1750) • W. Holder, *Elements of speech: an essay inquiring into the natural production of letters: with an appendix concerning persons deaf and dumb* (1669) • W. Holder, *A supplement to the Philosphical Transactions of July 1670, with some reflexions on Dr. John Wallis, his letter there inserted* (1678) • W. Holder, *A treatise of the natural grounds and principles of harmony* (1694) • W. Holder, *A discourse concerning time, for the better understanding of the Julian year and calendar* (1694)

Archives BL, Add. MSS 4275, fol. 294; 5871, fol. 49; 32352, fol. 44; MS Egerton 2231, fols. 195, 198 • BL, Harley MSS 7338–7339 • BL, Sloane MS 1338, fols. 56–180 • RS, Royal Society register book | Bodl. Oxf., MS Aubrey 12

Likenesses D. Loggan, line engraving, 1683, BM, NPG

Wealth at death legacies of £455; plus library, goods, and chattels: will, PRO, PROB 11/443, sig. 39

Holderness, Sir Thomas William, first baronet (1849–1924), administrator in India, came from a Yorkshire family, his grandfather Thomas Holderness being a timber merchant in Hull. His father, John William Holderness (d. 1865), settled for a time in New Brunswick, Canada, where he married Mary Ann Macleod and where, at St John's, Thomas Holderness, the eldest son, was born on 11 June 1849. Soon after his birth his parents returned to England, and in 1867 he was sent to Cheltenham College to be educated. The untimely death of his father two years previously left the family in straitened circumstances, but Holderness was able to maintain himself at Cheltenham by means of scholarships and prizes, and in 1869 he went as a scholar to University College, Oxford. In 1869 and again in 1870 he passed the open competitive examination for the Indian Civil Service, on the later occasion obtaining a place high enough to give him a choice of his province. In those days it was comparatively rare for Indian Civil Service probationers to pursue their university studies simultaneously with their preparation for India, but Holderness continued to read for classical honour moderations, in which he obtained a second class in 1871. Next year he obtained a second class in law and modern history.

After proceeding to India in the winter of 1872–3, Holderness spent his first three years in the small stations of Bijnor, Fatehpur, and Muzaffarnagar in what were then called the North-Western Provinces. As many others had done who had risen to distinction in the Indian service, he began to contribute to the press, and it was probably his writings as well as his exceptional administrative ability that attracted the notice of the lieutenant-governor, Sir John Strachey, and led to his being called in 1876 to the provincial capital, Allahabad, for secretarial duties in the offices of the government and the board of revenue. It is a coincidence that in later years he was entrusted with the work of revising and reissuing (4th edn, 1911) Sir John Strachey's classic work, *India: its Administration and Progress*. As a secretary he showed a capacity so obvious and outstanding that, during the rest of his Indian career, he never, except for one short interval, returned to executive work in the districts. At Allahabad he laid the foundations of a comprehensive knowledge of the revenue systems of

Sir Thomas William Holderness, first baronet (1849–1924), by
Walter Stoneman, 1920

India and an understanding of their impact on the well-being of agriculture. After five years' apprenticeship in the provincial offices, in 1881 Holderness was appointed under-secretary to the government of India in the revenue department, and there he remained, occasionally acting as secretary, until 1885. On 14 March 1885 he married Lucy Shepherd (d. 1948), daughter of George Robert *Elsmie CSI. They had a daughter and a son. In 1888, after being in charge of the district of Pilibhit for a short time, Holderness was appointed director of land records and agriculture, and later, secretary to the government of the United Provinces in both judicial and financial departments.

Although in 1894 Sir Antony MacDonnell, a member of the viceroy's council, told the viceroy, Lord Elgin, that Holderness had in fact 'done badly' as director of land records and agriculture, pointing out that the failure of the records in the provinces was 'primarily due to him' (MacDonnell to Elgin, 22 June 1894, Elgin MSS, MS Eur. F/84/64), Holderness's promotion was accelerated by his work in dealing with measures of relief in the disastrous series of famines with which the nineteenth century closed. The United Provinces were gravely affected as early as 1896, and Sir Antony MacDonnell who, as lieutenant-governor, directed the relief operations, summoned Holderness to assist him. Owing to the experience so gained, when the distress later on spread to other provinces, he was called by the viceroy, Lord Elgin, to Simla, as

adviser to the imperial government in the emergency. Holderness wrote the official *Narrative of the Famine in India, 1896–97*, which Lord Elgin regarded as 'a triumph', because it was 'so complete a narrative of so widespread a calamity', submitted at 'such an early date' (Elgin to Hamilton, 11 Nov 1897, Elgin MSS, MS Eur. F/84/15). For his services he was rewarded by the CSI (1898), and by the kaisar-i-Hind gold medal (1901). In 1898 he became secretary to the government of India, revenue and agricultural department, and was now in the recognized line of succession to the headship of a province. He was, in fact, offered such a post, but in order not to continue separated from his family, then resident in England, declined.

In 1901 Holderness retired from the Indian Civil Service and accepted the post of secretary in the revenue, statistics, and commerce department at the India Office, where Lord George Hamilton was the secretary of state. Lord Curzon, the viceroy, was instrumental in realizing the transfer of Holderness from the Indian Civil Service to the India Office; Curzon, who had a bitter relationship with the Council of India, was possibly expecting Holderness to forward the viceroy's views in the India Office. Soon, Hamilton found Holderness 'first rate also in the accuracy of his knowledge and its extent, and in the quickness of his work' (Hamilton to Curzon, 18 July 1901, Curzon MSS, MS Eur. F/811/160). Holderness was now in the wider stream of the world's affairs. International conferences on the sugar trade and on problems of sanitation claimed his attention, and the selection of the experts required by the great expansion of the scientific services, especially those connected with agriculture, during Lord Curzon's viceroyalty, came into his hands. He also attended the Colonial Conferences in 1902 and 1907 as a representative of the India Office. In recognition of his work as secretary he was created KCSI in 1907, and in 1912, on the death of Sir Richmond Ritchie, the permanent under-secretary of state, he was promoted to the vacant post, a unique distinction for an officer of the Indian services. To a former colleague still in the Indian service who had congratulated him on his promotion, Holderness wrote that '[We] are generally a despised race of sun-baked office-mongers in the thought of the average Briton, and anything that tends to contradict this notion is a consolation to us as a body' (Holderness to Butler, 15 Nov 1912, Butler MSS, MS Eur. F/816/45).

In June 1914 Holderness had reached the full retiring age of sixty-five, but he was granted an extended term of office, and after the outbreak of war his great experience and soundness of judgement made him an invaluable adviser, first in connection with the organization of munition supplies and the utilization of civil officers for war work, and later in connection with discussions on the Rowlatt bills and the Montagu–Chelmsford reforms. Accordingly, the further retention of his services was considered indispensable, and his term of office was extended by successive secretaries of state until 1919. In 1917, to the embarrassment of the secretary of state, Austen Chamberlain, Holderness was sympathetic to the view that Indian princes should be given more freedom in handling their affairs. To the Montagu–Chelmsford reforms he gave his cordial public support, being convinced that a liberal measure of political advance should be conceded in India. However, in fact Holderness was critical of the diarchy idea itself, because he thought that '[A] unitary government is more intelligible and more in accordance with the elementary principle of good government' (Holderness to Butler, 16 Jan 1919, Butler MSS, MS Eur. F/816/45).

In 1917 Holderness was appointed GCB (having been created KCB in 1914), and in 1920, after his retirement, a baronetcy was conferred on him. The secretary of state, Edwin Montagu, offered Holderness a peerage, but the latter refused on financial grounds. He was succeeded as permanent under-secretary by another former Indian civil servant, Sir William Duke. He devoted his retirement to reading, writing, and business in the City, where his keenness and sound judgement impressed his new colleagues. He was on the board of directors of the Bengal and North-Western Railways. Sanity of judgement was, indeed, his predominant trait; moreover, he had considerable literary gifts, and the works which he wrote or edited on Indian questions, such as *Peoples and Problems of India* (1912; rev. edn, 1920) and *India's Arduous Journey* in the series These Eventful Years (1924), in a lucid and persuasive style, commanded wide attention. He was of studious character, grave in demeanour, and simple, almost ascetic, in his habits of life.

Holderness died very suddenly on 16 September 1924, while walking on the golf-links at the heath, Walton on the Hill, near his home at Tadworth in Surrey. His wife survived him.   J. O. MILLER, *rev.* TAKEHIKO HONDA

Sources *The Times* (17 Sept 1924) · *India Office Lists* · private information (1937) · BL OIOC, Curzon MSS, MS Eur. F 111 · BL OIOC, Elgin MSS · BL OIOC, Chelmsford MSS, MS Eur. E. 264 · BL OIOC, Butler MSS, MS Eur. F 116 · B. M. Bhatia, *Famines in India: a study in some aspects of the economic history of India, 1860–1945* (1963) · P. G. Robb, *The government of India and reform: policies towards politics and the constitution, 1916–1921* (1976) · J. E. Kendle, *The colonial and imperial conferences, 1887–1911: a study in imperial organization* (1967) · S. R. Mehrotra, *India and the commonwealth, 1885–1929* (1965) · S. R. Ashton, *British policy towards the Indian states, 1905–1939* (1982) · Burke, *Peerage* (1967) · *CGPLA Eng. & Wales* (1924)

Archives BL OIOC, corresp. with Sir Harcourt Butler, MS Eur. F 116 · BL OIOC, Chelmsford MSS · BL OIOC, Curzon MSS · BL OIOC, Elgin MSS · Seton MSS · Bodl. Oxf., corresp. with Sir Aurel Stein · CUL, corresp. with Lord Hardinge and others · U. Birm. L., special collections department, corresp. with Austen Chamberlain

Likenesses W. Stoneman, photograph, 1920, NPG [*see illus.*]

Wealth at death £13,376 16s. 0d.: probate, 21 Oct 1924, *CGPLA Eng. & Wales*

Holdernesse. For this title name *see* Ramsay, John, earl of Holdernesse (c.1580–1626); D'Arcy, Robert, fourth earl of Holdernesse (1718–1778).

Holdich, Sir Thomas Hungerford (1843–1929), surveyor and geographer, was born at the rectory, Dingley, Northamptonshire, on 13 February 1843, the eldest son of Thomas Peach Holdich, rector of that parish, and Susan, daughter of William Atherton Garrard of Carisbrooke, Isle of Wight, and Olney, Buckinghamshire. After attending Godolphin Grammar School, Hammersmith, he went in 1859 to Addiscombe College, where he gained the sword of honour (1860). After training at the Royal Military Academy, Woolwich, he was commissioned in 1862 in the Royal Engineers and, after further training at Chatham, was sent to India in 1865 to become temporary assistant surveyor with the Bhutan expedition of 1865–6. This led to his permanent appointment to the survey department. From 1867 to 1868 he was lent to the Abyssinian expedition to conduct surveys. On 17 June 1873 he married Ada Maria, daughter of Captain John Heyning Vanrenen of the Indian army. They had two sons and two daughters, the elder son being Brigadier-General Harold Adrian Holdich.

In 1878 Holdich began a long connection with the north-west frontier as a survey officer with the southern Afghanistan field force. He served with distinction in the Second Anglo-Afghan War (1878–80), the Mahsud Waziri expedition of 1881, the Zhob field force of 1890, and the Afridi Tirah expedition of 1897–8, being several times mentioned in dispatches. He was promoted brevet major in 1881, brevet lieutenant-colonel in 1887, and brevet colonel in 1891. Fascinated by the prospect of filling out the very incomplete maps of the region, he surveyed and gathered intelligence both during military operations and when engaged to lay out roads and railways through the border passes of Baluchistan and Afghanistan. He proved not only technically competent and thorough, but also tactful in dealing with all those he came across in this politically sensitive region. His talents led to his appointment from 1884 to 1886 to the Pamir boundary commission which settled a long-vexed question by fixing and marking a buffer strip—barely 8 miles wide in one place—of Afghan and Chinese territory between the khanates under Russian domination on the north and the princely states of India on the south. For this work he received in 1887 the founder's medal of the Royal Geographical Society. From 1891 to 1898 he was superintendent of frontier surveys, and served on the Asmar and Pamir delimitation commission of 1894–6 and was chief commissioner of the Perso-Baluch boundary delimitations in 1895. He became a respected authority on boundaries, later outlining the principles on which he acted in *The Indian Borderland* (1901) and *Political Frontiers and Boundary Making* (1916). In 1898 he reached the age limit of fifty-five and consequently retired. He had been appointed KCIE in 1897 and was appointed KCMG in 1902.

In 1902 Holdich served on the tribunal appointed by the British government at the invitation of the governments of Chile and Argentina to interpret a treaty of 1881 which fixed their boundary in the south of the Andes mountains in a way which was simple and satisfactory on paper, but which the contorted geomorphology of the area made impossible to enforce in practice. Holdich insisted on investigating the terrain in person, and his geographical competence, tact, and industry so impressed the governments that they accepted his solution and invited him back to mark out the boundary on the ground.

Holdich was an active member of the Royal Geographical Society, served on its council under Sir Clements

Markham's presidency, and was himself president from 1916 to 1918, when he kept the society's activities going under conditions rendered difficult by the First World War. Deafness induced him to decline nomination for a third term, though he continued as vice-president until 1922. He wrote well-informed books on the geography of India (1904 and 1909). He died at his home, Parklands, Merrow, near Guildford, on 2 November 1929. His wife survived him. The practical results of his boundary work were enduring, as was his influence on political geography in its contemporary meaning as the geography of frontiers and boundaries.   ELIZABETH BAIGENT

Sources *The Times* (4 Nov 1929) · Burke, *Peerage* · H. R. Mill, *The record of the Royal Geographical Society, 1830–1930* (1930) · H. M. Vibart, *Addiscombe: its heroes and men of note* (1894) · *CGPLA Eng. & Wales* (1930) · K. Mason, 'Colonel Sir Thomas Hungerford Holdich', *GJ*, 75 (1930), 209–15 · [H. L. Crosthwait], *GJ*, 75 (1930), 215–17 · E. W. C. Sanders, *The military engineer in India*, 2 vols. (1933–5)
Archives RGS, corresp. with RGS; sketches and watercolours
Likenesses W. Stoneman, photograph, 1917, NPG
Wealth at death £8336 4s. 4d.: probate, 10 Jan 1930, *CGPLA Eng. & Wales*

Holding, Frederick (1817–1874). *See under* Holding, Henry James (1833–1872).

Holding, Henry James (1833–1872), landscape painter, the youngest son of Henry Holding, an amateur painter, was born at Salford, Lancashire, in November 1833. At an early age he was employed as a pattern designer to calico printers, but he soon began his career as an artist, following the example of three of his brothers. All the members of the family were artists, but none received any regular art training. While still a teenager he exhibited in Manchester, Liverpool, and London, his favourite subjects being marine landscapes and scenes featuring torrents, which he painted in both oil and watercolours. He was also noted for his historical scenes, especially his Tudor subjects. His last work, *Betws-y-coed*, exhibited in 1872, was considered his best. Another highly regarded picture, *Finding of the Body of Rufus by the Charcoal-Burners*, was exhibited in 1862. He died of consumption on 9 August 1872 in Paris while on a sketching tour, which had been expected to restore him to health. He was buried in the English cemetery (des.) at Paris. As his death left his wife and children in financial difficulties, an exhibition was held in Manchester for their benefit.

Holding's elder brother **Frederick Holding** (1817–1874), watercolour painter, born probably in Manchester, lived in Manchester for most of his life and painted watercolours, showing much skill in figure drawing. He also worked as an illustrator; the 1864 edition of Robert Southey's *Battle of Blenheim* includes some of his designs. Towards the end of his life he was the scene painter at the Theatre Royal and the Prince's Theatre in Manchester. He died in 1874, probably in Manchester. There is a Shakespearian scene by him in Manchester City Galleries.

    C. W. SUTTON, *rev.* SUZANNE FAGENCE COOPER

Sources *Art Journal*, 34 (1872), 255 · exhibition catalogues of Manchester Royal Institution, 1853–74 · Bryan, *Painters* (1903–5), 3.63 · Redgrave, *Artists*, 218 · Wood, *Vic. painters*, 3rd edn, 253 · G. W. Holding, *Manchester City News* (3 May 1890) · Mallalieu, *Watercolour artists* [Frederick Holding]
Archives Williamson Art Gallery, Birkenhead

Holding, Thomas Hiram (1844–1930), touring cyclist and promoter of recreational camping, was born on 29 December 1844 at Steel, Prees, Shropshire, the first son and first of nine children of Daniel Holding (1813–1857), a tailor, and his wife, Sarah, *née* Middleton (1823–1912). His parents became Mormons, and in February 1853 they sold their possessions and the family sailed for New Orleans, USA. Holding first experienced camping out 'above the wooded slope on the plateau behind Kairkock, on the Mississippi, which camp lasted about five weeks' (Holding, 3). On arrival in Salt Lake City in October 1853, word reached them that Daniel Holding's father, also a tailor and a wealthy man through his marriage, had died. After a perilous journey across the Rocky Mountains, during which another son was born, the family arrived back in Shropshire in 1854 to find that Daniel had been left with just £5 and no property. A relative lent them a cottage in which to live, but within three years Daniel had died, leaving Sarah penniless with five children to raise.

Holding lodged with George Shingler, a tailor of Prees, as a 'sojourner tailor', learning tailoring until he was sixteen years old. In 1862 he went to London to work at Hill's, Poole's, and Newton's before learning cutting from 'the famous Peter Middleton', after which he worked in Liverpool and Windsor. On 29 April 1869 he married Sarah Darlington (1839–1917) at Wem, Shropshire, and moved to Horncastle, Lincolnshire, as a foreman tailor, where their first child, Edgar Thomas Holding (1870–1952), later a renowned watercolour artist, was born. Subsequently the family moved to Lincoln and Banbury, and had three further sons and a daughter.

A keen cyclist and captain of the Banbury Bicycle Club in 1876, Holding wrote to *Bicycling News* suggesting a national touring club for cyclists, so that 'companiable men' could tour together (Lightwood, 42). As a direct outcome of that letter, the Bicycle Touring Club, later to become the Cyclists' Touring Club, was founded at Harrogate in 1878. He was president and chairman from 1880 to 1881, and was created an honorary member in 1899.

In 1877 Holding moved to Sunderland, where he was asked to lecture on 'Muscular Christianity'; this caused him to buy a canoe. 'The canoe led to camping, and camping led to a canoe-cruise in the Highlands of Scotland' (Holding, 3). The journey is recounted in his first book, *The Cruise of the Ospray*, published in October 1878. He was nicknamed 'the Skipper' after this trip, and canoeing and boating became his favourite pastime: on moving to Cheltenham about 1881 he kept his canoe at Tewkesbury and cycled there on his free days. Another canoe-camping voyage in Scotland in 1885, with three friends, is described in *Watery Wanderings mid Western Lochs*, published in 1886, when he became the editor of *The Canoeist* as a 'leisure time activity'. A founder member of the British Canoe

Association, he also won several canoe-camping competitions.

In 1883 Holding moved to London to take a position as a teacher of tailoring, connected with the trade journal the *Tailor and Cutter*, and set up in business for himself at Adelaide Street, Charing Cross, later moving to Maddox Street, off Regent Street. In 1884 he became editor of the *London Tailor and Record of Fashion*. In 1895 he purchased the magazine and renamed it the *London Tailor*. By this time he had built up a successful business and established his own cutting school attended by over one thousand students. He also lectured at the various foreman tailors' societies as far apart as Exeter and Dundee, at the same time also lecturing on church architecture. He continued as editor of the *London Tailor* until 1908, when he renamed it *London Tailor and Cutting*. Between 1885 and 1910 he wrote more than thirty books on tailoring subjects.

Despite his full working life, Holding continued with his cycling and boating holidays. With the advent of the 'safety' bicycle, and following a chance conversation with a friend, he designed a set of camping equipment which could be carried on a cycle, something which had been impossible on an 'ordinary'. With his younger son Frank and two friends he tried out the kit on a holiday in Ireland, the account of which he described in *Cycle and Camp*, published in 1897. As a direct result of this book, he founded the Association of Cycle Campers in 1901, being president and chairman until 1906. He added the design and manufacture of camping kit to his tailoring business in Maddox Street. In the first (1901) prospectus for the Association of Cycle Campers Holding told the thirty-five members:

> The freedom and the delight of camping ought to commend itself not only to those who are fond of travel, exploration and a healthy free life, but even to those with like tastes, who might stay at the best hotels, as the inventor himself (Holding) might, if he chose.   (Camping and Caravanning Club archive)

Numbers grew to 210 members. 'We organised great camps, almost every visitor attending becoming a disciple.' A disagreement led to his resignation from the association:

> But this big movement had life in it, so I formed the National Camping Club and to show that my work had taken deep root 150 members were enrolled in the new club within four months. Two thirds of this muster were of ladies and gentlemen who had only just begun, but none of them have an ill word to say of camping.   (Holding, 6–7)

He supplied enthusiasts for the new movement with a guide, *The Camper's Handbook* (1908). Thus under the guidance of this enthusiastic and practical man the camping movement became firmly established.

By 1910 Holding had left both organizations to fend for themselves and the two clubs amalgamated to form the Amateur Camping Club, with Robert Falcon Scott as its president, but he still lectured on the open-air life and camping. The *Daily Mirror* published a full-page illustrated feature about his 'wonderful contrivances' (24 Feb 1914). In 1919 the club changed its name to the Camping Club of

Great Britain and Ireland, and Sir Robert Baden Powell became its president. Holding was made an honorary member and vice-president in 1922. In 1983 the club was renamed the Camping and Caravanning Club, to emphasize that all types of campers were welcome within its ranks.

Holding gave up all his journalistic work in 1913, retired from business, and was made a county magistrate in London in 1915. A Congregationalist and a member of the Brotherhood movement, he was a sought-after speaker at various free churches. He died at his home, Hazeldean, 6 Fulham Park Gardens, Fulham, London, on 20 November 1930 and was cremated on 22 November at Golders Green.

An extraordinarily active man in all aspects of his life, with a strong but stubborn character, Holding's ideas for the organization of the two highly respected national clubs he founded have been followed by many similar organizations throughout the world. He is regarded as the father of modern recreational camping. His memory is perpetuated by a permanent campsite owned by the Camping and Caravanning Club in the Clent Hills near Birmingham, where a memorial stone is sited. There is a commemorative plaque on the bridge at Wantage, close to where the first Association of Cycle Campers' camp was held, and a plaque at Harrogate which commemorates the founding of the Cyclists' Touring Club.

HAZEL CONSTANCE

Sources private information (2004) [family] · Camping and Caravanning Club, Coventry, archive · T. H. Holding, *The camper's handbook* (1908) · H. Constance, *First in the field: a century of the Camping and Caravanning Club* (2001) · University of Warwick, national cycling archive · Hammersmith and Fulham Archive and Local History Centre, MSS · V&A NAL · *The Times* (24 Nov 1930) · *The Times* (28 Nov 1930) · J. T. Lightwood, *The Cyclists' Touring Club: being the romance of fifty years' cycling* (1928) · *Cyclists' Touring Club Gazette* (Jan 1931) · *Tailor's Magazine* (Jan 1914) · *CGPLA Eng. & Wales* (1930)
Archives Camping and Caravanning Club, Coventry, letters
Likenesses photograph, *c.*1858, Cyclists' Touring Club, Godalming, Surrey, photo library · sepia photograph, 1877 (with 'Ospray'), Camping and Caravanning Club, Coventry, archive · T. H. Holding, self-portrait, *c.*1907, Camping and Caravanning Club, Coventry, archive · probably E. T. Holding, photograph, *c.*1914, Camping and Caravanning Club, Coventry, archive · M. Hicks, oils, *c.*1915, Camping and Caravanning Club, Coventry, boardroom · A. Handford, photograph (in his seventies), Camping and Caravanning Club, Coventry, archive
Wealth at death £6668 17*s.* 4*d.*: probate, 29 Dec 1930, *CGPLA Eng. & Wales*

Holdingham [Haldingham], **Richard of** (d. 1278?), cartographic patron and supposed map maker, probably also named as Richard de Bello, is known for certain only as the author or at least the patron of the large and very detailed late thirteenth-century world map which is now preserved at Hereford Cathedral (known as the *Mappa mundi*). This bears an inscription in its lower left corner requesting prayers for 'Richard de Haldingham o de Lafford' ('Richard of Haldingham or of Lafford') who 'made and drew this history' ('fet e compasse cest estorie'). Holdingham is a hamlet in the parish of Lafford, Lincolnshire, and Richard is described as of either place in order to make his identity clear to people unacquainted with Holdingham. Lafford is a prebend of Lincoln Cathedral, and Richard has been assumed to be also identifiable as Richard de Bello (of Battle, almost certainly Battle in Sussex) who was prebendary of Lafford in 1277 and who was also treasurer of Lincoln Cathedral by October 1270, until at least April 1278. He is first found as a canon of Lincoln in 1265; he died on 4 November 1278.

The map gives some prominence to Lincoln and also names Lindsey (meaning either the later Lindsey or possibly the county of Lincoln), and the map's patron must have been just such a well-educated man with Lincolnshire connections as Richard de Bello, who was a master of arts. A link with the Augustinian priory of Kirkham, Yorkshire, is also suggested by the presence on the map of this relatively minor religious house. Although the map has very possibly been at Hereford since the later middle ages, and certainly since 1682, Hereford has an inconspicuous place on it, added at an early date in the abbreviated form 'H'ford'. There is no reason to associate Hereford with the prebendary of Lafford, the map's putative patron. One Richard de Bello was canon of Hereford from 1305 until he died in 1326, as well as being canon of Salisbury from 1298, but clearly he cannot be identified with his namesake, the canon of Lincoln. That the Hereford canon gave the map to Hereford remains a mere hypothesis; his ecclesiastical career was linked rather with the diocese of Salisbury, while the city of Salisbury is not included on the map.

World maps were not uncommon room furnishings in royal palaces and ecclesiastical institutions in the middle ages; one is listed in the mid-twelfth-century catalogue of the library of Lincoln Cathedral. Their ultimate source is maps from Roman imperial times, but in the twelfth and thirteenth centuries they received such modifications as the placing of Jerusalem in the centre, as on the Hereford map. The Hereford map is datable on stylistic and palaeographic grounds to about the very late thirteenth century. It includes Conwy and Caernarfon, whose castles were only begun in 1283 and not finished until about 1292, and it has therefore been suggested that it was made over a period of years. It does not have this appearance, however, and it may simply be a copy that updates but generally reproduces one that was written about the 1270s by, or rather for, Richard of Holdingham; despite the words 'made and drew' ('fet e compasse'), Richard of Holdingham is hardly likely to have actually written and drawn the map himself, since it has mistakes that show a lack of understanding of what was being copied.

The discrepancies of date between the life of Richard of Holdingham who was prebendary of Lincoln, and the map that is now at Hereford, are best explained by the hypothesis that Richard commissioned a world map in the 1270s, and that this was copied in every detail (down to the inscription that names him) but with some additions (such as Conwy and Caernarfon) in the late 1280s or 1290s, shortly before being brought to Hereford.

There remains also the faint possibility that Richard of Holdingham was not the same as the prebendary of Lincoln; it is perhaps significant that the inscription does not refer to him as a master (of arts).   NIGEL RAMSAY

Sources Emden, *Oxf.*, 1.556 · P. D. A. Harvey, *Mappa mundi: the Hereford world map* (1996) · *Fasti Angl., 1066–1300*, [Lincoln], 20, 73 · N. Morgan, *Early Gothic manuscripts*, 2 (1988), 195–200 · Sede vacante scrapbook, Canterbury Cathedral Archives, 1, p. 142 · N. Denholm-Young, *Collected papers of N. Denholm-Young* (1969), 74–82 · W. N. Yates, 'The authorship of the Hereford Mappa Mundi and the career of Richard de Bello', *Transactions of the Woolhope Naturalists' Field Club*, 41 (1974–5), 165–72 · *CEPR letters*, 1.370 · V. I. J. Flint, 'The Hereford map: its author(s), two scenes and a border', *TLS*, 6th ser., 8 (1998), 19–44
Archives Hereford Cathedral, 'Mappa mundi'

Holditch, Abraham (*bap.* 1639, *d.* 1678), naval officer and merchant adventurer, was baptized on 12 May 1639 at Totnes, Devon. He was probably the son of William Holditch (*d.* 1646?) and his wife, Agnes (*bap.* 1617), formerly Jakes. He married at St Magnus the Martyr, London, on 13 November 1661 Elizabeth (*bap.* 1644, *d.* 1702), daughter of Nathaniel Morecock.

Nothing is known of Holditch's early naval career prior to 1661 when he commanded the *Sophia*, one of the squadron led to the Gambia by Robert Holmes in search of goldmines. He is presumed to have accompanied Holmes on his second expedition to west Africa, and was appointed lieutenant on the *Revenge* on 14 March 1665, during the Second Anglo-Dutch War. After the battle off Lowestoft Holditch commanded several men-of-war before joining the Royal African Company. In the navy Holditch was regarded as a 'fitt man' and 'stout' (NMM, LBK/47), suitable for appointment by the duke of York to be captain of the *Mars* at the age of twenty-six. In 1671 he was sent by the Royal African Company to recover Cape Coast Castle, in Guinea, their west African headquarters which had been lost in a local insurrection. The success of the mission, for which he was awarded £500, was significant both for the company and for the subsequent development of the nation's trade. Holditch remained at the castle for a year as the company's agent-general.

In 1674 Holditch offered to command a ship to deter private trade on the Gold Coast and convey slaves to the West Indies, and in each of the following three years he was elected to the company's court of assistants, during which time he declined the offer of a second tour of duty as agent-general. He was active in the company's affairs, contributing his specialist knowledge to its administration until he was appointed chief searcher of London port shortly before his death, which occurred early in 1678. He was buried at St Dunstan and All Saints, Stepney, on 7 February. His widow later married John Chambers.

Holditch's son Richard became a director of the South Sea Company. His daughter Agnes (1671?–1749) married in 1689 **John Strong** (*c.*1654–1693); they had no children. Strong, a privateer and treasure seeker, was chief mate of the *James and Mary*, commanded by William Phipps, which in 1687 recovered treasure from a ship wrecked off the coast of Hispaniola. In 1689, armed with a royal commission, he sailed as commander of the *Welfare* to recover a Spanish treasure ship, the 1200 ton *Capitana Jesús Maria de* *la Limpia Concepción*, sunk in 1654 off the west coast of South America. He made the first undisputed landing on the Falkland Islands, giving the name of Falkland Sound to the channel between the two main islands. Strong passed through the Strait of Magellan in winter, with great difficulty and danger. He failed to find the ship and lost eleven men killed ashore; the capture of two prizes near Ireland on the way home was meagre compensation for his failure, for when the wreck was located in 1997 its bounty was estimated at £2.5 billion (*The Times*, 26 March 1997, 15d–h). Strong died at La Coruña on a voyage to the West Indies on 11 November 1693. E. W. L. KEYMER

Sources PRO, Royal African Company MSS, T 70/75–78; T70/100; T70/1211 · *CSP dom.*, 1671, 385; 1676, 105 · officers register, 1660–85, PRO, ADM 10/15 · W. A. Shaw, ed., *Calendar of treasury books*, 5, PRO (1911), 777; 8 (1923), 2062 · parish register, London, St Magnus the Martyr, 1661, GL · parish register, Stepney, St Dunstan and All Saints, 1678, LMA · PRO, PROB 11/356, sig. 14 [Abraham Holditch] · F. E. Dyer, 'Capt. John Strong', *Mariner's Mirror*, 13 (1927), 145–59 · depositions, PRO: *Gibbon v. Hendra*, 1668, C24/927/36; *Smith v. Albemarle*, 1687, C24/1109 · navy accounts, 1661, PRO, ADM 20/2/1066 · J. R. Tanner, ed., *A descriptive catalogue of the naval manuscripts in the Pepysian Library at Magdalene College, Cambridge*, 1, Navy RS, 26 (1903) · K. G. Davies, *The Royal African Company* (1957) · B. Capp, *Cromwell's navy: the fleet and the English revolution, 1648–1660* (1989); pbk repr. (1992) · PRO, PROB 32/32/86 [John Strong] · Albemarle letters, NMM, MS LBK/47

Archives BL, journal, Sloane MS 3295 · BL, journals, Sloane MSS 50 and 86 (or 672) · PRO, admiralty papers, ADM 10/15; ADM 20/2 · PRO, depositions, class C24 · PRO, high court of admiralty, classes HCA 25, 26, and 34 | NMM, Albemarle letters, LBK/47 · PRO, Royal African Company MSS, class T 70

Wealth at death £400—Royal African Company stock: PRO, Royal African Company MSS, T 70/78, Dec 1678; PROB 11/356, sig. 14 · over £1000—John Strong: PRO, PROB 32/32/86

Holdsworth, Edward (1684–1746), Latin poet, was born on 6 August 1684, the son of Thomas Holdsworth (*d.* *c.*1714?), rector of North Stoneham, Hampshire. He was educated at Winchester College, where in 1694, aged only nine, he was elected to a scholarship. On 14 December 1704 he matriculated at Corpus Christi College, Oxford; in July 1705, however, he was elected a demy of Magdalen College, where he remained for the next ten years. He graduated BA on 22 June 1708, and MA on 18 April 1711.

Holdsworth's most important (certainly his most celebrated) literary work was written soon after he became a BA. Dr Henry Sacheverell, Magdalen's most notorious member, is said to have encouraged its composition. This was a slightly scurrilous, and very funny, comic poem about the Welsh, entitled *Muscipula* (1709). A faulty, allegedly unauthorized, edition was rapidly followed by several correct ones, translations, and something of a literary furore. Softening the nationalistic blow, Holdsworth dedicated it to a Welsh gentleman commoner at Magdalen, Robert Lloyd: 'iracundioribus quibusdam vix in patriae tuae laudem confici videatur' ('this trifle, which to some pettish people may seem contriv'd not much to the honour of your country').

The story begins in heroic style:

> Monticolam Britonem, qui primus vincula muri
> Finxit, et exiguum vexavit carcere furem,
> Lethalesque dolos, et inextricabile fatum,
> Musa refer.
> ('Muse, tell of the Mountain-Briton who first caged the mouse, imposing on that little thief his deadly tricks and unavoidable death.')

Our hero is Taffy, an eater of cheese, the Welsh national dish; while Taffy slept off a cheese feast,

> mus audax sectatus, opinor, odores,
> Quos non concoctus pingui exalavit ab ore
> Caseus, accessit furtim.

In the version by F. T. (1709):

Edward Holdsworth (1684–1746), by James Russel, 1744 [right, in armchair, with (left to right) James Russel, Mr Marlowe, William Drake, and Dr Thomas Townson]

A Mouse, said he, pursuing as I guess
The scent of undigest[ed] toasted cheese
That from my mouth she smelt, which open lay,
Crept in and made strait down my throat her way.
Whilst she was feasting there, I did awake,
And as she try'd t'escape, her fast did take
Between my teeth.

Thus was the idea for the mousetrap born. Holdsworth effectively mixes elegant, vigorous Latin with gloriously low subject matter. We later meet a cat, who shares some characteristics with literary critics:

mentitur amorem
dum lacerare parat: varia sic arte jocosam
barbariem exercet, lepidaque tyrannide ludit.
(ll. 218–20)

In Hoadly's version (1749):

His neck now lightly pats with hurtless paw,
Dissembling love: but ruminates the while
To tear him limb from limb. The Mouser thus,
Witty in tyranny, with various art
Wanton barbarity enjoys …

Welsh pride demanded a reply. Thomas Richards of Jesus College, Oxford, rapidly produced *Hoglandiae descriptio* (1709), a satire on Hampshire (and another fine piece of Latin). Anthony Alsop, Oxford's most elegant Latin poet, and Edward Lhwyd, its most prominent Welshman, may have been involved. *Muscipula* was regularly reprinted, anthologized, and translated throughout the eighteenth century. The immediate stir caused by the poem led to four rival versions in 1709; others followed in 1712, 1715, 1718 (by Archdeacon Cobden), 1722, 1728 (published in Annapolis, Maryland), 1749 (by John Hoadly, a translation which Holdsworth greatly admired), and finally Richard Graves in 1793. Holdsworth's poem is firmly in the mock-heroic tradition, inspired by the pseudo-Homeric *Batrachomyomachia* ('Battle of Frogs and Mice'), a popular work in the Renaissance, as his Greek subtitle *Cambromyomachia* ('Battle of the Welsh and Mice') makes clear. Holdsworth's mock-heroic poem is a significant precursor to Alexander Pope's famous *Rape of the Lock*, which first appeared just a few years later, in 1712.

The fame of *Muscipula* spread to some surprising quarters. An interesting edition appeared in Florence in 1765; the anonymous Italian editor notes that he has received from England 'elegans quoddam ludicrum poemation manu exaratum' ('an elegant, humorous little poem in manuscript')—clearly he was unaware that *Muscipula* had been printed many times before. He has to explain many of Holdsworth's Welsh jokes laboriously to his audience, who have probably barely heard of Wales; yet he is still greatly impressed by the poem. Holdsworth himself, on his visits to Italy, or other Englishmen on the grand tour, may have helped the poem circulate; nevertheless, it is rare to find British neo-Latin of this period being read on the continent.

Holdsworth remained at Magdalen as a tutor, but rejected the opportunity to become a full fellow of the college, when his turn came in 1715, because he was not prepared to take the oath of allegiance to the new Hanoverian monarch. He therefore felt obliged to resign his post and leave the university; although he would have found many in Oxford to sympathize with him, and a few non-jurors, such as Thomas Hearne, did manage to retain some attachment to the university, it was more satisfactory to make a clean break. Holdsworth retained a strong affection for Magdalen; he planned the rebuilding of the college in the Palladian style. There have been doubts about his role, but 'Holdsworth's responsibility for the design … has now been fully established by letters and other documents recently discovered among the archives of Magdalen' (H. M. Colvin, in *Hist. U. Oxf.* 5: *18th-cent. Oxf.*, 840). A survey was made for his use in 1720; the fellows could finally contemplate building in 1729, when Holdsworth consulted the architect James Gibbs for help in revising the plans (the college paid Gibbs 20 guineas). The full scheme was approved, and illustrated in the 1731 *Oxford Almanack*; the college began to put it into practice in 1733. Only a single block, the majestic New Buildings, was ever completed.

For the rest of his life Holdsworth acted as a private tutor to the children of nonjuring or Jacobite families, or accompanied them on their travels in Europe. He remained in close touch with his extensive family (and the legacies in his will suggest that he had sufficient private means for a comfortable existence). He knew Pope, who wrote to him in December 1737 to ask for his vote for Harte in the election for professor of poetry at Oxford (*Correspondence of Alexander Pope*, 4.90). Holdsworth's travels encouraged his Virgilian studies. Joseph Spence declared him 'better acquainted with Italy as classic ground than any man' then living (Spence, *Polymetis*, quoted in *DNB*). He is said to have caught rheumatism, from which he never completely recovered, while exploring ancient drainage. He made many notes on Virgil, some incorporated in later editions. His *Pharsalia and Philippi* (1742) concentrated on explaining some contentious lines on the civil war battlefields; an expanded posthumous version (*Dissertation upon Eight Verses*, 1749) doubles the coverage to eight lines (*Georgics*, 2.65–72). Richard Bentley had shown how an apparently minor issue could produce a great dissertation; Holdsworth was no Bentley, but a respectable scholar none the less.

Holdsworth's scholarly and antiquarian interests did not, to the eighteenth-century mind, appear incompatible with his creative use of Latin verse, as the editor of his *Dissertation* (1749) asserts:

No reader, I hope, will think it at all improper, that the Dissertation should be accompanied by the Poem [*Muscipula*]; since, as that plainly shews, how well the Author understood Virgil, this is a demonstrative proof how well he could imitate him; a faculty very rare, and greatly superior to the other.   (p. xv)

In other words, it is better to write than to comment on Latin.

Holdsworth died of fever on 30 December 1746, at Lord Digby's house, near Coleshill, Warwickshire. He was buried in the church there on 4 January 1747. His friend Charles Jennens, of Gopsall in Leicestershire, placed a plain black marble stone above his grave. A more elaborate monument was erected in 1764, in a classical temple Jennens had built at Gopsall; this contained a long Latin inscription, and a statue by Roubiliac representing 'Religion'.

Holdsworth left his notes on Virgil to Jennens. 'I give to my dear friend Charles Jennens of Queen Square London … my interleaved Virgils with all my papers relating thereto and my pictures which now are in his custody.' His will bequeathed £100 to the building fund at Magdalen, towards the completion of his own architectural designs. Another £100 went to 'my nephew Robert Downes fellow of Magdalen College … to be employed in fitting up Chambers for him in the New Buildings there'. His brother Henry Holdsworth was chosen as executor; another brother, Winch Holdsworth DD, is mentioned, along with his sisters, Philadelphia Downes (who received £800) and Mary Ann Taylor. D. K. MONEY

Sources L. Bradner, *Musae Anglicanae: a history of Anglo-Latin poetry, 1500–1925* (1940) · D. K. Money, *The English Horace* (1998) · *DNB* · Holdsworth's will · [T. Richards], *Hoglandiae descriptio* (1709) · *The correspondence of Alexander Pope*, ed. G. Sherburn, 5 vols. (1956) · *Hist. U. Oxf.* 5: *18th-cent. Oxf.* · R. P. Bond, *English burlesque poetry, 1700–1750* (1932) · U. Broich, *The eighteenth-century mock-heroic poem* (1990)
Archives Magd. Oxf., papers relating to buildings · Yale U., Beinecke L., autograph draft of *Of the fountains of Egeria & the muses*
Likenesses C. F. Ponzone Milanese, sketch, 1741; copy, Magd. Oxf. · J. Russel, group portrait, 1744, priv. coll. [*see illus.*]

Holdsworth, Richard (1590–1649), Church of England clergyman and college head, was baptized in the parish of St Nicholas, Newcastle upon Tyne, in the year of his birth in that town, the youngest son of Richard Holdsworth (*d.* 1596), the vicar there, and his wife, whose maiden name was Pearson. After his father's death he was brought up by an uncle, William Pearson, who was a curate and lecturer in the town. Holdsworth may be assumed to have imbibed from this Newcastle background the moderate Calvinism often equated with puritanism—but somewhat misleadingly, since it was the dominant tendency in the Jacobean church of his youth. From grammar school he proceeded to St John's College, Cambridge, where he was admitted scholar on 2 November 1607. He graduated BA in 1610, was elected fellow on 20 March 1613, and was ordained deacon and priest at Peterborough in 1617. He was incorporated MA at Oxford in 1617 and in 1620 was appointed one of the university preachers. He became chaplain to Sir Henry Hobart, who presented him to a benefice in Yorkshire which he at once exchanged for the London rectory of St-Peter-le-Poer in Broad Street, his home base from 1624 and for the remainder of his life, which was spent split between London and Cambridge. In 1629 he became professor of divinity at Gresham College. He took his BD in 1622 and his doctorate in 1637.

Holdsworth gained a golden reputation as both tutor and preacher. The lawyer and parliamentarian Simonds D'Ewes left a number of snapshots of his 'loving tutor' as he led him through the standard texts in logic, ethics, and moral philosophy, and, for light relief, some history and Virgil's Eclogues. He remembers Holdsworth returning late from London and rousing the seventeen-year-old from his bed to share in a conversation which went on half the night with friends who, for their 'late watchings', were called 'noctuae Londinenses'. As tutors did, Holdsworth accompanied his pupil to his Suffolk home, where he preached for D'Ewes's father 'so sweetly and profitably' that Simonds 'began to love him better than ever', and almost forgot to mention the young man's debts of £13. A Suffolk contemporary of D'Ewes who was his opposite, the future Archbishop William Sancroft, wrote that at Emmanuel College (where he was master from 1637) Holdsworth was his 'card and compass', and that only his directions 'for study, for life, for all' had made Sancroft a scholar. These 'Directions for students in the university', while preserved at Emmanuel, doubtless record Holdsworth's practice at St John's. His curriculum was enlightened and perhaps novel, substituting for the year-by-year progression through grammar, logic, and rhetoric of the Elizabethan university statutes a varied day of studies, commencing with a morning of logic and philosophy and continuing with a more relaxed afternoon of poetry, classical oratory, and history, the fruits of which were to be stored in a commonplace book, full of 'choice and witty sayings, sentences and passages'. A gentler course was prescribed for gentlemen who had no need to make themselves scholars, readings mostly in English to provide 'such learning as may serve to delight and ornament'. This remarkable pedagogue amassed one of the largest private libraries of his time, estimated to contain more than 10,000 volumes by the time of his death.

Meanwhile, Holdsworth had become one of the most famous London preachers of the day. According to Thomas Fuller he 'dominated' the pulpit, a position marked by his presidency of the London clergy guild, Sion College (1639). D'Ewes says that his sermons were 'by general approbation deemed extraordinary' but, with a single exception, they were not published in a form which Holdsworth had himself authorized. The posthumous collection *The Valley of Vision* (1651) derived from inferior shorthand notes and appeared with a request that the reader make 'charitable allowances in things of this nature'. No such allowances were made, Fuller condemning the publication as 'none of his', with 'little vision therein' (Fuller, *Worthies*, 448). But Holdsworth's cousin Richard Pearson (grandson of William) was able to locate in Cambridge manuscript copies of the Latin sermons preached at Gresham College in the early 1630s, which he published in 1661 as *Praelectiones theologicae*, a folio volume of 737 pages. Six English sermons dating from 1634 and 1635 are also preserved (Bodl. Oxf., MS Tanner 331).

In 1633 the mastership of St John's fell vacant and while the vice-master, Robert Lane, received the support of the senior fellows and obtained a royal letter of recommendation, Holdsworth was elected by a clear majority of the governing body, presenting the vice-chancellor of the day with an embarrassing impasse. When a royal commission of the heads of other houses succeeded only in digging up a good deal of irregularity and some dirt (Lane was accused of 'singing drunken catches') Charles I took the matter into his own hands and appointed by mandate the

Arminian high-churchman William Beale. This *cause célèbre* lasted for months and soon even Archbishop Laud was weary of it. Holdsworth bore no resentment and presented the college with some books, before collecting his compensation prize, the archdeaconry of Huntingdon. The fact that on 26 April 1637 he was freely and without fuss elected master of Emmanuel, where earlier vacancies had seen cloak-and-dagger manoeuvres designed to protect the 'pure' traditions of the college, may or may not indicate a bad conscience in high circles for his treatment at St John's. Holdsworth may well have been the best and most popular master of Emmanuel in its history, receiving the full approbation of the foundation master, Laurence Chaderton, who lived on in the vicinity of the college into his hundredth year and beyond. In spite of other commitments, especially in London, his record of residence, which can be checked against a remarkable register of 'admonitions' for offences against the college statutes, was good.

By now, however, Holdsworth's more public life was entering stormy waters. He was a natural fence-sitter, from the most honourable of motives. When in 1637 Sylvester Adams of Peterhouse preached a sermon asserting the necessity of auricular confession, the heads of houses were divided, with five Arminian heads refusing to endorse the condemnatory sentence passed by the vice-chancellor, Ralph Brownrigg. Holdsworth believed that a recantation was necessary, but characteristically recommended 'that a longer time be given to Mr Adams to deliberate of it'. His misfortunes in England's gathering troubles he was to share with other moderate Calvinists, including the Emmanuel men Samuel Ward, master of Sidney Sussex College, Joseph Hall, bishop of Exeter, who recorded the 'hard measure' he received, and his particular friend and Hall's successor at Exeter, Brownrigg.

As a man of what had been the centre, Holdsworth was now raked by the vicious crossfire of an increasingly polarized political and ecclesiastical scene. Fuller wrote that when the times turned 'he, standing still, was left to the censure of factious innovators' (Fuller, *Worthies*, 447). No enemy of Laud, Holdsworth could write: 'His Grace Delights in Gentleness'. As archdeacon of Huntingdon, he was stricter than his diocesan, Laud's enemy John Williams, in insisting on the placing of the holy table altarwise and on reception of communion at the altar rails, and he was pleased to have achieved compliance in this respect at St Ives. But he confessed to 'weakness' when it came to dealing with scrupulous consciences. In his London parish he refused to read the Book of Sports. He was a natural choice to preach one of the fast sermons before the Short Parliament in 1640, and he opposed the continuation of convocation after the dissolution of that parliament, and the new canons which it legislated, especially the seventh, which enforced what he called 'these new taken up ceremonies'. By the early months of 1641 Holdsworth had joined with Archbishop James Ussher and Brownrigg in propounding a scheme for so-called 'reduced' episcopacy. Charles I made him a royal chaplain

and he was one of five anti-Arminian moderates, including Brownrigg, to be offered a mitre. Holdsworth was the only one to refuse, whether, according to Fuller, because he thought the appointment in the circumstances 'unsafe and unseasonable', or, as both Fuller and Holdsworth's nephew Pearson report, because the 'smallness' of the see in question, Bristol, would not allow him to maintain appropriate hospitality (Fuller, *Worthies*, 448).

The logic of the polarizing situation would now drive Holdsworth towards royalism, but for a time the Long Parliament did not know what to make of him. In December 1640 he was summoned to appear before it, it was thought because of his position on altar rails, but in May 1642 he was appointed to the Westminster assembly of divines, although in the previous October Oliver Cromwell, MP for Cambridge, had opposed the appointment of the five new bishops, and had spoken 'somewhat bitterly' against Holdsworth in particular, provoking Simonds D'Ewes to come to his old tutor's defence. According to D'Ewes himself, this business was debated 'with as great earnestness almost as I ever saw in the House'. Cromwell's hostility was perhaps provoked by Holdsworth's actions in contributing from his college, but really, it seems, from his own pocket, £100 towards the royal war chest.

As vice-chancellor (from 1640 to 1643) and head of his house, Holdsworth had already risked the ire of parliament in defending the interests of both university and college, particularly in his oration at the commencement in 1641. Now he could no longer avoid taking sides. In late March 1642 Charles I paid his last visit to Cambridge and Holdsworth preached before him in the university church. The sermon complained that the royal influence had been 'intercepted', and made much of 'manifold yieldings and recessions' on the part of the king, 'who knows how to recede from power, and in some cases, even from prerogative', the care of his people's happiness being 'radiant in our gracious Sovereign'. Charles having ordered the sermon to be published by the university printer, Holdsworth offered it as 'some little portion of that great happiness which this eighteen years we have enjoyed, under your blessed government' (*A Sermon Preached … the 27 of March*, 1642).

Holdsworth was now marked as 'delinquent'. In August 1642 the university published a pamphlet which called the resistance offered to the king by parliament 'unwarrantable', 'damnable', 'murder'. Holdsworth had to explain himself before the House of Commons, although he remained at liberty until May 1643, when he was arrested and imprisoned at Ely House, where he continued to live, and to preach, dangerously, and to license the republication of royal declarations. A parliamentary committee now wanted to know how he had become master of Emmanuel and wondered 'whether, by his demeanour since, he hath not forfeited the said place'. When the university provocatively elected Holdsworth Lady Margaret professor of divinity in succession to Samuel Ward, who had himself died in custody, Holdsworth was removed to the Tower, but not perhaps for long. In April 1646 he was at Carshalton in Surrey. There were rumours of a plot to enable Holdsworth to take up the Lady Margaret chair, which remained vacant, but he never returned to Cambridge, or only on fleeting visits. In 1647 he was in the king's presence at Hampton Court, and received the now empty honour of the deanery of Worcester. In September 1648 he made further unsuccessful attempts to attend the king, now weeks away from trial and execution. 'So here is their circle: first we are imprisoned because with the king, and then denied to be with the king because imprisoned.'

The earl of Manchester's visitation of the university had ejected Holdsworth from his master's lodge and had intruded as his successor Anthony Tuckney, but Tuckney was in no hurry to take possession, and in Emmanuel many regarded Holdsworth as, morally, still master. Sancroft, who had written 'I had not thought they would have beheaded whole colleges at a blow', was a constant correspondent, and looked for the time when Holdsworth would come back 'as the soul and life of this body, which hath been in a fainting and swooning condition ever since he was by violent hands snatched from us'. Holdsworth continued to feed Sancroft with prize gentry pupils ('you may please to take notice that he is a baronet'), hoped that Sancroft would be civil to Tuckney as man to man, if not as master, and was courtesy itself in all his dealings with Tuckney.

Holdsworth died, unmarried, on 22 August 1649 at his home in Broad Street, London, and was buried at St Peter-le-Poer. His final legacy to Cambridge was princely, but problematical: his huge library. It was gifted under the terms of a most unsatisfactory will, and come the Restoration, Emmanuel and the university were at legal loggerheads over the matter. Eventually the court of arches referred the dispute to the arbitration of three bishops, who found for the university, with some financial compensation for the college. Holdsworth's 10,000 books remained in the Cambridge University Library, but not, as the bishops' judgement required, 'distinguished from other books there by the name of Dr Holdsworth's library'.   PATRICK COLLINSON

Sources [R. Pearson], 'Authoris vita', in R. Holdsworth, *Praelectiones theologicae* (1661), sigs. A5–A7 · PRO, PROB 11/209, fols. 44v–45r [Holdsworth's will] · S. Bendall, C. Brooke, and P. Collinson, *A history of Emmanuel College, Cambridge* (1999) · J. Twigg, *The University of Cambridge and the English Revolution, 1625–1688* (1990) · T. Baker, *History of the college of St John the Evangelist, Cambridge*, ed. J. E. B. Mayor, 2 vols. (1869) · Bodl. Oxf., MSS Tanner 54–60, 65, 331 · H. Cary, ed., *Memorials of the great civil war in England from 1646 to 1652*, 2 vols. (1842) · Emmanuel College, Cambridge, MSS CHA.1.4.A, COL.9.1 (A & B), COL.9.8 · CUL, MS Mm.1.45 (Baker 34) · CUL, department of manuscripts and university archives, vice-chancellor's court, 1.57 · *Walker rev.* · *The journal of Sir Simonds D'Ewes from the first recess of the Long Parliament to the withdrawal of King Charles from London*, ed. W. H. Coates (1942) · T. Fuller, *The worthies of England*, ed. J. Freeman, abridged edn (1952), 447–8

Holdsworth, Sir William Searle (1871–1944), legal historian, was born at Beckenham, Kent, on 7 May 1871, the eldest son of Charles Joseph Holdsworth, solicitor, and his wife, Ellen Caroline Searle, whose descent could be traced

Sir William Searle Holdsworth (1871–1944), by Walter Stoneman, 1930

back to Oliver Cromwell. He was educated at Dulwich College and at New College, Oxford, where he was taught by H. A. L. Fisher and J. B. Moyle. He gained first classes in history in 1893 and in law in 1894, but obtained a second class, along with F. E. Smith (later Lord Birkenhead), in the BCL in 1896. On the results of the examination Smith was awarded the Vinerian scholarship ahead of him. They remained friends. Holdsworth won the Barstow scholarship to the inns of court in 1895, read for a short time in chambers and was called to the bar at Lincoln's Inn in 1896. But his heart was set on academic life and, after a period as a lecturer at New College from 1895, he was elected a fellow of St John's College, Oxford, in 1897. He taught law there for the next twenty-five years, covering the whole academic curriculum, as was then expected of college tutors. He combined his college duties with a chair of constitutional law at University College, London, from 1903 to 1908 and some lecturing at the London School of Economics. In 1910 he somewhat unexpectedly failed to succeed A. V. Dicey in Sir William Blackstone's chair as Vinerian professor of English law, W. M. Geldart being chosen instead. He was however appointed reader in English law in Geldart's place and on Geldart's retirement in 1922 he succeeded to the Vinerian chair, as expected, and became a fellow of All Souls.

Holdsworth proved himself a worthy holder of the premier chair of English law. A gifted and sympathetic teacher, he continued to do some tutorial teaching without pay after he became a professor. Indeed, he thought professors ought to do some private teaching besides lecturing. Though the college tutors and the professors in the Oxford law faculty had been at loggerheads, Holdsworth's eirenic personality did much to reconcile the two. Though a good tutor, Holdsworth was a poor lecturer, often inaudible except to those in the front row. On one occasion he took a young pupil to the theatre and remarked to him that he had yawned during the performance, though he never yawned when writing a lecture. 'No,' said the cheeky young man, 'but I have often yawned when listening to you lecture'—a remark that made the older man laugh.

From an early age Holdsworth, perhaps inspired by Sir Matthew Hale, the first historian of English law, wanted to write a large-scale history of the subject. The moment of destiny came in 1901, when Methuen, the publisher, who had asked Edward Jenks to write a one-volume history of English law, was referred by Jenks to the young tutor at St John's. Holdsworth seized the opportunity and planned a comprehensive history of English law from the earliest times to 1875. The first volume came out in 1903, the third in 1909. These early volumes were rather loosely written, but an improved version of them was published in 1922. They were followed by six more volumes in the 1920s, when as a professor Holdsworth had more time to write, and three in the 1930s, the last in 1938. The scope of the work grew broader and the detail richer as volume succeeded volume. As Plucknett puts it:

> Into that great work went gifts and qualities of the most varied sorts, and sympathies which were as broad as they were genuine. The rugged common law of Coke as well as the legal rationalism of Bacon, the subtleties of Fearne and Butler as well as the urbane cosmopolitanism of Mansfield and Blackstone, all received from him their due meed of appreciation.   (Plucknett, 5)

By 1938 he had, though not following a strict chronological sequence, brought the history up to the end of the eighteenth century. This was the period he most admired, when in his eyes the government was made up of separate units that checked and balanced each other, but when all were subject to a supreme law administered by independent judges. Holdsworth was more dubious of nineteenth- and twentieth-century developments, which seemed to concentrate too much power in the cabinet. But at his death he left drafts, often in a hand that was almost impossible to decipher, from which four more volumes were edited by A. L. Goodhart and H. G. Hanbury. These cover the period up to 1875, which he had from the start thought of as the end date of the work, though some topics, such as the law of conspiracy, are carried through into the twentieth century. The sixteenth and last volume is an index to the whole work.

No work of English legal history on this monumental scale has been produced before or since. Indeed it may never be wholly superseded. If any work deserves the title *magnum opus* it is Holdsworth's. Lord Wright wondered whether he 'could more properly be called a lawyer turned historian or a historian turned lawyer' (*Law Quarterly Review*, 60.145). In fact the enterprise required expertise in both. The author worked alone, made hardly any notes, and had no card index. His memory, energy, and accuracy were extraordinary. The only substantial help came from his friend and colleague A. E. W. Hazel, who read the proofs of the first twelve volumes and toned down some of their more stridently tory sentiments. Only a man of rare physique and tenacity of purpose could have carried the history to near completion over a period of forty years, besides writing many articles and reviews, especially in the *Law Quarterly Review*, and several other books. His *Sources and Literature of English Law* (1925), based on evening lectures delivered for the Council of Legal Education, is well informed and lucidly expressed. The *Historical Introduction to the Land Law* (1927) has been re-edited and kept abreast of recent research. *Some Lessons from our Legal History* came out in 1928. Three volumes express his deep interest in the human and personal aspects of legal history: *Historians of Anglo-American Law* (1927) comprised the Carpentier lectures delivered at Columbia; *Charles Dickens as a Legal Historian* (1928) the Storrs lectures at Yale; and *Some Makers of English Law* (1938) the Tagore lectures at Calcutta in 1938. He made several contributions to the publications of the Selden Society, the last of which (*Year Books*, vol. 22) was published posthumously.

How did Holdsworth find time to do so much? In the evenings, fortified by port, he would return to his rooms after dinner at St John's or All Souls and add to the 7000 or so pages of the *History* that were published before he died. He worked from published sources. He knew no German and did not tackle archival research, but his work takes account not merely of the English year books, statutes, and cases but of all the legal literature bearing on English law that had been published in English or French up to the time of writing. He displays a balanced grasp of the political and literary background and a keen interest in personalities. His written style is simple, nervous, and forthright, but at times pedestrian. The history is something to consult rather than to read through. Yet as John Simon says, his 'patience in investigation and balance in judgement often give the reader a satisfying sense of finality and impartiality' (*Law Quarterly Review*, 60.138). The shorter books and reviews are eminently readable.

Holdsworth kept in touch with his professional as well as his academic colleagues. He was for many years reader at the inns of court in equity and constitutional law. His advice was sought by the government, and he was a valued member of the Indian states inquiry committee in 1928 and the committee on ministers' powers (1929–32). In 1927 he made an extended lecture tour of the United States and in 1938 visited India as Tagore professor at Calcutta. He played a prominent part in the Society of Public Teachers of Law. He received several honours, being made king's counsel by his friend Lord Birkenhead, to whom the first nine volumes of his history were dedicated, in 1920. He became a bencher of Lincoln's Inn in 1924. In the same year he received the Swiney prize of the Royal Society of Arts and in 1927 the Ames medal of Harvard University. He was knighted, to his unaffected delight, on the India list in 1929. He had honorary degrees from universities in Britain (Cambridge, Birmingham, Edinburgh, Leeds), North America (Northwestern at Chicago and Southern California), Sweden (Uppsala), and India (Calcutta). When nearing death, in 1943 he was appointed to the Order of Merit.

Holdsworth stooped slightly but had a powerful frame and a luxuriant moustache of which he was not a little proud. In 1903 he married Jessie Annie Amelia Gilbert, daughter of Gilbert Wood of Bickley, Kent; they had a son. Though sometimes awkward in company, Holdsworth was a simple, convivial man, keenly interested in others and in the world outside Oxford. His genial social instincts made him a loyal and devoted companion in any institution engaged in the pursuit of learning, whether the ancient foundations of Oxford, the historic societies of the inns of court, or the younger metropolitan and provincial schools of law, and he contributed greatly to their activities in classroom, in committee, and on their festive occasions. He delighted in after-dinner conversation and was noted, says W. T. S. Stallybrass, for 'the indecent frequency with which he secured the "buzz"—the extra glass of port that falls to him with whom a bottle comes to an end' (*Law Quarterly Review*, 60.149). He was expert with a punt and drove a motor cycle and side-car in an age when that was not usual. No trouble was too great for him to help a young author, and he gave generously of his time to his colleagues, for example by reading the proofs of their books and articles. To the Birmingham University Law Society, which was named the Holdsworth Society in his honour, he left a pair of candelabra in recognition of many happy evenings spent at meetings there in the company of his wife and son. He was much liked by his colleagues, his pupils, and by the college staff at St John's and All Souls.

Holdsworth's son, Richard William Gilbert, had a meteoric career. He gained a first class in law, rowed three times in the Oxford boat against Cambridge, twice as stroke, and became Stowell civil law fellow of University College, Oxford. He was killed in action with the RAF in 1942. Holdsworth never recovered from his son's death and died after a long illness at his home, Grandpont House, Folly Bridge, Oxford, on 2 January 1944. He was buried in Wolvercote cemetery on 5 January and was survived by his wife.

H. G. HANBURY, rev. DAVID IBBETSON

Sources *The Times* (3 Jan 1944) · *The Times* (7 Jan 1944) · R. W. Lee and P. H. Winfield, 'Sir William Searle Holdsworth, 1871–1944', *PBA*, 30 (1944), 411–25, esp. 411, 414 · T. L. Ormiston, *Dulwich College register, 1619 to 1926* (1926), 193 · *The Times* (3 June 1929) · [F. W. F Smith, earl of Birkenhead], *F. E.: the life of F. E. Smith, first earl of Birkenhead* (1959); repr. (1960), 56 · A. L. Rowse, *All Souls in my time* (1993), 65, 73, 90 · 'In memoriam: Sir William Searle Holdsworth …, 1871–1944', *Law Quarterly Review*, 60 (1944), 138–59 · *CGPLA Eng. & Wales* (1944) · J. H. Baker, 'Holdsworth, Sir William Searle', *Biographical dictionary of the common law*, ed. A. W. B. Simpson (1984), 247–9 · T. F. P. Plucknett, 'Sir William Holdsworth, OM, KC, 1871–1944', *Year books of Edward II*, ed. J. P. Collas and W. S. Holdsworth, 22: 11 *Edward II*, 5–7, SeldS, 61 (1942)

Archives Bodl. Oxf., legal and literary papers, corresp. with A. L. Goodhart · Bodl. Oxf., corresp. relating to Society for the Protection of Science and Learning
Likenesses W. Stoneman, photograph, 1930, NPG [*see illus.*] · N. Cambier, oils, All Souls Oxf.
Wealth at death £6111 15s. 3d.: probate, 8 July 1944, *CGPLA Eng. & Wales*

Hole, Henry Fulke Plantagenet Woolocombe (1782–1852). *See under* Bewick, Thomas, apprentices (*act.* 1777–1828).

Hole, Matthew (1639/40–1730),

Church of England clergyman and religious writer, is of unknown origins. He matriculated as servitor from Exeter College, Oxford, on 18 March 1658 and graduated BA on 15 October 1661. Elected to a Devonshire fellowship on 30 June 1663 and to a full fellowship on 2 July 1664, he proceeded MA (1664), BD (1674), and DD (1716). Having taken deacon's orders he was appointed lecturer of St Martin's, Carfax, Oxford, on 18 December 1668. In June 1669 he was ordained priest by Bishop Walter Blandford at Christ Church Cathedral, Oxford, and held the vicarage of Bishops Lavington, Wiltshire, from 1673 to 1674. Through the influence of his friend Henry Godolphin, a fellow of Eton College, he was presented by the college to the vicarage of Stogursey, Somerset, in January 1688. He was made a prebendary of Wells Cathedral on 1 March 1688 and vacated his fellowship of Exeter in February 1689. From 1708 to 1711 he also held the living of Fiddington, Somerset.

Hole delighted in preaching and preached in many churches in Somerset as well as before the University of Oxford. His sermons were clear and straightforward and not overtly intellectual. He stirred up controversy, however, with a visitation sermon on a fixed form of liturgy that he delivered at Bridgwater on 19 August 1695. It provoked an exchange of pamphlets with John Moore (1642–1717), Presbyterian minister in Bridgwater, in 1698 and 1699. He continued to write in defence of the established church and published a two-part rejoinder, *An Antidote Against Infidelity* (1702, 1717), to William Coward's *Second Thoughts Concerning Human Soul* (1702).

Hole returned to Oxford after his election as rector of Exeter College on 8 March 1716. Two other candidates for the post had divided the college on party lines, and Hole had been chosen as a compromise. He was readmitted to a fellowship in 1718. He was unable to impose his will on the college and became embroiled in a long-running dispute with the fellows and the visitor over the plans of Richard Newton to turn Hart Hall, a tenant of Exeter, into a college. While rector he succeeded, however, in completing his most significant work, with publication of the fourth volume of his weighty *Practical Discourses upon the Communion Service* (1714–19). He continued to preach to within a year or so of his death and, according to Thomas Hearne, did not need spectacles even in his eighties. He never married and was cared for by two nieces who lived with him in his final years.

Hole died in his college lodgings on 19 July 1730, aged ninety, and was buried in the chapel on 21 July. He had a reputation for parsimony in his lifetime but left several charitable bequests in his will, including £200 for two charity schools in Oxford and £100 to his college towards building a new library.

W. P. COURTNEY, *rev.* S. J. SKEDD

Sources J. A. Giles, 'Memoir of Mathew Hole', in [M. Hole], *Practical discourses*, 4 vols. (1837–8), 1.vii–xiii · Foster, *Alum. Oxon.* · C. W. Boase, ed., *Registrum Collegii Exoniensis*, new edn, OHS, 27 (1894) · W. R. Ward, *Georgian Oxford* (1958) · will, PRO, PROB 11/639, sig. 239 · *Calamy rev.*
Likenesses M. Vandergucht, line engraving, BM, NPG; repro. in M. Hole, *Practical exposition of the catechism* (1715)

Hole, Richard (*bap.* 1746, *d.* 1803), poet and antiquary, was baptized on 2 June 1746 at St Peter's Cathedral, Exeter, the son of William Hole (*d.* 1791), archdeacon of Barnstaple and canon of Exeter Cathedral, and his wife, Thomasin. He was educated at the grammar school in Exeter before matriculating on 23 March 1764 at Exeter College, Oxford, where he graduated BCL on 3 May 1771. As a young man Hole involved himself with amateur theatricals, acting in *The Beaux' Stratagem* at grammar school and composing prologues and epilogues at college. While studying law at Oxford he circulated some facetious poems and began his *Poetical Translation of Fingal*, published in 1772. Under the influence of his friend General John Graves Simcoe, afterwards the first governor of Upper Canada, Hole briefly entertained the idea of a military career, though in the event he elected to enter the clergy. On 28 October 1776 he married Wilhelmina Katenkamp, daughter of a prosperous Exeter merchant, and the following year obtained the curacy of Sowton, near Exeter. He remained at Sowton after being presented in 1777 to the living of Buckerell, which lacked a suitable residence.

Hole's couplet adaptation of *Ossian* was the beginning of a literary career devoted to the more obscure corners of literature, history, and geography. His next literary enterprise, a translation of the *Homeric Hymn to Ceres* (1781) undertaken with the assistance of Samuel Badcock, proved more successful, being several times republished in the nineteenth century. Like his friend Richard Polwhele, Hole had a passion for Greek literature, local history, and religious superstitions. He contributed to the *Monthly Review*, *British Magazine*, and *Gentleman's Magazine*, and in 1782 contributed to the *London Magazine* a series of eight satirical dialogues entitled 'The Link Boy' in which the speakers include Don Quixote, Walter Shandy, Matthew Bramble, Clarissa Harlowe, and Sophie Western. Hole's humour also appears in a posthumously published farrago of scholarship and vulgarity, 'The Exmoor courtship, from the best editions, illustrated with notes critical, historical, philosophical, and classical', a Theocritean eclogue in the Exmoor dialect with a facing 'translation' into court pastoral.

Hole's major work, *Arthur, or, The Northern Enchantments* (1789), is a romance epic in seven books which in places imitates Homer, Virgil, Ariosto, and Spenser. But *Ossian* is the presiding influence in the first Arthuriad to recreate the manners and belief systems of fifth-century Britain. In an original story Arthur's Britons, allied with the Irish, repel a horde of invading Saxons and Scandinavians.

Supernatural forces figure largely as Merlin, whose daughter is betrothed to Arthur, is pitted against Urda and the Weird Sisters, who assist Hengist. The historical and geographical setting suggests that the Exeter poet was attempting to do for west Britain what Macpherson's *Ossian* had done for Scotland.

Hole was a founding member of the literary society at Exeter whose members included Richard Polwhele, Hugh Downman, and William Jackson (who set to music Hole's 'Ode to Imagination'). Writings by Hole (including Miltonic odes to terror, melancholy, and stupidity, and several philological essays) appear in the society's two publications, *Poems Chiefly by Gentlemen of Devonshire and Cornwall* (1792) and *Essays, by a Society of Gentleman at Exeter* (1796). Papers read before the Exeter literary society resulted in *Remarks on the Arabian Nights' Entertainments* (1797) which in turn led to a parallel work on Homer, a fragment of which was posthumously published in 1807 as *An Essay on the Character of Ulysses*. Hole displays a considerable if curious erudition in illustrating the monsters and marvels encountered by the two Mediterranean travellers. He left behind a commonplace book containing several original plays. Polwhele later quarrelled with Downman and Hole, and a review of the *Essays* which Hole erroneously attributed to Polwhele led to a falling-out and acrimonious exchanges in the *Gentleman's Magazine*. In 1792 Hole was promoted by the bishop of Exeter to the rectory of Faringdon, which he held with Buckerell, and afterwards to Inwardleigh, near Okehampton, which he held with Faringdon until his death. He died at Exmouth, after a painful illness, on 28 May 1803. He was survived by his wife of twenty-six years.

Hole's legacy as a poet and translator appears most obviously in the poetry of his nephew John Herman Merivale. While his personal character and literary abilities were highly esteemed in his Exeter circle, Hole's wry humour and antiquarian enthusiasms did not attract much attention elsewhere. In his 'Reply to *Blackwood's*' Byron catalogues 'Hoole, and Hole, and Hoyle' among the bards of wilted reputation (Byron, *Letters*, ed. R. E. Prothero, 1898–1904, 4.488). In the Devonshire *Essays* appear defences of Shylock and Iago, the irony of which, like that of Swift's *Modest Proposal*, was lost on several later critics. *Arthur, or, The Northern Enchantments* drew mixed reviews: while all approved of the subject, Nathan Drake objected to Hole's imitation of Ariosto, Egerton Brydges to his use of couplets, and Robert Southey, comparing *Arthur* to Wilkie's *Epigoniad*, to the departures from the Arthur of legend. Yet Southey's own ethnographic epics probably owe something to a childhood reading of Hole's romance. If his heroic couplets and Shandean wit belonged to the last age, Hole's imaginative reconstructions of exotic places and pagan beliefs anticipated much later romantic fabling.

DAVID HILL RADCLIFFE

Sources H. Downman, 'On reading Mr. Hole's Arthur', *Poems* (1790), 195–9 · N. Drake, 'On the poetry of the ages of Elizabeth and the Charleses, and of the present reign', *Literary hours* (1800), 1.146 · *GM*, 1st ser., 73 (1803), 599–600 · E. Brydges, *Censura literaria: containing titles, abstracts, and opinions of old English books*, 6 (1808), 214–

15 · R. Southey, 'Hole's *Arthur*', *Omniana* (1812), 1.83–5 · Nichols, *Lit. anecdotes*, 8.92–94n · *GM*, 1st ser., 87/1 (1817), 228–9 · R. Hole, 'The Exmoor courtship', *Blackwood*, 4 (1819), 530–41 · B. Parr, memoir, *Blackwood*, 5 (1819), 65–71 · R. Polwhele, *Traditions and recollections; domestic, clerical and literary*, 2 vols. (1826) · W. H. Kearley Wright, *West-country poets* (1896) · IGI

Archives Bodl. Oxf., corresp. with Francis Douce

Likenesses W. Daniell, etching, pubd 1809 (after G. Dance), BM, NPG

Hole, Samuel Reynolds (1819–1904), dean of Rochester and horticulturist, born at Ardwick, near Manchester (where his father was then in the cotton business), on 5 December 1819, was the only son of Samuel Hole (1778–1868) of Caunton Manor, Nottinghamshire, and his wife, Mary (*d.* 1852), daughter of Charles Cooke of Macclesfield. After attending Mrs Gilbey's Preparatory School at Newark, he went to Newark grammar school. At the age of sixteen he edited a periodical called the *Newark Bee*.

Foreign travel preceded Hole's admission to Brasenose College, Oxford, in 1840. Fox-hunting, to which he was devoted for fifty years, occupied much of his time at the university. He was, too, secretary to the Phoenix (the oldest social club in Oxford) in 1842, and presided at its centenary dinner on 29 June 1886. In 1843 he published a sprightly *jeu d'esprit* illustrating undergraduate life at Oxford, entitled *Hints to Freshmen*, which reached a third edition in 1853. He graduated BA in 1844 and proceeded MA in 1878.

Hole was ordained deacon in 1844 and priest in 1845. He became curate of Caunton in the former year, and in 1850 was appointed vicar by C. T. Longley, bishop of Ripon. He held the living until 1887. In 1865 he was appointed rural dean of Southwell, and in 1875 prebendary of Lincoln. He was chaplain to Edward White Benson from 1883, and in 1884 was elected proctor to convocation. At Caunton he instituted daily services and never omitted a daily visit to the village school; but this clerical duties were varied by hunting, shooting, and other rural sports, and he was an enthusiastic gardener. After the death of his father in 1868 he was squire of Caunton as well as vicar. He had married on 23 May 1861 Caroline (1840–1916), eldest daughter of John Francklin of Gonalston, Nottinghamshire, with whom he had one son.

In 1858 Hole came to know John Leech, the illustrator, and a close friendship followed. In the summer of 1858 the two, who often hunted together, made a tour in Ireland, of which one fruit was Leech's illustrated volume *A Little Tour in Ireland* (1859), with its well-informed and witty letterpress under the pseudonym Oxonian. A reprint of 1892 gives Hole as the author. Hole made many suggestions for Leech's pictures in *Punch*, and much correspondence passed between them (cf. John Brown's *Horae subsecivae*, 3rd ser., 1882, which contains Hole's biographical notes on Leech). Hole's friendship with Leech also led to his election to the *Punch* table in 1862, but he was never a regular contributor to the journal, writing only occasionally while Mark Lemon was editor. At Leech's house in Kensington Hole met Thackeray, who was, he wrote, of his own height (6 feet 3 inches). The novelist proposed him for the Garrick Club. At Thackeray's invitation Hole contributed some verses to the *Cornhill Magazine*.

Hole was long a rose-grower, and he came into general notice as promoter and honorary secretary of the first national rose show, which was held in the old St James's Hall, London, on 3 July 1858. Thenceforth he was an enthusiastic organizer of flower shows. At Caunton he grew upwards of 400 varieties of roses, and afterwards at Rochester had 135 in his deanery garden. He edited the *Gardener's Annual* for 1863, contributed to *The Garden*, founded by his friend William Robinson in 1871, and came to know the leading horticulturists in France and Italy as well as at home. The establishment of the National Rose Society in December 1876 was largely due to his efforts; his *Book about Roses, How to Grow and Show Them* (1869; 15th edn, 1896), though of no great scientific value, did much to popularize horticulture. The work was translated into German and circulated widely in America. Hole presided at the National Rose Conference at Chiswick in 1889, and Tennyson, in writing to him, hailed him as 'the Rose King'. Hole's more general work on gardening, *The Six of Spades* (the name of an imaginary club of six gardeners), appeared in 1872, and was reprinted, with additions, in 1892, as *A Book about the Garden and the Gardener*.

A moderate high-churchman who had been influenced at Oxford by E. B. Pusey, Hole proved popular as a preacher, especially to parochial home missions and as a platform orator. He spoke without notes. A rather raucous voice was atoned for by a fine presence, earnestness, plain language, and common sense. While he denounced drunkenness, gambling, and horse-racing, he frankly defended moderate drinking, at the church congress of 1892 (cf. John Kempster, *The Dean and the Drink*, 1892), and publicly justified the playing of whist for small stakes. He was president of the Industrial Home for Friendless Girls, and a supporter of the Society for the Prevention of Cruelty to Animals. For several years he was a midday preacher at St Paul's Cathedral during Lent, and he was a select preacher at Oxford in 1885–6.

In 1887 Hole was made dean of Rochester on the recommendation of Lord Salisbury. Besides popularizing the cathedral services and continuing for a time his home mission work, he made in 1894 a four months' lecture tour in the United States, by which he raised £500 for the restoration of his cathedral. He described his experiences in *A Little Tour in America* (1895). The crypt and west front of Rochester Cathedral were restored under Hole's supervision, the screen decorated, and vestries built. Hole received the Lambeth degree of DD in 1887, was appointed almoner of the chapter of St John of Jerusalem in 1895, and grand chaplain of freemasons in 1897. Hole died at Rochester deanery on 27 August 1904, and was survived by his wife and son, Samuel Hugh Francklin Hole (1862–1948). He was buried at Caunton.

A man of genial humour, Hole had a wide circle of correspondents including Leech, Millais, Thackeray, Dr John Brown, Dean Bradley, Sir George Grove, J. H. Shorthouse, and Archbishop Benson. A selection of his letters was published in 1907. Hole's *Memories* (1892) was prolific in good stories and wise observation; *More Memories* followed in 1894. Another rather more reflective volume of reminiscence, *Then and Now* (1901), was the author's favourite work. Hole wrote several hymns which were set to music by his friend Sir John Stainer. One of them, 'Father, forgive', had a sale of more than 28,000, and realized nearly £100 for the Transvaal war fund.

G. LE G. NORGATE, *rev.* M. C. CURTHOYS

Sources B. Massingham, *Turn on the fountains: the life of Dean Hole* (1974) • *The letters of Samuel Reynolds Hole*, ed. G. A. B. Dewar (1907) [with memoir by the ed.] • Burke, *Gen. GB* • *Men and women of the time* (1899) • *The Times* (29 Aug 1904) • *The Times* (31 Aug 1904) • *The Times* (1 Sept 1904) • *The Times* (2 Sept 1904) • *Gardeners' Chronicle*, 3rd ser., 36 (1904), 170–1 • *Nottingham Daily Express* (29 Aug 1904) • *Nottingham Daily Express* (30 Aug 1904) • [C. B. Heberden], ed., *Brasenose College register, 1509–1909*, 2 vols., OHS, 55 (1909)
Archives BLPES, corresp. • Newark Public Library, Newark-on-Trent, corresp. • Notts. Arch., papers
Likenesses engraving, *c.*1844, National Rose Society • double portrait, photograph, 1861 (with his wife), repro. in Massingham, *Turn on the fountains*, facing p. 116 • group portrait, photograph, *c.*1903 (with family), repro. in Massingham, *Turn on the fountains*, 209 • F. W. Pomeroy, marble effigy, exh. RA 1906, Rochester Cathedral • C. W. Furse, portrait, 1912?, Caunton, Nottinghamshire • Dawsons, photogravure, NPG • F. T. D. [F. T. Dalton], chromolithograph caricature, NPG; repro. in *VF* (18 July 1895) • photograph, repro. in Massingham, *Turn on the fountains*, 209 • portrait, repro. in *Nottingham Daily Express* (29 Aug 1904), 8 • two portraits, repro. in *Gardeners' Chronicle*, 170, 171
Wealth at death £29,305 2s. 9d.: probate, 10 Oct 1904, *CGPLA Eng. & Wales*

Hole [Holle], **William** (*d.* 1624), engraver, was the most versatile and prolific of the native-born members of his profession working in the reign of James I. Nothing is known of his origins or training, and the assumption that he was English is a deduction from his name. His first dated plates belong to 1607 and are the title-plate and nineteen of the maps for the second edition of William Camden's *Britannia*. The first edition had been engraved by William Rogers, the first significant native-born engraver, and Hole may have been his pupil.

As a copperplate-engraver Hole remained a specialist in engraving maps, music, and lettering. His figurative plates, mostly portrait frontispieces of the authors of books, are crude and wooden, especially by comparison with the work of Simon and Willem de Passe and Francis Delaram, the immigrants who displaced him in this field. His lettering is always delightful, and he stands at the head of the seventeenth-century tradition of engravers who worked for writing-masters. He engraved the plates to Martin Billingsley's *The Pens Excellencie, or, The Secretaries Delighte* of 1618, the first important English engraved copybook, dedicated to Charles as prince of Wales, and he was also responsible for the first engraved plates of music made outside Italy: the famous *Parthenia* of 1612–13 which contained music by William Byrd, John Bull, and Orlando Gibbons, and Angelo Notari's *Prime musiche nuove* of 1613.

In 1618 Hole was given a lifetime appointment to the office of head sculptor of the iron for money in the Tower and elsewhere. The steady stream of his dated portrait plates that begins in 1607 stops abruptly in 1619, and he henceforth confined himself to engraving coin dies. His salary of £30 was paid every year until his death in 1624: a document of 15 September that year granted his office as 'Chief Engraver of the Mint and Graver of the King's seals, ensigns and arms' to John Gilbert and Edward Green.

ANTONY GRIFFITHS

Sources A. M. Hind, *Engraving in England in the sixteenth and seventeenth centuries*, 2 (1955), 316–40 • H. A. Grueber, 'William Hole, or Holle, cuneator of the mint', *Numismatic Chronicle*, 4th ser., 7 (1907), 346–50 • H. Farquhar, 'A note on William Hole, cuneator of the mint', *Numismatic Chronicle*, 4th ser., 8 (1908), 273–7 • A. H. King, *Four hundred years of music publishing*, 2nd edn (1968), 18 • C. E. Challis, ed., *A new history of the royal mint* (1992), 298–9

Holes, Andrew (*d.* 1470), ecclesiastical administrator and book collector, was a younger son of Sir Hugh Holes of Cheshire. A Winchester scholar in 1408, he had become a scholar of New College, Oxford, by 1412, holding a fellowship from 1414 to 1420. By 1428 he was a bachelor in both laws; he lectured in Oxford in canon and civil law, taking a licentiate in canon law in 1433. Like many Wykehamists Holes entered public service. By November 1428 he was described as gentleman to the king. In July 1429 he was a delegate meeting ambassadors of the king of Aragon. In 1431 he was ambassador in Rome. In September 1432 he became proctor for the king in Rome, though without a formal appointment until 1437. His duties at the curia included securing papal confirmation of royal appointees to church offices, and representing the king in legal cases. The curia was in a state of crisis, with Pope Eugenius IV (*r.* 1431–47) at odds with the Council of Basel. By 1433 there was threat of a new schism. On 7 July 1433 Holes delivered a sermon to the English hospice before a congregation including seven cardinals and many prelates in which he showed himself sympathetic to church reform, arguing that priests should be chaste, abstemious, generous to the poor, and that they should preach.

Holes seems to have practised what he preached. Vespasiano da Bisticci included him in his memoirs of illustrious writers, bishops, and statesmen, describing him as a man of holy life who provided a model of charity, modesty, and temperance. However, the conciliar movement failed to implement necessary reforms, and by 1440 Holes had embraced a conservative viewpoint that accepted the divine origin of the papal office. A close friend of the pope, in June 1434 Holes had accompanied Eugenius when he fled Rome, taking the curia to Florence. He also accompanied him to Ferrara for negotiations with the Greek church in 1438, and returned to Florence in February 1439 after taking his doctorate in Padua. However, when Eugenius left Florence in March 1443, Holes remained in Florence conducting royal business at the curia.

During his thirteen years at the papal court Holes made friends with leading humanists and acquired a reputation as a scholar and book collector. Apart from William Grey (*d.* 1479), he is the only Englishman to be included in Vespasiano's *Memoirs*. According to this Florentine bookseller, Holes kept a vast number of scribes copying books, and after Eugenius quitted Florence he remained behind attending to his books. He also, according to Vespasiano, greatly favoured men of learning, and once made a feast to which he invited leading humanists like Manetti, Arezzo, and Palmieri. They debated a proposition of another of the guests, Giamozzo, that all things in scripture are true. When he left for England, Holes's collection of books, too numerous to be sent by land, was sent by sea. Twenty-four of these have now been identified. His taste was for Latin classics, including Cicero's speeches; early fathers like Jerome and Boethius; and modern works of Italian humanism such as Petrarch's *Letters*.

As befitted a friend of Thomas Beckington (*d.* 1465), Holes was a patron of learning. Beckington wrote to him soliciting his help on behalf of their old college, New College. He also named Holes in a commission to solicit the pope's aid on behalf of the free school of St Anthony's Hospital, London, which John Colet and Thomas More were later to attend. Holes left the bulk of his library to the colleges of Oxford, and also £100 for exhibitions. His interest in Latin classical literature reflects Wykehamist admiration for the Ciceronian ideal of combining scholarship with state service, and Holes fulfilled this role on his return from Italy at the end of 1444. In 1447 he was again a king's clerk, serving on a commission administering the mismanaged revenues of Ivychurch Priory in Salisbury diocese. When Adam Moleyns was murdered in 1450, his place as keeper of the privy seal passed to Holes, who held it until 4 April 1452.

The latter part of Holes's life was spent in scholarly seclusion in his home in the Salisbury Cathedral close (he was formally installed as chancellor in 1445). Vespasiano had observed that Holes, contrary to the ways of ordinary men, spurned honours and dignities such as might have accompanied a bishopric, and longed to leave the court of Rome to devote himself to contemplation. During Holes's eighteen years' retirement at Salisbury, the cathedral became a centre of intellectual activity, with its chapter including the physician Gilbert Kymer (*d.* 1463) and Nicholas Upton (*d.* 1457), author of *De studio militari*. Holes was also involved in the renewed efforts to secure the canonization of St Osmund, the first bishop of Salisbury (successfully concluded in 1457), in which he secured the help of Nicholas Upton and William Grey.

Holes died on 1 April 1470, and was buried in Salisbury Cathedral. His scholarly interests and achievements are reflected in his commemoration in an illustration to Thomas Chaundler's life of William Wykeham, in which Holes appears in a group of twelve distinguished alumni of New College, Oxford.   JONATHAN HUGHES

Sources M. Harvey, 'An Englishman at the Roman curia during the Council of Basle: Andrew Holes, his sermon of 1433 and his books', *Journal of Ecclesiastical History*, 42 (1991), 19–38 · J. W. Bennett, 'Andrew Holes, a neglected harbinger of the English Renaissance', *Speculum*, 19 (1944), 314–35 · Vespasiano da Bisticci, *Lives of illustrious men of the XVth century*, trans. W. G. Wales and E. Wales (1926) · R. Weiss, *Humanism in England during the fifteenth century*, 3rd edn (1967) · Emden, *Oxf.*, 2.949–50 · Österreichische Nationalbibliothek, Vienna, MS 4139, fols. 61r–69r

Archives Österreichische Nationalbibliothek, Vienna, MS 4139 fols. 61r–69r | Magd. Oxf., MS Lat. 141 · New College, Oxford, MS 155; MS 268

Likenesses portrait, repro. in *Hist. U. Oxf.* 2: *Late med. Oxf.*, pl. 3

Holford, Alice (*d.* 1455). *See under* Women traders and artisans in London (*act. c.*1200–*c.*1500).

Holford, Sir George Lindsay (1860–1926), landowner, was born on 2 June 1860 at Dorchester House, Park Lane, London, the fourth child and only son of Robert Stayner *Holford (1808–1892), MP and art and plant collector, of Westonbirt, Tetbury, Gloucestershire, and Dorchester House, London, and Mary Anne Lindsay (*d.* 1901), daughter of Lieutenant-General Sir James Lindsay. George Holford's maternal uncles were Sir Coutts Lindsay, bt (1824–1913), owner of the Grosvenor Gallery, London, Robert James Loyd-Lindsay, Baron Wantage, and (by marriage) Alexander Lindsay, twenty-fifth earl of Crawford. His father was reputedly the richest commoner in England.

After Eton College Holford was commissioned into the Life Guards. Despite a generous allowance from his father he ran up considerable debts and in 1883 had to be helped out by his future brother-in-law, the merchant banker Robert Henry *Benson. His other sisters married Albert *Grey, fourth Earl Grey, and Albert Parker, third earl of Morley. In 1888 he became equerry to the duke of Clarence, whom he accompanied on an official visit to India in 1889–90; for this he was appointed CIE. He was successively equerry to the prince of Wales, later Edward VII, an extra equerry to George V, and equerry-in-waiting to Queen Alexandra. He became colonel of the Life Guards' 1st battalion in 1908 and commanded its reserve battalion during the First World War. He was knighted in 1910.

Robert Holford died in 1892 and George Holford then came into an inheritance that included the fabled Holford picture collection, Westonbirt, Dorchester House, and over 16,000 acres. The collection remained vast, even though he sold the etchings and engravings, including a celebrated group of Rembrandt etchings, on 11–14 July 1893 at Christie, Manson, and Woods for £28,119. Further disposals included a painting by Meindert Hobbema to J. P. Morgan, privately; a portrait by Velázquez of the duke of Olivares, which passed through Duveen Bros. to the great American collector Arabella Yarrington, Mrs Collis P. Huntington; and a first folio Shakespeare to the New York dealer Dr Rosenbach. Holford's main interest, however, was in developing his father's arboretum at Westonbirt and in cultivating orchids. To this end he employed H. G. Alexander as his specialist grower. One result was *Cymbidium alexanderi* 'Westonbirt', which by 1993 had produced 381 first-generation hybrids, each of which had been used many times for second- and third-generation hybrids.

Holford's great-niece once asked his sister what Uncle George did and was told that he 'was at court and attended the king and he is the best backgammon player in London' (private information). It was discovered after his death that the drawers of his writing table at Dorchester House were crammed with IOUs. He had never tried to cash them as he had no need; nor, it was widely reported in his family, had he ever opened a business letter. He was amiable, generous, and even humble: it is as such a character that he made a fictional appearance in Dennis Wheatley's thriller *The Second Seal*.

On 17 December 1912 Holford married Susannah West Menzies, *née* Wilson (*d.* 1943), with whom he was reputed to have been in love for twenty years. He first met her at Tranby Croft, her father's home, during the weekend when Sir William Gordon Cummings was accused of cheating at cards in the presence of the future Edward VII. She was the widow of Jack Graham Menzies (*d.* 1911). Holford died, childless, on 11 September 1926 at Westonbirt. He left his orchids to Alexander. The rest of his wealth passed to his nephews and nieces, including his executor, Sir Reginald *Benson, and the estates were sold. Dorchester House was razed and the Dorchester Hotel built on the site while Westonbirt became a girls' school; the arboretum passed ultimately to the Forestry Commission.

The Greek vase, furniture, tapestries, Chinese porcelain, and objects of art at Westonbirt were sold there over five days in October 1927. The fabled picture collection was sold in two major sales; Christie, Manson, and Wood conducted all three auctions. The first picture sale, of Italian masters, took place on 15 July 1927 and realized nearly £156,000. The Dutch and Flemish pictures, together with a small number from the English school, were sold on 17–18 May 1928, and included Albert Cuyp's *Dordrecht at the Maas* (sold for 20,000 guineas), Rembrandt's *Portrait of a Man Holding the Torah* and *Portrait of the Young Man with a Cleft Chin* (48,000 and 44,000 guineas respectively), *The Elevation of the Cross* (5200 guineas) by Rubens, and Richard Wilson's *The River Dee* (4100 guineas). The first day's sale of seventy-eight paintings realized £364,094, a world record for a single day's sale of pictures by auction; a total of £416,197 was raised over the two days.   JEHANNE WAKE

Sources J. Wake, *Kleinwort Benson: a history of two families in banking* (1997) · private information (2004) · R. Benson, *The Holford collection* (privately printed, London, 1924) · R. Benson, *The Holford collection, Dorchester House*, 2 vols. (1927) · *The Times* (13 Sept 1926) · *WWW, 1916–28* · *DNB* · b. cert. · d. cert. · *Christie's season, 1927–8* (1928)
Archives U. Durham, Earl Grey papers
Likenesses J. S. Sargent, charcoal drawing, 1910, priv. coll.; repro. in Benson, *Holford collection, Dorchester House*, vol. 2
Wealth at death £374,663: probate, 1927, *CGPLA Eng. & Wales*

Holford [*married name* Hodson], **Margaret** (*bap.* 1778, *d.* 1852), poet and translator, was baptized on 1 June 1778 at St John the Baptist, Chester, Cheshire, the eldest of four daughters of Allen Holford of Davenham, Cheshire, and of Margaret, daughter of William Wrench, of Chester. Her father, who died while she was still a child, was the last male descendant of the ancient family of Holford of Davenham, a branch of the Holfords of Holford and Vale Royal. Her mother was a poet, Minerva Press novelist, and playwright, sufficiently prolific for the works of mother and daughter (both Margaret Holford) often to be confused in catalogues and dictionary entries. At the age of eight Margaret was taking volumes of Shakespeare to bed, reading early and late, writing poetry, and displaying an 'insatiable' appetite for all kinds of literature' (*N&Q*, 411). Her first published work, an anonymous and lengthy metrical romance, *Wallace, or, The Fight of Falkirk* (1809), was a

contemporary success in the wake of Walter Scott's *Marmion* (1808), which it blatantly imitates. She produced about the same time 'Lines Occasioned by Reading the Poetical Works of Walter Scott' (NL Scot.), the receipt of which Scott failed to acknowledge, causing resentment and the intervention of his friend Joanna Baillie on the side of the injured female poet, whom she described to Scott as a good 'military antiquarian' in his own style (*Letters of Sir Walter Scott*, 2.301 and n.). Scott's unchivalrous excuse for the slight was his horror of attaching to himself sentimental female poets.

Like Scott, other readers were less charitable than Baillie. *Poems* (1811), published under Holford's name and including an ode to Anna Seward, her mother's friend, and her second metrical romance, *Margaret of Anjou* (1816), were not favourably received. The latter, dedicated to her mother, from whom 'I have imbibed and inherited the taste which has devoted me to the service of the Muse', the *Monthly Review* declared to be 'tame and insipid … essentially deteriorated and deadened in spirit', when compared with *Wallace*, and unlikely to 'obtain a place of distinction in any but the *curious* and *rare* libraries of the twentieth century' (*Monthly Review*, 81, 1816, 354–5). A slim volume, *The Past, etc.* (1819) is a collection of overblown, indulgent pieces; the popular annuals, to which she was a regular contributor, continued to provide an outlet for such extravagant effusions. In 1820 she published *Warbeck of Wolfstein*, a novel with a medieval setting, and in 1823 she translated *Italian Stories*. On 16 October 1826, at South Kirkby, Yorkshire, she married the Revd Septimus Hodson [*see below*]. The only substantial work published after her marriage was a translation from the Spanish, *The Lives of Vasco Nunez de Balboa and Francisco Pizarro* (1832), which she dedicated to Robert Southey. She seems to have made up her quarrel with Scott, with whom she was corresponding in 1825, and her literary circle extended to S. T. Coleridge, Wordsworth, William Sotheby, and Savage Landor, who in 1845 was pressing her to reissue her one real success, *Wallace*. Margaret Hodson died at Plantation Terrace, Dawlish, Devon, on 11 September 1852.

Her husband, **Septimus Hodson** (1768–1833), Church of England clergyman and author, was born in Huntingdon, the seventh son of the Revd Robert Hodson (1725/6–1803). As a boy he attended St Ives School and Stilton School, and was admitted on 4 March 1779 as a pensioner to Gonville and Caius College, Cambridge, where he was a scholar from 1779 to 1784. He was ordained deacon on 25 April 1787 and priest on 3 June 1787. Hodson became perpetual curate of Little Raveley, Huntingdon, a post he held until his death. By his first marriage, on 15 March 1786, to Charlotte, the daughter of the Revd W. Affleck, a relative of Admiral Affleck, Hodson obtained, through the influence of Lord Sandwich, the rectory of Thrapstone, Northamptonshire, which he held from 1789 to 1828. He also became chaplain-in-ordinary to the prince of Wales and prebendary of Ripon Cathedral. In the 1790s he preached to the Asylum for Female Orphans at Lambeth, and several of his sermons as well as other religio-political addresses (*On the Scarcity and High Price of Provisions*, 1795, and *The Great Sin of Withholding Corn*, 1795) were published. The claim made in *A Biographical Dictionary of the Living Authors of Great Britain and Ireland* that he was forced to give up his preferments and flee to America 'in consequence of a discovery particularly disgraceful', seems to be unsubstantiated, although in 1789 he did publish *A Refutation of the Charges of Plagiarism Brought Against the Rev. Septimus Hodson*.

Hodson was married a second time, to Frances, the daughter of G. Burden, before his marriage to Margaret Holford in 1826. He settled with his third wife at Sharow Lodge, Ripon, where he died on 12 December 1833.

KATHRYN SUTHERLAND

Sources *N&Q*, 4th ser., 11 (1873), 411–12 · *GM*, 2nd ser., 38 (1852), 439 · *The letters of Sir Walter Scott*, ed. H. J. C. Grierson and others, centenary edn, 12 vols. (1932–79), vols. 2–3, 9 · *GM*, 2nd ser., 1 (1834), 338 [Septimus Hodson] · *BL cat.* [Septimus Hodson] · Venn, *Alum. Cant.* · [J. Watkins and F. Shoberl], *A biographical dictionary of the living authors of Great Britain and Ireland* (1816) · J. R. de J. Jackson, *Romantic poetry by women: a bibliography, 1770–1835* (1993), 161–2 [lists of M. Hodson's poetic pubns] · *IGI* · d. cert.

Holford, Robert Stayner (1808–1892), art and plant collector, was born at Westonbirt, Gloucestershire, on 16 March 1808, the only child of George Peter Holford, master in chancery, of Westonbirt, and his wife, Anne, daughter of the Revd Averill Daniel of Lifford, co. Donegal. Holford graduated BA from Oriel College, Oxford, in 1829. In 1838 he inherited £1 million from his uncle, Robert Holford.

Holford's earliest zeal was for landscape gardening. In 1829 he began the arboretum at Westonbirt, where a tract of sandy loam covering 114 acres allowed trees from almost any country in the world to be planted and raised. The increasing collection of different species of trees and plants—skilfully grouped by season or by collections of single types of tree, and designed in glades, avenues, and drives—caused the eventual expansion of the arboretum to 600 acres.

Holford began to collect works of art in 1839 and became one of the most distinguished collectors of his time, with an enthusiasm for the Italian Renaissance. The diarist A. N. L. Munby described him as 'a collector with an eye for quality and the means to indulge it without stint'. No doubt in tribute to the superb quality of his illuminated manuscripts and early printed books, he referred to Holford as the 'Ideal Connoisseur'. Apart from his pictures, manuscripts, and early printed books, Holford collected old-master prints and etchings by Rembrandt, sculpture, Della Robbia ware, bronze portrait busts, maiolica, porcelain, furniture, tapestries, and gold- and silver-smiths' work.

The picture collection, made with the help of the dealer William Buchanan, was formed chiefly between 1840 and 1860 from most of the important auctions in London and from Italian collections. Holford's collection included works by Rubens, Velázquez, Justus Sustermans, Van Dyck, and Rembrandt; French and Italian landscapes by Claude, Gaspard Dughet, Nicolas Poussin, and Salvator Rosa; Dutch landscape and genre painters; the early Flemish school; and English portraits.

In 1849 Holford purchased the freehold of the old Dorchester House, with its 100 yards of frontage to Park Lane, London: he chose Lewis Vulliamy as his architect to design the Italianate palazzo he planned for the site. He commissioned much of the interior decoration from Alfred Stevens; there was a special relationship between patron and sculptor, whereby Stevens was given a very free hand. The house, completed in 1856, was celebrated for its huge marble staircase and for the splendid series of staterooms on the *piano nobile*, designed for the reception and display of Holford's collections. Between 1863 and 1870 he rebuilt Westonbirt, again commissioning Vulliamy, but choosing an Elizabethan design.

Holford served as Conservative MP for East Gloucestershire from 1854 to 1872 and was a JP, but he took little interest in politics. He was an original member of the Burlington Fine Arts Club. On 5 August 1854 he married Mary Anne, daughter of Lieutenant-General James Lindsay MP of Balcarres, Fife, and thus became brother-in-law to three collectors: Alexander *Lindsay (twenty-fifth earl of Crawford), Robert *Lindsay (Baron Wantage), and the owner of the Grosvenor Gallery, Sir Coutts Lindsay. Holford and his wife had three daughters and one son, Lieutenant-Colonel Sir George *Holford (1860–1926). Holford died on 22 February 1892 at Dorchester House, London, and was buried in Westonbirt churchyard. The collection was sold after the death of his son, at Christies, London.

CHARLES SEBAG-MONTEFIORE, *rev.*

Sources R. Benson, *The Holford collection* (privately printed, London, 1924) · private information (1993) · G. L. Holford, *Catalogue of the trees and shrubs in the collection of the late Lieut.-Col. Sir George Lindsay Holford* (1927) · m. cert. · d. cert.
Archives Glos. RO, papers relating to West Gloucestershire election | RIBA, letters to Lewis Vulliamy
Likenesses photograph, 1862, repro. in Benson, *Holford collection* · E. Roberts, portrait, 1889, Westonbirt School, Tetbury, Gloucestershire
Wealth at death £422,432 18s. 0d.: probate, 7 May 1892, *CGPLA Eng. & Wales*

Holford, William Graham, Baron Holford (1907–1975), architect and town planner, was born in Berea, Johannesburg, Transvaal Colony, on 22 March 1907, the elder surviving child and second son of William George Holford (1866–1927) and his wife, Katherine Maud Palmer (1875–1966). Both parents came from Cape Colony. The Holford family, originally from Lancashire, was devoutly Wesleyan. The Revd William Holford (1831–1911) migrated to South Africa as a missionary; his son—Holford's father—became a railway engineer, mining engineer, then manager of Apex Mines, Johannesburg.

William Graham Holford was educated at Parktown School, Johannesburg, and, from 1920 to 1923, at the Diocesan College, Rondebosch, Cape Town. He became an enthusiastic rugby football supporter and amateur actor. Holford initially worked in a bank, before becoming an assistant to the Johannesburg architects Cowin, Powers, and Ellis. In September 1925 he sailed to England to enrol at the Liverpool University school of architecture. The

William Graham Holford, Baron Holford (1907–1975), by
Elliott & Fry, 1953

school, dominated by Charles Reilly, was modelled upon
Franco-American Beaux-Arts formal classicism, with over-
tones of approaching modernism. Holford travelled
widely in his vacations, and toured Italy in 1927. He
became close friends with Gordon Stephenson, and the
careers of the two men overlapped. In summer 1929 they
both worked for Voorhees and Walker in New York, then
travelled across the United States, before returning to Liverpool to prepare entries for the 1930 Rome prize, which
brought a year's study at the British School in Rome, with
a £250 premium. Holford's set-piece design for a museum
of archaeology won. He also graduated from Liverpool
with first-class honours.

Holford arrived in Rome in September 1930, and spent
three years in Italy. He studied Roman and baroque civic
design, and contemporary urbanism, influenced by Le
Corbusier. In February 1933 he was offered a senior lectureship at Liverpool (Stephenson had been appointed to
a junior post in October 1932). While in Rome Holford met
his future wife, also a Rome scholar (in mural painting).
Marjorie Brooks (1904–1980) was daughter of John Bunyan
Smedley Brooks (of Brooks perambulators), of Icklesham,
Sussex, and his wife, Caroline. The couple were married at
St Marylebone town hall on 28 August 1933. Marjorie Hol-
ford painted portraits of her husband, and of Sir Charles
Reilly.

In 1933, with Stephenson and Alex Adam, Holford
entered the Antwerp plan competition. Their submission
was unsuccessful, as was also their entry for the Bexhill

pavilion competition. However, Holford and Stephenson
were given an award in 1934, for semi-detached houses in
Gidea Park, Essex, a garden suburb, construction of which
was supervised by F. R. S. Yorke. A similar pair was built at
Icklesham, for Holford's mother-in-law, after two planning appeals.

Patrick Abercrombie had held the Lever chair of civic
design at Liverpool University since 1915, but in 1935 he
was appointed professor of town planning at University
College, London. Reilly and Holford hoped to attract Walter Gropius, the German Bauhaus architect, who had
recently left Nazi Germany, but this came to naught. Holford's appointment to the chair early in 1936 was a controversial choice: he had little planning experience, but
wished to develop architectural and socio-economic
dimensions to what had become a complex bureaucratic
procedure.

The economic depression of the 1930s profoundly
affected the country's heavy industries, and caused the
government, in 1935, to designate 'special areas' for
regeneration, in which state-supported 'trading estates'
were to be built. In August 1936 Holford was appointed
architect to the first of these, the North-Eastern trading
estates, the chief engineer of which was Hugh Beaver, of
Sir Alexander Gibb & Partners. Holford designed the layout, central block, and factory-type plans at the Team Valley trading estate, near Gateshead, co. Durham, a model
both for the north-east trading estates and for the industrial areas of the post-war new towns. In January 1939 Beaver brought Holford into preparatory war work in the
design and construction of the Kirkby munitions factory,
Lancashire. In 1941–2 he supervised a team of architects in
the design and construction of munitions workers' hostels for the Ministry of Works.

In 1941 Holford headed the reconstruction group serving Lord Reith at the Ministry of Works. His team, which
included Thomas Sharp, John Dower, Gordon Stephenson, and a career civil servant, H. L. G. Vincent, was a
model for subsequent groups. Lord Portal replaced Reith
in February 1942. During March of that year Holford
drafted an agenda for governmental planning research as
the basis of reconstruction. Local authorities were anxious to replan and reconstruct their blitzed areas,
although central-area redevelopment planning had
barely existed before 1939, and technical guidance was
urgently required. Central-area reconstruction planning
ventured beyond the elementary statutory process of the
1930s, which was concerned, if at all, largely with allocation of primary land-uses and definition of highway
improvement lines. Under Holford's guidance, consideration of building mass and volume—the third dimension—assumed increasing importance. Sharp drafted a
paper on civic design early in 1942. The 1944 Town and
Country Planning Act addressed the problems of 'blitz
and blight', and promoted the beginnings of comprehensive central-area redevelopment.

In 1943 a separate Ministry of Town and Country Planning was established, and Holford was its principal

adviser until 1947. Directed by Holford, Gordon Stephenson, Terry Kennedy, Peter Shepheard, Hugh Casson, Colin Buchanan, Percy Johnson-Marshall, Myles Wright, W. A. Allen, and others presented a formidable body of expertise. In 1946 Stephenson and Shepheard prepared the draft plan for Stevenage, the first new town. Myles Wright wrote *The Redevelopment of Central Areas* (1947) as a ministry handbook. It contained the key instrument of control for post-war urban redevelopment, the floor space index, which expressed the relationship between the curtilage of a site and the floor area of the buildings erected on it, later known as 'plot ratio'. The team also drafted the technical provisions of the 1947 Town and Country Planning Act.

In 1946, with Charles Holden, Holford was appointed planning consultant to the City of London. Their final report, *The City of London* (1951), was subtitled 'a record of destruction and survival'. They envisaged long-term redevelopment, involving a review of controls over building height and site coverage, a functional hierarchy of streets, and planning of traffic-free precincts, with a predominantly single-use office and business zoning. Rebuilding was slowed by the post-war continuation of building licences and the taxing of enhanced development value under the 1947 Town and Country Planning Act.

Holford now began to build up his private practice. He became planning consultant in 1946 to the University of Liverpool, and in 1953 to Exeter University, where, between 1956 and 1966, he designed the Queen's Building (arts faculties), refectory and union, and library. In 1948, with Myles Wright, he was appointed consultant to Cambridgeshire county council. In 1950 he became architect to Corby New Town Development Corporation, preparing the development plan (1951), town centre plan (1952), and layout for the first 500 houses in 1954. Holford also worked on plans for Pretoria and Durban, South Africa. From 1951 to 1957 he was consultant to the Australian government, and he updated and expanded Walter Burley Griffin's 1912–18 plan for the federal capital, Canberra, to a regional context.

The replanning of the precincts of St Paul's Cathedral and redevelopment plans for Piccadilly Circus attracted prolonged criticism. Holford's plan of March 1956 for the former featured a tower and wing which partly screened the cathedral's west front from Ludgate Hill. Although a public inquiry decision lowered the offending block, its general position was unchanged, and completion of the Paternoster precinct in 1967 rekindled the controversy. The quality of Holford's planning round the cathedral was let down by impoverished commercial architecture. Its mediocre, windswept squares never gained public acclaim; their redevelopment was mooted from the late 1980s, and was under way in 1999. Meanwhile, Piccadilly Circus by the late 1950s had become traffic-choked and surrounded by run-down buildings. Holford was brought in, following rejection of a tower and deck scheme by the London county council and the developer, Jack Cotton.

Holford's plan of early 1961, with office blocks and a central 'crystal palace', was subject to radical modification, and demands for greater traffic flow. His involvement ceased prior to redevelopment of the Trocadero site, south of the circus.

In 1948 Holford became professor of town planning at University College, London, upon Abercrombie's retirement. He served as president of the Town Planning Institute in 1953–4 and of the Royal Institute of British Architects in 1960–62, and received the gold medals of both (1961 and 1963). He became an associate of the Royal Academy in 1961, a member in 1968, and eventually its treasurer from 1970. He was a member (1943–69) of the Royal Fine Arts Commission and (from 1953) of the Historic Buildings Council; and he was a consultant to the Central Electricity Generating Board from 1949 to 1973, in which capacity he promoted high standards of architecture for power stations and improved environmental sensitivity with power lines passing through the countryside. He was also a trustee of the British Museum (and of the Soane Museum), and director of the Leverhulme trust from 1973 to 1975. He received honorary degrees from Durham, Liverpool, Oxford, and Exeter universities. Knighted in 1953, he was made a life peer in 1965, the first architect or town planner to be so honoured. Holford died in St Thomas's Hospital, London, on 17 October 1975. A memorial service in the crypt of St Paul's Cathedral on 30 September 1976 was addressed by Viscount Esher.

As a personality, Holford was genial and generous, affectionately recalled by generations of his students and colleagues. Professionally he was a brilliant speaker, a skilled draughtsman, and an able administrator, although he was not an outstanding architectural designer. He possessed an ability to build consensus opinion in order to resolve complex planning and civic design problems. His approach was in tune with the spirit of reconstruction and modernizing zeal which was prevalent in city centre replanning in the 1950s and 1960s but has since been eclipsed with the rising concern for conservation, and the emergence of post-modernism, since the early 1970s.

MERVYN MILLER

Sources G. E. Cherry and L. Penny, *Holford: a study in architecture, planning and civic design* (1986) · H. Myles Wright, *Lord Leverhulme's unknown venture: the Lever chair and the beginnings of town and regional planning* (1982) · H. Myles Wright, *The Holford partnership* (1982) · *Architects' Journal* (29 Oct 1975), 81 · *Building*, 229/6906 (24 Oct 1975), 53 · *The Guardian* (20 Oct 1975) · *The Planner*, 61/10 (Dec 1975), 386–7 · Lord Esher, 'Sir William Holford', *RIBA Journal*, 83 (Jan 1976), 37 · B. Collins, *The Times* (20 Oct 1975) · H. Myles Wright, *Town Planning Review*, 47/1 (Jan 1976), i–lv · *DNB* · R. Allan, 'The papers of the late Lord Holford', *University of Liverpool Recorder*, 84 (Oct 1980), 28–9 · E. D. Mills, 'Holford, William Graham', *Contemporary architects*, ed. M. Emmanuel (1980), 367–9 · 'Royal gold medal for architecture 1963', *RIBA Journal*, 70 (1963), 43

Archives Holford Associates, Fishmongers Chambers, London, practice records · U. Lpool, corresp. and papers | Rice University, Houston, Texas, Woodson Research Center, corresp. with Sir Julian Huxley · University of Strathclyde, Glasgow, corresp. with G. L. Pepler · Welwyn Garden City Central Library, corresp. with Sir Frederic Osborn

Likenesses Elliott & Fry, photograph, 1953, NPG [*see illus.*] ·
M. Brooks [Lady Holford], portraits · photographs, U. Lpool · presidential portrait, RIBA

Wealth at death £110,350: probate, 9 Jan 1976, *CGPLA Eng. &
Wales*

Holgate, Robert (1481/2–1555), archbishop of York, was
the youngest son of Thomas Holgate and his wife, Elizabeth, members of a family of lower gentry in Hemsworth,
Yorkshire.

Canon and bishop Holgate was educated in Cambridge,
where he proceeded BTh in 1524, and DTh in 1537, having
resided near Peterhouse in a study house belonging to the
Gilbertine order. He entered that order as a canon and was
to play an important role in the life of the community in
the years before the dissolution of the monasteries.
Appointed prior of St Catherine's-without-Lincoln in
1529, by 1534 he had been promoted to the position of
master of Sempringham, the head of the Gilbertine order.
His opponents were to claim that he owed this appointment to the agency of Thomas Cromwell, but Holgate's
career continued long after Cromwell's fall, as one of the
main players in the religious upheavals in England
between 1530 and 1555.

As master of the Gilbertines Holgate settled at the house
in Watton in Yorkshire as its prior, and he continued to
exercise this role even after his promotion to higher office
in the church. He was to be responsible for the surrender
of the Gilbertine order in December 1539, during the dissolution, and as prior of Watton he received a substantial
pension, amounting to some £68 per annum. In 1541 he
was granted priory land and eight of its manors, as well as
a house in the London parish of St Sepulchre. In March
1537 he was appointed as bishop of Llandaff, a position
that again seems to have been due to Cromwell's favour.
He was consecrated as bishop by John Hilsey, who had
replaced the executed John Fisher as bishop of Rochester,
and who had marked out his own evangelical credentials
in the campaign to expose the alleged fraud behind the
rood of Boxley and the blood of Hailes. It has been suggested that Holgate had gravitated towards the emerging
evangelical grouping in Cambridge during his time there,
and that the choice of Hilsey to officiate at the consecration was thus in keeping with Holgate's own views. He had
certainly been a contemporary of such men as Cranmer,
Barnes, and Ridley in Cambridge, and was not unsympathetic to the Reformation of the 1530s and 1540s.

The government of the north Holgate's position at Watton
had come under threat in 1536 when the house was targeted by the rebels leading the Pilgrimage of Grace. His
position was not without ambiguities. In his confession,
Robert Aske made it clear that he viewed Holgate as a protégé of Cromwell, but there were also charges that Holgate did little to ensure the defence of the house from the
rebels, and indeed he fled as the rebel army approached.
But the canons seem to have remained loyal to their prior,
and in fact Holgate was to benefit from the turbulent
events of 1536–7. In the aftermath of the defeat of the
rebels efforts were made to strengthen royal government
in the north of the county, and Holgate was appointed

president of the council of the north in 1538, a post he
held for eleven years. Despite his importance within the
Gilbertines he was not a major force in the politics of the
north, and probably for this reason he received upon his
appointment a number of instructions from the crown,
outlining the structure of the council and concerns of the
king. Most reflected the perceived need for 'good governance', including the collection of rents, the limitation of
liveries, and the suppression of pro-papal sentiments and
acts. After initial troubles, not least the fact that the new
lord president would need a residence in the north (the
former house of the abbot of St Mary's was provided), it is
clear that Holgate was a useful appointment for the
crown, in both practical and financial terms—after he
became archbishop Henry was able to cut by two-thirds
the payments made to him as lord president.

Following the death of Archbishop Lee on 13 September
1544, the earl of Shrewsbury recommended Holgate, as
'an honest and painstaking man', to be his successor (*LP
Henry VIII*, 19/2, no. 239), and Holgate was duly consecrated
at Lambeth on 26 January 1545, renouncing papal authority. Henry VIII was quick to seize the opportunities for
land transfer presented by Holgate's elevation, and one of
the latter's first actions as archbishop of York was to alien-
ate some sixty-seven diocesan manors, to the impoverish-
ment of the see. The baronies of Hexham, Ripon, Sherburn, Scrooby, and Churchdown were ceded to the crown,
in return for the rectories which made up what came to be
known as the 'great collection'. But Holgate escaped the
seizures of church land under Protector Somerset, and his
activities as archbishop suggest he was one of the more
competent of the former religious to rise to high office.
Certainly he made the best of the uncertain financial situation of his bishopric and the available lands. At his death
he was able to leave the estate of Sand Hutton to the hospital that he had founded at Hemsworth, and his will suggests strong investment in farming, showing that he possessed some 2500 sheep, about 100 horses, and quantities
of grain in store.

Theologian and reformer Archbishop Holgate was to be a
loyal servant of the crown, acting as both lord president
and archbishop for five years. He did much to assist the
military efforts of the duke of Somerset in Scotland in the
reign of Edward VI, at great personal cost. His policy of
co-operation with Somerset was built upon the relationship that the two men had developed during the latter's
time as lieutenant-general in the north in the latter years
of the reign of Henry VIII, but their alliance and friendship would cost Holgate dear after the fall of Somerset and
the rise to power of John Dudley, later duke of Northumberland. As someone who had worked closely with Somerset, Holgate was clearly an object of suspicion, even after
his removal from the presidency in 1550, and he himself
records that Northumberland taunted him as a papist. But
Holgate's own words and actions suggest that he was sympathetic to reform. He is listed in the commission for the
composition of the Bishops' Book in 1537, and in 1540 was
appointed a member of the committee that compiled the
Rationale of Ceremonial; the latter remained unpublished

until 1910, probably because the evangelical members of the committee, most notably Goodrich and Holgate, prevented any discussion of the eucharist. Holgate was also named to the doctrinal commission established by Henry VIII in April 1541, while in 1542, as part of the plan to produce a revised translation of the Bible, the epistles of Peter were assigned to him.

In his response to a set of questions sent to the bishops late in 1547 concerning matters of doctrine and practice, Holgate displayed an enthusiasm for the vernacular liturgy, arguing that it was appropriate to use 'such speech in the Mass as the people might well understand' (Burnet, 5.211–12). His injunctions for York Minster, issued in August 1552, display a strong commitment to the vernacular scriptures, and a clear concern that the clergy of the diocese should be well equipped to preach the word. All vicars and deacons were required to memorize parts of the Pauline epistles each week, and the choristers were to learn chapters of Acts or the gospels. All vicars were expected to possess a copy of the vernacular scriptures, and to read a chapter after dinner and after supper. The minster library was to be supplied with the works of the fathers, Lutheran literature, and works by Erasmus, Calvin, and Bullinger. Education was clearly important to the archbishop, who founded three schools, in York, Hemsworth, and Old Malton, and offered financial support to several others. Holgate was appointed to serve on the two Yorkshire chantry commissions, and his apparent friendship with the evangelical William Turner suggests that there was some common ground between the two men. The archbishop was also happy to find employment for the Scottish reformer John Rough in his diocese, securing a stipend for him at Hull.

Holgate's acceptance of doctrinal change in the reign of Edward VI is evidenced by the visible changes that he made to his cathedral. After his first visitation of the minster in 1547 Holgate had demanded that repairs be made to the fabric, and that the condition of ornaments and clerical vestments be improved. However as the Edwardian Reformation advanced Holgate was to oversee substantial changes, including the removal of images from above the high altar, and their replacement with texts from scripture. Organ music in the minster was abolished, and singing was expected to be plain and audible. The result of Holgate's work has been described as the transformation of the building from 'a resplendent if somewhat shabby edifice of late medieval Catholicism to a sombre temple of the new Protestantism' (Cross, 200).

Nevertheless there were signs that Holgate did not hold to some of the more radical opinions expressed in the reign of Edward. In response to the question on the eucharist put to him in 1547, Holgate's reply, buttressed with references to the New Testament, suggests a more conservative attitude than that of some of his fellow bishops, stating that:

> the oblations and sacrifice of Christ in the Mass is the presenting of the very body and blood of Christ to the heavenly father, under the forms of bread and wine, consecrated in the remembrance of his passion with prayer

and thanksgiving for the universal church. (Burnet, 5.201, 203)

Although he was appointed to the committee for the revision of the prayer book in 1551, Holgate's allegiance was given rather to the first Edwardian prayer book of 1549. But his evangelical credentials should not be doubted: he has been suggested as a plausible successor to Thomas Cranmer had the plot to subvert the succession in 1553 succeeded and the protestant Jane Grey secured the throne.

Marriage, deprivation, and death Doctrinal issues were not the only cause of conflict between Holgate and Dudley. The latter secured Holgate's removal from the presidency of the council of the north, and his designs on the archbishop's lands at Watton were to sour relations further. Moreover Holgate was later to claim that it was pressure from Northumberland that had led him to marry at the age of sixty-eight, and this marriage to Barbara Wentworth, celebrated in January 1550, threatened to become something of a scandal. The legality of the marriage was challenged by one Anthony Norman, who had been espoused to Wentworth in childhood. The law required that both parties give their consent to marriage on reaching the age of discretion, and this Barbara refused to do, instead pursuing a claim for annulment, evidently successfully. Perhaps inspired by the financial rewards reaped by the first husband of the wife of John Ponet, bishop of Winchester, Norman lodged a suit against Holgate, with the result that in November 1551 Holgate and his wife were summoned before the privy council. The order was then retracted, however, suggesting that the marriage of the archbishop was accepted by the government. But the same was not true of the more conservative laity and clergy of the diocese of York, including Robert Parkyn, curate of Adwick-le-Street, whose account of the Reformation made much capital out of the embarrassment of Holgate, and indeed of other married clerics. Holgate's position was to worsen dramatically with the accession of Mary in 1553. He was deprived of his see on 16 March 1554, alongside bishops Ferrar, Bird, and Bush, all married men and former monastics. The commissions of deprivation made it clear that marriage was their major offence, and when Holgate tried to recover his position later in 1554 in his *Apology*, his marriage provided the starting point.

The text of the *Apology*, addressed to the council through Sir Richard Southwell, is a valiant effort at self-justification, and sheds light upon both the character of the archbishop, and the events and controversies of the Reformation in the north of England. A. G. Dickens, writing in 1937, denounced it as a 'cringing' document, but later modified this position and, in recognition of the importance of the text, printed it in full. Probably writing late in 1554, Holgate uses his *Apology* to petition to be released from imprisonment in the Tower, and expresses the hope that he may be restored to sacerdotal functions. He was indeed released in January 1555, but that was the limit of his success. Holgate died on 15 November following, apparently in his London house, and was probably buried in the church of St Sepulchre nearby.

Holgate's *Apology* expresses regret on only one point—his marriage. The petition opens with an admission that he has married a 'gentilwoman' named Barbara Wentworth, but asserts that he did so only 'by the councell of Edwarde then the Duke of Somerset and for feare of the laite Duke of Northumberlande using to call him papiste and he thought verelye then that he myght have done soo by Godes lawes and the Kinges' (Dickens, *Reformation Studies*, 355). In contrast to this error of judgement, he outlines the able service that he has given to Henry VIII and Edward VI in the defence of order in the north, and promises that he will serve the queen if she grants him his freedom. Holgate points to the example of the other deprived bishops and claims that they were 'moche further gone amysse in religion then he was' (ibid., 357), although he does concede that by his marriage he has set a poor example to others, particularly those clergy in his diocese who have married. Holgate clearly hopes that he will be permitted to recover his lands and incomes, and concludes his petition by offering the queen the sum of £1000 as a token of his obedience and service. At the age of seventy-four, imprisoned in the Tower, Holgate had clearly decided to throw in his lot with the new regime. His career and more particularly his marriage point to sympathy with the ideals of the Edwardian Reformation, but his last months suggest a return to loyalties formed before the decade of more radical activity that did so much to shape his reputation.   H. L. PARISH

Sources A. G. Dickens, *Reformation studies* (1982) [incl. Holgate's *Apology*, 353–62] · A. G. Dickens, 'The marriage and character of Archbishop Holgate', *EngHR*, 52 (1937), 428–42 · G. Burnet, *The history of the Reformation of the Church of England*, rev. N. Pocock, new edn, 5 (1865) · *LP Henry VIII*, vols. 11–21 · Cooper, *Ath. Cantab.*, 1.164–5 · Venn, *Alum. Cant.*, 1/2.392 · *CPR, 1555–7* · D. MacCulloch, *Thomas Cranmer: a life* (1996) · F. Heal, *Of prelates and princes: a study of the economic and social position of the Tudor episcopate* (1980) · R. R. Reid, *The king's council in the north* (1921); facs. edn (1975) · C. Cross, 'From the Reformation to the Restoration', *A history of York Minster*, ed. G. E. Aylmer and R. Cant (1977), 193–232
Archives BL, corresp. with privy council, Henry VIII, and others, Add. MSS 32646–32656, *passim*
Likenesses J. Stowe, line engraving, pubd 1812, BM · engraving, Holgate's Hospital, Hemsworth, Yorkshire; repro. in Dickens, *Reformation studies*, 322
Wealth at death see *CPR, 1555–7*, 341–2, 471–2

Holiday, Henry George Alexander (1839–1927), painter and stained-glass artist, was born on 17 June 1839 at 2 Lower Southampton (now part of Conway) Street, Fitzroy Square, London, the second of four children of George Henry Holiday (1799–1884), a private tutor, and his wife, Climène Gerber (1804–1897), of Mulhouse, Alsace. Educated at home, he showed an early talent for drawing. After attending Leigh's Art School for a year (1854–5), he entered the Royal Academy Schools, aged only fifteen. There he absorbed elements of Pre-Raphaelitism—its historical realism, as in his first major painting *The Burgesses of Calais, A.D. 1347* (exh. RA, 1859; Guildhall Art Gallery, London), but also its decorative emphasis. Friendship

Henry George Alexander Holiday (1839–1927), by Henry Ashdown, 1870s

with Albert Moore and Simeon Solomon introduced him to D. G. Rossetti and the 'second-generation' Pre-Raphaelites Edward Burne-Jones and William Morris, with whom Holiday shared a similarly creative interest in art history. He also met the architect William Burges who, impressed by his virtuoso draughtsmanship, commissioned painted furniture and architectural decoration, initiating a long career devoted primarily to applied art.

In 1863 the stained-glass manufacturers James Powell & Sons invited Holiday to become their main designer, in succession to Burne-Jones. Work for other firms—Lavers and Barraud, and Heaton, Butler and Bayne—soon followed and the financial independence provided by numerous stained-glass commissions enabled Holiday on 13 October 1864 to marry Catherine Harriet (Kate) Raven (1839–1924), embroiderer, sister of landscape painter John Samuel Raven. Their only child, Winifred, was born in 1865.

Burges expected Holiday to be a compliant collaborator in his neo-Gothic decorative projects, but a visit to Italy in 1867, ironically at Burges's suggestion, led him to reject uncompromisingly the historicist tenets of the Gothic revival. Looking at Giotto's frescoes, he realized 'that all great art is modern when it is produced' (*The Builder*, 22 March 1890, 212). The fruits of this revelation soon appeared in his work. The I. K. Brunel memorial window (1868) in Westminster Abbey and the glazing scheme

(1869–1880s) at St Mary Magdalene, Rowington Close, Paddington, exemplify his powerfully original approach to stained glass, combining traditional technique with assertively contemporary figure-drawing.

Although gregarious and charming (especially in those social circles where patrons might be cultivated), Holiday could also be hot-tempered and polemical. Having fallen out with Burges, he began to see his career as 'a continued protest against medievalism' (Holiday, 164). By the 1870s, with the Gothic revival waning, he emerged as an influential force in British stained glass, leading a school of non-revivalist 'aesthetic' designers which included his former studio assistants H. E. Wooldridge and Carl Almquist.

Around 1870 Holiday's career seemed almost too successful. The frantic industry engendered by commissions for murals (Worcester College chapel, Oxford; Bradford and Rochdale town halls) and stained glass (all windows in Trinity College chapel, Cambridge), coupled with his excitable temperament, led to a breakdown. Respite came in 1871, when Holiday accompanied Sir Norman Lockyer's expedition to India to observe the solar eclipse. He produced meticulous drawings of the scientific phenomena and sketched local costumes and architecture, returning to London with a pet gazelle as a souvenir.

Holiday's *Reminiscences* (1914) chronicle the prodigious energy driving his artistic ideals, enriched by broad cultural and social interests. In March 1874 the Holidays moved to Oak Tree House, Branch Hill, Hampstead, designed in Queen Anne style by Basil Champneys. Ingeniously planned with ample studio space, the house proved equally suitable for regular musical and political gatherings. Alongside Henry's prolific output, Kate Holiday too developed a successful career. Her embroidery skills were ranked above 'all Europe' (Holiday, 266) by her collaborator William Morris, who exhibited her work in his firm's Oxford Street shop. The Holidays' friends included artists, musicians (especially fellow Wagnerites), and politicians, notably W. E. Gladstone.

Holiday's politics blended liberalism with idealistic socialism, derived from Edward Bellamy's utopian novel *Looking Backward* (1888). As with his friends Morris and Crane, conviction led to activism. He joined the Irish National League in the 1880s, designing banners, cartoons, even a home rule firework display, and several times visited Ireland, once to brief Gladstone on the unrest there. Other causes enlisting his propagandist talents were women's suffrage, infant crèches, and garden cities. In 1883 he was the first artist to testify to a parliamentary committee on an environmental issue, opposing the Ennerdale Valley Railway Bill. An aesthete to the core—but also a keen lakeland walker and cyclist—Holiday ardently promoted dress reform as editor of the Healthy and Artistic Dress Union's journal *Aglaia* (1893–4), castigating as 'the tubular system' (*English Illustrated Magazine*, Sept 1893, 909) the typical Victorian masculine garb of trousers, frock coat, and top hat. Holiday himself, a diminutive, bearded figure with a domed forehead and somewhat lugubrious expression, favoured Norfolk jackets and knee-breeches.

Holiday's artistic versatility was impressive, ranging from illustrations for his friend Lewis Carroll's *The Hunting of the Snark* (1876) to sculptural experiments such as *Jacob's Ladder* (exh. RA, 1884; Leighton House, London) and an innovative method of relief enamelling. For his paintings, research invariably entailed foreign travel. In 1881 he was in Italy, studying background details for *Dante and Beatrice* (1884; Walker Art Gallery, Liverpool), still his best-known work. A passion for Hellenic art was reinforced by his 1885 Greek trip, which resulted in *Aspasia on the Pnyx* (1888; Camden local studies collection, London). A lifelong interest in Egypt's culture culminated in an archaeological visit there in 1906.

Founder-membership of the designers' group The Fifteen, the Art Workers' Guild, and the Arts and Crafts Exhibition Society placed Holiday at the heart of the arts and crafts movement. A flood of stained-glass commissions, including the Robert E. Lee memorial in St Paul's, Richmond, Virginia, followed his 1890 trip to the USA and Canada, enabling him to terminate an increasingly unsatisfactory collaboration with Powells and establish his own workshop in Hampstead. With all processes of the craft under his personal supervision, he could implement the 'cordial and complete assimilation by the artist of the spirit of his material' (H. Holiday, *Stained Glass as an Art*, 1896, 93) which is conspicuously embodied in the windows of Holy Trinity Church, Manhattan, New York (1898–1925) and other late works.

After moving in 1920 to 18 Chesterford Gardens, Hampstead, Holiday suffered the double blow of his wife's death, soon after their sixtieth wedding anniversary, and failing eyesight. He died at home on 15 April 1927 and was cremated at Golders Green. Drawings and designs for stained glass by Holiday are held in the Victoria and Albert Museum, London, and the Birmingham Museum and Art Gallery.   PETER CORMACK

Sources H. Holiday, *Reminiscences of my life* (1914) · A. L. Baldry, 'Henry Holiday', *Walker's Quarterly* [whole issue], 31–2 (1930) · P. Cormack, *Henry Holiday, 1839–1927* (1989) [exhibition catalogue, William Morris Gallery, London] · C. Mill, 'Henry Holiday: eminent Hampstead Victorian', *Camden History Review*, 6 (1978), 24–7 · M. Harrison, *Victorian stained glass* (1980), 44–6, 79–80 · *The Times* (16 April 1927) · Graves, *RA exhibitors*, 4 (1906), 125–6 · B. R. Lövgren, 'Carl Almquist (1848–1924): his life and work', *Journal of Stained Glass*, 21 (1997), 11–40 · b. cert. · d. cert. · m. cert.

Archives NL Ire., corresp. and papers · priv. coll., diaries, photographs, and sketchbooks · William Morris Gallery, London, one stained-glass panel and an album of printed material by and about Henry Holiday, comprising political cartoons and copies of *Aglaia* compiled by his wife, Kate Holiday, cat. no. C197.1987; K2422.1990 | BL, corresp. with Macmillans, Add. MS 55234 · Herts. ALS, corresp. with Ebenezer Howard

Likenesses photograph, 1870, repro. in Holiday, *Reminiscences*, facing p. 168 · H. Ashdown, photograph, 1870–79, William Morris Gallery, London [*see illus.*] · J. Russell & Sons, photograph, *c.*1900, repro. in Holiday, *Reminiscences*, facing p. 2 · Swain, photograph, *c.*1900 (after Mendoza), repro. in Baldry, 'Henry Holiday', frontispiece · cabinet photograph, NPG

Wealth at death £4507 17s. 2d.: probate, 26 Aug 1927, CGPLA Eng. & Wales

Holinshed [Hollingshead], **Raphael** (*c.*1525–1580?), historian, was the son of Ralph Holinshed or Hollingshead of

Cophurst in the township of Sutton Downes, Cheshire. His cousin Ottiwell was a fellow of Trinity College, Cambridge, from 19 December 1546, and though a layman was a canon of Windsor from 24 September 1550 until Mary's accession. Cooper in the 1850s reported the belief that Raphael Holinshed had been educated at Cambridge, and cited Thomas Baker's opinion that he had attended Trinity Hall. But Anthony Wood gave credit to a report that Raphael Holinshed was 'a minister of God's word' (Wood, *Ath. Oxon.*, 1.714), thereby associating Holinshed with the growth of protestantism in England, and this may explain why during Mary's reign, when he was probably in his late twenties and early thirties, he found employment in the London printing house of Reyner Wolfe, a committed evangelical, rather than seeking a living in the church. Wolfe employed Holinshed to assist him in his grand plan to create 'a universal cosmographie', a vast historical and geographical description of the world, complete with maps.

Holinshed and his *Chronicles* The first edition of Holinshed's *Chronicles of England, Scotland, and Ireland* appeared in 1577. It formed part of a deliberate movement to elevate the status of England, English letters, and English language through writing and publishing maps, histories, national epics, and theoretical works on English poetry. In April 1547 Reyner Wolfe had received a royal privilege as the king's printer in Latin, Greek, and Hebrew that, according to its patent, included the exclusive right to provide charts and maps useful or necessary to the king and his countries. Although Wolfe's universal cosmology, according to Holinshed's preface to the *Chronicles*, 'wanted little to accomplishment' when Wolfe died in 1573, it was still incomplete a year later at the death of Wolfe's wife, Joan. Her will gave high priority to assuring Holinshed the 'benefit profit and commoditie' promised by her husband 'concerning the translating and prynting of a certaine Crownacle'; this was the first item after the bequest of Wolfe's substantial printing establishment to a son Robert and son-in-law, the haberdasher John Hun (Plomer, 19–23).

John Hun now joined John Harrison, the overseer of his mother-in-law's will and a prominent London printer, and together they formed a consortium with two members of the close-knit printing establishment at Wolfe's Brazen Serpent, Lucas Harrison and George Bishop, as the publishers of the *Chronicles*. For the printing they turned to Henry Bynneman, one of London's finest craftsmen and a man with considerable experience of printing histories—in 1580 Robert Dudley, earl of Leicester, and Sir Christopher Hatton secured for Bynneman the royal privilege to print 'all Dictionaries in all tongues, all Chronicles and histories whatsoever' (*CPR*, *1578–80*, no. 1594). In 1577 he completed the printing of Holinshed's monumental two-volume work, comprising 2835 small folio pages, besides preliminaries and indexes.

The *Chronicles* that appeared in 1577 fell short not only of Wolfe's projected 'Polychronicon' but also of Holinshed's expectations and the standards of some of the contributors. Holinshed's epistle dedicatory of 1577 to William

Cecil, Lord Burghley (also printed in the 1587 edition) suggests not only that Burghley may have been Wolfe's patron, but also that Holinshed was concerned that his own work might be censured for falling short of Wolfe's original conception—the 'universal cosmologie' illustrated with maps. The epistle dedicatory blames the work's relatively limited scope on Wolfe's executors, who although they brought the *Chronicles of England, Scotland, and Ireland* to fruition, earned little thanks from Holinshed for their efforts. William Harrison, the author of the 'Historicall description of the island of Britain', which prefaced the *Chronicles*, expressed concern that the speed with which he had written his contribution might have led to errors and omissions.

Whatever disappointments Holinshed himself may have felt about his published work, posterity has seen the *Chronicles* of 1577 as a commercial success. It was certainly both an expensive book and an important one. One of the books that Robert Devereux, later second earl of Essex, bought when he went up to Cambridge in 1577, at £1 6s. it was the most expensive volume among the young man's purchases (an investment equal to breakfast for the term). But its presence also suggests how informed Elizabethans were coming to place the understanding of their own history alongside the classics as part of the education of a young gentleman preparing for government service. How much 'benefit proffit and commoditie' Holinshed actually enjoyed as a result of the publication of his 'Crownacle' is not altogether clear. By 1 October 1578 he was in Bramcote, Warwickshire, acting as steward to Thomas Burdet, to whom he bequeathed his papers and books in a will that was proved on 24 April 1582. Wood reports that Holinshed probably died late in 1580.

The *Chronicles* after Holinshed In 1587 a second edition of Holinshed's *Chronicles* appeared. It was a substantial undertaking. The colophon to this text indicates that it was printed *cum privilegio*, that is, under a royal privilege, by Henry Denham at the sign of The Star in Aldersgate at the expense of John Harrison, George Bishop, Ralph Newbury, and Thomas Woodcocke. The 1587 *Chronicles* required the financial support of these backers as well as their co-operation. John Harrison and George Bishop owned the Stationers' Company's licence for the book, but in 1584 Ralph Newbury and Henry Denham held the exclusive right to print chronicles and histories under the queen's patent, which they obtained from the estate of Henry Bynneman, who had died in 1583. Thomas Woodcocke had purchased Lucas Harrison's share in the *Chronicles* from Harrison's widow. The stature of these printers and the extraordinary care they exercised in preparing the 1587 edition suggest that their concern to produce a distinguished history was as great as Wolfe's and Holinshed's had been, and since they controlled the project, they could produce a text that better met their expectations.

The seriousness with which Denham and the other publishers approached the second edition of Holinshed's

Chronicles can be seen in the care with which it was prepared. While Reyner Wolfe had worked along with Holinshed in compiling the 1577 edition, the second edition's publishers placed the project in the hands of Abraham *Fleming, a 'learned corrector' who worked extensively with Henry Denham (Donno, 'Abraham Fleming', 205). Acting as general editor between 1585 and 1587, Fleming revised the *Chronicles* and extended the English history to 1586. Among his inclusions were Thomas Churchyard's accounts of Elizabeth's progress to Suffolk and Norfolk in 1578 and of the elaborate tournament devised by Philip Sidney, Fulke Greville, and the earl of Arundel for the French ambassadors in 1581, Lord Burghley's pamphlet *The Execution of Justice* (1583), and parliament's demand in 1587 for sentence of death against Mary, queen of Scots, along with Elizabeth's refusal to execute her.

The *Chronicles* of 1587 were printed in three volumes in large-folio format gathered in six. William Harrison's 'Historical description' and the 'History of England' to 1066, both carried over from the 1577 edition and each signed and gathered independently, comprise the first volume. The second volume consists of the description and history of Ireland, revised and continued by John Hooker, and the description and history of Scotland, similarly treated by Francis Thynne. Again, each is signed and gathered independently. Volumes 1 and 2 are generally bound together. Volume 3 is the 'History of England' revised and continued by Fleming, although substantial parts of the continuation were contributed by John Stow.

The censored texts Both editions of the *Chronicles* underwent censorship. The first edition came to the privy council's attention in December 1577 because of Richard Stanyhurst's contribution to the 'History of Ireland'. The council ordered John Aylmer, bishop of London, to stay the sales until the text could be reformed, and he called upon the eleventh earl of Kildare to present Stanyhurst to the council. On 13 January 1578 the council ordered the bishop to release the stay once he received notice from Burghley as lord treasurer that the revisions Stanyhurst had agreed to make were completed. While the *Short title catalogue* (STC), second edition, notes three cancels in the *Chronicles* of 1577, only the F_7 gathering appears to contain significant changes. The revision toned down the text's strong bias against Kildare's grandfather, the ninth earl, and removed some disparaging remarks about Archbishop John Alen.

On 1 February 1587 the privy council wrote to Archbishop John Whitgift of Canterbury requesting 'the staye of furder sale and uttering' of a 'new booke of the Chronicles of England … until they shall be reviewed and reformyd' (APC, 1585–7, 311). The concern expressed in this order was specifically directed towards the recent additions made 'as an augmentation to Hollingsheades Chronicle' that contained

> sondry thinges which we wish had bene better considered, forasmuch as the same booke doth allso conteyne reporte of matters of later yeeres that concern the State, and are not therfore meete to be published in such sorte as they are delivered.

The order included the appointment of reviewers experienced in those state matters that warranted 'reformation': Henry Killigrew, Thomas Randolph, and John Hammond.

Holinshed's *Chronicles* of 1587 were castrated and reformed in three stages. The hands of Randolph, Killigrew, and Hammond clearly dictated the earliest stage of censorship evident in the earliest revised state of the text. Their work removed passages in the continuation of the Scottish history that might jeopardize Anglo-Scottish relations, especially those concerned with English intervention in Scottish factional politics. In the continuation of the 'History of England' their reforms enhanced the stature of Leicester, distanced England from the duc d'Alençon, who had recently offended the Dutch, and polished accounts of English legal practice to insist that trials and executions in England were administered fairly and according to due process of law. The censors apparently acted with the speed required by the privy council's order, since the first stage of the censorship was probably completed during the first week of February. This can be detected in one cancel in the 'History of Scotland', containing revised text that refers to the 'now imprisoned queene of Scotland' (p. 443, sig. A6–7). Since the page with this reference was reset, the initial review and reformation, including the resetting of the cancel leaves, must have taken place within a week of the initial order for censorship and before Mary's execution on 8 February 1587. Then, once the text had been reformed to meet Killigrew's, Randolph's, and Hammond's requirements, it was fine-tuned, probably by Whitgift, since at this stage censorship eliminated much of a long history of the archbishops of Canterbury.

The *Chronicles*' final revision, very likely dictated by political developments that followed the completion of the first and second reformations, reflects a careful attempt to cultivate good opinions both at home and abroad, and especially abroad, ahead both of English efforts to negotiate a settlement in the Low Countries and of the expected response to the execution of Mary, queen of Scots. Finally, in addition to the important matters of state reflected in the *Chronicles*' censorship and reform, the factional interests of certain councillors affected the text early and late, in particular the rivalry at court between the earl of Leicester, whose sympathies rested with international protestantism, and his more conservative opponents, notably William Brooke, Lord Cobham, and Thomas Sackville, Lord Buckhurst, who had both been appointed to the privy council in February 1586.

Textual variations All the castrations and cancels appear in the sections of the 1587 *Chronicles* that extended Holinshed's earlier histories of Scotland and England. Besides the few extant copies of the *Chronicles* that escaped castration and reformation, some copies exist that contain variant cancels together with more original leaves than the state of the text described in the STC. The greatest number of original leaves, formerly part of a broken copy of the *Chronicles*, survives in a fragment now in the Huntington Library, San Marino, California. This fragment represents the earliest state of the Holinshed text, and its cancels reflect the reformations indicated by Killigrew, Randolph, and Hammond. The second state of the 'reformed' text appears in a privately owned copy of the 1587 *Chronicles*. At each of these sites, when the original leaves, the Huntington Library fragment, and the private copy cancels and their adjacent leaves are compared with the *STC* cancels and their adjacent leaves, it can be seen that the textual reformations reflect a continuous process of revision, one completed by the time the book reappeared in the bookshops in 1587. Although *STC* suggests that the text was censored again in 1590 at the request of James VI of Scotland, in fact James relented in his demand and the *Chronicles* were not recalled.

Without a census of extant copies of Holinshed's 1587 *Chronicles*, it is unclear how many copies reflect each successive state of the text. Since the sale was stayed and the subsequent reformations made within a month of the book's completion and initial publication, copies with a fully uncensored text appear to be very rare. And although a particular copy may predominantly reflect a given state of the text of 1587, two circumstances may produce yet more variation. It is possible that in any one copy, where leaves should have been castrated and replaced with cancels, the site none the less may have been overlooked and the castration not made. Thus original leaves in one site (or more) may coexist in a copy with cancels elsewhere. Conversely, a castration may have been made, but the cancel not added. As a further complication, besides the variations that may have been produced in the sixteenth-century printing house, some copies of the *Chronicles* result from changes produced by antiquarian interests in the eighteenth century. Between 1723 and 1728 three facsimile reprints of the castrated leaves were sold, with the clear intention that they should be sophisticated into existing copies of the *Chronicles* to replace cancels and missing leaves. Consequently many copies of the 1587 edition have eighteenth-century leaves sophisticated at one or more of the castration sites. A third edition published in 1807–8 restored the censored passages but reordered the descriptions and histories and changed attribution practices.

Literary and historical significance Although Holinshed's *Chronicles* have been appreciated as a useful resource for sixteenth-century history, scholars have also tended to ignore their integrity. Their importance as a source for several of Shakespeare's plays—they underlie not only all the conventional English history plays, but also *King Lear*, *Macbeth*, and *Cymbeline*—has long been understood, but otherwise until late in the twentieth century historians were apt to consign the *Chronicles* to the margins of study, as either a vestige of medieval historiography or the sixteenth-century equivalent of a coffee-table art book, a commercial rather than an intellectual product. From the mid-1980s, however, the development of cultural studies has led to a renewed interest in Holinshed's *Chronicles* as the product of the emergent English nationalism of the end of the sixteenth century. The *Chronicles* may be regarded as a secular equivalent to John Foxe's *Acts and Monuments*, a massive and wide-ranging work of scholarship which served as a source for Holinshed, his colleagues, and successors.   CYNDIA SUSAN CLEGG

Sources Wood, *Ath. Oxon.*, new edn, 1.714 • C. S. Clegg, *Press censorship in Elizabethan England* (1997) • Cooper, *Ath. Cantab.*, 1.430, 568 • *APC*, 1585–7 • W. B. Devereux, *Lives and letters of the Devereux, earls of Essex … 1540–1646*, 2 (1853), 491 • state papers domestic, Elizabeth I, PRO, SP 12/235, 3, fol. 5 • E. S. Donno, 'Some aspects of Shakespeare's Holinshed', *Huntington Library Quarterly*, 50 (1987), 229–47 • E. S. Donno, 'Abraham Fleming: a learned corrector in 1586–87', *Studies in Bibliography*, 42 (1989), 200–11 • R. Holinshed, *Chronicles of England, Scotland, and Ireland* (1577); new edn (1587) • *STC, 1475–1640*, nos. 13568–9 • A. Patterson, *Reading Holinshed's 'Chronicles'* (1994) • F. Peck, *Desiderata curiosa* (1722) • H. R. Plomer, *Abstracts from the wills of English printers and stationers, from 1492 to 1630* (1903), 19–23 • C. Read, *Bibliography of British history, Tudor period, 1485–1603* (1933) • C. Read, *Mr Secretary Walsingham and the policy of Queen Elizabeth*, 3 (1925), 146–7 • Venn, *Alum. Cant.*, 1/2.148, 395 • K. I. Masters, 'Three eighteenth-century reprints of the castrated sheets of Holinshed's *Chronicles*', *The Library*, 5th ser., 12 (1958), 120–24

Holker, Jean-Louis (1770–1844). *See under* Holker, John (1719–1786).

Holker, John (1719–1786), Jacobite soldier and industrialist, was born on 14 October 1719 at Stretford, near Manchester, the son of John Holker, probably a blacksmith, and Alice, daughter of John Morris. His father died early; his mother was still alive in 1760. He was a partner with Peter Moss in a calendering business in Manchester while still in his twenties, and around 1740 he married Elizabeth Hilton, a Manchester woman. When the army of Charles Edward Stuart entered Manchester in 1746, Holker and Moss purchased commissions in the regiment raised there. He clearly stated that he was captured at Carlisle, though others in France later said it was at Culloden. He and Moss made a most daring escape from Newgate prison, and Holker made his way to France via the Netherlands. Once in France he joined a Jacobite regiment in the French army and saw service in Flanders. In 1750 he again showed the greatest courage in returning to England as Charles Stuart's sole companion, when he vainly urged the English Jacobites to rebel. Though given a sword of honour by Charles, Holker never seems to have claimed any merit for this act.

At this point Holker became known to Marc Morel, a French inspector of industry, who had examined the industrial situation in England. Morel drew him to the attention of Daniel-Charles Trudaine, the brilliant head of the bureau of commerce, who had a wide administrative brief. He and the scientist Mignot de Montigny, an industrial adviser to government, interviewed Holker. They concluded that he had the ability to raise the Rouen cotton industry to English standards. He was found capital and partners to set up two enterprises, one for spinning and weaving, and one for finishing cloth, particularly by calendering. Holker went to England, and to his native Lancashire, where his mother helped him to gather a well-selected group of workers, including some relatives. He successfully organized their removal to France, together with some machine models, and in many cases their families joined them. The two Rouen enterprises were very successful, and Holker gained the high esteem of Trudaine.

Holker submitted a scheme to the French government, probably with its strong encouragement, for the creation of a post that would encourage the seduction of workers from England, together with equipment, and, in the long term, would employ agents to continue this activity, and would then spread the industrial espionage beyond cotton. He was well aware of the British anti-suborning legislation of 1719 and after. He proposed that emigrant workers be encouraged by tax concessions and pensions. He himself would embark on tours through France to examine the industrial situation, and advise where it could be improved by an infusion of English technology and workers. The scheme was approved, and he became inspector-general of foreign manufactures in 1756.

Holker's tour reports are penetrating, often brilliant, and amazing, given his youth and limited industrial experience when he left England. For over quarter of a century he was the favoured and respected adviser of Trudaine and his son Trudaine de Montigny, who succeeded his father in 1769. One of his hardest tasks was to advise, direct, and comment on three other Englishmen, who were establishing themselves in France: John Badger, calenderer and maker of watered silks; Michael Alcock, a Birmingham metal manufacturer; and John Kay of fly-shuttle fame. All were difficult men to deal with, and the last two almost unreasonably so. Holker was largely responsible for setting up two large proto-industrial colonies of workers, at Sens and Bourges, based on the skills, and partly on the management, of British textile workers, many of whom he had secured himself. With his only son, John Holker [see below], he embarked on vitriol production after long preparations, which involved industrial espionage by his son in England. They established c.1768 the glass-globe process, and then c.1772 the lead-chamber process, the basis of much of the future heavy chemical industry.

In 1766 Holker and his wife took French nationality; in 1770 he received the cross of the military order of St Louis, and in 1774 he was granted letters of nobility because of his outstanding services to industry—there being a small preliminary charade of his proving gentility in England. Widowed by 1776, he took as his second wife Marie-Marguerite Thérèse Ribard, widow of Jean Testard, from a prominent Rouen business family claiming nobility.

During Holker's last years he was important in introducing English experts on the new textile machinery into France, particularly the Milnes of Stockport. Weeks before his death he gave greatly valued, and debated, advice on the potential terms of the Eden–Rayneval treaty of 1786 for freer trade between Britain and France. The 1780s were saddened for him by a bitter pamphlet attack on his achievements by his former protégé Roland de la Platière, and by his guaranteeing the vast debts which his son ran up as an envoy and then merchant and speculator in the United States.

Given Holker's limited industrial experience in England, his very poor written English, and his limited spoken French even in the 1770s, his achievements were remarkable. He was largely responsible for giving Rouen a significant cotton industry and France the basis of a heavy chemical industry, while intervening helpfully in many branches of French industry over much of the country. Able to maintain a successful rapport with some of the greatest and best French statesmen of the old regime, and become the respected friend of Jefferson and particularly Franklin, Holker remained sympathetic to the problems of the lowest worker. He died at Rouen on 27 April 1786.

John Holker's only child was his son, **John Holker** (1745–1822), born at Manchester. He had from 1764 received a specialized training to enable him to succeed his father, partly by studying science under Rouelle, Cadet, and others, partly by accompanying his father on industrial tours and inspections in France. In 1768 he was appointed *adjoint* to his father, and was deeply involved in obtaining the English technology of sulphuric acid (vitriol) manufacture; the Holkers started to produce the acid in Rouen by the globe process in 1769, and then by the lead-chamber process about 1772. The younger John Holker made major industrial espionage expeditions to Britain in 1767, 1770, and 1772; the 1770 visit brought the spinning jenny to France. He was made inspector-general of foreign manufactures in 1777. But in the same year he was sent on an ambitious but ill-defined diplomatic mission to the United States. He was appointed consul in Philadelphia and became concerned in the supply of the French fleet in America and that of the French and American land forces. He was also heavily involved with American finances and internal and external trade. He was unable to settle his accounts with the French navy, and unable to return to France until after his father's death, and then only very briefly. He became a land speculator in America on a large scale. His wife, Elizabeth Julie Quesnel, whom he had married in 1769, never joined him in America. He died there in 1822. His son, **Jean-Louis Holker** (1770–1844), seems not to have had any British connection. He was a major French chemical industrialist, largely responsible for the continuous production method in sulphuric acid, and extending into soda and chlorine bleach manufacture. J. R. HARRIS

Sources A. Rémond, *John Holker, manufacturier et grand fonctionnaire en France au XVIIIe siècle, 1719–1786* (Paris, 1946) · J. R. Harris, 'John Holker: a Lancashire Jacobite in French industry', *Transactions* [Newcomen Society], 64 (1992–3), 131–41 · S. Chassagne, *Le coton et ses patrons* (1991) · C. Ballot, *L'introduction du machinisme dans l'industrie française* (1923) · A. P. Wadsworth and J. de Lacy Mann, *The cotton trade and industrial Lancashire, 1600–1780* (1931) · J. G. Smith, *The origins and early development of the heavy chemical industry in France* (1979) · C. C. Gillespie, *Science and polity in France at the end of the old régime* (1980) · W. O. Henderson, *Britain and industrial Europe* (1954) · P. Boissonade, 'Trois mémoires relatives à l'amélioration des manufactures de France', *Revue d'Histoire Économique et Sociale*, 7 (1914–18) · F. J. McLynn, *Charles Edward Stuart: a tragedy in many acts* (1988); repr. (1991) · F. J. McLynn, *The Jacobite army in England, 1745: the final campaign* (1983) · H. T. Parker, *The Bureau of commerce in 1781 and its policies with respect to French industry* (Durham, NC, 1979) · H. T. Crofton, *A history of the ancient chapel of Stretford, in Manchester parish*, 3; Chetham Society, new ser., 51 (1903)

Archives Archives Nationales, Paris, series F12 · Bibliothèque Mazarine, Paris, Mignot de Montigny MSS · Conservatoire des Arts et Métiers, Paris · L. Cong., papers, incl. corresp. with his son John · various archives departementales, France

Likenesses portrait, 1770–1775?, Bibliothèque Municipale de Rouen, France; repro. in Smith, *Origins and early development*

Wealth at death fortune seriously affected in 1780s as guarantor of son's debts

Holker, John (1745–1822). *See under* Holker, John (1719–1786).

Holker, Sir John (1828–1882), judge and politician, was born in Bury, Lancashire, the son of Samuel Holker, a manufacturer there, and his wife, Sarah, daughter of John Brocklehurst of Clitheroe, Lancashire. He was educated at the Bury grammar school, and, though at first intended for the church, was articled to a solicitor by the name of Eastham of Kirkby Lonsdale, Westmorland. After some years he entered Gray's Inn, where he was called to the bar in 1854, and then became first a bencher and in 1875 treasurer. After a short time in London he joined the northern circuit, and settled in Manchester. For some time he got little work and was nicknamed 'sleepy Jack Holker' by his fellow barristers. According to an obituary in *The Times* he was a

> tall, plain, lumbering Lancashire man, who never seemed to labour a case nor to distinguish himself by ingenuity or eloquence, but through whom the justice of his cause appeared to shine as through a somewhat dull but altogether honest medium. (*The Times*)

On 5 September 1861 he married Janis, daughter of James Wilson of Eccles, Lancashire; they had no children.

After ten years building a miscellaneous practice, Holker finally distinguished himself through his work in a parliamentary committee on the Stalybridge and Ashton Waterworks Bill, and moved to London in 1864. He became queen's counsel in 1866, and at once took a leading position on his circuit; he was so successful in his first patent case at his first assize as a queen's counsel that patent became the mainstay of his practice.

In 1872 Holker won a by-election as a Conservative at Preston. The election was the first under the Ballot Act and attracted much attention. At the same time, the Tichborne case, which absorbed many of the best-known leaders at the bar, opened up opportunities for him in London where he was little known until then, and gave him a lot of work. After the death of his first wife, on 13 January 1874 he married Mary Lucia Richardson, daughter of Patrick McHugh of Cheetham Hill, Manchester; they had no children.

At the general elections in 1874 and in 1880 Holker was re-elected for Preston. He was appointed solicitor-general by the prime minister Disraeli and was knighted (1874). On the appointment of Sir Richard Baggallay to the Court of Appeal in November 1875, Holker became attorney-general. His practice became enormous, and his income for two consecutive years was £22,000 a year. Persuasiveness, shrewdness, and tact made him extraordinarily successful in winning verdicts.

In the House of Commons, Holker proved a successful law officer: he opposed Bass's bill to abolish committals for contempt in county courts, vigorously attacked W. E. Gladstone's eastern policy in 1877, introduced the Criminal Code Bill and Bankruptcy Bill, and carried the Summary Procedure Act and Public Prosecution Act in 1879. It was known that he was anxious to become lord chief baron, but Sir Fitzroy Kelly was unwilling to quit, so Holker returned to private practice on the fall of Lord Beaconsfield's government in 1880. The Liberal prime minister, William Gladstone, who appreciated Holker's close powers of reasoning, appointed him a lord justice of appeal in January 1882, but he sat for only a few months before failing health led him to resign on 19 May. He died on 24 May 1882 at his house, 46 Devonshire Street, Portland Place, London. He had suffered from heart and kidney trouble for some time but died of inflammation of the lungs after a cold. He was buried on 30 May in his mother's grave at Lytham, Lancashire. His widow, a Roman Catholic, became quite a close friend of Gladstone.

J. A. HAMILTON, rev. HUGH MOONEY

Sources *The Times* (25 May 1882) · *Law Journal* (27 May 1882), 286–7 · *Solicitors' Journal*, 26 (1881–2), 468 · Gladstone, *Diaries* · m. certs. · d. cert.

Likenesses Spy [L. Ward], watercolour cartoon, NPG; repro. in *VF* (9 Feb 1878) · wood-engraving (after photograph by Beattie of Preston), NPG; repro. in *ILN* (23 May 1874)

Wealth at death £26,457 0s. 8d.: resworn probate, May 1883, CGPLA Eng. & Wales (1882)

Holl family (*per. c.*1800–1884), printmakers, came to prominence with the engraver **William Holl the elder** (1771–1838), who was apparently of German origin and a pupil of Benjamin Smith, engraver. William Holl's prints were executed mainly in stipple and included many plates of portraits, decorative subjects, and statuary after contemporary artists, one of his best works being *The Boar which Killed Adonis Brought before Venus* after Richard Westall (1802). Although a man of retiring disposition, Holl was an advanced liberal in politics with strongly held views on social equality. At the time of the Spa Fields riots in 1816 he exposed himself and his family to great risk by concealing the ringleader, James Watson, son of the radical James Watson (1766–1836), and helping him escape to America. He was married to Mary Ravenscroft, who was recorded as the mother of his children in 1815. Holl was one of the first engravers to try out the new matrix of the steel plate for engraving banknotes in 1819. He also pioneered the use of stipple-engraving on steel, as seen in his *Portrait of the Reverend John Roadhouse* (1821). He died in London on 1 December 1838.

William Holl had four sons who were all apprenticed to their father as engravers. The eldest son, **William Holl the younger** (1807–1871), was born at Plaistow, London, in February 1807 and baptized on 6 August 1815 at St Mary's, St Marylebone, Middlesex. His independent plates date from 1835 with a series of portraits for E. Lodge's *Portraits of Illustrious Personages* (2nd edn, 1835). He also worked in line-engraving and mezzotint and between 1860 and 1871 he exhibited twenty-two engravings at the Royal Academy. He produced plates for the Art Union of London from

1851 and his plate after W. P. B. Frith's *An Old English Merry-making* (1849), was the first large engraving to be executed in the 'chalk' style. William Holl the younger was a founder member of the Chalcographic Society formed by several prominent engravers in 1830. He died at his home, 174 Adelaide Road, Haverstock Hill, London, on 30 January 1871, leaving a widow, Annie. His brother Charles Holl (c.1810–1882) worked in his studio for thirty years and completed several plates after William's death, including *Rebekah* after Frederick Goodall (1871) for the Art Union of London. Charles exhibited only one plate under his own name at the Royal Academy, in 1874.

Henry Benjamin Holl (1808–1884) was baptized on 6 August 1815 at St Mary's, St Marylebone, Middlesex. He was also a portrait engraver of merit whose plates date from 1828 to 1861. He was also an actor and a wine merchant and enjoyed a gregarious and cultured life. He was living at Broadstairs, Kent, with his wife and family in 1874 but apparently he died at Marisiana in the United States in 1884.

Francis Holl (1815–1884) was born on 23 March 1815 at Bayham Street, Camden Town, London, and baptized on 6 August that year with his brothers and sister, Isabella, at St Mary's, St Marylebone, Middlesex. He became a successful and fashionable engraver, working for book as well as print publishers. He frequently collaborated with his brother William, as in the four plates after J. Hayter for Finden's *Gallery of Beauty* (1841). He worked for twenty-five years engraving the queen's pictures and received royal commissions to execute private plates of portraits of the royal family. He engraved many plates after works by famous artists of the day. Two of his most popular engravings were *The Railway Station* (1862) and *Coming of Age in the Olden Time* (1854), both after paintings by W. P. B. Frith. Between 1856 and 1883 he exhibited twenty engravings at the Royal Academy and was finally elected an associate engraver in 1883. Francis Holl was also well known as an amateur actor and was a member of the Histrionics, who played at St James's Theatre, London. In 1846 and 1848 he played comic characters in performances in aid of the Artists' General Benevolent Fund, given by an amateur company of eminent artists which included George Cruickshank. He also sang well and played the cello. On 23 September 1841 he married Alicia Margaret, the daughter of Robert Dixon, a veteran of Trafalgar, and they had two sons and two daughters. The family lived for many years at 30 Gloucester Road, Regent's Park, London. In 1879 Francis Holl retired to live at Elm House, Milford, Surrey, where he died of peritonitis on 14 January 1884. He was buried on 19 January at Highgate cemetery, Middlesex. His wife survived him. His eldest son, Francis Montague Holl, known as Frank *Holl (1845–1888), showed artistic talent from an early age. He became a celebrated portrait painter and was elected a Royal Academician in 1883.

HILARY CHAPMAN

Sources DNB · Redgrave, *Artists* · R. K. Engen, *Dictionary of Victorian engravers, print publishers and their works* (1979) · B. Hunnisett, *Steel engraved book illustration in England* (1980) · B. Hunnisett, *An illustrated dictionary of British steel engravers*, new edn (1989) · A. M.

Reynolds, *The life and work of Frank Holl* (1912) · *Art Journal*, 10 (1871), 102–3 · A. Dyson, *Pictures to print* (1984) · *The Times* (16 Jan 1884) · H. Guise, *Great Victorian engravings* (1980) · J. H. Slater, *Engravings and their value* (1929) · Graves, *Artists*, new edn · IGI · CGPLA Eng. & Wales (1871) [William Holl] · CGPLA Eng. & Wales (1884) [Francis Holl]

Likenesses T. W. Harland, chalk drawing, 1830 (William Holl the younger), NPG · F. Holl, oils (Francis Holl), NPG · pencil drawing (William Holl the elder), NPG · photograph (Francis Holl), repro. in Reynolds, *Life and work*, 113 · wood-engraving (Francis Holl), repro. in *ILN*, 82 (1883), 469

Wealth at death under £3000—William Holl the younger: administration, 25 April 1871, CGPLA Eng. & Wales · £10,330 17s. 7d.—Francis Holl: probate, 7 Feb 1884, CGPLA Eng. & Wales

Holl, Francis (1815–1884). *See under* Holl family (*per. c.*1800–1884).

Holl, Francis Montague [Frank] (**1845–1888**), painter and illustrator, was born on 4 July 1845 at 7 St James's Terrace, in Kentish Town, London, the eldest among the four children of the well-known engraver Francis *Holl (1815–1884) [*see under* Holl family] and his wife, Alicia Margaret Dixon, who was the daughter of a naval officer and veteran of the battle of Trafalgar. His grandfather William *Holl the elder (1771–1838) and uncle William *Holl the younger (1807–1871) [*see under* Holl family] were also engravers.

Frank Holl learned the rudiments of drawing from his father. Because of a sickly constitution his formal schooling was limited, and the strain of ill health in boyhood may have contributed to his early death. Despite his apparent frailty, however, he exhibited a passion for cricket and tennis, playing the latter as an adult with considerable skill. Holl was accepted at fifteen as a student at the Royal Academy Schools, and won a gold medal for a religious painting, *Abraham about to Sacrifice Isaac*, in 1863. A year later two of his paintings were accepted for exhibition at the Royal Academy, where he showed work regularly until his death. (His election as associate of the Royal Academy in 1878 was followed by full membership in 1883.) On 16 May 1867 he married Annie Laura, daughter of the watercolourist and landscape painter Charles *Davidson (1824–1902). They had four daughters: Ada, Olive, Madeline, and Phillis.

The critical and public success of Holl's first great subject picture, *The Lord gave and the Lord hath taken away* (1869; Guildhall Art Gallery, London), which depicts a grief-stricken family praying together in their lowly cottage, resulted in the award of a travelling scholarship. In an unusual move Holl relinquished the scholarship after only a few months of travel abroad when he realized that he preferred to paint subjects from modern English life rather than to study Old Master paintings. On his return Queen Victoria commissioned from him *No Tidings from the Sea* (1871; Royal Collection), having been unable to purchase his first exhibited success, which was already sold. The subject matter endorsed Holl's reputation as an artist with a morbid temperament whose works often focused on themes of impending tragedy and death. Other melancholy images of family life from the 1870s include scenes of funeral processions, and maternal loss and grief, such

Francis Montague Holl (1845–1888), self-portrait, 1885

as *I am the Resurrection and the Life* (1872; Leeds City Art Gallery), *Her First Born* (1877; Sheffield City Art Galleries), and *Hushed* (1877; Tate Collection). While critical response to these lugubrious themes was often negative they remained extremely popular with the general public, and engravings after them extended their appeal to a wider audience.

Reviewers often compared Holl's mournful pictures to those of his contemporary the Dutch artist Jozef Israels (1824–1911), whose work, though admired by Holl in Antwerp while on his scholarship travels, was already well known in England. Holl's painting of prison life, based on his own observations—*Newgate: Committed for Trial* (1878; Royal Holloway Collection, University of London)—was another socially-aware image that obtained for the artist strong critical notice and public response. With Luke Fildes and Hubert von Herkomer, two artists with whom he worked at *The Graphic* magazine between 1872 and 1883, Holl became part of an informal school of social-realist painting that flourished during the 1870s; its aim was to draw attention to the everyday conditions of the working classes and the poor, and implicitly to criticize the social structures that maintained such conditions. Working intermittently for the periodical, Holl made some twenty illustrations either drawn especially for the magazine or based on paintings exhibited earlier at the Royal Academy. He also completed in 1874 a set of twenty-four illustrations for the novel *Phineas Redux*, by Anthony Trollope. Vincent Van Gogh collected several of Holl's social-realist engravings for his collection of works by English illustrators, now housed in the Vincent Van Gogh Museum and Foundation in Amsterdam.

When Holl exhibited a portrait of the engraver Samuel Cousins (Tate Collection; pen and wash drawing, NPG) at the Royal Academy in 1879 it created a sensation, and until his death in 1888 he painted a further 197 portraits, a staggering number in such a short period of time. It was thought that this feverish overwork aggravated the heart disease that eventually killed him. Holl painted many great men of his day (he painted only two female portraits); his most admired portrait work included *William Ewart Gladstone* (1888; Hawarden Castle, Flintshire), *The Earl Spencer* (1888; priv. coll.), *William Agnew* (1883; Thos. Agnew & Sons, Ltd, London), and *The Duke of Cleveland* (priv. coll., USA). One of his last portraits was of the American millionaire J. Pierpont Morgan (1888; Pierpont Morgan Library, New York), painted when Holl was mortally ill. It was this kind of conscientiousness in executing his commissions that exacerbated his already fragile health. His workload and exhausting schedule did, however, bring financial rewards that enabled Holl and his family to afford a lavish lifestyle resembling that of the illustrious figures whom he painted. He lived in two grand houses designed for him by the architect Richard Norman Shaw: Three Gables, Fitzjohn's Avenue, Hampstead, and Burrows Cross, Albury, Surrey.

Holl's success as a portraitist was often equated with that of his contemporaries John Everett Millais and George Frederic Watts. His portraits were distinctly sombre in hue, with a preponderance of black; the sober colouring of his work paid homage to his idols Velázquez and Rembrandt. Holl's technique, however, with its swiftly executed, sketchy brushwork also bears comparison with the then fashionable French portraitist Charles-Émile-Auguste Carolus-Duran. Holl felt privileged to meet the important people whom he painted and, wearing his signature checked suit, kept up a steady stream of conversation with his sitters, who numbered three a day. He was noted for capturing an excellent likeness and also for delineating in paint the essentials of his subjects' personality and character. *Sir John Tenniel* (c.1883) and *Joseph Chamberlain* (1886), both in the National Portrait Gallery, London, are good examples.

Holl died, of heart failure, at his home in Hampstead—Three Gables, Fitzjohn's Avenue—on 31 July 1888, and was buried in Highgate cemetery on 7 August. His wife survived him. In paying tribute to her father A. M. Reynolds wrote of 'his striking and vigorous intellect', remarking that he was 'gifted in many ways, of which painting was only one, and one into which he threw his whole soul'—a comment tempered by her observation that 'if one seeks for the dominant trait in his character … it was, perhaps, his extreme simplicity and modesty' (Reynolds, 315–16).

LEE MACCORMICK EDWARDS

Sources A. M. Reynolds, *The life and work of Frank Holl* (1912) • H. Quilter, 'In memoriam: Frank Holl', *Universal Review*, 1 (1888), 478–93 • J. Dafforne, 'The works of Frank Holl', *Art Journal*, 38 (1876), 9–12 • W. Meynell, 'Our living artists: Frank Holl, A. R. A.', *Magazine of Art*, 3 (1880), 187–91 • G. E. Campbell, 'Frank Holl and his works', *Art Journal*, 51 (1889), 85–91 • 'Celebrities at home: Mr. Frank Holl, R. A. at "The Three Gables", FitzJohns's Avenue', *The World* (21 Dec 1887) • J. Treuherz and others, *Hard times: social realism*

in Victorian art (1987) · R. Pickvance, *English influences on Vincent van Gogh* (1974) · b. cert. · m. cert. · d. cert. · *CGPLA Eng. & Wales* (1888)
Archives Hove Central Library, Sussex, letters to Lord Wolseley and Lady Wolseley · U. Birm. L., letters to H. G. Atkinson and Harriet Martineau
Likenesses F. M. Holl, self-portrait, oils, 1863, NPG · F. M. Holl, self-portrait, oils, 1885, Aberdeen Art Gallery [*see illus.*] · H. J. Brooks, group portrait, oils, 1889 (*Private view of the Old Masters Exhibition, 1888*), NPG · A. Gilbert, bronze bust, 1890, St Paul's Cathedral, London, The Crypt · Lock & Whitfield, photograph, woodburytype, NPG; repro. in T. Cooper, *Men of mark: a gallery of contemporary portraits* (1883) · photographs, repro. in Reynolds, *Life and work* · woodcuts, BM; NPG
Wealth at death £36,180 14s. 6d.: probate, 31 Aug 1888, *CGPLA Eng. & Wales*

Holl, William, the elder (1771–1838). *See under* Holl family (*per. c.*1800–1884).

Holl, William, the younger (1807–1871). *See under* Holl family (*per. c.*1800–1884).

Hollams, Sir John (1820–1910), lawyer, born at Loose, Kent, on 23 September 1820, was one of the two sons of John Hollams, curate in charge of Loose, and his wife, Mary Pettit; there were also several daughters in the family. His grandfather Sir John Hollams (knighted in 1831), was five times mayor of Deal. Hollams was educated privately, probably because of his delicate health. Consumption ran in the family, causing the death of his father in 1841 at the age of fifty-two, of his brother, and of three of his sisters. He was articled for a short time to a firm of solicitors in Maidstone, and in 1840 went to London. There he served the remainder of his articles with the firm of Brown, Marten, and Thomas in Mincing Lane. He was admitted a solicitor in 1844, and in the following year the firm took him into partnership. Hollams married on 30 July 1845 Rice (d. 1891), daughter of Edward Allfree, rector of St Andrew with St Mary Bredman, Canterbury, Kent. There were three sons of the marriage: John, who was born in 1846, Frederick William, born in 1848, and Edward Percy (always known as Percy) born in 1850. They were all educated at Blackheath proprietary school, followed, for John and Percy, by Trinity College, Cambridge, and for Frederick, by Trinity College, Oxford. John and Percy joined their father's firm as articled clerks and were admitted solicitors in 1871 and 1877 respectively. Frederick read for the bar and was called at the Inner Temple in 1872. The family lived in Blackheath from 1860 until 1874, when they moved to Eaton Square and, in the 1880s, Hollams bought Dene Park, a large country house and estate near Tonbridge in Kent; on the estate he had about forty people employed in 1910.

Hollams was a glutton for work. He wrote of his life: 'My own belief is that work, thought to be carried to an imprudent extent, really prolonged my life. I devoted the whole of my time to my profession' (Hollams, 240). According to his son Percy, he continued to work at home during the night and would often be going to bed as the servants got up to light the fires. Early in his career Hollams refused prestigious offers of salaried employment at the Admiralty and the court of chancery, building up instead a large litigation practice and a portfolio of mercantile and commercial clients, the latter including some of the private companies then supplying London's water—the New River Company, the Chelsea Water Company, and the Kent Water Works Company. He acted in such leading cases as that of *Vagliano Brothers v. Bank of England* (1887–91). Hollams was instrumental in the merger, in 1891, of the Central Bank (a long established client) and the Birmingham and Midland Bank which created the Midland Bank, for which he continued to act.

Hollams was also active on behalf of the fellow members of his profession. In 1866 he was elected to the council of the Law Society, serving as its president in 1878–9; his portrait by the Hon. John Collier was placed in the society's hall in Chancery Lane. He was a generous supporter of the Solicitors' Benevolent Society.

Hollams's other professional concern was law reform. Early in his career Hollams became acquainted with G. W. W. Bramwell and J. S. Willes; he noted the kindness and guidance he received from them. At their request he gave his views to the common law commission which reported in 1851 and resulted in the Common Law Procedure Acts of 1852 and 1854, simplifying the archaic court procedures still in use. In 1867 Hollams became a member of the judicature commission, the only London solicitor appointed to it. Its recommendations, after lengthy deliberations, provided the basis for the Judicature Act of 1873. This was introduced by Lord Chancellor Selbourne, who had secured the appointment of the commission and worked hard for the passage of the act. Selbourne himself named Hollams as one of the four men whose work on reform had been invaluable. In the 1880s and the 1890s Hollams continued to sit on committees concerned with law reform. In 1877 he was a member of the royal commission on the stock exchange, and in 1902 he was knighted. The crowning event in Hollam's career was the unique honour paid to him by the bench and bar in entertaining him at a dinner in the hall of the Inner Temple on 6 March 1903. The event was described, *inter alia*, in his collection of reminiscences, published under the title of *Jottings of an Old Solicitor* in 1906. He was made a deputy lieutenant for the county of London in 1882, and was a JP for the county of Kent. He died at Dene Park on 3 May 1910. Very shortly after the death of Sir John his two sons John and Percy, who were partners in the firm, retired. The firm continued under the name Coward and Hawksley, Sons, and Chance, later Coward Chance. In 1987 it merged with the firm of Clifford-Turner and, as Clifford Chance, it was in the 1990s the largest law firm in the City of London.

JUDY SLINN

Sources *Law Journal* (7 May 1910) · *Law Journal* (18 June 1910), 411 · J. Slinn, *Clifford Chance: its origins and development* (1993) · J. Hollams, *Jottings of an old solicitor* (1906) · *Solicitors' Journal*, 54 (1909–10), 472 · *The Times* (4 May 1910) · R. Palmer, first earl of Selborne, *Memorials. Part II: personal and political, 1865–1895*, ed. S. M. Palmer, 1 (1898), 46–7 · H. Kirk, *Portrait of a profession* (1976) · *DNB*
Likenesses J. Collier, oils, 1901, Law Society, London
Wealth at death £601,587 12s. 4d.: probate, 15 June 1910, *CGPLA Eng. & Wales*

Holland. For this title name *see* Florence (V), count of Holland (1254–1296); Jacqueline, *suo jure* countess of Hainault, *suo jure* countess of Holland, and *suo jure* countess of Zeeland (1401–1436); Rich, Henry, first earl of Holland (*bap.* 1590, *d.* 1649); Fox, Henry, first Baron Holland of Foxley (1705–1774); Fox, (Georgiana) Caroline, *suo jure* Baroness Holland of Holland (1723–1774); Fox, Elizabeth Vassall, Lady Holland (1771?–1845); Fox, Henry Richard, third Baron Holland of Holland and third Baron Holland of Foxley (1773–1840); Fox, Henry Edward, fourth Baron Holland of Holland and fourth Baron Holland of Foxley (1802–1859).

Holland, Abraham (*d.* 1626), poet, a son of Philemon *Holland (1552–1637) and his wife, Anne (1555–1627), daughter of William Bott, alias Peyton, was probably educated at the grammar school in Coventry, a school where his father was from 1608 an usher, in a town which Abraham's late epistle to him makes plain he had cause to be resentful of. He graduated BA in 1617 from Trinity College, Cambridge.

Holland's first published work advertises him as a scholar of Trinity; it is an elaborate Latin elegy on Lord Harington, presumably written close to the time of its subject's death in February 1614, but not printed before Holland's brother Henry added it to his *Herōologia* in 1620, the last item in the first folio volume. His *Naumachia*, not printed until 1622, but again presumably written earlier, describes a sea battle in the overblown manner associated with Lucan; it comes with prose and verse dedications, in English and Latin, to George Gordon, earl of Enzie, a favourite of King James, educated with the princes Henry and Charles, and, to judge from other dedications, the focus of a dominantly Scots courtly literary culture. The earl's father, the Catholic marquess of Huntly, also merits a set of complimentary verses. Verses to the author from Drayton and others commend the poem for its early promise. The prefatory 'Caveat to his muse', announcing Holland's preference for 'cabinet' poetry, nervously promotes this 'first Minerva' of his 'brain' and suggests he keeps darker verses in reserve.

A Continued Inquisition Against Paper-Persecutors by A. H., appended to John Davies of Hereford's *Scourge for Paper-Persecutors* (which had appeared in 1611 as the *Scourge of Folly*), republished by Holland's brother Henry in 1625, is a satire on popular print culture. The *Posthuma*, printed supposedly at Cambridge (actually in London) at Henry's expense, collects pieces belonging to the year of the poet's death: a fulsome elegy on King James which welcomes the new King Charles; one more distinctive on Henry, earl of Oxford; a long poem on the London plague of 1625, like the *Naumachia* indebted to Lucan's manner but here, particularly in the prefatory 'Envoy' to his friends in the country, informed by fine observation; an epistle to his sick father, Philemon, with a companion piece on his own sickness; and a miscellany of prose epistles (addressed to friends and relations) and meditations, verse translations of the psalms, and his own epitaph. The poems were marked as delivered to his brother by the dying poet on 18 February 1625 (that is, 1626), the day he died of the plague.

The *Naumachia*, with the sea battle now carefully identified as Lepanto, is reprinted in some copies of the *Posthuma*, and again in some copies of the 1632 edition of his father's translation of Xenophon's *Cyropaedia*. The poem on the plague from the *Posthuma* was reprinted under the title *London Looke-Backe*, along with related pieces by his brother Henry Holland and, from the previous century, by Thomas Phaer, as an appendix to *Salomon's Pest-House or Towre-Royall*, by J. D., 'Preacher of God's Word'. Crum identifies as autograph the versions in Bodleian Library, MS Rawlinson poet. 83, folios 1–4 and 5–17, of the *Caveat* (under the title *L'Envoy*) and the *Naumachia* (fragmentary towards the end); and also the versions in Bodleian Library, MSS Ashmole 36, 37 (an assembly of unrelated items), folios 151 and 152, of 'To my honest father Mr Michael Drayton, and my new, yet loved freind [*sic*], Mr Browne' and 'To Mrs E. F. in defence of a white blemish which lately grew in the sight of her ey [*sic*]', one of the few Cambridge poems later printed (but anonymously, and the address to 'E. F.' cancelled) in Abraham Wright's *Parnassus Biceps* (1656, 16–18). Newdigate (199) quotes from the manuscript poem to Drayton and Browne.

ROBERT CUMMINGS

Sources *Hollandi post-huma* (1626) · H. H. [H. Holland], *Herōologia Anglica* (Arnhem, 1620) · Venn, *Alum. Cant.* · J. Y., 'Holland's "Monumenta sepulchralia ecclesiae S. Pauli"', *N&Q*, 4 (1851), 125 · T. Corser, *Collectanea Anglo-poetica, or, A … catalogue of a … collection of early English poetry*, 8, Chetham Society, 102 (1878), 276–9 · B. H. Newdigate, *Michael Drayton and his circle* (1941) · M. Crum, ed., *First-line index of English poetry, 1500–1800, in manuscripts of the Bodleian Library, Oxford*, 2 vols. (1969) · *DNB*

Archives Bodl. Oxf., MSS Ashmole 36, 37 · Bodl. Oxf., MS Rawl. poet. 83

Holland, Charles (1733–1769), actor, was born on 12 March 1733 in Chiswick, the third of the three sons of John Holland (1697–1764), a baker, and his wife, Sarah (*d.* 1778). At the age of fourteen he was apprenticed to a turpentine merchant, but he later pursued an interest in the theatre: he applied to David Garrick, and made his début at Drury Lane on 13 October 1755 in the title role in Thomas Southerne's *Oroonoko*. By the end of the month he was performing as Dorilas in Aaron Hill's *Merope* and on 1 January 1756 he played George Barnwell in George Lillo's *The London Merchant*. Other roles in his first season at Drury Lane included Hamlet, and Florizel in *The Winter's Tale, or, Florizel and Perdita*, Garrick's adaptation from Shakespeare.

Holland was to remain at Drury Lane until his death in 1769, and he became renowned there as a capable performer of significant lead and secondary roles. In his fourteen years on that stage he tackled characters as diverse as Bajazet, Hotspur, Iago, Macbeth, Oakley, Prospero, Richard III, Romeo, Young Norval, and Ferdinand in *The Tempest*. Some of the original performances he gave included Hamlet in Murphy's *The Orphan of China* (21 April 1759), Moody in *The Country Girl*, Garrick's adaptation of Wycherley's *The Country Wife* (25 October 1766), Colonel Rivers in

Hugh Kelly's *False Delicacy* (23 January 1768), and Sir William Evans in Elizabeth Griffith's *The School for Rakes* (4 February 1769). He also enjoyed some success over the summer months in provincial theatres: he played at the New Concert Hall in Edinburgh in the summers of 1757 and 1758, at Birmingham in 1762, at Bath in 1762–3, and at the Smock Alley Theatre, Dublin, in 1763.

Holland maintained a close friendship with his fellow actor William Powell (1736–1769), and in 1766 they joined together (along with Matthew Clarke) in the management of the King Street Theatre, Bristol. As an acting team they were showered with praise, and their two summers' work together in Bristol enjoyed both financial and critical success. On hearing of Powell's untimely death on 3 July 1769, shortly before the curtain was to go up on his performance in *Richard III*, Holland apologized to his audience for being too overcome with grief to be able to tread the boards that evening.

Holland was a good-looking and masculine actor with a strong and resonant voice, and his talents developed and improved steadily as he gained more experience. He earned the trust and friendship of Garrick, whom he admired and emulated, and his style was frequently compared with that of his mentor (though not always favourably). The *Theatrical Review* of 1757–8 stated, for example, that he had 'all the merit a copy can pretend to; his face and voice are not disagreeable; and he cannot fail of being an actor of note'. Holland came to excel in Garrick's favourite roles, such as Chamont in Thomas Otway's *The Orphan*, Hastings in Nicholas Rowe's *Jane Shore*, and Tancred in James Thomson's *Tancred and Sigismunda*. His performances in 1767 in Bristol earned him the praise of Thomas Chatterton, who enthused in his poem 'To Holland' that 'No single part is thine, thou'rt all in all'. There is some doubt, though, over how accomplished an actor he truly was. Susceptible to the flattery of women, he was also prone to arrogance and overstatement under the influence of generous applause. Gentleman described him in the role of Iago as 'hunting after a meaning he never found' (Gentleman, 1.152), and Kelly described his style as 'sententious, dull, and heavy' (Kelly, 13).

Holland, an attractive young man, was not beyond a little philandering and engaged in romances with ease. His affair with the wife of William Earle landed him in court in 1765 on charges of criminal conversation. He never married though he was engaged for a brief time to the actress Jane *Pope (1744–1818). That relationship came to an end in 1768 following his being discovered with the actress Sophia *Baddeley (1745?–1786) on a boat on the river at Richmond. Holland left no known children, except that he made provision in his will for £200 to be placed in trust for a boy named as Harry should any inquiry prove the child to be his illegitimate son. The actor Charles *Holland (1768–1849) was his nephew.

Holland died of smallpox at the age of thirty-six in the early hours of 7 December 1769 in his house in Cecil Street, Strand, London. He was buried on 15 December in his family's vault at St Nicholas's Church, Chiswick. A monument was erected to his memory in the chancel of the church, though it was later moved to the wall of the north tower and accompanied by a bust. This carried an inscription by Garrick testifying to Holland's 'Talents to make entertainment instructive to support the credit of the Stage by just and manly Action'.   MARK BATTY

Sources Genest, *Eng. stage* · W. C. Russell, *Representative actors* [1888] · D. E. Baker, *Biographia dramatica, or, A companion to the playhouse*, rev. I. Reed, new edn, rev. S. Jones, 3 vols. in 4 (1812) · F. Gentleman, *The dramatic censor, or, Critical companion*, 2 vols. (1770) · H. Kelly, *Thespis, or, A critical examination into the merits of all the principal performers belonging to Drury-Lane Theatre* (1766) · Highfill, Burnim & Langhans, *BDA* · T. Chatterton, *Works*, 3 vols. (1803)
Likenesses J. Hutchinson, miniature on ivory, 1760, NPG · J. R. Smith, engraving, 1771 (after H. Barron), repro. in Highfill, Burnim & Langhans, *BDA* · J. R. Smith, mezzotint, pubd 1771 (after H. Barron), BM · J. S. Müller, line print, BM, NPG · V. S. Miller, engraving, Harvard TC · monumental bust, St Nicholas's Church, Chiswick, London · oils (after H. Barron), Garr. Club
Wealth at death £5000–£6000: Highfill, Burnim & Langhans, *BDA*

Holland, Charles (1768–1849), actor, the son of Thomas Holland of Chiswick, was a nephew of Charles *Holland (1733–1769), also an actor. After playing for some time in the provinces he appeared at Drury Lane on 31 October 1796, as Marcellus in *Hamlet*. He remained at this theatre until the season of 1819–20, but gained few opportunities and failed to improve his position. Some notice was taken of his opening performance, however, and his Trueman in George Lillo's *The London Merchant*, when he supported Sarah Siddons as Millwood, earned him praise. During the illness of Charles Kemble he performed Alonzo in Sheridan's *Pizarro*, in which piece he was the original Centinel (May 1799). He also attempted John Palmer's character of Sydenham in *The Wheel of Fortune* by R. Cumberland, and gradually began to make a name for himself. While at Drury Lane he took many subordinate parts in minor dramas, as well as roles such as Cassio in *Othello* and the Dauphin in *King John*. In June 1809, as Steinfort in Benjamin Thompson's *The Stranger*, he made his first appearance at the Haymarket. He went with the Drury Lane company in its move to the Lyceum, and on the opening of the new theatre, on 10 October 1812, was Horatio to R. W. Elliston's Hamlet. Holland supported Edmund Kean in many plays: he was York to the latter's Richard II, the original Mendizabel to his Manuel in Maturin's play *Manuel* (1817), and Buckingham to his Richard III (1819). He was the Earl of Angus in *Flodden Field*, an adaptation of *Marmion*, and Cedric in an adaptation of *Ivanhoe*. In April 1820 he played Gloucester to Kean's Lear, repeating the character on several succeeding nights. Holland was an educated and graceful actor, but his nervousness interfered with his success. He died on 5 December 1849 at St Peter's Cottage, Hammersmith. His sister Elizabeth married Joseph Constantine Carpue.

     JOSEPH KNIGHT, rev. NILANJANA BANERJI

Sources *The thespian dictionary, or, Dramatic biography of the present age*, 2nd edn (1805) · T. Gilliland, *The dramatic mirror, containing the history of the stage from the earliest period, to the present time*, 2 (1808) · Genest, *Eng. stage* · N&Q, 7th ser., 8 (1889), 486 · N&Q, 7th ser., 9 (1890), 66, 138, 341 · d. cert.

Holland, Compton (d. **1622**), print publisher, is first recorded in 1616, when he published a series of portrait engravings by Simon de Passe which revolutionized English print-making. Holland, as his will reveals, was the son of the translator Philemon *Holland (1552–1637) and his wife, Anne Bott (1555–1627), and brother to the printer Henry *Holland (b. 1583, d. in or after 1649) and the author Abraham *Holland (d. 1626). It was doubtless through Henry that he came into contact with Simon's father, Crispin de Passe, in Utrecht, for there is reason to think that Henry had taken over the position of London agent for Crispin from Hans Woutneel, who had died shortly before 1608.

Henry Holland was a member of the Stationers' Company, and secured copyright for some of Compton's plates by entering them in the Stationers' register (Compton himself was a member of the Leathersellers' Company). In 1618 the two men published in association the *Basiliologia*, the famous series of portrait engravings of English kings and queens. They were forced to use Renold Elstrack to engrave most of the plates, for Simon de Passe had gone over to work for the rival firm of Sudbury and Humble in 1617. Holland also published plates by Francis Delaram, as well as topical prints of monsters and salacious anti-Catholic propaganda. His address was always at the sign of the Globe in Cornhill, over against the Exchange.

The last date found on Holland's plates is 1620, and when he wrote his will in June 1621 he was seriously ill; he died in January the following year. Apart from minor bequests to the rest of the Holland family he left his estate to his wife Hester; it was probably she who continued to publish various plates from the Globe address, but without a name, from 1621 to 1623. Many of the plates later passed to John Hinde or to Roger Daniell. The sign and address were taken on by another print publisher, William Webb, who was working there from 1628.

ANTONY GRIFFITHS

Sources PRO, PROB 11/139 · *DNB*

Holland, Cornelius (1600–1671?), politician and regicide, the eldest son of Ralph Holland (1581–1625), Merchant Taylor, of London, and his wife, Joan (d. 1634), was born at St Laurence Pountney, London, on 3 March 1600; his family may have been that which had been prominent in the Merchant Taylors' Company since the fifteenth century. He was educated at Merchant Taylors' School from 1610 and Pembroke College, Cambridge, between 1614 and 1618. By 1627 he had married his wife, Sybill, shortly after which he moved to the parish of St Margaret, Westminster. This was occasioned by his having entered court service under Sir Henry Vane senior, and may have been effected through contacts forged by his own father, groom of the robes under Elizabeth and James. By 1626 he was a clerk in the cofferer's office, before becoming clerk of the acatry, and, by 1636, clerk comptroller of the household of the prince of Wales. In 1638–41 he acted as paymaster and clerk of the greencloth in the prince's court. Perhaps as a result of his refusal to provide money to finance the first bishops' war in 1639 he was replaced as cofferer in early

1641, although he remained clerk of the greencloth until at least the end of the year.

Holland was elected to the Long Parliament for New Windsor, and although the election was voided he succeeded in securing the seat at the second poll. He rapidly emerged as a prominent advocate of 'further reformation' in religion, and was prominent enough to be appointed to the 'recess' committee in 1641. Thereafter he emerged as a member of the war party in politics, hostile to negotiating with Charles other than from a position of great strength. He was undoubtedly motivated by religious zeal, in addition to which he displayed a pronounced political radicalism. It was these factors that led him to support parliament in the war, rather than the craven desire for self-advancement and financial gain that has generally been ascribed to him.

By 1643 Holland, along with men such as Henry Marten, was styled one of the 'fiery spirits' in the Commons. He was named to many of the most powerful committees, and became heavily involved in raising money for the war effort, and in the prosecution of delinquents. The issue with which he would become most clearly connected was the welfare of those who suffered most for their zeal in the war effort, in terms of maimed soldiers and their families. As an experienced courtier he was also involved in the care of the king's children, and this, together with an ongoing involvement in negotiations with the elector palatine, may indicate his willingness to consider replacing Charles with another king. On one occasion in late 1648 he was reported as having made a virulent speech against the Stuart monarchy, and in favour of banishing Charles. He also emerged as an opponent of a presbyterian church settlement, and a supporter of Independent 'dissenting brethren' and of toleration. By late 1648 he was perceived as being associated with the Levellers. He supported the army remonstrance calling for the king to be brought to justice, and may have been involved in planning Pride's Purge. He was certainly involved in preparing the king's trial, and attended its meetings assiduously. Although labelled a regicide for having been present on the day of sentencing, he did not sign the death warrant, which perhaps offers further evidence of his reticence to sanction the king's execution, if not his removal from power [see also Regicides].

Holland was extremely active on the first two councils of state (1649–50), as well as on the fourth (1651–2), and displayed enthusiasm for selling land and property of both crown and church. Thereafter he appears to have become disillusioned with political developments and the dominance of the army. There is little evidence that he opposed the protectorate, which he appears to have been willing to accommodate, but he was largely inactive in the mid-1650s. He may have sought election to Cromwell's parliament of 1656, but he was not returned, and only resumed his political work during the return of the Rump in 1659, when he was appointed to the committee of safety. After renewed army pressure in October, however, he withdrew from parliament. At the Restoration he fled to the continent, initially to the Low Countries, but by

1662 was with other regicides in Lausanne and Vevey under the alias John Ralfeson. There, he was free to exercise his dissenting beliefs in peace. He was clearly ill by early 1671, and probably died later in the same year.

J. T. PEACEY

Sources JHC · CSP dom., 1631–61 · D. Underdown, *Pride's Purge: politics in the puritan revolution* (1971) · B. Worden, *The Rump Parliament, 1648–1653* (1974) · Keeler, *Long Parliament* · G. E. Aylmer, *The king's servants: the civil service of Charles I, 1625–1642*, rev. edn (1974) · *The memoirs of Edmund Ludlow*, ed. C. H. Firth, 2 vols. (1894) · J. G. Muddiman, *The trial of King Charles the First* (1928) · E. Ludlow, *A voyce from the watch tower*, ed. A. B. Worden, CS, 4th ser., 21 (1978) · C. H. Firth and R. S. Rait, eds., *Acts and ordinances of the interregnum, 1642–1660*, 3 vols. (1911) · J. R. MacCormack, *Revolutionary politics in the Long Parliament* (1973) · *The letter books of Sir Samuel Luke, 1644–45*, ed. H. G. Tibbutt, Bedfordshire Historical RS, 42 (1963)

Holland, Sir Eardley Lancelot (1879–1967), obstetrician, was born on 29 October 1879 at Puttenham, Surrey, the eldest son of the rector there, the Revd Walter Lancelot Holland (1852–1936), and his wife, Edith, daughter of Canon Edward Revell Eardley-Wilmot. He was educated at Merchiston Castle, Edinburgh, and gained a Warneford entrance scholarship to King's College Hospital, London. He qualified in medicine in 1903 and in 1905 became MB BS (London) and FRCS (England). He held a number of resident house appointments at King's College Hospital, Paddington Green Hospital, Soho Hospital for Women, and Queen Charlotte's Maternity Hospital, and spent a year in Berlin where he worked with the distinguished gynaecologists Olhausen, Bumm, and Orth. In 1907 Holland was appointed obstetric registrar and tutor at King's College Hospital and in the same year obtained his London MD. In the following year he took the membership of the Royal College of Physicians. In 1913 Holland married Dorothy Marion (d. 1951), daughter of Dr Henry Colgate of Eastbourne; they had three daughters.

Holland was appointed to the honorary staff of King's College Hospital in 1914, but in 1916 moved to the London Hospital as obstetric and gynaecological surgeon, a more important appointment which offered greater facilities for research as well as a greater volume of clinical experience. He was unable to take up his appointment until 1919, serving in the meantime as a surgical specialist in France with the Royal Army Medical Corps.

Soon after his appointment to the London Hospital, Holland embarked on his research into the causes of stillbirth, encouraged therein by the Ministry of Health. In 1922 an official ministry report was published which contained the results of what was a classical piece of original research. Of particular importance was the establishment of the fact that in breech deliveries it was cerebral injury which was the major cause of the high stillbirth rate in those cases.

Holland also had an appointment to the staff at the City of London Maternity Hospital which he served for a number of years and in which he retained great interest. He held a number of public appointments of importance, serving as member of the royal commission on population, of the Central Midwives' Board, and of the council of King Edward's Hospital Fund. Between 1937 and 1940 he

Sir Eardley Lancelot Holland (1879–1967), by Sir James Gunn

was adviser in obstetrics and gynaecology to the Ministry of Health and when war broke out in 1939 he became responsible for organizing the evacuation of pregnant women from London to the country. He took charge of the emergency service in Hertfordshire and East Anglia, an experience which gave him many ideas about the development of a national maternity service. Many of these ideas were incorporated in a report made by the Royal College of Obstetricians and Gynaecologists and published in 1944, which was consulted by the Ministry of Health on various aspects of the maternity services in relation to the National Health Service which was to come into being in 1948. The British Medical Association took exception to remarks in the report about general practitioners 'which seemed to suggest a desire to exclude the general practitioner from midwifery practice' (*BMJ*, 313). Holland was president of the College of Obstetricians and Gynaecologists in 1943–6 and so had a very major say in the pattern of development of the maternity services at that time. Prior to his election as president Holland had served the college in many capacities: he had been active in its foundation in 1929, and as its honorary treasurer from 1930 to 1939 had played no small part in establishing its financial stability.

Professionally Holland's main interest and greatest contributions were in the field of obstetrics rather than gynaecology. He was not an outstanding abdominal surgeon but his skill in vaginal surgery was very considerable. This undoubtedly stemmed from his early training in Germany where this type of surgery was more frequently undertaken than in England. He always retained the closest links professionally with colleagues in Germany and established many firm friendships with leading gynaecologists there. Holland's teaching abilities were considerable as one might expect from a man who had such a very strong personality. He was extremely forthright and direct, found it difficult to suffer fools gladly, and was at times almost irascible and unreasonable. This did not always make him at one with his contemporaries and his colleagues. Nevertheless, his sincerity and the force of his personality made everyone realize the great contributions he had made to his speciality. He had a flourishing and successful private practice, which, however, he never allowed to divert him from his teaching, research, and public duties. Never, he advised, 'allow yourself to be crushed between the upper millstone of hospital work and the nether one of private practice' (Ross and Le Fanu, 164).

Holland's contributions to obstetric and gynaecological literature were considerable. For several editions he shared authorship with T. W. Eden of a *Manual of Obstetrics* and later became its sole author. For many years this textbook, which ran into twelve editions, was the one most widely read by undergraduates in all the British medical schools. In 1933 together with R. C. Jewesbury and W. Sheldon he wrote *A Doctor to a Mother: the Management of Material and Infant Welfare* and in 1926 with Janet Lane-Claypon he had published a study of 1673 stillbirths and neonatal deaths. He collaborated with Aleck Bourne in editing two volumes of a *British Obstetric and Gynaecological Practice* (1955) which also, at the time, had a very wide circulation. He served the *Journal of Obstetrics and Gynaecology of the British Empire* as editor for a number of years and played no small part in establishing it as one of the leading journals in the speciality's literature in the world. He was well known for his oft repeated correction 'My dear boy, an era commences but labour begins' (Ross and Le Fanu).

Holland made a special study of the obstetric details which surrounded the pregnancy and labour of Princess Charlotte of Wales who died in childbirth in 1817. The tragic circumstances which surrounded her death, which was followed by the suicide of Sir Richard Croft, the obstetrician in charge of the princess during her pregnancy, always fascinated him, and his knowledge of the intimate details which could be gleaned from all that had been written about this event was extensive. His lecture, *Princess Charlotte of Wales: a Triple Obstetric Tragedy*, was published in 1951. In 1952, after the death of his first wife the previous year, he married Olivia Marian (d. 1975), daughter of Leslie L. Constable JP of Fittleworth, Sussex.

Retirement at West Dean near Chichester was serene and pleasant for Holland. He enjoyed his family, his beautiful house, and even more beautiful garden. He continued in his literary activities long after his period of active medical practice had ended. His professional achievements received fitting recognition: honorary degrees from Dublin, Birmingham, and Leeds, an honorary MMSA and honorary FRCS of Edinburgh, and a knighthood in 1947, the year after he retired from the London Hospital. Holland died at West Dean on 21 July 1967. A memorial service was held in Chichester Cathedral.

JOHN PEEL, *rev.*

Sources J. Peel, *The lives of the fellows of the Royal College of Obstetricians and Gynaecologists, 1929–1969* (1976) · *BMJ* (29 July 1967) · J. P. Ross and W. R. Le Fanu, *Lives of the fellows of the Royal College of Surgeons of England, 1965–1973* (1981) · personal knowledge (1981) · Venn, *Alum. Cant.* [Holland, Walter Lancelot]
Archives Royal College of Obstetricians and Gynaecologists, London, corresp. and papers · Royal College of Obstetricians and Gynaecologists, London, memorandum · Royal College of Obstetricians and Gynaecologists, London, papers | Wellcome L., letters to G. Dick-Read
Likenesses J. Gunn, portrait, Royal College of Obstetricians and Gynaecologists, London [*see illus.*]
Wealth at death £95,393: probate, 4 Oct 1967, *CGPLA Eng. & Wales*

Holland, Edmund, seventh earl of Kent (1383–1408), magnate, was the third and youngest son of Thomas *Holland, fifth earl of Kent (1350–1397), and Alice (d. 1416), daughter of Richard (II) *Fitzalan, third earl of Arundel. He had two brothers: Thomas *Holland, sixth earl of Kent and duke of Surrey (c.1374–1400), and Richard, who died young; and six sisters: Eleanor (d. 1405), wife first of Roger (VII) Mortimer, earl of March, and then of Edward, Baron Charlton of Powys; Joan (d. 1434), wife of Edmund, duke of York, William, Lord Willoughby, Henry, Lord Scrope of Masham, and Henry Bromflete, Lord Vessy; Margaret (d. 1439), wife of John Beaufort, earl of Somerset, and Thomas, duke of Clarence; Eleanor (d. c.1420), wife of Thomas Montagu, earl of Salisbury; Elizabeth (d. 1423), wife of John, Lord Neville; and Bridget, a nun.

Holland's career as a court nobleman began in 1398 with his award, as 'king's nephew', of an exchequer annuity of 100 marks. He went to Ireland with Richard II in 1399 and was left there when the king with his close supporters, including Edmund's brother Thomas and his uncle John, returned to England to confront Henry Bolingbroke in August of that year. Edmund only finally returned from Ireland on 13 January 1400, and was seized on landing at Liverpool following the collapse of the rebellion of his brother and uncle against the new king, Henry IV. The death as a rebel of his brother Thomas left Holland as the heir to the Kent inheritance, but landless, since the inheritance was forfeited. However, Henry IV had a dearth of natural magnate support, and Holland, who was gradually making his mark at court, was restored to his estates and titles on 1 July 1403; he fought for the king against the Percys at the battle of Shrewsbury shortly afterwards. His brief career was dogged by impecuniosity: his inheritance was curtailed by the claims of three surviving dowager countesses of Kent, and in the aftermath of the 1400 rebellion some Kent estates were repossessed by the king, who claimed them to be rightfully part of his duchy of Lancaster inheritance. He did come to an advantageous agreement with one of the countesses, Joan, widow of his late brother Thomas, in January 1404, whereby she agreed to accept less than her full entitlement of dower estates, but his career continued to be dictated by the need to secure further royal patronage at court.

Holland first appeared in royal council in 1405 and he soon began to take up his father Thomas's reins on the south coast, acting as a JP in Dorset, Kent, Hampshire, Surrey, and Sussex, and investigating Beaulieu Abbey's problems in 1406 and 1407. Yet he impressed more militarily, serving at sea under Prince Thomas, Henry's second son, in 1405, and distinguishing himself at Sluys and along the Norman coast. He jousted against the earl of Mar at Smithfield in 1406 and was made a knight of the Order of the Garter. On 24 January 1407 he was married in St Mary Overie's, Southwark, to Lucia Visconti (1380–1424), one of the ten daughters of Bernabò Visconti, sometime lord of Milan. She should have brought a dowry of 70,000 florins to help Holland's finances, but her executor's executor was still pursuing claims for it in the 1470s. Holland was appointed admiral of the west and north in 1407. The piracy problem in the English Channel was an ever prevalent menace, and he received his first major independent command in March 1408 to sweep the channel in a series of patrols. This he did, though the successful assault on the Île de Bréhat, off Brittany, for Henry IV's queen, Joan, marked the end of his brief career: he discarded his helmet and was cut down by a crossbow quarrel through the head. He was buried at Bourne Abbey in Lincolnshire.

Holland left no heir, although he did have an illegitimate daughter, Eleanor, with Constance *Despenser (c.1375–1416), the daughter of Edmund, duke of York; Eleanor later married James Touchet, Lord Audley. Edmund Holland's widow, Lucia, remained in England and died in 1424. She was buried in the Austin Friars in London. The Kent inheritance was divided after 1408 between the four surviving dowager countesses of Kent and Holland's five sisters and their heirs. M. M. N. STANSFIELD

Sources M. M. N. Stansfield, 'The Holland family, dukes of Exeter, earls of Kent and Huntingdon, 1352–1475', DPhil diss., U. Oxf., 1987 • *Chancery records* • PRO, C53; C76; C137; E101; E401; E403; E404 • 'Annales Ricardi secundi et Henrici quarti, regum Angliae', *Johannis de Trokelowe et Henrici de Blaneforde ... chronica et annales*, ed. H. T. Riley, pt 3 of *Chronica monasterii S. Albani*, Rolls Series, 28 (1866), 155–420 • Rymer, *Foedera* • *Polychronicon Ranulphi Higden monachi Cestrensis*, ed. C. Babington and J. R. Lumby, 9 vols., Rolls Series, 41 (1865–86), vols. 8–9 • GEC, *Peerage* • N. H. Nicolas and E. Tyrrell, eds., *A chronicle of London* (1827), 91 • W. Dugdale, *The baronage of England*, 2 vols. (1675–6), vol. 2, p. 78

Wealth at death land, advowsons, and fees valued at £1219 7s. 2d.: PRO, C 137/74/51

Holland, Elizabeth (d. 1547/8). *See under* Howard, Thomas, third duke of Norfolk (1473–1554).

Holland, Francis James (1828–1907), promoter of Anglican girls' schools, was born in London on 20 January 1828, the second son of Sir Henry *Holland, bt (1788–1873), the celebrated royal physician, and his first wife, Margaret Emma (d. 1830), daughter of James Caldwell of Linley Wood, Staffordshire. Henry Thurstan *Holland, later first Viscount Knutsford, the Conservative politician, was his

elder brother. He was educated at Eton College (1842–7) and Trinity College, Cambridge, where he graduated in 1850. His ordination by the archbishop of Canterbury in 1852 and presentation as vicar of St Dunstan's, Canterbury, marked the beginning of his long close association with the diocese. He became one of the Six Preachers of Canterbury Cathedral in 1859. Assisted by his family networks, Holland was appointed in 1861 to the highly prized incumbency of the Quebec Chapel, Mayfair, which attracted a fashionable high-church congregation. His dignified services and the Tractarian tone of his preaching drew large numbers to the church, and on the strength of his success he was made chaplain-in-ordinary to Queen Victoria in 1873.

The families who attended Quebec Chapel encouraged Holland to establish the two Church of England schools for girls which still bear his name. The suggestion originated with his wife, **Mary Sybilla Holland** (1836–1891). She was born on 14 March 1836, the eldest daughter of the four daughters and seven sons of Alfred *Lyall (1796–1865) and his wife, Mary (d. 1878), daughter of James Tschudi Broadwood of Lyne House, Sussex. The Lyalls were a high-church clerical dynasty with Anglo-Indian connections: her uncle, William Rose Lyall, was dean of Canterbury, and two of her brothers, Alfred Comyn Lyall and James Broadwood Lyall (1838–1916), became Indian administrators. From 1848 the family lived at Harbledown, near Canterbury, where her father was rector, and where she met Francis Holland. They were married on 23 October 1855 and had five children: Lucy, Agnes, Bernard, Francis, and Michael.

In 1877 Mary Holland visited the schools for girls at Chelsea and Notting Hill recently founded by the Girls' Public Day School Company (GPDSC). She thought their non-denominational ethos unsatisfactory, believing that religion could not be treated as separate from the rest of education. From his congregation at Quebec Chapel Francis Holland also detected a reluctance on the part of parents to send their daughters to the GPDSC schools. The Hollands recognized a need for day schools for girls run on definite Anglican principles; a company was formed in 1877 to establish Church of England high schools for girls, with Francis Holland as its chairman. The first school founded by the company, in Baker Street, opened in 1878; Mary, who was greatly influenced by reading a history of the school founded at St Cyr by Madame De Maintenon, the governess to Louis XIV's children, attached great importance to 'selecting a set of really cultivated and high-tone schoolmistresses' (*Letters*, 57). A second school, in Sloane Square, opened in 1880.

Francis Holland invested much of his own private wealth in the scheme, and encouraged friends and family to do likewise. A friend gave £1500 for the endowment of a professorship for teaching scripture in the schools, a position which was given to Holland, who made weekly visits to the schools. He and his wife formed a Guild of Communicants, which was intended to unite past and present pupils. Parental fears that a secondary school would produce academic gaucheness in their daughters were allayed; Francis Holland reassured them that the schools encouraged refinement and emphasized the importance of preparing girls to be mothers. Although some girls entered the Cambridge local examinations, the majority did not, and most parents were anxious that they should not. While he spoke of improving women's education, he differed from the GPDSC in attaching a lower importance to training girls for university entry and the professions, though the Francis Holland schools did send girls to Oxford and took pride in their success.

In 1882 Gladstone, who had attended the Quebec Chapel, nominated Holland to a canonry of Canterbury. Holland maintained his close links with the girls' schools. In 1883 the company became the Church Schools Company, and sponsored the formation of other Anglican girls' schools, including Surbiton high school (1884). The most significant event of their Canterbury years was Mary Holland's conversion to Roman Catholicism. She had been moving towards Rome since the late 1870s, and made a public profession of faith on 20 August 1889. Her husband's reaction to her conversion was, she acknowledged, generous (*Letters*, 200). Mary Holland died at Harbledown, near Canterbury, Kent, on 23 September 1891. Francis Holland died at Sorrento, Italy, on 27 January 1907.   ELIZABETH COUTTS

Sources *Letters of Mary Sibylla Holland*, ed. B. Holland, 2nd edn (1898) · *The Times* (28 Jan 1907) · E. M. Bell, *Francis Holland School* (1938) · S. Hicklin, *Polished corners, 1878–1978* (1978) · C. Dewey, *The passing of Barchester* (1991) · *The Guardian* (30 Jan 1907) · Venn, *Alum. Cant.* · Burke, *Peerage* · d. cert. [Mary Sybilla Holland]

Archives Francis Holland School, Clarence Gate, London, various MSS

Wealth at death £51,655 3s. 8d.: resworn probate, 15 March 1907, CGPLA Eng. & Wales

Holland, George Calvert (1801–1865), physician, was born at Pitsmoor, Sheffield, on 28 February 1801, the second son of a respectable artisan who arranged for him to have a 'fair' elementary education. Originally intended for a trade he was apprenticed to a wig maker at the age of twelve. At sixteen he discovered an ability to write verse and contributed several poems to the *Sheffield and Rotherham Independent*, a local journal. As a result he developed a desire to educate himself. He read the classics and taught himself Latin, French, and Italian.

When Holland was twenty his ability was recognized by his elder brother and others, and he was placed under the tutelage of a Unitarian minister in Derby to study for the ministry of that church. However, after a year he turned to medicine and went to study in Edinburgh. A brilliant student, he graduated MD in 1827. He also studied for a year under R. T. H. Laënnec in Paris and took the degree of bachelor of letters. Holland went into practice in Manchester but after a year his enthusiasm for phrenology, possibly spurred by the examination of heads undertaken during his time as a wig maker, led to friction with his colleagues. He returned to Edinburgh where he undertook a year's research. It appears that it was at this time that he became president of the Royal Physical Society and of the Hunterian Society of Edinburgh. In 1828 he published *An Essay on Education, Founded on Phrenological Principles*, which was followed in 1829 by *An Experimental Inquiry into the Laws of Life*. In 1830 he returned to Sheffield and began to play an important part in the life of the town.

Holland next opened a dispensary for the poor, with Dr C. F. Flavell. He became lecturer in physiology and jurisprudence at the Sheffield Medical Institute but resigned the post in 1843. He also lectured regularly on phrenology and was enthusiastic about the revived science of mesmerism. In 1832 he was elected physician to the General Infirmary. In addition he became a member of the council of the Literary and Philosophical Society and lectured in aid of the formation of a mechanics' institute. He founded the Sheffield Physiological Society in 1837.

The next years were the most important of Holland's medical career. His *Inquiry into the Moral, Social and Intellectual Condition of the Industrious Classes of Sheffield* (1839) was followed by the publication in 1843 of his greatest work, *The Vital Statistics of Sheffield*, which won him recognition as a pioneer of industrial medicine. That same year saw the publication of the important but neglected *Diseases of the Lungs*, in which Holland described silicosis and silico-tuberculosis, and their cause by the silica dust raised in dry grinding. He described a system of dust extraction, which he correctly believed would prevent it.

Holland had a very successful practice but gave up medicine almost completely as he became increasingly involved in politics. Surprisingly, being a Liberal, he defended the corn laws, publishing *An Exposition of Corn-Law Repealing Fallacies and Inconsistencies* (1840) and *Suggestions towards Improving the Present System of Corn-Laws* (1841). This brought him a purse of 500 guineas from his new friends, but his actions probably cost him ten times that amount. He became a director of several railway companies at a time when there was a mania for such projects. He also became a director of the Leeds and West Riding Bank and the Sheffield and Retford Bank. Their failure led to his ruin. A writ against him for £54,000 resulted in his bankruptcy and he retired to Worksop until his affairs were settled. Here in 1848 Holland wrote what he regarded as his best work, *The Philosophy of Animated Nature*.

After an unsuccessful effort to establish himself in London, Holland returned to Sheffield in 1851. By this time he had been converted to homoeopathy, which destroyed his previously high reputation with the medical profession. He edited the *Sheffield Homoeopathic Lancet* in 1853. He was elected a member of the town council but lost his seat in 1858, as did all members of his party, due to their advocacy of the highly unpopular Local Improvement Act. However, in 1862 he was made alderman of the borough.

Holland was described as a man of courtly figure with full grey eyes and a thin intellectual face. A man of kindness and courtesy, his popularity was such that a public subscription was raised for him during his last illness, though at the time he was probably moderately well-to-do. He developed bronchitis, which according to his obituary 'supervened upon disease of the base of the brain brought on by close study and severe mental exertion'

(*Sheffield and Rotherham Independent*, 8 March 1865). He died in Broomhall Lodge, Broomhall Road, Sheffield, on 7 March 1865 and was buried on 13 March at Sheffield general cemetery. He was survived by his wife, Anne Martha, and a son and a daughter. In 1873, his wife having died, a petition was finally accepted for his daughter to receive a pension from the queen's bounty, in recognition of her father's work for industrial medicine.

BERNARD LEARY

Sources H. Cohen, 'George Calvert Holland', *North Wing* (winter 1955) · *Sheffield Daily Telegraph* (14 March 1865), 8 · *Sheffield and Rotherham Independent* (8 March 1865), 3 · *Sheffield and Rotherham Independent* (8 Dec 1881), 8 · census returns for Figtree Lane, Sheffield, 1841, 1861 · *Homoeopathic Medical Directory* (1853) · R. Cooter, *Phrenology in the British Isles: an annotated historical biobibliography and index* (1989) · *DNB*
Likenesses J. Brown, stipple (after J. Moore), Wellcome L.

Holland [Hoyland], **Gilbert of** (*d.* 1172), abbot of Holland, a Cistercian abbey which was itself called after the area of south Lincolnshire known as Holland; he was born of unknown parents, probably in England. The fact that his death was recorded in the late twelfth-century chronicle kept at Clairvaux may lie behind the tradition in the later Cistercian *Menologium* that he became a monk there. It has been suggested that he was in the group that established Rievaulx, North Riding of Yorkshire, Clairvaux's first English daughter house, in 1132, and in 1148 among the group of Rievaulx monks sent by Abbot Ailred to teach Cistercian customs at Swineshead soon after that house, and all the other Savigniac houses, were affiliated into the Cistercian order in 1147. One basis for this hypothesis is that Gilbert clearly knew Ailred well. Everything is, however, speculation until Gilbert witnesses as abbot some time in or after 1155, before which date he clearly must already have been a monk for some time.

Gilbert's abbey of Holland, usually now called Swineshead from the village where it was situated, was a daughter house of Furness, founded in 1135 by Robert de Gresley, a considerable landholder in Lancashire and the midlands. Its situation amid the fens, exposed to wind and water, is reflected in some of Gilbert's sermons. The scant evidence of his activity as abbot ends about 1167, while his successor is not mentioned before 1183–4. The Clairvaux chronicle records his death in 1172 at L'Arrivour, a daughter house of Clairvaux, from which it was not distant, being situated due east of Troyes. Its description of Gilbert as former (*quondam*) abbot may mean that he had resigned some time earlier, but it is possible that he became ill at L'Arrivour while on his way to, or from, general chapter at Cîteaux. The order's *Menologium* remembered him on 25 May, which must be the likely date of his death.

Gilbert is best known through his writings, the most famous of which are his forty-eight sermons on the Song of Songs. These took up the commentary started by Bernard of Clairvaux, who died in 1153. Before his own death Gilbert had expounded the Song of Songs from chapter 3: 1 to chapter 5: 10. Some of the sermons appear to have been originally given to nuns, and there is evidence of another version of the first sermons. He referred rarely to contemporary events, though sermon 41 contains a notable appreciation of Ailred, written soon after Gilbert heard of his death, which took place on 12 January 1167. For this Bernard's own lament for his brother Gerard, in sermon 26 of his series, provided a precedent. These sermons had considerable success all over western Europe, judging from surviving manuscripts. They were first printed at Venice in 1485, and were often reprinted along with the sermons of St Bernard, but were translated into many languages only in the twentieth century; the first scholarly edition was being prepared for Corpus Christianorum in the 1990s. Their affective spirituality reveals him as a true follower of Bernard, and, like him, dependent on the church fathers, particularly Augustine of Hippo. Gilbert wrote some treatises and letters which survive in far fewer manuscripts. These show him as a vigorous advocate of Cistercian life, and as being in touch with a number of other English Cistercians, including the abbots of Fountains and Byland. He was not, however, as the recent English translation of his works claims, the recipient of a work written for him by Roger of Byland. That work must be attributed to another Roger, monk at Forde, addressed to an otherwise unknown friend, Galienus. Gilbert's own writings reveal him as an impressive Cistercian abbot of the generation after Bernard.

CHRISTOPHER HOLDSWORTH

Sources *The works of Gilbert of Hoyland*, ed. and trans. L. C. Braceland, 4 vols. (1978–81) · D. Knowles, C. N. L. Brooke, and V. C. M. London, eds., *The heads of religious houses, England and Wales, 1: 940–1216* (1972) · J. Burton, 'The abbeys of Byland and Jervaulx, and the problems of the English Savigniacs, 1134–1156', *Monastic studies*, ed. J. Loades, 2 (1991), 119–31 · C. Holdsworth, 'John of Forde, 1191–1991', *A gathering of friends: the learning and spirituality of John of Forde*, ed. H. Costello and C. Holdsworth (1996), 17–41 · D. M. Smith, ed., *Lincoln, 1067–1185*, English Episcopal Acta, 1 (1980) · W. Farrer, ed., *Lancashire inquests, extents and feudal aids, 1205–1307*, Lancashire and Cheshire RS, 48 (1903) · C. W. Foster and K. Major, eds., *The registrum antiquissimum of the cathedral church of Lincoln*, 10 vols. in 12, Lincoln RS, 27–9, 32, 34, 41–2, 46, 51, 62, 67–8 (1931–73) · H. E. Hallam, *Settlement and society: a study of the early agrarian history of south Lincolnshire* (1965) · 'Chronicon Claraevallense', *Patrologia Latina*, 185 (1855), 1249–52 · C. Henriquez, ed., *Menologium Cisterciense* (1630) · *The life of Ailred of Rievaulx by Walter Daniel*, ed. and trans. M. Powicke (1950) · J. Vuong-Dinh-Lam, 'Gilbert de Hoyland', *Dictionnaire de spiritualité ascétique et mystique: doctrine et histoire*, ed. M. Viller and others (1937–95) · A. Dimier, 'Gilbert de Hoyland', *Dictionnaire d'histoire et de géographie ecclésiastiques*, ed. A. Baudrillart and others, 20 (Paris, 1984) · R. Sharpe, *A handlist of the Latin writers of Great Britain and Ireland before 1540* (1997), 145–6

Holland, Guy (1585/6–1660), Jesuit, was a native of Gainsborough, Lincolnshire. He was educated at St John's College, Cambridge, matriculating at Easter 1602 and graduating BA in 1606. Soon afterwards he became a Roman Catholic. He entered the English College at Valladolid on 26 November 1608, aged twenty-two, under the name of Guido Holt. At Valladolid he was ordained priest in 1613, and in May sent to England. A member of the Society of Jesus from 1615, his movements for the next years are not known, but it is likely that he was engaged on missionary work in England.

Certainly from 1621 to 1632 Holland was a missioner of the House of Probation of St Ignatius in London. He appears in John Gee's *A Foot out of the Snare* as a Jesuit resident in the city in 1623. On 15 March 1628 the house, at Clerkenwell, was raided. Holland and four colleagues were discovered hidden in a small enclosure created by a newly built brick wall. On 27 March the privy council issued a warrant for his imprisonment. Nothing discouraged, on 14 July he was professed of the four vows. In 1634 and 1636 he was still attached to the London house. In 1633 and in 1638, however, he worked under the supervision of the residence of St George (Worcestershire and Warwickshire).

From 1639 Holland acted as a missioner of the residence of St Mary (Oxfordshire), serving as its superior in 1645–6. A reply to the *Discourse of the Infallibility of the Church of Rome* by Lucius Cary (Lord Falkland) has been attributed to Holland, and *The Grand Prerogative of Human Nature* (1653), an attack on the belief that the soul dies with the body, is probably his work. Other writings remained unpublished because the censors considered 'that in one or two points he rather deviated from the common opinion of the doctors' (Foley, 7(1).365). He was attached to the Oxfordshire residence in 1655 and it seems likely that his last years were spent there. He died on 16 November 1660.

THOMPSON COOPER, *rev.* STEPHEN WRIGHT

Sources G. Anstruther, *The seminary priests*, 2 (1975) · E. Henson, ed., *The registers of the English College at Valladolid, 1589–1862*, Catholic RS, 30 (1930), 97 · T. M. McCoog, *English and Welsh Jesuits, 1555–1650*, 2, Catholic RS, 75 (1995), 209 · H. Foley, ed., *Records of the English province of the Society of Jesus*, 1–4 (1875–8); 7 (1882–3)

Holland, Henry, second duke of Exeter (1430–1475), magnate, the only son and heir of John *Holland, first duke of Exeter (1395–1447), and his first wife, Anne Stafford, dowager countess of March (*d*. 1432), was born in the Tower of London on 27 June 1430. Through his grandmother Elizabeth (*d*. 1425), sister of Henry IV, Henry Holland was closely related to the house of Lancaster—a connection which grew in importance as Henry VI's uncles died without heirs. His proximity to the royal line justified Earl John's creation in 1444 as duke of Exeter: his estates, worth only £1002 p.a. including his wife's dower in 1436, fell substantially short of the 2000 marks p.a. normally considered the minimum for a duke. Probably it was Holland's Lancastrian connections that prompted Richard, duke of York, to offer the enormous marriage portion of 4500 marks to marry his eldest daughter, Anne [*see below*], born in 1439, to Henry on 10 August 1445: at this time several great families were speculating on the succession. The marriage was completed in January 1446, before John Holland's death in 1447, when custody of the young second duke was granted to York. On 23 July 1450, while still under age, Henry Holland was granted special livery of his lands, perhaps in response to his inclusion among the ancient royal blood of the realm that Cade's rebels wished to see involved in government.

Duke Henry's reckless and violent conduct in the early 1450s may have been a desperate response to financial embarrassments. There was an obvious discrepancy between his royal blood and ducal title, which demanded a conspicuously ducal lifestyle, and his limited means. A customs annuity of 500 marks p.a. was resumed in 1451, his continental possessions were reconquered by the French, he did not even enjoy his whole patrimony until after the death of his stepmother in 1457, and he personally derived no direct benefit from his duchess's dowry which, if paid, passed to his father's executors. He had really needed to marry an heiress. Exeter bid with some success to supplement his Devon patrimony, securing the custody of the Gournay lands in Somerset and Dorset in 1450 and Lostwithiel, Restormel, and other duchy of Cornwall lands in 1451, but such gains were limited and temporary.

Exeter inherited eight Bedfordshire manors from a cousin in 1451, which he hoped to augment into a second endowment by securing Ampthill Castle and its members. A shadowy title was improved by fraud. False charges of treason were laid against the current occupant, the rich but ageing and childless former minister Lord Cromwell, and on 2 June 1452 Exeter seized the estate by force. He was in residence on 28 August following. With right on his side, and hence support from both government and the Lords, Cromwell was a formidable opponent: the treason charge was easily repudiated; on 15 July Exeter was bound in recognizances of £4000 to abide an award; and he and his agents were sued in the court of common pleas. Defeat faced Exeter if the law ran its course, so, besides initiating counter-suits, he overawed jurors and judicial officials both in Westminster Hall and Bedfordshire, where nobody would act as sheriff in 1453–4, and on 19 January 1454 allied himself to Lord Egremont, one of the Percy enemies of Cromwell, the Nevilles, and hence of Exeter's father-in-law, York. At this point a local dispute acquired national political dimensions. The onset of Henry VI's madness about August 1453 might have given Exeter, as the nearest relative of the king and the young prince, power as lord protector. Instead York was appointed in March 1454, a Neville (Salisbury) became chancellor, parliament backed Cromwell over Ampthill, and Cromwell, not Exeter, was appointed to the royal council. Exeter asserted his Lancastrian claims on 21 May 1454 at Spofforth in Yorkshire by rebelling and allegedly distributing Lancastrian livery, claiming the government and the duchy of Lancaster, and plotting with the Scots. It is true that Exeter was next heir to the duchy of Lancaster, but these indictments may be best seen as the exaggerated allegations of his enemies. The lord protector rushed northwards to quell the uprising. When the rebellion failed, Exeter appeared at Westminster to answer Cromwell in court. In July York removed him from Westminster Abbey to prison at Pontefract Castle and in September Cromwell finally re-entered Ampthill. The duke was released in March 1455 after Henry VI's recovery, but was incarcerated once again at Wallingford Castle in June following the Yorkist victory at St Albans. Cromwell's death in January 1456 fortunately ensured that Exeter escaped ruinous damages and was acquitted of treason, but Ampthill was irretrievably lost.

Exeter's alienation from York and the Nevilles was reinforced by Salisbury's subsequent appointment as keeper of the seas, an infringement of the duke's role as hereditary lord admiral, but he was not much better trusted by York's enemies at court. An attempt to seize Warwick in November 1458 resulted in his incarceration in Berkhamsted Castle, whence he was released only on bonds of £10,000 in February next year. Only then did Exeter commit himself politically to Henry VI. On the losing side at Bloreheath, he swore allegiance to Henry at Coventry on 11 December 1459, and was appointed constable of York's forfeited castle of Fotheringhay, Northamptonshire. On 19 March 1460 he indented to keep the sea with 3500 men against the Yorkist earls, but, uncertain of the loyalty of his men, dared not intercept Warwick on his return from Ireland. At the battle of Northampton Exeter was once again on the losing side; he was absent from the parliament of 1460, and joined Queen Margaret in the north, where on 20 January 1461 he was among those who guaranteed her treaty with the Scots. He marched south with her to the second battle of St Albans, retreated with her, and was on the losing side at Towton (29 March 1461). He was among those who attacked Carlisle in May, was with Jasper Tudor in Wales by July, and shared in his defeat at Twt Hill near Caernarfon on 16 October. He sailed with Queen Margaret from Edinburgh via Sluys to Burgundy, where he was in August 1463 and where Philippe de Commines allegedly saw him barefoot, begging from door to door. He was one of Margaret's impoverished court-in-exile at St Mihiel in Bar. Following Henry VI's restoration Exeter was encouraged to return to England by the duke of Burgundy, who saw him as a potential rival for Warwick. In England in February 1471, he was among those routed at Leicester on 3 April, and shared in Warwick's defeat on 14 April at Barnet, where he was wounded and left for dead. Exeter then took sanctuary in London, but was removed on 26 May and imprisoned in the Tower. Presumably Edward hesitated to execute a sick man, who had been taken from sanctuary, and was, furthermore, his brother-in-law. Exeter's wife secured a divorce on 12 November 1472 and his daughter had died by 1474, but he himself was released to join Edward IV's invasion of France in 1475, which might have led to his eventual restoration. Instead however he was drowned on the return journey, most probably by foul play; his rightful heir, Ralph Neville, later third earl of Westmorland, was not allowed to inherit.

Anne of York (1439–1476), eldest daughter of *Richard, duke of York, born at Fotheringhay on 10 August 1439, married Henry Holland in January 1446. Only one daughter was born of the union. Following the duke's attainder in 1461 the duchess was initially provided for, like the wives of other attainted Lancastrians, by the settlement of her jointure on feoffees to her use, to ensure that nothing passed to her husband. Very soon, however, she convinced her brother Edward IV of her loyalty and commitment, and enjoyed the favour and influence appropriate to the king's sister. In 1462 she was granted her husband's goods, his whole Exeter inheritance for life, Rochford and other forfeited lands in Exeter, Hadleigh, Essex, and other

forfeitures in 1465. In 1464 she was entrusted with the custody of the young Henry Stafford, duke of Buckingham. She contracted her daughter Anne, first to George Neville, infant son of the earl of Northumberland and male heir of Richard Neville, earl of Warwick (the Kingmaker), then to the queen's son Thomas Grey, later marquess of Dorset, and settled lands on Grey and Anne jointly: they were married in October 1466 but she had died by February 1474, when Dorset remarried. Anne of York's titles to her Exeter lands were repeatedly amended to ensure her estate for life, the performance of her will (1467), the inheritance of her daughter (1465), remainders to any further children born to the duchess herself (1467), and to the queen (1469). Such provisions suggest a new sexual liaison long before her divorce on 12 November 1472. She married Thomas St Leger, and the couple had a daughter, also called Anne, in 1475. The duchess died in January 1476 and was buried in St George's Chapel, Windsor. The sixteen-week-old Anne St Leger was regarded as the Exeter heir: in 1483 the inheritance was divided by act of parliament between the queen's younger son, Richard Grey, and Anne herself, who was contracted to Dorset's own son.

MICHAEL HICKS

Sources S. J. Payling, 'The Ampthill dispute: a study in aristocratic lawlessness and the breakdown of Lancastrian government', *EngHR*, 104 (1989), 881–907 · R. A. Griffiths, 'Local rivalries and national politics: the Percies, the Nevilles, and the duke of Exeter, 1452–55', *Speculum*, 43 (1968), 589–632 · M. Stansfield, 'John Holland, duke of Exeter and earl of Huntingdon (d. 1447) and the costs of the Hundred Years War', *Profit, piety and the professions in later medieval England*, ed. M. Hicks (1990), 103–18 · R. A. Griffiths, *The reign of King Henry VI: the exercise of royal authority, 1422–1461* (1981) · C. L. Scofield, *The reign of Edward IV*, 2 vols. (1923) · *Chancery records* · *RotP* · T. B. Pugh, 'Richard, duke of York and the rebellion of Henry Holand, duke of Exeter, in May 1454', *Historical Research*, 63 (1990), 248–62 · GEC, *Peerage*

Holland, Henry (1550–1625), Roman Catholic priest, was a native of Daventry, Northamptonshire, of whose family nothing is recorded except that he was related to the last abbot of Westminster, John Feckenham (1518–1585). Brought up at Worcester, he was sent for his further education to Eton College and on 24 March 1566 was admitted as scholar to St John's College, Oxford, where he was a contemporary of his future colleagues Edmund Campion and Gregory Martin. His education is aptly summed up in the epitaph recorded by Wood,

> Dantria me genuit, me clara Vigornia fovit,/Aetona me docuit, post docet Oxonium (Daventry bore me, famous Worcester reared me, Eton taught me, and now Oxford teaches me) (Wood, *Ath. Oxon.*, 2.386)

After receiving his BA in 1569 Holland was converted to Rome and made his way to the English College, Douai, in 1573. There, after studying theology, he was ordained deacon on 6 April 1577, graduated BD at the University of Douai in 1578 and, after the difficulties involved in moving the college from Douai to Rheims that year, was eventually ordained priest on 19 March 1580. He went on to win some fame as preacher there, while collaborating with Gregory Martin in the Rheims translation of the New Testament, which was published in 1582.

Once his task of translation was over Holland was sent on the English mission, where he laboured for several years while living with his sister at Cleeve, Gloucestershire. By 1587 he was back at Douai to receive a licentiate of theology from the university there. On again venturing into England, however, he was arrested in January 1600 at the house of a Mr Sweating in Yorkshire and was imprisoned for a time in York Castle.

From then on Holland seems to have spent the rest of his life in Flanders as divinity reader at the two monasteries of Marchiennes in Hainault and Anchine near Douai. To this period belong various Latin writings, notably his *Urna aurea, vel, In sacrosanctam missam … expositio*, which was published at Douai in 1612. Another issue, with the altered title of *Arca novi foederis in sacrosanctae missae canone representata*, was published at Antwerp in 1615. In the title he is accorded the rank of canon. He probably edited the collected works of Thomas Stapleton, with his own *Vita Thomae Stapletonii*; they appeared in four volumes at Paris in 1620, being the one substantial achievement of the group of Catholic controversialists at the college of Arras (founded in 1611). It was finally at the monastery of Anchine that, as Wood remarks, Holland 'gave way to fate in good old age' (Wood, *Ath. Oxon.*, 2.386) and died on 28 September 1625.

THOMPSON COOPER, *rev.* PETER MILWARD

Sources C. Dodd [H. Tootell], *The church history of England, from the year 1500, to the year 1688*, 2 (1739), 382 · Wood, *Ath. Oxon.*, new edn, 2.385–6 · Gillow, *Lit. biog. hist.*, 3.350–51 · G. Anstruther, *The seminary priests*, 1 (1969), 172–3

Holland, Henry (1555/6–1603), writer on witchcraft, was educated at Magdalene College, Cambridge, and graduated BA in 1579 or 1580. In 1580, aged twenty-four, he was ordained priest in the diocese of Ely and appointed vicar of Orwell, Cambridgeshire. In 1594 he moved to St Bride's, London.

Holland's theology was Calvinist. He was a firm predestinarian and placed a heavy emphasis on the active role of divine providence. Like many contemporary divines he was troubled by the failure of the bulk of the laity to comprehend the essential truths of Calvinism. Despite sermons and treatises the 'poor sheep', the 'seelie men', continued to adhere to a semi-pelagian position that confused the 'righteousness of faith and the righteousness of men' (Holland, *David's Faith and Repentance*). They also refused to respond properly to providential affliction. Rather than accept in patience and turn to God, they met misfortune with the resources of traditional magic as purveyed by the 'cunning-folk'. Holland shared other concerns with his clerical contemporaries. He was a sabbatarian, an opponent of dancing and of modern fashion—'misfiguring of head and face … following of strange attire' (Holland, *Christian Exercise of Fasting*, 192–3). After settling in the City of London he expressed his loathing for the capital's theatre, 'the nurceries of whoredome and uncleanesse' (Holland, *Spirituall Preservatives*, dedication; *The Historie of Adam*, fol. 93v).

Holland was a diligent parish minister; catechizing, expounding scripture, and preaching. Edward Topsell, the editor of his posthumous work *The Historie of Adam* (1606), attributed his death to his strenuous activity in his function. The bulk of his published works began as sermons: *David's Faith and Repentance* (1589), *The Christian Exercise of Fasting* (1596), and *Spirituall Preservatives Against the Pestilence* (1593, 1603). He was also a translator and an editor. His edition in 1599 and 1600 of the works of Richard Greenham (d. 1594), the great 'physician of the conscience' and his near neighbour in Cambridgeshire, cost him a good deal of effort in collecting and collating the manuscripts in which Greenham's 'cases of conscience' circulated. Holland's one scholarly treatise is his *Treatise of Witchcraft* (1590). This has a double inspiration. Like the related works of George Gifford and William Perkins, the *Treatise* was partly inspired by the 'brutish ignorance' of the 'rude people' that led them into 'a continuall trafficke and market' (Holland, *Witchcraft*, sig. A4) with the purveyors of folk magic. But Holland also sought to confute the sceptical arguments of Reginald Scot, and to do this he borrowed heavily from continental demonologists like Bodin, Daneau, and Hemmingsen: even the inquisitor authors of the *Malleus malificarum* receive favourable mention. In consequence Holland's tract, despite its populist intentions and solemn translations of all the Latin texts, has a curiously remote and academic flavour. The discussion of the diabolic covenant, sabbats, magical transformations, and transportations, sit as uneasily with the English popular beliefs and practices that he is ostensibly seeking to confute.

Throughout his life Holland was a conformist. He was not involved in any of the stirs instigated by many of the puritan ministers, his colleagues, in London in the 1590s. His works are dedicated to a variety of members of the Elizabethan lay establishment, from the court, legal, and civic hierarchies. He fulsomely praises Elizabeth's regime and, unlike Perkins, refuses to criticize overtly what he clearly viewed as the inadequacies of the legislation against witches and its enforcement. His unexpected death in London in August 1603 left his wife and children in some financial difficulties.

CLIVE HOLMES

Sources Venn, *Alum. Cant.*, 1/2. 393 · H. Holland, *A treatise against witchcraft* (1590) · [H. Holland], *David's faith and repentance* (1589) · H. Holland, *The Christian exercise of fasting, private and publike* (1596) · H. H. [H. Holland], *Spirituall preservatives against the pestilence* (1593) · H. Holland, *The historie of Adam*, ed. E. Topsell (1606)

Holland, Henry (b. 1583, d. in or after 1649), printer and bookseller, the son of Philemon *Holland (1552–1637) and his wife, Anne (1555–1627), daughter of William Bott, alias Peyton, was born at Coventry on 29 September 1583. His brothers were the poet Abraham *Holland (d. 1626) and the print publisher Compton *Holland (d. 1622). He went to London as a young man and usually designated himself 'Londonopolitanus'. Although he proved in later life a good classical scholar, and was clearly well educated, Holland was apprenticed to John Norton from 25 March 1599 and made free of the Stationers' Company on 5 December 1608. The first book published by him was Thomas Draxe's *Sicke Man's Catechisme* (1609), which was licensed to Holland and John Wright jointly on 4 February 1608–9. In 1610 he published, from a previously unprinted manuscript, Sir John Cheke's *A Royal Elegie*, on Edward VI; the book is now of great rarity. In 1613 he accompanied John, first Lord Harington, whose family had been on friendly terms with his father, to the Palatinate, when Harington accompanied Princess Elizabeth to the home of her husband, the elector palatine. In 1614 Holland published, in conjunction with Matthew Law, his compilation *Monumenta sepulchraria sancti Pauli: the monuments ... of kings, nobles, bishops, and others buried in the cathedrall church of St. Paul, London, untill this present yeare ... 1614, and a catalogue of all the bishops of London ... untill this present*. It was reissued as *Ecclesia sancti Pauli illustrata* in 1633 with a dedication by Holland, addressed to Laud, then bishop of London, and to the dean and chapter of St Paul's Cathedral.

Holland's reputation as a bookseller rested chiefly on two elaborately illustrated antiquarian works, with letterpress from his own pen. The earlier venture was *Baziliologia: a booke of kings, beeing the true and lively effigies of all our English kings from the conquest untill this present, with their severall coats of armes, impreses, and devises, and a briefe chronologie of their lives and deaths, elegantly graven in copper, printed for H. Holland, and are to be sold by Comp. Holland over against the Xchange*, 1618. The engravers employed included R. Elstracke, Simon Pass, and Francis Delaram, the last being responsible for the fine portraits of queens Mary and Elizabeth and princes Henry and Charles. Perfect copies include thirty-one portraits besides the title-page engraved with portraits of James I and Queen Anne.

Holland's second and more famous illustrated publication, *Heroologia Anglica, hoc est, clarissimorum et doctissimorum aliquot Anglorum qui floruerunt ab anno Christi M.D. usque ad presentem annum M.D.C.XX, vivae effigies, vitae, et elogia, duobus tomis, authore H. H., Anglo-Britanno, impensis Crispini Passaei calcographus et Jansoni bibliopolae Arnhemiensis* (1620), appeared in two folio volumes, the first dedicated to James I and the second to the universities of Cambridge and Oxford. There are sixty-five portraits, the first of Henry VIII, the last of Thomas Holland (*d.* 1612), regius professor of divinity at Oxford, and two engravings of monuments (of Prince Henry and Queen Elizabeth respectively). A presentation copy from Holland to Sir Thomas Holland is in the Grenville collection at the British Museum; another copy, with an inscription addressed by Holland to Robert Sidney, earl of Leicester, is described by Lowndes.

Holland seems to have carried on his publishing business until 1630. His less elaborate publications included *Newes from Frankfort* (1612) and *Newes from Gulick and Cleve* (1615) (jointly with G. Gibbs). In 1626 he printed at his own expense and published at Cambridge his brother Abraham's posthumous works as *Hollandi posthuma*. To *Salomon's Pest House*, by I. D., which he published with T. Harper in 1630, he added 'Mr. Hollands Admonition', a poem by his brother Abraham. Holland helped his father with his later publications. He wrote the dedication to Charles I of his father's *Cyropaedia* of Xenophon (1632), and edited after Dr Holland's death his Latin version of Bauderon's

Pharmacopoeia (1639), and his *Regimen sanitatis Salerni* (1649).

Holland's last days were spent in great poverty. A broadsheet issued on 26 June 1647, addressed 'to men, fathers, and brethren', appealed for charitable aid, stating that Holland had been 'a grandjury-man, and a subsidy-man, and one of the trained band charged with a corslet' (BL, 669, fol. 11, no. 34), and had acted as a commissioner under the great seal against bankrupts. His credit had been good, and he had rented a house in the parish of St Mary-le-Bow. During the plague in London in 1625 he and his wife, Susannah, had worked hard among the poor. She had since died (10 December 1635) at the Black Raven in Cheapside. As 'a zealous hater and abhorrer of all superstition and Popery and prelaticall innovations in church government' he had incurred the wrath of Laud, and had been imprisoned by order of both the high commission court and the Star Chamber. He declared himself adverse to 'all late sprung-up sectaries'. In 1643 he served in the life guards of Basil Feilding, earl of Denbigh, the parliamentary general, and was 'eldest man' of the troop, being sixty years old. Subsequently his eyesight and hearing had much decayed, he was crazy in his limbs, impotent in body, and so 'indigent in estate' owing to lawsuits that he had had to plead in a chancery suit *in forma pauperis*. The facts are attested by four persons, including William Gouge the puritan divine; but the facts that Holland dedicated his book about St Paul's Cathedral to Laud in 1633, and that his imprisonment has not been corroborated, throw some doubt on the details. The title-page of his father's posthumously published *Regimen* shows that Holland was still alive in 1649. The circumstances of his death are unknown. SIDNEY LEE, *rev.* ANITA McCONNELL

Sources Arber, *Regs. Stationers*, 2.237, 3.683 · Wood, *Ath. Oxon.*, new edn, 2.387 · T. Sharp, *Illustrations of the antiquities of Coventry* (1818), 1–37 · H. Holland, broadside petition, 1647, BL, 669, fol. 11, no. 34

Holland, Henry (1745–1806), architect, was born in Church Row, Fulham, on 20 July 1745, the eldest son of Henry Holland (1712–1785) and his wife, Mary (1716–1783), third child and only daughter of William Byrom of Fulham. Master of the Tylers' and Bricklayers' Company in 1772–3, Henry Holland senior was a prosperous Georgian builder who executed much of the architectural work of the celebrated landscape gardener Lancelot (Capability) Brown. After a modest architectural training, probably in his father's yard in Fulham, Holland entered into an informal but profitable partnership in 1771 with Brown, who lived not far away at Hampton Court. Gradually assuming responsibility for the architectural side of Brown's practice, Holland made the acquaintance of Brown's extensive and influential clientele. These contacts were particularly valuable for a young architect who had received the benefit of neither professional pupillage nor foreign travel.

Partnership with Lancelot Brown and marriage The first product of the partnership between Holland and Brown was the prestigious Claremont House, Esher, Surrey, built in 1771–4 for Robert Clive, first Baron Clive of Plassey, following his final return from India in 1767. Claremont is a very large Palladian house with a giant Corinthian portico, but somewhat spartan interiors with minimal classical trim. Representing a deliberate rejection of the elaborate ornament associated with the Adam brothers, this style was to reappear in Holland's later work. On 11 February 1773, while work was going forward on Claremont, Holland cemented the partnership with Brown by marrying his elder daughter, Bridget (1744–1828). They took up residence at 17 Hertford Street, Mayfair, recently built by Holland and his father. When Brown made his will in 1779, he named his son-in-law as one of his executors, and it was in the Hertford Street house that he died four years later.

Claremont was followed by a second collaboration between Brown and Holland, Benham Place, Berkshire (1774–5), for the sixth Baron Craven. Benham has a more interesting plan than Claremont, boasting a circular vestibule or tribune, two-storeyed and galleried, rising to a shallow dome containing a circular glazed lantern. Presumably contributed by Holland, this remarkable space made an impression on John Soane, who had indeed worked with Holland on the entrance hall at Claremont in 1772. Holland and Brown continued their collaboration at Cadland (1775–8), a modest 'marine villa' in the Palladian style overlooking the sea near Southampton. Holland's surviving sketches for interior decoration at Cadland are important because he noted the illustrated books on classical archaeology on which he drew for inspiration: Bernard de Montfaucon's *Antiquité expliquée* (1719–24), and *The Antiquities of Athens* by James Stuart and Nicholas Revett (vol. 1, 1762), a book to which Capability Brown was a subscriber.

Establishing himself independently: Brooks's Club, Hans Town and Place, and Sloane Place

The first important work which Holland undertook independently was Brooks's Club, St James's Street, London (1776–8), a club fashionable with the whig aristocrats who were to become his principal patrons; through them Holland met the prince of Wales who, in 1783, joined the club and appointed him as his architect. Behind a Palladian façade of pale yellow brick with stone dressings, like one of his country houses, Holland provided a suite of three first-floor rooms, the great subscription room, the small drawing-room, and the coffee (that is, dining) room, now the card room. With its segmental vaulted ceiling decorated with bands of guilloche ornament and chaste swags of husks, the great subscription room is one of the finest eighteenth-century rooms in London.

Holland was the obvious choice of architect for Brooks's, for not only did he own the site on which it was to be built, but his father had built the house in Pall Mall which the club had originally occupied. Like many eighteenth-century architects, Holland had taken to speculative building, purchasing in 1771 with money lent by his father a lease of 89 acres in Chelsea from Lord Cadogan. Here, from 1777 to c.1797, he built what was known as Hans Town, consisting of Sloane Street, Cadogan Place, and Hans Place. This urban development of simple terraced houses of stock brick, now largely demolished, immediately proved popular with the upper middle and professional classes for whom it was planned. As a piece of planned residential speculation, it found many imitators in London, though few as fashionable.

The octagonal Hans Place was left open at its south end to allow for an impressive view of a handsome detached villa with a large garden, the site of which is now partly occupied by Cadogan Square. Known as Sloane Place, this delectable residence was built by Holland for his own occupation between c.1782 and c.1789 as a public demonstration of his taste and professional success, in which role it is said to have attracted the favourable attention of the prince of Wales. Faced with the yellowish-white, thin imitation bricks known as mathematical tiles, it was U-shaped in plan with a colonnade of coupled Ionic columns along the south front. Behind this was a 113 foot enfilade of five intercommunicating rooms: drawing-room, dining-room, lobby, library, and music room, in which Holland displayed his collection of antique marbles and casts.

The miniature landscaped park at Sloane Place included a 16 acre meadow, formal flowers beds laid out in the French fashion, and an island containing a Gothic ice house. It was one of the very few detached mansions built in London in the second half of the eighteenth century with its own entrance courtyard and garden, an essentially Parisian form. It is known that Holland visited Paris in autumn 1785, but even before this he could have derived knowledge of contemporary French architecture and decoration from publications by Jacques Gondoin, Marie-Joseph Peyre, Pierre Patte, and Jean-François de Neufforge. It was partly Holland's Gallic tastes which made him sympathetic to his many whig clients, among whom it was fashionable to show some sympathy with the ideals of revolutionary France. The whig prince of Wales—to the annoyance of his father, George III—was a close friend of the duc de Chartres, who succeeded as duc d'Orléans in 1785; during the French Revolution, Orléans became known as Philippe Egalité. He was a frequent visitor to London, where he was a member of Brooks's.

Royal commissions: Carlton House, Brighton, and York House

In 1783 the prince of Wales employed Holland to rebuild his London residence, Carlton House, in Pall Mall. Holland brilliantly remodelled the rambling buildings which then occupied the site, creating a coherent façade of emphatically channelled rustication in the French manner with a central *porte-cochère*, the first in England. He screened the entrance court from Pall Mall by a low open colonnade of Ionic columns, a feature directly inspired by the colonnade which Peyre had proposed in 1763 for the Hôtel de Condé, and which Pierre Rousseau had built in 1782–5 at the Hôtel de Salm (now the Légion d'Honneur). These were a product of the opposition of French neo-classical theorists to the high, solid walls which had traditionally concealed aristocratic town mansions from the public gaze in both Paris and London.

By the end of 1783 Holland had engaged as draughtsmen

and interior decorators two French émigrés, Guillaume Gaubert, who stayed until 1787, and J.-P. Trécourt. They were soon joined by others, including Louis Delabrière and, about 1786, Dominique Daguerre, who remained until 1795. The interiors which, with their help, Holland created at Carlton House from 1783 to 1796 were among the most sophisticated in planning, design, furnishings, and craftsmanship ever created in England. The complicated plan of smallish interlocking rooms was French in origin, as at the Palais Bourbon in Paris, though the central octagonal tribune on which the whole complex plan pivoted may have been indebted to that proposed by Robert Adam in 1766 for Lord Bute at Luton Hoo. Holland's oval, top-lit staircase, one of the most dramatic in eighteenth-century England, was a baroque *tour de force* equalled only by William Kent's at 44 Berkeley Square (1742–4).

Carlton House was tragically demolished in 1826–7 by its creator (by then George IV), who by that date had turned his attention to the remodelling of Buckingham House and Windsor Castle. Something of its quality can be appreciated at Berrington Hall, Herefordshire (1778–81), built by Holland for the Hon. Thomas Harley, who was a tory, unlike most of his clients. The ambitious staircase incorporates coffered arches, free-standing columns on the first-floor gallery, and a tall glazed dome. The entrance front of Berrington shows Holland in a starker mood: a giant Ionic portico of startling abruptness carries a pediment pierced unconventionally by a Diocletian window.

In 1786 the prince of Wales acquired a farmhouse at Brighton, and employed Holland to expand it into a 'marine pavilion'. Holland gave it a Gallic flavour with a curved, domed bow, surrounded by engaged columns, as in the Hôtel de Salm in Paris. Faced with mathematical tiles, Holland's work was carried out in 1786–7, but was subsequently submerged by Nash's remodelling of the building as Brighton Pavilion in 1815–22.

In 1787–8 Holland rebuilt York (previously Featherstonhaugh, later Melbourne, and now Dover) House, Whitehall, for Frederick, duke of York, younger brother of the prince of Wales. Holland filled in the courtyard of the existing house, built in the 1750s, with a circular, galleried vestibule, 40 feet in diameter, a disposition inspired by French plans such as that for a town house published in Neufforge's *Recueil élémentaire d'architecture* (vol. 3, 1767). The vestibule is lit by a lantern above a shallow dome, and surrounded by eight pink scagliola columns. Holland added an entrance portico in Whitehall, featuring columns of the Greek Ionic order of the temple on the River Ilissus in Athens, as illustrated in *The Antiquities of Athens* (1762). This is set into a rusticated screen wall inspired by the library of Hadrian in Athens, again from a plate in the same volume of the *Antiquities*, where it is described as a 'Stoa or portico'.

Commissions from the whig élite: Althorp, Woburn Abbey, and Southill
In December 1786 Holland was commissioned to remodel Althorp, Northamptonshire, by the second Earl Spencer, one of the whig grandees who was a prominent member of Brooks's. Holland's handsome library is divided by two screens of his favourite Greek Ionic columns. The most exquisite room, however, is Lady Spencer's dressing-room with neo-classical painted pilasters and panels executed in 1790–91 by T. H. Pernotin. For Lord Spencer, Holland also remodelled Wimbledon Park House in 1799, adding a striking Tuscan portico with broadly projecting eaves, inspired by Inigo Jones's at St Paul's, Covent Garden.

While work at Althorp proceeded, Holland received a commission in 1787 from another whig nobleman, Francis Russell, the 21-year-old fifth duke of Bedford, to modernize Woburn Abbey, Bedfordshire. As at Althorp, Holland provided a fine tripartite library, divided with screens of columns. He also remodelled the east front, turning it into the main entrance front, which he marked by a deep *porte-cochère* in a version of Tuscan which borders closely on Greek Doric. At the same time he added the Chinese dairy, overlooking the pool to the north-east of the abbey. The pretty lantern with its finials is based on plates in Chambers's *Designs of Chinese Buildings* (1757), from which source Holland also drew inspiration for the interior decoration.

In 1789 Holland built a handsome greenhouse at Woburn with a Venetian window flanked by Louis XVI medallions and wreaths, carved in 1790 by Le Maison, who described himself on his bill as 'of Paris and London'. The duke subsequently decided to turn this building into a sculpture gallery, and commissioned Holland to set up the temple of liberty at one end in 1801. This was built to house busts of the duke's favourite political heroes, notably Nollekens's bust of Charles James Fox, who also presides over Brooks's Club and the prince of Wales's octagonal tribune at Carlton House. Holland's temple of liberty is an exceptionally refined creation with details based on two Athenian monuments, as recorded by Stuart and Revett: the Greek Ionic order from the Ilissus temple, and the frieze adorned with wreaths from the choragic monument of Thrasyllus in Athens. In 1788–92 the second Viscount Palmerston commissioned Holland to provide a handsome new Ionic portico in antis on the east front of Broadlands, Hampshire, as well as interior decoration; Brown had already worked on the house and park for the same client in 1766–8.

Holland's last major domestic commission came in 1796 from Samuel Whitbread, the wealthy brewer, for the remodelling of Southill House, Bedfordshire, where the grounds had been landscaped for a previous owner by Capability Brown. Holland's exteriors at Southill were understated, almost to the point of gracelessness, but he provided a series of varied but always exquisite astylar interiors, which are the climax of his personal style. Mrs Whitbread's room and boudoir, finished in April 1800, were the most French, with decorative painting in a Pompeian manner by A. L. Delabrière. The drawing-room has an almost sensuous beauty with its crimson silk wall panels, while the library has antique panels of griffins and candelabra.

Further works Both the Theatre Royal, Drury Lane, and the Covent Garden Theatre stood on land owned by the duke of Bedford, so that Holland was the obvious choice of architect in the 1790s to rebuild the former, and to make alterations to the latter. Turning for inspiration to recent publications on French theatre design by Pierre Patte and Étienne Dumont, Holland provided the Theatre Royal with chastely classical interior decoration and rich furnishing. Both theatres were burnt to the ground in 1808–9.

An unusual commission came in 1803 to remodel Melbourne House, Piccadilly, as residential chambers, and to add two ranges of apartments in the garden on the north. Built by Sir William Chambers for Lord Melbourne in 1771–4, the house had been the residence of the duke of York from 1792, and the decision to turn an aristocratic, and now royal, mansion into residential apartments, named the Albany, was highly unconventional. This commission involved the destruction of Chambers's magnificent staircase, but the two long ranges which Holland added were elegant and convenient, and serve the same purpose today as that for which they were erected. They flank an attractive covered way, known as the Ropewalk, which has a tent-shaped roof of narrow boarding with a faintly Chinese flavour.

Holland as a collector Holland's collection of antiquities, its arrangement and display, was an important part of his presentation of himself to the world as a man of taste; in this he followed the example of Adam as well as setting a precedent for Soane. In 1776 Holland made his first important purchase of casts from the antique, which were acquired for him in Italy by Christopher Ebdon, a former pupil of James Paine. In 1794 Holland sent his talented draughtsman Charles Heathcote Tatham to Rome to pursue his own studies and to collect for Holland decorative pieces such as fragments from antique altars, carved pilasters, and candelabra, as well as cinerary urns. For these services Holland made him an allowance of £60 a year, plus expenses. Holland thus made a vital contribution to the development of neo-classical taste in England: first, because Tatham's subsequent publications, beginning with *Etchings of Ancient Ornamental Architecture* (1799–1800), were to be influential on architects and furniture designers, and, second, because in 1816 Soane purchased the marbles which Tatham had acquired for Holland. He mounted them on the walls of the study at 13 Lincoln's Inn Fields, where they can be seen today.

Holland's brother John, who also spent much time in Italy, acquired further antique fragments for him. A sufficient quantity of objects were installed in Sloane Place by early 1796 for Holland to show them to experts, such as Charles Townley, who supported his election as a fellow of the Society of Antiquaries in December 1796. Holland offered them to the trustees of the British Museum who declined them, so they remained in his collection, passing on his death to his nephew.

Last years and death In 1799 Holland became surveyor to the East India Company, in which capacity he built the long neo-Palladian façade of East India House, Leadenhall Street (1799–1800), with interiors designed by his predecessor as surveyor Richard Jupp. His other official appointments included clerk of the works at the Royal Mews at Charing Cross (1775–82) and surveyor to the Bridewell and Bethlem hospitals (1782–93); he was appointed a JP for Middlesex in 1778. He acquired from Lord Spencer, seemingly in payment of debts, an estate at Okehampton, Devon, which was a political borough and a whig stronghold where the duke of Bedford played an important role. A committed whig, Holland secured the Okehampton seat in the House of Commons for his son Henry in 1802. He died in his London house, Sloane Place, on 17 June 1806, and was buried below the simple family tomb which he had designed for his parents in the churchyard of All Saints', Fulham. He left two sons, Henry and Lancelot, and five daughters. His drawings and papers seem to have been destroyed after his death by his nephew and executor, Henry Rowles.

Assessment It is hard to guess at Holland's personality for he was of a retiring disposition, and carefully avoided public notice. He chose not to exhibit his work at the Royal Academy, though he did take an active part in founding the Architects' Club in 1791 with George Dance, S. P. Cockerell, and James Wyatt. He took a practical interest in new materials and methods of construction for buildings of all types, such as mathematical tiles, fireproofing, Hartley's 'fire-plate', and *pisé* (rammed earth construction on brick or rubble foundations). He published papers in 1793 on the problems of fire prevention, and in 1797 on agricultural cottages and on *pisé*. His use of *pisé*, as in estate cottages supposedly built at Woburn in the early 1790s, was part of his admiration for France, for he was indebted to a publication on the subject by A. M. Cointereaux of Paris in 1791. The caustic Soane, who began his architectural career as an assistant in Holland's office, dismissed him, privately, as 'a bricklayer architect' (D. Watkin, *Sir John Soane: Enlightenment Thought and the Royal Academy Lectures*, 1996, 230).

Holland's principal stylistic debt was probably to Sir William Chambers, whose restrained Gallic tastes he echoed, though with the introduction of neo-Greek detail of which Chambers would have disapproved. It must also have been galling for Chambers to see Holland replace or succeed him at Melbourne House, Carlton House, and Woburn Abbey, while he was still in professional practice himself. But, as a whig, Holland was more acceptable to some patrons than the tory Chambers. Holland's opposite numbers as royal architects in France, Claude-Nicolas Ledoux and Richard Mique, were, respectively, imprisoned during the terror and guillotined, fates Holland would have been unlikely to have escaped had he too been French.   DAVID WATKIN

Sources [W. Papworth], ed., *The dictionary of architecture*, 11 vols. (1853–92) · H. B. Hodson, 'Holland, the architect', *The Builder*, 13 (1855), 437 · D. Stroud, *Henry Holland: his life and architecture* (1966) · Colvin, *Archs.* · J. M. Crook and M. H. Port, eds., *The history of the king's works*, 6 (1973), 307–12 · *Carlton House: the past glories of George*

IV's palace (1991) [exhibition catalogue, Queen's Gallery, Buckingham Palace, London] • A. E. Richardson and others, *Southill: a Regency house* (1951) • C. Hussey, *English country houses: mid-Georgian, 1760–1800* (1956) • *The parish of St James, Westminster*, 2/2, Survey of London, 32 (1963), 373–85 • J. Britton and A. Pugin, *The public buildings of London*, 2 (1828), 77–89, 193–201 • D. Watkin, *The royal interiors of Regency London* (1984), 98–126 • P. Ziegler and D. Seward, eds., *Brooks's: a social history* (1991), 153–9 • G. Richardson, *New Vitruvius Britannicus*, 1 (1802), pl. 6–7, 61–3 • N. Brawer, 'The anonymous architect of the India House', *Georgian Group Journal*, 7 (1997), 26–36

Archives NRA, priv. coll., plans and elevations of Cadland • RIBA, corresp. and papers | Birm. CL, letters to Boulton family • BL, letters to Lord Spencer • Hants. RO, papers relating to alterations of Stretton Park • Woburn Abbey, Bedfordshire, papers relating to work at Woburn Abbey

Likenesses G. Garrard, marble bust, 1803, Woburn Abbey, Bedfordshire • G. Garrard, marble bust, 1806, Southill, Bedfordshire • G. Garrard, woodcut, pubd 1806, BM, NPG • J. Opie, oils

Holland, Sir Henry, first baronet (1788–1873), physician, was born on 27 October 1788 at Knutsford, Cheshire, where his father, Peter Holland was a physician. He was related to Josiah Wedgwood, a keen patron of the arts, and to the novelist Elizabeth Gaskell. At Newcastle upon Tyne Holland was tutored by the Revd William Turner, from whom he acquired a love of natural science and travel. In 1803 he was sent to Dr John Prior Estlin's school in Bristol. As he records in *Recollections of a Past Life* his 'most intimate friend [there] was Richard Bright … who as Dr. Bright held such a high and well-merited place in the medical world' (*Recollections*, 11). The boys shared the same keen interest in science and geology. On leaving Estlin's school Holland walked the entire distance home to Knutsford, a precursor perhaps to his later obsession with adventure and travel. This probably led to his decision to follow a career in business which he believed would provide him with opportunity for travel; to this end he became an articled clerk with a major Liverpool merchant house. A family connection with the senior partner gave Holland the opportunity to enrol for two sessions at Glasgow University in 1804 and 1805 which in his own words 'virtually decided the course of my future life' (*Recollections*, 17). He was released from his articles and in 1806 embarked on a medical degree at Edinburgh. He also spent two winters at the United Hospitals of Guy's and St Thomas's in London. In 1810 his spirit of adventure was gratified by an expedition to Iceland in company with Sir George Mackenzie of Coul and Richard Bright. His study of the diseases of the Icelanders provided data for his doctoral thesis 'De morbis Islandiae' with which he graduated in 1811; it was dedicated to Bishop Geir Vidalin of Iceland. He contributed his accounts 'History and literature of Iceland' and 'Diseases of the Icelanders' to Mackenzie's *Travels in the Island of Iceland* (1811). Holland nearly lost his life when he and Bright made an abortive attempt to reach the summit of Snaefell Jokul. When retracing their steps Holland was the second to cross a precarious snow bridge; his foot broke through the ice and he just managed to save himself from being plunged into the deep chasm below. As he wrote in his journal this was not accomplished 'without much fear

and trembling whilst thus hazardously engaged!' (*Iceland Journal*, 195).

Having graduated Holland spent the next eighteen months travelling in Portugal, Gibraltar, Sardinia, Sicily, the Ionian Isles, and Greece. The publication in 1814 of an account of the eastern part of this journey, *Travels in the Ionian Isles, Albania, Thessaly, Macedonia etc. during 1812 and 1813*, provided him with an entrée to London society which would be of great benefit in a medical career which he determined would allow him to devote two months of every year to travel. In 1814 he again visited Europe, this time as medical attendant to the princess of Wales (later Queen Caroline). He was subsequently asked to testify at the inquiry of 1820 which sought the necessary evidence to divorce her from George IV.

Holland was made a licenciate of the Royal College of Physicians on 8 April 1816, and fellow in 1828. He commenced his professional life in 1816 in a fashionable practice at his home in Mount Street, London. Four years later he moved to Lower Brook Street where he lived until his death. Holland gave the Goulstonian lecture at the college in 1830 and served in numerous years as censor or consiliarius. He neither sought, nor apparently needed, a hospital appointment to further his career. He moved freely in society circles and his advice was much respected, albeit that a practised bedside manner was rather more in evidence than hard medical insight. At the end of the London season he visited the popular resort of Spa which further cemented his growing clientele of the rich and famous and allowed him to maintain his resolve to limit his professional work to that which afforded him an income of £5000 and gave him the freedom to pursue his great love of travel. In his lifetime he visited every European capital, made two visits to Iceland, and eight to America, covering more than 26,000 miles of that continent. The exploration of rivers afforded him particular pleasure:

> watching the flow of waters which come from unknown springs or find their issue in some remote ocean or sea. I have felt this on the Nile at its time of highest inundation, when crossing the Volga when scarcely wider than the Thames at Oxford and still more when near the sources of the streams that feed the Euphrates, south of Trebizond. (*Recollections*, 25)

On the accession of Queen Victoria in 1837 Holland was appointed physician-extraordinary, and in 1840 he became physician-in-ordinary to the prince consort. He declined the offer of a baronetcy made by Lord Melbourne in 1841 but happily accepted the offer in 1853. He received an honorary DCL from the University of Oxford and also from the University of Harvard, Massachusetts. As president of the Royal Institution Holland strove to popularize science by promoting the lectures to the élite of the fashionable circles in which he moved. He keenly supported the efforts of Faraday and Tyndall to improve the society and also set up the Holland Fund to which he contributed £40 each year for the promotion of scientific research. His *Recollections* not only provide interesting accounts of his travels but also record the diversity of leading figures of the times with whom he could boast intimacy. His Edinburgh days had brought him into contact with men such as Lord Brougham, Sydney Smith, and Francis Corner, while in London he was a frequenter of the soirées at Holland House and was acquainted with figures from the literary world such as Madame de Staël, Maria Edgeworth, and Joanna Baillie.

While Holland could not be described as a great physician, his medical text *Medical Notes and Reflections* (1839) is of some interest in its attempt to expose the relationship between mind and body. The book comprises several discrete essays on subjects relating to the philosophy and practice of medicine. The parts relating specifically to mental philosophy were published in 1851 in one volume entitled *Chapters on Mental Physiology*.

Holland was twice married, first in 1822 to Margaret Emma, daughter of James Caldwell of Linley Wood, Staffordshire. She died 2 February 1830 leaving two sons, Henry Thurstan *Holland, created Lord Knutsford in 1888, and Francis James *Holland, canon of Canterbury, and two daughters. In 1834 he married Saba (*d.* 1866), daughter of the Revd Sydney Smith; the couple had three daughters. Holland very determinedly carved out for himself exactly the life he wanted. Spare of stature but blessed with exceptionally good health, he was able to indulge his abiding love of travel right up to the time of his death. In the autumn of 1873 he journeyed with his son Francis from Nizhniy Novgorod in Russia to southern Italy. He returned to London on 25 October feeling somewhat unwell and gradually lost the power of speech over that weekend. He died peacefully at his home, 72 Brook Street, Grosvenor Square, on 27 October 1873.　　　DIANA BERRY

Sources Munk, *Roll*, 3.144–9 · *The Lancet* (1 Nov 1873), 650–51 · *BMJ* (1 Nov 1873), 532–3 · H. Holland, *Recollections of past life* (1872), 11, 17, 25 · H. Holland, *Medical notes and reflections* (1839) · *The Iceland journal of Henry Holland, 1810*, ed. A. Wawn, The Hakluyt Society (1987), 195 · d. cert.
Archives Ches. & Chester ALSS, letters of Knutsford · NL Scot., letters to his father · RCP Lond., original letters and prescriptions · Royal Society of Medicine, London, works · Wellcome L., works | BL, corresp. with W. E. Gladstone, Add. MSS 44393–44437, *passim* · BL, corresp. with Lord Holland, Add. MS 51814 · Ches. & Chester ALSS, letters to Sir J. T. Stanley · RS, corresp. with Sir John Herschel · Trinity Cam., letters to William Whewell · University of Rochester, New York, corresp.
Likenesses T. Brigstocke, oils, *c.*1860, NPG · Moira and Haigh, photographs, 1864, RCP Lond. · E. Edwards, photograph, 1867, Wellcome L. · Barraud and Jerrard, photograph, 1873, Wellcome L. · W. Theed, marble bust, 1873, NPG · wood-engraving, 1873, Wellcome L. · Maull and Polyblank, photograph, RCP Lond. · F. W. Wilkins, lithograph, RCP Lond. · F. W. Wilkins, lithograph, Wellcome L.
Wealth at death under £140,000: probate, 8 Nov 1873, *CGPLA Eng. & Wales*

Holland, Henry Scott (1847–1918), theologian and social reformer, was born on 27 January 1847 at Underdown, Ledbury, Herefordshire, the second of the six children of George Henry Holland and his wife, the Hon. Charlotte Dorothea Gifford, eldest daughter of Robert *Gifford, first Baron Gifford of St Leonards, Devon, attorney-general and deputy speaker of the House of Lords. His father was the

Henry Scott Holland (1847–1918), by Elliott & Fry

second son of Swinton Colthurst Holland of Dumbleton, Gloucestershire, a partner in a firm of merchant agents from whom he had received an inheritance sufficient to make him independent of any business or profession.

From his earliest childhood Holland exhibited an artistic imagination which was to affect all his preaching and writing. He was a friend of such artists as William Hunt and Edward Burne-Jones, a devotee of Wordsworth, and, in collaboration with William S. Rockstro, wrote the definitive two-volume memoir of his friend Jenny Lind. Yet it was only when he became a student at Balliol that he also began to show that intellectual ability which caused several contemporaries to describe him as one of the few authentic geniuses of his century.

After four years at Mr Bedford's private school in Allesley, near Coventry, Holland went to Eton College in 1860, the year when J. S. Mill's *On Liberty*, Charles Darwin's *The Origin of Species*, H. T. Buckle's *History of Civilisation in England*, and John Ruskin's *Unto this Last* were challenging many of the most cherished preconceptions of mid-Victorian England, and with the encouragement of his tutor William Johnson Cory, Holland enthusiastically adopted the new ideas, discovering that politics and economics, as well as theology, could be understood more by the intellectual imagination than by abstract science. When Holland went up to Balliol College, Oxford, in 1866, Thomas Hill Green gave him a philosophical language suited to this intellectual imagination, though he embraced Green's idealism more for its basic ethical stance than for those metaphysical principles which in the next century were to fall into such disfavour.

Holland had the exceptional ability of combining in himself the most disparate friendships and seemingly contrary attitudes. When he was ordained in 1872, Green and Richard Lewis Nettleship, Green's future biographer and one of Holland's closest friends, wondered if their friendship could possibly continue. At Oxford Nettleship drove Holland towards an expansive and liberal outlook while his other close friend, Stephen Freemantle, after whom St Stephen's Theological College was later named, urged him into high Anglicanism, confession, and ascetic discipline. Holland's contribution to the theological thought of his day was to demonstrate both intellectually and in his personality that such opposites were interdependent and that a rigid orthodoxy was the necessary foundation for a free and liberal spirit.

Holland reflected in himself diverse popular movements of his day: the new idealism of T. H. Green and the Romanticism of Ruskin; the conservatism of Tractarian orthodoxy and the theological breadth of F. D. Maurice; the political Liberalism of Gladstone and the radical socialism of some trade unionists. As the more perceptive recognized, these were not simply brought together in some eclectic fashion but were fused into an original and creative synthesis.

Following an outstanding first in *literae humaniores* in December 1870 Holland was elected by open examination to a senior studentship at Christ Church, where he remained for fourteen years. Though holding the university office of proctor in 1882–3 he never allowed himself to be swept into the stream of university business. His interests lay elsewhere, his mind ranging from incisive and penetrating theological studies of Justin Martyr and Dean Aldrich to critical articles on the opium trade in China and on various biblical and literary topics. He took an active interest in the founding of Lady Margaret Hall, the second Oxford college for women, and was instrumental in founding the Church of England Purity Society, the Christ Church Mission in Poplar, and the Oxford Mission to Calcutta.

Holland was always interested in developing new forms of community life within the church and through this helping the church transform society. Using the model of a Jesuit college, which he may have learned to appreciate from his early friendship with Gerard Manley Hopkins, he began to form plans in 1872 for a mission house at St Saviour's, Hoxton, where young men from Oxford could 'settle' before taking holy orders. Two years later, when Canon Barnett established the first 'settlement' house, Oxford House was also established by friends of Holland in Bethnal Green. Later, to train men to work in these settlements before ordination, Holland, with the support of Edward King, helped found St Stephen's House in Oxford as a kind of Oratorian community, and asked his friend R. C. Moberley to be its first principal.

On Gladstone's recommendation Holland was appointed canon of St Paul's in 1884 and immediately immersed himself in the social problems of London's East End. In 1889 he founded the Christian Social Union (CSU). Unlike other societies, such as the Guild of St Matthew, which existed, as he claimed, to take the Christian revelation into the world, the CSU existed to drag the social question into the church, and had much to do with the fact that England became one of the few countries where people did not think that Christianity and socialism were necessarily incompatible. Holland expounded his views on social reform not only through the pulpit and platform of the CSU but through a national parish magazine, *Goodwill*, and then through the pages of *Commonwealth*, a monthly periodical devoted to social issues which he helped found in 1896 and then edited until his death in 1918.

Holland always preferred working with others and, before moving to London, he initiated a small 'annual meeting of friends in council' which he ironically dubbed 'the holy party'. Meeting yearly for over forty years it became the germ of the Christian Social Union, the Community of the Resurrection in Mirfield, and the publication of *Lux mundi*, a controversial book of essays attempting to restate orthodox Christian doctrine in the language of contemporary society, which became the standard exposition of what Holland was to call 'Liberal Catholicism'. Holland wrote *Lux mundi*'s first essay, 'Faith'.

Though limited in later years by headaches he began to suffer when still in his early thirties, Holland was an avid reader, but the pulpit and short essay rather than the academic tome best suited his temperament. He published more than a dozen collections of sermons and essays, and well over 100 others were published in various books and periodicals. He was a gifted if somewhat florid orator, driving home his message by piling up verbal images one on top of another, so that a little girl once commented after one of his sermons, 'My, what a lot of adjectives that man knows'. A forceful hymnist, Holland's hymn 'Judge eternal, throned in splendour' remains popular. Charles Gore once said that, having learned all he knew from Holland, his task in life was to put scholarly footnotes to his genius.

In 1910 H. H. Asquith appointed Holland regius professor of divinity at Oxford. Though he hesitated at first, claiming that he had not been able to do any serious study for twenty-five years, his friends persuaded him to accept. In Oxford he wrote many of his most mature essays and began a scholarly study of St John. He very quickly had a large following, but then the university was decimated of students with the outbreak of the First World War, and Holland himself, no longer very well, was shattered by its horrors.

A few months before the war ended, after suffering from increasing ill health, Holland died in his house at Christ Church, Oxford, early on a Sunday morning, 17 March 1918, after reciting Wordsworth's *Yarrow Revisited* and having William Morris's *The House of the Wolfings* read to him. His funeral took place three days later in Christ Church Cathedral and his body was buried in the parish churchyard at Cuddesdon, Oxfordshire.

JOHN H. HEIDT

Sources DNB · J. H. Heidt, 'The social theology of Henry Scott Holland', DPhil diss., U. Oxf., 1975 · S. Paget, ed., *Henry Scott Holland, memoir and letters*, 2nd edn (1921) · C. Cheshire, ed., *Henry Scott Holland: some appreciations* (1919) · E. Lyttelton, *The mind and character of Henry Scott Holland* (1926) · G. W. E. Russell, *Prime ministers and some others* (1918), 87–105 · A. M. Ramsey, *From Gore to Temple: the development of Anglican theology between 'Lux mundi' and the Second World War,*

1889–1939 (1960) · W. J. Richmond, ed., *The philosophy of faith and the fourth gospel* (1920) · J. H. Foster, 'Henry Scott Holland: 1847–1918', PhD diss., U. Wales, 1970 · Gladstone, *Diaries*
Archives Balliol Oxf., letters · Borth. Inst., lectures, addresses, etc. · Community of the Resurrection, Mirfield, lecture notes and corresp. as regius professor · priv. coll. | BL, corresp. with Lord Gladstone, Add. MSS 46050–46069, *passim* · BL, Mary Gladstone MSS, vols. 29 and 30, Add. MSS 46247–46248 · Bodl. Oxf., letters to Herbert Asquith · Bodl. Oxf., corresp. with Sir Henry Burdett · Bodl. Oxf., Moberley MSS · Borth. Inst., corresp. with Mrs Edward Talbot · LPL, corresp. with Edward Benson · LPL, letters to Christopher Cheshire · NL Scot., corresp. with Lord Rosebery · Northants. RO, Cartwright (Edgecote) collection · U. St Andr. L., letters to A. L. Lilley · U. St Andr. L., letters to Wilfrid Ward
Likenesses Elliott & Fry, photograph, NPG [*see illus.*] · photographs
Wealth at death £21,320 4*s.* 0*d.*: probate, 17 May 1918, *CGPLA Eng. & Wales*

Holland, Henry Thurstan, first Viscount Knutsford (1825–1914), politician, belonged by descent to the family of Holland, derived, through the Hollands of Clifton and Mobberley, from the Hollands of Upholland. His ancestors owned various estates for many centuries in Lancashire and Cheshire. He was the elder son of Sir Henry *Holland, first baronet (1788–1873), a leading London physician, and his first wife, Margaret Emma, daughter of James Caldwell, of Linley Wood, Staffordshire. Francis James *Holland was his younger brother. He was born at his father's house, 72 Brook Street, London, on 3 August 1825. He was educated at Harrow School, at Durham University, and at Trinity College, Cambridge, where he took his degree in 1847. At Durham he won the Durham prize for Latin verse, and he coxed the Cambridge boat in the university four-oared race of 1846. He was called to the bar by the Inner Temple in 1849, and practised on the northern circuit.

In 1850 Holland acted as secretary to the royal commission on common law, and assisted in drafting the Common Law Procedure Acts of 1852 and 1854. He was offered by Lord Campbell the county court judgeship of Northumberland, but declined. In 1867 he was appointed by the fourth earl of Carnarvon to be legal adviser at the Colonial Office, and gave up private practice. In 1870 he became assistant under-secretary for the colonies. He held this office until August 1874, and then, having in 1873 succeeded to the baronetcy, resigned it in order to stand for parliament as Conservative candidate for Midhurst. His election was uncontested and he held the seat until 1885, when, under the Redistribution Act, Midhurst ceased to exist as a constituency. Holland then stood for the new constituency of Hampstead, where he defeated the marquess of Lorne. In that year he was for a month financial secretary to the Treasury in Lord Salisbury's administration, and from 17 September, vice-president of the committee of council on education. He held the same office again from 1886 in Lord Salisbury's second administration and on 14 January 1887 became colonial secretary and so head of the department in which he had served as a permanent official. He held that office until the fall of the Conservative government in 1892. In 1887 he organized and was president of the first colonial conference, held to coincide with celebrations for the Queen's jubilee.

Southern Africa was Holland's chief preoccupation as colonial secretary. He was responsible for the charter granted on 29 October 1887 to Rhodes's British South Africa Company, and consequently for the loose wording which led to confusion during the Matabele (Ndebele) crisis of 1892–4. He was horrified by aspects of Rhodes's plans, but was unable to control the early phase of Rhodes's drive to the north; his tenure of office ended in August 1892.

Holland had succeeded his father as baronet in 1873; in 1888 he was raised to the peerage under the title of Baron Knutsford, of Knutsford, Cheshire, and in 1895 he was created a viscount, not being included in Salisbury's government of that year. He was made a privy councillor in 1885; he was also a GCMG (1888), an ecclesiastical commissioner, a knight of justice of the order of St John of Jerusalem, and a bencher of the Inner Temple, and he served on several important royal commissions. He was noted for his good looks, social charm, and the energy which he put into any work that he had to do. He was not an orator, and confined his speeches in parliament to subjects with which he had, or had had, some official connection. He had a country residence for nearly forty years at Witley in Surrey, and, when not in office, took due part in local affairs.

Lord Knutsford married twice: first, in 1852 Elizabeth Margaret (*d.* 1855), daughter of Nathaniel and Emily Hibbert, of Munden House, Hertfordshire, and granddaughter of Sydney Smith; with her he had twin sons, one of whom, Sydney *Holland, succeeded him as second viscount, and a daughter; second, in 1858 Margaret Jean (*d.* 1906), daughter of Sir Charles Edward *Trevelyan and his first wife, Hannah, and niece of T. B. Macaulay, with whom he had three sons and one daughter. He died on 29 January 1914 at 75 Eaton Square, his London house, and was buried on 2 February at Witley.

B. H. HOLLAND, *rev.* H. C. G. MATTHEW

Sources GEC, *Peerage* · B. Holland, *The Lancashire Hollands* (1917) · W. F. Irvine, *A history of the family of Holland* (privately printed, Edinburgh, 1912) · R. Robinson, J. Gallagher, and A. Denny, *Africa and the Victorians* (1961) · R. I. Rotberg, *The founder: Cecil Rhodes and the pursuit of power* (1988) · C. Palley, *The constitutional history and law of Southern Rhodesia, 1888–1965* (1966) · G. Sutherland, *Policy-making in elementary education, 1870–1895* (1973)
Archives BL, corresp. with Lord Carnarvon, Add. MS 60796 · Bodl. Oxf., corresp. with Lord Kimberley · CCC Cam., corresp. with sixteenth earl of Derby · CKS, letters to Akers-Douglas · CKS, letters to Edward Stanhope · CUL, corresp. with Lord Hardinge · LPL, corresp. with Edward Benson · NA Scot., corresp. with first Baron Loch · NL Aus., corresp. with Alfred Deakin · Rhodes University, Grahamstown, South Africa, Cory Library for Historical Research, corresp. with Sir John Gordon Sprigg · Suffolk RO, Ipswich, corresp. with Lord Cranbrook · U. Leeds, Brotherton L., letters to E. Gosse
Likenesses A. S. Cope, oils, 1887; in possession of Lord Hambledon, 1927 · A. S. Cope, oils, 1906, NPG · Ape [C. Pellegrini], chromolithograph caricature, NPG; repro. in *VF* (29 Jan 1887) · A. S. Boyd, caricature, University of Cape Town, South Africa · J. Brown, stipple (after H. T. Wells; Grillion's Club series), BM · Russell & Sons, photograph, NPG · Walery, photograph, NPG · portrait, repro. in *Royal Academy Pictures*

Wealth at death £112,217: probate, 28 Feb 1914, *CGPLA Eng. & Wales*

Holland, Sir Henry Tristram (1875–1965), missionary and eye surgeon, was born on 12 February 1875 in the cathedral close, Durham, the second son in the family of three sons and one daughter of William Lyall Holland, then a cathedral canon, and Mary Gertrude, daughter of Canon Henry Baker Tristram, a naturalist. Holland spent most of his youth in his father's parsonage at Cornhill-on-Tweed in Northumberland, leading a rumbustious life which included hunting with five packs of hounds and bird-watching. He was educated at Loretto School, Edinburgh, from 1889 to 1894, and later, with distinction, at Edinburgh University medical school, where he became MB, ChB (1899). He was a medallist in anatomy and a prizeman in surgery.

While still an undergraduate Holland decided to be a medical missionary, and in 1900 he joined the Punjab mission of the Church Missionary Society (CMS), with which he remained for forty-eight years. Although he spent some time in Kashmir his main life's work was in the CMS hospital at Quetta, 5500 feet up in the mountains of Baluchistan, where he soon established a reputation for cataract surgery. Holland became FRCSE in 1907. In 1910 he married Florence Ethel (d. 1975), daughter of the Revd J. Tunbridge. They had two sons and a daughter. Both the sons became eye specialists.

In 1911 a Hindu philanthropist built a special hospital in Shikarpur, Sind, on condition that Holland worked there with a team especially to perform eye operations for six weeks every year. This work continued through the years, and Holland himself performed more than 60,000 operations for cataract alone. Visitors came from all over the world, and despite repeated offers of important posts elsewhere he always preferred to remain in the Punjab. Even so, he found time for travel throughout India and into Kashmir and Afghanistan on missionary and medical duties, and in the remoter parts of Baluchistan his name became a legend.

In 1935 Quetta Hospital was completely destroyed by an earthquake and Holland was buried in the ruins, but was rescued by his elder son. It was chiefly through his subsequent efforts that money was raised to erect, for the CMS and Church of England Zenana missionary hospitals at Quetta, much finer buildings than before. Holland's name will also be remembered in connection with temporary eye-camps that he used to establish in areas where blindness was rife. Over a period of some months Holland and a team of surgeons would then operate on hundreds of cases. In addition he was a founder member of the Royal Commonwealth Society for the Blind.

Holland was secretary of the CMS Punjab medical executive committee for thirty-two years, and also the society's medical adviser for that area. He had a very considerable share in the planning of medical policy, not only of the church but also of the government. He received the kaisar-i-Hind silver medal in 1910, the gold medal in 1925, and a bar to it in 1931. He was appointed CIE in 1929 and knighted in 1936.

After his official retirement from CMS missionary service in 1948 Sir Henry and Lady Holland returned to the north-west frontier a number of times at the invitation of local chieftains. On each occasion he performed cataract operations at Quetta or Shikarpur. In 1960 came the announcement that Holland and his son, Ronald W. B. Holland, had been honoured with the Ramon Magsaysay award, presented annually to outstanding persons who have served their fellow men with distinction. Both Sir Henry and Ronald Holland travelled to Manila to receive it. The citation stated that father and son had saved the sight of about 150,000 people. In his speech in reply Sir Henry concluded with the words, 'All that has been accomplished is only due to the Lord Jesus Christ, whose ambassadors we have tried to be.' Among his other distinctions, Holland was an honorary member of the section of ophthalmology of the Royal Society of Medicine, and of the Oxford Ophthalmology Congress. He was vice-president of the Pakistan Society. Holland died in Trimmers Hospital, Farnham, Surrey, on 19 September 1965.

P. D. TREVOR-ROPER, *rev.*

Sources H. Holland, *Frontier doctor* (1958) · *The Times* (20 Sept 1965) · *The Times* (25 Sept 1965) · *CGPLA Eng. & Wales* (1965) · d. cert.
Wealth at death £16,960: probate, 6 Dec 1965, *CGPLA Eng. & Wales*

Holland, Hezekiah (*fl.* 1638–1660), clergyman, was a native of Ireland who described himself as Anglo-Irish, and was almost certainly the Ezekias Holland who graduated BA at Trinity College, Dublin, in 1638. In a preface dated 10 July 1649 he made clear that he was new to England, 'a stranger, (a kind of a banished man) out of Ireland', explaining that 'five years ago I came out of that Kingdom into this' (Holland, *Looking Glasse*, 3, 7). It seems, then, that he had arrived in England about 1644. Following the sequestration of its vicar, Robert Smith, in March 1645, Holland was approved by parliament as the minister of Sutton Valence, Kent, and the preface cited above introduced a selection of his sermons preached there. In 1650 he published *An Exposition … of the most Choice Commentaries upon the Revelation of Saint John* (including those of St Augustine, Heinrich Bullinger, Thomas Brightman, and especially David Parens), which he had first delivered in his parish church. In Kent the General Baptists were building up a substantial following and it soon became necessary to engage in controversy with one of their most prominent Kentish leaders, George Hammon of Biddenden. For Hammon had 'gotten into great repute with those who know not how to contradict you', as his opponent admitted in the preface of his *Adam's Condition in Paradise Discovered*, signed from Sutton Valence on 3 February 1656. Since each side considered the other to be antichristian the controversy generated much acrimony. It seems from a work issued by Hammon in 1660 that Holland was still preaching at Sutton Valence in that year. After this time, however, nothing is known of him.

STEPHEN WRIGHT

Sources [J. H. Todd], ed., *A catalogue of graduates who have proceeded to degrees in the University of Dublin, from the earliest recorded commencements to … December 16, 1868* (1869) · *Walker rev.* · H. Holland, *A Christian looking glasse* (1649) [BL, E1376(2)] · H. Holland, *Adam's condition in paradise discovered* (1656)
Likenesses line engraving, 1650, BM, NPG; repro. in *Exposition of the Revelations* (1650)

Holland, Hugh (1563–1633), poet, was born in Denbigh, the younger son of Robert Holland and his wife, whose maiden name was Pain or Payne. He became a pupil of William Camden, for whom he retained a lifelong loyalty, and who numbered him with Philip Sidney, Edmund Spenser, Ben Jonson, and Michael Drayton as one of the 'most pregnant wits of these our times' (W. Camden, *Remaines*, 1614, 8). After attending Westminster School he was elected scholar of Trinity College, Cambridge, in 1589. He graduated BA in 1593–4 and MA in 1597. A Hugh Holland matriculated at Balliol College, Oxford, in March 1583. This is usually identified with the poet, although his cool references to Oxford in *A Cypress Garland* suggest that he felt little connection with that university. He retained close links with Wales, returning there for a period in 1601, probably in connection with the disturbances surrounding the Denbighshire elections in that year. While travelling through Germany and Holland in 1603 he heard news of the death of Elizabeth I. This journey, he said, fulfilled 'the desire I had but once in my life to see the world (for until then I had been always one of the Queen's deer)' (Holland, *Pancharis*, sig. D5r). Fuller reported that:

> he travailed beyond the seas and in Italy (conceiving himself without ear-reach of the English) let flie freely against the Credit of Queen Elizabeth. He went to Jerusalem, though there he was not made, or he would not own himself Knight of the Sepulchre (Fuller, *Worthies*, 16)

and that he was subsequently rebuked by Sir Thomas Glover, James I's ambassador in Constantinople, for his indiscretion. This detail dates the trip to 1606–13, the period of Glover's residence in Constantinople.

In London Holland was one of several poets and parliamentarians (including John Donne, Inigo Jones, and John Hoskyns) who met at the Mitre tavern about 1610. His ties with literary men remained strong throughout his life: Ben Jonson (whom Holland may have introduced to his near neighbour in Wales, Sir John Salusbury of Lleweni) wrote a dedicatory ode for Holland's *Pancharis* (1603), and Holland wrote dedicatory poems for Giles Farnaby's *Canzonets to Fowre Voyces* (1598), for Jonson's *Sejanus* (1605), Bolton's *Elements of Armory* (1610), *Parthenia* (1611), and Thomas Hawkins's *Odes of Horace* (1625). He also contributed mock-heroic verses to Thomas Coryate's *Odcombian Banquet* (1611) in Greek, Latin, and Welsh. In his last year he wrote Latin verses for the authorized edition of the Latin drama *Roxana* (1632), composed by his fellow student of Westminster and Trinity, William Alabaster. Fuller records that he also wrote a life of Camden, verses in description of the chief cities of Europe, and chronicles of the reign of Elizabeth.

Holland is chiefly remembered as the author of a dedicatory poem included in the First Folio of Shakespeare's plays, although his other works are of greater note. They include an elegy on the death of Henry, prince of Wales, an epitaph on Queen Elizabeth (printed in Camden's *Remaines*), *A Cypress Garland* (1625) on the death of James I, and an incomplete epic poem, *Pancharis*. This poem relates, in richly Spenserian language, and with many echoes of *Aeneid* 4, the courtship of Owen Tudor and Queen Katherine. Intended as a dynastic compliment to Elizabeth, and probably composed about 1601 (when several natives of Denbighshire sought to show their loyalty to the crown in the aftermath of the Essex rebellion), the poem was eventually printed in the summer of 1603, after the queen's death. The epistle appended to *Pancharis* promises further books which were to have recounted the martial exploits of Owen Glendower, and which would have been dedicated to Henry, prince of Wales.

Holland recorded that through the patronage of the duke of Buckingham he kissed the hand of James I three times in twenty weeks ('And with his snowy hand my lips he warmed'; *A Cypress Garland*, sig. A4r). There is no record that he ever received more material favours from the Stuarts, although Buckingham forwarded a suit of his to the king, and Holland's elegy for Prince Henry records that:

> oft, when as to Westminster I trudged
> About my fift yeers Suite (but yet unjudged)
> He [that is, Henry] cheered my heart that was full heavy.
> (*Sundry Funeral Elegies*, 1613, sig. D2v)

Fuller's claim that 'he grumbled out the rest of his life in visible discontentment' (Fuller, *Worthies*, 16) may have some truth in it: he had a lengthy legal dispute with John Reyноldes over the freehold of property in Paternoster Row and 'Ivey Lane'. This remained unresolved at his death.

Holland was a Catholic until April 1626, when he submitted to the national church after having been indicted for recusancy. He married Ursula, the widow of Robert Woodard of Burnham, Buckinghamshire. A daughter 'Phil' and a son Martin were dead by 1625; a son, Arbellin, or Arbellinus, lived to be his father's executor, and eventually, in 1638, resolved his father's legal battle with Reynoldes. Holland was made a freeman of the Mercers' Company by redemption, gratis, on 4 September 1621. Holland died intestate in London on or about 18 July 1633, presumably after a long illness, since reports of his death circulated as early as June 1632. He had suffered from gout. His son Arbellin was granted letters of administration on 31 August 1633. He was buried in Westminster Abbey in the south part of the church on 23 July 1633. No likeness survives, but his dark hair and skin (described in *Pancharis* as his distinguishing features) led Ben Jonson to describe his friend as the 'black swan'.   COLIN BURROW

Sources H. Berry, 'Some notes about Hugh Holland', *N&Q*, 209 (1964), 149–51 · D. Williams and A. S. Vaughan Thomas, *An essay on Hugh Holland* (1943) · B. Corney, 'Hugh Holland and his works', *N&Q*, 3 (1851), 427 · H. Holland, *A cypress garland: for the sacred forehead of our late soveraigne King James* (1625) · H. Holland, *Pancharis: the first booke, containing the preparation of the love betweene Owen Tudyr, and the Queene, long since intended to her maiden Majestie: and now dedicated to the invincible James* (1603) · *Brief lives, chiefly of contemporaries, set down by John Aubrey, between the years 1669 and 1696*, ed. A. Clark, 2

vols. (1898) · Fuller, *Worthies* (1662), 4.16 · Wood, *Ath. Oxon.*, new edn, 3.559 · B. Corney, 'A state paper rectified', *N&Q*, 3rd ser., 5 (1864), 5–6 · A. Shapiro, 'The Mermaid Club', *Modern Language Review*, 45 (1950), 6–17 · J. T. Curry, 'Epitaph on Queen Elizabeth', *N&Q*, 9th ser., 12 (1903), 3–4 · D. H. Bowler, ed., *London sessions record* · *DNB* · private information (2004) [D. Kathman]
Archives BL, Cotton MS Julius C. iii 15

Holland, James (1799–1870), watercolour painter, was born on 17 October 1799 in Burslem, Stoke-on-Trent, Staffordshire, the illegitimate son of Martha Holland (1777–1847). His father is believed to have been Timothy Edge (1776–1838), whom Martha Holland married in 1800, and who was employed in the Holland family pottery at Hill Top in Burslem. At the age of twelve James was taken on by John Davenport at Longport Hall as an apprentice pottery and porcelain painter, where he developed his skill in flower and bird painting. His apprenticeship was completed in the spring of 1819 and he decided to seek a career as an artist in London, while supporting himself through continued pottery painting. He found employment at one of the works in Deptford, which was at that time well outside London itself, and on 24 January 1820 he married a local girl, Elizabeth Mary Evans, at St Paul's parish church. By 1823 his circumstances had improved sufficiently to enable him to give up pottery painting, and to move to Marylebone, which was much closer to central London. A year later he moved again, this time to the St Pancras area of the city where, apart from an extended period in Greenwich, he was to spend the rest of his life.

Holland's first exhibition success came in 1824 when he had a flower painting accepted by the Royal Academy and thereafter he became a regular exhibitor both there and at the exhibitions of the Society of British Artists and the Society of Painters in Water Colours. Although his marriage was only brief—his wife died in 1828—they had three sons and two daughters; only the daughters survived into adulthood. In 1831 he travelled abroad for the first time, to Paris with fellow artist John Scarlett Davis, and in 1835 made the first of many trips to Venice, a city that he painted extensively, especially in watercolour. This work largely established his reputation. That same year, he was elected to the Society of Painters in Water Colours. About this time he met Charlotte Martha Morrant (1817–1909), with whom he had a relationship for the rest of his life, fathering a son who died in infancy and two daughters both of whom survived him. In 1837 he was commissioned by the *Landscape Annual* to travel to Portugal and produce illustrations for their forthcoming traveller's guide to that country. Many other overseas painting trips took him as far afield as Egypt, in addition to which he travelled and painted extensively throughout mainland Britain.

In 1842 Holland resigned from the Society of Painters in Water Colours to concentrate his efforts on gaining election to the Royal Academy which, curiously, he never achieved; he rejoined the society in 1856. His last continental painting trip was again to Venice in 1865 and thereafter he mainly worked only from his studio. He last had works accepted for exhibition at the society's winter exhibition in Pall Mall, London, in February 1870. He died on 13 February 1870 in his house, 8 Osnaburgh Street, St Pancras, of cirrhosis of the liver and exhaustion, and was buried in the family grave at Highgate cemetery, Middlesex. Well over two hundred of his works were exhibited during his lifetime, and several hundred were still in his studio when he died. Although best known as a watercolourist, he was equally talented in oils and is generally regarded as one of the finest artists of the English school, both a contemporary and an equal of the likes of R. P. Bonington and W. H. Hunt. His works can be found in most of the major collections in Great Britain, and many abroad, with particularly fine examples in the Victoria and Albert Museum, London; the City Art Gallery and Museum, Stoke-on-Trent; and the Huntington Library, San Marino, California.   STEVE J. BOND

Sources *Art Journal*, 32 (April 1870) · M. Tonkin, 'James Holland, 1799–1870', *Royal Watercolour Society Journal*, 42 (1967) · H. Stokes, 'James Holland', *Walker's Quarterly* [whole issue], 23 (1927) · J. L. Roget, *A history of the 'Old Water-Colour' Society*, 2 vols. (1891) · will, PRO · census returns · parish register (births), Burslem, 17/10/1799 · d. cert. · Graves, *RA exhibitors* · parish register, London, St Pancras, LMA · parish register, Greenwich, St Alfege, LMA
Archives Bankside Gallery, London, Royal Watercolour Society, corresp.
Likenesses W. Hunt, portrait, V&A · photograph, priv. coll.
Wealth at death under £6000: resworn probate, Nov 1870, *CGPLA Eng. & Wales*

Holland, John, first earl of Huntingdon and duke of Exeter (*c*.1352–1400), magnate and soldier, was the second son of Thomas *Holland, earl of Kent (*c*.1315–1360), and *Joan (*d*. 1385), daughter of *Edmund of Woodstock, earl of Kent. Holland became one of the premier nobles in the kingdom, one of the principal props of Richard II's regime in its later years, and a military figure of some renown with a considerable territorial base in the south-west. He had an elder brother, Thomas *Holland, earl of Kent (*d*. 1397), and two sisters, Maud (*d*. 1392), wife to Sir Hugh Courtenay and then Waleran, count of St Pol, and Joan (*d*. 1384), wife of Jean, duke of Brittany. Perhaps most significantly, Holland was half-brother of *Richard II, the son of Joan and Edward, the Black Prince, whom Joan married in 1361 after the death of Thomas Holland.

Although John Holland's precise date of birth is unknown, it was after 1350, and he was probably his father's youngest child. His stepfather, the Black Prince, assigned his yeoman John de la Haye to be Holland's guardian and he received royal household livery from 1371. He first came to prominence in 1378, shortly after his half-brother Richard's accession as king. Then he was awarded an annuity of £100 from the exchequer, served on John of Gaunt's abortive siege of St Malo in Brittany, and received his first grant of estates, the manors of Ardington and Philberds Court at East Hanney in Berkshire, to replace his annuity. He was given the Marensin lordship in Gascony in 1380. The award of the wardship of Rhys ap Gruffudd's estates, mainly in Staffordshire, Northwich in Cheshire, and Hope and Hopedale lordship in Flintshire, was extended by his first administrative appointment as justice of Cheshire for life on 6 May 1381.

In 1381 he was also made a knight of the Garter. A proposal to send him to Ireland as lieutenant in August 1382 was not carried out.

Holland came increasingly under the influence of John of Gaunt, duke of Lancaster, going on embassies with him to Calais in 1383 and again in 1384 when he was made a banneret. The Salisbury parliament in May 1384 witnessed the first indication of John Holland's violent temper. A friar who accused Gaunt of conspiring to kill the king was horribly murdered by Holland, and others, *propter amorem ducis* ('for love of the duke') according to the chronicler Walsingham. The fuller account of the monk of Westminster has Holland acting as a member of a household clique. Whatever his motive, this was his first real involvement in the politics of Richard II's court.

The grant in December 1384 of the reversion on their deaths of thirteen manors of Sir James Audley in Somerset, Devon, and Cornwall, and two manors of Sir Nigel Loryng in Devon provided Holland with the first properties in his later extensive south-western patrimony. He then joined Richard II's expedition to Scotland in July 1385. It had only reached York when in a brawl one of Holland's esquires was killed by an archer of the retinue of Ralph, son and heir to the earl of Stafford. Seeking the perpetrator, Holland happened upon Ralph Stafford and slew him without having ascertained properly who he was. He fled to claim sanctuary at Beverley Minster and was disgraced, losing many of his earlier awards. After suitably abject apologies he was pardoned in February 1386, at Gaunt's request according to the chronicler Knighton, and on condition that he establish three chaplains to pray for Ralph's soul.

Holland, still under a cloud at court, was now very much under Gaunt's aegis, and became constable of the army which Gaunt took to Spain in 1386 to win the crown of Castile. On 24 June of that year, near Plymouth, Holland married Gaunt's second daughter, Elizabeth [*see* Elizabeth of Lancaster (1364?–1425)], whom he had made pregnant while she was still married to the earl of Pembroke. The full importance of this marriage would only become apparent in 1471 when, on Henry VI's death, Holland's grandson, Henry, became the Lancastrian claimant to the throne. Gaunt's Spanish campaign was inconclusive, for which Holland as constable must take some blame. He featured extensively in the diplomatic engagements and his prowess in the jousts was lauded by the chronicler Froissart. He abandoned the army and returned by April 1388 to England, where he was wooed at court by Richard's appellant opponents, possibly in an attempt to gain, through Holland, Gaunt's support.

Holland was created earl of Huntingdon on 2 June 1388 with estates and revenues, mainly in the south-west and Suffolk, giving him an income of 2000 marks p.a. This was augmented by a number of grants of duchy of Cornwall estates, such as Berkhamsted Castle on 8 October 1388, Tintagel Castle on 6 January 1389, and Trematon Castle and manor in 1392. He used Berkhamsted Castle as a base but he then also built himself a considerable residence at Dartington Hall in Devon. Although regarded by Edward Courtenay, earl of Devon, as an intrusion into his area of authority, Holland's influence in the south-west grew further when he was made admiral of the west on 18 May 1389, and initiated a characteristically aggressive administration. On 1 June 1389 he was made captain of the Breton port of Brest, an English outpost requiring the leadership of an experienced, self-sufficient figure.

In addition to such military duties Holland was appointed chief chamberlain of England on 31 May 1390, a move prompted by Richard's increasing desire to build his own group of royal kin and supporters. This life award was augmented into a grant to him and the heirs male of his body on 2 February 1398. The post reflected Holland's chivalric renown, recorded and lauded by Froissart in tournaments at Calais in May and Smithfield in October 1390, and involved him in a number of ambitious foreign projects. He made preparations for a journey to Jerusalem and possibly Hungary in 1394, but joined the Irish expedition of 1395 late. He recruited troops for a projected expedition to Florence in 1397, when he was also appointed gonfalonier of the Roman church and captain-general of the papal troops on 1 March 1397, with the aim of ridding Italy of schismatics.

Despite the fact that Holland held an annuity of 200 marks from duchy of Lancaster estates in Norfolk by March 1391, his earlier ties with Gaunt seem to have cooled in the 1390s. One cause may have been the involvement of one of Holland's men, Sir Nicholas Clifton, in an anti-Gaunt rising in Cheshire in 1393; Holland also clashed with Gaunt over rival marital plans involving the duke of Brittany's children. Although Holland was Gaunt's son-in-law, he does not feature in Gaunt's will of 1398. By contrast, he was increasingly identified with the royal court. During the 1390s Richard handed to him a life interest in much of his duchy of Cornwall inheritance. The king further entrusted him with a series of castles to add to his south-western holdings: Rockingham on 19 April 1391, Horeston on 29 September 1391, Haverfordwest on 10 January 1392, and Conwy on 3 September 1394. After serving in Ireland on Richard's first expedition there in March and April 1395, Holland was appointed by Richard warden of the western march towards Scotland and custodian of Carlisle on 16 February 1397, as part of his policy of loosening the grip on that office of the Nevilles and Percys. His military exploits also encouraged Philippe de Mézières to enlist Holland's support as a patron for his order of the Passion and to present him with an abridgement of the order's rule, now Oxford, Bodleian, MS Ashmole 813. His violent intemperance and physical rashness were characteristics not then despised by contemporaries.

With his nephew Thomas, the new earl of Kent on his father's death in 1397, Holland was very firmly a supporter of Richard II in his actions to remove the appellants in his coup of 1397. In the absence of children of his own, Richard used his Holland relatives to bind his noble supporters closer to his cause and bring them within the royal kin. Holland's elder daughter, Constance, had been betrothed in 1391 to Thomas (II) Mowbray, the heir of one of

Richard's supporters, and his other daughter was married to Richard de Vere, the heir of the earl of Oxford, Holland's predecessor as king's chamberlain. The marriages of his nieces into the Mortimer, York, Beaufort, Montague, and Neville families, and of his nephew Thomas to a Stafford, all helped to tie these families closer to the king.

In July 1397 Richard II struck against the lords appellant of 1388. After dining with Holland in London, the king rode with him to Pleshey Castle to arrest the king's uncle, the duke of Gloucester. The earls of Arundel and Warwick were similarly seized. All their estates were forfeited. Holland was rewarded with the southern lordships of the earl of Arundel, including Arundel Castle, on 3 August 1397 and he was promoted duke of Exeter on 29 September. Thomas (I) Mowbray's banishment in 1398 brought Holland further southern Arundel estates, previously awarded to Mowbray, in Lewes Castle on 23 September 1398 and Reigate Castle on 15 January 1399. He was also established in south Wales with the wardship of the Mortimer estates there on the death of the earl of March in July 1398 and custody of Gaunt's powerful south Wales holdings on the death of his former mentor in February 1399.

Holland continued to help defend the peripheries of the kingdom, being appointed captain of Calais on 24 February 1398. He left Calais to serve on Richard's second Irish expedition in May 1399. On the news of Bolingbroke's landing in England, Holland accompanied Richard on his hasty journey to Pembroke in July and then on to Conwy Castle. Sent by Richard to negotiate with Bolingbroke, Holland was imprisoned in Chester, and Richard soon followed him into captivity. He was probably moved with Richard to London in September 1399, though he may have been at large to see to the birth of his youngest son, Edward, around this time, and his administration was still active in September.

Holland attended the parliament in October 1399 that formalized Richard's deposition. He denounced Richard's actions and assisted in Henry IV's coronation. He was then imprisoned in Hertford on 20 October, before being tried with fellow members of the previous regime on 3 November and stripped of all his gains since July 1397, so reverting to the status of earl of Huntingdon. Given the short time he had held these gains Holland's benefits from them had not been great, but the awards he had received before 1397 now also came under threat. He suffered from Richard's policy of passing on estates where the title was by no means absolute: his tenure had been secure while the king supported him, but now a number of rivals revived their claims to these lands. On 22 December Holland lost his Cornish duchy of Cornwall estates to the new prince of Wales. The abbey of St Mary Graces disputed his Devon lands and a claimant had seized from him Barford St Martin, a Wiltshire manor, in August. Other former supporters of Richard II, such as Holland's nephew Thomas, also saw their positions eroded after 3 November, with the result that a plot was hatched in the last days of 1399 to remove the new Henry IV.

The conspirators met at Kingston in Surrey on 4 January,

with the intention of surprising Henry at a tournament at Windsor. Henry had been forewarned and left Windsor for London. The rebels fled west to Cirencester where the earls of Kent and Salisbury were killed on 8 January. Holland had been waiting meantime to seize London on the news of success at Windsor. He escaped east on 6 January, but contrary winds drove his ship ashore in Essex. He received shelter at the de Vere castle of Hadleigh but was arrested at Prittlewell and imprisoned by the king's mother-in-law, the countess of Hereford, at Pleshey, Essex. In the presence of the new Fitzalan earl of Arundel, he was executed there by popular demand on 9 or 10 January. His head was displayed on London Bridge until it was buried with his body in the collegiate church at Pleshey in February 1400.

Holland left five children: Richard (d. 1400); John *Holland, earl of Huntingdon and duke of Exeter (1395–1447); Edward, count of Mortain (d. 1418); Constance (d. 1437), who married Thomas (II) Mowbray, earl of Nottingham, and then John Grey of Ruthin; and a daughter, name unknown, who married Richard de Vere, earl of Oxford. His widow, Elizabeth, married John Cornwall, later Lord Fanhope (d. 1443). She died on 24 November 1425 and was buried at Burford, Shropshire.   M. M. N. STANSFIELD

Sources M. M. N. Stansfield, 'The Holland family, dukes of Exeter, earls of Kent and Huntingdon, 1352–1475', DPhil diss., U. Oxf., 1987 · Chancery records · PRO, E 101, E 403, E 401, E 364, C 61, C 71, C 81, C 76, C 56, KB 27, KB 9, DL 29, E 159 · N. Saul, Richard II (1997) · Œuvres de Froissart: chroniques, ed. K. de Lettenhove, 25 vols. (Brussels, 1867–77) · Thomae Walsingham, quondam monachi S. Albani, historia Anglicana, ed. H. T. Riley, 2 vols., pt 1 of Chronica monasterii S. Albani, Rolls Series, 28 (1863–4) · B. Williams, ed., Chronicque de la traïson et mort de Richart Deux, roy Dengleterre, EHS, 9 (1846) · Polychronicon Ranulphi Higden monachi Cestrensis, ed. C. Babington and J. R. Lumby, 9 vols., Rolls Series, 41 (1865–86), vols. 8–9 · Chronicon Henrici Knighton, vel Cnitthon, monachi Leycestrensis, ed. J. R. Lumby, 2 vols., Rolls Series, 92 (1889–95) · 'Annales Ricardi secundi et Henrici quarti, regum Angliae', Johannis de Trokelowe et Henrici de Blaneforde … chronica et annales, ed. H. T. Riley, pt 3 of Chronica monasterii S. Albani, Rolls Series, 28 (1866), 155–420 · A. Roges, 'Henry IV and the revolt of the earls, 1400', History Today, 18 (1968), 277–83 · [J. Creton], 'Translation of a French metrical history of the deposition of King Richard the Second … with a copy of the original', ed. and trans. J. Webb, Archaeologia, 20 (1824), 1–423 · M. D. Legge, ed., Anglo-Norman letters and petitions from All Souls MS 182, Anglo-Norman Texts, 3 (1941) · M. Jones, Ducal Brittany, 1364–1399 (1970)
Likenesses manuscript, 1400–40 (with the duke of Surrey), BL, Harley MS 1319, fol. 25 · manuscript, BL, Harley MS 1319, fol. 30b
Wealth at death had £301 11s. 4d. of goods in flight from Essex (Jan 1400): PRO, E 101/355/7 · £2096 16s. 6d. of valuables used to pay off debts (Sept 1399): PRO, E 159/176, 177 · lands and annuities to value of 2000 marks as Earl of Huntingdon (1388)

Holland [Holand], **John, first duke of Exeter** (1395–1447), soldier and magnate, was born on 29 March 1395, at Dartington, Devon, the second son (his elder brother died in 1400) of John *Holland, duke of Exeter (c.1352–1400), who was Richard II's half-brother, and Elizabeth of Lancaster (d. 1425), Henry IV's sister. His father was executed and attainted for plotting against Henry IV. The younger John was brought up by his mother and her second husband (whom she married in 1400), Sir John *Cornwall (d. 1443), a dashing knight who served Prince Henry; in 1407 the king gave Cornewall 100 marks a year for the boy's maintenance. Holland was knighted in April 1413, on the eve of Henry V's coronation, and the new king appreciated his military potential, for he was 'brave and high spirited though young' (*Gesta Henrici quinti*, 46–7). He spent a lifetime in the French war, but captivity in France between 1421 and 1426 and the Lancastrians' unwillingness to endow him with substantial estates prejudiced his financial security.

Just before Henry V's departure for France in 1415, Holland sat on the tribunal that condemned the 'Southampton' plotters, including his own kinsman, Richard, earl of Cambridge. He accompanied the king to Normandy and, with his stepfather, led a force to reconnoitre Harfleur; at Agincourt on 25 October he was distinguished for his valour. He was elected to the Order of the Garter in May 1416, and in July became commander of the fleet to relieve Harfleur and patrol the seas. Holland had begun to style himself earl of Huntingdon, his father's title, earlier in 1416, and formal restoration came in parliament in October; yet he did not receive his father's dukedom of Exeter, which was pointedly granted to the king's uncle, Thomas Beaufort. Livery of his inheritance in the following March included only entailed estates. As a result, he did not enjoy his father's close links with Devon, and his resources were an inadequate foundation for his military career.

While commanding the fleet (ironically under Exeter as admiral), on 29 June 1417 Huntingdon captured Genoese ships, prisoners, and treasure, in an engagement off the Caux peninsula that was admired by contemporary chroniclers. This heralded Henry V's invasion of Normandy in which Huntingdon took the castle of Touques and besieged Caen; in the spring of 1418 he seized Coutances, Avranches, and other fortresses. He rejoined Henry V at the siege of Rouen (1418–19), where his brother, Edward Holland, was killed. He was accomplished alike in the field (as at Fresnay in March 1420) and at sieges, and his stepfather was usually at his side. Henry V rewarded him, notably in 1418 with the lordship of Bricqueville-sur-Mer, which he had subdued; in 1419 he was appointed captain of Gournay and Pontoise, and when Melun fell in November 1420 he became its governor. Following the treaty of Troyes (21 May 1420), Henry V made him constable of the Tower of London for life, with an annuity of £100 (20 August). Huntingdon entered Paris on 1 December with the two royal families: he was appointed captain of Vincennes and custodian of the infirm Charles VI.

Within months Huntingdon's fortunes had collapsed. He was captured at the battle of Baugé on 22 March 1421 and found himself the prisoner of a Scot, Sir John Sibbald; he spent five years in captivity in Anjou. Raising a ransom was his daunting priority: he was not well endowed with estates and parliament was told in 1424 that he was owed £10,500 from Henry V's day. His stepfather eventually negotiated, in 1425, an exchange with the count of Vendôme (captured at Agincourt and in Sir John Cornewall's hands), and Huntingdon returned to England by the beginning of 1426. He later claimed that his captivity cost him 20,000 marks.

Huntingdon's priorities on his return were to repair his fortunes; he also became a king's councillor in March 1426 and an ally of Humphrey, duke of Gloucester. In seeking a wife, a dowager would be more immediately profitable than a young heiress: by 15 July 1427 he had married Anne, daughter of Edmund Stafford, earl of Stafford, and widow of Edmund (V) Mortimer, earl of March (d. 1425), though he was fined 1200 marks for doing so without licence. After his mother's death in 1425 he inherited much of her property, and the king granted him the Norman county of Ivry in 1427. His place in noble society was less comfortable, for he may have quarrelled with the duke of Norfolk in 1428, and with his own brother-in-law, the earl of Stafford, when both came armed to parliament in 1429; he was one of several nobles requested to leave their large retinues at home when attending the parliament of 1430.

When Henry VI visited France in April 1430, Huntingdon accompanied him: he joined the duke of Burgundy at the siege of Compiègne but withdrew through lack of funds, and then, as captain of Gournay and Gisors, supported Bedford. At Paris he witnessed Henry's crowning as king of France in December 1431. During his absence from England, his son Henry *Holland was born in June 1430, but in September 1432 Anne Stafford died. Huntingdon quickly sought a new wife, and it is not surprising that he chose another dowager: in January 1433, on payment of 200 marks, he married Beatrice, illegitimate daughter of João I, king of Portugal and widow of Thomas Fitzalan, earl of Arundel (d. 1415).

With his affairs in fair order, Huntingdon resumed his military career, though it required 1300 marks in recognition of past services to persuade him to go to France in 1433; he displayed his usual flair and relieved Montargis. At the discussions with France and Burgundy at Arras in the summer of 1435, Huntingdon was an English envoy—a noble of repute and royal lineage rather than an experienced diplomat. A licence to take with him household goods worth £6000 reflected lavish tastes, which are confirmed by his will and an inventory of his possessions made after his death (Westminster Abbey muniments, 6643). Just before leaving for Arras, in July 1435 he and the earl of Northumberland were jointly appointed wardens of the east and west marches towards Scotland after the earl of Salisbury resigned as western warden. On his return he received the office of admiral of England on 2 October, and so helped to defend Calais against the Burgundians in August 1436.

After Henry VI came of age (1436–7), Huntingdon, like Gloucester, was eased out of the king's counsels, though his other services were still valued. In March 1439 he was appointed the king's lieutenant in Aquitaine for six years; £1000 was paid to him personally before he would sail for Bordeaux, accompanied by his wife, in August. He did not stay long, possibly because of inadequate resources: his own situation worsened after Beatrice's death at Bordeaux on 23 October 1439, although he was granted the wine-producing lordship of Lesparre in February 1440. After returning to England in December 1440 he sought an annual allowance, and in July 1441 was given 500 marks per annum in tail male to compensate for losses in France. At the same time, he was caught up in the Gloucester–Beaufort feud, perhaps as a king's councillor once again, and he sat in judgment on the duchess of Gloucester when she was charged with sorcery. His abilities in defence of the realm continued to be acknowledged: in November 1441 he received custody of Southampton Castle for life. He also found yet another wife, Anne Montagu (d. 1457), daughter of the earl of Salisbury and twice widowed. The king's grant of the royal manor of Berkhamsted, Hertfordshire, for life in December 1443 may have signalled Henry VI's affection for one of his closest male relatives and reliable commanders; it certainly brought him closer to the court, and on 6 January 1444 John Holland was created duke of Exeter, with precedence next to the duke of York. In 1445 he arranged that his son Henry should marry York's daughter, Anne, and York was prepared to offer a large dowry. The new duke's health may have been failing by 1446, for in February he associated his son with him as admiral, and then, a year later, as constable of the Tower. Exeter died on 5 August 1447 and was buried at St Katharine by the Tower, alongside his first wife and his sister Constance (d. 1437), the countess marshal.

John Holland's finances were precarious: his taxable income in 1436 was almost the lowest among the earls (a little over £1000 per annum). Three widows' dower estates were welcome, but they were hardly the basis for a sustained landed interest, and he never identified closely with the west country. His military reputation was high, despite his capture, and his royal blood was increasingly valued by Henry VI; but his political influence at court seems to have been modest.   R. A. GRIFFITHS

Sources Chancery, inquisitions post mortem, PRO, C138/21, no. 50 · *Chancery records* · Exchequer records, issue and receipt rolls, PRO, E403, 401 · GEC, *Peerage*, new edn, 5.208–11 · M. M. N. Stansfield, 'The Holland family, dukes of Exeter, earls of Kent and Huntingdon, 1352–1475', DPhil diss., U. Oxf., 1987 · M. Stansfield, 'John Holland, duke of Exeter and earl of Huntingdon (d. 1447) and the costs of the Hundred Years' War', *Profit, piety and the professions in later medieval England*, ed. M. Hicks (1990), 103–18 · Council records, council and privy seal, PRO, E28 · F. Taylor and J. S. Roskell, eds. and trans., *Gesta Henrici quinti / The deeds of Henry the Fifth*, OMT (1975) · C. L. Kingsford, ed., *The first English life of King Henry the Fifth* (1911) · [J. Nichols], ed., *A collection of … wills … of … every branch of the blood royal* (1780) · A. H. Thomas and P. E. Jones, eds., *Calendar of plea and memoranda rolls preserved among the archives of the corporation of the City of London at the Guildhall*, 4 (1943), 182–7 · J. Stevenson, ed., *Letters and papers illustrative of the wars of the English in France during the reign of Henry VI, king of England*, 2 vols. in 3 pts, Rolls Series, 22 (1861–4) · M. G. A. Vale, *English Gascony, 1399–1453: a study of war, government and politics during the later stages of the Hundred Years' War* (1970) · T. Twiss, ed., *Monumenta juridica: the Black Book of the admiralty*, 1, Rolls Series, 55 (1871), 246–75 · Westminster Abbey muniments, 6643 · T. B. Pugh and C. D. Ross, 'The English baronage and the income tax of 1436', *BIHR*, 26 (1953), 1–28

Wealth at death at least £1002 from land in 1436: Pugh and Ross, 'English baronage'

Holland, Sir John, first baronet (1603–1701), politician, was born in October 1603 in Ashwellthorpe, Norfolk, and baptized there the following November, the first son of Sir Thomas Holland (d. 1626) of Quidenham in the same county, and his first wife, Mary, daughter of Sir Thomas

Knyvett of Ashwellthorpe. He matriculated from Christ's College, Cambridge, in 1620, and went on to enter the Middle Temple in 1623. In 1629 he was created a baronet without fee. On 3 August the following year he married Alathea (d. 1679), widow of William Sandys, fourth Baron Sandys, and daughter of John Panton of Bryncunallt, Denbighshire. The couple had six sons and five daughters.

Holland was elected knight of the shire for Norfolk in the spring of 1640, his father having held the seat in 1624. He claimed later that he did not seek re-election for the county in the autumn because he wanted to avoid damaging 'sidings and faction' (Keeler, *Long Parliament*, 219). His fears may have arisen in consequence of doubts about the sincerity of his professed protestantism, largely informed by his marriage to a Catholic heiress, and perhaps also by his family's ancient association with the Howard family. He had been agent to the earl of Arundel for a number of years. When the Long Parliament met, Holland sat for Castle Rising in Norfolk, the earl's pocket borough. On 9 November he made a speech in which he decried the extension of the prerogative and the resurgence of the Catholic priesthood, as well as other grievances. However, a fortnight later he was put to publicly disavowing any sympathy for Catholicism on account of his wife's beliefs and practice. Holland sought vigorously for peace from the outset of the civil wars, attempting to arrange a neutrality pact in Norfolk. He came under fire in the Commons for his reluctance to take his share of responsibility for the sequestration of delinquents. He was a commissioner for the treaty at Oxford in 1643. When the talks failed, he withdrew to the Netherlands, where he joined the rest of his family, and did not return to Westminster until December 1645.

A parliamentary commissioner resident with the king at Holdenby in 1647, Holland long continued to believe and fervently to hope that Charles I 'was a prince under whose government we may yet be happy' (*DNB*). He was out of the country at the time of the purge of the Commons in December 1648 and absented himself from English politics until the readmission of the secluded members in 1660, whereupon he was elected to the council of state. He sought and obtained election to the convention for Castle Rising in 1660, and was considered a friend to the presbyterian interest by Lord Wharton. Returned to the Cavalier Parliament, this time for the Howard seat of Aldeburgh, he spoke against the revival of the temporal authority of episcopacy, and in favour of omitting a clause from the Act of Uniformity condemning the solemn league and covenant. Thereafter he periodically got himself a name as one who consistently opposed court interests, especially when they impinged on the taxpayers of Norfolk. However, he did oppose the bill prohibiting the import of Irish cattle, which would have curtailed one of the principal sources of his own income, derived from the fattening of such cattle for the London market. His opposition to the indulgence of nonconformity also waxed and waned somewhat. But his country sympathies were normally sufficiently to the fore to put Holland on successive ministries' lists of members worth cultivating. He spoke powerfully, and much to the distaste of the court, on the cost of government and the stop of the exchequer in October 1675. In a heavy-handed attempt to warn him off from making such overt criticism, court interests let it be known that William Ashburnham had claimed to remember hearing the same speech delivered by Holland in the Long Parliament. Eventually Holland was silenced by a £200 annual pension awarded to his son for the term of his father's life. 'He never addressed the House again' (Helms and Watson, 559).

In 1679 Holland declined to stand for Norfolk as a country candidate, on account, so it was said, of his wife's ill health; Lady Holland died in May that year. Along with the whig Sir Henry Hobart, Holland unsuccessfully opposed the court candidates for the county seats at the poll in 1685. Among those 'closeted' with James II in 1688, he told the duke of Norfolk that if he was elected to the next parliament:

> he could not (as his present judgment is) be for taking away the Penal Laws and the Tests, nor can contribute to the election of such as should; but he will live friendly with all persuasions as subjects of the same prince, and believes it to be his duty as a good Christian so to do. (Helms and Watson, 560)

He subsequently refused to serve on the newly modelled county bench, accepted the Williamite coup, and continued to act as a JP in the early 1690s. He died on 19 January 1701, the last surviving member of the Long Parliament, and was buried at Quidenham. He was survived by three sons and his five daughters.   SEAN KELSEY

Sources DNB · GEC, Baronetage, 2.74 · Keeler, Long Parliament · M. W. Helms and P. Watson, 'Holland, Sir John', HoP, Commons, 1660–90, 2.556–60 · Venn, Alum. Cant. · H. A. C. Sturgess, ed., Register of admissions to the Honourable Society of the Middle Temple, from the fifteenth century to the year 1944, 1 (1949), 114 · JHC, 2 (1640–42), 35 · will, PRO, PROB 11/481, fols. 71–3 · C. Robbins, 'Sir John Holland (1603–1701) in the convention of 1660', BIHR, 29 (1956), 244–52 · C. Robbins, 'Five speeches, 1661–3, by Sir John Holland, MP', BIHR, 28 (1955), 189–202 · C. Robbins, 'Election correspondence of Sir John Holland of Quidenham, 1661', Norfolk Archaeology, 30/2 (1947–52), 130–39 · The diary of John Milward, Esq., ed. C. Robbins (1938), appx 1 · Report on the manuscripts of the family of Gawdy, formerly of Norfolk, HMC, 11 (1885)

Archives Bodl. Oxf., papers, Tanner MSS 239, 321 | BL, Add. MSS · BL, Harley MSS · BL, Lansdowne MSS, Sloane MSS, and Stowe MSS · BL, letters to F. Gawdy, W. Gawdy, and O. Le Neve, Egerton MSS 2716–2718, passim

Wealth at death made major bequests totalling £8500, as well as many minor bequests worth several hundred pounds, all devised on extensive Norfolk real estate: will, PRO, PROB 11/481, fols. 71–3

Holland [Holand], **John** (1658–1721), merchant and banker, was born in the Bridewell precinct of the City of London, the elder son of Captain Philip Holland, a professional sailor whose family originated from Colchester, Essex, and who was captain, in the Cromwellian navy, of the *Assurance*, flagship of the earl of Sandwich's Baltic fleet in 1659. Philip Holland obtained a pardon under the terms of the declaration of Breda and initially retained his command. He remained a nonconformist and although appointed to the fireship *Loyal Merchant* in 1665, he deserted and joined the Dutch during the Medway raid in 1667. The family remained in England, and Philip Holland

was arrested but pardoned in 1672 in return for information about Dutch intentions during the Third Anglo-Dutch War.

John Holland was apprenticed to a London mercer in 1673, and there is evidence that in the mid-1670s he spent time in the Netherlands learning Dutch bookkeeping and accounting methods. In 1676 he was appointed clerk assistant to Francis Beyer, appointed auditor-general of the East India Company in 1675. The next twelve years were spent as a successful merchant, which cannot be explained by his salary of £40 a year as accountant for cotton imports in the company. A best guess is that he took shares in major voyages. In 1687 he married Jane Fowke (c.1669–1740), the only daughter of the second marriage of Walter Fowke MD, of Brewood Hall and Little Wyrley, Staffordshire. Brewood Hall became their principal home, and this was where their three surviving children, Richard Holland [see below], Jane (b. 1690), and Fowke (b. 1700), were brought up. After 1688 he became the friend and associate of a group of London-based Scottish merchants led by David Nairn, James Campbell, and Thomas Coutts, whose prime business was the supply of clothing and victuals for the newly raised Scottish regiments. After Francis Beyer's dismissal from the East India Company in 1692, he seems to have gone into semi-retirement, but in 1693 he was involved in a venture with the same group of Scots to introduce baize cloth into Scotland, a joint-stock project approved by the Scottish parliament.

Together with other London Scots John Holland secured the necessary political backing in Scotland in 1695 to obtain an act of parliament setting up a bank in Scotland under the name of the Governor and Company of the Bank of Scotland. It was founded on joint-stock principles, with limited liability for shareholders and a nominal capital of £100,000 sterling of which the initial trading capital was £10,000. It was also given a monopoly over banking in Scotland for a period of twenty-one years. Holland was appointed first governor, and it opened for business in February 1696. From the beginning there were problems. A few months earlier the Scottish Company had been set up in direct opposition to the East India Company as a general trading and banking company with a paid-up capital of £400,000 sterling. It moved into banking operations in Edinburgh and during the summer of 1696 nearly caused the collapse of the fledgeling bank. Holland's guidance, sagacity, and experience were vital ingredients in survival. It was in this context that he wrote and published the pamphlet *A short discourse on the present temper of the nation with respect to the India and Africa Company, and of the Bank of Scotland; also of Mr. Patterson's pretended fund of credit* (1696). At the general meeting in 1697 he stood down for two reasons: first, he was too closely associated with the East India Company; and second, the bank needed overt political protection in Scotland. This it found in the third earl of Leven, a professional soldier and governor of Edinburgh Castle. Thereafter Holland retired to Staffordshire, but in his writings and background advice helped to steer the bank through the difficulties of the next twenty years. In recognition of his many services the bank directors presented him with a silver cistern, which is mentioned in his will as a family heirloom (will, PRO, PROB 11/585/96).

Holland died at Brewood Hall, Brewood, Staffordshire, on 30 November 1721 and was interred in the Fowke family vault in the parish church at Brewood. His will was proved on 4 May 1722. Jane, his wife, died on 24 December 1740, having been predeceased by all her children.

His son **Richard Holland** (1688–1730), medical writer, was born in London and educated at St Catharine's College, Cambridge, where he graduated BA in 1709, MA in 1712, and MD in 1723. He and his father drew up a scheme for the establishment of a bank in Ireland similar to that in Scotland, but the scheme was not taken up. Holland inherited an estate in Ashdown Forest, Sussex. He was admitted as a candidate of the College of Physicians on 25 June 1724, a fellow on 25 June 1725, and was censor in 1728. He was elected a fellow of the Royal Society on 30 November 1726. He wrote *Observations on the Small Pox, or, An Essay to Discover a More Effectual Method of Cure* (1728), to which John Chandler wrote an anonymous reply in 1729. Holland died, unmarried, at Shrewsbury, Shropshire, on 29 October 1730. ALAN CAMERON

Sources will or R. Holland, PRO, PROB 11/64, sig. 333 · will, PRO, PROB 11/585, sig. 96 · R. Saville, *Bank of Scotland: a history, 1695–1995* (1996) · B. Capp, *Cromwell's navy: the fleet and the English revolution, 1648–1660* (1989) · Pepys, *Diary* · *The writings of William Paterson*, ed. S. Bannister, 2nd edn, 3 vols. (1859); repr. (1968) · W. Ferguson, *Scotland: 1689 to the present* (1968) · *APS*, 1689–1695 · S. G. Checkland, *Scottish banking: a history, 1695–1973* (1975) · J. Clapham, *The Bank of England: a history*, 2 vols. (1944) · J. H. Burton, ed., *The Darien papers*, Bannatyne Club, 90 (1849) · S. T. Jannsen, *A discourse concerning banks* (1697) · *CSP dom.*, 1652–72 · Venn, *Alum. Cant.* [Richard Holland] · Munk, *Roll* [Richard Holland] · T. Thomson, *History of the Royal Society from its institution to the end of the eighteenth century* (1812) [Richard Holland] · tombstone, parish church, Brewood, Staffordshire · *DNB* [R. Holland]
Archives Bank of Scotland, Edinburgh, archives department, minutes and papers · NA Scot., privy council registers and MSS | Coutts & Co., archive, letter book of John Campbell · NL Scot., Fletcher of Saltoun MSS
Wealth at death see will, PRO, PROB 11/585 sig. 96

Holland, John (1766–1826), Unitarian minister, was born in Manchester, the second son (and second child of four) of Thomas Holland and his wife and cousin, Anne Holland; the parents ran a boarding- and day school for girls. He entered Daventry Academy in 1783, and succeeded his uncle Philip *Holland as minister at Bank Street Chapel, Bolton, in 1789, though some in the congregation would have preferred a less outspoken Unitarian. Holland threw himself energetically into congregational affairs. He recommended the formation of a Sunday school on the plan of Robert Raikes, successfully repeating the first such effort in Bolton by the Methodists, and established a vestry library, prefixing 'Directions for a course of reading' to the printed catalogue. He also founded a short-lived periodical, the *Christian Miscellany* (1792).

Like many of his contemporaries he was a follower of Joseph Priestley. In *An Address to the Members of the Establishment in the Town and Neighbourhood of Bolton*, printed anonymously in 1790, he used Priestley's arguments to plead for repeal of the Test and Corporation Acts, an initiative then before parliament but with little hope of success. In 1791 he and several fellow ministers published *Letters to the Inhabitants of Wigan*, one of the earliest concerted defences of Unitarianism. Surviving doctrinal sermons hew to the Priestleyan line, emphasizing the humanity of Christ, the rejection of propitiatory atonement, the progress of humankind under a beneficent God, and the importance of avowing truth, but without distinction of either mind or rhetoric. Despite his evident seriousness and piety some in the congregation later criticized his preaching as 'abstruse and uninteresting', with insufficient attention to practical morality.

Philip Holland had run a well-known boarding-school; John Holland ran a co-educational day school, and published many teaching aids—on the Bible, geography, and history, among other subjects. The format was set in *Exercises for the Memory and Understanding* (1798), published jointly with his elder brother, Thomas, who had become a schoolmaster after blindness cut short a promising mercantile career. If the strategy of these publications brings to mind the insufferable Bitzer in M'Choakumchild's schoolroom, it is worth noting that the 'interrogative method' which they employ—William Turner *secundus*, a brother-in-law, credited it to Thomas—was accounted a novelty, and that Holland's books depart from strict catechetical form in omitting answers or printing them separately from questions, to encourage individual responses. A small surviving correspondence concerning two pupils, Robert and Hannah Heywood, shows him to have been a sensitive and caring teacher.

Holland was married to Esther Pilkington; there were no children. A growing temperamental irritability deepened into depression and reclusiveness, leading to his resignation in a sad letter of 20 August 1820. He took occasional services thereafter, but his decline into mental illness ended only with his death, in Bolton, on 25 June 1826. R. K. WEBB

Sources *Monthly Repository*, 21 (1826), 430, 495–6 · F. Baker, *The rise and progress of Nonconformity in Bolton* (1854) · W. E. Brown, *Robert Heywood of Bolton, 1786–1868* (1970) · V. F. [W. Turner], *Monthly Repository*, new ser., 3 (1829), 721–2 [obit. of Thomas Holland] · J. Hunter, *Familiae minorum gentium*, ed. J. W. Clay, 1, Harleian Society, 37 (1894) · letters to John Heywood, Bolton Public Library
Archives Bolton Public Library, Local History Collection

Holland, John (1794–1872), poet and writer, was born in Sheffield Park, Sheffield, on 14 March 1794, the son of John Holland, optical instrument maker, of Richmond Hill, in the parish of Handsworth, Yorkshire, and his wife, Elizabeth, daughter of Samuel Cox of Staveley, Derbyshire. He was brought up in his father's trade but soon abandoned it for literary pursuits, and was encouraged by James Montgomery, Sheffield's leading writer and evangelist, who became a close friend. As a prominent member of the Wesleyan Chapel in Carver Street, about 1818 he was appointed one of the secretaries of the Sheffield Sunday School Union.

As a young man he produced several volumes of poetry with a religious or moral purpose. Some, such as *Sheffield*

Park (1820) and *The Village of Eyam* (1821), had a local setting. His evangelical writings found a wide audience but are no longer read.

From 1825 to 1832 Holland was, in succession to Montgomery, editor of the radical newspaper the *Sheffield Iris*. In 1832 he became editor of the *Newcastle Courant*, but he returned to Sheffield in 1833 and acted as co-editor of the *Sheffield Mercury* from 1835 until the journal ceased publication in 1848. A lifelong interest in botany and geology led him to the publication of divers works on local flowers, gooseberries, and fossil fuels, and to the impressive *A Treatise on the Progressive Improvement and Present State of the Manufactures in Metals* (1831–49). He is chiefly remembered today for his historical and topographical writings, especially the *History, Antiquities and Description of the Town and Parish of Worksop* (1826) and the *Tour of the Don* (1837), and for various memoirs of the lives of poets, clergymen, and other notables, including *Memorials of Sir Francis Chantrey … in Hallamshire and Elsewhere* (1851) and *Memoirs of the Life and Writings of James Montgomery* (7 vols., 1854–6). He also wrote numerous sermons, hymns, and articles for *Notes and Queries* and *The Reliquary*, and for magazines and newspapers.

In acknowledgement of Holland's journalistic services an annuity of £100 was subscribed for by ten gentlemen of Sheffield and presented to him in 1870. He died, unmarried, at his residence at The Mount, Sheffield, on 28 December 1872 and was buried in the churchyard of the neighbouring parish of Handsworth.

THOMPSON COOPER, *rev.* DAVID HEY

Sources W. Hudson, *The life of John Holland of Sheffield Park* (1874) · Sheffield Central Library
Archives Sheff. Arch., corresp., papers, and literary MSS | BL, letters to Joseph Hunter and S. J. Junter, add. MS 24869 · Sheff. Arch., letters to Margaret Lawton · Sheff. Arch., corresp. with James Montgomery and Robert Leader
Likenesses H. Adlard, stipple, 1854 (after R. Smith), BM; repro. in J. Holland, *Memoirs of the life and writings of James Montgomery* (1854) · portrait, 1874, repro. in Hudson, *Life of John Holland*
Wealth at death under £1000: probate, 25 Jan 1873, *CGPLA Eng. & Wales*

Holland, John Charles Francis (1897–1956), army and intelligence officer, was born in India (probably in Calcutta) on 21 November 1897, the only son and elder child of Sir Thomas Henry *Holland (1868–1947), geologist, and his first wife, Frances Maud (*d.* 1942), daughter of Charles Chapman, deputy commissioner in Oudh. Close friends called him Jo.

Holland left Rugby School in 1914 for the Royal Military Academy, Woolwich, and from there he was commissioned into the Royal Engineers on 28 July 1915. He was posted to the eastern Mediterranean, arriving too late for the Gallipoli campaign, but serving on the Salonika front for most of the rest of the First World War. He was mentioned in dispatches in 1917, and in the summer of 1918 was awarded the DFC for gallantry in action with the Royal Air Force. He was badly wounded in Dublin during the troubles of 1919–21, in which he admired the technical skills of his Irish guerrilla opponents.

In 1922 Holland reverted from temporary major to lieutenant; he was promoted captain in 1924 and major seven years later. In 1924 he married Anne Christabel, daughter of Sir James Bennett Brunyate, of the Indian Civil Service; they had two sons and a daughter. Holland passed out from the Staff College, and held a staff captain's appointment in northern command in 1934–6. In 1938, again due for promotion but medically unfit, he took an appointment as a second-grade staff officer in the War Office to conduct research in any subject he chose. He chose irregular warfare. His branch, in which he was at first the only officer, was called GS (R).

Holland's Irish experiences led his lively imagination well outside the normal range of military thinking at the time. Early in 1939 his branch was renamed MI R, and placed in the military intelligence directorate, though Holland concentrated rather on operations. Encouraged by A. P. Wavell, he laid the foundations of several wartime secret services, and was one of the originators of the commandos. For a few months in the summer of 1939 he worked at 2 Caxton Street, Westminster, alongside L. D. Grand, a Woolwich contemporary who ran the then inadmissible section D of the secret service. On the outbreak of war in September Holland went back to the War Office.

Holland gathered like-minded officers round him, and dispatched each in turn to run the service for which he seemed fit: N. R. Crockatt, whose prowess he had admired at Rugby, to secure intelligence from prisoners of war; E. R. Coombe to form the inter-services security board, which handled code-names and deception as well as security; Gerald Templer to run the security of the expeditionary force; and M. R. Jefferis to invent and exploit secret gadgets. He sent Colin Gubbins to the independent companies in Norway, then to command projected stay-behind parties to damage the communications of any invading German forces, and eventually to run the Special Operations Executive (SOE). The latter was formed in July 1940 when Holland's staff, and Grand's, and a semi-secret propaganda branch of the Foreign Office were amalgamated.

Holland thereupon went back to regimental duty, on being offered a regular lieutenant-colonel's command. By July 1943 he was back in the War Office as deputy chief engineer and a major-general. He was appointed CB in 1945, and was admitted to the American Legion of Merit and received the medal of freedom with silver palm. In 1947–8 he was chief of staff, western command; in 1949–50 he was again employed, briefly, on secret planning; and he retired in 1951.

Holland was a shortish, burly man who went bald early; a heavy cigarette smoker; quick-tempered, but recovering fast from anger. He died at his elder son's house in Wimbledon on 17 March 1956.   M. R. D. FOOT, *rev.*

Sources *WWW* · private information (1993) · M. R. D. Foot, *SOE: an outline history of the Special Operations Executive, 1940–46* (1984) · *CGPLA Eng. & Wales* (1956) · W. J. M. Mackenzie, *The secret history of SOE* (2000) · J. B. Astley, *The inner circle* (1971)
Archives PRO, MI R papers, HS series
Likenesses photograph, repro. in Astley, *Inner circle*

Wealth at death £7991 13s. 8d.: probate, 22 May 1956, *CGPLA Eng. & Wales*

Holland, John Philip (1841–1914), inventor of the modern submarine, was born on 24 February 1841 in Castle Street, Liscannor, co. Clare, Ireland, the son of John Holland, a coastguard, and Mary Scanlon. Educated first at Limerick, he was prevented by poor eyesight from going to sea, so he took the initial vows of the teaching order of the Christian Brothers and studied at their schools in Ennistimon and Limerick. After 1858 he taught in a number of their schools in Ireland, but in 1872 his family emigrated to America and a year later he obtained a dispensation to quit the order on the grounds of ill health and followed his parents. He had become interested at an early age in the possibility of constructing submersible boats and, as an Irish patriot, saw how they might be used against the ships of the British navy in the fight for Irish independence. During the previous century there had been various proposals, of a more or less fanciful nature, for boats to go under water, but the technical problems were, at that time, insurmountable. By 1870 Holland had drawn up plans for such boats, and while working as a teacher in Paterson, New Jersey, he developed his projected submarine to the stage where he felt he could offer it to the United States Navy; in 1875 they rejected it as the fantastic scheme of a civilian landsman. The Fenians in America, through Clan na Gael, decided to finance his first experimental one-man craft which was tested with some success in 1878. They then gave him a further substantial sum to build a full-size submarine which they hoped would be capable of crossing the Atlantic and destroying the British fleet. He gave up teaching to build the *Fenian Ram*, completed in 1881, which was 31 feet long with a displacement of 19 tons and a crew of three. The first to be equipped with ballast tanks, horizontal rudders, and weight compensation, it was extensively tested in the waters of New York harbour and in 1883 dived to a depth of 60 feet. The Fenians were very impressed and took it out of the inventor's hands, but they were unable to achieve any of their objectives and abandoned it soon afterwards.

Holland was married on 17 January 1887 in Brooklyn, New York, to Margaret Foley of Paterson, New Jersey. He continued his work but encountered various difficulties until in 1895 the J. P. Holland Torpedo Boat Company, which he had set up in 1893, was awarded a contract for $150,000 to build a submarine for the United States Navy. The *Plunger* was, however, not built to his specification, the navy insisting on incorporating its own ideas, and it was not a success. With only $5000 of his own capital left he began to build the *Holland* to his own design, 54 feet in length, 10 feet in diameter and with a submerged displacement of 75 tons. It was fitted with a petrol engine for surface propulsion and electric storage batteries and motor for running submerged. Armed with one torpedo tube and a pneumatic dynamite gun, it was launched in 1898 and, after searching tests, was purchased in 1900 by the United States government. A few months later six more were ordered, and within a short time further orders were placed by Russia, Japan, and Britain; five submarines were built under licence by Vickers at Barrow in Furness in 1902–3. One of these, HMS *Holland No 1*, was lost under tow in 1913 but was raised and restored at the Royal Navy Submarine Museum in Gosport.

To Holland, therefore, belongs the credit for developing the submarine to a state of practical utility, and in December 1900 he contributed an article on 'The submarine boat and its future' to the *North American Review*, in which he foresaw many of the modern uses of the submarine in science, commerce, and exploration. This success was marred by animosity between Holland and the financial backers of the reorganized Electric Boat Company, and he turned his attention to other areas of research. In 1904 he invented a respirator for use in escaping from submarines underwater, and towards the end of his life he engaged in experiments in aeronautics. He died on 12 August 1914 in Newark, New Jersey, survived by his wife and four children.

RONALD M. BIRSE

Sources C. W. Mitman, 'Holland, John Philip', *DAB* · L. Day and I. McNeil, eds., *Biographical dictionary of the history of technology* (1996), 349–50 · H. Boylan, *A dictionary of Irish biography*, 2nd edn (1988) · R. Compton-Hall, *Submarine boats: the beginnings of underwater warfare* (1983)
Archives city park, Paterson, New Jersey, the *Fenian Ram*, 1881 [memorial] · museum, Paterson, New Jersey, first experimental craft of 1878 · Royal Navy Submarine Museum, Gosport, HMS *Holland I*, 1902
Likenesses photograph, repro. in Compton-Hall, *Submarine boats*, 32 · portrait, repro. in F. L. Darrow, *Masters of science and invention* (1923), 307–13

Holland, Joseph (d. 1605). See under Society of Antiquaries (act. 1586–1607).

Holland, Mary Sybilla (1836–1891). See under Holland, Francis James (1828–1907).

Holland, Sir (Edward) Milner (1902–1969), lawyer, was born on 8 September 1902 at Silverdale, Grange Road, Sutton, Surrey, the second son in the family of two sons and two daughters of Sir Edward John Holland DL JP (1865–1939), a publisher, and his wife, Selina Hobson. His father had a long career as a member of Surrey county council, of which he was chairman, and was knighted in 1929. His elder brother was killed in the Second World War.

Milner Holland was educated at Charterhouse School and at Hertford College, Oxford. At Charterhouse he was awarded a classical leaving exhibition and at Hertford, where he obtained a classical scholarship in 1921, he was junior and senior scholar and won the Gordon Whitbread prize and the Talbot gold medal (both in classics). He achieved second-class honours in classical moderations (1923) and a third in *literae humaniores* (1925). He was in the second class in jurisprudence (1926) and for the BCL degree in 1927. In the bar final examination of the Council of Legal Education he was awarded a certificate of honour. In addition he received from the Inner Temple as a law student a Profumo prize.

In 1927 Milner Holland was called to the bar by the Inner Temple. He became a pupil of Wilfrid Hunt, who had an exceptionally busy and varied practice as a Chancery junior. On finishing his pupillage he obtained a room in chambers in 7 New Square, Lincoln's Inn, and he remained a member of those chambers until his death. In the twelve years following his call to the bar he built up a substantial practice, mainly in the Chancery Division, and supplemented his income by lecturing for the Council of Legal Education. In 1931 he became assistant reader in equity to the council and in 1935 he was appointed reader. During this period he lectured on company law for the council. Following the outbreak of war he joined the Royal Army Service Corps as a second lieutenant and he served in the army until 1945. In 1943 he became deputy director of personal services at the War Office with the rank of brigadier, and in that capacity he was heavily engaged in the negotiations with the Treasury concerning army pay, allowances, and pensions. In recognition of his services in this field he was appointed CBE in 1945.

At the end of the war Holland returned to his practice at the bar. He was fortunate in finding his old chambers still available, together with a sufficient nucleus of pre-war barristers to constitute a viable set of Chancery chambers. He quickly re-established himself as an outstanding Chancery practitioner and in 1948 he took silk. He had in the meantime been called by Lincoln's Inn *ad eundem* and in 1953 he became a bencher of that inn. In 1951 he was appointed attorney-general of the duchy of Lancaster and attorney and sergeant within the county palatine. In 1957–8, and again in 1962–3, he was chairman of the general council of the bar and in 1957 he was elected a member of the Pilgrims. During this period he was a member of the 'bank rate' and 'Vassall' tribunals. From 1958 to 1962 he was a member of the Council on Tribunals and in 1962 he became vice-chairman of the inns of court executive council. In 1963 he was appointed chairman of the London rented housing survey which produced a valuable and exhaustive report (published in 1965) about the result of investigations into the housing shortage and the hardships suffered by tenants in the greater London area. He was knighted in 1959 and made a KCVO in 1965.

In the post-war period Milner Holland established his reputation as a great persuasive advocate not only at the Chancery bar but also in the field of local government and in the parliamentary corridors. The cases in which he was engaged as counsel, in the main successfully, were numerous and varied and included cases dealing with the Burmah Oil Company, the Fitzwilliam peerage, the will of George Bernard Shaw, and the litigation relating to 'Spanish champagne'.

Holland's success as an advocate was due partly to his extensive knowledge of the law but still more to his understanding of human nature, which enabled him to select and deploy the arguments most likely to attract whatever tribunal he was addressing at the time.

The mental strain of Milner Holland's practice would have been intolerable but for the recreations and hobbies in which he indulged. He was a keen golfer and had numerous other interests, including the construction of wireless sets and the study and photography of wild flowers. He was also a very popular and skilful after-dinner speaker. In all these pursuits Milner Holland was a perfectionist, and his concentration on any hobby in which he was for the time being absorbed no doubt helped him to bear the strain of his professional life.

It may seem surprising that in spite of his outstanding achievements in his profession as an advocate, and in spite of the judicial qualities that he had shown in the inquiries in which he had participated, Milner Holland did not accept appointment as a High Court judge. This may reflect his feeling that he had done his duty, so far as public work was concerned, by taking part in numerous inquiries and other unpaid activities which involved great expenditure of time and energy. But Holland also wanted to spend more time in the various non-legal pursuits which appealed to him and he preferred the independence which is in theory (but not always in practice) available to an advocate more often than to a judge. There can be no doubt that, had he been willing to accept a judgeship, he would have been a most valuable addition to the bench.

On 27 July 1929 he married Elinor Doreen (*b.* 1904/5), of Malvern, daughter of Frederick Archibald Leslie-Jones, a schoolmaster. They had two sons. Milner Holland died in a nursing home in Brighton Sussex, on 2 November 1969.

R. C-H. HORNE, *rev.*

Sources personal knowledge (1981) · *The Times* (3 Nov 1969) · *The Times* (6 Nov 1969) · b. cert. · m. cert.
Wealth at death £27,525: probate, 23 Jan 1970, *CGPLA Eng. & Wales*

Holland, Nathaniel. *See* Dance, Nathaniel (1735–1811).

Holland, Philemon (1552–1637), translator, was born in 1552, probably on 6 November, in Chelmsford, Essex, the son of John Holland (*d.* 1578), clergyman. He was a member of the same Norfolk family as Sir John Holland, first baronet (1603–1701); this family claimed to be related to the rather grander Hollands of Up Holland, Lancashire, from whom the nineteenth- and twentieth-century viscounts Knutsford were descended, but the connection is questionable.

Life before the publication of the translations, 1552–1599 When Philemon Holland was very young his father left England as a protestant exile, returning to be ordained by Edmund Grindal in 1559; he became rector of Dunmow Magna (Great Dunmow), Essex. Philemon attended the nearby Chelmsford grammar school and from about 1568 became a scholar of Trinity College, Cambridge, where he received the BA in 1571, and was elected to a minor fellowship in 1573 and to a major fellowship in 1574. On 10 February 1579 he married Anne (1555–1627), daughter of William Bott, alias Peyton, of Perry Hall, Handsworth, Staffordshire. His fellowship terminated on his marriage, and he moved to Coventry, about 25 miles from Perry Hall. There he became the usher, or junior of the two full-time masters, at the free school (now King Henry VIII School, Coventry, a position which brought him a salary of £10 a year and a house. He and his wife were famous for their hospitality, and brought up a family of ten children,

CYRUPÆDIA

OR

The Institution and
Life of CYRUS
King of
Persians.

Written in Greek by
Xenophon

Translated into English
BY
Philemon Holland.
Dr in Physick

Aᵒ Dom.1632.

Printed for Robert Allot

INTER PRES

CYRUS Maior Persarum
Rex Mundi Monarcha.

CAROLUS D.G. Britann:&
Rex Magna Britannia Monarcha.

Philemon Holland (1552–1637), by William Marshall, pubd 1632 (after H. H.)

among whom were the poet Abraham *Holland, the publisher and miscellaneous writer Henry *Holland, and the print publisher Compton *Holland. In 1585 he was incorporated MA at Oxford. In 1597 he received the degree of MD from Cambridge and began to practise medicine. Like other schoolmaster–physicians of the early modern period, such as Richard Argentine of Ipswich, he was able to combine his double profession with learned work. At some time before 1600 he began translating Livy's history of Rome.

The major folio translations, 1600–1610 Holland's first book, the first complete rendering of Livy into English, was published in 1600 when he was nearly fifty. It was a work of great importance, presented in a grand folio volume of 1458 pages, and dedicated to the queen. The translation set out to be lucid and unpretentious, and achieved its aim with marked success. It is accurate, and often lively, and although it does not attempt to imitate the terseness of Latin, it avoids prolixity. As part of his book Holland translated two other substantial works—an ancient epitome of Roman history which provides an outline of the lost books of Livy, and Bartolomeo Marliani's guide to the topography of Rome—as well as some smaller texts. These were taken from the edition of Livy published in

Paris in 1573; by translating them, Holland was making available in English a great learned compendium of historical knowledge, not simply a single ancient author. The Livy was followed in the next year by an equally huge translation, of the elder Pliny: *The Historie of the World, Commonly called, the Naturall Historie*. This encyclopaedia of ancient knowledge about the natural world had already had a great indirect influence in England, as elsewhere in Europe, but had not been translated into English before, and would not be again for 250 years. Indeed, after four centuries, Holland is still the only translator of this work to attempt to evoke its literary richness and beauty. Two years later Holland turned from Latin to Greek, publishing the first English translation of Plutarch's *Moralia*, a very large collection of miscellaneous essays and lectures which was widely read in the early modern period. This, together with Plutarch's *Lives*, had been translated into French by Jacques Amyot in the sixteenth century; whereas Sir Thomas North's English rendering of the *Lives* is directly from the French, Holland at least compared Amyot's translation, and a Latin translation, with the original. In all, over the four years 1600–1603, Holland published 4332 folio pages of translations of the very highest quality.

Holland's next translation, undertaken when an outbreak of plague in 1605 confined him to his house and published in the following year, was of a somewhat briefer work, *Historie of Twelve Caesars*, from the Latin of Suetonius, whose wealth of minute biographical detail lent itself very well to Holland's talent for conversational liveliness. Like his previous translations it was scholarly as well as vivid, with annotations drawn partly from Isaac Casaubon's edition of 1595. He dedicated it to Anne, Lady Harington, and his epistle to her suggests that he was on visiting terms at her house at Combe, a couple of miles from Coventry, where a former master of the free school, John Tovey, was chaplain and tutor; his son Henry travelled to the Palatinate in Lord Harington's retinue in 1613. In 1609 Holland published his translation of another Roman history, the extant books of Ammianus Marcellinus's history of the empire in the later fourth century, together with a chronology which had appeared in an edition of Ammianus printed in Paris in 1591, dedicating the translation to the corporation of Coventry. In 1610 he completed a translation of William Camden's *Britannia*, in the course of which he had corresponded with Camden and had also added some material from his own knowledge. This material was reprinted among the footnotes of the 1697 reworking of *Britannia*.

Subsequent translations, old age, and death, 1611–1637 In 1612 at the age of sixty, Holland was admitted to the freedom of the city of Coventry. Despite his local celebrity he was by no means rich enough to rest on his laurels, and over the next twenty years he kept working, though at a less astonishing rate than he had in his fifties. In 1615 he published a supplement to Thomas Thomas's Latin dictionary of about 6000 previously unrecorded words and meanings, of which many are from Pliny and Ammianus but others show a wide reading in ancient authors such as

Apuleius, Prudentius, and Varro, and moderns such as Pomponio Leto and Joseph Scaliger. This was followed the next year by a translation into Latin of John Speed's *The Theatre of the Empire of Great Britaine*, published in London and Amsterdam as *Theatrum imperii Magnae Britanniae*. In 1617 Holland translated the medieval medical verse text *Regimen sanitatis Salerni*, to be published with a new edition of Thomas Paynell's ninety-year-old translation of the commentary thereon by Arnaldus of Villanova, for a popular market, and when James I visited Coventry in that year Holland made a speech in his honour, which was subsequently printed. A second edition of the *Britannia* was entered in the Stationers' register in 1625, but was only published twelve years later. This was not the only piece of work which languished on Holland's desk in these years; he began work on Xenophon's *Cyropaedia* during the lifetime of Henry, prince of Wales, but completed the first draft only in 1621, and then continued reworking it for more than a decade.

In or before 1626 Holland fell dangerously ill, and his son Abraham addressed a poem to him in 1626 regretting that his merits have been unrewarded, and particularly that Coventry has been to him a

> lucklesse Cage
> Wherein you have bin cooped all your age
> And spent your golden yeares,

befriended only by those who wished to exploit him (Holland, sig. H2v). The following year, his wife, Anne, died. In 1628 he was appointed to the mastership of the school where he had taught for forty years, but he was too old to cope with the job and resigned it within a year; if the story that he taught Richard Allestree, who was born in 1619, is true, he may have returned to the position of usher. He became too infirm to practise as a physician. In 1632 his translation of Xenophon's *Cyropaedia* was published at last, together with a reprint of his son Abraham's poem on the battle of Lepanto, in a volume edited by Henry Holland. A treatise on the gout by another son, William (1592–1632), which was published in the following year as 'perused by P. H.' (*Gutta podagrica*, title-page) may also have been sent to the press by Henry, who also helped correct the second edition of *Britannia* for its eventual publication in 1637. In 1633 Philemon contributed a six-line epigram, in Greek, to a Cambridge collection celebrating Ralph Winterton's edition of Hippocrates.

From 1632 to 1636 Holland received an annual pension of £3 6s. 8d. from the city of Coventry. In 1635 he was authorized to receive charity from the members of his old university. He became bedridden in the following year and died, in Coventry, on 9 February 1637. He was buried in Holy Trinity Church, Coventry, under an epitaph which he composed in the last year of his life, in which he laments the deaths of six of his sons and describes himself as having entered a second childhood, nursed by his two unmarried daughters. Two years after his death his translation from French into Latin of Brice Bauderon's popular *Pharmacopoea* was published by Henry Holland, so that it could be read, as a conservative alternative to the

Pharmacopoea Londinensis of 1618, by learned medical practitioners who did not know French.

Holland's grandson remembered him as a hale old man—'his intellectuals and his senses remained perfect until the eighty fourth year of his age; and more especially his sight so good, that he never used spectacles in all his life'—adding that he was a remarkably moderate drinker, that he was 'always of a peaceable and quiet spirit, and hated contention as a serpent', and that he was 'most indefatigable in his study, saying often, that there was no greater burden and enemy to him than idleness' (Wood, *Ath. Oxon.: Fasti*, 234).

Posthumous reputation   Holland's translations were widely circulated and read into the eighteenth century. On their account Thomas Fuller included Holland in his *Worthies of England*, saying that he was 'the translator general in his age, so that those books alone of his turning into English will make a country gentleman a competent library for historians' (Fuller, *Worthies*, 287). Because he was a translator of large and learned works he became a byword for weighty erudition, perhaps especially among persons of limited education: the epigram:

> Phil: Holland with translations doth so fill us,
> He will not let Suetonius be Tranquillus
> (Bodl. Oxf., MS Tanner 466, fol. 66v)

evidently made up by a person proud of knowing Suetonius's cognomen, can be found in printed and manuscript collections. Even Pope made Holland's books, together with those printed by Caxton and Wynkyn de Worde, raw material for the altar erected to dullness in the first book of the *Dunciad*.

In the seventeenth and eighteenth centuries Holland was remembered not only as a translator but as a penman. The story that he wrote out the whole of his Livy with a single quill pen, which was then preserved as a precious relic by Lady Harington, survives in several versions, and suggests that he wrote with a particularly light and fastidious touch. A manuscript in his hand of the musical treatise ascribed to Euclid called *Harmonic* was said to have been one of the models shown to John Baskerville as he designed his Greek types for the University of Oxford.

In the nineteenth century Holland was still a living author. So, for instance, the readers for what became the *Oxford English Dictionary* were assiduous in gathering quotations from his works, of which 8095 were printed in the finished dictionary: only seven authors (Shakespeare, Scott, Milton, Wyclif, Chaucer, Caxton, and Dryden) are quoted there more often than Holland. Holland even became the object of sentimentality: 'Wherever the pestilence raged, or fever burned', wrote Charles Whibley in 1899, 'there went Holland, bringing with him the comfort of medicine and good counsel' (Whibley, viii); this overlooks the fact that when the pestilence raged Holland stayed at home and translated Suetonius. By the twentieth century his translations had (with a few minor exceptions such as that of Marliani's *Topographia*) been superseded for practical purposes, and very little has been written on him since 1900 except in general surveys. But he is doubly important. His classical translations made some of the major prose works to have survived from antiquity, together with some important recent European scholarly apparatus, available to the growing body of people who could read English fluently but Latin with difficulty if at all, and his translation of *Britannia* helped to bring the learned study of the British Isles and their antiquities into the mainstream of English vernacular culture: 'In this, through thee,' wrote John Davies of Hereford,

we see (as in a Glasse)
The wrinckled face of grave ANTIQUITY.
(Davies, 248)

JOHN CONSIDINE

Sources Wood, *Ath. Oxon.: Fasti* (1815) • C. Whibley, introduction, in Suetonius, *History of twelve Caesars*, trans. P. Holland, 1 (1899), vii–xxxviii • H. B. Lathrop, *Translations from the classics into English, 1477–1620* (1933) • A. Holland, *Hollandi posthuma* (1626) • R. Martin, '[Latin] history', *Oxford guide to literature in English translation*, ed. P. France (2000), 535–9 • Fuller, *Worthies* • *Brief lives, chiefly of contemporaries, set down by John Aubrey, between the years 1669 and 1696*, ed. A. Clark, 2 vols. (1898) • W. Dugdale, *The antiquities of Warwickshire illustrated* (1656) • S. Gillespie and R. Cummings, '[Latin] prose authors', *Oxford guide to literature in English translation*, ed. P. France (2000), 539–44 • J. Davies, *The scourge of folly* (1611) • B. Holland, *The Lancashire Hollands* (1917) • Venn, *Alum. Cant.* • J. Willinsky, *Empire of words: the reign of the OED* (1994) • IGI • Bodl. Oxf., MS Tanner 466 • R. A. Gerard, 'De Passe and early English natural history printmaking', *Print Quarterly*, 14/2 (1997), 174–9

Archives BL, letter, Cotton MS Julius CV

Likenesses W. Marshall, line engraving (after H. H.), BM, NPG; repro. in Xenophon, *Cyrupaedia*, trans. P. Holland (1632), additional title page [*see illus.*]

Holland, Philip (1721–1789), Presbyterian minister, eldest son of Thomas Holland (*bap.* 1690, *d.* 1753), dissenting minister, and Mary Savage, granddaughter of Philip Henry, was born at Wem, Shropshire. His grandfather was John Holland (*d.* 1713) of Dam Head House, Mobberly parish, Cheshire. The Hollands of Mobberly and Knutsford were local yeoman farmers and supporters of the protestant dissenting congregation that built the Brook Street Chapel at Knutsford. His father, a pupil of James Coningham, had been approved to preach by the Cheshire classis on 9 November 1711, and was ordained on 3 August 1714. About 1712, he succeeded Joseph Mottershead to the congregation at Kingsley, Cheshire, then moved to the congregation in Wem, Shropshire, around 1716–17.

Philip Holland entered Philip Doddridge's academy in 1739. He was followed in 1744 by his brother John, who ministered to the protestant dissenting congregations at Wem, Shropshire, and Allostock, Cheshire, before conforming to the Church of England in 1763. Another brother, Henry, entered Doddridge's academy in 1751 and transferred to Daventry upon Doddridge's death. He was minister in Prescot and Ormskirk, Lancashire, where he died on 10 December 1781. Philip Holland first preached at Wolverhampton, Staffordshire and succeeded his father to the pastorate at Wem. In 1755 he became the minister of Bank Street Chapel, Bolton, Lancashire, in succession to Thomas Dixon (1721–1754).

On 25 May 1758 Holland married his cousin, Catherine Holland (*b.* 1728) of Mobberley, the daughter of John Holland (1690–1770) of Dam Head House and Mary Colthurst;

she was a great-aunt of Mrs Gaskell. They had a son, Philip Henry Holland MD (*d.* 1788), and a daughter, Catherine, who married John Cole Rankin, merchant of Newcastle upon Tyne. The ministerial career of Philip's brother John Holland should not be confused with that of his wife Catherine's brother, John Holland (1720–1751), who ministered in Ormskirk and at the High Pavement Chapel, Nottingham. He was called to Chowbent, Lancashire, but died before commencing his work.

Philip Holland's theology was that of the Arminian Presbyterian divines of his day. At Wolverhampton he is described as being more liberal than his former tutor and out of step with the majority of the congregation, 'who were inclined for the most part to the tenets of Calvin' (Matthews, *Congregational Churches*, 152). He was influenced by John Seddon of Warrington, who introduced him to the moral philosophy of Francis Hutcheson. He was probably an Arian by the time of his Lancashire pastorate. During the 1750s in Bolton, a number of the Bank Street congregation left because of the tenets preached by Dixon and Holland, and joined John Bennet's Methodist chapel at Duke's Alley, which became Independent in 1759.

Holland's congregation none the less flourished, and the chapel was enlarged in 1760. Richard Arkwright, cotton-spinning entrepreneur and pioneer of the factory system, was a member of the Bank Street congregation between 1750 and 1767. Holland ran a boarding-school in Bolton, educating, among others, Josiah Wedgwood's son. He assisted Seddon in the foundation of the Warrington Academy in 1757 and contributed to the debate over the introduction of liturgical forms into dissenting worship, writing the third service in *A form of prayer and a new collection of psalms, for the use of a congregation of protestant dissenters in Liverpool* (1763), generally known as the 'Liverpool liturgy'. He was active in the movement to repeal (1779) the doctrinal subscription required by the Toleration Act, and was an advocate of independence for the American colonies. In the last decade of his life his views became somewhat more heterodox, Job Orton complaining that Holland had sunk 'the inspiration of the apostles and their epistles lower than I think he can justify' (Nightingale, 3.13). He published several sermons, including 'The importance of learning' (1760), which was reprinted in the *English Preacher*, volume 9 (1773), and his *Sermons on Practical Subjects* (2 vols., 1792) was printed posthumously, edited by John Holland and William Turner. Holland died at Bolton on 2 January 1789, aged sixty-seven. A mural monument was erected to his memory in Bank Street Chapel, where his nephew John *Holland (1766–1826) succeeded him.

ALEXANDER GORDON, *rev.* JONATHAN H. WESTAWAY

Sources W. F. Irvine, *A history of the family of Holland of Mobberly and Knutsford in the county of Chester, with some account of the family of Holland of Upholland and Denton in the county of Lancaster* (1902) [privately printed] • J. Hunter, *Familiae minorum gentium*, ed. J. W. Clay, 1, Harleian Society, 37 (1894) • F. Baker, *The rise and progress of nonconformity in Bolton: an historical sketch of a congregation … in Deansgate and afterwards in Bank Street* (1854) • B. Nightingale, *Lancashire nonconformity*, 6 vols. [1890–93], vol. 4, pp. 72, 106, 151–2, 193, 217, 218–19, 274;

vol. 3, pp. 12–13, 133, 287 · *Calendar of the correspondence of Philip Doddridge*, ed. G. F. Nuttall, HMC, JP 26 (1979) · A. Gordon, ed., *Cheshire classis: minutes, 1691–1745* (1919), 43, 45–8, 50, 52–61, 72, 75–80, 82, 86–7, 90–92, 181 · *Calamy rev.*, 272–3 · A. G. Matthews, *The Congregational churches of Staffordshire* (1924?), 152, 268 · H. McLachlan, *Warrington Academy: its history and influence*, Chetham Society, 107, new ser. (1943), 4, 6, 17–18, 47, 66, 93, 103, 109–14 · will, proved, Chester, 8 April 1793, Lancs. RO, MS WCW · J. Dixon, 'The burial list of the Ormskirk clergy and ministers', *Transactions of the Historic Society of Lancashire and Cheshire*, 3rd ser., 5 (1876–7), 125–38 · J. Orton, *The practical works of the Rev. Job Orton now first collected: consisting of discourses, sacramental meditations, and letters with copious indexes. To which is prefixed a memoir of the author*, 2 vols. (1842), 2.595 · W. Urwick, ed., *Historical sketches of nonconformity in the county palatine of Cheshire, by various ministers and laymen* (1864) · G. H. F. Vane, ed., *Diocese of Lichfield: Wem registers*, 9, Shropshire Parish Registers (1908) · 'Letters and papers of the Rev. John Seddon', *Christian Reformer, or, Unitarian Magazine and Review*, new ser., 10 (1854), 618–29, esp. 620–21 · 'Letters and papers of the Rev. John Seddon', *Christian Reformer, or, Unitarian Magazine and Review*, new ser., 11 (1855), 365–75 · J. Westaway, 'Scottish influences upon the reformed churches in north west England, c. 1689–1829: a study of the ministry within the Congregational and Presbyterian churches in Lancashire, Cumberland and Westmorland', PhD diss., 1997 · B. Holland, *The Lancashire Hollands* (1917) · S. Lawrence, *The descendants of Philip Henry, MA, incumbent of Worthenbury in the county of Flint, who was ejected therefrom by the Act of Uniformity in 1662* (1844); facs. edn [1972] · G. M. Ramsden, *A responsible society: the life and times of the congregation of Bank Street Chapel, Bolton, Lancashire* (privately printed, 1985) · C. Stell, *An inventory of nonconformist chapels and meeting-houses in the north of England*, Royal Commission on Historical Monuments (England) [1994] · C. J. Street and others, *Bank Street Chapel, Bolton, bi-centenary commemoration, 1696–1896* (1896), 41–4 · *DNB*

Archives DWL, Blackmore MSS · DWL, Seddon MSS, letters · JRL, letters to James Nicholson
Likenesses mural monument, Bank Street Chapel, Bolton, Lancashire · silhouette, repro. in P. Holland, *Sermons on practical subjects*, 2 vols. (1792)
Wealth at death between £2000 and £5000, incl. lands in Baddeley, Cheshire: *DNB*; will, 1793, Lancs. RO, MS WCW

Holland, Ralph (d. 1452), tailor and alderman of London, was possibly from Newington, Surrey, where he owned property. He had married a woman called Matilda by 1419, when he was already a successful cloth merchant. He owned shops in various parishes in London, and supplied cloth to, among others, Thomas of Lancaster, duke of Clarence (d. 1421). Like other ambitious London tailors involved in the cloth trade he was frequently described as a 'draper' and even became a member of the Drapers' Company. Despite this his loyalties clearly lay with the Tailors' Company, of which he became a liveryman in 1415–16 before being chosen master in 1419. He enrolled at least eleven apprentices during his career and made substantial contributions to the funds of the tailors' fraternity, dedicated to St John the Baptist, at a time when it was seeking to enhance its prestige in the City. His political career was controversial from the outset: in October 1426 he spoke out against the mayor who, drawing upon a royal writ of 1315, attempted to restrict participation in the mayoral and shrieval elections to those personally summoned by the mayor and aldermen. Holland declared the ordinance a fabrication, threatened several prominent citizens, and was sent to Ludgate prison. By 1429 he was a common councilman and was elected sheriff by the commonalty the same year, but failed in his first attempt to be elected an alderman. By 1434, when he was appointed one of the auditors of the accounts of London Bridge, he was probably the wealthiest member of his guild: he acquired two substantial houses, Basset's Inn and Pembridge's Inn, as well as other properties in London and Surrey which, in 1436, were assessed as being worth £24 per annum.

In 1435 Holland made the first of several loans to the crown and by October that year had finally been elected an alderman, for Bread Street ward. He subsequently served on several important civil committees. His election coincided with the intensification of the rivalry which existed between the tailors and the drapers, particularly over the right to search shops and stalls for defective cloth, a function normally delegated to guild officials by the mayor. In 1439, following an earlier statute, the tailors acquired a controversial new grant by letter patent, probably with the assistance of Humphrey, duke of Gloucester (d. 1447), with whom Holland and the tailors had established a strong connection. It was claimed by the drapers that this charter infringed the city's liberties concerning the 'search', and relations were further strained when the tailors claimed the right to scrutinize cloth sold at St Bartholomew's fair at Smithfield. In October 1439 Holland made the first of three bids for the mayoralty, knowing that success would greatly assist the ambitions of the predominantly artisan tailors, now in direct competition with the drapers. Holland was rejected on each occasion, but by 1441 his candidacy had become identified with the interests of a wider constituency of artisans in the capital, concerned at the gradual encroachment upon their rights as freemen by an overwhelmingly mercantile court of aldermen. At the election that October a large crowd of tailors, skinners, and other 'handycraftymen' greeted the election of Robert Clopton, a draper, with cries of 'nay, not that man but Raulyn Holland!' (Kingsford, 154–5), and in the ensuing disturbances six tailors and five skinners were arrested and sent to prison.

Over the next three years Holland continued to criticize the ruling oligarchy and leading citizens such as John Paddesley, a former mayor unpopular with the tailors, whom he accused of spending 1000 marks of the city's money on his private concerns. When a peace commission for London was established in 1443 Holland was at the forefront of the opposition to it, using the forum of the court of aldermen to declare it to be a commission 'not of peace but of war' (CLRO, Journal 4, fol. 4v), which would act against the interests of the city's artisans. The dissension came to a head at the election of the chamberlain in September, and a show of force was planned for the mayoral election on 13 October. Holland now rarely attended the court of aldermen and his house was used by the leaders of the artisans for conspiratorial meetings. The subsequent failure of the artisan movement resulted in Holland's own removal from the court of aldermen on 18 May 1444, after the aldermen had heard a lengthy account of his activities as an instigator of the unrest, and the accusations he had levelled at fellow aldermen over the years.

Holland took no further part in city politics and died before 23 October 1452, when the first of his wills was proved. His wife had died before March that year. In June he had received two tenements in Watling Street from the crown in recognition of his services to the present king and Henry V. Holland remembered his craft in his wills, leaving Basset's Inn, Pembridge's Inn, and other properties in London to the Tailors' guild. As well as funding his obit the income was to be used by the master and wardens to increase the amount paid to the almsmen and women of the guild by 1d. per week. He asked to be buried alongside his wife in the church of St Mary Aldermary. In 1454 the executors of that 'worshipful and notable man Raulyn Holand' (Anstey, 1.327) received a letter from Oxford University asking for a bequest for the new divinity schools. His son, also named Ralph, was likewise a tailor and appears to have predeceased him.   MATTHEW DAVIES

Sources C. M. Banon, 'Ralph Holland and the London radicals, 1438–1444', The English medieval town, ed. R. Holt and G. Rosser (1990), 160–83 · journals, CLRO · MS Records, Merchant Taylors' Company of London · M. P. Davies, 'The tailors of London and their guild, c.1300–1500', DPhil diss., U. Oxf., 1994 · PRO · C. L. Kingsford, ed., Chronicles of London (1905) · H. Anstey, ed., Epistolae academicae Oxon., 1, OHS, 35 (1898)

Wealth at death substantial wealth; landed property in Surrey and London valued at £24 p.a. in 1436

Holland, Richard [known as Sir Richard Holland] (d. in or after 1483), ecclesiastic and poet, is best remembered as the author of the alliterative verse The Buke of the Howlat. Of his background, education, and early career little is known. The records generally style him 'priest of Caithness'—probably a reference to the diocese in which he was ordained—and he may have been a native of Orkney, where he would later spend some ten years. It was his status as a priest which led to his being usually referred to as Sir Richard Holland. By 1444 he was in possession of the prebend of Kirkmichael in the diocese of Ross. He subsequently sought to exchange this for the archdeaconry of Caithness (1445), a move that led to an acrimonious three-year dispute with Alexander Sutherland, which he seems eventually to have lost. Holland was described as the rector of Halkirk, near Thurso, in 1450 and of Abriacher in the diocese of Moray in 1451. In 1452 he was provided to the canonry and prebend of Croy and a year later he was presented to the precentorship of Moray, another disputed benefice. His career was closely associated with the fortunes of the powerful Black Douglas family, in particular those of Archibald Douglas, earl of Moray, who in a charter of 1450 referred to Holland as his secretary. This charter was one of several witnessed and drawn up by Holland in his capacity as a notary public, which he had become no later than 1441. Although the exact circumstances surrounding the connection between Holland and his patron are unknown (it may have originated in the service of the earl's wife), he was clearly suited to this type of office.

Indeed, Holland's skills went beyond the secretarial, and some time about the year 1448 he composed The Buke of the Howlat, written, according to the final stanza, at Darnaway Castle and dedicated to the countess of Moray, Elizabeth Dunbar. Recognized as the earliest major poem of the Scottish alliterative revival, its 1001 lines are arranged in 13-line alliterative stanzas with wheel, a form which was to remain in use in Scotland throughout the fifteenth and sixteenth centuries. Holland's work offers a novel and amusing twist on the bird-assembly poems popularized in the fourteenth century, most notably Chaucer's Parliament of Fowls. The tale centres on a howlat (owl), who, lamenting his ugliness, is given a feather by each of his fellow birds. His overweening pride in his new appearance causes him to be stripped of his apparel, underlining the well-worn adage:

That pryde never yit left
His feir but a fall.
(Amours, 80)

As well as acting as moral exemplum, the poem is distinguished by the richness of its description, particularly of the two bird courts (papal and imperial), and provides vivid glimpses of contemporary opinion of clerical standards and of the life of a fifteenth-century aristocratic household.

The poem, its dating, and its possible allegorical significance have all been the subject of considerable debate. Internal evidence has led late twentieth-century critics to suggest dates of 1446, 1448, and 1450, while attempts to decode a hidden warning in the work have seen the unfortunate owl as James II, the powerful Livingston family, or the Douglases themselves. On balance, however, the poem seems less a warning to the Douglases than a passionate validation of the dynasty, celebrating its well-established tradition of loyal military service and glossing over the family rivalries of recent years. Certainly, if the poem was written in the summer of 1448, then it would have formed part of a programme of Douglas activity, of which the concluding event, a lavish tournament staged at Stirling Castle in 1449, also acted as a reminder of the family's carefully cultivated reputation as the 'wer wall', or rampart, of Scotland.

It was a message little appreciated by James II. He launched an aggressive campaign to destroy Douglas power in Scotland that culminated in royal victory at the battle of Arkinholm on 1 May 1455, when Moray was killed and his brothers forced into exile. Immediately following this Holland was at Darnaway, named among the countess's men placed under the protection of the earl of Huntly. The changed political climate of the late 1450s clearly rendered him uneasy, and by 1457 he had retreated to Kirkwall to serve as vicar of Ronaldsay and canon of Kirkwall Cathedral. A deed of collation dated 3 June 1467 refers to his demission of this benefice and it was probably then that he left for England, where he was apparently active in the Douglas cause. In 1480 a Richard Holland, clerk, was sent to Scotland by Edward IV, and the continuing support he gave his erstwhile patrons presumably explains his exclusion from an act of parliament of 1482 offering remission to all those who forsook the traitor James Douglas. Holland seems to have spent the rest of his life in political exile in England and in 1483 was placed under official royal protection. Thereafter he disappears from the records, and it is not known when he died. His literary reputation, however, survived. Praised by William Dunbar in his 'Lament for the Makaris' (between 1505 and 1508) and David Lindsay in *The Testament and Complaynt of our Souerane Lordis Papyngo* (1530), Holland's verse was preserved in the two great sixteenth-century manuscript collections Asloan (between 1513 and 1530) and Bannatyne (1565–8), and was also among the first works published by Scotland's nascent printing industry about 1508.

C. EDINGTON

Sources M. M. Stewart, 'Holland of the *Howlat*', *Innes Review*, 23 (1972), 3–15 · D. Laing, *Adversaria: notices illustrative of some of the earlier works printed for the Bannatyne Club*, Bannatyne Club, 115 (1867) · F. J. Amours, ed., *Scottish alliterative poems in riming stanzas*, 2 vols., STS, 27 (1897); 38 (1897) · W. Geddie, *A bibliography of Middle Scots poets, with an introduction on the history of their reputations*, STS, 61 (1912) · APS, 1124–1707 · CDS, vol. 4 · M. M. Stewart, 'Holland's *Howlat* and the fall of the Livingstones', *Innes Review*, 26 (1975), 67–79 · F. J. Riddy, 'Dating *The Buke of the Howlat*', *Review of English Studies*, new ser., 37 (1986), 1–10 · M. P. McDiarmid, 'Richard Holland's *Buke of the Howlat*: an interpretation', *Medium Aevum*, 38 (1969), 278–90 · J. Stuart, ed., *The miscellany of the Spalding Club*, 4–5, Spalding Club, 20, 24 (1849–52)

Holland, Richard (1596–1677), mathematician, was born at Lincoln. He was educated at Oxford, but appears not to have taken a degree. His life was mainly spent as a teacher of mathematics and geography at Hart Hall, Oxford, which included the instruction of his students in the use of globes and other mathematical instruments.

Holland wrote three books for the use of his pupils. The first—*An Explanation of Mr Gunter's Quadrant ... Enlarged*—appeared in 1676. The second, entitled *Globe Notes*, was published posthumously, in 1678 and again in 1684. It contains many of the simple propositions in astronomy, with definitions of such terms as colure, solstice, and equinoxial, and is clearly intended to be used in conjunction with the instruments themselves. The other book is *Notes how to Get the Angle of Parallax of a Comet or other Phenomenon at Two Observations* (1668). It contains diagrams, with practical directions implying some knowledge of trigonometry.

According to Wood, Holland was in such high demand as a teacher that he became a rich man. He died in Oxford on 1 May 1677, and was buried in the parish church of St Peter-in-the-East, Oxford. He should not be confused with another Richard Holland, of Emmanuel College, Cambridge, who was incorporated MA at Oxford in 1679, became rector of Stanford, Lincolnshire, and published five sermons between 1698 and 1702.

R. E. ANDERSON, rev. H. K. HIGTON

Sources E. G. R. Taylor, *The mathematical practitioners of Tudor and Stuart England* (1954) · Foster, *Alum. Oxon.* · Wood, *Ath. Oxon.*

Holland, Richard (1688–1730). *See under* Holland, John (1658–1721).

Holland, Sir Robert (c.1283–1328), baron, was the son of Sir Robert Holland of Upholland, Lancashire, and his wife Elizabeth, daughter of Sir William Samlesbury of Samlesbury, Lancashire. Robert Holland senior held moderately

extensive estates in his county and played an active part in its government, but his son's career was to be altogether more exceptional. Through his friendship with Thomas, earl of Lancaster, Edward II's cousin and the most powerful of his earls, he rose from the middle ranks of the gentry into the upper ranks of the baronage. Their connection probably began in 1298, when Holland served Lancaster as his *vallettus* on the Falkirk campaign. By 1305 he had been knighted.

From 1300, if not before, Holland began to receive a steady stream of lands from Lancaster, amounting eventually to some twenty-five manors worth perhaps £550 per annum. Lancaster was also responsible for his marriage, which took place about 1308 and led to still greater gains. His wife was Maud (d. 1349), one of the two daughters and coheirs of Alan de la Zouche, a prominent Leicestershire magnate, who brought to her husband, on Zouche's death in 1314, the greater part of her father's lands, worth nearly £720 a year. It was probably in consequence of this great accession of landed wealth that Holland was summoned to parliament for the first time in July 1314. At the height of his career his whole estate, including his patrimony, was probably worth rather more than £1300 a year.

In return for all this Holland became Lancaster's chief agent and confidant. According to the *Brut* chronicle, 'He truste more oppon him than oppon eny man alyve' (*Brut: England*, 216). Chronicles and records suggest that he exercised a general supervision over all Lancaster's affairs: directing his estate officials, receiving dubiously acquired lands to which the earl wished to bar legal claims, acting as Lancaster's intermediary with the king, and supporting him in his political and military ventures. He joined in the pursuit of Piers Gaveston in 1312 and served Lancaster in Scotland in 1318. He also served the king, acting for three periods as justice of Chester and holding the usual range of local commissions. It was to the king that Holland turned during the great crisis of 1321–2, when Lancaster rebelled against Edward. This was not the result of any long-standing arrangement with Edward, for Holland had played a leading part in Lancaster's actions against the Despensers in July 1321 and had begun to raise troops for him in the revolt that followed in the winter of 1321–2. But in early March 1322, when Lancaster was retreating through the north midlands before the royal army, Holland crossed over to Edward. His treachery cost Lancaster the campaign and ultimately his life, and Holland his reputation and his freedom. His motive in deserting his lord was obvious: to save his own life in what looked likely to be—and indeed became—a military catastrophe. He may have calculated that in the event of defeat his own position as Lancaster's henchman would make him more vulnerable than his lord, whose blood and ancestry might have been expected (too optimistically as it turned out) to protect him.

For the next five years Holland remained the king's captive, and only in December 1327, a year after the old reign had ended in a revolution, did Edward III order his release and the return of his lands. His restoration was short-lived. On 15 October 1328 he was murdered in Boreham-wood, near Elstree, in Hertfordshire, probably by a group of Lancastrian partisans and possibly with the connivance of Henry, earl of Lancaster, Thomas's brother. He was probably buried at the Greyfriars' Church, Preston, Lanca-shire. The bulk of his lands descended to his eldest son, another Robert, but it was his second son, Thomas *Hol-land, earl of Kent, who refounded the family's fortunes; he won fame in the French war, married *Joan (the Fair Maid of Kent), granddaughter of Edward I, and acquired the earldom of Kent in right of his wife.

Holland's linkage with the most powerful noble of his generation, and the scale of his consequent enrichment, made his career in some respects *sui generis*. In another way, however, it typified one of the main routes to social advancement in the middle ages: through service in the following of a great man. J. R. MADDICOTT

Sources J. R. Maddicott, 'Thomas of Lancaster and Sir Robert Hol-land: a study in noble patronage', *EngHR*, 86 (1971), 449–72 · F. W. D. Brie, ed., *The Brut, or, The chronicles of England*, 2 vols., EETS, 131, 136 (1906–8) · *Chancery records* · N. Denholm-Young, ed. and trans., *Vita Edwardi secundi* (1957) · GEC, *Peerage*, new edn, 6.528–31
Wealth at death approx. £1300 p.a.

Holland, Robert (1557–1622?), Church of England clergy-man and religious writer, was born at Conwy, Caernarvon-shire, the third son of Hew Gwyn Holland (d. 1584) and Jane, daughter of Hugh Conway of Bryneuryn. His father's family originated in Lancashire, but had been wealthy and influential in north Wales for centuries. Baptized at Conwy on 18 January 1557, Robert entered Clare College, Cambridge, at Easter 1577, graduated BA from Magdalene College in 1578, and proceeded MA from Jesus College in 1581. He was ordained deacon (on a title from his father) in early 1580 at Bangor and priest at Ely in the following April. In his paraphrase of the gospels he states that 'the race of his youth was unadvisedly run', but that after he had been 'four years or more tossed with sundry troubles', the hearts of his friends had been stirred up 'to favour his innocency, and to grant him breathing time after his travels' (Holland, *Holie Historie*, dedication).

Holland served for a time as curate of Weston Colville, and in 1580 was a schoolmaster in Dullingham, both in Cambridgeshire. In 1591 he returned to Wales, settling in Pembrokeshire, where he was presented to the rectory of Prendergast, north of Haverfordwest. He founded a dyn-asty in the nearby parish of Walwyn's Castle: with his wife, Jane, daughter and heir of Robert Meylir of Haver-fordwest, he had six sons, of whom Nicholas became rec-tor of Marloes in Pembrokeshire. The senior branch of the family remained at Walwyn's Castle until almost the mid-dle of the eighteenth century, when they settled in Eng-land.

Holland's ministry had important consequences for the course of the later Reformation in Wales. He has been described as one of the most 'fluent and prolific' of early Welsh protestant writers and is known to have written six books (Williams, 392). He first went into print in English, publishing *The holie historie of our lord and saviour Jesus Christ's nativitie, life, actes … gathered into English meter and*

published *to withdraw vaine wits from all unsaverie and wicked rimes and fables, to some love and liking of spirituall songs and holy scriptures* in 1594. But thereafter he turned his atten-tion to presenting the protestant message in the Welsh language. *Dau Gymro yn taring yn bell o'u gwlad* (probably c.1595) is a notable discussion, in dialogue form, of the cur-rent state of popular religion in Wales; it may have been modelled on the exercises in practical divinity, also in dia-logue, recently published by English writers like George Gifford. Tudur is in no doubt that everyone still believes in magic and expatiates on the subject, while drawing a dis-tinction between the white and black varieties. His oppon-ent, Cronw, remains unmoved by his arguments, exhort-ing him to study the Bible and to attend sermons. Impressed, Tudur is nevertheless forced to point out that he has never heard a sermon in his parish church, that the clergy are negligent in expounding biblical texts, and that most laymen are too poor to be able to buy a bible for study at home.

About 1600 Holland published at Oxford *Darmerth, neu, Arlwy i weddi*, a preparation for prayer and guide to exalt-ation, designed to guide the unlearned towards the true service of God; this was followed shortly afterwards by *Sail crefydd Gristionogol*, a translation of William Perkins's influential English catechism. In 1603 Holland embarked on a Welsh translation, with the help of George Owen Harry, of James I's *Basilikon doron*. If the project was com-pleted it was not published in full, perhaps because of the prevalence of plague in London that year. On 5 May 1607 Holland was presented to the rectory of Walwyn's Castle, and in 1612 to that of nearby Robeston West, both like Prendergast in the gift of the lord chancellor. He was also rector of Llanddowror, Carmarthenshire. Nothing is known of his later career, but he seems to have lived until 1622, when successors were appointed to his livings. Sev-eral of his writings survive only in late seventeenth-century reissues by Stephen Hughes.

LEONARD W. COWIE

Sources *Y bwygraffiadur cymreig hyd* (1940) · *DWB*, 360–62 · Venn, *Alum. Cant.*, 1/2.394 · W. Rowland, *Lly fryddiaethy Cymry*, ed. S. Evans (1869) · *Heraldic visitations of Wales and part of the marches … by Lewys Dwnn*, ed. S. R. Meyrick, 2 vols. (1846) · 'The Hollands of Conway', *Archaeologia Cambrensis*, 3rd ser., 13 (1867), 183–6 · B. H. Holland, *The Lancashire Hollands* (1917) · G. Williams, *Wales and the Reformation* (1997) · *DNB* · R. Holland, *The holie historie of our lord and saviour Jesus Christ's nativitie, life, actes …* (1594)

Holland, Saba (1802–1866). *See under* Smith, Sydney (1771–1845).

Holland, Samuel (1803–1892), slate industrialist and rail-way promoter, was born on 17 October 1803 in Duke Street, Liverpool, the youngest son and fifth child of Sam-uel Holland (1768–1851), merchant, and his wife, Kather-ine Menzies (d. 1847). He had two brothers and three sis-ters and was educated at the Revd William Lamport's school in Lancaster and then in Hanau, Germany (c.1815–1817). He was twice married: in 1850 he married Ann Rob-bins (d. 1877), and his second wife was Caroline Jane Burt (d. 1924). There were no children by either marriage.

In 1820 the elder Samuel Holland leased a slate quarry at

Rhiwbryfdir, in the parish of Ffestiniog, from W. G. Oakeley of Tan-y-Bwlch, Maentwrog, and in 1821 his son was put in charge of this quarry. He built a cart road down to his quay on the River Dwyryd, from which the slate was boated to the new harbour at Porthmadog. The quarry was sold in 1825 for £28,000 to what became known as the Welsh Slate Company. Another quarry above Rhiwbryfdir was taken over by the younger Samuel Holland in 1828, and was worked by him until 1877. In 1882 it became part of the complex of quarries called the Oakeley Quarry.

Holland played a crucial part in the rise and fall of the Ffestiniog Railway, designed for the carriage of slates from Blaenau Ffestiniog to Porthmadog. By chance, in 1829, he encountered Henry Archer (1799–1863), a Dubliner, who was interested in railways. Holland persuaded James Spooner (1789–1856) to survey the line with Thomas Pritchard, and Archer raised most of the capital in Dublin. Local opposition had defeated schemes in the 1820s and it took three attempts to get Archer's parliamentary bill through the House of Commons; it was finally approved on 25 May 1832. Archer became managing director of the railway. The gauge was 1 foot 11½ inches, and the line was 14 miles long. Opening day was 20 April 1836 and Holland was the first quarry owner to use the horse-drawn railway. By 1860 all the large quarries near Blaenau Ffestiniog were connected to it. In 1863 two steam locomotives, designed by Holland's nephew, Charles Menzies Holland, were in use and in 1869 R. F. Fairlie produced the *Little Wonder* with its double engine. In 1865 passenger trains were introduced; and from 1867 there was also a quarrymen's train, which ran twice weekly at first and then daily from 1881.

The Ffestiniog Railway brought prosperity, but Holland and other industrialists began to look for other outlets for their slate at lower rates. Holland was the chief promoter of the Ffestiniog and Blaenau Railway, which was opened in 1868 and went from the terminus of the Ffestiniog Railway to the village of Ffestiniog, a distance of 3½ miles. It was converted to standard gauge in 1883, and thereafter was worked by the Great Western Railway (GWR). Holland was also one of the directors of the Bala and Ffestiniog Railway, which was formed in 1873. This came to a working agreement with the GWR in 1879, and took over the Ffestiniog and Blaenau Railway in 1883.

Holland helped to get the tax on slate carried coastwise repealed in 1831, and, with other quarry owners, he persuaded the Board of Trade to include slate in the Anglo-French commercial treaty, which was negotiated by Cobden in 1860. Agreements with Norway, Sweden, and Denmark followed. In 1862 Holland was high sheriff of Merioneth. He was also deputy lieutenant for Merioneth and Caernarvonshire. He was a popular Liberal MP for Merioneth from 1870 to 1885 and was a JP and chairman of the board of guardians. He was opposed to trade unions and believed in a divide between employer and employee, but he had no confrontations with his quarrymen. In the 1850s he introduced gas lighting in his quarry, which, from 1840, had surface and underground workings. In 1873, a peak year, he employed about 500 men and 18,494 tons of slate were produced. Holland also invented a slate-dressing machine and he sent examples of his slate to the Paris Exhibition of 1854, gaining an honourable mention.

In partnership with John Whitehead Greaves, Holland founded the Porthmadog Mutual Ship Insurance Company, and in 1845 he promoted the Porthmadog Savings Bank, declaring it would instil habits of economy, industry, and self-dependence into the 'labouring classes'. He subscribed to the Oakeley hospital and built cottages at Tanygrisiau. In 1835 he founded a school at Penrhyndeudraeth, which was organized on the model of the British and Foreign Society schools. He also promoted Dr Williams's School for Girls, a fee-paying school and a nonconformist establishment which opened in Dolgellau in 1878. Holland's cousin Mrs Elizabeth Gaskell was staying with him in 1848 when *Mary Barton* was published. Photographs of him in maturity show a man of shrewd expression with imposing side-whiskers. Holland was resident at Cae'rdeon, Llanaber, near Barmouth, from the 1870s, and he died there on 27 December 1892. He was buried at Cae'rdeon church, and was survived by his second wife.

JEAN LINDSAY

Sources J. I. C. Boyd, *The Festiniog railway*, 2 vols. (1975) · M. J. T. Lewis, *How Ffestiniog got its railway* (1965) · J. Lindsay, *A history of the north Wales slate industry* (1974) · *DWB* · G. J. Williams, *Hanes plwyf Ffestiniog* (1882) · M. Burn, *The age of slate* (1972) · M. J. T. Lewis, ed., *The slate quarries of north Wales in 1873* (1987) · J. B. Edwards, 'Slates, steam and schools: Samuel Holland's contribution to Gwynedd', *Journal of the Merioneth Historical and Record Society*, 11 (1990–93), 94–7 · D. Thomas, 'Henry Archer', *Transactions of the Caernarvonshire Historical Society*, 11 (1950), 73–80 · J. Winton, *The little wonder: 150 years of the Festiniog Railway*, rev. edn (1986) · W. Davies, ed., 'The memoirs of Samuel Holland', *Journal of the Merioneth Historical and Record Society*, 1 (1952), suppl., 1–31 · E. Beazley, *Madocks and the wonder of Wales* (1967) · S. Holland, memoirs, NL Wales, MS 4983 · *WWBMP* · *CGPLA Eng. & Wales* (1893)

Archives Gwynedd Archives, Caernarfon, corresp. and papers · NL Wales, corresp., diary, and papers | Dolgellau RO, Breese, Casson, Jones MSS

Likenesses two photographs, NL Wales, photograph album

Wealth at death £12,638 19s. 0d.: probate, 1 May 1893, *CGPLA Eng. & Wales*

Holland, Seth (d. 1561), dean of Worcester, is of unknown parentage. He was educated at All Souls College, Oxford (BA 19 December 1534, MA 31 March 1539), and held a fellowship there from 1535 to at least 1542. In 1540 he took subdeacon's and deacon's orders, on 21 February and 13 March respectively. Shortly thereafter he served as chaplain to Richard Pates on embassy to Charles V, and may have accompanied Pates when he 'went to Pole' in early 1541. He is supposed to have been in Rome during Edward VI's reign. Perhaps after meeting Cardinal Reginald Pole at the English Hospice in Rome, Holland entered his service and undertook several missions to England for him. On 6 November 1554 he brought back the news of Pole's recall. Holland was well rewarded, beginning on 28 April 1555 with the second prebend in Worcester Cathedral. On 17 April 1556 he was elected warden of All Souls before receiving the prebend of Combe ix of Bath and Wells on 11 November. In the following year he gained further benefices after giving up the rectory of Upton Severn, Worcestershire (by March): rector of Newington, Oxfordshire,

1 July; of Fladbury, Worcestershire, 3 August (vacated by October 1558); and dean of Worcester, 21 August. As dean he handled some of his finances for Pates, who was now bishop. Two more rectories in Gloucestershire came to him after he resigned as warden of All Souls (by 9 June 1558), Bishops Cleeve on 5 September 1558 (institution bond 6 September; he gained the advowson as well; deprived by March 1559) and Naunton in 1559 (deprived 1561).

By October 1558 Holland had left Worcester and rejoined Pole's household at Lambeth. At some point he acted as secretary to Pole, transcribing some of his exegetical works, and being involved in the preparation of a projected new edition of Pole's *Pro ecclesiasticae unitatis defensione*, probably in 1554. Pole entrusted Holland with a final mission to Princess Elizabeth on 14 November 1558. He attended Pole's deathbed three days later, and was among those who were to see to the disposition of Pole's goods. Holland remained dean until at least 19 August 1559 (his replacement does not appear until 26 March 1560) although fairly shortly afterwards he must have refused the oath of supremacy and was committed to the Marshalsea in 1559. He died there before 6 March 1561, the day of his burial in St George's, Southwark. By his testament (of 1546) he left to Pates for poor English exiles Italian investments worth together about £700; these eventually came to the English colleges in Rome and Rheims/Douai. In March 1559 Holland had made contingent arrangements to transfer proceeds from the sale of these investments to England via the Buonvisi Bank.

T. F. Mayer

Sources *CSP Spain*, 1553, 441 · *CSP Venice*, 1557–8, nos. 1286–7 · Emden, *Oxf.*, 4.294 · *The Venerabile*, 21 (May 1962), 207 [sexcentenary issue: *The English hospice in Rome*] · *The diary of Henry Machyn, citizen and merchant-taylor of London, from AD 1550 to AD 1563*, ed. J. G. Nichols, CS, 42 (1848), 252 · Westm. DA, MS II, pp. 111, 113, 165 · Biblioteca Civica Angelo Mai, Bergamo, Archivio Stella in archivio Silvestri, 40/119 · Biblioteca Apostolica Vaticana, Vatican City, MS Vat. lat. 5968, fols. 195r–202v · Biblioteca Apostolica Vaticana, Vatican City, MS Vat. lat. 5969, fols. 1br–48r · Biblioteca Apostolica Vaticana, Vatican City, MS Vat. lat. 5970.2, fols. 239r–268v, 315r–328v · Archivio Segreto Vaticano, armaria 64:28, fol. 264r · Archivio Segreto Vaticano, Bolognetti, 95, fols. 296r–300r, 306v–307r · Archivio Segreto Vaticano, segreteria di stato, Inghilterra, 3, fol. 139r–139v · Bodl. Oxf., MS Tanner 106 · BL, Add. MS 35840 · BL, MS Cotton Vesp. F.iii, fol. 28 · Pole's register, LPL, fols. 67r, 78v · PRO, SP 15/8, fol. 239r · PRO, SP 15/8 no. 100, fols. 195r–196v · PRO, PROB 6/1, fol. 26v · Worcester Cathedral Library, A7(2), fols. 61v–62r, 66v · Glos. RO, GDR 1B, p. 15

Wealth at death approx. £700: Archives of the Archdiocese of Westminster, London, MS II, pp. 111, 113, 165

Holland, Sir Sidney George (1893–1961), prime minister of New Zealand, was born at Greendale, Canterbury, New Zealand, on 18 October 1893, the fourth son among the eight children of Henry Holland (1859–1944), a haulage contractor and later mayor of Christchurch and a member of parliament, and his wife, Jane Eastwood, a schoolteacher. After being educated at West Christchurch district school he was employed at 5s. a week in a hardware

firm at the age of fifteen, but then joined his father's haulage firm. He enlisted in the ranks in 1915, was later commissioned, but was invalided out in 1917. Following a lengthy convalescence he formed with his eldest brother the Midland Engineering Company and became extremely active in both business and conservative political circles in Christchurch.

In 1920 Holland married Florence Beatrice, the daughter of Arthur Fostyn Drayton of Christchurch. They had two sons and two daughters. He succeeded his father as member for Christchurch North in 1935. Although a new member of parliament, he spoke as an experienced businessman with a long record in local public affairs. His approach in parliament was direct and vigorous and appealed with uncomplicated ideas to the average man. He believed in free enterprise operated by enlightened employers. He strongly supported the empire, and the 'British way of life', and he thought that the best hope of world peace lay in co-operation between the empire and the United States, which he was willing to promote even by tariff reductions for America's benefit. He believed in healthy sport, in family life, in personal freedom within the limits of decency and law, and in the writing of legislation in plain language easily understood by those affected. He took up national politics with buoyant energy, a quick-wittedness, and an infectious optimism, and he revelled in the rough and tumble and the challenge and comradeship of parliamentary life.

The National Party opposition in 1935 had just suffered a shattering defeat. Its leaders had held office during depression-time distresses and were blamed both for what they had done and what they had left undone; its two main elements, farming and commerce, were in an uneasy alliance. Holland's robust, earthy common sense appealed to both camps, and under the conditions of war after 1939 he found a new role. The ruling Labour Party refused to have a coalition, but a war cabinet was set up alongside the domestic Labour cabinet. It comprised the senior members of both parties, leaving the junior members of the opposition free to campaign against Labour's domestic politics. Holland was the most effective member of this group, and in November 1940 he was elected leader of the National Party and of the parliamentary opposition. Thereafter party politics took on new life, though from June to September 1942 Holland and his leading supporters joined the short-lived two-party war administration. Over the next few years Holland welded together farmers and businessmen—he bought a farm and took a characteristically active personal interest in farming without losing touch with industry. He also helped to frame a Nationalist policy which was rather more than the mere negation of Labour's ideas. Both operations were achieved on a common-sense, practical level, with little regard for long-term theoretical problems. The National Party simply promised to preserve the material benefits of Labour's social security while restoring, under free enterprise, the spiritual values of liberty, individual initiative, and loyalty to the traditions of the empire.

This broad programme, designed to appeal to the ordinary man in the street, had been sketched while Holland was a back-bencher. He now promoted it with exuberant confidence and gained increasing support as the Labour Party seemed to have exhausted its mandate and as the electorate increasingly wearied of wartime controls. In November 1949 the National Party won an overwhelming victory, and Holland became prime minister; he also served, until 1954, as minister of finance. In office he remained consistently his practical, non-doctrinaire, cheerful self. His policies were derived less from principle than from shrewd reactions to problems as they arose.

In domestic matters Holland proclaimed the virtues of free enterprise and accelerated the dismantling of wartime controls; but there was no revolution. Indeed, when in power he realized that some pre-election policies must be modified, and he frankly acknowledged—and benefited from—the lessons of experience. Coalmining, broadcasting, and civil aviation, for example, remained under public ownership. Some long-standing promises were of course honoured, and certain fixed ideas were expressed with characteristic extravagance. In 1950, for example, the upper house of parliament, the nominated legislative council, was abolished with éclat, and in the following year an industrial dispute was handled as a section of the cold war, with New Zealand's communists seen as a traitorous fifth column. In 1942 Holland had destroyed the war administration in protest against the government's handling of a coalmining stoppage; in 1951 the battle against the waterside workers seemed part of a crusade against militant labour, preached with the vehemence of contemporary American witch-hunting, and fought with the traditional techniques of strike-breaking. Holland's government insisted on fighting this particular battle to total victory, sealed its triumph with a successful snap election which helped to secure a further six years of power, and proposed to follow overseas precedents with a drastic restriction of civil liberties. It appreciated the force of the resulting protests, however, and characteristically retreated to provisions that were middle-of-the-road conservative. The language of Holland and his colleagues could be virulently anti-'socialist', but the welfare state was not dismantled or even greatly modified.

A similar pattern appeared in New Zealand's foreign policies, which continued to be based on the hope that safety could still come from Commonwealth associations and on a worldwide system of collective security; but as the cold war intensified and a Japanese peace treaty appeared imminent there appeared to be an increasing need for an American guarantee. Holland's government responded promptly to the United Nations' call for help for American forces in the Korean War, and in 1951 New Zealand joined Australia and the United States in the ANZUS treaty of mutual guarantee. In 1954 New Zealand accepted the wider-based Manila pact, which also aimed at strengthening regional security. This was followed in 1955 by the little-noticed decision, reached as a result of Commonwealth discussions, to transfer New Zealand's military commitment from the traditional Mediterranean area to south-east Asia. Holland's government, however, saw these developments as entirely compatible with New Zealand's traditional relationships with Britain, America, and the United Nations. Holland himself used superlative—even embarrassing—language to describe New Zealand's devotion to the empire and to the United States.

Holland retained a firm grip over his cabinet and over New Zealand until his retirement through ill health in September 1957. His strength and buoyancy of personality, his friendliness and loyalty, his skill in parlour tricks and interest in sport, his success in parliamentary combat, fighting with 'the cutlass rather than the rapier', his directness, sincerity, and lack of subtlety, all helped to build a powerful public image. His life was in the world of action, not of the mind, and it is likely that he reflected the views—and prejudices—of a broad sector of New Zealand opinion. He was sworn of the privy council (1950) and was appointed CH (1951) and GCB (1957). He died at Wellington on 5 August 1961 and was cremated at the city's Karori crematorium on 8 August. F. L. W. WOOD, *rev.*

Sources *The Times* [Wellington] (5 Aug 1961) · *Evening Post* [Wellington] (5 Aug 1961) · M. Bassett, *Confrontation, 1951* (1972) · F. L. W. Wood, *The New Zealand people at war: political and external affairs* (1958) · R. S. Milne, *Political parties in New Zealand* (1966) · *New Zealand Listener* (18 Aug 1961) · K. Jackson, *The New Zealand legislative council* (1972) · *New Zealand ministry of foreign affairs: statements and documents, 1943–1957* (1972) · *The Times* (7 Aug 1961) · *New Zealand Herald* (7 Aug 1961) · A. H. McLintock, ed., *An encyclopaedia of New Zealand*, 3 vols. (1966) · J. Watson, 'Holland, Henry', *DNZB*, vol. 5 · *WW*
Archives FILM BFI NFTVA, news footage · BFI NFTVA, record footage
Likenesses group portrait, 1956, Hult. Arch.

Holland, Sydney George, second Viscount Knutsford

(1855–1931), hospital administrator and reformer, was born in London on 19 March 1855, the elder of the twin sons of Sir Henry Thurstan *Holland, second baronet and first Viscount Knutsford (1825–1914), and Elizabeth Margaret (1825–1855), elder daughter of Nathaniel and Emily Hibbert, of Munden, Hertfordshire, and a granddaughter of Sydney Smith; she died shortly after giving birth. His grandfather was Sir Henry *Holland (1788–1873), the physician. All through life the twins Sydney and Arthur were devoted to each other and for a long time it was hard to tell them apart. In 1858 their father married Margaret Jean, elder daughter of Sir Charles Edward *Trevelyan (1807–1886), sister of Sir George Trevelyan, and niece of Lord Macaulay; though she was a good mother to the twins, their unconventional and even prodigal outlook was not learned at her knee. Sir Henry, their father, a busy lawyer and later a statesman, was not able to see much of them, and they passed their summer holidays with their grandmother Mrs Hibbert or at Knutsford with their great-aunts Mary and Lucy Holland, the prototypes of the ladies in Elizabeth Gaskell's *Cranford*.

Holland was sent to Wellington School, where he came under the influence of the historian Osmund Airy, who opened the boy's mind and humanized his outlook, turning his thoughts to social service. Holland's father intended him for the army, but his educational standard proved too low for Woolwich. He fell back on the bar, to please his father, and in 1873 went to Trinity Hall, Cambridge, where he made many friends and spent his days in debates and rowing and swimming, in which last he became an expert. After leaving Cambridge with a third-class degree in 1876 he read for the bar and was called by the Inner Temple in 1879.

Holland next entered the chambers of George Baugh Allen, a well-known special pleader of the day. He began to interest himself in boys' clubs, did some competitive swimming, and learned conjuring from professionals. He achieved moderate success in the criminal courts and later at the parliamentary bar, but a flair for business and a call to social service decided, and divided, his life's activities. In the cause of temperance he helped to launch a scheme of coffee taverns. In 1882 he inherited a house and competence, and on 23 January 1883 he married Lady Mary Ashburnham (d. 1947), fourth and youngest daughter and tenth child of Bertram Ashburnham, fourth earl of Ashburnham (b. 1797).

Holland's name now began to be known through letters to the press and pamphlets on many social questions. In 1888 he was elected a director of the East and West India Dock Company, and in the dockers' strike of 1889 he took a leading part in voicing the employers' case, in which *The Times* and even John Burns acknowledged his fair-mindedness. His interest led him to visit various dock labourers at the Poplar Hospital in east London. Horrified by what he found, he launched without previous experience into hospital management in 1891. As a dock company director and chairman of Poplar Hospital at critical junctures he quickly put both concerns on their feet again. In four and a half years he raised enough money to turn the Poplar Hospital from a small, thirty-bed institution into one of the best of the smaller London hospitals, with more than 100 beds.

In 1896, at the suggestion of Miss Eva Luckes, matron of the London Hospital, Holland applied to be put on the London Hospital committee; in the same year he was elected chairman, an office he continued until his death. His fame rests on those thirty-five years. An obituary notice in *The Times* asserted:

> He was much more than 'the Prince of Beggars' who raised £5,000,000 for the 'London'. He was practically the founder of modern hospital efficiency. He raised the whole standard of nursing and hospital work from a very low to a very high level. (*The Times*, 28 July 1931)

After arriving he drew up a radical plan to modernize the hospital by renovating it throughout and by adding two new stories on the roof. His expertise as a fund-raiser came through in the massive donations he secured. The work took five years, during which services to patients continued as normal. As chairman he introduced drastic reforms in nursing at the hospital and built a new nurses' home next door. Although not medically trained, he was a public champion of progressive medicine, often speaking on the subject in the Lords.

As an administrator, Holland was autocratic and high-handed but very effective. His real genius was as a fund-raiser. He was no sentimentalist, though he knew how to play on the emotions. Publicity was his first weapon and he did not despise 'stunts'. His resource was remarkable: he was a great showman, a telling and touching speaker, and, with the actor's arts, a notable broadcaster.

Lord Knutsford, as he became on succeeding his father in 1914, loved the good things of life: he spent his City income royally on grouse moors and forests, made a pleasant home for his family at Kneesworth Hall, near Royston, and was happy in family life and friendships alike. He wrote innumerable articles and letters to the press and was himself a constant subject for press stories. In 1926 he published an autobiography, *In Black and White*, which had a popular success. He died in the London Hospital on 27 July 1931 and was survived by his wife and their two daughters.

Lord Knutsford was succeeded as fourth baronet and third Viscount Knutsford by his twin brother, Arthur Henry Holland-Hibbert (1855–1935).

JOHN GORE, rev. PATRICK WALLIS

Sources J. Gore, *Sydney Holland, Lord Knutsford* (1936) · S. G. Holland, *In black and white* (1926) · N. Langton, *The Prince of Beggars* (1921) · A. E. Clark-Kennedy, *The London: a study in the voluntary hospital system*, 2 vols. (1962–3) · Venn, *Alum. Cant.* · *The Times* (28 July 1931) · *BMJ* (8 Aug 1931), 277–8 · *The Lancet* (1 Aug 1931) · Burke, *Peerage* · *WWW* · personal knowledge (1949) · private information (1949)

Archives Royal London Hospital Archives and Museum, papers | BL, corresp. with Lord Northcliffe, Add. MS 62168 · Bodl. Oxf., corresp. with Sir Henry Burdett · NL Scot., letters to Lord Haldane

Likenesses O. Birley, oils, 1914, London Hospital, London · W. Stoneman, photograph, 1917, NPG · O. Birley, oils, 1930, Commercial Union, London · Spy [L. Ward], cartoon, chromolithograph caricature, NPG; repro. in *VF* (25 Aug 1904)

Wealth at death £77,634 6s. 1d.: probate, 25 Sept 1931, *CGPLA Eng. & Wales*

Holland, Thomas, earl of Kent (c.1315–1360), soldier, was the second son of Robert *Holland, Lord Holland (d. 1328) of Upholland, Lancashire, and Maud (d. 1349), daughter and coheir of Alan Zouche, Lord Zouche, of Ashby, Leicestershire. He had three brothers: Robert (d. 1373), who succeeded to the Holland estates in 1335 and resided at Thorpe Waterville in Northamptonshire, Alan, and Otto (d. 1359), who both followed Thomas into military service; and three sisters: Isabella, mistress of John de Warenne, earl of Surrey (d. 1347); Margaret (d. 1349), married to John de la Warr; and Matilda, possible sometime wife of John (II) Mowbray, Lord Mowbray.

Thomas Holland's soldiering probably began in Scotland in the early 1330s. He was in Bordeaux in 1337 with Robert d'Artois, was a knight of the royal household by 1338, served in Flanders in 1338–9 and 1340, at Sluys, and on the abortive Tournai campaign. Probably by this time he had made the considerable coup of marrying the king's cousin, *Joan (c.1328–1385), known as the Fair Maid of Kent. He was a landless young knight, son of a disgraced Lancastrian lord. She had also lost her father in disgrace and was not then the heiress she would become through the deaths without heirs of her uncle Thomas, Lord Wake, in 1349 and her brother John, earl of Kent, in 1352, but it seems a surprising match and may have been a reward by

Edward III to a loyal, energetic, young knight. Joan's mother, Margaret, countess of Kent, was not so favourable towards the match, and she may well have engineered Joan's marriage to the better connected William Montagu, heir to the earl of Salisbury, by February 1341, at a time when Holland was probably away on crusade in Prussia.

Holland fought in Brittany with the king in 1342–3, then went to Bayonne with Sir John Hardeshull, and probably on to Granada with the earl of Derby in 1343. He may have returned to Brittany in 1345. At the siege of Caen, in 1346, he captured the count of Eu, constable of France. Holland's reputation was apparently a factor in the count's choice of captor. This could have made Holland very wealthy as he sold the count to Edward III for 80,000 florins, but how much of this Holland ever received is unknown. The capture enhanced his eminence as a soldier on the Crécy campaign, when he also featured at Amiens and Rouen, was wounded at a castle on the Seine, commanded the rearguard on the march from Caen, and counted casualties after the battle at Crécy. His eminence led to his institution, in 1348, along with his brother Otto, often his associate and lieutenant in his military exploits, as one of the founder knights of the Order of the Garter.

Holland was now also able to institute proceedings at the papal court for the restoration of his wife, Joan. Their marriage was confirmed and publicized in November 1349; their first son, Thomas, was born in 1350. Their original union was declared to have been consummated; the 'marriage' with William Montagu had been null and void from the start. Holland's fortunes soon took a further rise as Joan's brother John, earl of Kent, died childless in 1352. Joan inherited his estates, spread over some sixteen counties. Holland was now, in the right of his wife, a landed lord of significant territorial resources. He was summoned to parliament as Lord Holland from 1354, and his military career burgeoned with a series of independent commands. Captain of Calais Castle in August 1352, he travelled again to Brittany in 1353 and in 1354 was made the king's captain and lieutenant there, with custody of the young heir to the duchy and funding from local revenues. He became keeper of the Channel Islands in June 1356, at a time when Castle Cornet there was in French hands; his able lieutenant, his brother Otto, soon recaptured it. Holland was appointed custodian of Crocy Castle in Normandy in November 1357 and then governor of the Harcourt lands in the Cotentin, based on St Sauveur le Vicomte, in October 1358. Custody of Barfleur in the Cotentin followed in October 1359, when he was also made joint lieutenant of Normandy with Philippe of Navarre. In September 1360 he received his most important post yet, when he was made Edward III's captain and lieutenant in Normandy and France. He was now accorded the title of earl of Kent to bolster his authority and prestige. He had the delicate, diplomatic task of carrying out the provisions of the treaty of Brétigny of October 1360, but while performing this duty he contracted some illness and died at Rouen on 28 December 1360. His body was initially interred in the church of the Friars Minor in Rouen,

and was later moved to the church of the Greyfriars, Stamford, Lincolnshire.

Holland left four children: Thomas *Holland, later earl of Kent; John *Holland, later earl of Huntingdon and duke of Exeter; Maud (d. 1392), who married first Hugh Courtenay and then Waleran, count of St Pol; and Joan (d. 1384), who married John de Montfort, duke of Brittany. Holland's widow, Joan, married Edward, the Black Prince, in 1361.   M. M. N. STANSFIELD

Sources M. M. N. Stansfield, 'The Holland family, dukes of Exeter, earls of Kent and Huntingdon, 1352–1475', DPhil diss., U. Oxf., 1987 · Chancery records · PRO, C135/155/117 · K. P. Wentersdorf, 'The clandestine marriages of the Fair Maid of Kent', Journal of Medieval History, 5 (1979), 203–32 · Œuvres de Froissart: chroniques, ed. K. de Lettenhove, 25 vols. (Brussels, 1867–77) · J. H. Le Patourel, The medieval administration of the Channel Islands, 1199–1399 (1937) · Chronique de Jean le Bel, ed. J. Viard and E. Déprez, 2 (Paris, 1905) · E. Perroy, The Hundred Years War, trans. W. B. Wells (1951) [Fr. orig., La guerre de cent ans (1945)]; repr. (1965) · G. Wrottesley, Crécy and Calais (1897) · S. Luce, ed., Chronique des quatre premiers Valois, 1327–1393 (Paris, 1862), 123
Wealth at death approx. £1281 17s. 2½d.: PRO, C 135/155/117

Holland, Thomas, fifth earl of Kent (1350–1397), magnate, was the elder son of Thomas *Holland, earl of Kent (c.1315–1360), and *Joan (c.1328–1385), daughter of Edmund of Woodstock, earl of Kent. After an early career soldiering abroad Holland became one of the less spectacular props of Richard II's regime, established mainly on the south coast, in and around Hampshire. He had a younger brother, John *Holland, earl of Huntingdon (c.1352–1400), and two sisters, Maud (d. 1392), wife to Hugh Courtenay and then Waleran, count of St Pol, and Joan (d. 1384), wife to John de Montfort, duke of Brittany. Perhaps most significantly, the second marriage in 1361 of his mother, Joan, to Edward, the Black Prince, meant that Holland had a younger half-brother, the future king *Richard II.

Thomas Holland's early career from 1366 was spent in military service abroad, first in Spain and then in France. He was knighted by his stepfather and godfather, the Black Prince, at Vitoria in Castile in 1367, and was made a knight of the Garter in 1376. His power and influence was restricted by the fact that his mother, Joan, held the estates of the Kent inheritance in her own right until her death in 1385. To help offset this somewhat, Thomas was married c.1364 to Alice (c.1350–1416), daughter of Richard (II) *Fitzalan, the wealthy earl of Arundel; Alice's dowry was 4000 marks, and the Black Prince enfeoffed the couple with lands worth 500 marks in three Yorkshire manors.

Richard II's accession in 1377 meant that Holland's half-brother was now king. To reflect this, he received a gift of 100 marks and an exchequer annuity of £200 in 1378, later augmented to 1000 marks in rents. He was also given custody of the royal forests south of the Trent in July 1377, and was appointed marshal of England in March 1380. The south was becoming his base: he resided much at Talworth Manor in Surrey (given him by his mother in October 1382); he became captain of Southampton in June 1380 to repel the French threat; and he served on the Surrey and Hampshire commissions of the peace. Late in 1380 he was accorded the title earl of Kent, which his father had held only briefly. His military experience was used to help suppress the peasants' revolt in Kent in 1381, and then as captain of the English bastion of Cherbourg from November 1384.

The death of his mother, Joan, in August 1385 brought to Holland the considerable estates of her inheritance. He was now a wealthy magnate, but played no great role in the political upheavals of 1386–9, having lost the post of marshal in June 1385. He was made constable of the Tower of London in May 1387, but then rather faded from the court scene in the 1390s, increasingly preferring his Hampshire residences at Lyndhurst and Brockenhurst. He became constable first of Corfe Castle (with his wife) in May 1391, and then of Carisbrooke Castle in July 1396, and was appointed to the Wiltshire commission of the peace in December 1390. The focus of his inherited estates lay less in the south than in the north-east midlands, especially Lincolnshire, and it was from there he dispensed his grants and patronage, yet even in the south his influence was not dominant, with no obvious nexus of Holland supporters in local posts. Thomas Holland died on 25 April 1397. He was buried shortly afterwards in Bourne Abbey, Lincolnshire, following a funeral in Westminster Abbey. According to Adam Usk, after Holland's death one of the earl's greyhounds spontaneously made its way to the king, and accompanied him everywhere, until the moment in 1399 when Richard deserted his army in Wales, whereupon the dog abandoned the king and joined the duke of Lancaster.

Holland had nine children, whose marriages brought many magnate families into Richard II's royal kin: Thomas *Holland, later earl of Kent and duke of Surrey; Richard (d. c.1396); Edmund *Holland, later earl of Kent; Eleanor (d. 1405) who married Roger (VII) *Mortimer, earl of March, and then Edward *Charlton, Baron Charlton of Powys; Joan (d. 1434), who married first *Edmund, duke of York, second William, Baron Willoughby, third Henry *Scrope, Baron Scrope of Masham, and fourth Henry Bromflete, Baron Vessy; Margaret (d. 1439), who married John *Beaufort, earl of Somerset, and then *Thomas, duke of Clarence; Eleanor (d. c.1420), who married Thomas *Montagu, earl of Salisbury; Elizabeth (d. 1423), who married John, Baron Neville; and Bridget, a nun. Holland's widow, Alice, remained constable of Corfe Castle until 1407 and then retired to Beaulieu Abbey; she died on 17 March 1416.   M. M. N. Stansfield

Sources M. M. N. Stansfield, 'The Holland family, dukes of Exeter, earls of Kent and Huntingdon, 1352–1475', DPhil diss., U. Oxf., 1987 · Chancery records · PRO, exchequer of receipt, issue rolls, E 403 · PRO, accounts various (king's remembrancer), E 101 · PRO, lord treasurer's remembrancer, enrolled accounts, E 364 · PRO, treaty rolls, C 76 · PRO, scotch rolls, C 71 · PRO, gaol delivery rolls, JUST/3 · PRO, lord treasurer's remembrancer, memoranda rolls, E 368 · PRO, inquisitions post mortem, C 136–138 · PRO, gascon rolls, C 61 · PRO, charter rolls, C 53 · PRO, special collections, ancient petitions, SC 8 · Essex RO, D/DRg 1/62 · CIPM, vol. 17 · M. C. B. Dawes, ed., Register of Edward, the Black Prince, 4 vols., PRO (1930–33) · Œuvres de Froissart: chroniques, ed. K. de Lettenhove, 25 vols. (Brussels, 1867–77) · A descriptive catalogue of ancient deeds in the Public Record Office, 2 (1894) · [J. Nichols], ed., A collection of … wills … of … every branch of the blood royal (1780), 118–19 · The chronicle of Adam Usk, 1377–1421, ed. and trans. C. Given-Wilson, OMT (1997)
Wealth at death estates worth approx. £1500: PRO, C 136/92

Holland [Holand], **Thomas**, sixth earl of Kent and duke of Surrey (c.1374–1400), magnate and courtier, was the son and heir of Richard II's half-brother Thomas *Holland, earl of Kent (1350–1397), and Alice, daughter of Richard *Fitzalan, earl of Arundel. He had two brothers and six sisters. John Holland, earl of Huntingdon and duke of Exeter, was his uncle. Thomas was not active in court circles until he reached adulthood, but he then became a leading supporter of Richard II.

Thomas Holland served on Richard II's Irish expedition in 1394, and he received two royal annuities, 200 marks in 1395, and £10 the following year. He had married Joan, daughter of Hugh *Stafford, earl of Stafford (d. 1386), in 1392, in spite of his uncle John's murder of her brother in 1385. His own father's death on 25 April 1397 brought the young earl into the vortex of the crises of Richard II's final years. He found the assumption of his inheritance greatly eased by royal favour. Not only was he made warden of his father's lands while they were nominally in the king's hands, but he was also granted all issues and reliefs due to his royal uncle. Moreover the earl was made a knight of the Garter in place of his father.

The new earl of Kent was immediately summoned to Nottingham where the king was planning the destruction of Thomas, duke of Gloucester, one of the lords appellant who had challenged the king's power a decade earlier. After Gloucester was in custody, Kent and the earl of Rutland were sent to arrest another of the appellants, Kent's uncle, the earl of Arundel. When Arundel and his former colleague the earl of Warwick were brought to trial in the parliament of September 1397, the earls of Kent and Huntingdon served as two of the eight appellants who appealed the former lords appellant of treason. Kent urged Arundel's execution, which was carried out. When Warwick was exiled, Kent received Warwick Castle with the custody of Warwick's heir, as well as the earl's stud of horses and cattle. On 29 September 1397 Thomas Holland was created duke of Surrey, and John Holland was created duke of Exeter. Selden noted that the virga aurea was first used on this occasion. Surrey and Exeter were two of five men elevated to dukedoms at the time, an inflation of honours which led to the derisive title of duketti.

When Henry Bolingbroke, duke of Hereford, accused his fellow dukettus and former appellant colleague the duke of Norfolk of attempting to enlist him in a conspiracy to act against Richard II before the king attacked them, Hereford reported that Norfolk warned him that Surrey was one of those out to destroy them both. Surrey replaced Norfolk as marshal of England on 31 January 1398 so that he might officiate at the scheduled duel between Hereford and Norfolk. Surrey's father had held this post in 1380, but the 1398 appointment gave Surrey specific power to arrest traitors found within the realm. The duel never took place; both men were banished. The duke of Surrey became marshal for life and shared in the spoils of Norfolk's estates. After the death of Hereford's father, John of Gaunt, duke of Lancaster, on 3 February 1399, Surrey received on 8 May custody of two Lancastrian manors until Bolingbroke or his heir should sue for livery. Surrey was also granted (on 18 February 1398) a licence to found a Carthusian priory called Mount Grace in his lordship of Bardelby in Cleveland; further grants to Surrey from the resources of alien priories helped to endow this house. The foundation of Mount Grace may demonstrate a degree of personal piety, but patronage of the Carthusians was also fashionable in court circles in the 1390s.

Richard II was greatly concerned to build up royal power in Ireland, and he hoped to employ Surrey in this endeavour. John Holland had had an abortive tenure as king's lieutenant in Ireland in 1382. Thomas Holland was now appointed to the office on 26 July 1398; the incumbent, Roger Mortimer, earl of March and Ulster, was ordered to have nothing to do with the office once Surrey arrived. Unknown to Richard at the time, Mortimer had been killed by the Irish on 20 July. An abstract of Surrey's indenture dated 10 April 1399 specifies that the duke was to command a retinue of 150 men-at-arms and 100 archers, including a mason and carpenter in every 20 archers. It has been argued that the indenture should be dated to 1398, but there seems no reason to assume such a scribal error so late in the regnal year. In May 1399 Surrey received 11,500 marks to support himself and his retinue in Ireland for one year. Surrey had been given wardship of the extensive Mortimer lands in Ireland; he was appointed keeper of Dublin Castle and of Drogheda; and he was given authority to present to all Irish benefices in the king's hands. On 16 May 1399, moreover, Thomas was appointed keeper of Carelogh Castle until the Mowbray heir sued for livery, and he was given the barony of Norragh while Art mac Murchada (d. 1417) remained a rebel. Norragh was one of the most prized estates of mac Murchada, the self-styled king of Leinster. The Lancastrian chronicler Adam of Usk improbably speculated that Richard II intended to crown Surrey king of Ireland. Richard II arrived in Ireland for his second campaign on 1 June 1399; Henry Bolingbroke landed in Yorkshire on 4 July.

Surrey returned with Richard to England, and he and the duke of Exeter attempted a reconciliation between Richard and Henry. Bolingbroke had no love for Surrey, and may have imprisoned him briefly at Chester, although the evidence is weak. On 20 October 1399 Surrey and other advisers of the deposed Richard II were arrested. Thomas Holland was committed to the Tower of London and then transferred to Wallingford. He was brought before parliament on 29 October where he pleaded his tender age as justification for his actions. On 6 November he and his uncle John were deprived of their dukedoms, and of the estates they had acquired after they had launched their appeal in 1397.

Once more earl of Kent, Thomas Holland joined his uncle John, the earl of Salisbury, and others in a plot to seize Henry IV and his sons at Windsor on 4 January 1400. The king had been warned and had withdrawn. Finding an empty nest, the conspirators rode to Richard's queen at Sonning. Kent announced that Richard II had escaped and was at Pontefract with 100,000 men. The conspiracy, betrayed by the earl of Rutland, soon collapsed. The conspirators fled to Cirencester where they were overcome by the townsmen. A priest in their company tried to cover their escape by torching a house. This further enraged the townsmen, who dragged the earls of Kent and Salisbury from the abbey in which they had sought refuge and beheaded them on the night of 7–8 January 1400. Kent's head was placed on London Bridge; his body was interred at Cirencester. Cooled by its stay on the bridge, the head was reunited with Kent's body; both were buried at his foundation, Mount Grace. According to Froissart, he was 'much lamented by several knights in England and other countries. He was young and handsome, and had very unwillingly taken part in this conspiracy; but his uncle and the earl of Salisbury had forced him into it' (Froissart, 2.706). The earls' conspiracy probably induced Henry IV to do away with the imprisoned Richard II. Kent's widow, Joan, was detained at Liverpool, probably while attempting to escape to Ireland, and was taken to London, but was not harmed by Henry IV. She lived until 1442; there were no children from her marriage to Thomas Holland. There are inquisitions post mortem for Thomas Holland for Leicester, Nottingham, Derby, Lincoln, and Middlesex, recording annual incomes in these counties amounting to nearly £650.   JAMES L. GILLESPIE

Sources J. L. Leland, 'Richard II and the counter-appellants', PhD diss., Yale U., 1979 · M. M. N. Stansfield, 'The Holland family, dukes of Exeter, earls of Kent and Huntingdon, 1352–1475', DPhil diss., U. Oxf., 1987 · A. Tuck, *Richard II and the English nobility* (1973) · N. Saul, *Richard II* (1997) · A. Goodman, *The loyal conspiracy: the lords appellant under Richard II* (1971) · G. F. Beltz, *Memorials of the most noble order of the Garter* (1841) · GEC, *Peerage* · A. B. Steel, *Richard II* (1941) · *Chancery records* · Thomae Walsingham, quondam monachi S. Albani, historia Anglicana, ed. H. T. Riley, 2 vols., pt 1 of *Chronica monasterii S. Albani*, Rolls Series, 28 (1863–4) · G. B. Stow, ed., *Historia vitae et regni Ricardi Secundi* (1977) · J. Froissart, *Chronicles of England, France, Spain, and the adjoining countries*, trans. T. Johnes, 2 vols. (1857) · *The chronicle of Adam Usk, 1377–1421*, ed. and trans. C. Given-Wilson, OMT (1997) · CIPM, 18, nos. 974–8 · CPR, 1391–6
Wealth at death over £642 18s. p.a.: CIPM, 18, nos. 974–8, 333–5

Holland, Thomas (d. 1612), university professor, was born in Ludlow, Shropshire, the second son of William Holland of Burwarton in the same county. He was educated at Oxford, where he gained an exhibition at Oriel College on 23 September 1569 and graduated BA on 9 December 1570. He probably entered the Middle Temple in 1571. On 13 January 1573 he was elected *socius sacerdotalis* or chaplain-fellow of Balliol College, where he was also college reader in rhetoric from 1575–7. He proceeded MA on 21 June 1575, and entered the faculty of theology; he graduated BTh on 13 July 1582 and DTh on 15 July 1584.

In 1585 Holland left Oxford for the northern Netherlands to work as a personal chaplain of Robert Dudley, earl of Leicester, a known patron of Calvinists in England. A renowned scholar as well as a loyal evangelical, on his return to Oxford in 1589 Holland was appointed regius professor of theology, a post he held until his death. On 9

June 1590 he was made a canon of Salisbury Cathedral on recommendation of the crown. A year later he was installed as rector of St Nicholas, Rotherfield Greys, Oxfordshire.

On 29 March 1592 Holland was elected to a fellowship at Exeter College, Oxford. In an attempt to bring religious conservatives among the fellowship to conformity, he was appointed rector of the college on the instigation of the queen and Sir John Petre. His election was disputed by the fellowship and not confirmed until 24 April, when his opponent 'who was really elected, resigned his claim at Lambeth, before Archbishop Whitgift, the Bishop of Oxford, and … the chancellor of the University' (Boase, *Registrum Collegii Exoniensis*, 84). He was noted as a skilled disputant in the university, and participated with his fellow doctors of theology at a debate in honour of Queen Elizabeth's visitation to the university in autumn 1592, and again thirteen years later during the visit of James I.

Holland was a gifted linguist, and frequently drew on the Hebrew scriptures and the Talmud in his sermons. At his suggestion John Prideaux, a good friend and protégé, compiled a Greek grammar for his students. His proficiency in biblical languages and his love for the scriptures were reason for his appointment in 1605 to translate, together with six other Oxford scholars, the prophetic books of the Old Testament (Isaiah–Malachi) for the Authorized Version of the Bible. He left two discourses in print: an oration on the occasion of Bishop Henry Cotton's graduation, *Oratio habita cum Henricus episcopus Sarisburiensis gradum doctoris susceperit*, was published in 1599; and a panegyric on the queen preached at St Paul's Cathedral, *Panēgyris D. Elizabethae Reginae: a sermon preached at Pauls in London the 17 of November*, appeared two years later. In 1612 Thomas Thompson, of Queen's College, edited and published the notaries' account of two disputations on monastic vows moderated in 1609 by Holland under the title, *Claviger ecclesiae: theses duae de votis monasticis*. On 2 February 1610, towards the end of his life, Holland was made an honorary member of Gray's Inn.

Throughout his life Holland remained a stalwart opponent of Catholicism. At his funeral oration the rector of Lincoln College, Richard Kilbie, recalled that 'a common farewell when he took any longer journey was this, Commendo vos dilectioni Dei, et odio papatus et superstitionis (I commend you to the love of God, and to the hatred of popery and superstition)' (Kilbie, 18). Holland died at Exeter College, Oxford, on 17 March 1612, and was buried on 26 March in the chancel of the university church of St Mary the Virgin. He was survived by his wife, Susanna, and was father to two children, Anne and William. J. ANDREAS LÖWE

Sources T. Holland, *Oratio habita cum Henricus episcopus Sarisburiensis gradum doctoris susceperit* (1599) • T. Holland, *Panēgyris D. Elizabethae … Reginae: a sermon preached at Pauls in London the 17 of November … 1599* (1601) • T. Thompson, *Claviger ecclesiae* (1612) • R. Kilbie, *A sermon preached in Maries Church in Oxford March 26. 1612* (1613), 16–18 • Wood, *Ath. Oxon.*, new edn, 2.111 • Foster, *Alum. Oxon., 1500–1714*, 2.731 • J. Foster, *The register of admissions to Gray's Inn, 1521–1889, together with the register of marriages in Gray's Inn chapel, 1695–1754* (privately printed, London, 1889), 122 • *Fasti Angl.*

(Hardy), 2.654 • *Fasti Angl., 1541–1857*, [Salisbury], 86 • C. W. Boase, ed., *Registrum Collegii Exoniensis*, new edn, OHS, 27 (1894), 83 • *Reg. Oxf.*, 1.281; 2/1.33, 230; 2/3.53 • *Hist. U. Oxf.* 3: *Colleg. univ.*, 318, 354 • J. Jones, *Balliol College: a history, 1263–1939* (1988), 289

Likenesses Passe, line engraving, BM, NPG; repro. in Holland, *Herōologia Anglica* (1620) • portrait?, Bodl. Oxf., Hope collection

Holland [*alias* Sanderson, Hammond], **Thomas** (1600–1642), Jesuit, was born at Sutton Hall, Prescot, Lancashire, the son of Richard Holland, gentleman, and Anne Ewers of Sutton Hall. He was educated to 1621 in the Jesuit college at St Omer and then at the English College, Valladolid. When Prince Charles visited Madrid in 1623 Holland, at the request of his fellow collegians, addressed the prince in a Latin oration, assuring him of the loyalty and good wishes of the English students in the seminaries of Spain. He entered the noviciate of the English province of the Society of Jesus at Watten on 16 May 1624, and afterwards studied theology at the college at Liège, where he was ordained priest about 1630, and was then at the Jesuit house at Ghent. Subsequently he was appointed prefect and confessor to the scholars at St Omer. In 1635 he was sent to England, and for seven years laboured on the mission in London, sometimes assuming the aliases of Sanderson and Hammond. At length, on 4 October 1642, he was arrested and committed to the New prison, and was then transferred to Newgate. On 7 December he was indicted for being a priest at the Old Bailey before Serjeant Phesant, was found guilty, and on 12 December 1642 was executed at Tyburn in the presence of a large crowd, including Count Egmont, the Spanish ambassador, and almost all his suite. Holland's quarters were displayed on London gates. He was beatified by Pope Pius XI on 15 December 1929. A manuscript book of his theological writings at Liège is preserved at Stonyhurst College.

THOMPSON COOPER, rev. G. BRADLEY

Sources W. F. Rea, 'Blessed Thomas Holland', *Stonyhurst Magazine*, 27 (1944) • A. Corby, *Certamen triplex a tribus societatis Jesu ex provincia Anglicana sacerdotibus, T. Hollando, R. Corbaeo, H. Morsaeo* (Antwerp, 1645) • H. Foley, ed., *Records of the English province of the Society of Jesus*, 1 (1877), 542–65 • J. H. Pollen, ed., *Acts of English martyrs* (1891), 357–67 • T. M. McCoog, *English and Welsh Jesuits, 1555–1650*, 2, Catholic RS, 75 (1995), 289 • G. Holt, *St Omers and Bruges colleges, 1593–1773: a biographical dictionary*, Catholic RS, 69 (1979) • R. Challoner, *Memoirs of missionary priests*, ed. J. H. Pollen, rev. edn (1924), 435–9 • Gillow, *Lit. biog. hist.*, 3.353

Archives Archives of the British Province of the Society of Jesus, Stonyhurst College, Lancashire, Stonyhurst MSS, Anglia, A vol 5

Likenesses engraving, repro. in Corbye, *Certamen triplex* • miniature, St Mawgan's Carmelite Convent, Lanherne, Newquay, Cornwall

Holland, Thomas Agar (1803–1888), Church of England clergyman and poet, was born on 16 January 1803 at Poynings rectory, near Steyning, Sussex, the eldest son of Samuel Holland (1772–1857), precentor of Chichester and rector of Poynings, and Frances Erskine, eldest daughter of Thomas *Erskine (1750–1823), lord chancellor. He was educated at Westminster School, London, from June 1816 to Christmas 1818, and then spent some time at Edinburgh University and later attended Worcester College, Oxford, matriculating in 1821. He took his BA in 1825, proceeding MA in 1828. He entered the church as deacon in 1826, becoming a priest the following year in Chichester. He was then instituted as vicar of Oving, Sussex (1827–38). In 1831 he married Magdaline Stewart, daughter of Major Philip Stewart. Their eldest son, the jurist Sir Thomas Erskine *Holland, was born in 1835. Holland became rector of Greatham, Hampshire, in 1838 and in 1846 he succeeded his father as rector of Poynings. In the same year he was a founder member of the Sussex Archaeological Society, to which he belonged until his death. It was for the society's publication that he wrote his *History of Poynings* in 1863.

Holland's first publication as a poet was anonymous: *The Colossal Statue of William Wallace: a Poem by an Undergraduate* (Oxford, 1824). His major claim to the title of poet was established by his collection *Dryburgh Abbey and other Poems* (1826). In his preface he talks of the title-poem:

> commenced in the winter, 1820–21 which the author (being yet in his 'teens') spent in Edinburgh, attending a session of the University (whence also the Latin prize) and occasionally visiting his grand-uncle, the late Earl of Buchan, at his mansion contiguous to the ruins of Dryburgh Abbey.

These visits inspired the lengthy piece, in octosyllabics, which reflects his actively anti-Catholic stance in its attitudes to idolatry. His anti-Catholic views were often in evidence in his preaching and writing, as he campaigned against the religion's revival in England. *Dryburgh Abbey* was a popular volume: it was issued in successive editions in 1829, 1845, and 1884. The volume was said by his son to have received the warm commendation of Sir Walter Scott, and there is evidence of Scott's influence on Holland's writing, especially in the Romantic appeal of Scottish history. The accompanying poems were rooted in the natural world and family, varying in tone from earnest to witty. Attended by his wife, Holland died at his beloved Poynings rectory on 18 October 1888 of senile decay and heart failure, leaving four surviving sons and three daughters.   ROSEMARY SCOTT

Sources DNB · Boase, *Mod. Eng. biog.* · Crockford · annual reports, 1846–8, Sussex Archaeological Society · *Transactions of the Sussex Archaeological Society* (1863) · BL cat. · Foster, *Alum. Oxon.* · *Old Westminsters*, vol. 1 · T. A. Holland, preface, in T. A. Holland, *Dryburgh Abbey and other poems* (1826) · d. cert.

Archives Bodl. Oxf., letters to Sir Thomas Phillipps · LPL, letters to Charles Golightly · NL Scot., letters to John Gough Nichols relating to Mar peerage case

Wealth at death £1106 8s. 6d.: probate, 31 Jan 1889, CGPLA Eng. & Wales

Holland, Sir Thomas Erskine (1835–1926), jurist, was born at Brighton on 17 July 1835, the eldest son of the Revd Thomas Agar *Holland (1803–1888) of Poynings, Sussex, and the great-grandson of Thomas Erskine, first Baron Erskine, lord chancellor. His mother was Magdaline, daughter of Major Philip Stewart. He attended Brighton College from 1847 to 1853. In 1854 he matriculated at Balliol College, Oxford, but in the following year migrated to Magdalen College as a foundation scholar. Holland obtained a second class in classical moderations in 1856 and a first class in *literae humaniores* in 1858. In his undergraduate days he joined the Old Mortality society, where he found intellectual companionship with other students

such as Albert Venn Dicey, James Bryce, and Thomas Hill Green. He was elected to a fellowship at Exeter College in 1859, and for a short time taught philosophy there.

Holland soon turned from philosophy to law, and going to London, read in chambers with W. H. Butterworth, the special pleader, with G. De Morgan, the conveyancer, with H. T. Erskine, and with A. Kekewich (in equity). In 1863 he was called to the bar by Lincoln's Inn and joined the home circuit. After some years of practice at the bar, combined with journalism and lecturing, he was elected Vinerian reader in 1874. Later in the same year he was elected to the Chichele chair of international law and diplomacy, a position which he held until his retirement in 1910, when he received the title of emeritus professor. In 1875 he was elected to a fellowship at All Souls College, which he held until his death. Holland completed his legal education by taking the bachelor of civil law degree in 1871 and the doctorate in civil law in 1876, both at Oxford. Among the other honours he earned was a knighthood in 1917. He took silk in 1901 and was an original fellow of the British Academy.

Holland was married twice. His first wife was Louise Henriette Delessert (d. 1891) of Passy; married in 1871, they had six sons and one daughter. Two of his sons predeceased Holland—one, tragically, was lost at sea. These losses took a toll on Holland's character, though they did not alter his commitment to his legal research and writing. In 1895 Holland married Ellen, widow of Stephen Edwardes, fellow of Merton College, Oxford; there were no children from the second marriage.

As the author of *The Elements of Jurisprudence*, which in his lifetime was widely regarded as the most successful book on jurisprudence ever written, Holland enjoyed an enviable reputation. This book first appeared in 1880, and Holland revised the thirteenth edition in 1924, in his eighty-ninth year. The influence of this work declined rapidly after Holland's death. It has been significant to later scholars simply as evidence of the direction analytical jurisprudence took under the guidance of a jurist whose interests were primarily academic. Holland belonged to that generation of the Oxford professoriate of the 1870s and 1880s which attempted to put the study of law on a scientific basis, central to the purposes of a modern university. In this endeavour he was joined by colleagues such as Dicey, Bryce, Sir William Anson, and Sir Frederick Pollock. Holland will always be remembered as the foremost interpreter in his generation of the analytical jurisprudence associated with Jeremy Bentham and John Austin.

The Elements of Jurisprudence repays reading because it still stands as a definitive commentary on the Bentham-Austin tradition of jurisprudence. Holland thought that he might rescue jurisprudence from the stylistic deficiencies that marred the writings of his forebears. He assumed, as did the others of his generation, that underneath the outward chaos of the common law, there existed internally consistent principles that represented the rational arrangement of legal categories. Holland thought of jurisprudence as the formal science of positive law, and this philosophical position enabled him to narrow dramatically the purview of legal speculation. Where Bentham and possibly Austin had regarded jurisprudence as a subject suitable for the reform of civil society Holland's definitions restricted law to a narrower, more formal search for legal principles. What *The Elements of Jurisprudence* gained in precision by this methodology, it lost in breadth of philosophical vision when compared with both Bentham and Austin. The book was, however, well suited for the emerging discipline of academic law, for it gathered in lucid form a body of legal knowledge that might be mastered by thorough study. The result was a comparatively short introduction to the study of law, presented in a logically organized way.

The gradual erosion of the book's influence, even in Holland's lifetime, resulted from his unwillingness to adapt the treatise to criticism and to changing intellectual fashion. As soon as Holland had published *The Elements of Jurisprudence*, he then turned for the rest of his professorial career to the study of international law. In succeeding editions of the book, he rarely acknowledged critics and made only minor changes despite the scholarly ferment within the field at the turn of the twentieth century. His passion for organization prevailed, and having expounded his views in magisterial fashion, Holland found no reason to change them.

Holland's contributions to the field of international law were less fundamental. This may have arisen from a basic philosophical conundrum that Holland never resolved. He had made the fundamental principle of his jurisprudence the positivist belief that a law unenforced by a sovereign authority was no law at all. By his own definition, international law, lacking an enforcing sovereign, was law only by courtesy or analogy, for it represented only the moral consensus of individual nations. His *Studies in International Law* (1898) did not place him among the modern founders of this legal discipline. His other publications in the area of international law were even more modest, and they certainly never equalled the fame earned by his work on jurisprudence.

Holland became best known to the general public as a frequent writer of letters to *The Times* on contemporary topics of international legal controversy. These letters were eventually collected and published in 1909 under the title, *Letters to The Times on War and Neutrality* and a third edition covering the period 1881–1920 appeared in 1921. Holland's concern for public service led him to rewrite for the Admiralty the official *Manual of Naval Prize Law* in 1888 and he prepared a handbook on the *Laws and Customs of War on Land* which was issued to the army in 1904. From 1903 to 1905 Holland served on the royal commission on the supply of food and raw material in time of war, and in 1906 he was one of the British plenipotentiaries to the conference at Geneva at which the Geneva Convention of 1864, dealing with the sick and wounded in land warfare, was revised.

Holland participated in university business at Oxford throughout his academic career. He served as assessor (sole judge) of the chancellor's court from 1876 to 1910,

and during his tenure of that office secured a thorough reform of the then antiquated procedure of that tribunal. His fixation on points of minor procedural importance at the expense of the practical issues at hand made him an ineffective operative in university politics. He rarely took notice of opposing views, made little effort to find common ground, and as a result forfeited whatever influence he might have won. His excessive insistence on points of form led Holland into one quixotic academic battle after another in which he invariably found himself on the losing side.

Holland was a handsome individual who in later life had a tonsure of silver hair that added distinction to the formality of his personality. His professorial dignity gave him an air of aloofness that precluded easy intimacy. For those who penetrated this façade, however, Holland proved a friend of warmth and support. Holland fought consistently for the improvement of undergraduate education and grew increasingly ambivalent about the increasing emphasis on research in the context of a professional discipline.

Holland was also among the founders of the *Law Quarterly Review*, the legal periodical that acted as a model for legal journals around the world. Frederick Pollock credited Holland with providing the intellectual leadership that made its appearance possible in 1885. For this alone Holland would merit the gratitude of ensuing generations of students and scholars. Holland remained active to the end of his long life. He was a keen walker and visited the Eggishorn regularly from the late sixties until just a year before his death. He died at Poynings House, 74 Woodstock Road, Oxford, on 24 May 1926 and was buried in Wolvercote cemetery. He was survived by his second wife. RICHARD A. COSGROVE

Sources W. S. Holdsworth, *Professor Sir Thomas Erskine Holland* (1927) • R. A. Cosgrove, *Scholars of the law: English jurisprudence from Blackstone to Hart* (1997) • T. E. Holland, *A valedictory retrospect* (1910) • Boston University, Mugar Memorial Library, Melville Madison Bigelow MSS • W. L. Morison, *John Austin* (1982) • F. H. Lawson, *The Oxford law school, 1850–1965* (1968) • *The Times* (25 May 1926) • CGPLA Eng. & Wales (1926)

Archives Bodl. Oxf., papers relating to Albericus Gentilis | All Souls Oxf., letters to Sir William Anson • Harvard U., Holmes MSS

Likenesses albumen print, c.1851–1859, NPG • H. G. Rivière, oils, exh. 1914, Athenaeum, London • W. Stoneman, photograph, 1917, NPG • photograph, All Souls Oxf.

Wealth at death £33,525 1s. 4d.: probate, 10 July 1926, CGPLA Eng. & Wales

Holland, Sir Thomas Henry (1868–1947), geologist and civil servant, was born at Helston Mills, Helston, Cornwall, on 22 November 1868, the son of John Holland, a miller, formerly of Springfield, Manitoba, and his wife, Grace Treloar, daughter of William Roberts, farmer. His Canadian family played a notable part in his life and in shaping his view of the world, its morphology, and its minerals. Educated at a local dame-school, at the age of sixteen he won a national scholarship to the Normal School of Science and Royal School of Mines, South Kensington, where he was taught by John Wesley Judd, professor of geology. In 1887 he won the Murchison medal and prize in geology, and in 1888 took the associateship of the Royal College of Science (RCS). At the RCS he began the college magazine (*The Phoenix*), and became a founder member of the student union. Holland developed a taste for research in chemical geology. His first scientific publications appeared in 1889 and in the same year he competed against older and more qualified men to win a three-year Berkeley fellowship at Owens College, Manchester. During his first year there, however, he accepted appointment as an assistant superintendent in the geological survey of India.

Holland sailed for Calcutta in October 1890—unusually via North America and Asia, where he took the chance to study local geological questions. As curator of the geological museum and laboratory of Calcutta he rearranged the rock collections in the mineral gallery to illustrate Precambrian formations. He entered energetically into colonial life, joining the Calcutta volunteer rifles (captain, 1891–1903) and the presidency battalion. Holland's early letters reveal him to be concerned with religious matters and he considered spending time in missionary work, but after initial hesitation, he became a part-time lecturer in geology at Presidency College, Calcutta, and in 1893 assisted the court of directors in inaugurating a chair of geology and mineralogy, of which he became the first incumbent. For the first time, Indian students could now take BA examinations in geology. A vigorous public scientist, Holland served repeatedly as president of the Microscopical Society of Calcutta (1893–6), and of the Mining and Geological Institute of India. His first-hand descriptions—published chiefly in the *Records* of the survey but also transmitted to London—challenged received views of Indian petrology and mineralogy. In 1894 he won local celebrity for predicting the rupture of a dam by a landslip at Gohna in the Himalayas. Subsequently he wrote on the mica-apatite-peridotites of the coalfields of Bihar and Bengal. His energy, personality, analytical talent, and eye for economic significance, commended him to the government of India. Over the heads of men senior to him he was appointed deputy superintendent of the survey in 1894, and in February 1903, director. He married, on 23 December 1896, at Moradabad, United Provinces, Frances Maud (*d.* 1942), daughter of Charles Chapman, deputy commissioner in Oudh, whose family were administrators and soldiers in India and Burma. Their son, John Charles Francis *Holland CB DFC, and daughter, Margaretta Victoria Elizabeth, later wife of Colonel A. G. Shea, were born in India.

From its creation in 1851 the survey had achieved a formidable scientific reputation, but one identified more with the interests of imperial rule than with local economic development. Holland's appointment coincided with a change of focus, accompanying growing interest in mineral investment throughout the world. Within a decade the economic value of India's mineral production almost doubled, and prospecting concessions increased sixfold. As director Holland overhauled the survey, increased its staff and their remuneration, and enhanced the status accorded to economic questions. He launched the survey's famous quinquennial reviews of economic minerals (the first covering the period 1898–1903), revived and extended its annual publication of mineral statistics, and secured for it the role of adviser to government on mining concessions. Under his administration the survey's scientific output also doubled, and the *Records of the Geological Survey* went to major scientific libraries throughout Europe and America.

Holland took a global view of his subject. Chafing at the difficulty of keeping up with original work, he obtained home leave in 1895 and 1898, during which he visited North America and Europe, and spoke to the British Association. In 1902 Holland again returned home, and received the Murchison medal of the Geological Society. Encouraged and assisted by his wife, who endured the trials of family life and separation, he published extensively. By 1903 he had written twenty-two papers on mineralogy, petrology, chemical geology, and physical geology in a variety of British journals, as well as in the *Records*. Nominated to the Royal Society by a dozen former teachers and contemporaries, representative of the leading geological departments of Oxford, Manchester, Cambridge, and Edinburgh, he was elected FRS in 1904.

As a practising geologist Holland became well known for his discovery of a suite of Archaean hypersthene-bearing rocks in Madras, which in 1900 he termed the charnockite series after Job Charnock (*d.* 1693), the founder of Calcutta, whose tomb in St John's churchyard is made of this material. In other directions Holland organized diamond-drilling in Singhbhum, which helped develop the copper industry there, and described the eleilite-syenites of Sivamalai (1901), as well as mica deposits (1902) valuable to the revenue of India. In 1903 he was among the earliest to recognize the essential identity of bauxite and laterite and three years later he introduced a new system of classification and nomenclature for Indian formations. His contribution to debates surrounding the putative existence of Gondwanaland raised the survey's profile. In 1905, at the request of the viceroy, Lord Curzon, Holland conducted experiments on the durability of the marbles of India and Europe, which cleared the way for the use of Makrana marble, similar to that used in the Taj Mahal, in the new Victoria Memorial Hall in Calcutta. In 1906, with William Henry Pickering, chief inspector of mines in India, Holland founded the Mining and Geological Institute of India and became its first president. He also became a member of the Institute of Engineers (India), and an honorary fellow of the Asiatic Society of Bengal (president, 1909). Between 1906 and 1909 he was chairman of the trustees of the Indian Museum in Calcutta. In 1908 his expertise, valued by government departments 'imperial, colonial and foreign', was recognized in his appointment as knight commander in the Order of the Indian Empire.

Increasing responsibilities brought heavier administrative work. In 1908 Holland observed that much of what he did had only an indirect connection with science, and had to force opportunities to keep in touch with what he called his 'real work'. In fact, he became widely known for his advocacy of practical science, especially as applied to the economic development of India. In 1910 he took early retirement from the survey and returned to Manchester as professor of geology at the Victoria University. There he taught applied geology, mineralogy, and petrology and introduced a new course in mineral economics. His ability to engage simultaneously in many things left him time for membership of the royal commission on navy fuel and engines (1911–13), and for service on the councils of the Institution of Mining Engineers (IME), the Institute of Mining and Metallurgy (IMM), and the Mineralogical Society. He continued his connection with India on the selection committee of the geological survey and represented the Indian government on the advisory committee of the Imperial Institute.

The coming of war in August 1914 found Holland in Australia, where he was sectional president for geology at the British Association's congress. Imperial geology, he noted, was really the 'science of the Earth' seen as a whole, and when the war created a huge demand for strategic minerals, Holland found himself again at centre stage. He remained in Manchester through 1915 but in early 1916 was recalled to India to serve as president of the Indian industrial commission (1916–18), and later as president of the Indian munitions board (1917). Professor John Simonsen, Manchester's distinguished organic chemist, became his chemical adviser. When published in 1919 the commission's report framed post-war imperial policy towards agriculture, industry, fisheries, energy, transportation, industrial investment, technical education, commercial intelligence, land acquisition, and labour welfare.

For his wartime services Holland was appointed KCSI in 1918. The next year the Indian munitions board was transformed into the department of munitions and industries of the government of India, and Holland was confirmed as its head, resigning from Manchester to become the youngest member of the viceroy's executive council. In July 1920 he was also appointed member for commerce and thus held two portfolios. At the end of 1921, however, this new career in India was cut short by a policy difference with the viceroy (Lord Reading). Accepting his resignation, both the secretary of state for India and the viceroy testified to the value of his imperial work. The following year Holland returned to South Kensington as rector of the Imperial College of Science and Technology.

In London, Holland warmed to what he called his 'old college', and added greatly to its public life. Within two years he secured agreement with the University of London to recognize the associateship examination as qualifying for the London BSc (with honours), and opened hostel accommodation for Imperial College students. In 1929, with his administrative reputation enhanced, he succeeded Sir Alfred Ewing as principal and vice-chancellor of the University of Edinburgh. The next fifteen years were happy, and his efforts met with conspicuous success. Confident and forceful, he appreciated those qualities in others. He negotiated the fusion of the university's faculty of divinity with the New College of the Church of Scotland, secured the affiliation of the Heriot-Watt College

and the Royal (Dick) Veterinary College, and presided over the university's 350th anniversary in 1933. As a mark of respect he was appointed deputy lieutenant for the county of the city of Edinburgh, and elected an honorary member of the Edinburgh Merchant Company. He retired from Edinburgh in 1944, at the age of seventy-six.

Almost continuously at work for fifty-four years, Holland is universally remembered for his astonishing energy. In Calcutta, Manchester, London, and Edinburgh, he played leading roles in several professional societies. He was president of the IME (1915–16), of the IMM (1925–7, gold medal 1930), and of the Institute of Petroleum Technologists (1925–7), as well as president of the Geological Society of London (1932–4, Bigsby medal, 1913), and of the Mineralogical Society of London (1933–6). He was a vice-president of the Royal Society (1924–5), and fellow (elected 1930) and vice-president (1932–5) of the Royal Society of Edinburgh. He was chairman of the Royal Society of Arts (1925–7, Albert medal 1939), and of the Empire Council of Mining and Metallurgical Institutions (1927–30). He was also a member of the Royal Cornwall Polytechnic Society and the Liverpool Geological Society. His imperial services were recognized by honorary DSc degrees from the universities of Calcutta, Melbourne, and the Witwatersrand, and he received LLD degrees from Manchester and Queen's (Ontario). Scotland outshone even these, giving him honorary LLD degrees from all four Scottish universities—Glasgow, Edinburgh, Aberdeen, and St Andrews.

Holland's most significant contribution to the study of mineral economics began with his experience of India, and continued at Manchester; it came to a focus in a paper for the IMM and culminated in his presidential address 'The international relationship of minerals' to the British Association in Johannesburg in 1929. In this he outlined the possibility of using 'mineral denial' as an instrument of peacekeeping among the industrial powers. His views, later expanded in *The Mineral Sanction as an Aid to International Security* (1935), were controversial, and in retrospect, politically impractical, but contributed significantly to the principle of economic sanctions.

Holland's abiding interest in geology as an instrument of economic development was equally well known. In 1928 he advised the Colonial Office on prospects for oil exploration in Trinidad, and was for many years a consultant to the Burma Oil Company. In the late 1930s he undertook an aerial survey of the oil fields of Mesopotamia, and served for twelve years on the geological advisory board of the Anglo-Iranian Oil Company. In retirement he retained a keen interest in resources policy, and, in June 1945, returned from a visit to the Soviet Union to report approvingly on Moscow's support for economic geology. He also continued to serve science as foreign secretary of the Geological Society and the Mineralogical Society. On 27 November 1946 Holland married Helen Ethleen (*b.* 1897/8), daughter of Frank Verrall, a retired brewer, of Bramley, near Guildford. She was active in local government, and served until 1954 as a member of Surrey county council. He died in Surrey County Hospital, St Helier, Carshalton, of prostate complications, on 15 May 1947. At the time of his death, he was president-designate of the Eighteenth International Geological Congress, held in Britain in 1948. ROY M. MACLEOD

Sources L. Fermor, *Nature*, 160 (1947), 11–13 · L. L. Fermor, *Obits. FRS*, 6 (1948–9), 83–114 · *The Times* (20 May 1947), 7 · *Transactions of the Institution of Mining and Metallurgy*, 57 (1947–8), 473–4 · C. S. Gibson, 'Thomas Henry Holland', *Journal of the Royal Society of Arts*, 95 (1946–7), 438–9 · *The Phoenix*, 24 (Dec 1911), 26–27 · RS, MS 768 · family letters, 1887–1918, ICL · T. G. Chambers, *Register of the associates and old students of the Royal College of Chemistry, the Royal College of Mines and the Royal College of Science* (1896) · *Records of the Geological Survey of India*, 41 (1912), 53–5 · E. Wedderburn and L. Fermor, *Year Book of the Royal Society of Edinburgh* (1946–8), 27–9 · *University of Edinburgh Journal*, 14 (1946–9), 117 · *University of Edinburgh Journal*, 27 (1975–6), 142 · J. H. Burnett, D. Howarth, and S. D. Fletcher, *The university portraits: second series* (1986), 110 · *The Record* [Old Students Association, Royal College of Science, London], 2nd ser., 2 (Jan 1930), 7–8 · *One hundred twenty five years of the Geological Survey of India (1851–1976): a short history* (1976) · M. Adams, ed., *Science in a changing world* (1933) · D. Kumar, 'Economic compulsions and the geological survey of India', *Indian Journal of History of Science*, 17/2 (1982), 289–300 · H. B. Charlton, *Portrait of a university, 1851–1951: to commemorate the centenary of Manchester University* (1951) · b. cert. · m. cert., 1946 · d. cert. · BL OIOC, IOR N/1/254 f. 59
Archives ICL, letters to his family · RS, corresp.
Likenesses S. Cursiter, portrait, U. Edin. · J. Wilke, portrait, Asiatic Society of Bengal, Calcutta
Wealth at death £55,005 4s. 4d.: probate, 27 Aug 1947, CGPLA Eng. & Wales

Holland, William (1711–1761), Moravian leader, was born on 16 January 1711 in Haverfordwest, Pembrokeshire, a son of Nicholas Holland. In March 1725 he was apprenticed to a relation in London, a house-painter. After completing his apprenticeship Holland returned to Wales to visit his relations, but when his former master died he moved back to London to take over the business, becoming a freeman of the City in July 1733.

Holland had joined one of the London religious societies in 1732. In 1736 he became a devotee of the devotional writer William Law, and it was when purchasing books by Law that he met James Hutton, the apprentice of the bookseller who sold them. He joined a new group formed by Hutton, and in April 1738 attended a meeting addressed by the Moravian Peter Böhler. Holland was out of town on 1 May, when Böhler formed a Moravian-style band which was to become the Fetter Lane Society. Later that month he showed Luther's *Commentary on the Epistle to the Galatians* to Charles Wesley and had an experience of liberation as Wesley read the preface aloud. Holland now joined one of the new bands stemming from Böhler's. Holland has been identified with the 'one' whose reading of Luther's *Preface to the Epistle to the Romans* occasioned John Wesley's 'heart-warming' experience.

Holland remained in the Fetter Lane Society after John Wesley withdrew, and in March 1741 the Moravians assumed its leadership. On 31 March 1741 he married Elizabeth (1710–1780), daughter of Peter and Elizabeth Delamotte and sister of the Moravian evangelist William Delamotte. Elizabeth had, in the previous year, refused a proposal of marriage from George Whitefield. She and Holland had six children, of whom four predeceased their father and only one daughter outlived their mother.

Elected one of two new society stewards in August 1741, Holland liquidated his large house-painting business in September to become a full-time 'labourer', moving from Basinghall Street to a room in the Moravians' headquarters in Little Wild Street. He was received into the Moravian church when its first English congregation was established in May 1742, and when the London congregation was founded in October 1742 Holland became its elder. In October 1743 he replaced the disaffected Richard Viney as warden of the Yorkshire congregation.

In 1744 Holland himself became dissatisfied, sympathizing with Viney, and from August 1744 another dispute arose, over a decision that the Moravians should register their places of worship as dissenting meeting-houses. Holland was a leading opponent of this, arguing that it was contrary to the assurance which he had secured in 1742 that Anglicans received into the Moravian church could remain members of the Church of England. Eventually he acquiesced in registration under the Toleration Act, but he held out, ultimately alone, against acceptance of the term 'dissenter'. In 1745 he was relieved of his office and summoned to Germany, leaving with his wife in September. In Germany he wrote an important account of the early years of the English revival to support his views.

After returning to England, Holland attended a Moravian general synod in the Netherlands in May 1746. He returned in August, and in November was sent on a mission to Wales. On his return in March 1747 he was re-admitted to the leadership's conference and sent temporarily to supervise work in Wiltshire. Back in London from July, Holland seems to have attempted to conform to the distinctive spirituality then prevailing in the Moravian church, but to no avail. In October 1747 he was told to cease preaching and resume his trade, and in December he withdrew from the Moravian church.

Holland now associated with, but did not join, the Wesleys. Instead he returned to the communion of the Church of England and mainly attended the preaching of evangelical clergy. His wife remained a Moravian, and her mother, Elizabeth Delamotte, who lived with the Hollands at the Rolls Buildings in Fetter Lane, became one. Holland supplied information to the anti-Moravian pamphleteer Henry Rimius in 1755, but he later became more friendly towards the Moravians, and in the later 1750s his eldest son was apprenticed to a leading Yorkshire Moravian. William Holland died suddenly of a stroke at his home in Fetter Lane on 23 February 1761. C. J. PODMORE

Sources W. Holland, 'An extract or short account of some few matters relating to the work of the Lord in England', MS, Moravian Church House, London · *DWB* · E. Holland, 'Memoir', in A. Dallimore, *George Whitefield*, 2 vols. (1970). 1.597–8 · C. J. Podmore, *The Moravian church in England, 1728–1760* (1998) · Fetter Lane congregation diary, Moravian Church House, 23 Feb 1761 · E. Griffiths, 'Moravians and Methodists: a sidelight on their early relations', *Cylchgrawn Cymdeithas Hanes Eglwys Methodistiaid Calfinaidd Cymru*, 16 (1931), 106–16 · E. Griffiths, 'A Moravian's diary: William Holland's journey through south Wales in 1746', *Cylchgrawn Cymdeithas Hanes Eglwys Methodistiaid Calfinaidd Cymru*, 16 (1931), 149–57 · E. Griffiths, 'A Moravian's diary: William Holland's journey through south Wales in 1746', *Cylchgrawn Cymdeithas Hanes Eglwys*

Methodistiaid Calfinaidd Cymru, 17 (1932), 6–11 • E. Griffiths, 'A Moravian's diary: William Holland's return from Wales in 1742 [*sic*]', *Cylchgrawn Cymdeithas Hanes Eglwys Methodistiaid Calfinaidd Cymru*, 17 (1932), 105–12 • city freedom admission bundle, July 1733, CLRO • D. Benham, *Memoirs of James Hutton* (1856)
Archives Fulneck Moravian Church, near Pudsey, Yorkshire, letters • Moravian Church House, London, letters and narrative accounts • Unitätsarchiv, Herrnhunt, Germany, letters

Holland, William (1837–1895), showman and music-hall and theatre entrepreneur, was born on 26 December 1837 at 58 Newington Causeway, London, the son of alderman William Holland, linen draper and wholesale upholsterer, and his wife, Mary, *née* Bayly. Though apprenticed to the family business, he was enamoured of amateur theatricals and left the trade while still young to promote minstrel shows, in which he played the interlocutor.

In 1866 in partnership with a publican uncle, Holland successfully revived Weston's music-hall in Holborn, a major venue fallen on hard times. He went into independent management in 1867 in the famous Canterbury music-hall in Lambeth, another ailing business rescued by the lavish refurbishments, aggressive publicity, and flamboyant self-promotion that were the trade marks of his career as 'the British Barnum'. At the Canterbury he laid the stalls with expensive Brussels carpet, compounding the misgivings of friends by inviting the public to 'Come and spit on Billy Holland's thousand guinea carpet' (H. G. Hibbert, *Fifty Years of a Londoner's Life*, 1916, 57). Here in 1868 Holland signed the biggest star of the day, George Leybourne, 'Champagne Charlie', to an exclusive contract, obliging him to maintain the lordly and extravagant style of his hit song off as well as on stage, while Holland placarded London with details of his sensational salary. 'We are', declared Holland, 'living in an age of luxury' ('Chat with William Holland', *The Era*, 6 Jan 1894), a luxury which he determined to extend to all classes, casting himself as 'the People's Caterer', and 'Emperor of Lambeth', an invocation of his personal hero, Napoleon III, whom he emulated in dress, manner, and carefully cultivated moustache.

In the 1870s Holland extended his entertainment empire to management of the Victoria and Surrey theatres and proprietorship of the North Woolwich Riverside Pleasure Gardens where his novel promotions included contests of trade skills for such as barmaids, postmen, and costers. 'The People's William' was himself frequently part of the show, riding on Blondin's back on tightrope at one of his halls and making surprise appearances in pantomime at the Surrey. Famously generous, he was a prominent freemason and ubiquitous figure at professional benefits and dinners, accompanied by his confidant and business adviser, fat Joe Pope, former army surgeon. Holland provided private entertainments for the prince of Wales, but also held benefits for Newcastle workers on strike for the nine-hour day in 1871 and provided soup for London's unemployed in 1886. Among his equally sensational failures were bull-fights at the Agricultural Hall over Christmas 1869, when imported Spanish bulls proved too meek to fight and Holland lost £7000 in three days—a notable improvidence for the then president of the Music Hall Provident Fund. Later ventures included management of Wilton's and the Alhambra, circus and variety bills at Covent Garden Opera House, and schemes to convert the Great Eastern steamship into an entertainment complex. Though he escaped one process-server by balloon from the North Woolwich, Holland was forced to declare bankruptcy in 1876 and again in 1881. In his last major metropolitan venture he took over the Albert Palace in Battersea, joining with the RSPCA in sponsoring a 3 mile parade of London carthorses as publicity. When the Albert proved 'not too cashful' (H. Chance Newton, *Idols of the Halls*, 1975, 89), Holland moved in 1887 to the new frontier of mass entertainments, Blackpool. Despite the timidity of fellow directors, his enterprising management of the Winter Gardens (and a similar operation in Morecambe) achieved popular and financial success and he commissioned the town's new opera house. Holland drove himself hard and died at his home, 46 Park Road, Blackpool, on 29 December 1895, following a talent scouting trip to the USA, his personal finances reportedly in a mess. He was buried in Blackpool and survived by his wife Mary Matilda, (to whom he had been married for more than thirty years), a daughter Matilda (Minnie), and a son Louis, also in theatre management.

Though his bravura style was being superseded by the bureaucratic disciplines of the large corporation, Billy Holland's quasi-aristocratic largesse and populist rhetoric of progress and plenty exemplified the confidence of liberal capitalism in an expanding modern leisure market.

PETER BAILEY

Sources Music-hall trade press and memorabilia, BL, Colindale, London, Newspaper Collection • P. Bailey, 'A community of friends: business and good fellowship in London music-hall management, c. 1860–1885', *Music hall: the business of pleasure*, ed. P. Bailey (1986), 3–52 • *The Era* (10 Feb 1906) • b. cert. • d. cert.
Archives BL, Colindale, London, Newspaper Library, music-hall trade press and memorabilia
Likenesses drawing, repro. in *Entr'acte Annual* (1886), 41 • portrait, repro. in *Artiste* (1 Jan 1887)

Holland, William Henry, first Baron Rotherham (1849–1927), textile manufacturer and politician, was born on 15 December 1849, at 68 Slater Street, Manchester, the younger of the two sons of William Holland (1823–1892), a warehouseman's son, and his wife, Ellen, daughter of Samuel Robinson, a coachman. William Holland was a self-made cotton master, a prominent Wesleyan, and a JP. William Henry was educated at Manchester grammar school and Bramham College, Tadcaster. At the age of eighteen he entered the family business and, in 1872, with his brother Samuel, was admitted as a partner. He married, on 30 September 1874, Mary Jane, eldest daughter of James Lund of Malsis Hall, near Bradford; they had three children.

William Holland & Sons were spinners of Egyptian and Sea Island cotton. In 1877 William Henry introduced the spinning of 'French cashmere' woollen yarn, and in 1878 he erected a mill for worsted spinning at Manchester. The Hollands were disciplinarians, but reputedly displayed a fairness that brought immunity from labour troubles. By the 1890s the firm was one of Manchester's largest; in 1898 its cotton interests were merged into the Fine Cotton Spinners' and Doublers' Association (FCSDA), subsequently the country's largest manufacturing company. Holland became vice-chairman and, in 1908, in succession to Sir William Houldsworth, chairman. From 1897 to 1910 Holland was a director of Williams Deacon and Manchester and Salford Bank Ltd, one of the FCSDA's bankers, and he may have played a part in the financial structuring of the new firm.

Holland had other interests. From 1886 he was a director of the Manchester chamber of commerce and sat on numerous of its subcommittees; he also helped to establish the conciliation board for dealing with trade disputes. In 1881 and 1891 Holland was selected to give evidence in London before the committees considering the French treaty negotiations, and in 1898 was a member of the Indian currency committee, where he defended the monetary *status quo*. He also served as a commissioner at the Brussels, Paris, and Milan exhibitions. The esteem in which he was held by his fellow businessmen is reflected in his election to the presidency of the Manchester chamber of commerce (1896–8), the Textile Institute (1910–12), and the Association of Chambers of Commerce (1904–07). He was also a member of the Machinery Users' Association (1908–10), and the Institute of Directors.

Holland developed an interest in politics during the 1874 general election, but became active only in the 1880s; his father had been a Lancashire county councillor. He established himself in local government, serving for ten years as an alderman of the city of Manchester (1889–99), was made president of the East Manchester Liberal Association in 1885 and the Manchester Reform Club in 1895, and was a member of the executive of the National Liberal Federation. Selected for the parliamentary constituency of Salford North in 1888 he was elected in 1892, and as an MP specialized in industrial and commercial questions. However, he was defeated by six votes at the 1895 election, suffering through his support for home rule and Indian cotton duties. In 1899 he returned as member for the Rotherham division of Yorkshire. He was a forceful advocate of the Manchester chamber of commerce's interests, and of free trade, albeit not the 'do nothing' variety—in 1904 with seven fellow MPs he wrote to Campbell-Bannerman, suggesting a programme of practical measures to combat overseas competitors that would appeal to businessmen and fight Chamberlain's proposals. The *Manchester Guardian* later acclaimed his contribution to 'winning … the industrial North' in 1906 (28 Dec 1927). In the Commons he advanced particular interests: the elevation of the president of the Board of Trade to more senior cabinet ranking, machine rating, limited partnership reform, and the Channel Tunnel Bill of 1907. He chaired several committees and spoke influentially on others, but did not serve in government. In February 1910 he took the Chiltern Hundreds, making his Rotherham seat available for J. A. Pease. Six months later he was raised to the peerage—he had been knighted in 1902 and created baronet in 1907—as Baron Rotherham of Broughton.

Elevation to the Lords marked a fresh phase in Rotherham's career. He became a director of the Royal Exchange Assurance Company in 1910, the London, City and Midland Bank in 1911, the Yorkshire Penny Bank in 1912, and, in 1913, a director of the Eagle Oil Transport Company, whose chairman was Lord Cowdray. He then engaged in riskier ventures: an electric-light company in Africa, oilfields in Russia, a colliery in Wales, and land in Canada. Loss-making stock exchange dealings, coupled with disastrous speculation in Manchuria and with Japanese bonds, plus war losses, brought him into the hands of moneylenders who, in July 1917, applied for a receiving order. Anticipating bankruptcy he resigned his appointments, including the FCSDA chairmanship. His assets, at first count £6105, could not meet liabilities of £332,516—later assessed at about £125,000—but he eventually obtained release with a composition of 6s. in the pound. From 1898 to 1917 Rotherham's annual income from cotton and banking was £20,000 to £25,000; he also shared in his father's £211,000 will and received £160,000 on the sale of William Holland & Sons to the FCSDA. But bankruptcy brought oblivion. Rotherham was to attribute his fall to the large sum of money received at the formation of the FCSDA, and his move to London where 'I was too trustful' (*The Times*, 28 Dec 1927).

Rotherham enjoyed a considerable career. He was not ungenerous with time or money and contributed to Mancunian and Indian charities. He was a JP for Manchester and Cheshire; a freeman of the borough of Rotherham; and officer of the order of Leopold, Belgium. Rotherham converted to the Roman Catholic church in 1924, following his wife who converted in 1905. He was able to keep a home at Lothersdale, Rottingdean, Sussex, where he died on 26 December 1927, leaving a mere £25. His wife died in 1931 leaving £2031 gross. Their only son, educated at Harrow and Oxford, joined the army and later became an inspector in the Ministry of Pensions; the peerage became extinct on his death in 1950.   J. J. MASON

Sources J. J. Mason, 'Holland, William Henry', *DBB* · *Manchester Guardian* (14 Nov 1892) · *Manchester Guardian* (28 Dec 1927) · *The Times* (31 Oct 1917) · *The Times* (7 Nov 1917) · *The Times* (30 Jan 1918) · *The Times* (27 Feb 1918) · *The Times* (6 March 1918) · *The Times* (28 Feb 1919) · *The Times* (4 April 1919) · *The Times* (28 Dec 1927) · *The Times* (11 Sept 1928) · *The Times* (15 Aug 1931) · *Spy* (12 July 1895) · W. B. Tracy and W. T. Pike, *Manchester & Salford at the close of the 19th century: contemporary biographies* (1899) · T. Swindells, *Manchester streets and Manchester men*, 5 vols. (1906–8) · *Salford Reporter* (25 June 1892) · *Salford Reporter* (6 July 1895) · *Salford Reporter* (13 July 1895) · 'Departmental committee to inquire into the dissemination of commercial information', *Parl. papers* (1898), vol. 33, C. 8962 · 'Report of the committee to inquire into Indian currency', *Parl. papers* (1899), 31.531, C. 9421 · *The cotton industry and the fiscal question: speeches by Sir W. H. Holland and Mr William Tattersall* (1909) · President's address, *Journal of the Textile Institute*, 1/1 (1910), 44–7 · *Annual Meeting* [Association of British Chambers of Commerce] (1904–7) · E. Helm, *Chapters in the history of the Manchester chamber of commerce* [1902] · Burke, *Peerage*

Archives Courtaulds Northern Spinning Division, Fine Cotton Spinners' and Doublers' Association Ltd, annual reports; executive board minutes; general board minutes · Man. CL, Manchester Archives and Local Studies, records of the Manchester chamber of commerce | BL, Campbell-Bannerman MSS, Add. MSS 41240,

41242 · BL, Herbert Gladstone MSS, Add. MS 46061 | FILM BFI NFTVA, propaganda footage (Hepworth Manufacturing Company)
Likenesses photograph, repro. in *Spy* · photograph, repro. in *Manchester Guardian* (28 Dec 1927)
Wealth at death £24 18s. 1d.: resworn administration, 21 Aug 1928, *CGPLA Eng. & Wales*

Hollar, Wenceslaus (1607–1677), etcher, was born in Clothmakers' Street, Prague, Bohemia, on 23 July 1607, the eldest of the three sons of Jan Hollar (d. 1630), an official of the land registry in Prague, and his wife, Marketa (d. c.1613), the daughter of David Löw of Löwengrün and Bareyt in the upper Palatinate. His father, from Horažd'ovice in southern Bohemia, was knighted by the emperor Rudolf II in 1600 and given the right to bear arms and style himself 'of Práchen'. The family were protestants connected with the evangelical Bohemian Brethren.

Early career Although intended for a bureaucratic or legal career, the young Hollar turned, against his father's wishes, to the arts. Beneath his etching (c.1649) of his portrait by Meyssens he is described as 'de nature fort inclin p[ou]r l'art de meniature principalement pour esclaircir, mais beaucoup retardé par son pere'. The few surviving early etchings and drawings, including copies after Dürer and Beham, show the influence of the etcher Aegidius Sadeler, but it is unlikely that Hollar had any formal training.

In 1627, aged twenty, Hollar left Prague, probably prompted by the edict of the emperor Ferdinand II of 31 July requiring the Bohemian nobility to convert to Catholicism or emigrate. From about November 1627 to Spring 1629 he was based at Stuttgart, from 1629 to 1630 at Strasbourg, and in 1631 at Frankfurt am Main, where he worked for Matthäus Merian. For four years from 1632 he lived in Cologne, whence he made extended tours up the Rhine to Mainz in 1632 and downstream to Amsterdam in 1634. Many drawings survive from these years, including a sketchbook now in the John Rylands University Library at Manchester. The Cologne publisher Abraham Hogenberg issued Hollar's first major productions, a set of views from Prague to the Dutch coast titled *Amoenissimae aliquot locorum in diversis provinciis iacentium effigies* ('Delightful likenesses of some places lying in various countries') (1635) and a set of small portraits entitled *Reisbuchlein* ('Little travel book') (1636).

Although Hollar must have left Prague with means sufficient to maintain his standing as a gentleman and had since become an accomplished landscape artist and proficient etcher, his work cannot have been remunerative. The arrival of Thomas Howard, second earl of Arundel, at Cologne on 2 May 1636 on an embassy to the emperor Ferdinand II was to change his life. On his departure on 8 May Arundel had, as he wrote to William Petty, 'one Hollarse wth me, whoe drawes and eches printes in strong water quickely, and wth a pretty spiritte' (BL, Add. MS 15970, fol. 26; Springell, 143). For eight months Hollar travelled in Arundel's retinue—he made a final visit to Prague and received confirmation of his father's grant of arms and the right to style himself 'Prachenberger von Löwengrün

Wenceslaus Hollar (1607–1677), self-portrait, 1647

und Bareyt' from the emperor at Regensburg on 16 October—before arriving in London on 28 December 1636.

It was intended that Hollar, who had lodgings in Arundel House, should reproduce paintings and drawings belonging to the earl and countess of Arundel, but the project never developed, and only four prints from his early years in London are based on their collections. From the start he courted other patrons, and his first major production in England, a panoramic view of Greenwich (1637), was dedicated to Queen Henrietta Maria and proudly signed 'Coelator' (*recte caelator*, engraver) to Arundel. A copy of the Wilton diptych (1639), dedicated to the king, is one of a few prints by Hollar bearing a royal privilege providing protection from copyists. At some time (according to Meyssens' portrait) he was appointed to the household of the young duke of York, presumably as a drawing master. Among Hollar's most ambitious early projects was a set of twenty-six plates of women's costumes, some deriving from Van Dyck, entitled *Ornatus muliebris Anglicanus, or, The severall habits of English women from the nobilitie to the country woman* (1640). He also made numerous portraits of political and religious figures, such as Thomas Wentworth, earl of Strafford, after Van Dyck (1640), whose trial and execution he also depicted (1641).

On 4 July 1641 Hollar married Margaret Tracy (d. 1653), a servant of the countess of Arundel and probably a daughter of Anthony Tracy, an agent of the earl's. She died in 1653 and was buried at St Giles-in-the-Fields, London, on 10 March. A son, James, was born on 8 April 1643 at Tart Hall, the countess's house in St James's Park. John Aubrey noted that he 'dyed in the Plague, an ingeniose youth, drew delicately' and that a daughter was 'one of the greatest Beauties I have seen' (*Brief Lives*, 163).

Middle career In February 1642 the earl and countess of Arundel left England for Antwerp. Hollar, now wholly dependent on his own means, continued to concentrate on women's costumes. A dark fur double muff was the first of nine versions of a favourite subject, and he also began work on a set of smaller female figures entitled *Aula Veneris*, or *Theatrum mulierum*. A set of full-length female figures as the four seasons (1643, 1644) are among his most famous prints and bring to an end his first English period, for, some time in 1644 he moved to Antwerp. There he joined the artists' Guild of St Luke as a free master, and by 1648 his friend from Frankfurt, the Arundels' art curator Hendrick van der Borcht the younger, was able to write to John Evelyn that Hollar 'is very much esteemd in these parts and Especially in Antwerp where he is nouw dwelling. Many Lovers of arts make Collections of all his worckes' (Harding, 41). To meet this demand Hollar turned for inspiration to his sketchbooks and the Arundel collections, now being dispersed. He produced copies of paintings and drawings by Holbein, Adam Elsheimer, Dürer, and Leonardo da Vinci, topographical and architectural prints—including, most importantly, the *Long View of London from Bankside* (1647) and the *Long View of Prague* (1649)—portraits, ships, a rare set of shells, sets of butterflies, and much more.

In late 1651 or early 1652 Hollar returned to London, where he was to be largely dependent on two men, the publisher John Ogilby and the antiquary and herald Sir William Dugdale. Ogilby's luxury edition of Virgil, with illustrations after Francis Cleyn (1654), and *Aesop's Fables* (1665) and Dugdale's *Monasticon Anglicanum* (1655), *Antiquities of Warwickshire* (1656), and *History of St Paul's Cathedral* (1658) all have numerous plates by Hollar.

At some time Hollar converted to Roman Catholicism. Evelyn noted that he 'was perverted at last by the Jesuits at Antwerp to chang his Religion' (Evelyn, 1.21), and Aubrey mentioned that he 'dyed a Catholique, of which religion, I suppose, he might be ever since he came to Arundel-howse' (*Brief Lives*, 163). In January 1656 he was bound over in the sum of £40 at the Middlesex sessions for hearing mass at the lodgings of the Venetian ambassador. On 3 July 1656 he married Honora Roberts at St Giles-in-the-Fields. Aubrey reported that they had several children. In 1658 Hollar was living in Holborn, near Gifford's buildings, and about 1661 he wrote to Aubrey that he was lodging 'without St Clemen[t]s Inne back doore' and to ask for 'the Frenchman Limmner for they know not my name perfectly' (Bodl. Oxf., MS Aubrey 12, fol. 175; Pennington, xli).

Later career In 1660 Hollar issued a prospectus for a large-scale map of London which he hoped would be his financial salvation, but the great fire of London in 1666 rendered his work obsolete. He quickly produced smaller maps and views depicting the damage, but he did not abandon his great map; its remains may be seen in Ogilby and Morgan's *Large Map of London* (1677). On 31 October 1666 he successfully petitioned the king for the 'Honour & Tittle of your Majesties Scenographer; or Designer of Prospects' (Godfrey, 29).

In March 1669 the sixty-two year old Hollar turned again to his old patrons and petitioned the king for permission to accompany Lord Henry Howard, Baron Howard of Castle Rising, on his embassy to Tangier as official artist. Some thirty-one drawings, including large panoramic watercolours, survive, and Overton issued a set of fifteen etchings by Hollar entitled *Divers Prospects in and about Tangier* (1673). On a voyage from Tangier to Salli in December 1669 they escaped an attack by Algerian pirates, which Hollar depicted in Ogilby's *Africa* (1670).

During all these years Hollar produced frontispieces, portraits, and maps for the book and print publishers, but the last years of his life were again filled by work for antiquaries: Elias Ashmole's *Institutions, Laws & Ceremonies of the Most Noble Order of the Garter* appeared in 1672 and the second and third volumes of Dugdale's *Monasticon Anglicanum* in 1661 and 1673. Francis Sandford's *Genealogical History of the Kings of England* and Robert Thoroton's *Antiquities of Nottinghamshire* appeared in 1677, after Hollar's death.

The recipe for Hollar's 'Ground for Etching in Copper or Brass; with his Directions how to use it' appeared in a number of artists' handbooks and was reprinted by Vertue (Vertue, *Description*, 133–6). The antiquary Richard Symonds 'saw Mr. Hollar etching' on 20 February 1649 and described his method of laying on the wax and acid (Vertue, *Note books*, 1.112). His friend Francis Place, an amateur artist, recalled that 'he did all by the hour, in which he was very exact, for if any body came that kep him from his business he always laid the hour glass on one side, till they were gone. he always recev'd 12d an hour' (ibid., 1.34). Hollar's only personal comments on his working methods are contained in a letter to Hendrick van der Borcht the elder in Frankfurt, on a proof of his copy of Holbein's *Solomon and the Queen of Sheba* (1642):

> Der Herr muss aber nicht denken dass das der beste abstrukh ist, von wegen dass ich sobal[d] als ich das Etzwasser abgeschitt had, disse Probe lassen truken, und es muss noch dz gantze Stuck nach dem Principal gekorrigirt werden, … Dan was der Herr hier sihet, dass ist nur dz wass dass Etzwasser gethan hatt, es wird aber noch mitt dem grabeissen verholffen werden. (But you must not think this is the best impression, because I had it printed as soon as I had shaken off the etching fluid, and the whole thing has still to be corrected according to the master. … For what you see here is only what the etching fluid has done, and now further work will be done with the graver.) (British Museum, department of prints & drawings, 1870-6-25-39; Griffiths, 167)

Contemporaries described Hollar as 'a very friendly good-natured man as could be, but Shiftlesse to the Worlde' (*Brief Lives*, 163) and 'a very passionate man easily moved' (Vertue, *Note books*, 1.34–5). Aubrey reported that he 'was very short-sighted' and 'When he tooke his Landskapes, he, then, had a glasse to helpe his Sight' (*Brief Lives*, 163). His portrait by Meyssens depicting him with his etching tools and an etched self-portrait (1647) show him with a neat moustache and small imperial beard.

Hollar died on 25 March 1677 at the age of seventy at his house in Gardener's Lane, Westminster, and was buried three days later at St Margaret's, Westminster. According to Francis Place's letter of 20 May 1719 to George Vertue he died 'of a Parraletick [or Apoplextick] fitt. & before his departure. the Bayliffs came and seiz'd all that he had, which gave him a great disturbance & he was heard to say they might have stayed till he was dead' (Vertue, *Note books*, 1.35). This cannot be strictly true, as an inventory of his possessions taken on 6 April valued the contents of the modestly furnished house and 'prints belonging to the decds: trade' ('Inventory of all the goods') (Westminster City Archives, inventories act book 6, no. 298) at £22. He died intestate, and administration of his estate was granted to his widow, Honora, on 25 May 1677. The date of her death is unknown, but she was apparently alive in 1701, when Sir Hans Sloane noted the purchase of a volume of Hollar's prints from her. Place said he left two daughters.

The variety of Hollar's work, his huge output (Pennington's *Descriptive Catalogue* runs to 2717 numbers), and his technical skill have ensured that his prints have always been keenly collected. Comprehensive collections are at the British Museum (based on Sir Hans Sloane's collection), the Royal Library in Windsor Castle (partly traceable to Queen Charlotte), University of Toronto Library (S. T. Fisher collection), and the National Gallery, Prague (Kinsky Palace). Some 400 drawings have survived, and important collections are at the British Museum, the Staatsmuseum, Berlin, the National Gallery, Prague, and the Royal Library, Windsor Castle.

ROBERT J. D. HARDING

Sources R. Pennington, *A descriptive catalogue of the etched work of Wenceslaus Hollar, 1607–1677* (1982) · F. Springell, *Connoisseur and diplomat: the earl of Arundel's embassy to Germany in 1636 as recounted in William Crowne's diary, the earl's letters and other contemporary sources with a catalogue of the topographical drawings made on the journey by Wenceslaus Hollar* (1963) · R. T. Godfrey, *Wenceslaus Hollar: a Bohemian artist in England* (1994) · V. Denkstein, *Hollar drawings* (1979) · *Aubrey's Brief lives*, ed. O. L. Dick (1949) · Vertue, *Note books* · Evelyn, *Diary* · J. Wussin, 'Das Hollar'sche Haus in Prag', *Archiv für die Zeichnende Kunst*, ed. R. Naumann, 10 (Leipzig, 1864), 363–9 · E. Ashmole, Bodl. Oxf., MS Ashmole 3, fol. 12 · E. Ashmole, Bodl. Oxf., MS Ashmole 243, fol. 180v · T. Howard, earl of Arundel, to the Revd William Petty, 27 May 1636, BL, Add. MS 15970, fol. 26 · H. van der Borcht the younger to John Evelyn, 1 April 1648, BL, Evelyn papers, bound letters, T–W 1319 · R. Harding, 'John Evelyn, Hendrick van der Borcht the younger and Wenceslaus Hollar', *Apollo*, 144 (Aug 1996), 39–44 · W. Hollar, letter to John Aubrey, c.1661, Bodl. Oxf., MS Aubrey 12, fol. 175 · *The life, diary, and correspondence of Sir William Dugdale*, ed. W. Hamper (1827) · W. Hollar to Hendrick van der Borcht the elder, [1642], BM, department of prints and drawings, 1870-6-25-39 · A. Griffiths, 'A Hollar rediscovery', *Print Quarterly*, 17 (2000), 167 · 'Inventory of all the goods & of all the goods chattles & houshold stuff of Wincislaues Holler late of the parish of St. Margarets in the City of Westminster decds taken & apprized the 6th day of April in the yeare of our Lord 1677 by Edward Lingly', City Westm. AC, inventories act book 6, no. 298 · G. Vertue, *A description of the works of the ingenious delineator and engraver Wenceslaus Hollar* (1759) · burial and marriage registers, St Giles-in-the-Fields, London · burial register, St Margaret's Church, Westminster, London **Archives** BL, engravings, letters, etc. | Bodl. Oxf., MSS Ashmole · Bodl. Oxf., MSS Aubrey **Likenesses** W. Hollar, etching, 1647, NPG [*see illus.*] · W. Hollar, etch and stipple, in or before 1661 (after J. Meyssens), BM, NPG; repro. in C. De Bie, *Het gulden cabinet* (Antwerp, 1661) · W. Hollar, etching (aged forty), BM, NPG · J. Meyssens, portrait **Wealth at death** £22: inventory, City Westm. AC, inventories act book 6, no. 298

Holles, Denzil, first Baron Holles (1598–1680), politician, was born on 31 October 1598, the second surviving son of John *Holles, first earl of Clare (d. 1637), and Anne (1576–1651), daughter of Sir Thomas Stanhope. His father was a substantial landowner in Nottinghamshire who also possessed important properties in London that brought in a quarter of his income at the time of Denzil's birth—his total income being between £5000 and £6000. His mother, daughter of another prominent Nottinghamshire gentleman, had brought a significant dowry with her. Denzil's father purchased the barony of Haughton in 1616 for £10,000 and the earldom of Clare in 1624 for £5000, but both titles passed to Denzil's older brother, John *Holles, second earl of Clare.

Early life and marriages Denzil, like other younger sons, was educated in a way that suggests that a career in the professions was in his family's mind. Like his father he attended Christ's College, Cambridge (matriculated June 1611), but unlike him graduated BA (*honoris causa* at the time of a visit by Prince Charles in 1613) and proceeded MA in 1616 and, also like his father, attended Gray's Inn, from 1615. But a proposed grand tour was twice abandoned. And successful activity in the marriage market spared him having to work for a living: first (on 4 June 1626) he married Dorothy (d. 1641), daughter of Sir Francis Ashley, a wealthy lawyer and king's serjeant. Dorothy was an only child and stood to bring a large fortune with her—the down payment on marriage consisted of lands worth £600 per annum. He married again, on 12 March 1642. His wife was Jane (d. 1666), wealthy widow of Sir Walter Covert, and eldest daughter of Sir John Shirley of Ifield, Sussex. Then on 16 September 1666 he married Esther (d. 1683), widow of Jacques Richer, seigneur de Cambrernon en Normandie; she was the severely Huguenot daughter of Gideon le Lou. Even a younger son could benefit from the marriage market, and an income of £300 settled on him by his father was swollen to some £4600 a year, principally as a result of choosing the right brides.

Holles was the angry younger son of a bitter and disappointed father. John Holles had been a gentleman pensioner under Elizabeth I but was sidelined in 1603 and despite endless attempts to draw attention to himself, not least by the extravagant purchase of peerages, he failed to get the positions at court he craved. His one big break was his appointment in 1610 as comptroller of the household of Prince Henry; no sooner had Holles settled in than the prince died and his household was dissolved. Holles attempted to tie himself to the interest of George Villiers, duke of Buckingham, in the years after 1617, but he was one of too many, and his sycophancy got him nowhere,

Denzil Holles, first Baron Holles (1598–1680), by unknown artist

while his pro-Spanish stance soon became a liability. His godly protestantism was going out of favour, too. His letter-books show a man whose ambition was consuming and counter-productive. He became a bitter, sour old man. It rubbed off on his son.

The 1620s parliaments and the personal rule Denzil was inconspicuous as MP for St Michael, Cornwall, in the parliament of 1624. He was returned in 1628 to Charles I's third parliament as MP for godly Dorchester where his then father-in-law was recorder. But although he had been privately expostulating to his brother-in-law Sir Thomas Wentworth about the miserable failures of the government to further the protestant cause—'every man knows, that since England was England, it received not so dishonourable a blow' as in the failure at the Isle of Ré (*Earl of Strafford's Letters and Despatches*, 1.41)—he seems to have been mute in the first session. But he found a new voice and a new resolve in the second session, speaking out against the customs farmers who had seized the goods of those merchants who had refused to pay non-parliamentary customs duties. When it became clear that the king would dissolve parliament rather than let this issue be pursued Holles was one of nine members who met privately in the Three Cranes inn in the City (but not so privately that the privy council did not get wind of it) to plan 'that we go not out like sheep scattered: but to testify to the world we have a care of their safety' (Crawford, *Holles*, 20). The outcome was the infamous mêlée on 2 March 1629 in which Holles and Benjamin Valentine held the speaker in his chair to prevent him from rising and thus adjourning the house (Holles allegedly crying 'God's wounds, he would sit until they pleased to rise'; Notestein

and Relf, 104). He also read to the house a digest of the paper denouncing as treasonous the collection of non-parliamentary customs duties and the promotion of Arminianism. Not surprisingly the nine conspirators were arrested. There followed a long struggle for bail. The king's lawyers, stymied by the petition of right, knew that they had to show cause for the imprisonment, but feared to allege that it was for words uttered and acts committed in the parliament house, lest the judges ruled that they were protected by parliamentary privilege. They therefore delayed and tried to bypass the courts by offering bail on bonds of good behaviour (which would imply an admission of guilt). In the end (29 October 1629), there was a fudge—Holles's bail was paid by his father-in-law and by his friend William Noy (whether with or without his foreknowledge and collusion is not clear). In January 1630 the attorney-general took the plunge and accused Sir John Eliot, Holles, and Valentine of conspiracy. They refused to plead on the ground that the court had no jurisdiction of them (a deeply ironic pre-echo of the king's plea precisely nineteen years later), and were found guilty on a *nihil dicit* and fined—in Holles's case 1000 marks (£666 13s. 4d.). He remained on bail, his fine unpaid, until it was cancelled by the Long Parliament.

Over the next decade Holles was a sullen country gentleman. He was living in a dower house close to Dorchester, and close to the hot-gospelling town minister, John White, whose *Commentary upon Genesis* (1656) was dedicated by White's son to Holles 'as an acknowledgment of your great friendship, and the severall Courtesies he had received from you' (sig. A2). Holles held some of the lesser offices associated with a man of his standing (commissioner for sewers in Dorset, 1636–8, a captaincy in the Dorset militia, from 1636) but he was not placed on the commission of the peace. He resisted (briefly) the second writ for ship money in 1635, he chased off some saltpetremen who came to dig up the soil around his dovecote (1638), and he refused to pay coat and conduct money towards the king's campaign against the Scots in 1639. His truculence had been enhanced rather than stilled by the events of 1629–30.

Member of parliament, 1640–1642 It is no surprise, therefore, to find that Holles was returned as MP for Dorchester in both the elections of 1640. Again he was a slow starter, playing little part in the Short Parliament or the early months of the Long Parliament—indeed Clarendon is quite clear in his *History of the Rebellion* that the king was planning in April 1641 to make Holles secretary of state as part of the plan for reconstructing his government with former critics. Holles's family ties caused him to take a back seat in the proceedings against Thomas Wentworth, earl of Strafford (indeed to work to save his life), and he backed John Pym's proposals for replacing the king's prerogative revenues with substantial parliamentary ones. But, as so often with the king, he was deterred from going the extra yard by Holles's surly puritanism. It was Holles who carried the Commons' articles of impeachment against Archbishop Laud to the Lords; it was Holles who showed most enthusiasm for a religious conformity between Scotland and England when it was proposed by the Scots commissioners in 1641 (indeed he showed himself consistently sympathetic in 1641 to all the Scots demands), and he was prominent on 9 February in supporting the London ministers' call for the abolition of episcopacy 'roots and branches'. By summer 1641 his position was largely indistinguishable from that of Pym and he shared the latter's paranoia about popish plots and the poisoning of the king's mind by evil counsellors. But there were differences. His opposition to episcopacy clearly arose not from an absolute objection to the office but from an alarm at the refusal of the existing bishops to accept a reduction of their powers—indeed his strongest speeches on religion were on measures to disbar the clergy from all manner of secular employment—and, unlike Pym, he showed a precocious dismay at the spread of sectarian activity: on 5 June 1641 he demanded that the houses take steps to silence 'mechanical men that preached now up and down' and to prevent 'this great disorder before it came to a higher pitch and degree' (Crawford, *Holles*, 52). Headstrong and outspoken on religious issues, and one of those first thought of whenever a message needed to be conveyed to the Lords (he was used on seven occasions in 1641), Holles was wobbling into the camp of those unwilling to accept the king's concessions as sufficient to safeguard liberties. But he *was* wobbling: he was omitted from the powerful executive committee that managed affairs during the autumn while the king was in Scotland and parliament was adjourned.

When the houses reconvened Holles was present, but again his role was largely one of making terse, intemperate speeches, especially on the need to remove evil counsellors (he pressed for another round of impeachments), and on the need to remove the clergy from all secular employments. Most dramatically, when thirteen bishops were impeached Sir Simonds D'Ewes wrote that on 26 October 1641 'Mr Denzil Holles ... move[d] us to give a name to our impeachment of the 13 Bishops and call it treason' (*Journal*, ed. Coates, 39). It is not surprising therefore that Charles (whose memory of 1629 was all too fresh, and who might have had leaked to him details of Holles's close links with the Scots over the preceding months) should exaggerate Holles's importance and intransigence, and that he should name him as one of the five members of the Commons whom he sought to pluck out and arraign on charges of treason on 5 January 1642 as the arch-incendiaries in a plot against his authority. What is more he had the evidence—both in their role in publishing the grand remonstrance and in their secret correspondence with the Scottish committee of the estates—to make it good in law.

Warrior for peace, 1642–1646 From that point to the outbreak of war in summer 1642 Holles had an enhanced status. He carried a number of peremptory requests from the Commons to the Lords, including a demand that the Lords join the Commons in a request to the king to appoint named persons to control the Tower of London and the militia: if they failed in their 'duty' he said, they would put peace at risk and 'they must not expect this House to come

to them again in this business' (BL, Harley MS 162, fol. 365v). In February the Commons made him deputy lieutenant of Bristol and in July he was appointed to help to organize the Dorset militia.

So there was never any prospect that Holles would leave Westminster for the king's headquarters. But there was also never a sign that he believed that the issues dividing the country needed to be settled by war. He was in 1642, and was to remain, committed to the view that a negotiated settlement was necessary and possible. In 1641 and 1642 twelve of his speeches were published and they reveal a consistent view: the king was a good but weak man misled by evil counsellors. He had been persuaded to subvert the rights and privileges of parliament and thereby to subvert the liberties of the people, which parliaments existed to defend and promote. Similarly, whenever he spoke of religion, he spoke of how the existing system had been discredited by a generation of bishops and their clerical cronies, and he accused them of introducing forms of worship and discipline evocative of the Roman Catholic church, thereby subverting true religion. He comes across as a strait-laced Calvinist internationalist.

Holles went reluctantly but unflinchingly to war against a king who was mentally ensnared by evil counsellors. He took up his responsibilities in the west, conducting a review of the Bristol militia, and then returned to London, raised a regiment of foot in the capital, and marched out with the earl of Essex. He was one of three colonels detached to attack Sherborne Castle, but was repulsed on 6 September, with a loss of more than half his men, albeit more by desertion than death. He limped back to Westminster, recruited his regiment back to strength, and rejoined the lord general in time to play an active and courageous part in the battle of Edgehill, where his men stood their ground on the left centre, while regiments on either side of his crumbled. The parliamentary commissioners singled him out for special commendation: 'through the valour of Colonel Holles's and the Lord General's they obtained a victory' (*England's Memorable Accidents*, 1649, 62). He soon encountered the bitterness of defeat. As the royalists made a push on London which was halted at Brentford on 11 November, Prince Rupert, launching a surprise attack through a thick morning fog, wiped out Holles's regiment, killing one third and taking two thirds captive, together with fifteen guns and eleven colours. Holles was absent, but his confidence was badly shaken. Although offered command of the army of the west, he declined. Henceforth he was committed to the essentially defensive strategy of the earl of Essex and to constantly seeking a route to peace. D'Ewes recorded, on 24 November, that Holles 'was much cooled in his fierceness by the great slaughter made in his regiment at Brentford' (Crawford, *Holles*, 84). He henceforth became recognized as the leader of the peace party.

That did not mean surrender. It meant having a clear set of principles for a settlement, but endlessly probing how to achieve them by negotiation. Whenever—as in spring 1643, winter 1644–5, summer 1646—the king was willing to talk Holles was prominent in formulating terms and in thinking of ways of addressing issues flexibly. The principles included: the nature of parliamentary control of those who advised the king and exercised authority in his name; those who were to be punished for their 'malignancy' and how; and the nature of the confessional state that would be established to secure the protestant interest. Thus as the negotiations on the Oxford articles ran into the sand in early March 1643, and D'Ewes feared that they would collapse, Holles 'very seasonably and fortunately' moved that they should treat on the propositions notwithstanding. He always sought to sustain or to reopen public treaties. And he opposed everything that would throw new difficulties in the way of a settlement: thus in May 1643 he opposed the proposal that the houses should have a new great seal made (the lord keeper having carried the original away to royalist headquarters). But more controversially he was willing to enter into secret treaties, using intermediaries to test the water for revised sets of proposals that he could lay before the houses. Thus in June 1643 he was clearly apprised of, and willing to go along with, the plans of Edmund Waller to seize control of the London militia using a royal commission of array, and thereby to restore royalist control of London as a prelude to the arrest of the most senior war party leaders including three of the five members attainted with Holles by Charles in January 1642, and the launch of conciliatory peace terms. When the king shortly afterwards issued a revised list of those he would exempt from pardon Holles's name was strikingly absent. Waller's plot failed, but when, in early August, Holles was teller for a motion that was defeated, to present to Charles new terms drawn up by the Lords, there is evidence that the war party contemplated his summary arrest. As about one third of the remaining Lords—including Holles's elder brother—departed from London for Oxford or for their estates, Holles applied for and was granted a pass to go to the continent so long as he took with him no plate and no children over sixteen. This warrant was revoked shortly afterwards, but it is a sign of the intolerable tensions within the Commons.

For the next twelve months Holles was much less active, much less visible, much less engaged. The groups he had led disintegrated, many deserting or fleeing abroad, or at any rate ceased attending regularly. Despite his earlier enthusiasm for Scottish involvement in the English settlement of 1641 he viewed with distaste the terms of the solemn league and covenant that brought them back into England bound by a solemn oath to impose certain conditions on the kingdoms. There are, indeed, signs that his religious views were modifying. His concern was with the purity of gospel preaching and a workable alliance of godly minister and magistrate, and he was not going to let forms of church government get in the way of peace. A straw in the wind was his surprisingly passionate defence of Daniel Featley, a 'reformed episcopate' man and ally of James Ussher, whom the firebrands in the Commons wished to expel from his living in Lambeth.

In the whole of 1644 Holles is most visible in his support for Lord General Essex against the more hawkish generals who criticized Essex's over-cautious strategy and in the long, slow thaw in his relations with the Scots. He shared their abhorrence of sectarianism and the promotion of free worship. He shared their political objectives. He was willing to abide the determinations of the Westminster assembly, subject to their open negotiation with the king when the time for settlement came.

By November 1644 there was an apparent military impasse and the houses set out on a dual strategy: the reorganization of their armies that resulted in the self-denying ordinance and the creation of the New Model Army, and a new push for peace, initiated by the supporters of Essex and those back-bench MPs whose lands lay in royalist territory. Holles, with others, was sent to Oxford with the preliminary version of what became (two months later) the Uxbridge articles. The commissioners took part in formal meetings, but two or three of them, Holles foremost among them, also took part in secret exploratory talks, brokered by Sabran, the French ambassador. So much Holles was later to admit. But one of those also involved, Lord Savile, was later to allege that Holles undertook to send secret reports to the king revealing what was really happening behind the scenes at Westminster (to assist in the peace process) and this Holles always strenuously denied. Certainly someone sent such letters to the king in 1645, but those who investigated the affair at the time and those who have studied it since have failed to find the smoking gun. Holles may well have gone further in his attempts to broker a peace than he ever admitted; but he probably did not go that far.

These revelations paralysed the Commons throughout June and July 1646. Savile accused Holles (and Bulstrode Whitelocke) of leaking secrets to the king; they responded by accusing Savile of being the agent of a plot masterminded by Henry Vane, Oliver St John, and Lord Saye and Sele to make their own private treaty with the king. Neither set of charges could ever be proven, for Savile could produce only an unsigned letter of disputed provenance; and the obvious explanation for the conduct of Vane, St John, and Saye was that, honestly believing that the king had a secret agent reporting to him from within the committee of both kingdoms, they were indeed engaged in following up possible ways of turning some leading royalists without the king finding out about it from disloyal parliamentarians. After weeks of investigation and mutual recrimination both sides admitted defeat, but Holles thought it best to seek leave to absent himself to the country for the high summer of 1645.

Whatever the truth behind these murky allegations, peace was not to be procured by negotiation or treachery. And the reorganization of armies constituted a political defeat. With Essex sidelined and Independent generals in control Holles formed an uneasy alliance with the Scots (it was their evidence which discredited Savile and made his testimony against Holles worthless). Holles thus worked closely with them in the months after the end of the war to shape and proffer the Newcastle propositions. By now he had identified himself with subversion of the *jure divino* schemes for presbyterian settlement propounded by the

Westminster assembly and the embracing of a 'lame, erastian presbytery' but this was clearly not his own first choice. It represented a form he hoped and believed that both the Scots and, eventually, the king could grudgingly live with.

Leader of counter-revolution, 1646–1647 Holles had fought and lost all the parliamentary battles of the war years; he was to win some parliamentary battles only to lose the war of the peace years. Weariness with war, economic and social ruin, and religious anarchy meant that most MPs wanted settlement. Holles emerged as the man to deliver it. He had a clear plan: to persuade the Scots to hand over Charles and to return to Scotland and disband; to promote a general demilitarization throughout Britain; and then to hold face-to-face talks with Charles and reach agreement. He had never been for a sell-out, only for talks with limited preconditions. His power base was in the committee for Irish affairs at Derby House, which was packed with his friends and allies and which took over effective control of the executive wing of government from the committee of both kingdoms.

Holles's plan had an inexorable logic to it. By paying the Scots to go home and to disband it became possible to argue for the large-scale disbandment of the English army (save those who would be sent to Ireland to undertake the gradual restoration of protestant hegemony there). The reduction of the English army to 6400 men, mainly drawn from regional armies rather than from the New Model, would begin the process of restoring traditional governance in England, with the general reduction of taxation and wartime bureaucracy. It would then be straightforward to enter into a personal treaty with the king leading to his restoration with enough restraints on his freedom of action to ensure long-term peace and stability. This plan cleared the first hurdle—sending home the Scots—but it fell at the second, persuading the New Model Army to disband. Holles simply could not raise enough money both to pay a reasonable proportion of the more than £2 million in arrears owed to soldiers still in service, and to pay for the reconquest of Ireland. And when the army protested Holles personally, in Edmund Ludlow's words, 'drew up a resolution upon his knee' (*Memoirs of Edmund Ludlow*, 1.149) and had it adopted by the Commons as what became known as the declaration of dislike. This, provocatively, challenged the right of soldiers to petition and threatened to cause any who did so to be prosecuted as disturbers of the peace. Nothing demonstrates better Holles's ability to be simultaneously resolute and reckless, courageous and crass. It set off a chain reaction with the defiance of the army, its refusal to be seen as 'a mere, mercenary army', and led to the organization of the general council of officers and adjutators, and in the late summer and autumn to the evolution of a full-scale programme of constitutional and social reform in the form of the *Heads of the Proposals* and *The Case of the Armie Truly Stated*. As army militancy escalated over the following months Holles responded with provocation upon provocation—for example by renewing the requirement that all remaining officers must have taken the covenant. He

showed a lack of sympathy and understanding for the material grievances of the army—their arrears, their concern for indemnity, for pensions for widows and the maimed, for future employment—and he could not see why they would not disband on the same meagre terms accepted by men in the regional armies disbanded in 1646. Just like Charles I in 1640–42 he alternated between sullen retractions and petulant threats of force. He attempted through the early summer months to raise a large force of troops to overbear the New Model (the London militia, the northern and western armies, thousands of reformadoes, decommissioned and disbanded men in London awaiting their pay-offs). While dozens of provincial MPs, driven on by a yearning for settlement, had backed him in the spring, they became alarmed at the prospect of confrontation between two rival armies raised by the parliament, and his majorities fell. In a final desperate gamble Holles appealed to the respectable tradesmen of London who were suffering most from the trade recession and crippling levels of taxation and asked them to support his plea for the king to be brought to London for a personal treaty. When their petition was rejected by a majority of MPs angry crowds swarmed around the Palace of Westminster, and on 26 July the speakers of both houses and some fifty-seven other commoners and seven other peers fled to the army. This was Holles's nemesis. The inevitable consequence was that the New Model marched on and occupied London, scattering the coalition of military forces that Holles had imprudently trusted and demanding the arrest and expulsion of the eleven incendiaries behind the events of 26 July. Holles hid for a few days and then applied to the speaker for a pass to go abroad. It was speedily granted. Eight of the eleven left the country, most of them settling in the Netherlands. But Holles settled in Normandy where (prudently enough) he had sent his mother, his eldest son, and £2000 some months beforehand.

Exile, regicide, exile, 1647–1660 Holles remained in Normandy for almost a year. And, like many political exiles before and since, he devoted his time to the composition of misleading accounts of his rise and fall. These were published in 1699, after his death, and with the slightly erroneous title (which he did not give them) of *Memoirs*. They offer little insight into his role and are consistently more interesting in the attribution of Machiavellianism to his opponents than as a reliable account of his own actions. They do, however, confirm the central folly of his political career: that Holles 'seriously overestimated the extent to which Charles could ever be persuaded to compromise' (Woolrych, 6).

After the king attempted to overturn the judgement of the first civil war by plunging the country into a new conflict, the vote against the eleven members was revoked (3 June 1648). Holles resumed his seat on 14 August following and worked, as ever before, for a personal treaty with the king that would limit his freedom to listen to bad advice or place trust in unreliable men, and that would secure control of the church in the hands of sound Calvinist protestants. He was central to the peace process that led to the proposal—which he presented to the Commons—on 4 December 1648 that the king's latest response represented a satisfactory basis for a settlement. It was action by Holles that had provoked both the king's arrest of seven members on 2 March 1629, and his attempted arrest of five members on 5 January 1642. His action had provoked the expulsion of eleven members of parliament on 1 August 1647. Now he provoked the greatest purge of all—Pride's Purge. On 6 December the army arrested as many as forty-five members of the Commons, and prevented as many as 186 from taking their seats. The way was cleared for the removal of Charles I by enforced abdication, by deposition, or by execution. This time Holles had really miscalculated. It would seem that he was not there to see it. He was not to be found, and his house in Covent Garden soon had troopers bivouacked in it. He had fled.

Holles's life throughout the interregnum is only sketchily recorded. He seems to have spent the early years wholly or mainly in Normandy, and his name recurs in royalist correspondence as a potential supporter. In March 1651, while he was at Caen, he received a royal summons and the offer of the post of secretary of state. He declined firmly. But within two months his servants were named as principals in the plot instigated by a group of London ministers to organize an uprising in London to coincide with the planned Scottish invasion (this was a plot that cost the leading presbyterian minister, Nicholas Love, his life). In March 1654 Lord Protector Cromwell offered an amnesty to presbyterian exiles like Holles and a free pass home, and Holles gratefully accepted. He retired to his estate in Dorset and kept himself to himself until the eve of the Restoration.

The Restoration, 1660–1663 As soon as General Monck permitted the return of men secluded at Pride's Purge to rejoin the restored Rump Parliament, Holles took his seat and within two days, on 23 February 1660, he was appointed to the council of state. When elections to the Convention were held in April he was again returned as MP for Dorchester and he was one of those who dragged Sir Edward Turner to the speaker's chair, for once a playful act. He worked hard to put the clock back to December 1648 and to admit Charles II on the terms accepted by Charles I on the eve of the purge. But the yearning for settlement upon the king's good-natured promise to leave all to parliament (since most, even of the old, parliamentarians believed that the problem of the 1640s had been a problem with Charles I, not a problem with monarchy, this is not surprising) meant that Holles was once more outvoted. The decision to send him to take the unconditional offer of Restoration to the king was intended to get him out of the way at a delicate moment—one cavalier told Edward Hyde that he had voted for 'the old ones' including Holles to be made the messengers since 'they would not be a trouble at home and might be sweetened by his Majesty's most excellent temper' (Crawford, *Holles*, 191). It worked all too well. Holles found sweetness too, and for once accepted defeat with a good grace. His reward for his mission and for a well-turned speech was a place on the privy council, although further reward, in the form of

a peerage as Baron Holles, came from the dregs of the Restoration cornucopia in June 1661.

Holles's role in the Restoration settlement was predictably erratic. He supported the principle of the Indemnity Bill, but was vindictive in his role on the high court trying the regicides. He was a key figure in the shaping of the Worcester House declaration of October 1660, which sought to re-establish bishops not as diocesan autocrats but as chairs of diocesan boards of governors and which re-established the old Book of Common Prayer but with freedom for individuals to dissent from the 'noxious ceremonies' that had troubled so many pre-war puritans. From early on he showed great sensitivity to the privileges of the two houses and to the full restoration of parliamentary procedures. He was precocious in supporting the restoration of the judicial powers of the houses, and especially the appellate jurisdiction of the Lords.

Diplomat and last years From 1662 to 1665 Holles was sent to Paris as Charles's ambassador. There his obsession with protocol and his determination to be accorded an exaggerated status as representative of the imperial crown of Britain caused irritated amusement to Charles II and cold fury in the French. Holles's comment that 'ceremony is substance, and who carries it in that will carry it in the essentials' (PRO, SP 78/119, fol. 110) was simply absurd in view of the calculated informality of Charles's own court and the king's own style. It rendered his embassy useless to the king; and all important negotiations with Louis XIV were conducted either via the French king's representative at St James, or via extraordinary ambassadors sent to Paris. In 1666–7 Holles was employed to negotiate a peace settlement with the Dutch at the end of the Second Anglo-Dutch War. Although much criticized at the time and since, this exercise in damage limitation was actually quite well managed in its outcome, if not in its 'too punctilious manner' (Crawford, *Holles*, 207).

The last decade or so of Holles's life saw the general conservative drift of his life continue. He had been an angry young man. He turned into a rather vain and querulous old man, complaining about the younger generation, forgetful of the fierce passions of his own youth. He became a respectable supporter of the established church, with a strong preference for a good sermon and an unfussy liturgy, ready to dismiss a chaplain for a sexual lapse, but increasingly intolerant of those who opted out for the sake of conscience. Those he patronized in later life included Henry Compton, who was to become bishop of London, and Gilbert Burnet, fashionable preacher and polemicist.

Holles's house in Covent Garden became (from early 1674) an early meeting place of those who were to become the leaders of the party that sought to place limitations on the power of the crown, including the exclusion of the Roman Catholic James, duke of York, from the succession. Thus he supported the first Test Act that drove hundreds of Catholics from office, but opposed Danby's attempt to bind protestants to uphold the existing structures in church and state. He wrote passionately in favour of the jurisdiction of the House of Lords during the impasse arising from the case of Shirley v. Fagg (1675) and he allowed his proxy to be used in an attempt to get a majority in favour of a parliamentary petition asking for a dissolution. In 1676 he was dropped from the privy council. He was sufficiently important for Charles to reinstate him when he was trying to curry favour at the height of the furore instigated by the Popish Plot revelations in 1679, but by then his shrill and querulous speeches were of little value to Charles's more potent opponents, especially as he, unlike Shaftesbury, was tempted to take up the king's offer of a bill to place limitations upon the power of a popish successor. His biographer claims that 'in the last years of his life Holles was a man out of his time' (Crawford, *Holles*, 218) and this seems an appropriate downbeat assessment. His piety was that of the pre-war aristocratic puritan, his politics were locked into the missed opportunities of the 1640s, his sense of personal honour and refined manners made him a fuddy-duddy on the fringes of the court of Charles II. Even his will, with its fussy traditionalist proclamation of his Calvinist reliance upon the 'merits and mediation of the Lord Christ my God and my Redeemer' (ibid., 210–11), is indicative of a man out of his time. Holles died on 17 February 1680 and was buried on 21 February in Westminster Abbey. A monument to him was erected in St Peter's, Dorchester, in 1699. His only surviving son, Francis, was from his first marriage and duly inherited the title. Holles's third wife, Esther, survived him by three years, seemingly having lived out her days in France. Denzil Holles was successful in almost everything he privately undertook, and unsuccessful in almost everything he publicly undertook. In particular, his passionate parliamentarianism was constantly counter-productive.

JOHN MORRILL

Sources P. Crawford, *Denzil Holles, 1598–1680: a study of his political career* (1979) · *Memoirs of Denzil, Lord Holles, baron of Ifield in Sussex, from the year 1641 to 1648* (1699) · S. Reyner, *A sermon preached at the funeral of the Right Honourable Denzell Lord Holles* (1680) · Clarendon, *Hist. rebellion* · S. R. Gardiner, *History of the great civil war, 1642–1649*, new edn, 4 vols. (1893) · D. Underdown, *Fire from heaven: life in an English town in the seventeenth century* (1992) · L. J. Reeve, *Charles I and the road to personal rule* (1989) · C. Russell, *The fall of the British monarchies, 1637–1642* (1992) · D. L. Smith, *Constitutional royalism and the search for settlement, 1641–1649* (1994) · M. A. Kishlansky, *The rise of the New Model Army* (1979) · I. Gentles, *The New Model Army in England, Ireland, and Scotland, 1645–1653* (1992) · A. Woolrych, *Soldiers and statesmen: the general council of the army and its debates, 1647–1648* (1987) · J. Hart, *Justice upon petition: the House of Lords and the reformation of justice, 1621–1675* (1991) · L. J. Reeve, 'The arguments in king's bench in 1629 concerning the imprisonment of John Selden and other members of the House of Commons', *Journal of British Studies*, 25 (1986), 264–87 · M. Mahony, 'The Savile affair and the politics of the Long Parliament', *Parliamentary History*, 7 (1988), 212–29 · P. Crawford, 'The Savile affair', *EngHR*, 90 (1975), 76–93 · J. Hart, 'The House of Lords and appellate jurisdiction in equity', *Parliamentary History*, 2 (1983), 49–70 · W. L. Grant, 'A puritan at the court of Louis XIV', *Bulletin of the Departments of Political and Economic Science in Queen's University, Kingston, Ontario*, 8 (1913), 24–42 · A. Collins, *Historical collections of the noble families of Cavendishe, Holles, Vere, Harley and Ogle* (1752) · *The journal of Sir Simonds D'Ewes from the first recess of the Long Parliament to the withdrawal of King Charles from London*, ed. W. H. Coates (1942) · G. Radcliffe, *The earl of Strafforde's letters and dispatches, with an essay towards his life*, ed. W. Knowler, 2 vols. (1739) · W. Notestein and F. H. Relf, eds., *Commons debates for 1629* (1921) · *The memoirs of Edmund Ludlow*, ed. C. H. Firth, 2 vols. (1894) · J. L. Chester, ed., *The marriage, baptismal, and burial registers of the collegiate church or abbey of St Peter, Westminster*, Harleian Society, 10 (1876) · Venn, *Alum. Cant.* · DNB

Archives BL, letters to Sir George Downing, Add. MS 22919 · BL, letters to first marquess of Halifax, C5

Likenesses R. White, line engraving, BM, NPG; repro. in Holles, *Memoirs* · oils, NPG [*see illus.*]

Wealth at death son's est. in 1684 incl. income of £4646, capital assets incl. timber valued at £12,000, several manor houses, about six advowsons

Holles, Sir Frescheville (1642–1672), naval officer, was born on 8 June 1642, the only son of Gervase *Holles (1607–1675), antiquary, and his second wife, Elizabeth Molesworth (d. 1662). Educated at the Middle Temple, he married Jane Crome (b. c.1632), widow, daughter of Richard Lewis of Marr, Yorkshire, in 1662—primarily, it was said, because of the fact that she brought £5000 to the marriage. He was a major in the Westminster militia (in 1664–7), while part owning and commanding the privateer *Panther* in 1665. His success in her brought him the recommendation of George Monck, duke of Albemarle, for a command in the navy, and on 2 October 1665 he became captain of the *Antelope*. Holles's conduct in the Four Days' Fight (1–4 June 1666) was widely praised and led to his knighthood, although he had lost his left arm during the engagement. He commanded the *Henrietta* from June to September 1666 (taking part in the St James's day fight on 25 July) before taking command of the *Cambridge*, remaining aboard her until January 1667. During the Dutch attack on the Medway in June 1667 he commanded the fireships guarding the Thames. He was returned to parliament for Great Grimsby on 22 November 1667, quickly becoming a leader of the attack on the naval administration's conduct of the war, allying himself with the duke of Buckingham's faction and speaking in favour of religious toleration. These activities hardly endeared him to the court, and in 1669 he was removed both from his captaincy in Albemarle's Coldstream regiment, which he had held since 1667, and from the place as a gentleman of the privy chamber that he had held since 1664. In 1670 he attempted unsuccessfully to enter the French service, then went to Ireland, where he bought timber for the navy. On his return to England he went over to the court, becoming a close ally of the duchess of Cleveland. With the outbreak of the Third Anglo-Dutch War he returned to the navy, rejoining the *Cambridge* on 20 January 1672 and taking part in the attack on the Dutch Smyrna fleet on 13 March. The *Cambridge* served as part of the admiral's division of the Red squadron at the battle of Solebay, on 28 May 1672, where Holles was killed. He was given a spectacular funeral on 29 June in Westminster Abbey.

Holles's two wills, the first dated 17 May 1665 and the second 25 April 1672, encapsulate his personality. Despite declaring in the first that he wanted no monument other 'than what my sword should raise for me of honour and fortune', the second was concerned chiefly with the planning of an impressive memorial in Westminster Abbey.

He made generous legacies to his friends, notably his executors, the banker Sir Robert Clayton and John Morris, and his former lieutenant Richard Carter. This combination of generosity, bravery, and vanity can also be seen in the famous 'double portrait' by Sir Peter Lely of Holles and Sir Robert Holmes, in which a swaggering Holles, sword in hand, is shown with no evidence of the lost left arm. Another of his former lieutenants recorded Holles's bravery and contemptuous disdain for his Dutch enemies ('so base a nation which were never guilty of any brave action'), as well as his recitation of poetry during a severe storm:

Blow winds, beat seas, in vain you spend your breath
My fate's too great by you to suffer death.
(Ingram, 33, 41)

Pepys's opinion of Holles was less complimentary. Virtually every reference to Holles in Pepys's diary is critical, if not abusive. Pepys described Holles's crew as 'the most debauched, damning, swearing rogues that ever were in the navy, just like their profane commander' (Pepys, *Diary*, 8.272) and the man himself as 'a conceited, idle, prating, lying fellow … as idle and insignificant a fellow as ever came into the fleet' (ibid., 8.275, 9.76). Holles wrote his wife out of his 1672 will, but her subsequent discovery of the 1665 will which named her as sole executor and beneficiary ensured that Holles's legal and financial affairs remained in a chaotic state well after his death.

J. D. DAVIES

Sources will and inventory, PRO, PROB 11/342, fol. 208 • will and inventory, PRO, PROB 5/2849 • J. D. Davies, *Gentlemen and tarpaulins: the officers and men of the Restoration navy* (1991) • P. Watson, 'Holles, Sir Frescheville', HoP, *Commons, 1660–90*, 2.564–5 • B. S. Ingram, ed., *Three sea journals of Stuart times* (1936) • J. L. Chester, ed., *The marriage, baptismal, and burial registers of the collegiate church or abbey of St Peter, Westminster*, Harleian Society, 10 (1876), 176 • PRO, ADM 10/15, p. 67 • *CSP dom., 1665–72* • W. A. Shaw, ed., *Calendar of treasury books*, [33 vols. in 64], PRO (1904–69) • NMM, MS LBK–47, MS AGC/6/3 • Pepys, *Diary* • *The manuscripts of his grace the duke of Portland*, 10 vols., HMC, 29 (1891–1931) • G. Holles, *Memorials of the Holles family, 1493–1656*, ed. A. C. Wood, CS, 3rd ser., 55 (1937) • J. L. Chester and J. Foster, eds., *London marriage licences, 1521–1869* (1887)
Likenesses P. Lely, double portrait, oils, c.1672 (with Sir R. Holmes), NMM; *see illus. in* Holmes, Sir Robert (c.1622–1692)
Wealth at death ready money to executors, out of which they paid funeral costs; £500 to Richard Carter and £200 each to Sir R. Clayton and J. Morris: will and inventory, PRO, PROB 11/342, fol. 208; PRO, PROB 5/2849 • owed the crown £1500 for Irish timber not delivered: Watson, 'Holles, Sir Frescheville'

Holles, Gervase (1607–1675), antiquary, was born at White Friars, Grimsby, Lincolnshire, on 9 March 1607, the only surviving son of Freschville Holles (1575–1630) and his wife, Elizabeth (1578–1608), daughter of John Kingston of Grimsby. His education which began at Grimsby grammar school was continued for nearly three years in the household of John Holles, first earl of Clare, who read logic and philosophy to him. After his father forbade him to enlist in Lord Vere's regiment in the Low Countries he entered Middle Temple in November 1628. Shortly after his father's death Holles married on 17 June 1630 Dorothy Kirketon and returned to Grimsby where for four years he was 'indulgent to my own contentment' and 'took great

pleasure in searching the records and investigating antiquities' (Wood, 228). Holles decided in September 1634 to move to Mansfield and recommence his study of the law but the sudden death of his wife the following January led him to return to Grimsby. After the death of his son George on 10 August 1635 he re-entered the Middle Temple for the Michaelmas term. He was chosen comptroller of the house and made a contribution of £200 to the Christmas festivities. As the mayor of Grimsby in 1636 and 1638 he collected ship money from the town. Holles was elected to represent Grimsby in March and October 1640. On 26 April 1641 he was suspended from the house after he attacked the Scottish proposals for peace 'as beyond all proportion' (BL, Lansdowne MS 207f, fols. 37v–38v). The order was rescinded on 2 December. In January 1642 a Commons committee investigated an incident between Holles and John Ogle in Westminster Hall and concluded that provocation had been given by Holles. After Holles ignored a summons of 18 April to attend the house he was eventually disabled from sitting and on 22 August 1642 a new writ of elections was issued (*JHC*, 2.128, 404, 537, 557, 734).

Holles who had moved to live at Newark in 1640 was appointed to the Nottinghamshire commission of the peace in March 1641. He was among the signatories of a letter in June 1642 to the Nottinghamshire MPs which warned parliament it should not conceive that their votes should be the law. In July he made a modest contribution to the appeal in Nottinghamshire to raise a troop of horse for the king. In the next month Holles was commissioned by the earl of Lindsey as a captain in the regiment of Sir Lewis Dives and when Charles raised his standard he brought 117 men to Nottingham. In September he was appointed sergeant-major of a regiment of foot and fought for the king at Edgehill. Holles was made an honorary MA by the University of Oxford and appointed to the parliament held in the town. In December he was given permission as a colonel to raise a regiment of foot from Lincolnshire which in the next month served at the seizure of Belvoir Castle and at the repulse of an attack on Newark. He joined the earl of Newcastle's troops at the battle of Adwalton Moor and fought at the first battle of Newbury. In February 1644 his regiment which was defending Muskham Bridge at Newark was broken by Meldrum's attack. Charles appointed Holles governor of King's Lynn in April 1644 but the town was and remained in parliamentary control. When Holles applied to compound in December 1645 his fine was set at £738 but it was not paid. After a proposal to raise troops for the doge of Venice failed, he enlisted in the service of the king of France. He returned to England to fight in the second civil war and was captured at the siege of Colchester and imprisoned. After his release in December 1649 Holles went to France but he eventually settled in Rotterdam. His penurious circumstances probably led to his request to compound but he failed to pay a fine of £860. Holles was impatient with the policy of waiting on events and in March 1657 he was reported to the commander of the English troops assembled for an invasion. Holles who lived in expectation of an invitation to go to England prepared a list of Lincolnshire peers and gentry who would support the king but the failure of Booth's rising prevented his return (BL, Egerton MS 2541, fol. 362r–v). In March 1660 Holles was informed that the king thought it was high time he returned to England. He was detained by lack of money and obligation to his landlady who had subsidized him for many years. Holles eventually returned in May 1660 and was in the next month appointed a master of requests. On 8 April 1661 he was elected to represent Grimsby in the House of Commons. Though he did not play an active role in the Commons he was listed among the dependants of the court in 1669 and 1671. Holles had been granted in January 1661 an annuity of £100 but the reward for which he was admirably suited, the keepership of the records in the Tower, eluded him (*Hastings MSS*, 2.313; *CSP dom.*, 1673–5, 473). Sir Frescheville *Holles, his son and heir by his second marriage (on 4 October 1637) to Elizabeth Molesworth (*d.* 1662), was killed in 1672 and this branch of the Holles family ended with Gervase's death in London on 10 February 1675. He was buried on 13 March at Mansfield.

Gervase Holles had originally intended 'to make a relation both historical and genealogical concerning Lincolnshire' by collecting many materials out of the records, charters, and church monuments of the shire. It was 'the damned and dire rebellion' which robbed him of his leisure and the greater part of his collection. Eight volumes of this collection now survive (BL, Lansdowne MSS 207a–f; Add. MSS 5531, 6118) but though parts of the work were transported to the Netherlands, Holles judged it was impossible to continue with his work on Lincolnshire. He decided to make a discourse of his family which now survives as the *Memorials of the Holles Family* (ed. A. C. Wood). The *Memorials* are the history of five generations of the Holles family whose position and prosperity were established by Sir William Holles, lord mayor of London in 1540. There are also genealogical accounts of the families with whom the Holleses married. It is the use of information from his contemporaries and his own experiences which, as in his account of John Holles, first earl of Clare, transforms his account from being mere tables of descent into a vivid portrait. It is regrettable that Gervase did not extend the brief account of his early life into the civil wars and their aftermath. P. R. SEDDON

Sources G. Holles, *Memorials of the Holles family, 1493–1656*, ed. A. C. Wood, CS, 3rd ser., 55 (1937) · *Calendar of the manuscripts of the marquis of Bath preserved at Longleat, Wiltshire*, 5 vols., HMC, 58 (1904–80), vol. 2 · BL, Lansdowne MSS 207a–f · BL, Add. MSS 5531, 6118 · *Report on the manuscripts of his grace the duke of Buccleuch and Queensberry ... preserved at Montagu House*, 3 vols. in 4, HMC, 45 (1899–1926), vol. 1 · *Report on the manuscripts of the late Reginald Rawdon Hastings*, 4 vols., HMC, 78 (1928–47), vol. 2 · *Newark on Trent: the civil war siegeworks*, Royal Commission on Historical Monuments (England) (1964) · *CSP dom.*, 1636; 1659–61; 1673–5 · *JHC*, 2 (1640–42) · M. A. E. Green, ed., *Calendar of the proceedings of the committee for compounding ... 1643–1660*, 3, PRO (1891) · R. W. Goulding, 'Gervase Holles: "a great lover of antiquities"', *Transactions of the Thoroton Society*, 26 (1923), 36–70 · U. Nott. L., department of manuscripts and special collections, Clifton CL LP.31 · *Calendar of the Clarendon state papers preserved in the Bodleian Library*, 3: 1655–1657, ed. W. D. Macray (1876); 4: 1657–1660, ed. F. J. Routledge (1932) · BL, Egerton MS 2541 · P. Watson, 'Holles, Gervase', HoP, *Commons, 1660–90*, 2.565–6

Archives BL, annotations to Lincolnshire church notes made by Francis Thynne, Add. MS 36295 · BL, Lincolnshire genealogical and antiquarian collections, Lansdowne MSS 207a–f · BL, Lincolnshire genealogical collections and papers, Add. MSS 5531, 6118, 6671 · BL, register book as master of requests, Add. MS 5759 · BL, register of petitions while master of requests, Add. MSS 5759, 15632 · Longleat House, Warminster, political corresp., incl. letters from Sir Edward Hyde, Sir George Radcliffe, and Thomas Ross · Northants. RO, family, official, and political papers

Holles, Gilbert, third earl of Clare (1633–1689), politician, was born on 24 April 1633 and baptized at Hackney on 18 May following, the second but only surviving son of John *Holles, second earl of Clare (1595–1666), and his wife, Lady Elizabeth Vere (*d.* 1683), eldest daughter and coheir of Horace *Vere, Baron Vere of Tilbury. During his father's lifetime Gilbert Holles held the courtesy title of Lord Haughton. In August 1645 he was permitted by parliament to travel overseas and he appears to have avoided formal education in England. On 12 July 1655 he was contracted to, and shortly after married, Grace Pierrepont (*d.* 1702), daughter of William Pierrepont of Thoresby, Nottinghamshire (the second son of Robert Pierrepont, first earl of Kingston).

In the Convention Parliament of 1660 Haughton represented Nottinghamshire; he made no speeches and was not elected to a committee. Appointed deputy lieutenant in 1660, he remained on the Nottinghamshire commission for a decade but rarely acted. He succeeded to the earldom in January 1666 and first attended the Lords the following December. A private act of 1667 enabled Clare to sell parts of his estate to pay inherited debts and raise marriage portions for his sisters. Clare came to notice in the Lords in January 1674 with his criticism of the king's attending the house and attempting to influence debates; after his second attack he had to ask the pardon of the king and the house. He was a supporter of the 1674 Comprehension Bill and, in the same session, of the proposal to exclude a Catholic from the succession if they married without parliamentary approval. As a result of these activities, Clare was seen by the court as one of the most 'forward' lords and an associate of Shaftesbury (Christie, 156–7). In September 1674 Clare, who admitted to being 'much addicted to a natural melancholly', was given a licence to travel abroad for his health (Newcastle deeds collection, Ne D 67). After his return to the Lords in February 1678 he fully justified Shaftesbury's rating of him as triple worthy, a rating he gave to only twelve peers. He remained a conscientious attender and consistent supporter of the country lords' policy. In December 1679 Clare joined the presenters of a petition to the king for the calling of a parliament. He supported the attempts in June 1680 of a Middlesex grand jury to indict James, duke of York, for recusancy. Clare was among the minority of thirty lords who voted for exclusion. The decision to call a parliament at Oxford saw Clare join in a protest of the leading whigs. At the parliament Clare dissented from the decision of the Lords that the legal proceedings against the informer Fitzharris should be by due course of law and not, as the whigs wanted, by impeachment. He continued a resolute supporter of Shaftesbury, standing surety at his trial in 1681, as he did for the duke of Monmouth the same year, and also spoke as a defence witness for Algernon Sidney in 1683. In the parliament of 1685 Clare joined the small group of whig lords in protests at decisions to reverse the impeachments of the popish lords of March 1679 and the attainder of Viscount Stafford, executed for his alleged participation in the Popish Plot. His last public act was to sign a petition of 17 November 1688 asking James to call a parliament. He died on 16 January 1689 at Warwick House, Holborn, and was buried at St James's Church, Haughton.

Though fined for conventicles held in his London properties, Clare was not an active patron of dissent. His will of 1686 shows him to have been an orthodox Calvinist and a critic of Arminianism. 'In this ill world', Clare complained, he found 'nothing but trouble and vexation of spiritt', and he particularly criticized his wife's frequent absences and love of London life. Despite his complaints about his indebted inheritance, which led to the sale of some London properties, he was able to retain the bulk of the estates he inherited. At his death they descended to his son John *Holles, who later became duke of Newcastle upon Tyne.   P. R. SEDDON

Sources *JHL*, 7–14 (1644–91) · U. Nott., Newcastle deeds collection, Ne D · A. Collins, *Historical collections of the noble families of Cavendishe, Holles, Vere, Harley and Ogle* (1752) · *CSP dom.*, 1673–89 · *Seventh report*, HMC, 6 (1879) [Sir Harry Verney] · A. Swatland, *The House of Lords in the reign of Charles II* (1996) · K. H. D. Haley, *The first earl of Shaftesbury* (1968) · E. S. de Beer, 'The House of Lords in the parliament of 1680', *BIHR*, 20 (1943–5), 22–37 · K. H. D. Haley, 'Shaftesbury's lists of the lay peers and members of the Commons, 1677–8', *BIHR*, 43 (1970), 86–105 · W. D. Christie, ed., *Letters addressed from London to Sir Joseph Williamson*, 2, CS, new ser., 9 (1874) · Notts. Arch., DDP 37/3 · W. Scott, ed., *A collection of scarce and valuable tracts … Lord Somers*, 2nd edn, 13 vols. (1809–15), vol. 8 · HoP, *Commons, 1660–90* · GEC, *Peerage*

Archives U. Nott., letters of the earl and his wife, PW 1 · U. Nott., Newcastle deeds and estates collections

Likenesses M. Verelst, portrait (after G. Holles), priv. coll.

Holles, John, first earl of Clare (*d.* 1637), landowner and politician, was the son of Denzel Holles (1538?–1590) and Eleanor, daughter of Edmund, Lord Sheffield. His year of birth is unknown. He matriculated at Christ's College, Cambridge, in 1579, was a fellow-commoner in 1580, and entered Gray's Inn in 1583. In April 1590 his father died, followed some nine months later by his grandfather Sir William Holles, 'by whose decease there devolved upon him a very fayre and opulent inheritance and with it the care of divers brothers and sisters' (Holles, *Memorials*, 89). Holles saw military service against the Armada in the Netherlands and Ireland where he was knighted by the earl of Essex in October 1593. He served as sheriff of Nottinghamshire in 1591–2. After his marriage in 1591 to Anne Stanhope (1576–1651), daughter of Sir Thomas Stanhope, Holles became an active supporter of his father-in-law in the latter's disputes with Gilbert Talbot, earl of Shrewsbury. Holles was twice challenged to a duel by Gervase Markham, a follower of Shrewsbury, but they did not fight until 1598. Although Markham was seriously wounded both men escaped punishment. In 1597, after he failed to

John Holles, first earl of Clare (*d.* 1637), by unknown artist

appear in Star Chamber when charged with infringing a proclamation forbidding new buildings in London, Holles was fined and criticized by Lord Burghley. Holles, who never let a public rebuke or insult pass unanswered, replied to Burghley's attack on the social status of his ancestors with a similar attack on the Cecils. Holles wisely ensured he was aboard the Azores expedition when the letter was delivered.

Elected MP for Nottinghamshire in 1604 and 1614, Holles was not a leading member of the Commons but his collection of the shire's views on the great contract consolidated his position in the county. Although he served as a gentleman of the king's privy chamber, it was not until his appointment, in the autumn of 1610, as comptroller of Prince Henry's household, that his quest for an important court office was rewarded. After Henry's death Sir John's hopes of office through his patron Robert Carr, earl of Somerset, were dashed when evidence emerged which implicated the earl in the murder of Sir Thomas Overbury. Holles was prominent in the attempts to clear Somerset. These culminated in his unsuccessful plea to Richard Weston, at his execution at Tyburn for Overbury's murder, to absolve the earl. For his temerity Holles was fined £1000 and imprisoned but it was Sir Edward Coke's stinging attack when he passed sentence which he never forgot and sought to avenge. After his release Holles hoped that appointment to office would recover his reputation. He was led to believe that £10,000 would purchase the treasurership of the king's household and a barony. By the time Holles discovered that only a barony was offered he was too deeply engaged to withdraw without dishonour. Though he complained it meant there was 'no use in me for the King and the state, then my purs' (*Letters*, 1.132), in July 1616 he paid £10,000 for the barony of Haughton.

As an adviser to Elizabeth, Lady Hatton, the estranged wife of Sir Edward Coke, Haughton seized every opportunity to attack his enemy. In 1617 he represented Lady Hatton in the negotiations for the marriage of her daughter Frances to Sir John Villiers, a brother of the earl of Buckingham. When it was discovered that Coke, who had been dismissed from the bench, also saw the marriage as a way of regaining favour, Frances was removed to the country. Coke, who accused but never proved that Haughton was responsible for his step-daughter's seclusion, seized Frances and his terms for the marriage were accepted by Buckingham. When Lady Hatton tried to defeat her husband by claiming there was a prior contract of marriage to the earl of Oxford, Haughton advised her to concede and seek the best available terms. She made her peace but Haughton found himself out of favour with Buckingham and James I. In 1618, when Margaret Langford accused Coke in Star Chamber of forcing her to sell lands in Derbyshire to him, Sir Edward accused Haughton of inciting the action. It was not until 1623 that this charge was withdrawn, by which time Haughton, who contested every legal move of his adversary, had been twice imprisoned for defying the orders of the privy council and the Star Chamber. He did become more cautious for in 1621 his refusal to join in a Star Chamber action brought against Coke, by Lepton and Goldsmith, two aggrieved patentees, was praised in the Commons.

In 1624 Buckingham's intermediary Bishop Williams, the lord keeper, offered Haughton an earldom for £6000. As a sign of his worth Haughton asked that office should accompany the honour. When he heard of Buckingham's 'willingness' to appoint him to the council of war, and after securing a reduction in the price, Haughton paid £5000 for the earldom of Clare (BL, Harley MS 7000, fols. 161r–162r; *Letters*, 2.296–7). Clare was not, however, appointed to the council of war and in his letters he became increasingly critical of the actions and influence of Buckingham. He joined the 'patriott' lords in their defence of the privileges of the nobility and the liberties of the subjects (*Letters*, 2.321, 334). In the 1626 parliament Clare was prominent in the attempts to free the earl of Arundel who had been imprisoned on the king's orders during the session. His fears that 'we gallopp all to the overthrow of Parliament …' were intensified when the crown tried to raise a forced loan. The nobility were expected to set an example by their subscriptions but Clare refused to lend for he believed the loan was unlawful and established a dangerous precedent. Although the realization that the king supported the loan perplexed him, he resisted all strategies to make it appear that he had contributed and was removed from the commission of the peace.

In the 1628 parliament Clare supported the attempts of the Commons to 'settle the propriety and liberty of the subject' and then to grant in subsidies a 'most bountifull retribution' for this was 'a better way' than 'either King or people be driven to extremes …' (*Letters*, 3.380). Clare played a leading role in the House of Lords debates, frequently arguing for accommodation with the Commons and the acceptance of the petition of right. In November 1629 Clare was imprisoned for possessing a pamphlet which urged the king to bridle the impertinency of parliaments and raise taxes by military force. It was eventually established that the proposals, which had been given to Clare by Somerset, had been rejected by James I and that the original was in Sir Robert Cotton's library. The charge that the pamphlet scandalized Charles I's government was now difficult to substantiate and the Star Chamber proceedings were withdrawn in May 1630. Clare believed he was prosecuted because of his opposition to the king's policies and his son Denzil *Holles's opposition in the Commons during the session of 1629. After a submission to the king, Clare was eventually restored to the commission of the peace and asked, in June 1630, to investigate the complaints of the town of Misterton. He continued to oppose what he believed were illegal proceedings and in his last year Clare was contesting his fines for building in London and enclosures in Nottinghamshire.

In 1629 Clare claimed he was unsuccessful in his search for court office because he was 'planted on the north side, where no court sunn shone, my nature advers to flatter greatnes, or to serve turns with base offices' (*Letters*, 3.390). This explanation forgets his successes: the comptrollership of Prince Henry's household, and, though it proved unlucky, his alliance with Somerset. As the years 1615–19 showed it was his combative temperament which led him to obstruct legal proceedings, and into unwise actions and his vendetta with Coke that undermined his search for office. It is no surprise that in 1618 James was reported to have 'no manner of liking to him in any sort' (*Letters of John Chamberlain*, 2.133) and his career never recovered from his actions in these years. His independence and determination to defend a cause did enable Clare in the years 1626–9 to make an important contribution to the principled opposition to the attacks on the liberties of the subjects.

From 1591, when he succeeded his grandfather, to his death in 1637 Clare spent at least £22,362 on the purchase of land in Nottinghamshire and Middlesex and £15,000 on the acquisition of peerages. In Nottinghamshire he concentrated on the consolidation of the properties he inherited around Haughton, the family seat. In Middlesex he followed a similar policy, adding to and improving his properties in and around the parish of St Clement Danes. As the profits from the lucrative London property market increased they came in the 1630s probably to amount to approximately half his rental income, which was about £4000 at his death (*Letters*, 1.xvii–xxiii). He died on 4 October 1637 at Thurland House, Nottingham, and was buried three days later at St Mary's, Nottingham. His son and namesake John *Holles succeeded to the earldom.

Despite the disappointments of his search for office Clare could console himself that though he became a 'chapman' to purchase titles, he had settled his house in honour (*Letters*, 1.135), and by his careful stewardship they had a more than sufficient income to maintain their status.   P. R. SEDDON

Sources *Letters of John Holles, 1587–1637*, ed. P. R. Seddon, 1, Thoroton Society Record Series, 31 (1975) · *Letters of John Holles, 1587–1637*, ed. P. R. Seddon, 2, Thoroton Society Record Series, 35 (1983) · *Letters of John Holles, 1587–1637*, ed. P. R. Seddon, 3, Thoroton Society Record Series, 36 (1986) · G. Holles, *Memorials of the Holles family, 1493–1656*, ed. A. C. Wood, CS, 3rd ser., 55 (1937) · U. Nott. L., department of manuscripts and special collections, Pw. V 4, 5; Ne D 1–9 · R. C. Johnson and others, eds., *Proceedings in parliament, 1628*, 5 (1983) · *Notes of the debates in the House of Lords, officially taken by Henry Elsing, clerk of the parliaments, AD 1624 and 1626*, ed. S. R. Gardiner, CS, new ser., 24 (1879) · W. Notestein, F. H. Relf, and H. Simpson, eds., *Commons debates, 1621*, 7 vols. (1935) · W. T. MacCaffrey, 'Talbot and Stanhope: an episode in Elizabethan politics', *BIHR*, 33 (1960), 73–85 · *The letters of John Chamberlain*, ed. N. E. McClure, 2 vols. (1939) · PRO, SP14, SP16 · *State trials* · commission of the peace, Birm. CL, Coventry MSS · BL, Harley MS 7000, fols. 161r–162r
Archives BL, commonplace and letter-book, Add. MS 70505 · BL, letter books of John Holles, Add. MS 32464 · Newcastle Deed Collection, letter books of John Holles, Portland Loan 29/239 N.U.M. D. Pw. V. 4, 5; Ne D. · U. Nott. L., corresp. · U. Nott. L., letter-books | Sheffield Central Library, Wentworth Woodhouse MSS, Strafford corresp.
Likenesses R. Clamp, stipple, BM, NPG; repro. in F. G. Waldren, *The biographical mirror*, 1 (1795) · oils, U. Nott., Newcastle collection [*see illus.*]
Wealth at death approx. £ 4000 p.a. in rentals: U. Nott. L., manuscripts department, Pw. V 4; Ne A 509–512

Holles, John, second earl of Clare (1595–1666), aristocrat, was born at Haughton, Nottinghamshire, on 13 June 1595, the son of John *Holles, first earl of Clare (d. 1637), and Anne Stanhope (d. 1651); Denzil *Holles, the politician, was a younger brother. Holles attended Christ's College, Cambridge, in 1611 and was admitted to Gray's Inn in February 1612. He lived in Paris in 1615–16. His 1621 election for Gatton, Surrey, was annulled by the House of Commons; when returned for both Mitchell, Cornwall, and East Retford in 1624 he chose to represent the latter, a Nottinghamshire borough. He was re-elected for East Retford in 1625 and 1626, when he was known as Lord Haughton following his father's elevation to the earldom of Clare, and on 24 September 1626 married Elizabeth Vere (d. 1683), daughter of Horace Vere, Baron Vere of Tilbury; he joined his father-in-law at the siege of Bois-le-Duc in 1629. He succeeded to the earldom in 1637.

Clare lacked political ambition and was accepted by the king to have 'no manner of relation to the Court' (Clarendon, *Hist. rebellion*, 3.142). In 1639 he claimed financial difficulties prevented him from producing the required equipage to attend on the king, then engaged against the Scots in the First Bishops' War. He joined the Lords in the 1640 Short Parliament, who voted that redress of grievances should precede supply. At the great council of peers held in September 1640 illness prevented him from acting as a commissioner to raise a royal loan from London, but he was appointed to advise the counties on the lending of money to the king. With the Long Parliament's 1641 impeachment of his brother-in-law, the earl of Strafford, Clare tried to counter the prosecution through his questioning of Secretary Vane over what Strafford had said at the crucial council meeting of 5 May 1640. When on 6 May 1641 the attack proceeded to voting on a bill of attainder against Strafford, he was excused for being absent from the upper house.

Thereafter Clare's stance showed some affinity with that of the 'popular' peers. He joined with five peers in September 1641 to protest at the Lords' decision to reissue their order of January 1641 upholding established church services, in opposition to the Commons' resolution ordering the removal of Laudian 'innovations'. In December 1641 his apprehension about the appointment of the royal nominee, Thomas Lunsford, to the sensitive military post of lieutenant of the Tower was recorded and in the next month he was among a substantial minority of the Lords who protested at the rejection of the Commons' proposal that parliamentary control of the militia was absolutely necessary. After these protests he was the obvious parliamentarian appointee as lord lieutenant of Nottinghamshire but he took no action to implement the militia ordinance. Instead, by June 1642 he had joined the king at York and signed a declaration that Charles had no intention to make war on parliament; Clarendon remembered that at this time he 'was looked upon as a man not only firm to the principles of monarchy but of duty to the person of the King' (Clarendon, *Hist. rebellion*, 3.153). Having learned of the king's resolution to raise his standard for war, however, Clare was among three peers who left York, having failed to persuade the king against this step. He returned to the residue of the Lords at Westminster in August when he was thanked for his carriage at York which 'tended to the preservation of the peace of the kingdom' (*JHL*, 5.284).

In the following month Clare was appointed to the committee for the safety of the kingdom and attended the Lords until August 1643. It was after the rejection of the Lords' peace propositions by the Commons that he followed the earls of Holland and Bedford to the king's court at Oxford. He was received by Charles at the siege of Gloucester, fought with the royalists at the battle of Newbury, and was admitted to the councils of war, yet royalist hostility to the peace proposals, in turn, opened his eyes and, 'undeceived', he left Oxford and eventually returned to London. In a letter of April 1644 to Essex which gives an explanation of his action he claimed it was 'the cause only and no other particular By-respects hath brought me back' (*JHL*, 6.495–6). Though the sequestration of his estates was rescinded and he took the covenant in April 1645, attempts to secure his readmission to the Lords failed. After his return Clare's political affiliations showed a consistency which had previously been absent. In June 1645 parliament appointed him to the Nottinghamshire committee of the northern association and in March 1646 warden of Sherwood Forest. After the first civil war he tried to restore order to Sherwood and continued during the Commonwealth and protectorate in his attempts to apply forest law and preserve the woods. He retained throughout these years his recordership of Nottingham.

It was not until April 1660, when he was reported to be ready to follow the earl of Bedford and take his seat in the

Lords, that Clare again began to consider taking a part in national politics. It needed a letter from the Lords asking him to attend before he took his seat on 5 May 1660 and he was a conscientious member of the Convention Parliament during its first few months and attended irregularly the Cavalier Parliament. The earl was more successful in persuading the king of his loyalty than the Nottinghamshire royalists. He was appointed to the standing council to consider the future regulation of the colonies but it needed the intervention of Charles II and Clarendon to defeat the attempts of the Nottinghamshire corporation commissioners to remove him from the recordership of Nottingham. Clare, they insisted, was a person whose 'good affection and zeale to our service we have no cause at all to doute' (U. Nott. L., MS Pw V 4, 286–7).

Clare had been taught by his father to be a careful steward of his inherited estates. They were concentrated in north Nottinghamshire and the parish of St Clement Danes, Middlesex, which was part of the rapidly growing London property market. He was purchasing land before his father's death and continued until the civil war the family's policy of seizing every opportunity to consolidate and enlarge its estates. He claimed in 1639 that his income was not near £4000, but his rental accounts showing £4069 0s. 2d. for that year prove that this estimate had been exceeded. During the interregnum Clare's major project was the improvement of and erection of new properties in and around St Clement Danes parish, for which he paid a fine in the protectorate of £1500 and spent £12,299 4s. 4d. before 1661. In 1657 he was given permission by parliament to hold a market and this privilege was confirmed in 1661. The last recorded rentals from Michaelmas 1664 to Lady day 1665 totalled £6626 3s. 1d. After Clare's death on 2 January 1666 the estate, which was encumbered by provision for dowries for his daughters and debts, descended to his son Gilbert *Holles, third earl of Clare. Clare was buried at St Mary's Church, Nottingham.   P. R. SEDDON

Sources JHL, 4–11 (1628–66) · A. Collins, Historical collections of the noble families of Cavendishe, Holles, Vere, Harley and Ogle (1752) · Letters of John Holles, 1587–1637, ed. P. R. Seddon, 3 vols., Thoroton Society Record Series, 31, 35–6 (1975–86) · Clarendon, Hist. rebellion, vols. 1–3 · U. Nott. L., MSS Pw.V 4, 5 · C. H. Firth and R. S. Rait, eds., Acts and ordinances of the interregnum, 1642–1660, 1–2 (1911) · W. Notestein, F. H. Relf, and H. Simpson, eds., Commons debates, 1621, 7 vols. (1935) · CSP dom., 1638–9; 1661–2 · C. R. Markham, The fighting Veres (1888) · P. Yorke [earl of Hardwicke], ed., Miscellaneous state papers, 1501–1726, 2 vols. (1778) · J. Rushworth, The tryal of Thomas earl of Strafford (1680) · JHC, 2 (1640–42) · DNB · R. W. Blencowe, ed., Sydney papers (1825) · B. Whitelocke, Memorials of English affairs, new edn, 4 vols. (1853) · G. Holles, Memorials of the Holles family, 1493–1656, ed. A. C. Wood, CS, 3rd ser., 55 (1937)

Archives U. Nott. L., Newcastle MSS, Ne C15,404 · U. Nott. L., Portland literary MS, Pw V2, 4, 5

Wealth at death £6626 3s. Michaelmas 1664–Lady day 1665, rentals: MSS Pw. V 4, p.2, U. Nott. L.

Holles, John, duke of Newcastle upon Tyne (1662–1711),

landowner and politician, was born on 9 January 1662, probably in Nottinghamshire, the eldest son of Gilbert *Holles, third earl of Clare (1633–1689), and his wife,

John Holles, duke of Newcastle upon Tyne (1662–1711), by Peter Cross

Grace (d. 1702), daughter of William Pierrepont of Thoresby, Nottinghamshire. From his father's accession to the earldom in 1666 he was known as Lord Haughton. Nothing seems to be known of his education beyond that he enjoyed 'all the advantages of education at home and abroad' (Collins, 178). He was the dedicatee of John Dryden's The Spanish Fryar in 1681, but there is no evidence that he was at court at this period.

In November 1688 Haughton waited on William of Orange as a representative of the supporters of the risings at York and Nottingham. He was elected to the Convention Parliament as a member for Nottinghamshire on 14 January 1689, but two days after his election his father died and he became fourth earl of Clare and inherited the Holles estates, mainly in Nottinghamshire and London. In the Lords he voted for the transfer of the crown to William and Mary, and was rewarded with the offices of gentleman of the bedchamber to William and lord lieutenant of Middlesex. Soon afterwards his mother suggested to her sister Frances, wife of Henry Cavendish, second duke of Newcastle, that he marry Newcastle's third but favourite daughter, Margaret (1661–1716). The marriage took place on 1 March 1690. By his will of May 1691 Newcastle left his estates, which were mainly in the east midlands and Northumberland, to Margaret and the heirs of her body, provided the estates remained undivided in the blood of the Cavendishes and that Margaret's descendants took the name of Cavendish in honour of the first duke of Newcastle. Clare vigorously defended the settlement in the court of chancery against Ralph Montagu, first earl of Montagu, who had married Newcastle's eldest daughter, Elizabeth, and Thomas Tufton, sixth earl of Thanet, who had married Newcastle's fourth daughter, Catherine. Chancery rejected all attempts to invalidate the will; the duel which Thanet and Clare fought on 13 May 1692 saw both wounded and did nothing to change the issue.

Clare, supported by his father-in-law, applied for a dukedom on 18 April 1691, but William III refused. The death of the duke on 26 July 1691 brought him the Newcastle estates, where he was able to pay an outstanding mortgage of £80,000. Disappointed at not receiving the dukedom he sought, Clare resigned as gentleman of the bedchamber and (in 1692) lord lieutenant of Middlesex, and retired to his estates, where he proved an informed and careful steward. On the death of his unmarried kinsman Denzil Holles, third Baron Holles of Ifield, on 25 January 1694, he succeeded to his property scattered throughout southern England. Clare also spent about £200,000 adding to the Nottinghamshire properties, re-creating the Holles interest in Lincolnshire, and acquiring substantial estates in Cambridgeshire, Bedfordshire and Huntingdonshire.

Clare was an informed and careful steward of his estates. He was, in the estimation of Bishop Burnet, 'the richest subject that had been in England for some ages' (*Bishop Burnet's History*, ed. Burnet and Burnet, 2.579), and on 14 May 1694 he was created marquess of Clare and duke of Newcastle upon Tyne. The next month he became lord lieutenant of Nottinghamshire. In October 1695 he reportedly spent £5042 on entertaining William III at Welbeck Abbey, inherited through his wife, which became his principal residence instead of the Holles family seat of Haughton. As long promised he was installed KG on 7 July 1698. His support for the junto ministry was rewarded in August 1699 with the lieutenancy of the East Riding of Yorkshire and the wardenship of the New Forest.

Newcastle became one of the leading electoral patrons of his day. At the core of his interest were East Retford in Nottinghamshire and Dorchester in Dorset, where he became high steward in January 1701. He purchased control of Aldborough, Yorkshire, and in neighbouring Boroughbridge his acquisitions in alliance with one of its leading families enabled him to significantly influence the return. In the first years of Anne's reign Newcastle voted with the whigs but, as before, he had little interest in major political office, until in March 1705 his friend Robert Harley persuaded him to join the Godolphin–Marlborough administration as lord privy seal. He was also sworn of the privy council and became lord lieutenant of the North Riding of Yorkshire, and from 1706 to 1707 was a commissioner for the union with Scotland. In the last two sessions of the parliament of 1705–8 Newcastle had a tight personal following of ten members, 'nearly all of whom were either mainly or entirely indebted' to him for their seats (Holmes, 225). His wealth and influence enabled him to act independently and he remained lord privy seal after the reconstruction of the ministry and tory victory in 1710. He was rewarded with more local offices, becoming chief justice in eyre, north of Trent, from September 1710, and lord lieutenant of Middlesex in July 1711. Newcastle seemed set to enjoy his extended influence; he was

trusted by Queen Anne and by Harley, although his adherence to the ministry had shaken his whig friends and was regarded with misgiving by some tories. However, on 13 July 1711 he fell from his horse while stag-hunting at Welbeck, and died there on 15 July. He was buried on 9 August 1711 at Westminster Abbey, 'under a sumptuous monument' (GEC, *Peerage*).

Newcastle's will of 29 August 1707 was the object of much critical comment by contemporaries, but underlines the priorities which governed his life. He attempted to keep the majority of his estates undivided and perpetuate his family's name. The bulk of his estate was left to his nephew, Thomas Pelham [see Holles, Thomas Pelham-, duke of Newcastle upon Tyne and first duke of Newcastle under Lyme], the son of his sister Grace who had married Thomas Pelham, first Baron Pelham of Laughton. The duchess of Newcastle received her jointure. Their only child, Henrietta (1694–1755) [see Harley, Henrietta Cavendish, countess of Oxford and Mortimer], was given a marriage portion of £20,000 and the former Cavendish properties in Staffordshire, Northumberland, and Yorkshire provided she did not enter upon or sue for any other parts of her father's real estate. The duchess and her daughter, who in 1713 married Edward *Harley, later second earl of Oxford and Mortimer, contested the will, claiming that Newcastle had no right to dispose of the Cavendish estate. After protracted litigation and the death of the duchess a settlement was agreed and given statutory form in 1719. Henrietta now received, with the exception of Nottingham Castle, all the properties that Newcastle had inherited from his father-in-law, the last Cavendish duke, in 1691, including Welbeck and Bolsover, and the acquisitions Newcastle had made since making his will in 1707. Henrietta had succeeded in increasing her share, but Newcastle had succeeded in keeping the majority of his possessions together which went, with the Yorkshire parliamentary boroughs, to Pelham.   P. R. SEDDON

Sources BL, Portland MSS, Add. MSS 70500–70502 · Notts. Arch., DD 3P 10/1–12; DD 4P 39 · U. Nott., Holles MSS, Pw 2 · BL, Pelham and Holles legal MSS, Add. MSS 33054, 33060, 33064 · G. S. Holmes, *British politics in the age of Anne* (1967) · A. S. Turberville, *Welbeck Abbey and its owners* (1938), 1 · O. R. F. Davies, 'The wealth and influence of John Holles, duke of Newcastle, 1694–1711', *Renaissance and Modern Studies*, 9 (1965), 22–46 · U. Nott. L., Newcastle MSS, Ne. D.; Ne. L. · E. Cruickshanks, D. Hayton, and C. Jones, 'Divisions in the House of Lords on the transfer of the crown and other issues, 1689–94', *BIHR*, 53 (1980), 56–87 · A. McInnes, *Robert Harley, puritan politician* (1970) · ER, vol. 1 · A. Browning, *Thomas Osborne, earl of Danby and duke of Leeds, 1632–1712*, 3 vols. (1944–51), vol. 2 · A. Collins, *Historical collections of the noble families of Cavendishe, Holles, Vere, Harley and Ogle* (1752) · *Memoirs of Sir John Reresby*, ed. A. Browning (1936) · R. Browning, *The duke of Newcastle* (1975) · *Bishop Burnet's History of his own time*, ed. G. Burnet and T. Burnet, 2 (1734) · *CSP dom., 1688–1712* · GEC, *Peerage*

Archives BL, Add. MSS 70500–70502 · BL, Add. MSS 500–502 · BL, corresp. and MSS, Harley MSS 2262–2264 · Notts. Arch., Portland MSS, DD 3P 10/1–12 · Notts. Arch., Portland MSS, DD 4P 39 · U. Nott., Holles MSS, Pw 2 | BL, Add. MS 33054 · BL, Add. MS 33060 · BL, Add. MS 33064 · CKS, letters to Alexander Stanhope · Hants. RO, corresp. · Notts. Arch., Portland MSS, DDP 1–4, 6 · U. Nott., letters to Sir Francis Molyneux · U. Nott., corresp. with Sir

Francis Molyneux and others • U. Nott., Newcastle MSS, Ne. D.; Ne. L. • U. Nott., Portland MSS, Cavendish MSS, Pw 1
Likenesses F. Bird, marble reclining effigy on monument, 1723 (after J. Gibbs), Westminster Abbey • P. Cross, miniature, priv. coll. [*see illus.*] • attrib. G. Kneller, oils, Malmö Museum, Sweden
Wealth at death £200,000 • £40,000 income: The English Reports • £33,060 p.a. rental income, 1701–11: Davies, 'Wealth'

Holles, Thomas Pelham-, duke of Newcastle upon Tyne and first duke of Newcastle under Lyme (1693–1768), prime minister, was born in Sussex on 21 July 1693, the eldest son of Thomas *Pelham (c.1653–1712) and his second wife, Lady Grace Holles (d. 1700). Thomas Pelham had two daughters by his first marriage; his subsequent union with Lady Grace produced, in addition, one son, Henry *Pelham, a later prime minister, and six daughters.

Childhood and education, 1693–1717 After attending Westminster School, young Thomas matriculated in 1709 at Clare College, Cambridge. Although he left the university before taking a degree, he retained throughout his life happy memories of his experiences at both Westminster and Cambridge and in later years assumed a measure of responsibility for governance at both institutions.

Pelham quickly became a wealthy man through two inheritances. The first came in July 1711, when his mother's brother, John Holles, duke of Newcastle upon Tyne, died, bequeathing Thomas a vast estate. The heir's only obligation was to append 'Holles' to his name, a duty Thomas fulfilled for the rest of his life. The astonished dowager duchess immediately launched a legal campaign to overturn the settlement. Although every judicial decision handed down on the case supported Thomas Pelham's right to the inheritance, he was inclined to be generous and proposed a compromise. By its terms he yielded a few choice properties to Lord Oxford, the dowager duchess's son-in-law. The second inheritance came in February 1712, on the death of Thomas's father. Thomas succeeded both to the title of Baron Pelham of Laughton, which his father had received in 1706, and to the Pelham estates in Sussex. As a consequence of these two inheritances the young Lord Pelham held lands in eleven counties and enjoyed an annual income of almost £32,000. He also either controlled or significantly influenced the selection of over a dozen members of parliament elected from Sussex, Yorkshire, and Nottinghamshire.

To his political influence Pelham added a fiery commitment to the whig cause. In the final years of Queen Anne's reign he joined the party's two leading social organizations, the Kit-Cat Club and the Hanover Club. In late 1714 the newly arrived George I appointed him to the lord lieutenancies of Middlesex and Nottinghamshire and raised him in the peerage with the titles of Viscount Houghton and earl of Clare, both formerly borne by his uncle. He promptly bought the land in Surrey upon which he would erect Claremont, his largest and favourite home. A year later, as a reward for Lord Clare's electoral support for the whigs in the general election of 1715, the king bestowed on him two additional titles that had belonged to John Holles: marquess of Clare and duke of Newcastle upon Tyne. On the outbreak of the Jacobite rising later in the

Thomas Pelham-Holles, duke of Newcastle upon Tyne and first duke of Newcastle under Lyme (1693–1768), by William Hoare, c.1752

year, Newcastle raised a voluntary defence force and led roving crowds in demonstrations on behalf of the king. When the whigs began to fissure in 1716, Newcastle, after some hesitation, threw his lot in with the victorious Sunderland–Stanhope camp. One facet of this decision was his marriage on 2 April 1717 to a woman with Sunderland ties, Lady Henrietta Godolphin (d. 1776). Less than two weeks after the wedding, on 13 April 1717, Newcastle received a political reward for his loyalty, taking the oath of office to become lord chamberlain. His public career was launched.

A whig politician, 1717–1730 In his new office Newcastle superintended the household 'above stairs', the largest section of the royal establishment. Frequent contact with George I allowed a friendship between the two men to emerge, and in March 1718 the duke was installed knight of the Garter. Meanwhile, in the House of Lords the duke gave vigorous support to the work of the government. He worried for his future when the government's defeat in the Commons on the Peerage Bill obliged the ministry to readmit Robert Walpole and Charles, Viscount Townshend. But the South Sea Bubble and the deaths of Stanhope and Sunderland so thoroughly recast the political world that, when the dust settled in 1722, Newcastle stood as the third most influential minister in the kingdom, overshadowed only by Walpole at the Treasury and Townshend as *de facto* foreign secretary. Many observers were surprised at this ascent. But, in addition to his good fortune, his rise was testimony to his affability, his diligence, his power as an electoral magnate, and his readiness to follow a leader. In 1724 Walpole completed the ratification of Newcastle's success by ousting the independent-minded Lord Carteret from office and installing the duke in the lucrative post of secretary of state for the southern department. Barely thirty, Newcastle now bore co-ordinate responsibility (with Townshend in the northern department) for the conduct of British foreign policy.

Even though Newcastle had never set foot on the European continent, he was not uninterested in foreign affairs. Townshend had adopted Stanhope's commitment to the maintenance of the friendship of France, and Newcastle followed the lead of his colleague. Where they parted ways was in trying to sort out the implications of that commitment for relations with other European states. The tension between the secretaries first arose when the unexpected juncture of Spain and Austria in the treaty of Vienna in 1725 raised the question: which country represented the greater threat to Britain? For Townshend, Vienna, with its new commercial interests in the East Indies, posed the greater challenge. For Newcastle, concerned to protect Gibraltar and British interests in American waters, Madrid deserved priority. The duke was also moved by the consideration that Britain and Austria had been allies against the France of Louis XIV, and he dreamed of restoring what he often styled the 'old system'—the alliance of London and Vienna against Versailles. When Walpole began to focus attention on this issue, he found himself more in sympathy with Newcastle's inclinations. Then when Spain adopted the belligerent course of interning a British ship and besieging Gibraltar, Newcastle's view received additional confirmation.

This incipient division in the ministry was abruptly eclipsed in June 1727, however, when George I died while in Hanover. The new monarch George II had, as prince of Wales, often quarrelled with his father, and a decade of strained relations in the royal family had given him ample occasion to hone a dislike of Walpole, Townshend, and Newcastle. His quarrel with the duke dated back to a public altercation between the two men at the baptism of the prince of Wales's son in 1717. In order now to protect their hold on office, the three ministers set aside their differences and, guided by Walpole's skilful efforts to prove his indispensability, sought to persuade the new king to retain his inherited servants. They were successful. Talk of saddling Newcastle with the purgatorial lord lieutenancy of Ireland quickly faded, and before the year was out the duke was expressing confidence that he had surmounted the danger.

The receding of the fear that he would be dislodged from office allowed Newcastle to return to his foreign policy disagreement with Townshend. He used his position as the secretary with responsibility for Spain to insist that London be unbending in negotiations with Madrid. In 1729 his hardline policy succeeded when, after the Vienna alliance fell apart, Spain abandoned its military harassment of Gibraltar and in the treaty of Seville, concluded in November, accepted a British construction of almost all of the points in dispute. This validation of Newcastle's policy left Townshend isolated within the ministry, and, when in May 1730 Walpole chose Newcastle's advice in negotiations with Austria as well, Townshend resigned the seals. Newcastle then crowned his triumph by filling the empty northern office with Lord Harrington, a man whom he believed could be trusted to be subservient to a senior secretarial colleague. With this latest ministerial reshuffle, Newcastle was the second most powerful politician in the kingdom.

Walpole's foreign minister, 1730–1739 No longer burdened with an unsympathetic secretarial colleague, Newcastle pressed ahead in his effort to restore the old system. The treaty of Vienna of March 1731 was a major triumph as Austria, in return for Britain's recognition of the so-called pragmatic sanction, abandoned its effort to use the Austrian Netherlands to try to challenge Britain's commercial dominance in Asian waters. Newcastle had thus overseen a reorientation of British foreign policy. In complimenting George II on having 'given peace to all Europe' (Coxe, *Robert Walpole*, 3.12), Newcastle was in fact hoping to praise himself.

But two years later the duke's commitment to Austria served as the basis for his first important foreign policy quarrel with Walpole. When the Bourbon states and Austria went to war in Italy, Newcastle believed that London should aid Vienna. But Walpole, with greater respect for the durability of the Habsburg state, and with an eye on an imminent general election, concluded that Britain's interests would be best served if the kingdom remained neutral, and, as chief minister, he prevailed. Newcastle, however, though acceding to Walpole's policy, was unconvinced of its wisdom: he feared that France and Spain would assume that Britain was ineffectual and that Austria would conclude that Britain was unreliable. Whatever good the treaties of Seville and Vienna had wrought was, he feared, being undone by Britain's neutrality in the War of the Polish Succession.

But if foreign affairs were tending to drive a wedge between Walpole and Newcastle after 1733, domestic affairs were solidifying their co-operation. At the opening of the decade, with Townshend's departure from office, Newcastle assumed responsibility for serving as the government's chief spokesman in the House of Lords. He was a ready and energetic, if not always coherent, speaker. When Walpole engineered a ministerial reshuffle after the excise tax crisis in 1733, the group that remained in office—especially the duke's close friend Lord Hardwicke and his brother Henry Pelham—comprised the nucleus of what Newcastle would later call the 'old corps'. Over the course of the next quarter of a century this group would have the fairest claim of all political factions to be the true repository, especially in domestic matters, of Walpolean whiggery, while during the same years Hardwicke became Newcastle's most trusted political adviser. Meanwhile, under the umbrella of this close domestic collegiality with Walpole, Newcastle steadily expanded the range of his influence and authority. He collected various offices in many of the counties with which he was associated. As early as 1725 the duke assumed nominal responsibility for Scottish affairs. After 1730 he slowly took control of appointments in the American colonies. After 1736 he extended his influence into the affairs of the Church of England. Having little interest in America, he used his colonial appointment powers largely to solve British (rather than American) political problems; deeply interested in the church, he exercised his powers of ecclesiastical appointment to advance the careers of churchmen of orthodox theological views and whiggish political sensibilities. Meanwhile, through his friendship with Princess Emily, he had access to court gossip and thinking. Thus, as the end of the decade approached, Newcastle sat at the centre of several extensive networks of patronage and information and enjoyed as full a measure of confidence as Walpole was ever likely to bestow on any governmental colleague.

In the final years of the decade another dispute with Spain, involving competing claims to various rights in America, tested the friendship. Two circumstances made it oddly intractable: the belief in Madrid that Britain would ultimately yield rather than go to war over disputes in distant America, and the intervention of the South Sea Company into what Walpole and Newcastle would have preferred to treat as an exclusively diplomatic matter. Neither minister wanted war. Newcastle's bona fides is evidenced by his willingness in 1738 to acknowledge Spain's right to search British ships in some circumstances and by his recall in the early months of 1739 of Nicholas Haddock's fleet from the Mediterranean. When negotiators finally completed the convention of Pardo in January 1739, Newcastle believed that war had been averted. But a severe public outcry, orchestrated by the South Sea Company, overwhelmed both Walpole and Newcastle: Pardo, all came to agree, was inadequate. The duke revealed his true feelings when, by way of explanation, he stated that 'we must yeild [sic] to the times' (BL, Add. MS 35406, fol. 111). The first formal intimations of war issued from Spain late in the spring of 1739. Soon thereafter Newcastle informed London's diplomat in Madrid of Britain's decision to 'pursue hostile measures' (BL, Add. MS 32801, fol. 67). The formal British declaration of war on 19 November transformed Newcastle from *de facto* foreign minister to *de facto* minister of defence.

Defence minister, 1739–1748 Over the course of the next nine years Newcastle, more than any other person, defined the contours of Britain's war policy. The conflict with Spain, conventionally called the War of Jenkins's Ear, became a sideshow in 1741 when, in reaction to the outbreak of continental hostilities between Austria on the one hand and France and Prussia on the other, Britain came to Austria's defence. For several years Britain remained technically an auxiliary to the Habsburg state, but in 1744 formal war with France was declared, and the

focus of the War of the Austrian Succession thereafter shifted from Germany towards the Atlantic. Throughout the belligerence Newcastle's chief foreign-policy goal was to conclude the war with the old system—which Newcastle later styled 'my doctrine and system' (BL, Add. MS 35412, fol. 16)—intact. In that aim, despite a number of stumbles along the way, he was finally successful.

That Britain went to Austria's assistance at all in 1741 was testimony to Newcastle's influence in the government; Walpole would have preferred to follow the non-involvement of 1733. But 1741 also delivered three blows to the ministry. First, the general election in May reduced the government's majority in the House of Commons to precarious levels. Then came word that the combined naval and military expedition against Cartagena in the New World had foundered with heavy loss of life. Finally, George II announced his decision, as elector of Hanover, to seek protection for his electorate by declaring its neutrality in the expanding war.

The climax of these set-backs came in February 1742, when Walpole, held responsible for military failures and diplomatic reverses, resigned his post at the Treasury. In the ensuing restructuring of the government, Newcastle, Pelham, and Hardwicke were obliged to admit some opposition politicians, including Lord Carteret, who accepted the seals for the northern department and pledged to inject a new vigour into Britain's war effort. Pleased at last to have a ministry of one mind about the need to push the war, Newcastle did not initially contest Carteret's control over the policy pursued. The new secretary even persuaded the king to restore Hanover's diplomatic co-operation with Britain, a step that Newcastle later called 'the best thing he ever did' (BL, Add. MS 32701, fol. 190). When Prussia left the war shortly after Carteret took office, his policy appeared to be succeeding. Meanwhile, Newcastle dealt in the House of Lords with the ceaseless complaining about what the opposition understood to be British coddling of Hanover. Against many expectations, Newcastle showed he could co-exist with Carteret.

By 1744, however, Newcastle was beginning to distance himself from his secretarial colleague. Carteret had set out to unite Europe against the Bourbon powers. His policy reached its apogee in September 1743, when the treaty of Worms effected an uneasy alliance between Austria and Piedmont-Sardinia. But Newcastle was suspicious of Carteret's grand design, predicting within months of Worms that 'our active secretary, will at last find out, that dexterity with princes, to seem to promise all, and intend nothing, will as little do, as with private persons' (BL, Add. MS 35407, fol. 280). Sure enough, in the first eight months of 1744, apparently as a reply to Worms, France redoubled its commitment to Spain and launched a fleet against Britain while Prussia rejoined the fray on the Bourbon side, forcing Austria to pull its army back from the Low Countries. The collapse of Carteret's foreign policy left the northern secretary politically vulnerable, and in December 1744, under duress, he resigned the seals. With Carteret's departure, the old corps triumvirate of Henry

Pelham, Lord Hardwicke, and Newcastle established themselves as the unchallenged directors of national politics, with command over foreign policy being the duke's particular province.

It was useful for Newcastle that four events of 1745 clarified the nature of the war. First, the battle of Fontenoy established France as the dominant power in the Low Countries. Second, Britain's capture of Louisbourg in North America gave London a valuable trophy for negotiating a peace with Versailles. Third, the failure of the French-supported Jacobite invasion of Britain confirmed that France could not reasonably hope to drive Britain from the war. Fourth, Prussia's final withdrawal from the war in December, by removing the ambiguity that Berlin's participation had imposed upon the belligerence, suggested that at the core of the conflict lay the old Habsburg–Bourbon rivalry for dominance on the continent.

The clarifications implicit in these events removed grounds for ministerial infighting about strategic matters, and the resultant united front emboldened the ministers to decide to teach a lesson to a monarch who had been quarrelsome and recalcitrant. In February 1746 Newcastle engineered a mass resignation of ministers which, by showing the political indispensability of the old corps, forced a stubborn George II to invite them back into office on their own terms. For the rest of the war the monarch forswore hampering the work of his ministers, and, as a result of this visible union of royal and ministerial wills, the government won a sweeping victory in the general election of 1747.

Meanwhile, with France establishing itself as unbeatable on land and Britain proving itself invincible at sea, the logic of a compromise peace settlement slowly emerged: London would hand Louisbourg back to Versailles, which in turn would return the Southern Netherlands to Vienna. In that way, the old system would be preserved. After much hesitation, the various combatants sent representatives to Aix-la-Chapelle in early 1748 to hammer out a treaty. Though Newcastle did not attend the negotiations, he so worried about losing influence if the monarch were left without his guidance that in the summer of 1748, having taken the reins in the northern department and given the southern department to the duke of Bedford, he endured the misery of seasickness to make his first visit to the continent in order to accompany the king to Hanover. The treaty of Aix-la-Chapelle was signed (by most powers) on 18 October. For Britain the principle underlying the settlement was *status quo ante bellum*. Such a dismal outcome left little room for anyone to claim that Britain had emerged triumphant, but at least the kingdom had not lost, and Newcastle, taking pride in this modest achievement, confided to his brother that 'I feel the joy of an honest man' (Coxe, *Pelham*, 2.325). Since the struggle had resolved none of the outstanding Anglo-French issues in America, however, its resumption in the coming years was widely predicted.

Pelham's foreign minister, 1748–1754 To prepare Britain for that conflict Newcastle turned his post-war energies to strengthening the old system through collective security,

thereby isolating France. He enjoyed a modest success in winning Spanish complaisance through the conclusion of a commercial treaty with Spain in 1750. But he had virtually no success at persuading Frederick II of the advantages of aligning Prussia with an anti-French coalition. Still, even if Prussia chose to stand aside, there were other German states whose support might be secured. Newcastle's problem was that these states were unlikely to commit themselves without a financial inducement to do so, and Henry Pelham at the Treasury was suspicious of the idea that subsidies paid in time of peace were a sound way to create a coalition that would operate in time of war. What Newcastle needed therefore was a reason to provide subsidies to German states which, without being bribes, nevertheless placed the recipients in the anti-French camp. From that dilemma emerged the strangest diplomatic initiative of his career—the plan to have Maria Theresa's son elected king of the Romans, and hence successor to his father Francis I when the reigning holy roman emperor should die.

Between 1749 and 1753 Newcastle directed a campaign to line up six of the nine imperial electors—a so-called eminent majority—to vote for young Joseph. Subsidies were paid to Bavaria and Saxony; a further subsidy was promised to the electoral Palatine. When Henry Pelham baulked at approving what he saw as reckless expenditure, Newcastle won his brother over by proclaiming the election plan 'the only means I can think of, of establishing any real, solid system for the preservation of peace and the maintenance of the liberties of Europe' (BL, Add. MS 32822, fol. 239). If money had been all that was needed, Newcastle would have realized his goal. But the basic problem with the scheme was that Austria, the presumed beneficiary of British largesse, was averse to it. Maria Theresa would have been happy to have had her son chosen as her husband's successor if the cost were reasonable. But the Austrian ministry feared that the project would needlessly antagonize France at a time when Austria needed the chance to recuperate and restructure its administration. Because Austria did not want to anger its British ally, it did not declare its opposition to the initiative openly, preferring to block its implementation through a variety of apparently minor obstructions. As a result, efforts to realize the election plan were protracted, dribbling away into inconsequentiality only in 1753. But Austria, which already nourished doubts about whether London's interests truly coincided with Vienna's, now had reason to ponder London's wisdom as well.

Still, if foreign politics were proving sticky, domestic politics in the years after 1748 were smooth and easy. When Newcastle eased the duke of Bedford out of the southern department office in 1751, replacing him with the thoroughly compliant Lord Holdernesse, he not only secured total control of foreign policy for himself but also removed from office the only whig grandee who sometimes charted a course at variance with the Pelhams. Fearful of reviving 'old Disputes & Distinctions, which are at present, quiet' (BL, Add. MS 32721, fol. 158), especially with a general election looming in 1754, he resisted any governmental action likely to unsettle some segment of the tranquil public. Only when the government secured passage of the Jewish Naturalization Act in the spring of 1753 did the tranquillity lapse, and the startled Pelhams moved quickly to reclaim the initiative late in the year by engineering the repeal of the very measure they had urged on the kingdom less than twelve months earlier. Sailing into 1754, all seemed serene. But then, on 6 March 1754, after a short illness, Henry Pelham died.

Prime minister, 1754–1756 Newcastle was quickly persuaded to protect old corps' interests by taking charge of affairs himself. But over the course of the next two and a half years he proved himself a disastrous prime minister, committing three fundamental errors. First, in order to retain for himself the fullest possible array of patronage power, he failed to give adequate support to his government's leader in the House of Commons. Second, in order to court an already reluctant Austria, he pursued a European policy that must finally be labelled fatuous. Finally, in order to spare himself the full weight of the blame for the misfortunes that befell his government, he sought to divert criticism by redefining his government into a set of autonomous departments and by recasting himself as little more than—perhaps even less than—*primus inter pares*. Together, the errors doomed his ministry.

Pelham's death necessitated several changes. Since Newcastle was unwilling to leave Treasury patronage to potentially critical colleagues, he assumed the office of first lord of the Treasury himself, calculating correctly that the expertise of the men who had served his brother would protect him from any gross financial errors. His difficulty lay in dealing with the House of Commons. As a peer, the duke could not personally assume his late brother's responsibility as leader of that house. Anxious lest he provide a political beachhead to a rival of talent, he bypassed such men as William Pitt, Henry Fox, and William Murray, persuading instead Thomas Robinson, whose experience lay in diplomacy rather than domestic politics, to become leader. The duke's deeper strategy was to govern the House of Commons indirectly, from the Lords. Because no ambition could have been more inimical to the self-definition of MPs, it was a fatally flawed strategy. But well before this deeper implication became clear, the general election was held in May, and the new government won a grand victory, allowing the duke to launch his prime ministership with a massive majority in the Commons.

The first sign of trouble came in July, when word arrived that a Virginian effort to dislodge the French from Fort Duquesne had failed. The engagement portended a wider Anglo-French conflict in America, and so Newcastle brought the king's son the duke of Cumberland, an experienced commander, into the government and began to pay more heed to the advice of Henry Fox, the secretary at war. After much hesitation and confusion, the ministry resolved to send Major-General Edward Braddock and Vice-Admiral Edward Boscawen to America to deal with the French challenge. But in the summer of 1755 word

arrived that Boscawen, though initiating hostilities by attacking a French fleet, had failed to prevent the landing of French troops at Louisbourg, while Braddock had been killed in an unsuccessful action in America. With this news Newcastle and his colleagues were compelled to acknowledge that an American crisis was at hand.

Meanwhile, the ministry's efforts to meet France's challenge in Europe were well under way. Although when he first learned of the clashes in the American wilderness Newcastle had hoped that the conflict might be confined to the New World, he had soon bowed to the logic of geopolitical reality: if border skirmishes should turn into war along the Appalachians, France would want to seize a trophy that might induce Britain to hand back any American winnings, and the most obvious candidate for trophy status was the king's German domain of Hanover. Therefore, by 1755 Newcastle was devoting attention to securing a commitment from Vienna that Austria would support Britain (and hence deter France) in any Anglo-French war. Austria, however, preferred to remain disengaged: its interest lay in recovering land lost to Prussia, and, if Britain was not willing to use troops to aid Vienna in recovering Silesia, Austria preferred not to commit itself to British ends. So Newcastle turned to a more circuitous strategy, and late in the summer of 1755 agreed to a treaty with Russia that committed St Petersburg, in return for a British subsidy of £100,000 in peacetime, to station troops on the east Prussian frontier and to launch them against Frederick II if Prussia attacked Britain or Hanover. If this move did not specifically deter France from attacking Hanover, it at least gave Prussia grounds for pause.

At this point the indirection of Newcastle's European policy began to cause the entire system to unravel spectacularly. The treaty of St Petersburg so alarmed Frederick II that Prussia suddenly warmed to the long-standing feelers from Britain. As a consequence, London and Berlin concluded the convention of Westminster in January 1756, with each state pledging itself to neutrality in Germany if a European war broke out. With this stroke Newcastle believed that he had secured Hanover against attack. But in fact the convention was a strategic disaster. First, it alienated Russia, which had understood its late-summer agreement with Britain to be the prelude to an attack on east Prussia. Now realizing that Britain was bent upon forestalling, not promoting, a war in Germany, Russia needed to look elsewhere for friends. Second, the British convention with Prussia finally convinced Austria that Britain was a useless ally. Vienna and Versailles soon began conversations that led, in May 1756, to an alliance between the two ancient enemies. Shortly thereafter Russia aligned itself with Austria and France. Newcastle's direction of British European policy had been so ill-conceived that he had contrived to provoke, in the so-called diplomatic revolution, what had once seemed impossible: the end of the Habsburg–Bourbon rivalry. The old system was gone.

Well before this unhappy dénouement, William Pitt and others had been complaining about the ministry's foreign policy. In the summer of 1755, in an effort to blunt these criticisms, Newcastle laboured to bring Pitt into the government without too dramatically compromising his own ability to direct affairs. When these negotiations faltered, the duke in desperation turned back to Henry Fox, winning a promise of his support for the work of the government in the Commons in return for Newcastle's commitment to name him southern secretary within a few months. For a while this solution succeeded: Fox secured easy passage of subsidy treaties and was soon given the seals. On 18 May 1756, with the situation in America deteriorating, Britain even declared war on France. But in June word arrived in London that Minorca had been lost to a French invasion and that Admiral John Byng had failed to use his squadron in defence of the island. Once again the wrath of the political nation boiled over, and while much of the anger was directed at Byng, who was arrested and brought home to face court martial, the real target of the national rage was Newcastle, whose policy since 1754 had shattered old alliances, left British possessions in America and the Mediterranean undefended, and led the kingdom into war. Then in August 1756 Prussia, deciding to move pre-emptively against the new Austro-French alliance, invaded Saxony; with this stroke the long-feared European war began.

Conversations with political allies quickly persuaded Newcastle that he could no longer remain in command of the government; parliament would not suffer such incompetence in the conduct of national affairs in an hour of national crisis. Moreover, given the failure of the duke's efforts to guide the House of Commons by indirect means, and the general belief that Fox, who resigned in October, was contaminated by his association with the floundering ministry, only William Pitt among possible candidates for leadership was understood to have the respect, standing, and independence for which the emergency called. Acknowledging that Pitt's claim to direct affairs could not be denied, Newcastle resigned the Treasury on 11 November 1756. A career that had extended over almost forty years seemed at an end.

Pitt's minister of finances, 1757–1762 This, however, was not the final outcome. Pitt was not an old corps whig and, without the duke's support to provide ballast for his ministry in the Commons, he risked parliamentary disapprobation virtually every time he brought a wartime measure forward. War under a Pitt ministry promised to be costly, for he proposed to win the battle for America, forestall France on the seas, and support Prussia in Europe. Newcastle meanwhile quickly recovered his love of office. He waited until various embarrassing matters had been resolved—the execution of Byng in March 1757, the ending of a parliamentary inquiry into his ministry in May—and then authorized close conversations with Pitt's followers. Lord Hardwicke found a formula that each party could agree to, and on 29 June 1757 Newcastle returned to the Treasury. Describing the arrangement, Lord Temple dubbed Pitt 'minister of measures' and Newcastle 'minister of numbers' (*Grenville Papers*, 1.405). The purpose of the coalition was to supply, through Newcastle's influence

with the old corps majority in the Commons, the parliamentary support necessary for winning the war. The duke's return in 1757 was his last great demonstration of political power.

For the next three years Newcastle was a fairly loyal supporter of Pitt's ministry and therefore the key enabler of its work. The Treasury over which he presided provided the funds that allowed Britain to send troops to America and Germany, fleets into the Atlantic, and subsidies to Prussia. Newcastle was pleased that Pitt, having built his popularity on hostility to Hanover, adopted a view closer to the duke's by seeing the electorate as the base for anti-French activity in Europe. Meanwhile, Newcastle handled patronage matters with his wonted enthusiasm. He did not always agree with Pitt, but in general he behaved like a subordinate and did not try to cripple Pitt's work. Thus the coalition ministry jogged along, happily accepting plaudits for the grand achievements of the army in America and the navy in the Atlantic. Then on 25 October 1760 George II, aged seventy-six but not in poor health, suddenly died. The duke's remark—that he had lost 'the best king, the best master, & the best friend, that ever subject had' (BL, Add. MS 32913, fol. 399)—was hyperbolic but not ill-cast, for the death of the second Hanoverian king implied the end of Newcastle's political *raison d'être*.

George III was the first Hanoverian monarch unconditioned by the party strife of the early decades of the eighteenth century. He tended, moreover, to take his cues from his former tutor, the earl of Bute, a politically inexperienced Scots peer. If Bute's influence was to rise in the new reign, it could do so only at the expense of the power of Newcastle and Pitt. That calculation suggested that Newcastle should have held firm to his new friendship with Pitt, which was the course that the duchess recommended. But a growing disagreement over the war was driving a wedge between the two men even as they needed to present a common front. Cheered by military and naval successes, Pitt wanted to redouble the kingdom's effort to crush France. Worried by the mounting cost of the belligerence, Newcastle wanted to use the triumphs already secured as a basis for negotiating an advantageous peace treaty that would release the kingdom from the financial burden of protracted warfare. Because the new reign triggered a general election, Newcastle had a quick opportunity to show his value, and the ministerial machine performed splendidly, bringing in another large majority for the government. But thereafter a three-cornered contest emerged, as the new king advanced Bute to the post of southern secretary while Newcastle and Pitt moved apart on strategic matters. The duke decided that his career was best served by aligning himself with Bute, who at least shared his view that the war was unbearably expensive. But he hopelessly compromised the clarity of his financial position by arguing that Britain ought not to desert Prussia. In doing so, he was trying, as he had (with Austria) in 1748, to assure that Britain did not find itself without a friend in a post-war world. But his position struck most observers as simply confused.

The first contender to fall in the three-way struggle was

Pitt. In September 1761 he wanted Britain to declare war on Spain, on the grounds that the new Franco-Spanish alliance portended eventual Spanish involvement: better, he argued, to wage the war by Britain's timetable, not Spain's. When he was unable to convince his ministerial colleagues of the wisdom of his proposal, he resigned. Pitt's October departure meant that Newcastle's continuation in the ministry was now a matter entirely at the discretion of Bute. When Newcastle opposed the royal favourite's proposal to end the massive subsidy to Prussia early in 1762, Bute decided to find a way to dislodge the duke, and, when an official in Newcastle's own Treasury supplied Bute with information suggesting that the Treasury had inflated its estimate of the level needed in the next vote of credit, Newcastle found himself not only badly outnumbered in the ministry but also beset by renegades in his own office. In a tearful meeting with the king, on 26 May 1762, he reluctantly resigned his leadership of the Treasury, declined the offer of a pension, and left an office of high responsibility for the last time.

Life in the wilderness, 1762–1768 Totally unhabituated to life out of office, Newcastle entered into opposition in full hope of returning yet again to government. In recognition of his age—almost seventy when he resigned the Treasury—he no longer aspired to a post that would require energy, aiming instead at an honorific position. Incredibly, he believed that he could command the loyalty of almost 40 per cent of the House of Commons, and he planned to use this political army to re-establish his command. The first indication of the feebleness of his new position came in the autumn of 1762 when, in protest against Bute's dismissal of the duke of Devonshire, he called upon persons committed to him to resign. It was embarrassing that only a few obeyed. But worse followed. The ministry, angry that Newcastle asked his followers to oppose the peace preliminaries, decided to dismiss almost all the Pelhamite loyalists still in office and then, visiting a final indignity on 23 December, stripped the duke of his lord lieutenancies and various other offices.

This 'massacre of the Pelhamite innocents', a purge unrivalled since 1714, compelled the old corps to give concentrated thought to how a party which had upheld the court should behave when out of office. Meanwhile, a younger generation of politicians was coming forward, ready to provide new leadership to the party. Newcastle often hosted the informal discussions among influential men who opposed Bute. But he was in no way regarded as the leader of the group. Though these men quickly concluded that they would need allies if they were to have any chance of regaining office, the alliance created when Pitt and Newcastle publicly resolved their differences in May 1763 foundered on the rocks of Pitt's touchiness and Newcastle's indecisiveness. Thus the government, directed after Bute's unexpected resignation by George Grenville, proved invulnerable to assaults. On 6 March 1764, with the party still out of office, Lord Hardwicke died. With the death of his closest friend the duke remained as the sole survivor of the old corps triumvirate that had directed British affairs in the decade after 1744.

The party's fortunes turned in 1765 when George III, reacting to Grenville's haughtiness, deputed the duke of Cumberland to find an alternative ministry. When Pitt proved unacceptably prickly, Cumberland turned to the whigs. At a meeting at Claremont on 30 June 1765, with Newcastle urging acceptance of the king's invitation, the party voted to form a government. The leader of the new ministry was the marquess of Rockingham; Newcastle happily became lord privy seal, with special responsibility for ecclesiastical affairs. But accident dealt unkindly with the new ministry. First, Cumberland, the important link with the king, died in October. Then American resistance to the Stamp Act forced the government to deal with an unforeseen colonial crisis. In a difficult compromise it decided to conjoin to its repeal of the offending measure a Declaratory Act that reaffirmed Britain's right to tax America. Newcastle energetically defended these decisions in the House of Lords; he also took the lead in convincing a doubtful George III that the ministry's course of conciliation was the right one. Ultimately, both measures passed. But the price that the party paid was high: royal distrust, renewed hostility from Pitt, and internal disagreement. These disabilities proved fatal, and in July 1766 the king invited Pitt (who soon became earl of Chatham) to form a government. On 30 July, again proudly spurning a proffered pension, Newcastle resigned his last major office under the crown.

Having just turned seventy-three, Newcastle was widely expected to retire from public life. Instead he plunged back into politics, and, adhering to the logic that only a coalition could marshal the power to oust a ministry that enjoyed royal support, he cast about for an ally, fixing his attention on the duke of Bedford. Inasmuch as the Bedfordites disagreed with the Rockinghams about America, inter-party negotiations were required, and Newcastle hosted several negotiating sessions in 1767 between the two faction leaders. Meanwhile, he led attacks against the government in the House of Lords. In many ways he did not understand the world into which he had survived, imposing on the unstable political landscape of the 1760s a dichotomous view of politics more suitable to the starker whig–tory distinctions of the earliest years of his public career and espying in the retired Bute an *éminence grise* behind the throne. Late in 1767 all of his energetic flailing came to naught when Bedford chose to align himself with the government. Newcastle had already learned that his initiative towards Bedford had failed when, in December, he suffered a stroke.

The private man The most important person in Newcastle's life was his wife. Henrietta suffered from poor health and, perhaps happily for her, was not fond of politics. But, because this disinterest gave her a measure of distance from the political scene, she was a counsellor to whom he often resorted. When he was away from her—and such occasions were frequent since she preferred Sussex to London—he wrote to her daily. Their marriage was a genuinely happy one. With his younger brother Henry, however, the duke had a far less placid relationship. The fraternal tie was grounded in sincere affection, but, as

Henry rose to independent political stature, the two proud men often found themselves at odds. Because Newcastle's marriage produced no children, he chose to lavish much affection on his five surviving sisters and their large tribe of children. He found parliamentary seats for some of his nephews and he applauded the marriages of his nieces. Sometimes this devotion was ill-paid, as for example when he had to endure denunciation from his nephew and principal heir, Lord Lincoln, for, in effect, living too long. This savaging was especially humiliating because, in 1756, Newcastle had secured an additional title—duke of Newcastle under Lyme—precisely to permit the 'Newcastle' dignity to be remaindered to Lincoln. Still, not all of the younger generation turned against him, and in his final years the duke rejoiced in the kind attentions of Tommy Pelham, a first cousin once removed to whom the specially delimited barony of Pelham of Stanmore would devolve.

In appearance Newcastle was a tall man. With his outsized head, erect posture, and amiable garrulousness, he was a pompous and dominating conversationalist, often taking hold of his auditor's lapels to drive home a point. He enjoyed staging vast entertainments, both at Claremont and at Newcastle House, his London home in Lincoln's Inn Fields. He was more than conventionally pious and more than conventionally eager to beautify his estates. He despised venality and prided himself on his honesty. Despite a reputation as a man who found pleasure only in politics, he patronized music and collected a useful and diverse library. His contemporaries snickered at some of his foibles—an aversion to beds not previously slept in, an abhorrence of drafts, a propensity to weep. Likewise they mocked the jealousy that drove him to dispense with so many of his secretarial colleagues over the years. Like many hypochondriacs, he was in fact quite healthy, able to enjoy outdoor activity until the last year of his life. Finally, in the conduct of public business he was remarkably orderly and hard-working, keeping memoranda of meetings and so tirelessly corresponding with friends and political colleagues that the so-called Newcastle papers comprise a treasure trove for historians.

Unhappily for Newcastle himself and many of his relatives, however, his management of his private financial affairs was a story of dramatic disorder. Newcastle saw his territorial holdings, and consequently his income from them, shrink through most of his life. In 1715 his estates brought in £32,000; by 1726 they were earning him only £24,000; by 1756 they were providing only about £12,000; and by 1762 his income was scarcely £9000. As the years passed he sold many of his lands, sometimes retaining the right to be a life tenant. In other instances he mortgaged properties. His indebtedness reached staggering levels. Advisers and relatives, appalled at his profligacy, sought to staunch the bleeding; some of Newcastle's bitterest quarrels with his brother turned on his fecklessness. Various trust devices were created to confine the duke, but none altered his habits of careless personal spending. Although much of the expenditure cannot now be accounted for, such categories as entertaining at his many homes, electioneering in his many constituencies, and the landscaping of his many grounds loom large. Munificence also played a role, as Newcastle was eager to bestow gifts on friends and relatives. What strikes the latter-day observer, however, is the monumental recklessness of the duke's cast of mind, for the very people he loved most— his wife, his nieces, his nephews—were the people whose long-term welfare was most damaged by this evisceration of his estate.

Death and judgement Impaired in memory and speech, lame of foot, and subject to episodes of fatigue after his stroke, Newcastle nevertheless recovered his appetite for politics. He returned to London early in November 1768 to prepare for the coming session. Soon thereafter, however, he collapsed, and on 17 November at Newcastle House, shortly after receiving the sacrament from Bishop John Hume, he died. With his death all his titles except the special remainders for Lord Lincoln and Tommy Pelham became extinct. His remains were interred in the family vault at Laughton, Sussex, on 27 November. Since the Nottinghamshire lands had already been assigned to Lord Lincoln, they were not part of the settlement after the duke's death. Most of what remained of the Sussex property went to Tommy Pelham; the rest passed to the dowager duchess. But the estate was encumbered by a debt that exceeded £300,000, and so it was liquidated through land sales to meet those obligations. Lord Clive, already one of the duke's major creditors, bought Claremont. The duchess lived on at Twickenham Park until her death on 17 July 1776. She protected the integrity of the duke's vast assemblage of papers, and late in the nineteenth century the earl of Chichester, a descendant of Lord Pelham of Stanmore, donated the collection intact to the British Library. It has served generations of scholars for over a century.

Because Newcastle and his eccentricities were frequent targets for ridicule, the duke's reputation languished for almost a century and a half in a historiographical world largely defined by the judgements of two celebrated contemporary memoirists, Lord Hervey and Horace Walpole. For many historians he was the classic example of incompetence elevated to power by virtue of wealth alone. A reappraisal began in earnest with the writings of Sir Lewis Namier, and by the 1970s many historians were contending, by way of extenuation, that no one could have continued to hold high office for four decades without ability. Drawing on a distinction suggested by another contemporary, Lord Waldegrave, they often added that, while the duke lacked the judgement and self-confidence to be a commander (hence his unsuccessful term as prime minister), he was well equipped by virtue of his diligence, his command of his details, and his skill with people to be a lieutenant. It is perhaps time to recede somewhat from that cautiously favourable view—not to return to the portrait of the ridiculous statesman but to reaffirm the more important truth that Newcastle all too often defended bad ideas. He was simply wrong when—to cite four examples—he urged that Britain go to war in 1733, refused opportunities to make peace in 1747, promoted the imperial election plan in 1750, and raised the stakes on the Prussian subsidy in 1762. Newcastle was not always guilty of poor judgement. But, leaving longevity aside, it is hard in surveying the entirety of his career to find substantive arguments for regarding it as anything other than an exercise in political mediocrity.

REED BROWNING

Sources DNB · R. Browning, *The duke of Newcastle* (1975) · P. C. Yorke, *The life and correspondence of Philip Yorke, earl of Hardwicke*, 3 vols. (1913) · W. Coxe, *Memoirs of the administration of the Right Honourable Henry Pelham*, 2 vols. (1829) · John, Lord Hervey, *Some materials towards memoirs of the reign of King George II*, ed. R. Sedgwick, 3 vols. (1931) · H. Walpole, *Memoirs of the reign of King George the Second*, ed. Lord Holland, 2nd edn, 3 vols. (1847) · W. Coxe, *Memoirs of the life and administration of Sir Robert Walpole, earl of Orford*, 3 vols. (1798) · *Memoirs from 1754 to 1758* (1821) · *Private correspondence of Chesterfield and Newcastle, 1744–1746*, ed. R. Lodge (1930) · *The correspondence of the dukes of Richmond and Newcastle, 1724–1750*, ed. T. J. McCann, Sussex RS, 73 (1984) · Walpole, *Corr.* · *A narrative of changes in the ministry, 1765–1767*, ed. M. Bateson, CS, new ser., 59 (1898) · *The Grenville papers: being the correspondence of Richard Grenville … and … George Grenville*, ed. W. J. Smith, 4 vols. (1852–3) · J. B. Owen, *The rise of the Pelhams* (1957) · R. Kelch, *Newcastle: a duke without money: Thomas Pelham-Holles, 1693–1768* (1974) · R. Middleton, *The bells of victory: the Pitt–Newcastle ministry and the conduct of the Seven Years' War, 1757–1762* (1985) · D. R. Hirschberg, 'The government and church patronage in England, 1660–1670', *Journal of British Studies*, 20/1 (1980–81), 109–39 · J. Black, *A system of ambition? British foreign policy, 1660–1793* (1991) · P. Langford, *A polite and commercial people: England, 1727–1783* (1989) · F. O'Gorman, *The emergence of the British two-party system, 1760–1832* (1982) · R. Browning, *The War of the Austrian Succession* (1993) · P. J. Kulisheck, *The duke of Newcastle, 1693–1768, and Henry Pelham, 1694–1754: a bibliography* (1997) · J. Walsh and others, eds., *The Church of England, c.1689–c.1833* (1993) · J. A. Henretta, *Salutary neglect: colonial administration under the duke of Newcastle* (1972) · P. Haffenden, 'Colonial appointments and patronage under the duke of Newcastle, 1724–1739', *EngHR*, 78 (1963), 417–35
Archives BL, biographical papers, Add. MSs 9202–9232 · BL, corresp. and papers, Add. MSS 32686–33078, 33157–33169, 33198–33201, 33325–33344, 33442, 69813 · BL, naval corresp., Kings MSS 55–59 · Derbys. RO, corresp. relating to Ireland · U. Nott., Newcastle (Clumber) MSS | BL, corresp. with James Dayrolle and Solomon Dayrolle, Add. MSS 15866–15875 · BL, letters to Lord Hardwicke, Add. MSS 34523–34525, 34713–35484 · BL, corresp. with Lord Holdernesse, Egerton MSS 3404–3412, 3427–3430 · BL, letters to Lord Holland, Add. MS 51379 · BL, corresp. with Lord Hyndford, Add. MSS 45117–45121 · BL, corresp. with Benjamin Keene, Add. MSS 43412–43430 · BL, corresp. with Andrew Mitchell, Add. MS 58283 · BL, Pelham MSS · BL, letters to Thomas Robinson, Add. MSS 23780–23828 · BL, corresp. with Walter Titley · BL, corresp. with Lord Tyrawley, Add. MSS 23627–23642, 28145–28157 · BL, corresp. with Edward Vernon, Add. MSS 40815–40817, 40827–40828 · BL, letters to James West, Add. MS 34729 · BL, letters to Charles Yorke, Add. MS 35429 · BL, naval corresp. · Bodl. Oxf., letters to Lord Guilford · Bodl. Oxf., corresp. with Benjamin Keene · Chatsworth House, Derbyshire, letters to dukes of Devonshire · Chewton House, Chewton Mendip, Somerset, corresp. with first Earl Waldegrave · CUL, corresp. with Sir Robert Walpole · Devon RO, letters to duke of Somerset · Hunt. L., letters to Lord Loudon · LPL, corresp. with Edmund Gibson · Mount Stuart Trust, Isle of Bute, corresp. with Lord Loudon and Bute · NA Scot., corresp. with Lord Marchmont · NA Scot., corresp. with Andrew Mitchell · NL Scot., corresp. with John Campbell · NL Scot., corresp. with Erskine family · NL Scot., corresp. with Duncan Forbes · NL Scot., letters to George Wade · NMM, corresp. with Lord Sandwich · NMM, corresp. with Edward Vernon · NRA, priv. coll., corresp. with Lord Hopetoun · PRO, letters to Lord Chatham, PRO 30/8 · Sheff. Arch., letters to Lord Rockingham · U. Cal., Berkeley, Bancroft Library, corresp. with Lord Chesterfield · U. Nott. L., corresp.

with Henry Pelham · U. Nott. L., letters to duke of Portland · W. Sussex RO, letters to duke of Richmond
Likenesses G. Kneller, portrait, *c.*1718, NPG · W. Hoare, chalk drawing, *c.*1752, NPG [*see illus.*] · W. Hoare, portrait, NPG; on loan to Gov. Art Coll.
Wealth at death over £321,000: Kelch, *Newcastle: a duke without money*

Holles, Sir William (1471?–1542), mayor of London, was one of three sons of Thomas Holles, yeoman, of Stoke. He was born at Stoke in Warwickshire, on the outskirts of Coventry. One brother, Thomas, became a priest. Holles was apprenticed to Robert Kervile, citizen and mercer of London, on 13 July 1493. He was admitted to the freedom of the Mercers' Company on 17 September 1499, entered the livery in 1507, was warden in 1518–19, and became master of the company in 1529. He married, before 1509, Elizabeth (*d.* 1544), daughter of John (or Thomas) Scopeham of London, and had sons John (who died young, possibly at the Guild of the Holy Trinity, Coventry), Thomas, William, and Francis, and daughters Anne and Joan. Holles was elected sheriff of London by the commonality in September 1527, and alderman for Aldgate ward on 31 March 1528; in August 1534 he transferred to Broad Street ward. A merchant of the staple and a supplier of fine imported cloth to Henry VIII, he attended the baptism of Princess Elizabeth on 10 September 1533 and was knighted the following month.

Considered to be London's most religiously conservative alderman, Holles was prevented from being selected as lord mayor in 1536, and the protestant Ralph Warren was elected instead. This led the city to petition the king to permit its accustomed free election, but royal intrusion again prevented Holles's selection in 1537 and 1538. He was allowed to assume the mayoralty on 13 October 1539. During his year in office Holles caused the moor ditch to be cleaned, and received Anne of Cleves in great state on 3 January 1540, but he was best known for the steadfast persecution of protestant heresy within the city. In July of 1540 as many as 500 Londoners were arrested and interrogated under the provisions of the Act of Six Articles (1539). This proved to be so divisive that restraints on the city's enthusiasm were imposed by the state.

Holles was also known for his sharp business practices. In 1536 he alienated Arthur Plantagenet, Viscount Lisle, when he conspired to transfer a long-disputed Somerset estate to Sir Edward Seymour by offering Lisle a short-term loan and then foreclosing on the estate. In a similar manner, Holles acquired property in Lincolnshire, Nottinghamshire, and Derbyshire for the inheritance of his younger son William by foreclosing in 1537 on his loan to Sir Ralph Langford. He purchased manors from, among others, William Fitzwilliam, earl of Southampton, Thomas Manners, earl of Rutland, and Sir Thomas Elliot, leased crown property, and speculated in the lands of the dissolved religious houses, as he built up landed estates for each of his three adult sons. On his deathbed he observed that he had:

> hughly and singulerly preferred and set forthe my three sones in my lyfe tyme and have given and assured unto every of theym Manors landes tenementes and heredytamentes

And whiche of them that hath least cost me foure
Thousande markes [£2666 13s. 4d.] and above.   (PRO, PROB
11/29, sig. 110)

The eldest son, Sir Thomas of Newstead, Lincolnshire, and
Flitcham, Norfolk, married Catherine Payne, a maid of
honour to Katherine of Aragon. The second, Sir William
(d. 1591), established a notable family seat at Haughton,
Nottinghamshire, on property purchased for him from
John Babington, married in 1535 Anne, daughter and
coheir of John Denzel, and served as sheriff of Nottinghamshire and Derbyshire under Mary I and Elizabeth I; his
grandson and heir, John Holles (1564–1637), was created
earl of Clare in 1624. The youngest son, Francis, of Hainton, Lincolnshire, esquire, married Katherine, daughter
of John Heneage of Hainton, but died in 1543 without
heirs. Anne, who predeceased her father, married Sir John
Whiddon, serjeant-at-law and later judge of queen's
bench. The extent of Holles's wealth is suggested by his
assessment for the royal subsidy of 1541; at £4000, the
mercer was rated second in the entire city.

Holles died in London, in the parish of St Helen,
Bishopsgate, on 20 October 1542; his remains were
interred in St Helen's. By his will, dated 25 December 1541
and proved on 18 December 1542, he requested requiem
masses for twenty years at the churches of St Thomas
Becket and St Helen, Bishopsgate, and in the mystery of
the Mercers' Company. He completed payment of £200 to
the city of Coventry for the erection of a 57-foot-high city
cross at Cross Chipping, which stood until 1771. His son
and heir, Thomas, was granted livery of his lands on 26
April 1543. Through improvidence he was said to have
wasted an inheritance estimated to be worth £10,000 per
annum and, according to family tradition, died in prison.
Dame Elizabeth Holles died on 13 March 1544. By her will
of 17 February 1544 she endowed almshouses for six aged
men or women beside the church of St Helen, Bishopsgate
(later called Sir Andrew Judd's Almshouses), and bestowed
the residue of her estate upon deeds of charity at the discretion of her executors, Andrew Judd and Thomas
Scopeham.   J. D. ALSOP

Sources G. Holles, *Memorials of the Holles family, 1493–1656*, ed. A. C.
Wood, CS, 3rd ser., 55 (1937) · *LP Henry VIII*, vols. 5–18 · will, PRO,
PROB 11/29, sigs. 109v–111v · will of Dame Elizabeth Holles, PRO,
PROB 11/30, fols. 37v–38 · S. Brigden, *London and the Reformation*
(1989), 240–41, 250, 320–2, 421 · repertories of the court of aldermen, CLRO, vols. 9–10 · M. St C. Byrne, ed., *The Lisle letters*, 6 vols.
(1981), vol. 3, pp. 490–3, 498–500, 613–15; vol. 5, pp. 46, 68 · M. L.
Bush, 'The Lisle–Seymour land dispute: a study of power and influence in the 1530s', *HJ*, 9 (1966), 255–74 · HoP, *Commons, 1509–58*,
2.377–8 · will of Francis Holles, PRO, PROB 11/29, fols. 177v–178

Holliday, John (1730/31–1801), barrister and writer, about
whose birth and parents nothing is known, entered Lincoln's Inn on 5 May 1759 and was called to the bar on 23
April 1771. By August 1789 he married Elizabeth, daughter
and sole heir of Elizabeth Harrison, widow, of Dilhorne
Manor, Staffordshire, with whom he had an only child,
Elizabeth Lydia. As well as acquiring Dilhorne through
marriage, Holliday purchased nearby Cheadle Park from
Sir Joseph Banks, and one or both properties incorporated

working coalmines. He also built a successful legal practice, specializing in conveyancing, and engaged in charitable occupations, becoming a governor of the royal hospitals Bridewell and Bedlam, and the Foundling Hospital.
Holliday also found time to indulge his eclectic interests.
He was elected fellow of the Royal Society on 9 March
1786, and he was an active member of the Society of Arts
and Manufactures, winning the society's gold medal in
1792 for having planted 118,000 mixed timber trees on his
estates.

Holliday cultivated his modest literary talent over many
years. He is said to have composed a translation of Virgil in
hexameter verse in his youth. Towards the end of his life
he published *The British Oak* (1800), a rambling poem, in
couplets, which celebrates selected episodes of local and
national history during the life of an ancient oak tree
planted in Cheadle Park. The poem was dedicated to
Nelson in gratitude for his victory at the Nile (1798).
Holliday's most significant prose publication is *The Life of
William Late Earl of Mansfield* (1797), a well researched biography of his friend and patron William Murray, the controversial judge and eminent politician. Holliday had
been in awe of Murray since the latter's appointment as
lord chief justice in 1756. Murray's vigorous toryism probably indicates Holliday's politics also. Holliday personally
gathered some of his materials for his biography from
among the most eminent lawyers of his day, confirming
his acceptance within the highest circles of the legal profession. He sat to George Romney, in London, between
1791 and 1793. At the end of the nineteenth century the
painting hung in Lupton House, Brixham, Devon, which
burnt down on 8 March 1926. The *Torquay Times* for 12
March disclosed that a Romney had been destroyed in the
blaze. Pictures and books which were salvaged from the
fire were subsequently stored on the first floor of a stable
block which also burnt down, on 23 February 1928. The
portrait survived, much damaged, and after restoration
was sold to a private buyer.

At the very end of his life Holliday wrote a brief memoir
of Owen Salusbury Brereton, a past vice-president of the
Society for the Encouragement of Arts, Manufactures and
Commerce, which appeared posthumously in the society's *Transactions* for 1801. By a curious irony Holliday was
expected to be selected for the same office but he died at
his house in Great Ormond Street, London, on 9 March
1801, a week before the election was due to take place.
According to an obituary he died 'in his seventy first year'
(*GM*, 71/1). In addition to his immediate family members,
Holliday made Charles Abbot, future lord chief justice,
one of the beneficiaries of his will. He also directed that
mourning rings should be sent to, among others, Nelson's
former commander in the Mediterranean Admiral John
Jervis, Earl St Vincent, and his wife, his neighbours in
nearby Meaford, Staffordshire.

JAMES WILLIAM KELLY

Sources will, PRO, PROB 11/1356, fols. 174r.–178v. · corresp. (May–
July 1797) from John Holliday to Lord Harwicke re his life of Mansfield, BL, Add. MS 35643, fols. 30, 35, 73 · letter from J. H. (as trustee
of the late John, second Earl Egmont) dated 28 January 1772 to

Lieutenant-Colonel Stephen Egan in Florida, BL, Add. MS 47054A, fol. 39 · probate, 15 September 1796, will of Elizabeth Harrison of Dilhorne, dated 1 August 1789, Lichfield RO · T. Cockin, *The Staffordshire encyclopedia: a secondary source index on the history of the old county of Stafford celebrating its curiosities, peculiarities and legends* (2000) · J. Foster, *The peerage, baronetage, and knightage of the British empire* [1880–82] · *VCH Staffordshire*, vol. 6 · registers, Lincoln's Inn, London · Nichols, *Lit. anecdotes*, 9.194–5, 203–4, 235 · T. H. Ward and W. Roberts, *Romney: a biographical and critical essay: with a catalogue raisonné of his works*, 2 vols. (1904), 2.79 · R. Plant, *History of Cheadle* (1881) · *GM*, 1st ser., 61 (1791), 582 · *GM*, 1st ser., 70 (1800), 1081–2 · *GM*, 1st ser., 71 (1801), 283–4 · *GM*, 2nd ser., 36 (1851), 670 · *Transactions of the Society for the Encouragement of Arts, Manufactures, and Commerce*, 19 (1801), iv–vii [memoir of Brereton] · *Torquay Times* (12 March 1926) · *Torquay Times* (24 Feb 1928) · *Paignton Observer* (23 Feb 1928), 8

Archives BL, corresp. with Lord Harwicke, Add. MS 35643, fols. 30, 35,73

Likenesses G. Romney, oils, *c*.1762, priv. coll.

Wealth at death Dilhorne Manor; possibly Cheadle Park; coal mines and pits within estates in Staffordshire; dwelling, coach house and stables in Great Ormond Street, London; three gold watches; wines; books, law books; horses and harness; over £300

Holliday, Read (1809–1889), chemical manufacturer, was born on 15 September 1809 in Bradford, the third child of Abraham Holliday (1745–1825), miller, wool spinner, and latterly a tinner, and his wife, Mary. Nothing is known of any formal education. Before he reached his teens Holliday went to work in a tannery and later at a Wakefield chemical works making ammonia products.

When Holliday was twenty-one he left to set up his own business processing liquid gasworks waste, producing ammonia and tar. The idea of using ammonia rather than urine for scouring woollen cloth was just beginning to gain acceptance, and he was able to sell his ammonia to surrounding woollen mills. He soon needed larger premises and moved to Turnbridge, Huddersfield, in 1839. In the same year he married Emma Copley (d. 1883) of Hunslet, Leeds; they had five sons and three daughters. Over the next few years he began to supply other ammonia products and acted as merchant for other makers' products needed by his customers, including natural dyes.

This small business, one of many dealing with gasworks waste, took a significant turn in the mid-1840s when Holliday began to distil coal tar to produce naphtha, creosote, and pitch. There was a ready market for creosote to pickle wooden railway sleepers and for pitch to bind coal dust into fuel briquettes. For naphtha, in 1848 Holliday designed and patented a wickless lamp which proved a considerable commercial success, gaining a prize at the Great Exhibition of 1851. It remained in demand, mainly for outdoor lighting, for half a century, although for most purposes it was superseded by paraffin lamps within a few years. Possibly because of his work on coal tar, Holliday got to know Charles B. Mansfield (1819–1855), one of a group of brilliant students from the newly established Royal School of Chemistry working on coal tar derivatives. Mansfield showed how valuable aromatic hydrocarbons, especially benzene, might be separated for further processing; Holliday applied this empirical research in what was still a hazardous and environmentally damaging cottage industry.

Another of the school's pupils, William Henry Perkin, began manufacture of the first 'coal tar' dye in 1857 and a couple of years later a third, Edward Chambers Nicholson, produced another aniline dye. As coal tar distillates were the starting point for these new products and demand was expanding rapidly, it was natural that Holliday should be interested. He began to produce his own magenta dye, soon to be followed by many other colours. There was an early set-back when Holliday was accused of infringing patents controlled by Nicholson; after protracted and costly litigation, the patents were ruled invalid. There was severe competition in the dye business.

Holliday's two eldest sons, Thomas (1840–1898) and Charles (1842–1893), joined their father in the early 1860s and played a significant part in developing the fine chemical and dye business. Holliday was sufficiently confident of their abilities to send them to New York in 1864 to set up production of aniline and dyes. The branch they set up was one of America's pioneer dye makers and became one of the firm's most valuable assets. It was later managed by his younger sons, Edgar (1847–1891) and John (1845–1894), while Thomas and Charles managed the firm's various English and one French works. The business had become the UK's largest chemical manufacturer and one of the largest dye makers, though dwarfed by the giant German chemical companies. In 1868, with the patents court case out of the way and the various branches of the business flourishing, Holliday sold the business to Thomas, Charles, and Edgar so that he could follow other interests.

Holliday was elected as a Liberal to the new Huddersfield town council but his blunt speaking and impatience with political ways made him unsuitable for a public career, and he soon resigned. He and his wife moved from their Huddersfield home, Lunn Clough Hall, to Queen's Road, Harrogate. He enjoyed building his new home so much that he went on to build virtually all the houses in Queen's Road. He was active to the end of his life, taking long cycle rides when he was well over seventy. He survived his wife by six years and died in his eightieth year, on 3 March 1889, following a stroke. He was buried in the family vault in Edgerton cemetery, Huddersfield.

FRANCIS GOODALL

Sources M. R. Fox, *Dye-makers of Great Britain, 1856–1976: a history of chemists, companies, products, and changes* (1987) · P. J. T. Morris and C. A. Russell, *Archives of the British chemical industry, 1750–1914: a handlist* (1988) · L. F. Haber, *The chemical industry during the nineteenth century* (1958) · D. W. F. Hardie and J. D. Pratt, *A history of the modern British chemical industry* (1966) · W. A. Campbell, *The chemical industry* (1971) · d. cert.

Likenesses portrait, repro. in Fox, *Dye-makers of Great Britain*

Wealth at death £19,099 11s. 1d.: probate, 18 Sept 1889, *CGPLA Eng. & Wales*

Hollier, Thomas (*bap.* 1609, *d.* 1690), surgeon, son of William Hollier, reputedly a poor shoemaker in Coventry, and his first wife, Susanna Foster (*d.* 1636), was baptized at Holy Trinity, Coventry, on 20 September 1609. He was taken to London by Dr Mathias, physician to Queen Anne; John Ward recorded his employment by Mathias, whose will as Mathews Hulsbos in April 1629 left Hollier books on medicine and surgery. He was soon apprenticed to the doctor's neighbour and friend James Molins (c.1580–1638), as whose assistant Hollier began fifty-three years of service at St Thomas's Hospital, where he was appointed surgeon for scald heads in October 1638. Free of the Barber-Surgeons' Company in May 1637, he was chosen for the livery in March 1639. By then he had been married twice, first on 21 December 1637 at Stepney to Joanna Saddocke of New Windsor and secondly, after her death, to Lucy Knowles on 3 January 1639 at Stoke Newington, a month after her grandfather James Molins had died there, leaving her £50. She was baptized on 20 March 1623, eldest daughter of Thomas Knowles (d. 1669), a linen draper in Holborn, and his wife, Lucy (d. 1647), eldest daughter of James and Aurelia Molins. The Holliers had four sons, of whom the eldest, Thomas (1643–1672) and the next, James (1650–1687) became surgeons, and five daughters. Lucy Hollier died on 15 August 1677 and was buried in Christ Church Greyfriars nine days later.

When Edward Molins (1610?–1663), who had succeeded to his father's hospital posts, joined the king's army in 1642 Hollier deputized for him. On Molins's dismissal by order of parliament in 1644 Hollier replaced him as surgeon to St Thomas's and as lithotomist there and at St Bartholomew's. With his great experience (the porter at St Thomas's told John Ward that he had cut thirty for the stone in a year, who all lived), Hollier was the appropriate surgeon to operate on Samuel Pepys on 26 March 1658. Anniversaries of the operation were celebrated by Pepys, who continued to consult 'Holliard' and enjoy his friendship throughout the *Diary* period.

Edward Molins was reinstated in his hospital posts in 1661, but Hollier remained a surgeon at St Thomas's and on Edward's death in 1663, when he was succeeded as surgeon by his son James Molins (1631–1687), the two hospitals' post as lithotomist was shared between Hollier and James Molins. Though briefly replaced by his son Thomas when he was ill in 1670, Hollier served St Thomas's until dismissed by order of the Quo Warranto commissioners in 1683, three years after he had retired from St Bartholomew's. He was an examiner of surgeons for his company and was elected to the court of assistants in 1657, becoming warden in the years 1664–6 and master in 1673.

Hollier's houses in Warwick Lane were destroyed by the great fire, but he sold the site to the College of Physicians for £1200 and moved to Rose Street, near Newgate Market. Besides a leased house near the gate of St Thomas's Hospital he probably had one in Camberwell, Surrey, in which parish three daughters and a son were married, and one daughter was buried between 1660 and 1679. Hollier died at Rose Street on 22 April 1690 and was buried a week later at Christ Church Greyfriars with his wife and two sons under a stone (destroyed with the church in 1940) bearing his and his wife's arms. He left no will. A portrait of Hollier, in the Royal College of Surgeons of England, has a severe expression on an elderly face.   G. C. R. MORRIS

Sources G. C. R. Morris, 'A portrait of Thomas Hollier, Pepys's surgeon', *Annals of the Royal College of Surgeons of England*, 61 (1979), 224–9 · Pepys, *Diary* · PRO, PROB 11/155 [will of Mathews Hulsbos, 1629], fol. 49 · parish register, Coventry, Holy Trinity, 20 Sept 1609, Warks. CRO, MS DR 581/1 [baptism] · 'Medical prescriptions circ. 1650', BL, Sloane MSS 1536, fol. 63 · F. G. Parsons, *The history of St Thomas's Hospital*, 2 (1934) · Barber-Surgeons' Company, freedoms, apprentices, wardens' accounts, masters, GL [microfilms] · D. Power, 'Who performed lithotomy on Mr Samuel Pepys', *The Lancet* (9 April 1904), 1011–12 · D. Power, 'The Rev. John Ward and medicine', *Transactions of the Medical Society of London*, 43 (1920), 253–84 · PRO, PROB 6/66, fol. 160 · A. J. Jewers, 'The monumental inscriptions and armorial bearings in the churches within the City of London', 1910–19, GL, MS 2480/1, 101 · A. W. C. Crawley-Boevey, *The 'perverse widow': being passages from the life of Catharina, wife of William Boevey* (1898) · parish register, marriage, Stepney, St Dunstan, 21/12/1637 · parish register, marriage, Stoke Newington, St Mary, 3/1/1639 · private information (2004)

Likenesses oils, RCS Eng.

Wealth at death gave four houses in Rose Street, Newgate, to son in 1676

Hollinghurst, Sir Leslie Norman (1895–1971), air force officer, was born at Vale Cottage, St James's Lane, Muswell Hill, Middlesex, on 2 January 1895, the younger son and second of the three children of Charles Herbert Hollinghurst, a master lithographer, of Brentwood, Essex, and his wife, Teresa Petty. His brother, Charles Stanley Hollinghurst MC DSM, served in the Royal Flying Corps in the First World War, and his sister, Phyllis, served in the WRAF in 1918. Hollinghurst was educated at schools in Essex and, riding his own motor cycle, enlisted in the Royal Engineers at the outbreak of war in 1914. He saw service in Gallipoli and was wounded at Salonika. In April 1916 he was commissioned to the 3rd battalion Middlesex regiment and later that year was seconded to the Royal Flying Corps. He learned to fly in Egypt. After a course at the Central Flying School he was posted to 87 squadron in France. To his proven courage and toughness he now added above-average flying skills, and he was awarded the DFC in October 1918.

Hollinghurst was given a permanent commission in the Royal Air Force in 1919 and served for three years with 5 (army co-operation) squadron in India, where he saw action in Waziristan. He became adjutant of the boys' wing at the RAF Cadet College, Cranwell, and then attended the RAF Staff College course (1925). His next interesting assignment was in China at the headquarters (RAF) of the Shanghai defence force (1927). He was back in India in 1929 and, having been appointed OBE (1932) and mentioned in dispatches, commanded 20 squadron with distinction (1933–4). His reputation was growing and he was clearly destined for high rank. He had a special interest in the athletic and sporting prowess of the airmen under his command.

On return to Britain Hollinghurst became a member of the directing staff of the RAF Staff College (1935–7). In 1938 he took the course at the Imperial Defence College. From there he joined the staff of the air member for supply and organization at the Air Ministry in 1939. He was promoted group captain the same year. In his posting as director of organization (1940) he revealed a remarkable administrative talent. He became air commodore in

1941 and acting air vice-marshal in 1942 (he attained substantive rank in 1946). In 1943, following his arduous staff duties as RAF director-general of organization (1941–3), he was given command of 9 group.

In November 1943 Hollinghurst was chosen by Air Marshal Sir Trafford Leigh Mallory to command a new formation—38 group. This was to provide the aircraft, gliders, and crews to airlift British airborne forces. Hollinghurst grappled brilliantly with the intricate problems of acquiring aircraft and experienced crews and of providing the necessary realistic training required for the D-day landings in June 1944. He learned to co-operate closely with the British parachute forces, especially those under his friend General Richard Gale, and with the American airborne forces. When the long-awaited invasion of Europe took place, the first pathfinder aircraft which left Harwell, at 23.03 hours on 5 June 1944, carried Air Vice-Marshal Hollinghurst as a passenger.

Hollinghurst's group made a major contribution to operation Market, the Arnhem landings, and he was awarded the American Distinguished Flying Cross for exercising command and control of his troop carrier fleet from a crew position in a Stirling aircraft on the initial glider lift of that operation.

In 1944 Hollinghurst was appointed air officer commanding base air forces, south-east Asia, and he then returned home to become air member for supply and organization from 1945 to 1948. In the chaotic post-war period his abilities were needed, and were evident. After a spell as inspector-general of the RAF (1948–9) he was appointed air member for personnel (1949), which post he retained until he retired (1952). He was promoted air chief marshal in 1950. His great abilities and diligence continued to be in demand, and he chaired two major investigations (1953–61) to produce reports on command and administration in the RAF and on technical matters such as pressure refuelling installations. He was appointed CB (1942), CBE (1944), KBE (1945), KCB (1948), and GBE (1952).

Hollinghurst remained a bachelor, dedicated to the service. He was a member of the Royal Air Force Club and of the East India and Sports Club, popular at both with his particular group of friends. His vast range of experience gave him an air of authority and command. His opinions were carefully formed and firmly expressed, but he was a man of good humour, fond of company. In his retirement he continued an early association with the Boy Scout movement in Essex. He died in London on 8 June 1971.

E. B. HASLAM, *rev.*

Sources Ministry of Defence, London, air historical branch (RAF) · RAF Museum archives, Hendon · *The Times* (9 June 1971) · *The Times* (12 June 1971) · *The Times* (15 June 1971) · private information (1986) · b. cert. · *CGPLA Eng. & Wales* (1971)
Archives IWM, reports of operations in Holland · Royal Air Force Museum, Hendon, papers
Likenesses C. H. Hollinghurst, portrait, priv. coll. · photographs, RAF Museum, Hendon
Wealth at death £26,622: probate, 25 Aug 1971, *CGPLA Eng. & Wales*

Hollings, Edmund (*c*.1556–1612), physician, born in Yorkshire, matriculated at Queen's College, Oxford, in 1573,

when he was aged seventeen, and was admitted BA on 7 February 1575. Renouncing protestantism, he moved to France, and on 14 May 1579 was received into the English College of Douai, then temporarily located in Rheims. On 21 August of the same year he left the college to travel on foot to Rome, in company with five other students, who were admitted into the English College there in the following October. Hollings, however, does not appear to have become a member of the college, though he certainly lived there for several years, and became an intimate friend of John Pits the biographer. An English spy, in his report to the government, stated that Hollings was one of the pope's scholars in the college in 1581 (Knox).

From Rome Hollings moved on to Ingolstadt in Bavaria, where he was created MD and appointed professor of medicine. He was 'highly venerated for his great knowledge, and the success he obtained in that faculty' (Wood, *Ath. Oxon.*).

All Hollings's works were published in Ingolstadt. They cover various aspects of medicine. The first was *De chylosi* (1592); the other works include *De salubri studiosorum victu* (1602), *Medicamentorum et oeconomia nova* (1610), and *Ad epistolam quandam a Martino Rulando, medico caesario, de lapide bezoar* (1611). There were also collections of poems, orations and letters. Hollings died in Ingolstadt on 26 March 1612.

THOMPSON COOPER, *rev.* SARAH BAKEWELL

Sources Gillow, *Lit. biog. hist.*, 3.357–8 · A. Seifert, ed., *Die Universität Ingolstadt im 15. und 16. Jahrhundert* (1973), 484 · Wood, *Ath. Oxon.* · T. F. Knox and others, eds., *The first and second diaries of the English College, Douay* (1878), 358

Hollings, John (*bap.* 1682, *d.* 1739), physician, was baptized at St Chad, Shrewsbury on 14 November 1682, the son of John Hollings (1635?–1712?), a physician of that town, and his wife, Anne. After attending Shrewsbury School, he entered Magdalene College, Cambridge, as a pensioner, on 27 March 1700, and graduated MB in 1705 and MD in 1710. He was admitted a candidate of the Royal College of Physicians on 25 June 1725, and became a fellow on 25 June 1726, having on 9 March previously been elected FRS.

Hollings rose to be physician-general to the army and physician-in-ordinary to the king. With his wife, Jane, he had two sons, John (*d.* 1739), a physician, and Richard (*d.* 1741), solicitor-general to the prince of Wales from 1736 to 1741, and two daughters. Hollings died at his home in Pall Mall, London, on 10 May 1739.

Hollings's reputation for classical scholarship and general culture was considerable among his contemporaries. His only publication was the Harveian oration for 1734, entitled *Status humanae naturae expositus in oratione coram medicis Londinensibus habita* (1734), of which an English translation appeared the same year.

GORDON GOODWIN, *rev.* PATRICK WALLIS

Sources Munk, *Roll* · *GM*, 1st ser., 9 (1739), 272 · *GM*, 1st ser., 9 (1739), 661 · will, PRO, PROB 11/696, sig. 106 · Venn, *Alum. Cant.* · *The record of the Royal Society of London*, 4th edn (1940) · IGI

Hollings, Michael Richard (1921–1997), Roman Catholic priest, was born on 30 December 1921 at Glerawly, Gordon

Michael Richard Hollings (1921–1997), by unknown
photographer

Road, Camberley, Surrey, the third child and younger son
of Lieutenant-Commander Richard Eustace Hollings
(1888–1928), a nephew of the composer Ethel Smyth, and
his wife, Agnes Mary (Molly; 1884–1945), daughter of Sir
Walter Hamilton-Dalrymple, bt. His father was Anglican,
and from an old Yorkshire family that would not allow
Catholics over the threshold; his mother was a devout
Scottish Catholic who was descended, unusually, from a
cardinal, Thomas Weld. His parents were unofficially separated when his father died of tuberculosis, in Switzerland. Michael was six and remembered meeting him only
once. He was sent to Avisford School in Sussex, then to St
John's, Egham, and on to its senior school, Beaumont College, Windsor, run by the Jesuits, before, at the outbreak
of the Second World War, begging himself a place at St
Catherine's Society, Oxford, where he spent two years
reading for a modern history war degree and looking after
his sick mother in Woodstock.

'God went out of my life', Hollings wrote, after he was
called up in 1941, sent to Sandhurst, and commissioned
into the Coldstream Guards. 'People came in' (Hollings,
1994, p. 19). Hollings had a tough two years fighting in
north Africa and Italy, being mentioned in dispatches and,
in 1943, winning the Military Cross for 'devotion to duty'
and 'outstanding powers of leadership' during a night
attack on Long Stop Hill, Tunis, on 22/23 December 1942.
He was shot through the throat and nearly died. Early in
1945 he volunteered for service in Japan in order to win
home leave to see his dying mother. He was sent not to
Japan, however, but to Palestine, and he was in Haifa
when he heard of her death in November 1945, and in
Jerusalem during Holy Week 1946 when God, according to
his account, came back in.

The three exemplars for Hollings the priest were St
Thérèse of Lisieux, the Carmelite nun (a favourite of his
mother) who died at the age of twenty-four, for her simplicity of devotion; St John Vianney, the Curé d'Ars, for his
humility and asceticism and incisive spiritual direction;
and, for his 'obedience' above all, Padre Pio, the stigmatic
Capuchin whom he first met in Italy in 1947. Hollings was

as passionate as he was sudden in embracing the idea of
priesthood. 'Why do you want to be a priest?' asked his
battalion chaplain. 'I said to help people', remembered
Hollings (Hollings, 1994). Cardinal Bernard Griffin, inter-
viewing him, thought he was thirty-four and sent him to
the Beda College in Rome, for late vocations. He was
twenty-four. In Rome the former army major turned his
discipline on himself. He enjoyed the *magnum silentium*, he
took to sleeping on the floor. Before his ordination in the
basilica of St John Lateran on 8 April 1950, he made a
retreat in the Trappist monastery at Tre Fontane.

This personal austerity was to be a distinguishing mark
of Michael Hollings's ministry. He believed that the gospel
was unambiguous: in following Christ a priest must suppress self, forgo comfort, spend hours a day in solitary
prayer. He must abandon himself to God. Hollings never
denied his own struggle for abandonment. That he was a
man of powerful appetites and no small ego made his self-
denial the more impressive. To the end of his life, he
would typically rise at five and pray for three hours before
the day began. He lived in one small room, working amid a
sea of books and papers ('Bless This Mess' read a sign on
his desk), sleeping on his sofa. He was a proponent of the
'open house' presbytery. Priests must be available, 'live
celibacy unselfishly' (ibid., 25). Junior clergy might be
turfed out of their beds for needy 'street women' (as Hollings called prostitutes) or 'men of the road'. Burglars
broke in and were given cups of tea.

Hollings's first posting was at St Patrick's, Soho (1950–
54), where he was told that a young priest should be seen
and not heard. His second posting, at Westminster Cathedral (1954–8), he described as largely dressing and
undressing the cardinal to music. In his third, as assistant
chaplain at London University (1958–9), he found leeway,
becoming a religious adviser to television. He came into
his own as Roman Catholic chaplain at Oxford University
(1959–70), where he established his first 'open house' and
pricked pomposities. He raised funds to acquire additional premises and commissioned new buildings to
replace the Nissen huts he had inherited. In 1970 he was
sent to the London parish of St Anselm, Southall, a difficult and mixed-race community, where he was responsible for bringing in Mother Teresa of Calcutta's Missionaries of Charity, their second community in Europe after
Rome. And in 1978 he moved to another mixed-race parish, St Mary of the Angels, Bayswater, where his open
house comprised the whole of Cardinal Manning's ambitious complex of 1857, and he was said to have stopped a
riot at the Notting Hill carnival single-handedly. In 1975 he
had been a contender to succeed Cardinal John Heenan as
archbishop of Westminster, and he was repeatedly tipped
for bishoprics, but he remained at St Mary's for the rest of
his life. His personal unorthodoxy was probably intimidating to the establishment and his private liberalism—
his obedience to his God being more apparent than his
obedience to the hierarchy—possibly exasperating.

Hollings was not, however, confined by the geographical limits of his west London parish. He had another
worldwide parish in the readers of his many books, which

included *Hey, you!* (1955), *The One who Listens* (with Etta Gullick, 1971), *Day by Day* (1972) and *Hearts not Garments* (1982), in the listeners to his broadcasts, and in the hundreds who received his hand-scrawled letters and who relied on his persistent practical exhortations: 'Press on!' he would say. Although he was volatile and could be crusty, he excelled at the one-to-one meeting, where his patience could tease out the most confounding problems, and his impatience cut abruptly through confusion. He was a spiritual director and inspiration to many priests, and perhaps the best of his books (though he distrusted literary polish and their style is roughshod) is *Living Priesthood* (1977).

Many of that worldwide parish, and many of his fellow priests, regarded him as a near saint. Hollings—tall, large-nosed and of somewhat patrician manner—would have snorted. But his example was both noble and daunting. Some have seen the last, awful phase of his life as a 'way of the Cross'. He was suspended from his parish for five months over a newspaper allegation of sexual impropriety twenty-five years previously, then reinstated. He endured painful ill health and months in hospital. He finally suffered the loss of a leg and spent his last three weeks in a coma. He died of pneumonia in St Mary's Hospital, Paddington, on 21 February 1997. 'Today', said Cardinal Basil Hume at his funeral in Westminster Cathedral on 28 February, 'we salute greatness in a man, we celebrate holiness in a priest, we admire a devoted shepherd'. Hollings was cremated at the West London crematorium and his ashes are buried in Kensal Green Roman Catholic cemetery. An eloquent portrait of him by Hector McDonnell hangs in the Catholic Chaplaincy at Oxford.

JAMES FERGUSSON

Sources *Daily Telegraph* (22 Feb 1997) · *The Independent* (22 Feb 1997) · *The Tablet* (1 March 1997) · *The Times* (24 Feb 1997) · M. Hollings, *Living priesthood* (1977); special edn (1994) · J. Dalrymple, J. McCrimmon, and T. Tastard, *Press on! Michael Hollings, his life and witness* (2001) · personal knowledge (2004) · private information (2004) · b. cert. · d. cert.

Likenesses H. McDonnell, portrait, Catholic Chaplaincy, Oxford · photograph, repro. in *Daily Telegraph* · photograph, repro. in *The Independent* · photograph, repro. in *The Tablet* · photograph, repro. in *The Times* · photograph, McCrimmon Publishing Company, Great Wakering, Essex [*see illus.*]

Hollingshead, John (1827–1904), journalist and theatre manager, born in Union Street, Hoxton, London, on 9 September 1827, was the son of Henry Randall Hollingshead and his wife, Elizabeth. The father failed in business, and was confined in the debtors' prison of Whitecross Street, but became in 1847 clerk to the secretary of the Irish society for administering the Irish estates of the London corporation, retiring on a pension in 1872 and dying the following year. Sarah Jones, great-aunt of John's mother, was long nurse to Charles Lamb's sister Mary, who lived for the last six years of her life (1841–7) under the care of Miss Jones's sister, a Mrs Parsons, at her house in Alpha Road, St John's Wood (E. V. Lucas, *Life of Lamb*, 1905, 2.285–6). Hollingshead as a child saw something of Lamb, and as a young man saw much of Mary Lamb and her literary

John Hollingshead (1827–1904), by unknown photographer

circle. After education at a Pestalozzian academy at Homerton, Hollingshead at an early age took a nondescript situation in a soft-goods warehouse in Lawrence Lane, Cheapside. A taste for literature early showed itself, and he read in his spare time at Dr Williams's Library (then in Cripplegate), and at the London Institution. He quickly developed an ambition to write for the press; at nineteen he contributed to *Lloyd's Entertaining Journal* an article called 'Saturday Night in London', and soon sent miscellaneous verse to *The Press*, a Conservative newspaper inspired by Benjamin Disraeli. After some experience as a commercial traveller, he entered into partnership as a cloth merchant in Warwick Street, Golden Square; the venture failed, and he turned to journalism for a livelihood. On 4 April 1854 he married Martha Charlotte, daughter of Daniel James, gentleman, of Kent Road, Camberwell, and his wife, Ann; they had two sons and a daughter.

In 1856 Hollingshead became a contributor to *The Train*, a shilling magazine founded and edited by Edmund Yates, and then joined his friend William Moy Thomas as part proprietor and joint editor of the *Weekly Mail*. In 1857 he sent to *Household Words*, then edited by Charles Dickens, a sketch of city life, called 'Poor Tom, a city weed'. The article pleased the editor, whose sentiment and style Hollingshead emulated, and he joined the staff. He was a voluminous contributor of lively articles, chiefly descriptive of current incident and of out-of-the-way scenes of London life. 'On the canal' was the title of several articles describing a journey in a canal boat from London to Birmingham, and he reported the classic boxing match between Tom Sayers and John C. Heenan. He collected many of his contributions to *Household Words* and other periodicals in volumes entitled *Bow Bells* (1859), *Odd Journeys In and Out of London* (1860), *Rubbing the Gilt off* (1860), *Underground London* (1862), and *Rough Diamonds* (1862). He published his recollections of Dickens as a reader in 1907. He was one of the first contributors to the *Cornhill Magazine*, founded in 1859. When W. M. Thackeray, the editor, asked him where he learned his 'pure style', he replied, 'In the streets, from costermongers and skittle-sharps.'

In 1861, during a period of extreme hardship for the London poor, Hollingshead wrote for the *Morning Post* 'London horrors' (republished as *Ragged London* the same year). He also wrote much in *The Leader* for his friend F. J. Tomlin, for the *London Review*, edited by Charles Mackay, and for *Good Words*, edited by Norman Macleod. Sir Charles Wentworth Dilke, a commissioner of the Great Exhibition of 1862, entrusted him with the historical introduction to the catalogue. From 1863 to 1868 he acted in succession to Yates as drama critic to the *Daily News*. He wrote from time to time for *Punch* when Shirley Brooks was editor, and in 1880, under Sir Francis Burnand's editorship, became an occasional contributor. In its pages he used satire to argue for improvements in the government of London, especially attacking the duke of Bedford, whom he christened the duke of Mudford, for his mismanagement of his Bloomsbury property. His articles entitled 'Mud salad (i.e. Covent Garden) market' and 'The gates of Gloomsbury' attracted wide attention. Many of his contributions to *Punch*, in verse and prose, reappeared in his volumes *Footlights* (1883), *Plain English* (1888), and *Niagara Spray* (1890).

Meanwhile Hollingshead took a spirited part in other public movements. In 1858 he became a member of the committee for the abolition of the paper duty, which was achieved in 1861. With Dion Boucicault he agitated in favour of free trade for theatres, and against the licensing regulations. In 1866, and again in 1892, a special committee of the House of Commons reported favourably on his general view, but no action was taken. To his efforts was largely due the Public Entertainments Act in 1875, sanctioning performances before five o'clock, which the act 25 Geo. II c. 36 had made illegal. In 1873 he led another agitation for the reform of copyright law so as to prevent the dramatization of novels without the author's sanction. A royal commission reported in 1878 in favour of the novelist. From 1860 onwards he fought the closing of the theatres on Ash Wednesday, and in 1885 the restriction was removed by Lord Lathom, then lord chamberlain.

Hollingshead helped to found the Arundel Club and the New Club, Covent Garden (Hollingshead, *My Lifetime*, 2.209), and joined with zest in Bohemian society. He first turned theatrical manager in 1865. Although he did not abandon journalism, his main interest lay for nearly a quarter of a century in theatrical projects. From 1865 to 1868 he was stage director of the Alhambra, where he thoroughly reformed the performances. For acting a pantomimic sketch in contravention of the theatrical licensing law he was fined £240 or £20 a performance.

On 21 December 1868 Hollingshead, as manager, opened the Gaiety Theatre in the Strand, which had been newly built by Charles John Phipps for Lionel Lawson. A theatre and restaurant were now combined for the first time in London in one building. At the Gaiety, Hollingshead made many innovations, including the system of 'no fees', and inaugurated continual Wednesday and Saturday matinées. In August 1878, outside the theatre, he first introduced the electric light into London, and later was the first to make use of it on the stage. He mainly devoted himself to burlesque, which he first produced in three acts. In his own phrase, he kept 'the sacred lamp of burlesque' burning at the Gaiety for eighteen years. His chief successes in burlesque were Robert Reece's *Forty Thieves*, Hervé's and Alfred Thompson's *Aladdin*, H. J. Byron's *Little Dr Faust* and *Little Don César de Bazan*, and *Blue Beard*, *Ariel*, and other pieces by Sir Francis Burnand. His actors included John Lawrence Toole, Edward Terry, Nellie Farren, Fred Leslie, and Kate Vaughan. His scene-painters were Thomas Grieve, Telbin & Son, John O'Connor, and W. Hann, and his musical conductor was Meyer Lütz.

Hollingshead did not confine himself to burlesque. He produced serious new plays by T. W. Robertson, W. S. Gilbert, H. J. Byron, Charles Reade, and Dion Boucicault, as well as operas and operettas (in which Charles Santley and Emmeline Cole sang) by Hérold, Hervé, Offenbach, Lecocq, and Suppé. Shakespeare and old and modern English comedy were interpreted by, among others, Samuel Phelps, Charles Mathews, Toole Compton, Hermann Vezin, Forbes Robertson, Ada Cavendish, Matilda Vining, and Rose Leclercq. He produced *Thespis* on 26 December 1871, the first work in which Gilbert and Sullivan collaborated, and was the first English manager to stage a play by Ibsen (*Quicksands, or, Pillars of Society*, 15 December 1880). Some of the work which he produced was from his own pen. He wrote the farce *The Birthplace of Podgers*, first performed at the Lyceum on 10 March 1858, in which J. L. Toole acted the part of Tom Cranky for thirty-six years; the plot was suggested by Hollingshead's investigations in early life into the identity of the house in which the poet Chatterton died in Brook Street, Holborn (Hatton, *Reminiscences of Toole*, 1889, 1.96). In 1877 he adapted *The Grasshopper* from *La cigale* by Meilhac and Halévy. In 1879 he arranged through M. Mayer for the complete company of the Comédie Française, including Sarah Bernhardt, Got, Delaunay, the two Coquelins, Febvre, and Mounet Sully, to give six weeks' performances (forty-two showings) from 2 June to 12 July. He paid £9600 in advance, and the total receipts were £19,805 4s. 6d., an average of £473 for each performance. 'Practical John' was his theatrical nickname. With characteristic public spirit, benevolence, and success, he organized many benefits for old actors and public causes.

At Christmas 1874, in addition to the Gaiety, Hollingshead took and managed for a short time the Amphitheatre in Holborn and the Opéra Comique in the Strand.

In 1888 he resigned the management of the Gaiety to George Edwardes. The receipts from the theatre, which contained 2000 seats, were, for fifteen years of his control (1869–83), £608,201. The theatre was closed for only eighteen weeks in seventeen years. Hollingshead was responsible for 959 matinées in the period. In eighteen years Hollingshead made £120,000 profit, after paying out about £1.25 million. His salaries were high: he paid Samuel Phelps, Toole, and Charles Mathews £100 a week each for appearing in a revival of Colman's *John Bull* in 1873.

On 12 March 1888, at a hall near Queen Anne's Gate, Westminster, Hollingshead started a spectacular panorama of Niagara, which he carried on until 29 November 1890. In his later years he contributed a weekly letter to *The Umpire*, a Manchester sporting paper. His practicality deserted him at this time and the fortune which he had derived from the Gaiety was lost in speculation in theatres and music-halls.

Hollingshead published several volumes of miscellanies between 1865 and 1900, recorded his life at the Gaiety in *Gaiety Chronicles* (1898), and in 1895 published *My Lifetime* in two volumes. His recreations included 'trampling into every hole and corner of London, or any other city' (*Who Was Who*). He died of heart failure at his house in the Fulham Road on 10 October 1904, and was buried in Brompton cemetery near Sir Augustus Harris and Nellie Farren.   A. F. SIEVEKING, rev. H. C. G. MATTHEW

Sources J. Hollingshead, *My lifetime*, 2 vols. (1895) · J. Hollingshead, *Gaiety chronicles* (1898) · *The Times* (11 Oct 1904) · *The Times* (15 Oct 1904) · *WWW* · W. Tinsley, *Random recollections of an old publisher*, 2 vols. (1900) · *The life and adventures of George Augustus Sala*, 2 vols. (1895) · E. H. Yates, *Edmund Yates: his recollections and experiences*, 2 vols. (1884) · F. C. Burnand, *Records and reminiscences, personal and general*, 2 vols. (1904) · J. B. Booth, *Life, laughter, and brass hats* (1939) · m. cert.

Archives Hunt. L., corresp. and papers

Likenesses A. N. King, carte-de-visite, NPG · E. L. Sambourne, drawing (for *Punch*) · caricature, repro. in Hollingshead, *Gaiety chronicles* · photograph, NPG [*see illus.*] · photogravure, repro. in Hollingshead, *My lifetime* · prints, Harvard TC, NPG

Hollingsworth, Dorothy Frances (1916–1994), nutritionist and civil servant, was born on 10 May 1916 at 15 Honister Avenue, Newcastle upon Tyne, the daughter of Arthur Hollingsworth, pharmacist, and his wife, Dorothy Coldwell. After secondary education at Newcastle upon Tyne Church High School she entered King's College, Newcastle (Durham University), where she achieved a second-class BSc honours degree in chemistry in 1937. She dropped her original intention of becoming a teacher and, at the suggestion of her general practitioner who regarded nutrition as an up-and-coming field, decided to take the diploma of dietetics at the school of dietetics in the Royal Infirmary, Edinburgh, under the pioneer dietician Sister Ruth Pybus. This course involved three months at the domestic science college at Atholl Crescent, as well as some teaching by members of Edinburgh University's biochemistry department, and some nursing experience.

Hollingsworth qualified in 1939 and three months later obtained a temporary unpaid summer locum post in the Royal Northern Hospital, London. After the outbreak of war, however, she stayed on, becoming the senior dietician running the hospital's dietetics department, before successfully applying for a job with the Ministry of Food in 1941. She joined a group in the ministry's statistics division, working on the Wartime Food Survey, based at Colwyn Bay in north Wales. The aim of the survey, begun in July 1940, was to find out how well the population was coping with wartime food rationing. Hollingsworth learned about statistics and economics from her colleagues in the ministry and was initially responsible for working out, from the survey findings, the nutritional composition of the food consumed and the implication of the results. The data were collected by the London Press Exchange on behalf of the ministry, and at first only urban working-class households in seven cities were included. In 1945 the exercise was continued as the Family Food Survey, and in 1950 it was extended to a national sample of the population, becoming the National Food Survey. The survey was used to assess the effects of the end of rationing in 1954, and gave rise to some concern about the deterioration of the diet of poorer and larger families. It became a valued resource not only for government, but also for scientists and the food industry. Hollingsworth was associated with the survey throughout her period in government service, and later continued to be a member of and consultant to the National Food Survey Committee.

In 1945 Hollingsworth and the nutritional part of the food survey were transferred to the scientific adviser's division of the Ministry of Food under Sir Jack Drummond. In 1949 she succeeded Magnus Pyke as principal scientific officer in the division in charge, and took charge of its nutrition bureau. She remained responsible for a range of nutrition-related work for the next twenty-one years, during which time there was a series of divisional reorganizations. Other administrative changes included the merger of the Ministry of Food with the Ministry of Agriculture and Fisheries to form the Ministry of Agriculture, Fisheries and Food in 1955. Latterly Hollingsworth's title was head of food science advice branch. Her remit covered all aspects of scientific information in nutrition, and aspects of food science, statistics, and education. Her responsibilities varied over time but included a laboratory concerned with the nutritional value of food, an experimental kitchen and taste-panel studies, an experimental factory in Aberdeen which made dehydrated foods, and food defence work. In 1958 she was appointed OBE.

In 1970 Hollingsworth left the civil service and was appointed director of the British Nutrition Foundation (BNF), an organization which aimed to emulate a body funded by the food industry in the United States. The BNF had been founded in 1967 on the initiative of Alastair Frazer, professor of medical biochemistry and pharmacology at Birmingham University, who was the first director-general. Hollingsworth succeeded Frazer after he died in 1969, and she remained in the post until 1977. The BNF hoped to disburse funds for nutritional research donated from industry, on the basis of the advice of an independent scientific committee. However, insufficient money was forthcoming for this objective to be pursued on any scale. The organization then began to concentrate on educational activities. Hollingsworth had to keep up to date with knowledge while responding to enquiries from the press and other sources and organizing events on behalf of the foundation. With only a small staff she found this frustrating and tiring.

Hollingsworth edited two volumes based on BNF conferences, *Nutritional Problems in a Changing World* (1973) and, with Elizabeth Morse, *People and Food Tomorrow* (1976). Earlier, in 1957, she published the revised edition of a work by Jack Drummond and Anne Wilbraham, *The Englishman's Food: a History of Five Centuries of English Diet*. This had first been published in 1939, and Hollingsworth added a chapter updating the book. In 1969, with Hugh Sinclair, she published *Food and the Principles of Nutrition*, a revised edition of Robert Hutchison's *Food and the Principles of Dietetics*.

Hollingsworth was a member of many professional and scientific organizations. She served as chairman of the British Dietetic Association (1947–9) and as honorary secretary of the Nutrition Society (1962–5). She was a member of the dietetics board of the Council for Professions Supplementary for Medicine (1962–74), and the joint Agricultural Research Council and Medical Research Council committee on food and nutrition research (1970–74). She was a fellow of the Royal Institute of Chemistry, the Institute of Biology, and the Institute of Food Science and Technology. After her formal retirement she served as secretary-general of the International Union of Nutritional Sciences. Her recreations as given in *Who's Who* included talking to intelligent and humorous friends, appreciation of music, theatre, countryside, and gardening—interests reflected in her membership of the University Women's Club and the Arts Theatre Club. She died at Bromley Hospital, Bromley, Kent, on 16 February 1994. She was unmarried. DAVID F. SMITH

Sources *Who's who in British science* (1953) · *Who's who of British scientists* (1969–70) · *Who's who of British scientists* (1980–81) · D. F. Hollingsworth and D. F. Smith, interview, 6 Nov 1979 [partial transcript and tape in possession of D. F. Smith] · *WWW* · b. cert. · d. cert.
Archives SOUND taped interview by the author, 6/11/79
Wealth at death £293,198: probate, 4 May 1994, *CGPLA Eng. & Wales*

Hollingworth, Richard (1639?–1701), royalist writer, was born in Lincolnshire, perhaps the son of Simonde Hollingworth of Stewton, near Louth, and baptized on 6 October 1639. He entered Emmanuel College, Cambridge, as a sizar on 5 February 1655 and graduated in 1659; he proceeded MA in 1662 and DD in 1684. He was ordained by Robert Sanderson, bishop of Lincoln, and in 1663 was licensed to a lectureship in London by Gilbert Sheldon, bishop of London, on the recommendation of John Dolben, archbishop of York. On 18 April 1672 he became vicar of West Ham, Essex, and between 1673 and 1681 he published several sermons attacking nonconformists as

well as one at the execution of John Marketman at Chelmsford gaol (1680). In 1682 Hollingworth resigned West Ham to become curate to James Adern, rector of St Botolph, Aldgate, London, where he officiated at the marriage, by special licence, of Daniel Defoe on 1 January 1684. Following Adern's resignation Hollingworth succeeded to the living, but he was ejected after an action by Samuel Brewster, the impropriator, in 1693. Hollingworth may have been involved in the trade of clandestine marriages, and was summoned before the ecclesiastical commission on 2 October 1686 for marrying people without licences. From 22 January 1691 he was also vicar of Chigwell, Essex, where he moved in 1693 on his ejection from St Botolph.

Hollingworth is remembered for his part in the complex and heated exchange of pamphlets between 1691 and 1693 debating the authorship of *Eikon basilike: Pourtraicture of his Sacred Majestie in his Solitudes and Sufferings*. Doubts over the authorship of *Eikon basilike*, popularly ascribed to Charles I, had been expressed since its appearance in 1649, but were rekindled in 1690 by the insertion of the 'Anglesey memorandum' in a new edition of John Milton's *Eikonoklastes*, asserting that the work had been written by John Gauden, later bishop of Worcester. This claim was supported by Anthony Walker of Bocking, Gauden's former curate. The following year an anonymous republican pamphleteer, using the name of the regicide Edmund Ludlow, published *A Letter from Major-General Ludlow to Sir E[dward] S[eymour]*, in Amsterdam, which criticized Charles I, comparing his tyranny with that of James II. Hollingworth was incensed by these claims and attacked both Walker and Ludlow in equally intemperate terms in *A Defence of King Charles I: Occasion'd by the Lyes and Scandals of many Bad Men of this Age*, in December 1691. (Another work on the same subject, *Vindiciae Carolinae*, published in 1692 and once attributed to Hollingworth, is now ascribed to John Wilson, author of *A Discourse of Monarchy*.) Anthony Walker responded to Hollingworth's attack with modesty and obvious sincerity in *A true account of the author of a book entitled 'Eikon basilike' … proved to be written by Dr. Gauden … with an answer to all objections made by Dr. Hollingsworth and others*. Edmund Ludlow responded in less measured terms with *A Letter from General Ludlow to Dr. Hollingworth* (1692), accusing him of hypocrisy in defending a cause he had formerly reviled.

Walker died before his book appeared in May 1692, but nevertheless Hollingworth returned to attack him with *Dr. Hollingworth's defence of K. Charles the First's holy and divine book … against the rude and undutiful assaults of the late Dr. Walker*. Likewise he responded to Ludlow with *A second defence of King Charles I by way of reply to an infamous libel called Ludlow's letter to Dr. Hollingworth*. This work called forth another largely scurrilous reply entitled *Ludlow no lyar, or, A detection of Dr. Hollingworth's disingenuity in his second defence of King Charles I … together with a reply to the false and malicious assertions in the doctor's lewd pamphlet* (1692); it was addressed to Luke Milbourne, described as a minister of Great Yarmouth and 'Assistant to Dr Hollingworth in his mighty undertakings', who later achieved notoriety as a satirist and for his high-church sermons. The Ludlow pamphlets have since been variously attributed to Slingsby Bethel, John Phillips, Thomas Percival, and more recently John Toland, the editor and biographer of Milton. Hollingworth again responded in kind with *The character of King Charles I from the declaration of Mr. Alexander Henderson … with a further defence of the king's holy book: to which is annex'd some short remarks upon a vile book, call'd Ludlow no lyar*. Late in 1692 Thomas Long, prebendary of Exeter, joined the debate with *Dr Walker's true, modest and faithful account … strictly examined, and demonstrated to be false, impudent and deceitful*. Both of these works were answered by an anonymous work *The plain dealer: an essay wherein are some remarks upon Mr. Thomas Long, but more particularly upon Dr. Hollingworth's book*. Ludlow also responded with *Truth brought to light, or, The gross forgeries of Dr. Hollingworth, in his pamphlet intituled, The character of King Charles the First … detected, being a vindication of Mr. Henderson and Dr. Walker, from the Aldgate chaplain's vile scandals*, which appeared early in 1693.

Hollingworth attempted to reply yet again in a sermon commemorating the anniversary of the execution of Charles I, entitled *The Death of King Charles I Proved a Down-Right Murder*, which was published in February 1693, but thereafter he appears to have withdrawn from the continuing pamphlet war, possibly due to his ejection from his London living.

Hollingworth died at Chigwell in October 1701, and his widow, Margaret, was granted the administration of the estate on the 28th of that month. The controversy over *Eikon basilike* had the effect of bringing to light a range of conflicting evidence and the testimonies of several surviving witnesses (details of which are discussed in an appendix to Madan, 126–63), but without resolving the matter. Hollingworth's heated and outspoken language and unsubstantiated accusations against his enemies did not endear him to contemporaries. According to Richard Baxter, some of the accusations in his sermons were 'a meer fiction' (*Reliquiae Baxterianae*, 3.180).

DAVID STOKER

Sources F. F. Madan, *A new bibliography of the Eikon basilike of King Charles the First* (1950), 126–63 • Venn, *Alum. Cant.* • *Reliquiae Baxterianae, or, Mr Richard Baxter's narrative of the most memorable passages of his life and times*, ed. M. Sylvester, 1 vol. in 3 pts (1696), pt 3, p. 180 • *ESTC* • parish register, Stewton, 6 Oct 1639, Lincs. Arch. [baptisms] • E. Ludlow, *A voyce from the watch tower*, ed. A. B. Worden, CS, 4th ser., 21 (1978) • administration, PRO, PROB 6/77, fol. 177 [Chigwell, Essex]
Archives BL, Add. MS 5871

Hollingworth, Sydney Ewart (1899–1966), geologist, was born on 7 November 1899 in Floore, Northamptonshire, the son of Charles Hollingworth, a foreman in the army ordnance department, and his wife, Alice Masters. After attending Northampton School he joined the army shortly before the end of the First World War; he saw active service and was wounded. After demobilization he entered Clare College, Cambridge, where he took a first in both parts of the natural sciences tripos and was awarded the Harkness scholarship in 1921. At Cambridge he came

under the strong influence of John Edward Marr, the Woodwardian professor, and Alfred Harker, reader in petrology.

In 1921 Hollingworth joined the staff of the Geological Survey of Great Britain. He was soon assigned to the new unit being formed in Cumberland, which was designed primarily to resurvey the west Cumberland coal and iron-ore fields. His official work took him to the Brampton (near Carlisle), Whitehaven, Gosforth, and Cockermouth districts of Cumberland, and he was a contributor to the revised 1 inch maps and the published memoirs covering each of these districts. At Brampton, with F. M. Trotter, he worked in the north-eastern part of the northern Pennines. The collaboration not only produced a controversial correlation of Upper Carboniferous strata, but also the concept of the Alston Block that profoundly influenced the interpretation of the structure of these mountains. At Cockermouth he was concerned with the Skiddaw slates and Borrowdale lavas, and particularly with the Carrock Fell gabbro, where his detailed mapping brought out conclusions at variance with those of his former teacher Harker. The description in the Cockermouth memoir, published posthumously in 1968, is a memorial to Hollingworth's work in the best tradition of the Cambridge school. In his spare time he had become interested in the glaciation and drumlin development in Edenside and the Solway basin, and the subject formed the basis of his 1931 London DSc. Several years previously, in 1927, Hollingworth had married Anne Mary Lamb of Egremont. The couple later had two sons.

In 1934, Hollingworth was transferred to the west midlands unit of the geological survey, and he commenced fieldwork in the Cambridge district. At the same time he completed his Cumbrian studies—synthesizing the information on the gypsum-anhydrite deposits of the Eden valley and comparing it with the salt deposits of south Durham and north Yorkshire. He was among the first to recognize the rhythmic character of the chemical sedimentation, and he was an advocate of rhythmic clastic sedimentation in the Carboniferous.

With the onset of the Second World War, Hollingworth became a member, with James Hawerd Taylor, of a team formed to update and amplify geological knowledge of the Jurassic ironstones, particularly those in Northamptonshire. These were the chief domestic source of iron ore, playing an important part in the expansion of steel production necessary for the war effort. His contribution to the problems of superficial structure was particularly significant.

When war ended Hollingworth became Yates-Goldsmid professor of geology at University College, London. There it quickly became apparent that, as well as being an exceptional fieldworker, he was also an inspiring teacher. He increased the department's space, equipment, and standing, and also embarked upon new areas of research, firstly in the Caledonian mountains of Norway, and later in Chile. Here he began to relate his long-standing interest in geomorphology to the stages of enrichment of the 'porphyry'-type copper deposits. He died on 23 June 1966 in University College Hospital after attending his last London University senate meeting before retiring. Hollingworth's affection for the high Andes had grown with the years, and his ashes were scattered among them. He was survived by his wife and sons.

Hollingworth is remembered for his quick-witted contributions to discussion at the Geological Society of London, of which he became a fellow in 1922. He served on its council for a total of seventeen years, was secretary from 1949 to 1956, twice its vice-president (1956–8 and 1962–4), and president between 1960 and 1962. His work was recognized with the award from the Lyell fund in 1938, and the Murchison medal in 1959. He was active in promoting the engineering geology group of the society, and was himself a consultant to the Metropolitan Water Board. In 1964 the Geologists' Association, for which he had led a number of field meetings, took the unusual step of electing him an honorary member.   KINGSLEY DUNHAM, rev.

Sources [M. K. W.], 'Sydney Ewart Hollingworth', *Proceedings of the Geological Society of London* (1965–6), 192–6 • E. B. Bailey, *Geological survey of Great Britain* (1952), 257 • personal knowledge (1981) • *CGPLA Eng. & Wales* (1967)
Archives UCL, student notes
Wealth at death £12,526: probate, 13 March 1967, *CGPLA Eng. & Wales*

Hollins, John (1798–1855), portrait and subject painter, was born in Birmingham on 1 June 1798, the son of a glass-painter in that town. He showed an early artistic talent, and sent two portraits to the Royal Academy exhibition in 1819 and three more in 1821. In 1822 he moved to London, where he produced oil paintings and occasionally miniatures. He travelled to Italy in 1825 and studied art there for two years. On his return in 1827 he resumed practice in London, and became a frequent exhibitor at the Royal Academy and the British Institution. Besides portraits he painted numerous historical subjects from the works of Shakespeare, Goethe, and other writers. Later in life he applied himself to landscapes and figure subjects. He was successful in his colour and grouping, and his portraits were considered good likenesses. Hollins was elected an associate of the Royal Academy in 1842. Between 1836 and 1838 he had painted an important memorial picture, now in the National Portrait Gallery's collection, called *A consultation previous to an aerial voyage from London to Weilburg in Nassau on November 7th, 1836*. In this composition Hollins introduced portraits of various people of note, namely W. Prideaux, the lawyer and poet; W. M. James; T. Monck Mason, the musician and writer; Charles Green, the balloonist; Robert Holland, lawyer and MP for Hastings from 1837 to 1852; Sir William Milbourne, lord justice of appeal; and himself (exh. RA, 1838; Bodelwyddan Castle, Flintshire). In 1854 he painted and exhibited (in conjunction with F. R. Lee RA) *Salmon Fishing on the Awe*, in which he also portrayed several people notable at the time (exh. RA, 1854). Another painting by Hollins in the collection of the National Portrait Gallery is a portrait of Charles Abbott, Lord Tenterden, copied by Hollins in 1850 from a portrait by William Owen (originally exh. RA, 1819). Hollins died unmarried at his home, 47 Berners Street, London, on 7

March 1855 and was buried in Kensal Green cemetery. William *Hollins (1763–1843) (architect and sculptor) and Peter *Hollins (1800–1886) [see under Hollins, William] were his cousins.   L. H. CUST, rev. RUTH STEWART

Sources Redgrave, *Artists* • Graves, *RA exhibitors* • Graves, *Artists* • R. Ormond, *Early Victorian portraits*, 2 vols. (1973) • H. Ottley, *A biographical and critical dictionary of recent and living painters and engravers* (1866) • administration, PRO, PROB 6/231, fol. 363r
Likenesses J. Hollins, group portrait, oils (*A consultation previous to an aerial voyage from London to Weilburg*, 1836), NPG
Wealth at death £5000: administration, PRO, PROB 6/231, fol. 363r

Hollins, Peter (1800–1886). *See under* Hollins, William (1763–1843).

Hollins, William (1763–1843), architect and sculptor, was born at Shifnal, Shropshire, on 18 March 1763, the son of John and Mary Hollins. He married c.1783 Catherine (1764–1831), daughter of Peter and Betty Holbrook of Middlewich, Cheshire, with whom he had sixteen children. They settled at 17 Great Hampton Street, Birmingham, which remained William's, and then his son Peter's, home and studio until 1886. Originally a journeyman stonemason, William Hollins taught himself drawing and perspective, learned the rudiments of classical architecture in the London office of George Saunders, and in 1792 assisted Saunders with the working drawings for the rebuilding of the Birmingham Theatre Royal.

Hollins had established his own practice in Birmingham by 1798, when he designed the old buildings of the Union Street Library. In 1808 he built the old Dispensary, also in Union Street; and in 1813 the Birmingham Proof House, Banbury Street. Other Birmingham buildings by Hollins survive only in prints: the earliest parts of the public offices and prison in Moor Street (1805), the Institute for Promoting the Fine Arts, and the Egyptian Conduit in the Bull Ring (1807). Though Hollins's architecture is predominantly Greek revival in style, he experimented with Gothic, notably in the restoration of Handsworth parish church (c.1819), and additions to the earl of Shrewsbury's Staffordshire residence, Alton Abbey, including ornamental stone carving; in 1817 he was working on a new Gothic entrance hall at Alton, and the installation of a steam heating system. Hollins's ideas of architectural style were associational ones. When building the Egyptian Conduit at Birmingham, he justified the placing of a pyramid at the side of the Gothic church of St Martin's by arguing that the pyramid was the Egyptian symbol of the deity.

As a sculptor, Hollins was outshone by his son Peter, though he exhibited at the Birmingham Society of Artists and the Royal Academy. Several of his buildings included carved figures, and he designed memorials for a number of churches in the Birmingham area. His studies of Roman lettering were used to formulate a set of rules for their construction: *The British Standard of Capital Letters Contained in the Roman Alphabet* (1813). In addition he prepared drawings for the new royal mint at St Petersburg, having declined, it is said, an invitation from the empress Catherine II to join her team of imperial architects. Hollins died at his home on 12 January 1843 and was buried in the churchyard at St Paul's, Birmingham. A memorial inside the church incorporates a portrait bust carved by his son Peter.

Peter Hollins (1800–1886), sculptor, was born on 1 May 1800 at 17 Great Hampton Street, Birmingham, the fourth surviving son of William Hollins, an elder Peter having died in infancy. He took drawing lessons at J. Vincent Barber's academy in Newhall Street, and trained in his father's studio until about 1822, when he went to work under Sir Francis Chantrey before returning to assist in his father's practice. While his father was employed at Alton Abbey, Peter carved much of the marble statuary and other ornamental work in the gardens, including a bust of Charles Talbot, fifteenth earl of Shrewsbury. About 1831 he established a London studio in Old Bond Street, before finally returning to Great Hampton Street following William's death in 1843. He restored the tower front of St Philip's Church (now the cathedral) in his father's memory. For thirty-seven years he was vice-president of the Royal Birmingham Society of Artists.

Hollins's best work is considered to be equal to that of Chantrey, fine examples being his monuments to Sophia Thompson at Malvern Priory, Worcestershire (1838), and to the countess of Bradford at Weston under Lizard, Staffordshire (1842). He produced over sixty major works including several exhibited at the Royal Academy. Crippled with rheumatism in later years, he died at 17 Great Hampton Street on 16 August 1886 and was buried in the family plot in St Paul's churchyard, Birmingham.

MICHAEL FISHER

Sources Colvin, *Archs.* · R. Gunnis, *Dictionary of British sculptors, 1660–1851* (1953); new edn (1968) · 'A gifted Birmingham family', *Birmingham Post* (7 Nov 1953) · *Birmingham Daily Post* (18 Aug 1886) · Alton Abbey accounts, Staffs. RO, D240 · Staffs. RO, Shrewsbury papers, D240 · F. Greenacre, 'William Hollins and the Gun Barrel Proof House, 1813', 1968, Birm. CL, local studies dept.
Archives Birm. CA, letters to Boulton family
Likenesses P. Hollins, bust, 1843, St Paul's Church, Birmingham · H. J. Whitlock, photograph, *c.*1880, Birm. CL
Wealth at death £24,219 1*s.* 6*d.*: Peter Hollins: catalogue of Birmingham wills, Birm. CL, 22 Nov 1886

Hollinworth, Richard (*bap.* 1607, *d.* 1656), Church of England clergyman, son of Francis Hollinworth (*d.* 1657) and his wife, Margaret Wirrall or Worrall (*d.* 1642), was born at Manchester and baptized on 15 November 1607 at Manchester collegiate church. He was educated at the Manchester grammar school and Magdalene College, Cambridge, graduating BA in 1627, and proceeding MA in 1630. His Cambridge contemporaries included other future Lancashire and Cheshire puritan ministers—John Angier, Christopher Hudson, and Samuel Torshell.

Hollinworth's first clerical appointment after his ordination was to a curacy at Middleton, Manchester. He had moved to the new chapel at Salford by 1636 (having preached at its dedication service on 20 May 1635) and remained there until the 1640s. He succeeded William Bourne as fellow of the collegiate church, Manchester, in 1643. During the suspension of the corporate body of the college by the parliament he officiated, along with Richard Heyrick, the warden, as a 'minister' and dropped his

title of fellow, although the college was not actually dissolved until 1650. The protestation of the people of Salford in 1642 had been taken before him as minister of the town. In 1644 he was named in an ordinance of parliament for ordaining ministers in Lancashire. During an outbreak of plague in Manchester in 1645 he worked unstintingly among the people, his duties being increased through Heyrick's absence in London at the Westminster assembly.

Hollinworth, as a staunch presbyterian, was vocal both in preaching and in print in his opposition to the idea of religious toleration and to the Independents of the Manchester region in particular. *An Examination of Sundry Scriptures alleadged by our Dissenting Brethren* (1645) and *Certain Queres Modestly (though Plainly) Propounded to such as Affect the Congregational Way* (1646) were two such products of this pamphlet warfare, and Samuel Eaton and Timothy Taylor of Dukinfield were their principal targets. He corresponded on this subject with Thomas Edwards who incorporated Hollinworth's disclosures in his *Gangraena* (1646, 3.67, 166).

Hollinworth and Heyrick played a prominent part in ensuring that the presbyterian experiment in Lancashire, established by parliamentary ordinance on 2 October 1646, was much more vigorous than that enacted elsewhere. Held in high esteem by his co-religionists—Henry Newcome, for instance, sang his praises and was still invoking his memory in the 1670s—Hollinworth readily assumed the role of a local leader. His name is the second of those appended to the harmonious consent of the Lancashire ministers with the ministers of London, in 1648, in which toleration is strongly condemned. He evidently assisted in preparing the Lancashire answer to the Levellers' *Agreement of the People* in 1649, and in that year also he wrote a popular work in favour of the presbyterian system, entitled *The main points of church government and discipline plainly and modestly handled by way of question and answer*. The short introductory epistle was signed by Christopher Love.

After the battle of Worcester in September 1651, Hollinworth, along with Heyrick and Angier, was imprisoned on suspicion of 'some correspondence with the King his going through the country' (*Autobiography of Henry Newcome*, 1.33), but he was soon released and returned to Manchester. He was centrally involved in the discussions which lay behind a succession of collective statements by the Lancashire presbyterian ministers in the 1650s. Along with Newcome and Angier he took a leading part in local debates on the taking of the engagement oath. In the Manchester classis he generally acted as moderator during Heyrick's absence. He was named in the parliamentary ordinance of 29 August 1654 as a commissioner for ejecting scandalous and ignorant ministers and schoolmasters in Lancashire.

When Humphrey Chetham drew up his will for the foundation of the public library known by his name, he nominated Hollinworth one of his feoffees and as one of his chosen instruments for the setting up of smaller libraries in outlying churches and chapels in the Manchester area. Hollinworth continued to publish and to confront the destabilizing errors of the Quakers and other sects. *The Catechist Catechised* and *The Holy Ghost on the Bench* appeared in 1653 and 1657 respectively. In a modest way he was also a historian. He compiled *Mancuniensis*, a history of the town in which he had been born and with whose leading commercial families—the Mosleys, Chethams, Nugents, and Hollands—he was connected. Unfinished at the time of his death, it was belatedly published in Manchester in a very inadequate edition in 1839.

Hollinworth died suddenly in Manchester on 3 November 1656, aged forty-nine, and was buried two days later in Manchester collegiate church, where his wife, Margaret, had been interred two years before. Of his five children only one, Ann, survived him. His own father, however, lived to be over 100 and died in 1657. At the meeting of the Manchester classis on 11 November 1656 it was agreed that a day of fasting should held on 3 December with sermons from Edward Gee and John Tilsey 'upon the occasion of the sad breach made in the congregation by the death of Mr Hollinworth, late minister there, to desire the Lord's guidance in the election of a minister to succeed him' (Shaw, 2.253). C. W. SUTTON, *rev.* R. C. RICHARDSON

Sources F. R. Raines, *The fellows of the collegiate church of Manchester*, ed. F. Renaud, 1, Chetham Society, new ser., 21 (1891) · W. A. Shaw, ed., *Minutes of the Manchester presbyterian classis*, 3 vols., Chetham Society, new ser., 20, 22, 24 (1890–91) · *The autobiography of Henry Newcome*, ed. R. Parkinson, 2 vols., Chetham Society, 26–7 (1852) · R. C. Richardson, *Puritanism in north-west England: a regional study of the diocese of Chester to 1642* (1972) · A. D. Meikle, 'The Lancashire presbyterian ministers, 1640–1662', MPhil diss., University of Manchester, 1990 · J. J. Barber, *The Booth charities* (1972), 102

Archives Chetham's Library, Manchester, MS copy of 'Mancuniensis' · Man. CL, annotated copies of some of Hollinworth's publications

Hollis, Aiskew Paffard (1764–1844), naval officer, entered the navy in 1774, under the protection of Captain Parry, and in 1778 was present on the *Vigilant* in Keppel's action off Ushant. In January 1781 he was promoted lieutenant, and, continuing in active service during the peace, was appointed in July 1793 to the *Queen*, flagship of Rear-Admiral Gardner. In her he took part in the battle of 1 June 1794, where he was seriously wounded in the head by a splinter, and the encounter off Lorient on 23 July 1795. In November 1796 he was promoted to command the *Chichester* (44 guns), employed as a storeship. On 10 November 1797, at the Cape of Good Hope, he was ordered to take temporary command of the *Jupiter* and bring in the frigate *Crescent*, then in a state of mutiny at Robin Island. This delicate service was well performed, and the *Crescent* towed into Table Bay, under the batteries. Six days afterwards he was given an acting commission as captain of the flagship *Tremendous* (74 guns), from which he was shortly moved to the frigate *Vindictive* and sent home in charge of an East Indies convoy. On his arrival his commission was confirmed by the Admiralty.

In June 1801 Hollis was appointed to the frigate *Thames* (32 guns), and commanded her in the action in the Gut of Gibraltar on 12 July, and in the operations on the coast of Egypt. The *Thames* was paid off in January 1803, and in the following autumn Hollis was appointed to the *Mermaid*, in which he served in the West Indies under the flag of Sir John Duckworth. He returned to England in 1807, and in March 1809 joined the *Standard* (64 guns), forming one of the fleet up the Baltic under Sir James Saumarez, and in which he was detached in command of the squadron which in May occupied the Isle of Anholt. Early in 1811 the *Standard* went out to Lisbon in charge of a large convoy, and for a short time assisted in the defence of Cadiz. In April Hollis was moved into the *Achilles* (80 guns), attached to the fleet before Toulon, and later employed in the Adriatic, returning to England in the summer of 1813. After the peace Hollis commanded the *Rivoli* (74 guns) from 1816 to 1817, and the *Ramillies* from 1818 to 1821, as guardships at Portsmouth. He saw no further service, though he became in course of seniority rear-admiral in 1825 and vice-admiral in 1837. He died at his residence, Highfield, Southampton, on 23 June 1844.

J. K. LAUGHTON, *rev.* ROGER MORRISS

Sources J. Marshall, *Royal naval biography*, 2/1 (1824), 115 · *GM*, 2nd ser., 22 (1844) · W. James, *The naval history of Great Britain, from the declaration of war by France in 1793, to the accession of George IV*, [5th edn], 6 vols. (1859–60), vol. 4, p. 431 · P. Mackesy, *The war in the Mediterranean, 1803–1810* (1957) · R. Muir, *Britain and the defeat of Napoleon, 1807–1815* (1996)

Likenesses H. W. Pickersgill, portrait, exh. 1838, NMM

Hollis, (Maurice) Christopher (1902–1977), author and politician, was born at Axbridge in Somerset on 29 March 1902, the second of four sons (there were no daughters) of George Arthur Hollis (1868–1944), later bishop-suffragan of Taunton, and his wife, Mary Margaret, the daughter of Charles Marcus Church, canon of Wells, a grand-niece of R. W. *Church, dean of St Paul's. Sir Roger Henry *Hollis (1905–1973) was his brother, (James) Martin *Hollis (1938–1998), philosopher, his nephew.

Hollis went to Eton College as a scholar in September 1914 and then to Balliol College, Oxford (1920), where he won a Brackenbury scholarship. He was elected president of the Oxford Union Debating Society in 1923 and he subsequently toured the USA, New Zealand, and Australia as a member of the union debating team. He obtained a third class in *literae humaniores* in 1924. From 1925 to 1935 he taught history at Stonyhurst College. In 1929 he married Margaret Madeleine, daughter of the Revd (William) Richard (Cambridge) King, of Cholderton rectory, Salisbury. They had three sons and one daughter. In 1935 he became a visiting professor at Notre Dame University, Indiana, USA, having attracted attention by his writings on monetary theory. He was engaged on economic research there from 1935 to 1939. With the outbreak of the Second World War he returned to England and served with the Royal Air Force as an intelligence officer throughout the war.

From 1945 to 1955 Hollis was Conservative MP for the Devizes division of Wiltshire. In parliament he showed independence—for example, in his abolitionist views on capital punishment, which was not the received doctrine of the Conservative Party. He was popular on both sides of the house and when he left he became an observant and able reporter of its happenings for *Punch*, where he became a member of the Table. When he resigned his seat in parliament he retired to his beloved Somerset, passionately interested in the future of the Somerset County Cricket Club and all that concerned the county. At home in Mells, near Frome in Somerset, he devoted himself to authorship and occasional journalism as well as having a somewhat tenuous relationship with the publishing firm which carried his name, Hollis and Carter, a subsidiary company of the publishers Burns and Oates. He averaged a book a year on a wide variety of historical and political subjects.

Hollis's wide-ranging mind had led him throughout his working life to embark on such diverse subjects as Lenin and the origins of Soviet communism, St Ignatius of Loyola and the foundation of the Jesuits, Erasmus, Thomas More, Dryden, Dr Johnson, monetary reform, and foreign policy, as well as some works of fiction. His intuitive approach and clarity of expression was marred by a somewhat slapdash style in this great output of some thirty books. They were all honest endeavours and he could not be accused of special pleading.

Hollis recounted his life in two autobiographical works: *Along the Road to Frome* (1958) and *The Seven Ages* (1974). He can hardly be said to have pursued the seven ages of the Shakespearian sequence himself because he seemed to live simultaneously in all of them: he had a youthful zest and sense of fun in his old age, whereas he was rather doctrinaire, precocious, and opinionated in his youth.

Undoubtedly the turning point in Hollis's life was his conversion to the Roman Catholic church as an undergraduate in 1924. Through his close friend Douglas Woodruff, he had, as he put it himself, fallen 'a victim to the theories of the "Chesterbelloc", to Belloc's theses of the Catholic Church as Europe's creative force and of the coming of the Servile State, to Chesterton's ... rhetorical verse and the vision of the Distributist society'. It was a dramatic step from a deeply respected Anglican background. He never regretted it, but, in the words of T. S. Eliot, he came to see it as 'the right deed for the wrong reason'. He described himself later as an Anglican parson *manqué* and in his later years attached much more importance to the spiritual bond between Christians than to denominational divisions.

Hollis had a warmth of heart and a range of sympathy rare in men of fixed ideas and passionate convictions. He loved life and in his autobiographical writings he showed this by his constant delight in anecdotes, describing the small details of friendly occasions. He was a family man above all but also had a genius for friendship with all sorts of people, often with those his junior by many years.

In religion, beginning with a convert's over-zealous ecclesiastical outlook, he ended with a benign view of the varieties of religious experience, totally convinced of his own position but equally aware of the rights of others to have opinions, some of which he would certainly have challenged in his youth.

Hollis was a man who loved life but was always conscious of its transient quality. He had no worldly ambitions or acquisitive instincts. An impatient mind and an abrasive manner disguised a character that was essentially humble, diffident, and affectionate. His characteristic loud laugh certainly did not bespeak an empty mind but a confidence in the goodness of creation. His last book was *Oxford in the Twenties* (1976), recollections of Maurice Bowra, Leslie Hore-Belisha, Evelyn Waugh, R. C. Robertson-Glasgow, and Sir Harold Acton. Hollis died suddenly as he was watching television, at his home, Claveys, Mells, near Frome, Somerset, on 5 May 1977.

T. F. BURNS, *rev.*

Sources C. Hollis, *Along the road to Frome* (1958) · C. Hollis, *The seven ages* (1974) · personal knowledge (1986)
Archives SOUND BL NSA, performace recording
Wealth at death £24,413: administration with will, 13 July 1977, *CGPLA Eng. & Wales*

Hollis, Sir (Alfred) Claud (1874–1961), colonial governor, was born on 12 May 1874 at Cumberland Villa, Highgate Road, London, the second son of George Hollis (1843–1919), a barrister of the Inner Temple, and his wife, Susannah Smith (1843–1921). A pioneer of British administration in east Africa from the 1890s, he also served in Sierra Leone (1913–16) and Trinidad (1930–36). He was educated privately at St Leonards (to 1890) and in Switzerland (1891) and Germany (1892). In March 1897, after working for a commercial company in German East Africa (1893–6), he was appointed assistant collector in the British East Africa Protectorate. He quickly made his mark, through his energetic work as a district officer at the coast, his linguistic ability—he became government examiner in Swahili in 1901—and his publications on local history and anthropology. Invited to join the staff of the commissioner and consul-general, Sir Arthur Hardinge, he was subsequently appointed private secretary to Hardinge's successor, Sir Charles Eliot, and to the new post of secretary to the protectorate administration.

Hollis took part in the expeditions to Jubaland (1900–01) and against the Nandi (1905), receiving the Africa general service medal. His real concern, however, was the protection of African interests, especially from the demands for land and labour from incoming European settlers. Official recognition came in 1907 with his appointment as secretary for native affairs and membership of the legislative council. His pioneering and authoritative works on the Maasai (1905) and the Nandi (1908)—to both of which Eliot contributed introductions—received wide acclaim. Eliot's successor, Sir Donald Stewart, had little time for studious officials. He nevertheless appreciated Hollis's skills at shooting and cricket. Hollis's work continued to be commended by successive governors, Sir James Hayes-Sadler and Sir Percy Girouard. In 1911 he was appointed CMG, receiving congratulations from, among others, Winston Churchill, who had strongly supported Hollis in his defence of African interests when he visited the protectorate as under-secretary of state for the colonies in 1907.

Promotion came in January 1913, when Hollis took up the post of colonial secretary, Sierra Leone. Initially he was not accompanied by his wife, Enid Mabel Longman (1888–1939), whom he had married on 17 September 1910 at St Michael's Church, Highgate. She followed later, leaving their small daughter, Christian Ainslie (b. 29 June 1911), with grandparents at Worthing. Enid was to prove a constant support, spending the majority of time with her husband overseas, while also caring for the family, first at Highgate and then at Bishops, Widdington, near Saffron Walden, Essex. Mark William was born on 25 April 1914 and Prunella on 8 April 1923.

Following the outbreak of the First World War in 1914, Freetown, the capital of Sierra Leone, became a port of call for troopships from the south, as a result of which Hollis's responsibilities were greatly increased. But the tide of war in east Africa, following the defeat of German forces near Kilimanjaro, led to Hollis's recall. He became secretary to the administrator of the occupied territory of German East Africa and in 1920, chief secretary in the newly created Tanganyika territory, and was made CBE in 1919. Further promotion came in 1924 when he became British resident in Zanzibar. These years proved enjoyable and constructive. He developed cordial relations with the sultan and with leaders of the local community, concentrating on road and harbour improvements and also assisting schools, dispensaries, and the local clove farmers. In January 1927 he was appointed KCMG (promoted GCMG in 1934).

In 1930 Hollis was made governor of Trinidad, a post he held until his retirement in 1936. In addition to dispensing generous hospitality to numerous guests, he concentrated on improving Trinidad's lot in the years following the great depression. Major public works, installing a central water supply scheme, an electricity scheme, and work on a deep water harbour all contributed significantly to economic recovery. 'In spite of … difficulties', wrote a historian of Trinidad, 'Sir Claud Hollis appears to have been one of the Colony's most popular Governors' (Craig, 48).

Hollis's early years of retirement, though fully occupied with a range of activities including membership of the imperial communications advisory committee, were marked with sadness. His devoted wife Enid died in 1939 at the early age of fifty-one and his only son, Mark, was killed in action in 1941. He nevertheless remained active for many years, serving as a JP and as master of the Leathersellers' Company (1945–6), and enjoying English country life. He died, aged eighty-seven, on 22 November 1961, at the Evelyn Nursing Home in Cambridge.

G. H. Mungeam

Sources A. C. Hollis, autobiography, Bodl. RH, MSS Brit. Emp. S.293–304 [12 vols.] · A. C. Hollis, The Masai, their language and folklore (1905) · A. C. Hollis, The Nandi, their language and folklore (1908) · G. H. Mungeam, British rule in Kenya, 1895–1912: the establishment of administration in the East Africa Protectorate (1966) · The Times (23 Nov 1961) · R. Coupland, East Africa and its invaders (1938) · R. Coupland, The exploitation of east Africa, 1856–1890 (1939) · W. S. Churchill, My African journey (1908); repr. (1962) · H. Craig, The legislative council of Trinidad and Tobago (1952) · A. C. Hollis, account of the village of Widdington, 1950, CUL · CGPLA Eng. & Wales (1962) · d. cert. · WWW, 1961–70

Archives Bodl. RH, MS autobiography · Bodl. RH, papers relating to the Wasegeju · CUL, account of the village of Widdington · Royal Anthropological Institute, London, genealogical notes relating to East African peoples
Likenesses photographs, Bodl. RH, MSS Brit. Emp. S.293–304
Wealth at death £9760 11s. 10d.: probate, 3 Jan 1962, CGPLA Eng. & Wales

Hollis, George (1793–1842), engraver, of whose parents nothing is known, was born at Oxford and from about 1807 until about 1815 was apprenticed to George Cooke in London. He worked mainly on topographical subjects, the earliest of which to attract notice, in 1818, were six views of Chudleigh, Devon, drawn before the destructive fire of 1807 by Henry Francis de Cort. Further views appeared in works on Greece (1819), Hallamshire in the West Riding of Yorkshire (1819), Cheshire (1819), Wiltshire (1824), Shrewsbury (1825–6), and Glastonbury (1826). J. Hakewill's Picturesque Tour of Italy (1818–20) contained some engravings worked up by J. M. W. Turner from the author's drawings. In 1821 W. B. Cooke held his first exhibition of engravings at 9 Soho Square, London, which included six plates by Hollis (whose address was given as Oxford)—two of Rome after Turner, two architectural studies in Oxford and Edinburgh, and two landscapes. Engravings done by him for the publications of the Society of Dilettanti and the Gentleman's Magazine were admired, and he also engraved views of Oxford colleges and halls, some after his own designs. From about 1830 to 1834 he lived in Montmartre, Paris, where he probably obtained the commission to engrave on steel two plates for L. Bechstein's Thüringen (vol. 4 of Das malerische und romantische Deutschland, 1836). These were two of his few engravings on steel, probably a reflection of his master's extreme dislike of the metal; other engravings using steel appeared in J. H. Caunter's Scenes in India (vol. 1 of the Oriental Annual, 1834), and a single plate after G. Pickering, dated 1835, was published in E. Baines's History of the County Palatine and Duchy of Lancaster (1836). Some engravings by G. and T. Hollis were done for Cumberland's British Theatre, 6 (1834). In 1837 Hollis engraved Turner's St Mark's Place, Venice—Juliet and her Nurse on copper, signed, as usual, 'G. Hollis'; exhibited at the Royal Academy in 1838, it remained unpublished at his death, but was issued by Agnew in 1842. Hollis etched some drawings by his son Thomas for Monumental Effigies of Great Britain in 1839 (continuing an earlier work by Charles Stothard), the first part of which was published in 1840. Only five parts were completed at his death, which occurred on 2 January 1842 at Gloucester Buildings, Walworth, London, at the age of forty-nine.

Thomas Hollis (1818–1843), George Hollis's only son, was born in London and about 1830 moved with his family to France. As a schoolboy he sketched scenes around Montmartre, Paris, and in 1832 copied paintings in the Louvre. At the age of sixteen he helped his father to produce some engravings for Cumberland's British Theatre, 6 (1834). A self-taught artist, he continued his studies in the British Museum and National Gallery on his return to England, and in April 1836 was admitted as a student at the Royal Academy, where he trained to become a historical painter. He was later a pupil of the portrait painter H. W. Pickersgill. Hollis is known as the painter of many landscape views around Dulwich. On his father's death he tried to provide for his widowed mother, and etched as well as drew a few more plates for *Monumental Effigies of Great Britain*, but as a result of overwork he died of consumption on 14 October 1843 at Apollo Buildings, Walworth, aged only twenty-five.

L. H. CUST, *rev.* B. HUNNISETT

Sources GM, 2nd ser., 17 (1842), 333–4 • GM, 2nd ser., 21 (1844), 101–2 • Redgrave, Artists, 220 • W. G. Rawlinson, The engraved work of J. M. W. Turner, 2 (1913), 206 • Wood, Vic. painters, 2nd edn

Hollis, Sir Leslie Chasemore [Jo] (1897–1963), marine officer, was born at Walcot, Bath, on 9 February 1897, the son of Charles Joseph Hollis (1866–1941), curate of Bath Abbey church (1894–1900), vicar of Holy Trinity, Worthing (1900–41), and rural dean of Worthing (1925–41), and his wife, Marion (*née* Chasemore). Hollis received a classical education at St Lawrence College, Ramsgate, which was, however, insufficient preparation for the Royal Marines entrance examination. So he was coached in mathematics and science by a crammer who made him memorize the answers to 150 previous examination questions: he passed, and was commissioned probationary second lieutenant, Royal Marine light infantry, in April 1915.

In November 1915 Hollis was posted acting lieutenant to the *Duke of Edinburgh*. The ship was one of four coal-burning cruisers forming the 1st cruiser squadron, commanded by Sir Robert Arbuthnot, part of the Grand Fleet based on Scapa Flow. Hollis's action station was in the foretop, where he had a clear view of events at the battle of Jutland (31 May 1916). It was disastrous for the squadron, three of the four ships being sunk. Only the *Duke of Edinburgh* survived, fortunately with no casualties. Later in the war Hollis took over his first command, as lieutenant in charge of the Royal Marine detachment in the *Coventry*, in the Harwich force. Hollis married on 18 September 1923 Rose May (*d.* 12 May 1978), daughter of Alfred Fraser of Folkestone: they had no children. She had obtained a divorce from her previous husband, Juan de la Torre Bueno, with whom she had had two daughters.

After the war Hollis served in various ships—becoming captain, Royal Marines, in 1921—until in 1927 he was selected for the naval staff course (1927–8) at the Royal Naval College, Greenwich; he passed out in December 1928, and was then appointed intelligence officer on the staff of the commander-in-chief Africa station, with headquarters at Simonstown (1929–32). This was the first of a succession of staff appointments and Hollis always thereafter regarded those three years as the happiest of his life. In 1932 he was brought home to the plans division of the Admiralty (1932–36) as a captain in the local defence section which dealt with the sea defences of ports at home and abroad, including Singapore; this brought him into contact with his War Office and Air Ministry counterparts. After four years in plans division (major, 1935), Hollis expected to go to sea again and was to join the *Hood*. However, Sir Maurice Hankey, secretary to the cabinet and to

Sir Leslie Chasemore Hollis (1897–1963), by Bassano, 1946

the committee of imperial defence (CID), and himself a Royal Marine officer, 'hand-picked' (Roskill, 3.423) and requested him, and thus in the spring of 1936 Hollis became secretary of the joint planning subcommittee, and one of the military assistant secretaries of the CID.

The CID had a small, specially selected, staff from the three services, which formed part of the cabinet office. Hankey was the secretary and head of the whole office, but when he retired in 1938 the responsibilities were divided, Edward (later Lord) Bridges becoming secretary of the cabinet, and Hastings (later Lord) Ismay becoming secretary of the CID. Ismay had been Hankey's deputy, and so Hollis served under him (from 1936) for the important years of preparation for war (becoming his deputy in 1938), and then through the war itself, before succeeding him when he retired at the end of 1946—nearly eleven unbroken years in all. Hollis continued a close friend of Hankey.

The tempo of work steadily quickened with the inevitable approach of war, and as the size of the office was rigidly controlled, the load on each assistant secretary became heavier. When war came in 1939 Hollis had already proved his capacity, and had enough experience to take his place as a key member of the machinery for the conduct of worldwide operations. When Churchill became prime minister in 1940 he also assumed the title of minister of defence, and appointed Ismay as his chief staff officer, military deputy secretary to the war cabinet, and an additional member of the chiefs of staff committee. Hollis took over as secretary of this committee, and as Ismay's deputy, he became responsible for the organization and efficiency of the military side of the war cabinet secretariat, which became known as the office of the minister of defence. He remained in this position for six years, and was promoted lieutenant-colonel, colonel, brigadier, and in November 1943 acting major-general.

Ismay relied on Hollis to keep the office going at maximum efficiency, so that he, Ismay, would be free to serve Churchill and the chiefs of staff in ways which fell outside the daily routine. Increasingly, as the scope of the war widened, Hollis found himself acting as Ismay's alternate, and the two played Box and Cox on the many journeys abroad taken by Churchill and the chiefs of staff. The system was such that, wherever the prime minister, war cabinet members, and the chiefs of staff were, they were served with the same efficiency and, as in London, this was largely due to Hollis.

At the end of 1946 Hollis succeeded Ismay as deputy military secretary to the cabinet and as chief staff officer to A. V. Alexander, who had been appointed to the newly established Ministry of Defence. Hollis was promoted major-general in 1947 and lieutenant-general in 1949, the year in which he was also appointed commandant general, Royal Marines. His appointment surprised some, as he had been for so many years on the staff, but his knowledge of persons in high position enabled him to play a decisive role in saving the corps from the abolition proposed after the war. He had been appointed CBE (1942), CB (1943), and KBE (1946), and was promoted full general, and made KCB, in 1951. He retired in 1952, and wrote two books of reminiscences, *One Marine's Tale* (1956) and *War at the Top* (1959), and a biography of Prince Philip, duke of Edinburgh, *The Captain General* (1961). He also served the English-speaking union as director of current affairs, and became director of some commercial companies. But he suffered increasingly from ill health, and gradually gave up his occupations.

Jo Hollis was full of common sense, loyal, reliable, calm, imperturbable and hard-working, cheerful, and unflurried. He estimated afterwards that he had attended more than 6000 meetings of chiefs of staff during those years, and innumerable other meetings and conferences. Although no intellectual, he had the ability to deal with even the most stubborn or truculent, from the prime minister downwards, without losing his balance and with unfailing tact; Churchill described him as 'a tower of strength'. His mind was practical, he had a dry and lively sense of humour, excelled as a raconteur, and he was Ismay's constant ally in creating a relaxed and confident atmosphere, even in the darkest hours; there was no bickering under their aegis, and no such division between 'frocks' and 'brass hats' as in the previous war. He suffered from asthma, but never allowed this to affect his work: he was rarely away for even one day throughout the war—days which normally began at 7.30 a.m. and ended in the small hours of the next morning. Hollis was stocky—about 5 feet 8 inches tall—and of upright carriage; his

brown hair was brushed back and parted in the middle, and he wore a short moustache. Brisk in his movements, he was impassive when working. Hollis died at Cuckfield Hospital, Cuckfield, Sussex, on 9 August 1963.

IAN JACOB, rev. ROGER T. STEARN

Sources L. Hollis, *One marine's tale* (1956) · L. Hollis, *War at the top* (1959) · personal knowledge (1980) · private information (1980) · WWW · Burke, *Peerage* (1959) · B. Bond, *British military policy between the two world wars* (1980) · M. Dockrill, *British defence since 1945* (1988) · W. Jackson and D. Bramall, *The chiefs: the story of the United Kingdom chiefs of staff* (1992) · Venn, *Alum. Cant.* · S. W. Roskill, *Hankey, man of secrets*, 3 (1974) · CGPLA Eng. & Wales (1963)
Archives IWM, typescript memoirs | HLRO, corresp. with Lord Beaverbrook
Likenesses Bassano, photograph, 1946, NPG [*see illus.*] · W. Stoneman, photograph, 1946, NPG · photograph, repro. in Hollis, *One marine's tale*, facing p. 64
Wealth at death £20,837 13s. 0d.: probate, 26 Nov 1963, CGPLA Eng. & Wales

Hollis, (James) Martin (1938–1998), philosopher, was born on 14 March 1938 in St Mary's Hospital, Paddington, London, the son of (Hugh) Marcus Noel [Mark] Hollis, an advertising agent and later a member of the Foreign Office, and his wife Ruth Margaret, née Colthurst. (Maurice) Christopher *Hollis (1902–1977), author and politician, and Sir Roger Henry *Hollis (1905–1973), director-general of MI5, were his uncles. He won a scholarship to Winchester College, and did his national service in the Royal Artillery before going up to New College, Oxford, on a classics scholarship. At Oxford he read philosophy, politics, and economics, and was inspired by the teaching of A. J. Ayer, Wykeham professor of logic and a fellow of New College. He graduated with a second-class degree in 1961. After spending two years in the United States on a Harkness fellowship, studying sociology at Harvard University (where he first came across W. V. O. Quine and John Rawls, two philosophers who greatly influenced his work) and the University of California at Berkeley, he joined the Foreign Office, having come top in the entrance examination. Although still working at the Foreign Office until 1966, he found the life of a civil servant unstimulating, and was also a college lecturer in philosophy at New College from 1964 to 1965, and at Balliol College, Oxford, from 1965 to 1967. On 18 September 1965 he married Patricia Lesley (b. 1941), a historian and later a Labour politician, daughter of (Harry) Lesley George Wells, a civil servant. She was leader of Norwich city council from 1983 to 1988, and was created Baroness Hollis of Heigham in 1990. They had two sons, Simon (b. 1969) and Matthew (b. 1971).

In 1967 Martin and Patricia Hollis were both appointed to lectureships at the new University of East Anglia in Norwich, and he remained there for the rest of his career: he was promoted to senior lecturer in 1972, and in 1981 became professor of philosophy. He also served as dean of the school of economic and social studies from 1983 to 1986, and while pro-vice-chancellor (1992–5) he had to administer the change from the traditional three-term academic year to a two-semester system on the American model. A brilliant lecturer, he held visiting lectureships and professorships in universities in North America and

Germany, and taught at the philosophy summer school near Guangzhou, in China. He loved philosophical debate, and founded the East Anglia Philosophy Triangle, which held regular informal meetings in Norwich, Cambridge, and Colchester.

Hollis's main field of interest was the philosophy of social science, and central to his thought was a concern with the nature of rationality. He sought to broaden the notion of instrumental rationality, prevalent in economics, to include not just the means chosen but the ends sought. This enriched notion of 'expressive rationality' embraced moral as well as intellectual virtues while remaining compatible with economics. He saw this approach as counter-acting the individualism of economic theory and as accommodating values of social co-operation and mutual trust. Also, by including goals and values within the framework of reason, he hoped that this notion of rationality would help to oppose any form of epistemological or cultural relativism. Much of his published work in philosophy consisted of explorations of the nature of rational choice in various academic disciplines, including anthropology, politics, economics, and history. *Rational Economic Man: a Philosophical Critique of Neo-Classical Economics* (1975, written with Edward J. Nell), was followed by *Models of Man: Philosophical Thoughts on Social Action* (1977), in which he dealt with the philosophy of sociology, and *The Cunning of Reason* (1988). With Steve Smith he examined the philosophy of international relations in *Explaining and Understanding International Relations* (1990). In his last book, *Trust within Reason*, published posthumously in 1998, he looked at moral and political philosophy. He also wrote two widely used textbooks, *An Invitation to Philosophy* (1985) and *The Philosophy of Social Science: an Introduction* (1994). He edited several collections of essays, including *Philosophy and Economic Theory* (1979) with Frank Hahn; *Rationality and Relativism* (1982) with Steven Lukes; and *Reason in Action: Essays in the Philosophy of Social Science* (1996); and wrote over ninety articles and reviews. A member of the editorial boards of *Cambridge Studies in Philosophy* from 1978 and the *Journal of Applied Philosophy* from 1984, he edited the Anglo-German philosophical journal *Ratio* from 1980 to 1987. He was elected a fellow of the British Academy in 1990, and served on the council and as chairman of the philosophy section.

A JP in Norwich for ten years, Hollis also helped his wife in her political career on Norwich city council. He was a very strong chess player, often using chess to illustrate his philosophical points, and he also enjoyed playing bridge. For many years he set brain-teasers for the *New Scientist*, some of which were published as *Tantalisers* (1970). During the final months of his life, when he was suffering from a brain tumour and was confined to a wheelchair, he continued to take part in meetings and seminars. He died on 27 February 1998 at his home, 30 Park Lane, Norwich, and was survived by his wife and their two sons. The first of a series of Martin Hollis memorial lectures at the University of East Anglia was delivered on 5 May 1998.

ANNE PIMLOTT BAKER

Sources *The Times* (4 March 1998) · *The Guardian* (3 March 1998) · *The Independent* (11 March 1998) · 'Martin Hollis—a bibliography', www.uea.ac.uk/soc/phil/martin_hollis, 23 April 2002 · *WW* · b. cert. · m. cert. · d. cert.
Likenesses photograph, repro. in *The Times* · photograph, repro. in *The Independent*
Wealth at death £125,122: probate, 30 June 1998, *CGPLA Eng. & Wales*

Hollis, Sir Roger Henry (1905–1973), intelligence officer, was born at Wells, Somerset, on 2 December 1905, the third of the four sons (there were no daughters) of the Revd George Arthur Hollis (1868–1944), vice-principal of Wells Theological College and later bishop-suffragan of Taunton, and his wife, Mary Margaret, the daughter of Charles Marcus Church, canon of Wells, a great-niece of R. W. Church, dean of St Paul's. His elder brother, (Maurice) Christopher *Hollis (1902–1977), one-time Conservative MP for Devizes, has described the early years of his family life in his autobiography: 'I grew up not merely as a clergyman's son, but in a cleric-inhabited society—in a sort of Trollopean world' (Hollis, 4).

Roger Hollis was educated at Leeds grammar school, Clifton College, and Worcester College, Oxford. At school he was a promising scholar who went to Oxford with a classical exhibition. But at Oxford he read English and in the view of his contemporaries seemed to prefer a happy social life to an academic one. In the memoirs of Evelyn Waugh he appears as 'a good bottle man' and in Sir Harold Acton's as an agreeable friend. Because of this easy-going approach, and for no more dramatic reason, he went down four terms before he was due to take his finals.

After barely a year's work in the dominions, Commonwealth, and overseas branch of Barclays Bank, Hollis left England to become a journalist on a Hong Kong newspaper. This too proved a brief assignment, and in April 1928 he transferred to the British American Tobacco Company (BAT), in whose service he remained for the following eight years of his residence in China. His work enabled him to travel widely in a country torn by the almost continuous conflict between Chinese warlords and Japanese invaders. His letters home provide dry and witty accounts of life in China, free of the travel romanticism then so much in vogue. A lecture he gave to the Royal Central Asian Society in October 1937 (and published in its journal in January 1938) provides further insights into his Chinese experiences. Entitled 'The conflict in China', it showed a considerable grasp of a complex situation. The nine formative years in China were terminated by an attack of tuberculosis which led to his being invalided out of BAT. He returned to England in 1936 for a further brief spell with the Ardath Tobacco Company, an associate of BAT. On 10 July of the following year he was married in Wells Cathedral to Evelyn Esmé, daughter of George Champeny Swayne, of Burnham-on-Sea, Somerset, solicitor in Glastonbury. Their one child, Adrian Swayne Hollis, became a fellow and tutor in classics at Keble College, Oxford, and a chess player of international reputation.

Hollis began a new career in the Security Service, MI5, in 1938. It lasted twenty-seven years and constituted his most absorbing interest. By qualities of mind and character he was in several ways well adapted to it. He was a hard and conscientious worker, level-headed, fair-minded, and always calm. He began as a student of international communism, a field in which he became an acknowledged authority in the service. During the war—when the bulk of the service's talents and resources were committed to German, Italian, and Japanese counter-intelligence—he managed with small resources to ensure that the dangers of Russian directed communism were not neglected. Consequently, when the war was over and the Security Service turned to face the problems of the cold war, he had already become one of its key figures. In 1953 he was appointed deputy director-general and three years later, when his predecessor was unexpectedly transferred to other work, he inherited the top position as director-general of MI5.

Hollis held the post with quiet efficiency for the next nine turbulent years. Throughout that time the cold war was at its height, and was especially manifest in the field of Soviet espionage. Spy case followed spy case at the Old Bailey: Anthony Wraight, W. J. Vassall, George Blake, Harry Houghton, Ethel Gee, Gordon Lonsdale, and the Krogers became notorious figures, while in a different context the case of John Profumo caused great political consternation. Parallel with these events new sources of information became available to the Security Service from defectors arriving in the West from Russia and other communist countries. These depicted the KGB in vast and threatening terms, but were difficult to assess and only rarely provided sure and certain guidance. In the light of these events and circumstances the governments of the day felt the need to allay public and parliamentary concern over national security standards, and during his nine-year tenure of office as director-general Hollis had to face on behalf of his service three major official inquiries which he and the service survived with considerable credit. Lord Denning, in memoirs later serialized in *The Times*, commented on the confidence he felt in Hollis during the inquiry for which he was responsible. By the time he retired in 1965 Hollis had become a respected figure in Whitehall. He was appointed OBE (1946), CB (1956), was knighted (1960), and was created KBE (1966). He was respected inside his own service and by others within the intelligence community, though he did not enjoy easy personal relations with its ordinary members, who tended to find him reserved and aloof. Outside these two fields he was hardly known at all; this was exactly how he would have wished things to be, and how they would have remained but for the misfortune that clouded the last years of his life.

On his retirement Hollis moved first to a house in Wells, which he occupied only until 1967. In 1968 his first marriage was dissolved and he married Edith Valentine Hammond, his former secretary, the daughter of Ernest Gower Hammond, of Stratford upon Avon. They moved to a new home in the Somerset village of Catcott, where Hollis indulged his formidable skills as a golfer and undertook some modest jobs in local government. He was then suddenly asked to visit his old service, where he learned

that—as a result of information tending to imply a high-level Soviet penetration of the service—he, among others, had become a subject of investigation. He was asked to submit himself to interrogation and agreed. Members of a service in the front line of attack by the KGB can appreciate the need for secret inquiries of this kind at whatever rank they may apply. Unfortunately some of the details of the investigation became public knowledge after his death, at Catcott on 26 October 1973, because of internal leaks, and in 1981 *Their Trade is Treachery*, by Chapman Pincher, was published. This book's picture of the Hollis investigation implied that the former director-general of the Security Service had probably been a Russian spy throughout his career in the service. Not unnaturally it provoked such an outcry in press and parliament that Margaret Thatcher, the prime minister, had to intervene. On 25 March 1981 she informed the House of Commons that the outcome of the last Hollis investigation (by Lord Trend, secretary of the cabinet from 1963 to 1973) had been the clearance of his name and reputation. The great public interest in the matter was a severe ordeal for Hollis's family.

A further case for Hollis being a Soviet agent was made in 1989 by W. J. West in *The Truth about Hollis*. However, the testimony of ex-Soviet KGB agents (Oleg Gordievsky and Yuri Modin) has cast doubt on this, as they deny he was the so-called 'fifth man'. The balance of opinion appears to suggest that Sir Roger was indeed innocent of the accusations levelled against him. DICK WHITE, *rev.*

Sources C. Hollis, *The seven ages* (1974) · WWW · *The Times* (30 Oct 1973) · personal knowledge (1986) · private information (1986) · C. Pincher, *Their trade is treachery* (1981) · W. J. West, *The truth about Hollis: an investigation* (1989) · R. Deacon, *The greatest treason: the bizarre story of Hollis, Liddell and Mountbatten* (1990) · 'Mrs Thatcher says inquiries failed to incriminate Hollis', *The Times* (27 March 1998) · 'Hollis innocent, ex-KGB man says', *The Times* (2 Oct 1991) · 'A spy mystery with no ending', *The Times* (19 Dec 1999) · CGPLA Eng. & Wales (1974)

Likenesses photograph, c.1960, Hult. Arch.

Wealth at death £40,355: probate, 7 Jan 1974, CGPLA Eng. & Wales

Hollis, Thomas (1720–1774), political propagandist, was born in London on 14 April 1720, the only child of Thomas Hollis (d. 1735) and the daughter of a Mr Scott of Wolverhampton, in whose household he lived until he was four or five years old. His great-great-grandfather had been a Baptist whitesmith in Rotherham, Yorkshire, and his great-grandfather established a London branch of the cutlery business. Hollis was educated at the free school in Newport, Shropshire, until the age of nine or ten, then in St Albans, and for fifteen months in Amsterdam, where he learned Dutch, French, writing, arithmetic, and accounts in preparation for a business career. He lived with his father, who died in 1735, and then under the guardianship of John Hollister, and was trained to public service partly by John Ward of Gresham College, London. He took chambers in Lincoln's Inn, though without reading law, from February 1740 to 1748. By then he was rich, having inherited from his uncle as well as his father and, in 1738, his grandfather. In 1748–9 he toured Europe with his friend Thomas Brand (later Brand Hollis), and, during 1750–53, largely on his own, meeting many leading French *philosophes* and several Italian painters. Back in England he was an ardent member of the Society of Arts, for a time chairing its committee on the polite arts. A member himself, he proposed Piranesi for membership of the Society of Antiquaries, gave numerous commissions to Cipriani, and, as one of Canaletto's best friends in England, commissioned six paintings from him. He was elected a fellow of the Royal Society in 1757. Sometimes accused of being an atheist, Hollis was a rational dissenter who supported Caleb Fleming's ministry at Pinners' Hall. In common with many contemporaries he was rabidly anti-Catholic and campaigned vigorously against popery; he became convinced that he was the intended victim of a Catholic plot. He had many connections, among them liberal churchmen such as Francis Blackburne and Theophilus Lindsey, John Wilkes, several peers, and especially the elder William Pitt (though this friendship was suspended when Pitt accepted a peerage in 1766 and resumed only about 1771).

Hollis believed citizenship should be active: individuals had an important role to play in public life. He partly fulfilled this responsibility by charitable work as a governor of Guy's and St Thomas's hospitals, and a guardian of the asylum and Magdalen Hospital. Applauding Wilkes's cause privately, he deplored political bribery and declined to stand for parliament at Dorchester in 1761. He believed that legitimate government was contractual, and that the people as constituent authority were entitled to replace tyrants by new governments. As a republican Hollis provided material for Catharine Macaulay's *History of England*. Yet he was also a patriotic Englishman and warm supporter of the house of Hanover. His heroes were Elizabeth I, Oliver Cromwell, and Pitt, all of whom extended England's international standing, as well as John Milton, his particular hero.

Convinced of the decadence of his own times but hopeful for the future, Hollis's principal contribution to public service was the protection and advancement of English liberty by circulating appropriate books on government, for he argued that 'if government goes right, all goes right' (Robbins, 'Library', 8). From 1754 onwards he reprinted and distributed literature from the seventeenth-century republican canon, thus keeping the cause of parliamentary reform alive during a difficult period. Among the works were Toland's *Life of Milton*, tracts by Marchmont Nedham, Henry Neville, and Philip Sidney, and John Locke's *Two Treatises of Government*; they were elegantly bound to give them greater effect and tooled with libertarian ornaments such as the liberty cap and owl. He also designed and distributed medals based on Greek and Roman models and prints as part of his plan. Initially the tracts were directed towards libraries throughout Britain and continental Europe; later he turned his generosity to America.

Continuing his great-uncle Thomas's practice, Hollis was a great benefactor to American colleges, especially Harvard, sending donations and numerous books, often decorated with libertarian symbols. From 1755 his principal American correspondent was Jonathan Mayhew of Boston, and, after his death in 1766, Andrew Eliot. He also followed worsening Anglo-American political relations during the 1760s. Declining to participate directly in politics he published short pieces in the newspapers and printed and circulated colonial tracts in Britain, frequently subsidizing the printers to ensure their appearance. In particular he contributed to the successful campaign against the appointment of an American bishop by reprinting sermons by Mayhew and others. He also compiled *The True Sentiments of America* in 1768; it incorporated John Adams's *Dissertation on the Canon and the Feudal Law*, which he greatly admired. But he denied inciting the colonies to independence.

Horace Walpole considered Hollis 'as simple a poor soul as ever existed' (Robbins, 'Strenuous whig', 409). Cipriani, who described him as over 6 feet tall, Herculean in size and strength, and possessing bright brown eyes, a short nose, and laughing mouth, remarked on his gentleness and sweetness of manner. His diet was eccentric, but he kept himself fit by walking, riding, and fencing. Exhausted by the effort of what he originally intended as only a ten-year campaign to disseminate libertarian tracts, Hollis retired in 1770 to Urles Farm, at Corscombe, Dorset, where he owned about 3000 acres. He died there suddenly on 1 January 1774, and was buried in one of his fields and the grave ploughed over. He was unmarried, and after minor legacies left his estates to Thomas Brand, who added Hollis's name to his own.

COLIN BONWICK

Sources [F. Blackburne], *Memoirs of Thomas Hollis, esq*, 2 vols. (1780) • C. Robbins, 'The strenuous whig: Thomas Hollis of Lincoln's Inn', *William and Mary Quarterly*, 7 (1950), 407–53 • C. Robbins, 'Library of liberty: assembled for Harvard College by Thomas Hollis of Lincoln's Inn', *Harvard Library Bulletin*, 5 (1951), 5–23, 181–96 • T. Hollis, diary, Harvard U., Houghton L. • 'Thomas Hollis and Jonathan Mayhew: their correspondence, 1759–1766', ed. B. Knollenberg, *Proceedings of the Massachusetts Historical Society*, 69 (1947–50), 102–93 • W. H. Bond, *Thomas Hollis of Lincoln's Inn: a whig and his books* (1990) • P. D. Marshall, 'Thomas Hollis, 1720–74: the bibliophile as libertarian', *Bulletin of the John Rylands University Library*, 66 (1983–4), 246–63 • W. T. Whitley, *Artists and their friends in England, 1700–1799*, 1 (1928) • 'Letters from Andrew Eliot to Thomas Hollis', *Collections of the Massachusetts Historical Society*, 4th ser., 4 (1858), 398–461 • C. Robbins, *The eighteenth-century commonwealthman* (1959) • W. H. Bond, 'Letters from Thomas Hollis of Lincoln's Inn to Andrew Eliot', *Proceedings of the Massachusetts Historical Society*, 99 (1987), 76–167

Archives BL, corresp. and papers, Add. MSS 4310, 4443, 4724–4725, 5821, 5872, 6179–6180, 6210, 22674, 26889, 34733 • BL, printed works with his MS notes and additions • DWL, annotated book, *Civil war colours, standards and bearings* • Harvard U., Houghton L., diary, MSS • Mass. Hist. Soc., corresp. and papers | Boston University, Jonathan Mayhew MSS • Harvard U., Houghton L., corresp. with Timothy Hollis • PRO, letters to first earl of Chatham, PRO 30/8

Likenesses A. Pozzi, ivory miniature bas-relief, 1752, Harvard TC • R. Wilson, oils, 1752, Harvard TC • G. B. Cipriani, crayon drawing, 1769, Harvard TC • W. Bromley, line print, BM, NPG; repro. in *European Magazine* (1788) • Canaletto, portrait (*Old Walton Bridge*) • G. B. Cipriani, line print, BM, NPG; repro. in Blackburne, *Memoirs* (1780) • J. Greenwood, pen-and-pencil drawing, BM • engravings, Bodl. Oxf. • portraits, priv. coll.

Hollis, Thomas (1818–1843). *See under* Hollis, George (1793–1842).

Hollis, Thomas Brand (*c*.1719–1804), radical, was born Thomas Brand at The Hyde, near Ingatestone, Essex, the only son among three children of Timothy Brand (*d.* 1734), who had retired from his mercer's business in London, and Sarah (*d.* 1744), daughter of Thomas Michell of Rickling, Hertfordshire. He attended Brentwood and Felsted schools and, excluded from the English universities as a protestant dissenter, matriculated at Glasgow University, where Richard Baron was a friend; both were greatly influenced by Francis Hutcheson. His admission to the freedom of Glasgow in 1741 probably ended his academic career. Finding law uncongenial he declined a place at the Inner Temple in London the same year. He toured continental Europe in 1748–9 with Thomas Hollis, whom he had met at the inns of court, and largely alone in 1750–53. Thereafter he divided his time between London and The Hyde, which Sir William Chambers remodelled in 1761. He inherited almost all Hollis's property in 1774, adding his benefactor's surname to his own. The inheritance strengthened Brand Hollis's already comfortable patrimony.

Brand Hollis's connections, principally among dissenters, political radicals, and in the intellectual and charitable world, steadily expanded after returning to London. He was elected fellow of the Royal Society in 1756 and of the Society of Antiquaries in 1757, became a member of the Academy of Arts, Manufactures, and Commerce two years later, and was appointed a governor of Guy's and St Thomas's hospitals in 1754 and 1755 respectively. Partly through friendships with liberal Anglicans such as Francis Blackburne and John Jebb he became a Unitarian. He supported Theophilus Lindsey's Essex Street Chapel and contributed to the dissenters' college at Hackney from its foundation in 1786 to its demise ten years later. Brand Hollis was especially concerned for religious liberty and supported the 1787, 1789, and 1790 campaigns against the Test and Corporation Acts, but was strongly anti-Catholic; contrary to Caroline Robbins he published nothing.

Above all, Brand Hollis advocated political reform. His first foray ended in humiliating disaster. Hoping to promote the cause in parliament he purchased the rotten borough of Hindon, Wiltshire, at the 1774 general election, but the election was challenged. He was convicted of corruption, unseated, fined 1000 marks, and jailed for six months. Undeterred, he joined the parliamentary reform movement precipitated by the American War of Independence. He was a founder member of the Society for Constitutional Information in 1780, and as a member of the Essex and Dorset county associations collaborated with Christopher Wyvill of Yorkshire, whose modest programme of reform at the St Alban's tavern conference in March 1780 he supported without success. Brand Hollis was especially influential on the Westminster Committee, which appointed him and Jebb to a subcommittee authorized to consider general electoral matters. Using arguments drawn from James Burgh and other Commonwealthsmen, they persuaded it to recommend a complete recasting of the representative system, including annual parliaments, equal electoral districts, universal male suffrage, and the ballot. Such advanced proposals also came to nothing and possibly damaged the cause of moderate reform. Somewhat eccentrically he considered the City of London as the epitome of the English constitution, insisting that its officers were ultimately dependent on popular choice and declaring that its frequent elections provided a balance against usurpation and tyranny.

In 1788 Brand Hollis was a founder member of the Revolution Society and a steward at its commemoration of the revolution of 1688, arguing that another revolution in Britain could be averted by following its principles. Initially Brand Hollis approved of the French Revolution, but was horrified by its later course and feared a similar catastrophe in England. He denied assisting publication of Thomas Paine's *Rights of Man* in 1791 and giving him money the following year. Withdrawing from the Society for Constitutional Information in 1791 after its capture by more extreme reformers, but alarmed by ministerial attacks on free expression, he joined the moderate Society of the Friends of the People, and the Society of Friends to the Liberty of the Press in 1792–3.

Brand Hollis deeply admired America. Deploring government policy towards the colonies before the revolution, he condemned the use of force and feared that both English and American liberty were at risk. He named trees at The Hyde after George Washington and other Americans and welcomed independence. Afterwards he became a close friend of John Adams, the first American minister in London, and his family. He also met and corresponded with several other Americans, including Benjamin Franklin and Thomas Jefferson, whose Virginia statute for religious freedom he printed in the *Chelmsford Gazette* during the repeal campaign. A benefactor to New England institutions, he was elected to the American Academy of Arts and Sciences in 1783 and awarded an honorary doctorate by Harvard College in 1787. He greatly admired the United States constitution, which he reprinted.

Brand Hollis was said to possess every characteristic of a gentleman. Mild in disposition, amiable in temper but somewhat naive, he was averse to business of any kind, including the minutiae of his own affairs; his knowledge of virtu and antiquities was considered particularly chaste and correct. His health deteriorated from 1800 onward, and he left London the following year. He died on 9 September 1804 at The Hyde, and was buried at Ingatestone parish church, leaving the bulk of his property to John Disney, his friend since the 1780s. His sister Elizabeth kept house for him; he never married.

COLIN BONWICK

Sources J. Disney, *Memoirs of Thomas Brand-Hollis* (1808) · C. Robbins, 'Thomas Brand Hollis (1719–1804): English admirer of Franklin and intimate of John Adams', *Proceedings of the American Philosophical Society*, 97 (1953), 239–47 · Mass. Hist. Soc., Adams MSS · 'Letters of Joseph Willard', *Proceedings of the Massachusetts Historical Society*, 43 (1909–10), 609–46 · N. Yorks. CRO, Wyvill papers · Westminster Committee minutes, BL, Add. MSS 38593–38595 · treasury solicitor's papers, PRO · *GM*, 1st ser., 74 (1804), 888–9 · C. K. Shipton, *Sibley's Harvard graduates: biographical sketches of graduates of Harvard University*, 17 vols. (1873–1975), vol. 11

Archives BL, Westminster Committee minutes, Add. MSS 38593–38595 · Mass. Hist. Soc., Adams MSS · N. Yorks. CRO, Wyvill MSS · PRO, Treasury solicitor's papers

Likenesses A. Pozzi, engraving, 1752 (after a drawing), Harvard TC · Canaletto, portrait (*Old Walton Bridge*) · portrait, repro. in Disney, *Memoirs of Thomas Brand-Hollis*, frontispiece

Hollister, Dennis (d. 1676), Quaker leader, lived in Bristol, where he owned a prosperous grocery business in the High Street. Married to Bridget Popley (d. 13 Oct 1671), he had one son and five daughters, the eldest of whom, Hannah, married Thomas Callowhill and became the mother of William *Penn's second wife, also Hannah. Both before and after their 1699 return from Philadelphia, Hollister's granddaughter and Penn lived on the Hollister family estate.

A member of the Bristol city council in 1645, Hollister sided with parliament during the civil wars, serving as a militia commissioner in 1648 and 1659. Significant because of his radical politics and religious activism in seventeenth-century Bristol, Hollister was a founding member, in 1640, and elder of the Baptist Broadmead Church of Christ. His involvement in sectarian politics resulted in an invitation to sit for Bristol in Cromwell's nominated parliament, which convened on 4 July 1653. On 14 July Hollister was elected to the council of state and served sporadically for three months. Major-General Thomas Harrison and Sir Henry Vane, high steward of Bristol in 1650, may have been instrumental in securing his appointment as an admiralty and navy commissioner. During the nominated assembly's debate to abolish the court of chancery, Hollister spoke passionately in favour of the motion. He was among the radical MPs who proposed the abolition of tithes and considered discontinuing the universities, which they regarded as inapt for producing spiritual ministers.

While in London, Hollister became discontented with Cromwellian politics and enamoured of Quaker principles. When he returned to Bristol, he alienated his brethren after saying scripture blinded souls, and that the source of truth was, the central Quaker tenet, the inner light of Christ. After the preachers John Audland and John Camm visited the city in 1654, Quakers, including the large number of former Baptists who followed Hollister, began to meet on his property, the former Dominican friary.

Hollister was critical of the pro-royalist sympathizers in Bristol who, despite Commonwealth legislation, openly participated in local affairs. In the July 1654 parliamentary election, the 'godly' party's candidates lost to two pro-royalists more disposed to the traditional interests of the maritime community. Hollister's contention that the 'Instrument of government' had been violated prompted secretary of state John Thurloe to investigate the election, as well as local officials' complaints regarding the growing number of Quakers.

Hollister and four Bristol Quakers, including captains George Bishop and Edward Pyott, documented the violence that had accompanied the introduction of the Quaker movement. *The Cry of Blood* (1656) catalogues their grievances against certain ministers and magistrates they regarded as hypocrites to the spiritual, political, and legal issues that had necessitated the civil wars. Like other radical literature of the period, the tract infuses the spiritual within the literal, and anxiously defends beliefs that were tolerated after the dismantling of the Anglican church. Hollister's 1656 *The Skirts of the Whore Discovered* and his 1658 *Harlot's Vail Removed*, prompted by a letter delivered to him by three members of the Broadmead congregation, are didactic polemics aimed at the Baptists' censuring of Quaker principles and practices.

In January 1661 sixty-five persons were taken from a meeting at Hollister's. Because of his social standing Hollister and his *The Cry of Blood* co-author, George Bishop, had been released until they commented they 'might as well think to hinder the sun from shining, or the tide from flowing' than to stop meeting (Besse, 1.42). In the face of the prohibition of nonconformity included in the Clarendon code and the 1662 Quaker Act, Hollister continued in a position of leadership among Bristol Quakers, safeguarding Fox from arrest during his 1662 visit, planning the building of a meeting-house on the north side of the River Avon, and, after Bishop's death, continuing the account of Quaker 'sufferings' in New England, which drew the attention of the king.

Hollister died in Bristol on 13 July 1676. He owned considerable property in and outside the city, and chose four Quakers to oversee the execution of his will, which included bequests for Fox and several brethren.

MARYANN S. FEOLA

Sources R. Hayden, ed., *The records of a church in Christ in Bristol, 1640–1687*, Bristol RS, 27 (1974) · R. Mortimer, ed., *Minute book of the men's meeting of the Society of Friends in Bristol*, Bristol RS, 26 (1971) · A. Woolrych, *Commonwealth to protectorate* (1982) · J. Besse, *A collection of the sufferings of the people called Quakers*, 1 (1753) · Greaves & Zaller, *BDBR*, vol. 2 · 'Dictionary of Quaker biography', RS Friends, Lond. [card index], fol. H · H. E. Nott and E. Ralph, eds., *The deposition books of Bristol*, 2, Bristol RS, 13 (1948) · A. B. Beavan, *Bristol lists, municipal and miscellaneous* (1899) · PRO, PROB 11/351, sig. 91, fols. 292–6

Wealth at death substantial property in Bristol and London; much cash: will, PRO, PROB 11/351, sig. 91

Hollond [*née* Teed], **Ellen Julia** (1822–1884), salon hostess, philanthropist, and author, was born at Madras on 28 September 1822, only child of the lawyer Thomas Teed (1797–1843) and his Scottish wife, Julia Jane Jordan (1800–1866), afterwards Lushington. Sent to England at an early age, she was later joined by her parents, who in 1835 bought Stanmore Hall at Great Stanmore, Middlesex. On 18 March 1840 she married at Great Stanmore **Robert Hollond** (1808–1877), Liberal MP for Hastings.

Of an Anglo-Indian background like herself, Robert Hollond was born in London on 5 January 1808, fourth son of William Hollond (d. 1836), a wealthy Bengal civil servant, and his wife, Harriet Pope. He graduated from Corpus Christi College, Cambridge, in 1831 and was called to the bar at Lincoln's Inn in 1834, but became absorbed by aeronautics and financed the *Great Nassau* balloon voyage from London to Weilburg on 7–8 November 1836; undertaken with Charles Green and Thomas Monck Mason, this was logged by himself at the time, described scientifically in Mason's *Aeronautica* (1838) and more flippantly in R. H. Barham's *Ingoldsby Legends* (1840), and celebrated in a painting by John Hollins at the National Portrait Gallery. In 1837 Hollond was elected to parliament as a 'Reformer, pledged to support the ballot'. During his fifteen years there he made only one speech (on balloon-conveyed projectiles) and uttered some sentences of protest when the cleanliness of Hastings was impugned, but both he and his wife became known as unsparing benefactors to local and national causes, including the welfare of children.

The Hollonds made a handsome pair, he dark and aristocratic in appearance, she tender-looking, with glossy brown hair and splendid large blue eyes. They resided chiefly at 63 Portland Place and counted W. M. Thackeray among their intimates, but after the revolution of 1848 they wintered increasingly in Paris, in the rue Basse-du-Rempart and later in the rue d'Astorg. Among their earliest French friends was Ary Scheffer, who painted a graceful portrait of Ellen (1852) and used her as a model for a copy (1854) of his *St Augustine and St Monica*; both pictures are in the National Gallery. Before the *coup d'état* of December 1851 Ellen Hollond had started to host gatherings of democratic figures such as Odilon Barrot and Charles de Rémusat who, together with other eminent if disparate representatives of the 'ligue libérale', including Prévost-Paradol, Lanfrey, Mignet, Laboulaye, Dufaure, and the Catholic but Stanmore-born comte de Montalembert, later formed in her salon a tacit opposition to Napoleon III, the common ground of which, according to her obituarist Edmond de Pressensé, was 'love of freedom and hatred of empire'.

Another distinguished guest was the philosopher Victor Cousin, who delighted in Ellen Hollond's company at Cannes, where Robert purchased in 1864 the pretty Villa Allegria, with a magnificent sea view, to enjoy the winter seasons and rest Mrs Hollond's weak constitution. There too she secured her greatest prize, Prosper Mérimée. Though at first suspicious of this bluestocking with Britannic prejudices, he came to respect her mind and warmly admired her books. The first two of these had appeared anonymously in Paris. In *Channing: sa vie et ses oeuvres* (1857) she presented the views of the Unitarian philosopher with an ecumenical intent seen also in the chatty but charming *La vie de village en Angleterre, ou, Souvenirs d'un exilé* (1862), which eulogized various aspects of protestant English life, including cricket. Under her own name she published in London in 1864 *A Lady's Journal of her Travels in Egypt and Nubia*, and in Paris in 1870 *Les Quakers*, a short but well-written plea for religious tolerance.

Meanwhile Robert Hollond, whose great wealth permitted the childless couple to commute among five desirable addresses, to buy paintings including a Boucher, and to entertain on an unusually grand scale, was perplexed by the conversation in his drawing-room and kept to himself and his whisky. He is said to have had little French; where English could be spoken, participation was easier. This would have been so in the quiet, Anglophile Paris home of the émigré Russian historian Nikolay Turgenev, where the Hollonds met the novelist Ivan Turgenev, or even in the more famous salon of Julius and Mary Mohl, which Mrs Hollond had to some extent been emulating. Mary Mohl herself was quite attached to her, but felt uncomfortable at her receptions as French politics always predominated. Less sympathetic critics attacked Mrs Hollond's taste for the new and fashionable, saying that she used her beauty and charm to attract anyone with talent or a name. It is true that, unlike Mary Mohl, she was an informed listener rather than a compelling conversationalist, but she doubtless preferred brilliant minds to speak to each other rather than to herself. Moreover, her generosity was never in question, and received its best practical expression in the home that she founded for English nurses at Cannes.

In 1877 Robert Hollond was taken ill while they were staying at the Turgenevs' at 97 rue de Lille, Paris, and he died there on 26 December; he was buried at Great Stanmore on 3 January 1878 in the imposing family mausoleum that he had built in the ruins of the old church. He left most of his estate of some £350,000 to or for the lifetime use of his widow, including properties in Devon and the south of France, the lease of 1 Upper Berkeley Street, and Stanmore Hall, which he had acquired in 1847. In broken health and aged beyond her years, Ellen Hollond retained Villa Allegria but spent the warmer months at Wonham in Devon or at Stanmore Hall, where she died from pneumonia on 29 November 1884; she was buried at Great Stanmore on 5 December. From her estate of some £60,000 she left benefactions for this parish which she loved and for her dozen servants, as well as £5000 to continue her work of providing English nurses for invalids in France.

PATRICK WADDINGTON

Sources E. de Pressensé, 'Mme Robert Holland', *Journal des Débats* (6 Dec 1884) · P. Mérimée, *Correspondance générale*, ed. M. Parturier, P. Josserand, and J. Mallion, 17 vols. (Paris, 1941–64) · E. Grenier, *Souvenirs littéraires* (1894) · *Hansard 3* (1847), 93.933–5; (1851), 117.1066, 1458 · M. C. M. Simpson, *Letters and recollections of Julius and Mary Mohl* (1887) · N. W. Senior, *Journals kept in France and Italy from 1848 to 1852*, ed. M. C. M. Simpson (1871) · N. W. Senior, *Conversations with M. Thiers, M. Guizot, and other distinguished persons*, ed. M. C. M. Simpson, 2 vols. (1878) · N. W. Senior, *Conversations with distinguished persons during the Second Empire from 1860 to 1863*, ed. M. C. M. Simpson, 2 vols. (1880) · M. Kolb, *Ary Scheffer et son temps* (1937) · *The letters and private papers of William Makepeace Thackeray*, ed. G. N. Ray, 4 vols. (1945–6) · M. E. G. Duff, *Notes from a diary, 1851–1872*, 2 vols. (1897) · M. E. G. Duff, *Notes from a diary, 1873–1881*, 2 vols. (1898–9) · WWBMP · *Literaturnoye Nasledstvo*, 76 (1967) · C. de Rémusat, *Mémoires de ma vie*, ed. C. H. Pouthas (1958–62) · m. cert. · d. cert. · Boase, *Mod. Eng. biog.* · parish records (burial), Great Stanmore, Middlesex, 5 Dec 1884 · Venn, *Alum. Cant.* [Robert Hollond] · IGI [Robert Hollond]

Likenesses A. Scheffer, portrait, 1852, National Gallery, London · L. Haghe, lithograph (aged nineteen), BM, NPG · J. Holling, group portrait, oils (Robert Hollond; *A consultation prior to the aerial voyage to Weilburg, 1836*), NPG · J. H. Robinson, engraving (Robert Hollond; after Holling), NPG

Wealth at death £60,302 14s. 3d.: probate, 5 Jan 1885, CGPLA Eng. & Wales · under £350,000—Robert Hollond: probate, 24 Jan 1878, CGPLA Eng. & Wales

Hollond [Holland], **John** (*fl. c.*1624–*c.*1661), naval official, was from an obscure background, but may have originally come from London or the surrounding areas. He first entered the navy about 1624 in the humble capacity of a clerk at Chatham. In 1626 and again in 1627 he was recommended, unsuccessfully, for a purser's place and also failed to obtain the position of clerk of the check at Portsmouth, which would have amounted to a significant promotion. The position went to his long-term rival, John Brooke, much to Hollond's annoyance. Hollond was argumentative but undoubtedly competent and by 1635 had risen to become paymaster of the navy, probably through the patronage of Kenrick Edisbury, surveyor of the navy. In this position he was directly responsible to the navy treasurer and wielded considerable influence, which he used to secure the dismissal and short-term imprisonment of Brooke for malpractice.

In 1636 the earl of Northumberland, the admiral of the ship money fleet, presented a document to Charles I containing thirteen articles outlining current abuses in the navy. Hollond was implicated for his refusal to pay the wages of men transferred from one ship to another unless they could produce tickets as proof of service. These tickets often proved impossible to obtain, and many seamen were defrauded of legitimate wages. He had also allegedly accepted gratuities for payment on such tickets. He was, however, found guilty only of the offence of charging 2s. in the pound for the practice of stopping slops money (for clothing) out of the seamen's wages, his defence being that this had been common practice for the previous thirty years. He was ordered to stop the practice and it appears that no further action was taken.

In his manuscript entitled 'A discourse of the navy' of 1638 (published in 1896) Hollond examined in detail, and in a rough style, the navy's endemic material abuses, inefficiencies, and corruption. The emphasis of the 'Discourse' was on the administration of wages, victuals, stores, and personnel. There is no definite reference to Hollond between the publication of the 'Discourse' and the defection of the fleet to parliament in 1642, but he was an active partner in the timber trade and was probably the same John Hollond who sold timber to the navy in 1639. In 1642 he became one of parliament's six professional navy commissioners, at a salary of £100 p.a. He was particularly active as a commissioner in this early period of hostilities when administration at the senior level was being radically reorganized, but his abrasiveness soon brought him into conflict with the other commissioners.

In February 1644 Hollond was nominated as a commissioner for the sale of prize goods, another potentially lucrative position, but this was balanced by the loss of his place as a navy commissioner in late 1645. He was said to have absented himself from this post for fourteen months in 1644–5, while he, in turn, alleged that differences with colleagues obliged him to stay away from his duties, and it seems impossible to establish the truth of the matter. One of the main causes of friction was the hire (or freight) by parliament of vessels for service in the navy, owned or part owned by members of the navy's administration. The freight rate established after the outbreak of hostilities of £3 15s. 6d. per man per month (allowing thirty men per hundred tons) was more complicated than the previous arrangement of a set amount per ton, and was particularly susceptible to exploitation. A significant number of vessels owned by naval administrators and officers (up to and including the earl of Warwick, lord admiral) received freight and it was to become a focus of Hollond's criticism of the navy commissioners. He named Giles Green, chairman of the navy committee, as the chief culprit in this abuse, though navy commissioners such as Samuel Vassall, Richard Crandley, and Alexander Bence also owned shares in vessels hired by the state. The sums involved can best be judged by the freight record of the *Mayflower*, the owners of which (including Vassall) received £22,947 19s. 2d. over a three-year period. While it was only natural that those with a maritime background should form the nucleus of the navy commissioners it would also appear that they used their positions to unfair advantage. Hollond's replacement, Thomas Smith, was yet another shipowner whose vessels received freight.

Although this marked a temporary end to Hollond's administrative career he returned to naval affairs following the execution of the king and the reorganization of naval administration. In January 1649 he was appointed to the committee of merchants established to remodel the navy and the customs, and in February as navy surveyor in place of Sir William Batten, and again as a commissioner. He resigned in December 1652 following charges against him by his colleagues, which he vigorously denied, and in the wake of a clash with the powerful Pett clan. He later denounced the committee of merchants, asserting that the 'welfare of the English navy was of no more concern to them than was the navy of the great Turk, unless it were to settle a brother and a friend in two or three of the best places thereof' (Capp, 50), though his criticisms cannot be taken at face value. Following his departure from office he moved from his official residence at Tower Hill to Deptford and resumed his timber trade.

Hollond did not completely disappear from public life for in August 1654 he was appointed one of the commissioners to resolve problems in the allocation of land among the adventurers for Ireland. He appears to have invested in the adventure himself on such a scale as to secure an allocation of 2666 acres in King's county. Alongside these duties he maintained his interest in the timber trade and was engaged in the preparation of his second 'Discourse'. Although written largely before 1658 it finally appeared with a dedication to the duke of York (perhaps with an eye to future employment), which dates it to about 1661. (Again, it remained unpublished until 1896.) The second 'Discourse' attracted some attention. Longer, more polished, and more systematic than the first, it covered a range of new topics, particularly with regard to victualling. It was highly regarded by Pepys, who used it as a source for his ideas on naval administration, and by Sir William Penn. In November 1660 Hollond's proposals to allow for the immediate discharge of the Commonwealth fleet, hampered by lack of ready money, were considered by the Admiralty but not implemented. He appears to have died shortly afterwards, though his widow may have survived until 1692, residing at Deptford where two of Hollond's daughters are recorded as having died, Mabel in 1666 and Mary in 1670.

Hollond had sought to pursue his dual callings as state servant and businessman without overt political commitments, and avoiding conflicts of interest. In the second 'Discourse' he stood upon his professional integrity, noting that he had avoided supplying timber to the navy while acting as a commissioner. Instead he denounced profiteering through contracts for victuals and ships and, though some comments in the second 'Discourse' targeted the 'godly', thus playing to a Restoration audience, the focus of Hollond's criticisms remained the structures which bred corruption within the administration of the navy.   ROY McCAUGHEY

Sources *Two discourses of the navy, 1638 and 1659, by John Holland*, ed. J. R. Tanner, Navy Records Society, 7 (1896) · *The naval tracts of Sir William Monson*, ed. M. Oppenheim, 5 vols., Navy RS, 22–3, 43, 45, 47 (1902–14) · M. Oppenheim, *A history of the administration of the Royal Navy* (1896) · A. Burrell, *The humble remonstrance of Andrewes Burrell for a reformation of England's navy* (1646) · *JHC* · *CSP dom.* · C. H. Firth and R. S. Rait, eds., *Acts and ordinances of the interregnum, 1642–1660*, 3 vols. (1911) · admiralty bill books, PRO · Bodl. Oxf., MS Rawl. A. 220 · R. McCaughey, 'The English navy, politics and administration, *c.*1640–1649', PhD diss., University of Ulster, 1983 · Pepys, *Diary* · G. E. Aylmer, *The king's servants: the civil service of Charles I, 1625–1642*, rev. edn (1974) · K. R. Andrews, *Ships, money and politics* (1991) · B. Capp, *Cromwell's navy: the fleet and the English revolution, 1648–1660* (1989) · K. S. Bottigheimer, *English money and Irish land* (1971) · *CSP Ire., 1642–59* · *DNB*

Marjorie Hollond (1895–1977), by Elliott & Fry

Hollond [*née* Tappan], **Marjorie** (1895–1977), economist and academic administrator, was born in New York city, USA, on 31 October 1895, the elder daughter of Herman Tappan of Gloucester, Massachusetts, and his wife, Beatrice, *née* Haslitt. She was educated at Bryn Mawr College, Pennsylvania, from 1911 to 1915. After completing her doctoral degree at Columbia University, she came to England. She worked at the Galton Laboratory at University College, London, 1920–22, and lectured part-time at the London School of Economics, 1921–6. In 1923 she was appointed director of studies in economics at both Newnham and Girton colleges, Cambridge. She held the post at Newnham for ten years; at Girton she remained director of studies in economics until her retirement in 1963. In 1926 she was appointed university lecturer in economics, under new statutes that established the faculty structure at Cambridge, although at this time women were still barred from university membership and degrees. On 7 September 1929 she married Henry Arthur Hollond (1884–1974), fellow of Trinity College, Cambridge, and reader of English law; he had himself opposed the admission of women to university membership and degrees earlier in the decade. He later became Rouse Ball professor of English law and vice-master of Trinity College. They had no children.

During the war years Marjorie Hollond held appointments at the Treasury, the Ministry of Economic Warfare, and the Ministry of Agriculture and Fisheries, and served for four months with the United Nations mission at a food and agriculture conference in Washington in 1943. On her return to Girton in 1946, she was appointed bursar, a post that she held until retirement. When women were admitted to degrees and membership of Cambridge University in 1948, the status of their colleges also altered, becoming that of colleges of the university. This entailed not only the adjustment of their account procedures to harmonize them with university practice but also the rewriting of the college statutes. As bursar, Hollond was responsible not only for the necessary adjustment of accounting procedures but also for the college's investments on which its future expansion depended. The drafting of the 1954 college statutes owes much to her work and the assistance on legal matters given by her husband. The university recognized her financial talent and she was appointed to the financial board in 1951, remaining a member until 1962. She worked on many subcommittees, notably the investment subcommittee and on the syndicate examining the financial relationship between the university and the colleges. Her published work consisted of articles and reviews in academic journals and she was the author of reports for college, university, and government purposes.

As an American in Cambridge in the 1920s Hollond made a striking impact—a tall, slim, and elegant figure lecturing in a variety of stylish hats. She was hardworking, chain-smoking with a long, beautiful cigarette holder, filled with nervous energy, and passionate, and she could infuriate people with her lack of punctuality and exaggerated opinions. An early enthusiasm for riding was later transformed into a passion for fast cars. A loyal and caring friend, she was also known for acts of great kindness. She had a special interest in the history and art of the Middle East and Asia, especially Russia and China, travelling widely and making many friends throughout the world. Her rooms in college and later her house, which she purchased without ever having set foot in it, were exquisitely furnished with fine antiques collected over her lifetime. She died at home at the Stone House, Madingley Road, Cambridge, on 30 January 1977, and was cremated at Cambridge crematorium; her ashes were scattered in Girton College.

RITA McWILLIAMS TULLBERG

Sources K. T. Butler and H. I. McMorran, eds., *Girton College register, 1869–1946* (1948), 655 · *The Times* (1 Feb 1977) · private information (2004)
Archives Girton Cam., personal corresp., lecture notes, diaries, publications, and reviews, papers from period at the Ministry of Agriculture and Fisheries, and photographs. | Bodl. Oxf., Henry Arthur Hollond MSS
Likenesses Elliott & Fry, photograph, Girton Cam. [*see illus.*] · photographs, Girton Cam.
Wealth at death £127,454: probate, 23 March 1977, *CGPLA Eng. & Wales*

Hollond, Robert (1808–1877). *See under* Hollond, Ellen Julia (1822–1884).

Holloway, Benjamin (1690/91–1759), religious controversialist and Church of England clergyman, was born at Stony Stratford, Buckinghamshire, the son of Joseph Holloway (d. c.1720), a maltster. Holloway was educated under Dr Thomas Knipe at Westminster School, where he was a bishop's boy, and matriculated from St John's College, Cambridge, on 4 February 1708, aged seventeen. In 1713 he graduated LLB and on 5 July was ordained deacon by William Wake, bishop of Lincoln. He was appointed vicar of Willington and of Renhold, both in Bedfordshire, and was ordained priest on 27 May 1716. By this time Holloway had made the acquaintance of John Woodward. In 1715 he began work on a translation from Latin into English of a reply to Elias Camerarius, who had criticized Woodward's ideas about the geological history of the earth. From Bedford, where he was also acting as tutor to a noble family, Holloway wrote to Woodward on 6 July 1723 about a visit that he had made to the fuller's-earth pits at Wavendon, near Woburn. In this letter, which was subsequently published in the *Philosophical Transactions*, he provided evidence for Woodward's theories concerning the laying down of rocks and minerals in strata. With the support of Sir Hans Sloane, he was elected a fellow of the Royal Society on 30 November 1723.

Holloway's translation of Woodward's answer to Camerarius was published as *The Natural History of the Earth* in 1726. In this volume, which was translated into French by Jean Pierre Niceron in 1735 and into Italian in 1739, he also printed several of Woodward's letters and papers, concerning ancient mythology, biblical history, and the importance of the blood for sustaining life. On 17 March

1726 Holloway was presented by the crown to the second portion of the rectory of Waddesdon, Buckinghamshire, which he held together with the rectory of Middleton Stoney, Oxfordshire, where he had taken up residence in 1725. He resigned the living of Waddesdon on his preferment by Charles Spencer, third duke of Marlborough, to the rectory of Bladon in March 1736. In 1739 he handed the care of Bladon on to one of his sons, also called Benjamin Holloway.

From Middleton Stoney, Holloway composed an account of the pits at Headington, near Oxford, which he sent to the Royal Society in 1729, but he was prevented from attending the society's meetings by the distance that he lived from London. In the early 1730s he wrote annotations to Ecclesiastes 'in which there is a good deal that is Philosophical' (BL, Sloane MS 4051, fols. 105–6) and tried unsuccessfully to persuade Sloane to publish parts of them in the *Philosophical Transactions*. By this time Holloway had begun to espouse some of the views of John Hutchinson about the interpretation of the Hebrew Bible and its implications for an understanding of nature. In particular, he now distrusted the use made by many divines of the Septuagint (the Greek Old Testament). In 1727 Holloway had published a work of controversial divinity, *An after-Commendation of the New-Lutheran's Answer*, and during the following decade he continued to write critically about contemporary theology. *The Commemorative Sacrifice*, a sermon that he preached at Woodstock on 8 October 1736, was based on his unpublished criticisms of Benjamin Hoadley, to whom he also addressed *Some Remarks* in 1741. *The Nullity of Repentance without Faith* (1739), which published three of his sermons, replied to the ideas of the deist Thomas Chubb. In a supplement to this work, Holloway deployed some of the ideas of Hutchinson and his followers about the significance of figurative language in the Old Testament, in particular suggesting that Melchizedek was a manifestation of Christ before the incarnation. Unable to print it at Oxford because of the opposition of the vice-chancellor, Theophilus Leigh, Holloway published *The True Doctrine of Repentance Vindicated* ([1739]) in London. Towards the end of 1744 he lived in the house of John Spencer, Marlborough's younger brother, acting as tutor to Spencer's son, John, afterwards first Earl Spencer. He became increasingly involved in the academic controversies that were developing over Hutchinson's theories, criticizing Thomas Hunt, Laudian professor of Arabic at Oxford, and his allies, who argued that knowledge of Arabic might help to explain the true meaning of obscure terms in the Old Testament. In 1750 his *Marginal Animadversions on Mr. Costard's Two Late Dissertations* appeared, followed in 1751 by *Remarks on Dr Sharp's Pieces on the Words Elohim and Berith*, to which both Thomas Sharp and George Kalmar replied, and in 1754 by *The Primaevity and Preeminence of the Sacred Hebrew*. Holloway's own version of Hutchinsonian biblical criticism, *Originals Physical and Theological Sacred and Profane*, was composed during the 1740s with the encouragement of Duncan Forbes and published in two volumes in 1751, with a dedication to John

Carteret, second Earl Granville, to whose mother Holloway had been chaplain in the 1720s. This work was largely concerned with the exposition of the meaning of the Hebrew text of Genesis, as was *Letter and Spirit* (1753), in which Holloway again relied on Hutchinsonian principles for the interpretation of the roots from which Hebrew words were derived. The reflections on the allegorical and spiritual interpretation of scripture that Holloway included in *Letter and Spirit* were a response to the work of the French critic Charles François Houbigant.

Holloway's links with the Hutchinsonians and their ideas, which were generally hostile to contemporary Judaism, may also help to explain his opposition to the Jewish Naturalization Act. Because of this, he voted against the whig candidate supported by his patron, the duke of Marlborough, at the Oxfordshire election in 1754. By this time, however, Holloway was in poor health and he died at Middleton Stoney on 10 April 1759. He was buried at the church there on 13 April. George Horne, who had been encouraged by Holloway during his studies for ordination, afterwards sorted through Holloway's unpublished papers and remarked on 'the example of his indefatigable industry & primitive devotion' (CUL, Add. MS 8134, A/2, p. 90).   SCOTT MANDELBROTE

Sources Bodl. Oxf., MS Gough Wales 8, fols. 29–48 · J. Woodward, *The natural history of the earth*, ed. B. Holloway (1726) · J. M. Levine, *Dr Woodward's shield: history, science, and satire in Augustan England* (1977) · CUL, Add. MS 8134, A/2 · BL, Sloane MS 4047, fols. 108–109; 4050, fols. 294–295; 4051, fols. 105–106; 4052, fols. 42–43, 111–112 · letterbooks, RS, vol. 16, fols. 509–12; vol. 22, fol. 443 · B. Holloway, *Originals physical and theological sacred and profane*, 2 vols. (1751) · G. Horne, *Works*, ed. W. Jones, 4 vols. (1831), vol. 1, pp. xlii–xliv · J. E. B. Mayor, ed., *Admissions to the College of St John the Evangelist in the University of Cambridge*, pts 1–2: *Jan 1629/30 – July 1715* (1882–93), pt 2, p. 187 · *Old Westminsters*, 1.472 · T. W. Perry, *Public opinion, propaganda, and politics in eighteenth-century England* (1962), 169

Archives BL, letters, MSS Sloane 4047, 4050–4052 · Bodl. Oxf., letters, Gough Wales MS 8, Eng. Lett. d. 122 · RS, MSS, letters

Wealth at death over £25: will, PRO, PROB 11/848, sig. 268

Holloway, Sir Charles (1749–1827), army officer, was born on 17 April 1749; nothing is known of his parents. On 7 February 1764 he entered the drawing room of the Board of Ordnance at the Tower of London and in 1773 he went to Portsmouth to assist the commanding royal engineer with the plans of the new fortifications. There, on 17 January 1776, he was commissioned second lieutenant of engineers, and in 1777 he was sent to Gibraltar. When the great siege began in 1779, the chief engineer, Colonel (later Sir) William Green (1725–1811), appointed Holloway his staff officer, and on Green's promotion to brigadier in 1781, his brigade major. Holloway's diaries, of which there is a partial transcript among the Conolly papers at Chatham, describe the siege and his role in it. Having been promoted first lieutenant on 1 January 1783, he was wounded by a shell splinter three days later, and in June, after Gibraltar's defence had been successfully concluded, he was publicly thanked by the governor, General Sir George Augustus Eliott.

On 1 October 1784 Holloway joined Major-General William Roy and for three years assisted him in his survey triangulations in Kent. He married, on 15 December 1785, Helen Mary (d. 11 April 1798), daughter of his former commanding officer General Sir William Green; they had six children. From 1788 onwards Holloway superintended fortification work at Landguard and Yarmouth, Gravesend and Tilbury, and Woolwich. On 16 January 1793 he was promoted captain-lieutenant and, after succeeding as commanding engineer Thames division, was promoted captain on 31 December 1795. His company of artificers was roughly handled when a riot broke out among the artillerymen at Woolwich in May 1797.

In October 1798 Holloway was chosen as second in command, with the local rank of major, of a military mission under Brigadier-General G. F. Koehler to assist the Turks in repelling the French invasion of Egypt. After arriving at Constantinople in March 1799, Holloway was sent to report on the Dardanelles fortifications. In June 1800 he went with the mission to Jaffa in Syria where the Ottoman army was regrouping after being repulsed from Egypt. News of the arrival in the eastern Mediterranean of a British army under General Sir Ralph Abercromby—coincidental with the death from plague of General Koehler on 29 December 1800—meant that the urgent task of ensuring that the Turks returned to Egypt in support of Abercromby's expedition now fell to Holloway. Despite the ravages of the plague, the lack of supplies, and the chronic indiscipline of the Ottoman army, Holloway spurred his hosts forward, and in March 1801, organized in three divisions as he had suggested, the army began its slow advance from Gaza across the desert. On 16 May the Turks encountered the French under General Belliard at al-Khanka, outside Cairo. Holloway, knowing the British army on the Nile was approaching, had wished the Turks to avoid combat, but the French were unable to defeat the masses of horsemen swirling about them and after seven hours they withdrew. The surrender of the French in Egypt, first in Cairo and then Alexandria, followed within months.

Although in his dispatches Holloway, who on 1 January 1801 was promoted major with the local rank of lieutenant-colonel, modestly played down his own contribution, the ambassador in Constantinople, Lord Elgin, informed the government that the successful advance of the Turks, and their victory at al-Khanka, were due to Holloway's influence. On his return to England Holloway received a knighthood (2 February 1803) to add to the five pelisses of honour and a gold medal already awarded him by the Turks.

In March 1803 Holloway was appointed commanding royal engineer (CRE) at Cork where, to secure the defences of the harbour, he constructed a large new fort on Spike Island. On 20 July 1804 he was promoted lieutenant-colonel and a year later was one of a committee of military engineers appointed to recommend a system of defence for Ireland. He returned to Gibraltar as CRE in 1807. He reported on the defences of Cadiz, Algeciras, and Ceuta in 1809, and in 1810, with Spanish agreement, he demolished by mines the old forts and lines to the north of the neutral ground of the Gibraltar isthmus to prevent their use by the French. In October 1813 one of the recurrent outbreaks of fever at Gibraltar killed Holloway's son Charles, an artillery lieutenant, and a daughter, Helen Smith, wife of an officer in the garrison. Holloway was promoted colonel on 1 May 1811 and major-general on 4 June 1814, and in September 1817 he left Gibraltar for England. He retired by sale of his commission on 17 July 1824 and died at his home at Stoke Cottage, Stoke Damerel, Devonport, Devon, on 4 January 1827. His will instructed that he be buried near his daughter Augusta Jane in Exeter Cathedral.

Holloway's eldest son, **William Cuthbert Elphinstone-Holloway** (1787–1850), was born on 1 May 1787 and, after attending the Royal Military Academy, Woolwich, joined the Royal Engineers as a second lieutenant on 1 January 1804. He served with his father at Cork before spending the year of 1808 with the British garrison on Madeira. In 1810, having been employed in the eastern military district in England, he left for the Peninsular War. His conduct as a second captain at the capture of Badajoz, during which he was severely wounded, was mentioned in Wellington's dispatch of 27 March 1812 (*LondG*, 1812, 702). He was awarded a wound pension, and after further duties in Britain he was posted to the Cape of Good Hope in 1818, served in the Cape Frontier War of 1819, and conducted military surveys before returning home in 1831. He took from his wife, Amelia (*d.* 12 July 1874), daughter of Captain Thomas Elphinstone RN, the additional surname of Elphinstone in February 1825. He was made a companion of the Bath on 26 September 1831. His subsequent duties in Ireland were followed by promotion to colonel on 23 November 1841 and an appointment as CRE in Canada between 1843 and 1849. He died as CRE western district at Plymouth Citadel, Devon, on 4 September 1850, and was buried in Plymouth cemetery.

R. H. VETCH, *rev.* ALASTAIR W. MASSIE

Sources T. W. J. Connolly, 'Notitia historica of the corps of royal engineers', *c.*1860, Royal Engineers' Library, Chatham · J. Philippart, ed., *The royal military calendar*, 3rd edn, 5 vols. (1820) · W. Porter, *History of the corps of royal engineers*, 1 (1889) · 'The British military mission in Egypt, 1798–1802', *Royal Engineers Journal*, new ser., 14 (1911), 91–102, 149–62 · W. Wittman, *Travels in Turkey, Asia Minor, Syria, and across the desert in Egypt* (1803) · T. W. J. Connolly, *History of the royal sappers and miners*, 2nd edn, 2 vols. (1857) · P. Mackesy, *British victory in Egypt, 1801: the end of Napoleon's conquest* (1995) · R. T. Wilson, *History of the British expedition to Egypt* (1802) · will, PRO, PROB 11/1724, 237 · E. W. C. Sandes, *The royal engineers in Egypt and the Sudan* (1937) · R. F. Edwards, ed., *Roll of officers of the corps of royal engineers from 1660 to 1898* (1898)
Likenesses J. S. Copley, oils, 1783, Guildhall Art Gallery, London
Wealth at death £2800 in taxable cash legacies; also home, effects, and some annuities: PRO, death duty registers, IR 26/1129, 274; will, PRO, PROB 11/1724, 237

Holloway, Sir Henry (1857–1923), builder, was born on 5 August 1857 at Littleton, West Lavington, Wiltshire, the fourth of the five sons of Thomas Holloway, jobbing builder and bricklayer, of West Lavington, and his wife, Elizabeth Orchard. After the family moved to London, Holloway went to a church school in Pimlico. For a short time he worked for a firm of timber merchants, but in 1876 he, his father, and three brothers joined Holloway's

eldest brother, James, who had set up his own building and contracting business in Wandsworth Road in 1875. Holloway was the office manager. On 16 February 1881 he married Annie Jane, eldest daughter of John Gollop of Clapham. They had seven children. In 1882 he and his older brother, (Henry) Thomas (1853–1914), left the firm after James had refused to make them partners, and started their own company, Holloway Brothers, in Battersea. After James's premature death in 1889, Henry and Thomas took over his business, and their father and other two brothers joined Holloway Brothers.

The business became very successful very rapidly. The first important contract came in 1891 for the new Battersea Polytechnic, designed by E. W. Mountford in the Flemish Renaissance style. After the company won the contract for the new naval barracks at Chatham in 1897 contracts for the construction of large public buildings poured in. Among these were the Admiralty building in Horse Guards Parade (1898), the Central Criminal Court, the Old Bailey (1900–7), the United Universities Club, Pall Mall (1905–6), and the new General Post Office (1907–10), an early example of the use of reinforced concrete in a major public building in London. Whiteleys store in Bayswater (1908–12) was one of the first buildings to be built with a steel frame, allowing much larger display windows. Holloways also won several important housing contracts, including a housing scheme for Wandsworth borough council at Earlsfield, and the building of a garden city at Rosyth for the Admiralty.

In 1900 the expanding business moved to a larger site at Victoria Wharf, Belvedere Road, on the south bank of the Thames. This meant that stone, bricks, and other materials could be landed directly onto the wharf, and timber was shipped directly from Scandinavia. New joinery and stonemasonry works were built, and it was the first London firm of builders to use electricity to drive its machinery. In 1902 Holloway Brothers (London) Ltd was registered as a private limited company, with Henry and Thomas Holloway as governing directors. Also in 1902 they opened a West End branch at 43 South Audley Street to provide craftsmen to decorate houses in Mayfair. This later became a leading interior decorator for large buildings.

From 1906 Holloway Brothers began to take on civil engineering contracts. The first project was to build a covered reservoir in reinforced concrete for the Luton Water Company. The company went on to win dock contracts, such as that for the London docks improvement scheme, starting in 1912, railway contracts, including a new power station for the London and North Western Railway in 1914, and contracts for sea defence works such as the construction of a new sea wall at Rottingdean in 1907–13. Its first major bridge-building contract was in 1914, for a three-span reinforced concrete bridge over the River Esk at Gretna.

Holloway Brothers was forced to move again, in 1915, because London county council wanted the Belvedere Road site for County Hall and managed to get a bill through parliament permitting this. The new site, at

Bridge Wharf on the corner of Vauxhall Bridge and Grosvenor Road, on Millbank, was too small for all the works, and the joinery works had to be moved to Earlsfield, and the masonry works to Nine Elms. A branch office opened in Newcastle in 1917 to handle the growing business in the north-east.

Holloway was knighted in 1917 for his contribution to solving the problem of the shortage of housing for the labour force needed to work in the new wartime factories. David Lloyd George, minister of munitions, approached Holloway, and he undertook to provide the necessary housing within six months. This he did, after touring the country in 1916 as director of housing construction in the labour supply department of the Ministry of Munitions, and putting local architects and builders to work, a brilliant feat of organization.

It was Henry Holloway's drive and organizational ability that had made the company so successful so quickly. He was highly respected by his colleagues, and served as president of the Institute of Builders and of the London Master Builders' Association. A JP for the county of London, Holloway also took an interest in politics, and campaigned for John Moulton (later Baron Moulton), elected Liberal MP for Clapham in 1885, and for Reginald McKenna, who contested Clapham unsuccessfully in 1892. He was a fervent member of the Wesleyan Methodist church (his father had been a local preacher), and supported the temperance movement.

Holloway died at his home, Draxmont, Wimbledon Hill, Surrey, on his birthday, 5 August 1923. He was survived by his wife. His youngest brother, Samuel, succeeded him as chairman of Holloway Brothers (London) Ltd. He was buried at Upper Tooting Wesleyan Church, Balham High Road, London, three days later.

The other member of the family who was to lead the firm was Sir Henry's nephew, **Sir Henry Thomas Holloway** (1876–1951), builder. Born on 29 March 1876, at 3 Tipthorpe Road, Battersea, London, H. T. Holloway was the fifth in the family of eight children of (Henry) Thomas Holloway, co-founder of the company, and his wife, Phebe Jane Holt. Nothing is known about his education but he married Brucine Mildenhall Pimm in 1911. They had two sons.

H. T. Holloway was a director from 1912, and chairman from 1933 until his death. Under his chairmanship the civil engineering side of the business expanded, starting with the new Chelsea Bridge in 1934–7, its first steel bridge. The company also took on a number of civil engineering projects in the Middle East from the 1930s onwards, including the King Ghazi and King Feisal bridges across the Tigris in Baghdad in 1936, and Baghdad railway station in 1946–52.

During the Second World War the company built ordnance depots and factories, hospitals, army camps, and RAF stations. It also built sea forts and floating docks, and its expertise contributed significantly to the success of the Mulberry harbour project. To improve coal supplies, it built opencast coal mines from 1942 onwards in the Dukeries and Newcastle coalfields. Holloway was knighted in 1945 for his contribution to the war effort. After the war, the company was greatly involved in postwar reconstruction, including that of Trafalgar Square, completed in 1948. Holloway was a member of the council of the London Master Builders' Association, a president of the Institute of Builders, and president (1940–46) of the Federation of Civil Engineering Contractors. He served on the joint consultative council of building and civil engineering institutes at the Ministry of Works in 1941–6.

Sir Henry Thomas Holloway died on 18 September 1951 at St Peter's Hospital, Westminster. He was buried in the churchyard of All Saints' Church, West Lavington, Wiltshire. His wife survived him.   ANNE PIMLOTT BAKER

Sources L. T. C. Rolt, *Holloways of Millbank. The first seventy-five years* (1958) • *The Builder*, 125 (1923), 262 • *The Times* (6 Aug 1923) • *The Times* (25 Sept 1951) • *WWW* • C. Whitaker, ed., *Whitaker's Almanack* (1916) • Burke, *Peerage* • *WWBMP* • *CGPLA Eng. & Wales* (1923) • *CGPLA Eng. & Wales* (1952) [Sir Henry Thomas Holloway] • b. cert. • b. cert. [Sir Henry Thomas Holloway] • d. cert. • d. cert. [Sir Henry Thomas Holloway]

Likenesses J. Gunn, portrait (Sir Henry Thomas Holloway), repro. in Rolt, *Holloways of Millbank* • F. O. Salisbury, portrait, repro. in Rolt, *Holloways of Millbank*

Wealth at death £95,502 0s. 3d.: probate, 2 Oct 1923, *CGPLA Eng. & Wales* • £203,491 8s. 2d.—Sir Henry Thomas Holloway: probate, 23 Feb 1952, *CGPLA Eng. & Wales*

Holloway, Sir Henry Thomas (1876–1951). *See under* Holloway, Sir Henry (1857–1923).

Holloway, James [alias John Milward] (d. 1684), conspirator, learned the linen trade as an apprentice to the iconoclast Walter Stephens of Bristol. On 17 September 1677 Holloway married Martha Stevens, possibly a kinswoman of his former master. As an established linen draper and merchant, he saw an opportunity to expand England's linen production when trade with France was embargoed in 1678. He travelled to London in the hope of persuading parliament to establish linen manufactories that would employ the indigent. Although he founded such an establishment in Warwickshire, hiring hundreds, the effort failed because his linen was not competitive with foreign imports. Holloway returned to London in the spring of 1679 to renew his quest for parliamentary backing. On 8 May, Bristol's common council approved his plan to erect a workhouse for 500 spinners from the city's Bridewell prison, but it had second thoughts after Sir John Knight, MP for Bristol, warned that the French embargo would expire in March 1681. About June 1680 Holloway told the earl of Essex about his vision of linen manufactories spread over 40,000 acres, employing 80,000, and providing £200,000 p.a. to royal coffers. Essex sent him to Laurence Hyde, the lord treasurer, who introduced Holloway to Sir Edward Dering; he received money and advice to attend the next parliament. He did so, displaying some of his linen in the speaker's chamber, but members were preoccupied with the succession issue. At the Oxford parliament, the earl of Clarendon and others suggested he draft a bill to implement his plan, which he did, though once more his plans fell victim to the succession struggle.

Throughout this period, political fears had troubled Holloway. Allegations of the Popish Plot prompted him to worry that Englishmen might be enslaved if James, duke of York, became king. Allegations of a Catholic threat continued to trouble him at the time he attended parliament. A member of the whig Horseshoe Club in Bristol, Holloway brooded about the treatment of Stephen College in his trial at Oxford, the controversy surrounding Slingsby Bethel's efforts to empanel pro-whig jurors in London, Charles's desire to recall London's charter, and the disputed election of Dudley North and Peter Rich as sheriffs of London in July 1682.

Shortly after the London election, the Bristol clothier Joseph Tiley told Holloway about Shaftesbury's scheme for an insurrection in the autumn to rescue Charles from his 'evil' counsellors. Confirmation came when Holloway met the Bristol attorney Nathaniel Wade in August; they concluded that 350 men, including 150 from the Taunton area, were needed to secure Bristol. To clear the streets, Holloway offered small ordnance from his shipping yard. However, the uprising was postponed. On 3 March 1683 Holloway went to London, where Wade informed him that planning was in the hands of Essex, Lord Howard of Escrick, Ford, Lord Grey, Lord William Russell, Algernon Sidney, John Hampden, John Wildman, and Francis Charlton. Before Holloway left London on the 6th, Wade introduced him to another plotter, Colonel John Rumsey. When Holloway returned to London on 5 April, he met the attorney Robert West. Swearing Holloway to secrecy, West outlined the plot to assassinate Charles and James as they returned from Newmarket. After his arrest in 1684, Holloway insisted he had condemned assassination as dishonourable and cowardly. On the 6th, the Bristol merchant John Row took Holloway to the house of Zachary Bourne, where he met Robert Ferguson. The latter apprised Holloway of current plans for a general insurrection, including the arrival of key Scottish dissidents in London. The same day Holloway conferred with Rumsey, who reputedly indicated he knew of the assassination scheme; after Holloway's execution in 1684, Rumsey denied this allegation. Holloway returned to Bristol on the 7th, but in early May he travelled to London, where he conferred again, independently, with West, Rumsey, and Ferguson, still professing, he later insisted, his opposition to assassination. Later the same month, Holloway participated in strategy sessions with West, Rumsey, Wade, Richard and Francis Goodenough, Edward Norton, and Thomas Walcott to enlist 3000 men in the London area. In the last meeting Holloway attended, he reiterated his objections to killing the royal brothers, pledging instead to support an uprising in Bristol. On his return there, he and others planned a surprise attack utilizing 350 men, scheduling it for 4 a.m. to avoid bloodshed. Some ninety men would suppress the mayor's guards while the rest secured strategic posts.

Holloway's difficulties commenced before Josiah Keeling disclosed the plotting to the government on 12 June. Holloway had fallen into substantial debt and feared incarceration. Moreover, about 1 May, Ralph Ollive, mayor of Bristol, had falsely accused him of attending a conventicle of open-membership Baptists and had him arrested

and bound over to the Gloucester quarter sessions. Following Keeling's disclosure, Holloway disguised himself as a wool merchant and travelled through Somerset, Gloucestershire, and Oxfordshire. On 12 July a grand jury indicted him for high treason, the state having three witnesses against him. In mid-August he returned to Bristol, where, with his wife's assistance, he hired a small ship to take him to France and the West Indies. He sailed on 23 August, stopped at St Ives to repair a broken mast, and reached La Rochelle on 17 September. With a cargo of brandy and other merchandise, he left for the West Indies on 4 October, arriving at Barbados on 11 November. Using the alias John Milward, Holloway conducted his business in Antigua, Montserrat, Nevis, St Kitts, St Eustatius, and Anguilla. Reported by his own factor, he was apprehended in January 1684 and returned to England in chains, his ship reaching Bristol on 4 April. Upon his arrival he wrote a jeremiad in verse form, warning England of its sins and wondering,

> Who could have thought in seventy eight that we
> Soe much enslav'd by eighty four should be.
> (PRO, SP 29/437/91)

If he were now to die, he thought, he had done his part to free England from Catholicism. Examined by the privy council on the 10th, he was ordered to compose a narrative of his involvement, but he failed to convince the government he was confessing everything he knew. An appeal for mercy to Sir Leoline Jenkins on the 14th was unsuccessful, and Holloway appeared in the king's bench a week later. Although a trial was unnecessary because he had been attainted by outlawry on an indictment of high treason, the attorney-general offered him one. Holloway refused, throwing himself on the king's mercy. He appealed to Charles and Sidney Godolphin, telling the latter that had the king 'not been Mercifull to popish Plotters I had never been a Plotter' (PRO, SP 29/437/127). On the scaffold at Tyburn on 30 April he proclaimed himself a member of the Church of England, insisted he had made a full confession, and averred he had never favoured assassination. He gave the sheriffs an account of the plotting dated 26 April, lamenting that he had brought ruin on his wife and children, censure on his friends, and great losses to his creditors. (After his death, officials in the West Indies discovered debts owed to Holloway of between £400 and £500.) Holloway also left a statement condemning reputedly illegal actions in recent years to establish arbitrary government and Catholicism. On 5 May the government ordered that his head and quarters be sent to Bristol for display on the city gates. Almost to the end Holloway had hoped for mercy, in return for which he promised to pursue his proposal to establish linen manufactories in England. He also offered a new plan to resettle hundreds of dissidents on an island in the West Indies.

RICHARD L. GREAVES

Sources BL, Add. MSS 62453 · PRO, SP 29/425, 430, 433, 436–7 · State trials, 10.1–30 · PRO, SP 44, entry books 54, 64 · R. L. Greaves, Secrets of the kingdom: British radicals from the Popish Plot to the revolution of 1688–89 (1992) · R. Hayden, ed., The records of a church in Christ in Bristol, 1640–1687, Bristol RS, 27 (1974), 251, 295 · T. Sprat, A true account and declaration of the horrid conspiracy against the late king

(1685) • J. Holloway, *The free and voluntary confession of James Holloway* (1684) • *CSP dom.*, 1684–5 • *The manuscripts of his grace the duke of Portland*, 10 vols., HMC, 29 (1891–1931), vol. 2 • *CSP col.*, 11.754 • E. Ralph, ed., *Marriage bonds for the diocese of Bristol*, Bristol and Gloucestershire Archaeological Society Records Section, 1 (1952) • N. Luttrell, *A brief historical relation of state affairs from September 1678 to April 1714*, 1 (1857), 266–67, 305–6

Archives PRO, state papers 29/437

Wealth at death died in debt; was owed £400–£500 by debtors in the West Indies: *CSP America and West Indies, 1681–85*, 754

Holloway, John (1666?–1734), lawyer and politician in America, was born in England. Having emigrated to America about 1700 Holloway typified a narrowing group of men who achieved positions of power and influence in early eighteenth-century Virginia without the benefit of family background, status, or inherited wealth. Little is known of his early years, although he may have been attracted to Virginia by distant relatives who settled there in the 1630s. He probably had no formal education but he clearly learned to read and write early in life and eventually he acquired a working knowledge of the law. While still young he served a clerkship, had a brief stint with the army in Ireland, became an attorney at the Marshalsea court in London, and tried and failed at several business ventures. Whatever his background, successes, or failures in England he arrived in Virginia with the kind of practical legal knowledge and experience needed in the relatively new colonial capital of Williamsburg.

Holloway first appears in the records of Virginia in September 1704, when he replaced the attorney-general as the crown's advocate in a trial of Native Americans. Over the next thirty years he represented provincial and county governments in a wide variety of legal matters, prosecuting cases, giving opinions on points of law, and arguing on behalf of local jurisdictions. His private law practice involved the legal affairs of Virginia's most prominent citizens, including Robert 'King' Carter, Colonel Edmund Jenings, and the widow of Governor Hugh Drysdale. Holloway also represented common folk as an executor or trustee of their estates and once assisted the settlers of Germanna in a petition against their former benefactor Governor Alexander Spotswood. Holloway apparently argued cases with such persistence that he often won, despite much evidence to the contrary. His services were thus highly prized, although a fellow lawyer, Sir John Randolph, thought he took considerable advantage of his reputation and charged excessive fees.

Holloway's public career began in 1710, when King and Queen county elected him to the house of burgesses, the lower house of the Virginia legislature; they elected him again in 1712. Holloway immediately sought the top leadership positions in the house; he stood unsuccessfully for the position of speaker but soon chaired a number of major committees, including one supervising the construction of the governor's palace. He either did not run or suffered defeat in the elections of 1715 and 1718, possibly because he had favoured Governor Spotswood's controversial tobacco bill.

While out of the house Holloway pursued other political avenues: in 1714 he became a justice of the peace of King and Queen county, a judge of the Admiralty court, and naval officer of the lower James River; about 1718 he joined the York county court and the vestry of Bruton parish. These positions in turn provided the springboard for his return to the house in 1720 as a burgess from York. The house immediately selected him speaker, and from 1720 to 1734 his leadership initiated a gradual increase in the stature and influence of the burgesses, which culminated many decades later in their stubborn stand against royal governors and parliament. In addition to serving as the first mayor of Williamsburg in 1722 Holloway was one of five prominent lawyers tasked with the compilation of all the laws passed by the house, which was published in 1732. He also served as Virginia treasurer from 1723 to 1734 but left the colony's finances in much disarray at his death.

Holloway's personal affairs concerned the acquisition and improvement of his landholdings in York, Elizabeth City, King and Queen, King William, Nansemond, Henrico, and possibly Prince George counties, as well as the city of Williamsburg. In the early 1720s he appears to have married Elizabeth (d. 1755), widow of Dr William Cocke (d. 1720) and sister of the naturalist Mark Catesby (1683–1749); they had no children. Holloway's health deteriorated in early 1734; he resigned as speaker and treasurer in August and died in York county on 14 December, after suffering an epileptic seizure. He was buried in Williamsburg.   JOHN G. KOLP

Sources G. Wythe, etymological praxis in Greek and Latin of part of Homer's Iliad, and notes on John Holloway and William Hopkins copied by an unidentified person from Sir John Randolph's breviate book, Virginia Historical Society [reprinted in part as 'Two old lawyers', *Virginia Historical Register*, 1 (1848), 119–23, and in *Southern Literary Messenger*, 1 (1834–5), 353–4] • J. Kukla, *Speakers and clerks of the Virginia house of burgesses, 1643–1776* (1981) • G. E. Hopkins, *Colonial cousins, being the history, genealogy … of the family of Holloway … York county, Virginia* (1940) • H. R. McIlwaine and J. P. Kennedy, eds., *Journals of the house of burgesses of Virginia, 1619–1776*, 13 vols. (1905–15) • H. R. McIlwaine and others, eds., *Executive journals of the council of colonial Virginia*, 6 vols. (1925–66) • J. P. Greene, *The quest for power: the lower houses of assembly in the southern royal colonies, 1689–1776* (1963)

Wealth at death substantially wealthy; possibly 20,000 acres in at least six counties

Holloway, Sir Richard (*bap.* 1627, *d.* 1699), judge, was baptized on 21 October 1627 at St Aldates, Oxford, the second son of John Holloway BCL (*d.* 1675) of Oxford and Susan Anyan (*d.* 1685) of Sandwich, Kent, sister of Dr Thomas Anyan. Holloway's father was an official to the archdeacon of Berkshire and a 'covetous civilian and public notary' (*DNB*). Holloway matriculated at New College, Oxford, in March 1643; he was expelled by the parliamentary visitors in 1648 and is not known to have taken a degree. He was admitted to the Inner Temple in 1646 and called to the bar on 24 November 1658. His name does not appear in any law reports, and he probably practised locally in Oxford, where he lived opposite the Blue Boar in St Aldates parish. On 10 November 1659 he married Alice (*d.* 1672), daughter of John Smith MP, of Kennington, Berkshire.

In February 1666 Holloway was elected recorder of Wallingford. Having been called to the bench of his inn in 1670 he was made a serjeant-at-law in October 1677. He was one of the counsel for the prosecution of Stephen College at Oxford in 1681 on a charge of high treason. On 18 April 1683 he was made a king's serjeant, and was knighted on 24 May. On 25 September 1683 he was made a judge of king's bench, and in November was one of the judges before whom Algernon Sidney was tried. In January 1684 the earl of Danby described Holloway as being particularly under the influence of Lord Chief Justice Jeffreys. Holloway's judicial patent was confirmed on the accession of James II. He also concurred in the sentence on Titus Oates and on the earl of Devonshire for assaulting Colonel Thomas Colepeper in the royal presence. Holloway was in favour of the dispensing power, and appears to have given the king advice on the way to proceed over the Magdalen College affair. However, he resisted James II's attempts to have martial law imposed on the army in time of peace without the consent of parliament. Further, during the trial of the seven bishops in June 1688 he defended the right of the subject to petition the monarch and believed that the bishops were not guilty of seditious libel as there was no intent to be seditious. As a consequence of his actions at this trial he received his quietus on 2 July 1688. Following the revolution he was summoned before the House of Lords to explain his judgments in the Oates and Devonshire cases, and before the Commons to explain why he was turned out of office. He was excepted from the Act of Indemnity in 1690 because of his support for the dispensing power. Holloway lived in retirement in Oxford until his death in 1699, his will being proved in 1700.

STUART HANDLEY

Sources Sainty, *Judges*, 34 · Baker, *Serjeants*, 447, 518 · Foster, *Alum. Oxon.* · F. A. Inderwick and R. A. Roberts, eds., *A calendar of the Inner Temple records*, 3 (1901), 308 · *The life and times of Anthony Wood*, ed. A. Clark, 2, OHS, 21 (1892), 250, 308; 3, OHS, 26 (1894), 120, 200, 268, 272, 331 · IGI · Foss, *Judges*, 7.223–5 · J. R. Bloxam, ed., *Magdalen College and James II, 1686–1688: a series of documents*, OHS, 6 (1886), 95 · *The manuscripts of the earl of Buckinghamshire, the earl of Lindsey … and James Round*, HMC, 38 (1895), 438–9 [Lindsey MSS] · N. Luttrell, *A brief historical relation of state affairs from September 1678 to April 1714*, 1 (1857), 447–9, 530, 547–8 · *State trials*, 9.867, 10.1318, 12.426 · G. W. Keeton, *Lord Chancellor Jeffreys and the Stuart cause* (1965), 220, 272, 278, 294–5 · *The autobiography of Sir John Bramston*, ed. [Lord Braybrooke], CS, 32 (1845), 272, 310–11 · DNB

Holloway, Stanley Augustus (1890–1982), actor and singer, was born on 1 October 1890 at 30 Wentworth Road, Manor Park, London, the younger child and only son of George Augustus Holloway, a law clerk, and his wife, Florence Bell. His family was fairly prosperous and he attended the Carpenters' Company School, where his 'big moment at school was joining The Choir' (Holloway, 44). Local engagements as a boy soprano encouraged him to contemplate a career in singing. After a short time in positions as a junior clerk Holloway joined a concert party at Walton on the Naze, and continued with this work for a few seasons before studying singing in Milan in 1914 and then serving with the Connaught Rangers, in Ireland during the Easter rising in 1916 and then in France.

Stanley Augustus Holloway (1890–1982), by Houston Rogers

In November 1913 Holloway married Alice Mary-Laure (Queenie; *c*.1892–1937), daughter of John Thomas Foran, who lived on the income from inherited property. They had three daughters and a son. On 2 January 1939 he married Violet Marion, an actress, daughter of Alfred Lane, civil engineer. They had one son.

In 1921 Holloway became a utility-man-cum-baritone for a West End success—the Co-Optimists' pierrot show. The show ran until 1927, then was revived in 1929. In 1927 he first introduced the monologue into his work, with the story of 'Sam "pick oop tha musket" Small'. He delivered comic narratives such as these in a flat, unemotional Lancastrian fashion. The droll accounts, both in variety and on 12 inch records, of Albert Ramsbottom, who was swallowed by the lion at Blackpool Zoo, and other such tales, were extremely popular, and were described as becoming 'part of English folklore during the 1930s' (*The Times*, 1 Feb 1982, 10).

Holloway also appeared in light theatre. His first West End showing was in 1919 as Captain Wentworth in *Kissing Time*, by Guy Bolton and P. G. Wodehouse, and his first pantomime was in Birmingham in 1934, where he was Abanazar in *Aladdin*. He performed in variety as well as musical comedy and revue, and had other theatre successes, notably in Shakespeare, as First Gravedigger in *Hamlet* (with Alec Guinness, 1951) and Bottom in the Old Vic's *A Midsummer Night's Dream* (1954) at the Edinburgh Festival and an American coast-to-coast tour. In the Shaw Festival at Niagara-on-the-Lake, Canada, he appeared as Burgess in G. B. Shaw's *Candida* (1970) and William in his *You Never can Tell* (1973). He also played Pooh Bah in an impressive USA television production of Gilbert and Sullivan's *The Mikado*. As late as 1977 he toured Australia and Hong Kong with Douglas Fairbanks junior.

A generation of cinema audiences also learned to appreciate Holloway's delightful comedy acting, and he appeared in more than sixty films, beginning with *The Rotters* in 1921, and including *This Happy Breed* (1944), *Brief Encounter* (1945), *The Way to the Stars* (1945), *The Lavender Hill Mob* (1951), and *The Titfield Thunderbolt* (1952). On American television he appeared with his son, Julian, in the series *Our Man Higgins* (1962–3).

He perhaps crowned his career with his performance as Alfred Doolittle the philosophical dustman in *My Fair Lady*, Lerner and Loewe's musical version of *Pygmalion* by G. B. Shaw. Holloway starred in the Broadway première (1956–8), the London production at Drury Lane (1958–9), and the film version of 1964. With his cockney authenticity, his splendid baritone voice, and his wealth of comedy experience, he made a great success of this role, and, as he said, it put him 'bang on top of the heap, in demand' again (Holloway, 12) at a time when, in his mid-sixties, his career was beginning to wane. He was appointed OBE in 1960, and was awarded the Variety Club of Great Britain special award in 1978. He published his autobiography, *Wiv a Little Bit o'Luck* in 1967 and three anthologies of monologues in 1979, 1980, and 1981. He died at the Nightingale Nursing Home, Beach Road, Littlehampton, Sussex, on 30 January 1982. He was cremated, and his remains were buried in the churchyard in East Preston, Sussex.

ERIC MIDWINTER, rev.

Sources S. Holloway, *Wiv a little bit o' luck: the life story of Stanley Holloway* (1967) · R. Walding, *An arm of iron: the life and times of the entertainer Stanley Holloway* (1996) · *The Times* (1–2 Feb 1982) · J. Fisher, *Funny way to be a hero* (1973) · L. Halliwell, *The filmgoer's companion*, 5th edn (1976) · personal knowledge (1990) · private information (1990) · J. Parker, ed., *Who's who in the theatre*, 6th edn (1930) · I. Herbert, ed., *Who's who in the theatre*, 16th edn (1977) · *CGPLA Eng. & Wales* (1982)
Archives FILM BFI NFTVA, *Those British faces*, Channel 4, 6 May 1997 · BFI NFTVA, performance footage · BFI NFTVA, propaganda film footage (ministry of information) | SOUND BL NSA, documentary recording · BL NSA, performance recording
Likenesses H. Rogers, photograph, Theatre Museum, London [see illus.] · photographs, repro. in Holloway, *Wiv a little bit o' luck*
Wealth at death £94,001: probate, 6 April 1982, *CGPLA Eng. & Wales*

Holloway, Thomas (1748–1827), engraver, was born at 74 Broad Street, London, the eldest child of the two sons and two daughters of Thomas Holloway (*c.*1727–1759), ironmonger, and his wife, Ann (1724–1776). His brother, John, achieved some fame as a lecturer in animal magnetism. Since his mother's portrait was painted by John Russell (1745–1806), it is possible that Thomas Holloway was encouraged by him. In due course he was articled to a seal engraver named Stent, and then in 1773 enrolled at the Royal Academy Schools. From the family home, between 1773 and 1777, he exhibited a variety of works at the Royal Academy, including seals, engraved gems, and portraits in crayon and oil. From 1781 to 1784 he lived at 88 Fleet Street and then from 1784 to 1792 at 11 Baches Row, City Road, Hoxton. In 1793 and 1795 he engraved Shakespearian

paintings by Robert Smirke and Gavin Hamilton for Boydell's *Shakspeare Gallery*.

Holloway's largest project, however, was the English edition of J. C. Lavater's *Essays on Physiognomy*, translated by Dr Henry Hunter and published in five volumes (1789–98). This work was illustrated with about 800 plates, executed by Holloway himself (about 300), Francesco Bartolozzi, William Blake, Daniel Chodowiecki, and others under the direction of Henry Fuseli. However, Holloway had overall control of the engravings, illustrated by his observation in an inscription to his engraving of J.-P. Bouchardon's bust of Charles XII of Sweden: 'The English artist has endeavoured … to excel the French original … but felt himself obliged to copy it correctly enough to support the ingenious Author's remarks' (Lavater, 1.229). His tailpieces reveal a lively imagination: one depicts seven human skulls, representing the ages from young to old, arranged in a circular group in a grassy plot. His skill in surface textures is seen in his engraving of John Brown's drawing of the marble head of Homer found at Baiae in 1780, also in the *Essays*.

In 1800—with three young ex-pupils—Holloway commenced a folio edition of engravings after the seven cartoons of Raphael then at Windsor (now in the Victoria and Albert Museum); as a result of his initial work he was appointed historical engraver to the king. In 1820, with four plates completed, the group moved to Coltishall, near Norwich; Holloway lived to see the fifth plate finished in 1824. He died, unmarried, at Coltishall on 19 February 1827. His nephew, John Holloway, wrote of him that he 'never [lost] the art of expressing himself gracefully and of reading elegantly … a person of short stature, and rather muscular form, he was yet graceful and dignified' (Holloway, 9).

The last plate of the Raphael cartoons, issued in 1839, sold for 10 guineas (the price for each of the first four had been 3 guineas), but even in 1848, when the value of the set was much higher, there was little demand. This was not the only ambitious artistic project to founder in this period of change.

PETER TOMORY

Sources [J. Holloway], *Memoirs of the late Mr Thomas Holloway by one of his executors* (1872) · A. E. Goodman, 'A half-hour with the Holloways', [n.d.], Society of Genealogists, London · *DNB* · G. K. Nagler, ed., *Neues allgemeines Künstler-Lexikon*, 22 vols. (Munich, 1835–52) · Bryan, *Painters* (1903–5) · Graves, *RA exhibitors* · Waterhouse, *18c painters*
Archives BM, department of prints and drawings

Holloway, Thomas (1800–1883), manufacturer of patent medicines and philanthropist, was born on 22 September 1800 at Devonport, the eldest of six children and elder of two sons of Thomas Holloway (*d.* 1836), a baker formerly in the Royal Navy, and his wife, Mary (*d.* 1843), daughter of John Chellew, a carpenter of Lelant, Cornwall. He was educated at Camborne and later at Mr John Spasshat's school in Penzance, to where the family moved in 1816. After leaving school, he assisted his mother in a grocer's shop, his father by then keeping a public house. He did not leave home until 1828, when he began a mercantile career in northern France.

Thomas Holloway (1800–1883), by William Scott, 1845

After Holloway's return to Britain, in 1836 he set up unsuccessfully as a merchant in London, supplementing his meagre earnings by acting as interpreter at a nearby hotel. There he met Felix Albinolo from Turin, hawking his St Cosmas and St Damian ointment. After having obtained testimonials from a number of eminent London medical men, Holloway offered to go into partnership with him, but failed to provide the needed capital. In October 1837 he began advertising Holloway's Universal Family Ointment in the *Sunday Times* and other London newspapers. Hostile accounts written soon afterwards charged him with having stolen Albinolo's formula, or at least the idea and the testimonials.

For more than a year in 1838–9, the enraged Albinolo and Holloway battled in the advertising columns of *The Times* and elsewhere, each bankrupting himself in the process. Holloway was committed to a debtors' prison, being released with his mother's financial assistance. He thereafter paid his debts—including wages—on the day of incurring them. Albinolo was also gaoled, and subsequently vanished from the scene. During 1839 Holloway began to make digestive pills, and moved to large premises at 244 Strand. On 12 January 1840 he married Jane Pearce (1814–1875), elder daughter of John Driver, a shipwright of Rotherhithe. A plain-faced but cheerful and robust young woman, fifteen years his junior, she was expected to work very long hours, which he later claimed to have been from 4 a.m. to 10 p.m. By chance or design they had no children, and indeed during the years of struggle, Jane could scarcely have been spared for child-

bearing. In later life he refused to have any children in his home, preferring the less rumbustious company of dogs and horses.

Holloway's success as a businessman lay in his grasp of the power of publicity in an era when newspapers were springing up in Britain and throughout the world. He therefore spent on advertising all the money he could spare, this expenditure rising, according to his own publicity, from £5000 in 1842 to £20,000 in 1851. He regularly visited the London docks to bring his products to the notice of ships' officers and passengers, and to gain information about overseas markets. Similarly, he wrote thousands of letters to missionaries and other foreign residents, to discover the names of overseas papers in which to advertise.

Although Holloway freely quoted figures showing how his advertising outlay rose steadily to £50,000 in 1883, no figures survive to show the proportion spent overseas or the value of his sales there. He apparently did well in the colonies. However, an attempt to manufacture in the United States, effective for a while (notably during the civil war of 1861–5), ultimately failed through poor and sometimes corrupt local management and pertinacious counterfeiting by Americans, so that by 1883 he no longer had any sales there. According to the revenue stamps he bought, home turnover rose from £18,000 in 1851 to about £60,000 in the 1860s, dipping slightly to £57,000 in the 1870s, then rising to no higher than £65,000 on average in his four final years. He scarcely troubled to overhaul his products as the years passed. Technology was backward in the absence of steam machinery, pill masses and ointment being inadequately mixed, and the advertising copy seemed dated.

With no sons to succeed him, Holloway made up with his brother, Henry, manager of the factory, despite having taken out an injunction in 1850 to prevent his selling separately made brands of Holloway's pills and ointment. When the Strand premises were demolished to make way for the new law courts in 1867, the business removed to New Oxford Street. After the death of Henry in 1874, Thomas's brother-in-law, Henry Driver, took over as manager. The workforce grew from twenty-nine in 1851 to about a hundred in 1883.

Holloway's second career was as a financier. Once money poured in regularly from his medicines, he strove to make it work for him. There was never a Holloway's Bank as such, but he did in some ways operate as a banker. He regularly advanced money to private individuals in need of cash, against life-insurance policies which he held, disregarding pleas from dependants who found themselves penniless when the debtor died. Although he had an account with Coutts's Bank from 1845 onwards, every afternoon he arranged for all surplus funds in his possession to be lent out on the money market overnight. He was also famous for his skilful investment in British and overseas stocks and shares.

Holloway, his wife, and some close relatives moved to Tittenhurst Park, Sunninghill, Berkshire, in the 1860s.

There he devoted many hours a day to poring over the daily returns from the firm and his stock and share papers. Afternoons were spent on carriage rides or billiards and the evenings on piano playing or reading aloud. An abstemious man, he drank only claret and water; the days of his earlier impromptu suppers and sing-songs were long gone, as was his urge to travel. He had no interest in organized religion or in politics.

Holloway's third career was as a philanthropist. He offered to set up a charitable foundation at Devonport, only to be cold-shouldered by the town fathers. With the advice of Anthony Ashley Cooper, seventh earl of Shaftesbury, he planned a sanatorium at Virginia Water for 240 middle-class mental patients, costing £300,000. This was opened by the prince and princess of Wales (later Edward VII and Queen Alexandra), in June 1885; it closed in 1981. Jane Holloway, who had lived in gilded idleness ever since the firm had become prosperous, put on much weight and died of heart trouble and bronchitis in 1875, aged sixty. Holloway, in memory of his wife, decided to endow a college for women, to house 250 students. The exotic building, of white marble and red brick, comprised a double quadrangle with two lofty parallel blocks, and was of French Renaissance design, largely modelled on the Château de Chambord in France. Costing £700,000, it dominated the skyline at Egham Hill. Holloway closely supervised every aspect of construction, remarking that he worked harder to spend his money than to generate it. Queen Victoria opened what she dubbed Royal Holloway College in 1886. Holloway also spent £83,000 on building up a collection of paintings, some by Turner and Constable but most reflecting the best (and worst) of high Victorian artistic taste.

Holloway died of congestion of the lungs at Tittenhurst, on 26 December 1883, and was buried at St Michael's, Sunninghill, on 4 January 1884. He left a personal estate of £596,335, plus a considerable amount of freehold property. His patent medicine business gradually declined and in 1930 was taken over by the rival Beechams Pills Ltd.

T. A. B. CORLEY

Sources C. Bingham, *The history of Royal Holloway College, 1886–1986* (1987) · A. Harrison-Barbet, *Thomas Holloway: Victorian philanthropist* (1994) · R. Davis, 'Thomas Holloway, entrepreneur and philanthropist', *Surrey History*, 3 (1985–6), 67–75 · G. C. Boase, 'Thomas Holloway, pill maker and philanthropist', *The Western Antiquary*, 4 (1884–5), 183–7 · 'The anatomy of quackery: Holloway's pills and ointment', *Medical Circular and General Medical Adviser*, 11 (1853), 45, 67–8, 86–7 · H. Johnstone, 'The founder', *The Royal Holloway College, 1887–1937*, ed. M. J. Powell (privately printed, Egham, [1937]), 9–15 · *The story of Thomas Holloway (1800–1883)* (1933) · L. Smith, *Thomas Holloway and the establishment of Holloway Sanatorium, Virginia Water, Surrey* (1932) · 'The puffing system', *The Town* (28 July 1838), 485 · 'The puffing system', *The Town* (11 Aug 1838), 501 · *Manchester Guardian* (29 Dec 1883) · *The Times* (28 Dec 1883) · *The Times* (29 Dec 1883) · *The Times* (31 Dec 1883) · *Pall Mall Gazette* (9 Jan 1884) · *Pall Mall Gazette* (11 Jan 1884) · m. cert.
Archives Egham Museum · Royal Holloway College, Egham, Surrey, corresp. and papers · Surrey HC
Likenesses W. Scott, portrait, 1845, Royal Holloway College, Egham, Surrey [*see illus.*] · photographs, Royal Holloway College,

Egham, Surrey · statue (with Jane Holloway), Royal Holloway College, Egham, Surrey
Wealth at death £596,335 8s. 5d.: resworn probate, Aug 1885, *CGPLA Eng. & Wales* (1884)

Holloway, William Cuthbert Elphinstone- (1787–1850).
See under Holloway, Sir Charles (1749–1827).

Hollowell, James Hirst (1851–1909),
advocate of non-sectarian education, was born in St Giles's Street, Northampton, on 25 February 1851, the son of William Hollowell, shoemaker and a local preacher in the Reformed Wesleyan denomination, and his wife, Mary Anne (*née* Swinfield). Sent to the British school at Northampton at the age of six, Hollowell left school early to earn a living, but read widely by himself, and also attended a class which met three times a week from five to six in the morning.

In early youth Hollowell showed a gift for public speaking, and at eighteen became a temperance agent and lecturer. Joining the Congregationalists at Dumfries, he decided to study for the Congregational ministry. In 1870 he married Sarah Ann, daughter of James Lacey of Crewkerne, Somerset. The following year he entered Nottingham (Congregational) Institute, going on from there in 1872 to Cheshunt College, where he won a scholarship. From 1875 to 1882 he was pastor at Bedford Chapel, Camden Town, London, and from 1882 to 1889 was minister of Park Hill Congregational Church, Nottingham. At Nottingham he was first drawn into politics, publishing an attack on the financial bondage into which Egypt had been reduced by Conservative policy between 1874 and 1880. In 1885 he produced a defence of the Gladstone government's handling of the General Gordon crisis. He was elected to the Nottingham school board, of which he became chairman in 1888. Subsequently he was pastor of Milton church, Rochdale, from October 1889 until December 1896. This charge he relinquished in order to devote himself to the work of organizing secretary of the Northern Counties Education League, founded in 1896 to oppose Sir John Gorst's Education Bill and to promote non-sectarian state education.

Hollowell was one of the prime movers in the Nonconformist Parliamentary Council, established in 1898 to exercise electoral pressure on issues of concern to the free churches. A campaigner at by-elections in favour of non-sectarian education and temperance, he took a pro-Boer position in 1900, believing the war to have been promoted by financial interests. In 1903 he took a leading part in organizing with the Revd John Clifford 'the passive resistance movement' against the payment of rates and taxes, on the ground that the Conservative government's Education Act of 1902 gave an inequitable support at state expense to church schools which taught church doctrine. Learned in educational legislation, he was a forcible speaker and an untiring pamphleteer, always alert to what he considered the schemes of supporters of church schools. In February 1904 he unsuccessfully stood against the Liberal Unionist Viscount Morpeth in a by-election for Birmingham South. After the 'Liberal landslide' of 1906 he was an unrelenting critic of the Liberal government's concessions to denominationalism in the education bills of 1906 and 1908, and was criticized for his uncompromising militancy. Contemporaries saw in him the spirit of the puritan warrior.

Hollowell wrote a novel entitled *Ritualism Abandoned, or, A Priest Redeemed* (1899), under the pseudonym of K. Ireton, and *What Nonconformists stand for* (1901; 2nd edn, 1904). A representative at the International Congregational Council meeting at Boston, USA, in 1899, he was elected chairman of the Lancashire Congregational Union in 1908. Hollowell's exertions broke down his health, and he died of cerebral apoplexy at his home, Castlemere, Rochdale, on 24 December 1909, and was buried at Milton Chapel, Rochdale, four days later. He had one son and five daughters. C. W. SUTTON, rev. M. C. CURTHOYS

Sources W. Evans and W. Claridge, *James Hirst Hollowell and the movement for civic control in education* (1911) · *Congregational Year Book* (1911), 176 · *Manchester Guardian* (27 Dec 1909) · S. Koss, *Nonconformity in modern British politics* (1975)
Likenesses J. Cassidy, bust, 1911, Congregational Church House, Manchester · photograph, repro. in Evans and Claridge, *James Hirst Hollowell*, frontispiece · photograph (in youth), repro. in Evans and Claridge, *James Hirst Hollowell*, facing p. 9
Wealth at death £3,578 3s. 9d.: probate, 18 Jan 1910, *CGPLA Eng. & Wales*

Hollyer, Frederick (1838–1933), photographer and art publisher, was born on 17 June 1838 at 34 Penton Place, Clerkenwell, London, the youngest son of Samuel Hollyer, assistant sealer to the first Lord Brougham, the lord chancellor, and his wife, Mary Ann Hudson. Like his father and two of his brothers, he was trained as a reproductive engraver in mezzotint, and he engraved two paintings by Edwin Landseer, *The Shepherd's Grave* (1868) and *The Shepherd's Chief Mourner* (1869). He began his career in photography about 1860 and was elected a member of the Photographic Society of London in 1865. He was also a member of the Solar Club, founded by G. Wharton Simpson and H. P. Robinson in 1865. In the 1860s he photographed a series of drawings by Simeon Solomon, *A Dream of Love in Sleep*. In this early work he used wet collodion glass-plate negatives and printed on unglazed salted paper, but he began printing in platinum as soon as the process became available in the mid-1870s.

In 1873 Hollyer moved from Kentish Town in north-west London to a studio in Pembroke Square, Kensington. He was commissioned in the 1870s to photograph the paintings of Frederick Leighton; he also photographed many of those of Edward Burne-Jones in different stages of production. With its delicacy of tone and matt paper surface, the platinotype produced facsimiles of drawings by artists such as Burne-Jones so perfect as to be later mistaken for originals. He soon became well known for these art reproductions of the work of other contemporary English artists such as Albert Moore, Dante Gabriel Rossetti, Ford Madox Brown, Holman Hunt, Frederick Sandys, and George Richmond, as well as the old masters.

Hollyer's platinum prints of paintings are said to have been so subtly evocative as to have suggested modifications to the painters. G. F. Watts credited them as largely responsible for bringing to the notice of the general public both his own work and that of Rossetti and Burne-Jones. At the turn of the century his platinum reproductions were praised as equalling the mezzotint in richness but surpassing it in fidelity to the original and thereby preserving the individual expression of the painter. Catalogues of 'platinotype reproductions of pictures' exhibited at Hollyer's studio and later at the Dudley Gallery in London were issued regularly from 1893 to 1911, and again after 1918. These art reproductions, some as large as 40 inches by 30, are now found in art collections worldwide.

For thirty years, beginning in 1882, Hollyer's studio was reserved on Mondays for portraits, which he considered to be his creative work. In 1892 he became a member of the Linked Ring Brotherhood, a group which aspired to artistic photography and held exhibitions independent of the Photographic Society. Most of his work exhibited at the salons of the Linked Ring consisted of portraits or figure studies. By 1906 his eldest son, Frederick Thomas Hollyer, had joined the business, with a series of photographic reproductions of portrait paintings from The Hague. In 1913 Hollyer retired from his studio at 8–9 Pembroke Square, Kensington, and left his two sons, Frederick Thomas and Arthur Samuel, in charge of the business. In 1920 he compiled for his daughter Eleanor three small albums of platinum portraits, of prominent artists, writers, and statesmen from the previous decades of his career—including William Morris, W. B. Yeats, Lord Kelvin, and General Smuts—which are now in the collection of the Victoria and Albert Museum in London. Frederick Hollyer died on 21 November 1933 in Blewbury, Berkshire, at Meers Parcel, the home of his son. The name of his wife, and whether she outlived him, is not known.

ANNE HAMMOND

Sources M. Harker, *The Linked Ring* (1979) · *The Times* (24 Nov 1933), 19 · b. cert. · d. cert. · *CGPLA Eng. & Wales* (1934)
Likenesses F. Hollyer, self-portrait, photograph, 1920, V&A
Wealth at death £10,287 16s. 9d.: probate, 15 Jan 1934, *CGPLA Eng. & Wales*

Holm [*née* Gray], **Helen Warren** (1907–1971), golfer, was born on 14 March 1907 at 3 Manor Road, Jordanhill, Partick, one of two daughters of Thomas Gray (1869–1932), professor of technical chemistry at the Royal Technical College, Glasgow, and his wife, Violet Irene Emma Warren. She married Andrew Mackie Holm, a farmer, with whom she had a son.

Holm twice won the (British) ladies' championship in a playing career that spanned three decades and is cited as an example of the golfing longevity often attributed to the Scots. Her first championship title came at Porth-cawl in 1934, with an emphatic victory over the young Pam Barton in the final. This was the first time the championship had been won by a Scot since 1911. She repeated her success at Burnham in 1938, defeating Miss Corlett 4 and 3 in the final. Holm was also a member of three Britain and Ireland Curtis cup teams. In May 1936 she played in the drawn match at the King's course, Gleneagles, and was on the losing side at Essex Country Club, Massachusetts, in

September 1938. When the match resumed after the war she was included in the British side to face the Americans at Birkdale in May 1948, and once again the visitors triumphed, extending their impressive record in the series.

Holm was the dominant figure of her generation in Scottish women's golf, reaching at least the semi-final round of the national championship no fewer than fifteen times between 1929 and 1964, winning the title five times and losing in five other finals. Her first victory was at Turnberry in 1930, and she won again in 1932, 1937, and 1948, securing her final title at St Andrews in 1950 at the age of forty-three. Appropriately her last appearance in the final was very close to home, at Troon in 1957. She won numerous regional championships and represented Scotland in international matches for a quarter of a century from 1932. She also played annually for the British Isles against France from 1933 to 1938 and from 1947 to 1949, and was non-playing captain of the British teams that faced France and Belgium in 1951.

Writing in *Golf between Two Wars* (1944), Bernard Darwin thought Mrs Holm 'the most striking lady player since Miss Wethered had left the lists', than which there could be no higher praise: 'She was not the most consistent and was capable of unexpected and perhaps light-hearted mistakes, but when in full tide of play she had a majestic power and a capacity for playing the counting shot rarely seen' (p. 132). Holm was 'exceptionally tall and possessed a slow, graceful swing that was given extra propulsion by moving on to her toes at impact' (Crane, 101). Her longevity in championships can be attributed to a deftness of touch which she retained into her fifties, when her strength and stamina naturally declined. It gave her a continued edge over younger opponents, and Belle Robertson, who lost to her at Turnberry in the Scottish championship of 1960, acknowledged her mastery: 'the sheer brilliance of her touch on a course which was that week dry and bouncy had to be seen to be believed' (Mair, 56). And like all enduring champions, Holm was both mentally and physically tough: she won the second of her five Scottish titles in 1932 with a victory at the fifth extra hole.

Holm died of lung cancer on 14 December 1971 at Broomfield Nursing Home, Ayr, her husband having predeceased her. Two years later the Helen Holm trophy event was begun at Holm's beloved Troon Portland, where she once held the ladies' record with 69 and had holed the fourteenth in one. Now one of the premier stroke-play events in the ladies' calendar, with a very high calibre entry, the final round of the trophy is played over the open championship links of Royal Troon, and the victor is awarded Holm's putter as the trophy. MARK POTTLE

Sources L. Mair, *One hundred years of women's golf* (1992) • *Golfer's Handbook* (1967) • E. Wilson, *A gallery of women golfers* (1961) • R. Cossey, *Golfing ladies: five centuries of golf in Great Britain and Ireland* (1984) • M. Crane, *The story of ladies' golf* (1991) • B. Darwin, *Golf between two wars* (1944) • b. cert. • d. cert.
Likenesses photographs, repro. in Cossey, *Golfing ladies*, pp. 65, 171

Wealth at death £108,499.17: confirmation, 28 Feb 1972, *CCI*

Holman, Francis (*bap.* 1729, *d.* 1784), marine painter, was born in Ramsgate and baptized there on 14 November 1729 at St Laurence-in-Thanet, the eldest son and second of six children of Francis Holman (*bap.* 1696, *d.* 1739), master mariner, and his wife, Anne Long (*bap.* 1707, *d.* 1757). His paternal grandfather was a Ramsgate cooper; he believed that his ancestors had come from Dorset to St Nicholas-at-Wade in Thanet in 1564. A younger brother, Captain John Holman (1733–1816), to whom Francis evidently remained close, continued the family shipping business. In a letter of 1800 Captain Holman included the reference 'in 1758 by Francis Holman Herald Painter', indicating that his brother may have begun his career in that branch of painting (MS Letter, priv. coll.). By then Francis Holman lived in Wapping, the main base of Ramsgate's merchant shipping families; all his five known addresses are in or around what are now Wapping High Street and Wapping Lane. Surviving records of St George's-in-the-East document his wife, Elizabeth, and son John (b. 1757), and two more sons, both named Francis, who died in infancy. Holman was a widower by 1781, when on 7 May he married Jane Maxted (c.1736–1790); the Maxteds of Ozengell Grange were a Thanet landowning family. He was apparently childless when he wrote his will in 1783.

Holman's earliest pictures are ship's portraits, often commissioned for ships' masters, a genre in which he continued to paint throughout his career. *The 'John and Mary' and the 'Three Sisters' off the Coast of Dover*, inscribed under the lining 'The John & Mary and 3 Sisters. Painted by Francis Holman of Wappen. 1763 for Capt Maudbe', is a good example (Sotheby sale catalogue, 16 July 1993, p. 12, lot 10). Many paintings show the distinctive landmarks of the Kentish coast, especially the distinctive profile of the line of cliffs around Dover and Deal, that he knew well. From 1767 to 1772 he exhibited eleven pictures at the Free Society of Artists, showing an increasing interest in capturing the mood of the sea in different weathers. The first painting he sent for exhibition was entitled *A Sea Convoy in a Storm* (exh. Free Society, 1767); his later *A Sudden Squall, with Ships Sailing through the Narrow Channel Near Reculver in Kent* (exh. RA, 1777) was described in 1906 by H. Wilson Holman, to whom it then belonged, as a masterly treatment of sea and sky. By 1773 Holman had taken on an apprentice, Thomas Luny, who exhibited from his master's address in Johnson Street, St George's, Wapping.

In his later years Holman switched to patriotic themes. Between 1774 and 1784 he sent seventeen pictures, mostly of the Royal Navy or sea battles, for exhibition at the Royal Academy. He painted all the important naval engagements of the American War of Independence, most notably a dramatic moment, *The Moonlight Battle off Cape St Vincent, 16th January 1780* (exh. RA, 1780; NMM) and *The Battle of the Saints, 12th April 1782* (exh. RA, 1783). He also depicted the shipbuilding programme engendered by that war, one of his best-known paintings being the striking *Blackwall Shipyard from the Thames* (exh. RA, 1784; NMM). Holman died in Wapping on 29 November 1784. Captain Holman brought his body back to Ramsgate for burial on 4 December in the Maxted family vault at St Laurence, where the vicar recorded his death as due to lethargy.

Since Sir Lionel Cust wrote in the *Dictionary of National Biography* that Holman's work had 'met with unmerited neglect' several of his paintings have surfaced in sales and been acquired by museums, and his reputation as a major marine painter has consequently grown. Holman knew his subject matter intimately and approached his chosen profession as a craftsman. His skilful depiction of the seafaring trade in which he grew up provides an entrancing record of many aspects of eighteenth-century naval life.

MICHAEL STEED

Sources Graves, *Soc. Artists* · Graves, *RA exhibitors* · H. W. Holman, 'Francis Holman, marine painter', *Devon Notes & Queries*, 4, 118–22 · J. Holman, letter, 1800, priv. coll. · parish register, Ramsgate, St Laurence-in-Thanet, 14 Nov 1729 [baptism]; 7 May 1781 [marriage]; 4 Dec 1784 [burial] · parish register, London, St George-in-the-East, 1757– [baptism, burial: children] · E. H. H. Archibald, *Dictionary of sea painters*, 2nd edn (1989) · will, PRO, PROB 11/1124, sig. 648
Wealth at death bequeathed money in stocks, no specific amount stated in will

Holman, James Baptiste (1785/6–1857), traveller, was the fourth child of a chemist and druggist of Fore Street, Exeter, where he was born on 15 October in 1785 or 1786. Like his brother William he entered the navy, as a first-class volunteer on the *Royal George* on 7 December 1798. From September 1799 to April 1805 he served in the *Cambrian* on the home and North American stations and then on the *Leander* and the *Cleopatra*, of which last frigate he was appointed lieutenant on 27 April 1807. From October 1808 to November 1810, when he was invalided, he served on the *Guerrière* off the coast of North America. He was invalided out at the age of twenty-four and became totally blind not long afterwards for reasons which are not clear.

Despite his blindness Holman studied briefly at the University of Edinburgh. On 29 September 1812 he was appointed a naval knight of Windsor but, finding life there intolerably quiet, he obtained leave to travel abroad. His first trip, from 1819 to 1821, took him to familiar parts of Europe, but his subsequent journeys were ever more adventurous. His second, from 1822 to 1824, took him as far as Siberia, where he was imprisoned as a spy. He then set off round the world, reaching Africa, Asia, Australasia, and America. In 1826 he was elected fellow of the Royal Society and founder fellow of the Raleigh Club, forerunner of the Royal Geographical Society. His accounts of his travels, although not of lasting worth, were extremely popular at the time, reaching many editions and earning him the name 'the blind traveller'. His fourth and last journey was through Iberia, the Balkans and into Turkey. While preparing his notes for publication he died at his lodgings, 11 Crutched Friars, near the Minories, London, on 28 July 1857; his death certificate gives his age as seventy-one. He left his manuscripts to a literary friend who had helped him compile his earlier works, but they were never published.

Holman was energetic and restless. In London he was usually accompanied by a servant, but when travelling usually went alone, trusting to his own judgement and the kindness of others. His election to the Raleigh Club signified that the foremost travellers of the day esteemed his experience irrespective of his blindness, although it was his braveness in overcoming his disability which won the sympathy of the public.

ELIZABETH BAIGENT

Sources C. R. Markham, *Some account of the Geographical Club*, 6th edn (1905) · C. R. Markham, *The fifty years' work of the Royal Geographical Society* (1881) · N. H. Robinson, *The Royal Society catalogue of portraits* (1980) · J. Wilson, *Biography of the blind, or, The lives of such as have distinguished themselves as poets, philosophers, artists, etc.*, 4th edn (1838) · O'Byrne, *Naval biog. dict.* · d. cert.
Likenesses G. Chinnery, oils, 1830, RS · W. Brockedon, chalk drawing, 1834, NPG · J. R. Jackson, mezzotint, pubd 1849 (after J. P. Knight), BM · R. Cooper, stipple (after Fabrioni), NPG · E. Finden, stipple (after T. Wageman), NPG

Holman, Joseph George (1764–1817), actor and playwright, born in August 1764, was the son of John Major Holman of the parish of St Giles-in-the-Fields, Middlesex, an officer in the British army, who died when his son was two years old. He was sent by his uncle to Dr Barwis's school in Soho Square, where annual theatrical productions were popular. He matriculated on 7 February 1783 at the Queen's College, Oxford, but took no degree. On 26 October 1784, at Covent Garden, he made his first appearance on the stage, as Romeo. An occasional address, the opening lines of which were

> From Isis' banks just wing'd his daring flight
> A College Soph presents himself to-night,

was spoken by Thomas Hull, who played Friar Lawrence. Holman performed a number of other leading roles in his first season, including Richard III, Hamlet, and Lothario. His original characters during his first spell at Covent Garden included Harry Thunder in John O'Keeffe's *Wild Oats* (16 April 1791). At the end of his third season Holman left Covent Garden owing to a dispute over salary, and acted in Dublin and in the principal English and Scottish towns; but he soon returned to his former theatre.

In the season of 1799–1800 a serious quarrel took place between the proprietors of Covent Garden and eight of the principal actors. A pamphlet entitled *A statement of the differences subsisting between the proprietors and performers of the Theatre-Royal, Covent-Garden ...* was published in 1800, and went through several editions. The authorship of the pamphlet, which printed correspondence and memoranda between the proprietors and the actors, was attributed to Holman. The grievances of the actors were submitted to the lord chamberlain, the marquess of Salisbury, whose verdict went against them. Some newspaper correspondence and disturbance in theatrical circles followed. Seven actors accepted the decision and remained at Covent Garden, but Holman either resigned or was dismissed. He appeared a few times at the Haymarket, where he produced his *What a Blunder*, a comic opera in three acts, in which he acted Count Alphonso d'Esparza. He then went to Dublin, where he had sufficient success to take for a time a share with Frederick Edward Jones in the management of Crow Street Theatre. After a while, however, he resigned, and took up farming. On 31 July 1806 he played in Dublin for his benefit Antony in Dryden's *All for Love*. On 22 August 1812 he reappeared at the Haymarket, after eleven years' absence, and played a few parts.

In 1798 Holman had married Jane, the youngest daughter of the Hon. and Revd Frederick Hamilton; she died on 11 June 1810. No mention of a previous marriage is traceable, but, when Holman went to America in 1812 he took with him a daughter old enough to play Lady Townly in Vanbrugh's *The Provoked Husband* in New York to his Lord Townly; she supported him throughout his American career. In a letter of introduction he took out he was erroneously described as a fellow of Queen's College. In 1813 Holman and his daughter performed at the Chestnut Street Theatre, Philadelphia. He undertook the management of the Walnut Street Theatre in that city, but was unsuccessful. In 1815 he managed a theatre in Charleston. In 1817 he married a Miss Lattimer, a singer 'of great talent and distinguished beauty and merit'; she afterwards married C. W. Sandford, and died in 1859. Holman himself died, probably of apoplexy, at Rockaway on Long Island, New York, on 24 August 1817.

Several of Holman's theatrical works were performed; the earliest, the comic opera *Abroad and at Home*, was among the best known. His reputation as an actor was established when he was a young man, and remained high throughout his lifetime. W. C. Macready, in his *Reminiscences*, described him as 'remarkably handsome, though inclined to obesity, his tendency to which he endeavoured to combat by a chicken diet' (1.58).

JOSEPH KNIGHT, *rev.* JOHN WELLS

Sources D. E. Baker, *Biographia dramatica, or, A companion to the playhouse*, rev. I. Reed, new edn, rev. S. Jones, 1 (1812) · J. N. Ireland, *Records of the New York stage, from 1750 to 1860*, 1 (1866) · *The thespian dictionary, or, Dramatic biography of the present age*, 2nd edn (1805) · J. Johnstone and others, *A statement of the differences subsisting between the proprietors and performers of the Theatre-Royal, Covent-Garden* (1800) · *Macready's reminiscences, and selections from his diaries and letters*, ed. F. Pollock, 1 (1875) · Foster, *Alum. Oxon.* · [J. Watkins and F. Shoberl], *A biographical dictionary of the living authors of Great Britain and Ireland* (1816)

Likenesses J. Sayers, etching, pubd 1786, NPG · S. De Wilde, four portraits, Garr. Club · D. Dodd, ink miniature, V&A · G. Dupont, oils (in *King Lear*), Garr. Club · J. Heath, engraving (after bust? by H. Bone), Harvard TC · engravings, Harvard TC · oils (as Hamlet), Garr. Club · prints, BM, NPG

Holman, William (*bap.* 1669, *d.* 1730), county historian, was baptized on 15 December 1669, at Whitchurch Canonicorum, Dorset, the son of William Holman. He had migrated to London by 1690, when he was received into the Stepney Independent meeting, as 'chaplain to Mr Fletcher' (*Holman's Halstead*, vii). In 1700 he became pastor of the Old Independent Chapel, Parsonage Street, Halstead, Essex, where he ministered successfully until his death. His congregation, which in 1716 numbered 500, including 39 county voters and 13 gentlemen, built a new chapel in 1718.

From 1708 to 1728 Holman lived in the Chantry House, High Street, Halstead, formerly part of Bourchier's chantry or college (founded 1412; dissolved 1551), a fitting home

for an antiquary. About 1711 he began compiling a history of Halstead and the surrounding hundred of Hinckford, under the patronage of John 'Carcase' or 'Merchant' Morley of Munchensies (now Blue Bridge House), Halstead, butcher, land-jobber, and agent to Robert Harley, earl of Oxford.

Holman entered into the labours of earlier Essex antiquaries, particularly Thomas Jekyll, a king's bench official with a country house at Bocking, Essex, who had collected from the public records many references to Essex, Norfolk, and Suffolk. Most of Jekyll's manuscript notes had passed to his grandson Nicholas Jekyll of Castle Hedingham, Essex, who put them at the disposal of John Ouseley, rector of Panfield, and later of Springfield and Little Waltham, all in Essex. Ouseley planned a history of Essex, which by 1695 was said to be well advanced, but it never appeared. His death opened the way for a younger historian. Holman, encouraged and helped by Nicholas Jekyll, acquired much of Thomas Jekyll's Essex collection, and also that of Ouseley. With financial backing from John Morley, and also, it seems, from Lord Oxford, he extended his studies to the whole of Essex, undertaking fieldwork as well as documentary research, and corresponding with the antiquaries Peter Le Neve and Thomas Wotton, and in Essex with Thomas Cox, William Derham, Charles Gray of Colchester, and Anthony Holbrook, Ouseley's son-in-law. Humfrey Wanley, Lord Oxford's librarian, gave Holman advice and hospitality, receiving in return original documents and gifts of oysters. Holman's principal assistant over many years was the apothecary and physician Samuel Dale, who sent him manuscripts, pedigrees, and notes from parish registers, and toured the country on horseback, recording monumental inscriptions.

Holman planned a history of Essex consisting mainly of brief histories of each of the 400 parishes, arranged under hundreds. His friends urged publication, but this had not begun when he collapsed and died on 4 November 1730 in the porch of Colne Engaine church, near Halstead. He had been hampered by gout, and, it seems, by lack of experience in writing and publishing, by preoccupation with the details of inscriptions, and by a stubborn refusal to be rushed. He left behind, besides many letters and papers, a set of manuscript booklets containing annotated histories of nearly all the parishes in the county, in each of which is given the Domesday references, the descents of the manors, the parochial charities, and the history of the church and its monuments. The set does not, however, include the ancient borough of Colchester, then the largest town in Essex.

Holman was buried in the chapel where he had ministered, and where his wife, Rebekah (*d.* 1727), already lay. Their son William (*d.* 1748) and his wife, Francis (*d.* 1770), are also buried there. All four are commemorated by a stone tablet in the present United Reformed church in Parsonage Street.

Holman's Essex collection was later used by the antiquaries Nicholas Tindal, Nathanael Salmon, and Philip Morant, whose *History and Antiquities of the County of Essex* was based mainly on Holman's parish booklets. Holman's history of *Halstead* was published finally in 1902, with a memoir by T. G. Gibbons. W. RAYMOND POWELL

Sources Essex RO, Chelmsford, Holman MSS, D/Y 1 · W. Holman, 'History of Essex', Essex RO, Chelmsford, T/P 195 · *Holman's Halstead*, ed. T. G. Gibbons (1902) · C. F. D. Sperling, *Essex Review*, 3 (1894), 261–6 · *VCH Essex*, bibliography [articles in *Essex Review*] · C. E. Cobbold, 'The writing of Essex county history, *c*.1600–1768', *Essex Journal*, 8 (1973), 2 · P. Morant, *The history and antiquities of the county of Essex*, 2 vols. (1768); repr. with introduction by G. H. Martin (1978) · W. J. Evans, *Old and new Halstead* (1886) · W. F. Monk and others, *Congregationalism in Halstead, 1662–1962* (1962) · R. C. Fowler, 'The college of Halstead', *VCH Essex*, 2.192–3 · D. W. Clark, 'The college of Halstead or Bourchier's chantry', *Transactions of the Essex Archaeological Society*, new ser., 14 (1915–17), 311–37 · *Blue Bridge House, Halstead* (*c*.1970)
Archives BL, genealogy of the Harley family, Add. MS 70468 · Bodl. Oxf., Essex collections · Essex RO, catalogue of Nicholas Jekyll papers; corresp. and antiquarian papers | BL, misc. letters to Thomas Wotton and others · BL, Holman's catalogue of MSS of Nicholas Jekyll, Egerton MS 2382, fols. 153–176

Holme, Benjamin (1683–1749), Quaker minister, was born of Quaker parentage at Penrith, Cumberland, in January 1683 NS and brought up as a Friend. In his autobiography he says that 'he grew up in wildness' (*Collection of the Epistles*) but that when he was about fourteen years of age he prayed, and that somewhat later he testified at Quaker meetings for worship. While still very young he was recognized as a minister and travelled to 'visit Friends'. In 1699 he made a journey with Leonard Fell and Joseph Kirkbride, an American Friend, through the north of England. Two years later he visited a number of meetings in the east and west of England and in Wales, and in 1703 he went to Scotland, where he was imprisoned for a night at Glasgow for travelling on the sabbath. The following year he visited Ireland for the first time.

In April 1706 Holme went to live at York, where he appears to have been engaged in business, but he continued to spend a large part of each year in ministerial journeys. In 1712 he again visited Ireland; he was imprisoned at Longford for holding a Quaker meeting, and was ill-treated at Londonderry. In the following year he published *A Tender Invitation and Call to All People, to Embrace the Offers of God's Love*. In 1714 he visited the Friends in the Netherlands, and in the following year those in New England, travelling thence down the eastern colonies to the Carolinas. While in America he debated in public with various ministers but he escaped persecution; he also wrote a tract against mixed marriages, which were then common among American Quakers. In 1719 he visited the West Indies for a few months and was received with kindness by the governors of various islands. He returned to England via Ireland in 1720.

In 1722 Holme took an active part in obtaining from parliament a less objectionable form of affirmation than that then prescribed for Quakers. During the following year he again went to the Netherlands and while there he visited the Baptists and wrote *A Serious Call*, a treatise giving a succinct account of Quaker principles, which was first printed in Dutch and published in 1723; it was subsequently reprinted twenty-four times in English and translated into Latin, French, and Welsh. The following two and a half years were chiefly spent in a minute investigation of the Quaker meetings in Ireland. In a letter to David Bull of Tottenham, dated December 1725, Holme states that he was arrested at Letterkenny for refusing to make a declaration of fidelity in a form that was unacceptable to Quaker thinking, but that he was released after some time at the instance of the bishop of Raphoe. After his return from Ireland, Holme was chiefly occupied in ministerial journeys in England and Scotland. He visited Ireland again in 1734 and once paid a visit to Jersey, where a small meeting was much oppressed by the magistrates, and sought to obtain redress for their grievances.

It is not known whether Holme married. He died at Swansea on 14 April 1749 NS, following an illness brought on by attending a meeting when in bad health, and was buried there. He was widely esteemed, plain, simple, and charitable. His writings are extremely practical and broad in tone, while their style is pleasant and lucid. An autobiographical work, *A collection of the epistles and works of Benjamin Holme, to which is prefixed an account of his life and travels in the work of the ministry, through several parts of Europe and America, written by himself*, was published posthumously in 1753 and reprinted in 1754.

A. C. BICKLEY, *rev.* ROB GOODBODY

Sources *A collection of the epistles and works of Benjamin Holme ... written by himself* (1753) · J. Rutty, *A history of the rise and progress of the people called Quakers in Ireland* (1751) · J. Smith, ed., *A descriptive catalogue of Friends' books*, 2 vols. (1867); suppl. (1893)
Archives RS Friends, Lond., letters

Holme, Bryan (*bap.* 1776, *d.* 1856), lawyer and a founder of the Law Society, was baptized on 29 December 1776 at Tunstall, near Lancaster, the son of William Holme and his wife, Elizabeth. He attended a school at nearby Wray and was articled in 1793 to John Baldwin, a solicitor in Lancaster. On admission in 1800 he worked in Lancaster for a short time before moving to London about 1803 where he entered the offices of Bleasdale and Alexander, solicitors of Hatton Court, Threadneedle Street, and New Inn. Bleasdale and Alexander was a well-established firm which acted for the London Assurance Corporation and the Hudson Bay Company. Holme began as a managing clerk, specializing in chancery work, but he soon became a partner in 1806. The following year he married Anne Simpson, a daughter of Samuel Simpson, shipowner and merchant of Lancaster. In 1810 Holme was elected a member of the Society of Gentlemen Practisers, an exclusive London-based solicitors' association, but he did not become involved in its activities.

By the early 1820s Holme had become the senior partner of the eminent firm of Holme, Frampton, and Loftus. In 1823 he emerged as the leading figure in the project to establish a permanent society for the solicitors' profession, to be called the Law Institution. Until this time the associations for solicitors had been confined either to the metropolis or to localities in the provinces. None had achieved a major impact on the profession as a whole. The

Law Institution represented a new departure and an attempt to form a country-wide professional organization. A number of prospectuses were issued and subscriptions invited to raise a fund for the institution and the building of a hall and library. In 1825 meetings of the subscribers were held in London which led to the formation of the Law Institution. A committee of management, of which Holme was an original member, was appointed to put the scheme into effect. A site in Chancery Lane, at the heart of London's legal quarter, was purchased in 1828 for the construction of the hall, which was completed in 1832. In 1831 a royal charter was obtained and the institution became the Society of Attorneys, Solicitors, Proctors and others, not being Barristers, practising in the Courts of Law and Equity of the United Kingdom, or more simply, the Incorporated Law Society. The name was altered to the Law Society in 1906.

After his initial central role in the formation of the society, Holme played a less conspicuous part in its subsequent development. He became neither chairman of the committee of management nor president. However, he continued as a member of the committee of management (and later the council) until his death, and served on several subcommittees, particularly those which reflected his professional and personal interests, such as the library and chancery subcommittees. His role as the principal architect of the society was recognized in a resolution passed at the special general meeting for accepting the charter in January 1832, and was further celebrated by the raising of a subscription for a full-length portrait by Henry William Pickersgill which was hung in the society's hall in 1834.

Holme continued to practise and quietly pursued his interests in literature and book collecting. He presented many books to the society's library. Late in life, in 1854, he again became involved in professional matters, when plans for establishing a benevolent institution for the relief of aged and infirm London solicitors were broached. Holme was chairman of the provisional committee, but before matters could proceed beyond the circulation of a prospectus, his health declined and the scheme came to nought. Holme died at his residence in Brunswick Square, London, on 15 July 1856 of heart disease and was buried at Kensal Green cemetery. It is curious that his death passed largely unremarked by the Incorporated Law Society and the profession. He was survived by his wife.

ANDREW ROWLEY

Sources 'Memoir of Bryan Holme', *Legal Observer*, 52 (1856), 280–85 · Law Society, 113 Chancery Lane, London, Law Society Archives · Boase, *Mod. Eng. biog.*

Likenesses H. W. Pickersgill, oils, *c*.1834, Law Society, London

Holme, Charles (1848–1923), magazine editor, was born in Derby on 7 October 1848, the younger son of George Holme, silk manufacturer, and his wife, Anne, *née* Brentnall. Educated at a private school in Derby, he was put to his father's trade, but at about the age of twenty-three he went to Bradford and set himself up in the woollen business. His sound commercial transactions brought him financial success, and through the extension of his business to the East he developed an interest in art. A lecture by Robert Barkley Shaw, the oriental traveller, at the Bradford chamber of commerce about 1873, led him to exchange Bradford goods with products from Turkestan and, later, India, China, and Japan. Holme travelled into central Asia and India in 1876. In 1879 he joined Christopher Dresser in the firm of Dresser and Holme, trading in Asian merchandise for the home interior market. Dresser, eighteen years Holme's senior, was a designer, writer, and dealer in Middle Eastern and Asian art objects and art manager of the Art Furnishers' Alliance, also backed by Arthur Liberty. By the 1880s Holme was a buyer for Liberty's department store. He was profoundly struck by the perfection of Japanese craftsmanship. When he toured around the world in 1889, Holme spent some months in Japan; in 1892 he became one of the founders of the Japan Society. He amassed a large collection of old books, prints, letters, drawings, paintings, documents, embroidery, Kelmscott books, and oriental art objects, later sold at Sothebys in 1923 and 1924.

In 1893, after his retirement in 1892, Holme founded *The Studio: An Illustrated Magazine of Fine and Applied Arts* to serve commercial interests and to promote good design. The magazine first cost 6*d.*, then 8*d.*, and then a shilling by the late 1890s. Annual subscriptions before the First World War cost 16*s.* in England (38*s.* abroad) and included three special numbers and the *Year Book of Decorative Art*. Writers included professional critics such as Marcus Huish (editor of the *Art Journal*), D. S. MacColl, and Aymer Vallance, and they worked freelance, also writing for other periodicals. C. Lewis Hind was the first editor, for only four months, followed by Gleeson White, editor until 1895, who continued to write for the magazine until his death in 1898. Walter Shaw Sparrow was art editor from 1899 to 1904. *The Studio*'s intended audience was middle class and its contents sympathetic to mass production. Its advertising was extensive (occupying up to one-third of its total pages) and diverse: home appliances, medicines, artists' supplies, and classifieds. The magazine promoted selected galleries and artists, thus also appealing to a specialized clientele. *The Studio* attained a very wide circulation before the First World War. One innovation was the special number; these appeared three times a year and were written by specialists on such topics as crafts, etching, architecture, photography, and theatre design. In 1906 the magazine began its *Year Book of Decorative Art*; later other annuals appeared.

The Studio held competitions (for drawings, glass, photos, furnishings), a device of the 'new journalism', the methods of which—conversational style, human-interest stories, interviews, and glimpses inside artists' studios (one of its most popular series)—*The Studio* shared with other periodicals, such as the *Magazine of Art*. Art students were encouraged to participate in the magazine's competitions. Appearing when photo-engraving made possible new continuous tone reproduction, *The Studio* promoted the camera (including advertisements for Kodak).

Printmaking techniques were common subjects for articles written by master artists, such as Whistler.

Despite sympathies with journalism and commercial interests and his dual role as proprietor and editor after 1895, Holme was also influenced by William Morris, into whose Red House at Bexleyheath, Kent, he moved in 1889. Holme believed architecture and the applied arts to be as valuable as the fine arts. *The Studio* maintained a high standard of production; lavishly illustrated special numbers were, in effect, books. *The Studio's* fashionableness co-existed with insular resistance to continental modernism. It advocated works by Charles Rennie Mackintosh and Charles F. A. Voysey, and Japanese design, but promoted furniture made from stock patterns and condemned post-impressionism (J. J. Shannon, *The Studio*, 8, 1896, 72) and early Picasso (*The Studio*, 56, 1912, 65). *The Studio* struggled to combine progressive attitudes with commercial appeal to a domestic audience. The first issue had a cover by Aubrey Vincent Beardsley and work by Frank Brangwyn, then unknown artists. Despite their appearance, the editor censored Beardsley's cover design and, subsequently, *Studio* reviewers condemned his illustrations in *The Yellow Book* (*The Studio*, 3, 1894, 131). *The Studio* included articles on women artists and their education and had a large female readership.

Holme hoped to improve international understanding through art and design. The magazine had worldwide distribution, covered foreign art, and published in foreign editions abroad. Foreign correspondents' reports from Paris appeared in the first issue. *The Studio* soon had correspondents in all continental capitals and throughout the British empire, America, and Japan.

Holme had married, in 1873, Clara, daughter of George Benton, brass founder, of Birmingham; they had four children. He continued to participate in *The Studio* work until ill health compelled him to retire in 1922. He died at his house, Upton Grey, near Basingstoke, Hampshire, on 14 March 1923. His only son, Geoffrey Holme, succeeded to the editorship of *The Studio*. JULIE F. CODELL

Sources A. Brothers, *A Studio portrait: the marketing of art and taste, 1893–1918* (1993) · B. Holme, 'Introduction', in B. Holme, *The Studio: a bibliography: the first fifty years* (1978) · D. J. Gordon, 'Dilemmas: The Studio in 1893–4', *Studio International*, 175 (1968), 175–83 · C. Ashwin, 'The Studio and modernism: a periodical's progress', *Studio International*, 193 (1976), 103–13 · WWW · C. Holme, *General index to the first twenty-one volumes of The Studio* (1901) · Sotheby, Wilkinson, and Hodge sale catalogues (1923–4) · W. S. Sparrow, *Memories of life and art* (1925)

Likenesses P. A. de Laszlo, portrait, 1908, repro. in *The Studio* (1911)

Wealth at death £88,447 17s. 7d.: probate, 14 June 1923, CGPLA Eng. & Wales

Holme [*married name* Punchard], **(Edith) Constance** (1880–1955), novelist and short story writer, was born on 7 October 1880 at Owlet Ash, Milnthorpe, Westmorland, the youngest of the fourteen children of John Holme (1829–1905), land agent and, after his retirement in 1880, local magistrate and deputy lord lieutenant of Westmorland,

and his wife, Elizabeth Cartmel (1836–1931), whose parents owned land in nearby Farleton. Constance Holme's parents were both of long-established northern stock. John Holme represented the third generation of a family branch which had settled in Milnthorpe in the late eighteenth century and had acted since then as land agents for the nearby Dallam Tower estate. Both her parents were impressively handsome and had a local reputation for stand-offishness, John Holme being an intimidating figure to the village children. Constance Holme inherited some of their looks and some of their remoteness: a photograph taken when she was eighteen shows a clear-eyed, long-nosed, sensitive-lipped face narrowing to a dimpled, rather weak chin. She loved and admired both her parents and in middle life made periodic visits to Somerset House to trace her ancestry.

Constance Holme's formal education, of the conventional 'young lady' variety, began about 1888. She was first a weekly boarder at a small Methodist school, Oakfield Place, in nearby Arnside. From about 1893 she attended Buckingham House, a school in Birkenhead, finishing her education at Cedar Lodge, Blackheath, London, a school run on strict lines and Church of England principles. Her few years of education in the south constituted the longest period Constance Holme was absent from the estuary and hill landscape she loved, which provided the inspiration and setting for all her work. She achieved national publication first with a poem in the *Westminster Gazette* (5 October 1907), but for some years her larger-scale successes were entirely local: two full-length novels, *Staggie Three* (1905) and *Hugh of Hughsdale* (1906), serialized in the *Kendal Mercury* between 1909 and 1911; and a dialect play, *Duck Egg Dick*, performed in Kendal before a capacity audience in 1912. Her deepest wish was to attain success as a playwright, but this largely eluded her: only two of the many plays she wrote achieved performance in London, *The Home of Vision* in 1919 and *I Want* in 1931. The poetry she wrote throughout her life, and occasionally published in *Country Life*, is skilful but minor.

Constance Holme aroused metropolitan critical interest when she was almost thirty-three with her novel *Crump Folk Going Home* (1913). This and her next two novels, *The Lonely Plough* (1914) and *The Old Road from Spain* (1916), were set in the immediate Milnthorpe area and drew their material from the upper- and middle-class worlds of land-owning and land agency which she knew intimately and described with both realistic accuracy and poetic feeling. *The Lonely Plough*, its dramatic climax drawn from the great River Kent flood of 1907, established her national reputation as a regional novelist of uncommon force and distinction, and became the book most identified with her name.

Constance Holme's ties with the world into which she had been born were strengthened by her marriage to Frederick Burt Punchard (1867–1946) of Kearstwick, Westmorland. The wedding, a grandly feudal local occasion, largely attended, took place at St Peter's, Heversham, on 8 February 1916. Like John Holme, Frederick Punchard was a land agent: educated at Sedbergh School, he had succeeded his father in 1906 as agent at Underley Hall, the estate outside Kirkby Lonsdale of Lord Henry Bentinck. Marriage brought Constance Holme an indulgent if far from handsome husband thirteen years older than herself, and a visit in 1917 to Garsington Manor: Lady Ottoline Morrell, the literary hostess who lived there, was Lord Henry Bentinck's sister, and Constance Holme was by now a minor literary lion. Soon after her marriage, she settled at The Gables, Kirkby Lonsdale, where she spent the next twenty years. Though only 10 miles from Milnthorpe, she was frequently homesick.

Retaining her maiden name as author, Constance Holme published five more novels while living at Kirkby Lonsdale: *Beautiful End* (1918); *The Splendid Fairing* (1919), for which she was awarded the Femina Vie Heureuse prize (later won by Mary Webb and Virginia Woolf) in May 1921; *The Trumpet in the Dust* (1921), arguably her finest work; *The Things which Belong* (1925); and *He-who-Came* (1930). All five novels differ from their predecessors in having a tighter, often single-day time scheme, and in concentrating on characters from a humbler social level. This shift of focus is accompanied by an increase in psychological intensity: the restricted, often disappointed lives with which Constance Holme chooses to deal are presented with a penetration, and an austere beauty, sometimes reminiscent of Hardy and Conrad, the latter of whom she admired passionately.

Constance Holme's novels were reviewed regularly, and with consistent respect, by *The Athenaeum*, *The Spectator*, and the *Times Literary Supplement*. This respect was shared by the publisher to Oxford University, Humphrey Milford, who not only reprinted all of them in the Oxford World's Classics series during the 1930s, but also took the unusual step of putting straight into the series, in 1937, Constance Holme's collection of short stories entitled *The Wisdom of the Simple*. This proved to be her last published book, although over the final decades of her life she almost succeeded in completing one more novel, *The Jasper Sea*, which had as its protagonist a village handyman and gravedigger.

When her husband retired from land agency in 1937, Constance Holme returned with him to Milnthorpe, to live again at Owlet Ash. Recurring ailments (nervous disorders of the stomach, sciatica, neuritis, tetany) made her later years difficult, as did her sense that the world was changing out of recognition, and for the worse. During the Second World War she became more reclusive; on 25 April 1946 her husband died of bronchopneumonia; and by the autumn of 1953 she was living, alone and much shrunk physically, in a single room of the Georgian house she could no longer afford to maintain. In February 1954 she moved to a small terraced house, 13 Orchard Road, Arnside. By a sad irony reminiscent of some of her novels, her eldest sister, Annie, whom she had hoped to be living next to, died at the age of ninety-two, just as she moved in. She herself died in the following year, on 17 June 1955, of cancer. The funeral, attended by fewer than twenty people, took place on 20 June 1955 at St Thomas's, Milnthorpe; she joined her husband in a grave just across the road from the family home she had had to sell. Structural alterations were already in progress.

Philip Gardner

Sources private information (2004) · Ransom HRC, Constance Holme archive · B. Rota, 'Some uncollected authors XI: Constance Holme', *Book Collector*, 5 (1956), 250–55 · R. K. Bingham, *The chronicles of Milnthorpe* (1987) · D. McCall, *When that I was* (1952) · C. Holme, 'Preface', *The old road from Spain*, World's Classics edn (1932) · A. L. Brown, 'Constance Holme (1880–1955)', *Sérif* (April 1964), 21–4 · *Westmorland Gazette* (12 Feb 1916) · *Westmorland Gazette* (25 June 1955)

Archives Ransom HRC, MSS and literary papers, letters · University of Bristol Library, special collections, corresp. and literary papers

Likenesses photographs, priv. coll.

Wealth at death £26,744 16s. 9d.: probate, 17 Sept 1955, CGPLA Eng. & Wales

Holme, Edward (1770–1847), physician, son of Thomas Holme, farmer and mercer, was born at Kendal, Westmorland, on 17 February 1770. After attending Sedbergh School he spent two years at the Manchester Academy, from 1787 to 1789, and then went on to study at the universities of Göttingen and Edinburgh. He graduated MD at Leiden in December 1793, with a thesis entitled 'De structura et usu vasorum absorbentium'.

Early in 1794 Holme began in practice at Manchester and he was elected one of the physicians to the infirmary there in April that year. He joined the Literary and Philosophical Society on settling in Manchester and was one of its vice-presidents from 1797 to 1844, when he succeeded his friend John Dalton as president. He became a member of the Linnean Society in 1799. Holme was one of the founders of the Portico Library, and its president for twenty-eight years. He was also a founder and the first president of both the Manchester Natural History Society and the Chetham Society. He was the first president of the medical section of the British Association at its inaugural meeting at York in 1831, and he presided over the Provincial Medical and Surgical Association in 1836.

Holme struggled to build up his practice for many years, but it was not until after the death of John Ferriar that he became a leader in the medical profession in Manchester, and the recognized head in all the local literary and scientific societies. He was well known for his extensive learning, which earned him the sobriquet, 'the walking dictionary', from Thomas Percival (*The Lancet*, 637), and he possessed a large and valuable library at his house on King's Street. Nevertheless, though he was known to 'get "impetuously warm" in discussions with some of his friends', he found expressing himself in writing difficult (Brockbank, 195). Of the fourteen essays contributed to the Literary and Philosophical Society on a range of antiquarian and literary topics, he published only one, the short 'Note on a Roman inscription found at Manchester' (*Memoirs of the Literary and Philosophical Society of Manchester*, 2nd ser., 5 1831), refusing to allow the publication of the others. Another essay, 'On the history of sculpture to the time of Phidias', was printed after his death.

Holme died unmarried on 28 November 1847 at Manchester, and was buried at Ardwick cemetery on 13 December, leaving property worth over £50,000. The greater part of this he bequeathed, together with his large library, to the medical department of University College, London.   C. W. SUTTON, rev. PATRICK WALLIS

Sources R. W. Innes Smith, *English-speaking students of medicine at the University of Leyden* (1932) • W. C. Henry, 'A biographical notice of Edward Holme', *Transactions of the Provincial Medical and Surgical Association*, 16 (1849), 99–114 • E. M. Brockbank, *Sketches of the lives and work of the honorary medical staff of the Manchester Infirmary: from its foundation in 1752 to 1830* (1904) • *The Lancet* (11 Dec 1847) • *Manchester Guardian* (1 Dec 1847) • *Manchester Guardian* (4 Dec 1847) • *Manchester Guardian* (8 Dec 1847) • A. Brooks and B. Haworth, *Boomtown Manchester, 1800–1850* (1993) • T. Baker, *Memorials of a dissenting chapel* (1884)
Archives Chetham's Library, Long Millgate, Manchester, corresp. and medical papers
Likenesses J. R. Jackson, mezzotint (after W. Scott), Wellcome L. • W. Scott, portrait, Manchester Literary and Philosophical Society
Wealth at death over £50,000

Holme, Randle (1570/71–1655), herald, was born in Chester, son of Thomas Holme (*d.* 1610), a blacksmith descended from a prosperous gentry family from Tranmere, Cheshire, and his wife, Elizabeth Devenett of Kinnerton, Flintshire. He was the first of four generations, all named Randle, who were members of the Stationers' Company of Chester and who worked as herald painters and genealogists. Holme was apprenticed to Thomas Chaloner (*d.* 1598), deputy to William Flower (1498?–1588), Norroy king of arms, on 10 January 1578. In 1598 he married Chaloner's widow, Elizabeth (*d.* 1635), *née* Alcock; they raised three children, William, Randle [*see below*], and Elizabeth, in a leased house on the Bridge Street corner of Castle Lane, St Mary's on the Hill, Chester.

Holme was elected an alderman by 1604 and was appointed as a servant to Prince Henry by May 1607. More importantly, on 1 March 1600 and again on 20 May 1606 Norroy appointed Holme deputy herald in Cheshire, Lancashire, and north Wales. A change of rules governing deputies in 1618 effectively annulled his office, but in 1619 after persistent lobbying he was reappointed deputy to the College of Arms for Cheshire and north Wales.

Besides his main role of arranging funerals of those entitled to bear arms, Holme made money painting hatchments and marshalling funerals, about which he made detailed notes, completing 121 heraldic and genealogical funeral certificates and collecting the fees payable to the heralds, earning 2s. in the pound for his trouble. However, as his grandson once wrote, 'gentlemen … will order their own concerns' (Earwaker, 143) and Holme certainly had great difficulty overcoming their reluctance to pay—it took twelve years to collect Sir Thomas Ireland's fee—and this led to frequent discord with his masters in London.

From the early 1620s, when he suffered from a rupture that made long journeys painful, Holme delegated the annual Easter trips to report to the College of Arms to his son Randle. Thus he was fined for not attending Charles I's coronation, and for refusing a knighthood in 1631. Holme was sheriff of Chester in 1628, alderman in 1629, and in

October 1633 he was elected mayor. On 19 July 1634 he was so busy overseeing the Saturday market that he failed to attend the arrival of the earl of Arundel; the earl summoned Holme, berated him furiously, and fined him. On 11 September 1635 Holme married his second wife Catherine Browne (*d.* 1672), formerly Ellis, daughter of Ralph Allen, alderman of Chester.

Holme remained in the city during the siege of Chester, from September 1645 to February 1646, and the ensuing plague of 1648. Sir William Brereton, who captured the city for parliament, called him a 'friend of trust' and, having taken the covenant in 1645, he became a commissioner of the peace and oversaw the repair of the city walls. Despite this, the committee for compounding fined him £160 on the strength of a petition submitted, apparently without Holme's authority, by his nephew Thomas Alcock. Claiming he had 'never acted against Parliament', Holme disputed the fine and produced testimony from Brereton and others, which seems to have led to his being let off.

Holme died on 16 January 1655 at the age of eighty-four and was buried on 30 January 1655 at St Mary's on the Hill, Chester, where he and his family are commemorated by memorials, leaving a house in Eastgate to his wife and the rest of his estate, including the manuscript collection he had inherited from Chaloner and to which he had added voluminously, to his son Randle.

Randle Holme (*bap.* 1601, *d.* 1659), herald, was baptized on 15 July 1601 at St Mary's on the Hill, Chester; he married in the same church on 29 September 1625 Catherine (*d.* 1640), a granddaughter of his future stepmother and daughter of Mathew Ellis of Overleigh: their eldest son, Randle *Holme (1627–1700), followed his father as a herald. Other children who survived infancy were William, Elizabeth, Amy, Alice, and Ralph. He married secondly, in September 1643, Elizabeth Martyn (*d. c.*1671), daughter of Thomas Dodd of Chester. They lived at Elizabeth's house in Watergate Street, Holy Trinity, from 1643 until Randle Holme the elder's death, when they returned to Castle Lane.

Holme worked closely with his father, becoming deputy herald for Lancashire in 1627. He was city treasurer in 1633, clerk to the Stationers' Company in 1641, and mayor for a year from October 1643, working with the royalist governor to defend the city from parliamentarians under Sir William Brereton. Following the city's fall to Brereton, parliament dismissed him from his offices of alderman and JP. Permission for him to compound for his estate was withdrawn in November 1651; there is no record of whether he paid his fine. He worked latterly as a genealogist, admitting he had insufficient learning to compile proper pedigrees. He was buried at St Mary's on the Hill on 1 September 1659.   ANTHONY R. J. S. ADOLPH

Sources G. Ormerod, *The history of the county palatine and city of Chester*, 2nd edn, ed. T. Helsby, 3 vols. (1882) • memorial inscription, St Mary's on the Hill, Chester • parish register, Chester, St Mary's on the Hill, 29 May 1635 [burial] • will of Elizabeth Holme, BL, Harley MS 2022, fols. 148ff. • J. P. Earwaker, 'The four Randle Holmes of Chester, antiquaries, heraldists and genealogists, c.1571 to 1707',

Chester Antiquarian Society, 4 (1892), 113–70 · G. D. Squibb, 'The deputy heralds of Chester', *Journal of the Chester Archaeological Society*, 56 (1969), 23–36 · F. R. Raines, ed., 'Letters on the claims of the College of Arms in Lancashire in the time of James the First', *Chetham miscellanies*, 5, Chetham Society, 96 (1875) · W. H. Godfrey, A. Wagner, and H. Stanford London, *The College of Arms, Queen Victoria Street* (1963) · J. P. Rylands, ed., *Cheshire and Lancashire funeral certificates, AD 1600 to 1678*, Lancashire and Cheshire RS, 6 (1882) · T. W. King and F. R. Raines, eds., *Lancashire funeral certificates*, Chetham Society, 75 (1869), 50 · M. A. E. Green, ed., *Calendar of the proceedings of the committee for compounding … 1643–1660*, 5 vols., PRO (1889–92) · A. Wagner, *Heralds of England: a history of the office and College of Arms* (1967) · R. F. Gould, *The history of freemasonry: its antiquities, symbols, constitutions, customs*, 3 (1887)
Archives BL, Harley MSS 1920–2177, 5955, 7568–7569 · Coll. Arms, MSS

Holme, Randle (*bap.* 1601, *d.* 1659). *See under* Holme, Randle (1570/71–1655).

Holme, Randle (1627–1700), herald painter, was born on 24 December 1627 and baptized on 30 December at St Mary's on the Hill, Chester, the son of Randle *Holme (*bap.* 1601, *d.* 1659) [*see under* Holme, Randle (1570/71–1655)], herald, and his wife, Catherine (*d.* 1640). He married on 23 August 1655 Sarah (*bap.* 1629, *d.* 1665), daughter of the Revd Henry Soley; they had five children, Randle [*see below*], Sarah, Elizabeth, Katherine, and Rachel. On 31 July 1666 he married Elizabeth (1643–1685), daughter of George Wilson of Chester, with whom he had eight more children, George (*d.* 1667), George, William, Raphe, Thomas, John, Amy, and Alice. In 1689 he married Ann (Birkenhead?).

Holme was steward to the Stationers' Company in 1656 and alderman from 1659, when he moved to Bridge Street, Chester. In 1664 Charles II granted him a sinecure, the position of sewer of the chamber in extraordinary, but he worked as an unlicensed herald painter, incurring the wrath of Dugdale, who tore down the hatchments he had made and sued him for £20. However, by 1675 he was taking funeral certificates for Dugdale, and by 1678 he was deputy herald for Chester, Lancashire, and north Wales, apparently only for a couple of years, after which he continued to be a herald painter. A freemason, he made records of a lodge in Chester about 1665.

Holme wrote *The Academie of Armorie* (anagramatizing his name as 'Lo Mens Herald'), 'a fascinating encyclopaedia masquerading as a book of heraldry' (Wagner, 240). In 1688 he printed books 1 and 2 and part of book 3 at his house, giving up owing to expense and 'Gentlemen's coldness of zeal' (*Academie*, conclusion). The remainder of book 3 and book 4 were published by the Roxburghe Club in 1905. Holme died on 12 March 1700 and was buried at St Mary's on the Hill, Chester, on 15 March.

Holme's son **Randle Holme** (*c.*1659–1707), herald painter, married Margaret (*d.* 1733), daughter of Griffith Lloyd of Llanarmon, Denbighshire, about 1687 and had five children who all died young. Holme worked in partnership with his father; he seems not to have been a deputy herald but was sheriff of Chester in 1705. He died on 30 August 1707 and was buried at St Mary's on the Hill on 2

September, leaving benefactions of £300. The family manuscript collection of 261 volumes is catalogued as Harley MSS 1920–2180 in the British Library.

ANTHONY R. J. S. ADOLPH

Sources J. P. Earwaker, 'The four Randle Holmes of Chester, antiquaries, heraldists and genealogists, c.1571 to 1707', *Chester Antiquarian Society*, 4 (1892), 113–70 · G. Ormerod, *The history of the county palatine and city of Chester*, 2nd edn, ed. T. Helsby, 3 vols. (1882) · G. D. Squibb, 'The deputy heralds of Chester', *Journal of the Chester Archaeological Society*, 56 (1969), 23–36 · W. H. Godfrey, A. Wagner, and H. Stanford London, *The College of Arms, Queen Victoria Street* (1963) · J. P. Rylands, ed., *Cheshire and Lancashire funeral certificates, AD 1600 to 1678*, Lancashire and Cheshire RS, 6 (1882) · T. W. King and F. R. Raines, eds., *Lancashire funeral certificates*, Chetham Society, 75 (1869), 50 · M. A. E. Green, ed., *Calendar of the proceedings of the committee for compounding … 1643–1660*, 5 vols., PRO (1889–92) · A. Wagner, *Heralds of England: a history of the office and College of Arms* (1967) · R. F. Gould, *The history of freemasonry: its antiquities, symbols, constitutions, customs*, 3 (1887) · will, proved consistory court of Chester, 1707
Archives BL, Cheshire collection, Harley MSS 1920–2177, 5955, 7568–7569 · Ches. & Chester ALSS, pedigree roll · Coll. Arms, MSS

Holme, Randle (*c.*1659–1707). *See under* Holme, Randle (1627–1700).

Holme, Thomas (1626/7–1666), Quaker missionary, was born at Kendal in Westmorland to parents at present unknown, and was by trade a weaver. In 1652 he was convinced by William Gibson and later became 'the apostle of Quakerism in South Wales' (Braithwaite, *Beginnings*, 92). In 1653 he began his first missionary tour of Cumberland, Westmorland, co. Durham, Lancashire, Staffordshire, and Cheshire where, although he experienced success in gaining converts, he occasionally met violent opposition. In October 1653, while preaching at a conventicle at Durham, he was 'violently pulled downe … from the seat on wch he stood' (Penney, 89), but was rescued by other Friends at the meeting. Similarly on 28 August 1655 while in prison at Chester, Holme wrote to Margaret Fell noting that prior to his arrest he had 'suffered sum percution … stones & durt cast upon mee' (RS Friends, Lond., Swarthmore MSS, 1.197). In a letter of 10 December 1655 Holme observed that William Bell, vicar of Huyton near Liverpool, had threatened to confront the Quakers and 'have our blood' (ibid., 1.194).

In earlier letters written from Chester between March and October 1654 to George Fox, Thomas Willan, and Margaret Fell, Holme noted that he was in prison along with other Friends, notably **Elizabeth Leavens** (*d.* 1665) who was to become his wife and fellow Quaker missionary. In March 1654 he noted that before he was arrested the officer sent to apprehend him fainted, which was taken by Friends as a sign that Holme had received God's favour. To assist his missionary work in northern England and on the Welsh borders the Society supplied him with a pair of shoes and breeches worth 10s. 6d. from a fund for travelling Quaker preachers, while Thomas Storey, another early Quaker, bequeathed £5. During his confinement at Chester Holme was often moved by the Lord to sing loudly at any hour of the day or night; as he wrote to Margaret Fell on 5 April 1654:

And the power was so great it made all my fellow-prisoners amazed, and some were shaken, for the power was exceeding great, and I scarcely know whether I was in the body, yea or no, and there appeared light in the prison and astonished me, and I was afraid, and trembled at the appearance of the light, my legs shook under me: and my fellow-prisoners beheld the light and wondered, and the light was so glorious it dazzled my eyes. (Braithwaite, *Beginnings*, 125)

Apart from his preaching and singing, in August 1655 Holme walked the streets of Chester 'naked as a sign' which led to a further period of imprisonment in the city gaol. It seems that his preaching was successful and occasioned 'a remarkable revival in Cheshire and South Lancashire, where his excitable nature had awakened a condition in his hearers' (Brailsford, 149).

It was, however, in Wales that Holme made his greatest impact. He held open-air meetings or 'threshing meetings' in Wales and frequently harangued clergymen. As a consequence he was constantly imprisoned and received 'many hardships, as scoffing, scorneing, beatinge, and Imprisonmt' (Penney, 257). On 16 October 1654 he married Elizabeth Leavens, after they had seen visions that this was the will of God. Their marriage and Elizabeth's subsequent pregnancy in 1656 caused Margaret Fell to rebuke the couple as she felt that they were undermining their missionary work and burdening recently 'convinced' members in south Wales. Yet both continued to preach after their marriage and ensured that they conducted separate preaching tours. They had three children who remained with fellow Friends, but who after the death of Thomas and Elizabeth 'walked not in the steps of theire honrable parents' (ibid., 260).

The preaching of Holmes and his wife quickly converted many Welsh people to Quakerism. In 1655 Thomas Willan of Kendal wrote to Margaret Fell about the success of their missionary work, and on 27 February 1656 Holme himself wrote to Fox that his arrival in Radnor had led to the conversion of many Welsh Baptists and consequently 'many of the Churches ar[e] broken in pecses' (RS Friends, Lond., Swarthmore MSS, 4.247). He had, he continued, held two further meetings in Abergavenny in Monmouthshire, the first at an inn and the second, the following day, in the market place where he 'drew the peopell into A convenient place & spok A prety time to them' (ibid.). Such meetings, he felt, 'cast A sund thoraw the town & country for not any frind had spoken ther before …' and '… the Lord is gathering A peopell in Munmuthshir & Glamorganshir' (ibid.). Similarly he informed Margaret Fell the following April that in Monmouthshire and Glamorgan Friends were able to hold at least ten meetings on a regular basis and 'in many places hear is breakings thorow A peopell the lord … is gathering' (RS Friends, Lond., Swarthmore MSS, 1.203).

With the assistance of Holme's wife, Elizabeth, and Alice Birkett, another itinerant preacher, further meetings were held throughout south Wales, and among the first attenders were two justices of the peace, one at Newport and Walter Jenkins of Llanfihangel Ystum Llywern. More conversions soon followed. As the meetings increased in size Holme was able to organize small communities of worshippers to meet in family homes or at other suitable venues.

In 1657 Holme complained about Welsh Friends who had accompanied James Nayler to Bristol. He criticized the constant interruptions of Nayler's devotees to the Welsh meetings and noted their 'tumbling on floors' and their preference for sackcloth and ashes (RS Friends, Lond., Swarthmore MSS, 1.196). In response George Fox visited Wales and, with the assistance of Holme, helped to convince many of 'Truth' and established new meetings. On 16 April 1657 Holme expressed his fervent piety in a letter to Margaret Fell:

I know that hee that hath delivered me will alsoe deliver mee, from every evell worke, hee hath not left my soull in hell, but hath redemed it by his precious blood, of which I daily drinke, wher by I am dayly refreshed. (ibid.)

The following year Holme was imprisoned at Usk, Monmouthshire, for disturbing a minister during divine service at Caer-went, and continued to preach against 'hireling' ministers throughout the remaining years of the interregnum. Outdoor meetings continued to be held: in March 1660 Holme recorded both that at several meetings in south Wales 'many was convinced of the truth … and unclean spirits are cept down … the power of god is on top of that which would have been on top of it' and the continuing animosity that such meetings generated; soldiers had violently broken up a meeting in Monmouthshire and 'threatened to pistol one or two of us', later imprisoning nineteen Friends at Usk gaol (RS Friends, Lond., Swarthmore MSS, 4.253, 252). He was again imprisoned at Cardiff in 1661. The persecution of Friends had not abated by 1663 when Holme wrote to Fox on 11 June noting the various meetings that had been established in Wales as well as the occasional violence encountered by Friends.

Holme, along with other missionary Friends from the north of England, was 'instrumentall to the Convincemt of many, and to strengthen in the Truth those that were convinc't before' (Penney, 323). On 10 September 1665 Elizabeth Holme died at Kendal and on 2 October 1666 Thomas died, at St Fagans, near Cardiff, aged thirty-nine. On 4 October he was interred at the Pont-y-Moel burial-ground in Pontypool. According to Friends his death was 'greatly Lameneted … his service amongst them haveing bene so great that he was highly Esteemed & beloved by them above most' (ibid., 257). RICHARD C. ALLEN

Sources 'Great book of sufferings', RS Friends, Lond., vol. 2, fol. 2 · RS Friends, Lond., Swarthmore papers · 'Dictionary of Quaker biography', RS Friends, Lond. [card index] · F. Gawler, *A record of some persecutions … in south Wales* (1659), 6 · J. Besse, *A collection of the sufferings of the people called Quakers*, 1 (1753), 735–62 · N. Penney, ed., *'The first publishers of truth': being early records, now first printed, of the introduction of Quakerism into the counties of England and Wales* (1907), 16n., 37, 89, 90, 147, 209n., 218, 230, 257, 260, 323–4, 368 · T. M. Rees, *A history of the Quakers in Wales* (1925), 17–18, 22–5, 35, 40, 73, 175 · M. F. Williams, 'The Society of Friends in Glamorgan, 1654–1900', MA diss., U. Wales, Aberystwyth, 1950, 17–19, 31–2, 35, 56, 61–2 · R. C. Allen, 'The Society of Friends in Wales: the case of Monmouthshire, c.1654–1836', PhD diss., U. Wales, Aberystwyth, 1999, 38, 61–4, 66–7, 71–2, 201, 220, 230–31, 240–41 · M. F. Williams, 'Glamorgan Quakers, 1654–1900', *Morgannwg*, 5 (1961), 49–75 · M. R.

Brailsford, *Quaker women, 1650–1690* (1915), 48, 148–56 · R. Jones, *Crynwyr Bore Cymru, 1653–1699* (1931), 16, 19, 20–25, 27, 32, 35, 62, 68 · W. C. Braithwaite, *The beginnings of Quakerism*, ed. H. J. Cadbury, 2nd edn (1955), 92–3, 105n., 114, 120, 125–6, 155, 207, 236–7, 249n., 270, 347, 375 · W. C. Braithwaite, *The second period of Quakerism*, ed. H. J. Cadbury, 2nd edn (1961), 353 · *The journal of George Fox*, rev. edn, ed. J. L. Nickalls (1952), 174, 290 · R. Nichols, 'More about early Quakers in Monmouthshire', *Anglo-Welsh Review*, 25 (spring 1976), 97–113 · D. Salmon, 'The Quakers of Pembrokeshire', *Transactions of the Historical Society of West Wales*, 9 (1920–23), 1–32 · G. F. Nuttall, *The Welsh saints, 1640–1660* (1957), 57–63 · Society of Friends registers, Pont-y-moel burials, 1662–1787, PRO, RG6/1010, no.667

Archives RS Friends, Lond., Swarthmore papers, letters to Margaret Fell, George Fox, and Thomas Willan

Holme, Vera Louise (1881–1969), actress and suffragette, was born on 29 August 1881 at 6 Lulworth Road, Birkdale, Lancashire, the daughter of Richard Holme, a timber merchant, and his wife, Mary Louisa (*née* Crowe). Nothing is known for certain of her education; she may have spent some of her youth in a convent school in France. She was an accomplished violinist and singer and by 1908 was a member of the chorus of the D'Oyly Carte Opera Company. Vera Holme became involved in the militant women's suffrage movement, joining the Women's Social and Political Union (WSPU) and, in 1908, the Actresses' Franchise League. Sylvia Pankhurst described her as 'a noisy, explosive young person, frequently rebuked by her elders for lack of dignity' (Pankhurst, 225).

The 7 May 1909 issue of *Votes for Women*, the WSPU's weekly paper, contained a poem, 'An Organ Record', written by Vera Holme to commemorate her escapade on 2 May, when, with another suffragette, she hid after an evening concert inside the organ in the Colston Hall, Bristol, staying there all night and the next day in order to call out 'Votes for women' during the course of a meeting being held by a government minister that evening. She was an adept horsewoman and appeared, mounted, as a marshal at many WSPU demonstrations. In late 1909 she became chauffeur to the leaders of the WSPU, Mrs Pankhurst and Mrs Pethick-Lawrence, wearing a striking uniform in the WSPU colours, with a smart peaked cap, decorated with her RAC badge of efficiency. Her hair was now cut decidedly short and in November 1909 she appeared as Hannah Snell, the woman who went to war disguised as a soldier, in Cicely Hamilton's *Pageant of Great Women*, a propaganda play staged by the suffrage societies. In November 1911 Vera Holme was sentenced to five days' imprisonment on a charge of stone-throwing; this appears to have been her only prison sentence. Through the suffrage movement she met and became a very close friend of the Hon. Evelina Haverfield, with whom she lived in Devon from 1911. It was probably about this time that she acquired the nickname Jack or Jacko.

On the outbreak of the First World War Vera Holme joined the Women's Volunteer Reserve, and was commissioned a major on 1 October 1914. She served in the transport unit of the Scottish Women's Hospital from 1915 to 1916, in charge of horses and trucks, working with Mrs Haverfield. In October 1917 Vera Holme was entrusted by Dr Elsie Inglis with the details of a report on the situation

Vera Louise Holme (1881–1969), by Dorothy Johnstone, 1919

of the Serb army at the Romanian front. She and another member of the Scottish Women's Hospital team were instructed when they returned to England to present the full report in person to Lord Robert Cecil of the Foreign Office and Lord Derby, the secretary of state for war. After the end of the war and the death of Evelina Haverfield, who left her a small annuity, Vera Holme was the administrator of the Haverfield Fund for Serbian Children. She kept in touch with Serbian friends and visited the country again in 1934. She lived in Scotland, at Allt Griannach, Lochearnhead, Perthshire, and was associated with the artistic set that centred on Kirkcudbright. Its leader, Jessie M. King, designed a most appropriate book-plate for her, depicting an armoured Joan of Arc figure with the legend 'O Freedom Beautiful Beyond Compare Thy Kingdom is Established', presumably marking women's emancipation. She was twice painted by the Edinburgh artist Dorothy Johnstone. Vera Holme had been an acting member of the Pioneer Players from 1914 to 1915 and from 1917 to 1920, and remained a lifelong friend of Edith Craig, the daughter of Ellen Terry, for many years helping to stage the annual Ellen Terry memorial performance in the Barn

Theatre at Smallhythe in Kent. Vera Holme died at 50 St Andrew's Drive, Glasgow, on 1 January 1969 of renal failure and arteriosclerosis.   ELIZABETH CRAWFORD

Sources L. Leneman, *In the service of life: the story of Elsie Inglis and the Scottish women's hospitals* (1994) · E. S. Pankhurst, *The suffragette movement: an intimate account of persons and ideals* (1931) · E. S. McLaren, *A history of the Scottish women's hospitals* (1919) · D. Atkinson, *The suffragettes in pictures* (1996) · b. cert. · d. cert. · private information (2004)
Archives Women's Library, London | FILM BFI NFTVA, news footage
Likenesses D. Johnstone, *c.*1918, repro. in McLaren, *History of the Scottish women's hospitals* · D. Johnstone, portrait, 1919, priv. coll. [*see illus.*] · photograph, Museum of London, Suffragette Fellowship collection; repro. in Atkinson, *The suffragettes*, 33

Holme, Wilfrid (*d.* 1538), author, was the son of Thomas Holme (*d.* 1520), gentleman, of Huntington near York, and his wife, Margaret, daughter of Sir Thomas Bolton of Huby. The Holme family had acquired the manor of Huntington in the later fifteenth century and had close connections with the ruling élite in the city of York, where the family held lands and where another branch was active in civic life. The estate at Huntington was settled on Wilfrid in 1511 on the occasion of his marriage to Elizabeth, daughter of Philip Constable of Skirton, a member of a junior branch of the Flamborough Constables.

Few details are known of Holme's life beyond his authorship in 1537 of a lengthy poem of 269 stanzas entitled *The Fall and Evill Success of Rebellion*, which recalled the events and issues surrounding the recent rising in the north known as the Pilgrimage of Grace. The poem takes the form of a medieval dream allegory, a form much favoured by more famous contemporary court poets such as John Skelton, and reveals Holme as a man familiar with classical and English history, though there is no evidence to suggest where he acquired this learning. Holme's poem takes a strongly reformist line, claiming that while some gentry were compelled to join the rising by the Commons, more were 'seduced with the Papistes devise' (Dickens, 118), and goes on to attack the state of the monasteries and to oppose saints' days, miracles, and the doctrine of purgatory. Holme strongly defends the royal supremacy, likening Henry VIII to the Old Testament kings of Israel, and praises the monarch for abolishing mortuary fees and other clerical privileges.

Holme's poem provides a provincial reflection of the concerns expressed to parliament in 1529 in Simon Fish's influential pamphlet *The Supplicacyon for the Beggars*. Holme's protestant views led him to support clerical marriage, while he denounces as a dog who has returned to his vomit Sir Francis Bigod, formerly a fellow reformer who had become involved with the rebels and who was executed on 2 June 1537. The poem finishes with a reference to the Mouldwarp prophecy of Merlin, recorded in Geoffrey of Monmouth's *History* and, with other such prophecies, current among the rebels, and with a resounding acclamation of King Henry. The text of the poem, with its mixture of archaic forms and sources and its knowledge of humanist and protestant ideas, stands as a corrective to

an oversimplified view of the north as a bastion of conservatism at this time, and demonstrates how cultural and religious debates in the capital and at court could reach the modest provincial gentry. Holme died before the end of July 1538, leaving lands at Haxby and Huntington which were held in trust by his kinsmen Sir Marmaduke Constable and Seth Snawsell for his eight-year-old son, Seth. His poem remained unpublished until it was printed in 1572 and again in 1573, when it formed part of the government's propaganda campaign in the wake of another recent rising in the north, which had the express ambition of deposing Elizabeth I and restoring Catholicism.

WILLIAM JOSEPH SHEILS

Sources A. G. Dickens, *Lollards and protestants in the diocese of York, 1509–1558*, 2nd edn (1982) · *VCH Yorkshire North Riding*, vol. 2 · D. M. Palliser, *Tudor York* (1979)

Holmes, Abraham (*d.* 1685), army officer and conspirator, was perhaps from co. Durham, though nothing definite is known of his background. He first appears during the early years of the civil war as a lieutenant in Robert Lilburne's regiment of arquebusiers in Lord Ferdinando Fairfax's parliamentarian army in Yorkshire. In 1646 Holmes was a captain in Lilburne's foot regiment in the New Model Army and in the following year was prominent as one of its regimental agitators. From August 1648 to March 1650 Holmes served with the regiment, now under the command of Sir Arthur Hesilrige, at Newcastle and Tynemouth. In June 1650 Holmes's foot company formed part of the new regiment under George Monck, and by August, Holmes, who was reputedly a Baptist by faith, had risen to the rank of major. He fought in Scotland that same year and was eventually appointed JP for Edinburgh and Haddingtonshire.

In December 1654 Holmes was approached by the ringleaders of what became known as Overton's plot, who expected him to mobilize those disaffected with the protectorate among Monck's officers. Instead Holmes revealed their plans to Monck, who sent him to London for further interrogation. Convinced of his loyalty, Cromwell returned Holmes to Scotland. In July 1659 the restored Rump promoted Holmes to lieutenant-colonel of Roger Sawrey's regiment stationed at Ayr. In December of that year, in anticipation of Monck's purge of unreliable officers, Holmes joined Sawrey in a futile attempt to hold Ayr for the army in England. Holmes eventually fled to Carlisle, but was displaced from the army in early 1660.

Holmes remained an outspoken republican and nonconformist following the Restoration, keeping company with London's disaffected. In 1664 he was arrested at a tavern near the Exchange for his alleged involvement in a plot to raise a rebellion with Dutch arms. He was imprisoned without trial in Windsor Castle for at least three years. The date of his release is unknown, but he was active in whig circles in the early 1680s. In 1681 Holmes hid the earl of Argyll, who had escaped from Edinburgh where he was being held for high treason. In August 1682 Argyll fled to the Netherlands, and Holmes remained his agent in London, passing ciphered letters between Argyll and the whig lords active in the Rye House plot. In June

1683 Holmes was arrested and committed to the Gatehouse, charged with treason. Argyll's encoded letters along with some of their keys were found in his possession. On 29 June Holmes confessed that the letters concerned negotiations between Argyll and the whig leaders, including Monmouth and Lord Russell, to raise an insurrection in Scotland. Holmes, whose wife was granted permission to visit him in gaol, was not brought to trial, nor is it clear whether he escaped his imprisonment or if he was released.

Holmes was in the Netherlands by 1684, however, consorting with the whigs and dissenters gathered around Monmouth and Argyll. He sailed to Lyme Regis with Monmouth in 1685 as lieutenant-colonel of the Green regiment. His son, Blake, who joined him from London, was made a captain. Both fought at Norton St Philip, where Abraham's arm was shattered and Blake was killed. On 6 July Holmes valiantly led the Green regiment into action at Sedgemoor. He was captured on the battlefield, stripped, and carried to the house of a JP. There he amputated his own mangled arm with a carving knife in the justice's kitchen. He was sent back to London and interrogated on 20 July, mentioning only Captain Foulkes and Major Thomas Venner. James II attended his interrogation and offered Holmes his life if he would promise to live in peace. Holmes reportedly replied, 'I am an aged man and what remains to me of life is not worth a falsehood or a baseness. I have always been a republican; and I am still' (Macaulay, 2.636).

Holmes was tried on a charge of high treason by Judge Jeffreys at Dorchester on 10 September 1685; he pleaded guilty and was hanged at Lyme Regis on 12 September. According to whig martyrologists, writing after the revolution, onlookers at his execution were amazed as the horses that were first to pull the sledge of prisoners refused to stir and their replacements broke it to pieces. Holmes and the others walked to the gallows. There Holmes sat at the foot of the ladder and addressed the spectators, asserting that he had joined Monmouth because he 'believed the Protestant religion was bleeding, and in a step towards extirpation'. He continued that while God had not appointed them to be 'the instruments in so glorious a work; yet notwithstanding he … doubted not but that God would make use of others that should meet with better success' (J. Tutchin, *The Western Martyrology*, 1705, 170–71).   MELINDA ZOOK

Sources CSP dom., 1660–61, 269; 1661–2, 487; 1663–4, 542; 1667, 459–60, 465; 1667–8, 349; Jan–June 1683, 292, 325, 333–4, 370, 385; July–Sept 1683, 23, 34, 36, 55–7, 286, 296, 287, 303, 345; 1683–4, 104, 252, 27, 137 · *The letters and journals of Robert Baillie*, ed. D. Laing, 3 vols. (1841–2), vol. 3, pp. 438–9 · *State trials*, 9.334–5 · J. Lowther, *Memoir of the reign of James II*, ed. W. Lowther (1808), 12 · Thurloe, *State papers*, 3.46; 7.248 · *The diary of Bulstrode Whitelocke, 1605–1675*, ed. R. Spalding, British Academy, Records of Social and Economic History, new ser., 13 (1990), 586–7 · J. Nicoll, *A diary of public transactions and other occurrences, chiefly in Scotland, from January 1650 to June 1667*, ed. D. Laing, Bannatyne Club, 52 (1836), 285 · *Sixth report*, HMC, 5 (1877–8), 633 · *Ninth report*, 3, HMC, 8 (1884), 5a · *Seventh report*, HMC, 6 (1879), 364 · N. Luttrell, *A brief historical relation of state affairs from September 1678 to April 1714*, 1 (1857), 352 · T. B. Macaulay, *The history of England from the accession of James II*, new edn, ed.

C. H. Firth, 6 vols. (1913–15), vol. 2, p. 636 · R. Wodrow, *The history of the sufferings of the Church of Scotland from the Restauration to the revolution*, 2 vols. (1721–2), vol.3, p.339 · R. L. Greaves, *Secrets of the kingdom: British radicals from the Popish Plot to the revolution of 1688–89* (1992), 102–05, 163, 169, 176, 194, 242, 244, 288 · P. Earle, *Monmouth's rebels* (1977), 32, 100, 128, 129, 130, 133, 148, 165, 175–6 · 'Wade's narrative (of the Monmouth rebellion)', W. MacDonald Wigfield, *The Monmouth rebellion: a social history* (1980), 149–171 · *Corrections and additions to the Dictionary of National Biography*, Institute of Historical Research (1966) · C. H. Firth and G. Davies, *The regimental history of Cromwell's army*, 2 (1940), 438, 456, 459, 479–80, 535–6, 539, 540–41
Archives BL, confession, Lansdowne MS 1152A | PRO, Calendar of state papers, domestic, Charles II

Holmes, Alfred (1837–1876), violinist and composer, was born on 9 November 1837 in London, the son of Thomas Holmes of Lincoln and his wife, Eliza, *née* Sutch. He was given his first, and perhaps only, violin lessons by his father, concentrating on the study of Spohr's *Violin School*, followed by the practice of works by Pierre Rode, Pierre Baillot, and Rodolphe Kreutzer. It is reported that this intensive study made him a finished player before he was twenty. In 1847 he was principal boy soprano at the oratory, King William Street in the Strand, and on 13 July of the same year he and his younger brother, Henry *Holmes (1839–1905), also taught by his father, and Alfred's apparent equal in talent, gave their début performance at the Haymarket Theatre for Benjamin Webster's benefit in a duet arrangement of the overture to Auber's *Masaniello* (*La muette de Portici*). In 1852 they played duets by Spohr for the composer when he visited London, and the latter was delighted by their renderings.

However, their formal introduction to the public as violinists was delayed until 5 May 1853, when the brothers appeared at the Beethoven Rooms. Their performance of J. W. Kalliwoda's double concerto and of solos by various composers (including Vieuxtemps's *Fantasie caprice*) won high praise. In 1855 they made the first of a series of concert tours on the continent, beginning in Brussels, where they greatly impressed C. A. de Bériot and Hubert Léonard. In 1856 they visited Germany, and in Kassel were once again heard by Spohr. His recognition of the outstanding quality of their playing was so thoroughly confirmed that he dedicated to them his three grand duos for two violins, opp. 148, 150, and 153. It is also thought that Spohr's own Guadagnini violin of 1780 was later owned by Alfred and Henry in turn. The brothers went on to visit Vienna (1857), Sweden (1857–9), Denmark (1860), and Norway and Holland (1860–61).

After some successful concerts in Paris in the autumn of 1864 the two men parted. Alfred Holmes settled in Paris and, early in 1866, under the auspices of the ministry of public education, established a series of Sunday fortnightly concerts. The following year he toured through Belgium, the Netherlands, Germany, and finally, Russia. Perhaps encouraged by Berlioz, Holmes had already decided to devote himself chiefly to composition, and the first performance of his first symphony, *Jeanne d'Arc*, was produced in April 1867 at St Petersburg. He then returned to Paris, where this work, scored for solo voices, chorus, and orchestra, was enthusiastically received at the Théâtre Italien in 1870. Two other symphonies, *The Siege of Paris* and *Robin Hood*, were given in Paris in the same year. During one of Holmes's occasional visits to London the concert overture *The Cid* was performed at the Crystal Palace (21 February 1874), and the first symphony was given at the same venue (27 February 1875). Another symphony, entitled *The Youth of Shakespeare*, formed part of the programme at a concert populaire in Paris, though his opera *Iñez de Castro* (1869, five acts, libretto by Louis Uhlbach) was accepted but never staged at the Grand Opéra. Other works include a further two programmatic symphonies, *Charles XII* and *Romeo and Juliet*; a concert overture, *The Muses*; and pieces for violin and piano (1857), solo piano, and songs.

Holmes died in Paris on 4 March 1876. A sympathetic notice of him by D. Nisard, a member of the Académie Française, appeared in *La Patrie* on the 7th of the same month.   L. M. MIDDLETON, *rev.* DAVID J. GOLBY

Sources J. D. Brown, *Biographical dictionary of musicians: with a bibliography of English writings on music* (1886), 328 · concert announcement, *MT*, 5 (1852–4), 177 · concert review, *MT*, 5 (1852–4), 205 · D. Nisard, 'From the "Patrie", 7th March', *Musical World* (18 March 1876), 205 · A. Pougin, ed., *Biographie universelle des musiciens, et bibliographie générale de la musique: supplément et complément*, 1 (Paris, 1878), 480 · W. H. Husk and A. Mell, 'Holmes, Alfred', *New Grove*
Likenesses wood-engraving, NPG; repro. in *ILN* (1 April 1876)

Holmes, Arthur (1890–1965), geologist and geophysicist, was born on 14 January 1890 at 62 Glen Terrace, Hebburn, Newcastle upon Tyne, the only child of David Holmes (1865–1941), hardware shop assistant, and Emily Dickinson (1869–1952?), schoolteacher, both from Newcastle. Educated at Gateshead higher grade school, he was introduced to geology and the age of the earth controversy between Lord Kelvin and the geologists by his inspirational physics teacher, James McIntosh. In 1907 he gained a scholarship to study physics at the Royal College of Science (Imperial College), London, where he became interested in the newly emerging science of radioactivity and its application to dating minerals. He graduated BSc in physics in 1909, but with a growing interest in geological problems, and believing that job opportunities were greater for geologists than physicists, he transferred to geology and gained associateship of the Royal College of Science in 1910. Notwithstanding the transfer, he remained under the guidance of Robert J. Strutt, professor of physics, researching the measurement of geological time. Results of this early work were read to the Royal Society when Holmes was only twenty-one.

Early research and *The Age of the Earth* Throughout his early life Holmes struggled against financial hardship and frequently sought alternative means to support himself and his research. Thus in 1911 when offered a short contract with Memba Minerals prospecting in Mozambique he accepted with alacrity, having recently suffered the ignominy of being unable to take up a nomination to the Geological Society because he could not afford the £5 membership fee: 'Money will be the necessity. Influence I have in plenty for these Societies' (Holmes, diary, 1911). The

expedition to Mozambique formed the foundation stone for his three lifelong research interests: the radiometric dating of rocks and the age of the earth; the petrology of igneous rocks with particular reference to Africa, the Pre-Cambrian and Tertiary alkaline volcanics; and the evolution of the earth. In Mozambique he conceived his vision of building a geological time-scale based on radioactive ages determined on common rocks of a known stratigraphic age. He also contracted blackwater fever, a severe and often fatal form of malaria; fortunately he recovered, despite a report of his death being telegraphed to England, although debilitating attacks recurred throughout his life.

In 1912, as an assistant demonstrator at Imperial College, Holmes wrote the first of three editions of his celebrated booklet *The Age of the Earth* (1913, 1927, 1937). Greatly influenced by the work of the American geologist Thomas Chamberlin and his 'planetesimal hypothesis' for the formation of the earth, Holmes then examined the radium content of meteorites believing that they were representative of a primeval earth—'meteorites allow us to read at our leisure many of the secrets which are otherwise locked up in the Earth's interior' (A. Holmes, 'The terrestrial distribution of radium', *Science Progress*, 9, 1914, 33). This work became the basis for his later ideas on crustal differentiation and continental drift.

Following the discovery of isotopes in 1913 Holmes pursued increasingly accurate uranium-lead age measurements with his schoolfriend Robert Lawson, then at the Vienna Institute of Radium. Unfortunately the time-consuming atomic weight determinations demanded by the chemical-lead method severely hampered progress of the technique, leading Holmes eventually to abandon it and search for an easier method. In 1926 Holmes and Lawson recognized the possibility of using the decay scheme of potassium to calcium, and in 1932 Holmes published a seminal paper 'The origin of igneous rocks' (*Geological Magazine*, 69, 1932, 543–8) in which he demonstrated the significance of initial isotope ratios when investigating the source of igneous melts. However, because the work erroneously assumed the decay scheme to be $^{41}K/^{41}Ca$, the importance of initial ratios was overlooked for thirty years.

During the early 1940s refinement of the mass spectrometer by Alfred Nier at the University of Minnesota led Holmes to renew his interest in a geological time-scale, and by 1947 he had pushed back the age of the earth, which for decades had remained at 2000 million years, to 3350 million years. This estimate was based on Nier's terrestrial lead ratios, then considered to represent a primeval earth, but in 1953 Clair C. Patterson (1922–1995) showed that in fact meteorites were more representative of the primeval earth, as Holmes had suggested forty years earlier, and the age of both the meteorites and the earth was finalized at 4550 million years.

Holmes married Margaret (Maggie) Howe (1885–1938) on 14 July 1914, three weeks before the outbreak of the First World War, and his son Norman was born in 1918. Holmes escaped active service because of poor health and was seconded to naval intelligence. After the war, despite his growing reputation, prolific publications, two influential books (*Nomenclature of Petrology*, 1920, and *Petrographic Methods and Calculations*, 1921), and having obtained his doctorate in 1917, by 1920 Holmes was still only a demonstrator at Imperial College on £200 a year. An unambitious man who lived only for his research, financial necessity finally compelled him to accept a post in Burma as chief geologist to the Yomah Oil Company (1920) Ltd. In 1921 he was made up-country manager, but by 1922 Yomah Oil was in severe financial difficulties, with Holmes having to sell his own shares to meet immediate needs. In a desperate bid to save the company by finding new oil, he stayed on when others resigned, a decision he always regretted. Six weeks before leaving for England three-year-old Norman caught dysentery and died. Holmes and his wife returned to Gateshead childless and penniless. Nine months of unemployment followed, during which time Holmes gave piano recitals and, it is rumoured, sold vacuum cleaners. Eventually he opened a shop in the centre of Newcastle with his wife's cousin. She traded in furs and he in Far Eastern crafts, but the business was short lived.

Geology at Durham and continental drift In 1924 science was reborn at Durham University. Four new departments were created and seven new appointments made. One of eighteen applicants, Holmes was offered the readership in geology, becoming the head of a one-man department. With his fortunes thus revived, and enhanced by the birth of his son Geoffrey in February that year, this period saw an invigorated renewal of his research activities. An immediate supporter of the continental drift theory originally proposed by Wegener in 1912, Holmes saw at once that it explained why identical palaeoflora, palaeofauna, and rock formations occurred on either side of the Atlantic, doing away with the absurd notion of a 5000 mile land bridge linking Brazil and west Africa. But opposition to continental drift from establishment geology was hard to overcome. In Britain a particularly vocal opponent was the eminent mathematician and physicist, Harold Jeffreys, who argued that it was 'out of the question' (H. Jeffreys, *The Earth*, 2nd edn, 1929, 305) as no force was adequate to move continental slabs over the surface of the globe. However, Holmes's profound understanding of radioactivity—the amount of heat it generated and the enormous time it bestowed on geology for infinitely slow processes—coupled with his work on crustal differentiation, placed him in a unique position to formulate a mechanism for continental drift. In December 1927 he read a ground-breaking paper to the Edinburgh Geological Society, 'Radioactivity and geology', which proposed that differential heating of the earth's interior, generated by the decay of radioactive elements, caused convection of the mantle (substratum as he called it), which could produce a force sufficient to drag continents sideways, allowing the substratum to rise up and take its place in the ocean floor.

In the United States opposition was even greater than in Britain, and leading geologists were exasperated by such ideas: 'Holmes brings out a new thought which is even more impossible than Wegener's. That is that the submerged ridge through the Atlantic Ocean is the place at which North and South America separated from Europe and Africa' (Bowie to Schuchert, 11 Oct 1928, Yale Archive, Schuchert MSS 435, box 38, book 1). Nevertheless, in 1932 Holmes was invited to the United States by Reginald Daly to give the Lowell lectures on geology and radioactivity. Daly expressed the opinion that 'Holmes was one of the few English geologists with ideas on the grand scale' (Dunham, 293). It was not until 1965, the year of Holmes's death, that his ideas on convection currents in the mantle were shown to be fundamentally correct, and it was even longer before he was given credit for them.

The hallmark of Holmes's lectures and writing was clarity and simplicity, coupled with an enthusiasm for his subject that never failed to motivate his students who, if unwittingly, were privileged to hear his original and unorthodox views. His genuine interest in their wellbeing and willingness to 'talk geology' with them as though they were colleagues inspired long-term devotion. In 1931, on a field excursion to Ardnamurchan in Scotland, Holmes met Doris Livesey Reynolds (1899–1985), a brilliant geologist then working at University College, London. A loud and boisterous personality, she was the complete antithesis of Holmes, who was always quietly spoken, even retiring. Nevertheless, it was a meeting of minds, their individual interests in geology dovetailing perfectly. Two years later Holmes engineered a lectureship for her in the Durham department, and she was installed on the opposite side of his enormous desk, ostensibly because there was no room for her elsewhere. (Later, through the 1940s and 50s, they became embroiled in the 'granitization' controversy on the origin of granites, a theory fiercely advocated by Reynolds. But although he accompanied her on multiple trips to Ireland to study the problem in the field, Holmes kept his distance regarding the theory which ultimately proved untenable.)

Holmes's marriage to Maggie, from whom he had become estranged although they 'kept up appearances', ended in 1938 when she died of cancer, leaving Holmes and Reynolds free to marry, only nine months later, on 30 June 1939. Ironically, it was the formalization of their relationship that gave the university authorities an opportunity to voice their disapproval of its previously illicit nature. They questioned the validity of husband and wife working in the same department and Reynolds's contract was renewed for one 'experimental' year only, instead of the normal five years. It was time to move on.

Professor at Edinburgh, recognition, and death Recognition of Holmes's outstanding contributions to geology came when he was elected FRS in 1942 and a year later appointed to the regius chair in geology at Edinburgh University, where he continued to make research a priority, refusing to succumb to administrative overload. He retired from Edinburgh in 1956 when he began to have attacks of auricular fibrillation, and was elected professor emeritus. A special minute adopted at a meeting of the senatus academicus included the telling words: 'If his seat at times has been vacant at Senatus, his absence must be weighed against his contributions to Science' (Stewart to Holmes, 19 Oct 1956, Royal Holloway University Library, Doris Reynolds MSS, box 2).

During the Second World War Holmes was commissioned to write a book on physical geology for RAF cadets which he wrote while on fire watching duty. His celebrated *Principles of Physical Geology*, first published in 1944, soon became known simply as 'Holmes'. Reprinted in English eighteen times it was an international best-seller, becoming the geological bible for generations of geologists and doing much to revive failing interest in the geological sciences. When he retired in 1956 he set out to rewrite the book completely but with his health failing it was a mammoth task, completed only months before he died. This second edition was published in 1965 and reprinted six times. Doris Reynolds wrote a third edition (1978) and her student, P. Donald Duff, a fourth edition in 1993.

Holmes was a deep thinker on the broad philosophical aspects of geology, with ideas far ahead of his time. He often erected 'wickets to be bowled at', considering speculation justified if it stimulated a search 'for the more elusive pieces of the jigsaw'. He published over 200 papers and books, seventy of which were on radioactive age dating, a field he dominated for fifty years. As early as 1926 he became a founder member of the United States National Research Council's committee on the measurement of geological time.

The Geological Society of London awarded Holmes its Murchison medal in 1940 and its highest honour, the Wollaston medal, in 1956. In the same year he received the Penrose medal from the Geological Society of America. He was honoured by many foreign societies including those of America, Belgium, France, the Netherlands, and Sweden. His final and most prestigious accolade was the Vetlesen award, the geologist's equivalent of the Nobel prize, presented to him in 1964 by Columbia University for his 'uniquely distinguished achievement in the sciences resulting in a clearer understanding of the Earth, its history, and its relation to the universe'.

Originally from a Methodist background, by the age of twenty-one Holmes had thrown off all religious shackles. Always of smart appearance he was a 'gentleman' of quiet charm and unfailing kindness. He had an exceptional talent for playing the piano which saw him through many difficult times in his life; he was fascinated by history, and he loved poetry. Despite early financial difficulties, lessons on investing learned around the camp fire in Mozambique resulted in considerable success on the stock exchange. Holmes died of bronchial pneumonia on 20 September 1965 at Bolingbroke Hospital, Battersea, leaving everything to his beloved wife, Doris, who survived him by twenty years, but nothing to his son, Geoffrey.

CHERRY L. E. LEWIS

Sources A. Holmes, diaries, 1911–12, GS Lond., Arthur Holmes MSS · K. C. Dunham, *Memoirs FRS*, 12 (1966), 291–310 · A. Holmes, 'Response by Arthur Holmes [presentation of the Penrose medal to Arthur Holmes]', *Proceedings Volume of the Geological Society of America for 1956* (1957), 74–6 · private information (2004) · W. Bowie, letter to C. Schuchert, 11 Oct 1928, Yale Archive, Schuchert MS 435, box 38, book 1 · H. Stewart, letter to A. Holmes, 19 Oct 1956, Royal Holloway College, Egham, Surrey, Doris Reynolds MSS, box 2 · C. C. Patterson, 'The isotopic composition of meteoric, basaltic and oceanic leads, and the age of the earth', *Proceedings of the conference on nuclear processes in geologic settings, Williams Bay, Wisconsin, September 21–23, 1953* (1953), 36–40 · Royal Holloway College, Egham, Surrey, Doris Reynolds MSS · b. cert. · m. certs.

Archives NHM, departmental corresp., letters to various keepers of minerals · RGS, diaries; letters to his parents and Bob Lawson, etc. · U. Durham, department of geology, lantern slides deposit · U. Edin. L., accession no. E88.13 | Harvard U., Pusey Library, Reginald A. Daly MSS · RGS, Leonard Hawkes' corresp., LDGSL 1047 · Royal Holloway College, Egham, Surrey, Doris Reynolds MSS · University of Chicago, Thomas Chrowder Chamberlin MSS · University of Minnesota, Minneapolis, Walter Library, corresp. with A. O. Nier · Yale U., Sterling Memorial Library, Charles Schuchert MSS | SOUND GS Lond., Arthur Holmes Collection, taped interviews with people who knew Arthur Holmes

Likenesses photograph, 1956, repro. in H. Hedberg, 'Presentation of Penrose medal to Arthur Holmes', *Proceedings Volume of the Geological Society of America for 1956* (1957), 68–74 · R. Geary, oils, 1984, GS Lond. · photograph, repro. in Dunham, *Memoirs FRS*

Wealth at death £34,043: probate, 29 Nov 1965, CGPLA Eng. & Wales

Holmès [*née* Holmes], **Augusta Mary Anne** (1847–1903), composer, born in the rue de Berri, Paris, on 16 December 1847, was the daughter of Captain Dalkeith Holmes, an Irishman who had settled in Paris in 1820 and married Augusta Shearer in 1827. Her godfather was the poet Alfred de Vigny, who may, according to gossip of the time, have been her true father. She was brought up in Versailles, where her mother died in 1857. The following year her father allowed her to take up music seriously. From 1859 to 1865 she attracted attention as a piano prodigy and singer of French songs of her own composition. As early as 1862 she published some pieces under the pseudonym Hermann Zenta.

After instruction from the organist Henri Lambert, the bandmaster Klosé, and Saint-Saëns, she became a pupil of César Franck in 1875, having previously acquired no little fame by her setting of *In exitu Israel* in 1873. Her studies with Franck bore fruit in her dramatic symphonies *Orlando Furioso* (1877) and *Lutèce*, which was awarded second place in the competition offered by the city of Paris in 1878. In 1879 she became a French citizen, and thenceforth wrote her name as Holmès. Another dramatic symphony, *Les Argonautes*, was performed under the direction of Jules Étienne Pasdeloup at the Concerts Populaires (24 April 1881), and was followed by the symphonic poem *Irlande* (2 March 1882), which was described by Adolphe Jullien as 'a creation of great worth, evincing by turns a charming tenderness, ardent passion, and masculine spirit', and firmly established Holmès's reputation. Many other critics remarked on her music's virile qualities, and the influence of both Franck and Wagner was strong. Another patriotic symphony, *Pologne*, was given at the Concerts Populaires on 9 December 1883, and in 1884 she published a volume of songs, *Les sept ivresses*. Her symphonic ode *Ludus pro patria* was well received at the concerts of the Conservatoire on 4 March 1888. Its reception was, however, surpassed by that of her *Ode triomphale*, performed by a very large chorus and orchestra at the Paris Exhibition in 1889. She wrote a *Hymne à la paix* for the Florence Exhibition in 1890, and a symphonic suite, *Au pays bleu*, in 1891.

Holmès then turned her attention to the lyric stage and composed a four-act opera, *La montagne noire*, given at the Paris Opéra on 8 February 1895. The failure of this work hastened her withdrawal from composition and darkened her last years. Three other operas, *Héro et Léandre*, *Astarté*, and *Lancelot du lac*, were never performed. Holmès's interest in Ireland grew, and after reading much about the country she revised her symphonic poem *Irlande* for production at the first Feis Ceoil, in Dublin, on 18 May 1897. She was admired by a wide circle of musicians and poets, and was for many years the mistress of the novelist Catulle Mendès (1841–1909), with whom she had three daughters. For a time a theosophist and afterwards a spiritualist, she finally became a Roman Catholic, and was baptized in the Dominican friary church in the Faubourg St Honoré in 1902. She died at Versailles on 28 January 1903, and was buried in the St Louis cemetery there, where a monument to her memory was erected in 1904. Recordings were made of some of Holmès's works, including *Irlande*.   W. H. G. FLOOD, *rev.* HUGH MACDONALD

Sources R. Myers, 'Augusta Holmès: a meteoric career', *Musical Quarterly*, 53 (1967), 365–76 · H. Macdonald, 'Holmès, Augusta (Mary Anne)', *New Grove* · H. Imbert, *Nouveaux profils de musiciens* (1892), 137–59 · A. Jullien, 'Holmès, Augusta', Grove, *Dict. mus.* (1906) · W. H. G. Flood, *A history of Irish music*, 4th edn (1927), 332–3 · A. Pungin, *Le Ménestrel* (3 Feb 1903)
Archives Bibliothèque municipale de Versailles
Likenesses photograph, repro. in J. A. Sadie and R. Samuel, eds., *New Grove dictionary of women composers* (1994)

Holmes, Charles (*bap.* 1711, *d.* 1761), naval officer, fourth son of Henry Holmes, governor of the Isle of Wight, and his wife (and cousin), Mary, the illegitimate daughter of Admiral Sir Robert *Holmes, was baptized at Yarmouth, Isle of Wight, on 19 September 1711. In 1727 he entered the *Captain* as an ordinary seaman. He was made lieutenant on 18 June 1734. Four years later he was serving in the *Sunderland*, and in 1740 in the *Pembroke*, one of the Mediterranean Fleet, under Nicholas Haddock. He then went to the West Indies as a lieutenant of the *Tilbury* and there moved into the *Princess Caroline*, Edward Vernon's flagship. On 24 February 1741 he was promoted to the command of the fireship *Stromboli*, and he served with the fleet in the expedition to Cartagena (March–April 1741).

On 9 June 1741 Holmes was moved into the *Success*; he returned in her to England and was, on 20 February 1742, posted to the *Sapphire*, and employed during the next two years in cruising against Spanish privateers. In December 1743 he was moved into the *Cornwall*, and in the following June into the *Enterprise*, which he commanded for the next three years in the West Indies. In May 1747 he was transferred to the *Lennox* (70 guns) which, in September 1748, sailed from Jamaica in charge of the homeward trade. In the Gulf of Florida, on 29 September, they fell in with the

Spanish squadron under Reggio, on which Holmes directed the convoy to make the best of their way while he went himself in the *Lennox* to give the news to Rear-Admiral Charles Knowles, whom he believed to be off Havana, and to reinforce him, in case of an action. On the following evening he fell in with Knowles, and at daylight on 1 October the Spanish squadron came in sight.

In the action that ensued the *Lennox*, by reason of her reduced armament, was stationed to windward of the line as a frigate. Knowles afterwards complained that several captains had been prone to error, and that Holmes especially had been guilty of disobedience and neglect of signals. From these events there came a series of courts martial, from which Holmes alone came out clear, the court not only acquitting him of the charges laid against him, but also passing a warm eulogium on his conduct and zeal in joining Knowles before the action.

In January 1753 Holmes was appointed to the *Anson*, guardship at Portsmouth, and in 1755 to the *Grafton*, one of the squadron sent out with Rear-Admiral Francis Holburne as a reinforcement to Edward Boscawen in North America. In the following year he was again on the coast of North America, this time with orders to prevent reinforcements from reaching Louisbourg. He arrived off Nova Scotia on 26 June, just after Richard Spry, who had wintered in Halifax harbour with several ships, was forced off the station owing to sickness in his crews. A month later Holmes failed to prevent four French ships under Louis-Joseph, Comte Beaussier de l'Isle, from entering Louisbourg harbour. An indecisive action lasting three hours was fought, when the French squadron came out, forcing Holmes to retreat to Halifax for repairs. Thereafter he confined his squadron to attacking defenceless French fishing craft and settlements in the Gulf of St Lawrence.

Holmes returned to England for the winter, and sat as a member of the court martial on Admiral John Byng, but in the summer of 1757 he was again in the *Grafton* on the North American station, and was with Holburne off Louisbourg when the fleet was shattered by the storm of 24 September. In addition to the loss of her masts the *Grafton* lost her rudder, and being obliged to bear away for England she fitted a jury rudder made of a spare topmast. Early in the following year Holmes in the small frigate *Seahorse*, in company with the *Stromboli*, was sent to the coast of Friesland, where the French and Austrians had taken possession of Emden with a force of 3000 men. On 18 March these two little vessels took up a position in the Ems that cut the enemy's communications. The French and Austrian forces at once decided that the place was no longer tenable, and evacuated it the next day.

On his return to England Holmes was appointed to the *Warspite* for a few months, and on 6 July he was promoted rear-admiral of the blue. The following year, with his flag in the *Dublin*, he was third in command of the fleet in the St Lawrence, under Sir Charles Saunders, in the expedition to capture Quebec. In August he commanded a small force which raided extensively and forced some of the French troops guarding the town to march after him. On 6

September General James Wolfe came aboard to reconnoitre the shore upriver from Quebec. When he selected
the Anse au Foulon landing site it was Holmes's task to
guarantee the army's safe landing, a task he described as
'the most hazardous and difficult task' he had ever
attempted. Late in September Holmes returned to England.

In March 1760 Holmes was appointed commander-in-
chief at Jamaica. He arrived there in May, and during the
next eighteen months seized all vessels leaving Monte
Christi and the French ports of Hispaniola, major termini
for American illegal trade. He died at Jamaica on 21
November 1761. There is a monument to his memory in
Westminster Abbey.

J. K. LAUGHTON, rev. JULIAN GWYN

Sources W. A. B. Douglas, 'Holmes, Charles', *DCB*, vol. 3 · D. W.
Grinnell-Milne, *Mad, is he? The character and achievement of James
Wolfe* (1963) · W. Wood, ed., *The logs of the conquest of Canada* (1909),
vol. 4 · C. P. Stacey, *Quebec, 1759: the siege and the battle* (1959)
Archives PRO, ADM1/480–482, ADM1/1892, ADM1/236
Likenesses attrib. N. Dance, oils, after 1758, NMM · J. Wilton,
marble statue, Westminster Abbey

Holmes, Sir Charles John (1868–1936), landscape painter
and art critic, was born at Preston on 11 November 1868,
the elder son of Charles Rivington Holmes (*d.* 1873), vicar
of St Michael's Church, Bromley by Bow, later vicar of
Stratton, Cornwall, and his wife, Mary Susan, eldest
daughter of Joseph Briggs Dickson, solicitor, of Preston.
He was the grandson of the antiquary John *Holmes and
nephew of Sir Richard *Holmes, librarian at Windsor
Castle. After early schooling at St Edmund's School, Canterbury, Holmes went as a scholar to Eton College in 1883,
and as an exhibitioner to Brasenose College, Oxford, in
1887. From 1889 to 1903 he worked in London as a publisher's and printer's assistant: first with his cousin Francis
Rivington and later at the Ballantyne Press; with John
Cumming Nimmo; and with Charles Ricketts and Charles
Shannon at the Vale Press. For some years he had been
teaching himself to draw; now direction was given to his
efforts by Ricketts, and he was encouraged to etch by William Strang. Laurence Binyon prompted his first essay in
art criticism, 'Hiroshige', published in *The Dome* for September 1897. Other early publications, *Hokusai* (1899), *Constable* (1901), and art journalism in *The Realm* and the *Athenaeum*, culminated in the major book *Constable and his Influence on Landscape Painting* (1902). In 1900, as a landscape
painter himself, Holmes began exhibiting with the New
English Art Club.

On 21 July 1903 Holmes married his cousin Florence
Mary Hill (*b.* 1872/3), a violinist and composer, only daughter of Charles Robert Rivington, solicitor, of London; they
had two sons. That same year Holmes became co-editor,
with Robert Dell, of the newly established *Burlington Magazine*. By the time of his resignation in 1909 he had transformed the fortunes of the journal, which benefited vastly
from his experience of publishing and printing. In 1904 he
was elected Slade professor of fine art at Oxford and continued in this post until 1910. Some of his Slade lectures

Sir Charles John Holmes (1868–1936), by Elliott & Fry

are the basis of *Notes on the Science of Picture-Making* (1909)
and *Notes on the Art of Rembrandt* (1911). His standing as a
painter was recognized in 1904, when, on the same day as
J. S. Sargent, he was elected a member of the New English
Art Club. The only other London art society which he
joined was the Royal Society of Painters in Water Colours,
of which he was elected an associate in 1924 and a member in 1929. His paintings of mountain scenes and industrial subjects belong to no school or movement but his
own. They were inspired by strong personal emotion, but
in execution disciplined by constant analysis of the methods of previous exponents of both Eastern and Western
art.

On the retirement of Lionel Cust in 1909 Holmes
became director of the National Portrait Gallery. His
prime concerns were remodelling and rearranging the
exhibition rooms, and starting a national photographic
record. In 1916 he was appointed director of the National
Gallery, in succession to Sir Charles Holroyd. The constitution of the gallery was then a vexed question. Alternative
solutions were to give the director unfettered responsibility for the purchase of pictures, subject to Treasury control; or but one vote on a board of many amateurs. The second policy was in favour, though the new director was
hardly supple enough gladly to subordinate what he
regarded as a trust of scholarship to the prejudice or taste
of less exacting standards. Holmes resigned himself to
working within this arrangement, but made clear what he
thought was wrong with it in his evidence before the royal
commission on national museums and galleries in 1928.

Meanwhile his wide experience as critic, administrator, and publisher was focused on familiarizing the public with the contents and significance of the National Gallery. Photograph and publications departments were organized, Holmes personally contributing the admirable *Illustrated Guide to the National Gallery* (1921) and *Old Masters and Modern Art in the National Gallery* (3 vols., 1923–7). He was knighted in 1921 and appointed KCVO in 1928, the year in which he retired from the directorship of the National Gallery. He continued to paint and write and his last book was his autobiography, *Self and Partners* (1936).

Holmes's achievement as a writer, and the distinction of his art, are due to an unusual integration of theory and practice. He learned to draw and paint through unremitting experiment and analysis of the old masters. His painter's insight gave him a special grasp of those masters' problems and their ways of solving them. Other writings of his, notably 'Leonardo da Vinci' (*PBA*, 9, 1919), *An Introduction to Italian Painting* (1929), and *A Grammar of the Arts* (1931), offered lucid, concrete explanation of the great artists' thought and practice. He received honorary degrees from the universities of Cambridge and Leeds, and was elected an honorary fellow of Brasenose College in 1931. He died at his home, 19 Pembridge Gardens, Kensington, London, on 7 December 1936. Works by Holmes are in many public collections, including the Tate Collection, British Museum, Victoria and Albert Museum, London; the Fitzwilliam Museum, Cambridge; the Ashmolean Museum, Oxford; and galleries in Adelaide, Johannesburg, Melbourne, and Sydney.

C. H. C. BAKER, rev. MARK POTTLE

Sources Mallalieu, *Watercolour artists*, vol. 1 · Wood, *Vic. painters*, 2nd edn · J. Johnson and A. Greutzner, *The dictionary of British artists, 1880–1940* (1976), vol. 5 of *Dictionary of British art* · G. M. Waters, *Dictionary of British artists, working 1900–1950* (1975) · F. Spalding, *20th century painters and sculptors* (1990), vol. 6 of *Dictionary of British art* · *The water-colours of C. J. Holmes* (1920) [with a foreword by M. Sadleir] · X. B. [C. H. Collins Baker], *Charles Holmes* (1924) · C. J. Holmes, *Self & partners (mostly self): being the reminiscences of C. J. Holmes* (London, 1936) · *The Times* (8 Dec 1936) · A. M. Hind, 'The sketch-books of Sir Charles Holmes', *Burlington Magazine*, 77 (1940), 45–52 · A. M. Hind, 'The etchings of Sir Charles Holmes', *Burlington Magazine*, 72 (1938), 176–82 · *CGPLA Eng. & Wales* (1937) · m. cert. · d. cert.
Archives NPG, diaries and notebooks | BL, corresp. with Lord D'Abernon, Add. MS 48930 · U. Glas. L., letters to D. S. MacColl
Likenesses G. H. B. Holland, oils, 1934, NPG · Elliott & Fry, photograph, NPG [*see illus.*] · P. Evans, caricature, ink, NPG · photograph, repro. in *The Times* (7 Dec 1936)
Wealth at death £16,812 6s. 1d.: probate, 17 Feb 1937, *CGPLA Eng. & Wales*

Holmes, David (1843–1906), trade unionist, was born on 16 November 1843 at Nelson Street, Manchester, the illegitimate son of Mary Holmes, a hand-loom weaver. His mother came from north-east Lancashire, and Holmes was weaving by the time he was eight. At the age of ten he absconded to live with an uncle in Padiham. Here, he turned to power-loom weaving, made up for his earlier lack of schooling by attending Sunday and evening classes at the Unitarian chapel, and in 1859 became involved in his first strike. He married in the early 1860s and removed to nearby Burnley, where he lived for the rest of his life.

The 1850s had seen both the final transition from outwork to factory production in cotton and the first attempts by weavers' unions in the different Lancashire towns to secure uniform lists of piece-rates for their industry. However, the cotton 'famine' of the early 1860s seriously damaged the fledgeling unions, and when industrial expansion was resumed the task of devising a regular system of industrial relations had to begin all over again. Holmes played a leading part in setting up the Burnley Weavers' Association, and served as its president from 1871 until his death. During the union's early years, the peculiarly fragmented structure of the weaving industry around Burnley meant difficulties in persuading employers and weavers alike of the merits of collective bargaining. Holmes was blacklisted for his activities, and the union, too poor to pay a regular salary, set him up as a rag-and-bone man. A lengthy, violent, and unsuccessful county-wide strike to prevent wage reductions during the recession of 1878 demonstrated the need for more effective co-operation between the weavers of the different towns. How this might be achieved became apparent when the employers demanded a further cut at the end of 1883: the Burnley weavers were persuaded by Holmes to accept the reduction and remain at work in order to be able to subsidize the Blackburn weavers, who struck against it. This tactic convinced both the local unions and the leading employers of the advantages of uniform wage-rates agreed by formal negotiation and enforced by the threat of partial strike action. The Northern Counties Amalgamated Association of Weavers, set up under Holmes's presidency in 1884 to pursue these objectives, steadily increased its membership and built up an impressive strike fund. In 1892 collective bargaining finally produced a comprehensive uniform list of piece-rates for cotton weaving, and the industry remained free from further major strikes until after Holmes's death.

By the early 1890s the cotton industry was held up as a model of good labour relations and David Holmes was the acknowledged master of one of the country's largest, richest, and most effectively organized trade unions. At home in Burnley he had become a figure of considerable consequence: member of the school board, town councillor, JP, vice-president of the Liberal Association, and a man whose name was seriously discussed on several occasions as a possible parliamentary candidate. His impact on the national trade union movement was even more significant, thanks to his role on the parliamentary committee of the Trades Union Congress, on which he served almost continuously between 1892 and 1904 and which he chaired in 1894–5. A zealous opponent of socialism and a hard-nosed critic of both the pretensions and the practices of the so-called 'new unions' which had emerged in 1889–90, Holmes was the key figure in the back-stage *coup* which forced the system of card-voting on the 1895 congress and thereby demonstrated the weakness of the new unions, compared with the real 'mass unions' in coal and cotton. His stature within British trade unionism was reflected in the international conferences and delegations in which he was involved during the 1890s.

After 1900 Holmes gradually withdrew from many of his outside activities in favour of his protégé, David Shackleton, and by the time he died he was regarded in the rapidly changing labour movement as a relic of an earlier age. He remained personally loyal to the Liberal Party, while insisting that political partisanship and state intervention had no place in the narrow world of industrial relations. Tough, pragmatic, and unimaginative, Holmes took most of the traditions and assumptions of the cotton trade as he found them. Because an exporting industry such as cotton had to remain internationally competitive, he opposed the statutory eight-hour working day and compulsory arbitration. At the same time, he accepted the industry's need for a largely female and juvenile labour force which, although protected from the worst forms of exploitation by the Factory Acts, was both over-worked and—relative to men—under-paid. Such a limited vision was increasingly criticized at a time when class war, public ownership, and women's rights were becoming prominent on the political agenda; the wave of labour unrest which struck the cotton industry just before the First World War marked the widespread rejection of the cautious and compromising tactics which Holmes and his generation had pursued.

David Holmes was taken ill while attending the Trades Union Congress at Hanley in September 1905, and died of cardiac disease and dropsy at his home, 11 Lawn Street, Burnley, on 14 January 1906. He left a widow and eleven surviving children out of a family of fourteen. His quasi-public funeral at Burnley cemetery made an appropriate end to a career which symbolized the growth of mass trade unionism and its gradual incorporation into the mainstream of British public life during the last thirty years of the nineteenth century.   DUNCAN BYTHELL

Sources *Burnley Gazette* (22 June 1878) · *Burnley Gazette* (14 Aug 1895) · *Burnley Gazette* (14 Sept 1895) · *Burnley Gazette* (20 May 1905) · *Burnley Gazette* (17 Jan 1906) · *Cotton Factory Times* (6 May 1892) · *Cotton Factory Times* (27 Feb 1903) · *Cotton Factory Times* (20 Jan 1905) · *Cotton Factory Times* (19 May 1905) · *Cotton Factory Times* (19 Jan 1906) · *Annual Report* [Trades Union Congress] (1887–1906) · 'Royal commission on labour: minutes of evidence, group C', *Parl. papers* (1892), 35.711, C. 6708-VI · H. A. Clegg, A. Fox, and A. F. Thompson, *A history of British trade unions since 1889*, 1 (1964) · H. A. Turner, *Trade union growth, structure, and policy: a comparative study of the cotton unions* (1962) · D. Howell, *British workers and the independent labour party, 1888–1906* (1983) · B. C. Roberts, *The Trades Union Congress, 1868–1921* (1958) · E. Hopwood, *The Lancashire weavers' story* (1969) · *Burnley Express* (17 Jan 1906) · b. cert. · d. cert.

Holmes, Edmond Gore Alexander (1850–1936), inspector of schools, was born at Moycashel, co. Westmeath, Ireland, on 17 July 1850, the fourth son of Robert Holmes (1803–1870) and his wife, Jane, daughter of William Henn, a master in chancery, of Dublin. He had four brothers, including T. R. E. *Holmes, and two sisters. He was educated at Merchant Taylors' School, London (1863–8), and at St John's College, Oxford (1869–74), where he gained first classes in classical moderations and *literae*

humaniores. He taught for a short time at Repton and Wellington before becoming tutor to the family of the eleventh earl of Winchilsea. A Conservative politician, Winchilsea was responsible for advancing Holmes's claim for an inspectorship after the return of the Disraeli government in 1874. Holmes was appointed as one of her majesty's inspectors of schools the following year at the age of twenty-four. He served in the West Riding of Yorkshire (1875–9), Kent (1879–97), Oxford (1897–1903), and Northumberland (1903–5). Touring the elementary schools of his districts, he observed and noted the effects of the 'payment by results' system on both teachers and pupils. The system led to the undue concentration on the 'three Rs'; mechanical methods were employed and the curriculum was largely confined to 'paying' subjects. As he wrote in his general report for 1878–9, 'I do not reproach them [the teachers] for this defect. I only wonder that it is not more striking and more disastrous than it is. Circumstances are against the teacher from first to last.' Holmes believed that it was through the teaching of English, especially literature and poetry, that the emotions could be cultivated and the child's imagination stimulated.

In 1880 Holmes married Florence Mary, daughter of Captain P. M. Syme RA. They had two daughters and a son, Maurice Gerald *Holmes, who entered the Board of Education in 1909 and was permanent secretary from 1937 to 1945.

When Holmes was appointed chief inspector of elementary schools in 1905, he had thirty years' experience of inspecting. In that year, the Board of Education issued a volume entitled *Suggestions for the Use of Teachers and Others Concerned with the Work of Elementary Schools* (later retitled *Handbook of Suggestions for Teachers*), which encouraged teachers to apply the teaching methods that were most suitable to the needs of their school. He had been largely involved in the final form of the *Handbook*. In the course of one of his many visits to elementary schools, in 1907 he discovered a school at Sompting, Sussex, which was a living embodiment of his philosophy. The headmistress, Harriet Finlay-Johnson, whom he called his 'Egeria', had created an atmosphere in which the children were engaged in all forms of self-expression through an imaginative approach that included respect for each individual.

On his retirement in November 1910, Holmes published *What is and What Might Be* (1911), a condemnation of the existing education system, which stressed competition rather than co-operation, emphasized visible results, and demanded the mechanical obedience of the child. The book attracted wide public attention. In 1912 he spent some time in Rome visiting the infant schools of Maria Montessori, an account of which was published by the Board of Education. Shortly before his retirement, he became involved in the furore over the so-called 'Holmes–Morant circular', a highly confidential memorandum which he had issued in January 1910 to inspectors, criticizing the quality of the local inspectorate. Its disclosure in parliament in March 1911 led to changes in office of the permanent secretary of the board, Robert Morant, and the president, Walter Runciman.

Holmes was influenced by the idealist philosophy of T. H. Green, though differing from it in some aspects. He wrote extensively on education, philosophy, and religion, and was also a poet. He had become interested in theosophy in his youth and, inspired by the work of Madame Blavatsky, became president of the Quest Society in 1921. But his main interest was in education. He arranged a large conference for educational progressives with the Montessorian Society in 1914 at East Runton, Norfolk. Out of this grew the New Education Fellowship which became a world-wide movement. He was the main moving force of its annual conferences, in which he regularly participated until his death. He died at 108 Cromwell Road, London, on 14 October 1936.   PETER GORDON

Sources R. W. Macan, 'A memorial of Edmond Holmes', *Conference on new ideals in education: report* (1937), 1–16 • P. Gordon, 'The writings of Edmond Holmes: a reassessment and bibliography', *History of Education*, 12 (1983), 15–24 • E. G. A. Holmes, *In quest of an ideal* (1920) • E. G. A. Holmes, 'The confessions and hopes of an ex-inspector of schools', *Hibbert Journal*, 20 (1922), 231–9 • E. Sharwood Smith, *The faith of a schoolmaster* (1935) • WWW
Wealth at death £1781 5s. 8d.: probate, 11 Jan 1937, *CGPLA Eng. & Wales*

Holmes, Edward (1797?–1859), music critic, was probably born in London in 1797, though his death certificate gives his age in 1859 as fifty-nine. At John Clarke's school, Enfield, he became friends with Keats, whose respect he won first as a fighter but subsequently for his literary taste. He was in turn influenced by the headmaster's son, Charles Cowden Clarke, who introduced them both to the music of Mozart. After a brief apprenticeship to the bookseller R. B. Seeley he lodged in Vincent Novello's house as a music student; there he met Shelley, Hazlitt, Leigh Hunt, and Charles and Mary Lamb, and musicians including Mozart's pupils Thomas Attwood and Hummel, as well as Mendelssohn and Liszt.

On the foundation of the weekly *Atlas* in November 1826, Holmes became its music critic, and in the following year he set off on a continental tour that led to his first book, *A Ramble among the Musicians of Germany* (1828). Somewhat influenced by the work of Hazlitt and the Lambs, this is an individual, entertaining, and sharply observed account of his travels, which included encounters with famous musicians, such as the singers Henriette Sontag and Luigi Lablache, as well as elderly members of the Prague orchestra who had played in the first performance of *Don Giovanni*. There are also detailed specifications of the organs Holmes was able to examine. Holmes contributed to various other journals, especially the *Foreign Quarterly Review* (1829–31), the *Monthly Chronicle* (1838–9), the *Musical World* (1838–9), *The Spectator* (from 1843), *Fraser's Magazine* (from 1848), and, from its foundation in 1845 by Novello, over many years to the *Musical Times*. From 1833 he was organist of All Saints' Church, Poplar, and later of Holloway Chapel; he also taught the piano.

A second continental journey led to *The Life of Mozart* (1845). The first adequate account of Mozart in English,

this still valuable book was based on such printed sources as existed in German, together with Holmes's own researches and those of Vincent Novello, as well as close study of the music. Holmes's admiration for Mozart was based on what he saw as an ideal artistic balance between elegance of form and originality of feeling, and some of his judgements (for instance, his view of *Idomeneo* as 'an opera of the first magnitude and complexity') were far ahead of their time. For some time his 'classical' response to Mozart excluded appreciation of the new Romantic music, and he was reserved about Weber, resistant to some of Beethoven, and hostile to Meyerbeer. However, he lived up to his principles of empirical criticism by allowing his prejudice against Berlioz's *Symphonie fantastique* to be overcome by the experience of hearing the work at the composer's first London concert on 7 February 1848, and wrote candidly of being won over by 'the original and poetic effects of the music' (*The Atlas*, 12 Feb 1848). He became a friend of Berlioz, for whom he was a 'savant amateur de musique de mes amis' ('a knowledgeable music-lover among my friends'; undated letter of 1855), and whose reputation he did much secure in England, both with articles and with practical support.

Holmes's writings were based on sound technical knowledge, and, particularly in his essays on the masses of Haydn, Mozart, and Beethoven, he supported his arguments with copious use of music examples. However, he resisted what he saw as some of the more limiting attitudes of the musical academics of his day, and lost few opportunities to attack 'the crowd of heavy professors'. He saw himself as a mediator between composer and public, in particular in fighting British insularity, in gaining a hearing for unfamiliar music, and in arousing his countrymen to an awareness of the greater richness of German musical life. However, he also struck blows for his contemporaries John Field and George Onslow, and was one of the first critics to argue a case for Purcell (whom he regarded as worthy of comparison with Mozart), for Restoration composers, and for the madrigalists. His style, at its best lively, colourful, and vigorous, helped to give English music criticism new intellectual respectability.

In 1849 Holmes visited America, returning in the following year. On 15 July 1857 he married Louisa Sarah Webbe, granddaughter of the composer Samuel Webbe. He published a few original compositions, in particular songs. He died in London on 28 August 1859.   JOHN WARRACK

Sources J. Warrack, 'Holmes, Edward', *New Grove* • M. Cowden Clarke, *The life and labours of Vincent Novello, by his daughter* (1864) • C. Cowden Clarke and M. Cowden Clarke, *Reminiscences of writers* (1878) • H. E. Rollins, ed., *The Keats circle: letters and papers, 1816–1878* (1948) • A. W. Ganz, *Berlioz in London* (1950) • MT, 9 (1859–61), 125–6 • E. D. Mackerness, 'Edward Holmes (1797–1859)', *Music and Letters*, 45 (1964), 213–27 • d. cert. • m. cert.

Holmes, George (1661/2–1749), archivist, was born at Skipton in Craven, in the West Riding of Yorkshire, to unknown parents. He was for many years a protégé of William Petyt (1641?–1707), keeper of the records in the Tower of London from 1689 to 1706. Both were educated at Skipton grammar school, and about 1691 Holmes was appointed one of Petyt's clerks at the Tower; until about 1705 he lodged in his house. Petyt bequeathed him £200 in 1707. In 1699 Holmes married Elizabeth Marshall (d. in or after 1749), the daughter of a Fleet Street sword-cutter; they had one son, George.

Petyt's successor as keeper, Richard Topham, made Holmes his chief clerk in September 1706, and six months later appointed him his deputy. Holmes was reappointed by Topham's successor, Polhill. As deputy keeper, Holmes effectively was head of the office, and thus was in charge of most of the older records of the chancery and parliament; in 1731 he was formally appointed keeper, and he retained this office until his death. For a time his son was clerk under him, but he predeceased his father.

In 1704 Holmes acted as secretary of a House of Lords subcommittee that prepared a scheme for housing, sorting, and calendaring certain of the records in the Tower; the final report of this committee (1707) was followed a few months later by Holmes's permanent appointment to methodize and digest—in other words, to calendar—the Tower records, at a yearly salary of £200.

Holmes's professional competence was displayed in the compilation of a general calendar of the Tower records (of which a copy is perhaps identifiable as BL, Stowe MS 543, fols. 1–38), and in his revision of the first seventeen volumes of Thomas Rymer's Foedera. For the second edition of this enormous collection of historical texts he collated the printed versions with the originals in the Tower and made many hundreds of corrections. The revised volumes were published between 1727 and 1729; in addition he issued a separate listing of his corrections as The Emendations in the New Edition of Mr Rymer's Foedera (1730). He also made some of the transcripts, and certified others, for an intended edition of the rolls of parliament, which was finally published in six volumes as Rotuli parliamentorum (1767–83). He was always highly regarded for his helpfulness to historical researchers.

Holmes was a sociable man, with a wide circle of friends in the antiquarian world. In 1698 the palaeographer Humfrey Wanley encountered him at the Cotton Library:

> we never saw one another before, and yet he was pleas'd to entertain so good an opinion of me at first sight, that he would needs have me dine with him, which I did: his lodgings being not 200 yards from mine: there he entertain'd me very kindly, &c. (Letters, 90)

He was a member of the Society of Antiquaries from almost its beginning, being brought to its third meeting, in January 1708, by Peter Le Neve, and he was a founder member when it was revived in 1717. He was also elected a fellow of the Royal Society (1741).

Holmes was a keen numismatist, and in 1722 undertook to catalogue the Saxon coins of John Hill, as part of a project planned by Le Neve for catalogues of all the ancient coins relative to Great Britain; the project never came to fruition, however. Holmes himself in 1692 had shown some Dutch medals of the sixteenth and seventeenth centuries to a group of friends at the Mitre tavern.

Holmes died, aged eighty-seven, on 16 February 1749, and was survived by his wife. He was buried in the chapel of the Tower of London. His library, consisting of books and some manuscripts and books of prints, and his collection of coins and medals were both sold by auction in December 1749. In tribute to his memory a portrait of him was engraved by George Vertue in the same year, at the charge of the Society of Antiquaries; the painting on which this was based, by R. van Bleeck, was itself presented to the society in 1766 by his friend James West.

NIGEL RAMSAY

Sources Nichols, Lit. anecdotes, 5.353–4 • J. Conway Davies, ed., Catalogue of manuscripts in the library of the Honourable Society of the Inner Temple, 3 vols. (1972), vol. 1, pp. 16–19, 24–5 • J. Evans, A history of the Society of Antiquaries (1956), 37, 47, 51–2, 67, 72, 115 • Letters of Humfrey Wanley: palaeographer, Anglo-Saxonist, librarian, 1672–1726, ed. P. L. Heyworth (1989), 90, 382 • H. G. Richardson and G. O. Sayles, eds., Rotuli parliamentorum Anglie hactenus inediti, MCCLXXIX–MCCCLXXIII, CS, 3rd ser., 51 (1935), xxiii–xxv • BL, Add. MSS 4633–4637 • 'Registrum palatinum Dunelmense': the register of Richard de Kellawe, lord palatine and bishop of Durham, ed. T. D. Hardy, 4 vols., Rolls Series, 62 (1873–8) • will, PRO, PROB 11/769, fols. 159–160r • BL, Add. MS 5853, fol. 77r • BL, Add. MS 5833, fol. 163v • BL, Sloane MS 3961, fol. 15r–v • ESTC • M. M. Condon and E. M. Hallam, 'Government printing of the public records in the eighteenth century', Journal of the Society of Archivists, 7 (1982–5), 348–88, esp. 365–70

Archives BL, collections, Add. MSS 4633–4637

Likenesses R. van Bleeck, oils, 1743, S. Antiquaries, Lond. • G. Vertue, line engraving, 1749 (after R. van Bleeck, 1743), BM, NPG • oils, S. Antiquaries, Lond.

Holmes, George (d. 1721), organist and composer, may have been related to the cathedral musicians John Holmes (d. 1629) and Thomas Holmes (d. 1638). In 1698 he was organist to the bishop of Durham, and in 1704 succeeded Thomas Allinson as organist of Lincoln Cathedral. His surviving music includes two settings of the Magnificat for five voices, and two anthems, 'Arise, shine, o daughter of Zion' (composed on the union of England with Scotland), and 'I will love thee, o Lord'. These latter are in Tudway's collection in the British Library (Harleian MS 7341). His setting of the burial sentences was in use in Lincoln Cathedral as late as 1937, and was republished by Novello, edited by G. J. Burnett. Holmes's Ode for St Cecilia's Day has been dated by its contents to between 1703 and 1713. He also published several songs: 'Tell me, little wanton boy' and 'Celia's Invitation' have been ascribed to him. The catches by a George Holmes in Hilton's Catch as Catch can (1652) are possibly by his father. Holmes died at Lincoln in 1721.						L. M. MIDDLETON, rev. K. D. REYNOLDS

Sources New Grove • Grove, Dict. mus. (1927) • W. H. Husk, An account of the musical celebrations on St Cecilia's day (1857)

Holmes, Sir Gordon Morgan (1876–1965), neurologist, was born in Dublin on 22 February 1876, one of three sons and a daughter of Gordon Holmes and his wife, Kathleen, daughter of John Morgan, from whom she inherited Dellin House, Castlebellingham, co. Louth, which his father farmed. From Dundalk Educational Institute he went on to Trinity College, Dublin, where he displayed both academic and athletic prowess. Having won a scholarship he graduated BA in 1897 as senior moderator in natural science and gold medallist. He qualified in medicine in 1898 and the following year, funded by the Stewart scholarship, studied in the neurological department of the Senkenberg Institute at Frankfurt-am-Main under Karl Weigert and Ludwig Edinger. The latter soon made Holmes an instructor in his university course of neuro-anatomy and eventually urged him warmly to remain as his assistant, but Holmes decided to return to Ireland. On his way through London he heard of a vacancy as house physician in the National Hospital for Nervous Diseases, Queen Square, for which he successfully applied in 1901. At this time there were two world centres for neurological study: Paris, at the Salpêtrière, and London, with its National Hospital. Holmes, who proceeded MD in 1903 and was elected FRCP in 1914, moved up from house physician to resident medical officer, then in 1904 to the new post of pathologist and director of research. In 1909 he became honorary physician to the hospital and in 1912 he turned over the pathology laboratory to S. A. Kinnier Wilson, who was in turn followed in 1914 by a permanent pathologist, J. G. Greenfield. Holmes was also associated for a long period with the Charing Cross and Seamen's Hospital and also Moorfields.

Holmes had become a restless, indefatigable investigator and this was the time for the pathological and physiological analysis which was to pave the way for more adequate therapy. The physicians of the National Hospital brought their independent skills and differing genius to this neurological centre, long called the National Hospital for the Paralysed and Epileptic. Advancing up the ladder of seniority on the staff they served patients without remuneration and conducted graduate teaching, like the early Greeks, without university organization.

When Holmes entered the clinical field, with his knowledge of anatomy and neuropathology, he proceeded to make of neurological examination a relatively exact science. At the same time, like Sir William Gowers and J. Hughlings Jackson, he collected and recorded his observations of patients with neurological lesions. From 1901 to 1911 his publications dealt in general with neuropathology and neuroanatomy. By 1911 he had turned to clinical neurophysiology, working with Henry Head of the London Hospital, a neurologist of great vision and originality. They studied the role of the human cerebral cortex in sensory perception, using the critical, sometimes quantitative, methods devised by Head. Holmes applied these tests with scrupulous exactitude. The formidable study which he and Head wrote in *Brain* (34, 1911, 102–254) showed that the optic thalamus was the seat of physiological processes which underlie crude sensations of contact, heat and cold, while the cortex had to do with the more discriminative aspects of sensation.

With the outbreak of war in 1914 Holmes became consulting neurologist to the British army. His Goulstonian lecture, 'The spinal injuries of warfare' (1915), showed how quickly he had changed the focus of his attention. A brilliant series of publications followed, which dealt with the function of man's cerebellum and the effect of cortical lesions on vision and on somatic sensation. In conjunction with the surgeon Percy Sargent, Holmes made various studies of battle casualties which involved the nervous system. He was appointed CMG in 1917 and CBE in 1919.

In 1920 he wrote a chapter for *Nelson Loose-Leaf Medicine* including F. M. R. Walshe in the authorship. It was entitled 'An introduction to the study of diseases of the nervous system'. From 1922 to 1937 Holmes was editor of *Brain*, following Head in this highly influential editorial post. He was elected a fellow of the Royal Society in 1933, gave the Ferrier lecture in 1944 and was a member of council in 1945–6. In 1935 he was president of the Second International Congress of Neurology when it met in London.

Holmes rarely referred to his own philosophy of life. But in 1934 when he was principal speaker at the Opening Exercises when the Montreal Neurological Institute was founded, he said:

> The student of neurology must equip himself with that intellectual honesty and independence which refuse to submit to authority or to be controlled by preconception ... But on the other hand, he must have the courage to formulate, when ready to do so, observations into hypotheses or rational generalisations, for, as Francis Bacon had told us, 'truth can emerge sooner from error than from confusion'.

His contributions to the physiology of the cerebral cortex, thalamus, and cerebellum of man were important, and the role he played as critic and editor was of great value, but his contribution as a teacher of teachers was outstanding, and he attracted many postgraduate students from abroad. He was formidable man, of driving energy, with little use for diplomacy or compromise, still less for committees or after dinner speeches. But his logical thinking and lucid exposition made him unsurpassed, especially as a teacher of small groups.

In 1918 Holmes married Rosalie (d. 1963), daughter of the late brigade surgeon William Jobson; she was a charming woman with an unfailing sense of humour who had studied at Oxford and had later qualified in medicine. They found a house, 9 Wimpole Street, large enough for their home and consulting rooms. There, three daughters were born to them. The house was damaged by bombs during the Second World War and Holmes moved to Farnham, Surrey, where, alongside his interests in ecclesiastical history, gothic style, and Irish geology, he enjoyed cultivating a large garden. He retired from the National Hospital in 1941 and gradually gave up his London commitments, but he continued to serve throughout the war as a consultant for the Emergency Medical Service. He was knighted in 1951; received several honorary degrees, and honorary membership of many foreign neurological societies; was awarded the Conway Evans prize in 1952; and was an honorary fellow, gold medallist, and Hughlings Jackson medallist of the Royal Society of Medicine.

In 1946 Holmes published *Introduction to Clinical Neurology* and in 1954 he wrote a short history of the National Hospital. In 1956 his *Selected Papers* were edited by Sir F. M. R. Walshe in a volume dedicated to Holmes for his eightieth birthday by the guarantors of *Brain*. Holmes died at his home, Sirmoor, 29 Shortheath Road, Farnham, on

29 December 1965. A memorial service was held on 4 February 1966 in the chapel of the National Hospital for Nervous Diseases in London.   WILDER PENFIELD, rev.

Sources F. M. R. Walshe, *Memoirs FRS*, 12 (1966), 311–19 · *BMJ* (8 Jan 1966), 111–12; (15 Jan 1966), 177; (29 Jan 1966), 302 · W. Penfield, *Journal of the Neurological Sciences*, 5 (1967) · Munk, *Roll*, vol. 5 · *Nature*, 209 (1966), 853–4 · d. cert.
Wealth at death £52,800: probate, 5 April 1966, *CGPLA Eng. & Wales*

Holmes, Henry (1839–1905), violinist and composer, was born on 7 November 1839 at 1 Cross Street, Westminster, London, the second son of Thomas Holmes of Lincoln, a shoemaker, and his wife, Eliza, *née* Sutch. He went to school at the oratory, King William Street, Strand. His early career followed the same path as that of his brother Alfred *Holmes (1837–1876): he studied the violin, from an early age played in public with his brother, and toured the continent, until in 1865 he left Paris, alone, first for Copenhagen and then for Stockholm. He then settled in London, where, having established a reputation as a solo violinist and quartet player, he initiated a series of highly popular chamber concerts (known as Musical Evenings) in 1868. During the 1870s and 1880s he was also a regular participant in Edward Dannreuther's semi-private subscription concerts at Orme Square, Bayswater, and promoted other public concerts in London, one of which, at St George's Hall on 27 November 1872, included the first English performance of Brahms's sextet no. 2 in G, op. 36. Holmes was also active as a composer, producing five symphonies, three violin concertos, a cello concerto, numerous chamber works, and much choral music (his cantata *Christmas Day* was given at the Gloucester Three Choirs festival in 1880). In recognition of his achievements he was invited by George Grove to join the staff of the newly founded Royal College of Music as a professor of violin in 1883. However, within a few years of his appointment at the college, Grove became uncomfortably aware of his 'radical unbelieving views' and of his inclination to lecture his students on atheism and socialism. In December 1893 he was dismissed from his position after he was accused of seducing several of his female students. This episode created a notable scandal at the Royal College and signalled the end in 1894 of Grove's directorship.

After his dismissal Holmes fled to Europe, where, in the Balkans, he wrote a pamphlet, *Man's Faith: his God-Given Attributes; the Creed of an Artist* (under the pseudonym Ilex Illuminati), in which he attempted to outline the basis of his philosophical and artistic beliefs. In 1896 he briefly resettled in London in order to set up a private practice teaching violin and viola, but it was not long before his presence was discovered by those who still remembered the scandal of 1893. In an article entitled 'The re-appearance of Henry Holmes', in *Truth* (14 May 1896), his pamphlet was publicly berated as 'indecent and demoralising'; the writer added that 'no-one who had seen this delectable brochure would ever allow any young person in whose moral welfare he was interested to associate with Holmes on any footing—least of all in the relationship of teacher and pupil'. Unable to establish his teaching practice, and effectively hounded out of London, Holmes moved to San Francisco, where he died on 9 December 1905.   JEREMY DIBBLE

Sources W. H. Husk and A. Mell, 'Holmes, Henry', *New Grove* · P. M. Young, *George Grove, 1820–1900: a biography* (1980) · J. Dibble, *C. Hubert H. Parry: his life and music* (1992) · 'The re-appearance of Henry Holmes', *Truth* (14 May 1896) · Ilex Illuminati, *Man's faith: his God-given attributes; the creed of an artist* (1895) · C. L. Graves, *The life and letters of Sir George Grove* (1903) · b. cert.
Archives Royal College of Music, London

Holmes, Hugh (1840–1916), judge, was born in Dungannon, co. Tyrone, on 17 February 1840, the son of William Holmes, a private gentleman, and his wife, Anne Maxwell. He was educated at the Royal School, Dungannon (where he was a contemporary of Richard Henn Collins, the future Baron Collins of Kensington) and at Trinity College, Dublin, where he matriculated on 1 July 1857. He graduated BA in 1861, with a senior moderatorship in history and English literature, and took his MA in 1879.

Holmes was admitted to the Middle Temple on 16 January 1864 and was called to the Irish bar in Michaelmas Term 1865. He joined the north-west circuit, rapidly acquired a substantial practice, and took silk in 1877. His practice continued to grow—he was frequently instructed in cases arising under the Land Law Acts—and he became the acknowledged leader of his circuit. In 1877 he was appointed law adviser to the crown, and on 14 December 1878 he was appointed solicitor-general for Ireland in Lord Beaconsfield's administration. He was elected a bencher of King's Inns shortly afterwards. He held the junior law officer's post until the Liberal election victory in 1880.

As former law officer Holmes was debarred from rejoining his old circuit, but his workload nevertheless continued to increase rapidly, and by 1885 he was reputed to have the largest practice at the Irish bar. In that year he was elected one of the two MPs for Dublin University, taking the seat vacated by Edward Gibson, who had been appointed to the Irish woolsack as first Baron Ashbourne. Salisbury appointed Holmes attorney-general for Ireland, a post which he held with considerable distinction. He was responsible for steering a number of important bills (many of which he had helped to draft) through the Commons, including the Educational Endowments (Ireland) Act and the Criminal Law Amendment (Ireland) Act of 1887. He also had the arduous task of defending government policy on Ireland at a particularly turbulent period in her history. Although his was not perhaps a great parliamentary presence Holmes carried out his work with considerable ability; T. H. Burke, the Irish under-secretary, adjudged him the best law officer that he had ever known, and he enjoyed considerable influence with both Lord Randolph Churchill and Sir Michael Hicks Beach—the latter described him as his 'closest political associate' (R. F. Foster, *Lord Randolph Churchill: a Political Life*, 1981, 342).

In 1887 Holmes resigned both the attorney-generalship (which he had had to relinquish during the brief Liberal administration in 1886) and his parliamentary seat on his elevation to the Irish high court bench. The vacancy arose when Michael Morris (subsequently Baron Morris of Spiddal and first Baron Killanin) was promoted from chief justice of the Common Pleas to chief justice of the Queen's Bench. As attorney-general Holmes would ordinarily have had the right to succeed as chief justice of the Common Pleas, but as Ashbourne sought to abolish the post and fuse the Common Pleas Division with that of the Queen's Bench Holmes, with immense good grace, accepted only a puisne judgeship. He was initially appointed a justice of the Common Pleas but transferred to the Queen's Bench Division in 1888. He sat as a judge of first instance for ten successful years, until the death of Lord Justice Barry created a vacancy in the Court of Appeal, which Holmes was appointed to fill in 1897; as the *Irish Law Times* noted, his 'success as a judge of first instance completely justified his promotion'.

On first being appointed to the bench Holmes took some time to settle into his new judicial role; criticism was voiced of his initially harsh attitude towards counsel and his habit of lolling in his seat, which was attributed to his years in the Commons. He eventually acquired a measure of the requisite judicial urbanity, but while he learned to become a fairly patient tribunal he was never wholly able to subdue his irritation with counsel who he felt were wasting his time. He was an able trier of complicated commercial cases, and held great sway with juries, civil and criminal. He was a strict (some would have said savage) criminal judge and took a particularly severe view of agrarian crime, which was rife at the time. However, Serjeant Sullivan noted that Holmes was wont to hand down severe sentences from the bench to serve as a warning to the prisoner and the public when the actual sentence recorded in the crown book often was less draconian. In any event Holmes's harsher sentences were reserved for those who genuinely deserved them; an offender who had not in fact caused much harm could expect some leniency. He was strictly impartial regarding protestants and Catholics, although there were still party riots when he went on circuit in the north; his physical courage, and that of his fellow judges who travelled the country dispensing justice in very dangerous times, should not be overlooked.

As a lord justice of appeal Holmes was given a greater opportunity to display his intellectual ability and his remarkable knowledge of the law, although, as the *Law Times* observed, 'he could be terribly severe upon a judge in the divisional court when he was reversing his decision'. Holmes often sat with Gerald Fitzgibbon in the Court of Appeal, and while the two men were equally able lawyers their approaches were markedly different. Fitzgibbon, like Ashbourne, would assess the justice of the case and use his ingenuity to apply the law so as to achieve a fair result. Holmes, like Chief Baron Palles, insisted instead upon a strict application of settled legal principles to the facts—'if these same principles were strained or tampered with, all our law, and with it our civilisation, he thought, would fall into a Serbonian bog' (Ross, 201). Despite these differences of approach these two 'brilliant' men (ibid.) worked well together.

On a personal level the *Law Times* opined that Holmes's manner could on occasion be 'chilling and severe', and Maurice Healy described him (not inaccurately) as 'short, bearded and look[ing] like a severe edition of Father Christmas attempting to disguise himself as a retired admiral' (Healy, 276). By way of explanation for the severity of his aspect Holmes's biographer noted that he was often afflicted with continuous and extreme pain. His judgments, however, were often notable for their general good humour and flashes of wit. Holmes encountered many situations, ranging from the banal to the bizarre, and he considered them all with the good-natured cynicism that is readily apparent from his reported judgments; that on *Duffy* v. *Duffy* (1906) begins: 'The Duffy family was very sickly; it was also rather fraudulent, and the illness from which its members suffered in turn gave the convalescents opportunities to try to over-reach the invalids'.

Privately Holmes was not at all the gruff figure that he seemed to some who had seen him only in public. He enjoyed several strong friendships, and for many years he took a country house (usually in England or Scotland) for the long vacation, where he entertained 'hosts of friends' (Ross, 201), a practice that he carried on until his death. His belief in the importance of the family comes across clearly in his judgment in *Re Harriet O'Hara* ([1900] 2 IR 232), where he confessed to being 'strongly impressed with the importance, in the interests of children, of maintaining, where it is possible, the bond of the family, with the duties and affections that spring therefrom'. He himself had seven children with Olivia (d. 1901), daughter of John Watkins Moule of Elmley Lovett, in Worcestershire, whom he married on 17 March 1869. Among their sons were Sir Valentine *Holmes, an eminent king's counsel in practice at the English bar, and Hugh Holmes, a judge in Egypt. Their daughter Violet married Denis Henry, subsequently the first lord chief justice of Northern Ireland, and another daughter married E. S. Murphy, subsequently a judge of the Northern Irish court of appeal.

Holmes was also a man of 'very deep feelings, which he rarely showed' (Healy, 276) but his fundamental humanity can often be discerned from his judgments, whether it took the form of returning a young child to the mother who had been forced by poverty to give her up for adoption (*Re Harriet O'Hara* 1900) or condemning vivisection and animal cruelty (*Re Cranston* 1898). He was a member of the Church of Ireland synod but afforded the deepest respect to the beliefs of those who did not share his creed (see his discussion of the celebration of the mass by Roman Catholic clergy in *O'Hanlon* v. *Logue* (1906).

In his final years on the bench Holmes's health deteriorated sharply, and he retired in December 1914. He died at his Dublin residence, 3 Fitzwilliam Place, on 20 April 1916. His loss was keenly felt by the Irish bench, for he ranked in ability alongside men like Fitzgibbon and Palles. Even *Freeman's Journal*, a longstanding political foe, acknowledged that he 'gave evidence that he was a first rate lawyer, imbued with sound principles of law, permeated with equally sound common sense'. Such praise was well merited. Holmes's judgments are clearly and tersely written, often humorous, sometimes touching, but always learned and well reasoned. His dicta continue to be discussed and relied upon, not just by the Irish courts but also the English, and at the highest level (see, for instance, the decisions of the House of Lords in *IRC* v. *Crossman*, 1937, *Beswick* v. *Beswick*, 1968, *J* v. *C*, 1970, and *R* v. *Oxfordshire City Council, ex parte Sunningwell Parish Council*, 2000). It is fair to say, as did the *Irish Law Times*, that 'with Lord Ashbourne, Sir Samuel Walker and Lord Justice Fitzgibbon as colleagues the Court of Appeal was at its best'.

NATHAN WELLS

Sources *Irish Law Times and Solicitors' Journal* (22 April 1916) · *Irish Law Times and Solicitors' Journal* (24 June 1916) · *Law Times* (29 April 1916) · J. Ross, *The years of my pilgrimage* (1924) · A. M. Sullivan, *The last serjeant* (1952) · M. Healy, *The old Munster circuit* (1939) · The Irish reports · F. E. Ball, *The judges in Ireland, 1221–1921*, 2 (New York, 1927) · Rhadamanthus, *Our judges* (1890) · Burtchaell & Sadleir, *Alum. Dubl.*, 2nd edn · *WWBMP*, vol. 2 · *WWW*, 1916–28 · H. A. C. Sturgess, ed., *Register of admissions to the Honourable Society of the Middle Temple, from the fifteenth century to the year 1944*, 2 (1949) · E. Keane, P. Beryl Phair, and T. U. Sadleir, eds., *King's Inns admission papers, 1607–1867*, IMC (1982) · B. M. Walker, ed., *Parliamentary election results in Ireland, 1801–1922* (1978) · T. W. Moody and others, eds., *A new history of Ireland*, 9: *Maps, genealogies, lists* (1984) · *RSD Magazine* (1917–24) · m. cert.

Archives PRO NIre., memoirs

Likenesses photograph, repro. in Rhadamanthus, *Our Judges*

Wealth at death £52,572 18s. 0d.: probate, 1916, Ireland, *CGPLA Ire.*

Holmes, James (1777–1860), miniature painter, was 'born in a humble sphere of life', the son of a dealer in precious stones in Clerkenwell, London, who died when James was about seven (Story, 3). At school he showed a talent for drawing, and a master gave him a copy of Aesop's fables, from which he copied woodcut illustrations. His mother, a Catholic, sent him to the Abbé de la Touzé to learn French, and had him apprenticed to the engraver R. M. Meadows, with whom he remained until he was twenty-one. Aged '19½' he entered the Royal Academy Schools on 19 March 1796 to study engraving. He engraved Richard Westall's *Storm in Harvest* and Sir Thomas Lawrence's portrait of the duke of Leeds. In 1800 he engraved in stipple a portrait of the radical author and bookseller Thomas Clio Rickman, after W. Hazlitt. He became friends with his fellow apprentice Thomas Heaphy and also with the painters Richard and William Westall, the engraver Luke Clennell, and the miniature painter Henry Richter, who showed him how to use small clay or wax models to arrange a composition and from whom he learned colouring techniques. In the early part of his career Holmes, who was a good draughtsman, assisted Richard Westall, whose works were then popular, with acquatints after his drawings, and worked especially on the heads of figures.

His apprenticeship completed, Holmes gave up engraving and turned to watercolour painting. He received several portrait commissions in Worcester, where he also taught drawing, for which he charged 1 and then 2 guineas an hour, and returned to London as a popular instructor in watercolour painting. As his miniatures gained in popularity he gave up teaching. He became a member of the Associated Artists in Water Colours and exhibited with them twenty-two works, of which six were portraits from 1808, until 1812, when the society was dissolved. At the last exhibition he showed *The Doubtful Shilling*, which was much admired and acquired for the duchess of York by Beau Brummell, with whom Holmes became friends. The work was reproduced by Holmes in acquatint and finished by hand, and was very popular. In 1813 Holmes became a member of the Society of Painters in Water Colours, which had recently changed its rules to admit painters in oil, and sent two works—*Hot Porridge* and *The Married Man*—to their exhibition that year, and further small subject pictures and a few portraits to their exhibitions until 1821, when the society's rules reverted to admitting only painters in watercolour. *The Michaelmas Dinner* (exh. 1817; Royal Collection), which 'allied [him] to the Dutch school', Holmes regarded as among his best works (Story, 86). In 1824 he was a founder member of the Society of British Artists, of which he was president in 1829, and exhibited with them for nearly thirty years.

In 1814 Holmes moved from 9 Delancey Place, Camden Town, where he had lived for some years, to 1 Upper Titchfield Street, Fitzroy Square, a change that was probably the result of his marriage at that time. In 1815 he moved again, to 9 Upper Titchfield Street, and then in 1817, to 9 Cirencester Place, where he remained until his move to 15 Wilton Street, Belgrave Square, in 1828. Holmes, whose wife's identity is unknown, had three surviving sons: George Augustus and Edward, who became painters—the former of figure and animal subjects, the latter of portraits in miniature and landscape—and Henry, who emigrated to Australia. (His first son, James, died young.) Holmes and his family enjoyed a lifelong friendship with the Leigh family—George Augustus was the godson of Augusta Leigh, half-sister of the poet Lord Byron. Holmes painted a miniature portrait of Augusta (priv. coll.) and several of Byron, with whom he was intimate.

Princess Esterházy, of whom Holmes painted about twelve portraits, introduced him to her cousin George IV, of whom he painted four portraits, including in 1828 a reduced-size copy of a whole-length by John Hoppner (oils; Temple Newsam, Leeds), which was subsequently engraved; his reduced-size copy in oil of a portrait of George III after James Northcote is also at Temple Newsam. He also made a portrait of the duke of Clarence, later William IV, in uniform as lord high admiral, and miniatures of the Princess Sophia. His miniature of Princess Mary of Russia, grand duchess of Saxe-Weimar-Eisenbach, signed and dated 1821, is in the Royal Collection. Holmes was invited to the coronation of George IV and later made a sketch of this from a pencil drawing that he had made on the spot. He painted three or four portraits of Maria II, queen of Portugal, and in 1828 the duc d'Orléans sat to him in Wilton Street. 'Holmes's suavity of manners and invariable good humour, joined to his talents as an artist and as a miniaturist had rendered him a great favourite at Court, and he became a frequent guest at His Majesty's evening parties' (Story, 90–91). A talented flautist (he had been encouraged by Novello, founder of the well-known music publishing firm, to give up painting for music), Holmes was often invited to play for the king; Marquess Conyngham commented that 'Mr. Holmes had become the King's hobby' (ibid., 91). He was also patronized by the brewer Sir Henry Meux and the society hostess Lady Sarah Sophia, countess of Jersey, of whom he painted a whole-length portrait in oil (1834; priv. coll.). Other sitters included Charles John Gardiner, first earl of Blessington (NPG), Thomas Grenville (exh. Society of British Artists, 1837), and F. J. Robinson, first earl of Ripon (c.1844). At the height of his career Holmes was earning in excess of 2000 guineas a year but his temperate nature led him always to be short of funds.

In 1835 Holmes made a two-month visit to Italy with the painter F. Y. Hurlstone, with whom he became acquainted in 1823–4. He accompanied Hurlstone as far as Milan and then went on separately to Venice, where in 1818 Byron had invited him to paint portraits of his mistress and his natural daughter, Allegra. In later years Holmes stood surety for the builder of his studio, whose firm subsequently went bankrupt, and at seventy he was financially ruined. He gave up his home in Wilton Street and moved to Hendon. In 1853 his wife died, and he passed several years visiting friends in Shropshire and Worcestershire, before living with his sons George and Edward. He died in London on 24 February 1860.

Holmes was 'comparatively short of stature and inclined to spareness of figure'; he was 'very strongly built', 'quick of motion', and noted for his 'vivacity of temperament' and 'perpetual good spirits' (Story, 107–8). Basil Long commented that although he was more successful with his watercolours than in oil 'the few miniatures by Holmes which I have seen were not such as to justify the reputation he appears to have enjoyed' (Long, 217). Daphne Foskett noted the large amount of gum arabic Holmes used to obtain a varnish-like finish to his miniatures in watercolour but commented more favourably that his miniatures signed 'J. Holmes' or 'Js Holmes Pt' or 'J. H.', followed by a date, 'are well-drawn and expressive' (Foskett, 568). Holmes was much in demand, and his sitters commissioned from him many copies of miniature portraits that he had painted from life. The quality of his work varies greatly, depending on whether the status of a miniature is that of a prime version or a copy after a studio template. (George Augustus Holmes is also known to have made copies of miniatures painted by his father.) At his best—for example, in the prime versions of his portraits of Lord Byron of 1813 and 1815–16—Holmes's work shows great sensitivity in rendering the sitter's facial expression as well as his physical appearance. Byron wrote that 'Holmes made (*I think the very best*) one of me in 1815—or 1816—and from this there were some good engravings taken … I prefer that likeness to any which has been done of me by any artist whatever' (*Byron's Letters and Journals*, 10.175). ANNETTE PEACH

Sources A. T. Story, *James Holmes and John Varley* (1894) • A. Peach, 'Portraits of Byron', *Walpole Society*, 62 (2000), 1–144 • artist's file, NPG, Heinz Archive and Library • *Byron's letters and journals*, ed. L. A. Marchand, 12 vols. (1973–82) • B. S. Long, *British miniaturists* (1929) [with MS annotations by Carl Parker made in the copy in the print room of the V&A] • M. Elwin, *Lord Byron's wife* (1962) • D. Foskett, *Miniatures: dictionary and guide* (1987) • R. Walker, *The eighteenth and early nineteenth century miniatures in the collection of her majesty the queen* (1991) • *Engraved Brit. ports.* • *Graves, RA exhibitors* • J. Johnson, ed., *Works exhibited at the Royal Society of British Artists, 1824–1893, and the New English Art Club, 1888–1917*, 2 vols. (1975)
Likenesses E. Holmes, drawing • autotype (after E. Holmes), repro. in Story, *James Holmes and John Varley*, frontispiece
Wealth at death financially ruined, c.1847

Holmes, James Headgoose (1861–1934), trade unionist, was born at Kirton, near Boston, in Lincolnshire, on 19 March 1861, the son of Maria Holmes. No father appears on the birth certificate. Between the ages of nine and seventeen he worked on the land, except for a period at sea. Following a spell in a stables, he joined the Great Northern Railway at Spalding in 1882. After transferring to the signalling grade, he moved up the promotional ladder. In 1891 he was appointed a class one signalman at Retford. An activist in the Amalgamated Society of Railway Servants (ASRS), he became in July 1892 the subject of a victimization case. His refusal to accept two transfers at reduced wages led to dismissal. Holmes claimed political victimization: he had supported the local Liberal candidate in the recent general election. The company insisted that he had been in breach of a safety regulation. Holmes acknowledged an error but claimed differential treatment.

The ASRS accepted his victimization claim, thereby allowing him to retain union membership as he developed a successful career with the Singer Sewing Machine Company. His new employment involved a move to Doncaster, where he was elected to the board of guardians and sat on the Trades and Labour Council as an ASRS delegate. Increasing prominence in the union culminated in his election as a full-time organizer at the union's 1898 annual general meeting. He was given responsibility for Wales and the west of England.

Over the next few years Holmes played a significant role in the emergence of the Labour Representation Committee (LRC), subsequently the Labour Party. At the 1899 Plymouth Trades Union Congress, he moved on behalf of his union the decisive resolution which led in February 1900 to the formation of the LRC. The ASRS was committed to political independence, and the resolution had originated in the union's Doncaster branch, where Holmes had recently been active. Yet his own political position was ambiguous. His municipal interventions in Doncaster politics had enjoyed local Liberal support.

The durability of the LRC depended on a significant level of trade union affiliations. The Taff Vale legal judgment of 1901 provided a strong incentive. The judgment followed a strike on the Taff Vale Railway in August 1900 and established that trade unions could be sued by employers for losses arising out of industrial action. The Taff Vale Railway came within Holmes's district. Following his appointment as organizer, Holmes soon found himself in conflict with the union's recently elected general secretary, Richard Bell. In part the clash was strategic. Bell, mindful of the union's weakness, advocated a cautious policy of developing support for a national programme. Holmes was more ready to encourage militant initiatives directed at specific companies. Their personalities also clashed. Bell was shrewd and autocratic; Holmes volatile and verbally combative. The result was suspicion in the prelude to the strike and acrimony in its aftermath. When the trial for damages was held late in 1902, Bell succeeded in separating his and the union's defence from that of Holmes. Mr Justice Willis reserved his most severe criticisms for Holmes, characterizing him as 'a stormy petrel'. The affair split the union. A special general meeting in January 1903 passed a resolution critical of Holmes but acknowledging that his actions did not merit dismissal.

Holmes remained as an organizer with the ASRS and, from 1913, with the National Union of Railwaymen (NUR) until he retired in 1922. Politically active, he fought three lively but unsuccessful campaigns as a Labour parliamentary candidate. Despite his strong support for the 1914–18 war, he was prosecuted at Barnsley under the Defence of the Realm Act following an incident on 6 January 1916. An argument between Holmes and an unsympathetic company official had exploded after Holmes had opposed military conscription. He was fined £25 with the option of two months in prison. The fine was paid by members of the NUR.

Holmes died at his home, 16 Brunner Road, Brentham, Ealing, Middlesex, on 1 October 1934, and was buried at Westminster cemetery, Hanwell. He was survived by his wife, Elsie May. George Alcock, the union's first historian, recalled Holmes on the platform: 'Humour, pathos, irony, scorn, invective mingled with his gift of speech. His audiences have laughed and cried in turn' (*Railway Review*, 12 Oct 1934). Another contemporary was more down to earth: 'Holmes was all right to have a drink with, but if he went on the platform, he would set the world on fire' (*Railway Review*, 5 Oct 1934). Apart from his role in the formation of the Labour Party, he was a talented union organizer in an industry where managements were often paternalistic and sometimes authoritarian.

DAVID HOWELL

Sources P. S. Bagwell, *The railwaymen: the history of the National Union of Railwaymen*, [1] (1963) · D. Howell, *Respectable radicals: studies in the politics of railway trade unionism* (1999) · G. W. Alcock, *Fifty years of railway trade unionism* (1922) · *Railway Review* (5 Oct 1934) · *Railway Review* (12 Oct 1934) · *Doncaster Gazette* (4 Oct 1934) · *West Middlesex Gazette* (6 Oct 1934) · *Doncaster Chronicle* (1890–99) · *Doncaster Gazette* (1890–99) · *TUC report of proceedings* (1899) · *Labour Pioneer* (c.1900) · *Gloucestershire Journal* (1900) · *Barnsley Chronicle* (8 April 1916) · *Doncaster Gazette* (7 April 1916) · People's History Museum, Manchester, Labour Party archive, LRC letter files 28/82, 180–81 · Labour Party general corresp., 1906–7, People's History Museum, Manchester, 21 · National Museum of Labour Party, Manchester, Labour Party Archive, LP/HEN/811 · b. cert. · d. cert. · *CGPLA Eng. & Wales* (1934)
Archives Labour History Archive and Study Centre, Manchester · PRO, Taff Vale Company's file, RAIL 1057/1791 · U. Warwick Mod. RC, NUR collection, corresp. and MSS relating to Taff Vale, MSS 127/AS/TV

Likenesses photograph, repro. in Alcock, *Fifty years of railway trade unionism*
Wealth at death £6476 3s. 2d.: probate, 22 Nov 1934, *CGPLA Eng. & Wales*

Holmes, John (d. 1629), musician, is of unknown parentage. Although the archival sources are fragmentary, it is certain that Holmes spent the early part of his adult working life at Winchester Cathedral. He is first mentioned on 18 December 1599, in circumstances which suggest that he may have served from the outset as organist, when he was admitted a lay vicar. Holmes served as organist at installation ceremonies in January 1611, June 1613, and August 1621; and further confirmation is found in an indenture dated 20 January 1616, relating to the lease of a house in Kingsgate parish, Winchester.

Holmes's association with Salisbury Cathedral is first attested in August 1613, when he took two of his Winchester choristers to augment the choir during James I's visit there; but in 1621 Holmes accepted a probationary lay vicar's place at Salisbury, and was also appointed instructor of the choristers, a post in which he was shortly afterwards confirmed. He is first styled 'M[aste]r of the Choristers' on 25 July 1622, in the baptismal record of one of his sons, James. His wife's name was Dussabella.

Probably an able teacher as well as an accomplished composer, Holmes had as his most famous pupil the composer Adrian Batten, once a chorister of Winchester. A manuscript known as the Batten organ book states that its copies of Holmes's anthems, some of which are dated between 1602 and 1610, were 'prict [i.e. copied] from his owne hand prickinge [that is, Holmes's autograph] in the yeare: 1635' (Tenbury MS 791, fol. 400r). His second protégé was the Salisbury chorister Edward Lowe, subsequently organist of Christ Church, Oxford, and professor of music there.

Sadly, Holmes's church music (comprising full-choir settings of the preces and Psalm 89 and two evening services, and seventeen verse anthems) is now incomplete; but the surviving fragments reveal a competent technique and a love of rich sonorities, and his verse compositions are some of the earliest provincial examples of the type. Holmes's other works (which include an untexted five-part anthem, perhaps intended for viols, a madrigal, and a short keyboard pavan) are less significant.

Holmes made his will on 27 January 1629 and died soon afterwards, probably at his home (thought to have been the choristers' house) in the close, Salisbury. His burial at Salisbury Cathedral on 30 January 1629 was followed by a bitter dispute as to whether he should be succeeded as the choristers' instructor by his son Thomas or by Giles Tomkins; the latter triumphed, and on 5 November an order of the court of chancery had to be produced to secure possession of the choristers' house from Holmes's widow.

Thomas Holmes (bap. 1606, d. 1638), organist, singer, and composer, was baptized in St Swithun's parish, Winchester, on 11 April 1606, a son of John and Dussabella Holmes. While it is reasonable to assume that he was a chorister at Winchester under his father, there is no proof of this, and he first appears in the records relating to the dispute over his father's successor at Salisbury Cathedral in 1629, which Thomas Holmes appears to have lost. He was admitted lay vicar and organist at Winchester on 5 April 1631, at the dean's special request, and on 17 September 1633 was appointed a gentleman of the Chapel Royal. His royal duties may by the following month have made him the subject of a dispute, when they were apparently causing him to be absent from Winchester, much to the chapter's annoyance. Apparently the archbishop of Canterbury had taken Holmes's side in the matter, and the chapter would have written 'to his Grace and to represent the necessity our church had of his presence' (Shaw, 296) had not the king intervened to prevent such a petition. The situation was probably rectified, for two years later one visitor to the cathedral praised Holmes as 'one of the rarest Organists … that this Land affoords' (Hammond, 46). Meanwhile, his court connections probably qualified him to take part, as a bass singer, in James Shirley's masque *The Triumph of Peace* on 13 February 1634. Perhaps this was the occasion of his meeting with the composer John Jenkins, who reported a story about his having 'one false Eye of Glasse' and his bizarre sense of humour in accommodating it (Ashbee and Lasocki, 582). Holmes died in Salisbury on 25 March 1638 and was buried in the close there later that month.

Holmes's extant compositions include five verse anthems, music for three viols, and a single song; but it is for his three-part catches and canons, published between 1651 and 1680, that he is best known.

His most unusual work, however, is the solo bass song 'Oberon, or, The Madmans Songe, sung in a comedy at Cambridge before the king & queene by the author'. Preserved in British Library Add. MS 11608, fol. 18r, and beginning 'Newly from a Poatcht Toad & a broyl'd Viper', it begins with strikingly athletic vocal leaps, seasoned with florid ornamentation, and concludes in a smooth and melodious triple metre.　　　　　　　　　　　　IAN PAYNE

Sources H. W. Shaw, *The succession of organists of the Chapel Royal and the cathedrals of England and Wales from c.1538* (1991), 261–2, 294–6 · A. Ashbee and D. Lasocki, eds., *A biographical dictionary of English court musicians, 1485–1714*, 1 (1998), 581–2 · D. H. Robertson, *Sarum Close: a history of the life and education of the cathedral choristers for 700 years* (1938) · Salisbury Cathedral, Salisbury chapter muniments, Shuter's register contents list, 189–90 · private information (2004) [archivists of Winchester and Salisbury cathedral archives] · Bodl. Oxf., MS Tenbury 791 · *New Grove* · [Lieutenant Hammond], 'A relation of a short survey of the western counties made by a lieutenant … in 1635', ed. L. G. W. Legg, *Camden miscellany, XVI*, CS, 3rd ser., 52 (1936), 46 · BL, Add. MS 11608 [facs. in *English song, 1600–1675*, ed. E. Jorgens, British Library MSS, 4 (1986)] · will and probate inventory, Wilts. & Swindon RO, records of the dean of Sarum

Archives Longleat House, Wiltshire, Whitelock MSS, signature of Thomas Holmes, Parcel II, no. 6

Wealth at death £52 15s. 8d.—household goods: will and probate inventory, Wilts. & Swindon RO, records of the dean of Sarum

Holmes, Sir John (1639/40–1683), naval officer, was the son of Henry Holmes of Mallow, co. Cork, and a younger brother of Admiral Sir Robert *Holmes. The reference to him as a 'land officer' in the duke of Albemarle's letter-book for 1665 (NMM, LBK-47) suggests that, like Robert, he probably served as a mercenary in the late 1650s. In 1664

he was lieutenant to his brother in the *Jersey*, taking part in her expedition to Guinea, and he served as lieutenant of the *Centurion* in the 1665 campaign, including at the battle of Lowestoft on 3 June. In September 1665 he was made captain of the *St Paul*, commanding her at the Four Days' Fight on 1–4 June 1666; Holmes was wounded and the ship disabled and subsequently burnt by her own side in that action. He moved shortly afterwards to the *Bristol*, serving under his brother in the St James's day fight on 25 July, and again served under Sir Robert in the raid on the Dutch shipping in the Vlie in August. He remained in command of the *Bristol* until October 1667; an elevation to the second-rate *Triumph*, referred to in several accounts, was in fact only a temporary command for three days at the tail end of the Four Days' Fight. He briefly commanded the *Falcon* and *Kent* in 1668, and in 1669–72 he commanded successively the *Nonsuch*, *Bristol*, and *Diamond* in the Mediterranean Fleet, engaged in the war against the Algerine corsairs. In January 1672 he took command of the *Gloucester*, one of the ships which took part in his brother's attack on the Dutch Smyrna convoy, and was badly wounded by a shot in the chest, although his ship successfully took the *Klein Hollandia*, killing the Dutch flag officer Aert van Nes. His reward for this service was a knighthood and command of the *Rupert*, in which he served in all the major engagements of the Third Anglo-Dutch War. On 14 August 1673, thanks largely to the patronage of Prince Rupert, he became rear-admiral of the blue, flying his flag in the *Royal Charles*, and remained aboard her until October.

Following the end of the war Holmes exploited his brother's governorship of the Isle of Wight by obtaining the reversion of that office in December 1675, purchasing the governorship of Hurst Castle for £500, serving as mayor of Yarmouth in 1678–9, and becoming MP for Newtown (Isle of Wight) in his brother's interest, first at a distinctly dubious by-election in 1677 and then in the elections for the three Exclusion Parliaments. Regarded at the time as a strong supporter of the court, although both he and Sir Robert went into opposition in the final session of the Cavalier Parliament, he was denounced by his political opponents as a syphilitic coward who had won his seat on the vote of one burgess, cast in the middle of the night. He returned to sea as commander-in-chief in the Downs, flying the union flag at the main in the *Mountague*, from April 1677 to May 1678, and escorted William of Orange on his return to Holland after his marriage to Princess Mary. He became rear-admiral of the fleet sent out in the French war scare of 1678, flying his flag in the *Charles*. His final sea-going command was that of the *Captain*, again as commander-in-chief in the Downs, from September 1678 to September 1679. In June 1679 he fought a duel with his fellow MP for Newtown, John Churchill, later duke of Marlborough, over Holmes relating to the king a story about Churchill 'beating an orange wench' (*Seventh Report*, HMC, 473); Holmes successfully disarmed the future victor of Blenheim.

Holmes married Margaret (b. c.1648, d. after 1692), daughter of Alderman Robert Lowther, draper of London, in April 1668. Pepys noted that the marriage was:

by stealth; which I was sorry for, he being an idle rascal and proud, and worth little I doubt, and she a mighty pretty, well-disposed lady, and good fortune … but the sport is, Sir Rob. Holmes doth seem to be mad too with his brother and will disinherit him, saying he hath ruined himself, marrying below himself and to his disadvantage.   (Pepys, 9.157)

In the event, however, Sir Robert ultimately became guardian of Sir John's six children, and in his will bequeathed annuities to the three survivors, Robert, John, and Elizabeth, and to their widowed mother. Sir John Holmes died at his brother's house near the Horse Guards in London on 28 May 1683 and was buried on 23 June at Yarmouth church.   J. D. DAVIES

Sources R. Ollard, *Man of war: Sir Robert Holmes and the Restoration navy* (1969) • Pepys, *Diary*, 9.157 • J. D. Davies, *Gentlemen and tarpaulins: the officers and men of the Restoration navy* (1991) • PRO, ADM 10/15, 67 • NMM, LBK-47 • J. R. Powell and E. K. Timings, eds., *The Rupert and Monck letter book, 1666*, Navy RS, 112 (1969) • R. C. Anderson, ed., *Journals and narratives of the Third Dutch War*, Navy RS, 86 (1946) • *CSP dom.*, 1665–83 • *Seventh report*, HMC, 6 (1879), 473 • *Le Neve's Pedigrees of the knights*, ed. G. W. Marshall, Harleian Society, 8 (1873), 3 • J. L. Chester and J. Foster, eds., *London marriage licences, 1521–1869* (1887), 702 • P. Watson, 'Holmes, Sir John', HoP, *Commons, 1660–90*, 2.568–9 • parish register, Isle of Wight Record Office, Yarmouth [burials]

Holmes, John (1702/3–1760), schoolmaster and writer on education, is of unknown family background. He is described in a 1729 broadsheet of his Latin verses as 'ex schola Holtensis'. Following the death in 1729 of David Dunscombe, the headmaster of Gresham's School in Holt, Norfolk, the governors of the Fishmongers' Company (who administered the school) appointed Holmes in his place from 1730. This appointment broke with tradition since he was not in holy orders, and recognized the neglect of the school by previous office holders. Holmes restored the school's reputation and broadened the curriculum to include 'Arithmetic in all its parts, Bookkeeping by Double Entry … the Use of Globes and writing in all the hands used in Great Britain' according to the advertisement in *A new grammar of the Latin tongue … freed from the many obscurities, defects, superfluities, and errors, which render the common grammar an insufferable impediment to the progress of education*, which he published in 1732. His Latin grammar went through thirteen editions before 1788, and was followed by *A Greek Grammar* in 1735 (seven editions published by 1771) and his *Clavis grammaticalis … or, Examination of the Latin and Greek Grammars* in 1739.

Holmes also taught oratory and drama, and in 1738 published *The art of rhetorick made easy … to meet the needs of the time when schoolboys are expected to be led, sooth'd and entic'd to their studies … rather than by force and harsh discipline drove, as in days of yore*. This work 'maintained a degree of popularity for well over a hundred years after its publication' (Howell, 137). He simultaneously published an engraved taxonomy of the subject called *Rhetorick Epitomiz'd*, with the optimistic sub-title 'whereby the principles of the whole art may be learned in an hour'. The annual school play became a notable public occasion in the town, and his dramatized *History of England* (published in Latin and English in 1737) was 'Performed by the Gentlemen of the … Grammar School … at their Christmas breaking up' (title-

page). The school entertainment for 1741 was a masque entitled 'The Constellations Reformed' performed by the boys in costume. Holmes likewise pioneered the teaching of modern languages, geography, and astronomy, publishing a French grammar in 1741 and twenty lectures entitled *The Grammarian's Geography and Astronomy Ancient and Modern* in 1751. *The Grammarian's Arithmetic: a Compendious Treatise of the Art of Ciphering* was advertised in 1755, but either was not published or else may not have survived. He corresponded with Francis Blomefield, historian of Norfolk, and supplied him with notes and descriptions of churches and other buildings in Holt hundred, and some fine drawings, though these were not ultimately used in the published work. In return Blomefield supplied information relating to the history of his school and its foundation by the Gresham family.

Holmes's headmastership is regarded as 'a period of outstanding success' (Linnell and Douglas, 20), and the Fishmongers' Company presented him with a silver tankard, acknowledging his merit. However, Holmes and his Greek grammar were subjected to a concerted vitriolic campaign of denigration in the London and Norwich press, and in contemporary pamphlets published in 1738–40. The criticisms were voiced by Robert Hankinson and the mathematician Robert Heath. Holmes successfully answered his critics in a series of letters to the press under the pseudonym Patroclus, and was supported by (among others) the mathematician Thomas Simpson.

Holmes was married to Jane (d. 1767), and they had a daughter, Jane, who married John Burrell, rector of Letheringsett; she was the mother of the lepidopterist and entomologist John Burrell. Holmes died in Holt on 22 December 1760 aged fifty-seven, and was buried in Holt church.   DAVID STOKER

Sources D. Stoker, 'The grammarians' battleground: controversies surrounding the publication of John Holmes' *Greek grammar*', *Paradigm: the Journal of the Textbook Colloquium*, 17 (1995), 1–14 • C. L. S. Linnell and A. B. Douglas, *Gresham's School history and register, 1555–1954* (1955), 16–20 • E. G. R. Taylor, *The mathematical practitioners of Hanoverian England, 1714–1840* (1966), 162 • W. S. Howell, *Eighteenth-century British logic and rhetoric* (1971), 125–37 • *Norwich Mercury* (3 Jan 1761) • *The correspondence of the Reverend Francis Blomefield, 1705–52*, ed. D. Stoker, Norfolk RS, 55 (1992) • [J. Chambers], *A general history of the county of Norfolk*, 2 (1829), 779 • Philomathematicus, *A battle fought with the boasters, or, Patroclus's weak defence by force defeated* (1738)

Holmes, John (1800–1854), antiquary, son of Nathaniel Holmes (1761/2–1840), was born on 17 July 1800 in Deptford, Kent. He was brought up in the house of a bookseller, John Lepard, 108 Strand, London, and for a short time had his own business in Derby. Catalogues of manuscripts that he prepared for the bookseller John Cochrane in 1829 attracted the notice of Lord Bexley and Lord Glenelg, and through their influence he was appointed temporary assistant in the department of manuscripts at the British Museum on 15 January 1830. On 8 September 1832 he married Mary Anne, eldest daughter of Charles *Rivington (1754–1831), publisher [see under Rivington family], of St Paul's Churchyard, and sister of the publisher Francis Rivington; she died at Highgate on 8 February 1870. They had five children, one of whom, Richard Rivington *Holmes, became librarian at Windsor Castle. Their eldest son, the Revd Charles Rivington Holmes, was father of Sir Charles John Holmes, director of the National Gallery.

Holmes was promoted to senior assistant in the manuscripts department in April 1837, and to assistant keeper on 6 May 1850. His most valuable official work was the *Catalogue of Maps, Plans and Topographical Drawings*, of which the first two volumes were published in 1844. The third volume was printed in 1861 with a preface, additions, and corrections by Sir Frederic Madden, the keeper of manuscripts, but the trustees of the museum refused to sanction publication, as Madden's corrections might have been thought to imply some inadequacy in the previous volumes: Sir Antony Panizzi, the principal librarian, told Madden that he 'must not cry *stinking fish*' (Madden, 12 June 1861). The whole impression, already bound, was almost entirely destroyed in a bindery fire in 1865, but some surviving sheets were published lithographically as volume 3 in 1961. Descriptions made by Holmes for a fourth volume have since disappeared. He began a classified index to the manuscript collections, of which a specimen was submitted to the trustees in 1836. It was evident, however, that the project could not be pursued until the collections were adequately catalogued, and the idea came to fruition only in the keepership of Sir E. A. Bond (1866–78). He gave evidence to the royal commission on the British Museum which reported in 1850. After the British Museum had failed to purchase the manuscripts of Guglielmo Libri in 1846, he negotiated their purchase for Lord Ashburnham; a transaction of doubtful propriety, as it was already suspected that many of them were stolen. Holmes was elected FSA in 1832. He published little original work apart from articles in *The Athenaeum* and *Quarterly Review*, but he produced new editions of George Cavendish's *Life of Cardinal Wolsey* (1852) and Christopher Wordsworth's *Ecclesiastical Biography* (1853), and contributed notes to the 1854 edition of Lord Braybrooke's *Diary and Correspondence of Samuel Pepys* and to Samuel Wilberforce's edition of John Evelyn's *Life of Mrs. Godolphin* (1847).

Obituarists described Holmes as a learned and kindly man, generous in his help to scholars. Madden, however, thought that he was lazy and neglected his duties in favour of social climbing, a view no doubt coloured by his subordinate's close friendship with Panizzi, whom Madden detested. Holmes tried, unsuccessfully, to effect a reconciliation between the two men in 1852. After Holmes's death Madden nevertheless welcomed the appointment of Holmes's second son, Richard, as junior assistant in his department, 'a proper and gracious act on the part of the Trustees in consideration of Mr. H.'s period of service' (Madden, 5 April 1854). Holmes died suddenly at his home, 4 Park Terrace, Highgate, Middlesex, on 1 April 1854. His library was sold by Puttick and Simpson on 15 June 1854. The British Museum bought his antiquarian papers from his widow in 1855 (BL, Add. MSS 20751–20777).

MICHAEL BORRIE

Sources *GM*, 2nd ser., 42 (1854), 87–8 · *The Athenaeum* (15 April 1854), 465 · F. Madden, journal, Bodl. Oxf., MSS Eng. hist. c. 140–182 · M. A. F. Borrie, 'Panizzi and Madden', *British Library Journal*, 5 (1979), 18–36, esp. 31–3 · *DNB*
Archives BL, catalogue, lists, notes, Add. MSS 20751–20777, 22589 · CUL, catalogue of MSS owned by the duc d'Ammale, with coat of arms | Bodl. Oxf., corresp. with Sir Thomas Phillipps · E. Sussex RO, letters to fourth earl of Ashburnham relating to MS collections
Likenesses R. C. Lucas, wax relief sculpture, S. Antiquaries, Lond.

Holmes, John Beck [*formerly* Johanes Holm] (1767–1843), Moravian bishop, was born at Copenhagen on 3 November 1767. In 1780 he was sent to the academy at Nisky in Silesia, and subsequently attended the Moravian Academy at Barby in Wittenberg. In 1791 he was appointed a teacher at the Seminary of the United Brethren, Fulneck, near Leeds, where he remained until 1799, also serving as minister to the single men of the community. He then became minister of one of the small churches of the district at Wyke, and about this time he married. In 1812 he was appointed minister of the congregation at Dublin, and then on 18 August 1825 he was ordained a bishop of the church at Herrnhut in Saxony, being stationed at Fulneck and serving there as minister to the Moravian church's most significant congregation in the north of England. He presided at the 1835 British provincial synod of the church. While he was in Dublin he studied the history of the Moravians, and several of his works, including *Historical sketches of the missions of the United Brethren for propagating the gospel among the heathen* (1818) and *History of the Protestant Church of the United Brethren* (2 vols., 1825–30), became standard accounts. He died at Fulneck on 3 September 1843, and was buried there.

PETER J. LINEHAM

Sources J. T. Hamilton and K. G. Hamilton, *History of the Moravian church* (1983) · Fulneck Moravian Diary, Moravian Archives, Fulneck, Yorkshire · R. V. Taylor, ed., *The biographia Leodiensis, or, Biographical sketches of the worthies of Leeds* (1865) · d. cert.
Archives Moravian Archives, Fulneck, Yorkshire

Holmes, Sir Maurice Gerald (1885–1964), civil servant and educationist, was born on 14 June 1885, the son of Edmond Gore Alexander *Holmes (1850–1936), chief inspector of elementary schools for England, and his wife, Florence Mary (d. 1927), eldest daughter of Captain P. M. Syme RA. He had two sisters, one of whom was the engineer Verena Winifred *Holmes. He went to school at Sutherland House, Folkestone (1894–6), and then at Stanmore Park, Middlesex (1896–9), before going on to Wellington College (1900–04). He studied law at Balliol College, Oxford, from 1904 until 1908, when he was awarded a first-class degree in jurisprudence. He entered for the bar at the Inner Temple in 1908 (being called to the bar in 1909) and at this stage appeared destined for a legal career. When he applied in October 1908 to the Board of Education for a temporary position as a junior examiner he was already about to enter a barrister's chambers to gain further expertise in this area. He had no training or experience as a teacher, and his appointment came at a time when the board was heavily criticized for recruiting by patronage.

However, his legal background and knowledge proved highly valuable throughout the rest of his long career in the department.

Holmes's early employment at the board consisted of a range of junior positions; he worked as a temporary barrister and then examiner in the technological branch, then as a junior examiner at assistant principal level at a salary of £230 per annum. During the First World War he served in France, Belgium, Egypt, and Palestine, and rose to lieutenant-colonel in the Army Service Corps. He was appointed OBE for his military service in 1919. In 1917 he married Ivy Marie Beatrice (b. 1892), the daughter of Brigadier-General Francis Pearson Shaw Dunsford. They lived for most of their married life at 7 Sloane Street, London, and raised two daughters.

After the war Holmes rose swiftly within the Board of Education. He was entrusted with important duties in which, as the then permanent secretary of the board, L. A. Selby-Bigge, observed, he 'made good', and demonstrated 'great aptitude for Establishment work' (PRO, ED 36/4). In 1919 Selby-Bigge appointed him to the post of chief clerk of the Board of Education at the level of principal. Among the sensitive tasks for which he assumed much responsibility was the moving of Board of Education staff from the Victoria and Albert Museum to Whitehall in 1920. He also assisted with supply and transport in north Wales in view of a threatened strike of railway and transport workers in April 1921, a situation in which he apparently displayed 'great energy, capacity and resource' in dealing with difficulties (ibid.). In 1922 he became private secretary to the president of the Board of Education, initially H. A. L. Fisher and then Edward Wood. The following year, still in his thirties, he became director of establishments to the board, a prime-ministerial appointment. After the retirement of Sir Edward Chambers in 1926 he was appointed principal assistant secretary (secondary schools). Five years later he became deputy secretary of the board, and in 1937 he succeeded Sir (Edward) Henry Pelham, also a Balliol graduate, as permanent secretary at a fixed salary of £3000 per annum. He was appointed KCB in 1938.

During his eight years as permanent secretary Holmes was largely responsible for managing the board's involvement in the major educational debates which culminated in the Education Act of 1944. He exhibited a shrewd capacity for working with the key figures on whom the board depended to construct reasoned positions on educational reform, and for developing the potential role of committees in specific areas of inquiry, such as the Norwood committee on the secondary-school curriculum and examinations and the Fleming committee on the public schools. He generally preferred the role of the board itself to be developed, and in fact strengthened during this period, out of the public eye rather than as part of a political debate. In 1941 the circulation of the so-called green book entitled Education after the War, a prototype statement of educational reconstruction composed by senior officials of the board, with a foreword by Holmes, was restricted to a small circle of insiders. His own opinions on key issues relating to reform carried a great deal of weight within

the board, or the ministry as it became after 1944. He advised the president of the Board of Education, R. A. Butler, in 1942 that the duration of the war itself would largely determine the outcome of educational reforms: 'The longer it lasts, the more clamant the demand for social equality is likely to be' (PRO, ED 136/294).

Holmes could express his views precisely and often in strong terms, for instance in attributing the 'woefully inadequate' provision of technical education to the lack of interest taken by industry and to external financial pressures (PRO, ED 136/132). At the same time he avoided becoming involved in public controversies such as those to which his father had become attracted towards the end of his career. In this respect he also differed from his Edwardian predecessor Sir Robert Morant, who had been strongly influential in the debates that led to the Education Act of 1902 but had himself become a focus of contention. Behind the scenes Holmes's authority and experience as an administrator constituted a key factor in the success of the Board of Education in negotiating a safe passage for the Education Act in 1944, and stands as his major contribution to the development of educational and social policy in twentieth-century Britain. It also helped to ensure not only broad social and political support but also lasting agreement around measures that were potentially divisive, a combination that was to elude attempts to recast the educational system later in the century.

Immediately after the war, in semi-retirement, Holmes remained influential, for example in his advice to the new education minister in the Labour government, Ellen Wilkinson, that, despite what he called 'constant pressure to secure that this or that subject is included in the curriculum of schools', it was better to resist such proposals on the ground that 'in this country' the details of the curriculum were not controlled or dominated by the ministry, but were left to the determination of the local education authorities and the teachers (PRO, ED 147/21). He retired in 1945 and was promoted GBE.

In 1947 Holmes served on the east African salaries commission and in 1948–9 chaired the Caribbean public services commission. He also undertook a number of local inquiries for the Ministry of Transport. He was a governor of Wellington College and chairman of the Oxford and Cambridge Club. He maintained a keen interest in the work of George Bernard Shaw and in the life of Captain James Cook, and published bibliographies on both. He died at his London home, Flat 8, 7 Sloane Street, on 4 April 1964.

GARY MCCULLOCH

Sources The Times (6 April 1964) · P. H. J. H. Gosden, Education in the Second World War: a study in policy and administration (1976) · P. Gosden, 'Putting the act together', History of Education, 24 (1995), 195–207 · I. Elliott, ed., The Balliol College register, 1900–1950, 3rd edn (privately printed, Oxford, 1953) · WW · P. Gosden, 'From board to ministry: the impact of the war on the education department', History of Education, 18 (1989) · P. Gordon, 'The writings of Edmond Holmes: a reassessment and bibliography', History of Education, 12 (1983), 15–24 · R. Aldrich and P. Gordon, Dictionary of British educationists (1989) · M. Barber, The making of the 1944 Education Act (1994) · G. McCulloch, Educational reconstruction: the 1944 Education Act and the twenty-first century (1994) · R. G. Wallace, 'The origins and authorship of the 1944 Education Act', History of Education, 10 (1981), 283–90 · K. Jefferys, 'R. A. Butler, the board of education and the 1944 Education Act', History, new ser., 69 (1984), 415–31 · CGPLA Eng. & Wales (1964) · London, board of education papers, PRO, ED 36/4, ED 136/294, ED 136/132, ED 147/21

Archives PRO, Board of Education papers, ED 36/4 | BL, letters to Albert Mansbridge, Add. MS 65253
Likenesses W. Stoneman, photographs, 1938–48, NPG · W. H. Alden, photograph, 1966 (with Barbara Castle), Hult. Arch.
Wealth at death £28,582: probate, 10 Aug 1964, CGPLA Eng. & Wales

Holmes, Nathaniel. See Homes, Nathaniel (1599–1678).

Holmes, Sir Richard Rivington (1835–1911), librarian, born in London on 16 November 1835, was the second of five children of John *Holmes (1800–1854), assistant keeper of manuscripts at the British Museum, and his wife, Mary Anne, eldest daughter of Charles *Rivington (1754–1831) [see under Rivington family], bookseller, and sister of Francis Rivington (1805–1885). An elder brother, the Revd Charles Rivington Holmes (d. 1873), was father of Sir Charles John *Holmes. Richard Rivington Holmes was educated at Highgate School (1843–53), where he obtained a foundation scholarship, and after spending a short time in a merchant's office he assisted his father unofficially at the British Museum until the latter's death in April 1854, when he was appointed an assistant in the manuscript department. Here he acquired a knowledge of palaeography, which, combined with his skill as a draughtsman, led to his selection for the post of archaeologist to Lord Napier's Abyssinian expedition of 1867–8. On the capture of Magdala, Holmes obtained for the British Museum approximately 400 manuscripts, which King Theodore had gathered in a church in Magdala, as well as the gold crown of the sovereigns of Abyssinia and a sixteenth-century chalice, which are now housed in the Victoria and Albert Museum. Six of the manuscripts were given to Queen Victoria and are in the Royal Library, Windsor Castle. These transactions were severely criticized by Gladstone, but Holmes's conduct won the approval of the authorities, and he was awarded the war medal.

In 1870, on the recommendation of the dean of Windsor, Gerald Wellesley, Queen Victoria appointed Holmes librarian at Windsor Castle in succession to Bernard Bolingbroke Woodward. Although more of an antiquary than a bibliographer, Holmes showed a collector's zeal for the acquisition of books connected with the history of the castle and of the royal family, and he took a special interest in the drawings, miniatures, and etchings at Windsor. Under his supervision the rearrangement of drawings by Holbein, Leonardo da Vinci, and other old masters was completed, and on his advice the collection of royal and historical miniatures was enriched by important purchases. He took advantage of his personal friendship with J. A. M. Whistler to secure an almost complete set of that artist's etchings, but these were subsequently sold.

Holmes was always a favourite of the royal family, although some of his colleagues in the royal household

Sir Richard Rivington Holmes (1835–1911), by Robert Jefferson Bingham, c.1861

considered him lazy. He wrote popular and slight biographies of Victoria and Edward VII: Queen Victoria (1897; new edn, 1901) and Edward VII, his Life and Times (1910). Nominated serjeant-at-arms to Queen Victoria in 1898, he was continued in that office, as well as in that of librarian at Windsor Castle, by Edward VII. He was made MVO in 1897, CVO in 1901, and promoted KCVO in 1905. He retired from the Royal Library in the following year but continued to live in his house close to the castle, 5 Park Street. In 1908 he published a book, Windsor, illustrated by George M. Henton.

Holmes shared with his brothers a natural aptitude for drawing, but received no regular training. While an assistant at the British Museum he executed two series of Outlines for Illumination, and in 1860 he assisted Henry Le Strange and Thomas Gambier Parry in the decoration of Ely Cathedral. In 1873 Queen Victoria approved his designs for two stained-glass windows for Crathie church, near Balmoral Castle, to commemorate Dr Norman MacLeod, one of the queen's chaplains. The windows were moved to the Barony Chapel, Glasgow, when the new Crathie church was built in 1895. He also executed five stained-glass windows in 1867 and three more in 1889 for Highgate School chapel. At Windsor he devoted his leisure to designing bookbindings for the Royal Library and to landscape painting in watercolour. In 1893 he had published *Specimens of Royal, Fine and Historical Bookbinding Selected from the Royal Library, Windsor Castle*. There are twelve of his drawings and watercolours in the Royal Library. He was a frequent exhibitor at the Royal Academy, the Grosvenor Gallery, and the New Gallery, and drew a series of illustrations for Margaret Oliphant's *Makers of Venice* (1887).

Holmes married on 27 October 1880 Evelyn, eldest daughter of Richard Gee, canon of Windsor; they had two daughters, of whom the elder predeceased her father in 1904. Holmes, who was a keen volunteer, attained the rank of lieutenant-colonel in the 1st volunteer battalion of the Berkshire regiment, and received the volunteer decoration. Elected fellow of the Society of Antiquaries on 22 March 1860, he became vice-president in 1907. In his last years he was a treasurer of the Royal Literary Fund. He died at his home, 16 St Thomas's Mansions, Westminster Bridge, London, on 22 March 1911, and was buried at Upton, Buckinghamshire. His wife survived him.

G. S. WOODS, rev. OLIVER EVERETT

Sources *The Times* (23 March 1911) · *The Athenaeum* (25 March 1911), 333 · private information (1912) · T. L. Southgate, 'The late Sir Richard R. Holmes', *The Cholmeleian*, 34/172 (1911), 180–82 · Royal Arch. · Royal Library, Windsor Castle · *CGPLA Eng. & Wales* (1911)
Likenesses R. J. Bingham, carte-de-visite, c.1861, NPG [*see illus.*] · H. von Angeli, drawing, 1877; in possession of his widow, 1912 · W. Gibb, oils, c.1895; in possession of Mrs Johnstone of Anne Foord's House, Windsor, 1912 · A. Legros, silverpoint drawing, c.1902 · W. Strang, chalk drawing, 1907, Royal Collection · A. S. Watson, carte-de-visite, NPG
Wealth at death £120 5s. 8d.: probate, 13 April 1911, *CGPLA Eng. & Wales*

Holmes, Sir Robert (c.1622–1692), naval officer, was the third son of Henry Holmes of Mallow, co. Cork. His grandfather, a Lancastrian, had been an officer in Elizabeth I's Irish wars. By 1643 he was a cornet in Prince Maurice's regiment of royalist horse, helping to rescue the prince when he was briefly captured, and subsequently fought at the battle of Roundway Down. He seems to have entered the service of Maurice's brother, Prince Rupert of the Rhine, by the mid-1640s, and was certainly in the English force which Rupert commanded in the French army in 1647. He suffered a serious leg wound in a skirmish in July, during the attempted Spanish relief of La Bassée. In 1648 part of the parliamentarian fleet revolted and defected to the royalists in the Netherlands. Rupert took command of the royalist squadron towards the end of the year and sailed to Kinsale in January 1649; Holmes was almost certainly with him at this time, and during the squadron's subsequent series of escapades. On 29 February 1652 he was given command of a prize, the *John*, which had been taken in the Gambia River, and later commanded the four prizes which Rupert's last remaining warship, the *Swallow*, brought back to France in March 1653. He handled the disposal of the ships and goods for Rupert, but his movements from then until the Restoration are obscure. It was reported in 1658 that he had obtained a commission for a Spanish privateer; his monument in Yarmouth church hints at military service in France, Flanders, and Germany, perhaps as an imperial mercenary.

By early 1660 Holmes was active as a royalist agent, serving as an intermediary with Edward Mountagu, general-at-sea, during April, and after the Restoration he was granted £600 for unspecified services rendered. From June 1660 to November 1660 he commanded successively the Medway guardships *Bramble* and *Truelove* before taking command of the *Henrietta*, intended for a voyage to Guinea to search for a 'mountain of gold' which Rupert had learned of in the 1650s. Holmes would also command a squadron containing four other ships, with orders to assist the new Royal African Company's trade in the region. He sailed from Portsmouth on 25 January 1661, reaching the Gambia on 4 March. On 18 March he forced the surrender of the Dutch fort of St Andreas, and after an unsuccessful attempt to find the legendary store of gold, he returned to the Downs on 28 July. The cruise made a loss and brought a storm of diplomatic protest from the Dutch, but it led to Holmes's elevation to captain of the *Royal Charles*, the flagship of the expedition intended to bring Catherine of Braganza from Lisbon. However, he was dismissed in November for failing to make a Swedish vessel strike her colours in salute. At much the same time he first became well known to Samuel Pepys:

he seems to be very well acquainted with the King's mind and with all the several factions at court … being a cunning fellow, and one (by his own confession to me) that can put on two several faces and look his enemies in the face with as much love as his friends. But good God, what an age is this, that a man cannot live without playing the knave and dissimulation. (Pepys, 2.169)

Their relations were soon marred by an apparent attempt by Holmes to seduce Mrs Pepys (Pepys, 2.237, 3.4), and by Samuel Pepys's consequent suspicion of Holmes's easy charm and liking for fine clothing.

Tumult of war Holmes became captain of the new third-rate *Reserve* on 9 August 1662, taking her on a voyage to the Mediterranean before returning to Chatham in March 1663. His contempt for his ship's master, Pepys's protégé Richard Cooper, exacerbated his feud with the diarist: Pepys feared for days that his attempt to defend Cooper would lead Holmes to run him through in a duel. The matter was glossed over, and Holmes took the *Reserve* back south, calling at Lisbon and Tangier before finally paying her off in September. Two months later Holmes received a commission for the *Jersey* and instructions for another voyage to Guinea. Although ostensibly intended to protect the African Company's trade, the real purpose of the expedition was to disrupt that of the Dutch and to seize Dutch possessions on the Guinea coast. Holmes sighted Cape Verde on 25 December 1663 and two days later captured the *Brill*, a Dutch West Indiaman, off the Isle of Goree. The next few weeks were spent in preparations for the inevitable local war with the Dutch. On 21 January Holmes attacked Goree, sinking two ships and taking two others, and the island surrendered on the following day. Sailing on to Sierra Leone and Cape Palmas, he took the thirty-gun Dutch vessel *Walcheren* on 28 March, arriving at

Takoradi on 9 April and taking the Dutch fort of Anta on the following day. He attacked Cape Coast Castle on 20 April, although it did not surrender until 1 May, and then took a number of other Dutch positions along the Gold Coast before sailing for England on 16 June. The *Jersey* reached Plymouth on 6 December and the Downs on the twenty-seventh. By the time of his return, a substantial Dutch fleet under De Ruyter had retaken virtually all of his conquests, and, in turn, a large English fleet under Rupert was fitting out to oppose it. The African Company was baying for compensation, there was a widespread feeling that Holmes had exceeded his instructions, and he was committed to the Tower from 9 to 23 January 1665, and then from 14 February to 6 March. He was examined twice (on 14 January and 3 March), but his final release and eventual pardon on 23 March can be attributed to the fact that due largely to his activities in Africa, England had gone to war with the Netherlands on 22 February. Indeed, even before his pardon was finalized, Holmes had become captain of the third-rate *Revenge* (14 March 1665).

At the battle of Lowestoft on 3 June 1665, the *Revenge* was immediately astern of Rupert's flagship of the White squadron. The death of the rear-admiral of the white in the battle created a vacancy which Rupert requested for Holmes, but the duke of York gave it instead to his own flag captain, John Harman. Holmes bitterly resented the slight and gave up his commission, with Pepys believing that he was 'a rash, proud coxcomb' who was 'rich, and hath, it seems, sought an occasion of leaving the service' (Pepys, 6.129). He returned to the fleet for the 1666 campaign, when Rupert was one of the joint admirals. On 27 March he attended the launch at Deptford of his new command, the *Defiance*, and was knighted on that day. On 29 May Rupert was detached to counter an imaginary French threat from the west, and Holmes became rear-admiral of

the red, playing a leading role in the four days' battle that followed. He moved his flag to the *Henry* on 9 June, fighting in her during the St James's day fight (25 June). On 8 August Holmes was detached from the main fleet, flying his flag in the *Tiger*, with orders to attack the islands of Vlie and Schelling, along with Dutch shipping in the Vlie anchorage. On the following day his force attacked with longboats and fireships, burning between 110 and 160 Dutch vessels, together with the town of Westerschelling: the action became known to posterity as 'Holmes's bonfire'. The fleet returned to harbour in October, and Holmes immediately resumed his feud with the duke of Albemarle's leading naval client, Sir Jeremy Smith, over their respective conduct in the St James's day fight. The submissions made to the king on 21 October were resolved largely in Holmes's favour. In April 1667 Holmes became commander-in-chief of a squadron operating from Portsmouth and the Isle of Wight, sailing west in June to escort homeward-bound merchantmen from the Mediterranean before paying off in October. During this period he was loaned a prize ship, the *Saint George*, as a privateer for three months, but got into trouble with the prize commissioners for keeping her to windward of his squadron in order to seize prizes off the coast of Ireland, 'even in sight of the King's ships under your command' (BL, Harleian MS 1510, fol. 193).

During 1668 Holmes commanded the *Cambridge* (from March to September) but also became more heavily involved in politics ashore. In January he acted as second to the duke of Buckingham during the latter's duel with the earl of Shrewsbury, receiving a pardon for his part in the earl's death. His quarrel with Smith was carried over into the House of Commons, forming a part of the house's inquest into the naval miscarriages of the war (October 1667, February–March 1668). By December 1668 Pepys

Sir Robert Holmes (*c.*1622–1692), by Sir Peter Lely, *c.*1672 [right, with Sir Frescheville Holles]

believed that 'Holmes and [Sir Edward] Spragge now rule all with the duke of Buckingham, as to sea-business, and will be great men' (Pepys, 9.382). In September of the same year Holmes agreed to purchase the governorship of the Isle of Wight from Sir John Culpepper, assuming the position on 28 December. He had been governor of Sandown Castle since 1660, and on 26 October 1669 he was elected MP for Winchester, serving there until 1679. On 16 January 1672 he became captain of the 90-gun *St Michael*, sailing with his squadron in March to cruise in the channel with orders to seize Dutch merchantmen. On 13 March he sighted the inward-bound Dutch Smyrna convoy and summoned them to surrender. When the Dutch refused, a general engagement began. The English ships came off badly, with Holmes having to move to the *Cambridge* because the *St Michael* was disabled. The action resumed on the next day, but despite being reinforced (by, among others, the *Gloucester*, commanded by Holmes's brother John) the English were unable to prevent most of the Dutch vessels escaping. The attack on the Smyrna convoy signalled the beginning of the Third Anglo-Dutch War, but also provided ammunition for Holmes in his quarrel with another of his rivals for high command, Sir Edward Spragge, whom he accused of deliberately not bringing his independent squadron to support him. For the remainder of the 1672 campaign, Spragge was a flag officer and Holmes a mere captain. He served at the battle of Solebay (28 May), where the duke of York briefly flew his flag in the *St Michael* before she became as disabled as his previous flagship, the *Royal Prince*. Although the ship was repaired and Holmes commanded her for the remainder of 1672, he was overlooked for a flag post and did not serve at sea at all in 1673, despite persistent attempts by the then admiral of the fleet, Prince Rupert, to secure his services. The duke of York, Spragge's patron, steadfastly refused to employ Holmes, and also rejected his candidacy for the governorship of Tangier in 1673. York's removal from the Admiralty and Spragge's death (11 August) came too late to revive Holmes's naval career, and he never served at sea again.

Isle of Wight governorship For the rest of his life Holmes concentrated on his governorship of the Isle of Wight. His wealth from prize money, from rents, his flag officer's pension of £500 a year, and the perquisites due to him as vice-admiral of Hampshire and the Isle of Wight, attracted much comment, as in the famous jibe of 1677 often attributed to Andrew Marvell: 'Sir Robert Holmes, first an Irish livery-boy, then a highway-man, now Bashaw of the Isle of Wight, got in boons and by rapine £100,000. The cursed beginner of the two Dutch wars' (Ollard, 14-15). On several occasions he was censured for over-zealous attempts to secure the cargoes of ships wrecked on the island, especially if they were carrying wine. In the spring of 1684 Holmes was threatened with a court martial for making false musters in his regiment, a charge brought by one of his captains, Joseph Brent, and plans were made for the duke of Grafton to succeed him as governor. Holmes attempted stalling tactics, enlisting the support of William Blathwayt, the secretary of war, but the court met at Horse Guards on 27 May under the presidency of the earl of Craven. Holmes was accused of drawing pay illicitly for his steward, two of his gardeners, his coachman, and for men who had been at sea when allegedly present at musters; although the verdict is not recorded, it was almost certainly favourable, as Holmes retained the governorship. There were also positive aspects to his governorship: throughout the 1670s and 1680s he was chiefly responsible for a gradual upgrading of the defences of the island's forts. He moved from Winchester to the parliamentary seat of Newport, Isle of Wight, in March 1679, did not serve in the second or third Exclusion Parliaments, represented Newport again in 1685, Yarmouth in 1689, and Newport once more in 1690–92. Holmes had been a staunch supporter of the court until the mid-1670s, but in 1676 he publicly disagreed with Pepys in parliament over the projected dimensions of thirty new ships, and in 1678 he went over to the opposition, making an ill-judged attempt to reconcile the king and the duke of Monmouth in 1682. Holmes was soon reconciled to the legitimate royal family, and entertained the king when he visited the Isle of Wight in 1684. In August 1687 Holmes was granted a commission to command a squadron to suppress piracy in the West Indies, but the ill health which had dogged him for years prevented him assuming the command. He spent the summer of 1688 preparing the Isle of Wight against an expected Dutch invasion, and was at Bath recovering from gout on 27 September when he received an urgent letter from the king ordering him to return to his post. On 4 November Holmes watched William of Orange's fleet pass the island, and over the next few days he sent a rapid succession of reports to the secretary of state, Preston, recording Dutch movements (including his mistaken opinion that they had to be bound for France) and his pessimism about the state of the island's defences: 'I shall not be able to oppose these people … part of the militia is grown mutinous already … Yarmouth and Hurst I put my stress upon, and will defend both to the last' (*Seventh Report*, HMC, 1.414). The king's flight, and Lord Dartmouth's subsequent surrender of the fleet at Spithead to William, meant that Holmes had no alternative other than to draft the surrender of the island (17 December).

Final years Holmes continued to hold the governorship after the revolution, despite unjustified charges of Jacobitism against him. In parliament he opposed the offer of the crown to William and Mary and campaigned vigorously for the removal of Irish troops which had been billeted on the island before being shipped to Germany. Throughout the summer of 1689 Holmes made repeated requests to go to Bath for his health—'I only go to refresh my limbs and get strength to serve him [William III] … I am now so ill of my limbs that I have not been out of my chamber these two days' (Isle of Wight RO, GW 10/49, Holmes to Blathwayt, 22 July 1689). He was finally given leave for a month on 25 November 1689. In January 1690 he had the additional stress of having to entertain the queen of Spain (at considerable personal expense). No sooner had he obtained another spell of leave and crossed to the mainland (24 June 1690) than he had to hurry back to the island to defend it against Tourville's French fleet, which he could see clearly from his headquarters at Appuldurcombe both before and after the battle of Beachy Head (30 June). Holmes was increasingly ill during 1691, and died at Yarmouth on 18 November 1692. He was buried at Yarmouth church, where a grand monument was erected to him; the marble statue was allegedly intended to be of Louis XIV, taken from a ship bound for France but wrecked on the island, with Holmes's head substituted for that of *le roi soleil*. By his will, dated 28 October 1692, Sir Robert made over most of his lands and property to his nephew Henry, the son of his brother Thomas Holmes of Kilmallock, co. Limerick, on condition that Henry married Sir Robert's illegitimate daughter Mary (*b.* c.1678). The condition was met, and their eldest son was eventually created Lord Holmes of Kilmallock in 1760. Smaller bequests were left to the sons of another brother, Admiral Sir John *Holmes (1639/40–1683), although it was a sign of the chaotic nature of Sir John's finances that Sir Robert was still owed many debts from his estate, some of them dating back twenty years. Inventories were made of Holmes's many properties: two houses at Yarmouth (the newer being now the George Hotel, next to the castle), another at Park, Isle of Wight; one at Inglefield Green, Surrey; another at Bath; and the grandest of all, a house in Whitehall which fully reflected the extravagant tastes which Pepys had attributed to Holmes years before.

Holmes's image in history suffered over the years, primarily because of his clashes with Pepys and his reputation as the begetter of two wars. The old canard that he had been responsible for capturing New Amsterdam in 1664, and renaming it New York, took many years to scotch, and was even repeated in the *Dictionary of National Biography*. Holmes's reputation was finally rehabilitated by Richard Ollard in his biography *Man of War* (1969). Undoubtedly brave and passionately loyal to his monarchs, despite propensities for quarrelling, exceeding orders, and self-aggrandizement, he tended to excite strong opinions: Sir William Coventry thought that he possessed 'an understanding fit to make a war' (Longleat House, Coventry MS 102, p. 6), but Clarendon, in many ways Holmes's antithesis, thought him 'a very bold and expert man' (Ollard, 14).   J. D. DAVIES

Sources R. Ollard, *Man of war: Sir Robert Holmes and the Restoration navy* (1969) • Pepys, *Diary* • Holmes's will, PRO, PROB 11/412, fol. 69v • letters by Holmes, Isle of Wight RO, MS GW 10/49 • inventory of Holmes's properties, Isle of Wight RO, MS JER/HBY/104/2 • J. D. Davies, *Gentlemen and tarpaulins: the officers and men of the Restoration navy* (1991) • J. R. Powell and E. K. Timings, eds., *The Rupert and Monck letter book, 1666*, Navy RS, 112 (1969) • F. L. Fox, *A distant storm: the Four Days battle of 1666* (1996) • journals of Holmes's Guinea voyages, Magd. Cam., Pepys Library, Pepys MS 2698 • J. R. Tanner, ed., *A descriptive catalogue of the naval manuscripts in the Pepysian Library at Magdalene College, Cambridge*, 4 vols., Navy RS, 26–7, 36, 57 (1903–23) • A. W. Tedder, *The navy of the Restoration* (1916) • Prince Rupert's corresp., BL, Add. MS 18982 • court martial records, 1684, PRO, WO 26/6, 36–9 • MSS relating to privateer *Saint George*, BL, Harleian MS 1510 • *The manuscripts of his grace the duke of Portland*, 10 vols., HMC, 29 (1891–1931), vol. 1 • HoP, *Commons, 1660–90* • PRO, Admiralty MSS • A. M. Coleby, *Central government and the localities: Hampshire, 1649–1689* (1987) • *Seventh report*, HMC, 6 (1879)

Archives Isle of Wight RO, Newport, MS GW 10/49 • PRO, admiralty MSS | Magd. Cam., Pepys MSS

Likenesses P. Lely, double portrait, oils, c.1672 (with F. Holles), NMM [*see illus.*] • marble monument, St James' Church, Isle of Wight; repro. in Ollard, *Man of war*, following p. 184

Wealth at death left nephew extensive lands on Isle of Wight; five houses (Inglefield Green, Bath, London, and two at Yarmouth) to nephews and illegitimate daughter; inventory goods in houses: new house at Yarmouth, £34 5s.; old house at Yarmouth, £39; Inglefield Green, £60 2s. 6d.; Whitehall, £126 1s.; Bath, £37 4s. 4d.; sundry goods in houses totalled £245 9s. 5d.; ready money, £321 6s.; plate, £422 3s.; £1500 owed to him, plus many debts from late brother: will, PRO, PROB 11/412, fol. 69v; inventory, Isle of Wight RO, Newport, MS JER/HBY/104/2

Holmes, Robert (*bap.* 1748, *d.* 1805), biblical scholar, was baptized at St Martin-in-the-Fields, London, on 30 November 1748, the son of Edmund Holmes of the parish and his wife, Mary. He became a scholar of Winchester College in 1760, and matriculated from New College, Oxford, on 3 March 1767. In 1769 he won the chancellor's prize for Latin verse, the subject being 'Ars pingendi'. He graduated BA in 1770, was elected fellow of the college, and graduated MA in 1774, BD in 1787, and DD in 1789.

Holmes was appointed to the college rectory of Stanton St John, Oxfordshire, and held the post until his death. He became prebendary of Lyme and Halstock in Salisbury Cathedral on 23 May 1790, prebendary of Moreton-with-Whaddon in Hereford Cathedral on 12 August 1791, prebendary of the seventh stall in Christ Church, Oxford, on 28 April 1795, and dean of Winchester on 20 February 1804. In addition to these positions, Holmes was professor of poetry at Oxford, 1783–93. He was the Bampton lecturer for 1782, and gave a fast-day sermon to parliament on 9 March 1796. On 14 December 1797 he was elected FRS.

Holmes's works are wide-ranging: he published *Alfred: an Ode* (1778) and an ode for the duke of Portland which was set to music by Philip Hayes (1793), as well as his Bampton lectures (1782), the fast-day sermon (1796), a sermon on the resurrection (1777), and various tracts. In 1788 he began his weightiest work: the collation of the manuscripts of the Septuagint. The work was intended to draw on all the known manuscripts of the Greek text, including oriental versions, and for seventeen years, despite the difficulties caused by the wars, he managed to collate various readings from manuscripts in libraries throughout Europe. The delegates of the Clarendon Press allowed him £40 a year for three years on condition that he exhibited his work annually, and deposited it in the Bodleian Library. He received additional support from annual subscriptions for the project, which attracted financial contributions from academia, the clergy, and the aristocracy. Major donors in 1789 included the universities of Cambridge and Dublin, Beilby Porteus, and nineteen other members of the bishop's bench. Annual accounts of the progress of the work, with lists of subscribers, were published from 1789, and in 1795 Holmes published specimens of the Septuagint together with Latin letters to Shute Barrington. Part of Genesis was published in 1798. Holmes's last volume (numbered 142) of collations was deposited in the Bodleian Library in 1805. Following Holmes's death at his home in St Giles', Oxford, on 12 November 1805 the work was continued by James Parsons, and completed in 1827. It was not published, despite attempts by Oxford University Press to raise funds for its publication in 1816.

GORDON GOODWIN, *rev.* EMMA MAJOR

Sources Foster, *Alum. Oxon.* · *GM*, 1st ser., 75 (1805), 1086 · R. Holmes, *The first annual account of the collation of the MSS of the Septuagint-version* (1789) · *ESTC* · *IGI* · W. F. Hook, *An ecclesiastical biography*, 8 vols. (1845–52) · A. Chalmers, ed., *The general biographical dictionary*, new edn, 18 (1814), 82–4 · W. D. Macray, *Annals of the Bodleian Library, Oxford*, 2nd edn (1890), 207
Archives Bodl. Oxf., corresp.; MSS Greek and papers

Holmes, Robert (1765–1859), barrister, was born in Dublin, the son of Hugh Holmes, a miller from Belfast. He was taught at a school in Belfast, where the family was living, and was then sent to a public school. He entered Trinity College, Dublin, on 4 November 1782, and graduated BA in 1787. Despite an early interest in medicine, he was called to the bar in 1795. In the same year he married Mary Emma, *née* Emmet, the sister of Robert Emmet. They had one child before Mary died, allegedly of a brain fever after hearing of her brother's execution in 1803.

Holmes was an opponent of the union, and in 1798 he withdrew his membership of the lawyer corps of yeomanry. He feared that the placing of the corps under the military authorities might result in violence towards civilians. He was imprisoned for three months for having challenged a barrister who made imputations of cowardice against him. In 1799 he published a satirical pamphlet, *A Demonstration of the Necessity of the Legislative Union of Great Britain and Ireland*, and he was imprisoned for some months after the rising of his brother-in-law, Robert Emmet, on 23 July 1803. Despite the fact that he had had no connection with the rebellion his association with radicalism and scandal slowed his professional progress.

Holmes declined to receive any favours from the government, refusing in succession the offices of crown prosecutor, king's counsel, and solicitor-general; he never took silk, not wanting to receive a compliment through William Plunket, who had led the prosecution against Emmet. Despite his refusal to accept favours from the government, his was for many years the largest practice of any member of the Irish courts. He was renowned as a fine lawyer and his arguments were always learned. He was a powerful and impressive advocate, and several of his speeches to juries—particularly his speeches in *Watson v. Dill*, in defence of the *Nation* newspaper, and his oration on behalf of John Mitchel, tried for treason-felony on 24 May 1848—earned him a good deal of professional respect. During the course of his practice he was said to have made over £100,000. Nor did he refrain from continuing to write about his political opinions on Ireland: he published *An Address to the Yeomanry of Ireland, Demonstrating the Necessity of their Declaring their Opinions upon Political Subjects* and in 1847 *The Case of Ireland Stated*, on the repeal of the union. When old age prevented his continuing on circuit, the members of the north-east bar presented him with an address and presented a bust to the bar mess-room. Holmes retired formally in 1852, choosing to live in London with his only child, Elizabeth, who had married George William Lenox-Conyngham, chief clerk of the Foreign Office. Holmes died at 37 Eaton Place, Belgrave Square, London, on 30 November 1859.

G. C. BOASE, *rev.* SINÉAD AGNEW

Sources J. R. O'Flanagan, *The Irish bar*, 2nd edn (1879), 273–87 · Burtchaell & Sadleir, *Alum. Dubl.* · A. J. Webb, *A compendium of Irish biography* (1878), 253 · *N&Q*, 3rd ser., 12 (1867), 188–9 · Boase, *Mod. Eng. biog.* · J. S. Crone, *A concise dictionary of Irish biography*, rev. edn (1937), 97 · *Dublin University Magazine*, 31 (1848), 122–33
Likenesses E. Hayes, chalk drawing, 1844, NG Ire. · H. Griffiths, stipple, pubd 1848, NG Ire. · S. Bellin, mezzotint (after E. Hayes), NG Ire. · portrait, repro. in *Dublin University Magazine*, 122–3

Holmes, Thomas (*bap.* 1606, *d.* 1638). *See under* Holmes, John (*d.* 1629).

Holmes, Thomas (1846–1918), police-court missionary and philanthropist, was born on 25 January 1846 at the small village of Pelsall, near Walsall, Staffordshire, the son of William Holmes, an iron-moulder, and his wife, Cecilia, the daughter of Thomas Withington. At the age of twelve Thomas became an iron-moulder himself, working fourteen hours a day and earning 3*d.* per week. His education consisted of Bible readings with his father and general instruction from a teacher at the church school at Rugeley, Staffordshire. He continued to work as an iron-moulder until he was thirty-three. On his scant earnings he married in 1872 Margaret, the daughter of Ralph Brammer, a carpenter of Rugeley; they had five sons. Meanwhile he was winning a reputation for community service by devoting himself after his long day's labour to the education of his fellow workers in evening classes and at the Sunday school.

In 1877 Holmes had a serious accident which eventually made it impossible for him to continue his work as an iron-moulder. His friends, who appreciated his gift for gentle persuasion, advised him in 1885 to apply for the post of police-court missionary at Lambeth police court. To his surprise Holmes was appointed, and found there his true vocation. In 1889 he was transferred to the North London police court. Over the course of his twenty years' service as a police-court missionary for the Church of England Temperance Society, he dealt with thieves, drunkards, prostitutes, and outcasts of every description, devoting himself with single-minded zeal to their reformation. His popular first book, *Pictures and Problems from London Police Courts* (1900), offered readers a tour of the 'horrible wonderland' where summary justice was rendered amid 'the sickening whiff of stale debauch'. Holmes became known both in England and abroad as a practical criminologist with sound judgement, and gained profit as well as reputation from his writings. Some of his police-court associates believed that he resembled Dickens, whose memory Holmes held dear.

In 1905 Holmes retired from the police courts in order to become secretary to the Howard Association, England's leading pressure group concerned with the administration of the criminal law. In this capacity he worked for ten years, and earned the gratitude of a succession of home secretaries for his advice on prison reform. As a police-court missionary Holmes had stressed the extent to which alcohol weakened moral resolve and so promoted criminal behaviour; as secretary of the Howard Association he pushed this environmental analysis further, arguing against the proposition that criminals are 'born'. Holmes insisted in such studies as *London's Underworld* (1912) and *Psychology and Crime* (1912) that inequalities of wealth, unemployment, and bad housing were the true incubators of crime. In 1910 he was sent to the United States as the British representative at the Penological Congress.

The latter part of Holmes's life was devoted to a new philanthropic endeavour. In 1904, before he left the police courts, he founded the Home Workers' Aid Association, which soon developed into an important voluntary effort. The association's aims were to improve the conditions under which such unregulated labour as costume-sewing and artificial flower-making took place, and to provide the women engaged in these sweated trades with annual holidays and recreational facilities. Before the establishment of the trades board in 1909, home workers faced terrible privation: the women who made boxes, toothbrushes, or babies' bonnets worked up to sixteen hours per day yet earned less than 2s. It was this state of affairs which Holmes set out to remedy. In 1910 he was able to establish Singholm, a guest house with flower and fruit gardens at Walton on the Naze, where forty women during their fortnight's holiday could relax in healthy surroundings. Holmes spent much of his own time there on the Essex coast after retiring from the Howard Association in early 1916. He died of heart failure on 26 March 1918 at 33 Beaumont Street, London.

C. M. CHAPMAN, rev. GEORGE K. BEHLMER

Sources *The Times* (27 March 1918) • G. Rose, *The struggle for penal reform* (1961) • M. J. Wiener, *Reconstructing the criminal* (1990) • *CGPLA Eng. & Wales* (1918)
Wealth at death £2937: probate, 22 June 1918, *CGPLA Eng. & Wales*

Holmes, Thomas Rice Edward (1855–1933), historian and classical scholar, was born at Waterstown House, near Athlone, co. Westmeath, on 24 May 1855. He was the fifth son (the fourth was E. G. A. *Holmes) and seventh child of Robert Holmes (1803–1870), owner of the property of Moycashel, in the parish of Kilbeggan, co. Westmeath, and tenant of Waterstown House, and his wife, Jane, daughter of William Henn, a master in chancery, of Dublin. From Merchant Taylors' School in London he passed in 1873 to Christ Church, Oxford. At Oxford, where he obtained a second class in classical moderations (1875) and a first class in modern history (1877), he was greatly influenced by S. J. Owen, then university teacher of Indian law and history.

In 1878 Holmes became a master at Lincoln grammar school; in 1880 he moved to Blackheath proprietary school. Six years later he went to St Paul's School where he remained until 1909, in which year he retired, his grant of a civil-list pension having been sponsored by Asquith. He received honorary degrees from the universities of Dublin

(1904) and Oxford (1922), and was elected a fellow of the British Academy in 1925. In 1888 he married Eliza Isabel, daughter of Lionel and Caroline Isabella Isaacs, of The Grove, Mandeville, Jamaica: they had no children. Much of his retirement was probably spent in Roehampton, but he died at Upper Richmond Road, Putney, on 4 August 1933. He was survived by his wife.

Throughout his career Holmes devoted his leisure, and during the twenty-four years of his retirement his whole working time, to historical research. First, he developed an interest acquired at Oxford by writing an account of the events in India during the years 1857 and 1858, using original sources as well as contemporary works. His *History of the Indian Mutiny* appeared in 1883 and was well considered during his lifetime, being reprinted several times. Secondly, having published various subsidiary studies on the history of British India, he attempted to enliven the study of classics for his pupils by examining the life and works of Julius Caesar. It was as a Caesarean scholar, and as a historian of Rome in the times of Caesar and Augustus, that he became most widely known. In these fields his main publications were *Caesar's Conquest of Gaul* (1899; 2nd edn, 1911), *Ancient Britain and the Invasions of Julius Caesar* (1907), *The Roman Republic and the Founder of the Empire* (3 vols., 1923), and *The Architect of the Roman Empire* (2 vols., 1928–31). He was considered instrumental in challenging the influence of the work of Napoleon III, and in leading Caesarean studies into a new era.

[ANON.], rev. MYFANWY LLOYD

Sources 'Materials for a bibliography of the writings published by T. R. E. Holmes', *PBA*, 22 (1936), 358–79 [incl. obit.] • Allibone, *Dict.* • G. P. Gooch, *History and historians in the nineteenth century*, 4th edn (1928) • Burke, *Gen. Ire.* • Foster, *Alum. Oxon.* • *CGPLA Eng. & Wales* (1933)
Likenesses W. Stoneman, photograph, 1925, NPG
Wealth at death £3320 17s. 2d.: probate, 26 Aug 1933, *CGPLA Eng. & Wales*

Holmes, Timothy (1825–1907), surgeon, born on 9 May 1825 at his parents' home in Colebrooke Row, Islington, London, was the son of John Holmes, warehouseman, and his wife, Elizabeth. He entered Merchant Taylors' School in London in November 1836, and gained a Stuart's exhibition to Pembroke College, Cambridge, in 1843. In 1845 he was admitted a scholar of the college, and he graduated BA in 1847 as forty-second wrangler and twelfth classic. He obtained his MA in 1850; in 1900 the further degree of master in surgery was conferred upon him, and in the same year he was made an honorary fellow of Pembroke College. Holmes returned to London after completing his initial studies at Cambridge and became a student at St George's Hospital; he was admitted FRCS on 12 May 1853 without previously taking the usual diploma of membership. He then served as house surgeon and surgical registrar at St George's Hospital. He acted for a time as curator of the museum and demonstrator of anatomy until in June 1861 he was elected assistant surgeon and lecturer on anatomy; he became full surgeon in December 1867. Together with John William Ogle he founded the *St George's Hospital Reports* (1866–79). He retired in 1887 owing to a time limit on service and was appointed consulting surgeon. In 1894 he accepted the position of honorary treasurer, and was appointed a vice-president on his retirement from active work in 1904. In addition he was elected assistant surgeon to the Hospital for Sick Children in Great Ormond Street in May 1859, and he was full surgeon there from 1861 to 1868. He published *A Treatise on the Surgical Treatment of the Diseases of Infancy and Childhood* (1868), drawn from this experience. For twenty years he was also chief surgeon to the Metropolitan Police.

In 1872 Holmes was elected Hunterian professor of surgery and pathology at the Royal College of Surgeons. A member of the court of examiners from 1873 to 1883, he joined the newly appointed board of examiners in anatomy and physiology, and in 1880 he was a surgical examiner on the board of examiners in dental surgery. In 1877 Holmes was elected a member of the council of the college, but he did not seek re-election at the end of his first term of office in 1885. He took an active interest in the Royal Medical and Chirurgical Society of London (later merged in the Royal Society of Medicine), and in 1900 he was elected president of the society, having filled all the subordinate offices. He also played important roles in the Clinical Society and the Pathological Society of London. He married Sarah Brooksbank, who predeceased him; they had no children.

Holmes edited the third to ninth editions of Gray's *Anatomy* and designed and edited (with J. W. Hulke) *A System of Surgery, Theoretical and Practical* (4 vols., 1860–64). He wrote *A Treatise on the Principles and Practice of Surgery* (1875), which became a textbook for students, and a biography of Benjamin Brodie (1898). He also prepared with John Syer Bristowe a valuable report on hospitals and their administration, published as an appendix to the sixth annual report of the public health department of the privy council.

Holmes was a scientific surgeon possessed of an unusually clear and logical mind. Gifted with the power of incisive speech, he was fearless in expressing his conclusions, and exposed the fallacy in an argument mercilessly. The loss of an eye as a result of an accident during his hospital work, a harsh and somewhat monotonous voice, and a manner carefully cultivated to hide any interest he might feel in those whom he examined, made him a terror to students.

After a long residence in London at 18 Great Cumberland Place, Holmes moved to 6 Sussex Place, Hyde Park, where he died on 8 September 1907. He was buried at Hendon.   D'A. POWER, rev. CHRISTIAN KERSLAKE

Sources *St George's Hospital Gazette*, 15 (1907), 127 · *The Lancet* (14 Sept 1907), 803–7 · *BMJ* (14 Sept 1907), 704–5 · Venn, *Alum. Cant.* · personal knowledge (1912)
Likenesses photograph, 1888, repro. in *The Lancet*, 803 · W. B. Richmond, portrait, exh. 1889; formerly at St George's Hospital, London · H. J. Brooks, group portrait, oils (*Council of the Royal College of Surgeons of England, 1884–85*), RCS Eng.
Wealth at death £28,125 3s. 10d.: probate, 22 Oct 1907, CGPLA Eng. & Wales

Holmes, Sir Valentine (1888–1956), barrister, was born on 24 July 1888 in Blackrock, co. Dublin, the third son of Sir Hugh Holmes (1840–1916), who was successively solicitor and attorney-general, judge, lord justice, and privy councillor in Ireland, and his wife, Olivia Moule (d. 1901). He was educated at Charterhouse and Trinity College, Dublin, where he was awarded a senior moderatorship in classics with gold medal in 1911. He was called to the bar at both the Inner Temple and the Middle Temple in 1913. In 1915 he married Gwen, daughter of Andrew Armstrong of Dublin; they had one son and one daughter. During the First World War Holmes served as an officer in the Royal Artillery.

After the war Holmes joined the chambers of Sir Leslie Scott, where he had devilled after being called. His first brief was before a county court judge. Because the sum claimed in the action was not more than £10 he had to ask for what is still called a certificate for counsel, normally awarded more or less as a matter of course. But the judge refused it, saying he had not been assisted by counsel; Holmes said he had to wait some time for another brief (private information, Andrew Leggatt). However, he quickly developed a large practice, whose spark may have been a war damage reparations case in the divisional court. He had two leaders; but when the case was called on neither was present and he had to open it himself. He was able to do this, having worked on the case (so he said) for six months. It was perhaps just as well, for he was not a natural born advocate. He had a hesitant manner, and himself used to say that he had to fight against court nerves throughout his career.

From first to last Holmes's capacity for work was prodigious; this, his profound knowledge of the law, and not least his good judgement quickly recommended him. He was to acquire a special reputation in the law of libel, but was early involved in other heavy work. In 1926 he was led by Scott in a fifty-six-day hearing, a mammoth case in those days, where the issue was whether the Swansea corporation's reservoir endangered the Graigola Merthyr Company's colliery. During this period also he was associated with Scott as adviser to some of the Indian princes in connection with constitutional changes in India which were then taking place.

In 1929 Holmes established chambers of his own. His clerk, Frank Connett, was a close friend for the rest of his time in the law. In 1935 Holmes was elected a bencher of the Inner Temple and appointed first junior counsel to the Treasury in common law, the 'Treasury devil'; it meant—as it still means—that he undertook all the leading cases on behalf of the government in civil matters. The office may go back to the end of the eighteenth century. By the late twentieth century, largely owing to the growth of judicial review and the impact of European law, the job was so heavy that it was impossible to combine it with private work. Lord Bridge of Harwich, Treasury devil from 1964 to 1968, kept one private brief from his previous practice, a House of Lords appeal; since then no Treasury devil has retained any private cases. Holmes carried it off with no abatement of his private practice, and though the work was not as considerable as it later became, this was remarkable. There was a great increase in government litigation during the Second World War, the demands of Holmes's libel practice were severe, and two members of the bar who devilled for him departed for war service. He worked harder than ever. In his years as Treasury devil he had the biggest practice at the junior bar. Perhaps his most celebrated wartime case was *Liversidge* v. *Anderson* (1942), in which the House of Lords had to construe the home secretary's powers of detention under regulation 18B of the defence (general) regulations, 1939. Holmes was led by the attorney-general, Sir Donald Somervell, for the crown.

Conventionally the Treasury devil is appointed directly to the High Court bench after five years or so without taking silk. Holmes did ten years, and spanned them with a consistent intellectual brilliance. When he relinquished the post in the spring of 1945, however, he did not become a judge. He was very fond of going to the greyhound races at the White City with his clerk, enjoyed the casinos at Deauville during the vacation, and was said to drink whisky in bed. There was a welcome bohemian streak in him, and it was presumably on this account that he declined his reward on the bench, which he could certainly have obtained.

Holmes was appointed king's counsel in 1945 on ceasing to be Treasury devil, in which office he was succeeded by Hubert Parker. He was the only Treasury devil in the twentieth century to have taken silk save for Gordon Slynn (later Lord Slynn of Hadley), who did so in 1974 but was appointed to the Queen's Bench in 1976. Holmes was knighted in 1946, at the same time as his elder brother Hugh Holmes (1886–1955) who served as procurator-general of the mixed court of appeal in Egypt from 1929 to 1949.

Holmes practised at the bar for only three years more. He was at once one of the two or three leading silks. His defamation practice continued unabated. He was in great demand for heavy cases generally in the common law and commercial fields. He was one of the counsel for the Australian banks in their successful appeal to the privy council on the question whether legislation which provided for their nationalization was unconstitutional. He appeared for the defendants in a libel action brought by a newspaper photographer where the plaintiff had forced his way into a private house on the occasion of a wedding. Holmes's cross-examination was a brilliant performance and Sir Malcolm Hilbery, giving judgment for the defendants, had some trenchant things to say about the standards required of editors and press reporters. But for thirty years Holmes had worked too hard, and in 1949 decided to retire from the bar when he was still very much at the top. In the following year he was appointed legal consultant to the Shell Oil group. There he quickly won the confidence of the directors and his colleagues, and applied himself to the work with all the energy he had displayed at the bar. He remained with Shell until his death in London on 19 November 1956.

Holmes's judgement was sound and deep, and it was probably for this quality that his services were most greatly valued. He expressed himself on paper very tersely but with great clarity. His opinions as Treasury devil were always brief, and handwritten on the inside of a backsheet. Before the Second World War he worked from 9 a.m. one morning until 1 a.m. the next. During the war he worked from 3 a.m. until 6 or 7 p.m.—and firewatched as well. His opinion in one case was thirteen words long—'The judgment of the Court of Appeal is wrong and will be reversed' (private information, Lord Bridge): and so it was. On another occasion, he was presented with an enormous set of papers by his clerk and told that the solicitors wanted his opinion immediately after the weekend. On the following Monday the clerk came to collect the papers. The opinion was written on the backsheet. It consisted of the words 'No'—crossed out; then 'Yes'; then Holmes's signature (private information, Sir William Gage). Peter Bristow (later Mr Justice Bristow), who had been his pupil in 1936, described him as a 'great master of his art and a humble and lovable man' (*The Times*, 23 Nov 1956), and Geoffrey Tribe, who knew him at Shell, wrote of his kindliness and humility: apt tributes for a brilliant barrister who eschewed the judicial ermine for the dogs at the White City.   JOHN LAWS

Sources personal knowledge (2004) · G. Tribe and P. Bristow, postscripts to obit., *The Times* (23 Nov 1956) · *DNB* · *The Times* (20 Nov 1956) · private information (2004) [Lord Bridge of Harwich; Rt Hon. Sir Andrew Leggatt; Mr Justice Gage]

Wealth at death £69,725 1s. 2d.: probate, 20 Dec 1956, *CGPLA Eng. & Wales*

Holmes, Verena Winifred (1889–1964), engineer, was born on 23 June 1889, at Highworth, Ashford, Kent, the daughter of Edmond Gore Alexander Holmes, schools inspector and author, and his wife, Florence Mary, *née* Syme. Verena's brother was the prominent educational reformer Sir Maurice *Holmes (1885–1964). The family was of Irish extraction. Though reared in artistic and literary surroundings Holmes showed scientific leanings early, dismantling her dolls to see how they worked. Upon leaving Oxford High School for Girls she studied photography, doing fine work, but she yearned for engineering. The First World War opened the door.

After building wooden propellers at the Integral Propeller Co., Hendon, with evening classes at Shoreditch Technical Institute, Holmes joined Ruston and Hornsby, in Lincoln, where she attended the technical college. Engaged as a supervisor she was able to exchange this position for a formal apprenticeship before male employees returned from war. Though advanced from fitting to draughting, she resolved to become a first-class designer. She entered Loughborough Engineering College, where in 1922 she received her BSc(Eng.).

In engineering Verena Holmes was versatile, working on marine engines, locomotive engines, heavy oil, diesel, and internal combustion engines. During the 1920s, with employment scarce, she worked briefly for a marine engineering firm and tried her hand at technical journalism in the United States. Back in England she became an associate of the Institution of Marine Engineers (1924), worked for the North British Locomotive Co., and was the first woman admitted to the Institution of Locomotive Engineers (1931). During the Second World War she worked on rotary gyro valves for torpedoes, new superchargers, and other apparatus for the Admiralty, designing much of the complicated mechanism for Lord Mountbatten's station keeping system.

Verena Holmes was a versatile inventor, too, holding at least twelve patents for items ranging from medical devices (the Holmes and Wingfield pneumo-thorax apparatus for treating tuberculosis, a surgeon's headlamp, and an aspirator) to a safety paper cutter for school use, and rotary valves for internal combustion engines. Like most inventors she also had numerous unpatented inventions, such as the Bantam shearing machine, the Bantam rod cutter, and several wartime devices. Her years (1932–9) at Research Engineers Ltd, where invention was her job and Lord Mountbatten a frequent client, were probably her happiest. Here she built the model of her most ambitious invention, the poppet valve for steam locomotives. Holmes's pneumo-thorax apparatus was widely used, notably in prisons, and her Safeguard guillotine (manufactured by her own firm) was acknowledged best of its kind. The poppet valve, however, despite praise for her introductory paper, was rejected by the major railway companies.

Holmes's first venture into the family field of education was her highly successful programme to train women for munitions work during the Second World War. It brought actresses, housewives, architects, and fishwives alike to high levels of efficiency—and fascination. The queen deplored that she could not take the course herself, and Holmes was appointed headquarters technical officer with the Ministry of Labour (1940–44). Always innovative, she advocated the sandwich course, alternating periods of work experience and college study, as an improvement on standard apprenticeships.

Never complacent about her success—the Institution of Mechanical Engineers waited twenty years to raise her from associate (1924) to member (1944)—Holmes sought to ease the path of talented girls and women in engineering. Outstanding among her protégés was Kathleen Cook (later Goodwin), who became chief engineer and managing director of Wilman Engineering Ltd. Holmes was a founding member, with Caroline Haslett and Claudia Parsons, of the Women's Engineering Society (1919), which she served as president (1930, 1931), council member, and honorary secretary (until 1960). Her own engineering firm, Holmes and Leather, founded in 1946, employed only women, and she created the Women's Technical Service Register, where girls could enrol to train for such positions as junior draughtsman and laboratory assistant.

Slim and elegant, a brilliant speaker and a good writer, Holmes read many papers before professional societies, including one on mechanical fuel injection for diesel engines at the first Women's Engineering Society conference, and in 1958 she published an important booklet, *Training and Opportunities for Women in Engineering.*

Verena Holmes never married, devoting herself to her career, and finding lodgings wherever work took her. She never completely recovered from her exhausting wartime stint at the Ministry of Labour, where she sometimes visited four factories or shipyards in one day. She died of heart disease in a nursing home, Whitehanger, Fernhurst, Sussex, on 20 February 1964.

Holmes never sought fame, and it never found her; her memorial must be the Women's Engineering Society Verena Holmes lectures. AUTUMN STANLEY

Sources C. Parsons, 'Verena through the eyes of her friends', *The Woman Engineer*, 9 (1964), 2–6 · *The Woman Engineer*, 5 (1940), 70 · *The Chartered Mechanical Engineer*, 11 (1964), 304 · *The Woman Engineer*, 9 (1945), 2f · private information (2004) · b. cert. · d. cert.
Likenesses photographs, repro. in Parsons, 'Verena through the eyes of her friends', 2, 6
Wealth at death £9365: probate, 5 May 1964, *CGPLA Eng. & Wales*

Holmes, William (1689–1748), college head, was born in the parish of St Swithin London Stone on 5 April 1689, the son of Thomas and Margaret Holmes of London. He was admitted into Merchant Taylors' School, London, on 12 September 1701 and was elected to St John's College, Oxford, on 11 June 1707, whence he matriculated on 2 July. He was admitted fellow in 1710, graduated BA on 16 May 1711, and proceeded MA on 9 April 1715. After filling the office of proctor in 1721 he took the degree of BD on 13 April 1722 and that of DD on 5 March 1725. He held in succession the livings of North Leigh, near Oxford (1725–6), and of Henbury, Gloucestershire (1726–8), and was elected president of St John's College on 3 June 1728. On 24 September he was appointed rector of Boxwell, Gloucestershire, and to the college living of Hanborough, Oxfordshire. From 1731 to 1737 he was proctor for the clergy of the diocese of Oxford in convocation.

From 1732 to 1735 Holmes was vice-chancellor of Oxford University and, as such, was appealed to by John Wesley to allay the fears of critics of the Holy Club. In 1734 he was appointed one of the king's chaplains. In the same year, as vice-chancellor, he presented addresses from the university on the occasion of the marriage of the princess royal to the prince of Orange, who during his time at Oxford had been partly under Holmes's care. From 1736 to 1742 Holmes was an energetic regius professor of history. As president of St John's he had printed, so that it might be given to every scholar on entry, the last letter of Sir Thomas White, founder of the college, in which he urges the fellows to live at peace with each other and bids them 'take a coppye of yt for my sake'. Holmes is ridiculed as time-serving in an imitation of the first satire of Juvenal, printed in London in 1740, and in a letter purporting to be written from Oxford and published in *British Champions, or, The Impartial Advertiser* (10 January 1743); 'that ornament of learning and politeness H—es' is given as an example of those who 'steer judiciously between all extremes'. He was certainly the first president to be loyal to the house of Hanover. He seems to have supported sound learning and was civil to Thomas Hearne, the antiquary, who wished to see a plan adopted for printing Oxford manuscripts. While vice-chancellor Holmes revived, on 9 July 1733, the ceremony of 'the act', which had been discontinued, and invited Handel to play before and after the ceremony. He offended Hearne and probably other traditionalists, however, by allowing Handel to perform on his own account in the Sheldonian Theatre on several occasions and to charge 5s. for admission; Hearne refers scathingly to 'Handel and (his lousy crew) a great number of foreign fiddlers' (*Reliquiae*, 778). On the other hand Holmes prohibited a company of players from visiting Oxford. On 4 June 1742 he was nominated by the crown to the deanery of Exeter.

The only work ascribed to Holmes is *The Country Parson's Advice to his Parishioners … of the Younger Sort*, published anonymously in 1742; other editions, with slightly different titles, were published in 1764, 1769, and 1783. Holmes died on 4 April 1748, at the age of fifty-eight, leaving considerable property (two farms and £200 a year) to St John's College, and was buried in the college chapel. He was survived by his wife, Sarah, formerly the widow of Robert England; she died on 3 December 1750. She was also a benefactor to the college, where her portrait still hangs, in St Giles's House. A monument was erected to Holmes in the college chapel, at her direction.

WILLIAM HUNT, rev. JOHN D. HAIGH

Sources private information (1891, 2004) · *Reliquiae Hearnianae: the remains of Thomas Hearne*, ed. P. Bliss, 2 (1857), 778–80, 852–4 · Foster, *Alum. Oxon.* · *Hist. U. Oxf.* 5: 18th-cent. *Oxf.*, 118, 451–2, 474, 860, 871 · C. J. Robinson, ed., *A register of the scholars admitted into Merchant Taylors' School, from AD 1562 to 1874*, 2 (1883), 5 · Nichols, *Lit. anecdotes*, 2.215; 8.404 · A. Wood, *The history and antiquities of the colleges and halls in the University of Oxford*, ed. J. Gutch (1786), 546; appx (1790), 166–7 · G. Oliver, *Lives of the bishops of Exeter, and a history of the cathedral* (1861), 277 · Bodl. Oxf., MSS Rawl. · *IGI* · monument, St John's College, Oxford
Likenesses E. Seeman, oils, c.1742, St John's College, Oxford
Wealth at death two farms; £200 p.a. to St John's College, Oxford: will

Holmes, William (1779–1851), politician, was the fifth son of Thomas Holmes, a rich brewer in co. Sligo, and his wife, Anne; and of a family long settled in King's county, Ireland. He was born in Sligo, and graduated BA of Trinity College, Dublin, in 1795. He entered the army, served in the West Indies, and was there military secretary to Sir Thomas Hislop. He later developed his West Indian connections as agent for Demerara from 1820 to 1833. He left the army in 1807 upon his marriage on 27 October that year to Helen, Lady Strong, widow of the Revd Sir James Strong, bt, and daughter of John Tew of Dublin and Margaret Muswell. He entered parliament for Grampound, Cornwall, in March 1808, and sat for that place until 1812, then for Tregony, Cornwall (1812–18), Totnes, Devon (1818–20), Bishop's Castle, Shropshire (1820–30), Haslemere, Surrey (1830–32), and Berwick upon Tweed (1837–41). From 1832 to 1837 he was not in parliament, though in 1835 he unsuccessfully contested Ipswich. In 1841 he stood for Stafford, but was not elected, and he then quitted parliamentary life.

For thirty years 'Black Billy' Holmes was the adroit and dexterous whip of the tory party, and his great knowledge of the tastes, wishes, idiosyncrasies, weaknesses, and family connections of all the members on the tory side of the house made him a most skilful party manager and dispenser of patronage. His position was of especial importance as Peel, the tory leader in the Commons, took little interest in party business. His Charles Street headquarters developed into the Carlton Club and the 'Charles Street fund' was an important precedent in the development of party organization. Very unusually for a whip, Holmes was not a lord of the Treasury, but was treasurer of the ordnance from 1818 to 1830. He was classed as an 'ultra-tory' but reported on the ultras to the party leadership. Though often violently attacked, his personal honour remained unquestioned in the midst of a life of intrigue, and he was not unpopular with his opponents. A fanatical protestant, by special permission from the duke of Wellington he was allowed in 1829 to vote against the ministerial Roman Catholic Relief Bill. He died at his home in Grafton Street, London, on 26 January 1851, leaving one son, Thomas Knox Holmes.

J. A. HAMILTON, rev. H. C. G. MATTHEW

Sources GM, 2nd ser., 35 (1851), 315 · HoP, Commons · R. Stewart, *The foundation of the conservative party, 1830–1867* (1978) · N. Gash, *Politics in the age of Peel* (1953)
Archives BL, letters to Sir Robert Peel, Add. MSS 40245, 40258–40259, 40402–40403, 40420–40421, 40423–40424, 40427 · Niedersächsisches Hauptstaatsarchiv Hannover, Hanover, letters to duke of Cumberland · U. Southampton L., letters to first duke of Wellington
Likenesses S. Freeman, stipple, pubd 1832 (after J. Moore), BM, NPG

Holmes, William Anthony (1782–1843), Church of Ireland clergyman, was born in Drogheda, co. Louth, the son of Joseph Holmes. He was educated privately, and then entered Trinity College, Dublin, on 7 January 1799 and was elected a scholar in 1801. He graduated BA in 1803 and BD and DD in 1834. Having been ordained a priest in 1806, he became incumbent of Holywood, co. Down, in 1810. While there he played an important part in establishing an institute for beggars in Belfast by publishing the tract *A Plan for a Mendicity Institution* (c.1817–1819). In 1818 he was promoted to the rectory of Ballyroan in the diocese of Leighlin; for some years he was preacher of Cashel Cathedral, and in 1822 became rector of Hore Abbey in the diocese of Cashel. On 22 May 1832 he was collated to the chancellorship of Cashel, and in 1837 to the rectory of Templemore. He was described by a contemporary archdeacon as 'an eloquent preacher, and a person of active mind and literary habits'.

Besides sermons and contributions to periodicals, Holmes published several works including *The Time of the End; being a Series of Lectures on Prophetical Chronology* (1833) and *The Queen's Declaration Against Popery, and the Coronation Oath Discussed* (1843). He was married to Caroline (d. 1838), daughter of John Bond, of Newbridge House, near Bath, and they had two sons. He died at the rectory, Templemore, on 30 December 1843, and was buried in St John the Baptist's churchyard, Cashel.

B. H. BLACKER, rev. DAVID HUDDLESTON

Sources J. B. Leslie and H. B. Swanzy, *Biographical succession lists of the clergy of diocese of Down* (1936), 130 · H. Cotton, *Fasti ecclesiae Hibernicae*, 3 (1849), 118–19 · *Irish Ecclesiastical Gazette* (23 March

1876), 77 • L. M. Ewart, *Handbook of the united diocese of Down and Connor and Dromore* (1886), 50 • St J. D. Seymour, *The succession of parochial clergy in the united diocese of Cashel and Emly* (Dublin, 1908), 24, 47–9 • [J. H. Todd], ed., *A catalogue of graduates who have proceeded to degrees in the University of Dublin, from the earliest recorded commencements to … December 16, 1868* (1869), 280 • Burtchaell & Sadleir, *Alum. Dubl.*, 2nd edn • *GM*, 2nd ser., 21 (1844), 214

Holmyard, Eric John (1891–1959), teacher and historian of science, was born at Midsomer Norton, Somerset, on 11 July 1891, the son of Isaac Berrow Holmyard, a teacher in a national school, and his wife, Alice Cheshire. His early life was spent in Somerset—a county for which he had a deep affection and to which he returned in his retirement—where he was educated at Sexey's School, Bruton. From there he went to Sidney Sussex College, Cambridge, reading history and science, for both of which he had displayed an aptitude at an early age and which were to remain his lifelong interests. He obtained a first class in both parts of the natural sciences tripos (1910–12) and a second in part two of the history tripos (1911). He next spent a year at Rothamsted Experimental Station, where he was one of the board of agriculture's first research scholars. In 1916 Holmyard married Ethel Elizabeth Britten (d. 1941), a schoolmistress, with whom he had two sons.

Holmyard decided that his real vocation was teaching and after a brief appointment at Bristol grammar school and at Marlborough College (1917–19) he became in 1919 head of the science department at Clifton College at Bristol, in which post he remained for some twenty years. Under his guidance Clifton established a reputation for science teaching probably unequalled, and certainly not surpassed, by any other British school. In 1926 he was chairman of the Science Masters Association. His influence extended far beyond Clifton, for during his time there he wrote a series of school textbooks, especially of chemistry, which were widely used throughout the English-speaking world.

An important factor in the success of these books was that through them Holmyard gave expression to his profound knowledge of the history of science, especially of alchemy. In order to be able to read original Islamic manuscripts, from which much alchemical lore derives, he taught himself Arabic; he also had a fair knowledge of Hebrew. He edited several Arabic alchemical texts, including Richard Russell's translation (1678) of the works of Geber (Jabir ibn Hayyan), published in 1928. In that year his important contributions to this field of scholarship were recognized by Bristol University by the award of the degree of DLitt. Subsequently he held office as chairman of the Society for the Study of Alchemy and Early Chemistry and was a corresponding member of the Académie Internationale d'Histoire des Sciences. His *Alchemy* (1957) was recognized as an important addition to the literature.

The outbreak of war in 1939 launched Holmyard on a new career. The severe air raids on Bristol compelled Clifton to evacuate to Bude in 1940. Preferring not to move, Holmyard resigned just at the time when Imperial Chemical Industries (ICI) conceived the idea of *Endeavour* as a new multilingual journal which would tell the story of Britain's contribution to the progress of science. He became the first editor, and established its reputation so firmly that when the war ended it was decided to continue its publication; Holmyard remained as editor until 1954. Meanwhile, however, ICI had given him further opportunity to contribute to international scholarship. In 1950 the company undertook to sponsor the preparation of a comprehensive *History of Technology*, to be published by the Clarendon Press, Oxford, under the joint editorship of Holmyard and Charles Singer. The first volume appeared in 1954 and the fifth and final volume of this work, to which some 150 scholars of international reputation contributed, in 1958, only a year before Holmyard's death. The success of the venture owed much to his meticulously careful editorial work and his remarkably far-ranging historical knowledge.

Despite his gifts, Holmyard was of an unassuming and retiring disposition and his influence on the world of learning was made far more through his extensive writing than through personal contact. Although he rarely sought the company of his fellow men, those who came to him for information or advice unfailingly received it in full measure. Throughout his life, his greatest joy was in the simple pleasures of the countryside; in particular he was fond of horses and was a good judge of them; he was a founder, and member of council, of the Somerset Horse Association. Gardening and walking were among his other leisure pursuits. No portrait of Holmyard exists, but there is a good photograph of him at Clifton College. He died at his home, Deefa, Princes Road, Clevedon, Somerset, on 13 October 1959. TREVOR I. WILLIAMS, *rev.*

Sources *The Times* (15 Oct 1959) • *The Times* (23 Oct 1959) • *Endeavour*, 19 (1960), 3 • *Nature*, 184 (1959), 1360 • *Chemistry and Industry* (2 Jan 1960) • *ICI Magazine* (1959) • personal knowledge (1971) • private information (1971) • *CGPLA Eng. & Wales* (1960)
Archives Bodl. Oxf., letters to O. G. S. Crawford
Likenesses photograph, Clifton College, Bristol
Wealth at death £10,692 8s. 7d.: probate, 6 Jan 1960, *CGPLA Eng. & Wales*

Holroyd, Sir Charles (1861–1917), etcher and museum director, was born in Potternewton, near Leeds, Yorkshire, on 9 April 1861, the eldest son of William Holroyd, a damask merchant, and his wife, Lucy Woodthorpe. He was educated at Leeds grammar school and at the Yorkshire College of Science, where he studied mining engineering. In 1880 he changed course and went to the Slade School of Fine Art, London, where he studied for four years under Alphonse Legros. From 1885 to 1889 he taught at the school, and he spent the years 1889–91 in Italy—much of the time in Rome—on a travelling scholarship. On 7 September 1891 he married another former student of the Slade whom he had met in Rome: Fannie Fetherstonhaugh (1864/5–1924), daughter of the Hon. John Alexander Macpherson of Melbourne, at one time premier of Victoria.

Sir Charles Holroyd (1861–1917), by Alphonse Legros, c.1905

In 1885 Holroyd sent his first picture to the Royal Academy, *Painting the Sail*, which was painted at the artists' colony of Newlyn in Cornwall where he lived for half that year. In the same year he was elected a fellow of the Society of Painter-Etchers, to whose annual exhibitions he was a regular contributor. Although he continued to exhibit at the Royal Academy until 1895, he mainly produced etchings, a medium he learned while under Legros at the Slade and for which he is now chiefly known. He also became a member of the Art Workers' Guild in 1898 and master in 1905. He was knighted in 1903.

In subject matter Holroyd's etchings ranged from landscapes to subjects taken from religion, allegory, and mythology, such as *The Prodigal Son* (1887), *The Flight into Egypt* (c.1899), and the Icarus series which he worked on from 1895 to 1902. These figure subjects distinguished Holroyd from other English etchers of the period, who tended to concentrate on picturesque landscapes and architecture. He was also very much influenced by both Italian scenery and artists of the Italian Renaissance, especially Giorgione, whose pastoral landscapes he imitated with the burin. Among the large number of views of Italy can be cited the Monte Oliveto series, inspired by a visit to the monastery of that name not far from Siena during his first sojourn in Italy. He also etched many views of Italian towns, notably Rome and Venice. Examples of etchings based directly on a work of a master of the Italian Renaissance are *Eve Finding the Body of Abel* (1901) and *The Dead Christ* (1912) which were inspired in composition by Piero di Cosimo's *A Satyr Mourning over a Nymph* (National Gallery). Holroyd's later etchings tended to be less figure-based, and he favoured landscapes, for example scenes on the Medway, in the New Forest, and in the Lake District, views of Siena, Venice, Belluno, and Rome. For these he would etch directly from nature rather than work from studies back in the studio. He was also noted for his etched studies of trees. His complete etchings were catalogued by Campbell Dodgson in the *Print Collector's Quarterly* (October and December 1923). About 1900, also under the influence of Legros, he began to practise as a medallist. Portrait medals of the novelist George Meredith and the painter George Frederic Watts are in the National Portrait Gallery, London.

In 1897 Holroyd was appointed the first keeper of the National Gallery of British Art at Millbank (now Tate Britain). In 1906 he succeeded Sir Edward Poynter as director of the National Gallery, a position which he held until 1916. He was one of the last practising artists appointed to this position and much debate in the press over the relative merits of the artist or connoisseur for the directorship surrounded his appointment. During his keepership at the Tate he did much to promote neglected British artists, for example founding a collection of works by Alfred Stevens. During his directorship of the National Gallery one of his most notable achievements was to bring out from storage and have transferred to the Turner gallery at Millbank the unfinished paintings in the Turner bequest. He also made some noteworthy acquisitions, despite the rise in prices at this period and difficulties with the trustees of the gallery, a legacy of Sir Edward Poynter's stewardship when the powers of the director in making acquisitions had been curtailed. Two major bequests came to the gallery during Holroyd's directorship: that of George Salting in 1910 comprised British, Dutch, Italian, and French paintings, and did much to increase the representation of French nineteenth-century painting in the gallery; the important collection of Renaissance paintings of Sir Austin Henry Layard came in 1916. Some notable gifts were also made by the National Art Collections Fund, particularly Holbein's *Christina of Denmark, Duchess of Milan* in 1909 and Velázquez's *The Toilet of Venus* ('Rokeby Venus'). As an art historian his strongest interest and knowledge lay in the Italian Renaissance, and his only major book, *Michael Angelo Buonarroti*, which included a new translation of Ascanio Condivi's life of the artist, was published in 1903.

From 1915 onwards Holroyd suffered from heart disease, for which reason he resigned from the National Gallery in June 1916. He spent most of his time in Sturdie House, Ballands Park, Walton, Surrey, the house he had built for himself in 1901–3, and where he died on 17 November 1917. He was survived by his wife, who died in 1924, and their only son, Michael, who was a fellow of Brasenose College, Oxford.   SARAH HERRING

Sources C. Dodgson, 'Sir Charles Holroyd's etchings', *Print Collector's Quarterly*, 10/3 (1923), 309–44 · C. Dodgson, 'Sir Charles Holroyd's etchings', *Print Collector's Quarterly*, 10/4 (1923), 347–67 · S. Brinton, 'Sir Charles Holroyd als Radierer', *Zeitschrift für Bildenden Kunst*, 18 (1907), 3–21 · S. Brinton, 'Etchings by Sir Charles Holroyd', *The Connoisseur*, 17 (1907), 85–91 · S. Brinton, 'Later etchings of Sir Charles Holroyd', *The Connoisseur*, 53 (1919), 85–90 · A. L. Baldry, 'The paintings and etchings of Sir Charles Holroyd', *The Studio*, 30 (1903–4), 285–92 · M.A., 'A monthly chronicle', *Burlington Magazine*, 31 (1917), 250 · C. D. [C. Dodgson], *Burlington Magazine*, 31 (1917), 251 · F. Wedmore, *Etching in England* (1895), 81–8 · A. M. Hind, 'Sir Charles Holroyd's radierung', *Die Graphische Künste*, 29 (1906), 7–13 · F. Wedmore, 'Giorgione at Asolo', *Art Journal*, new ser., 22 (1902), 272 · M. Hopkinson, 'No day without a line', in *The history of the Royal Society of Painter-Printmakers, 1880–1998*, Ashmolean Museum (1999), 16, 28, 29, 30, 31, 56 · C. J. Holmes, *Self and partners (mostly self) being the reminiscences of C. J. Holmes* (1936), 189, 222, 223, 272, 287, 313, 315, 318, 320, 321 · *CGPLA Eng. & Wales* (1918) · b. cert. · m. cert. · d. cert.
Likenesses W. Strang, etching, 1887, NPG · W. Strang, drypoint etching, 1901, NPG · A. Legros, engraving, c.1905, NPG [*see illus.*] · G. C. Beresford, photograph, c.1907, NPG · A. Legros, drawing, Art Workers' Guild, London
Wealth at death £13,221 8s. 7d.: probate, 8 Feb 1918, *CGPLA Eng. & Wales*

Holroyd, Sir George Sowley (1758–1831), judge, was born on 31 October 1758 in York, the eldest son of George Holroyd and Eleanor, *née* Sowley, of Appleby, Westmorland, and a distant relative of John Baker Holroyd, first earl of Sheffield. His comfortable expectations as a boy were shattered by his father's losses from speculation. Instead of going to university, in April 1774 he had to be removed from Harrow School and articled to a London attorney, Mr Borthwick. Having determined on a career at the bar he entered Gray's Inn in 1777 and two years later set himself up as a special pleader. In eighteenth-century common law, the drawing of pleadings was an ancillary but significant craft and Holroyd seems to have been well fitted to its recondite niceties. With Samuel Romilly, Edward Christian, and John Baynes, Holroyd formed a mooting group where each argued a problem case for one party or gave a reasoned judgment. This exercise in mutual training must have been particularly useful at a time when formal legal education scarcely existed.

By 1787 Holroyd was in a position both to be called to the bar and, on 10 September that year, to marry Sarah Chaplin (*bap.* 1768) at St Paul's Covent Garden. Baptized a Roman Catholic, she was the daughter of Amos Chaplin of Brydges Street, Covent Garden, and his wife, Maria Anna. They had fourteen children, six of whom lived to survive their father. His career prospered; according to Foss 'his fee-book shows the rapid increase in his practice, proving also the advance of his reputation by the number and importance of the cases submitted to his direction' (Foss, *Judges*). It was an advance built upon a quiet, judicious temperament, a fund of knowledge, and a natural ability for putting things in convincing perspective. Chief Justice Campbell would later proclaim Holroyd's 'genius for the law' (Campbell, 356) and Lord Brougham, for once in agreement, described him (on his memorial in Wargrave church) as 'one of the most able, most learned, and most virtuous men that ever … adorned the profession of the law'.

A rather shy man, Holroyd did not seek appointment as king's counsel, but his skills were well enough appreciated, notably by Edward Law, first Baron Ellenborough, the domineering chief justice of king's bench. In 1812 the democrat Sir Francis Burdett published what the Commons decided was a libel upon it, and it ordered his arrest. Holroyd appeared for Burdett in a subsequent action against Speaker Charles Abbot for damages, and argued the case for the absence of such a power in the Commons alone by an exhaustive survey of precedent and practice from the thirteenth century onwards. Ellenborough, while clearly determined to uphold what had been done, treated the counter-arguments with great attention. Four years later, on 14 February 1816, he secured Holroyd's accession to his court.

Holroyd served as one of the three puisne judges of king's bench with, first, Ellenborough and then Charles Abbott, first Baron Tenterden, as his chiefs. Sitting with Sir John Bayley and Sir Joseph Littledale, both men of notable learning, the court enjoyed a decade of strong reputation. At this period king's bench continued to have a much greater flow of causes laid in it than either of its rivals, the courts of common pleas and of exchequer. This preference, which turned upon a number of factors, was certainly enhanced in those periods when the bar and attorneys placed their trust in the membership of the court.

Holroyd can be seen in typical form in the case of *Blundell v. Catterall* (1821); holding that a member of the public has no directly enforceable right to cross the foreshore in order to bathe in the sea, his display of legal learning is notable both for its depth and its analytic dissection. Many similar instances of decisions on matters of private right could be given. Occasionally Holroyd was also drawn back into political dramas. In *Redford v. Birley* (1822) he had to try a civil action for assault by one of the victims of the Peterloo riots against the yeomanry members who mowed him down. He directed the jury at York assizes with calm persistence and secured a verdict exonerating the defendants that clearly he thought justified. The full bench upheld his conduct of the proceedings, as to which nice questions arose about the admissibility of evidence, and the jury's verdict.

Holroyd remained in office until the age of seventy, when ill health forced his retirement, on 17 November 1828. He died at his home, Hare Hatch, Wargrave, Berkshire, on 21 December 1831, leaving his widow in less than comfortable circumstances, and was buried at Wargrave parish church.   W. R. CORNISH

Sources DNB · E. Foss, *Biographia juridica: a biographical dictionary of the judges of England … 1066–1870* (1870), 350–51 · A. W. B. Simpson, ed., *Biographical dictionary of the common law* (1984), 254 · T. Starkie, *Report of cases, determined at nisi prius, in the courts of king's bench and common pleas, and on the circuit*, 3 vols. (1817–23), vol. 3, p. 76 [*Redford v. Birley* (1822)] · E. H. East, *Reports of cases argued and determined in the court of king's bench*, 16 vols. (1805–18), vol. 14, p. 1 [*Burdett v. Abbot* (1812)] · 'Blundell v. Cotterell', *Barnewall and Cresswell's king's bench reports*, 10 vols. (1823–32), vol. 5, pp. 268, 288–304 [B & C] · John,

Lord Campbell, *The lives of the chief justices of England*, 3rd edn, 4 (1874), 356 · D. Duman, *The judicial bench in England, 1727–1875* (1982), 160–61 · Holdsworth, *Eng. law*, 12.86 · Holdsworth, *Eng. law*, 13.505 · *EdinR*, 69 (1839), 1–49, esp. 3–7 · memorial, Wargrave church, Berkshire · *IGI*
Likenesses S. W. Reynolds, mezzotint, pubd 1834, BM, NPG · attrib. T. Phillips, oils, Gray's Inn, London

Holroyd, Henry North, **third earl of Sheffield** (1832–1909), patron of cricket, was born on 18 January 1832 at 58 Portland Place, St Marylebone, Middlesex, the elder surviving son of George Augustus Frederick Charles Holroyd, second earl of Sheffield (1802–1876), and his wife, Harriet (1802–1889), eldest daughter of Henry Lascelles, second earl of Harewood. Until he succeeded to the earldom in 1876 he bore the courtesy title of Viscount Pevensey. After being educated at Eton College, he entered the diplomatic service and was attached successively to the embassies at Constantinople (1852), at Copenhagen (1852–3), and again at Constantinople (1853–6). From 1857 to 1865 he sat in the House of Commons as Conservative MP for East Sussex.

A keen club cricketer for thirty years, Sheffield failed to trouble the scorers in either of his innings for the Gentlemen of Sussex against those of Kent in 1856, his sole representative appearance. His main contribution to cricket was his patronage, not least of the Sussex county club, of which he was president from 1879 to 1897. He spent thousands of pounds on the provision of coaching for young players and in aiding the club financially and was instrumental in securing for it the services of William Murdoch, the Australian test captain. In 1904 he accepted the presidency again and in 1907 he inaugurated the Sheffield Park cricket association for local village clubs. He also had a cricket ground of international standard laid out in 1864 at Sheffield Park, his 2400 hectare seat at Fletching, Sussex. In subsequent years several Australian touring teams played there against 'English' elevens raised by the earl.

In 1891–2 Sheffield financed at a net cost of £2700 a tour to Australia of a team under the captaincy of W. G. Grace, thus enabling him to combine his enthusiasm for cricket with a winter away from Britain, which was deemed likely to improve his ailing health. He presented the Australian cricketing authorities with £150 with which they commissioned the Sheffield shield, still the prize for the premier team in inter-state first-class cricket. His gift forced the colonial bodies to work together to develop a structured domestic competition which replaced previous *ad hoc* arrangements. Originally involving only Victoria, New South Wales, and South Australia, the Sheffield shield tournament eventually encompassed all the Australian states and remained the financial lifeblood of the country's cricket until the emergence of World Series cricket in the 1970s.

Sheffield's generosity extended beyond the cricket field, with the regular provision of holiday entertainment for his tenants and the Fletching villagers, clothes and food for the indigenous poor, and education for local children whose fathers had been killed in the Second South African War. He was particularly beneficent to the people of Newhaven, Sussex, in the creation of a recreation ground at the cost of £4000 and the donation of a site for the port's town hall.

Sheffield's grandfather John Baker *Holroyd, first earl of Sheffield (1741–1821), was the patron and friend of Edward Gibbon, the historian. Following his example, in 1894 Sheffield served as president of the Gibbon commemoration committee of the Royal Historical Society and lent the Gibbon manuscripts and relics in his possession to the centenary exhibition in the British Museum. He sold the manuscripts to the museum in 1895, having previously allowed the publication of material omitted from his grandfather's edition of Gibbon's *Autobiography*. This editorial licence, although contrary to the first earl's injunction that no further publication be made from the manuscripts, Sheffield justified by the passage of time. He also contributed introductions to *The Autobiographies of Edward Gibbon*, edited by John Murray (1896), and to the two-volumed *Private Letters of Edward Gibbon*, edited by Rowland E. Prothero (1896).

Sheffield was camera-shy throughout his life, and descriptions suggest that he dressed for comfort rather than fashion. An Australian journal summed him up as

> a little fat, stumpy man, for all the world like an English farmer of the old standard type. Hair long and straggly, lips and face roughly shaven, and a little fringe of a beard left under the chin, eyes small and cute, thick-necked, heavy jowled, obstinate, good-natured and shrewd, his Lordship is just the sort of man that would make a fine landlord for a bush pub. (*The Bulletin*, 12 Dec 1891)

There would have been no landlady, as Sheffield never married.

In 1908 Sheffield's health declined seriously and he lost interest in public affairs and even in his beloved cricket. A move to France's warmer climes was to no avail and he died at Beaulieu on 21 April 1909. He was buried in the family vault in Fletching churchyard.

PERCEVAL LUCAS, rev. WRAY VAMPLEW

Sources B. Green, ed., *The Wisden book of obituaries* (1986) · *The Bulletin* [Sydney, NSW] (12 Dec 1891) · C. Harte, *The history of the Sheffield shield* (1987) · *Sussex Daily News* (22 April 1909) · *Daily Telegraph* (22 April 1909) · *The Field* (24 April 1909) · W. G. Grace, *Cricket* (1891) · J. Pollard, *The formative years of Australian cricket, 1803–1893* (1897) · annual reports of Melbourne Cricket Club, Victorian Cricket Association, and South Australian Cricket Association
Likenesses bust, Melbourne cricket ground, Australia · cartoon, repro. in *The Bulletin*
Wealth at death £126,994 12s. 6d.: probate, 14 June 1909, *CGPLA Eng. & Wales*

Holroyd, John Baker, **first earl of Sheffield** (1741–1821), politician, was born on 21 December 1741, the second son of Isaac Holroyd (1707–1778), a lawyer, and his wife, Dorothy Baker (d. 1777). His father was from a Yorkshire family which had settled in Ireland in the seventeenth century. Holroyd was educated at Dr Ford's school in Dublin and may have contemplated an army career, since he was a cornet in the 21st dragoons in 1760 and captain by the end of 1761. His prospects changed when his elder brother Daniel was killed in 1762, and after the war he began a long continental tour. In 1768 he succeeded to the estates

John Baker Holroyd, first earl of Sheffield (1741–1821), by Henry Edridge, 1798

of his mother's brother, the Revd Jones Baker, and took the name Baker before Holroyd. The following year he purchased Sheffield Park in Sussex for £31,000. Much of his fortune he devoted to the improvement of his estate: he employed James Wyatt to rebuild the house in gothick and Capability Brown and Humphry Repton to lay out the park. On 26 May 1767 he married his first wife, Abigail Way (bap. 1746, d. 1793), the daughter of Lewis Way of Richmond, and the sister of Benjamin Way MP.

Holroyd's friendship with Edward Gibbon commenced at Lausanne in September 1763. Gibbon's first impression was that his new acquaintance was 'très suffisant' ('very self-important'), but soon he took to him (Le journal, 21). They remained fast friends and were both buried in Fletching church, near Sheffield Park. Gibbon leaned heavily on Holroyd's business acumen, in return offering Holroyd sensible advice (rarely taken) on political questions. Holroyd was a small, restless, ambitious man. His wide circle of friends included William Eden (later Lord Auckland), John Foster (later Lord Oriel), a prominent member of the Irish House of Commons, and Alexander Wedderburn, later lord chancellor. Despite lecturing his friends on their political blunders, Holroyd remained on good terms with most of them, and a stream of visitors made their way to Sheffield Park.

Holroyd's first attempt to enter parliament was in 1774 for Sussex. Gibbon advised against: 'I cannot yet think you

ripe for a county member … Five years are very little to remove the obvious objection of a *novus homo*' (*Letters of Edward Gibbon*, 2.26). Holroyd put forward his name but was obliged to withdraw. He remained anxious to play a public role, and when the American war broke out raised a regiment of light dragoons (the 22nd or Sussex regiment) and became colonel. A posting to Coventry made him familiar with the politics of that turbulent borough, and he resolved to stand at a by-election in February 1780. Once more Gibbon advised caution: a general election was due and holding the seat would be difficult and expensive. Holroyd was returned unopposed and entered parliament determined to make his mark, 'indefatigable and eager' (*Letters of Edward Gibbon*, 2.241). Perhaps he overdid it. Having been returned on 15 February, on 17 March he moved that Temple Luttrell's attack on Lord North for corruption at Milborne Port was 'ill-founded and injurious' (Cobbett, *Parl. hist.*, 21, 1780, 292). Although his motion was carried, so prominent an action from a brand new member was unbecoming, and in his next speech Holroyd admitted ruefully that 'the part he had taken in the Milborne Port business' (ibid., 21, 1780, 335) had been held against him. But before the general election his stock had risen dramatically. When Lord George Gordon's monster petition was presented to parliament in June 1780, with the protestant mob howling outside, Holroyd dogged Gordon, prevented him from inciting his supporters, and threatened to run him through if any attempt was made to storm the building. In the savage rioting in London that followed, Holroyd, 'among the flames with the Northumberland militia' (*Letters of Edward Gibbon*, 2.243), defended the bank from assault.

The contest for Coventry which Gibbon had predicted took place at the general election in October 1780, when North's government found £2000 towards Holroyd's expenses. The campaign was riotous, the poll interrupted, but Holroyd was seated on petition. The reward for his exertions, political and military, was an Irish peerage—he became first Baron Sheffield of Dunamore in January 1781—that allowed him to retain his Commons seat. He was acquiring a reputation also in economic questions: his attack upon Pitt's proposal to relax the navigation laws ('the palladium of Britain') against the new United States of America was widely reported and issued as a pamphlet. Sheffield supported the Fox–North coalition and was granted a new Irish barony in September 1783 with succession to his two daughters, since his only son had died aged five. His attitude was always quasi-independent, but in the tense spring of 1784, when the coalition's majority was melting, he wrote to Eden to deny any intention of ratting: 'you seem to be a little suspicious of me, but it is exactly the moment … when according to my nature, it is impossible to be off' (*Journal and Correspondence of … Auckland*, 1.71–2). Pitt's government sponsored an attack upon his position at Coventry at the general election, and he lost his seat, 'swept away in the general unpopularity' (*Letters of Edward Gibbon*, 2.405).

Out of parliament from 1784 until 1790, Sheffield gave

independent support to the opposition. He attacked Pitt's commercial propositions in a pamphlet, *Observations on the Manufactures, Trade and Present State of Ireland* (1785). His precocious daughter Maria wrote in March 1786: 'I went last Thursday to my first play … Papa was too busy importing and exporting to think of such things' (Holroyd, *Girlhood*, 12). His strong opinion that black slavery was essential for the cultivation of Britain's sugar islands suggested a possible political home at Bristol, which had grown rich on the slave trade. In the spring of 1790 he published *Observations on the Project for Abolishing the Slave Trade* and at the June general election was returned after only a token contest. 'The duties of a Bristol member', wrote Gibbon, 'which would kill me in the first session, would supply your activity with a constant fund of amusement' (*Letters of Edward Gibbon*, 3.192).

Like most of the remaining Northites, Sheffield gravitated towards government as the French Revolution unfolded. Its violence agitated him greatly—France was 'the vilest of all nations' he told the Commons in 1792 (Cobbett, *Parl. hist.*, 80, 1792, 81)—and he and his wife spent much time helping French refugees. In 1793 the government found employment for him on the new board of agriculture and as chairman of the commission to issue exchequer bills. But he pined for greater recognition. Wedderburn, now Lord Loughborough, reported to Eden that Sheffield was convinced that 'until he is more consulted things will always go wrong'. 'He is of a very active, bustling temper and turn of mind', wrote Sylvester Douglas, 'but I fear he has mistaken that turn for genius' (HoP, *Commons*).

In 1796 Sheffield was returned top of the poll at Bristol and resumed his idiosyncratic support of government, for he disliked many of its financial proposals. His opinion of the proposed union with Ireland fluctuated, but on 22 April 1799 he spoke strongly in favour of the principle, publishing his speech as another pamphlet. After the sudden death of his first wife, on 3 April 1793, he married twice more into political families. On 26 December 1794 he married Lucy Pelham (1763–1797), the daughter of Thomas Pelham, first earl of Chichester, and Anne Frankland, and the sister of Thomas Pelham, a Sussex neighbour and chief secretary for Ireland. His third wife, whom he married on 20 January 1798, was Lady Anne North (1764–1832), one of the daughters of Lord North and Anne Speke; they had two children, including the much wanted son. After Gibbon's death in 1794, Sheffield began the task of editing his *Miscellaneous Works*, among them the autobiography (1796), treating the text with great freedom.

Sheffield's campaign for promotion continued unabated. In 1801 he asked for the presidency of the Board of Trade, observing that 'I have some reputation with the public from John o'Groats to the Land's end on several subjects' (HoP, *Commons*). Importunity triumphed in 1802 when Addington recommended a United Kingdom peerage, and he was created Baron Sheffield of Sheffield, in the county of York. The following year he was made president of the board of agriculture, a post he held until 1806. His

ambition merely whetted, he pressed for an Irish earldom, which he obtained in 1816. In 1806 he begged Grenville to appoint him to the Board of Trade. Eden's comment was deadly:

> Though he is friendly, honourable, well-informed and sedulous … those qualities alone are not sufficient to facilitate the business of a Board which is in danger of being overwhelmed by the variety of applications crowding into it. That business can only be kept down and efficiently discharged by quiet consideration and enquiry such as to authorize prompt decisions, without being exposed to eternal discussions about the navigation laws, and long reasonings (and 'rechauffées') from pamphlets. (*Fortescue MSS*, 8.29)

In 1809 Sheffield was at last admitted to the privy council and the Board of Trade, and he held office until his death. His stream of pamphlets continued to the end, one on the corn laws in 1815, another on the poor laws in 1819. His last intervention in the Lords was in November 1820, and he died at his home in Portland Place, London, on 30 May 1821. He was buried in Fletching church, near Sheffield Park.   JOHN CANNON

Sources J. Brooke, 'Holroyd, John Baker', HoP, *Commons* • D. R. Fisher, 'Holroyd, John Baker', HoP, *Commons* • *Letters of Edward Gibbon*, ed. J. E. Norton, 3 vols. (1956) • Cobbett, *Parl. hist.*, 21.292, 335; 30.81 • *The journal and correspondence of William, Lord Auckland*, ed. [G. Hogge], 4 vols. (1861–2) • Walpole, *Corr.* • *Le journal de Gibbon à Lausanne, 17 août 1763 – 19 avril 1764*, ed. G. Bonnard (Lausanne, 1945) • *The girlhood of Maria Josepha Holroyd*, ed. J. H. Adeane (1896) • *The early married life of Maria Josepha Holroyd*, ed. J. H. Adeane (1899) • *The manuscripts of the marquess of Abergavenny, Lord Braye, G. F. Luttrell*, HMC, 15 (1887) • *The manuscripts of J. B. Fortescue*, 10 vols., HMC, 30 (1892–1927) • *The diaries of Sylvester Douglas (Lord Glenbervie)*, ed. F. Bickley, 2 vols. (1928) • GEC, *Peerage* • *GM*, 1st ser., 91/1 (1821), 563 • *DNB* • N. W. Wraxall, *Historical memoirs of his own time*, new edn, 4 vols. (1836) • N. W. Wraxall, *Posthumous memoirs of his own time*, 2nd edn, 3 vols. (1836) • H. Brougham, *Lives of men of letters and science who flourished in the time of George III*, 2 vols. (1845–6) • *An Anglo-Irish dialogue: a calendar of the correspondence between John Foster and Lord Sheffield, 1774–1821* [1976] • J. E. Norton, *A Gibbon bibliography* (1940)

Archives BL, corresp. and papers, Add. MSS 34883–34885, 34887 • BL, travel journal, corresp., and papers, Add. MSS 61979–61983 • Ches. & Chester ALSS, corresp. and papers • CKS, corresp. and notebooks • Coventry Central Library, corresp. and papers relating to Coventry elections • E. Sussex RO, corresp. and papers • LUL, corresp. and papers; drafts and working papers • NAM, papers as troop commander • PRO NIre., corresp. and papers relating to Ireland | BL, corresp. with Lord Auckland, Add. MSS 34412–34471 • BL, letters to earls of Chichester, Add. MSS 33093–33130, *passim* • BL, letters to Edward Gibbon, Add. MS 34886 • BL, corresp. with earls of Liverpool, Add. MSS 38217–38311, *passim* • BL, letters to Andrew Young, Add. MSS 35126–35133, *passim* • FM Cam., letters to William Hayley; literary MSS • NRA Scotland, priv. coll., letters to Sir John Sinclair • priv. coll., letters to Lord Egremont • PRO, letters to William Pitt, PRO 30/8 • PRO NIre., corresp. with John Foster • Yale U., Beinecke L., Sheffield Park MSS

Likenesses H. Walton, oils, 1773, repro. in Bonnard, ed., *Le journal de Gibbon*, 232 • J. R. Smith, mezzotint engraving, pubd 1777 (after A. Kauffman), NPG • J. Downman, engraving, 1780, repro. in Bonnard, ed., *Le journal de Gibbon*, 2.256 • J. Reynolds, oils, 1788, repro. in Norton, ed., *Letters of Edward Gibbon*, 730, 732, 752, 757, 759 • J. Jones, stipple engraving, pubd 1789 (after G. Reynolds), BM, NPG • H. Edridge, pencil drawing, 1798, NPG [*see illus.*] • M. A. Shee, oils, exh. RA 1806 • J. Jones, stipple (after J. Downman), BM • line print, BM, NPG; repro. in *European Magazine* (1784)

Wealth at death £4000 p.a. in Sussex (1807); also estates in Buckinghamshire, Yorkshire, Ireland: Faringdon, *Diary*, 4.158

Holst, Gustav Theodore (1874–1934), composer and teacher of music, was born on 21 September 1874 at 4 Pittville Terrace, Cheltenham, the elder son of Adolph von Holst (1846–1901) and his first wife, Clara Cox (1841–1882), daughter of Samuel Lediard, solicitor, of Cirencester. He was baptized Gustavus Theodore, but for the latter part of his career used the single forename Gustav professionally, and he dropped the 'von' (to which his branch of the family was never really entitled) by deed poll on 25 September 1918. His great-grandfather Matthias (c.1767–1854) was of Scandinavian origin; he lived in Riga, composed, and taught the harp to the imperial family in St Petersburg, but moved to London with his Russian wife, Katharina (*née* Rogge), and their son Gustavus Valentine (1799–1871) early in the nineteenth century. Gustavus Valentine became a pianist and composer, and married Honoria Gooderich; his younger brother Theodor became a painter. Gustavus Valentine settled in Cheltenham as a music teacher; his sons Gustavus Matthias and Adolph were also pianists and music teachers.

Early career A weak child, suffering from asthma and poor eyesight, Holst showed musical aptitude and began studying the violin and the piano at an early age. From 1886 to 1891 he was at Cheltenham grammar school. Here, given Macaulay's *Horatius* to learn, he set it to music for an eccentric combination of instruments without any training apart from a reading of Berlioz's *Treatise on Orchestration*. He abandoned the work after attempting to play the results on the piano. His father discouraged composition, hoping he would become a pianist; nevertheless, when the neuritis that was to be a lifelong burden caused problems, he was allowed at the age of seventeen to spend four months in Oxford studying counterpoint with G. F. Sims, organist of Merton College. Failing to win scholarships to any London music colleges, he took up his first professional appointment, while still seventeen, as organist at Wyck Rissington, Gloucestershire, also conducting a choir at Bourton on the Water. The success of an operetta, *Lansdowne Castle*, on its performance at Cheltenham Corn Exchange on 7 February 1893 encouraged his father to borrow £100 and send him to the Royal College of Music in London.

Here Holst responded especially to the teaching of Stanford, above all the insistence on sincerity and on technical security. With a fellow pupil, Fritz Hart, he was overwhelmed by the experience of Wagner, later also by hearing Bach's B minor mass in Worcester. Troubled by his neuritis and hand cramps, which made it difficult to hold a pen, he abandoned the piano for the trombone, feeling that the instrument might both strengthen his lungs and give him inside orchestral experience. It also provided him with a modest income, and in February 1895 he won an open scholarship to the Royal College, together with a maintenance grant of £30 a year. This he continued to supplement with trombone playing, especially in Stanislaus Wurm's White Viennese Band. That autumn he met Ralph

Gustav Theodore Holst (1874–1934), by Herbert Lambert, pubd 1923

Vaughan Williams, who was to be a lifelong friend. According to Vaughan Williams, they 'would spend whole days discussing their compositions. Holst declared that his music was influenced by that of his friend: the converse is certainly true' (*DNB*).

Holst continued to compose, writing works including some short operas to texts by Fritz Hart, but much of the music of this early phase suggests that his intoxication with Wagner had left him unsteady on his own creative feet. He interested himself in the socialism of William Morris and Bernard Shaw, joining the Kelmscott House Socialist Club, and in 1896 became conductor of the Hammersmith Socialist Choir, giving them Morley and Purcell as well as Wagner to sing. Here he met (Emily) Isobel Harrison (1876–1969), to whom he became engaged. His music was beginning to be published and performed, he was organist at several London churches, and he continued to play in theatre orchestras, in 1898 becoming first trombonist and répétiteur with the Carl Rosa Opera Company. He also toured with the Scottish Orchestra, and while not a brilliant player was good enough to win praise from Hans Richter.

Drawn to Hindu literature and mysticism in 1899, Holst studied the Rig-Veda, the *Ramayana*, and the *Bhagavad Gita*, and in order to set parts of them to music began to learn Sanskrit at the School of Oriental Languages with Dr Mabel Bode. Though never proficient, he felt able to draw closer to the originals by laboriously making his own translations, and produced versions of twenty hymns from the Rig-Veda as well as poems by Kalidasa. In 1900 he also completed his largest work to date, the *Cotswolds Symphony*, whose slow movement, an elegy in memory of William Morris, 'has moments in it where the intensity of his thought breaks through the inadequacies of his language' (Holst, *The Music of Gustav Holst*, 6). Financially more secure, on 22 June 1901 he married Isobel Harrison. He gave up the trombone in 1903 and began teaching at James Allen's Girls' School, Dulwich, remaining until 1921; he also taught at the Passmore Edwards (later Mary Ward) Settlement, where he introduced Bach cantatas. From 1905 he was also director of music at St Paul's Girls' School, Hammersmith, a post he filled with originality and distinction until his death, and from 1907 director of music at Morley College (until 1924).

Emergent individuality Meanwhile, a more individual voice was beginning to be heard in Holst's music, not only the Sanskrit works but also the settings of poets who had begun to absorb him, Walt Whitman and especially Robert Bridges, who became a friend, and Thomas Hardy. In 1904 he composed *The Mystic Trumpeter*, a Whitman setting in which there begins to emerge his characteristic interest in bitonality, the use of two keys simultaneously. Another characteristic, born of his interest in the natural flow of words in setting English poetry, was the frequent use of uneven metres, with five or seven beats to a bar. The discovery of English folk-song, prompted by Vaughan Williams, added a love of modes other than the familiar major and minor keys. Attempts to compose original music making use of folk-song met with mixed results, being most successful when he did not try to incorporate them into larger forms for which they were little suited and in turn presented structural problems for which he had no answer. The unevenness of the *Somerset Rhapsody* reflects these fascinations and difficulties.

The influence of Wagner is still intrusive in *Sita*, the three-act opera based on the *Ramayana*, which Holst completed in 1906 and which he later dismissed as 'good old Wagnerian bawling'. Submitted for the Ricordi opera prize in 1908, it was placed second; his neuritis was causing much pain; he was seriously overworked; and it was difficult to concentrate at home, his only child, Imogen *Holst, having been born on 12 April 1907. When his doctor ordered a holiday in a warm climate, he was given £50 by Vaughan Williams to go to Algeria at Easter, and here his musical impressions found an outcome in his suite *Beni Mora* (1910) as well as in later works.

The second of his Sanskrit operas was in complete contrast to the first. *Savitri*, based on an episode in the *Mahabharata*, uses only three singers, a small hidden chorus of female voices, and a dozen instruments. Death, coming for the woodman Satyavan, encounters instead his wife Savitri but is defeated by her love and forced to retreat. The economy of means extends to the musical language, which though spare is constructed with extraordinary expressive subtlety, so that the two unaccompanied vocal lines opening the work skilfully convey the relationship

between Death, steadily advancing through the forest, and Savitri, her frightened answers fluttering round him, unable to escape his harmonic pull. It was the most original and also the most consistent work Holst had yet written, and was achieved during ten months in which he resumed teaching and conducting at his two schools (including a performance of Purcell's *King Arthur* at Morley). He also wrote the *Choral Hymns from the Rig Veda* and *The Cloud Messenger*. Here, too, his characteristic style continues to assert itself more strongly over the weak or awkward passages that seldom quite left his music, witness to the struggle he had to affirm his true originality. Choirs and orchestras, apart from those with whom he worked, were as slow as publishers were to respond to this, though he was beginning to make some headway.

Another important enterprise at Morley College, in 1911, was the preparation of the first performance since 1697 of Purcell's *The Fairy Queen*. The effort bore heavily on his health, but he was enabled to pay for a short walking holiday in Switzerland with a commission to score some morris dances for the newly formed English Folk Dance Society. On his return he conducted the first performances of *Beni Mora* and *The Cloud Messenger* in two concert series organized by a new friend and generous patron, Henry Balfour Gardiner. Demands for occasional music, for military band suites, and especially for choir and school music were readily met, and found no lowering of creative standards in a composer whose work was always grounded in practical considerations. The volume of work did, however, affect his health, and once again he was grateful to accept the offer of a holiday, this time an invitation from Balfour Gardiner to accompany him with Clifford and Arnold Bax to Majorca, where they stayed from 27 March to 22 April 1913. On his return to St Paul's Girls' School, he found that in the new music wing (opened on 1 July) there had been built for him a specially heated and sound-proof music room. His gratitude was immediately expressed in the *St Paul's Suite*, but also in the amount of music he was henceforth able to compose in these favourable conditions.

War and *The Planets* On the outbreak of war in 1914 Holst tried to enlist, but was rejected on health grounds. He had already begun work on what was to be his largest and most popular work, *The Planets*. A mild interest in astrology provided the idea of seven movements for full orchestra reflecting the astrological character of each planet. However, this served as no more than a stimulus to his invention and to solving the problem of creating an extended work, which had so far baffled him. Some of the aspects of his idiom are here put to brilliant new use. Uneven rhythms give an emphatic, disquietingly insistent impetus to 'Mars, the Bringer of War' but also sketch the speeding flight of 'Mercury, the Winged Messenger'. The bitonal opposition of unrelated keys provides an unresolved, discordant clash in 'Mars' and a swerving unpredictability in 'Mercury'; it also creates a mysterious, unresolved timelessness in the final movement, 'Neptune, the Mystic', with its haunting close on a receding wordless female chorus chanting two chords, never ending, since space does not end, but drifting away into eternal silence. 'Saturn, the Bringer of Old Age', Holst's preferred 'planet', also opposes chords, in an inexorable advance in what he called the 'sad procession' that occurs in much of his music. The noble central melody of 'Jupiter, the Bringer of Jollity' has suffered from the association which later, exhausted and against his better judgement, he allowed to be made with Cecil Spring-Rice's poem 'The Two Fatherlands' ('I vow to thee, my country'). But Holst asserted the unity of *The Planets* when he resisted performance of individual movements. His own incapacity to master traditional methods of symphonic composition reflected a general crisis in the form to which the work is a positive and original response (Schoenberg's *Five Orchestral Pieces* of 1909 had also confronted the problem, and partly influenced *The Planets*). The work's enduring stature owes more to this than to the appeal of its sensational orchestration and beguiling tunefulness.

A move in 1914 for weekends and school holidays to a cottage at Thaxted, in what was then still a rural part of Essex, brought not only conditions for work on *The Planets* but the opportunity to put into practice a new-found enthusiasm for Tudor music. The vicar, Conrad Noel, described by Imogen Holst as 'a socialist with a sense of humour' (Holst, *The Music of Gustav Holst*, 42), became a friend. His enthusiasm led to the first Whitsun festival on 10–12 June 1916, during which Byrd's three-part mass was sung liturgically by Holst's students from Morley and St Paul's augmenting the local choir, and much other music-making filled the weekend. He also wrote for the festival an unaccompanied motet, a setting of the medieval poem 'Tomorrow shall be my dancing day', which not only reflects the excitement that possessed him in the wake of his discovery of Tudor and Elizabethan music but touched on a latent interest in the connection between music, dance, and ritual. Composing music for Thaxted had a deep appeal for him, and Imogen Holst has written perceptively of:

> one of his most far-reaching contributions to the musical life of England during the difficult first quarter of the century, this reminder that the fundamental necessities of music are shared alike by the original thinker piercing the distances and by the amateur struggling to learn his notes.   (ibid., 44)

December 1916 saw the first performance of the opera *Savitri*, at the London School of Opera, and the completion of *The Planets*. Persistent problems with his writing arm led to Holst's recruiting two of the music staff of St Paul's, Nora Day and Vally Lasker, and his pupil Jane Joseph, to act as what he called 'scribes' in preparing this and some later scores. Jane Joseph also helped him to learn some Greek when the interest in dancing and ritual led him to the early Christian poem known as *The Hymn of Jesus*. Forming part of the apocryphal New Testament writings, and almost certainly spurious, the text appealed to Holst for its atmosphere of mystic dance ritual, and he prefaced it with two plainchant hymns, *Pange lingua* and *Vexilla regis*. His liking for repeated figures in the bass, or ostinatos (in this case, steadily pacing scale figures), serves a ritual effect, but also made the physical pain of writing easier

when the repeats could be simply indicated. Again, it is with an uneven metre (here, five beats to the bar) that the exultation of the dance is signified. Harmonically, the work is also very advanced, as when Holst reaches the words, 'To you who gaze, a lamp am I', and moves to a searing discord then clearing onto a plain chord—an extraordinary aural image of eyes at first blinded by an explosion of light and then, growing accustomed, discovering it to be new illumination. The *Hymn* is scarcely religious in any specific sense, but it uses various devices of ritual to create its own, completely individual atmosphere of mystery and celebration.

As the war moved into its third year, Holst became increasingly frustrated at being repeatedly rejected for any form of service, especially with his wife finding employment as a hospital driver, Vaughan Williams serving in France, and several friends, among them George Butterworth, having been killed in action. Eventually the YMCA offered him the post of musical organizer for troops in the Near East. As a parting present, Balfour Gardiner gave him a private performance of *The Planets* with the New Queen's Hall Orchestra under Adrian Boult on 29 September 1918. On 31 October Holst sailed for Salonika, from where he later moved on to Constantinople. His work, on which he reported enthusiastically in his letters home, included teaching and putting on concerts for demobilized troops; he set out for home again on 17 June. In his absence, *The Planets* received its first public performance on 27 February 1919, omitting 'Venus' and 'Neptune' since the conductor, again Adrian Boult, felt that the music was too novel for the public to absorb at a first hearing. The first complete performance was given by the London Symphony Orchestra under Albert Coates at a Queen's Hall Promenade Concert on 15 November 1920.

Later works Back in England, Holst resumed his teaching at Morley College and St Paul's Girls' School, but gave up his post at James Allen's Girls' School on being appointed professor at University College, Reading (a post he held until 1923). Also in 1919 he joined the teaching staff of the Royal College of Music (until 1924). Returning to Whitman's poetry, he composed a setting of the *Ode to Death* (1919), a work which reflects some of the choral writing in *The Hymn of Jesus* and also expresses, in a brief space, the mood of aloof tranquillity that was increasingly a central part of his idiom. He conducted the first performance of *The Hymn of Jesus* in a Royal Philharmonic Society concert on 25 March 1920, to wide acclaim. He then turned his attention to an opera. The idea for *The Perfect Fool* had occurred to him as early as 1908, and he had composed in 1918 music for a play by Clifford Bax, *The Sneezing Charm*, which he now converted into a ballet opening the opera, also incorporating some scenes he had devised for his Morley students. However, the libretto is cumbersomely arch, the music uneven; and he was honest enough to admit later to Jane Joseph that 'the libretto of the Fool wants a light touch, and I find I haven't one' (Holst, *Gustav Holst*, 79).

In February 1923 Holst had a fall from the rostrum while conducting in Reading, an accident from which he took some time to recover. However, he accepted an invitation to travel to America and conduct at a festival at the University of Michigan. He sailed with his wife in April. In his absence the opera was poorly received at its first performance, at Covent Garden, London, on 14 May 1923. Much though he enjoyed himself in America, he felt unable to accept the offer of a professorship, and returned in June. The autumn brought more performances of his music than he had ever had, with huge acclaim for *The Planets*. However, this popularity brought him, characteristically, little pleasure, though an anonymous admirer (in fact, Claude Johnson, a director of Rolls Royce) presented him with enough money to enable him to cut down on his teaching. Having already composed *A Fugal Overture* (played as the overture to *The Perfect Fool*) and *A Fugal Concerto* for flute, oboe, and strings, he retreated, on the verge of a nervous breakdown, to Thaxted to work on his first choral symphony (he began but never completed a second). Here, a recluse for a year, he at last lived what he called 'the life of a real composer'.

The symphony is entirely based on Keats. The finest music in it, the movement setting the 'Ode on a Grecian Urn', can match the best in Holst's whole output, and there is much to admire in the scherzo ('Ever let the fancy roam') and parts of the first movement. But his structural problems with extended movements admitted some slack passages after the fine prelude, 'Invocation to Pan'; and he was not the only symphonic composer to find insuperable problems with a finale. It is still an impressive achievement, and, as has often been the case with his music, time diminishes the weaknesses and renders them more acceptable as part of his idiom.

Declaring that 'as the critics have decided that I can't write a libretto, the words of my new opera have been written by Shakespeare', Holst conceived the idea of compressing the tavern scenes from the two Henry IV plays, with minor additions, into a Falstaff opera, drawing for his musical sources on folk tunes, mostly from Playford's *English Dancing Master* (1651). The idea is ingenious, and Holst's musical ingenuity is admirable, but there is a dramatic problem in compressing originally separate scenes that leave little room for more expansive, lyrical comic qualities. The opera was first performed in Manchester by the British National Opera Company under Malcolm Sargent.

Holst had by now returned from his Thaxted isolation. He was awarded Yale University's Howland memorial prize, and elected (before he could refuse) a fellow of the Royal College of Music. A terzetto for flute, oboe, and viola is an interesting experiment in writing in three keys at once, a drier exercise than the succeeding set of partsongs setting Robert Bridges. After a failed attempt at another choral symphony (on Meredith), a number of lesser and occasional pieces followed, among them the *Moorside Suite* for brass band, but also his late masterpiece *Egdon Heath* (1927). Based on Hardy's description in *The Return of the Native*, this short tone poem drew the criticism of bleakness which Holst was increasingly encountering, for all the subtlety and refinement of the ideas. The year also saw

a Holst festival in his native Cheltenham. As antidote to an event which overwhelmed him, he went on a walking tour of Yorkshire, and that August was driven round Dorset by Hardy (who, typically, regretted that they were not seeing it in November). He also went on a prolonged holiday to Germany, Austria, and Czechoslovakia, and on an Italian tour in the winter of 1928–9 before accepting an invitation from the American Academy of Arts and Sciences.

There followed in 1929 a group of songs setting poems by Humbert Wolfe—one of which, at least, 'On Betelgeuse', recaptures the sense of uncanny peace in 'Neptune'—and a bitonal double concerto for two violins, somewhat in the manner of the earlier *Fugal Concerto* and the terzetto, before Holst's last opera, *The Wandering Scholar*. Clifford Bax's libretto, taking a story in Helen Waddell's study of medieval wandering scholars, provided Holst with a fast-moving narrative of a young man frustrating a portly friar's seduction of a vigorous young wife. Though the racy tale may seem little suited to the weary, increasingly remote Holst, he responded to its liveliness with some of his sharpest and most swiftly paced music.

Death and reputation The works of Holst's last few years were slow to win full appreciation, but have come to be recognized as among his finest achievements. They include the *Choral Fantasia* (1930) on a text by Robert Bridges; *Hammersmith* (1930), a brilliantly original portrait of the Thames and its lively bank-dwellers (originally for military band, later rescored for orchestra); some beautifully written partsongs and canons on Helen Waddell translations; the *Brook Green Suite* for the St Paul's Girls' School junior orchestra (1933); a *Lyric Movement* for viola and orchestra (1933); and finally a vigorous scherzo that was part of a planned symphony. Holst refused to accept most titles and honours—other than the gold medal of the Royal Philharmonic Society (1930) and Yale University's Howland memorial prize for distinction in the arts.

Following a duodenal ulcer with attendant complications in March 1932 while at Harvard University as visiting lecturer, Holst returned home to eighteen months spent largely in clinics, with his activity much restricted. Despite a successful operation for the ulcer on 23 May 1934, he died of heart failure on 25 May at Beaufort House, Grange Park, Ealing. He was cremated at Golders Green three days later, and his ashes were buried in the north transept of Chichester Cathedral on 24 June.

Holst was short and slight, with thick spectacles and hair that whitened and receded with the increasingly haggard appearance that came to affect him through overwork and illness. This belied the vitality of his personality, as a St Paul's pupil testified: 'He was thin and looked shy; he was rather short-sighted, and his voice was so exceedingly quiet in class that his laughter came as a surprise. It was the most robust thing about him' (Bonnett). He resisted, even feared, publicity and success, once encouraging a pupil who had failed a scholarship with a kindly letter including the advice, 'The truth is that failure is a most important part of an artist's training, and one that you cannot afford to do without' (ibid.). He had a gift for drawing his pupils into practical music-making, always insisting on learning by doing, and the music through which he taught introduced them to the Tudor and Elizabethan composers which meant much to him, and especially to Purcell. Vaughan Williams wrote that 'intense idealism of conception coupled with complete realism in practice, guided by his strong sense of humanity … made Holst a great teacher as they made him a great composer' (Vaughan Williams, 'Gustav Holst: man and musician', 79).

These qualities inform Holst's music even where there are flaws in the realization of the vision. Such flaws never arise from a failure in honesty or craftsmanship, but occasionally from some error of artistic judgement, perhaps admitting a cliché alongside a passage of astonishing originality. That a certain coldness entered his idiom cannot be denied, though it could be turned to effects of extraordinary beauty, as in 'Saturn' and 'Neptune', or the 'Grecian Urn' movement of the choral symphony and the whole of *Egdon Heath*. Towards the end of his life he became aware of this, and there are signs, for instance in the *Lyric Movement*, that a new manner might have lain ahead. He was, in fact, in a number of ways ahead of his time, notably in his rediscovery of earlier English music, in its own right but also as a source of so much artistic nourishment. He was a strong influence on the two most important English composers of a succeeding generation, Michael Tippett and Benjamin Britten, as they always acknowledged; and with the passage of time his own music continues to grow in stature.   JOHN WARRACK

Sources I. Holst, *Gustav Holst* (1938) • I. Holst, *Gustav Holst: a biography*, 2nd edn (1969) • I. Holst, *The music of Gustav Holst* (1951) • I. Holst, *The music of Gustav Holst*, rev. and augmented 3rd edn (1986) • I. Holst, *A thematic catalogue of Gustav Holst's music* (1974) • U. Vaughan Williams and I. Holst, eds., *Heirs and rebels* (1959) • R. Vaughan Williams, 'Gustav Holst: man and musician', *RCM Magazine*, 30/3 (1934), 78–80 • I. Bonnett, 'Mr Holst in school', *RCM Magazine*, 30/3 (1934), 86–8 • *DNB* • M. Short, ed., *Gustav Holst (1874–1934): a centenary documentation* (1974) • M. Short, *Gustav Holst: the man and his music* (1990) • A. Foster, 'Holst and the amateur', *RCM Magazine*, 30/3 (1934), 88–90 • W. Mellers, 'Holst and the English language', *Music Review*, 2 (1941), 228–34 • personal information, 2004 [Imogen Holst, daughter; others] • *CGPLA Eng. & Wales* (1934)
Archives BL, corresp., compositions, and notebooks, Add. MSS 47804–47838, 52915, 57863–57910 • BL, papers, Add. MS 56726 • Britten–Pears Library, Red House, Aldeburgh, Suffolk, Holst Foundation archives • Cheltenham Art Gallery and Museum, papers and scrapbooks • Holst Birthplace Museum, 4 Clarence Road, Cheltenham, Gloucestershire • Royal College of Music, London, Add. MSS 47804–47838, 52915, 56726, 57863–57910 • State University of New York, Buffalo, compositions and corresp., incl. corresp. with Imogen Holst | BL, letters to A. C. Boult and his wife, Add. MS 60498 • BL, letters to H. L. Brooke, Add. MS 57953 • BL, letters to Linetta Palamidessi de Castelvecchio, Add. MS 61951 • BL, letters to Ralph Vaughan Williams and A. Vaughan Williams, Add. MS 57953 • U. Glas. L., corresp. with W. G. Whittaker | FILM BFI NFTVA, actuality footage | SOUND BL NSA, documentary recordings • BL NSA, 'Gustav Holst', 2 March 1970, T483W, M4426WC1 • BL NSA, performance recordings • BL NSA, *Talking about music*, 87, 1LP0152104 S1 BD1 BBC TRANSC • BL NSA, *Talking about music*, 175, 1LP0200950 S1 BD1 BBC TRANSC • BL NSA, *Talking about music*, 302, 1LP0205246 S1 BD1 BBC TRANSC
Likenesses M. Woodforde, oils, *c*.1910–1911, NPG • photograph, 1916, Hult. Arch. • W. Rothenstein, pencil drawing, 1920, Morley College, London • H. Lambert, photograph, pubd 1923, NPG [*see illus.*] • M. Roberts, group portrait, drawing, 1925 (*Holst and St Paul's School Orchestra*), Holst Birthplace Museum, Cheltenham • M. Stern, photographs, *c*.1929–1930, NPG • E. Kapp, chalk drawing, 1931, Man. City Gall. • E. Kapp, drawing, 1932, Barber Institute of Fine Arts, Birmingham • C. Mackail, caricature, repro. in Vaughan Williams and Holst, eds., *Heirs and rebels* • B. Munns, oils, Cheltenham Art Gallery and Museum • pen-and-ink drawing, Cheltenham Art Gallery and Museum • photographs, repro. in Holst, *Gustav Holst*
Wealth at death £9318 0s. 4d.: resworn probate, 24 Sept 1934, *CGPLA Eng. & Wales*

Holst, Imogen Clare (1907–1984), musician, was born at 31 Grena Road, Richmond, Surrey, on 12 April 1907, the only child of the composer Gustav Theodore *Holst (1874–1934) and his wife, (Emily) Isobel Harrison (1876–1969). Imogen was brought up in west London (with a holiday home from 1915 in, or near, Thaxted, Essex) and educated at St Paul's Girls' School, where Gustav Holst was director of music. She worked with Herbert Howells before entering the Royal College of Music in 1926 to study composition with George Dyson and Gordon Jacob, the piano with Kathleen Long, harmony and counterpoint with Ralph Vaughan Williams, and conducting with William H. Reed. Membership of Penelope Spencer's ballet class and its stage productions made up for the fact that she had not been physically strong enough to become a dancer. Imogen Holst had a close relationship with her father, who, while watching her progress, never interfered but gave excellent advice when needed. She gained several awards for composition including the Cobbett prize for a 'Phantasy' string quartet (1928) and a travelling scholarship on leaving the Royal College of Music in the summer of 1930. She never forgot the experience of being on the continent of Europe at that time.

In 1931 Holst began earning her living as a freelance musician, though her hopes of being a concert pianist were dashed by incipient phlebitis in her left arm. From 1932 to 1938 she was on the staff of the English Folk Dance and Song Society, of which she had been an active member since 1923. Her compositional skills were constantly put to use in the editions and arrangements made for those she taught, and after the death of Gustav Holst her talent for writing emerged in her 1938 biography of him.

In April 1939 Holst went to Switzerland to study, and she returned just before the outbreak of war. She served on the Bloomsbury House Refugee Committee, working for musicians from Austria and Germany, and in January 1940 was appointed by Sir Walford Davies to be one of six musicians charged with inspiring and organizing musical activities among civilians in rural areas. The scheme, originally funded by the Pilgrim Trust, was taken over by the newly formed Council for the Encouragement of Music and the Arts, forerunner of the Arts Council of Great Britain. Holst's region, formidable for a non-driver, was southwest England from Oxfordshire to Land's End. She worked heroically, lifting the spirits of those she met, but by July 1942 was completely exhausted and had to resign.

Invited by Dorothy Elmhirst to recuperate at Dartington Hall, Devon, Holst started a music training course there in

Imogen Clare Holst (1907–1984), by Mary Potter, 1954–5

September 1943 with four young students. Like her father she was above all a practical musician and inspirational teacher, and in eight years she established a remarkable music school (ultimately to become Dartington College) with students including near-beginners and conservatory graduates. Her second book, *The Music of Gustav Holst* (1951), was written there, a hard-hitting appraisal of her father's work. At the beginning of 1951, sabbatical weeks at Santiniketan (Sir Rabindranath Tagore's university in West Bengal) fulfilled her long-held ambition to study Indian music.

Imogen Holst left Dartington in July 1951 to resume a freelance career, and when in the autumn of 1952 the composer Benjamin Britten asked her to come to Aldeburgh, Suffolk, to help with his opera *Gloriana*, she unhesitatingly accepted. She had first met him and the tenor Peter Pears at Dartington in the 1940s, and mutual respect for each other's musicianship and gifts led to real friendship. She lived in Aldeburgh for the rest of her life, initially working closely with Britten both as his music assistant and for the Aldeburgh Festival, of which she was an artistic director from 1956 to 1977. On her arrival in Suffolk, Pears asked her to form and conduct a chamber choir of young singers in London; with this group, the Purcell Singers (1953–67), she gave concerts and broadcasts of well-designed programmes ranging from seldom heard medieval music (via the madrigalists, Purcell, Schütz, Bach, and their contemporaries) to twentieth-century pieces.

In 1964 Imogen Holst relinquished her work for Britten to concentrate on the music of Gustav Holst, for which she

felt uniquely responsible. She supervised and conducted recordings; with the aid of the composer Colin Matthews she prepared and revised scholarly editions of her father's works (including four volumes of facsimiles) and compiled *A Thematic Catalogue of Gustav Holst's Music* (1974). She wrote introductory biographies of composers and other books on music, and returned to composition, writing original works mainly for amateurs. From 1977 she considered herself to be retired, with few outside engagements.

Imogen Holst was of medium height and build, with blue eyes, fair hair, and oval face inherited from her father. Her speaking voice was clear and well projected, and her movements, especially when conducting, revealed the discipline of dance. She had great warmth and generosity of spirit and an astute business sense, and although frugal in habit and solitary by nature (she never married) enjoyed friendship and good company. Entirely devoted to the service of music and with absolute professional standards, she had a retentive, enquiring mind which remained open and always ready to learn.

Appointed CBE in 1975, Imogen Holst became a fellow of the Royal College of Music in 1966 and an honorary member of the Royal Academy of Music in 1970; she received honorary doctorates from the universities of Essex (1968), Exeter (1969), and Leeds (1983). She died of a coronary heart attack at her home in Aldeburgh, 9 Church Walk, on 9 March 1984, and was buried at Aldeburgh parish church cemetery on 14 March.   ROSAMUND STRODE

Sources Britten–Pears Library, Aldeburgh, Suffolk, Holst Foundation archives, Imogen Holst papers · R. Strode, *RCM Magazine*, 80/2 (1984), 69–72 · personal knowledge (2004) · *CGPLA Eng. & Wales* (1984) · b. cert. · d. cert. · C. Tinker, 'Imogen Holst's music, 1962–84', *Tempo*, 166 (1988), 22–7 · J. A. Sadie and R. Samuel, eds., *The new Grove dictionary of women composers* (1994) · parish register, London, Barnes, St Michael's, 9 June 1907 [baptism] · gravestone, Aldeburgh parish church cemetery

Archives Britten–Pears Library, Red House, Aldeburgh, Suffolk, Holst Foundation archives, MSS, diaries, letters, personal papers, etc. · Dartington College of Arts, Totnes, Devon, Dartington Hall archives, letters, etc. relating to her time as director of music in the arts department | Bodl. Oxf., corresp. with Lord Bridges | FILM BFI NFTVA, home film footage | SOUND BL NSA, documentary recordings · BL NSA, oral history interviews · BL NSA, performance recordings

Likenesses M. Potter, oils, 1954–5, Britten–Pears Library, Aldeburgh, Suffolk [*see illus.*] · E. Seago, oils, 1962, priv. coll. · M. Cosman, etching, 1981, priv. coll. · photographs, priv. coll.

Wealth at death £245,186: probate, 22 June 1984, *CGPLA Eng. & Wales*

Holst, Theodor Richard Edward von (1810–1844), literary painter, born in London on 3 September 1810, was the fourth of the five children of Matthias von Holst (*c*.1767–1854), professor of music and composer, who was of Livonian descent, and his Russian wife, Katharina Rogge (*d.* 1838). His precocious talent for drawing was quickly recognized by Henry Fuseli and Sir Thomas Lawrence, the latter buying the first of many drawings from von Holst when he was only ten years old. However, the subsequent commission of erotic drawings, of which some were purportedly destined for George IV, provoked posthumous criticism of Lawrence's patronage. Von Holst became a favourite pupil of Fuseli and spent some time copying from the antique in the British Museum before his admission as a student to the Royal Academy Schools in 1824. His early instruction by Fuseli exerted such a powerful influence on his artistic development that some of his work is almost indistinguishable from that of his master.

As with Fuseli, almost all von Holst's subjects were derived from literature: Virgil, Dante, Shakespeare, Shelley, and Victor Hugo each inspired at least one major work, but it was the German Romantics, particularly Goethe, E. T. A. Hoffmann, and Baron de la Motte-Fouqué, which provided the themes for almost half his output. Thus von Holst became the most prolific English illustrator of German Romance, making his exhibition début with *Witches Hastening to the Hartzgebirg* (exh. RA, 1827) from Goethe's *Faust*, his favourite source throughout his life. While his exceptional imagination and draughtsmanship were widely praised, his choice of subjects were out of step with the age and public taste. His penchant for the demonic, supernatural, and erotic led to a degree of neglect that was otherwise undeserved.

Von Holst exhibited forty-nine paintings at the major London exhibitions and the most successful of these, his later romanticized female portraits, were bought by some of the leading aristocratic collectors of the day. He was awarded a premium of 50 guineas for *The Raising of Jairus's Daughter* by the British Institution in 1841; this work was later engraved. In the same year, he married Amelia Thomasina Symmes Villard (b. 1820), at Marylebone on 17 August. Little is known about their relationship apart from a comment by William Bell Scott that von Holst desired an open marriage but his wife 'a wild creature … returned him an unconquerable jealousy' (*Autobiographical Notes*, 1892, 163).

Von Holst's greatest admirer was Dante Gabriel Rossetti, who considered him a significant link between the older generation of English Romantic painters, such as Fuseli and William Blake, and the Pre-Raphaelite circle. Early drawings by Rossetti show a considerable debt to von Holst, as does his poem 'The Card-Dealer', inspired by von Holst's portentous portrayal of *The Wish* (exh. British Institution, 1841). His medievalism, jewel-like colours, and firm drawing were much admired by the Pre-Raphaelites, who patronized Campbell's Scotch Stores restaurant in Soho because it was adorned with von Holst's pictures.

Von Holst was the first to illustrate Mary Shelley's *Frankenstein* by contributing two designs for Henry Colburn's Standard Novels edition of 1831. The following year Edward Bulwer-Lytton bought *The Drinking Scene from 'Faust'* and later based his novel *Lucretia, or, The Children of Night* (1846) on a close friend of von Holst's and fellow disciple of Fuseli, the infamous Thomas Griffiths Wainewright. Von Holst was attempting to finish a gratis portrait of Bulwer-Lytton when he died from disease of the liver at his home, 2 Percy Street, Bedford Square, London, on 14 February 1844; he was buried on 21 February. He was a pipe-smoker and is also likely to have indulged in opium,

a particular fad of the time. The sale of his remaining works took place at Christie and Manson on 26 June. His great-nephew was the composer Gustav *Holst.

MAX BROWNE

Sources M. Browne, *The romantic art of Theodor von Holst (1810–44)* (1994) · *Art Union*, 6 (1844), 87 · *People's Journal*, 111 (20 Feb 1847), 101f. · A. Gilchrist, *Life of William Blake, 'Pictor ignotus'*, 1 (1863), 379 · *The Athenaeum* (27 July 1844), 701 · *DNB* · m. cert. · d. cert.
Archives BM, department of prints and drawings, drawings and MSS · Gustav Holst Birthplace Museum, Cheltenham, family memorabilia and pictures
Likenesses T. von Holst, self-portrait, oils, c.1835 (with his brother Gustavus), Gustav Holst Birthplace Museum, Cheltenham · T. von Holst, self-portrait, watercolour, c.1835, V&A, Department of Prints and Drawings · T. von Holst, self-portrait, pen and watercolour (aged sixteen), Gustav Holst Birthplace Museum, Cheltenham
Wealth at death £100 to widow; sale of remaining works (£97 19s. 6d.); many pictures remained unsold: will, PRO

Holstocke [Holstock], **William** (d. 1589), naval commander and administrator, sailed as page to Richard Gonson in 1534 on a voyage to Candia (Crete) and Chios in the ship *Matthew Gonson*. In the following year he made another voyage to the islands as purser of the same ship. His association with the Gonson family led to his appointment, upon the establishment of the navy board on 24 April 1546, as one of two 'extra officers' at a retainer of 1s. per day. By the following year he was assisting Robert Legge, treasurer of the navy; and in 1549 he was appointed as keeper of the storehouses, with a salary of £26 13s. 4d. per year. He held this post until 1561, having also been jointly appointed in 1560 with Edward Baeshe as surveyor of the victuals. On 12 December 1561 he succeeded William Brooke as controller of the navy, an office he held for the remainder of his life.

Like his fellow principal officers of the navy, Holstocke was not simply an administrator. In September 1551, commanding one of Edward VI's ships, he was admonished for his men's rather less than gentle treatment of mariners in suspected privateering vessels that he intercepted. He commanded naval vessels during the Anglo-French war of 1557–8, and appears to have remained at sea for most of 1559. In the ship *Swallow* he was Sir William Winter's vice-admiral during the brilliant Scottish campaign of 1559–60, during which he was obliged to loan £175 of his own money to feed the fleet's mariners. In August 1561 he commanded a squadron to attend Queen Elizabeth at Harwich, and some days later intercepted the vessels carrying Mary Stewart from France to Scotland, though these were searched courteously and dismissed thereafter. In August 1563 Holstocke commanded fourteen vessels in assisting Winter to evacuate the English garrison at Le Havre following its surrender, and was appointed vice-admiral of the narrow seas thereafter, while fear of a French invasion remained high.

In the years of peace that followed Holstocke was closely involved with the rebuilding or replacement of many of the queen's ships. In 1572 he was at sea once more, having command of three vessels with orders, as vice-admiral, to clear the channel of privateers. He is said to have seized or recovered thirty-six ships within six weeks. He was on active service again during 1575–6; on 10 August 1576 he sailed as admiral of the narrow seas to pursue a fleet of privateers operating from Flushing. By the end of the month, too many of his prisoners had begun to arrive in England for interrogation; a council order of 7 September pointedly urged him to 'forbeare to impeache any of the shippes of Holland and Zealande' unless he was sure of their complicity. By 10 September he had taken eight ships as prizes.

This appears to have been Holstocke's final term of duty at sea. Perhaps considered overzealous in action, he was thereafter kept busy with administrative duties, though as late as 5 January 1586 he was still being named as a man 'fit to command ships' (PRO, SP 12/186, 8). On 9 December 1587, with Sir William Winter, he signed a note certifying John Hawkins's good service as treasurer of the navy. During the Armada campaign he was engaged in preparing the queen's ships for duty, but saw no active service therein. He was still living in August 1589; on 19 August Joachim Ortel, agent of the states general in London, wrote to Burghley to complain of Holstocke's pressing of certain Dordrecht ships and threatening their Dutch mariners with imprisonment in the Marshalsea if they resisted. William Borough's patent to succeed Holstocke was issued before the end of the same year. He was buried at St Mary-at-Hill, Billingsgate ward, London.

JAMES MCDERMOTT

Sources PRO, E351/2196, 2197, 2199 [declared accounts of the treasurer of the navy] • APC, 1547–52, 1575–7 • M. Oppenheim, A history of the administration of the Royal Navy (1896) • T. Glasgow, 'The navy in Philip and Mary's war, 1557–1558', Mariner's Mirror, 53 (1967), 321–42 • T. Glasgow, 'The navy in the first Elizabethan undeclared war, 1559–1560', Mariner's Mirror, 54 (1968), 23–37 • T. Glasgow, 'The navy in the French wars of Mary and Elizabeth I [pt 2]', Mariner's Mirror, 54 (1968), 281–96 • R. Hakluyt, The principal navigations, voyages, traffiques and discoveries of the English nation, 5, Hakluyt Society, extra ser., 5 (1904) • PRO, SP/12/186, 206 • J. K. Laughton, ed., State papers relating to the defeat of the Spanish Armada, anno 1588, 2 vols., Navy RS, 1–2 (1894) • W. L. Clowes, The Royal Navy: a history from the earliest times to the present, 7 vols. (1897–1903), vol. 1 • D. M. Loades, The Tudor navy (1992) • CSP, 1 • J. Stow and E. Howes, The annales, or, Generall chronicle of England … unto the ende of the present yeere, 1614 (1615)

Holt, Alfred (1829–1911), engineer and shipowner, was born on 13 June 1829 at 2 Rake Lane, Liverpool, third of the six children of George Holt (1790–1861), cotton broker, and Emma, daughter of William Durning, a prosperous Liverpool merchant, and his wife, Jane. George Holt was born in Rochdale and bred to the family mill and dyeworks, but in 1807 he was apprenticed to Samuel Hope, a leading Liverpool cotton broker. His marriage into the Durning family drew him into the influential circle of Unitarian businessmen. Having set up his own broking business, he helped to found the Bank of Liverpool and the Liverpool and London Assurance Company and became fully involved in the public life of Liverpool, especially in the dock and water committees.

Education and early career From childhood Alfred Holt showed an adventurous spirit (he once escaped from a dame-school). From 1838 to 1844 he attended a private boys' school kept by a Unitarian minister at Knutsford, Cheshire. One of the pupils was George Fairbairn, son of the engineer Sir William Fairbairn, who, by giving Alfred his own working model steam engine, generated his lifelong interest in steam. On 1 July 1846 Alfred began a five-year apprenticeship to Edward Woods, engineer to the Liverpool and Manchester Railway. During that time, in his own workshop, he made model steam engines and took lessons in mathematics, chemistry, and drawing, and also in literature, which may have accounted for the Homeric names of his ships. However, by the time his apprenticeship had ended the railway industry was in depression and job prospects bleak. Fortunately Holt was able to find clerical employment with the shipowners Lamport and Holt, in which his brother Philip Henry (1830–1915) was a partner. Alfred Holt soon learned the basic principles of marine engineering and, by sailing to the Mediterranean in the steamship Orontes as supernumerary engineer, its practical aspects. In January 1852 Holt set up as a consulting engineer in an office in India Buildings (built by his father in 1834 and occupied by Holt until his retirement), finding work testing locomotives for his old master and supervising the construction of iron steamships.

The Ocean Steam Ship Company Holt soon abandoned locomotive work to concentrate on the problems that beset iron steamships in the early days, mainly connected with the screw propeller, the iron construction, and the compound engine. His golden opportunity came when Thomas Ainsworth of Cleator, Cumberland, sought his advice on the defective engines of his steam-powered hybrid brig, Alpha, built for the iron-ore trade between Whitehaven and Cardiff. Holt became engineer and agent to Ainsworth and, most importantly, got to know Isaac Middleton (d. 1878), who became his pioneer captain in all his undertakings. Such mutual respect between managers and captains was to be a keystone in the Holt management style for a century. Holt's success with Alpha led his father to invest with Ainsworth in another steamer, the Dumbarton Youth, of which Holt was also engineer and agent; its blue funnel became the symbol of the line that carried Holt's name around the world. Holt also designed the Cleator, built in Liverpool.

In 1855 Alfred and Philip Holt invested in five larger vessels for the competitive and therefore risky West India trade. At one stage Alfred even considered giving up and going into the family cotton-broking business, but he held out until 1864 before selling out to a rival firm, keeping only the Cleator. In January 1864 Philip left his partnership in Lamport and Holt and joined Alfred permanently. Together they considered possible trade routes and decided on China. Because of the vast distance involved China was considered beyond the reach of steamships, which required frequent rebunkering, but the thrill of beating the clipper, the most prestigious sailing ship of its time, appealed to Alfred's adventurous spirit. With American vessels out of the running because of the civil war, freight rates for tea rose dramatically. Alfred fitted the *Cleator* with a new, compact, vertical compound tandem engine whose boiler could take a pressure of 60 lb p.s.i., a major breakthrough in that for the first time the Board of Trade accepted such high pressures at sea. The gains in practical and commercial efficiency were immense. After trials the first three steamers of the Ocean Steam Ship Company were ordered from Scotts of Greenock (at a total cost of £156,000) bearing the majestic names of *Agamemnon*, *Ajax*, and *Achilles*, Homeric heroes all. The company was registered on 11 January 1865, with 51 per cent of the shares held by the two brothers and the rest by family, friends, and the three captains. Each vessel carried about 3000 tons of cargo and could sail non-stop from Liverpool to Mauritius in thirty-seven days, some 8500 miles, carrying sufficient coal for an average speed of 10 knots. On 16 January 1866 the first public circular was issued. The route was to be Mauritius, Penang, Singapore, Hong Kong, and Shanghai, taking seventy-six days and returning via Foochow (Fuzhou); it was to be the mainstay of the business for more than a century.

The opening of the Suez Canal brought the Mecca pilgrim traffic, but success bred rivalry and by 1876 competition was intense. Unlike their competitors, who acquired larger and faster vessels, Alfred and Philip kept to their original schedules as the China trade sank into depression. Although the Holts had been reared in the classic Liberal ethos of free trade, John Swire, Holts' Shanghai agent, was convinced that a conference system was desirable, so by 1879 an outward and homeward conference was formed, with Swire as chairman, to secure freight rates and a fair division of cargoes. The Holt brothers were slow to be convinced and, having joined, did not always play by the rules. In 1891 Alfred Holt met the competition by ordering faster and larger ships capable of carrying heavier and more varied freight, and twenty-two steamers were added to his fleet between 1894 and 1902. In 1895 direct trade with the Dutch colonies was secured by the formation of a subsidiary company registered in the Netherlands; paid managers were appointed, including Holt's nephew Richard Durning Holt [*see below*]. Philip, who was responsible for the commercial side, changed the accounting system so that each voyage carried its own overheads. He promoted profitable feeder services and invested in banks and various subsidiary ventures before retiring in 1897. In 1902 Holts became a limited liability company, a move initially resisted by both brothers. Alfred retired in 1904.

Other interests Outside work Holt's chief joy was sailing. His steam yacht, the *Argo*, built in 1875 and designed by himself, was originally intended to be a fast mail-carrier to the Far East in hope of getting the government contract. In 1876 it was used for a Liverpool Museum scientific expedition. The honour Holt most prized was his election as a member of the Institution of Civil Engineers in February 1875, earning him both a Watt medal and a Telford premium. He was also a member of the Institution of Naval Architects. Locally he was an active member of the Mersey Docks and Harbour Company, serving as its chairman in 1889–90, chairman of the Liverpool Underwriters' Register of Iron Vessels, president of the Liverpool Engineering Society, and a director of the Liverpool Institute, an educational foundation. He loyally supported the Unitarian churches and their social outreach through the domestic mission. Although not politically active he was a committed Liberal and long-standing member of the Reform Club. He felt the greatest affinity with John Bright, as a fellow businessman strongly opposed to government interference in the form of factory legislation. On similar grounds Holt opposed Plimsoll's Merchant Shipping Act of 1875–6. His ships were all built to a higher class than Lloyds A1; indeed, 'Holts class' became an official designation, so he argued that attempts to enforce standards, even on humanitarian grounds, would result in standards generally slipping to the legal minimum.

Holt also enjoyed fell-walking, shooting, theatre, horse races, and Christmas parties. He wrote a pamphlet about the burial-place of his hero, Oliver Cromwell, which was published in 1899. He was married first to Catherine Long on 20 September 1865. They had a daughter, Jane, who married Professor Sir William Herdman, eminent marine biologist and benefactor of Liverpool University; a son, George, who became one of the firm's managers; and another son, who died in his teens. After Catherine's death in 1869 Alfred Holt married her cousin Frances Long, on 4 July 1871, and had two more sons. Active to the last, he died of a seizure at his home, Crofton, Sudley Road, Aigburth, Liverpool, on 28 November 1911. He was cremated as one might expect of a founder of the local crematorium; his ashes were interred at Brook Street Unitarian Chapel, Knutsford.

Sir Richard Holt: shipping career Philip Holt died in 1914, but ever since Alfred's retirement Richard Durning Holt had been senior partner and held the reins. **Sir Richard Durning Holt**, baronet (1868–1941), was born at 29 Edge Lane, West Derby, Liverpool on 13 November 1868, one of the five sons of Robert Durning Holt (1832–1908), Alfred's brother and a cotton broker in the family business as well as a leader of the Liberal Party on the Liverpool city council. His mother was Lawrencina (Lally), daughter of Richard Potter of Manchester and sister of the Fabian socialist Beatrice Webb [*see* Webb, (Martha) Beatrice]. Richard attended Winchester College and New College, Oxford, and in 1889 entered his uncle's firm. He served in various departments to learn the business, and in 1892 undertook an extensive tour of the Far East, becoming familiar with the work done in Singapore, Hong Kong, and Shanghai. In 1895 he was promoted to manager. His career was regarded as a model. Described as 'a great financier' (*Journal of Commerce*), he showed almost instinctive commercial acumen, coupled with a strength of personality that enabled him to hold together 'a powerful management team of varied and often warring individuals who gave their complete loyalty to the company' (Falkus, 21).

Two years after being admitted to partnership Richard Durning Holt married Eliza Lawrence Wells, an American, and with their three daughters they shared an idyllic family life, though their hoped-for son was stillborn in 1904.

Beatrice Webb noted that 'Dick ... under the influence of a charming American wife [has] developed into a shrewd pleasant, public-spirited man'. However, she added 'he retains his parrot-like prejudices against all new ideas; in political intelligence he is still a child' (Dutton, xiv). Holt nevertheless remained very much the archetypal shipowner and very much a Liverpool man. In April 1939 he reflected in a speech at Liverpool town hall:

> It has been work that has been a real true pleasure, and I have enjoyed living in Liverpool. I was brought up to the idea that we were Liverpool people and that was where I was expected to work ... if I didn't like it I had got to make myself like it and do it properly.   (Falkus, 14)

Political career In 1904 Holt debated whether he should seek a political career. In his political convictions he adhered to the creed of free trade Liberalism in which the family business had been nurtured. He was unsuccessful in Liverpool by-elections in 1903 and 1906, but in 1907 he won Hexham, Northumberland, joining a parliamentary party with a massive majority. In 1909 he recorded that 'Parliament is very attractive to me' (Dutton, 19). However, the Liberal Party was not wholly in agreement with his traditionalist views. Holt opposed Lloyd George's social policies, not because he lacked sympathy for the workers but because he disbelieved in government interference with business. None the less, he professed himself largely converted to the idea of a minimum wage in 1900. Likewise in 1929 he at first opposed the idea of public works to provide employment, contending that it would put up prices. Then, reflecting that it might result in the unemployed having to earn their keep, he changed his line.

Holt's principal pre-1914 activity was organizing the 'Holt cave', a group of like-minded businessmen still wedded to Liberal watchwords of peace, retrenchment, and reform. During the First World War Holt opposed conscription and the government's controls. He even took the head of the Ministry of Shipping to court over the legality of the government's claim to command the services of shipowners. From 1916 he favoured peace negotiations and advocated milder terms of surrender for Germany. He rejected the idea of the 'knock-out blow', as a result of which he was rejected by the Hexham Liberal Party for the 1918 election. He made other attempts to recover a parliamentary seat without success.

By now Holt thoroughly distrusted most of the leading Liberals, especially Lloyd George. He also saw that the Liberal Party was now the third runner politically and that without proportional representation, which he strongly advocated, it was doomed. He nevertheless had some sympathy for the grievances of workers and criticized the methods by which other shipowners repressed a strike in London in 1912. He advocated recognition of trade unions and, like his brother Lawrence, wished to end the degrading system of casual labour for dockers.

As his political star sank Holt found increased satisfaction in his shipping interests. The takeover of the China Mutual Steam Navigation Company in 1902, the development of his firm's Australian, Pacific, and American trades, and the expansion of property holdings in the Far East had already been largely his initiatives. Holt played a key role at the time of the Royal Mail Shipping Group crisis, so that Elder Dempster, the west Africa shipping company, as well as Glen Line, came under his chairmanship in 1932. In 1923 he became chairman of the Liverpool Steamship Owners' Association and chairman of Martins Bank, which incorporated the Bank of Liverpool, of which his grandfather had been a founder in 1831.

Holt was a JP for the county of Lancaster, made an honorary LLD of Liverpool University in 1933, and received a baronetcy in 1935 in recognition of his outstanding contribution to the shipping industry. Despite the strains of war and loss of profits in the subsequent depression, he brought his firm and with it, to some extent, Liverpool's shipping through both, largely on the basis of Victorian virtues rather than technical expertise. R. H. Thornton, a manager of Ocean until 1953, wrote of Holt as 'the dominating, outstanding personality of it all, shrewd, vigorous and witty, and a very warm heart ... A man of extremely high commercial principles, dogmatic mind, ungracious in argument, invariably loyal in defeat' (Falkus, 22). Beatrice Webb's description of him as a conventional capitalist is unfair. His diary, which reveals both his strengths and his blind spots, shows how much he cherished principles as opposed to commercial expediency.

Holt's main relaxation was shooting and fishing at Abernethy in the Cairngorms. Traditional, even in domestic life, he always dressed for dinner, was shaved by his valet, and never learned to drive his Blue Funnel blue Daimler. He also furiously disapproved of smoking. He remained a staunch Unitarian all his life and in 1918 was elected president of the British and Foreign Unitarian Association. He died at his home, 54 Ullet Road, Liverpool, on 22 March 1941. His wife survived him.   J. GORDON READ

Sources A. Holt, *Fragmentary autobiography* (privately printed, 1911) · C. Jones, *Pioneer shipowners*, 2 (1938), 107–38 · F. E. Hyde, *Blue Funnel: a history of Alfred Holt and Company of Liverpool from 1865 to 1914*, another edn (1957) · M. Falkus, *The Blue Funnel legend: a history of the Ocean Steam Ship Company, 1865–1973* (1990) · J. R. Harris, 'Holt, Alfred', *DBB* · *Odyssey of an Edwardian liberal: the political diary of Richard Durning Holt*, ed. D. J. Dutton, Lancashire and Cheshire RS, 129 (1989) · *Fifty years: a commemoration of the association of Sir Richard D. Holt with the Blue Funnel line* (1939) · S. W. Roskill, *A merchant fleet in war, Alfred Holt & Co., 1939–1945* (1962) · *Journal of Commerce* (24 March 1941) · d. cert. · d. cert. [Richard Durning Holt] · *CGPLA Eng. & Wales* (1941) · b. cert. [Richard Durning Holt]

Archives Lpool RO, corresp., diaries, and papers | Liverpool Central Library, Liverpool Overhead Railway archives · Merseyside Maritime Museum, Liverpool, Employers' Association of the Port of Liverpool archives · Merseyside Maritime Museum, Liverpool, Mersey docks and harbour board archives · Merseyside Maritime Museum, Liverpool, Ocean archives

Likenesses photograph (Richard Durning Holt), repro. in Falkus, *Blue Funnel legend* · portrait, repro. in Hyde, *Blue Funnel*

Wealth at death £155,566 3s. 6d.: probate, 8 Feb 1912, *CGPLA Eng. & Wales* · £104,228 3s. 2d.—Richard Durning Holt: probate, 26 July 1941, *CGPLA Eng. & Wales*

Holt, Emily Sarah (*b.* 1836, *d.* in or after 1904?), novelist and author of religious tracts, was born at Stubbylee, Lancashire, and baptized on 25 June 1836 at Bacup, Lancashire, the daughter of John Holt and his wife, Judith, whose maiden name was probably Maden. Beyond this bare information on her background she is known only by the subjects and contents of her many works. These suggest that she was very well educated, especially in history and literature, with a strong emphasis on the English past and the history of the Christian church.

Her first publication, *Memoirs of Royal Ladies* (2 vols.), appeared in 1861. It was one of many collective biographies of women published in the nineteenth century. Most of these works focused on great and famous figures; Holt, however, provided biographies of largely unknown or little-noticed women who were not always good role models. Several, such as Jeanne de Valois and Charlotte de Montmorency, were forced to marry for political or dynastic reasons; nearly all suffered from a loveless or a brief marriage. For an introduction to such women as Ela de Rosman, Alicia de Lacy, Joan of Kent, or Constance, second wife of John of Gaunt, this work is still probably a useful starting place. The essays are documented and show a wide knowledge of the sources.

Holt's next published work was *Mistress Margary: a Tale of the Lollards*, which appeared in 1868. This was the first of forty-five books which were published regularly until 1897. They were historical novels for girls aged about ten to sixteen. Published by John F. Shaw, these books were clearly successful. They move at a brisk pace and incorporate historical information while telling a story of everyday life, families, love, and marriage to which girls could relate. An indication of their long print life was given by the advertisements for variously priced editions included with each new publication. The more expensive editions were touted as gift books, the less expensive as Sunday school prizes.

These works were based on Holt's historical research; she usually acknowledged her sources in the preface and often pointed out which characters were entirely her own invention and which were based on fact. Girls and women were always leading characters in these books. Her message to her readers was consistent: what females do is important; marriage is not their only option. A forced or a mercenary marriage is not likely to be successful. Holt's other message, also stressed by her good female characters and their male counterparts, was a total commitment to evangelical Anglican Christianity. Heroes and heroines were persecuted, imprisoned, even killed for their beliefs, but in the end they were victorious either on earth or in heaven.

Holt was probably brought up in an evangelical family, and from her works it is clear that she was adamantly opposed not only to Roman Catholicism but also to the Puseyite movement in the Church of England. *Memoirs of Royal Ladies* hints at anti-Catholicism, although as a historian the author admitted that most of the women she included had no alternative to Rome. More strident was the preface to *Robin Tremayne of Bodmin: a Story of the Marian Persecution* (1872), in which she wrote, 'For 43 years [since the emancipation of Roman Catholics in 1829] England has been creeping gradually closer to the outstretched arms of the great enchantress'. Given her religious opinions, it is not surprising that the fourteenth, fifteenth, and sixteenth centuries were the periods on which she most frequently focused. She wrote about the Lollards, several other medieval proto-reform movements, and the religious upheavals of the Tudor era. She also created books out of several medieval legends, such as that of Thomas Becket's mother, as well as such unlikely subjects as Piers Gaveston.

In addition to her steady production of books for girls, in the 1880s Holt published a book about medieval daily life as well as a biography of John Wyclif. In *Light in the Darkness* (1896) she returned to collective biography, in this case of King Alfred and other Englishmen. She also wrote several instructive religious tracts for young people and two guides to manners, the *Encyclopaedia of Etiquette* (1901) and *The Secret of Popularity: how to Achieve Social Success* (1904). The latter was her last-known published work. Her death date, however, has not been established.

Holt is scarcely ever noticed in works about nineteenth-century children's literature. When she is mentioned it is only as a minor Sunday school writer. While there is certainly a didactic religious tone to her books, she was also telling a good and, so far as she could, historically accurate story. It is probable that she influenced at least as many girls as did Charlotte Yonge, and she may also have inspired in many girls an interest in history.

BARBARA BRANDON SCHNORRENBERG

Sources R. C. Alston, *A checklist of women writers, 1801–1900: fiction, verse, drama* (Boston, MA, 1991) · G. Avery, *Childhood's pattern: a study of the heroes and heroines of children's fiction, 1770–1950* (1975) · B. Smith, 'The contributions of women to modern historiography in Great Britain, France, and the United States, 1750–1940', *American Historical Review*, 89 (1984), 709–32 · Allibone, *Dict.* · IGI · National union catalog, Library of Congress

Holt, Emma Georgina (1862–1944), philanthropist and supporter of women's higher education, was born on 10 January 1862 at Bradstones, Sandfield Park, West Derby, Liverpool, the only child of George Holt (1825–1896), merchant and shipowner (co-founder of the Lamport and Holt Line), and his wife, Elizabeth (1833–1920), daughter of Samuel Bright, merchant, of Liverpool, and his wife, Elizabeth Anne Bright. Educated at home by a governess, she was brought up to a life of cultured and elegant gentility; she produced her first specimen of needlework at the age of four and could speak French at eight. She was a day student at University College, Liverpool (of which her father was a major benefactor), during the Lent and summer terms of 1884 and spent two further terms in 1900–01 attending lectures on the history of architecture at the college. (She later endowed a travelling scholarship in the university's school of architecture.) She was born into a family whose members were prominent Liberals and Unitarians and her religious, moral, and educational development was strongly influenced by the Revd John H. Thom (1808–1894), minister of Renshaw Street Unitarian Chapel, Liverpool. Described by Thom in 1894 as 'almoner' to the chapel's 'decayed members or families', she was one of the leaders of the chapel and of its successor, Ullet Road (Unitarian) Church.

On her father's death in 1896, Emma Holt became joint tenant, with her mother, of his estate, and continued his public work. A life governor of both University College and the University of Liverpool (which received its charter in 1903), she was also, unusually for a woman, a member of the university's council from 1909 to 1915 and from 1916 to 1934. She took a particular interest in the welfare of women students and was a founder (together with her cousins Eva Melly and Jane Herdman, wife of Professor W. A. Herdman) and the principal benefactress of a hostel for women students at the college, University Hall, which opened in 1899 and was presented to the university in 1921. Besides her substantial donations to the hall and its building fund, there were her gifts of furniture, paintings, and books, in order to provide the hall with a collegiate life in surroundings of beauty, dignity, and comfort. She contributed generously to the cost of the women's wing of the university's students' union (completed in 1913), including paying for the installation of an oak staircase. Besides her substantial gifts to University Hall prior to 1921, her recorded monetary gifts to the university over the period 1904–42 total £33,813 (of which £8950 was given jointly with her mother). In recognition of 'the large and far-reaching benefactions, in which she has maintained the princely practice of her family', the university in 1928 awarded her the degree of doctor of laws, *honoris causa*.

In 1910 Emma Holt persuaded the university's council to appoint a committee to consider the advisability of increasing the proportion of women on the university's staff; the report of the committee (whose members included Emma Holt and Eleanor Rathbone, also a member of council) supported the case, which was also accepted by the council but taken little notice of by the senate. In 1915 she supported the recommendation, accepted by the university court, that Latin should cease to be a compulsory subject at matriculation for medical students, recognizing that women students were particularly handicapped by the regulation.

Emma Holt also contributed her services as counsellor and voluntary worker to a number of Liverpool charities. Of the Liverpool Queen Victoria District Nursing Association, she was not only a subscriber from its foundation in 1898 but also joint, later sole, lady superintendent of one of the busiest districts from 1915 to 1943. The Holt and Rathbone families were closely associated with both this association and other charities including (in the persons of Eleanor Rathbone and Emma Holt) the Liverpool Council of Social Service and the Liverpool Personal Service Society. Emma Holt was an early supporter of the Victoria Women's Settlement, whose honorary secretary from 1904 onwards was Eleanor Rathbone. She took a particular interest in the Girls' Own Club of the Liverpool Domestic Mission (one of whose founders was the Revd J. H. Thom) and was lady president of the Liverpool Home for Incurables. During the First World War she converted the former Liverpool residence of an uncle, Alfred Holt (1829–

1911), into a war hospital and supported it when afterwards it became a women's hospital.

In 1940 failing health led Emma Holt to leave Liverpool and spend her last years at her Lake District home, Tent Lodge, in her beloved Coniston, at whose parish church she worshipped. She died there, unmarried, on 19 December 1944 and was buried on the 22nd in the Holt family burial-ground, Toxteth Unitarian Chapel, Liverpool. She bequeathed her Liverpool home, Sudley, Mossley Hill, to the city to be used as a public garden and park; a total of 146 paintings in Sudley, collected by her father, were also left to Liverpool, to be kept together as a collection, on condition that the public were allowed to view them free of charge. Besides bequests to relatives and servants, she left £13,500 to named Liverpool charities, including the university and University Hall.

Of short stature, Emma Holt was plain featured, with a long face. Portraits of her in later life show a stately and gracious lady but inadequately convey her character. 'Modest, simple, invariably kind and friendly, yet with a shrewd judgement of men and things', wrote Eleanor Rathbone of her in the *Liverpool Daily Post* of 21 December 1944. A devoted Unitarian, her inherited wealth was regarded as held in trust, to support those not so fortunate as herself.
ADRIAN R. ALLAN

Sources J. H. Thom, letters to E. G. Holt, 1867–94, Lpool RO · Wills of Miss Holt and her parents, Principal Registry of the Family Division, London · Records of University Hall, University Council, Vice-Chancellor, and Registrar, U. Lpool L., special collections and archives · records, Lpool RO [Ullet Road Church, Liverpool Queen Victoria District Nursing Association, Liverpool Domestic Mission, Liverpool Personal Service Society, and Liverpool Home for Incurables] · Records of Victoria Settlement and University Settlement, U. Lpool L., special collections and archives · L. Redfern, memorial address, 1944, Lpool RO [Emma Georgina Holt] · *Liverpool Daily Post* (20 Dec 1944) · *Liverpool Daily Post* (21 Dec 1944) · L. Redfern, *Liverpool Post* (23 April 1949) [appreciation of Miss Holt] · *The Emma Holt bequest: Sudley, illustrated catalogue and history of the house* (1971) · C. Dyhouse, *No distinction of sex? Women in British universities, 1870–1939* (1995) · T. Kelly, *For advancement of learning: the University of Liverpool, 1881–1981* (1981) · G. Melly, *Scouse Mouse or I never got over it* (1984), 111–19 · census returns, 1871, 1881, 1891 · D. Butterworth, *The parish of Church Coniston, 1586–1986* (1986) · b. cert. · *Gore's Directory of Liverpool* (1862) · Lpool RO, 920 DUR 1/4 · d. cert.
Archives Lpool RO, travel diaries and memorial address | U. Lpool L., records of University Hall, Liverpool
Likenesses P. Bigland, oils, 1889, Walker Art Gallery, Liverpool · D. Muirhead, oils, 1909, U. Lpool · R. de l'Hôpital, oils, 1928, U. Lpool
Wealth at death £667,718 2s. 4d.: probate, 6 April 1945, CGPLA Eng. & Wales

Holt, Francis Ludlow (1779–1844), legal writer, was born at Watford, Hertfordshire, the son of the Revd Ludlow Holt, author of some sermons published in 1780–81, and his wife, Jane. He was elected a king's scholar of Westminster School in 1794, matriculated at Christ Church, Oxford, in 1798, and was admitted to Trinity Hall, Cambridge, in 1807. He did not graduate at either university. He was called to the bar at the Middle Temple on 27 January 1809. In the early part of his professional career he went on the northern circuit, but after a few years he resigned the circuit practice altogether, confining himself thereafter to an extensive chamber practice. He became a king's counsel (on Henry Brougham's recommendation) and bencher of the Inner Temple in 1831, and treasurer of that inn in 1840. He was for some time an exchequer-bill loan commissioner. He succeeded Sir Giffin Wilson as vice-chancellor of the county palatine of Lancaster in 1826 and held the post until his death. He married a niece of John Bell, proprietor of *Bell's Weekly Messenger*, of which he was for many years the principal editor.

Holt was the author of several law treatises and also produced a set of *nisi prius* reports between 1815 and 1817. He was the author of *The Law of Libel*, one of the first treatises on its subject, written at a time when the libel laws were under much criticism for hindering the freedom of the press. His work merely summarized the existing law in a superficial way, however, and was seen by critics of the law, such as James Mill, as work of a tory lawyer. It was largely superseded by that of Thomas Starkie. His other main treatise was *A System of the Shipping and Navigation Laws of Great Britain*, published in 1820. Although it was comprehensive and well-written, it was superseded by the work of Charles Abbott, later Lord Tenterden. He also wrote a treatise on the bankruptcy laws, and on *The Law and Usage of Parliament, in Cases of Privilege and Contempt* (1810). In addition to his legal writings Holt wrote some plays, publishing in 1804 a comedy, *The Land We Live In*. Though successful as a literary work (reaching a third edition by 1805), it was unsuitable to the stage, the author having sacrificed plot to dialogue; it was performed at Drury Lane on one night in 1805. Holt died at his residence, 13 Earl's Terrace, Kensington, on 29 September 1844.   MICHAEL LOBBAN

Sources GM, 2nd ser., 22 (1844), 650 • *Annual Register* (1844), 272 • Holdsworth, *Eng. law*, 13.437, 481, 488 • J. Welch, *The list of the queen's scholars of St Peter's College, Westminster*, ed. [C. B. Phillimore], new edn (1852) • *IGI* • d. cert.
Archives UCL, Brougham MSS

Holt [*née* Wiseman], **Jane** (*fl. c.*1682–1717), playwright and poet, is of obscure origins, though her maiden name appears to have been Wiseman. The prompter John Downes notes that a 'Mrs. Wiseman' inherited the part of Roxolana in the earl of Orrery's tragedy *Mustapha* from Mary Betterton some time after 1665 (Downes, 26), and this may have been the writer. A 'Mrs. Wiseman' was listed as a member of the Duke's Company about the time of the union of theatrical companies in 1682, and the United Company revived *Mustapha* in October 1686, though no cast list from this production has survived. Wiseman may indeed have acted the part in 1686 as Betterton had reduced her schedule in the mid-1680s.

The actress named Wiseman is probably the Jane Wiseman who appears late in 1701 when her play, *Antiochus the Great, or, The Fatal Relapse*, was acted at the New Theatre, Lincoln's Inn Fields. The exact date of the première remains unknown, but the play was performed in the week of 11 November, and it was published on 25 November 1701 (but dated 1702). According to Giles Jacob, Wiseman worked as a servant in the family of William Wright, recorder of Oxford, before her success with *Antiochus*. In

Wright's household she read novels and plays from his library which apparently sparked her first attempt at composition (Jacob, 301). In the dedication to John, Lord Jeffries, Wiseman provides only a general hint that *Antiochus* is the product of a self-taught, labouring-class type as she describes her work as 'the first Fruits of a Muse, not yet debas'd to the Low Imployment of Scandal or Private Reflection'. Some time after the success of *Antiochus*, according to Jacob, Wiseman married 'a young Vintner' named Holt and retired from the stage, using the profits from her play to open a tavern in Westminster with her husband (ibid.).

In 1717 a 'Mrs Holt' published a short book of verse titled *A Fairy Tale Inscrib'd, to the Honourable Mrs. W—, with other Poems*. The many detailed references to the Restoration stage and to fellow playwrights among the verses serve to connect the poet Holt to the actress-playwright Wiseman. The author is more explicit about her humble origins, referring to herself as 'the meanest of the Muses Train' and describing her poetic efforts as 'artless Song' (*Fairy Tale*, 26). But there are several accomplished poems in this volume, and Holt also presents herself, perhaps imaginatively, as a retiring country type, content with a 'few choice books' and her female 'Friends', far removed from the strife of London. No details of Holt's death and burial appear to have survived.   WILLIAM J. CHRISTMAS

Sources J. Downes, *Roscius Anglicanus, or, An historical review of the stage* (1708), 126 • [G. Jacob], *The poetical register, or, The lives and characters of the English dramatick poets*, [1] (1719), 301 • M. Summers, *The playhouse of Pepys* (1935), 109 • E. L. Avery, ed., *The London stage, 1660–1800*, pt 2: 1700–1729 (1960), 16–17 • W. Van Lennep and others, eds., *The London stage, 1660–1800*, pt 1: 1660–1700 (1965), 352 • J. Wiseman, *Antiochus the Great, or, The fatal relapse* (1701) • *Post Man* (11 Nov 1701) • *Post Man* (13 Nov 1701) • J. Holt, *A fairy tale inscrib'd, to the Honourable Mrs. W—, with other poems* (1717)

Holt, Sir John (d. 1418/19), justice, is of obscure origins. He trained as a lawyer, and from 1 October 1375 was paid as a king's serjeant, even though he did not formally become a serjeant-at-law until Hilary term 1376. His pleadings are often recorded in the year-books. He formed other important connections at court. By the mid-1370s he was involved in the property affairs of William, Lord Latimer, the king's chamberlain, and he also entered the service of John of Gaunt, duke of Lancaster, who in 1377 appointed him steward of his lordship of Higham Ferrers, Northamptonshire, an office he held at least until October 1382. By 20 February 1376 he had married a woman named Alice, probably the heir of the Islip family; on 28 March property in Islip, Aldwincle, Grafton by Cranford, and Woodford, all in Northamptonshire, was quitclaimed to them, and the manor of Sacombe in Hertfordshire, which Holt had purchased, was conveyed to the couple jointly. Other acquisitions made by Holt were the manor and advowson of Brampton, Huntingdonshire, property in Lincoln, and an inn in Southwark, the Angel in the Hope. On 21 May 1382 he was granted the wardship of John Stonor, a minor who was heir to estates in Oxfordshire, but soon relinquished it to the chief justice of the common pleas, Sir Robert Bealknap.

On 4 November 1383 Holt was appointed to the common bench, and by 3 May following he had been knighted. He was a trier of petitions in the parliaments of 1384, 1385, and 1386. In August 1387 he was one of the justices who responded to Richard II's questions about the legitimacy of proceedings in the previous year's parliament, which had placed royal authority under conciliar control, by declaring that they were derogatory to the king's prerogative, and that those responsible for them were traitors. When the earls of Derby and Nottingham rose in arms against Richard II's favourites in December 1387, they detained Holt while he was holding sessions at Newmarket Heath. In January 1388 he was among the justices deprived of office at the instigation of the two earls and their fellow lords appellant, and on 2 March he was one of six of them who were brought before parliament, to be impeached by the Commons for the opinions to which they had subscribed in 1387. Holt claimed that he had complied as a result of dire threats from Archbishop Alexander Neville, Robert de Vere, duke of Ireland, and Michael de la Pole, earl of Suffolk, and that because of his hesitancy he was physically assaulted. The Lords were divided on sentencing the former justices, but on 6 March they were condemned to hanging and forfeiture, then granted their lives at the supplication of the bishops. At the end of parliament their banishment to Ireland was agreed upon. Holt (like Bealknap) was to stay in Drogheda or its vicinity: in July arrangements were made for his transportation from Chester with two of his servants, the first instalment of his annuity (to be raised from what had been his own lands) of £26 13s. 4d., sufficient raiment, and a bed. On 7 July 1390, with the great council's assent, his forfeited properties were sold for £500 to his eldest son, John. The latter and his brothers Hugh and Richard (a cleric) experienced difficulties in making the annual payments: in 1395 the debt was rescheduled.

Then in the first parliament of 1397 the former justices' banishments were rescinded, and in January 1398 parliament reversed their sentences. Holt was back in England that year. In Henry IV's first parliament, in 1399, the sentences were reinstated. The new king disregarded the Commons' pity for the surviving offenders' old age and poor health. However, on 20 February 1400 Holt was licensed to live in England, and his petitions to parliament in 1401 and 1402 (made jointly with his former colleague and fellow exile William Burgh) resulted in his receiving royal permission to sue for his former estates. Sir John Holt died in either 1418 or 1419. His eldest son, John, had predeceased him, as had his wife, and his second son, Hugh, succeeded to the recovered estates.

ANTHONY GOODMAN

Sources *Chancery records* · *CEPR letters*, vol. 5 · M. McKisack, ed., 'Historia, sive, Narracio de modo et forma Mirabilis Parliamenti apud Westmonasterium', *Camden miscellany, XIV*, CS, 3rd ser., 37 (1926) · L. C. Hector and B. F. Harvey, eds. and trans., *The Westminster chronicle, 1381–1394*, OMT (1982) · *Knighton's chronicle, 1337–1396*, ed. and trans. G. H. Martin, OMT (1995) [Lat. orig., *Chronica de eventibus Angliae a tempore regis Edgari usque mortem regis Ricardi Secundi*, with parallel Eng. text] · *VCH Hertfordshire*, vol. 3 · *RotP*, vol. 3 · Sainty, *King's counsel* · R. Somerville, *History of the duchy of Lancaster, 1265–1603* (1953) · Tout, *Admin. hist.*, vol. 3

Holt, John (*d.* 1504), schoolmaster and grammarian, was the son of William Holt (or Smyth), sometime mayor and tradesman of Chichester, Sussex, and, apparently, his first wife, Joan. His schooling may have taken place in Chichester, but he is first recorded being admitted as a probationary fellow of Magdalen College, Oxford, on 27 July 1490, becoming a full fellow one year later. He graduated MA in 1494, and by Michaelmas of that year was employed as usher or second master of Magdalen College School, then in its heyday as a pioneer centre of humanist Latin teaching. Holt left this post at Easter 1496 (having been ordained priest in the previous year) to become grammar master of the boys and youths of Archbishop Morton's household at Lambeth Palace. There he wrote his surviving grammatical work, *Lac puerorum*.

In 1498 Morton rewarded Holt with the valuable rectory of Smarden, Kent, and after the archbishop's death in 1500 Holt appears to have withdrawn to this parish. In September 1501, however, he accepted a new full-time teaching appointment from the dean and chapter of Chichester Cathedral as master of Chichester prebendal (or cathedral) school. The school had been endowed two years previously by Bishop Story of Chichester with the cathedral prebend of Highleigh, providing the master with a salary to teach without charging fees. Holt held the post for only about a year before leaving, by the end of 1502, for a fourth scholastic appointment as grammar master to Prince Henry (later Henry VIII), in succession to John Skelton. In 1502 he was also presented to the rectory of Week St Mary, Cornwall, by Sir Edmund Arundell, possibly through the influence of Arundell's relative the bishop of Exeter, a colleague of Morton and Story. This benefice (which he held with Smarden by papal dispensation) made him a wealthy man, but by 21 March 1504 he had fallen sufficiently ill to make his will at St Paul's, London, and he was dead by 14 June.

Holt was one of a group of schoolmasters associated with Magdalen College School, including John Anwykyll (*d.* 1487), William Lily (*d.* 1522), and John Stanbridge (*d.* 1510), who were influential in spreading the teaching of humanist Latin to schools in England through the publication of school textbooks. His own published work, *Lac puerorum*, subtitled *Mylke for Chyldren*, survives only in editions printed after the author's death, the earliest about 1505, but it contains a dedication to Morton, then dead, and verses by Holt which state that it was written with the archbishop's approval in the hall of Lambeth Palace: evidently between 1496 and 1500. It was prefaced and concluded by complimentary Latin verses by Thomas More (*d.* 1535), whose earliest surviving letter was also written to Holt in 1501. *Lac puerorum* is an elementary textbook in English, introducing pupils to Latin accidence, grammatical definitions, and syntax. Though traditional in form, it tries to help children in the first stages of learning Latin by the novel practice of using pictures to present the declensions of nouns and by employing simple words ('showing', 'asking', 'bidding', and 'wishing') to explain the moods of the verb. The work had a modest success, being published at least five times before about 1511 in London and Antwerp, before it lost the field to grammars like those of Stanbridge and Lily. NICHOLAS ORME

Sources N. Orme, 'John Holt (d. 1504), Tudor grammarian', *The Library*, 6th ser., 18 (1996), 283–305 • Emden, *Oxf.*, 2.953 • J. R. Bloxam, *A register of the presidents, fellows … of Saint Mary Magdalen College*, 8 vols. (1853–85), vol. 3, pp. 7–10 • W. D. Macray, *A register of the members of St Mary Magdalen College, Oxford*, 8 vols. (1894–1915), vol. 1, p. 120 • *STC, 1475–1640*, nos. 13603.7–13606.5 • J. Holt, *Lac puerorum* [1508] • A. W. Reed, 'The young Thomas More', *Under God and the law*, ed. R. O'Sullivan (1949), 1–27 • PRO, PROB 11/11, fol. 309 [will of William Holt] • PRO, PROB 11/14, fol. 81v [will of John Holt]

Holt, John (d. 1540), bishop, was probably a member of the Holt family of Bury St Edmunds, though he does not appear in its heraldic pedigree of 1561. In his will he styled himself 'Master', suggesting that he had graduated from a university, but it is not known which. Although he may have been the 'Master Holte of London' recorded in September 1526 as supplying money to Thomas Cromwell for works on Cardinal College, Oxford, the first certain reference to him comes from 15 June 1528, when as bishop of Lydda *in partibus* he laid the foundation stone of Cardinal Wolsey's projected college at Ipswich, as the stone itself, preserved in the chapter house of Christ Church Cathedral, Oxford, records. Holt's episcopal style is puzzling, for there was already a bishop of Lydda active in England, namely Thomas Bele, who was suffragan in the diocese of London from no later than September 1521 until at least 17 December 1529. And Bele's tenure of the 'diocese' overlapped with that of Roger Smith, abbot of Dorchester, who was papally provided to it in 1513 and may have held it until his death c.1535. Probably neither popes nor bishops were particularly careful about the titles borne by English suffragans.

Holt was most likely employed as suffragan in East Anglia, as is suggested by his role at Ipswich and again by his performing ordinations at Norwich on 22 May 1535. His will, which he drew up on 11 August 1540, shows that he was then living in Bury and had property at Great Barton near by. Still styling himself bishop of Lydda, he made a traditional bequest of his soul to God, the Virgin, and the heavenly host, and requested burial in St Mary's parish church, Bury, 'in our Ladys Ile next unto the hedde of John Holt gent' (will). The latter, who must have been the John Holt whose memorial stone in that church records his death on 13 July 1539 and his interment in its south chancel aisle, is the only man of that surname referred to in the will. Bishop Holt's most substantial bequests, including his property in Great Barton, were to two servants. He also left money to three parish guilds, and disposed of chimere, mitre, and rochets, largely to pay for his funeral and for a distribution of alms to the poor. He had died at Bury St Edmunds by 19 August, when his will was proved. HENRY SUMMERSON

Sources will, PRO, PROB 11/28, fol. 75r–75v • J. R. Bloxam, *A register of the presidents, fellows … of Saint Mary Magdalen College*, 8 vols. (1853–85) • GL, MSS 9531/9–10 • *LP Henry VIII*, 4/2, no. 2538 • Norfolk RO, ORR/1/1, fol. 25 [information from Dr K. Carleton] • W. Hervey, *The visitation of Suffolk, 1561*, ed. J. Corder, 1, Harleian Society, new ser., 2 (1981), 52–4 • *CEPR letters*, 18.602 • M. Bowker, *The secular clergy in the diocese of Lincoln, 1495–1520* (1968)

Holt, Sir John (1642–1710), judge, was born at Thame, Oxfordshire, on 30 December 1642, the first son of Sir Thomas Holt and of Susan, daughter of John Peacock of Chawley, Berkshire. Holt's father, a barrister of Gray's Inn, was recorder of Abingdon as well as its member of parliament during the 1650s. The younger Holt attended the free school in Abingdon. He was admitted to his father's inn in November 1652 when he was not yet ten years old. On 31 July 1658 he matriculated from Oriel College, Oxford, where he took no degree. Though reportedly a dissolute youth, he was called to the bar in February 1664.

Holt as barrister, 1664–1688 By late 1664 Holt had begun to plead in king's bench, the court where he made his greatest mark, and by 1668 he had begun to earn mention in the law reports. On 28 June 1675 he married Ann (c.1657–1712), daughter of Sir John Cropley. From the late 1670s Holt's prominence in his profession was underscored by his regular appearance as counsel in suits before the House of Lords.

Unlike many leaders at the bar in the late 1670s and 1680s, Holt defies easy labelling as a whig or tory. He represented clients such as the Norwich alderman who lost his office after allegations that he had not observed the terms of the Corporation Act and the Ipswich justices of the peace who would not support collecting fines from dissenters, suggesting Holt's sympathy for nonconformity. But he also provided advice to the leaders of Leicester who wanted to understand better the actions they could take to enforce the conventicle acts. He provided counsel in 1679 to the king's adviser, the earl of Danby, and in 1683 to the accused traitor Lord Russell. Holt performed a supporting role in crown prosecutions, appearing in trials for seditious libel in 1680 and against Slingsby Bethel in 1681 for his alleged assault at Southwark's parliamentary election. On the other hand, Holt represented the whig leader Lord Grey of Werk during his trial for debauching his sister-in-law, Lady Henrietta Berkeley. Holt also joined prominent whig lawyers Francis Pollexfen, William Williams, and Sir Francis Winnington in their unsuccessful defence of Thomas Pilkington, Samuel Shute, Lord Grey, and others for their riot at the election of London's sheriffs in 1682.

While Holt supported these whigs in court in the 1680s, he just as consistently promoted royal authority in the crown's legal battles with the urban corporations. He did not appear in the *quo warranto* trial against London's corporation, but was among those consulted by the City about how it should respond after judgment came down against it in June 1683. Though Holt advised surrender, the City followed other counsel and ultimately forfeited its charter. Holt likewise advised Berwick to surrender its charter after the town initially decided to fight a *quo warranto*. In both instances Holt premised his advice on the idea that all franchises—including corporations—derive from the king and would thus survive in royal matter, Holt alone contended that the soldier could not be executed when the kingdom was not at war. Later, in his absence, judgment was given and the soldier was indeed executed. Holt asked to be dismissed from the recordership and in May 1687 the king obliged.

Holt remained a king's serjeant and thus refused to appear as counsel in court against the king throughout 1687 and 1688. But he continued active before the bench, right through the autumn of 1688. In October he was among those convened to investigate whether the prince of Wales, born the previous June, was indeed the queen's child. After James II fled in December Holt was one of the legal counsel consulted by London's leaders and later by the provisional government about how to summon a parliament in the king's absence.

When the convention met in January 1689 the House of Lords asked Holt to serve as one of its legal advisers. Hinting that government was by contract, not *jure divino*, he was among those who suggested that James II had abdicated because his departure was a violation—and thus a renunciation—of his trust as king. On 31 January Bere Alston returned Holt to the Commons, where he spoke often, served on two dozen committees, and helped to manage the conference with the Lords about the crown—in which he promoted William of Orange's claim to the throne independent of any right by his wife, Mary. During the November debate on the Bill of Rights Holt also argued that the king possessed the authority to grant *non obstantes*—a dispensing power—though he added that this power did not permit making exceptions to the Test Act. Holt also supported the new monarch's right to collect revenues granted by parliament to the previous king. In short, while he accepted that a king like James might forfeit the throne by breaking his trust, Holt continued to accord the monarch significant authority as a matter of law.

Holt as jurist, 1689–1710 Holt's brief Commons career was ended by his appointment as chief justice of king's bench on 17 April 1689. As a jurist Holt exercised greater sway over the law than any judge between Hale and Mansfield. Unlike Hale, he extended this influence exclusively through his reported opinions rather than by authoring legal treatises, which perhaps explains Holt's concern about the accuracy of most reports. In criminal law Holt was notable for the attention he gave to how evidence was presented before him, though perhaps William Holdsworth's pronouncement that Holt 'established the modern attitude of the judge to the criminal' (Holdsworth, *Eng. law*, 6.518) overstates the matter. Holt's summation of the case against Richard Hathaway at Surrey assizes for giving false evidence of witchcraft shows his scepticism of those who sought convictions by questionable means. Similarly Holt refused to countenance evidence of a defendant's character prior to the events in question, though he carefully applied this rule when such evidence might have helped a defendant as well as when it might not.

Holt's care with evidence reveals the precision of his mind in applying law, not a peculiar sensitivity for the

Sir John Holt (1642–1710), by Richard van Bleeck, *c.*1700

hands if seized after judgment or upon surrender. The same view of regal power over franchises appeared in Holt's arguments in the East India Company case, in which he found Pollexfen, Williams, and Sir George Treby arrayed against him. In a learned argument, drawn not only from statute and law reports but from scripture, Grotius, John Selden, and other treatise authors, Holt justified the company's privileges by justifying the king's power to grant them a monopoly by royal charter: 'by the law of the land, no subject of England can trade with infidels without license from the king' (*State trials*, 10.373).

Holt was made serjeant-at-law in February 1684, at which time he was again advising Danby in his effort to win release from the Tower. Though he aided the former royal minister and had just received the crown's favour, in the same period Holt joined Pollexfen to defend William Sacheverell and other alleged whig rioters from Nottingham, without success. In February 1686 James II knighted Holt and made him recorder of London, the City's charter being still in abeyance and its officers acting by the king's nomination. He was promoted to king's serjeant in April. Holt's reported reluctance to accept the recorder's place only grew when he sat in the Old Bailey in the trial of a soldier accused of desertion. Of nine judges hearing the accused. This was apparent in his handling of the treason case against Sir William Parkyns. Parkyns complained that he had not had sufficient time to gather his witnesses. None the less, Holt denied his request for a delay, saying that Parkyns had had ample time, even though he had received notice of trial just six days earlier and had been delayed in meeting with his solicitor. Parkyns next asked for counsel in court, pointing to a statute providing for counsel in treason trials due to take effect the day following his arrest. Holt again refused: 'we are to proceed according to what the law is, and not what it will be'. Parkyns responded that the preamble to the new law noted that the change thereby enacted was simply 'declarative of the common law' because it was a provision that was 'always just and reasonable'; Parkyns reasoned that 'what is just and reasonable tomorrow, sure is just and reasonable today'. Holt stood firm: 'We cannot alter the law till lawmakers do it … it is not a law till the time comes that the parliament hath appointed' (*State trials*, 13.72–3). Holt denied Robert Charnock the same request. 'We are not here in a court of equity, but must proceed according to the rules of law' (ibid., 12.1382). Both men were executed.

Holt proved as ready as most of his contemporaries on the bench to chastise jurors when he disagreed with their verdicts. When the jury hearing one of the first actions of criminal conversation—brought by the duke of Norfolk against John Germaine for adultery with his duchess—Holt approved the jury's finding of adultery but berated them for fining Germaine only 100 marks with costs. In 1700, in another adultery action, Holt rejected the jury's first verdict and scolded them again when their second verdict was little better.

Holt's judgments in a few slavery cases have traditionally been celebrated as much as his conduct of criminal cases, though again the legacy appears more mixed upon closer analysis. Holt proclaimed in 1701, 'as soon as a negro comes into England, he becomes free: one may be a villein in England, but not a slave'. While this applied to England itself, Holt by no means negated laws elsewhere that made chattel slavery legal. As he put it, 'the sale was in Virginia, and, by the laws of that country, negroes are saleable; for the laws of England do not extend to Virginia; being a conquered country their law is what the king pleases' (91 ER 566). Holt recommended that the plaintiff simply amend his declaration in order to make good on his plea of debt for the sale of a slave.

Holt's rulings were less ambiguous in three other areas: commerce, corporations, and administrative law. His impact on commercial law was made largely in the area of negotiable bills of exchange. Posterity has judged him harshly for his judgments in *Clerke* v. *Martin* (92 ER 6) and in *Buller* v. *Crispe* (87 ER 793), condemning his unwillingness to countenance the same procedures for disputed promissory notes as were available for bills of exchange. But Holt's reluctance to accept the imposition of bankers' innovations on the common law arose not only from his precise application of common law, but also from his sense that providing the same remedies in both instances would be to conflate non-commercial with commercial

money transfer and lending practices. Holt feared this would give undue power to creditors by sweeping away the old law of debt with all its procedural protections for debtors. His unwillingness to accept alleged mercantile custom in the handling of notes also arose from his hesitance to innovate from the bench in a matter that would have such important implications for law and commerce. He felt that such innovation could only be made by statute, thus revealing the respect he accorded acts made by king-in-parliament. It has been suggested for this reason that Holt himself promoted the statute of 1704 governing the law of notes and bills by which they came to be handled in a similar fashion.

Elsewhere, Holt clarified principles concerning employer liability, declaring in 1697 that when a servant did some damage, 'it shall be intended, that the servant had authority from his master, it being for his master's benefit' (91 ER 1073). Holt carried this broad vicarious liability into the commercial setting, noting that 'the master at his peril ought to take care what servant he employs; and it is more reasonable, that [the master] should suffer for the cheats of his servant than strangers' (ibid., 91.797). In his judgment in *Coggs* v. *Barnard* of 1703, Holt separated problems associated with bailment from contract and tort by outlining clear categories by which to assess bailees' obligations. 'It is of great consequence, that the law should be settled in this point.' In a rather rare display of modesty, he added, 'I don't know whether I may have settled it, or may not rather have unsettled it' (ibid., 92.114).

In corporation law, Holt's pronouncements built upon extensive experience. Both before and after he rose to the bench he consistently viewed all franchises, including corporate ones, as deriving only from the king. As such, where the liberties granted by the king were injurious to others or were abused by those holding them they could be seized by the king, by judgment either on *scire facias*, or, more commonly and controversially in the 1680s, on *quo warranto*. As Holt put it in 1692, 'a corporation is a trust reposed in several persons for the better ordering and managing the affairs of the city or town which is incorporated, and if that trust be broken, it incurs a forfeiture' (BL, Add. MS 35982, fol. 23).

Holt's 1683 advice that London should surrender its charter arose from this position. Holt reiterated this view of the royal origin of franchises—and thus of the legality of charter surrenders—in the parliamentary debates of 1689–90 concerning London and the other corporations that had lost their charters, and again in Sir James Smith's case of 1691–2. Though politically suspect after 1689 for their use in the 1680s to control the corporations, *quo warranto* was thus preserved by Holt for future use to constrain arbitrary behaviour in corporations. With the Hertford *quo warranto* of 1698–9, Holt made clear what would be the practice in the years ahead: that individuals rather than the corporation as a whole would be liable for misdeeds. Since corporation members acted according to privileges granted by the king, it would continue to be the role of the king's principal court to inspect—by *quo warranto*—the use of those privileges and to oust or punish those who used them wrongly.

Holt's view of individual accountability for wrongs committed by corporations points to the active role he accorded his court in supervising other jurisdictions. In 1699 he grandly proclaimed: 'it is by the common law that this Court will examine if other Courts exceed their jurisdictions' (91 ER 1212). He reinforced the point in the case of *Cardiff Bridge*: 'wherever any new jurisdiction is erected … they are subject to the inspections of this Court by writ of error, or by certiorari and mandamus' (91 ER 135). Holt strengthened his court's broad power to review the work of other tribunals by clarifying procedure in the use of *certiorari* and *mandamus*, by vigorously imposing fines and attachments on those who were slow to return these writs, and by speaking forcefully to questions about where these writs lay. In particular, Holt largely resolved the question about the rationale for granting *mandamus*, a question on which the court had vacillated throughout the previous century: namely whether it was granted to help gain restitution to office conceived as a type of private property, or whether restoration to office and other uses of *mandamus* should arise from the public quality of office and official actions. Holt was clear: *mandamus* lay only where the matter in question concerned the public. By stressing this aspect of local office-holding, he sharpened the distinction between private property and public duties and justified the broad authority over other jurisdictions he accorded his court. For Holt, only parliament acting legislatively stood above such review. No other agencies or courts had 'a sovereign power. Therefore all their acts … are subject to the review of the king's courts, which [acts] are so far valid as they are agreeable to law and right reason' (Hamburger, 2140). Agreement with law and reason were for Holt and his judicial peers to determine.

Though Holt held statutes made by king-in-parliament as the highest law, he was never shy about challenging arbitrary commands of the separate houses when not acting legislatively. Thus he quashed a murder indictment against Charles Knollys after Knollys argued that he was the earl of Banbury and that he had thus been misnamed in the indictment. Knollys's claims to the earldom had been rejected by the House of Lords. The Lords thus considered it a contempt that Holt had dismissed the charge against Knollys on grounds that he was a peer. But when the house demanded an explanation for the decision, Holt grandly refused, stating that 'I gave my judgment according to my conscience' (*State trials*, 12.1179) and that he owed an account to no one for what he did judicially. Rumours circulated that Holt might be imprisoned for this further contempt, but the matter was silently dropped.

The case of *Ashby* v. *White* occasioned a similar conflict with the House of Commons. Matthew Ashby had been denied his vote at Aylesbury's parliamentary election, so he sued Mayor William White and won the verdict. White then appealed to queen's bench, where all the judges, except Holt, reversed the initial result, contending that the Commons alone determined rights of election. Ashby next turned to the House of Lords on a writ of error in 1703–4. Holt's view—that this concerned rights of Englishmen for which only the courts could provide relief, and that the Lords, as the highest court, could proceed on a writ of error—now prevailed. The Commons responded by declaring that by pursuing the matter in the House of Lords Ashby had committed a breach of their privilege.

Disputes only intensified as five more Aylesbury voters sued White too. The Commons summoned all five, examined them, and then imprisoned them for breach of privilege. The Aylesbury voters now resorted to queen's bench for writs of habeas corpus. Again, three of the court's justices refused to bail them because they stood committed by the Commons, which commitments they said were beyond their review. Again, Holt disagreed:

> Neither House of Parliament hath power, no, not both together, to dispose, limit, or diminish the liberty or property of the subject, because by law (which is superior to the actions or determinations of either House) that liberty or property is established, and cannot be diminished or infringed by a less[er] authority than the legislature of the kingdom, which is the Queen, the Lords, and Commons assembled in Parliament.   (Hamburger, 2145)

Holt always recognized that statute made by queen-in-parliament stood above judicial review. But the pronouncements of each house when acting otherwise than by legislation were not beyond the law applied in his court. Holt had challenged both the Commons' claim to determine all rights of election and their power to imprison. Such bold assertions, consistent with his other views as a jurist, failed to sway his contemporaries.

Holt outside court, 1689–1710   Holt's commitments as a jurist in no way diminished his political commitments to the revolution settlement and to the king, who made him a privy councillor—on 26 September 1689—as well as a judge. While he presided in numerous treason trials and investigated various plots, his reports to the privy council often served to constrain those in government who hoped to stretch legal principles or practices to ensnare as many of the regime's enemies as possible. But like justices of previous generations, Holt often used his place on the bench to defend the crown from its critics. As he noted during the 1704 trial of John Tutchin for seditious libel:

> To say that corrupt officers are appointed to administer affairs, is certainly a reflection on the government. If people should not be called to account for possessing the people with an ill opinion of the government, no government can subsist.   (*State trials*, 14.1128)

It is a sign though of Holt's concern for the precise application of law that he then agreed to quash a guilty verdict of which he clearly approved once it was seen that the writ on which Tutchin was tried had been misdated.

The king asked Holt to be lord chancellor in April 1700. He refused, saying he did not know enough of equity to hold the office, though he did serve for one month as one of the commissioners of the great seal until Sir Nathan Wright became lord keeper. In the years following, Holt was troubled by occasional bouts of illness, though this did not prevent his continuing to ride the assize circuits.

In 1708 the queen herself shared fears for his health and implored him to rest. A brief spell in Bath may have helped, and Holt was soon back in his post. Rumours now circulated that he might receive a peerage, but by the winter of 1710 his health declined sharply. He died on 5 March 1710 at his house in Bedford Row, London, and was buried on 20 March in the church at Redgrave, Suffolk, the manor of which he had purchased from Sir Robert Bacon. He was survived by his wife; common report suggested that neither enjoyed the union. Having no children, Holt left the bulk of his estate to his brother Rowland, reserving a £700 per annum rent charge for his widow's maintenance. Throughout, Holt had shown great loyalty to his brother, appointing him as master of king's bench—which occasioned a battle with the duchess of Grafton over the right of appointment—and helping him gain the post of comptroller of the customs.

Holt never lacked confidence in his opinions, which permitted him to hold out against the threats of both houses of parliament at different times. When the countess of Anglesey came to Holt and showed him the bruises inflicted by her husband, Holt imposed a bond of £8000 on the earl to keep the peace. A man of Holt's confidence was also quick to protect his dignity, as in 1696 when he ordered the arrest of the bookseller Brabazon Aylmer for his account of Sir John Friend's trial, which had offended Holt. Holt likewise reprimanded three clergymen in 1699 for their criticism of his condemnation of a coiner at Kingston assizes. No less a figure than Daniel Defoe felt it necessary to publish an apology in 1706 when Holt imposed a £200 bond on him after Defoe wrote a piece that was generally understood to reflect negatively on the chief justice.

A monument in the church at Redgrave, carved by Thomas Green, shows Holt seated in his robes, flanked by Justice and Mercy. For twenty-one years on the bench he had served both virtues, though perhaps in less perfect balance than later hagiographers have ascribed to him. But this is not to diminish his accomplishments. Holt's rulings contributed significantly to the development of the law of commerce, of corporations, and of public administration. His collisions with both Lords and Commons highlighted the dangers of peremptory parliamentary behaviour as parliament moved increasingly to the fore in the constitution. Though he wrote no great treatises, his opinions—available in printed reports as well as in his manuscripts in the British Library and the Harvard law school—show his erudition, the neatness of his mind, and the force of his ideas. Holt not only possessed a comprehensive knowledge of the statutes and reports from which common law was constructed, he also read deeply in the civil law and was well acquainted with the ideas of John Locke and other natural law theorists. Presiding over the kingdom's leading court for two decades after the political transformations wrought in 1688–9, Holt was peculiarly positioned by learning and experience to make a deep and lasting imprint on the law. PAUL D. HALLIDAY

Sources State trials, vols. 7–14 • N. Luttrell, A brief historical relation of state affairs from September 1678 to April 1714, 6 vols. (1857) • HoP, Commons, 1660–90, 2.572 • Foss, Judges • W. N. Welsby, Lives of eminent English judges of the seventeenth and eighteenth centuries (1846) • [J. Rayner], The life of … Sir John Holt (1764) • Sainty, Judges • Sainty, King's counsel • J. H. Baker, An introduction to English legal history, 3rd edn (1990) • Holdsworth, Eng. law • Fifth report, HMC, 4 (1876) • Seventh report, HMC, 6 (1879) • Eighth report, 1, HMC, 7 (1907–9) • The manuscripts of his grace the duke of Rutland, 4 vols., HMC, 24 (1888–1905), vol. 2 • Report on the manuscripts of the marquis of Downshire, 6 vols. in 7, HMC, 75 (1924–95), vol. 1 • Report on the manuscripts of Allan George Finch, 5 vols., HMC, 71 (1913–2003), vols. 2–3 • The manuscripts of the House of Lords, 4 vols., HMC, 17 (1887–94) • CSP dom., 1683–5, 1695–6, 1698, 1700–04 • PRO, KB 21/15–27 • JHL, 13 (1675–81) • E. G. Henderson, Foundations of English administrative law: certiorari and mandamus in the seventeenth century (1963) • P. D. Halliday, Dismembering the body politic: partisan politics in England's towns, 1650–1730 (1998) • J. S. Rogers, The early history of the law of bills and notes (1995) • D. Coquillette, 'Legal ideology and incorporation: the nature of civilian influence on modern Anglo-American commercial law', Boston University Law Review, 67 (1987), 877ff. • P. A. Hamburger, 'Revolution and judicial review: Chief Justice Holt's opinion in City of London v. Wood', Columbia Law Review, 94 (1994), 2091–153 • E. Cruickshanks, 'Ashby v. White: the case of the men of Aylesbury, 1701–4', Party and management in parliament, 1660–1784, ed. C. Jones (1984), 87–103 • D. Lemmings, Gentlemen and barristers: the inns of court and the English bar, 1680–1730 (1990) • J. Levin, The charter controversy in the City of London, 1660–1688, and its consequences (1969) • The autobiography of Sir John Bramston, ed. [Lord Braybrooke], CS, 32 (1845) • The correspondence of Henry Hyde, earl of Clarendon, and of his brother Laurence Hyde, earl of Rochester, ed. S. W. Singer, 2 vols. (1828) • R. Beddard, ed., A kingdom without a king: the journal of the provisional government in the revolution of 1688 (1988) • R. North, The lives of … Francis North … Dudley North … and … John North, new edn, 3 vols. (1826) • H. Horwitz, Parliament, policy and politics in the reign of William III (1977) • Foster, Alum. Oxon. • will, PRO, PROB 11/516, fols. 197v–201v

Archives BL, case book reports, Add. MSS 34125, 35979–35982 • Harvard U., law school, reports • University of Chicago Library, papers regarding administration of his estate | BL, Redgrave Hall papers, Add. MSS 40061–40072

Likenesses R. White, line engraving, 1689 (after G. Kneller), BM • R. van Bleeck, oils, c.1700, NPG [see illus.] • T. Green, statue on monument, Redgrave Church, Suffolk • G. Kneller, oils, Harvard U., law school

Wealth at death land in Suffolk, Berkshire, and other counties: will, PRO, PROB 11/516, fols. 197v–201v

Holt, John (bap. 1743, d. 1801), author, was born at Hattersley, near Mottram in Longdendale, Cheshire, where he was baptized on 24 May 1743, the son of John Holt. He was educated with a view to becoming a dissenting minister, but changed his beliefs and became a member of the Church of England. About 1757 he settled at Walton on the Hill, near Liverpool, where for many years he acted as parish clerk, highway surveyor, and master of the free grammar school. He married in 1767 Elizabeth France, with whom he set up a girls' school. They had no children. He published in 1786–8 Characters of Kings and Queens of England, in three volumes. A few years later he made the agricultural survey of Lancashire, and published his report, a General View of the Agriculture of the County of Lancaster, with Observations on the Means of its Improvement, in 1794. It was reprinted with additions in 1795. A paper 'On the curle in potatoes' procured him the medal of the Society of Arts. He compiled a few books for the use of schools, wrote one or two novels, and collected materials for a history of Liverpool, which he bequeathed to Matthew Gregson. He contributed many papers to the Gentleman's Magazine, and

John Holt (*bap.* 1743, *d.* 1801), by H. Rogers, 1800

for a long period communicated the monthly 'Meteorological diary' to that periodical. He died at Walton on 21 March 1801.   C. W. SUTTON, *rev.* ANITA MCCONNELL

Sources *GM*, 1st ser., 71 (1801), 285–6, 370, 793 · H. Smithers, *Liverpool, its commerce, statistics and institutions; with a history of the cotton trade* (1825), 424 · IGI

Archives Lpool RO, notebook incl. journal of a trip to London

Likenesses H. Rogers, etching, 1800, BM, NPG [*see illus.*]

Holt, John (1777/8–1852). *See under* Rochdale Pioneers (*act.* 1844).

Holt, Joseph (1756x9–1826), Irish nationalist, was born in Ballydonnell, co. Wicklow, the second eldest of six children of John and Mary, of a Church of Ireland farming family of English ancestry. His tombstone records his date of birth as 1756, yet he was baptized in Castlemacadam in July 1759 close to Ballymoneen, where the family moved in the 1780s. His brothers, William, Thomas, and Jonathan, joined him in the ranks of the republican United Irishmen in 1797. When a youth Joseph Holt worked in Bray as a gardener for a magistrate named Sweeney and later received agricultural training in the north of Ireland. From his earliest days Holt professed an interest in military affairs and he was briefly a member of the 32nd foot until recalled home by his parents about 1779. He then joined a patriotic 'volunteer' unit raised in Arklow.

Holt's marriage to the widowed Hester Long in 1782 occasioned a shift to her small but well-appointed farm at Mullinaveigue (Roundwood). He gained work as a wood ranger, bailiff, and billet master; his most important appointment was as deputy aulnager, or cloth assessor, in a county undergoing a massive textile boom. Attendance at fairs and travel throughout adjacent counties gave Holt a reputedly unrivalled knowledge of regional geography which he put to good use during the 1798 rising. He served as a baronial constable, primarily in his native Ballinacor North district, but also in Dublin in the early 1790s. In August 1794 he captured the notorious gaolbreaker Patrick Rogers and his fame as a zealous 'thief taker' was soon unsurpassed in the province of Leinster.

The Holts were heavily engaged in the building industry and Joseph Holt procured several grand jury contracts in the 1790s for road maintenance and bridge building near Roundwood. Financial irregularities embroiled him in disputes with county officials which proved dangerous when Wicklow society became disturbed by political ferment. Contrary to the false impression given in his disingenuous memoirs, Holt was an early, willing, and prominent United Irishman and an elected captain prior to the close of 1797. He may well have come to resent the prevailing barriers to social and commercial advancement. Wicklow activists like Holt succeeded in disaffecting 'protestant, catholic and dissenter' in an area that boasted the largest, rural non-Catholic population outside Ulster. He evidently used his cover as a cloth assessor to recruit in the Wicklow mountains and liaise with city-based committees that later supplied his forces with munitions. Information regarding his activities reached the authorities in early May 1798 and Holt became an armed fugitive in the mountains after his farm was burnt on 10 May.

Holt's first known act as a rebel commander took place on 29 May 1798 when he led 300 men to burn the home of loyalist magistrate Thomas Hugo. They were dispersed by cavalry and did not reform in time to participate in the failed attempt to capture Newtownmountkennedy the following day. This check stalled the rising in the north of the county and Holt was one of several Wicklow militants who ventured south into Wexford to avail of more propitious circumstances. His men were supplied by the commissary of the forces that attacked New Ross on 5 June but evidently did not participate in that mismanaged assault. Holt returned to his native county to await the breakthrough at Arklow on 9 June and, when this failed to materialize, launched a highly destructive attack on loyalist properties around Roundwood on the 14th.

Mountain skirmishes with yeomanry and Reay Highlanders ensued for several days in which both sides enjoyed minor victories of little strategic consequence. Holt's flair for guerrilla-style fighting consolidated his position as the principal leader of insurgent forces in north Wicklow. They joined the more substantial forces from south Wicklow and north Wexford on 24 June and attacked Hacketstown on the 25th. Holt's horse was shot under him in the course of this pyrrhic victory. Much greater success was enjoyed on 30 June, however, when Holt laid a highly effective ambush at Ballyellis in which a large cavalry patrol sustained forty-nine fatalities.

Holt fought again on 2 July at Ballyrahan Hill, co. Wicklow, where nineteen yeomen officers and men were killed, after which he withdrew his faction to the north of the county. This evinced Holt's independent frame of mind and stemmed from his opposition to campaigning once more in Wexford, where terrain, logistics, and enemy strength militated against the insurgents' success. His judgement was soon vindicated and from 5 July harried parties of insurgents made their way towards his camp at Whelp Rock above Blessington. By then the vast majority of active insurgents were availing themselves of a liberal amnesty offered by the newly instated viceroy, Lord Cornwallis. A much diminished hard core of about 4000 relocated to the remote Wicklow mountains.

It was with great reluctance that Holt agreed on 8 July to accompany an expedition from the mountains into the

Joseph Holt (1756x9–1826), by Robert Jacob Hamerton, pubd 1838 (after unknown artist, 1798)

exposed lowlands of Kildare and co. Meath. Insurgent commanders hoped to reignite the virtually dormant rising in the midlands and locate other small fugitive bodies presumed to be hiding there ahead of an attempt on Dublin. A costly repulse at Clonard on 11 July and assault on the camp at Rynville Hill on the 12th put paid to this gambit. Holt singularly distinguished himself by organizing a rear guard action, in which he sustained two minor wounds to his head and arm. Left for dead by the rump mainforce that was defeated at Knightstown on 14 July, he was guided through Dublin city to Wicklow by United Irish sympathizers.

Following the midlands débâcle Holt was the only leader of note willing to fight on. From mid-July he led up to 2000 men in one of the first guerrilla campaigns in Europe and held off vastly superior forces until November. His tactical skill and innovation during this period were remarkable and he took pains to discipline his irregulars to the greatest degree possible. They burnt over 400 loyalist-owned houses and premises to punish local enemies and to deny the army the use of strategic stone buildings. While attrition, factionalism, and the amnesty steadily sapped Holt's ranks, the critical mass necessary for meaningful resistance was sustained by their ideological commitment and expectation of French military assistance. Losses were compensated for by 150 or so militia and army defectors who rallied to Holt in the autumn of 1798.

A major upsurge of fighting in Wicklow in late August coincided with French army landings in Mayo but continued long after their surrender on 8 September. Fatal clashes occurred near Coolgreany, Clone Hill, Mucklagh

Hill, Blessington, Greenan, Keadeen, and Glenmalure. In a rare feat Holt's men captured the defended town of Aughrim on 19 September and occupied it overnight. Their depredations and the political instability they engendered troubled a government that was keen to usher in the Act of Union while presenting a confident face to the French. Illness, wounds, and the prospect of a difficult winter campaign with a price on his head clearly disposed Holt to contemplate capitulation in October 1798. He ultimately accepted a deal brokered by the La Touche family of Delgany after Dublin United Irish leaders informed him that there was no prospect of further French aid. On 10 November 1798 he surrendered to Lord Powerscourt on the understanding that his life would be spared, a concession that outraged many Irish conservatives.

When held in Dublin Castle Holt made statements implicating associates who had engaged in brigandage but refused offers to act against fellow United Irishmen. He was consequently obliged to finance his family's passage to New South Wales on the convict ship *Minerva*. His infant daughter, Marianne, was left in the care of Ann La Touche's school and a second son, Joseph Harrison, was born on board the transport in early 1799. Much to the concern of the colonial authorities, Holt arrived in Sydney as a free man in January 1800. He accepted work as an overseer on Captain William Cox's Brush Farm and evidently enjoyed his considerable status in the sizeable community of Irish political prisoners. Hester Holt, meanwhile, obtained a land grant of 100 acres in her own name and this property was subsequently increased by a number of purchases and exchanges.

Holt frequently ran foul of the colonial administration and was strongly suspected of involvement in the rebellious 'Irish plots' of September and October 1800 which were nipped in the bud. Cox's influence and a short hunger strike in Sydney gaol, however, enabled him to escape severe punishment. Holt was also cleared in December 1803 of plotting to kill Judge-Advocate Richard Atkins but soon afterwards entered into the planning stages of the Castle Hill revolt. On being warned of betrayal Holt pulled out of the plot and fended off rebel efforts to conscript him at Brush Farm on the night of 4 March 1804. He was, nevertheless, deemed culpable and was banished to the feared penal outpost of Norfolk Island. Holt was allowed back to the mainland in March 1806 after a short stay on Van Diemen's Land and from that point his avoidance of sedition paved the way for success as a colonist.

Holt received an absolute pardon in January 1811 and upon settling his affairs he and his family took passage home on the *Isabella*. The ship was wrecked in the Falkland Islands in February 1813 and its passengers marooned until rescued by an American ship, *Nannina*, on 4 April. The ship was almost immediately made a prize of by HMS *Nancy* and it was not until February 1814 that the Holts reached Liverpool, arriving in Dublin on 5 April. Resettlement in Wicklow was out of the question in view of Holt's notoriety and he instead opened a pub in Kevin Street, Dublin. By 1819 police harassment and allegations from rivals that he was an informer became intolerable. Holt sold the business and moved to the coastal suburb of Dún Laoghaire, where he apparently built several houses in York Street. He died there on 16 May 1826 and was buried in a family plot in Carrickbrennan cemetery, Monkstown. He was survived by his wife.

Holt's manuscript autobiography passed from his friend Sir William Betham to the noted folklorist Thomas Crofton Croker, who edited it for publication in 1838. The work proved unpopular with nationalists, who were unaware that Croker had gentrified and censored Holt's narrative and, most seriously, interpolated passages which portrayed its ostensible author as a loyalist apologist. This badly damaged Holt's reputation and that of the Wicklow theatre of the 1798 rising until the 1980s, when his historical importance was reassessed.

RUÁN O'DONNELL

Sources Memoirs of Joseph Holt, general of the Irish rebels in 1798, edited from his original manuscript in the possession of Sir William Betham, ed. T. C. Croker, 2 vols. (1838) · R. O'Donnell, The rebellion in Wicklow, 1798 (1998) · R. O'Donnell, 'General Joseph Holt', Exiles from Erin: convict lives in Ireland and Australia, ed. B. Reece (1991), 27–56 · P. O'Shaughnessy, ed., A rum story: the adventures of Joseph Holt, thirteen years in New South Wales (1800–12) (Sydney, 1988) · P. O'Shaughnessy, ed., Rebellion in Wicklow: General Joseph Holt's personal account of 1798 (1998) · A. M. Whitaker, Unfinished revolution: the United Irishmen in New South Wales, 1800–1810 (Sydney, 1994) · Mitchell L., NSW, Holt MS A2024A
Archives Mitchell L., NSW, autobiography
Likenesses R. J. Hamerton, engraving (after unknown artist, 1798), NPG [see illus.] · oils, priv. coll.
Wealth at death two or three houses in Dublin

Holt, Sir Richard Durning, baronet (1868–1941). See under Holt, Alfred (1829–1911).

Holt, Thomas (1577/8–1624), carpenter, was born in Yorkshire. He was one of the group of northern craftsmen, including the Halifax masons John Akroyd and John Bentley, who were invited to Oxford by Sir Henry Savile, warden of Merton College, at a time when the university was in dispute with the city building crafts, and who undertook some of the most prestigious projects of the first two decades of the seventeenth century. Despite the assumption that he came from Halifax, Holt's birthplace in Yorkshire is unknown and it is likely that he first became associated with Akroyd during building work in the 1590s at either Methley Hall or Howley Hall, Yorkshire, both of which were owned by the Savile family. In May 1609 he was appointed master carpenter for the Fellows Quadrangle at Merton, where Akroyd and Bentley were already engaged on the masonry. Building was completed in 1610 and later that year the team moved on to build the arts end of the Bodleian Library. In August 1611 Holt was working with another group of masons who had come from Somerset to build Wadham College under the direction of William Arnold. He subsequently rejoined Akroyd and Bentley to work on the Schools Quadrangle of the Bodleian which had been commenced in March 1613. In 1618, aged forty, following the deaths of his former partners, he took over the direction of the works and was still engaged on the site after 1621 when he was working on the gates. His other commissions within the university included unspecified contracts for Jesus College and Hart Hall for which payments were outstanding at the time of his death.

Holt's wife, Margaret Facer, probably came from Britwell Salome near Watlington, Oxfordshire, and they established their home and workshop in Oxford at 17 Holywell Street at a house leased from Merton College. Holt died there, comparatively wealthy, on 9 September 1624. He left instructions in his will that his two eldest sons, Thomas and John, should be apprenticed 'as soon as may be' and made provision for three younger children. He was buried in St Cross churchyard, Holywell, where Anthony Wood recorded a monument erected by Margaret which described him as 'Scholarum publicarum architect[us]' (Wood, Survey, 190). This has led to claims that he designed both the Schools Quadrangle and Wadham College, neither of which can be substantiated. Holt was not an architect in the modern sense but rather a skilled and successful carpenter. When he was registered a privileged person of the university in 1618 it was as 'faberlignarius Coll. Novi' (Reg. Oxf., 2/1.404). The reference is to the new college of Wadham, and the conservative hammerbeam roof in the hall can be considered his most visible achievement.

MALCOLM AIRS

Sources T. W. Hanson, 'Halifax builders in Oxford', Transactions of the Halifax Antiquarian Society (1928), 253–317 · A. Wood, Survey of the antiquities of the city of Oxford, ed. A. Clark, 3, OHS, 37 (1899), 190–91 · Colvin, Archs. · Reg. Oxf., 2/1.404 · I. G. Philip, 'The building of the Schools Quadrangle', Oxoniensia, 13 (1948), 39–48 · C. Cole, 'The building of the Tower of Five Orders', Oxoniensia, 33 (1968), 89–107 · VCH Oxfordshire, 3.45–7, 102 · Hist. U. Oxf. 4: 17th-cent. Oxf., 150, 156–7 · will, 23 Nov 1624, U. Oxf., chancellor's court
Wealth at death £196 4s. 2d.; plus debts owed of £37 15s. 0d. and a bond of £10: Hanson, Halifax builders, 312–13

Holt, William (1545–1599), Jesuit, was born on 28 September 1545 at Ashworth, Lancashire. He was privately educated before attending Oxford between 1562 and 1572. He took his BA and MA degrees at Oxford, and then converted to Catholicism. He was at Douai in 1574 to study theology. After his ordination he continued his studies in Rome until 8 November 1578, when he entered the Society of Jesus.

Robert Persons sent Holt in the summer of 1581 to minister to the Catholics of northern England, and subsequently asked him to meet a secular priest, William Watts, for discussions with Catholic lords at Edinburgh in December. Over the next six months Holt learned of the ambitious plans of Lennox and a group of Catholic peers, which required his return to London to brief the Spanish ambassador, Mendoza, in February 1582. He then travelled north to Dalkeith in March to meet Lennox and a Scottish Jesuit, William Crichton. In April the two Jesuits went to France to see William Allen, the duke of Guise, Persons, and other Catholic exiles. At this stage the leaders, hoping for the conversion of the young James VI, were presuming strong financial backing from the pope and Philip II for foreign troops, and an active role for the Catholics of Scotland and England in a vague 'enterprise' in the north to secure their own freedom. Since many problems remained to be resolved, Holt went back to Scotland in June 1582 to visit recusants in safe areas. He was initially assisted by Alexander Gordon, twelfth earl of Sutherland; later he turned to George, fifth Lord Seton, to minister to families in the south-east. William Allen was impressed by this early success.

Aware of Holt's priesthood, the English ambassador, Robert Bowes, arrested him at Leith in March 1583 and brought him to King James, who was at Edinburgh Castle in the hands of the 'Ruthven raiders'. For months a tug-of-war went on between the king and the ambassador, who insisted that Holt be handed over to be tried in England. Since James refused Bowes asked to interrogate him 'intensely'—a euphemism for torture if needed—at which the French ambassador, the sieur de Mainville, protested. Asserting his independence, on 27 April James assured Henri III: 'William Holt will not receive any harm … nor be transported into England, nor placed under any other authority … but mine' (Hicks, 202 n. 5). After James's liberation from the raiders, he adroitly connived at Holt's escape from the castle, to the chagrin of Bowes. Equally valuable for Holt was the personal safe conduct from King James, which enabled him to prolong his stay in Scotland. In June 1584 Persons wrote: 'Holt is very well in Scotland, secured against the ministers by the public protection of the king', and still hopeful for a conversion 'of this young man' (Hicks, 213).

From then on Holt looked for a friendly Scottish peer as a patron, although upon his release Seton advised him to return to France. Instead, Holt went north with George Gordon, sixth earl of Huntly, visiting other Catholic enclaves, and later toured Dumfriesshire with help from John Maxwell, earl of Morton. This itinerary sheds light on the survival of recusancy in Scotland despite the kirk's hostility. As there was no clear leader of the Catholic minority Holt sought a peer with local influence who could protect him. He was convinced of the staunch belief of the peers he met, although some, such as Huntly, practised occasional conformity. Similarly, his personal encounters with James led him to expect a tolerance of Catholics, but the king found it expedient to change this policy. In March 1586 Holt left Scotland for good since Persons required his diplomatic skill in Rome.

For the next year and a half, as rector of the English College, Holt tried to appease a student faction critical of Allen and Persons for their Hispanophile preference and neglect of the imprisoned queen of Scots. Since Holt was well aware of the Scottish scene no quarrels erupted. Then in early 1588 Holt and Joseph Creswell were called to Flanders to serve as chaplains in Parma's army. After the failure of the Armada, Creswell went back to Rome but Holt stayed in Flanders as a military chaplain for ten years. Assisted by Henry Walpole in 1590–91 he paid visits to companies of English, Irish, and Italian soldiers deployed in the siege warfare against the Dutch forces. During these years in service Holt saw the morale of the entire army plummet, due to the failure to provide back pay and vital supplies, so that scattered mutinies occurred as well as desertions. Holt also regularly visited the court of the governor-general in Brussels to seek the arrears of pensions due to English exiles, who were paid from a near empty treasury of the army. At length, in 1596, Holt with two others prepared a list of the names of known pensioners, citing their years of service and the arrears due to them, and commenting on their loyalty to the crown; this was sent to Madrid. However, the crown's bankruptcy, the illness of Philip II, and greater problems elsewhere prevented relief at that time.

Meanwhile Holt wrote, probably at the request of his friend Richard Barret, president of Douai College, a lengthy advisory essay in Latin, entitled 'How the Catholic religion was maintained in England'; it chronicled the survival of the Catholic clergy since 1559 and suggested how their lot might be improved. He stressed that new leadership was needed by appointing an English prelate in Rome, with a second in England to provide confirmation for the faithful, guidance for the clergy, and chrism for the sacraments. However, Clement VIII did not consider it then prudent to nominate prelates from the English clergy, subsequently preferring an archpriest. For those preparing for ordination in the colleges Holt urged closer scrutiny both before admission and during studies, which seemed to aim at reducing the disruptive factions. Lastly, because of the higher numbers of priests and students travelling in Flanders, he advised that a priest should be designated to assist them in their needs, but none could be spared to do it.

Since Holt had become prominent as a leader among the exiles and at the court of Archduke Albert by this time, Charles Paget, widely known as an indefatigable opponent of the Jesuits, sent an accusation with thirty-six charges of abuses of power by Holt to the archduke and the pope. When visiting Rome, Barret was astounded when Clement VIII asked about 'a certain Jesuit father who dominates there and tyrannizes', so that he returned at once to Douai to gather a large number of signatures in support of Holt. The career of Paget, as an informant of the court of Elizabeth and a troublesome divisive presence in Flanders, was familiar to many Catholics, but not to the unsuspecting archduke, who conferred with Oliver Mannaerts, the Jesuit superior, and Juan Baptista de Tassis, a veteran diplomat. After close questioning they exonerated Holt of all charges, but he later commented: 'I never lost even one hour's sleep in the midst of all that tumult'. He continued to serve as a military chaplain with the additional post of vice-prefect of the English Jesuits in Flanders after April 1598. In November he set out for Spain but first visited Milan in January 1599 to meet Archduke Albert. This proved to be his final discussion of the problems of the English in Flanders, for he died about 25 May 1599, probably during an epidemic, at Barcelona, where he was buried, probably that month.

A. J. LOOMIE

Sources T. M. McCoog, *The Society of Jesus in Ireland, Scotland, and England, 1541–1588* (1996) · L. Hicks, ed., *Letters and memorials of Father Robert Persons*, Catholic RS, 39 (1942) · *Letters of William Allen and Richard Barret, 1572–1598*, ed. P. Renold, Catholic RS, 58 (1967) · 'The memoirs of Father Persons', ed. J. H. Pollen, *Miscellanea, II*, Catholic RS, 2 (1906), 12–218 · A. J. Loomie, *The Spanish Elizabethans*

(1963) · H. Foley, ed., *Records of the English province of the Society of Jesus*, 7 vols. in 8 (1875–83) · *The Elizabethan Jesuits: Historia missionis Anglicanae Societatis Jesu (1660) of Henry More*, ed. and trans. F. Edwards (1981) · M. H. B. Sanderson, 'Catholic recusancy in Scotland in the sixteenth century', *Innes Review*, 21 (1970), 87–107 · *The letters and memorials of William, Cardinal Allen (1532–1594)*, ed. T. F. Knox (1882), vol. 2 of *Records of the English Catholics under the penal laws* (1878–82) · G. Parker, *The army of Flanders and the Spanish road, 1567–1659* (1972) · T. M. McCoog, *English and Welsh Jesuits, 1555–1650*, 2 vols., Catholic RS, 74–5 (1994–5) · letters, PRO, SP 12/137, fol. 2, SP 12/268, fol. 79

Archives Archives of the British Province of the Society of Jesus, Stonyhurst College, London, corresp. · Archivum Romanum Societatis Jesu, Rome, corresp.

Holtby, Richard (1552–1640), Jesuit, was born at Fryton, Yorkshire, the second son of Lancelot Holtby of Fryton and Ellen Butler of Nunnington in Ryedale. He went to the University of Cambridge, studying first at Christ's College and then at Gonville and Caius. In 1573 he moved on to Oxford where he studied at Hart Hall, whose principal favoured the old religion. Alexander Briant, the future Jesuit, was there at the time. His next stop was the English College in Douai, where he arrived in August 1577. There he was received into the Roman Catholic church. He was ordained a priest at nearby Cambrai on 29 March 1578. The next year he went on the English mission and he laboured with good results in his home county. In 1581 Edmund Campion paid him a visit. It was Holtby who provided Campion with a suitable place where he could write his *Decem rationes*.

The following year Holtby felt that despite his many years of schooling he needed more expertise in theological controversy. He thought that joining the Jesuits would solve this problem. After Lent 1582 he travelled on horseback to London to find the Jesuit superior. When his search was fruitless he sold his horse and bought a passage to the continent. He was admitted to the Society of Jesus in Verdun on 5 October 1582. After finishing his noviciate he was sent to Pont-à-Mousson to study theology and serve as superior of the Scots College there. He also worked with victims of the plague. He was sent to England in late 1588 or early 1589. By January 1590 he was back in the north, and from that time until his death in 1640 he was one of the bulwarks of the English Catholic church. Holtby was then in his late thirties and a brilliant apostolic career lay ahead of him. He never used his extra years of training to write books of controversial theology, but he was an enthusiastic admirer of the controversial writings of Robert Persons as was apparent from the annual report he sent to Rome in 1609.

Holtby worked closely both with the secular clergy and with the lay Catholics of northern England. With their help he was able to find places where new priests for the English mission could disembark on the Tyne. He also supplied many of these new recruits with horses, cash, and a place to stay. On one occasion he met Henry Garnet, the superior of the mission, and Nicholas Owen in order to devise a way to make better priest's holes. Holtby himself was an excellent carpenter and fashioned many hiding

places. He also used a number of aliases to avoid arrest, including Andrew Ducket, Robert North, and Richard Fetherston.

In 1603 Holtby professed the four Jesuit vows. After the arrest of Henry Garnet in 1604 he succeeded him as superior of the Jesuits on the English mission, and when Garnet was executed in 1606 Holtby was named his successor. He held the office until he was succeeded in 1609 by Robert Jones. A government spy described Holtby as 'a little man with a reddish beard', and he has the reputation for having been one of the toughest missionaries in England. He once escaped some would-be captors by lying quietly in the grass for two days and nights. Holtby also appreciated the key role that Catholic women played in evangelization. He was a close friend of Dorothy Lawson, whose house at St Anthony's near Newcastle was built 'as a centre for the Jesuits in the far north-east' (Bossy, 157). It all began when Lawson, whose husband spent most of his time in London, asked Holtby to give her and her maid an eight-day retreat. Holtby was also a spiritual adviser of Mary Ward, who later founded a religious order for women.

One of Holtby's hobbies was needlework. He made not only vestments and altar cloths, but jerkins and everyday wear. He also wrote two long memoranda concerning the persecution of Roman Catholics in the north of England. He was one of the few priests on the English mission in the early seventeenth century who died in his bed. Not only did he escape the death penalty, he was never jailed. He died in the Durham district between 15 and 25 May 1640.

Thomas H. Clancy

Sources H. Foley, ed., *Records of the English province of the Society of Jesus*, 3 (1878), 3–16 · J. Morris, ed., *The troubles of our Catholic forefathers related by themselves*, 3 (1877), 118–230 [memoranda by Holtby] · J. Bossy, *The English Catholic community, 1570–1850* (1975) · B. Basset, *The English Jesuits, from Campion to Martindale* (1967) · T. M. McCoog, ed., *Monumenta Angliae*, 1–2 (1992)

Holtby, Winifred (1898–1935), novelist and feminist reformer, was born at Rudston, Yorkshire, on 23 June 1898, the younger daughter of David Holtby, a prosperous farmer, and his wife, Alice Winn, who served as alderman in the East Riding. An independent and precocious child, Holtby was encouraged in her literary ambitions while at Queen Margaret's School, Scarborough (1909–16). After a year as a probationer nurse in a London nursing home, she went up to Somerville College, Oxford, in 1917, but she left in the following year to join the Women's Army Auxiliary Corps, and served in France until August 1919 as a hostel forewoman.

Returning to Somerville that October, Holtby encountered in her modern history tutorials the woman who was to become her closest friend and colleague—Vera Brittain. Initial hostility gave way to a deep understanding in which their literary talent and ambition, similarity of experience (especially in war service), and leftist social and political views allowed them to help and encourage each other creatively. Physically and temperamentally

Winifred Holtby (1898–1935), by F. Howard Lewis, 1936

they were very different, however: Holtby tall, fair, confident, gregarious, and equable; Brittain small, dark, pretty, shy, and volatile. These differences complicated and strengthened their friendship.

They left Oxford in 1921, with second-class degrees, and shared a flat in London while establishing parallel careers. Holtby's lively, stylish, witty articles and reviews soon gained her a high reputation as a journalist. She became a regular contributor (and from 1926 a director) of the feminist journal *Time and Tide*, and a friend of its founder and editor, Margaret Haig Thomas, Viscountess Rhondda. Joining Rhondda's Six Point Group, Holtby and Brittain quickly established themselves as influential young feminists. In her article 'Feminism divided', 1926, Holtby wrote:

> Personally, I am a feminist ... because I dislike everything that feminism implies. ... I want to be about the work in which my real interests lie ... But while ... injustice is done and opportunity denied to the great majority of women, I shall have to be a feminist.

Holtby and Brittain also joined the League of Nations Union, lecturing widely on world peace, and in 1922 toured Europe to investigate post-war conditions. Both joined the Labour Party. Both published novels in 1923 and 1924. During 1926 Holtby visited South Africa for over five months to speak on behalf of the League of Nations Union. Appalled by the racism she observed there, she worked energetically against it for the rest of her life, giving moral and financial support to the black trade union movement. On her return to London she was invited by Brittain, who was now married, to join a household soon

further enlivened by two children, one of them Shirley Williams, to whom Holtby became a beloved 'aunt'. The two women had a wide circle of friends and acquaintances, many prominent as writers, feminists, and socialists.

Extremely generous and dutiful, Holtby sacrificed much time and energy to her friends and family. Yet her literary career of less than fifteen years was notably prolific. Her first two novels—*Anderby Wold* (1923) and *The Crowded Street* (1924)—established a recurrent theme: the quest for independence, and its cost. Realistic regional novels, they incorporated satire, an element which strengthened in her next three novels, *The Land of Green Ginger* (1927), *Poor Caroline* (1931), and *Mandoa, Mandoa!* (1934). Increasingly ambitious, all these novels are unpretentiously direct and witty in style, imaginative in using Holtby's own experience, and firmly focused on social and political problems. The latter two novels also moved away from Yorkshire, to London and an imagined Abyssinia respectively. Among the other seven books she published are a fine pioneering critical study of *Virginia Woolf* (1932); *The Astonishing Island* (1933), a satire; a feminist treatise, *Women and a Changing Civilisation* (1934); *Truth is not Sober* (1934), a collection of short stories; and a collection of poems, *The Frozen Earth* (1935). A play attacking the rise of fascism, *Take Back Your Freedom*, was published posthumously, as were a further volume of short stories and two selections from her lively correspondence.

During the last four years of her life Holtby fought gallantly against the depredations of renal sclerosis (Bright's disease). Before she completed *Mandoa, Mandoa!* she had been warned that her time was short, and her final novel was begun in the knowledge that she might not be able to complete it. Her courage and consideration were so remarkable that even close friends had no idea, until near the end, that she was seriously ill. Equally remarkable were the ambition and determination that pushed *South Riding* (published posthumously in 1936 and awarded the James Tait Black memorial prize) to completion. Her final novel is also her masterpiece. Returning to a Yorkshire setting, Holtby wrote a rich regional study of social change and local government, drawing to some extent on her mother's experiences as the first woman alderman in the East Riding. Like George Eliot's *Middlemarch*, Holtby's novel weaves together a large number of characters and several plots to represent a complex society; illness and death are repeatedly present, but balanced against a characteristically vigorous optimism; and the quest for individual independence and fulfilment—that long-established theme—is here given its fullest and most impressive expression.

On her deathbed in a London nursing home at 23 Devonshire Street, Marylebone, Winifred Holtby was betrothed to the man she loved, Harry Pearson. She died on 29 September 1935, and was buried in Yorkshire at Rudston churchyard on 2 October 1935, one day after a memorial service in St Martin-in-the-Fields, London.

ALAN BISHOP

Sources V. Brittain, *Testament of friendship* (1940) · G. Handley-Taylor, *Winifred Holtby* (1955) · P. Berry and A. G. Bishop, eds., *Testament of a generation* (1985) · V. Brittain, *Chronicle of friendship*, ed. A. G. Bishop (1986) · P. Berry and M. Bostridge, *Vera Brittain: a life* (1990) · P. Berry, 'Holtby, Winifred', *The Europa biographical dictionary of British women*, ed. A. Crawford and others (1983) · personal knowledge (2004) · CGPLA Eng. & Wales (1936)
Archives BL, corresp. with Society of Authors, Add. MS 56726 · Bridlington Library, collection · Fisk University Library and Media Center, Nashville, Tennessee, corresp., literary MSS, and papers · Hull Central Library, corresp. and papers | Bodl. RH, letters to Arthur Creech Jones · JRL, corresp. with Robert Donat · McMaster University, Hamilton, Ontario, Vera Brittain Archive · U. Reading L., letters to Bodley Head Ltd · UCL, letters to Arnold Bennett · University of Cape Town Library, Cape Town, corresp. with W. G. Ballinger
Likenesses F. H. Lewis, oils, 1936 (after photograph), Somerville College, Oxford [see illus.]
Wealth at death £24,730 17s. 5d.: probate, 27 Jan 1936, CGPLA Eng. & Wales

Holte, John. *See* Holt, John (d. 1504).

Holte, Sir Thomas, first baronet (1570/71–1654), landowner and royalist sympathizer, was the eldest surviving son of Edward Holte (d. 1592) and his wife, Dorothy Ferrers (d. 1594). At the time of his birth the Holtes had been in possession of estates at Duddeston and Aston in Warwickshire for over a century. On 9 February 1588 Holte matriculated, aged seventeen, at Magdalen College, Oxford, but did not apparently graduate. He was, however, later described as 'a gentleman well read in most parts of learning, and versed in several languages' (Dugdale, 2.872). In 1590 he was admitted to the Inner Temple.

Succeeding his father upon the latter's death on 3 February 1592, Holte substantially increased the family estates through his marriage to Grace, daughter of William Bradburne of Hough, Derbyshire, perhaps in 1598 or 1599. In 1598 he bought the rectory of Aston and its appended properties for £1870. The following year he served as sheriff of Warwickshire. On 18 April 1603 he was knighted by James I during his passage from Scotland to Westminster. In addition to his estates in Warwickshire, Holte acquired or rented a house in Islington, Middlesex, where he baptized a son, Richard, in 1604 and buried a daughter, Katherine, in 1605. In 1606 he was accused of brutally murdering a man employed by him as a cook. Neither he, nor anyone else, was brought to trial, and the victim has remained nameless. Yet the Victorian historian of the family of Holte reluctantly concluded that there is 'a very strong degree of probability' that Sir Thomas was guilty of the killing, which took place at Duddeston, and reconstructed the likeliest sequence of events thus:

> Sir Thomas, when returning from hunting, in the course of conversation, laid a wager to some amount as to the punctuality of his cook, who most unfortunately, for once was behind time. Enraged at the jeers of his companions, he hastened into the kitchen, and seizing the first article at hand, avenged himself on his domestic. (Davidson, 24–5)

Holte afterwards reportedly sought to conceal the deed, and sued for slander William Ascrick or Ascherig of Birmingham, whom he charged with publicly claiming on 20 December 1605 that:

> Sir Thomas took a cleaver and hit his cook with the same cleaver upon the head and clave his head that one side there fell upon one of his shoulders and the other side on the other shoulder; and this I will verify to be true. (Davidson, 25)

At the Warwick assizes in July 1608 Ascrick was found guilty and damages of £30 were awarded against him. Ascrick fought back and launched an appeal in king's bench that autumn. There the judges found for him, concluding that, whatever the implication of his words, Ascrick had not actually directly accused Holte of murder but merely of splitting the cook's skull in two, and the man might have recovered from his wounds: 'it is not averred that the cook was killed, but argumentative slander ought to be direct … notwithstanding such wounding, the party may yet be living; and then it is but trespass. Wherefore it is adjudged for the defendant' (*Reports*, 184). By this device the court, faced with a dispute between two pillars of Warwickshire society, was able simultaneously to acquit Ascrick and avoid ruining Holte, who was himself a JP. The cook's failure to demonstrate the remarkable recuperative powers on which the eminent judges based their decision seems not to have caused any further legal difficulties for Holte (though it may explain why he took the precaution of obtaining a blanket pardon from Charles I in 1626 for offences committed in the previous reign). Local tradition had it that Holte was forced, in a symbolic punishment for his crime, to wear a blood-red hand on his coat of arms. The truth is less edifying. Holte was created a baronet on 25 November 1612 for the standard price of £1095, a sum supposedly intended towards the defence of Ulster; all baronets, accordingly, wore the red hand of Ulster on their shields. The emblem was a badge of honour, not of shame.

Holte prospered exceedingly and his income has been estimated as in excess of £1000 per annum. In 1618 he began the building of Aston Hall. The architect John Thorpe had a hand in the elaborate design of a house which 'for beauty and state much exceedeth any in these parts' (Dugdale, 2.872); the building was occupied in 1631 but was not completed until four years later. The portrait of Holte which survives at Aston Hall duly portrays him the lord of his domain, in the deer park created out of enclosed open fields in 1621, with the house in the background. Holte continued to act as a JP in his local division, served as a subsidy commissioner in the 1620s, and was a commissioner for the distraint of knighthood in Hemlingford hundred in 1630–32. He served as a deputy lieutenant in 1638–9. In religion he was a moderate Calvinist.

Holte's marriage to Grace Bradburne produced fifteen children, of whom only a daughter, Grace (d. 1677), who married Sir Richard *Shuckburgh, survived him. After the death of his first wife Holte married Anne (d. 1697), daughter of Sir Edward Littleton of Pillaton Hall, Staffordshire; they had no children. In his dealings with his eldest son Holte acted the part of an implacable patriarch. When Edward (1600–1643) fell in love with Elizabeth King, the daughter of John *King (d. 1621), bishop of London, Holte forbade the match, and when the couple married anyway, he threatened to disinherit Edward. It took the intervention of Charles I to make Holte withdraw his threat: in August 1627 the king wrote to Holte urging, 'The interest we have in all our subjects, and especially the families of the best quality, giveth us cause to interfere in this, while a severe proceeding against your son would endanger the overthrow of your house' (Colville, 424). Charles further promised to make provision for Edward if his father provided poorly for him, and it is reported that he later kept his word by appointing the young man as a groom of his bedchamber. Henry *King, Elizabeth's brother, recalled in 1653 that 'the unnatural usage of an implacable father denied them competent means whereby they might subsist' (Davidson, 22). Typically Holte proved able to have the last word by outliving his heir. Edward was wounded at the battle of Edgehill and, though he recovered sufficiently to take part in the defence of Oxford, he died there of a fever on 28 August 1643. Sir Thomas, in his will of 1650, left not a penny to the widow. He was somewhat more mellow towards his granddaughter Katherine, to whom he left £300, 'although she hath undone herself by her marriage without consent which her husband shall have nothing to do with' (Hughes, 38).

At the outbreak of the civil war Holte himself was at first uncommitted in the struggle for allegiance in the west midlands between the parliamentarian Lord Brooke and the royalist earl of Northampton in the summer of 1642. By late August, however, he was reported to have joined other royalists at Lichfield. In mid-October, just before the battle of Edgehill, the king stayed at Aston Hall for two days. On 12 December 1643, at Holte's request, a royalist garrison was put into the house; on 28 December it fell to an overwhelming parliamentarian force.

Holte was sequestered by the county committee but discharged by the Lords and Commons in December 1646. The following March, however, he was threatened with renewed sequestration and in October 1648 this was put into effect. In 1650 Holte applied to compound for his sequestered properties, pleading that 'having had houses in Birmingham worth £1000 burned by the king's horses, all his goods taken, so that he had neither a bed nor a shirt left, to the loss of £6000 and being 80 years old his fine may be set at 1/10th' (Green, 4.2556–7). The committee for compounding were perhaps aware that in 1647 the bedless and shirtless Holte had acquired from Viscount Hereford the manor of Erdington, Warwickshire. On 3 February 1652 his fine was set at £4492 2s. 4d., which was paid within three weeks and the estate discharged. Holte died in mid-November 1654 but was not buried until 14 December at Aston. By his will he assigned £300 for the building and endowment of an almshouse at Aston for the maintenance of ten aged poor, five of each sex. He also provided for a monument to the memory of himself and his second wife in Aston church. His baronetcy and the bulk of his estate passed to Edward's eldest son, Robert.

STEPHEN WRIGHT

Sources A. Davidson, *The Holtes of Aston* (1854) · A. Hughes, *Politics, society and civil war in Warwickshire, 1620–1660* (1987) · will, PRO, PROB 11/249, sig. 336 · M. A. E. Green, ed., *Calendar of the proceedings of the committee for compounding … 1643–1660*, 4, PRO (1892) · W. Dugdale, *The antiquities of Warwickshire illustrated*, rev. W. Thomas, 2nd edn, 2 vols. (1730) · *VCH Warwickshire*, vols. 2, 7 · Foster, *Alum. Oxon.* · *Reports of Sir George Croke, knight: formerly one of the justices of the courts of king's bench and common pleas*, ed. and trans. H. Grimston, 4th edn, ed. T. Leach, 4 vols. (1790–92) · *The life, diary, and correspondence of Sir William Dugdale*, ed. W. Hamper (1827) · W. H. Cooke, ed., *Students admitted to the Inner Temple, 1547–1660* [1878] · F. L. Colvile, *The worthies of Warwickshire who lived between 1500 and 1800* [1870] · E. Kimber and R. Johnson, *The baronetage of England*, 3 vols. (1771), 1.131 · J. H. Gleason, *The justices of the peace in England, 1558 to 1640* (1969) · V. M. Larminie, *Wealth, kinship and culture: the seventeenth-century Newdigates of Arbury and their world*, Royal Historical Society Studies in History, 72 (1995)

Archives Birm. CA, papers
Likenesses oils, Birmingham Museums and Art Gallery
Wealth at death £1631—apparently moveable possessions: Davidson, *The Holtes*, 27–8; will, PRO, PROB 11/249, sig. 336

Holttum, (Richard) Eric (1895–1990), botanist, was born on 20 July 1895 in Linton, Cambridgeshire, the eldest in the family of two sons and one daughter of Richard Holttum, grocer and owner of a village general store, and his wife, Florence Bradley. His parents being Quakers, he was educated at the Friends' school, Saffron Walden, Essex, and then at Bootham School, York. He wrote in 1980 that his Quaker schooling 'conveyed a sense of responsibility and of respect for other people based on some appreciation of the spiritual basis of all living'. His long life of public service and research had that foundation. In 1914 he entered St John's College, Cambridge, with a scholarship to study botany, physics, and chemistry. He obtained a first class in part one of the natural sciences tripos in 1916. The horror of the First World War led him to join in 1916 the Friends' Ambulance Unit, in which he served with the French army on the western front. In 1919 he received the Croix de Guerre. He returned to Cambridge, gaining first-class honours in part two of the tripos (botany) in 1920 and was awarded the university's Frank Smart prize.

In 1920 Professor Albert C. Seward appointed Holttum as his assistant and as a junior demonstrator in botany at Cambridge, and together they went to Greenland in 1921 to investigate in fossil deposits its former tropical flora. Holttum was appointed assistant director of the botanic gardens, Singapore, in 1922. The Singapore herbarium was in a chaotic state and the general state of fern taxonomy was likewise unsatisfactory, with current classifications inconsistent, genera ill-defined, and specific descriptions inadequate. Holttum's research to remedy this led to his extensive fundamental pteridological publications. In 1925 he became director of the Singapore Botanic Gardens. An indefatigable field botanist, he was also a far-sighted, energetic administrator, intent on both botanical investigation and the encouragement of gardening in Malaya. Holttum used the method of raising orchid seedlings on nutrient media in glass test-tubes and flasks to raise new orchid hybrids. Out of his enterprise grew the important orchid-growing industry of Malaya. In 1927 he married an artist, Ursula (d. 1987), daughter of

John William Massey, gentleman farmer at Finchingfield, Essex. They had two daughters.

After the Japanese conquest of Singapore in July 1942, Holttum's fate and that of the Singapore Botanic Gardens were determined by Emperor Hirohito's instruction that such scientific institutions be maintained. Professor Hidezo Tanakadate ordered Holttum and the assistant director to continue their work. Later in 1942 Professor Kwan Koriba took over the administration. He treated Holttum 'with much kindness', as Holttum gratefully acknowledged, and for the next three years encouraged his scientific research on orchids, gingers, ferns, and bamboos, for which he previously had had too little time. Conscious, however, of the hardships of internees while he himself was exceptionally privileged, Holttum requested to be interned also, but Koriba ordered him to continue with research. Nevertheless his isolation caused him acute mental distress, near to utter despair. After the Japanese surrender in September 1945 Holttum returned to England to recuperate. He then resumed direction of the neglected Singapore Botanic Gardens, resigning in 1949 to become the first professor of botany in the newly founded University of Singapore, where he proved to be an enthusiastic and inspiring teacher. Never wasting time, he published *Plant Life in Malaya* (1954), *Gardening in the Lowlands of Malaya* (1953), and *Orchids of Malaya* (1953). With his department established and thriving, Holttum retired in 1954, returned to England, settled at Kew, and worked in the herbarium of the Royal Botanic Gardens, Kew, principally on tropical ferns, until his death. His *Ferns of Malaya* (1955) was the prelude to major work on the ferns of Malaya, Indonesia, New Guinea, and the Philippines for the *Flora Malesiana* (section Pteridophyta). About 110 of his 500 or more publications on botany and horticulture relate to ferns, and all manifest his meticulous attention to detail, originality, and breadth of outlook.

Holttum was made an honorary Cambridge ScD (1951) and an honorary DSc at Singapore (1954); he was awarded the Victoria medal of honour of the Royal Horticultural Society (1972), the gold medal of the American Orchid Society (1963), and the gold medal of the Linnean Society of London (1964). The University of Malaya, which created him an honorary DSc in 1949, awards an Eric Holttum medal to an outstanding student of botany. At least twenty-three botanical specific names with the epithet *holttumi* or *holttumianus* commemorate him.

A lifelong member of the Society of Friends, Holttum joined the society's Brentford and Isleworth meeting in 1955. His spoken ministry there had its background in an extensive acquaintance with religious and philosophical literature, deep spiritual insight, and much thought. He published in 1975 *A Personal Christology* (reprinted 1995). His religious views also found expression in Quaker magazines and journals. From 1962 onwards he became increasingly deaf, and was ultimately completely deaf, although his eyesight, patience, and intellect remained unimpaired to the end. He had a modest, unassuming manner, and was helpful to all. Physically he was short and sparse in build, with sharp and alert features, a high forehead, and ginger hair. Holttum died from pneumonia on 18 September 1990 in Queen Mary's Hospital, Roehampton, London. WILLIAM T. STEARN, rev.

Sources *Flora Malesiana Bulletin*, 30 (1975), 2477–500 [autobiography and list of publications] · *Kew Bulletin*, 41 (1986), 484–9 · *The Friend* (25 Jan 1991) · W. T. Stearn, 'Richard Eric Holttum … botanist and religious thinker', *The Linnean*, 7/3 (1991), 12–18 · *The Times* (25 Sept 1990) · *CGPLA Eng. & Wales* (1991) · personal knowledge (1996) · private information (1996)
Archives RBG Kew, letters and notes about Bougainvillea; scientific papers
Wealth at death £155,015: probate, 4 Jan 1991, *CGPLA Eng. & Wales*

Holtzapffel, Charles (1806–1847), mechanical engineer and technical writer, was the son of a German immigrant, John Jacob Holtzapffel, who, in 1787, settled in London as a tool and lathe maker. In addition to a thorough training in workshop practice, Holtzapffel received a good general education and, by assiduous study and practice, became a skilled mechanical engineer. He was married and had children. In 1838 he published his *New system of scales of equal parts applicable to various purposes of engineering, architecture and general science*, followed by *List of Scales of Equal Parts* suitable for his system. His principal work, *Turning and mechanical manipulation, intended as a work of general reference and practical instruction on the lathe*, was designed to fill five volumes, but only three, published in 1843, were completed. The final two volumes were completed by his son, John J. Holtzapffel. The family business was Holtzapffel & Co., 64 Charing Cross Road, London. They made lathes and other machines, and published a number of works in connection with woodworking. They also marketed an amateur printing press, about which they published a number of booklets.

In his writing, Holtzapffel throughout displayed a masterly knowledge of technical art and of the scientific principles underlying it. He was a member of the Institution of Civil Engineers and a member of its council. He was for a time chairman of the mechanics' committee of the Society of Arts. He died on 11 April 1847. He was survived by his wife and family. R. E. ANDERSON, rev. R. C. COX

Sources *PICE*, 7 (1848), 14–15 · *GM*, 2nd ser., 28 (1847), 213
Archives BL, letters to Charles Babbage, Add. MSS 37189–37194
Wealth at death widow and young family inherited business

Holwell, John (*b.* 1649, *d.* in or after 1686), astrologer and mathematician, born in London on 24 November 1649, was probably the John Holwell, son of Thomas and Catherine Holwell, who was baptized at St James's, Clerkenwell, on 28 November 1649. According to a family tradition he was descended from the Holwells of Holwell House, near Tavistock, Devon; his father and grandfather were allegedly engaged in Penruddock's plot in 1655, fell in the royalist cause, and forfeited the family estates. His namesake, a John Holwell of Sampford, was indeed sequestered in 1655, and in 1652 a Captain John Holwell, perhaps the same person, appears as giving information against alleged papists to the officers of the Commonwealth. The connection between this John Holwell and John Holwell the astrologer is unclear.

Holwell studied astrology under Henry Coley, and achieved considerable notoriety through his bold political predictions. His first work in this vein was *A New Prophecy … of the Blazing Star* (1679), in the form of a letter on the comet that had appeared in April 1677. Holwell put forward a Paracelsian view of comets as 'composed by the Spirits of the Air', at God's command, 'to forewarn this Evil World'. His text hinted at another great fire of London, 'by the hands of an Enemy' (ibid., 4), and the overthrow of the French monarchy. In his major astrological work, *Catastrophe mundi, or, Europe's many Mutations until the Year 1701* (1682), he explored the likely effects of the triple conjunction of Saturn and Jupiter in the fiery trigon in 1682–3. Holwell explained that the two great planets entered the fiery triplicity (the three 'hot' houses of the zodiac), where their conjunctions had the greatest effect, only after intervals of 794 years. Extraordinary results might therefore be expected. His work drew on Richard Edlin's study of the 1663 conjunction, and also borrowed heavily from William Lilly and from the *De mundi catastrophe* (1625), by the Italian astrologer Giovanni Spina. Sheltering behind these authors Holwell felt free to publish sensational prophecies with an apocalyptic flavour. Some were provocative, including one (borrowed from Lilly) that God would curb 'Monarchical Pomp'. Holwell explained that the tyrannical behaviour of rulers, from kings to justices of the peace, would drive their subjects to rebel and call them to account, an inflammatory comment in the wake of the exclusion crisis. These remarks led to his indictment for seditious libel before the Middlesex quarter sessions in May 1683. Abandoning an initial plea of not guilty he confessed the charge at his trial on 9 July, and was fined.

The *Catastrophe* also promised that popery could never triumph in England, and included highly dramatic prophecies on the Ottomans, a controversial subject in the context of their invasion of Austria. Holwell predicted that the Ottoman armies would sweep through Germany, France, Spain, and Italy, capturing the emperor and toppling the pope. After years of upheaval and misery a 'great Conquerour' would suddenly appear in 1699 (*Catastrophe*, 90), bringing universal peace and paving the way for the conversion of both Turks and Jews. In *An Appendix*, published six months later, he printed a nativity of Louis XIV, predicting that the French king was likely to die soon or be driven out by the Turks or his own enraged subjects. Holwell's predictions made him a highly controversial figure. His claims on the Turkish threat were answered in print by several rivals, including John Gadbury, John Merrifield, and Henry Krabtree.

Holwell was married, and had a son and a daughter. When he published his *Catastrophe* in 1682 he was living on the east side of Spitalfields, near the Red Lion, by Dorset Street, and he advertised his services and tuition there in 'astronomy, navigation, dyalling, surveying, geography, perspective, and gunnery'. He achieved considerable prominence in these less febrile activities, especially in surveying. In 1678 he published *A Sure Guide to the Practical Surveyor*, dedicated to John Wildman, politician and one-time leveller, which gave detailed instructions on surveying land, roads, and rivers. He used the instruments of Walter Hayes, the foremost instrument maker of the time. Earlier, he had been one of the team working with John Ogilby on his pioneering surveys of English roads, and he used some of this material in his book. In pressing his credentials as a surveyor he confidently asserted that he had 'the most experience of any man in England' (ibid.). In 1684 he was employed to survey disputed property in Wapping for Thomas Neale, and gave evidence in the celebrated trial that followed between Neale and Lady Ivy, heard by Lord Chief Justice Jeffreys. He also published *Trigonometry Made Easie* (1685), referring readers to the works of Henry Gellibrand and Isaac Newton for more advanced studies. His *Clavis horologiae, or, A Key to the Whole Art of Dialling* was issued in 1686, by public subscription; the subscribers included the diallist and surveyor Robert Baker and the king's hydrographer, John Seller, who also shared Holwell's radical politics and had been implicated in the republican Tong plot of 1662.

Holwell's skill as a practical mathematician commanded respect; he could refer in 1686 to Edmond Halley as his very good and very loving friend. However, he was never far from controversy. In the month of James II's accession, February 1685, an anonymous correspondent warned the privy council of rumours circulating among the 'fanatics' of an imminent great battle on a Yorkshire moor between the duke of York (James II) and Monmouth, which would result in James's death. The report implicated Holwell with these predictions, hinting that he had calculated the nativities of both Charles II and James II, and had surveyed the Yorkshire moor in question, and made cryptic statements about it. According to a family tradition published in 1799, James II's government sent Holwell to America late in 1685 (thus after Monmouth's execution) to survey and map New York, with secret orders that he was not to be allowed to return. He is said to have died there very suddenly, after drinking poisoned coffee, soon after completing the work. Holwell has not been traced after 1686, and it is quite possible that he died about that time while on a surveying mission in the New World.

Holwell's Predictions (1690), published in Cambridge, Massachusetts, and *John Holwell's Strange and Wonderful Prophesies* (1696), both drawn from his *Catastrophe mundi*, show that his name lived on. Holwell left a widow whose name is unknown, a son, and a daughter, and his estate was divided equally among them. His son Zephaniah (d. 1729), a London timber merchant, was the father of John Zephaniah Holwell, scholar and governor of Bengal.

BERNARD CAPP

Sources E. G. R. Taylor, *The mathematical practitioners of Tudor and Stuart England* (1954) • B. S. Capp, *Astrology and the popular press: English almanacs, 1500–1800* (1979) • 'An account of the late Governor Holwell', *Asiatic Annual Register*, 1 (1799), 25–6 • Bodl. Oxf., MSS Ashmole 237, 240, 436, 475 • J. C. Jeaffreson, ed., *Middlesex county records*, Middlesex County RS, 4 (1892) • *CSP dom.* • parish register (baptism), Clerkenwell, St James, 28 Nov 1649 • 'The famous tryal in B.R. between Thomas Neale, Esq., and the late Lady Theodosia Ivy, on 4th of June 1684', 1696, GL

Holwell, John Zephaniah (1711–1798), East India Company servant, was born on 17 September 1711 in Dublin, the son of Zephaniah Holwell (*d.* 1729), timber merchant of London, and his wife, Sarah Bott, and grandson of the astrologer John *Holwell. He was educated at Richmond Green, Surrey, and Iselmond, near Rotterdam, and was then employed as a clerk by a banker and ship's husband in Rotterdam. His enthusiasm for this work waned and he left for Ireland before being summoned to London by his father, where he embarked upon a career in surgery and was apprenticed to a surgeon in Southwark. He was later placed under Andrew Cooper, senior surgeon at Guy's Hospital. In 1732 he sailed for India as surgeon's mate on an Indiaman. Following his arrival in Calcutta he travelled to the Middle East, serving as surgeon on ships sailing to the Persian Gulf and to Jiddah and Mocha. In Bengal he acted briefly as surgeon to the East India Company's factory at Dacca before settling more permanently in Calcutta in late 1736. There he became assistant surgeon to the hospital in 1740 and principal physician and surgeon to the presidency in 1746. During this period he also became involved in civic affairs, being elected as an alderman in the mayor's court and as mayor in 1747 and 1748. Intellectually Holwell found much stimulation in India; his travels gave him the opportunity to learn Arabic, in which he became quite fluent, and he acquired knowledge of other languages. He also began to research Hindu theology.

In 1750 Holwell left India, but he was back in Bengal by early July 1752. During his brief stay in England he had drawn on his knowledge and experience to convince the company's directors of the need to reform the post of *zamindar* in Calcutta. The *zamindar*, appointed by the company since 1698, was responsible for revenue collection and law and order, and Holwell had been nominated to that office by the directors, who had placed him twelfth in the Fort William council with the stipulation that he rise no higher. Following his arrival in Bengal Holwell enquired into the state of the revenues and investigated the activities of Govindaram Mitra, who had been involved in the management of the revenues for over thirty years and who was suspected of having committed frauds. His efforts were warmly praised by the directors, who applauded the increase in revenues which had been achieved without the introduction of new duties, and the restriction on his promotion within the council was removed. Holwell's work was, however, met with much less enthusiasm by other members of the council, who were slow to act on his findings.

In June 1756 the nawab of Bengal, Siraj ud-Daula, attacked Calcutta, and Fort William was abandoned by Governor Drake and other senior company servants, leaving Holwell and others to their fate. It was agreed that Holwell should take charge, and he proceeded to lead the defence of the fort, but was eventually compelled to surrender to the nawab's forces and, along with the remnants of the garrison, was placed under arrest. On the night of 20 June he and others were incarcerated in a cell within the fort known as the Black Hole; this event was to become infamous, mainly as a result of propaganda put about by Holwell. Two years later an account by him was published which claimed that 146 individuals were crammed into the cell and that of these 123 died (*A genuine narrative of the deplorable deaths of the English gentlemen and others, who were suffocated in the Black Hole*); research has, however, suggested that those imprisoned numbered sixty-four and that twenty-one survived. Some years later Holwell erected an obelisk in Calcutta in memory of those who had died. After his release from the cell Holwell was taken with three others to Murshidabad, where they were held prisoner until the middle of July; he then rejoined Drake (whose authority as governor he eventually accepted) and other council members, and plans were made for the recapture of Calcutta, which was achieved by Robert Clive in January 1757.

Holwell remained in Bengal until February 1757, when he returned to England. Before he left he wrote the directors a lengthy narrative of events in which he was critical of the conduct of Drake and the other senior company servants during the attack on Calcutta; such remarks were the product of his own ambition and did nothing for his personal popularity in Bengal. He referred to his incarceration in the Black Hole as 'a night of horrors I will not attempt to describe, as they bar all description' (Holwell to directors, 30 Nov 1756, ed. Datta, 1088). Once in England he was able to provide the directors with first-hand accounts of events in Bengal, to advise them on the reorganization of their affairs there, and to cultivate a following among them which included John Payne, the chairman of the company. In November 1757 he was appointed to fourth place in the council and governor by fourfold rotation, but after two revisions of these arrangements his interest suffered when, at the election of directors in April 1758, his supporters lost power. In consequence he was reduced to ninth place in the council and was therefore distanced from the governorship.

In November 1758 Holwell, having returned to Bengal, took his seat in the council, which was now presided over by Clive, whose victory over Siraj ud-Daula at Plassey over a year earlier had been followed by the accession of Mir Jafar as nawab of Bengal. He was again involved in administrative reform, being appointed to a committee which considered orders from the directors which dealt with various matters including the post of *zamindar*. His position in the council was altered dramatically by the departure of a large number of councillors, and when Clive resigned the governorship in January 1760 it was Holwell who succeeded him until Henry Vansittart became governor in July of that year. Holwell's administration coincided with growing dissatisfaction with Mir Jafar and he devised a plan whereby the nawab would surrender power to his son-in-law Mir Kasim but retain his title; this scheme was implemented by Vansittart in October 1760 with the result that Mir Jafar resigned completely and Mir Kasim became nawab. It is likely that Holwell was motivated by a desire for personal financial reward in his dealings with Mir Kasim; he was certainly promised £20,000 by him at some point, of which at least £5000 was paid.

Some claimed he was worth £96,000 upon his departure from office.

Holwell returned to England in 1761; for a time his country residence was Chilton Lodge, near Hungerford, Berkshire. The rest of his life was taken up with literary pursuits; during the 1760s he published several defences of his conduct in India, notably *Important Facts Regarding the East India Company's Affairs in Bengal from 1752 to 1760* (1764). Of greater significance were his historical and theological works, whose importance lay in their popular appeal rather than their content; his *Interesting Historical Events, Relative to the Provinces of Bengal and the Empire of Indostan* (3 vols., 1765–71) was translated into German and French and earned him praise from Voltaire. A Christian with eccentric beliefs and an advocate of vegetarianism, Holwell also issued writings on other subjects including smallpox inoculation and crime prevention.

Holwell was twice married and three children survived him. He died at his home in Pinner, Middlesex, on 5 November 1798. D. L. PRIOR

Sources court minutes, committee of correspondence records, Bengal public consultations, mayor's court records, BL OIOC • K. K. Datta and others, eds., *Fort William–India House correspondence*, 1–2 (1957–8) • *Asiatic Annual Register*, 1 (1799) • L. S. Sutherland, *The East India Company in eighteenth century politics* (1952) • P. J. Marshall, *East Indian fortunes: the British in Bengal in the eighteenth century* (1976) • P. J. Marshall, *The British discovery of Hinduism in the eighteenth century* (1970) • C. A. Bayly, ed., *The raj: India and the British, 1600–1947* (1990) [exhibition catalogue, NPG, 19 Oct 1990 – 17 March 1991] • J. M. Holzman, *The nabobs in England* (1926) • M. Bence-Jones, *Clive of India* (1974) • M. Edwardes, *Plassey: the founding of an empire* (1969) • J. P. Losty, *Calcutta, city of palaces* (1990) • *The Times* (16 Nov 1798)
Archives BL OIOC, corresp., MSS Eur. Orme
Likenesses platinotype print (after attrib. Reynolds), BL OIOC
Wealth at death see will, PRO, PROB 11/1319, 118

Holwell, William (1725/6–1798), Church of England clergyman and writer, was baptized on 11 May 1726 in Exeter Cathedral, the elder son of William Holwell (*bap.* 1699) of Exeter and his wife, Ann (*d.* 1783), daughter of Bishop Ofspring *Blackall (*d.* 1716). Holwell's father died early; his mother remarried on 26 December 1738.

On 26 June 1740 Holwell was nominated to a canoneer studentship at Christ Church, Oxford, by his stepfather Peter Foulkes (1676–1747), canon of that house; he matriculated on 17 December 1741, aged fifteen, and took his BA in 1745 and MA in 1748. He became a lecturer, a tutor, censor, librarian, and catechist at Christ Church, and was university proctor in 1758; he took his BD in 1760. His pupil William Petty (1737–1805), future earl of Shelburne, patronizingly called him 'a narrow-minded tutor', but 'not without learning' (Fitzmaurice, 17, 18). Holwell's learning was first published in editions of Aristotle's *Rhetoric* (1759) and of selected literary essays by Dionysius of Halicarnassus (1766).

Holwell was instituted as vicar of Thornbury, Gloucestershire, a Christ Church living, on 11 January 1762. By the early 1770s he was married to a woman named Martha; by 1775 he was a chaplain-in-ordinary to King George III; he became a prebendary of Exeter on 26 June 1776. Horace Walpole describes his encounter, in August 1774, with the obsequious Holwell and his lean wife, suckling a child, after he had mistaken the vicarage for the sexton's mean cottage, but Walpole probably improved the tale, for, according to Holwell's own account, the living in 1778 was more than £150 and improvable; according to his successor in 1800 it was worth £250; and Holwell was able, in his will of 12 December 1796, to dispose of over £5300 together with evidently valuable household goods.

At Thornbury, Holwell became a compiler and popularizer, with a selection of 'beauties' from Homer's *Iliad* (1775), a corresponding selection from Alexander Pope's Homer translation (1775), and a *Mythological Dictionary* (1793), extracted from Bryant's *New System … of Ancient Mythology* (1774–6) and rearranged alphabetically for the benefit of 'the young beginner' (preface). Holwell later contributed to Ralph Bigland's *Historical … Collections* on Gloucestershire, and in 1789–90 read and corrected proofs of John Wilkes's edition of Theophrastus's *Characters*. His letters to Wilkes unconvincingly imply that Holwell too was a radical. Holwell died on 13 February 1798 at Thornbury. He was survived by his wife and two children, Edward Ofspring Holwell (1773/4–1832) and Charlotte Eleonora. William Holwell *Carr (1758–1830) was his nephew. JAMES SAMBROOK

Sources *GM*, 1st ser., 68 (1798), 259 • private information (2004) [J. Curthoys, archivist, Christ Church, Oxf.] • will, PRO, PROB 11/1310, sig. 482 • *Fasti Angl.* (Hardy), 1.430, 3.499 • Walpole, *Corr.*, vol. 1, pp. 345 • R. Bigland, *Historical, monumental and genealogical collections, relative to the county of Gloucester*, ed. B. Frith, 3 (1992), 1313 • E. G. W. Bill, *Education at Christ Church, Oxford, 1660–1800* (1988), 53, 127, 284n., 345 • *Life of William, earl of Shelburne … with extracts from his papers and correspondence*, ed. E. G. P. Fitzmaurice, 1 (1875), 17–19 • Foster, *Alum. Oxon.* • *The registers of baptisms, marriages, and burials of the city of Exeter*, 1, ed. W. U. Reynell-Upham and H. Tapley-Soper, Devon and Cornwall RS (1910)
Archives BL, letters to J. Wilkes, Add. MSS 30873, fols. 193, 202–8, 30874, fols. 6, 8, 12, 19, 20, 25
Wealth at death over £5300; plus silver, books, pictures, etc.: will, PRO, PROB 11/1310, sig. 482

Holworthy, James (*bap.* 1780, *d.* 1841), watercolour painter, was baptized in Market Bosworth in Leicestershire on 26 December 1780, the son of James Holworthy, a monumental stone mason, and his wife, Mary. As a young man Holworthy moved to London where he lived at 4 Mount Street, Berkeley Square; Joseph Farington recorded in his journals that in May 1804 another Leicestershire artist, John Glover, was lodging with Holworthy and instructing him. Holworthy also taught drawing; in a self-portrait as a young man entitled *The Drawing Master* in the Paul Mellon collection he sits sketching out of doors between two female pupils. He exhibited at the Royal Academy in 1803 and 1804, and showed five drawings at the first exhibition of the recently formed Society of Painters in Water Colours in 1805. Holworthy continued to exhibit with the society until 1813. In the National Art Library there are papers relating to his membership, including a letter of 13 February 1815 from Copley Fielding stating that other members 'could not divest themselves of the idea that Mr Holworthy was only an absent and not a "ci devant" member'. In all he showed only twenty-nine drawings, mostly Welsh views and castles, and priced up to £9. His work is similar to Glover's. Martin Hardie called him the 'least significant' of the first members of the society. Monkhouse, a contemporary critic, described Holworthy as 'an elegant artist, very skilful in the use of Indian Ink but not venturing far in the colour process' (Hardie, 2.134). The Victoria and Albert Museum has two watercolours and three sketchbooks by him. Holworthy's low output as a painter must in part have been as a result of defective eyesight but he was sufficiently wealthy not to have to earn a living.

On 15 October 1821 Holworthy married Anne Wright (1777–1842) in Hastings; she was the daughter of Richard Wright, a doctor with a considerable practice in Derby and elder brother of the artist Joseph Wright of Derby. They lived at Greenhill House in Derby with Anne's elder sister Hannah. However, Holworthy was ambitious to be a country gentleman and, according to a notebook kept by him (now in Derby Local Studies Library), Holworthy decided after a visit to the Peak District in autumn 1823 that he wished to move into the country: 'I have often decided that there are only two places to live—one in London and the other in the country far from the hurry of the world'; in 1824 he bought the Brookfield estate at Hathersage in Derbyshire, 'a district uncultivated and uncivilised', with 1401 acres, a grouse moor, farm houses, and a substantial house, which he rebuilt.

Holworthy was a close friend of J. M. W. Turner, some of whose most intimate surviving letters are to Holworthy. Turner stayed at his house at 29 York Buildings, New Road, in St Marylebone, when his own was being repaired in 1820. Two drawings, *Mountainous Landscape* and *Coast Scene Sunrise*, given by Turner in 1824, a *Liber Studiorum*, and a snuff box 'made out of Lava from Mount Vesuvius' used by Turner as a pallet are listed in the Brookfield sale catalogue of March 1868; the catalogue also includes 5000 engravings, 4000 books, and paintings by Watteau (formerly in the collection of Sir Joshua Reynolds), Chardin, and Joseph Wright, as well as oil and watercolour landscapes by Holworthy and a watercolour by Glover.

Holworthy was appointed a justice of the peace for Derbyshire in July 1827, but in May the following year in *R. v. Holworthy*, held in Westminster Hall, he was accused of irregularities in the conviction of three men for poaching partridges; the lord chief justice dismissed the case. Towards the end of his life Holworthy brought an action against the *Sheffield Iris* over an alleged libel in an anonymous letter. He died from bronchitis at 3 St John Street, Gray's Inn, London, on 13 June 1841 aged sixty-one, and was buried at Kensal Green cemetery on 19 June. His wife died on 28 November 1842 aged sixty-five, and was buried among the Wright family graves at St Alkmund's Church, Derby. There were no children. Brookfield continued to be occupied by Hannah Wright until her death in 1867 after which the estate was sold.   SIMON FENWICK

Sources R. C. Timms, 'James Holworthy (1780–1841)', *OWCS Club*, 58, 9–13 · MSS notes by Timms, New Walk Museum and Art Gallery, Leicester · Brookfield sale catalogue (1868) · M. Hardie, *Water-colour painting in Britain*, ed. D. Snelgrove, J. Mayne, and B. Taylor, 2: *The Romantic period* (1967), 134 · will, PRO, PROB 11/1985, sig. 635 · Anne Holworthy's will, PRO, PROB 11/1985, sig. 639 · Farington, *Diary* · W. Bemrose, *The life and works of Joseph Wright, A.R.A., commonly called 'Wright of Derby'* (1885), 4

Archives Derbys. RO, corresp. | Derbys. RO, notebook; *R. v. Holworthy* case papers; Hannah Wright MSS; Brookfield sale catalogue · V&A NAL, corresp. relating to Society of Painters in Water Colours, London

Likenesses J. Holworthy, self-portrait (as young man in *The drawing master*), Yale U. CBA, Paul Mellon collection; repro. in Hardie, *Water-colour painting*

Holyday [Holiday], **Barten** (1593–1661), Church of England clergyman and poet, was born in the parish of All Saints, Oxford, the son of Thomas Holiday, a tailor. He was educated at St Paul's School, London, before going to Christ Church, Oxford, in 1605, perhaps as a chorister, matriculating on 13 December. He graduated BA on 14 May 1612 and proceeded MA on 15 June 1615, already being recognized as a gifted orator and poet. He was ordained and given two benefices in Oxford diocese. In 1616 he published his well-received verse translation of Persius's *Satires*, noted for its smoothness; by 1650 it had reached its fifth edition. From 1617 to 1621 he served as praelector in rhetoric and philosophy and, while a student of Christ Church, he produced *Technogamia, or, The Marriages of the Arts*, which was acted in the hall on 13 February 1617 and published in 1618. It was intended to be a comedy in which characters representing the range of studies in the university argue for their positions, but the wordy laboured speeches included allusions that were not always grasped by the audience.

In 1618 Holyday made a more favourable impression when he went to Spain as chaplain to Sir Francis Stewart, who accompanied Count Gondomar on his return home after many years as ambassador. Three years later, on 26 August 1621, *Technogamia* was performed before James I at Woodstock, Oxfordshire, but the king was not impressed. He found it tedious and had to be persuaded to stay to the end. Some epigrams on the Woodstock performance were circulated by Cambridge wits, and Holyday's Oxford friends, including Henry King, later bishop of Chichester, had to come to his support.

In 1623 Holyday became vicar of Ashleworth, Gloucestershire, and Brize Norton, Oxfordshire, and in 1625 archdeacon of Oxford. Sermons preached at Paul's Cross on 5 August 1623 and 24 March 1625 and three sermons delivered in Oxford on the passion, resurrection, and ascension of Christ were published in 1626. These were the first of many that appeared in his lifetime, their subjects ranging from examinations of texts taken from the Old and New Testaments to considerations of motives for a godly life and the nature of faith. On 14 August 1628 Holyday married Elizabeth Wickham at Garsington, Oxfordshire; they had three sons and two daughters. In 1633 his *Philosophiae polito-barbarae specimen*, a Latin tractate, was published, and he continued to write verse, typical being his commendatory verses prefixed to the 1640 edition of Jonson's poems and his comic epitaph on the death of the proctor Edward Wood in 1655. By 1638 he was rector of Emmington, with Iffley and Littlemore, Oxfordshire.

Holyday remained in Oxford when it became the royalist headquarters in the autumn of 1642, and it was probably about this time that he became a chaplain to the king. On 1 November he was created DD by royal command. According to his later account, he was sequestered in 1646; on 17 June 1647 the committee for plundered ministers referred articles against him to the committee for compounding. He apparently remained in Oxfordshire, and on 9 August 1649, as a widower, married at Radley, just over the border in Berkshire, Margaret, *née* Sheppard (*d.* 1661), widow of Francis Dewey, minister of Chippenham, Wiltshire; they had a son, Barten, and a daughter. By 1652 Holyday was curate of Iffley, and on 31 October 1655 he was admitted to the rectory of Chilton, Berkshire. Continuing his writing, he published an edition of Horace in 1652, *Of the Nature of Faith* (1654), and *Motives to a Good Life* (1657).

In 1660 Holyday returned to Oxford and the position of archdeacon, living in Iffley. He might well have become a bishop had he not been thought to have had too great a sense of his own importance. In 1661 his *Survey of the World*, a substantial poetic work in ten books, possibly drafted earlier in his life, was published in Oxford. In his preface and elsewhere, taking an overview of the world and using iambic pentameter couplets, Holyday reveals an alertness to the beauty of a landscape through the combination of nature and art. He died at Iffley on 2 October 1661 and was buried three days later in Christ Church, Oxford. His widow survived him for only a few weeks, dying on 16 December.   F. D. A. BURNS

Sources Foster, *Alum. Oxon.* · Wood, *Ath. Oxon.*, new edn, 3.520 · M. J. C. Cavanagh, introduction, in B. Holyday, *Technogamia* (1942) · *Walker rev.*, 297 · *IGI* [parish register of Radley] · *Remarks and collections of Thomas Hearne*, ed. C. E. Doble and others, 1, OHS, 2 (1885), 267

Holy Island, Robert of [Robert de Insula] (*d.* 1283), bishop of Durham, took his name from Holy Island off the coast of Northumberland. His origins were humble, and his mother, described as a poor little woman (*paupercula*), was later said to have been discomforted by the provision of servants made for her by her son when bishop. Having become a monk of Durham, he was sacrist between 1265 and 1269, and prior of the highly favoured dependent cell at Finchale by 1272. He represented his community in the outside world on a number of occasions, at the royal court in 1265, in borrowing from Sienese merchants and repaying them in London in 1266, and as a proctor to the legatine council in London in 1268 and to the second Council of Lyons in 1274. He was elected bishop on 24 September 1274, the temporalities were restored on 8 November, and he was consecrated on 9 December at York. Among other benefactions to Durham's cell at Finchale he appropriated the church of Bishop Middleham, co. Durham, in 1278, to increase the number of monks at the cell by six. Synodal statutes are extant with an ascription to Bishop Robert and dated 1276; largely derived from older statutes, they relate almost entirely to matters of tithe and ecclesiastical censures.

In 1277 Bishop Robert complained of Scottish encroachments on the march, presumably into the northern part of the palatinate of Durham, along the south bank of the Tweed. After the issue was raised in parliament, and then in the royal council, Edward I appointed a commission of oyer and terminer in February 1279 to deal with the disputes between the bishop and the Scots, but this apparently came to nothing. While the bishop was in the vicinity of the border in March 1281 Archbishop William de Wickwane of York (*d.* 1285) announced his intention of conducting a visitation of the diocese of Durham, starting with the cathedral priory; the Durham monks immediately resolved to resist the archbishop, and their bishop, who was already in dispute with Wickwane, joined them, although possibly with less uncompromising fervour. By the time the archbishop arrived in Durham on 25 June to find the gates closed against him, the bishop had apparently left for the papal curia, and he was not immediately involved in the subsequent complicated litigation. During the early months of 1283 Antony (I) Bek, acting on the authority of Edward I, achieved a temporary compromise, but this collapsed when Bishop Robert died shortly afterwards, and the dispute resumed with increased violence. Technically it was never finally resolved, so qualifying as the longest law case on record, with Archbishop William Temple (*d.* 1944) echoing Wickwane's claims in 1939.

The Lanercost chronicle reports that Robert kept two monkeys 'in the fashion of modern prelates to provide some relief from anxieties' (*Chronicon de Lanercost*, 114). He died at Bishop Middleham on 7 June 1283 and was buried in the cathedral chapter house on 10 June. His heavy borrowings from the cathedral priory left him very substantially in debt when he died. His brother Henry was one of his executors.   A. J. PIPER

Sources *Chancery records* · *Historiae Dunelmensis scriptores tres: Gaufridus de Coldingham, Robertus de Graystanes, et Willielmus de Chambre*, ed. J. Raine, SurtS, 9 (1839) · F. Barlow, ed., *Durham annals and documents of the thirteenth century*, SurtS, 155 (1945) · Durham Cath. CL, Loc.XIV:1k, Loc.II:7, Loc.I:60, Misc. Ch. 4109f, 1.2. Archid.Dunelm.7 · R. Brentano, *York metropolitan jurisdiction and papal judges delegate, 1279–1296* (1959) · D. Whitelock, M. Brett, and C. N. L. Brooke, eds., *Councils and synods with other documents relating to the English church, 871–1204*, 2 (1981), 817–20 · J. Stevenson, ed., *Chronicon de Lanercost, 1201–1346*, Bannatyne Club, 65 (1839)
Archives Durham Cath. CL
Likenesses engraving, 1838 (after seal), repro. in R. Surtees, *History and antiquities of the County Palatine of Durham*, 4 (1840) · seal (as bishop of Durham), repro. in W. Greenwell and C. H. Hunter Blair, *Catalogue of the seals in the treasury of the dean and chapter of Durham*, 2 (1911–21), 449–50, pl. 49, no. 3124

Holy Maid of Kent, the. *See* Barton, Elizabeth (*c.*1506–1534).

Holyman, John (1495–1558), bishop of Bristol, was a native of Cuddington, near Haddenham in Buckinghamshire. He was admitted a scholar at Winchester College in 1506, aged eleven, and then went to New College, Oxford, where, in 1512, he became a fellow. He graduated BA in 1514, MA in 1518, and BTh in 1526. He left his college about 1526, and became rector of Colerne, Wiltshire, but for the sake of books and literary society settled in Exeter College, Oxford, where he was charged for the rent of a room in 1525–6 and 1534–5. There he soon acquired a great reputation for learning and sanctity, and was university preacher on Easter day in both 1527 and 1530. In 1530 he took the degree of DTh. A letter of December that year from Hugh Farindon, abbot of St Mary's, Reading, in support of Holyman's supplication that a sermon preached by him at Paul's Cross, London, might count in place of a statutory sermon preached in St Mary's, Oxford, was misunderstood by Anthony Wood as suggesting that Holyman had become a monk of that abbey. He opposed the divorce of Henry VIII from Queen Catherine, advocating the validity of their marriage by writing and preaching and being described as 'an enemy to the King's cause' in a letter of Richard Croke to Thomas Cromwell of 26 January 1534 (*LP Henry VIII*, 7, no. 101). He was obliged in consequence to remove to Handborough, near Woodstock, of which he was rector, living partly there and partly in Exeter College. He became vicar of Wing, Buckinghamshire, on 3 May 1546.

Following Mary's accession Holyman was promoted to the bishopric of Bristol, and was consecrated in the chapel of the bishop of London on 18 November 1554. The temporalities were restored ten days later. Little is known of his episcopate, from which no register survives, but Holyman, who was firmly committed to the Catholic cause, appears to have been a satisfactory bishop. He was included with John White and James Brooks in a commission to try Ridley and Latimer for heresy, and took part at Oxford in the disputation with Cranmer (1554) and in the trial of Bishop Hooper. He appears to have shown no great zeal for prosecuting heretics, and few burnings took place in his diocese. He is not mentioned by Foxe as present when William Dalby, his chancellor, sent three men to the stake at Bristol for their religious beliefs. Anthony Wood attributes a number of works to him, including 'Tractatus contra doctrinam M. Lutheri' and 'Defensio matrimonii Reginae Catharinae cum Rege Henrico octavo'. These are not known to have survived.

Holyman died on 20 December 1558 and was buried not in his cathedral but in the chancel of Handborough church. By his will, dated 4 June 1558, and proved on 16 February 1559, he bequeathed £20 to New College, Oxford, and to Winchester College the writings of St Augustine, St Jerome, St Cyprian, and other works of church history, which were afterwards chained in the library.

B. H. BLACKER, rev. KENNETH CARLETON

Sources *Fasti Angl.* (Hardy), vol. 1 • Emden, *Oxf.*, 4.295–6 • *LP Henry VIII*, 7, no. 101 • *VCH Gloucestershire*, vol. 2 • *The acts and monuments of John Foxe*, ed. S. R. Cattley, 8 vols. (1837–41) • Wood, *Ath. Oxon.*, new edn, 1.275–6 • *Fasti Angl., 1541–1857*, [Bristol]
Wealth at death £20 to New College, Oxford, books to Winchester College: Emden, *Oxf.*, 4.295–6

Holyoake, Austin (1826–1874), freethought printer and publisher, was born on 27 October 1826 in Birmingham into an artisan household, the seventh child and fifth son of George Holyoake (1790–1853), a printer, and Catherine Groves (1792–1867), a horn-button maker. Influenced by his older brother George Jacob *Holyoake he became an Owenite, and from 1842 worked as a printer on radical papers in Birmingham and then London. In October 1847 he took charge of the printing of G. J. Holyoake's weekly periodical, *The Reasoner*, at 54 Exmouth Street, Clerkenwell. Two years later the brothers went into partnership, operating from James Watson's premises at 3 Queen's Head Passage until 1853, when they acquired their own premises at 147 Fleet Street. Here, with Austin responsible for the printing and, from 1858, the publishing, they attempted to give leadership to the freethought movement. In 1862 the venture failed but two years later Austin revived the business, trading as Austin & Co. at 17 Johnson's Court, Fleet Street. He was also active in radicalism during these years, with a reputation for fairmindedness and much in demand as a chairman of meetings. He was a member of the Association for the Repeal of the Taxes on Knowledge and the last printer in England to be prosecuted under the Newspaper Stamp Act, repealed in 1855. He was also on the recruiting committee for the Garibaldi Legion (1860) and a member of the Reform League (1866). From 1866 until his death he was sub-editor of Bradlaugh's *National Reformer* and a vice-president and first treasurer of the National Secular Society, founded in 1866. From the mid-1850s he was a convinced atheist and published over a dozen tracts and lectures, including *Thoughts on Atheism, or, Can Man by Searching Find out God?* (1870) and a neo-Malthusean pamphlet, *Large or Small Families? On which Side Lies the Balance of Comfort?* (1870). He edited with Charles Watts *The Secularist's Manual of Songs and Ceremonies* (1871), to which he contributed secular marriage and burial services. In 1871 he presided over the formation of a republican committee in London, and two years later published his lecture *Would a Republican Form of Government be Suitable to England?*

Austin Holyoake married twice. His first wife, whom he met at the Owenite John Street Institute, was Lucy, daughter of Robert Pettigrew, a tailor. They were married on 5 August 1851, but she died in childbirth on 23 September 1855, aged twenty-seven years. His second wife, Jane, the daughter of James Baker, a coach-maker, was a professional singer, performing as Alice Austin. They were married on 20 November 1858, and had one son, Percy (b. 1861), and one daughter. After Holyoake's death, his widow married Theodore Wright and became a well-known London actress.

Austin Holyoake's importance in radical freethought has been overshadowed by that of his elder brother, George Jacob, but he was an easier personality than the latter and his hard work behind the scenes did much both to launch the secularist movement and to smooth the difficult relations between his brother and Charles Bradlaugh. By 1872 his health was failing and consumption was diagnosed. He died on 10 April 1874 at 17 Johnson's Court, Fleet Street, and was buried a week later in Highgate cemetery, with Charles Watts reading Austin's own burial service over the grave.   EDWARD ROYLE

Sources G. J. Holyoake, *National Reformer* (10 May 1874) • A. Holyoake, 'Thoughts in the sick room', *National Reformer* (19 April 1874) •

G. J. Holyoake, *In memoriam. Austin Holyoake, died April the 10th, 1874* (1874) • A. Holyoake, 'Republican committees—what qualifies for membership?', *Eastern Post* (15 April 1871) • C. M. Davies, 'An atheist's funeral', *Heterodox London, or, Phases of free thought in the metropolis*, 2 vols. (1874), 397–408 [an account of Holyoake's funeral, repr. from the *Sun*, 25 April 1874] • H. T. Law, *Secular Chronicle* (24 Feb 1878) • E. Royle, *Victorian infidels: the origins of the British secularist movement, 1791–1866* (1974) • E. Royle, *Radicals, secularists and republicans: popular freethought in Britain, 1866–1915* (1980) • *The Reasoner* (22 Dec 1847) • J. M. Wheeler, *A biographical dictionary of freethinkers of all ages and nations* (1889), 175 • m. cert. • d. cert. • *CGPLA Eng. & Wales* (1874)

Archives Co-operative Union, Holyoake House, Manchester, G. J. Holyoake MSS

Likenesses engraving, repro. in Law, *Secular Chronicle*

Wealth at death under £450: probate, 2 June 1874, *CGPLA Eng. & Wales*

Holyoake, Francis (1566×73–1653), Church of England clergyman and lexicographer, was born at Nether Whitacre, Warwickshire. He was admitted to Queen's College, Oxford, as a commoner in 1582, but is not recorded as being admitted to a degree. Wood claims that he had been a schoolteacher. However, Holyoake commenced study at Cambridge as a sizar at Emmanuel College on 1 April 1594, and moved to Peterhouse in Lent 1596. He was admitted BA in 1599 and was ordained priest on 29 June 1601, when he was noted as aged twenty-eight.

In 1604 Holyoake became curate of Thames Ditton, and then rector of Southam, Warwickshire, a living in the gift of the crown, where he lived until his death. At some point he married Judith, the daughter of Edmund Dalby of Brookhampton in Combrook, Warwickshire. A son, **Thomas Holyoake** (1616–1675), was born on 26 December 1616, probably at Stoneythorpe Hall in Long Itchington, and baptized by his father on 12 January 1617 at Southam.

Holyoake's first venture into lexicography, *Riders Dictionarie, Corrected and Augmented* (1606), was a revision of John Rider's *Bibliotheca scholastica* (1589). Holyoake took Rider's Latin index and created a genuine double dictionary by borrowing freely from Thomas Thomas's successful *Dictionarium linguae Latinae et Anglicanae* (1587). The rights to Rider's dictionary had recently passed from a London stationer, Cuthbert Burby, to a powerful London booktrade syndicate, and the work immediately became embroiled in the ongoing tussle between the Cambridge University printer, John Legate, and the Stationers' Company in London, since Thomas's dictionary had been published in Cambridge. A 'reprehensible agreement' (McKitterick, 119) was struck over the production of these competing works; editions of both dictionaries were published in 1606.

Holyoake's second work was entitled *A Sermon of Obedience Especially unto Authoritie Ecclesiasticall*, preached and published in 1610. The work was dedicated to Sir C. Throckmorton, and was reprinted in 1613. Holyoake's next version of Rider, entitled *Riders Dictionarie Corrected, and with the Addition of about Five Hundred Words Enriched*, only slightly augmented, appeared in 1612. It included an etymological component, largely taken from Ambrogio

Calepino's *Dictionarium*. The next edition of the dictionary, in 1617, added some Greek terms, many again from Thomas.

Holyoake was elected to the southern convocation in 1625. His dictionary was again published in 1626 as *Dictionarium etymologicum Latinum*, but this time with augmentation and many improvements by Nicholas Gray. Undeterred by the grant in 1621 of a new patent for the Thomas dictionary to the Cambridge publisher John Legate junior, Holyoake himself produced a new edition in 1627, and further editions during Holyoake's lifetime appeared in 1633, 1639, and 1648. He was granted a fourteen-year patent for his dictionary in 1635.

Holyoake's life was, however, abruptly disrupted in his old age by the civil war. Royalist sympathies led to his home being raided by parliamentary forces in 1642. A roundhead subaltern, Nehemiah Walton, describes Southam as 'a very malignant town, both minister and people', relating that 'we pillaged the minister, and tooke from him a drum and severall armes' (*Archeologia*, 316). Holyoake was also described as of 'very evil and dissolute conversation' (Tennant, 36). His son's petition at the Restoration for compensation claimed that a servant was killed and the death of his mother hastened, and that the family was reduced to living on charity.

Holyoake had his estate, valued at £300 per annum, sequestrated on 22 April 1647 for inciting his parishioners and keeping arms in his house; he was permitted to retain one-fifth of his income, as was normal in cases of deprivation, in view of his age. There were also disputes with parishioners and sequestrators over the felling of timber on the glebe in 1646, and an action for trespass in 1648. Nevertheless, a new edition of the dictionary duly appeared in 1648. At this time Holyoake also presented a manuscript to Queen's College Library entitled 'Hugguccionis, seu Huguitionis, Pisani, ep. Ferrariensis, lexicon alphabeticum'.

Francis Holyoake was buried in St Mary's, Warwick, in 1653, when his age was given as eighty-six, and his monument was placed in the north transept. His character is suggested both by his staunch royalism and by his refusal to desist from blatant and repeated plagiarism of Thomas's dictionary.

Holyoake's son Thomas went to Coventry grammar school and then Queen's College, Oxford; having commenced in Michaelmas term 1632, he graduated BA in 1636 and MA in 1639. He became a chaplain of Queen's in 1637, and in 1641 was presented to the living of Birdingbury, Warwickshire. At the outbreak of the civil war he was commissioned to lead an infantry company consisting largely of scholars. The king rewarded him for his services with a doctorate of divinity, a title used in his will. Holyoake was licensed by the university in 1647 to practise medicine following the surrender of the garrison at Oxford in 1646.

On 27 July 1660 Holyoake petitioned the king for restitution of the harm done by the sequestration of his father's estate, and asked to be presented to the rectory of Tatenhill, Staffordshire, pointing out the family's difficulties, and that he had had to care for his aged father. Another petition followed, requesting confirmation of the grant of the living of Nuneaton, in which he complained about the anti-royalist sermons of the incumbent, Richard Pyke. He petitioned a third time in October 1660, requesting presentation to both parishes. However, he was presented to Whitnash, near Warwick, and was also made a prebendary of the collegiate church of Wolverhampton. In 1674 he received the donative of Breamore, Hampshire. He died there of a fever on 10 June 1675. His will, which was proved on 5 June 1678, provided amply for his family since he had acquired property in both Warwickshire and Breamore, which he left to his wife, Anne, and his sons. He was also able to leave £200 to both his daughters. Thomas Holyoake revised and enlarged his father's dictionary, but the work was published posthumously by his own eldest son, Charles, in 1677.   R. W. McConchie

Sources DNB · De W. T. Starnes, *Renaissance dictionaries: English–Latin and Latin–English* (1954) · W. Camden, *The visitation of the county of Warwick in the year 1619*, ed. J. Fetherston, Harleian Society, 12 (1877), 369 · W. L. Smith, *Historical notices and recollections relating to the parish of Southam* (1895) · *Notices of the churches of Warwickshire* (1847), vol. 1 · *Walker rev.* · 'Letters from a subaltern officer of the earl of Essex's army, written in the summer and autumne of 1642', *Archeologia*, 35 (1853) · P. Tennant, *The civil war in Stratford-upon-Avon: conflict and community in south Warwickshire, 1642–1646* (1997) · D. McKitterick, *A history of Cambridge University Press*, 1 (1992) · A. Hunt, 'Book trade patents, 1603–1640', *The book trade and its customers, 1450–1900: historical essays for Robin Myers*, ed. A. Hunt, G. Mandelbrote, and A. Shell (1997), 27–54 · G. Stein, *The English dictionary before Cawdrey* (1985) · H. O. Coxe, ed., *Catalogus codicum MSS qui in collegiis aulisque Oxoniensibus hodie adservantur*, 2 vols. (1852); facs. edn under title *Catalogue of the manuscripts in the Oxford colleges* (1972) · will, PRO, PROB 11/357, fols. 69v–70r · PRO, SP 29/8, fol. 89 · PRO, SP 29/12, fol. 160 · PRO, SP 29/20, fols. 175–7

Archives PRO, HO 107/1748/2 fl

Holyoake, George Jacob (1817–1906), freethinker and co-operator, was born at 1 Inge Street, Birmingham, on 13 April 1817, the second of thirteen children and eldest son of George Holyoake (1790–1853), a printer, and Catherine Groves (1792–1867), a horn-button maker. He received a basic education at a dame-school and Carr's Lane Sunday school. For thirteen years until 1839 he worked at the Eagle Foundry, becoming a skilled whitesmith, and in 1836 joined the Mechanics' Institute, where he developed an interest in arithmetic, geometry, astronomy, and phrenology. On his marriage on 10 March 1839 to Eleanor (Helen) Williams (1819–1884), daughter of Thomas Williams, a small farmer from Kingswinford, he looked for a teaching post. Despite his experience as an assistant at the Birmingham Mechanics' Institute, he found promotion there and elsewhere blocked by his association with Robert Owen, to whom he had been attracted in 1836. He therefore sought employment from the Owenite Central Board, which appointed him stationed lecturer at Worcester in October 1840, moving him on to Sheffield the following May. The couple's first child, Madeline, was born in May 1840, and a second daughter, Helen (Eveline), followed in December 1841.

Holyoake's views at this time were radical but not

George Jacob Holyoake (1817–1906), by Walter Sickert, exh. New English Art Club 1892

extreme. In religion he was probably Unitarian, but religious controversies within Owenism redirected his life when, in November 1841, Charles Southwell, the Bristol social missionary, started a weekly atheistic publication, the *Oracle of Reason*. A month later he was arrested for blasphemy and Holyoake volunteered to edit the paper. On his way to visit Southwell in Bristol gaol in May 1842 he stopped in Cheltenham to lecture on Owenite socialism. A flippant reply to a question about the place of religion in the proposed socialist communities led to his prosecution for blasphemy at the assizes in August 1842, where he was sentenced to six months in Gloucester gaol. The death of Madeline in October 1842 put an emotional seal on his intellectual conversion to atheism.

On release Holyoake taught and lectured among the Owenites in London until May 1845, when he went to Glasgow for a year. Two sons were added to the family at this time, Manfred (1844) and Maltus (1846). As Owenism collapsed with the failure of the Queenwood community, remnants of the movement looked to Holyoake's obvious organizational talents to provide a new lead. He had already edited *The Movement* (1843–5) and the *Circular of the Anti-Persecution Union* (1845) but his greatest achievement was *The Reasoner*, which ran weekly from June 1846 until June 1861 and intermittently thereafter. Around this paper he developed the social teachings of Owen into a new movement which in 1851 he called secularism.

Holyoake's public image at this time was far more extreme than the reality. In London he was moving among those advanced liberals who wrote for and supported Thornton Hunt's *Leader* and were associated with the freethinking South Place Chapel. His acquaintances now included John Stuart Mill, George Henry Lewes, Francis Newman, and Harriet Martineau, while some former colleagues accused him of prevarication in religious and political matters. Although still an atheist, he wished secularism neither to deny nor assert the existence of God. Those who believed religion a barrier to progress thought this a betrayal of principle. For Holyoake the sole principle was individual freedom of thought and expression without interference from state, church, or society.

In 1849 Holyoake, with his brother Austin *Holyoake, established a printing firm which in 1853 took over James Watson's publishing business, conducted by the brothers at 147 Fleet Street until 1862. Here in 1855, as members of the Association for the Repeal of the Taxes on Knowledge, they helped secure—through defiance of the law—the repeal of the Newspaper Stamp Act. *The Reasoner* collected funds to support European republicanism, and in 1860 Holyoake was secretary of the committee formed to send volunteers to assist Garibaldi in Italy. In politics he was a member of nearly every leading society for reform from the revived Birmingham Political Union in 1837 to the Reform League in 1867, including the last executive of the National Charter Association in 1852. Through his correspondence and personal acquaintance with Liberal MPs he began to build those bridges which created the popular Liberal alliance of the 1860s. Above all, collaborating with former Owenites and Christian socialists, he worked to establish the co-operative movement. His most effective propaganda, *Self Help by the People* (1858), told the story of co-operation in Rochdale since 1844 and largely created the myth of the *Rochdale Pioneers.

In 1861, after twenty years of writing and provincial lecture tours, Holyoake was physically and emotionally exhausted. Many secularists were turning to the more vigorous leadership of Charles Bradlaugh. He had family responsibilities and social and intellectual aspirations beyond his limited means. His wife, who retained her religious beliefs and took little part in his public life, was bronchitic and in the mid-1860s moved out to Harrow, while her husband retained lodgings in London. They had three further children: Maximilian Robespierre (1848–1855), Francis George (b. 1855), and Emilie (b. 1861), of whom only the last was later to join him in his public work.

Increasingly Holyoake's life was spent in journalism, writing and lecturing for Liberalism and the co-operative movement. He offered himself for parliament in 1857 (Tower Hamlets), 1868 (Birmingham), and 1884 (Leicester), but each time withdrew before the poll. He was acquainted with most of the leading Liberals of the day, and in 1893 was made an honorary member of the National Liberal Club. As a consistent supporter of co-operation he was elected to the first central board in 1869, published a two-volume *History of Co-Operation* (1875, 1879), and presided over the Co-operative Congress at Carlisle in 1887. He was a staunch advocate of co-partnership in industrial production and of the international co-operative movement, attending the inaugural congresses of the French and Italian movements in Paris

(1885) and Milan (1886) respectively. He also visited North America in 1879 and 1882 to collect information for a settlers' guide book.

Though no longer fully active in the secularist movement Holyoake continued to champion moderation against what he interpreted as Bradlaugh's dogmatic atheism, debating the subject with Bradlaugh in 1870 and reiterating his position in *The Origin and Nature of Secularism* (1896). When Bradlaugh republished the *Fruits of Philosophy* in 1877 Holyoake supported Charles Watts and the British Secular Union, and in 1899 became first chairman of Charles Albert Watts's Rationalist Press Association.

Holyoake was a shrewd observer and had a dry wit, but his thin, high-pitched voice made him a poor orator. His writings are readable but unreliable, and he frequently overestimated his own importance. His reputation, overstated during his lifetime, thereafter suffered undeserved neglect. In the later twentieth century historians have rediscovered his importance in the making of Liberalism and a liberal society in Victorian Britain.

Holyoake died on 22 January 1906 at his home, 36 Camelford Street, Brighton, Sussex, where he had moved with Emilie shortly before his marriage on 25 May 1886 to his second wife, Mary Jane Pearson (1845–1906), daughter of George Shaw, clothier, and a widow twenty-eight years his junior. He was cremated at Golders Green on Saturday 27 January and, after a service conducted the following day by J. A. Hobson at the South Place Chapel, his ashes were buried on 29 January in Highgate cemetery. On 9 November 1907 a memorial was placed over the grave by the co-operative movement. EDWARD ROYLE

Sources J. McCabe, *Life and letters of George Jacob Holyoake*, 2 vols. (1908) · L. E. Grugel, *George Jacob Holyoake: a study in the evolution of a Victorian radical* (1976) · *George Jacob Holyoake (1817–1906) and the development of the British co-operative movement* (1988) · G. J. Holyoake, *Sixty years of an agitator's life*, 2 vols. (1892) · G. J. Holyoake, *Bygones worth remembering*, 2 vols. (1905) · C. W. F. Goss, *A descriptive bibliography of the writings of George Jacob Holyoake* (1908) · *The Times* (23 Jan 1906) · C. T. Gorham, *Literary Guide* (Feb 1906) · E. Royle, *Victorian infidels: the origins of the British secularist movement, 1791–1866* (1974) · E. Royle, *Radicals, secularists and republicans: popular freethought in Britain, 1866–1915* (1980) · m. cert., 1839 · m. cert., 1886 · d. cert.

Archives Bishopsgate Institute, London, corresp., diaries, and other papers · Co-operative Union, Holyoake House, Manchester, corresp. and papers · Duke U., Perkins L., letters and papers | Bishopsgate Institute, London, corresp. with Charles Bradlaugh and Hypatia Bradlaugh · Bishopsgate Institute, London, letters to George Howell · BL, letters to W. E. Gladstone, Add. MSS 44403–44786, passim · BL, corresp. with and relating to Harriet Martineau, Add. MS 42726 · Co-operative Union, Holyoake House, Manchester, letters to E. O. Greening · Co-operative Union, Holyoake House, Manchester, letters to Robert Owen · JRL, letters to John Howard Nodal

Likenesses W. Holyoake, oils, 1876, Birmingham Museums and Art Gallery · W. Sickert, ink line drawing, 1890–93, repro. in Holyoake, *Sixty years of an agitator's life*, 3rd edn, 2 vols. (1893), vol. 1, frontispiece · W. Sickert, oils, exh. New English Art Club 1892, NPG [see illus.] · W. Sickert, crayon and watercolour sketch, 1897, Co-operative Union, Holyoake House, Manchester · R. Holyoake, oils, 1902, Rationalist Press Association, London · C. Chabot, line print, 1903 (after a medallion), NPG · photograph, 1905, repro. in Holyoake, *Bygones worth remembering*, vol. 2 · A. Toft, bust, 1907, Highgate cemetery, London · W. & D. Downey, woodburytype photograph, NPG; repro. in W. Downey and D. Downey, *The cabinet portrait gallery*, 4 (1893) · F. von Kamptz, oils, National Liberal Club, London · photograph (as a younger man), repro. in Holyoake, *Sixty years of an agitator's life*, vol. 1 · photograph (as an older man), repro. in Holyoake, *Sixty years of an agitator's life*, vol. 2 · photograph (as an old man), repro. in Holyoake, *Bygones worth remembering*, vol. 1 · plaster replica (after bust by A. Toft), Conway Hall, London

Wealth at death £2946 19*s*. 8*d*.: probate, 7 April 1906, *CGPLA Eng. & Wales*

Holyoake, Henry (1657–1731), headmaster, was probably born in Warwickshire, the son of Thomas *Holyoake (1616–1675) [*see under* Holyoake, Francis], physician and former clergyman, and Anne his wife; his grandfather was Francis *Holyoake (1566x73–1653). In 1672 he was elected to a choristership at Magdalen College, Oxford; he matriculated on 12 March 1674 at the age of seventeen. From 1676 to 1681 he was a clerk and sub-librarian there. He graduated BA on 22 October 1678, proceeded MA on 4 July 1681, and was chaplain of his college from 1681 notionally until 1690, although he left with the fellows ejected by James II and did not return.

On 7 February 1688 Holyoake was appointed headmaster of Rugby School. Despite the smallness of his salary and other disadvantages, he was credited with 'recovering the creditt and reputation of the schoole' (Rouse, 377), and was the first to engage an assistant master. Among his pupils was Edward Cave, whose precocity led to his becoming a general scapegoat, until eventually even the headmaster turned against him and (allegedly) sent him away. Cave, however, would recall Holyoake as 'universally esteem'd for his singular learning and humanity' (*GM*, 126). Meanwhile Holyoake was instituted successively to the Warwickshire rectories of Bourton upon Dunsmore on 30 June 1698, Bilton on 31 August 1705, and Harborough Magna on 9 November 1712.

Holyoake died unmarried at Rugby on 10 March 1731 and was buried in St Mary's Church, Warwick, where he had erected an inscription written by himself to his own memory and that of his father and grandfather. His domestic establishment had been managed by his cousin Judith Holyoake, to whom he left a legacy on the express ground of her having been 'very serviceable and seemingly kind' to the boys. He bequeathed £30 to the daughter of Widow Harris, his 'tripe-woman', the interest on £200 to the poor of Rugby after the death of his cousin Elizabeth Holyoake, and all his books and family portraits (none of either being extant) to Rugby School (Colvile, 430).   GORDON GOODWIN, *rev.* C. S. KNIGHTON

Sources J. R. Bloxam, *A register of the presidents, fellows … of Saint Mary Magdalen College*, 8 vols. (1853–85), vol. 1, pp. 95–6; vol. 2, p. 77 · W. D. Macray, *A register of the members of St Mary Magdalen College, Oxford*, 8 vols. (1894–1915), vol. 4, p. 52 · Nichols, *Lit. anecdotes*, 5.2–3 · *GM*, 1st ser., 1 (1731), 126 · F. L. Colvile, *The worthies of Warwickshire who lived between 1500 and 1800* [1870], 428–30 · W. H. D. Rouse, *A history of Rugby School* (1898), 88–100

Wealth at death see will, Colvile, *Worthies of Warwickshire*

Holyoake, Sir Keith Jacka (1904–1983), prime minister of New Zealand, was born on 11 February 1904 at Scarborough (Mangamutu), near Pahiatua, in the Wairarapa district of the North Island of New Zealand, the third of

Sir Keith Jacka Holyoake (1904–1983), by unknown photographer, *c*.1964

seven children of Henry Victor Holyoake (1875–1954), storekeeper, labourer, and farmer, and his wife, Esther, *née* Eves (1873–1954). Soon afterwards his parents moved to Hastings, and then to a farm at Omokoroa, near Tauranga. In 1914 they moved to the Holyoake family farm at Riwaka, in the Nelson region in the South Island. Apart from encouragement from his mother, a former schoolteacher, Holyoake's education was brief and elementary. At the age of twelve he left his local one-room Brooklyn primary school to help on the farm. By his twenties he had taken over the farm, joined local producer associations, and was excelling in sport—cycle racing, tennis, and rugby. In 1930–33 he was president of the Golden Bay Rugby Union.

In a by-election on 1 December 1932 Holyoake became parliament's youngest member as the Reform Party representative for his local constituency, having failed to win the seat the previous year. The Reform/United coalition government was trounced in 1935 elections; Holyoake was one of a handful of MPs left. On 24 September 1934 he had married Norma Janet Ingram (1909–1984), a shop assistant. Although brought up in a strict Open Brethren environment, in later years he attended the Presbyterian church, in irregular fashion, and a registry wedding in Wellington was followed, in the summer recess, with a Presbyterian church wedding in his home district on 11 January 1935.

In 1938 boundary changes cost Holyoake his seat. A united National Party had been formed from the coalition parties, and he was one of its most promising new generation politicians: a leading office-holder in the Farmers' Union, on the executives of local Progress Leagues, of his district Fruit Exporters' Association and of the New Zealand Tobacco Growers' Federation; for a number of years he was vice-president of the New Zealand Rugby Union. In 1940 party supporters helped finance him into a sheep and cattle farm at Waitahora to follow the retiring member in the safe rural constituency of Pahiatua (named after the town). The Holyoakes subsequently moved to Dannevirke. Holyoake could not be in contention in 1940, when the party chose a new leader, S. G. Holland, but following war-deferred elections in 1943 he was back in parliament and was immediately promoted to the front bench. After the 1946 elections Holland made Holyoake his deputy. Holyoake continued his association with the Farmers' Union, including seven years as national vice-president, and participated in the establishment of the Federated Farmers of New Zealand in 1944; in 1946 he represented New Zealand at the London conference which established the International Federation of Agricultural Producers.

In the Holland government of 1949 Holyoake became minister of agriculture, minister in charge of the Department of Scientific and Industrial Research (1949–50), and minister of marketing until April 1953 and abolition of the department. His family, now comprising two sons and three daughters, moved to a ministerial house in central Wellington in 1950. He led missions to London to negotiate new price levels for New Zealand meat and dairy products, still, until 1954, sold under wartime bulk trading agreements, and in 1957 to seek assured continued access. In 1955 he chaired the Food and Agricultural Organization conference in Rome.

Holland retired on 29 September 1957, weeks before the triennial elections. There was no challenge to the succession of his deputy, but change of leader did not save the government. It lost, by 39 to 41 seats, and Holyoake resigned on 12 December. He proved a vigorous opposition leader, stumping the country, exploiting the Labour government's notorious 'black budget' of 1958, which increased both direct and indirect taxes contrary to election eve promises. On 12 December 1960 Holyoake regained power. For the next few years he dominated his government's economic policy, and ensured that it did not repeat his predecessors' abrupt fiscal measures. He made a virtue of not making excessive election promises and a practice of fulfilling those that were made.

Short of stature—but wearing built-up shoes—the public Holyoake had a pompous manner and plummy voice. The private Holyoake, however, was unpretentious, frugal, and with a puckish sense of humour. The telephone at the prime ministerial residence was publicly listed and might be answered by the prime minister himself. On state papers secretaries might have to do with a prime ministerial pencil tick. His proudest achievement was to have broken in new farm land from 1953 at Kinloch, Lake Taupo.

Holyoake won four successive elections to become one of the Commonwealth's senior statesmen; he served as his own foreign affairs minister. Yet it was only in his last years that political commentators came to recognize his political skills: skills which won him the respect of his colleagues in government and parliament. Like his predecessors he was himself leader of the house. A consensus builder, he was in command as chair in party caucus and in cabinet.

The first years of Holyoake government were reform years. Restructuring in the public services followed a royal commission inquiry, Holyoake himself being minister of state services, 1963–72. Parliamentary reforms included steps to improve scrutiny of public expenditure, and of regulations, and introduction of a daily oral question period. An ombudsman was appointed, the first in a Westminster system. Censorship was placed with an independent tribunal; broadcasting was taken out of direct ministerial control. As minister in charge of the security intelligence service Holyoake made public its existence and its budget. In taking up a government report on race relations and its compilation of scandalous statistical comparisons between people of European and Maori descent, the Holyoake government acknowledged more than previously the racial inequalities of New Zealand society. His government also ended the practice of New Zealand rugby touring teams accepting a South African veto of Maori players, declared that New Zealand should be free of nuclear weapons, and protested against nuclear tests in the Pacific. It faced, too, the long challenge posed by potential British entry into the European Economic Community. A free trade agreement was negotiated with Australia in 1965, and in 1971 special concessions for butter and cheese were obtained in tandem with British entry negotiations.

Holyoake's final years of premiership were his least successful. By the late 1960s years of prosperity and growth had ended, even if this was not necessarily apparent at the time. His sixteen-man cabinet team had included some able ministers and some inspired portfolio allocations. In the course of 1969 he lost two key lieutenants. Previously, in 1967, after the death of his first minister of finance, Rob Muldoon was given that portfolio; pugnacious and outspoken, increasingly he was a leading and divisive member of the government.

The government promoted national development planning, a concept whose time appeared to have come, but which quickly passed. It failed to respond to new pressures: from women's groups, Maori, environmentalists. While supporting the United States' involvement in Vietnam, Holyoake skilfully kept New Zealand's contribution to a minimum. But Vietnam was an election issue in 1966, and its polarizing effects remained for the rest of his premiership.

When Holyoake retired and was succeeded by his deputy, Jack Marshall, on 9 February 1972, his government appeared to be out of tune with the community and to have a leader whose long-discussed retirement was politically debilitating. Holyoake remained as minister of foreign affairs until 8 December 1972 and defeat of the government. In 1975 the National Party under Muldoon returned to office and Holyoake was appointed minister of state. He abruptly resigned, on 7 and 10 March 1977, from government and parliament; he had been named next governor-general of New Zealand.

During Holyoake's premiership the first New Zealand-born governors-general had been appointed. This was in line with his policy of increasingly, if undramatically, asserting the autochthonous identity of his country, which included expanding its relations with other countries, particularly in the Pacific. But Holyoake's own nomination outraged the Labour Party opposition. Subsequent governments took pains to ensure that no future appointment would be so controversial.

From 26 October 1977 to 27 October 1980 he performed his viceregal duties with dignity and without political contention. Honoured as CH in 1963 and GCMG in 1970, in 1980 he was made a knight of the Garter. He did not long outlive his last public office. Suffering from high blood pressure he had his first stroke while governor-general, and died of a stroke in Wellington Public Hospital on 8 December 1983. He was cremated at the Karori cemetery in Wellington on 13 December and his ashes were scattered at Kinloch. His widow died twelve months later.

G. A. WOOD

Sources R. A. Doughty, *The Holyoake years* (1977) • M. Clark, ed., *Sir Keith Holyoake: towards a political biography* (1997) • B. Gustafson, *The first 50 years: a history of the New Zealand national party* (1986) • N. McMillan, *Top of the greasy pole* (1993) • *New Zealand Parliamentary Debates* (8 Dec 1983), 4718–32 • *Who's who in New Zealand* • I. Templeton and K. Eunson, *Election '69: an independent survey of the New Zealand political scene* (1969) • R. Chapman, 'From labour to national', *The Oxford history of New Zealand*, ed. G. W. Rice, 2nd edn (1992), 351–84 • K. J. Holyoake, 'The task of the prime minister', *Political Science*, 15 (1963) [reprinted in Cleveland and Robinson, *Readings in New Zealand government* (1972)] • A. V. Mitchell, ed., *Government by party: parliament and politics in New Zealand* (1966) • R. D. Muldoon, *The rise and fall of a young Turk* (1974) • Radio New Zealand, *Spectrum* programme, 'Minding the ministers', 10 and 17 Aug 1997 • J. Marshall, *Memoirs, 1960 to 1988* (1989), vol. 2 of *Memoirs* • R. M. Chapman, W. K. Jackson, and A. V. Mitchell, *New Zealand politics in action: the 1960 general election* (1962) • G. Chapman, *The years of lightning* (1980) • B. Edwards, ed., *Right out: labour victory '72: the inside story* (1973) • [A. E. Woolf], *The 7 oaks* (New Zealand, 1977) [Holyoake Family Reunion Committee] • G. Mallaby, *From my level: unwritten minutes* (1965) • E. McLeay, *The cabinet and political power in New Zealand* (1995) • R. D. Muldoon, *Muldoon* (1977) • W. P. Riley, 'Room at the top', *Management*, 8/9 (1961), esp. 18–21 • 'Sir Keith Holyoake interviewed by J. M. Barr, 7 January 1973', typescript, priv. coll. • *Stone's Directory* (1904) • *New Zealand Post Office directory* (1910–11); (1914) • *New Zealand Gazette* • b. cert. • m. cert. • d. cert. • d. cert. [Dame Norma Janet Holyoake] • private information (2004)
Archives NL NZ, Turnbull L., MSS | U. Birm. L., corresp. with Lord Avon | SOUND NL NZ, Turnbull L.
Likenesses photograph, c.1964, NL NZ, Turnbull L. [see illus.] • F. Szirmay, bronze bust, 1972, National Party Headquarters, 57 Willis Street, Wellington • R. Burgess, statue, 1990, Molesworth Street, Wellington • W. Dargie, oils, Museum of New Zealand (Te Papa), Wellington • P. Grugeon, photograph (as governor-general), Government House, Wellington • S. Hope, portrait, National Party Headquarters, 57 Willis Street, Wellington • cartoons, NL NZ, Turnbull L. • photograph (as prime minister), Parliament House, Wellington • photographs, NL NZ, Turnbull L.
Wealth at death not wealthy; $10,000 lump sum and $5000 monthly annuity to wife: will, 8 July 1982

Holyoake, Thomas (1616–1675). *See under* Holyoake, Francis (1566x73–1653).

Holywood [à Sacro Bosco], **Christopher** (1559?–1626), Jesuit, was probably born in 1559 at Artane, near Dublin, the son of Nicholas Holywood, a landowner in counties Dublin, Meath, and Wexford, and his wife, Elizabeth Plunkett, granddaughter and heir-general of Robert Plunkett, fifth Baron Dunsany. He studied at the University of Padua and in 1584 became a member of the Society of Jesus at Verdun, entering the noviciate at Dôle in France. He was ordained at Pont-à-Mousson in 1593, and over the next few years taught theology there and at Dôle, and philosophy and scripture in Italy, at Ferrara and Padua, where he met the influential Cardinal Bellarmine. On 26 September 1598 he was appointed to the mission of the Jesuits in Ireland. Disguised as a merchant he sailed for England, but was arrested on landing at Dover. He declined to take the oath of supremacy, was examined before Robert Cecil, the secretary of state, and was detained in custody at the Gatehouse, London. From February 1600 he was detained at Wisbech, where he occupied himself with literary work and theological disputation. After the death of Elizabeth I he was transferred to Framlingham in Suffolk and then banished to the continent.

Holywood spent time in the Spanish Netherlands and northern France in 1603–4 and arranged for the publication of two works of theology, which appeared under the name à Sacro Bosco, a Latin form of his name in traditional use in his family. His *Defensio decreti Tridentini et sententiae Roberti Bellarmini, S. R. E. cardinalis, de authoritate Vulgatae editionis Latinae, adversus sectarios, maxime Whitakerum* (1604), re-issued with additions in 1619, was a defence of Bellarmine's views on the Vulgate in reply to William Whitaker and other protestant controversialists. He also wrote *De investiganda vera ac visibili Christi ecclesia libellus* (1604) and the unpublished treatise 'Opusculum de virtutibus' (1619). There is some evidence that he was the author of a work of natural philosophy entitled *De meteoris tractatus lucidissimus in quinque partes distinctus*, apparently also an early work, but revised in 1612 and published in Paris in 1613 under the pseudonym Johannes Geraldinus.

In Ireland from March 1604 until his death, Holywood acted as superior of the Jesuit mission. He spent his time in Dublin and the surrounding areas actively promoting the Jesuit mission and normally lived with relatives, including his cousin Sir Christopher Plunkett in Dublin, and members of the Holywood family in co. Meath. Wise reported that Holywood was 'generally in and about the court of Dublin' (Hogan, *Distinguished Irishmen*, 459) and was no stranger to political controversy, though he insisted the society focus on its spiritual mission. Though he spent time in co. Meath to avoid persecution in Dublin and Drogheda he regarded it as a 'remote' place and was reported to have rarely travelled beyond the pale because he spoke little Irish and did not enjoy good health. As provincial he corresponded regularly with fellow Jesuits, usually signing his name as John Bushlock before 1618, and after that date regularly using the alias Thomas Lawndrie

(Lawndaeus); elsewhere his name was recorded by contemporaries as Holividus or Holivodius. During his time as superior the Jesuit presence in Ireland grew considerably, both numerically, with more than forty Jesuits in the country, and geographically, with the establishment of a network of residences and an Irish mission to the western isles of Scotland. He died in Ireland on 4 September 1626.

J. T. GILBERT, *rev.* BERNADETTE CUNNINGHAM

Sources E. Hogan, ed., *Ibernia Ignatiana, seu, Ibernorum Societatis Jesu patrum monumenta* (1880) · E. Hogan, *Distinguished Irishmen of the sixteenth century* (1894), 395–501 · Jesuit Archives, Dublin, MacErlean transcripts · F. O'Donoghue, 'The Jesuit mission in Ireland, 1598–1651', PhD diss., Catholic University of America, Washington, DC, 1981 · J. J. Corboy, 'The Jesuit mission to Ireland, 1596–1626', MA diss., University College Dublin, 1941 · notes and correspondence of Fergus O'Donoghue, Jesuit Archives, Dublin · J. Geraldinus, *De meteoris*, 1613, TCD, DD f. 5, no. 2 [contains important MS notes on Holywood]
Archives Archives of the Irish Province of the Society of Jesus, Dublin, MSS A/1–89 · Archivum Romanum Societatis Jesu, Rome, annual letters as superior | Archives of the Irish Province of the Society of Jesus, Dublin, MacErlean transcripts
Wealth at death property assigned to brother, 1587: Hogan, *Distinguished Irishmen*, 400

Holywood, John of. *See* Sacrobosco, John de (d. c.1236).

Homan [*née* Waterlow], **Ruth** (1850–1938), educationist and women's welfare campaigner, was born on 8 August 1850 at 5 Gloucester Terrace, Hoxton Old Town, London, the eldest daughter of the three sons and five daughters of Sir Sydney Hedley *Waterlow (1822–1906), stationer and MP, and his first wife, Anna Maria (d. 1880), the younger daughter of William Hickson, London merchant and manufacturer. She spent her childhood at Waterlow Park; little else is known of her early life. On 7 May 1873 she married Francis Wilkes Homan, the son of Ebenezer Homan of Wormwood Street. Left a widow in 1880, with one daughter, she accompanied her father, sister Hilda, and brother Paul on a tour of Canada and the United States in 1881. Widely travelled, she had by 1896 been round the world three times.

Ruth Homan's candidature for the London school board in 1891 was practically her first experience of public work, though her upbringing in a politically active family obviously facilitated the process of learning how to 'work' the existent political machinery. Her father's friends included four board members: Sir Edmund Hay Currie, T. H. Huxley, Samuel Morley, and the Revd William Rogers. Her brother, David Waterlow (1857–1924), later became a county councillor and Liberal MP. Her interest in education had been aroused while presiding over a girl teachers' club in the East End, and she took exceptional pains to qualify herself for school board work. She first became a school manager in Chelsea in 1887, then, to extend her knowledge of cookery, health, and hygiene, followed the course of artisan and scullery cooking classes at South Kensington School of Cookery, going on to serve as a probationer at St Bartholomew's Hospital, of which her father was treasurer. Finally her work for a charity called the Country Holidays Fund gave her a personal acquaintance with some of the poorest and most unfortunate children attending the board schools.

Ruth Homan was elected at the head of the poll for Tower Hamlets division of the London school board in 1891, temporarily leaving her home at 52 Addison Mansions, Kensington, to take lodgings in the midst of the constituency. She held the seat until the 1903 London Education Act abolished the board, transferring its responsibilities to the London county council (LCC). A Liberal who supported the school and Progressive Party policy, she endorsed the development of the higher grade and evening continuation schools, the teaching of temperance principles in board school, and special teaching for 'afflicted' and delicate children. She took an active interest in the work of Elizabeth Miriam Burgwin, superintendent of London's special schools for physically and mentally handicapped children and was a keen advocate of the kindergarten system. She also promoted the teaching of cookery and laundry-work and went on to succeed Rosamond Davenport-Hill as chair of the domestic subjects subcommittee. Hard-working, active, and efficient, both women were frequently depicted as 'typical' women members by the contemporary media. On 16 March 1896 she gave evidence to the departmental committee on reformatory and industrial schools. She recommended industrial schools for both boys and girls, women inspectors, varied industrial training, and the cottage home system of organization.

Ruth Homan gave all her spare time to the work of the board. This amounted to five or six days a week while the board was sitting, and incalculable time during the recess as she visited schools both at home and abroad. She also extended her charitable work in the East End—an interest she had first displayed in the late 1880s. She continued to run a boot and clothing help society in the schools, and used her position as a member of the committee of the London School Dinners Association to supply free school meals to needy East End children during the winter months. She was also vice-president of the Pupil-Teachers Association and member of a Club of Working Girls in the City. Co-opted to the education committee of the LCC following the dissolution of the London school board in 1904, she served on the day schools and special schools subcommittee.

In 1897 Ruth Homan was elected president of the Cornish Union of Women's Liberal Associations. Qualifying for election on the basis of her property at Tintagel (her daughter married Arthur Greig Chapman, the vicar of Tintagel), she was also president of the Hammersmith Women's Liberal Association and officer of Poplar Women's Liberal Association. A member of the Somerville Club for Women, she and four other women members of the London school board—Margaret Eve, Susan Lawrence, Emma Maitland, and Hilda Miall-Smith—belonged to the Women's Local Government Society (WLGS), an upper-middle-class, liberal, London-based feminist group, which supported the claims of all women to elected local office, whatever their politics. Ruth herself contributed to the fight against the Education Acts of 1902–3 which, until 1907, disqualified women for election to the new local education authorities. Possessing an attractive personality and with an established reputation as an easy, fluent speaker, she was an ideal person to publicize the work of women in local government. She wrote and spoke on both school board work and public work more generally in an open letter entitled *Women as Candidates for Local Elections*, published by the WLGS in November 1908. She herself continued to act as a role model for other women. In 1910 she was elected a poor-law guardian for Ewell, Surrey, and served for eleven years. Latterly she lived mainly in Cornwall and died at Camelford on 6 November 1938.   JANE MARTIN

Sources M. Bateson, ed., *Professional women upon their professions* (1895), 48–51 • *Young Woman*, 4 (1895–6), 129–32 • *School Board Chronicle* (1891–1904) • *The Board Teacher* (1 Nov 1892), 236 • 'Departmental committee on reformatory and industrial schools', *Parl. papers* (1896), 45.788–92, C. 8204 • G. Smalley, *The life of Sir Sydney Waterlow bart* (1909) • A. Wright, ed., *The Argus guide to municipal London: a poll-book and a year-book combined* (1903), 130 • b. cert. • m. cert. • CGPLA Eng. & Wales (1939)
Archives LMA, Women's Local Government Society records, pamphlets and references to political activities
Likenesses photograph, repro. in *Board Teacher* • portrait, repro. in Election Manifestos, 1891–1900 • sketch, repro. in Bateson, ed., *Professional women*, 48
Wealth at death £20,168 10s. 2d.: resworn probate, 25 Jan 1939, CGPLA Eng. & Wales

Home. *See also* Hume.

Home family. *See* Hume family (*per.* 1424–1516).

Home, Alexander, **fifth Lord Home** (*c*.1525–1575), nobleman, was the eldest son of George *Hume or Home, fourth Lord Hume (*d.* 1549), and his wife, Dame Mariota Haliburton. He was probably sixteen when his curators were chosen, about 1541. He had acquired his father's titles and estates by March 1550, though these were not ratified by retour until 16 April 1551. There was a rumour that he would be offered the earldom of March in June 1565, but this never materialized. About 1558 he married Margaret Ker of Cessford, who died on 24 June 1565, leaving a daughter Margaret who married George Keith, fifth Earl Marischal, about 1581. Home's second wife, whom he married in October 1565, was Agnes Gray (*d.* 1583×6), daughter of Patrick, Lord Gray, and widow of Robert Logan of Restalrig. They had one son, Alexander *Home, sixth Lord Home and later first earl of Home, and two daughters including Isobel, who later married Sir James Home of Eccles. Agnes later married Sir Thomas Lyon of Baldukie, after Lord Home's death. Home also had a bastard son, John, provost of Dunglass, who was legitimized by the privy council in 1565.

Alexander Home is first noticed as the fourth lord's son and heir in a land grant of June 1535. Eager to placate James V at the time of the latter's general revocation of all land grants in 1538, his father granted Alexander's marriage agreement to the king. Alexander was to 'contract marriage with ane dochtir naturale of his hienes' and could not marry elsewhere without the king's consent (Hannay, 468–9). The king had in mind a daughter of his

liaison with Elizabeth Beaton, but this wedding never happened. The rights to Alexander's marriage were then passed successively to James Douglas, third earl of Morton, in October 1541, and to Margaret Stewart, sister of the earl of Lennox, in 1542. There were rumours that he would marry a daughter of George, Lord Seton, in 1543, as Seton had acquired the rights from Margaret Stewart. It was not until 1550 that Alexander had his choice of bride given to him by Mary of Guise in return for good service on the borders. He thereafter chose to marry the daughter of a border laird instead of a fellow nobleman's daughter.

In the 1540s, as master of Home, Alexander served bravely alongside his father in the wars against England. The English falsely claimed that 'Master Howme' had assured to their allegiance in October 1543. Lord Home and his son would never betray the Scots throughout the troubled 1540s, though a few of their kinsmen did capitulate. Henry VIII demanded Alexander as a hostage in July 1544 to stop Scottish retribution for the earl of Hertford's raid on Scotland that May. Home defied him by evading capture on several occasions, and he and his kin signed an assurance to defend the Merse and Teviotdale from English attack at the parliament of October 1545. Alexander's luck had run out by May 1546, however, when he was listed as an English prisoner, though there was some discussion of exchanging him for the earl of Cumberland's brother, Thomas Clifford. The master was probably released later in 1546, as he attended parliament that year with his father, but he was recaptured after the Scottish defeat at the battle of Pinkie on 10 September 1547. By November 1547 Lady Home was begging Protector Somerset (formerly Hertford) to let her son come home while she was secretly negotiating the surrender of Hume Castle. The master of Home and his mother were now seen to be important in their own right as the fourth Lord Home had been badly injured at Pinkie. After a licensed return to Scotland on 6 December 1548 Alexander probably assisted with the recapture of Hume Castle from the English on 16 December. He went on to help recapture the occupied town of Kelso as well. By July 1549 he and his father were receiving pensions for themselves and regular salaries for the Hume garrison. By October 1559 these salaries amounted to £75 Scots per month.

Alexander Home was acting as his father's executor by March 1550, and it was as Lord Home that he accompanied Mary of Guise on her voyage to France in the summer of 1550. Once in France he was amply rewarded for his family's service to both Scotland and France during the 1540s. His French pensions were paid regularly throughout the 1550s, but dried up after Mary's death in 1560. After he returned from France, Home took a leading role in the administration of the Anglo-Scottish borders throughout the 1550s and 1560s. He was warden and justiciar of the Scottish east march during 1550–58 and 1559–70 and was temporarily joint warden of the east and middle marches in 1557–8. He was additionally a border commissioner in 1550 and 1559 and a guardian of Liddesdale in 1562. During 1554, when he was 'trublit with infirmitie', he asked his brother Andrew, commendator of Jedburgh, to deputize (*Reg. PCS*, *addenda*, 122). Home also held local offices as bailie and chamberlain of the crown lands in the Merse, steward and receiver of the earldom of March, bailie of Coldingham, Eccles, and Dryburgh, heritable bailie of Coldstream Priory (from 1566), and sheriff of Berwickshire and bailie of Lauderdale after the downfall of the fourth earl of Bothwell in 1567. The latter appointment gave Home particular pleasure as he had viewed Bothwell as a territorial rival, even though the Home kindred was firmly entrenched in Berwickshire by the mid-sixteenth century.

At a national level Home attended parliaments in 1546, 1558, 1560, 1561, 1567, when he was elected one of the lords of the articles, and 1568. He was also a privy councillor from 1561 until 1570. His political role at the centre of Scottish government took off after he attended the Reformation Parliament of 1560. Home had previously been in the pro-French faction in Scotland, and he entertained Mary of Guise at Hume Castle in 1557. He was never destined to become a committed supporter of the protestant cause, yet like many of the Scottish élite he dallied with Reformation politics during the late 1550s and 1560s. He sometimes appeared to play each side against the other in *politique* fashion. After the return of Mary, queen of Scots, in 1561, he continued to keep Hume Castle garrisoned for her, yet appeared to lean towards the pro-English protestant lords. And despite entertaining the queen at Hume in 1567 he became one of the rival 'king's men' that year, supporting the faction surrounding the fledgeling James VI. During 1567 he besieged the queen, tried to arrest her husband Bothwell, and joined forces against her at the defeat of Carberry. He signed the order to imprison Mary in Lochleven Castle, witnessed her abdication, and assisted at the subsequent coronation of James VI. Home subsequently fought with Regent Moray's forces against those of the queen until she went into exile after the battle of Langside on 13 May 1568, when he apparently fought on foot and sustained many injuries. Home undoubtedly achieved greater power and influence as a result of this politicking, but he was privately unhappy about the turn of events.

In 1569 Home dramatically changed sides again to assist the supporters of the now exiled Queen Mary. Why he did this is unclear, but he must have felt remorse about his earlier opposition to the queen. Perhaps he had fallen out with the politically ascendant earl of Morton, whom he had stood beside at Carberry? He may also have reclaimed his Roman Catholicism, and with it an image of Mary as the victim of oppression and the rightful claimant to both the Scottish and the English thrones. The clearest manifestation of this change of heart came when Home gave shelter at Hume Castle to fugitives from the doomed English northern rising of 1569, including the countess of Northumberland, whom he treated 'honourablie' (T. Thomson, 154). There was a heavy price to pay for this hospitality as Queen Elizabeth then ordered the earl of Sussex to attack Hume Castle with all possible force. Home could do little to stop the English, either from taking the castle and ransacking it, or from garrisoning

Hume for the next three years, gathering Lord Home's crops for their own profit without any local opposition.

Home had made a major political blunder, for most of his kinsmen in the Merse had remained in the king's party. The politically ambitious Homes of Manderston and Cowdenknowes, in particular, were now openly hostile, and competed with the fifth lord for power in the locality. Other lairds, more subdued in their opposition, simply refused to join him. An erroneous English report of 1570 stated that 'my lord Hume and almost all the gentlemen in Tevydale Marsh and Lowdyan were knitt together in such frendship' (Clifford, 2.114). In truth Home had very few friends at this time, especially among his own kinsmen. Unable to return to the Merse, he became increasingly embroiled in the affairs of the Marians during the confused years of 1570–73. The centre of Scottish politics was split between king's men and Marians, with rival parliaments meeting and political leaders forfeiting each other. Home was taken prisoner in 1571 and warded in Tantallon Castle, only to be released in an exchange a few weeks later. During 1572 he demanded the return of the Hume and Fastcastle properties but without success, and in disillusion he then joined William Kirkcaldy of Grange, William Maitland of Lethington, and their supporters, in Edinburgh Castle. Home prepared himself for a lengthy siege as he took a large entourage with him, including his wife, his sister-in-law, his servitor Mr John Home, a dozen hagbutters (gunners), 'Marten the cooke' and his two boys, a tailor, a brewer, a shoemaker, and 'Esabell the wessher' (PRO, SP 52/25, fols. 68–9). The Edinburgh Castle Marians were then besieged for eleven days in May 1573 by Regent Morton's forces backed up by English reinforcements, until they reluctantly surrendered.

Home was taken prisoner and transferred to Holyrood. Morton lost no time in executing the rebels, but now the Homes of Manderston and Cowdenknowes changed their tactics, and along with Home of North Berwick successfully pleaded with Morton for Lord Home's life. Home then had to find £10,000 Scots security to secure this clemency, together with a pardon for his children. As his finances were precarious, his kinsmen—the lairds of Polwarth, North Berwick, Huttonhall, and Manderston—obliged him as sureties when he borrowed the money from Andrew Ker of Faldonside. Home was nevertheless forfeited of his lands and titles and imprisoned back in Edinburgh Castle for the next two years. He became so ill that in June 1575 Morton released him from the castle to his lodging in Friar Wynd. Too weak to walk, Home was 'cariit thairto in ane bed' (T. Thomson, 348). He died there on 11 August 1575, probably having discovered the treachery of Manderston and Cowdenknowes. In his will he asked the lairds of Wedderburn, Ayton, and Polwarth to protect his widow, son, and daughters.

MAUREEN M. MEIKLE

Sources NA Scot., testaments CC8/8/1 · NRA Scotland, 859, Home of the Hirsel · PRO, State Papers Scotland, SP52/25 · *Manuscripts of the duke of Atholl … and of the earl of Home*, HMC, 26 (1891) · *Report on the manuscripts of Colonel David Milne Home, of Wedderburn Castle,*

HMC, 57 (1902) · *Calendar of the manuscripts of the most hon. the marquis of Salisbury*, 24 vols., HMC, 9 (1883–1976) · *APS, 1424–1592* · *CSP Scot.*, 1547–81 · J. M. Thomson and others, eds., *Registrum magni sigilli regum Scotorum / The register of the great seal of Scotland*, 11 vols. (1882–1914) · *Reg. PCS*, 1st ser., vols. 1–2 · M. Livingstone, D. Hay Fleming, and others, eds., *Registrum secreti sigilli regum Scotorum / The register of the privy seal of Scotland*, 8 vols. (1908–82) · *LP Henry VIII* · J. B. Paul and C. T. McInnes, eds., *Compota thesaurariorum regum Scotorum / Accounts of the lord high treasurer of Scotland*, 6–13 (1905–78) · R. K. Hannay, ed., *Acts of the lords of council in public affairs, 1501–1554* (1932) · *CSP dom.*, 1547–80; *addenda, 1547–79; 1566–79* · *CSP for.*, 1558–77 · G. Burnett and others, eds., *The exchequer rolls of Scotland*, 23 vols. (1878–1908), vols. 16–20 · J. Lesley, *The history of Scotland*, ed. T. Thomson, Bannatyne Club, 38 (1830) · T. Thomson, ed., *A diurnal of remarkable occurrents that have passed within the country of Scotland*, Bannatyne Club, 43 (1833) · *Scots peerage*, 4.458–60 · *The state papers and letters of Sir Ralph Sadler*, ed. A. Clifford, 3 vols. (1809) · *The Scottish correspondence of Mary of Lorraine*, ed. A. I. Cameron, Scottish History Society, 3rd ser., 10 (1927) · J. Bain, ed., *The Hamilton papers: letters and papers illustrating the political relations of England and Scotland in the XVIth century*, 2 vols. (1890–92) · *The historie and cronicles of Scotland … by Robert Lindesay of Pitscottie*, ed. A. J. G. Mackay, 3 vols., STS, 42–3, 60 (1899–1911) · *CSP Rome, 1558–78* · M. M. Meikle, 'Lairds and gentlemen: a study of the landed families of the Eastern Anglo-Scottish Borders, *c*.1540–1603', PhD diss., U. Edin., 1989 · T. I. Rae, *The administration of the Scottish frontier, 1513–1603* (1966)

Wealth at death see *APS*, 3.282–3; will, 1575, Milne Home manuscripts, 240–43

Home, Alexander, first earl of Home (*c*.1566–1619),

nobleman, was the eldest son of Alexander *Home, fifth Lord Home (*c*.1525–1575), and his second wife, Lady Agnes Gray (*d*. 1583x6), daughter of Patrick, fourth Lord Gray, and widow of Robert Logan of Restalrig and Fastcastle, who later married Sir Thomas Lyon of Balduikie. Because of his involvement in rebel action on behalf of the exiled Mary, queen of Scots, the fifth Lord Home and Alexander, as master of Home, took the unusual step of choosing curators for their estates on 16 February 1571, but to no avail as the lands and title were forfeited in October 1573. The younger Alexander Home was at St Leonard's College, St Andrews, in 1578–9, but did not take a degree. He was restored to his father's estates and title, as sixth Lord Home, by parliament on 25 July 1578 and was retoured heir to these lands on 18 August 1579. Probably as part of the restitution deal his ward and marriage had been granted on 6 August 1578 to William, Lord Ruthven, who acted as Home's tutor Andrew Home as curator for his estates until he was twenty-one. Andrew Ker of Faldonside had held the lease of most of the Home estates during the forfeiture and had resisted the temptation to asset-strip the properties because of his friendship with Home's father. Others who benefited from the fifth lord's downfall, including kinsmen and even the new sixth Lord Home's stepfather, were, however, less willing to return his property. Home took back the semi-ruinous Hume Castle by force and used the privy council to evict the others.

In 1581, although only fifteen, Home attended his first of many sittings of parliament and assumed his father's roles as warden of the Scottish east march, sheriff of Berwickshire, and bailiff of Lauderdale. In the following year the privy council ordered him to hold his first judiciary court. Home had shown early responsibility by arbitrating a feud between some of the Homes and the Niddries of Wauchope in 1580, yet he became embroiled in the infamous 1582–3 Ruthven raid that kidnapped the young King James VI from the earl of Lennox's faction, probably owing to his being a ward of Lord Ruthven, now earl of Gowrie. Gowrie imposed his feudal rights to arrange the marriage of his ward. On 31 May 1582 Gowrie proffered either Lilias or Dorothy, his daughters. Home's aunt Mary Gray had refused Gowrie's hand in the 1560s and Home now rejected his daughters. On 9 January 1586 he married Christian (*d*. 1604), daughter of William Douglas of Lochleven (earl of Morton from 1588) and widow of Lawrence, master of Oliphant. Her tocher (dowry) was a mere thirty chalders of victual from the Oliphant estates and though Christian had children by her first marriage, she had none during her second union. This may have been linked to irreconcilable social and religious differences as Home would have children from his second marriage. According to court gossip in October 1595 there was 'appearance of a seperacon between my Lord Home and my Lady who hathe taken the platte and beste stuffe at Dunglass and caryed with her to fife to her lyving there' (PRO, SP 52/57/37).

In 1584 Home was warded in Tantallon Castle by order of the earl of Arran, chancellor of Scotland, for his part in various property disputes and feuds. Resentment at this led to Home's involvement with the return of the banished protestant lords in 1585, who subsequently toppled Arran's regime. By 1587 Home was in trouble again as he challenged to combat Lord Fleming, brother-in-law of Home's territorial rival Maitland of Thirlestane. However, the most damaging alliance for Home was his turbulent on-off friendship with the maverick earl of Bothwell. From 1583 to 1593 both their petty feuding and Home's reconciliations with the eventually outlawed earl alarmed the government. Home was warded several times and even ordered to remain within his Scottish east march during 1589–90, when the king sailed to Denmark to collect his bride, Princess Anne. He foolishly joined Bothwell's rebel band in 1591, yet by July the lure of Bothwell's escheat and the advice of kinsmen made it politically expedient for Home to make his peace with the king. James also insisted that he sign a bond of friendship with Maitland to prevent further trouble in the borders. The Homes of Huttonhall, Broxmouth, North Berwick, and Wedderburn did not want Home to suffer the same fate as his father and probably instigated Home's self-imposed exile during 1591–2 which kept him far from Bothwell's influence and Maitland's meddling. James welcomed Home upon his return and bestowed lands and honours on him for forsaking Bothwell's allegiance. These included the lands of Coldingham Priory and the offices of privy councillor, grand master stabler, gentleman of the bedchamber, and captain of the king's guard. He was, in addition, a lord of the articles at the parliaments of 1593, 1594, and 1612. Home signed James VI's declaration against Bothwell in 1593 and was a commissioner to hound Bothwell out of his bounds in 1594. He had an inconclusive sortie with the disgraced earl near Edinburgh in April 1594, but 1595 saw both Bothwell's departure into exile and the death of Maitland of Thirlestane. These events gave Home great power in the borders and at court, but his triumphs would be marred by his adherence to Roman Catholicism.

Until 1588 Home's religious affiliation had not given cause for concern. Church authorities were beginning to suspect Home, though, for not repairing churches and for keeping well-known Jesuit sympathizers such as Andrew Clark and Thomas Tyrie in his household, and tried to have him cast out of royal circles. James VI, however, refused to be dictated to by the kirk and Home avoided the wrath of the presbytery of Dunbar by going abroad during 1591–2. The presbytery of Edinburgh ordered him to appear before them in January 1593 when he 'professed himself a Catholik Roman, but desired conference' (Calderwood, 5.221). That October he was provocatively excommunicated by the synod of Fife against the express wishes of the king. He appeared before the general assembly on 17 May 1594 and absolved himself from excommunication by promising to adhere to protestantism. When the riding of parliament took place that month it was very obvious to the crowd that the king had placed Home at his left hand, a position of great honour. Evidence of royal favour was apparent at the baptismal celebrations for Prince Henry in August 1594, when Home carried a diamond crown in the procession and sat near Queen Anne at the banquet, and where his Turkish-attired team won the tournament.

Even so, the sceptical presbytery of Edinburgh alerted the presbytery of Duns to watch Home. They cited his shortcomings and excommunicated him in 1598 for killing William Lauder, who had murdered an ally of Home's in front of his stepsister, Lady Marischal. James VI could not persuade the kirk to change its mind so Home left the country for another year-long exile, taking both his protestant kinsman Alexander Home of Huttonhall and Thomas Tyrie with him. Lady Home stayed at home and there is no indication that she was ever Catholic. Home was never far from church scrutiny as he modified payments to the church from the third of benefices of Coldingham Priory and Jedburgh Abbey, of which he had become commendator in 1597. In 1602 the general assembly deliberately planted a minister in his household, but this was to no avail for Tyrie was still in his household in 1604. In 1606 the kirk ordered Home to remain in Edinburgh as 'a suspected Papist' (Calderwood, 6.248, 608). He continued to provoke the authority of the kirk by non-payment of taxes in 1607, though he shrewdly took the 1608 oath of allegiance to keep all his offices.

Home's lifelong service to the crown proved to be his ultimate defence against the kirk. He was James VI's ambassador to Henri IV of France between April 1599 and May 1600, and for three months in the autumn of 1602. He had been to France on four occasions between 1591 and 1602, which prompted the derogatory comment that he was 'sore grieved with the French pokis and being every year occasioned to go beyond sea for his health' (CSP Scot.,

1597–1603, p. 1017). He was praised for his diplomatic skills by Henri IV and received an audience with Queen Elizabeth I while travelling back to Scotland in 1602. She thanked him for his excellent border service as an exemplary warden of the generally peaceful Scottish east march who never failed to give good justice to his opposite English wardens. Home had salvaged Anglo-Scottish friendship after a disastrous day of truce in 1597 when during a fracas he gathered his kinsmen around the English commissioners to protect them, escorted them into Scotland for hospitality, and persuaded the worst Scottish middle march recalcitrants to hand themselves over to the English commissioners after this event.

After the union of the crowns Home was a natural candidate to be lieutenant and justiciar over all three Scottish marches. He was appointed on 7 July 1603 and set about his wide-ranging commission from August 1603, after he returned from accompanying James VI and I to London. He had no qualms about torturing and executing persistent thieves, which made him few friends outside his east march domain. The Maxwells and Armstrongs, for instance, attacked some of Home's property and tenants in retribution for his actions. Although his Catholicism lost him this office in 1607 he returned in 1618 to lead the Scottish commissioners in a new commission for the pacification of the so-called middle shires and remained active in border affairs until his death. Much of the credit for the eventual pacification of the marches belongs to Home and his deputies.

In 1603 James VI and I spent the first night of his journey to England at Home's house of Dunglass. Home was rewarded in 1605 with the new British title of earl of Home—for reasons unknown he had turned down the Scottish earldom of March in 1600. As a mark of favour his ecclesiastical properties at Jedburgh and Canonbie were amalgamated into a temporal lordship in 1606, with Coldingham and various kirklands being officially added to the lordship in 1610. He was possibly made an English privy councillor at Theobalds in May 1603. Home remained an active member of the Scottish privy council, yet his overall political powers were in slow decline after 1603. He acknowledged that he had become a client of his kinsman the supremely ascendant earl of Dunbar and after Dunbar's death in 1611 sought the patronage of the earl of Salisbury. Salisbury's death in 1612 left him further removed from British court politics since he had no particular ties to the king's subsequent favourites, Somerset and Buckingham. The king still honoured Home during his return visit to Scotland in 1617 by spending his first night in Scotland at Dunglass, where Home's kinsman poet Alexander Home of Logie delivered an impressive welcome speech in Latin, after which Home lavishly entertained the king and his company.

As Home had no heirs at his first wife's death in 1604, he provided a tailzie of his titles to his closest kin, the Homes of Cowdenknowes. However, on 11 July 1605 he married Mary Sutton (1586–1645), daughter of the ninth Lord Dudley. They had a happy marriage that produced two sons and two daughters. Home died in London on 5 April 1619, where he had gone to accompany his wife at the forthcoming funeral of Queen Anne. His body was brought back to Scotland and was buried in May at his family chapel in Dunglass collegiate church. He was succeeded by his eldest son, James, seventh Lord Home and second earl of Home. His widow remained in Edinburgh, building a magnificent house in the Canongate now known as Moray House.   MAUREEN M. MEIKLE

Sources NA Scot., Edinburgh commissary court: testaments, CC8/8; gifts and deposits, GD16, GD205, GD206, GD237, GD267; register of deeds, 1st ser., RD1 · PRO, state papers Scotland, SP52; state papers Borders, SP59 · BL, Cotton MS, Caligula CV, DI, DII; Stowe MS 574 · NRA Scotland, 859, Home of the Hirsel · *Manuscripts of the duke of Atholl … and of the earl of Home*, HMC, 26 (1891) · *Calendar of the manuscripts of the most hon. the marquis of Salisbury*, 24 vols., HMC, 9 (1883–1976) · *APS · CSP Scot.* · J. Bain, ed., *The border papers: calendar of letters and papers relating to the affairs of the borders of England and Scotland*, 2 vols. (1894–6) · *CSP dom.* · J. M. Thomson and others, eds., *Registrum magni sigilli regum Scotorum / The register of the great seal of Scotland*, 11 vols. (1882–1914) · *Reg. PCS*, 1st ser. · *Reg. PCS*, 2nd ser. · *Reg. PCS*, 3rd ser. · M. Livingstone, D. Hay Fleming, and others, eds., *Registrum secreti sigilli regum Scotorum / The register of the privy seal of Scotland*, 8 vols. (1908–82) · J. Kirk, ed., *The records of the synod of Lothian and Tweeddale, 1589–1596, 1640–1649*, Stair Society, 30 (1977) · *Scots peerage* · D. Calderwood, *The history of the Kirk of Scotland*, ed. T. Thomson and D. Laing, 8 vols., Wodrow Society, 7 (1842–9) · J. Nichols, *The progresses, processions, and magnificent festivities of King James I, his royal consort, family and court*, 3 (1828), 300–05 · J. M. Anderson, ed., *Early records of the University of St Andrews*, Scottish History Society, 3rd ser., 8 (1926) · M. M. Meikle, 'Lairds and gentlemen: a study of the landed families of the Eastern Anglo-Scottish Borders, c.1540–1603', PhD diss., U. Edin., 1989
Wealth at death £43,830 3s. 4d. Scots—incl. moveable goods £13,598 3s. 4d. Scots; debts owed by Home £6032 6s. 8d. Scots; debts owed to Home £36,274 8s. Scots: NA Scot., CC8/8/51, 20 March 1621

Home, Alexander Frederick [Alec] **Douglas-, fourteenth earl of Home and Baron Home of the Hirsel** (1903–1995), prime minister, was born in London on 2 July 1903, the first child in a family of five sons and two daughters of Charles Cospatrick Archibald Douglas-Home, thirteenth earl of Home (1873–1951), and his wife, Lilian, *née* Lambton (1881–1966), second daughter of Frederick William Lambton, fourth earl of Durham. In 1918, on his grandfather's death, he became Lord Dunglass, the courtesy title of the eldest son of the earl of Home. His father had inherited two Scottish estates amounting to 100,000 acres, divided between the Hirsel on the Tweed in Berwickshire and Douglas in Lanarkshire. The thirteenth earl, a likeable and straightforward man, was no politician and advised his eldest son against a political career. The duties and pleasures which befell the twenty-fifth largest landowner in the country were in his view ample to fill a normal lifetime. Although he ignored this advice, Home never abandoned or strayed far in his thoughts from the border country in which he was brought up. The knowledge of the countryside which he acquired as a boy was fundamental to his later life and loyalties. The flight of birds, the moods of a river, the lie of a hill, the changes of the sky were familiar and dear to him throughout his life, and are well caught in Suzie Malin's portrait (1980) in the National Portrait Gallery. From the same source came a strong sense of family, and an easy self-confidence

Alexander Frederick Douglas-Home, fourteenth earl of Home and Baron Home of the Hirsel (1903–1995), by Vivienne, 1950s

which showed itself in consideration for others. The three most courteous men I knew in politics were Lord Home, King Hussein of Jordan, and President Nelson Mandela. All three had ease of birth, in the sense that they never needed to worry about who they themselves were and so had more time to concern themselves with the feelings of others.

Childhood and youth Although the family's history was in Scotland, there was nothing narrow about its perspective. The heir to the earldom was born in a specially rented house in London, the imperial capital, that being the custom of the time. His preparatory school (Ludgrove), his public school (Eton College), and his university (Oxford) were all in the south of England, in accordance with the family tradition. At Eton he coincided with an entirely different kind of boy, Cyril Connolly, who produced an early example of those exposés of public school life which became somewhat tedious as the century wore on. In *Enemies of Promise* (1938) Connolly vividly described Alec Dunglass:

> He was a votary of the esoteric Eton religion, the kind of graceful tolerant sleepy boy who is showered with favours and crowned with all the laurels, who is liked by the masters and admired by the boys without any apparent exertion on his part, without experiencing the ill effect of success himself or arousing the pangs of envy in others. In the eighteenth century he would have become Prime Minister before he was thirty; as it was he appeared honourably ineligible for the struggle of life. (Connolly, 294)

Little in Dunglass's record at Eton or Oxford contradicted this verdict. He distinguished himself at cricket, taking four Harrow wickets at Lord's for thirty-seven runs on a rain-sodden pitch in his last year before a crowd of about 20,000. He moved smoothly up the ladder to become president of Pop, the self-elected society whose members wore coloured waistcoats and were at that time, according to Connolly, the true rulers of Eton. At Christ Church he was tutored by J. C. Masterman, an important and long-lasting influence. He managed only a third-class degree in history (in 1925), hampered partly by illness but to a greater extent by a range of non-academic activities, which included hunting, cricket, bridge, and champagne, of which cricket remained the most important. He did not bother with the debates of the Oxford Union.

But something had been stirring beneath that pleasant and easy-going surface. Years later Home wrote an airy account of his life called *The Way the Wind Blows* (1976), a book full of anecdotes about politicians, grouse, and salmon. With one or two exceptions it did not probe deep into the author's emotion. But near the beginning of the book Home described his father's departure for Gallipoli in 1915 with the Lanarkshire yeomanry. The earl took his son down to London from Scotland for the start of his prep school term at Ludgrove. Father and son spent the night in a hotel, parting at bedtime because the earl had to leave early for Southampton next morning to join his regiment. 'I shall never forget the long night of agony in the King's Cross Station Hotel which I somehow came through; squeezed of all emotion but fear and rage at the folly to which man could descend.' This is strong stuff for a lad of twelve, but no one who knew Home could doubt its truth. 'Ever since then, while I revere the patriot, I have detested the jingo tub-thumper, the narrow nationalist and the advocates and practitioners of violence' (Home, 43).

Early career in politics After Oxford, Dunglass toured South America playing cricket for the MCC before returning to Scotland to pick up the threads of a laird's traditional life—the Boys' Brigade, the yeomanry, Burns clubs, and nine 20-pound salmon in one morning. But for a perceptive young man these activities so close to the central belt of Scotland could not be separated from the experience of many fellow Scots nearby who were losing their jobs in coal and shipbuilding. Against his father's wishes Dunglass became involved in politics. It might seem from the background so far described that his loyalties would automatically be tory, but that would be to misread both the man and his family. His mother was a Liberal by instinct, his father unpolitical, and much of his early admiration went to Lloyd George, who was entering the sunset of his own political career as a powerful advocate of strong measures against unemployment. But these choices, then as now, often depend on the luck of direct personal magnetism. Dunglass was drawn into the circle of an up-and-coming Scottish Conservative, Noel Skelton, MP for Perth. Skelton was a contemporary and friend of Anthony Eden. It was Skelton who in one of the essays published in his book *Constructive Conservatism* (1924) coined the phrase 'property owning democracy', which Eden later made his own. If he had not died of cancer in 1935 Skelton would have been a leading figure alongside

Eden, Butler, and Macmillan in the post-war renaissance of the Conservative Party. Skelton encouraged Dunglass to fight the 1929 election as the Conservative candidate for Coatbridge, a mining town 10 miles east of Glasgow. Labour had held the seat in 1924 and the tide in Scotland had swung markedly towards Labour since then. So it was no surprise that Dunglass was defeated. An uncertain apprentice in public speaking, he had a rough time from hecklers. He lost decisively, but was not deterred. Not for the last time, luck was on his side. Almost at once the more promising, though narrowly Labour seat of Lanark lost its Conservative candidate, and Dunglass was adopted. He was swept into the House of Commons in the landslide of 1931, standing as a National Unionist. He was immediately asked by Skelton, now a junior minister at the Scottish Office, to serve as his unpaid parliamentary private secretary.

So in his late twenties the form of Dunglass's Conservatism was set. It remained unchanged through his life. He valued deeply the traditional values into which he had been bred. At the same time he was a shrewd observer of reality, of the way the wind was blowing. He distrusted abstract philosophizing, whether of left or right. He had no rigid devotion to the free market or to any other economic or social creed. He disagreed with those who regarded each ditch as the one in which they had to die. He favoured defence in depth, believing that Conservatives should use their traditional skills not to avert change but to guide it. Thus he believed that Churchill was wrong in the early 1930s to oppose the constitutional concessions in India. At different times in his career he favoured a degree of protection for industry, an elected Scottish assembly, and the banning of the hereditary peerage from the House of Lords. During his premiership in 1963–4 he was caricatured by the left as an unthinking reactionary, but the facts of his career speak otherwise.

Chamberlain and Munich That career moved decisively forward in February 1936 when Dunglass was appointed parliamentary private secretary to the chancellor of the exchequer, Neville Chamberlain, who kept him in that position when he succeeded Baldwin as prime minister the following year. Chamberlain excelled in the competent transaction of business, a political talent which Dunglass valued highly and practised when he himself briefly became prime minister. But Chamberlain lacked the personal charm which makes competent administration palatable to wayward colleagues—a gift which his parliamentary private secretary possessed in abundance. He developed a strong admiration for the prime minister, tacked on to the loyalty which he would have shown anyway. The premiership was short and disastrous. Chamberlain took Dunglass with him to his final meeting with Hitler at Munich in September 1938. Dunglass went as an aide-de-camp rather than a policy adviser, and sat in outer rooms while the talks proceeded, eating unwanted food and watching the repeated changes in Goering's uniform. He travelled with Chamberlain on the fateful return journey through London, when the king made the mistake of inviting the prime minister to appear on the balcony of

Buckingham Palace, followed by Chamberlain's even greater mistake of proclaiming, quite out of character, 'peace for our time' from his own first-floor window in Downing Street. Dunglass defended the Munich settlement all his life. He believed that there was no possibility of successfully defying Hitler in 1938, and that the year gained was essential for the military preparations which Chamberlain had set in hand. But he was not at the time required to justify Munich in public. In this respect he was luckier than Butler, junior minister at the Foreign Office; the label of Munich was only lightly attached to him in later years. But he accepted immediately a quite different burden, the care of an exhausted prime minister. Chamberlain, walking in the woods at Chequers, suddenly felt that he was on the edge of a nervous breakdown. Dunglass persuaded his father to issue an invitation, and Chamberlain spent ten days at the Hirsel in October, at first fishing, then shooting, then beginning on the red boxes as the cloud of exhaustion lifted. Dunglass was in charge of the hospitality. This was easy, for he shared to the full Chamberlain's enthusiasms as a naturalist and an outdoor sportsman. Twice in later years, in 1956 and 1963, he had further occasion to support and advise a failing prime minister. 1940 was the bleakest year of his own life. He joined in the bitterness which Chamberlain's supporters felt in the immediate aftermath of his fall in May—a bitterness focused not on Churchill, the new prime minister, but on the raffish types who accompanied him into his office, such as Bracken and Boothby. Dunglass continued to serve Neville Chamberlain in his last and powerless office as lord president of the council. But in the autumn Chamberlain was dead of cancer, and a sudden thunderbolt struck Dunglass. He presented himself for a medical examination in Edinburgh as a prelude to rejoining the Lanarkshire yeomanry for active service. A hole was discovered in his spine surrounded by severe tuberculosis. A new and dangerous operation was performed, after which Dunglass was encased in plaster for nearly two years. For a physically active man, this sentence of almost total immobility during the decisive years of the war was an appalling blow: 'I often felt that I would be better dead' (Home, 86).

Marriage and the Second World War But there was strong help at hand. Four years earlier, on 3 October 1936, Dunglass had married Elizabeth Hester Alington (1909/10–1990), second daughter of the Very Revd Cyril Argentine *Alington, dean of Durham and former headmaster of Eton. They had four children: (Lavinia) Caroline (b. 1937), Meriel Kathleen (b. 1939), Diana Lucy (b. 1940), and David Alexander Cospatrick (b. 1943). The serene success of their marriage, which lasted fifty-four years, was evident to anyone who saw them together or who heard either speak of the other. Elizabeth was gentle and invariably courteous in manner, but there was no doubting her strength, which was exercised in the cause of whatever was straightforward. She rarely expressed strong political views, but her skill as a judge of individuals was added to the native shrewdness of her husband to make a formidable combination. Her support during these two testing years was

decisive in securing his recovery. The experience reinforced one of the fundamental facts about his life, namely that his family and its background were more important to him than political success.

Dunglass used his years in plaster to re-educate himself. He read books for which there had been no time during the cheerful years of champagne and cricket at Christ Church. It was a turning point. No one who knew him would suppose that the reading list was entirely solemn; characteristically in his autobiography he provides a long list of novelists whom he devoured, beginning with John Buchan and ending with Dorothy Sayers and Ngaio Marsh. But these were overshadowed by Marx, Engels, Dostoyevsky, and Koestler, together with the classics of nineteenth-century English political biography. On this reading he built an unpretentious but solid foundation of belief which went deeper than politics. He thought about the religion which he had hitherto taken for granted, one result being the declaration of faith which appeared rather unexpectedly in the middle of his autobiography. He called this 'a weak witness of Christianity' (Home, 81–2), but in fact it was a firm though modest statement based on God the creator and the two commandments of Christ. Perhaps no other modern politician could convincingly have slipped such a chapter into a book about family, sport, and politics.

At this time another theme took deep root in Dunglass's mind—partly from his reading, partly from a friendship formed during his illness with a Count Starzenski, who was serving as a tank gunner after escaping from Poland, where he had worked before the war as private secretary to the foreign minister. The books and his new Polish friend persuaded him that the main threat to Britain after the defeat of Hitler would be Soviet imperialism. Nothing which happened during his later career shook this well-researched conviction, which he had formed well before it became fashionable and which became the mainspring of many of his later decisions on foreign policy.

After his recovery and return to parliament in 1944 Dunglass found early evidence to justify his suspicions. He was bold enough to criticize the Yalta agreement in the Commons because it transferred Polish territory to the Soviet Union and fell short of elementary standards in international behaviour. Churchill bore no grudge and appointed Dunglass as under-secretary at the Foreign Office in the caretaker government of summer 1945. The prospect of a period of steady work in what had become his main interest was shattered when he lost Lanark by nearly 2000 votes in the Labour landslide of July 1945.

Opposition and office For the next five years Dunglass relapsed, without complaint, into the kind of life which would naturally have been his had he never felt the pull of politics. A directorship of the Bank of Scotland, a few articles in the press, increasing care of the two Scottish estates as his father grew old—to these he added continued cultivation of the Lanark constituency. In the general election of February 1950 his persistence was rewarded when he recaptured the seat by 685 votes. The sitting member, Tom Steele, had five years earlier written to the *Daily Worker* thanking the local communists for their support. A connection which had seemed harmless in 1945 looked more sinister in 1950; Dunglass republished the letter and exploited it to the full. This was a legitimate election tactic, but it showed what was sometimes forgotten, that beneath the surface of a gentle, even simple manner he possessed the instincts of a shrewd political operator.

Once again the road of a promising career in the Commons was open, but once again it was blocked. Dunglass had to give up his newly regained seat when he became the fourteenth earl of Home on his father's death in July 1951. By now his main patron was James Stuart, a chief whip of legendary skill who was the leading political figure in Scotland, becoming secretary of state when the Conservatives won the election of October 1951. Churchill took little interest in junior ministerial appointments and Stuart had no difficulty in allocating to Home the new post of minister of state at the Scottish Office. His work lay in Scotland rather than the House of Lords, and must have been thoroughly enjoyable. For this was a golden age of Conservative strength in Scotland based on political and economic contentment, before the collapse of traditional industries and the resurgence of nationalism. Home built up a reputation for steady good sense and skill in handling people, which led the next prime minister, Anthony Eden, to promote him to the cabinet as Commonwealth secretary in April 1955. Eden understood that the usefulness of the Commonwealth depended not on any pretensions to political or economic strength as an institution but on the personal contacts which enabled it to act as a lubricant in the world's affairs. The Homes undertook a huge tour of the Commonwealth between August and November 1955. But the prime minister who had made such a shrewd appointment dealt the Commonwealth a near fatal blow in the botched Suez enterprise of 1956. As at Munich in 1938, Home was quietly there, near but not quite at the centre of disastrous events. Though himself loyal to Eden, he warned him of the unhappiness of cabinet colleagues, in particular Butler. His correspondence with Eden when the latter fell shows a genuine sadness and sympathy. By the imperceptible process characteristic of British politics he found himself month by month, without any particular manoeuvre on his part, becoming an indispensable figure in the government. Harold Macmillan confirmed him in office, and for the next few years his main preoccupation was to bind up the wounds dealt by Suez to the idea of a modern multiracial Commonwealth. As this task came to an end, another subject began to fill his red boxes, which in turn became the next testing strain for the Commonwealth. The effort spent by British politicians on the future of central Africa between the start of the federation in 1953 and Lord Carrington's final settlement of the Rhodesian question in 1980 was immense. The strains in the federation were becoming formidable while Home was at the Commonwealth Office. He respected and supported the efforts of Roy Welensky to bridge the gap between black aspiration and the interests of the white settlers, but showed no particular passion in anyone's

cause. For him it was a matter of managing as decent a transition as possible from British sovereignty to a successor regime. Home worked in close friendship with the colonial secretary, Alan Lennox Boyd, but could never strike up a good relationship with his successor, Ian Macleod. This was a matter of temperament rather than belief. Macleod was a hard, tense, imaginative party politician, far removed from the atmosphere of calm, unintellectual discussion leading to reasonable compromise in which Home naturally thrived.

Foreign secretary In the summer of 1960 Harold Macmillan wished to transfer his foreign secretary Selwyn Lloyd to the Treasury. On grounds of talent and experience Home would have been a natural successor if he had still been in the Commons. There had been no example since the war of a foreign secretary in the Lords. When despite this Macmillan announced Home's appointment as foreign secretary on 27 July, there was an uproar in the press which the Labour Party prolonged with enthusiasm. Like all such artificial commotions it died down after a time (and indeed was not renewed with any strength nineteen years later when Margaret Thatcher appointed another peer, Lord Carrington, to the same post). The argument that the government's foreign policy must be presented in the Commons by a member of the cabinet was met by the promotion of Ted Heath as lord privy seal, based with particular responsibility in the Foreign Office. Thus began a close fifteen-year partnership between Home and Heath which served both men well—indeed, helped each of them to the premiership. Home was as different in character and upbringing from Heath as he was from Macleod, but with Heath his relationship ran smoothly from the start. Neither man lived in the other's pocket nor attempted a social relationship which would have been artificial. But Heath felt and, equally important, required from others a consistent respect for the elder man, and Home gave Heath steady support in the various scrapes in which the latter found himself over the years. Because each had given serious thought to getting the relationship right, Home moved in relation to Heath from superior to subordinate without any serious friction.

During his periods as foreign secretary from 1960 to 1963 and from 1970 to 1974, Home saw himself essentially as a navigator. He did not regard it as his job to scale high peaks and plant his personal flag on them. Rather, his purpose was to steer a vessel without mishap down a river made dangerous by imperfectly charted rocks and rapids. As Commonwealth secretary he was already familiar with the task of managing with skill the decline of the British empire. To this he now added the task of frustrating the attempt of the Soviet Union to dominate the world, which he had foreseen and analysed during his wartime illness. This was the consistent theme which ran through his principal decisions and speeches. He did not believe in noisy diplomacy or theatrical flourishes. Indeed he relished and used the amusements and small adventures of traditional diplomacy. For example, he formed a cautious though friendly relationship with the Soviet foreign minister, Andrey Gromeko. But he wrote:

> Such are the amenities of international public life, and they are necessary to sanity. But one must always force oneself to remember—odious and boring though it is—that all Communists are devoted to a single end—victory over every other creed and every other way of life.   (Home, 250)

Practical examples were not slow to come. Khrushchov as Soviet leader compensated for his relative moderation compared to Stalin with occasional rash and dangerous lunges against the West. In January 1961 he lodged an unprovoked ultimatum against the western portion of Berlin. The West refused to budge. Khrushchov followed in 1962 with the dispatch of missiles to Cuba, an act bound to test to the full the courage of the new American president, John Kennedy. Historians will continue to argue about the importance of the role played by Harold Macmillan and his colleagues in keeping Kennedy steady yet strong during the critical weeks of October 1962. What is not in doubt is Home's role in keeping Macmillan steady. The two men got on well together, but were very different. Macmillan's calm was assumed with difficulty by a skilled actor who knew its importance as a political technique. Beneath his calm at moments of crisis bubbled all manner of anxieties and complex emotion. To Home, by contrast, calm came so naturally that he could effectively communicate it to others. He was not capable of Macmillan's flights of imagination but was by now expert in keeping policy close to the ground, making full use of its contours. The combination worked well. Home earned the respect of skilled practitioners like Dean Rusk, and also of the foreign service. He was customarily brief in speech and on paper. He did not skimp the detailed work in his boxes, but had the gift of extricating from each document the essential point, and communicating a clear decision on what should be done.

Prime minister   The Macmillan administration lost impetus in 1963, becalmed in a sea of satire and scandal. Home was not particularly involved in the Profumo affair. His main enterprise that year was the negotiation and signature in Moscow of the nuclear test ban treaty, one of the most significant staging posts on the road to *détente*. But he privately advised Harold Macmillan to step down as prime minister before the next election, which had to be held at latest by autumn 1964. Macmillan did not resent this advice from a friend, but it was not welcome; indeed he persuaded himself that Home's real view was that he should stay. There is no need to record here the story of Macmillan's indecision during the autumn of 1963, both as regards his own future and the identity of his successor once illness appeared to force his hand. Clearly Home during most of this period had virtually excluded from his mind the thought that he would or could succeed Macmillan as prime minister. This was not because he doubted his own ability, for in this he always had quiet confidence. Nor was his peerage any longer an obstacle since, as a result of Anthony Wedgwood Benn's efforts, the law had been changed to enable hereditary peers to renounce their titles. But Home, though by now widely respected among those who knew him, was not yet a household name. A general election could not be more than a year away, and the Conservative Party badly needed a well-known leader to rally it from the setbacks of 1963. This might be Hailsham, well qualified as a trumpeter; or Butler, with his subtle intelligence and unrivalled experience; or conceivably Maudling, an up-and-coming new man. At cabinet on 8 October when the succession was discussed Home said that he was not a candidate. This was the only notable occasion in his life when he acted in a way which some criticized later as not honourable. The criticism was unwarranted. What Home said on 8 October was a statement of present fact, not a pledge for the future; but Ian Macleod and Enoch Powell later regarded it as misleading and therefore wrong. Events moved rapidly. Senior members of the party began to put it into Home's mind that he should stand. Luck put cards into his hand. Macmillan charged him as the president that year of the National Union of Conservative and Unionist Associations to tell the party conference at Blackpool on 10 October of Macmillan's decision to resign. This propelled Home to the centre of the stage. His own foreign affairs speech at the conference went well, whereas in different ways Butler and Hailsham mismanaged their own opportunities. The party conference had no say in electing the party leader, but the publicity which it generated influenced the outcome. Meanwhile soundings in the traditional manner were being made among Conservative MPs and peers, and the results reported to Harold Macmillan in his hospital sickbed, so that he could make the decisive recommendation to the queen. Macmillan himself had earlier favoured Hailsham, but doubts about Hailsham's judgement were increased by American unhappiness over the way he had handled his part in the test ban negotiations. The soundings pointed to the less than emphatic conclusion that Home would have less difficulty in forming and carrying on a government than any of his rivals. Macmillan was content with this, and advised the queen to ask Home to form a government, which she did on 18 October. He had already checked with his doctor that his health could stand the strain. By another stroke of luck the safe Commons seat of Kinross and West Perthshire was vacant. The remaining hazard was that Butler would refuse to join a Home government and so make his task impossible. Macleod and Powell were for this reason anxious that Butler should indeed refuse; but Butler, true to his own tradition of diffident but determined public service, agreed to serve as foreign secretary. Home became prime minister on 18 October 1963. Five days later he disclaimed his peerage for life, becoming Sir Alec Douglas-Home (having been made a knight of the Thistle the previous year).

The twelve months of Home's premiership were not dramatic in British history. The prime minister scaled no peaks; his vessel hit no rocks. The most striking world event was the assassination of President Kennedy in November 1963. Home had worked well with Kennedy but found it hard to build a relationship with his successor, Lyndon Johnson; indeed the two governments staged a substantial row on the issue of British trade with Cuba.

Rhodesian affairs drifted slowly in the wrong direction. The Commonwealth prime ministers met in London. In domestic as well as foreign affairs the prime minister was quietly competent in the transaction of business. The main argument of substance concerned Heath's proposal to abolish retail price maintenance. The plan roused fierce opposition inside the Conservative Party, many of whose members thought it folly to antagonize small shopkeepers in the run-up to a general election. Heath showed his determination. Home would almost certainly not have originated the measure himself, but he was persuaded of its merits, and Heath had served him well. As a result Home staunchly supported his colleague. Thus the first and one of the most important acts of liberalizing the British economy, in a series later known as 'Thatcherite', was carried through by Heath and Home, neither of whom rate in the history books as disciples of Margaret Thatcher.

But the main preoccupation of British politicians was the forthcoming election. Everything pointed to a substantial Labour victory. Labour was led with skill, sometimes with brilliance, by Harold Wilson. The Conservatives had been in office for thirteen years. They were caricatured as old-fashioned and upper class; they seemed to play into the hands of their opponents by choosing a grouse-shooting earl as their leader. Home had once admitted that he used matchsticks to do his sums; Wilson promised in contrast to mobilize for Britain the white heat of the technological revolution. Home disliked television appearances and found the quarrelsome noise of the House of Commons distasteful, whereas Wilson thrived on both. But when the contest came, right up against the deadline of October 1964, it did not go entirely as expected. The campaign was noisy, and the prime minister fared particularly badly at the hands of hecklers in the Bull Ring at Birmingham. Labour won, but narrowly, winning 317 seats against the Conservatives' 304. It was enough, but not a walkover, and the Conservative Party was not demoralized as in 1945 and 1997. During his premiership Home had gradually asserted himself as an honourable leader, albeit in an unfashionable tradition. The poisons of 1963 slowly drained out of British political life in 1964, making possible a straightforward election with no backdrop of scandal or what was later called sleaze. Home's decent, matter-of-fact premiership helped to bring this about, and his riposte to Harold Wilson gained him a place in the quotation books and scored a palpable hit: 'As far as the fourteenth Earl is concerned, I suppose Mr Wilson, when you come to think of it, is the fourteenth Mr Wilson' (*Oxford Book of Quotations*).

Opposition, and return to the Foreign Office But a defeat was a defeat. Back in opposition Home quickly changed the rules for electing a Conservative leader. He responded to the widespread criticism of the secretive way in which he himself had been chosen in 1963 by what Macleod in a famous *Spectator* article had called the 'magic circle'. The new rules, which placed the power firmly and openly with Conservative MPs, lasted with one revision until they were in turn criticized after the fall of Margaret Thatcher

in 1990. Home did not at once resign as leader of the Conservative Party. Many of his friends as well as his wife wanted him to continue. But the criticisms which he had felt bound to endure while governing the country became intolerable to him once that responsibility had passed. 'My reaction', he wrote, 'was boredom with the whole business' (Home, 220). On 22 July 1965 he told the 1922 committee of the parliamentary party that he intended to step down. Ted Heath was elected to succeed him under the new rules. Home served as shadow foreign secretary during the following five years of opposition, travelling the world, maintaining his foreign contacts, and wrestling as president of the MCC with the baleful influence of apartheid on the aborted English cricket tour of South Africa. Returning to his earlier involvement in Scottish politics, he supported Heath's declaration at Perth in favour of devolution and chaired a commission which produced a plan for a Scottish assembly. Much pain and damage to the union would have been avoided if the Heath government had later acted on that report.

Home was by now the unrivalled elder statesman of the Conservative Party. His appearance at each year's party conference was greeted with tumultuous applause, in which guilt mingled with affection. Senior members of the shadow cabinet turned to him in early June 1970 when it looked as if Labour would win a third election victory in a row, an outcome which would have condemned Heath to failure and compelled him to resign as leader. Home refused to discuss the issues in advance, and Heath confounded all expert opinion by winning a satisfactory majority on 18 June. Home returned with pleasure to a second stint at the Foreign Office.

As during Home's previous tenure of that office between 1960 and 1963, Britain's desire to enter the European Economic Community quickly came to the fore of events. Once again Home had alongside him a fellow cabinet minister, this time Geoffrey Rippon, who handled the actual negotiations under the active supervision of the prime minister. But Home was more than a bystander. By temperament and background he was some distance removed from Heath's passionate commitment to a united Europe. All the more important was his steadfast support for British entry, which he based on a clear assessment of Britain's place in the modern world, and in particular her relationship with France and Germany on the one hand and the United States on the other. Home brought the traditional analysis of Foreign Office diplomacy to bear on the European issue, and reached the same conclusion as Heath by another route, thus providing the right of the Conservative Party with much needed assurance. Otherwise his main concerns at the Foreign Office were again the Soviet Union and Africa. In September 1971, after much unproductive correspondence with Gromeko, Home created a sensation by expelling 105 Soviet spies from Britain. This worked well. The KGB suffered a heavy blow and the roof did not fall in on Britain's relationship with the Soviet Union. Largely as a result of his efforts a compromise agreement was reached with Ian Smith, the rebel white prime minister of Rhodesia, which would have led in stages to African majority rule. To Home's great disappointment a commission led by Lord Pearce reported in May 1972 that most Africans rejected the proposals, which then fell.

Retirement After Heath's defeat in the election of February 1974 Home's active political career came to an end. He accepted a life peerage, as Baron Home of the Hirsel, in October 1974, and re-entered the House of Lords. Two years later he published a good-natured autobiography, with perhaps more anecdotes than insights, which he called *The Way the Wind Blows*; it was an instant success. As the years passed he spent more time in Scotland, with his family and the country pursuits which gave spice to his life. There was no sudden moment when he abandoned politics, but his interventions became fewer and fewer. In 1990 his wife died two months before her eighty-first birthday. The gap thus torn in his life could never be repaired. Margaret Thatcher rightly wrote: 'Goodness and kindness radiated from Elizabeth to all the people she came in contact with' (Thorpe, 460). For five years he lived on at the Hirsel, well nursed and cared for, but with the light gradually fading. He died of bronchopneumonia at the Hirsel at the age of ninety-two on 9 October 1995.

Home was the fourteenth earl of Home, the thirteenth prime minister of this country to be educated at Christ Church, Oxford, and the eighteenth prime minister to be educated at Eton. Such a combination, surprising at the time, has become even less probable. Home represented the last flowering of a highly sympathetic tradition of political service based on a mixture of patriotic duty, personal ambition, and inherited land. During the frenetic days of October 1963 Macmillan had written a private memorandum in hospital which he never sent to the queen but which expressed frankly his views on the different men who might succeed him. His comments on Home will serve as a summary:

> Lord Home is clearly a man who represents the old governing class at its best ... He is not ambitious in the sense of wanting to scheme for power, although not foolish enough to resist honour when it comes to him ... He gives that impression by a curious mixture of great courtesy, and even if yielding to pressure, with underlying rigidity on matters of principle ... This is exactly the quality that the class to which he belongs have at their best because they think about the question under discussion and not about themselves. (Thorpe, 301)

DOUGLAS HURD

Sources Lord Home, *The way the wind blows* (1976) · J. Dickie, *The uncommon commoner: a study of Sir Alec Douglas-Home* (1964) · E. Hughes, *Sir Alec Douglas-Home* (1964) · K. Young, *Sir Alec Douglas-Home* (1970) · D. R. Thorpe, *Alec Douglas-Home* (1996) · C. Connolly, *Enemies of promise* (1938) · *The Times* (10 Oct 1995) · *The Guardian* (10 Oct 1995) · *The Independent* (10 Oct 1995) · *Daily Telegraph* (10 Oct 1995) · *The Scotsman* (10 Oct 1995) · *WWW*, 1991–5 · Burke, *Peerage* · d. cert.
Archives NRA, priv. coll., papers | Bodl. Oxf., corresp. with Lord Monckton · Bodl. RH, corresp. with Sir R. R. Welensky and papers relating to Rhodesia · NL Scot., corresp. with Lord and Lady Tweedsmuir · U. Birm. L., corresp. with Lord Avon
Likenesses Vivienne, photograph, 1950–59, NPG [see illus.] · E. Arnold, bromide print, 1964, NPG · J. Musgrave-Wood, pen-and-

ink, 1967, NPG · A. Newman, print, c.1978, NPG · S. Malin, oils, 1980, NPG · A. Arikha, portrait, 1988, Scot. NPG · M. Cummings, pen-and-ink, NPG · W. Papas, pen-and-ink, NPG · W. Weist, pen-and-ink, NPG · photograph, repro. in *The Times* · photograph, repro. in *The Guardian* · photograph, repro. in *The Independent* · photograph, repro. in *Daily Telegraph* · photograph, repro. in *The Scotsman* · photographs, repro. in Lord Home, *Way the wind blows*
Wealth at death £430,296.61: confirmation, 27 Feb 1996, CCI

Home, Cecil. *See* Webster, (Julia) Augusta (1837–1894).

Home, Charles Cospatrick Douglas- (1937–1985), newspaper editor, was born in London on 1 September 1937, the second son and youngest of three children of Henry Montagu Douglas-Home (1907–1980), ornithologist, known as the BBC 'bird man', the second son of the thirteenth earl of Home. His mother, Lady (Alexandra) Margaret Elizabeth Spencer (1906–1996), was the daughter of Charles Robert Spencer, the sixth Earl Spencer. Douglas-Home was a cousin of *Diana, princess of Wales. He won a foundation scholarship as king's scholar at Eton College. For his national service he was selected for a commission in the Royal Scots Greys, becoming an unruly subaltern. After leaving the army he did not try for university, but spent nine months in Canada, supporting himself by selling encyclopaedias. He then took up the post of aide-de-camp to Sir Evelyn Baring, the governor of Kenya, at the climax of the Mau Mau insurgency. He later wrote Baring's biography, entitled *Evelyn Baring: the Last Proconsul* (1978). During that year (1958–9) Douglas-Home found his taste for international politics.

Douglas-Home then applied for the novel job of television commentator. But the BBC and then independent television instantly rejected him on the grounds that his approach and accent were both wrong, and because he lacked journalistic experience. So he took a job as a general reporter for the *Scottish Daily Express*, and learnt his trade in the notoriously tough school of Glasgow journalism, where he earned a reputation as a 'hard news man'.

In 1962 Beaverbrook Newspapers promoted Douglas-Home to London as deputy to Chapman Pincher, defence correspondent for the *Daily Express*. In this position he developed his taste for political intrigue and spycatching melodrama. He was also told that he must give up drink if he wanted to live. Douglas-Home, who had acquired the habit of breakfasting on claret, gave up alcohol. He subsequently gave up meat and tobacco also. The *Express* promoted him to political and diplomatic correspondent. In this post and through his family connections (his uncle, Sir Alec Douglas-Home [*see* Home, Alexander Frederick Douglas-], was Conservative prime minister, 1963–4), Douglas-Home built a network of contacts through parliament and Whitehall.

In 1965 Douglas-Home was appointed defence correspondent of *The Times*. The young man with his flowered ties brought a breath of fresh air to Printing House Square. Instead of writing 'think pieces' on strategy from official briefings, Douglas-Home reverted to the older *Times* tradition set by William Howard Russell. He followed the sound of the guns, and reported from the front line. In 1967 he covered the Six Day War, and in 1968 the Soviet invasion of Czechoslovakia. On the latter assignment the Russians arrested him as a spy while he was examining one of their tanks. They held him for eight hours before expelling him. In 1966 Douglas-Home married Jessica Violet Gwynne, a strong-minded artist and stage designer, the daughter of Major John Nevile Wake Gwynne of Gloucestershire. They had two sons.

At *The Times*, Douglas-Home rose through the *cursus honorum*. He became features editor (1970), home editor (1973), and foreign editor (1978). In May 1981, after Rupert Murdoch had bought *The Times*, Douglas-Home was appointed deputy editor under Harold Evans. Within a year Evans's editorship collapsed in confusion for reasons that are still controversial. Douglas-Home, who had been negotiating to escape to the *Daily Telegraph*, took over the editorship in a raging storm, with panic and mutiny below decks, and *The Times* in danger of foundering. He was the only *Times* man trusted by the proprietor, the old guard known in Lord Northcliffe's contemptuous compliment as the 'Blackfriars', Evans's young turks, and the readers (because of his aristocratic provenance). His editorship lasted for only three years, a short period to occupy the editor's chair in those days. But it was as crucial as any for the survival of the paper.

Douglas-Home steered *The Times* sharply to the right, supporting most Thatcherite policies and the Reagan administration, especially in its Star Wars initiative. He gave the paper a clear sense of direction instead of moderate drift, while still allowing opposing views a place in its 'Oped' columns. Typical leading articles of the 'Thunderer' no longer perorated 'On the one hand A. On the other hand B. Only time will tell'. He carried on Evans's programme of modernization and demystification, while introducing many more features, and fuller coverage of crime and sport. He also introduced a top person's version of Bingo, called Portfolio, a stocks and shares game for money prizes, which he considered to be respectable for a paper such as *The Times*. High-minded 'Blackfriars' disapproved of his populist tendencies. But they saved the paper, and doubled its circulation to 500,000.

Douglas-Home suffered from chronic arthritis, caused by injuring his spine when he fell from horses while hunting. He was often confined to a wheelchair. After he became editor he developed myeloma, cancer of the bone marrow. He continued to edit through a telephone 'squawk box' connected to an amplifier in the conference room, while he was at the Royal Marsden Hospital undergoing radium treatment. He carried on editing and writing leaders with the tenacity of a border reaver until the end.

Widely known as Charlie, Douglas-Home was informal and mischievous, but at the same time a highly professional and political journalist. He was without personal vanity, surprising the Heythrop hunt by turning out in a yellow cardigan and his colleagues by wearing handed-down clothes and his son's shoes. Charlie Douglas-Home served *The Times* well through a crisis of nearly mortal turbulence. He died in the Royal Free Hospital, London, on 29 October 1985. PHILIP HOWARD

Sources *The Times* (30 Oct 1985) • News Int. RO, *The Times* archive • J. Grigg, *The history of The Times*, 6 (1993) • H. Evans, *Good times bad times* (1983) • W. Shawcross, *Murdoch* (1992) • *Daily Telegraph* (30 Oct 1985) • *Sunday Times* (3 Nov 1985) • *The Observer* (3 Nov 1985) • *CGPLA Eng. & Wales* (1986) • *DNB* • Burke, *Peerage* (1999)

Archives King's Lond., Liddell Hart C., corresp. and papers • News Int. RO | King's Lond., Liddell Hart C., corresp. with Sir B. H. Liddell Hart

Likenesses photographs, Times Picture Library

Wealth at death £212,382: probate, 24 Jan 1986, *CGPLA Eng. & Wales*

Home, Daniel Dunglas (1833–1886), medium, was born at Currie, near Edinburgh, on 20 March 1833, the third son of William Home (c.1810–1882), a labourer, and his wife, Elizabeth, *née* McNeil (c.1810–1850), and was raised as a Presbyterian. He seems to have added his middle name later because of his belief that his father was the illegitimate son of the tenth earl of Home. Hostile biographers have alleged that he invented this story; but there is documentary evidence that the earl paid for William Home's apprenticeship and upkeep. Daniel Home was adopted in infancy by his mother's sister, Mrs Mary Cook, and with this lady and her husband emigrated about 1842 to the United States, settling in Greeneville, now part of Norwich, Connecticut. Here he attended school, receiving a sound basic education. His own family shortly settled in nearby Waterford, Connecticut.

Home was a studious, dreamy, and sensitive boy, often ill. A vision in 1850 of the unexpected death of his mother awoke in him religious interests that led to friction with his aunt. That lady, a strict Presbyterian, was further shocked early the following year when poltergeist phenomena, in the form of inexplicable raps and object movements, broke out around him. This was the period of the Fox sisters and the rapid spread of 'spirit-rapping' in the eastern United States. Daniel's rappings soon began to take the form of ostensible communications from the dead, and the terrified Mrs Cook threw out her nephew, still not quite eighteen, to fend for himself. The strange phenomena went with him.

In this way Home was precipitated into a mode of life that he pursued for many years. He did not become a professional medium, but almost a professional guest, moving from one hospitable family to another, mostly of spiritualists. At first they were solid middle-class folk, but after his return to Europe he moved increasingly among the cosmopolitan upper classes. Usually there was a tacit understanding that he would, if 'in power', hold séances for his hosts and their friends. He would never sit for money, though he did receive indirect benefits over and above hospitality—for instance travelling expenses and gifts, especially of jewellery (which he retained rather than sold).

During Home's residence in the United States most of his characteristic phenomena were already in evidence. The company generally sat with their hands on a table, often a large and heavy one. Raps would come from it,

Daniel Dunglas Home (1833–1886), by Maull & Co.

spelling out messages from the 'spirits', who sometimes produced information which the medium could hardly have known. Commonly the table would move about, rock, and rise clear of the floor, sometimes to a considerable height. Or it might tilt steeply while objects on it remained as if glued in position. Surrounding items of furniture might be moved, or small objects carried through the air. These phenomena would often occur in good light, and sitters were at liberty to search beneath levitated tables. Dimmer, though usually passable, light was required for the playing of musical instruments by unseen hands, and for the visible or tangible manifestation of the hands themselves. Near, though not total, darkness was needed for the relatively frequent phenomenon of 'spirit lights' and the much rarer one of levitation of the medium's body. Later developments included the unscathed handling of red-hot coals, the supposed elongation of his body, once by as much as 11 inches, and the materialization of dim or misty phantom figures. During all these happenings (which were by no means confined to séance situations) Home might be awake, or sleepy, or ostensibly in a trance state. When in trance he might clairvoyantly 'see' spirits and deliver messages from them (some of which profoundly impressed the recipients) or be 'taken over' and speak as if controlled by them.

Meanwhile friends at Newburgh, New York, had been urging him to resume his education. Early in 1853 he went as a boarder to the Newburgh Theological Institute, and began the private study of French and German. That autumn he commenced medical studies in New York, but after a few months his health broke down. A second attempt the following autumn had the same result. In January 1855 pulmonary consumption was diagnosed and a voyage to Europe recommended. On 31 March he sailed for England, probably subsidized and furnished with introductions by prosperous American spiritualists.

In the spring and summer Home stayed for extended periods with two spiritualist sympathizers, Mr William Cox of Cox's Hotel, Jermyn Street, London, and Mr J. S. Rymer, a solicitor of Ealing. Invitations to his sittings were eagerly sought. Among notables who attended and were impressed were Sir Edward Bulwer Lytton, Robert Owen, Lord Brougham, Sir David Brewster (who later denied that he had seen anything remarkable), J. J. Garth Wilkinson (a well-known Swedenborgian), T. Adolphus Trollope and his mother, and Elizabeth Barrett Browning. However Elizabeth's husband, Robert, conceived a violent loathing of Home and later lampooned him viciously in 'Mr Sludge the Medium' (1864).

In autumn 1855 Home travelled to Florence at the invitation of the Trollopes. There 'the manifestations were very strong', and hostesses were eager to secure him. But he became the subject of obscurely unfavourable gossip, and on 10 February 1856 the spirits informed him that his power would depart for a year. Shortly afterwards he visited Naples and Rome with friends, and while at Rome was received into the Catholic church. In June 1856 he went to Paris and remained there through the winter, despite serious lung ailments. On 10 February 1857 his powers duly returned. The emperor, Louis Napoleon, immediately summoned him, and for much of the next year he was frequently at court, where his virtuoso displays caused amazement and his supposed influence over the emperor and empress dark rumours. Towards the end of March he returned briefly to America to fetch his sister, Christine, whose education the empress had offered to arrange; in August and September he visited Baden Baden, and there gave three sittings to Friedrich Wilhelm, the crown prince of Prussia (later emperor of Germany). In February 1858 he was taken to Holland for sittings with a rationalist group, De Dageraad, and also gave sittings to the queen of Holland. On his return to Paris he received medical advice to seek a warmer climate, and in March went to Rome. There he met, and after a swift courtship became engaged to, Alexandrina (Sacha) de Kroll, a diminutive, vivacious, and charming Russian girl of seventeen, the daughter of Count de Kroll, and a goddaughter of the tsar. They were married at St Petersburg on 1 August 1858.

For almost a year they remained in Russia, where Home gave sittings to many in high society, including the tsar. On 8 May 1859 the Homes had a son, Gregoire (Gricha). In the autumn they made their way to England, staying there for the best part of the next two years. Home was now famous, and much in demand by fashionable hostesses. Persons of greater intellectual consequence also showed some interest, especially following publication of Robert Bell's article 'Stranger than fiction' in the *Cornhill Magazine* for August 1860. Sacha Home, by now a total convert to spiritualism, frequently attended her husband's sittings, but she was consumptive, and her health was failing. Visits to health resorts in England and abroad did not halt the disease, and she died in France on 3 July 1862.

On returning to London, Home found himself in financial difficulties. Sacha's modest estate had been seized by relatives. To raise funds he produced, with the help of two recent converts, W. M. Wilkinson, a solicitor, and Robert Chambers, his autobiographical *Incidents in my Life* (1863). He also embarked on a disastrous attempt to train as a sculptor in Rome. He arrived there in November 1863, but early in January was summarily expelled as a practitioner of the black arts. In England again, he decided to earn his living by giving public readings, and in the summer of 1864 successfully toured America. On his return in May 1865 he set out for Russia, where his phenomena were very powerful and he became the guest of the tsar and of Count Aleksey Tolstoy. Back in England later in the year his health deteriorated, and he spent several periods at the Malvern hydropathic establishment of another convert, Dr James Manby Gully. In the summer of 1866 Gully joined Mr and Mrs S. C. Hall and other well-wishers in establishing a spiritualist centre, the Spiritual Athenaeum, at 22 Sloane Street, London, of which Home became resident secretary without any obligation to hold sittings.

This comfortable arrangement was upset after a few months by the intrusion into Home's life of a dominating and emotionally disturbed elderly widow, Mrs Jane Lyon, who pressed upon him £60,000 by deeds of gift on condition that he added her surname to his own. Home foolishly agreed. In the summer of 1867 Mrs Lyon changed her mind, accused Home of swindling her, and instituted a chancery suit. At the hearing in April 1868 she was detected in numerous lies and contradictions, but the vice-chancellor, although refusing to award her costs, found against Home on the curious but legally correct grounds that the onus was on the defendant to prove that he had not exercised undue influence.

Home was befriended during this difficult period by Lord Adare (later fourth earl of Dunraven) and the master of Lindsay. He spent much time in the company of Adare, whose accounts (and his father's) of seventy-eight sittings from November 1867 to July 1869 (*Experiences in Spiritualism with D. D. Home*) constitute the most extensive, and the most controversial, record of the phenomena Home produced both within and between séances.

The Lyon lawsuit left Home heavily in debt, and in 1869 and 1870 he toured England and Scotland giving highly successful public readings. On the outbreak of the Franco-Prussian War in July 1870 he travelled to France as war correspondent for the *San Francisco Chronicle*. In February 1871 he accepted an invitation to recuperate in Russia. There he was investigated by a number of savants, including A. Butlerov, professor of chemistry at St Petersburg. He also met Butlerov's sister-in-law, Miss Julie De Gloumeline, a keen spiritualist, and almost immediately became engaged to her.

Before the marriage, however, Home returned to England to fulfil a promise to William Crookes, the eminent chemist. Between April and July 1871 Crookes conducted the only attempts ever made to record Home's phenomena on self-registering instruments. In the most remarkable of these experiments Home, watched and held in sufficient light, was several times able to depress, without contact, a pivoted board and a parchment drum.

Home (now received into the Greek Orthodox church) and Miss De Gloumeline were married in Paris on 16 October 1871. She was a person of considerable worldly competence and took total charge of their affairs. She came from a well-to-do and well-connected family, and Home had by this time obtained the residuum of his first wife's estate. They travelled a good deal around Europe, visiting friends and health resorts. Their only child, a daughter Marie, born in April 1872, died a few months later. Though Home's health problems, pulmonary and arthritic, grew steadily worse, he still gave occasional sittings. He kept up a large correspondence, and published two more books, a second series of *Incidents in my Life* (1872) and *Lights and Shadows of Spiritualism* (1877), which shocked spiritualists by its attacks on mediumistic fraud. He died at Auteuil in France on 21 June 1886, survived by his second wife, and was buried at St Germain-en-Laye.

Home was about 5 feet 10 inches in height, slim, blue-eyed and red-haired, often tired or ill, but always fastidious in dress. There are many photographs of him. He had no immediately obvious faults of character, unless one counts a somewhat marked vanity, an occasional prickliness, a delight in wearing jewellery, and a willingness to be cossetted by the ladies; he was often accused of effeminacy. He was a pleasant guest, musically talented, a fair linguist, kind, humorous, sociable, and happy to participate in parlour games and amateur dramatics. Scandalous rumours about him sometimes circulated, but are difficult to trace to any satisfactory source.

Of the strange happenings that surrounded Home many contemporary reports remain which, though varying in value, raise considerable problems. If the phenomena were as described, the framework of conventional science cannot accommodate them. But explaining them away presents its own difficulties. That (as sometimes suggested) Home hypnotized his sitters could be maintained only by someone who knew nothing of hypnosis. That he was a clever conjuror there is little evidence. The few allegations that he was detected in fraud were second- or third-hand, or were related long after the event, or both, and are of unclear significance. The conjuring hypothesis is almost pure speculation and generally involves passing over many of Home's performances, and supposing that others were radically different from the reports of them. He remains a puzzle.   ALAN GAULD

Sources G. Zorab, *D. D. Home il medium* (1976) · E. Jenkins, *The shadow and the light: a defence of Daniel Dunglas Home the medium* (1982) · J. Burton, *Heyday of a wizard: Daniel Home the medium* (1948) ·

J. Home, *D. D. Home, his life and mission* (1888) • J. Home, *The gift of D. D. Home* (1890) • D. D. Home, *Incidents in my life*, 2 vols. (1863–72) • F. W. H. Myers and W. F. Barrett, 'D. D. Home, his life and mission', *Journal of the Society for Psychical Research*, 4 (1889–90), 101–36 • E. J. Dingwall, *Some human oddities: studies in the queer, the uncanny and the fanatical* (1947), 91–128, 187–93 • F. Podmore, *Modern spiritualism: a history and a criticism* (1902), 2, 223–43 • *Crookes and the spirit world*, ed. M. R. Barrington and others (1972) • Viscount Adare [W. T. Wyndham-Quin], *Experiences in spiritualism with D. D. Home* (1870) • F. W. H. Myers, 'The character of Mr D. D. Home', *Journal of the Society for Psychical Research*, 6 (1893–4), 176–9 • *Report on spiritualism of the committee of the London Dialectical Society* (1871), 187–94, 206–16, 213–17, 359–71 • W. Crookes, *Researches in the phenomena of spiritualism* (1874) • W. Crookes, 'Notes of séances with D. D. Home', *Proceedings of the Society for Psychical Research*, 6 (1889–90), 98–127 • J. S. Rymer, *Spirit manifestations* (1857) • P. P. Alexander, *Spiritualism: a narrative with a discussion* (1871) • F. Podmore, *The newer spiritualism* (1910), 31–86 • A. Lang, *Historical mysteries* (1904), 170–92 • J. Oppenheim, *The other world: spiritualism and psychical research in England, 1850–1914* (1985), 10–16, 34–5 • G. Stein, *The sorcerer of kings* (1993) • T. H. Hall, *The enigma of Daniel Home: medium or fraud?* (1984)

Archives CUL, Society for Psychical Research archives, corresp. • NA Scot., earl of Home MSS

Likenesses J. Durham?, bronze bust, *c.*1860, Society for Psychical Research, London • H. W. Pickersgill, oils, 1866, College of Psychic Studies, London • Maull & Co., photograph, London Library [*see illus.*] • photographs, CUL, SPR Archives • photographs, Mary Evans Picture Library, London • prints, NPG

Wealth at death £40: probate, 30 Aug 1886, *CGPLA Eng. & Wales*

Home [Hume], Sir David, of Crossrig, Lord Crossrig

(1643–1707), judge and diarist, was born on 23 May 1643, the second son of Sir John Home (*d.* 1656) of Blackadder, Berwickshire, and of Mary (*d.* 1678), daughter of Sir James Dundas of Arniston. He was only thirteen years old when his father died in October 1656, leaving a legacy that should have been enough to see him through his education, despite his elder brother's characteristic tardiness in payment. In 1657 Home entered the University of Edinburgh, from which he eventually graduated in 1662 after being excluded for part of his first year because he had attended an illicit football match. In 1664 he travelled to France and began studying the civil law at Poitiers, but when France allied with the Netherlands in the Second Anglo-Dutch War in January 1666 he had to cut his stay short and return to Edinburgh. Others in the same predicament at once petitioned for admission of the bar, but Home lacked confidence in his learning and determined to continue studying on his own. In 1672 he finally decided that he would never be suitably qualified and, 'judging it an undecent and evil thing to be altogether idle', embarked on a series of unsuccessful commercial ventures (Hume, *Domestic Details*, 17). In debt for the first time, he nevertheless decided to marry Barbara Weir (*d.* 1678), widow of William Laurie of Reidcastle, on 28 April 1674. In the following year his brother died, leaving him with responsibility for the care of his nephew, and by the time his wife died in 1678 he also had two daughters to look after. He found it convenient to move to Blackadder and to lead the life destined originally for his brother and now for his nephew.

Some time in 1680 Home married a woman he called 'Mrs Smith' (*née* Hepburn), widow of James Smith, an Edinburgh merchant, who gave birth to two sons in 1681 and 1683. Throughout these years at Blackadder, Home was so frequently involved in legal wrangles that by 1687 he felt sufficiently experienced to make another attempt at entering the legal profession. Although too 'rusted in the study of law' to have any prospect of passing the examination imposed on intrants to the bar, he was allowed into practice by the lords of session without going through the usual procedure, agreeing to pay the Faculty of Advocates twice the usual admission fee (Hume, *Domestic Details*, 43). His legal wrangles continued, and it was in consequence of one protracted dispute, relating to debts owed since 1636, that he eventually acquired the lands of Crossrig. His claim to the lands was jeopardized in 1700 when his deeds were lost in the great fire that swept through the Edinburgh meal market, but he was able to obtain an act of parliament in 1701 making up their tenor. By the time he died in 1707 he had managed to secure his financial position.

The foundation of this new security was his surprising appointment to judicial office as a lord of session on 1 November 1689 and a lord of justiciary on 27 January 1690. His late arrival at the bar, together with his known commitment to presbyterian church government and suspected involvement in plots against the rule of James VII, made him an attractive appointment to William III (who knighted him shortly afterwards), though his presence in the session did not assist those who had to defend the bench against charges of incompetence and insufficiency. Unlike some of his colleagues, he was at least excused from the charge of corruption and was remembered after his death for being 'Upright in judgment, in decisions sure', a friend to the weak who dispensed justice 'without bribes' (Brunton and Haig, 440).

Seven years after his appointment to the bench, and two years after he was knighted, Home began to keep the diary from which most of the interest in and information about his life derives, starting with a lengthy account of his past experiences 'for my own and my successors information' (Hume, *Domestic Details*, 1). The diary is largely a record of the financial affairs of a Scottish laird in the latter half of the seventeenth century, full of interesting detail on how estates were acquired, relatives provided for, disputes conducted, and settlements made. Occasionally more weighty matters of politics creep in, as well as a good deal of personal detail on topics that are not obviously financial. Some remarks are frustratingly succinct, like the note on 13 April 1681: 'I gott my hurt that occasioned the cutting off my leg' (ibid., 29).

In 1701 Home wrote a letter of consolation to one of his children which, although not particularly interesting, was printed in 1771 as *Advice to a Daughter*. Between 1700 and his death on 13 April 1707 he compiled a record of the proceedings of the last Scottish parliament and of the privy council which, although not based on his own active involvement in politics, has proved useful to historians of the union.

J. D. FORD

Sources D. Hume, *Domestic details* (1843) • D. Hume, *A diary of the proceedings in parliament and the privy council of Scotland, May 21, 1700 – March 7, 1707*, Bannatyne Club, 27 (1828) • G. Brunton and D. Haig,

An historical account of the senators of the college of justice, from its institution in MDXXXII (1832) · *APS, 1696–1701,* 292
Archives Royal College of Physicians of Edinburgh, diaries
Likenesses oils, U. Edin. · portrait; formerly in the possession of Mr Charles Kilpatrick Sharpe, possibly no longer survives
Wealth at death see Hume, *Domestic details*

Home, David Milne [*formerly* David Milne] (1805–1890), advocate and scientist, was born on 22 January 1805 at Inveresk, Musselburgh, near Edinburgh, the elder son of Admiral Sir David *Milne (1763–1845) and his first wife, Grace Purves (1776?–1814). He was educated at home, then at Musselburgh grammar school, and Edinburgh high school from 1819 to 1820. Milne showed high intellectual capacity and developed an early interest in science, most notably in geology, but after graduating MA at Edinburgh University in 1825 he studied law and became an advocate in 1826. He quickly became established in his profession and was advocate-depute from 1841 to 1845. On 30 July 1832 he married Jean Forman Home (1811?–1876) of Paxton. They had five daughters and a son.

Despite a heavy legal workload Milne maintained his interest in science and became a fellow of the Royal Society of Edinburgh in 1828. His researches in geology were published mainly in the society's *Transactions* and included papers on the geology of Berwickshire (1834) and Roxburghshire (1842–3), the coalfields of East Lothian and Midlothian (1839), and earthquakes in Great Britain (1841–3). He studied the terraces known as the parallel roads in Glen Roy and concluded that they marked the former levels of lakes, but never accepted the glaciation theory for their formation or for the distribution of boulders (erratics) in Scotland. He was a prominent member of the Highland and Agricultural Society of Scotland.

In 1845 Milne inherited from his father the estate of Milne-Graden, near Coldstream, Berwickshire. He gave up legal practice and became a country gentleman, devoting as much time as possible to science. He took the name Milne Home in 1852, when his wife inherited the properties of Wedderburn, Billie, and Paxton in Berwickshire. Milne Home was instrumental in the formation of the Edinburgh Geological Society and was elected a vice-president in 1871 and president in 1874. He was vice-president of the Royal Society of Edinburgh more than once and in 1870 was made an honorary LLD by the University of Edinburgh for his services to science.

Milne Home's contribution to meteorology in Scotland was primarily as a facilitator. In 1855 he and Sir John Forbes of Fettercairn drew up a prospectus for a meteorological association, which later became the Scottish Meteorological Society (SMS) and from 1858 to 1883 Milne Home was chairman of its council before becoming vice-president until his death. The surviving council minute books (1859 to 1881) show that he conducted the business most efficiently and gave every support to Alexander Buchan, the distinguished meteorological secretary, who was appointed in December 1860. From 1855 the SMS organized and ran the Scottish climatological network, but received no payment from government, although some computations were made by the astronomer royal

David Milne Home [David Milne] (1805–1890), by unknown artist

for Scotland. Milne Home played a major role in repeated attempts by the SMS to obtain a government grant, but this was refused until 1877. In 1877, as a means of obtaining upper air measurements, he proposed the setting up of a meteorological observatory on Ben Nevis, the highest mountain in Scotland and the next year he climbed the mountain to ascertain that this was feasible. Since no government support could be obtained a successful public appeal was launched in 1883. At the celebratory dinner for the opening Milne Home welcomed a situation which prevented government interference with Scottish management of the observatory, and 'he for one was in favour of local Scottish management of local affairs' (*The Scotsman*, 18 Oct 1883).

In politics Milne Home was a Conservative. He was convenor of Berwickshire county council from 1876 to 1889, and was the chief promoter of a fund which raised £26,000 for dependants of the Eyemouth fishermen who drowned in the terrible gale of 14 October 1881. Religion was of great importance to him: he was ordained an elder of the Church of Scotland at Inveresk in 1828 and he frequently spoke at the general assembly. He was a tall, dignified, somewhat autocratic man, who believed that 'What is worth doing at all, is worth doing well' (Home, 145). His wife died on 14 April 1876 and in 1885 he suffered an illness from which he never fully recovered. He died on 19 September 1890 at Milne-Graden from epithelioma and pneumonia and was buried on the 24th in Hutton churchyard.

MARJORY G. ROY

Sources G. M. Home, *Biographical sketch of David Milne Home* (1891) · R. Richardson, *Transactions of the Geological Society of Edinburgh*, 6 (1890), 119–27 · Scottish Meteorological Society, minute books of the council, 1859–81 • 'Reports of the council to the general meeting of the Scottish Meteorological Society', *Proceedings of the Scottish Meteorological Society* (1856–63) • 'Reports of the council to the general meeting of the Scottish Meteorological Society', *Journal of the Scottish Meteorological Society*, 1–9 (1864–90) • A. Watt, 'The early days of the society', *Journal of the Scottish Meteorological Society*, 15 (1911), 304–12 • *The Scotsman* (18 Oct 1883) • *Glasgow Herald* (18 Oct 1883) • *The Scotsman* (22 Sept 1890) • parish register (baptism), Inveresk, Musselburgh, Scotland, 22 Feb 1805 • d. cert.

Archives NL Scot., family corresp. • NRA Scotland, priv. coll., corresp. and papers | U. Edin. L., special collections division, letters to Sir Archibald Geikie • U. Edin. L., special collections division, letters to Sir Charles Lyell

Likenesses pencil drawing, Edinburgh Meteorological Office archives [*see illus.*]

Wealth at death £121,226 4*s*. 11*d*.: confirmation, 14 Nov 1890, *CCI*

Home, Sir Everard, first baronet (1756–1832), surgeon, was born at Hull, Yorkshire, on 6 May 1756, the son of Robert Boyne Home (*d*. 1786), army surgeon, later of Greenlaw Castle, Berwickshire, and his wife, Mary, daughter of Colonel Hutchinson. Robert *Home, the painter, was his brother. Educated at Westminster School where he was a king's scholar, Home gained a scholarship to Trinity College, Cambridge, in 1773, but chose instead to become a surgical pupil of his brother-in-law John *Hunter (1728–1793), surgeon at St George's Hospital, London. Hunter had married Home's sister Anne [*see* Hunter, Anne] in 1771 after a seven-year courtship during which Home had come to know him well. Home qualified through the Company of Surgeons in 1778 and was appointed assistant surgeon in the new naval hospital at Plymouth. In 1779 he went to Jamaica as staff surgeon with the army, but on returning to England on half pay in 1784 he rejoined Hunter at St George's as assistant in teaching, research, and clinical practice, living in Hunter's house in Green Street, Leicester Square. He was elected FRS on 15 February 1787 and in the same year he became assistant surgeon at St George's Hospital. For his first published medical work, *A Dissertation on the Properties of Pus* (1788), he received the gold medal of the Lyceum Medicum Londinensis, a medical society founded by Hunter and George Fordyce. In 1790–91 Home read lectures for Hunter and in the following year he succeeded Hunter as lecturer in anatomy. Also in 1792 he married Jane Thompson, daughter of the Revd Dr Tunstall, and widow of Stephen Thompson. They lived in Leicester Square near Hunter's house and there were two sons and four daughters.

Home joined the army in Flanders in the spring of 1793, but returned just before Hunter's sudden death on 16 October 1793. He then became surgeon at St George's Hospital and was also joint executor of Hunter's will with Matthew Baillie, Hunter's nephew. In 1793–4 they saw Hunter's important work, *On the Blood, Inflammation and Gun-Shot Wounds*, through the press and in 1794 Home approached Pitt's government to secure the purchase for the nation of Hunter's large collection of anatomical and pathological specimens. After protracted negotiations the collection was purchased for £15,000 in 1799 and presented to the College of Surgeons. In 1806 the collection was moved from Hunter's gallery in Castle Street to form

Sir Everard Home, first baronet (1756–1832), by Thomas Phillips, 1829

the Hunterian Museum at the new site of the college in Lincoln's Inn Fields. Home was chief curator and William Clift, who had worked with Hunter since 1792, was retained as resident conservator. Clift also had charge of Hunter's numerous folios, drawings, and accounts of anatomical and pathological investigations, which were essential for a clear understanding of the collection.

In the years following Hunter's death Home built up a large surgical practice and published more than one hundred papers of varying quality, some very good, mainly in the *Philosophical Transactions of the Royal Society*. He gave the Croonian lectures fifteen times between 1794 and 1826. As Hunter's brother-in-law and executor he had great influence at the Royal College of Surgeons where he was elected to the court of assistants in 1801, an examiner in 1809, master in 1813 and 1821, and its first president in 1822. Having, with Matthew Baillie, endowed the Hunterian oration, he was the first Hunterian orator on 14 February 1814 and again in 1822. He became keeper and a trustee of the Hunterian Museum in 1817 and was professor of anatomy and surgery at the college from 1804 to 1813 and again in 1821. His *Lectures on Comparative Anatomy* were published in 1814 with a volume of plates from drawings by Clift. A further volume of lectures followed in 1823 accompanied by microscopical and anatomical drawings by Bauer and Clift. Two more volumes appeared in 1828. This work, although lacking in structure, is an important record of Hunter's investigations, especially the last two volumes.

Home drew heavily on Hunter's work in the papers and books which he published after Hunter's death. Before the collection was presented to the Company of Surgeons in 1799 Home arranged for Clift to convey to his own house Hunter's folio volumes and fasciculi of manuscripts containing descriptions of the preparations and investigations connected with them. He promised to catalogue the collection, refusing help, but, despite repeated requests, only a synopsis appeared in 1818. B. C. Brodie says that Home was busily using Hunter's papers in preparing his own contributions for the Royal Society. Home himself later stated that he had published all of value in Hunter's papers and that his one hundred articles in *Philosophical Transactions* formed a *catalogue raisonée* of the Hunterian Museum. Home destroyed most of Hunter's papers in 1823.

A select committee was set up by parliament after Home's death to enquire into the details of this act of vandalism. Clift told this committee in 1834 that Home had used Hunter's papers extensively and had claimed that Hunter, when he was dying, had ordered him to destroy his papers. Yet Home, who was not present at Hunter's death, had kept the papers for thirty years. Clift also declared that he had often transcribed parts of Hunter's original work and drawings into papers which appeared under Home's name. Home produced a few of Hunter's papers which he had not destroyed and Clift had copied about half of the descriptions of preparations in the collection, consequently enough of Hunter's work survives to suggest that Home had often published Hunter's observations as his own. Although the full extent of Home's plagiarism cannot be determined, there is little doubt that it was considerable and this seriously damaged his reputation.

Home's friend Astley Cooper said that he had a good deal of genius and great mental quickness. He was a competent surgeon; his examinations at the college were good and he was an excellent teacher, but his destruction of Hunter's papers was unwise as it led to the unfounded belief that he did nothing himself. Home's best work is in his surgical books, especially his *Practical Observations on the Treatment of Ulcers on the Legs* (1797), based on his military experience. In character he was vain, overbearing, and violent in language. He wanted to be recognized as the equal of Hunter and tried without success to fill his place. Yet, although disappointed, he received many honours never accorded to Hunter. In 1808 Home was appointed sergeant-surgeon to George III. He also established a personal friendship with the prince regent who on 2 January 1813 created him baronet. In 1821 Home became surgeon to the Royal Chelsea Hospital and in 1827 he resigned the surgeoncy at St George's Hospital, becoming consulting surgeon. He died in his apartments at Chelsea Hospital on 31 August 1832 and was buried in the hospital burial-ground.   N. G. COLEY

Sources T. H. Sellors, 'Some pupils of John Hunter [pt 2]', *Annals of the Royal College of Surgeons of England*, 53 (1973), 206–10, esp. 208–9 · J. M. Oppenheimer, *New aspects of John and William Hunter*, 1/1: *Everard Home and the destruction of the John Hunter manuscripts* (1946) · *GM*, 1st ser., 102/2 (1832), 384–5 · A. Keith, 'Life and times of William Clift', *BMJ* (15 Dec 1923), 1127–31 · *Autobiography of the late Sir Benjamin C. Brodie*, ed. B. C. B. [B. C. Brodie], 2nd edn (1865), 29–31 · B. B. Cooper, *The life of Sir Astley Cooper*, 2 vols. (1843) · W. Clift, 'Abstract of the evidence of members of the Royal College of Surgeons … taken before the parliamentary medical committee in 1834', *The Lancet* (11 July 1835), 471–6 · W. Le Fanu, 'Home, Everard', *DSB*, 6.478–9 · D. C. L. Fitzwilliams, 'The destruction of John Hunter's papers', *Proceedings of the Royal Society of Medicine*, 42 (1949), 871–6 · J. Dobson, *William Clift* (1954) · private information (2004) · Z. Cope, *The Royal College of Surgeons of England: a history* (1959) · *The record of the Royal Society of London*, 4th edn (1940)

Archives BL, lecture notes, Add. MS 34407 · College of Physicians of Philadelphia · CUL, lecture notes · NHM, corresp. and papers; lecture notes and corresp. · RCS Eng., corresp. and papers · RS, papers · U. Edin. L., special collections division, lecture notes · Wellcome L., notes on his lectures | Académie des Sciences, Paris, corresp. with Baron de Cuvier · RCS Eng., letters to J. E. Home

Likenesses W. Beachey, oils, 1810, RCS Eng. · F. Chantrey, marble bust, exh. RA 1816, RCS Eng. · T. Phillips, oils, 1829, RS [*see illus.*] · F. Chantrey, pencil drawing, NPG · W. Clift, pencil sketch (in presidential robes), RCS Eng. · W. H. Clift, pencil drawing, BM · W. Sharp, line engravings (after W. Beechey), Wellcome L.

Home, Francis (1719–1813), physician, was born in Edinburgh on 9 November 1719, the second son of James Home, an advocate of Eccles, Berwickshire, and Jean Kinloch. Home's early schooling was in Duns with the respected classical scholar and teacher Mr Cruickshanks, who instilled in his pupil the love of classical literature and skill in Latin that remained with him throughout his life. After this early schooling he was apprenticed to Mr Rattray, an eminent Edinburgh surgeon. Next came studies at the new medical faculty of the University of Edinburgh, where he was an early member of the influential Royal Medical Society. However, before graduating he became a surgeon with the 6th Inniskilling regiment of dragoons and served with them in Flanders during the War of the Austrian Succession. During the campaign Home drew up regimental orders for the prevention of fevers, which stated that the soldiers should not drink water unless it had been boiled. He used the winter campaign breaks to attend Leiden medical school (popular with Scots wishing to study medicine) and still flourishing in this period twelve years after Herman Boerhaave's death.

After the war Home settled in Edinburgh, where he finally graduated MD from the university in 1750. He put his army experience to good use by incorporating medical data on the remittent fevers (malaria) collected while tending troops at Worms into his inaugural dissertation, *De febre remittente*. The next twenty years were very productive and Home's interests ranged widely. In 1751 he published an essay on the chemical properties of 'Dunse Spa' (Duns), proposing that the waters had an anthelminthic effect. The year 1751 also saw Home becoming a fellow of the Royal College of Physicians of Edinburgh and starting to build up his medical practice. In 1758 an Edinburgh measles epidemic prompted him to experiment with the use of a measles vaccine. In *Medical Facts and Experiments* (1759) he stated 'I should do no small service to mankind if I could render this disease more mild and safe in the same way as the Turks have taught us to mitigate the small-pox'. Home took blood from the cutaneous veins found among the measle spots of his most feverish patients and tried it out on both children with measles and those without. He concluded that the inoculated patients had milder cases of measles. He also published important observations on diphtheria in the first clinical description of croup, *An Inquiry into the Nature, Cause and Cure of the Croup* (1765). This publication detailed the development of laryngeal and tracheal involvement in the disease. Home described the 'white, soft, thick prenatural coat or membrane' lining the upper respiratory tract and vividly observed that it lay loose, resembling the 'blankets of a bed that has been lain in' (pp. 16–19). He suggested that tracheotomy should be used in desperate cases.

In 1756 Home turned his attention to chemistry and in *Experiments on Bleaching* recommended that bleachers should use dilute sulphuric acid instead of sour milk. This publication greatly increased the profitability of bleaching and the Honourable Board of Trustees for the Improvement of Manufactures in North Britain paid him £100 and presented him with a gold medal. In 1757 it was agriculture that benefited from his research. In his book *The Principles of Agriculture and Vegetation* he applied chemistry to farming, describing the growth of plants potted in soils treated with compounds like magnesium sulphate and potassium nitrate. He also showed that plants gain nutrition from air.

Home was not neglecting medicine and in 1758 he published the first edition of his scientific history of disease, *Principia medicinae*, which included a description of his discovery that yeast ferments diabetic urine. *Principia medicinae* increased his reputation—especially in Europe and America, where the publication was widely used as a textbook. It went through several editions and was still consulted well into the nineteenth century. In 1768 Home obtained the first professorship of materia medica in the University of Edinburgh. The subject had previously been studied as a subset of botany. To meet the student need for a syllabus of drugs Home published in 1770 *Methodus materia medicae* based on his lecture notes. During this period Edinburgh University had an official relationship with the Royal Infirmary of Edinburgh (established in 1756) and Home was one of the professors responsible for patient care and bedside teaching in its teaching ward. Clinical observation was always one of his interests and he promoted the methodology for history taking and physical examination formulated by the medical faculty. He stated that 'many symptoms cannot be described by the patient himself, these we must discover by our senses' ('Clinical lectures', 8). The publication of a course of clinical lectures in 1780, *Clinical Experiments Histories and Dissections*, rounded off his publishing career.

Home was one of his majesty's physicians in Scotland and he followed William Cullen as president of the Royal College of Physicians of Edinburgh from 1775 to 1777. During his presidency he oversaw the problematic construction of the college's George Street Hall, designed by James Craig. In 1798 James *Home succeeded his father, becoming the second professor of materia medica. Francis himself lived for another fourteen years. Contemporary statements and the evidence of his manuscript cashbook suggest that he was mentally active until within a short

period of his death on 15 February 1813 in his ninety-fourth year. He was buried at Earlston, Berwickshire.

Francis Home was in many ways the quintessential establishment Scottish Enlightenment physician, whose long life spanned the period when Edinburgh medicine was at its most influential.   IAIN MILNE

Sources E. E. Hume, 'Francis Home, MD (1719–1813), the Scottish military surgeon who first described diphtheria as a clinical entity', *Bulletin of the History of Medicine*, 11 (1942), 48–68 · W. E. Home, 'Francis Home (1719–1813), first professor of materia medica in Edinburgh', *Proceedings of the Royal Society of Medicine*, 21 (1927–8), 1013–15 · J. F. Enders, 'Francis Home and his experimental approach to medicine', *Bulletin of the History of Medicine*, 38 (1964), 101–12 · J. Kay, *A series of original portraits and caricature etchings … with biographical sketches and illustrative anecdotes*, ed. [H. Paton and others], new edn [2nd edn], 1 (1842), 249–51 · 'Francis Home (1719–1813), practitioner of experimental medicine', *Journal of the American Medical Association*, 209 (1969), 412–13 [editorial] · J. J. Byrne, 'Dr Francis Home and puerperal sepsis', *The New England Journal of Medicine*, 251 (1954), 440–42 · S. A. Plotkin, 'Vaccination against measles in the 18th century', *Clinical Pediatrics*, 6 (1967), 312–15 · J. D. Comrie, *History of Scottish medicine*, 2nd edn, 1 (1932), 317–19 · J. D. Comrie, *History of Scottish medicine to 1860* (1927), 118–19 · A. Doig, J. P. S. Ferguson, I. A. Milne, and R. Passmore, eds., *William Cullen and the eighteenth century medical world* (1993), 20 · D. T. Rice and P. McIntyre, *The university portraits* (1957), 107–8 · G. B. Risse, *Hospital life in Enlightenment Scotland: care and teaching at the Royal Infirmary of Edinburgh* (1986) · 'Clinical lectures by Dr Francis Home King's physitian at Edinburgh taken by John Goodsir', 1769, Royal College of Physicians of Edinburgh, Home MS (F) 5, 8 · *IGI*

Archives Edinburgh Central Reference Library, casebook · Royal College of Physicians of Edinburgh, casebooks and lecture notes · U. Edin. L., clinico-medical cases and lecture notes · Wellcome L., casebook

Likenesses J. Kay, caricature, etching, 1787, BM · D. Allan?, oils, U. Edin.

Home, George. *See* Hume, George, fourth Lord Hume (*d.* 1549).

Home, George, earl of Dunbar (*d.* 1611), courtier and administrator, was the fourth son of Alexander Home of Manderston (*d.* 1593) and Janet Home (*d.* 1593), daughter of George Home of Spott. The date of his birth is uncertain. There were many divisions among the Homes as a family, including religious divisions. The Manderston sept was firmly protestant. The head of the family, Alexander, sixth Lord Home, was a Catholic, and in 1590 George Home married Elizabeth, daughter and heir of the Catholic Sir George Gordon of Gicht. His ties to both religious parties stood Home in good stead in the occasionally overheated religious atmosphere of Jacobean Scotland.

The courtier At some point in the early 1580s Home made his way to court. In March 1585 he was cleared of a charge, brought by a kinsman, of being in touch with the Ruthven raiders, a group of nobles and lairds who had seized the young James VI and taken control of government in 1582–3; shortly thereafter he became a gentleman of the bedchamber. In 1589 Home accompanied King James on his voyage to Denmark to claim his bride. While there Home engineered his first major promotion, to the office of master of the wardrobe. James was annoyed at the incumbent, Sir William Keith, because, James said, Keith dressed better than he did. More importantly, the king was annoyed

George Home, earl of Dunbar (*d.* 1611), by unknown artist

at the head of the family, George Keith, fourth Earl Marischal, his ambassador to the Danish court, who resented having to yield precedence there to the lord chancellor, John Maitland of Thirlestane, whom Marischal regarded as an upstart. In making his profit from circumstances for which he was not responsible, Home showed a sure touch and an ability to read the king's moods which he never lost. He became a favourite with James, but not of the usual kind. He was not a pretty young man. He did not share the king's passion for hunting. But he was good company, discreet, cautious, and, above all, loyal. As George Nicolson, the English agent in Edinburgh, who knew him well, put it in January 1603, Home acted 'by the King's good direction, without which he is noted to deal in nothing' (*CSP Scot.*, *1597–1603*, 1055–6).

In the faction-ridden Scottish court of the 1590s Home became the quintessential courtier. As early as August 1590 Chancellor Maitland thought it worth while to have Home's support for requests he made of the king. On 4 November 1590 Home was knighted; he and Alexander Lindsay, who became Lord Spynie in that same month, were described as James's 'special favourites', who received 'a promise of a great part' of the annual pension James received from England 'before it be arrived' (*CSP Scot.*, *1589–93*, 419, 473). Spynie was a rival. Both became privy councillors in June 1592, but by August they had quarrelled, and Spynie found himself accused of being friendly with Francis Stewart, first earl of Bothwell, the king's cousin but now the object of James's hatred and fear. Home was Bothwell's enemy, and had been ever since 1584, when Bothwell 'hewed Davy Hume [George's

brother] all to pieces' (*CSP Scot.*, *1584–5*, 330), because Bothwell claimed the priory of Coldingham, currently in the possession of George's eldest brother, Alexander. Home solidified his position as the king's confidant. James frequently used him to carry messages to the English agents at court, one of whom described him in December 1591 as 'very wise and very honest' (*CSP Scot.*, *1589–93*, 595). Those in James's bad books, such as Bothwell's associate John Colville, found that the surest way to regain the king's goodwill was to enlist Home's support. In June 1594 Home in his capacity as master of the wardrobe received £4000 Scots to buy cloth, chairs, and stools, and repair tapestries, in anticipation of the baptism of James's son and heir, which took place in August. A month later an English agent reported that Bothwell, who in 1592 had publicly urged that Home be killed, planned to seize the king and hang Home, in imitation of the aristocracy's treatment of James III's alleged favourite, Thomas Cochrane, in 1482. Within six months Bothwell had left Scotland forever. During these years Home managed to avoid denunciation by the kirk on account of his friendship with the Catholic earl of Huntly—he was alleged to have obtained the notorious blank commission for Huntly before the latter's murder of the earl of Moray in 1592—and indeed Home helped to persuade his kinsman Lord Home to submit to the kirk and follow the king's wishes.

Lord treasurer The appointment of the Octavians in 1596 to bring order out of the chaos of James's finances threatened not only the incomes of those like Home whom the contemporary historian David Calderwood described as 'cubicular courtiers' (Calderwood, 5.510), but also Home's ambition, which had surfaced as early as 1592, to become lord treasurer himself. It is possible, as Calderwood alleges, that Home had a hand in prodding some clergymen to take action against the Octavians, many of whom were regarded, accurately, as Catholics. The resulting anti-Catholic riot in December 1596 served Home well. James now viewed the Octavians, efficient though they were, as a political liability. Successive lords treasurer who replaced them were incompetent; so James finally turned to Home, whom Nicolson described in October 1600 as 'the only greatest courtier' (*CSP Scot.*, *1597–1603*, 720). On 1 October 1601 Home became lord treasurer. He retained the office until his death, although after 1603, when he followed the king to London and remained there, he exercised his authority through deputies.

During his eighteen months of direct supervision of the treasury Home acted with vigour. The collection of arrears of taxation was speeded up; Home himself received a share of what was collected. He tightened up the administration of acts of caution. In the interest of law and order as well as the treasury he ordered all sheriffs and their subordinates to pursue all those at the horn (outlawed) since 1596 and to seize their moveables until they found caution to appear in court. Paradoxically, his own record as sheriff of Berwick was none too good; the privy council in December 1599 cited him for negligence in pursuit of those charged with crimes, especially if their names happened to be Home.

These activities, and regular attendance at meetings of the privy council, kept Home busy, but never so busy that he neglected his principal occupation: constant attendance on the king. He had a reputation for ruthlessness in undercutting potential rivals; so much so that when in February 1601 the earl of Mar was preparing to go to London on special embassy, he had his cousin Thomas Erskine, one of the heroes of the Gowrie conspiracy, remain behind to be sure Home attempted nothing prejudicial to Mar's interests while he was gone. Only Home had the courage and tact to discuss with James the rumours of Queen Anne's possible involvement with Gowrie. When the royal couple's baby son died in June 1602 Home brought the body quietly at night to Holyrood Abbey for burial—neither parent was there—and then rode off to Dunfermline to comfort the king. He was not one of those officially involved in James's private correspondence with Robert Cecil in the last years of Elizabeth's reign, but he could foresee what would happen, and knew that it would pay him to have a good reputation among English officials. So he cultivated Nicolson, who in 1595 used him to urge James to write to Elizabeth about the situation in Ireland; he was helpful, wrote Nicolson, in keeping aid from going to the Irish rebels. Nicolson regularly praised him as 'a very good instrument for the peace and amity' (*CSP Scot.*, 1595–7, 39–40), and as regularly pointed out his closeness to the king: he followed James's wishes absolutely, 'so dutiful and observing of the king is he' (*CSP Scot.*, 1597–1603, 924). His power was steadily growing; in July 1602 Nicolson wrote that Home and Comptroller David Murray of Gospertie, his colleague in the financial administration, were the dominant figures in the government.

The union of the crowns When James succeeded to the English throne Home and Murray loaned him large sums to pay the expenses of his journey south. And they accompanied James, along with many others. Most of the officials in James's entourage eventually returned to Scotland; Home did not. His power depended on personal contact with the king, and he was determined not to relinquish it. James wanted him to stay; he appointed Home to the English privy council, made him keeper of the great wardrobe, put him in charge of Norham Castle, raised him to the English peerage as Baron Home of Berwick on 7 July 1604, and in the spring of 1608 made him a knight of the Garter. Home established an excellent working relationship with Sir Robert Cecil, and in effect acted as James's principal gatekeeper: access to the king could be most readily obtained through him. Perhaps in anticipation of the successful conclusion of the union he had so much at heart, James also made Home chancellor of the exchequer, one of two Scots named to an English governmental office. The appointments were widely resented, especially as Scots monopolized those positions, such as bedchamber posts, that involved personal access to the king. In 1606 Home, who on 3 July 1605 became earl of Dunbar in the Scottish peerage, stepped down from his English office.

Dunbar took no part in the union negotiations of 1604.

In the first two years after his removal to London he concentrated on another cause dear to James's heart: improved law and order in Scotland, especially on the borders. James could now afford a police force; Dunbar's ally, Comptroller Murray, was authorized to raise one. A separate border police was established in 1605, as was a joint Anglo-Scottish commission of justiciary. There were complaints on both sides of lack of co-operation; finally, in December 1606, James appointed Dunbar as chief of a revamped border commission with virtually full power to reorganize border administration and crack down on malefactors. Dunbar's crackdown was savage and efficient, so much so that his police chief, Sir William Cranston, was almost lynched in Dumfries. But by August 1609, following a mass hanging at Dumfries—one of several over which Dunbar had presided in the previous three years—Lord Chancellor Dunfermline could write to James comparing Dunbar's work to Hercules's cleansing of the Augean stables. His task was facilitated by the existence after 1608 of a refuge in the Ulster plantations for border reivers on the run from Cranston's police. By the time of Dunbar's death in 1611, writes one authority, 'there was no more Borderland in the old, wild, independent sense of the word' (Fraser, 327).

That Dunbar rather than one of the Edinburgh-based members of the privy council was put in charge of the borders was not surprising. By 1606 he had prevailed over Dunfermline, the head of the administration in Edinburgh, in their rivalry for the position of James's principal agent for Scottish business in the wake of the failed plans for Anglo-Scottish union. Once again Dunbar profited from circumstances not of his own making: Dunfermline's mishandling of an act of defiance by a group of ministers, who insisted on holding an unauthorized general assembly in 1605 in spite of a royal prohibition. James was very angry, and sent Dunbar north to deal with the ringleaders. In January 1606 six of the ministers were tried for treason and convicted by a jury packed with Dunbar's kinsmen which, even so, had to be bullied into its verdict. Dunbar returned to court to report and, if possible, to undermine the king's confidence in Dunfermline. In May 1606 Dunbar returned to Scotland to conduct a hearing that might have led to the chancellor's dismissal. Dunfermline saved himself, but had lost the power struggle. Dunbar's victory was facilitated by the technique he developed for exercising his influence: he travelled. From 1606 on he went back and forth between James's court and Scotland, as often as was necessary. When in Scotland he employed a combination of abruptness, violence, and distribution of favours which stimulated the fear and the greed of the Scottish political class. The method was extremely effective: Dunbar's appearances in Edinburgh had something of the impact of a royal visit.

The revival of episcopacy Dunbar was first, last, and always the courtier. He had no discernible views on public issues: what James wanted, he wanted. So he concentrated on James's priorities: the union, about which he could do little save to advise the passage of a parliamentary act prohibiting anti-English speeches, plays, and other writings;

law and order; and the reimposition of the power of the bishops in the Scottish church. The first step toward the achievement of the last goal was taken in parliament in July 1606, with the repeal of the 1587 act of annexation of the temporalities of benefices to the crown, an action accompanied by lavish rewards to many members of the landed classes, and ratifications of their existing possessions, in order to allay their fears for their own holdings of church property. For the clergy there was the creation of a commission to improve clerical stipends. Dunbar was instrumental in implementing James's decision to exile his principal clerical opponents, including Andrew and James Melville, and the six ministers convicted of treason.

The next step was to convene a clerical conference in Linlithgow in December 1606, ostensibly to deal with Catholics and increase clerical harmony. Dunbar, amply provided with cash, went north to manage it—his third trip of the year. He got the gathering to accept the king's proposal that each presbytery should have a permanent moderator appointed by the king. On being assured that this was a temporary measure, the gathering accepted it. When the record of the meeting emerged a few months later, however, it had been altered to declare that the meeting had been a general assembly, and that synods as well as presbyteries were to have constant moderators, namely, the bishops. Under pressure the synods and presbyteries, one by one, accepted this, and so did a properly convened general assembly in July 1608. Dunbar once again managed the meeting. He was accompanied north by his chaplain, George Abbot, and another English cleric 'to persuade the Scots that there was no substantial difference in religion betwixt the two realms' (Calderwood, 6.735). In January 1609 a convention of estates adopted a series of measures against Catholics and authorized the bishops to enforce them; in June parliament restored the bishops' jurisdiction over commissary courts; in February 1610 James created courts of high commission in the two archiepiscopal provinces, in imitation of England. Finally, in June 1610 a general assembly held at Glasgow approved the restoration of episcopal authority, subject only to the power of the assembly to censure or deprive a bishop, with the king's consent—if the assembly ever met again: there was no guarantee that it would. Dunbar managed all these meetings with his usual combination of intimidation and bribery. When parliament ratified the actions of the Glasgow assembly in 1612, after Dunbar's death, there was no mention of episcopal accountability to the assembly. Thanks to James's determination and Dunbar's tactical skills diocesan episcopacy returned to Scotland after a lapse of fifty years.

The final years With the question of episcopacy on its way to solution, Dunbar tightened his grip on power by a reorganization of the privy council. In February 1610 it was reduced substantially in size, and Dunbar swept out virtually all the judges of the court of session save those who were also officials: as lawyers they were more apt to be Dunfermline's allies than his. In August 1610 Dunbar

took advantage of the death of the comptroller to combine that office with his own, thus monopolizing financial authority. Two months later he and Dunfermline persuaded James to approve a plan to revise customs rates and end free trade with England in order to increase the crown's income. Dunbar's power in Scotland was at its apogee when he suddenly died, at Whitehall, on 20 January 1611. There was evidence that he was beginning to interest himself in English politics, with the decline in the influence of Robert Cecil, now earl of Salisbury, after the failure of the 'great contract' in the previous year. He recommended his former chaplain, Bishop George Abbot of London, for the vacant archbishopric of Canterbury; James made the appointment two months after Dunbar's death. After a funeral service at Westminster in April 1611 Dunbar's body was sent back to Scotland for burial in Dunbar collegiate church, where a splendid monument was raised to his memory.

There were no more earls of Dunbar. With his wife Elizabeth Gordon, whom he married in 1590, George Home had two daughters. The elder, Anne, married Sir James Home of Whitrig; their son James *Home succeeded to the earldom of Home in 1633. The younger daughter, Elizabeth, married Theophilus *Howard, the heir of Thomas Howard, first earl of Suffolk, one of Salisbury's political allies. Calderwood, who detested Dunbar for his role in restoring episcopacy, rejoiced that he died before he could occupy his 'sumptuous and glorious palace' in Berwick:

> But the curse was executed upon him that was pronounced upon the builders of Jericho. He ... left nothing undone to overthrow the discipline of our church ... But none of his posterity enjoyeth a foot broad of land this day of his conquist in Scotland. (Calderwood, 7.153)

Even Archbishop Spottiswoode was hardly effusive:

> a man of deep wit, few words, and in his majesty's service no less faithful than fortunate. The most difficult affairs he accomplished without any noise, and never returned when he was employed without the work performed that he was sent to do. (History of the Church, 3.214)

What can be said of Dunbar is that during his years of power Scotland saw greater change than at any other time in James's twenty-two years of absentee rule. There is a splendid portrait, painted in his last years, in the Scottish National Portrait Gallery. MAURICE LEE JUN.

Sources M. Lee, *Government by pen: Scotland under James VI and I* (1980) · G. Donaldson, *Scotland: James V to James VII* (1965), vol. 3 of *The Edinburgh history of Scotland* (1965–75) · J. Wormald, *Court, kirk, and community: Scotland, 1470–1625* (1981) · *CSP Scot., 1581–1603*, 6–13 · *Reg. PCS*, 1st ser., vols. 3–9, 14 · *Calendar of the manuscripts of the most hon. the marquis of Salisbury*, 24 vols., HMC, 9 (1883–1976) · *APS, 1567–1625* · *Report on the manuscripts of the earl of Mar and Kellie*, HMC, 60 (1904); suppl. (1930) · D. Calderwood, *The history of the Kirk of Scotland*, ed. T. Thomson and D. Laing, 8 vols., Wodrow Society, 7 (1842–9) · *State papers and miscellaneous correspondence of Thomas, earl of Melros*, ed. J. Maidment, 2 vols., Abbotsford Club, 9 (1837) · J. Maidment, ed., *Letters and state papers during the reign of King James the Sixth*, Abbotsford Club, 13 (1838) · *CSP dom., 1603–25* · J. Spottiswood, *The history of the Church of Scotland*, ed. M. Napier and M. Russell, 3 vols., Bannatyne Club, 93 (1850) · *Scots peerage*, vol. 3 · GEC, *Peerage*, 4.5, 10–11 · G. M. Fraser, *The steel bonnets: the story of the Anglo-Scottish border reivers* (1971)

Home, George, of Wedderburn (*fl.* 1779–1810). *See under* Mirror Club (*act.* 1776–1787).

Home, Henry, Lord Kames (1696–1782), judge and writer, was born at Kames, near Duns, Berwickshire, the first son of George Home of Kames (*d.* 1741) and his wife, Agnes (*b.* 1675), daughter of John Walkinshaw of Barrowfield, near Glasgow. His father was an impecunious border laird, much burdened by debt and a large family (by 1715 he had nine children). Home was educated at home by private tutors, first John Wingate and then a Mr Anderson, who taught him Greek, Latin, mathematics, and natural philosophy. Both tutors were nonjuring clergymen. Aged sixteen Home was apprenticed to John Dickson, a Berwickshire neighbour, who was a writer to the signet in Edinburgh. He also enrolled at the private civil law college of James Craig. Two years of learning law by rote followed, but then came an important switch in direction into advocacy. It was prompted, or so Home said, by a chance visit to the home of Sir Hew Dalrymple, lord president of the court of session, whose affluent lifestyle whetted Home's appetite for a branch of the legal profession in which the returns to the successful were so very much more obvious. He continued to study with Craig for a further year, but having resolved on the change to advocacy, he had to make up the deficiencies in his education, notably in the classics, although he also took up French and Italian. Home was a prodigiously hard worker, a man of energy and drive to complement his native intelligence, and after a public examination on 19 January 1723, he was duly admitted to the Faculty of Advocates three days later.

Early career Home lacked a powerful patron so the early years of his practice as an advocate proved difficult. At first he seems to have led a carefree existence, but he soon found himself in debt and had to concentrate on establishing a career. He gained little employment, but was able in his free time to continue his education, and he also began to play a role in the Faculty of Advocates. In January 1725 his name appears on the faculty's list of public examiners for the first time. He also began to write on legal topics. His *Remarkable Decisions of the Court of Session from 1716 to 1728* (1728) was followed by a stream of further writings, which helped both to chart the development of the Scottish legal system in this period and to shape it. He was first taken notice of at the bar in the bankruptcy case of Charles Belches in 1730, owing to the efficient job he made of scheduling the debts on the estate which earned the congratulation of the presiding judge, Sir Gilbert Elliot, second baronet, Lord Minto. No doubt in order to supplement his income, in August 1732 he applied unsuccessfully for the chair in Roman law at the University of Edinburgh, vacant by the death of his old teacher, James Craig. His application was coterminous with the publication of *Essays upon Several Subjects in Law* (1732), which demonstrated the philosophical cast of his approach to the law.

By 1736 Home had acquired a reasonable legal practice.

In July 1736 he was defence counsel in the high profile trial of Captain John Porteous. Following the lynching of Porteous by the Edinburgh mob, the subsequent inquiry at Westminster sent for Home, who spent April and May 1737 in London although he was not called upon to give evidence. He took the opportunity to call upon Dr Joseph Butler, author of *Analogy of Religion*, for conversation on deism and Christianity. The appointment in 1737 of his friend Charles Erskine as lord advocate led to his own appointment as advocate-depute. He continued to write, and in 1741 published *Decisions of the court of session, from its first institution to the present time. Abridged and digested under heads in the form of a dictionary*, in two volumes. This had originated as an idea of an Edinburgh bookseller, who had approached Home on the recommendation of the Faculty of Advocates when his first author withdrew. The combination of abridgements of reports and accounts of issues of law in one dictionary had proved popular in England, but Home used the dictionary to emphasize his belief that the reasons upon which judges made their decisions must be examined, and that precedent was worthless if the decision was founded upon wrong principles. Two further volumes were published in 1778 and 1797, edited by Alexander Fraser Tytler.

Marriage and the bench In April 1741 Home's father died. This was followed by Home's marriage on 24 August 1741, 'at the prudent age of forty-seven' (Chambers, Scots., 275), to Agatha (1711–1795), daughter of James Drummond of Blair Drummond, Perthshire, with a portion of £1000. They had one son, George, born in November 1743, and one daughter, Jean, born in 1744. During the Jacobite rising of 1745 Home stayed at Kames, surely the action of a prudent man, given that he had been accused of Jacobite sympathies in the past. Enforced absence from Edinburgh, where the courts were not sitting, led Home to write another book, published in 1747 as *Essays upon Several Subjects Concerning British Antiquities*, which eventually went through four editions. It contained several pieces critical of Jacobite political thought. In August 1746 he subscribed £300 to the British Linen Company, a key project of Archibald Campbell, third duke of Argyll, and Andrew Fletcher, Lord Milton, important members of the Scottish whig establishment.

Home was now a candidate for the Scottish bench. Upon the death of James Graham, Lord Easdale, in August 1750, the duke of Argyll recommended Home for the vacant seat on the Scottish bench, but to no avail. The next vacancy occurred in August 1751, but Home's promotion was delayed by a political smear that his father had been a Jacobite—in fact George Home had been in arms for the Hanoverians in 1715. Although his maternal uncle John Walkinshaw had been an active Jacobite (Clementine Walkinshaw, mistress of Prince Charles Edward Stuart, was Home's first cousin), this smear was easily refuted, and Home was appointed an ordinary lord of session on 6 February 1752, taking the title Lord Kames. In consequence of his appointment, he resigned as a public examiner and as a member of the council of the dean of the Faculty of Advocates.

Kames's next published work, *Essays on the Principles of Morality and Natural Religion* (1751), produced a furore among the more high-flying members of the Scottish church, and there were some who wished to see the author excommunicated. Kames's friendship with, and support for, David Hume made him a target, although the *Essays* were not an uncritical endorsement of Hume's views. Kames's fault was to suggest that man had a 'deceitful … feeling of liberty' (Ross, 103)—that all was determined, but that this was not evident to men who made choices as if they were free. At the general assembly of the Church of Scotland in May 1755 Kames escaped censure by name as that body contented itself with generalities. However, the controversy did cause Kames to rethink some of his more controversial opinions, which appeared in December 1756 as *Objections Against the 'Essays on Morality and Religion' Examined*. However, he retained a dislike of the 'popular Scottish clergy' (Ross, 165) and what he perceived as their bigotry and intolerance.

After Kames's promotion to the bench, other appointments followed: to the commission for forfeited estates (1752), to the board of trustees for fisheries and manufactures (1754), and as a director of the British Linen Company (1754–6). In May 1754 Kames became a founder member of the Select Society and its offshoot, the Edinburgh Society for Encouraging Arts, Sciences, Manufactures, and Agriculture in Scotland, which were part of the flourishing intellectual life of Edinburgh. In 1755 he served as vice-president of the Philosophical Society, having been involved with that body and its forerunners since the 1730s.

Kames was still ambitious for advancement in the legal profession. In 1759 he was disappointed not to be chosen to succeed Sir James Fergusson, second baronet, Lord Kilkerran, on the justiciary court. This prompted him to return to his literary efforts and in 1760 he published *Principles of Equity*, his principal work in the eyes of Scottish legal historians. It drew on an extensive body of historical and philosophical material, and made comparisons with theory and practice in England: he considered that each legal system could learn with advantage from the other. Although it was a theoretical work, Kames also dealt with practical issues, including the rules relating to bankruptcy. The work was well received, not least by William Murray, Baron Mansfield, lord chief justice of the king's bench in England, who in a letter to Kames in February 1762 regretted the lack of any equivalent English writer: 'I wish we had a pen and genius and diligence like your lordship's to do it' (Ross, 238). A second edition appeared in 1767, and a third in 1778, with a section on workers' combinations, then an issue very much under discussion.

In 1761 Kames befriended the young James Boswell, then in Edinburgh studying to be an advocate, in what can be seen as the latest of a long line of friendships with able younger men which began in the 1730s and included David Hume, Adam Smith, and the poet William Hamilton as well as foreign dignitaries such as Benjamin Franklin who visited Kames in 1759. It is Boswell who provided

much intimate and colourful detail on Kames. He recognized the formidable powers of concentration deployed by the judge to secure his professional advancement: 'women and wine are only your amusements and mislead you no more from your main aims than an evening walk or a game at whist' (Ross, 90).

In *Elements of Criticism* (1762) Kames sought to propound the fundamental principles of criticism drawn from human nature. That year saw Kames's involvement in one legal case and the beginning of another with which his name would be associated. In January 1762 Kames found in favour of Peter Williamson, who had been kidnapped as a boy some twenty years earlier by local merchants in Aberdeen and sent to North America. On his return to Scotland, Williamson had told the story of the trade in boys, which brought down on him the wrath of the Aberdeen mercantile community, outraged by the slur on them. Williamson was forced by the magistrates of Aberdeen to disown his account and was temporarily gaoled. However, on being reunited with his relatives he took the magistrates before the court of session and won damages. December 1762 saw the beginning of the 'Douglas cause' before the court of session, between rival claimants to the vast Douglas inheritance. It continued before the court in July 1767 when Kames supported the claim of Archibald Douglas against that of James George Hamilton, seventh duke of Hamilton, before being settled on appeal to the House of Lords in February 1769.

Kames finally reached the criminal court following his appointment on 15 April 1763 as a commissioner of justiciary, taking his seat on 3 May. This also meant going on circuit. His favourite circuit was the northern, including sittings at Perth, Inverness, and Aberdeen, but he also took his turn on the two other circuits, the western and the southern. Kames had the reputation as a judge keen to secure convictions, with a somewhat cruel wit: according to George Fergusson, later Lord Hermand, defence counsel in the case, in 1780 he greeted a verdict against Matthew Hay, an old chess partner found guilty of murder, with the quip, 'that's checkmate to you, Matthew!' (Ross, 311).

Industrial and agricultural improvement In 1764 and 1765 Kames was the central figure in the committee of proprietors appointed by the British Linen Company to review its affairs and which produced a report which saved the company from financial disaster. The encouragement of linen was the central element of the government's strategy for the economic development and political passivity of Scotland, particularly the highlands. Kames was to become an expert in the possibilities and problems of this industry, publishing an anonymous pamphlet, *Progress of Flax-Husbandry in Scotland* (1766). He explained that he regarded linen as Scotland's principal manufacture stimulating the circulation of currency, and providing work for otherwise idle hands. Kames was most involved through his membership of the board of trustees for fisheries, manufactures, and improvements in Scotland, although the commission for forfeited estates also took an interest. He used a network of correspondents to get first-hand expert advice for the board, corresponding with William Cullen about the chemistry of linen bleaching, with William Tod over the quality of Scottish linen on sale at London, and with George Young of Coupar Angus on the role of small merchants and hawkers. Not all of his suggestions and proposals turned out well. The Linen Hall established at Edinburgh in 1766, which was a scheme that Kames persuaded the board of trustees to support with the intention of assisting individual linen dealers against large wholesalers, proved an expensive failure, but it was widely approved by experienced merchants in the trade whom Kames had consulted.

Kames continued his legal writing during this period. In 1766 he published a further volume of *Remarkable Decisions of the Court of Session*, covering the period 1730 to 1752; his work in collecting decisions of the court was ongoing, and *Select Decisions of the Court of Session*, covering the period from 1752 to 1768, appeared in 1780. After 1768 the court of session appointed a clerk to take over Kames's work.

In 1766 the death of her brother and his infant son saw Kames's wife inherit Blair Drummond, in Perthshire but near Stirling, an estate worth nearly £2000 per annum. Henceforth his wife was known as Mrs Home Drummond, and the double surname was adopted by their descendants in the male line. This estate was to provide a focus of Kames's quest for agricultural improvement, setting in train a scheme to clear moss land of its unproductive top layers of moss and peat. His enthusiasm for improvement bore fruit with the publication of a 400-page tome, *The Gentleman Farmer*, in 1776. This book offered both an attempt to bring together agricultural change and technique into a coherent theoretical system and some very practical observations based on experience about crops, rotations, buildings, and stock. He observed how much progress there had been, and how very different the condition of agriculture in Scotland was from forty years previously, but called for the creation of a board for improving agriculture: centralized direction had benefited the linen industry, and would, in his view, do the same for agriculture. In 1778 the *Present State of Husbandry in Scotland* was published. This was the result of an initiative from Kames in the commission for forfeited estates to authorize a series of surveys in the highlands to investigate what agricultural practice was in the north and how it might be improved. Kames wrote the preface in which he welcomed turnpike roads, bridge construction, and canal projects as measures to promote development. In 1777 Kames published his last legal book in what had become a prolific and significant career as a writer on Scots law, *Elucidations Respecting the Common and Statute Law of Scotland*. This was a detailed and systematic analysis, with a strong autobiographical flavour, of areas which had long exercised his mind such as how to rank creditors on a bankrupt estate. His last major work was *Loose Hints on Education, Chiefly Concerning the Culture of Children* (1781), which with its emphasis on training to develop sensibility unsurprisingly drew the criticism that it showed a lack of respect to Christianity.

Death and family In October 1782 Kames's son, George, married Janet Jardine at Blair Drummond. By December Kames was visibly ailing. On 21 December Boswell recorded his last appearance in the court of session: 'like a ghost, shaking hands with Lord Kennet in the chair, and lords Alva and Eskgrove patting him kindly on the back as if for the last time' (Ross, 370). Traditionally, Kames's parting from his fellow judges was recorded with his characteristic earthiness as 'fare ye a' weel, ye bitches' (Ross, 370). Kames died on 27 December 1782 at his house in New Street, Canongate, Edinburgh. He was buried at Blair Drummond, probably on 30 December 1782. His wife died on 18 June 1795.

Kames was succeeded in his estate by his son, George, who had been educated away from his father's eye at St Andrews University, followed by the grand tour and a period in business in London. He had then taken over as laird of Blair Drummond, where he completed the work of his father in draining the moss land by utilizing Meikle's great wheel which he had installed in 1787. Kames's daughter, Jean, married in 1761, and within a month she had embarked on an affair with James Boswell. After that ended, other affairs followed, and in January 1772 her husband obtained a divorce on the grounds of adultery. Kames found the court proceedings wounding with her own servants giving evidence against her, and he could not forgive Jean, whom he sent away to France. Father and daughter were never reconciled, and Jean receives no recognition on the family memorial in the churchyard of Kincardine in Menteith.

Kames was a striking figure physically—it was said that he was tall enough to have made a Prussian guard—and robust featured. He was bitingly sharp tongued and on occasion showed the warmth of temper to which the epitaph raised by his son refers. He could and did blow hot and cold, and could be by turns convivial and studious, sentimental and clear eyed, coarse and refined, vain and quirky. As a writer on Scots law his output of eight books plus essays and collections was prolific and significant, even if his style of writing lacked fluency. In John Ramsay of Ouchtertyre's judgement had Kames devoted himself fully to the law, he would have been one of the greatest and most enlightened judges of his time. As it was, he made important contributions to many other areas of Scottish life.

ALASTAIR J. DURIE and STUART HANDLEY

Sources I. S. Ross, *Lord Kames and the Scotland of his day* (1972) · A. F. Tytler, Lord Woodhouselee, *Memoirs of the life and writings of venerable Lord Kames*, 2 vols. (1807–9) · A. J. Durie, *The British Linen Company, 1745–1775* (1996) · L. Leneman, *Alienated affections: the Scottish experience of divorce and separation* (1998) · Chambers, *Scots.*, rev. T. Thomson (1875) · J. M. Pinkerton, ed., *The minute book of the Faculty of Advocates, 1713–1750*, Stair Society, 32 (1980) · A. Stewart, ed., *The minute book of the Faculty of Advocates*, 3: *1751–1783*, Stair Society, 46 (1999) · F. J. Grant, ed., *The Faculty of Advocates in Scotland, 1532–1943*, Scottish RS, 145 (1944), 103 · *IGI* · memorial, Blair Drummond church, Perthshire · epitaph, graveyard, Blair Drummond, Perthshire

Archives NA Scot., corresp. · NL Scot., letters | BL, letters, and literary MSS, to Catharine Gordon and her mother, Add. MS 40635 · Hunt. L., letters to Elizabeth Montagu · NA Scot., letters to

Sir Archibald Grant · NL Scot., corresp., mainly with Lord Milton · NRA priv. coll., letters to Dr John Walker and others · NRA, priv. coll., corresp. with William Creech · Yale U., Beinecke L., corresp. with James Boswell

Likenesses D. Martin, oils, Scot. NPG; repro. in Ross, *Lord Kames* · W. Miller, portrait, repro. in Ross, *Lord Kames* · engraving (after D. Martin), repro. in A. F. Tytler, Lord Woodhouselee, *Memoirs of the life and writings of the honourable Henry Home of Kames*, 2nd edn, 1 (1814), frontispiece · etchings, repro. in J. Kay, *A series of original portraits and caricature etchings*, nos. 5 and 132 · portrait, Scot. NPG

Home, James, third earl of Home (1615–1666), politician, was born in the summer of 1615, the eldest son of Sir James Home of Cowdenknowes (*d.* 1618x20) and his wife, Lady Anne (*d.* 1621), eldest daughter and coheir of George *Home, earl of Dunbar. With the death on 13 February 1633 of his distant cousin James Home, second earl, he became third earl of Home. During his lifetime the second earl had obtained a decreet in favour of his sisters Lady Doune and Lady Maitland against Sir James Home of Cowdenknowes. This decreet reduced the contract of tailzie made between the second earl's father, Alexander, first earl of Home, and Sir John Home of Cowdenknowes and his son Sir James (the third earl's grandfather and father respectively), dated 18 December 1604, in which Lord Home entailed his estates of Home to himself and his heirs-male, whom failing to Sir John Home and Sir James Home and their heirs-male, whom failing to Lord Home and his heirs-female. James Home of Cowdenknowes was able to secure a reversal of the decreet of reduction, after litigation, in March 1634. However, a new patent was not issued by Charles I until 22 March 1636 (dated at Hampton Court), ratifying to him and his heirs-male of the honours, privileges, and precedencies enjoyed by Alexander and James, earls of Home. On 31 July 1637 he had a charter of the barony of Duns, and on 14 July 1638 he had a charter of the lands and the baronies of Dunglas and others. On 1 July 1641 he was served heir male of Alexander, first earl of Home, of Alexander, fifth Lord Home, and of James, second earl of Home.

Home signed the petition against the king's and Archbishop Laud's introduction of the new liturgy in Scotland, and was present in Edinburgh on 20 September 1637 when the petition was presented to James Stewart, duke of Lennox, to be sent to Charles I. Together with John Lindsay, Lord Lindsay, he protested openly at the market cross of Edinburgh against the king's proclamation of 19 February 1638, in the name of the nobility, ministry, barons, and burgesses. John Gordon classes him among those of the commissioners in 1638 who were professed covenanters, or who quickly afterwards declared for the covenant. That year Home served as an elder at the Glasgow general assembly, and on 24 September was appointed by the privy council to oversee the subscription of the national covenant in the sheriffdom of Berwick. Sir James Balfour referred to Home as being among 'some of the chieffe covenanters' in March 1639 (*Historical Works of Balfour*, 2.321). On 22 March, accompanied by other leading covenanters, Home went at the head of 1000 musketeers to Dalkeith House and forced the lord treasurer, John Stewart, earl of Traquair, to surrender it, when they discovered concealed

in it an immense quantity of ammunition and arms, and also the regalia, crown, sceptre, and sword, which they then carried with them to Edinburgh. He was appointed colonel of horse in the covenanting army, and towards the end of the month raised a force of 600 horse. During the second bishops' war (1640–41) he was a colonel of foot. He also attended both the 1639 parliament and the parliamentary sessions of 1640–41.

By contract dated 13 July 1640 Home married Lady Jane, fourth daughter of William Douglas, earl of Douglas. Meanwhile he had become alienated by the radical leadership of Archibald Campbell, earl of Argyll, and he signed the 1640 Cumbernauld bond, drawn up by the earl of Montrose. On 17 November 1641 he was nominated a member of the privy council, but his name was deleted by parliament on the ground that he was opposed to the covenanters. Home presented the royalist 'cross petition', articulated in 1642 and designed to win over moderate covenanting opinion, to the privy council on 10 January 1643, as part of the ongoing struggle in Scotland over whether or not to support Charles I in his conflict with the English parliamentarians. He became sheriff of Berwickshire and he was also present in the 1643 convention of estates. Similarly, he was present in the 1644 convention of estates on 16 April, when he was appointed to the committee for the south for governing the country. That year he was fined £20,000 Scots for violently dispossessing Sir Patrick Hepburn of Waughton of Fast Castle and the adjacent lands of Wester Lumsden. With five other noblemen he voted against rendering the 'raising of armes' punishable by 'forfaultry', and also against a similar punishment for 'holding houses against the estates of the country' (*Historical Works of Balfour*, 3.200). Home sat in the parliamentary sessions of 1644–6, and was a member of the shire committee of war for Berwickshire in 1644, 1647, and 1648. His increasingly royalist stance was reflected in his attendance at the Engagement Parliament on 2 March 1648, his appointment as colonel of the Berwickshire foot on 4 May, and his membership of the committee of estates on 8 June. He was instructed to levy 1200 men and they crossed the border in July 1648. Home's infantry were involved in the military action of the engagement invasion, but the earl escaped to Scotland following the surrender of the infantry at Warrington Bridge. The English captured 277 of his men, including his lieutenant-colonel.

In 1650, during Home's absence, Home Castle was captured and garrisoned by Cromwellian troops. He repented for his involvement in the engagement, allowing for his political rehabilitation. This was reflected in his appointments to the committee for regulating the affairs of the army on 28 March 1651 and to the committee of estates on 3 June. On 28 March he was also appointed colonel of Berwickshire. On 7 May 1651 he raised a regiment of horse which was part of the 7th cavalry brigade, though it appears that it suffered heavy losses in the Cromwellian victories of that summer. With the Cromwellian conquest of Scotland, Home's estates were forfeited.

At the Restoration, Home went to London as one of a

special deputation to represent to the council and to parliament 'the grievances of this opprest kingdom' (Nicoll, 279). In the autumn and winter of 1660 he attended the meetings of the committee of estates, which acted as a provisional government in Scotland until parliament was convened on 1 January 1661. That year he was reinstated in his estates, and was named a member of the Scottish privy council. He was present in the parliamentary sessions of 1661, 1662, and 1663, and on 8 January 1661 was appointed as a member of the standing committee, the lords of the articles. Parliamentary proceedings of April and May 1661 indicate that he was called as a witness in the trial against Archibald Campbell, marquess of Argyll. In November 1661 and July 1663 Home was a member of privy council committees to consider the prevention of theft and robbery in the borders, while in November 1661 he had been appointed to a privy council committee to consider the activities of the minister Robert Blair. In September 1664 he was ordered by the privy council, along with the earls of Haddington and Roxburghe, to provide twenty-six men for service in the English navy. That year he was appointed a member of the high commission for the execution of the law in church affairs, and in February 1663 and November 1664 he was also involved, in his capacity as sheriff of Berwick, in the apprehension in the borders of two Quakers, Andrew Hague and Andrew Robertson. Home sat in the 1665 convention of estates and on 2 August 1665 he was appointed as a member of the committee for inbringing taxation. Shortly before his death, which occurred in December 1666, he had been instructed by the privy council in November to assist in the government preparations against the expected rebel insurrection which came to be known as the Pentland rising.

Home was survived by his wife, who was still alive in 1683. They had a daughter and four sons, of whom Alexander (d. 1674), James (d. 1687), and Charles (d. 1706) successively succeeded their father as fourth, fifth, and sixth earls of Home.   JOHN R. YOUNG

Sources Scots peerage · APS · register of the committee of estates, August–October 1660, NA Scot., PA.11/12 · minute book of the committee of estates, October–December 1660, NA Scot., PA.11/13 · Reg. PCS, 2nd ser., vol. 7 · Reg. PCS, 3rd ser., vol. 2 · Reg. PCS, 3rd ser., vol. 1 · The historical works of Sir James Balfour, ed. J. Haig, 4 vols. (1824–5) · The letters and journals of Robert Baillie, ed. D. Laing, 3 vols. (1841–2) · E. M. Furgol, A regimental history of the covenanting armies, 1639–1651 (1990) · J. Nicoll, A diary of public transactions and other occurrences, chiefly in Scotland, from January 1650 to June 1667, ed. D. Laing, Bannatyne Club, 52 (1836) · J. Gordon, History of Scots affairs from 1637–1641, ed. J. Robertson and G. Grub, 3 vols., Spalding Club, 1, 3, 5 (1841) · J. Spalding, The history of the troubles and memorable transactions in Scotland and England, from 1624 to 1645, ed. J. Skene, 2 vols., Bannatyne Club, 25 (1828–9) · DNB

Home, James (1760–1844), physician, son of Francis *Home (1719–1813), studied medicine at Edinburgh University and succeeded his father as professor of materia medica at Edinburgh in 1798. He was so successful that he raised the attendance at his class from 50 to 310 students, even though his lectures were given at 8 a.m. in winter. In 1821, on the death of James Gregory, he obtained the professorship of physic after a severe contest; his tory political views agreed with those of the majority of the town council, who were the patrons. He was, however, more than sixty years old, and failed in his new post from the first. In later years his classroom was a scene of great disorder. Nevertheless, he continued to lecture until his death on 5 December 1844. A good clinical teacher, Home was president of the Royal College of Physicians of Edinburgh and was elected a fellow of the Royal Society of Edinburgh in 1787.   G. T. BETTANY, rev. CLAIRE L. NUTT

Sources The life of Sir Robert Christison, 2 vols. (1885–6) · A. Grant, The story of the University of Edinburgh during its first three hundred years, 2 (1884), 412, 424 · F. Bennet and M. Melrose, Index of fellows of the Royal Society of Edinburgh: elected November 1783 – July 1883, ed. H. Frew, rev. edn (1984) · L. Rosner, Medical education in the age of improvement: Edinburgh students and apprentices, 1760–1826 (1991)
Archives Royal College of Physicians of Edinburgh, corresp., lecture notes, and papers · U. Edin. L., lecture notes and papers
Likenesses A. Geddes?, portrait, U. Edin.

Home, John (1722–1808), Church of Scotland minister and playwright, was born in Leith on 21 September 1722, the son of Alexander Home, town clerk of Leith, and Christian Hay, daughter of John Hay, writer in Edinburgh. Home was a distant relative of both the earl of Home and David Hume.

Education and the Jacobite rising of 1745 Home was educated at Leith grammar school and Edinburgh University, where he graduated MA on 18 March 1742. He trained for the ministry alongside William Robertson (soon leader of the moderate faction in the Church of Scotland), Hugh Blair, Alexander Carlyle, and Adam Ferguson. Carlyle records that Home was 'a great favourite with his companions', and 'his entry to a company was received like letting in the sun into a darkened room' (Carlyle, 24, 114). Contemporaries testified that he 'was from childhood delighted with the lofty and heroic ideas which embody themselves in the description or narrative of poetry' (Mackenzie, 6).

On 13 September 1745 Home enlisted in the college company of volunteers to defend Edinburgh against the Jacobite army. With the opening of the city to the rebels, Home and a few companions joined the army of Sir John Cope at Dunbar. As lieutenant in a regiment of volunteers raised by Glasgow, Home joined Hawley's army: he was taken prisoner at Falkirk on 17 January 1746 and held in Doune Castle, from which he led an escape by means of blanket-ropes.

With the patronage of Sir David Kinloch of Gilmerton, Home was ordained minister of Athelstaneford, in the presbytery of Haddington, on 17 July 1746, succeeding Robert Blair, author of The Grave. He was inducted on 11 February 1747. Kinloch's encouragement of farming on his estate fostered a prosperous and enlightened community.

Douglas and other early works Home found in Plutarch inspiration for his first tragedy, Agis (1749), which dealt with the sufferings of the king of Sparta. His addition of a romantic sub-plot 'to suit the prevailing dramatic taste'

John Home (1722–1808), by Sir Henry Raeburn, c.1795–1800

(Mackenzie, 34) prompted David Hume to allege he 'had corrupted his taste by imitation of Shakespeare, whom he ought only to have admired' (*Letters of David Hume*, 1.204). Home took the play to London at the end of 1747. When David Garrick rejected the play as not well adapted to the stage (Mackenzie, 35), the author vented his mortification in 'Verses Written by Mr. Home, with a Pencil, on Shakespeare's Monument in Westminster Abbey'. Returning via Winchester, Home was introduced to William Collins, who inscribed to him his 'Ode on the Popular Superstitions of the Highlands of Scotland', in which he predicts Home's success in tragedy and enjoins him to find subject matter in his native land.

The ballad 'Gil Morrice' provided the inspiration for Home's most famous tragedy, *Douglas*. There, according to his biographer Henry Mackenzie, Home found material 'which happily suited the bent of his imagination, that loved to dwell amidst the heroic times of chivalry and romantic valour, particularly amidst those in which the great names of our ancient Scottish Worthies were distinguished' (Mackenzie, 91–2). Heeding criticisms of *Agis*, Home eschewed romantic sub-plot and focused on maternal tenderness and youthful honour in a plot comparable to that of Voltaire's *Merope* (c.1743), but 'as simple and natural as that of the French author is complicated and artificial' (Scott, 346). The project found favour with the literati, eager to validate in terms of tragic drama Scotland's right to cultural partnership with England. Drafts circulated among Blair, Robertson, Carlyle, Lord Elibank, and Sir Gilbert Elliott of Minto, corrections were made, and, later, names were changed (Douglas for Norval, Randolph for Barnet). Hume's endorsement (*Letters of David Hume*, 1.215) represented 'only the sentiment of the whole Republic of Belles Lettres' (Carlyle, 152). The view was not shared by Garrick who, in February 1755, rejected the play as totally unfit for the stage (Mackenzie, 37).

Home's introduction by Lord Milton to Archibald, third duke of Argyll, helped get *Douglas* staged in Edinburgh at the theatre in the Canongate on 14 December 1756, with Digges as Douglas and Mrs Ward as Lady Randolph. Though then a boy, Mackenzie recalled that 'the applause was enthusiastic; but a better criterion of its merits was the tears of the audience' (Mackenzie, 38). The Edinburgh prologue, appealing for 'no common tear' for a renowned Scottish hero, identifies Caledonia and ancient Athens in terms of topography, learning, and the finer feelings such as pity, so establishing *Douglas* as a key text in the Scottish literature of sensibility. Here, unlike his classically derived tragedies, Home discovered 'a beautiful talent for painting genuine nature and the manners of his country' (*Letters of Horace Walpole*, 3.298). The equation of proximity to nature with emotional intensity, combined with the analogies between human and natural experience, anticipates James Macpherson's *Poems of Ossian*. The sustained evocation of pity for Lady Randolph, locating the play within the tradition of the pathetic tragedy of Thomas Otway and Nicholas Rowe, long proved effective with audiences—Robert Burns wrote of 'the horrors I felt for Lady Randolph's distresses' (*Letters of Robert Burns*, 2.64)—and the clash between the heroic code and her maternal protectiveness provides dramatic tension.

From Dublin, Thomas Sheridan sent Home a gold medal, an action which Dr Johnson found incomprehensible (Boswell, *Life*, 2.320, 5.360), and the play inspired Frances Sheridan in writing her *Memoirs of Miss Sidney Bidulph* (1761). Approving of *Douglas*'s adherence to the unities and seeing it as a standard-bearer for Scottish tragedy, Hume dedicated his *Four Dissertations* (1757) to its author thus: 'you possess the true theatric genius of Shakespeare and Otway, refined from the unhappy barbarism of the one, and the licentiousness of the other'. Not all agreed: witness *The Philosopher's Opera* (1757), an anonymous satire, and Oliver Goldsmith's demurring (*Monthly Review*, 16, May 1757). Even Hume had misgivings, including questioning why Lady Randolph should break her silence regarding her lost child after eighteen years (*Letters of David Hume*, 1.215–16). The language was widely praised (for example, Gray, 2.515; *Complete Works*, 9.94), but, with most of the action taking place either in the past or off-stage, it is a play of words rather than deeds.

The staging of *Douglas* sparked a religious controversy. Presbyterian opposition to drama was exacerbated by the circumstances: the dramatist was a clergyman and performances were attended by ministers. Charges were brought against Alexander Carlyle, and Thomas White of Liberton was suspended, though with mitigated sentence on his pleading 'that he attended the representation only once, and endeavoured to conceal himself in a corner to avoid giving offence' (Mackenzie, 44). Between the high-flying and moderate factions a war of pamphlets ensued. Defences came from Adam Ferguson and Carlyle, whose *An argument to prove, that the tragedy of Douglas ought to be publicly burnt by the hands of the hangman* was an ironical piece in the manner of Swift. Carlyle also circulated *A Full and True History of the Bloody Tragedy of Douglas*, which added two nights to the run. Home pre-empted prosecution by the presbytery of Haddington by resigning as minister of Athelstaneford on 7 June 1757. Soon 'manners overcame the law of the church' (ibid., 49): in 1784 Mrs Siddons played Lady Randolph to the severe detriment of attendances at the general assembly of the Church of Scotland.

Bute's private secretary and later works Having moved to London in March 1757, Home lodged in Chapel Court, South Audley Street. Bute installed him as his private secretary and as tutor to the prince of Wales, whose mother awarded him £100 a year. It was said that Home was 'entirely at the command of Lord Bute, whose nod made him break every engagement' (Carlyle, 170). *Douglas* was staged by John Rich at Covent Garden on 14 March 1757, with Spranger Barry as Douglas and Peg Woffington as Lady Randolph. Its success, and its author's new-found eminence, induced Garrick to stage *Agis* at Drury Lane (21 February 1758), himself playing Lysander. Attended twice by Bute and the prince of Wales, it ran for nine nights and 'the author made some hundreds by it' (ibid., 182). *The Siege of Aquileia* followed at Drury Lane on 21 February 1760, with Garrick as Aemilius and Mrs Cibber as Cornelia. Though the events relate to the siege of Berwick by Edward III in 1333, Home, politically alert on this occasion, relocated the action in Roman times. While the play suffers from Home's characteristic weakness—predominance of declamation over action—he achieves a measure of psychological realism: the dilemma of Aemilius, who must surrender the city or his two captive sons will die, dramatizes the conflicting demands of public duty and personal loyalty.

In 1760 Home published *Douglas*, *Agis*, and *The Siege of Aquileia* in a volume dedicated to the prince of Wales, who, on his succession, bestowed on him an annual pension of £300. Home, it was claimed, 'might have been said to have been the second man in the kingdom while Bute remained in power' (Carlyle, 208). Others have questioned his qualifications for such eminence, alluding to his vanity, inattention to money matters, and lack of reserve (Mackenzie, 52–5), and designating him 'like many other bards, in every respect the reverse of a man of method' (Scott, 317). However, far from abusing his position of power to his own advantage, Home was active in the interest of his friends (Knapp, 246; *Letters of David Hume*, 1.429). So unpopular was the Bute ministry, and such the preponderance of eminent Scots in the capital, that Hume wrote in March 1763 of 'the general rage against the Scots' (*Letters of David Hume*, 1.382). When Bute's administration fell in April 1763 Home resigned as his secretary, but they remained close.

Home was a member of the *Poker Club, founded in 1762, so named by Adam Ferguson to stir resentment at the refusal to grant Scotland the right, allowed to England, to raise a militia. In 1763 Home was appointed conservator of Scottish privileges at Campvere, a sinecure worth £300 a year which he held until 1770, entitling him to attend the general assembly of the Church of Scotland. These visits may have prompted his notion of standing for parliament in August 1765 on the death of Sir Harry Erskine, a plan which Hume deemed 'wild and extravagant' (*Letters of David Hume*, 1.518) and which came to nothing. In 1767 Home leased land from Kinloch and built a villa at Kilduff. His grateful former parishioners 'insisted on carting the [building] materials free of charge' (*Fasti Scot.*, new edn, 1.354). On 15 July 1770 he married Mary (*d.* 1816), daughter of a relation, William Home, minister of Foggo (1758–85); the marriage was childless. Until 1779 they lived at Kilduff, where the young Walter Scott was a frequent guest (Lockhart, 1.153).

Home had three further plays staged. *The Fatal Discovery* opened at Drury Lane on 23 February 1769. Originally titled *Rivine*, it was inspired by one of the fragments—whose authenticity he steadfastly accepted—translated to Home by Macpherson when they met at Moffat in October 1759. Alert to anti-Scots feeling, Garrick presented an Oxford undergraduate as its author, but so favourable was its reception that Home acknowledged the authorship, terminating its run. *Alonzo* ran for eleven nights from 27 January 1773, with Mrs Barry as Ormisinda. With slight variations in plot, it transposed the material of *Douglas* to the Spain of the Moorish invasions. Eliciting pity for maternal tenderness, it proved the most popular of Home's plays after *Douglas*. Walpole thought otherwise, threatening to send it to a correspondent as a punishment (*Letters of Horace Walpole*, 5.445). First staged on 21 January 1778, *Alfred* was one of Home's least successful, but most ambitious, plays. Its failure may be attributed to what Adam Ferguson termed 'the substitution of a love-interest for an interest of state, which the audience expected from the name of Alfred' (Mackenzie, 117); yet, with language relatively free of bombast and ornament, the play depicts Alfred as human being rather than figure-head.

At Morpeth in April 1776 Home and Adam Smith met Hume, now ailing and heading south. Home accompanied him to London, Bath, Buxton, and back to Edinburgh. In a letter of 13 May 1776 to Blair, Hume testified to the beneficial effect of Home's company (Mackenzie, 162–3). The codicil to Hume's will makes reference to the two bones of jocular contention between them—the orthography of the surname, and their respective preferences for claret and port (ibid., 163).

Home's interest in matters military led in 1778 to his commission in a new regiment of the Midlothian fencibles, with the duke of Buccleuch as colonel. A fall from his horse had the consequence that, even after convalescence, 'his intellectual powers were never restored to their original state' (Mackenzie, 66). In 1779 Home and his wife moved to Edinburgh.

After the failure of *Alfred* Home occupied himself with his *History of the Rebellion, 1745*, which he had begun as early as 1746. Finally published in 1802 with a dedication to George III, the history 'breaks off abruptly at the battle of Culloden, without giving us any account of the manner in which that victory was used' (Scott, 352). Mackenzie lists among Home's papers an unfinished tragedy, 'Alina, or, The Maid of Yarrow', and two acts of an unfinished, untitled play based on an East India story; there is also reference in a letter of Macpherson to a comedy, 'The Surprise, or, Who would have thought it?' (Mackenzie, 118–20). Home also wrote occasional verse.

John Home died at Merchiston, Edinburgh, on 5 September 1808. He was buried in South Leith churchyard.

KENNETH SIMPSON

Sources H. Mackenzie, *An account of the life and writings of John Home esq.* (1822) · A. Carlyle, *Anecdotes and characters of the times*, ed. J. Kinsley (1973) · W. Scott, 'Life and works of John Home', *Miscellaneous prose works of Sir Walter Scott, bart*, 28 vols. (1835), vol. 19, vol. 3, article 8 [from *QR*, 36 (1827), 167–216] · *Fasti Scot.*, new edn, vol. 1 · J. Home, *Douglas*, ed. G. Parker (1972) · J. Sinclair, *The statistical account of Scotland, 1791–99* (1975), vol. 2 · *DNB* · *The letters of David Hume*, ed. J. Y. T. Greig, 2 vols. (1932) · *The letters of Horace Walpole, fourth earl of Oxford*, ed. P. Cunningham, 9 vols. (1906) · J. G. Lockhart, *The life of Sir Walter Scott* (1903) · Boswell, *Life* · O. Goldsmith, *Monthly Review*, 16 (May 1757), 426–9 · *The philosopher's opera* (1757) · *The letters of Robert Burns*, ed. J. de Lancey Ferguson, 2nd edn, ed. G. Ross Roy, 2 vols. (1985) · L. Mansfield Knapp, *Tobias Smollett: doctor of men and manners* (Princeton, 1949) · *Correspondence of Thomas Gray*, ed. P. Toynbee and L. Whibley, 3 vols. (1935) · *The complete works of William Hazlitt*, ed. P. P. Howe, 21 vols. (1930–34)
Archives Hunt. L., letters · NL Scot., corresp. and papers · NL Scot., letters · NL Scot., papers incl. account of journey to Bath with David Hume in 1776 · U. Edin. L., letters and literary MSS | NL Scot., corresp. with Lord Milton · NL Scot., corresp. with Andrew Stuart
Likenesses W. Millar, oils, 1762, Scot. NPG · J. Tassie, paste medallion, 1791, Scot. NPG · H. Raeburn, oils, *c.*1795–1800, NPG [*see illus.*] · W. Ridley, stipple (after S. Drummond), BM, NPG; repro. in *Monthly Mirror* (1799) · W. Yellowlees, oils (after H. Raeburn), Perth Museum and Art Gallery · miniature, Scot. NPG · oils, Scot. NPG · watercolour on ivory (after H. Raeburn), Scot. NPG

Home, Robert (1752–1834), portrait painter, was born in Hull on 6 August 1752, and baptized on 15 September that year at Holy Trinity, Kingston upon Hull. The son of Robert Boyne Home (*d.* 1786), an army surgeon, and Mary, daughter of Colonel Alexander Hutchinson, Robert Home was one of seven children, not all of whom survived infancy: his brother was the surgeon Sir Everard *Home, first baronet; his sister Anne Home [*see* Hunter, Anne], poet, married the anatomist John Hunter; and another sister, Maria (*d.* 1797), married the architect and engineer Robert *Mylne.

At the age of twelve or thirteen Home stowed away to Newfoundland in order to avoid parental pressure to enter medicine. Put off the ship eighteen months later, he returned with a badly disabled left arm, which, when treated by John Hunter, was immobilized across his chest and ossified in that position. Reunited with his family, who were by then settled at Pall Mall in London, Home developed an aptitude for anatomical drawing with instruction from John Hunter. He received encouragement from Angelica Kauffmann and entered the Royal Academy Schools on 14 February 1769. He first exhibited there in 1770, contributing twenty-three paintings intermittently until 1813. In 1773 Home departed for Rome, visiting Paris and Florence *en route*, and remained there until August 1777. He met the artists William Miller and

Thomas Jones, undertook small commissions, and made studies of antiquities, now in the Victoria and Albert Museum.

Having tried, unsuccessfully, to establish a practice in London, Home moved, in 1780, to Dublin under the patronage of Lord Lifford the Irish chancellor. There he exhibited twenty-two paintings at the Artists' Exhibition in 1780, and, in 1782, undertook eight portraits, at 35 guineas each, for Trinity College theatre, including copies of portraits of Elizabeth I and Dean Swift, and Henry Grattan from life. Home married Suzanna (*d.* 1790), daughter of the painter Solomon *Delane on 8 September 1783. They had one daughter, Anne (*d.* 1829), and between three and five sons. With the arrival of a rival portrait painter, Gilbert Stuart, in Dublin, and Suzanna's failing health, Home returned to London in 1789.

Suzanna died in London in 1790, and Home left for India, where he had connections. Leaving his children with relatives, he departed without permission from the East India Company, reaching Madras in January 1791. There he met the artists John Smart and William Hickey, and found work painting theatrical scenery. Having sought and secured permission to accompany the grand army to Bangalore during the Third Anglo-Mysore War, Home reached the troops on 5 March. He remained with them until early April 1792, sketching captured forts, officers, and the local countryside (examples are in V&A). He was present at, and later painted, the handing over of the hostage princes to Lord Cornwallis (*Lord Cornwallis Receiving the Sons of Sultan Tipu as Hostages* 1794–5, exh. RA, 1797; NAM).

Home's contact with the British military proved enduring and lucrative. Within six months of returning to Madras, a subscription was raised and Home was commissioned to paint the death of Colonel Joseph Moorhouse (*The Death of Colonel Moorhouse at the Storming of the Pettah Gate of Bangalore, 7 March 1791*, 1793–4, exh. RA, 1797, engraved by E. Stalker, 1811, NAM) and several notable portraits including *Charles, Second Earl Cornwallis* (1792; Banqueting Hall, Madras). Home's style combined careful drawing with simplicity and dignity, and his intimate knowledge of Indian topography enlivened his large-scale paintings with local detail and colour. After travelling with the artists Thomas and William Daniell he depicted a number of local monuments, including *Sculptured rocks: penance of Arjuna, Mahabalipuram* and *Dharmaraja Rath, Mahabalipuram* (both 1793; Asiatic Society of Bengal, Calcutta). Twenty-nine of his earlier sketches were engraved and published, with written descriptions, as *Selected views of Mysore, the country of Tippoo Sultan* (1794) and *A Description of Seringapatam* (1796), containing six coloured aquatints.

Home sailed for Calcutta on 28 May 1795, and arrived on 4 June. On 17 September he married (Anna) Alicia Patterson (*d.* 1817), sister-in-law to his close friend James Colvin, and was later joined by his daughter and sons. In 1797 he was elected a member of the Asiatic Society, and secretary from 6 March 1802 to April 1804. His practice flourished, William Baille writing to Ozias Humphry in 1795 that Home was 'much employed, and has handsome prices' (MS, RA archive, London). Home's accounts ledger, June

1795–August 1814 (NPG archive), lists eight portraits of Richard, first Marquess Wellesley, when governor-general and fourteen of his brother Sir Arthur Wellesley (later first duke of Wellington), begun between September 1804 and August 1806. Examples are at Apsley House, London; Stratfield Saye, Hampshire; the Royal Collection; and the National Portrait Gallery, London. Other significant subjects were *Lord Lake and his Son on Horseback* (1805; Victoria Memorial, Calcutta), *Gilbert Elliot, Lord Minto* (1811–12; Rashtrapati Bhavan, New Delhi, and 1812; Victoria Memorial).

Home's prosperity was due to his willingness to accept commissions large and small. He repaired paintings for Wellesley's rebuilt Government House in 1803, although a group of ceiling paintings was not completed. He also recorded indigenous mammals, birds, and reptiles. Two volumes of watercolours are at Victoria Memorial Hall, Calcutta, and *A White Leopard* (1805) is in the Royal Collection. In 1814 Home moved to Lucknow as historical and portrait painter at the court of Oudh, where his son John was equerry and European aide-de-camp, 1820–25. He received 5000 sicca rupees per annum, and was also responsible for designing and superintending the making of carriages and other court attributes. Bishop Heber, visiting Lucknow in 1824, noted that:

> Mr. Home would have been a distinguished painter had he remained in Europe, for he had a great deal of taste and his drawing is very good and rapid; but it has been of course a great disadvantage to him to have only his own work to study, and he probably finds it necessary to paint in glowing colours to satisfy his Royal masters. (Heber, 1.395)

Alicia Patterson died in 1817, and in 1825 Home resigned and moved to Cawnpore with his daughter and granddaughter, Jean. Home died in Cawnpore on 12 September 1834 and was buried there at Cutcherry cemetery. On 5 November 1834, Home's sons presented their father's collection of paintings to the Asiatic Society.

TINA FISKE

Sources R. Home, sitter book, Calcutta, 1795–1814, NPG, Heinz Archive and Library · E. Cotton, 'Robert Home', *Bengal Past and Present*, 35 (1928), 1–24 · M. Archer, *India and British portraiture, 1770–1825* (1979) · W. G. Strickland, *A dictionary of Irish artists*, 2 vols. (1913) · J. Ingamells, ed., *A dictionary of British and Irish travellers in Italy, 1701–1800* (1997) · D. Foskett, *A dictionary of British miniature painters*, 2 vols. (1972), vol. 2 · W. Y. Carmen, 'The storming of Bangalore and the death of Colonel Moorhouse', *The Connoisseur*, 178/717 (1971), 161–5 · R. Heber, *Narrative of a journey through the upper provinces of India from Calcutta to Bombay, 1824–25*, 2 vols. (1828) · H. D. Love, ed., *List of pictures in Government House, Madras* (1903) · S. C. Hutchison, 'The Royal Academy Schools, 1768–1830', *Walpole Society*, 38 (1960–62), 123–91 · IGI · RA, Ozias Humphry MSS · *National Gallery of Ireland: illustrated summary catalogue of paintings* (1981) · R. Walker, *National Portrait Gallery: Regency portraits*, 2 vols. (1985) · Graves, *RA exhibitors* · P. Rohatgi, *Portraits in the India Office Library and records* (1986)

Archives NPG, sitter book, Calcutta

Likenesses T. Banks, terracotta sculpture, exh. RA 1781 · J. Smart, miniature, 1791; Christies, 27 Aug 1983, lot 354 · self-portrait, *c.*1810; Christies, 1 March 1991, lot 15 · self-portrait, oils, *c.*1810–1820, NPG · R. Gregory, portrait, Asiatic Society of Bengal, Calcutta · self-portrait (painting an Indian dock scene); Sothebys, 12 March 1980, lot 116

Wealth at death collection of paintings given by sons to Asiatic Society, Bengal, 5 November 1834: Cotton, 'Robert Home'

Home, Robert (1837–1879), army officer, born in Antigua, West Indies, on 29 December 1837, was eldest son of Major James Home, who served for some years in the 30th regiment, and afterwards settled in Ireland as a land agent. Robert Home was early thrown on his own resources, and when, for a short time during the Crimean War, commissions in the artillery and engineers were opened to public competition without the necessity of passing through the Royal Military Academy, Woolwich, he obtained one in the Royal Engineers, and was commissioned lieutenant on 7 April 1856. After serving at Chatham and in Nova Scotia, in 1858 he was one of the first to join the new Staff College at Sandhurst. After the course there, he was attached at Aldershot to the other three arms of the service successively, to complete his training for the staff. In 1862 he went to Portland, and was employed in the new defences. He married, in February 1864, Anne Josephine, daughter of J. Hunt, a Dublin barrister, who survived him with four sons and two daughters.

After his promotion to captain on 9 December 1864 Home was sent to Canada, where he wrote an able report on the defence of the frontier against invasion, which attracted the attention of the authorities at home. The following year he was appointed to the staff at Aldershot as deputy assistant quartermaster-general. The ability he showed led to further special employment. In 1870 he became secretary of the Royal Engineers committee (a standing scientific committee), and in 1871 he was appointed to the topographical and statistical department of the War Office, which in 1873 developed into the intelligence branch.

In 1873 Home was selected by Garnet Wolseley to be the commanding royal engineer of the Asante expedition, and he became a member of the Wolseley 'ring'. In the Second Anglo-Asante War he proved himself capable in the field, his energy and force of character enabling him to overcome manifold difficulties in preparing the way for the march to Kumasi. He used 6000 local labourers to clear a road through 70 miles of bush, build seven way stations, and construct the forward base at Prasu. He received a brevet lieutenant-colonelcy and a CB. On his return he resumed his duties at the intelligence branch, assisting its head, Major-General Sir Patrick MacDougall (deputy adjutant-general for intelligence). Home was able, energetic, and far-sighted, and the 1875 mobilization plan for the army and the 'regulations for the organisation of the communications of an army in the field' were his work. He also rendered good service as the secretary and moving spirit of several War Office committees. On 1 April 1876 he succeeded Major Charles Wilson as assistant quartermaster-general of the intelligence branch, the post he retained until his death.

During the Russo-Turkish War, when there was risk of Britain intervening, Home's opinion was frequently sought, and reportedly great weight attached to it in military circles. Towards the end of 1876 he was sent to Turkey to report on the defence of Constantinople. His dispatches gained him a brevet colonelcy, and the knowledge he had acquired of the politico-military situation reportedly made him the trusted adviser of the highest authorities. He was appointed British commissioner for the delimitation of the frontier of the principality of Bulgaria, under article 2 of the treaty of Berlin, on 10 September 1878. He had hardly begun the work when he contracted typhoid and came home.

Home's real work, according to *The Times* of 31 January 1879, was known to

> a comparatively limited circle, but that circle comprised most of those to whose hands the destinies of the empire have been entrusted during the last two administrations. … most of the statesmen who have been engaged in the difficult work of the last few years attribute no small importance to the assistance derived from Colonel Home's genius and grasp of facts.

Home published a small anonymous pamphlet on army administration. His principal work, *A Précis of Modern Tactics* (1873), was when published one of the few English books on the subject, and continued for some years the best, becoming an official textbook. In 1872 he translated Baron Stoffel's *Military Reports* and a French work on the 'law of recruiting'. He also contributed to the *Quarterly Review*, *Macmillan's Magazine*, and other periodicals. He was a FRGS and an associate of the Society of Telegraph Engineers. Home died of typhoid at his residence, 21 Regent's Park Terrace, London, on 29 January 1879. A stained-glass memorial window was placed in Rochester Cathedral by public subscription. A civil-list pension of £300 a year was conferred on his widow, in recognition of his services.

R. H. VETCH, *rev.* ROGER T. STEARN

Sources *The Times* (31 Jan 1879) · *LondG* · corps records, Royal Engineers Institution, Chatham · Ward, *Men of the reign* · T. G. Fergusson, *British military intelligence, 1870–1914* (1984) · 'Correspondence respecting … the demarcation of frontiers under the treaty of Berlin', *Parl. papers* (1880), 80.147, C. 2471 [Turkey] · B. Bond, ed., *Victorian military campaigns* (1967) · J. Luvaas, *The education of an army: British military thought, 1815–1940*, new edn (1965) · E. M. Spiers, *The late Victorian army, 1868–1902* (1992) · A. Lloyd, *The drums of Kumasi: the story of the Ashanti wars* (1964) · Boase, *Mod. Eng. biog.* · *CGPLA Eng. & Wales* (1879)
Archives BL, letters to A. H. Layard: reports on defences of Constantinople, Add. MSS 39022–39024, 39162, *passim*
Likenesses engraving, repro. in *Graphic*, 19 (1879), 372 · wood-engraving (after photograph by A. Bassano), NPG; repro. in *ILN* (22 Feb 1879)
Wealth at death under £4000: probate, 24 March 1879, *CGPLA Eng. & Wales*

Home, William, eighth earl of Home (*d.* 1761), army officer, was the second but first surviving son of Alexander seventh earl of Home (*d.* 1720), and his wife, Lady Anne (*d.* 1727), second daughter of William Kerr, second marquess of Lothian. Having succeeded his father in 1720, Home embarked on a military career, obtaining a cornet's commission in the 2nd regiment of dragoon guards on 13 May 1735 and a troop in Churchill's dragoons in May 1740. At the election of 1741 he was chosen a Scottish representative peer, a place which he continued to hold until his death, no doubt because of his support for the Argyll interest, he being described about 1757 as one of the third duke's 'greatest favourites' (Carlyle, 166). He married at Hampstead on 25 December 1742 Elizabeth (1703/1704–

1784), daughter and heir of William Gibbons, of Vere, Jamaica, the widow of James Lawes, who was the son of Sir Nicholas Lawes, governor of Jamaica. Although she had a jointure of £7000 p.a. from her first husband, Home apparently deserted her in February 1743. They had no children.

In July 1743 Home received a captain's commission in the 3rd regiment of dragoon guards, with which he served on the continent. Home was in Scotland when the Jacobite rising of 1745 broke out and volunteered his services to the army under the command of Sir John Cope, distinguishing himself at the battle of Prestonpans on 21 September 1745. He was given command of the Glasgow volunteer regiment of foot which was dispatched to defend Stirling, and he was very active in Scotland while the bulk of the rebel forces were in England. In 1749 Home was promoted major of the 3rd regiment of foot guards; on 11 August 1750 he became colonel of the 48th foot and on 29 April 1752 colonel of the 29th foot. Home's local power base was in Berwickshire where he faced the intense rivalry of the Hume family of Polwarth, earls of Marchmont. Early in April 1757 Argyll procured for Home the lord lieutenancy of the county, and on 16 April he was named governor of Gibraltar. He was made a lieutenant-general in 1759. He died in Gibraltar on 28 April 1761, on the eve of his departure for England, and was succeeded by his brother Alexander. His widow died in London on 15 January 1784 and was buried in Westminster Abbey.

T. F. HENDERSON, *rev.* STUART HANDLEY

Sources GEC, *Peerage* · J. L. Chester, ed., *The marriage, baptismal, and burial registers of the collegiate church or abbey of St Peter, Westminster*, Harleian Society, 10 (1876), 437 · *GM*, 1st ser., 54 (1784), 74 · *GM*, 1st ser., 31 (1761), 284 · *Scots peerage* · N. B. Leslie, *The succession of colonels of the British army from 1660 to the present day* (1974), 67, 84 · E. Haden-Guest, 'Berwickshire', *HoP, Commons, 1754–90* · A. Carlyle, *Anecdotes and characters of the times*, ed. J. Kinsley (1973), 166 · *Descriptive lists of secretaries of state: state papers Scotland, ser. 2, 1688–1782*, List and Index Society (1996), 262–4 · J. S. Shaw, *The management of Scottish society, 1707–1764* (1983), 183, 198
Archives Hunt. L., letters to the earl of Loudon · West Highland Museum, Fort William, letters relating to the '45

Home, William Douglas (1912–1992), playwright, was born on 3 June 1912 at 23 Moray Place, Edinburgh, the third son and fifth of the seven children of Charles Cospatrick Archibald Douglas-Home, Lord Dunglass, later thirteenth earl of Home (1873–1951), and his wife, Lady Lilian (1881–1966), daughter of Frederick William Lambton, fourth earl of Durham. After an infancy spent at the ancestral homes of the Hirsel, near Coldstream, Berwickshire, and Douglas Castle, Lanarkshire, Will disliked going to Ludgrove School in Hertfordshire in 1921. He was a shy nervous child who learned to hide behind a mask of flippancy. His characteristic mode of speech would later be a light, allusive banter, accompanied by whimsical half-smiles. He became a teller of anecdotes and also the subject of them, emerging as a practical joker at Eton College (1926–31) and New College, Oxford (1931–4).

On leaving university with a fourth in history, the Hon. William Douglas Home—he dispensed with the hyphen— spent two years at the Royal Academy of Dramatic Art in

William Douglas Home (1912–1992), by Bassano, 1936

London before making his stage début in Brighton in 1937. He looked an acceptable leading man, with his slender build, high brow, straight nose, and small eyes, but his acting ability was insufficient to launch a career. In any case writing interested him more. His first full-length play, *Great Possessions*, appeared at the Q Theatre in London in March 1937. Subsidized by his father, he shared a flat in South Eaton Place with his friends Jo Grimond and Brian Johnston.

Having been an idealistic supporter of appeasement, Douglas Home helped Kenneth de Courcy produce *Intelligence Digest* in 1939–40, a newsletter that some deemed defeatist. Douglas Home described himself as 99 per cent pacifist, yet, when drafted into the Royal East Kent regiment (the Buffs) in July 1940, he went on to serve as a second lieutenant in what became the Royal Armoured Corps. However, the Second World War brought out his stubborn and opinionated side. Douglas Home contested three parliamentary by-elections between 1942 and 1944 as an Independent Progressive, denouncing Churchill's objective of unconditional German surrender. He then refused in September 1944 to participate in the assault on Le Havre after the allies turned down a German request for a ceasefire to allow civilian evacuation. When Acting-Captain Douglas Home publicized this in the press, he was court-martialled and sentenced to a year's hard labour, first at Wormwood Scrubs and then at Wakefield. He defended his conduct ever after, though his eventual

appeal for a review of the case failed in 1991. Will was not simply a charming jester.

On his release in June 1945 Douglas Home wrote *Now Barabbas …*, a compassionate prison drama which made his name as a playwright when it opened in London in February 1947. This was followed at the Vaudeville Theatre in August 1947 by another hit, more typical of subsequent ones. *The Chiltern Hundreds* exploited the comic potential of an upper-class socialist facing the family butler as his tory opponent in a by-election. Douglas Home based the benignly eccentric aristocrats on his own relations. Thoroughly good-humoured, with easy conversational dialogue, the piece gave rise to a film, an American version, and two sequels. His next few plays fared less well, however; audiences booed the anti-war fantasy *Ambassador Extraordinary* (1948).

In 1950 Douglas Home was Conservative prospective parliamentary candidate for Kirkcaldy Burghs, but only briefly: he opposed the Korean War. Grimond later induced him to contest Edinburgh South as a Liberal in 1957 and 1959. On 26 July 1951 Douglas Home married Rachel Leila Brand (*b.* 1929); she succeeded as Baroness Dacre in 1970. They had one son and three daughters and lived for thirty years (1954–85) at Drayton House, East Meon, Hampshire.

The Reluctant Debutante, a polished light comedy, proved highly popular at the Cambridge Theatre, London, where it received 752 performances (1955–6), with Wilfrid Hyde White, Celia Johnson, and Anna Massey, prior to success on Broadway and on film. Then came the backlash: drama critics, exhilarated by John Osborne's *Look Back in Anger* (1956), suddenly turned Douglas Home into an Aunt Sally who symbolized everything snobbish, out-of-date, and shallow in British theatre. Kenneth Tynan, especially, aimed to drive 'the Honourable William' off the stage. Douglas Home held out doggedly against the 'new wave' of social realism. His *Aunt Edwina* (1959) made fun of a retired colonel changing sex after mistakenly taking equine hormone pills. Incensed by vitriolic reviews, the author backed it with his own money and lost.

Douglas Home's dramatic range was broader than many allowed. He wrote serious works on contemporary moral themes (though maybe not very effectively), topical skits, and a string of plays about historical figures, such as *The Thistle and the Rose* (King James IV of Scotland) in 1949, *Caro William* (Melbourne) in 1952, *Betzi* (Napoleon) in 1965, and *The Queen's Highland Servant* (John Brown) in 1967. Nevertheless, he remained pigeon-holed as a purveyor of 'bourgeois' drawing-room comedies. The mid-1960s were lean years. The appointment of his brother Sir Alec Douglas-Home (1903–1995) [*see* Home, Alexander Frederick Douglas-] as prime minister ensured a fair London run for *The Reluctant Peer* (1964). Otherwise he had to retreat into the provinces, whence he contrived his comeback in 1967. *The Secretary Bird*, a comedy of marital infidelity, premièred in Swanage, Dorset; it went on to achieve 1463 performances in the West End, showing impresarios that audiences and critics were not the same. Fresh commercial successes followed: *The Jockey Club Stakes* (1970), *Lloyd*

George Knew my Father (1972), and *The Kingfisher* (1977). Actors of the calibre of Kenneth More, Alastair Sim, Rex Harrison, and Ralph Richardson starred in his shows.

Douglas Home was prolific, writing memoirs, verse, and magazine columns, as well as forty-five performed plays. Interest in his stage works slowly faded from the late 1970s, but they appeared at regional venues, in amateur productions, and in France (where they retained high critical esteem). Never financially prudent—he was a lifelong devotee of the turf—he felt obliged to take a smaller house in 1985, when heart trouble required the fitting of a pacemaker. Still he kept creating well-crafted new dramas; the last to be staged was *The Christmas Truce* (1989). William Douglas Home died at his home, Derry House, Kilmeston, near Alresford, Hampshire, on 28 September 1992. He was buried four days later in the churchyard of All Saints, East Meon, Hampshire.   JASON TOMES

Sources D. Fraser, *Will: a portrait of William Douglas Home* (1995) • W. Douglas Home, *Old men remember* (1991) • W. Douglas Home, *Mr Home pronounced Hume* (1979) • *Daily Telegraph* (30 Sept 1992) • *The Times* (30 Sept 1992) • *The Guardian* (30 Sept 1992) • *The Independent* (30 Sept 1992) • D. Kirkpatrick, ed., *Contemporary dramatists*, 4th edn (1988) • W. Douglas Home, *Sins of commission* (1985) • P. Ziegler, 'The case for moderation', *Daily Telegraph* (2 Dec 1995) • I. Gilmour, 'A gentleman of the theatre', *Sunday Times* (29 Oct 1995) • b. cert. • d. cert.
Archives NL Scot., corresp., papers, and literary MSS | King's Lond., Liddell Hart C., corresp. with Sir B. H. Liddell Hart
Likenesses Bassano, photograph, 1936, NPG [*see illus.*] • R. Sturgis, bronze sculpted head • photographs, repro. in Fraser, *Will* • photographs, repro. in Douglas Home, *Old men remember*
Wealth at death £362,003: probate, 21 July 1993, CGPLA Eng. & Wales

Homer, Arthur (*bap.* 1758, *d.* 1806). *See under* Homer, Henry Sacheverell (*bap.* 1719, *d.* 1791).

Homer, Henry (*bap.* 1752, *d.* 1791), classical scholar, was baptized on 27 November 1752 at Birdingbury, Warwickshire, the eldest of the seventeen children of Henry Sacheverell *Homer (*bap.* 1719, *d.* 1791), rector of Birdingbury, and his wife, Susannah Pitts (*d.* in or after 1806). From 1758 he was educated at Rugby School, where aged fourteen he became head boy. Afterwards he studied for three years at Birmingham. In November 1768 he was admitted to Emmanuel College, Cambridge, under Richard Farmer, where he became acquainted with Samuel Parr, who helped to direct his studies. Other intimate college friends included William Bennet, afterwards bishop of Cloyne, and George Dyer, poet and political reformer. He graduated BA (1773), MA (1776), and BD (1783). Homer was elected a fellow of the college in 1778, and returned to the university from Warwickshire, where he had been living for about three years, soon after his election.

About this time Homer was admitted into deacon's orders. He now resided chiefly at Cambridge, and spent much time in the university library, turning his attention to philological studies. In 1787 he joined with Parr in the republication of Bellenden's *Tracts*, and prepared editions of several classical authors, all remarkable for the accuracy and elegance of the typography. On Parr's suggestion he undertook a variorum edition of Horace, but died

before its completion. It was finally published by Charles Combe, and this occasioned an angry literary altercation between Combe and Parr. In consequence of religious scruples Homer declined to take priest's orders in compliance with the college statutes, and his fellowship was therefore declared vacant in June 1788. Among Homer's other publications are editions of works by Livy, Tacitus, Sallust, Cicero, Pliny, Ovid, and Julius Caesar. He died at Birdingbury after a short illness on 4 May 1791, and was buried in the family tomb in the parish churchyard. Those works, including an edition of Quintilian, which he left unfinished were completed by his brothers Arthur *Homer [*see under* Homer, Henry Sacheverell] and Philip Bracebridge *Homer.

     THOMPSON COOPER, *rev.* PHILIP CARTER

Sources Foster, *Alum. Oxon.* • IGI • GM, 1st ser., 61 (1791), 492 • GM, 1st ser., 76 (1806), 1209 • *The works of Samuel Parr ... with memoirs of his life and writings*, ed. J. Johnstone, 8 vols. (1828) • Nichols, *Illustrations*, 4.704 • Nichols, *Lit. anecdotes*, 3.163, 660 • W. T. Lowndes, *The bibliographer's manual of English literature*, 4 vols. (1834) • PRO, PROB 11/1209, fols. 352r–356r [will of Henry Sacheverell Homer]
Likenesses J. Jones, stipple, pubd 1791 (after S. Harding), BM, NPG • S. Harding, portrait • T. Walker, etching (after P. S. Lambourn), BM

Homer, Henry Sacheverell (*bap.* 1719, *d.* 1791), writer, son of Edward Homer, of Sutton Coldfield, Warwickshire, and godson of Henry Sacheverell, from whom he received his Christian name, was baptized in Sutton Coldfield on 19 November 1719, and educated at Oxford, where he matriculated on 26 June 1736 as a member of University College. He became a demy of Magdalen College in 1737, and graduated BA in 1740, MA in 1743. On 11 February 1751 he married Susannah Pitts (*d.* in or after 1806) at Birdingbury. He was appointed rector of Birdingbury, Warwickshire, and vicar of Willoughby in 1764; and chaplain to Edward, Lord Leigh, high steward of the University of Oxford. From 1774 to 1779 he also held the vicarage of Anstey, Warwickshire.

While Homer was a clergyman, he was also a Warwickshire commissioner of enclosure. His name 'appears in Acts for at least twenty enclosures in surrounding counties alone' (Beresford, 131) and he dedicated his *Essay on the nature and method of ascertaining the specific shares of proprietors upon the inclosure of common fields* (1766) to his fellow commissioners. According to J. A. Yelling, Homer's work on enclosure 'gives perhaps the most detailed view of the procedure from the commissioners' point of view' (Yelling, 135). Homer's other major work, *An Enquiry into the Means of Preserving and Improving the Publick Roads of this Kingdom* (1767), examines the importance of inland navigation to the British economy. Its anonymous reviewer in the *Monthly Review* called it 'a masterpiece of its kind' (1767, 403). Homer also wrote in 1788 a memoir of the archdeacon of Richmond, Thomas Townson, which later appeared in the *Gentleman's Magazine* in 1792 (587–8).

Homer died on 14 July 1791 'suddenly, as he was returning from his hay-field', and was buried in the family tomb 'near the east end of the church at Birdingbury' (*GM*, 1791, 685; 1806, 1209). His seventeen children included Arthur [*see below*], Henry *Homer, and Philip Bracebridge *Homer.

Arthur Homer (*bap.* 1758, *d.* 1806), the fourth son of Henry Sacheverell Homer and his wife, Susannah Pitts, was baptized at Birdingbury, Warwickshire, on 9 August 1758, and educated at Rugby School and at Magdalen College, Oxford. He graduated BA (1778), proceeded MA (1781), BD (1790), and DD (1797); from 1782 to 1802 he was a probationary fellow of Magdalen. In 1802 the college presented him to the rectory of Standlake, Oxfordshire, where he died on 4 June 1806. There is a monument to his memory, with an inscription supposed to have been written by Samuel Parr, on the south wall of the chancel of Standlake church. In 1799 Homer published a proposal and prospectus, *Bibliotheca Universalis Americana, or, An Universal American Library*, a work that was to consist of 'two quarto volumes … and to be dedicated to Gen. Washington' (*GM*, 1806, 1208). The proposal was revised twice (in 1800 and 1801) but in 1803 Homer issued a printed letter to his prospective subscribers announcing that he had suspended work on the project indefinitely. His work never did appear in print, though Leman Thomas Rede's *Bibliotheca Americana* (1789) was later thought to be the first volume of it and misattributed to Homer.

THOMPSON COOPER, *rev.* JEFFREY HERRLE

Sources *GM*, 1st ser., 76 (1806), 1208–10 · Foster, *Alum. Oxon.* · *GM*, 1st ser., 61 (1791), 685 · *GM*, 1st ser., 61 (1791), 1156 · M. W. Beresford, 'Commissioners of enclosure', *Economic History Review*, 16 (1946), 130–40 · J. A. Yelling, *Common field and enclosure in England, 1450–1850* (1977) · review of *Enquiry into the means of preserving and improving the publick roads*, *Monthly Review*, 36 (1767), 402–3 · IGI · will, PRO, PROB 11/1454, fol. 307r [Susannah Homer]

Homer, Philip Bracebridge (1765–1838), schoolmaster and poet, was the tenth son of the Revd Henry Sacheverell *Homer (*bap.* 1719, *d.* 1791), rector of Birdingbury, Warwickshire, where Philip was born, and Susannah Pitts (*d.* in or after 1806). He went to Rugby School in 1772, and was distinguished for his classical attainments. He matriculated as a member of University College, Oxford, on 31 October 1781, aged fifteen, and was elected a demy of Magdalen College in 1783 (BA 1785, MA 1788, BD 1804). In 1785 he returned to Rugby, where he was an assistant master for thirty-seven years. He was better regarded for his scholarship than for his abilities at maintaining discipline among the boys, who gave him the sobriquet Philly. He entered holy orders and was a probationer fellow of Magdalen College, Oxford, from 1802; he gave up his fellowship in 1806, having married in the previous year. His wife, Caroline, died on 21 February 1815. The terms of his will (20 June 1834) indicate that he remarried. In 1825 he was elected a fellow of Rugby School, being the first of the newly created fellows on the foundation. He died at Rugby on 26 April 1838.

While at Oxford, Homer gained a literary reputation, contributing in 1787 to the miscellany *Olla Podrida* edited by his Magdalen contemporary Thomas Monro. A collection of poems, *The Garland*, followed in 1788, and his *Anthologia* (1789), including verse which he had previously published in the *Gentleman's Magazine*, gained the high

opinion of Thomas Burgess, who was then a fellow of Corpus Christi College. Some light-hearted aspersions by Samuel Parr on the quality of his verse only temporarily interrupted their friendship. With his brother Arthur *Homer (*d.* 1806) [*see under* Homer, Henry Sacheverell] he completed and prepared for publication the editions of the Latin classics which their brother Henry *Homer, had left unfinished. In the 1820s he published two schoolbooks, an edition of the Eton Greek grammar (1825) and a school text on Christian evidences (1827). A manuscript English–Hebrew lexicon which he had compiled was presented by Henry Homer (1819–1911), his son by his second marriage, to the library of Magdalen College, Oxford.

THOMPSON COOPER, *rev.* M. C. CURTHOYS

Sources J. R. Bloxam, *A register of the presidents, fellows … of Saint Mary Magdalen College*, 8 vols. (1853–85), vol. 7, pp. 76–81 · *GM*, 2nd ser., 9 (1838), 661–2 · F. L. Colvile, *The worthies of Warwickshire who lived between 1500 and 1800* [1870], 437 · PRO, PROB 11/1895/324
Archives Magd. Oxf., Hebrew lexicon · U. Birm. L., poems and copies of letters

Homes [Holmes], **Nathaniel** (1599–1678), Independent divine, was born in Wiltshire, the son of the Revd George Homes of Kingswood. He matriculated as a fellow-commoner at Magdalen Hall, Oxford, on 11 April 1617, but wishing to study with John Prideaux (later bishop of Worcester), took his BA at Exeter College, where he graduated on 19 October 1620. He received his MA from Magdalen on 18 June 1623, his BD from Exeter on 27 June 1633, and the DD on 28 June 1637. During the period 1631 to 1642 he was rector of Whipsnade, Bedfordshire, and subsequently, in 1642, became rector at St Mary Staining in London, where he also held a lectureship at St Michael Bassishaw. By 1633 he had married Elizabeth (*d.* 1666), with whom he baptized at least two daughters at Whipsnade.

In co-operation with Henry Burton, Homes founded one of the first Independent gathered churches, which by 1643 was refusing to celebrate Easter. This came to the attention of John Vicars, who, in *The Schismatic Sifted*, accused Homes of excluding 'all his foresaid loving parishioners from Christian communion in their own parish church, except they would enter into a covenant with him' (Tolmie, 110). According to the well-known controversialist Thomas Edwards, Homes was active outside London and regularly attended to the needs of parishes between London and Dover 'going twice or thrice a year to visit' (Edwards, 72). He was nominated by the House of Lords on 30 October 1643 to be a member of the Westminster assembly, but he never sat in the assembly.

During his lifetime Homes maintained an avid interest in the last and final days of the world and produced a wealth of material containing his interpretations of the prophetic texts. His main concern was predicting the imminent downfall of the antichristian forces and the expected future glorious state of the church on earth. He adhered closely to Joseph Mede's millenarian interpretation of a spiritual reign of Christ through his saints, rather than the more radical interpretations that expected Christ to reign in person for a thousand years. His vision of a new world was forcefully expounded in his fast sermon before parliament in 1641, published as *The New World*. It was here that he linked his vision of a renewed society with a theory of congregationalism. As he declared, 'we, therefore, by new heavens and a new earth understand a new form of worship, religion in the expression thereof reformed, brought more close to the rule of the gospel, made more spiritual and heavenlike' (N. Homes, *The New World*, 1641, 7). Homes was very knowledgeable in Hebrew thought and his eschatological outlook was informed by the ancient Jewish doctrine that the world would last six thousand years and the seventh thousand would be the eternal sabbath. In a tract published in 1650 an opponent, Thomas Hall, denounced Homes's eschatological views and accused him of bringing 'forth the malignant fruit of Schisme in the Church, and Sedition in the State', and branded him *Chiliastorum Achilles* (Hall, sig. *4v).

Between 1650 and 1666 Homes's output of eschatological material was immense and in 1653 his tract *The Resurrection Revealed* was ordered to be presented to the council of state for its judgment. Joseph Caryll, who read the tract on behalf of the council before publication, subsequently qualified Homes's interpretation of the thousand-year reign of Christ upon earth by upbraiding those who expected a state of 'carnal liberty and worldly glory' and praised Homes for showing 'the exceeding spiritualness and holiness of this state, to which, as none but the truly holy shall attain' (Homes, *Resurrection*, sig. A3v). Such an interpretation of the future millennium stands in stark contrast to that elaborated by, for example, the Fifth Monarchy Men, who desired significant changes to the economic, political, and social structures of society. During this time Homes's fear of social and political unrest is reflected in his attacks on precisely these radical religious sects and his calls for laws to be implemented against judicial astrology. The appearance of these 'wicked agents of Satan' convinced Homes that the final days were imminent (Homes, *Daemonologie*, 24). During the interregnum he continued to find favour with the government and in 1659 was appointed preacher to the council of state with lodgings in Whitehall.

After the Restoration, Homes continued in his ministry and in 1661 he is found together with George Cockayne holding weekly meetings in an alehouse in Ivy Lane. Their congregational activity attracted the attention of the authorities and it was suggested, in a communication from a Mr Ashmole to Secretary Nicholas that it was likely that 'if their studies were searched papers of consequence might be found' (*CSP dom.*, 1661–2, 128). Because of his adherence to congregationalism Homes did not comply with the provision of the Act of Uniformity in 1662 and was subsequently ejected from his living at St Mary Staining. His wife died on 29 July 1666 and a son, Nathaniel, was buried on 29 August. The following year on 28 October, Homes married Sarah Lander at St James's, Duke's Place, London. On 16 May 1672 he took advantage of the declaration of indulgence and was granted a licence as a congregationalist to hold meetings at his house in Horseshoe Alley, Upper Moorfields. He died in June 1678 at St Giles Cripplegate, leaving bequests to Sarah and a daughter, Bithiah, and was buried at St Mary Aldermanbury on 2 July.

KENNETH GIBSON

Sources *Calamy rev.* · B. Ball, *A great expectation: eschatological thought in English protestantism to 1660* (1975) · M. Tolmie, *The triumph of the saints: the separate churches of London, 1616–1649* (1977) · J. Vicars, *The schismatic sifted* (1646) · *CSP dom.*, 1659–62 · N. Homes, *The resurrection revealed* (1653) · N. Homes, *Daemonologie and theology* (1650) · T. Edwards, *Gangraena, or, A catalogue and discovery of many of the errours, heresies, blasphemies and pernicious practices of the sectaries of this time*, 3 vols. in 1 (1646) · T. Hall, *Chiliasto-mastix redivivus* (1657) · Foster, *Alum. Oxon.* · will, PRO, PROB 11/357, sig. 77
Wealth at death property in London

Homfray family (*per.* 1702–1833), ironmasters, of Wollaston and Penydarren, came to prominence with **Francis [i] Homfray** (1674–1737), who was born at Wales, near Rotherham, Yorkshire, on 23 September 1674. He was the first member of his family to be employed in the iron trade. He moved from Yorkshire to Old Swinford, near Stourbridge, where he became involved in the local iron industry, rising to become nail-keeper in the large Crowley family business, which made and sold iron goods. Francis [i] Homfray left the Crowleys in 1702 to set himself up as a dealer in iron goods and later as a slitter, turning wrought iron bars into thin rods ready for nail manufacture. In 1704 he married Sarah Baker (d. 1715), and then in 1717 Mary Jeston [**Mary Homfray** (d. 1758)]. He had four sons and five daughters. After his death on 1 March 1737, the business was carried on by Mary Homfray. Various members of the family were now working mills and forges along the River Stour and around Kidderminster.

Francis Homfray's sons followed their father into the iron industry. His fourth son, John Homfray (1731–1760), of Wollaston Hall, died leaving one son, John Homfray [**John Addenbrooke** (1759–1827)], who in 1792 assumed the maiden name of his mother, Mary, the daughter and heir of Jeremiah Addenbrooke, a local landowner. John Addenbrooke was involved with his Homfray relatives in the iron industry of Shropshire and the Black Country. In 1780 he married Elizabeth Grazebrook. He was high sheriff of Worcestershire in 1798.

However, of the second generation, it was to be Francis [i] Homfray's second son, **Francis [ii] Homfray** (1725–1798), of Broadwaters and Stourton Castle, who was to achieve fame in the iron trade. Born on 9 September 1725, he greatly extended the family's undertakings along the Stour and invested in the Shropshire coke iron industry. This period of expansion was related to his two marriages. In 1751 he married Hannah Popkin (d. 1754), a member of an important ironmaking family based in south Wales. After her death in 1754, he married in 1756 Catherine (d. 1766), the daughter of Jeremiah Caswell, one of the principal iron manufacturers operating on the River Stour. By 1787 Francis [ii] Homfray and John Addenbrooke owned the Lightmoor ironworks in Shropshire. In 1778 Francis [ii] was a partner in the Calcutts ironworks, also in Shropshire, at which cannon were manufactured during and after the American War of Independence.

Two of Francis [ii] Homfray's sons continued to be involved in the midlands iron industry, operating a series of forges and mills along the River Stour. Francis [iii] Homfray (1757–1809), of The Hyde, married Mary Pidcock in 1778, and their two elder daughters married into the Crawshay family; Jeston Homfray (1752–1816) married Sarah Pidcock in 1776. After Jeston Homfray's death in 1816 his wife continued to run the Stourton mill as Widow Homfray & Son.

However, a crisis in the ironmaking business of Anthony Bacon (*bap.* 1717, *d.* 1786) was to draw Francis [ii] Homfray to south Wales. Bacon, a successful merchant who was manufacturing cannon at Cyfarthfa, was also MP for Aylesbury. When in 1782 Clerke's Act was passed prohibiting government contractors from sitting in the House of Commons, Bacon circumvented this problem by subletting the mill and forge to another operator, with the stipulation that the concern had to purchase his Cyfarthfa iron. He turned to Francis [ii] whose wide experience in slitting iron and manufacturing nails, selling iron and iron goods, operating forges and blast furnaces, and boring cannon had gained him all the necessary skills to work the forge and the mill. Bacon persuaded Homfray to lease the Cyfarthfa undertakings in 1784 with rather restrictive terms.

Francis [ii] Homfray worked the forge and mill until March 1786. However, after a disagreement with Bacon over the supply of iron, he gave up the lease of the Cyfarthfa property. While working at Cyfarthfa, he had seen the potential for ironmaking at Merthyr Tudful. As a result, he encouraged two of his other sons—**Samuel Homfray** (1762–1822), who was born on 16 February 1762, and **Sir Jeremiah Homfray** (1759–1833), born on 16 February 1759—to lease land at Penydarren and build an ironworks. The partnership was soon expanded when their brother Thomas Homfray (1760–1825) and members of the *Forman family invested in the Penydarren ironworks. William Forman, one of the new partners, was an ordnance agent at the Tower of London and had become acquainted with the Homfrays through cannon manufacture.

In 1795 Samuel Homfray was the chief promoter of the Glamorgan Canal. While managing the Penydarren ironworks he appears to have worked closely with Richard Crawshay (1739–1810) in improving Henry Cort's puddling process for making wrought iron. Crawshay and Homfray were both abrasive characters: Crawshay described Homfray as 'so ungrateful and litigious that I cannot be on neighbourly terms with him' (R. Crawshay to the Revd George Maber, 16 Nov 1795, Gwent RO, D2/162, fol. 169). However, both families found common ground when they combined to cast doubts over the originality of Cort's patent for his puddling process.

A quarrel between Samuel and Jeremiah Homfray concerning expenditure on the Penydarren ironworks saw the management of the business fall completely on Samuel Homfray's shoulders. As sole manager of the works he could pursue his own deep interest in steam power. He installed Boulton and Watt engines to increase output and also manufactured boiler plate and engine parts. His interest in steam power brought him into contact with Richard

Trevithick (1771–1833) in May 1803. The result of this meeting was that Samuel Homfray bought a one-quarter share in Trevithick's high-pressure steam patent. Homfray encouraged Trevithick to develop his high-pressure engine and one of Trevithick's engines was constructed at Penydarren in 1804 as a tram road locomotive. This locomotive is acknowledged as the world's first steam locomotive and it made several trips along the Penydarren tram road before being converted to stationary use.

In 1787 Jeremiah Homfray married Mary Richards (*d.* 1830). Barred from active management at Penydarren, he turned his talents to the development of other ironworks along the northern outcrop of the south Wales coalfield. He was involved in the early development of ironworks at Ebbw Vale, Aber-nant, and Hirwaun, and, in fact, seems to have made a profitable career in setting up ironworks and then selling them as going concerns. He was also later involved in leasing land for coalmining, but this proved to be less successful than his ventures in the iron trade and led to his bankruptcy. Sir Jeremiah Homfray, who was knighted in 1809, died on 9 January 1833.

Samuel Homfray seems, like many of his family, to have had a restless nature and about 1813 he left the Penydarren Iron Company to concentrate his resources on developing the Tredegar ironworks in Monmouthshire. Handicapped at Penydarren by a shortage of coal on the property, he faced no such problems when he built his new works. In 1793 Samuel Homfray married Mary Jane (*d.* 1846), widow of Captain Henry Ball RN and the elder daughter of Sir Charles Gould Morgan of Tredegar. The marriage saw Homfray's fortunes tied closely to those of one of the most important landowning gentry families in south-east Wales. In 1800 Morgan leased to Homfray land at Bedwellte Common, Tredegar, on which he developed the Tredegar ironworks. By 1823 Tredegar had five furnaces in blast, producing over 16,000 tons of iron each year. Homfray's connection with Penydarren continued, however, for his daughter Amelia married one of the works' owners, William *Thompson (1793–1854). Samuel Homfray's success as a businessman led him to become high sheriff of Monmouthshire, and he served as MP for Stafford from 1818 to 1820. He is thought to have been the 'Mr. H' who harassed Wilberforce on a coach journey on 13 November 1816, who 'with stentorian voice left me no peace till his whole tale was told. Inventor of tram roads, founder of all great iron works in Monmouthshire, etc.' (HoP, *Commons, 1790–1820*, 220).

After Samuel Homfray's death on 20 May 1822 his sons, Watkin Homfray (1796–1837) and Samuel Homfray (1795–1883), continued to take an active role in the management of the Tredegar ironworks. The Homfray family's involvement with the Tredegar ironworks continued until 1868, when the family sold its shares to the Fothergill and Forman families, who were co-partners.

The Homfray family played a major part in the changes introduced in the south Wales iron industry during the industrial revolution. Members of the family were highly involved in promoting the adoption in south Wales of coal-using technology in the iron industry. Furthermore, the Homfrays' story exemplifies the migration of skills to Wales from the west midlands and clearly demonstrates the rise of steam power in the British iron industry.

LAURENCE INCE

Sources L. Ince, *The south Wales iron industry, 1750–1885* (1993), 73–81 · M. S. Taylor, 'The Penydarren ironworks, 1784–1859', *Glamorgan Historian*, 3 (1966), 75–88 · Burke, *Gen. GB*, 309–13 · C. Evans, *The labyrinth of flames* (1993), 143 · letter-book of Richard Crawshay, 1788–97, Gwent RO, Cwmbrân, D2.162, fol. 169 · HoP, *Commons, 1790–1820* · private information (2004)
Archives NL Wales, MSS | Glamorgan RO, Cardiff, Penllyn Castle MSS · Gwent RO, Cwmbrân, letter-book of Richard Crawshay, D2.162, fol. 169
Likenesses W. Williams, portrait, *c.*1784 (Samuel Homfray), priv. coll. · portrait (Samuel Homfray), NL Wales

Homfray, Francis (1674–1737). *See under* Homfray family (*per.* 1702–1833).

Homfray, Francis (1725–1798). *See under* Homfray family (*per.* 1702–1833).

Homfray, Sir Jeremiah (1759–1833). *See under* Homfray family (*per.* 1702–1833).

Homfray, Mary (d. 1758). *See under* Homfray family (*per.* 1702–1833).

Homfray, Samuel (1762–1822). *See under* Homfray family (*per.* 1702–1833).

Homrigh, Esther Van [*known as* Vanessa] (1688–1723), correspondent and lover of Jonathan Swift, was the elder daughter of a leading Dublin citizen, Bartholomew Van Homrigh (d. 1703), and Esther, *née* Stone (d. 1714). At their majority or marriage each daughter was entitled to £250 annually, and after Bartholomew's decease possibly as much as £5000 apiece. Vanessa's sister was Mary (*c.*1696–1721), her brothers Ginkell (1694–1710) and Bartholomew jun. (1693–1715). In 1707 the family moved from Dublin to London, where their circle included Sir Andrew Fountaine, diplomat and friend of Leibniz, and Erasmus Lewis, friend of Pope, Prior, Arbuthnot, and Gay. Jonathan *Swift met up with them *en route* for London at Dunstable in December that year. In 1713 (6 June) and 1720 (12 August) he recalled the precise occasion when Vanessa spilled coffee in the fireplace of the inn at Dunstable. Although he may have known the family before 1707, it was here that their serious, seventeen-year relationship began.

Esther Johnson dismissed the Van Homrighs as 'of no consequence' in a letter to Swift (*c.*24 Feb 1711, Swift, *Journal to Stella*, 202), but she had been seriously misled. By May 1711 the Van Homrighs set aside a room for Swift's use in their London house in Bury Street, St James's. At this period in 1711–12 he sometimes visited twice daily. Described as 'a closet' when writing to Stella, with Vanessa their private space was called the 'Sluttery, which I have so often found to be the most agreeable Chamber in the World' (18 Dec 1711, *Correspondence of Jonathan Swift*, 1, no. 149). Here they enjoyed privacy, sugared oranges, and coffee. Each referred to drinking coffee as a symbol of social intimacy, and in 1766 Horace Walpole suggested that this was a coded reference to sexual intercourse. The

family moved to Park Place, off St James's Street, in August and September 1712.

Twenty-eight of Swift's letters to Vanessa (the first dated 18 December 1711) and seventeen drafts of Vanessa's to Swift survive. Mere friendship was insufficient, and Vanessa demanded a passionate, even a sexual involvement, which Swift was psychologically and perhaps also physically incapable of managing, least of all of reciprocating. Their clandestine communication was aided by Erasmus Lewis and Charles Ford. In November 1714, after his installation as dean of St Patrick's and in spite of Swift's warning (12 August 1714) that he could seldom see her because of risks to their reputations, Vanessa followed him to Dublin, where she was acutely miserable. Gossip about his visit to Vanessa with 'little master' (20 Dec 1714, *Correspondence of Jonathan Swift*, 2, nos. 371–2), has been interpreted by those wishing to normalize Swift's sexual psyche as an allusion to a natural son of Swift and Stella (possibly Bryan M'Loghlin), or to an unnamed natural son by Vanessa.

Of independent means, but burdened by debts accumulated by her mother and spendthrift brother Bartholomew (for his will, see Le Brocquy, *Cadenus*, 143–9), Vanessa lived at Celbridge (later Marlay Abbey), 11 miles from Dublin and on the way to Charles Ford's estate at Wood Park, and, more dangerously if more conveniently for Swift, at the family's town house, Turnstile Alley, near College Green. 'You have taught me to distinguish and then you leave me miserable', she wrote (18 Dec 1714?, *Correspondence of Jonathan Swift*, 2, no. 370), and it may have been six years before Swift visited her at Celbridge. *Cadenus and Vanessa* had been written for Vanessa perhaps at Windsor between August and September 1712, and not intended for publication. Manuscript copies circulated before publication first in Dublin in 1726 and then in London on 19 May 1726, and eventually an authoritative text appeared in the 1727 *Miscellanies*. A passage cancelled by Swift reveals the essential and problematic dynamic in their relationship, from Swift's viewpoint:

> She wish'd her Tutor were her Lover;
> Resolv'd she would her Flame discover.
> (Swift, *Journal*, xliii)

Her name is Swift's invention, a compound of 'Van' and 'Hessy'.

Swift's last letter, of 7/8 August 1722, was written nine months before Vanessa made her will. His liaison with Stella perhaps caused Vanessa to confront him with the necessity of choosing between or acknowledging the status of one or the other. Vanessa died on 2 June 1723, probably from tuberculosis contracted from nursing her sister Mary (her will, signed 1 May 1723, is in Le Brocquy, *Cadenus*, 152–4). After her death Swift disappeared from Dublin on a two-month visit to southern Ireland, and in June at the parish of Skull he composed a Latin poem, 'Carberiae rupes', full of apocalyptic imagery. Poems attributed to Vanessa are: 'To Love', 'Ode to Spring', 'Ode to Wisdom', and a 'Rebus' on Swift's name. Shortly after Stella's death, a scandal novel based transparently on the Swift-Stella-

Vanessa story appeared (*Some Memoirs*), giving some insight into public speculation of the time.

Vanessa was determined to be remembered. Erasmus Lewis, Francis Annesley, Archbishop William King, Archbishop Theophilus Bolton, Dr Bryan Robinson (probably her Dublin physician), and five others received £25 each for a mourning ring. Most of her estate went to two heirs and sole executors whom she hardly knew, Robert Marshall, law student of Clonmel, and the Revd Dr George Berkeley, fellow of Trinity College, Dublin. Swift is not mentioned, perhaps a final retaliation against a man whose neglect made her 'live a life like a languishing Death' (November/December 1720, *Correspondence of Jonathan Swift*, 2.524). The story of deathbed instructions for publication of her letters is apocryphal, but Marshall and Berkeley nevertheless began the publication process until Sheridan intervened.   CLIVE PROBYN

Sources *Some memoirs of the amours and intrigues of a certain Irish dean*, pt 2 (1728) • A. M. Freeman, ed., *Vanessa and her correspondence with Jonathan Swift* (1921) • S. Le Brocquy, *Cadenus: a reassessment in the light of new evidence of the relationships between Swift, Stella, and Vanessa* (1962) • S. Le Brocquy, *Swift's most valuable friend* (1968) • J. Swift, *Journal to Stella*, ed. H. Williams, 2 vols. (1948); repr. (1963) • *The poems of Jonathan Swift*, ed. H. Williams, 3 vols. (1937); 2nd edn (1958) • *The correspondence of Jonathan Swift*, ed. D. Woolley, 4 vols. (1999–2004)
Archives BL, corresp. with J. Swift, Add. MS 39839
Likenesses attrib. C. Jervas, oils, NG Ire.
Wealth at death see will, 1 May 1723, quoted in Le Brocquy, *Cadenus: a reassessment*

Hondelink, Englebert Roger (1890–1972), civil engineer and railway consultant, was born on 13 September 1890 at Dieren, Netherlands, son of Gerrit Hendrik Hondelink (1865–1930x34), stationmaster, and his wife, Gerarda Jacoba Immink (1865–1919). He was educated at Winterswyk high school, followed by a pupillage with the Holland Railway Company while he studied at Delft Engineering University. In 1911 he gained an MSc degree and joined the Holland Railway Company. On 26 May 1919 he married Anna Katerina Lucretia Voges (1894–1967). They had a daughter, Victoria Ann, and a son, Henry Roger.

After wide experience in all aspects of civil engineering, Hondelink went in 1921 to China to build the eastern division of the Longhai Railway which runs westward from Lianyungang on the Yellow Sea to Langhou, a distance of 1759 km; he became chief engineer and general manager of the Longhai, for the Chinese state railway. Construction—including road, harbour, and ancillary works—was completed in 1925 at a cost of £5 million. Based at Richmond upon Thames from 1926 to 1936 Hondelink was consultant to governments and syndicates worldwide on road, water, and railway construction, operation, equipment, and transport. Projects in which he was involved included the Arigna development in Ireland, the Jiangsu Railway in China (interrupted by civil war), and a detailed survey of the Chinese Eastern Railway (formerly the Trans-Siberian through Harbin) with advice to purchase from Russia with a plan for gauge conversion.

In 1936 Delft University appointed Hondelink professor of transport engineering and operation, a position he held until 1948, when he became emeritus professor. Using the Netherlands as example, he initiated research into rail, road, and air services. He was in Brussels in 1940 when Germany invaded the Low Countries, and went from there to London to advise British ministries, working from the Railway Research Office. There he met Brigadier-General Sir Osborne Manse and became a close friend of its head, C. E. R. Sherrington, who also held appointments in the International Union of Railways (UIC). In 1942 Hondelink was appointed chairman of the inter-allied technical advisory committee on transport, part of Sir Frederick Leith Ross's study for post-war redevelopment. In 1945 he became director-general of the European Central Inland Transport Organization (ECITO); its function was to restore communications, especially rail, in co-operation with the allied armies as they liberated Europe, an immense task with bridges destroyed, lines blocked, and usable rolling stock in short supply. For his work with ECITO he was made a member of the Légion d'honneur and the order of George I of Greece. When ECITO completed its work in December 1947 and international rail affairs returned to UIC, Hondelink became consultant on transport, later senior consultant, to the United Nations and to the World Bank. Also in 1948 he became a British citizen. Among his assignments were the Turkey–Iran rail link and applications for loans from countries all over the world, including Iraq, Japan, British Guiana, Malaya, Mexico, and Nigeria.

Britain's railway problems troubled Hondelink greatly, especially the top-heavy management structure set up under the 1947 Transport Act, when there were ten levels. He urged in letters to MPs, civil servants and other influential people that there should never be more than four levels between the top and persons in contact with the public. The 1953 Transport Act (1 & 2 Eliz. 2) showed some ground gained. 'In 1962 the Marples–Beeching axis began to define their territorial ambitions about rural railways; they laid it down in general that they did not pay, which was true; and never could pay, which was false' (Fiennes, 114). So Gerard Fiennes summed up the position at the time of the 1962 Transport Act (10 & 11 Eliz. 2).

Hondelink offered his services as honorary consultant to the Great Central Association, defenders of a threatened main line, and to the National Council on Inland Transport, which had a wider remit. The presidents of the latter—Lord Stonham (a Labour life peer) and the earl of Kinnoull (Conservative)—were able to ask parliamentary questions and arrange debates, supported widely by other members of both houses. Hondelink contended that government's rail closure policy was completely wrong. It treated rail in isolation from other transport. The financial case was spurious because traffic that branch lines contributed to main lines went uncounted. Possible economies were not made. The public was allowed to protest only about the hardship that would be incurred if a present often run-down service were closed. Hondelink correctly saw that closures would lead to a catastrophic loss of traffic. To the Geddes committee on carriers' licensing, set up by Ernest Marples in 1963 to examine the licensing of road haulage, he contended that a rail loss of £82 million in 1963 was matched by a road transport loss of £300 million if all relevant costs were included; and even that did not include a return to the nation on the capital value of 220,000 miles of highway. He discussed with Professor Kolbusewski of Birmingham University the coming population explosion which would require more railways, not fewer. Louis Armand, a French academician, whom Hondelink met in ECITO days, wrote:'The further ahead you look, the greater are the public needs for railroads. We face the possibility of the railways being dismantled in the near future only to be rebuilt later at vastly greater cost' (*Railway Gazette*, 26 July 1963). At a social function Dr Beeching met Hondelink's son, and told him that his father was 'a major thorn in my side; as fast as I close one railway line, he comes along and gets it open again' (private information). On being told this, Hondelink said he regarded it as one of the greatest compliments he had ever received. Had he lived to see the events at the turn of the century he might have sought to remind the Department of Transport of what he wrote to the minister of transport from the World Bank on 17 April 1958: '[such a] combination [as you propose] of modernization and retrenchment can only have a disastrous effect, namely a few spectacular services here and there, but the railway system as a whole becoming a perpetual burden on the tax payer' (Calvert, *Switches and Crossings*, 33). Hondelink died on 2 October 1972 at his home, Linthwaite, Bois Avenue, Chesham Bois, Buckinghamshire, and the cremation of his remains took place at Amersham crematorium.

ROGER CALVERT

Sources R. Calvert, ed., *Switches and crossings* (1981) · R. Calvert, *The rape of Britain's railways and waterways* (1991) · G. F. Fiennes, *I tried to run a railway* (1967) · *Railway Gazette* (26 July 1963) · b. cert. · *CGPLA Eng. & Wales* (1973) · personal knowledge (2004) · private information (2004) [Mrs A. Hondelink, daughter-in-law; Mrs V. A. Glossop, daughter] · *Modern Transport* (15 Oct 1960)
Archives Inst. CE, records of Institution of Civil Engineers | Doncaster Central Library, National Council on Inland Transport corresp. · priv. coll., records of the Great Central Association
Likenesses photograph, repro. in *Modern Transport*
Wealth at death £31,418: probate, 20 March 1973, *CGPLA Eng. & Wales*

Hondius [de Hont, de Hond], **Abraham Danielszoon** (*c.*1631–1691), painter, was born probably in Rotterdam, the eldest of six children (four boys and two girls) of Daniel Abrahamszoon de Hond (*d.* 1664), master mason, and Crijntgen Alewijnsdochter Pancrasz (*d.* 1673). His brother Isaac de Hond (*c.*1646–1716) also became a painter. Although Hondius was already a skilled master by the age of about twenty—his earliest known painting, *Sportsman Outside an Italianate Inn*, signed and dated 1651, was described as a work of consummate skill—nothing is known of his youth or of how or with whom he learned his trade. On 27 April 1653 he married Geertruyd Willemsdochter van den Eijck (*d.* 1681), of Rotterdam. The date of birth of their only child, a daughter named Geertruyd, is not known; a son, Abraham, also a painter, is mentioned in Hondius's will.

The signed and dated *œuvre* of Hondius is large and varied. A break in his work, according to where the paintings were made, is evident: in his Netherlandish work, made before he settled in England, the subject matter is varied and includes hunting scenes with and without figures, domestic scenes, history paintings based on stories from the Old and New Testaments, historical and mythological works. He often painted on panel, and the dimensions of his paintings are on the whole modest. A key work is his monumental altar piece *Adoration of the Shepherds*, signed and dated 1664 (Museum Catharijneconvent, Utrecht). At that time he was living at the Oppert, in Rotterdam; since a clandestine Roman Catholic church was an integral part of the buildings it can be inferred that he himself was a Catholic.

In Hondius's signed and dated work after 1671–2 the variety of subject matter has disappeared, as has the use of panel as support. He now almost exclusively paints savage hunting scenes without figures on canvas, generally of very large dimensions. A subject unusual for Hondius but very popular in England appears in his *œuvre*, namely large town views that refer to a specific event; *The Frozen River* (1677; Museum of London) is a good example of this development. The quality of his canvasses depicting hunting scenes declined at this time.

These changes in his *œuvre* indicate that Hondius left the Netherlands in 1671–2, a time of great economic crisis. In his *Diary*, which covers the period 1672–80, the scientist and architect Robert Hooke mentions that he is involved with Hondius on two projects, for the Guildhall (1674) and for the Royal College of Physicians (1674). Sequences in Hooke's *Diary* indicate that their partnership fell apart for financial reasons that were mainly due to Hondius's awkward temperament. His biographer Jacob Campo Weyerman (1729–1769), also a painter, who might have known him in London, describes Hondius as 'a great man in his profession but quite unfortunate in his temperament which was not well served by his behaviour' (Weyerman, 3.157–8). Weyerman further notes:

> he left for England with someone else's wife with whom he lived as his genuine spouse. After the death of this lady he married a frump who, with a basket on her head, earned her living in the vegetable market. (ibid.)

Hondius died at the Blackamoor's Head, near Water Lane, Fleet Street, London, in September 1691 and was buried on 17 September. His wife, Sarah, inherited 'two peices of landskipp, halflenghts. And eight of his best small peices with his own picture' (Croft-Murray and Hulton, 370). To his son Abraham he left his prints, books, and drawings 'for his own proper use'; the remaining paintings were intended to be sold to pay for his funeral. Weyerman recorded that he 'painted Portraits, Trojan devastations, candlelight scenes, statuary, deerhunts, hounds—and bearfights, hawking parties, horses and dogs … an Amsterdam Dog Market by his hand, with more than thirty different types of dogs, [was] beautifully drawn and lovingly painted' (Weyerman, 157–8).

M. PEYSER-VERHAAR

Sources M. Peyser-Verhaar, 'Abraham Hondius: his life and background', *Oud Holland*, 112 (1998) · *The diary of Robert Hooke … 1672–1680*, ed. H. W. Robinson and W. Adams (1935) · J. C. Weyerman, *De levens-beschryvingen der Nederlandsche konst-schilders en konst-schilderessen*, 4 vols. (The Hague, 1729–69), vol. 3, pp. 157–8 [typescript trans. by M. Peyser] · E. Croft-Murray and P. H. Hulton, eds., *Catalogue of British drawings*, 1 (1960), 369–70 · Vertue, *Note books*, 2.13, 74 · GL, MS 6540/2
Likenesses J. Houbraken, line engraving (after A. Hondius), NPG · J. C. Smith, mezzotint (after self-portrait by A. Hondius), BM, NPG; repro. in J. C. Smith, *British mezzotinto portraits*, 4 vols. (1883), vol. 3, p. 1180

Hondius, Jodocus [Joost de Hondt] (1563–1612), engraver and cartographer, was born on 12 October 1563 at Wackene, near Ghent, in Flanders, one of several children born to Olivier de Hondt (*d.* 1580), engraver, and his wife, Petronella van Havertuyn. Two years later his parents moved to Ghent, where Hondius was educated. By the age of eight he was able to reproduce his own designs by engraving on ivory and copper, and in due course his father apprenticed him to Hendrick van der Keere, an engraver and typecutter at Ghent. Hondius's formal education ceased with the death of both his father and van der Keere in 1580, but he had shown sufficient proof of his talents to be offered commissions by Alexander Farnese, duke of Parma, commander of the Spanish forces in what was then the Spanish Netherlands. As his family was protestant, Hondius declined this invitation, and another to go to Rome, and applied himself to the study of Greek and Latin and to cosmography. When Parma's troops captured Ghent in 1583 Hondius and the family of van der Keere were among those who fled to London.

In London, Hondius adopted the Latin form of his name, settled in the parish of St Thomas the Apostle, Southwark, and was soon at work engraving maps and charts bearing the latest information brought back by mariners venturing new routes into distant seas. His work for the map publisher Edward Wright brought him into contact with the great explorers, among them Sir Francis Drake, Sir Walter Ralegh, and Thomas Cavendish. In 1589 he associated with De Bry and Augustin Ryther to engrave maps for the English version of *The Mariner's Mirror*, and he produced a world map in hemispheres measuring some 7½ by 6 feet. He cut type, illustrated the voyages of Drake and Cavendish, and engraved their portraits and those of Queen Elizabeth, Henry IV, and Gerardus Mercator, signing his prints H. J. A set of five circular thematic maps, probably designed as book illustrations, may date from this period. On 11 April 1587, at the Dutch church in London, Hondius married Colette van der Keere, daughter of his late master. Of their thirteen children, two sons and four daughters survived infancy.

Celestial globes had long been familiar, and the first terrestrial globes had been produced on the continent about 1500. The depiction of topographic information on globes grew in popularity as voyages of discovery extended to distant regions and high latitudes, for it was difficult to project such large areas realistically on a flat map. William Sanderson (1548?–1638?), a merchant who had funded several of the northern voyages, paid for the manufacture of a pair of large globes (of 62 cm diameter), the terrestrial being the first to be made in England. Emery Molyneux compiled the maps and Hondius engraved the copper plates in the richly embellished style of the Southern Netherlands. They were published in 1592 and the first pair were presented to Queen Elizabeth at Greenwich. A second pair, bearing Sanderson's newly acquired arms, are now in the library of Middle Temple, London.

In 1593 Hondius left London for Amsterdam, now part of the United Provinces and a prosperous trading city. Hondius was fully employed, obtaining a privilege to publish in 1597 the first pair of his own globes. The celestial globe was the first to show those constellations newly invented by Petrus Plancius, based on a recent survey by Dutch navigators. In the same year Hondius brought out a Dutch translation of Robert Hues's *Tractatus de globis* (1594), updated and corrected as *Tractaet Ofte Handelinge van het Genbrijk der Himelscher ende Aertscher Globe*, to serve users of his own terrestrial globe. His smaller map of the world of 1596/1597, known as the 'Christian knight' from a prominent figure in the margin, was one of the first produced before 1600 to Gerardus Mercator's projection. It led to trouble with Edward Wright, who complained that Hondius had stolen this projection when he was shown in confidence the manuscript of Wright's 'Certaine errors in navigation' (1599). The argument turned on whether Hondius had used the method of calculation published by Mercator in 1569, or that of Wright. Hondius was, moreover, in competition with other map makers, first with Jacob Floris van Langren and later with the Blaeu family. In 1602 he bought the plates of Mercator's famous *Atlas*, adding fifty more plates in a new edition published in 1606. In his later years Hondius was described as tall and stout, but sober, pious, gentle, and hardworking. He died at Amsterdam on 10 February 1612. The business continued in the hands of his widow and their eldest son, Jodocus de Hondt (1593–1629), later joined by the younger son, Hendrik de Hondt (1597–1651). ANITA MCCONNELL

Sources E. Dekker, *Globes at Greenwich* (1999), 357–63 · P. van der Krogt, *Globi Neerlandici: the production of globes in the Low Countries* (1993) · F. G. Waller, *Biographisch woordenboek van Noord Nederlandsche graveurs* (1938), 147–8 · *Biographie des hommes remarquables de la Flandre occidentale*, 4 (1849), 106 · P. van der Krogt, 'The globes of Hondius', *Antiquariat Forum Catalogue*, 98 (1991), 29–32 · G. Schilder, 'An unrecorded set of thematic maps by Hondius', *Map Collector*, 59 (1992), 44–7 · H. Wallis, 'Emigrant map-makers of the late 16th century and the protestant New World', *Proceedings of the Huguenot Society*, 24 (1983–8), 210–20 · R. E. G. Kirk and E. F. Kirk, eds., *Returns of aliens dwelling in the city and suburbs of London, from the reign of Henry VIII to that of James I*, Huguenot Society of London, 10/2 (1902), 332
Likenesses J. Hondius or workshop, double portrait, line engraving (with Gerardus Mercator), NPG; repro. in G. Mercator, *Atlas*, 4th edn (Amsterdam, 1613)

Hone, Eva Sydney [Evie] (1894–1955), artist and craftswoman, the youngest daughter of Eva Eleanor, *née* Robinson (*d.* 1894), and Joseph Hone (1850–1908), maltster and banker, was born on 22 April 1894 in Roebuck Grove, co. Dublin. Her family had been merchants, painters and manufacturers in Dublin since the early seventeenth century. In 1905, a fall while decorating her local church for

Eva Sydney Hone (1894–1955), by Hilda van Stockum

Easter resulted in the paralysis which physically disabled her but encouraged the inner spiritual quest which informed all aspects of her life. Trips all over Europe in search of medical treatment led to her deep interest in art. In 1914, still severely incapacitated, she took her first art lessons with Walter Sickert at the Westminster School of Art, London (where she met her lifelong friend and fellow painter, Mainie Jellett), with Byam Shaw, and with Bernard Meninsky, who encouraged her to continue her studies in Paris. During this period she also studied at the Central School of Arts and Crafts, London. She went to Paris in 1920, to be joined by Jellett. They studied for a year with the semi-cubist painter and writer André Lhôte, before persuading the purely abstract, intransigently cubist painter and theorist Albert Gleizes, to take them on as students for an annual period over the next ten years. There began their systematic disregard of perspective in favour of a strictly two-dimensional surface based on what Gleizes called the translation and rotation of form and on the rainbow spectrum of colour. With Gleizes, they found direct parallels between the forms and construction of early Christian art and cubism in what Hone described as 'a direction to the spirit to contemplate the Divine Author of the rhythm and form of all created life by a composition of form and colour, by a circular movement symbolic of eternity, by a sublimity of form, by simplicity and severity of colour' (MacCarvill, 112).

This highly disciplined search for a creative response to the mystical, contemplative strength and movement underlying the universe governed all Hone's work and found its theological counterpart in her withdrawal to the Anglican Community of the Epiphany in Truro, Cornwall, between 1925 and 1927. In 1937 she converted to Roman Catholicism.

Hone's travels continued, particularly to Gleizes' artists' colony in the south of France, throughout the 1920s when she also exhibited with avant-garde groups including the Society of Dublin Painters (twice in Dublin in 1924 when over fifty of her paintings were displayed in a joint show with Jellett); in Paris in 1925; with the Seven and Five Society, London during 1926–7 and in a solo exhibition in Dublin in 1929. Just as her pioneering role, with Jellett, in introducing a purely abstract art into Ireland was recognized in the Brussels 1930 'Exposition d'Art Irlandais', in a journal, *abstraction création art non-figuratif*, and in the 1931 Dublin painters' exhibition, Hone began to develop a more lively, figurative, representational idiom. In 1932, this led her to stained glass. Her application to work at the Dublin stained glass co-operative studio An Túr Gloine rejected, she went to London to learn the foundations of the craft with Wilhelmina Geddes. The resulting small, richly coloured, abstract panels (the first of around 150 she would make) were leaded into a figurative composition *The Annunciation* (1933–4; Taney church, co. Dublin). She had found her vocation.

Hone worked at An Túr Gloine between 1935 and 1943, guided by her fellow painter Michael Healy, and Thomas Kinsella, her glazier, until his death in 1953. There she introduced a new, expressionist intensity into stained glass, forging a carefully articulated, freely painted, glowingly chromatic link between the early medieval glass painters and modernism. From 1944 all her windows were produced in a studio beside her residence, the Dower House, Marlay Grange, Rathfarnham, co. Dublin. At Marlay she made her finest series of full-scale windows: for the Jesuit chapel, Tullabeg, Offaly (1946); for University Hall Chapel, Hatch Street, Dublin (1947); for Kingscourt church, co. Cavan (1947–8) and, her best-known, the huge and cumbersome eighteen-light Eton College chapel *Crucifixion and Last Supper* window (1949–52).

This commission for the bomb-damaged chapel was the most important of Evie Hone's works and was awarded after her work at Tullabeg was shown by the painter Derek Hill to the connoisseur and trustee of art David Lindsay, earl of Crawford and Balcarres, and Sir Jasper Ridley. A short film, *Hallowed Fire*, recorded the artist completing the window in 1952, and it has since been described by Patrick Reyntiens as 'a dramatic breakthrough … the herald of a new period of co-operation between the eye of the painter and the eye of the artist in stained glass' (Reyntiens, 13).

While Hone's work is seen to bridge the arts and crafts achievements of Michael Healy, Harry Clarke and Wilhelmina Geddes and the post-war painters Patrick Pye and Patrick Pollen (both deeply influenced by her work), John Piper compared her artistic expression through glass to work by Georges Rouault, Fernand Léger, Henri Matisse, and Georges Braque.

Evie Hone died while attending mass in her parish church on 13 March 1955, and was buried at St Maelruan's church, Tallaght, Rathfarnham, near Dublin, on 15 March. Shy and contemplative, loyal and kind, impishly humorous among friends, she possessed a quiet strength and an indomitable commitment to her work which may be seen in churches in Ireland, England and America; the Tate collection; the Victoria and Albert Museum, London; the Stained Glass Museum, Ely, Cambridgeshire; the National Gallery of Ireland and the Hugh Lane Municipal Gallery, Dublin; and the Ulster Museum, Belfast.

NICOLA GORDON BOWE

Sources C. P. Curran, 'Evie Hone: stained glass worker, 1894–1955', *Studies*, 44 (1955), 129–42 · S. Frost, ed., *A tribute to Evie Hone and Mainie Jellett* (1957) · N. G. Bowe, D. Caron, and M. Wynne, *Gazetteer of Irish stained glass* (1988) · A. Wrigley, ed., *Evie Hone, 1894–1955* (1992) [exhibition catalogue, Ballyroan Library, Dublin, March 1992] · E. MacCarvill, *Mainie Jellett, the artist's vision: lectures and essays on art* (1958) · E. Rivers, 'Evie Sydney Hone', *Journal of the British Society of Master Glass Painters*, 12/1 (1956), 71–3 · M. Wynne, 'Stained glass in Ireland, principally Irish stained glass, 1760–1963', PhD diss., University of Dublin, 1975 · J. White, *Evie Hone, 1894–1955* (1959) [exhibition catalogue, Arts Council Gallery and Tate Gallery, London, 2 Jan – 15 Feb 1959] · M. Wynne, 'A life concerned with glass: Evie Hone, 1894–1955', *Country Life*, 175 (1984), 1740–42 · N. G. Bowe, *20th century Irish stained glass* (1983) · P. Pollen, 'Thoughts on the art and life of Evie Hone', *University Review*, 1 (1956), 38–44 · S. B. Kennedy, *Irish art and modernism, 1880–1950* (1991) [exhibition catalogue, Hugh Lane Municipal Gallery of Modern Art, Dublin, 20 Sept – 10 Nov 1991 and Ulster Museum, Belfast, 22 Nov 1991 – 26 Jan 1992] · P. Reyntiens, *The technique of stained glass* (1967) · CGPLA Eng. & Wales (1955) · CGPLA Éire (1955) · J. Piper, 'Abstraction to creation', *A tribute to Evie Hone and Mainie Jellett*, ed. S. Frost (1957), 43–5
Archives Ballyroan Library, Dublin, archive · National Cathedral Archive, Washington, DC · National College of Art and Design, Dublin, Hone Library | TCD, McGreevy MSS | FILM BAC Films and Irish Film Board archive, Dublin, *Hallowed fire* (1952) · Irish Film Archive, Dublin
Likenesses F. Boland, portrait, c.1935, priv. coll. · O. Kelly, bronze bust, St Mary's, Emo, Ireland, Jesuit noviciate · H. van Stockum, oils, NG Ire. [see illus.] · photograph, repro. in Frost, ed., *Evie Hone*, frontispiece
Wealth at death £46,545: probate, 28 May 1955, CGPLA Éire · £16,203 6s. 3d. in England: administration with will, 1955, CGPLA Eng. & Wales

Hone, Horace (1754–1825). *See under* Hone, Nathaniel (1718–1784).

Hone, John Camillus (1759–1836). *See under* Hone, Nathaniel (1718–1784).

Hone, Nathaniel (1718–1784), painter, was born on 24 April 1718 at Wood Quay in Dublin. He was descended from a family of goldsmiths. His father was Nathaniel Hone, a merchant in Dublin and treasurer of the congregation of Eustace Street Presbyterian Chapel, and his mother, Rebeckah, was the daughter of Samuel Brindley of Staffordshire. Hone, if not self-taught, may have studied with Robert West, who had an art school in St George's Lane. He moved in his youth to England, where he worked as an itinerant portrait painter. In 1742 (February or 9 October) he married Mary (Molly) Earle (d. 1791), a woman endowed with a small fortune, in York Minster. His marriage may have obviated his need to travel, as soon afterwards he settled in St James's Place, London. He produced both oil paintings and miniatures and quickly established

a sizeable clientele. His works on enamel are of particularly high quality. Contrary to popular accounts, Hone did not travel to Italy. His younger brother Samuel, also an artist, having been elected a member of the Accademia del Disegno in Florence in September 1752, arranged for Nathaniel to be elected *in absentia* on 14 January 1753. Nathaniel's application was endorsed by Ignazio Hugford, one of two consuls of the academy.

Hone exhibited a total of twenty-eight paintings at the Society of Artists of Great Britain between 1760 and 1768, was one of the artists who signed a petition for incorporation in 1766, and was among the first directors of the new Society of Incorporated Artists. However, he defected in 1768 to become one of the two Irish foundation members of the Royal Academy. He was a prolific exhibitor at the academy, showing sixty-nine oil paintings and miniatures there between 1769 and 1784, the year of his death. Hone wished to be identified principally as a painter in oils, and gradually relinquished working on miniatures to concentrate on easel painting. He developed a reputation for irreverence, submitting to the Royal Academy in 1770 a picture of Francis Grose and Theodosius Forrest masquerading as Capuchin monks feasting at a table. The treatment of the subject, which featured one character stirring a bowl of punch with a crucifix, was deemed inappropriate for the academy. Hone agreed to amend the painting for exhibition, but engraved it subsequently in its original state. In 1775 he painted *The Conjuror*, a blatant attack on Sir Joshua Reynolds, president of the Royal Academy. It appears that Hone was suspicious of Reynolds's reliance on Italian artistic models for his own work, and also resented his adversary's pre-eminent status among portrait painters. *The Conjuror*'s implicit suggestions of plagiarism, and alleged scurrilous references to an intimate relationship between Reynolds and Angelica Kauffman led to its removal, at Kauffman's behest, from the Royal Academy exhibition. Hone denied all allegations and painted out the figure of Angelica Kauffman, but the painting was not reinstated. Hone duly made it the centrepiece of his one-man show, probably the first of its kind, at 70 St Martin's Lane, London, which featured sixty-five other works. Formally entitled *The exhibition of pictures by Nathaniel Hone: mostly the works of his leisure, and many of them in his own possession*, the exhibition was accompanied by a catalogue, which itself featured a deliberately pedantic introduction by the artist.

Among Hone's principal sitters were Captain Thomas Baillie; Edmund Burke; John, fourth earl of Bute; Lady Caroline Curzon; Henry, first Earl Digby; Sir John Fielding; Lord Fortescue; Francis Grose; Lord and Lady Middlesex; Frederick, prince of Wales; Horace Walpole; John Wesley; and Signora Zamperini. A large number of his portraits were engraved, often by Hone himself.

Though best-known as a portrait painter, Hone also produced a number of genre paintings, and pictures with theatrical, mythological, and biblical themes, many of which he exhibited. Among these were *The Brickdust Man* (exh. Society of Artists of Great Britain, 1760); *Diogenes Looking for an Honest Man* (exh. Society of Artists of Great Britain,

1768); and *A Historical Sketch of Nathan in his Reply to David the King* (RA; 1783). Hone also executed a large number of self-portraits during his career, both miniatures and easel paintings, in which he presented himself in a variety of guises, from cavalier to country squire. He referred to his wife in a number of his self-portraits by various means, such as the introduction of a relief, an easel portrait in the background, or a miniature. Hone was a mercurial character, but his portraits of other members of his family demonstrate his affection for them. He painted his sons **Horace Hone** (1754–1825) and **John Camillus Hone** (1759–1836), both of whom became highly accomplished miniature painters in their own right. Hone's celebrated painting *A Piping Boy* (1789; NG Ire.) and *The Spartan Boy* (1775; priv. coll.) featured his son John Camillus, and *David the Shepherd Boy* (1771) his son Horace. Horace Hone was born in Frith Street, Soho, London, the second son of Nathaniel Hone and Mary. On 19 October 1770 he entered the Royal Academy Schools when his age was recorded as '17 11th Febry next' (Hutchison, 136), indicating that he was born on 11 February 1754. He exhibited at the Royal Academy from 1772 to 1822 and was elected an associate of the academy in 1779. In 1782 he went to Dublin, where he established a successful practice, living in Dorset Street. He painted in watercolour and enamel as well as producing engravings. In 1795 he became miniature painter to the prince of Wales. After the union of England and Ireland his practice declined, and he returned to London in 1804. His sitters included the actress Mrs Siddons (NG Ire.), Mrs Elizabeth Prentice, wife of Thomas Prentice of Dublin (enamel, priv. coll.), the fourth duke of Rutland, and Lord Edward Fitzgerald. Daphne Foskett noted that 'Hone's style of painting varies a great deal; it is usually elegant and his miniatures of ladies are attractive and well posed' (Foskett, 568). He was a friend of the painter and diarist Joseph Farington, in whose diary he is mentioned. He suffered from mental health problems from about 1807. Hone died at 20 Dover Street, London, on 24 May 1825,

leaving both a widow and a daughter, Sophia Matilda. He was buried in the grounds of St George's Chapel, Bayswater Road, London. A self-portrait by Horace Hone is in the National Portrait Gallery, London, and another in the National Gallery of Ireland. Further examples of his work are in the Victoria and Albert Museum, London, and the Fitzwilliam Museum, Cambridge.

John Camillus Hone was a younger son of Nathaniel Hone and studied under his father. He exhibited at the Royal Academy and the Free Society of Artists from 1775 to 1780, after which date he worked in India for about ten years. He was teaching drawing in Calcutta in 1785. Following his return home about 1790 he settled in Dublin, where he became engraver of dies in the stamp office. In October 1807 he married his cousin Abigail (d. 1855), daughter of Joseph Hone of York Street and widow of the Revd John Conolly of York Street. He painted miniatures and oil portraits. John Camillus Hone died at his house in Summerhill, Dublin, on 23 May 1836.

Nathaniel Hone also painted his daughters Lydia (*bap.* 1756) and Amelia, his granddaughter Eleanor (or Mary) Metcalfe, his brother Samuel, and his mother. He is believed to have had at least seven other children, Samuel Augustus (*bap.* 1748), Herbert, Apelles Earl (*bap.* 1750), Mary, Charles, Sophie, and Floretta Augusta (*bap.* 1751). Hone was also a competent etcher and an enthusiastic art collector, and could count within his collection drawings by and prints after works by such artists as Maratti, Rubens, Rembrandt, Watteau, and Vernet, and a large number after Hogarth. A number of his drawings and prints carry his mark, a human eye. His collection was sold in two auctions in February and March 1785. Hone was also associated, with Captain William Baillie, in the formation of Lord Bute's collection.

Hone moved to Pall Mall in 1774, and then to north Soho in 1780. He may have maintained contact with his family in Dublin, but remained in London until his death at his

Nathaniel Hone (1718–1784), self-portrait, *c.*1775

home, 44 Rathbone Place, on 14 August 1784. He was buried six days later on 20 August in Hendon churchyard, where five of his children had already been interred. In his will Hone mentions that his 'dear wife Ann Hone's fortune is in her own power' (will, PRO, PROB 11/1121, sig. 509). This suggests that Ann was probably identical with the Mary Earle whom Hone married in 1742. Hone's portraiture was solid, and sometimes exceptional. He was particularly adept at depicting children, and often afforded his sitters a distinctly soft expression. Though he was not universally admired, and his use of colour was often adversely criticized, he commanded an enviable profile among his peers.   BRENDAN ROONEY

Sources N. Figgis and B. Rooney, *Irish paintings in the National Gallery of Ireland*, 1 (2001) · W. G. Strickland, *A dictionary of Irish artists*, 1 (1913) · E. Edwards, *Anecdotes of painters* (1808); facs. edn (1970) · A. Pasquin [J. Williams], *An authentic history of the professors of painting, sculpture, and architecture who have practiced in Ireland … to which are added, Memoirs of the royal academicians* [1796]; facs. edn as *An authentic history of painting in Ireland* with introduction by R. W. Lightbown (1970) · N. Hone, *The exhibition of pictures by Nathaniel Hone: mostly the works of his leisure, and many of them in his own possession* (1775) [exhibition catalogue, London, 1775] · M. Wynne, 'Members from Great Britain and Ireland of the Florentine Accademia del Disegno, 1700–1855', *Burlington Magazine*, 132 (1990), 535–7 · Redgrave, *Artists* · J. T. Smith, *Nollekens and his times*, 2 vols. (1828) · M. Butlin, 'An eighteenth-century art scandal: Nathaniel Hone's *The conjuror*', *The Connoisseur*, 174/699 (1970), 1–9 · J. Newman, 'Reynolds and Hone—the conjuror unmasked', *Reynolds*, ed. N. Penny (1986) [exhibition catalogue, RA, 16 Jan – 31 March 1986] · F. Lugt, *Répertoire des catalogues de ventes publiques*, 1 (The Hague, 1938) · G. Walkley, *Artists' houses in London, 1764–1914* (1994) · will, PRO, PROB 11/1121, sig. 509 · A. Le Harivel, *Nathaniel Hone the elder, 1718–1784* (Dublin, 1992) · D. Foskett, *Miniatures: dictionary and guide* (1987) · S. C. Hutchison, 'The Royal Academy Schools, 1768–1830', *Walpole Society*, 38 (1960–62), 123–91, esp. 136 · IGI · J. J. Foster, 'A few notes upon the diary of Nathaniel Hone, R. A., for the years 1752 and 1753', *The Antiquary*, 9 (June 1884), 244–50 · H. J. M. Milne, 'Two diaries of Nathaniel Hone', *British Museum Quarterly*, 10/3 (1936), 108–9

Archives BL, memorandum books, Add. MSS 44024–44025 · RA, corresp.

Likenesses N. Hone, self-portrait, oils, c.1747, NG Ire. · N. Hone, self-portrait, enamel miniature, 1749 · N. Hone, self-portrait, oils, c.1760, NPG · N. Hone, self-portrait, enamel miniature, 1760–69, NPG · N. Hone, self-portrait, oils, 1760–69, NG Ire. · N. Hone, self-portrait, drawing, 1764, BM · N. Hone, self-portrait, oils, c.1765, RA · N. Hone, self-portrait, oils, c.1775, NG Ire. [*see illus.*] · E. Fisher, mezzotint (after N. Hone), BM, NPG · H. Hone, self-portrait (Horace Hone), NPG · H. Hone, self-portrait (Horace Hone), NG Ire. · N. Hone, portrait (John Camillus Hone), NG Ire. · N. Hone, self-portrait, oils, Man. City Gall. · N. Hone, self-portrait, sketch, BM · J. Sanders, watercolour (after J. Zoffany, *The academicians of the Royal Academy*), NPG · J. Zoffany, group portrait, oils (*Royal Academicians*, 1772), Royal Collection

Wealth at death left two houses in Dublin, one each to his sons; money in the 3 per cents to daughters; money to grandchildren: will, PRO, PROB 11/1121, sig. 509

Hone, Sir (Herbert) Ralph (1896–1992), army officer and colonial official, was born on 3 May 1896 at 89 Sackville Road, Hove, Sussex, the son of Herbert Hone, schoolmaster, and his wife, Miriam Grace, *née* Dracott. He was educated at Varndean Grammar School, Brighton, where he was senior prefect. His mother died while he was still in his teens; his father, who was 'a man of character' (*The*

Independent), went on to become mayor of Brighton in 1937.

Hone passed the civil service examination in April 1915 before joining the Inns of Court regiment, from which he was commissioned and gazetted to the London Irish Rifles later that year. He was posted to the 1/18th battalion, a sporting unit which had kicked a rugby football ahead when it attacked in the murderous battle of Loos in autumn 1915. He served in the Notre Dame de Lorette sector and then at Vimy Ridge, where incessant rain made the trenches insanitary, but where everyone was expected to shave every day. Acute trench fever and impetigo put him in hospital, but after discharge he returned to the trenches, and to endless bombardment including by mustard gas shells. He was present when the Germans opened their offensive on 21 March 1918 with 6000 guns. Hone's company checked the first infantry assault near Couillet valley and took twenty-five German prisoners. In the ensuing fighting Hone anticipated and foiled several German attempts to infiltrate their lines, and led several counter-attacks. When the Germans sited a machine-gun where it could enfilade his company lines, he took a Lewis gun on to the parapet and promptly silenced it. In doing so he was badly wounded in the arm. Although losing blood fast, he was sent to walk several miles back to the casualty clearing station, where, with his bones fractured and the ulnar nerve severed, he was registered as 'slightly wounded'. However, he was sent back to England and his courage and conduct in the action was recognized by the award of an MC. He ended the war as a captain. On 12 November 1918 he married Elizabeth Daisy (b. 1894/5), daughter of James Herbert Matthews, master tailor of Brighton. They had a son and a daughter.

After the war Hone served as a staff captain in the Ministry of Munitions from 1918 to 1920, when he resigned his commission to join the colonial service as assistant treasurer in Uganda. He used his spare time to qualify as a barrister, and was called to the bar by the Middle Temple in 1924. He also sat the London LLB externally. From 1924 to 1925 he practised on the south-eastern circuit, but in 1925 he returned to Africa as registrar to the high court (1925–8) and resident magistrate (1928–30) in Zanzibar. In 1930 he was appointed crown counsel in Tanganyika territory. From January to August 1933 he returned to Britain as assistant legal adviser to the colonial and dominions offices. He was then appointed attorney-general in Gibraltar, where he was commissioner for the revision of the laws of Gibraltar in 1934 and chairman of the Gibraltar government commission on slum clearance and rent restriction in 1936. He was also occasionally acting chief justice of Gibraltar. His next posting was as attorney-general of Uganda from 1937 to 1943.

Shortly after the outbreak of the Second World War, and while still attorney-general of Uganda, Hone was made commandant of the Uganda defence force. In 1941 he was transferred to general headquarters Middle East, first as legal adviser (advising notably on law in the conquered Italian territories) and then (from 1942) as chief political officer. In March 1943 he was promoted to major-general, 'to ease his command over the Brigadiers under him' (*The Independent*); he was also appointed CBE. Later that year he returned to London, where he served on the general staff at the War Office, dealing in particular with the war in Asia. He travelled frequently between London and SEAC headquarters, and struck up a close friendship with Louis Mountbatten, Lord Mountbatten of Burma.

In August 1945 Hone was appointed chief civil affairs officer in Malaya, overseeing the transition to civilian rule. He was present at the Japanese surrender at Singapore on 12 September. On 25 October 1945 (he and his first wife having divorced earlier in the year) Hone married Sybil Mary, daughter of Auguste Alfred Collins, and widow of Wing Commander G. Simond. There was one son of this second marriage. Mountbatten pressed for Hone to be offered the post of governor-general of Malaya in 1946, and was extremely annoyed when the Colonial Office vetoed the appointment on the grounds that divorced people should not become colonial governors. Mountbatten took up the point with George VI, who then abolished the rule about divorce. In consequence Hone, who was appointed KBE in 1946, and served as secretary-general to the governor-general of Malaya from 1946 to 1948, and deputy commissioner-general in south-east Asia from 1948 to 1949, was appointed governor and commander-in-chief of North Borneo in 1949. Mountbatten wrote to him saying that he was sure he would make a great success of the post, 'for it will help to establish the principle that the Governorship should be open to all suitable people, irrespective of old-fashioned rules' (*Daily Telegraph*). However, the Colonial Office did not bow out gracefully, and in their letter of congratulation on his appointment the deputed official said,

> It may interest you to know that in this respect you are establishing a precedent and I have been asked to make it clear to you that your appointment will not automatically entitle you to receive an invitation to social entertainments, such as Garden Parties at Buckingham Palace, and this particular embargo is not, I am told, to be waived. (*Daily Telegraph*)

As governor of North Borneo, Hone was, in the event, a great success, encouraging the country's recovery from the ravages of the Japanese occupation, expanding trade in rubber, timber, and copra, and travelling to remote villages which no governor had visited before. He was appointed KCMG in 1951. In 1954 he returned to Britain to become head of the legal division of the Commonwealth Relations Office. He remained there until 1961, advising and producing reports on a wide range of constitutional and legal issues. In 1961 he retired from the civil service, and resumed practice at the bar. Nevertheless, he also held many important advisory posts both at home and overseas, his ability at bringing new ideas to solve apparently intractable problems being very much appreciated. He was constitutional adviser to the Kenyan government from December 1961 to January 1962, to R. A. Butler (on central Africa) from July to October 1962, to the South Arabian government from October 1965 to January 1966, and to the Bermudan government from July to November 1966.

The key to Hone's success was hard work, meticulous attention to detail, and good-humoured leadership. He relaxed with tennis, badminton, and philately. He was an active freemason, and was bailiff grand cross of the order of St John. He died at his home, 56 Kenilworth Court, Lower Richmond Road, Putney, London, on 28 November 1992, of pneumonia; he was survived by his second wife and by his three children. A memorial service was held on 8 February 1993 at the Grand Priory Church, St John's Square, Clerkenwell Road, London.   PHILIP WARNER

Sources *Daily Telegraph* (7 Dec 1992) · *The Times* (7 Dec 1992) · *The Times* (10 Feb 1993) · *The Independent* (4 Dec 1992) · Burke, *Peerage* · *WWW* · b. cert. · m. cert. [Elizabeth Daisy Matthews] · d. cert.
Archives Bodl. RH, papers, MSS Brit Emp S 407, MSS Ind Ou S 271
Likenesses photograph, repro. in *The Independent* (4 Dec 1992) · photograph, repro. in *The Times* (7 Dec 1992)
Wealth at death £265,824: probate, 22 Dec 1992, *CGPLA Eng. & Wales*

Hone, William (*d.* 1683), conspirator, is of unknown origins and background. He first became visible in the late 1670s as a carpenter in London, a reputed member of the Green Ribbon Club, and a signatory of the 'monster' petition of January 1680 urging Charles II to summon a new parliament. Two years later he attracted attention by posting a copy of Magna Carta on Temple Bar gate, and was henceforth called '"Magna Charta" for so doing' (*CSP dom.*, 1682, 245). About the same time he allegedly told a government informer that James, duke of York, should not inherit the throne because he had been indicted as a Catholic, and that the duke of Monmouth was Charles's legitimate son. A protestant himself, Hone variously worshipped in presbyterian, congregational, and Anglican services. In February 1683 Sir Robert Viner obtained information that Hone and other dissidents were acquiring weapons. Their intent, alleged the tobacconist John Harrison, was to resist the court and the Catholics, who threatened their religion and liberties. By April Hone reportedly could find little work and 'Thirst[ed] for Blood' (PRO, SP 29/423/98).

In early 1683 the whig attorney Richard Goodenough recruited Hone to participate in a plot to assassinate Charles and James, promising to give him £20 to purchase a horse and weapons. At various times in the preceding four years he had been employed by Goodenough and his fellow conspirator, the attorney Robert West. Although he was never part of the inner circle of conspirators around West he met on several occasions in taverns and coffee houses with several of the plotters, including Goodenough, Josiah Keeling, Richard Rumbold, and the dyer Thomas Lee. By his own subsequent admission, on one of these occasions he told Keeling that he 'would depose the King & had rather see that Effected, than that Any Hurt should come to the Kings Brother' (PRO, SP 29/429/71). Yet he would also confess that initially he had supported the assassination of both Charles and James. After Keeling informed on his co-conspirators the government issued a proclamation, on 23 June 1683, offering a reward of £100 for the apprehension of each one. Having fled London, Hone was arrested at Fordham, in the fens, on the 24th and imprisoned in Cambridge Castle, before the proclamation reached there, for having stolen a horse. Transferred to London he confessed, adding that several years ago he had told Sir Nicholas Butler that he and others could assassinate Charles and James at St Mary-le-Bow church during the lord mayor's show. Butler subsequently testified to this at Hone's trial, though Hone then claimed that he only reported what he had heard.

When he was arraigned at the Old Bailey on 12 July, Hone sought to plead guilty to having conspired to murder Charles but not to providing weapons. However, when the chief justice, Sir Francis Pemberton, refused to permit the distinction Hone pleaded not guilty. During his trial the following day, Keeling, West, and Butler were the principal witnesses against him. Following their testimony Pemberton recommended that the jury find him guilty, and it did so without leaving the room. Having confessed on 1 and 2 July, Lee could also have testified against him. Sentenced on the 14th to be hanged, drawn, and quartered, Hone received permission for his friends, presumably including his wife, as he is known to have been married, to visit him. From the scaffold on 20 July he expressed remorse, admitted that he had agreed to participate in the assassination scheme, but insisted that he had never attended meetings of the principal conspirators. After his execution his head was affixed to Aldgate, where it remained until 1689, but his body was buried. Numerous accounts of his trial and execution were rushed into print, including *The Tryal of William Hone*, published in Dublin, *Eigentlicher Bericht*, probably printed in Frankfurt or Leipzig, and the song 'A Terror for Traitors'. He was imaginatively linked to Stephen College, another carpenter who had been executed for treason, in *The Protestant Joyner's Ghost* (1683), and in *Strange News* (1683) a satirist included Hone in a 'Commonwealth of Fiends' with Shaftesbury, Monmouth, Essex, and other dissidents.

RICHARD L. GREAVES

Sources PRO, SP 29/419/93; 29/442, 88, 152; 29/423/98; 29/425/85, 86, 87, 87.1; 29/426, pt 2, fol. 45; 29/427/49; 29/429/71, 184; 29/433/7 · BL, Lansdowne MS 1152, fol. 243v · *CSP dom.*, 1682–3 · *State trials*, 9.571–8 · *Copies of the informations and original papers* (1685) · R. L. Greaves, *Secrets of the kingdom: British radicals from the Popish Plot to the revolution of 1688–89* (1992) · *LondG* (21–5 June 1683) · *LondG* (12–16 July 1683) · *A true narrative of the whole proceedings at the sessions-house in the Old-Bayly* (1683) · *The last speech and behaviour of William Late Lord Russel … also … Capt. Thomas Walcot, John Rouse gent. and William Hone joyner* (1683) · M. S. Zook, *Radical whigs and conspiratorial politics in late Stuart England* (1999) · *The proceedings to execution of the sentence awarded against Captain Thomas Walcot, William Hone, and John Rouse, for high-treason* (1683)
Archives BL, Lansdowne MS 1152 · PRO, State Papers, domestic, SP 29

Hone, William (1780–1842), political writer and publisher, was born on 3 June 1780 at Bath, the first child of William Hone (1755–1831) and his wife, Frances Maria Stawell (*d.* 1833).

William Hone (1780–1842), by William Patten, in or before 1818

Background and early life Little is known of Hone's mother. Hone's father was the eldest son of a farmer from Surrey, who, after an apprenticeship with a law stationer and a short-lived ambition to act in the theatre, became a clerk, initially to a solicitor, then to a corn merchant in Bath. Hone was baptized on 26 August in the parish of St James, and in 1783 the family moved to London in order that Hone's father, a devout Calvinist Methodist, could attend the congregation of the well-known preacher William Huntington. They lived first in Grafton Street, Paddington, then briefly in Tottenham Court Road, before settling in Warren Street, while Hone's father resumed his career as a solicitor's clerk. The environment of Hone's early years, spent on the edge of a rapidly expanding London, allowed him to witness the poverty of urban life alongside the rural scenery of nearby dairy farms and Hampstead Heath. His parents taught him to read from the Bible (although Hone claimed his first book was 'Nature'), and before he was six he was sent to a local dame-school, where he showed an aptitude for reading. At seven he was sent to a day school for boys, and shortly afterwards contracted a dangerous smallpox; this, followed by another move—to Old North Street, Red Lion Square—led to a cessation of his formal education. At twelve he attended another boys' school for a short period before a bullying incident led his father to remove him permanently. Thereafter the only instruction he received was from his father and his own reading.

Hone's love of books was evident from an early age. His home held only a few devout volumes, but he garnered reading material from a variety of sources, saving his meagre pocket money in order to buy secondhand copies, borrowing books from friendly booksellers and neighbours, gathering odd sheets from printers, and even collecting old printed papers used for wrapping. In 1792, at the age of twelve, he witnessed the arrest of Thomas Spence for allegedly selling Paine's *Rights of Man*, an event prefiguring his future persecution as a champion of the free press. At this time, however, Hone's incipient politics were conservative, and in 1793, encouraged by his parents, he wrote an anti-Jacobin poem comparing the liberties of England to the tyrannies of revolutionary France, which was privately printed as a single sheet. Its distribution brought small gifts of money from admirers. In the same year Hone began employment as a solicitor's assistant before becoming a clerk in the office which his father supervised, and then, in turn, a clerk to a solicitor named Pelletti. Hone held this position until he was seventeen, when his father arranged for him to take up a similar post in Chatham, probably as a result of his worries about the political and social life which his son was developing: Hone had become infatuated with the theatre, interested in Unitarianism and subsequently intrigued by rationalism, a member of the London Corresponding Society, and a follower of Holcroft and Godwin. His exile was short-lived. He returned to London the next year, took lodgings at Lambeth, and on 19 July 1800 married his landlady's daughter, Sarah Johnson (1781–1864). With the help of Sarah's mother he set up as a bookseller and stationer with a circulating library on Lambeth Walk.

Early publishing and philanthropic ventures Hone's life in business was always a struggle, and a large family compounded his difficulties: the first of his thirteen children was born in 1801. Bankrupted twice, and permanently beset by debt, he spent the greater part of the next thirty years engaged in publishing ventures ranging from outright flops to popular successes, but he was never able to convert the latter into significant financial gain. About 1806 he became involved in an elaborate and ambitious scheme known as 'tranquillity', and inaugurated by John Bone, one-time secretary of the London Corresponding Society. This aimed to end the poor law by establishing a fund by subscription to provide for the deserving poor. Bone, together with the radical publisher J. S. Jordan, also set up the Society for the Gradual Abolition of the Poor's Rate, and Hone acted as the secretary. The venture collapsed within a year. In 1808, a year in which a severe bout of rheumatic fever led Hone to learn to write with his left hand, he went into partnership with Bone to take over Jordan's publishing and bookselling business. Until 1810, when the business went bankrupt, they were active in publishing reformist works, and in providing support for the financial backing of the 'Old Price' riots against an increase in theatre admission prices in 1809. These activities drew Hone into the Westminster circle of reformists and radicals, an association which lasted some ten years, and led to his friendship with Francis Place, and his acquaintance with Bentham, Mill, and John Cam Hobhouse, among others. In 1810 Hone was prominent among

organizers of the triumphal procession planned to accompany Sir Francis Burdett's release from the Tower of London, following his controversial confinement there by the House of Commons on a breach of privilege charge (Burdett's case had become a focal point for the radical cause, and a large crowd had gathered along the route planned by Hone and his associates, only to be disappointed by Burdett's decision to take a quiet exit route along the Thames). By the end of 1810 Hone's family were living with his wife's mother, while he opened a small bookshop in Bloomsbury. By 1811 Hone was a trade auctioneer in Ludgate Hill, but his continuing impecuniosity forced the whole family to move into the Old Bailey, whence Hone contributed articles to such publications as the *Critical Review* and the *British Lady's Magazine* as a means of securing some income.

Hone's strong public-spirited and reformist tendencies are evident in his campaign of 1814 to improve the condition of lunatic asylums. Together with Edward Wakefield and James Bevans the architect, he formed a self-appointed and voluntary committee to investigate asylums and present a report to parliament. The committee simply visited asylums and compiled an account of what they saw. Their most famous exposure was that of William Norris, confined in Bethlem Hospital for twelve years with an elaborate system of chains and manacles permitting only minimal movement. Wakefield presented the report to a selected group of MPs while Hone extracted the illustration of Norris and published it priced at a shilling. The etching was by George Cruikshank, and it marks the beginning of Hone's fruitful partnership with this famous caricaturist and illustrator. Hone's efforts were undoubtedly influential in the subsequent asylum reforms. Following the case of Norris, he espoused two other famous causes in 1814 and 1815: that of Lord Cochrane, who had been tried and convicted of alleged fraud in 1814 as a result (it was widely believed) of his reformist politics and his anti-Admiralty stance; and that of Elizabeth Fenning, who was convicted and hanged for murder. Hone took a major part in the Cochrane affair, collecting a public subscription to pay his £1000 fine.

The case of Fenning—who was convicted on circumstantial evidence—attracted large public sympathy. Before she was hanged Hone was active in compiling a petition for mercy; after the event, he published accounts of the case and a hurriedly produced but highly successful satirical pamphlet with illustrations by Cruikshank, based on a popular drama showing at the time, entitled *The Maid and the Magpie*. In 1815 Hone also witnessed the shooting of a corn-law rioter, Edward Vyse. Having become editor of the *Critical Review* in the previous year, Hone used the journal to publicize this brutality, and made other political critiques. This led to his dismissal in June 1815, and the loss of a salary. Undeterred as ever, Hone went on to lend his support to the lord mayor, Matthew Wood, in his exposure of the spy network and blood money system in London.

The blasphemy trials of 1817 December 1817 marked Hone's moment of eminence, for it was then that he was put on trial for blasphemy, in one of the great case histories of all blasphemy trials. The provocation was three parodies written and published by him in 1817: *The Late John Wilkes's Catechism of a Ministerial Member*, *The Political Litany Diligently Revised to be Said or Sung until the Appointed Change Come*, and *The Sinecurists' Creed or Belief, as the Same Can or May be Said*. The trials—a separate trial for each publication—attracted enormous publicity, and they were clearly a strategic and malicious attempt by the government to make an example of Hone, who, at this time, may have seemed an easy target. Although reasonably well known, he was not regarded as among the most dangerous of radicals. He had placed himself—with some political acumen—apart from the ultra-radicals in 1816 when he distributed posters advising against carrying arms at the time of the Spa Fields riots, and he was not, unlike many radicals of his time, a great public speaker. Nevertheless, he had begun publishing the *Reformists' Register* in February 1817, and he had entered the controversy surrounding the suspension of habeas corpus in 1817, which had been provoked by a stone thrown at the regent's carriage in January. The stone was at first adjudged to be a bullet, and the event, therefore, an assassination attempt, and this in turn had called forth a form of thanksgiving that was published and read in churches. Hone's quick-witted response was another parody of litany entitled *The Bullet Te Deum*, a publication not included in the charges against him, almost certainly because the affair had become so farcical.

Hone knew he was being watched. He withdrew his parodies, and when seditious materials were planted on his premises, he simply took them up and handed them in at the Treasury. Yet on 3 May 1817 he was arrested on grounds of blasphemy and sedition, and was brought before Lord Ellenborough, the lord chief justice, who demanded that he plea without seeing a copy of the indictment. A punitively high bail was set at £2000, and Hone was sent to await trial in prison. He was released on 2 July after protests against the grounds of his arrest and amid challenges to special juries (generally acknowledged to be packed) by Charles Pearson, a young lawyer acting on his behalf. The campaign against special juries continued in the *Reformists' Register*. In November 1817 the case against Hone was reinstated, and the first trial was set for 18 December. Hone elected to speak for himself, a decision that brought with it the entitlements to call witnesses, cross-examine, and review the case for the jury. The courtroom was full to the brim with a large crowd outside; *The Times* gave a figure of 20,000. Most of the special jury did not arrive, and unvetted jurors were therefore conscripted.

The three trials were—vindictively—held on successive days and Hone was acquitted at each one. Justice Abbot presided over the first, and was promptly replaced on the bench by Ellenborough himself for the second and third, a ploy which increased the prosecution's humiliation, as also did the attorney-general's decision to go on to a subsequent trial after each acquittal. Hone's defence in each case was quite simple, although all accounts of the trials testify to his masterly control and strong sense of theatre.

Shabbily dressed, and surrounded by literary evidence, he complained purposefully that his trial was unjust because he was not allowed to see the indictment without paying an extortionate fee. He claimed that parodies were of two kinds: those that ridiculed the form imitated, and those that, like his own, used the form as a means of ridiculing another subject. As he had been charged with blasphemy and not sedition, he found himself in the unique position of being able to frame his defence against a vituperative government by claiming that it, and not religion, was the subject of his ridicule. Further, he remarked on the number of parodies of scripture and litany in a vast range of literary and other texts, including those of Canning, the anti-Jacobin poet—who, ironically, sat in the ministry that endorsed Hone's persecution. Quoting extensively, and rising in confidence though ailing in health as each trial proceeded, Hone won three unmitigated victories and stated that he stood not just for himself but for 'the liberty of the press'. His exoneration was celebrated wildly and vigorously by a London public fired up by the transparency of vituperative government tactics, and delighted by Hone's unlikely virtuoso performance in court. The trials also stood for the restitution of the credibility of the jury system, each concluding with shouts of 'Long live an honest jury! An honest jury for ever!' Hone was therefore acclaimed as champion of the people's rights on a dual account.

Later publishing ventures Following the trials came rallies of support for Hone in the form of visits from eminent sympathizers, contributions of money, press coverage, and a proliferation of popular literature about the trials themselves and the discomfited ministers. On 29 December a public meeting for the 'Friends of Liberty of the Press and Trial by Jury' was held at the London tavern, organized by Robert Waithman, who had assisted Hone with the asylum project, and was later to become lord mayor. The meeting set up a subscription list for Hone which excited a national response, and the money he received allowed him to move his household to 45 Ludgate Hill, where he set up in business. Hone was now famous, and the subsequent publishing ventures brought in sales but not financial security. He sought now to set himself up as a publisher of collectable editions as well as popular items. To this end, he proposed to develop his antiquarian interests by investigating the collections in the British Museum, and made an application for access in 1818 that was granted in 1820. The *Trials* themselves were published early in 1818, and in February 1819 Hone announced his most ambitious project to date: an edition of the *Trials* that would also serve as a history of parody, providing full versions of all the parodies cited in his defence. An extensive library of materials for this history was collected by Hone, and was auctioned in 1827 when he was imprisoned for debt: the publication was never finished. *The Political House that Jack Built* (1814), however, was highly successful, with sales in excess of 100,000 copies in fifty-four editions. This satire, a response in part to the atrocities of Peterloo, was a poem by Hone based on the similarly fitted nursery rhyme, accompanied by thirteen woodcuts by Cruikshank. An attack on Liverpool's cabinet (specifically Canning, Castlereagh, and Sidmouth), the regent, and other well-known figures of the day involved in government repression (such as Robert Gifford, the attorney-general from July 1819), the parody extolled the virtues of a free press and reform as guardians of a traditional British liberty. The piece is carefully pitched, like so much of Hone's work. The levity established in the nursery-rhyme structure provided a protection against persecution, which necessarily would invoke trivia and farce. Simultaneously, the parody is vehemently critical of its targets, of the violent oppression of the people, and uncompromising in its defence of a subversive free press.

In the same year Hone and Cruikshank collaborated on an imitation of a £1 note, entitled the *Bank Restriction Note*, a copper-plate engraving displaying a line of figures on the gallows. The note was an attack on the legislation which permitted the death penalty for the forging or passing of imitation paper money, a law which was popularly deemed too savage given the temptations involved and the opportunity for the persecution of innocent people, including children. The note attracted much attention, as too did another joint parodic production, *A Slap at Slop and the Bridge Street Gang* (1820), a burlesque of John Stoddart's newspaper, the *New Times*. Stoddart had attempted to influence the jury in Hone's trials by circulating false reports that someone had been tried and convicted for publishing Hone's parodies. *A Slap at Slop* ('Slop' being Hone's nickname for Stoddart) was his revenge, much of the imitation being taken up by mischievous mockery of the newspaper itself, and a good proportion dedicated to a vicious biography of Stoddart. The years from 1819 to 1822 were perhaps Hone's most prolific period as a political satirist, during which he published such popular successes as *The Queen's Matrimonial Ladder*, *Hone's Political Showman—at Home!*, and *Buonapartephobia*.

Hone had always nurtured a scholarly antiquarianism alongside his politics. In 1820 and then again in 1823 he published two books with impacts in both fields, raising questions about biblical canonicity: *The Apocryphal New Testament* and *Ancient Mysteries Described*. He wryly claimed that his interest in the medieval mystery plays was stimulated by a comment by Lord Ellenborough about them at his trial. Investigating the manuscripts at the British Museum led to the discovery of the little-known New Testament apocrypha, which he very rapidly published, to the great discomfort of Christian orthodoxy; the book had a stormy reception. *Ancient Mysteries Described* was less controversial, but by no means innocent: both books constituted a challenge to the limits of knowledge, and in particular scriptural knowledge. Hone was also accused of stepping beyond his class position in his invasion of theology, an exclusive field of scholarship.

However, these controversial books mark Hone's passage into the more generally acceptable antiquarian publishing activities which led to his fame in the nineteenth century, in the form of the *Everyday Book* (1825), the *Table Book* (1827), and the *Year Book* (1832). Admired by Southey

and Dickens among others, these works began as weekly publications before being bound into volumes. Each was a miscellany, including short articles from various contributors including Hone on fairs and customs, folklore, memories, accounts of urban rambles or travels, trade and working practices, natural history, and local life. There were also illustrations from a variety of sources. These publications were at once popular, educational, quaint, and socially pertinent. They constructed an inclusive readership not restricted by class boundaries, and they were affordable.

Final years: conversion to Christianity As ever, Hone's sensitivity to the public taste was not matched by his financial abilities. In April 1826 he was arrested for debt, evicted from Ludgate Hill, and placed under the rules of the king's bench prison requiring him to live in Southwark, where he remained with his family until declared bankrupt in 1828, when he moved to Newington Green. Friends and benefactors then raised a sum to help the Hone family set up in a coffee house in Gracechurch Street near London Bridge which opened in April 1830, and ran for three years before the inevitable bankruptcy. Thereafter the family went to live in a cottage on Peckham Rye Common before Hone's appointment as a sub-editor of *The Patriot* required a removal to the paper's office at Bolt Court in 1836. The newspaper was an organ of evangelical nonconformism under the editorship of Josiah Condor, and Hone was well regarded there, although he found the work onerous, not least because of his declining health. In 1832 Hone became a Christian, and soon afterwards, a regular member of the congregation of the Weigh House Chapel, where he became a friend and admirer of the preacher the Revd Thomas Binney. The ecclesiastical historian John Fuller Russell met Hone in 1833, and described him as 'rather corpulent, dressed very plainly, and his lofty forehead, keen eye, grey and scanty locks, and very expressive countenance, commanded respect'; by then he reportedly believed that the 1832 Reform Act had gone too far and that the political unions should have been forcibly put down. In June 1840, after a string of convalescent breaks, Hone retired and soon after moved to Tottenham, eventually settling there at 8 Grove Place. In 1841 he published a work of autobiography, *The Early Life and Conversion of William Hone*. He died at home in Tottenham on 6 November 1842, having been visited on his deathbed by Cruikshank (with whom he had quarrelled some fifteen years before) and Dickens, of whose novels he had grown particularly fond. He was buried in Abney Park cemetery, Stoke Newington. A collected edition of his output entitled *Hone's Works* (4 vols., 1882) is not comprehensive: a full bibliography is included in F. W. Hackwood, *William Hone: his Life and Times* (1912).

Until recently, Hone's fame rested largely on the achievements of the *Everyday Book*, *Table Book*, and *Year Book*, the antiquarian charm of which appealed to his Victorian readers. Undoubtedly these works were important, and they retain their value as forms of social commentary and records of popular life. In addition, their serialized production and their form—that of the essay-sketch—influenced the genres and styles of later writers. Latterly, Hone has been increasingly recognized as a key figure for those historians recovering the radical milieux of early nineteenth-century Britain on account of his strong advocacy of the liberty of the press and the rights of individuals and the persecuted. He dedicated himself to these causes to the detriment of his own self-interest and financial security, and his literary and political influence is still underestimated.   PHILIP W. MARTIN

Sources F. W. Hackwood, *William Hone: his life and times* (1912) · J. Marsh, *Word crimes: blasphemy, culture and literature in 19th century England* (1998) · K. Grimes, 'The William Hone bio-text', www.uab.edu/english/hone · J. A. Hone, 'William Hone (1780–1842), publisher and bookseller', *Historical Studies: Australia and New Zealand*, 16 (1974–5), 55–70 · J. Wardroper, *The world of William Hone* (1997) · J. A. Hone, *For the cause of truth: radicalism in London, 1796–1821* (1982) · H. Mackey, 'Hone, William', *BDMBR*, vol. 1 · O. Smith, *The politics of language* (1984) · W. Hone, *Three trials* (1818) · I. McCalman, *Radical underworld: prophets, revolutionaries, and pornographers in London, 1795–1840* (1988) · D. Worrall, *Radical culture* (1982) · *DNB*
Archives Adelphi University, New York, archive · BL, letters to Royal Literary Fund, loan 96 · BL, papers, Add. MSS 40108–40122, 40856, 41071, 50746 · Bodl. Oxf., corresp. · GL, scrapbook · Hunt. L., letters and literary MSS · UCL, corresp. · Washington State University Libraries, Pullman, Washington, papers · Wolverhampton Archives and Local Studies, Wolverhampton, papers | BL, corresp. with Samuel Butler, Add. MSS 34585–34586
Likenesses E. H. Landseer, pencil drawings, 1806?, priv. coll. · W. Patten, oils, in or before 1818, NPG [*see illus.*] · A. Hone, bust, *c.*1836 · G. Cruikshank, double portrait, engraving (with Cruikshank), repro. in Hackwood, *William Hone* · G. Cruikshank, pencil, pen, and ink drawing, NPG · Rogers, stipple (after G. Cruikshank), BM

Honey, George (1822–1880), actor and singer, was born on 25 May 1822. In 1843 he became a call-boy at the Adelphi in London. He was later given the opportunity to sing some verses of a comic duet as the singing mouse in *Harlequin Blue Beard*, and made his acting début in London at the Princess's Theatre, in November 1848, as Pan in *Midas*. In the summer of 1851 he began to appear in comic operas such as *Good Night* and *Signor Pantalon* at the Adelphi, and continued at the Lyceum and at Covent Garden with the Pyne and Harrison opera company. In 1860 he played at Her Majesty's in G. A. Macfarren's *Robin Hood*. Honey then quit the lyric for the dramatic stage. He appeared at the Strand in October 1863 in H. T. Craven's *Miriam's Crime*, in which he played a disreputable lawyer, and gave a good presentation of drunkenness. Thereafter he performed mainly in comedies and extravaganzas, his most notable roles being Turco the Terrible in William Brough's burlesque *Prince Amabel* (Royalty, 1865), Annibal Locust, a bibulous sergeant, in Watts Phillips's *The Huguenot Captain* (Princess's, 1866), and Eccles in T. W. Robertson's *Caste* (Prince of Wales's, 1867). In the opening performance at the Vaudeville, on 16 April 1870, he was Major Buncombe in Andrew Halliday's *For Love or Money*. He had played Graves in Bulwer-Lytton's *Money* at the Holborn in 1869 under Barry Sullivan, but attracted more attention in this part when the play was revived at the Prince of Wales's in 1872, and again in 1875. Among his later creations the most successful was Cheviot Hill in W. S. Gilbert's *Engaged* at the Haymarket, on 3 October 1877. Honey also acted in America. He was a useful singer and a clever comic performer, and was most successful in the presentation of eccentric and dissipated characters. After a paralytic seizure in 1879 his only theatrical appearances were in minor parts for benefits. He died in London of aneurysm of the heart on 28 May 1880, and was buried in Highgate cemetery, where a medallion surmounts his grave.

JOSEPH KNIGHT, *rev.* NILANJANA BANERJI

Sources *The Era* (30 May 1880) · *The life and reminiscences of E. L. Blanchard, with notes from the diary of Wm. Blanchard*, ed. C. W. Scott and C. Howard, 2 vols. (1891) · C. E. Pascoe, ed., *The dramatic list*, 2nd edn (1880) · E. D. Cook, *Nights at the play* (1883) · Hall, *Dramatic ports.*
Likenesses R. Waller, oils, 1880, Garr. Club · Fradelle & Marshall, carte-de-visite, NPG · H. B.?, lithograph (in *Miriam's Crime*), NPG · bust, repro. in *Our Boys* (1875) [music sheet] · medallion, Highgate cemetery, London · photograph, repro. in *Illustrated Sporting and Dramatic News* (23 Jan 1879) · prints, Harvard TC · woodbury-type, NPG

Honey [*née* Young], **Laura Martha** (1816?–1843), actress, said to have been born on 6 December 1816, was the daughter of Mrs Young, an actress at Sadler's Wells, and as a girl worked in the wardrobe of that house. She first appeared on the stage there, under the name of Laura Bell, in some juvenile parts. In 1826 she was with her mother at the Olympic, and in 1827 played a midshipman in Bayle Bernard's *Casco Bay*. After a brief engagement at the Surrey, where she took lessons in music, she returned to Sadler's Wells in 1829. At the age of sixteen she married William Honey, a lawyer's clerk, from whom she soon separated; he continued to live on her earnings. He was accidentally drowned in the Thames in 1836. Mrs Honey went in 1832 with Harriet Waylett to the Strand, where she first appeared in Leman Rede's *The Loves of the Angels*. In 1833 she was at the Queen's (subsequently the Prince of Wales's) Theatre, under Mrs Nisbet. At the Adelphi under F. H. Yates she made a great success as Psyche in a burlesque called *Cupid* with John Reeve, and as Lurline in the fairy drama of that name.

After a season at the Haymarket, where she played in J. B. Buckstone's *Open House*, and a tour in the provinces, Laura Honey went to the Olympic under Madame Vestris. She was described as 'the delicious Mrs Honey, beautiful as a houri, with the throat of a nightingale' (Baker, 2.148). In 1837 she undertook the management of the City of London Theatre, where she played Tom Tug in *The Waterman*, Myrtilla in Planché's *Riquet with the Tuft*, and in *The Spirit of the Rhine* by Morris Barnett, in which she sang with great effect 'My Beautiful Rhine', which long remained popular. In her last season she performed at the Haymarket and in the provinces, and returned to the City of London. She died on 1 April 1843, from 'ulcers in the chest', at her home, 149 Albany Street, Regent's Park, and was buried on the 6th in the churchyard of the Old Church, Hampstead. She bequeathed her property by will to two children aged respectively ten and three. She was a pleasing and graceful actress, particularly in breeches roles, and a delightful ballad singer, but her performances were practically confined to the lightest class of entertainment.

JOSEPH KNIGHT, *rev.* J. GILLILAND

Sources Ward, *Men of the reign* · H. B. Baker, *The London stage: its history and traditions from 1576 to 1888*, 2 vols. (1889) · *The Era* (9 April 1843) · Hall, *Dramatic ports.* · *N&Q*, 7th ser., 9 (1890), 93, 157 · T. C. Davis, *Actresses as working women: their social identity in Victorian culture* (1991) · d. cert.
Archives Theatre Museum, London, letter file
Likenesses prints, BM, Harvard TC, NPG

Hongi Hika (1772–1828), Maori tribal leader and war chief, was, by his own account, born in the year of the death of the French explorer Marion du Fresne, 1772, near Kaikohe in central Northland in the North Island of New Zealand. He was the second of several children of Te Hotete of the three *hapu* ('clans or descent groups'), Te Uri-o-Hua, Ngati Tautahi, and Ngai Tawake of the Nga Puhi people. Te Hotete was an *ariki* ('chief'), a *tapu* or sacred person descended from the founding ancestors and the gods by senior lines of descent, but Hongi was the son of his junior wife, Tuhikura of Ngati Rehia. Hongi's elder half-brother, Kaingaroa, inherited their father's status as *ariki*, but after their father's death, and even before that of Kaingaroa in 1815, Hongi was always the real leader of his people. After his death and following his numerous military victories in which he became famed throughout New Zealand, the general name for Hongi's various *hapu* from Kaikohe to Kerikeri, Nga Puhi, came to be extended as a tribal name to include all his wider kin and allies from a much larger area, including Hokianga, Whangaroa, the Bay of Islands, and Whangarei. This was Hongi's main though unintended achievement, although in the eyes of generations of New Zealanders he has also epitomized the warrior leader bringing blood-soaked mayhem to Maori in the 'muskets wars' through his early adoption and successful use of European weaponry.

Hongi Hika grew to *toa* ('warrior') status and leadership at a time when the Maori people were first experiencing the perils and benefits of contact with Europeans. While he was young, other than epidemics of introduced diseases, and the beneficial spread of pigs and the white potato as new resources, these were relatively minimal. In his youth his people conquered Waimate North and Kerikeri at the Bay of Islands, and, following disputes, fought wars with the Te Roroa and Ngati Whatua peoples, whose various divisions occupied lands from the Dargaville area to Waitemata Harbour. Wars with these people culminated in a disastrous defeat of the allied Bay of Islands and Hokianga peoples at the battle of Moremonui about 1807, at Maunganui Bluff. A few muskets purchased from Europeans were used in this battle by Hongi's group, but the clumsy contemporary weapons took time to reload, and the opposing war leader, Murupaenga, used this delay to win using traditional weapons. In this battle, a formative influence on Hongi, he lost many relatives, and saw some of the most important chiefs of his people killed; he himself only escaped by fleeing.

Hongi Hika (1772–1828), by unknown artist, *c.*1820 [centre, with Waikato (left) and the missionary Thomas Kendall (right)]

Maori warfare obliged the defeated to seek *utu* ('payment') for their dead through inflicting at least an equivalent defeat on their foes, or suffer a loss of *mana* ('authority, prestige'). Hongi's numerous war campaigns were carried out for these traditional purposes; they were not, for example, attempts to conquer new territory or create an expanded polity with himself as its king, even though this was suggested to him by missionaries, probably keen to obtain influence over Maori through one ruler as had been done in Tahiti. Although his aims were traditional, Hongi was an innovative tactician, and his early campaigns against northern peoples convinced him of the military value of the new weapons. He adapted his great *pa* ('fort') at Waimate for musket warfare, introducing flanking angles, loop-holes, and other modifications. He also embraced the opportunities for trade with Europeans for iron tools, iron weapons, and muskets and powder, and unlike some other chiefs, quickly perceived that he would best achieve his aims by protecting rather than attacking European shipping—whalers and others were ready to trade for the commodities he needed—and from the second decade of the nineteenth century Hongi greatly expanded his people's potato production and reserved all his pigs for barter. Maori were used to the cultivation of root crops only; it was typical of Hongi's intelligence that he persisted in experimenting with the wheat introduced by his nephew, Ruatara of Rangihoua; other chiefs had destroyed their first crops when they failed to produce tubers. The Church Missionary Society missionaries, who first arrived in 1814, lived (after the death of Ruatara) under Hongi's protection, although Hongi himself was quite uninterested in Christianity. He was interested in the missionaries' tools and skills as carpenters and gunsmiths, and particularly their techniques for growing wheat and producing flour. Far from being the stereotypical bloodthirsty warrior often portrayed in secondary sources, Hongi was quietly spoken, mild-mannered, and solicitous of his family, and the head of the Church Missionary Society mission, Samuel Marsden (1765–1838), thought him a very fine character.

By 1818 Hongi's people were armed with significant numbers of muskets, and he led his first major war expedition against southern tribes as yet unfamiliar with the new weapons. The possession of firearms by one side only tended to produce panic, and assisted Hongi to obtain unprecedented success in the pursuit of *utu*, through the large numbers killed and captured. His prisoners became his slaves, and their labour helped him to increase the land under cultivation with crops for trade. Hongi had visited Port Jackson (later Sydney) in the mission vessel, the *Active*, in 1814. In 1820 he visited England, travelling with the missionary Thomas Kendall and a young relative, Waikato. Hongi's aim was to obtain more guns; Kendall's aim was to convince the influential Hongi of the benefits of civilization, including Christianity. While in England Hongi worked with Professor Samuel Lee (1783–1852) of Cambridge, who established the standard method of writing Maori and compiled a Maori dictionary. Hongi and Waikato were lionized in society and introduced to George IV, although Hongi quickly became offended when he realized that he was regarded as a curiosity. He got no guns, but was presented with many other gifts, including a suit of armour and helmet which protected him in his later campaigns, giving him a reputation for invincibility. At Port Jackson on his way home he sold most of the gifts and purchased a significant quantity of muskets.

With his new firearms and those his people had acquired through trade, Hongi was able to enthuse his northern allies to undertake combined war expeditions against southern tribes from 1821 to 1823, taking various major *pa* near the Tamaki River, near Thames, in Waikato, and on the island in Lake Rotorua. The missionaries (and later scholars) tended to regard these large expeditions and the scale of the battles they fought as unprecedented (as in fact they were in the missionaries' short time in the Bay of Islands), but Hongi was obtaining *utu* for similar campaigns against his people in the late 18th century, as well as for the losses in his recent battles. Scholars have tended to exaggerate the attrition directly and indirectly resulting from war, especially the numbers killed in battle and eaten. (At that time Maori consumed their slain enemies, mainly for ritual purposes, and preserved their heads for display.) However, Hongi's campaigns from 1821 to 1823, and his wars against the people of Kaipara in 1825, continuing in 1826 into the Waikato as he pursued those who fled from Kaipara because of the loss there of his eldest son, had a ripple effect: attacked peoples migrated inland for safety, often provoking further wars with their new hosts; the dislocation contributed to the death toll.

Hongi's last campaign, in January 1827, was against the people of Whangaroa; he had determined to retake lands once dominated by his father, and to punish the tribes there for attacks on European shipping. His blind senior wife, Turikatuku, died in 1827 during this campaign. While pursuing the fleeing tribesmen (who, in passing, sacked the Wesleyan mission), he was wounded by a musket ball which passed through his chest. After lingering through the following year as an invalid, he died in Whangaroa from his bullet wound on or about 3 March 1828. Although survived by several children, his heir at Waimate was the chief Rewa or Manu, while his cousin Ururoa led the Whangaroa division of his people. After a year, a *hahunga* ('ritual cleaning and mourning ceremony') was held; his bones were concealed in a hidden location.

ANGELA BALLARA

Sources J. R. Elder, ed., *Letters and journals of Samuel Marsden* (1932) • A. Earle, *Narrative of a residence in New Zealand*, ed. E. H. McCormick (1966) • L. M. Rogers, ed., *The early journals of Henry Williams, 1826–1840* (1961) • J. Binney, *The legacy of guilt* (1968) • J. Sissons, W. W. Hongi, and P. Hōhepa, *The Pūriri trees are laughing: a political history of Ngā Puhi in the inland Bay of Islands* (1987) • papers of Hamiora Maioha, Auckland Institute and Museum, MS 585 • C. Baker, letters and journals, 1827–67, Auckland Institute and Museum • C. Davis, journals, 1827–8, Auckland Institute and Museum • J. Hamlin, journals, 1826–37, NL NZ, Turnbull L. • J. Hobbs, diaries, 1823–30, Auckland Institute and Museum • J. Kemp, journals, 1823–34, Auckland Public Library • J. Shepherd, journals, 1822–4, Auckland Institute and Museum [microfilm] • W. Williams, journals, 1825–55, Auckland Institute and Museum • northern minute books, native land court, vols. 1–5, micro MS collection 06, A.T.U. • J. Butler, *Earliest New Zealand* (1927) • J. L. Nicholas, *A narrative of a voyage to New Zealand*, 2 vols. (1817) • journals of the ships *Recherche*, *Espérance* and *Coquille*, 1793 and 1824, *Early eyewitness accounts of Maori life*, 3–6 (Wellington, 1986)
Likenesses group portrait, oils, *c*.1820, NL NZ, Turnbull L. [*see illus.*] • A. Earle, oils, 1828 (*Meeting of the artist and Hongi*)

Honner, Maria (1808–1870). *See under* Honner, Robert William (1809–1852).

Honner, Robert William (1809–1852), actor and theatre manager, the youngest son of John Honner (d. 1817), solicitor, in the partnership of Fletcher and Honner, of the parish of St Anne, Soho, was born at 24 Percy Street, Tottenham Court Road, London, on 18 January 1809. He was educated at a private school at Pentonville, where Joseph Grimaldi the younger and Thomas Hamblin were his schoolfellows. His father gave up his profession to become proprietor of the Heathcock tavern, Heathcock Court, close to the Sans Pareil Theatre (later known as the Adelphi) in the Strand. There Robert Honner found opportunities for indulging his taste for theatricals. His father soon died, leaving his mother unprovided for.

In 1817 Honner was articled for three years to the ballet master Charles Leclercq, and shortly after appeared for his master's benefit at the Sans Pareil in a ballet called *The Crown of Roses*. In 1820 he went as a dancer with Kinloch to the Pantheon Theatre, Edinburgh, but the enterprise was a failure, and he was left destitute. He visited south and west England, then joined the corps de ballet at the Coburg Theatre, London, and in 1824 went to the Surrey. In 1825 Honner was again at the Coburg, and soon afterwards joined Andrew Ducrow, with whom he remained a long period, although he still undertook provincial tours, during which he played every character, from leading business to harlequin, clown, and pantaloon. He acted subsequently at Sadler's Wells under Grimaldi (1827), at the Surrey, first with R. W. Elliston and then with Charles

Elliston and D. W. Osbaldiston, and at the Old City Theatre in Milton Street under Benjamin Webster (1829). At later dates he returned to the Coburg, was one of G. B. Davidge's company at Liverpool, was stage-manager for George Almar at Sadler's Wells (1833), and from 1835 to 1838 was lessee of Sadler's Wells, as well as acting-manager for Davidge at the Surrey. He also often appeared at the latter house at short notice for John Reeve, T. P. Cooke, and others who happened to be indisposed.

On 21 May 1836 Honner married the actress Maria Macarthy [see below], and they appeared together at the Surrey until 1838. As lessee of Sadler's Wells from 1838 to 1840 Honner tried to establish a taste for the legitimate drama. He managed the Surrey from 1842 to 1846, and after a short lease of the City of London Theatre in Norton Folgate he joined John Douglass as stage-manager of the Standard Theatre, where he remained until his death.

Honner was a good actor, his chief roles being Richmond, Laertes in *Hamlet*, Fag in Richard Cumberland's *The Jew*, Scrooge the Miser in *A Christmas Carol*, and Jemmy Twitcher in *The Golden Farmer*. He died at his home, Nichols Square, Hackney Road, London, on 31 December 1852. His death was registered in the name Robert Walter Honner.

His wife, **Maria Honner** (1808–1870), actress, born at Enniskillen, Ireland, on 21 December 1808, was the daughter of Eugene Macarthy, actor–manager, who died in the Dramatic College at Maybury, Surrey, on 14 May 1866, aged seventy-eight. She was educated at Cork and lost her mother at an early age. Being left to her own resources at her father's second marriage, with a younger brother to support, she made her first appearance on the stage at the age of fifteen, at a theatre in the south of Ireland. She afterwards played in Dublin, and as the hero of juvenile tragedy attracted the notice of Charles Kean and W. C. Macready. Her first important character was Rosalie Somers, which she played to Edmund Kean. An engagement in Scotland followed, and she became a popular favourite. In 1831 she was taken on by John Farrell for the Pavilion Theatre, London, where for two seasons she was the leading attraction. In 1833 she transferred her services to the Coburg Theatre, and, on the retirement of Davidge, the lessee, moved to Sadler's Wells, where Honner was the manager. After the termination of two successful seasons she went to the Surrey. In June 1835 she played Julia in Sheridan Knowles's *The Hunchback* with great success at Drury Lane, for the benefit of 'Jerry-Sneak Russell'. On 21 May 1836 she married Honner.

Maria Honner continued acting with her husband at the Surrey until Whitsuntide 1838, when he became lessee of Sadler's Wells; they played together at the latter house for about five years to much acclaim. At the request of Davidge she returned to the Surrey, where she remained until September 1845, and then went to the City of London Theatre. She was a good actress in pathetic roles, and after the retirement of Elizabeth Yates was for a time without a rival. She was excellent in many Shakespearian parts, as well as in the roles of Mary in *Paul the Pilot*, Susan in *The Kohal Cave*, Felix in *The French Revolution*, and Clemency in

Dickens's *The Battle of Life*. She died of paralysis on 4 January 1870, at the residence of her second husband, Frederick Morton, stage-manager of the Charing Cross Theatre. G. C. BOASE, *rev.* NILANJANA BANERJI

Sources H. B. Baker, *The London stage: its history and traditions from 1576 to 1888*, 2 vols. (1889) · Hall, *Dramatic ports.* · *The Era* (9 Jan 1870) · *Actors by Daylight* (24 Nov 1838) · *Theatrical Times* (27 March 1847) · *Theatrical Times* (10 Oct 1846) · *Actors by Gaslight* (4 Aug 1838) · [G. Daniel], *Cumberland's Minor theatre*, 15 (1828–44), 3–4
Likenesses portrait, repro. in *Theatrical Times* (27 March 1847) · portrait (Maria Honner), repro. in *Theatrical Times* (10 Oct 1846) · portrait (Maria Honner), repro. in *Actors by Gaslight* · portrait (Maria Honner), repro. in *Actors by Daylight* · portrait (Maria Honner), repro. in Cumberland, *Cumberland's minor theatre* · prints, Harvard TC

Honorius [St Honorius] (*d.* 653), archbishop of Canterbury, was, according to Bede, one of the 'disciples of St Gregory' sent to England in either 597 or 601 with the missionary groups under Augustine and Mellitus. After the death of Archbishop Justus, Honorius was consecrated to the see of Canterbury as the fifth archbishop by Paulinus, bishop of York, at some date between 628 and 631. The ceremony took place in the stone church which the reeve Blæcca had built at Lincoln. In 630 or 631 Honorius sent the exiled Burgundian bishop, Felix, to preach to the East Angles. He also collaborated with Paulinus and with King Eadwine in requesting Pope Honorius I to establish a metropolitan see at York so that when a vacancy occurred at either Canterbury or York the surviving archbishop might ordain to the empty metropolitan see. The pope wrote to him on 11 June 634 acceding to these wishes and sending palls both to him and to Paulinus. The terms of the pope's letter and the equal gifts sent to both are sufficient to discredit the spurious privilege, forged at Canterbury after the Norman conquest and purporting to have been written by Pope Honorius on the same day, which declares the primacy of Canterbury over York. By 634, however, the Roman mission in Northumbria had already been overthrown by the defeat and death of Eadwine in the previous year. Honorius received Paulinus in Kent and with the concurrence of King Eadbald appointed him to the vacant see of Rochester. With the accession of Eorcenberht in Kent in 640 Honorius gained a zealous helper, for the king compelled the destruction of all the idols and the observance of the Lenten fast in his kingdom. Honorius's authority was limited to Kent, where he ordained Ithamar as bishop of Rochester in 644, and to East Anglia, where he ordained (in succession to Felix) Thomas in 647 or 648 and the Kentishman Berhtgils, in 652 or 653. He died on 30 September 653, and was buried in the west porch of St Peter's and St Paul's Monastery at Canterbury (later St Augustine's). The see of Canterbury remained vacant until the consecration of Deusdedit eighteen months later. Neither the brief life by Goscelin (*d.* after 1107) in the form of ten lections, nor the summary late medieval versions in verse or prose add anything to Bede's account.

WILLIAM HUNT, *rev.* N. P. BROOKS

Sources Bede, *Hist. eccl.*, 2.3; 3.15–18, 20; 5.19 · A. W. Haddan and W. Stubbs, eds., *Councils and ecclesiastical documents relating to Great Britain and Ireland*, 3 (1871), 82–93 · N. Brooks, *The early history of the*

church of Canterbury: Christ Church from 597 to 1066 (1984), 65–7, 265 • T. D. Hardy, *Descriptive catalogue of materials relating to the history of Great Britain and Ireland*, 1, Rolls Series, 26 (1862), nos. 657–9

Honorius (*d. c.*1213), canonist, was of unknown origins. He may have been rector of Willesborough, Kent, from 1184 or 1185, but was more certainly first a clerk (from *c.*1191) and then official (from 1195) of Archbishop Geoffrey (*d.* 1212) of York. He acted as administrator of the see during Geoffrey's absences between 1195 and 1198, and became archdeacon of Richmond on 8 March 1198. His York career was marred by the bitter three-sided disputes between Archbishop Geoffrey, the kings (Richard I and John), and the dean and chapter of York. His appointment as archdeacon was revoked by King Richard in favour of Roger of St Edmund in 1198, and he was subsequently excommunicated by the dean (Simon de Apulia) and forced to defend his rights not only against Roger and King John, but also against his own archbishop, and to plead his case in person before Pope Innocent III (*r.* 1198–1216), who confirmed Honorius's institution as archdeacon in June 1202. But he had had to offer 300 marks to King John for letters of protection and permission to pursue his case against Roger, a debt not cleared until 1208; an additional debt of a palfrey occurs from 1206 to 1210 when it, too, was cleared.

From *c.*1201 to 1205 Honorius was a member of the household of Archbishop Hubert Walter (*d.* 1205) at Canterbury, where he joined the company of Richard de Morins (Ricardus Anglicus; *d.* 1242), and other leading canonists; but his change of allegiance from York to Canterbury was already under way between 1198 and 1200, when, as *clericus noster*, he received the Kent churches of Tarring and Patching from Hubert Walter, in a document witnessed by his former Oxford colleagues, Simon of Sywell and John of Tynemouth, both distinguished canonists; and his own professional skill was attested by his successful presentation of Hubert Walter's case against Robert, former abbot of Thorney, in Innocent III's presence in 1202.

Honorius's Canterbury career was undermined by Hubert Walter's death. He appears briefly in the circle of Bishop John de Gray of Norwich (King John's candidate for the vacant archbishopric) in late 1205, but although in 1206 he represented the king in the opening phase of the Canterbury election dispute, he was despoiled and imprisoned at Gloucester in 1208, perhaps in consequence of the general interdict. The last years of his life are obscure, but he was acquitted of his debt to the king at the exchequer in 1210, and may have served Bishop Bernard of Carlisle. His death date of *c.*1213 has been deduced from the appearance of Master Richard Marsh (*d.* 1226) as archdeacon of Richmond from before 4 July 1213.

Honorius's scholarly career embraced two phases: from 1185 to *c.*1191 or 1192 he studied and perhaps taught canon law at Paris; from 1191 or 1192 to 1195 he taught and practised law in Oxford (with Simon of Sywell and John of Tynemouth), where Thomas of Marlborough (*d.* 1236) was one of his pupils. His two canonical commentaries, written between *c.*1185 and 1190, date from his Parisian phase,

and place him among the most distinguished English canonists of the time. Although only one manuscript of *De iure canonico tractaturus* (1188–90) has survived (Laon, Bibliothèque de la ville MS 371, fols. 83–170v), copies of the important *Summa decretalium quaestionum* (1185–6) are now found in six continental libraries (Bamberg, Douai, Laon, Leipzig, Paris, and Zwettl), while a seventh copy (from Königsberg) has been lost. Divided into three distinctions (on rescripts, orders and offices, and marriage), this 'most successful piece of English canonistic writing of the twelfth century' (Kuttner and Rathbone, 296) combined elements of the systematic *summa* with the dialectical technique of the *quaestiones*: proposing, discussing, and solving disputed questions, in a manner similar to that employed by Gratian in his *dicta*, although it departed from Gratian's order. Derived from teaching (it was the fruit of a series of Friday lectures), the *Summa* constituted a new type of canonical treatise, whose method stimulated the literary treatment of cases and problems by Bolognese masters and others. The vicissitudes of Master Honorius's career exemplify the vulnerability of legal professionals to the impact of political factors.

CHARLES DUGGAN

Sources *Chronica magistri Rogeri de Hovedene*, ed. W. Stubbs, 4, Rolls Series, 51 (1871), 44, 52, 89, 158, 176–85 • *Pipe rolls*, 3–12 John • C. R. Cheney and E. John, eds., *Canterbury, 1193–1205*, English Episcopal Acta, 3 (1986), nos. 338, 384, 401, 445, 484, 533, 536, 619, 656 • C. Harper-Bill, ed., *Norwich, 1070–1214*, English Episcopal Acta, 6 (1990), nos. 332, 338, 407 • M. Lovatt, ed., *York, 1154–81*, English Episcopal Acta, 20 (2000) • *The letters of Pope Innocent III (1198–1216) concerning England and Wales*, ed. C. R. Cheney and M. G. Cheney (1967), nos. 249n., 250, 270–73, 283, 284, 303–5, 330, 365, 382, 415–21, 699 • S. Kuttner and E. Rathbone, 'Anglo-Norman canonists of the twelfth century', *Traditio*, 7 (1949–51), 279–358, esp. 296, 304–10, 344–7 • B. Grimm, 'Die Ehelehre des Magister Honorius: ein Beitrag zur Ehelehre der anglo-normannischen Schule', *Studia Gratiana*, 24 (1989), 231–387 • R. Weigand, *Die bedingte Eheschliessung im kanonischen Recht*, 1 (1963), 189–97 • R. Weigand, 'Bemerkungen über die Schriften und Lehren des Magister Honorius', *Proceedings of the Fifth International Congress of Medieval Canon Law, Salamanca, 21–25 September 1976*, ed. S. Kuttner and K. Pennington (1980), 195–212 • R. Weigand, 'Die anglo-normannische Kanonistik in den letzten Jahrzehnten des 12. Jahrhunderts', *Seventh International Congress of Medieval Canon Law* [Cambridge 1984], ed. P. Linehan (1988), 249–63 • Emden, *Oxf.*, 2.956–57 • A. H. Thompson, 'The registers of the archdeaconry of Richmond', *Yorkshire Archaeological Journal*, 25 (1918–20), 129–268, esp. 131–5

Archives Bibliothèque de la Ville, Laon, MS 371 (*bis*), fols. 171–176v • Bibliothèque de la Ville, Laon, MS 371, fols. 83–170v • Bibliothèque de la Ville, Douai, MS 640, fols. 1–42a • Bibliothèque Nationale, Paris, MS Lat. 14591, fols. 50–83ra • Staatsbibliothek, Bamberg, Can. 45, fols. 23–39 • Universitätsbibliothek, Königsberg, MS 21, fols. 44–75 • Universitätsbibliothek, Leipzig, MS 984, fols. 90–110 • Zwettl, Austria, MS 162, fols. 179–213

Honorius [Henricus, Heinricus] **Augustodunensis** (*d. c.*1140), scholar and author, was long believed to have come from Autun in Burgundy, in consequence of the name by which he was generally known in Latin: Honorius Augustodunensis. However, it is now impossible to associate Honorius with Autun. The only direct and contemporary biographical information about Honorius appears in the final chapter of his own *De luminaribus ecclesiae*, published *c.*1133. This describes Honorius as priest and *scholasticus* of the church *Augustodunensis*, assigns his floruit to the reign of the Emperor Heinrich V of Germany (r. 1106–25), and lists twenty-two of his writings in this order: *Elucidarius, Sigillum, Inevitabile, Speculum ecclesiae, Offendiculum, Summa totius, Gemma animae, Sacramentarium, Neocosmum, Eucharistion, Cognitio vitae, Imago mundi, Summa gloria, Scala coeli, De anima et de Deo, Expositio Psalterii, Cantica Canticorum, Evangelia, Clavis physicae, Refectio mentium, Pabulum vitae, De luminaribus ecclesiae*. All but the *Evangelia, Refectio mentium,* and *Pabulum vitae* have survived. Another ten may, through manuscript attribution and inner associations, be added to the list, together with many, as yet unedited, fragments and *quaestiones*. Over 260 manuscript copies of Honorius's works remain from the twelfth century alone, the majority from religious houses sympathetic to the reforming ideals of the monasteries of Gorze and Fruttuaria.

Honorius was possibly of south German or Savoyard origin, and arguably a kinsman of Archbishop Anselm of Canterbury (d. 1109). He spent his formative years (c.1096–1110) as a reforming canon in England, many of them in the archbishop's immediate circle. He was an ardent supporter of Anselm's battle for papal reform against the Anglo-Norman kings. At, or shortly after, the archbishop's death Honorius left England for Regensburg, in Bavaria. The puzzling name Augustodunensis may be a toponym, derived from his later career (c.1110–1133) as canon *scholasticus*, or teacher in the school, of the Alte Kapelle in Regensburg. He remained an advocate of the papal cause, and earned the favour of Bishop Cuno of Regensburg (1126–32).

The immediate influence of Anselm's teaching is especially marked in the first three of the works listed in the *De luminaribus*, above all in the most popular of these, the catechetical *Elucidarius*. Honorius's teaching career in Regensburg allowed him to continue to communicate Anselm's views, notably through the *Offendiculum* and the *Cognitio vitae*. Honorius was thus one of the main vehicles whereby Anselm's writings and reforming sentiments gained early currency, both in England and in Europe. In England, the dioceses of Canterbury, Rochester, Worcester, and Winchester showed an especially early interest in Honorius's writings. He may have spent time in each one, perhaps leaving Canterbury for the other southern dioceses during Anselm's exiles, between 1097 and 1100, and between 1103 and 1107. Honorius's abandonment of England for Regensburg, and his preferment there, is probably connected with the betrothal in 1110 of Matilda, daughter of Henry I of England, to the Emperor Heinrich V of Germany (d. 1125). The betrothal is noted in an important early copy of Honorius's *Imago mundi* (Cambridge, Corpus Christi College, MS 66). The first recension of this work is dated 1110, and was dedicated to one Henricus. The earliest surviving copy of the *Imago mundi* (Bodl. Oxf., MS Rawl. B. 484) comes from Winchester, home of Archdeacon Henry, Princess Matilda's chaplain. This connection would account, too, for Honorius's associating his own floruit with the reign of the emperor.

Honorius's works may be divided by content into four main groups: polemical (primarily in support of the celibate priesthood), liturgical, cosmological, and exegetical. Many remain inadequately edited. A desire to extend the influence throughout the Christian church of reforming bishops, especially monastic bishops such as Anselm or Cuno of Regensburg, pervades his immense literary output and is perhaps the fundamental reason for it.

The name Honorius is an unusual one for the period. This fact, together with the interest in the works of John Scottus (Eriugena) manifest in many of his writings, and the dedication of certain of these to Christian, Irish abbot (c.1133–1152) of the Schottenkloster of St Jakob of Regensburg, have been used to support the idea that Honorius was himself an Irishman. This idea has little substance. The name Honorius appears rather to have been adopted, perhaps in honour of Honorius, archbishop of Canterbury (627–52). Honorius's original name was probably He[i]nricus, a name that occurs not merely in early manuscripts of his works, but also in a twelfth-century gift of books containing, out of a collection of some forty-seven treatises, twenty-two known to be by him. This same donation, together with surviving Lambach codices of certain of the works on the list, connects He[i]nricus with the abbey of Lambach. In many other early manuscript copies of Honorius's writings their author is described as *inclusus* or *solitarius*. This combined evidence suggests that He[i]nricus, or Honorius, entered a Benedictine abbey late in life (possibly in 1133)—perhaps Lambach or St Jakob of Regensburg, home of such other famous solitary monks, or monks *inclusi*, as Marianus of Regensburg. The precise date of his death is unknown, but is likely to have been about 1140.   VALERIE I. J. FLINT

Sources V. I. J. Flint, *Honorius Augustodunensis of Regensburg* (1995) • 'Honorius Augustodunensis: opera omnia', *Patrologia Latina*, 172 (1854) [collected works] • J.-A. Endres, *Honorius Augustodunensis* (1906) • M.-O. Garrigues, 'L'oeuvre d'Honorius Augustodunensis: inventaire critique [pts 1–3]', *Abhandlungen der Braunschweigischen Wissenschaftlichen Gesellschaft*, 38 (1986), 7–138; 39 (1987), 123–228; 40 (1988), 131–90 • J.-A. Endres, *Das St Jakobsportal in Regensburg und Honorius Augustodunensis* (1903) • 'Honorius Augustodunensis. Imago mundi', ed. V. I. J. Flint, *Archives d'Histoire Doctrinale et Littéraire du Moyen Âge*, 49 (1982), 7–153 • H. Menhardt, 'Der Nachlass des Honorius Augustodunensis', *Zeitschrift für Deutsches Altertum*, 89 (1958–9), 23–69 • E. Rooth, 'Kleine Beiträge zur Kenntnis des sogenannten Honorius Augustodunensis', *Studia Neophilologica*, 12 (1939), 120–35 • R. Bauerreiss, 'Zur Herkunft des Honorius Augustodunensis', *Studien und Mitteilungen zur Geschichte des Benediktiner Ordens*, 53 (1935), 28–36 • E. M. Sanford, 'Honorius, *presbyter* and *scholasticus*', *Speculum*, 23 (1948), 397–425 • *Honorius Augustodunensis 'Clavis physicae'*, ed. P. Lucentini (1974) • *Das Elucidarium des Honorius Augustodunensis*, ed. D. Gottschall (Tübingen, 1992)
Archives Bayerische Staatsbibliothek, Munich • Bodl. Oxf., MS Rawl. B 484 • CCC Cam., MS 66

Honyman, Sir George Essex, fourth baronet (1819–1875), judge, was born at Strawberry Hill, Middlesex, on 22 January 1819, the eldest son of Sir Ord Honyman, third baronet (1794–1863), who became lieutenant-colonel commanding the Grenadier Guards in 1850, and his wife, Elizabeth Essex *née* Bowen (d. 1864) of Coton Hall, Shropshire.

Honyman joined the firm of Martineau, Malton, and

Trollope, solicitors, of Lincoln's Inn in 1838 and in 1840 became a pupil of Sir Fitzroy Kelly. He afterwards read with David Octavius Gibbons, the special pleader. In 1842 he commenced his own practice as a pleader, gaining few clients for seven years, but studying hard to master commercial law. On 8 June 1849 he was called to the bar at the Middle Temple, and practised on the home circuit, where by 1853 he was thought to be the best commercial lawyer of the day. On 26 November 1860 he married Annie Johanna Thirkettle (d. 13 Jan 1881).

Honyman was not considered a great orator, but he had a quick intellect, a tenacious memory, and was industrious and conscientiously thorough. On his father's death he became fourth baronet; and on 23 July 1866 was appointed a queen's counsel. He became a bencher of his inn in November 1866, and a serjeant-at-law on 23 January 1873. On the recommendation of Lord Selborne he became a judge of the court of common pleas on 23 January 1873. He resigned in February 1875, and died at Tunbridge Wells on 16 September 1875. His brother, the Revd Sir William Macdonald Honyman, succeeded as fifth baronet.   G. C. BOASE, rev. SINÉAD AGNEW

Sources Boase, *Mod. Eng. biog.* • *Law Times* (9 Oct 1875), 383 • *Law Magazine*, 4th ser., 1 (1875–6), 122–7 • J. Hutchinson, ed., *A catalogue of notable Middle Templars: with brief biographical notices* (1902), 124 • *Men of the time* (1875), 545 • *The Times* (20 Sept 1875), 7 • *Morning Post* (20 Sept 1875), 5 • *ILN* (25 Sept 1875), 319 • *ILN* (2 Oct 1875), 333 • *ILN* (4 Dec 1875), 566 • E. Kilmurray, *Dictionary of British portraiture*, 3 (1981), 96 • F. W. Hamilton, *The origin and history of the first or grenadier guards*, 3 (1874), 149, 150, 425, 506
Likenesses wood-engraving (after photograph by London Stereoscopic Co.), NPG; repro. in *ILN* (2 Oct 1875)
Wealth at death under £60,000: probate, 20 Nov 1875, *CGPLA Eng. & Wales*

Honywood [*née* Waters], **Mary** (1527–1620), matriarch and sustainer of protestant martyrs, was the daughter and coheir of Robert Waters, esquire, of Lenham, Kent, where she was born. In 1543 Mary married Robert Honywood, esquire, of Charing and later of Marks Hall, Essex. The couple had 16 children and by the time of her death she had 114 grandchildren, 228 great-grandchildren, and 9 great-great-grandchildren. As Fuller remarks, 'thus she had a child for every day in the (though leap) year, and one over' (Fuller, *Worthies*, 2.86). Her many grandchildren included Michael Honywood (1596–1681), the post-Restoration dean of Lincoln, and his brother Sir Thomas Honywood of Marks Hall (1587–1666), a leading Essex parliamentarian. However, the same writer regarded Mary as 'more memorable on another account, viz., for the patient weathering out the tempest of a troubled conscience' (ibid., 2.85–6). According to Simeon Foxe, the son of the martyrologist, Mrs Honywood languished 'sick of a consumption through melancholy' from the age of forty, and during this time 'consulted with the gravest Divines and the best Physitians' including his own father, John Foxe. Previously she had also sought spiritual solace from the martyr John Bradford and the renowned puritan preacher Edward Dering, both of whom corresponded with her. In 1592 it was reported that she had believed that she was possessed by a devil for some fourteen years and that in

1591 she had endured exorcism at the hands of the religious charlatan William Hacket. Simeon Foxe later recorded a meeting between Mrs Honywood and John Foxe, at which the latter assured her that she would recover and live to a great age. To which she replied 'as well might you have said … that if I should throw this glasse against the wall, I might beleeve it would not break to pieces' and 'threw it forth'. The glass hit a chest before falling to the ground without either breaking or cracking (Foxe, sig. B3*r–v*).

Other contemporary and later authors, including Fuller, cast this story as a miraculous test by Mrs Honywood of her salvation, for which Foxe gently reproved her. According to Fuller her encounter with Foxe did not cure Mrs Honywood, but some time later she suddenly received comfort 'like lightening into her soul' and spent the rest of her life in 'spiritual gladnesse' (Fuller, *Worthies*, 2.86). Although most authors have concentrated on stories of Mary Honywood's numerous descendants and of her religious despair, she also played an important role as one of the female 'sustainers' of the Marian martyrs. She corresponded with John Bradford, although they had never met, and Fuller records that 'in the days of Queen Mary she used to visit the prisons, and to comfort and relieve the confessors therein' (ibid.). He also states that Mrs Honywood was determined to see the end of John Bradford's sufferings and was present at his burning in 1555, when the press of people was so great that her shoes were trodden off and she was forced to walk barefoot from Smithfield to St Martin's before she could purchase a new pair.

Mary Honywood died at Marks Hall on 12 May 1620, in her ninety-third year, and was buried at Lenham on the 20th. A portrait of her which descended in the Mildmay family, showing her holding the Venetian glass that failed to break, was reported in the early nineteenth century, but its present whereabouts is unknown. But pictures of her made in 1597 and 1605 survive in the Colchester and Essex Museum and Wren Library respectively.

JACQUELINE EALES

Sources Fuller, *Worthies* (1662), 2.85–6 • T. Freeman, '"The Good Ministrye of Godly and Vertuouse Women": the Elizabethan martyrologists and the female supporters of the Marian martyrs', *Journal of British Studies*, 39 (2000), 8–33 • P. Collinson, 'A mirror of Elizabethan puritanism: the life and letters of "Godly Master Dering"', *Godly people: essays on English protestantism and puritanism* (1983), 288–324, 289–324 • E. Dering, *Certaine godly and comfortable letters full of Christian consolation* (Middelburg, 1590), sigs. A6–B3, CIv–2v • J. Foxe, *The second volume of the ecclesiastical history containing the acts and monuments of martyrs*, 8th edn (1641), sig. B3r–v • bishops' transcripts, Lenham parish, Canterbury Cathedral, archives, DCb/BT1/141 • J. G. Nichols, ed., *The topographer and genealogist*, 1 (1846), 397–8 • *DNB*
Likenesses portrait, 1597, Colchester and Essex Museum; copy, 1640, Lincoln Cathedral • portrait, 1605, Trinity Cam., Wren Library • stipple, pubd 1813, NPG • line engraving, NPG • oils, Oriel College, Oxford

Honywood, Michael (1596–1681), dean of Lincoln, was born on 1 October 1596 in the parish of St Helen in London, the sixth son and ninth child of Robert Honywood (1545–1627), esquire, of Charing, Kent, and later of Marks

Hall, Essex, and his second wife, Elizabeth (d. 1631), daughter of Sir Thomas Browne of Betchworth Castle, Surrey; he was the grandson of Mary *Honywood (1527–1620) and younger brother of Sir Thomas *Honywood (1587–1666). He was admitted to Christ's College, Cambridge, graduated BA in January 1615 and proceeded MA in 1618. In 1618, through the patronage of Elizabeth, queen of Bohemia, he became fellow of his college. He was ordained deacon in the same year and priest in 1619. He assisted Richard Crakanthorpe with his Logicae libri quinque (1622), help gratefully acknowledged by the author. He served the university offices of taxor in 1623 and of proctor in 1628. Among the fellows of Christ's during his years of residence were Thomas Bainbridge (master of the college), Henry More, Joseph Mede, and Edward King, whose early death was commemorated by the publication of a collection of verses, including two Latin poems by Honywood, and 'Lycidas' by John Milton, a former student of Christ's. Honywood took an active part in the management of the college. He was probably the instigator of the erection of the new fellows' buildings, completed in 1644; he gave money to the project, lent more, and was active in raising funds for it.

In 1636 Honywood proceeded BD and in 1639 he was appointed to the lucrative college living of Kegworth, Leicestershire, but he was exempted from the requirement to reside by his appointment as president, or deputy master, of the college. In January 1643 he crossed to the Low Countries, and by August he was in Leiden. Although Thomas Bainbridge wrote to him in August of that year urging him to return and expressing the wish that Honywood should succeed him as master of Christ's, Honywood remained abroad. During his exile he lived mainly at Utrecht, enjoying the friendship of William Sancroft and devoting himself to the collection of books. The notebook in which he recorded his purchases reveals the breadth of his interests, including theology, politics, travel, antiquities, linguistics, science, and mathematics. He acted as a lending library to the circle of exiled Anglican clergy in the Netherlands, many of whom were writing books of their own. For some time he was able to retain the rectory of Kegworth, employing a curate to carry out his duties there, but by 1649 the benefice was finally sequestered by the Leicester county committee and a new minister, William Moore, appointed.

At the Restoration, Honywood returned to England. Some of the fellows of Christ's College vainly petitioned that he might be appointed master, in place of Dr Ralph Cudworth. He was restored to his living of Kegworth, which he held until his death. Although it was necessary for him in 1667 to bring a suit against one Richard Gibson, a Quaker, for non-payment of tithes, the parish was not much frequented by nonconformists and it was reported in 1669 that there was no conventicle there. Honywood gave £20 to the repair of the schoolhouse. On 29 September 1660 the king presented him to the deanery of Lincoln; he was installed in person on 12 October. He proceeded DD in 1661. As dean Honywood set vigorously to work to repair the damage done to the fabric of Lincoln Cathedral and its precincts during the civil war and interregnum, contributing liberally from his own purse. He also acted swiftly to re-establish the long-suspended choral services, and by the end of 1660 vicars and choristers had been appointed. With all English cathedrals in a similar position, skilled musicians were in short supply. In 1663 Honywood brought a Dutch organist, Andreas Hecht, to Lincoln, and in 1666 he was in correspondence with Sancroft, then dean of St Paul's, in search of duly qualified voices for the Lincoln choir at a time when the choir of St Paul's was unemployed as a result of the fire of London. The rebuilding of the ruined houses of the vicars choral and the education of the singing boys also occupied Honywood's attention. He earnestly defended the long-suspended rights of the dean and chapter, resumed the practice of decanal visitations of the prebendal churches and estates, and reasserted the franchises of the close. Honywood's chief work in connection with his cathedral was the erection at his own cost (£780) of the library from the designs of Sir Christopher Wren, on the site of the ruined north walk of the cloister. In this building he placed his extensive collection of books, which he eventually bequeathed to the chapter. The collection contains incunabula, an invaluable series of rare seventeenth-century tracts, and other works on a wide range of subjects and in a great variety of languages. Although the library's collections have continued to grow since his death, Honywood's own books are distinguished by the monogram 'MH'.

Besides Sancroft, Honywood's friends included Herbert Thorndike and Samuel Pepys. The latter speaks of him as 'a good nature, but a very weak man; yet a Deane and a man in great esteem', and 'a simple priest … though a good well-meaning man' (Pepys, Diary, 29 June, 6 Aug 1664). Honywood died unmarried at his deanery on 7 September 1681; he was buried in the cathedral. John Walker describes him as 'a Holy and Humble Man, and a Living Library for Learning' (Walker, 2.269).

NICHOLAS BENNETT

Sources J. Peile, Biographical register of Christ's College, 1505–1905, and of the earlier foundation, God's House, 1448–1505, ed. [J. A. Venn], 1 (1910) · J. H. Strawley, Michael Honywood dean of Lincoln (1660–81), rev. edn (1981) · N. Linnell, 'Michael Honywood and Lincoln Cathedral Library', The Library, 6th ser., 5 (1983), 126–39 · J. Nichols, The history and antiquities of the county of Leicester, 3/2 (1804) · Pepys, Diary · J. Walker, An attempt towards recovering an account of the numbers and sufferings of the clergy of the Church of England, 2 pts in 1 (1714) · Elizabeth, queen of Bohemia, letter to the earl of Suffolk, Lincs. Arch., D and C Ciij/13/2/22, D and C Wills 15/103 (Michael Honywood), 19 June 1618 · C. W. Foster, 'Admissions to benefices … in the county of Leicester', Associated Archaeology Society Reports and Papers, 37 (1923–5), 144–76 · R. H. Evans, 'Nonconformity in Leicestershire in 1669', Transactions of the Leicestershire Archaeological Society, 25 (1949), 98–143 · N. Linnell, 'A unique copy of Richard Crakanthorp's Logic', The Library, 6th ser., 4 (1982), 323–6 · B. W. Greenfield, ed., 'Honywood evidences' [2], The topographer and genealogist, ed. J. G. Nichols, 2 (1853), 169–73 · Walker rev. · private information (2004)

Archives Lincoln Cathedral, catalogues of books and MSS, and papers

Likenesses attrib. A. Hanneman, oils, Lincoln Cathedral library · W. Holl, stipple (after C. Johnson), BM; repro. in T. F. Dibdin, The *bibliographical decameron*, 3 vols. (1817) • oils, Christ's College, Cambridge

Honywood, Sir Robert (1601–1686), diplomat and translator, was born on 3 August 1601 at Hollingbourne, Kent, the second of twenty children, and eldest surviving son, of Sir Robert Honywood of Petts Court, Charing, Kent, and Alice Barnham, daughter of Sir Martin Barnham of Hollingbourne. Robert Honywood the elder was knighted by Charles I at Canterbury on 15 June 1625. The younger Honywood received the same honour at Oakfields on 7 July 1627, when he is described as 'servant to the Queen of Bohemia' (Shaw, 192). Elizabeth refers to him as her steward and his duties evidently included staging entertainments for her household—Elizabeth mentions Honywood's participation in a production of Francis Beaumont's and John Fletcher's *The Scornful Lady*—and carrying messages on Elizabeth's behalf to her friends and allies in England, including Charles I and Archbishop Laud. In a letter to Laud, Elizabeth describes Honywood as honest and faithful, and thus suitable to be trusted with confidential information (*Letters*, ed. Baker, 78; *CSP dom.*, 1635–6, 338, 402, and 222). The appointment of Sir Charles Cotterell as steward to Elizabeth '[a]bout 1652' (*DNB*) may indicate that by this date Honywood had left her service.

Honywood married Frances Vane (1614–1688), daughter of Sir Henry *Vane, on 3 April 1631, at Shipbourne, Kent. The historian Edward Hasted says that they had sixteen children (BL, Add. MS 5480, fol. 69r), but only seven are recorded by name, four in Kent parish registers (Robert, Henry, Frances, and Edward). In her will, dated 26 January 1688, Frances Vane mentions three further children, Elizabeth, Ann, and Charles, all deceased. (Frances, her mother's executor, seems to have been the only one of the Honywood children to outlive the parents.) At least one of the children appears to have been born in the Netherlands, where Honywood is said to have owned three houses (*CSP dom.*, 1635, 435).

Honywood's sympathies during the civil war are unclear. Through his father-in-law and brother-in-law, also named Sir Henry Vane, he had close connections with the parliamentary side; and he continued to correspond with the elder Vane even while the latter was serving as a parliamentary commissioner to Scotland in 1645. In a friendly letter to the elder Vane, dated 13 October 1645, Honywood appears to refer to Fairfax's forces as 'our army', and to foreign animadversions against parliament as an 'ill office' (*CSP dom.*, 1645–7, 188–90). However, Honywood also maintained his links with Elizabeth of Bohemia, who records his presence, with his son Robert and brother-in-law Walter Vane, at The Hague in August 1655 (*Letters*, ed. Baker, 239). In the later 1650s he apparently served as a captain in one of the English cavalry regiments in the army of the states general, for in 1659, while on leave in England, he wrote to De Witt requesting that his company be transferred to his son, then on duty with the Dutch forces at Copenhagen (Rowen, 159). On 19 May 1659 he was appointed a member of the council of state, and in June 1659 Honywood, Algernon Sidney, Edward Montague, and Thomas Boone were chosen as plenipotentiaries to negotiate a peace between the kings of Sweden and Denmark. The English party arrived at Elsinore in July 1659 and remained in Denmark until after the Restoration. With Sidney, Honywood was among the signatories to the peace treaty signed between Sweden and Denmark, dated 27 May 1660. He returned to England in August 1660.

Honywood's involvement with the council of state evidently caused him some embarrassment with his erstwhile employer, the queen of Bohemia, to whom he wrote, probably in autumn 1660, to say that he had seen King Charles and received assurances 'that he had nothing of objection against my person nor in relation to the employment I had been in, knowing well that I had followed my instructions, and beleeving that having lived so long in y^r Ma^{stys} service, I could not in any thing be forward to disoblige y^r family' (BL, Add. MS 18744). Further distress ensued when his son Robert was attainted for treason in 1667, having refused to answer a proclamation recalling him from service with the Dutch forces against the English in the Second Anglo-Dutch War.

In 1673 Honywood published *The history of the affairs of Europe in this present age, but more particularly of the republick of Venice*, a translation of the *Historia della republica Veneta* by the Venetian diplomat Giovanni Battista Nani (first published in 1662). In his dedicatory letter to Walter Vane (identified as 'Colonel of His Majesties Holland-Regiment'), Honywood writes that he had begun this translation 'in the Circumstances of an uncomfortable old Age and ruined Fortune, brought upon me, rather by publick Calamity than private Vice, or domestick Prodigality. And I undertook it to divert the melancholy hours, arising from the consideration of either' (sig. A1r). There may have been a domestic political motivation in Honywood's choice of Nani's history of Venice. From the civil war period onwards, the government and institutions of Venice had been of especial interest to Englishmen of parliamentarian and oppositional sympathies, including Honywood's erstwhile colleague Algernon Sidney. Such men admired Venice as a mixed polity, in which the head of state ruled in collaboration with an enlightened aristocracy, and which had, uniquely among Italian states, successfully resisted tyranny. Interest in Venice seems to have been especially intense in the middle and later years of Charles II's reign: Honywood's translation is one of ten books on the government of the Serene Republic to have been published by Englishmen during this period (Fink, 125). Since Nani's history explicitly honours the institutions of Venice and celebrates liberty, it is probable that Honywood's translation would have carried anti-monarchical and possibly republican connotations in the fraught English politics of the 1670s.

Honywood died on 15 April 1686, and was buried at Charing church. By his will, dated 10 December 1672, he left all his possessions to his wife. She died on 17 February 1688 and was buried with her husband.

GILLIAN WRIGHT

Sources R. Honywood, *The history of the affairs of Europe in this present age, but more particularly of the republick of Venice* (1673) • *The letters*

of Elizabeth, queen of Bohemia, ed. L. M. Baker (1953) · CSP dom., 1635–73 · H. H. Rowen, John de Witt, grand pensionary of Holland, 1625–1672 (1978) · BL, Add. MS 18744, fols. 17–18 · parish register, Hollingbourne, Kent [birth] · parish registers, Charing and Shipbourne, Kent · BL, Add. MS 5480, fol. 69 · W. A. Shaw, The knights of England, 2 (1906) · P. Parsons, The monuments and painted glass of upwards of one hundred churches, chiefly in the eastern part of Kent (1744) · R. Manley, The history of the late warres in Denmark (1670) · Thurloe, State papers, vol. 6 · A. Everitt, The community of Kent and the great rebellion, 1640–60 (1973) · J. G. Nicholls, Topographer and genealogist, 1 (1848) · Z. S. Fink, The classical republicans: an essay in the recovery of a pattern of thought in seventeenth-century England (1945) · DNB

Archives BL, Add. MS 18744 · BL, Add. MS 33084, fols. 44, 49, 73
Wealth at death personal possessions only; estate at Charing had seemingly already passed to eldest son: will, 10 Dec 1672

Honywood, Sir Thomas, appointed Lord Honywood under the protectorate (1587–1666), parliamentarian army officer and local politician, was born on 15 January 1587 at Betchworth Castle, Surrey, the second son of Robert Honywood, esquire (1545–1627), and his second wife, Elizabeth (d. 1631), daughter of Sir Thomas Browne, whose seat Betchworth was. His paternal grandmother was the long-lived and devout Mary *Honywood, who died aged ninety-three in 1620. Michael *Honywood, royalist and dean of Lincoln, was a younger brother.

Honywood was possibly a student of the Inner Temple in 1605, when a man of his name is described as of South Mimms, Middlesex, gentleman. He inherited Marks Hall, Essex, in 1631 and was knighted on 22 November 1632. Honywood married Hester (1606/7–1681), widow of John Manning of Hackney and daughter of John Lamotte of London, both merchants, on 10 May 1634. They had seven children of whom only three, Thomas, John, and Elizabeth, survived their father.

Honywood was not active as magistrate or deputy lieutenant in the 1630s, perhaps out of antipathy to Charles I's political and religious policies. War with the Scots saw him named as an Essex commissioner for the collection of subsidies; fear of Irish insurgents saw him appointed commissioner for the £400,000 tax of 1642.

Honywood was a committed puritan. He appointed a puritan to Markshall rectory in 1646 and befriended the puritan minister Ralph Josselin of Earls Colne. Driven by his religious proclivities he became a stalwart supporter of the parliamentarian cause. Named on every major ordinance relating to taxation, sequestration, and the militia he was a committed county committee man and a key divisional commissioner around Colchester. He was appointed a member of the Essex committee for scandalous ministers in both 1644 and 1654 and was nominated as an elder on the stillborn presbyterian classis of 1645–8. In 1650 he was appointed commissioner for the Commonwealth church survey. He upheld the authority of parliament and its successor regimes as magistrate at quarter sessions, c.1645–59 and was custos rotulorum between 1656 and 1659. He was keen to see local fortifications maintained.

Yet while acknowledging local concerns and expressing concerns to parliament about excessive demands (in 1643 describing his local administrative division as being 'infinitely oppressed'), Honywood saw beyond any narrow county provincialism (BL, Egerton MS 2647, fol. 199). In June 1643 he backed the attempt by the earl of Essex at a levee en masse 'for the defence of Religion and libertie' (BL, Stowe MS 189, fol. 10). He saw 'forwardness' in Essex as potentially inspirational to the well affected in other counties (BL, Egerton MS 2647, fol. 146). In spring 1643, as colonel of a regiment of foot, he took Essex trained bands to Reading and in July 1644 took them out again to the siege of Greenland House. The committee of both kingdoms consequently acknowledged his 'very good service to the public' in preventing the enemy from entering the very 'bowels of the Association' (CSP dom., 1644, 346). Significantly he had been one of the Essex signatories at the inception of the eastern association in February 1643 and was active in supporting both it and the subsequent New Model Army.

Honywood was decisive in undermining local support for the royalists during the second civil war in 1648 through his rapid deployment of the trained bands. He preserved the magazine at Coggeshall. He joined Thomas, Lord Fairfax, on 11 June and subsequently formed part of the forces besieging Colchester. He appears to have headed the signatories to the articles of surrender at the end of August. Honywood's hostility towards the defeated was implacable; he opposed indemnity and demanded that enemy estates should be sequestrated and the money arising used to secure Essex from 'like imbroilments' (Portland MSS, 1.480, 473–4). He insisted on the right of the Essex county committee and not Goldsmith's Hall to compound with them so that those suffering losses at Colchester could be compensated. Honywood was appointed to the high court of justice for trying Charles I in 1649, but did not attend.

Trouble flared again in Colchester and neighbouring counties at the end of 1650. Since Honywood had disobeyed orders by not dismantling the fortifications at Colchester the council of state was obliged to appoint him governor of its garrison with the power to raise militia forces and disarm suspects. In 1651 Honywood again came to the defence of the Commonwealth when Charles II threatened at Worcester. At the battle Honywood was in charge of a regiment of foot from Essex; his forces allowed Lieutenant-General Fleetwood 'to advance close up' (Mercurius Politicus, 28 Aug–4 Sept 1651, 1042). For this he was created a doctor of civil law by Oxford University. Locally, during 1655, Honywood, appointed a militia commissioner, zealously supported Cromwell's major-general, Hezekiah Heynes, by finding malignants; he and his fellow commissioners used godly rhetoric to request tough action against rebels and was 'most forward' in his support of the decimation tax (Thurloe, 4.320). That year Honywood stayed in Colchester to influence the elections there to ensure 'a good magistracy' (ibid., 320).

Honywood was elected MP for Essex in 1654 and 1656. He was appointed to several committees, from the committee for printing to a committee which considered abuses in alehouses; occasionally he acted as a teller. In

December 1657 Honywood was made a peer and appointed to the upper house.

At the Restoration political settlement was all, and although excluded from the earl of Oxford's commission for deputy lieutenants for Essex and from the county bench Honywood received his pardon and paid his 'free and voluntary present' in 1661, while drifting into a healthy political obscurity. He died aged seventy-nine at Cotton House in Westminster, the house of his son-in-law, on 26 May 1666 'taken with a vomiting &c' (Bodl. Oxf., MS Rawl. Essex 23, fol. 300). He was interred on 1 June in the chancel of Markshall church by Ralph Josselin.

BILL CLIFTLANDS

Sources BL, Barrington family papers, Egerton MSS 2643, 2646–2648, 2651 · Essex RO, Morant MSS D/Y 2/2, 2/7, 2/9 · Essex parliamentarian committee papers, BL, Stowe MS 189 · Essex county committee papers, PRO, SP 28/227 · judgments and orders of the standing committee of Essex, BL, Harleian MS 6244 · miscellaneous county committee papers and accounts, PRO, SP 28/332 · *CSP dom.*, 1644–60 · *JHC*, 3–7 (1642–59) · *JHL*, 8–15 (1646–93) · C. H. Firth and R. S. Rait, eds., *Acts and ordinances of the interregnum, 1642–1660*, 3 vols. (1911) · D. H. Allen, ed., *Essex quarter sessions and order book, 1652–1661*, Essex Record Office Publications, no. 65 (1974) · pardon of Sir Thomas Honywood, 12 Chas. II, Essex RO, D/DM F20/5 · free and voluntary present, 13 Chas. II, PRO, E 179/246/7 · Essex committee book for scandalous ministers, BL, Add. MS 5829 · M. C. [M. Carter], *A … true … relation of that as honourable as unfortunate expedition of Kent, Essex, and Colchester* (1650) · J. Rushworth, *Historical collections*, new edn, 7 (1721), 1150, 1244 · *An exact narrative of every dayes proceedings since the insurrection in Essex … till the 18 of June present, 1648* (1648) [Thomason tract E 448(18)] · *A Perfect Diurnall* (10–20 July 1648) [Thomason tract E 448(23)] · *Mercurius Politicus* (28 Aug–4 Sept 1651) [Thomason tract E 641(4)] · *The manuscripts of his grace the duke of Portland*, 10 vols., HMC, 29 (1891–1931), vol. 1, pp. 119–20, 145, 161, 187, 268, 295, 458, 470, 473, 480 · Thurloe, *State papers*, 3.228, 247, 253, 285, 688; 4.317, 320, 329 · *Diary of Samuel Pepys*, ed. H. B. Wheatley, 1 (1962), 167, 205 · B. Whitelocke, *Memorials of English affairs*, new edn, 4 vols. (1853) · J. G. Nichols, ed., *The topographer and genealogist*, 2 (1853), 171 · *The manuscripts of the earl of Buckinghamshire, the earl of Lindsey … and James Round*, HMC, 38 (1895), 282 · A. Everitt, *Suffolk and the great rebellion, 1640–60*, Suffolk Records Society, 3 (1960) · Foster, *Alum. Oxon.* · H. Smith, *The ecclesiastical history of Essex under the Long Parliament and Commonwealth* [n.d.] · C. Fell Smith, 'Markshall and the Honywoods', *Essex Review*, 7 (1898), 156–75 · extracts from the diary of John Sparrow of Dynes Hall, Essex, Bodl. Oxf., MS Rawl. Essex 23, fol. 300 · Holman's notes for Markes Hall, 1717, PRO, T/P 195/11/25 · earl of Oxford's commission for the deputy lieutenants of Essex, 1660, Essex RO, D/DQ25 · *The writings and speeches of Oliver Cromwell*, ed. W. C. Abbott and C. D. Crane, 4 vols. (1937–47), vol. 3, pp. 672–3; vol. 4, pp. 683–5 · *Mercurius civicus*, 11–17 July 1644, BL, E2 (16), 579 · letter of the county committee of Essex to the committee for compounding, 10 May 1649, PRO, SP 23/248/14 · *The diary of Ralph Josselin, 1616–1683*, ed. A. MacFarlane, British Academy, Records of Social and Economic History, new ser., 3 (1976) · *The Clarke Papers*, ed. C. H. Firth, 2, CS, new ser., 54 (1894), 26–7 · R. Bell, ed., *Memorials of the civil war … forming the concluding volumes of the Fairfax correspondence*, 2 (1849), 35 · will, PRO, PROB 11/321, sig. 129, fol. 298 · P. Morant, *The history and antiquities of the county of Essex*, 2 (1768), 166–79 · GEC, *Peerage*

Likenesses portrait, repro. in *Essex County Standard* (18 March 1933) · portrait, Hollytrees Museum, Colchester

Hood. For this title name *see* individual entries under Hood; *see also* Mackenzie, Mary Elizabeth Frederica Stewart-, Lady Hood (1783–1862).

Hood, Alexander, **Viscount Bridport** (1726–1814), naval officer and politician, was born on 2 December 1726, second son of Samuel Hood (d. 1777), vicar of Butleigh, Somerset, and Mary, daughter of Richard Hoskins of Beaminster, Dorset. He was the younger brother of Samuel *Hood (later Viscount Hood), who also entered the Royal Navy, Alexander preceding him by a few months, the protégé of Captain Thomas Smith.

Early naval and parliamentary career Hood was entered on 19 January 1741 as captain's servant to Smith in the *Romney*, in which he remained with Captain Thomas Grenville until 22 April 1743, when he transferred to the *Princess Mary*, again with Smith, who rated him midshipman. He followed Smith to the *Royal Sovereign* (December 1744), the *Exeter* (March 1745), and the *Hawk* (May 1746); from her he was promoted lieutenant on 2 December to the *Bridgewater* in which he remained until she was paid off in October 1748.

Hood remained on half pay until January 1755 when he was appointed lieutenant in the *Prince* (Captain Charles Saunders); he was then (23 March 1756) appointed to the command of the sloop *Merlin*, fitting in the River Thames, and subsequently (10 June) was made post captain in the *Prince George*, in which Saunders, now a rear-admiral, hoisted his flag and proceeded to the Mediterranean station as second-in-command. Hood remained Saunders's flag captain for the next two years, following him successively to the *Prince*, the *Culloden*, and the *St George*. Following his return to England, on 5 January 1759 Hood was appointed to the frigate *Minerva*, attached to the fleet off Brest under Sir Edward Hawke, whence she was placed in October and November in a small squadron commanded by Captain Robert Duff cruising on the Morbihan coast of Brittany. In the latter month the squadron was chased by the French fleet, which was then itself pursued by Hawke and defeated on 20 November 1759 in Quiberon Bay where Hood was present. He remained with the Channel Fleet for two more years, distinguishing himself on 23 January 1761 in the Bay of Biscay when the *Minerva* fell in with the *Warwick*, a British 60-gun ship captured by the French in 1756 and now used as a transport. Although reduced in her armament, the *Warwick's* size and scantling posed a challenge to the 32-gun frigate, and indeed the contest proved roughly equal. In an engagement lasting six hours, each ship lost two of three masts, and each had about forty-six dead and wounded. But, to Hood's credit, the *Warwick* was captured.

In summer 1761 Hood married Mary, known as Molly (c.1706–1786), daughter of Richard West, prebendary of Winchester; her mother was Maria, daughter of Sir Richard Temple, connected to the Lyttelton and Grenville families. Lord Lyttelton gave away the bride. Mary was twenty years older than Hood, but the match proved a happy one and his genuine tenderness to this 'glorious girl' was touching (Wyndham, 2.278). That August, Lord Anson, first lord of the Admiralty, honoured Hood by taking the *Minerva* with him in a small squadron that escorted Princess Charlotte, the future queen, on her sea crossing from

Alexander Hood, Viscount Bridport (1726–1814), by Sir Joshua Reynolds, 1763

Mecklenburg to Harwich. In September 1761 Hood transferred to the *Africa* (64 guns), launched the previous month, in which he served in the Mediterranean until the peace in 1763. In December 1763 he was appointed to the royal yacht *Katherine*, a command he retained until December 1777. His income was supplemented from 23 September 1766 when he succeeded Sir Charles Saunders as treasurer of Greenwich Hospital. The fortune of his wife, which Hood insisted she retain, and his several incomes permitted the couple to maintain a country house, Cricket Lodge at Cricket St Thomas, near Chard, Somerset, and a house in Harley Street, London.

In December 1777 Hood was appointed to the *Robust* (74 guns). On 27 July of the following year she formed one of Vice-Admiral Sir Hugh Palliser's rear division of the fleet under Admiral Augustus Keppel which indecisively engaged the French off Ushant. The ensuing controversy, involving courts martial of both Keppel and Palliser, almost ruined Hood's career, for at Keppel's trial he was forced to admit that he had directed the log book of the *Robust* to be altered, by the insertion of signal, after the court martial was ordered. Hood made the perfectly reasonable assertion that the book had been written up carelessly and that his additions, which were not suspicious, merely improved and corrected the master's rough draft. Other log books had also been amended and the court did not condemn the insertion. George III was also inclined to put a favourable interpretation on the alteration: he recalled Hood had hitherto

> always borne the character of a man of strict honour. I therefore trust the affair will be explained and that his

conduct will rather be proved to have been actuated by over-niceness than any inclination to alter the complexion of a document. (Hood, 47–8)

But the public noise in favour of Keppel was vociferous; Hood was hissed in court and the word 'hooded' for a short while meant being subject to false evidence.

To restore his reputation after the court martial Hood appealed in February 1779 either for promotion or for a colonelcy of marines, his wife and brother adding their weight to his request. The 'most friendly act' Lord Sandwich, first lord of the Admiralty, felt he could do was to order the *Robust* to the North American station. But, determined to face hostile opinion at home, Hood resigned his command of the *Robust*, and was re-appointed to the royal yacht *Katherine*. He was promoted rear-admiral on 26 September 1780 but it was another two years before he was appointed to a real command, following the death of Rear-Admiral Richard Kempenfelt, in the Channel Fleet under Lord Howe. He hoisted his flag on the *Queen* (90 guns) and took part in the final relief of Gibraltar and the subsequent skirmish with the Franco-Spanish fleet off Cape Spartel, on 19 October 1782.

At the general election in 1784, under the patronage of the fourth Earl Poulett, Hood was elected member for Bridgwater. He spoke in parliament for the first time on 23 June 1784, and thereafter on three or four other occasions, all on naval matters. He voted with the government on the regency question, but abandoned his seat in 1790 on failing to agree terms with his patron. He was nevertheless re-elected for Buckingham in December 1790, and represented that constituency until 1796, though virtually without utterance, by the influence of the marquess of Buckingham, to whom he was related through his first wife, Mary. She had died in 1786 and on 4 May 1788 he married Maria Sophia (*c*.1746–1831), daughter of Thomas Bray of Edmonton. He had been promoted vice-admiral on 24 September 1787, and three days after his second marriage he was nominated a knight of the Bath.

Commander at sea During the Spanish armament of 1790 Hood hoisted his flag for a short while on the *London* at Spithead. However, significant further service only recommenced in February 1793 when he was appointed third in command of the Channel Fleet under Lord Howe and hoisted his flag on the *Royal George*. He was promoted admiral on 24 April 1794; and for his part in the battle of 1 June 1794 he was created Baron Bridport in the Irish peerage (two years later he was created Baron Bridport of Cricket St Thomas in the peerage of Great Britain). Following the battle Bridport became second in command of the Channel Fleet; and from mid-1795, when Howe's weakening health obliged the Admiralty to permit him to command from on shore, Bridport took the fleet to sea in the invidious position of responsibility without power. On 12 June he sailed in escort of the British expedition to support a royalist rising in Brittany, parting company from the troop convoy and escort under Sir John Borlase Warren close to Belle Île. The French fleet was reported to have left Brest, and it was sighted by Warren off Belle Île; taking evasive action, Warren immediately sent word to Bridport who sighted the French fleet on 22 June. Villaret-Joyeuse, the French admiral, had only twelve of the line; Bridport, with Warren's ships of the line, a potential seventeen. Bridport gave chase, and on 23 June, Isle de Groix east 6 or 7 miles, captured three French battleships before Villaret-Joyeuse took refuge in Lorient.

Since Howe had been forced ashore to recuperate from the battle of 1 June, Bridport had revealed jealousy of the favourable treatment of his commander-in-chief who was only a year older than himself and with whom he did not enjoy a close relationship. Bridport too had health problems, complaining in 1794 of gout. To retain Howe as nominal commander-in-chief, yet to reward and encourage Bridport for remaining at sea, in July 1795 Earl Spencer, first lord of the Admiralty, proposed the latter be appointed commander-in-chief of a squadron to be employed on a particular service, which carried higher emoluments. Bridport reported honestly that the new commission, which he thought overdue, failed to arouse in him either a sense of honour or feeling of gratitude, and that he still expected some further mark of royal approbation for his services. Irritating to Spencer, the reply prompted George III to observe that his remarks revealed Bridport's true priorities; 'in his family self value is so predominant that all other objects are not sufficiently attended to' (to Spencer, 16 Aug 1795, *Later Correspondence of George III*, 2.380). Yet the arrangement proved unsatisfactory. Remaining overall commander-in-chief, Howe still shared in prize money even though he served on shore, while Bridport, probably deliberately, failed to keep him informed of his proceedings. The new commission was suspended in October and Bridport retired on shore on half pay.

Bridport did not again volunteer his services until October 1796, when Spencer was ready to employ him. Under the necessity to defend the Quiberon expedition from interference, the close blockade of Brest and Lorient had begun in June 1795. Since then detachments of the British fleet had relieved one another on station off Brest and this arrangement remained adequate throughout autumn 1796, though enhanced activity in the port steadily raised the demand for larger scale deterrence. In a move that coincided with the reinforcement of the Brest fleet from Rochefort, Bridport rehoisted his flag on 18 December 1796, though still nominally under the shore command of Howe. The French expedition to Ireland had sailed two days earlier; on 20 December the Admiralty dispatched orders to Bridport to put to sea from Spithead; an easterly wind and adverse tide contributed to collisions involving five ships on 25 December and eventually he sailed on 3 January 1797. However, though he remained at sea for a month, Bridport contributed little directly to the failure of the French expedition which returned into port on 13 January, having lost a quarter of its force through foundering, grounding, or capture by frigates.

The Spithead mutiny and the blockade of Brest Following a brief cruise in March 1797 Bridport was at Spithead on 15 April when, on account of discontent in Ireland and intelligence of preparations in Brest, the fleet was ordered to make ready for sea and the seamen of the fleet, led by those in the *Queen Charlotte*, refused to unmoor. The Spithead mutiny took Bridport by surprise. In March the seamen had sent petitions to Howe who had referred them to Lord Hugh Seymour in the fleet; he had assured Howe that there was no general sign of discontent and sent the petitions to the Board of Admiralty where they had been ignored. Rather the board simply hoped that officers of the fleet would take steps to nip the mutiny in the bud. This placed the responsibility on Bridport, for Howe had finally resigned as commander-in-chief of the Channel Fleet on 8 April. Bridport was angry that measures had not been taken earlier to pacify the men; he also realized the scale of the mutiny and the impossibility of forcing the seamen to sail against their will. He accordingly ignored directions to proceed to sea and committed the Admiralty to answer the petitions. That answer was noncommittal, and as further petitions reached him, he placed responsibility squarely with the board to state to the seamen precisely how their grievances were being answered.

In the ensuing negotiations Bridport consistently took the part of the mutineers. After the board migrated to Portsmouth to settle matters on the spot and seamen's delegates met on Bridport's flagship, the *Royal George*, on 21 April he was obliged to strike his flag. But on 23 April he was able to report to the mutineers that their demands had been conceded and he was permitted that day to rehoist his flag. At this time six ships became operational and dropped down to St Helens, the outer anchorage. However, further demands promptly emerged from them; before sailing the seamen also wished to secure the concessions they had won. Following Bridport's example, Spencer was willing to keep the seamen informed of the progress made in meeting their requirements. By 6 May order seemed to have been re-established. Yet again discontent revived, the St Helens ships refusing to sail without confirmation of the funds granted by the House of Commons towards their increased pay and provisions. Evidence of this was sent down from London. Bridport ensured its acceptability by insisting that the date the increases would take effect should be not the date set in London by order in council, but that which he had used in negotiating with the seamen. He also insisted that officers opposed by the men be replaced by others and that authority in ships be restored before he took the fleet to sea. He graciously accepted the diplomatic mediating mission of Howe, through whose reassurances the mutiny was finally settled by 15 May. The delegates expressed to Bridport their gratitude for his 'open and generous manner' and for the 'humanity' with which he employed his authority. Their letters of thanks were retained in his personal papers.

Bridport did not arouse similar feelings either at the Admiralty or with some of his officers. Since mid-March 1797 Spencer had maintained the need to keep a more strict and systematic watch on the port of Brest. To more closely co-ordinate Falmouth-based frigate squadrons (hitherto reporting directly to the Admiralty) with the battle fleet operating from Spithead, in May 1797 the frigate squadron commanders, Sir John Borlase Warren and Sir

Edward Pellew, were placed directly under Bridport's command. Both resented their loss of independence and found relations with Bridport difficult. At the same time, despite having the command of more frigates, Bridport denied being able to keep Brest under close watch, especially in easterly winds which drove blockading ships off shore while permitting the French to pass through the narrow neck of Brest harbour. He also wished to grant favoured captains cruising voyages within the limits of his command as a reward for past services while the Admiralty, short of ships and having to ration both frigates and ships of the line within every command, wished to understand and specify precisely the stations ships would fill, and have their captains keep those stations with absolute regularity. On other matters, such as officer appointments, the Board of Admiralty did what it could to satisfy him. But Bridport's dissatisfaction was by now accepted as characteristic: hence the secretary of the Admiralty observed in September 1797 he 'ought to be pleased, though he is never likely to be so' (Sir Evan Nepean to Spencer, 11 Sept 1797, BL, Althorp papers).

Bridport became more reconciled to more strict Admiralty control after March 1798 when discontent in Ireland and mass manning of ships in Brest appeared extremely threatening. Nevertheless he did not refrain from complaint at losses of ships to other stations or deficiencies of flag officers. While short of ships, he denied an ability to defend convoys passing through the mouth of the channel while also blockading Brest. Undoubtedly after May 1798 he felt the strain of having to maintain station off Ushant. His correspondence with the Admiralty became acrimonious; he had a reputation at the Admiralty for putting 'a stronger and unfavourable construction on some things than they were meant to convey' (Bridport to unknown Admiralty commissioner, 2 July 1798, BL, Add. MS 35199). In the event, the blockade failed to prevent French ships sailing for Ireland from Rochefort in August and from Brest in September. Moreover, though seven of the nine vessels that escaped from Brest were captured, the credit did not fall to Bridport, most being taken by ships under the commander-in-chief on the Irish coast. A third expedition sailed from Rochefort in October but, on learning the fate of its predecessors, it returned safely into Rochefort.

Through winter 1798–9 the blockade was reduced to squadrons, occasionally even fewer ships, and Bridport remained on shore. He returned to sail from Spithead on 13 April 1799 and was off Ushant when, under the cover of fog, Vice-Admiral Eustache Bruix with eighteen ships of the line slipped out of Brest, was reinforced from Lorient, and sailed for the Mediterranean. The threat of the loose fleet was momentarily exacerbated by an obvious *ruse de guerre* contained in messages captured on 27 April on the French lugger *Black Joke*. By now elaborate instructions were in place for the defence of Ireland, while reinforcements were sent to the Mediterranean. Yet it was not until 10 May that the Admiralty knew for certain that Bruix had gone south. He did little harm in the Mediterranean, but was able to unite with his fleet Spanish squadrons from both Cartagena and Cadiz which in July returned north. After leave on shore Bridport took station off Brest but could not prevent the re-entry of an enemy fleet of forty ships of the line.

During autumn 1799 Bridport presided over thirty-two ships of the line off Brest; in March 1800 he was directed to keep twenty-eight always with him. Inshore the blockade by frigates focused as much on preventing the entry of stores as on the departure of warships. With the necessity to maintain the largest possible Channel Fleet at sea, the emphasis in maintenance and victualling had shifted from Portsmouth to Plymouth. Special efforts were made to improve victualling arrangements, especially to the fleet anchorage in Torbay. These included the provision of fresh vegetables and lemon juice, issued since 1796, to deter scurvy. The disease was not entirely beaten. Because lemon juice was still issued only as a cure, scurvy continued to break out, as much a psychological worry for fleet commanders as a physical problem.

In April 1800 severe weather drove Bridport into Torbay and he took the opportunity to strike his flag for the final time. He was by then seventy-three and had for some time been feeling frail. He nevertheless lived until 2 May 1814. He was still not favoured by George III, but in justice was honoured by his advancement in 1800 to the dignity of viscount in the peerage of Great Britain. His titles in the peerage of Great Britain became extinct at his death, but his Irish barony descended to his great-nephew.

ROGER MORRISS

Sources D. Hood, *The Admirals Hood* [n.d.] · R. Morriss, *The channel fleet and the blockade of Brest*, Navy Records Society (2001) · W. James, *The naval history of Great Britain, from the declaration of war by France in 1793, to the accession of George IV*, [5th edn], 6 vols. (1859–60) · *The later correspondence of George III*, ed. A. Aspinall, 5 vols. (1962–70), vol. 2 · BL, Althorp papers · BL, Bridport papers, Add. MSS 34933, 35194–35210 · PRO, admiralty in-letters, ADM 1 · PRO, admiralty out-letters, ADM 2 · M. M. L. Wyndham, *Chronicles of the eighteenth century: founded on the correspondence of Sir Thomas Lyttelton and his family*, 2 vols. (1924)
Archives BL, corresp. and MSS, Add. MSS 35191–35202 · NMM, corresp. and MSS | BL, MSS of George Spencer, second Earl Spencer, first lord of the admiralty [uncatalogued] · CKS, letters to William Pitt · Devon RO, corresp. with Viscount Sidmouth · PRO, letters to William Pitt and Lord and Lady Chatham, 30/8
Likenesses J. Reynolds, oils, 1763, NMM [*see illus.*] · L. F. Abbott, oils, 1795, NMM; sketch, NMM · J. R. Jackson, mezzotint, pubd 1867 (after J. Reynolds), BM, NPG · J. Reynolds, portrait, exh. South Kensington 1867; formerly in possession of Lord Hood, 1891 · L. F. Abbott, oils, NPG · attrib. M. Brown, chalk drawing, Scot. NPG · K. A. Hickel, group portrait, oils (*The House of Commons, 1793*), NPG

Hood, Alexander (1758–1798), naval officer, was born on 23 April 1758 at Netherbury, Dorset, the second son of Samuel Hood (*fl.* 1720–1780) of Kingsland, Dorset, and Anne (*d.* 1775), daughter of James Bere of Westbury, Wiltshire. His father was a purser in the navy and first cousin of Samuel Hood, Viscount Hood, and of Alexander Hood, Viscount Bridport. His elder brother, Arthur, also served in the navy, and was lost in the sloop *Pomona* in August 1776. His younger brother was Sir Samuel *Hood, baronet, naval officer. Alexander's entry into the navy is a matter of uncertainty, as an Alexander Hood appears on the books of two ships simultaneously, namely the *Romney*, carrying his cousin Samuel's broad pendant on the North American station, between 15 April 1767 and 9 November 1770, and the yacht *Katharine*, commanded by his father, from 4 July 1768 to 4 March 1772. Although the *Dictionary of National Biography* places him in the *Romney*, it is not known by what authority, as his passing certificate for lieutenant mentions only the yacht, from which he was discharged into the *Resolution* (Captain James Cook) for the latter's second voyage of exploration.

In 1776 Hood went to North America under the patronage of Lord Howe, by whom he was promoted lieutenant in the *Raisonable* on 18 July 1777. In March 1780 he was appointed to command the cutter *Ranger*, which in the early part of 1781 was sent to the West Indies, where Sir George Rodney gave him the rank of commander on 17 May 1781. On 27 July he was appointed to the *Barfleur* as flag-captain to his cousin Sir Samuel Hood, then in temporary command of the station. As captain of the *Barfleur* he took part in the action off Cape Henry on 5 September 1781, and again in that at St Kitts on 25–6 January 1782. A few days later he was appointed to the frigate *Champion*, one of the repeating ships in the actions off Dominica on 9 and 12 April, specially attached to the Red squadron under Sir Samuel Hood, with whom she was afterwards sent to the Mona passage; there she had the fortune to capture the corvette *Cérès*, with whose captain, the baron de Parois, a nephew of the comte de Vaudreuil, Alexander Hood became very friendly. On the arrival of the squadron at Port Royal he was moved into the *Aimable*, another of the prizes, which he took to England in the summer of 1783. He then visited France at the invitation of the comte de Vaudreuil. In 1790–92 and again in 1793 he commanded the frigate *Hebe* in the channel, and in the following year he was appointed to the *Audacious*, but was compelled by ill health to leave her. He was unable to resume active service until February 1797, when he was appointed to the *Mars* (74 guns), attached to the Channel Fleet, then commanded by Lord Bridport. He experienced the mutinies at Spithead and St Helens, and was one of the captains sent on shore by the mutineers on 11 May. In the following spring the *Mars* was with the fleet off Brest, and late on the morning of 21 April 1798, in company with the other ships of the inshore squadron, the *Ramillies* and the *Jason*, discovered a French ship, the *Hercule* (74 guns), making for the harbour. About 9 p.m. the *Mars*, by herself, found the *Hercule* at anchor off the Pointe du Raz, waiting for the tide to turn. The darkness and the strength of the current prevented any attempt at manoeuvring. After an interchange of broadsides the *Mars* fell alongside the *Hercule* with the effect that the anchors at the bows became hooked together with the two ships touching, and the guns, which could not be run out, were fired in many cases from inboard. Such conditions led to the *Hercule*'s losing 315 men killed or wounded and with her guns dismounted she struck her colours. Casualties on the *Mars*, a similarly sized but older ship, totalled no more than ninety. Early in the action Hood had been shot in the thigh by a musket-bullet which cut the femoral artery. He was carried below,

and expired just as the sword of the French captain, who also died later, was placed in his hand. Hood's body was taken to England, and buried in the churchyard of Butleigh, Somerset, beneath a monument erected by his widow, Elizabeth, daughter of John Periam of Butleigh. Although Hood undoubtedly benefited by his family connections, and he also showed some signs of being excessively strict, which resulted in his being put ashore in 1797, examples of his consideration also exist, and he was clearly an officer of ability and good powers of leadership.

His will, leaving all to his wife, was made after he received his fatal wound, and gives no indication of his financial position. He was survived by their two children, of whom Alexander (*d.* 1851) succeeded to the baronetcy conferred on his uncle Sir Samuel Hood; his children in turn included Sir Arthur William Acland *Hood, naval officer. J. K. LAUGHTON, *rev.* A. W. H. PEARSALL

Sources The private papers of John, earl of Sandwich, ed. G. R. Barnes and J. H. Owen, 4, Navy RS, 78 (1938), 154, 262 • *Private papers of George, second Earl Spencer*, ed. J. S. Corbett and H. W. Richmond, 2, Navy RS, 48 (1924), 126, 163–8, 486 • W. H. Dillon, *A narrative of my professional adventures (1790–1839)*, ed. M. A. Lewis, 2 vols., Navy RS, 93, 97 (1953–6) • J. Ralfe, *The naval biography of Great Britain*, 4 vols. (1828) • W. James, *The naval history of Great Britain, from the declaration of war by France in 1793 to the accession of George IV*, [7th edn], 6 vols. (1886) • PRO, ADM 107/6, 343 • PRO, ADM 36/8426, 7847–9 • Burke, *Peerage* (1967)
Archives NMM, corresp. and papers • PRO • Som. ARS, naval corresp. and papers
Likenesses oils (after portrait, *c.*1790), NMM

Hood, Sir Alexander (1888–1980), army medical officer and colonial governor, was born on 25 September 1888 at 68 Easter Road, Leith, Edinburgh, the son of Alexander Hood, clerk, and his wife, Agnes Marshall, *née* Cunningham. He was educated at George Watson's College, Edinburgh, and in 1910 graduated MB, ChB, from the medical school of the University of Edinburgh. He was awarded his MD in 1931. In 1912 he was commissioned into the Royal Army Medical Corps as a lieutenant. He achieved rapid promotion, especially for the time, by being made a captain after just three years. In India by 1914, he was quickly returned to France where he spent the opening two years of the First World War. He then returned to India and over the next five years served on the north-west frontier and in Afghanistan. Staff duties returned him for two years to the newly formed British army of the Rhine, in which he served from 1922 to 1924. His main interest was pathology, and the next five years back in India allowed him to develop this. He was graded as a specialist in pathology in 1924, serving in military hospitals in Meerut and Bangalore before undertaking staff duties as deputy assistant district pathologist for the Madras region. He returned as assistant district pathologist, southern command, in 1929—his first home posting since being commissioned seventeen years before.

During the next decade Hood served in Aldershot, Hampshire, and the Middle East, as he alternated between

Sir Alexander Hood (1888–1980), by Bassano, 1946

staff and clinical pathology posts. The outbreak of the Second World War saw him achieve the rank of colonel and deputy director of medical services, Palestine. Within a year he was made deputy director of medical services for the British expeditionary force in France and had been mentioned in dispatches three times. In less than a year he had also held the rank of acting brigadier three times. His reward was an increase in staff work and, in March 1941, the post of deputy director-general, Army Medical Services at the War Office, this time with the rank of temporary brigadier. By August of that year he was confirmed as director-general with the rank of lieutenant-general and honorary physician to George VI. This rapid promotion was most unusual, and he remained professional head of the military medical services until 1948—double the usual time. The significance of Hood's contribution was such that on retirement he was appointed governor and commander-in-chief, Bermuda, a unique appointment for a doctor. His duties were twice extended and he served until 1955. This covered the withdrawal of troops in 1953 from what had been a garrison since 1701.

Hood was married twice: first to Evelyn Dulcia, daughter of George Ellwood of Kensington, London, and second to Mrs Helen Winifred Wilkinson of Hamilton, Bermuda. He died in Bermuda on 11 September 1980. His service with the Royal Army Medical Corps was commemorated at the training depot by the naming in his honour of the foremost lecture theatre, which was opened shortly after his death. Hood was awarded numerous honorary degrees. He was also appointed knight of the order of Orange Nassau (Netherlands), commander of the Legion of Merit (USA), Belgian order of the crown (commander),

and knight of the order of the White House (Czechoslovakia). He was appointed KCB in 1943 (CB, 1942), GBE in 1946 (CBE, 1939), and KCVO in 1953.

JOHN D. C. BENNETT

Sources R. Drew, *Commissioned officers in the medical services of the British army, 1660–1960*, 2 (1968) · officers' original records, Royal Army Medical Corps, Keogh barracks, Aldershot, Hampshire · *The Times* (15 Sept 1980), 14g · *WWW* · b. cert.
Archives Wellcome L., autobiography and papers
Likenesses Bassano, photograph, 1946, NPG [*see illus.*] · portrait, Royal Army Medical Corps, Millbank, London

Hood, Arthur William Acland, Baron Hood of Avalon (1824–1901), naval officer, born at Bath on 14 July 1824, was the second son of Sir Alexander Hood, second baronet (1793–1851), and his wife, Amelia Anne, youngest daughter and coheir of Sir Hugh Bateman, baronet, of Hartlington Hall, Derbyshire. Alexander *Hood (1758–1798) was his grandfather. Entering the navy in 1836, he served on the north coast of Spain, and on the coast of Syria at the capture of Acre. In January 1846 he was promoted lieutenant of the *President*, on the Cape station, from which he was paid off in 1849. In 1850 he was appointed to the *Arethusa*, and in the channel, the Mediterranean, the Black Sea, and ashore in the Crimea before Sevastopol, remained attached to her for nearly five years. On 27 November 1854 he was promoted commander, for service with the naval brigade. Hood married on 2 October 1855 Fanny Henrietta (d. 29 Aug 1919), third daughter of Sir Charles Fitzroy Maclean bt; she survived him with two daughters, Emily Isabel and Fanny Sophia.

In 1856 Hood went to China in command of the brig *Acorn*. He was engaged at Fatshan (Foshan) on 1 June 1857, and at the capture of Canton (Guangzhou) on 27–28 December 1857, for which he was promoted captain on 26 February 1858. After nearly five years on shore he was appointed in December 1862 to the *Pylades*, for the North American station, from which in the autumn of 1866 he was ordered home to take command of the *Excellent* and the Royal Naval College, Portsmouth. The *Excellent* was the school of gunnery, and after three years there Hood was appointed director of naval ordnance; he remained for five years, a careful, painstaking, and essentially conservative officer in technology as in politics.

In May 1871 Hood was made a CB; and in 1874 was appointed to the *Monarch* in the Channel Fleet. In March 1876 he became rear-admiral, and from January 1877 to December 1879 was naval lord of the Admiralty and for much of 1879 the effective senior naval lord. He was then appointed to command the Channel Fleet, where he remained until April 1882, becoming vice-admiral in July 1880. In June 1885 he was appointed first naval lord in succession to Sir Astley Cooper Key, being promoted admiral on 1 July 1885, and nominated KCB in December 1885.

As a gunnery officer and technologist Hood appreciated the power of modern artillery, and placed a very high priority on protection. His views remained consistent from the 1871 Admiralty committee on designs to the year he left office. In a period when the size and cost of new ships were arbitrarily constrained he favoured low freeboard turret battleships as the most powerful fighting ships that could be built on a limited displacement. He designed the Nile class of 1885 despite the opposition of the outgoing and incoming directors of naval construction, Nathaniel Barnaby and William White, the latter of whom he had personally brought back to the Admiralty. These ships were highly regarded by naval officers, because they gave priority to protection and firepower. Hood's ideas were still influential in 1889, when one of the Naval Defence Act battleships, the *Hood*, was designed to meet his criteria. At the strategic level Hood has been described as 'an irascible if not a stupid man' (Ranft, 7) on the basis of his evidence to the 1888 select committee on naval estimates. Here Hood and the first lord refused to be drawn on their plans, while Hood was not enamoured of theoretical speculation on a public platform, particularly one set up by Lord Charles Beresford. By contrast, once he was told to prepare for war with France and Russia he drew up the Naval Defence Bill and, with Lord George Hamilton, secured the assent of the prime minister, Lord Salisbury. The restatement of the 'two power standard' was the crowning achievement of his term at the Admiralty, and made him an important architect of the naval revival of the 1890s.

On 11 July 1889, having attained the age limit of sixty-five, Hood was placed on the retired list, and resigned his seat at the Admiralty. In September 1889 he was appointed GCB, and in February 1892 was created Baron Hood of Avalon. He continued to take an active interest in naval affairs, and showed, in occasional letters in *The Times* and in the House of Lords a correct appreciation of the problems of naval supremacy. He resided at 19 Queen's Gate Place, South Kensington, London. He died at Wootton House, Glastonbury, the residence of his nephew, Sir Alexander Hood, fourth baronet, on 16 November 1901, and his peerage became extinct. He was buried at Butleigh, Somerset, on 23 November 1901.

Although a stern man, lacking any touch of humour, Hood was highly regarded by those who served with him. His first lord, Lord George Hamilton, considered him the finest administrator he had ever served with, and relied on him entirely on naval and technical issues. A political Conservative, his reputation suffered from the posthumous criticism of Liberal progressives, beginning with Laughton's memoir in the *Dictionary of National Biography*.

ANDREW LAMBERT

Sources G. Hamilton, *Parliamentary reminiscences and reflections*, 2 vols. (1916–22) • B. M. Ranft, *Technical change and British naval policy, 1860–1939* (1977) • A. J. Marder, *The anatomy of British sea power*, American edn (1940) • R. A. Burt, *British battleships, 1889–1904* (1988) • 'Committee on designs for ships of war', *Parl. papers* (1872), 14.501, C. 477; 14.581, C. 477-I • W. H. Boys, *Memoir of Admiral Henry Boys* (1913) • *Navy List* • *The Times* (18 Nov 1901) • Burke, *Peerage* (1900) • W. L. Clowes, *The Royal Navy: a history from the earliest times to the present*, 7 vols. (1897–1903), vol. 7 • GEC, *Peerage* • DNB • CGPLA *Eng. & Wales* (1902) • P. Smith, 'Ruling the waves: 1885–99', *Government and armed forces in Britain, 1856–1990*, ed. P. Smith (1996)
Archives NMM, corresp. and papers
Likenesses J. S. Hodges, portrait, NMM
Wealth at death £85,355 5s. 9d.: resworn probate, May 1903, CGPLA *Eng. & Wales* (1902)

Hood, Charles (1826–1883), army officer, was educated at the Royal Military College, Sandhurst. He obtained an ensigncy by purchase in the 3rd Buffs on 26 June 1844. In 1846 he was secretary to the mission sent to settle the dispute between Great Britain and France and General Rosa, governor of Buenos Aires. He became lieutenant in the Buffs on 20 November 1846, and captain on 7 November 1851.

Hood arrived in the Crimea in May 1855. He was senior officer of his regiment in the trenches before Sevastopol, and led the ladder party in the attack on the Redan on 8 October 1855, and was wounded. He commanded the regiment from 13 September to 27 December 1855, and was at its head when it marched with colours flying into the Korabelnaya suburb after the fall of Sevastopol. He was rewarded with promotion to brevet major (8 January 1856) and with the Mejidiye (fifth class).

After serving as major of the depot battalion at Templemore, Hood became lieutenant-colonel 58th (Rutlandshire) foot on 23 November 1860, and from 1864 to 1874 commanded the regiment in Bengal. He became a major-general on 25 July 1870. On 23 May 1874 he retired on half pay. He was promoted lieutenant-general (retired list) on 1 July 1881. He died at his home, 29 Belsize Road, Hampstead, London, on 8 February 1883.

H. M. CHICHESTER, rev. ALEX MAY

Sources *Army List* • *Hart's Army List* • *FO List* (1847) • C. R. B. Knight, *Historical records of the Buffs, east Kent regiment (3rd foot): 1704–1914*, 2: *1814–1914* (1935) • E. F. Hall, *A short history of the buffs* (1950) • A. R. Traylen, ed., *The Services of Rutland* (Rutland Local History Society, Oakham, 1978) • '58th foot (Rutlandshire foot): typed outline history', NAM • CGPLA *Eng. & Wales* (1883)
Wealth at death £12,074 7s. 7d.: probate, 14 Dec 1883, CGPLA *Eng. & Wales*

Hood, Edwin Paxton (1820–1885), Congregational minister and writer, son of Thomas Hood, an able seaman who had served under Nelson on the *Téméraire*, and a maidservant to Bishop Beilby Porteous's brother, was born in the latter's home, Half Moon Street, Piccadilly, on 24 October 1820. The child was fostered by Mr Simpson, a heraldic painter, and his wife, of Deptford, members of Greenwich Road Tabernacle. Edwin attended Union Chapel, Lewisham, and then Midway Place Chapel, Deptford. He also sat at the feet of Thomas Binney at the King's Weigh House Chapel: here he imbibed the romantic, liberalized theology later conspicuous in his own preaching. He began to lead worship and to lecture on temperance and peace, and in 1840 became a full-time temperance worker. In York in 1847 he met and married Jane Wagstaff (b. 1824/5), who died in childbirth the following year. He was a delegate to the Paris peace conference in 1848. From 1852 to 1857 he was Congregational minister at North Nibley, Gloucestershire: he described this appointment as his 'college training'. In 1853 he married Elizabeth Atkin Barnly (b. 1824/5) of Hull, but she died of consumption two years later. At Nibley he began to write hymns for Sunday school anniversaries, and these rank among his best compositions.

From 1857 to 1862 Hood served at Offord Road Church,

Islington, a new cause which he built up as a thriving middle-class congregation with a strong working-class fringe. In 1857 he married his third wife, Lavinia, daughter of the Revd S. Oughton of Kingston, Jamaica—she outlived him. Offord Road was troubled by a serious burden of debt, and in 1862 he moved to Queen Street, Brighton, where the church had to be enlarged to house his growing congregation. Surprisingly he returned to Offord Road in 1873, even though the surrounding area was deteriorating and the debt problem remained. In 1877 he was called to the prestigious pulpit of Cavendish Street, Manchester. He began badly by fiercely attacking Disraeli's foreign policy from the pulpit. This so divided his flock that his health became impaired and he resigned in 1880, preaching to his supporters for a short time in Hulme town hall. He visited the USA and then for four years pastored the historic Falcon Square Chapel, London, where he seems to have found a peace which had long eluded him.

Hood, a restless, quixotic and inspirational activist, wrote many books, popular biographies, temperance and peace literature, textbooks for young people, and appreciations of his own age. Two of these last are particularly notable: *The Age and its Architects* (1852), in which he famously defines and explores his own times as 'an age of experiment' with an absence of 'all present faith and belief', and *The Throne of Eloquence* (1885), a keenly observed introduction to earlier, but especially Victorian, preachers and preaching. He was for eight years editor of the *Eclectic Review* and for two years edited the *Preachers' Lantern*. He played some part in putting the poetry of Robert Browning on the literary map. The British Library catalogue lists more than sixty of his publications. He was a great friend of, and fund-raiser for, the Hospital for Incurables, but after his death was best known as a hymn writer, particularly for children. He edited *Our Hymn Book* (1862) and *The Children's Choir* (1870). Though a later age found many of his hymns too cloying, some, especially 'I love to think though I am young' and 'God who hath made the daisies', were still being anthologized in the mid-twentieth century.

He took his last services at Falcon Square Chapel on 7 June 1885 and then departed on a tour of Italy; he had reached only Paris when he died on 12 June 1885. He was buried in Abney Park cemetery.

J. M. RIGG, rev. IAN SELLERS

Sources G. H. Giddins, *Edwin Paxton Hood* (1886) · *Congregational Year Book* (1886) · *The Times* (16 June 1885) · *The Times* (5 Feb 1886) · m. certs.
Archives DWL, letters to Henry Allon
Likenesses portrait, repro. in Giddins, *Edwin Paxton Hood*
Wealth at death £1419 0s. 9d.: probate, 18 Aug 1885, CGPLA Eng. & Wales

Hood, Francis Grosvenor (1809–1854), army officer, born on 4 March 1809, was the second son of Lieutenant-Colonel Francis Wheler Hood (1781–1814), son of Henry, second Viscount Hood. His mother was Caroline (d. 11 March 1858), only daughter of Sir Andrew Snape *Hamond. His father was killed in action in his thirty-third year, on the heights of Aire in France, on 2 March

1814, and was, in the words of Wellington, 'an officer of great promise and merit' (*Despatches*, ed. J. Gurwood, 7, 1837, 346; *GM*, 1st ser., 84/1, 1814, 413, 492). Francis joined the Grenadier Guards in 1827, was promoted to his lieutenancy and captaincy in 1830, became captain and lieutenant-colonel on 31 December 1841, and on 27 June 1854 was gazetted major of the 3rd battalion. He married on 8 September 1842 his first cousin, Elizabeth Jane (d. 15 Jan 1910), second daughter of Sir Graham Eden *Hamond; they had no children.

Hood went with the 3rd battalion to the Crimea, and led it at the battle of the Alma on 20 September 1854, when his bravery and judgement contributed to the defeat of the Russian counter-attack, and he received the special thanks of Lord Raglan. On 18 October 1854 he was in command of the covering party guarding the trenches and guns before Sevastopol, and was killed by a Russian roundshot. Lord Raglan, in his dispatch of 23 October, described Hood as an excellent officer, and wrote that he was 'deeply lamented'.   [ANON.], rev. JAMES FALKNER

Sources *Army List* · *GM*, 2nd ser., 43 (1855), 83–4 · *Hart's Army List* · F. W. Hamilton, *The origin and history of the first or grenadier guards*, 3 (1874), 206 · P. Young and H. Harris, *The Alma* (1971) · A. W. Kinglake, *The invasion of the Crimea*, 8 vols. (1863–87), vols. 3, 4 · Boase, *Mod. Eng. biog.* · Burke, *Peerage*
Archives NAM, military papers

Hood, Henry (*fl.* 1777–1811). *See under* Hood, John (c.1721–1784).

Hood, Sir Horace Lambert Alexander (1870–1916), naval officer, was born at 40 South Street, London, on 2 October 1870, the third of five sons of Francis Wheler Hood, fourth Viscount Hood (1838–1907), and his wife, Edith (d. 1911), daughter of Arthur W. Ward, of Tunbridge Wells. He was a descendant of Samuel, first Viscount Hood, whose younger brother was Alexander Hood, first Viscount Bridport—names famous in British naval history. He joined the *Britannia* as a naval cadet at the age of twelve, and left her, after the customary two years' training, with the highest classes obtainable in all subjects. He served in the *Temeraire*, of the Mediterranean squadron, from September 1885 to June 1886, then in the *Minotaur* until January 1887, when he joined the *Calliope*, and in her was present at Samoa in the hurricane of 16 March 1889. In the examinations for his promotion to lieutenant in 1890 he set what was then a record of 4398 out of a possible 4600 marks. He has been described as 'the beau ideal of a naval officer, spirited in manner, lively of mind, enterprising, courageous, handsome, and youthful in appearance ... His lineage was pure Royal Navy, at its most gallant' (Hough, 241).

Hood had a year's service in the *Trafalgar* (June 1891 – September 1892), and then spent three years ashore studying gunnery and acting as a staff officer; he next served successively in the *Royal Sovereign*, *Wildfire*, *Sanspareil*, and *Cambrian*. In June 1897 he was lent to the Egyptian government for the Nile campaign, where he had his first experience of active service, in command of a river gunboat. He was present at the battles of the Atbara and Omdurman, and at the end of the campaign was promoted to commander (1898). On the outbreak of the Second South African

Sir Horace Lambert Alexander Hood (1870–1916), by unknown photographer

War he was employed for three months on transport duties. After serving as commander (1900–03) of the *Ramillies*, flagship of Lord Charles Beresford, second in command in the Mediterranean, he was promoted captain, and in July 1903 was appointed to the *Hyacinth*, flagship of Rear-Admiral G. L. Atkinson-Willes in the East Indies. He led the force sent against the Dervishes at Illig, Somaliland, in April 1904, when 627 officers and men of the *Hyacinth*, *Fox*, and *Mohawk*, with a detachment of 127 men of the Hampshire regiment, dislodged the Dervishes after landing in a heavy surf in the dark. He took a prominent part in the hand-to-hand fighting, and was appointed DSO for his services. Hood next commanded the *Berwick* (1906–7) and, after serving one year as naval attaché at Washington, the *Commonwealth* (1908–9). On 19 January 1910 he married Ellen (*d*. 1950), daughter of A. E. Touzalin and widow of George Nickerson, of Dedham, Massachusetts. They had two sons.

After commanding the Royal Naval College at Osborne from October 1910 to January 1913, Hood was promoted to rear-admiral (May 1913) and hoisted his flag on board the *Centurion* for three months. In June 1914 he became naval secretary to the first lord of the Admiralty, Winston Churchill.

In October 1914 Hood was placed in command of a small naval force assisting the British and Belgian armies in stemming the German advance towards the channel ports. In May 1915 he took command of the 3rd battle-cruiser squadron of the Grand Fleet, with his flag on board the *Invincible*.

On 30 May 1916 Hood's squadron sailed with the main body of the fleet from Scapa Flow, and on the 31st, during the preliminaries of the battle of Jutland, was stationed 25 miles ahead of the battle fleet. When news arrived at 3.40 p.m. that Admiral Beatty's cruiser squadron was engaged, Hood was detached to the east-south-eastward at full speed to support. Two hours later he came into action in support of the light cruiser *Chester*, which, hard pressed by Rear-Admiral Boedicker's second scouting group (light cruisers), was retiring under heavy fire to the westward. Hood, hearing the gunfire to the north-west, turned towards it. His appearance surprised Boedicker, who, abandoning chase of the *Chester*, gave his commander-in-chief, Admiral Scheer, information by wireless that the British main body was to the north-eastward. At the same time, Vice-Admiral Hipper, with the German battle cruisers, believing himself headed by the whole British fleet, turned south-west to rejoin his own battleships. This was a decisive moment in the battle, and it has been said that by his intervention 'Hood was the magician that pulled off the trick' that prevented the near destruction of the British fleet (Hough, 243). Hood found Beatty's squadron, and turned to form the vanguard of the Battle-Cruiser Fleet. Within a few minutes he was closely engaged with Hipper's battle cruisers, now coming up again from the southward.

After about ten minutes of battle, in which the flagship had been hit several times, Hood called to his gunnery officers: 'Your fire is very good. Keep at it as quickly as you can; every shot is telling' (Hough, 246). Five minutes later (6.34 p.m.) a shell from the *Derfflinger* burst in the *Invincible*'s 'Q' turret. The flash went down to the magazine, which immediately exploded, and the ship, breaking in half, sank in a cloud of smoke, leaving her bow and stern standing out of the water to mark where she lay. Hood, and all his ship's company save six, perished.

In Hood the navy lost an officer of exceptional quality. A remarkable seaman and 'one of the best brains in the service' (Marder, 3.40), Arthur Marder has suggested that 'had he lived he would have been practically certain of reaching the rank of Admiral of the Fleet' (ibid., 3.99). He was posthumously appointed KCB.

H. W. RICHMOND, *rev*. MARC BRODIE

Sources *The Times* (5 June 1916) · Burke, *Peerage* (1980) · R. Hough, *The great war at sea, 1914–1918* (1986) · A. J. Marder, *From the Dreadnought to Scapa Flow: the Royal Navy in the Fisher era, 1904–1919*, 5 vols. (1961–70) · *WWW* · *CGPLA Eng. & Wales* (1916) · personal knowledge (1927)

Archives CAC Cam., papers | NMM, corresp. with Sir Julian S. Corbett

Likenesses A. S. Cope, group portrait, oils, 1921 (*Naval officers of World War I, 1914–1918*), NPG · photograph, repro. in Hough, *Great war at sea*, pl. 13 [*see illus.*]

Wealth at death £7681 7*s*. 0*d*.: probate, 17 Nov 1916, *CGPLA Eng. & Wales*

Hood, John (*c*.1721–1784), land surveyor, was born at Moyle, co. Donegal. He was the first known in a family of land surveyors active in the north-west of Ireland in the eighteenth and early nineteenth centuries. In 1772 he published in Dublin his *Table of Difference of Latitude and Departure for Navigators, Land Surveyors, &c.*, which he had 'compiled at the insistence of the Dublin Society' (title-page). In it he also gives an account of the diurnal variation of the compass needle and its correction following the work of a 'Mr Anderson' and a description of his new combined theodolite and compass, known as Hood's compass theodolite, which was sold by Edward Spicer and James Lynch, both instrument makers of Dublin. This is the earliest known description of such an instrument. Hood is also said to have anticipated the invention of Hadley's quadrant, but he took out no patents. In the *Proceedings of the Dublin Society* (1777) he advocated the use of a chain of 1/100th of an Irish mile. He died in 1784.

John Hood had at least one son, **John Hood** (*fl.* 1768–1803), land surveyor, to whom Bendall attributes the publication and instrument which others have ascribed to the father. Two other land surveyors, the brothers **Henry Hood** (*fl.* 1777–1811) and **Matthew Hood** (*fl.* 1800–1804) were contemporaries of John the younger and may also have been his brothers, and therefore John the elder's sons. All produced estate maps, of which several are extant in collections in Ireland and Britain. Henry was in the 1790s employed by the first marquess of Abercorn, whose agent considered that he spent too much time studying and was too diffident and abstemious. Henry and John the younger developed a complex system of land classification for recording the type and quality of land they surveyed. The family was noted for the high quality of its work but did not achieve prosperity thereby: Matthew noted that even so successful a surveyor as his brother Henry had only one instrument. Matthew was a farm manager at Baronscourt on the Abercorn estate from October 1796 to May 1806 and his 200 letters to Lord Abercorn, account book, and map of Baronscourt (all at the Public Record Office of Northern Ireland) give a detailed picture of his management of the land.

Samuel Hood (*c.*1800–1875), legal writer, the son of Matthew Hood and Margery Risk, was born in Moyle, co. Donegal, about 1800, emigrated to the USA in 1826, and was called to the bar in Philadelphia. He published a treatise, *On the Law of Decedents* (1847), and wrote, among other works, *A Brief Account of the Society of the Friendly Son of St Patrick* (1844) for the Hibernian Society of Philadelphia. He died at Philadelphia in 1875, survived by three sons and his wife, Ellen Gowen.   ELIZABETH BAIGENT

Sources J. H. Andrews, *Plantation acres: an historical study of the Irish land surveyor* (1985) • PRO NIre., Abercorn MSS • F. W. Steer and others, *Dictionary of land surveyors and local map-makers of Great Britain and Ireland, 1530–1850*, ed. P. Eden, 2nd edn, ed. S. Bendall, 2 vols. (1997) • E. G. R. Taylor, *The mathematical practitioners of Hanoverian England, 1714–1840* (1966) • G. R. Crowe, *Maps and their makers* (1953) • private information (2004) [S. Bendall, J. Andrews] • DNB • A. J. Webb, *A compendium of Irish biography* (1878) • Allibone, *Dict.*

Hood, John (*fl.* 1768–1803). *See under* Hood, John (*c.*1721–1784).

Hood, Matthew (*fl.* 1800–1804). *See under* Hood, John (*c.*1721–1784).

Hood, Robin (*supp. fl.* late 12th–13th cent.), legendary outlaw hero, is wellnigh impossible to identify, first because of the sparsity and peculiar nature of the evidence, and second because Robin quickly became a composite figure of an archetypal criminal, and then an outlaw hero.

Historical foundation Only three early writers attempted to place Robin in a historical context. Andrew Wyntoun, who by 1420 had completed a rhyming chronicle of Scotland up to 1408, referred to Robin Hood and Little John under the years 1283–5. In the 1440s Walter Bower inserted a notice of Robin Hood and Little John into his continuation of Fordun's *Scotichronicon* under the year 1266. Then in 1521, in his *Historia majoris Britanniae*, John Mair assigned Robin and Little John to the years of Richard I's captivity in Germany, 1193–4. All three writers were Scots. On this matter they are independent of one another. Their sources for these statements are unknown. They were not copied by English historians, and no medieval English historian made any such attempt to identify Robin Hood. Of the three, John Mair's date is the best. This is because Robin Hood, in all probability, was already a legendary criminal by 1261–2.

The earliest indication of the legend is to be found in the surname Robinhood and its variants (Rabunhod, Robehod, and so on), which first appear in the late thirteenth century. Some eight examples, widely scattered, have so far been discovered. Such a name formation is rare, and the most likely explanation of it is that one so called, or those who gave him the name, knew something of the legend of Robin Hood. The earliest example, coming from Berkshire in 1261–2, is crucial. It begins with an entry on the king's remembrancer's memoranda roll of Easter 1262 which notes a pardon of a penalty imposed on the prior of Sandleford for seizing without warrant the chattels of William Robehod, fugitive. The same case occurs on the roll of the justices on eyre in Berkshire in 1261, which records the indictment and outlawry of a criminal gang suspected of robberies and the harbouring of robbers. The gang included one William, son of Robert le Fevre (Smith), whose chattels had been seized by the prior of Sandleford. Without any doubt William Robehod of the memoranda roll and William, son of Robert le Fevre, of the plea roll were one and the same person. Someone along the administrative channel from the justices on eyre to the king's remembrancer changed the name. He probably did so because William, son of Robert, had Robert in his name and was a member of an outlaw gang. So he became William Robehod. It follows that whoever changed the name knew of Robin as an exemplary outlaw.

The discovery of this evidence by Dr David Crook in 1984 was decisive. The original Robin Hood, if such there was, must have lived before 1261 and probably some considerable time before, sufficient at any rate to generate this kind of fame. This gives some credence to John Mair's date. It is further supported by the appearance of a Robert Hod, fugitive, who failed to appear before the justices at the York assizes in 1225 and whose chattels, worth 32s. 6d., were accordingly forfeit at the account of the exchequer in Michaelmas 1226. Finally, and much later, Thomas Gale, dean of York (1697–1702), left among his papers a note of an epitaph which recorded that Robin died on 24 Kalends December 1247. This is late evidence, and there is no such date in the Roman calendar; yet the interval between 1225 and 1247 exactly matches the final twenty-two years of his life which, in legend, Robin spent in the greenwood. So, in a somewhat tendentious reconstruction, a shadowy biography emerges: Robin was an active outlaw in 1193–4, outlawed again in 1225, dead in 1247, and already a legendary figure by 1261–2. In that outline the dates 1225 and 1261–2 are firm; and this Robert Hod is the only possible original who is known to have been an outlaw. There is even a hint that he became legendary: when the account for his chattels was repeated in 1227 he was recorded as 'Hobbehod'. The only other morsel of information is that the account was due from the liberty of St Peter's; Robert Hod must accordingly have been a tenant of the archbishopric of York.

However, what the evidence of 1261–2 gives with one hand it takes away with the other. Certainly it provides a *terminus ante quem* for a prototype Robin Hood. Yet it also demonstrates how Robin Hoods were made. If William, son of Robert le Fevre, could become a Robin Hood, so could others. In the case of Robert Hod of 1226–7 the real name and nickname coincided; it is the only case where this is certainly so, and he could well have started the legend. But in many other cases criminals could have used or attracted the nickname without its leaving any trace of itself in the record of their crimes. It is only through luck that the flash of illumination from the case of William, son of Robert le Fevre exists. So it could well be, and almost certainly was, that the legend as it is now originated in multiple Robin Hoods, a composite person embodying real people and real incidents all brought together under the umbrella of a single persona. There were other outlaws with other names—some real, some legendary. This one snowballed, absorbing other legends and continuing to gather new material down to the present day.

Early tales of Robin Hood In this context the evidence from 1261–2 ceases to be a touchstone. Instead scholars have attempted to match real incidents and real people with the legend of Robin Hood as it first appeared in written form in the fifteenth century. The first tales to survive in manuscript come from about 1450. 'Robin Hood and the Monk', found in a manuscript collection that includes a prayer against thieves and robbers, is a thriller, a story of treachery and revenge. Robin is betrayed to the sheriff by a knavish monk while at worship in the church of St Mary, Nottingham. He is then rescued from Nottingham Castle by Little John and the rest of the gang. 'Robin Hood and the Potter', part of a manuscript collection of romances and moralistic pieces probably written shortly after 1503, is by contrast a burlesque. Robin, after challenging and fighting a travelling potter, takes the potter's dress and wares in order to inveigle his way into Nottingham Castle and lure the sheriff to the outlaw lair in Sherwood. The *Gest of Robyn Hode*, assembled in the fifteenth century,

most probably after 1450, is a collection of tales then current, which it presents as an integrated *geste* in a roughly constructed chronological sequence. It attracted the attention of the early printers, in no fewer than five editions produced between the last years of the fifteenth century and the middle of the sixteenth century. It is in effect a minstrel's serial, designed to be recited at intervals. It includes what is perhaps the earliest story of all, the tale of the impoverished knight. In this story, Robin assists a knight who has mortgaged his lands to the abbot of St Mary's, York, by robbing the monks themselves to repay the loan. The knight later becomes Sir Richard of the Lee who fortifies his castle to protect Robin and his men from the vengeful sheriff. The *Gest* includes much else, including two archery contests held in Nottingham, also an encounter between the king and Robin in Sherwood, and a summary tale of Robin's death at Kirklees Priory in the West Riding of Yorkshire, which was later amplified in a seventeenth-century version. The main setting of the *Gest* is Wentbridge and Barnsdale (West Riding), but it is partly obscured by the intrusion of a tale of Little John and the sheriff of Nottingham, and by the setting of the meeting of Robin and the king in Sherwood. The canon is completed by a separate tale, 'Robin Hood and Guy of Gisborne', which is the story of a medieval bounty hunter whom Robin defeats and kills. This also is set in Barnsdale. Its early date is confirmed by a dramatic fragment of *c*.1475 which covers much the same ground.

Together these tales make up the authentic medieval legend. The *Gest* is much the largest and most important item, a long poem of 456 four-line stanzas. The thematic material of the *Gest* is generally accepted as coming earlier rather than later in the development of the legend. Partly because of this, it is primarily in the *Gest* that scholars have sought to find the traces of real people. However, 200 years, and more, separated the composition of the *Gest* from the William Robehod of 1261–2, and very little is known of the development of the legend in that interval. The only landmark is William Langland who, in 1377, had Sloth declare that he could recite rhymes of Robin Hood and Ranulf, earl of Chester. That remains the earliest literary reference. So the search for real individuals is made more difficult by the total ignorance of when and how the surviving tales were generated. There is only one point of certainty. In the *Gest* the king has no other name but Edward. In 1852 Joseph Hunter established that the circuit of 'Edward our comely king' through the royal forests of Yorkshire and Lancashire and thence to Nottingham, as described in the *Gest*, fitted only one royal progress, namely that of Edward II between April and November 1323. Nothing that has been discovered since has disturbed Hunter's conclusion. This part of the *Gest* is based on Edward II's journey and must have been composed after 1323. It may, nevertheless, be intrusive.

The search for authenticity It is within these parameters that the search for real people has been carried out. It has yielded some real probabilities, some possible candidates, one disappointing rejection in which for a time great confidence was placed, and a rag-bag of assertive speculations which do not merit serious consideration. The first concerns Eustace of Lowdham, who acted as sheriff or deputy in Yorkshire and Nottinghamshire at various times between 1217 and 1233. He combined in these offices the two geographic locations of the Robin tales. In this respect he fits the bill of the legendary sheriff; he is one of the few sheriffs to do so. In 1225, as sheriff of Yorkshire, he was instructed to seek, take, and behead one Robert of Wetherby as an outlaw and evil-doer. Robert was quickly caught and his body suspended in chains, an outlaw at the right time, in the right place, and with the right forename, but by Robin Hood's standards a failure. Yet incidents lying behind these bare records may have contributed to the legend, especially perhaps to the violent tale of Guy of Gisborne. Another possible contributor was Roger Godberd, who led an outlaw gang which terrorized Nottinghamshire, Derbyshire, and Leicestershire in the years after the Montfortian rebellion of 1265. He was pursued by various posses and, after evading capture for many years, ended his days in Newgate Prison in 1276. The final charges against him were that he and other malefactors had robbed an abbey, taking money, stock, and horses, and slain one of the monks (though of Stanley, Wiltshire, not St Mary's, York). Roger gained some protection from a local knight of some prominence named Richard Foliot, who in 1272 was accused of harbouring Godberd and had to surrender his castle of Fenwick and find sureties of good behaviour. Like Sir Richard of the Lee he was a knightly patron of outlaws, and his land lay in the right place: Fenwick is 6 miles or so from Barnsdale, and Foliot also held estates on the eastern bounds of Sherwood. So he too fits the bill. He surrendered his castle; Sir Richard of the Lee fortified and defended his; otherwise their roles are identical, and the coincidence of outlaw and knightly patron is remarkable. A third set of possible originals has been advanced from a later period: Thomas Moulton, abbot of St Mary's, York, 1332–59, as the abbot of the *Gest*; Geoffrey Scrope, chief justice of the king's bench, 1324–38, as the corrupt justice; and John Oxenford, sheriff of Nottingham for most of the years 1334–9, as the vicious sheriff. These are less acceptable. Such strength as the case has depends on the coincidence of the three, and the context does not include an outlaw leader as a possible contributor to Robin.

These suggestions have all arisen since 1955, some since 1980. None of them has gained anything like the acceptance of the hypothesis put forward by Joseph Hunter in 1852. He identified Robin Hood with a Robert Hood of Wakefield, who is well recorded in the rolls of the manor court up to 1317. The crux of his argument was that Robert Hood vanished from the Wakefield records by 1323 (there being no surviving rolls for 1317–23), while a Robyn Hod appeared as one of the porters of the king's chamber in 1324. This seemed to occur at just the right place and moment—at Nottingham, at the end of Edward II's northern progress which matches so exactly the king's journey in the *Gest*, after which Robin made his peace with the king and entered the royal service as a yeoman. This concordance seemed utterly convincing, and it has been

much embroidered, partly by Hunter who advanced the guess that Robert Hood had been outlawed as a supporter of Thomas, earl of Lancaster, who had been defeated at the battle of Boroughbridge in 1322, but mainly by later antiquaries who have compounded their enthusiasm with bad judgement, worse understanding of record, and, on occasion, rank mistranslation of Latin. But it scarcely matters, for Hunter missed crucial evidence which put beyond doubt that Robyn Hode, porter of the chamber, was already in the royal service six months before Edward came to Nottingham. That is sufficient to bring the whole edifice tumbling down. The last heard of the porter is that he retired through incapacity (either of age or health) with a grant of 5s. in November 1324. There were two men, then, not one: Robert Hood of Wakefield and Robyn Hode, porter of the chamber; and there is no evidence that either of them contributed to the legendary Robin.

The development and enrichment of the legend The legend had a life of its own. New personae were constantly absorbed. The early tales contain no Friar Tuck and no Maid Marion. The friar is of special interest because he demonstrates once again how the doings of real people were pressed into service for the story. The original was Robert Stafford, parson of Lindfield, Sussex, who gathered around him a band of evil-doers who committed murders and robberies and threatened the peace of Surrey and Sussex between 1417 and 1429. He assumed the name of Friar Tuck, and puzzled royal officials recorded that he was 'newly so called in common parlance'. By 1475 the friar figured in the first surviving fragment of a Robin Hood play. Maid Marion in contrast was a literary and dramatic figment. She originated in a French pastoral play, *Robin et Marion*, composed c.1283 by Adam de la Halle; she was then taken over in Gower's *Mirour de l'omme* of 1376–9 where she participates in rustic festivals; and by 1500 or shortly afterwards Robin Hood and Marion had come to figure as king and queen of May in the May games. But Marion was by no means the first literary component. Once the story had become an entertainment in the hands of minstrels it was contaminated by other tales. The earliest written versions share analogues and topoi with romances of other outlaw heroes—Hereward the Wake, Eustace the Monk, Fulk Fitzwarine (d. 1256). These all belong to the thirteenth century. All Robin's literary links are with adventures of this kind, all concerned with real men. The argument that he was some kind of woodland sprite, linked with Robin Goodfellow or the Green Man, which originated with Thomas Wright (1846) and culminated in Margaret Murray's *God of the Witches* (1931), is no longer seriously entertained.

One other element is also missing from the earliest versions. All the early notices of Robin treat him as a criminal. In 1433, for the first time, he is described as 'Goodman'. The early written tales contain little if anything of what has become Robin's best-known characteristic, that he robbed the rich to give to the poor. This was foisted on the legend in the sixteenth and seventeenth centuries and was further developed by the radical antiquary Joseph

Ritson in his edition of the tales of 1795. The notion probably originated in the Robin Hood plays. These are first recorded in Exeter in 1425. By the beginning of the sixteenth century they were widespread in southern England as a feature of the spring festival. They were licensed by ecclesiastical authority, and in some centres Robin and his players conducted charitable collections, sometimes far from gently. The churchwardens met the expenses for dress and entertainment and received an account of the collection. In effect, and under licence, Robin was taking from the rich and giving to the poor.

The claim that Robin Hood was of noble birth is derived from Leland, later much expanded in Anthony Munday's *Downfall of Robert Earl of Huntington* (1598). It has no further warrant. In the medieval legend he is a yeoman, nothing else. His association with Saxon resistance to the Normans stems from Sir Walter Scott's *Ivanhoe* (1819) and is equally fictitious. Scott's depiction of Robin of Locksley in this, his most popular novel, ensured Robin's prominence in the age of mass culture. Many plays and popular stories about him appeared in the nineteenth century (though Tennyson's verse play, *The Foresters*, failed disastrously in 1892). The legend lent itself easily to film and television, with *The Adventures of Robin Hood* (1938), starring Errol Flynn, the best of a long series.

Robin Hood was supposedly buried at Kirklees. Nathaniel Johnston in 1665 sketched a grave slab which is now much damaged. As with Little John's supposed grave at Hathersage, no body lies underneath. At Castle Hill near Wentbridge, the most exact of all the locations in the *Gest*, Johnston also sketched a plan of what he took to be a small motte and bailey castle. This has not been excavated.   J. C. HOLT

Sources J. C. Holt, *Robin Hood*, 2nd edn (1989) · R. B. Dobson and J. Taylor, *Rymes of Robyn Hood*, 2nd edn (1979) · D. Crook, 'Some further evidence concerning the dating of the origins of the legend of Robin Hood', *EngHR*, 99 (1984), 530–34 · D. Crook, 'The sheriff of Nottingham and Robin Hood: the genesis of the legend?', *Thirteenth century England: proceedings of the Newcastle upon Tyne conference* [Newcastle upon Tyne 1987], ed. P. R. Coss and S. D. Lloyd, 2 (1988), 59–68 · J. R. Maddicott, 'The birth and setting of the ballads of Robin Hood', *EngHR*, 93 (1978), 276–99 · M. H. Keen, *The outlaws of medieval legend*, 2nd edn (1977) · E. J. Hobsbawm, *Primitive rebels*, 3rd edn (1971) · F. J. Child, *The English and Scottish popular ballads*, 5 vols. (1882–98) · A. Freeman, *Robin Hood, the 'Forresters' manuscript* (1993) · D. Wiles, *The early plays of Robin Hood* (1981) · W. H. Clawson, *The gest of Robin Hood* (1909) · J. H. Gable, *Bibliography of Robin Hood* (1939) · J. Hunter, *Mr. Hunter's Critical and historical tracts*, 4: *The great hero of the ancient minstrelsy of England, Robin Hood* (1852) · S. Knight, *Robin Hood* (1994) · M. Ikegami, 'The language and the date of *A Gest of Robyn Hode*', *Neuphilologische Mitteilungen*, 3/96 (1995), 271–81 · J. Richards, *Swordsmen of the screen* (1977) · S. Knight, ed., *Robin Hood: an anthology of scholarship and criticism* (1999)
Likenesses J. Woodford, statue, 1949, Castle Green, Nottingham

Hood, Samuel, first Viscount Hood (1724–1816), naval officer, born on 12 December 1724 in Butleigh, Somerset, was the eldest son of Samuel Hood (*d.* 1777), vicar of Butleigh and prebendary of Wells, and Mary Hoskins. Both parents came from Dorset, the father being a younger son of Alexander Hood, squire of Mosterton, and the mother a daughter of Richard Hoskins of Beaminster. The sea was

Samuel Hood, first Viscount Hood (1724–1816), by James Northcote, 1784

nowhere in Hood's background. Samuel and his younger brother Alexander *Hood may well have been charmed by Captain Thomas Smith's tales of navy life when he stayed overnight at Butleigh in 1740. Smith is known to have occasionally visited Butleigh Court, the country house of his cousin James Grenville. Alexander went aboard Smith's *Romney* (50 guns) a few months before Samuel, who was entered for pay on 6 May 1741 but must have joined the ship in March before she sailed for Newfoundland. At sixteen he was somewhat older than most boys who aspired to be naval officers and thus had time to become more broadly educated.

Early naval career, 1742–1755 Smith was arguably the best guardian and mentor that a youngster entering the navy could have. Thomas Grenville succeeded Smith as the *Romney*'s captain in 1742 in the Mediterranean, and Hood followed Grenville to the *Guarland* in April 1743. In November Hood was rated a midshipman in the *Sheerness*, under Captain George Bridges Rodney. He moved with Rodney to the *Ludlow Castle*, leaving her on 23 January 1746 for service under Smith who had just been given command of a squadron patrolling the coast of Scotland in consequence of the Jacobite rising of 1745. As commodore, Smith was able to appoint Hood acting lieutenant of the *Winchelsea* (20 guns) on 17 May; the promotion, seconded by her captain, Henry Dyve, was confirmed by the Admiralty a month later.

The ship was ordered from the North Sea to the channel where, during a fierce and ultimately successful action near the Isles of Scilly with the *Subtile* (26 guns), Hood was wounded in the hand. In March 1748 he went on the *Greenwich* (50 guns) under Captain John Montagu, but Smith was quickly able to persuade Rear-Admiral Charles Watson to take Hood as third lieutenant of his flagship, the *Lyon* (60 guns), on a voyage to North America. On her return in November, the *Lyon* was paid off.

While on half pay at Portsmouth Hood married, on 25 August 1749, Susannah Linzee (1726–1806), daughter of Edward Linzee, a prominent surgeon and apothecary who was active in borough politics and frequently held the office of mayor. She was twenty-three and within a year a son was born, named Samuel. Hood plunged into Portsmouth politics with gusto. In October 1750 the infant was elected a junior burgess of the corporation but he died six months later. Hood remained in close touch with Admiral Smith and in January 1753 he was appointed a lieutenant of the guardship *Invincible*, from which he transferred in May to the *Terrible*, also a guardship at Portsmouth. A squadron preparing for the East Indies offered hopes of promotion and Hood was eager to go if he could be placed favourably for filling a vacancy, but a better option arose in early 1754 when his father-in-law got word that the captain of the sloop *Jamaica*, stationed at South Carolina, was 'as far gone as a man can be and alive'. There may have been help from Sir Richard Lyttelton, but it seems clear that Edward Linzee, who went up to London to solicit Lord Anson personally, was the main cause of Hood's gaining the rank of master and commander. Towards the end of June he took passage to Charles Town. Although career advantage may have been in his mind when he married Susannah Linzee, he found, as he confided to Smith, the parting 'very severe. I did not think it would have affected me so much, but I find I love my sweet wench better than I thought for' (Wyndham, 2.102).

Hood arrived in America on 8 August 1754. He had anticipated that South Carolina's warm climate would soothe his intestinal disorders and found that he liked 'the face of the country' and was 'treated with … civility and respect by all the best of the people'; they were 'all prodigiously kind'. Only one thing was missing, he told Smith: 'if Susan should come to me (which I have earnestly desired if no war) I shall then be happy indeed!' (Wyndham, 2.106). He wrote this from Hampton Roads in early May 1755 in company with Commodore Augustus Keppel who had been assisting General Braddock, so he well knew that war with the French was possible; yet his extravagant optimism regarding the upcoming British and colonial operations in North America allowed him to hope that the French might give up. Susan stayed in Portsmouth, and the sloop *Jamaica* was placed under Commodore Charles Holmes. After Hood distinguished himself in an action with a French squadron off Louisbourg on 27 July 1756, Holmes posted him as captain of his flagship *Grafton* (70 guns), not knowing that the Admiralty had already posted Hood for the *Lively* (20 guns).

Post captain, 1756–1780 The *Grafton* came home in late 1756. At thirty-two Hood was not a young captain, yet not too old for good career prospects. Highly regarded by first-rate professional mentors (Smith, Watson, Holmes), he could also look to his father-in-law's influence and his connection through Smith and James Grenville to the 'cousin-hood'—Lytteltons, Grenvilles, and Pitts—who had just moved into high offices of state. Lord Temple (Richard Grenville) was now first lord, and Hood—'no ways inclined to be idle ashore'—wrote that he would be happy to take over temporarily for any captain required ashore for the court martial of Admiral Byng. Consequently in spring 1757 he commanded three ships in rapid succession: the *Torbay* (70 guns), the *Tartar* (35 guns), and the *Antelope* (50 guns). In the last he found an opportunity to prove himself in command when, on 14 May 1757, he espied three sail off Brittany. Pursuing the largest, the *Aquilon* (50 guns), he chased, engaged, and drove her on the rocks in Audierne Bay, where she became a total wreck. A week later he captured a 'small snow' bound from Bordeaux to Canada, and on 25 May a 16-gun privateer. The Admiralty rewarded him on 14 July with permanent command of the *Bideford* (20 guns), attached to Sir Edward Hawke's squadron cruising in the Bay of Biscay.

On 7 February 1758 Hood was given command of the *Vestal* (32 guns); he took part in Hawke's second foray into Basque Roads and the destruction of the fortifications on the Isle of Aix, but during most of the year he cruised the channel approaches between Ushant and Ireland. Early in 1759, on the way out to North America with Commodore Holmes's squadron, Hood encountered off Cape Finisterre (21 February) the French frigate *Bellona*, also carrying 32 guns. He chased and engaged; in a running battle of more than three hours the *Bellona* was devastated and she struck. The *Vestal*, heavily damaged, returned to Portsmouth with her prize; her victorious captain was presented to the king by Lord Anson. After refitting, the *Vestal* patrolled off Le Havre, where an invasion flotilla of flat-bottomed boats had been collected. She formed part of a bombardment squadron that succeeded in destroying them (4 to 6 July 1759). Rodney, who supervised from on board the *Vestal*, gave all credit for positioning the bomb vessels in darkness to Hood and two other officers, the assigned pilots proving useless. By spring 1760 the war in the Atlantic was winding down, and on 30 April Hood asked to be sent to the Mediterranean, mainly, it appears, for genuine reasons of health. 'For ten years past,' he explained, 'I have been afflicted more or less with a bilious disorder, which has been very severe within these nine months as to confine me to my cabin for many days together' (*DNB*). Again he looked for a warmer climate. The *Vestal* carried out Sir Charles Saunders's orders to scour the Spanish coast and then headed for the Levant. Hood was occupied mainly in Mediterranean convoy service until the war ended.

On his return home in 1763 Hood found that his most important naval patrons had died, yet his service reputation was well established and he was soon employed in the privileged position of captain of the guardship *Thunderer* at Portsmouth. In February 1764 he requested leave to take the waters at Bath, and again in September when he asked for two months 'to fortify my stomach against the winter', something to which he felt entitled because he had 'served the whole of the last war, without asking a single day's' absence from duty (PRO, ADM 1/1898, 13 February and 2 Sept 1764). In summer 1765 the ship carried a regiment of foot from Ireland to Halifax. Edward Linzee became mayor of Portsmouth for a fifth time in 1766 and Sir Edward Hawke, the first lord, was one of the borough's MPs; it was not surprising that Hood should be favoured by appointment to the North American station in April 1767 as commander-in-chief.

Hood's base was Halifax and except for the cold climate the assignment promised to be pleasant, quiet, and advantageous (Robert and John Linzee were with him and he secured promotions for both), but it came to be dominated by the storm of protest aroused in Boston by the 'Townshend duties'. Hood sent the *Romney* there in May 1768 but did not go himself until November. He planned to stay only through that winter but remained in Boston until late July 1769. To provide him with enough warships for moving troops, since transports for the purpose could not be hired locally, his authority was extended to encompass the entire Atlantic coast. Initially Hood favoured strict enforcement of the revenue laws, but by February 1769 he had observed the spread of opposition throughout the colonies and was 'apprehensive it will be a task no ways easy to bring America to acknowledge (I mean the assemblies) the Power of Great Britain's Parliament to tax it'. He therefore became 'very circumspect … not to widen, but rather to heal, the unhappy breach' (PRO, ADM 1/483, 27 February and 26 March 1769). Thereafter his dispatches aimed at dissuading the home government from acting provocatively; he did not believe there would be armed rebellion. Later in 1769 Hood was at Halifax supervising improvements to the yard facilities, and he did not return to Boston until ordered there in September 1770; his successor arrived on 10 October.

Hood commanded the guardship *Royal William* at Portsmouth from January 1771 to November 1773. During this time he settled into a country house at Catherington, near Horndean, and rode 10 miles to work. Spending very little time on half pay, he was next appointed to the guardship *Marlborough*. As she was clearing for the dock on 5 July 1776 she suffered a powder explosion that killed almost twenty people (men, women, and children) and wounded fifty. Turned over with officers and crew into the *Courageux* (74 guns), Hood spent most of 1777 at sea, first in raising men, then in cruising to protect trade from Cape Finisterre to the channel. Hood was happy to find that despite her size she chased extremely well and could frighten off American privateers, though he made no captures. Upon returning to port in early February 1778 he accepted a civil appointment as resident commissioner of the navy and governor of the Royal Naval Academy at Portsmouth. He was now fifty-three and thinking about his health, but he accepted the position on condition that it would not preclude an eventual return to active service as a flag officer. Also, by soliciting and obtaining command of the *Courageux* for his unemployed brother, Alexander, he was able to give some continuity to the careers of his followers, one of whom was the earl of Chatham's third son,

whom Lady Chatham had entrusted to his care (James, who died of disease in the West Indies in 1781).

Spring 1778 was a time of feverish mobilization for impending war with France. George III journeyed to Portsmouth in May to witness the preparations and took the occasion to discuss with Hood the entry into the navy of his third son, Prince William. He took notice of Hood's energy in forwarding 'the business of the Dockyard' (*Extracts*, ed. Laughton, 1.225) and forthwith created Hood a baronet. As Sir Samuel, an officer very favourably noticed by the king, he could not help looking at his career from a new perspective. Upon declaration of war with France he wrote to Lord North reminding him that he was still available for sea service, further remarking that he had not politically identified himself with the Pitts and Grenvilles but had instead both publicly and privately supported the government. For whatever reason, he was kept on as commissioner. Two years later, as promotions to rear-admiral were speeding up, he wrote to Lord Sandwich, the first lord, expressing his 'very great desire of hoisting [his] flag and serving in the military line' (*Private Papers of … Sandwich*, 3.161) and claiming that he had accepted the commissionership not out of inclination but to accommodate the government. After some very impatient waiting Hood's plea finally got results. In mid-September 1780 a letter from the Admiralty arrived asking him whether, if there was a promotion of admirals, he would accept his flag and go to the West Indies. Lord Sandwich needed someone to serve as second-in-command to the demanding, irascible Rodney after Hyde Parker, unable to stand him any more, resigned. Faced with a defection of opposition whig officers and the reluctance of others to serve under Rodney, the first lord remembered Hood, who had twice served under Rodney without serious friction.

Amazingly Hood turned the offer down; he cited 'bodily infirmities' so long continued that he was without 'spirits' and would 'only be the shadow of a flag officer'. Two days later, however, he wrote again, rather urgently, saying that he would like to accept; he added: 'a warm climate will tend more towards removing my complaints than any assistance I can get at home' (*Private Papers of … Sandwich*, 3.228–9). Reconsideration of his health prospects may have been linked to news that Edward Linzee was sure to be elected mayor again, making Hood's presence less critical, yet this flag promotion and assignment was the chance of a lifetime, so a third explanation seems more compelling. For more than a year, in the wake of the notorious Keppel–Palliser court martial, Sir Samuel had been striving to rescue the career of his younger brother, who had corrected his ship's log, perhaps legitimately, but in a way that favoured Palliser's accusations. Alexander was castigated for this by the officer corps and the public, and Lord Sandwich found it prudent to turn his back on him. In refusing the offer Hood had asked Sandwich to protect and favour Alexander. No record of a promise from the first lord regarding Alexander survives, but in the extensive promotion of 26 September the brothers were elevated to rear-admiral simultaneously.

West Indies and North America, 1781–1783 As rear-admiral of the blue Hood hoisted his flag in the *Barfleur* (98 guns) and departed with eight of the line and the trade on 19 November to join Rodney in the West Indies. After leading an advanced division in the expedition against St Eustatius in January 1781 he took station to windward of Martinique with eighteen of the line in imminent expectation of an arriving French squadron and convoy. Because Rodney remained at St Eustatius looking after the booty Hood held independent command. Hood was not free to decide where to position his force, however; he chose the windward station, but after five weeks of futile cruising (the French force was much delayed) Rodney ordered him to leeward. Hood repeatedly wrote to try to reverse his chief's decision, knowing that from leeward he would have little chance of preventing the enemy from gaining shelter under Martinique's guns should the escort commander choose to avoid battle. But Rodney held him to leeward. Hood believed that Rodney's main motive was to ensure that the six warships already at Martinique were blockaded, to prevent them from attacking the loot to be transported from St Eustatius.

On the morning of 29 April the French squadron, twenty of the line, came round the southern end of the island, the storeships hugging the shore. Although Hood had got word of their arrival from one of his frigates during the night, his attempt to close was frustrated by the adverse current and very light, sometimes non-existent breezes. Four of the line from Fort Royal joined Admiral de Grasse's already strong squadron. Outnumbered and with crews weakened by lack of refreshment, Hood had to be wary. De Grasse chose not to press an attack, but during a long-range skirmish six of Hood's ships were damaged and he had to retire to Antigua for repairs.

Everyone knew that the battle fleets would go to North America for the hurricane season, but no one on the British side anticipated that de Grasse, co-operating with the American army in a secret plan that required assured naval superiority, would take his entire fleet. Before sailing for home Rodney gave Hood most of the available ships, fourteen of the line. With these Hood left Antigua on 10 August and reached the American coast before de Grasse. Not finding him in the Chesapeake or Delaware bays he went to New York to join the ships of Rear-Admiral Thomas Graves. Clearly, the best course was to attack de Grasse's squadron before seven French warships at Rhode Island could join it; only after vehement remonstrations could Hood persuade Graves of the urgency. Graves, slightly senior to Hood, was in command when the British fleet, numbering nineteen of the line, arrived off the entrance to the Chesapeake on the morning of 5 September 1781. As soon as the tide permitted (around noon), de Grasse began to work his twenty-four of the line out of the bay.

Afterwards Hood claimed that the obvious move would have been for Graves to fall upon the French van speedily, concentrating the entire British line upon it as soon as it came out. This would undoubtedly have been a wise proceeding since the remaining French ships were only slowly getting clear of Cape Henry. But Graves tried to execute an orthodox form of battle and spent hours in manoeuvring to achieve the parallel extended line that he wanted. All the while the French were assembling their superior force, and not until 4.15 p.m. did firing begin. The vans clashed, but most of Graves's line, approaching on an angle, was beyond range. He realized that he must try to bring his whole force into action, but the manoeuvring example set by his flagship in the centre was inadequate (it turned parallel and began firing at too great a distance), and his signals, based on complex and unfamiliar fighting instructions inherited from his predecessor, sowed confusion. Time ran out as sunset ended the battle.

Hood commanded the rear division. His decision to remain in line ahead until the battle was almost over kept the rear entirely out of action and does not cast him in a good light. Granted, he felt constrained by Graves's line ahead signal which, until it was hauled down at 5.30 p.m., seemed to negate (remembering Graves's many signals for dressing the line) the simultaneous signal to engage. The next day Graves issued a clarifying instruction which amounted to admission of a problem. Both admirals knew that when sea battles went awry the burden of censure almost always fell upon an officer who failed to adhere to the discipline of the line. Yet posterity must find it difficult to forgive a man of Hood's temper and energy for allowing tactical confusion to trump a signal for close action, even though little could have been done to hurt a retiring enemy so late in the day. By the end of September it was realized that Lord Cornwallis's situation was desperate and the navy could do nothing to help him.

Hood's record as an admiral had thus far not shown anything commendable. His overblown claim that he was 'conscious of no one omission' in managing his ships prior to or during the action off Martinique (*Private Papers of … Sandwich*, 4.155–9) suggests the opposite. With regard to the battle of the Chesapeake it cannot be assumed that if the chief responsibility had been his, he would have had the quick perception and resolve to attack the French van with an improvised line. (Neither he nor Graves was aware on 5 September of Cornwallis's dire predicament.) When he returned to the Caribbean as a commander-in-chief, however, his actions began to disclose the qualities of leadership for which he is remembered. Even before leaving New York he began to reveal some of them: he persuaded Graves's successor, Rear-Admiral Robert Digby, to release four battleships for Caribbean operations until spring, making the bargain attractive by a generous offer to share all prize money until the ships were returned. In consequence Hood commanded a substantial squadron, and he raised it to a high level of fighting efficiency by exercises on voyage. Although still outnumbered, he was nevertheless confident. 'I will seek and give battle to the Count De Grasse,' he wrote to the Admiralty, 'be his numbers as they may' (*Letters*, ed. Hannay, 62).

This he did. When the French attacked St Kitt's, Hood proceeded with his twenty-two of the line against de Grasse's twenty-nine. His plan, carefully confided to the whole squadron in advance, was to attack the three rear ships of the French line at the Basseterre anchorage in succession. It was frustrated by a collision between his lead battleship and a frigate, enabling de Grasse to stand out to sea, and next morning, 25 January 1782, Hood decided that the best chance to save the island was to seize the anchorage. He made a feint towards the French fleet, drawing it seaward, and then raced towards the anchorage. Belatedly de Grasse sought to thwart him, but Hood sent a frigate ahead to give his van precise instructions for entering and anchoring in succession. The plan provided mutual cover for his divisions and resulted in a tight line sealing Frigate Bay. Thus Hood had interposed his ships between the French fleet and their army ashore. With springs to their cables they could direct their broadsides and de Grasse's attacks were driven off. The British land force, however, even using Hood's marines, was insufficient, and when the Brimstone Hill garrison capitulated Hood knew that the French would bring shore batteries against his squadron, trapping it between them and the French fleet, which now numbered thirty-two. After re-embarking his marines, Hood on 14 February summoned flag officers followed by lieutenants from the whole squadron to his cabin and required them to synchronize their watches by his chronometer. At 11 o'clock that night every ship cut its cable without signal and departed, the enemy remaining unaware until near dawn that the anchorage was empty. This campaign though futile was the making of Hood's reputation, and its daring and superb execution were noted by the French as well. Mahan has described the three-week operation at St Kitt's as 'the most brilliant military effort of the whole war' (Mahan, 470).

Rodney arrived at Barbados with twelve of the line to resume command on 19 February and Hood joined him. Both admirals were aware that de Grasse at Martinique was awaiting a convoy of troops and stores necessary for offensive operations. On 22 March the British squadron numbered thirty-six of the line, and because the French convoy escort was unlikely to number more than fourteen Hood was gratified when Rodney initially placed the fleet (to windward) athwart both the northern and southern approaches. But Rodney changed his mind and ordered a southern concentration. The French convoy, escorted by only three of the line, reached Fort Royal safely by the unguarded northern route. Hood was livid; only a 'madman' in command of the French squadron would have come 'in sight of St Lucia, knowing, as he must, the force of the British fleet, which would naturally be on the lookout' (*Letters*, ed. Hannay, 97).

When de Grasse left Fort Royal for St Domingue with thirty-six of the line escorting a vast convoy of troops and trade, Rodney pursued. Hood's division was in the van, which became isolated on 9 April when the rest of the squadron lay becalmed in the lee of Dominica; the *Barfleur* received fire from five French ships for over an hour before support could come up. De Grasse, retreating towards Guadeloupe while shepherding battle-damaged ships, was brought to engagement near the Saints on 12 April with his fleet reduced to thirty against the British thirty-six. Hood's division, now placed in the rear because

of the damage it had suffered, was in a position to emulate Rodney in breaking through the French line. But this left him becalmed in the lee of Dominica and only in late afternoon could he rejoin the action. By this time de Grasse in the shattered *Ville de Paris* (110 guns) was looking for a flag officer to whom to surrender with honour. Hood obliged, and after a brief but bloody ten minutes of fire from the *Barfleur* de Grasse struck. Five French ships were taken and the rest fled. Knowing the French were in disarray, Hood pleaded with Rodney to let him chase, but permission was not given until 17 April, upon which Hood hurried to the Mona Passage with ten of the line. It took only two days, but the French had got through one day before; still, he captured two of the line that came from Guadeloupe plus a frigate and a sloop. Yet all he could think about was the opportunity that had been lost—'a great fleet … so *completely beaten* and *routed* and *not pursued*'. He vented his feelings in letters bemoaning the capriciousness of Rodney and the irresolution of Rodney's captain of the fleet, who was 'no more fit for the station he fills than I am to be an archbishop' (*Letters*, ed. Hannay, 136–7; *Letters and Papers of … Barham*, 1.163). He was advised to tone his letters down, but declared he could not.

In June Hood supervised fleet repairs at Jamaica. In July Rodney was superseded by Admiral Hugh Pigot, inexperienced and sluggish but agreeable; Hood deluged him with advice, but they got along rather well. The hurricane season of 1782 was spent at New York. Hood, whose marriage was a happy one, wrote to Susannah that he would 'not let slip any opportunity' to return to her (Hood, *Admirals Hood*, 81) and drafted a letter of resignation, but, finding that the king had sent out Prince William to serve under his care, knew he must stay on and threw 'the letter into the fire' (*Letters and Papers of … Barham*, 1.249). When Hood left New York on 22 November the *Albemarle*, commanded by young Captain Horatio Nelson, went with him, Nelson having asked Pigot to let him serve under Hood in the West Indies. Nelson was soon elated: 'He treats me as if I was his son' (*Dispatches and Letters*, 1.72). Hood held semi-independent command off Jamaica (Pigot was at the Leeward Islands) and spent the rest of the war trying to intercept and bring to battle French and Spanish squadrons that had no wish to meet him.

Peace and war, 1783–1795 Hood returned to England in late June 1783. The warm relationship with Captain Nelson continued; after having him to dinner at his London house, 12 Wimpole Street, Hood declared that it was always open to him, and the oftener Nelson came the happier it would make him. In 1784 Hood helped Nelson obtain command of the *Boreas*, assigned to the West Indies. That same year, as a popular admiral (the City of London had presented him with its freedom in a gold box), he was nominated for Westminster, and though he had considered himself lucky to escape from an earlier attempt to nominate him, this time he could not refuse because Pitt the younger (and the king) truly needed him to oppose Charles James Fox. The election in May 1784 was notoriously marked by violence and fraudulent voting. Hood later described it as 'the most arduous and unpleasant business I ever took in hand' (*Rutland MSS*, 3.134). He topped the poll but was not comfortable in parliament, and the expense of being in London exhausted his finances, for he had never set his sights on making a fortune in prize money. He requested a sinecure, which was denied, but was appointed commander-in-chief at Portsmouth during 1786–8 and again in 1791–3.

In September 1782 Hood had been given an Irish peerage as Baron Hood of Catherington. Certainly he deserved royal favour, not least because responsibility for Prince William was a difficult assignment. The father himself cautioned that 'it would not be proper he should be left to the sole guidance of his volatile imagination' (*Extracts*, ed. Laughton, 1.228). When the time came for William to be captain of a ship Hood saw that Lieutenant Isaac Schomberg was placed on board as a 'minder'. At Antigua in 1787 a dispute erupted between the captain and his lieutenant over a petty matter and Schomberg demanded a court martial, which Nelson, then the commodore on station, unwisely granted. Thereafter Hood was unable to do anything for Nelson for five years, but he took the risk of offending Prince William by appointing Schomberg, 'a deserving officer with no prospect of promotion but by him', first lieutenant of his flagship. The prince was deeply wounded by this and wrote angry, censorious letters. Hood composed beautifully tactful replies, making clear, nevertheless, that he was unrepentant and judged Schomberg to be 'a very excellent officer, and a sensible well-behaved man' (Ranft, 4.290–3). This mark of determination to support professional merit even under the most trying circumstances was noticed in the service.

Hood was not averse to the idea of going to sea again. He had been offered the East Indies command in 1784, but refused it. As he confided to Prince William,

> I should run a great risque of losing that character, which has cost me forty years labour to obtain, and besides, had I lived, I must have returned poorer than I went out, unless I did one of two things, either connive at trade in the Kings ships, or plunder government by contracts, neither of which I could bring myself to do. (NMM, HOO/2, 2 Aug 1784)

Yet he strongly defended Warren Hastings in a parliamentary speech that stressed how dangerous a restraint would be placed upon persons in 'stations abroad of high difficulty' if fear of impeachment hung over them (Brooke, 2.637). Too many of his speeches, however, were thought indiscreet, a factor that evidently prevented his being appointed first lord upon the retirement of Lord Howe. Instead Pitt asked him to take a seat on the board so that Lord Chatham 'should have the best Professional assistance' (NMM, HOO/2, 21 June 1788). Thus, from 1788 to 1795, he served on the Admiralty board; nevertheless, when war came in February 1793 he was appointed commander-in-chief in the Mediterranean. He left Portsmouth on 22 May in the *Victory* with a talented group of protégés, among whom was Horatio Nelson.

The Mediterranean command had always required strategic and diplomatic wisdom. Supremacy was to be exerted over a broad expanse while simultaneously keeping the French fleet at Toulon in check. At this time the only British base was Gibraltar, so the navy's operational viability greatly depended upon diplomacy. Hood was soon complaining that he was almost blind from writing to so many ministers and other correspondents.

Quickly, however, the situation became highly unusual. Hood had scarcely arrived off Toulon when he was approached by envoys from Marseilles and the naval base at Toulon, fearfully seeking his protection from the ruthless Jacobin army sent south from Paris. Their rather amazing offer was to place the Toulon forts and fleet in British hands in trust, to be restored after the war. Hood accepted on condition that the French declare for constitutional monarchy as the price of his assistance, a stance not formally adopted by the British government. Yet Hood had had to act quickly, and as Nelson commented, he had secured a strongly fortified port and twenty-two sail of the line without firing a shot. Pitt publicly hailed the event, but the opportunity had come too early, before British troops could be made available. Having only 1500 to land, Hood had to scrape together what foreign troops he could and hope to hang on until help arrived. Sir Gilbert Elliot came out to assist him politically and administratively; assistance that was welcome, the variety of tasks being well beyond the powers of one man. Yet Hood, though almost seventy, displayed vigour and alertness; Nelson commented that 'he possesses the mind of forty years of age' (*Dispatches and Letters*, 1.378).

However, Hood proved too vigorous, devoting much of his naval force to carrying out manifold tasks all over the Mediterranean according to his original orders. The unfortunate consequence was that when the French launched a major attack on Toulon in December he had only a third of his fleet present to resist it and to remove the French warships and refugee royalists when resistance crumbled. Moreover his excessive optimism led to hanging on too long in hopes of military relief. He ignored the urgings of both his own and the Spanish government to begin preparations for taking the French warships out of harbour. In consequence the final evacuation on 17 December was hastily improvised: only three French battleships were removed, and attempts to burn the rest were botched, with only nine of the line, three frigates, and two sloops being destroyed.

None the less, it was a prodigious naval victory. The French lost a total of thirteen of the line and the Toulon arsenal was ravaged. Hood refused to be discouraged. After carrying the refugees to Italian ports he mounted an expedition to occupy Corsica as a base. Frustrated by the caution of the generals, he intervened in their business. On this occasion Hood's positive thinking yielded success. Assaults from the sea mounted by his marines (they were actually soldiers assigned to the fleet as marines), assisted by a blockade and Pasquale Paoli's independence movement, helped the army complete the conquest, which was sealed by the French garrison's surrender (4500 men) on 22 May 1794. But the army commanders, two of whom resigned in protest, did not hide their resentment of his imperious direction and sometimes ill-informed criticism.

Hood went home in early November 1794, intending to return the next spring. In recognition of his services he was made an elder brother of Trinity House, his wife was given a British peerage as Baroness Hood of Catherington, and on 4 April 1795 he was promoted admiral of the blue. He did not return to the Mediterranean because when he insisted, going over the first lord's head, that the number of ships assigned to him by the Admiralty was seriously inadequate, Earl Spencer, seeing a threat to naval discipline, got him dismissed from the command. This ended Hood's naval career. In 1796 he was appointed governor of Greenwich Hospital, and, on vacating his Westminster seat at the general election, he was elevated to Viscount Hood of Whitley in the British peerage.

The man and his profession Deeply regretting the loss of Hood to the service in 1795, Horatio Nelson remarked that he was 'the best Officer, take him altogether, that England has to boast of, … equally great in all situations which an Admiral can be placed in' (*Dispatches and Letters*, 2.146). Few naval officers at that moment in time would have disagreed with this assessment. Although before 1781 Hood had had no experience of fleet command, he rapidly identified the countless things conducive to success, things that required professional knowledge and imagination, clarity of communication (Hood could write as well as speak clearly), forethought, attention to detail, and vigilant monitoring. Some men's minds, he wrote in 1782, 'are full of anxiety, impatience, and apprehension, while others, under similar circumstances, are perfectly cool, tranquil, and indifferent. Mine is of the former cast' (*Letters*, ed. Hannay, 145). Naturally he set a high standard for himself and despised indolence or negligence in others whether superiors or subordinates. One is not surprised to hear that he inspired awe. As his former secretary wrote in 1799, he displayed 'the sternness of the old school …, but then, the whole is tempered by a tenderness and urbanity, that prevents its ever being oppressive, or tyrannical' (*Naval Chronicle*, 2.45).

Hood's leadership of a fleet in battle was never fully tested, either because he was second in command or, later, because opposing squadrons were intent on keeping their distance. Instead, he should be remembered as a consummate naval strategist. Gathering information was a fundamental duty; a commander who did not take steps to discover what he needed to know could 'do nothing but from the chapter of accidents' (*Letters and Papers of … Barham*, 1.205). Hood's active mind weighed intelligence reports, worried through the possibilities, and produced reasoned appreciations. He was uncannily accurate in forecasting French moves in the Caribbean in 1781–3, often to an unreceptive superior. Working through his anxieties and apprehensions to a reasoned plan, he was then strongly disposed to act, and one may easily detect in him a perpetual offensive spirit, one of his most striking attributes. It was also, however, principled: as he commented to Digby after asking for the four battleships, he wished to be on the offensive; on the defensive he could

not 'prevent mischief' (PRO, ADM 1/313, 2 Nov 1781). This offensive spirit he carried to excess during the Toulon occupation, but Hood's inability to exercise it as second in command in 1781–2 was unfortunate.

Some historians have been disgusted by the relentless stream of advice and criticism appearing in Hood's letters. Although most of the advice was issued beforehand and most of the criticism was provoked by advice not taken, it still seems, at least to the modern eye, excessive and insubordinate. At one point he admitted that he had 'probably gone too far in hints … thrown out' to Admiral Pigot (*Letters*, ed. Hannay, 140). At times he certainly went too far when his criticisms touched elements of personal character, as they frequently did in the case of Rodney. Some of this amounted to backbiting but most of it was in the open and may be characterized as effrontery (when asked to tone down his letters he remarked that it would be pointless because his views were known throughout the fleet). He was so often guilty of the crime of being right that the king's personal regard may have played a role in saving him from the usual hierarchical consequences.

On the other hand, there is no evidence that 'the fleet' disagreed with his criticisms or thought that he should have suppressed them, and it should be recalled that Hood's relations with his chiefs were not, except in the case of Graves, disruptive. Rodney exhausted the patience of many who had to work with him and his temperament was as unlike Hood's as can be imagined, but Hood recognized Rodney's merit as a combat leader. He remarked to Sir Charles Middleton that if Rodney had been in command at the Chesapeake 'the 5th of September would I think have been a most glorious day for Great Britain' (*Letters and Papers of … Barham*, 1.125). At the time he wrote this he had recently experienced four months of Sir George in other respects, at his worst. But there was never a breach; in fact there was co-operation, and considering their differences of temperament this was a commendable achievement for both admirals, less common in that century than is sometimes supposed. Hood also worked well with Pigot and Digby. But he did not mend relations with Graves, and Rodney kept them apart. In the end, one should remember that the ablest of Hood's naval contemporaries judged him by his actions.

They also admired his deep respect for the profession. Fellow officers realized that he was not pure. He helped his relatives to promotions—they all did—and accepted the role of patronage. On the other hand, he was confident that performance would always earn approbation and respect, 'for no commanding officer, however overbearing he may be, dare take any liberty with an inferior who does his duty like an officer and a gentleman' (Hotham, 1.32). As for politics, Hood was not really averse, despite his discomfort with the hurly-burly of electioneering at Westminster. He proclaimed that he was not 'a *party man*'; if so perceived, he said, 'I must … expect to lose every consideration in the line of my profession' (*Letters*, ed. Hannay, 155–6). His loyalty to the regime during the American war and thereafter to the younger Pitt manifested a strong disposition to support the government in power and avoid partisanship. This disposition seems to have enabled Keppel, when first lord in 1782, to re-establish good relations with the Hood brothers. Finally, there was the matter of prize money, to which Samuel Hood was relatively indifferent. He did not become rich in the service—unusual for an admiral active in wartime. He therefore felt that he needed (and deserved) a public pension to enable him to support his peerage, because, as he informed Pitt in 1798, 'the greatest part of my income arises from the governorship I hold; and when I drop, Lady Hood, possessing every shilling I am worth, will not have more than £800 a year to maintain her' (PRO, 30/8/146, fols. 27–8). The pension was awarded in 1800.

Throughout retirement Hood's mind remained active; he seldom gave way to bitterness, though a great blow fell when Susannah died on 25 May 1806, in the apartments at Greenwich. Hood wrote: 'A better woman, a better mother, or better wife never existed' (GEC, *Peerage*, 6.569). His health problems, so much heard about earlier, were remarkably minor; at eighty-five he still rode every day and had 'no complaint but deafness' (*Diaries of Sylvester Douglas*, 2.34). He died at 5 Queen's Square, Bath, on 27 January 1816 after suffering a fall. Upon feeling weak and retiring to lie down, he made a last accurate forecast: the accident, he remarked, would be the 'finishing blow'.

The viscountcy passed to his third and only surviving son, Henry (1753–1836), whose marriage to Jane Wheler of Whitley Abbey had brought Warwickshire lands to the family. Hood was buried next to his wife at Greenwich Hospital. Among distinguished admirals of the eighteenth century he is almost unique in that no monument has been erected to his memory, but there can hardly be a more impressive one than beautiful Mount Hood in Oregon, sighted and named in October 1792 by a lieutenant with George Vancouver's expedition. Worldwide Hood is remembered for the majestic battle cruiser that carried his name; inadequately armoured and penetrated by a German salvo, she blew up and sank in May 1941.

DANIEL A. BAUGH and MICHAEL DUFFY

Sources M. Duffy, 'Samuel Hood, first Viscount Hood, 1724–1816', *Precursors of Nelson: British admirals of the eighteenth century*, ed. P. Le Fevre and R. Harding (2000) · D. A. Baugh, 'Sir Samuel Hood: superior subordinate', *George Washington's opponents: British generals and admirals in the American Revolution*, ed. G. A. Billias (1969) · D. Hood, *The Admirals Hood* (1942) · *Letters written by Sir Samuel Hood (Viscount Hood) in 1781-2-3*, ed. D. Hannay, Navy RS (1895) · *Letters and papers of Charles, Lord Barham*, ed. J. K. Laughton, 3 vols., Navy RS, 32, 38–9 (1907–11) · J. Holland Rose, *Lord Hood and the defence of Toulon* (1922) · M. Wyndham, *Chronicles of the eighteenth century*, 2 vols. (1924), vol. 2 · *The private papers of John, earl of Sandwich*, ed. G. R. Barnes and J. H. Owen, 4 vols., Navy RS, 69, 71, 75, 78 (1932–8) · K. Breen, 'Graves and Hood at the Chesapeake', *Mariner's Mirror*, 66 (1980), 53–64 · J. A. Sulivan, 'Graves and Hood', *Mariner's Mirror*, 69 (1983), 175–94 · GEC, *Peerage*, 6.568–70 · *DNB* · flag officers' letters, North America, 1767–72, PRO, ADM 1/483 · captains' letters, 1774–8, PRO, ADM 1/1898–1904 · flag officers' letters, Leeward Islands, 1780–87, PRO, ADM 1/313 · J. Creswell, *British admirals of the eighteenth century: tactics in battle* (1972) · D. Syrett, *The Royal Navy in American waters, 1775–1783* (1989) · A. T. Mahan, *The influence of sea power upon history, 1660–1783*, 12th edn (1918) · B. McL. Ranft, ed., 'Prince William and Lieutenant Schomberg, 1787–1788', *The naval miscellany*, 4, Navy RS, 92 (1952), 270–93 · 'Biographical memoirs of the Right Honourable Samuel Viscount Hood', *The Naval Chronicle*, 2 (July–Dec 1799), 1–50 · *The dispatches and letters of Vice-Admiral Lord Viscount Nelson*, ed. N. H. Nicolas, 7 vols. (1844–6) · NMM, HOO/2, 20 May, 2 Aug 1784, 21 June 1788 · 'Extracts from the papers of Samuel, first Viscount Hood', ed. J. K. Laughton, *The naval miscellany*, 1, Navy RS (1892), 221–58 · J. Brooke, 'Hood, Samuel', HoP, *Commons, 1754–90* · *Pages and portraits from the past: being the private papers of Sir William Hotham*, ed. A. M. W. Stirling, 2 vols. (1919) · *The diaries of Sylvester Douglas*, ed. F. Bickley, 2 vols. (1928) · N. W. Surry and J. H. Thomas, eds., *Book of original entries, 1731–51*, Portsmouth Record Series, 3 (1976) · *The manuscripts of his grace the duke of Rutland*, 4 vols., HMC, 24 (1888–1905)

Archives BL, signal book, Add. MS 47467 · CAC Cam., corresp. and papers · NMM, corresp. and papers · Wilts. & Swindon RO, letters | BL, letters to Lord Bridport, Add. MSS 35193–35202, *passim* · BL, letters to Francis Drake, Add. MS 46825 · BL, letters to George Jackson, Add. MS 9343 · BL, corresp. with Lord Nelson, Add. MSS 34902–34937, *passim* · Bucks. RLSS, corresp. with Scrope Bernard · Devon RO, corresp. with first Viscount Sidmouth · Glos. RO, letters to Francis Reynolds · NL Scot., corresp. with Robert Liston · NMM, letters to William Hamilton · NMM, letters to Samuel Hood · NMM, letters to Charles Middleton · NMM, letters to Lord Sandwich · NMM, letters to Charles Yorke · PRO, corresp. with F. J. Jackson, FO353 · PRO, letters to William Pitt and second earl of Chatham, PRO 36/8 · PRO, corresp. with Lord Rodney, boxes 12, 26

Likenesses J. Wollaston, oils, 1746, NMM · J. Reynolds, oils, 1783, Man. City Gall. · J. K. Sherwin, line engraving, pubd 1783 (after T. Gainsborough), NPG · J. Northcote, oils, 1784, NMM [*see illus.*] · L. F. Abbott, oils, 1794–5, NMM; version, NPG · Abbott, print, repro. in Hood, *Admirals Hood*, facing p. 112 · T. Gainsborough, oils, Ironmongers' Hall, London · K. A. Hickel, group portrait, oils (*The House of Commons, 1793*), NPG · J. C. Lochée, Wedgwood medallion, Wedgwood Museum, Stoke on Trent · J. Northcote, oils, the Admiralty, Portsmouth · J. Tassie, paste medallion, Scot. NPG · B. West, portrait, priv. coll.; repro. in Hood, *Admirals Hood*, facing p. 24

Wealth at death pension of £2000 p.a. from 1800

Hood, Sir Samuel, first baronet (1762–1814), naval officer, third son of Samuel Hood of Kingsland, Dorset, and Anne (d. 1775), daughter of James Bere of Westbury, Wiltshire, was born on 27 November 1762. Captain Alexander *Hood (1758–1798) was his brother. He entered the navy in 1776 on the *Courageux* with his cousin Samuel (afterwards Lord) Hood. In 1778 he was moved to the *Robust* with Alexander Hood, the future Lord Bridport, and was present at the action off Ushant on 27 July. In 1779–80 he served in the sloop *Lively* in the channel. When Sir Samuel Hood was appointed second in command in the West Indies he took Samuel into his flagship, the *Barfleur*, on which he was promoted lieutenant on 11 October 1780. He was present in the several actions with De Grasse—off Martinique on 29 April 1781; at the Chesapeake on 5 September 1781; and at St Kitts on 25–6 January 1782.

On 31 January 1782 Hood was promoted by his cousin to the nominal command of the sloop *Renard*, then a hospital ship at Antigua. Hood remained in the *Barfleur* as a volunteer until the end of the war, and was thus at the actions off Dominica on 9 April, at the battle of the Saintes on 12 April, and in the Mona passage on 19 April 1782. He brought the *Renard* back to England at the end of the war. He lived two years in France, acquiring an intimate knowledge of the language. In 1785 he was appointed to the sloop *Weasel* on the Halifax station, where he surveyed the coasts and harbours, and on 24 May 1788 he was posted to the command of the frigate *Thisbe*, which he brought home and paid off in the autumn of 1789. In May 1790 he commissioned the frigate *Juno* (32 guns) in which he went out to Jamaica. On 3 February 1791, while lying in St Anne's harbour, he rescued three men from a wreck during a violent storm. With his bargemen reluctant to man his captain's barge, Hood himself jumped in, saying, 'I never gave an order to a sailor in my life that I was not ready to undertake and execute myself', and shoved off. For this the house of assembly of Jamaica voted 100 guineas for a sword to be presented to him.

The *Juno* returned to England in the summer of 1791, and through the autumn and the following year was stationed at Weymouth, in attendance on the king. Early in 1793 she went out to the Mediterranean with the fleet under Lord Hood, and was with it at the occupation of Toulon. However, the *Juno* was absent at Malta when Toulon fell, and Hood, unaware of developments, brought her back to the inner harbour on the dark and drizzling night of 9 January 1794; but then he made a dashing escape, under fire.

Soon after this Hood was engaged in the operations on the coast of Corsica, and after the capture of S. Fiorenzo Lord Hood transferred him to the fine frigate *L'Aigle* (36 guns), and sent him in 1795 in command of a small squadron into the archipelago to protect the trade and watch some French frigates which had taken refuge in Smyrna. In April 1796 Hood was moved into the *Zealous* (74 guns), one of the fleet with Sir John Jervis (afterwards the earl of St Vincent) off Toulon, and in 1797 off Cadiz. He won the confidence of his new commander (who had little love for Hood's cousins) by establishing discipline in a previously disorderly ship. He missed the battle of Cape St Vincent because the *Zealous* was refitting at Lisbon; but in July she was one of the squadron with Nelson in his disastrous attack on Santa Cruz. With the assault force almost out of ammunition and surrounded in a square, Hood was employed by Troubridge to conduct the extraordinary negotiations which extricated the survivors. Hood demanded of the Spanish governor that they be provided with boats to return to their squadron within ten minutes or they would burn the town; he stood with watch in hand until the Spaniard backed down.

In early 1798 the *Zealous* was in the Bay of Biscay and off Rochefort; but having again joined the fleet before Cadiz, she was one of the ships sent in May to reinforce Nelson in the Mediterranean. In the battle of Abu Qir Bay the *Zealous*'s role was particularly brilliant: closely following the *Goliath*, Hood let go his anchor on the bow of the *Guerrier*, the leading French ship; he than heartened the oncoming British line by dismasting her within twelve minutes. After a three-hour pounding *Guerrier* surrendered, completely shattered, and Hood passed on to engage other ships. When Nelson quitted the coast of Egypt, Hood was senior officer commanding the squadron which continued to blockade the French army, and captured or destroyed some thirty of their transports. In February 1799 he rejoined Nelson at Palermo, and was employed during the spring in the defence of Salerno, and

afterwards as governor of Castel Nuovo at Naples. The king of the Two Sicilies awarded him the order of St Ferdinand and of Merit.

In May 1800 the *Zealous* was paid off, and Hood was appointed to the *Courageux*, in the squadron under Sir John Borlase Warren off Ferrol. In January 1801 he was moved into the *Venerable*, which after a few months in the channel joined Sir James Saumarez (afterwards Lord de Saumarez) in time to take prominent parts in the unfortunate action at Algeciras on 6 July, and in the brilliant victory in the straits on 12 July. When leading the pursuit next day, the *Venerable* had all her masts shot away; she went ashore, and was later refloated with difficulty. The *Venerable* was paid off at the peace, and in October 1802 Hood was sent out as joint-commissioner for the government of Trinidad. By the death of Rear-Admiral Totty he became commander-in-chief of the Leeward Islands station, hoisting a broad pennant on board the *Centaur*; and on the renewal of the war he captured, together with the land forces, the islands of St Lucia and Tobago in June 1803, and, on the mainland, Demerara, Essequibo, and Berbice (September), and Surinam (May 1804). Under his command also a large number of the enemy's privateers and warships were captured or destroyed, to the great advantage of the English trade; and in January 1804 the Diamond Rock at the entrance to Fort Royal harbour, Martinique, was occupied, armed, and commissioned as 'a sloop of war'. Hood's services were acknowledged by complimentary addresses from the legislative assemblies of the islands, and the present of plate of the value of 300 guineas; he was also nominated a KB (26 September 1804). On 6 November he married the Hon. Mary Elizabeth Frederica *Mackenzie (1783–1862), eldest daughter of Lord Seaforth, governor of Barbados; they had no children.

Early in 1805 Hood returned to England, where he was further rewarded with a colonelcy of the marines; continuing in the *Centaur* he was sent off Rochefort in command of a squadron of six battleships. On 25 September he fell in with a French squadron of five large frigates and two brigs bound for the West Indies with troops, but while his ships were capturing the four largest of these Hood's right elbow was smashed by a musket ball, entailing the amputation of the arm; for this he was awarded a pension of £500 per annum. In the 1806 election the government nominated him a 'naval hero' candidate for the Westminster seat once held by Lord Hood, and he topped the poll. His lust for active service afloat led him to decline a proffered seat on the Admiralty board. At the May 1807 election his friend Sir Evan Nepean provided him with a seat, Bridport, which he was to hold until 1812. Hood returned to sea in the *Centaur* in 1807, and was in Lord Gambier's fleet at Copenhagen. On 2 October Hood was promoted rear-admiral of the blue, and later, with his flag in the *Centaur*, he had naval command of the force which captured Madeira on 26 December 1807. In the following year he advanced to rear-admiral of the white and was second in command of the fleet in the Baltic, under Sir James Saumarez. On 26 August the *Centaur* was with the *Implacable* (Captain Thomas Byam Martin), pursuing far ahead of the Swedish fleet to which they were attached; Hood cut off the *Sevolod* (80 guns) from the Russian line, and captured her after a stubborn defence in which the two ships, locked together, ran aground. The *Sevolod* had to be burnt, but the *Centaur* was saved from the Russian fleet by Byam Martin's intervention. The king of Sweden awarded him the grand cross of the order of the Sword.

In January 1809 Hood was second in command at Corunna during the re-embarkation of the army, for which he received the tumultuous thanks of the House of Commons in his seat as member for Bridport. He was created a baronet on 13 April 1809, and for the next two years he commanded a division in the Mediterranean. On 31 July 1810 he became rear-admiral of the red. On 1 August 1811 he was advanced to vice-admiral of the blue, and towards the end of the year was appointed commander-in-chief in the East Indies, where he arrived in the early summer of 1812. His command was uneventful, the war having been brought to an end with the capture of Java and Mauritius; and the time was mainly occupied in regulating and reforming points of organization or discipline and the methods of victualling, in which his reforms reportedly effected a saving to the government of something like 30 per cent. On 4 January 1814 he was appointed vice-admiral of the white. He died at Madras on 24 December 1814, of malaria, after three days' illness.

A life which, with few and short intermissions, was spent in active service left Hood short of social polish. Even service friends thought him 'reserved to a distressing degree' (*Letters and Papers of … Thos. Byam Martin*, 1.154) and 'awkward and ungraceful' (Hotham, 1.270). The latter thought him the only man he ever knew 'who appeared to like a sea life *par excellence*, and who was never happy out of it' (ibid., 1.269). In his own element he was a thorough professional and a popular commander with all ranks. The 'occasional streak of obstinacy about him if what he heard did not coincide with his opinion or suit his wishes' (ibid., 1.269), also made him an unrelenting opponent in combat, the archetypal fighting captain that commanders wanted when action loomed. Because Hood died without children, the baronetcy, by a special clause in the patent, passed to the son of his brother Alexander.

J. K. LAUGHTON, rev. MICHAEL DUFFY

Sources 'Biographical memoirs of Commodore Sir Samuel Hood', *Naval Chronicle*, 17 (1807), 1–37 · *Naval Chronicle*, 34 (1815), 30–32 · D. Hood, *The Admirals Hood* [1942] · *Pages and portraits from the past: being the private papers of Sir William Hotham*, ed. A. M. W. Stirling, 2 vols. (1919), vol. 1, pp. 268–71 · *Letters and papers of Admiral of the Fleet Sir Thos. Byam Martin, GCB*, ed. R. V. Hamilton, 1, Navy RS, 24 (1903) · *Letters and papers of Admiral of the Fleet Sir Thos. Byam Martin, GCB*, ed. R. V. Hamilton, 2, Navy RS, 12 (1898) · W. James, *The naval history of Great Britain, from the declaration of war by France in 1793, to the accession of George IV*, [3rd edn], 6 vols. (1837) · HoP, *Commons, 1790–1820*, 4.225 · D. Syrett and R. L. DiNardo, *The commissioned sea officers of the Royal Navy, 1660–1815*, rev. edn, Occasional Publications of the Navy RS, 1 (1994) · Burke, *Peerage* (1967) [St Audries]
Archives NMM, letterbooks, logbooks, and papers | BL, letters to Lord Bridport, Add. MSS 35196–35202, *passim* · BL, corresp. with T. B. Martin, Add. MSS 41365–41367 · BL, letters to Lord Melville, Add. MS 63102 · BL, letters to Lord Nelson and Captain Troubridge, Add. MSS 34907–34932, *passim* · NA Scot., corresp. with Lord and Lady Seaforth · NL Scot., letters to Lord Minto · Som. ARS, corresp. and papers
Likenesses G. Clint, engraving, *c.*1776–1800 (after J. R. A. Hoppner), Walmer Castle, Kent · C. Turner, mezzotint, pubd 1806 (after J. Downman), BM · J. Hoppner, oils, exh. RA 1807, NMM · oils, *c.*1808–*c.*1811, NMM · W. Beechey, oils (before loss of his arm) · E. Bocquet, stipple (after W. Beechey), BM, NPG; repro. in *The British gallery of contemporary portraits* (1813) · Downman, oils (after loss of his arm) · Hopper, oils (after loss of his arm), priv. coll. · Ridley & Blood, stipple (after miniature), BM, NPG; repro. in *European Magazine* (1807) · engraving, repro. in *Naval Chronicle*, 17 (1807), 1

Hood, Samuel (*c.*1800–1875). *See under* Hood, John (*c.*1721–1784).

Hood, Thomas (*bap.* 1556, *d.* 1620), mathematician and physician, was baptized at St Leonard Eastcheap on 23 June 1556, the son of Thomas Hood, a Merchant Taylor. He entered the Merchant Taylors' School on 7 November 1567 and matriculated at Trinity College, Cambridge, in November 1573. Having gained his BA in 1577–8 he was elected fellow of the college and completed his MA in 1581. Four years later the university granted him a licence to practise medicine.

In the aftermath of the Spanish armada of 1588, concern for a greater knowledge of the mathematical sciences among military officers and naval commanders was voiced by members of the privy council. In consequence, Sir Thomas Smith and Lord Lumley instituted a mathematical lectureship in London, and Hood was invited to become 'Mathematical Lecturer to the City of London'. He gave his first lecture on 4 November 1588 in Smith's House, Gracechurch Street. This lecture was published within the next few months: it listed the reasons for establishing the lectureship and spoke of the importance of the mathematical sciences to people in all walks of life. It included a brief history of mathematics from Adam to contemporary scholars. Hood was particularly anxious to stress the centrality of mathematical principles to all parts of creation. Later lectures took place in the Staplers' Chapel in Leadenhall Street, where copies of Hood's textbooks were made available to students. Judging from the title-pages, his lectures ceased at some point in 1592.

At this time Hood was living in Abchurch Lane, but he later moved to a house in the Minories. He continued to teach privately, but turned his attention increasingly to navigational problems and to designing new instruments as aids for navigators and surveyors. He applied for a licence to practise medicine in London from the Royal College of Physicians, but this was denied him owing to his having an insufficient knowledge of Galen. The college finally granted him a conditional licence on 5 August 1597. At some time after this Hood moved to Worcester and established a medical practice. He also had a residence at the nearby village of Shrawley. Hood was married; his wife's name was Frances. He died at Worcester in March or April 1620.

Hood's works demonstrate both his wide range of interests and his skill as a teacher. He wrote two texts concerning globes, which were just beginning to become widely available: *The Use of the Celestial Globe in Plano, Set Foorth in*

Two Hemispheres (1590) was largely intended to help the student astronomer to recognize the stars and their constellations; *The Use of Both the Globes Celestiall and Terrestriall* (1592) supplied definitions and applications for both astronomy and geography. Parts of his writing on the myths associated with the constellations were published more than sixty years later as 'Ancient poeticall stories of the starres' in Joseph Moxon's *Tutor to Astronomie* (1659).

There were also two books on the use of instruments which he had designed, *The Use of the Jacobs Staffe* (1590, republished in 1596 as *Two Mathematicall Instruments, the Crosse-Staffe and the Jacobs Staffe*) and *The Making and Use of the Geometricall Instrument called a Sector* (1598). The latter marked the appearance in England of this type of instrument, which was to be popularized by Edmund Gunter twenty years later.

Most of Hood's original writing was set in the form of a dialogue between master and scholar. He showed himself able to bring a clarity of expression to complicated topics and the diagrams in his final book, *The Making and Use of the … Sector*, allowed a straightforward presentation of an instrument whose uses cannot easily be explained by the written word. He also did much work as an editor. He produced *Elements of Geometry* (1590), a translation of the work by Peter Ramus, and the *Arithmetic* (1596) of an obscure Swiss mathematician, Urstisius. His interest in navigation led him to prepare a new version of William Bourne's *A Regiment for the Sea* (1592), subsequently reissued twice.

H. K. HIGTON

Sources S. Johnston, 'Mathematical practitioners and instruments in Elizabethan England', *Annals of Science*, 48 (1991), 319–44 · E. G. R. Taylor, *The mathematical practitioners of Tudor and Stuart England* (1954) · Venn, *Alum. Cant.* · T. Hood, *A copie of the speache made by the mathematicall lecturer* (1588) · C. J. Robinson, ed., *A register of the scholars admitted into Merchant Taylors' School, from AD 1562 to 1874*, 2 vols. (1882–3)

Hood, Thomas (1799–1845), poet and humorist, was born on 23 May 1799 at 31 Poultry, London. His father, also Thomas Hood (1759–1811), bookseller and publisher, was a Scot from Tayside. His mother, Elizabeth Sands (*d*. 1821), came from a well-known London family of engravers. Hood was the third of six children, the second of two sons. The family moved to Islington, then pleasantly rural. Hood attended a dame-school in Tokenhouse Yard and, later, Dr Wanostracht's Alfred House Academy in Camberwell. When Hood was twelve both his father and brother died and he moved to a modest day school run by an elderly Scot, afterwards gratefully remembered. By fourteen he was working in a City office but became ill and, possibly apprenticed to his uncle Robert Sands, or Le Keux, began to learn engraving. When his health deteriorated in 1815 he was sent north to relatives in Dundee, where he stayed for about two years. He was already writing prose and verse and contributing anonymously to local papers.

Hood returned to London in the autumn of 1817, much improved in health. He was busy engraving, working from home, and he joined a literary society. In one of his entertaining letters he wrote in 1821: 'Truly I am T. Hood Scripsit et sculpsit—I am engraving and writing prose and

Thomas Hood (1799–1845), by unknown artist, *c*.1832–4

poetry by turns' (Hood, 27). 1821 was a year of mixed fortune. His mother died. That summer, however, Taylor and Hessey (Keats's publishers) took over the *London Magazine* after the death of its editor in a duel. John Taylor had worked for Hood's father and invited the young Thomas to become sub-editor. Hood was in his element: 'I dreamt articles, thought articles, wrote articles … The more irksome parts of authorship, such as the correction of the press, were to me labours of love' (Jerrold, 99). His career as a literary journalist had begun.

Apart from a novel, *Tylney Hall* (1834), some unremarkable prose, and minor writing for the stage, nearly all Hood's work, verse and prose, first appeared in magazines and annuals catering for the growing middle-class market. From 1821 to 1845 Hood was closely involved, as contributor or editor, with many of them, particularly the *London Magazine*, *The Athenaeum*, *The Gem*, the *New Monthly Magazine*, and *Punch*. He wrote—and illustrated, inventing visual puns—a series of *Comic Annuals* (1830–9), collected his magazine contributions into *Whims and Oddities* (1826 and 1827) and *Whimsicalities* (1844), and also published *Hood's Magazine* (1844–5). Hood wrote for a living, and was keenly alive to contemporary life and popular taste. His work provides insight into domestic reading and the development of periodical publishing in the first half of the nineteenth century.

As a young man at the *London Magazine*, Hood found himself 'in rare company': among the contributors were Charles Lamb, William Hazlitt, Thomas De Quincey, and his own contemporary, Keats's friend John Hamilton Reynolds. His 'Literary reminiscences' in *Hood's Own* (1839) contain lively descriptions of the principal figures of the Romantic movement. Lamb became his mentor. In 1825 he collaborated with Reynolds in a successful volume of light satirical verse, *Odes and Addresses to Great People*, and published what Lamb termed his Hogarthian etching, *The Progress of Cant*. On 5 May 1825 he married Reynolds's sister Jane (1791–1846).

Hood's appearance accords oddly with his destined role of literary buffoon and laughter-maker: slight, unassuming, dressed in black, with what he himself on several occasions called 'a Methodist face' (Hood, 348). The Hoods settled at 2 Robert Street, Adelphi, London. Lamb's poem 'On an Infant Dying as Soon as Born' mourned their first child, but a daughter, Frances (1830–1878) [*see* Broderip, Frances Freeling], was born soon after they moved to Winchmore Hill; and, after they moved in 1832 to Lake House, Wanstead, a son, Tom *Hood (1835–1874), was born; he was to follow his father's profession. Although constantly worried about money and health, the Hoods were a devoted, affectionate family as *Memorials of Thomas Hood* (1860), based on his letters and compiled by his children, testifies.

In the year Tom was born the Hoods faced financial ruin. Hood, happy in family and friends, inept or unfortunate in business dealings, invested in a publishing venture that failed. To economize and pay his debts the family moved to Koblenz in 1835; they remained in Europe for five years, the last three in Ostend. Hood worked on courageously although chronically ill. His rheumatic heart condition became much worse and he returned to London in 1840 to the care of his own doctor. The family lived first in various lodgings, finally settling at Devonshire Lodge, New Finchley Road, St John's Wood. Briefly, when he was editor of the *New Monthly Magazine* (1841–3), Hood's financial position improved, but became precarious again when he initiated a lawsuit over copyright (settled favourably after his death). One of Thackeray's *Roundabout Papers* gives a touching recollection of this 'true genius and poet' at this time. In 1844 several of his fellow writers, distressed by his financial hardship and rapidly deteriorating physical condition, petitioned Peel to grant him a civil-list pension; it was settled on his wife. Hood died at his London home, Devonshire Lodge, on 3 May 1845, his wife on 4 December 1846. He was buried on 10 May. In 1854 a memorial, paid for by public subscription, was erected over their grave in Kensal Green cemetery.

Hood had endeared himself to the reading public. Although his early Keatsian collection of serious verse, *The Plea of the Midsummer Fairies* (1827), was not well received, much in the volume was distinctive: some of the shorter poems, 'I remember, I remember', 'Silence', and 'Ruth', for example, have a haunting quality that places them in many anthologies. The light-hearted banter and agile puns of *Odes and Addresses*, however, sold well. Hood, as he frequently said, became 'a lively Hood for a livelihood'. Years of inventive comic verse followed, its boisterous fun and terse puns uncongenial to later tastes. It does, however, exhibit Hood's extraordinary technical virtuosity in handling form, metre, and language. Here Hood is wholly individual, 'major' not 'minor', as W. H. Auden judged: 'like nobody but himself and serious in the true sense of the word' (Auden, 17).

Hood was never wholly clown. Light and dark coexist in his world, and often a crude reality punctures the hilarious. He wrote sombre ballads such as *The Dream of Eugene Aram* (1829), and tender lyrics such as 'The Death Bed'. 'The Haunted House' and 'The Elm Tree' share contemporary taste for the macabre. Hood preferred laughter to preaching as a vehicle for social criticism: before Dickens or Thackeray the serialized, manic history of *Miss Kilmansegg and her Precious Leg* (1840–41) attacked with comic vigour society's vulgar display of wealth. His *Ode to Rae Wilson* (1837) reacted sharply to attacks on his levity, revealing the generous humanitarian impulses behind his writing: love of his fellow men, compassion, a tolerant non-sectarian Christianity, and a strong preference for a cheerful philosophy of life. Hood spoke out early against slavery, campaigned for a copyright law, and drew attention to the poor, the rejected, the oppressed, those exploited, and those harshly judged in the midst of Victorian prosperity.

Near his death Hood engaged the hearts and consciences of his readers directly in a number of poems prompted by real incidents: 'The Song of the Shirt' (*Punch*, Christmas 1843) highlighted the plight of the underpaid seamstresses of the day; in 1844 'The Workhouse Clock' addressed the hardship of the poor laws; 'The Lay of the Labourer', the suffering of the agricultural poor. 'The Bridge of Sighs', the purest poem of these public verses, sprang from a newspaper report of a suicide.

In his short life Hood saw 'Romantic' change into 'Victorian': he took tea with Wordsworth, dined with Dickens. Hood's work mirrors this change. Much of his writing has intrinsic merit; some is memorable, its range impressive, its style often forward-looking, and all is valuable to anyone concerned with the transitional period, literary and social, which it reflects.   JOY FLINT

Sources W. Jerrold, *Hood: his life and times* (1907) · *The letters of Thomas Hood*, ed. P. F. Morgan (1973) · F. F. Broderip and T. Hood, *Memorials of Thomas Hood*, 2 vols. (1860) [rev. with additions (1884)] · J. C. Reid, *Thomas Hood* (1963) · J. Clubbe, *Victorian forerunner: the later career of Thomas Hood* (1968) [incl. *The progress of cant*] · W. Jerrold, *Thomas Hood and Charles Lamb* (1930) [repr. 'Literary reminiscences', from *Hood's own* (1839), and Lamb's reviews of *The progress of cant*] · L. Brander, *Thomas Hood* (1963) · W. M. Thackeray, 'On a joke I once heard from the late Thomas Hood', *Roundabout papers* (1863) · W. H. Auden, introduction, *Nineteenth century British minor poets*, ed. W. H. Auden (New York, 1966) · A. Elliott, *Hood in Scotland* (1885) · J. Shattock, ed., *The Cambridge bibliography of English literature*, 3rd edn, 4 (1999)

Archives Col. U., Rare Book and Manuscript Library, letters · Harvard U., Houghton L., papers · Hunt. L., letters · Morgan L., papers · NYPL, papers · priv. coll. · Ransom HRC, papers · U. Cal., Los Angeles, William Andrews Clark Memorial Library, papers · Yale U., Beinecke L., papers | BL, letters to Sir Charles Dilke and Maria Dilke, Add. MS 43899 · BL, corresp. with Sir Robert Peel, Add. MSS 40553–40554, 40560 · Bodl. Oxf., letters to Bradbury and Evans · Bristol Public Library, John Wright MSS · NL Scot.,

corresp. · NL Scot., letters to William Blackwood and Sons · University of Bristol, de Franck MSS
Likenesses oils, *c*.1832–1834, NPG [*see illus.*] · portrait, *c*.1835, NPG · T. Lewis, oils, 1838, NPG · E. Davis, bust, 1844 · M. Noble, bust on monument, 1854, Kensal Green cemetery, London · F. Croll, line engraving, BM, NPG; repro. in Hogg, *Weekly Instructor* · Heath, engraving (after bust by Davis), repro. in *Hood's Magazine* (1845) · W. Holl, stipple (after T. Lewis), BM, NPG; repro. in Hood, *Complete works*, ed. W. Jerrold (1935) · D. Maclise?, drawing, priv. coll. · portrait, repro. in Jerrold, *Thomas Hood*
Wealth at death negligible; appears to have died in debt: Reid, *Thomas Hood*; Clubbe, *Victorian forerunner*

Hood, Thomas [Tom; *known as* Thomas Hood the younger] (1835–1874), humorist and journal editor, was born on 19 January 1835 at Lake House, Wanstead, Essex, the son of the poet and humorist Thomas *Hood (1799–1845) and his wife, Jane, *née* Reynolds (1791–1846). After the death of his parents, Hood was supported by a civil-list pension. He attended the University College School in London, then Louth grammar school, and finally Pembroke College, Oxford, in 1853. He passed his examinations, but ran up huge debts, and never received his degree.

Living in Cornwall from 1856 to 1859, Hood wrote for and then edited the *Liskeard Gazette*. A collection of humorous writing, *Pen and Pencil Pictures*, appeared in 1857. Three years later he and his sister Frances *Broderip (1830–1878) published their father's *Memorials* (1860). After friends found Hood a position in the War Office, he became a London literary jack of all trades, publishing *Quips and Cranks* (1861), a poetry collection entitled *The Daughters of King Daher* (1861), illustrations for children's books written by his sister, a reissue of his father's 1839 collection *Hood's Own* (1861), and contributions to such periodicals as *Cornhill Magazine*, the *Comic News*, and *Temple Bar*.

Hood was best known as a writer, an illustrator, and ultimately the editor for the weekly penny comic paper *Fun*. A contributor almost from its inception in September 1861, he replaced H. J. Byron as editor in May 1865. Hood's staff included Ambrose Bierce, E. L. Blanchard, Matt Morgan, George Rose ('Arthur Sketchley'), the dramatist T. W. Robertson, and W. S. Gilbert, whose 'Bab Ballads' first appeared in *Fun*. Hood edited *Fun* until he died, making it *Punch's* foremost competitor.

Hood issued various collections of his father's works, and wrote fiction, including the sensation novels *A Disputed Inheritance* (1863), *Vere Vereker's Vengeance* (1865), *Captain Masters's Children* (1865), *A Golden Heart* (1867), *The Lost Link* (1868), and *Love and Valour* (1871), the last containing Oxford scenes which may be partly autobiographical. *Tom Hood's Comic Annual* began appearing in 1867, and he edited collections of anecdotes, comic readings, stories, and puzzles for children. *The Rules of Rhyme* (1869) was frequently reprinted.

As a writer and illustrator, Hood was prolific but seldom more than competent. He was more impressive as an editor and champion of his father's reputation. Hood was tall, handsome, and famously convivial. Literary friends recalled fondly his Friday suppers in his lodgings in Brompton during the 1860s. Other contemporaries saw

Hood as proof that literary greatness cannot be inherited, and attributed his early death to dissipation.

Hood's first wife, Susan, often called 'Mrs Tom', died in 1873, aged thirty-seven. He married his second wife, Justine Rudolphine Charotton (*b.* 1844/5) on 15 August 1874, only a few months before his death at his home, Gloucester Cottage, Peckham Rye, on 20 November 1874, from a liver ailment. He was buried in Nunhead cemetery.

CRAIG HOWES

Sources E. S. Lauterbach, '*Fun* and its contributors: the literary history of a Victorian humor magazine', PhD diss., University of Illinois, Urbana, 1961 · F. F. Broderip, 'Memoir', *Poems humorous and pathetic by Thomas Hood the younger, edited, with a memoir, by his sister* (1877) · H. W. Lucy, 'Tom Hood: a biographical sketch', *GM*, 5th ser., 14 (1875), 77–88 · H. W. Lucy, 'Table talk', *GM*, 5th ser., 14 (1875), 127–129 · C. Scott, *The drama of yesterday and today*, 2 vols. (1899) · J. Clubbe, *Victorian forerunner: the later career of Thomas Hood* (1968) · W. Tegg, 'Thomas Hood', *N&Q*, 8th ser., 7 (1895), 84–5 · S. C. Hall, *Retrospect of a long life, from 1815 to 1883*, 2 vols. (1883) · J. C. Reid, *Thomas Hood* (1963) · *Fun* (28 Nov 1874) · *ILN* (28 Nov 1874) · m. cert. [Tom Hood and Justine Rudolphine Charotton] · P. Mann, 'The Reynolds family', *Keats–Shelley Journal*, 5 (1956), 6 · tombstone, Nunhead cemetery
Archives *Punch*, London, archive · Bristol Reference Library, letters, speeches, and fragmentary MSS · FM Cam., letters · University of Bristol Library, sketchbooks and scrapbooks | Yale U., Beinecke L., letters to Frederick Locker-Lampson
Likenesses Elliott & Fry, carte-de-visite, NPG · Tradells & Marshall, photograph, repro. in 'Memoir', Broderip · S. A. Walker, carte-de-visite, NPG · J. & C. Watkins, cartes-de-visite, NPG · engraving (after photograph by C. Watkins), repro. in *ILN* · portrait (after photograph by C. Watkins), NPG
Wealth at death under £300: probate, 15 Dec 1874, *CGPLA Eng. & Wales*

Hook, James (1746–1827), organist and composer, was born in 1746, probably on 3 June, in the parish of St John, Maddermarket, Norwich, the son of a cutler. He was taught by Thomas Garland, organist of Norwich Cathedral, and possibly also by Charles Burney when Burney was resident at King's Lynn. He began playing in public concerts while still a boy—he was performing concertos at the age of six—and later taught music at a local boarding-school. About 1763 he moved to London and became organist at White Conduit House, a tea house in Clerkenwell, where he played daily. He soon established himself as a composer too, and won a Catch Club medal in 1765. On 29 May 1766 at St Pancras, Middlesex, he married Elizabeth Jane Madden (*d.* 1795), a miniature painter, and five months later they visited Norwich, where Hook played in a benefit concert for his widowed mother. Hook and his wife had two sons: James *Hook (1772?–1828), later dean of Worcester and father of the clergyman Walter Farquhar Hook, and Theodore Edward *Hook (1788–1841), a writer. In 1769 Hook became organist and composer at Marylebone Gardens and about this time also he was appointed organist at St John's, Horsleydown, Bermondsey. Five years later he moved to the more prestigious Vauxhall Gardens, where he became well known particularly for his keyboard concerto performances given each evening during the summer season.

Hook's output was extensive. Of about thirty stage

James Hook (1746–1827), by Lemuel Francis Abbott, c.1800

works, written for the main London theatres as well as for the gardens, the operas *Il dilettante* (Marylebone, 1772), *The Lady of the Manor* (Covent Garden, 1778), and *The Double Disguise* (Drury Lane, 1784, to a libretto by his wife) are among the better examples, but Hook's dramatic sense was not well developed. His music for Vauxhall also included keyboard concertos, cantatas, and more than 2000 songs, some of them written in the fashionable Scottish folk style. His popularity there—he stayed for almost half a century—was dependent not least on his ability to turn out musical ephemera in the simple, light, easy-going idiom that suited the relatively unsophisticated tastes of the clientele. He kept abreast of continental compositional trends, from the new orchestral techniques of the Mannheim composers in the 1760s to the symphonic writing of Haydn thirty years later, and was quick to incorporate them in his own music, to the extent that he was considered by some to be little more than an expert plagiarist. Yet he was among the more accomplished English practitioners of the *galant* style, which, with its lucid phraseology and uncomplicated harmonic gestures, appealed to Vauxhall audiences, and, significantly, he was one of the first English composers of the period for whom the music of Handel ceased to be the main stylistic impetus. In 1768, at a concert in Hickford's room in Brewer Street, he performed a concerto on the newfangled pianoforte, perhaps the first person to do so in public in England, and some of his later keyboard works show a development towards a specifically pianistic technique. Hook was a prosperous teacher, and his *Guida di musica* instruction manuals, as well as the large amount of chamber and keyboard music he published, must have had a considerable impact on domestic music-making in late eighteenth- and early nineteenth-century Britain.

With Vauxhall Gardens falling out of fashion, Hook left suddenly in 1820, and he died in Boulogne in 1827. His second wife, Harriet, whose surname may have been Horncastle (*d.* 1873), outlived him by many years, and they may have had a son. The oboist William Parke recalled Hook in his *Memoirs*: a good-humoured character, he walked with a limp, having been born club-footed, and was 'a very agreeable companion', an inveterate leg-puller who had 'a happy knack of punning' (Parke, 2.255).

PETER LYNAN

Sources *New Grove* · B. Matthews, 'James Hook and his family', *MT*, 131 (1990), 622–5 · W. T. Parke, *Musical memoirs*, 2 vols. (1830) · T. Fawcett, *Music in eighteenth-century Norwich and Norfolk* (1979) · R. Fiske, *English theatre music in the eighteenth century*, 2nd edn (1986) **Archives** BL, music collections, musical MSS and papers, Add. MSS 19647, 28971 · RA, letters and bills **Likenesses** L. F. Abbott, portrait, *c.*1800, NPG [*see illus.*] · T. Blood, stipple, pubd 1813 (after S. Drummond), BM, NPG; repro. in *European Magazine*, 66 (1813)

Hook, James (1772?–1828), dean of Worcester, was the son of James *Hook (1746–1827), organist, and his first wife, Elizabeth Jane Madden (*d.* 1795); he was brother of Theodore Edward *Hook. He was born in London, probably in 1772 (his son's biographer says June 1771, but as he is recorded to have entered Westminster School in 1788 at the age of fifteen, and to have died in February 1828, aged fifty-five, this cannot be the case). While at Westminster he edited the school magazine, *The Trifler*, and by an unlucky attempt to satirize Eton provoked a blistering response from George Canning on the 'heavy fellows' of Westminster in *The Microcosm*, the Etonian magazine. He inherited his father's skill in music and his mother's skill in painting: as a young man he wrote the librettos of two of his father's musical entertainments, 'Jack of Newbury' and 'Diamond Cut Diamond', which were performed, but never printed; his juvenile sketches, which included a set of caricatures of leading public men, induced Sir Joshua Reynolds to recommend that he should be educated as an artist. In 1792 he was a candidate for election from Westminster School to Christ Church, Oxford, but was excluded for 'acts of insubordination', to which he had also invited others. He proceeded to Oxford nevertheless, and graduated from St Mary Hall in 1796. In the same year, yielding to the strong wish of his mother, he took holy orders, and in the following year contracted an advantageous marriage with Anne (*d.* 1844), daughter of Sir Walter *Farquhar, bt, physician and confidential friend of the prince of Wales, whose private chaplain he became.

Hook's rise in the church was consequently very rapid. After having held livings in Gloucestershire, Leicestershire, Lincolnshire, and Hertfordshire he became in 1814 archdeacon of Huntingdon, in 1817 rector of Whippingham in the Isle of Wight, and in 1825 dean of Worcester, an appointment bringing with it two valuable livings. He did not enjoy it long, dying at the deanery, Worcester, on 5 February 1828. He was buried in the south aisle of the cathedral, and his epitaph was written by the bishop (Folliott

H. W. Cornewall). Notwithstanding his accumulated preferment, he left his family in straitened circumstances. Walter Farquhar *Hook was his son.

Hook published *Anguis in herba* (1802), a defence of the clergy against certain imputations and an attack on Methodism and Jacobinism; he also published sermons and charges. The review of Thomas Moore's 'Loves of the Angels', published among his brother's works, is probably from his pen. He was also author of a pamphlet against Thomas Paine and other revolutionary writers, signed Publicola; of *Al Kalomeric: an Arabian Tale* (1814), satirizing Napoleon; and of *The Good Old Times, or, The Poor Man's History of England* (1817). His anonymous novels, *Pen Owen* (1822) and *Percy Mallory* (1824), are similar in style to his brother's. The former, which is considerably the better, has a lively portrait of R. B. Sheridan as Tom Sparkle, and a spirited description of the Cato Street conspiracy.

RICHARD GARNETT, rev. H. C. G. MATTHEW

Sources *GM*, 1st ser., 98/1 (1828), 369–70 · R. H. D. Barham, *The life and remains of Theodore Edward Hook*, 2 vols. (1849) · W. R. W. Stephens, *The life and letters of Walter Farquhar Hook*, 2 vols. (1878) · J. Welch, *The list of the queen's scholars of St Peter's College, Westminster*, ed. [C. B. Phillimore], new edn (1852) · *The correspondence of George, prince of Wales, 1770–1812*, ed. A. Aspinall, 8 vols. (1963–71) · Burke, *Peerage*

Archives NRA, priv. coll., corresp.

Likenesses S. W. Reynolds, jun., mezzotint, pubd 1836 (after R. Evans), BM, NPG

Hook, James Clarke (1819–1907), landscape and history painter, born in Northampton Square, Clerkenwell, London, on 21 November 1819, was the eldest son of James Hook, who was at first a draper in London, and after a bankruptcy became judge of the mixed commission court in Sierra Leone; his mother was Eliza Frances, the second daughter of Dr Adam *Clarke (1762–1832), a Bible commentator and leading Methodist. After a general education at the North Islington proprietary school (*c*.1830–1834), he studied art in London, first privately at the British Museum, and then in the Royal Academy Schools, to which he was admitted in December 1836. As a boy he was introduced to John Jackson and, through Jackson, to John Constable.

Hook first exhibited at the Royal Academy as early as 1839, and a work of his was included in the exhibition of cartoons for the Westminster frescoes in 1844, though he did not win a prize. In 1845 *The Body of Harold* (engraving in *ILN*, 2, 1845, 88) won the RA gold medal for historical painting. On 13 August 1846 he married the painter Rosalie Burton (*d*. 1897), daughter of James Burton, a London solicitor, and in the same year won a travelling scholarship to Italy, where he spent two years studying Venetian art. His wife, who accompanied him on the sometimes impecunious Italian trip, increasingly dealt with the practicalities of life, allowing him to concentrate on painting. They had two sons, Allan James and Bryan, who both became artists.

Hook was elected an ARA and a member of the Etching Club in 1850, at which time works such as *The Rescue of the Brides of Venice* (exh. RA, 1851; Harris Museum and Art Gallery, Preston) indicated that he intended to make a career as a history painter. In 1853, however, he visited the picturesque village of Abinger in Surrey and, possibly under the influence of the Pre-Raphaelites, began to paint from nature, identifying themes of rural labour as being of particular interest, as in *A Few Minutes to Go before Twelve O'Clock* (exh. RA, 1854; reproduced in Bethel, pl. 16a). The Pre-Raphaelite painter Ford Madox Brown wrote of 'Hook, who for colour and indescribable charm is pre-eminent, even to hugging him in one's arms. A perfect poem is each of his little pictures' (*The Diary of Ford Madox Brown*, ed. V. Surtees, 1981, 174).

Hook found his true voice in seashore landscapes with fishermen and -women, many of which were painted in the vicinity of Clovelly, Devon; examples can be found in many public collections. *Wreckage from the Fruiter* (exh. RA, 1889; Tate collection), is a wild seascape, with minimal narrative interest. Sometimes, however, his seashore subjects took on the character of genre paintings: in *Word from the Missing* (exh. RA, 1877; Guildhall Art Gallery, London), fatherless children discover a message in a bottle while their mother scavenges for driftwood. Many of these paintings celebrate the virtues of labour and the affectionate bonds of the family. John Ruskin, an admirer of Hook's work, found in *A Signal on the Horizon* (exh. RA, 1857) 'the sweetest and most pathetic picture of an English boy that has been painted in modern times' (*Academy Notes*, 1857; repr. in *Ruskin on Pictures*, 2, 1902, 87). Unlike most landscapists of his generation, Hook was unafraid to expose the industrialization of rural life: *From under the Sea* (exh. RA, 1864; Manchester City Galleries) is a frank depiction of Cornish tin miners at Botallack, documenting steam-powered haulage.

From 1852 Hook lived at Tor Villa, Campden Hill, but in 1857 he left London for the villages of Hambledon and Witley, near Godalming in Surrey. In 1866 he built Silverbeck, an elaborate country house near Churt, Surrey, incorporating two well-lit studios into the plan. A lifelong Methodist, he was described by G. D. Leslie as 'like William Morris, somewhat of a socialist' (Leslie, 105) and by F. G. Stephens as 'a Liberal, or rather an advanced radical' who held regular public meetings in Churt, at which he 'endeavoured to educate his humbler neighbours in knowledge of what he thinks they ought to know' (Stephens, 32). Millais's portrait of Hook (exh. RA, 1883; priv. coll.) presents him as a countryman, wearing a suit of grey homespun, with a 'ruddy visage, which tells of a healthy life, and almost constant exposure to air and sunlight' (ibid.).

James Clarke Hook died at Silverbeck on 14 April 1907. In 1966 Graham Reynolds noted: 'To be praised by Baudelaire [as Hook had been at the Paris Universal Exhibition of 1855] and Ruskin is no common achievement and Hook's work will some day emerge from the obscurity in which it temporarily rests' (*Victorian Painting*, 1966, 153). Although his best work bears comparison with the marine paintings of the celebrated nineteenth-century American painter Winslow Homer, he has yet to benefit from the general revival of interest in Victorian art.

TIM BARRINGER

Sources R. Allwood, 'Hook, James Clarke', *The dictionary of art*, ed. J. Turner (1996) · D. Bethel, 'James Clarke Hook RA, 1819–1907', MA diss., Courtauld Inst., 1975 · A. J. Hook, *The life of James Clarke Hook RA* (privately printed, 1929–32) · F. G. S. Stephens, 'J. C. Hook: his life and work', *Art Annual* (1888) [whole issue] · R. Spencer, 'Whistler and James Clarke Hook', *Gazette des Beaux-Arts*, 6th ser., 104 (1984), 45–7 · G. D. Leslie, *The inner life of the Royal Academy* (1914) · *CGPLA Eng. & Wales* (1907)
Archives Bodl. Oxf., letters to F. G. Stephens · Cornell University, Ithaca, New York, letters to Violet Hunt
Likenesses C. H. Lear, chalk drawing, 1845, NPG · G. Reid, oils, 1881, Aberdeen Art Gallery, MacDonald collection · J. Millais, oils, exh. RA 1883, priv. coll. · O. Leyde, etching, pubd 1884 (after J. E. Millais, exh. RA 1883), BM, NPG · J. C. Hook, self-portrait, oils, 1891, Uffizi Gallery, Florence · J. C. Hook, self-portrait, oils, 1895, Aberdeen Art Gallery, MacDonald collection · R. Cleaver, group portrait, pen-and-ink (*Hanging committee, Royal Academy, 1892*), NPG · Elliott & Fry, carte-de-visite, NPG · Lock and Whitfield, woodbury-type photograph, NPG; repro. in T. Cooper, *Men of mark: a gallery of contemporary portraits* (1880) · R. W. Robinson, photograph, NPG; repro. in *Members and associates of the Royal Academy of Arts, 1891*
Wealth at death £112,108 11s. 4d.: probate, 16 May 1907, *CGPLA Eng. & Wales*

Hook, Theodore Edward (1788–1841), writer and hoaxer, was born on 22 September 1788 at 3 Charlotte Street, Bedford Square, London, the son of James *Hook (1746–1827), composer, and his wife, Elizabeth Jane Madden (d. 1795). Theodore Hook was educated at private schools, and subsequently for a short time at Harrow School. He was, according to his own account, principally distinguished at school for mischief, deceitfulness, and a lack of serious application. Such a natural talent for raillery was fostered by an early introduction to the theatrical world as author of the words for the songs of his father's comic operas, a predilection he shared with his mother and elder brother James *Hook (1772?–1828). Theodore Hook's libretto for the *Soldier's Return, or, What Can Beauty Do?* (1805), a comic opera in two acts, earned him £50 when he was only sixteen. Sometimes in conjunction with his father, sometimes independently, he produced during the next five or six years a number of farces and melodramas. One of the latter, *Teleki*, in which the hero is hidden in a barrel on the stage, was ridiculed by Byron in *English Bards and Scotch Reviewers* but proved a popular success. Hook's achievements as a writer, however, were at least matched by his penchant for clever practical jokes and, in particular, by his skill in perpetrating hoaxes.

The most celebrated of Hook's hoaxes was the Berners Street hoax of 1809. This hoax, aimed at a Mrs Tottenham, against whom Hook had grievances, was undertaken with two accomplices and was six weeks in preparation. Having falsely ordered a range of goods and sent out bogus invitations to dignitaries and notables, Hook and his accomplices watched from a room opposite as wagonloads of coal from the Paddington wharves, upholsterers' goods in cartloads, organs, pianofortes, linen, jewellery, and all types of furniture arrived in unison at the woman's Berners Street door. The lord mayor of London, governor of the Bank of England, chairman of the East India Company, and the duke of Gloucester were equally tricked into making an appearance. An amused crowd blocked

Theodore Edward Hook (1788–1841), by Daniel Maclise, 1834

the street for the entire day; yet, although he was suspected, Hook escaped without his involvement being proved.

Hook next took up residence at St Mary Hall, Oxford University, but left after two terms to resume his high-spirited life. He became acquainted with the Revd E. Cannon and other favourites of the prince of Wales and it was probably through their influence and that of his brother that, at twenty-four and utterly unacquainted with business, he obtained the post of accountant-general and treasurer at Mauritius, where he arrived in October 1813. This apparently miraculous piece of good fortune proved his ruin. An examination into the state of the treasury in 1817 revealed a shortfall of $62,000, for which Hook could offer no explanation. His property was confiscated and he was sent home. On his return to England the case was investigated by the Treasury who, though discovering no grounds for criminal proceedings, seized his remaining property. He was imprisoned from 1823 to 1825. Despite for many years receiving an ample income from his writing, he never attempted to discharge any portion of his admitted liability.

Long before his release from gaol Hook began making his living with his pen. In 1811 the two farces *Trial by Jury* and *Darkness Visible* were staged, and in 1819 and 1820 appeared the clever farce *Exchange No Robbery*, brought out under the pseudonym Richard Jones, along with *The Arcadian*, a short-lived magazine, and *Tentamen, or, An Essay towards the History of Whittington, Sometime Lord Mayor of London*, a satire on Queen Caroline and Alderman Wood. The latter achieved great success and, combined with the general recommendation of Sir Walter Scott, saw Hook appointed as the editor of the *John Bull*, established in late 1820 to counteract the popular enthusiasm for Queen Caroline. Hook's penchant for comedy and faculty for improvisation were never displayed to so much advantage as in this scurrilous, but irresistibly facetious, journal. He was the prince of lampooners, exuberant, polished, and energetic and *John Bull*, along with *The Craftsman* and the *North Briton*, can be counted as one of the most influential English publications of its time. 'It is impossible to deny', said the *Quarterly Review*, 'that "Bull" frightened the Whig aristocracy from countenancing the Court of Brandenburg House. The national movement was arrested and George IV had mainly "John Bull" to thank for that result' (*QR*, 77). It also produced another, far less satisfactory result: when Hook's long concealed identity leaked out it became impossible for the Treasury to ignore his previous financial mismanagement.

In the meantime Hook was dissipating his energies in a number of abortive literary projects, rather than concentrating them in the journal, so much so that, despite some years of unparalleled success, it eventually ceased to be financially viable. Between 1826 and 1829 he did, however, produce nine novellas under the collective title of *Sayings and Doings*, for which he received almost £3000. The best known are 'Martha the Gypsy', in which a respectable Londoner is cursed by a Gypsy for refusing to give alms, 'Passion and Principle', 'Cousin William', a story about dark passion, and 'Gervase Skinner', about a miser who loses his money. Hook well understood his method of framing story in humorous incident and social observation. 'Give me', he said, 'a story to tell, and I can tell it, but I cannot create' (Barham, 169). The hero of *Maxwell* (1830), his next and most carefully constructed novel, is a close portrait of his friend Cannon, while his later works *Gilbert Gurney* and *Gurney Married* (1836 and 1838) are thinly disguised portraits and a string of anecdotes from real life. They appeared in the *New Monthly Magazine*, of which he became editor, in 1836. In the interval he had written *The Parson's Daughter* (1833) and *Love and Pride* (1833); *Jack Brag*, published in 1836, is a satire on freeloading. Turning to biography, he published in 1832 a life of Sir David Baird, rewrote reminiscences of Michael Kelly, and began a life of Charles Mathews, which was discontinued following differences with his family. Hook's last novel of importance was *Births, Marriages and Deaths* (1839), a novel about jealousy. His health failing, works after this are believed to be only partially from his own hand.

Hook died at his house, Egmont villa, in Fulham on 24 August 1841, 'done up', as he said, 'in purse, in mind and in body' (*QR*, 100). His effects were seized by the crown as preferential creditor, but his family were provided for by

subscription (although he never married, he and Mary Anne Doughty, with whom he lived, had six children). Tellingly, except for support from the king of Hanover, this subscription did not include support from his aristocratic patrons. He was, wrote John Gibson Lockhart, editor of the *Quarterly Review*, 'human, charitable, generous. … and there was that about him which made it hard to be often in his society without regarding him with as much of fondness as of admiration' (ibid., 104). He appears in Disraeli's *Coningsby* as Lucian Gay and in Thackeray's *Vanity Fair* as Lord Steyne's toady Mr Wagg. Coleridge, a contemporary, described him as being 'as true a genius as Dante' (ibid., 66). Hook's genius lay in his extremely sharp wit and his clever improvisations. His hoaxes are as indicative of this as his prose. GRAEME HARPER

Sources R. A. Jones, 'Theodore Hook: his life and works', MA diss., U. Wales, Bangor, 1932 · B. N. Dunn, *The man who was John Bull: the biography of Theodore Edward Hook* (1996) · *QR*, 72 (1843), 53–108 · R. H. D. Barham, *The life and remains of Theodore Edward Hook*, rev. edn (1853) · *DNB* · will, PRO, PROB 11/1956, sig. 30

Archives Hammersmith and Fulham Archives and Local History Centre, London, diary; letters; papers · Hunt. L., letters · NRA, priv. coll., corresp. | Hammersmith and Fulham Archives and Local History Centre, London, corresp. with T. Baylis and T. Croker · NL Wales, letters to William Blackwood & Sons · University of Chicago Library, letters to John Wilson Croker

Likenesses T. E. Hook, self-portrait, drawing, c.1831, Yale U. · D. Maclise, pencil drawing, 1834, NPG [*see illus.*] · R. J. Lane, lithograph, pubd 1839 (after Count D'Orsay), BM, NPG · stipple and line engraving, 1839, BM, NPG · stipple and line engraving, 1841, BM, NPG · W. Brockedon, chalk drawing, NPG · E. U. Eddis, oils, NPG · S. Freeman, stipple (after Bennett), BM; repro. in *Monthly Mirror* (1807) · D. Maclise, lithograph, NPG; repro. in *Fraser's Magazine* (1834)

Hook, Walter Farquhar

Hook, Walter Farquhar (1798–1875), dean of Chichester, was born on 13 March 1798 in Conduit Street, London, the eldest child of the Revd James *Hook (1772?–1828) and his wife, Anne Farquhar. His early childhood was spent at his father's rectory of Hertingfordbury.

Education and early career At the age of nine Hook was sent with his only brother, Robert, to Dr Michael Henry Thornhill Luscombe's school at Hertford, and two years later to Tiverton School, where the discipline was severe but the teaching indifferent. In 1812 he was entered as a commoner at Winchester College, where he formed his lifelong friendship with William Page Wood. Although weak at both formal scholarship and games, he acquired at Winchester a deep love for the works of Shakespeare and Milton, and his physical strength ensured that he was never bullied. Indeed, he retained his substantial and robust physique for the rest of his life. By working diligently he passed the examination to enter the sixth form, and twice won the silver medal for speech-day recitations.

In 1817 Hook's grandfather, Sir Walter *Farquhar (1738–1819), obtained a nomination for him from the prince regent to a studentship at Christ Church, Oxford. Here he had an undistinguished career, leading a rather isolated and reclusive life, with little interest in the formal course of studies; he became a keen reader of the works of Sir Walter Scott, and made his first, rather tentative, contacts with some of the future leaders of the Oxford Movement, such as E. B. Pusey and J. H. Newman. His failure in 1821 to win the Newdigate prize for an English poem, the only university honour which he tried to obtain, was a great disappointment to him, and he was glad to leave Oxford after graduating BA in 1821. He subsequently obtained his MA in 1824, and his BD and DD in 1837.

This life of comparative indolence changed completely after Hook's ordination as deacon on 30 September 1821. He now acquired a sense of purpose and direction that had previously been absent, and his time as his father's curate from 1821 to 1825 at Whippingham in the Isle of Wight was spent in an intensive programme of study. He built a small hut for himself where he spent up to ten hours a day working through a detailed reading plan of church history and theology, which confirmed his high-church interpretation of Anglicanism. His ideas were clearly outlined in his first published sermon in 1822, and at Christmas that year he was ordained priest. At the same time he discovered a talent for pastoral work. In the village of East Cowes, some 2 miles from the rectory and with no church of its own, Hook improvised Sunday evening services in a sail-loft, and for the first time in his life came into intimate contact with working people.

This growing self-confidence was demonstrated in 1825 when Hook's former schoolmaster, Dr Luscombe, pointed to the absence of episcopal supervision for the scattered Anglican congregations on the continent. After the initial proposal of a suffragan to the bishop of London was rejected for constitutional reasons, it was Hook who pointed to the precedent of the Scottish Episcopal church consecrating the first bishop for the American republic in 1785. His idea was adopted, and on 20 March 1825 Dr Luscombe was himself consecrated at Stirling, Hook preaching the sermon. This was subsequently published as *An attempt to demonstrate the Catholicism of the Church of England and other branches of the episcopal church*, in form and content marking an advance in his thinking over the sermon of 1822. In May 1826 Hook defended the consecration of Luscombe in an article in the *Christian Remembrancer*, which further demonstrated his recently acquired command of church history.

With the departure of his father to the deanery of Worcester in 1825 Hook left Whippingham and was appointed perpetual curate of Moseley, near Birmingham. Here he established a village school and experienced the first opposition to his work from local evangelicals. His appointment to a lectureship at St Philip's, Birmingham, in 1827 enabled him to appoint a curate at Moseley, while he established a penitentiary in Birmingham.

Vicar of Coventry In 1828 Hook became vicar of Holy Trinity, Coventry, and it was here that he had his first contact with a large urban parish, an experience that was to prepare him for his later work in Leeds. He arrived at Coventry in a period of great economic distress among the textile workers of the town, with much consequent poverty, and from this point onwards Hook's ministry always combined spiritual revival with a strong social concern. By 1830 he had begun evening services, and in 1831 a course of lectures. When he arrived in Coventry there were only 120 children in the Sunday schools; by the time he left in 1837 there were 1200. He increased the frequency of holy communion, and founded a savings bank and the Religious and Useful Knowledge Society. In all this work he was now supported by his wife, Anna Delicia (*d.* 1871), eldest daughter of Dr John *Johnstone, whom he married on 4 June 1829. They had several children, the eldest son dying in 1836.

It was while Hook was at Coventry that the Oxford Movement gained momentum with the first of the Tracts for the Times appearing in September 1833. His relationship to the Tractarians was often misunderstood at the time, and has sometimes been misinterpreted subsequently. Hook's theological position had been clearly formed in the years before the movement began, and, while he showed much sympathy with its earlier manifestations, distributing the tracts among his flock in Coventry, he also had some clear areas of disagreement with the movement's leaders, valuing the church establishment and its sixteenth-century Reformers more highly than many of them did. Over the years his reservations matured into distrust, especially with what he saw as the increasingly Roman tendencies of the more extreme members of the movement. Hook always remained a traditional high-churchman, and, unlike some of that persuasion such as Henry Newland, he never departed from his original views.

Vicar of Leeds and dean of Chichester In 1837 Hook became vicar of Leeds: it was his work there over the following twenty-two years as a pioneer in restoring the position of the Church of England in the new industrial towns that marked it as one of the most important parochial ministries of the nineteenth century. However, even before his formal election by the trustees, Hook encountered opposition in the form of a petition against his appointment signed by 400 of his future parishioners, and he was attacked in the local press as a Tractarian. At that time Leeds was a town of very decided protestant sympathies; as Hook himself wrote to Samuel Wilberforce in 1837: 'the *de facto* established religion is Methodism'. Between 1770 and 1840 some twenty-two Wesleyan Methodist chapels had been founded in the outer townships of Leeds alone. In contrast in 1825 the Church of England had its parish church, thirteen chapels of ease, and only eighteen clergy, many of whom were non-resident, for a parish of 125,000 souls. It was a system which had proved unworkable in the eighteenth century, and was now totally inadequate for an industrial town of the nineteenth. In the years immediately before Hook's arrival in Leeds, Anglicans had lost control of the improvement commission in 1829 and of the town council following the Municipal Corporations Act of 1835. In 1827 the nonconformist majority in the vestry had voted against any further payments towards the building of new Anglican churches, and by 1833 the majority of the churchwardens were nonconformists; not surprisingly the sums raised by the church rate fell from £2611 in 1818, to £614 in 1833, and from that latter year no further rate was raised.

Hook's achievements in Leeds fall into three broad

areas. First of all, he largely overcame the suspicion and opposition which he faced in 1837; secondly, he reconstructed the material resources of the Church of England; and thirdly, he developed a new concept of pastoral mission for an urban community. Upon his arrival the ratepayers deliberately elected seven churchwardens hostile to him who refused to pay to replace the tattered surplices and service books. However, Hook's first success came as early as 19 August 1837, at a meeting in the Old Cloth Hall called to fix a church rate. He effectively found himself faced by a hostile mob of 3000 persons, but with shrewdness, good humour, wit, and tolerance brought the meeting to an end with a vote of thanks to himself carried by acclamation. During the following years Hook encountered opposition on many occasions, notably in March 1841, when it became known that he had defended Newman's publication of Tract 90 in letters to Newman and others, and again faced a hostile audience at a meeting of the Pastoral Aid Society in Leeds. But gradually the opposition subsided in the face of his tireless work in Leeds, and his departure in 1859 was marked by a testimonial collection of 2000 guineas.

Hook knew that the material resources at his disposal when he first arrived in Leeds were totally inadequate to the demands made of them. Nevertheless, one of his first decisions was to build a new parish church, which was completed in 1841 at a cost of £28,000, and which had a capacity of nearly 4000 persons, many of them in free seating. He also embarked on a parallel programme of church building throughout the town, and by the time he left Leeds he had doubled the number of Anglican churches to thirty-six. In addition, he increased the number of parsonages from six to twenty-nine, and the number of church schools from three to thirty. In all of this work he found a ready ally in Charles Thomas Longley, the first bishop of the newly reconstructed diocese of Ripon in 1836; the Diocesan Church Building Society gave grants of up to 30 per cent of the cost for building many of the new churches in Leeds. In many ways the centrepiece of this aspect of Hook's work was the Leeds Vicarage Act of 1844, by which the chapels of ease were reconstituted as parishes in their own right, the former vicar sacrificing not only control but also about one-third of his income.

The liturgical and pastoral life of the town's Anglican churches also underwent a transformation, with Hook increasing the frequency and dignity of the services. His new parish church was specifically designed for a surpliced choir and sacramental worship. When he arrived in Leeds the parish church could barely muster fifty communicants; within four years he had raised that to nearly 500, and could count former Methodist ministers among their number. However, as well as gaining friends by his work Hook could also on occasion arouse equal measures of hostility. His open support for the Ten Hours Movement for factory reform as demonstrated in his speech to a public meeting in Leeds in 1844, when he defended the proposed bill then before parliament on medical, moral, and educational grounds, caused a temporary rift with some of his supporters among the Leeds merchants and manufacturers. In 1846 he published a pamphlet, in the form of a letter to the bishop of St David's, outlining his views on education: he argued that only the state had the capacity to educate all the nation's children, but as there was no longer a common religion in England, secular and religious education should be separated and no one denomination favoured over another. Such ideas led to criticism of him by other high-churchmen, the National Society, and some nonconformists. On the other hand, his frequent lectures at mechanics' institutes and his friendly relations with his churchwardens who were Chartists made him popular with the working population of Leeds. In his early life Hook had been a natural tory, but by the early 1850s he had become sceptical of all organized political parties; the one politician with whom he retained friendly relations throughout his career was William Gladstone, who shared his educational views.

Hook's relationship with his fellow Tractarians also underwent change in the 1850s. His one major disappointment at Leeds was the building of St Saviour's church by E. B. Pusey as a Tractarian centre in the town. His initial support for this was shaken in 1847 when the first clergy from this church converted to Roman Catholicism, followed by further waves of converts into the early 1850s. Indeed, this whole episode was crucial in confirming his own growing disillusionment with the Oxford Movement. By 1859 Hook's energies were clearly waning, and in that year he accepted the offer of the deanery of Chichester, where he could retire to compose his most significant work of scholarship, the *Lives of the Archbishops of Canterbury*, of which ten volumes were completed before his death. This, his *Church Dictionary*, and *A Dictionary of Ecclesiastical Biography* (8 vols., 1845–52) were his major academic works. Although well regarded in their time, they were soon overtaken by more advanced historical scholarship. Many of his sermons were collected into two volumes entitled *The Church and her Ordinances* (1876). On 5 May 1871 his wife died, and he followed her on 20 October 1875, dying at the deanery in Chichester and being buried next to her at Mid Lavant, Sussex, on 27 October.

GEORGE HERRING

Sources W. R. W. Stephens, *The life and letters of Walter Farquhar Hook*, 2 vols. (1878) · D. Fraser, ed., *A history of modern Leeds* (1980) · N. Yates, *The Oxford Movement and parish life: St Saviour's, Leeds, 1839–1929*, Borthwick Papers, 48 (1975) · C. J. Stranks, *Dean Hook* (1954) · R. J. Wood, *Church extension in Leeds* (1964) · A. D. Gilbert, *Religion and society in industrial England* (1976) · A. Briggs, *Victorian cities* (1968) · A. Briggs, ed., *Chartist studies* (1959) · J. T. Ward, *The factory movement, 1830–1855* (1962)

Archives Leeds Central Library, records of forty Anglican churches · Leeds Leisure Services, sermon preached at Leeds · priv. coll. · Pusey Oxf., corresp. | BL, corresp. with Samuel Butler, Add. MSS 34588–34591, *passim* · BL, corresp. with W. E. Gladstone, Add. MS 44213 · Bodl. Oxf., letters to Robert Wilberforce · Bodl. Oxf., corresp. with Samuel Wilberforce · JRL, letters to E. A. Freeman · LPL, letters to C. T. Longley · LPL, corresp. with A. C. Tait · LPL, letters to Cecil Wray

Likenesses C. E. Wagstaff, mezzotint, pubd c.1838 (after F. Rosenberg), BM, NPG · W. Holl?, stipple, pubd 1849 (after G. Richmond), BM, NPG · W. K. Briggs, portrait, repro. in Stephens, *Life and letters*, frontispiece · W. D. Keyworth, effigy, St Peter's Church, Leeds ·

F. W. Pomeroy, bronze statue, City Square, Leeds · D. J. Pound, stipple and line (after photograph by Navey), NPG · Russell & Sons, cartes-de-visite, NPG

Wealth at death under £5000: probate, 3 Dec 1875, CGPLA Eng. & Wales

Hook, William. *See* Hooke, William (1600/01–1678).

Hooke, John (*bap.* 1634, *d.* 1710). *See under* Hooke, William (1600/01–1678).

Hooke, John (1655–1712), judge, was born in Drogheda, Ireland, the eldest son of John Hooke, a merchant, and his wife, Margaret, daughter of Christopher Hooke of Alway, Gloucestershire. The Jacobite politician Nathaniel *Hooke (1664–1738) was his brother. John was educated at Kilkenny School and on 28 June 1672 entered as a pensioner at Trinity College, Dublin, under the tuition of Richard Acton of Drogheda. He was admitted to Gray's Inn on 3 February 1675 and was called to the bar on 8 February 1681. His wife, Elizabeth (*d.* 1736), was the daughter of Major-General John Lambert. Their son, Nathaniel *Hooke (*d.* 1763), wrote a history of Rome.

Following the revolution of 1688 Hooke achieved office on 15 August 1689 as second justice of Anglesey, Caernarfon, and Merioneth, rising to chief justice there on 2 May 1695. Also in 1695 he became deputy to Sir J. Coombes as chief justice of Chester. On 8 March 1699 a meeting was held at Hooke's house in Lincoln's Inn which resulted in the foundation of the Society for Promoting Christian Knowledge (SPCK). Hooke was the organization's first treasurer, and it continued to meet in his residence for the next three years. In November 1700 he was made a serjeant-at-law, his patrons being Lord Guilford (another founder member of the society) and Sir Nathan Wright (the new lord keeper). However, Hooke was not reappointed a Welsh judge on the accession of Queen Anne.

Hooke returned to office as chief justice of Anglesey in May 1706, although he was still practising as a barrister in Chester in August of that year. In 1707 he was accused by Lord Bulkeley of demanding presents, which was examined by a committee of the House of Commons. Hooke's explanation that it was merely a customary present from the town of Beaumaris was not sufficient to sway the committee which found him guilty, but when the matter was reported to the house he was exonerated by a vote of 178 to 130. Hooke's politics are difficult to determine, and he himself rejected a party label, informing Robert Harley, the new chief minister, that 'I cannot list myself under either of the two common denominations, Whig or Tory'. Further he did not support 'an absolute unlimited Toleration', but opposed 'persecuting good loyal Protestants who agreed with the Church in fundamentals' (Rose, 173, 188). Hooke was removed from office in 1711 and died in 1712, affirming in his will of February 1711 (proved in May 1712) his 'zeal for true and pure Christianity and moderation' (Woolrych, 2. 467).   STUART HANDLEY

Sources Baker, *Serjeants*, 452, 519 · Burtchaell & Sadlier, *Alum. Dubl.*, 409 · J. Foster, *The register of admissions to Gray's Inn, 1521–1889, together with the register of marriages in Gray's Inn chapel, 1695–1754* (privately printed, London, 1889), 320 · H. W. Woolrych, *Lives of eminent serjeants-at-law of the English bar*, 2 vols. (1869), 2.467 · W. R. Williams, *The history of the great sessions in Wales, 1542–1830* (privately printed, Brecon, 1899), 111 · W. K. L. Clarke, *A history of the S.P.C.K.* (1959), 10, 91 · C. Rose, 'The origins and ideals of the SPCK, 1699–1716', *The Church of England, c.1689–c.1833*, ed. J. Walsh and others (1993), 172–90, 173, 188 · will, PRO, PROB 11/526, sig. 92 · *GM*, 1st ser., 6 (1736), 56 · R. J. Fletcher, ed., *The pension book of Gray's Inn*, 2 (1910), 67 · *The diary of Henry Prescott, LLB, deputy registrar of Chester diocese*, ed. J. Addy and others, 1, Lancashire and Cheshire RS, 127 (1987), 113 · *DNB*

Hooke, Luke Joseph (1714–1796), Roman Catholic theologian, was born in Dublin, one of three children of Nathaniel *Hooke (*d.* 1763), historian of Rome, and his wife, Mary Gore, an English protestant. He was brought to Paris in the 1720s probably by his father, who acted as secretary to his uncle, Nathaniel Hooke (1664–1738), Jacobite and French diplomatic agent. When his father quit Paris for England, his son remained with his grand-uncle and his wife, Lady Eleanor McCarthy Reagh (1683–1731), in the rue St Jacques du Haut-Pas.

Hooke took the degree of master in arts in 1734, and it is likely that he got to know Denis Diderot at this time. The following year he entered the Seminary of St Nicolas du Chardonnet, as a student for the Dublin archdiocese. A bachelor of theology of Paris University in 1737, he succeeded as prior of St Germain-des-Vaux in 1738. In 1739 his thesis for the licence in theology, which defended the ecumenicity of the Council of Florence, was referred to the *parlement* of Paris. He received his licence in 1740 and was appointed professor of theology in 1742 to succeed his countryman James Wogan (*d.* 1742). He supported the Jacobite rising of 1745. Building up a reputation as a modernizing theologian and keeping abreast of intellectual developments in England, he prepared his lecture notes for publication in 1751. However, before the text appeared Hooke agreed to preside over the examination of the thesis of Jean Martin De Prades, a priest of Montauban diocese and contributor to the second volume of the *Encyclopédie*. Although the faculty awarded the grade, De Prades was subsequently charged with deism. Hooke was implicated and, a victim of faculty politics, lost his chair. Despite this set-back he published two volumes of his *Religionis naturalis et revelatae principia* in 1752, a third appearing two years later with a *Monitum lectori*.

The *Principia*, often mistaken for mere apology, actually sought to build bridges between traditional theology and the new science. It abandoned the scholastic system of presentation and attempted to integrate the work of Isaac Newton into its theological system. It included a remarkably positive assessment of human desire. There were Venetian (1763) and German (1783) editions. Reprinted in Jacques Paul Minge's *Theologiae cursus completus* (1860) it influenced generations of Catholic theological textbooks. In 1762 Hooke was appointed chairman of a faculty of theology committee set up to examine J. J. Rousseau's *Émile*. Buoyed up by the successful conclusion of this charge, he put his name forward for election to a vacant theology chair. Nevertheless, his election was contested by the archbishop of Paris, who later ordered a boycott of his lectures. In the ensuing legal wrangle Hooke published his *Lettre de M. l'Abbé Hooke à Mgr l'archevêque de Paris* (1763). He was forced to resign his chair in 1766; however, he retained the support of many of his colleagues, and in 1767 was appointed professor of Hebrew and Chaldean.

Hooke developed strong links with the English Benedictines resident in Paris. Among these was Dom John Bede Brewer, who in 1774 undertook to republish and expand the *Principia*. Hooke translated into French some of his father's writings on Roman history under the title *Discours et réflexions critiques sur l'histoire et le gouvernement de l'ancienne Rome* (1770–84). He participated in public debates concerning Roman history. In 1775 he welcomed Samuel Johnson to Paris. 'We walked round the palace and had some talk', wrote Johnson, and the next day Hooke returned his call at Johnson's inn (Boswell, *Life*, 2.397). Hooke edited *Les mémoires du maréchal de Berwick* in 1778. In the same year he was appointed chief librarian at the Mazarine Library, and under his enlightened rule the collection grew considerably. In 1791 he refused to take the oath to the civil constitution of the clergy. This exposed him to a plot mounted by his assistant, Le Blond, to remove him from the library. He fought back through a series of published letters and petitions to the king, the national assembly, and, later, the provisional executive of the French Republic. In 1791 he published *Principes sur l'origine, la nature, la souveraineté, l'étendue et l'alliance des deux puissances*, an important pamphlet on the relations between ecclesiastical and civil powers. It contains a strong argument for an independent state church. Deprived of his position at the Mazarine he retired to St Cloud where he died, in poverty, on 12 April 1796.

THOMAS O'CONNOR

Sources T. O'Connor, *An Irish theologian in Enlightenment France: Luke Joseph Hooke, 1714–96* (1995) • T. O'Connor, 'Surviving the civil constitution of the clergy: Luke Joseph Hooke's revolutionary experiences', *Eighteenth-Century Ireland*, 11 (1996), 129–45 • A. Gwynn, 'A forgotten Irish theologian', *Studies: an Irish Quarterly Review*, 63 (1974), 259–68 • L. W. B. Brockliss and P. Ferté, 'Biographical register of Irish clerics educated at the universities of Paris and Toulouse–Cahors', Royal Irish Acad. • Boswell, *Life* • R. R. Palmer, *Catholics and unbelievers in eighteenth century France* (1939) • série E, Notariat de Saint Cloud, Archives Départementales, Hauts-de-Seine, 27 Germinal AN IV • *Correspondence of Colonel N. Hooke*, ed. W. D. Macray, 2 vols., Roxburghe Club, 92, 95 (1870–71)
Archives Archives Nationales, Paris, MM 257–259 | Bibliothèque Nationale, Paris, Collection Joly de Fleury, 194, f.5 • Royal Arch., Stuart
Likenesses bust, 1760–99, Mazarine Library, Paris
Wealth at death died in poverty; odd clothes, a wig, five books in English, two assignats of 5 livres, one of 25 sols: Archives Départementales, Hauts-de-Seine, série E, Notariat de Saint Cloud, 27 Germinal AN IV

Hooke, Nathaniel, Jacobite first Baron Hooke (1664–1738), Jacobite politician, was born at Corballis, co. Meath, the third son of John Hooke, a merchant of Drogheda, and his wife, Margaret, the daughter of Christopher Hooke of Alway, Gloucestershire. His grandfather Thomas Hooke was a merchant and alderman of Dublin. John *Hooke, serjeant-at-law, was his eldest brother. In 1679 he entered

Trinity College, Dublin, but he left almost immediately, possibly on account of his religious opinions, which were puritan. He went to Glasgow University in 1680, but soon moved to Sidney Sussex College, Cambridge, where he was admitted a sizar on 6 July 1681, leaving Cambridge as he had left Glasgow, without taking a degree. He then went abroad, joining the earl of Argyll in the Netherlands. In 1685 he landed with the duke of Monmouth at Lyme Regis, acting as the duke's private independent chaplain. When Monmouth passed into Somerset at the beginning of July, Hooke was sent secretly to London with Henry Danvers to raise an insurrection in the city. He was exempted from the general pardon issued on 10 March 1686, but in 1688 he gave himself up and was pardoned after what later enemies would claim were 'some services' involving 'a good deal of treachery' (*Stuart Papers*, 6.548).

Hooke then became a loyal servant of James II and converted to Roman Catholicism, though it was said that his conversion did not occur until the court went into exile at St Germain-en-Laye (ibid.). After James's abdication Hooke joined Viscount Dundee in Scotland, but in May 1689 was captured at Chester and committed to the Tower of London. He was released on 12 February 1690 and travelled to Ireland, where he served in the Jacobite army at the battle of the Boyne, and then entered the French service in the Irish regiment of Galmoy. He was examined regarding Jacobite plots in March 1696. Hooke was in attendance upon King James in 1701, but received a discharge from his service in that year so that he could take service 'under other princes' (ibid., 4.3). In 1702 Hooke entered into communication with the duke of Marlborough; the next year he held a command in the regiment of Sparre, and served with the French army in Flanders and on the Moselle. In 1704 he married Eleanor Susan, sometime maid of honour to the exiled queen-dowager. She was the daughter of Donogh, or Denis, MacCarthy and Catherine Douvns. They had one son, James Nathaniel Hooke (1705–1744), and a daughter, Louise Sophia Françoise (*bap.* 1710), sometime governess of the royal children of France. In August 1705 Hooke went on a mission to the Scottish Jacobites in company with his brother John, and in 1706 he obtained letters of naturalization in France and took part in the battle of Ramillies. In April 1707 he again went to Scotland, with Lieutenant-Colonel John Murray, to confer with the Jacobites. The next year he became a brigadier in the French army (3 March 1708), was created Baron Hooke of Hooke Castle, co. Waterford (in the Jacobite peerage), and was present at the Dunkirk expedition of that year, and at Malplaquet in the next.

Hooke had now wearied of negotiating schemes for rebellion with the Jacobites in Scotland, and refused in 1709 to go again as an emissary. He is probably the Mr Hooke who appears as a correspondent of the duke of Marlborough in 1710, and in 1711 he went to Dresden on a diplomatic mission from Louis XIV to Frederick Augustus, king of Poland and elector of Saxony, but this negotiation was superseded by the general arrangements for peace at Utrecht. Hooke took no active part in the Jacobite rising of 1715. He communicated in that year with John Dalrymple, second earl of Stair, British ambassador in Paris, but there is nothing to prove that he turned traitor to the Jacobite cause; it is more probable that in his relations with Stair he was acting as a spy in the Jacobite interest. Plans were, however, afoot in 1716 to appoint him Jacobite ambassador to the holy Roman emperor. On 18 March 1718 he became a *maréchal de camp* in the French army, though he was at this time heavily afflicted with rheumatism. Despite his protestations he was accused of being, and, on account of his support for Marischal, probably was, the active leader of the court opposition against Mar, Kellie, and Middleton, who in 1718 described him as 'no good man' (*Stuart Papers*, 6.548). He was still in favour with James III (James Francis Edward Stuart), who appointed him envoy to Prussia on 12 May 1718, perhaps because he was still active in organizing his relations in London to cause trouble for the Hanoverian regime. On 1 January 1720 his letters of French naturalization were confirmed and registered, and on 27 February 1721 he became a knight commander of the order of St Louis. Hooke married his second wife, Helen de St Jean, widow respectively of the Sieur O'Brien and the Sieur MacCarthy, shortly before his death in France on 25 October 1738.

Lord Hooke's correspondence from 1703 to 1707, partly transcribed by his nephew, Nathaniel Hooke (*d.* 1763), the historian of Rome, is now in the Bodleian Library in Oxford. This was edited, with a memoir by W. D. Macray, for the Roxburgh Club in 1870–71. Portions of Hooke's correspondence had previously appeared in *Révolutions d'Écosse et d'Irelande en 1707, 1708, et 1709*, published at The Hague in 1758, and in James Macpherson's *Original Papers* (1775).   W. A. J. ARCHBOLD, rev. M. R. GLOZIER

Sources DNB · lettres de noblesse, 1669–1790, Centre Accueil de la Recherche des Archives Nationales, Paris, O¹54 · lettres d'anoblissement de confirmation ou de maintenu de noblesse, enregistrées à la chambre des comptes de Paris, de 1635 à 1787, Centre Accueil de la Recherche des Archives Nationales, Paris, pp. 146/bis · lettres de naturalité et lettres de légitimation, 1635–1787, Centre Accueil de la Recherche des Archives Nationales, Paris, pp. 151/bis · Louise Sophia Françoise Butler, *née* Hooke, Centre Accueil de la Recherche des Archives Nationales, Paris, O¹670, fol. 320 · *Calendar of the Stuart papers belonging to his majesty the king, preserved at Windsor Castle*, 7 vols., HMC, 56 (1902–23), vol. 1, p. 217; vol. 3, p. 149; vol. 5, pp. 498–9 · J. Macpherson, ed., *Original papers: containing the secret history of Great Britain*, 2 vols. (1775) · M. H. Massue de Ruvigny, ed., *The Jacobite peerage* (1904); repr. (1974) · *Third report*, HMC, 2 (1872), 328

Archives Bodl. Oxf., corresp., dispatches, and papers [copies]

Hooke, Nathaniel (*d.* 1763), writer, was the eldest son of John *Hooke (1655–1712), serjeant-at-law, and Elizabeth, *née* Lambert (*d.* 1736). He was the nephew of Nathaniel *Hooke. The younger Nathaniel is thought by the antiquary John Kirk to have studied with Alexander Pope at Twyford School, near Winchester, and formed a lifelong friendship with the poet. He was admitted to Lincoln's Inn on 6 February 1702. Writing to the earl of Oxford on 17 October 1722, Hooke spoke of how 'the late epidemical distemper' (that is, interest in the stocks of the South Sea Company) had 'seized him', and that 'he was in some measure happy to find himself at that instant just worth nothing'. In the letter Hooke sought employment and also

permission to dedicate to Oxford his *Life of Fénelon* (1723), a translation from the French of the work by Andrew Michael Ramsay. The permission was granted, and from 1723 until his death Hooke enjoyed the confidence and patronage of many distinguished men, including Oxford, the earl of Marchmont, Arthur Onslow, speaker in the House of Commons, Pope, the physician George Cheyne, and Dr King, principal of St Mary Hall, Oxford. In 1741 Hooke was recommended by Lord Chesterfield to Sarah, dowager duchess of Marlborough, as someone able to assist her in the publication of her memoirs. The elderly duchess recounted a narrative of her time at court which Hooke wrote up and published in book form in 1742. During the book's compilation Hooke lived with the duchess and the two developed a friendship. As Pope told Lady Marlborough, Hooke's respect for his employer was of 'such a degree that I doubt whether he can be Impartial enough to be your Historian' (Harris, 332). For his work on her memoirs Hooke received £5000 from the duchess. During Hooke's residence with her Lady Marlborough commissioned him to negotiate with Pope for the suppression, in consideration of the payment of £3000, of the character of 'Atossa' in his *Epistles*. Hooke's Catholicism created tension in his relationship with the resolutely agnostic duchess. Finally, in 1743, Hooke's religious convictions became too irksome and the duchess ended their friendship. Hooke also brought a Roman Catholic ecclesiastic to take Pope's confession on his deathbed, angering Lord Bolingbroke who flew into a great passion on learning what had happened.

Bishop Warburton described Hooke as 'a mystic and quietist, and a warm disciple of Fénelon', Samuel Johnson observed that he 'was a virtuous man, as his history shows', and Pope suggested that Hooke and Conyers Middleton were the only two contemporary prose writers whose works were worth consulting by an English lexicographer. Other works by Hooke include *The Roman History, from the Building of Rome to the Ruin of the Commonwealth* (4 vols., 1738–71), a highly regarded study, reprinted in 1830; *Travels of Cyrus, with a Discourse on Mythology* (1739), translated by Hooke in twenty days while at Bath; *Observations* (1758), dedicated to Speaker Onslow, and 'Six Letters to a Lady of Quality', first published in *The contrast, or, An antidote against the pernicious principles disseminated in the letters of the late earl of Chesterfield* (1791). With his wife, Mary, *née* Gore, Hook had three children. At his death at Cookham, Berkshire, on 19 July 1763 he was survived by two sons, Thomas, a Church of England clergyman, and Luke Joseph *Hooke. His daughter, Jane Mary, died in April 1793 and was buried at Hedsor churchyard in Buckinghamshire where her father had also been buried thirty years earlier.   THOMPSON COOPER, rev. ADAM I. P. SMITH

Sources Nichols, *Lit. anecdotes* · Watt, *Bibl. Brit.* · W. T. Lowndes, *The bibliographer's manual of English literature*, 4 vols. (1834) · *N&Q*, 2nd ser., 7 (1859), 258, 375, 423 · F. Harris, *A passion for government: the life of Sarah, duchess of Marlborough* (1991) · *GM*, 1st ser., 33 (1763), 362 · will, PRO, PROB 11/890, sig. 386

Likenesses B. Dandridge, oils, NPG

Wealth at death see will, PRO, PROB 11/890, sig. 386

Hooke, Robert (1635–1703), natural philosopher, was born on 18 July 1635 in the village of Freshwater on the Isle of Wight, the son of the Revd John Hooke (*d.* 1648), minister of the parish, and his wife, Cecily Gyles (*d.* 1665). According to some autobiographical notes reported by Richard Waller in *The Posthumous Works of Robert Hooke* (1705), young Robert's constitution was so weak and sickly that his parents feared for his life for at least his first seven years. He was nursed at home, in contrast to his brother and sisters who were nursed abroad. Hooke reports himself to have been sprightly and active in running and leaping, though incapable of more robust exercise. His quick capacity to learn initially led his father to instruct him towards the ministry, but young Hooke's severe headaches interfered with his studies and this plan was abandoned. Left to his own interests, he constructed mechanical toys and devices, including a wooden clock 'that would go' and a ship model about a yard long complete with rigging and some small guns that could fire as it sailed. He also exhibited talent in drawing.

Robert Hooke's father died in October 1648. John Aubrey reports in his *Brief Lives* that the thirteen-year-old Robert received an inheritance of £100, but according to the actual will Robert's inheritance amounted to £50 (including £10 from Robert's grandmother on his mother's side) and all his father's books (Nakajima). Hooke was sent to London to study with the painter Sir Peter Lely, his inheritance used to secure his apprenticeship. Waller reports that the smell of the oil paints increased Hooke's headaches, curtailing this activity, while Aubrey ascribes the brevity of this association to young Hooke's conclusion that he could teach himself this art and save the apprentice fee. Aubrey adds that Hooke also received instruction in drawing from Samuel Cowper. Hooke subsequently went to live in the house of Richard Busby, master of Westminster School. Though he attended school infrequently, he actively pursued his education, learning Latin and Greek and gaining an acquaintance with Hebrew and with oriental languages. By Aubrey's account, Hooke mastered the first six books of Euclid in a week and 'learned to play twenty lessons on the organ', which presumably means that he learned to play the organ in twenty lessons.

Introduction to science In 1653 or 1654 Hooke went to Christ Church, Oxford, where his musical training was sufficient to secure the post of chorister. He served as assistant to the chemist Thomas Willis and subsequently to Robert Boyle. Working for Boyle, Hooke was exposed to active scientific research: he was responsible for Boyle's first workable pneumatic engine (vacuum pump) and assisted Boyle in his experiments on the spring and weight of the air. At Oxford, Hooke was brought into contact with many other of the finest natural philosophers of the day, including John Wilkins, Seth Ward, William Petty, John Wallis, and Christopher Wren. Among his scientific endeavours there were the pursuit of astronomy and, instigated by Ward, the development of clockwork for recording observations. Hooke later ascribed his invention of a spring-regulated watch to this time. He did not receive a bachelor's degree, but was granted his MA degree in 1663.

In November 1662 Hooke was formally proposed as curator of experiments for the newly formed Royal Society of London, his task being to provide three or four experiments at each meeting. This post was to be without recompense until the society could afford to provide a salary. Hooke lost no time in fulfilling his responsibilities, producing his first set of experiments before the society on 18 November. While not always providing the full complement of three or four experiments at every meeting, he almost invariably presented some demonstration or commentary. The value of this activity was soon recognized by the council of the Royal Society, which included Hooke on its list of 20 May 1663 of persons to be admitted as fellows.

The range of Hooke's demonstrations and commentaries in this early period was remarkable. Indeed, virtually all his later publications had their roots in work performed at this time, in enquiries which Hooke would address and then put aside, sometimes repeatedly over the years. These various endeavours were recorded week by week in the journal books of the Royal Society and eventually printed in Thomas Birch's *History of the Royal Society of London* (1757). In these volumes, as well as in the many brief references in Hooke's diaries (in the London Guildhall Library), Hooke addresses very different areas of science from week to week, day to day, and even within a single day. While his published accounts in the *Micrographia*, in his Cutler lectures, and in various articles, appear successively over many years, his actual practice involved a more complicated diversity of simultaneous endeavours. This diversity is even more remarkable given his responsibilities in the years following the great fire of London of 1666 as one of the official surveyors for the rebuilding.

Hooke's employment with the Royal Society gained him respect in the scientific community but his post continued to be without remuneration. An opportunity for a salaried position presented itself in 1664 with the resignation of Isaac Barrow as professor of geometry of Gresham College. On 20 May the committee for the college met to decide on Barrow's replacement, selecting Arthur Dacres over Hooke. A month later, a delegation from the Royal Society was ordered to speak to Sir John Cutler about his promise to pay £50 a year for life to Mr Hooke to lecture at Gresham College on the histories of trades. A formal statement of Hooke's appointment to the Cutler lectureship was made before the Royal Society on 9 November. The next week Hooke was proposed as 'curator by office' to the society, a salaried position corresponding to the volunteer post he had been holding. Although the council had decided some months previously on a yearly salary of £80 for the curator, this now became £30 in view of the £50 per year to be supplied by Cutler. This appointment in effect makes Hooke the first professional research scientist, employed specifically to enquire into the phenomena and principles of nature. On the other hand, as a salaried employee, distinct from the many volunteer curators for specific experiments drawn from the other fellows of the society, Hooke's social position was in principle one of servant. Thus he was frequently 'ordered' to try an experiment or to bring in an account, whereas other members of the society were 'desired' to carry out corresponding tasks. Hooke was, however, so successful in his experimental pursuits that within a couple of years he had made himself indispensable, and for the most part was allowed to determine his own experimental programme.

The 'Philosophical history' Hooke moved into Gresham College in September or October 1664 to lecture on the history of nature and art under the endowment provided by Cutler. Francis Bacon had insisted throughout his works that a history of nature was a necessary prerequisite to the formulation of a new natural philosophy. In his *New Atlantis* (1627) Bacon imagined an organization, 'Salomon's House', that would carry out this programme. To many of its early members the Royal Society was a realization of Salomon's House, and Hooke's promotion of a new natural history through his lectures was therefore an appropriate activity. Some of his ideas for this new natural philosophy are found in a series of manuscripts which are probably the texts of these early lectures (London, Guildhall Library, MS 1757/11; RS, classified papers 20.50a, 50b).

For Hooke as for Bacon the improvement of natural philosophy must rest on a suitably collected and arranged body of knowledge which Hooke calls the 'Philosophical history'. He divides the subjects of this history into art or trades versus natural phenomena, with the latter further divided and subdivided. Each investigation into a specific phenomenon is to be guided by an extended series of queries, the order of which serves to organize the observations being recorded. Should observations be found to favour contrary hypotheses, further queries are required to reach an 'experimentum crucis' sufficient to decide between the alternatives. Both here, and when he uses this term in the *Micrographia*, Hooke attributes this phrase to Francis Bacon. While Bacon presents in his *Novum organum* the idea of observations intended to distinguish between different supposed causes, he refers to these as 'instantias crucis'. The specific phrase 'experimentum crucis', best known for its use by Isaac Newton in his 1672 letter a 'New theory about light and colours', appears to have originated with Hooke.

Hooke elaborates upon Bacon's views on spreading among many investigators the work of compiling the history of nature and art. His list of qualifications for the 'Philosophical historian' provides insight into the body of learning he presumably hoped to attain. The historian must have a knowledge of mechanics and other mathematical learning and must have experience in experimental procedures and in the techniques of various trades. Since these last would be difficult for any one person to gain first hand, Hooke proposes that detailed accounts of specific trades be collected, an effort to which he himself made several contributions over the ensuing years. He suggests that the techniques of the tradesmen

themselves could benefit from the careful scrutiny of capable men not already set in the established procedures of that trade. He expects his historian to be familiar with the full range of current explanatory hypotheses and theories, but free from dogmatic adherence to any of them. The historian ought to repeat all experiments and observations at least two or three times, describing his instruments and manner of experimenting as well as recording the observations themselves.

The ideas presented in these lectures are restated in more polished form in Hooke's posthumously published essay 'A general scheme, or idea of the present state of natural philosophy, and how its defects may be remedied by a methodical proceeding in the making experiments and collecting observations, whereby to compile a natural history, as the solid basis for the superstructure of true philosophy' (Hooke, 1–70). This essay stands as the most compelling rendition of Baconian principles into a solid programme of scientific investigation.

The 'Philosophical algebra' Shortly after arriving at Gresham College, Hooke learned of an irregularity in the election which he had lost the year before. According to John Ward's manuscript 'Memoires relating to Gresham College', Hooke petitioned the college committee about this on 20 March 1665. The committee found that of the ten men present at the election the previous May, five had voted for Hooke and five for Dacres. Among this second group was the lord mayor, who then used his tie-breaking vote to declare the election in Dacres's favour. Since, however, the lord mayor was not actually a member of the committee and should not have voted unless there was a tie, Hooke had actually won the election by five votes to four, as was now recognized; he duly ascended to the geometry lectureship of Gresham College in June.

In both his lecture series of 1665 and his 'General scheme' of 1668, Hooke promises to provide a 'Philosophical algebra' or method for raising general principles of nature from the philosophical history. While he does not deliver on this promise, leaving the 'General scheme' unfinished, he does, however, provide hints about the nature of this method, claiming that it would bring to the study of nature the benefits which mathematical algebra brings to geometry. These last benefits are treated in detail by Hooke in a series of Latin manuscripts in the London Guildhall Library and in the English translation of one of these at the Royal Society (London, Guildhall Library, MS 1757/12; RS, classified papers 20.39). The Royal Society manuscript is dated June 1665, and the lectures show a smooth transition from his previous lectures on the philosophical history to a more mathematical topic fitting his new position.

In these lectures Hooke represents geometry and arithmetic as the studies of continuous and discontinuous quantities, respectively. Algebra is introduced, not as a third field of mathematics, but as an ancillary means of solving problems in geometry and arithmetic. For Hooke the power of algebra is that it facilitates the procedures of 'comparing, compounding and separating' elements of a problem leading towards the discovery of a solution. Algebra achieves this by:

> comprising in a small space a whole series of ratiocination so, as to a small cast of an eye as it were, and in an instant almost, one is enabled to examine and compare and change and transpose and order any part of it, as he pleases, with very little trouble and the greatest certainty.   (RS, classified papers 20.39, fol. 65v)

Hooke suggests that problems in the understanding of nature could likewise be solved if these same advantages were available to natural philosophy.

Near the end of the 'General scheme', after advocating the use of simple language in registering natural histories, Hooke suggests recording philosophical histories in a shorthand or abbreviated form. As in mathematical algebra, the use of 'obvious and plain symbols' is to help the mind to reach new insights in natural philosophy. Hooke's ideas in this area reflect the influence of Ward and Wilkins, his acquaintance with whom had carried on from Oxford to the Royal Society. These two scholars advocated the formulation of a universal character as part of a universal language, intended to replace Latin as the language of international communication. Ward and Wilkins, however, felt that this language should have a logical structure such that the words or symbols for objects and relations would reflect the essence of the things being represented. Hooke was much in contact with Wilkins during the years when the latter was composing *An Essay towards a Real Character and a Philosophical Language* (1668). Samuel Pepys mentions in his diary entry for 4 June 1666 that Hooke accompanied him home from Gresham College and borrowed some tables of nautical terms for Wilkins's book. Hooke praises Wilkins's invented language at the end of his Cutler lecture on helioscopes (1676) and prints a description of the principle of his spring-regulated watch in Wilkins's *Real Character*. Some years later Leibniz and Hooke engaged in a correspondence in which the former expresses views remarkably similar to Hooke's about the inventive power of a well-conceived set of symbols for representing objects and relations in nature. Hooke's statements within that correspondence exactly parallel his earlier claims for the philosophical algebra:

> My aims have always been much higher, viz. to make it not only useful for expressing and remembering of things and notions but to direct, regulate, assist and even necessitate and compel the mind to find out and comprehend whatsoever is knowable.   (RS, early letters, H.3.64)

The *Micrographia* Hooke's ideas about the collecting of observations of nature and art and the philosophical understanding to be adduced from them are exemplified in his most famous work, *Micrographia, or, Some physiological descriptions of minute bodies made by magnifying glasses, with observations and inquiries thereupon* (1665). This book initiated the field of microscopy. Just as Galileo, on turning his telescope to the heavens, had made one remarkable observation after another, so Hooke, applying his microscope to inanimate and animate objects, revealed equally remarkable features about their structure. His talent for drawing and attention to detail is evident in the many plates that adorn the volume, especially those of the fly,

gnat, and flea. His text provides clear and precise descriptions of observations, but also provides explanations of the things observed. A description 'Of the colours observable in muscovy glass [mica], and other thin bodies' serves as an introduction to a lengthy discussion of his two-colour (blue and red) theory of light. According to this theory, light is a motion transmitted through a medium, the source of which is the rapid vibration of the minute parts of the shining body. This vibration produces pulses in the surrounding medium which, according to Hooke, may be oblique to the line of propagation. If this obliqueness results in the weaker side or edge of the pulse arriving before the stronger, then the light registers on the eye as blue; if the stronger side precedes the weaker, then the light appears red. While Hooke's theory contains many ambiguous features, it does allow him to explain how white light can become coloured through refraction in prisms and through refraction and reflection in thin plates.

Hooke's observations of kidney stones and of crystals found in flint lead to a discussion of the regular form of crystals and the way these can arise from arrangements of tightly packed spherical particles. In his observations of petrified wood, Hooke notes the presence of small regular compartments which he terms cells, thereby introducing that term into the biological sciences. In his observations of cork he elaborates on his description of cells, ascribing to them a diameter of less than a thousandth of an inch. In treating fossils he proposes a process by which once living substances fossilize, thereby setting the stage for his later geological speculations in which fossils serve as a record of past life.

Observations of charcoal lead to a general discussion of combustion. Hooke contends that there is no element of fire present in combustible objects, but rather that combustion is a process in which a substance mixed in the air combines with some part of the combustible material. While Hooke does not discuss respiration in the *Micrographia*, his later treatments of this subject refer to the same substance in the air as being required for respiration. His experiments in this area came to include attempts to keep a vivisected dog alive by blowing air into its lungs with a bellows. In 1668 he showed that a bird remained healthy in a container of compressed air longer than in the same volume of common air, as does a burning lamp. Hooke later engaged in some experiments involving a large chamber in which he placed himself. He reports that the evacuation of a quarter of the air in the chamber caused him to experience pain in his ears and to become temporarily deaf, but that he suffered no other ill effects.

Hooke describes the glass drops (formed by dropping molten glass into cold water) which shatter entirely when their stems are broken. This leads him to a general discussion of heat, which he regards as arising from the agitation of the parts of a body. Greater agitation results in expansion or, as in the case of water heated in a sealed container, in a tendency to expand which can cause the container to burst. Hooke describes his work with sealed thermometers and his introduction of a scale with zero corresponding to the freezing point of distilled water.

Hooke includes in the *Micrographia* descriptions of a variety of instruments that he has recently invented. He describes the wheel barometer and a device based on the beard of a wild oat attached to a dial to register humidity in the air. He describes a device for measuring the refraction of light passing through a transparent liquid, which instrument he reports having used to verify the law of refraction that had been published by Descartes. He also proposes a design, making clear that he has not yet built it, for a device for grinding lenses of large diameter and long focal length. Large lenses of long focal length are ideal for astronomical telescopes, though the suspension of long telescopes presents considerable difficulties. Hooke does not address this last problem in the *Micrographia*, but he subsequently devises a system of braces for suspending long telescopes, and has one of 40 foot length constructed in the Gresham College quadrangle. In the late 1670s Hooke describes an aerial telescope in which object lens and eyepiece are aligned by a rope and pulley, without the need for a massive tube and support. The final sections of the *Micrographia* deal with astronomical observations of stars and of the surface of the moon; over the course of his career he also made observations of the large spot on Jupiter, of the rotation of Mars, of double stars, and other astronomical phenomena reported in his Cutler lectures and in the *Philosophical Transactions of the Royal Society*.

In the *Micrographia* Hooke provides a calculation of the height of the atmosphere based on the inverse relation between pressure and volume of gases, a relation now known as Boyle's law. Hooke had been Boyle's assistant at the time Boyle published this relation in *A Defence of the Doctrine Touching the Spring and Weight of the Air* (1662). Boyle acknowledges that Richard Towneley had originally suggested this relation, but his account suggests that Towneley had not produced an experimental verification of the relation. Boyle supplies this demonstration with two experiments involving the compression and rarefaction of a sample of air by a column of mercury. A question exists of the degree to which Hooke deserves credit for the design and execution of these experiments. In the *Micrographia* he uses the first person in describing the same experiments. He credits Towneley with having originally suggested the hypothesis, but refers to 'the most illustrious and incomparable Mr. Boyle' only in connection with the value for the density of the air near the earth's surface. Hooke would hardly have failed to give more credit to Boyle for the demonstration of this hypothesis if he had felt that Boyle, or other members of the Royal Society, would find fault with the present version, and in fact was not criticized at the meetings following publication of the *Micrographia*. Years later Newton, who was always reticent about crediting Hooke, ascribes to Hooke the demonstration of this relation (Cohen, 'Newton, Hooke and "Boyle's law"', 620).

Hooke as surveyor Hooke's financial situation improved considerably as a result of the fire of London in 1666. Less than a week after it had ceased he produced before the Royal Society a model for the rebuilding of the destroyed portion of the city. While his grid-work plan was not adopted, Hooke was made one of three official surveyors for the rebuilding, which lasted decades. Recent studies of his detailed activity in this capacity reveal no evidence that Hooke was anything but perfectly scrupulous and responsible in all of his duties (Cooper). His contributions to the rebuilding included acting as architect on a number of projects, some of which have traditionally been associated with Christopher Wren. The most notable of these (and the only one still standing) was the monument to the great fire, a particular feature of which is the open interior column which Hooke hoped to use for a variety of experimental researches. Some of these experiments were carried out, but vibrations from nearby traffic precluded many others. Another such building was the Royal College of Physicians on Warwick Lane which survived well into the nineteenth century. Hooke was also responsible for Bethlem Hospital in Moorfields, a building that was much admired until it was pulled down in 1814. Hooke's involvement with a variety of other well-known building is more ambiguous, largely because it is difficult to separate out his involvement as surveyor.

The Cutler lectures A decade after the publication of the *Micrographia* Hooke began publishing a series of tracts based on lectures delivered at Gresham College before the Royal Society under Cutler's endowment. In *An Attempt to Prove the Motion of the Earth by Observation* (1674) he describes the fixed zenith telescope he had mounted in his lodgings at Gresham College, with which he had attempted to measure a shift in position of the brightest star of the constellation Draco over the course of the year as a demonstration of the earth's motion round the sun. While his measurements were later called into question, his method was universally praised and served as both instigation and model for the later measurements of Samuel Molyneux and James Bradley. Hooke ends this lecture with a promise to publish an account of the system of the world based upon three suppositions of celestial mechanics: first, that all celestial bodies have a gravitating power towards their centre whereby they attract not only parts of their own bodies, but also all other celestial bodies 'within the sphere of their activity'; second, that all moving bodies travel in straight lines unless their path is deflected into a circle, ellipse, or other curve; third, that the attractive power diminishes with distance from a body's centre.

In *Animadversions on the … Machina Coelestis of … Johannes Hevelius* (1674), Hooke argues for the advantages of telescopic sights over plain sights for making astronomical measurements. He was not the first inventor of the micrometer for telescopic use, nor ever claimed to be, but he did invent a form of this device that received particular praise from the Royal Society. He describes in detail a split-image mural quadrant in which a pair of telescopes with sites mounted to a frame may be used to measure angles between astronomical objects. This quadrant features a spirit level so that altitudes may be measured accurately from the horizontal. Hooke describes this level in detail, apparently unaware that Thevenot had anticipated him in its invention. Hooke describes an alternative level, explicitly crediting Wren as its inventor. He devises what may have been the first dividing engine for graduating the limb of his quadrant by a screw. He also describes an equatorial mount driven by clockwork and regulated by a conical pendulum. While this is probably the earliest description of a clockwork-driven telescope, there is no evidence that it was ever constructed. Hooke also describes a quadrant mounted on a platform to which rotary motion is transmitted by another of Hooke's inventions, the universal joint.

In *A Description of Helioscopes and some other Instruments* (1676) Hooke describes a series of telescopes in which the path of light is folded within the telescope tube by means of one or more flat mirrors. He discusses the common flaws of mirrors for astronomical purposes and his experiments to improve them. Though the universal joint had figured in his previous lecture, he now elaborates on its various applications, and in a postscript promises to publish a theory of elasticity or springiness, presenting its key principle in the form of an anagram: 'ceiiinossssttuu'. The promised tract is his *Lectures de potentia restitutiva, or of spring* (1678), where he reveals the meaning of this anagram to be 'Ut tensio sic vis'. This principle, that a spring's extension or displacement from its neutral position is directly proportional to the force applied, has come to be known as Hooke's law. Hooke establishes this principle experimentally for a variety of configurations of springs and springy bodies. A corresponding anagram is revealed as 'Ut pondus sic tensio': the weight is proportional to the extension. This is the principal of another Hooke invention which he called the 'philosophical scale'—today's spring balance.

A major premise of the mechanistic philosophers of the seventeenth century was that natural phenomena are to be explained in terms of matter and motion, and that so-called occult qualities such as nature's abhorrence of a vacuum are to be dismissed. Hooke had assisted Boyle in experiments that had gone far towards banishing from the science of pneumatics such occult principles. For Hooke the key motion to the understanding of a wide range of natural phenomena is that of vibration. In *Lectures de potentia restitutiva* he suggests that the vibrations of the smallest parts of matter account for the overall volume of objects. He is not specific about the details, but the different rates at which the parts of different substances vibrate give rise to a greater or lesser tendency of these parts to pack together, a phenomenon he referred to as the congruity and incongruity of different kinds of matter. Although not mentioned in this lecture, he believed that gravity might be caused by vibrations of a surrounding ether impelling one gross body towards another. He demonstrated using water in vessels and powder on plates how imparted vibrations can cause bodies to be attracted towards the source of the vibration. In the course of these and related experiments Hooke anticipated Chialdni's experiments in the visualization of vibrating modes of

vessels and plates. In other experiments involving vibration and sound he anticipated Savart in the production of tones by the rotation of a toothed wheel.

The spring-regulated watch Among Hooke's most notable inventions was the idea of using a balance wheel vibrating by the action of a spring to regulate portable timekeepers. Like a swinging pendulum, a vibrating spring has the feature that the period of oscillation is the same over a wide range of sizes of oscillation. In his lecture *Of Spring* he presents a theoretical analysis of the motion of a released spring intended to show that it had this property; but the analysis is flawed. While Hooke never published a corrected version, he did compose one which is preserved in manuscript in the library of Trinity College, Cambridge (MS 0.11 a.1/16).

In the same postscript to *Helioscopes* in which he published his anagram on springs Hooke presented his case for having invented the spring-regulated watch:

> About *seventeen years since* [that is, about 1659], being very inquisitive about the *regulating the measure of Time*, in order to *find the Longitude*, I did from an Art of Invention, or mechanical *Algebra* (which I was then Master of) find out and perfect this contrivance, both as to the Theory and Experimental verification thereof, of which I then discoursed to *divers of my Friends*, but concealed the *modus*. (Gunther, *Cutler Lectures*, 146)

There was apparently no working model. Waller confirms having seen a draft of an agreement with Lord Brouncker, Robert Boyle, and Sir Robert Moray guaranteeing Hooke an income in return for revealing his invention. According to Hooke's account, negotiations broke down over a clause that would have denied to him any benefit of his invention should anyone else improve the device. He was aware that there were a large variety of ways that springs could be applied to regulate timekeepers, and that any of these could be regarded as improvements for specific applications, and therefore withheld details of his invention. In January 1675 Christiaan Huygens invented the spiral balance and in February he obtained a French patent. Huygens then offered the rights of any English patent to the society but this offer was not mentioned when Oldenburg read Huygens's letter at the society meeting of 18 February 1675. Hooke protested his priority and, when he heard of the patent offer, accused Oldenburg of treachery. Thereafter the matter degenerated into a personal battle between Oldenburg and Lord Brouncker on one side and Hooke on the other, both sides seeking to obtain a patent. As part of his unsuccessful attempt Hooke had Tompion construct a presentation watch for Charles II with the engraved legend, 'Robert Hook inven. 1658. T. Tompion fecit 1675'.

Orbital motion Following Oldenburg's death in 1677, Hooke was elected as one of two secretaries to the Royal Society. In this capacity he initiated correspondence with a number of members who had not been heard from in recent years, among them Isaac Newton. In 1672, when Newton had submitted his 'New theory about light and colours' to the Royal Society, it had sparked heated debate and exchanges of letters. Hooke had been particularly critical of Newton's underlying view that light consisted of a stream of particles, though Newton had insisted that his conclusions did not depend upon that hypothesis. In spite of that earlier dispute the exchange of letters in 1677, which also dealt with the refraction of light, was thoroughly cordial.

In November 1679 Hooke again entreated Newton to communicate his thoughts on philosophical matters, inviting him to comment on Hooke's work:

> And particularly if you will let me know your thoughts of that of compounding the celestiall motions of the planets of a direct motion by the tangent & an attractive motion towards the centrall body, Or what objections you have against my hypothesis of the lawes or causes of Springinesse. (Correspondence of Isaac Newton, 2.297)

Newton replied that he had not heard of these hypotheses. He proposed an experiment to detect the effects of the earth's rotation on a falling body, including a diagram in which the path of fall is extended within the body of the earth. Hooke corrected Newton's diagram only to be corrected in turn by Newton with a new diagram based on the assumption of a constant force towards the centre of the earth. Hooke replied that his own supposition was that gravitational attraction acted 'in a duplicate proportion to the Distance from the Center Reciprocall' (ibid., 2.309), that is, as the inverse square of distance. Given this correspondence it is not surprising that Hooke felt that Newton had learned the inverse square law of gravity from him. He could not know that over a decade earlier Newton had not only supposed this relation, but had tested it by calculation two different ways. Hooke's insistence that he deserved some credit from Newton for this proposition, and Newton's refusal to acknowledge any debt to Hooke whatsoever, led to mutual resentment that never abated. While Newton had good reason not to acknowledge a debt to Hooke for the inverse square relation, recent scholarship credits Hooke with introducing Newton to the idea of analysing orbital motion as the sum of a tangential velocity and a deflection towards a centre (Westfall; Cohen, 'Newton's discovery'). This became a key feature of Newton's subsequent analysis of orbital motion in the tract De Motu and in the Principia (1687), while it had not figured in his earlier demonstrations on the inverse square law.

Earth sciences In 1663 Hooke laid before the Royal Society a detailed proposal for making a history of the weather, a version of which was printed in Sprat's History of the Royal Society (1667). He invented or improved several of the instruments commonly associated with meteorology. Best known of these is the wheel barometer, for which he had at least three slightly different designs. He also developed multi-liquid barometers for increased precision, credit for which must be shared with Huygens. Hooke's so-called marine barometer (actually a manometer) was intended to serve on board a moving ship, where the mercury barometer was impractical. Other instruments devised by him include rain gauges, hygroscopes for determining the humidity of the air, and a wind speed instrument. He was also involved in the development of a weather-clock which would automatically record a number of different instrument readings. While the general Baconian goal of collecting data and raising theories from revealed correspondences did not lead to advances in weather prediction either for Hooke or for his successors in the centuries to follow, he was among the first to recognize the barometer's ability to predict storms.

Hooke's analysis of the height of the atmosphere distinguishes clearly between the two factors of height and density that contribute to the pressure of a surrounding medium. He demonstrated these two effects by immersing a mercury barometer to various depths in vessels of salt and fresh water. In an effort to focus on this second factor as it applies to the atmosphere, he produced an air poise or aerostatic balance, a device previously described by Robert Boyle and Otto Von Guericke. Hooke used the idea of variable atmospheric density, again illustrated by using fresh and salt water, to explain the floating of clouds. Among the experiments carried out by him at the Monument was a series of measurements of air pressure at various altitudes intended as a check on his analysis of the height of the atmosphere.

Following the society's declared interest in the depth and salinity of the seas and oceans, Hooke developed instruments for sounding the depths and for bringing up water from the bottom. His geological ideas are summarized in a series of tracts collected by Waller in Hooke's Posthumous Works. In 1668 he declared his conviction that fossil shells derive from once-living bodies, by no means a universal view at the time. The presence of these aquatic forms in regions now remote from the sea is explained at some length as being due to the rising from and settling into the sea of bodies of land through the action of earthquakes and, to a lesser extent, erosion by the sea and by weather. In a series of lectures delivered early in 1687, Hooke explains the major upheavals suffered by the earth in terms of the dynamics of a rotating body. Supposing the earth to have consisted originally of concentric layers of earth and water, the uneven stresses caused by its daily rotation would cause fissures as matter is forced away from the axis, most strongly near the equator, least strongly near the poles. Shifts in the axis of rotation, which Hooke believes to have taken place even in historical times, would introduce changes in the portion of the globe subject to the greatest forces. Thus, mountains may form where there had previously been seas, explaining the presence of fossil shells in mountainous regions.

Character and final years As curator of experiments for the Royal Society, Hooke's contribution in establishing a strong role for empirical approaches to the understanding of nature was considerable. He also served the society as secretary and publisher of the Philosophical Collections, the short-lived successor to the Philosophical Transactions, in the late 1670s and early 1680s. He remained as lecturer in geometry at Gresham College until his death, residing in his rooms at the college and carrying out all duties responsibly, including during periods when other professors were failing to deliver lectures and were even renting out their rooms. The only major exception to this was between July 1665 and March 1666 when the plague was most severe in London; during this period Hooke and some others attended Wilkins in Surrey, carrying out philosophical investigations that were later reported to the Royal Society. Hooke's reputation as a natural philosopher and experimenter was widespread. In 1691 he received from the bishop of Lambeth a licence to practise medicine, in recognition of his medical enquiries into relieving his own long-term ill health, and for his earlier anatomical, physiological, and microscopic researches. Thomas Shadwell created the character of Sir Nicholas Gimcrack in his play *The Virtuoso* as a parody of scientific practitioners of the day, and of Hooke in particular. After attending a performance on 2 June 1676, Hooke recorded in his diary, 'Damned Dogs. *Vindica me Deus*. People almost pointed' (Robinson and Adams, 235). While Hooke was not pleased at being the object of parody, the incident shows that he was so well known that Shadwell's audience recognized him as the model.

Three charges against Hooke's character arise in accounts of his life and work. The first is that he was a 'universal claimant', whose response to being told of some invention or discovery was to claim to have accomplished the same work himself years before. The second is that he was miserly. The third is that he was cantankerous and had an ill-natured disposition. The first of these has some justice as there are a large number of minor cases recorded in the minutes of Royal Society meetings of exactly this taking place. There are also a small number of celebrated cases of extended disputes over priority: most notably with Huygens over the invention of the spring-regulated watch and some other devices and with Newton over the discovery of the principles of gravity and orbital motion. When the disputes are individually examined, Hooke's claims are never without foundation, though he does not always appreciate the extent to which others had progressed his ideas, or rendered them practical. Moreover, there are also cases where Hooke makes no claims even when he deserves more credit than he received. Hooke's regard for Robert Boyle, in part a measure of their great disparity in rank but probably also due to his loyalty and gratitude towards one who was so important in launching his career, precludes any hints that Boyle owed him credit for the work they had accomplished together. Halley, a junior friend of social position comparable to Hooke, is never challenged over his paper on the upward extension of the atmosphere in spite of Hooke's earlier, seminal work on this topic.

Hooke's reputation for being miserly has little foundation. After his death a chest that had been unopened for thirty years, containing several thousand pounds, was found in his rooms. Hooke presumably regarded this money, earned during the most lucrative period of his activities as surveyor, as his savings account, and lived day to day on his income. He was frugal, but no more so than one would have expected of a self-made man in a profession that was not well established. He was involved in a major law suit over money, that against the estate of John Cutler for unpaid salary under the Cutler endowment.

This was but the culmination of years of difficulty in obtaining his promised salary. Hooke's initial failure to obtain the position of professor of geometry at Gresham College, in spite of having properly won the election, presumably served as an early reminder that he would obtain what was due to him only by pursuing his claims.

While Hooke's acrimonious disputes with Newton and Oldenburg have occasionally been ascribed to a cantankerous nature, he is far from alone in being on ill terms with these particular individuals. His disputes with Huygens over matters of priority become acrimonious only with respect to Hooke's belief that Oldenburg was revealing features of Hooke's work that were learned in confidence. His dispute with Hevelius is a technical one over the accuracy of plain versus telescopic sights, in the midst of which Hooke remains free in his praise of Hevelius's accomplishments. Hooke's diaries and correspondence make it clear that he had a goodly number of friends and acquaintances who were pleased to share his company at coffee houses and in his rooms. On the other hand, Hooke did suffer from a range of digestive and other maladies which placed considerable strains upon his disposition. There is no indication of the effect upon him of the death by suicide of his brother John, but Waller reports that after the death of his niece Grace (1660–1687), John's daughter, he became melancholy and cynical, and remained so until his own death (Hooke, xxiv). Grace had lived in Hooke's care at least since she was eleven, and had eventually become his mistress. (An earlier liaison with a married woman, Nell, *née* Young, a maid and seamstress, had ended in September 1673.)

No portrait of Hooke remains, though one is reported to have existed. Waller describes him as crooked and low of stature, though:

> by his Limbs he shou'd have been moderately tall. He was always very pale and lean, and laterly nothing but Skin and Bone, with a meagre Aspect, his Eyes grey and full, with a sharp ingenious Look whilst younger; his Nose but thin, of a moderate height and length; his Mouth meanly wide, and upper Lip thin; his Chin sharp, and Forehead large; his head of middle size. He wore his own Hair of a dark brown colour, very long and hanging neglected over his Face uncut and lank, which about three Year before his Death he cut off, and wore a Periwig. (Hooke, xxvii)

Following his death on 3 March 1703 those members of the Royal Society then in London attended his burial at St Helen, Bishopsgate. His grave is not marked.

PATRI J. PUGLIESE

Sources E. N. da C. Andrade, '"Robert Hooke", Wilkins lecture, December 15, 1949', *PRS*, 201A (1950), 439–73 · M. I. Batten, 'The architecture of Dr Robert Hooke', *Walpole Society*, 25 (1936–7), 83–113 · T. Birch, *The history of the Royal Society of London*, 4 vols. (1756–7), repr. with an introduction by A. R. Hall (1968) · I. B. Cohen, 'Newton, Hooke and "Boyle's law". (Discovered by Power and Towneley)', *Nature*, 204 (1964), 618–21 · I. B. Cohen, 'Newton's discovery of gravity', *Scientific American*, 244 (1981), 166–79 · M. A. R. Cooper, 'Robert Hooke's work as surveyor for the City of London in the aftermath of the great fire', *Notes and Records of the Royal Society*, 51 (1997), 161–74; 52 (1998), 25–38, 205–20 · M. 'Espinasse, *Robert Hooke* (1956); repr. (1962) · L. Rostenberg, *The library of Robert Hooke* (1989) · P. Gouk, 'The role of acoustics and music theory in the scientific work of Robert Hooke', *Annals of Science*, 37 (1980), 573–605 ·

R. Hooke, diaries, GL, MS 1757 · R. T. Gunther, *Early science in Oxford*, 6–7: *The life and work of Robert Hooke* (1930) · R. T. Gunther, *Early science in Oxford*, 8: *The Cutler lectures of Robert Hooke* (1931) · R. T. Gunther, *Early science in Oxford*, 4 (1925), 122, 130; 10 (1935), 114, 195; 12 (1939); 14 (1945) · R. T. Gunther, *Early science in Oxford*, 13: *The life and work of Robert Hooke* (1938) · A. R. Hall, 'Newton on the calculation of central forces', *Annals of Science*, 13 (1957), 62–71 · M. Hesse, 'Hooke's philosophical algebra', *Isis*, 57 (1966), 67–83 · M. Hunter and S. Schaffer, eds., *Robert Hooke: new studies* [London 1988] (1989) · R. Iliffe, 'Material doubts: Hooke, artisan culture, and the exchange of information in 1670s London', *British Journal for the History of Science*, 28 (1995), 285–318 · G. Keynes, *A bibliography of Dr. Robert Hooke* (1960) · H. Nakajima, 'Robert Hooke's family and his youth: some new evidence from the will of the Rev. John Hooke', *Notes and Records of the Royal Society*, 48 (1994), 11–16 · *The correspondence of Isaac Newton*, ed. H. W. Turnbull and others, 7 vols. (1959–77) · D. R. Oldroyd, 'Some writings of Robert Hooke on procedures for the prosecution of scientific enquiry, including his "Lectures of things requisite to a Ntral History"', *Notes and Records of the Royal Society*, 41 (1986–7), 145–67 · S. Pumfrey, 'Ideas above his station: a social study of Hooke's curatorship of experiments', *History of Science*, 29 (1991), 1–44 · *The diary of Robert Hooke … 1672–1680*, ed. H. W. Robinson and W. Adams (1935) · RS, classified papers, vol. 20 · RS, early letters, H.3.64 · *The posthumous works of Robert Hooke*, ed. R. Waller (1705), repr. with introduction by R. S. Westfall, 1969 · J. Ward, *The lives of the professors of Gresham College* (1740) · R. S. Westfall, 'Hooke and the law of gravitation', *British Journal for the History of Science*, 3 (1966–7), 245–61 · M. Hunter, 'Science, technology and patronage: Robert Hooke and the Cutlerian lectureship', *Establishing the new science: the experience of the early Royal Society* (1989), 297–338 · P. J. Pugliese, 'The scientific achievement of Robert Hooke', PhD diss., Harvard U., 1982

Archives BL, papers and corresp., incl. essay on the inflection of a direct motion into a curve, 1666, discourse concerning Newton's theory of light, account of Burnet's 'Archaeologiae philosophicae', method for making a history of the weather, and drawings, Sloane MSS 698, 917, 1039, 1676–1677, 1942, 3823, 4062, 4067, Add. MSS 5238, 6193–6209 · GL, papers, incl. diary, travel journals, reports as surveyor for rebuilding London after the great fire, anatomical observations, lectures, and therapeutical notes · RS, corresp. and papers · Trinity Cam., papers, incl. 'Philosophicall scribbles', and some corresp.

Wealth at death 'many thousands of pounds': *Posthumous works*, ed. Waller, xiii

Hooke, Samuel Henry

Hooke, Samuel Henry (1874–1968), biblical scholar and orientalist, was born at 1 Chesterton Villas, Cirencester, on 21 January 1874, the elder son of Henry Mann Hooke, a Plymouth Brother, and his wife, Elizabeth Loudoun. Educated at Wirksworth and at St Mark's School, Windsor, he left school early, after his father's death, in order to help support his mother and brother by teaching in a preparatory school in Clifton and by setting courses and examining for Wolsey Hall (then called the Diploma Correspondence College). He was thirty-three when he went on a scholarship to Jesus College, Oxford, where he took a first in theology (1910) and a second in oriental languages (1912) and won five university prizes, also playing cricket, rugby, hockey, and tennis for Jesus College and golf for the university. There he joined the Church of England and began the radical critique of the Christian faith which, with his undiminished passion for the Bible, was to make him an exciting and beloved teacher for nearly sixty years.

In 1913 Hooke became Flavelle associate professor of oriental languages and literature at Victoria College, Toronto, where during the First World War he also taught English literature and history. Through his leadership in the Student Christian Movement, then a centre of religious ferment, and his progressive views he had a powerful influence over his students; this eventually upset their more conservative parents and he was encouraged to resign in 1925. In 1926, having built his own summer cottage on an island in Lake Muskoka, he returned to London with a Rockefeller fellowship in anthropology, to study Babylonian, Assyrian, Hittite, and Egyptian texts from which he derived his distinctive ideas about myth, ritual, and kingship. In 1930 he was appointed to the Samuel Davidson chair of Old Testament studies at London. Retirement in 1942 brought only a change of activity. He became a master at Blundell's School and was then appointed examining chaplain to the bishop of Coventry. In 1958 he went to Ghana as a visiting professor, and four years later he was lecturing in Rhodesia.

Hooke was Schweich lecturer in 1935, president of the Folk Lore Society in 1936–7, a fellow of the Society of Antiquaries from 1937, president of the Society for Old Testament Study in 1951, and Speaker's lecturer at Oxford in 1956–61. He was awarded the British Academy Burkitt bronze medal for biblical studies (1948), the honorary degree of DD (Glasgow, 1950), and an honorary doctorate of theology from Uppsala (1957), and was elected honorary fellow of Jesus College, Oxford, in 1964.

Hooke was an indefatigable writer, constantly contributing articles and reviews to dictionaries and periodicals. For twenty-three years he edited the *Palestine Exploration Quarterly*; he also produced 100,000 chain references for new editions of the Bible, and translated the Bible into basic English, as well as writing fourteen books on the Christian faith and on the Old Testament and its background. But he was most famous as the innovator and pioneer of what others called the 'myth and ritual school'. He edited two symposia, *Myth and Ritual* (1933) and *The Labyrinth* (1935), in which the contributors set forth the evidence for the existence of recurring patterns in the religions of the ancient Near East and for the influence of these patterns on the Old Testament. His aim, as he said in *Myth and Ritual*, was 'to build a bridge between the three disciplines of Anthropology, Archaeology, and Biblical Studies', an ambition which he continued to pursue in his Schweich lectures and later writings. As with so much scholarship of the period, modern scholars are not keen to draw parallels between Hebrew and other cultures with such confidence as was previously the case, although Hooke's work helped to alter later attitudes to religion in the Old Testament.

Hooke had married, but his first wife, Alice Ellen (1869/70–1945), a Yorkshire school teacher, became a permanent invalid soon after their marriage and grew increasingly dependent on him until she finally died. They had not had any children. In 1946 he married Beatrice Emily Wyatt, the daughter of Louis Holland Kiek, a London banker, who had been married before and brought with her the children of her first marriage. From 1958 the family lived in Buckland, Berkshire, where

Hooke took enthusiastically to gardening and village life. He died at his home, Westbrook Cottage, Buckland, on 17 January 1968, just before his ninety-fourth birthday.

G. B. CAIRD, rev. GERALD LAW

Sources E. C. Graham, *Nothing is here for tears: a memoir of S. H. Hooke* (1969) · private information (1981) · W. R. Matthews, *The Times* (24 Jan 1968), 10 · *The Times* (19 Jan 1968), 10 · b. cert. · m. cert. [Beatrice Emily Wyatt] · d. cert. · d. cert. [Alice Ellen Hooke]
Wealth at death £4777: probate, 21 March 1968, *CGPLA Eng. & Wales*

Hooke [Hook], **William** (1600/01–1678), Independent minister, was the second son of William Hooke of Hook, Hampshire. He matriculated at Trinity College, Oxford, on 19 May 1620, aged nineteen, graduated BA that year, and proceeded MA in 1623. He became rector of Upper Clatford, Hampshire, on 4 May 1627. In May 1630 he married Jane (*fl.* 1622–1681), daughter of Richard Whalley of Kirketon and Screveton, Nottinghamshire, and his wife, Frances Cromwell. She was sister to Edward Whalley the future regicide, niece to Joan, Lady Barrington, and cousin of Oliver Cromwell; the Barrington family papers include letters from William and Jane Hooke. In 1631 they moved to Axmouth, Devon, where Hooke became vicar on 26 July 1632. He took his family to New England some time after October 1637.

Hooke settled at Taunton (Cohannet), Massachusetts, within the Plymouth patent. He gathered a church and, according to Thomas Lechford, was reordained by a schoolmaster and a husbandman. On 23 July 1640 he preached on the first official fast day for England observed in New England. The sermon was printed as *New Englands Tears for Old Englands Feares* (1641), one of the first tracts to reach the London press from the puritan colonies. Its publication was part of a strategy to reassure the godly in England that colonists, though absent, had not deserted their homeland. Hooke's sequel, *New Englands Sence of Old-England and Irelands Sorrows*, appeared in 1645.

In 1644 Hooke moved to be teacher to the New Haven church, alongside its pastor, John Davenport. By 1653 New Haven faced threats from the Dutch and from Indians, and was in serious economic difficulties. Hooke wrote to Oliver Cromwell about the colony's straits, and its consequent loss of settlers: many, he reported, liked Cromwell's plans to move colonists to Ireland; others were 'more willing … once more (if God will) to salute their native soyle' (Thurloe, *State papers*, 1.564–5). Hooke's son John Hooke [*see below*] had already left, and Hooke and Davenport were on the brink of returning to England. In July 1654 Davenport wrote that Hooke would stay another year until new ministers could be found, 'though he thinkes to send his family before, for the good of his posterity, whereunto he hath strong encouragements' (*Letters of John Davenport*, 93). Davenport in the end remained in New England. Jane Hooke returned to England in 1654 with her remaining children: William, Walter, Caleb, Eliazar, Ebenezer, Jane, Elizabeth, and Mary. Her husband followed in October 1656.

On 13 April 1657 Hooke wrote to John Winthrop the younger 'I am not, as yet, settled, the protector having

engaged me to Him, not long after my landing.' He told of Cromwell's 'desire … that a church may be gathered in his family', but predicted difficulties (*Massachusetts Historical Society Collections*, 3rd ser., 1, 1846, 182). He acted as one of Cromwell's chaplains. On 24 October 1657 he was appointed an assistant to the Middlesex commission. Early in 1658 he became master of the Savoy, London, which Cromwell was using to accommodate members of his court. Later that year representatives from congregationalist churches met there, for the Savoy conference. In 1659 Hooke printed the catechism he and Davenport had used in New Haven.

Following the Restoration, the Act for Confirmation of Leases of 18 December 1660 prevented Hooke from continuing as master of the Savoy. He remained in London and in 1661 published with Joseph Caryl Davenport's *The Saints Anchor-Hold*. He and Jane Hooke maintained contact with New England by letter, and probably influenced Edward Whalley's decision to emigrate there with William Goffe. Hooke went into hiding in March 1663 when a letter to Davenport, reporting English news, was intercepted: John Winthrop the younger, visiting London to resolve a dispute between New Haven and Connecticut, met the parties at Hooke's secret lodgings. Jane Hooke collected money and clothing for colonists. On 20 April 1672 Hooke was licensed as a congregationalist minister at Richard Loton's house, Spital Yard, Bishopsgate. The following year he published *The Priviledge of the Saints on Earth*, a discourse on Hezekiah and the building of the new Jerusalem on earth. He died on 21 March 1678 and was buried at Bunhill Fields. His final work, *A Discourse Concerning the Witnesses*, appeared in 1681.

John Hooke (*bap.* 1634, *d.* 1710), Independent minister, second son of William, was baptized at Axmouth, Devon, on 9 February 1634 and grew up in New England. He left Harvard without taking a degree, matriculated at Magdalen College, Oxford, in 1652, and graduated BA in 1654. He was rector of Kingsworthy, Hampshire, from 3 November 1658 until some time before 29 January 1661, when his successor was instituted. Thereafter, he never took a parish living, although he conformed; he subscribed on 21 August 1662 as of the Savoy Chapel, London (surprisingly, but no doubt because of his father's connections). He was admitted as a chaplain there on 30 July 1663, and held office until 1702 when the Savoy Hospital foundation was dissolved. He had lived for a time in Berkshire, but after 1702 lived in Basingstoke, Hampshire, preaching 'to a separate congregation from the Church' (*Calamy rev.*). He died in 1710 and was buried there on 26 April. He was survived by his wife, Elianor (*d.* 1714), and three daughters.

SUSAN HARDMAN MOORE

Sources *Calamy rev.*, 15, 27 · *Letters of John Davenport*, ed. I. M. Calder (1937) · *Collections of the Massachusetts Historical Society*, 4th ser., 7 (1867) [*The Winthrop papers*, vol. 2] · *Collections of the Massachusetts Historical Society*, 4th ser., 8 (1868) [*The Mather papers*, ed. T. Prince] · *Collections of the Massachusetts Historical Society*, 5th ser., 7 (1882) · *Collections of the Massachusetts Historical Society*, 5th ser., 8 (1882) · A. G. Matthews, 'A censored letter: William Hooke in England to John Davenport in New England', *Transactions of the Congregational Historical Society*, 9 (1924–6) · T. Lechford, 'Plain dealing, or, Newes from

New England', *Collections of the Massachusetts Historical Society*, 3rd ser., 3 (1833), 54–128, esp. 95–6 [1642] • A. Searle, ed., *Barrington family letters, 1628–1632*, CS, 4th ser., 28 (1983) • C. J. Hoadley, ed., *Records of the colony and plantation of New Haven, 1638–1649* (1857) • C. J. Hoadley, ed., *Records of the colony and plantation of New Haven, 1653–1665* (1858) • F. B. Dexter, ed., *New Haven town records, 1649–1662* (1917)

Archives Bodl. Oxf., MSS Rawl. A, Thurloe state papers, MS Rawl. A 60, fol. 484, Hooke to Thurloe; MS Rawl. A 61, fol. 335, Hooke to Thurloe • Boston PL, Mather MSS • Mass. Hist. Soc., Winthrop MSS, papers, letters

Hooker [Vowell], **John** (*c*.1527–1601), antiquary and civic administrator, was born at Bourbridge Hall, Exeter, the second son of Robert Vowell or Hooker of Exeter (*c*.1500?–1537) and his third wife, Agnes Doble (1502?–1537) of Woodbridge, Suffolk. The Vowell family had originated in Pembrokeshire, acquiring the name Hooker through marriage to a Hampshire heiress in the fifteenth century; however, John's forebears usually styled themselves Vowell, and John himself was known by that name for much of his life. By the early sixteenth century the family had been prominent in Exeter for several generations.

Education and early career John Hooker's parents both died in summer 1537. The education of their son, who was aged about ten, was then entrusted to Dr John Moreman, vicar of Menheniot, Cornwall, of whom Hooker retained affectionate memories—'of a verye honest and good nature, lovinge to all men and hurtefull to none' (BL, Harley MS 5827, fols. 45v–46r). Hooker is also the principal source for the rest of his own education. He proceeded to Oxford to read civil law, most likely at Corpus Christi College, but left without taking a degree and went abroad, studying law at Cologne and afterwards theology at Strasbourg, where he stayed with Pietro Martire Vermigli (known as Peter Martyr). After a brief visit to England he crossed to France, but the outbreak of war, presumably that of 1544, dashed his hopes of further travel and he returned home, where he was 'dryven to take a wyffe' (ibid., fol. 51r–v). She was Martha (*b*. *c*.1500?), daughter of Robert Toker or Tucker of Exeter; they had three sons and two daughters.

His staying with Vermigli and many passages in his own writings make it clear that John Hooker was evangelical in religion. He was in Exeter when the city was besieged for several weeks during the western rebellion of 1549, and left a vivid account of events—'where at I the writer was present and testis oculatus [eyewitness] of the things ther donne' (Hooker, *Description*, 1.55). The moving force behind the rising was religion in the form of traditional Catholicism, which had its adherents within the city as well as among the rebels. Hooker denounces those who chose 'to supporte the authoritie of the Idoll of Rome whome they never sawe in contempte of their trewe & lawfull kinge, whom they knewe and oughte to obeye' even though he admits that they were in a majority in Exeter, and makes it clear that his own place was in that minority which 'wholye replyed them selffes to the reformed religion: and to the kinges proceedings' (ibid., 67, 71). But his religious partisanship cannot conceal his pride in the valour of the westerners in their resistance to the king's army, and he reflects sadly on the fate of

John Hooker (*c*.1527–1601), by unknown artist, 1601

Robert Welsh, the vicar of St Thomas, who had saved the city from burning but was nevertheless hanged in his vestments from his own church tower: 'he was a companyon in anye exercises of activitie & of a courtuose and gentle behavio[r] … he had benne a good member in his commonwelthe had not the weedes overgrowne the good corne' (ibid., 91–4).

In 1551 Hooker was in the employment of Miles Coverdale, newly appointed bishop of Exeter, on whose behalf he went to Oxford and there obtained for the bishop the services of Robert Weston as his vicar-general. But following Mary's accession Coverdale went abroad, and in 1555 Hooker found secular employment, as the first chamberlain of Exeter. His important office was central to the civic finances—the chamberlain was responsible for the administration of the city's properties, for example—and Hooker can hardly have exaggerated when he wrote that it required a man 'wyse and lerned and of great modestie and sobrietie' (Hooker, *Description*, 1.814). In 1559 he gave legal advice to the city's merchant adventurers in a dispute with the craft guilds over the former's new charter of incorporation, and two years later oversaw the rebuilding of Exeter's high school. He applied himself to beautifying Exeter by planting trees, and above all he collected and arranged the city's records, producing what he described as:

> An Abstracte of all the Orders & ordynances extent made, enacted & ordayned by the Maiors & Common Councell of the Citie of Excester for the tyme beinge for the good goverment of the sayde Citie & Commonwelth of the same. (ibid., 863)

The labour was a considerable one, involving documents from the reign of Henry III onwards.

Ireland Given his efforts on Exeter's behalf, Hooker regarded himself as underpaid, and also as underappreciated in some quarters—there were men 'who most unkyndly and agaynst all humanitie have traduced and most bitterly Chardged me wi^th and false reports' (Hooker, *Description*, 1.5). This may help explain why in 1568 he went to Ireland in the service of Sir Peter Carew, who after an adventurous career in England and on the continent had decided to rebuild his fortunes by establishing himself on lands held by his ancestors across the Irish Sea. Carew had a substantial body of written evidence, but was unable to read it, and therefore turned to Hooker as a man who was 'greatly given to seek and search old records and antient writings, and was very skilful in reading of them' (Hooker, *Carew*, 71). Hooker put the Carew papers in order and drew up a pedigree for Sir Peter, who was so pleased that he persuaded Hooker to go to Ireland with him as his legal adviser. In Dublin Hooker also found relevant documents in Dublin Castle, and committed himself so wholeheartedly to Carew's cause—principally directed towards securing the barony of Idrone, co. Carlow—that in 1569 he was returned to the Irish parliament as member for Athenry, and made a speech in defence of an impost on wine that led to his being threatened with violence.

The principal source for Hooker's activities in Ireland is his own life of Carew, a remarkable exercise in biography and also a highly original one, in recounting the story of a man whose status was only that of a gentleman. That originality extends to Hooker's treatment of his subject, for Sir Peter is presented as combining the stereotypical virtues of the English landowner with new elements of Renaissance culture; thus he is not only a bold and straightforward man of action, but also a jouster, courtier, and traveller who makes his way (always at his ease, whatever the risk) across Europe as far as Constantinople. In his eagerness to present Sir Peter as a man of honour (and perhaps also because he was heavily dependent on the latter for evidence), Hooker almost certainly underplays the violence and chicanery behind Carew's Irish venture, which had a seriously unsettling effect upon Munster, in particular, and thus also understates his own supporting role. He probably helped provoke a quarrel with the Butlers, who held the western part of Idrone, and, though he sometimes returned to Exeter, he nevertheless acted variously as Carew's rent collector, representative, and trustee. In 1574 he found houses for his employer in Cork and Kinsale.

Authority on parliament, reviser of Holinshed Carew died on 27 November 1575, and Hooker, who had attended Sir Peter's exequies, returned to England for good. His parliamentary experience was not confined to Ireland, for in 1571 he had been returned to the English parliament as one of the burgesses for Exeter. He kept a journal of proceedings (which only lasted a few weeks), the first of its kind. It accurately relates the business of the session, shedding valuable light on such aspects of parliamentary procedure as the role of the judges during deliberations. His experiences in the Irish and English parliaments led to his writing a treatise on parliamentary practice, *The Order*

and Usage how to Keepe a Parlement in England, which was published in two different editions in 1572. One, with a preface addressed to Sir William Fitzwilliam, who was then governor of Ireland, was overtly intended to bring order to the Irish assembly, and seems to have had that effect, becoming the principal authority for proceedings at Dublin for decades afterwards. The other, addressed to the Exeter city authorities, was presumably for the benefit of Hooker's successors as parliamentary burgesses, at a time when the rules and procedures of the House of Commons were 'to most men hidden and unknowen' (Snow, 125). The treatise is historiographically important for printing the early fourteenth-century treatise *Modus tenendi parliamentum*; the fact that Hooker misdates it to the reign of Edward the Confessor is a reflection of his high view of the status of parliament, and of the House of Commons within it. The monarch was the moving force in parliament, which Hooker saw as above all a court, but under her the Commons constituted the essential element—he argued that if necessary queen and Commons could disregard the Lords to enact legislation.

Hooker represented Exeter in parliament again in 1586. By this time he was engaged in another historiographical enterprise, the second edition of Raphael Holinshed's *Chronicles*, which appeared in 1587. Hooker was at one time considered to have been the principal editor; that position is now more often ascribed to Abraham Fleming, but Hooker's contribution was certainly a major one. Not only was his *Order and Usage* incorporated in the English section, but he also provided an updated history of Ireland, which included both a translation of the late twelfth-century *Expugnatio Hibernica* of Gerald of Wales and a condensed version of Hooker's own life of Sir Peter Carew. His Irish section sheds revealing light on Hooker's political and religious views. In his dedicatory epistle he makes a direct link between loyalty to the established order and God's blessing, as he compares the desolate condition of the native Irish with the prosperity of the English pale: 'Two notable examples (I saie) and worthie to be throughlie observed; the one of Gods just judgment against the rebels and traitors, and the other of mercie and love towards the obedient and dutifull subject'. And in accordance with this viewpoint he repeatedly denounces the Catholicism of the Irish, which he sees as the prime cause of their persistent rebelliousness, with a virulence unmatched anywhere else in his writings. Rome is 'the pestilent hydra', the pope 'the sonne of sathan, and the manne of sinne, and the enimie unto the crosse of Christ, whose bloodthirstiness will never be quenched' (Holinshed, 2.168, 182).

The historian of Devon In his other writings Hooker shows himself a loyal protestant, but in writing about the Catholic past, as opposed to present-day adherents of Rome, he adopted a less extreme position. In his later years he continued to serve his native city, becoming coroner there in 1583 and recorder in 1590, and he was also appointed steward of Bradninch by Sir Walter Ralegh in 1587. But his energies seem to have been increasingly devoted to historical research and writing. He became a member of the

*Society of Antiquaries, and a friend of Richard Carew, who in his *Survey of Cornwall* refers to 'the commendable painful antiquary, and my kind friend Master Hooker' (Snow, 24). Of his writings, his *Description of the Citie of Excester* was published in 1919–47, but others remain wholly or partly unprinted, including his 'Catalogue of the bishops of Excester' (partly printed, like a number of his writings, in Holinshed) and a 'Synopsis chorographicall of Devonshire' (several manuscripts, including BL, Harley MS 5827). The latter was never finished, but was nevertheless highly influential for later Devon historians. Its structure is indebted to William Harrison, whose *Description of England*, a pioneering work of social and economic analysis, supplied the preface to Holinshed. Hooker was no mere plagiarist, however, but a diligent and affectionate observer of his native city and county. Like other chorographers he devoted much space to the history and heraldry of gentry families, but he also noted the wealth of particular places, for instance by giving the subsidy assessments for the county's boroughs, and did not miss the importance of fishing in the local economy, especially that of pilchards during the summer months.

Interested in sources of wealth, Hooker also observed the uses to which it was put, for instance praising the third earl of Bath for his lavish spending at Tawstock, where he 'dothe contynewally keepe in most bountefull order to his greate honor & to the great good of the countri and to the releafe of the poor' (BL, Harley MS 5827, fol. 126v), while at Plymouth he noted the immense labour involved in Sir Francis Drake's project to give the town its first supply of fresh water. In his comments on the bishops of Exeter, too, he especially praises those who were builders, while denouncing John Veysey for giving away so much of the endowment of his see. Hooker is fair-minded in his accounts of the pre-Reformation bishops; Edmund Lacy, for instance, is allowed to have been 'a good a modest & a discrete man … He was very devoute in the religion in those dayes' (ibid., fol. 70r). But his warmest praise is reserved for the protestant prelates of his own time, notably William Alley, where his character sketch has something of the same vividness as his life of Carew:

> He seemed at the first appeerance to be a rough and an austere man, but in verie truth, a verie courteous, gentle, and an affable man … All his exercises, which for the most part was at bowles, verie merrie and pleasant, void of all sadnesse … he was somewhat credulous, of a hastie beleefe, and light of credit, which he did oftentimes mislike & blame in himselfe. (Holinshed, 3.1309)

The same warmth informs almost everything Hooker writes about Exeter, which is repeatedly praised for the beauty of its position and buildings, led by the cathedral—'a verie fayre and a sumptuose buyldinge' (Hooker, *Description*, 2.35). Unsurprisingly, he was responsible for the first map of the city, a splendid one engraved by Remigius Hogenberg at Hooker's expense in 1587. By this time his wife, Martha, had died, and Hooker had married Anastryce (c.1540?–1599), daughter of Edward Bridgeman of Exeter. They had seven sons and five daughters. One of his daughters, Alice, married the godly clergyman John Travers. Hooker's health began to fail, and he wrote to the corporation of Exeter describing himself as 'Drawen in to yeres and bearinge the borden of sondry infirmities … for my sight waxeth Dymme my hyringe [hearing] very thycke my speache imperfecte and my memory very feeble' (ibid., 2.4). He died in Exeter in 1601, some time between 26 January and 15 September, and was probably buried in the cathedral.   S. MENDYK

Sources BL, Harley MS 5827 · F. Barlow, ed., *Exeter and its region* (1969) · W. J. Blake, 'Hooker's *Synopsis chorographical of Devonshire*', *Transactions of the Devonshire Association for the Advancement of Science*, 47 (1915), 334–68 · M. Brayshay, ed., *Topographical writers in south-west England* (1996) · J. S. Brewer and W. Bullen, eds., *Calendar of the Carew manuscripts*, 6 vols., PRO (1867–73) · C. Carlton, 'John Hooker and Exeter's court of orphans', *Huntington Library Quarterly*, 36/4 (1973), 307–16 · C. S. Clegg, 'Which Holinshed? Holinshed's *Chronicles* at the Huntington Library', *Huntington Library Quarterly*, 55 (1955), 559–77 · *'Description of England' by William Harrison*, ed. G. Edelen (Cornell, NY, 1968) · R. Dudley Edwards, 'Ireland, Elizabeth I and the Counter-Reformation', *Elizabethan government and society: essays presented to Sir John Neale*, ed. S. T. Bindoff, J. Hurstfield, and C. H. Williams (1961), 315–39 · W. J. Harte, *Gleanings from the common place book of John Hooker, relating to the city of Exeter (1485–1590)* (1926) · HoP, *Commons, 1558–1603*, 2.333–5 · R. Holinshed and others, eds., *The chronicles of England, Scotland and Ireland*, 2nd edn, ed. J. Hooker, 3 vols. in 2 (1586–7) · J. Hooker, *An original manuscript of John Hooker* (1892?) [intro. H. E. Reynolds] · J. Hooker, 'Diary, or journal, January 17 to February 23, 1568–69', in C. Litton Falkiner, *Essays relating to Ireland* (Port Washington, NY, 1970), appx C · J. Vowell [J. Hooker], *The description of the citie of Excester*, ed. W. J. Harte, J. W. Schopp, and H. Tapley-Soper, 3 pts in 1, Devon and Cornwall RS (1919–47) · J. Hooker, *The dyscourse and dyscoverye of the lyffe of Sir Peter Carew*, ed. J. Maclean (1857) · W. G. Hoskins, 'The Elizabethan merchants of Exeter', *Elizabethan government and society: essays presented to Sir John Neale*, ed. S. T. Bindoff, J. Hurstfield, and C. H. Williams (1961), 163–87 · [M. R. James], 'The Carew manuscripts', *EngHR*, 42 (1927), 261–7 · *The letters of Sir Walter Ralegh*, ed. A. Latham and J. Youings (1999) · F. J. Levy, *Tudor historical thought* (San Marino, CA, 1967) · W. T. MacCaffrey, *Exeter, 1540–1640: the growth of an English county town* (Cambridge, MA, 1958) · A. Patterson, *Reading Holinshed's 'Chronicles'* (1994) · A. Patterson, 'Rethinking Tudor historiography', *South Atlantic Quarterly*, 92/2 (spring 1993), 185–206 · D. B. Quinn, 'Government printing and publication of the Irish statutes in the 16th century', *Proceedings of the Royal Irish Academy*, 49C (1943–4), 45–79 · W. Ravenhill, 'Bird's-eye view and bird's-flight view', *Map Collector*, 35 (June 1986), 36–7 · F. Rose-Troup, *The western rebellion of 1549* (1913) · V. F. Snow, *Parliament in Elizabethan England: John Hooker's 'Order and usage'* (1977) · V. Treadwell, 'The Irish parliament of 1569–71', *Proceedings of the Royal Irish Academy*, 65C (1966–7), 55–89 · J. A. Wagner, *The Devon gentleman: the life of Sir Peter Carew* (1998) · D. R. Woolf, *The idea of history in early Stuart England* (1990) · J. Youings, *Early Tudor Exeter* (1974) · J. Youings, 'John Hooker and the Tudor bishops of Exeter', *Exeter Cathedral: a celebration*, ed. M. Swanton (1991) · J. Youings, 'Some early topographers of Devon and Cornwall', *Topographical writers in south-west England*, ed. M. Brayshay (1996) · W. Ravenhill and M. Rowe, 'A decorated screen map of Exeter based on John Hooker's map of 1587', *Tudor and Stuart Devon … essays presented to Joyce Youings*, ed. T. Gray, M. Rowe, and A. Erskine (1992), 1–12 · J. L. Vivian, ed., *The visitations of the county of Devon, comprising the herald's visitations of 1531, 1564, and 1620* (privately printed, Exeter, [1895]) · F. T. Colby, ed., *The visitation of the county of Devon, 1564* (1881) · DNB

Archives BL, star chamber papers, etc. *temp* Eliz. I, Add. 48025 (Yelverton MS 29) [copies, fols. 154–161b, J. Hooker, 'The order and usage of the keeping of a parlia.', 1571–72] · BL, papers relating to parliament, Add. MS 48110 (Yelverton MS 122) [copies, fols. 2–42, tracts on parliament] · BL, MS copy of collection of Irish statutes,

Cotton MS, Titus B.IX · CUL, diary or journal, MS Mm · Devon RO, commonplace book, MS history of Exeter, charter book, etc. · Exeter City Records, commonplace book, Bk55 | BL, miscellaneous tracts and papers, Add. MS 48020 (Yelverton MS 21) [sixteenth-century copies, fols. 26–52, two tracts on parliament by John Hooker; also see BL, Harley MS 1178, fols. 19–27, 33–52b.] · Exeter Cathedral Archives, collections for history of Exeter · 'A catalogue of the bishops of Excester', Exeter Dean and Chapter MS 3548E · transcripts and papers relating to Exeter and St Sidwell's, Exeter Dean and Chapter MS 3530

Likenesses oils, 1601, Royal Albert Memorial Museum, Exeter [see illus.] · portrait, repro. in Harte, *Gleanings*

Hooker, Sir Joseph Dalton (1817–1911), botanist, was born at Halesworth, Suffolk, on 30 June 1817, the younger son of Sir William Jackson *Hooker (1785–1865), regius professor of botany at Glasgow University, and his wife, Maria Sarah (1797–1872), daughter of Dawson *Turner. Hooker attended his father's university botany lectures from the age of seven and formed an interest in plant distribution. Another early enthusiasm was travellers' tales—he recalled sitting on his grandfather's knee looking at the pictures in Captain Cook's *Voyages*. He was particularly struck by one showing Cook's sailors killing penguins on Kerguelen's Land, and he remembered thinking that, 'I should be the happiest boy alive if ever I would see that wonderful arched rock, and knock penguins on the head' (Huxley, 6). He was educated at Glasgow high school and at Glasgow University, where he graduated MD in 1839.

The *Erebus* voyage, 1839–1843 Hooker's passions for botany and travel were combined when he was appointed assistant surgeon aboard HMS *Erebus*, which—commanded by James Clark Ross and accompanied by its sister ship, the *Terror*—was to spend four years exploring the southern oceans. The ships wintered in New Zealand and Van Diemen's Land (Tasmania), and also visited the numerous tiny islands around Antarctica. These included Kerguelen's Land, where Hooker was finally able to gratify his desire to knock penguins on the head. More important, the sojourns ashore allowed him to collect plants in relatively unexplored regions. Before Hooker set sail Charles Lyell of Kinnordy (father of the geologist) had given him the proofs of Charles Darwin's *Voyage of the Beagle*, which he read eagerly, excited but a little overwhelmed at the 'variety of acquirements, mental and physical, required in a naturalist who should follow in Darwin's footsteps' (F. Darwin, 19–20). Hooker was not alone in seeing Darwin as a role model: Ross wanted 'such a person as Mr. Darwin' as the expedition's naturalist, but felt that Hooker had not yet proved himself of Darwin's calibre. After Ross appointed him to the inferior position of expedition's botanist Hooker complained to his father 'what was Mr. D. before he went out? he, I daresay, knew his subject better than I now do, but did the world know him? the voyage with Fitz-Roy was the making of him (as I hoped this exped. would me)' (Huxley, 41).

Travel was a major way in which aspiring men of science like Hooker and Darwin could gain themselves a reputation. Although Ross was a friend of William Hooker and encouraged Joseph's botanical work during the voyage,

Sir Joseph Dalton Hooker (1817–1911), by Julia Margaret Cameron, 1868

William's income would not allow Joseph to travel as a self-financed, gentlemanly companion to the captain—as Darwin had done. Instead Joseph sailed as a lowly assistant surgeon, subject to naval discipline and with many shipboard duties to perform.

When the *Erebus* returned to England in 1843 Hooker needed to find paid botanical employment. Two years earlier his father had been appointed first director of the Royal Botanic Gardens at Kew, which had just been brought under government control. The appointment brought William Hooker to the centres of scientific life in London but reduced his income and he was still unable to give his son much financial support. Fortunately his influence was sufficient to secure an Admiralty grant of £1000 to cover the cost of the *Botany of the Antarctic Voyage*'s plates, and Joseph received his assistant surgeon's pay while he worked on it. The book eventually formed six large volumes: two each for the *Flora Antarctica*, 1844–7; the *Flora Novae-Zelandiae*, 1851–3; and the *Flora Tasmaniae*, 1853–9. None the less Hooker's Antarctic publications never made any money, and much of his time in the 1840s was taken up with searching for paid employment. In 1845 he was an unsuccessful candidate for the chair of botany at the University of Edinburgh. His father's contacts helped him secure work at the geological survey from 1847 to 1848, but he still had no permanent position.

Friendship with Darwin Shortly after his return from the Antarctic, Hooker received a letter from Darwin congratulating him on his achievements, offering specimens from Tierra del Fuego, and asking whether Hooker would be interested in classifying the plants Darwin had gathered in the Galápagos. At this time the two men hardly knew each other, having met only once, shortly before Hooker set sail. Nevertheless Hooker was flattered by his scientific hero's attention and began the Galápagos work. These first letters marked the beginning of a lifelong correspondence, through which the two became friends and collaborators, and debated their many scientific interests—notably over questions of plant distribution. The rapid deepening of their friendship is evident from a letter Darwin wrote on 14 January 1844: 'I am almost convinced', he told his new acquaintance '(quite contrary to opinion I started with) that species are not (it is like confessing a murder) immutable', adding 'I think I have found out (here's presumption!) the simple way by which species become exquisitely adapted to various ends' (*Correspondence*, 3.2). The 'simple way' (ibid.) was, of course, natural selection, and Hooker was the first in the world to hear of Darwin's secret. In the early nineteenth century, the origins and nature of species, including humans, were two of the most contentious topics naturalists faced. So, despite his tongue-in-cheek description of himself as confessing a murder, Darwin genuinely feared that Hooker might be appalled by his ideas; he must have been relieved when Hooker replied that there might well have been 'a gradual change of species,' adding, 'I shall be delighted to hear how you think that this change may have taken place, as no presently conceived opinions satisfy me on the subject' (*Correspondence*, 3.6–7).

Hooker's calm reply was probably shaped by some degree of deference, but also suggests a pre-existing interest in the species question. Although Hooker said little about his own opinions until the late 1850s his willingness to listen to Darwin's ideas opened the way to a long and fruitful correspondence. As Darwin worked out the details of his theory over the next fourteen years the two men regularly discussed natural selection and Darwin would later acknowledge Hooker as 'the one living soul from whom I have constantly received sympathy' (*Correspondence*, 7.174). Yet Hooker never hesitated to criticize Darwin when he disagreed with him. Writing to Lyell in 1866 Darwin noted that Hooker's 'mind is so acute and critical that I always expect to hear a torrent of objections to anything proposed; but he is so candid that he often comes round in a year or two' (*More Letters*, 138).

Imperial botany The geographical distribution of plants was a central concern for Hooker. He was puzzled, for example, by the species he had seen growing on widely scattered islands; like other naturalists he wondered how they had got there. One option was simply to assume that God had created them several times in their existing locations, but Hooker rejected this theory of multiple centres of creation, and sought a more law-like explanation. He assumed that each species had been created (by an unknown means) at a single time and place from where it had spread. However, this did not explain how species travelled over huge expanses of ocean. Hooker's solution drew on the work of his friend and colleague, Edward

Forbes, Britain's most vociferous proponent of single centres of creation. Forbes argued that the plants had migrated at a time when the isolated islands had been connected, but that sea levels had since risen—as proposed by Lyell's geological theories—leaving disconnected lands with common floras. Hooker explained the distributional puzzles of the Southern Ocean by hypothesizing that a much larger Antarctic continent had once linked many of the now isolated lands. Darwin proposed instead that anomalous distributions were better explained by seeds having been carried by birds and animals, or wind and ocean currents. He and Hooker argued over their competing theories for many years.

Studying plant distribution promised to shed light on the origins of species, but also had more practical implications. The wealth of Britain's empire was largely based on plants: from cotton and timber, spices, indigo and other dyes, to the gutta-percha (natural latex) so essential to Britain's dominance of cable telegraphy. Voyages like Hooker's were partly concerned with mapping these vital natural resources and discovering new ones. But it was also hoped that such mapping would eventually reveal the laws that explained why particular plants grew where they did. Such laws would aid the search for new plants, and make transplanting crops between colonies much easier. However, plant distribution studies required a global survey of vegetation and even after his voyage Hooker needed many more specimens before he could write his floras. Unfortunately the government's funding of Kew during the middle decades of the century did not include provision for professional collectors, and neither William nor Joseph Hooker could afford to pay them out of their own pockets. Instead they had to rely on a diverse group of unpaid enthusiasts who eventually supplied the tens of thousands of specimens that allowed Joseph to complete his books while building his herbarium and reputation.

The imperial context and importance of Hooker's work is also evident in his trip to the central and eastern Himalaya (1847–9). Hooker obtained a government grant for the trip and the Admiralty gave him free passage on the ships taking Lord Dalhousie, the newly appointed governor-general, to India. After visiting Calcutta, Hooker went to Darjeeling, where he met Brian Houghton Hodgson who was an expert on Nepalese culture and Buddhism, a collector of Sanskrit manuscripts, and also a passionate naturalist. The two became close friends and Hodgson helped Hooker prepare for his trip into the Himalaya. However, by the time Hooker was ready to set off for Sikkim in 1848 Hodgson was too ill to accompany him and Dr Archibald Campbell, the British government agent, went instead.

Sikkim—a small and impoverished state—was bordered by Tibet, Nepal, and Bhutan, as well as British India. Its raja was understandably anxious not to annoy any of his powerful neighbours, so he and his chief minister, the *diwan*, were particularly suspicious of travellers like Hooker who surveyed and made maps during their travels. (Their suspicions proved well founded, as Hooker's maps later proved to have both economic and military importance to the British.) When Hooker first sought permission to enter Sikkim the *diwan* made considerable efforts to prevent him, and even after pressure from the British administration forced the *diwan* to submit he obstructed their progress in various ways. He particularly urged them not to cross the northern border with Tibet during their explorations, but Hooker and Campbell knowingly ignored his order and the border violation was used by the *diwan* as a pretext to arrest and imprison them in November 1849. The British government secured their release within weeks by threatening to invade Sikkim. The elderly raja was punished with the annexation of some of his land and the withdrawal of his British pension, a response that even some of the British thought excessive.

Following his release Hooker spent 1850 travelling with his old university friend Thomas Thomson in eastern Bengal and the two returned to England in 1851. Together they wrote the first volume of a projected *Flora Indica* (1855), which was never completed because of a lack of support from the East India Company. However, the introductory essay on the geographical relations of India's flora was to be one of Hooker's most important statements on biogeographical issues.

Altogether Hooker collected about 7000 species in India and Nepal and on his return to England managed to secure another government grant while he classified and named them. The first publication was the *Rhododendrons of the Sikkim-Himalaya* (1849–51), edited by his father and illustrated by Walter Hood Fitch, whose fine drawings enriched many of both the Hookers' publications. Hooker's and Campbell's travels added twenty-five new rhododendrons to the fifty already known and the spectacular new species they introduced into Britain helped create a rhododendron craze among British gardeners. Hooker's journey also produced his *Himalayan Journals* (1854), which were dedicated to Darwin.

The consolidation of a career On 15 July 1851 Hooker married Frances Harriet (1825–1874), eldest daughter of John Stevens Henslow, the Cambridge professor of botany who had taught Darwin. Joseph and Frances had four sons and two surviving daughters, but Hooker's favourite daughter, Minnie (Maria Elizabeth), died in September 1863 when she was just six years old. He wrote to Darwin (who had suffered a similar blow a dozen years earlier when his daughter Annie had died) that 'It will be long before I cease to hear her voice in my ears, or feel her little hand stealing into mine; by the fireside and in the garden, wherever I go she is there' (Turrill, 191). Hooker was close to his children and enjoyed playing with them. He also followed Darwin's suggestion and not only attended their births but gave his wife the anaesthetic chloroform during labour, as Darwin had done for Emma—a procedure the two men agreed was as soothing for themselves as for the mother. Frances died in 1874 and on 22 August 1876 Joseph married Hyacinth Jardine (1842–1921), only daughter of William Samuel Symonds, with whom he had two more sons.

The 1850s also saw the appearance of several of Hooker's most important publications. These were largely taxonomic, concerned with classifying and naming new species and with reclassifying previously known ones. Hooker was a taxonomic 'lumper', a proponent of large, broadly defined species that encompassed many varieties that others classified as separate species. Hooker's lumping was undoubtedly a product of his global plant surveys—compiling these imperial inventories was made nightmarishly complex by those he called hair-splitters, who gave a new name to every minor variation they spotted, thus multiplying species and names. In an effort to overrule the splitters Hooker claimed that the size of Kew's herbarium (which contained about 150,000 species by the early 1850s) allowed global comparisons that made his judgements superior to those of botanists who only knew the plants of their locality.

The herbarium and gardens at Kew had grown substantially since William Hooker had been put in charge. When the government finally agreed that the director could not cope alone their decision gave Joseph the secure, paid employment he sought: he was appointed assistant director on 5 June 1855.

While Hooker was travelling, publishing, and making his name, Darwin was still working in secret on his 'big species book'; only his close friends knew that he was planning a comprehensive account of his long-held theory. On 15 June 1858 Darwin received a letter from Alfred Russel Wallace, then in the Celebes Islands (Sulawesi), in which Wallace asked for Darwin's help in publishing his own theory of the transmutation of species—a theory that largely anticipated Darwin's own. Darwin was anxious not to lose priority for his idea, but was equally concerned not to treat Wallace unjustly. As he and several of his children were ill he left Hooker and Lyell to decide what to do. They arranged for Wallace's paper to be read at a meeting of the Linnean Society on 1 July, but to be accompanied by an abstract of Darwin's theory (which Hooker had read in 1844) and by a letter to Asa Gray, the American botanist, which substantiated Darwin's claim to priority. After the meeting Hooker wrote to Gray that he was 'Most thankful … that I can now use Darwin's doctrines—hitherto they have been kept secrets I was bound in honor to know, to keep, to discuss with him in private—but never to allude to in public' (Porter, 32–3).

Although the Linnean Society paper did not create much public interest Wallace's letter persuaded Darwin to publish a shortened, more accessible version of his theory immediately, and the *Origin of Species* appeared in November 1859. A month later Hooker published his 'Introductory essay on the flora of Tasmania' (the final part of the *Flora Tasmaniae*), in which he announced his public support for 'the ingenious and original reasonings and theories by Mr. Darwin and Mr. Wallace' (Hooker, 3.ii). As evidence for natural selection Hooker offered a detailed analysis of the distribution of the Australian flora, arguing that a combination of his earlier Forbesian geological theories and Darwin's could best explain the observed distribution of plants.

Kew under Hooker In 1865 Hooker's father died and Joseph succeeded him as director of Kew. Hooker was by this time a highly regarded botanist with a worldwide reputation, though he might not have secured the position without his father's constant assistance: William Hooker had offered to leave his vast private herbarium to the nation as long as Joseph was appointed to succeed him. Hooker remained director of Kew until his retirement in 1885. These twenty years were marked by the continuation and expansion of Kew's imperial role. In 1859–60 William Hooker and Kew had provided essential assistance in the transfer of *Cinchona* (the tree from whose bark quinine was made) from South America to India. This enabled this crucial crop to be grown in a British colony with plentiful supplies of cheap labour, resulting in cheaper, more reliable supplies of a drug essential to combat the malaria endemic to many tropical colonies. The cinchona transplantation was emulated under Joseph Hooker's direction in the 1870s when rubber trees (*Hevea brasiliensis*) were removed (entirely without the knowledge or permission of the Portuguese government of Brazil) to be grown in British colonies, especially in Ceylon (Sri Lanka), Singapore, and Malaya.

The public function of Kew became a source of controversy in various ways during Hooker's tenure as director. He asserted that the garden's 'primary objects are scientific and utilitarian, not recreational' and complained about the need to create elaborate floral displays for those he regarded as 'mere pleasure or recreation seekers … whose motives are rude romping and games' (Desmond, *Kew*, 230, 234). Given these views it is hardly surprising that he continued the tradition of allowing only serious botanical students and artists to enter the gardens during the morning, and resisted all attempts to extend the garden's opening hours for the general public.

Behind this opposition to admitting the public and providing better facilities for them lay an anxiety about the scientific standing of Kew and of botany more generally. Botany continued to enjoy enormous popularity with non-professionals and was associated in the public mind with respectable middle-class activities, such as gardening and flower painting. It was also particularly popular with women—at a time when the world of Victorian science was almost entirely dominated by men. Hooker's long struggle to find a paid botanical appointment may have made him peculiarly sensitive to issues about the status of his studies. His concern to transform botany into a properly 'philosophical' study, one concerned with the laws of distribution and the origin of species, helps explain his opposition to the pleasure seekers and 'rude rompers'.

In the 1870s anxieties over the status of Kew—and over his personal standing in the scientific world—drew Hooker into conflict with Acton Smee Ayrton, the first commissioner of the Office of Works (which had taken over control of Kew from the Office of Woods and Forests in 1850). Hooker's notorious irritability—even Darwin described him as 'impulsive and somewhat peppery in temper' (*Autobiography*, 105)—probably contributed to the

conflict, but the immediate focus of what became known as the Ayrton controversy was Richard Owen's natural history museum at South Kensington. The new building was to house the natural history collections of the British Museum, including the vast herbarium of Sir Joseph Banks. In 1868 Hooker had proposed that the Banksian herbarium be transferred to Kew, citing mismanagement at the British Museum as his justification. Owen, then keeper of the British Museum's natural history collections, opposed Hooker's plan, which would have jeopardized his new museum. Sharp ideological differences lay behind the dispute: Hooker was one of Darwin's best-known public defenders, while Owen was a vociferous opponent.

By 1872 Ayrton had already made several attempts to cut public spending on scientific institutions and had clashed with Hooker several times as he tried to assert his authority over Kew. He now privately consulted Owen on the future of the rival herbaria and Owen, not surprisingly, proposed that Kew's collections be transferred to the natural history museum—a proposal that would have reduced Kew to a mere public park. Hooker resisted this strongly, calling in every prominent British man of science he knew, including Darwin and Lyell, to protest publicly against the proposed change. After debates in both houses of parliament Hooker and the Darwinians succeeded in getting Ayrton transferred to the office of judge advocate-general. Both Kew and the British Museum (Natural History) retained their respective collections, and at the general election of 1874 Ayrton lost his seat.

Yet despite Hooker's autocratic opposition to anything he regarded as diluting Kew's scientific role he did not oppose widening public participation in science. In 1866 he addressed the British Association for the Advancement of Science (BAAS), whose meetings the general public were encouraged to attend, and delivered a lecture, 'Insular floras', in which he finally gave up what he now called 'sinking imaginary continents' and instead adopted Darwin's theory of plant distribution by migration. Hooker's involvement with the BAAS also included presiding over the department of zoology and botany in 1874 and over the geographical section in 1881. In 1873 Hooker was elected president of the Royal Society, where he instituted various reforms designed to broaden public participation in the society, including the ladies' soirées. When he retired from the presidency in 1878 Hooker was particularly proud of the £10,000 he had helped raise which allowed the restrictively high membership dues to be reduced.

In public Hooker was extremely reticent about his political and religious views. However, in a letter to Gray he described himself as a whig and elsewhere referred to himself as 'a philosophic conservative, a strong Unionist, but not a Tory' (Turrill, 197). However, he never expressed much interest in party politics and was similarly discreet about his religious views. He refused to give public support to Sir John Lubbock's petition in support of the authors of the *Essays and Reviews* (a collection of essays by liberal clergymen that questioned traditional readings of scripture) because he claimed to be unsure about the benefits of Lubbock's campaign. He was similarly cautious in the controversy over the work of John William Colenso, the bishop of Natal, whose doubts about the historical accuracy of parts of the Old Testament led to his excommunication in 1863. Hooker gave money to Colenso's defence fund provided that his name was not published; he told Darwin he was anxious to avoid upsetting his devout, traditionalist mother. In private Hooker's religious views were close to the agnosticism of his friend Thomas Henry Huxley; in a letter to his friend, the clergyman and amateur naturalist James Digues de la Touche, Hooker expressed praise for Huxley's concept of 'a religion of pure reason' (Turrill, 198). Huxley and Hooker were among the founders of the X Club, a private dining society that supported Darwinism and opposed those they saw as obstructing scientific progress, especially traditional churchmen. In letters to Huxley, Hooker was forthright about his dislike of theological dogmatism, sacerdotalism, and ceremony, but nevertheless remained a churchgoing Anglican and agreed to act as godfather for Huxley's son.

Hooker's place in history According to his son-in-law William Thiselton-Dyer, Hooker was 'five feet eleven inches in height and spare and wiry in figure' (there are portraits of him at the Royal and Linnean societies and numerous photographs and drawings at Kew) and 'in temperament he was nervous and high-strung'. Thiselton-Dyer also attested to Hooker's capacity for hard work, a claim borne out by the full list of his publications, which fills twenty pages (Huxley, 486–506). Some of the more important later ones include: 'Outlines of the distribution of Arctic plants' (1862); the *Student's Flora of the British Isles* (1870); *Genera plantarum* (with George Bentham, 1860–83); the *Flora of British India* (1855–97); editing the *Journal* of Joseph Banks (1896); completing Trimen's *Handbook of the Flora of Ceylon* (1898–1900); and, finally, writing a sketch of the life and labours of his father (1902). As well as writing he continued to travel and visited Syria (1860), Morocco (1871), and the Rocky Mountains of Colorado and Utah (1877).

Hooker was highly regarded in his lifetime and received numerous honorary degrees including ones from Oxford and Cambridge. He was created CB in 1869; KCSI in 1877; GCSI in 1897; and received the OM in 1907. The Royal Society gave him their royal medal in 1854, the Copley in 1887, and the Darwin in 1892. He received numerous prizes and awards from both British and foreign scientific societies; the full list of his honours runs to ten pages (Huxley, 507–17).

Although botanists have long recognized Hooker's taxonomic skills and his pioneering work on distribution, his wider reputation has been somewhat obscured by his close relationship with Darwin. When Hooker appears in histories of nineteenth century science, it is almost invariably as a minor character in Darwin's story and his own work, attitudes, and opinions have been neglected as a result. However, recent scholarship has begun to recognize that Hooker's preoccupations—especially taxonomy,

botanical distribution, and the disciplinary status of botany—are central to understanding the material practices of nineteenth-century natural history, particularly in its imperial context. Hooker's correspondence with his colonial collectors illustrates how the practices of nineteenth century natural history need to be seen as a complex series of negotiations, rather than in terms of straightforward metropolitan dominance; much existing historiography has assumed that those in the colonies were passive servants of imperial science, and as a result their interests and careers have been neglected. Hooker's career also casts doubt over standard accounts of the professionalization of British science, particularly over the assumption that he and the other young professionalizers (especially those in the X Club) were determined to replace institutions based on patronage with those based on merit: Hooker inherited Kew from his father and bequeathed it to his son-in-law—and the role of patronage in these transitions is unmistakable. Likewise, Hooker's equivocation over Darwinism undermines the assumption that it functioned as a unifying ideology for the professionalizers. While he welcomed and embraced natural selection as allowing naturalists to form 'more philosophical conceptions', he also stressed that both Darwinists and non-Darwinians 'must employ the same methods of investigation and follow the same principles' (Hooker, *Flora Tasmaniae*, iv). This apparent ambivalence probably resulted from his need to maintain good relations with his diverse collecting networks, whose members were often deeply divided over the species question. As is illustrated by the Ayrton controversy, conflicts over Darwinism were potentially dangerous to a man in Hooker's position.

Hooker died in his sleep at midnight at his home, The Camp, Sunningdale, on 10 December 1911 after a short and apparently minor illness. His widow, Hyacinth, was offered the option of having him buried alongside Darwin in Westminster Abbey but perhaps she understood that—despite the importance of his relationship with Darwin—it was botany, Kew Gardens, and his father which should determine his final resting place; Hooker was buried, as he wished to be, alongside his father in the churchyard of St Anne's on Kew Green on 17 December.

JIM ENDERSBY

Sources L. Huxley, *Life and letters of Joseph Dalton Hooker* (1918) · R. Desmond, *Sir Joseph Dalton Hooker: traveller and plant collector* (1999) · W. B. Turrill, *Joseph Dalton Hooker: botanist, explorer and administrator* (1963) · M. Allan, *The Hookers of Kew, 1785–1911* (1967) · *The correspondence of Charles Darwin*, ed. F. Burkhardt and S. Smith, [13 vols.] (1985–), vols. 3, 5, 7 · *The life and letters of Charles Darwin, including an autobiographical chapter*, ed. F. Darwin, rev. edn, 3 vols. (1888), vol. 2 · *More letters of Charles Darwin*, ed. F. Darwin and A. C. Seward, 2 vols. (1903), vol. 2 · D. Porter, 'On the road to the *Origin* with Darwin, Hooker, and Gray', *Journal of the History of Biology*, 26 (1993), 1–38 · R. Desmond, *Kew: the history of the Royal Botanic Gardens* (1995) · J. Endersby, '"From having no Herbarium": local knowledge vs. metropolitan expertise: Joseph Hooker's Australasian correspondence with William Colenso and Ronald Gunn', *Pacific Science* [forthcoming] · R. H. Drayton, *Nature's government: science, imperial Britain and the 'improvement' of the world* (New Haven, CT, 2000) · J. D. Hooker, *The botany of the Antarctic voyage of H. M. discovery ships Erebus and Terror*, 6 vols. (1844–60), vols. 2–3 · E. J. Browne,

'C. R. Darwin and J. D. Hooker: episodes in the history of plant geography, 1840–1860', PhD diss., U. Lond., 1979 • R. MacLeod, 'The Ayrton incident: a commentary on the relations between science and government in England, 1870–1873', *Science and values: patterns of tradition and change*, ed. A. Thackray and E. Mendelsohn (New York, 1983), 45–78 • J. Browne, *The secular ark: studies in the history of biogeography* (New Haven, CT, 1983) • *The autobiography of Charles Darwin, 1809–1882*, ed. N. Barlow (1958) • R. Barton, 'Huxley, Lubbock, and half a dozen others: professionals and gentlemen in the formation of the X Club, 1851–1864', *Isis*, 89 (1998), 410–44 • P. Rehbock, *The philosophical naturalists: themes in early nineteenth-century British biology* (Madison, WI, 1983) • A. Desmond and J. Moore, *Darwin* (1991) • J. Browne, *Charles Darwin: voyaging* (1995) • J. A. Secord, *Victorian sensation: the extraordinary publication, reception, and secret authorship of 'Vestiges of the natural history of creation'* (2000) • A. Desmond, *The politics of evolution: morphology, medicine, and reform in radical London* (Chicago, IL, 1989)

Archives American Philosophical Society Library, Pennsylvania, letters and papers • Boston PL, letters • Carnegie Mellon University, Pittsburgh, papers • Linn. Soc., corresp. and papers • RBG Kew, corresp. and papers • RBG Kew, letters • Sci. Mus., corresp. | Archives New Zealand, Wellington, corresp. with Sir James Hector • Auckland Public Library, letters to Sir George Grey • Bath Royal Literary and Scientific Institution, letters to Leonard Blomefield • BL, letters to Alfred Wallace, Add. MSS 46435–46438 • BL OIOC, letters to Sir Mountstuart Grant Duff, MS Eur. F 234 • CUL, letters to Sir Henry Barkly • CUL, corresp. with Charles Darwin • CUL, letters to Sir George Stokes • Dorset RO, letters to J. C. Mansel–Pleydell • Harvard U., letters to Asa Gray • ICL, letters to Sir Andrew Ramsey • LUL, letters to Sir Edward Frankland • LUL, letters to Sir Francis Galton • LUL, corresp. with Thomas Huxley • Mitchell L., Glas., Glasgow City Archives, letters to Sabrina Paisley • NHM, letters to A. C. L. G. Gunther and R. W. T. Gunther • NL Scot., letters to William Gourlie • NRA, priv. coll., letters to Sir R. H. I. Palgrave • RBG Kew, corresp. with Thomas Anderson • RBG Kew, letters to W. E. Darwin • RBG Kew, corresp. with Asa Gray • RBG Kew, letters to W. La Touche • RGS, letters to John Hogg • RGS, letters to Royal Geographical Society • Royal Botanic Gardens and National Herbarium of Victoria, letters to Sir Ferdinand von Mueller • Royal Horticultural Society, London, corresp. with George Maw • Royal Institution of Great Britain, London, letters to John Tyndall • U. Newcastle, Robinson L., letters to Sir Walter Trevelyan

Likenesses T. H. Maguire, lithograph, 1851, BM, NPG; repro. in T. H. Maguire, *Portraits of the honorary members of the Ipswich Museum* (1852) • W. Walker, mezzotint, pubd 1854 (after F. Stone), BL OIOC • Maull & Polyblank, albumen print, c.1855, NPG • G. Richmond, oils, 1855, priv. coll. • J. M. Cameron, photograph, 1868, National Museum of Photography, Film and Television, Bradford, Royal Photographic Society collection [*see illus.*] • J. Collier, oils, 1880?, RS • H. von Herkomer, oils, 1889, Linn. Soc. • F. Bowcher, silvered copper medallion, 1897, NPG • F. Bowcher, Wedgwood medallion, 1897, NPG • W. Rothenstein, pencil drawing, 1903, NPG • F. G. M. Gleichen, drawing, 1908, Royal Collection • E. Cook, oils, 1909, RBG Kew • E. Edwards, photograph, NPG; repro. in L. Reeve, ed., *Portraits of men of eminence*, 2 (1864) • U. Eustafieff, group portrait, Down House, London • C. H. Jeens, stipple, BM, NPG • Lock & Whitfield, woodburytype photograph, NPG; repro. in T. Cooper and others, *Men of mark: a gallery of contemporary portraits* (1881) • H. J. Whitlock, carte-de-visite, NPG • medallions, Linn. Soc., RS • photogravure (aged eighty), BM

Wealth at death £36,861 5s. 1d.: probate, 1912, *CGPLA Eng. & Wales*

Hooker, Richard (1554–1600), theologian and philosopher, was born in or near Exeter in early April 1554. The original name of the family was Vowell, but in the fifteenth century its members began calling themselves Vowell, alias Hooker or Hoker, and in the sixteenth century the original name was generally dropped. Hooker's

great-grandfather, John Hooker (*d.* 1493), and his grandfather, Robert Hooker (*d.* 1537), were mayors of Exeter, the former in 1490 and the latter in 1529. But his father Roger Vowell, alias Hooker, was relatively poor.

Education and early career Richard was educated at Exeter grammar school, where according to Izaak Walton he was 'an early questionist, quietly inquisitive' (Walton, 7). His progress was rapid, and at the schoolmaster's commendation his uncle John *Hooker, alias Vowell, resolved to provide him with means for a university education. The uncle, 'Exeter's resident humanist for half a century' (Hill, xiii), was intimate with Bishop John Jewel of Salisbury, and urged his friend to look favourably on his poor nephew. Jewel summoned the lad and his teacher to Salisbury, was impressed by Richard's promise, and obtained a place for him at Corpus Christi College, Oxford, where he matriculated in late 1569.

The president of the college, William Cole, took an interest in Hooker, who sometimes journeyed on foot from Oxford to Exeter, on the way visiting Jewel, whom he later extolled as 'the worthiest Divine that Christendome hath bred for the space of some hundreds of yeres' (Hooker, *Laws*, 2.6.4). Jewel died in September 1571, and his place as Hooker's patron was taken by Edwin Sandys, then bishop of London, who sent his son Edwin to be Hooker's pupil at Oxford. Sandys and another Oxford pupil, George Cranmer, great-nephew of the archbishop, became two of Hooker's closest friends. In 1573, when he was nearly twenty years old, Hooker was elected a disciple of his college. The statutable limit of age for this was nineteen, but it was permissible according to the founder's statutes to make an exception for a candidate of unusual attainments. Corpus was a Renaissance foundation, with a humanistic curriculum combining classical with Christian wisdom (including that of the Greek fathers). Hooker's education there was accordingly very wide. Theology was his chief study, but he was well acquainted with music (he had been a chorister) and poetry, 'all which he had digested and made useful' (Walton, 19). His friends at university included Henry Savile and his tutor, John Rainolds, a moderate and immensely learned puritan, to whom Hooker submitted some of his later anti-puritan writings for criticism.

While Hooker was at Oxford, his father, then in Sir Peter Carew's service in Ireland, was captured by rebels. He had died by 1582, when his son was granted a pension of £4 by the corporation of Exeter. By then Richard had graduated in January 1574 and proceeded MA on 29 March 1577. He became a scholar (probationary fellow) of Corpus on 16 September 1577 and a full fellow in 1579. In July 1579, on the recommendation of Robert Dudley, earl of Leicester, Hooker was appointed deputy professor of Hebrew. On 14 August of the same year he was ordained deacon by John Aylmer, bishop of London.

In October 1580 Hooker, with Rainolds and three other fellows, was briefly expelled from the college for opposing a manoeuvre to replace Cole as president with John Barfoot, the vice-president, a rigorous enforcer of conformity to the Book of Common Prayer. On 15 January 1583 the chapter of Canterbury Cathedral, persuaded by letters from Leicester and another staunch defender of the protestant cause, Sir Francis Walsingham, granted Hooker an annual bursary of £5 6s. 8d. Two sermons on the epistle of Jude survive from Hooker's Oxford years, and a Latin letter to Rainolds may also come from this period. All three compositions express anguish and trepidation at Roman Catholic attacks on the English church, especially those made by Englishmen themselves. In October 1584 Hooker was presented to the living of Drayton Beauchamp in Buckinghamshire, but there is no evidence of his presence in this parish. Walton's tale of his friends Sandys and Cranmer finding him there tending sheep while reading Ovid and then rocking the cradle under orders from a shrewish wife is certainly false, since Hooker was not yet married. He resigned this living in October 1585.

Personality The few known remarks made by contemporaries on Hooker's personal characteristics and the many offered in Walton's *Life* (first published in 1665), must be assessed in the light of his writings and the course of his life. Allowances must also be made for bias in Walton's sources—family connections no doubt resented a suit brought against Sandys for Hooker's daughters, and hence entertained a low opinion of his wife and in-laws—and for Walton's readiness to model Hooker as the proleptic defender of an English church very different from the one to which he was actually devoted. When these filters are applied, parts of Walton's account must be rejected outright, such as Mrs John Churchman's entrapment of a naïve and rain-soaked Hooker as a husband for her ill-favoured daughter Joan, and the visit of Cranmer and Sandys to a henpecked Hooker at Drayton Beauchamp. Other features in Walton's portrait must be redrawn. The meekness attributed to Hooker by his first editor, John Spenser, and amplified by Walton into being his dominant trait cannot, on the evidence of his writings, have been docile submission to authority as such. If, however, meekness is construed as a notable lack of arrogance or personal animus, the attributions are evidence that Hooker's usual fraternal stance towards his puritan antagonists in his defence (or reconstruction) of the Elizabethan religious and political establishment was an expression of his character, not merely a rhetorical device. As Walton reports it, Hooker meditated on his deathbed, with his friend Adrian Saravia in attendance, on the obedience of the angels and wished it were so on earth. Hooker may have thought of the angels at his end, but their perfect obedience was not as central in his vision of them as it may have been for Walton or for the absolutist Saravia. Angelic delight in beholding God would also have been before his mind (Hooker, *Laws*, 1.4.1).

It is also possible that some features of the image of Hooker presented by Walton deserve more prominence than the latter actually gave them. Walton has Hooker jesting memorably with young people while beating the parish bounds at Bishopsbourne, a pleasant complement to C. S. Lewis's discovery of 'plenty of humour, almost a mischievous humour' in his writing (Lewis, 462). There is reason to believe that Hooker attended a performance of

Shakespeare's *Julius Caesar*, a sign that the taste for poetry Walton ascribes to him at Oxford was not purely classical and bookish. Walton's report that Hooker died of a cold caught on a trip from London is one of the few indications in the *Life* of the cosmopolitanism that is perhaps C. J. Sisson's most important single addition to the received image of the man. What, then, of Hooker's marriage? He valued silence in women, counting their propensity to gossip (as well as their relatively weak understanding) a factor in the spread of puritanism and going out of his way in a funeral sermon to commend the reticence of the deceased for emulation by others of her sex (*Works of Hooker*, ed. Hill, 5.373). Signs of dissatisfaction with Joan? Yet he made 'my wel beloved wife' sole executor of his will (*Works of Hooker*, ed. Keble, Church, and Paget, 1.89n.). She is known to have had six children with him (the four daughters who survived him and two boys who died as infants), and it may be supposed that personal experience lay behind his remark that 'that kind of love which is the perfectest ground of wedlock is seldome able to yeeld anie reason of it selfe' (Hooker, *Laws*, 5.73.2). Although an image of Hooker that is both rounded and reliable is not to be had, there are grounds for believing that he was a livelier and more interesting man than the early testimonials may suggest.

Rhetorical and literary style Hooker's preaching style was evidently not entertaining. In Fuller's account of Hooker's preaching in the 1580s:

> his voice was low, stature little, gesture none at all, standing stone-still in the Pulpit, as if the posture of his body were the emblem of his minde, unmoveable in his opinions. Where his eye was left fixed at the beginning, it was found fixed at the end of his Sermon: In a word, the doctrine he delivered, had nothing but it self to garnish it. (Fuller, *Church-history*, bk 9, 216)

The style thus reported was emblematic not only of Hooker's mind but of the attitude towards preaching he expressed in a discussion of sermons some years later. Arguing first for public reading of scripture as the primary form of Christian preaching, he went on to contend that in sermons themselves the essential elements were 'substance of matter, evidence of thinges, strength and validitie of argumentes and proofes', attributes, he pointed out, perfectly retained in reading them. Hence, he contended, it would follow from the puritan denial that bare reading of scripture, homilies, or sermons can save souls, that

> the vigor and vitall efficacie of sermons doth grow from certaine accidentes which are not in them but in theire maker; his virtue, his gesture, his countenance, his zeale, the motion of his bodie, and the inflection of his voice who first uttereth them as his own, is that which giveth them the forme, the nature, the verie essence of instrumentes availeable to eternall life. (Hooker, *Laws*, 5.22.19)

Hooker's ironic downgrading of pulpit oratory does not mean that he considered sermons unimportant. He left money in his will for a new pulpit in his last parish. Nor would it be correct to say that he eschewed the use of rhetorical devices in his own preaching. The point is that rhetoric was to serve the purpose of instruction rather than emotional arousal. Thus reorientated, rhetoric contributed much to Hooker's discourse. If his doctrine had nothing but itself to garnish it, there was considerable art in the internal garnishing. As Fuller also attests, those 'who would patiently attend … had their expectations *over-paid* at the close' (Fuller, *Worthies*, 264).

Attentive readers of Hooker's prose have ranked it among the best in the English language. There are more citations of Hooker in the first volume of Samuel Johnson's Dictionary than of any other author save Locke, and Swift found that he wrote so naturally that his English had survived all changes of fashion. More recently, his style in the *Laws* has been praised as apt rather than natural, as:

> for its purpose, perhaps the most perfect in English … The beauty of Hooker's prose is functional … His characteristic unit is the long, syntactically latinized, sentence, unobtrusively garnished with metaphor, anaphora, and chiasmus. The Latin syntax is there for use, not ornament; it enables him, as English syntax would not, to keep many ideas, as it were, in the air, limiting, enriching, and guiding one another, but not fully affirmed or denied until at last, with the weight of all that thought behind him, he slowly descends to the matured conclusion.   (Lewis, 462)

Preaching and controversy at the Temple Hooker's public career began with the preaching of a sermon at Paul's Cross, London, probably in autumn 1584. On the recommendation of Bishop Aylmer and the elder Edwin Sandys, now archbishop of York, he was appointed master of the Temple in early 1585, receiving letters patent from the crown on 17 March. According to Fuller, Hooker's sermons 'followed the inclination of his studies, and were for the most part on controversies, and deep points of School Divinity' (Fuller, *Church-history*, 216). This is not the impression given by the sermons that survive. These show Hooker as primarily concerned to address the pastoral needs of his congregation. In *A Learned and Comfortable Sermon of the Certaintie and Perpetuitie of Faith in the Elect* he seeks to show that faith may endure even in those who are not aware of having it, to reassure his auditors that the experience of uncertainty in faith (as compared, say, with the certainty that accompanies the testimony of our senses) is not conclusive evidence that one in fact lacks the enduring faith granted the elect in Reformed theology. There is no exploration of deep theological points here but rather a picture of God as so merciful to human weakness and wavering that even anxiety about not having faith can be taken as a sign of having it.

In the sermons from this period comprised in the posthumously published *A Learned Discourse of Justification, Workes, and how the Foundation of Faith is Overthrowne* Hooker's pastoral care was directed to a different sort of anxiety, one that might have been felt by anyone looking back over the previous millennium of Christian history. After laying out the differences between the doctrines of justification taught by the churches of England and Rome, Hooker ventured to suggest that 'God was mercifull to save thousandes of our fathers living in popishe superstitions, in as muche as they synned ignorantlie' (*Works of Hooker*, ed. Hill, 5.165). Here he touched on some deep theological points, but his aim was to diminish the salvific

importance of such points, to show that even if an individual holds beliefs logically incompatible with faith in Christ, this does not demonstrate lack of such faith. Although the 'popish' doctrine that good works are necessary to salvation is logically incompatible with the 'foundation' of faith in Christ, Hooker the logician does not demand perfect logic from his fellow Christians. Rather, he is concerned 'leste if we make too many waies of denying christe we scarse leave any waie for our selves truly and soundly to confesse him' (ibid., 5.149). Hooker never adopts a relaxed attitude towards Christian believing, but for him that believing was emphatically not a matter of giving impeccable answers to theological inquisitors, even Reformed ones.

For his apparent leniency towards both weak believing and false beliefs, Hooker came into conflict in his first year at the Temple with his kinsman by marriage Walter Travers, the Temple lecturer. Without personal animosity, Travers, who later declared that Hooker was 'a holy man' (Fuller, *Church-history*, 218), attacked Hooker's views relentlessly in his afternoon lectures for several months, until in March 1586 Archbishop John Whitgift forbade him to continue preaching. Fuller's characterization of the dispute as one in which 'the Pulpit spake pure Canterbury in the Morning, and Geneva in the Afternoon' (Fuller, *Worthies*, 264) can mislead. There is no reason to suppose that Whitgift was closer to Hooker than to Travers on the nature of faith or the possibility of salvation in the Roman church—the issues disputed between them. But Fuller saw the exchanges as a combat between the 'champions' of the 'Prelaticall Party' and the 'Presbyterian power' (Fuller, *Church-history*, 213–14), and it was indeed Travers's suspected role as an advocate of presbyterianism that sealed the archbishop's judgement against him. Travers appealed against his suspension to the privy council, but, although 'The Councell table was much divided about Travers his petition' (ibid., 218), Whitgift prevailed.

Hooker held his post at the Temple for five more years. Throughout this period he seems to have lived in the house of John Churchman, a then prosperous London merchant whose daughter Joan he married on 13 February 1588. It is most likely that it was in these years that an attack on his character was made. Fuller touches on it cryptically: 'Spotless was his conversation, and though some dirt was cast, none could stick on his reputation' (Fuller, *Church-history*, 214). Henry King, bishop of Chichester, relates in a letter to Izaak Walton that he had heard from his father, John King, bishop of London from 1611, 'all the circumstances of the plot to defame him [Hooker]; and how Sir Edwin Sandys outwitted his accusers, and gained their confession' (Walton, 82–3, 102–3). Gauden devotes more than a page to the story, as he had it from 'some well advised men of former years'. A prostitute and her accomplice arranged to accost Hooker on a walk in the fields near London and blackmailed him, until Sir Edwin Sandys, whose father had been similarly ensnared, came to know of it, had Hooker's tormentors imprisoned, and secured a confession. Gauden, like Bishop King, suggests that it was 'a *plot* and *practice* laid by some of Mr. *Hookers …* more cowardly *Enemies*' (*Works of Hooker*, ed. Gauden, 32).

Of the Laws of Ecclesiastical Polity: conception On the ground that Travers had caused or allowed his petition to the privy council to be made public and that his own silence might be taken 'as an argument that I lake what to speake trewlie, and justlie, in myne owne defence' (*Works of Hooker*, ed. Hill, 5.227), Hooker addressed to Whitgift in March or April of 1586 an *Answer* to Travers's supplication which itself became public, gaining respect for him in some quarters but by no means mollifying Travers's supporters—according to Walton these caused Hooker 'extreme grief' with their opposition after their champion's departure (Walton, 66). His response was to begin what came to be published as *Of the Laws of Ecclesiastical Polity: Eight Books*, the first major work in the fields of theology, philosophy, and political thought to be written in English. In its professed aim of resolving the consciences or enlisting the affections of those who could or would not accept the religious settlement of 1559, the *Laws* can be read as a continuation of Hooker's earlier pastoral efforts. It can also be read as an attempt to resolve his own conscience against the charge that 'if we maintain things that are established … we serve the time, and speak in favour of the present state, because thereby we either hold or seek preferment' (*Laws*, 1.1.1).

Given the scale on which Hooker conceived the work, it required more time and peace than his position at the Temple afforded. On 21 June 1591 he became subdean of Salisbury and prebendary of Netheravon, livings joined to that of Boscombe, Wiltshire, where he was instituted as rector by Whitgift on 17 July. His appointment at the Temple ended on 10 November. In the next few years he was occasionally active at Salisbury and perhaps at Boscombe. The first drafting of some or all of the *Laws* was done, however, at his father-in-law's houses in Watling Street in London and at Enfield, Middlesex. Hooker worked in close consultation with his former pupils Cranmer and Sandys, and publication of the preface and first four books early in 1593 was subsidized by Sandys, who signed a contract with Hooker's cousin John Windet for the printing of the work on 26 January. Hooker sent a copy to Lord Burghley on 13 March, in time to be used in support of legislation in that year's parliament that was for the first time directed against protestant separatists as well as Catholic recusants.

The timing was not accidental. Chapter 8 of the preface, singularly harsh and directly apposite to the measures under consideration, seems to have been a late addition written at the urging of George Cranmer. It was later testified that the printing had been 'hastened by such eminente persons whome the cause did moste speciallie concerne' (Sisson, 145). These must surely have included Whitgift, who had apparently placed his library at Lambeth at Hooker's disposal, would naturally have been kept informed from the beginning, at least in general terms, of what he was writing, and had personally licensed the work's publication; and very likely Richard Bancroft, who

was at the time particularly active in pursuing nonconformists and separatists. Burghley, by contrast, had for years opposed Whitgift's repression of nonconformists. The dispatch of Hooker's work to him was thus presumably meant to steel him for action contrary to his personal sympathies. How far Hooker moved him is unknown, but in the event Burghley was the government's chief spokesman in the Lords for the bill that retrospectively legitimated the execution of the separatists Henry Barrow and John Greenwood on 6 April 1593.

Whatever forces were active at its first publication, the germ of the *Laws* can be detected in *A Learned Sermon of the Nature of Pride* preached at the Temple, probably after the controversy with Travers. In it Hooker urges that the divine origin of a law does not entail its immutability. The point is expanded in book 3 of the *Laws* to refute the necessity of a particular form of church government even if it was the polity of the primitive church. Hooker goes further than this, however. In the course of its eight books, the *Laws* deals with issues between conformists and nonconformists, episcopalians and presbyterians, and Rome and the Church of England in greater depth than any previous treatment.

The idea of law That depth came primarily from Hooker's allocation of the first four books to 'generall meditations' or first principles, before he came directly to grips in the last four with the particular issues concerning worship and governance that so agitated the church when he wrote. Lest this plan call for more patience than those interested in the disputed issues could muster, Hooker prefaced his work with an address 'To them that seeke (as they tearme it) the reformation of Lawes, and orders Ecclesiasticall, in the Church of England' in which he dealt obliquely and historically with the reformist movement, while promising to provide later a direct theological treatment of its particular demands. This preface presents Calvin's establishment of a clerical–lay consistory at Geneva as an astute response to chance circumstances, not the fulfilment of a divine imperative, and attributes enthusiasm for the Genevan model in England to factors other than biblical inspiration or rational persuasion. Early critics noted indignantly the irony in some of his references to Calvin. For example: 'Divine knowledge he gathered, not by hearing or reading so much, as by teaching others' (Hooker, *Laws*, preface, 2.1).

The ruling idea in Hooker's 'generall meditations' is law. The laws with which he was most crucially concerned are indicated early in book 1. On one hand there are 'the lawes whereby we live', that is, 'the rites, customes, and orders of Ecclesiasticall governement' currently in force in the English church. On the other hand, there is divine law, presented by advocates of Genevan presbyterianism as a radically incompatible alternative. 'We are accused as men that will not have Christ Jesus to rule over them, but have wilfully cast his statutes behind their backs, hating to be reformed, and made subject unto the scepter of his discipline' (*Laws*, 1.1.3). Hooker's strategy for defusing the potentially explosive clash between these alternatives was to enrich the very idea of law to include 'any kind of rule or canon, whereby actions are framed'. More precisely, since 'all things that are' have some characteristic operation or work aiming at an end, which cannot be achieved 'unlesse the worke be also fit to obteine it by', a law is that which specifies how a thing must operate in order to achieve its end: 'That which doth assigne unto each thing the kinde, that which doth moderate the force and power, that which doth appoint the forme and measure of working, the same we tearme a *Lawe*' (ibid., 1.2.1). In the sixteen chapters of book 1 Hooker does in fact apply this conception of law to 'all things that are': God, the angels, natural (non-voluntary) agents, and human beings; and human beings are considered both as individuals and in societies and as guided by the law of reason, by the supernaturally revealed law of salvation found in scripture, and by laws of their own making.

In setting forth this legal cosmology Hooker's own aim was to show how much more complex were the issues involved in regulating church life than the proponents of the presbyterian discipline believed. He concludes by showing how each sort of law discussed has a bearing on issues in the life of the church. In this demonstration and in appeals to the whole range of normative considerations in the course of his work, Hooker substitutes devotion to the ideal of law as intelligible direction towards an understood end for devotion to what he regards as a narrow and ill-founded conception of Christ's statutes. Exaltation of 'the scepter of Christ's discipline' is echoed by Hooker in an encomium of law itself, of which, he says:

there can be no lesse acknowledged, then that her seate is the bosome of God, her voyce the harmony of the world, all thinges in heaven and earth doe her homage, the very least as feeling her care, and the greatest as not exempted from her power, but Angels and men and creatures of what condition so ever, though ech in different sort and maner, yet all with uniforme consent, admiring her as the mother of their peace and joy. (*Laws*, 1.16.8)

Hooker's conception of a diversity of laws allows him to mount in book 2 a powerful response to the contention 'That scripture is the onely rule of all things which in this life may be done by men' (*Laws*, bk 2, title). Scripture contains all things necessary to salvation, it is perfect in relation to the actions it directs towards the end for which God provided it, but in directing to salvation it presupposes and acknowledges the validity of natural human reason. The same division of directive labour refutes the thesis 'that in scripture there must be of necessitie contained a forme of Church-politie the lawes whereof may in no wise be altered' (ibid., bk 3, title), the subject of book 3. For first, scripture's specific aim of showing the way to salvation through faith in Christ does not require for its fulfilment the laying down of a form of church polity, and further, if a particular polity should be found in scripture, even with divine inspiration or endorsement, that would not by itself show that the designated form was binding on the church in perpetuity. It is not the maker of a law but its nature that determines whether it is immutably binding. The nature of church polity, as Hooker saw it, is not such as to require that it always take a single form. In book 4 Hooker responds to the charge 'that our forme of

church-politie is corrupted with popish orders rites and ceremonies banished out of certaine reformed Churches whose example therein we ought to have followed' (ibid., bk 4, title). He argues that conformity with Roman Catholic ceremonial usage is no reason for the Church of England to abandon otherwise effective devotional forms. To make distance from Rome the criterion for adopting a ceremony is to make an incidental feature essential and thus to distort the purpose of ceremonies. 'The end which is aimed at in setting downe the outward forme of all religious actions is the edification of the Church' (ibid., 4.1.3). In Hooker's view, for a church to define itself by difference from other churches does not build it up:

Where Rome keepeth that which is ancienter and better; others whome we much more affect leavinge it for newer, and changinge it for worse, we had rather followe the perfections of them whome we like not, then in defectes resemble them whome we love. (ibid., 5.28.1)

The public duties of religion There is reason to believe that Hooker had drafted all eight books of the *Laws* by 1593, when the first four were published. At the end of this first publication, however, he announced that 'for some causes' he had thought it fit to 'let goe these first foure bookes by themselves, then to stay both them and the rest, till the whole might together be published'. In line with his earlier description of the design of the work, he suggested that the 'generalities of the cause' handled in books 1–4 might well be considered apart, 'as by way of introduction unto the bookes that are to followe concerning particulars'. By the time book 5 was published, about December 1597, Hooker's base of operations had shifted. On 7 January 1595 he was presented by the queen to the living of Bishopsbourne, Kent.

Book 5 of the *Laws* is a detailed exposition of the worship and ministry prescribed in the Book of Common Prayer. It is longer than the preface and first four books combined. There is evidence, however, of a shorter earlier form of the book, one less exhaustive in replying to reformist objections. Even in its full form book 5 is as much constructive as defensive. In controversy with Thomas Cartwright in the 1570s Whitgift had collected ancient precedents for the disputed usages, but his decisive argument was that these were 'things indifferent' (*adiaphora*) and hence fell under the authority of the Christian magistrate. In effect, when Hooker wrote, the church's ceremonies were seen as 'there because they were there' (Lake, *Anglicans and Puritans?*, 164). Hooker made explicit the many ways in which the prescribed devotional forms could serve the important aim of building up the church.

This construction project had two dimensions, one broadly social, the other transcendently spiritual. Book 5 begins with a chapter on 'True Religion' as 'the roote of all true virtues and the stay of all well ordered commonwealthes'. The second main section of the book begins with the contention that 'happines not eternall only but also temporall' depends upon a proper Christian ministry (Hooker, *Laws*, 5.76). Godliness, Hooker maintains, is the 'cheifest top' and the 'welspringe' of all true virtues (ibid., 5.1.2). In spelling out this thesis with regard to the cardinal virtues of justice, courage, and prudence his emphasis is more on motivating good behaviour from those in power than on securing obedience from those below. This is one of many signs scattered through Hooker's work of his critical attitude towards the personal qualities of those currently administering the laws he defended. His moral earnestness about the social significance of religion—and the ill effects of irreligion—is his strongest link with evangelical Christianity.

Hooker's conception of the dynamics of worship shows how he expected it to achieve its aim. In instruction and prayer (including the prayer that all may be saved) there is an 'entercorse and comerce betwene God and us' (Laws, 5.23.1) which prepares a congregation for participation in Christ in the sacraments, and Hooker accordingly thought of public worship as effecting an ongoing personal transformation shaping the whole of life.

But for Hooker the aim of Christian worship was not limited to improvement of character for the benefit of society. In book 1 of the Laws he had approached the religious dimension of life by way of the dissatisfaction felt with even the best things a purely natural existence can offer. The human soul seeks 'that which exceedeth the reach of sense; yea, somwhat above capacitie of reason, somewhat divine and heavenly, which with hidden exultation it rather surmiseth then conceyveth' (Laws, 1.11.4). This seeking can only end

> when fully we injoy God, as an object wherein the powers of our soules are satisfied even with everlasting delight: so that although we be men, yet by being unto God united we live as it were the life of God.   (ibid., 1.11.2)

It is in the centre of book 5, and in the central idea of participation in Christ, that Hooker points most directly to such a living of the life of God. The 'union or mutuall participation which is betweene Christ and the Church of Christ in this present worlde' is 'that mutuall inward hold which Christ hath of us and wee of him, in such sort that ech possesseth other by waie of speciall interest propertie and inherent copulation' (ibid., 5.56.1). Seen from a later century, the sacramentalism Hooker built on this theology of mutual participation has looked distinctively catholic, but at the time it was an authentic part of Reformed tradition. A nice sign of this is the conclusion of Hooker's discussion of the eucharist (ibid., 5.67.12), a rhapsodic translation of a twelfth-century Latin text edited by a French Reformed pastor. Most of the particulars of worship discussed in book 5 are indeed, technically, adiaphora, but in both its details and its Christocentric structure the book offers a theology of public devotion of extraordinary depth.

Last years: the mystery of the missing books Hooker's one known invitation to preach at court was during Lent 1598, a few months after the publication of book 5. Whether or not the queen appreciated the fact, Hooker appears to have come 'uncannily close to what we can glean of the idiosyncratic private religious opinions of this very private woman' (MacCulloch, 781).

In his few remaining years Hooker was an exemplary pastor at Bishopsbourne, while continuing to work on the Laws. After a long and painful illness, which began on a trip from London to Gravesend, he died at Bishopsbourne on 2 November 1600. He was buried in the church, under a slab that had formerly been the altar. A monument, with the most nearly contemporary likeness of him (it was the source of several engravings from the 1650s onwards), was set up by William Cowper in 1635. Hooker's estate was substantial, including what must have been a magnificent library, valued at £300. The whole amounted to nearly £1100, enough for £100 towards the dowry of each of his daughters, £3 for the pulpit at Bishopsbourne, £5 5s. to the poor of Barham and Bishopsbourne, and a handsome residue for his wife, with which she soon made an unfortunate marriage to Edward Nethersole, a former mayor of Canterbury.

There is good evidence that Hooker finished the last three books of the Laws, but it is clear that the surviving texts, though undoubtedly Hooker's work, are not in finished form. On 7 November 1600, within a week of Hooker's death, Lancelot Andrewes instructed Henry Parry, who had informed him of the event, to 'have a care to deal with his Executrix or Executor … that there be speciall care and regard for preserving such papers as he left, besides the three last books expected' (Works of Hooker, ed. Hill, 3.xiii–xiv). Perhaps on Parry's initiative, Hooker's father-in-law, designated in his will as his overseer (with Sandys), sent his servant Philip Culme to Bishopsbourne to collect 'all such written books, writings, and written papers as he … could find' (ibid.). Churchman later called together Parry, Sandys, and John Spenser (president of Hooker's Oxford college) to examine the papers that Culme had salvaged. In a division of the papers made at another meeting, at which Andrewes was present, Spenser was given the manuscripts pertaining to the three last books, with a view to publishing them. In a note to the reader prefacing a second edition of Laws, books 1–5, published in 1604, Spenser testified with regard to books 6–8 that Hooker had 'lived till he sawe them perfected' and announced that, although the 'perfect Copies' had been 'smothered', 'the importunities of many great and worthy persons will not suffer them quietly to dye and to be buried', and so 'it is intended they shall see them as they are'. When and why the project was abandoned is matter for conjecture. The content of book 7 and still more of book 8 ran strongly against the tide of divine right views of episcopacy and kingship current under the early Stuarts, and this may be why the latter was first published (along with the surviving portion of book 6) only in 1648, when a more moderate conception of royal authority might reasonably have hoped for acceptance, while book 7 appeared only in 1662 under the auspices of John Gauden, bishop of Exeter.

The status of the surviving texts of the three last books has been much debated. There are two distinct questions here. First, did Hooker actually finish these books, and if so, what happened to the 'perfect Copies'? Second and more important, are the surviving texts of Laws, books 6–8, genuinely Hooker's work?

On the first question, besides Spenser's assertion in

1604 that Hooker lived to see his work completed, there is testimony to the same effect a year earlier by William Covel in his *A Just and Temperate Defence of the Five Books of Ecclesiastical Policie*. Covel referred to the three last books 'which from his own mouth, I am informed that they were finisht' (*Works of Hooker*, ed. Hill, 3.xvii). What happened, then? When Andrewes urged Parry to 'have a care' to preserve Hooker's papers, he explained that:

> By preserving I meane, that not only they be not embezelled, and come to nothing, but that they come not into great hands, whoe will only have use of them quatenus et quousque [as far and as long (as they wish)], and suppresse the rest, or unhappily all.   (ibid., 3.xiv)

Spenser in 1604 confirms what Andrewes had feared, informing his readers with regard to the three last books of the *Laws* that 'some evill disposed mindes, whether of malice, or covetousnesse, or wicked blinde Zeale, it is uncerteine … smothered them, and by conveying away the perfect Copies, left unto us nothing but certaine olde unperfect and mangled draughts, dismembred into peeces'.

Who might these 'evill disposed mindes' have been? There are two sets of candidates. Edmund Parbo, a London lawyer, of Staple Inn, testified in 1614 (in the suit brought against Sandys on behalf of Hooker's daughters for such proceeds as might be owing them from the sale of their father's works) that he had 'Credibly heard' that Nethersole, Joan Hooker's new husband, Roger Raven, a Canterbury schoolmaster, and a Mr Aldridge gained possession of various of Hooker's 'written woorks' and burnt or caused to be burnt all or most of them (Sisson, 138). Walton gives an account similar to Parbo's but names different culprits. Here Hooker's widow is said to have testified that she had allowed one Mr Chark and another local minister access to Hooker's study and that they burnt and tore many of his writings, assuring her that they were not fit to be seen. C. J. Sisson, whose research brought to light a wealth of information about the writing and publication of books 1–5 of *Laws*, the hard circumstances of Hooker's daughters (their mother dead in 1603 and her father bankrupt), and the suit against Sandys, was disturbed by imprecisions and inconsistencies in the preceding testimonies—and perhaps by their degree of support for the negative picture of Joan Hooker that he had done much to efface. He accordingly argued, somewhat strainedly, not only that the tales of vandalism were baseless, but even that Covel's and Spenser's direct assertions that Hooker had finished the *Laws* should be rejected. There had not been any 'perfect Copies'. The manuscripts divided up at John Churchman's house in 1600 contained Hooker's last words on the last books. Since Sisson wrote, however, another incident involving the defacing of books by Roger Raven has been discovered.

The second, more material question about the surviving texts of *Laws*, books 6–8, that of their authenticity, can be dealt with more briefly. What is extant of these three last books is indeed by Hooker. There is no suggestion by Spenser that the manuscripts brought to London after Hooker's death had included addition or other alteration to what Hooker had written, only that what remained were 'olde unperfect and mangled draughts, dismembred into peeces'. The possibility of alteration in these manuscripts between their assignment to Spenser and their publication by others decades later must be addressed, but such alteration does not appear to have occurred. Each of the three books is authentic as far as it goes, and all are of some importance.

Penance, prelates, and princes In the plan of the *Laws* laid out in the preface, book 6 was to deal with the presbyterian polity urged upon the English church by Travers, Cartwright, and their followers, and in particular with the power of jurisdiction enjoyed by lay elders in that scheme. From comments made on it by Cranmer and Sandys it is certain that Hooker had completed, probably by 1593, a draft of such a book. The text printed as book 6 in all editions of the *Laws* since 1648 begins in accordance with the announced plan but soon turns into a treatise on 'the virtue and discipline of repentance'. This book 6 is certainly not a revision of the early draft. It has been suggested, however, that a discussion of penance would have been a reasonable preliminary to a revised treatment of the eldership, since, as Hooker avers at the beginning of the book as it survives, repentance is the aim of ecclesiastical jurisdiction. This suggestion receives support from a body of autograph working notes for books 6 and 8 discovered during preparation of the Folger edition of Hooker's works (*Works of Hooker*, ed. Hill, 3.462–523; 6.233–48, 1055–99). These notes show him working towards an account of existing English ecclesiastical law in response to a comment by Sandys on the lost draft. Such an account, along with a revision of the earlier draft and the existing treatise on penance could have yielded an extensive but coherent book 6. The surviving treatise is largely historical; it argues against the Roman Catholic view of penance as a sacrament and differs from some Reformed conceptions in making the sinner's cure or repentance, rather than the church's purity, the aim of spiritual discipline.

The absence of a full book 6, along with the evidence that Hooker completed the *Laws*, supports Spenser's charge of vandalism. A refutation of presbyterianism would have been the part of Hooker's work above all others that overly zealous disciplinarians would have been tempted to destroy. Conversely, there is no reason to suppose that Spenser or his associates would have wished to suppress it.

Book 7 as it survives in Gauden's edition of 1662 is the most finished of the posthumous books. Fourteen chapters in nuanced defence of the authority of bishops are followed by eight in defence of episcopal 'honours', especially ample endowment with lands and livings. Hooker's assertion that 'if any thing in the Churches Government, surely the first institution of Bishops was from Heaven, was even of God, the Holy Ghost was the Author of it' (*Laws*, 7.5.10) makes a strong claim on behalf of *jure divino* episcopacy, but the 'if' which begins this much quoted statement should not be ignored, and even granting Hooker's probable acceptance of divine inspiration as the origin of episcopacy, it would not follow, on his principles, that the office was immutable. He makes this point in book 7 in an exegesis of St Jerome's declaration that bishops owe their power to the custom of the church, not to any commandment of the Lord. Hooker's exposition of Jerome is complex in itself; it was rendered more complex by inclusion in the text published by Gauden of what appears to be a warning comment from one of Hooker's advisers. The suggestion that episcopacy, even if of divine institution, could in some (very extreme) circumstances be abolished is compatible with Hooker's contention in his sermon on pride and in book 3 of the *Laws* that not all divine commandments are immutable. The presence of the obscuring comment in the manuscript in Gauden's possession and some signs of hasty composition or imperfect editing elsewhere may indicate that Gauden's manuscript was not a fair copy of the book. A part of book 7 that puritans certainly would not have objected to is the beginning of chapter 24, with its scathing animadversions on the faults of contemporary bishops. 'No other apologist for the Elizabethan *status quo* chose to be as critical as Hooker of the institution he was supposed to be defending' (Collinson, 171). Hooker's defence of episcopacy in book 7 of the *Laws* is thus, for all its vigour, a qualified one with regard both to the office and to its present incumbents.

Hooker's defence of the royal headship of the English church—the 'power of Ecclesiastical Dominion as by the Lawes of this Land belongeth unto the Supreme Regent thereof' (*Laws*, bk 8, title)—is also significantly qualified. In the dedication of book 5, he had ranked 'those questions which are at this daie betweene us and the Church of Rome about the actions of the body of the Church of God' as second in importance only to the controversies over the person of Christ in the patristic period (ibid., bk 5, dedication, 3). Accordingly, book 8 and the autograph notes pertaining to it are occupied at least as much with Rome as with domestic presbyterianism. Hooker indeed emphasizes the 'body' of the English church, 'personally' identical with the 'independent multitude' which is the commonwealth of England, in his account of the royal supremacy.

> We say that the care of religion being common unto all *Societies* politique, such *Societies* as doe embrace the true religion, have the name of the *Church* given unto every of them for distinction from the rest. So that every body politique hath some religion, but the *Church* that religion, which is only true. (ibid., 8.1.2)

The royal supremacy, as Hooker saw it, was a wholly legitimate institution with which the body politic that was the English church cared for its religion. Besides depending on law emanating from the community for its initial legitimacy, the crown's power of dominion was limited in its operations by laws made in and with a parliament in which all the monarch's subjects were present either in person or by proxy. Hooker was unique among his contemporaries in his emphasis on law—and not only divine and natural law but 'municipal' law, the law of the land—as a restraint on royal action. He distanced himself

from the newly fashionable concept of sovereignty in book 8 and has accordingly been criticized for holding an illogical notion of twin majesty, but just such a consensual idea of political authority might have been useful in the fateful political debates of the next century.

None of the ten known manuscript versions of book 8 appears finished. If Hooker filled out some of the hints in the autograph notes, the result would have been, or perhaps was (if vandals disposed of a finished version) even more constitutionalist than the extant text. The surviving text, for example, argues for the king's exemption from ordinary ecclesiastical censure of the sort proposed by the disciplinarians. The autograph notes suggest an intention to lay out arguments on both sides of the general question of sovereign immunity, the ultimately decisive issue of the civil war.

Editions Besides the first editions of the preface and first four books of the *Laws* in 1593 and book 5 in 1597, there were five early seventeenth-century editions of the first five books together, Spenser's in 1604, printed by Windet, and four printed by William Stansby (1616–17, 1622, 1632, and 1638–9). *The answere of Mr. Richard Hooker to a supplication preferred by Mr. Walter Travers to the HH. lords of the privie counsell*, edited by Spenser's associate, Henry Jackson, was printed at Oxford by Joseph Barnes in 1612. Jackson also edited and Barnes published *A learned and comfortable sermon of the certaintie and perpetuitie of faith in the elect; especially of the prophet Habbakuks faith* (1612); *A learned discourse of justification, workes, and how the foundation of faith is overthrowne* (1612, 2nd edn 1613); *A learned sermon of the nature of pride* (1612); *A remedie against sorrow and feare, delivered in a funerall sermon* (1612); and *Two sermons upon part of S. Judes epistle* (1614). The first collected edition of these writings, *Certayne divine tractates, and other godly sermons*, was printed in London by Stansby in 1618. This was issued with the 1616–17 edition of *Laws*, books 1–5, and was reprinted in 1622, 1632, 1635–6, and 1639. A fragment, possibly of a sermon, was published as 'A discovery of the causes of the continuance of these contentions touching church-government: out of the fragments of Richard Hooker' in a publication arranged by Archbishop Ussher, *Certain briefe treatises … concerning the … government of the church* (1641). Ussher was also responsible for the first edition of *Laws*, books 6 and 8: *Of the lawes of ecclesiasticall politie; the sixth and eighth books … now published according to the most authentique copies* (1648; reissued 1651). Fragments of book 8 were published as 'Mr. Hookers judgment of the kings power in matters of religion, advancement of bishops &c.' in *Clavi trabales*, edited by Nicholas Bernard (1661). Book 7 was first published in Gauden's edition of *The works of Mr. Richard Hooker … in eight books of 'Ecclesiastical polity': now compleated, as with the sixth and eighth, so with the seventh … out of his own manuscripts, never before published* (1662). Numerous later editions were published, most notably that of John Keble, the first critical edition, which appeared in three volumes in 1836. The seventh edition of Keble (1888) was the standard reference text until the appearance, with new material, of *The Folger Library Edition of the Works of Richard Hooker* published in seven volumes between 1977 and 1998 under the general editorship of W. Speed Hill.

Hooker and Anglican identity Hooker presents himself in the *Laws* as offering posterity 'information … concerning the present state of the Church of God established amongst us' lest 'their carefull endevour which woulde have upheld the same' be permitted to 'passe away as in a dreame' (preface, 1.1). He is commonly read as not merely an informant but a defender of the established church: as '*par excellence* the apologist of the Elizabethan Settlement of 1559 and perhaps the most accomplished advocate that Anglicanism has ever had' (Cross and Livingstone, 789); or, in a less amiable statement, as providing 'window dressing for the command structure of Elizabethan society' (Eccleshall, 63). A closer look at the reception of Hooker's work across the centuries raises questions about such characterizations. There is the question whether he was 'not so much defensively recapitulating Anglicanism as inventing it' (Collinson, 151), and, if the latter, there is a further question as to what sort of Anglicanism it is that he invented.

The first published reaction to the *Laws* (that is, to the five books published in their author's lifetime) was the anonymous *Christian Letter* of 1599. Its author or authors certainly saw something new in Hooker, not simply information about, much less defence of, the Church of England as defined by the Thirty-Nine Articles. The *Letter* attacked Hooker on one article after another, to his very great annoyance. Complementing this protestant attack was the positive reception accorded the work in Catholic circles. When the crypto-papist John Good attacked puritans in the parliament of 1604 as being 'no better than Protestant sectaries' he quoted the 'absolute and unanswerable works of reverend Mr. Hooker' (MacCulloch, 787). About the same time Elizabeth, Lady Falkland, anticipated James II in attributing her conversion to Catholicism to reading Hooker. He

> had left her hanging in the air; for having brought her so far (which she thought he did very reasonably) she saw not how, nor at what, she could stop, till she returned to the Church from whence they were come. (ibid.)

Covel in his *Just and Temperate Defence* of 1603 had sought to rescue Hooker as a loyal member of the English church, as did Henry Jackson in his editions of Hooker's sermons. Covel, however, confirms the impression of Hooker's defence of prescribed practices as being at the same time a shift in their interpretation, a sort of 'avant-garde conformism' moving away from the Reformed mainstream of the rest of Europe and towards the sacramentalism of the Laudian church. Yet in this same period Samuel Ward of Sidney Sussex College, Cambridge, 'a hero of the godly and a disciple of William Perkins', strongly commended Hooker's views on the eucharist as healthier than the general run of English protestant sacramental discussion (ibid., 789–90).

Moderation has been a watchword in eulogies of Hooker, but it seems to have been the Laudians, hardly moderate by Hooker's standards in their ideas or exercise

of authority, who first made much of the adjective 'judicious' which eventually came to characterize the man. Hooker's defence of reason against what might be called forensic biblicism also won him admirers in the first half of the seventeenth century. He was a hero for the group of genuinely moderate intellectuals who gathered around the second Viscount Falkland (son of Lady Elizabeth) at Great Tew; he was especially admired by William Chillingworth, author of *The Religion of Protestants a Safe Way to Salvation*. By the outbreak of the civil war, then, Hooker had achieved iconic status in at least some respects for a remarkable range of persuasions: 'godly' as well as moderate and rationalist protestants, high-flying Laudians, and converts to Roman Catholicism.

Publication of book 8 of the *Laws* in 1648 significantly altered what there was to approve or reject in Hooker. Manuscripts of the book had been circulating for some years. According to Dugdale's *A Short View of the Late Troubles*, constitutionalist passages in some copies (insertions, he thought) had 'miserably captivated' many well-meaning people and drawn them to the parliamentary side. At length they

> were not ashamed, in that Treaty which they had with his Majesty [Charles I] in the Isle of Wight [1648], to vouch the authority of this venerable man, in derogation of his Supremacy, and to place the Soveraign power in the People …. Whereunto the good King answered; that *though those three Books, were not allowed to be Mr. Hookers; yet he would admit them so to be, and consent to what his Lordship* [William, Viscount Saye and Sele] *endeavoured to prove out of them, in case he would assent to the judgment of Mr. Hooker, declared in the other five books, which were unquestionably his.* (Dugdale, 39)

Charles especially commended Hooker's *Laws* to his children, though presumably not book 8. When book 7 was published at the Restoration, the stage was set for a minuet of selective appropriations of Hooker in which each claimant chose for a partner either the Hooker of books 1–5 of *Laws*, the serene expositor of orderly liturgy and an ordered society, or the ecclesio-political rationalist of the last two books. John Locke, the most influential student of Hooker's teachings on consent as the basis of political authority and law as supreme in its exercise, was careful to quote only from the undoubtedly authentic earlier books, but public awareness of the later ones could only confirm his interpretation of the others. Suspicions of the three last books, kept alive by inclusion of Walton's *Life* in editions of Hooker's works from 1666, preserved him for tory use, however, and as an implicit nonjuring defender of the church's apostolic government.

Hooker maintained his double identity as whig and tory into the eighteenth century, when, however, the weakening hold on political reality of his ideal of a church organically connected with the nation's civil polity led Warburton to propose in 1736, in explicit disagreement with Hooker, an 'alliance' rather than an identity of church and state. Reacting a century later against the secularization of society, Coleridge, a great admirer of Hooker, 'creatively misunderstood him'. In his *On the Constitution of Church and State* of 1830, he saw the national church as bearer of a nation's civilization, echoing Hooker's thesis that political communities are properly concerned with goods of the soul, not merely material welfare—but Coleridge went lightly on the divine character of the institution. In the same period there were competing Tractarian and evangelical presentations of Hooker. Keble sought to rescue Hooker from 'the rationalists … and the liberals of the school of Locke and Hoadly', but Benjamin Hanbury, in his edition, had already criticized the high-church treatment of Hooker as 'the smoke of incense obscuring the truth'.

At the turn of the millennium perceptions of Hooker were still diverse. An American political philosopher proclaimed his importance as a pioneer of enlightenment:

> If there is any single point that must be chosen as the beginning of the English Enlightenment, as the first glimmering of its dawn, then that would have to be the publication in 1593 of the first four books of Richard Hooker's *Of the Lawes of Ecclesiasticall Politie*. (Beiser, 46)

In a volume marking completion of the Folger edition an eminent historian of Elizabethan puritanism confirmed Lake's account of Hooker as the inventor of Anglicanism but with a negative twist. Hooker did indeed confront the English church with an original account of its identity, but it was a 'disturbing and destabilizing' one (Collinson, 181). In the same volume, however, Hooker is presented as 'an Apologist of the Magisterial Reformation in England' and his position is praised by a catholic-minded Anglican bishop as one of 'contemplative pragmatism'.

Such an assemblage of Hooker's admirers and critics through the centuries may suggest that he was either a thoroughly confused thinker or a deeply ambiguous author. But if Hooker's work is read, rather than read about, a different impression may form. His views are complex, but they are the outcome of engagement with a wider range of ideas than those who would appropriate or reject him usually consider. His style is complex, too, but not unreadable, once both its art and its naturalness are appreciated. Hooker thought that undue concern with positioning the Church of England as an antagonist of Roman Catholicism was a distraction from the proper tasks of Christian life. Possibly the attempt to pigeon-hole Hooker himself is, similarly, a distraction from the best use and enjoyment of his work. A. S. McGRADE

Sources *The Folger Library edition of the works of Richard Hooker*, ed. W. S. Hill, 7 vols. (1977–98) • D. MacCulloch, 'Richard Hooker's reputation', *EngHR*, 117 (2002), 773–812 • C. S. Lewis, *Poetry and prose in the sixteenth century* (1990), vol. 4 of The Oxford History of English Literature • C. J. Sisson, *The judicious marriage of Mr Hooker and the birth of 'The laws of ecclesiastical polity'* (1940) • A. S. McGrade, ed., *Richard Hooker and the construction of Christian community* (1997) [includes bibliography of Hooker's works and works with significant reference to him] • W. S. Hill, ed., *Studies in Richard Hooker: essays preliminary to an edition of his works* (1972) [includes bibliography of Hooker's works and commentary on them] • R. Keen, ed., 'Inventory of Richard Hooker, 1601', *Archaeologia Cantiana*, 70 (1956), 231–6 • T. Fuller, *The church-history of Britain*, 11 pts in 1 (1655) • Fuller, *Worthies* (1662) • *The works of Mr. Richard Hooker … in eight books of 'Ecclesiastical polity': now compleated, as with the sixth and eighth, so with the seventh … out of his own manuscripts, never before published*, ed. J. Gauden (1662) • [W. Dugdale], *A short view of the late troubles in England* (1681) • I. Walton, 'The life of Mr. Richard Hooker', in *The works of Mr. Richard Hooker*, ed. J. Keble, 7th edn, revised, ed. R. W. Church and F. Paget (1888) • *DNB* • J. Martin, *Walton's 'Lives': conformist commemorations and the rise of biography* (2001) • R. R. Eccleshall, 'Richard Hooker and the peculiarities of the English: the reception of the 'Ecclesiastical polity' in the seventeenth and eighteenth centuries', *History of Political Thought*, 2 (1981), 63–117 • *The works of Mr. Richard Hooker*, ed. J. Keble, 7th edn, rev. R. W. Church and F. Paget (1888) • P. Lake, *Anglicans and puritans? Presbyterianism and English conformist thought from Whitgift to Hooker* (1988) • P. Lake, 'Business as usual? The immediate reception of Hooker's *Ecclesiastical polity*', *Journal of Ecclesiastical History*, 52 (2001), 456–86 • P. Collinson, 'Hooker and the Elizabethan establishment', *Richard Hooker and the construction of Christian community*, ed. A. S. McGrade (1997), 149–81 • F. L. Cross and E. A. Livingstone, eds., *The Oxford dictionary of the Christian church*, 3rd edn (1997) • CKS, PRC 32/38/291 • P. B. Secor, *Richard Hooker, prophet of Anglicanism* (1999) • F. C. Beiser, *The sovereignty of reason: the defense of rationality in the early English Enlightenment* (1996)

Archives NRA, corresp. and papers

Likenesses relief bust on monument, 1635, St Mary Virgin, Bishopsbourne, Kent • W. Faithorne, line engraving, BM, NPG; repro. in *The works of Mr. Richard Hooker*, ed. J. Gauden (1662) • W. Hollar, etching (aged fifty), BM • W. Hollar?, etching, BM, NPG; repro. in A. Sparrow, *A rationale upon the Book of Common Prayer* (1657)

Wealth at death £1092 9s. 2d.: *Works*, ed. Keble (1888), 1.89; L. Yeandle in ed. Hill, 5, xiv n. 5

Hooker, Sir Stanley George (1907–1984), engineer and aero-engine designer, was born on 30 September 1907 at the Crooked Billet, Eastchurch, Isle of Sheppey, Kent, the fifth son and ninth and youngest child of William Harry Hooker, flour miller and later a carrier, and his wife, Ellen Mary Russell, of Ruckinge, Ashford, Kent. From village schools and Borden grammar school a royal scholarship took him in 1926 to Imperial College, London, to read mathematics. He won the Busk studentship in aeronautics (1928) and the Armourers and Brasiers research fellowship (1930), and gained his DPhil at Brasenose College, Oxford, in 1935.

From Oxford Hooker went to the Admiralty laboratories, Teddington, to Woolwich arsenal, and then in 1938 to Rolls-Royce at Derby. After suggesting improvements which raised the efficiency of Merlin superchargers from 68 to 76 per cent, Hooker found himself in charge of supercharger development. Under his leadership progress was rapid, and by 1941 a two-speed, two-stage intercooled supercharger for the Merlin 60 engine was provided. This increased the speed of the Spitfire aircraft from 300 to 400 m.p.h. at 30,000 feet, and also increased the rate of climb from 650 to 2,300 feet per minute. This development was prominent in enabling the RAF to win the air war against the German air force.

By August 1940 the Rover Company had ministry contracts to produce Frank Whittle's jet engine at Barnoldswick and Clitheroe, but progress was slow. In November 1942 S. B. Wilks of Rover agreed with Ernest Walter Hives of Rolls-Royce to exchange the work on the Whittle jet engine for the Rolls-Royce tank work at Nottingham, and in January 1943 a Rolls-Royce team, with Hooker as chief engineer and Leslie Buckler as works manager, took over the Rover workshops. Buckler quickly overcame turbine blade shortages which had delayed progress and Hives turned production resources over to development, thus increasing the effort tenfold, with the result that a squadron of RAF Meteors was delivered in July 1944. The B37 turbo-jet, the Nene, and the Derwent 5 engines, all centrifugals, were rapidly developed at Barnoldswick under Hooker, but the Avon axial flow turbo-jet which followed gave trouble for years. Believing that turbo-jets would be unsuitable for transport aircraft, Hooker started turbo-prop work in 1943. The Trent became the world's first turbo-prop to fly, in 1944. The two-shaft Clyde turbo-prop, with axial flow low pressure and centrifugal high pressure compressors, became the first to do the 150-hour military/civil type test.

By 1946 Hooker was suffering from overwork. The war over, Hives sent him to Argentina to recuperate, and moved Barnoldswick Engineering to Derby. On his return Hooker struggled with stubborn Avon troubles but failed to solve them quickly. Hives, whose first priority had to be the health of Rolls-Royce, found himself in an awkward situation. He put A. Cyril Lovesey in charge of the Avon and made Hooker chief research engineer. As a result, the relationship between Hives and Hooker was permanently soured. In September 1948 Hooker left Rolls-Royce for Bristol Siddeley.

January 1949 found Hooker tackling the Bristol Proteus turbo-prop, power plant of the Bristol Britannia. Proteus pioneered the use of gas turbines in the navy and in the Central Electricity Generating Board. The two-shaft Olympus turbo-jet went to test in 1950, as Hooker became chief engineer. It powered the Vulcan bomber, the cancelled TSR2, and Concorde. In 1953 Bristol started the Orpheus turbo-jet for the Gnat fighter designed by W. E. W. Petter. Rolls-Royce pursued vertical take-off with small multiple jet engines but Hooker at Bristol Siddeley preferred the Gyroptère concept of Michel Wibault. Using the Orpheus compressor, Bristol created the Pegasus vectored thrust vertical take-off turbo-fan, which emerged as the world's first operational VTOL (vertical take-off and landing) fighter engine, and was used in the Harrier in the Falklands war.

In 1966 Rolls-Royce acquired Bristol but did not appoint Hooker to the main board and in September 1970 he retired. A month later he returned as technical director to help the Derby works with RB211 troubles, which bankrupted Rolls-Royce soon afterwards. The government acquired the aero assets of Rolls-Royce and continued to fund RB211 development.

During the 1960s the supply of Viper turbo-jets to Romania enabled Hooker to develop a relationship with Romanian communism, which gave him an entrée to China. An honorary professorship of Peking Institute of Aeronautical Sciences followed in 1973, and substantial business later. Of his many distinctions and medals only fellowship of the Royal Society (1962) was nearer to his heart than this Chinese professorship. Hooker was appointed OBE (1946) and CBE (1964), and was knighted in 1974.

Mechanical engineering was not Hooker's forte. He excelled in the physics of aviation, in procuring funding, in salesmanship, and in exposition to laymen. His charisma, and his humour, ensured an easy relationship with people in all walks of life.

On 16 October 1937 Hooker married the Hon. Margaret, daughter of John Swanwick *Bradbury, first Baron Bradbury, civil servant. They had one daughter. The marriage broke down under Hooker's pressure of work and was dissolved in 1950. In the same year, on 1 May, Hooker married Kate Maria, daughter of Herbert George Pope, licensed victualler, and former wife of Gordon Garth. They also had one daughter. After retirement his interest in Rolls-Royce only yielded to terminal illness. Hooker died on 24 May 1984 in the Chesterfield Hospital, Clifton, Bristol. He was survived by his second wife.

LIONEL HAWORTH, rev.

Sources P. H. J. Young and others, *Memoirs FRS*, 32 (1986), 277–319 · S. G. Hooker, *Not much of an engineer* (1984) · *Annual Obituary* (1984), 261–2 · personal knowledge (1990) · m. certs. · d. cert.
Likenesses photograph, repro. in *Memoirs FRS*
Wealth at death £63,226: probate, 19 Sept 1984, *CGPLA Eng. & Wales*

Hooker, Thomas (1586?–1647), minister in America, was probably born in 1586, possibly on 7 July, the son of Thomas Hooker (d. 1635), of Marfield (now Markfield), Leicestershire, a yeoman farmer and overseer of the Digby family's properties. His mother's name is unknown. Pre-seventeenth-century church records from Marfield are lost, but it is known that he had a brother, John, and two sisters, one perhaps called Anne, and Dorothy.

Education At some point Hooker was sent to the grammar school endowed by Sir Wolfstan Dixie at Market Bosworth, some 10 miles from Marfield, where he prepared for Cambridge. He matriculated there at Queens' College in 1604, but soon migrated to the decidedly puritan Emmanuel College, where he graduated BA early in 1608 and proceeded MA in 1611. In 1609 he was elected to a Dixie fellowship, one of two at the college endowed by Dixie and reserved to his relatives or to former pupils of Market Bosworth School. Hooker's contemporaries included such other future puritan lights as John Cotton, Anthony Tuckney, Zechariah Symmes, Simeon Ashe, and Nathaniel Rogers. During his years at Emmanuel, Hooker experienced an extended period of spiritual struggle that eventually resulted in his assurance of God's grace. This 'most experimental acquaintance with the truths of the gospel', as Cotton Mather described it (Mather, 1.304), was later the basis for his vivid representation of the conversion process in his central series of sermons.

The college's account books indicate that Hooker left Emmanuel College's employ in the early autumn of 1618. Fourteen years in a university setting had provided him with a thorough grounding in the literature of church history and theology. He was deeply read in the Bible itself as well as in the writings of the church fathers, medieval Catholic churchmen, logicians such as Aristotle, Aquinas, and Ramus, Reformation leaders, and recent protestant commentators and disputants. His personal library at the time of his death was valued at £300, indicating a large collection that comprised more than one-quarter of the value of his estate. Yet, despite his love for scholarship, he believed that no amount of learning could bring an individual soul closer to God. As he colourfully insisted, 'A dram of spirituall wisdome … is worth a thousand cartloads of that dung-hill, carnall wisdome' (Hooker, *The Soules Exaltation*, 1638, 86). His long experience in academic circles led him to warn that 'Men of the greatest ability for depth of brain and strength of understanding are most hardly brought to brokennes of heart' (Hooker, *The Application of Redemption, the Ninth and Tenth Books*, 1656, 98).

English ministry After leaving Cambridge, Hooker gave occasional sermons in his home county of Leicestershire, but his first settled post-academic position was as rector of St George's in Esher, Surrey. The patrons of that church were Sir Francis Drake and Joan, Lady Drake. Hooker became an important counsellor to Lady Drake, who was spiritually distraught, believing she had committed the unpardonable sin. Despite her previous care by several puritan ministers, including the venerable John Dod, it was Hooker, apparently drawing on the experience of his own recent spiritual struggles, who succeeded in bringing her relief. The case was witnessed by one Jasper Heartwell, a London barrister, whose pseudonymous *Trodden Down Strength* (1647) records the story, up to the moment of Lady Drake's death on 18 April 1625 in a state of assurance of her salvation.

On 3 April 1621 Hooker had married her woman-in-waiting, Susannah Garbrand, in Amersham, Buckinghamshire, Joan Drake's birthplace. Two daughters were born to the Hookers in the early 1620s: Joanna (*d.* 1647), named for Hooker's patron and later the second wife of the Revd Thomas *Shepard (1605–1649) of Cambridge, Massachusetts, and Mary, who later married the Revd Roger Newton, pastor at Milford, Connecticut. At some point in Hooker's Esher ministry, the bishop of Winchester, Lancelot Andrewes, silenced him 'on the complaint of King James' himself (PRO, SP 16/151/12), perhaps for his criticism of Prince Charles's proposed match with the Spanish infanta, Maria.

Some time after Joan Drake's death in 1625, Hooker accepted a post as lecturer and curate to John Michaelson, the rector of St Mary's, Chelmsford, Essex. In this location, Hooker's outspoken puritan principles soon earned him a reputation as one of England's most powerful and prominent voices of Independency. He strengthened devotion to the nonconformist cause by organizing a monthly conference of similarly inclined Essex ministers. Although as a lecturer, paid by privately donated moneys, he escaped the usual requirement of subscribing to the church's Act of Uniformity, he was nevertheless under the close surveillance of the church authorities. Despite great popularity and the support of many colleagues, he eventually felt the force of the established church's intolerance of puritanism.

The earliest preserved sermon from Hooker's Chelmsford years was for the funeral of the Revd Robert Wilmott of Clare, Suffolk, a King's College graduate whom Hooker had known at Cambridge. Hooker took the occasion to lament the current crackdown by church authorities on nonconformists. It was also a period when the armies of Spain were crushing protestants in the Low Countries and an invasion of England itself was widely feared. Other sermons by Hooker from this period reflect a combination of sharp criticism of lax believers and pointed allusion to oppressions of ministers by church and state officials. This combination of spiritual and political concerns is expressed in such sermons as *The Faithful Covenanter* (1644), *The Stay of the Faithful* (1638), and *The Danger of Desertion* (1641).

Like many other puritans, Hooker was increasingly opposed to the English church's ecclesiastical hierarchy and to the use of 'human inventions'—scripturally unauthorized ceremonies—in the church's forms of worship. Still, his overarching message was one of spiritual encouragement. In the market town of Chelmsford, his audience included the full range of society. Hooker intentionally 'chose to be where great numbers of *the Poor* might receive the *Gospel* from him.' 'His lecture was exceedingly frequented' as 'his ministry shone through the whole county of *Essex*' (Mather, 1.304). His audience included 'some of great quality among the rest', the most prominent being 'the truly noble Earl of *Warwick*' (ibid., 1.304–5), a friend and protector of puritans, including, eventually, Hooker and his family. As Mather further notes, Hooker developed a reputation for special power in the 'Use' or 'Application' section of his sermons, the final, and often very long, section where the biblical exegesis and rational explanations of the text were 'brought home' through practical admonitions to the congregation.

Hooker's great popularity among his listeners was based on this ability to speak the language of the people while conveying the high truths of scripture. Since his ministry in England and later in New England was always focused on encouraging his listeners to think positively and actively about realizing God's 'promise' of salvation in their own lives, he stayed close to the experiences of their lives in the figures of speech that characterized his preaching. He preached in a plain style, eschewing the use of classical languages, in which he was fluent, enlivening his sermons instead with such dramatic tools as imagined dialogue, 'character' sketches, and invitations to his listeners to imagine themselves in real-life situations to which he gave deep spiritual meaning. During his Chelmsford ministry (1625–30) he preached the sermons called *The Poor Doubting Christian Drawn unto Christ*, published anonymously in 1629. The title indicates his desire to give encouragement to those inclined to see themselves as hopeless cases. His message was directed at the 'poor soul' who 'mourns and cries to heaven for mercy, and prays against a stubborn hard heart; and he is weary of his life because his wild heart remains' (Williams and others, 185). Such listeners, in spite of human helplessness, were told they should 'expect power from Christ to pluck thee out of thyself' (ibid., 159). *The Poor Doubting Christian* was his most popular book, going through at least seventeen editions by 1700, including a Dutch translation.

Silencing At some point during his Chelmsford period, Hooker opened a school in his home, a farmhouse called Cuckoos, in Little Baddow. His assistant was John Eliot, later known as 'the Apostle to the Indians'. Eliot reported that it was in this place that he experienced God's saving grace and that 'when I came to this blessed family, I then saw, and never before, the power of godliness, in its lively vigour, and efficacy' (Mather, 1.305). During these years of Hooker's Essex ministry, four more children were born, two of whom, Anne and Sarah, died in infancy while a second Sarah and John both survived to adulthood.

By 1629 Hooker's notoriety had attracted the full attention of the anti-puritan forces in Essex, including William Laud, bishop of London from 1628. Conformist ministers in the region wrote letters to the bishop warning that Hooker was acquiring great influence with the people, and in particular with the younger ministers, for whom he was 'an oracle, and their principal library' (*CSP dom.*, 1628–9, 554). A letter from Samuel Collins, vicar of Braintree, warned Laud that 'all men's eares are now filled with the obstreprous clamours of his [Hooker's] followers against my Lord [Laud] … as a man endeavouring to suppress good preaching and advance Popery' (Davids, 150). Hooker had become a flashpoint in the increasingly vehement puritan struggle against the strict enforcers of conformity in the forms of worship. So prominent was Hooker's voice, and so intently were East Anglians attuned to ecclesiastical matters, that Collins claimed the question of Hooker's continuance in the active ministry 'drowns the noise of the greate question of Tonnage and Poundage … I dare be bold to say that if he be once quietly gone, my Lord hath overcame the greatest difficulty in governing this parte of his diocese' (ibid., 152). In a June 1629 meeting with Laud, Hooker expressed a willingness to depart from the diocese so long as he was not called before the court of high commission. Late in 1629 petitions to Laud both for and against Hooker's ministry followed, with over forty clerical signatures on each. When in 1630 he was finally summoned to appear before the court, he elected to forfeit bond and go into hiding.

Despite his preference for a tone of hopeful encouragement in his preaching, one of Hooker's most powerful sermons was a rousing jeremiad. It was his farewell sermon in England, *The Danger of Desertion*, in which he warned his hearers that 'England hath seen her best days' (Williams and others, 245) and that 'As sure as God is God, God is going from England' (ibid., 244). His warning that 'God is packing up of his gospel, because none will buy his wares' (ibid., 246) carried visual immediacy in the market town of Chelmsford. His own imminent departure was implied as he further warned that:

> God begins to ship away his Noahs, which prophesied and foretold that destruction was near; and God makes account that New England shall be a refuge for his Noahs and his Lots, a rock and a shelter for his righteous ones to run unto. (ibid., 246)

His accusations of guilt for this situation include both the simple half-hearted believers in his audience who have taken God's blessings too much for granted and the king himself, about whom:

> Some may say: 'Surely kings and monarchs are exempted, they need not fear that such torments will come upon them.' But God will say, be he a king that rules or reigns, yet as he hath rejected God, so God will reject him. He is a King of Kings, and Lord of Lords. (ibid., 243)

The Netherlands Pursuivants actively sought Hooker until he escaped on a vessel to the Netherlands in June 1631. He expected a call to the English church in Amsterdam's Begijnhof, whose congregation had encouraged him to come. But the incumbent minister there, John Paget, put twenty questions to Hooker to test his opinions on church government, baptism, and separatism. Paget found him too strongly congregational in his opinions on church government, so Hooker moved on to Delft and became the assistant to the Scottish minister, John Forbes, in the Prinsenhof church, where he served until 1633. Early in that year he was briefly with William Ames, the puritan exiled from Cambridge in 1609 and subsequently professor and rector at Franeker, whose earlier work had helped form Hooker's theology and ecclesiology. Hooker wrote a lengthy 'Preface' to Ames's *Fresh Suit Against Human Ceremonies* (1633) before covertly returning to England. In a 1633 letter to John Cotton dissuading him from coming to Holland, Hooker reported a low level of 'heart religion' and 'the power of godliness' there, adding that his own affliction with ague had helped to discourage him from remaining (Williams and others, 297). On returning to England, he was reunited with his family, who had remained there on the earl of Warwick's estate during Hooker's exile. Together with Cotton, Samuel Stone, and their families, about 10 July 1633 the Hookers boarded the *Griffin* off the Downs, arriving in Boston in the Massachusetts Bay colony eight weeks later, on 4 September 1633.

Massachusetts Bay Hooker soon settled as pastor of a new church at Newtown (later called Cambridge) while Cotton became the teacher of the already established church at Boston and Stone became the teacher at Newtown. Some of Hooker's followers from Essex, led by his friend William Goodwin, had preceded him to Newtown in 1632 and were known there as 'Mr. Hooker's company' before he arrived. Many of these same faithful again followed him just three years later when he moved to Connecticut.

About a year after arriving in New England, Hooker was reluctantly drawn into a controversy in Salem over the impetuous John Endecott's cutting a part of St George's cross from a military banner, on the grounds that it was an idolatrous icon. When his opinion was sought by the general court of the colony, Hooker expressed reluctance to disagree with his brethren, but nevertheless rendered a lengthy opinion, thirteen pages in manuscript, 'Touching the crosse in the banners', in which he argued that the cross in the flag was a civil use of the symbol, not a religious one, and therefore was not idolatrous. This view, despite dissent from some colonial leaders, ultimately carried the day. At about the time this issue was resolved,

Hooker's friend John Haynes, a member of his congregation, was elected governor of the Massachusetts Bay colony, placing Hooker in a position to have considerable influence in colonial affairs if he chose. But in the next year, members of the Newtown church and community, dissatisfied with what they considered inadequate land for farming, sent an advance party 100 miles to the southwest to investigate the possibility of a move to the banks of the Connecticut River. In May 1636, just as Haynes was being replaced in the governorship by the newly arrived Henry Vane, the Newtown church, led by Hooker and Stone, decided to move to the site known by the native population as Suckiaug, but renamed Hartford by the English settlers in honour of Samuel Stone's English birthplace. The reasons for this removal have been much debated. The seventeenth-century historian William Hubbard believed that Hooker and Cotton needed more geographical distance between them because 'Nature doth not allow two suns in one firmament' (*Collections*, 6.306). Yet, although there were differences between them, including some of their views on the process of grace in the believer's soul and on admission to church membership, the reason Hooker gave for the move was economic—too little good meadow and grazing land for cattle and too great constriction of Newtown residents between Watertown and Charlestown, both of which had been established and laid out before Newtown. This restriction in farmland and the consequent limitation on productivity, as the Newtowners said, made it difficult to pay their ministers adequately.

Hartford, Connecticut The five-day journey to Hartford began on 31 May 1636. Hooker made occasional return visits to the Bay colony thereafter, but Hartford was his home for the rest of his life. His family at this time included five children, Samuel having been born in Newtown about 1633. The Hookers' eighth and last child, a son, had been born and died in Newtown in late 1634. Their mother, Susannah, was infirm at the time of the move and was transported to Connecticut on a litter, though she ultimately outlived her husband, dying on 17 May 1676. Hooker's ministry and his influence on civil affairs thrived at Hartford. He returned in August of 1637 to be co-moderator with Peter Bulkeley at the synod that took up the antinomian controversy then reaching full development. His reputation as both a disputant and a negotiator was well established by this time. He is known to have maintained a correspondence with both John Winthrop, governor of the Massachusetts Bay colony, and Roger Williams, the exiled radical living in Providence plantation, though fewer than a dozen of Hooker's letters have survived.

When representatives from the new Connecticut towns met to organize a colonial confederation in 1638, Hooker preached to them on the subject of government. Although some enthusiastic historians called him the first American democrat, this is far from accurate. As Perry Miller has shown, his understanding of the relationship between people and authority is based on the model of the church covenant that every New England church

adopted. But Hooker reminded his audience that civil magistrates are selected by the people they govern and that these people can limit the power of their rulers. Connecticut's fundamental orders were more liberal than the Massachusetts laws, however, in not restricting the ability to hold public office to church members, though this requirement still held for the governor. The new laws confirmed the *status quo* of a colony already in existence for three years.

Their reputations in England led to the invitation from members of parliament to Hooker, Cotton, and John Davenport to represent New England's churches at the newly convened Westminster assembly in 1642. Hooker firmly declined, however, realizing that they would be among a small minority of Independent churchmen, vastly outnumbered by the predominantly presbyterian views of many of the reform-minded English and Scottish churchmen. He did, however, send for publication in England four works through which he probably intended to influence the assembly's work on a confession of faith and a catechism: *A Briefe Exposition of the Lords Prayer*, *An Exposition of the Principles of Religion* (published together), *The Immortality of Mans Soule*, and *The Saints Guide in Three Treatises*, all published in London in 1645. His strength in argument also made him a logical choice by his New England brethren to write a defence of the New England way of church organization in response to challenges from home in the mid-1640s. Specifically in answer to the Scottish presbyterian Samuel Rutherford's *Peaceable and Temperate Plea for Pauls Presbyterie* (1642) and *The Due Right of Presbyteries* (1644), he wrote *A Survey of the Summe of Church Discipline* and sent it over in an ill-fated vessel that sank without survivors. He rewrote the book, which was eventually published posthumously in 1648.

Preaching But the central work of Hooker's career, a series of sermons preached in Cambridge, Chelmsford, and Hartford, was his epic account of the psychological process of the sinner's inner journey to salvation. Anticipating John Bunyan's allegorical *The Pilgrim's Progress*, Hooker's masterful analysis of the motions of faith describes a journey from the first awareness of one's own captivity by sin beginning with the preparatory stages of contrition and humiliation, and extending through vocation, adoption, faith, justification, sanctification, and glorification. The sermons were first published from auditors' notes as *The Soules Preparation* (1632), *The Soules Humiliation* (1637), *The Soules Effectuall Calling* (1637), *The Soules Implantation* (1637), *The Soules Exaltation* (1638), and *The Soules Possession of Christ* (1638). Although not published from his own texts, these books often capture the dynamic force of his actual delivery. In New England, Hooker revised these sermons for publication as *The Application of Redemption, the First Eight Books* and *The Application of Redemption, Books Nine and Ten*, both of which were published posthumously in 1656, as was his treatise on glorification, the final stage in the soul's ascent to heaven, *A Comment upon Christs Last Prayer*. This is the fullest account of the sequence of spiritual stages in the life of the soul produced in Hooker's generation. In it, Hooker's capacity for capturing a strong sense of spiritual adventure, of the need for constant 'application' to the challenge of subduing sin and 'labouring' in the hope of receiving God's essential help in the task, is brilliantly evident.

Hooker's importance rests on these dramatic examples of his pulpit mastery. His fellow Connecticut minister, Henry Whitfield, captured an essential characteristic in Hooker's ministry in saying:

> That he had the best command of his own spirit, which he ever saw in any man whatever. For though he were a Man of a Cholerick Disposition, and had a mighty vigour and fervour of spirit, which as occasion served, was wondrous useful unto him, yet he had ordinarily as much government of his choler, as a man has of a mastiff dog in a chain; he *could let out his dog, and pull in his dog, as he pleased.*   (Mather, 1.313)

Another contemporary simply said, 'He was a person who while doing his master's work, would put a king in his pocket' (ibid.).

Although no authentic likeness of Thomas Hooker exists, he is represented in a bronze statue created by Frances L. Wadsworth in downtown Hartford, the city where he died of an epidemic sickness on 7 July 1647 and was buried in the Central Church burying-ground.

SARGENT BUSH, JUN.

Sources C. Mather, *Magnalia Christi Americana*, 7 bks in 2 vols. (1820) • F. Shuffelton, *Thomas Hooker, 1586–1647* (1977) • S. Bush, *The writings of Thomas Hooker: spiritual adventure in two worlds* (1980) • R. C. Anderson, *The great migration begins: immigrants to New England, 1620–1633*, 2 (1995), 982–5 • G. H. Williams and others, eds., *Thomas Hooker: writings in England and Holland, 1626–1633*, Harvard Theological Studies, 28 (1975) • G. H. Williams, 'Called by thy name, leave us not: the case of Mrs Joan Drake, a formative episode in the pastoral career of Thomas Hooker in England', *Harvard Library Bulletin*, 16 (1968), 111–28, 278–300 • S. Bush, 'Thomas Hooker and the Westminster assembly', *William and Mary Quarterly*, 29 (1972), 291–300 • S. Bush, 'The growth of Thomas Hooker's *Poor doubting Christian*', *Early American Literature*, 8 (1973), 3–20 • G. L. Walker, *Thomas Hooker: preacher, founder, democrat* (1891) • T. Webster, *Godly clergy in early Stuart England: the Caroline puritan movement, c.1620–1643* (1997) • J. H. Ball, *Chronicling the soul's windings: Thomas Hooker and his morphology of conversion* (1992) • M. J. A. Jones, *Congregational commonwealth: Connecticut, 1636–1662* (1968) • *Collections of the Massachusetts Historical Society*, 2nd ser., 5–6 (1817) [*A general history of New England*, by W. Hubbard] • T. W. Davids, *Annals of evangelical nonconformity in Essex* (1863) • P. Miller, 'Thomas Hooker and the democracy of Connecticut', *Errand into the wilderness* (1956) • K. L. Sprunger, 'The Dutch career of Thomas Hooker', *New England Quarterly*, 46 (1973), 17–44 • J. Knight, *Orthodoxies in Massachusetts: rereading American puritanism* (1994) • E. Emerson, 'Thomas Hooker: the puritan as theologian', *Anglican Theological Review*, 44 (1967) • N. Pettit, *The heart prepared: grace and conversion in puritan spiritual life* (1966) • W. Herget, 'Preaching and publication: chronology and the style of Thomas Hooker's sermons', *Harvard Theological Review*, 65 (1972), 231–9 • Venn, *Alum. Cant.*

Archives Connecticut Historical Society, Hartford, MS book, 'Hooker family memorial' • Yale U., letters | Mass. Hist. Soc., Winthrop papers, letters • Massachusetts State Archives, Boston, Hutchinson papers, letters and MS

Likenesses F. L. Wadsworth, bronze statue, Hartford, Connecticut

Wealth at death £1136 15s.: Walker, *Thomas Hooker*, 181–3

Hooker, William Dawson (1816–1840). *See under* Hooker, Sir William Jackson (1785–1865).

Hooker, Sir **William Jackson** (1785–1865), botanist, was born on 6 July 1785 at 71–7 Magdalen Street, Norwich, the second of the two children of Joseph Hooker (1754–1845) and his wife, Lydia, *née* Vincent (1759–1829). Joseph Hooker was distantly related to the Baring brothers and was a confidential clerk in their Norwich office, trading in worsted and bombazine. He was also an amateur botanist and gardener, with a collection of succulent plants. Lydia Hooker came from a family of worsted weavers and artists in Norwich. William Jackson Hooker was named after his godfather William Jackson (1757–1789), his mother's cousin, and son of John Jackson (1710–1795), a wealthy brewer and farmer, three times mayor of Canterbury, Kent. He bequeathed his estate to William Jackson Hooker who inherited in 1806 when he was twenty-one.

Education and early career Hooker attended Norwich grammar school from about 1792 until 1802 or 1803. He then went to Starston Hall, 18 miles south-east of Norwich, as a pupil in estate management, probably so that he could manage the estates inherited through his godfather. Hooker's father encouraged his interest in natural history, especially in botany and entomology; he made many field trips in Norfolk and Suffolk and got to know the principal naturalists in East Anglia. His most important patrons were Sir James Edward Smith (1759–1828), who owned Linnaeus's herbarium and library; Dawson *Turner (1775–1858), banker and botanist, who became Hooker's friend and father-in-law; and Sir Joseph Banks (1743–1820), president of the Royal Society, to whom Dawson Turner introduced him in 1806. In 1805 Hooker made his first important botanical discovery when he found a species of moss not previously recorded in Britain, *Buxbaumia aphylla*, at Rackheath, near Sproston, Norfolk. He studied mainly mosses, liverworts, and ferns, and became an expert in a difficult group of liverworts, the Jungermanniae, on which in 1816 he published a monograph.

On his election to the Linnean Society of London in 1806 Hooker felt committed to a life of botany. He read his first paper to the society in 1807, on the mosses of Nepal from Buchanan Hamilton's specimens in Smith's herbarium. He toured Scotland, the Hebrides, and the Orkneys in 1807 and 1808. In 1809 he went to Iceland to make a botanical survey for Banks; his collections were lost in a fire at sea on the way home but with the aid of Banks's notes from his own journey there in 1772 Hooker was able to produce an account which was published in 1811. Sir James Smith named a new genus of mosses (*Hookeria*) after him.

Hooker helped Turner with his botanical work, preparing 234 of the 258 coloured plates in Turner's book on seaweeds (*Fuci*, 4 vols., 1808–19), which went unacknowledged. In 1809–20 he managed a brewery in Halesworth, Suffolk, for Turner. He made his first visit to Kew Gardens on 5 June 1811; with Thomas Taylor (1786–1848) he began work on a new book on mosses, *Muscologia Britannica* (1818; 2nd edn, 1827; 3rd edn, 1855). In 1812 he was elected a fellow of the Royal Society of London.

In 1814 Hooker travelled in Europe for nine months, going to Paris with the Turner family, then continuing

Sir William Jackson Hooker (1785–1865), by Spiridione Gambardella, 1843

alone to Switzerland, the south of France, and Italy. On this tour he met with leading botanists and laid the foundations of many long-term friendships. In Paris Baron von Humboldt invited him to write up the cryptogamic plants he had collected in South America; Hooker's text and plates were published in 1816 as *Plantae cryptogamicae, quas in plaga orbis novi aequinoctali collegerunt &c.*, with some mosses being published in his *Musci exotici* (1818–20).

On 12 June 1815 Hooker married Turner's eldest daughter, Maria Sarah (1797–1872). Their first son, **William Dawson Hooker** (1816–1840), was born at Halesworth on 4 April 1816. He graduated MD at Glasgow in 1839 and married in the same year Isabella Whitelaw Smith. In 1837 he visited Norway. He published *Notes on Norway* (1837 and 1839) and his dissertation on cinchona before leaving for the West Indies, where he died at Kingston, Jamaica, on 1 January 1840. A second son, Joseph Dalton *Hooker (1817–1911), was born on 30 June 1817, and three daughters followed. Hooker's life at this time consisted of 'brewery, books and babies' (Allan, 72), but many botanists visited him at Halesworth and consulted his herbarium. The brewery was neither successful nor congenial to Hooker, and he sought paid botanical work. Eventually, in 1820, with Banks's recommendation he was appointed regius professor of botany at Glasgow University.

Professor of botany at Glasgow When Hooker arrived at Glasgow there were thirty botany students and 8000 plants in the botanical garden in Sauchiehall Street; when he left in 1841 he had more than 100 students and the garden had been relocated and contained 20,000 plants. Many years later his son said:

He had never lectured, nor even attended a course of lectures; … the botanical chair was and always had been held by a graduate in medicine … his appointment was … unfavourably viewed by the medical faculty …. But he had resources that enabled him to overcome all obstacles: familiarity with his subject, devotion to its study, energy, eloquence, and a commanding presence with urbanity of manners, and above all the art of making the student love the science that he taught.   (J. D. Hooker, 'Opening of the new botanical department', 551)

Some of his students went on to achieve fame at home or overseas; many were to make valuable contributions to his herbarium and library in later years. Hooker was always prompt to thank them and to respond to their queries. Thousands of herbarium sheets were added to his herbarium every year, all identified, labelled, and filed.

In Glasgow Hooker lectured and took his students on field trips. He wrote *Flora Scotica* (1821), prepared *Botanical Illustrations* (1822) as a pioneering visual aid, and initiated summer courses in botany for the general public. He was awarded the university's LLD in 1821. Between 1823 and 1840 he prepared and illustrated seven major works, on the plants of Frederick Beechey's voyage of 1825–8 to the Pacific and Bering's Strait, on the plants of North America, and on ferns. He described numerous new plants and in 1827 became editor of *Curtis's Botanical Magazine*, a journal which described plants from round the world suitable for cultivation in Britain, with a finely drawn coloured plate for each. In 1829 Hooker started *Botanical Miscellany—Journal of Botany*, which continued with some title modifications until 1857, and *Icones plantarum* in 1834 which continued until 1990. He employed Walter Fitch (1817–1892) to prepare drawings for reference and publication, training him in the requirements of botanical work, and employed helpers to curate his herbarium. During this time Hooker wrote a *Catalogue of the Plants in the Royal Botanic Garden of Glasgow* (1825), *Directions for Collecting and Preserving Plants in Foreign Countries* (1828), *The British Flora* (1830; 7th edn, 1855), and *Perthshire illustrated, a series of select views … a general introduction illustrative of the scenery, botany &c.* (1833). He was knighted in 1836 in the Royal Guelphic Order by William IV, in recognition of his work at Glasgow and services to botany.

Director of Kew Gardens Throughout the years in Scotland Hooker remained hopeful of employment in London or East Anglia. His dream was Kew, which had a magnificent collection of plants; it had been founded in 1759 by Princess Augusta, but after the deaths of George III and Banks had declined. A parliamentary working party set up in 1838 to review the management and expenditure of the various royal gardens recommended the development of Kew as a national botanical garden providing information and plants to the new colonies, and aiding the mother country, Britain, in everything useful in the vegetable kingdom. In April 1841 Sir William Hooker was appointed the first full-time director of the royal gardens at Kew. He was now fifty-seven, but he told Turner he felt 'as if I were going to begin life over again' (Allan, 109).

The botanic garden at Kew then comprised 11 acres. In his first year Hooker extended the opening hours, and that year 9174 visitors went. By 1845, 271 acres had been added, a new arboretum planted, glasshouses repaired and extended where possible, and a new palm house begun, built to pioneering design in wide-span wrought iron by Decimus Burton (1800–1881) and Richard Turner (c.1798–1881), to replace the old Great Stove designed by William Chambers (1723-1796). Queen Victoria and Prince Albert both took a keen practical interest in Hooker's work at Kew, visiting on many occasions with their children. Hooker continued his worldwide correspondence, received plants from every continent, sent out plant collectors to gather specifically for Kew, and established further education lectures and a reading-room for Kew's gardeners. The public loved it all, and went in their thousands: in 1851, the year of the Great Exhibition in London, 331,210 people went to Kew Gardens; in 1865, the year he died, there were 529,241.

Hooker's annual reports from 1844 detailed the progress made, the plants and herbarium specimens received, the books and periodicals acquired, and the research visitors who came to consult his collections which from 1847 increasingly included samples of plant products for the new Museum of Economic Botany. He continued to edit Curtis's Botanical Magazine, still illustrated by Fitch who had accompanied him from Glasgow. It covered a wide range of plants from round the world, including many orchids, and the giant water lily, Victoria amazonica. Hooker wrote many of the articles himself with the horticultural notes contributed by John Smith (1798–1888) until 1852. Smith, a fern enthusiast, had worked at Kew since 1820, then as curator from 1841 to 1864. Joseph Hooker said that it was entirely due to him 'that the Royal Botanic Gardens maintained any position … between the death of Sir Joseph Banks in 1820 and the appointment of the new Director in 1841' (J. D. Hooker, 'Sketch', xlvii). Smith was experienced, knowledgeable, and outspoken, but sometimes clashed with Hooker. On one occasion, when Hooker and his landscaper William Nesfield ignored his advice on the siting of the palm house in relation to the pond, Smith was proved right. Smith and Fitch commiserated with each other on the perceived injustices they suffered, but stayed and were invaluable in the development of the gardens and its useful publications.

The contacts Hooker had already developed at Glasgow with governments, the India Office, and the colonies benefited Kew considerably, and enabled it to take on its new role quickly. A highly significant and effective worldwide network of botanical gardens and herbaria grew up, centring on Kew but also communicating directly with each other. Hooker was consulted when they needed senior staff, and often recommended young Kew-trained gardeners for posts overseas, or to accompany exploring expeditions. Kew became the botanical arm of the Foreign Office and was always consulted when questions arose about plants, new crops, forestry, and useful natural products. These questions all presumed the accurate identification of plants, and to assist in this critical work Hooker initiated a series of inexpensive colonial flora volumes

describing the plants of various territories, written for the educated layman. He was also appointed local commissioner for the Great Exhibition in London in 1851, advising particularly on economic botany.

Useful new plants were propagated and sent to the botanical gardens overseas where they were most likely to flourish, and many became regular crops. One of the most important was the transfer of Cinchona plants to India in 1859–60 at the request of the India Office, as a remedy for malaria. Hooker also established contacts outside the colonies, notably in Japan. In Britain, Kew-trained gardeners took up appointments in other botanical gardens and the new municipal horticultural departments. Kew propagated plane trees for distribution to London boroughs, and sent suitable new plants to both private and public gardens elsewhere.

The donation of the herbarium and library of W. A. Bromfield (1801–1851), a former student at Glasgow, permitted Hooker to move Kew's herbarium specimens and his own collections from his former home at West Park, Mortlake, into Hunter House on Kew Green, while Hooker himself took up residence in another nearby house. This brought the collections closer to hand, gave space for expansion, and demonstrated the government's commitment to botany; it also attracted other donations, including George Bentham's library and herbarium in 1854. During this time the need grew for an assistant director; Hooker eventually succeeded in getting the post created, and his son Joseph appointed. It was one of Hooker's main ambitions to see his son take over as director at Kew. Father and son worked closely for many years, and is not always easy to attribute responsibility for development at Kew correctly.

Character and final days   Sir Joseph Dalton Hooker described his father as over 6 feet tall:

> erect, slim, muscular; forehead broad and high but receding, hair nearly black, complexion sanguine, eyes brown, nose aquiline—it had been broken in a school fight; his mobile face, and especially mouth, was the despair of artists … He was a vigorous pedestrian, covering 60 miles a day with ease. (J. D. Hooker, 'Sketch', lxxxv)

The marble bust of William Hooker by Thomas Woolner in 1859 was regarded by his son as an excellent likeness. He was generally very healthy, but a little deaf after an attack of scarlet fever in Glasgow, and subject to eczema and throat infections. In character he was well-mannered, affable, and immediately impressed people with his energy and ability. He had a good memory and worked fast, was prudent and judicious, and knew his strengths. He worked long hours throughout his life, usually until midnight. He was not often seen at great social functions, society meetings, or on committees and suchlike—he did not enjoy them and anyway had his own very wide network of contacts. Besides his Glasgow degree and his knighthood, Hooker received the DCL from Oxford in 1845, and was a corresponding member of the Académie Française, and companion of the Légion d'honneur of France, as well as a member of other leading academies in Europe, Russia, and America.

In summer 1865 there was an epidemic of septic disease of the throat, probably caused by streptococcal bacteria. On Monday 7 August Hooker and his son walked about 5 miles to Battersea Park, to see some sub-tropical plants, and later he showed people around the gardens at Kew; the next day he fell ill. His family were on holiday at Yarmouth, as it had been very hot in London: Lady Hooker was summoned home, but everyone else was advised to stay away for fear of infection. Joseph then became ill with a bad attack of rheumatic fever (also probably caused by *Streptococcus*) and close friends were called in to help; Sir William died on Saturday 12 August, from a septic paralysis of the throat. He was buried in the family tomb in St Anne's churchyard, Kew Green, on 17 August, and commemorated by a Wedgwood plaque within the church. His wife, Maria, died at Torquay in 1872.

George Bentham and Thomas Thomson completed Hooker's unfinished articles for the next issue of the *Botanical Magazine*. In accordance with Hooker's will, his personal herbarium and library were offered for sale to the nation, and were purchased for Kew in 1866; they contained over 1 million herbarium specimens, 4000 volumes of publications, and about 29,000 letters dating from 1810 from over 4400 correspondents, bound in 76 volumes.

SYLVIA FITZGERALD

Sources J. D. Hooker, 'A sketch of the life and labours of Sir William Jackson Hooker, with portrait', *Annals of Botany*, 16 (1902), lxc-ccxxi · M. Allan, *The Hookers of Kew, 1785–1911* (1967) · F. A. Stafleu and R. S. Cowan, *Taxonomic literature: a selective guide*, 2nd edn, 4, Regnum Vegetabile, 110 (1983), 283–301 · R. Desmond, *Kew: the history of the Royal Botanic Gardens* (1995) · J. D. Hooker, 'The opening of the new botanical department at the Glasgow University', *Annals of Botany*, 15 (1901), 551–8 · G. Bentham, diary, 1865, RBG Kew · W. J. Hooker, diplomas granted, etc., RBG Kew · R. Desmond, *A celebration of flowers: two hundred years of Curtis's Botanical Magazine* (1987) · F. O. Bowen, 'Sir William Jackson Hooker', *Makers of British botany*, ed. F. W. Oliver (1913), 127–49 · *Sir William Jackson Hooker … 1785–1865*, RBG Kew (1965) · L. Huxley, ed., *Life and letters of Joseph Dalton Hooker* (1918) · G. Bentham, 'Sir William Jackson Hooker, 1785–1865', *Proceedings of the Linnean Society of London* (1865–6), lxvi–lxxiii · *DNB* · *IGI*
Archives Boston PL, letters · Carnegie Mellon University, Pittsburgh, Hunt Botanical Library, letters · NHM, notes and drawings · NL Scot., letters · NRA, priv. coll., letters · RBG Kew, corresp. and MSS · RBG Kew, official records in registered files | Auckland Public Library, letters to Sir George Grey · BL, letters to Robert Brown, Add. MSS 32439–32440 · Bucks. RLSS, letters to duke of Somerset · Elgin Museum, letters to George Gordon · Harvard U., Houghton L., letters to Asa Gray · Linn. Soc., letters to William Swainson; letters to Sir James Smith · NHM, letters to members of the Sowerby family · Norfolk RO, letters to Hudson Gurney · Oxf. U. Mus. NH, letters to J.O. Westwood · PRO, CRES, WORKS, Admiralty, Foreign Office, Colonial Office and India Office collections · RBG Kew, letters to Richard Spruce · RGS, letters to Royal Geographical Society · RS, corresp. with Sir John Herschel · Suffolk RO, Ipswich, letters to Robert White · U. Newcastle, Robinson L., letters to Sir Walter Trevelyan
Likenesses H. Cook, stipple, 1834 (after T. Phillips), BM, NPG; repro. in W. Jerdan, *National portrait gallery of illustrious and eminent personages* (1834) · W. Drummond, lithograph, pubd 1837, BM · S. Gambardella, oils, 1843, Linn. Soc. [*see illus.*] · T. H. Maguire, lithograph, 1851, BM, NPG · T. Woolner, marble bust, 1859, RBG Kew; plaster cast, NPG · Wedgwood medallion, 1866 (after model by T. Woolner), NPG · E. Edwards, photograph, NPG; repro. in

L. Reeve, ed., *Portraits of men of eminence* (1863) · D. Macnee, drawing, RBG Kew· Maull & Polyblank, carte-de-visite, NPG · T. Phillips, pastel drawing, RBG Kew · D. Turner, etching (after J. S. Colman), BM, NPG · T. Woolner, Wedgwood memorial plaque, St Anne's Church, Kew Green; copy, V&A · engraving (after photograph by E. Edwards), repro. in *ILN* (26 Aug 1865)
Wealth at death under £40,000: resworn probate, April 1867, *CGPLA Eng. & Wales*

Hookes, Ellis (*bap.* 1635, *d.* 1681), Quaker administrator, was born in the Woodyard Lodgings within the environs of the Palace of Westminster, and was baptized on 12 March 1635 at St Margaret's Church, near Westminster. His father, Thomas Hookes of Conwy, Denbighshire, a courtier to Charles I, held the post of yeoman of the woodyard and servant to the prince. His mother was Elizabeth Chudleigh, and through her the family had important connections: Thomas Clifford, first Baron Clifford of Chudleigh, was Ellis's first cousin; Philip Herbert, earl of Pembroke, was the family patron; and other relatives included John Williams, later archbishop of York. Following the execution of Charles I the Hookes family moved to the Round Court, Thieving Lane, Westminster. The education of Ellis is uncertain; in his will he is described as a scrivener and so it is likely that he was apprenticed at some point in his teenage years.

The precise date and circumstances of Hookes's conversion to Quakerism are unclear. It has been suggested that there may have been links with the Baptist leader, William Kiffin, who, according to Honneyman, came from Conwy, and whose family had connections through marriage with the Hookes family. Another suggestion is that he may have become involved with people at court who were attracted to Quakerism, such as Nicholas Bond, who was a steward at Whitehall. Certainly it appears that Hookes was 'convinced' by at least 1658, for at this time he delivered a letter to his mother (who was residing at Stanton Harcourt, the residence of her friend Sir William Waller, who lived nearby to Cogges Manor Farm, near Witney in Oxfordshire, the Hookes's rented home since the 1650s), but 'because he did not pay the Knight and his lady the Hat-honour, and customary Compliments, was by them, and their Servants, beaten and abused'. Hookes suffered further when, 'by their Influence, his own Father was so incensed against him, that he turned him out of Doors' (Besse, 564). Hookes came to grief again for his beliefs the following year when he and seventy others were pulled out of a Westminster meeting and 'beaten, bruised, and had their Clothes torn by soldiers' (ibid., 366).

Hookes's work for the Society of Friends began about 1657, as Quaker records state that he was clerk to the society for twenty-four years and he was to remain so until his death in 1681. During this time, he compiled the first two manuscript volumes of sufferings, which survive in his handwriting and amount to about 1300 pages. Relations between Hookes and other leading Quakers were not always harmonious, and a dispute occurred about 1660–61 in relation to sufferings when some London Friends pressed for his resignation, and he gave in his notice. It appears, however, that George Fox and other leading

Friends intervened and he was retained as clerk. Hookes became a key figure in the Quaker central organization which grew up in London from the early 1670s and served on all of the important meetings: the meeting for sufferings, the second-day morning meeting, and the yearly meeting, as well as other smaller meetings. He worked in a 'chamber', an office or committee room at 3 King's Court, near Lombard Street, London, and had an assistant to help him. His work for Friends was often arduous: for example, after the issue of the declaration of indulgence in March 1672 when leading Friends sought to release imprisoned Quakers, Ellis wrote:

> The weakness of my body is such that it makes the exercises I meet with much more hard: I am often ready to fall under by reason thereof. G. W. and myself have been much employed this summer in the business of the prisoners' liberty; and it is such a troublesome business to got through as I have not met with the like. (Braithwaite, *Second Period*, 83)

His efforts and those of other London Friends were rewarded, however, when the king issued the great pardon in September 1672.

Hookes published over twenty works, a number of which were co-written with George Fox, such as *A Primer and Catechism for Children* (1670) and *An Instruction for Right Spelling* (1673). In addition to these works of an educational nature he wrote a number of works relating to persecution, perhaps his most important one being *The Spirit of the Martyrs Revived* (n.d.), a lengthy historical work which went through many reprints. In this he places Quakerism firmly in the tradition of the early church and looks back to the creation, the fathers, patriarchs, prophets, Christ, and the apostles, as well as providing an account of persecution through the ages, in which he states that 'Satan ... in all Ages used all his Power to stop the increase and growth of this holy *seed*, by Persecuting, Murdering and Destroying their Bodies' ('To the reader'). He also found time to edit the works of other Quakers such as Edward Burrough, Francis Howgill, Samuel Fisher, and William Smith.

Hookes seems never to have married. According to his will he lived with the Quaker and widow Anne Travers for twenty years at her home in Southwark. Before living in London it is thought that he resided at Odiham, Hampshire, then at various addresses: Edward Man's, Bishopsgate; John Staploe's, close to the Three Cups in Aldersgate; and also at 3 King's Court, near Lombard Street.

Hookes died from consumption on 12 November 1681, when Quakers recorded his residence as Horsley Down, Southwark, and he was buried on 15 November at Chequer Alley (Bunhill Fields), London. On 3 December 1681 his will was proved by Anne Travers, and in it he is recorded as a scrivener of Newington Butts, Surrey. Hookes left various sums of money to Travers, other Friends, and to some of his relations.

CAROLINE L. LEACHMAN

Sources D. J. Honeyman, 'Ellis Hookes (1635–1681), first recording clerk of the Society of Friends', *Quaker History*, 72 (1983), 43–54 · J. Besse, *A collection of the sufferings of the people called Quakers*, 1 (1753) · W. C. Braithwaite, *The beginnings of Quakerism*, ed. H. J. Cadbury, 2nd edn (1955); repr. (1981) · W. C. Braithwaite, *The second period of Quakerism*, ed. H. J. Cadbury, 2nd edn (1961); repr. (1979) · N. Penney, 'Our recording clerk', *Journal of the Friends' Historical Society*, 1 (1903–4), 12–22 · J. Smith, ed., *A descriptive catalogue of Friends' books*, 1 (1867) · J. Pennyman, *A short account of the life of Mr John Pennyman* (1703) · R. Moore, *The light in their consciences: the early Quakers in Britain, 1646–1666* (2000) · Quaker digest registers, RS Friends, Lond.
Archives RS Friends, Lond., 'Great book of sufferings', vols. 1–2 | RS Friends, Lond., Swarthmore MSS [vol. 1: 44–61, 385–6, vol. 4: 117–18, 121–2, 122a]
Wealth at death approx. £130: will, PRO, PROB 11/368, sig. 183

Hookes, Nicholas (1632–1712), poet, was born in London, the son of Thomas Hookes of London. He was a king's scholar at Westminster School under Richard Busby. He was elected to a scholarship at Trinity College, Cambridge, in 1649; his tutor was Alexander Akehurst and he took his BA degree in 1653.

In his graduation year Hookes published *Amanda, a sacrifice to an unknown goddess, or, A free-will offering of a lovinge heart to a sweet-heart*, dedicated to Edward Montagu, a fellow *alumnus* of Westminster School and an undergraduate at Sidney Sussex College, the son of Lord Montagu of Boughton. There are commendatory verses by Richard Moyle, Charles Ireton, and Thomas Adams, all of Trinity College, and Matthew Palmer of the Middle Temple. The last three had attended Westminster School. Hookes attempted to secure the attention of two potential patrons; in addition to Edward Montagu he addressed a pair of poems to Sir Thomas Leventhorp, an undergraduate at Christ's College (54–6, 81–3). In the same year as *Amanda*, Hookes also published *Miscellanea poetica*; they are usually found bound together. The latter volume mainly consists of Cambridge elegies in Latin. Most of *Amanda* consists of verses on various occasions addressed to an imaginary mistress. For the most part they are unexceptional exercises in the amatory Cavalier mode, varied with moments of idiosyncrasy, such as the lines from 'To Amanda Going to Bed':

> Make me thy maiden-chamber-man,
> Or let me be thy warming-pan
> ... Then i'th morning ere I rose
> I'd kisse thy pretty pettitoes.

However, the very act of publishing verses in this overtly royalist style was potentially very provocative in the 1650s.

Hookes's bids for patronage and college preferment (the ostensible aim of *Miscellanea poetica*) were unsuccessful, and after his *annus mirabilis* of 1653, nothing more is known of him until his death almost sixty years later. He died in Lambeth on 7 November 1712 and was buried in St Mary's, Lambeth, on the south side of the north aisle. A Latin inscription describes him as 'virum qui summam dubiis probitatem sincera in Deum pietate, spectata in utrumque Carolum fide, eximia in omnes charitate, moribus suavissimis et limatissimo ingenio, omnibus elegantioris literaturae ornamentis exculto, mire adornavit' ('a man who wonderfully adorned his age in sincere piety towards God, in the greatest probity towards men, in outstanding loyalty to both Charleses, in exceptional charity towards all, by the great elegance of his wit and his great cultivation in all things that adorn the *belles-lettres*'). The phrasing of the epitaph suggests that he must have died in comfortable circumstances. Hookes's wife, Elizabeth (d. 1692?), was buried in the same grave, as were other family members.

PETER DAVIDSON and IAN WILLIAM MᶜLELLAN

Sources DNB · W. W. Rouse Ball and J. A. Venn, eds., *Admissions to Trinity College, Cambridge*, 2 (1913) · *Old Westminsters*, vol. 1 · H. A. C. Sturgess, ed., *Register of admissions to the Honourable Society of the Middle Temple, from the fifteenth century to the year 1944*, 1 (1949) · J. A. Winn, *John Dryden and his world* (1987)

Hoole, Charles (1610–1667), schoolmaster and author, was born in Wakefield, the son of Charles Hoole. He attended Wakefield Free Grammar School under Robert Doughty, and in 1628, supported by his kinsman Robert Sanderson (the future bishop of Lincoln), entered Lincoln College, Oxford. He graduated BA in 1632, proceeded MA in 1636, and was ordained. Through Sanderson's influence he was appointed master of the free grammar school at Rotherham and began the work which was to make him one of the most noted of seventeenth-century teachers and educational writers. In 1642 he became rector of Great Ponton in Lincolnshire, but his royalist sympathies led to his sequestration and departure for London about 1646, although he was cited before the committee for plundered ministers on 21 July 1647 for trying to collect tithes from his former parish. On his returning to educational work, he was successively master of two private grammar schools in London, one off Aldersgate and the other in Lothbury, near the Royal Exchange. At an unknown date he seems to have married: the preface to his 1659 publication mentions a child who had died.

Hoole's numerous educational works comprise grammars, translations, and a book on educational method and structures. His adaptation of Lily's 'authorized' grammar, *The Latine Grammar Fitted for the Use of Schools* (1651), is more attractively presented than the original, with English and Latin on opposite pages. This method is also used in his *Aesop's Fables, English and Latin* (1689) and *Publii Terentii Carthaginiensis Afri': Six Comedies of … Terentius* (1676). In 1659 he published a translation of Comenius's *Orbis sensualium pictus* and recommended the pictorial method for the teaching of younger children as an antidote to the prevailing manner of '[teaching them] as we do parrots, to speak they know not what' (*Orbis pictus*, preface).

Hoole's most notable work, *A New Discovery of the Old Art of Teaching Schoole* (1660), not only sets out his views on what education should be but also paints a vivid picture of education as it actually was in the mid-seventeenth century and is an essential source for educational historians of the period. The book stresses the value 'to Church and Commonwealth' of an efficient and progressive system of education with widely available elementary instruction and, alongside the grammar schools, practical schools for older children who lacked the academic bent. His ideas on the curriculum were traditional—Greek, Latin, and some Hebrew for the grammar school; English and Latin grammar for the 'petty school'; and basic English and arithmetic for the 'writing school'. However, he insisted that the means of instruction must vary to fit the capacity of the scholar, and teachers must rely on proper preparation and method rather than (particularly for younger children) the rod.

In 1660 Hoole became chaplain to Sanderson, who tried on 5 March 1661 to get him a prebend at Lincoln. He gained the rectory of Stock, near Chelmsford, and died there on 7 March 1667. He was buried in the chancel of the parish church.

W. R. MEYER

Sources Wood, *Ath. Oxon.*, new edn, 3.758–9 · C. Hoole, *A new discovery of the old art of teaching schoole* (1660); facs. edn, ed. E. T. Campagnac (1913) · Foster, *Alum. Oxon.* · W. A. L. Vincent, *The state and school education, 1640–1660* (1950), 8–9, 17–18, 66–7, 69, 91–2 · F. Watson, *The English grammar schools to 1660: their curriculum and practice* (1908), 64–7, 271–2, 278, 315–16, 479–82, 513 · J. A. Comenius, *Orbis sensualium pictus*, trans. C. Hoole (1659) · *Walker rev.*, 252 · *VCH Lincolnshire*, 2.63–4

Hoole, Elijah (1798–1872), missionary, was born in Manchester on 3 February 1798, the second son of Holland Hoole, shoemaker and lay Wesleyan preacher, and his wife, Sarah. He was educated at Manchester grammar school (1809–13) and he then studied Greek and Hebrew privately. He was a devout Wesleyan and in 1819, after he had served as a probationer with the Wesleyan Methodist Missionary Society (WMMS) in London, the society selected him to found a mission at Bangalore in south India. He was shipwrecked on the outward voyage and settled initially at Negapatam, but in May 1821, with seven months of intensive Tamil study behind him, he finally arrived at Bangalore. Barely ten months later, however, he was ordered to Madras to work on a new Tamil translation of the Bible for the Bible Society and in September 1822 he became secretary of the society's translations committee.

In 1828 ill health forced Hoole back to Britain. While recuperating he wrote up his journal, *Personal Narrative of a Mission to the South of India* (1829; 2nd edn, 1844), and then accepted the job of superintending the Wesleyan schools in Ireland. He was appointed assistant secretary to the WMMS in 1834, and in 1836 general secretary, a post he held until his death. In 1835 he married Elizabeth, third daughter of Charles *Chubb (1772–1846), lock- and safe-maker of London; they had two sons, Charles Holland and Elijah. Elizabeth became effectively the women's secretary of the WMMS. She played mother to the many missionaries passing through her house, corresponded with their wives all over the world, and for twenty years edited *Juvenile Offering*, the Wesleyans' first missionary magazine for children.

Hoole's efficiency and diligence in transacting WMMS business were universally admired; nevertheless, in correspondence he could be abrasive and he often intervened forcefully in controversial issues such as the baptism of polygamists. Outside the WMMS he was honorary secretary of the British Society for the Propagation of the Gospel among the Jews and of the Home for Asiatics in London. He was also a member of the Royal Asiatic Society, in whose journal he published several pieces on Tamil philology and folklore. He frequently edited the *Wesleyan Missionary Notices*, as well as several individual missionary memoirs and histories.

Hoole died at his home, 8 Myddleton Square, Pentonville, London, on 17 June 1872, and was buried in Highgate cemetery on 22 June. His widow held office in the WMMS women's auxiliary until 1878; she died on 3 June 1880, aged seventy-four.   KATHERINE PRIOR

Sources *The Wesleyan Missionary Notices*, 4th ser., 4 (1872) · E. Hoole, *Personal narrative of a mission to the south of India* (1829) · G. G. Findlay and W. W. Holdsworth, *The history of the Wesleyan Methodist Missionary Society*, 5 vols. (1921–4) · J. F. Smith, ed., *The admission register of the Manchester School, with some notes of the more distinguished scholars*, 2, Chetham Society, 73 (1868) · W. Moister, *A history of Wesleyan missions, in all parts of the world* (1871) · B. H. Badley, *Indian missionary directory and memorial volume*, 3rd edn (1886) · d. cert. [Hoole, Elizabeth Chubb]
Archives SOAS, Archives of the Methodist Church Overseas Division, records of the Wesleyan Methodist Missionary Society, journal, and corresp. as society secretary
Likenesses Dean, stipple (after Lovatt), NPG
Wealth at death under £3000: probate, 7 Nov 1872, *CGPLA Eng. & Wales*

Hoole, John (1727–1803), translator, was born in December 1727 in Moorfields, London, one of six children of Samuel Hoole (*b.* 1692), mechanician, and his wife, Sarah (*c.*1700–*c.*1793), daughter of James Drury, clockmaker, of Clerkenwell, London. He attended James Bennet's school at Hoddesdon, Hertfordshire, after being educated by an uncle (the '*metaphysical taylor*', according to Johnson; *Boswell's Life of Johnson*, 4.187). Hoole enjoyed languages and studied Italian for pleasure. After an unsuccessful attempt to join the theatre, he went as clerk to the East India Company in 1744 where he gained promotion to auditor, wrote *Present State of the English East India Company's Affairs* (1772) and remained there until his retirement.

On 25 May 1757 he married Susanna Smith (*c.*1730–1808), a 'handsome Quakeress' (W. Foster, 156) of Bishop's Stortford. They had one son, Samuel *Hoole. In 1760 John Hoole's first publication *A Monody: to the Memory of Mrs Margaret Woffington* appeared. However, it was his interest in translating Italian literature, encouraged by George Oldmixon, a colleague and Italian scholar, as well as his friendship with Dr Samuel Johnson, that forwarded Hoole's reputation. In 1763 he published *Jerusalem Delivered* (a translation of Tasso's *Gerusalemme liberata*), having had the first book printed in 1761 for his friends. His labours on Tasso's works (*Rinaldo* was published in 1792) earned him the nickname Tasso Hoole. Although *Jerusalem Delivered* was generally favourably received, Sir Walter Scott, introduced to Tasso 'through the flat medium of Mr Hoole's translation', said the translator was 'a noble transmuter of gold into lead' (Lockhart, 1.29 and 5.9). Charles Lamb, wishing to 'gain some idea of Tasso from this Mr

Hoole, the great boast and ornament of the India House … found him more vapid than smallest small beer "sunvinegared"' (Fitzgerald, 1.357). Hoole's later *Works of Metastasio* (1767) pleased Metastasio himself, although the poet expressed the difficulty of translating Italian poetry effectively.

Samuel Johnson was introduced to Hoole by John Hawkesworth in 1761, and helped the translator's literary career, participating in nearly every publication in some way. He wrote dedications to *Jerusalem Delivered* and *Works of Metastasio*, urged Warren Hastings, then governor of Bengal, to promote Hoole's works, and encouraged Hoole to adapt plays for the stage. In return Hoole gathered members 'who were not *patriots*' (*Boswell's Life of Johnson*, 4.87) for Johnson's City Club, belonged to the Essex Head Club which, dominated by literary figures, had its rules set by Johnson and, with his wife and son, the Revd Samuel Hoole, attended Johnson on his deathbed. Jeremy Bentham viewed such intimacy cynically, calling Hoole one of Johnson's 'lickspittles' (*Letters of Samuel Johnson*, 2.363). Johnson bequeathed a book apiece of their choosing to Hoole and his son, while in his own will Hoole left a writing desk formerly belonging to Johnson. Following Johnson's death Hoole published a detailed narrative of his friend's last days.

Hoole's three tragedies, *Cyrus* (first performed 1768), *Timanthes* (1770), and *Cleonice* (1775), were enacted at the Theatre Royal, Covent Garden. The failure of *Cleonice*, in spite of Johnson's being sure of its success, prompted Hoole to return much of the advanced copyright money for he reasoned that, it being unlikely to be profitable for booksellers, it should not be a loss. *Cyrus* and *Timanthes* were reasonably successful due, contemporaries implied, to the popularity of the cast members, Mrs Mary Ann Yates in particular.

Having lived in and around London at Wandsworth, Clement's Inn (about 1768), then Shire Lane (1775), Hoole moved to Great Queen Street. From here in 1783 he published his translation of Ariosto's *Orlando Furioso*. Included in this first edition was his portrait by Frances Reynolds (sister of Sir Joshua) who temporarily lived with the Hoole family at Great Queen Street. In 1785 Hoole added a biographical sketch to John Scott's *Critical Essays* (1785). The following year, having retired from the East India Company, he moved with his wife to live with their son at Abinger, near Dorking, where Samuel had a curacy. Shortsighted, 'of middling stature and of athletic make', a contemporary described Hoole as 'gentle, unassuming and affectionate' (W. Foster, 162). Several portraits were made, including one engraved by his nephew Anker Smith. Most of Hoole's works were reprinted several times but now he is regarded primarily as one of Johnson's circle rather than for his own endeavours. He died on a visit to Dorking on 2 August 1803 and was buried there.

VIVIENNE W. PAINTING

Sources W. Foster, *The East India House* (1924) · *Boswell's Life of Johnson*, ed. G. B. Hill, 1–4 (1887) · *Letters of Samuel Johnson*, ed. G. B. Hill, 2 (1892) · selection of material from Tower Hamlets, London, Local

History Library and Archives, cuttings box, ref. TH/8204/6–7 · *DNB* · C. Drury, 'John Hoole, poet', *N&Q*, 12th ser., 5 (1919), 327 · *IGI* · A. M. D., 'John Hoole', *N&Q*, 8th ser., 9 (1896), 518–19 · J. G. Lockhart, *Memoirs of Sir Walter Scott*, 5 vols. (1900) · C. J. Stratman, ed., *Bibliography of English printed tragedy, 1565–1900* [1966] · C. Leech, T. W. Craik, L. Potter, and others, eds., *The Revels history of drama in English*, 8 vols. (1975–83), vol. 6 · *Annual Register* (1773), 68–75 · P. Fitzgerald, ed., *Life, letters and writings of Charles Lamb* (1882), vol. 1 · *GM*, 1st ser., 31 (1761), 422 · Foster, *Alum. Oxon.* (1886) · John Hoole's will, PRO, PROB 11/1398, fols. 374*v*–376*r* · *BL cat.*

Archives BL, biographical writings about Samuel Johnson, RP252 [copies] | Yale U., Beinecke L., corresp. with James Boswell **Likenesses** F. Reynolds, oils?, *c.*1783, repro. in J. Hoole, *Orlando furioso* (1783), frontispiece · A. Smith, line engraving, 1792, BM, NPG; repro. in *European Magazine* (March 1792) · G. Dance, pencil drawing, 1793, NPG · W. Daniell, engraving (after G. Dance), BM · O. Humphry, portrait; Sothebys, June 1920 · Mrs. D. Turner, etching (after O. Humphry), BM, NPG

Wealth at death annuity from East India Company: will, PRO, PROB 11/1398, fols. 374*v*–376*r*

Hoole, Samuel (1757/8–1839), poet, was baptized on 31 January 1758 at Bartholomew Close and Pinners Hall Independent, London, the son of John *Hoole (1727–1803), the translator of Ariosto, and Susanna Smith (*c.*1730–1808) of Bishop's Stortford, Hertfordshire. The elder Hoole was then employed as auditor of the India accounts for the East India Company; he kept chambers at Clement's Inn while his family resided at suburban Wandsworth. Nothing is recorded of Samuel Hoole's early life; possibly he attended a private boarding-school like his father. He would have grown up amid an extensive circle of family acquaintances: friends from the East India House, Quaker society through the mother's connections, including John Scott of Amwell, and distinguished literary friends of his father's, including Samuel Johnson. From his parents Samuel Hoole learned to temper a basic sobriety with an easy and pleasing social manner. In July 1780 he entered Magdalen College, Oxford, to prepare for the ministry at the late age of twenty-two. While at Oxford he published his first poem, *Modern Manners* (1782), a novel in verse that cleverly imitates Christopher Anstey's *New Bath Guide*. This was followed by *Aurelia, or, The Contest: an Heroi-Comic Poem* (1783). In November 1783 Johnson, who seems to have had a particular affection for Samuel Hoole, unsuccessfully attempted to get him a place as reader to the Inner and Middle temples; in January 1784 his father sought Bishop Percy's assistance in getting Samuel a fellowship at Dulwich College. For this purpose he was granted a Lambeth degree by the archbishop of Canterbury, though in the event the fellowship was awarded by a lottery in which Hoole was not successful. He was in orders by September 1784, and afterwards worked as a private tutor and preached at St Alban, Wood Street. One of his first clerical duties was to attend Samuel Johnson in his final illness; Johnson left his 'reverend friend' a bequest of books.

In 1786 Hoole published a volume of sermons and in April moved with his parents to Surrey, where he served as a curate for Abinger Wotton, near Dorking. The following year he published *Edward, or, The Curate*, a tragic tale

written in stanzas after the sentimental manner of James Beattie's *Minstrel*. Like his earlier poetry this was well received, and Hoole's collected poems were published in two volumes in 1790. The Hooles were frequent visitors at the homes of Charles Burney and Arthur Young. In her journals for 1787 Susan Burney describes Hoole as conversable, entertaining, and fond of children. In his autobiography Arthur Young describes him as a moral man of strict integrity, and fond of his second daughter Elizabeth (1768–1794), whom Samuel Hoole married in September 1791. Charles Burney thought this marriage to a young poet of uncertain means not splendid in point of circumstances, but wrote to Young that he hoped that 'they will gain a prize in the fortuitous distribution of such happiness as reasonable mortals have a right to expect' (*Autobiography of Arthur Young*, 198). It was not to be; Mrs Hoole contracted consumption and after bearing the illness with characteristic patience died on 1 August 1794.

An augmented collection of Hoole's sermons was published in 1795. John Hoole, who since retiring on his pension had lived a peripatetic life, died at Abinger in 1803, the year Samuel was belatedly promoted to the rectory of Poplar Chapel in Middlesex. On 10 December 1803 he married Catherine Wainford of Dorking, near his former residence. Hoole had long complained of failing eyesight, and after publishing a sermon to mark the refitting of the chapel at Poplar in 1804 he published nothing until a final collection of sermons in 1833. In 1827 John, his eldest son from the second marriage, became his father's curate at Poplar after completing his BA at Oxford. Samuel Hoole died aged eighty-one on 26 February 1839 in Tenterden, Kent.

While he was never so famous as his father, Samuel Hoole's contemporary literary reputation was considerable. In a 1783 letter to James Beattie, Scott of Amwell described him as a 'rising genius'; in a 1787 letter Anna Seward bestowed high praise on *The Curate* and described Hoole as a 'risen-genius'. In his *Table Talk* Samuel Rogers, who knew the poet when he was working as a tutor in London, described *The Curate* as 'by no means bad'. Hoole was a fine craftsman in several kinds of verse. His poems blend genial satire and pious sentiment in the late Augustan manner pursued by his contemporaries William Hayley, Richard Tickell, Anna Seward, and Hannah More. If the fashion for such verse passed quickly, Hoole's narrative adaptation of Beattie's *Minstrel* struck out a path that several later imitators would follow.

DAVID HILL RADCLIFFE

Sources *European Magazine and London Review*, 21 (1792), 163–5 · *GM*, 1st ser., 64 (1794), 769 · *GM*, 1st ser., 73 (1803), 793, 1184 · D. Rivers, *Living authors*, 2 vols. (1798) · W. Forbes, *An account of the life and writings of James Beattie*, 2 vols. (1806) · *Letters of Anna Seward: written between the years 1784 and 1807*, ed. A. Constable, 6 vols. (1811) · Nichols, *Lit. anecdotes* · Nichols, *Illustrations* · [J. Watkins and F. Shoberl], *A biographical dictionary of the living authors of Great Britain and Ireland* (1816) · S. Rogers, *Table Talk* (1856) · Foster, *Alum. Oxon.* · *DNB* · *The autobiography of Arthur Young*, ed. M. Beetham-Edwards (1898) · R. B. Johnson, *Fanny Burney and the Burneys* (1926) · *The journals and letters of Fanny Burney (Madame D'Arblay)*, ed.

J. Hemlow and others, 12 vols. (1972–84) · *The letters of Samuel Johnson*, ed. B. Redford, 5 vols. (1992–4) · *IGI*

Hoole, William [Bill] (1894–1979), railway engine driver, was born on 27 July 1894 at 69 Kew Street, St Martin's, Liverpool, the second eldest in the family of seven of William Hoole (*d.* early 1930s), greengrocer and later a miner, and his wife, Martha, *née* Coy. He was educated at Kirkdale Day Industrial School in Liverpool, and spent his school holidays exploring the city, its port, and railway stations. On leaving school he found work as a dock messenger with the Midland Railway. He worked a 66-hour week, beginning each day by hitching a ride at dawn on the footplate of one of the Great Central line dock pilots. Soon he was allowed to help with the shovel and even handle the regulator of the small engine: 'from then on steam was just what he wanted' (Semmens, 17). In 1911 he became a locomotive cleaner with the Great Central line, moving south to Neasden in May 1913 to accelerate his progress onto the footplate.

Bill Hoole, as he was always known, volunteered for the army soon after the outbreak of war in 1914. He joined the Royal Field Artillery and saw action in Flanders as a signals corporal in a gun battery. After being demobilized in 1919 he returned to the Great Central line and to a fireman's job. On 26 February 1921, at Willesden register office, he married Dorothy (Dolly) May (*b.* 1899/1900), a laundry packer, the daughter of Richard Ratley, an engine driver; Hoole had lodged with her family before the war. They had two daughters. A lifelong union man, Hoole was assistant secretary of the Neasden branch of the Associated Society of Locomotive Engineers and Firemen. He was also active in the Labour Party in Paddington and raised funds for Manor House Hospital at Golders Green, the 'labour hospital' started by volunteers during the First World War. He gave up his political work when he moved from Neasden in 1927, primarily because of family commitments.

In January 1923 the Great Central line, with 223,000 staff and 7000 miles of track, became part of the London and North Eastern Railway (LNER). Cloth caps and mufflers began to disappear from the footplate, replaced by peaked caps and overalls. Against this background Hoole worked his way up the firing 'links', graduating from local runs to the 200-mile journey to Manchester. The fireman's job involved skill and precision rather than heavy labour. Each shovelful carried only a few pounds of coal, but had to be delivered through the narrow aperture of the firebox while the locomotive pitched at high speed. It required upper body strength and the footwork of a boxer; at 10 stone, Hoole had the near-perfect build. In 1926 he passed his driver's exam and in 1927 moved to 'top shed' at King's Cross, where he remained until his retirement in 1959.

Hoole began his driving on the junior links, undertaking shed duties and shunting in the first 6 miles out of King's Cross. The work, though unglamorous, provided excellent training, with a wide variety of locomotive types and complex signal workings. He drove passenger trains for the first time in 1935. The LNER was now approaching the zenith of its pre-war operations, when new locomotives—such as *Silver Link*, the first of Sir Nigel Gresley's A4s—set record speeds in a blaze of publicity. The advent of war put an end to this era of fast running. In 1939 Hoole was made air-raid warden of top shed, but he soon found a way back to the footplate, continuing his steady ascent through the driving links. In 1953 he realized his ambition of promotion to the top or 'no. 1' link. For the remainder of his career he drove express passenger trains, generally lodging in a distant city overnight. His wages reflected his élite status: some weeks he paid as much in income tax as a new driver might earn in total.

Years of training had taught Hoole how to use his engine and the geography of the track to achieve sustained high speeds. He relished a late departure, which offered the challenge of making up time, and was always ready to help his fireman with a stint on the shovel. The 'Hoole philosophy' 'aimed at getting to the other end of the journey as quickly as possible' (Semmens, 135). Like all enginemen he developed a sixth sense about his locomotive and had the reputation of pushing his engines hard: in the opinion of some critics, too hard. And because he was always trying to run ahead of schedule he caused difficulties for signalmen and controllers. Occasionally he overran a signal and would exaggerate the effect for his fireman, sitting 'with his hands pressed together as if in prayer' (ibid.).

The lack of automated warning systems in this era exposed drivers and passengers alike to great risks. The multiple collision at Harrow and Wealdstone station, on 8 October 1952, in which 112 people died, accelerated the introduction of safety mechanisms in drivers' cabs. Hoole had his share of 'incidents', but his disarming honesty in admitting mistakes often lessened the disciplinary consequences. The most serious incident of his career was the derailment of the *Duke of Rothesay* on 17 July 1948. Faulty track maintenance caused the bogie to derail near Barnet, tearing up the track and overturning the locomotive and tender. Hoole's fireman, Albert Young, was thrown from the footplate and killed, and Hoole and several passengers were injured. He resumed driving ten days later and made light of the incident, but it nevertheless affected him deeply.

For almost a decade after the war the railways struggled to recapture their pre-war running. After nationalization, on 1 January 1948, managers sought greater flexibility from the workforce. Drivers found their schedules changed during a shift, and perhaps hours added to their day. Hoole felt that footplate crews were being exploited and disobeyed some instructions in protest. In five years he collected a number of 'severe personal reprimands', which might later have ended his footplate career. But while he was unafraid to court the disapproval of his superiors, he also had their respect, and this often saved him.

Hoole drove many locomotives on top link but his favourite was the A4 engine *Sir Nigel Gresley*. In November

1955 he achieved probably the highest speed of his career on the London-bound 'Tees-Tyne Pullman'. 'Sir Nigel Gresley was in particularly fine condition and Bill gave it the works descending Stoke Bank' (Semmens, 134). Unknown to him, however, the trip was being logged by the civil engineering department. According to the Hallade recorder in the last coach he topped 117 m.p.h., well over the 110 m.p.h. limit. The run became the talk of messrooms throughout the region, but doubts about the accuracy of the recorder meant that Hoole escaped with only a reprimand. On another occasion a turn of speed earned him praise. In November 1956 a bomb hoax delayed the 'Talisman' Anglo-Scottish express by 25 minutes. Hoole nevertheless reached Newcastle on time, giving British Railways a welcome publicity coup. The incident helped to gain him celebrity, and he attracted a growing following among railway enthusiasts, or 'platform enders'. Many of his runs were documented by their stop watches and tabulated in the railway magazines.

In July 1958 Hoole drove his first diesel locomotive. He was far from being dismissive of the new 'Deltic' engines, but found diesel locomotion impersonal compared to steam. As he approached his own retirement it became clear that the days of the A4 were also numbered. On Saturday 23 May 1959 a high-speed enthusiasts' special was organized: a farewell to the A4 and a celebration of the golden jubilee of the Stephenson Locomotive Society. Hoole was invited to drive Sir Nigel Gresley on this run. Every seat of the eight-coach train was taken and a public address system gave a running commentary from the footplate. After turning at Doncaster the train left for King's Cross two minutes late—Hoole later confessed that he had wished it was more. He had studied the 126 m.p.h. record-breaking run of Mallard in 1938 and was convinced that Sir Nigel Gresley could go faster. He held 75 m.p.h. to the summit of Stoke Bank and then began racing down the incline: 'Excitement in the train was intense, and a wave of clicks from the massed stop watches greeted the passage of each milepost' (Semmens, 171). With fireman Alf Hancox keeping the boiler pressure well up, Hoole pushed his locomotive over 100 m.p.h. A tap on the shoulder from the inspector, however, forced him to ease off with 7 miles of the bank left to run. The top speed was officially 112 m.p.h., a post-war record for steam traction: 'Steam power on the East Coast Route could not have had a more fitting grand finale' (Semmens, 172).

Hoole made his last run on Tuesday 7 July 1959 on the Scotland to London 'Elizabethan'. A small crowd greeted him at King's Cross, including his wife Dolly, daughter Irene, and a BBC interviewer. His departure was greeted by managers there with sadness tinged with relief. As one put it: 'There are no characters left now, only drivers' (Semmens, 190). He faced potentially a difficult retirement, having to supplement his pension by part-time work, until an invitation from Allan Garraway enabled him to join the Festiniog narrow-gauge railway in north Wales, where 'Bill's disarming manner, his perennial smile and cheerfulness, and his willingness to help as

much as he could, soon made him an inseparable part of the Festiniog scene' (Semmens 178). Latterly he lived in Birmingham, where he died, on 7 June 1979, at Moseley Hall Hospital. He was buried in Minffordd cemetery, 'in sight and sound of trains on both the Festiniog and British Railways' (Railway Magazine, August 1979, 410).

MARK POTTLE

Sources P. W. B. Semmens, Bill Hoole: engineman extraordinary (1966) · Railway Magazine, 125/940 (Aug 1979) · N. McKillop, How I became an engine driver (1953) · b. cert. · m. cert. · d. cert. · The Guardian (1 May 2002), suppl., pp. 2–3
Likenesses E. Treacy, photograph, National Railway Museum, York · photographs, repro. in Semmens, Bill Hoole

Hooley, Edgar Purnell (1860–1942), surveyor and road builder, was born on 5 June 1860 at Brunswick Street, Swansea, the son of Charles Hooley, commercial traveller, and his wife, Elizabeth Phillips, née Purnell. Nothing is known about his education, but following a short period in the office of the surveyor to the Neath (south Wales) highway board, Hooley was articled in 1876 to James Craik, civil engineer and surveyor, Bristol. He spent a further year, 1879–80, as an assistant, before returning to Neath, and entering a general partnership with Francis Lean. In 1881, he became surveyor to the Stow on the Wold highway board, and took a similar position with the rural sanitary authority for Maidstone in Kent, in 1884, where he was also responsible for the design of water and sewerage schemes, as well as for roads and bridges. In a tract published by the Institution of Civil Engineers in 1892, Sanitary Work in Rural Districts, Hooley wrote of how outbreaks of disease caused by the poor drainage of such districts might excite less public interest, but proportionately they were just as commonplace as in urban areas.

Hooley was appointed surveyor and architect to the newly established Nottinghamshire county council in 1889. Together with his chief assistant, he designed and built between 1896 and 1902 the county asylum, at a cost of £147,000. Drawing heavily on his experience at Maidstone, he put into effect a bookkeeping and contractual system for the maintenance of the county's main roads. An outline of the system, which he gave to the newly empowered district councils, was later published as a book, Management of Highways (1894). In 1902, Hooley took the further position of road engineer for the Kesteven county council of Lincolnshire. However, the work of the two counties, together with private practice, led to a breakdown in his health, and his resignation from the Kesteven position. He later served as acting county surveyor for Oxfordshire, and as consulting county surveyor for Buckinghamshire.

Hooley was keenly interested in the materials used in road construction and maintenance. During his time at Maidstone, he had substituted granite for local stone. Although more expensive to purchase, and import to the county, its hard-wearing qualities brought longer term savings. His priority in the early 1890s was to remedy damage wrought by earlier short-term economies. Roads had been 'starved' of materials to the point where their foundations showed through. Again, there were significant, long-term savings to be made from large-scale and immediate expenditure. The increasing number of heavy traction engines placed further demands on road construction and maintenance. Even where the foundations were sound, and the traditional water-based macadam surface well maintained, the 'sucking-up' action of the pneumatic tyres of the rapidly growing number of motor cars created a crisis in road management. Not only was there public outcry over the dust and mud nuisance, but the road surface disintegrated even more rapidly.

Convinced that the future lay with the car—it made less dirt, and was quicker and more convenient than either the horse or traction engine—Hooley saw no alternative but to design an entirely new road surface. There had been numerous trials with various forms of tarmacadam. Hooley is generally credited with being the first to discover ways of mixing tar with slag mechanically at the blast furnace in such a way as to produce an impervious and hard-wearing surfacing material. The re-formation of a 5 mile length of the Radcliffe Road, south of Nottingham, and its covering with tarmac, demonstrated what such investment could achieve in terms of a dust- and mud-free surface, that lasted considerably longer than conventional surfaces. Hooley obtained a patent in 1902, and registered a company to exploit it in June 1903. The venture was secured, however, only by the intervention of Sir Alfred Hickman MP (the owner of a blast furnace), who became chairman, in 1905, of the company which now called itself Tarmac.

Hooley was elected to the Incorporated Association of Municipal and County Engineers in 1884, was a contributor to its journal, and its president in 1908–9. He was elected an associate member of the Institution of Civil Engineers in December 1886, and member in January 1906. For many years, he was an outstanding figure as an expert witness in the committee room of the House of Commons, in the law courts, and at Local Government Board inquiries. He served as a member of the advisory committee of the roads board.

Hooley resigned as county surveyor in January 1915, after he had offered his professional services to the Sherwood Foresters. Never one to tolerate ill-informed criticism of his profession, Hooley was described as immensely popular with all who knew him. He died at home in Oxford, at Greyroofs, 16 Davenant Road, on 26 January 1942. He was survived by his wife, Matilda Fanny, two daughters, and two sons. He was cremated on 28 January 1942.   JOHN SHEAIL

Sources *Journal of the Institution of Municipal and County Engineers*, 68 (1942), xii · *Nottingham Journal* (6 Feb 1942) · J. B. F. Earle, *Black top: a history of the British flexible roads industry* (1974) · J. B. F. Earle, *A century of road materials: a history of the roadstone division of Tarmac Ltd* (1971), 101–2, 108–9 · 'Departmental committee … to inquire into the subject of highways authorities and administration in England and Wales', *Parl. papers* (1904), 24.363–576, Cd 1794 · d. cert. · b. cert. · *CGPLA Eng. & Wales* (1942) · E. P. Hooley, *Sanitary work in rural districts* (1892) · E. P. Hooley, *Management of highways* (1894)

Archives Inst. CE | Notts. Arch., highways, bridges, and county buildings committee papers · Notts. Arch., reports of county surveyor, CC/SV
Likenesses photograph, repro. in Earle, *Black top* · portrait, repro. in *Proceedings of the Incorporated Association of Municipal and County Engineers*, 35 (1908–9), frontispiece
Wealth at death £3954 7s. 9d.: probate, 15 April 1942, *CGPLA Eng. & Wales*

Hooley, Ernest Terah (1859–1947), financier, was born on 5 February 1859 in Sneinton, Nottinghamshire, the only child of Terah Hooley, lacemaker, and his wife, Elizabeth, *née* Peach. In his autobiography he claimed that the family had been farmers at Long Eaton, Derbyshire, since the eighteenth century. At the age of twenty-one he joined his father's lace business, and in the following year (1881) he married Annie Maria, *née* Winlaw, the daughter of a baker, with whom he had four daughters and three sons. His earnings in his father's business (possibly helped by an inheritance from his mother) enabled him in 1888 to buy Risley Hall in Derbyshire for £5000. In 1889 he left the lace business in search of larger fortunes and set up as a stockbroker in Nottingham.

In an age devoid of regulations to oversee the scrupulousness of share prospectuses and flotations, Hooley discovered a talent for making large sums of money by selling off companies at inflated prices and pocketing a sizeable percentage of the proceeds. Among them was his first public flotation in 1894—that of an American subsidiary of Humber & Co. Ltd, cycle manufacturers—as well as household names such as Raleigh, Singer, Swift, and above all the Dunlop Pneumatic Tyre Company, bought by Hooley and M. D. Rucker in 1896 for £3 million and promptly floated at £5 million (which was 80 per cent over-subscribed). Other celebrated companies to pass through Hooley's hands included Schweppes and Bovril (both in 1897). He also caused a stir with his purchase in 1896 and resale in segments of the Trafford Park estate in Manchester.

Partly for reasons of image-building, Hooley moved his business to London in 1896. He cultivated members of the aristocracy and sprinkled them among his company boards to impress potential investors. He affected a lavish lifestyle, purchasing Papworth Hall in Cambridgeshire for £70,000 in 1895, and later adding several adjacent estates costing £210,000. His entertainment featured abundant wine and cigars, although he himself was a non-smoking teetotaller.

Hooley's gilded years came to an abrupt end in June 1898, when he himself filed a petition for the first and most sensational of his four bankruptcies. The background to this was the ending of the cycle boom in the previous year. The specific causes of Hooley's failure remain obscure, owing partly to deliberate obfuscation and partly to the erratic nature of his business methods, including a total absence of accounts. He was certainly faced with claims for large commission payments arising out of his company promotions; and he alleged that his partner Martin Rucker had removed £506,000 from the business (in addition to shares) in six months.

Bankruptcy sharply lowered Hooley's social position,

but made less difference to his lifestyle, not least because before his crash he had made over to his wife both Papworth and Risley Hall and their contents. He was also allowed to continue trading, on condition that he kept his trustee supplied with a record of his financial affairs, so as to facilitate repayment of outstanding creditors. In the years 1899–1904 Hooley was involved in a series of dubious companies concerned with exploiting concessions on foreign territories. It was in relation to one of these, the Siberian Goldfield Development Company formed in May 1900, that Hooley and his associate H. J. *Lawson were charged in 1904 with fraudulent share promotion. Hooley was acquitted, but Lawson received a twelve-month gaol sentence.

Thereafter Hooley steered clear of companies for some time, concentrating on land deals. In 1911–12 he was involved almost simultaneously in three distinct sets of legal proceedings. First, his trustee, Mr Basden, charged him with contempt of court for failing to produce statements of his financial affairs over the preceding five years, and Hooley was eventually committed to Brixton prison for a month. Secondly, in October 1911 he faced a charge of obtaining money on false pretences in connection with an abortive land deal in Nottinghamshire, which ended with a twelve-month gaol sentence. Thirdly, he was declared bankrupt for the second time in 1912 on a creditor's petition.

During the boom which followed the end of the First World War, Hooley became involved in trading shares in the cotton industry. In 1921 he and five others were charged with fraudulent misrepresentation in floating shares of Jubilee Cotton Mills Ltd in 1919–20. Hooley, as ringleader, received a three-year gaol sentence. He was also declared bankrupt for the third time in September 1921. His fourth bankruptcy followed in January 1939 on a petition of the Inland Revenue for an income-tax claim of £699 17s. 5d.

For all his legal transgressions, Hooley was not an unattractive character: warm-hearted, dynamic, musically gifted (he played the piano and the organ), and with a contagious sense of humour. His enduring legacy was on the Papworth estate, where he left behind not merely a reputation for kindness and generosity, but a series of 'new model cottages' for farmworkers, which continued to be appreciated several decades after his death. He died on 11 February 1947, at 197 College Street, Long Eaton, Derbyshire.   P. M. OPPENHEIMER, rev.

Sources J. Dicks, *The Hooley book: the amazing financier, his career and his crowd* (1904) • E. T. Hooley, *Hooley's confessions* (1925) • R. Parker, *On the road: the Papworth story* (1977) • P. L. Payne, 'The emergence of the large-scale company in Great Britain, 1870–1914', *Economic History Review*, 2nd ser., 20 (1967), 519–42 • *DBB* • d. cert. • J. Armstrong, 'Hooley and the Bovril Company', *Business History*, 28/1 (1986), 18–34

Hooper, Edmund (c.1553–1621), organist and composer, was born in Halberton, near Tiverton, Devon. He was brought up at nearby Bradninch, and at Greenwich, where he received his schooling. By 1582 he had joined the choir of Westminster Abbey and on 3 December 1588 he succeeded Henry Leeve as master of the choristers. He was appointed abbey organist by patent dated 9 May 1606. His responsibilities included repairing the organ and copying music for the choir. The abbey muniments suggest that his appointment was not an unqualified success. In December 1603 there was indiscipline among the choristers, and Hooper may also have been involved in financial irregularities; in 1606 he was relieved of the teaching of the choristers. He remained as organist, however, and the patent renewing his organist's post for life, which was drawn up in 1616, refers to his 'good and faithful service' (Shaw, 328). On 1 March 1604 he was sworn in as a gentleman of the Chapel Royal, holding this post in plurality with that at Westminster. He received part of the salary due to John Bull, the first Chapel Royal musician to be entitled organist, when Bull left to work abroad in 1613. In an entry dated 2 November 1615 in the Chapel Royal cheque book Hooper is named as joint organist with Orlando Gibbons, although he may already have been partially performing the functions of that office for several years.

Except for a small number of keyboard pieces, Hooper's surviving music is exclusively for liturgical use. Much of it is in the 'verse' style, exploiting soloists in addition to full choir. The presence of his compositions in virtually every pre-Restoration source of Anglican church music attests to their popularity. Several of his more elaborate works, such as 'Hearken, ye nations' (for gunpowder treason day) and 'O God of Gods' (for the anniversary of the king's accession), are incomplete. He contributed two pieces to Sir William Leighton's *Teares or Lamentacions of a Sorrowful Soule* (1614), and three anthems were printed posthumously in John Barnard's *First Book of Selected Church Musick* (1641). Hooper died in London on 14 July 1621 and was interred two days later beside his first wife (who had died by 1604) in the cloisters of Westminster Abbey. His will, which dates from 1620, was proved on 31 July 1621 by his second wife, Mary (d. 1652). It contains a legacy to sixty-seven poor people, and probably reflects his age. Judging from other bequests of property and money, he would appear to have been a person of substance.

JOHN MOREHEN

Sources E. F. Rimbault, ed., *The old cheque book, or book of remembrance of the Chapel Royal, from 1561 to 1744*, CS, 3rd ser., 3 (1872); 2nd repr. (New York, 1966) • H. W. Shaw, *The succession of organists of the Chapel Royal and the cathedrals of England and Wales from c.1538* (1991) • A. Ashbee and D. Lasocki, eds., *A biographical dictionary of English court musicians, 1485–1714*, 1 (1998), 583–5 • J. Morehen, 'Hooper, Edmund', *New Grove* • P. Le Huray, *Music and the Reformation in England, 1549–1660* (1967); repr. with corrections (1978), 128–9, 390–91 • C. S. Knighton, ed., *Acts of the dean and chapter of Westminster*, 2 (1999), 130, 204–5, 217 • E. Pine, *The Westminster Abbey singers* (1953) • R. T. Daniel and P. le Huray, *The sources of English church music, 1549–1660* (1972) • *IGI* • will, PRO, PROB 11/138, sig. 67
Wealth at death substantial: will, PRO, PROB 11/138, sig. 67

Hooper, Sir Frederic Collins [Eric], **first baronet** (1892–1963), industrialist, was born at Bruton, Somerset, on 19 July 1892, the only son of Frederic Stephen Hooper, wine merchant, and his wife, Annie Collins. He was educated at Sexey's School, Bruton, and at University College, London, where he read botany and graduated in 1913. On the outbreak of war in 1914 he was commissioned into the Dorset regiment and served on the western front.

Demobilized in 1919, Hooper spent the next two years in Athens with the Ionian Bank. In 1922 he was recruited to Lewis's, the Liverpool department store, by F. J. Marquis (later the earl of Woolton), its managing director and a pioneer in the training of university graduates for industry. Marquis later wrote of Hooper: 'he was successful in everything except his personal relationship with his seniors. I promoted him to the board so that he had nobody to quarrel with except me—and I felt I could take it.' In 1942, after two years as joint managing director of Lewis's, Hooper resigned in quest of a political career. At the invitation of Sir Kingsley Wood, chancellor of the exchequer, he set up the Political Research Centre. Designed to keep Conservative doctrine alive during the wartime party truce, it produced several papers on postwar policy: and in conjunction with Lord Hinchingbrooke's Tory Reform Committee it published a series of pamphlets, *Forward—by the Right!*, which sold 250,000 copies. Some of the more senior Conservatives, however, found its doctrines disobligingly radical. The death of Wood in 1943 removed Hooper's most powerful patron, and in the following year the Political Research Centre was extinguished from above. Nor could Hooper find a Conservative constituency association willing to adopt him. But it was during those wartime years that he made his reputation as a broadcaster, succeeding Sir Norman Birkett in the use of the pseudonym Onlooker.

From 1945 to 1946, as director of business training at the Ministry of Labour, Hooper speeded the resettlement of returning ex-service men. That task completed, he formed his own business consultancy firm. His first client happened to be Schweppes, the mineral water company; and when he recommended that they find a new managing director, he was promptly invited to accept the appointment himself. He did so (in 1948) on the understanding that a modest salary should be supplemented by a commission on the company's annual profits. Fifteen years later, on the eve of his intended retirement in 1963, the prosperity to which he had raised Schweppes was reflected in personal emoluments approaching £100,000 a year.

Hooper was far-sighted in labour relations. 'The time', he wrote, 'is no longer opportune—even if it were desirable—for management to insist on mechanical obedience or the sack.' He laid down that his employees should be told at the earliest possible moment of changes in company policy or fluctuations in its fortunes; and that all businesses should establish profit-sharing schemes and a promotion structure flexible enough to satisfy both ambition and enthusiasm. Strikes and other disturbances, he maintained, were nearly always the fault of bad managers. Such doctrines, which have since become the platitudes of harmonious industrial relations, were not widely accepted in Hooper's day. Many of them he embodied in his dynamic *Management Survey*, published in 1948 and since reprinted several times. A contented labour force was his first concern; advertising was his plaything and delight. With that master of puns Stephen Potter and the artist George Him, he added an entirely new county, Schweppeshire, to the map of England. It was under his leadership, too, that the company built up an international reputation for its soft drinks.

Hooper gave an increasing amount of his time to public service, particularly to problems of national defence. Between 1954 and 1956 he sat on committees of inquiry into the organization of the Royal Air Force and into the employment of national servicemen. In 1957 he became chairman of the advisory board set up by the Ministry of Labour to ensure the smooth transition to civilian life of officers and other ranks, many of whom had been obliged to retire prematurely as a result of cuts in defence expenditure. He was successful in persuading retired officers not to despise industry, and industrialists not to regard officers as 'Colonel Blimps'. In 1960 he became adviser on recruiting to the minister of defence. Again he dispelled the myth that service in the regular forces was the last refuge of the bone-headed or the destitute; and the imaginative use of television advertising which he recommended sent recruiting figures soaring. Ashridge Trust, the Royal Academy of Dancing, the Royal College of Nursing, and the Institute of Directors were other bodies whose fortunes he helped to guide. He became a fellow of University College in 1957. He was knighted in 1956 and received a baronetcy in 1962.

Eric Hooper held, indeed he flourished, opinions not always found in a boardroom. He had a particular regard for trade unionists, journalism, the regular army, the wines of St Émilion, the brisk wit of the United States, and the therapeutic qualities of egg farming. He detested tax fiddlers, pop singers, ostentation, and the fizzy drinks upon which the prosperity of his firm depended. He collected modern pictures, designed a beautiful garden at his house, The Dandy, Tenterden, in Kent, and loved the ballet. He also supported the contemporary theatre both as a patron and as an increasingly disenchanted playgoer. A tall, heavily built man with several chins, he was nevertheless a nimble ballroom dancer, and a cunning but sometimes bad-tempered tennis player.

His first marriage, in 1918, was to Eglantine Irene, daughter of Thomas Augustine Bland, of Yelverton, Devon. They had one son, Anthony Robin Maurice (*b.* 1918), who succeeded him to the title, and a daughter. The marriage was dissolved in 1945, when he married Prudence Avery, daughter of Basil Elliott Wenham, of Barnt Green, Worcestershire, with whom he had a daughter. He died at his London flat in Clive House, Connaught Place, Paddington, on 4 October 1963. KENNETH ROSE, *rev.*

Sources *The Times* (5 Oct 1963), 10e · *WWW* · private information (1981) · personal knowledge (1981) · *CGPLA Eng. & Wales* (1963) · d. cert.

Likenesses W. Bird, photograph, 1962, NPG

Wealth at death £109,387 14s. 11d.: probate, 15 Nov 1963, *CGPLA Eng. & Wales*

Hooper, George (1640–1727), bishop of Bath and Wells and scholar, was born on 18 November 1640 at Grimley, Worcestershire, the son of George Hooper, of a lesser landed gentry family, and his wife, Joan, daughter of Edmund Giles of White Ladies Aston, Worcestershire. The Hoopers were royalist, but the Giles family was parliamentarian by inclination—Hooper's uncle became a master in chancery under Cromwell.

Education Hooper was educated briefly at St Paul's School, London, and then from about 1653, as king's scholar, at Westminster School. Richard Busby, the headmaster, well known for his exacting standards, thought highly of him: 'the boy is the least favoured in features of any in the school, but he will be the most extraordinary of any of them' (Cassan, 2.172). Later he described Hooper as 'the best scholar, the finest gentleman and will make the completest bishop that was ever educated at Westminster' (*DNB*). Here Hooper first learned Hebrew, Arabic, and Aramaic, which were to be for him a lifelong pursuit. He entered Christ Church, Oxford, in 1657 as a scholar, graduated BA in 1660, and became a don. He proceeded MA in 1663, BD in 1673, and DD in 1677. He now not only developed into a competent classical and mathematical scholar, but under Edward Pococke, the leading Arabist of his day, Hooper also became a notable oriental linguist. He played his full part in college life, while in the university he deputized for the public orator, and in 1669 for both Thomas Willis, Sedleian professor of natural philosophy, and John Wallis, Savilian professor of geometry. During that year he also wrote a mathematical treatise which interested Nicholas Mercator. A recently discovered brass Gunter quadrant, made by him and bearing his inscription, confirms his proficiency in that field. He was still writing to Robert Hooke about quadrants in 1676. Already a multifaceted academic, Hooper had also been ordained deacon on 23 December 1666 and priest early in 1668 by Walter Blandford, bishop of Oxford.

Early career Apart from his scholarly work Hooper's career for thirty years after 1670 followed two other intertwining paths—as cleric and as royal confidant. In 1670 George Morley, bishop of Winchester, invited him to be his chaplain and a year later rector of Havant. But the damp there soon so affected his health that his fellow chaplain, Thomas Ken, destined to be a close friend and colleague for the next forty years, vacated East Woodhay, Hampshire, in his favour in November 1672. As incumbent there until 1691 and assisted by a competent curate, he earned an exemplary reputation as parish priest. In fact, Isaac Milles, incumbent at nearby Highclere, always admired him: he was 'the perfect gentleman, the thorough scholar and the venerable and skilful divine' (Milles, 92–3). His time as Morley's chaplain, however, ended abruptly. Hooper's daughter, Abigail Prowse, records how Archbishop Sheldon cajoled Morley into releasing him to be his chaplain at Lambeth. Nevertheless letters of autumn 1672 emphatically suggest otherwise. Morley, a

George Hooper (1640–1727), by Thomas Hill, 1723

staid bachelor, was so appalled at the possibility of Hooper's marriage to a Winchester woman that he determined to be rid of him, and persuaded the primate to promote him.

Consequently in 1673 Hooper went to Lambeth as Sheldon's chaplain. This was to be a key moment in his career. In October 1675 the primate likewise offered him the rectory of St Mary, Lambeth, which he held until 1703. Here Hooper was much respected, and the church underwent major refurbishment. In the long run this move to Lambeth paid handsome dividends, for it introduced Hooper to London's exceptionally gifted clerical circle—the future archbishops Tillotson, Tenison, Wake, and Sharp were his fellow incumbents—whose spirituality, scholarship, and dedicated pastoral care provided a 'luminous interlude', a 'Small Awakening' in the church (Rupp, 51). Significantly, Hooper's move introduced him to the royal family. Circumstantial evidence suggests he may even have joined Gilbert Burnet's discussions with Tsar Peter the Great at Lambeth in 1698.

In spring 1678 Bishop Compton of London chose Hooper to succeed William Lloyd at The Hague as almoner to Princess Mary, recently married to William III of Orange. He was to preserve Mary's Anglican faith from Dutch Calvinist contagion, an essential task because Mary seemed likely to inherit the English throne. More punctilious than Lloyd, whom several contemporaries suspected of letting her attend English Congregationalist meetings at The Hague, Hooper provided suitable reading matter, including Eusebius and Hooker, and a chapel complete with Anglican furnishings which Mary used twice daily. William jibbed at these fripperies and frostily kicked the altar steps, asking what they were for and, when told, 'he answered with a hum' (Prowse, 5). Later he showed his disapproval: 'Well, Dr. Hooper, you will never be a bishop' (ibid., 6). On 2 May 1679 Hooper married Abigail Guilford (1654/5–1726), daughter of Richard Guilford, a notable Lambeth brewer. Soon after his marriage, in October 1679, he left for England. Ken succeeded him.

Hooper's contacts with royalty developed further. In 1681 he became chaplain to the king. In 1685 James II asked him to accompany the duke of Monmouth with Tenison, Ken, and Lloyd the night before his execution. Hooper talked privately with the duke, solely to prepare him for death, and was one of the four who witnessed his declaration of illegitimacy. As Monmouth was to die the next morning Hooper 'thought it teasing rather than necessary' to try to get a confession of rebellion from him (Prowse, 9). All were with the duke the next morning on the scaffold.

Ken, now bishop of Bath and Wells, was Hooper's guest in 1688 during the trial of the seven bishops and during the Convention Parliament the following spring. One night Hooper almost persuaded Ken to swear allegiance to William and Mary, but eventually they agreed to differ. Though a high-churchman, Hooper took the oaths. Nevertheless his relations with William were at best cool, but he remained on close terms with Mary and her sister, Anne. Though clearly in line for a bishopric, Hooper's fortunes only changed after William's death in 1702.

In 1677 Hooper had been appointed precentor of Exeter Cathedral, a post he held until 1704. His spells of duty, though infrequent—once every two or three years—were lengthy, up to three months. By the standards of the day he certainly fulfilled his role, and often presided at chapter meetings in the dean's absence. Then in 1691, during William's absence abroad, Mary hastily appointed him dean of Canterbury, much to the king's later irritation. Regular in attendance at chapter meetings, unlike at Exeter, he masterminded extensive cathedral refurbishment. Significantly he was often host to William and Mary—and after Mary's death in 1694 to William alone—when they were en route for the Netherlands.

In 1701 Hooper achieved notoriety as prolocutor of the lower house of the revived convocation, a position where Ken hoped he would take a lead in church affairs. This predominantly high-church body set out to thwart the upper house, presided over by Archbishop Tenison. In the ensuing dispute Hooper displayed not only competence, but combative and high-handed belligerence in defying the primate. His actions momentarily earned Atterbury's acclamation, but once the session was over Hooper returned to his usual restraint. He not only joined Henry Aldrich in writing A Narrative of the Proceedings of the Lower House of Convocation, less strident than Atterbury's pamphlets, but he refused to stand for re-election as prolocutor for 1702. To a disgusted Atterbury this was treachery; he heaped vitriolic abuse upon him. Hearne later branded him as 'a Complyer'.

Bishop With William dead and Anne queen, Hooper's relationship with Robert Harley, the speaker and now the mainspring of ecclesiastical preferments, became more intimate. This soon yielded fruit. In 1703, after reluctantly accepting and being consecrated to the impecunious Welsh see of St Asaph on 31 October 1703, he was nominated to the more prestigious bishopric of Bath and Wells in succession to Richard Kidder. At first he refused, hoping that Ken, the nonjuring bishop deprived in 1689, would return to the see, now that both William III and the 'usurping' Kidder were dead. But Ken, already in poor health at Longleat, approved of Hooper as one 'most able and willing to preserve the Depositum' (Plumptre, 2.141) and agreed to cede the bishopric to him. Ken no longer signed himself 'Thomas Bath and Wells', thereby personally acknowledging the cession to Hooper (LPL, MS 2872, fols. 76 and 78). Though extreme nonjurors felt a sense of betrayal, Hooper was enthroned by proxy on 3 April 1704. In later years Ken visited Hooper at Wells.

Hooper was a conscientious pastor of his diocese. He conferred orders, usually at least twice every year, on fifty-five occasions, all in the diocese. Even in June 1727, shortly before his death, he ordained nine priests and three deacons. He was meticulous but considerate over ordinands' academic standards; only 14 of the 369 he ordained were non-graduates. An underachiever would return home for further study, encouraged by 'guineas in his pocket to subsist on' (Prowse, 34). The few visitation records that remain show that he fulfilled visitations regularly throughout his episcopate, and in his use of patronage he normally gave benefices only to those from within the diocese. A competent administrator, he pursued rights over episcopal manors, broke down nepotism in the cathedral chapter and defended the rights of the College of Vicars. His relationships with recusants, nonjurors, and rationalists, such as Whiston, were not only firm, but humane and tolerant. One incumbent, Thomas Coney, writing soon after Hooper's death, recorded that he was always accessible to his clergy: each 'had the favour of a son, the access of an equal and the reception of a friend' (Coney, appendix, 31).

The scholar Above all Hooper was a scholar—linguist, mathematician, and theologian—with an insatiable thirst for all types of knowledge. Noted as such by Busby at Westminster, and also at Oxford, he earned applause from many quarters. Reportedly he refused the regius professorship of divinity in 1680. Twells, Pococke's biographer, claimed that Hooper had no superior in 'piety, extent of learning and every good quality that could adorn a bishop, a gentleman or a scholar' (Twells, 273). Ken, who wrote a poem in his honour, regarded him as one of the most eminent intellects he knew, who could do 'excellent service to our sinking church' (Marshall, 95). As an ecclesiastical lawyer, linguist, and theologian, he could hold his own against the best in the country, but he was far from being a dilettante.

Hooper's use of Arabic was significant throughout his life. Using it to help solve problems in the Bible, he was still actively working with Arabic in the 1720s when he was over eighty years of age. He was then buying and annotating recently printed books in Arabic, a psalter and

The Life and Activities of the Prophet Mohammed. Furthermore, his study of Genesis 49, published at his request after his death, but first conceived before 1681, owed much to his Arabic. Mathematics was still an active interest then too. As late as 1721, at the age of eighty, he published *An Enquiry in to Ancient Weights and Measures, the Attic, the Roman and the Jewish*. The library of almost 300 books he bequeathed to Wells Cathedral confirms his remarkable breadth of interest. Besides books in Latin and Greek, tools usual for a scholar, there are many in Arabic, including some on medicine. There are also books in Hebrew, annotated by him, Syriac, Anglo-Saxon, even a *Grammatica Russica*, and books on optics and astronomy.

Apart from two brief poems written in 1660, Hooper's first publications did not appear until the 1680s. These related to the major uncertainty of the day, the threat from Rome—*The Church of England Free from the Imputation of Popery* (1682), *The Infallible Guide* (1689), and the *Credibility of Human Testimony* (1699). Other academic studies followed: *A Discourse Concerning Lent* (1695), *De Valentinianorum haeresi conjecturae* (1711), and *De benedictione patriarchae Jacobi Gen. XLIX conjecturae*. Though Hooper was no Romanist, scholarly enthusiasm drew him into friendly contact with Catholic academics in France. His study of the origins of the Benedictines caught the attention of the order, especially the congregation of St Maur in Paris, among whom were Bernard Montfaucon and Edmond Martène, with whom he corresponded and whose books he possessed. Likewise he corresponded with a French Jesuit, Tournemaine, to whom latterly he sent a copy of each work as it was published. Other writings included *The Parson's Case under the Present Land Tax* (1689) and his *Narrative of the Proceedings of the Lower House of Convocation*.

Hooper had a notable reputation as a preacher. John Evelyn, who often heard his sermons, regarded him as 'one of the first rank of pulpit men in the nation' (Evelyn, 4.260). Of the eight sermons Hooper published, probably the most notable was that preached in St Paul's on 7 July 1713 to celebrate the end of the war. In this he supported the contemporary tory policy of peace. Later, when the Hanoverian succession hung in the balance, he preached a sermon on 13 June 1714, significantly anti-Roman in tone. Two manuscript volumes of other sermons still exist.

Politics Politically Hooper was no enthusiast. In the turbulence of the late seventeenth and early eighteenth centuries he was a moderate, at most a reluctant, politician. Hearne's accusations of trimming are unjust, for Hooper was more interested in his scholarship and his diocese; but in politics, so far as it concerned him, he was a pragmatist. Though no admirer of William and close in his thinking to Ken, Hooper's pragmatism persuaded him to swear allegiance to the joint monarchs. In the 1690s his intimacy with Harley, the rising country tory, was the source of mutual support. Indeed the two had several clandestine discussions on a boat in mid-river. In 1701 as prolocutor he found himself miscast as a hostile, pugnacious assailant of the whig episcopal bench, a role totally foreign to him. As soon as he could, he withdrew from such exposure. In

1702 Godolphin had vetoed Rochester's nomination of him as primate of Ireland—Hooper then lacked the necessary episcopal experience—but it was Harley who was instrumental in his elevation to the episcopate in the following year. Though initially Hooper was punctilious in attending the Lords—he voted for the second Occasional Conformity Bill (1703)—he soon displayed a prickly independence, much to the irritation of Godolphin and Harley. He defected, voting and speaking more with the high tory opposition over such matters as 'the Church in Danger' and Scottish union. From 1707 his Lords attendance declined dramatically. Refusing repeated requests from Weymouth and, after 1710, from Harley, now earl of Oxford, he rarely attended the Lords. In fact, a lack of political enthusiasm, combined with his refusal to answer frequent government calls for support in the Lords, cost him the prestigious sees of both London and York. Nevertheless, as problems with the succession to Anne grew larger, he adhered once more to Oxford, still a friend, and began to attend more regularly. In speech and sermon he solidly supported the Hanover tories in their peace strategy in Europe and for a Hanoverian succession in England. Had he been prepared to involve himself more politically, he would indeed have scaled greater ecclesiastical heights in the service of the 'sinking church', as Ken had envisaged.

Conclusion Hooper was primarily a scholar and a diocesan bishop. Believing in political moderation and pragmatism, he was a man of consistency, moral rectitude, and humanity in an age of turbulence and change. Of his nine children only two survived childhood. Rebecca, the younger daughter, died aged twenty, but the elder, Abigail, who married John Prowse of Axbridge, survived to write the 'memorandums' on her father's life. Hooper died at Berkeley, Gloucestershire, on 6 September 1727, a year after his wife. He was buried in Wells Cathedral ten days later alongside her and their younger daughter. A memorial was erected in the cloister.

WILLIAM MARSHALL

Sources W. M. Marshall, *George Hooper, 1640–1727, bishop of Bath and Wells* (1976) · A. Prowse, 'Some memorandums concerning Bishop Hooper', LPL, MS 3016 · T. Ken to G. Hooper, Dec 1703, LPL, MS 2872, fols. 76–82 · E. H. Plumptre, *The life of Thomas Ken*, 2 vols. (1888) · *The works of George Hooper*, ed. T. Hunt (1757) · G. Hooper, sermons, LPL, MS 3345 · G. Hooper to R. Harley, BL, Portland loan MS 29/147 · Hooper's episcopal register, Som. ARS · T. Coney, *Twenty five sermons preached upon several subjects and occasions, to which is annex'd a short character of … Dr. George Hooper* (1730) · E. G. R. Taylor, *The mathematical practitioners of Tudor and Stuart England* (1954) · D. J. Bryden, 'Made in Oxford: John Prujean's 1701 catalogue of mathematical instruments', *Oxoniensia*, 58 (1993), 263–85 · G. Rupp, *Religion in England, 1688–1791* (1986) · S. H. Cassan, *The lives of the bishops of Bath and Wells*, 2 vols. (1829–30) · L. Twells and S. Burdy, *The lives of Dr Edward Pocock … Dr Zachary Pearce … Dr Thomas Newton … and of the Rev Philip Skelton*, 2 vols. (1816) · Evelyn, *Diary* · T. Milles, *An account of the life and conversation of Isaac Milles, late rector of Highclere* (1721) · Foster, *Alum. Oxon.* · *Fasti Angl.* (Hardy) · Oxford episcopal registers, Oxon. RO, Oxford diocesan papers, e.14 · House of Lords proxy books, 1685–1733, HLRO [esp. 1713–14] · *DNB*

Archives BL, corresp., index of MSS, V, 1985 · LPL, corresp., MS 2872 · LPL, sermons and biography, MS 3345 · U. Birm. L., sermons,

1957/ii/7 | BM, brass Gunter quadrant (signed 'GH Fecit 1665') · Bodl. Oxf., MS Rawl. D373 · Bodl. Oxf., MS Tanner 21, 24, 27, 30, 43, 460 · LPL, Gibson MS 942

Likenesses M. Dahl?, oils, 1691–1704, deanery, Canterbury · oils, c.1700–1710, Royal Collection, Windsor · oils, c.1704–1710, vicars' hall, Wells, Somerset · oils, c.1710, town hall, Wells, Somerset · T. Hill, oils, 1723, Christ Church Oxf. [see illus.] · G. White, mezzotint, 1728, BM, NPG · oils, bishop's palace, Wells

Hooper [married name Dening], **(Emma) Geraldine Henrietta Hamilton** (1841–1872), preacher, was born on 30 March 1841 in Paris, the daughter of Thomas Clarence Hooper, a descendant of the Marian martyr John Hooper, bishop of Gloucester. Born into comfortable middle-class circumstances, as a child Geraldine Hooper lived mainly in Green Park, Bath. Possessing a 'clear, sweet, and powerful voice' (Guinness, 11), which made her an attractive singer, and fond of dancing, she entered society early. However, under the preaching of J. M. Dixon, rector of Trinity Church, Bath, she underwent an evangelical conversion about 1861 and withdrew from society pleasures. She devoted herself to cultivating piety, conducting a Bible class and a prayer meeting for the poor in Avon Street, Bath, in association with the revivalist Church of England clergyman William Haslam.

Geraldine Hooper began preaching in 1862, at first speaking only when no clergyman was available but soon drawing crowds attracted by her ability. In 1863 she held her first large mission in Buckenham, Norfolk, owing to the encouragement of the wife of William Haslam, by then rector of Buckenham and Hassingham. From that time until her death she itinerated widely in southern England and the west country, becoming possibly the most celebrated of the female preachers of the 1860s. Her acceptance into the British revivalist network was confirmed by her joint mission with Hay Macdowall Grant of Arndilly, a prominent Scottish evangelist, in 1867 in Torquay. On 2 October 1868 she married (Thomas) Henry Frickey Dening, a gentleman of independent means from Ottery St Mary, who was an evangelist in Devon. They moved to Bath in 1869, and in that year her only child, a daughter, was born. While remaining members of the Church of England they opened a mission in Bath, St James's Hall, with wife and husband sharing the preaching. Several of her sermons were published as popular tracts.

Geraldine Hooper's preaching was made possible by currents within mid-Victorian protestant evangelicalism, particularly its revivalist enthusiasm and its adventism—women preaching being interpreted by their supporters as a sign of the last days. She conformed to contemporary ideas of femininity. An account of her preaching describes her as 'the perfect lady' with a *petite* oval countenance', her voice 'pleasing and irresistibly moving' (Guinness, 163). She also used Victorian sentimentality to her advantage, and her preaching was accompanied by frequent outbursts of weeping among the audience. Although her activities owed nothing to feminism, it has been argued that the activities of women such as Geraldine Dening were important at a popular level in making expanded roles for women possible.

During the ten years in which she was active Hooper preached about 4000 times. She was prone to frequent illnesses which were exacerbated by her strenuous life. She contracted erysipelas in the face, which with septicaemia and meningitis was given as the cause of her death on 12 August 1872, aged thirty-one, at 20 Green Park Buildings, Bath. She was survived by her husband, and was buried in Bath.   NEIL DICKSON

Sources Mrs G. Guiness [F. E. Guinness], 'She spake of him'; being recollections of the loving labours and early death of Mrs Henry Dening (1872) · O. Anderson, 'Women preachers in mid-Victorian Britain: some reflexions on feminism, popular religion and social change', HJ, 12 (1969), 467–84 · W. Haslam, 'Yet not I', or, More years of my ministry (1882) · m. cert. · d. cert.
Likenesses photograph, repro. in Guiness, 'She spake of him', frontispiece

Hooper, Henry (c.1687–1767), planter, lawyer, and politician in America, was born in Dorchester county, Maryland, the son of Henry Hooper (c.1643–1720), planter and politician, and his second wife, Mary (1663–1740), daughter of Roger Woolford. A third-generation Marylander, Hooper was a member of a prominent eastern shore family and a man of considerable influence. While little is known about his early life and formal education, he was a practising member of the Church of England and apparently worked as a mariner during his youth. By 1712 he had married Mary, daughter of Joseph Ennalls (d. 1709). They had one son and two daughters. Their son, also Henry Hooper (1727–1790), was active during the American revolutionary era. He sat on several of the Maryland provincial conventions that met during 1775 and 1776, served on the eastern shore Council of Safety, and was brigadier-general of the region's lower district.

On his father's death in 1720 Henry Hooper inherited 1281 acres of land in Dorchester and Calvert counties. This constituted the original core of his extensive landed estate, but in the same year he also purchased a large tract known as My Lady Sewall's Manor from Major Nicholas Sewall for £250. This was later resurveyed along with several other adjacent plots and eventually became incorporated into a property which he named Warwick Fort Manor. These acquisitions made him a wealthy planter, and shortly afterwards he embarked upon a distinguished public career. This began in 1722 when Hooper was elected to the Maryland lower house as a representative from Dorchester county. He served in that capacity until 1763, even acting as speaker from 1754 until 1763 with a brief break because of illness in 1756. He was also active at the local level, serving as a Dorchester county justice in 1723, from 1732 to 1734, and from 1751 at least until 1764. As an attorney he was admitted to Dorchester county court by August 1742 and to Talbot county court by August 1744. Hooper was a judge of the eastern shore assize court from 1734 to 1739, in 1743, and in 1747, and served at the provincial court, eventually becoming chief justice by 1766. During 1765–6 his political career reached its peak when he was appointed to the upper house because of his loyal support for the colony's proprietary executive interests.

Hooper died on 20 April 1767 at his home plantation in

Dorchester county. On the same day his brick dwelling house burnt to the ground, and his body 'being then in the house was with much difficulty saved from the flames'. He was buried in Dorchester county. His personal estate, which included twenty-four slaves, a collection of books, and new silver plate imported from England, was valued at £1551 16s. 9d. At his death Hooper also owned at least 2900 acres in Dorchester county, possibly 500 acres in Calvert county, and one lot in Georgetown, Kent county.

KEITH MASON

Sources E. C. Papenfuse and others, eds., *A biographical dictionary of the Maryland legislature, 1635–1789*, 2 vols. (1979–85) · E. Jones, *New revised history of Dorchester county, Maryland* (1966) · D. C. Skaggs, *Roots of Maryland democracy, 1753–1776* (1973) · R. Hoffman, *A spirit of dissension: economics, politics, and the revolution in Maryland* (1973) · C. B. Clark, ed., *The eastern shore of Maryland and Virginia*, 3 vols. (1950) · K. Mason, 'A region in revolt: the eastern shore of Maryland, 1740–90', PhD diss., Johns Hopkins University, 1984 · W. H. Browne and others, eds., *Archives of Maryland* (1883–) · A. Pedley, *The manuscript collections of the Maryland Historical Society* (1968) · R. J. Cox and L. E. Sullivan, eds., *Guide to the research collections of the Maryland Historical Society* (1981)

Archives Maryland Historical Society, Baltimore, Jones collection of Dorchester county land papers, MS 1744

Wealth at death £1551 16s. 9d.; plus at least 2900 acres in Dorchester county; possibly 500 acres in Calvert county; lot in Georgetown, Kent county: Papenfuse and others, eds., *Biographical dictionary*, 1.457

Hooper, John (1495x1500–1555), bishop of Gloucester and Worcester and protestant martyr, was born some time between 1495 and 1500. Little can be said for sure about either his place of origin or his parents. According to Hooper himself, his father was wealthy; there is some evidence to suggest that he had prospered in the cloth trade. Tradition has always claimed that Hooper was a native of Somerset, but there is little evidence to support this assertion, first made by Thomas Tanner in 1748 and repeated ever since. There is, however, good reason to suppose that Hooper was born and raised either in Devon or Oxfordshire. Whatever the exact location of his birth, Hooper's connections with the west country seem sure.

Education and early career Hooper was educated at Oxford, graduating BA in 1519. His college is unknown, and his association with Merton College is the result of confusion with another John Hooper (d. 1522), sometimes wrongly thought to be a relation. Foxe claims that Hooper was 'a student and graduate in the university … after the study of sciences wherein he abundantly profited' (Foxe, 2.1502). But there is little evidence to indicate that Hooper proceeded beyond a BA, although he was styled 'professor of divinity' by Edward VI and on the patent rolls, usually a reliable source. Speculation that he received a doctorate at a continental university is also without foundation, despite the claim made by Richard Hilles in the 1540s, that Hooper was studying at Zürich.

The period between his BA at Oxford and his emergence as a heterodox thinker in 1539 remains vague. Foxe places Hooper at Oxford for most of this period where he encountered difficulty at the time of the Act of Six Articles (1539) from 'certain rabbins', most especially Dr Richard Smith (Foxe, 2.1502). However, it is known from the charges brought against him in 1555 that Hooper was a Cistercian monk at the monastery in Cleeve, Somerset, and he seems to have been resident there. Hooper himself kept silent about this part of his life, but it is likely that he left Oxford some time after 1519 and entered the monastery at Cleeve, leaving in 1537 after the visitation of Sir Thomas Arundell, one of Cromwell's commissioners for the suppression of religious houses. This possibility is strengthened by Hooper's being found in 1538 as rector of Liddington, Wiltshire, a benefice in Arundell's gift. He was certainly a non-resident incumbent, for he appears to have served Arundell as his steward. His conflict with Smith and other Oxford 'rabbins' may date from this period but is more likely to have occurred later, when he was in the service of Sir John St Loe after his flight to and return from Paris.

Conversion and its consequences While in the service of Arundell, Hooper encountered the works of Huldrich Zwingli and Heinrich Bullinger for the first time and they changed his life. Hooper himself regarded his encounter with the writings of the Swiss reformers as a kind of 'road to Damascus' experience and he was eager thereafter to portray himself as a reprobate renewed and rescued from living 'too much of a court life at the palace of our king' by the works of these two divines (Robinson, *Original Letters*, 1.33–4). Quite how much of a reprobate Hooper had in fact been must remain open to question—he had little time or opportunity to experience much of court life. But Hooper seems always to have been a rather severe personality and a harsh judge of the behaviour of others and himself. His conversion to a Zwinglian form of reformed Christianity seems to have served to reinforce and affirm his harsher qualities, ones which all too often made him irascible, stubborn, uncompromising, and even unapproachable.

Arundell was conservative in his religious views, and some time between June 1539 and November 1540 he became concerned about Hooper's new opinions and sent him to Stephen Gardiner, bishop of Winchester, for examination and correction. Their encounter lasted four or five days and was a highly charged affair: neither man had an easy personality, and Hooper's characteristic refusal to alter or compromise his opinions only served to enrage the bishop. Despite Gardiner's promise that he would send Hooper back safely to Arundell, Hooper received intelligence that he was now in danger. According to Foxe, Hooper fled to Paris for an unspecified period, before returning to England and entering the service of Sir John St Loe, constable of Thornbury Castle, Somerset, and a man of evangelical sympathies despite being Arundell's nephew. Hooper himself records nothing of any of these events.

It was not long before Hooper found himself in danger again, though the reasons for his subsequent flight from England remain obscure. It may be that his controversy with Richard Smith at Oxford took place at this time. Despite the protection offered him by Arundell and his affinity, Hooper's encounters with ecclesiastical authorities tended to be explosive, and he seems to have found it impossible not to speak his mind regardless of the consequences. This second flight from England appears to have occurred some time in 1544, and he was certainly in Strasbourg by 1546, in the company of English expatriates and merchants like Richard Hilles, John Burcher, and John Butler. His associations with merchant communities were lifelong and there is some evidence to suggest that Hooper supported himself, at least in part, by trading in cloth. By now he had established contact with most of the major protestant thinkers in Basel, Strasbourg, and Zürich, including Martin Bucer, Theodore Biliander, Simon Grinaeus, and Conrad Pelican. But the most important and long-lasting contact he made was with Heinrich Bullinger.

By January 1546 Hooper had already decided to move to Zürich permanently. First, however, he returned to England to secure his inheritance from his father, a man he knew to be hostile to reforming ideas. Hooper claimed that he was imprisoned twice while in England (probably at Exeter) and that this depleted his fortune significantly, but there is no other record of these imprisonments. His account also suggests that he became involved in lecturing or preaching to underground protestants. After leaving England he married Anna de Tscerlas, a Belgian attached to the household of Jacques de Bourgogne, seigneur de Falais. The marriage probably took place in February 1547. They had two children: Rachel, born in 1548, and Daniel, born some time after they returned to England in 1549. Anna Hooper died on 7 December 1555 at Frankfurt during an outbreak of plague and was followed shortly afterwards by her daughter. Daniel seems to have survived only a little longer: nineteenth-century claims for direct descendants from Hooper are without the least foundation.

Once he had returned to the continent Hooper quickly moved to Zürich, where he lived near and studied with Bullinger, developing a deep and lasting friendship. Hooper remained in Zürich for two years, during which he published three books, *An Answer to my Lord of Wynchesters Booke Intytlyd a Detection of the Devyls Sophistry* (1547); *A Declaration of Christ and his Office* (1547); and *A Declaration of the Ten Holy Commandments* (1548). He appears to have been in no hurry to return to England, although he was aware of the changes in religion begun following the accession of Edward VI. In Zürich he found a Christian community that most closely matched his own ideas of the pure and primitive church and it was an environment that he admired. Here he developed his ideas on theology and church polity, influenced by Zwingli and Bullinger, that he brought back with him to England and, eventually, to his dioceses. By 1549, however, Hooper was coming under pressure to return to England, and there seems to have been some expectation that he would be made a bishop.

Evangelical reformer Hooper arrived in London on 3 May 1549 and was immediately taken into the household of the duke of Somerset. This was probably by prior arrangement, as Hooper seems to have been gathering intelligence for the government about the emperor Charles V as he passed through Brussels, and he was also in contact with the English ambassador Sir Philip Hoby. Once settled in London, Hooper became a leader among the more advanced protestants and his influence appears to have been decisive in the foundation of the two 'Stranger Churches' for Dutch and French refugees in London and Glastonbury, which were considered to be models of the Zwinglian form. Hooper was friendly with both the duke of Somerset and the earl of Warwick (later duke of Northumberland) and was useful to them in a variety of ways. Apart from his extensive contacts among the foreign protestant community, most notably his friendship with John à Lasco, he took part in the trial of Bishop Bonner in 1549 as a witness for the prosecution, an act which Bonner seems never to have forgiven.

Hooper was very popular in London as a preacher and lecturer, although the enthusiasm with which Anabaptists flocked to his addresses annoyed and embarrassed him. So effective was he in the pulpit that his old adversary Richard Smith reported that he was regarded as 'a prophet, nay they looked upon him as some deity' (Strype, *Ecclesiastical Memorials*, 2/1.66). He took part in several disputes, including a long and bitter argument with Bartholomew Traheron on predestination—a doctrine with which Hooper seems to have had a great deal of difficulty, leading to accusations of Pelagianism. He also worked to move Thomas Cranmer to a more Zwinglian position theologically, and to mitigate the influence of Martin Bucer—a man for whom Hooper had only the most grudging respect.

Untouched by the fall of the duke of Somerset in October 1549, Hooper still enjoyed favour at court where his sermons before the king during Lent 1550 moved Edward to offer him the see of Gloucester. The programme of reform that he outlined in his Lenten sermons on the book of Jonah was clear on two points: the oath bishops were required to take and ecclesiastical vestments. Hooper found both impious and papistical and declined the king's offer. While references to the saints in the oath were expunged by the king in person, the issue of vestments proved more difficult, and underlined the extent to which Hooper's aggressive stands on matters of principle and his desire to see all reforms instituted immediately could make him a difficult ally. Generating considerably more heat than light, the dispute—a considerable embarrassment to the church establishment—involved most of the leading divines of the day. A caustic debate between Hooper and Ridley saw Ridley emerge as the clear winner and the support that Hooper had counted on from Bullinger, Pietro Martire Vermigli, and Bucer evaporated; only John à Lasco stood by him. Cranmer and Ridley successfully managed to shift the focus of the debate away from the vestments themselves and on to the question of authority and good order. Against the background of the risings of 1549, this argument proved decisive. When Hooper obstinately refused to shift he was imprisoned early in 1551, first at Lambeth Palace and then in the Fleet. However Bullinger, like most of the other divines, did not see the vestments issue as worth the division it was causing. His intervention finally induced Hooper to relent and he was consecrated bishop on 8 March 1551, in vestments (though whether these ever saw the light of day again is doubtful).

Bishop of Gloucester and Worcester Hooper arrived in his diocese soon after Easter 1551. Hardly on the cutting edge of the Reformation, the diocese had a limited protestant presence although part of it had been under Hugh Latimer's direction from 1535 to 1539. A relatively new diocese (founded in 1541), it had been administered without much vigour by Bishop John Wakeman, and the clergy, when not openly hostile, did no more than acquiesce in the changes brought about under Edward VI. Hooper brought with him fifty articles of religion, thirty-one injunctions, twenty-seven interrogatories to be asked of the clergy, and sixty-one interrogatories to be asked of the laity. These articles and interrogatories served as the foundation for Hooper's programme of reform within the diocese and went beyond anything seen before, anywhere in England. They have much in common with the forty-two articles, promulgated in 1552, which Hooper had a hand in formulating.

Hooper also drew up a further nine questions to put to the diocesan clergy. The findings of this examination have been interpreted in the past as justifying a reformer's criticism of an ignorant clerical body, but this overstates the case. Few incumbents were disciplined or removed following this examination, but Hooper did institute a programme of clerical education and also took steps to improve communications between the parish clergy and their bishop. Sensibly recognizing that it would be impossible to create a church in Gloucester along the lines he had known in Zürich, Hooper's injunctions concentrated on creating an environment in his parishes that would encourage piety, church attendance, and good order. His advanced reforming ideas are clear in his articles but he was judicious about enforcing them. He was undoubtedly responsible for the destruction of altars, images, and other components of traditional worship, but he was not an indiscriminate purifier and expressed detestation for those who enriched themselves by despoiling churches.

Hooper's moderation and personal attention to his diocese made him popular and respected there, if not loved. He was no respecter of status and applied his principles to all classes equally. A violent altercation with Sir Anthony Kingston of Painswick, who refused to attend a hearing in the bishop's court after being accused of adultery, came to blows but Hooper was not intimidated: Kingston later claimed that Hooper had changed his life.

In April 1552, after the deprivation of Nicholas Heath, bishop of Worcester, the diocese of Gloucester was dissolved and created as an archdeaconry within the diocese of Worcester to which Hooper was translated. The change meant a net loss for Hooper as he had to surrender much of the income of Gloucester to the government. By December 1552, Gloucester and Worcester were united as one diocese, 'like that of Coventry and Lichfield or that of Bath and Wells' (*CPR, 1550–53*, 231). Hooper was to spend half the year in each diocese and to provide for preaching and services in the church from which he was separated.

Hooper attempted to institute the same reforms in Worcester as in Gloucester and undertook a similar visitation. Although he met stiff resistance in Worcester, his efforts in his two dioceses were herculean. He made two circuits of each between 1551 and 1553 in addition to fulfilling his responsibilities in parliament and acting as a member of commissions to review ecclesiastical laws and to survey and inventory parish goods in the city of Gloucester. He seems also to have been involved in preparing the 1552 prayer book and in the planned revision of the canon law.

Protestant martyr Following the death of Edward VI on 6 July 1553, Hooper opposed Northumberland's attempt to put Jane Grey on the throne and supported Mary Tudor both in writing and materially, sending Sir John Talbot and William Ligon with a troop of horse to her aid. Nevertheless, by August Hooper had been summoned before the privy council and by 1 September he was imprisoned in the Fleet. As the law had not as yet been changed to allow his arrest for heresy, he was imprisoned on the charge of owing the crown £509 5s. 5d. in unpaid first fruits. Hooper denied this and claimed that he was himself owed more than £80 by the government. The truth of the claims and counter-claims in this dispute was irrelevant and everyone knew it: Hooper was in custody because of his radical protestant views. Although he had ample time to escape, he chose to remain in England and face certain imprisonment and possible death. His wife and children, however, escaped to Frankfurt where they remained until their deaths.

Hooper remained in custody until his death. His imprisonment was harsh and he suffered a variety of physical ailments, notably sciatica. He was able to communicate with the outside world with surprising ease and encouraged the formation of protestant cells in London; notable among these was a congregation that met in Bow churchyard. In all some thirty letters survive from the period of his imprisonment and he probably wrote considerably more that were intercepted, lost, or otherwise destroyed.

On 15 March 1554 Hooper was deprived of his bishopric. A concerted effort was made to discredit him by circulating rumours that he had recanted, but the effort failed. On 22 January 1555 he was arraigned at St Saviour's Church; examined on the 28th, he proved obstinate. Next day the sentence of the court was read by Stephen Gardiner, and along with John Rogers Hooper was taken to Newgate to await execution. On 4 February he was degraded by Bonner and left for Gloucester early the next morning. He was burnt at the stake at 9 o'clock in the morning on 9 February 1555, his sufferings protracted by faggots of green wood which long failed to catch fire.

A copious writer, Hooper's books and letters were collected into two volumes by the Parker Society (1843, 1845). Additional correspondence was published in *Original Letters Relative to the English Reformation* (1846–7). All attest the radical and uncompromising personality which made him as much an enigma to his contemporaries as he remains today.   D. G. NEWCOMBE

Sources *Early writings of John Hooper DD*, ed. S. Carr, Parker Society, 15 (1843) · *Later writings of John Hooper DD*, ed. C. Nevinson, Parker Society, 16 (1852) · S. Brigden, *London and the Reformation* (1989) · *CPR, 1547–55* · Emden, *Oxf.*, 4.296–7 · J. Foxe, *Actes and monuments*, 4th edn, 2 vols. (1583) · D. MacCulloch, *Thomas Cranmer: a life* (1996) · D. G. Newcombe, 'The life and theological thought of John Hooper, bishop of Gloucester and Worcester, 1551–1553', PhD diss., U. Cam., 1990, no. 16115 · D. G. Newcombe, 'John Hooper's visitation and examination of the clergy in the diocese of Glouces-ter, 1551', *Reformations old and new*, ed. B. Kumin (1996) · A. Pettegree, *Foreign protestant communities in sixteenth-century London* (1986) · T. Phillips, ed., *Institutiones clericorum in comitatu Wiltoniae*, 1297–1810, 2 vols. (1825) · J. H. Primus, *The vestments controversy* (Kampen, 1960) · H. Robinson, ed. and trans., *Original letters relative to the English Reformation*, 1 vol. in 2, Parker Society, [26] (1846–7) · J. Strype, *Ecclesiastical memorials*, 3 vols. (1822) · J. Strype, *Memorials of the most reverend father in God Thomas Cranmer*, new edn, 2 vols. (1840) · Tanner, *Bibl. Brit.-Hib.*

Likenesses H. B. Hall, engraving, pubd 1839 (after J. Childe), NPG · J. Faber junior, mezzotint (after unknown artist), NPG

Sir Leonard James Hooper (1914–1994), by unknown photographer

Hooper, Sir Leonard James [Joe] **(1914–1994)**, intelligence officer and civil servant, was born on 23 July 1914 at 67 East Dulwich Road, Camberwell, London, the only child of James Edmund Hooper, copywriter for a pharmaceutical firm, and his wife, Grace Lena, *née* Pitts, a headmistress. He was educated at London choir school, Alleyn's School, Dul-wich, and Worcester College, Oxford, where, after a half-blue in cross-country running, he obtained a first-class honours degree in modern history in 1936. He then began, but did not complete, a DPhil thesis on English Jesuits in the seventeenth and eighteenth centuries.

In August 1938 Hooper was recruited via the Air Ministry as a junior assistant at the Government Code and Cypher School, Bletchley Park, the national signals intelligence organization and predecessor of the post-war Govern-ment Communications Headquarters (GCHQ). He was based throughout the war in Bletchley Park (transferring to Foreign Office employment in October 1943) and remained with the organization through its subsequent moves to north-west London and Cheltenham. On 17 Octo-ber 1942 he married Hilda Sefton Jones (*b.* 1920/21), a sec-tion officer in the Women's Auxiliary Air Force, and daughter of the Revd Sidney Herbert Jones. There was one son of the marriage, which was dissolved in 1949. On 29 September 1951 Hooper married Ena Mary Osborn (*b.* 1920/21), an executive-class officer in the Foreign Office, and daughter of Hugh John Osborn, farmer; they had no children. Hooper was early on spotted as a 'high-flyer' (*The Times*, 24 Feb 1994) and after the war he achieved rapid pro-motion. He was appointed a divisional head in January 1949, attended the Imperial Defence College in 1953–4, and became GCHQ's assistant director in February 1954, deputy director in June 1960, and director in January 1965. He was appointed CBE in 1951, CMG in 1962, and KCMG in 1967.

Hooper applied the mental qualities of an outstanding organizer and negotiator to the esoteric craft of signals intelligence. In the war he worked initially on cryptanaly-sis and other communications analysis on the Italian and Japanese air forces, but in that fluid and rapidly expand-ing organization he quickly emerged as a manager, orchestrating efforts that spanned the UK, the US, and the Far East. After 1945 he joined in the planning of the post-war British signals intelligence effort, and throughout the 1950s and early 1960s was a prime influence upon it. The fact that his eight years from 1965 as GCHQ's director seemed a period largely of consolidation reflected the powerful impact he had already had there.

To all his work Hooper brought unusual energy and dedication; work was his passion. It was said of him that 'the one item always missing from [his] desk was a pend-ing tray: he never left for home until everything had been cleared' (*The Times*, 24 Feb 1994). As director he had the great advantage, not shared by his predecessors, of having performed analytical work himself in the crucible of war-time experience; from this came a professional empathy that never deserted him. Throughout his career he was on remarkably good terms with junior staff in what became an organization of some 6000 civilians of variegated occu-pations and backgrounds. One of his few recreations was supporting the local civil service rugby club, and he could be found in the evenings painting the clubhouse with other volunteers. He was clubbable and sociable, espe-cially with his American allies. He was not a delegator, and his professional intensity and attention to detail produced difficulties for subordinates, although this professional dominance was balanced by approachability and infor-mality.

Hooper's main contribution, before and during his dir-ectorship, was in putting the vital signals intelligence effort of the Second World War on to a firm basis as the UK's principal intelligence source, and in developing a tightly controlled organization over a long period of expansion and technical change. He was successful in his relationships with the armed services, and saw what after 1945 was still a loose federation of military and civilian elements evolve into a more tightly knit signals intelligence structure. He paid particular attention to his transatlantic and Commonwealth relationships. He took the maintenance of the UK–US alliance to be the keystone of intelligence policy, and supported a variety of joint UK–US operations. Other overseas connections, within Europe and elsewhere, were of far less importance to him.

Perhaps Hooper's biggest personal imprint on GCHQ's organization was in its administration. GCHQ's scale after 1945 made it inevitable that it should be gradually assimilated into mainstream civil service practices. Hooper enthusiastically supported this process against the inclination of many of his colleagues. He could eventually take some pride in the paradox that GCHQ, despite its unavowed function and secret activities, was regarded as a well-managed civil service department. In financial matters he was a reluctant expansionist. In Whitehall's eyes, including those of the Treasury, he was a model head of a secret agency. It was indeed in administration that Hooper figured in an episode with controversial consequences. Two unions, representing two bodies of junior staff, worked to rule in 1969 in protest against a civil service arbitration ruling on their pay claim. Hooper intervened personally to obtain a re-hearing which led to a better pay award. Repetitions of union action or threats of it followed in the 1970s and early 1980s, leading eventually to the government's controversial banning of national unions at GCHQ in 1984. With hindsight a tougher management line in 1969 might have been justified, yet in the national spirit of the time it was hardly an option.

Hooper retired as director of GCHQ in November 1973 in order to take up a position as the government's intelligence co-ordinator, with the rank of deputy secretary in the Cabinet Office. He was the first full-time holder of this post and his tenure shaped its development. He maintained a relatively low profile, assisting with budgetary matters and specific issues referred to him but not encroaching on the independence of heads of agencies. Arguably the post might have developed a more interventionist style. He deserves great credit, however, for having become convinced while at GCHQ that revelations of Bletchley's wartime code-breaking successes could no longer be resisted as endangering current sources and methods. He subsequently took a lead in Whitehall in formulating and implementing policy for the release of this wartime signals intelligence material, a policy that led eventually to the publication of the official history of intelligence in the Second World War, and to a fuller public appreciation of intelligence's national role and value.

Hooper retired from the Cabinet Office in 1978, and settled in Cheltenham. His second marriage ended in divorce early that year and on 28 July he married Mary Kathleen (Kate) Horwood, née Weeks (b. 1922/3), retired civil servant (also at Bletchley Park and GCHQ), and daughter of Albert Weeks, a farmer. In retirement Hooper was active as chairman of the governors of Dean Close School, Cheltenham, which named a new quadrangle after him. He was also chairman of Alleyn's School committee from 1974, and of the south-west area of the Civil Service Sports Council Association. He died of pneumonia at the Charlton Lane unit, Cheltenham, on 19 February 1994; he was survived by his third wife, Kate. His body was cremated at Cheltenham, and a memorial service was held in the chapel of Dean Close School on 22 March 1994.

British intelligence since 1945 has not produced towering figures but for twenty-five years Hooper was held in unusually high regard nationally and internationally. He was a major figure in the peacetime development of signals intelligence as a well-managed, large-scale, high-technology enterprise with an intimate transatlantic relationship. He and Sir Dick White were the two leading British intelligence professionals of the second half of the twentieth century.   MICHAEL HERMAN

Sources *The Times* (24 Feb 1994) · *The Times* (22 March 1994) · *WWW*, 1991–5 · personal knowledge (2004) · private information (2004) · b. cert. · m. certs. · d. cert.
Likenesses photograph, News International Syndication, London [*see illus.*]
Wealth at death under £125,000: probate, 11 April 1994, *CGPLA Eng. & Wales*

Hooper, Louisa (1860–1946). *See under* White, Lucy Anna (1848–1923).

Hooper, Robert (1773–1835), physician and medical writer, son of John Hooper of Marylebone, was born in London and educated by Dr William Rutherford of the academy at Uxbridge. After a course of medical study in London Hooper was appointed apothecary to the Marylebone workhouse infirmary, where he made an extensive collection of anatomical preparations. He entered Pembroke College, Oxford, on 24 October 1796, graduated BA in 1803, and MA and MB in 1804. Some difficulty—instigated, it is said, by members of the Royal College of Physicians who would not 'tarnish its hallowed walls with the flame of the workhouse laboratory' (*Lancet*, 494)—prevented his proceeding DM at Oxford, but he was created MD of St Andrews University on 16 December 1805, and admitted LRCP in London on 23 December 1805. After settling in Savile Row, he lectured there on the practice of medicine for many years to large classes.

Hooper built an extensive practice and was a prolific writer, and his books had a large sale. His writings include *Observations on the structure and economy of plants; to which is added the analogy between the animal and vegetable kingdoms* (1797), and *A compendious medical dictionary, containing an explanation of the terms in anatomy, physiology, surgery* (1798), of which numerous American editions were issued. The edition of 1811 was issued as a new edition of John Quincy's *Lexicon medicum*, a work of long-standing repute which had gone through thirteen editions and had been largely copied by Hooper. Subsequent editions bore the title *Lexicon medicum, or, Medical Dictionary*, without reference to Quincy. *The anatomist's vade mecum, containing the anatomy, physiology, and morbid appearances of the human body* (1798) was published in America in Boston in 1801 and 1803. Other works were *Anatomical plates of the bones and muscles, reduced from Albinus, for the use of students and artists* (1802),

The London Dissector (1804), and *The physician's vade mecum, containing the symptoms, causes, prognosis, and treatment of diseases* (1809).

Hooper retired from practice in 1829, having made a fortune, and lived at Stanmore, Middlesex. He died from a disease of the bladder in Bentinck Street, Manchester Square, London, on 6 May 1835. He left a fine collection of paintings, part of the estate bequeathed to his brothers.

G. T. BETTANY, *rev.* MICHAEL BEVAN

Sources Munk, *Roll* · *The Lancet* (11 July 1835), 493–4 · Foster, *Alum. Oxon.* · *GM*, 2nd ser., 3 (1835), 667 · *GM*, 2nd ser., 4 (1835), 670
Likenesses attrib. P. Reinagle, oils, *c*.1813, RCP Lond.
Wealth at death wealthy; owned fine collection of paintings

Hooper, William Hulme (1827–1854), naval officer, after passing his examination at Portsmouth was in November 1847 appointed mate of the *Plover*, under Commander Thomas E. L. Moore. *Plover* was one of the earliest vessels sent out to search for and relieve Sir John Franklin. Her orders were to pass through the Bering Strait and examine the coast eastwards. She sailed from Plymouth on 30 January 1848, and from Honolulu on 25 August. On 15 October she was off Chutsky Nos, and the next day went into Port Providence, where she wintered. Hooper led a party along the coast as far as Cape Atcheen, and through the winter mixed with the local people, whom he called Tuski, and whose language he learned. The following summer the *Plover* moved over to Kotzebue Sound, and near Icy Cape, on 25 July 1849, her two boats, under the command of Lieutenants Pullen and Hooper (who, though he did not know it, had been promoted lieutenant on 12 May), left the ship for a voyage along the coast. This they examined as far as the mouth of the Mackenzie River, and, going up it, Hooper wintered (1849–50) on the shores of Bear Lake, close to Fort Franklin; Pullen travelled a little further up the river and wintered at Fort Simpson. In the summer of 1850 they travelled down river and examined the coast as far as Cape Bathurst. They returned to Fort Simpson, where they both wintered (1850–51). Leaving their boats they later travelled overland to New York, and reached England in October 1851.

Hooper's health had given way under the hardships of three Arctic winters, and he became a confirmed invalid, relieving the tedium of his illness by writing an account of the expedition: *Ten months among the tents of the Tuski, with incidents of an Arctic boat expedition in search of Sir John Franklin* (1853). Hooper died, reportedly from the effects of his Arctic service, at Brompton, London, on 19 May 1854, aged twenty-seven.

J. K. LAUGHTON, *rev.* ROGER MORRISS

Sources W. H. Hooper, *Ten months among the tents of the Tuski, with incidents of an Arctic boat expedition in search of Sir John Franklin* (1853) · *GM*, 2nd ser., 42 (1854), 91 · *Journal of the Royal Geographical Society*, 24 (1854), 84 · C. Holland, *Arctic exploration and development, c. 500 BC to 1915: an encyclopedia* (1994) · T. H. Levere, *Science and the Canadian Arctic: a century of exploration, 1818–1918* (1993) · M. Graf, *Arctic journeys: a history of exploration for the north-west passage* (1992) · Boase, *Mod. Eng. biog.*

PICTURE CREDITS

Hickeringill, Edmund (*bap.* 1631, *d.* 1708)—© Copyright The British Museum

Hickes, George (1642–1715)—© National Portrait Gallery, London

Hickman, Henry (1800–1830)—private collection

Hicks, Baptist, first Viscount Campden (1551?–1629)—© National Portrait Gallery, London

Hicks, Edward Lee (1843–1919)—© National Portrait Gallery, London

Hicks, Sir John Richard (1904–1989)—© National Portrait Gallery, London

Hicks, William [Hicks Pasha] (1831–1883)—© National Portrait Gallery, London

Hicks, William Joynson-, first Viscount Brentford (1865–1932)—© National Portrait Gallery, London

Hickson, Joan Bogle (1906–1998)—© News International Newspapers Ltd

Higden, Ranulf (*d.* 1364)—© The Bodleian Library, University of Oxford

Higgins, Francis (1669/70–1728)—© National Portrait Gallery, London

Higgins, Matthew James (1810–1868)—© National Portrait Gallery, London

Higgins, Reynold Alleyne (1916–1993)—© reserved; News International Syndication; photograph National Portrait Gallery, London

Highmore, Joseph (1692–1780)—National Gallery of Victoria, Melbourne, Australia

Highmore, Susanna (1689/90–1750)—Art Gallery of South Australia, Adelaide

Higinbotham, George (1826–1892)—La Trobe Picture Collection, State Library of Victoria

Hildyard, Sir Henry John Thoroton (1846–1916)—© National Portrait Gallery, London

Hill, Alfred Hawthorne [Benny] (1924–1992)—© Bob Collins; collection National Portrait Gallery, London

Hill, Archibald Vivian (1886–1977)—by kind permission of the Provost and Fellows of King's College, Cambridge

Hill, Charles, Baron Hill of Luton (1904–1989)—© National Portrait Gallery, London

Hill, David Octavius (1802–1870)—© National Portrait Gallery, London

Hill, Dame Elizabeth Mary (1900–1996)—The Mistress and Fellows, Girton College, Cambridge

Hill, Frank Harrison (1830–1910)—© National Portrait Gallery, London

Hill, (Norman) Graham (1929–1975)—© Klemantaski Collection; collection National Portrait Gallery, London

Hill, Sir John (*bap.* 1714, *d.* 1775)—© National Portrait Gallery, London

Hill, Leonard Raven- (1867–1942)—© Estate of Leonard Raven-Hill; collection National Portrait Gallery, London

Hill, Matthew Davenport (1792–1872)—© National Portrait Gallery, London

Hill, Octavia (1838–1912)—© National Portrait Gallery, London

Hill, Sir Roderic Maxwell (1894–1954)—© National Portrait Gallery, London

Hill, Rowland (1744–1833)—© National Portrait Gallery, London

Hill, Rowland, first Viscount Hill (1772–1842)—© National Portrait Gallery, London

Hill, Sir Rowland (1795–1879)—© National Portrait Gallery, London

Hill, Thomas Wright (1763–1851)—© National Portrait Gallery, London

Hill, William (1903–1971)—© Popperfoto

Hill, William Noel-, third Baron Berwick (1773–1842)—National Trust Photographic Library / John Hammond

Hill, Wills, first marquess of Downshire (1718–1793)—private collection. Photograph © Ulster Museum. Photograph reproduced with the kind permission of the Trustees of the National Museums & Galleries of Northern Ireland

Hillary, Richard Hope (1919–1943)—© National Portrait Gallery, London

Hilliard, Nicholas (1547?–1619)—V&A Images, The Victoria and Albert Museum

Hillier, Sir Harold George (1905–1985)—Royal Horticultural Society, Lindley Library; photograph National Portrait Gallery, London

Hillyar, Sir James (1769–1843)—© National Maritime Museum, London

Hillyard, Blanche (1863–1946)—Getty Images - Hulton Archive

Hilton, Roger (1911–1975)—Snowdon / Camera Press; collection National Portrait Gallery, London

Himsworth, Sir Harold Percival (1905–1993)—© National Portrait Gallery, London

Hind, James (*bap.* 1616, *d.* 1652)—© National Portrait Gallery, London

Hindmarsh, Robert (1759–1835)—© National Portrait Gallery, London

Hingeston, John (*c.*1606–1683)—Faculty of Music, University of Oxford

Hingley, Noah (1796–1877)—taken from original held at Dudley Archives & Local History Service

Hinshelwood, Sir Cyril Norman (1897–1967)—© reserved; © reserved in the photograph

Hinsley, Arthur (1865–1943)—Archbishop's House, Westminster; photograph National Portrait Gallery, London

Hinton, Christopher, Baron Hinton of Bankside (1901–1983)—© National Portrait Gallery, London

Hinton, James (1822–1875)—© National Portrait Gallery, London

Hinton, Paula Doris (1924–1996)—© Roger Wood / The Independent; photograph National Portrait Gallery, London

Hirschell, Solomon (1762–1842)—© National Portrait Gallery, London

Hirst, Francis Wrigley (1873–1953)—© National Portrait Gallery, London

Hirst, Olive Mirzl (1912–1994)—© National Portrait Gallery, London

Hirst, Thomas Archer (1830–1892)—DH70, College Collection Photographs, UCL Library Services

Hitchcock, Alfred Joseph (1899–1980)—© Karsh / Camera Press; collection National Portrait Gallery, London

Hitchcock, Sir Eldred Frederick (1887–1959)—© reserved; unknown collection

Hoadly, Benjamin (1676–1761)—© Tate, London, 2004

Hoare, Sir (Richard) Colt, second baronet (1758–1838)—National Trust Photographic Library / John Hammond

Hoare, Henry (1677–1725)—Stourhead, The Hoare Collection (The National Trust). Photograph: Photographic Survey, Courtauld Institute of Art, London

Hoare, Henry (1705–1785)—Stourhead, The Hoare Collection (The National Trust). Photograph: Photographic Survey, Courtauld Institute of Art, London

Hoare, Louisa Gurney (1784–1836)—© National Portrait Gallery, London

Hoare, Samuel John Gurney, Viscount Templewood (1880–1959)—© National Portrait Gallery, London

Hoare, William (1707/8–1792)—© Clive Quinnel / Royal National Hospital for Rheumatic Diseases, Bath

Hobart, John, second earl of Buckinghamshire (1723–1793)—The National Trust; photograph National Portrait Gallery, London

Hobart, Sir Percy Cleghorn Stanley (1885–1957)—© National Portrait Gallery, London

Hobart, Robert, fourth earl of Buckinghamshire (1760–1816)—private collection; photograph National Portrait Gallery, London

Hobbes, Thomas (1588–1679)—© National Portrait Gallery, London

Hobbs, Sir John Berry [Jack] (1882–1963)—Surrey C.C.C. Photo Library

Hobday, Sir Frederick Thomas George (1870–1939)—The Historical Collection, The Royal Veterinary College

Hobhouse, Emily (1860–1926)—© National Portrait Gallery, London

Hobhouse, Henry (1854–1937)—© National Portrait Gallery, London

Hobhouse, John Cam, Baron Broughton (1786–1869)—© National Portrait Gallery, London

Hobhouse, Leonard Trelawny (1864–1929)—British Library of Political and Economic Science

Hobson, John Atkinson (1858–1940)—British Library of Political and Economic Science

Hobson, Thomas (1545–1631)—© National Portrait Gallery, London

Hobson, (Babette Louisa) Valerie (1917–1998)—© National Portrait Gallery, London

Hoby, Sir Edward (1560–1617)—© National Portrait Gallery, London

Hoby, Sir Philip (1504/5–1558)—The Royal Collection © 2004 HM Queen Elizabeth II

Hoby, Sir Thomas (1530–1566)—The Conway Library, Courtauld Institute of Art, London

Hoccleve, Thomas (*c.*1367–1426)—The British Library

Hoddesdon, John (*c.*1632–1659)—© National Portrait Gallery, London

Hodge, Sir William Vallance Douglas (1903–1975)—© National Portrait Gallery, London

Hodges, Charles Howard (1764–1837)—© Rijksmuseum, Amsterdam

Hodges, Sir William, first baronet (*c.*1645–1714)—© National Portrait Gallery, London

Hodgkin, Sir Alan Lloyd (1914–1998)—© Derek Hill; collection Royal Society

Hodgkin, Dorothy Mary Crowfoot (1910–1994)—© National Portrait Gallery, London

Hodgkin, Thomas (1798–1866)—© reserved

Hodgkin, Thomas (1831–1913)—© National Portrait Gallery, London

Hodgkin, Thomas Lionel (1910–1982)—© reserved; private collection

Hodgson, James (*bap.* 1678?, *d.* 1755)—© National Portrait Gallery, London

Hodson, Henrietta (1841–1910)—© National Portrait Gallery, London

Hodson, William Stephen Raikes (1821–1858)—© National Portrait Gallery, London

Hoffnung, Gerard (1925–1959)—© Peter Keen; collection National Portrait Gallery, London

Hofmeyr, Jan Hendrik (1845–1909)—© National Portrait Gallery, London

Hogarth, Ann (1910–1993)—Getty Images - Hulton Archive

Hogarth, David George (1862–1927)—private collection

Hogarth, William (1697–1764)—© Tate, London, 2004

Hogg, James (*bap.* 1770, *d.* 1835)—Scottish National Portrait Gallery

Hogg, Quintin (1845–1903)—© National Portrait Gallery, London

Hogg, Thomas Jefferson (1792–1862)—© Bodleian Library, University of Oxford

Holbein, Hans, the younger (1497/8–1543)—Collection Uffizi Museum, Florence; © reserved in the photograph

Holberry, Samuel (1814–1842)—© Sheffield Galleries & Museums Trust

Holcroft, Thomas (1745–1809)—© National Portrait Gallery, London

Holden, Sir David Charles Beresford (1915–1998)—Universal Pictorial Press

Holden, Edith Blackwell (1871–1920)—© RS & RW 2004

Holderness, Sir Thomas William, first baronet (1849-1924)—© National Portrait Gallery, London

Holdsworth, Edward (1684-1746)—photograph © English Heritage Photo Library

Holdsworth, Sir William Searle (1871-1944)—© National Portrait Gallery, London

Holford, William Graham, Baron Holford (1907-1975)—© National Portrait Gallery, London

Holiday, Henry George Alexander (1839-1927)—William Morris Gallery, London

Holl, Francis Montague (1845-1888)—Aberdeen Art Gallery and Museums Collections

Holland, Sir Eardley Lancelot (1879-1967)—Estate of the Artist; reproduced by permission of the Archives of the Royal College of Obstetricians and Gynaecologists

Holland, Henry Scott (1847-1918)—© National Portrait Gallery, London

Holland, Philemon (1552-1637)—© National Portrait Gallery, London

Hollar, Wenceslaus (1607-1677)—© National Portrait Gallery, London

Holles, Denzil, first Baron Holles (1598-1680)—private collection; on loan to the National Portrait Gallery, London

Holles, John, first earl of Clare (d. 1637)—Department of Manuscripts and Special Collections, University of Nottingham; Newcastle Collection Ne 4P 24

Holles, John, duke of Newcastle upon Tyne (1662-1711)—private collection; photograph National Portrait Gallery, London

Holles, Thomas Pelham-, duke of Newcastle upon Tyne and first duke of Newcastle under Lyme (1693-1768)—© National Portrait Gallery, London

Hollings, Michael Richard (1921-1997)—© McCrimmon Publishing Company Ltd., Great Wakering, Essex, UK

Hollingshead, John (1827-1904)—© National Portrait Gallery, London

Hollis, Sir Leslie Chasemore (1897-1963)—© National Portrait Gallery, London

Hollond, Marjorie (1895-1977)—The Mistress and Fellows, Girton College, Cambridge

Holloway, Stanley Augustus (1890-1982)—V&A Images, The Victoria and Albert Museum

Holloway, Thomas (1800-1883)—Archives, Royal Holloway, University of London (RHC PH/281/4/3)

Holme, Vera Louise (1881-1969)—© Estate of the Artist; private collection; photograph courtesy The Fine Art Society, London

Holmes, Sir Charles John (1868-1936)—© National Portrait Gallery, London

Holmes, Sir Richard Rivington (1835-1911)—© National Portrait Gallery, London

Holmes, Sir Robert (c.1622-1692)—© National Maritime Museum, London

Holroyd, Sir Charles (1861-1917)—© National Portrait Gallery, London

Holroyd, John Baker, first earl of Sheffield (1741-1821)—© National Portrait Gallery, London

Holst, Gustav Theodore (1874-1934)—© Jenny Letton, administered by

Composer Prints Ltd.; collection National Portrait Gallery, London

Holst, Imogen Clare (1907-1984)—courtesy of The Britten-Pears Library, Aldeburgh; photograph Nigel Luckhurst; reproduced by permission of the Mary Potter Estate

Holt, Sir John (1642-1710)—© National Portrait Gallery, London

Holt, John (bap. 1743, d. 1801)—© National Portrait Gallery, London

Holt, Joseph (1756x9-1826)—© National Portrait Gallery, London

Holtby, Winifred (1898-1935)—Somerville College, Oxford

Holyoake, George Jacob (1817-1906)—© Estate of Walter Sickert / National Portrait Gallery, London

Holyoake, Sir Keith Jacka (1904-1983)—Alexander Turnbull Library, National Library of New Zealand, Te Puna Matauranga o Aotearoa

Home, Alexander Frederick Douglas-, fourteenth earl of Home and Baron Home of the Hirsel (1903-1995)—© National Portrait Gallery, London

Home, Daniel Dunglas (1833-1886)—Mary Evans / Society for Psychical Research

Home, David Milne [David Milne] (1805-1890)—Edinburgh Meteorological Office archives

Home, Sir Everard, first baronet (1756-1832)—© The Royal Society

Home, George, earl of Dunbar (d. 1611)—Scottish National Portrait Gallery

Home, John (1722-1808)—© National Portrait Gallery, London

Home, William Douglas (1912-1992)—© National Portrait Gallery, London

Hone, Eva Sydney (1894-1955)—© reserved; by courtesy of the National Gallery of Ireland

Hone, Nathaniel (1718-1784)—National Gallery of Ireland

Hone, William (1780-1842)—© National Portrait Gallery, London

Hongi Hika (1772-1828)—Alexander Turnbull Library, National Library of New Zealand, Te Puna Matauranga o Aotearoa (G-618)

Hood, Alexander, Viscount Bridport (1726-1814)—© National Maritime Museum, London, Greenwich Hospital Collection

Hood, Sir Alexander (1888-1980)—© National Portrait Gallery, London

Hood, Sir Horace Lambert Alexander (1870-1916)—© reserved

Hood, Samuel, first Viscount Hood (1724-1816)—© National Maritime Museum, London

Hood, Thomas (1799-1845)—© National Portrait Gallery, London

Hook, James (1746-1827)—© National Portrait Gallery, London

Hook, Theodore Edward (1788-1841)—© National Portrait Gallery, London

Hooker, John (c.1527-1601)—Exeter City Museums & Art Gallery

Hooker, Sir Joseph Dalton (1817-1911)—Royal Photographic Society

Hooker, Sir William Jackson (1785-1865)—by permission of the Linnean Society of London

Hooper, George (1640-1727)—Christ Church, Oxford

Hooper, Sir Leonard James (1914-1994)—© reserved; News International Syndication; photograph National Portrait Gallery, London

Oxford dictionary of
national biography